■ THE RESOURCE FOR THE INDEPENDENT TRAVELER

"The guides are aimed not only at young budget travelers but at the indepedent traveler; a sort of streetwise cookbook for traveling alone."

—The New York Times

"Unbeatable; good sight-seeing advice; up-to-date info on restaurants, hotels, and inns; a commitment to money-saving travel; and a wry style that brightens nearly every page."

—The Washington Post

"Lighthearted and sophisticated, informative and fun to read. [Let's Go] helps the novice traveler navigate like a knowledgeable old hand."

—Atlanta Journal-Constitution

"A world-wise traveling companion—always ready with friendly advice and helpful hints, all sprinkled with a bit of wit."

—The Philadelphia Inquirer

■ THE BEST TRAVEL BARGAINS IN YOUR PRICE RANGE

"All the dirt, dirt cheap."

—People

"Anything you need to know about budget traveling is detailed in this book."

—The Chicago Sun-Times

"Let's Go follows the creed that you don't have to toss your life's savings to the wind to travel—unless you want to."

—The Salt Lake Tribune

■ REAL ADVICE FOR REAL EXPERIENCES

"The writers seem to have experienced every rooster-packed bus and lunar-surfaced mattress about which they write."

—The New York Times

"A guide should tell you what to expect from a destination. Here Let's Go shines."

—The Chicago Tribune

LET'S GO PUBLICATIONS

TRAVEL GUIDES

Alaska & the Pacific Northwest 2003
Australia 2003
Austria & Switzerland 2003
Britain & Ireland 2003
California 2003
Central America 8th edition
Chile 1st edition **NEW TITLE**
China 4th edition
Costa Rica 1st edition **NEW TITLE**
Eastern Europe 2003
Egypt 2nd edition
Europe 2003
France 2003
Germany 2003
Greece 2003
Hawaii 2003 **NEW TITLE**
India & Nepal 7th edition
Ireland 2003
Israel 4th edition
Italy 2003
Mexico 19th edition
Middle East 4th edition
New Zealand 6th edition
Peru, Ecuador & Bolivia 3rd edition
South Africa 5th edition
Southeast Asia 8th edition
Southwest USA 2003
Spain & Portugal 2003
Thailand 1st edition **NEW TITLE**
Turkey 5th edition
USA 2003
Western Europe 2003

CITY GUIDES

Amsterdam 2003
Barcelona 2003
Boston 2003
London 2003
New York City 2003
Paris 2003
Rome 2003
San Francisco 2003
Washington, D.C. 2003

MAP GUIDES

Amsterdam
Berlin
Boston
Chicago
Dublin
Florence
Hong Kong
London
Los Angeles
Madrid
New Orleans
New York City
Paris
Prague
Rome
San Francisco
Seattle
Sydney
Venice
Washington, D.C.

USA

INCLUDING COVERAGE OF CANADA

2003

BRENNA C. FARRELL EDITOR
SCOTT M. ROWEN ASSOCIATE EDITOR
MEGAN SMITH ASSOCIATE EDITOR

RESEARCHER-WRITERS

ANNIE ANTAR
SARA BARNETT
STEPHANIE BUTLER
AARON HAAS
KRISTIN KITCHEN

KATE MCFARLIN
NASSIRA NICOLA
MATTHEW SHEA O'HARE
JULIA REISCHEL
MOLLY M. SIMMONS
JAKUB WRZESNIEWSKI

ARIEL BENJAMIN ERGAS SHWAYDER MAP EDITOR
CHRISTOPHER BLAZEJEWSKI MANAGING EDITOR
ANKUR GHOSH TYPESETTER

ST. MARTIN'S PRESS ✽ NEW YORK

HELPING LET'S GO

If you want to share your discoveries, suggestions, or corrections, please drop us a line. We read every piece of correspondence, whether a postcard, a 10-page email, or a coconut. Please note that mail received after May 2003 may be too late for the 2004 book, but will be kept for future editions. **Address mail to:**

Let's Go: USA
67 Mount Auburn Street
Cambridge, MA 02138
USA

Visit Let's Go at **http://www.letsgo.com,** or send email to:

feedback@letsgo.com
Subject: "Let's Go: USA"

In addition to the invaluable travel advice our readers share with us, many are kind enough to offer their services as researchers or editors. Unfortunately, our charter enables us to employ only currently enrolled Harvard students.

Maps by David Lindroth copyright © 2003 by St. Martin's Press.
New York City Subway Map © Metropolitan Transportation Authority. Used with permission.

Distributed outside the USA and Canada by Macmillan.

ISBN: 0-312-30598-2

First edition
10 9 8 7 6 5 4 3 2 1

Let's Go: USA is written by Let's Go Publications, 67 Mount Auburn Street, Cambridge, MA 02138, USA.

HOW TO USE THIS BOOK

ORGANIZATION. Welcome to *Let's Go USA 2003!* This book will walk you (and probably ride with you) state by state and province by province through the USA and Canada, starting on the east coast and heading west. The black tabs on the side of the book should help you navigate your way through.

PRICE RANGES & RANKINGS. Our researchers list establishments in order of value from best to worst, except gay establishments, which are listed at the end of each section. Our favorites are denoted by the Let's Go thumbs-up (🗹). Since the best value is not always the cheapest price, we have incorporated a system of price ranges in the guide. The table below lists how prices fall within each bracket.

USA	❶	❷	❸	❹	❺
ACCOMMODATIONS	under $30	$30-45	$46-70	$71-100	over $100
FOOD	under $6	$6-8	$9-12	$13-16	over $16
CANADA	❶	❷	❸	❹	❺
ACCOMMODATIONS	under CDN$45	CDN $45-67	CDN $68-105	CDN $106-150	over CDN$150
FOOD	under CDN$7	CDN$7-12	CDN$13-18	CDN$19-24	over CDN$24

PHONE CODES & TELEPHONE NUMBERS. Area codes for each region appear opposite the name of the region and are denoted by the ☎ icon. Phone numbers in text are also preceded by the ☎ icon.

WHEN TO USE IT

TWO MONTHS BEFORE. The first chapter, **Discover the United States and Canada,** contains highlights of the US and Canada, including Suggested Itineraries that can help you plan your trip. The **Essentials** section contains practical information on planning a budget, making reservations, and renewing a passport, and has other useful tips about traveling in the US and Canada.

ONE MONTH BEFORE. Take care of insurance, and write down a list of emergency numbers. Read through the coverage and be sure you understand the transportation requirements of your itinerary. Make any reservations if necessary; many campsites fill up very quickly, as do hostels and hotels during special events.

TWO WEEKS BEFORE. Leave an itinerary and a photocopy of important documents with someone at home. Take some time to peruse the **Life and Times** (see p. 8), which has info on history, culture, recent political events, and more.

ON THE ROAD. Our new **Roadtrips** and **Walking Tours** can help you make the most of the continent's natural scenery and bustling cities, and other features will entertain you as you go. Now, arm yourself with a travel journal and hit the road!

A NOTE TO OUR READERS The information for this book was gathered by *Let's Go* researchers from May through August of 2002. Each listing is based on one researcher's opinion, formed during his or her visit at a particular time. Those traveling at other times may have different experiences since prices, dates, hours, and conditions are always subject to change. You are urged to check the facts presented in this book beforehand to avoid inconvenience and surprises.

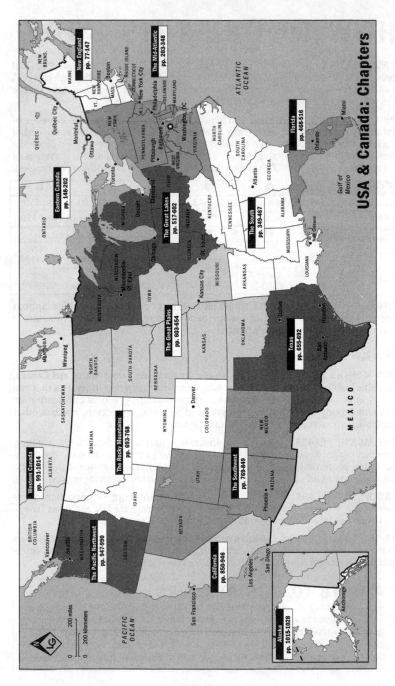

USA & Canada: Chapters

New England pp. 77-147

The Mid-Atlantic pp. 203-348

Eastern Canada pp. 148-202

Florida pp. 468-516

The Great Lakes pp. 517-602

The South pp. 349-467

The Great Plains pp. 603-654

Texas pp. 655-692

Western Canada pp. 991-1014

The Rocky Mountains pp. 693-768

The Southwest pp. 769-849

The Pacific Northwest pp. 947-990

California pp. 850-946

Alaska pp. 1015-1028

CONTENTS

**DISCOVER THE USA
& CANADA** 1
When to Go 1
Things to Do 1
Suggested Itineraries 5
LIFE & TIMES 8
THE UNITED STATES 8
History 8
Culture 14
Additional Resources 26
CANADA 26
O Canada! A Brief History 27
Canuck Culture 28

ESSENTIALS 30
Facts for the Traveler 30
Accommodations 42
Getting There 53
Getting Around 56
Specific Concerns 67
The World Wide Web 71

ALTERNATIVES TO TOURISM 72
Studying Abroad 72
Working 74
Volunteering 76

NEW ENGLAND 77
MAINE 78
MAINE COAST 78
Portland 79
South of Portland 81
Mt. Desert Island 82
Northern Maine Coast 84
NEW HAMPSHIRE 87
Portsmouth 87
WHITE MOUNTAINS 89
Franconia Notch Area 92
VERMONT 95
Burlington 96
Middlebury 99
Stowe 101
MASSACHUSETTS 104
BOSTON 105
Near Boston 121
CAPE COD & ISLANDS 127
WESTERN MASSACHUSETTS 135
The Berkshires 135
RHODE ISLAND 137
Providence 137
Newport 140
CONNECTICUT 143
Hartford 143
New Haven 144

EASTERN CANADA 148

NOVA SCOTIA 148
Lighthouse Route 150
Halifax 151
Cape Breton Island 153
NEW BRUNSWICK 155
Saint John 155
Fundy National Park 157
PRINCE EDWARD ISLAND 160
Charlottetown 160
NEWFOUNDLAND 162
St. John's 163
QUÉBEC 166
MONTRÉAL 166
Québec City 178
ONTARIO 185
TORONTO 187
Ottawa 196

MID-ATLANTIC 203
NEW YORK 203
NEW YORK CITY 205
Long Island 243
The Catskills 245
Albany 247
Cooperstown 248
Ithaca & the Finger Lakes 250
Buffalo 252
Niagara Falls 253
NORTHERN NEW YORK 256
NEW JERSEY 261
Atlantic City 261
Cape May 264
PENNSYLVANIA 266
PHILADELPHIA 266
Lancaster County 279
Gettysburg 281
Pittsburgh 283
DELAWARE 288
Lewes 288
Rehoboth Beach 289
MARYLAND 290
Baltimore 291
Annapolis 297
Assateague & Chincoteague 300
Ocean City 302
WASHINGTON, D.C. 304
VIRGINIA 322
Richmond 323
Fredericksburg 327
Williamsburg 330
Virginia Beach 333
Charlottesville 335
Shenandoah National Park 338
New River Gorge 341
WEST VIRGINIA 345

THE SOUTH **349**
KENTUCKY 349
Louisville 352
Lexington 356
TENNESSEE 359
Nashville 359
Knoxville 365
Great Smoky Mountains 367
Chattanooga 370
Memphis 372
NORTH CAROLINA 378
The Research Triangle 379
Winston-Salem 382
Charlotte 383
CAROLINA MOUNTAINS 384
Asheville 384
NORTH CAROLINA COAST 387
Outer Banks 387
SOUTH CAROLINA 390
Charleston 391
Columbia 395
GEORGIA 400
ATLANTA 401
Athens 413
Macon 415
Savannah 418
ALABAMA 421
Montgomery 422
Birmingham 426
Mobile 430
MISSISSIPPI 433
Jackson 433
Vicksburg 435
Oxford 437
LOUISIANA 439
NEW ORLEANS 439
Baton Rouge 458
Natchitoches 459
ACADIANA 461
Lafayette 463
ARKANSAS 465
Little Rock 466
FLORIDA **468**
Jacksonville 468
St. Augustine 471
Daytona Beach 474
Orlando 475
Walt Disney World 479
Palm Beach & West Palm Beach 485
Fort Lauderdale 487
Miami & Miami Beach 492
Everglades 499
FLORIDA KEYS 502
GULF COAST 507
GREAT LAKES **517**
OHIO 517
Cleveland 518
Columbus 523

Cincinnati 525
INDIANA 529
Indianapolis 529
Bloomington 532
MICHIGAN 533
Detroit 533
Ann Arbor 540
Grand Rapids 543
LAKE MICHIGAN SHORE 544
UPPER PENINSULA 550
ILLINOIS 553
Chicago 553
Springfield 571
WISCONSIN 573
Milwaukee 573
Madison 579
Door County 583
Apostle Islands 585
MINNESOTA 588
Minneapolis & St. Paul 588
Duluth 597
Iron Range 599
Voyageurs National Park 600
GREAT PLAINS **603**
NORTH DAKOTA 603
Fargo 605
Bismarck 606
Theodore Roosevelt National Park 608
SOUTH DAKOTA 610
The Badlands 612
BLACK HILLS REGION 615
IOWA 620
Des Moines 620
Iowa City 624
NEBRASKA 627
Omaha 628
Lincoln 630
KANSAS 633
Wichita 634
MISSOURI 637
St. Louis 637
Kansas City 644
OKLAHOMA 650
Tulsa 650
Oklahoma City 652
TEXAS **655**
San Antonio 656
Austin 661
Dallas 670
Houston 676
Corpus Christi 684
WEST TEXAS 686
ROCKY MOUNTAINS **693**
IDAHO 693
Boise 694
Ketchum & Sun Valley 696
Sawtooth National Recreation Area 698

MONTANA **701**	Tijuana 881
Helena 701	THE CALIFORNIA DESERT 884
Bozeman 702	THE CENTRAL COAST 888
Red Lodge 704	Santa Barbara 888
Missoula 705	San Luis Obispo 891
WATERTON-GLACIER PEACE PARK 708	Monterey 893
Glacier National Park 709	Santa Cruz 894
Waterton Lakes National Park, AB 714	SAN FRANCISCO 897
WYOMING **715**	THE BAY AREA 919
Yellowstone National Park 715	WINE COUNTRY 925
Grand Teton National Park 724	Mendocino 932
Jackson 729	Redwood National & State Parks 933
Cheyenne 735	THE NORTHERN INTERIOR 935
COLORADO **738**	THE SIERRA NEVADA 937
Denver 739	Lake Tahoe 937
Mountain Resorts on I-70 745	Yosemite National Park 941
Boulder 747	
Rocky Mountain National Park 750	**PACIFIC NORTHWEST** **947**
Vail 753	**WASHINGTON** **947**
Aspen 756	SEATTLE 948
Colorado Springs 758	Olympia 961
SAN JUAN MOUNTAINS 760	San Juan Islands 962
Telluride 762	OLYMPIC PENINSULA 964
Durango 765	Olympic National Park 965
Mesa Verde 767	CASCADE RANGE 968
	Mount St. Helens 968
THE SOUTHWEST **769**	Mount Rainier National Park 972
NEVADA **769**	**OREGON** **974**
Las Vegas 771	Portland 974
Reno 775	Mount Hood 982
UTAH **777**	Columbia River Gorge 983
SALT LAKE CITY 778	INLAND OREGON 984
Moab 786	Eugene 984
UTAH'S NATURAL WONDERS 787	Hells Canyon & Wallowa 989
Arches 788	
Capitol Reef 789	**WESTERN CANADA** **991**
Bryce Canyon 790	**BRITISH COLUMBIA** **991**
Zion National Park 793	Vancouver 993
ARIZONA **795**	Victoria 999
GRAND CANYON 795	Prince Rupert 1001
South Rim 797	Alaska Approaches 1003
North Rim 801	**THE YUKON TERRITORY** **1004**
Flagstaff 803	**ALBERTA** **1007**
Sedona 808	THE ROCKIES 1009
NAVAJO RESERVATION 810	Banff National Park & Lake Louise 1009
Petrified Forest National Park 813	Jasper National Park 1011
Lake Powell & Page 814	Calgary 1013
Phoenix 817	
Tucson 823	**ALASKA** **1015**
NEW MEXICO **830**	Anchorage 1016
Santa Fe 831	Fairbanks 1022
Taos 836	SOUTHEAST ALASKA 1024
Albuquerque 839	Ketchikan 1024
Truth or Consequences 845	Juneau 1026
White Sands National Monument 847	
CALIFORNIA **850**	**INDEX & APPENDIX** **1030**
LOS ANGELES 850	Distances (Mi.) & Travel Times (by Bus) 1030
Orange County 872	Index 1031
San Diego 876	Map Index 1052

RESEARCHER-WRITERS

Annie Antar   *New England and Upstate New York*

The indefatigable Annie, despite suffering a broken pelvic bone, battled through a rough-and-tumble itinerary traveling across New England. A top level rugby player, Annie's hardy outdoor skills propelled her along oceanside hikes in Maine and sustained her during camping expeditions in the Adirondack Mountains. Yet even while roughing it, Annie found time for small niceties: her thoughtful postcards delighted her editors all summer.

Sara Barnett   *Mid-Atlantic Coast*

A Baltimore native, Sara has previously worked in Washington, D.C. as a newspaper reporter in Dupont Circle. Her background in the mid-Atlantic region, along with her natural diplomacy and interviewing skills, made her the perfect choice to research the center of American government and history. A connoisseur of regional cuisine, Barnett demonstrated her expertise during an epicurean foray into the world of New Jersey salt water taffy.

Stephanie Butler   *Great Lakes*

Starting from her home in Chicago, Stephanie set on a course across Middle America, determined to bring the underestimated cities of the Heartland into the limelight. A writer for Harvard's *FM* magazine, she plowed through the the Midwest pen in hand (or "trusty" computer in lap). With an innate ability to connect to local culture, Stephanie wove stories out of the experiences she gleaned from the land—from Door County, WI to Pittsburgh, PA.

Kristin Kitchen   *Great Plains, South Carolina, Florida*

Hailing from Florida, Kristin trekked through her itinerary with all the spirit and animation of her former cheerleading days. From Florida to Wyoming, and from the Seven Dwarves of Disney to the Munchkins of Minnesota, Kristin charmed her way across the country and back with a heartening appreciation for American kitsch. Her astronomical stamina and down-to-earth humility brought a fresh perspctive and refreshing tone to all that she researched.

Matthew Shea O'Hare   *The Rocky Mountains*

Matt is familiar with the inner workings of *Let's Go*, having written for *Australia 2002*. Researching during the winter and spring in the Rockies, Matt connected with the mountainous terrain, finding hidden deals, outdoor adventures, and a few crazy characters in a still-wild west. Traveling across several months, he updated coverage of America's most imposing mountains, skiied her most coveted slopes, and trekked through the grandeur of Yellowstone.

Julia Reischel   *The Deep South*

We're not sure whether Julia was more charmed by the South or the South was more charmed by Julia. If only we had a whole book to devote to her stories! She had us laughing all summer long with her tales of cockfights, hobos, and being flashed ("and not in the good New Orleans sort of way"). Julia's unbounded enthusiasm and a keen ability to evaluate her surroundings made for great coverage and scored her lots of new friends, several of which were not sleazy.

Molly M. Simmons   *North Carolina, Tennessee, Kentucky, Atlanta*

Molly was a "natural" choice for handling coverage of the Great Smoky Mountain region. A former ski instructor at Vail and an avid rower on the waters of Boston's Charles River, she was born to be in the outdoors. After expanding our North Carolina coverage, she shagged in West Virginia, found fellow country music lovers while walkin' in Memphis, and swung by Hotlanta to have some fun. Even more impressively, she did it all with her arm in a full cast.

Jakub Wrzesniewski   *Altantic Canada*

Veteran RW Jakub, alias "Kuba," has trotted the globe for *Let's Go: Southwest USA 2002* and *Southeast Asia 2001*. In 2003, Kuba was the USA's renaissance man, using his travel experience, Canadian know-how (he's from BC, eh?), and sunny Polish disposition to expand our coverage into Newfoundland. *Let's Go: USA* was greatly enriched by Kuba's off-beat sense of humor, and his willingness to always come through in the crunch.

Aaron Haas   *Texas, Oklahoma, Kansas*

Like a strong and silent cowboy hero of yore, Aaron Haas rode into the West with a good eye and a steady hand to rope the best the region had to offer. A judicious researcher, Aaron put down his law books for the summer to reflect on the Oklahoma City Stockyards and to study the music scene in Austin, TX. After some inititial skepticism, this man of few words learned to love the open roads of Kansas, rattlesnake paraphernalia, and bronco busting.

Kate McFarlin   *Southern Florida*

We like to think of Kate as our style consultant. A Tampa native, she's been navigating the ins and outs of beach culture for years, so she handled the glam party scenes of SoBe and the Keys like a pro. Kate came through in the clutch, providing fashion updates and revising our coverage to give it a hip spin all her own. Going where no budget traveler has gone before, she even blended into the aristocracy of Palm Beach to find deals and bargains all along the way.

Nassira Nicola   *Québec and Ontario*

Not merely studying, but truly living linguistics, Nassira has a passion for human language. From her enthusiasm for *québécois* culture to her knowledge of and involvement in the Deaf community, she prides herself (and rightly so) on her ability to blend into communities other than her own—often being mistaken for a native. Nassira went undercover in Québec, talking with locals and consulting with friends, and infusing her copy with insider knowledge.

REGIONAL RESEARCHER-WRITERS

Posy Busby, Carleton Goold, Catherine Gowl, Sarah Murphy, James Pinto, Greg Schmeller
Alaska & The Pacific Northwest

Sheila Baynes, Robert Cacace, Dustin Lewis, Evan North, Jonathan Sherman *Southwest USA*

Sara Clark, Eliza Dick, James Kearney, Kevin Yip   *California*

Stephanie Stallings   *Columbia, SC*

Daniel F. Chen, Hollin N. Kretzmann	*Washington, D.C.*
Loran C. Fredric, Mandy M. Hu, Michael C. Wheeler	*New York City and environs*
Shawn H. Snyder, Laura E. Spence, James L. Stillwell	*San Francisco and environs*
Ankur Ghosh and friends	*Boston and environs*

REGIONAL EDITORS

Benjamin G. Wells	Editor, *Let's Go: Alaska & The Pacific Northwest*
Robert J. Dubbin	Associate Editor, *Let's Go: Alaska & The Pacific Northwest*
Eli Ewing	Editor, *Let's Go: Southwest USA*
Jakub Wrzesniewski	Editor, *Let's Go: Southwest USA*
Nitin Shah	Editor, *Let's Go: California*
Ariel Fox	Associate Editor, *Let's Go: California*
Brian Wansley Flanagan	Editor, *Let's Go: Washington, D.C.*
Judy S. Kwok	Editor, *Let's Go: New York City*
Antoinette C. Nwandu	Editor, *Let's Go: San Francisco*
Ankur Ghosh	Editor, *Let's Go: Boston*

CONTRIBUTING WRITERS

Sarah Haskins was a Researcher-Writer for *Let's Go: Ireland 2001*. She now lives in Chicago, supporting her improv comedy habit by writing commercials.

T.J. Kelleher associate edited *Let's Go: USA 1999*, edited *USA 2000*, and a Researcher-Writer for *Australia 2001*. He is now a magazine editor for the American Museum of Natural History.

Jane A. Lindholm has worked for *Let's Go* guides to Central America, Mexico, Spain, and Chile. She is producer for National Public Radio in Washington, D.C.

Dinaw Mengestu has written for the Princeton Review and SparkNotes, and is in the process of writing a novel for his master's thesis.

Benjamin Paloff was a Researcher-Writer for *Let's Go: Eastern Europe 1998*, edited *Eastern Europe 1999*, and was a Managing Editor for the series in 2000.

Stephanie L. Smith was a Researcher-Writer for *Let's Go: California 1997* and *New Zealand 1998*. She has worked as a freelancer for CitySearch Los Angeles, reviewing restaurants, bars, and attractions.

ACKNOWLEDGMENTS

TEAM USA THANKS: Our persevering and entertaining group of RWs! May you never have to travel our barbaric nation with a broken laptop ever again. Blaz for always having a sense of humor. Ari, our reliable, infallible mapper. Kuba, Eli, Chairman Dubbinwells, Nitin, Ariel, Ankur, Flanagan, Judy, and Antoinette, for returning to their books when they least wanted to. West B, it's a hard knock life. Huge thanks to those who helped last-minute: Jesse, Scrobins, Emma, Mangela, Cody, Judy, Ariel, Nitin, Michelle, Megha, Abi, and Leichtman.

BRENNA THANKS: Scott for his fine-tooth-comb mentality, big-picture perspective, and Guffman channeling. Megan for her formatting genius, decisiveness, and blazing line dancing. Kuba for his charming morbidity. Erin, Jen, Dad, Mom, and Larry for their love. The Voorhees for stamina. East B. for honky-tonk, West B. for swank. Huma and Matt, my best friends. Johnny Cash, my best role model.

SCOTT THANKS: Brenna for guiding the ship through stormy waters, MrSmith for white-girl dancing, & "Jake" for Coke cans. God and my family for constant love and support. The dysfunctional East B: Eli, Wells, Nitin, Dubbin, & Ariel, you guys are awesome. West B for laughs, and Axis for putting up with me. TL, PL, & MH, my two best friends; LS, BM, TD, LH, SR, SM, RG, MG, & MS, for being "family."

MEGAN THANKS: My family who will have *Let's Go USA: 2003* on their coffeetable for years to come. Durks, Lo, and O'doyle, who kept me sane with their tales from the road. Scotty R. for opening my eyes to Guffman. Brenna for taking it to the end in style. Kuba just for being a comrade. Tesh, I'd never have made it without Tommy's value. The basement: Wild horses couldn't drag me away.

ARI THANKS: My roommates who made this a most enjoyable summer. Mapland for keeping it real and entertaining. Julie for answering my barage of questions. Love to ACL.

Editor Brenna C. Farrell
Associate Editors Scott M. Rowen, Megan Smith
Managing Editor Christopher Blazejewski
Map Editor Ariel Benjamin Ergas Shwayder

WHO WE ARE

A NEW LET'S GO FOR 2003

With a sleeker look and innovative new content, we have revamped the entire series to reflect more than ever the needs and interests of the independent traveler. Here are just some of the improvements you will notice when traveling with the new *Let's Go*.

MORE PRICE OPTIONS

Still the best resource for budget travelers, *Let's Go* recognizes that everyone needs the occassional indulgence. Our "Big Splurges" indicate establishments that are actually worth those extra pennies (pulas, pesos, or pounds), and price-level symbols (❶ ❷ ❸ ❹ ❺) allow you to quickly determine whether an accommodation or restaurant will break the bank. We may have diversified, but we'll never lose our budget focus—"Hidden Deals" reveal the best-kept travel secrets.

BEYOND THE TOURIST EXPERIENCE

Our Alternatives to Tourism chapter offers ideas on immersing yourself in a new community through study, work, or volunteering.

AN INSIDER'S PERSPECTIVE

As always, every item is written and researched by our on-site writers. This year we have highlighted more viewpoints to help you gain an even more thorough understanding of the places you are visiting.

IN RECENT NEWS. *Let's Go* correspondents around the globe report back on current regional issues that may affect you as a traveler.

CONTRIBUTING WRITERS. Respected scholars and former *Let's Go* writers discuss topics on society and culture, going into greater depth than the usual guidebook summary.

THE LOCAL STORY. From the Parisian monk toting a cell phone to the Russian *babushka* confronting capitalism, *Let's Go* shares its revealing conversations with local personalities—a unique glimpse of what matters to real people.

FROM THE ROAD. Always helpful and sometimes downright hilarious, our researchers share useful insights on the typical (and atypical) travel experience.

SLIMMER SIZE

Don't be fooled by our new, smaller size. *Let's Go* is still packed with invaluable travel advice, but now it's easier to carry with a more compact design.

FORTY-THREE YEARS OF WISDOM

For over four decades *Let's Go* has provided the most up-to-date information on the hippest cafes, the most pristine beaches, and the best routes from border to border. It all started in 1960 when a few well-traveled students at Harvard University handed out a 20-page mimeographed pamphlet of their tips on budget travel to passengers on student charter flights to Europe. From humble beginnings, *Let's Go* has grown to cover six continents and *Let's Go: Europe* still reigns as the world's best-selling travel guide. This year we've beefed up our coverage of Latin America with *Let's Go: Costa Rica* and *Let's Go: Chile;* on the other side of the globe, we've added *Let's Go: Thailand* and *Let's Go: Hawaii*. Our new guides bring the total number of titles to 61, each infused with the spirit of adventure that travelers around the world have come to count on.

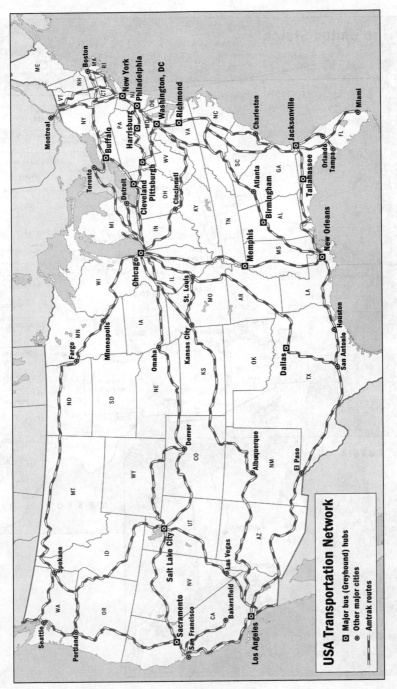

USA Transportation Network

☒ Major bus (Greyhound) hubs
◉ Other major cities
〰️ Amtrak routes

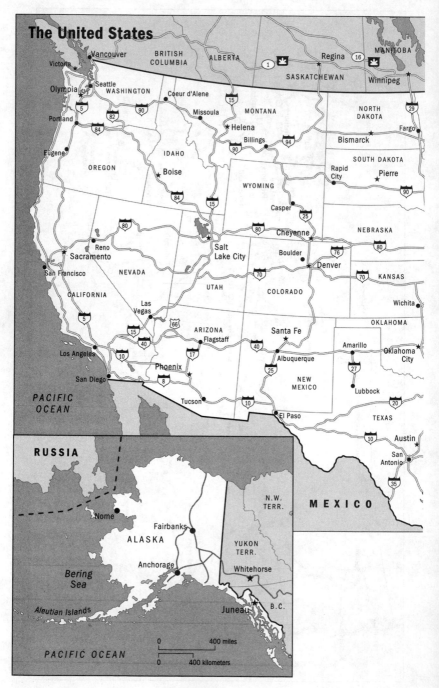

The United States

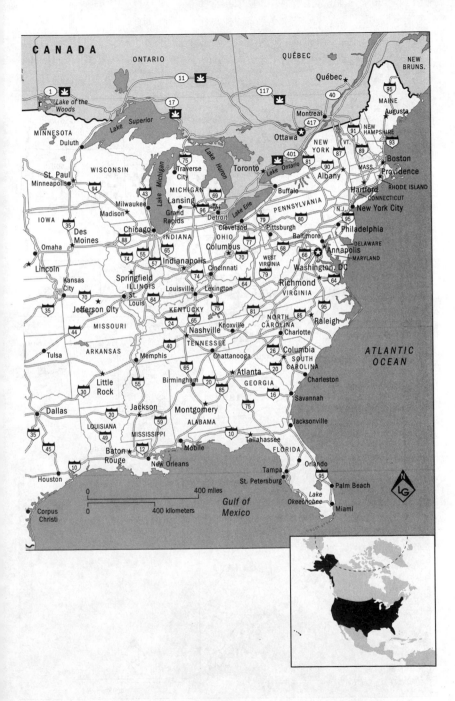

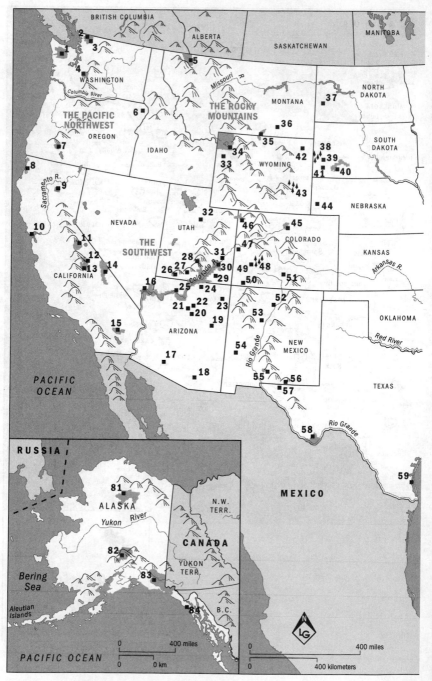

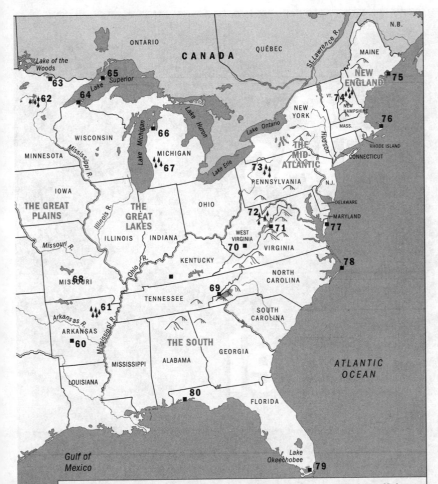

USA National Park System

National Monuments
Bandelier, NM, **52**
Black Canyon, CO, **49**
Canyon de Chelly, AZ, **23**
Colorado, CO, **47**
Devils Tower, WY, **42**
Dinosaur, CO, **46**
Gila Cliff Dwellings, NM, **54**
Great Sand Dunes, CO, **51**
Lassen Volcanic, CA, **9**
Little Bighorn, MT, **36**
Mt. Rushmore, SD, **39**
Natural Bridges, UT, **29**
Navajo, AZ, **24**
Organ Pipe, AZ, **17**
Petroglyph, NM, **53**
Scotts Bluff, NE, **44**
Sunset Crater, AZ, **21**
Timpanogos Cave, UT, **32**
Walnut Canyon, AZ, **20**
White Sands, NM, **55**
Wupatki, AZ, **22**

National Parks
Acadia, ME, **75**
Arches, UT, **31**
Badlands, SD, **40**
Big Bend, TX, **58**
Bryce Canyon, UT, **27**
Canyonlands, UT, **30**
Capitol Reef, UT, **28**
Carlsbad Caverns, NM, **56**
Crater Lake, OR, **7**
Death Valley, CA, **14**
Denali, AK, **82**
Everglades, FL, **79**
Gates of the Arctic, AK, **81**
Glacier, MT, **5**
Glacier Bay, AK, **84**
Grand Canyon, AZ, **25**
Grand Teton, WY, **33**
Great Smoky Mts., TN, **69**
Guadalupe Mts., TX, **57**
Hot Springs, AR, **60**
Isle Royale, MI, **65**

Joshua Tree, CA, **15**
Kings Canyon, CA, **12**
Mammoth Cave, KY, **68**
Mesa Verde, CO, **50**
Mt. Rainier, WA, **4**
New River Gorge, WV, **70**
North Cascades, WA, **2**
Olympic, WA, **1**
Petrified Forest, AZ, **19**
Redwood, CA, **8**
Rocky Mt., CO, **45**
Saguaro, AZ, **18**
Sequoia, CA, **13**
Shenandoah, VA, **71**
Theodore Roosevelt, ND, **37**
Voyageurs, MN, **63**
Wind Cave, SD, **41**
Wrangell-St. Elias, AK, **83**
Yellowstone, WY, **34**
Yosemite, CA, **11**
Zion, UT, **26**

National Recreation Areas
Bighorn Canyon, MT, **35**
Golden Gate, CA, **10**

Hell's Canyon, OR, **6**
Lake Mead, NV, **16**
Ross Lake, WA, **3**

National Forests
Allegheny, PA, **73**
Black Hills, SD, **38**
Chippewa, MN, **62**
Grand Mesa, CO, **48**
Manistee, MI, **67**
Medicine Bow, WY, **43**
Monongahela, WV, **72**
Ozark, AR, **61**
White Mts., NH, **74**

National Lakeshores
Apostle Islands, WI, **64**
Sleeping Bear Dunes, MI, **66**

National Seashores
Assateague, MD, **77**
Cape Cod, MA, **76**
Cape Hatteras, NC, **78**
Padre Island, TX, **59**
Gulf Islands, FL, **80**

DISCOVER THE USA & CANADA

Stretching from below the Tropic of Cancer to above the Arctic Circle, the United States is a country defined by open spaces and an amazing breadth of terrain. From sparse deserts to lush forests and snow-capped peaks to rolling fields of grain, the American landscape sprouts new views in every region.

America's accumulation of wealth and prestige since WWII has heightened both its patriotism and its interior divisions. In this fair country, world-class creature comforts exist minutes away from acres of country quiet—and most of it is accessible, at least in theory, to everyone. However, the contrast between the overall abundance of wealth and the many who struggle to make ends meet is a constant confrontation. Wealthy people may run the big show, but the middle-class masses inspire America's ideology toward unpretentious family values. Through centuries of immigration, the US has absorbed and integrated millions of immigrants to create the cultural amalgamation that now defines the population and contributes to the diversity that pervades the country.

While thousands of airplanes stream in and out of America's massive airports, the most rewarding way to see the country is still by car. The road trip is an authentic American institution that has captured the imagination of statesmen, writers, and lowly college students alike.

USA FACTS AND FIGURES

POPULATION: 287,504,665.

LARGEST CITIES: New York City, Los Angeles, Chicago, Houston, Philadelphia.

RELIGIOUS AFFILIATION: Protestant 56%; Roman Catholic 28%; Jewish 2%; other 4%; non-religious 10%.

MILES DRIVEN EACH YEAR: 1½ trillion (to the sun and back 7500 times).

URBAN/RURAL POPULATION: City mice 77%; country mice 23%.

ETHNICITY: White 75%; Black 12%; Hispanic 12.5%; Asian and Pacific Islander 3.7%; Native American 1%.

WHEN TO GO

In general, the US tourist season comprises the summer months between Memorial Day and Labor Day (May 26-Sept. 1, 2003); the Canadian tourist season starts around mid-June. National parks flood with visitors during the high season, but cities are less affected by seasonal variation. For regions where winter sports are big or where winters are mild, the tourist season is generally inverted (Dec.-Mar.).

THINGS TO DO

Neither the following few pages nor this book's one thousand pages can do justice to the vibrant and diverse offerings of the North American continent. No two trips to the New World are ever the same, and visitors to different regions may feel like they've visited different countries. There are, however, a few common themes in the US and Canada that deserve mention and that should be a part of any thorough exploration.

SCENIC DRIVES

News commentator and stalwart American patriot Charles Kuralt once said, "Thanks to the interstate highway system, it is now possible to travel from coast to coast without seeing anything." The interstate system is the fastest, most efficient, most sensible way of driving through America—and also the least rewarding. The incredible network of backroads in the US affords a genuine view of the country. Unobstructed by vision-blocking soundproofers and gas-spewing trailers, the rest stops on back roads possess more character than the next Burger King. The **Blue Ridge Parkway, VA** (p. 343), connects two national parks—Shenandoah and Great Smoky Mountains—passing tremendous green mountains and rustic Appalachian wilderness. In the North, the **Lake Superior North Shore Drive, MN** (p. 601) traces the dramatic, cliff-lined shore of the most massive Great Lake, revealing waterfalls, lighthouses, and forests. Connecting San Antonio with Austin, TX, the **Texas Hill Country Drive** (p. 663) goes deep into the heart of broad-rim hat and dusty jean country, where the landscape is dotted with historical immigrant communities and pristine vineyards. Just outside Phoenix, AZ, the **Apache Trail** (p. 822) curves around the stark cactus-laden desert mountains that loom over deep blue artificial lakes. The **San Juan Skyway** (p. 764), in southern CO, ascends to breathtaking heights under snow-capped mountains and past bottomless gorges. **Going-to-the-Sun Road** (p. 712), in the Waterton-Glacier Peace Park, MT, skirts mountainous landscape as it passes bubbling waterfalls and steep escarpments before descending into the rainforest. **I-87** winds through the tree-carpeted Adirondacks (p. 256).

MUST-SEE CITIES

Sure, everyone knows the major cities: New York has...well, everything; nothing tops the vivacity, glamour, great weather, and unbeatable smog of Los Angeles; and the multicultural metropolis of Toronto offers unparalleled opportunities. However, the real reasons to buckle up for the great American journey are the smaller, less obvious cities and towns. The magnificent fortifications and twisting alleyways of **Québec City, QC** (p. 178) testify to the city's unmatched old-world character. The "staid" American Midwest boasts **Minneapolis-St. Paul, MN** (p. 588), a sprawling and unsung urban center with the sights and diversity to rival even the most famous of American cities. Travelers to **Savannah, GA** (p. 418) are rewarded with lush gardens, antebellum homes, and old-timey Southern charm. The legendary nightlife of **Austin, TX** (p. 670) thrives on the city's mix of Southwestern grit, collegiate energy, and dot-com optimism. Only the most liberal-minded and fun-loving traveler need stop in the eclectic town of **Boulder, CO** (p. 753), a place of all sorts of Rocky Mountain highs. Countless adventurers find a warm welcome in **Flagstaff, AZ** (p. 803), perhaps the greatest crossroads in the US. The spirited city of **Portland, OR** (p. 974), known as the microbrewery capital of North America, is quickly becoming one of the most sought-after destinations on the continent.

COLLEGE TOWNS

America's colleges, from sprawling state universities to tiny liberal-arts academies, have engendered unique communities with youthful vitality and alternative spirit. Lost between the twin giants of New York and Boston, the smaller college town of **Providence, RI** (p. 137), beckons with a slower, more inviting pace. The mountain hamlet of **Middlebury, VT** (p. 101) combines rural charm with a touch of collegiate rowdiness. An increasingly diverse student community gives the Southern establishment a run for its money in **Charlottesville, VA** (p. 336), a gorgeous town characterized by its rolling hills and splendid architecture. The student population of **Laramie, WY** (p. 738) has put a new spin on the region's traditional cowboy chic, while **Missoula, MT** (p. 705) has become one of the most fascinatingly cosmopolitan cities in the Prairie. The liberal haven of **Berkeley, CA** (p. 919), which has become much more than a college town, is always worth a visit.

AMERICANA

America vaunts the biggest, smallest, and zaniest of almost everything. Kitschy roadside attractions dot the country's dusty roads, putting on public display a vast and truly baffling material culture—for a modest fee. Out west in Polson, MT (p. 708), the **Miracle of America Museum** enshrines reg'lar old American living. **Wall Drug's** (p. 612) notorious billboards lure tourists to the Badlands of South Dakota from as far away as Amsterdam—that's right, in Holland—and have turned their marketing ploy into a cultural phenomenon. The **Beer Can House** in Houston, TX (p. 682) needs no explanation. Further evidence of American architectural ingenuity can be found at the **Corn Palace** in Mitchell, SD (p. 611); this gargantuan structure is rebuilt every year with a fresh crop. America also claims the world's largest **folding pocketknife** in Natchitoches, LA (p. 461) and **wooden cross** in Petoskey, MI (p. 550), neither of which can quite compete with the magnitude of **Carhenge**—a scale model of Stonehenge built from 36 old cars just north of Alliance, NE (p. 630). Bigger and brighter still are the casinos of **the Strip** in Las Vegas, NV (p. 771) and **the Boardwalk** in Atlantic City, NJ (p. 263). No tribute to the American value of individual rights stands so proud as **"The Tree That Owns Itself"** in Athens, GA (p. 414). And, of course no tour of American kitsch would be complete without a trip to the heart and soul of all Americana—Elvis's **Graceland** (p. 375).

NATIONAL PARKS

From ancient glaciers to an endless sea of blinding white gypsum, from haunting red buttes to endless pitch-black caves, the national parks of the US and Canada protect some of the most phenomenal natural beauty in the world. While much of the land's beauty can be seen along the byways, the truly miraculous works of nature are cared for by the National Park Service. The easternmost park in the US, **Acadia National Park,** ME (p. 84) features unspoiled rocky beaches and dense pine forests. **Shenandoah National Park,** VA (p. 339) made its way into history as America's first land reclamation project, and today lures travelers with its mountain vistas. **Great Smoky Mountains National Park,** TN (p. 367), the largest national park east of the Mississippi, also holds the distinctions of International Biosphere Reserve and World Heritage Site.

The most popular parks, however, lie out west. Arguably the most famous (and most crowded) park in the US, **Yellowstone National Park,** WY (p. 731), has attractions such as the Old Faithful geyser. **Grand Canyon National Park,** AZ (p. 795) wows visitors with...well, the Grand Canyon, while **Yosemite National Park,** CA (p. 941) draws hordes of trekkers, trailers, and tourists with its steep mountains and stunning waterfalls. Smaller—but no less breathtaking—are the otherworldly hoodoos (pillar-like rock formations) of **Bryce Canyon National Park,** UT (p. 790), the varied and dramatic terrain of **Waterton-Glacier International Peace Park,** MT (p. 709), and the awesome mountains of **Grand Teton National Park,** WY (p. 724).

Canada also possesses a highly developed and well-maintained national park system. At **Fundy National Park,** NB (p. 157) the world's largest tides ebb and flow, while nearby **Kouchibouguac National Park** (p. 159) features sandy beaches and acres of marshland. On Newfoundland, the UNESCO world heritage site of **Gros Morne National Park** (p. 165) sees more moose than tourists...for now. The Canadian Rockies also play host to gorgeous parklands, including the expansive ice fields of **Jasper National Park,** AB (p. 1011). The isolated **Pacific Rim National Park,** BC (p. 1001) offers some of the best hiking, surfing, and diving on the continent.

DISCOVER

☑ LET'S GO PICKS

BEST OPPORTUNITIES FOR PUBLIC BATHING: Hot springs are a therapeutic diversion from the hard work of travel; some of the best are Lolo Springs, MT (p. 707); Saratoga, WY (p. 737); and Calistoga, CA (p. 928). For just plain skinny dippin', try Hippie Hollow in Austin, TX (p. 668).

BEST SUN SPOTS: For a great East Coast sunrise, head to Cadillac Mt. in Acadia National Park, ME (p. 84). For a sunset celebration, go to the pier in Clearwater, FL (p. 509).

BEST FOR SPELUNKERS: Don't forget to explore the underground. Highest marks go to Mammoth Cave, KY (p. 355) and Carlsbad Caverns, NM (p. 849).

BEST GATORS: America's most impressive creatures. Get up close and scarily personal in places like Nachitoches, LA (p. 459); the Everglades, FL (p. 499); and St. Augustine, FL (p. 468).

MOST APPETIZING BEER NAMES: Montana's Moose Drool (p. 721), Florida's Dolphin's Breath (p. 472), and Louisiana's funkybuttjuice (p. 453) definitely rank among the nation's finest.

BEST BIG ART: Everything's big in America. Twenty-seven factory buildings are needed to hold the exhibits at the Museum of Contemporary Art in North Adams, MA (p. 135). The world's largest painting, a 360° mural, is housed in Atlanta, GA (p. 407). Still unfinished, the sculpture of Crazy Horse (p. 617) will be 563 ft. when completed, thus making the 60 ft. presidential heads on nearby Mt. Rushmore (p. 616) seem like child's play.

LONGEST PUB STREET: George St., NF (p. 164). Learn to drink like a Canadian.

BEST WAY TO ESCAPE AMERICA (OTHER THAN CANADA): Tibetan cuisine, rare in the US, is served in Bloomington, IN (p. 532) at the Snow Lion restaurant, owned by the Dalai Lama's nephew. Made in Tajikstan and shipped to Boulder, CO (p. 753), the building of the Dushanbe teahouse is a gift between sister cities—a tasty tribute to international relations.

BEST EXTRATERRESTRIALS: Many claim Roswell, NM (p. 848) and Sedona, AZ (p. 808) have hosted a few *really* long-distance travelers.

SUGGESTED ITINERARIES

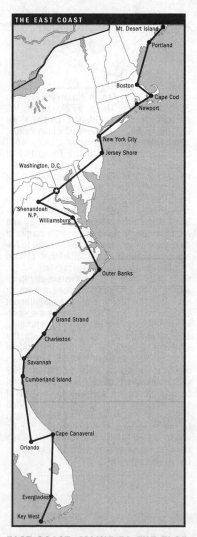

THE EAST COAST

Mt. Desert Island
Portland
Boston
Cape Cod
Newport
New York City
Jersey Shore
Washington, D.C.
Shenandoah N.P.
Williamsburg
Outer Banks
Grand Strand
Charleston
Savannah
Cumberland Island
Cape Canaveral
Orlando
Everglades
Key West

EAST COAST: MAINE TO THE FLORIDA KEYS (6 WEEKS) I-95 and the sometimes commercial, sometimes scenic U.S. 1 parallel each other from the northern wilds of Maine down to the gorgeous Florida Keys. Despite the many state-levied tolls, this strip gives a true cross-section of American life and culture, and encourages on-a-whim diversions. Begin on Mt. Desert Island, ME (p. 82) where mountain and ocean meet with spectacular results, then head down the coast. The youthful Portland, ME (p. 79) will whet your appetite for city life, and the thriving culture of Boston, MA (p. 105) will satisfy it. Cape Cod (p. 127) awaits with pristine beaches, while Newport, RI (p. 140) preserves the must-see summer estates of America's wealthiest industrialists. From there, cruise over to larger-than-life New York City (p. 245). The Jersey Shore (p. 266) deals out boardwalks and beaches for a quintessential summer experience. Washington, D.C. (p. 304) merits a few days, as does the placid Shenandoah National Park (p. 339). See colonial history acted out in Williamsburg, VA (p. 330), or find solitude on long stretches of sand in the Outer Banks (p. 387). The more built-up Grand Strand (p. 398) and the city of Charleston, SC (p. 391) beckon partyers back to the mainland. Savannah (p. 418) and stunning Cumberland Island (p. 420) will leave Georgia on your mind, but Disney World (p. 479) will leave you blissfully mind-numb. Give the Space Coast of Florida (p. 484) a fly-by, and make a brief stop to explore the vast, mysterious Everglades (p. 499). Celebrate the end of your journey with umbrella drinks on sugar-white beaches in Key West (p. 503).

THE NORTH: TRACING THE US-CANADIAN BORDER (6 WEEKS) Crossing the continent at higher latitudes affords travelers time in the unique cities and less touristed parks of the North. Begin north of the border and take a whirlwind tour of Canada's cosmopolitan eastern cities. Québec City (p. 178) and Montréal (p. 166) are predominantly French-speaking and overflow with culture. Toronto (p. 187) boasts huge ethnic quarters and refreshing tidiness for such a big city. Cross the border at the spectacular Niagara Falls (p. 253) and motor over to the oft-stigmatized and under-estimated city of Detroit (p. 533). Sail on to the Windy City of Chicago (p. 553). Wind down in the friendly and scenic lakeside

DISCOVER

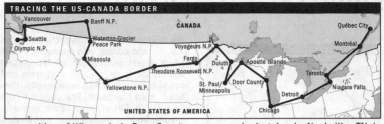

TRACING THE US-CANADA BORDER

communities of Wisconsin in Door County (p. 583) and the Apostle Islands (p. 585). Next, head to the surprisingly hip twin cities of St. Paul and Minneapolis (p. 588). The charming city of Duluth, MN (p. 597) combines a thriving shipping industry with endless waterfront recreation. Before leaving Minnesota, park the car and boat into the unspoiled expanse of Voyageurs National Park (p. 600). Stop in Fargo (p. 605), then speed out to the breathtaking Theodore Roosevelt (p. 608) and Yellowstone (p. 731) National Parks. Young and fresh, Missoula, MT (p. 705) provides a much-needed stop before heading north to Waterton-Glacier Peace Park (p. 709) and the popular Banff National Park (p. 1009) in Canada. Out on the Pacific coast, visit the lively city scenes of Vancouver (p. 993) and Seattle (p. 948), or the serene wilderness of one of world's last remaining old-growth temperate rainforests at Olympic National Park (p. 965).

SOUTH BY SOUTHWEST (8 WEEKS)

Striking straight across the American South from sea to shining sea—and even dipping into Mexico—this route highlights old-fashioned Southern flavor, Mexican-infused Southwestern culture, and canyon country. It can be driven year-round. Warm up with big cities tempered by Southern hospitality in the triangle of Charleston, SC (p. 391), Savannah, GA (p. 418) and Atlanta, GA (p. 401). Trace the roots of virtually all Ameri-

can musical styles in Nashville, TN (p. 359); Memphis, TN (p. 372); Oxford, MS (p. 437); and New Orleans, LA (p. 439). Experience the unadulterated Cajun culture of the Deep South in Acadiana, LA (p. 461) before heading out to the Texan trio of Houston (p. 676), San Antonio (p. 656), and Austin (p. 670). New Mexico offers the otherworldly White Sands National Monument (p. 847), and the phenomenal mineral baths of Truth or Consequences (p. 845). The cities of Santa Fe (p. 831) and Albuquerque (p. 839) are worth a couple of days each. After having your fill, head to Arizona's astonishing Petrified Forest and Painted Desert (p. 812). Flagstaff, AZ (p. 803) is an inviting Southwestern city in its own right, and makes a convenient base for exploring the region near the magnificent Grand Canyon (p. 795). Stop by the enormous Lake Powell (p. 814) for stunning scenery and great boating. To the north, the idyllic wilderness of Utah's Zion National Park (p. 793) and the startling rock pillars of Bryce Canyon (p. 790) provide travelers with a last gasp of clean air and natural beauty before the plunge into the glitz of Las Vegas (p. 771). In California, Joshua Tree National Park (p. 885) is a worthy stop in the desert on the way to the Pacific coast. Savor sunny San Diego (p. 876) before becoming star-struck in glamorous Los Angeles (p. 850).

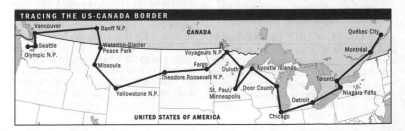

TRACING THE US-CANADA BORDER

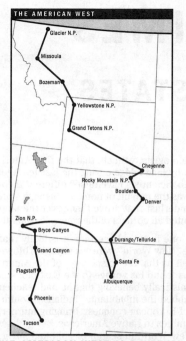

THE AMERICAN WEST

Glacier N.P.
Missoula
Bozeman
Yellowstone N.P.
Grand Tetons N.P.
Cheyenne
Rocky Mountain N.P.
Boulder
Denver
Zion N.P.
Bryce Canyon
Durango/Telluride
Grand Canyon
Santa Fe
Flagstaff
Albuquerque
Phoenix
Tucson

THE AMERICAN WEST (3-6 WEEKS)

Saddle up; the American West has blown the minds of generations of wanderers. Sidle up to the region with tours of Tucson, AZ (p. 823), Phoenix, AZ (p. 817), and Flagstaff, AZ (p. 803). Hit the must-see Grand Canyon (p. 795) from the South Rim, and then mosey through the more tranquil Bryce Canyon (p. 790) and Zion (p. 793) National Parks In Utah. Cllmb on toward Albuquerque, NM (p. 839) and Santa Fe, NM (p. 831) on the way to more mountainous terrain. Spend some time in the authentic Western towns of Durango (p. 765) and Telluride, CO (p. 762). After taking on the mile-high city of Denver (p. 739) and the youthful Boulder (p. 753), get lost among the peaks of Rocky Mountain National Park (p. 750). Stop over in Cheyenne, WY (p. 735) for a boot-stompin' good time on your way to the impressive Tetons (p. 724). The immensely popular Yellowstone National Park (p. 731) warrants an extra couple of days. The towns of Bozeman (p. 704) and Missoula, MT (p. 705), culturally straddling East and West, make pleasant and unique stops for the weary. Cap off your trip with the purple mountains' majesty of rugged Glacier National Park (p. 709).

THE WEST COAST: FROM L.A. TO VANCOUVER (2-6 WEEKS).

Between sunny, boisterous Los Angeles, CA and lush, mellow Vancouver, BC lies much natural (and artificial) diversion. America's western outpost of high culture, L.A. provides access to Hollywood (p. 855), famous art, and beach culture. Las Vegas, NV (p. 771), Tijuana, Mexico (p. 881), and Joshua Tree National Park, CA (p. 885) are worthy side trips. The 400 mi. stretch of shore-hugging Rte. 1 between L.A. and San Francisco—through Big Sur (p. 893) and Santa Cruz (p. 894)—is pure California: rolling surf, secluded beaches, dramatic cliffs, and eccentric locals. San Francisco (p. 896), a groovin' city in itself, is only 3-4hr. from Yosemite National Park (p. 941). From SF, the slightly inland Rte. 101 hits Napa Valley wine country (p. 925) before reuniting with Rte. 1 (and the coast) and passing through the primordial Redwood National Park (p. 933). Rejoin I-5 for a trip to Portland, OR (p. 974), Crater Lake (p. 986), and Mt. Hood (p. 982). Before getting too settled with a latte in Seattle (p. 948), commune with nature at Mt. St. Helens (p. 968) and Olympic National Park (p. 965), or trek over to Vancouver, BC (p. 993) and the outdoor havens of Vancouver Island (p. 999).

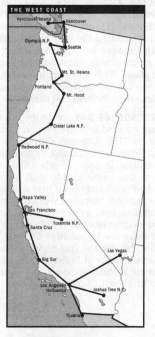

THE WEST COAST

Vancouver Island
Vancouver
Olympic N.P.
Seattle
Mt. St. Helens
Portland
Mt. Hood
Crater Lake N.P.
Redwood N.P.
Napa Valley
San Francisco
Yosemite N.P.
Santa Cruz
Las Vegas
Big Sur
Los Angeles/Hollywood
Joshua Tree N.P.
Tijuana

DISCOVER

LIFE & TIMES

THE UNITED STATES

HISTORY

BRIDGE OVER TROUBLED WATER. Archaeologists estimate that the first Americans crossed the Bering Sea from Siberia by **land bridge** during the last Ice Age, somewhere from 10,000 to 15,000 years ago. Scientists have raised different theories to explain this migration. Whether it was the pursuit of nomadic bison, a shift in living conditions in Asia, or simple wanderlust that drove them over the land bridge, the Asiatic peoples gradually inhabited all corners of their new continent.

(UN)WELCOME EUROPEANS. Though no one is entirely certain, it is likely that the earliest Europeans to stumble upon the "New World" were sea voyagers blown off-course by storms. History textbooks tell us that the "discovery" of the Americas was in 1492, when **Christopher Columbus** found his voyage to the East blocked by Hispaniola in the Caribbean Sea. Optimistically believing that he had reached the spice islands of the East Indies, he dubbed the inhabitants "Indians." Columbus's arrival unleashed the unhappy tide of European conquest, bringing murder, disease, forced conversion, and other calamities to Native Americans.

Many Europeans high-tailed it to the New World in search of gold and silver. Even though most were unsuccessful, colonial fever took hold. The Spanish expanded into the Southern regions of the modern-day US, while the French and Dutch created more modest empires to the north. The English, meanwhile, successfully settled the vast New World. After a few failed attempts, the English finally managed to establish a colony at **Jamestown** in 1607. Their success hinged on a strain of indigenous weed called tobacco, which quickly became all the rage in England. While the Virginia settlements were founded for economic purposes, settlers came to the New World for different reasons. A group of religious separatists known as **Puritans** fled persecution to settle in present-day Massachusetts.

INDEPENDENCE DAY. In order to protect her holdings in the Americas, Great Britain entered into the French and Indian War against France (and her Indian allies) in 1754. Although ultimately successful, the struggle more than doubled Great Britain's government expenditures and raised awareness of the high price of colonialism. In order to offset the burden of this price on British taxpayers, the powers that be decided to shift more responsibility onto the American colonies, who had previously been taxed lightly. These new taxes angered colonists, who rallied against "taxation without representation." The leaders of the First Continental Congress were divided as to a course of action, but continued fighting between colonists and British troops convinced the Second Continental Congress to prepare the 13 colonies for war. In 1776, a **Declaration of Independence** was drafted. **July 4th,** the date on which the declaration was adopted, remains the most important national holiday for Americans. After eight years of fighting up and down the Eastern seaboard, British troops sailed off, and the colonists had a country of their own.

LIFE, LIBERTY, & THE CONSTITUTION. After achieving its independence, the country experimented with a loose confederated government until 1787, when the state legislatures sent a distinguished group of 55 men to draft what was to become the world's first written **Constitution.** The **Bill of Rights,** a set of ten constitutional amendments passed shortly after the Constitution, has remained a cornerstone of the American political system. This document included the rights to free speech, freedom of the press, and freedom of religion—along with the controversial right to bear arms. The original words of the document's authors are still interpreted differently according to the political climate of each era. Therein lies the power of the Constitution: it has the ability to be both timeless and timely, to represent the hopes of the nation's founders while accommodating the values of subsequent generations.

MANIFEST DESTINY. Looking beyond the Mississippi River, President Thomas Jefferson purchased the **Louisiana Territory** from Napoleon in 1803 for less than 3¢ an acre. The next year, Jefferson sent the Lewis and Clark expedition to explore the territory and to find an aqueous trade route to the Pacific Ocean. Lewis and Clark never did find a trade route, but they did chart the vast extent of land that lay west of the Mississippi. Droves of people migrated west in covered wagons along the grueling Oregon Trail in search of land, fortune, and a new life.

The **Homestead Act** of 1862 prompted the cultivation of the Great Plains by distributing government land to those who would farm it and live on it. This large-scale settlement led to bloody battles with the Sioux, Hunkpapas, and Cheyenne tribes who had long inhabited the Plains. From 1866 to 1891, the US fought a continuous war against the remaining 300,000 Native Americans The Native Americans were routed out, their land taken away, and their communities relegated to reservations. Much of the legend surrounding the **Wild West** revolves around tall tales of brave white settlers and stoic cowboys rounding up cattle and fending off Indian attacks.

AMERICA'S PECULIAR INSTITUTION. The first **Africans** were brought to America in 1619, prisoners aboard a Dutch slave ship headed for Jamestown, Virginia. The infusion of African slave labor led to the decline of indentured servitude, a system by which poor Europeans would provide seven years of labor in exchange for their Atlantic crossing. From the late 16th century and into the 17th century, as the demand for cheap labor increased, white settlers systematically invaded and terrorized Native American communities in search of slaves. As white indentured servitude tapered off and Native Americans suffered fatally from European diseases, colonial America relied heavily on the African slave trade to fill the gap. Thousands of Africans were taken from their homes and forced across the Atlantic in the dark holds of slave ships, a harrowing journey known as the **Middle Passage.** Once in the US, they were auctioned. This practice would last until 1807, when the slave trade was abolished. Slave ownership would continue until the late 19th century, forming one of the most brutal chapters in the country's short history.

Slavery exacerbated existing ideological differences between the North and the South. Because the federal government was designed to be relatively weak in order to prevent the "tyranny" of pre-Revolution days from reoccurring, each state could decide to allow or prohibit slavery independently. As the Northern states became more insistent that territories and new states should be kept free of slavery, the Southern states counteracted by citing the Revolutionary ideal of states' rights to self-determination. Northern abolitionists also joined with free African Americans to form the elusive **Underground Railroad,** an escape route in which "conductors" secretly transported slaves in covered wagons into the free northern states. Southerners who invaded the North to retrieve their "property" fueled existing tensions between these two separate halves of a nation split by socioeconomic differences. It would take a fierce and bloody conflict to decide which identity would prevail.

"A HOUSE DIVIDED": THE CIVIL WAR. Tensions between the North and South came to a head when an anti-slavery Senator and future national hero **Abraham Lincoln**, forever memorialized in the public consciousness as the President who saved the Union and abolished slavery, was elected President in 1860—the same year that South Carolina seceded from the Union. Lincoln refused to officially recognize the secession, though, and twelve states followed suit in 1861, with 1862 witnessing the birth of a united **Southern Confederacy** under the lead of Jefferson Davis. Most federal forts in the South were converted to Confederate control. On April 12, 1861, Southern troops fired at the fort, and the Civil War began. For four years the country endured a savage and bloody war, fought by the North to restore the Union and by the South to break it.

Lincoln led the North to victory, but the price was high. The war claimed more American lives than any other in history, and many families were divided against each other as brothers took up different uniforms and loyalties. Lincoln was assassinated on April 14, 1865, by a Southern sympathizer named John Wilkes Booth.

RECONSTRUCTION & INDUSTRIALIZATION. The period after the war brought Reconstruction to the South and Industrial Revolution to the North. The North's rapid industrialization rendered it a formidable contender in the world economy, while the South's agricultural economy began a slow decline. Injured and embittered by the war and dependent on an outdated agricultural tradition, Southerners struggled to readjust to the new economic and social situations forced upon them. The newly freed blacks faced a difficult transition from plantation to free life. **Jim Crow** laws continued to restrict blacks' freedom, while white politicians espousing the "separate but equal" doctrine prohibited blacks from frequenting the same establishments and schools as whites. Even drinking fountains were classified according to race. Though black colleges were founded and prominent blacks were able to gain some degree of political power, others were relegated to a life of share-cropping for white landowners.

During the North's **"Gilded Age"** of the 1870s, captains of industry such as Cornelius Vanderbilt, Andrew Carnegie, and John D. Rockefeller built commercial empires and enormous personal fortunes amid an atmosphere of widespread political and economic corruption. The burden of the concentration of massive wealth in a few hands landed most heavily on the powerless masses—on hapless farmers toiling in a dying agricultural economy and on workers facing low wages, violent strike break-ups, and unsafe working conditions. Yet the fruits of the industrial age, including railroads, telegraphs, and telephones, made transportation and communication across the vast nation easier.

IMPERIALISM & WWI. The racism expressed in Jim Crow laws and Native American genocide didn't end at domestic borders. The United States' victory in the **Spanish-American War** in 1898 validated America's sense of white superiority, and the belief that its influence could be extended worldwide. The United States caught imperial fever, acquiring colonies in the Philippines, Puerto Rico, and Cuba. Meanwhile, large industrial monopolies came under attack from the Progressive Party. A new breed of journalists, the "muckrakers," began exposing the corruption rampant in big business.

In 1901, at age 42, **Teddy Roosevelt** became the youngest president in history. In response to the corrupt, monopolistic practices of big business, Roosevelt promoted anti-trust reforms to regulate large companies. In foreign affairs, Roosevelt established the US as an international police power, and recommended that the nation "speak softly and carry a big stick."

After vowing to keep the US out of "Europe's War," President **Woodrow Wilson** reluctantly entered **World War I** in its closing stages. US troops landed in Europe in 1917 and fought until Germany's defeat the next year. Though the metal-consuming war jump-started America's industrial economy and established the United States as a major international power, the toll of the Great War—10 million people dead, including 130,174 Americans—disillusioned and shocked the nation.

ROARING 20S, GREAT DEPRESSION, & WWII. Americans returned their attentions to their own continent, bursting with money but ruffled by the winds of change. Labor unrest and racial tension were blamed on communist influences, and the US would experience increased paranoia of communism (a **"Red Scare"**) over the course of 1919. The same year, the perceived moral decline of America was addressed with the immensely unpopular **Prohibition**, which outlawed all alcohol. Among the younger generations, however, restrictive conventions were exuberantly tossed aside. In celebration of the free-wheelin', booze-smugglin' **"Jazz Age,"** women shucked their undergarments aside and bared their shoulders to dance the Charleston. Women **suffragists** also mobilized for the right to vote, which the 19th Amendment to the Constitution granted in 1920.

The **"Roaring 20s"** were largely supported by overextended credit. The facade crumbled on "Black Thursday," October 24, 1929, when the New York Stock Exchange crashed, launching the **Great Depression.** In an urbanized, mechanized age, millions of workers (25-50% of the work force) were left unemployed and struggled to provide food and housing for their families. The United States was unable to rebound from the Great Depression as it had from previous depressions. The Depression imprinted a generation of Americans with a compulsion to hoard, an appreciation of money, and a skepticism of the economy. Under the guidance of President **Franklin D. Roosevelt,** the US began a decade-long recovery.

As the German Nazi regime plowed through Europe, anxious Americans largely stood aside and watched, unaware of the Holocaust. The Japanese attack on Pearl Harbor, Hawaii on December 7, 1941, brought America reluctantly into **World War II.** The war existed on two fronts, as the Allied powers fought both the Germans in Europe and the Japanese in the Pacific. The European front was resolved with the German surrender on May 8, 1945. The war in the Pacific continued until August, when the US dropped two newly developed **nuclear bombs** on Japan, at Hiroshima on August 6, 1945, and at Nagasaki three days later, killing 80,000 civilians.

DUCK & COVER: THE COLD WAR. Spared the wartime devastation faced by Europe and East Asia, and empowered by nationalist pride, the US economy boomed in the post-war era and secured the nation's status as the world's dominant economic and military power. While the 1950s are often nostalgically recalled as a time of prosperity, traditional values, and contentedness, the decade certainly experienced its fair share of tumult and angst.

While Elvis Presley shook his hound dog and Americans sported Buddy Holly glasses, the ideological gulf between the two nuclear powers—the democratic, capitalist America and the totalitarian, communist Soviet Union—initiated a half-century of **Cold War** between the two nations. Tension with the Soviet Union heightened as President Harry Truman exaggerated the Soviet threat in order to gain support for his foreign policy of **Communist containment.** Amid the anti-Communist hysteria, **McCarthyism** took root. A powerful congressional committee, labeled the House Un-American Activities Committee and led by Senator Joseph McCarthy, conducted witch-hunts in every facet of American public life. Reaching from politics to the film industry, McCarthyism was a move to expose all communists, though most accusations were groundless.

Fear of communism gained a feverish intensity during the McCarthy era, and ultimately led to American military involvement in Asia, where communism was beginning to take hold. From 1950 to 1953, the United States fought the **Korean War** on behalf of the South Koreans, who had been attacked by the Communist North Korean government. The precedents set in Korea were carried over to the Vietnam conflict. The Soviet launch of Sputnik, the first artificial satellite, in 1957 rekindled fears that communism was getting ahead. The **Cuban Missile Crisis** in 1962, during which President John F. Kennedy narrowly negotiated the removal of Soviet missiles from a Cuban base, reinforced the notion that the United States must protect the world from Soviet invasion and nuclear assault.

In 1963, Lee Harvey Oswald assassinated **President Kennedy** during a campaign parade in Dallas, Texas (see p. 670). The assassination of the young, charismatic President seemed to mirror America's larger loss of innocence and optimism. Throughout the rest of the decade, cultural revolution refashioned the nation's social fabric with the long-fought Civil Rights movement and the turmoil of the bloody Vietnam War.

ALL YOU NEED IS LOVE...AND PROTEST. High on its role as global policemen staying the tide of communism, the United States became embroiled in Vietnamese politics, culminating in a large-scale deployment of combat troops in 1965 to protect the South Vietnamese government from Ho Chi Minh's socialist government to the north. The **Vietnam War** became a symbol for America's credibility as a protector of nations struggling with communism, making retreat difficult even when it became apparent that the situation in Vietnam was not clear-cut and that victory was unlikely. Though many Americans supported the war at first, opposition grew as it dragged on and its moral premises were questioned. The use of TV and photographic media to cover the war contributed to the harsh and hopeless vision of the situation in Vietnam. The mounting human costs of Vietnam—and growing suspicion of America's motives—catalyzed wrenching generational clashes reflected vividly in the stacks of burning draft cards and anti-war demonstrations on college campuses. The mantra "Make Love, Not War," shouted among long-haired, scantily-clad bodies rolling in the mud at the 1969 **Woodstock** music festival, came to symbolize the hippie generation.

The Vietnam War was not the only cause that captured the hearts and lungs of idealistic young Americans. Rosa Parks's refusal to give up a bus seat in Montgomery, Alabama, in 1955 contributed to the **Civil Rights movement,** a time of intense protests by African Americans and other supporters, who organized countless demonstrations, marches, and sit-ins in the heart of a defiant and often violent South. Activists were drenched with fire hoses, arrested, and even killed by local mobs and policemen. The movement peaked with the March on Washington in 1963, where **Dr. Martin Luther King, Jr.** delivered his famous "I Have A Dream" speech, calling for non-violent racial integration. The tone of the Civil Rights movement changed as blacks became fed up with peaceful moderation and turned to the more militant rhetoric of **Malcolm X,** a converted Black Muslim who espoused separatist "Black Power." The gun-toting Black Panthers resorted to terrorist tactics to assert the rights of African-Americans.

The second wave of the **women's movement** accompanied the Civil Rights movement. Sparked by Betty Friedan's landmark book *The Feminine Mystique,*

American women sought to change the delineation between men's and women's roles in society, and demanded access to male-dominated professions and equal pay. The sexual revolution, fueled by the introduction of the birth control pill, heightened debate over a woman's right to choose to have an abortion. The 1973 Supreme Court decision *Roe v. Wade* legalized abortion, but the battle between abortion opponents and pro-choice advocates still divides the nation today.

Despite a spate of Civil Rights legislation and anti-poverty measures passed under President Lyndon B. Johnson's **Great Society** agenda, the specter of the war overshadowed his presidency. By the end of these tumultuous years, the nation had dropped 7 million tons of bombs on Indochina—twice the amount used against America's World War II enemies—and victory was still unattainable. In 1972, as President Richard Nixon was attempting to "honorably" extricate the United States from Vietnam, five burglars were caught breaking into the Democratic National Convention Headquarters in the **Watergate** apartment complex. Their botched attempt to bug the Democratic offices eventually led to a broader scandal involving the President himself. Caught by his own audiotape, Nixon fought Congress but ultimately resigned from the Presidency.

By the mid-1970s, America was firmly disillusioned with the idealistic counter-culture of the previous decade. More frivolous forms of fun, such as dancing in platform shoes and powder blue suits under flashing colored lights—a phenomenon known as **"disco"**—became the mark of a generation that just wanted to have fun. Unfortunately, the international situation continued to be tenuous. The oil-rich Arab nations boycotted the US, causing an **energy crisis** that drove up gas prices, frustrated autophile Americans, and precipitated an economic recession. The oil crisis also forced the US to develop more energy-efficient technology, lending economic credibility to the environmentalist movement.

THE 1980S. In 1980, **Ronald Reagan,** a politically conservative actor and former California governor, was elected to the White House. Reagan knew how to give the people what they wanted: money. He cut government spending on public programs and lowered taxes. Though the decade's conservatives did embrace certain right-wing social goals like school prayer and the campaign against abortion, the Reagan revolution was essentially economic. **Reaganomics** handed tax breaks to big business, spurred short-term consumption, and deregulated savings and loans. Yet all was not well—whereas the US had been a creditor nation in 1980, the end of the decade saw the nation as the world's largest debtor.

On the foreign policy front, Reagan aggressively expanded the military budget and sent weapons and aid to right-wing "freedom fighters" in Guatemala, Nicaragua, and Afghanistan.

THE 1990S: "SLICK WILLY". The US remained an active police force in the world through the early 1990s, as President Bush instigated **"Operation Desert Storm"** in 1990 as a response to Iraq's invasion of neighboring Kuwait. The war freed Kuwait, but its popularity in the US was compromised by the recession that followed. The public replaced Bush in the 1992 Presidential election with the young, saxophone-tooting Democrat **Bill Clinton,** who promised a new era of government activism after years of laissez-faire rule.

Meanwhile, Clinton's young administration began to find itself plagued with its own problems: a suspicious Arkansas real estate development called **Whitewater,** an alleged extramarital affair with Gennifer Flowers, and accusations of sexual harassment from Paula Jones. Yet Clinton's public approval remained high, especially after the nation supported him in a struggle against the Congressional

Republicans whose attempts to balance the budget led to two government shutdowns between 1995 and 1996. Clinton was re-elected in 1996.

A new scandal erupted in 1998, as reports of an inappropriate relationship between Clinton and 24-year-old White House intern **Monica Lewinsky** were plastered across American newspapers, magazines, and television. Clinton initially denied the allegations, but he later admitted that he lied. Eventually, he was **impeached** for perjury and obstruction of justice on the recommendation of Independent Counsel Kenneth Starr. The resulting trial in the Senate ended with a vote for informal censure over conviction, and Clinton remained in office.

RECENT NEWS

SEPTEMBER 11, 2001. On September 11th, the most severe terrorist attack in US history occurred when four planes were hijacked. The site of the most violent crash was the World Trade Center in New York City, where almost a thousand lives were taken. Osama bin Laden and the Taliban, the Islamic ruling body of Afghanistan, were deemed responsible for the attacks. Since September 11th, President Bush has waged a "War on Terrorism" designed to identify and capture known terrorists, particularly those of Al-Qaeda, an international terrorist network. The "War on Terrorism" became controversial among the US public when President Bush instituted military tribunals and US Attorney General John Ashcroft threatened the civil liberties of "immigrants" and "non-citizens."

ECONOMIC RECESSION. The first months of the Bush administration witnessed a sharp decline in the stock market, ending six years of economic prosperity under Bill Clinton. Inflated technology stocks plummeted in value, causing the NASDAQ to fall. Further economic trouble came after September 11th when the travel industry saw a dramatic decrease in travelers resulting from fears of terrorism. In recent months, the US economy has shown signs of rebounding, but the possibility of a recession remains.

CATHOLIC CHURCH CONFESSIONS. Numerous accusations of clergy sexually abusing minors led to an investigation of the Catholic Church's policies toward sexually deviant members of the cloth. Studies suggested that the Catholic Church had a history of allowing clergy to remain in the priesthood even after they were known to be sexual offenders. This revelation has led to a review of church policy in dealing with cases of abuse.

CULTURE

FOOD

There is more to American food than McDonald's and KFC. Due to the geographic and ethnic diversity of the States, however, it is not easy to nail down exactly what American food is. The truth is that real American food is best found at the regional level, where agricultural production, immigration patterns, and local culture have resulted in food that goes beyond the fast food stereotype.

NORTHEAST. America's English settlers first landed in the Northeast, combining their staples of meats and vegetables with uniquely American foodstuffs such as turkey, maple syrup, clams, lobster, cranberries, and corn. The results yielded such treasures as Boston brown bread, Indian pudding, New England clam chowder, and Maine boiled lobster. The shellfish in the Northeast are second to none.

SOUTHEAST. Be prepared for some good ol' home cookin'. Fried chicken, biscuits, mashed potatoes, grits, and collard greens are some of the highlights of Southeastern cuisine. Virginia ham is widely renowned, and ham biscuits provide a savory supplement to lunch and dinner dishes.

LOUISIANA. Chefs in New Orleans are among the best in the country, and creole or Cajun cooking tantalizes the taste buds. Locals and tourists alike regard smothered crawfish, fried catfish, jambalaya (rice cooked with ham, sausage, shrimp, and herbs), and gumbo (a soup with okra, meat, and vegetables) as delicacies. The faint of taste buds beware: Cajun and creole cooking can fry the mouth.

TEXAS. From juicy tenderloins, to luscious baby back ribs, to whole pig roasts, Texans like to throw it on the grill. Eat at any of the many BBQ joints, though, and they'll tell you that the real secret's in the sauce. For those in the mood for something ethnic, enchiladas, burritos, and fajitas are scrumptious Tex-Mex options.

SOUTHWEST. Strongly influenced by Mexican cuisine, the Mexican foodstuffs of corn, flour, and chilies are the basic components of Southwestern grub. Salsa made from tomatoes, chilies, and *tomatillos* adds a spicy notes to nearly all dishes, especially cheese- and chicken-filled quesadillas and ground beef tacos.

CUSTOMS & ETIQUETTE

TABLE MANNERS. In the US, good table manners means quiet eating. Loud chewing, talking with food in your mouth, or slurping are seen as rude, and burping is not seen as complimentary to the chef. When eating in a restaurant, servers usually expect to be tipped 15%.

PUBLIC BEHAVIOR. Dress in the US tends to be more modest than in Europe. Toplessness, particularly in women, should be avoided. The most acceptable forms of public affection are hugging and holding hands. Kissing in public will usually draw a few glances. Although most cities are tolerant of homosexuality, gay or lesbian couples should be aware that they may receive unwanted attention for public displays of affection.

GESTURES. One of the most offensive gestures in the US is extending your middle finger at someone. Otherwise known as "giving someone the finger," this gesture is considered not only rude, but obscene. On the other hand, a "thumbs up" gesture is a sign of approval and a widely recognized signal for hitchhiking.

THE ARTS

While early US artistic endeavors owed much to age-old European traditions, it did not take long for hearty American individualism to make its mark on the global canon. From the 19th century Transcendentalist literature of New England to the unique musical stylings of bluegrass and jazz, America has established itself time and again as an innovator in the world of creative arts.

LITERATURE

THE FIRST FEW PAGES. The first best-seller printed in America, the *Bay Psalm Book*, was published in Cambridge, MA, in 1640. Reflecting the Puritanical culture of much of 17th- and 18th-century America, it was religious in nature. Very few enduring classics were created until the early 1800s, when artists began to explore the unique American experience in their writing. **James Fenimore Cooper**'s *Last of the Mohicans* (1826), **Nathaniel Hawthorne**'s *The Scarlet Letter* (1850), and **Herman Melville**'s *Moby Dick* (1851)—among the first great American novels—all feature strong yet innocent individualists negotiating the raw American landscape. By the mid-nineteenth century, the work of **New England Transcendentalists** like **Henry David Thoreau** (*Walden*) and **Ralph Waldo Emerson** embodied a spirit of anti-materialism by focusing on self-reflection and a retreat into nature. Meanwhile, **Mark Twain** became one of America's best-loved storytellers with his homespun tales out of Hannibal, Missouri. His *Adventures of Huckleberry Finn* (1885) uses a young boy's journey to express social criticism and a treatment of the human spirit.

Literature also provided 19th-century American women the opportunity both to express themselves and to comment critically on their society. In 1852, **Harriet Beecher Stowe** published *Uncle Tom's Cabin*, an exposé of slavery that, according to some scholars, may have contributed to the outbreak of the Civil War. Poet **Emily Dickinson** secretly scribbled away in her native Amherst, Massachusetts, home; her untitled, unpunctuated, and uncapitalized verses weren't discovered until after her death in 1886.

EARLY 20TH CENTURY EXPLORATIONS. The 1920s marked a time of economic prosperity, while a reflective, self-centered movement fermented in American literature. **F. Scott Fitzgerald**'s works (*The Great Gatsby*) portray restless individuals who are financially secure but unfulfilled by their conspicuous consumption. During this tumultuous time, many writers moved abroad in search of refuge; this **Lost Generation** included Fitzgerald, **Ernest Hemingway** (*The Sun Also Rises*), **T.S. Eliot** ("The Waste Land"), **Ezra Pound**, and **e.e. cummings**, whose sophisticated works conveyed the contemporary American experience. The **Harlem Renaissance**, a gathering of African-American artistic energy in New York City, fed off the excitement of the Jazz Age. **Langston Hughes, Nella Larsen,** and **Zora Neale Hurston** (*Their Eyes Were Watching God*) brought awareness of an African-American presence to a broad audience while revealing the depths of black creativity and intellectualism.

As America struggled to recover from the Great Depression, the plight of decaying agricultural life and faltering industry of the Deep South and West began to infiltrate literature. **William Faulkner** (*The Sound and the Fury*) juxtaposed avant-garde stream-of-consciousness techniques with subjects rooted in the rot and decay of the rural South. Nobel prize recipient **John Steinbeck** is known for his 1939 novel *The Grapes of Wrath*, an epic story about a family of laborers migrating from Oklahoma to California. The plays of **Tennessee Williams** (*A Streetcar Named Desire*) often portray family dynamics within lower-class, uprooted Southern families. In his remarkable autobiography, *Black Boy* (1945), **Richard Wright** recounts growing up black in the Jim Crow South.

POST-WAR MALAISE. In the conformist 1950s, literature provided alternative commentary on America's underlying social problems. **Ralph Ellison**'s *Invisible Man*, published in 1952, confronted a broad audience with the division between white and black identities in America. In 1955, **Vladimir Nabokov**, a Russian émigré, redefined English prose style for a whole generation of writers with his controversial story about unconventional love, *Lolita*. **Gwendolyn Brooks**, the first black writer to win a Pulitzer Prize, published intense poetry that highlighted social problems such as abortion, gangs, and drop-outs. The **Beats**, spearheaded by cult heroes **Jack Kerouac** (*On the Road*) and **Allen Ginsberg** ("Howl"), lived wildly and proposed a more free-wheeling attitude. Playwright **Arthur Miller** delved into the American psyche with *Death of a Salesman* (1949), in which he explored the frailty of the mythical American dream.

As the rules of established society began to crumble in the 1960s, writers began to explore more outrageous material. **Anne Sexton** uncovered the depths of her own mental breakdown, while **Sylvia Plath** paved the way for feminist authors; exposed her psychological deterioration and hinted at her suicide in *The Bell Jar* (1963). The essays and stories of **James Baldwin** (*The Fire Next Time*) warned both white and black Americans about the self-destructive implications of racial hatred. **Flannery O'Connor** exposed the eerie, grotesque underbelly of the contemporary South in her stories, such as "A Good Man is Hard to Find."

In more recent fiction, the search for identity and the attempt to reconcile artistic and social agendas has continued. **E.L. Doctorow**'s *Ragtime* (1975) evokes vibrant images of a turn-of-the-century America, weaving together historical and fictional figures. **Toni Morrison** (*Beloved*) won the Nobel Prize for her visceral interpretations of the tension between gender, ethnic, and cultural identities. **Don DeLillo**'s *White Noise* (1985) carries on the American absurdist tradition by heating up the tune of a chemical holocaust. Many stories have also focused on the fast pace and commercialism of modern society. In *Bright Lights Big City* (1987), **Jay McIntire** exposes the fast-living Wall Street of the 1980s, while the plays of **David Mamet** (*Glengarry Glen Ross*) are known for explosively confronting the gritty underside of American business.

REGIONAL READS

Many American writers have gained notoriety through their association with a particular region of the country. For those travelers seeking to add a literary component to their cross-country journey, *Let's Go* recommends the following regional picks:

New England: *The Scarlet Letter* (1850), by Nathaniel Hawthorne. The classic tale of sin and repression, set in colonial Massachusetts.

New York: *The Age of Innocence* (1920), by Edith Wharton. Set in the Golden Age of New York City, this novel explores the power of desire within the rigorously structured world of high society.

The South: *As I Lay Dying* (1930), by William Faulkner. Describes the odyssey of a Southern family across the landscape of rural Mississippi.

Texas: *Lonesome Dove* (1985), by Larry McMurtry. This epic novel presents a fresh and innovative take on the mythical Texas.

The Midwest: *Winesburg, Ohio* (1919), by Sherwood Anderson. A collection of short stories exploring the colorful lives of inhabitants of small town mid-America.

The Plains: *O Pioneers!* (1913), by Willa Cather. The story of one woman's grit and determination, set against the backdrop of the Nebraska farmlands.

The Rockies: *The Virginian* (1925), by Owen Wister. The Western novel *par excellence*, this cowboy classic set the stage for an entire genre of writing.

The Southwest: *All the Pretty Horses* (1992), by Cormac McCarthy. This rich, elegant novel spins a tale of adventure and romance on both sides of the Mexican border.

California: *East of Eden* (1952), by John Steinbeck. A modern interpretation of the classic struggle between good and evil, this novel—set mainly in rural California—follows the story of two sets of brothers.

The Pacific Northwest: *Snow Falling on Cedars* (1994), by David Guterson. Set on an isolated island in Washington state, this novel explores the tragic legacy of the WWII Asian-American internment camps.

MUSIC

The United States has given birth to a plethora of musical genres and artists, whose styles and songs have intermingled to produce the many distinct styles that can be heard today. **Scott Joplin** meshed African-American harmony and rhythm with classical European style to develop the first American piano form, ragtime. From this rich, upbeat, piano-banging dance music of the 19th century to the Deep South's tradition of mournful blues, early African-American music defined soul. As soul and gospel music evolved into rhythm and blues, jazz, and funk, American music came to reflect the legacy of a resilient African-American voice.

SINGIN' THE BLUES. The blues can be described as the epitome of soul music. Like ragtime, black Southerners were primarily responsible for the blues, which was originally a blend of Northwest African slave calls and Native American song and verse forms. Blues songs were popularized by **W.C. Handy;** his "St. Louis Blues" remains one of the most recorded songs ever. As Southern blacks migrated during the early 20th century, the blues found an audience in the North, as the contributions of women like **Mamie Smith, Billie Holiday,** and **Bessie Smith** were substantial in bringing the flattened, minor chords of the blues into the American consciousness. The blues heavily influenced the development of other popular American musical styles, most notably jazz and rock 'n' roll.

AND ALL THAT JAZZ. Ragtime, blues, and military brass combined in New Orleans in the early 20th century to create America's classical music, jazz. Jazz's emphasis on improvisation and unique tonal and harmonic rules distinguished it from all other previous genres. The work of all-time jazz greats like **Louis Armstrong** and **Ella Fitzgerald** influenced the later work of classical composers; **Leonard Bernstein**'s classical orchestrations and **George Gershwin**'s jazzy theatrical style both evoke strong images of poetic Americana. Early jazz also expanded into big band music, of which the incomparable **Duke Ellington** and the swing orchestra of **Glenn Miller** reigned supreme.

O, BROTHER. Country music has its roots in the Appalachian Mountains, among a poor rural white population that was putting a new spin on ancestral European folk traditions. Sentimental, often spiritual lyrics were placed to simple melodies to create a characteristically honest American sound. The genre owes much of its attitude and sound to classic heroes: **Hank Williams** cultivated an air of tragic, honky-tonk mystique, while **Johnny Cash** left his mark with a brazen, devil-may-care honesty. Commercially, country didn't catch on until it was given a boost by radio, and Nashville's famous 1930s program the **Grand Ole Opry.** Today, country artists like **Tim McGraw** and **Martina McBride** have captured both Southern and Northern audiences; roadtrippers should be aware that country music now dominates the radio waves across the country.

Another similar genre carrying on a distinctly American style is folk. Folk music has often embraced political and social activism through its direct lyrics and honest spirit. **Woody Guthrie**'s diverse music touched upon issues of patriotism in the midst of the Great Depression ("This Land is Your Land") as well as commenting on union labor organization issues. Thanks to artists like **Bob Dylan** and **Joan Baez,** folk music popularly caught on in the sixties and spoke to social protesters across the nation. The **Grateful Dead** also grew out of the sixties; more than just a band, they were an entire lifestyle that celebrated drugs and counterculture. Folk still survives today in coffee shops and on street corners, as folk musicians remain some of the most lucid social commentators.

PUT ANOTHER DIME IN THE JUKEBOX, BABY. No one can say exactly how rock 'n' roll was started, although it originally grew out of African-American traditions of gospel and rhythm and blues. One thing is for certain, though: **Elvis Presley** was the first to be crowned "King." His rock kingdom of **Graceland** is a popular attraction for Memphis tourists (see page Graceland, p. 375). During the fifties and sixties, rock 'n' roll's driving, danceable rhythms, rebellious attitude, and fascination with electric instruments would dominate the popular music charts. Rock 'n' roll reflected the new post-World War II optimism and innocence throughout America, as teenagers looked for something more exciting and daring to express their style. The genre has produced most of America's more famous music icons—before Elvis, there was **Chuck Berry** and **Jerry Lee Lewis**, who ushered in a new era of poodle skirts and slicked-back hair. Today, the general category of "rock" could be divided chronologically into oldies (the **Beach Boys, Buddy Holly**), classic rock (**Bruce Springsteen, Pink Floyd**), and modern rock.

The 1970s will be forever remembered for being the era of disco. Disco divas like **Gloria Gaynor** ("I Will Survive") and funk bands like those of **George Clinton** dominated the American nightlife and fostered a culture that celebrated dancing, drugs, and excess. Spawned by East Coast stars **Public Enemy** and the **Beastie Boys,** the eighties witnessed a rap revolution which is still going strong today through the efforts of bad boy **Eminem**. The 1980s also ushered in the popularity of "hair bands" like **Poison** and punk rockers like **The Ramones,** not to mention a little entertainer named **Madonna.** In the early nineties, grunge music made a short appearance largely because of Seattle's **Nirvana** and **Pearl Jam,** while hip-hop acts like the late **Notorious B.I.G.** infiltrated styles around the world. The West Coast birthed the "gangsta rap" movement (**Dr. Dre, Snoop Doggy Dogg**) in the nineties as well, which has sparked much debate over the heavy espousal of violence and excessive misogyny in the lyrics.

DIRTY POP. The late 1990s and new millennium have been dominated by a resurgence of bubblegum pop and dance tunes. The new MTV generation of consumer teens has sustained the popularity of young singers like **Britney Spears** and boy bands such as ***N-Sync.** Although many criticize the genre for being full of copycat songs with essentially the same musical structure and dance beat, legions of screaming fans, weaned on the energetically choreographed music videos of current superstars, don't seem to mind.

FILM

SILENT FILMS & PRE-CODE TALKIES. Before sound was wedded to image in the first "talkie"—*The Jazz Singer*, 1927—silent films ruled the screen. Though silent films quickly went out of fashion once sound entered the picture, they still hold a place of prominence in film history and the hearts of film buffs. **Hollywood,** California, owing to its sunny, film-friendly climate, proximity to a variety of photogenic terrain, and previous prominence as a theater center, quickly became the center of the movie business. By the period just after World War I, actors like Charlie Chaplin, Buster Keaton, and Mary Pickford were household names. Free from the control of domineering studios, these film artists brought a playful, exuberant, and innovative attitude to their work. Films such as *Sunrise* and *The Crowd*, meanwhile, combined innovative cinematography and compelling stories that remain vibrant to this day.

Between 1930 and 1934 American cinema enjoyed a rollicking, saucy period of artistic freedom that came to be known as Pre-Code Hollywood. Movies from this period bristled with robust doses of sex, violence, and brash humour. Films such as *Freaks*, *Morocco*, and *Scarface* took advantage of the free-spirited times and portrayed aspects of life that would soon be ignored when pressure to clean up the screen brought about the enforcement of the moral Production code in 1934.

CLASSIC ERA. It was not long, however, before the wild success of the movies gave rise to expansion of the **studio system**. Giant production houses like Paramount, MGM, and Warner took up residence on the West Coast and turned movies into big business. American film's **golden age** took place during the height of the studio era, fueled by those who transcended the studio system's confines. Victor Fleming's *Gone with the Wind* (1939), a Civil War epic, was the first large-scale movie extravaganza, redefining the bounds of cinematic scope. Frank Capra, in his surprisingly probing morality plays like *It's a Wonderful Life* (1946) and *Mr. Smith Goes to Washington* (1939), brought a conscience to entertainment. Michael Curtiz's *Casablanca* (1942), starring the moody Humphrey Bogart, fine-tuned the art of creating cinematic romance. In 1941, Orson Welles unveiled his intricate masterpiece, *Citizen Kane*, a landmark work whose innovations expanded contemporary ideas about the potential of film. Fantasy, however, still sold tickets: Walt Disney's animated *Snow White* (1937) and Fleming's *The Wizard of Oz* (1939) kept producers well-fed.

PRETTY BOYS, MONSTERS, & BOMBSHELLS. Heightened tensions with the Soviet Union and conflicts against communism abroad led to widespread communist witch-hunts at home. The film industry, under government pressure, took up the policy of **blacklisting** any artists with suspected ties to communism (or even leftism). The result of constant paranoia and dwindling box office returns—due to competition with television—resulted in a slew of films that were sensational enough to draw crowds away from their television. Films such as *Invasion of the Body Snatchers* and *The Incredible Shrinking Man* used the genre of **science fiction** to grapple with cultural anxieties about communism and nuclear weapons while larger than life **westerns** such as *Giant* and *The Searchers* galloped across the screens. Meanwhile, master of suspense Alfred Hitchcock (*Strangers on a Train*) and the ever-free-thinking Orson Welles (*The Lady from Shanghai*) threw an element of suspense into the mix.

The 1950s also saw the emergence of a cult of **glamour** surrounding the most luminous stars. Cloaked in glitz and scandal, sex symbols Marilyn Monroe, James Dean (*Rebel Without a Cause*), Elizabeth Taylor, and Rock Hudson drew audiences to movies by name recognition alone. Along with actors Marlon Brando (*A Streetcar Named Desire*) and Audrey Hepburn (*Breakfast at Tiffany's*), these stars brought their own personal mystique to the screen, while adding much to the art of cinematic performance.

SOCK IT TO ME. The 1960s and early 1970s saw widespread **social upheaval** and tension between generations. The studio system proved entirely incapable of responding to the demands of the young, more liberal-thinking audiences. Rethinking their battle plans, many studios enlisted directors influenced by the French New Wave as well as artists from other media to direct features, including Sidney Lumet, John Frankenheimer, and Robert Altman. With the studios more willing to take a gamble, and the introduction of a movie ratings board (MPAA) to replace censorship, the work of a number of **innovative filmmakers** began to enter the mainstream. Stanley Kubrick, in *Dr. Strangelove* (1964), *2001: A Space Odyssey* (1968), and *A Clockwork Orange* (1971), brought a literary importance to filmmaking. Dennis Hopper's *Easy Rider* (1969), a film about countercultural youth rebellion, and the acclaimed documentary *Woodstock* (1970) opened the door to social critique. Meanwhile, during the first half of the 1970's the short-lived genre of **blaxploitation**—sensationalized portrayals of urban African-American lifestyles—enjoyed its time in the limelight with films such as *Shaft*, and *Superfly*.

Throughout the 1970s, experimentalism largely gave way to more polished treatment of equally serious issues. Film-schooled directors like Martin Scorsese (*Taxi Driver*), Francis Ford Coppola (*The Godfather*), and Michael Cimino (*The Deer Hunter*) brought technical skill to their exploration of the darker side of humanity. An influx of foreign filmmakers, like Milos Forman (*One Flew Over the Cuckoo's Nest*) and Roman Polanski (*Chinatown*), introduced a new perspective to American film.

TAKING CARE OF BUSINESS. Driven by the global mass distribution of American cinema and the development of high-tech special effects, the late 1970s and 1980s witnessed the revitalization of the **blockbuster.** Directors like George Lucas with the *Star Wars* trilogy, and Steven Spielberg with *E.T.* (1982) and *Raiders of the Lost Ark* (1981), created enormously successful movies whose success spanned the globe. Though such films were often criticized for their over-reliance on special effects and lack of story line, they almost single-handedly returned Hollywood to its former status as king.

Despite the profit-orientation of Hollywood, quite a bit of highly imaginative work came out of the period, including *Rain Man*, a thoughtful critique of 1980s materialism and self-absorption, as well as David Lynch's *Blue Velvet*, a disturbing exploration of the primal terror beneath the tranquil surface of suburbia.

INDIE FEVER. The revival of the blockbuster continued strong into the 1990s, with such high-budget money makers as the dinosaur extravaganza *Jurassic Park* and the decadent marine love-story *Titanic* drawing the largest crowds.

Yet the recognition of independent, or **indie,** films—films that are either produced independently of any major studio or at least do not follow standard studio conventions—marks the most interesting turn for cinema in the last several years. Brothers Joel and Ethan Coen have created some of the most creative and original work of late, including the gruesome comedy *Fargo* and the hilarious, off-beat *The Big Lebowski*. Quentin Tarantino's cool yet hyper-charged action (*Reservoir Dogs, Pulp Fiction*), Steven Soderbergh's vibrant visual style (*Traffic*), and Wes Anderson's darkly quirky humor (*Rushmore, The Royal Tenenbaums*) have all injected new life into American cinema.

FINE ARTS

American art has often been glossed over as a pale reflection of European trends. Despite this stereotype, American art has a rich history rooted in the country's expansion from colonial America to the present day. Its raw and uncontrolled nature is reflected not only in the grandiose 19th-century landscape paintings that sought to capture the beauty of the untamed West, but also in the unwieldy lines and shapes of American 20th-century **abstract expressionism**.

Colonial America produced art in two main genres—portraiture and landscape painting. Early American artists, like George Fuller and Winslow Homer, captured intimate portraits, sweeping seaside scenes, and Civil War farmscapes. Emerging from these narrow genres was the surrealist work of painters like Georgia O'Keefe. By the 1940s, abstract expressionism, originating in Europe, had been reborn in the US. Country-wide anxiety over international unrest and the threat of war bore heavily on the American psyche. In drip paintings and figurative images, painters like Jackson Pollock and Mark Rothko reflected the ironic mix of swaggering confidence and frenetic insecurity that characterized Cold War America.

Ushering in the age of **pop art**, Andy Warhol used graphic, cartoonish images to satirize the icons of American popular culture. Warhol mass-produced loud, colorful images of American cultural icons. The 1980s art boom, stationed around private galleries in New York City and L.A., ushered in a decade of slick, idyllic paintings.

PHOTOGRAPHY. Beginning in the early 20th century, photography became the medium of choice for artists with a social conscience. American photographers captured everything from the urban poor to destitute farmers to crisp landscapes. In the 1970s, photography came into its own as the back-to-basics 35mm photographs pushed the boundaries of defined art. Eventually a backlash against 1980s materialism led artists to produce ultra-realistic, bare-all photographs of the harshness in human life.

ARCHITECTURE & PUBLIC ART. American architecture of earlier days may have scraped together the leftovers of passé European styles, but the 20th-century architect **Frank Lloyd Wright** gave America its own architectural mode. His works, including the Fallingwater house in Pennsylvania (see p. 287) and the Robie House in Chicago (see p. 565), demonstrate an angular aesthetic and attention to environmental cohesiveness. Contemporary architects like Frank Gehry have moved the craft of architecture into the 21st century with feats of seemingly impossible engineering and optical effects.

In most American cities, public art has an established role. Not only do sculptures and installations adorn city parks and the lobbies of public buildings, but experiential walk-through environments like Maya Ying Lin's Vietnam Veterans Memorial in Washington, D.C. (see p. 313) are often commissioned in large cities.

THE MEDIA

America is wired. Images, sounds, and stories from the television, radio, Internet, and magazines infiltrate every aspect of the American lifestyle. Fads have been popularized and fortunes have been made thanks solely to the power of mass media, but because of this intense power, constant debate rages over who should be held responsible for content. Despite controversy about policing the industry, American consumption of new media is continually growing.

TELEVISION. Television sets are found in 99% of US homes. Competition between the six national **networks** (ABC, CBS, NBC, Fox, UPN, and WB), cable television, and satellite TV has triggered exponential growth in TV culture over the past few years. Some of the most popular shows airing during prime time (8-11pm EST) include the political drama *The West Wing* (NBC), the hip comedy *Will and Grace* (NBC), the dysfunctional family of *Malcolm in the Middle* (Fox), and the bitingly witty cartoon *The Simpsons* (Fox). One need not be bound to the networks, however, as **cable** provides special-interest channels that cover every subject from cooking to sports to science fiction. Meanwhile, **premium stations** air recently released movies along with regular programming; one favorite is HBO, which boasts the bawdy, cosmopolitan *Sex and the City* and the mobster drama *The Sopranos*. Travelers will find that some hotel rooms come equipped with basic cable, while others offer premium stations or even pay-per-view channels.

Although **reality television** surged in popularity a few years ago, many network programs have suffered from the effects of an over-saturated market in 2002, and even the granddaddy of them all, *Survivor* (CBS), has dropped in popularity. Still, cable station MTV seems to have gotten it right, as teenagers and young adults spend hours glued to reality programs *The Real World* and *The Osbournes*. Special comedy programs also dominate much of TV-land. Americans and Canadians alike have contributed to the successes of the long-running *Saturday Night Live* (NBC), while late-night television is sustained by the comic stylings of talk-show hosts like David Letterman on *The Late Show* (CBS). Daytime programming is less-watched and less-respected but still fills the hours with tawdry soap operas and frequently trashy talk shows.

Television is the point of entry to **world wide news** for most Americans. Twenty-four hour news coverage is available on CNN and MSNBC, both cable stations. Each network presents local and national nightly news (usually at 5 and/or 11pm EST), while prime-time "newsmagazines" like *60 Minutes* (CBS), *Dateline* (NBC), and *20/20* (ABC) specialize in investigative reports and exposés.

The Public Broadcasting Station (PBS) is commercial-free, funded by viewer contributions, the federal government, and corporate grants. Its repertoire includes educational children's shows like *Sesame Street* and *Mister Roger's Neighborhood*, nature programs, mystery shows, and British comedies.

PRINT. Despite the onset of more sophisticated technologies like TV and the Internet, Americans still cherish the feel of glossy pages and the smell of newsprint. Today, newsstands crowd city corners and transportation terminals throughout the country. Publications cover all areas of society, culture, and politics; whether it's for lounging away a Sunday afternoon at home or passing time in a doctor's waiting room, print media dominate the market.

Some of the most well-respected daily newspapers include *The New York Times* and *The Washington Post*, although every city has at least one major paper. Another popular rag, *USA Today*, is a more informal daily. Fashion magazines such as *Cosmopolitan* and men's magazines like *Maxim* feature articles and photos about sex and fashion, while *The New Yorker* amuses its pretentious subscribers with short stories and essays. Entertainment magazines such as *People* chronicle American gossip, while *Rolling Stone* focuses on the music industry. Those interested in the ups and downs of the stock market swear by the *Wall Street Journal* and *Forbes*; those who prefer statistics about their favorite sports franchise surf the pages of *Sports Illustrated*. Ranging from trashy tabloids like the *National Enquirer* to the most influential and respected news organs, American media is notably diverse but also subject to criticism for being exploitative and sensational. Despite this, many Americans consume and trust their news sources with a blind and undying faith.

RADIO. Before television transformed American culture, the radio was the country's primary source of entertainment and news. Classic comedy programs like *The Jack Benny Show* and the crackly sounding news coverage of Edward R. Murrow amused and informed Americans for decades. Even though the moving images and crisper sounds of television have reduced radio's earlier, widespread popularity, it remains a treasured medium. Radio is generally divided into AM and FM; talk radio comprises most of the low-frequency AM slots, and the high-powered FM stations feature most of the music. Each broadcaster owns a four-letter call-name, with "W" as the first letter for those east of the Mississippi River (as in WJMN), and "K" to the west (as in KPFA).

Radio is on everyone's wavelength. The more intellectually minded listen to **National Public Radio (NPR).** Full of classical music and social pundits debating important issues, the station gives even *Car Talk*, a show about car repair, an academic flair. Supplying the country's regional needs, local area channels give up-to-the-minute news reports and air a wide range of music, from country western to the latest pop. College radio stations often play more alternative styles of music to appeal to younger listeners.

LIFE & TIMES

SPORTS & RECREATION

For Americans, sports are inseparable from commercialism and regional allegiances. Dressed in colorful uniforms and covered with face-paint, Americans fill stadiums or lounge at home to cheer on their local teams.

BASEBALL. The slow, tension-building game of baseball captures the hearts of dreaming Little League children and earns its place as America's national pastime. Baseball in the US and Canada centers on the **Major League Baseball (MLB)** season. With teams in most major cities, the MLB baseball season ends with the **World Series,** a seven game series between the leagues' two best teams.

(AMERICAN) FOOTBALL. Nowhere is the commercialism of American sports more spectacularly displayed than in the **Super Bowl.** Every January, the **National Football League (NFL)** season ends in grandiose style with a championship featuring the league's two best teams and commercial campaigns costing millions of dollars. The American-rules game is especially dear to middle America, where the padded warriors of the gridiron are applauded for their brute athleticism.

BASKETBALL. Professional basketball teams hail from almost every major city, making up the **National Basketball Association (NBA).** NBA players have come a long way since the first teams were playing with peach baskets and Converse All-Star sneakers. Today, professional basketball games are fast-paced, aerial shows. Enthusiasm for college hoops, however, often surpasses that for the pros. Sticking with their school allegiances, many Americans are known to live and die by—and bet large amounts of money on—their college's basketball team in the NCAA tournament, fondly called **March Madness.**

ICE HOCKEY. Though not as popular as other sports in the US, hockey is somewhat a national religion for Canadians. The **National Hockey League (NHL),** comprised of both American and Canadian teams, features great ice hockey and some of the best fights in professional sports. As NHL teams vie for the **Stanley Cup,** the tension of competition often results in crowd-pleasing team brawls.

OTHER SPORTS. Other sports claim smaller niches of the American spectatorship. Both golf and tennis have internationally publicized tournaments known as the **US Open.** The horse racing of the **Kentucky Derby** hones the betting strategies of seasoned gamblers and tries the tolerance of seasoned boozers. **NASCAR auto racing** draws droves of fans to Daytona Beach, Florida in February with the Daytona 500. Here, the cars tear around a banked track hundreds of times, while wide-eyed and open-mouthed fans throw down countless beers and hot dogs. **Major League Soccer (MLS)** and women's basketball **(WNBA)** are both up-and-coming but not yet widely followed sports.

HOLIDAYS & FESTIVALS

USA: NATIONAL HOLIDAYS	
DATE IN 2003	**HOLIDAY**
January 1	New Year's Day
January 20	Martin Luther King, Jr. Day
February 17	Presidents Day
May 26	Memorial Day
July 4	Independence Day
September 1	Labor Day
October 13	Columbus Day
November 11	Veterans Day
November 27	Thanksgiving
December 25	Christmas Day

CANADA: NATIONAL HOLIDAYS	
DATE IN 2003	**HOLIDAY**
January 1	New Year's Day
April 20	Easter Sunday
April 21	Easter Monday
May 19	Victoria Day
July 1	Canada Day
September 1	Labour Day
October 13	Thanksgiving
November 11	Remembrance Day
December 25	Christmas Day
December 26	Boxing Day

FESTIVALS 2003

From music to magic, culture to kitsch, the USA and Canada are home to a remarkably varied selection of festivals. Some of the most popular American and Canadian festivals are listed below, along with the page numbers of their respective descriptions in the guide. This list is far from exhaustive; refer to the Sights and Entertainment sections of specific cities for more festivals.

USA	
MONTH	**FESTIVAL**
January	**Western Stock Show, Rodeo, and Horse Show,** Denver, CO (p. 744)
	Winter Carnival, St. Paul, MN (p. 596)
February	**Mardi Gras,** New Orleans, LA (p. 439)
	Oregon Shakespeare Festival, (through October) Ashland, OR (p. 987)
March	**South by Southwest,** Austin, TX (p. 670)
	Rattlesnake Round-up, Sweetwater, TX (p. 677)
	Gasparilla Pirate Festival, (Tampa, FL (p. 507)
April	**New Orleans Jazz and Heritage Festival,** New Orleans, LA (p. 439)
	Fiesta San Antonio, San Antonio, TX (p. 686)
May	**Memphis in May International Festival,** Memphis, TN (p. 372)
	Spoleto Festival USA, Charleston, SC (p. 391)
June	**Portland Rose Festival,** Portland, OR (p. 979)
	Chicago Blues Festival, Chicago, IL (p. 553)
	Summerfest, Milwaukee, WI (p. 578)
	Aspen Music Festival, (through August), Aspen, CO (p. 756)
	Tanglewood, Lenox, MA (p. 136)
July	**Frontier Days,** Cheyenne, WY (p. 736)
	Aquatennial, Minneapolis, MN (p. 596)
August	**Newport Folk Festival and JVC Jazz Festival,** Newport, RI (p. 140)
	Elvis Week, Memphis, TN (p. 376)
September	**La Fiesta de Santa Fe,** Santa Fe, NM (p. 831)
October	**Hot Air Balloon Festival,** Albuquerque, NM (p. 839)
November	**Macy's Thanksgiving Day Parade,** New York, NY (p. 220)
CANADA	
MONTH	**FESTIVAL**
January	**Annual Polar Bear Swim,** Vancouver, BC (p. 993)
February	**Winterlude,** Ottawa, ON (p. 196)
	Winter Carnival, Québec City, QC (p. 178)
May	**Stratford Shakespeare Festival** (through Nov.), Stratford, ON (p. 196)
	Canadian Tulip Festival, Ottawa, ON (p. 196)
July	**Nova Scotia International Tattoo Festival,** Halifax, NS (p. 150)
	International Jazz Festival, Montréal, QC (p. 166)
August	**Canadian National Exhibition,** Toronto, ON (p. 194)

LIFE & TIMES

ADDITIONAL RESOURCES

GENERAL HISTORY

Gail Bederman, *Manliness and Civilization*. A cultural history of gender and race in America from 1880 to 1917, this book investigates the way ideas of manhood changed at the turn of the century by focusing on the lives of Theodore Roosevelt, educator G. Stanley Hall, Ida B. Wells, and Charlotte Perkins Gilman.

James W. Loewen, *Lies My Teacher Told Me*. This work, subtitled "Everything Your American History Textbook Got Wrong," exposes misrepresentations and misinterpretations of common historical accounts, attempting to correct fallacies and provide more thorough context for well-known facts.

Richard Slotkin, *Fatal Environment*. This work discusses the significance of the West in American culture, focusing on ways in which the challenges presented by the ever-advancing American frontier permanently shaped American culture.

Howard Zinn, *A People's History of the United States*. With a broad scope spanning from Columbus's first steps in the New World to the first term of President Clinton, Zinn's massive book focuses on previously ignored figures, giving a voice to marginalized Americans and providing a new perspective to major historical events.

DOCUMENTARIES

Eyes on the Prize. Henry Hampton. A stunning, heart-wrenching film on the American Civil Rights movement. 1987.

The Civil War. Ken Burns. A gripping series on the American Civil War. 1990.

Paris is Burning. Jennie Livingston. A look into the lives of a community of NYC drag queens in the 1980s who wrestle with class, gender, and sexual identities as they compete on the ball scene. 1990.

The Atomic Cafe. A playful, quirky, and intelligent look at 1960s footage on how to survive a nuclear attack, and how radiation effects people and the environment. 1982.

Harlan County, USA. Barbara Kopple. Delves into the struggles of a Kentucky miner's strike. 1976.

The History of Rock 'n' Roll. A ten-part series on rock 'n' roll with amazing interviews with many of the genres superstars. 1995.

CANADA

Geographically speaking, Canada is the second largest country in the world, sprawling over almost 10 million square kilometers (3.85 million sq. mi.). Still, just over 30 million people—roughly the population of California—inhabit Canada's ten provinces and three territories. Well over half the population crowds into the southern provinces of Ontario and Québec, while the newly declared territory, Nunavut, has under 30,000 people. Framed by the Atlantic to the east and the Pacific to the west, Canada extends from fertile southern farmlands to frozen northern tundra. The early French and English colonists were both geographically and culturally distant from one another. To this day, **anglophones** and **francophones** fight to retain political dominance in the Canadian government. The concerns of the First Nation peoples and an increasing immigrant population have also become intertwined in the struggle.

O CANADA! A BRIEF HISTORY

Although archaeologists are uncertain about the exact timing, recent data indicates that the **first Canadians** arrived at least 10,000 years ago by crossing the Asian-Alaskan land bridge. Their descendents flooded the continent, fragmenting into disparate tribes. The first **Europeans** known to explore the area were the Norse, who settled in northern Newfoundland around the year 1000. England came next; John Cabot sighted Newfoundland in 1497. When Jacques Cartier, landing on the gulf of the St. Lawrence River, claimed the mainland for the French crown in 1534, he touched off a rivalry that persisted until Britain's 1759 capture of Québec in the Seven Years' War and France's total capitulation four years later.

During the Revolutionary War, when the thirteen colonies on the American seaboard opted for independence and revolted from Britain, the Canadian settlements—upper and lower Canada (modern Quebec and Ontario) and the maritimes (Newfoundland, Nova Scotia, New Brunswick and Prince Edward Island)—remained loyal to the crown. Their populations boomed as thousands of Empire Loyalists fled the newly-formed United States to remain within the British Empire. The English-speaking colonies of North America were thus split in two, with the North remaining loyal to Britain and the thirteen colonies federating independently. In early America, there was hope that the breach could be repaired and that the Canadian colonies could be induced to enter the Union. The federalist papers included articles arguing for the unconditional right of statehood to any British North American colony willing to enter the Union. During the War of 1812, Thomas Jefferson anticipated the wholehearted entry of the Canadians—English and French—into the ranks of the US. Tensions between the US and the British North American colonies continued right up until the Civil War, which diverted American interest permanently from the North.

The movement to unify the British North American colonies gathered speed after the American Civil War, when US military might and economic isolationism threatened the independent and continued existence of the British colonies. On March 29, 1867, Queen Victoria signed the **British North America Act** (BNA), uniting Nova Scotia, New Brunswick, Upper Canada, and Lower Canada (now Ontario and Québec). Though still a dominion of the British throne, Canada at last had its country—and its day: the BNA was proclaimed on July 1, Canada Day.

Since that time, Canada has expanded both territorially and economically. The years following consolidation witnessed sustained economic growth and expansion. Westward travelers, often trekking toward the Pacific in search of gold, were greatly aided by the completion of a trans-continental railway in 1885. During this period, Canada grew to encompass most of the land it covers today. Participation in World War I earned the Dominion international respect and a charter membership in the League of Nations. It joined the United Nations in 1945 and was a founding member of the **North Atlantic Treaty Organization** in 1949. The Liberal government of the following decade created a national social security system and a national health insurance program. Pierre Trudeau's government repatriated Canada's constitution in 1981, freeing the nation from Britain in constitutional legality (though Elizabeth II remains nominal head of state). Free to forge its own alliances, the country signed the controversial **North American Free Trade Agreement** (NAFTA) in 1992 under the leadership of Conservative Brian Mulroney.

In recent years, Canada has faced internal political tensions as well as an ever-increasing pressure to Americanize. Mulroney strove hard to mold a strong, unified Canada, but he will probably go down in Canadian history as the leader who nearly tore the nation apart in an effort to bring it together. His numerous attempts to negotiate a constitution that all ten provinces would ratify (Canada's present constitution lacks Québec's support) consistently failed, fanning the flames of century-old regional tensions and leading ultimately to the end of his government.

The **québécois separatist movement** has a long and not entirely pleasant history. Though francophone nationalism has roots as far back as the colonial period, the separatist impulse truly took hold in 1960, when nationalist Liberals took power in Québec. In 1970, after a decade of bombings and robberies, the Front de Liberation du Québec kidnapped two Canadian officials, killing one. The crisis, which prompted Trudeau to declare a brief period of martial law, brought the issue of Québec's separation to a head. Support for the newly formed Parti Québécois was not universal, however, and a 1980 referendum saw 60% of *québécois* opposed to separation from the Dominion. In a more recent (1996) referendum, however, separation was rejected by a mere 1.2% margin. The struggle for an independent Québec thus continues in both the cultural and parliamentary arenas.

Canada has also locked horns with its **aboriginal peoples,** know as the First Nations. The Inuit and other peoples in the Northwest Territories have struggled for more political representation and have been largely successful: the 1999 creation of Nunavut represented a huge gain for First Nations in the north. The newly formed territory covers approximately 2 million sq. km (770,000 sq. mi.). About 85% of the region's 26,000 inhabitants are Inuit. While Nunavut's government mirrors that of the other provinces and territories, the new territory's political system is greatly influenced by Inuit customs and beliefs.

In addition to fretting over the independence wishes of their numerous constituents, Canadian policy-makers continue to struggle for Canada's **cultural independence** from the US. Media domination by their southern neighbor has put a bit of a strain on Canadian pride, so much so that Canada's radio stations are required by law to play 30% Canadian music.

CANUCK CULTURE

Canada has two official languages, English and French. The *québécois* pronunciation of French can be perplexing to European speakers, and the protocol is less formal. There are also numerous native languages. Inuktitut, the Inuit language, is widely spoken in Nunavut and the Northwest Territories.

Most noted **Canadian literature** is post-1867. The opening of the Northwest and the Klondike Gold Rush (1898) provided fodder for the adventure tale—Jack London (*The Call of the Wild, White Fang*) and Robert Service (*Songs of a Sourdough, The Trail of '98*) both authored stories of prospectors and wolves based on their mining experience in the north. In the Maritimes, L.M. Montgomery penned one of the greatest coming-of-age novels of all times, *Anne of Green Gables* (1908). Prominent contemporary English-language authors include Margaret Atwood, best known for the futuristic best-seller *The Handmaid's Tale* (1986), and Sri Lankan-born novelist Michael Ondaatje, whose *The English Patient* (1992) received the prestigious Booker Prize. Canada also boasts three of the world's most authoritative cultural and literary critics: Northrop Frye, Hugh Kenner, and pop phenom Marshall McLuhan. The *québécois* literary tradition is becoming more recognized, and has been important in defining an emerging cultural and political identity.

Canada's contributions to the world of **popular music** encompass a range of artists and genres. Canadian rockers include Neil Young, Joni Mitchell, Bruce Cockburn, Rush, Cowboy Junkies, Barenaked Ladies, k.d. lang, Bryan Adams, Crash Test Dummies, Sarah McLachlan, and pop icons the Tragically Hip. Chart-toppers of the last few years include the inimitable (and who would want to?) Céline Dion, country cross-over Shania Twain, and Alanis Morissette. Canada is also home to *québécois* folk music and several world-class orchestras, including the Montréal, Toronto, and Vancouver Symphonies.

On the **silver screen**, Canada's National Film Board (NFB), which finances many documentaries, has gained worldwide acclaim. The first Oscar given to a documentary went to the NFB's 1941 *Churchill Island*. Recent figures of note include indie director Atom Egoyan, whose haunting film *The Sweet Hereafter* (1997) scored two Oscar nominations. *Québécois* filmmakers have also met with success. Director Denys Arcand caught the world's eye with the striking *Jésus de Montréal* (1989), a reflection of the filmmaker's disillusionment with the Church, and the Oscar-nominated movie *Le déclin de l'empire américain* (1985).

The *Toronto Globe and Mail* is Canada's national newspaper, distributed six days a week across the entire country. Every Canadian city has at least one daily paper; the weekly news magazine is *Maclean's*. The publicly owned **Canadian Broadcasting Corporation (CBC)** provides two national networks (one in English, one in French) for both radio and TV. The CBC is supplemented by a private broadcaster, CTV, as well as specialty cable channels and American networks.

In the realm of sports, Canada possesses an athletic heritage befitting its northern latitudes. Popular sports include ice skating, skiing, and the perennial favorite, ice hockey. Canadians also enjoy a spirited game of **curling,** which involves pushing a 20kg stone across a sheet of ice. Some of Canada's other popular sports are derived from those of the First Nations. Lacrosse, the national game of Canada, was played long before the Europeans arrived. Sports played in the United States have crossed the border in full force; in addition to the **Canadian Football League (CFL),** Canada has one NBA team and soon will have only one Major League Baseball outfit.

ESSENTIALS

ENTRANCE REQUIREMENTS

Passport (p. 32). Required of all visitors to the US and Canada.

Visa (p. 33). Usually required to visit the US and Canada, but can be waived.

Work Permit (p. 72). Required of all foreigners planning to work in the US or Canada.

Driving Permit (p. 61). Required for all those planning to drive.

FACTS FOR THE TRAVELER

EMBASSIES & CONSULATES

Contact your nearest embassy or consulate for information regarding visas and passports to the United States and Canada. The **US State Department** provides contact info for US embassies and consulates abroad at http://usembassy.state.gov. Foreign embassies in the US are located in Washington, D.C. For more detailed information on embassies, consult www.embassyworld.com.

AMERICAN CONSULAR SERVICES ABROAD

US EMBASSIES

Australia, Moonah Pl., Yarralumla **(Canberra)** ACT 2600 (☎02 6214 5600; fax 6214 5970; http://usembassy-australia.state.gov/embassy).

Canada, 490 Sussex Drive, **Ottawa** ON K1N 1G8 (☎613-238-5335; fax 688-3091; www.usembassycanada.gov).

Ireland, 42 Elgin Rd., Ballsbridge, **Dublin** 4 (☎01 668 8777 or 668 7122; fax 668 9946; www.usembassy.ie).

New Zealand, 29 Fitzherbert Terr. (or P.O. Box 1190), Thorndon, **Wellington** (☎64+4 462 6000; fax 478 1701; http://usembassy.org.nz).

South Africa, P.O. Box 9536, Pretoria 0001, 877 Pretorius St., **Pretoria** (☎012 342 1048; fax 342 2244; http://usembassy.state.gov/pretoria).

UK, 24 Grosvenor Sq., **London** W1A 1AE (☎ 0207 499 9000; fax 495 5012; www.usembassy.org.uk).

US CONSULATES

Australia, 553 St. Kilda Rd., **Melbourne** VIC 3004 (☎03 9526 5900; fax 9510 4646); 16 St. George's Terr., 13th fl., **Perth** WA 6000 (☎08 9202 1224; fax 9231 9444). MLC Centre, 19-29 Martin Pl., 59th fl., **Sydney** NSW 2000 (☎02 9373 9200; fax 9373 9125).

Canada, 615 Macleod Trail SE, Room 1000, **Calgary** AB T2G 4T8 (☎403-266-8962; fax 264-6630); 1969 Upper Water St., Purdy's Wharf Tower II, suite 904, **Halifax** NS B3J 3R7 (☎902-429-2480; fax 423-6861); Street Address: 1155 St. Alexandre St., **Montréal** QC H3B 3Z1. Mailing Address: P.O. Box 65, Postal Station Desjardins, Montréal QC H5B 1G1 (☎514-398-9695; fax 398-9748);street address: 2 Place Terrasse Dufferin, **Québec City** QC G1R 4T9 Mailing Address: B.P. 939, Québec City QC (☎418-

692-2095; fax 692-4640); 360 University Ave., **Toronto** ON M5G 1S4 (☎416-595-1700; fax 595-0051); Street address 1075 West Pender St., Mezzanine, **Vancouver** BC. Mailing address: 1095 West Pender St. 21st fl., Vancouver BC V6E 2M6 (☎604-685-4311; fax 685-7175).

New Zealand, Street Address: Citibank Building, 3rd fl., 23 Customs St., **Auckland.** Mailing Address: Private Bag 92022, Auckland (☎64+9 303 2724; fax 366 0870).

South Africa, Street Address: Monte Carlo Bldg., 7th fl., Heerengracht, Foreshore, **Cape Town.** Mailing Address: P.O. Box 6773 ROGGEBAI, 8012 (☎021 421 4351; fax 425 3014); 2901 Durban Bay Building, 333 Smith St., **Durban** 4000 (☎031 304 4737; fax 301 0265); Street Address: 1 River St., Killarney, **Johannesburg.** Mailing Address: P.O. Box 1762, Houghton, 2041, Johannesburg (☎011 644 8000; fax 646 6916).

UK, Queen's House, 14 Queen St., **Belfast,** N. Ireland BT1 6EQ (☎028 9032 8239; fax 9024 8482); 3 Regent Terr., **Edinburgh,** Scotland EH7 5BW (☎0131 556 8315; fax 557 6023).

CANADIAN EMBASSIES

Australia, Commonwealth Ave., **Canberra** ACT 2600 (☎02 6270 4000; fax 6273 3285; www.dfait-maeci.gc.ca/australia).

Ireland, 65 St. Stephen's Green, **Dublin** 2 (☎01 417 4100; fax 01 417 4101).

New Zealand, Street Address: 61 Molesworth St., 3rd fl., Thorndon, **Wellington.** Mailing Address: P.O. Box 12049 Thorndon, Wellington (☎04 473 9577; fax 471 2082; www.dfait-maeci.gc.ca/newzealand).

South Africa, 1103 Arcadia St., Hatfield 0028, **Pretoria** (☎012 422 3000; fax 422 3052).

UK, Canada House, Trafalgar Sq., **London** SW1Y 5BJ (☎0207 258 6600; fax 258 6333; www.dfait-maeci.gc.ca/london).

US, 501 Pennsylvania Ave. NW, **Washington, D.C.** 20001 (☎202-682-1740; fax 682-7726; http://canadianembassy.org).

CANADIAN CONSULATES

Australia, 267 St. George's Terr., 3rd fl., **Perth** WA 6000 (☎08 9322 7930; fax 9261 7706); Quay West Bldg., 111 Harrington St., 5th fl., **Sydney** NSW 2000 (☎02 9364 3000; fax 9364 3098).

New Zealand, Street Address: Jetset Centre, 9th fl., 48 Emily Pl., **Auckland.** Mailing Address: P.O. Box 6186, Auckland (☎09 309 3690; fax 307 3111).

South Africa, Street Address: Reserve Bank Bldg., 60 St. George's Mall, 19th fl., **Cape Town** 8001. Mailing Address: P.O. Box 683, Cape Town 8000 (☎021 423 5240; fax 423 4893); Street Address: 14 Nuttall Gardens, Morningside, **Durban** 4001. Mailing Address: P.O. Box 712, Durban 4000 (☎031 303 9695; fax 309 9694).

UK, 378 Stranmillis Rd., **Belfast,** N. Ireland BT3 5BL (☎232 660 212; fax 687 798); Port Rd., Rhoose, **Vale of Glamorgan,** Wales CF62 3BT (☎1446 719 172; fax 710 856); 30 Lothian Rd., **Edinburgh,** Scotland EH1 2DH (☎0131 220 4333; fax 245 6010).

US, 3 Copley Pl., #400, **Boston** MA 02116 (☎617-262-3760; fax 262-3415); 2 Prudential Plaza, 180 N. Stetson Ave., #2400, **Chicago** IL 60601 (☎312-616-1860; fax 616-1877); 750 N. St. Paul Street, #1700, **Dallas** TX 75201 (☎214-922-9806; fax 922-9296); 550 S. Hope St., 9th fl., **Los Angeles** CA 90071 (☎213-346-2700; fax 620-8827); 200 S. Biscayne Blvd. #1600, **Miami** FL 33131(☎305-579-1600; fax 374-6774); 1251 Ave. of the Americas, **New York** NY 10020 (☎212-596-1628; fax 596-1790); 555 Montgomery St., #1288, **San Francisco** CA 94111 (☎415-834-3180, fax 834-3189).

CONSULAR SERVICES IN THE US AND CANADA

IN WASHINGTON, D.C. (US)

Australia, 1601 Massachusetts Ave., 20036 (☎202-797-3000; fax 797-3168; www.austemb.org). **Ireland,** 2234 Massachusetts Ave., 20008 (☎202-462-3939; fax 232-5993; www.irelandemb.org). **New Zealand,** 37 Observatory Circle, 20008 (☎202-328-4800; fax 667-5227; www.nzemb.org). **UK,** 3100 Massachusetts Ave., 20008 (☎202-588-6500; fax 588-7870; www.britainusa.com/consular/embassy). **South Africa,** 3051 Massachusetts Ave., 20008 (☎202-232-4400; fax 265-1607); http://usaembassy.southafrica.net).

IN OTTAWA, ONTARIO (CANADA)

Australia, 50 O'Connor St., #710, K1P 6L2 (☎613-236-0841; fax 236-4376; www.ahc-ottawa.org). **Ireland,** 130 Albert St. #1105, K1P 5G4 (☎613-233-6281; fax 233-5835). **New Zealand,** 99 Bank St., #727, K1P 6G3 (☎613-238-5991; fax 238-5707; www.nzhcottawa.org). **UK,** 80 Elgin St., K1P 5K7(☎613-237-1303; fax 237-2400; www.britain-in-canada.org). **South Africa,** 15 Sussex Drive, K1M 1M8 (☎613-744-0330; fax 741-1639).

DOCUMENTS & FORMALITIES

PASSPORTS

REQUIREMENTS. All foreign visitors except Canadians need valid passports to enter the United States and to re-enter their own country. Returning home with an expired passport is illegal and may result in a fine. Canadians need to demonstrate proof of Canadian citizenship, such as a citizenship card with photo ID. The US does not allow entrance if the holder's passport expires in under six months.

NEW PASSPORTS. File any new passport or renewal applications well in advance of your departure date. Most passport offices offer rush services for a steep fee. Citizens living abroad who need a passport or renewal should contact the nearest consular service of their home country.

Australia: Citizens must apply for a passport in person at a post office, a passport office, or an Australian diplomatic mission overseas. Passport offices are located in Adelaide, Brisbane, Canberra, Darwin, Hobart, Melbourne, Newcastle, Perth, and Sydney. New adult passports cost AUS$144 (for a 32-page passport) or AUS$204 (64-page), and a child's is AUS$68/AUS$102. Adult passports are valid for 10 years and child passports for 5 years. For more info, call toll-free (in Australia) 13 12 32, or visit www.passports.gov.au.

Canada: Citizens may cross the US-Canada border with any proof of citizenship.

Ireland: Citizens can apply for a passport by mail to either the Department of Foreign Affairs, Passport Office, Setanta Centre, Molesworth St., Dublin 2 (☎01 671 1633; fax 671 1092; www.irlgov.ie/iveagh), or the Passport Office, Irish Life Building, 1A South Mall, Cork (☎021 27 2525). Obtain an application at a local *Garda* station or post office, or request one from a passport office. 32-page passports cost IR£45/€57 and are valid for 10 years. 48-page passports cost IR£55/€69. Citizens under 16 or over 65 can request a 3-year passport (IR£10/€12).

New Zealand: Application forms for passports are available from any travel agency or Link Centre. Applications may be forwarded to the Passport Office, P.O. Box 10-526, Wellington, New Zealand (☎0800 225 050 or 04 474 8100; fax 474 8010; www.passports.govt.nz). Standard processing time is 10 working days. Adult passports (NZ$80) are valid 10 years; passports for children under 16 (NZ$40) are valid 5 years.

South Africa: Department of Home Affairs. Passports are issued only in Pretoria, but all applications must still be submitted or forwarded to the nearest South African consulate. Processing time is 3 months or more. Passports around SAR190; valid for 10 years. Under 16 around SAR140; valid for five years.

United Kingdom: Application forms are available at passport offices, main post offices, travel agencies, and online (www.ukpa.gov.uk). Apply by mail or in person to one of the passport offices, located in London, Liverpool, Newport, Peterborough, Glasgow, or Belfast. Adult passports (UK£30) are valid for 10 years; under 16 (UK£16) are valid for 5. The process takes about 4 weeks. The UK Passport Agency can be reached by phone at 0870 521 0410.

United States: Citizens may cross the US-Canada border with any proof of citizenship.

PASSPORT MAINTENANCE. Be sure to photocopy the page of your passport with your photo, passport number, and other identifying info, as well as any visas, travel insurance policies, plane tickets, or traveler's check serial numbers. Consulates also recommend that you carry an expired passport or an official copy of your birth certificate in a part of your baggage separate from other documents.

If you lose your passport, immediately notify the local police and the consulate of your home government. To expedite its replacement, it helps to have a photocopy of the passport to show as ID and to provide proof of citizenship. In some cases, a replacement may take weeks to process, and it may be valid only for a limited time. Any **visas** stamped in your old passport will be irretrievably lost. In an emergency, ask for **temporary traveling papers** that will permit you to re-enter your home country. Your passport is a public document belonging to your nation's government. You may have to surrender it to a US government official, but if you don't get it back in a reasonable amount of time, inform your country's nearest mission.

VISAS

Citizens of South Africa and some other countries need a visa—a stamp, sticker, or insert in your passport specifying the purpose of your travel and the permitted duration of your stay—in addition to a valid passport for entrance to the US. See http://travel.state.gov/visa_services.html for more information. To obtain a visa, contact a US embassy or consulate.

Citizens of most European countries, Australia, and New Zealand can waive US visas through the **Visa Waiver Pilot Program.** Visitors qualify if they are traveling only for business or pleasure (*not* work or study) and are staying for fewer than 90 days. In addition, travelers must provide proof of intent to leave (such as a return plane ticket) and an I-94 form.

All travelers planning a stay of more than 90 days (180 days for Canadians) need to obtain a visa; contact the closest US embassy or consulate. The **Center for International Business and Travel (CIBT),** (☎800-925-2428; www.cibt.com), secures **B-2** (pleasure travel) visas to and from all possible countries for a variable service charge. If you lose your I-94 form, you can replace it at the nearest **Immigration and Naturalization Service (INS)** office (☎800-375-5283; www.ins.usdoj.gov), though it's unlikely that the form will be replaced during your stay. **Visa extensions** are sometimes attainable with a completed I-539 form; call the forms request line (☎800-870-3676). Be sure to double-check on entrance requirements at the nearest US embassy or consulate.

Citizens of Australia, Ireland, New Zealand, the UK, and the US may enter Canada without visas for stays of 90 days or less if they carry proof of intent to leave. South Africans need a visa to enter Canada (CDN$75 for a single person, CDN$400 for a family). Citizens of other countries should contact their Canadian consulate for more info. Write to Citizenship and Immigration Canada for the booklet *Apply-*

ing for a Visitor Visa at Information Centre, Public Affairs Branch, Jean Edmonds Tower S, 365 Laurier Ave. W, Ottawa ON K1A 1L1 (☎888-242-2100; http://cicnet.ci.gc.ca). Visa extensions are sometimes granted; phone the nearest Canada Immigration Centre.

IDENTIFICATION

When you travel, always carry two or more forms of identification on your person, including at least one photo ID. A passport combined with a driver's license or birth certificate is usually adequate. Never carry all your forms of ID together; keep them in separate places in case of theft or loss.

TEACHER, STUDENT, & YOUTH IDENTIFICATION. The **International Student Identity Card (ISIC)** provides discounts on sights, accommodations, food, and transport; access to 24-hour emergency helpline (in North America ☎877-370-ISIC); and insurance benefits for US cardholders (see **Insurance**, p. 41). Applicants must be degree-seeking students of a secondary or post-secondary school and must be at least 12 years old. Because of the proliferation of fake ISICs, some services (particularly airlines) require additional proof of student identity.

The **International Teacher Identity Card (ITIC)** offers teachers the same insurance coverage and similar but limited discounts. For travelers who are 25 years old or under but are not students, the **International Youth Travel Card (IYTC)** offers many of the same benefits as the ISIC.

Each of these cards costs $22 or equivalent. ISIC and ITIC cards are valid for sixteen months; IYTC cards are valid for one year from the date of issue. Many student travel agencies (see p. 54) issue the cards, including STA Travel in Australia and New Zealand; Travel CUTS in Canada; usit in the Republic of Ireland and Northern Ireland; SASTS in South Africa; Campus Travel and STA Travel in the UK; and Council Travel and STA Travel in the US.

CUSTOMS

Upon entering the United States or Canada, you must declare certain items from abroad and pay a duty on the value of those articles that exceed the allowance established by the US or Canada's customs service. Goods and gifts purchased at **duty-free** shops abroad are not exempt from duty or sales tax at your point of return; you must declare these items as well. "Duty-free" merely means that you need not pay a tax in the country of purchase. For more specific information on customs requirements, contact the following info centers.

> **AMERICAN & CANADIAN CUSTOMS DECLARATIONS.** Entering the **US** as a *non-resident,* you are allowed to claim $100 of gifts and merchandise if you will be in the country for 72hr. *Residents* may claim $400 worth of goods. If 21, this may include 1L of wine, beer, or liquor. 200 cigarettes, 100 cigars (steer clear of Cubans), or 2kg of smoking tobacco are also permitted for those over 18. Entering **Canada,** *visitors* may bring in gifts, each of which may not exceed CDN$60 in value. *Residents* who have been out of the country for 24hr. may claim an exemption of CDN$50. After 48hr. they may claim CDN$200, and after 7 days CDN$750. If you are of the legal drinking age in the province, and have been out of the country for 48hr. or more, you may bring in 1.5L of wine, 1.14L of liquor, or 24x355mL cans or bottles of beer or ale. You may also bring in 200 cigarettes, 50 cigars, or 200g of manufactured tobacco.

MONEY

CURRENCY & EXCHANGE

US DOLLARS		CANADIAN DOLLARS	
CDN$1 = US$0.63	US$1 = CDN$1.58	US$1 = CDN$1.58	CDN$1 = US$0.63
UK£1 = US$1.53	US$1 = UK£0.65	UK£1 = CDN$2.42	CDN$1 = UK£0.41
EUR€1 = US$0.97	US$1 = EUR€1.03	EUR€1 = CDN$1.53	CDN$1 = EUR€0.66
AUS$1 = US$0.53	US$1= AUS$1.87	AUS$1 = CDN$0.84	CDN$1= AUS$1.19
NZ$1 = US$0.45	US$1 = NZ$2.20	NZ$1 = CDN$0.72	CDN$1 = NZ$1.39
ZAR1 = US$0.10	US$1 = ZAR10.40	ZAR1 = CDN$0.15	CDN$1 = ZAR6.58

The currency chart above is based on August 2002 exchange rates between local currency and Australian dollars (AUS$), Canadian dollars (CDN$), Irish pounds (IR£), New Zealand dollars (NZ$), South African Rand (ZAR), British pounds (UK£), US dollars ($), and European Union Euros (EUR€). Check financial websites, such as www.bloomberg.com, or a newspaper for the latest exchange rates.

As a general rule, it's cheaper to convert money in the US than at home. While currency exchange will probably be available in your arrival airport, it's wise to bring enough foreign currency to last for the first 24 to 72 hours of a trip.

When changing money abroad, try to go only to banks or other establishments that have at most a 5% margin between their buy and sell prices. Since you lose money with every transaction, **convert large sums** (unless the currency is depreciating rapidly), **but no more than you'll need.**

If you use traveler's checks or bills, carry some in small denominations (the equivalent of $50 or less) for times when you are forced to exchange money at poor rates, but bring a range of denominations since charges may be levied per check cashed. Store your money in a variety of forms.

Many Canadian shops, as well as vending machines and parking meters, accept US coins at face value. Stores often convert the price of your purchase for you, but they are not legally obligated to offer a fair exchange. In almost all circumstances, you will receive Canadian change in return. (During the past several years, the Canadian dollar has been worth roughly 30% less than the US dollar.)

TRAVELER'S CHECKS

Traveler's checks are one of the safest and least troublesome means of carrying funds. American Express and Visa are the most widely recognized brands. Many banks and agencies sell them for a small commission. Check issuers provide refunds if the checks are lost or stolen, and many provide additional services, such as toll-free refund hotlines abroad, emergency message services, and stolen credit card assistance. They are readily accepted throughout the US.

CREDIT CARDS

Where they are accepted, credit cards often offer superior exchange rates. Credit cards may also offer services such as insurance or emergency help, and are sometimes required to reserve hotel rooms or rental cars. **MasterCard** and **Visa** are the most welcomed; **American Express** cards work at some ATMs and at AmEx offices and major airports. ATM cards and machines are found throughout the US. ATMs get the same wholesale exchange rate as credit cards, but there is often a limit on the amount of money you can withdraw per day (around $500) and typically a surcharge of $1-5 per withdrawal.

GETTING MONEY FROM HOME

If you run out of money while traveling, the easiest and cheapest solution is to have someone back home make a deposit to your credit card or cash (ATM) card. Failing that, consider one of the following options.

WIRING MONEY. It is possible to arrange a **bank money transfer**, which means asking a bank back home to wire money to a bank in your region. This is the cheapest way to transfer cash, but it's also the slowest, usually taking several days or more. Note that some banks may only release your funds in local currency, potentially sticking you with a poor exchange rate; inquire about this in advance. Money transfer services like **Western Union** are faster and more convenient than bank transfers—but also much pricier. Western Union has many locations worldwide. To find one, visit www.westernunion.com or call: in the US ☎ 800-325-6000; in Canada ☎ 800-235-0000; in the UK ☎ 0800 83 38 33; in Australia ☎ 800 501 500; in New Zealand ☎ 800 27 0000; in South Africa ☎ 0860 100031. To wire money within the US using a credit card (Visa, MasterCard, Discover), call ☎ 800-225-5227. Money transfer services are also available at **American Express** and **Thomas Cook** offices.

COSTS

STAYING ON A BUDGET. Accommodations start at about $12 per night in a hostel bed, while a basic sit-down meal costs about $10 depending on the region. If you stay in hostels and prepare your own food, you'll probably spend from $30-40 per person per day. A slightly more comfortable day (sleeping in hostels/guest houses and the occasional budget hotel, eating one meal a day at a restaurant, going out at night) would run $50-65. **Gas** prices in the US have risen over the past year. A gallon of gas now costs about $1.60 (40¢ per L), but prices vary widely according to state gasoline taxes. In Canada, gas costs CDN70¢ per L (CDN$2.65 per gallon).

TIPPING & BARGAINING

In the US, it is customary to tip waitstaff and cab drivers 15-20% (at your discretion). Tips are usually not included in restaurant bills, unless you are in a party of six or more. At the airport and in hotels, porters expect at least a $1 per bag tip to carry your bags. Tipping is less compulsory in Canada; a good tip signifies remarkable service. Bargaining is generally frowned upon and fruitless in both countries.

TAXES

In the US, sales tax is similar to the European Value-Added Tax and ranges from 4-10% depending on the item and the place. In many states, groceries are not taxed. *Let's Go* lists sales tax rates in the introduction to each state; usually these taxes are not included in the prices of items.

In Canada, you'll quickly notice the 7% goods and services tax (GST) and an additional sales tax in some provinces. See the introductory sections for info on provincial taxes. Visitors can claim a rebate of the GST they pay on accommodations of less than one month and on most goods they buy and take home, so be sure to save your receipts and pick up a GST rebate form while in Canada. Total purchases must be at least CDN$200 and made within ten months of the date of the purchase; further goods must be exported from Canada within 60 days of purchase. A brochure detailing restrictions is available from local tourist offices or through Revenue Canada, Visitor's Rebate Program, 275 Pope Rd. #104, Summerside, PE C1N 6C6 (☎ 902-432-5608 or 800-668-4748).

SAFETY & SECURITY

> **EMERGENCY = 911.** For emergencies in the US and Canada, dial 911. This number is toll-free from all phones, including coin phones. In a very few remote communities, 911 may not work. If it does not, dial 0 for the operator. In national parks, it is usually best to call the park warden in case of emergency.

PERSONAL SAFETY

EXPLORING

Crime is mostly concentrated in the cities, but being safe is a good idea no matter where you are. Newark, NJ; Atlanta, GA; St. Louis, MO; New Orleans, LA; Detroit, MI; Baltimore, MD; Miami, FL; and Washington, D.C. are the most dangerous cities in the United States, but that does not mean you should not visit them. Common sense and a little bit of thought will go a long way in helping you to avoid dangerous situations. Wherever possible, *Let's Go* warns of neighborhoods that should be avoided when traveling alone or at night.

Tourists are especially vulnerable to crime because they tend to carry large amounts of cash and tend not to be as street-savvy as locals. Avoid unwanted attention by blending in as much as possible; the gawking camera-toter is a more obvious target for thieves than the low-profile traveler. Familiarize yourself with the area before setting out; if you must check a map on the street, duck into a cafe or shop. Always carry yourself with confidence. Be sure that someone at home knows your itinerary and *never admit that you are traveling alone.*

GETTING AROUND

If you are using a **car,** learn local driving signals and wear a seatbelt. Children under 40 lb. should ride only in a specially-designed carseat, available for a small fee from most car rental agencies. **Sleeping in your car** is one of the most dangerous (and often illegal) ways to get your rest.

Interstate **public transportation** is generally safe. Occasionally, bus or train stations can be unsafe; *Let's Go* warns of these stations where applicable. Within major US cities, the quality and safety of public transportation vary considerably. It is usually a good idea to avoid subways and intra-city buses late at night; if you must use these forms of transportation, try to travel in a large groups.

Let's Go does not recommend **hitchhiking** under any circumstances, particularly for women—see **Getting Around,** p. 56 for more info.

TERRORISM

In light of the September 11, 2001 terrorist attacks in the Eastern US, there is an elevated threat of further terrorist activities in the United States. Terrorists often target landmarks popular with tourists; however, the threat of an attack is generally not specific or great enough to warrant avoiding certain places or modes of transportation. Stay aware of developments in the news and watch for alerts from federal, state, and local law enforcement officials. Also, allow extra time for airport security and do not pack sharp objects in your carry-on luggage, as they will be confiscated. For more information on the terror threat to the US, visit http://www.terrorismanswers.com.

ESSENTIALS

TRAVEL ADVISORIES. The following government offices provide travel information and advisories by telephone, by fax, or via the web:

Australian Department of Foreign Affairs and Trade: ☎ 1300 555135; faxback service ☎ 02 6261 1299; www.dfat.gov.au.

Canadian Department of Foreign Affairs and International Trade (DFAIT): In Canada and the US call ☎ 800-267-6788, elsewhere call ☎ +1 613-944-6788; www.dfait-maeci.gc.ca. Call for their free booklet, *Bon Voyage...But*.

New Zealand Ministry of Foreign Affairs: ☎ 04 494 8500; fax 494 8506; www.mft.govt.nz/trav.html.

United Kingdom Foreign and Commonwealth Office: ☎ 020 7008 0232; fax 7008 0155; www.fco.gov.uk.

US Department of State: ☎ 202-647-5225; faxback service 202-647-3000; http://travel.state.gov. For their free booklet *A Safe Trip Abroad*, call ☎ 202-512-1800.

FINANCIAL SECURITY

PROTECTING YOUR VALUABLES. First, **bring as few belongings and as little cash with you as possible.** Second, buy a few combination **padlocks** to secure your belongings either in your pack or in a hostel or train station locker. Keep your traveler's checks and ATM/credit cards in a **money belt**—not a "fanny pack"—along with your passport and ID cards. Fourth, **keep a small cash reserve separate from your primary stash.**

CON ARTISTS & PICKPOCKETS. In large cities **con artists** often work in groups, and children are among the most effective. Beware of certain classics: sob stories that require money or rolls of bills "found" on the street. **Don't ever let your passport out of your sight.** Don't let your bags out of sight. Beware of **pickpockets** in city crowds, especially on public transportation.

ACCOMMODATIONS & TRANSPORTATION. Never leave your belongings unattended; crime occurs in even the most demure-looking hostel or hotel. Be particularly careful on **buses** and **trains.** Carry your backpack in front of you where you can see it. When traveling with others, sleep in alternate shifts. When alone, use good judgment in selecting a train compartment: never stay in an empty one, and use a lock to secure your pack to the luggage rack. Try to sleep on top bunks with your luggage stored above you (if not in bed with you), and keep important documents and other valuables on you. If traveling by **car,** don't leave valuables (such as jewelry or luggage) in it while you are away.

DRUGS & ALCOHOL

In the US, the drinking age is 21; in Canada it is 19, except in Alberta, Manitoba, and Québec, where it is 18. Drinking restrictions are particularly strict in the US. The youthful should expect to be asked to show government-issued identification when purchasing any alcoholic beverage. Drinking and driving is prohibited everywhere, not to mention dangerous and idiotic. Open beverage containers in your car will incur heavy fines; a failed breathalyzer test will mean fines, a suspended license, imprisonment, or all three. Most localities restrict where and when alcohol can be sold. Sales usually stop at a certain time at night and are often prohibited entirely on Sundays. Narcotics like marijuana, heroin, and cocaine are highly illegal in the US and Canada. If you carry prescription drugs while you travel, keep a copy of the prescription with you, especially at border crossings.

HEALTH

BEFORE YOU GO

In your **passport**, write the names of any people you wish to be contacted in case of a medical emergency, and list any allergies or medical conditions. Carry up-to-date, legible prescriptions or a statement from your doctor stating the medication's trade name, manufacturer, chemical name, and dosage.

IMMUNIZATIONS & PRECAUTIONS

Travelers over two years old should be sure that the following vaccines are up to date: MMR (for measles, mumps, and rubella); DTaP or Td (for diptheria, tetanus, and pertussis), OPV (for polio), HbCV (for haemophilus influenza B), and HBV (for hepatitis B).

USEFUL ORGANIZATIONS & PUBLICATIONS

The US **Centers for Disease Control and Prevention (CDC;** ☎877-FYI-TRIP/394-8747; fax 888-232-3299; www.cdc.gov/travel) maintains an international travelers' hotline and an informative website. The CDC's comprehensive booklet *Health Information for International Travel*, an annual rundown of disease, immunization, and general health advice, is free online or $25 via the Public Health Foundation (☎877-252-1200). For detailed information on travel health, including a country-by-country overview of diseases (and a list of travel clinics in the US), try the **International Travel Health Guide** ($20; www.travmed.com). For general health info, contact the **American Red Cross** (☎800-564-1234; www.redcross.org).

MEDICAL ASSISTANCE ON THE ROAD

In case of medical emergency, dial **911** from any phone and an operator will send out paramedics, a fire brigade, or the police as needed. Emergency care is also readily available in the US and Canada at any emergency room on a walk-in basis. If you do not have insurance, you will have to pay for medical care. (see **Insurance** p. 41) Appointments are required for non-emergency medical services.

ONCE IN THE US & CANADA

ENVIRONMENTAL HAZARDS

Heat exhaustion and dehydration: Heat exhaustion can lead to fatigue, headaches, and wooziness. Continuous heat stress can eventually lead to heatstroke, characterized by a rising temperature, severe headache, and cessation of sweating. Victims should be cooled off with wet towels and taken to a doctor.

Hypothermia and frostbite: Hypothermia occurs when someone is overexposed to the cold. Symptoms include a rapid drop in body temperature, shivering, exhaustion, poor coordination, slurred speech, hallucinations, and/or amnesia. *Do not let hypothermia victims fall asleep.* To avoid hypothermia, keep dry, wear layers, and stay out of the wind. When the temperature is below freezing, watch out for frostbite. If skin turns white, waxy, and cold, do not rub the area. Drink warm beverages, get dry, and slowly warm the area with dry fabric or steady body contact.

High altitude: Allow your body a couple of days to adjust to less oxygen before exerting yourself. Note that alcohol is more potent and UV rays are stronger at high elevations.

INSECT-BORNE DISEASES

Many diseases are transmitted by insects—mainly mosquitoes, fleas, ticks, and lice. Be aware of insects in wet or forested areas. Use insect repellents, such as

DEET, and soak or spray your gear with permethrin (licensed in the US for use on clothing). To stop the itch after being bitten, try Calamine lotion or topical cortisones (like Cortaid). Ticks—responsible for Lyme and other diseases—can be particularly dangerous in rural and forested regions. They are most common in the Northeast, the Great Lakes region, and the Pacific Northwest.

Lyme disease: A bacterial infection carried by ticks and marked by a circular bull's-eye rash of 2 in. or more. Later symptoms include fever, headache, fatigue, and aches and pains. Antibiotics are effective if administered early. Left untreated, Lyme can cause problems in joints, the heart, and the nervous system. Ticks should be removed with tweezers. Grasping the tick's head as close to the skin as possible, apply slow, steady traction. Do not try to remove ticks by burning them or coating them with nail polish remover or petroleum jelly.

FOOD- & WATER-BORNE DISEASES

Prevention is the best cure: be sure that your food is properly cooked and the water you drink is clean. The tap water in the United States and Canada is treated to be safe for drinking.

Traveler's diarrhea: Results from drinking untreated water or eating uncooked foods. Symptoms include nausea, bloating, and urgency. Try quick-energy, non-sugary foods with protein and carbohydrates to keep your strength up. Over-the-counter anti-diarrheals (e.g. Imodium) may counteract the problems. The most dangerous side effect is dehydration; drink 8 oz. of water with ½ tsp. of sugar or honey and a pinch of salt, try caffeinate-free soft drinks, or eat salted crackers.

Dysentery: Results from a serious intestinal infection caused by certain bacteria. The most common type is bacillary dysentery, also called shigellosis. Symptoms include bloody diarrhea (sometimes mixed with mucus), fever, and abdominal pain and tenderness. Bacillary dysentery generally only lasts a week, but it is highly contagious. Amoebic dysentery, which develops more slowly, is a more serious disease and may cause long-term damage if left untreated. Dysentery can be treated with the drugs norfloxacin or ciprofloxacin (commonly known as Cipro).

Parasites: Microbes, tapeworms, etc. that hide in unsafe water and food. **Giardiasis,** for example, is acquired by drinking untreated water from streams or lakes. Symptoms include swollen glands or lymph nodes, fever, rashes or itchiness, and digestive problems. Boil water, wear shoes, and eat only cooked food.

OTHER INFECTIOUS DISEASES

Rabies: Transmitted through the saliva of infected animals; fatal if untreated. By the time symptoms (thirst and muscle spasms) appear, the disease is in its terminal stage. If you are bitten, wash the wound thoroughly, seek immediate medical care, and try to have the animal located. A rabies vaccine, which consists of 3 shots given over a 21-day period, is available but is only semi-effective.

Hepatitis B: A viral infection of the liver transmitted via bodily fluids or needle-sharing. Symptoms may not surface until years after infection. A 3-shot vaccination sequence is recommended for health-care workers, sexually-active travelers, and anyone planning to seek medical treatment abroad; it must begin 6 mo. before traveling.

Hepatitis C: Like Hepatitis B, but the mode of transmission differs. IV drug users, those with occupational exposure to blood, hemodialysis patients, and recipients of blood transfusions are at the highest risk, but the disease can also be spread through sexual contact or sharing items that may have traces of blood on them.

AIDS, HIV, & STDS

For detailed information on **Acquired Immune Deficiency Syndrome (AIDS)** in the United States, call the **US Centers for Disease Control's** 24hr. hotline at ☎ 800-342-2437, or contact the **Joint United Nations Programme on HIV/AIDS (UNAIDS),** 20 Ave. Appia, CH-1211 Geneva 27, Switzerland (☎ +41 22 791 3666; fax 22 791 4187).

The Council on International Educational Exchange's pamphlet *Travel Safe: AIDS and International Travel* is posted on their web site (www.ciee.org/Isp/safety/travelsafe.htm), along with links to other online and phone resources. According to US law, HIV positive persons are not permitted to enter the US. However, HIV testing is conducted only for those who are planning to immigrate permanently. Travelers from areas with particularly high concentrations of HIV positive persons or those with AIDS may be required to provide more info when applying. Travelers to Canada who are suspected of being HIV positive will be required to submit to HIV testing.

Sexually transmitted diseases (STDs) such as gonorrhea, chlamydia, genital warts, syphilis, and herpes are easier to catch than HIV, and some can be just as deadly. **Hepatitis B** and **C** are also serious sexually transmitted diseases (see above). Though condoms may protect you from some STDs, oral or even tactile contact can lead to transmission.

INSURANCE

Medical insurance (especially university policies) often covers costs incurred abroad; check with your provider. **Canadians** are protected by their home province's health insurance plan for up to 90 days after leaving the country; check with the provincial Ministry of Health or Health Plan Headquarters for details. **Homeowners' insurance** (or your family's coverage) often covers theft during travel and loss of travel documents (passport, plane ticket, railpass, etc.) up to $500.

Travel insurance generally covers four basic areas: medical/health problems, property loss, trip cancellation/interruption, and emergency evacuation. You might consider purchasing travel insurance if the cost of potential trip cancellation/interruption is greater than you can absorb. Prices generally run about $50 per week for full coverage, while trip cancellation/interruption may be purchased separately at a rate of about $5.50 per $100 of coverage.

ISIC and **ITIC** (see p. 34) provide basic insurance benefits, including $100 per day of in-hospital sickness for up to 60 days, $3000 of accident-related medical reimbursement, and $25,000 for emergency medical transport. Cardholders have access to a toll-free 24hr. helpline (run by the insurance provider **TravelGuard**) for medical, legal, and financial emergencies (☎ 877-370-4742). **American Express** (☎ 800-528-4800) grants most cardholders automatic car rental insurance (collision and theft, but not liability) and ground travel accident coverage of $100,000 on flight purchases made with the card.

PACKING

LUGGAGE. If you plan to cover most of your itinerary by foot, a sturdy **frame backpack** is unbeatable. (For the basics on buying a pack, see p. 51.) Toting a **suitcase** or **trunk** is fine if you plan to live in one or two cities or can store things in your car, but otherwise can be burdensome. In addition to your main piece of luggage, a **daypack** (a small backpack or courier bag) is a must.

CLOTHING. The climate in the US and Canada varies widely according to region. For most regions it's a good idea to bring a warm jacket or wool sweater, a rain jacket (Gore-Tex® is both waterproof and breathable), sturdy shoes or hiking boots, and thick socks. Flip-flops or waterproof sandals are must-haves for grubby hostel showers.

WASHING CLOTHES. Laundromats are common in North America, but it may be cheaper and easier to use a sink. Bring a small bar or tube of detergent soap, a small rubber ball to stop up the sink, and a travel clothesline.

CONVERTERS & ADAPTERS. In the United States, electricity is 110V. 220/240V electrical appliances are not compatible with 110V current. Appliances from anywhere outside the US and Canada will need to be used with an **adapter** (which changes the shape of the plug) and a **converter** (which changes the voltage, $20).

FIRST-AID KIT. For a basic first-aid kit, pack: bandages, pain reliever, antibiotic cream, a thermometer, a Swiss Army knife, tweezers, moleskin, decongestant, motion-sickness remedy, diarrhea or upset-stomach medication (Imodium or Pepto Bismol), an antihistamine, sunscreen, insect repellent, burn ointment, and a syringe for emergencies (get an explanatory letter from your doctor).

ACCOMMODATIONS

HOSTELS

Hostels are generally dorm-style accommodations, often in single-sex large rooms with bunk beds, although some hostels do offer private rooms for families and couples. They sometimes have kitchens and utensils for your use, bike or moped rentals, storage areas, and laundry facilities. There can be drawbacks: some hostels close during certain daytime "lockout" hours, have a curfew, don't accept reservations, impose a maximum stay, or, less frequently, require that you do chores. In the US and Canada, a bed in a hostel will average around $15.

HOSTELLING INTERNATIONAL

Joining the youth hostel association in your own country (listed below) automatically grants you membership privileges in **Hostelling International (HI),** a federation of national hosteling associations. HI hostels are scattered throughout the US and Canada and may accept reservations via the **International Booking Network** (www.hostelbooking.com). HI's umbrella organization's web page (www.iyhf.org) lists the web addresses and phone numbers of all national associations. Other hostelling websites include www.hostels.com and www.hostelplanet.com.

Most HI-AYH hostels also honor **guest memberships**—you'll get a blank card with space for six validation stamps. Each night you'll pay a nonmember supplement (one-sixth the membership fee) and earn one guest stamp; get six stamps, and you're a member. Most student travel agencies (see p. 54) sell HI-AYH cards, as do all of the national hosteling organizations listed below. All prices listed below are valid for **one-year memberships** unless otherwise noted.

Australian Youth Hostels Association (AYHA), 10 Mallett St., 3rd fl., Camperdown NSW 2050 (☎02 9565 1699; fax 9565 1325; www.yha.org.au). AUS$52, travelers under 18 AUS$16.

Hostelling International-Canada (HI-C), 400-205 Catherine St., Ottawa, ON K2P 1C3 (☎800-663-5777; fax 237-7868; www.hostellingintl.ca). CDN$35, under 18 free.

An Óige (Irish Youth Hostel Association), 61 Mountjoy St., Dublin 7 (☎830 4555; fax 830 5808; anoige@iol.ie; www.irelandyha.org). IR£10, under 18 IR£4.

Youth Hostels Association of New Zealand (YHANZ), P.O. Box 436, 193 Cashel St., 3rd Floor Union House, Christchurch 1 (☎03 379 9970; fax 365 4476; info@yha.org.nz; www.yha.org.nz). NZ$40, under 17 free.

Hostels Association of South Africa, 3rd fl. 73 St. George's St. Mall, P.O. Box 4402, Cape Town 8000 (☎021 424 2511; fax 424 4119; www.hisa.org.za). SAR45.

Scottish Youth Hostels Association (SYHA), 7 Glebe Crescent, Stirling FK8 2JA (☎01786 89 14 00; fax 89 13 33; www.syha.org.uk). UK£6.

Youth Hostels Association (England and Wales) Ltd., Trevelyan House, 8 St. Stephen's Hill, St. Albans, Hertfordshire AL1 2DY, UK (☎0870 870 8808; fax 01727 84 41 26; www.yha.org.uk). UK£12.50, under 18 UK£6.25, families UK£25.

Hostelling International Northern Ireland (HINI), 22-32 Donegall Rd., Belfast BT12 5JN, Northern Ireland (☎02890 31 54 35; fax 43 96 99; info@hini.org.uk; www.hini.org.uk). UK£10, under 18 UK£6.

Hostelling International-American Youth Hostels (HI-AYH), 733 15th St. NW, #840, Washington, D.C. 20005 (☎202-783-6161; fax 783-6171; hiayhserv@hiayh.org; www.hiayh.org). $25, under 18 free.

HOTELS

HOTEL CHAIN	TELEPHONE	HOTEL CHAIN	TELEPHONE
Best Western	☎800-780-7234	La Quinta Inn	☎800-531-5900
Comfort Inn	☎800-228-5150	Motel 6	☎800-466-8356
Days Inn	☎800-325-2525	Ramada Inn	☎800-272-6232
Econolodge	☎800-446-6900	Red Carpet Inn	☎800-251-1962
Embassy Suites Hotel	☎800-362-2779	Select Inn	☎800-641-1000
Hampton Inn	☎800-426-7866	Sleep Inn	☎800-221-2222
Hilton Hotel	☎800-445-8667	Super 8 Motel	☎800-800-8000
Holiday Inn	☎800-465-4329	Travelodge	☎800-255-3050
Howard Johnson	☎800-654-2000	YMCA	☎800-922-9622

Hotel rooms in the US vary widely in cost depending on the region in which the hotel is located. The cheapest hotel single in the Northeast would run about $60 per night, while it is possible to stay for $30 per night in a comparable hotel in the South, West, or Midwest regions. You'll typically have a private bathroom and shower with hot water, though some cheaper places may offer shared restrooms.

OTHER TYPES OF ACCOMMODATIONS

YMCAS AND YWCAS

Young Men's Christian Association (YMCA) lodgings are usually cheaper than a hotel but more expensive than a hostel. Not all YMCA locations offer lodging; those that do are often located in urban downtowns. Many YMCAs accept women and families; some will not lodge those under 18 without parental permission.

YMCA of the USA, 101 North Wacker Dr., Chicago, IL 60606 USA(☎888-333-9622 or 800-872-9622; fax 312 977-9063; www.ymca.net). Provides a listing of the nearly 1000 Ys across the US and Canada. Offers info on prices, services available, telephone numbers and addresses. Free reservations can be made at www.travel-ys.com.

YMCA Canada, 42 Charles St. E, 9th fl., Toronto, ON M4Y 1T4 Canada(☎416-967-9622; fax 413-9626; services@ymca.ca; www.ymca.ca), offers info on Ys in Canada.

YWCA of the USA, Empire State Building, #301, 350 Fifth Ave., New York, NY 10118 USA (☎212-273-7800; fax 465-2281; www.ywca.org). Publishes a directory (US$8) on YWCAs across the USA.

BED & BREAKFASTS

For a cozy alternative to impersonal hotel rooms, B&Bs (private homes with rooms available to travelers) range from the acceptable to the sublime. Rooms in B&Bs generally cost $50-70 for a single and $70-90 for a double in the US and Canada, but on holidays or in expensive locations, prices can soar. For more info on B&Bs, see **Bed & Breakfast Inns Online,** P.O. Box 829, Madison, TN 37116 (☎615-868-1946; info@bbonline.com; www.bbonline.com); InnFinder, 6200 Gisholt Dr. #100, Madison, WI 53713 (☎608-285-6600; fax 285-6601; www.inncrawler.com); or InnSite (www.innsite.com).

UNIVERSITY DORMS

Many **colleges and universities** open their residence halls to travelers when school is not in session (May-Sept.)—some do so even during term-time. Rates tend to be low, and many offer free local calls.

FURTHER READING: ACCOMMODATIONS

Campus Lodging Guide (19th Ed.). B&J Publications ($15).

The Complete Guide to Bed and Breakfasts, Inns and Guesthouses in the US, Canada, and Worldwide, Pamela Lanier. Ten Speed Press ($17).

CAMPING & THE OUTDOORS

Camping is probably the most rewarding way to slash travel costs. Considering the sheer number of public lands available for camping in both the United States and Canada, it may also be the most convenient. Well-equipped campsites (usually including prepared tent sites, toilets, and water) go for $5-25 per night in the US and CDN$10-30 in Canada. **Backcountry camping,** which lacks all of the above amenities, is often free but can cost up to $20 at some national parks. Most campsites are first come first served.

USEFUL PUBLICATIONS & RESOURCES

A variety of publishing companies offer hiking guidebooks to meet the educational needs of novice or expert. For information about camping, hiking, and biking, write or call the publishers listed below to receive a free catalog.

Automobile Association, Contact Ctr., Car Ellison House, William Armstrong Dr., Newcastle-upon-Tyne NE4 7YA, UK. (General info ☎0870 600 0371; fax 0191 235 5111; www.theaa.co.uk).

Family Campers and RVers/National Campers and Hikers Association, Inc., 4804 Transit Rd., Bldg. #2, Depew, NY 14043 (☎/fax 716-668-6242). Membership fee ($25) includes their publication *Camping Today.*

Sierra Club Books, 85 2nd. St., 2nd fl., San Francisco, CA 94105 (☎415-977-5500; www.sierraclub.org/books). Publishes general resource books on hiking, camping, and women traveling in the outdoors, as well as books on hiking in Arizona, Florida, Arkansas, the Rockies, the California Desert, and hikes of northern California.

The Mountaineers Books, 1001 SW Klickitat Way, #201, Seattle, WA 98134 (☎800-553-4453 or 206-223-6303; fax 223-6306; www.mountaineersbooks.org). Over 400 titles on hiking, biking, mountaineering, natural history, and conservation.

The US Geological Survey, Branch of Information Services, P.O. Box 25286, Denver Federal Center, Denver, CO 80225 (☎888-275-8747; fax 303-202-4693; http://mapping.usgs.gov/mac/findmaps.html). The USGS provides excellent topographical maps of the US that are ideal for hiking and other wilderness activity. All maps are $4-14.

Wilderness Press, 1200 5th. St., Berkeley, CA 94710 (☎800-443-7227 or 510-558-1666; fax 558-1696; www.wildernesspress.com). Over 100 hiking guides/maps, mostly for the western US.

Woodall Publications Corporation, 2575 Vista Del Mar Dr., Ventura, CA 93001 (☎800-323-9076 or 805-667-4100; www.woodalls.com). Woodall publishes the annually updated *Woodall's Campground Directory* ($22) as well as regional directories for the US and Canada ($7).

NATIONAL PARKS

National Parks protect some of the most spectacular scenery in North America (see p. 3). Though their primary purpose is preservation, the parks also host recreational activities such as ranger talks, guided hikes, marked trails, skiing, and snowshoe expeditions. For info, contact the **National Park Service,** 1849 C St. NW, Washington, D.C. 20240 (☎202-208-6843; www.nps.gov).

Entrance fees vary. The larger and more popular parks charge a $4-20 entry fee for cars and sometimes a $2-7 fee for pedestrians and cyclists. The **National Parks Pass** ($50), available at park entrances, allows the passport-holder's party entry into all national parks for one year. National Parks Passes can also be bought by writing to National Park Foundation, P.O. Box 34108, Washington, D.C. 20043 (send $50 plus $3.95 shipping and handling) or online at www.nationalparks.org. For an additional $15, the Parks Service will affix a **Golden Eagle Passport** hologram to your card, which will allow you access to sites managed by the US Fish and Wildlife Service, the US Forest Service, and the Bureau of Land Management. US citizens or residents 62 and over qualify for the lifetime **Golden Age Passport** ($10 one-time fee), which entitles the holder's party to free park entry, a 50% discount on camping, and 50% reductions on various recreational fees for the passport holder. Persons eligible for federal benefits on account of disabilities can enjoy the same privileges with the **Golden Access Passport** (free).

Most national parks have both backcountry and developed **camping.** Some welcome RVs, and a few offer grand lodges. At the more popular parks in the US and Canada, reservations are essential, available through MISTIX (☎800-365-2267; http://reservations.nps.gov) no more than five months in advance. Indoor accommodations should be reserved months in advance. Campgrounds often observe first come, first served policies, and many fill up by late morning.

NATIONAL FORESTS

Often less accessible and less crowded, **US National Forests** (www.fs.fed.us) are a purist's alternative to parks. While some have recreation facilities, most are equipped only for primitive camping—pit toilets and no water are the norm. When charged, entrance fees are $10-20, but camping is generally free or $3-4. Necessary wilderness permits for backpackers can be obtained at the US Forest Service field office in the area. *The Guide to Your National Forests* is available at all Forest Service branches, or call or write the main office (USDA, Forest Service, P.O. Box 96090, Washington, D.C. 20090; ☎202-205-8333). This booklet includes a list of all national forest addresses; request maps and other info directly from the forest(s) you plan to visit. Reservations, with a one-time $16.50 service fee, are available for most forests, but are usually only needed during high season at the more popular sites. Call up to one year in advance to National Recreation Reservation Center (☎877-444-6777; international 518-885-3639; www.reserveusa.com).

CANADA'S NATIONAL PARKS

Less trammeled than their southern counterparts, these parks boast at least as much natural splendor. Park entrance fees range from CDN$3-7 per person, with family and multi-day passes available. Reservations are offered for a limited number of campgrounds with a CDN$7 fee. For these reservations, or for info on the over 40 parks and countless historical sites in the network, call Parks Canada (☎888-773-8888) or consult the web page (http://parkscanada.pch.gc.ca). Regional passes are available at relevant parks; the best is the Western Canada Pass, which covers admission to all the parks in the Western provinces for a year (CDN$35 per adult, CDN$70 per group—up to seven people).

WILDERNESS SAFETY

THE GREAT OUTDOORS. Stay warm, stay dry, and stay hydrated. The vast majority of life-threatening wilderness situations can be avoided by following this simple advice. Prepare yourself for an emergency, however, by always packing raingear, a hat and mittens, a first-aid kit, a reflector, a whistle, high energy food, and extra water for any hike. Dress in wool or warm layers of synthetic materials designed for the outdoors; never rely on cotton for warmth, as it is useless when wet. See **Health,** p. 39, for information about outdoor ailments and basic medical concerns.

WILDLIFE. If you are hiking in an area that might be frequented by **bears,** keep your distance. No matter how cute bears appear, don't be fooled—they're powerful and dangerous animals. If you see a bear at a distance, calmly walk (don't run) in the other direction. If the bear pursues you, back away slowly while speaking in low, firm tones. If you are attacked by a bear, get in a fetal position to protect yourself, put your arms over your neck, and play dead. In all situations, remain calm and don't make any loud noises or sudden movements. Don't leave food or other scented items (trash, toiletries, the clothes that you cooked in) near your tent.Putting these objects into canisters is now mandatory in some national parks in California, including Yosemite. **Bear-bagging,** hanging edibles and other good-smelling objects from a tree out of reach of hungry paws, is the best way to keep your

ENVIRONMENTALLY RESPONSIBLE TOURISM. The idea behind responsible tourism is to leave no trace of human presence behind. A campstove is the safer (and more efficient) way to cook than using vegetation, but if you must make a fire, keep it small and use only dead branches or brush rather than cutting vegetation. Make sure your campsite is at least 150 ft. (50m) from water supplies or bodies of water. If there are no toilet facilities, bury human waste (but not paper) at least four inches (10cm) deep and above the high-water line, and 150 ft. or more from any water supplies and campsites. Always pack your trash in a plastic bag and carry it with you until you reach the next trash receptacle. For more information on these issues, contact one of the organizations listed below.

Earthwatch, 3 Clock Tower Pl., #100, Box 75, Maynard, MA 01754 (☎800-776-0188 or 978-461-0081; fax 978-461-2332; info@earthwatch.org; www.earthwatch.org).

Ecotourism Society, P.O. Box 668, Burlington, VT 05402 (☎802-651-9818; fax 802-651-9819; ecomail@ecotourism.org; www.ecotourism.org).

National Audobon Society, Nature Odysseys, 700 Broadway, New York, NY 10003 (☎212-979-3000; fax 212-979-3188; audobon@neodata.com; www.audobon.org).

Tourism Concern, Stapleton House, 277-281 Holloway Rd., London N7 8HN, UK (☎020 7753 3330; fax 020 7753 3331; info@tourismconcern.org.uk; www.tourismconcern.org.uk).

toothpaste from becoming a condiment. Bears are also attracted to any **perfume,** as are bugs, so cologne, scented soap, deodorant, and hairspray should stay at home.

Poisonous **snakes** are hazards in many wilderness areas in the US and Canada and should be carefully avoided. The two most dangerous are coral and rattlesnakes. Coral snakes reside in the Southwestern US and can be identified by black, yellow, and red bands. Rattlesnakes live in desert and marsh areas and will vigorously shake the rattle at the end of their tail when threatened. Don't attempt to handle or kill a snake; if you see one, back away slowly. If you are bitten, apply a pressure bandage and ice to the wound and immobilize the limb. Seek immediate medical attention for any snakebite that breaks the skin.

Mountain regions provide the stomping grounds for **moose.** These big, antlered animals have been known to charge humans, so never feed, walk toward, or throw anything at a moose. If a moose charges, get behind a tree immediately. If it attacks you, get on the ground in a fetal position and stay very still.

For more info, see *How to Stay Alive in the Woods* (Macmillan Press, $8).

CAMPING & HIKING EQUIPMENT

WHAT TO BUY...

Good camping equipment is both sturdy and light. Camping equipment is generally more expensive in Australia, New Zealand, and the UK than in North America.

Sleeping Bag: Sleeping bags come in a number of materials and varieties specialized for season. Prices range $80-210 for a summer synthetic to $250-300 for a good down winter bag.

Tent: The best tents are free-standing (with their own frames and suspension systems), set up quickly, and only require staking in high winds. Good 2-person tents start at $90, 4-person at $300. Seal the seams of your tent with waterproofer, and make sure to check that it has a rain fly.

Backpack: Internal-frame packs mold better to your back, keep a lower center of gravity, and flex adequately to allow you to hike difficult trails. **External-frame packs** are more comfortable for long hikes over even terrain, as they keep weight higher and distribute it more evenly. Sturdy backpacks cost anywhere from $125-420—this is one area in which it doesn't pay to economize.

Boots: Be sure to wear hiking boots with good **ankle support.** They should fit snugly and comfortably over 1-2 pairs of wool socks and thin liner socks. Break in boots over several weeks first in order to spare yourself painful and debilitating blisters.

Other Necessities: Synthetic layers, like those made of polypropylene, and a **pile jacket** will keep you warm even when wet. A **"space blanket"** will help you to retain your body heat and doubles as a groundcloth ($5-15). Plastic **water bottles** are virtually shatter- and leak-proof. Bring **water-purification tablets** for when you can't boil water. For those places that forbid fires or the gathering of firewood, you'll need a **camp stove** (the classic Coleman starts at $40) and a propane-filled **fuel bottle** to operate it. Also don't forget a **first-aid kit, pocketknife, insect repellent, calamine lotion,** and **waterproof matches** or a **lighter.**

CAMPERS & RVS

Much to the chagrin of more purist outdoorsmen, the US and Canada are havens for the corpulent, home-and-stove on wheels known as **recreational vehicles (RVs).** Most national parks and small towns cater to RV travelers, providing campgrounds with large parking areas and electric outlets ("full hook-up"). The costs of RVing compare favorably with the price of staying in hotels and renting a car (see **Rental Cars,** p. 63), and the convenience of bringing along your own bedroom, bathroom, and kitchen makes it an attractive option.

ORGANIZED ADVENTURE TRIPS

Organized adventure tours offer another way of exploring the wild. Activities include hiking, biking, skiing, canoeing, kayaking, rafting, and climbing. Consult tourism bureaus, which can suggest parks, trails, and outfitters. Other good sources for organized adventure options are the stores and organizations specializing in camping and outdoor equipment listed above.

Specialty Travel Index, 305 San Anselmo Ave., #313, San Anselmo, CA 94960 (☎800-442-4922 or 415-459-4900; fax 415-459-9474; info@specialtytravel.com; www.specialtytravel.com). Tours worldwide.

AmeriCan Adventures & Roadrunner, P.O. Box 1155, Gardena, CA 90249 (☎800-TREK-USA or 310-324-3447; fax 310-324-3562; UK ☎01295 756 2000; www.americanadventures.com). Organizes group adventure camping and hostelling trips (with transportation and camping costs included) in the US and Canada.

The Sierra Club, 85 2nd. St., 2nd fl., San Francisco, CA 94105 (☎415-977-5522; national.outings@sierraclub.org; www.sierraclub.org/outings), plans many adventure outings at all of its branches throughout Canada and the US.

TrekAmerica, P.O. Box 189, Rockaway, NJ 07866 (☎800-221-0596; www.trekamerica.com), operates small group adventure tours throughout the US, including Alaska, Hawaii, and Canada. Tours are for 18- to 38-year olds and run 1-9 weeks.

KEEPING IN TOUCH

BY MAIL

First-class letters sent and received within the US take 1-3 days and cost $0.37; Priority Mail packages up to 1 lb. generally take 2 days and cost $3.85, up to 5 lb.

$7.70. All days specified denote business days. For more details, see www.usps.com.

SENDING MAIL FROM THE US & CANADA

Aerogrammes, printed sheets that fold into envelopes and travel via airmail, are available at post offices. The marking "par avion" is universally understood. The cost is 70¢; a simple postcard is also 70¢. A **standard letter** can be sent abroad in about 4-7 business days for $1.50. For packages up to 4 lb., use **Global Priority Mail,** for delivery to major locations in 3-5 business days for a flat rate ($5).

If regular airmail is too slow, **Federal Express** (☎800-247-4747) can get a letter from New York to Sydney in two business days for a whopping $30. By **US Express Mail,** a letter would arrive within four business days and would cost $15.

Surface mail is by far the cheapest and slowest way to send mail. It takes one to three months to cross the Atlantic and two to four to cross the Pacific—appropriate for sending large quantities of items you won't need to see for a while. When ordering books and materials from abroad, always include one or two **International Reply Coupons (IRCs)**—a way of providing the postage to cover delivery. IRCs should be available from your local post office and those abroad ($1).

RECEIVING MAIL

Mail can be sent to the US through **General Delivery** to almost any city or town with a post office. Address letters to:

Elvis PRESLEY
General Delivery
Post Office Street Address
Memphis, TN 38101 or Kelowna, BC V1Z 2H6
USA or CANADA.

The mail will go to a special desk in the central post office, unless you specify a post office by street address or postal code. As a rule, it is best to use the largest post office in the area, and mail may be sent there regardless of what is written on the envelope. It is usually safer and quicker to send mail express or registered. When picking up your mail, bring a form of photo ID, preferably a passport.

BY TELEPHONE

PLACING INTERNATIONAL CALLS. To call the US or Canada from home or to call home from the US or Canada dial:
1. The **international dialing prefix.** To dial out of **Australia,** dial 0011; the **Republic of Ireland, New Zealand,** or the **UK,** 00; **South Africa,** 09; out of **Canada** or the **US,** 011.
2. The **country code** of the country you want to call. To call **Australia,** dial 61; the **Republic of Ireland,** 353; **New Zealand,** 64; **South Africa,** 27; the **UK,** 44; **Canada** or the **US,** 1.
3. The **city/area code.** *Let's Go* lists the city/area codes for cities and towns opposite the city or town name, next to a ☎.
4. The **local number.**

CALLING HOME FROM CANADA & THE US

A **calling card** is probably your cheapest bet. Calls are billed collect or to your account. You can often also make **direct international calls** from pay phones, but if you aren't using a calling card, you may need to drop your coins as quickly as your words. Where available, prepaid phone cards (see below) and occasionally major credit cards can be used for direct international calls, but they are still less cost-effective. (See the box on **Placing International Calls** (p. 52) for directions on how to place a direct international call.)

CALLING WITHIN CANADA & THE US

The simplest way to call within the country is to use a coin-operated pay phone which charges 35 cents for local calls. You can also buy **prepaid phone cards,** which carry a certain amount of prepaid phone time. Phone rates tend to be highest in the morning, lower in the evening, and lowest on Sunday and late at night.

Let's Go has recently formed a partnership with ekit.com to provide a calling card that offers a number of services, including email and voice messaging services. Before purchasing any calling card, always be sure to compare rates with other cards, and to make sure it serves your needs (a local phonecard is generally better for local calls, for instance). For more information on this card, visit www.letsgo.ekit.com.

BY EMAIL & INTERNET

Most public libraries in the US and Canada offer free Internet access, and Internet cafes abound. Check the **Practical Information** sections of major cities for establishments with Internet access. For lists of additional cybercafes the US and Canada, check out www.cybercaptive.com.

GETTING THERE

BY PLANE

When it comes to airfare, a little effort can save you a bundle. If your plans are flexible enough to deal with the restrictions, courier fares are the cheapest. Tickets bought from consolidators and standby seating are also good deals, but last-minute specials, airfare wars, and charter flights often beat these fares. The key is to hunt around, to be flexible, and to persistently ask about discounts. Students, seniors, and those under 26 should never pay full price for a ticket.

DETAILS AND TIPS

Route: Round-trip flights are by far the cheapest; "open-jaw" (arriving in and departing from different cities) and round-the-world, flights are pricier but reasonable alternatives. Patching one-way flights together is the least economical way to travel. Flights between capital cities or regional hubs will offer the most competitive fares.

Gateway Cities: Flights between capitals or regional hubs will offer the cheapest fares. The cheapest gateway cities in North America are typically New York, Chicago, Atlanta, Houston, and Los Angeles.

Fares: Round-trip fares from Western Europe to the US range from $100-400 (during the off season) to $200-550 (during the summer). Fares from Australia tend to the $900-1200 range. If the US or Canada is only 1 stop on a more extensive globe-hop, consider a round-the-world (RTW) ticket. Tickets usually include at least 5 stops and are valid for about a year; prices range US$1200-5000. Try **Northwest Airlines/KLM** (US ☎800-447-4747; www.nwa.com) or **Star Alliance,** a consortium of 22 airlines including United Airlines (US ☎800-241-6522; www.star-alliance.com).

ESSENTIALS

BUDGET & STUDENT TRAVEL AGENCIES

A knowledgeable agent specializing in flights to the US and Canada can make your life easy and help you save, too, but agents may not spend the time to find you the lowest possible fare—they get paid on commission. Those holding **ISIC and IYTC cards** (see **Identification,** p. 34) qualify for big discounts from student travel agencies. Most flights from budget agencies are on major airlines, but in peak season some may sell seats on less reliable chartered aircraft.

> **usit world** (www.usitworld.com). Over 50 **usit campus** branches in the UK, including 52 Grosvenor Gardens, **London** SW1W 0AG (☎0870 240 10 10); **Manchester** (☎0161 273 1880); and **Edinburgh** (☎0131 668 3303). Nearly 20 **usit NOW** offices in Ireland, including 19-21 Aston Quay, O'Connell Bridge, **Dublin** 2 (☎01 602 1600; www.usit-now.ie), and **Belfast** (☎02 890 327 111; www.usitnow.com). Offices also in Athens, Auckland, Brussels, Frankfurt, Johannesburg, Lisbon, Luxembourg, Madrid, and Paris.

> **CTS Travel,** 44 Goodge St., **London** W1T 2AD, UK(☎0207 636 0031; fax 0207 637 5328; ctsinfo@ctstravel.co.uk).

> **STA Travel,** 7890 S. Hardy Dr., Ste. 110, Tempe AZ 85284 (24hr. reservations and info ☎800-781-4040; www.sta-travel.com). A student and youth travel organization with over 150 offices worldwide, including US offices in Boston, Chicago, L.A., New York, San Francisco, Seattle, and Washington, D.C. Ticket booking, travel insurance, rail-passes, and more. In the UK, walk-in office 11 Goodge St., **London** W1T 2PF or call 0207-436-7779. In New Zealand, Shop 2B, 182 Queen St., **Auckland** (☎09 309 0458). In Australia, 366 Lygon St., **Carlton** Vic 3053 (☎03 9349 4344).

> **Travel CUTS (Canadian Universities Travel Services Limited),** 187 College St., **Toronto,** ON M5T 1P7 (☎416-979-2406; fax 979-8167; www.travelcuts.com). 60 offices across Canada. Also in the UK, 295-A Regent St., **London** W1R 7YA (☎0207-255-1944).

COMMERCIAL AIRLINES

The commercial airlines' lowest regular offer is the **APEX** (Advance Purchase Excursion) fare, which provides confirmed reservations and allows "open-jaw" tickets. Generally, reservations must be made seven to 21 days ahead of departure, with seven- to 14-day minimum-stay and up to 90-day maximum-stay restrictions. These fares carry hefty cancellation and change penalties (fees rise in summer). Book peak-season APEX fares early; by May you will have a hard time getting your desired departure date.

Although APEX fares are probably not the cheapest possible fares, they provide a sense of the average commercial price. Low-season fares should be appreciably cheaper than peak-season (mid-June to Aug.) fares.

AIR COURIER FLIGHTS

Those who travel light should consider courier flights. Generally, couriers must travel with carry-ons only and deal with complex flight restrictions. Most flights are round-trip with short fixed-length stays (usually one week) and a limit of a one ticket per issue. Most flights operate only out of major gateway cities: New York, Los Angeles, San Francisco, or Miami in the US; and Montreal, Toronto, or Vancouver in Canada. Generally, you must be over 21 (in some cases 18). In summer, the most popular destinations usually require an advance reservation of about two weeks (you can usually book up to two months ahead). Super-discounted fares are common for "last-minute" flights (three to 14 days ahead).

ESSENTIALS

STANDBY FLIGHTS

Traveling standby requires considerable flexibility in arrival and departure dates and cities. Companies dealing in standby flights sell vouchers rather than tickets, along with the promise to get to your destination (or near your destination) within a certain window of time (typically one-five days). To check on a company's service record in the US, call the Better Business Bureau (☎212-533-6200).

TICKET CONSOLIDATORS

Ticket consolidators, or **"bucket shops,"** buy unsold tickets in bulk from commercial airlines and sell them at discounted rates. The best place to look is in the Sunday travel section of any major newspaper, where many bucket shops place tiny ads. Call quickly, as availability is typically extremely limited. Not all bucket shops are reliable, so insist on a receipt that gives full details of restrictions, refunds, and tickets, and pay by credit card so you can stop payment if you never receive your tickets. For more info, see www.travel-library.com/air-travel/consolidators.html.

CHARTER FLIGHTS

Charters are flights a tour operator contracts with an airline to fly extra loads of passengers during peak season. Charter flights fly less frequently than major airlines, make refunds particularly difficult, and are almost always fully booked. Schedules and itineraries may also change or be cancelled at the last moment (as late as 48 hours before the trip, and without a full refund), and check-in, boarding, and baggage claim are often much slower. However, they can also be cheaper.

Discount clubs and **fare brokers** offer members savings on last-minute charter and tour deals. Study contracts closely; you don't want to end up with an unwanted overnight layover. **Travelers Advantage,** Trumbull, CT, USA (☎203-365-2000; www.travelersadvantage.com; $60 annual fee includes discounts and cheap flight directories) can provide more information.

> ✈ **FLIGHT PLANNING ON THE INTERNET.** Many airline sites offer special last-minute deals on the Web. Other sites do the legwork and compile the deals for you—try www.bestfares.com, www.flights.com, www.hotdeals.com, www.onetravel.com, and www.travelzoo.com.
>
> ▨ **StudentUniverse** (www.studentuniverse.com), **STA** (www.sta-travel.com), **Council** (www.counciltravel.com), and **Orbitz.com** provide quotes on student tickets, while **Expedia** (www.expedia.com) and **Travelocity** (www.travelocity.com) offer full travel services. **Priceline** (www.priceline.com) allows you to specify a price, and obligates you to buy any ticket that meets or beats it; be prepared for antisocial hours and odd routes. **Skyauction** (www.skyauction.com) allows you to bid on both last-minute and advance-purchase tickets.

GETTING AROUND
BY TRAIN

Locomotion is still one of the least expensive (and most pleasant) ways to tour the US and Canada, but discounted air travel may be cheaper, and much faster, than train travel. As with airlines, you can save money by purchasing your tickets as far in advance as possible, so plan ahead and make reservations early. It is essential to travel light on trains; not all stations will check your baggage.

AMTRAK

Amtrak is the only provider of intercity passenger train service in the US. (☎800-872-7245; www.amtrak.com.) Most cities have Amtrak offices which directly sell tickets, but tickets must be bought through an agent in some small towns. The web page lists up-to-date schedules, fares, arrival and departure info, and makes reservations. **Discounts** on full rail fares are given to: senior citizens (15% off), Student Advantage cardholders (15% off; call 800-962-6872 to purchase the $20 card), travelers with disabilities (15% off), ages 2-15 accompanied by a paying adult (50% off), children under 2 (free), and current members of the US armed forces, active-duty veterans, and their dependents (25% off; www.veteransadvantage.com). "Rail SALE" offers online discounts of up to 90%. Amtrak also offers some **special packages**—check the website or call for more information.

VIA RAIL

VIA Rail, 3 Place Ville-Marie, Suite 500, Montreal, Quebec H3B 2C9 (☎888-842-7245 or 800-561-3449 from the US; www.viarail.ca), is Amtrak's Canadian analog. **Discounts** on full fares are given to: full-time students with ISIC cards (35% off full fare), seniors 60 and over (10% off), ages 2-11 accompanied by an adult (50% off), ages 12-17 (35% off). Reservations are required for first-class seats and sleep car accommodations. The **Canrailpass** allows unlimited travel on 12 days within a 30-day period. Between early June and early October, a 12-day pass costs CDN$678 (seniors and youths and students with an ISIC, CDN$610). Off-season passes cost CDN$423 (seniors, youths, and students, CDN$381). Add CDN$34-50 per extra day up to 3 days. Call for info on seasonal promotions.

BY BUS

Buses generally offer the most frequent and complete service between the cities and towns of the US and Canada. Often a bus is the only way to reach smaller locales without a car. In rural areas and across open spaces, however, bus lines tend to be sparse. *Russell's Official National Motor Coach Guide* ($16 including postage) is an invaluable tool for constructing an itinerary. Updated each month, Russell's Guide has schedules of every bus route (including Greyhound) between any two towns in the United States and Canada. Russell's also publishes two semiannual Supplements which are free when ordered with the main issue; a Directory of Bus Lines and Bus Stations, and a series of Route Maps (both $9 if ordered separately). To order any of the above, write **Russell's Guides, Inc.,** P.O. Box 178, Cedar Rapids, IA 52406 (☎319-364-6138; fax 362-8808).

GREYHOUND

Greyhound (☎800-231-2222; www.greyhound.com) operates the most routes in the US, and provides service to parts of Canada. Schedule information is available at any Greyhound terminal or agency and on their web page.

> **Advance purchase fares:** Reserving space far ahead of time ensures a lower fare, but expect smaller discounts between June 5 and Sept. 15. Fares are often lower for 14-day, 7-day, or 3-day advance purchases. For 3-day advance purchase M-Th, 2 people ride for the price of 1 ticket. Call for up-to-date pricing or consult their web page.

> **Discounts on full fares:** Senior citizens with a Greyhound Senior Club Card (10% off); children ages 2-11 (50% off); Student Advantage card holders (up to 15% off); disabled travelers and their companions receive two tickets for the price of one; active and retired US military personnel and National Guard Reserves (10% off with valid ID). With a ticket purchased 3 or more days in advance during the spring and summer months, a friend can travel along for free (with some exceptions).

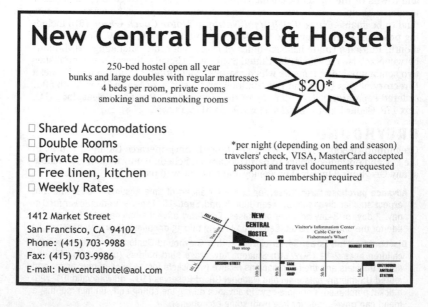

Ameripass: ☎800-454-7277. Allows adults unlimited travel through the US. 7-day pass $220; 10-day pass $269; 15-day pass $340; 30-day pass $450, 45-day pass $499; 60-day pass $625. Student discounts available. Children's passes are half-price. Before purchasing an Ameripass, total up the separate bus fares between towns to make sure that the pass is more economical or at least worth the flexibility it provides.

International Ameripass: For travelers from outside North America. ☎800-454-7277 for info. 7 days ($204), 10 days ($254), 15 days ($314), 30 days ($424), 45 days ($464), or 60 days ($499). International Ameripasses are not available at the terminal; they can be purchased in foreign countries at Greyhound-affiliated agencies; telephone numbers are listed on the website. Passes can also be ordered at the website, or purchased by calling ☎800-229-9424 in the US.

GREYHOUND CANADA TRANSPORTATION

Greyhound Canada Transportation, (☎800-661-8747; www.greyhound.ca), is Canada's main intercity bus company. The web page has full schedule info.

Discounts: Seniors 10% off; students 25% off with an ISIC; 10% off with other student cards; If reservations are made at least 7 days in advance, a friend travels half off, while children under 16 ride free with an adult.

Canada Pass: Unlimited travel from the western border of Canada to Montréal on all routes for North American residents, including some links to northern US cities. 7 day advance purchase required. 7-day pass CDN$264, 10-day pass CDN$334, 15-day pass CDN$404, 21-day pass CDN$444, 30-day pass CDN$474, 45-day pass CDN$564, 60-day pass CDN$634. Discovery Passes are available for non-US, non-Canadian travelers.

BY CAR

"I" (as in "I-90") refers to Interstate highways, "U.S." (as in "U.S. 1") to US highways, and "Rte." (as in "Rte. 7") to state and local highways. For Canadian highways, "TCH" refers to the Trans-Canada Hwy., while "Hwy." or "autoroute" refers to standard automobile routes.

INTERNATIONAL DRIVING PERMIT

If you do not have a license issued by a US state or Canadian province or territory, you might want an International Driving Permit (IDP)—it may help with police if your license is not written in English. You must carry your home license with your IDP at all times. You must be 18 to obtain an IDP, it is valid for a year, and must be issued in the country in which your license originates.

CAR INSURANCE

Most credit cards cover standard insurance. If you rent, lease, or borrow a car, you will need a **green card,** or **International Insurance Certificate,** to certify that you have liability insurance and that it applies abroad. Green cards can be obtained at car rental agencies, car dealers (for those leasing cars), some travel agents, and some border crossings. Rental agencies may require you to purchase theft insurance in countries that they consider to have a high risk of auto theft.

AUTOMOBILE CLUBS

Most automobile clubs offer free towing, emergency roadside assistance, travel-related discounts, and random goodies in exchange for a modest membership fee. Travelers should strongly consider membership if planning an extended roadtrip.

ESSENTIALS

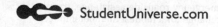

■ **American Automobile Association (AAA).** Provides emergency road service (☎800-222-4357) in the US. Free trip-planning services, maps, and guidebooks, and 24hr. emergency road service anywhere in the US.US Free towing and commission-free American Express Traveler's Checks from over 1000 offices across the country. Discounts on Hertz car rental (5-20%), Amtrak tickets (10%), and various motel chains and theme parks. Basic membership $45, Associate Membership $24. To sign up, call 800-564-6222 or go to www.aaa.com.

Canadian Automobile Association (CAA), 1145 Hunt Club Rd., #200, Ottawa, ON K1V 0Y3 (☎800-222-4357; www.caa.ca). Affiliated with AAA (see above), the CAA provides the same membership benefits, including 24hr. emergency roadside assistance, free maps and tourbooks, route planning, and various discounts. Basic membership is CDN$68 and CDN$33 for associates; call 800-564-6222 to sign up.

ON THE ROAD

While driving, be sure to buckle up—seat belts are **required by law** in many regions of the US and Canada. The **speed limit** in the US varies considerably from region to region. Most urban highways have a limit of 55 mph (89kph), while rural routes range from 65 mph (104kph) to 75 mph (120kph). Heed the limit; not only does it save gas, but most local police forces and state troopers make frequent use of radar to catch speed demons. The **speed limit in Canada** is 50kph (31mph) in cities and 80kph (49 mph) on highways. On rural highways the speed limit may be 100kph (62 mph).

HOW TO NAVIGATE THE INTERSTATES

In the 50s, President Dwight D. Eisenhower envisioned a well-organized **interstate highway system.** His dream has been realized: there is now a comprehensive, well-maintained, efficient means of traveling between major cities and between states. Luckily for travelers, the highways are named with an intuitive numbering system. Even-numbered interstates run east-west and odd ones run north-south, decreasing in number toward the south and the west. North-south routes begin on the West Coast with I-5 and end with I-95 on the East Coast. The southernmost east-west route is I-4 in Florida. The northernmost east-west route is I-94, stretching from Montana to Wisconsin. Three-digit numbers signify branches of other interstates (e.g., I-285 is a branch of I-85) that often skirt around large cities.

RENTING. Car rental agencies fall into two categories: national companies with hundreds of branches, and local agencies that serve only one city or region. National chains usually allow you to pick up a car in one city and drop it off in another (for a hefty charge, sometimes in excess of $1000). The drawbacks of car rentals include steep prices (a compact car rents for $25-45 per day) and high minimum ages for rentals (usually 25). Most branches rent to ages 21 to 24 with an additional fee, but policies and prices vary from agency to agency. **Alamo** (☎800-327-9633; www.alamo.com) rents to ages 21 to 24 with a major credit card for an additional $20 per day. **Enterprise** (☎800-736-8222; www.enterprise.com) rents to customers ages 21 to 24 with a variable surcharge. **Dollar** (☎800-800-4000; www.dollar.com) and **Thrifty** (☎800-367-2277; www.thrifty.com) locations do likewise for varying surcharges. **Rent-A-Wreck** (☎800-944-7501; www.rent-a-wreck.com) specializes in supplying vehicles that are past their prime for lower-than-average prices; a bare-bones compact less than eight years old rents for around $20 to $25. There may be an additional charge for a **collision and damage waiver (CDW),** which usually comes to about $12 to 15 per day. Major credit cards (including MasterCard and American Express) will sometimes cover the CDW if you use their card to rent a car; call your credit card company for specifics.

Because it is mandatory for all drivers in the US, make sure with your rental agency that you are covered by **insurance**. Be sure to ask whether the price

ESSENTIALS

includes **insurance** against theft and collision. Some credit cards cover standard insurance. If you rent, lease, or borrow a car, and you are not from the US or Canada, you will need a **green card,** or **International Insurance Certificate,** to certify that you have liability insurance and that it applies abroad. Green cards can be obtained at car rental agencies, car dealerships, some travel agents, and some border crossings. If you are driving a conventional vehicle on an **unpaved road** in a rental car, you are almost never covered by insurance. National chains often allow one-way rentals, picking up in one city and dropping off in another, although there is often a steep additional charge. There is usually a minimum hire period and sometimes an extra drop-off charge of several hundred dollars.

AUTO TRANSPORT COMPANIES. These services match drivers with car owners who need cars moved from one city to another. Would-be travelers give the company their desired destination and the company finds a car that needs to go there. Expenses include gas, tolls, and your own living expenses. Some companies insure their cars; with others, your security deposit covers any breakdowns or damage. You must be over 21, have a valid license, and agree to drive about 400 mi. per day on a fairly direct route. The following are popular transport companies:

Auto Driveaway Co., 310 S. Michigan Ave., Chicago, IL 60604-4298 (☎800-346-2277/312-341-1900; www.autodriveaway.com).

Across America Driveaway, 9839 Industrial Dr., Highland, IN 46322 (☎800-619-7707; www.schultz-international.com). Offices in L.A. (☎800-964-7874).

BY BICYCLE

Before you pedal furiously onto the byways of America astride your banana-seat Huffy, remember that safe and secure cycling requires a quality helmet and lock. U-shaped **Kryptonite** or **Citadel** locks ($30-60) carry insurance against theft for 1 or 2 years if your bike is registered with the police. **Bike Nashbar,** P.O. Box 1455, Crab Orchard, WV 25827 (☎800-627-4227), will beat any nationally advertised in-stock price by 5¢, and ships anywhere in the US or Canada. Their techline (☎800-888-2710; open M-F 8am-6pm ET) fields questions about repairs and maintenance.

Adventure Cycling Association, P.O. Box 8308, Missoula, MT 59807 (☎800-755-2453; www.adv-cycling.org). A national, nonprofit organization that researches and maps long distance routes and organizes bike tours (75-day Great Divide Expedition $2800, 6-9 day trip $650-800). Annual membership ($30), includes access to maps and routes and a subscription to *Adventure Cyclist* magazine

The Canadian Cycling Association, 702-2197 Riverside Dr., Ottawa, ON K1H 7X3 (☎613-248-1353; fax 248-9311; general@canadian-cycling.com; www.canadian-cycling.com). Provides info for cyclists of all abilities. Distributes The Canadian Cycling Association's Complete Guide to Bicycle Touring in Canada.

BY MOTORCYCLE

The wind-in-your-face thrill, burly leather, and revving crackle of a motorcycle engine unobscured by windows or upholstery has built up quite a cult following, but motorcycling is the most dangerous of roadtop activities. Of course, safety should be your primary concern. Helmets are required by law in California; wear the best one you can find. Those considering a long journey should contact the **American Motorcyclist Association,** 13515 Yarmouth Dr., Pickering, OH 43147 (☎800-262-5646; www.ama-cycle.org), the linchpin of US biker culture. And of course, take a copy of Robert Pirsig's *Zen and the Art of Motorcycle Maintenance* (1974) with you.

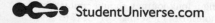

BY THUMB

Let's Go urges you to consider the great risks and disadvantages of **hitchhiking** before thumbing it. Hitching means entrusting your life to a randomly selected person who happens to stop beside you on the road. While this may be comparatively safe in some areas of Europe and Australia, it is generally *not* so in the US or Canada. We strongly urge you to find other means of transportation and to avoid situations where hitching is the only option.

SPECIFIC CONCERNS

WOMEN TRAVELERS

Women exploring on their own inevitably face some additional safety concerns, but it's easy to be adventurous without taking undue risks. Always carry extra money for a phone call, bus, or taxi. **Hitchhiking** is never safe especially for women travelling alone.Your best answer to verbal harassment is no answer at all; feigning deafness, sitting motionless, and staring straight ahead will usually be effective. *Let's Go: USA* lists emergency numbers (including rape crisis lines) in the **Practical Information** listings of most cities, and you can always dial **911.**

INFORMATION SERVICES

National Organization for Women, or **NOW** (now@now.org; www.now.org), can refer women travelers to rape crisis centers and counseling services. Main office: 733 15th St. NW, 2nd fl., Washington, D.C. 20005 (☎202-628-8669).

FURTHER READING

A Journey of One's Own: Uncommon Advice for the Independent Woman Traveler, Thalia Zepatos. Eighth Mountain Press ($17).

Active Women Vacation Guide, Evelyn Kaye. Blue Panda Publications ($18).

TRAVELING ALONE

There are many benefits to traveling alone, including independence and greater interaction with locals. On the other hand, any solo traveler is a more vulnerable target of harassment and street theft. As a lone traveler, try not to stand out as a tourist, look confident, and be especially careful in deserted or very crowded areas. If questioned, never admit that you are traveling alone. Maintain regular contact with someone at home who knows your itinerary.

INFORMATION SERVICES

Connecting: Solo Traveler Network, 689 Park Rd., Unit 6, Gibsons, BC V0N 1V7 (☎604-886-9099; info@cstn.org; www.cstn.org). Bimonthly newsletter features going solo tips, single-friendly tips, and travel companion ads. Membership $35.

Travel Companion Exchange (TCE), P.O. Box 833, Amityville, NY 11701 (☎800-392-1256 or 631-454-0880; www.whytravelalone.com) Subscription $48.

FURTHER READING

Traveling Solo, Eleanor Berman. Globe Pequot ($17).

The Single Traveler Newsletter, P.O. Box 682, Ross, CA 94957 (☎415-389-0227). 6 issues $29.

OLDER TRAVELERS

Senior citizens are eligible for a wide range of discounts on transportation, museums, movies, theaters, concerts, restaurants, and accommodations. If you don't see a senior citizen price listed, ask.

FURTHER READING

No Problem! Worldwise Tips for Mature Adventurers, Janice Kenyon. Orca Book Publishers ($16).

Unbelievably Good Deals and Great Adventures That You Absolutely Can't Get Unless You're Over 50, by Joan Rattner Heilman. NTC/Contemporary Publishing ($13).

INFORMATION SERVICES

ElderTreks, 597 Markham St., Toronto, ON M6G 2L7 (☎800-741-7956; www.eldertreks.com). Adventure travel programs for the 50+ traveler.

Elderhostel, 11 Ave. de Lafayette, Boston, MA 02111 (☎877-426-8056; www.elderhostel.org). Organizes 1- to 4-week "educational adventures" on varied topics for those 55+.

The Mature Traveler, P.O. Box 15791, Sacramento, CA 95852 (☎800-460-6676). Deals, discounts, and travel packages for the 50+ traveler. Subscription $30.

Walking the World, P.O. Box 1186, Fort Collins, CO 80522 (☎800-340-9255; www.walkingtheworld.com), organizes trips for 50+ travelers to the USA.

BISEXUAL, GAY, LESBIAN TRAVELERS

American cities are generally accepting of all sexualities, and thriving gay and lesbian communities can be found in most cosmopolitan areas. Most college towns are gay-friendly as well. In rural areas, however, homophobia can be rampant. In light of the anti-gay legislative measures narrowly defeated in various states, and not-so-isolated gay-bashing incidents, homophobia is still all too common.

INFORMATION SERVICES

Damron Company, P.O. Box 422458, San Francisco, CA. (☎415-255-0404 or ☎800-462-6654; www.damron.com). Publishes the *Damron Men's Guide, Damron Women's Traveller, DamronRoad Atlas,* and *Damron's Accommodations* ($14-19).

Giovanni's Room, 345 South 12th St., Philadelphia, PA. Mail Order: 1145 Pine St., Philadelphia, PA 19107 (☎215-923-2960; www.queerbooks.com). An international lesbian/feminist and gay bookstore with mail-order service.

International Lesbian and Gay Association (ILGA), 81 rue Marché-au-Charbon, B-1000 Brussels, Belgium (☎+32 2 502 2471; www.ilga.org). Provides political information, such as homosexuality laws of individual countries.

Out & About, 995 Market St., 14th Floor, San Francisco, CA 94103. (☎415-644-804; www.outandabout.com). Offers a bi-weekly newsletter addressing gay travel concerns.

FURTHER READING

Spartacus International Gay Guide 2002-2003. Bruno Gmunder Verlag ($33).

Ferrari Guides' Gay Travel A to Z, Ferrari Guides' Men's Travel in Your Pocket, Ferrari Guides' Women's Travel in Your Pocket, and *Ferrari Guides' Inn Places.* Marianne Ferrari. Ferrari Guides ($16-20).

Gayellow pages USA/Canada, Frances Green. Gayellow pages ($16). Order by phone (212-674-0120) or online at www.gayellowpages.com.

TRAVELERS WITH DISABILITIES

Federal law dictates that all public buildings should be wheelchair accessible, and recent laws governing building codes have made disabled access more the norm than the exception. Businesses, transportation companies, national parks, and public services are compelled to assist the disabled in using their facilities. All the same, those with disabilities should inform airlines, buses, trains, and hotels of their disabilities when making arrangements for travel; some time may be needed to prepare special accommodations. Call ahead to restaurants, hotels, parks, and other facilities to find out about the existence of ramps, the widths of doors, the dimensions of elevators, etc.

In the US, both Amtrak and major airlines will accommodate disabled passengers if notified at least 72 hours in advance. Amtrak offers a 15% discount to physically disabled travelers (☎800-872-7245, TDD/TTY 800-523-6590). Greyhound buses will provide free travel for a companion; if you are without a fellow traveler, call Greyhound (☎800-752-4841, TDD 800-345-3109) at least 48 hours, but no more than one week, before you plan to leave and they will make arrangements to assist you. For information on transportation availability in individual US cities, contact the local chapter of the Easter Seals Society.

If you are planning to visit a national park or attraction in the US run by the National Park Service, obtain a free **Golden Access Passport,** which is available at all park entrances and from federal offices whose functions relate to land, forests, or wildlife. The Passport entitles disabled travelers and their families to free park admission and provides a 50% discount on all campsite and parking fees.

USEFUL ORGANIZATIONS

Mobility International USA (MIUSA), P.O. Box 10767, Eugene, OR 97440, USA (☎541--343-1284, voice and TDD; www.miusa.org). Sells *A World of Options: A Guide to International Educational Exchange, Community Service, and Travel for Persons with Disabilities* (US$35).

Society for Accessible Travel & Hospitality. (SATH), 347 5th Ave., #610, New York, NY 10016, USA (☎212-447-7284; www.sath.org). Publishes free online travel information and the travel magazine *OPEN WORLD* (US$18, free for members). Annual membership $45, students and seniors $30.

TOUR AGENCIES

Directions Unlimited, 123 Green Ln., Bedford Hills, NY 10507, USA (☎800-533-5343). Books individual and group vacations for the physically disabled; not an info service.

The Guided Tour Inc., 7900 Old York Rd., #114B, Elkins Park, PA 19027, USA (☎800-783-5841; www.guidedtour.com). Organizes travel programs for persons with developmental and physical challenges throughout the US and Canada.

MINORITY TRAVELERS

While general attitudes towards race relations in the US and Canada differ drastically from region to region, racial and ethnic minorities sometimes face blatant and, more often, subtle discrimination and/or harassment. Verbal harassment is now less common than unfair pricing, false info on accommodations, or inexcusably slow or unfriendly service at restaurants. Report individuals to a supervisor and establishments to the **Better Business Bureau** for the region (www.bbb.org, or call the operator for local listings); contact the police in extreme situations. *Let's Go* always welcomes reader input regarding discriminating establishments.

FURTHER RESOURCES

United States Department of Justice (www.usdoj.gov/civilliberties.htm).

Go Girl! The Black Woman's Book of Travel and Adventure, Elaine Lee. Eighth Mountain Press ($18).

The African-American Travel Guide, Wayne Robinson. Hunter Publishing ($10).

TRAVELERS WITH CHILDREN

Restaurants often have children's discounts. as do virtually all museums and tourist attractions. Children under two generally fly for free or 10% of the adult airfare on domestic flights (this does not necessarily include a seat). Fares are usually discounted 25% for children 2 to 11 years old.

FURTHER READING

Kidding Around Boston; San Francisco; Washington, D.C.; Indianapolis; Austin; Chicago; Cleveland; Kansas City; Miami; Milwaukee; Minneapolis/St. Paul; Nashville; Portland; Seattle. various authors ($8).

How to take Great Trips with Your Kids, Sanford and Jane Portnoy. Harvard Common Press ($10).

Have Kid, Will Travel: 101 Survival Strategies for Vacationing With Babies and Young Children, Claire and Lucille Tristram. Andrews McMeel Publishing ($9).

DIETARY CONCERNS

Most major US cities are vegetarian-friendly, and the West Coast is especially so. While **vegetarians** should have no problem finding suitable cuisine as they travel, **vegans** may still meet with some confused, blank stares, especially in small-town America. For more info, consult:

North American Vegetarian Society, P.O. Box 72, Dolgeville, NY 13329 (☎518-568-7970; navs@telenet.com; www.navs-online.org). Publishes Transformative Adventures, a Guide to Vacations and Retreats ($15), and the Vegetarian Journal's Guide to Natural Food Restaurants in the US and Canada ($12).

FURTHER READING

The Vegetarian Traveler: Where to Stay if You're Vegetarian, Vegan, Environmentally Sensitive, Jed and Susan Civic. Larson Publications ($16).

Travelers who keep **kosher** should contact synagogues in larger cities for info on kosher restaurants; your own synagogue or college Hillel should have access to lists of Jewish institutions across the nation. You may also consult the kosher restaurant database at www.shamash.org/kosher.

The Jewish Travel Guide lists synagogues, kosher restaurants, and Jewish institutions in the US and Canada. Available in the US ($16) from ISBS, 5804 NE Hassallo St., Portland, OR 97213 (☎800-944-6190).

THE WORLD WIDE WEB

Almost every aspect of budget travel is accessible via the web. Listed here are some budget travel sites to start off your surfing; other relevant web sites are listed throughout the book. Because website turnover is high, use search engines (such as www.google.com) to strike out on your own.

OUR PERSONAL FAVORITE...

 WWW.LETSGO.COM Our newly designed website now features the full online content of all of our guides. In addition, trial versions of all nine City Guides are available for download onto Palm OS™ PDAs. Our website also contains our newsletter, links for photos and streaming video, online ordering of our titles, info about our books, and a travel forum buzzing with stories and tips.

THE ART OF BUDGET TRAVEL

How to See the World: www.artoftravel.com. A compendium of great travel tips, from cheap flights to self defense to interacting with local culture.

Rec. Travel Library: www.travel-library.com. A fantastic set of links for general information and personal travelogues.

Lycos: travel.lycos.com. Introductions to cities and regions throughout the US and Canada, accompanied by links to applicable histories, news, and local tourism sites.

Shoestring Travel: www.stratpub.com. An alternative to Microsoft's huge site. A budget travel e-zine that features listings of home exchanges, links, and accommodations info.

INFORMATION ON THE USA AND CANADA

CIA World Factbook: www.odci.gov/cia/publications/factbook/index.html. Tons of vital statistics on the US and Canada's geography, government, economy, and people.

Tourism Offices Worldwide Directory: www.towd.com. Lists tourism offices for all 50 states and Canada, as well as consulate and embassy addresses.

ESSENTIALS

ALTERNATIVES TO TOURISM

VISA INFORMATION

Visa. Visitors from most of Europe, Australia, and New Zealand can travel in the US for up to 90 days without a visa, although you may need to show a return plane ticket. Citizens of South Africa need a visa.

Work Permit. Required for all foreigners planning to work in the US.

Traveling from place to place around the world may be a memorable experience, but if you are looking for a more rewarding and complete way to see the world, you might want to consider Alternatives to Tourism. Working, volunteering, or studying for an extended period of time can be a better way to understand life in the US and Canada. This chapter outlines some of the different ways to get to know a new place, whether you want to pay your way, or just get the personal satisfaction that comes from studying and volunteering. In most cases, you will partake in a more meaningful and educational experience—something that the average budget traveler often misses out on.

All travelers planning a stay of more than 90 days (180 days for Canadians) need to obtain a visa. **The Center for International Business and Travel (CIBT),** 23201 New Mexico Ave. NW #210, Washington, D.C. 20016 (☎800-925-2428; www.cibt.com), or 6300 Wilshire Blvd., #1520, Los Angeles, CA 90048 (☎323-658-5100), secures "pleasure tourist" or B-2 visas to and from all possible countries for a variable service charge (6-month visa around $45). If you lose your I-94 form, you can replace it at the nearest **Immigration and Naturalization Service (INS)** office (☎800-375-5283; www.ins.usdoj.gov), though it's unlikely that the form will be replaced within the time of your stay. Visa extensions are sometimes attainable with an I-539 form; call the forms request line (☎800-870-3676).

Foreign students who wish to study in the US must apply for either an M-1 visa (vocational studies) or an F-1 visa (for full-time students enrolled in an academic or language program). If English is not your native language, you will probably be required to take the Test of English as a Foreign Language (TOEFL), which is administered in many countries. The international students office at the institution you will be attending can give you the specifics. Contact **TOEFL/TSE Publications,** P.O. Box 6151, Princeton, NJ 08541 (☎609-771-7100; www.toefl.org).

If you are a foreigner, you need a **work permit** or "green card" to work in the US. Your employer must obtain this document, usually by demonstrating that you have skills that locals lack. Friends in the US can sometimes help expedite work permits or arrange work-for-accommodations exchanges. Obtaining a worker's visa may seem complex, but it's critical that you go through the proper channels—the alternative is potential deportation.

STUDYING ABROAD

Study abroad programs range from basic language and culture courses to college-level classes, often for credit. In order to choose a program that best fits your needs, you will want to find out what kind of students participate in the program

STUDYING ABROAD ■ 73

and what sort of accommodations are provided. In programs that have large groups of students who speak the same language, there is a trade-off. You may feel more comfortable in the community, but you will not have the same opportunity to practice a foreign language or to befriend other international students. For accommodations, dorm life provides a better opportunity to mingle with fellow students, but there is less of a chance to experience the local scene. If you live with a family, there is a potential to build lifelong friendships with natives and to experience day-to-day life in more depth, but conditions can vary greatly from family to family and university to university.

Although getting college credit may be more difficult, Those relatively fluent in English may find it cheaper to enroll directly in a university abroad. Some American schools still require students to pay them for credits they obtain elsewhere. Most university-level study-abroad programs are meant as language and culture enrichment opportunities, and therefore are conducted in English. Still, many programs do offer classes in English and beginner- and lower-level language courses. A good resource for finding programs that cater to your particular interests is **www.studyabroad.com,** which has links to various semester abroad programs based on a variety of criteria, including desired location and focus of study. The following is a list of organizations that can help place students in university programs abroad, or have their own branch in the US.

PROGRAMS IN THE USA
In order to live the life of a real American college student, consider a visiting student program lasting either a semester or a full year. The best method by far is to contact colleges and universities in your home country to see what kind of exchanges they have with those in the US; college students can often receive credit for study abroad. A more complicated option for advanced English speakers is to enroll directly, full-time in an American institution. The US hosts a number of reputable universities, among them Stanford, Yale, and Duke, and Harvard. Apart from these, each state maintains a public state university system, and there are innumerable community, professional, and technical colleges. Unfortunately, tuition costs are high in the US and a full course of undergraduate study entails a four-year commitment.

LANGUAGE SCHOOLS
Unlike American universities, language schools are frequently independently-run international or local organizations or divisions of foreign universities that rarely offer college credit. Language schools offer a deeper focus on language, and/or a slightly less-rigorous course load. These programs are also good for younger high school students who might not feel comfortable with older students in a university program.

> **Eurocentres,** 101 N. Union St. #300, Alexandria, VA 22314 (☎703-684-1494; www.eurocentres.com) or in Europe, Head Office, Seestr. 247, CH-8038 Zurich, Switzerland (☎+41 1 485 50 40; fax 481 61 24). Language programs for beginning to advanced students with home stays in the US.

> **Nomen Global Language Center,** 63 North 400 West, Provo, UT 84601 (☎801-375-7878; www.nomenglobal.com). $1510 for a 15-week course, $325 for a 2-week short course, with corresponding costs for shorter and longer programs. Housing can also be arranged; home stays $110, accommodation rentals $225-1000.

> **American Language Programs,** 56 Hobbs Brook Rd., Weston, MA 02493 (☎781-888-1515; fax 894-3113; www.alp-online.com). ALP runs programs in the US that include home stay and intensive English training. $900-1080 per week (15-25hr.) for 1 person, $1600-1960 for 2 people.

Osako Sangyo University Los Angeles (OSULA) Education Center, 3921 Laurel Canyon Blvd., Los Angeles, CA 91604 (☎818-509-1484; www.osula.com). Offers intensive and general English classes in the suburbs of Los Angeles, in a residential college setting.

ART PROGRAMS & ARTISTS COLONIES

Those of a more creative persuasion can pursue artistic expression in the US— bohemian quarters of New York and San Francisco, as well as the wide open spaces of the American interior, beckon with artistic organizations of all stripes.

New York Film Academy, 100 E. 17th St., New York, NY 10003 (☎818-733-2600; www.nyfa.com). NYFA allows would-be actors, filmmakers, and screenwriters the chance to hone their skills on studio sets. Program lengths vary from 4 weeks to a year, with classes in acting, screenwriting, digital imaging, filmmaking, and 3-D animation. Program costs $2,000-22,500.

Arcosanti, HC 74 BOX 4136, Mayer, AZ 86333 (☎928-632-7135; tminus@arcosanti.org; www.arcosanti.org.) Founded by Frank Lloyd Wright's disciple Paolo Soleri, who still lives here, Arcosanti is an experimental community based on Soleri's theories of architecture and urban organization. It hosts 5-week workshops ($950) in which participants help expand the settlement while learning about Soleri's project and developing their skills at construction and planning. For those with some background in construction or architecture, an expense-paid internship is available for a 3-month commitment.

Institute for Unpopular Culture (IFUC), PMB#1523, 1850 Union St., San Francisco, CA 94123 (☎415-986-4382; fax 415-986-4354; www.ifuc.org). The IFUC accepts volunteers to help with its mission of funding unconventional and neglected art forms and artists. Free volunteering consists mainly of office support work.

Santa Fe Art Institute, 1600 St. Michael's Dr., Santa Fe, NM 84505 (☎505-424-5050; fax 505-424-5051; www.sfai.org). A world-class artistic center, the Santa Fe Art Institute offers 1- and 2-week workshops ($1000-1800) giving participants the opportunity to work with professional resident artists in Santa Fe.

Denver Center Theater Company, 1245 Champa St., Denver, CO 80204 (☎303-893-400; www.denvercenter.org). The Tony-award winning Denver Center Theatre Company offers a number of technical and administrative internships every year, as well as offering volunteering opportunities and inexpensive ($200-$300) theater classes.

The Wilma Theater, 265 S. Broad St., Philadelphia, PA 19107 (☎215-893-0895; www.wilmathater.org). Wilma offers unpaid internships and paid fellowships to young people with theater experience.

WORKING

Some travelers want long-term jobs that allow them to get to know another part of the world in depth (such as teaching their native language or working in the tourist industry), while other travelers seek out short-term jobs to finance their travel. This section discusses both short-term and long-term opportunities for working in the US. Make sure you understand the United States' **visa requirements** for foreign workers (see the box on p. 72).

LONG-TERM WORK

If you're planning on spending a substantial amount of time (more than three months) working in the US, search for a job well in advance. International placement agencies are often the easiest way to find employment abroad, especially for teaching English. If you don't mind an unconventional job, try **www.coolworks.com.** for a database of colorful, off-beat work opportunities. **Internships,** usually for college students, are a good way to segue into working abroad. Although they are often poorly paid, if paid at all, many say the experience is well worth it. Be wary of advertisements or companies that claim the ability to get you a job abroad for a fee—often times the same listings are available online or in newspapers, or even out of date. It's best, if going through an organization, to use one that's somewhat reputable. Some good ones include:

Council Exchanges, 52 Poland St., London W1V 4JQ, UK (☎020 748 2000; www.councilexchanges.org.uk). They have a database of jobs and internships for US positions.

Camp Counselors USA, Green Dragon House, 64-70 High St., Croydon CRO 9XN, UK (☎+44 020 8668 9051; www.workexperienceusa.com), places people (ages 18-30) as counselors in summer camps in the US.

Alliances Abroad, 702 West Ave., Austin, TX 78701 (☎888-6ABROAD/227623; www.alliancesabroad.com) sponsors internships in San Francisco.

AU PAIR WORK

Typically women ages 18-27, au pairs work as live-in nannies—caring for children and doing light housework in foreign countries in exchange for room, board, and a small stipend. Drawbacks often include long hours, being constantly on-duty, and mediocre pay. Much of the au pair experience depends on the family you're placed with. In the US, weekly salaries typically fall well below $200, with at least 45hr. of work expected. Au pairs in the US are expected to speak English and have at least 200 hr of childcare experience. The agencies below are a good starting point for looking for employment as an au pair.

Childcare International, Ltd., Trafalgar House, Grenville Pl., London NW7 3SA, UK (☎+44 020 8906 3116; fax 8906 3461; www.childint.co.uk).

InterExchange, 161 Sixth Ave., New York, NY 10013 (☎212-924-0446; fax 924-0575; www.interexchange.org or www.aupair.tripod.com).

International Educational Services, Calle Los Centelles 45-6-11, 46006 Valencia, Spain (☎+34 96 320 6491; fax 320 7832, US fax 707-281-0289; www.ies.ciberia.com).

SHORT-TERM WORK

Traveling for long periods of time can get expensive, and many travelers defray costs by trying their hand at odd jobs. The type of short-term work available varies substantially from region to region. In Western Canada, there is tree-planting or fruit-picking; in Alaska, the canneries are a good place to start looking for work; in the Southwest, agricultural work is gruelling and pays poorly, but is usually available; and in most large cities and tourist towns an ongoing demand exists for waiters, dishwashers, salespeople, and other service workers. Another popular option is to work a few hours a day at a hostel in exchange for free or discounted room and/or board. Most often, these short-term jobs are found by word of mouth, or simply by talking to the owner of a hostel or restaurant. Many places, especially due to the high turnover in the tourism industry, are always eager for help, even if only temporarily. *Let's Go* tries to list temporary jobs like these whenever possible; check the Practical Information sections in larger cities, or the index under **short-term work** to find individual listings.

VOLUNTEERING

Volunteering can be one of life's most fulfilling experiences, especially if you combine it with travel in a foreign land. Many volunteer services charge a fee to participate in a program, and these fees can be surprisingly hefty (although they frequently cover airfare and most, if not all, living expenses). Try to research programs before committing and find out exactly what you're getting into. Talk to people who have previously participated—living and working conditions can vary greatly, and different programs are geared toward different ages and levels of experience. Most people choose to go through a parent organization that takes care of logistical details, and in many cases, provides a group environment and support system. There are two main types of organizations—religious (often Catholic) and non-sectarian—but there are rarely restrictions on participation.

Amizade, Ltd., 367 S. Graham St., Pittsburgh, PA 15232 (☎888-973-4443; fax 412-648-1492; www.amizade.org). Sends individuals or groups (over age 18) to work in Montana or on the Navajo Reservation on short-term community-oriented projects, such as building schools and health centers and giving vocational training to children. Cost $475.

Archaeological Institute of America, 656 Beacon St., Boston, MA 02215, USA (☎617-353-9361; www.archaeological.org). The *Archaeological Fieldwork Opportunities Bulletin*, available on the organization's website, lists field sites throughout the US.

Bike Aid, (☎800-743-3808, brooke@globalexchange.org, www.globalexchange.org/bikeaid), organizes cross-country bicycle tours to raise money and awareness of international trade issues. Fundraising required.

Earthwatch, 3 Clocktower Pl. Suite 100, Box 75, Maynard, MA 01754 (☎800-776-0188 or 978-461-0081; www.earthwatch.org). Arranges 1- to 3-week programs in the US and Canada to promote conservation of natural resources. Fees vary based on program location and duration, costs average $1700 plus airfare.

Habitat for Humanity International, 121 Habitat St., Americus, GA 31709 (☎229-924-6935 x2551; www.habitat.org). Volunteers build houses throughout the US for anywhere from 2 weeks to 3 years. Short-term program costs range from $1200-4000.

Mobility International USA, P.O. Box 10767, Eugene, OR 97440 (☎541-343-1284; fax 541-343-6812; www.miusa.org). Travel programs for people with and without disabilities. Also serves as database of international disabled travel opportunities.

Volunteers for Peace, 1034 Tiffany Rd., Belmont., VT 05730 (☎802-259-2759; www.vfp.org). Arranges placement in work camps in the US. Membership required for registration. Annual *International Workcamp Directory* $20. Programs average $200-500 for 2-3 weeks.

FOR FURTHER READING ON ALTERNATIVES TO TOURISM

Alternatives to the Peace Corps: A Directory of Third World and U.S. Volunteer Opportunities, by Joan Powell. Food First Books, 2000 ($10).

International Directory of Voluntary Work, by Whetter and Pybus. Peterson's Guides and Vacation Work, 2000 ($16).

Work Your Way Around the World, by Susan Griffith. Worldview Publishing Services, 2001 ($18).

Hello! USA, Everyday Living for International Residents and Visitors, by Judy Priven. Hello America, Inc., 2002 ($22).

NEW ENGLAND

New England fancied itself an intellectual and political center long before the States were United, and still does today. Students and scholars funnel into New England's colleges each fall, and town meetings still evoke the spirit of popular government that once inspired American colonists to create a nation. Numerous historic landmarks recount every step of the country's break from "Old" England.

The region's unpredictable climate can be particularly dismal during the harsh, wet winter from November to March, when rivers, campgrounds, and tourist attractions freeze up. Nevertheless, today's visitors find adventure in the rough edges that troubled early settlers, flocking to New England's dramatic, salty coastline to sun on the sand or heading to the slopes and valleys of the Green and White Mountains to ski, hike, bike, and canoe. In the fall, the nation's most brilliant foliage bleeds and burns, transforming the entire region into a kaleidoscope of color.

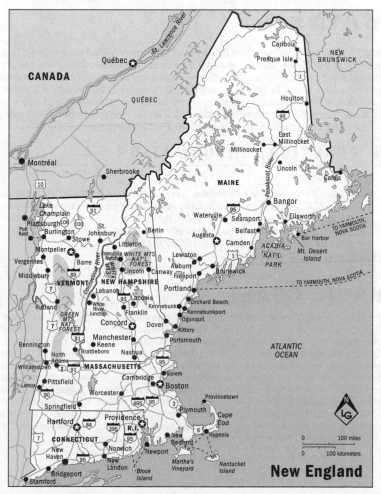

New England

HIGHLIGHTS OF NEW ENGLAND

SEAFOOD. Head to Maine (see below) for the best lobster around, and don't forget to try New England clam "chowda" before you leave.

SKIING. Enthusiasts flock to the mountains of New Hampshire and Vermont; the most famous resorts include Stowe (p. 101) and Killington (p. 95).

BEACHES. Cape Cod (p. 127) and Nantucket, MA (p. 133) have the region's best.

COLONIAL LANDMARKS. They're everywhere, but a walk along the Freedom Trail in Boston, MA (p. 105) is a great place to start.

SCENIC NEW ENGLAND. Take a drive along Rte. 100 in the fall, when the foliage is at its most striking, or hike the Appalachian Trail (p. 85) for a view on foot.

MAINE

Nearly a thousand years ago, Leif Erikson and his band of Viking explorers set foot on the coasts of Maine. Moose roamed the sprawling evergreen wilderness, the cry of the Maine coon cat echoed through towering mountains, and countless lobsters crawled in the ocean deep. A millennium has changed little. Forests still cover nearly 90% of Maine's land, an area larger than all the other New England states to the south. The inner reaches of the state stretch on for mile after uninhabited mile, while some more populated locales break up a harsh and jagged coastline.

ⓘ PRACTICAL INFORMATION

Capital: Augusta.

Visitor Info: Maine Tourism Information, 325B Water St., P.O. Box 2300, Hallowell 04347 (☎207-623-0363 or 888-624-6345; www.visitmaine.com). **Bureau of Parks and Lands,** State House Station #22 (AMHI, Harlow Bldg.), Augusta 04333 (☎207-287-3821). **Maine Forest Service,** Bureau of Forestry, State House Station #22, Harlow Bldg., 2nd fl., Augusta 04333 (☎207-287-2791).

Postal Abbreviation: ME. **Sales Tax:** 5%.

MAINE COAST

The Maine coast, if measured straight from Kittery to Lubec, spans 228 mi. But if all of the shoreline's inlets and rocky promontories are untangled, the distance stretches out to 3478 mi. The meandering, two-lane **U.S. 1** hugs the coastline, stringing the port towns together, and is the only option for accessing most coastal towns north of Portland. Be prepared to take your time; the traffic pace is often slow in the summer, especially through towns and villages. Lesser roads and small ferry lines connect the remote villages and offshore islands. **Visitor info: Maine Information Center,** in Kittery, 3 mi. north of the Maine-New Hampshire bridge. (☎207-439-1319. Open July-early Oct. daily 8am-6pm; mid-Oct. to June 9am-5pm.) **Greyhound** serves points between Portland and Bangor along I-95, as well as the town of Brunswick, but to truly explore the coast, a car is necessary.

PORTLAND ☎ 207

The Victorian architecture in the Old Port Exchange forms a rather ironic backdrop to Portland's spirited youth culture. Teenagers and twenty-somethings gather in bars, restaurants, and cafes near the wharf, and flood the streets in talkative groups or couples, even after stores close down. Outside the city, ferries run to the Casco Bay Islands while Sebago Lake provides sunning and water-skiing.

◪ ⁊ ORIENTATION & PRACTICAL INFORMATION. Downtown sits near the bay, along **Congress St.** between State and Pearl St. A few blocks south lies the **Old Port,** on Commercial and Fore St. These two districts contain most of the city's sights and attractions. **I-295** (off I-95) forms the western boundary of downtown. **Concord Trailways,** 295 Thompson Pt., on Connector Rd., off Congress St. (☎828-1151; office open daily 4:30am-8:30pm), runs to Bangor (2hr., 3 per day, $22) and Boston (2hr., 11 per day, $18). Metro buses run to and from the station. The **Greyhound/Vermont Transit** station (☎772-6587) is located at 950 Congress St., on the western outskirts of town. *Be cautious here at night.* Buses run to Bangor (2½-3½hr., 7 per day, $19) and Boston (2hr., 9 per day, $15). **Prince of Fundy Cruises,** 468 Commercial St., sends ferries to Yarmouth, NS from the Portland International Ferry Terminal, on Commercial St., near the Million Dollar Bridge. Boats run May to mid-June and mid-September to late October. Ferries depart Portland at 8pm for the 11hr. trip. (☎775-5616 or 800-341-7540. Cabins available. Fare mid-Sept. to late June $70, ages 5-14 $35; car $90, bike $10. Late June to mid-Sept. $98/45/110/20. Reservations strongly recommended.) **Metro Bus** services downtown Portland. Routes run 5:30am-11:50pm, depending on route. (☎774-0351. $1, seniors with Medicaid card 50¢, under 5 free; transfers free.) **Visitors Information Bureau:** 305 Commercial St., at Center St. (☎772-5800. Open mid-May to mid-Oct. M-F 8am-6pm, Sa 10am-6pm; mid-Oct. to mid-May M-F 8am-5pm, Sa 10am-5pm.) **Internet access: JavaNet Cafe,** 37 Exchange St. (☎773-2469. Open M-Th 7am-10pm, F 7am-11pm, Sa 8am-11pm, Su 8am-9pm. $8 per hr.) **Post Office:** 125 Forrest Ave. (☎871-8426. Open M-F 7:30am-7pm, Sa 9am-1pm.) **ZIP code:** 04101. **Area code:** 207.

⁆ ACCOMMODATIONS. Portland has some inexpensive accommodations, but prices jump during the summer. **The Inn at St. John ❸,** 939 Congress St., is not located in an especially appealing neighborhood, but its upscale decor makes it an elegant alternative. (☎773-6481 or 800-636-9127. Continental breakfast included. Laundry facilities, bike storage, free local calls, and free parking. Rooms with private bath are available. Singles and doubles in summer from at M-Th $60, F-Su $70; in winter $55.) **Wassamki Springs ❶,** 56 Saco St., in Scarborough, is the closest campground to Portland. Drive 6 mi. west on Congress St. (which becomes Rte. 22, then County Rd.), then turn right on Saco St. Flocks of migrant Winnebagos nest among cozy, fairly private sites bordering a lake encircled by sandy beaches. (☎839-4276. Free showers and flush toilets. Reserve 2 weeks in advance, especially July-Aug. Open May to mid-Oct. Sites with water and electricity for 2 adults $28, with hookup $30; each additional person $5; lakefront sites $3 extra.)

◻ FOOD. Portland's harbor overflows with the ocean's fruits, but non-aquatic and vegetarian fare aren't too hard to find either. A favorite among Portland's youth, **Federal Spice ❶,** 225 Federal St., just off Congress St., spices all its entrees (all under $6) with fiery Caribbean, South American, and Asian ingredients. (☎774-6404. Open M-F 11am-9pm, Sa 11am-6pm.) **Gilbert's Chowder House ❷,** 92 Commer-

cial St., is the local choice for seafood. A large bowl of chowder in a bread bowl ($7) is a meal in itself. (☎871-5636. Open June-Sept. Su-Th 11am-10pm, F-Sa 11am-11pm; Oct.-May call for hours.) The homemade, organic pizza pies at the **Flatbread Company ❸**, 72 Commercial St., are tasty and healthy treats ($7.75-13.50). Sit and enjoy the ocean view as your meal is fired in a huge clay oven. (☎772-8777. Open in summer M-Th 11:30am-9:30pm, F-Sa 11:30am-10:30pm; in winter M-Th 11:30am-9pm, F-Sa 11:30am-10pm.)

◨ **SIGHTS.** Offshore islands with secluded beaches and relatively undeveloped interiors lie just a ferry ride from the city proper. **Casco Bay Lines,** on State Pier near the corner of Commercial and Franklin, runs year-round to nearby islands. Daily **ferries** depart approximately every hour for **Peaks Island.** (☎774-7871. Operates M-Sa 5:45am-11:30pm, Su 7:45am-11:30pm; last return 11:55pm. Round-trip $6, seniors and ages 5-9 $3.) On the island, **Brad's Recycled Bike Shop,** 115 Island Ave., rents out bikes. (☎766-5631. Open daily 10am-6pm. $5 per hr., $8.50 for 3hr., $12 per day.) Casco Bay Lines also runs ten ferries a day to **Long Island,** where waves crash on to a quiet, unpopulated beach. Starting at Long Island, island-hop by catching later ferries to other islands (same price as Peaks ferry), but you can really only get to two islands in one day. Try **Two Lights State Park,** across the Million Dollar Bridge on State St., then south along Rte. 77 to Cape Elizabeth, for an uncrowded spot to picnic or walk alongside the ocean. (☎799-5871. $2.50.)

In addition to the call of the sea, Portland has land activities. The **Portland Museum of Art,** 7 Congress Sq., at the intersection of Congress, High, and Free St., collects American art by John Singer Sargent and Winslow Homer. (☎775-6148 or 800-639-4067. Open June to mid-Oct. M-W and Sa-Su 10am-5pm, Th-F 10am-9pm; mid-Oct to May closed M. $8, students and seniors $6, ages 6-12 $2; F 5-9pm free. Wheelchair accessible.) The **Wadsworth-Longfellow House,** 489 Congress St., was the home of 19th-century poet Henry Wadsworth Longfellow. Presently, it stands as a museum of social history and US literature, focusing on late 18th- and 19th-century antiques as well as the life of the poet. (☎879-0427, ext. 208. Open June-Oct. daily 10am-4pm. $7, students and seniors $6, ages 5-17 $3. Price includes admission to a small neighboring history museum with rotating exhibits. Tours every 30-40min.)

◨◨ **ENTERTAINMENT & NIGHTLIFE.** Portland's vibrant, youthful culture shows in its many summer theater and orchestra performances. Signs for productions decorate the city, and schedules are available at the Visitors Center (see **Practical Information,** p. 79). The **Portland Symphony** presents concerts renowned throughout the Northeast. (☎842-0800, 10-15% student discount.) Info on Portland's jazz, blues, and club scene packs the *Casco Bay Weekly* and *FACE,* both of which are free in many restaurants and stores. Traditionally on the first Sunday in June, the **Old Port Festival** (☎772-6828) fills the blocks from Federal to Commercial St. with as many as 50,000 people. On summer afternoons from late June to August, the **Noontime Performance Series** (☎772-6828) hosts a variety of bands performing in Portland's Monument and Congress Squares.

The Old Port area, known as "the strip"—especially **Fore St.** between Union and Exchange St.—livens up after dark as pleasant (if touristy) shops stay open late and a few good pubs start serving beer. **Brian Boru,** 57 Center St., provides a mellow pub scene with top-notch nachos for $5. (☎780-1506. Su $2 pints. Open daily 11:30am-1am.) **Gritty MacDuff's,** 396 Fore St., brews its own beer ($3 pints) for adoring locals and entertains with live bluegrass and jazz two to three times a week. (☎772-2739. No cover. Open daily 11:30am-1am.) The English pub around the corner, **Three Dollar Dewey's,** 241 Commercial St., serves over 100 different beers (36 on tap, $3-3.50) along with great chili (cup $3.50) and free popcorn. (☎772-3310. Open M-Sa 11:30am-1am, Su noon-1am.) With an outside bar and fantastic waterfront view, the **Dry Dock Restaurant & Tavern,** 84 Commercial St., is an ideal place to relax with a few drinks and friends. (☎774-3550. Open daily 11am-11:30pm.)

SOUTH OF PORTLAND   ☎207

KENNEBUNK

Kennebunk and its coastal counterpart 8 mi. east, **Kennebunkport,** are popular hideaways for wealthy authors and artists—Kennebunkport reluctantly grew famous as the summer home of former President George Bush. Rare and used bookstores line U.S. 1 just south of Kennebunk, while art galleries fill the town. You could spend a day (and a fortune) exploring all the little shops in town. Even more scary than its monied homogeneity is the **Maritime Productions' Chilling and Unusual Theater Cruise,** a 2hr. cruise and performance narrating true tales of haunted lighthouses, ghost ships, and cannibalism in New England's maritime past and present. (☎967-4938. Departs twice daily from Kennebunkport Marina on Ocean Ave. Matinee cruise: 3:30pm; $26, over 65 $24, ages 6-16 $22. Sunset cruise: 6:30pm; $30.) The 55 ft. gaff-rigged **Schooner Eleanor,** leaving from Arundel Wharf, Ocean Ave., provides a relaxed 2hr. yachting experience. (☎967-8809. $38. Call for reservations and times.) The **Kennebunk-Kennebunkport Chamber of Commerce,** 17 U.S. 9/Western Ave., in Kennebunkport, has a free area guide. (☎967-0857. Open in summer M-F 9am-5pm, Sa 9am-2pm, Su 9am-1pm; off-season closed Su.)

WELLS

The **Rachel Carson National Wildlife Refuge,** ½ mi. off U.S. 1 on Rte. 9 East, provides a secluded escape from the throngs of tourists. A trail winds through the salt marsh that is home to over 200 species of shorebirds and waterfowl. (☎646-9226. Trail open daily sunrise-sunset. Office open in summer M-F 8am-4:30pm, Sa-Su 10am-2pm; off-season M-F 8am-4:30pm. Free.) Sprawling across meadows and beaches, the **Wells Reserve at Laudholm Farm,** at the junction of U.S. 1 and Rte. 9, offers tours of the estuary, bird life, and wildflowers. (☎646-1555. Trails open mid-May to Aug. daily 8am-8pm; Sept. to mid-May 8am-5pm. Visitors Center open May-Oct M-Sa 10am-4pm, Su noon-4pm; mid-Jan. to Apr. and Nov. to mid-Dec. M-F 9am-4pm. $2, under 13 free.) **Wheels and Waves,** U.S. 1 on the Wells/Ogunquit border, rents mountain bikes. (☎646-5774. Open daily 7am-7pm. Bikes $20 per day, $25 for 24hr.; kayaks $35 per half-day, $45 per day.)

OGUNQUIT

South of Kennebunk on U.S. 1 lies Ogunquit, which means "beautiful place by the sea." True to its name, the long, sandy shoreline is probably the best beach north of Cape Cod. Ogunquit also has one of New England's largest (although seasonal) gay communities. The **Ogunquit Welcome Center and Chamber of Commerce,** on U.S. 1, has info about the town. (☎646-2939. Open June-Aug. Su-Th 9am-5pm, F 9am-8pm, Sa 9am-6pm; early Sept. to late May daily 9am-5pm.) Nearby **Perkins Cove,** accessible only by a very winding and narrow road, charms the argyle socks off the polo-shirt crowd with boutiques hawking seashell sculptures. The two **Barnacle Billy's ❹** restaurants, about 60 ft. apart on Oar Weed Rd., practice an interesting division of labor. The original broils, bakes, and sautées lobsters, but the newer, full-service location has a bigger menu. (☎646-5575. Sandwiches $3-6. Lobster roll $13. Dinners $14-26. Both open daily 11am-9pm.) Weather permitting, biking is the best way to travel Maine's rocky shores and avoid the thick summer traffic.

NEW ENGLAND

MT. DESERT ISLAND ☎ 207

Roughly half of Mt. Desert Island is covered by Acadia National Park, which harbors some of the last protected marine, mountain, and forest environments on the New England coast. During the summer, the island swarms with tourists lured by the thick forests and mountainous landscape. Bar Harbor, on the eastern side, is by far the most crowded and glitzy part of the island. Once a summer hamlet for the affluent, the town now welcomes a motley melange of R&R-seekers. However, while the well-heeled wealthy have fled to the more secluded Northeast and Seal Harbor, the town still maintains its overpriced traditions.

▟▞ ORIENTATION & PRACTICAL INFORMATION. Mt. Desert Island is shaped roughly like a big lobster claw, 14 mi. long and 12 mi. wide. To the east, on Rte. 3, lie **Bar Harbor** and **Seal Harbor.** South on Rte. 198 near the cleft is **Northeast Harbor.** Across Somes Sound on Rte. 102 is **Southwest Harbor,** where fishing and shipbuilding thrive without the taint of tourism. **Rte. 3** runs through Bar Harbor, becoming **Mt. Desert St.** Rte. 3/Mt. Desert St. and **Cottage St.** are the major streets for shops, restaurants, and bars in Bar Harbor. **Rte. 102** circuits the western half of the island. There is a $10 park pass, which can be avoided by hiking, biking, or taking an Island Explorer bus onto the island.

Greyhound (☎ 945-3000 or 800-231-2222) leaves Bar Harbor once daily from the Villager Motel, 207 Main St., for Boston (4½ hr., $53.50) via Bangor (1½ hr., $9.25). **Beal & Bunker** (☎ 244-3575; open late June to early Sept. daily 8am-4:30pm; call for winter hours) runs ferries from the Northeast Harbor town dock to Great Cranberry Island (15min.; 6 per day; $12, under 12 $6). **Bay Ferries** (☎ 888-249-7245), in Bar Harbor, runs to Yarmouth, NS (2¾hr.; 1-2 per day; $55, seniors $50, ages 5-17 $25; cars $95, bikes $10. Reservations recommended, $5 fee; car price does not include passengers.) Free **Island Explorer** buses depart from Bar Harbor green and are the best way to get around the park and its campgrounds. Schedule can be found in *Acadia Weekly*. **Acadia Bike & Canoe,** 48 Cottage St., in Bar Harbor, rents bikes, canoes and kayaks, and leads sea kayaking tours. (☎ 288-9605, for tours ☎ 800-526-8615. Open May-Oct. daily 8am-6pm. Bikes $13 per half-day, $18 per day; children $10/10. Canoes $30 per day, $25 each additional day; one-person kayaks $45 per day, tandems $55. Sea kayak tours $34 per 2½ hr., $45 per half-day, $69 per full day; includes kayaking lessons. Inquire for advanced tours or multi-day tours.) **Acadia National Park Visitors Center,** 3 mi. north of Bar Harbor on Rte. 3., has a huge topographical map, a small bookstore, and rangers ready and willing to help. (☎ 288-5262. Open mid-June to mid-Sept. daily 8am-6pm; mid-Apr. to mid-June and mid-Sept. to Oct. 8am-4:30pm.) The **Park Headquarters,** 3 mi. west of Bar Harbor on Rte. 233, can provide visitor info during the off-season. (☎ 288-3338. Open year-round M-F 8am-4:30pm.) **Bar Harbor Chamber of Commerce,** 93 Cottage St. (☎ 288-5103; open June-Oct. M-F 8am-5pm, Nov.-May M-F 8am-4pm), operates an **Info booth** at 1 Harbor Place (mid-May to mid-Oct. daily 9am-5pm). **Hotlines: Downeast Sexual Assault Helpline,** ☎ 800-228-2470; operates 24hr. **Emergency: Acadia National Park Law Enforcement,** ☎ 288-3369. **Internet access: The Opera House,** 27 Cottage St. (☎ 288-3509. Open May-Oct. daily 7am-11pm. $2 first 17min., 10¢ each additional min.) **Post Office:** 55 Cottage St. (☎ 288-3122. Open M-F 8am-4:30pm, Sa 9am-noon.) **ZIP code:** 04609. **Area code:** 207.

▛ ACCOMMODATIONS. Though grand hotels and prices recall the island's exclusive resort days, a few reasonable establishments do exist, particularly on Rte. 3 north of Bar Harbor. The perennially popular **█Bar Harbor Youth Hostel ❶,** 321 Main St., accommodates 30 people in two dorm rooms and two private rooms. The hostel's friendly manager gives out free baked goods and discounts on kayak rentals. A book-swap and movie nights keep travelers entertained. (☎288-5587. Linen $2. Lockout 10am-5pm. Curfew 11pm. Reservations accepted if pre-payment as a check or money order is sent to P.O. Box 32, Bar Harbor. Open May-Nov. $17, nonmembers $20. No credit cards; cash or travelers check only.) Sleep tight at **Briarfield ❹**, 60 Cottage St., a B&B just a short walk from downtown Bar Harbor. (☎288-5297 or 800-228-6660. A/C and private bath; some rooms have fireplaces. Rooms in summer $90-175; off-season $65-125.)

Camping spots cover the island, especially on **Rte. 102** and **Rte. 198,** well west of town. **White Birches Campground ❶**, in Southwest Harbor, on Seal Cove Rd. 1 mi. west of Rte. 102, has 60 widely-spaced, wooded sites in a remote location. (☎244-3797. Free hot showers, bathrooms, laundry, and pool. Reservations recommended, especially in summer. Open mid-May to mid-Oct. daily. Sites for 1-4 people $20, with hookup $24; weekly $120/144; each additional person $4.) **Acadia National Park campgrounds** include **Blackwoods ❶**, 5 mi. south of Bar Harbor on Rte. 3. More than 300 wooded sites seem tightly packed when the campgrounds reach full occupancy in summer. When the throngs depart, however, the charm of the campground's thick, deep, dark woods returns, as do the larger wildlife. (☎800-365-2267. Reservations recommended in summer. Open mid-Mar. to Oct. $20; mid-Dec. to mid-Mar. lower rates.) **Seawall ❶**, located off Rte. 102A on the western side of the island, 4 mi. south of Southwest Harbor and a 10min. walk from the ocean, is slightly more rustic, with toilets but no hookups. (☎800-365-2267. Open daily late May to Sept. Sites $14; drive-in and RV sites $20.)

◖ FOOD. To watch some flicks and chow down on a few slices, head over to **▨Reel Pizza ❸**, 33 Kennebec Pl., at the end of Rodick off Main St. This movie theater-*cum*-pizzeria shows two films each evening for $5 and serves up creative pizza pies ($8.50-18), such as the "fantastic voyage," heaped with smoked salmon, roasted red peppers, and artichoke spread. The first four rows of the "theater" are comfy couches. (☎288-3828. Open daily 5pm to end of last screening.) The walls and ceilings at **Freddie's Route 66 Restaurant ❸**, 21 Cottage St., in Bar Harbor, are absolutely crammed with campy license plates, wind-up metal cars, and boob tubes showing Casper the Friendly Ghost in black and white. The Cadillac burger is a well-spent $9. (☎288-3708. Seafood pie $18. Open mid-May to mid-Oct. daily 11am-3pm and 4:30-10pm.) **Beal's ❸**, off Main St., at the end of Clark Point Rd., in Southwest Harbor, goes easy on the frills, offering lobster at superb prices on an outdoor, picnic-tabled patio overlooking the pier. Pick a live crustacean from a tank ($9.75/lb.), and it'll be buttered and steaming red in minutes. (☎244-3202 or 800-245-7178. Open May-Oct. daily 7am-8pm; Nov.-Apr. 7am-4pm. Seafood sold year-round daily 9am-5pm. Hours vary with weather.) **The Colonel's Deli Bakery and Restaurant ❷**, on Main St. in Northeast Harbor, fixes sandwiches so big that it's hard to get one into your mouth ($6-11). Take one for the road as a cheap dinner in the National Park. (☎276-5147. Open mid-Apr. to Oct. daily 6:30am-9pm.) **Ben and Bill's Chocolate Emporium**, 66 Main St., near Cottage St., boasts 48 flavors of homemade ice cream, including—no kidding—lobster. (☎288-3281. Fudge $12 per lb. Cones $3-4. Open mid-Feb. to Jan. daily 9am-11:30pm.)

◙ SIGHTS. The staff at the **Mt. Desert Oceanarium**, at the end of Clark Pt. Rd. near Beal's in Southwest Harbor, have their sea shtick down. The main museum is small and geared for children, but the hands-on display fascinates all ages. Its sister oceanarium, off Rte 3. on the northeast edge of the island, teaches everything there is to know about lobsters. (☎244-7330. Open mid-May to mid-Oct. M-Sa 9am-5pm. Main oceanarium $7, ages 4-12 $5. Ticket for both facilities $13/10.) For a relaxing drive, **Sargent Dr.** runs along Somes Sound. For travelers on foot, head to Bar Island at low tide, when a gravel path leads the way from the end of Bridge St.

NEW ENGLAND

in Bay Harbor to Bar Island. Tide times are published in the free and widely distributed *Acadia Weekly*. **Wildwood Stables,** along Park Loop Rd. in Seal Harbor, takes tourists on explorations of the island via horse and carriage. (☎276-3622. 1hr. tour $13.50, seniors $12.50, ages 6-12 $7, ages 2-5 $4. 2hr. tour $17.50/16.50/8/5. Reservations recommended. Wheelchair accessible if notified in advance.)

🎭🎬 **ENTERTAINMENT & NIGHTLIFE.** Most after-dinner pleasures on the island are simple and cluster in Bar Harbor. **Geddy's Pub,** 19 Main St., gives a backwoods backdrop of weathered wooden signs, beat-up license plates, and moose head trophies to the dancing frenzy that breaks out nightly as tables are moved aside for a DJ and dance floor. (☎288-5077. No cover. Live music daily 7-10pm. Open Apr.-Oct. M-Sa 11:30am-12:30am, Su 11:30am-11pm; winter hours vary. Pub-style dinner served until 10pm.) Locals adore the **Lompoc Cafe & Brew Pub,** 36 Rodick St., off Cottage St., which features Bar Harbor Real Ale and live jazz, blues, Celtic, rock, and folk on the weekends. (☎288-9392. Th open mic. Shows F-Sa nights. No cover. Open May-Oct. daily 11:30am-1am.) The Art Deco **Criterion Theater,** on Cottage St., shows mainstream movies in the summer. (☎288-3441. 2 movies nightly. Box office opens 30min. before show. $7.50, seniors $6.50, under 13 $5.50; balcony seats $8.50.)

ACADIA NATIONAL PARK ☎207

The jagged, rocky, oceanside perimeter of Acadia National Park's 38,500 acres is gradually obscured, then completely enveloped by thick pine forests further inland. Fern-shrouded streams and 120 miles of hiking trails criss-cross the rugged, coastal terrain. Fearing the island would one day be overrun by cars, millionaire John D. Rockefeller funded the creation of 51 miles of carriage roads, now accessible to hikers and mountain bikes.

With views of Long Pond, Echo Lake, and a watchtower that crowns the summit, **Beech Mountain** (½ mi.) is a pleasant trail for amateur hikers. **Precipice Trail** (1½ mi.), one of the most popular and strenuous hikes, is closed June to late August to accommodate nesting peregrine falcons; be ready to use the iron ladders that are needed to finish off the meandering cliff and ledge trail. To reach the top of Cadillac Mountain (1530 ft.), hike either the **Cadillac Mountain North** (4½ mi.) or **South Ridge** (7½ mi.) trail, or cruise up the paved **auto road.**

About 4 mi. south of Bar Harbor on Rte. 3, **Park Loop Rd.** runs along the shore of the island, where great waves crash against steep granite cliffs. The sea comes into **Thunder Hole** with a bang at three-quarters tide. Brave the chilly water at **Echo Lake** or **Sand Beach,** both of which have lifeguards in the summer. Also along Park Loop Rd. are Wildwood Stables (see **sights,** above) and **Jordan Pond House ❹,** a restaurant at the south edge of Jordan Pond where travelers can have afternoon tea (with 2 popovers $7.25) on a lawn facing the pond. (☎276-3316. Lunch $12.50-18. Dinner $14-20. Open mid-May to late Oct. daily 11:30am-9pm; hours can vary.)

Touring the park by auto costs $10 for seven days. Seniors can purchase a lifetime pass for $10 (the best years or weeks of your life). The *Biking and Hiking Guide to the Carriage Roads* ($6), available at the Visitors Center and in bookstores, offers invaluable directions for the more labyrinthine trails. To spend the night in or near the park, see Mt. Desert Island's **Accommodations** (p. 82).

NORTHERN MAINE COAST ☎207

Much like the coastal region south of Portland, the north offers the traveler unforgettable beaches, windswept ocean vistas, and verdant forests—for a price. Lodging in L.L.Bean country isn't cheap, but just passing through allows you to taste the

NEW ENGLAND

area's proverbial milk and honey without buying the cow. U.S. 1 is northern coastal Maine's only thoroughfare, and be warned, traffic barely creeps along on rainy weekends in Freeport.

FREEPORT

Freeport is known as the factory outlet capital of the world, with over 100 downtown stores attracting urbanites sick of the woods. The granddaddy of them all, **L.L. Bean,** began making Maine Hunting Shoes here in 1912. The megamogul now sells everything in outdoor gear and outfits America's youth with lifetime-guaranteed backpacks. The **factory outlet,** 11 Depot St., behind Nine West Shoes, is the place for bargains. (☎552-7772. Open June-Dec. daily 9am-10pm; Jan. to late May 9am-9pm.) The gigantic multi-storied **retail store,** 95 Main St., generates a madness that could transform even the biggest city slicker into a backwoods renegade. (☎865-4761. Open 24hr. 2hr. kayak trips $12. Fly fishing casting lessons $10.)

CAMDEN

In the summer, khaki-clad crowds flock to Camden, 100 mi. north of Portland, to dock their yachts alongside the tall-masted schooners in Penobscot Bay. Cruises are generally out of the budgeteer's price range, but the **Camden-Rockport Lincolnville Chamber of Commerce,** on the public landing in Camden behind Cappy's Chowder House, can tell visitors which are most affordable. They also have info on where to find one of Camden's sparse budget accommodations. (☎236-4404 or 800-223-5459. Open mid-May to mid-Oct. M-F 9am-5pm, Sa 10am-5pm, Su 10am-4pm; mid-Oct. to mid-May closed Su.) The **Camden Hills State Park ❶,** 1¼ mi. north of town on U.S. 1, is almost always full in July and August, but sites are usually available for arrivals before 2pm. This beautiful coastal retreat offers more than 25 mi. of trails, including one which leads up to Mt. Battie and provides a great harbor view. (☎236-3109, reservations ☎800-332-1501. Open mid-May to mid-Oct. Free showers. Sites $20, ME residents $15; day use $2.50.) The folks at **Maine Sports,** on U.S. 1 in Rockport, just south of Camden, rent and sell a wide array of sea-worthy vehicles. Kayaks will only be rented to those with paddling experience, but anyone can join a tour. (☎236-7120. Open June-Aug. daily 8am-9pm; Sept.-May 9am-6pm. 2hr. harbor tour $45. Singles $35-50 per day, doubles $45-65, depending on whether it's a sea or lake kayak. Ask about overnight trips. Canoes $35-40 per day, bikes $15, snowboards $30.) The **Maine State Ferry Service,** 5 mi. north of Camden in Lincolnville, floats over to Islesboro Island. (☎800-491-4883. 30min.; 5-9 per day, last return trip 4:30pm. Round-trip $5.25, with bike $9.25, car and driver $15. Parking $6 per day.) The ferry also has an agency at 517A Main St., on U.S. 1 in Rockland, that runs to Matinicus, North Haven, and Vinalhaven. (☎596-2202. Rates and schedules change with the weather; call ahead.)

THE APPALACHIAN TRAIL Stretching 2160 mi. from Mt. Katahdin, ME, to Springer Mountain, GA, the **Appalachian Trail (AT)** follows the path of the Appalachian Mountains along the eastern United States. Use of the AT is free, although only foot travelers may traverse it. The trail cuts through 14 states, 8 national forests, and 6 national parks. Generally, the AT is very accessible, crossed by roads along its entire length except for the northernmost 100 mi. Although many sections make excellent day hikes or overnights, about 2500 "through-hikers" attempt a continuous hike of the AT annually. Three-sided shelters (first come, first served) dot the trail, spaced about a day's journey apart. Hikers take advantage of streams and nearby towns to stock up on water and supplies. White blazes on rocks and trees mark the length of the main trail, while blue blazes mark side trails.

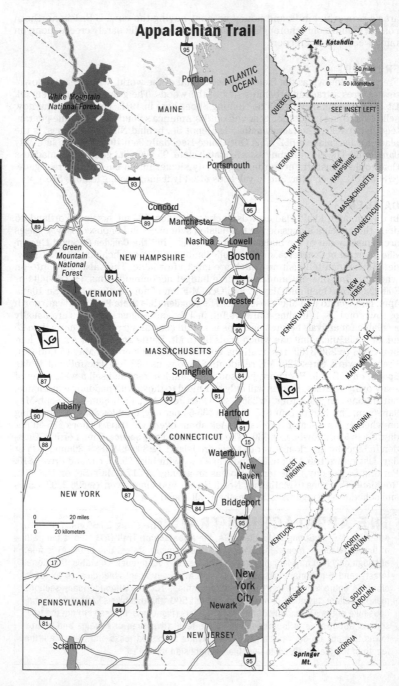

NEW HAMPSHIRE

There are two sides to New Hampshire: the rugged landscape and natural beauty of the White Mountains, and the tax-free outlets, tourist traps, and state liquor stores that line most of the highways. The first colony to declare its independence from Great Britain, New Hampshire has retained its backwoods libertarian charm along with its motto, "Live Free or Die!"

◪ PRACTICAL INFORMATION

Capital: Concord.

Visitor Info: Office of Travel and Tourism, P.O. Box 856, Concord 03302 (☎603-271-2666 or 800-386-4664; www.visitnh.gov). **NH Parks and Recreation,** ☎271-3556. **Fish and Game Dept.,** 2 Hazen Dr., Concord 03301 (☎603-271-3421), furnishes info on hunting and fishing regulations and license fees. **U.S. Forest Service,** 719 North Main St., Laconia 03246 (☎603-528-8721). Open M-F 8am-4:30pm.

Postal Abbreviation: NH. **Sales Tax:** 8% on meals and lodgings. **Area Code:** 603.

PORTSMOUTH ☎603

Although New Hampshire's seacoast is the smallest in the nation, with only 13 miles fronting the Atlantic Ocean, the state makes the most of its toehold on the water. Portsmouth, once the colonial capital, is one of the nicest seaside towns in New England. Most buildings date to the 18th century, while a handful were built in the mid-17th century. Although not large by any standards, Portsmouth is exceptionally cultured—and expensive. History is the main attraction, seafood reigns supreme, and a pint of local ale is the mainstay after dinner.

◪ **PRACTICAL INFORMATION.** Just 57 mi. north of Boston, Portsmouth is at the junction of U.S. 1, 1A, and I-95. Leave cars in the inexpensive lots ($1 per hr.) downtown; the town is best navigated by foot. State St. runs north-south through downtown and is bisected by Pleasant and Fleet St. **Vermont Transit/Greyhound,** 10 Ladd St. (☎436-0163), 1 block from Market Sq., heads to Portsmouth from Boston (4 per day, 1¼hr., $12.50-13.50). **Seacoast Trolley** (☎431-6975) runs in summer every hour 10am-5pm, with 17 stops in and around Portsmouth (Fare $2.50). **Taxis: Blue Star Taxi,** ☎436-2774. **Visitor Info: Greater Portsmouth Chamber of Commerce,** 500 Market St., outside downtown. (☎436-1118. Open M-F 8:30am-5pm.) **Medical Services: Portsmouth Regional** (☎433-4006), a few miles from town at 333 Borthwick Ave. **Violence and Rape Hotline,** ☎800-336-3795. **Post Office:** 80 Daniel St. (☎431-287. Open M-F 7:30am-5:30pm, Sa 8am-noon.) **ZIP code:** 03801. **Area code:** 603.

⌐Cↄ **ACCOMMODATIONS & FOOD.** Portsmouth is not the best place for the budget traveler to spend the night; accommodations in town are pricey. Try U.S. 1A south of Portsmouth for typically drab motels. A nice alternative is **Camp Eaton ❷**, in York Harbor, ME, about 15 mi. north of Portsmouth off Rte. 1. Although the wooded sites are still expensive, oceanside vistas and immaculate bathrooms ease the pain. (☎207-363-3424. 2-person sites $31-45, $3 each additional person.) Portsmouth's great nightlife may be worth the splurge to stay in town.

Portsmouth offers plenty of dining options, with many fine establishments peppering Market St. Unfortunately, great deals may be in short supply. ◪**The Friendly Toast ❶,** 121 Congress St., a block and a half from Market Sq., is a local landmark, cluttered with the most ghastly artifacts the 1950s could produce: mannequin limbs, pulp novels, formica furniture, and stroke-inducingly bad art. Most menu items, such as the "mission burrito" ($6.25), are nearly impossible to finish. (☎430-2154. Entrees $6-7. Breakfast served all day. Open M-Th 7am-11pm, F 7am through Su 9pm.) Grab a free slice of gourmet bread at **Me & Ollie's Honest Bread ❶**, 10 Pleasant St., and stay for the generous $5-7 sandwiches. (☎433-6588. Open M-Sa 7am-6:30pm, Su 8am-5pm.) At **Gilly's Lunchcart ❶**, 175 Fleet St., semi-inebriated folk trail out the door of a nearby pub and into the street for heavenly hot dogs, burgers, and sandwiches into the wee hours of any given night. (Fries $1.25; chili cheese fries $3. Open M-Sa 11:30am-2:30am, Su 4pm-2:30am.)

◙⚎ SIGHTS & ENTERTAINMENT. Modern Portsmouth sells itself with its colonial past. The most prestigious and well-known example is **Strawbery Banke Museum**, on the corner of Marcy and Hancock St. The museum is a collection of original buildings from the town's colonial days. To find the museum, follow the signs that lead toward the harbor and through a charming maze of shops. (☎433-1100. Open May-Oct. M-Sa 10am-5pm, Su noon-5pm. $12, seniors $11, ages 7-17 $8; families $28. Tickets good for 2 consecutive days.) Right across the street, **Prescott Park** snuggles the Piscataqua River. A great place to picnic or lounge, these small, well-tended gardens offer shade, fountains, and a pleasant respite from a day of travel. For something more technological, try the **USS Albacore**, off Exit 7, a research submarine built locally at the Portsmouth Naval Shipyard. (☎436-3680. Open May-Oct. daily 9:30am-5pm; winter hours vary. $5, over 62 or military with ID $3.50, ages 7-17 $2; families $10.) One of Portsmouth's oldest graveyards, North Cemetery, holds the burial sites of some of the city's most important skeletons. **Gravestones by Dusk** offers a 1hr. historical tour of the cemetery. (☎436-5096. Open Apr.-Oct. M-Su. $10 per person for 2, $8 per person for more than 2; $20 min. Times vary; call for reservations.)

NEW HAMPSHIRE SKI RESORTS   ☎603

The various ranges within the White Mountains offer numerous opportunities for skiing. **Ski New Hampshire**, P.O. Box 517, Lincoln 03251, is a service that provides information and reservations for five resorts in the White Mountains. (☎745-8101 or 800-937-5493; www.skinh.com.) Winters in New England are long, meaning skiing is usually available from November through April, depending on the weather.

Cranmore, in North Conway (see p. 94), offers 39 trails and ski vacations complemented by great shopping. The 350 ft. half-pipe and Children's Summer Camp are huge warm weather draws. The slopes open in late November. (☎800-786-6754. Lift operates M-F 9am-4pm, Sa-Su 8:30am-4pm. Lift tickets $29, ages 6-12 $15.) Located along U.S. 302 near North Conway, **Attitash** is expensive but offers two mountains, 68 trails (20% beginner, 47% intermediate, 33% expert), and 25 acres of glades. Mountain biking, horseback riding, waterslides, a climbing wall, trampolines, and an alpine slide keep visitors busy in summer. (☎374-2368. Lift tickets M-F $42, Sa-Su $48, holidays $50; children $30/27/30. Alpine slide open in summer daily 10am-6pm. Single ride $10, double $16. Summer all-day $25, ages 2-7 $10.)

Just outside Pinkham Notch on Rte. 16, **Wildcat Mountain** offers 44 trails (25% beginner, 40% intermediate, 35% expert) and mountainscape views from its 4062 ft. peak. (☎888-754-9453. Lift tickets M-F $39, Sa-Su $49; seniors and ages 13-17 $34/39; ages 6-12 $27/29. In summer gondola rides $9.50.) Three miles east of Lincoln on Rte. 112, **Loon Mountain** guarantees less crowded conditions on their 43 trails by limiting ticket sales. During warm weather, biking and horseback riding hit the slopes, and the third week in September sees the annual Highland Games. (☎745-8111. Lift tickets M-F $40, Sa-Su $47; ages 13-19 $33/41; under 13 $25/29.) Just off I-93 in Franconia Notch State Park, **Cannon Mountain** has 42 trails (30% beginner,

30% intermediate, 40% expert) at slightly lower prices than other local resorts. Summer hiking, biking, and swimming keep athletes in shape, while the Aerial Tramway (see p. 93) schleps non-athletes up the mountain. (☎823-8800. Lift tickets M-F $30, Sa-Su $42; ages 13-19 $30/35; seniors and under 13 $20/27.)

WHITE MOUNTAINS ☎603

Consisting of 780,000 acres of mountainous national forest maintained by the US Forest Service, the White Mountains provide a playground for outdoor enthusiasts. Year-round hiking and camping, as well as warm weather alternatives like canoeing, kayaking, and fishing, supplement the White Mountains' intense winter skiing options. The White Mountain National Forest also holds dozens of geological wonders and preserves a mostly undisturbed refuge for some awe-inspiring and dangerous animals, like the moose and black bear.

■ ⁊ ORIENTATION & PRACTICAL INFORMATION. The White Mountains can be daunting to an unfamiliar traveler. The immense forest, spanning both New Hampshire and Maine, is bordered by a dozen or so distinctive towns and contains several commercial ski resorts. Many of the region's highlights can be found within three areas: **Pinkham Notch** (see p. 91), the popular center of the region; **Franconia Notch Area** (see p. 92), northwest of the National Forest; and **North Conway** (see p. 94), a buzzing gateway town.

Any unattended vehicle parked on White Mountain National Forest land must display a **parking pass,** sold by the US Forest Service and the AMC; vehicles parked at national forest campground sites are an exception. (☎528-8721. $5 per week, $20 per year.) The **US Forest Service** operates four **ranger stations,** each providing free information on recreational opportunities, camping, and safety precautions in the White Mountains. The **Ammonoosuc/Pemigewasset,** on Rte. 175 in Plymouth near exit 25 of I-93, covers the southwest region of the forest. (☎536-1315. Open M-F 8am-4:30pm.) **Androscoggin,** 5 mi. south of Gorham on Rte. 16, oversees the northern half. (☎466-2713. Open in summer daily 8am-5pm; in winter M-Sa 8am-4:30pm.) **Evans Notch,** 18 Mayville Rd., in Bethel, ME, covers the Maine section of the national forest. (☎207-824-2134. Open in summer daily 8am-4:30pm; in winter Tu-Sa 8am-4:30pm.) **Saco,** 100 yards west of the junction with Rte. 16 on Hwy. 112 (Kancamagus Hwy.), oversees the southeast section of the forest. (☎447-5448. Open daily 8am-4:30pm.)

The **White Mountain Attraction Center,** P.O. Box 10, N. Woodstock 03262, at Exit 32 from I-93, has info on recreation in the mountains. (☎745-8720. Open daily 8:30am-5:30pm.) The **Appalachian Mountain Club (AMC)** is a nonprofit conservation and recreation organization that maintains 1400 miles of trails in the Northeast. They offer outdoors skills workshops and provide lodging at backcountry huts, shelters, camps, and roadside lodges. The AMC's **Pinkham Notch Visitors Center,** 10 mi. north of Jackson on Rte. 16, is the area's best source of info on weather and trail conditions. They handle lodging reservations and have comprehensive information on White Mountain trails, safety, and *Leave No Trace* backpacking. (AMC headquarters: ☎617-523-0636; www.outdoors.org. Visitors Center: ☎466-2727. Open daily 6:30am-10pm.)

▐ TRANSPORTATION. The scenery along the ride to the White Mountains gives only a taste of the breathtaking views you'll drink in upon arrival. **Concord Trailways** 30 Stickney Ave. (☎228-3300 or 800-639-3317), runs from Boston to Concord (14 per day, $12), Conway (1 per day, $26), and Franconia (1 per day, $27). **Vermont Transit** (☎800-451-3292) runs from Boston, stopping in Concord (4 per day, $12.50) at the Trailways terminal. The **AMC** runs a **shuttle** between locations on the Appalachian Trail in the White Mountains. Consult AMC's *The Guide* for a complete map of routes and times. (☎466-2727. Service operates June to mid-Oct. daily 8am-4pm. Reservations recommended for all stops; required for some. $9.)

✝ ACCOMMODATIONS. Other than ski resorts, most accommodations within the National Forest are controlled by the AMC. Just outside the borders of the forest, usually within an hour's drive from the most central region, plentiful accommodations range from hostels and motels to high-end resorts. For a guide and price range of the motels and hotels near the White Mountains, pick up the small, yellow *White Mountains Travel Guide*, available at any **info booth.**

The **AMC** operates seven full-service **huts** and one self-service hut, all of which are only accessible via trail. The free *AMC Huts and Lodges*, available at the Pinkham Notch Visitors Center or from the AMC main line, has descriptions and locations. At the huts, all bunks are in co-ed bunkrooms. There are no showers, electric lights, or electrical outlets at any of the huts. The **full-service ❸** huts provide bunk, mattress, pillow, and three wool blankets. There are toilets, washrooms separated by gender, and cold running water. Bring sleeping gear and a flashlight. Dinner and breakfast are served daily. At the **self-service ❶** huts, guests must provide their own food but have use of a kitchen stocked with cookware. Blankets are not provided—bring a warm sleeping bag. (☎466-2727; www.outdoors.org. No pets. No smoking. Open June to mid-Sept. Two huts open in winter. Full service huts: AMC members $65, under 15 $42; nonmembers $69/46. Self-service huts: members $19, nonmembers $21.)

For car-accessible lodging, the AMC currently runs the **Joe Dodge Lodge** (see **p. 91**). In addition, the **Highland Center at Crawford Notch,** currently under construction, should be completed by September 2003. It will have 120 beds and serve as an outdoor program center. Contact the AMC for more information. Another lodging option is the **White Mountains Hostel** (see p. 94).

▣ CAMPING. The US Forest Service maintains 23 designated **National Forest campgrounds ❶,** all of which are accessible by car. Four remain open in winter. All campgrounds keep some sites available on a first come, first served basis. On weekends, get to the campsite around check-out time (usually 10-11am) to snag a site. Bathrooms and firewood are usually available at campsites. (Reservations: ☎877-444-6777; www.reserveusa.com. Reservations accepted beginning Jan. 1. Sites $12-16; reservation charge $9, fee to change or cancel reservation $10. Cars parked at campsite do not require a parking pass.)

Camping is less expensive or free of charge at the many **backcountry campsites,** which are only accessible via hiking trails. Regulations prohibit camping and fires above the tree line (approximately 4000 ft.), within 200 ft. of a trail and certain bodies of water, or within ¼ mi. of roads, huts, shelters, tent platforms, lakes, or streams. Rules are even more strict in the Great Gulf Wilderness—no wood or charcoal fires at all. Consult the US Forest Service's *Backcountry Camping Rules 2003/2004* for the complete run-down.

Finally, there exist a plethora of private campgrounds just outside the borders of the forest, the majority of which cater to RVs and families. Pick up a copy of *New Hampshire's Guide to Camping* from any highway rest stop or info booth in the state for a map, prices, and phone numbers of private and state park campgrounds.

▨ OUTDOOR ACTIVITIES. If you intend to spend a lot of time in the area and are planning to do a significant amount of **hiking,** the *AMC White Mountain Guide* ($22; available in most bookstores and huts) is invaluable. The guide

> ❗ No matter where you camp, **bears** are a threat. Stop by a ranger station or the AMC Visitors Center to pick up information on minimizing the risk of danger. Keep food hung and well away from sleeping areas. Do not keep anything with the scent of food on it in or near your tent (clothes worn while eating, for example). But animals are not only a danger when camping; **moose** can be problematic to drivers, so keep a watchful eye.

includes full maps and descriptions of all the mountain trails. Hikers should bring three layers of clothing in all seasons: one for wind, one for rain, and at least one for warmth, preferably fleece or wool but not cotton. Carry insect repellent; black flies and swarms of mosquitoes can ruin a trip, particularly in June.

After hiking, **cycling** is the next most popular way to tour the White Mountains. Many areas are accessible by bike, and some locations have specific bike paths. *The White Mountain Ride Guide* ($13), the US Forest Service's **bike trail guides** (available at info centers), or *30 Bicycle Tours in New Hampshire* ($13 at local bookstores and outdoor equipment stores) can help with planning. **Great Glen Trails Outdoor Center,** just north of Mt. Washington Auto Rd. on Rte. 16, rents bikes for use on their trails only. (☎ 466-2333. Open daily 9am-5pm. Trail fee $7. Bikes $15 for 2hr., half-day $20, full-day $30; under 18 $12/15/20.)

To see the National Forest without much exertion, drive the ⧄**Kancamagus Scenic Highway (Rte. 12),** which connects the towns of Lincoln and Conway. The 35 mi. drive requires at least an hour, though the vistas typically lure drivers to the side of the road for a picnic. Check gas at Lincoln or North Woodstock, as no gas is available for 35 mi., then head east on the clearly marked Kanc to enjoy the scenic splendor stretching all the way to Conway.

PINKHAM NOTCH   ☎ 603

Pinkham Notch, New Hampshire's easternmost notch, lies in the shadow of the tallest mountain in the Northeast—the 6288 ft. Mt. Washington. Pinkham's proximity to the peak makes it more crowded and less peaceful than some neighboring areas. The **AMC's Pinkham Notch Visitors Center** lies between Gorham and Jackson on Rte. 16.

Stretching from just behind the Pinkham Notch Visitors Center all the way up to the summit of Mt. Washington, **Tuckerman's Ravine Trail** demands 4-5hr. of steep hiking each way. *Authorities urge caution when climbing—Mt. Washington claims at least one life every year.* A gorgeous day here can suddenly turn into a chilling storm, with whipping winds and rumbling thunderclouds. It has never been recorded to be warmer than 72°F atop Mt. Washington, and the average temperature on the peak is a bone-chilling 26.7°F with an *average* wind speed of 35 mph. The summit of Mt. Washington boasts the highest wind speed ever recorded at 231 mph. With proper measures, however, the trek up is stellar. Clouds covering the summit make the view from the top foggy, but the view on the way up makes up for it. The **Lion's Head Trail** is a slightly less daunting hiking option with more stable treadway. Motorists can take the **Mt. Washington Auto Rd.,** a paved and dirt road that winds 8 mi. to the summit. Motorists scaling the mountain by car receive bragging rights in the form of a free "This Car Climbed Mt. Washington" bumper sticker; delay affixing it to said bumper until your car has proven that its engine and brakes can handle the challenge. The road begins at **Glen House,** 3 mi. north of the Visitors Center on Rte. 16. (☎ 466-3988. Road open June-Aug. daily 7:30am-6pm; May-June and Sept.-Oct. 8am-5pm. $16 per car and driver; $6 each additional passenger, ages 5-12 $4.)

NEW ENGLAND

Many of the region's lodging options are on or near Mt. Washington. The **Joe Dodge Lodge ❸**, immediately behind the Pinkham Notch Visitors Center, includes a comfortable bunk with delicious and sizeable breakfasts and dinners. The lodge offers over 100 bunks. (☎466-2727. In summer bunks $53, under 16 $36; AMC members $49/33. Off-season $50/34; AMC members $46/32. 2-person private rooms, not including food, $70, AMC members $66; for 3 or more $93/84. Reservations recommended.) Situated about 2hr. up the Tuckerman Ravine Trail, **Hermit Lake Shelter ❶** has bathrooms but no showers, and sleeps 72 people in eight lean-tos and three tent platforms ($8; buy nightly passes at the Visitors Center). **Lakes of the Clouds** hut, just 1.5 mi. from Mt. Washington's summit, is one of AMC's most popular huts.

FRANCONIA NOTCH AREA ☎603

Located in the northwestern expanse of the forest, Franconia Notch is not actually part of the White Mountain National Forest, but a state park—owned and maintained by the state of New Hampshire. Imposing granite cliffs, formed by glacial movements that began during an ice age 400 million years ago, tower on either side of the Franconia Notch Parkway. Waterfalls, endless woodlands, and the famous rocky profile better known as the "Old Man of the Mountain" all call the state park home.

🛈 PRACTICAL INFORMATION. Most of the area highlights are directly accessible from I-93. The **Franconia Notch Chamber of Commerce** (☎800-237-9007; www.franconianotch.org), on Main St. in Franconia, has maps of the region and brochures on nearby campgrounds and sites. A note for those using old maps: recently, the highway exit numbering system changed. Old Exit 1 on the FN Parkway corresponds to new 34A, Exit 2 to 34B, and Exit 3 to 34C.

🖪🍴 CAMPING & FOOD. The beauty of Franconia Notch makes it an ideal place for camping. The extremely popular **Lafayette Place Campground ❶**, off I-93 south between Exits 34A and 34B, has nearly 100 sites with coin-operated showers nestled in the middle of Franconia Notch State Park. From the campground, the scenic Pemi Trail winds 2 mi. through the Notch forest and drops hikers at the Old Man of the Mountain Viewing Area. (☎823-9513; www.nhparks.state.nh.us. Reservations strongly recommended. Open mid-May to mid-Oct., weather permitting. 2-person sites $16; $8 per additional adult, children no extra charge.) For more privacy, set up a tent at one of the 91 sites in **Fransted Campground ❶**, 3 mi. north of the Notch on Rte. 18. Facilities include showers and a bathroom. (☎823-5675. Open Apr.-Oct. Tent sites $20-24; full hookup RV sites $26.)

Woodstock Inn & Station ❹, on Rte. 3, offers a comfortable (read: jacuzzi and health club privileges), though expensive, alternative to camping. (☎745-3951. Rooms from $87, breakfast included.) Even if the Inn's prices are too steep, the endless menu at the **Woodstock Inn Brewery ❷**, housed in the Inn & Station, is sure to please, with everything from not-so-standard sandwiches and salads ($6-8) to Mexican fare and seafood. **Polly's Pancake Parlor ❷**, on Rte. 117 in Sugar Hill, just 2 mi. from Exit 38 off I-93, is a homey cabin restaurant with a dining room overlooking Mt. Washington. The parlor offers a stack of six superb pancakes for $6 or unlimited pancakes for $11, which come topped with maple syrup, maple spread, or maple sugar from the restaurant's own product line. (☎823-5575. Open May-Oct. daily 7am-3pm; Apr. and Nov. Sa-Su 7am-2pm.)

◉ **SIGHTS.** Traveling north from Lincoln on I-93, ◪**The Flume,** Exit 34A on I-93, is a 2 mi. walk, part of which cuts through a spectacular granite gorge. The moss-covered canyon walls are 90 ft. high, and the walk takes visitors over centuries-old covered bridges and past the 45 ft. Avalanche Falls. Buy tickets from the **The Flume Visitors Center,** which also shows an excellent free 15-minute film that acquaints visitors with the area. (☎745-8391; www.flumegorge.com. Open May-June and Sept.-Oct. daily 9am-5pm; July-Aug. daily 9am-5:30pm. $8, ages 6-12 $5.) A 9 mi. **bike path** begins at the Visitors Center and parallels I-93 north. Between Exits 34A and 34B on I-93, visitors can find a well-marked turn-off for **The Basin,** a whirlpool along the Pemigewasset River that has been carved out of a massive base of granite by a 15 ft. waterfall. It's fully accessible with a paved path to viewing areas.

Franconia is best known for the **Old Man of the Mountain,** Exit 34B on I-93, with wheelchair accessible viewing between Exit 34A and 34B heading north. Gracing state license plates and US quarters as the symbol of the Granite State, the Old Man is a 40 ft. human profile formed by five ledges of stone atop a 1200 ft. cliff on Cannon Mountain. A 10-minute walk down the designated path brings viewers to the banks of **Profile Lake,** which affords the best available view of the mountain. The 80-passenger **Cannon Mountain Aerial Tramway,** Exit 34B, climbs over 2000 ft. in 7min. and carries visitors to the summit of the Great Cannon Cliff, a 1000 ft. sheer drop into the cleft between Mt. Lafayette and Cannon Mountain. The tram offers unparalleled vistas of Franconia Notch along its ascent. At the top stands an **observation tower** (elevation over 4200 ft.), while trails wind between miniature trees. (☎823-8800. Open June-Oct. daily 9am-5pm. Trains run every 15min. One-way $8, round-trip $10, ages 6-12 $6.) Rather than riding the tramway, skilled mountaineers enjoy climbing via the aptly named "Sticky Fingers" or "Meat Grinder" routes. In winter, the tram takes skiers up the mountain, which has 40 trails. (Ski pass M-F $32, Sa-Su $44.) Right next to the tramway station sits the one-room **New England Ski Museum.** (☎823-7177. Open June-Aug. and Dec.-Mar. daily noon-5pm. Free.) On summer days, the lifeguard-protected beach at **Echo Lake,** just off Exit 34C on I-93, offers cool but crowded waters. The lake is accessible until 10pm. (☎823-5563. Lifeguard on duty mid-June to early Sept. daily 10am-5pm. $3, seniors and under 12 free. Canoe or paddleboat rental $10 per hr. Last rental 4:30pm.)

◪ **HIKING.** Myriad trails lead up into the mountains on both sides of Franconia Notch, providing excellent day hikes and views. Be prepared for severe weather, especially above 4000 ft. The **Lonesome Lake Trail,** a relatively easy hike, winds its way 1½ mi. from Lafayette Place Campground to **Lonesome Lake,** where the AMC operates its westernmost summer hut. The **Greenleaf Trail** (2½ mi.), which starts at the Aerial Tramway parking lot, and the **Old Bridle Path** (3 mi.), beginning from Lafayette Place, are more ambitious. Both lead up to the AMC's Greenleaf Hut, near the summit of Mt. Lafayette and overlooking Echo Lake. This is a favorite destination for sunset photographers. From Greenleaf, a 7½ mi. trek east along **Garfield Ridge** leads to the AMC's most remote hut, the **Galehead.** This area can keep trekkers occupied for days; get adequate supplies and equipment before starting out. Campsites on Garfield ridge cost $5.

NEAR FRANCONIA: LOST RIVER

Outside of Franconia Notch State Park, ◪**Lost River,** located 6 mi. west of North Woodstock on Rte. 112, is a glacial gorge with numerous caves and rock formations. The reservation also maintains an elaborate nature garden and a forestry

NEW ENGLAND

museum. The walk through the gorge on a wooden walkway is less than 1 mi., but can take a while; each creatively-named cavern (such as the Lemon Squeeze) is open for exploration to those agile (and willing) enough to wrench through. (☎745-8031. Open July-Aug. daily 9am-6pm; May-June and Sept.-Oct. 9am-5pm. $9, children 6-12 $6.)

NORTH CONWAY & CONWAY ☎603

The town of North Conway serves as one of New Hampshire's most popular vacation destinations because of its proximity to ski resorts in winter, foliage in the fall, and hiking and shopping year-round. Rte. 16, the traffic-infested main road, houses outlet stores from big-buck labels. The town of Conway, several miles south, has fewer touristy shops but several excellent meal and lodging options.

A number of stores in the North Conway area rent outdoor equipment. For ski goods in winter or biking gear during other seasons, **Joe Jones,** 2709 White Mtn. Hwy. at Mechanic St. in North Conway, has it all. A second branch lies a few miles north of town on Rte. 302. (☎356-9411. Open July-Aug. daily 9am-8pm; Sept.-Nov. and Apr.-June Su-Th 10am-6pm, F-Sa 9am-6pm; Dec-Mar. M-F 8:30am-6pm, Sa-Su 8:30am-8pm. Alpine skis, boots, and poles $20 for 1 day, $36 for 2 days; cross-country equipment $15/26; snowboards $20/38.) **Eastern Mountain Sports (EMS),** just north on White Mtn. Hwy. in the lobby of the Eastern Slope Inn, distributes free info on the area, sells camping equipment, and rents tents (2-person $15 for 1 day, $20 for 3 days; 4-person $20/25), sleeping bags ($15/20), snowshoes, packs, and skis. The knowledgeable staff provides first-hand info on climbing and hiking in North Conway, and offers their own summer climbing school. (☎356-5433. Open June-Sept. M-Sa 8:30am-9pm, Su 8:30am-6pm; Oct.-May Su-Th 8:30am-6pm, F-Sa 8:30am-9pm.)

The ▨**White Mountains Hostel (HI-AYH) ❶**, 36 Washington St., off Rte. 16 at the intersection of Rte. 153 in the heart of Conway, is maintained by incredibly friendly folk, kept meticulously clean, and proud to be environmentally friendly. The hostel has 43 comfy bunks on several floors, a kitchen, and Internet access. Each bed comes with clean linen and a pillow. (☎447-1001. Light breakfast included. Laundry $3. Reception daily 7-10am and 5-10pm. Check-out 10am. Reservations recommended during the summer and peak foliage season. Open Dec.-Oct. Bunks $21.60, nonmembers $24.60; private rooms $48/51.) The hostel at the beautiful **Cranmore Mt. Lodge ❶**, 859 Kearsarge Rd., in North Conway, has 40 bunks. The lodge is a few miles from downtown, but its recreation room, pool, jacuzzi, trails, cable TV, refrigerator, microwave, and duck pond are all at the disposal of guests. A delicious full breakfast, included with each overnight stay, makes up for the tight bunkrooms and thin mattresses. Be sure to bring a warm blanket to ward off the nightly temperature drop. (☎356-2044 or 800-356-3596. Linen and towel available for a small fee. Check-in 3-9pm. Check-out 11am. $19.)

As for eateries, **Horsefeathers ❷**, on Main St. in North Conway, offers burgers for about $7 and an array of other entrees—including several meatless options—for a few bucks more. (☎356-6862. Kitchen open daily 11:30am-11:45pm; bar open until 1am.) Across the way, adjacent to Olympia Sports, **Morning Dew,** 2686 Main St., caffeinates a great percentage of the local populous. This hole-in-the-wall coffee shack offers bagels, juice, and the daily paper in addition to a variety of coffees ($1-2.50) and teas. (☎356-9366. Open daily 7am-8pm.) Stay wired with a bagful of penny candy from **Zeb's General Store,** which also sells everything New England has to offer, from pure maple syrup to wooden signs and moose memorabilia. Thirsty tourists might wish to partake of their homemade soda. (☎356-9294. Open mid-June to Dec. 9am-10pm; Jan.-May hours vary.) Several miles south in Conway, pink, green, and purple pastels decorate **Cafe Noche ❷**, 147 Main St., which offers authentic Mexican food with many vegetarian choices. Mexican tunes filter through the restaurant and onto the outdoor patio, shaded by a giant maple and colorful umbrellas. Local patrons recommend the Montezuma Pie (Mexican lasagna, $7.25) or the garden burger ($4.25), but they warn against filling up on the unlimited chips and salsa. (☎ 447-5050. Open daily 11:30am-9pm.)

VERMONT

In 1609 Samuel de Champlain dubbed the area "green mountain" in his native French, and the name Vermont stuck. Today, the Green Mountain range defines Vermont, spanning the length of the state from north to south and filling most of its width as well. Over the past few decades, ex-urbanite yuppies have invaded, creating some tension between the original, pristine Vermont and the packaged Vermont of trendy businesses. Fortunately, the former still prevails, and small towns sprinkle the unpopulated mountains to create a friendly, rural atmosphere.

⌘ PRACTICAL INFORMATION

Capital: Montpelier.

Visitor Info: Vermont Information Center, 134 State St., Montpelier 05602 (☎802-828-3237; www.vermontvacation.com). Open daily 8am-8pm. **Dept. of Forests, Parks and Recreation,** 103 S. Main St., Waterbury 05676 (☎802-241-3670). Open M-F 7:45am-4:30pm. **Vermont Snowline** (☎802-229-0531) gives snow conditions Nov.-May, 24hr.

Postal Abbreviation: VT. **Sales Tax:** 5%, meals and lodgings 9%. **Area code:** 802.

VERMONT SKI RESORTS   ☎802

Every winter, skiers pour into Vermont and onto the Northeast's finest slopes; in the summer and fall, these same inclines melt into the stomping grounds of hikers and cyclists. Towns surrounding each of the mountains make their livelihood on this annual avalanche, offering a range of accommodations options. For information, contact **Ski Vermont,** 26 State St., P.O. Box 368, Montpelier 05601. (☎223-2439; www.skivermont.com. Open M-F 7:45am-4:45pm.) The Vermont Information Center (see **Practical Information,** above) provides helpful info. Cheaper lift tickets can be found off-season before mid-December and after mid-March.

Just north of Stowe on Rte. 108 W. lies **Smuggler's Notch,** with three mountains, 72 trails, and the only triple-black-diamond run in the East. A hot spot in winter, the resort's package deals and warm-weather canoeing, kayaking, children's programs, fishing, tennis, golf, and hiking options attract visitors throughout the year. (☎644-8851 or 800-451-8752. Lift tickets M-F $48, Sa-Su $52; children $34/36. In winter, five-day lodging and lift packages start at $119/229 per day.) Just down the road, The **Stowe Mountain Resort** offers one-day lift tickets for $58. Stowe offers 48 trails (16% beginner, 59% intermediate, 25% expert). Stowe's summer facilities are impressive: a golf course and country club, mountain biking, alpine slides (single ride $8, seniors and ages 6-12 $7), and a skate park with a half-pipe. (☎253-3000 or 800-253-4754. All-day pass $15, seniors and children $12; half-day $8/6.50.) West of Brattleboro on Rte. 100, in the town of West Dover, **Mt. Snow** boasts 134 trails (25% beginner, 53% intermediate, 22% expert), 26 lifts, excellent snowmaking capabilities, and the first snowboard park in the Northeast. In the summer, mountain bikers take advantage of 45 mi. of trails. (☎800-245-7669. Open mid-Nov. to late Apr. M-F 9am-4pm, Sa-Su 8am-4pm; May-early Nov. daily 9am-4pm. Lift tickets M-F $49, Sa-Su $55; ages 13-19 $46/44; seniors and under 13 $33/31. $30 per day in summer.)

NEW ENGLAND

At the junction of U.S. 4 and Rte. 100 N in Sherburne, **Killington's** seven mountains and 205 trails cover the most terrain and entertain the East's longest ski and snowboarding season (mid-Oct. to early June). Hiking, biking, and an adventure center (2 alpine slides, 2 waterslides, golf, mini-golf, and tennis) keep visitors busy in the summer. (☎ 800-621-6867. Lift tickets M-F $59, Sa-Su $62; ages 13-18 $54; ages 6-12 $36. $26 per day in summer.) For some of the most reasonable lift ticket prices in Vermont, head to **Burke,** off I-91 in northeastern Vermont. Burke features 35 trails (30% beginner, 40% intermediate, 30% expert). They operate a campsite in summer, when visitors can fish, hike, and bike 200 mi. of trails. (☎ 626-3322. Lift tickets $42, ages 13-18 $32, under 13 $28; rates slightly lower on non-peak days and months. Tent sites $12, lean-tos $15, no hookups.) Near the US-Canadian border in Vermont's Northeast Kingdom, **Jay Peak,** in Jay on Rte. 242, catches more annual snowfall than any other New England resort. With some of the East's best glades and ample opportunities for woods-skiing, Jay Peak is an appealing option for thrill-seekers (75 trails; 40% expert). Excellent fishing and mountain biking are available in summer. (☎ 988-2611 or 800-451-4449. Lift tickets $53, ages 7-17 $39; after 2:45pm $15.)

Other resorts include **Stratton** (☎ 297-2200 or 800-787-2886; 120 trails, 12 lifts), on Rte. 30 N in Bondville, and **Sugarbush** (☎ 583-6100 or 800-537-8427; 4 mountains, 112 trails, 18 lifts), in Warren. Cross-country resorts include the **Von Trapp Family Lodge** (see **Stowe,** p. 101); **Mountain Meadows,** Killington (☎ 775-7077; 90 mi. of trails); and **Woodstock** (☎ 457-1100; 40 mi. of trails).

BURLINGTON ☎ 802

Tucked between Lake Champlain and the Green Mountains, the largest city in Vermont offers spectacular views of New York's Adirondack Mountains across the sailboat-studded waters of Champlain. Five colleges, including the University of Vermont (UVM), give the area a youthful, progressive flair. Along the bustling downtown marketplace of Church St., numerous sidewalk cafes offer a taste of middle-class hippie atmosphere and a chance for people-watching.

⏸ PRACTICAL INFORMATION. Three miles east of Burlington, **Burlington International Airport** flies to a handful of major cities. **Chittenden County Transit Authority (CCTA):** U Mall/Airport shuttles to the airport. **Amtrak,** 29 Railroad Ave., Essex Junction (☎ 879-7298; open daily 8:30am-noon and 8-9pm), 5 mi. east of Burlington on Rte. 15, chugs to New York (9¾hr., 1 per day, $59) and White River Junction (2hr., 1 per day, $16). **Vermont Transit,** 345 Pine St. (☎ 864-6811 or 800-552-8737; open daily 5:30am-7:30pm), at Main St., buses to: Albany (4¾hr., 3 per day, $35); Boston (4¾hr., 5 per day, $46.50); Middlebury (1hr., 3 per day, $7.50); Montréal (2½hr., 4 per day, $19); and White River Junction (2hr., 5 per day, $15). CCTA provides unbeatable access and frequent, reliable service. Pick up connections to Shelburne and other outlying areas downtown at the intersection of Cherry and Church St. (☎ 864-2282. Buses operate at least every 30min. M-Sa 6:15am-9:20pm, depending on routes. $1; seniors, disabled, and under 19 50¢; under 6 free.) **Ski Rack,** 85 Main St., rents bikes. (☎ 658-3313 or 800-882-4530. Open M-Th 10am-7pm, F 10am-8pm, Sa 9am-6pm, Su 11am-5pm. Mountain bikes $10 for 1hr., $16 for 4hr., $22 per day; helmet and lock included. In-line skates $10 for 4hr., $14 per day. Credit card required.) **Visitor Info: Lake Champlain Regional Chamber of Commerce,** 60 Main St., Rte. 100. (☎ 863-3489; 5pm-midnight ☎ 877-686-5253, then dial 0 for a receptionist. Open M-F 8am-5pm, Sa-Su 9am-5pm; Oct.-May closed Sa-Su.) **Post Office:** 11 Elmwood Ave., at Pearl St. (☎ 863-6033. Open M-F 8am-5pm, Sa 8am-1pm.) **ZIP code:** 05401. **Area code:** 802.

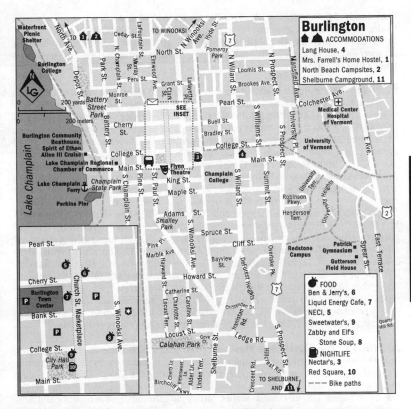

Burlington

▲ ▲ ACCOMMODATIONS

Lang House, **4**
Mrs. Farrell's Home Hostel, **1**
North Beach Campsites, **2**
Shelburne Campground, **11**

■ FOOD
Ben & Jerry's, **6**
Liquid Energy Cafe, **7**
NECI, **5**
Sweetwater's, **9**
Zabby and Elf's
  Stone Soup, **8**

■ NIGHTLIFE
Nectar's, **3**
Red Square, **10**
— — — Bike paths

NEW ENGLAND

⚑ ACCOMMODATIONS. The Chamber of Commerce has the complete rundown on area accommodations. B&Bs are generally found in the outlying suburbs. Reasonably priced hotels and guest houses line **Shelburne Rd./Rte. 7,** south of downtown, and **Main St./Rte. 2,** east of downtown. ◪**Mrs. Farrell's Home Hostel (HI-AYH) ❶,** 27 Arlington Ct., 3 mi. north of downtown via North Ave., is a welcoming abode for the homesick traveler. In keeping with the local hippie slant, posters about everything from nuclear waste to vegan lifestyle make it a haven for peace, justice, and harmony. Six beds are split between a clean, comfortable basement and a lovely garden porch. Light breakfast included. (☎865-3730, call between 4-6pm. Check-in before 5pm. Linen $1. Dorms $20.50, nonmembers $22.50.) For a more upscale experience, stay at the **Lang House ❺,** 360 Main St., a 3-year-old B&B less than a minute's walk from Church St. and downtown. Chefs prepare a gourmet breakfast daily, and the view of Lake Champlain from the third floor rooms is stunning. (☎652-2500 or 877-919-9799. Rooms $135, $160, or $195.) The **North Beach Campsites ❶,** on Institute Rd., 1½ mi. north of town by North Ave., have 137 sites with access to a pristine beach on Lake Champlain. Take Rte. 127 to North Ave., or the "North Ave." bus from the main terminal on Pine St. The beach is open to non-campers and rents canoes and kayaks. (☎862-0942 or 800-571-1198. Beach open 24hr; beach parking closes at 9pm. Campgrounds open May to mid-Oct. Showers 25¢ per 5min. Sites $21, full hookup $2; $5 parking fee for non-campers.) The **Shelburne Campground ❶,** on Shelburne Rd., lies 1 mi. north of Shelburne and

5 mi. south of Burlington by Rte. 7; CCTA buses to Shelburne South stop right next to the campground. Campground amenities include pool, showers, and laundry. (☎985-2540. Open May-Oct. 2-person sites $19, with water and electricity $21, full hookup $30; $5.25 each additional adult, $2.10 each additional child.) See **Champlain Valley** (p. 99) for more camping options.

◖ FOOD. **Church Street Marketplace** and its adjacent sidestreets make Burlington a food lover's paradise with approximately 85 restaurants. Visitors could eat downtown for weeks without hitting the same place twice—not bad for a city of only 40,000. A mostly vegetarian cafe, ■**Zabby and Elf's Stone Soup ❶**, 211 College St., specializes in the homey, hearty, and healthy. Sandwiches on freshly baked breads ($5) and hefty veggie meals from the hot and cold bars are perfect to go. (☎862-7616. Open M 7am-7pm, Tu-F 7am-9pm, Sa 8am-7pm. No credit cards.) At the **Liquid Energy Cafe ❶**, 57 Church St., nonchalant staff and patrons define "chill" while concocting delicious smoothies ($3-5) with unconventional ingredients and restorative powers: custom-build yours to cure anything from acne to asthma. (☎860-7666. Live music daily. Open daily 9am-2am.) The **New England Culinary Institute ❹**, 25 Church St., is a proving ground for up-and-coming chefs. All food is prepared by student chefs, and most of the waitstaff is also students taking a serving class. (☎862-6324. Dinner entrees from $14. Lunch daily 11:30am-2pm; bistro M-Su 2-4pm, Su brunch 11am-3pm; dinner M-Th 5:30-10pm, F-Sa 5:30-10:30pm, Su 5:30-9:30pm; in winter dinner closes ½hr. earlier.) At **Sweetwater's ❷**, 120 Church St., incredibly high ceilings and vast wall paintings dwarf those who come for delicious soups ($3-3:50) and sandwiches ($6-7). In the summer, ask to be seated outdoors to observe Church St. Marketplace. (☎864-9800. Open M-Sa 11:30am-midnight, Su 10:30am-11am; bar open M-Sa until 1:30am, Su until 12:30am.)

◙ SIGHTS. The ■**Shelburne Museum**, 7 mi. south of Burlington in Shelburne, houses one of the best collections of Americana in the country. A 19th-century General Store and an adjacent apothecary are among the 37 buildings composing the splendid 45-acre museum. A covered bridge, lighthouse, and 1950s house are displayed beside Degas, Cassat, Manet, Monet, Rembrandt, and Whistler paintings. (☎985-3346. Open mid-May to Oct. daily 10am-5pm. Tickets valid for 2 days $17.50, ages 6-18 $8.75; after 3pm $10/5.) Five mi. farther south on U.S. 7, the **Vermont Wildflower Farm** has a seed shop, bookstore, and six acres of wildflowers. A gravel path winds through a field and wood, while signs identify the flora. (☎951-5812. Open May to late Oct. daily 10am-5pm. $4, seniors and AAA $3.45, under 12 free.)

Amateur historians delight in Victorian **South Willard St.**, where **Champlain College** and the **University of Vermont** reside. **City Hall Park**, in the heart of downtown, and **Battery St. Park**, on Lake Champlain near the edge of downtown, are charmingly pastoral. The **Burlington Community Boathouse**, at the base of College St. at Lake Champlain, is open to rents rhodes 19s and lasers (sailboats) for a cruise on the lake. (☎865-3377. Open mid-May to mid-Oct. 24hr.; rentals 10am-6pm. Sailboats $25-35 per hr.) The **Spirit of Ethan Allen III** scenic cruise departs from the boathouse at the bottom of College St. Live commentary complements the close-up view of the famous **Champlain Thrust Fault**, a geological wonder not visible from land. (☎862-8300. Cruises late May to mid-Oct. daily 10am, noon, 2, and 4pm; sunset cruise 6:30pm. $10, ages 3-11 $4. Sunset cruise $13/5.) One mi. south of Shelburne on Rte. 7, seven mi. south of Burlington, take the ½hr. tour of the **Vermont Teddy Bear Factory** to learn how teddy bears are born—but be prepared to hear every beary bad bear pun that ever existed. (☎985-1319 or 800-829-2327. Open May-Dec. M-Sa 9am-6pm, Su 10am-5pm; Jan.-Apr. M-Sa 9am-5pm, Su 10am-5pm. Tours leave every 15-30min. Tours $2, under 13 free.) The **Ethan Allen Homestead** rests northeast of Burlington on Rte. 127. In the 1780s, Allen and his Green Mountain Boys forced the surrender of Fort Ticonderoga and helped establish the state of Vermont. He built his cabin in what is now the Winooski Valley Park. (☎865-4556. Open May-Oct. M-Sa 10am-5pm, Su 1-5pm; Sept.-Apr. Sa 10am-5pm, Su 1-5pm. $5, seniors $4, ages 5-17 $2.50; families $14.)

◪ ◪ **FESTIVALS & NIGHTLIFE.** UVM and several other nearby colleges fuel Burlington's youthful, kickin' atmosphere. The town's locus is, yes, Church St. Marketplace, a pedestrian haven for tie-dye seekers and ice cream lovers that nurtures off-beat puppeteers and musicians who entertain the crowds. Pick up a free *Seven Days* newspaper to get the skinny on what's happening in town. In the summer, the **Vermont Mozart Festival** (☎862-7352 or 800-639-9097) brings Bach, Beethoven, and Mozart to local barns, farms, and meadows. The **Discover Jazz Festival** (☎863-7992) features over 1000 musicians in both free and ticketed performances. The **Flynn Theater Box Office**, 153 Main St., handles sales for the Mozart and jazz performances. (☎863-5966. Open M-F 10am-5pm, Sa 11am-4pm.) The **Champlain Valley Folk Festival** (☎800-769-9176) croons in early August. **Nectar's**, 188 Main St., rocks with inexpensive food, including the locally acclaimed gravy fries ($3), and nightly live tunes. (☎658-4771. No cover. Open M-F 5:45am-2am, Sa-Su 7:30am-2am.) The **Red Square**, 136 Church St., is one of Burlington's most popular night spots with live music nightly. Bands play in the alley if the crowd gets large. (☎859-8909. No cover. Open daily 4pm-2am.)

▣ **DAYTRIP FROM BURLINGTON: CHAMPLAIN VALLEY. Lake Champlain,** a 100 mi. long lake between Vermont's Green Mountains and New York's Adirondacks, is often referred to as "Vermont's West Coast." You can take a bridge or ferry across the lake; the ferry offers fantastic views. The **Lake Champlain Ferry,** located on the dock at the bottom of King St., sails 1hr. each way daily from Burlington to Port Kent, NY, and back. (☎864-9804; www.ferries.com. July-Aug. 11-13 per day 7:30am-7:30pm; mid-May to late June and Sept. to mid-Oct. 9 per day 8am-6:35pm. $3.50, ages 6-12 $1.25; car $13.25.) Throughout the day, service from Grand Isle to Plattsburg, NY and from Charlotte, VT, 14 mi. south of Burlington, to Essex, NY is also offered. (Each route $2.50, ages 6-12 50¢; car $7.50.)

Mt. Philo State Park ❶, 15 mi. south of Burlington, off Rte. 7, offers pleasant camping on its seven sites and gorgeous views of the Champlain Valley and the Green Mountains; take the Vermont Transit bus from Burlington south along U.S. 7 toward Vergennes. The area is available for day use, and the lookout point at the top of Mt. Philo is well worth the 2-3 mi. walk or drive. (☎425-2390 or 800-658-1622. Min. stay 2 nights. Open mid-May to mid-Oct. daily 10am-dusk. 7 sites without hookups $13; 3 lean-tos $20. Entrance fee $2.50, ages 4-14 $2.) The marsh of the **Missisquoi National Wildlife Refuge** sits at the northern end of the lake west of Swanton, VT along Rte. 78. Also north of the lake, **Burton Island State Park ❶** is accessible only by ferry from Kill Kare State Park, 35 mi. north of Burlington and 3½ mi. southwest off U.S. 7, near St. Albans Bay. (☎524-6353 or 800-252-2363. Open late May-early Sept. daily 8am-8pm; call for schedule. Day use $4. 19 tent sites $13, 26 lean-tos $19; $4 each additional person.) The state park on **Grand Isle ❶,** just off U.S. 2, north of Keeler Bay, also offers lakeside camping. (☎372-4300. Reservations strongly recommended, especially for summer weekends. Open mid-May to mid-Oct. 4-person sites $13, $3 each additional person; lean-tos $17/4; cabin $34.)

MIDDLEBURY ☎802

"Vermont's Landmark College Town" basks in the energy and culture stimulated by Middlebury College. The result is a traditional Vermont atmosphere tinged with both vitality and history.

7 PRACTICAL INFORMATION. Middlebury stretches along U.S. 7, 42 mi. south of Burlington. **Vermont Transit** stops at the Exxon station, 16 Court St., west of Main St. (☎388-4373. Station open M-Sa 6am-9pm, Su 7am-9pm.) Buses run to: Albany (3hr., 3 per day, $28); Boston (6hr., 3 per day, $43); Burlington (1hr., 3 per day, $7.50); and Rutland (1½hr., 3 per day, $7.50). The **Addison County Transit Resources** provide free shuttle service from the station to the immediate Middlebury vicinity (☎388-1946). The downtown area may best be explored by foot, but for those who prefer wheels, the **Bike Center,** 74 Main St., rents bikes. (☎388-6666. Open M-Sa 9:30am-5:30pm. Bikes from $17 per day.) The staff at the **Addison County Chamber of Commerce,** 2 Court St., in the historic Gamaliel Painter House, has area info. (☎388-7951. Open M-F 9am-5pm; late Sept.-Oct. also Sa-Su 9am-5pm.) **Internet access: Ilsley Public Library,** 75 Main St. (☎388-4095. Open M, W, and F 10am-6pm; Tu and Th 10am-8pm; Sa 10am-4pm.) **Post Office:** 10 Main St. (☎388-2681. Open M-F 8am-5pm, Sa 8am-noon.) **ZIP code:** 05753. **Area code:** 802.

🛏 ACCOMMODATIONS. Lodging with four walls and no mosquitoes does not come cheaply in Middlebury. The **Sugar House Motor Inn ❸,** 1395 Rte. 7 S, just north of Middlebury, offers basic motel rooms with free local calls, refrigerators, microwaves, and cable TV. (☎388-2770 or 800-784-2746. Make reservations in advance. Rooms start at $69.) On the southern edge of Middlebury, the **Greystone Motel ❸,** 2 mi. south of the town center on Rte. 7, has ten recently decorated, basic rooms with cable TV and refrigerator. (☎388-4935. Breakfast included. Reservations recommended. Singles $55; doubles Nov.-Apr. $75, May-Oct. $95.) The best budget accommodations are to be found in the great outdoors. **Branbury State Park ❶,** 7 mi. south on U.S. 7, then 4 mi. south on Rte. 53, stretches along Lake Dunmore, offering 40 sites among the idyllic fields. (☎247-5925. Open late May to mid-Oct. Sites $13, lean-tos $19. Showers 25¢ per 5min. Canoe rentals $5 per hr., $30 per day; paddle boats $5 per 30min.) **River's Bend Campground ❶,** 1000 Dog Team Rd., 4 mi. north of Middlebury off Rte. 7. in New Haven, has 65 clean sites and sits on a picturesque stream. (☎388-9092 or 888-505-5159. Sites for 2 adults and 3 children with water and electricity $22, river sites $26; $10 each additional adult, $3 each additional child under 16. Showers 25¢ per 6min. Fishing, swimming and picnicking facilities $4. Canoe rental $6 per hr.)

🍴🌙 FOOD & NIGHTLIFE. Middlebury's many fine restaurants cater chiefly to plump wallets, but the year-round presence of students ensures the survival of cheaper places. **Noonie's Deli ❶,** 137 Maple St., in the Marbleworks building just behind Main St., is a student favorite and makes terrific sandwiches ($4-5) on homemade bread. (☎388-0014. Open M-Sa 8am-8pm.) Students also flock to **Mister Up's ❷,** a popular nighttime hangout on Bakery Ln., just off Main St., for a sizeable menu including sandwiches ($6-7) and an extensive salad bar. (☎388-6724. Open M-Sa 11:30am-midnight, Su 11am-midnight.) Decked with cacti, **Amigos ❸,** 4 Merchants Row, offers fajitas, burritos, and other Mexican favorites. (☎388-3624. Live music F-Sa. Lunch $5-7. Dinner entrees $8-13. Open M-Th 11:30am-9pm, F-Sa 11:30am-10pm, Su 4-9pm; bar open daily until midnight.) Night owls should check out **Angela's Pub,** 86 Main St. Whether it's live music, the jukebox, or karaoke, this hot spot jumps with musical accompaniment at night. (☎388-0002. Th karaoke, F live band, Sa DJ. Open Tu-F 4pm-2am, Sa 7pm-2am.)

🎨 SIGHTS. The **Frog Hollow Vermont State Craft Center,** 1 Mill St., exhibits and sells the artistic productions of Vermonters. (☎388-3177. Open M-Th 9:30am-5:30pm, F-Sa 9am-6pm, Su 11am-5pm.) Just behind the Center, the **Marbleworks Memorial Bridge** provides a terrific view of the crumbling mills that once generated the town's power. **Middlebury College** hosts the town's cultural events; the concert hall in the college **Arts Center,** just outside of town, has a terrific concert series. The campus **box office** has details on events sponsored by the college. (☎443-6433. Open Sept.-May M-F noon-5pm, also 1hr. before start of show.) Tours from the **Admissions Office,** in Emma Willard Hall on S. Main St., showcase the campus. (☎443-3000. Tours Sept.-late May daily 9am and 1pm. Call for reservations. July-Aug. self-guided tour brochures available.) Too poor for a pint? Trek ¾ mi. north of town to the **Otter Creek Brewery,** 793 Exchange St., for free samples and a tour. (☎800-473-0727. Tours daily at 1, 3, and 5pm.) Fifteen miles east of the Middlebury College campus, the **Middlebury College Snow Bowl** (☎388-4356) entertains skiers in winter with 15 trails and lifts.

STOWE ☎802

Stowe curls gracefully up the side of Mt. Mansfield (Vermont's highest peak, at 4393 ft.). The village self-consciously fancies itself an American skiing hot spot on par with its ritzier European counterparts. In fact, Stowe has something of an obsession with all things Austrian, which may account for the proliferation of Austrian-type chalets and restaurants sprouting off the mountain's ascending road.

🖊 **PRACTICAL INFORMATION.** Stowe is 12 mi. north of I-89 Exit 10, 27 mi. southwest of Burlington. The ski slopes lie along **Rte. 108** (Mountain Rd.), northwest of Stowe. **Vermont Transit** (☎244-7689 or 800-872-7245; open daily 5am-9pm) comes only as close as **Depot Beverage,** 1 River Rd., in Waterbury, 10 mi. from Stowe. **Peg's Pick-up/Stowe Taxi** (☎253-9490 or 800-370-9490) will take you into Stowe for around $15, but call ahead. In winter, the **Stowe Trolley** runs irregularly up and down Mountain Rd., picking up passengers. (☎253-7585. 1¼hr. tours leave from town hall in summer daily 11am; trolley runs in winter 7:30am-10pm. $1, weekly pass $10, season pass $20.) **Visitors Info: Stowe Area Association,** 51 Main St. (☎253-7321 or 800-247-8693; www.gostowe.com. Open in summer and winter M-Sa 9am-8pm, Su 9am-5pm; in spring and fall M-F 9am-5pm.) **Post Office:** 105 Depot St., off Main St. (☎253-7521. Open M-F 7:15am-5pm, Sa 9am-noon.) **ZIP code:** 05672. **Area code:** 802.

📍 **ACCOMMODATIONS.** Easy access is one of many reasons to stay at the **Snow Bound Lodge ❶,** 645 S. Main St., located about half a mile south of the intersection of Rte. 100 and 108. The friendly owners, make even the most weary travelers feel at ease with their engaging conversation and homemade breakfast. (☎253-4515. $25 per person.) **Foster's Place ❷,** 4986 Mountain Rd., offers dorm rooms with a lounge, game room, and hot tub/sauna in a recently renovated school building. (☎253-9404 or 800-330-4880. Reservations recommended. Singles $35-39, with private bath $49-59; quads $55. Call for seasonal rates.) **Smuggler's Notch State Park ❶,** 7248 Mountain Rd., 8 mi. west of Stowe, just past the hostel, keeps it simple with hot showers, tent sites, and lean-tos. (☎253-4014. Reservations recommended. Open late May to mid-Oct. 4-person sites $13, lean-tos $18; each additional person $4.) **Gold Brook Campground ❶,** 1½ mi. south of the town center on Rte. 100, is the only camping area open year-round in Stowe. Facilities include showers, laundry, and horseshoes. (☎253-7683. 2-person sites $20, with hookup $22-29; each additional person $5.)

🍴 **FOOD.** The ▨**Depot Street Malt Shoppe ❶,** 57 Depot St., is reminiscent of decades past. Sports pennants and 45s deck the walls, while rock 'n' roll favorites liven up the outdoor patio seating. The cost of a 1950s-style cherry or vanilla Coke has been adjusted for inflation, but prices remain reasonable. (☎253-4269. Meals

$3-6. Open daily 11:30am-9pm.) Located in Mac's Stowe Market, on S. Main St. by the intersection of Rte. 100 and Rte. 108, **Mac's Deli ❶** has tasty sandwiches ($3) and subs ($4) but no seating. They also serve piping hot soups for $2.40 per lb. (☎253-4576. Open M-Sa 7am-9pm, Su 7am-8pm.) The **Sunset Grille and Tap Room ❸**, 140 Cottage Club Rd., off Mountain Rd., is a favorite among sports fans with its 20 TVs (including 3 big screens) and pool and air hockey tables. The restaurant adjacent to the bar offers barbecue fare. (☎253-9281. Lunch $4-9. Dinner $10-15. Kitchen open daily 11:30am-midnight; bar open until 2am.) The pub-like atmosphere of **The Shed,** 1859 Mountain Rd., along with six potent homemade microbrews and unbeatable M-F specials, make it another nighttime hot spot. (☎253-4364. Tu night $2.50 pint night. Open daily 11:30am-midnight.)

⛷ **SKIING.** Stowe's ski offerings include the **Stowe Mountain Resort** (☎253-3000 or 800-253-4754) and **Smuggler's Notch** (☎644-8851 or 800-451-8752; see **Vermont Ski Resorts,** p. 95). The hills are alive with the area's best cross-country skiing at the **Von Trapp Family Lodge,** on Luce Hill Rd., 2 mi. off Mountain Rd. Don't stay here unless you have a rich uncle in Stowe—prices for lodging climb to $845 in the high season. There's no charge to visit, however, and the lodge offers fairly cheap rentals and lessons for their cross-country ski trails. (☎253-8511 or 800-826-7000. Trail fee $14, ski rentals $16, lessons $14-40 per hr. Ski school package includes all 3 for $35. Discounts available.) **AJ's Ski and Sports,** at the base of Mountain Rd., rents ski equipment in winter and bikes and in-line skates during other seasons. (☎253-4593 or 800-226-6257. Open in winter Su-Th 8am-8pm, F-Sa 8am-9pm; in summer daily 9am-6pm. Skis, boots, and poles: downhill $24 per day, $46 for 2 days; cross-country $12/22, snowboard and boots $24 per day. 20% discount with advance reservations. Mountain bike or in-line skates $7 per hr., $16 per half-day, $24 full-day; helmet and map included. Call to reserve a 2-3½hr. mountain bike tour $30-45.)

🎿 **OUTDOOR ACTIVITIES.** In summer, Stowe's frenetic pace drops off, as do its prices. **Action Outfitters,** 2160 Mountain Rd., serves your recreation needs. (☎253-7975. Open daily 9am-6pm. Mountain bikes $6 per hr., $14 per half-day, $20 full day; in-line skates $6/12/18. Canoes $25 per half-day, $30 full day; includes life jackets, paddles, and car rack.) Stowe's 5½ mi. asphalt **recreation path** runs parallel to the Mountain Rd.'s ascent and begins behind the church on Main St. in Stowe. Perfect for cross-country skiing in the winter, the path accommodates biking, skating, and strolling in the summer. A few miles past Smuggler's Notch lies **Rte. 108/Mountain Rd.** This newly paved, one-lane road winds past huge boulders, trees, and 1000 ft. high cliffs. Several trails branch out from the highway.

Fly fishermen should head to the **Fly Rod Shop,** 3 mi. south of Stowe on Rte. 100, to pick up the necessary fishing licenses ($15 per day, $30 per week, $41 per year, $20 per year for VT residents) and to rent fly rods and reels. There are also free fly fishing classes in the shop's pond. (☎253-7346 or 800-535-9763. Classes W and Sa 4pm. Open Apr.-Oct. M-F 9am-6pm, Sa 9am-4pm, Su 10am-4pm; Nov.-Mar. M-F 9am-5pm, Sa 9am-4pm, Su 10am-4pm. Rods and reels $15 per day.) Named after a unique type of kayak used by the Inuit, **Umiak,** on Rte. 100, 1 mi. south of Stowe Center, rents kayaks and canoes in the summer and offers a full-day river trip. (☎253-2317. Open Apr.-Oct. daily 9am-6pm; winter hours vary. River trip $38 per person; rental and transportation to the river included. Sport kayaks $10 per hr., $20 for 4 hr.; canoes $15/30.) Located in a rustic red barn, **The Nordic Barn at Topnotch,** 4000 Mountain Rd., offers 1hr. horseback-riding tours through woods and streams. No experience is necessary. (☎253-8585. Tours late May-Nov. daily 11am, 1, and 3pm. $30. Reservations required.)

ME & MY CHUNKY MONKEY

In 1978, Ben Cohen and Jerry Greenfield enrolled in a Penn State correspondence course in ice cream making, converted a gas station into their first shop, and launched themselves on the road to a double- scoop success story. Today, ⊠**Ben and Jerry's Ice Cream Factory,** north of Waterbury on Rte. 100, is a mecca for ice cream lovers. Whether you're into "Karamel Sutra" or just "Makin' Whoopie Pie," the 30min. tour of the facilities gives you a taste of the founders' passion. The tour tells Ben & Jerry's history, showcases the company's social consciousness, and awards a free sample at the end. (☎882-2586. Tours June daily every 20min. 9am-5pm; July-Aug. every 10min. 9am-8pm; Sept.-Oct. every 15min. 9am-6pm.; Nov.-May every 30min. 10am-5pm. $2, seniors $1.75, under 12 free.)

NEAR STOWE: ROUTE 100 GLUTTONY

Rte. 100 features a bona fide food fiesta south of Stowe. Begin at Ben & Jerry's (see **graybox,** above) and drive north on Rte. 100 towards Stowe. The first stop is the **Cabot Annex Store,** home to rich chocolate truffles and Vermont's best cheddar. (☎244-6334. Free cheddar samples. Open daily 9am-6pm.) Leave room for **Cold Hollow Cider Mill;** in addition to the potent beverage, cider spin-offs include the 44¢ jelly and doughnuts. Free cider tastings and fudge samples go down easy in the adjacent building. (☎800-327-7537. Call for a cider-making schedule. Open daily 8am-7pm.) Finally, maple is everywhere at the **Stowe Maple Products.** March and April is syrup season, but they sell their home-harvested goods all year. (☎253-2508. Open M-Sa 9am-5pm, Su 10am-4pm.)

BRATTLEBORO   ☎802

The colonial brick facade of Brattleboro's Main St. contains plenty of sporting goods stores, with good reason: the town is popular as a starting point for adventures in the southern Green Mountains and along the Connecticut River. Foliage season in October is the most beautiful (and the most expensive) time to visit this region of Vermont. The region can be explored by canoe from the **Vermont Canoe Touring Center,** 1 mi. north of town, 451 Putney Rd./Rte. 9. (☎257-5008. Open late May to early Sept. daily 9am-6pm; otherwise call for reservations. Rentals $10 for 1hr., $15 for 2hr., half-day $20, full-day $35. River tours $20 per person.) The **Brattleboro Museum and Art Center,** 10 Vernon St., resides in the old Union Railroad Station at the lower end of Main St. and houses a changing and eclectic collection of very modern art. (☎257-0124. Open mid-May to Nov. Tu-Su noon-6pm. $3, students and seniors $2, under 12 free.) The **Gallery Walk** is a free walking tour of Brattleboro's plentiful art galleries; start at any gallery. (First F of every month 5-7pm.)

Economy lodgings proliferate on Rte. 9 (singles generally $49-69), although privately-owned establishments can offer slightly better deals. The simple **Molly Stark Motel ❸,** 829 Marlboro Rd., sits 4 mi. west on Rte. 9. (☎254-2440. Singles in winter from $40; in summer from $55.) **Fort Dummer State Park ❶** is 2 mi. south of town on U.S. 5; turn left on Fairground Ave. just before the I-91 interchange, then right on S. Main St., which becomes Old Guilford Rd. The park offers 51 campsites with fireplaces, picnic tables, bathroom facilities, hiking trails, a playground, and a lean-to with wheelchair access. (☎254-2610. Day use of park $2.50, children $2. Firewood $2.50 per armload. Hot showers 25¢ per 5min. Reservations accepted. Sites $13, $4 each additional person; ten lean-tos $20/4.) **Molly Stark State Park ❶,** 15 mi. west of town on Rte. 9, in a secluded location, provides similar facilities. (☎464-5460. Open May to mid-Oct. RV sites $13, no hookup.)

The casual **Marina Restaurant ❷** perches atop the bank of the West River, 1 mi. north of town on Rte. 5, across Putney Rd. from the Vermont Canoe Touring Center. Enjoy an unsurpassed view from the porch or outdoor terrace along with such favorites as the $5.75 shrimp and chips basket and the $6 "rajun" Cajun chicken. (☎257-7563. Live music Su 3-6pm and W 7-10pm. Open in summer M-Sa 11:30am-10pm, Su 11am-9pm; winter hours vary.) With locally grown fruits, vegetables, and cider, the **Farmers Markets** have what you need. (☎254-9567. Open W 11am-2pm on Main St.; Sa 9am-2pm on Rte. 9 2 mi. west of town.) At night, rock, blues, R&B, and reggae tunnel through the **Mole's Eye Cafe ❷**, downstairs at 4 High St., off Main St. Offering pub fare for under $7, the Mole's Eye is more bar than cafe and frequently hosts live entertainment. (☎257-0771. Live music F-Sa 9pm. Cover F-Sa $4. Open M-Th 4pm-midnight, F-Sa 11:30am-1am; kitchen open until 9pm.)

The **Amtrak** (☎254-2301) train from New York and Springfield, MA stops in Brattleboro behind the museum on Vernon St. Trains depart once per day for New York (6hr., $50) and Washington, D.C. (9¾hr., $79). **Greyhound** and **Vermont Transit** roll into town at the parking lot behind the Citgo station, off Exit 3 on I-91, on Putney Rd. (☎254-6066. Open M-F 8am-4pm, Sa-Su 8am-3:20pm.) Buses run to: Boston (3hr., 2 per day, $25-31.50); Burlington (3½hr., 5 per day, $31); Montréal (6½hr., 4 per day, $59); and New York (5hr., 4 per day, $41). The **Chamber of Commerce,** 180 Main St., provides the *Brattleboro Main Street Walking Tour,* detailed town maps, and brochures galore for outdoor activities. (☎254-4565. Open M-F 9am-5pm, Sa 10am-2pm.) In summer and fall, an **info booth** (☎257-1112) operates on the Town Common off Putney Rd. (Open W-M 9am-5pm.) **Post Office:** 204 Main St. (☎254-4110. Open M-F 8am-5:30pm, Sa 8am-noon.) **ZIP code:** 05301. **Area code:** 802.

MASSACHUSETTS

Massachusetts regards itself, with some justification, as the intellectual center of the nation. Since the 1636 establishment of Cambridge's Harvard College, the oldest college in America, Massachusetts has been a breeding ground for academics and literati. The undisputed highlight of the state is Boston, the birthplace of the American Revolution (a.k.a. the "Cradle of Liberty") and later self-proclaimed "Hub of the Universe," a small, diverse city packed full of cultural and historical attractions. Resplendent with bright colors during the fall, the Berkshire Mountains fill western Massachusetts with a charm that attracts thousands of visitors. The seaside areas—from Nantucket to Northern Bristol and including scenic Cape Cod, New England's premier vacation destination—illuminate the stark beauty that first attracted settlers to these shores.

⑦ PRACTICAL INFORMATION

Capital: Boston.

Visitor Info: Office of Travel & Tourism, 10 Park Plaza, Suite 4510, Boston, MA 02116 (☎617-973-8500 or 800-227-6277; www.mass-vacation.com). Free, comprehensive *Getaway Guide* available online or in person. Open M-F 8:45am-5pm.

Postal Abbreviation: MA. **Sales Tax:** 5%; no tax on clothing and pre-packaged food.

BOSTON
☎ 617

Perhaps more than any other American city, Boston reveals the limits of the "melting pot" metaphor. The corporate sanctuaries of the Financial District are visible from the winding streets of the North End. Snootily aristocratic Beacon Hill is just across Boston Common from the nation's first Chinatown. The South End, trendy and increasingly gay, abuts the less gentrified neighborhoods of Roxbury and Dorchester. While walking Boston's famed Freedom Trail will expose you to some of the earliest history of the United States—in which Boston played a starring role—wandering the streets of Boston's neighborhoods lends a glimpse of a still-evolving metropolis, where old colonial history is often less important (and less interesting) than the lives of the 800,000 people who call Boston home. For more info on Boston, see ▧*Let's Go: Boston 2003.*

⊠ INTERCITY TRANSPORTATION

Airport: Logan International (☎ 800-235-6486), 5mi. northeast of Downtown. T: Airport (Blue); a free shuttle connects all 5 terminals with the T stop. **Shuttle King** (☎ 877-748-8853; www.us-shuttle.com) runs 24hr. door-to-door service to and from the airport (24hr. advanced reservation required). A **taxi** to Downtown costs $15-20.

Trains: South Station, Summer St. at Atlantic Ave. T: South Station (Red). **Amtrak** runs frequent daily service to: **New York City** (4-5hr., $55-64); **Philadelphia** (6hr., $63-74); **Washington, D.C.** (8hr., $69-81).

Buses: Buses depart South Station. T: South Station (Red). **Bonanza Bus** (☎ 888-751-8800) runs daily to: **Newport** (1½hr., every 2hr., $16.75); **Providence** (1hr., every 1-2hr., $9); **Woods Hole** (1½hr., every 1-2hr., $22). **Greyhound** runs to: **New York City** (4-5hr., every 30min., $42); **Philadelphia** (7-8hr., every hr., $55); **Washington, D.C.** (10hr., every 1-2hr., $66). **Peter Pan Trailways** (☎ 800-237-8747) runs to **Albany** (4hr., 5 per day, $32-34) and **New York City** (4-5hr., every ½-1hr., $20-42). **Plymouth & Brockton St. Railway** (☎ 746-0378) goes to **Plymouth** (1hr., $9) and all over **Cape Cod,** including **Hyannis** (1½hr.; M-F 24 per day 7am-midnight, Sa-Su 17 per day 7am-midnight; $14) and **Provincetown** (3¼hr.; $23, round-trip $45). **Vermont Transit** (☎ 800-552-8737) goes north to: **Burlington** (5hr., 5 per day, $50); **Montréal** (8hr., 6 per day, $62); **Portland** (2hr., 9 per day, $15).

⊞ ORIENTATION

Boston is the capital of Massachusetts and the largest city in New England. The city's patchwork of distinct neighborhoods is situated on a peninsula jutting into the Massachusetts Bay (bordered to the north and west by the **Charles River** and to the east by **Boston Harbor**). The city proper is centered on the grassy expanse of **Boston Common;** the popular **Freedom Trail** (p. 112) begins here and links most of the city's major sights. The Trail heads east through crowded **Downtown** (still the same compact three sq. mi. settled in 1630), skirting the city's growing **Waterfront** district to the southeast. The Trail then veers north to the charming **North End,** Boston's "Little Italy"—cut off from Boston proper by the **Fitzgerald Expwy. (I-93)**—then crosses the river to historic **Charlestown.**

Boston Common is sandwiched between aristocratic **Beacon Hill** to the north and the nation's first **Chinatown** to the south. Much of Chinatown overlaps the nightlife-heavy **Theatre District,** to the west. Just west of the Common are the grand

IN RECENT NEWS

DIG THIS

There is construction, and then there's the **Big Dig.** The local nickname for the ambitious Central Artery/Tunnel project, the Big Dig sounds crazy because it is crazy: how else do you explain a plan to drive a dilapidated six-lane highway (the Central Artery) underground and underwater, while simultaneously expanding it into a speedy ten-lane expressway?

The Big Dig has already cost Boston $15 billion, making it, per mile, the most expensive building project in the history of mankind. If you drove or took a taxi from the airport (passing through the heart of the Big Dig), you know the cost to residents: 10 years of headaches, noisy construction, and snarled traffic. Though under construction since late 1991, constant delays, skyrocketing budgets, and general confusion have plagued the project from the start. It's scheduled for completion late next year, but we'll believe it when we see it. The Big Dig has now surpassed even the cursed Red Sox as the favorite thing for Bostonians to gripe about.

Despite its many problems, the Big Dig does have a few welcome side effects. Aside from making the trip to and from the airport bearable, the Big Dig will reconnect neighborhoods cut off from Boston by the Central Artery—namely the charming North End and fast-growing Waterfront. Big Dig bigwigs also promise 40 acres of lush waterfront parks at the mouth of the Charles River—presided over by the elegant 10-lane Zakim Bunker Hill Bridge, whose opening in 2002 gave Bostonians new hope for the Big Dig.

boulevards and brownstones of the chic **Back Bay,** centered on beautiful Copley Sq. and home to Boylston St., a bar-hoppers' paradise. The **Mass. Turnpike (I-90)** separates the Back Bay from the artsy and predominantly gay **South End,** to its south, which has a lion's share of the city's best restaurants. West of the Back Bay are **Kenmore Sq.** and **the Fenway,** home to baseball's Red Sox, the city's major museums, and the clubs of Lansdowne St. South of the Fenway is vibrant, gay-friendly **Jamaica Plain,** filled with countless green spaces and cheap restaurants.

▐⁼ LOCAL TRANSPORT

Public Transit: MBTA or **Massachusetts Bay Transportation Authority** (☎222-5000; www.mbta.com). Known as the T, the subway has 5 colored lines—Red, Blue, Orange, Green, and Silver (Green also splits into lettered lines B-E)—that radiate out from Downtown. "Inbound" trains head toward T: Park St. or T: Downtown Crossing; "outbound" trains head away from those stops. All T stops have maps and schedules, as does the front of this book. Lines run daily 5:30am-12:30am; "Night Owl" system of above-ground buses run F-Sa until 3am. Fare $1, seniors 25¢, ages 5-11 40¢. **Visitor passes** for unlimited subway and bus use are good for 1 day ($6), 3 days ($11), or 7 days ($22). **MBTA Commuter Rail** trains run from T: North Station (Green/Orange) to: **Concord** (Fitchburg line; $4); **Plymouth** (Plymouth/Kingston line; 1hr., $5); **Salem** (Newburyport/Rockport line; 30min., $3).

Taxis: Boston Cab, ☎536-5010. **Checker Taxi,** ☎495-8294. **Town Taxi,** ☎536-5000.

Car Rental: Dollar Rent-a-Car (☎634-0006), at the airport. Open 24hr. Under 25 $30 surcharge per day. 10% AAA discount. Must be 21+ with major credit card. All other agencies have desks at the airport.

🛈 PRACTICAL INFO

Visitor Info: Greater Boston Convention & Visitors Bureau (☎536-4100; www.bostonusa.com) has a booth at Boston Common, outside T: Park St. (Green/Red). Open daily 9am-5pm. Downtown's **National Historic Park Visitor Center,** 15 State St. (☎242-5642), has Freedom Trail info and tours. T: State (Blue/Orange). Open daily 9am-5pm.

Tours: Boston Duck Tours (☎723-3825; www.bostonducktours.com). Wacky con-DUCKtors drive WWII amphibious vehicles past major sights before splashing down in the Charles, offering cheesy commentary and vigorous quacking all the way. 80min. tours depart from the Prudential Ctr., T: Prudential (Green), daily every 30min. 9am to 1hr. before sunset. $23, students and seniors $19, ages 4-12 $13. Tickets sold online; at the New England Aquarium, T: Aquarium (Blue); and the Prudential Ctr. Apr.-Nov. M-Sa 8:30am-8pm, Su 8:30am-6pm. Credit cards accepted only at Aquarium and online.

Hotlines: Rape Crisis Ctr., ☎492-7273. 24 hr. **BGLT Help Line,** ☎267-9001. M-F 6-11pm, Sa-Su 5-10pm.

Post Office: 25 Dorchester Ave. (☎267-8162), behind South Station at T: South Station (Red). Open 24hr. **ZIP code:** 02205. **Area code:** 617. 10-digit dialing required.

⌂ ACCOMMODATIONS

Finding truly cheap accommodations in Boston is very hard. Rates and bookings are highest in summer and during college-rush times in September, late May, and early June. Reservation services promise to find discounted rooms, even during sold-out periods. Try **Boston Reservations** (☎332-4199), **Central Reservation Service** (☎800-332-3026 or 569-3800), or **Citywide Reservation Services** (☎267-7424 or 800-468-3593). **Room tax** in Boston is 12.45%.

▨ **HI–Boston Fenway (HI-AYH),** 575 Commonwealth Ave. (☎267-8599, in Fenway. T: Kenmore (Green-B,C,D) lets out onto Comm. Ave. The best hostel in Boston, housed in a former luxury hotel, with 155 bright and airy 3-bed dorm rooms and a penthouse common room with a 360° view of Boston. Each room has private bath and A/C. Same lineup of freebies at HI-Boston (see below). Free linen. Check-out 11am. Open June-Aug. Individual bed $35, nonmembers $38; 3-bed room $99. ❷

463 Beacon St. Guest House, 463 Beacon St. (☎536-1302), in Back Bay. From T: Hynes/ICA (Green-B,C,D), walk up Massachusetts Ave. and turn right onto Beacon St. Clean, calm, rambling old townhouse in the heart of the Back Bay, with 20 spacious rooms. Private bath, cable TV, telephone, A/C, and kitchenette. Check-in 1-3pm. Check-out noon. Doubles $69-129. ❸

HI–Boston (HI-AYH), 12 Hemenway St. (☎536-9455), in Back Bay. From T: Hynes/ICA (Green-B,C,D), walk down Massachusetts Ave., turn right onto Boylston St., then left onto Hemenway St. Central location, spotless bathrooms, quiet dorms, and an amazing lineup of nightly events, including free movie screenings and complimentary entrance to museums and dance clubs. Free linen, lockers, and kitchen use. Laundry $1 per lb. Check-in noon. Check-out 11am. Dorms $29, nonmembers $32. ❶

Beantown Hostel & Irish Embassy Hostel, 222 Friend St., 3rd fl. (☎723-0800). Exit T: North Station (Green/Orange) onto Causeway St. and turn left onto Friend St. in Downtown. These 2 connected, party-hardy hostels are Boston's cheapest and most dilapidated. Co-ed and single sex dorms (110 beds). Beantown curfew 2am; Irish Embassy (above a pub) curfew-less. Free linen, lockers, and kitchen use. Free buffet Tu and Th 8pm. Laundry (wash/dry) $3.50. Check-out 10am. Dorms $25. Cash only. ❶

YMCA of Greater Boston, 316 Huntington Ave. (☎927-8040). T: Northeastern (Green-E) lets out onto Huntington Ave. in Back Bay. Access to their world-class athletic facilities and Boston's major cultural attractions nearby. A long-term men-only residence that goes co-ed and short-term July-Aug. 6 fl. of sterile but serviceable rooms (with shared hallway bathrooms). Breakfast included. Reception 24hr. Check-out 11am. Must be 18+. Singles $45; doubles $65. $5 discount with HI card. ❷

YWCA Berkeley Residence, 40 Berkeley St. (☎375-2524), at Appleton St. in South End. From T: Back Bay (Orange), follow traffic down Clarendon St. and turn left onto Appleton St. Hostel-style accommodations for women only, with cramped quarters and 2 bathrooms on each fl. Breakfast included. Reception 24hr. Singles $56, doubles $86, triples $99 (discounts for stays longer than 14 days). ❸

NEW ENGLAND

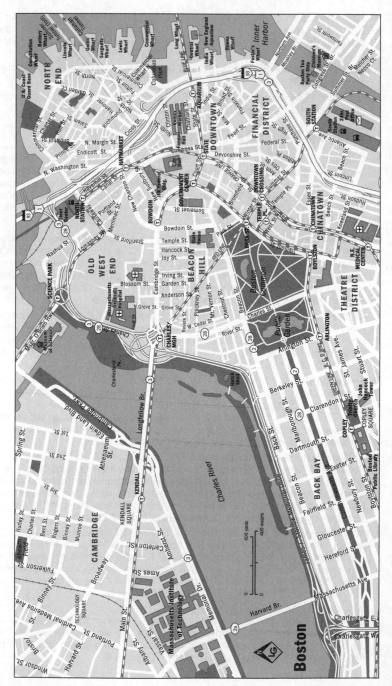

MidTown Hotel, 220 Huntington Ave. (☎262-1000 or 800-343-1177), at Cumberland St. in Back Bay. Exit T: Prudential (Green-E) onto Huntington Ave. and walk with the Prudential Colonnade on the right. A typical mid-range hotel of mid-range quality. All rooms have private bath, TVs, phones, and A/C. Free toiletries, daily housekeeping service, free parking, and a pool. Check-in 3pm; check-out noon. Doubles (2 double beds) $119-199; $15 per additional person. ❸

◖ FOOD

Once a culinary dead zone whose only claim to fame was baked beans, Boston is now a paradise of food. Trendy bistros, fusion restaurants, and a globetrotting array of ethnic eateries have taken their place alongside the long-standing "chowda" shacks, greasy-spoons, soul-food joints, and welcoming pubs.

DOWNTOWN

Downtown is the most heavily touristed part of Boston, so expect mediocre food, big crowds, and high prices. The best and most affordable food options are the identical sandwich shops (sandwiches $5-7) found on almost every street corner and the more diverse food court inside **Quincy Market** (p. 112; most dishes $5-7). Downtown is also near the fresh seafood shops lining Boston's **Waterfront** district.

No Name, 15½ Fish Pier (☎338-7539), the next pier over from the World Trade Ctr. Take the free shuttle to the WTC from T: South Station (Red). One of Boston's best and cheapest Waterfront seafood spots, with fish sent fin-flapping fresh from the boats to your table. Entrees $8-12. Open M-Sa 11am-10pm, Su 11am-9pm. Cash only. ❸

Durgin Park, Quincy Market (☎227-2038). T: Government Ctr. (Blue/Green). Boston's most touristed restaurant, Durgin Park has been serving (rightfully) rare old New England dishes—like fried seafood and lobster, Yankee pot roast, and Indian pudding— since 1827. Meat entrees $9-13. Seafood entrees $13-15. Lobster from $20. Open Su 11:30am-9pm, M-Th 11:30am-10pm, F-Sa 11:30am-10:30pm. ❸

Country Life Vegetarian, 200 High St. (☎951-2685). Entrance on Broad St. From T: State (Blue/Orange), walk against traffic down State St. and turn right onto Broad St. It's a chain, it's far, it's dreary, and it feels like a high school cafeteria, but it also happens to serves the best vegan deal in Boston: $7 ($8 at dinner) gets you an all-you-can-eat buffet of filling, animal product-free fare, plus salad bar. Popular vegan brunch ($9; Su 10am-3pm). Open Su 10am-8pm, M and F 11:30am-3pm, Tu-Th 11:30am-8pm. ❸

Legal Sea Foods, 255 State St. (☎617-227-3115), opposite the New England Aquarium, near T: Aquarium (Blue). Now a national chain, Legal Sea Foods remains Boston's finest seafood restaurant. High-quality cuisine at high prices (raw bar $8-9; entrees $18-30), alongside the best clam chowder ($4-6) in the city, if not the world. Open Su noon-10pm, M-Th 11am-10pm, F-Sa 11am-11pm. ❹

NORTH END

Boston's Italian-American enclave is the place to come for authentic Italian fare, with over 100 nearly identical red sauce restaurants packed into one sq. mi. Quality doesn't vary drastically from place to place, but price does. Most establishments line **Hanover St.,** accessible from T: Haymarket (Green/Orange). After dinner, follow the crowds to one of Hanover St.'s countless Italian *caffès.* For *cannoli* to go ($2-3), try **Mike's Pastry,** 300 Hanover St., or **Modern Pastry,** 257 Hanover St.

Trattoria Il Panino, 11 Parmenter St. (☎720-1336), at Hanover St. The classic romantic North End *trattoria*—warm lighting, exposed brick, intimate seating, and jovial staff—with equally classic fare in gigantic portions. *Antipasti* $11-13. Pastas $10-15. Chicken

THE BIG SPLURGE

BOMBOA

With food as scandalous, sensual, and unique as its decor (complete with a zinc bar, bright clashing colors, and zebra-striped seats), **Bomboa** is a breath of fresh Caribbean air in the often too-similar and too mediocre high-end Boston dining scene. The orchestration of flavors, techniques, and colors on the plate delight all senses.

Most importantly, Felino Samson's tropical, Franco-Brazilian and Latin fusion cuisine will awaken tastebuds tired of French bistro knock-offs. Delights include prawns and honey-braised rutabagas in a spicy coconut crab broth or mackerel *ceviche* with avocados, popcorn, and pineapple wasabi. Even the *feijoada*—a traditional Brazilian black bean dish—gets the celebrity chef treatment thanks to crispy yucca and the aptly-termed "papaya mojo."

Bomboa is also one of the city's hottest drinking destinations. You shouldn't miss their signature tropical cocktails, like the passionfruit *caipirinha*, a super-sweet take on Brazil's national rum drink. *(35 Stanhope St.* ☎ *236-6363; www.bomboa.com. In the South End. From T: Back Bay (Orange), walk 1 block up Clarendon St. (with the T on your left), then right onto Stanhope St. Entrees $22-28. 3-course prix fixe Su-Th $28. Open daily 5:30pm-2am; food served until midnight.* ❺ *)*

dishes $16. Open Su-Th 11am-11pm, F-Sa 11am-midnight. ❸ Il Panino also runs the cheaper lunch counter **Il Panino Express,** 264 Hanover St. Calzones, 1 ft. subs, and salads $5-8. Open daily 1, down the street. 1am-11pm. Cash only. ❷

L'Osteria, 104 Salem St. (☎723-7847). Turn left off Hanover St. onto Parmenter St., then right onto Salem St. A simple, reliable *trattoria* that serves all the robust Italian favorites found on Hanover St., but at lower prices. *Antipasti* $8-10. Pastas $10. Chicken dishes $14. Open Su-Th noon-10pm, F-Sa noon-11pm. ❸

Pizzeria Regina, 11 Thatcher St. (☎227-0765). Turn left off Hanover St. onto Prince St., then left again onto Thatcher St. Since 1926, the North End's best pizza comes gooey, greasy, and always piping hot. Worth the lengthy wait. Open Su-Th 11am-11pm, F-Sa 11am-midnight. Cash only. ❶

Dolce Vita, 221 Hanover St. (☎720-0422). Chatty owner Franco Graceffa works the dining room nightly and spontaneously bursts into love songs from the Old Country, accompanied by his brothers (F-Sa). *Antipasti* $5-10. Pastas $11-13. Meat dishes $14-18. Open daily 11am-11pm. ❸

CHINATOWN

Chinatown is *the* place for filling and cheap Asian food (not just Chinese) anytime. Most places stay open until 3-4am, and even though "blue laws" only allow alcohol to be served until 2am, it's rumored that if you ask for "cold tea," you'll get a teapot filled with something that's brewed, but not from tea leaves. All establishments below are accessible from T: Chinatown (Orange).

■ **Shabu-Zen,** 16 Tyler St. (☎292-8828), off Beach St. Spartan Shabu-Zen is named for its signature DIY dish *shabu-shabu*. Waitresses offer plates of thinly sliced meats and vegetables that you cook yourself in pots of boiling hot water. 2-person combo plates $10-15, à la carte $5-8. Open daily noon-11pm. ❸

Jumbo Seafood Restaurant, 5-7-9 Hudson St. (☎542-2823). Greet your dinner swimming in the tanks by the entrance at the best of Chinatown's Hong Kong-style seafood spots, with huge plates, a light touch, and a glowing velvet mural of HK on the wall. Dinner entrees $9-13. Lunch specials $5-6. Open M-Th 11am-1am, F-Su 11am-2am. ❸

Grand Chau Chow, 41-45 Beach St. (☎292-5166). Despite its ritzy name, this dimly lit spot is one of Chinatown's cheapest. Rice and noodle dishes $6-8. Meat and seafood $9-10. Open Su-Th 11am-3am, F-Sa 11am-4am. ❷

Buddha's Delight, 3 Beach St., 2nd fl. (☎451-2395). Refreshingly airy, clean, and quiet Buddha's Delight (with fat buddhas smilingly benevolently down) features an all-vegan menu soothing to the stomach and the soul. Tofu-based entrees (flavored to taste like meat) $8-10. Open Su-Th 11am-9:30pm, F-Sa 11am-10:30pm. ❸

BACK BAY

The diverse eateries of the elegant Back Bay line chic **Newbury St.,** accessible from T: Hynes/ICA (Green). Though Newbury is known as Boston's expensive shopping district, the street does contain affordable eateries.

Kashmir, 279 Newbury St. (☎536-1695), at Gloucester St. Boston's best Indian. Marble floors, traditional carpets, and plush red seats create a setting as light and exotic as the subtly flavored curries ($13-15) and *dosas* (lentil-and-curry crêpes; $6-9). All-you-can-eat buffet (11am-3pm) M-F $9, Sa-Su $12. Open daily 11:30am-11pm. ❸

Island Hopper, 91 Massachusetts Ave. (☎266-1618), at Newbury St. Encyclopedic menu lives up to its name, with a country-hopping array of Chinese and pan-Southeast Asian dishes—from General Gau's Chicken to *pad thai* to Burmese Noodles. Entrees $8-10. Lunch specials and all-day combos $7-8. Open Su noon-11pm, M-Th 11:30am-11pm, F-Sa 11:30am-midnight. ❸

Shino Express, 144 Newbury St. (☎262-4530). A subterranean sushi counter swiftly making fresh rolls for incredibly cheap. 6pc. rolls $1-5. Open daily until 9pm. ❷

Steve's Greek Cuisine, 316 Newbury St. (☎267-1817), at Hereford St. Decent, amply proportioned Greek food in a cozy cafeteria setting. Stick to hefty *gyros* ($5-7) or vegetarian classics like *tabbouleh,* hummus, and delightful vegetarian *moussaka* (eggplant, potato, and zucchini; all $6-9). Open Su 10am-10pm, M-Sa 7:30am-11pm. ❷

SOUTH END

Prices here continue to rise as lines grow ever longer, but the wait and hefty bill are worth it: the South End's restaurants creatively meld flavors and techniques from around the world to create amazing meals. Most eateries line **Tremont St.,** accessible from T: Back Bay (Orange).

▨ **Addis Red Sea,** 544 Tremont St. (☎426-8727). Spicy, curry- and veggie-heavy Ethiopian cuisine in an intimate and sophisticated (but still casual) setting are not to be missed. All entrees are served utensil-free on traditional *mesob* tables, to be scooped up with spongy, slightly sour *injera* bread. Entrees $8-10; 2-person combos $11-17. Open Su noon-10pm, M-F 5-10:30pm, Sa noon-11pm. ❸

Flour, 1595 Washington St. (☎267-4300), at Rutland St. T: Newton St. (Silver). Harvard-educated chef/owner Joanne Chang bakes the most mouth-watering cakes, cookies, and pastries ($1-3) in the city, all nothing short of transcendent. Gourmet sandwiches $6-7. Open Su 9am-3pm, M-F 7am-7pm, Sa 8am-6pm. ❷

Laurel, 142 Berkeley St. (☎424-6711), a few blocks up Columbus St. from T: Back Bay (Orange). All entrees at gourmet Laurel are $10—half the price they'd be anywhere else for this quality. For less than a museum ticket, you get artful culinary masterpieces like duck confit with sweet potatoes or shrimp and prosciutto ravioli—and all in gigantic portions. Open daily 5:30-10pm. ❸

Le Gamin Café, 550 Tremont St. (☎654-8969), at Waltham St. Tucked into a comfy underground grotto, the casual Boston branch of NYC's trendy, celebrity-frequented Les Deux Gamins attracts locals and visitors alike with sweet and savory crêpes ($4-10). Open daily 8:30am-midnight. Cash only. ❸

JAMAICA PLAIN

Restaurants in "JP" are some of the best bargains in the city, with a variety of ethnic cuisines (especially Mexican). Many places also cater to the neighborhood's large vegetarian and vegan population. The action is centered on **Centre St.**, which runs parallel to the Orange Line (between T: Jackson Sq. and T: Forest Hills).

■ **Bella Luna,** 405 Centre St. (☎524-6060). T: Green St. (Orange). Crispy gourmet pizza (toppings from asparagus to zabaglione) in a funky setting—complete with hand-decorated plates, local art on the walls, and crayons at the tables. Medium pizzas $7-12, large $10-16. Upstairs from the **Milky Way Lounge & Lanes,** a bowling alley-*cum*-karaoke bar. Open Su noon-10pm, M-W 11am-10pm, Th-Sa 11am-11pm. ❸

Tacos El Charro, 349 Centre St. (☎522-2578), at Westerly St. T: Jackson Sq. (Orange). Delicious tacos, burritos, tostadas, and quesadillas ($1.50-5) dished up amidst sombreros, piñatas, and *musica mexicana* to locals and gringos alike. Live mariachi music F-Su 7-10pm. Cover $1. Open M-Th 5-11pm, F-Su 11am-midnight. ❶

Centre St. Café, 669 Centre St. (☎524-9217). T: Green St. (Orange). At the forefront of Jamaica Plain's artsy/crunchy revival, Bohemian Centre St. dishes up a creative rotating menu that works miracles with locally grown organic ingredients. Vegetarians and carnivores alike will rejoice at the healthful, fresh dishes ($10-15). Open Su 9:30am-9:30pm, M-F 11:30am-10pm, Sa 9am-10pm (closed daily 3-5pm). ❸

El Oriental de Cuba, 416 Centre St. (☎524-6464). T: Stony Brook (Orange). No Asian food here—the Oriental of this divey restaurant's name is the Cuban Oriente, home to a hearty, plantain-loving, meat-heavy cuisine. Don't miss the pressed Cuban sandwiches ($5), plantains and beans, or Puerto Rican *mofongo* (mashed garlicky plantains). Entrees $7-10. Open Su 8am-10pm, M-Th 8am-8pm, F-Sa 8am-9pm. ❸

◉ SIGHTS

THE FREEDOM TRAIL

Passing through many of the landmarks that put the city on the map in colonial times, the 2½ mi. red-painted path of the Freedom Trail is a great introduction to Boston's history. Even on a trail dedicated to freedom, though, some sights charge admission. Starting at their **Visitors Center,** the National Park Service offers free 90min. guided tours of the portion of the Trail from the Old South Meeting House to the Old North Church. *(15 State St., opposite Old State House. ☎242-5642; www.thefreedomtrail.org. Tours mid-June to Aug. daily 10, 11am, 1, 2, 3pm. Sept. to mid-June M-F 2pm; Sa-Su 10, 11am, 2pm. Arrive 30min. before tour start time to get a required ticket. Limit 30 people per tour.)* The Freedom Trail begins at another **Visitors Center,** on Boston Common, outside T: Park St. (Green).

BEACON HILL. The Trail first runs uphill to the **Robert Gould Shaw Memorial,** which honors the first black regiment of the Union Army in the American Civil War and their Bostonian leader, made famous by the movie *Glory.* Opposite the memorial is the gold-domed **State House.** *(☎727-3676. Open M-F 10am-4pm. Free; self-guided tour pamphlet available at entrance.)*

DOWNTOWN. Passing the **Park St. Church** (☎523-3383), the trail reaches the **Granary Burial Ground,** where John Hancock, Samuel Adams, Elizabeth Goose (of "Mother Goose" fame), and Paul Revere rest. **King's Chapel & Burying Ground** is America's oldest Anglican church (they ran out of money before they could build a steeple); the latest inhabitants are Unitarian. The burying ground next door is the city's first and the final resting place of midnight rider William Dawes. *(58 Tremont St. ☎227-2155. Chapel open in summer daily 9:30am-4pm. Burying Ground open in summer daily 8am-5:30pm; in winter 8am-3pm. Chapel $1. Burying Ground free.)* The Charles

Bulfinch-designed **Old City Hall,** around the corner on School St., is the original site of the country's first public school, the Boston Latin School, which has since relocated to the Fenway. Now a tourist trinket shop, the **Old Corner Bookstore** was once the heart of the city's intellectual and literary scene. *(1 School St. ☎ 367-4000. Open M-Sa 9am-6pm, Su noon-5pm.)* The **Old South Meeting House** was the site of the preliminary meeting that set the mood for the Boston Tea Party. *(310 Washington St. ☎ 482-6439. Open Apr.-Oct. daily 9:30am-5pm; Nov.-Mar. 10am-4pm. $3, students and seniors $2.50, ages 6-18 $1.)* Formerly the seat of British government in Boston, the ▧**Old State House** now serves as a fascinating museum chronicling the history of Boston and its place in American history. *(20 Washington St. ☎ 720-1713. Open daily 9am-5pm. $5, students and seniors $4, ages 6-18 $1.)* The Trail passes a circle of bricks marking the site of the **Boston Massacre** en route to **Faneuil Hall and Quincy Market,** Boston's most visited tourist sights. A former meeting hall and current mega-mall, the complex is home to a food court and carts selling Boston tourist dreck. *(☎ 242-5675. Open daily 9am-5pm. Tours of Faneuil Hall every 30min. on the 2nd fl.)*

NORTH END. Heading into the Italian-American North End, the Trail crawls through Big Dig rubble to the **Paul Revere House.** *(19 North Sq. ☎ 523-2338. Open mid-Apr. to Oct. daily 9:30am-5:15pm; Nov.-Dec. and mid-Apr. 9:30am-4:15pm; Jan.-Mar Tu-Su 9:30am-4:15pm. $2.50, students and seniors $2, ages 5-17 $1.)* The **Old North Church** is where Robert Newman was instructed by Revere to hang lanterns—"one if by land, two if by sea"—warning patriots in Charlestown that the British were coming. The church itself is uninteresting, but the back room of the gift shop next door houses such Revolutionary relics as George Washington's hair and tea from the Boston Tea Party. *(193 Salem St. ☎ 523-6676. Open June-Oct. daily 9am-6pm; Nov.-May 9am-5pm. Free.)* **Copp's Hill Burying Ground,** up Hull St. from the church, is a final resting place for numerous colonial Bostonians, and was an important vantage point in the Battle of Bunker Hill.

CHARLESTOWN. The Battle of Bunker Hill is the focus of much of the rest of the Trail, which heads across the Charles River to the **USS Constitution** (a.k.a. "Old Ironsides") and its companion museum. *(Ship open daily 10am-4pm. Museum open May-Oct. daily 9am-6pm; Nov.-Apr. 10am-5pm. Free.)* The Trail winds through residential Charlestown toward the suggestive **Bunker Hill Monument,** which is actually on Breed's Hill—fitting given that the entire Battle of Bunker Hill was actually fought on Breed's Hill. A grand view awaits at the top of the monument's 294 steps. *(Monument Sq. Open daily 9am-5pm.)* The Trail loops back to Boston from Monument Sq., passing **City Sq.,** the site of the Puritans' original settlement, begun in 1629 when they first arrived in the Boston area.

DOWNTOWN

In 1634, Massachusetts Bay colonists designated the **Boston Common** as a place for their cattle to graze. These days, street vendors, runners, and tourists roam the green, and many congregate near the **Frog Pond,** a children's wading pool in summer and an ice-skating rink in winter. *(T: Park St. Green line.)* Across Charles St. from the Common is the lavishly laid out **Public Garden,** the nation's first botanical garden. Bronze versions of the title characters from the children's book *Make Way for Ducklings* (in the book, they live in the Public Garden) point the way to the **Swan Boats,** graceful paddle-boats that float around a quiet pond lined with shady willows. *(☎ 522-1966. $2-3 for a 15min. ride. Boats open daily until 4pm.)* Just steps from the Common is the pedestrian mall at **Downtown Crossing.** The city's biggest budget shopping district—with countless discount shoe stores and department stores—is centered around legendary **Filene's Basement,** a chaotic three-floor bargain feeding frenzy. *(426 Washington St. T: Downtown Crossing. Orange/Red line. ☎ 542-2011. Open M-Sa 9:30am-8pm, Su 11am-7pm.)*

N E W   E N G L A N D

BEACON HILL

Looming snootily over the Common is aristocratic Beacon Hill, an exclusive residential neighborhood that was the first spot on the Shawmut Peninsula settled by Puritans. Antique shops, pricey cafés, and ritzy boutiques now line charming **Charles St.**, the neighborhood's main artery. For generations, the Hill was home to Boston's intellectual, political, and social elite, christened the "Boston Brahmins." For a taste of Brahmin life, visit the **Nichols House**, preserved as it was in the 19th century. *(55 Mt. Vernon St. Off Charles St. T: Charles/MGH. Red line. ☎ 227-6993. Open May-Oct. Tu-Sa noon-5:30pm; Nov.-Apr. Th-Sa noon-5:30pm. $5. Entrance by 30min. guided tour only, given every 30min. until 4:30pm.)* Quiet **Louisburg Sq.** was the birthplace of door-to-door Christmas caroling.

The city was the first in America to outlaw slavery, and many blacks moved to the Beacon Hill era after the Civil War. The **Black Heritage Trail** is a free 2hr. (1.6 mi.) walking tour through Beacon Hill sights that were important during Boston's abolitionist era. The tour begins at the foot of Beacon Hill, near the Shaw Memorial (p. 112), and ends at the free **Museum of Afro-American History.** *(46 Joy St. ☎ 720-2991. Museum open June-Aug. daily 10am-4pm; Sept.-May M-Sa 10am-4pm. Heritage Trail tours June-Aug. daily 10am, noon, 2pm; Sept.-May by appointment.)* Also at the foot of the hill is the cheesy **Bull & Finch Pub,** the inspiration for the bar in *Cheers. (84 Beacon St.)*

WATERFRONT

The Waterfront district is made up of the wharves along Boston Harbor from South Station to the North End. The excellent ◙**New England Aquarium** presents cavorting penguins, an open animal hospital, and a bevy of briny beasts in a four-story, 200,000 gallon tank. *(Central Wharf at T: Aquarium. Blue line. ☎ 973-5200. Open July-Aug. M-Tu and F 9am-6pm, W-Th 9am-8pm, Sa-Su 9am-7pm; Sept.-June M-F 9am-5pm, Sa-Su 9am-6pm. $13.50, over 60 $11, ages 3-11 $7. W 4-8pm $1 off. IMAX $7.50.)* The Long Wharf, north of Central Wharf, is the departing point for **Boston Harbor Cruises,** which leads history-minded sightseeing cruises and various whale-watching excursions; they also charter boats to the Harbor Islands. *(☎ 227-4321. Open May-Oct. Cruises: Sightseeing 90min.; 3 per day; $17. Whale-watching 3hr., $29.)* Though closed due to fire through 2002, the **Boston Tea Party Ship** will someday reopen and offer its tongue-in-cheek reenactments of the rebellious event *(T: South Station. Red line.)*

BACK BAY

Now one of Boston's most desirable and eminently walkable districts, the Back Bay was an uninhabitable tidal flat tucked into the "back" corner of the bay west of the Shawmut Peninsula until the late 19th century. A 37-year land reclamation project—impressive even for Boston, home of the multi-billion dollar Big Dig (see p. 106)—began in 1857 and filled the tidal flat with dirt from surrounding hills. Today the elegant Back Bay is lined with stately brownstones and spacious, shady promenades laid out in an easily navigable grid. Cross-streets are labeled alphabetically from Arlington to Hereford St. Running through the Back Bay, **Newbury St.,** accessible from T: Hynes/ICA (Green), is an eight-block parade of everything fashionable, form-fitting, and fabulous.

COPLEY SQUARE. Named for painter John Singleton Copley, Copley Sq. is popular with both lunching businessmen and busy Newbury St. tourists looking for a place to rest their feet and credit cards. The square is dominated by H.H. Richardson's Romanesque fantasy, **Trinity Church,** reflected in the 14 acres of glass used in I.M. Pei's stunning **John Hancock Tower.** The tower is now closed to the public. *(T: Copley. Green line. Church ☎ 536-0944. Open daily 8am-6pm. $3.)* Facing the church, the dramatic ◙**Boston Public Library** is a library disguised as a museum; don't miss John Singer Sargent's mural or the quiet, hidden courtyard. Of the library's seven million odd books, 128 are copies of *Make Way for Ducklings*. (☎536-5400. *Open M-Th 9am-9pm, F-Sa 9am-5pm, Oct.-May Su 1-5pm. Free. 7 terminals of free Internet access.)* The 50th fl. of the **Prudential Center** mall next door to Copley Sq. is home to the **Prudential Skywalk,** which offers a 360° view of Boston from a height of 700 ft. *(T: Prudential. Green E line. ☎859-0648. Shops open M-Sa 10am-8pm, Su 11am-6pm. Skywalk open daily 10am-10pm. Skywalk $7, over 62 and ages 3-10 $4.)*

CHRISTIAN SCIENCE PLAZA. Down Massachusetts Ave. from Newbury St., the 14-acre Christian Science Plaza is the most well-designed and underappreciated public space in Boston. This epic expanse of concrete, centered on a smooth reflecting pool, is home to the Byzantine-revival "Mother Church," a.k.a. **First Church of Christ, Scientist,** a Christian denomination of faith-based healing founded in Boston by Mary Baker Eddy. *(T: Symphony. Green-E line. ☎450-3790. Open June-Aug. M-Sa 10am-4pm; Sept.-May M-F 10am-4pm. Entrance by free 30-45min. tours only. Tours depart on the hr. M-F 10am-3:30pm and Su 11:30am; no tour W noon.)* The adjacent **Mary Baker Eddy Library,** another of Boston's library-*cum*-museums, has exhibits on Mrs. Eddy's life and a surreal "hologram fountain," where holographic words pour out of a spout and crawl all over the walls. The ▓**Mapparium,** a glowing, humming, multistory stained-glass globe, depicts the world as it was in 1935, and the globe's perfect acoustics let you whisper in the ear of Pakistan and hear it in Suriname. *(☎222-3711. Open Tu-F 10am-9pm, Sa 10am-5pm, Su 11am-5pm. $5; students, seniors, and children $3.)*

JAMAICA PLAIN

Jamaica Plain offers the quintessentially un-Bostonian: ample parking, good Mexican food, and Mother Nature. Although it's one of Boston's largest green spaces (over 265 acres), many residents never make it to the lush fields of the **Arnold Arboretum.** A popular spot for bikers, skaters, and joggers, the Arboretum has countless flora and fauna from all over the world, including over 500 lilacs that bloom but once, on the second or third Sunday in May—a.k.a. Lilac Sunday. *(T: Forest Hills. Orange line. ☎524-1718. Open daily dawn-dusk.)* The Arboretum is the next-to-last link in Frederick Law Olmsted's Emerald Necklace, a ring of nine parks around Boston. Near the Arboretum, **Jamaica Pond** is a glacier-made pond (Boston's largest), a popular illicit skinny-dipping spot, and a great place for a quick sail. *(T: Green St. Orange line. boathouse craft rentals $10-20 per hr.)* For an "educational" end to your JP junket, swing by the **Sam Adams Brewery.** At the end of the tour, those with 21+ ID learn how to "taste" beer and can even try brews currently being tested in their labs. *(30 Germania St. T: Stony Brook. Orange line. ☎522-9080. Tours May-Aug. W and Th 2pm; F 2, 5:30pm; Sa noon, 1, 2pm. Sept.-Apr. Th 2pm; F 2, 5:30pm; Sa noon, 1, 2pm. Free.)*

🏛 MUSEUMS

If you're planning a museum binge, consider a **CityPass** (www.citypass.com), which covers admission to the JFK Library, MFA, the Museum of Science, Harvard's Museum of Natural History (p. 122), the Aquarium (p. 114), and the Prudential Center Skywalk (p. 114). Passes, available at museums or online, are valid for nine days. ($30.25, ages 3-17 $18.50.)

▓ **Isabella Stewart Gardner Museum,** 280 The Fenway (☎566-1401), in Fenway. T: Museum (Green-E). This astounding private collection remains exactly as eccentric Mrs. Gardner arranged it over a century ago. Empty frames even remain where stolen paintings once hung. The Venetian-style *palazzo* architecture gets as much attention as the Old Masters, and the courtyard garden alone is worth the price of admission. Highlights include an original of Dante's *Divine Comedy* and Titian's *Europa*, considered the most important Italian Renaissance work in North America. Open Tu-Su 11am-5pm. M-F $10, Sa-Su $11; students $5; under 18 free.

FROM THE ROAD

RUNNING THE BOSTON

My relationship with the Boston Marathon began early. My childhood home was in sight of the halfway point in Wellesley, MA; on Marathon Mondays, we neighborhood kids would hang around high-fiving the stragglers even as the frontrunners were accepting the laurel wreaths. For the 100th running of the Boston Marathon, I skipped school and headed to Copley Sq. with my stepfather. At one point he turned to me and asked if I thought I would ever be among those crossing the yellow finish line. "Sure," I said, nodding my head; when what I really felt was "what, are you crazy?"

The idea did appeal to me. Completing the Boston is a long-distance runners' highest achievement. Although competition is fierce, there is a unique camaraderie among runners and spectators as complete strangers encourage each other the whole way. The more I thought about it, the more I wanted to be a part of this. So in Nov. 2000, I began running along the banks of the Charles every day to train.

I can't say it went by too quickly. I almost sprinted with happiness the first few miles. I gritted my teeth and crossed six mi. of hills (including brutal Heartbreak Hill). When I finally saw the glittering Hancock Tower and turned the last corner, it was all I could do to keep from crying. i couldn't believe I had run a marathon. After watching it 14 times, I had tried it for myself—and I had finished.

—Jane A. Lindholm, now a producer for National Public Radio in Washington, D.C., has worked for the Let's Go guides to Central America, Mexico, Spain, and Chile.

Museum of Fine Arts, 465 Huntington Ave. (☎267-9300; www.mfa.org), in Fenway. T: Museum (Green-E). The exhaustive MFA showcases a globe-spanning array of artwork from every tradition known to mankind—from samurai armor to contemporary American art to medieval instruments. The ancient Egyptian and Nubian galleries (lots of mummies), Impressionist paintings (the largest collection outside France), and the colonial portrait gallery (includes the painting of George Washington found on the $1 bill) are in the collection. Open M-Tu and Sa-Su 10am-4:45pm, W-F 10am-9:45pm (Th-F only West Wing open after 5pm). $15; students and seniors $13; ages 7-17 M-F $5, after 3pm free. Free W after 4pm, $2 off Th-F after 5pm.

Sports Museum of New England, Fleet Ctr. (☎624-1235), in Downtown. T: North Station (Green/Orange). A must for all who understand or want to understand Boston's fanatical sports obsession. Interactive exhibits each dedicated to a different Boston sports franchise. Archival footage, authentic gear, awards, and other artifacts, plus reconstructions of lockers belonging to Boston's all-time greats. Don't miss Larry Bird's size 14 shoes. Open by tour only, usually M-Sa on the hr. 11am-3pm, Su noon and 2pm. $6, seniors and ages 6-17 $4, under 6 free.

John F. Kenney Library & Museum (☎929-4500 or 877-616-4599), Columbia Point, just off I-93 in Dorchester, south of Boston. From T: JFK/UMass (Red), take free shuttle #2 "JFK Library" (daily every 20min. 8am-5:30pm.) Housed since 1993 in a stunning glass tower designed by I.M. Pei, the JFK Library is a thoughtful monument-cum-museum to Boston's favorite son, 35th US President John Francis Fitzgerald Kennedy. Exhibits trace JFK's career from the campaign trail to his tragic, unexplained death. Plenty of exhibits on his fashion plate wife Jackie. Open daily 9am-5pm. $8, students and seniors $6, ages 13-17 $4, under 12 free.

Institute of Contemporary Art (ICA), 955 Boylston St. (☎266-5152). in Back Bay. T: Hynes/ICA (Green-B,C,D). Boston's lone outpost of the avant-garde attracts major and minor contemporary artists. Thought-provoking (though hardly provocative) exhibits rotate every 3-4 months. Open W and F noon-5pm, Th noon-9pm, Sa-Su 11am-5pm. $7, students and seniors $5. Free Th 5-9pm.

Museum of Science, Science Park (☎723-2500). T: Science Park (Green). Seeks to educate and entertain children of all ages with countless permanent and rotating interactive exhibits, divided up among 3 color-coded wings. The must-sees are the giant *Tyrannosaurus rex*; the wacky Theater of Electricity; and the Soundstair, stairs that sing when you step on them. An IMAX

Theater and trippy laser shows are at the Hayden Planetarium. Open Sept.-June Sa-Th 9am-5pm, F 9am-9pm; July-Aug. Sa-Th 9am-7pm, F 9am-9pm. $11, seniors and ages 3-11 $8. IMAX or laser show tickets $8, seniors and ages 3-11 $6; $1.50 discount on shows Su-Th after 6pm.

Children's Museum Boston, 300 Congress St. (☎426-8855), in Waterfront. From T: South Station (Red), follow traffic up Atlantic Ave. and turn right onto Congress St. Children under 10 can run wild making bubbles, climbing, visiting wigwams, playing dress-up, weaving, performing, and seeing the TV/book series *Arthur the Aardvark* come to life. Open Su-Th and Sa 10am-5pm, F 10am-9pm. $8, seniors and ages 2-15 $6, ages 1-2 $2, under 1 free. F 5-9pm $1 for everyone.

🎵 ENTERTAINMENT

The best publications for entertainment and nightlife listings are the *Boston Phoenix* (published every Th; free from streetside boxes) and the *Boston Globe* Calendar section (50¢, included with Th *Boston Globe*). In addition to selling tickets to most major theater shows, **Bostix** sells half-price, day-of-show tickets for select shows from booths at Faneuil Hall (p. 113) and Copley Sq. (p. 114); the website and booths post which shows are on sale each day. (☎723-5181. Tickets daily 11am. Cash only.)

THEATER

Boston's tiny two-block Theater District, near T: Boylston (Green), west of Chinatown, was once the nation's premier pre-Broadway tryout area. Today it remains a stop for touring Broadway and West End productions, not to mention a sexy nightlife district. The **Charles Playhouse,** 74 Warrenton St., is home to the wacky whodunit *Shear Madness* and the dazzling performance *Blue Man Group.* (*Shear:* ☎426-5225. $34; *Blue Man:* ☎426-6912. $43-53. Half-price student rush tickets available 1hr. before showtime. Volunteer to usher *Blue Man Group* and watch for free.) The giant **Wang Center,** 270 Tremont St., hosts various Broadway productions and the nation's most-watched performance of the Christmastime favorite *The Nutcracker.* (☎482-9393 or 800-447-7400. Box office open M-Sa 10am-6pm.) For more avant-garde productions, check out the **Boston Center for the Arts,** 539 Tremont St. (☎426-2748), in the South End, near T: Back Bay (Orange).

CLASSICAL MUSIC

Modeled on the world's most acoustically perfect music hall (the Gewandhaus in Leipzig, Germany), **Symphony Hall,** 301 Massachusetts Ave., T: Symphony (Green-E), is home to both the well-respected **Boston Symphony Orchestra (BSO)** and its light-hearted sister the **Boston Pops.** Beloved conductor Seiji Ozawa left in 2002, and the NYC Met's James Levine takes over in 2004, so this year's season will feature guest conductors. Every 4th of July, the Pops gives a free evening concert at the Esplanade's **Hatch Shell,** near T: Charles/MGH (Red), bursting with patriotic music, fireworks, and a performance of Tschaikovsky's *1812 Overture* using real cannons. (☎266-1492. Box office open daily 10am-6pm. BSO: Season Oct.-Apr. $22-67; general seating at open rehearsals W night, Th morning. $12. Rush Tu and Th 5pm, F 9pm $10. Pops: Season May-July. $14-53.)

SPORTS

Tourists may think Boston is the Freedom Trail, but Bostonians know that—despite the supposed "Curse of the Bambino" placed on the Boston Red Sox by Babe Ruth—the true heart of the city beats within the gates of storied **Fenway Park.** The nation's oldest, smallest, and most expensive baseball park, Fenway is also home to the Green Monster (the in-play left field wall) and one of only two manual scoreboards left in the major leagues (the other's at Chicago's Wrigley Field; p. 569). Get tickets from the **Ticket Office,** 4 Yawkey Way, T: Kenmore (Green-B,C,D). (☎482-4769. Bleachers $18-20; grandstands $25-44; field boxes $60.) If you are a basketball or hockey fan, head to the **Fleet Center,** 50 Causeway St., at T: North Station (Green/Orange). Built on the site of the legendary Boston Garden in 1995, this 20,000-seat complex hosts concerts and games for basketball's **Celtics** and hockey's **Bruins.** (☎624-1750. Box office in summer M-F 10am-5pm; in season daily 10am-7pm. Celtics $10-140. Bruins $20-140.)

Raced every Patriot's Day, the **Boston Marathon** (Apr. 21, 2003), the nation's oldest foot race, is a 26.2 mi. run that snakes from Hopkinton, MA in the west, passes over "Heartbreak Hill," and ends amid much hoopla at Copley Sq. For over 100 years, the marathon has attracted countless runners and spectators from all over the world. Since 1965, the **Head of the Charles Regatta**—the world's largest crew regatta—has drawn preppies past and present to the banks of the river. (See www.hocr.org; Oct. 18-19, 2003.)

🌙 NIGHTLIFE

Before you set out to paint the town red, there are a few things to keep in mind. Boston bars and clubs are notoriously strict about age requirements (usually **21+**), so bring back-up ID. Arcane zoning laws require that all nightlife shuts down by **2am.** The **T** stops running at 1am, so bring extra cash for the taxi ride home. The T tried out a late-night "Night Owl" service in 2002 (with trains running F-Sa until 3am), but as of press time, they had not decided if the service would continue in 2003.

DANCE CLUBS

Boston is a town for pubbers, not clubbers. What few clubs Boston has are on or near Kenmore Sq.'s **Lansdowne St.,** near T: Kenmore (Green-B,C,D).

Avalon, 15 Lansdowne St. (☎262-2424). The flashy, trashy grand dame of Boston's club scene and the closest Puritan Boston gets to Ibiza. World-class DJs, amazing light shows, an oxygen bar (flavored oxygen hits $9 for 7min.), gender-bending cage dancers, and throngs of hotties pack the giant dance floor. Su gay night. Th-F 19+, Sa-Su 21+. Cover $10-20. Open Th-Su 10pm-2am.

Axis, 13 Lansdowne St. (☎617-262-2437). Smaller, less popular little sister of Avalon has a similar techno beat and identical sweaty college crowd. Popular drag shows M night, hosted by sassy 6 ft. drag diva Mizery. 19+. Cover M $7, Th and Sa $10, F varies. Open M and Th-Sa 10pm-2am.

Sophia's, 1270 Boylston St. (☎351-7001). From T: Kenmore (Green-B,C,D), walk down Brookline Ave., turn left onto Yawkey Way, then right onto Boylston St. Far from Lansdowne St. in distance and style, Sophia's is a fiery Latin dance club with 4 fl. of salsa, merengue, and Latin music from a mix of live bands and DJs. Trendy, international crowd. 21+. Cover $10; no cover before 9:30pm W-Th and Sa. Open W-Sa 5pm-2am.

The Modern/Embassy, 36 Lansdowne St. (☎536-2100). Swanky Euro/house dance club (Embassy) with an ultra-cool lounge downstairs (The Modern). 19+. Cover $15. Open Th-Sa 10pm-2am.

BARS AND PUBS

Boston's large student population means the city is filled with great bars and pubs. Most tourists stick to the many faux Irish pubs around **Downtown,** while the **Theatre District** is the premier after-dark destination of the city's international elite. The shamelessly yuppie meat markets along Back Bay's **Boylston St.** are also popular.

Pravda 116, 116 Boylston St. (☎482-7799), in the Theatre District. T: Boylston (Green). The caviar, red decor, long lines, and 116 brands of vodka may recall Mother Russia, but capitalism reigns supreme at commie-chic Pravda, the favored haunt of Boston's upwardly-mobile twenty-somethings. Full Top 40 dance club and 2 bars (1 made of ice). 21+. Cover W $15, F-Sa $10. Bars open Tu-Sa 5pm-2am; club W-Sa 10pm-2am.

Bukowski's Tavern, 50 Dalton St. (☎437-9999), in Back Bay off Boylston St., 1 block south of T: Hynes/ICA (Green). Named for boozer poet Charles Bukowski, Bukowski's casual atmosphere and 99+ bottles of beer on the wall (plus 15 on tap) is the antithesis of Boylston St. chic. Pints $3-15. 21+. No cover. Open daily until 2am. Cash only.

Emily's/SW1, 48 Winter St. (☎423-3649), in Downtown. T: Park St. (Green). A fun college crowd throngs to this hopping dark Top 40 dance club that was catapulted to fame as the hangout of choice for the cast of MTV's *Real World: Boston,* who lived across the Common in Beacon Hill. Beer $4. Cover $5. Open Tu-Th until midnight, F-Sa until 2am.

Mantra/OmBar, 52 Temple Pl. (☎542-8111), in Downtown. T: Temple Pl. (Silver). Seductive. Scandalous. Incomprehensible...and that's just the bathroom, which has 1-way mirrored stalls and ice cubes in the urinals. Pricey fusion restaurant by day, Mantra becomes OmBar by night, complete with a thumping bar in the bank vault downstairs and a "hookah den" upstairs—a surreal Ottoman hideaway with plush couches and tobacco-filled hookah pipes ($25). Cocktails $9. Open daily 5:30pm-2am.

Purple Shamrock, 1 Union St. (☎227-2060), in Downtown. From T: Government Ctr. (Blue/Green), walk through City Hall Plaza to Congress St., parallel to Union St. This faux pub is popular with college kids. Karaoke Tu starts 9:30-10pm. 21+. Cover Th-Su $5. Open daily until 2am.

Delux Café, 100 Chandler St. (☎338-5258), at Clarendon St. 1 block south of T: Back Bay (Orange), in the South End. Dine or drink (or both) among kooky decorative distractions like Elvis shrines, blinking Christmas trees, and continuously looped cartoons. Popular with everyone from bike messengers to businessmen. Cocktails $4-5. No cover. Open M-Sa 5pm-1am; food until 11:30pm. Cash only.

The Littlest Bar, 47 Province St. (☎523-9766), in Downtown. T: Park St. (Green). This very cozy, predominantly local watering hole draws curious tourists and celebrities (note the "Seamus Heaney peed here" sign) hoping for a spot inside what is, in fact, the littlest bar in Boston (just 16 ft. from end to end). Open daily until 2am. Cash only.

LIVE MUSIC

The live music scene in Boston is impressive—no surprise for the town that gave the world such rockin' acts as Aerosmith, the Dropkick Murphys, and the Mighty Mighty Bosstones. The best acts often play across the river in **Cambridge** (p. 123).

Limbo, 49 Temple Pl. (☎338-0280), in Downtown. T: Temple Pl. (Silver). Ultra-sophisticated 3 fl. bar and jazz club, where the only thing smoother than the nightly live jazz (9pm) is the well-heeled crowd. W-Sa DJ spins upstairs. Open daily 5pm-2am.

Wally's Café, 427 Massachusetts Ave. (☎424-1408), at Columbus Ave. in the South End. Turn right out of T: Massachusetts Ave. (Orange) or T: Symphony (Green). Established in 1947, Wally's is Boston's longest-standing jazz joint—and it only improves with age. Nightly live music daily 9pm-2am. 21+. No cover. Cash only.

GAY & LESBIAN NIGHTLIFE

For up-to-date listings of gay and lesbian nightlife, pick up a free copy of the South End-based *Bay Windows,* a gay weekly available everywhere, or check the lengthy listings in the free *Boston Phoenix* and *Improper Bostonian.*

The **South End's** bars and late-night restaurants, accessible from T: Back Bay (Orange), are all gay-friendly (sorry ladies, these are mostly spots for the boys).

NEW ENGLAND

$$$ **THE BIG SPLURGE**

OH OH OLEANA

If you can only splurge once, make it at Oleana. Named one of the five best new restaurants in the entire country last year by the prestigious James Beard Foundation, Oleana seems like nothing special at first—just a few simple beige rooms (with exotic accents) tucked away on an unassuming residential street. But just one taste and you'll realize what all the fuss is about. Ana Sortun's note-perfect Mediterranean menu (think Turkish, Greek, and Middle Eastern favorites with a few intelligent French flourishes) is exquisite but simple, with light grilling the technique of choice and complex, tongue-tingling spices dusting everything. The crown achievement? Sortun's signature lamb, grilled with Turkish spices and served with a divine fava bean *moussaka*.

And then there's Maureen Kilpatrick's sumptuous dessert menu. Your trip to Boston isn't complete without a taste of the dramatically plated baked Alaska—a spiky macaroon and coconut confection drizzled with passionfruit caramel—the perfect ending to a perfect meal. *(134 Hampshire St., Inman Sq. From T: Harvard (Red), walk or take bus #69 up Cambridge St. and turn right onto Hampshire St. ☎ 661-0505. Entrees $19-24. Open Su-Th 5:30-10pm, F-Sa 5:30-11pm. ⑤)*

The sports bar **Fritz**, 26 Chandler St. (☎ 482-4428), and divey **The Eagle**, 520 Tremont St. (☎ 542-4494), are exclusively for gay men. Boston's other major exclusively gay bar/clubs are the Theatre District's **Vapor**, 100 Warrenton St. (☎ 695-9500); **Jacque's**, 71 Broadway (☎ 426-8902); and **Europa/Buzz**, 51-67 Stuart St. (☎ 482-3939). In Fenway is **Ramrod**, 1256 Boylston St. (☎ 266-2986), a Leather & Levis spot that spawned a non-fetish dance club known as **Machine**. Popular gay nights at breeder clubs include Avalon's Sunday bash (p. 118)—preceded by the early evening "T-Dance" at Vapor—and sassy drag night at Axis on Monday (p. 118).

Lesbians flock to **Jamaica Plain's** bookstores and cafés, many of which are queer-owned. On Thursdays, the girls all trek out to **Midway Café**, 3496 Washington St. (☎ 524-9038), south of T: Green St. (Orange), for the phenomenally popular (and very cruisy) ■**Dyke Night**. On Fridays, queer women flock to **"Circuit Girl"** at Europa/Buzz, then rest on Saturday in preparation for Sunday's **"Trix"** lesbian night at Machine.

⚠ OUTDOOR ACTIVITIES

For such a major urban center, Boston has a surprising number of green spaces and outdoor opportunities—thanks largely to the **Emerald Necklace**, a continuous string of nine parks ringing the city. Designed by Frederick Law Olmsted (1822-1903), who also created New York's Central Park (p. 222) and San Francisco's Golden Gate Park (p. 910), the Necklace runs from Boston Common and the Public Garden along the Commonwealth Avenue Mall, the Back Bay Fens and Riverway, Jamaica Plain's Olmsted Park, Jamaica Pond, and Arnold Arboretum (p. 115), ending finally at far-flung Franklin Park. The spots in Jamaica Plain, especially the Arboretum, are the most popular with bikers, skaters, runners, and picnickers.

The **Charles River** separates Boston from Cambridge and is popular with outdoors enthusiasts. Though swimming is strongly discouraged, runners, bikers, and skaters crowd the **Charles River Esplanade** park, which runs along the Charles' banks. The Esplanade is home to the **Hatch Shell**, where Boston's renowned 4th of July festivities take place. Rent watercraft from **Charles River Canoe & Kayak**, beyond Eliot Bridge in the west. (☎ 462-2513. Canoes $11 per hr., $44 per day; kayaks $12/56. Open May-Oct. F 1pm to 30min. before sunset, Sa-Su and holidays 10am to 30min. before sunset.)

Serious hikers should consider the **Harbor Islands National Park,** made up of the 30-odd wooded islands floating in Boston Harbor that are ringed with pristine beaches and blanketed with miles of hiking trails. The most popular islands include Lovell's (with the islands' best beach) and Bumpkin (wild berry paradise). **Boston Harbor Cruises** runs ferries from Long Wharf at T: Aquarium (Blue) to George's Island. (☎227-43121; www.bostonislands.com. Open May-Oct. daily 9am-sunset, hours vary by island. Ferries run May-June and Sept.-Oct. daily 10am, 2, 4pm; July-Aug. daily on the hr. 9am-5pm. Ferry ticket $10, seniors $8, children $7; includes free shuttles to other islands from George's Island.)

NEAR BOSTON

CAMBRIDGE ☎617

Although it is separated from Boston by only a small river, Cambridge (pop. 100,000)—often referred to as Boston's "Left Bank" for its liberal politics and Bohemian flair—has always been worlds away from conservative in both history and temperament. The city has thrived as an intellectual hotbed since the colonial era, when it became the home of prestigious **Harvard University,** the nation's first college. The **Massachusetts Institute of Technology (MIT),** the country's foremost school for the study of science and technology, moved here in the early 20th century. Cambridge's counterculture vibe has long died down since its 1960s heyday, but the city remains a vibrant and exciting place to be, with dozens of bookstores and shops, a large student population, and superior food and nightlife options.

🛈 **PRACTICAL INFORMATION.** Across the Charles River from Boston, Cambridge is best visited as a daytrip, easily reached by a 10min. T ride from Downtown. Accommodations are expensive; it's best to stay in Boston. Cambridge's main artery, **Massachusetts Ave.** ("Mass. Ave."), runs parallel to the T's Red Line, which makes stops along the street. The **Kendall/MIT** stop is just across the river from Boston, near MIT's campus. The Red Line continues to: **Central Sq.,** a bar-hoppers' paradise; **Harvard Sq.,** the city's chaotic heart; and largely residential **Porter Sq.** Harvard Sq. sits at the intersection of Mass. Ave., Brattle St., JFK St., and Dunster St. The **Cambridge Office For Tourism** runs a booth outside T: Harvard (Red) with plenty of maps and info. (☎497-1630 or 617-441-2884; www.cambridge-usa.org. Open M-F 9am-5pm, Sa 10am-3pm, Su 1-5pm.) **Internet access: Adrenaline Zone,** 40 Brattle St., in Harvard Sq. (☎876-1314. Open daily 11am-11pm. $5 per hr., $3 for 30min.) **Post Office:** 770 Massachusetts Ave. (☎876-0550), in Central Sq., and 125 Mt. Auburn St. (☎876-3883), in Harvard Sq. (Both open M-F 7:30am-6pm, Sa 7:30am-3pm.) **ZIP code:** 02138. **Area code:** 617; 10-digit dialing required.

🍴 **FOOD.** Cambridge is a United Nations of ethnic eateries, from Mexican to Tibetan. Most visitors stick to the spots in Harvard Sq. The all-you-can-eat lunch buffets ($7-9, served daily 11:30am-3pm) at Cambridge's many Indian restaurants are as much cherished local institutions as Harvard or MIT. One of the best is **Tanjore ❷,** 18 Eliot St. (☎868-1900), off JFK St. 🔳**Pho Pasteur ❷,** 35 Dunster St., serves cheap, delicious Vietnamese food, including *bun* (vermicelli plates, $6) and their namesake *pho* (beef noodle soups, $6) and has plenty of vegetarian options. (☎864-4100. Open Su-W 11am-10pm, Th-Sa 11am-10:30pm.) **Spice ❸,** 24 Holyoke St., at Mt. Auburn St., has swift service and epic portions of high-quality Thai food. (☎868-9560. Entrees $8-12. Open M-F 11:30am-3pm and 5-10pm, Sa-Su noon-10pm.) For over 40 years, **Bartley's Burger Cottage ❸,** 1246 Mass. Ave., has been serving some of the area's best and juiciest burgers, all named after American politicians and celebrities. Try the Ted Kennedy, a "plump liberal" burger. (☎354-6559. Burgers $8-12. Open M-Tu and Sa 11am-9pm; W-F 11am-10pm. Cash only.) **Darwin's Ltd. ❷**, 148 Mt. Auburn St., (☎617-354-5233), is a 5min. walk from Harvard Sq. proper: exit the T onto Brattle St. and turn right at the Harvard Sq. Hotel onto Mt. Auburn St.; it's 6-7 blocks up on the left. The attractive, Bohemian staff at this busy deli counter (with quiet attached café) craft Boston's best gourmet sandwiches ($5-6.25), all served on fresh bread and named after nearby streets. (☎354-5233. Open Su 7am-7pm, M-Sa 6:30am-9pm. Cash only.) Cool off after a hot day with a so-smooth-it's-illegal scoop from **Toscanini's ❶**, 1310 Mass. Ave. Will it be burnt caramel, cassis sorbet, or Vienna finger cookie? (☎354-9350. Scoop $3. Open Su-Th 8am-11pm F-Sa 8am-midnight.)

◪ **SIGHTS.** Harvard Sq. is of course named after Harvard University. The student-led tours offered by **Harvard Events & Information,** Holyoke Ctr. Arcade (across Dunster St. from the T), are the best way to tour the university's dignified red-brick-and-ivy campus and learn about its sometimes tumultuous history. They also have pamphlets ($1-3) for self-guided tours. (☎485-1573. Open M-Sa 9am-5pm. Tours Sept.-May M-F 10am and 2pm, Sa 2pm; June-Aug. M-Sa 10, 11:15am, 2, 3:15pm.) **Harvard Yard,** just off Mass. Ave., is the heart of undergraduate life at Harvard and the site of the university's annual commencement. The massive **Harry Elkins Widener Memorial Library,** in Harvard Yard, houses nearly 5 million of Harvard's 13.3 million book collection, making it the world's largest university library collection.

Harvard's many museums, just outside Harvard Yard, are worth a visit. The disorganized **Arthur M. Sackler Museum,** 485 Broadway, at Quincy St. just off Mass. Ave., has four floors of non-Western art, including East Asian, pre-Columbian, Islamic, and Indian treasures. Across the street, the **Fogg Art Museum,** 32 Quincy St., offers a small survey of North American and European work from the Middle Ages to the early 20th century, with a strong Impressionist collection and several great van Gogh portraits. Inside the Fogg, the excellent **Busch-Reisinger Museum** is dedicated to modern German work. (All 3 museums: ☎495-9400. Open M-Sa 10am-5pm, Su 1-5pm. $5, students $3, seniors $4, under 18 free. Free all day W and Sa 10am-noon.) Continue your artistic education next door at the Le Corbusier-designed **Carpenter Center,** 24 Quincy St., which displays the hottest contemporary art by both students and professionals. The **Harvard Film Archive,** in the basement of the Carpenter, has a great art-house film series. Schedules are posted outside the door. (☎495-3251. Open M-Sa 9am-11pm, Su noon-11pm. Galleries free. HFA $7, students $5.) The **Harvard Museum of Natural History,** 26 Oxford St., has interesting exhibits on botany, comparative zoology, and geology, including the famous **Glass Flowers,** over 3000 incredibly life-like, life-sized glass models of plants. (☎495-3045; www.hmnh.harvard.edu. Open daily 9am-5pm. $6.50, students and seniors $5, children 3-18 $4. Free year-round Su 9am-noon and Sept.-May W 3-5pm.)

Kendall Sq., T: Kendall/MIT (Red), is home to the **Massachusetts Institute of Technology (MIT),** the world's leading institution dedicated to the study of science and technology. Free campus tours begin at the **MIT Info Ctr.,** 77 Mass Ave., in Lobby 7/Small Dome building, and includes visits to the Chapel and Kresge Auditorium, which touches the ground in only three places. (☎253-1000. Tours M-F 10am and 2pm.) The ◪**MIT Museum,** 265 Mass. Ave., features cutting-edge technological innovations presented in dazzling multimedia exhibitions. Highlights include a gallery of "hacks" (nerdy campus pranks) and the world's largest hologram collection. (☎253-4444; web.mit.edu/museum. Open Tu-F 10am-5pm, Sa-Su noon-5pm. $5; students, seniors, and ages 5-18 $2.)

⊡ ENTERTAINMENT. Some of the Boston area's best live music spots are also in Central Sq, T: Central (Red). **The Middle East,** 472-480 Mass. Ave. (☎864-3278), and **T.T. the Bear's Place,** 10 Brookline St. (☎492-2327), at Mass. Ave., feature live music every night, from the nation's hottest indie rock acts. Harvard Sq.'s **Club Passim,** 47 Palmer St., at Church St., off Mass. Ave., is a folk music legend: a 17-year-old Joan Baez premiered here, while Bob Dylan played between sets, and countless acoustic acts have hit this intimate venue before making it big. (☎492-7679. Tu 7pm open mic. Cover $10-20. Box office open daily 6:30-10pm.)

⊠ NIGHTLIFE. On weekend nights, **Harvard Sq.** is equal parts gathering place, music hall, and three-ring circus, with tourists, locals, and pierced suburban punks enjoying the varied street performers, from magicians to Andean flute players. During the school year, stressed Harvard students unwind as much as they can in the square's many bars, but Cambridge's best nightlife options are in **Central Sq.,** a bar-hopper's heaven not yet overrun by yuppies or tourists. All bars are open until 1am. The harem-like ⊠**Enormous Room,** 567 Mass. Ave., unmarked save an outline of a bull elephant on the window, is too seductive to resist. Amidst sultry arabesque lighting and couches and floor pillows for lounging, a well-scrubbed mixed crowd jives to music from a hidden DJ. (☎491-5550. Beer $4. Mixed drinks $6-9. Cash only.) **The Field,** 20 Prospect St., off Mass. Ave., is the best of Central Sq.'s many faux Irish pubs. An attractive crowd gathers in three warmly and eclectically decorated rooms. (☎354-7345. Beer and mixed drinks $4-5.) A typical-looking Irish pub on the outside, **The Phoenix Landing,** 512 Mass. Ave., literally throbs with the sounds of some of the area's best electric and downtempo grooves. (☎576-6260. Su and W-Th 19+, M-Tu and F-Sa 21+. Cover $3-5.) **The Good Life,** 720 Mass. Ave., is a snazzy nightspot with a casual crowd and high-class atmosphere—jazz, plush booths, and 1950s-era cocktails. (☎868-8800. Drinks $5-7.)

LEXINGTON ☎781

"Stand your ground. Don't fire unless fired upon, but if they mean to have a war, let it begin here," said Captain John Parker to the colonial Minutemen on April 19, 1775. Although no one is certain who fired the "shot heard 'round the world," the American Revolution did indeed erupt in downtown Lexington. The site of the fracas lies in the center of town at Battle Green, where a Minuteman Statue still stands guard. The fateful command itself was issued from across the street at the **Buckman Tavern,** 1 Bedford St. (☎862-5598), which housed the Minutemen on the eve of their decisive battle. The nearby **Hancock-Clarke House,** 36 Hancock St. (☎861-0928), and the **Munroe Tavern,** 1332 Mass. Ave. (☎862-1703), also played significant roles in the birth of the Revolution. All three can be seen on a 30min. tour that runs continuously. (All open Mar.-Nov. M-Sa 10am-5pm, Su 1-5pm. $5 per site, ages 6-16 $3; combo ticket for all 3 $12/7.) The **Museum of Our National Heritage,** 33 Marrett Rd./Rte. 2A, emphasizes a historical approach to understanding popular American life, especially at the time of the Revolution. (☎861-6559. Open M-Sa 10am-5pm, Su noon-5pm. Free.)

The road from Boston to Lexington is easy. Drive straight up Mass. Ave. from Boston or Cambridge, or bike the excellent **Minuteman Trail** to downtown Lexington (access off Mass. Ave. in Arlington, or Alewife St. in Cambridge). MBTA bus #62/76 from T: Alewife (Red) runs to Lexington (20min., 75¢). An excellent model and description of the Battle of Lexington decorates the **Visitors Center,** 1875 Mass. Ave., opposite Battle Green. (☎862-1450. Open Apr.-Oct. daily 9am-5pm, Nov.-Apr. 10am-4pm.) **Area code:** 781.

CONCORD

☎978

Concord, site of the second conflict of the American Revolution, is famous both for its military history and for its status as a 19th-century intellectual center. The The period rooms at the **Concord Museum**, 200 Lexington Rd., on the Cambridge Turnpike, move through Concord's three centuries of history. Highlights include the original lamp from Paul Revere's midnight ride and an exhibit of Ralph Waldo Emerson's study, which is curiously missing from his well-preserved 19th-century home across the street. (☎369-9609. Open Apr.-Dec. M-Sa 9am-5pm, Su noon-5pm; Jan.-Mar. M-Sa 11am-4pm, Su 1-4pm. $7, students and seniors $6, ages 5-18 $3; families $16. Emerson House by 30min. guided tour only. $6, seniors and ages 7-17 $4.) Down the road from the museum, the **Orchard House**, 399 Lexington Rd., was once home to the multi-talented Alcotts, whose daughter Louisa May wrote *Little Women*. (☎369-4118. Open Apr.-Oct. M-Sa 10am-4:30pm, Su 1-4:30pm; Nov.-Mar. M-F 11am-3pm, Sa 10am-4:30pm, Su 1-4:30pm. $7, students and seniors $6, ages 6-17 $4; families $16. Guided tour only.) Farther down the road lies **Wayside**, 455 Lexington Rd., the former residence of the Alcotts and Hawthornes. (☎369-6975. Open May-Oct. Th-Tu 10am-5pm. $4, under 17 free. Guided tour only.) Today, Alcott, Hawthorne, Emerson, and Thoreau reside on "Author's Ridge" in the **Sleepy Hollow Cemetery** on Rte. 62, three blocks from the center of town.

The spot from which "the shot heard 'round the world" was fired is over the **Old North Bridge**. From the parking lot, a five-minute walk brings visitors to the **North Bridge Visitors Center**, 174 Liberty St., to learn about the town's history, especially its involvement in the Revolutionary War. (☎369-6993. Open Apr.-Oct daily 9am-5pm; Nov.-Mar. 9am-4pm.) The **Minuteman National Historical Park**, off Rte. 2A between Concord and Lexington, best explored along the adjacent 5½ mi. **Battle Rd. Trail**, includes an impressive **Visitors Center** that presents battle reenactments and a multimedia presentation on the "Road to Revolution." (☎781-862-7753. Off Rte. 2A between Concord and Lexington. Open Apr.-Nov. daily 9am-5pm; Dec.-Mar. 9am-4pm.) Concord, north of Boston, is served by the Fitchburg commuter rail train ($4) that runs from T: North Station (Green/Orange). **Area Code:** 978.

NEAR CONCORD: WALDEN POND

☎978

In 1845, Thoreau retreated 1½ mi. south of Concord "to live deliberately, to front only the essential facts of life" (though the harsh essence of *his* life was eased from time to time by his mother's home cooking; she lived within walking distance of his cabin). In 1845, he published his thoughts on his time here under the title *Walden*, now considered one of the major works of the Transcendentalist movement. The **Walden Pond State Reservation**, 915 Walden St., off Rte. 126, draws picnickers, swimmers, and boaters and is mobbed in summer. No camping, pets, or "novelty flotation devices" are allowed. Although visiting after the pond closes is forbidden, it has become something of a rite of passage for local college students to break in after dark and go skinny-dipping. (☎369-3254. Open daily dawn-dusk. Parking $5.) When Walden Pond swarms with crowds, head east from Concord center on Rte. 62 to another of Thoreau's haunts, **Great Meadows National Wildlife Refuge**, on Monsen Rd. (☎443-4661. Open daily dawn-dusk. Free.)

NEW ENGLAND

SALEM ☎ 978

Salem isn't trying that hard to free itself from certain stereotypes. The **Salem Witch Museum,** 19½ Washington Sq. N., gives a melodramatic but informative multimedia presentation detailing the history of the infamous 17th-century witch trials. It also presents an interesting exhibit on the role of scapegoating throughout history. (☎745-1692. Open July-Aug. daily 10am-7pm; Sept.-June 10am-5pm. $6, seniors $5.50, ages 6-14 $4. Cash only.) Escape the witch kitsch at the **Witch Trials Memorial,** off Charter St., where engraved stones commemorate the trials' 19 victims.

Salem's **Peabody Essex Museum,** East India Sq., on the corner of Essex and New Liberty St., recalls the port's former leading role in Atlantic whaling and merchant shipping. Admission includes tours of four historic Salem houses. (☎800-745-4054 or 745-9500. Open Apr.-Oct. M-Sa 10am-5pm, Su noon-5pm; Nov.-Mar. Tu-Sa 10am-5pm, Su noon-5pm. $10, students and seniors $8, under 17 free.) Built in 1668 and officially named the Turner-Ingersoll Mansion, Salem's **House of Seven Gables,** 54 Turner St., became the "second most famous house in America" after the release of Concord-born Nathaniel Hawthorne's Gothic romance of the same name. (☎744-0991. Open July-Nov. daily 10am-7pm; Dec.-June M-Sa 10am-5pm, Su noon-5pm. $10, seniors $9, ages 5-12 $5.50, under 5 free. By 30min. guided tour only.)

The **Salem Visitors Center,** 2 New Liberty St., has free maps, public restrooms, historical displays, and a gift shop. (☎740-1650. Open July-Aug. daily 9am-6pm; Sept.-June 9am-5pm.) Salem, 20 mi. northeast of Boston, is accessible by the Newburyport/Rockport commuter rail train (30min., $3) from Boston's North Station, by MBTA bus #450 or 455 (45min., 75¢) from T: Haymarket (Green/Orange), or by car from I-95 or U.S. 1 N. to Rte. 128 and Rte. 114. **Area code:** 978.

PLYMOUTH ☎ 508

Despite what American high school textbooks say, the Pilgrims' first step onto the New World was *not* at Plymouth. They stopped first at Provincetown (see p. 129), then promptly left because the soil was so inadequate. **Plymouth Rock** is actually a small stone that has dubiously been identified as the actual rock on which the Pilgrims disembarked. It served as a symbol of liberty during the American Revolution; since then, it has moved three times before ending up at its current home, beneath an extravagant portico on Water St., at the foot of North St. After several vandalization episodes, it's under tight security.

Three miles south of town off Rte. 3A, the historical theme park **≋Plimoth Plantation** recreates the Pilgrims' early settlement. In the **Pilgrim Village,** costumed actors play the roles of actual villagers carrying out their daily tasks, while **Hobbamock's Homesite** represents a Native American village of the same period. (☎746-1622. Open Apr.-Nov. daily 9am-5pm. $20, ages 6-12 $12; $2 AAA discount.) Docked off Water St., the *Mayflower II* was built in the 1950s to recapture the atmosphere of the original ship. (Open Apr.-Nov. daily 9am-5pm. $8, ages 6-12 $6. Admission to both sights $22, students and seniors $20, ages 6-12 $14; $3 AAA discount.) The nation's oldest museum in continuous existence, the **Pilgrim Hall Museum,** 75 Court St., houses Puritan crafts, furniture, books, paintings, and weapons. The main hall is dominated by the ship *Sparrow-Hawk,* preserved for 250 years in Cape Cod sands. (☎746-1620. Open Feb.-Dec. daily 9:30am-4:30pm. $5, seniors $4.50, ages 5-17 $3; families $14.)

NEW ENGLAND

Plymouth, 40 mi. southeast of Boston, requires a car; take Exit 6A from Rte. 3, off I-93. **Plymouth & Brockton Bus** (☎746-0378) runs from T: South Station (Red) to the Exit 5 Info Ctr. (1hr., $9). Plymouth/Kingston commuter rail train goes from T: North Station (Green/Orange) to the Cordage Park Station (1hr., 3-4 per day, $5). From the info center and Cordage Park Station, catch a local GATRA bus (75¢, seniors and children 35¢) to Plymouth center. **Plymouth Visitors Center** is at 170 Water St. (☎747-7525 or 800-872-1620. Open Apr.-May and Sept.-Nov. daily 9am-5pm; June 9am-6pm; July-Aug. 9am-9pm.) **Area code:** 508.

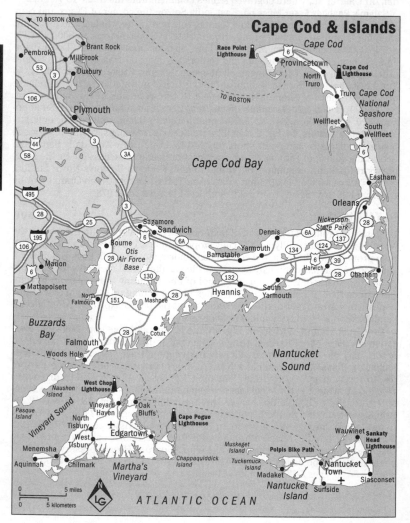

Cape Cod & Islands

CAPE COD & ISLANDS ☎ 508

Writer Henry David Thoreau once said of Cape Cod: "It is wholly unknown to the fashionable world, and probably will never be agreeable to them." Thoreau couldn't have been more wrong. When Englishman Bartholomew Gosnold landed on this peninsula in 1602, he could not have guessed that a population of tourists and summer escapees from the big city would come to outnumber the plentiful cod population for which he had named the peninsula. Now New England's premier vacation destination, this thin strip of land draws tourists by the droves with its charming small towns and diverse, sun-drenched landscapes—everything from cranberry bogs and sandy beaches to deep freshwater ponds carved by glaciers and desert-like dunes sculpted by the wind. Though parts of the Cape are known as the playground of the rich and famous—and the peninsula is in general geared toward bigger spenders—it can be an option for budget travelers, thanks to an emphasis on free activities, like sunbathing and hiking, and a decent hostel and budget B&B system.

🔆 ORIENTATION

Stretching out into the Atlantic Ocean south of Boston, Cape Cod resembles a bent arm, with **Woods Hole** at its armpit, **Hyannis** at its bicep, **Chatham** at its elbow, the **National Seashore** tattooed on its forearm, and **Provincetown** at its clenched fist. The southern islands **Martha's Vineyard** (p. 131) and **Nantucket** (p. 133) are accessible by ferries from Woods Hole or Hyannis.

Cape locations can be confusing. **Upper Cape** refers to the suburbanized, more developed area closer to the mainland. Proceeding eastward away from the mainland and curving up along the Cape, you travel **Down Cape** through **Mid-Cape** (where the Cape's two hostels are, near **Eastham** and **Truro**), finally hitting the **Lower Cape** and the National Seashore. In summer, traffic to and from the Cape is hell: vacationers drive out on Friday and return Sunday afternoon, so avoid traveling then.

Cycling is the best way to travel the Cape's gentle slopes. The park service has free trail maps and the highly recommended and detailed *Cape Cod Bike Book* ($3), also available at most Cape bookstores. The 135 mi. **Boston-Cape Cod Bikeway** connects Boston to Provincetown, and the trails that line either side of the **Cape Cod Canal** in the National Seashore rank among the country's most scenic, as does the 25 mi. **Cape Cod Rail Trail** from Dennis to Wellfleet. For discount coupons good throughout the Cape, pick up a free *Official 2003 Guide to Cape Cod* or *Cape Cod Best Read Guide*, available at most Cape info centers. **Area code:** 508.

HYANNIS ☎ 508

Tattooed midway across the Cape's upper arm, Hyannis is not the Cape Cod most people expect. Though JFK spent his summers in nearby Hyannisport, Hyannis proper is little more than a transportation hub (ferries to Nantucket depart from here) with a depressing Main St. and tacky mall—a far cry from the quaint villages further out on the Cape. **Kalmus Park,** on Ocean St. in Hyannisport, is popular with windsurfers, while **Orrin Keyes,** on Sea St., attracts more of a local crowd. **Veteran's Park Beach,** off Ocean St., is great for families. All have parking ($10), lifeguards, bathhouses, snack bars, picnic areas, and wheelchair accessibility. Hyannis is full of cookie-cutter motels and inns. The immense **Hyannis Inn Motel ❸,** 473 Main St., has large, clean rooms with cable TV and mini-fridges. (☎ 775-0255. Open mid-Mar. to mid-Oct. Doubles $62-126; deluxe rooms $72-141, with whirlpool $97-165.) For inexpensive, delicious sandwiches ($4-6), head to ▩**Box Lunch** ❶, 357 Main St., a local Cape Cod chain. (☎790-5855. Open M-F 9am-6pm, Sa 10am-10pm, Su 10am-5pm.) Identical upscale seafood restaurants line Main St., with entrees averaging $12-20. **Plymouth & Brockton** (☎746-0378) runs from Boston's South Station to Hyannis Bus Station, on Elm St. (1½hr.; M-F 24 per day 7am-midnight, Sa-Su 17 per day 7am-midnight; $14).

EASTHAM   ☎508

Situated just north of the elbow of the Cape, Eastham marks the beginning of the extensive **Cape Cod National Seashore,** and is also home to the only of the Cape's two HI-accredited hostels accessible by public transportation. The still-functional **Eastham Windmill,** on Rte. 6 at Samoset Rd., has had its nose to the grindstone since 1680, but has only been at this location for 191 years. (Open June-Aug. M-Su 10am-5pm. Free.) Off Rte. 6, **Fort Hill** overlooks Nauset Marsh and the ocean. Eastham's **Mid-Cape Hostel (HI-AYH)** ❶, 75 Goody Hallet Dr., close to the bike path known as the **Cape Cod Rail Trail,** features communal bungalow living in a woodsy location. From Rte. 6, take the Rock Harbor exit at the Orleans Ctr. rotary, turn right onto Bridge Rd., then right again onto Goody Hallet Dr. By P&B bus, ask the drive to let you off as close as possible, and call the hostel for the "shortcut" directions along walking paths. (☎255-2785, toll-free ☎888-901-2085. Shared bathrooms, kitchen, and BBQ facilities. Bike rental $5 per day. Max stay 7 days. Open late June-early Sept. Dorms $19, nonmembers $22.) **Plymouth & Brockton** (☎746-0378) runs buses from Boston's South Station to Eastham (2½hr.; $18, round-trip $35). By car, take Rte. 3 to Rte. 6 west, cross the Sagamore Bridge, and follow signs.

CAPE COD NATIONAL SEASHORE   ☎508

As early as 1825, the Cape had suffered so much man-made damage that the town of Truro required local residents to plant beach grass and keep their cows off the dunes. These conservation efforts culminated in 1961, when the National Park Service created the Cape Cod National Seashore. The seashore includes much of the Lower and Outer Cape from Provincetown south to Chatham. The National Seashore has six beaches: **Coast Guard** and **Nauset Light,** in Eastham; **Marconi,** in Wellfleet; **Head of the Meadow,** in Truro; and **Race Point** and **Herring Cove,** in Provincetown. There are 11 self-guided nature trails and 3 bike trails. Parking at the beaches is expensive. (In summer Sa-Su and off-season holidays $10 per day, $30 per season; different rates for Marconi and Head of the Meadow.) Among the best of the seashore's 11 self-guided **nature trails** are the **Great Island Trail** and the **Atlantic White Cedar Swamp Trail.** The Great Island Trail, in Wellfleet, traces an eight-mile loop through pine forests and grassy marshes and has views of the bay and Provincetown. The **Atlantic White Cedar Swamp Trail,** a 1.3 mi. walk, starts at Marconi Station in south Wellfleet and trickles pasᵗ swampy waters and under towering trees. There are also three bike trails: **Nauset Trail** (1.5 mi.), **Head of the Meadow Trail** (2 mi.), and **Province Lands Trail** (5 mi.). Park rangers at the **National Seashore's Salt Pond Visitors Ctr.,** at Salt Pond, off Rte. 6 in Eastham, provide maps, schedules for guided tours, and additional information about the park. (☎255-3421. Open July-Aug. daily 9am-5pm; Sept.-June 9am-4:30pm.) Camping in the National Seashore is illegal.

PROVINCETOWN ☎508

At first glance, Provincetown may seem like a typical Cape Cod village with a slight cosmopolitan twist. What sets it apart is its popularity as one of the premier gay and lesbian vacation spots on the East Coast. The first landing site of the Pilgrims in 1620, Provincetown was a key fishing and whaling center in the 1800s, attracting a large Portuguese population. In the early 20th century, the town's popularity soared with artists and writers like Norman Mailer, Tennessee Williams, and Edward Hopper. Provincetown's tradition of tolerance and open-mindedness soon began to attract the gay community, who now fill the town to its rim in summer. Though far from inexpensive, P-town has better options for outdoors, dining, and nightlife than much of Cape Cod. It's easily accessible by public transportation and just as easily navigated on foot.

7 PRACTICAL INFORMATION. Plymouth & Brockton (☎746-0378) runs buses from Boston's South Station to Provincetown (3¼hr.; $23 one-way, $45 round-trip). All but officially known as the "Fairy Ferry," **Boston Harbor Cruises** (☎617-227-4321 or 877-733-9425; www.bostonharborcruises.com) runs catamarans from Long Wharf, near T: Aquarium (Blue) in Boston. (1½hr. $28, round-trip $49; students and seniors $21/35.)

Most people in P-town are very sure of their orientation, but maybe you need help. **Commercial St.**, the town's main drag—home to countless art galleries, novelty shops, and trendy bars and eateries—runs along the harbor, centered on **MacMillian Wharf. Bradford St.**, the other main street, runs parallel to Commercial St., one block inland. Standish St. divides P-town into the **East End** and **West End**. Take the **Provincetown Shuttle** to outlying areas including Herring Cove Beach and North Truro. Buy tickets on the bus or at the Chamber of Commerce. (☎800-352-7155. late June to Aug. daily every hr. 7am-9am, every 20min. 9am-12:30am. $1; seniors, ages 6-16 50¢; under 6 free. One-day pass $3; seniors, disabled, and children $1.50.)

Rent bikes from **Ptown Bikes**, 42 Bradford St. (☎487-8735. Open daily 9am-7pm. 2hr. min. $3.50 per hr., $10-17 per day.) **Arnold's**, 329 Commercial St., also has bikes. (☎487-0844. Open daily 9am-7pm. 2hr. min. $3-4 per hr., $14-19 per day.) The helpful **Provincetown Chamber of Commerce**, 307 Commercial St., is on MacMillian Wharf. (☎508-487-3424; www.ptownchamber.com. Open June-Sept. daily 9am-7pm; reduced off-season hours.) Head to the **Province Lands Visitors Center**, on Race Point Rd. off Rte. 6, for park info. (☎508-487-1256. Open May-Oct. daily 9am-5pm.)

🏠 ACCOMMODATIONS. Provincetown teems with expensive places to rest your head. **🏠Somerset House ❹**, 378 Commercial St., is a fun and fabulous 12-room guesthouse with a very social, sassy atmosphere—and with a motto like "Get Serviced," you'd expect nothing less. (☎487-0383 or 800-575-1850. Doubles May-Aug. $110-245; Sept.-Apr. $75-177. Nov.-Apr. 50% off 2nd day.) **Dexter's Inn ❹**, 6 Conwell St., just off Bradford St., offers hotel-quality rooms for quite reasonable prices, plus a lush garden, large sundeck, and free parking. (☎487-1911. Mid-June to mid-Sept. min. stay 4 nights. Mid-June to mid-Sept. $75-115; late May to mid-June and mid-Sept. to mid-Oct. $70-90; mid-Oct. to late May $50-65.) **Sunset Inn ❹**, 142 Bradford St., was the inspiration for Edward Hopper's painting *Rooms for Tourists*. It's lost some of the romance of Hopper's painting, but still has simple and well-kept rooms, plus a "clothing optional" sundeck. (☎487-9810 or 800-965-1801. June-Sept. rooms with shared bath $79-89; Apr.-May and Oct. $59-99.) The only truly budget accommodation is **Outermost Hostel ❶**, 28 Winslow St., with 5 cramped cottages and less than pristine bathrooms. (☎487-4378. Linen $3. Key deposit $10. Reception daily 8-9:30am and 5:30-10pm. Open May to mid-Oct. Dorms $19.)

◪ **FOOD.** Sit-down meals in Provincetown tend to be expensive. A number of fast food joints line the Commercial St. extension (next to MacMillian Wharf) and the Aquarium Mall, farther west on Commercial St. Get groceries at the **A&P**, 28 Shankpainter Rd., in the West End. (☎508-487-4903. Open M-Sa 7am-11pm, Su 8am-9pm.) Though the post office theme at the **Post Office Café ❸**, 303 Commercial St., is somewhat inconsistently executed, the seafood, pasta, and sandwiches are consistently good. Their clambake special (1¼lb. lobster and steamers) is the best deal is town at $14. (☎487-3892. Entrees $7-20. Open daily 7am-midnight.) **Tofu A Go-Go ❷**, 338 Commercial St., is a casual restaurant with deliciously fresh vegetarian, vegan, and macrobiotic options. (☎487-6237. Entrees $5-8. Lunch F-M 11:30am-4pm, dinner served after 5:30pm.) **Karoo Kafe ❷**, 338 Commercial St., is a self-described "fast food safari," serving up South African and Mediterranean favorites from falafel to tofu with *peri-peri* sauce. (☎487-6630. Most entrees $5-7. Open daily 10am-9pm.) **Café Edwidge ❸**, 333 Commercial St., delivers an elegant but casual dining experience in an airy candlelit dining room or outdoor terrace. Though the dinner menu is delicious, it's the Edwidge's breakfast that draws crowds. (☎487-4020. Breakfast $6-10. Dinner $8-22. Open May-Oct. daily 8am-1pm and 6-10pm.) **Spiritus ❶**, 190 Commercial St., serves up spirit-lifting whole-wheat pizzas with various toppings. (☎487-2808. Slices $2-3. Open Apr.-Oct. daily noon-2am.)

◙ **SIGHTS.** The **Pilgrim Monument**, the tallest all-granite structure in the US at 253 ft., and the **Provincetown Museum**, on High Pole Hill just north of the center of town, commemorate the Pilgrims' first landing. Hike up to the top of the tower for stunning views of the Cape and the Atlantic; on a clear day, you can see Boston. (☎487-1310. Open Apr.-Nov. daily 9am-5pm; July-Aug. 9am-7pm. $6, ages 4-12 $3, under 4 free.) A large bas-relief **monument,** in the small park at Bradford St. and Ryder St. behind the town hall, depicts the signing of the Mayflower Compact on Nov. 11, 1620 in Provincetown Harbor.

◪ **OUTDOOR ACTIVITIES.** Provincetown's miles of shoreline provide spectacular scenery and more than enough space to catch some sun. **National Seashore** park (2mi. from town) stretches out from Race Point Rd. with its beaches, forest, and sand dunes. At **Race Point Beach,** waves roll in from the Atlantic, while **Herring Cove Beach,** at the west end of town, offers calm, protected waters. The **Visitors Center** offers free daily guided tours and activities during the summer. Directly across from Snail Rd. on Rte. 6, an unlikely path leads to a world of rolling **sand dunes;** look for shacks where writers such as Tennessee Williams, Norman Mailer, and John Dos Passos spent their days. At the west end of Commercial St., the 1.2 mi. **Breakwater Jetty** takes you away from the crowds to a secluded peninsula, where there are two working lighthouses and the remains of a Civil War fort.

Today, Provincetown seafarers have traded harpoons for cameras, but they still enjoy whale-hunting—**whale-watching cruises** rank among P-town's most popular attractions. Most companies guarantee whale sightings. (3hr. tour $18-20. Discount coupons at the Chamber of Commerce.) **Boston Harbor Cruises Whale Watch** (☎617-227-4321 or 877-733-9425), **Dolphin Fleet** (☎349-1900 or 800-826-9300), and **Portuguese Princess** (☎487-2651 or 800-422-3188) all leave from MacMillian Wharf.

☒ NIGHTLIFE. It's no surprise that nightlife in P-town is almost totally gay- and lesbian-oriented. The establishments listed are 21+. **Crown & Anchor,** 247 Commercial St., is a complex with a restaurant, two cabarets, the chill Wave video bar, and the techno-filled Paramount dance club, where the boys flock nightly. (☎487-1430. Beer $3-4, mixed drinks $4-8. Sa "Summer Camp." Cover $10; no cover for Wave. Open Sa-Su 11pm-1am, in summer daily 11pm-1am.) Founded in 1798 by gay whalers, the **Atlantic House,** 6 Masonic Pl., just off Commercial St., still attracts its fair share of seamen. Choose from three different scenes: the low-key "little bar;" the Leather & Levis "macho bar;" and the "big room," where you too can be a dancing queen. (☎487-3821. Beer $3. Mixed drinks $4. Cover $10. Open daily 9pm-1am; "little bar" 11am-1am.) The only major club for women is **Vixen,** 336 Commercial St., with a casual bar out front and a steamy dance floor out back. (☎487-6424. Beer $3, mixed drinks $4-5. Cover $5. Bar open daily noon-1am; club open daily 10pm-1am.) Don't be fooled by the traditional decor at **Governor Bradford,** 312 Commercial St.; the Governor has a wild side, hosting drag karaoke nightly after 9:30pm. (☎487-2781. Beer $3-4. Mixed drinks $4-8. No cover. Open daily noon-1am.)

MARTHA'S VINEYARD ☎508

Martha's Vineyard is a favorite summertime escape from Boston, although such escape doesn't come cheap. In the past decade, the Vineyard has become one of the most popular vacation destinations for the area's rich and famous, but the island hasn't always been so popular. In the 1800s, the island profited from successful whalers and fishermen. By the 1960s, it had become a liberal hippie haven; aging boomers still appreciate the remaining "clothing-optional" beaches. From July to August, the population swells to over 105,000—up from the 15,000 year-round Islanders. Savvy travelers might consider a weekend visit to the Vineyard in the spring and fall, when many private and town beaches are open, and B&B and inn prices plunge.

☒ TRANSPORTATION. The island is accessible by ferry or airplane only; the latter is prohibitively expensive (flights begin at $130 each way), so stick to ferries. **Bonanza Bus** (☎888-751-8800) runs from Boston's South Station to Woods Hole on Cape Cod (1½hr., $16.50), where the **Steamship Authority** (☎693-9130 on Martha's Vineyard, ☎477-8600 elsewhere) sends 24 boats per day to either **Vineyard Haven** (45min.; daily 7am-9:30pm; $5.50, ages 5-12 $2.75; bikes additional $3) or **Oak Bluffs** (45min., May-Oct. 10:45am-6:15pm, same prices as Vineyard Haven). **Martha's Vineyard Regional Transit Authority** runs summer shuttles between and within the 6 towns on the island (☎627-7448. $1.) Pick up a free **schedule and map** of all 15 routes at the ferry terminal, Chamber of Commerce, or info booths. **Bikes** are the cheapest way to get around; rent from **Martha's Bike Rental,** in Vineyard Haven, at Beach St. and Beach Rd. (☎693-6593. Open Mar.-Nov. daily 8am-6pm. $20 per day.) **Taxis: AdamCab,** ☎800-281-4462. **Atlantic Cab,** ☎877-477-8294. **All Island,** ☎800-693-8294.

☒ ORIENTATION & PRACTICAL INFORMATION. Six communities make up Martha's Vineyard. The rural towns of West Tisbury, Chilmark, and Aquinnah (Gay Head) take up the western side of the island, called **up-island** because sailors tack up-wind to get to it. The three **down-island** towns are Oak Bluffs, Edgartown, and **Vineyard Haven.** Only Oak Bluffs and Edgarton sell alcohol. Vineyard Haven is home to the main ferry port and the **Chamber of Commerce,** on Beach Rd. (☎693-0085. Open M-F 9am-5pm.) **Post Office:** Across from the Chamber of Commerce. (☎693-2818. Open M-F 8:30am-5pm, Sa 9:30am-1pm.) **ZIP code:** 02568. **Area code:** 508.

NEW ENGLAND

ᖴ ACCOMMODATIONS. Budget accommodations are almost nonexistent in the Vineyard; always reserve far in advance. **Attleboro House ❹**, 42 Lake Ave., in Oak Bluffs, has a homey, no-frills atmosphere in one of Oak Bluffs' famous gingerbread houses, built in 1874. From the ferry terminal, walk 4 blocks straight down Lake Ave. (☎ 693-4346. Open June to mid-Sept. Doubles $85-95; suites $125-135; each additional person $15.) **Nashua House ❸**, 30 Kennebec Ave., in Oak Bluffs, is cozy and convenient with 15 rooms (all with shared bath) in an old Victorian. From the ferry terminal, walk straight ahead along Lake Ave. and turn left onto Kennebec Ave. (☎ 693-0043. Singles and doubles with shared bath $59-109; each additional person $20.) **Martha's Vineyard Hostel (HI-AYH) ❶**, Edgartown-West Tisbury Rd., right next to a bike path in West Tisbury, has the 74 cheapest beds on the island. From Vineyard Haven, take MVRTA bus #3 or 3a to West Tisbury and then #6 to the hostel. (☎ 693-2665 or 888-901-2087. Free linen. Lockers 75¢. Bike rental $15 per day. Open Apr.-Nov. Dorms $22, nonmembers $25; off-season $19/22.)

◖ FOOD. Vineyard food is mostly mediocre and overpriced, though cheap lunch places dot Vineyard Haven and Oak Bluffs. Popular seafood shacks sell fried fish, clams, and shrimp for $10-15. **Zapotec ❹**, Kennebec Ave., in Oak Bluffs, brings the Southwest to New England in the form of swordfish fajitas, lobster quesadillas, and burritos. (☎ 693-6800. Entrees $12-17. Open May-Oct. daily noon-10pm.) **Fresh Pasta Shoppe ❸**, 206 Upper Main St., in Edgartown, is actually known for serving the best pizza ($10-16) around. (☎ 627-5582. Open M-Sa 11am-9pm, Su 4-9pm.) **Linda Jean's Restaurant ❷**, 34 Circuit Ave., in Oak Bluffs, is popular with locals for their cheap breakfasts (under $7) and friendly service. (☎ 693-4093. Sandwiches $3-5. Entrees $10. Open daily 6am-8pm.) The **Black Dog Tavern ❹**, 21 Beach St. Extension, in Vineyard Haven, has tasty if uninventive classics like herb chicken and linguini, not to mention their notorious t-shirts. (☎ 693-9223. Entrees $11-30. Open daily 7am-10pm.) **Mad Martha's ❶**, 117 Circuit Ave., in Oak Bluffs with branches in Edgartown and Vineyard Haven, is an island institution serving outstanding homemade ice cream. (☎ 693-9151. 2 scoops $3. All branches open in summer daily 11am-11pm. Cash only.)

◙ SIGHTS. Oak Bluffs, 3mi. west of Vineyard Haven on Beach Rd., is the most youth-oriented of the Vineyard villages. A tour of **Trinity Park,** near the harbor, includes the famous **Gingerbread Houses,** elaborate pastel Victorian cottages, and the **Flying Horses Carousel,** the oldest carousel in the nation. Snatch the brass ring and win a free ride. (☎ 693-9481. Open June-Aug. daily 10am-10pm. $1.) **Chicama Vineyards,** a one-mile walk up a dirt road from the MVRTA #3 bus stop, in West Tisbury, has free tours and wine tastings. (☎ 693-0309; www.chicamavineyards.com. Open June-Oct. M-Sa 11am-5pm, Su 1-5pm; Nov.-May M-Sa 1-4pm. Tours June-Oct. M-Sa noon, 2, 4pm; Su 2 and 4pm.) **Vineyard Haven** has more artsy boutiques and fewer tacky t-shirt shops than some of the other towns on the island.

⚠ OUTDOOR ACTIVITIES. Exploring the Vineyard can involve more than pedaling around—hit the beach or trek down one of the great trails. ◙**Felix Neck Wildlife Sanctuary,** on the Edgartown-Vineyard Haven Rd., offers five trails that meander through 350 acres and lead to water. (☎ 627-4850. Open June-Sept. M-Sa 8am-4pm, Su 12:30-3pm; Oct.-May Tu-Sa 8am-4pm, Su 10am-3pm. $3, seniors and ages 3-12 $2.) **Menemsha Hills Reservation,** off North Rd. in Menemsha, has 4 mi. of trails along the rocky Vineyard Sound beach, leading to the island's 2nd-highest point. **Cedar Creek Tree Neck,** off Indian Hill Rd. on the western shore, harbors 250 acres of headland with trails throughout, while the Long Point park in West Tisbury preserves 633 acres and a shore on the Tisbury Great Pond. The 20-acre ◙**Polly Hill**

Arboretum, 809 State Rd., in West Tisbury, is a must for anyone with an interest in flora and fauna. (☎ 696-9538. Open in summer Th-Tu 7am-7pm, off-season sunrise to sunset. $5, under 13 free.)

Two of the best beaches on the island, **South Beach,** at the end of Katama Rd., 3 mi. south of Edgartown (shuttle from Edgartown $2), and **State Beach,** on Beach Rd. between Edgartown and Oak Bluffs, are free and open to the public. South Beach boasts sizeable surf but an occasionally nasty undertow. State Beach's warmer waters once set the stage for parts of *Jaws,* the granddaddy of classic beach-horror films. For the best sunsets on the island, stake out a spot at ▨**Aquinnah Beach,** New England's best clothing-optional spot, or **Menemsha Town Beach.** The native Wampanoag frequently saved sailors shipwrecked on the breathtaking **Gay Head Cliffs,** near Aquinnah. The 100,000-year-old precipice shines brilliantly and supports one of the island's five **lighthouses,** a favorite sunset spot. (☎ 645-2211. Open F-Su 1½hr. before sunset to 30min. after sunset. $3, under 12 free.)

NANTUCKET   ☎ 508

Nantucket has entered modern lore as Martha's Vineyard's conservative little sister. Rampant affluence has given the islands' residents an influential stance in fighting for the preservation of its charms: dune-covered beaches, wild flowers, cobblestone streets, and spectacular bike paths. Even with all this privilege, it is possible to enjoy a stay on the island without holding up a convenience store.

▨ PRACTICAL INFORMATION. As any fan of the American TV show *Wings* (set in Nantucket's Tom Nevers Field airport) knows, flights are out-of-reach pricey, so take one of the ferries from Hyannis, on Cape Cod (both are near the bus station). **Hy-Line Cruises,** Ocean St. Wharf (☎ 778-2600), runs to Straight Wharf on slow boats (2hr. in summer 5 per day; off-season 1-3 per day; $13.50, ages 5-12 $6.75) and fast boats (1hr., year-round 6 per day, $33/25). The **Steamship Authority,** South St. Wharf (☎ 477-8600), goes to Steamboat Wharf on slow boats (2hr. May-Oct. 6 per day; Oct.-Dec. 3 per day; $13, ages 5-12 6.50) and fast boats (1hr.; year-round 5 per day 6am-7:20pm; $26/19.50). Both charge $5 extra for bikes.

Steamship Authority ferries dock at Steamboat Wharf, which becomes **Broad St.** inland. Turn left off Broad St. onto S. Water St. to reach **Main St.,** at the base of which **Hy-Line** ferries dock. **Nantucket Regional Transit Authority** (☎ 228-7025; www.town.nantucket.ma.us) has shuttle buses to destinations throughout the island. Buses to **Siasconset** and **Surfside** leave from Washington and Main St. (near the lamppost). Buses to **Miacomet** leave from Washington and Salem St., a block up from Straight Wharf; and those to **Madaket** and **Jetties Beach** leave from Broad St., in front of the Peter Foulger Museum. (Buses every 30min. 7am-11:30pm; the Surfside bus every 40min. 10am-5:20pm. Fare 50¢-$2, seniors half-price, under 6 free.) Bikes are the best way to see Nantucket. The cheapest rentals are at **Cook's Cycle,** 6 S. Beach St., right off Broad St. (☎ 228-0800. Open Apr.-Nov. daily 9am-5pm. $10 per 4hr.) Get bus maps at **Nantucket Visitor Services,** 25 Federal St., off Broad St. (☎ 508-228-0925. Open summer daily 9am-6pm; winter M-Sa 9am-5:30pm.)

▨ ACCOMMODATIONS. There once was a hostel on Nantucket—and there still is. Across the street from the beach the **Nantucket Hostel (HI-AYH) ❶,** 31 Western Ave., a 3½ mi. bike ride from town at the end of the unlit Surfside Bike Path, is housed in a gorgeous 128-year-old lifesaving station, with 3 large, clean, single-sex dorm rooms. (☎ 228-0433 or 888-901-20-84. Taxi to the hostel $8. Full kitchen. Free linen. Check in 5-10pm. Lockout 10am-5pm. Curfew 10pm. Max. stay 7 days. Open Apr.-Oct. Dorms $22, nonmembers $25.) Unfortunately, most other accommodations on Nantucket are expensive; cheap options are listed with the **Nantucket**

Accommodations Bureau (☎228-9559) or **Nantucket & Martha's Vineyard Reservations** (☎800-649-5671). **Nesbitt Inn ❸,** 21 Broad St., one block from the wharf, is the oldest and one of the least expensive inns on Nantucket. Small rooms with fan, sink, and shared baths explain the low price, but guests are kept comfortable with a fireplace, deck, common room with TV, and continental breakfast. (☎228-0156. Reception 7am-10pm. Open Mar.-Dec. Singles $75; doubles $85, with king-sized bed $95; quads $125. Mar.-Apr. and Oct.-Dec. $20 less.)

🍴 **FOOD.** Sit-down restaurants are pricey (entrees average $15-20). The cheapest options are the takeout places on Steamboat Wharf. Get groceries at the **A&P** off Straight Wharf. (☎228-9756. Open M-Sa 7am-10pm, Su 7am-7pm.) **The Atlantic Café ❸,** 15 S. Water St., is nautical *and* nice, with an aquatic theme, friendly employees, and American pub fare. (☎228-0570. Sandwiches $8-15. Entrees $13-22. Open May-Oct. daily 11:30am-1am; Nov.-Apr. Tu-Su 11:30am-1am. Food until 11pm.) **Mac's Place ❸,** 6 Harbor View Way, at the Children's Beach, off S. Beach St., a right off Steamboat Wharf, has full breakfasts (under $8) and all-American lunches ($4-11) on the patio of a small house. (☎228-3127. Open May-Sept. daily 7am-2pm, ice cream and light snacks until 5pm. Cash only.) The sandwich shop **Henry's ❶** is the first place visitors see getting off the ferry at Steamboat Wharf. (☎228-0123. Sandwiches $4-5.25. Open May to mid-Oct. daily 8am-10pm. Cash only.)

📷 **SIGHTS.** The popular **Nantucket Whaling Museum,** 7 Broad St., explores the glories and hardships of the old whaling community. Next door, the **Peter Foulger Museum** has a rotating exhibit on Nantucket history. (Whaling Museum ☎228-1736, Peter Foulger ☎228-1894; www.nha.org. Both open June to early Oct. M-Sa 10am-5pm, Su noon-5pm; early Oct. to May Sa-Su noon-4pm. Whaling museum $10, ages 6-17 $6, under 6 free. Admission to Foulger Museum only available with a History Ticket: $15, ages 6-17 $8, under 7 free; family pass $35.) For a panorama of the island, climb the 92 stairs to the top of the bright white **Congregational Church Tower,** 62 Centre St., the third right off Broad St. On a clear day, visitors can see 14 mi. out to sea. (☎228-0950. Open mid-June to Oct. M-Sa 10am-4pm; Apr. to mid-June F-Sa 10am-2pm. $2.50, ages 5-12 50¢.)

🏄 **OUTDOOR ACTIVITIES.** The silky public beaches of Nantucket are the highlight of the island. The northern beaches (Children's, Jetties, and Dionis) are calmer than the southern beaches (Cisco, Surfside, Nobadeer). **Madaket** is one of the few places on the eastern seaboard where you can see the sun set over the ocean. **Dionis** and **Jetties** near town are the most popular (and busiest) beaches, while **Siasconset** and **Wauwinet** to the east are isolated and quiet. The biggest waves are at **Nobadeer** and **Cisco. Nantucket Community Sailing,** at Jetties Beach, rents water craft. (☎228-6600. Open late June to Aug. daily 9am-5pm. Kayaks $15 per hr., $80 per day.) **Barry Thurston's,** 5 Salem St., at Candle St., left off Straight Wharf, rents rods and reels. (☎228-9595. Open Apr.-Dec. M-F 8am-6pm, Su 8am-5pm. Equipment $20 per 24hr.)

There are two popular bike routes on Nantucket. From Steamboat Wharf, turn right on N. Water St., and bear left onto Cliff Rd., headed for **Madaket Beach** (6.2 mi. each way). Many combine this with the **Sanford Farm hike,** a single trail made up of several loops running through the brushy flatlands and hills of the old Sanford Farm, a preserved area at the heart of the island. A longer bike route runs to **Siasconset** (8.2 mi.) from the Straight Wharf. Head up Main St. and turn left onto Orange St.; signs to the bike path begin after the rotary. To see more of the island, return from Siasconset Beach on the **Polpis Rd.** path (10 mi.).

WESTERN MASSACHUSETTS

THE BERKSHIRES   ☎413

Cultural events in the summer and rich foliage in the fall make the Berkshires an attractive destination for a weekend getaway. Sprinkled with small New England towns, the Berkshires offer fudge shops, country stores, and scenic rural drives, as well as pristine colleges and their local towns and art museums.

✳ ▮ ORIENTATION & PRACTICAL INFORMATION

Comprising the western third of Massachusetts, the **Berkshire** region is bordered to the north by Rte. 2 (the Mohawk Trail) and Vermont and to the south by the Mass. Pike and Connecticut. **Peter Pan Bus Lines** (☎800-343-9999) runs buses from Boston to Springfield, where there is a **Bonanza** connection to Williamstown (4hr., daily 10am, $35). **Visitor Info: Berkshire Visitors Bureau,** 2 Berkshire Common, Plaza Level, in Pittsfield. (☎443-9186 or 800-237-5747; www.berkshires.org. Open M-F 8:30am-5pm.) An **Information booth** is located on the east side of Pittsfield's rotary circle (open M-F 9am-5pm). Berkshire County's twelve state parks and forests cover 100,000 acres and offer numerous camping and hiking options. For info, stop by the **Region 5 Headquarters,** 740 South St., in Pittsfield. (☎442-8928. Open M-F 8am-5pm.) **Area code:** 413.

NORTH ADAMS

Once a large industrial center (100 trains per day passed through its state-of-the-art Hoosac Tunnel), the prestige and popularity of North Adams have declined over the years. Bolstered by a new art museum, however, the city is on the upswing again as it finds new uses for its many factory buildings. The four-year-old ▨**Mass. MoCA,** 1040 Mass MoCA Way, comprises 27 old factory buildings and is the largest center for contemporary visual and performing arts in the country. The museum exhibits art that, because of its complexity, can't be exhibited anywhere else in the US. (☎662-2111. Open June-Oct. daily 10am-6pm; Nov.-May M and W-Su 11am-5pm. June-Oct. $9, ages 6-16 $3; Nov.-May $7, students and seniors $5, ages 6-16 $2.) The **Contemporary Artists Center,** 189 Beaver St. (Rte. 8 N), also displays stunning modern art. (☎663-9555. Open W-Sa 11am-5pm, Su noon-5pm. Free.)

The **Western Gateway,** on the Furnace St. bypass off Rte. 8, is a small complex comprising a railroad museum, a gallery, and one of Massachusetts's five Heritage State Parks. (☎663-6312. Open daily 10am-5pm. Live music in summer Th 7pm. Free; donations appreciated.) On Rte. 8, ½ mi. north of downtown North Adams, lies **Natural Bridge State Park,** home to a white marble bridge formed during the last Ice Age. (May-Oct. ☎663-6392; Nov.-Apr. ☎663-6312. Open late May to mid-Oct. daily 9am-5pm. Parking $2.) **Clarksburg State Park ❶,** a few miles north of town on Rte. 8, has 44 wooded campsites, a brand-new bathroom/shower complex, and over 3000 acres of woods and water. (☎664-8345. Camping $12, MA residents $10; day use $5.) Bring empty water bottles and jugs to fill with **Red Mills Spring Water,** on the side of Rte. 8 between the North Adams Country Club and Natural Bridge State Park, just before East Rd. heading north. A fountain with four heads by the side of the road continuously spouts pure, ice-cold spring water for townies and tourists alike to drink. There is a **Visitors Center** on Union St. (Rte. 2 and 8), on the east side of town. (☎663-9204. Open daily 10am-4pm.)

WILLIAMSTOWN

Williams College injects youth and preppiness into what would otherwise be a quaint little town surrounded by beautiful hills. Nicknamed "Ephs" (after college founder Ephraim Williams), Williams students rally behind their mascot, the purple cow, when competing with rival **Amherst College**. Maps of the scenic campus are available from the admissions office, 33 Stetson Ct., in Bascom House. (☎597-2211. Open M-F 8:30am-4:30pm. Tours daily M-F; June-early Nov. also daily M-Sa.) While on campus, pay a visit to the **Williams College Museum of Art,** 15 Lawrence Hall Dr., #2, which houses medieval to contemporary works of art, with a focus on American and contemporary works. (☎597-2429. Open Tu-Sa 10am-5pm, Su 1-5pm. Free. Wheelchair accessible.)

Located ½ mi. down South St. from the info booth, the immaculate **Clark Art Institute,** 225 South St., displays a collection of 14th- to 16th-century European and American works. (☎458-2303. Open July-Aug. daily 10am-5pm; Sept.-June Tu-Su 10am-5pm. Nov.-May free; June-Oct. $10, discounts for students and children under 19. Wheelchair accessible.) In summer, check out the Tony-award winning ▓**Williamstown Theater Festival,** which hosts plays and musical on three stages, one of which is free. (☎597-3400, info line 597-3399. Box office open June-Aug. Tu-Sa 11am-after curtain, Su 11am-4pm. Performances Tu-Su. Main Stage $35-45; Nikos Stage $20-25, F afternoons $3.)

The wooded hills surrounding Williamstown beckon from the moment visitors arrive. The **Hopkins Memorial Forest** (☎597-2346) offers 2250 acres of free hiking and cross-country skiing. Take Rte. 7 N (North St.), turn left on Bulkley St., follow Bulkley to the end, and turn right onto Northwest Hill Rd. For bike, snowshoe, or cross-country ski rentals, check out **The Mountain Goat,** 130 Water St. (☎458-8445. Bike and ski rentals $20 per day, $30 for 2 days.)

Williamstown has many affordable motels east of town on Rte. 2. The welcoming **Maple Terrace Motel ❹,** 555 Main St./Rte. 2, has bright rooms with cable TV and VCRs, a heated outdoor pool, and continental breakfast. (☎458-9677. Reception daily 8am-10:30pm. Check-in 1pm. Check-out 11am. Rooms in summer $75-104; off-season $53-63.) Comfortable **Chimney Mirror Motel ❷,** 295 Main St., is a cheaper, less lavish choice with A/C and breakfast. (☎458-5202. Rooms in summer Su-Th $45-50, F-Sa $72-99; off-season $45-60.) For affordable meals, take a stroll down Spring St. **Pappa Charlie's ❶,** 28 Spring St., invites you to sink your teeth into $5 sandwiches like the "Gwyneth Paltrow" and "Mary Tyler Moore," named after famous actors and actresses who have appeared at the WTF. (☎458-5969. Open Su-Th 8am-8pm, F-Sa 8am-9pm, Su 9am-8pm. Cash only.) Serving up Herrell's ice cream ($1.75) and delightful lunchtime specials, **Lickety Split ❶,** 69 Spring St., is hopping in the early afternoon. (☎458-1818. Sandwiches $5. Quiche $3. Open May-Oct. daily 11:30am-10pm; Nov.-Apr. 11:30am-4pm; lunch until 3pm. Cash only.)

LENOX

Tanglewood, south on Rte. 7, a short distance west of Lenox Center on Rte. 183 (West St.), is one of the Berkshires' greatest treasures. Tanglewood showcases a variety of concerts spanning many musical genres, but as the famed summer home of the **Boston Symphony Orchestra,** its bread-and-butter is top-notch classical music. Lawn tickets and picnics make for a great evening or Sunday afternoon. Chamber concerts entertain on Thursday evenings, the Boston Pops give three summer concerts, and the young musicians of the Tanglewood Music Center, a premier training institute, perform throughout the summer. The summer ends with a **jazz festival** over Labor Day weekend. (☎637-5165. Orchestral concerts held late June to early Sept. F 8:30pm with 6pm prelude, Sa 8:30pm, Su 2:30pm; open rehearsals Sa 10:30am. Auditorium/"Music Shed" $17-88; lawn seats $14-17, under 12 free. Students with valid ID should inquire about discounts. Call for schedule.)

Though best known for her foundational fiction, **Edith Wharton** also dabbled in architecture, designing and building her own home in 1902. Newly restored, **The Mount,** 2 Plunkett St., at the southern junction of Rte. 7 and 7A, offers tours, special events, and lecture series. (☎637-1899. Open late May-late Oct. daily 9am-5pm; tours M-F every hr. and Sa-Su every ½hr. from 9:30am-3:30pm. $16, students $8, under 12 free.) Visit **Shakespeare & Company,** 70 Kemble St. (Rte. 7A), at the new Founders Theater to enjoy enchanting productions of Shakespeare's plays as well as those written by Berkshires authors like Wharton and Henry James. (☎637-3353. Box office open late May-late Oct. daily 10am-2pm or until performance. $10-100.) At **Pleasant Valley Wildlife Sanctuary,** amble through the 1500 acres and 7 mi. of trails in this Massachusetts Audubon Society Sanctuary. (☎637-0320. Open July-Sept. daily dawn-dusk.)

RHODE ISLAND

Though you can drive through the whole of Rhode Island in 45 minutes, the Ocean State's 400-mile coastline deserves a longer look. Founded during colonial days by the religious outcast Roger Williams, Rhode Island still exudes pure New England charm. Small, elegant hamlets speckle the shores winding to Connecticut, while numerous bike trails and small highways cut into the scenic interior.

⁊ PRACTICAL INFORMATION

Capital: Providence.

Visitor Info: Dept. of Tourism, 1 West Exchange St., Providence 02903 (☎401-222-2601 or 800-556-2484; www.visitrhodeisland.com). Open M-F 8:30am-4pm. **Division of Parks and Recreation,** 2321 Hartford Ave., Johnston 02919 (☎401-222-2632). Open M-F 8:30am-4pm.

Postal Abbreviation: RI. **Sales Tax:** 7%.

PROVIDENCE   ☎401

Providence, at the mouth of the Seekonk River, is a compact and walkable city. Cobbled sidewalks, historic buildings, and modern art sculptures share space in Down City, while the area around the colleges supports a plethora of inexpensive restaurants and shops. The native working class community is joined by students, artists, academics, and state representatives, making Providence a city with a little of everything.

▛ **TRANSPORTATION. T.F. Green Airport,** south of the city at Exit 13 off I-95, is a Southwest Airlines hub. **Amtrak,** 100 Gaspee St., operates from a gleaming white structure across the street from the state capitol. (☎727-7379 or 800-872-7245. Luggage storage. Wheelchair accessible. Station open daily 5am-10:45pm; ticket booth open 5am-9:45pm.) Trains set out for Boston (1hr., high-speed Acela train 30min.; 11 per day, Acela 4 per day; $17-19) and New York (4hr., Acela trains 3¼hr.; 12 per day, Acela 4 per day; $44-63). **Greyhound,** 102 Fountain St., in downtown Providence, offers a free companion ticket for purchases made four or more days in advance. (☎454-0790. Station open M-Sa 6:30am-6pm, Su 6:30am-7pm.) To: Boston (1hr., 12 per day, round-trip $16.25) and New York (5hr., 13 per day, round-trip $39). **Bonanza Bus,** 1 Bonanza Way, at Exit 25 off I-95 and at the RIPTA information booth (☎888-751-8800; station open daily 4:30am-11pm), also has frequent ser-

IN RECENT NEWS

WHAT'S ALL THE RACKET ABOUT BUDDY CIANCI?

Vincent A. "Buddy" Cianci began his career in government as a state prosecutor before going on to spend 26 years as the mayor of Providence. During his time in office, Buddy was often credited with cleaning up the city. Recently, the tables were turned, as the prominent mayor has returned to the courtroom as a defendant in the **Plunder Dome Case.** When the FBI began investigating allegations that Providence officials were accepting bribes to lower taxes, one of the numerous accusations hurled was that Buddy Cianci had conspired to racketeer. Indictments against the mayor came in April 2001, and he was finally convicted in the summer of 2002. Buddy now awaits sentencing— a feeling with which he is not unfamiliar. This is not the first time the Providence leader has had a brush with the law. In 1984, he was forced to give up his office as mayor after being found guilty of felony assault for attacking his estranged wife's lover with a **burning log.** After his first conviction, Buddy managed to retake his office as mayor, but this most recent conviction has led to the longstanding municipal leader's announcement that he will not seek reelection.

vice to Boston (1hr., 18 per day, $9) and New York (4hr., 6 per day, $37). **Rhode Island Public Transit Authority (RIPTA),** 265 Melrose St., runs an **info booth** at Kennedy Plaza that provides route assistance and free bus maps. (☎781-9400. Open M-F 7am-7pm, Sa 8am-6pm.) RIPTA's service includes Newport and other points. (Hours vary, buses run daily 5am-midnight; 25¢-$5, base fare $1.25, within Providence 50¢.) **Providence Link,** run by RIPTA, has happy tourist trolleys (50¢) that run through the city with stops at major sights. **Yellow Cab** (☎941-1122) provides taxi service in the Providence metro area.

🛈 🗺 ORIENTATION & PRACTICAL INFORMA-TION. I-95 and the **Providence River** run north-south and split Providence into three areas. West of I-95 is **Federal Hill;** between I-95 and the Providence River is **Down City;** and east of Providence is **College Hill,** home to **Rhode Island School of Design (RISD)** and **Brown University.** Walking or taking the Providence Link are the best ways to see the city during daylight hours. Federal Hill, Down City, and College Hill are, at most, within a fifteen minute walk from each other. **Providence/Warwick Convention and Visitors Bureau:** 1 Sabin St., in downtown (☎274-1636 or 800-233-1636. Open M-Sa 9am-5pm). The **Providence Preservation Society,** 21 Meeting St., at the foot of College Hill, has info on historic Providence. (☎831-7440. Open M-F 9am-5pm.) **Post Office:** 2 Exchange Terr. (☎421-4361. Open M-F 7:30am-5:30pm, Sa 8am-2pm). **ZIP code:** 02903. **Area code:** 401.

🏨 ACCOMMODATIONS. Downtown motel rates make Providence an expensive overnight stay. Rooms fill up well in advance for the graduation season in May and early June. Head 10 mi. south on I-95 to **Warwick** or **Cranston** for cheaper motels or to **Seekonk, MA** on Rte. 6.

Catering largely to the international visitors of the universities, the stained-glass-windowed **International House of Rhode Island ❸,** 8 Stimson Ave., off Hope St. near the Brown campus, has three comfortable, welcoming rooms that fill up quickly. Reservations are required and should be made far in advance. Amenities include kitchen, private bath, TV, and a fridge. (☎421-7181. Reception Aug.-June M-F 9:30am-5pm, July M-F 9:30am-4pm. Singles $50, students $35; doubles $60/$45; $5 per night discount for stays of 5 nights or more; $550/month.) The **Town 'n' Country Motel ❸,** 1 mi. after entering Seekonk, MA on Rte. 6, has clean, comfortable rooms. (☎336-8300. Singles $57, doubles $60.) The nearest **campgrounds** lie 30 minutes from downtown. One of the closest, **Col-**

well's Campground ❶, in Coventry, RI, provides showers and hookups for 75 sites along the Flat River Reservoir, a perfect place to swim or water ski. From Providence, take I-95 S. to Exit 10, then head west 8½ mi. on Rte. 117 to Peckham Ln. (☎ 397-4614. Check-in 9am-3pm. Sites $14, with electricity $16.)

❒ **FOOD.** Three areas in Providence present the hungry with a range of inexpensive options. **Atwells Ave.** is in the Italian district, on Federal Hill just west of downtown; **Thayer St.**, on College Hill to the east, is home to off-beat student hangouts and ethnic restaurants; and **Wickenden St.**, in the southeast corner of town, has many inexpensive international eateries.

Julian's ❷, 318 Broadway, near Federal Hill, is a funky sit-down eatery with plenty of vegetarian options. On Thursday nights, a DJ spins in an open-mic format. (☎ 861-1770. Wraps and sandwiches $7. Open M 9am-5pm, Tu-F 9am-1am, Sa 9am-3pm and 5pm-1am, Su 9am-3pm and 9pm-1am.) **Geoff's Superlative Sandwiches ❶**, 163 Benefit St., in College Hill, attracts a diverse clientele with 102 creatively-named sandwiches ($4-6), such as the "Buddy Cianci," the "Marlene Dietrich," and the "Embryonic Journey." Grab a green dessert from the huge pickle barrel on the way out. (☎ 751-2248. Open M-F 8am-9pm, Sa-Su 9:30am-9pm.) Offering quick service and cheap homestyle breakfasts and lunches, **Seaplane Diner ❶**, 307 Allen's Ave., five minutes from downtown near I-195, is a classic diner. (☎ 941-9547. Entrees under $5. Open M-Th 5am-3pm, F 5am-3pm and midnight-4am, Sa 5am-1pm and midnight-4am.) **Loui's Family Restaurant ❶**, 286 Brook St., serves specials like the "Henry Hample" ($3), a vegan eggplant Florentine sub, to scores of local college students. (☎ 861-5225. Open daily 5:30am-3pm.)

◙ **SIGHTS.** A jaunt down Benefit St. in College Hill reveals notable historic sights and art galleries. The world-renowned RISD occasionally shows the work of its students and professors at the ▨**RISD Museum of Art,** 224 Benefit St. The museum's 5-floor maze of well-lit galleries also exhibits a smattering of Egyptian, Indian, Impressionist, medieval, and Roman artwork, as well as a gigantic 12th-century Japanese Buddha. (☎ 454-6500. Open Tu-Su 10am-5pm. $5, students $2, seniors $4, ages 5-18 $1. Free Su 10am-1pm, every 3rd Th 5-9pm, and last Sa of month.) Established in 1764, **Brown University** includes several 18th-century buildings. Formerly the home of the inventor of the elevator, the historic **Carliss-Brackett House,** 45 Prospect St., is now the Office of Admission for Brown. (☎ 863-2378. Free 1hr. walking tours of the campus leave from here M-F 10, 11am, 1, 3, and 4pm. Open M-F 8am-4pm.) From atop the hill, gaze at the impressive marble dome of the **Rhode Island State Capitol.** (☎ 222-2357. Open M-F 8:30am-4:30pm. Free guided tours M-F 9am-noon. Reservations recommended for groups. Free self-guide booklets available in room 38.)

In addition to founding Rhode Island, in 1638 Roger Williams founded the *first* **First Baptist Church of America.** Rarely crowded, its 1775 incarnation stands today at 75 N. Main St. (☎ 454-3418. Open M-F 10am-noon and 1-3pm, Sa 10am-noon. Free.) Nearby, the **John Brown House Museum,** 52 Power St., sits in tranquil elegance. Tour guides and a short film introduce visitors to 18th-century Providence and its old families, whose historic houses line the streets outside. (☎ 331-8575. Open Tu-Sa 10am-5pm, Su noon-4pm. $7, students and seniors $5.50, ages 7-17 $3, family $18.) The factory that started the industrial revolution in America is preserved in Pawtucket at the **Slater Mill Historic Site,** 67 Roosevelt Ave. Situated by the rushing waters of the Blackstone River, the site has working water-powered machinery. (☎ 725-8638. Open June-Nov. Tu-Sa 10am-5pm, Su 1-5pm. Call for winter hours. Tours leave roughly every 2hr. $8, seniors $7, ages 6-12 $6, under 6 free.)

NEW ENGLAND

🎦📺 ENTERTAINMENT & NIGHTLIFE. For film, theater, and nightlife listings, read the "Weekend" section of the *Providence Journal* or the *Providence Phoenix*. About fifteen summer evenings per year, the floating bonfires along the River are set ablaze during **Water Fire,** a public art piece and festival with music, entertainment, and slow boats meandering down the river. (☎272-3111; www.waterfire.org. Free.) The regionally acclaimed **Trinity Repertory Company,** 201 Washington St., typically offers $12 student rush tickets two hours before performances. (☎351-4242. $34-42.) The **Providence Performing Arts Center,** 220 Weybosset St., hosts a variety of higher-end productions such as concerts and Broadway musicals. (☎421-2787. Box office open M-F 10am-6pm, Sa noon-5pm. Half-price tickets for students and seniors sometimes available 1 hr. before weekday showtimes; call ahead to confirm.) The **Cable Car Cinema and Cafe,** 204 S. Main St., one block down from Benefit St., shows artsy and foreign films in a small theater outfitted with comfy couches. Sandwiches are served up for around $4. (☎272-3970. $7.50, M-W students $5.50.)

Brownies, townies, and RISDs rock the night away at several hot spots throughout town. Something's going on every night at **AS220,** 115 Empire St., between Washington and Westminster St., a cafe/bar/gallery/performance space. (☎831-9327. Cover $3-5. Open M-F 10am-1am, Sa 1-6pm and 7pm-1am, Su 7pm-1am.) Head over to the **Custom House Tavern,** 36 Weybosset St., in Down City, to hear local talent perform rock, jazz, or funk. (☎751-3630. Open M-Th 11:30am-1am, F 11:30am-2am, Sa 8pm-2am, Su 8pm-1am.) In a whitewashed shack near Federal Hill, **White Electric Coffee,** 150 Broadway, serves a young, alternative crowd with occasional shows in a small, funky setting. (☎453-3007. Open M-F 7am-5:30pm, Sa 8am-5:30pm.) Gay and straight alike favor **Gerardo's,** 1 Franklin Sq., on Allen's Ave., where DJ beats and karaoke fill a neon pink and blue disco dance hall. (☎274-5560. Th-Su cover varies. Open daily 6pm-2am.)

NEWPORT ☎401

Money has always found its way into Newport. Once supported by slave trade profits, the coastal town later became the summer home of America's elite and thus sports some of the nation's most opulent mansions. Today, Newport is a high-priced tourist town, but its numerous arts festivals—and the awe-inspiring extravagance of its mansions—are reason enough to visit.

🗐 PRACTICAL INFORMATION. Running parallel to the shore, **Thames St.** is home to the tourist strip and the wharves, while **Bellevue Ave.** contains many of Newport's mansions. For free maps and information, visit the **Newport County Convention and Visitors Bureau,** 23 America's Cup Ave., two blocks from Thames St., in the Newport Gateway Center. (☎845-9123 or 800-976-5122; www.gonewport.com. Open Su-Th 9am-5pm, F-Sa 9am-6pm.) **Bonanza Buses** (☎846-1820) depart from the Center as do the buses of **Rhode Island Public Transit Authority** (**RIPTA;** see p. 137). If using the RIPTA bus, parking at the Center is a cheap option ($1 per day). **Ten Speed Spokes,** 18 Elm St., rents bikes. (☎847-5609. Open M-Th 10am-6pm, F-Sa 9am-6pm, Su 11am-5pm. Mountain bikes $5 per hr., $25 per day. Credit card and photo ID required.) **Post Office:** 320 Thames St. (☎847-2329. Open M-F 8:30am-5pm, Sa 9am-1pm). **ZIP code:** 02840. **Area code:** 401.

🛏 ACCOMMODATIONS. Guest houses account for the bulk of Newport's accommodations. Most places offer a bed and continental breakfast with colonial intimacy—though not at colonial prices. Those willing to share a bathroom or forego a sea view might find a double for $75; singles are almost nonexistent.

Many hotels and guest houses book solid two months in advance for summer weekends. The best deal in the area is at the family-owned and built ⚫Twin Lanterns ❶, 1172 W. Main Rd., 7 mi. north of Newport. In the process of expanding, they currently offer four clean one-room cabins with two single beds and eight tent sites with hot shower facilities. (☎682-1304 or 866-682-1304. Cabins $40. Tent sites $15.) A few minutes from Newport's harborfront, the **Newport Gateway Hotel** ❺, 31 W. Main Rd., has clean, comfortable doubles with A/C and cable TV. (☎847-2735. Su-Th $95-115, F-Sa $175-195.) An inexpensive option is the **Pineapple Inn** ❸, 372 Coddington Hwy., near the military base. Rooms are clean and offer A/C and cable TV. (☎847-2600. Must be 21+. In summer Su-Th $50; in winter Su-Th $35. Weekend rates vary.) **Fort Getty Recreation Area** ❶, on Fort Getty Rd. on Conanicut Island, provides a peaceful respite. (☎423-7264, reservations ☎423-7211. Showers and beach access. Reservations recommended 1-2 months in advance. RV sites $30; tent sites late May-Oct. $20.)

⬛ **FOOD.** While many Newport restaurants are pricey, cheap food does exist. Most line up on Thames St., along with several ice cream parlors. A drive north down W. Main Rd. reveals typical chains and the **Newport Creamery.** Good, hearty breakfasts like the "Portuguese Sailor" (chorizo sausage and eggs $5) are prepared before your eyes at the **Franklin Spa** ❶, 229 Spring St. (☎847-3540. Open M-W 6am-2pm, Th-Sa 6am-3pm, Su 7am-1:30pm.) Shack up with some choice mollusks at **Flo's Clam Shack** ❸, on Rte. 138A/Aquidneck Ave., across from Easton Beach. (☎847-8141. Fried clams $11. Open Su-Th 11am-9pm, F-Sa 11am-10pm; call for off-season hours.) **Dry Dock Seafood** ❸, 448 Thames St., serves fresh fish. (☎847-3974. Entrees $7-15, baked fish of the day $9. Open in summer daily 11am-9pm; off-season Tu-Su 11am-9pm.) **Mel's Cafenio** ❶, 25 Broadway St., is the place to find locals skimming newspapers and enjoying cheap non-seafood fare. (☎849-6420. Lunch $4-5. Open daily 6am-3pm.)

⬛ **SIGHTS.** George Noble Jones built the first "summer cottage" in Newport in 1839, thereby kicking off the creation of an extravagant string of palatial summer estates. Five of the mansions lie south of downtown on Bellevue Ave. A self-guided walking tour or a guided tour by the **Preservation Society of Newport,** 424 Bellevue Ave., provides a chance to ogle the decadence; purchase tickets at any mansion. (☎847-1000. Open M-F 9am-5pm; mansions open M-F 10am-5pm. $10-15, ages 6-17 $4. Combination tickets available.) **The Marble House,** containing over 500,000 cubic ft. of marble, silk walls, and rooms covered entirely in gold, is the must-see of all the mansions. (☎847-1000. Open Apr.-Oct. M-F 10am-5pm; Jan.-Mar. Sa-Su 10am-4pm. $9, ages 6-17 $4.)

A notorious Red Sea pirate opened the **White Horse Tavern** ❺ at Marlborough St. and Farewell St. in 1687, making it the oldest continuously operated drinking establishment in the country. The tavern makes off like a bandit with its entrees ($30) but serves up beer for $3-4. (☎849-3600. Open daily 6-10pm for dinner; also M and W-Su 11:30am-2:30pm for lunch.) The oldest synagogue in the US, the restored Georgian **Touro Synagogue,** 85 Touro St., dates back to 1763. (☎847-4794. Tours only, every 30min. Late May to late June M-F 1-2:30pm, Su 11am-2:30pm; early July to early Sept. Su-F 10am-4:30pm. Call for off-season tour schedule. Free.)

Die-hard tennis fans will feel right at home at the **Tennis Hall of Fame,** 194 Bellevue Ave. (☎849-3990. Open daily 9:30am-5pm. $8, students and seniors $6, under 17 $4, families $20.) Eight miles north of Newport in Portsmouth, the **Green Animals Topiary Gardens,** on Cory's Lane, holds 21 shrubs amazingly sculpted as giraffes and lions. (☎683-1267. Open May-Oct. daily 10am-5pm. $10, ages 6-17 $4.)

Newport's gorgeous beaches are frequently as crowded as the streets. The most popular is **Easton's Beach,** or First Beach, on Memorial Blvd. (☎848-6491. Open late May to early Sept. M-F 9am-9pm, Sa-Su 8am-9pm. Parking M-F $8, Sa-Su $10; before 10am $6.) Other beaches line Little Compton, Narragansett, and the shore between Watch Hill and Point Judith; for more details pick up a free *Ocean State Beach Guide,* available at the **Visitors Center.** Starting at Easton's Beach or Narragansett Ave., the **Cliff Walk** traverses Newport's eastern shore as a 3½ mi. walking/running trail. Wildflowers and a rocky shoreline mark one side while gorgeous mansions border the other side of the trail. **Fort Adams State Park,** south of town on Ocean Dr., 2½ mi. from the Visitors Center, offers showers, picnic areas, and two fishing piers. (☎847-2400. Park open sunrise to sunset.) While in the Fort Adams area, **Ocean Drive** is a breathtaking 5-10 minute car ride along the coast.

⚑ ENTERTAINMENT. From June through August, Newport gives lovers of classical, folk, blues, jazz, and film each a festival to call their own. One of the oldest and best-known jazz festivals in the world, the **Newport Jazz Festival** has seen the likes of Duke Ellington and Count Basie; bring beach chairs and coolers to Fort Adams State Park to join the fun. Also at Fort Adams State Park, folk singers entertain at the **Newport Folk Festival,** where former acts include Bob Dylan, Joan Baez, and the Indigo Girls. (Both festivals ☎847-3700. Jazz Festival Aug. 15-17, 2003; Folk Festival Aug. 8-10, 2003. Tickets around $50 per day, under 12 $5.) The **Newport Music Festival** brings classical musicians from around the world for two weeks of concerts in the ballrooms and on the lawns of the mansions. (☎846-1133; box office ☎849-0700. July 11-27, 2003. Box office open daily 10am-6pm. $35-40.) For information on the **Newport International Film Festival,** visit newportfilmfestival.com.

A number of pubs and clubs line Thames St., making it a happening area at night. **One Pelham East,** 274 Thames St., showcases alternative cover bands. (☎324-6111. Live music nightly. Cover varies. Open M-F 3pm-1am, Sa-Su 1pm-1am.) **The Newport Blues Cafe,** 286 Thames St., has rocking blues music seven nights a week. (☎841-5510. Open 6pm-1am; dinner until 10pm; live music after 9:30pm. Cover varies; only passports and US IDs accepted.) The **Jane Pickens Theater,** 49 Touro St., screens art films. (☎846-5252. $7, seniors $4.) For more mainstream flicks, head across the street to **Opera House Cinema,** 19 Touro St. (☎847-3456. $7, children $4.)

▶ NEAR NEWPORT: BLOCK ISLAND

A popular daytrip 10 miles southeast of Newport in the Atlantic Ocean, sand-blown **Block Island** possesses an untamed natural beauty. One-quarter of the island is protected open space; local conservationists hope to increase this figure to 50%. The 11 sq. mi. island is less hyper-social than Martha's Vineyard and Nantucket; here there are fewer bars and celebrities, and more nature- and family-oriented activities. All beaches are free, but the less crowded ones are a bit of a hike from the ferry stops. The **Interstate Navigation Co.** (☎783-4613) provides **ferry service** to Block Island from Galilee Pier in Point Judith, RI. (1¼hr.; 8-9 per day; $8.40, ages 5-11 $4.10. Cars by reservation $26.30, driver and passengers extra; bikes $2.30.) Additional summer service runs from New London, CT. (2hr.; mid-June to mid-Sept. Sa-Th 1 per day, F 2 per day; $15, ages 5-11 $9.)

The island does not permit camping; it's best to take a daytrip unless you're willing to shell out $60 or more for a room in a guest house. Moderately priced restaurants hover near the ferry dock in Old Harbor, while others New Harbor, 1 mi. inland. **Rebecca's Seafood Restaurant ❶,** on Water St. across from the dock, opens early for breakfast and stays open late to serve up some of the cheapest eats in the area. (☎466-5411. Sandwiches $4. Open M-Th 7am-8pm, F-Su 7am-2am.)

Cycling is the ideal way to explore the tiny island; the **Old Harbor Bike Shop,** directly to the left of the ferry exit, rents all manner of conveyances from mountain bikes to Geo Trackers to kayaks. (☎466-2029. Mountain bikes $5-8 per hr., $20-30 per day; mopeds $35/$120. Tracker SUVs $80 half-day, $140 full-day. Kayaks $20 per hr. Must be 21+ with credit card. Open mid-May to mid-Oct. daily 8:30am-7pm.) **Ballard's Inn**, 42 Water St. (☎466-2231), hires for summer work in May. The **Block Island Chamber of Commerce** (☎466-2982) is located at the ferry dock in Old Harbor Drawer D. (Open in summer daily 9am-5pm; off-season hours vary.) **Area code:** 401.

CONNECTICUT

Connecticut is like a patchwork quilt; industrialized centers like Hartford and New Haven are interspersed with serene New England villages, a vast coastline, and lush woodland beauty. Home to Yale University and the nation's first law school, Connecticut has a rich intellectual history. However, this doesn't mean that the people of Connecticut don't know how to let their hair down—this is the state that also brought us the lollipop, the three-ring circus, and the largest casino in the United States.

◪ PRACTICAL INFORMATION

Capital: Hartford.

Visitor Info: Connecticut Vacation Center, 865 Brook St., Rocky Hill 06067 (☎800-282-6863; www.ctbound.org). Open M-F 9am-4:30pm.

Postal Abbreviation: CT. **Sales Tax:** 6%.

HARTFORD   ☎860

Hartford may be the world's insurance capital, but it has more to offer travelers than financial protection, including several high-quality museums, a lively theater scene, and the only hostel in all of Connecticut and Rhode Island. As Mark Twain—a prized former resident of 17 years—boasted, "of all the beautiful towns it has been my fortune to see, this is the chief."

◪ **PRACTICAL INFORMATION.** Hartford marks the intersection of the **Connecticut River, I-91,** and **I-84.** Union Place, between Church and Asylum St., houses **Amtrak,** which runs trains north and south (☎727-1778; office open M-F 6am-7:30pm, Sa-Su 6:30am-7:30pm) and **Greyhound** (station open daily 5:45am-10pm). Greyhound runs buses to New York (2½hr., 34 per day, $20) and Boston (2½hr., 14 per day, $21). **Greater Hartford Convention and Visitors Bureau**, 1 Civic Center Pl., 3rd fl. (☎728-6789 or 800-446-7811; open M-F 9am-4:30pm). The **Old State House**, 800 Main St., provides free Internet access and tourist info. (☎522-6766. Open M-F 10am-4pm, Sa 11am-4pm.) **Connecticut Transit's Information Center**, at State and Market St. (☎525-9181; www.cttransit.com. Open M-Sa 6:30am-6:30pm, Su 7am-6pm.) **Taxi: Yellow Cab,** ☎666-6666. **Post Office:** 141 Weston St. (☎524-6074. Open M-F 7am-6pm, Sa 7am-3pm.) **ZIP code:** 06101. **Area code:** 860.

▸◖ **ACCOMMODATIONS & FOOD.** The cozy **Mark Twain Hostel (HI-AYH) ①,** 131 Tremont St., offers welcoming accommodations not far from the center of town. Head west on Farmington Ave., then turn left on Tremont St., or take the "Farmington Ave." bus west. (☎523-7255. Check-in 5-10pm. Reservations recommended. Dorms $18, nonmembers $21.) In the heart of downtown, the **YMCA ①,** 160 Jewell St., near the capitol in the lush Bushnell Park, offers dorm-like rooms for men and women at reasonable rates, as well as use of the gym, pool, and racquetball courts. (☎246-9622. $10 key deposit. Must be 18+ with ID. Check-in 7:30am-10pm. Check-out noon. No reservations. Singles $20, with private bath $25.) Many restaurants lie within a few blocks of downtown. Hartford's oldest eatery, the **Municipal Cafe ❶**, 485 Main St., is a friendly lunch diner. Make it past the wooden alligator at the door, and reap the benefits of delicious $4-6 entrees. (☎241-1111. Open M-F 10am-2:30pm.) **Black-Eyed Sally's BBQ & Blues ❷**, 350 Asylum St., serves down-home cooking. A picture of Sally warns patrons that the only thing worse than a barbecue sandwich without sauce is "skinny dippin' with yer mother." (☎278-7427. Sandwiches $7. Half-rack of ribs $12. Open M-W 11:30am-10pm, Th 11:30am-11pm, F 11:30am-midnight, Sa 5pm-midnight, Su 5-9pm. Live blues W-Sa nights.)

◙ SIGHTS. The **▧Wadsworth Athenaeum**, 600 Main St., has collections of contemporary and Baroque art, including one of three Caravaggios in the US. Rotating exhibitions, a breathtaking collection of American landscapes, and a room dedicated to Calder's sculpture are other delights contained in the museum. (☎278-2670. Open Tu-F 11am-5pm, Sa-Su 10am-5pm. $7, students and seniors $5, ages 6-17 $4; additional $7 for special exhibits. Free all day Th and Sa before noon. Free weekend parking. Call ahead for tour and lecture info.) Designed by Charles Bulfinch in 1796, the gold-domed **Old State House**, 800 Main St., housed the state government until 1878. Now, historic actors welcome tourists into the small chambers, and into a museum of oddities that includes a two-headed calf, and—not to be outdone—a two-headed pig. (☎522-6766. Open M-F 10am-4pm, Sa 11am-4pm. Free.) Colorfully reflecting the lives and times of their owners, the **Mark Twain House**, 351 Farmington Ave., and the **Harriet Beecher Stowe House**, 77 Forest St., sit side-by-side just west of the city center on Farmington Ave. From the Old State House, take any "Farmington Ave." bus west. An entertaining tour of the intricately textured **Twain** homestead, where the author penned *The Adventures of Huckleberry Finn*, poignantly recalls Twain's energetic life and family tragedies. (☎247-0998. Open M-Sa 9:30am-5pm, Su noon-5pm; Jan.-Apr. and Nov. closed Tu. $9, seniors $8, ages 13-18 $7, ages 6-12 $5.) **Stowe's** homey cottage housed the author—whom Abraham Lincoln called "the little lady that started the big war"—after the publication of *Uncle Tom's Cabin*. (☎522-9258. Open June to early Oct. M-Sa 9:30am-4:30pm, Su noon-4:30pm; early Oct.-May closed M. $6.50, seniors $6, ages 6-16 $2.75.)

◪ ENTERTAINMENT. The **Hartford Stage Company**, 50 Church St., a Tony Award-winning regional troupe, stages productions of classics and contemporary works. (☎527-5151. $25-55. Call for showtimes.) **TheaterWorks**, 233 Pearl St., is an off-Broadway-style theater that presents recent American plays. (☎527-7838. $18-25. Performances Tu-Sa 8pm, Su 2:30pm.) For more show options, head to **The Bushnell**, 166 Capitol Ave., home of Hartford's symphony, ballet, and opera companies. (☎987-5900. Box office open M-Sa 10am-5pm, Su noon-4pm. Rush tickets sometimes available.)

NEW HAVEN ☎203

Simultaneously university town and depressed city, New Haven maintains an uneasy tension between academic types and a working-class population living in close quarters. While most of New Haven continues to decay, the area around the Yale campus sustains a plethora of tiny ethnic restaurants, galleries, pizza dives, and coffee shops.

⁊ PRACTICAL INFORMATION. New Haven lies at the intersection of I-95 and I-91, 40 mi. south of Hartford, and is laid out in nine squares. Between Yale University and City Hall, the central square, called **the Green,** provides a pleasant escape from the hassles of city life. *At night, don't wander too far from the immediate downtown and campus areas; surrounding sections are notably less safe.* **Amtrak,** at Union Station on Union Ave., Exit 1 off I-91 (☎773-6178; ticket office open daily 6:30am-9:30pm), runs to: New York (1½hr., 13 per day, $41); Boston (2½hr., 8 per day, $33); Washington, D.C. (6hr., 13 per day, $69); and Mystic (1¼hr., 6 per day, $23). Also at Union Station, **Greyhound** (☎772-2470; ticket office open daily 7am-8pm) runs frequently to: New York (2½hr., 11 per day, $21); Boston (4hr., 13 per day, $29); and Providence (2½hr., 13 per day, $21.25). **Taxi: MetroTaxi,** ☎777-7777. **Greater New Haven Convention and Visitors Bureau,** 59 Elm St. (☎777-8550. Open M-F 8:30am-5pm.) **Internet access: New Haven Public Library,** 133 Elm St. Free access 30 minutes per day with photo ID. (☎946-8130. Open M-Th 9am-9pm, F-Sa 9am-5pm, Su 1-5pm. Closed Sa-Su in July and Aug.) **Post Office:** 50 Brewery St. (☎782-7000; open M-F 8am-6pm, Sa 8am-1pm). **ZIP code:** 06511. **Area code:** 203.

⌐ ACCOMMODATIONS. Inexpensive lodgings are sparse in New Haven; the hunt intensifies around Yale Parents Weekend (mid-October) and Commencement (early June). Head 10 mi. south on I-95 to **Milford** for affordable motels. **Hotel Duncan ❸,** 1151 Chapel St., located in the heart of Yale's campus, exudes old-fashioned charm—guests enjoy rides in the oldest manually operated elevator in the state. (☎787-1273. Singles $50; doubles $70. Reservations recommended for F-Su.) **Motel 6 ❸,** 270 Foxon Blvd., Exit 8 off I-91, keeps 58 rooms at good prices. (☎469-0343 or 800-466-8356. $56 per person, $6 each additional person.) **Hammonasset Beach State Park ❶,** twenty minutes east on I-95 N from New Haven, Exit 62 in Madison, offers 558 sites just a few minutes from woods and a sandy beach. (☎245-1817. Office open mid-May to Oct. daily 8am-11pm. Sites $12.)

◖ FOOD. For great authentic Italian cuisine, work your way along Wooster St., in Little Italy ten minutes east of downtown. **▨Pepe's ❸,** 157 Wooster St., claims to be the originator of the first American pizza. Try a small red or white sauce clam pie for $9. (☎865-5762. Open M and W-Th 4-10pm, F-Sa 11:30am-11pm, Su 2:30-10pm.) No condiments are allowed at **Louis' Lunch ❶,** 263 Crown St. Cooked vertically in original cast iron grills, these burgers ($3.75)—and burgers are all they make—are too fine for ketchup or mustard. (☎562-5507. Open Tu-W 11am-4pm, Th-Sa 11am-2am.) Indian restaurants dominate the neighborhood southwest of downtown, by Howe St. The all-you-can-eat lunch buffet ($7) at **India Palace ❷,** 65 Howe St., is one of the best deals in town. (☎776-9010. Open daily 11:30am-10:30pm; lunch served 11:30am-3pm.) For Thai cravings, **Thai Taste ❷,** 1151 Chapel St. (☎776-9802), serves up *Tom Kar Gai* (chicken coconut soup) for $2.50. (☎776-9802. Entrees $7-10. Open daily 11:30am-3pm and 5-10pm.) **Claire's Corner Copia ❷,** 1000 Chapel St., serves hearty portions of kosher vegetarian cuisine. Claire's offerings include Italian, Mexican, and Middle Eastern dishes and desserts. (☎562-3888. Entrees around $7. Open M-F 8am-9pm, Sa-Su 8am-10pm.)

◪ SIGHTS. The Yale University Campus provides the bulk of the city's sights and museums. Each campus building was designed in the English Gothic or Georgian Colonial styles, many of them with intricate moldings and a few with gargoyles. The **Yale Visitors Center,** 149 Elm St., faces the Green. (☎432-2300. Open M-F 9am-4:45pm, Sa-Su 10am-4pm. Free 1¼hr. campus tours M-F 10:30am and 2pm, Sa-Su 1:30pm.) Bordered by Chapel, College, Elm, and High St., the charming Old Campus contains Connecticut Hall, the university's oldest building. One block north, on the other side of Elm St., **Sterling Memorial Library,** 120 High St., is designed to resemble a monastery—even the telephone booths are shaped like confessionals. Paneled with Vermont marble cut thin enough to be translucent, **Beinecke Rare Book and Manuscript Library,** 121 Wall St., is a massive modern white structure with no windows. The building protects one of five Gutenberg Bibles in the US and an extensive collection of William Carlos Williams's writings. (☎432-2977. Open M-F 8:30am-5pm, Sa 10am-5pm. Closed Sa in Aug.)

Open since 1832, the **Yale University Art Gallery,** 1111 Chapel St., on the corner of York St., holds over 100,000 pieces from around the world, including works by Monet and Picasso. (☎432-0600. Open Tu-W and F-Sa 10am-5pm, Th 10am-8pm, Su 1-6pm. Free.) The **Peabody Museum of Natural History,** 170 Whitney Ave., Exit 3 off I-91, houses Rudolph F. Zallinger's Pulitzer Prize-winning mural depicting the North American continent before European settlement. Check out the 100 million-year old, three-ton turtle and a mummy residing in the "house of eternity." (☎432-5050. Open M-Sa 10am-5pm, Su noon-5pm. $5, seniors and ages 3-15 $3.)

🎵 🎬 **ENTERTAINMENT & NIGHTLIFE.** Pick up a free copy of *The Advocate* for the latest nightlife options. **The Shubert Theater,** 247 College St., brings in popular Broadway productions, and often acts as a test market before shows make it to Broadway. (☎562-5666 or 800-228-6622. Box office open M-F 10am-6pm, Sa 10am-2pm, Su 11am-3pm.) **The Yale Repertory Theater,** 1120 Chapel St., boasts illustrious alums like Meryl Streep, Glenn Close, and James Earl Jones. (☎432-1234. Open M-F 10am-5pm. $22-39. Half-price student rush tickets on the day of a show, except Sa evenings.) In summer, various concerts are held on the Green (☎946-7821), including the **New Haven Symphony.** (☎865-0831, box office ☎776-1444. Open M-F 10am-5pm.) During the last two weeks of June, New Haven hosts the **International Festival of Arts & Ideas,** an extravaganza of theater, music, visual arts, dance, and "ideas." (☎888-278-4332; www.artidea.org. Many events free.)

Toad's Place, 300 York St., has hosted gigs by Bob Dylan, the Rolling Stones, and George Clinton. (☎562-5694, recorded info ☎624-8623. Box office open daily 11am-6pm; buy tickets at the bar after 8pm. Open Su-Th 8pm-1am, F-Sa 8pm-2am; closed when there is not a show.) **Bar,** 254 Crown St., is a hip hangout, replete with pool table, lounge room, dance floor/theater, homemade beer, and brick-oven pizza. The party every Tuesday night attracts a large gay crowd. (☎495-8924. Open Su-Tu 4pm-1am, W-Th 11:30am-2:30am, F 11:30am-2am, Sa 5am-2am.)

MYSTIC & THE CONNECTICUT COAST ☎ 860

Connecticut's coastal towns were busy seaports in the days of Herman Melville and Moby Dick, but the days of dark, musty inns filled with tattooed sailors swapping stories are long gone. Today, sea lovers of a different breed fill these lodgings, as sailing enthusiasts and vacationers seek the Connecticut coast.

Mystic Seaport, 1 mi. south on Rte. 27 from I-95 at Exit 90, offers a look back at 18th century whaling Connecticut, with 17 acres of recreated village, a working, wood-only shipyard, and 3 splendid ships. (☎888-973-2767. Open Apr.-Oct. daily 9am-5pm; Nov.-Mar. 10am-4pm. $17, seniors $16, ages 6-12 $9. Audio tours $3.50.) A few dollars more entitles visitors to **Sabino Charters'** steamboat cruise on the **Mystic River.** (☎572-5351. 30min. trips on the hr. mid-May to early Oct. daily 11am-4pm. $5, ages 6-12 $4.) For some indoor aquatic life, don't miss the seals, penguins, sharks, and dolphins that await at one of the Northeast's finest aquariums, the **Mystic Marinelife Aquarium,** 55 Coogan Blvd., at Exit 90 off I-95. (☎572-5955. Open July-early Sept. 9am-6pm; early Sept.-July daily 9am-5pm. $16, seniors $15, ages 3-12 $11.) The **Denison Pequotsepos Nature Center,** 109 Pequotsepos Rd., 1½ mi. east of downtown offers a relaxing refuge from the droves of tourists, with great bird watching and 10 mi. of scenic trails. (☎ 536-1216. Visitor center open M-Sa 9am-5pm, Su 10am-4pm. Park open dawn-dusk. $6, seniors and ages 6-12 $4.)

It is almost impossible to find budget-friendly lodgings in Mystic, and reservations need to be made well in advance. Reasonably priced rooms are available at the **Windsor Motel ❸**, 345 Gold Star Hwy./Rte. 184, 7 mi. west of Mystic in Groton. (☎ 877-445-7474. Singles $40-45, F-Sa $75; doubles $50/85.) Close to Mystic are the well-facilitated **Seaport Campgrounds ❶**, on Rte. 184, 3 mi. north on Rte. 27 from Mystic. (☎ 536-4044. Open mid-Apr. to mid-Nov. daily. Sites $28, with water and electricity $32; $7 each additional person over 2 adults and 2 children. Seniors and AAA members 10% discount.)

Mystic Pizza ❷, 56 W. Main St., the town's most renowned eatery, has been serving its tasty "secret recipe" pizzas since 1973. Its popularity stems from the 1988 Julia Roberts movie that was set and filmed in the restaurant. (☎ 536-3737. Small pizza $6.15; large $11. Open 10am-11pm.) For consistently good seafood, **Cove Fish Market ❹** resides in a take-out shack 1 mi. east of downtown on Old Stonington Rd. (☎ 536-0061. Entrees $3-11. Open mid-May through early Sept. M-Th 11am-7pm, F-Su 11am-8pm. Fish market open year-round M-Sa 9am-6pm, Su 10am-4pm.) There are also several hot places for kicking back a cold one. **Margarita's**, 12 Water St., in downtown, is a Mexican restaurant that hosts the younger Mystic crowd at night. (☎ 536-4589. W night is college night; a student ID will get you 2-for-1 deals on food. Happy Hour 4-7pm. Open Su-Th 4pm-1am, F-Sa 4pm-2am; kitchen closes at 11pm.)

The **Mystic Tourist and Information Center,** Bldg. 1d in Old Mystick Village, off Rte. 27, has a friendly staff and information on activities in the area. (☎ 536-1641. Open M-Sa 9am-5:30pm, Su 10am-5pm.) **Post Office:** 23 E. Main St. (☎ 536-8143. Open M-F 8am-5pm, Sa 8:30am-12:30pm.) **ZIP code:** 06355. **Area code:** 860.

EASTERN CANADA

! All prices in this chapter are listed in Canadian dollars unless otherwise noted.

A diverse and unique country, Canada is a destination for many international travelers. The eastern stretches of this country abound in unique, world-renowned destinations. Some travelers are attracted to the gleaming, ultra-modern metropolis of Toronto, the United Nations' "most international city," while others follow the jazz musicians up to Montréal for festivals, a sexy nightlife, a vibrant bilingual arts scene, and some of the finest dining to be had on the western shore of the Atlantic. The city of Québec brings together Old World charm with Canadian value, and the port of Halifax draw ships from around the world. Cape Breton and Newfoundland's rolling green hills are alive with the sound of Celtic music, and the islands' fjords and forests promise blissful traquility and amazing vistas. As an added bonus, Canada can be enjoyed on the cheap—due to a favorable exchange rate, American dollars will go 30% further in Canada.

HIGHLIGHTS OF EASTERN CANADA

FOOD. Fresh seafood abounds, particularly on Prince Edward Island (p. 160). Delicious *québécois* cuisine fills the restaurants of Québec City, QC (p. 181).

COASTAL TOWNS. Say "cheese" in the photo-opportune towns of Yarmouth, NS (p. 150) and Fundy, NB (p. 157).

NIGHTLIFE. Québec offers up terrific nightlife opportunities in Montréal (p. 166). What's more, the drinking age is a mere 18.

TORONTO. Ethnic neighborhoods and fabulous museums provide fodder for long days of exploration (p. 187).

NOVA SCOTIA

Around 1605, French colonists joined the indigenous Micmac Indians in the Annapolis Valley and on the shores of Cape Breton Island. During the American Revolution, Nova Scotia declined the opportunity to become the 14th American state, establishing itself as a refuge for fleeing British loyalists. Subsequent immigration waves infused Pictou and Antigonish Counties with a Scottish flavor. As a result of these multinational immigrants, Nova Scotia's population is a cultural "mixed salad." This diversity is complemented by the four breathtaking geographies found in the province: the rugged Atlantic coast, the lush Annapolis Valley, the calm Northumberland Strait, and the glorious highlands of Cape Breton Island.

◪ PRACTICAL INFORMATION

Capital: Halifax.

Visitor info: Nova Scotia Department of Tourism and Culture, P.O. Box 456, Halifax B3J 2R5 (☎ 902-425-5781 or 800-565-0000; www.explore.gov.ns.ca).

Drinking Age: 19. **Postal Abbreviation:** NS. **Sales Tax:** 15% HST.

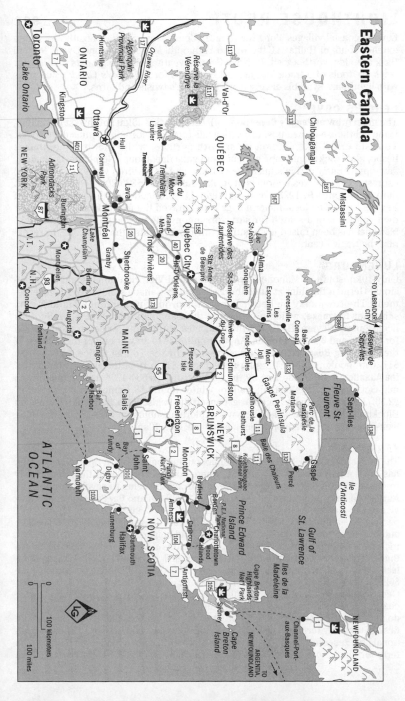

Eastern Canada

EASTERN CANADA

LIGHTHOUSE ROUTE   ☎902

Linking coastal villages along the Atlantic Coast, Nova Scotia's Lighthouse Route extends south of Halifax all the way to Yarmouth. Mahone Bay and Ovens Natural Park are also worth a visit. In Nova Scotia, weathered fishing boats and lobster traps are tools of a trade, not just set dressings for *Dawson's Creek*. Blue signs with lighthouse symbols clearly mark the route's twists and turns.

PEGGY'S COVE

The main draw at **Peggy's Cove** (pop. 60), off Hwy. 333 43km southwest of Halifax, is the lighthouse-turned-post office that sits atop an enormous peninsula of rocks. Tourists crawl like ants on its smooth surface, while picturesque houses bespeckle a rocky landscape as mammoth gulls flap about. (No phone. Open daily 9am-6pm.) Early arrivals miss the crowds, and early birds wake up with $2.50 espresso and 75¢ fresh cookies at **Beales Bailiwick.** (☎823-2099. Open Apr.-Nov. daily 9am-8pm.) In 1998, Swissair flight 111 plunged into the waters just off Peggy's Cove. The local fishermen gallantly braved the fog and rain to take their own boats out in a search for survivors among the wreckage. The **Swissair 111 Memorial** has been raised just south of town, overlooking the crash site, to recognize the tragic event.

LUNENBURG

Only 10km south of Mahone Bay, dark-trimmed Victorian houses and the occasional German flag hint at Lunenburg's status as Canada's oldest German settlement. The town may be better known for producing the undefeated racing schooner **Bluenose**, which now adorns the Canadian dime and Nova Scotia's license plate. Several B&Bs dot the roadsides in this area; prices are around $55 for singles and $65 for doubles. Another option is to stay at one of the 55 sites of the **Lunenburg Board of Trade Campgrounds ❶,** by the Tourist Office. (☎634-8100. $17, with hookup $21-22.) Explore ocean-going history at the **Fisheries Museum of the Atlantic,** 68 Bluenose Dr., by the harborfront. (☎634-4794. Open mid-May to mid-Oct. daily 9:30am-5:30pm; call for winter hours. $8, seniors $6.50, ages 6-17 $2.50.) For more info on Lunenburg, consult the **Tourist Office,** in the blockhouse on Blockhouse Hill Rd. (☎634-8100; www.explorelunenburg.ca. Open daily May-June 9am-7pm; July-Aug. 9am-8pm; Sept. 9am-6pm; Oct. 10am-6pm.)

YARMOUTH

The port of Yarmouth, 339km from Halifax on the southwestern tip of Nova Scotia, has a major **ferry terminal,** 58 Water St., where boats set out across the Bay of Fundy to Maine. (Open daily 8am-5pm.) Life in Yarmouth seems to revolve around the ferries. All ferry and cruise prices are listed in US dollars: **Bay Ferries** provides service to Bar Harbor, ME. (☎742-6800 or 888-249-7245. 2½hr.; 2 per day; off-season 1 per day. In summer $55, seniors $50, ages 5-12 $25; off-season $45/40/20. Bikes $20; automobiles from $85, depending on length and height, passengers and driver not included. $3 departure/arrival tax. Reservations recommended.) **Scotia Prince Cruises** sail 11hr. from Yarmouth to Portland, ME. (☎866-871-3560. 11hr. To **Portland:** daily 9am Atlantic time. Late June-Oct. $70, ages 5-12 $35; Nov. to mid-June $52/26. Bikes $20/10, autos $65/55. To **Yarmouth:** daily 8pm Eastern time. Late June-Oct. $90, ages 5-12; off-season $70/35. Bikes $20/10; autos $110/90. $5 passage charge per person, additional $2.50 per automobile. $3 US departure tax. Car fares do not include passengers and driver.) **Avis** has rental cars at 42 Starr's Rd. and at a desk in the ferry terminal. (☎742-3323. $30-60 per day. 200 free km, 15¢ each additional km. Reserve ahead. 21+.) The **Visitors Center,** 228 Main St., up the hill from the ferry terminal, houses both **Nova Scotia Information** (☎742-5033) and **Yarmouth Town**

and County Information. (☎ 742-6639. Both open May to mid-Oct.; Th-Tu 7:30am-9pm, W 7:30am-5pm.) The **Ice House Hostel ❶** and adjacent **Churchill Mansion Inn ❸** overlook Darling Lake, 15km from Yarmouth on Hwy. 1 E; turn left on Old Post Rd.; the hostel and inn are on the right. Inn guests stay in the Inn proper; hostelers are housed in the converted carriage house. Guests have access to all inn facilities, including the restaurant. Pickup from ferry upon request. (☎ 649-2818. Shared bath, laundry, kitchen, and Internet access. Restaurant meals $6.50-14. Reservations recommended. Open May-Nov. Dorms $14; Inn rooms $59-140.)

HALIFAX ☎ 902

Once upon a time there was a little peninsula in Nova Scotia. On that peninsula there stood a hill, and upon that hill was built a star-shaped fortress that became a strategic stronghold for the British in their ongoing skirmishes with the French. This Halifax Citadel, finished in 1749, took 28 years to complete. Today, the buzzing seaport city attracts droves of linen-clad wayfarers in search of maritime souvenirs. Despite being Atlantic Canada's largest city and having first-rate nightlife, Halifax is manageable, tree-filled, and laid-back.

⚑🖫 ORIENTATION & PRACTICAL INFORMATION. The major north-south thoroughfare, **Barrington St.,** runs straight through downtown. Approaching the Citadel and the Public Garden, **Sackville St.** cuts east-west parallel to **Spring Garden Rd.,** Halifax's shopping thoroughfare. Downtown is flanked by the blue-collar North End and the mostly quiet and arboreal South End, on the ocean. Traffic is light, and parking is available by the waterfront for $3-7. **VIA Rail,** 1161 Hollis St. (☎ 494-7920 or 800-561-3952; open daily 9am-5:30pm), at South St. in the South End, near the harbor, has trains to Montréal ($146, students $127) and Québec City ($173/116). **Acadian Lines** shares the VIA Rail terminal and covers most of Nova Scotia. (☎ 454-9321. Open daily 6:30am-7pm. Students 10% discount, seniors 25%, ages 5-11 50%.) To: Annapolis Royal (3-5hr., 1 per day, $35); Charlottetown, P.E.I. (8½hr., 2-3 per day, $67); and North Sydney (6-7½hr., 2 per day, $63). For public transportation, **Metro Transit** is efficient and thorough; maps and schedules are available at any Visitors Center. (☎ 490-6600. Buses run daily roughly 6am-11pm. Bus info M-F 7:30am-10pm. $1.65, seniors and ages 5-15 $1.15, under 5 free.) **FRED (Free Rides Everywhere Downtown)** operates during the summer. (☎ 423-3848. Daily 11am-6pm.) **Dartmouth/Woodside-Halifax Ferry,** on the harbor front, departs every 15-30min. (☎ 490-6600. Open June-Sept. M-Sa 6:30am-11:30pm, Su noon-6pm; Oct.-May M-Sa 6:30am-11:30pm. $1.65, seniors and ages 5-15 $1.15, under 5 free.) **Visitor info: Halifax International Visitors Center,** 1595 Barrington St. (☎ 490-5946. Open in summer daily 8:30am-8pm; off-season M-F 8:30am-4:30pm. Free Internet access.) **Royal Canadian Mounted Police:** ☎ 426-1323. **Hotlines: Sexual Assault,** ☎ 425-0122. **Crisis Center,** ☎ 421-1188. Both 24hr. **Post Office:** 1680 Bedford Row. (☎ 494-4000. Open M-F 7:30am-5:15pm.) **Postal code:** B3K 5M9. **Area code:** 902.

🏠 ACCOMMODATIONS. Affordable summer accommodations come easy, but popular ones, like the universities and hostels, are usually booked. Expect crowds during major events, such as the Tattoo Festival (see **Entertainment,** below). The **Halifax Backpackers Hostel ❶,** 2193 Gottingen St., attached to a coffee shop, exemplifies the grassroots community spirit that makes Halifax worth visiting. (☎ 431-3170. TV/VCR in common room, full kitchen, free coffee and tea, a coffee shop, Internet, bike rental/storage, and laundry. F-Sa live music. Check-in noon-5pm; early or late arrivals call ahead. Dorms $19; singles $35 per person; doubles $25 per person; family room $65. Rooms almost always co-ed.) The **Halifax Heritage House Hostel (HI-C) ❶,** 1253 Barrington St., is a 3-minute walk from the heart of downtown. Behind the brick facade is a newly renovated hostel with a high-ceilinged TV room, kitchen, laundry facilities, and four- to eight-bed dorms. (☎422-3863. Office open 7am-1am. Check-in after 2pm. Dorms $18, nonmembers $23. Parking $5.) Just a short distance from pubs and clubs, **St. Mary's University ❶**, 923 Robie St., has hundreds of rooms in the summer. (☎420-5049. Free linen, towels, and local calls. Reservations recommended. Open May-Aug. Singles $28; doubles $43.) Open May-Aug. Singles $37, students $25; doubles $56/43.) **Laurie Provincial Park ❶**, 25km north of Halifax on Hwy. 2, offers rustic campsites on Grand Lake. (☎861-1623. No showers. Check-in before dusk. Open June-Sept. Sites $10.)

◖ FOOD. Dozens of downtown restaurants double as nightspots after dusk. Grab a bite before 9 or 10pm, as most places close their doors (and kitchens) when the sun goes down. After eating, let the drinking and music commence. **Henry House/Granite Brewery ❶**, 1222 Barrington St., produces five of their own micro-brewed beers and traditional pub grub. The "Peculiar" brew (pints $5.75) is a sweet, smooth, and potent complement to the hearty $5.25 beef-and-beer stew. (☎423-5660. Open M-Sa 11:30am-1am, Su noon-11:30pm.) At **Mediterraneo Restaurant ❶**, 1571 Barrington St., students, professionals, and savvy backpackers gather over Middle Eastern dishes. (☎423-4403. Falafel sandwich $4-5. Full breakfast, served until closing, $2.50-5. Open M-Sa 7am-10pm, Su 7am-9pm. Discount with HI or ISIC card.) For great food in a fun, casual atmosphere, try **The Atrium ❷**, 1740 Argyle St., which is also a popular nightspot. (☎422-5453. Seafood dishes around $6-8. Daily specials $6-7. Famous 15¢ wings daily 4-9pm. Open M-Tu 11am-2am, W-Su 11am-3:30am; kitchen closes at 9pm.)

◪ SIGHTS. Citadel Hill, the city's major landmark, offers a fine view of the city and harbor and houses the star-shaped **Halifax Citadel National Historical Park,** on Sackville St., as well as the old **Town Clock.** A 1hr. film tells the history of the British fortress. Come any day at noon to see the preparation for the **noonday cannon firing.** Guided tours lasting 45min. are the best way to take in the little-known stories about the fort's history; call for schedule. (☎426-5080. Open mid-June to early Sept. daily 9am-6pm; mid-May to mid-June and early Sept. to mid-Oct. 9am-5pm. May-Oct. $6, seniors $4.50, ages 6-16 $3, family $14.75. Parking $2.75. Nov.-Apr. admission free, no tours.) The **Halifax Public Gardens,** across from the Citadel, near the intersection of South Park and Sackville St., are ideal for strolling, lounging, or picnicking. The Roman statues, Victorian bandstand, gas lamps, exquisite horticulture, and overfed loons on the pond are all properly British. (☎424-4248. Open daily 8am-sunset. Concerts July-Sept. Su 2pm.)

The 186 car-free wooded acres of **Point Pleasant Park** is at the southern tip of Halifax; take bus #9 from Barrington St. downtown. Leased to the city of Halifax for 999 years at the bargain rate of one shilling per year, the park remains one of England's last imperial holdings. Inside the park, the **Prince of Wales Martello Tower,** an odd fort built by the British in 1797, honors Prince Edward's obsession with round buildings—with no corners, there's no place for ghosts to hide. (☎426-5080. Open July-Sept. daily 10am-6pm.) A little farther from downtown, **The Dingle** or **Sir Sandford Fleming Park,** on Dingle Rd., provides ocean access for escaping the occasionally scorching summer heat. If you're really *hot*, go to **Crystal Crescent Beach,** off Hwy. 349, Halifax's clothing-optional locale.

◪◪ ENTERTAINMENT & NIGHTLIFE. The **Neptune Theater,** 1593 Argyle St., presents the area's most noteworthy professional stage productions. (☎429-7070. Box office open Tu-Sa 9am-9pm, Su 11am-9pm. $18-33; student and senior discounts available.) Those who like fifes, drums, and men in kilts should check out the **Nova Scotia International Tattoo Festival,** Halifax's biggest summer event. The Tattoo brings together military groups and international performers for a week in

BOOM! What do you get when you cross 200 tons of TNT, a few barrels of butane, a hell of a lot of picric acid, and one lone spark? On Dec. 6, 1917, the citizens of Halifax discovered the answer—the biggest explosion before the Atomic Age. Tragically, over 2000 people lost their lives when *Mont Blanc*, a French ship heavy with acid and TNT, collided with *Imo*, a Belgian relief ship. Both vessels began to burn, luring hapless spectators to the docks. An hour later, the blast leveled 325 acres of the city. The **Maritime Museum of the Atlantic** has an exhibit and short film on the disaster. *(1675 Lower Water St. ☎ 424-7490. Open June to late Oct. M-Sa 9:30am-5:30pm, Su 1-5:30pm; late Oct. to May Tu-Sa 8:30am-5pm, Su 1-5pm. June to late Oct. $6, seniors $5, ages 6-17 $2, families $15. Late Oct. to May free.)*

late June-early July. At noon, the Metro area fills with free entertainment, while at 7:30pm, a 2hr. show begins in the Metro Centre. (☎ 420-1114, ticket info ☎ 451-1221. $18-29, seniors and under 13 $10-22.) The **Atlantic Jazz Festival** (☎ 492-2225 or 800-567-5277) jams for a week in mid-July with ticketed and free concerts. In mid-September, street performers display random talents from magic tricks to chalk art at **Buskerfest** (☎ 429-3910). At the end of September, the **Atlantic Film Festival** (☎ 422-3456) shows Canadian and international films. The **Halifax Event Line** (☎ 451-1202) and **Civic Events and Festivals Line** (☎ 490-6776, ext. 2) offer info.

Halifax boasts an intoxicating nighttime scene—the pub per capita ratio is "the highest in North America," which makes bar-hopping common and easy. The free *Coast* lists special goings-on. **Ginger's**, 1662 Barrington St., is a growing favorite among the folk and folk-rock set as much for its scrumptious maple-glazed salmon ($11.50) as for its nightly live concerts. (No cover. Shows start 9-9:30pm. Open M-Sa 11:30am-11pm.) **The Dome**, 1740 Argyle St., is an entertainment complex that offers a little of everything and attracts a twenty- and thirty-something party crowd at night. (☎ 422-5453. Cover $2-7. Open M-F 11am-4pm, Sa-Su 8pm-4am; last call 3:30am.) The **Seahorse Tavern**, 1665 Argyle St., is the oldest tavern in Nova Scotia. Purple-haired students chat with paralegals in a dark basement room with carved woodwork and benches aplenty. (☎ 423-7200. Open M-W noon-1am, Th-Sa noon-2am.) Amid nautical decor, the **Lower Deck,** in the Historic Properties region, on Upper Water St., offers excellent Irish folk music. (☎ 425-1501. Cover $2-5. Open daily 11am-12:30am.) The city's best sound system throbs at **Reflections Cabaret,** 5184 Sackville St., a hot gay spot where pounding bass overtakes dancers' heartbeats. (☎ 422-2957. Open nightly until 4am.)

EASTERN CANADA

CAPE BRETON ISLAND ☎ 902

Located north of Halifax and set against the awesome canvas of the Atlantic Ocean, Cape Breton Island offers wonderful vistas and overflows with Acadian and Gaelic heritage. To top it all off, the impressive mountains and valleys of Cape Breton Highlands National Park accentuate the Island's natural grandeur.

🛈 PRACTICAL INFORMATION. The **Port Hastings Visitor Information Centre,** just up the hill from the Canso Causeway in Port Hastings, hands out info. Pick up a copy of *Dreamers and Doers* to find out the latest happenings. (☎ 625-4201. Open July-Aug. daily 8am-8:30pm; mid-May to June and Sept. to mid-Oct. 9am-5pm.) **Acadia Bus Lines,** 99 Terminal Rd., in Sydney (☎ 564-5533 or 800-567-3151), runs buses to Halifax (6hr., 2 per day, $40-60). Even though Cape Breton lacks any public transportation, there are a number of privately-owned (read: expensive) **shuttle services** from which to choose; check the *Cape Breton Post* and the Visitors Center for listings. **Taxis: Guy's Taxi,** ☎ 625-1434. **Post Office:** 11 Lover's Ln. (☎ 625-1677. Open M-F 8:30am-5pm, Sa 9am-2pm.) **Postal code:** B9A 1N2. **Area code:** 902.

⌐⌐ ACCOMMODATIONS & FOOD. To avoid the pricey bed and breakfasts on the island, head to the town of Mabou. The newly-renovated ▧**Mabou River Hostel and Guest House (HI-C)** ❶, 19 Mabou Ridge Rd., is kept immaculate and welcoming by the gracious owners. With its restaurant, hair salon, and bike and kayak rental, the Mabou exceeds the expectations of even the most demanding hostelers. Also included are the usual hostel facilities: full continental breakfast ($4), Internet access ($1 per 10min.), laundry service ($3 per load), kitchen, and parking. (☎ 945-2356 or 888-627-9744. Check-in 2-10pm. Dorms $20; private rooms $85-95; suites $105. Bike rental $6 per 4 hours, $10 per day. Kayak rental singles $10 per hr., doubles $12.) For a taste of pub food ($4-8) and rich Celtic music, the **Red Shoe Pub** ❶, just down the street from the hostel, crams in locals and visitors alike who come to see live nightly performances. (☎ 945-2626. Beer $3.25. Occasional cover charge depending on the entertainment. Open Su-W noon-11pm, Th-Sa noon-1am; kitchen closes 9pm.) A trip to Cape Breton would be incomplete without sampling the area's seafood. At **Baddeck Lobster Suppers** ❹, 17 Ross St., the famished can dig into a salmon (hot-planked $22; cold-poached $18) or 1 lb. lobster meal ($27) before filling up on all-you-can-eat mussels and chowder. (☎ 295-3307. Lunch $3-8. Open 11:30am-1:30pm and 4-9pm.)

◙ ♬ SIGHTS & ENTERTAINMENT. Cape Breton's most appealing quality is its natural splendor. By car, the best way to take in the surrounding scenery is the ▧**Cabot Trail.** With more than its fair share of awe-inspiring moments, the drive winds along steep rocky cliffs by the coast and takes as long as two days to complete. A parks pass is required for the northern two thirds of the Trail from May to mid-October. (1 day $3.50, seniors $2.50, ages 6-16 $1.50; 4 days $10.50/7.50/4.50.) If you want to view the coast by kayak, stop in at **Scotia Sea Kayaking,** in Chéticamp at the west entrance to Cape Breton Highlands National Park on the Cabot Trail. Tours range from afternoon jaunts to three-day excursions. (☎ 235-2679 or 800-564-2330. Half-day tours $45, ages 13-17 $35, ages 6-12 $25; food and camping equipment rental included. Reservations recommended.) Tourists aren't the only ones attracted to Cape Breton's unique maritime environment—whales migrate in during the summer months. **Wesley's Whale Watch** organizes 2hr. tours from Pleasant Bay on the northern tip of the Island, and will refund your money if you come back without spotting anything. (☎ 866-999-4253. Each tour 5 per day. Zodiac tour: $36, ages 7-16 $18. Trawler tour: $24/12. 25% discount on first tour of the day, 15% discount on last. Reservations recommended.) A worthy stop along the Trail is the area of Baddeck on Hwy. 105 North of Port Hastings. Here, at the **Alexander Graham Bell Museum,** 559 Chebacto St., visitors can learn about the creative genius of the "queerest man fooling around the live-long day," as his neighbors here once referred to him. The museum delves into Bell's personal life and work with the deaf. (☎ 295-2069. Open June daily 9am-6pm; July-Aug. 8:30am-7:30pm; Sept. to mid-Oct. 8:30am-6pm; mid-Oct. to May 9am-5pm. $5, seniors $3.75, ages 6-16 $2.50; family $12.50.) Another sight off the Trail, **Meat Cove** is a fishing village which serves as a prime spot for whale-watching and picnicking. In the Acadian village of **Chéticamp,** on the west coast of the island, art collectors can procure pieces of traditional folk art. For those more interested in critiquing art than buying it, **Les Trois Pignons,** 15584 Main St., displays some of the finest local works and provides Internet access. (☎ 222-2642. Open July-Aug. daily 8am-6pm; Sept.-June 9am-5pm. $3.50, students $2.50, seniors $3. Internet access M-F 9am-5pm. $2 per hr.)

CAPE BRETON HIGHLANDS NATIONAL PARK

While driving in the area is breathtaking, exploring the national park area on foot or bike reveals mountain passes, steep descents, and rocky coastal vistas that dwarf visitors in their grand majesty. There are 27 hiking and walking trails ranging from 20min. family strolls to challenging overnight adventures. The **Skyline Loop** (7km., 2-3hr.), an especially popular trail of intermediate difficulty, is known for moose sightings. **Black Brook Beach** is a gorgeous spot to stop for lunch or relax in the sun. A parks pass is required mid-May to mid-October. There are two **Visitors Centers,** one at the entrance to the park in the east at Ingonish and the other at the entrance just beyond Chéticamp on the west coast. (Ingonish ☎285-2335; Chéticamp ☎224-2306. Both open June-Aug. daily 8am-8pm; Sept.-Oct. and mid-May to June 9am-5pm.) The park also has six serviced **campgrounds ❶** and two wilderness grounds. Each has 10-20 sites ($15-21).

NEW BRUNSWICK

Powerful South Indian Ocean currents sweep around the tip of Africa and ripple thousands of kilometers through the Atlantic before coming to a spectacular finish at New Brunswick. The Bay of Fundy witnesses the world's highest tides, which can ebb and flow through a staggering 48 ft. cycle. Away from the ocean's violent influence, vast unpopulated stretches of timeless wilderness swathe the land. While over a third of the province's population is French-speaking, English is widely used throughout the province.

🔢 PRACTICAL INFORMATION

Capital: Fredericton.

Visitor info: Dept. of Tourism and Parks, P.O. Box 12345, Main Station, Cambellton E3N 3T6 (☎800-561-0123; www.TourismNewBrunswick.ca).

Drinking Age: 19. **Postal Abbreviation:** NB. **Sales Tax:** 15% HST.

SAINT JOHN   ☎506

The city of Saint John (never abbreviated, in order to distinguish it from St. John's, Newfoundland) was literally founded overnight on May 18, 1783, by the United Empire Loyalists, a band of roughly 10,000 American colonists holding allegiance to the British crown. Today, the town draws thousands of nature enthusiasts who flood here to witness the Bay of Fundy's tides and the "Reversing Falls."

🔢🔢 ORIENTATION & PRACTICAL INFORMATION. Saint John's downtown is bounded by **Union St.** to the north, **Princess St.** to the south, **King Sq.** to the east, and **Market Sq.** and the harbor to the west. Fort Latour Harbour Bridge (toll 25¢) on Hwy. 1 links Saint John to West Saint John, as does a free bridge on Hwy. 100. If driving, reasonably priced lots are located at Water St. and Chipman Hill; free streetside parking can be found outside of downtown. **Via Rail** (☎857-9830) has a station in Moncton that services eastern Canada; take an SMT bus from Saint John to reach the station. **SMT,** 300 Union St. (☎648-3500; open daily 7:30am-9pm), sends buses to Halifax (6-6½hr., 5 per week, $65), Moncton (2hr., 2-4 per day, $23), and Montréal (14hr., 2 per day, $94). **Saint John Transit** runs local transport until roughly 12:30am. (☎658-4700. $1.75, under 15 $1.45.) They also offer a 2hr. tour of historic Saint John, leaving from Reversing Falls, the Rockwood Park Campsite, and Barbours General Store at Loyalist Plaza. (Late June to early Oct. $16, ages 6-14 $5.) **NFL Bay Ferries** (☎888-249-7245), on Lancaster St., after Exit 109 from Hwy. 1 (follow signs), float to Digby, NS. (3hr.; 2-3 per day; $30, seniors $25, ages 5-12 $15; cars $60). The **City Centre Information Centre,** at Market Sq., has info. (☎658-

2855. Open June-Aug. daily 9am-8pm; Sept.-May 9am-6pm.) **Taxis: Century Taxi,** ☎ 696-6969. **Post Office:** Station B, 41 Church Ave. W, in West Saint John. (☎ 672-6704. Open M-F 8am-5pm.) **Postal code:** E2L 3W9. **Area Code:** 506.

⌂ ACCOMMODATIONS. There are a number of nearly identical motels on the 1100 to 1300 blocks and farther along on the 1700 block of **Manawagonish Rd.**, in the western part of town. Singles cost $35-50. Take Hwy. 100 into West Saint John, turn right on Main St., and head west until it turns into Manawagonish Rd., or just take Fort Latour Harbour Bridge. The **University of New Brunswick at Saint John ❶**, on Tucker Park Rd., offers neat, furnished rooms a 10min. drive from downtown. Take Somerset St. onto Churchill Blvd. and turn left onto Tucker Park Rd. (☎ 648-5768. Reception M-F 8am-4pm. Open May-Aug. Singles $29, students $18; doubles $42/30.) Partially wooded tent sites at the **Rockwood Park Campground ❶**, off Lake Drive S in Rockwood Park; take the "University" bus to Mt. Pleasant and follow the signs. (☎ 652-4050. Showers. Open May-Sept. Sites $15, with hookup $18; weekly $65/95.)

⊡ FOOD. The butcher, baker, fishmonger, produce dealer, and cheese merchant sell fresh goodies at **City Market,** 47 Charlotte St., between King and Brunswick Sq. The market may be the best place to get your daily **dulse,** sun-dried seaweed from the Bay of Fundy that is best described as "ocean jerky." (☎ 658-2820. Open M-Th 7:30am-6pm, F 7:30am-7pm, Sa 7:30am-5pm.) **Billy's Seafood Company ❷**, 49-51 Charlotte St., is delicious, though pricey—splurge for the lobster. (☎ 672-3474. Fresh oysters 6 for $10. Fish and chips $11. Open M-Th 11am-10pm, F-Sa 11am-11pm, Su 4-10pm.) **Reggie's Restaurant ❶**, 26 Germain St., the local hub, provides homestyle North American fare. The plentiful breakfast special ($4.25) is served all day. (☎ 657-6270. Open M-Tu 6am-7pm, W-F 6am-8pm, Sa-Su 6am-6pm.)

◎ SIGHTS. Saint John's main attraction is the ▨**Reversing Falls,** a natural phenomenon caused by the powerful Bay of Fundy tides (for more on the tides see **Fundy,** below). Though the name suggests upward-running 100 ft. walls of gravity-defying water, the "falls" are actually beneath the surface of the water. Two hours before and after high tide, patient spectators see the flow of water at the nexus of the Saint John River and Saint John Harbour slowly halt and change direction. As amazing as the event itself is the huge number of people captivated by it. The **Reversing Falls Tourist Centre,** 200 Bridge St., at the west end of the Hwy. 100 bridge, distributes tide schedules and shows a 12min. film on the phenomenon. Take the westbound "East-West" bus from the Scotia Bank facing Billy's Seafood. (☎ 658-2937. Open May-Oct. daily 8am-8pm. Screenings every 15 min. $1.75.) At **Reversing Falls Jet-Boat,** in Fallsview Park, thrill-seekers might consider riding the falls in a jet boat or running through the rapids in a plastic bubble. (☎ 634-8987. Open June to mid-Oct. Boat $25; bubble $97. Reservations required for the Whitewater Bubble.) The more culturally inclined will prefer a visit to the **New Brunswick Museum,** in Market Sq. Three floors are devoted to the art and history of the province. (☎ 643-2300. Open M-W and F 9am-5pm, Th 9am-9pm, Sa 10am-5pm, Su noon-5pm. $6, students $3.25, seniors $4.75.) **Moosehead Breweries,** 89 Main St., in West Saint John, is the oldest independent brewery in Canada. (☎ 635-7000. 1hr. tours with samples mid-June to Aug. M-Th 1 and 3pm. Tours limited to 20 people; make reservations 2-3 days in advance. Free.)

FUNDY NATIONAL PARK ☎506

Twice each day, the world's largest tides withdraw over one kilometer into the Bay of Fundy, leaving a variety of aquatic lifeforms high and dry on a vast stretch of seashore. The dramatic contrast between the two tidescapes and the rapidity with which the waters rise and fall (1m per 3min.) is enough to draw thousands of tourists each year to Fundy National Park. An hour's drive southeast of Moncton on Hwy. 114, the park occupies 260 square kilometers of New Brunswick's coast and offers exquisite campgrounds and recreation facilities, in addition to a variety of wooded, oceanside, and swampy hiking trails. Visitors to the park in chillier September and October will avoid the crush of vacationers.

🔢 PRACTICAL INFORMATION. The park requires an entrance fee. ($4 per day, seniors $3, ages 6-16 $2; family $8) **Park Headquarters,** P.O. Box 1001, Alma, in the southeastern corner of the Park facing the Bay, includes an administrative building and the **Visitors Center.** (☎887-6000. Open mid-June to early Sept. daily 8am-10pm; mid-May to mid-June and early Sept. to early Oct. M-F 8am-4:30pm, Sa-Su 8am-5pm; mid-Oct. to early May M-F 8am-4:30pm, Sa-Su 9am-4pm.) Entrance fee for the park. Another Visitors Center, **Wolfe Lake Information,** is at the northwest entrance, off Hwy. 114. (☎432-6026. Open late June to early Sept. daily 10am-6pm.) No public transportation serves Fundy; the nearest bus depots are in Moncton and Sussex. The free and invaluable park newspaper *Salt and Fir,* available at the entrance stations and Visitors Centers, includes a map of hiking trails and campgrounds. **Weather info:** ☎887-6000.

📷 CAMPING. The park operates four **campgrounds** and over 600 sites. Getting a site is seldom a problem, but finding one at your campground of choice may be difficult. (☎800-414-6765. Reservations are highly recommended.) **Headquarters Campground ❶** is closest to civilization with a washer and dryer, kitchen, shower, and playground but is usually in highest demand. (Open year-round. Sites $12, with hookup $19. Wheelchair accessible.) **Chignecto North Campground ❶,** off Hwy. 114, 5km inland from the headquarters, provides more private, wooded sites. (Open mid-May to mid-Oct. Sites $13, with hookup $17-19. Partial wheelchair access.) **Point Wolfe Campground ❶,** along the scenic coast, 7km west of headquarters, stays cooler and more insect-free than the inland campgrounds and has direct access to several beautiful oceanside hikes. (Open late June to early Sept. Sites $12.) Year-round wilderness camping is also available in some of the most scenic areas of the park, especially **Goose River** along the coast. The campsites, all with fireplaces, wood, and outhouses, require **permits** ($3 per person per night). Opt for a more domestic alternative while remaining burrowed within the park's splendor at the **Fundy National Park Hostel (HI-C) ❶,** near Devil's Half Acre, about 1km south of the park headquarters. The 24-bed hostel has a full kitchen, showers, laundry facilities, and a common room. (☎887-2216. Check-in 8-10am and 5-10pm. Open June-Sept. Dorms $12, nonmembers $17. Wheelchair accessible.)

🍴 FOOD. Refuel with basic groceries or a home-cooked meal at **Harbor View Market and Coffee Shop ❶,** 8598 Main St., in Alma. The breakfast special of two eggs, toast, bacon, and coffee sets customers back a mere $4.50. (☎887-2450. Open July-Aug. daily 7am-10pm.) A trip into Alma is more than worthwhile if only for a sticky bun ($1) from **▨Kelly's Bake Shop,** 8587 Main St. Replenish lost hiking calories (and

IN RECENT NEWS

AN UNEXPECTED LAYOVER

By now, there is no shortage of stories about September 11th heroism—but Moncton's story, at once harrowing and heartwarming, deserves to be added to the mix as an example of what's best about small towns.

In the days after the attacks, the modest population of Moncton swelled, as thousands of airplane passengers were stranded in what they believed to be the middle of nowhere. Because Moncton holds a reasonably central location in relation to northeastern North American flights and was unlikely to be a terrorist target, many commercial flights were instructed to land there until security was re-established. This forced passengers to find shelter in a town that was filled to capacity.

Monctonians rose to the occasion. The Red Cross provided basic supplies, while local bed-and-breakfast owners mobilized to welcome unexpected visitors. Many B&Bs canceled reservations and proudly added these newly-vacant rooms to the Red Cross vacancy tallies. Hosts found themselves shopping for food and cooking more than just breakfast—restaurants were crowded, and many guests either couldn't afford to go out or couldn't bear to.

Meanwhile, the common sense and practical heroism of the B&B owners was often matched by other Monctonians who pitched in during the crisis. When asked to discuss those intense days in September, townspeople respond with the utmost modesty about their communities' response to human need.

then some!) with fresh baked bread, cookies, pies, and peanut butter balls. (☎ 887-2460. Open July-Aug. 7am-8pm; Sept.-June 10am-5:30pm.) For seafood caught locally and hauled in daily, **Collins Lobster ❷**, just behind Kelly's Bake Shop, is a well-known favorite. The takeout lobster ($8 per lb. live, $8.75 cooked) is a fine catch. (☎ 887-2054. Open daily 10am-6pm.)

🏔 OUTDOOR ACTIVITIES. The park maintains 104km of trails year-round. Though no rental outfits serve the island, about 35km are open to mountain bikes. *Salt and Fir* contains detailed descriptions of all trails, including where to find waterfalls and ocean views. Moose are most common along Hwy. 114 between Wolfe Lake and Caribou Plain. Hike the 🏔**Caribou Plain Trail** (3½km loop) at dusk and you'll likely spot several of the beasts dining in the swamps. Deer live throughout the park while thieving raccoons run thick; the peregrine falcons are harder to spot. Most recreational facilities operate only during the summer season (mid-May to early Oct.) and include daily free interpretive programs designed to help visitors get to know the park. The park staff leads beach walks and evening theater and campfire gatherings, usually involving storytelling, forest education, and singing. Visitors can take a three-hour nocturnal tour through the woods. (Tours two times per week. $12, children $8, families $33.)

MONCTON   ☎ 506

This pleasant town was a controversial choice for host of the 1999 *Sommet de la Fancophonie* (Francophone Summit). Moncton, however, has proven itself against larger neighbors, with a recently revived downtown and a couple of the most peculiar natural attractions found in all of Eastern Canada.

The **Petitcodiac River** that flows through the center of Moncton is usually nothing more than red mud flats, but twice a day the tidal bore rushes in as two dramatic waves, raising the river at the rate of three meters per hour. This strange phenomenon can best be viewed near the end of Main St. at the suitably named **Tidal Bore Park**, where tide schedules are available. Still a mystery after all these years, **Magnetic Hill**, at the corner of Mountain Rd. and Trans-Canada Hwy., wows visitors with its seemingly outright defiance of physics. Though a bit hokey, the thrill of rolling "uphill" puzzles the mind and is well worth the cost of $3 per car. (☎ 853-3540. Open late June to early Oct. daily 8am-8pm.) The **Acadian Museum,** on the campus of the Université de Moncton, has an **art gal-**

lery attached to the museum showcases new works by some of the best artists in the "picture province." (☎858-4088. Open M-F 10am-5pm, Sa-Su 1-5pm. $2, students and seniors $1. Su free.)

Although there are no registered hostels in Moncton, the **Université de Moncton ❶** rents well-appointed rooms in the summer at two of its residences. Reception is at Résidence Lefebvre, near the center of campus. (☎858-4008. Private bath, microwave, and fridge. Singles $40-60.) The cozy, charming **▧Downtown Bed & Breakfast ❷**, 101 Alma St., with its sunroom and French toast breakfast, is conveniently located and extremely well-priced. They also have fast, free Internet access, which is otherwise nonexistent in Moncton. (☎855-7108. Shared but uncrowded bath, towels, and TV/VCR in common room. Singles $58; doubles $69.) More intrepid travelers can try the sites at **Magnetic Hill Campground ❶**, near the intersection of the Trans-Canada Hwy. and Mountain Rd. (☎384-0191. Showers and laundry. Open May-Oct. Sites $16.)

The Pump House ❶, 5 Orange Ln., is a firehouse-themed brewery that churns out eight original beers on-site. Plenty of vegetarian options and wood-fired brick oven pizzas ($3-8) satisfy any hunger. (☎855-2337. Open M-W 11am-midnight, Th 11am-1am, F-Sa 11am-2am, Su noon-midnight.) **Graffiti ❷**, 897 Main St., designs good-sized portions of Greek and Mediterranean fare in a funky atmosphere. (☎382-4299. *Souvlaki* dishes and filet mignon shish kebabs $5-9. Open Su-Th 11am-11pm, F-Sa 11am-midnight.) For a popular student hangout with both a lively nightlife and rejuvenating breakfast, head to **Doc Dylan's ❷**, 841 Main St. (☎382-3627. Lunch specials about $8. Open daily 11am-2am, Sa-Su 10:30am-4pm.)

SMT, 961 Main St. (☎859-5060), on the corner of Bonacord, runs buses to Halifax (4hr., 3 per day, $45); Montréal (9hr., 2 per day, $105); and Saint John (2hr., 3 per day, $23). **Codiac Transit** is the local bus line. (☎857-2008 for schedules and fares. Open M-F 6am-4:30pm. Operates M-Sa 7am-6pm.) **Bike Rental: Gary's**, 239 Weldon St., provides two-wheeled transportation. (☎855-2394. $25 per day.) **Taxi: Air Cab** (☎857-2000) drives from the airport to town for $15. The **Tourist Information Center**, newly relocated to the Treitz Prince Lewis House in Tidal Bore Park, informs. (☎800-363-4558. Open late May daily 8:30am-4:30pm; early June 9am-7pm; late June to Aug. 9am-8pm; other seasons hours vary.) **Post Office:** 281 St. George St. (☎857-7240. Open M-F 8am-5:30pm.) **Postal code:** E1C 1G9. **Area code:** 506.

NEAR MONCTON: KOUCHIBOUGUAC NATIONAL PARK

Unlike Fundy's rugged forests and high tides, **Kouchibouguac National Park** (the name means "river of the long tides") features warm lagoon waters, salt marshes, peat bogs, and white sandy beaches. Bask in the sun along the 25km stretch of barrier islands and sand dunes, or float down canoe waterways. **Ryans Rental Center**, in the park between the South Kouchibouguac Campground and Kelly's Beach, rents canoes, kayaks, and bikes. (☎876-8918. Open June-Aug. daily 8am-9pm; May Sa-Su 8am-5pm. Canoes or kayaks $6 per hr., $30 per day. Bikes $4 per hr., $26 per day.) The park runs two campgrounds in the summer. **South Kouchibouguac ❶** has 311 sites with showers. (Reservations recommended. Late June to early Sept. $16.25, with hookup $22; mid-May to late June and early Sept. to mid-Oct. $13/18.) **Côte-à-Fabien ❶** has 32 sites ($14) but no showers. Off-season campers stay at **primitive sites ❶** within the park and campgrounds just outside the park. (Entrance fee $3.50, ages 6-16 $1.75.) The **Visitors Center** is at the park entrance on Hwy. 117, just off Hwy. 11, 90km north of Moncton. (☎876-2443. Open mid-June to mid-Sept. daily 8am-8pm; mid-Sept. to mid-June 9am-5pm. Park administration open year-round M-F 8am-4:30pm.)

EASTERN CANADA

PRINCE EDWARD ISLAND

Prince Edward Island, host to the 1864 conference setting Canada on the path to nationhood, is the smallest province in Canada, Prince Edward Island, more commonly called "P.E.I." or "the Island," attracts most of its visitors with the beauty made famous by the novel *Anne of Green Gables*. The fictional work did not exaggerate the wonders of natural life on the island; the soil, made red by its high iron-oxide content, contrasts with the green crops and shrubbery, turquoise waters, and purple roadside lupin. Some of Canada's finest beaches stretch across the shores, while quaint towns checker the rest of the island.

🛈 PRACTICAL INFORMATION

Capital: Charlottetown.

Ferries: Northumberland Ferry (☎ 888-249-7245 from P.E.I. and Nova Scotia), in Wood Islands, 61km east of Charlottetown on the Trans-Canada Hwy. To **Caribou, NS** (1¼hr.; 6-10 per day; $12, seniors $10; vehicles $49).

Toll Bridges: Confederation Bridge (☎ 437-7300 or 888-437-6565) connects the cities of Borden, P.E.I. and Bayfield, NB across the Northumberland Strait. Tourists pay no fee crossing into P.E.I., but must shell out a $37.75 passenger car toll when leaving.

Visitor info: P.E.I. Visitor Information Centre, P.O. Box 940, Charlottetown C1A 7M5 (☎ 368-4444 or 888-734-7529). Open June daily 8am-8pm; July-Aug. 8am-10pm; Sept. to mid-Oct. 9am-6pm; mid-Oct. to May M-F 9am-4:30pm.

Drinking Age: 19. **Postal abbreviation:** PEI. **Sales Tax:** 10% PST, plus 7% GST.

CHARLOTTETOWN ☎ 902

Most of Charlottetown's sights center on its role in Canadian history, as the site of the Charlottetown Confederation Conference. In addition to history, the coastal Prince Edward Island National Park contains an incredible landscape. The town is also home to the **University of Prince Edward Island (UPEI).** Between these elements Charlottetown is one of the most visited spots on Prince Edwards Island.

🖪 🛈 ORIENTATION AND PRACTICAL INFORMATION. Queen St. and **University Ave.** are the main thoroughfares, straddling **Confederation Centre** on the west and east, respectively. The most popular beaches—**Cavendish, Brackley,** and **Rustico Island**—lie on the north shore in the middle of the province opposite Charlottetown. The longest continuous marine span bridge in the world, **Confederation Bridge** meets P.E.I. at Borden-Carleton, 56km west of Charlottetown on Hwy. 1. **Charlottetown-Cavendish Shuttles** (☎ 566-3243) picks up passengers at the Information Center and the hostel (call for additional points) and drops them off in Cavendish. (45min. July-Aug. 4 per day; June and Sept. 2 per day. $10, same-day round-trip $18.) Taxis: **City Cab,** ☎ 892-6567 (24hr.). **Bike Rental: MacQueens,** 430 Queen St. (☎ 368-2453. Open M-Sa 8:30am-5:30pm. Hybrid road and mountain bikes $25 per day, $125 per week; under 12 $20/80. Must have credit card or $100 deposit.) **Visitor info: P.E.I. Visitor Information Centre,** 178 Water St. (See **Practical Information,** above.) **Internet access: CyberDeck Cafe,** 115 Queen St. (☎ 569-2787. Open M-Sa 10am-midnight, Su noon-5pm.) **Hotline: Crisis Center,** ☎ 566-8999 (24hr.). **Post Office:** 135 Kent St. (☎ 628-4400. Open M-F 8am-5:15pm.) **Postal Code:** C1A 7K2. **Area Code:** 902

⌐ ACCOMMODATIONS. B&Bs and country inns crowd every nook and cranny of the province; some are open year-round, but the most inexpensive are closed off-season. Rates hover around $35-40 for singles and $50 for doubles. To land those prices call in advance. Many of the island's Visitors Centers, including Charlottetown's, display daily vacancy listings for the island's inns, B&Bs, campgrounds, and other accommodations. The **Charlottetown International Hostel (HI-C)** ❶, 153 Mt. Edward Rd., across the yard from the University of P.E.I. (UPEI), is housed in a large blue barn. Take Belvedere Ave. one block east of University Ave., then turn left onto Mt. Edward Rd. (☎894-9696. Kitchen facilities, showers, and TV lounge. Check-in 7-10am and 4pm-midnight. Lockout 10am-4pm. Curfew midnight. Open June to early Sept. Dorms $16.50, nonmembers $19.50. Bike rental $15.) Off Belvedere Ave., the **UPEI** runs a dorm-style B&B without the Victorian frills in two resident halls: **Marian Hall** ❶ (☎566-0486; June-Aug. ☎566-0442. July-Aug. singles $38; doubles $48. May-June $32/39) and **Bernardine Hall** ❷ (☎566-0486; June-Aug. ☎566-0442. July-Aug. $51/58; May-June $46/48). Check-in is at Bernardine Hall. The **Woods Motel and Cottages** ❸, in Orwell out of town toward Wood Island, lets guests experience a stay in a country farm setting. (☎651-2620. Doubles from $45.)

◻ FOOD. The quest for food often boils down to the search for **lobster.** The coveted crustaceans start around $9 per lb. Fresh seafood, including world-famous **Malpeque oysters,** is sold along the shores of the island, especially in North Rustico on the north shore. The back of the *P.E.I. Visitor's Guide* lists fresh seafood outlets. (☎368-4444. Open July-Aug. W and Sa 9am-2pm; Sept.-June Sa 9am-2pm.) The young clientele at **Beanz** ❶, 52 University Ave., basks on a sunny terrace and washes down homemade sandwiches ($3-4) with great espresso. (☎892-8797. Open M-F 6:30am-6pm, Sa 8am-6pm, Su 9am-5pm.) **Shaddy's** ❹, 44 University Ave., has lobsters (seasonal $20-24) and Lebanese and Canadian fare. (☎368-8886. Sandwiches $3-8. Open daily 10am-9:30pm.)

◧ SIGHTS. Embracing some of Canada's finest beaches, **Prince Edward Island National Park** consists of a 32km coastal strip. Wind-sculpted sand dunes and salt marshes undulate along the park's terrain, which is home to many of the Island's 300 species of birds. (☎963-7830. Campgrounds, programs, and services early July to mid-Aug.) The stretches of beach on the eastern coast of P.E.I. are less touristed than those in the west, perhaps due to the rougher surf. **Lakeside,** a beach 35km east of Charlottetown on Hwy. 2, is unsupervised and often nearly deserted on summer weekdays. Trot along the surf atop a sturdy steed from **Gun Trail Ride,** located beside the golf course. (☎961-2076. Open June to early Oct. daily 9am-8pm. $15 per hr.) **Basin Head Beach,** 95km east of Charlottetown, makes a relaxing daytrip, with over 11km of uncrowded white sand. Celtic concerts and Scottish *ceilidhs,* with bagpipes and traditional dance, are held throughout the summer at the ▧**College of Piping,** 619 Water St. E, in Summerside. Call for a full schedule. (☎877-224-7473. *Ceilidhs* M and F 7pm. $12, seniors $11, students and children $7.)

Proving that Americans don't have a monopoly on garish nationalism, **Founder's Hall,** 6 Prince St., leads visitors through an orgiastic multimedia spectacle that traces Canada's history from the Charlottetown Confederation conference to the present. (☎368-1864. Open mid-May to late June and Sept.-Oct. daily 9am-4pm; July-Aug. M-F 9am-8pm, Sa-Su 9am-6pm. $7, seniors $5.50, ages 6-17 $3.75.) A walk up Great George St. will take you to **Province House,** site of that first conference. (☎566-7626. Open daily 8:30am-6pm. Free.)

CAVENDISH ☎902

Green Gables House, off Hwy. 6 in Cavendish just west of Hwy. 13, is a shrine for readers adoring Lucy Maud Montgomery's *Anne of Green Gables*, a surprising number of whom are from Japan. The traditionally furnished house and its surroundings served as inspiration for this P.E.I. native's first novel. After seeing a few sappy L.M. Montgomery films and memorabilia, most visitors can't escape without purchasing a special edition copy of *Anne* or a commemorative thimble. Arrive early morning or in the evening to escape crowds. (☎963-3370. Open July-Aug. daily 9am-8pm; May-June and Sept.-Oct. 9am-5pm. $5.50, seniors $4.50, ages 6-16 $2.70; families $13. Cheaper off-season.)

Prince Edward Island National Park ❶ operates three campgrounds during the summer and one off-season. Reservations are strongly recommended and must be made at least three days in advance. (☎672-6350 for info; ☎800-414-6765 for reservations. Showers, toilets, kitchen access, and laundry facilities. In summer, primitive sites $15-19; in winter $8; with hookup $21.) **Cavendish Campground** has a beachside location, so reservations are particularly handy. Privately-owned campgrounds fill the island and provide an alternative when campsites are unavailable at the national park; info is available at Visitors Centers.

NEWFOUNDLAND

Perched off the Eastern shore of North America, Newfoundland had the earliest encounter with European civilization on the continent. In the 10th century, 500 years before Columbus, Viking seafarers established at least one outpost on the north shore of the island. The area's legendary stock of codfish later lured British and Irish colonists to the ports and harbor of Newfoundland's craggy coast. For the next few centuries, Newfoundland incubated a distinct maritime culture, combining elements from Irish and British seafaring traditions in a unique music, accent, and way of life. Geographic remoteness hardly dampened the Islanders' enthusiasm for Great Britain—Newfoundland was the last province to, reluctantly, join the Confederation in 1949. To this day, Newfoundland maintains a fiercely independent spirit as well as gorgeous vistas, rugged fjords, the longest pub street in North America, and the friendliest folks east of Iowa.

⏻ PRACTICAL INFORMATION

Capital: St. John's.

Visitor Info: Tourism Newfoundland & Labrador, P.O. Box 8700, St. John's A1B 4J6 (☎800-563-6353; www.gov.nf.ca/tourism).

Newfoundland Ferries: Marine Atlantic (☎800-341-7981) runs service from **North Sydney, NS** to **Argentia** (15 hr.; late June to mid-Sept. 3 per week; late Sept. M only; $64.25, seniors $58; ages 5-12 $32; bicycles $21, automobiles $140.25) and **Port aux Basques** (1-2 per day; 6-8 hours; $23.50/21.25/11.75/10.50/69.75). Reservations recommended.

Drinking Age: 19. **Postal Abbreviation:** NF. **Sales Tax:** 15% HST.

ST. JOHN'S ☎709

One of the oldest ports in North America, St. John's has grown from a 16th-century strategic harbor to the capital of Canada's easternmost province. The city's heart continues to be its harbor, which is still crammed with freighters and fishing boats from all around the world. Despite this traffic, the downtown has maintained a residential, fishing-town feel while also sustaining countless pubs, world-class restaurants, and swank Scandinavian clothing stores.

◼🛈 ORIENTATION & PRACTICAL INFORMATION. The Trans-Canada Hwy., becoming **Kenmount Rd.** as it enters the city limits, is packed with strip malls, fast food restaurants, and chain motels. From the end of Kenmount St., Freshwater Rd. leads into the downtown core. The downtown itself hugs the harbor. **Harbour Dr., Water St.,** and **Duckworth Rd.** run parallel to one another and host the lion's share of stores, pubs, and restaurants.

Provincial Airlines (☎800-563-2800 or 709-576-1666; www.provair.com) flies from St. John's to locations throughout Atlantic Canada, including **Halifax** (daily, 5hr., prices vary with season). **Air Canada** (☎888-247-2262; www.aircanada.ca) flies into St. John's daily from **Montréal** and **Toronto**. Newfoundland is not friendly to those without cars—its remoteness has left it neglected by all the major transport companies. **DRL Coachlines** (☎888-269-1852), a regional firm, runs buses to Port aux Basques on the far end of the island. Numerous local taxi shuttles service the more remote communities; ask at the Visitors Center. **St. John's Metrobus** buses locally within the city. (☎570-2020. Buses daily 6:30am-11pm. $1.50, school children $1, under 3 free.) Cars can be rented at **Rent-a-Wreck** (☎753-2277 or 800-327-0116), on Pippy Place, off Kenmount Rd.

From June to September, there is a **Visitors Center** in a converted railcar on Harbour Dr. (☎576-8514. Open daily 9am-5pm.) **Medical services: General Hospital,** Prince Philip Pkwy. (☎737-6300). **Hotline: Crisis line,** ☎726-1411. 24hr. **Post Office:** 354 Water St. (☎758-1003. Free Internet access. Open M-F 8am-5pm.) **Postal Code:** A1C 1C4. **Area code:** 709.

🛏 ACCOMMODATIONS. Most of the accommodations in St. John's take the form of Victorian B&Bs. Although quality is very high and the charm is undeniable, the prices (starting at $55 and going straight up) discourage many budget travelers. Fortunately, there are a few other options. **The Hostel on the Hill ❶,** 65 Longs Hill, 3 blocks north of Duckworth St. up Queens Rd., offers free breakfast, Internet access ($4 per hour), kitchen, cycle storage, and a TV lounge. (☎754-7658. Dorms $15; private rooms $30.) **Memorial University ❶,** on Elizabeth Ave. off Kenmount Rd., rents rooms during the summer season. Check-in M-Th 2pm-midnight, F-Su 2pm-1am. Open May-Aug. Singles $18, non-students $30; doubles $30/38.) **The Roses B&B ❸,** 9 Military Rd., two streets from Duckworth St., has a gorgeous harbor view and rooms that are downright proper. (☎726-3336. Open year-round. Singles $70; doubles $80. Suites $90-95.)

🍴 FOOD. The golden-arch school of American cuisine can be found along Kenmount Rd. near the University. Hipper restaurants cluster around Water St. For the budget-minded, 📷**Steele Mountain Records Bar ❶,** on Water St., is a sure bet for thrift and taste. During the day, graze on a vegetarian-friendly menu of wraps and salads ($3.50-8) washed down with fresh fruit smoothies ($3.50). By night, Steele Mountain becomes a chatty, intimate bar with a laid-back feel and $3.75 beers. (Open daily 11am-4:45pm and W-Su 8pm-3am.) **The Classic Cafe ❷**, 364 Duckworth St., is a St. John's classic with tasty Island grub available 24hr. (☎ 579-4444. Dinner menu $9-20. 24hr. menu $2-12.) For a bite of homestyle local food, **Velma's Traditional Newfoundland Food ❸**, 264 Water St., does amazing things to cod. (☎ 576-2264. Cod tongues $15. Open M-F 8:30am-9:30pm, Sa 8am-10pm, Su 9am-9pm.)

◖ SIGHTS. A trip up **Signal Hill**, on Signal Hill Rd. just east of Duckworth St., grants gorgeous views of the harbor, the city, and the bleak insanity of the Atlantic Ocean. The commanding views from this height are the key to commanding the harbor—numerous bloody battles were fought by the French and English for this bit of maritime real estate. **The Queen's Battery,** a number of ancient canons, date from those conflicts. The hill has seen its share of peaceful moments too. It earned its name by being the site where Marconi received the first trans-Atlantic radio transmission in 1901. With a grand view, **Cabot Tower,** at the peak of the hill, houses exhibits about that technological breakthrough. (Tower open year-round daily 8:30am-9pm.) Bi-weekly during the summer the **Signal Hill Tattoo** reenacts 19th-century military exercises in full period costume. The informative Visitors Center gives performance times and sells admission tickets to the site. (☎ 772-5367. $2.50, over 65 $2, ages 6-16 $1.50; family $6; 1 day pass for Signal Hill and Cape Spear $4/ 3/2/9. Open in summer June-Sept. daily 8:30am-8pm; Oct. 8:30am-5pm.)

Eleven kilometers out of town on Blackhead Rd., off Water St., **Cape Spear** promontory is the easternmost land in North America. White lighthouses stand out against a green, rocky point and the slate-gray Atlantic. Paths meander around the jagged shore and up through the heath to the lighthouses, past two run-down bunkers from World War II. The paths alone are worth the trip, and the view on a clear day is breathtaking. (☎ 772-4210. Visitors Center open May-Oct. daily 10am-6pm.) The **Irish Loop,** a scenic drive around the southern tip of the Avalon Peninsula, grants views of passing icebergs, seasonal Atlantic Puffin, and the rugged Avalon Peninsula Reserve. The trip can be done in a day, and numerous towns and hamlets provide services along its length. For thrills by sea rather than land, head to Cape Broyle on the Irish Loop and dive into a sea kayak. **Stan Cook Sea Kayaking,** 67 Circular Rd., a family-run tour operation, has tours for all skill levels. (☎ 579-6353 or 888-747-6353. 2hr. $40, 4hr. $60, all-day $90.)

◖◪ ENTERTAINMENT & NIGHTLIFE. The entertainment options in and around St. John's are surprisingly varied. Traditional Newfoundland dinner parties ("times") include folk music, dancing, and occasionally theater; check at the Visitors Center for the *Soirees & Times* listings. More organized theater may be had just off Water St. at the converted **Longshoremen's Protective Union Hall,** 3 Victoria St. (☎ 753-4531), which puts on shows and organizes functions throughout the year. Every other summer, St. John's hosts the **Soundsymposium** (☎ 754-5409; www.soundsymposium.com), a festival of experimental and bizarre music. The next one is due July 2004. Events occur throughout the city, including the daily performance of the world's only symphony for boat whistles.

Less organized fun can be had in the legendary pub scene. **George St.,** or Pub Street, contains the longest continuous chain of pubs and bars in North America and has themes and music to suit any partygoer's tastes. **The Ship Inn,** 265 Duckworth St. at Solomon's Lane, is legendary in St. John's for its phenomenal live music and relaxed feel. (☎ 753-3870. Occasional cover. Open Su-W noon-midnight, Th-Sa noon-3am.) **O'Reilly's Irish,** 15 George St., packs in the twenty-somethings with a booming mix of Top 40 and Newfoundland music. (☎722-3735. Open Su-Th 11am-2am, F-Sa 11am-3am.) **Zone 216,** 216 Water St., attracts a gay crowd with its intense, all-night music and drag shows. (☎754-2492. Th no cover; F-Sa 11pm-midnight $3, after midnight $5. Open Th 9pm-2am, F-Sa 9pm to sunrise.)

GROS MORNE NATIONAL PARK   ☎709

On precisely the opposite side of Newfoundland from St. John's, Gros Morne encompasses more than 1800 square kilometers of fjords, conifer forests, and mountainsides. Designated a UNESCO world heritage site in 1987, Gros Morne preserves some of the wildest scenery and animal life in North America.

▚▐ ORIENTATION & PRACTICAL INFORMATION. Tucked against the Gulf of St. Lawrence on the west coast of Newfoundland, Gros Morne is reached by taking the **430 spur (Viking Trail)** off the Trans-Canada Highway in Deer Lake. There is no public transportation to Gros Morne, although a local shuttle taxi goes as far as Deer Lake. Inside the park, the town of **Rocky Harbour** is the main service center. The main **Visitors Center** is at the center of the park, near Rocky Harbour; pick up the invaluable *Tuckamore* guide, along with good advice from the knowledgeable staff. From mid-May to mid-October, there are fees for admittance to the National Park, charged at either the entrance kiosk or the Visitors Center. (☎458-2066; www.parkscanda.gc.ca/grosmorne. Open mid-June to Aug. daily 9am-9pm; May to mid-June and Sept. to mid-Oct. 9am-5pm; mid-Oct. to Jan. M-F 9am-4pm. Daily pass $7.50, seniors $6, ages 6-16 $3.75; family $15. Seasonal rates available.)

▟ CAMPING. Gros Morne contains five developed **campgrounds ❶** (☎800-563-6353) comprising dozens of sites. Although popular during the summer months, Gros Morne rarely operates to capacity. Nevertheless, the cautious camper can pay a reservation fee to avoid disappointment. The developed campgrounds contain the usual amenities—pit toilets, running water, and close proximity to picnic grounds. **Shallow Bay, Green Point,** and **Lomond** campgrounds are on the coast with unsupervised beach access; Lomond has a boat launch. **Trout River** campground is on a pond and has freshwater swimming and a sheltered boat launch. **Berry Hill** campground is set off the beach, close to a number of trailheads. Most campgrounds are open mid-June to September. Notable exceptions are Lomond, which is open mid-May to October, and Green Point, which is open year-round but has no water from October to April. **Backcountry camping** is allowed with a permit along some of the longer trails. Campers pay a reduced entry fee to the park, but must pay a daily rate for camping. (Entry for campers $5.50, seniors $4.25, ages 6-16 $3; family $11. Campsites $18, except at Green Point $13; backcountry camping $12.) For the less rugged and/or more thrifty, the **Juniper Campground ❶**, in Rocky Harbour, runs a **hostel.** (☎458-2917. Kitchen. Dorms $12.)

▟ OUTDOOR ACTIVITIES. The easiest way to take in the Gros Morne scenery is onboard a **boat tour** of the fjords and shoreline. A number of private operators work out of Trout River, Western Brook Pond, and Boone Bay. Prices vary with demand, but usually hover between $15-25 for adults. For those with the will to hike, there are hundreds of kilometers of trails to enjoy. **Gros Morne Mountain** (16km, 7-8hr.) is one of the most rigorous hikes in the park. Although it is possible to complete the hike in one day, primitive campsites along the route break up the trek. The view from the peak is awe-inspiring, but snowbound until late June. The **Tablelands Trail** (6km, 2hr.) is less demanding and affords great canyon views.

QUÉBEC

Originally populated by French fur trading settlements along the St. Lawrence River, Québec was ceded to the British in 1759. Ever since, anti-federalist elements within *québécois* society have rankled under control of the national government. Visitors may be tipped off to the underlying struggles for independence by the occasional cry for "Liberté!" scrawled across a building or sidewalk, but the tensions are mostly kept behind closed doors in Ottawa. Instead, Montréal's renowned nightlife and Québec City's centuries-old European flair distinguish Québec among Canada's provinces.

🛈 PRACTICAL INFORMATION

Capital: Québec City.

Visitor info: Tourisme Québec, C.P. 979, Montréal H3C 2W3 (☎800-363-7777, in Montréal 514-873-2015; www.tourisme.gouv.qc.ca). Open daily 9am-5pm. **Canadian Parks Service,** Québec Region, 3 Passage du D'or, C.P. Box 6060, Haute-Ville GIR 4V7 (☎800-463-6769, in Québec City 418-648-4177).

Drinking Age: 18. **Postal Abbreviation:** QC. **Sales Tax:** 7.5% PST, plus 7% GST.

MONTRÉAL ☎514

This island city, named for the royal mountain in its midst, has been coveted territory for over 300 years. Wars and sieges have brought governments in and out like the tide. Today, the invaders are not British, French, or American generals, but rather visitors eager to experience a diverse city with a cosmopolitan air. An hour from the U.S. border, Montréal has grown to be the second largest French-speaking city in the world. Fashion that rivals Paris, a nightlife comparable to London, and cuisine from around the globe all attest to a prominent European legacy. Whether attracted to Montréal's global flavor or its large student population, it is hard not to be swept up by the vibrancy coursing through the *centre-ville*.

✈ INTERCITY TRANSPORTATION

Airports: Dorval (☎394-7377; www.admtl.com), 25min. from downtown by car. Many area hostels run airport shuttles for an average of $11; call hostels in advance for information. By Métro, take bus #211 from the Lionel Groulx (green and orange lines) to Dorval Train Station, then transfer to bus #204. **L'Aérobus** (☎931-9002) runs a minivan to Dorval from 777 rue de la Gauchetière Ouest, at rue de l'Université, stopping at any downtown hotel if notified in advance. Vans run every 20min. M-F, every 30min. Sa-Su 5:20am-11pm. $12, under 5 free. Taxi to downtown $30-35. Another airport, **Mirabel International** (☎450-476-3010 or 800-465-1213), is 45min. from downtown by car. Taxi to downtown $60.

Trains: Gare Centrale, 895 rue de la Gauchetière Ouest, under Queen Elizabeth Hotel. Métro: Bonaventure. Served by **VIA Rail** (☎989-2626 or 800-561-9181), open daily 7am-9pm. To: **Ottawa** (2hr.; 4 per day; $40, students $26, seniors $36, ages 2-11 $20); **Québec City** (3hr., 3-4 per day, $51/33/46/26); and **Toronto** (4-5½hr., 6 per day, $97/63/87/49). Discount tickets can be bought 5 or more days in advance. **Amtrak** (☎800-842-7275), open daily 8am-5pm. To **Boston** (13hr., 1 per day, US$115) and **New York** (10hr., 1 per day, US$65).

Buses: Voyageur, 505 bd. de Maisonneuve Est (☎842-2281). Métro: Berri-UQAM; from the main level of the station (near the hockey puck-shaped bench), follow the gray "Autobus-Teminus" signs upstairs to the bus station. To: **Ottawa** (2½hr., 17-18 per day, $29); **Québec City** (3hr.; 15 per day; $40, students $30); and **Toronto** (6¾hr., 5 per day, $78/54). **Greyhound USA** (☎287-1580). To **Boston** (7hr., 7 per day, $84) and **New York City** (7½-8¾hr., 7 per day, $103.50). Book Greyhound tickets 7 days in advance for the best prices. On shorter notice, ask the front desk at your hostel or B&B if they offer $5 discount coupons.

Driver/Rider Service: Allô Stop, 4317 rue St-Denis (☎985-3032). Open daily 9am-6pm. Matches passengers with member drivers; part of the rider fee goes to the driver. To: **Boston** ($42); **New York City** ($50); **Québec City** ($15); **Sherbrooke** ($9); and **Toronto** ($26). Riders and drivers fix their own fees for rides over 1000 mi. Annual membership fee required ($6, drivers $7).

■ ORIENTATION

Two major streets divide the city, making orientation simple. The one-way **bd. St-Laurent** (also called **"le Main,"** or **"The Main"**) runs north through the city, splitting Montréal and its streets east-west. The Main also serves as the unofficial French/English divider; English **McGill University** lies to the west, while **St-Denis,** a street running parallel to St-Laurent, lies to the east and defines the French student quarter (also called the *quartier latin* and the "student ghetto"). **Rue Sherbrooke,** which is paralleled by **de Maisonneuve** and **Ste-Catherine** downtown, runs east-west almost the entire length of Montréal. The **Underground City** runs north-south, stretching from **rue Sherbrooke** to **rue de la Gauchetière** and **rue St. Antoine.** A free map from the tourist office helps navigation. **Parking** is expensive and often difficult to find along the streets. Meters are 25¢ for 10min., and $30 tickets are common; watch out for signs saying *"Remorquage à vos frais"*—that is, "Towing at your own expense." Try the lots—especially those on the outskirts—for more reasonable parking prices.

NEIGHBORHOODS

When first founded, Montréal was limited to the riverside area of present-day **Vieux Montréal.** It has since evolved from a settlement of French colonists into a hip, cosmopolitan metropolis. A stroll along **rue Ste-Catherine,** the flashy commercial avenue, is a must. This is where European fashion teases Canada, overheard conversations mix English and French, and upscale retail shops intermingle with tacky souvenir stores and debaucherous nightclubs. Its assortment of peep shows and sex shops has earned it the nickname "Saint-Vitrine" (holy windows).

A small **Chinatown,** packed with specialty markets, occupies rue de la Gauchetière, just north of Métro: Place d'Armes. **Little Greece,** a fairly long walk from downtown, is just southeast of the Outremont Métro; stroll by rue Hutchison between avenue Van Horne and avenue Edouard-Charles. At the northern edge of the town's center, **Little Italy** occupies the area north of rue Beaubien between rue St-Hubert and Louis-Hémon. Walk east from Métro: Beaubien. Rue St-Denis, home to the city's elite at the turn of the century, still serves as the **Quartier Latin's** main street. Restaurants of all flavors are clustered along rue Prince Arthur (Métro: Berri-UQAM or Sherbrooke). Nearby, **Square St-Louis** (Métro: Sherbrooke) hosts a beautiful fountain and sculptures. **Bd. St-Laurent,** north of Sherbrooke, is perfect for walking or biking. A little further north, at **Jean-Talon,** Montréal shows its multicultural flair as a welcome wagon for Greek, Slavic, Latin American, and Portuguese immigrants among others. Many attractions surround **Mont-Royal** and the **Fleuve St-Laurent** are free. **Le Village,** the gay village, is located along rue Ste-Catherine Est between rue St-Hubert and Papineau. Both the Quartier Latin and the area along rue St-Denis foster a very liberal, gay-friendly atmosphere.

EASTERN CANADA

Montréal

🏠 ACCOMMODATIONS

Auberge de Jeunesse (HI-C), **17**
Hôtel le Breton, **9**
Hôtel de Paris, **7**
McGill University, **3**
Université de Montréal, **8**

🍎 FOOD

Brûlerie St. Denis, **2**
Étoile des Indes, **12**
L'Oiseau Bleu, **5**
La Crême de la Crême
  Bistro Café, **18**
La Creperie Bretanne
  le Trishell, **6**
Restaurant l'Académie, **1**

🍸 NIGHTLIFE

Café Campus, **4**
The Dome, **14**
Le Drugstore, **15**
O'Donnells Pub, **13**
Pub McKibbins, **11**
Sir Winston Churchill's, **10**
Sisters, **16**

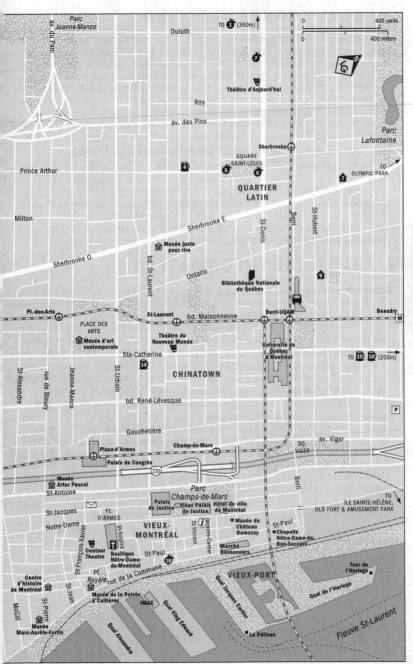

⌐ LOCAL TRANSPORTATION

Public Transit: STM Métro and Bus (☎288-6287). The world's most advanced public transit system when it was built for the 1976 World's Fair, Montréal's Métro is still comprehensive, logical, and safe. The 4 Métro lines and most buses run daily 5:30am-12:30am; some have early morning schedules as well. Get maps at the tourist office or any Métro station booth. Buses are well-integrated into the system; transfer tickets (*correspondances*) from bus drivers are valid as subway tickets and vice versa. Fare for métro or bus $2.25, 6 tickets $9. Between April and October, buy a Tourist Card at any downtown station, Sherbrooke, Mont-Royal, Pie-IX, Jean-Talon, or Longueuil. One-day unlimited access $7, 3-day $14. Québec university students are eligible for discounts.

Taxis: Taxi Coop de Montréal, ☎725-9885. **Champlain Taxi Inc.,** ☎273-2435.

Car Rental: Via Route, 1255 rue MacKay (☎871-1166), at Ste-Catherine. Métro: Guy-Concordia. Rates from $40 per day; special 4hr. rental $25. Must be 21+ with credit card. Open M-F 7am-7pm, Sa 7:30am-5pm, Su 9am-9pm.

Bike Rental: Cycle Pop, 1000 rue Rachel Est (☎526-2525). Métro: Mont-Royal. Open M-W 10am-6pm, Th-F 10am-9pm, Sa-Su 9am-5pm. 21-speeds $20 per day, $40 per weekend. Credit card or $250 deposit required. Much of the Métro system allows bikes during designated hours. Before trying, check the policy of the route.

🛈 PRACTICAL INFORMATION

Visitor info: Infotouriste, 1001 rue de Square-Dorchester (☎873-2015 or 800-363-7777; www.tourisme-montreal.org), on Ste-Catherine between rue Peel and rue Metcalfe. Métro: Peel. Open July-Aug. daily 7am-8pm; Sept.-June 9am-6pm. In **Vieux-Montréal,** 174 rue Notre-Dame Est, at Place Jacques Cartier. Open July-Aug. daily 9am-7pm; late Mar. to early June and Sept.-Oct. 9am-5pm; Nov. to early Mar. Th-Su 9am-5pm.

Budget Travel: Tourisme Jeunesse, 4800 rue St-Denis (☎252-3117). Métro: Sherbrooke. A non-profit organization that inspects and ranks all officially recognized youth hostels in Québec. Open M-W and Sa 10am-6pm, Th-F 10am-9pm, Su 10am-5pm. **Travel CUTS/Voyages Campus,** McGill Student Union, 3480 rue McTavish (☎398-0647). Métro: McGill. Specializes in budget travel for college students. Open M-F 9am-5pm.

Currency Exchange: Currencies International, 1250 rue Peel (☎392-9100). Métro: Peel. Open in summer M-W 8:30am-8pm, Th-F 8:30am-9pm, Sa 8:30am-7pm, Su 9am-6pm; call for winter hours. **Thomas Cook,** 777 rue de la Gauchetière Ouest (☎397-4029). Métro: Bonaventure. Open M-F 8:30am-7pm, Sa 9am-4pm, Su 10am-3pm. Rue Ste-Catherine is lined with other small *bureaux de change*—watch out for high commissions. Most ATMs are on the PLUS system and charge only the normal transaction fee for withdrawals abroad; ask your bank about fees.

American Express, 1141 bd. de Maisonneuve (☎284-3300), at Peel. Métro: Peel. Travel agency, traveler's checks, and currency exchange. Open M-F 9am-5pm.

Hotlines: Tél-Aide, ☎935-1101. **Gay and Lesbian Hotline,** ☎252-4429. **Sexual Assault Hotline,** ☎934-4504. **Suicide-Action,** ☎723-4000. All operate 24hr. **Rape Crisis,** ☎278-9383. Operates M-F 9:30am-4:30pm; call Tél-Aide after hours.

Post Office: Succursale (Postal Station) "B," 1250 ave Université (☎395-4539), at Cathcart St. Open M-F 8am-5pm. **Postal code:** H3B 3B0. **Area code:** 514.

⌂ ACCOMMODATIONS

The **Infotouriste** (☎800-363-7777) is the best resource for info about hostels, hotels, and *chambres touristiques* (rooms in private homes or small guest houses). B&B singles cost $25-40, and doubles run $35-75. Inquire directly about B&Bs at the

Downtown Bed and Breakfast Network ❶, 3458 av. Laval, H2X 3C8, near Sherbrooke; the managers run their own modest hideaway and maintain a list of 80 other homes downtown. (☎289-9749 or 800-267-5180; www.bbmontreal.qc.ca. Open daily 9am-9pm. Singles $40-65; doubles $45-75.) The least expensive *maisons touristiques* and hotels cluster around **rue St-Denis**. The area, which abuts Vieux Montréal, flaunts lively nightclubs and a number of funky cafes and bistros.

▨ **Auberge de Jeunesse, Montréal Youth Hostel (HI-C),** 1030 rue MacKay (☎843-3317). Métro: Lucien-L'Allier; from the station exit, cross the street and head right. The hostel is down the first real street on the left, across from the parking lot. Airport shuttle drivers will stop here if asked. With a full bathroom in every room, a complete kitchen, laundry facilities, pool tables, Internet access, and a *petit café* whipping up gourmet creations, the Montréal Youth Hostel is synonymous with heaven. The 250 beds (4-10 per room) fill quickly in summer; reservations are strongly recommended. Pub crawl Tu and F 8:30pm. Some parking. Linen $2.30; no sleeping bags. 1 week max. stay. Reception 24hr. Dorms $21, nonmembers $25; private doubles $26/32 per person. ❶

Hôtel Le Breton, 1609 rue St-Hubert (☎524-7273), around the corner from the bus station and 2 blocks east of St-Denis. Métro: Berri-UQAM. On a street lined with inexpensive, interchangeable hotels, Le Breton's comfort and conveniences make it a standout. The 13 clean and comfortable rooms come with cable TV. Some rooms have A/C. Complimentary coffee and croissants. Reception 8am-midnight; front door remains locked. Reservations recommended 2 weeks in advance. Rooms $35-75. ❶

McGill University, Bishop Mountain Hall, 3935 rue de l'Université (☎398-6367). Métro: McGill. Follow Université along the edge of campus; when the road seems to end in a parking lot at the top of the steep hill, bear right—it is the circular grey stone building with lots of windows. Kitchenettes on each floor. 1000 beds. Free Internet access, common room with TV, towels and linen provided, and laundry facilities. Full breakfast M-Th 7:30-9:30am $6. Reception daily 7am-10pm; there is a guard for late check-in. Open mid-May to mid-Aug. Singles $45, students and seniors $40.50; weekly $230/200. ❷

Université de Montréal, Residences, 2350 rue Edouard-Montpetit (☎343-6531), off Côte-des-Neiges. Métro: Edouard-Montpetit. Located in a tranquil, remote neighborhood on the edge of a beautiful campus, the East Tower affords a great view. Newly renovated. Free local calls. Laundry facilities. Cafe with basic foods open M-F 7:30am-2:30pm. Reception 24hr. Check-out noon, strictly enforced. Parking $7. Open mid-May to early-Aug. Singles $35. ❶

Hôtel de Paris, 901 rue Sherbrooke E (☎522-6861 or 800-567-7217). Métro: Sherbrooke. This European-style 19th-century flat houses a score of pleasant hotel rooms with private bath, TV, telephone, and A/C. Some rooms contain fireplaces or kitchenettes. There are also about 100 hostel beds, which, while cheaper than the hotel rooms, are not as good a deal as Montréal's other hostels. Linen $3. Single-sex dorm rooms $19. Hotel rooms $80-90. ❶

Camping Alouette, 3449 rue de l'Industrie (☎450-464-1661), 30km from the city. Follow Autoroute 20, take Exit 105, and follow the signs to the campground. Find the privacy that is missing from Montréal's bustling hostels. Pool, laundry facilities, a small store, and a daily shuttle to and from Montréal. Showers 25¢. Sites for 2 $19, with hookup $27; each additional person $2. Shuttle $10 per person round-trip. ❷

☯ BON APPÉTIT

Montréal is a diner's city, where chic restaurants rub shoulders with funky cafés, and everyone can find something to fit their taste. Expect nothing less than excellent food, but don't hold your breath for speedy service. **Chinatown** and **Little Italy** boast outstanding examples of their culinary heritage, and **rue Prince Arthur** adds a cheerful blend of Greek and Polish to the mix. The western half of **Ste-Catherine** and the area of **bd. St-Laurent** north of Sherbrooke offer a large range of choices. By far the best and most consistently affordable restaurants cluster on **rue St-Denis.**

Many restaurants, even upscale ones, have no liquor license; head to the nearest **dépanneur** or **SAQ** (*Societé des alcools du Québec*) to buy wine to have with dinner. All restaurants are required by law to post their menus outside. For further guidance, consult the free *Restaurant Guide*, published by the **Greater Montréal Convention and Tourism Bureau** (☎844-5400), which lists over 130 restaurants by type of cuisine.

If you feel like cooking, head to one of the **markets.** (☎937-7754. All markets open M-W 8am-6pm, Th 8am-8pm, F 8am-9pm, Sa-Su 8am-5pm; on nights of special events, the Marché Maisonneuve is often open later.) **Marché Jean-Talon** has a vibrant selection of ethnic goodies in addition to the usual fare, while the **Marché Maisonneuve,** 4375 rue Ontario Est (Métro: Pie-IX), is great for produce and traditional *québécois* gems.

■ **Restaurant l'Académie,** 4051 rue St-Denis (☎849-2249), on the corner of av. Duluth. Métro: Sherbrooke. An elegant culinary heaven where lunchtime self-indulgence is reasonably priced. People-watch from the glass walls as you fill up on Italian and French cuisine. L'Académie is most recognized for their *moule frites,* which are mussels steamed and served in a variety of sophisticated sauces (around $10). Open daily noon-10pm. ❷

■ **Brûlerie St. Denis,** 3967 rue St-Denis (☎286-9158). Métro: Sherbrooke. A fun student cafe where the food and coffee are excellent, the waiters are friendly, and the patrons seem to already know each other. While adventurous types will find themselves quickly caught up in conversation, you won't feel out of place sitting with a newspaper. Café du jour $1.35. Bagel "Belle Hélène" $4. Shockingly large slices of raspberry cheesecake $4.75. Open daily 8am-11pm. ❶

Étoile des Indes, 1806 Ste-Catherine Ouest (☎932-8330), near St-Mathieu (parking on St-Mathieu). A local favorite for Indian food. Their spicy Bangalore *phal* dishes are only for the brave, but the homemade cheese in their *paneer* plates is for everyone. Dinners $5-15. Lunch specials $5-8. Open M-Sa noon-2:30pm and 5-11pm, Su 5-11pm. ❷

La Crêperie Bretonne le Trishell, 3470 rue St-Denis (☎281-1012). Métro: Sherbrooke. Montréalers have been known to line up for a taste of le Trishell's melt-in-your-mouth crêpes and fondues. Asparagus-cheese crêpe $6. Open M-W 11:30am-11pm, Th-F 11:30am-midnight, Sa noon-midnight, Su noon-11pm. ❶

La Crème de la Crème Bistro Café, 21 rue de la Commune Est (☎874-0723), in Vieux-Montréal. A cozy brick cafe on the waterfront which combines Greek cuisine and Provençal decor, La Crème de la Crème serves up tasty baguette sandwiches (with salad $7-9) and generous slices of cake ($4). Open June-Sept. daily 11am-midnight; Oct.-June hours vary. ❷

Au Pain Doré, 5214 Côte des Neiges (☎342-8995), near rue Jean Brillant. Delicious pastries, filling sandwiches (the grilled veggies are especially good), and a well-stocked retail cheese section. Another location is on St-Denis near Roy. Baguettes $1.50-4. Open M-W 8:30am-7pm, Th-F 8:30am-7:30pm, Sa-Su 8:30am-5:30pm. ❶

L'Oiseau Bleu, 3603 av. Laval (☎286-6654), in Sq. Saint-Louis. This ice cream parlor sells great licks to the kids, lovers, punks, and others who meander through the park. Cones $1.50-2.50. Wraps and sandwiches $4-6. Open May-Nov. daily noon-11pm. ❶

PRIME MINISTER'S CHOICE During the American Presidential Campaign of 2000, a Canadian television show convinced then-Governor George W. Bush that Jean Poutine was Prime Minister of Canada (it's actually Jean Chrétien). In reality, poutine is the *québécois* snack food of choice. The basic recipe produces a gooey, salty, addictive mess and involves french fries, spicy brown gravy, and curd cheese. Travelers to Montréal will find it for about $2.25 at almost any low-key eatery, and most fast-food chains will "poutine their fries" for 75¢-$1.

◎ SIGHTS

MONT-ROYAL, LE PLATEAU, & THE EAST

Package tickets *(forfaits)* for the Funiculaire, Biodôme, and Gardens/Insectarium are a decent deal. Tickets are good for 30 days, so feel free to pace yourself. *(Any 2 sights $16, students and seniors $12, children 5-17 $8. All 3 sights $24/18/12.)*

BIODÔME. The fascinating ▨Biodôme is the most recent addition to Olympic park. Housed in the former Olympic Vélodrome, the Biodôme is a "living museum" in which 4 complete ecosystems have been reconstructed: the Tropical Forest, the Laurentian Forest, the St-Laurent marine ecosystem, and the Polar World. Stay alert to spot some of the more elusive of the 6200 vertebrates subsisting here. *(4777 av. Pierre-de-Coubertin. Métro: Viau. ☎ 868-3000. Open in summer daily 9am-7pm; off-season 9am-5pm. $10, students and seniors $7.50, ages 5-17 $5.)*

ST. JOSEPH'S. The dome of ▨St. Joseph's Oratory, the second highest dome in the world after St. Peter's Basilica in Rome, stands in testimony to the chapel's grandeur. An acclaimed religious site that attracts pilgrims from all over the globe, St. Joseph's is credited with a long list of miracles and unexplained healings. The **Votive Chapel,** where the crutches and canes of thousands of healed devotees hang for all to see, keeps warm with the heat of 10,000 candles. *(3800 ch. Queen Mary. Métro: Côte-des-Neiges. ☎ 733-8211. Open daily 6am-9:30pm.)*

OLYMPIC PARK. The world's tallest inclined tower (called *le Tour Olympique* or *le Tour de Montréal*) is the crowning glory of the ultra-modern **Olympic Park,** built for the 1976 summer Olympic games. Take the **Funiculaire** to the top of the tower for a breathtaking view of Montréal. *(3200 rue Viau, less than a minute's walk from the Biodôme. Métro: Viau, Pie-IX. ☎ 252-8687. Four tours of the stadium offered daily, 2 in French and 2 in English. Call for times. Tour $5.50, students and seniors $5, ages 5-17 $4.25; tour not included in "forfait" package—see above. Funiculaire open mid-June to Sept. M noon-9pm, Tu-Th 10am-9pm, F-Su 10am-11pm; early Sept. to mid-June M noon-5pm, Tu-Su 10am-5pm. $10, students and seniors $7.50, ages 5-17 $5; included in forfait package.)*

BOTANICAL GARDENS & INSECTARIUM. In the summer, a free shuttle runs across the park to the **Jardin Botanique (Botanical Gardens).** The Japanese and Chinese landscapes showcase the largest *bonsai* and *penjing* collections outside of Asia. Beware: the gardens also harbor an **insectarium** with astounding collections of mounted and live exotic bugs, including at least a dozen fist-sized spiders. *(4101 rue Sherbrooke Est. Métro: Pie-IX. ☎ 872-1400. Open July-Aug. daily 9am-7pm; Sept.-June 9am-5pm. $10, students and seniors $7.50, ages 5-17 $5.)*

EASTERN CANADA

PARC DU MONT-ROYAL. Designed by Frederick Law Olmstead, who also designed New York's Central Park, the 127-year-old Parc du Mont-Royal surrounds and includes Montréal's namesake mountain. Though the hike from rue Peel up the mountain is longer than it looks, the view of the city from the observation points rewards the hardy. The **30m cross** at the top of the mountain is a replica of the cross placed there in 1643 by de Maisonneuve, the founder of Montréal. In winter, locals gather here to ice-skate, toboggan, and cross-country ski. In summer, Mont-Royal welcomes joggers, cyclists, picnickers, and amblers. *(The park is loosely bordered by ch. Remembrance, bd. Mont-Royal, av. du Parc, and ch. de la Côte des Neiges. Métro: Mont-Royal or Bus #11. ☎844-4928. Open daily 6am-midnight.)*

CATHÉDRALE MARIE REINE DU MONDE & ENVIRONS. On the block bordered by René-Lévesque, Cathédrale, and Metcalfe, **Cathédrale Marie Reine du Monde** is a scaled-down replica of St. Peter's in Rome. A Roman Catholic basilica, it stirred tensions when it was built in the heart of Montréal's Anglo-Protestant area. *(☎866-1661. Open M-F 6am-7:30pm, Sa 7:30am-8:30pm, Su 8:30am-7:30pm. At least 3-4 masses offered daily. Free.)* Across rue Cathédrale, the soothing **Place du Canada** comprises a lovely park and modest war memorial.

MCGILL. The **McGill University** campus extends up Mont-Royal and is composed predominantly of Victorian-style buildings set on pleasant greens. For a look around campus, stop by the **McGill Welcome Center** for a tour. *(Burnside Hall Building, Room 115. ☎398-6555. Open M-Sa 9am-5pm.)* The campus also includes the site of the 16th-century Native American village of **Hochelaga** and the **Redpath Museum of Natural History**, containing rare fossils and two genuine Egyptian mummies. *(Main gate at rue McGill and Sherbrooke. Métro: McGill. ☎398-4086. Open July-Aug. M-Th 9am-5pm, Su 1-5pm; Sept. to late June M-F 9am-5pm, Su 1-5pm. Free.)*

THE UNDERGROUND CITY

Not content with being one of the best shopping spots on the planet, Montréal has set its sights lower. Twenty-nine kilometers of tunnels link Métro stops and form the ever-expanding "prototype city of the future," connecting railway stations, two bus terminals, restaurants, banks, cinemas, theaters, hotels, two universities, two department stores, 1700 businesses, 1615 housing units, and 1600 boutiques. Here, residents bustle through the hallways of this sprawling, mall-like, "sub-urban" city.

MCGILL. At the McGill stop lie some of the Underground City's finest and most navigable offerings. The **Promenades de la Cathédrale** take their name from their above-ground neighbor, **Christ Church Cathedral.** However, the Underground City's primary shopping complex is more interested in your pocketbook than your soul. *(635 rue Ste-Catherine Ouest. Church: ☎843-6577. Open daily 8am-6pm. Promenades: ☎849-9925.)* Three blocks east, passing through **Centre Eaton**, the **Place Montréal Trust** offers even more commercial decadence amidst beautiful modern architecture.

PLACE BONAVENTURE. While much of this shopping wonderland is caught in the throes of a never-ending renovation, the accessible areas are worth exploring, especially on a rainy day. Follow the signs marked "Restaurants et Commerce" through the maze of shops under rue de la Gauchetière Ouest. The tourist office supplies treasure maps of the tunnels and underground attractions. *(900 rue de la Gauchetière Ouest. Métro: Bonaventure. ☎397-2325. Shops open daily 9am-9pm.)*

VIEUX MONTRÉAL (OLD MONTRÉAL)

In the 17th century, the city of Montréal, while struggling with Iroquois tribes for control of the area's lucrative fur trade, erected walls encircling the settlement for defense. Today the remnants of those ramparts delineate the boundaries of Vieux Montréal, the city's first settlement, on the stretch of river bank between **rue**

McGill, Notre-Dame, and **Berri.** The fortified walls that once protected the quarter have crumbled, but the beautiful 17th- and 18th-century mansions of politicos and merchants have retained their splendor.

CHAPELLE NÔTRE-DAME-DE-BON-SECOURS. Marguerite Bourgeoys was the first teacher in Montréal, founder of the first order of non-cloistered nuns, and the driving force behind the construction of the first stone chapel, built on the waterfront as a sailor's refuge. This chapel now houses the museum that bears her name and displays archaeological treasures illuminating Montréal's history. *(400 rue St-Paul Est. Métro: Champ-de-Mars. ☎ 282-8670. Museum and chapel open May-Oct. Tu-Sa 10am-5pm; Nov. to mid-Jan. Tu-Su 11am-3:30pm. $6, seniors $4; call for child, group, and family rates. Play presented mid-May to early Sept. Th-Su; English 1:30pm, French 3:30pm. Call for ticket info.)*

CHÂTEAU RAMEZAY. The grand Château Ramezay presides over Vieux-Montréal as a testament to the power of the French viceroy for whom it was built. Constructed in 1705, converted to a museum in 1895, and renovated in the summer of 2002, the Château is a living record of Québec's heritage. Don't miss the 18th-century Governor's garden and the outdoor cafe. *(280 rue Notre-Dame Est. Métro: Champ-de-Mars. ☎ 861-3708. Open June-Sept. daily 10am-6pm; Oct.-May Tu-Su 10am-4:30pm. $6, students $4, seniors $5, under 18 $3, and families $12. Tours available by reservation. Partially wheelchair accessible; assistance may be required.)*

BASILIQUE NOTRE-DAME-DE-MONTRÉAL. A couple blocks south of the Place d'Armes, Notre-Dame-de-Montréal towers above the memorial to de Maisonneuve in the bordering square. One of North America's largest churches and a historic center for the city's Catholic population, the neo-Gothic basilica has hosted everyone from Québec separatists to the Pope. The extremely ornate and detailed hand-painted designs covering the pillars and ceiling are most impressive as well as the sound-and-light spectacular *Et la lumière fut*—"And then there was light." *(116 rue Notre-Dame Ouest. Métro: Place-D'Armes. ☎ 842-2925. Open Su-M 7am-6pm, Tu-Sa 7am-5pm. Free for prayer; tours $2, ages 7-17 $1. Light show ticketed separately; call for details.)*

OTHER ATTRACTIONS. The **St-Sulpice Seminary,** built in 1685, is the oldest building in Montréal, and the clock over the facade, built in 1701, is the oldest public timepiece in North America. Today, St-Sulpice is a monument to continuity; it is still a functioning seminary, and the clock still chimes as it has for hundreds of years. *(130 rue Notre-Dame Ouest. Métro: Place D'Armes.)* In 1967, Charles de Gaulle stood in the balcony of the **Hôtel de Ville de Montréal** and cried "Vive le Québec libre!," thrilling separatists, embarrassing the Canadian government, and injecting a little historical fun into an otherwise ordinary city hall. *(275 rue Notre-Dame Est. Métro: Champ-de-Mars. ☎ 872-3355. Guided tours daily 8:30am-4:30pm. Free.)* **Place Jacques Cartier** is the site of Montréal's oldest market. Here the modern European character of Montréal is most evident. Cafes line the square, and street artists strut their stuff during the summer. *(Rue St. Paul. Métro: Champ-de-Mars.)*

ÎLE STE-HÉLÈNE & ST-LAURENT

By car, take either of two bridges to Île Ste-Hélène: the Pont Jacques Cartier or the Pont de la Concorde. To avoid traffic and the hassle of finding parking, take the yellow Métro line to Île Ste-Hélène and catch a bus to the island's attractions.

LA RONDE. The best among many good reasons to visit Île Ste-Hélène, **La Ronde** amusement park boasts a free-fall drop and one of the largest wooden roller coasters in North America. *(Métro: Jean-Drapeau. ☎ 397-2000. Rides open in summer daily 11am-11pm, grounds open until midnight; hours vary off-season. Unlimited one-day pass $29.)* Every Saturday night in June and July, La Ronde hosts the **Mondial SAQ,** the world's most prestigious fireworks competition—view the sky explosions free from Mont-Royal or the crowded Pont Jacques-Cartier. *(Tickets ☎ 800-361-4595, info ☎ 872-7044.)*

LE VIEUX FORT. Originally built in 1820 to defend Canada's inland waterways from the imperialistic Americans to the south, Le Vieux Fort now protects the **Stewart Museum.** The museum houses a large collection of weapons, war instruments, and strategic maps and stages a musket firing by costumed colonials. *(Métro: Jean-Drapeau. ☎861-6701. Open mid-May to mid-Oct. daily 10am-6pm; late Oct. to early May M and W-Su 10am-5pm. Musket firing in summer daily 3pm. $7, students and seniors $5, under 7 free; families of 4 $14.)*

🏛 MUSEUMS

McCord Museum, 690 rue Sherbrooke Ouest (☎398-7100). Métro: McGill or bus #24. An absorbing collection of textiles, paintings, and artifacts trace Canada's history from Confederation onward. The museum features a unique First Nations collection, Canada's largest costumes collection, and an immense photographic archive. Open June-Sept. daily 10am-5pm; Oct.-May Tu-F 10am-6pm, Sa-Su 10am-5pm. $9.50, students $5, seniors $7, ages 7-12 $3, families $19. Free Sa 10am-noon.

Musée des Beaux-Arts, 1380 rue Sherbrooke Ouest (☎285-2000). Métro: Guy-Concordia. Located about 5 blocks west of the McGill entrance, this museum's small permanent collection touches upon all major artistic periods and includes Canadian and Inuit work. Open Tu-Su 11am-6pm. Permanent collection free. Temporary exhibits $12, students and seniors $6, under 12 $3; half-price W 5:30-9pm.

Musée d'Art Contemporain, 185 rue Ste-Catherine Ouest (☎847-6226), at Jeanne-Mance. Métro: Place-des-Arts. Canada's major contemporary art museum showcases the avant-garde in almost every imaginable medium. Open Tu and Th-Su 11am-6pm, W 11am-9pm. $6, students $3, seniors $4, under 12 free; W 6-9pm free.

Pointe-à-Callière: Montréal Museum of Archaeology and History, 350 Place Royale (☎872-9150), off rue de la Commune near Vieux-Port. Métro: Place d'Armes. This museum and national historic site uses the products of more than 10 years of archaeological digs in an innovative tour of the city's history. Open late June to early Sept. M 10am-6pm, Tu-F 10am-5pm, Sa-Su 11am-5pm; off-season closed M. $9.50, students $5.50, seniors $7, ages 6-12 $3, under 5 free.

Canadian Centre for Architecture, 1920 av. Baile (☎939-7026). Métro: Guy-Concordia or Atwater. Houses one of the world's most important collections of architectural prints, drawings, photographs, and books. Open in summer Tu-W and F-Su 11am-6pm, Th 11am-9pm; off-season hours vary. $6, students $3, seniors $4, under 12 free.

Montréal Museum of Decorative Arts, 2200 rue Crescent (☎284-1252). Métro: Guy-Concordia, then transfer to bus #24 "Pie-IX." Stop by for a slew of innovative and absurd decorative pieces. Open Tu-Su 11am-6pm, W 11am-9pm. $4, students $3, under 12 free.

🌙 NIGHTLIFE

Combine a loosely enforced drinking age of 18 with thousands of taps flowing unchecked till 3am and the result is the unofficially titled "nightlife capital of North America." Most pubs and bars offer a happy hour, usually from 5-8pm, when bottled drinks may be two-for-one and mixed drinks may be double their usual potency. In summer, restaurants spill onto outdoor patios and streets clog with strollers, thespians, and couples holding hands. Avoid crowds of drunken American college students by ducking into one of the laid-back local pubs along **rue St-Denis** north of Ste-Catherine. Alternatively, *be* a drunken American college student on **rue Ste-Catherine,** especially around **rue Crescent.** Tamer fun can be found in the pedestrian-only section of **rue Prince Arthur** at **rue St-Laurent.**

▒ **Café Campus,** 57 rue Prince Arthur (☎844-1010). Unlike the more touristy meat-market discothèques, this hip club gathers a friendly student and twenty-something crowd. Regular theme nights include: Su French music, Th "Tabasko" (Latin groove), and the fun and happy Retro Tu (hits from the 1980s and 1990s). Drinks $4-5.50. Cover $2-4, live music $5-15. Open M-Sa 7pm-3am, Su 8:30pm-3am.

▒ **Pub McKibbins,** 1426 rue Bishop (☎288-1580). Fine fermented drinks are served within the dark mahogany confines of this Irish pub. Trophies and brass tokens ornament the walls and dartboards entertain the crowds, while a fieldstone fireplace warms the quarters in winter. Ground yourself with the Shepard's Pie ($9) before the next Guinness. Open daily 11am-3am; kitchen closes 10pm.

O'Donnells Pub, 1224 rue Bishop (☎877-3128), south of rue Ste-Catherine. Enticing weekday dinner specials (F fish and chips $7). The tartan stools and cozy booths are quickly claimed W-Sa, when live traditional Irish music filters into the street. Open daily noon-3am; kitchen closes 10pm.

Sir Winston Churchill's, 1459 rue Crescent (☎288-0616). Perhaps the most impressive ratio of counter length to total area of any bar in Montréal—every wall is covered and ready to serve. This multi-story restaurant/pub attracts a crowd of English-speaking Montréalers and out-of-towners. Open daily 10:30am-3am.

The Dome, 32 rue Ste-Catherine Est (☎875-5757), at the corner of St-Laurent. Attracts an international crowd to bump and grind. Cover $5. Open F-Sa 10pm-3am.

GAY & LESBIAN NIGHTLIFE

Most of Montréal's gay and lesbian hot spots can be found in the **gay village**, along rue St-Catherine between St-Hubert and Papineau. While most of the village's establishments cater to men, a few lesbian-friendly locales are interspersed throughout the neighborhood.

Le Drugstore, 1366 rue Ste-Catherine Est (☎868-9278). Métro: Beaudry. A 3-story gay megaplex basking in the glow of multicolored neon lights. Crowd is mostly male, though women are welcome. Ground floor is wheelchair accessible. Open M-F 7pm-6am.

Sisters, 1333 rue Ste-Catherine Est (☎522-4717). Métro: Beaudry. Since the closing of several popular girl bars in 2000, Sisters has picked up the slack, offering intimate tables, disco dancing, and a well-equipped bar. Tu "Boyz in the House" night. Cover F-Sa $5. Open Th-Sa 10pm-3am.

◪ ENTERTAINMENT

THEATER

Montréal lives up to its cultured reputation with a vast selection of theater in both French and English. The **Théâtre du Nouveau Monde,** 84 rue Ste-Catherine Ouest (☎866-8667; Métro: Place-des-Arts), usually stages French productions. In mid-June, however, the theater is turned over to the bilingual **Festival Juste pour Rire/Just for Laughs** (☎790-4242). The friendly **Théâtre du Rideau Vert,** 4664 rue St-Denis (☎844-1793; Métro: Mont-Royal), puts on both *québécois* works and French adaptations of English plays. The hip **Théâtre d'Aujourd'hui,** 3900 rue St-Denis (☎782-3900; Métro: Sherbrooke), produces original, eccentric *québécois* shows. For English theater, a good bet is the **Centaur Theatre.** (453 rue St-François-Xaviers. Métro: Place-d'Armes. ☎288-1229, ticket info 288-3161. Performances mostly Sept.-May.) The hyper-competitive, well-renowned **National Theatre School of Canada,** 5030 rue St-Denis (☎842-7954), stages excellent "school plays" throughout the academic year. The city's exciting **Place des Arts,** 260 bd. de Maisonneuve Ouest

(☎842-2112), at rue Ste. Catherine Ouest and rue Jeanne Mance, houses the **Opéra de Montréal** (☎985-2258), the **Montréal Symphony Orchestra** (☎842-9951), and **Les Grands Ballets Canadiens** (☎849-8681). **Théâtre Saint-Denis,** 1594 rue St-Denis (☎849-4211), hosts Broadway-style traveling productions—like *Cats*. Theatergoers should peruse the *Calendar of Events*, available at tourist offices and newspaper stands, or call **Telspec** for ticket info. (☎790-2222. Open M-Sa 9am-9pm, Su noon-6pm.) **Admission Ticket Network** also has tickets for various events. (☎790-1245 or 800-361-4595. Open daily 8am-midnight. Credit card required.)

MUSIC, FESTIVALS, & SPORTS

Montréal might also be in the running for festival capital of the world. To keep track of all the offerings, it's a good idea to pick up a copy of *Mirror* (in English) or *Voir* (in French). In summer, keep your eyes peeled for *ventes-trottoirs*, "sidewalk sales" that shut down a major Montréal street for a day and night of pedestrian-only outdoor fun. In June, Montréal reels from the effects of its always-entertaining **fringe-theater festival** (☎849-3378), at various spots throughout the Plateau Mont-Royal. Meanwhile, it wouldn't be Montréal without the high-spirited **Fête Nationale** (☎849-2560), on St-Jean-Baptiste Day, June 24, a celebration of Quebec pride. The best place to catch the spirit is Parc Maisonneuve.

Two of Montréal's signature summer festivals draw crowds from all over the world. During the third week in June, Montreal swoons during the **Mondial de la Bière,** when over 75 beers are available for tasting and visitors discover the happy marriage of spirits, music, and cuisine. (☎722-9640; www.festivalmondialbiere.qc.ca. Day pass $10.) The first week of July, jazz fiends take over the city for the **Montréal International Jazz Festival** (☎871-1881; www.montrealjazzfest.com). From traditional jazz artists to last year's Lauryn Hill appearance, the show typically brings together a variety of over 300 performers. Events cluster near Métro station **Place-des-Arts.** One month later, **Divers/Cité** (www.diverscite.org), the gay pride week, rocks the city in or around Emilie-Gamelin Park.

Montréal also has its share of sporting events. Between October and April, hockey's **Montréal Canadiens** (nicknamed Les Habitants—"the locals"—or Les Habs) play at the **Molson Centre,** 1250 rue de la Gauchetière Ouest. (☎932-2582. Métro: Bonaventure. Call well in advance to reserve tickets.) Dress and behavior at games can be quite formal; jackets and ties are not uncommon. If you'd rather get into the action than watch from the sidelines, perhaps the one-day **Tour de l'Île** is more your speed. This 64km circuit of the island has over 45,000 mostly amateur cyclists pedaling their wares. (☎521-8356. Register by Apr. to participate. Separate days for adults and children.)

Like much of the city, Vieux Montréal is best seen at night. Street performers, artists, and *chansonniers* in various *brasseries* set the tone for lively summer evenings of clapping, stomping, and singing along. Real fun goes down on **St-Paul,** near the corner of St-Vincent. For a sweet Sunday afternoon, **Parc Jeanne-Mance** reels with bongos, dancing, and handicrafts. (May-Sept. noon-7pm.)

QUÉBEC CITY ☎418

Dubbed the "Gibraltar of America" because of the stone escarpments and military fortifications protecting the port, Québec City (generally shortened to just "Québec") sits high on the rocky heights of Cap Diamant, where the St. Laurence narrows and is joined by the St. Charles River. Passing through the portals of North America's only walled city is like stepping into a European past. Horse-drawn carriages greet visitors to the winding maze of streets in the Old City (Vieux Québec), and there are enough sights and museums to satisfy even the most voracious history buff for weeks. Canada's oldest city also boasts a thriving French culture, standing apart from Montréal as the center of true *québécois* culture.

⌐ TRANSPORTATION

Airport: Jean Lesage International Airport (☎692-0770) is far out of town and inaccessible by public transit. Taxi to downtown $30. By car, turn right onto Rt. de l'Aéroport and then take either bd. Wilfred-Hamel or Autoroute 440 to get into the city. **Autobus La Québécoise** (☎872-5525) runs a shuttle service between the airport and the major hotels of the city. Operates M-F 6 per day 8:45am-9:45pm, Sa 7 per day 9am-8:45pm, Su 7 per day 9am-11:35pm. $9, under 12 free.

Trains: VIA Rail, 450 rue de la Gare du Palais (☎692-3940), in Québec City. Open daily 6am-8:30pm. To: **Montréal** (3hr.; M-F 4 per day, Sa-Su 3 per day; $53, students $34, seniors $48, ages 2-11 $26); **Ottawa** (3hr., 3 per day, $77/50/69/39); and **Toronto** (8hr., 4 per day, $133/86/120/67). Nearby stations: 3255 ch. de la Gare, in Ste-Foy. Open M-F 6am-9pm, Sa-Su 7:30am-9pm. 5995 St-Laurent, Autoroute 20, in Lévis. Open Th-M 4-5am and 8-10:30pm, Tu 4-5am, W 8-10:30pm.

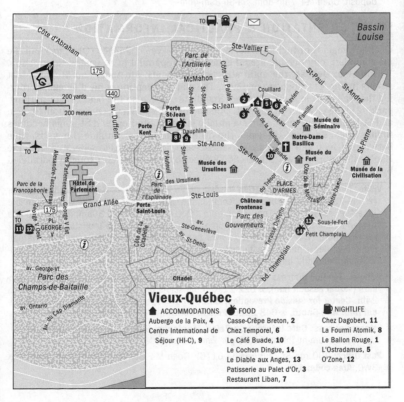

Vieux-Québec

⌂ ACCOMMODATIONS
Auberge de la Paix, **4**
Centre International de Séjour (HI-C), **9**

🍴 FOOD
Casse-Crêpe Breton, **2**
Chez Temporel, **6**
Le Café Buade, **10**
Le Cochon Dingue, **14**
Le Diable aux Anges, **13**
Patisserie au Palet d'Or, **3**
Restaurant Liban, **7**

🍸 NIGHTLIFE
Chez Dagobert, **11**
La Fourmi Atomik, **8**
Le Ballon Rouge, **1**
L'Ostradamus, **5**
O'Zone, **12**

Buses: Orléans Express, 320 rue Abraham Martin. (☎525-3000). Open daily 5:30am-1am. Outlying stations: 3001 ch. des Quatre-Bourgeois, in Ste-Foy (☎650-0087). Open M-Sa 6am-1am, Su 7am-1am. 63 Hwy. Trans-Canada Ouest, also called Hwy. 132 (☎837-5805), in Lévis. Open daily 6am-2am. To: **Montréal** (3hr.; every hr. 6am-8pm and 9:30-11pm; $35, seniors $26, ages 5-11 $17); **Ste-Anne-de-Beaupré** (25min., 3 per day, $5); and the **US** via Montréal.

Public Transit: Société de Transport de la Communauté Urbaine de Québec (STCUQ), 270 rue des Rocailles (route and schedule info ☎627-2511). Open M-F 6:30am-10pm, Sa-Su 8am-10pm. Buses operate daily 6am-1am, although individual routes and hours of operation vary significantly. Many bus routes, in fact, may be interrupted or discontinued during the summer. $2.25, students $1.50, seniors and children $1.30; advance-purchase tickets $1.60/1/1; under 5 free.

Taxis: Coop Taxis Québec, ☎525-5191.

Driver/Rider Service: Allô Stop, 665 rue St-Jean (☎522-0056), will match you with a driver heading for Montréal ($15). Must be a member ($6 per year, drivers $7). Open M, W-Th and Sa-Su 9am-6pm, Tu and F 9am-7pm.

Car Rental: Pelletier, 900 bd. Pierre Bertrand (☎681-0678). $35 per day, $50 with insurance; 250km free, 11¢ each additional km. Must be 25+ with 20% credit card deposit. Open M-F 7am-8pm, Sa-Su 8am-4pm.

◼◼ ORIENTATION & PRACTICAL INFORMATION

Québec's main thoroughfares service both the *Vieux Québec* (Old City) and the more modern city outside it, and generally run parallel in an east-west direction. Within **Vieux Québec,** the main streets are **St-Louis, Ste-Anne,** and **St-Jean.** Most streets in Vieux Québec are one-way. The major exception is **rue d'Auteuil,** bordering the walls inside Vieux Québec. Rue d'Auteuil is also the best bet for parking; parking in the city can be difficult. Outside the walls of Vieux Québec, both St-Jean and St-Louis continue. St-Jean eventually joins ch. Ste-Foy, and St-Louis becomes **Grande Allée. Bd. René-Lévesque,** the other major street outside the walls, runs between St-Jean and St-Louis. The Basse-ville (lower town) is separated from the Haute-ville (upper town, a.k.a. Old Québec) by an abrupt cliff roughly paralleled by rue St-Vallier Est.

Visitor info: Bureau d'information touristique du Vieux-Québec, 835 av. Wilfred Laurier (☎649-2608; www.quebecregion.com), in the Old City just outside the walls. Open late June-Aug. daily 8:30am-7pm; Sept. to mid-Oct. daily 8:30am-6:30pm; mid-Oct. to late June M-Th and Sa 9am-5pm, F 9am-6pm, Su 10am-4pm. **Centre Touriste de Québec,** 12 rue Ste-Anne (☎877-266-5687; www.bonjourquebec.com), across from Château Frontenac, deals primarily with provincial tourism. Open late June-Aug. daily 8:30am-7:30pm; Sept.-mid June 9am-5pm.

Hotlines: Tél-Aide distress center, ☎686-2433. Operates daily noon-midnight. **Viol-Secours (sexual assault line),** ☎522-2120. Counselors on duty M-F 9am-4pm and on-call 24hr. **Center for Suicide Prevention,** ☎529-0015. Operates daily 8am-midnight. **Medical info: Info-Santé,** ☎648-2626. **Poison Control,** ☎656-8090. 24hr.

Internet access: Café Internet du Palais Montcalm, 995 rue d'Youville (☎692-4909). Open daily 7am-midnight. $3.50 per ½hr., $6 per hr.

Post Office: 300 rue St-Paul (☎694-6176). Open M-F 8am-5:45pm. **Postal code:** G1K 3W0. **Area code:** 418.

EASTERN CANADA

ACCOMMODATIONS

There are a number of B&Bs in Québec, many of which can be a good deal. **Le Transit,** 1050 av. Turnbull, G1R 2X8 (☎647-6802; call 8am-noon or 4-9pm), will help with bed and breakfast referrals. Rooms start at $50 for one or two people, and hosts are usually bilingual. You can obtain a list of nearby **campgrounds** from the Maison du Tourisme de Québec, or write to **Tourisme Québec,** C.P. 979, Montréal H3C 2W3. (☎800-363-7777. Open daily 9am-5pm.)

▨ **Centre International de Séjour (HI-C),** 19 rue Ste-Ursule (☎694-0755). From the bus station, take rue St-Nicolas uphill; stay with it as it changes to rue St-Vallier E and then to Côte du Palais. Turn right onto St-Jean, then left onto Ste-Ursule. If driving, follow St-Louis into the Old City and take the 2nd left past the walls onto Ste-Ursule. Diverse, young clientele, a fabulous location. Laundry, microwave, TV, pool table, ping-pong tables, living room, kitchen, Internet access, and in-house theater. The 250 beds fill up fast in July-Aug. Reduced-rate parking at a city garage. Check-out 10am. Lockout 11pm, but the front desk will let you in if you flash your key. Reservations recommended. $18, nonmembers $23; private rooms $46/50. ❶

Auberge de la Paix, 31 rue Couillard (☎694-0735). Take St-Jean into Vieux Québec; when it splits into 3, keep to the far left and you'll be on Couillard. Check yourself into this friendly, conveniently located "peace hostel" (look for the peace sign suspended above the door). There are no locks on the doors, but this doesn't seem to be a problem. Continental breakfast 8-10am. Linen $2.50. Curfew 2am, but 24hr. access to facilities. Reservations required July-Aug. 60 beds in 14 co-ed rooms $19. ❶

Montmartre Canadien, 1675 ch. St-Louis (☎686-0867). Take bus #25 or 11 if service hasn't been interrupted; best reached by car. On the outskirts of the city near Sillery, this small white house is ideal for those willing to trade proximity for privacy. Located in a religious sanctuary run by Assumptionist monks, the relaxing grounds verge on asceticism. Common showers. Reservations recommended 2-3 weeks in advance. Dirt-cheap, immaculate singles $17; doubles $30; triples $42. ❶

Municipal de Beauport, 95 rue de la Serenité (☎666-2228), in Beauport. Take Autoroute 40E, get off at Exit 321 at rue Labelle onto Hwy. 369, turn left, and follow the signs marked "camping." Bus #55 through 800 will also take you to this 135-site campground on a hill over the Montmorency River. Swimming pool and laundry facilities. Canoes $8 per hr. Showers 50¢ per 5min. Open June-early Sept. Sites $20, with hookup $25; $120/150 per week. ❶

L'HAUTE CUISINE

In general, rue Buade, St-Jean, and Cartier, as well as the **Place Royale** and **Petit Champlain** areas, offer the widest selection of food and drink. The **Grande Allée** may seem like heaven to the hungry, but its prices may encourage you to keep strolling. One of the most filling yet inexpensive meals is a *croque monsieur*, a large, open-faced sandwich with ham and melted cheese (about $6), usually served with salad. French onion soup, slathered with melted cheese, can be found in virtually every restaurant and cafe. It usually comes with baguettes or *tourtière*, a thick meat pie. Other specialties include the ever-versatile crepe.

▨ **Le Diable aux Anges,** 28 bd. Champlain and 39 rue du Petit-Champlain (☎692-4674). Absorbs the European aura of its dimly lit, colonial interior. A number of traditional *québécois* dishes and sinfully-named desserts add a seldom-found variety to the usual bistro cafe. Try the *oeuf gaspésien* (an English muffin topped with smoked salmon, poached egg, and hollandaise sauce; $10) with herbed potatoes and beans. Open daily 10am-11pm. ❷

▧ **Casse-Crêpe Breton,** 1136 rue St-Jean (☎ 692-0438), offers mix-and-match dinner crepes ($3.85-6.40) and mouth-watering desserts ($3-3.75). Grab a spot at the counter to watch the chef in action. Open daily 7:30am-midnight. ❶

Restaurant Liban, 23 rue d'Auteuil (☎ 694-1888), off rue St-Jean. Grab a falafel sandwich ($4.50) to go, or sit on the terrace and munch *tabouleh* (with pita $3.50) while watching the world go by. Open daily 9am-4:30am. ❶

Chez Temporel, 25 rue Couillard (☎ 694-1813). Stay off the touristy path at this genuine *café québécois*, discreetly tucked in a side alley off rue St-Jean, near the Auberge de la Paix. Besides the usual cafe staples, it offers some unique drinks ($4.50). Alcoholic drinks available with food. Salads and soups $4-7. Excellent quiches $6. Open daily 7am-2am. ❶

Le Café Buade, 31 rue Buade (☎ 692-3909), is renowned for its succulent prime rib ($15-20). For those a little shorter on money, breakfast ($4) and lunch specials ($11) are large and delicious. Open daily 7am-midnight. ❸

Le Cochon Dingue, 46 bd. Champlain (☎ 692-2013), which means "crazy pig," is quickly becoming a culinary landmark in Québec. Go hog-wild with a few extra chocolate pear pies ($4). Entrees $10. Open June-Aug. M-Th 7am-midnight, F 7am-1am, Sa-Su 8am-1am; Sept.-May M-F 7am-11pm, Sa-Su 8am-11pm. ❷

Pâtisserie au Palet d'Or, 60 rue Garneau (☎ 692-2488), at the juncture of Charlevoix, St-Jean, Couillard, Garneau, and de la Fabrique, is likewise affordably delicious. Score the *menu du jour* for $6.45: an entree, salad, beverage, and one of 40 sweet, doughy desserts. Open daily 7am-9pm. ❷

◉ SIGHTS

Inside the **Fortifications of Québec,** a 6.5km stretch of wall surrounding Vieux Québec, are most of the city's historic attractions. Monuments are clearly marked and explained, usually in French; you'll get more out of the town by consulting the *Greater Québec Area Tourist Guide*, available at any Visitors Center. Although it takes one to two days to explore all of Vieux Québec's narrow, hilly streets and historic sites on foot, this is by far the best way to absorb its charm. The ubiquitous **horse-drawn carriage tours,** while pricey ($50-70 per tour) can be fun. Find carriages on the Grande Allée, or call *Calèches du Vieux-Québec* (☎ 683-9222). The **Funiculaire** carries passengers between Upper-Town, Place Royal, and the Quartier Petit-Champlain. (☎ 692-1132. Open 7:30am-midnight. $1.25.)

BATTLEFIELDS. The **Parc des Champs-de-Bataille,** or **Plains of Abraham,** adjacent to the Citadel along av. George-VI accessible from Grande Allée, has on its grounds an astounding assortment of historical, cultural, and natural offerings. The **Discovery Pavilion,** near St-Louis Gate and the Manège Militaire, is the primary information desk for the park and houses the new multimedia **Canada Odyssey,** a virtual tour of Canadian history. *(Pavilion: ☎ 648-4071. Open mid-June to mid-Oct. daily 9am-5:30pm; mid-Oct. to mid-June 9am-5pm. $6.50, seniors and ages 13-17 $5.50, families $20. Canada Odyssey: ☎ 648-4071. Open mid-May to early Sept. daily 10am-5:30pm; call for off-season times. Multimedia show $3.50, seniors and ages 13-17 $2.75; families $10.)* To enjoy the beautiful natural setting of the battlefields, visit the **Jardin Jeanne d'Arc,** a serene spot with over 150 flower species. The **Martello Towers** present a look at the more personal side of military history, including exhibits in Tower 1 on the day-to-day lives of soldiers and in Tower 2 the "Council of War," an award-winning period mystery dinner. *(Tower 1: Open mid-June to Aug. daily 10am-5:30pm; Sept. to mid-Oct. Sa-Su 10am-5:30pm. $3.50, seniors and ages 13-17 $2.75, families $10. "Council of War:" ☎ 649-6157. Runs July-Aug. Sa in French, Su in English at 6pm; also on some holidays. $31.75, seniors and ages 13-17 $28.75. Reservations required.)* On the ground of the battlefields, the **Musée du Québec** houses eclectic modern and colonial art, focusing on the works of *québécois* artists. A permanent tactile exhibit is designed for blind visitors. *(☎ 643-2150. Open June-early Sept. M-Tu and Th-Su 10am-6pm, W 10am-9pm; mid-Sept. to May Tu and Th-Su 10am-5pm, W 10am-9pm. Free; special exhibits $10, students $5, seniors $9, ages 12-16 $3.)*

PLACE-ROYALE & QUARTIER PETIT-CHAMPLAIN. One of Old Québec's highlights is the crowded thoroughfare of **Rue du Petit-Champlain.** Along either side of this narrow passageway, visitors will find a host of cafes, craft shops, trendy boutiques, and restaurants. Each evening, the **Théâtre Petit Champlain** presents *québécois* music, singing, and dancing. *(68 rue du Petit-Champlain. ☎ 692-2631. Call for schedules. Most shows $25-30.)* The **Centre d'interprétation Place-Royale** provides free 45min. tours of **Place-Royale,** home to the oldest permanent European settlement in Canada (dating from 1608). *(Take rue Sous-le-Fort from the bottom of the Funiculaire. ☎ 643-6631. Open daily 10am-5pm.)* Dating back to 1688, **L'Eglise Notre-Dame-des-Victoires** is the oldest church in Canada. *(32 rue Sous-le-Fort. ☎ 692-1650. Open May to mid-Oct. M-F 9:30am-5pm, Sa-Su 9:30am-4:30pm; mid-Oct. to Apr. daily 10am-4:30pm. Admission and tours free.)* The **Musée de la Civilisation** celebrates Québec's past, present, and future with elaborate, themed exhibits. Follow the series of signs at the bottom of the Funiculaire. *(85 rue Dalhousie. ☎ 643-2158. Open late June-early Sept. daily 10am-7pm; mid-Sept. to mid-June Tu-Su 10am-5pm. $7, students $4, seniors $6.)*

CAP DIAMANT. Climbing to the top of Cap Diamant for a view of the city is a good way to get oriented. Just north is the **Citadel,** the largest North American fortification still guarded (somewhat inexplicably) by troops. *(On rue St-Louis at Côte de la Citadelle. Take Terrasse Dufferin to the Promenade des Gouverneurs. ☎ 694-2815. Open Apr. to mid-May daily 10am-4pm; mid-May to mid-June 9am-5pm; mid-June to Aug. 9am-6pm; Sept. 9am-4pm; Oct. 10am-3pm. Changing of the guard daily 10am. Beating of the retreat W-Sa 6pm. $6, seniors $5, under 18 $3, families $14.)*

PARLIAMENT HILL. Finished in 1886, the **Assemblée Nationale,** just outside the wall of the city, was designed in the style of Louis XIV. Lively debates can be observed from the visitors' gallery; simultaneous translation earphones are available for both English and French speakers. *(At ave. Dufferin and Grande Allée Est. ☎ 643-7239. Open late June to early Sept. M-F 9am-4:30pm, Sa-Su 10am-4:30pm; mid-Sept. to mid-June hours vary. 30min. tours free. Reservations recommended.)* The **Capital Observatory** offers breathtaking views of the city from 230m above sea level, the highest observing place in town. *(1037 rue de la Chevrotière, off Grande Allée. ☎ 644-9841. Open daily 10am-5pm. $4, students and seniors $3.)*

CHÂTEAU FRONTENAC. The **Château Frontenac,** with its grand architecture and green copper roofs, is perhaps the most recognizable structure in the city and is thought to be the most photographed hotel in the world. A costumed guide leads visitors through the former Governor's Palace, highlighting its place in history with photographs of famous visitors. *(1 rue des Carrières. ☎ 692-3861. Tours mid-May to mid-Oct. daily every hr. 10am-6pm; mid-Oct. to mid-May Sa-Su 1-5pm. Reservations highly recommended. $6.50, seniors $5.50, under 16 $3.75.)*

OTHER ATTRACTIONS. With its shimmering golden altar and ornate stained-glass windows, the **Basilique Notre-Dame de Québec** is one of the oldest and most stunning cathedrals in North America. The Basilique shows a fantastic 45min. light show, the **"Act of Faith,"** which relays the history of the church. *(At rue de Buade and rue Ste-Famille. ☎ 694-4000. Basilique open daily 9:30am-4:30pm. Free. Shows daily May-Oct.; times vary. $7.50, students and seniors $5, families $20.)* The **Musée de l'Amérique-française,** on the grounds of the **Québec Seminary** just down the street from the Basilica, is an excellent museum whose informative exhibits recount the details of Francophone settlement in North America. *(9 rue de l'Université. ☎ 692-2843. Open Tu-Su 10am-5pm. $4, students and seniors $3.)*

THE HIDDEN DEAL

FACE THE MUSIC

In the mood for music, Québec City style? Step into a *boîte aux chansons*, or "song bar," where live local musicians serenade the crowd every night (for animatronics see Disney World, p. 479). The selection ranges from rock and pop favorites *à la québécoise*—with hits by francophone stars like Jean Leloup and Daniel Bélanger—to original works by the artist of the night. Sometimes American oldies and *québécois* folk work their way into the program, and believe us, a bar full of Québeckers singing "California Dreamin'" is an experience not to be missed. The local favorite seems to be ◨ **Les Yeux Bleux**, where *chansonniers* sing from a candlelit stage dripping with the red wax of concerts past. Everyone feels like a regular in this cozy nook, which is definitely a high-energy, low-pressure introduction to the *boîte aux chansons* phenomenon. *(1117½ rue St-Jean.* ☎ *694-9118. No cover. 2-for-1 Beer May-Aug. F-Sa before 9pm and Su-Th before 10pm. Open daily 8pm-3am; arrive between 9-10pm for 10pm shows.)*

▣ FESTIVALS

Images of "Le Bonhomme de Neige" plaster the snow-covered city in anticipation of the raucous annual **Winter Carnival** (☎ 626-3716), which will break the tedium of northern winters from January 31 to February 16, 2003. The 36th annual **Summer Festival**, or **Festival d'Été** (☎ 529-5200), with free outdoor concerts, packs hostels and crowds the streets in mid-July. Throughout the summer, the **Plein Art** (☎ 694-0260) exhibition floods the Pigeonnier on the Grande-Allée with arts and crafts. Now in its 11th season, the **Edwin Bélanger Bandstand** hosts free outdoor concerts throughout the summer. (☎ 648-4050; www.ccbn-nbc.gc.ca. Parking during concerts $3.) **Les nuits Black**, Québec's main jazz festival, bebops the city for two weeks in late June. But Québec's most festive day of the year—eclipsing even Canada Day—is June 24, **la Fête nationale du Québec** or St-Jean-Baptiste Day (☎ 640-0799). This celebration of *québécois* culture features several free concerts, a bonfire, and 5 million rip-roaring drunk acolytes of John the Baptist.

◪ NIGHTLIFE

The Grande Allée's many restaurants are interspersed with *bar discothèques*, where twenty-somethings dance until dawn. Quebéc City's young, visible punk contingent clusters around rue St-Jean and several nearby sidestreets, but more laid-back nightclubs find a niche here, too. The gay scene in Québec City is limited.

Chez Dagobert, 600 Grande Allée Est (☎ 522-0393), saturates the air with pop and dance sounds that can be heard for blocks. Two dance floors and an adjoining bar give plenty of room to mingle. Outside bar open daily 2pm-2am; inside club 10pm-3am.

O'Zone, 570 Grande Allée (☎ 529-7932), is a bit less hectic than its neighbors. Folks linger at the bars (both the conventional and the fusion-sushi) before going to the 2nd-story dance floor for rock, dance, and hip-hop. Open M-Sa 11am-3am, Su 1pm-3am.

Le Ballon Rouge, 811 rue St-Jean (☎ 647-9227), several blocks beyond the walls of the Old City, is a favorite dance club where dimly lit pool tables coexist with neon rainbows. No cover. Open daily 5pm-3am.

La Fourmi Atomik, 33 rue d'Auteuil (☎ 694-1473), has underground rock and themed music nights. 18+. Open June-Sept. daily 1pm-3am; Oct.-May 4pm-3am.

L'Ostradamus, 29 rue Couillard (☎ 694-9560), injects live jazz and techno into its smoke-drenched, "spiritual" ambience. Cover $4. Open daily 8pm-3am.

▶ DAYTRIPS FROM QUÉBEC CITY

ÎLE-D'ORLÉANS

Originally named in honor of the god of wine (and sex), the **Île-d'Orléans** was first called *Île de Bacchus* because of the multitude of wild grapes fermenting there. The Île-d'Orléans remains a sparsely populated retreat made up of small villages and endless strawberry fields. The island is about 10km downstream from Québec on the St-Laurent, making it an ideal excursion by car (public transportation doesn't access the island, and the highway stretch to the island makes biking impossible). Take Hwy. 75 to Autoroute 440 Est, on to Hwy. 368, and cross over the only bridge leading to the island, Pont de l'Île. A tour of the island covers 64km.

STE-ANNE-DE-BEAUPRÉ

On the way out of Île-d'Orléans, turn east onto Hwy. 138/bd. Ste-Anne to view the splendid **Chute Montmorency** (Montmorency Falls). In winter, vapors from the falls form a frozen mist that screens the running water. About 20km farther along Hwy. 138 lies **Ste-Anne-de-Beaupré** (Orléans Express buses link it to Québec City for $5, see **Practical Information**). This small town's *raison d'être* is the famous double-spired **Basilique Ste-Anne-de-Beaupré,** 10018 av. Royale, which houses the alleged forearm bone of St. Anne, mother to the Virgin Mary. How did it get to Canada? The pilgrims who visit by the hundreds of thousands each year don't question the logistics; the racks of discarded crutches inside speak to the church's miraculous healing power. (☎ 827-3781. Open early May to mid-Sept. daily 6am-9:30pm.)

ONTARIO

Sitting in uneasy political tension with French Québec, this populous central province raises the ire of peripheral regions of Canada with its high concentration of power and wealth. In the south, world-class Toronto shines—multicultural, vibrant, clean, and generally safe. Middle-class suburbs, an occasional college town, and farms surround the city. On the Québec border sits the national capital Ottawa. To the north, layers of cottage country and ski resorts give way to a pristine wilderness that is as much French and Native Canadian as it is British.

▶ PRACTICAL INFORMATION

Capital: Toronto.

Visitor Info: Customer Service Branch of the **Ontario Ministry of Tourism, Culture, and Recreation** (☎ 800-668-2746; www.tourism.gov.on.ca; Tourism and Recreation, Hearst Block, 900 Bay St., Toronto, ON M7A 2E1).

Drinking Age: 19. **Postal Abbreviation:** ON. **Sales Tax:** 8% PST (rooms 5%), plus 7% GST.

EASTERN CANADA

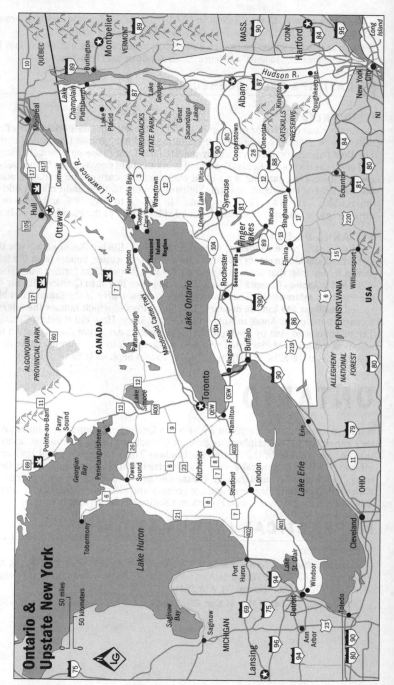

TORONTO ☎416

There's no denying that Toronto is a major city. When walking down the streets, however, it's difficult to tell which one. The skyscrapers and bustling financial district suggest New York, while the theater district recalls London. Conversations on the street could take place in Athens, Beijing, Paris, or Rio. In short, Toronto has earned its recent designation by the United Nations as the world's most multicultural city. A city so diverse might be expected to have something of an identity crisis, but residents are unified by their justifiable hometown pride.

✈ INTERCITY TRANSPORTATION

Airport: Pearson International (☎247-7678), about 20km west of Toronto via Hwy. 401. Take bus #58A west from Lawrence W subway. **Pacific Western Transportation** (☎905-564-6333) runs buses to downtown hotels every 20min. 5:30am-12:15am. $14.25, round-trip $24.50.

Trains: All trains leave from **Union Station,** 65 Front St. (☎366-8411), at Bay and York St. Subway: Union. Station open M-Sa 5:30am-12:45am, Su 6:30am-12:45am. **VIA Rail** (☎366-8411). Ticket office open M-F 6am-11:30pm, Sa 6am-6:30pm, Su 7am-11:30pm. To: **Chicago** (11hr., 1-2 per day, $160); **Montréal** (5½hr., 7 per day, $99); **New York City** (12hr., 1-2 per day, $95); and **Windsor** (4hr., 4-5 per day, $74).

Buses: Trentway-Wagar (☎393-7911) and **Greyhound** (☎367-8747) operate from the **Bay Street Terminal,** 610 Bay St., just north of Dundas St. Subway: St. Patrick or Dundas. Ticket office open daily 5am-1am. Trentway-Wagar has service to **Montréal** (7hr., 7 per day, $82). Greyhound goes to: **Calgary** (49hr., 3 per day, $161); **New York City** (11hr., 6 per day, $108); **Ottawa** (5½-7hr., 9 per day, $59); and **Vancouver** (2½ days, 3 per day, $182).

Jump-On/Jump-Off Service: Moose Travel Co. Ltd. (☎905-853-4762 or 888-816-6673). A series of expeditions, founded by former backpackers, lets you hop on and off a bus at dozens of destinations throughout Eastern Canada. Travel time as short as 4 days can spread over 5 months. Three routes through Ontario and Québec ($239-399) and discounted rail connections to western routes.

✦ ORIENTATION

Toronto's streets form a grid pattern. Addresses on north-south streets increase toward the north, away from **Lake Ontario. Yonge St.** is the main north-south route, dividing the cross streets into east and west. Numbering for both sides starts at Yonge St. and increases moving away in either direction. West of Yonge St., the main arteries are **Bay St., University Ave., Spadina Ave.,** and **Bathurst St.** The major east-west routes include, from the water moving northward, **Front, Queen, Dundas, College, Bloor,** and **Eglinton St.** For an extended stay or travel outside the city center, it is best to buy the *Downtown and Metro Toronto Visitor's Map Guide* from a drug store or tourist shop ($3). The *Ride Guide*, free at all TTC stations and info booths, explains metro area transit.

NEIGHBORHOODS

Downtown Toronto splits into many distinctive neighborhoods. **Chinatown** centers on Dundas St. W between Bay St. and Spadina Ave. Formerly the Jewish market of the 1920s, **Kensington Market,** on Kensington Ave., Augusta Ave., and the western half of Baldwin St., is now a largely Portuguese neighborhood with many good restaurants, vintage clothing shops, and an outdoor bazaar. The strip of old factories,

EASTERN CANADA

EASTERN CANADA

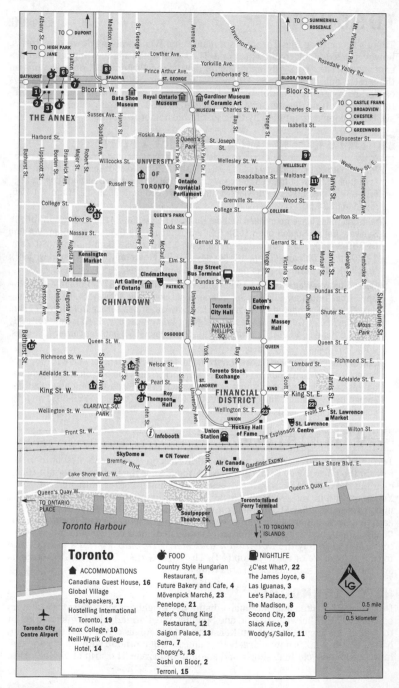

Toronto

🔺 **ACCOMMODATIONS**

Canadiana Guest House, **16**
Global Village
Backpackers, **17**
Hostelling International
Toronto, **19**
Knox College, **10**
Neill-Wycik College
Hotel, **14**

✈ **Toronto City
Centre Airport**

🍎 **FOOD**

Country Style Hungarian
Restaurant, **5**
Future Bakery and Cafe, **4**
Mövenpick Marché, **23**
Penelope, **21**
Peter's Chung King
Restaurant, **12**
Saigon Palace, **13**
Serra, **7**
Shopsy's, **18**
Sushi on Bloor, **2**
Terroni, **15**

🍸 **NIGHTLIFE**

¿C'est What?, **22**
The James Joyce, **6**
Las Iguanas, **3**
Lee's Palace, **1**
The Madison, **8**
Second City, **20**
Slack Alice, **9**
Woody's/Sailor, **11**

0   0.5 mile
0   0.5 kilometer

stores, and warehouses on **Queen St. W,** from University Ave. to Bathurst St., is a good place to shop during the day and go club-hopping at night. The ivy-covered Gothic buildings and magnificent quadrangles of the **University of Toronto (U of T)** occupy about 200 acres in the center of the city. **The Annex,** on Bloor St. W, at the Spadina subway, has an artistic ambience and an excellent range of budget restaurants. Afterwards, hit the numerous bars and nightclubs along Bloor St. heading west. **Yorkville,** just north of Bloor between Yonge St. and Avenue Rd., was once the communal home of flower children and folk guitarists. **Cabbagetown,** just east of Yonge St., bounded by Gerrard St. E, Wellesley, and Sumach St., takes its name from the Irish immigrants who used to plant the vegetable in their yards. The **Gay and Lesbian Village,** around Church and Wellesley St., has fine outdoor cafes.

On Front St. between Sherbourne and Yonge St., the **Theater District** supports enough venues to whet any cultural appetite. Music, food, ferry rides, dance companies, and artists all dock at the **Harbourfront** (☎973-3000), on Queen's Quay W along the lake from York to Bathurst St. The three main **Toronto Islands,** accessible by ferry (see **Local Transportation,** below), offer beaches, bike rentals, and an amusement park. East from the harbor, the beaches along and south of Queen's St. E, between Woodbine and Victoria, boast a popular boardwalk. 5km east of the city center, the rugged stretch of **Scarborough Bluffs** rises over the lakeshore. Three more ethnic enclaves lie 15-30min. from downtown by public transit. **Corso Italia** surrounds St. Clair W at Dufferin St.; take the subway to St. Clair W and bus #512 west. **Little India** is at Gerrard St. E and Coxwell; ride the subway to Coxwell, then take bus #22 south to the second Gerard St. stop. Better known as **"the Danforth,"** **Greektown** (subway: Pape) is on Danforth Ave. at Pape Ave.

⬕ LOCAL TRANSPORTATION

The **Toronto Transit Commission's (TTC)** subway and streetcars are the easiest way to get around the city, but if you must drive, avoid rush hour (4-7pm). A flashing green light means that you can go straight or turn left freely, as the opposing traffic has a red light. Pedestrians should exercise caution when crossing the streets; they do not necessarily have the legal right of way. **Parking** on the street is hard to find and usually carries a 1hr. limit, except on Sunday and at night (until 7am), when spaces are free and abundant. Day parking generally costs inbound daytrippers $3-4 at outlying subway stations; parking overnight at the subway stations is prohibited. Parking lots within the city run at least $12 for 24 hours (7am-7pm). Free parking is available in **Rosedale,** a residential neighborhood northeast of Bloor and Sherbourne St., about 3km from downtown. To combat transportation problems, city officials enforce traffic and parking regulations zealously—don't tempt them. Towing is a common occurrence, even for locals; the **non-emergency police number** (☎808-2222) has an answering system to help recover towed cars.

Ferries: Toronto Island Ferry Service (☎392-8194, recording ☎392-8193). Ferries to Centre Island, Hanlans Point, and Wards Island leave from the foot of Bay St. Service daily every 1-1½hr.; call for exact schedule. Round-trip $5; students, seniors, and ages 15-19 $3; ages 2-14 $2.

Public Transit: Toronto Transit Commission (☎393-4636) has a network of 2 long subway lines, supplemented by and connected to many bus and streetcar routes. Buses are required to stop anywhere along a route at a female passenger's request 9pm-5am. Subway service begins M-Sa 6am, Su 9am; last trains leave downtown at 1:30am. Buses cover subway routes after 1:30am. Fare $2.25, 11 tokens for $20; students with ID and seniors $1.50; under 13 50¢, 10 tokens for $4. M-Sa 1-day travel pass $7.50. Su and holidays unlimited travel for families $7.50. Free transfers at stations among subway, buses, and streetcars.

Taxis: Co-op Cabs, ☎ 504-2667.

Bike Rental: Brown's Sports and Bike Rental, 2447 Bloor St. W (☎ 763-4176). $22 per day, $45 per weekend, $55 per week. $300 deposit or credit card required. Open M-W 9:30am-6pm, Th-F 9:30am-8pm, Sa 9:30am-5:30pm.

🚹 PRACTICAL INFORMATION

Visitor info: The **Metropolitan Toronto Convention and Visitors Association (MTCVA),** 207 Queens Quay W (☎ 203-2500 or 800-363-1990), mails out information packets and provides a comprehensive automated phone system for answering questions.

Budget Travel: Travel CUTS, 187 College St. (☎ 979-2406), just west of University Ave. Subway: Queen's Park. Open M and Th-F 9am-5pm, Tu 9:30am-5pm, W 9am-7pm, Sa 10am-3pm.

Currency Exchange: Toronto Currency Exchange, 363 Yonge St. (☎ 598-3769), at Dundas St., offers the best rates around. Open M-Sa 10am-8pm, Su 11am-7pm. Another location at 2 Walton St. (☎ 599-5821). Open daily 10am-7pm. **Royal Bank of Canada,** 200 Bay St. Plaza (☎ 800-769-2511), exchanges around the city. Branches generally open M-F 10am-4pm; call for each branch's specific hours.

Hotlines: Rape Crisis, ☎ 597-8808. **Services for the Disabled, Info Ability,** ☎ 800-665-9092. Both 24hr. **Toronto Gay and Lesbian Phone Line,** ☎ 964-6600. Open M-F 7-10pm.

Post Office: Adelaide Station, 31 Adelaide St. E (☎ 214-2353). Subway: King. Open M-F 8am-5:45pm. **Postal code:** M5C 1J0. **Area code:** 416 (city), 905 (outskirts). In text, 416 unless noted otherwise.

🏠 ACCOMMODATIONS

Cut-rate hotels concentrate around Jarvis and Gerrard St. The University of Toronto provides cheap sleep for budget travelers; contact the **U of T Housing Service,** 214 College St., at St. George St. (☎ 978-8045. Open M-F 8:45am-5pm. Rooms $20-45.) The **Downtown Association of Bed and Breakfast Guest Houses** places guests in renovated Victorian homes. (☎ 483-8032. Singles $50-85; doubles $75-130.) It is difficult to regulate these registries, so visit a B&B before committing.

Canadiana Guest House & Backpackers, 42 Widmer St. (☎ 598-9090 or 877-215-1225), off Adelaide St. W. Subway: Osgoode. An assortment of young, adventurous professionals populate the Canadiana, whose wooden beds and Victorian facade create a calm, refined atmosphere. Its central location is near several hot. 70 beds, A/C, kitchen, and Internet access. Lockers $1. Laundry $3. Check-in 8am-11pm. Check-out 10:30am. Dorms $27; private doubles $60. Discounts for ISIC or HI cardholders. ❶

Global Village Backpackers, 460 King St. W (☎ 703-8540 or 888-844-7875). Subway: St. Andrew. 195 beds and an in-house bar make this former hotel a prime piece of backpacking real estate. Kitchen, Internet, and a Travel CUTS branch. Nightly barbecues 7-9:30pm Lockers $1. Laundry $1.50. Reception 24hr. Bed in dorm for 6-10 people $25, in 4-person dorm $27; private doubles in summer $60, slightly less off-season. $2-4 off for ISIC or HI members. ❶

Neill-Wycik College Hotel, 96 Gerrard St. E (☎ 977-2320 or 800-268-4358). Subway: Dundas. Tucked into the heart of the city, the hotel offers tidy rooms and an unbeatable panoramic view. Enjoy a relaxing and picturesque lounge on the roof deck. Kitchen on every floor. Sauna, family rooms, and lockers available. Breakfast cafe open early May-late Aug. 7-11am. Open early May to late Aug. Laundry $2. Check-in after 4pm. Check-out 10am. Dorms $24.40. Singles $42.50; students, seniors, and HI members $34. Family rooms $70, HI members $56. ❶

Knox College, 59 St. George St. (☎978-0168). Subway: Queen's Park or St. George. This genteel Presbyterian seminary boasts huge rooms, wooden floors, and a location right on the U of T campus. Office open M-F 10am-5pm. Reserve rooms at least 3 weeks in advance. Open mid-May to late Aug. Singles $56, students $40; doubles $70. ❷

Hostelling International Toronto (HI-C), 76 Church St. (☎971-4440 or 877-848-8737), at King St. Subway: King. Recently relocated hostel in a great downtown location. Kitchen, outdoor patio, and Internet access. Linen $2. Laundry $3. Reception 24hr. Check-in after noon. Check-out 11am. Reservations recommended in the summer. Dorms $20, nonmembers $24. Additional location June-Aug. at 160 Mutual St. (☎971-7073). Dorms $22.50/27. ❶

◨ FOOD

Toronto's multiculturalism is most gloriously evident in its culinary scene. With over 5,000 metropolitan-area restaurants trying to out-cook each other, an amazing meal is found on almost any street. "L.L.B.O." (for "Liquor Licensing Board of Ontario") signs indicate that alcohol is available. **Village by the Grange,** at McCaul and Dundas near the Art Gallery of Ontario, is home to a super-cheap restaurants and food stands. For fresh produce, try **Kensington Market** or the **St. Lawrence Market,** at King and Sherbourne St., six blocks east of the King subway stop.

THE ANNEX

▨ **Serra,** 378 Bloor St. W (☎922-6999). Subway: Spadina. Cool but not intimidating, slightly upscale but not exorbitant, and delicious beyond all expectations, Serra is an oasis amid the bustle of the Annex. Goat cheese *angolotti* with basil cream sauce $14. Open daily noon-10pm; closing times vary. ❸

Country Style Hungarian Restaurant, 450 Bloor St. W (☎537-1745). Subway: Bathurst. Plan to arrive famished and leave stuffed—the generous cooks load your plate with enough schnitzel ($9.75) and other traditional Hungarian goodies to feed you for days. Daily specials $9.50-$12. Raspberry soda $1.95. Open daily 11am-10pm. ❷

Future Bakery & Cafe, 483 Bloor St. W (☎922-5875). Subway: Bathurst. Fresh cakes ($4) and huge breakfast pastries charge up the young student crowd by day, and beer ($4-5) on the patio winds them down after dark. Open Su-Th 7:30am-12:30am, F-Sa 7:30am-1:30am. ❶

Sushi on Bloor, 515 Bloor St. W (☎516-3456). Subway: Bathurst. One of the many sushi joints crowding into the Annex, Sushi on Bloor stands out with its pleasantly bright lighting and friendly staff. Fresh sushi (6 pieces) $4-5. Lunch and dinner specials from $5.50. Open M-Th noon-10:45pm, F-Sa noon-11pm, Su noon-10pm. ❶

CHINATOWN

▨ **Peter's Chung King Restaurant,** 281 College St. W (☎928-2936). Subway: Spadina. A picture of Chris de Burgh (of "Lady in Red" fame) adorns the window, with a note proclaiming "Wonderful Food!" Chris is not the only one who thinks so—Peter's is consistently named one of Toronto's best Chinese restaurants. Garlic shrimp $9. Soy-sauteed green beans $7. Open M-Th noon-10pm, F noon-11pm, Sa 1-11pm, Su 1-10pm. ❷

Saigon Palace, 454 Spadina Ave. (☎968-1623), at College St. Subway: Spadina. An inexpensive Vietnamese restaurant with great spring rolls and a wide array of exotic juices ($3). Be sure to specify if ordering vegetarian rolls. Beef or vegetable dishes over rice $4-8. Open M-Th noon-10pm, F noon-11pm, Sa 1-11pm, Su 1-10pm. ❶

THEATER/ST. LAWRENCE DISTRICT

▓ **Terroni,** 720 Queen St. W (☎ 504-0320). Named for a derogatory description of Southern Italians (*terroni* means "people of the earth" or, basically, "dirty, muddy people"), Terroni brings a gentle irreverence to both its food and its atmosphere. Imagine someone's no-nonsense Italian granny catering a Fortune 500 luncheon to get an idea of the mixture of hearty portions and sophisticated cuisine. They're most famous for their pizzas ($9-13), but their *rigatoni al gorgonzola* ($14) is truly excellent. The deli section is also well worth a visit. Open daily 11am-11pm. ❷

▓ **Penelope,** 225 King St. W (☎ 351-9393 or 877-215-4026). Subway: St. Andrew. Attentive service and mouth-watering food in the relaxing atmosphere of a Grecian resort. Pre-theater dinner special around $11. Roast lamb $13. Open M-W 11:30am-10pm, Th-F 11:30am-11:30pm, Sa 4:30-11:30pm. ❷

Mövenpick Marché, 161 Bay St. (☎ 366-8986), in BCE Place at Yonge and Front St. A combination restaurant and produce market the size of some department stores (and every bit as complex), Mövenpick allows diners to browse through 14 culinary stations in order to customize their meals. Avoid lines by taking a meal to go. Entrees $8-10. Open in summer daily 7:30am-4am; in winter 7:30am-2am. ❷

Shopsy's, 284A King St. W (☎ 599-5464). Other locations at 33 Yonge St. (☎ 365-3333), and 1535 Yonge St. (☎ 967-5252). The definitive Toronto deli, with 300 seats and snappy service. Hot dog $3.79. Open M 6:30am-10pm, Tu-W 6:30am-11pm, Th-F 6:30am-midnight, Sa 8am-midnight, Su 8am-9pm. ❶

◎ SIGHTS

One of Toronto's most interesting activities is also its cheapest thrill: walking through the busy streets. Streetside conversations change languages frequently, architectural wonders dazzle pedestrians, and the main thoroughfares are usually full of frenetic activity. For an organized expedition, the **Royal Ontario Museum** leads ten **free walking tours.** (☎ 586-5513. Tours June-Sept. W 6pm and Su 2pm. Destinations and meeting places vary; call for specific info.) Free 1hr. walking tours of the **University of Toronto,** Canada's largest university, depart from the Nona MacDonald Visitors Centre at King's College Circle. (☎ 978-5000. Tours June-Aug. M-F 11am and 2pm, Sa-Su 11am.)

CN TOWER. Toronto's **CN Tower** stands as the world's tallest free-standing structure. It also contains the world's highest wine cellar and longest metal stairway. The mammoth concrete symbol of human ingenuity is visible from nearly every corner of the city. The tower offers a heavenly view, and despite the frightening void below, trusting souls can lie down on the observation deck's sturdy glass floor. (*301 Front St. W. Subway: Union.* ☎ *360-8500. Tower open daily 8am-11pm; inside attractions 9am-9pm. $16, seniors $14, ages 4-12 $11; additional $7.50 for the Sky Pod. Combined admission to tower, attractions, and Sky Pod available; call to inquire.*)

GOVERNMENT. Curving twin towers and a two-story rotunda make up the innovative **City Hall,** brochures available for self-guided tours of this 1960s creation. (*Subway: Osgoode.* ☎ *338-0338. Open M-F 8:30am-4:30pm.*) In front of City Hall, **Nathan Phillips Sq.** is home to a reflecting pool that becomes a skating rink in winter. Numerous events, including live music every Wednesday (June to early Oct. noon-2pm), also happen on the square. The Ontario government meets in the stately **Provincial Parliament Buildings,** at Queen's Park in the city center. (*Subway: Queen's Park.* ☎ *325-7500. 30min. tours late May-early Sept. daily 9am-4pm. Call ahead for Parliamentary schedule. Free gallery passes available at south basement door when the House is in session.*)

SPADINA HOMES. Straight from a fairy tale, the 98-room **Casa Loma,** atop a hill near Spadina, is a classic tourist attraction. An eerie underground tunnel and two imposing towers add to the grandeur of this display of late-Victorian opulence. *(Subway: Dupont, then walk a few blocks north.* ☎ *923-1171. Open daily 9:30am-4pm. $13, seniors and ages 14-17 $9, ages 4-13 $7. Parking $2.30 per hour.)* Visitors are treated to a tour of 19th-century Toronto next door at the **Spadina House,** a six-acre estate relic from 1866. *(285 Spadina Rd.* ☎ *392-6910. Open Apr.-Sept. Tu-Su noon-5pm. $5, seniors and ages 12-17 $3.25, ages 6-11 $3.)*

WILDLIFE. The **Metro Toronto Zoo** keeps over 6600 animals in a 710-acre park that re-creates the world's seven geographic regions and features rare wildlife including a Tasmanian devil. *(Meadowvale Rd. off Exit 389 on Hwy. 401. Take bus #86A from Kennedy Station.* ☎ *392-5900. Open late May to early Sept. 9am-7:30pm; mid-Oct. to mid-Mar. daily 9:30am-4:30pm; mid-Mar. to mid-May and early Sept. to mid-Oct. 9am-6pm. Last entry 1hr. before closing. $15, seniors $11, ages 4-14 $9. Parking $6.)*

HOCKEY. No trip to Toronto is complete without a visit to the **Hockey Hall of Fame,** the cathedral for Canada's religiously-devoted sports fans. A beautiful stained glass dome in the 100-year-old **Great Hall** houses hockey's Holy Grail, the Stanley Cup. If not in the mood for idle veneration, interactive exhibits and play-by-plays of historical hockey moments provide an opportunity for more active enjoyment. *(In BCE Place, 30 Yonge St. Subway: BCE Place.* ☎ *360-7765. Open mid-June to early Sept. M-Sa 9:30am-6pm, Su 10am-6pm; mid-Sept. to early June M-F 10am-5pm, Sa 9:30am-6pm, Su 10:30am-5pm. $12, seniors and under 18 $7.)*

🏛 MUSEUMS

Art Gallery of Ontario (AGO), 317 Dundas St. (☎ 979-6648), on 3 blocks of University Ave. downtown. Subway: St. Patrick. Showcases an enormous collection of Western art from the Renaissance to the 1990s, with a particular focus on the works of Canadian artists. Last year's special exhibits featured dog portraitist William Wegman and masterworks of Surrealism. Open Tu and Th-F 11am-6pm, W 11am-8:30pm, Sa-Su 10am-5:30pm. $12, students with ID and seniors $9, ages 6-15 $6; W 6-8:30pm free. Admission to special exhibits extra; call for specifics.

Royal Ontario Museum (ROM), 100 Queen's Park (☎ 586-5549), across the street from the Gardiner Museum. Subway; Museum. Houses artifacts from ancient civilizations, a bat cave, and a giant *T. rex.* Open M-Th and Sa 10am-6pm, F 10am-9:30pm, Su 11am-6pm. $15, students and seniors $10, ages 5-14 $8; F after 4:30pm free. Admission to special exhibits extra; call for specifics.

Ontario Science Center, 770 Don Mills Rd. (☎ 696-3127), at Eglinton Ave. E, presents more than 650 interactive exhibits showcasing humanity's greatest innovations. Open daily 10am-6pm. $13, seniors and ages 13-17 $9, ages 5-12 $7; with Omnimax film $18/12/10.

Bata Shoe Museum, 327 Bloor St. (☎ 979-7799). Subway: St. George or Spadina. Walk a mile in a medieval knight's metal boots or in the tiny Chinese slippers that once contained bound feet. The diverse collection focuses on the often stepped-over role of footwear in human culture. Open M-W and F-Sa 10am-5pm, Th 10am-8pm, Su noon-5pm. $6, students and seniors $4, ages 2-14 $2, families $13; 1st Tu of every month free.

George R. Gardiner Museum of Ceramic Art, 111 Queen's Park (☎ 586-8080). Subway: Museum. Traces the history of ceramics. Open M, W, and F 10am-6pm; Tu, Th 10am-8pm; Sa-Su 10am-5pm. $10, students and seniors $6; 1st Tu of every month free.

> **GET OFF MY BACK** If you find the subway crowded but don't want to hail a cab, rickshaws will sweep you off your feet. Originally from Hong Kong, these human-drawn carriages have caught on all over Canada. In Toronto, companies like **Rickshaw Services of Toronto** (☎410-4593) will cart you through the city streets courtesy of other people's backs. Rates are about $3 per block per person.

🎭 ENTERTAINMENT

The monthly *Where Toronto*, available free at tourist booths, gives the lowdown on arts and entertainment. **T.O. Tix**, 208 Yonge St., north of Queen St. at Eaton's Centre, sells half-price tickets on performance day. (Subway: Queen. ☎536-6468. Open Tu-Sa noon-7:30pm; arrive before 11:45am for first dibs.) **Ticketmaster** (☎870-8000) offers tickets for many Toronto venues but requires a hefty service charge.

Ontario Place, 955 Lakeshore Blvd. W, features cheap summer entertainment, including music and light shows. (☎314-9811, recording ☎314-9900. Park open mid-May to early Sept. daily 10:30am-midnight.) Top pop artists perform in the **Molson Amphitheater**, 909 Lakeshore Blvd. W. (☎260-5600. Tickets through Ticketmaster $20-125.) **Roy Thompson Hall**, 60 Simcoe St., at King St. W, is both Toronto's premier concert hall and the home of the **Toronto Symphony Orchestra** from September to June. (Subway: St. Andrews. ☎593-4828, box office ☎872-4255. Open M-F 10am-6pm, Sa noon-5pm, Su 2hr. before performances. $25-85; matinees $25-50. $15 rush tickets available on concert days M-F 11am and Sa 1pm.)

The **St. Lawrence Centre**, 27 Front St. E, stages excellent drama and chamber music recitals. (☎366-7723. Box office open in summer M-Sa 10am-6pm; in winter performance days 10am-8pm, non-performance days 10am-6pm. Some student and senior discounts.) **Canadian Stage** performs free summer Shakespeare ($12 donation suggested) at **High Park**, on Bloor St. W, at Parkside Dr. Year-round shows at the St. Lawrence Centre include new Canadian works and classics. (Subway: High Park. Box office ☎368-3110. Open M-Sa 10am-6pm. Call for schedule.) Several blocks west in the Harbourfront Centre, the **Soulpepper Theatre Company**, 231 Queen's Quay W, presents famous masterpieces. (☎973-4000. $21-45, students $25, rush tickets $18.)

Canada's answer to Disney is **Canada's Wonderland**, 9580 Jane St., 1hr. from downtown. Splash down water rides or ride on coasters at Canada's premier amusement park. (☎905-832-7000. Open late June to early Sept. daily 10am-10pm; in fall Sa-Su, times vary. Waterpark open in summer daily 11am-7pm. $45, seniors and ages 3-6 $24.) The park is accessible by public transit; take **Vaughn Transit** (☎905-762-2100) from the Richmond Hill area or the **Go Bus** (☎869-3200; one-way $3.75) from the Yorkdale or York Mills subway station.

From April to early October, the **Toronto Blue Jays** play hardball at the enormous, modern **Sky Dome**, at Front and Peter St. (Subway: Union, follow the signs. ☎341-1111, tickets ☎341-1234. $7-42.) To get an inside look at the Sky Dome, take the tour. (☎341-2770. Times vary. $12.50, seniors and under 16 $8.50.) The Sky Dome is also the home to the **Toronto Argonauts** (☎489-2746) of the Canadian Football League, as well as concerts (☎341-3663) and other events throughout the year. Hockey fans head for **The Air Canada Centre**, 40 Bay St., to see the **Maple Leafs**. (Subway: Union. ☎815-5700. Tickets $30-160.)

Film fans choose the **Bloor Cinema**, 506 Bloor St. W (☎532-6677), at Bathurst St., or the **Cinématheque Ontario**, 317 Dundas St. W (☎923-3456), at McCaul St. **Cineforum**, 463 Bathurst (☎605-6643), offers an eccentric selection of obscure classics and art films; call for current schedule. Toronto's rich cultural offerings include several world-class **festivals**. The ten-day **Toronto International Film Festival** (☎967-

7371), Sept. 4-13, 2003, is one of the most prestigious festivals on the art-house circuit, with its showings of classic, Canadian, and foreign films. In June, the **Toronto International Dragon Boat Race Festival** (☎598-8945) continues a 2000-year-old Chinese tradition replete with great food and performances. In late August, the **Canadian National Exhibition (CNE)**, the world's largest annual fair, brings an international carnival to Exhibition Place. (☎393-6000. Open daily 10am-midnight. $9, seniors and under 6 $6.) In late June, the city also rocks with the second-largest **Gay Pride celebration** in the world, while in mid-July a growing **street festival** and **fringe theater festival** come to the city.

☑ NIGHTLIFE

Toronto offers a seemingly limitless selection of bars, pubs, dance clubs, and late-night cafes, including the **Second Cup Coffee Co.**, which has branches all over town. The city stops alcohol distribution nightly at 2am, which is when most clubs close down. New clubs are always opening on trendy **Queen St. W** in the **Entertainment District**, on **College St. W**, and on **Bloor St. W.** The free entertainment magazines *Now* and *Eye* come out every Thursday. The gay scene centers on **Wellesley** and **Church St.** For info, pick up the free, biweekly *fab*.

THE ANNEX

▨ **The James Joyce,** 386 Bloor St. (☎324-9400). Subway: Spadina. Live Celtic music every night makes this traditional Irish pub even more Irish than its expatriate namesake. Open daily noon-2am.

The Madison, 14 Madison Ave. (☎927-1722), at Bloor St. Subway: Spadina. One pool room, 4 patios, and a laid-back but crowded atmosphere attract students and yuppies. 16 beers on tap. Pints $5. Wings $9. Open daily 11am-2am.

Lee's Palace, 529 Bloor St. W (☎532-7632). Subway: Bathurst, then walk east. Live alternative music nightly downstairs. Box office opens 8pm, shows begin 10pm. Cover $3-20. Open M-Sa 10pm-2am. A batcave-like DJ dance club, the **Dance Cave,** swings upstairs. Cover after 10pm $4. Open M and Th-Su 9pm-3am, sometimes later.

Las Iguanas, 513 Bloor St. W (☎532-3360). Subway: Bathurst. This kitschy, friendly Mexican bar and grill offers a break from yuppiedom with faux-calfskin booths and beer ($4-5). Sa is cheap nachos night. Open M-F noon-2am, Sa-Su 11am-2am.

DOWNTOWN

▨ **The Second City,** 56 Blue Jays Way (☎343-0011 or 888-263-4485), at Wellington St., just north of the Sky Dome. Subway: Union. One of North America's wackiest, most creative comedy clubs that has spawned comics Dan Akroyd, John Candy, Martin Short, Mike Myers, and a hit TV show (SCTV). Free improv sessions M-Th 9:30pm and Sa midnight. Free F midnight howl with guest improv troupe. Shows M-Th 8pm $21, F-Sa 8pm and 10:30pm $25-27, Su touring company's production $14. Reservations required.

C'est What?, 67 Front St. E (☎867-9499). Subway: Union. This mellow cafe/pub is a great showcase for local and underground musical talent, as well as local alcohol—try their homemade microbrews and wines while listening. Open M-F noon-2am, Sa-Su 11am-2am.

THE GAY & LESBIAN VILLAGE

Woody's/Sailor, 465-467 Church St. (☎972-0887), by Maitland St. Subway: Wellesley. *The* gay bar in the Church and Wellesley area, famous throughout Canada. Don't miss "Bad Boys Night Out" Tu and "Best Chest" Th at midnight. Bottled beer $4.75. Open daily noon-2am.

Slack Alice, 562 Church St. (☎969-8742). Subway: Wellesley. This cafe and bar offers international food, a patio, and a happy hour from 4-7pm. The crowd is mostly gay and lesbian, but straight-friendly. DJ and dancing on weekends. Entrees $9-27. Open daily 11am-2am.

⚄ DAYTRIPS FROM TORONTO

ONATION'S NIAGARA ESCARPMENT

As beautiful as its name is strange, Onation's Niagara Escarpment passes west of Toronto as it winds its way from Niagara Falls to Tobermory at the tip of the Bruce Peninsula. Along this rocky 724km ridge, the **Bruce Trail** snakes through parks and private land. Hikers are treated to spectacular waterfalls, the breathtaking cliffs along **Georgian Bay,** and unique flora and fauna. Because the Escarpment is registered as a UN world biosphere reserve, future land development must exist symbiotically with the natural environment. For maps and Escarpment info, write or call the **Niagara Escarpment Commission,** 232 Guelph St., Georgetown, ON L7G 4B1 (☎905-877-5191). Specifics on the Bruce Trail can be obtained from the **Bruce Trail Association,** P.O. Box 857, Hamilton, ON L8N 3N9 (☎905-529-6821).

STRATFORD

The **Stratford Shakespeare Festival,** held in nearby Stratford since 1953, has proven to be the lifeblood of this picturesque town, named for the Bard's own village. The renowned festival runs from early May to early November with about 15 Shakespearean and non-Shakespearean plays performed in three theaters. The **Festival Theatre,** 55 Queen St., the **Avon Theatre,** 99 Downie St., and the **Tom Patterson Theatre,** 111 Lakeside Dr., host most of the action. (☎800-567-1600; www.stratfordfestival.ca. Box office open M-Sa 9am-8pm, Su 9am-2pm. July-Aug. up to 6 shows per day Tu-Su. Matinees 2pm, evening performances 8pm. $49-79. Rush tickets $38-50 at 9am on the morning of the show at the box office or theater, 9:30am by phone. Sept. and Nov. matinees student and senior tickets from $22; general student discounts $27. Some performances in the fall are half-price.)

OTTAWA ☎613

Legend has it that in the mid-19th century, Queen Victoria chose Ottawa as Canada's capital by closing her eyes and pointing a finger at a map. In reality, perhaps political savvy, rather than blind chance, guided her to this once remote logging town. As a stronghold for neither the French nor English, Ottawa was the perfect compromise. Faced with the tough task of forging national unity while preserving local identities, Ottawa continues to play cultural diplomat to larger Canada.

▰ TRANSPORTATION

Airport: Ottawa International (☎248-2125), 20min. south of the city off Bronson Ave. Take bus #97 from MacKenzie King Bridge. Info desk in arrival area open 9am-9pm. **Kasbary Transport, Inc.** (☎736-9993) runs shuttles between the airport and all downtown hotels every 30min. 4:40am-2am; call for later pickup. $9, seniors and ages 11-18 $6. Call for pickup from smaller hotels.

Trains: VIA Rail, 200 Tremblay Rd. (☎244-8289), east of downtown, off the Queensway at Alta Vista Rd. Ticket office open M-F 5am-9pm, Sa 6:30am-7pm, Su 8:20am-9pm. To: **Montréal** (2hr., 4 per day, $40); **Québec City** via Montréal (7hr., 2 per day, $75); and **Toronto** (4hr., 5 per day, $85).

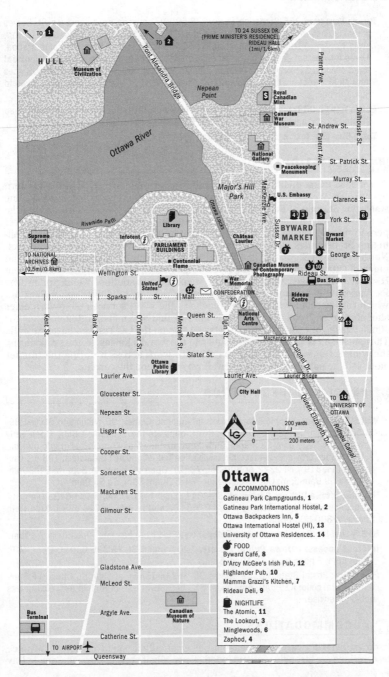

EASTERN CANADA

Ottawa

🏠 ACCOMMODATIONS
Gatineau Park Campgrounds, **1**
Gatineau Park International Hostel, **2**
Ottawa Backpackers Inn, **5**
Ottawa International Hostel (HI), **13**
University of Ottawa Residences. **14**

🍴 FOOD
Byward Café, **8**
D'Arcy McGee's Irish Pub, **12**
Highlander Pub, **10**
Mamma Grazzi's Kitchen, **7**
Rideau Deli, **9**

🌙 NIGHTLIFE
The Atomic, **11**
The Lookout, **3**
Minglewoods, **6**
Zaphod, **4**

Buses: Voyageur, 265 Catherine St. (☎238-5900), between Kent and Lyon St. Serves primarily Eastern Canada. Station open daily 6:30am-12:30am. To **Montréal** (2½hr., every hr. 7am-11pm, $29). **Greyhound** (☎237-7038) leaves from the same station, bound for Western Canada and southern Ontario, and runs to **Québec City** via **Montréal** (6hr., every hr., $64.20) and **Toronto** (5hr., 7 per day, $56.50). Service to the US goes through Montréal or Toronto. Blue **Hull City** buses (☎819-770-3242) connect Ottawa to Hull, Québec, across the river.

Public Transit: OC Transpo, 1500 St. Laurent (☎741-4390). Buses congregate at Rideau Centre. $2.25, ages 6-11 $1.25; express (green buses) $3.50.

Taxis: Blue Line Taxi, ☎238-1111. **Capital,** ☎744-3333.

ORIENTATION

The **Rideau Canal** divides Ottawa into the eastern lower town and the western upper town. West of the canal, Parliament buildings and government offices line **Wellington St.**, one of the city's main east-west arteries, running directly into the heart of downtown and crossing the canal. **Laurier** is the only other east-west street permitting traffic from one side of the canal to the other. East of the canal, Wellington St. becomes **Rideau St.**, surrounded by a fashionable shopping district. North of Rideau St., the **Byward Market** hosts a summertime open-air market and much of Ottawa's nightlife. **Elgin St.**, a primary north-south artery stretching from Hwy. 417 (the Queensway) to the War Memorial just south of Wellington nearby Parliament Hill, is also home to a number of pubs and nightlife spots. **Bank St.**, which runs parallel to Elgin three blocks to the west, services the town's older shopping area. Parking downtown is hard to find and meters often cost 25¢ for 10min. Stash your car near the hostels and hop on the OC Transpo buses or walk. The canal itself is a major access route and the world's longest skating rink during the winter; thousands of Ottawans skate to work across it during the frostier months. Bike paths and pedestrian walkways also line the canals.

PRACTICAL INFORMATION

Visitor info: National Capital Commission Information Center, 90 Wellington St. (☎239-5000 or within Canada ☎800-465-1867), opposite the Parliament Bldg. Open early May to early Sept. daily 9am-9pm; early Sept. to early May 9am-5pm. For info on Hull, in the Québec province, contact the **Association Touristique de l'Outaouais,** 103 rue Laurier, Hull (☎819-778-2222 or 800-265-7822). Open mid-June to Sept. M-F 8:30am-8pm, Sa-Su 9am-6pm; Oct. to early June M-F 8:30am-5pm, Sa-Su 9am-4pm.

Hotlines: Ottawa Distress Centre, ☎238-3311 (English). **Tél-Aide,** ☎741-6433 (French). **Sexual Assault Support Centre,** ☎234-2266. **Disability Info,** ☎724-5886. **Kids Help Phone,** ☎800-668-6868.

Bi-Gay-Lesbian Resource: Gayline-Telegai (☎238-1717) has info. Open daily 7-10pm.

Internet access: Ottawa Public Library, 120 Metcalf St. (☎236-0301). Open M-Th 10am-8pm, F noon-6pm, Sa 10am-5pm.

Post Office: Postal Station B, 59 Sparks St. (☎844-1545), at Elgin St. Open M-F 8am-6pm. **Postal code:** K1P 5A0. **Area code:** 613 in Ottawa; 819 in Hull. In text, 613 unless noted otherwise.

ACCOMMODATIONS

In downtown Ottawa, economical options exist only if you avoid hotels. Advance reservations are strongly recommended, especially if staying through Canada Day

(July 1). **Ottawa Bed and Breakfast** represents ten B&Bs in the Ottawa area. (☎563-0161. Singles $49-54, doubles $59-64.) A complete list of B&Bs can be found in the *Ottawa Visitors Guide.*

▨ **Ottawa International Hostel (HI-C),** 75 Nicholas St., (☎235-2595), in downtown Ottawa. The site of Canada's last public hanging, the former Carleton County Jail now incarcerates travelers. Cells contain 4-8 bunks and minimal personal space. Communal showers, kitchen, Internet access, laundry facilities, lounges, jail tours, and a friendly, tongue-in-cheek atmosphere. Linen $2. In winter, doors locked 2-7am. Dorms $20, nonmembers $25; private rooms from $46/50. Parking $4.30 per day. ❶

Gatineau Park International Hostel (HI-C), 66 Carman Rd. (☎819-459-3180), 20min. from downtown Ottawa. Take Hwy. 5 north to its end and turn left at the intersection; the hostel is 5km down the road on the left. Take bus #1 "Maniwaki" and ask the driver to stop at the intersection of Hwy. 105 and Chemin Carman. Call the hostel in advance for shuttle service from here. Dorms $17, nonmembers $20. ❶

University of Ottawa Residences, 90 University St. (☎564-5400), in the center of campus, an easy walk from downtown. From the bus and train stations, take bus #95. Clean dorms in a concrete landscape. Free linen and towels. Check-in 4:30pm. Parking $10 per day. Open early May to late Aug. Singles $40, doubles $50; singles or doubles for students with ID $40. Rooms in New Residence $99 for up to 4 people; tasty breakfast included. ❶

Ottawa Backpackers Inn, 203 York St. (☎241-3402 or 888-394-0334). This friendly 32-bed heritage abode has both a prime downtown location and free coffee, tea, and linen. Facilities include a full kitchen, television, and Internet access. Reception 7am-midnight. No curfew. Geographically-themed 4- and 6-bed dorms $19. ❶

Gatineau Park (☎819-827-2020, reservations ☎819-456-3016), northwest of Hull. Three rustic campgrounds within 45min. of Ottawa: **Lac Philippe Campground,** 248 sites with facilities for family camping, trailers, and campers; **Lac Taylor Campground,** 33 semi-rustic sites; and **Lac la Pêche,** 36 campsites accessible only by canoe. Lac Philippe and Lac Taylor open in summer daily 9am-6pm; in winter 9:30am-6pm. La Pêche is available mid-May to mid-Oct. **Camping permits** (mid-Oct. to mid-June $19; mid-June to mid-Oct. $21), available at the campground entrance, are required for Philippe and Taylor. Pay for a site at La Pêche ($19) on Eardley Rd. ❶

◪ FOOD

Ottawa's **Byward Market,** on Byward St. between York and Rideau St., is full of tables with fresh produce and plants, chatty locals, and sweet-smelling maple syrup. (☎562-3325. Open in warmer weather daily 8am-5pm; boutiques open later.)

▨ **Mamma Grazzi's Kitchen,** 25 George St. (☎241-8656). This little Italian hideaway is located in a stone building in one of the oldest parts of Ottawa. The thin-crust pizza ($8-13) is well worth the wait. Open Su-Th noon-10pm, F-Sa noon-11pm. ❷

Byward Café, 55 Byward Market (☎241-2555), at the very south end of the market. Fun pop background music, a huge array of savory treats, and a prime location for people-watching bring both young and old to eat, drink, and relax on the breezy covered patio. Sandwiches around $4.50. Football-sized piece of ring cake $2.65. Open in summer daily 8am-11pm; in winter 8am-6pm. ❶

Highlander Pub, 115 Rideau St. (☎562-5678). A humorous menu playfully complements Highlander's sophisticated, nouveau-Scottish cuisine, including a stylish *haggis* ($12). Soak up the regimental, tartan atmosphere—or try one of the 46 single-malt scotches or 17 on-tap beers available. Live music weekly; schedule varies. Open M-Th 11am-midnight, F-Su 11am-2am. ❷

D'Arcy McGee's Irish Pub, 44 Sparks St. (☎230-4433). Whether lured in by the traditional Celtic music or chased in by the traditional Canadian rain, visitors to D'Arcy's are never sorry they came. Hearty pub food $8-15. Live music W nights. Open Su-Tu 11am-1am, W-Sa 11am-2am. ❷

Rideau Deli, 113 Rideau St. (☎562-8147). Tasty quick-stop sandwiches $2. Open M-W 9:30am-6pm, Th-F 9:30am-7pm, Sa 9:30am-5pm, Su 11:30am-5pm. ❶

👁 SIGHTS

THE HUB. Parliament Hill, on Wellington at Metcalfe St., towers over downtown with its distinguished Gothic architecture. Warm your hands over the **Centennial Flame** at the south gate, lit in 1967 to mark the 100th anniversary of the Dominion of Canada's inaugural session of Parliament. The Prime Minister can occasionally be spotted at the central Parliament structure, **Centre Block,** which contains the House of Commons, Senate, and Library of Parliament (library accessible only to Parliament officials). Free tours of Centre Block depart every 30min. from the white **Infotent** by the Visitors Center. *(☎992-4793. Tours mid-May to Sept. M-F 9am-8pm, Sa-Su 9am-5pm; Sept. to mid-May daily 9am-3:30pm. Infotent open mid-May to mid-June daily 9am-5pm; mid-June to Aug. 9am-8pm.)*

When Parliament is in session, you can watch Canada's government officials debate. Visitors with luck and stamina may be able to see **Question Period,** the most interesting debates of the day. *(☎992-4793. Mid-Sept. to Dec. and Feb. to mid-June M-Th 2:15-3pm, F 11:15am-noon. Plan to arrive about 2hr. in advance. Passes required.)* On display behind the library, the bell from Centre Block is one of few remnants of the original 1859-66 structure that survived a 1916 fire. According to legend, the bell crashed to the ground after chiming at midnight on the night of the blaze, now a carillon of 53 bells hangs in the Peace Tower.

Those interested in trying to make a statuesque soldier smile should attend the 30min **Changing of the Guard** on the broad lawns in front of Centre Block. *(☎993-1811. Late June to late Aug. daily 10am, weather permitting.)* At dusk, Centre Block and its lawns transform into the background for **Sound and Light: Wind Odyssey,** a show that relates the history of the Parliament Buildings and the nation. *(☎239-5100. Shows mid-May to early Sept. Performances alternate between French and English; call for specifics or check the information board behind the Centennial Flame.)* A five-minute walk west along Wellington St., the **Supreme Court of Canada** cohabits with the **Federal Court.** *(☎995-5361. Open daily 9am-5pm; Sept.-May hours vary. Tours every 30min.; tours alternate between French and English. No tours Sa-Su noon-1pm.)*

CONFEDERATION SQUARE. East of the Parliament Buildings at the junction of Sparks, Wellington, and Elgin St. stands **Confederation Sq.** and the enormous **National War Memorial,** dedicated by King George VI in 1939. The structure symbolizes the triumph of peace over war—an ironic message on the eve of World War II. **Nepean Point,** several blocks northwest of Rideau Centre and the Byward Market, behind the National Gallery of Canada, promises a panoramic view of the capital. While this spot is theoretically accessible by car, it is much easier to park the car elsewhere and simply walk up.

ROYAL RESIDENCES. The **Governor General,** the Queen's representative in Canada, resides at **Rideau Hall.** The public is welcome to take a guided tour of the house, gardens, and art collection, and many visitors run into the ever-gracious Governor General as they walk through the halls. *(1 Sussex Dr. ☎991-4422 or 800-465-6890. Guided tours 10am-3pm; self-guided tours 3-4:30pm.)* The next stop in the series of political homes is the **Prime Minister's residence.** Free tours of the premises leave from the main gate at 1 Sussex Dr. *(24 Sussex Dr. ☎ 800-465-6890 for tour info.)* See the production of "loonies" ($1 coins) at the **Royal Canadian Mint.** *(320 Sussex Dr. ☎ 993-8990 or 800-276-7714. Tour schedule varies.)*

OUTDOOR ACTIVITIES. Ottawa has managed to skirt the traditional urban vices of pollution and violent crime; the many parks and recreation areas have visitors forgetting they're in a city at all. A favorite destination for Ottawans who want to cycle, hike, or fish, is **Gatineau Park** (see **Accommodations,** p. 198), occupying 356 sq. km in the northwest. Artificial **Dow's Lake,** accessible by the Queen Elizabeth Driveway, extends off the Rideau Canal 15min. south of Ottawa. **Dow's Lake Pavilion** rents pedal boats, canoes, and bikes in the summer and ice skates and sleighs during the winter. *(101 Queen Elizabeth Driveway, near Preston St. ☎ 232-1001. Open mid-May to Sept. daily 8am-8pm. Rentals by the hr. and half-hour, prices vary.)*

🏛 MUSEUMS

Geographically concentrated and manageable, many of Ottawa's notable museums double as architectural marvels. Most are wheelchair accessible.

National Gallery, 380 Sussex Dr. (☎ 990-1985 or 800-319-2787). A spectacular glass-towered building adjacent to Nepean Pt. holds the world's most comprehensive collection of Canadian art, complemented by outstanding European, American, and Asian works. The facade—a work of art in itself—is a modern reinterpretation of the nearby neo-Gothic Library of Parliament. Open May-Oct. M-W and F-Su 10am-6pm, Th 10am-8pm; off-season hours vary. Free; special exhibits $12, seniors $10, ages 12-19 $5. Reservations required for special exhibits.

Canadian Museum of Civilization, 100 Laurier St., Gatineau, QC (☎ 819-776-7000). Housed in a striking sand dune-like structure across Pont Alexandra Bridge from the National Gallery, the museum offers life-sized dioramas and an outstanding series of events and live performances exploring 1000 years of Canadian history. Open Apr.-Oct. M-W and F-Su 9am-6pm, Th 9am-9pm; off-season hours vary. $10, students $6, seniors $7, ages 2-12 $4; families $22. Free after 4pm on Th; half-price on Su.

Canadian Museum of Contemporary Photography, 1 Rideau Canal (☎ 990-8257), on the steps between the Château Laurier and the Ottawa Locks. Time stands still here as modern Canadian life is freeze-framed in the museum's impressive collection. Open in summer M-W and F-Su 10am-6pm, Th 10am-8pm; in winter W and F-Su 10am-5pm, Th 10am-8pm. Free.

Canadian War Museum, 330 Sussex Dr. (☎ 776-8600), next to the National Gallery. Outside stands a poignant exhibit of Canadian citizens at war, from colonial skirmishes to UN Peacekeeping missions. Open M-W and F-Su 9:30am-5pm, Th 9:30am-8pm; mid-Oct. to May closed M. $4, students and seniors $3, children $2; free after 4pm on Th and half-price on Su. Free for Canadian veterans, retired military personnel, and their families.

Canadian Museum of Nature, 240 McLeod St. (☎ 566-4700), at Metcalfe St. A multimedia exploration of the natural world. For something creepy-crawly, check out the bug petting zoo, where nothing bites...hard. Open May to early Sept. M-W and F-Su 9:30am-5pm, Th 9:30am-8pm; off-season hours vary. $6, students and seniors $4, ages 3-12 $2.50, families $13; Th after 4pm free.

National Museum of Science and Technology, 1867 St. Laurent Blvd. (☎ 991-3044, TDD ☎ 991-9207). The entrance is on Lancaster Rd., 200m east of St. Laurent. Explore the world of modern technology with hands-on exhibits. Open May-Sept. daily 9am-5pm; Oct.-Apr. Tu-Su 9am-5pm. $6, students and seniors $5, ages 4-14 $3, families $14.

Laurier House, 335 Laurier Ave. E (☎992-8142). Liberal Prime Minister William Lyon Mackenzie King governed from this elegant house for most of his lengthy tenure. Admire all that he accumulated, including the crystal ball he used to consult his long-dead mother on matters of national importance. Open Apr. to mid-Oct. Tu-Sa 9am-5pm, Su noon-5pm. $2.25, students $1.25, seniors $2, under 5 free.

National Archives of Canada, 395 Wellington St. (☎995-5138 or 866-578-7777). History buffs can get lost in Canadian publications, old maps, photographs, letters, and historical exhibits. Reading room open M-F 8:30am-10pm, Sa-Su 8am-6pm. Exhibitions open daily 9am-9pm. Call ahead for a tour. Free.

🎵 NIGHTLIFE

Ottawa nightlife once meant trekking into Hull for a lower drinking age and longer drinking hours, but many nightclubs have recently been bought out due to increasing crime. Because of Ottawa's decision to allow nightspots to serve alcohol until 2am, the capital city is now where it's at. For a taste of it, stroll around **Byward Market** and the nearby area, where streets overflow with pedestrians in the evening.

The Atomic, 137 Besserer St. (☎241-2411), lures clubbers through its silver doors with the most up-to-date music scene in Canada, spinning techno and rave tunes still virgin to the airwaves. Cover Th $5; F $7, after 1am $10; Sa $10, after 1am $12. Open Th 10pm-3am, F 10pm-5am, Sa 10pm-8am.

Zaphod, 27 York St. (☎562-1010), in Byward Market. While not in the classiest area, this popular alternative club will help you experience life, the universe, and a bit of everything else. Pangalactic Gargle Blasters $6.50. Live bands on weekends, music on weekdays. Cover $2-10 depending on performer. Open daily 3pm-2am.

The Lookout, 41 York St. (☎789-1624), next to Zaphod's. A hoppin' gay club with intense dancing. Though the Thursday-evening crowd is mostly male, women flock in on Fridays. Open daily 3pm-2am.

Minglewoods, 101 York St. (☎562-2611), on the corner of Dalhousie, has a slew of domestic beers on tap. The 3 levels include a bar, pool room, and dance floor. Open daily 11:30am-2am.

🌑 FESTIVALS

Ottawans seem to celebrate everything, even the bitter Canadian cold. All-important **Canada Day,** July 1, involves fireworks, partying in Major's Hill Park, concerts, and all-around merrymaking. During the first three weekends of Feb., **Winterlude** (☎239-5000) lines the Rideau Canal. Ice sculptures illustrate how it feels to be an Ottawan in the winter—frozen. For a week in mid-May, the **Tulip Festival** (☎567-5757) explodes with a kaleidoscope of more than a million buds around Dow's Lake. Music fills the air during the **Dance Festival** (☎237-5158), in mid-June, and the **Jazz Festival** (594-3580), in mid-July; both hold free recitals and concerts as well as pricier events. During Labor Day weekend, hundreds of international balloons take to the sky at the **Hot Air Balloon Festival** (☎819-243-2330).

MID-ATLANTIC

From the Eastern seaboard of New York south through Virginia, the mid-Atlantic states claim not only a large slice of the nation's population, but also several of its major historical, political, and economic centers. This region has witnessed the rotation of US capitals: first Philadelphia, PA; then Princeton, NJ; Annapolis, MD; Trenton, NJ; New York City, and finally Washington, D.C. During the Civil War, the mid-Atlantic even housed the Confederacy's capital, Richmond, VA. Urban centers (and suburban sprawl) cover much of the land, but the great outdoors have survived. The Appalachian Trail meanders through the region, and New York's Adirondacks compose the largest national park outside of Alaska.

HIGHLIGHTS OF THE MID-ATLANTIC

NEW YORK, NY. The Big Apple combines world-class museums (p. 226) with top-notch arts and entertainment venues (p. 231).

WASHINGTON, D.C. The impressive Smithsonian Museum (p. 317), the White House (p. 314), the Capitol (p. 312), and a slew of monuments (p. 313) comprise some of the coveted attractions of the nation's capital.

SCENIC DRIVES. The long and winding Blue Ridge Pkwy. (p. 342) is justifiably famous.

HISTORIC SITES. Four-time battlefield Fredericksburg, VA (p. 328); Harper's Ferry, WV (p. 345); and Gettysburg, PA (p. 281) are the best places to relive the Civil War. Philadelphia, PA (p. 266) abounds with colonial landmarks.

NEW YORK

This state offers a little bit of everything: the excitement of New York City, the grandeur of Niagara Falls, and the fresh natural beauty of the Catskills and the Adirondacks. While "The City" attracts cosmopolitan types looking for adventure year-round, those seeking a more mellow New York experience head upstate. Here, surrounded by the beauty of some of the state's landscape, you may find it difficult to remember that smog and traffic exist. The cities of upstate New York have a sweet natural flavor contrasting the tang of the Big Apple.

⚑ PRACTICAL INFORMATION

Capital: Albany.

Visitor info: Division of Tourism, 1 Commerce Plaza, Albany 12245 (☎518-474-4116 or 800-225-5697; www.iloveny.state.ny.us). Operators available M-F 8:30am-5pm. **New York State Office of Parks and Recreation and Historic Preservation,** Empire State Plaza, Agency Bldg. 1, Albany 12238 (☎518-474-0456). Open M-F 9am-5pm.

State Muffin: Apple. **Postal Abbreviation:** NY. **Sales Tax:** 7-9%, depending on county.

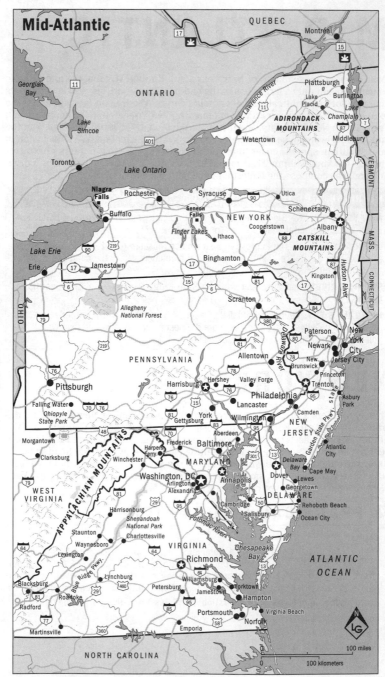

Mid-Atlantic

NEW YORK CITY ☎ 212

Since its earliest days, New York has scoffed at the timid offerings of other American cities. It boasts the most immigrants, the tallest skyscrapers, the biggest museum in the Western Hemisphere, and plenty of large landfills. Even the vast blocks of concrete have their own gritty charm. With a population of eight million, New York City's five boroughs teem with something much better than fresh air: constant, varied, and thrilling action. There's flamenco at an outdoor cafe, jazz in a historic speakeasy, house and techno in a flashy club. For more on the Big Apple, see 📖*Let's Go: New York City 2003*.

New Yorkers were awakened to both horror and heroism on September 11, 2001, when Osama bin Laden's suicide hijackers crashed American Airlines 11 and United Airlines Flight 175—both from Boston—into the two towers of the World Trade Center. The city has returned to normal with resilience, but it hasn't forgotten. Corporate skyscrapers and government buildings are heavily guarded, and several sites are closed indefinitely. Nevertheless, don't let heightened security keep you from appreciating the glamour and excitement of *the* ultimate big city.

◪ INTERCITY TRANSPORTATION

Airports: 3 airports serve the New York metropolitan area.

John F. Kennedy Airport (JFK) (☎718-244-4444), at the end of the Van Wyck Expwy., in southern Queens. JFK handles most international and many domestic flights. The airport is located 15 mi. from Midtown Manhattan, but the drive can take up to 1hr. Bus service is available 24hr. from any airport terminal to the Howard Beach-JFK subway station (60-75min., every 15-20min., $1.50). From there, take the Far Rockaway A train to Manhattan (1hr.). A taxi to Manhattan costs $35 (plus tolls and tip).

LaGuardia Airport (☎718-533-3400), off Exit 7 on the Grand Central Pkwy., in northern Queens. LaGuardia is 9 mi. from Midtown Manhattan; the drive is around 20-25min. Domestic flights leave from here. The MTA M60 bus connects to Manhattan subway lines 1 at 110th St./Broadway; A, B, C, D at 125th St./St. Nicholas Ave.; 2, 3 at 125th St./Lenox (Sixth) Ave.; 4, 5 6 to at 125th St./Lexington Ave. The Q33 bus goes to Jackson Heights/Roosevelt Ave. in Queens for E, F, G, R, V, 7; the Q48 bus goes to 74th St.-Broadway in Queens for E, F, G, R, V, 7. (Allow at least 1½hr. for all routes. M60 runs daily 5am-1am, Q33 and Q48 24hr.; all buses $1.50.) Taxis to Manhattan are $16-26 (plus tolls and tip).

Newark International Airport (☎973-961-6000), 16 mi. west of midtown in Newark, NJ, on I-95 at Exit 14. Domestic and international flights. Olympia Airport Express (☎973-964-6233) travels from the airport to Port Authority, Grand Central Terminal, and Penn Station 24hr., leaving every 15-30min. (Trip takes 40-50min. $11.) Bus #107 by the New Jersey Transit Authority (☎973-762-5100) covers Newark, Newark International Airport (North Terminal) and Port Authority (25min.; every 30-45min. 6am-midnight; $3.60).

Trains: Grand Central Terminal, 42nd St. and Park Ave. (Subway: 4, 5, 6, 7, S to 42nd St.-Grand Central), handles **Metro-North** (☎800-638-7646) commuter lines to Connecticut and NY suburbs. **Amtrak** (☎800-872-7245) runs out of **Penn Station,** 33rd St. and Eighth Ave. (Subway: 1, 2, 3 to 34th St.-Penn Station/Seventh Ave.; A, C, E to 34th St.-Penn Station/Eighth Ave.) To: **Boston** (4-5 hr., $64); **Philadelphia** (1½hr., $48); **Washington, D.C.** (3-4hr., $72). The **Long Island Railroad (LIRR)** (☎718-217-5477) and **NJ Transit** (☎973-762-5100) commuter rails also chug from Penn Station. Nearby at 33rd St. and Sixth Ave., **PATH** trains depart for New Jersey (☎800-234-7284).

Buses: Greyhound (☎800-231-2222) buses leave the **Port Authority Terminal,** 42nd St. and Eighth Ave. (☎212-564-8484; subway: A, C, E to 42nd St.-Port Authority). Watch for con artists and pickpockets, especially at night. Greyhound covers **Boston** (4-6hr., $42); **Philadelphia** (2-3hr., $21); **Washington, D.C.** (4½hr., $42).

MID-ATLANTIC

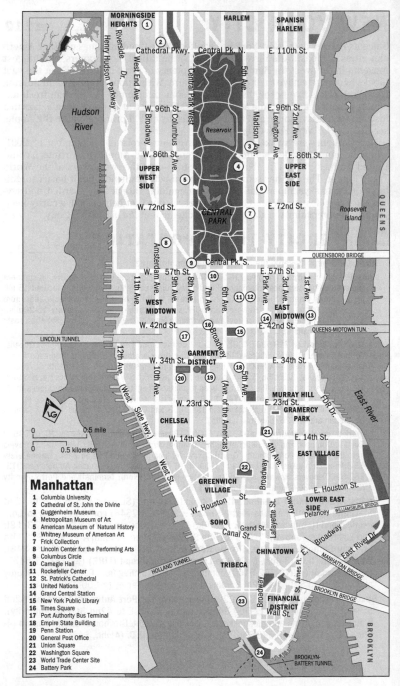

MID-ATLANTIC

Manhattan

1 Columbia University
2 Cathedral of St. John the Divine
3 Guggenheim Museum
4 Metropolitan Museum of Art
5 American Museum of Natural History
6 Whitney Museum of American Art
7 Frick Collection
8 Lincoln Center for the Performing Arts
9 Columbus Circle
10 Carnegie Hall
11 Rockefeller Center
12 St. Patrick's Cathedral
13 United Nations
14 Grand Central Station
15 New York Public Library
16 Times Square
17 Port Authority Bus Terminal
18 Empire State Building
19 Penn Station
20 General Post Office
21 Union Square
22 Washington Square
23 World Trade Center Site
24 Battery Park

■ ORIENTATION

NYC is comprised of **five boroughs:** the Bronx, Brooklyn, Manhattan, Queens, and Staten Island. Flanked on the east by the "East River" (actually a strait) and on the west by the Hudson River, **Manhattan** is a sliver of an island, measuring only 13 mi. long and 2½ mi. wide. **Queens** and **Brooklyn** are on the other side of the East River. Residential **Staten Island,** southwest of Manhattan, has repeatedly sought secession from the city. North of Manhattan sits the **Bronx,** the only borough connected by land to the rest of the US. The five boroughs united to form one city in 1898.

BOROUGHS

MANHATTAN

Above 14th St., Manhattan is an organized grid of avenues running north-south and streets east-west. Streets run consecutively, and their numbers grow as you travel north. Avenues are slightly less predictable: some are numbered while others are named. The numbers of the avenues increase as one goes west. **Broadway,** which follows an old Algonquin trail, defies the rectangular pattern and cuts diagonally across the island, veering east of Fifth Ave. at 23rd St. Central Park and Fifth Ave. (south of 59th St., north of 110th St.) separate the city into the East Side and West Side. **Washington Heights** is located north of 155th St.; **Morningside Heights** (above 110th St. and below 125th St.) is sandwiched between the grittiness of **Harlem** (150s to 110th St.) and the bourgeois glamorous **Upper West Side** (110th St. to 59th St., west of Central Park). The museum-heavy **Upper East Side** is directly across Central Park, above Fifth Ave., Times Square, and the Theater District in glittering **Midtown** (59th St. to 42nd St.). **Lower Midtown** (41st St. to 14th St.) includes **Herald Square, Chelsea,** and **Union Square.**

Below 14th St., the city dissolves into a confusing tangle of old, narrow streets that aren't numbered south of Houston St. The rebellious, bohemian **East Village** and **Alphabet City** are grid-like, with alphabetized avenues from Ave. A to Ave. D, east of First Ave. More established but still intellectual **Greenwich Village,** only slightly less confusing, is especially complicated west of Sixth Ave. Moving south, trendy **SoHo** (South of Houston St.) and **TriBeCa** (Triangle Below Canal St.) are just west of historically ethnic enclaves **Little Italy, Chinatown,** and the **Lower East Side.** The **Financial District/Wall St. area** at the tip of Manhattan, set over the original Dutch layout, is full of narrow, winding, one-way streets.

BROOKLYN

The **Brooklyn-Queens Expwy. (BQE)** pours into the **Belt Pkwy.** and circumscribes Brooklyn. Ocean Pkwy., Ocean Ave., Coney Island Ave., and diagonal Flatbush Ave. run from the beaches of southern Brooklyn (**Coney Island** and **Brighton Beach**) to the heart of the borough in **Prospect Park.** The streets of western Brooklyn (including **Park Slope**) are aligned with the western shore and thus collide at a 45-degree angle with central Brooklyn's main arteries. In northern Brooklyn (including **Williamsburg, Greenpoint, Brooklyn Heights,** and **Downtown Brooklyn**), several avenues—Atlantic Ave., Eastern Pkwy., and Flushing Ave.—travel from downtown Brooklyn east into Queens.

QUEENS

The streets of Queens resemble neither the orderly grid of Upper Manhattan nor the haphazard angles of Greenwich Village; instead, a mixed bag of urban planning techniques has resulted in a logical—but extremely complicated—system. Streets generally run north-south and are numbered from west to east, from 1st St. in **Astoria** to 271st St. in **Glen Oaks.** Avenues run perpendicular to streets and are numbered from north to south, from Second Ave. to 165th Ave. The address of an establishment or residence often tells you the closest cross-street (for example, 45-07 32nd Ave. is near the intersection with 45th St.). Pick up the very useful Queens Bus Map, free and available on most Queens buses.

THE BRONX

Major highways cut the Bronx up into many pieces. The **Major Deegan Expwy. (I-87)** runs up the western border of the borough, next to the Harlem River. The **Cross-Bronx Expwy. (I-95)** runs across the borough before turning north on its easternmost edge. Up the center of the borough runs the **Bronx River Pkwy.** Several avenues run north-south, including **Jerome Ave.** on the western side of the borough and **White Plains Rd.** and **Boston Rd.** on the eastern side of the borough. Streets running east-west include **Tremont Ave.** and **Fordham Rd.** and the **Bronx** and **Pelham Pkwy.**

STATEN ISLAND

Unlike the rest of the city, Staten Island is quite spread out. Pick up much-needed maps of Staten Island's bus routes as well as other pamphlets at the **Chamber of Commerce,** 130 Bay St. (718-727-1900), left from the ferry station onto Bay St.

▐▄ LOCAL TRANSPORTATION

Public Transit: The **Metropolitan Transit Authority (MTA)** runs the city's subways, buses, and trains. The extensive subway system is open daily 24hr. Once inside, a passenger may transfer onto any other train without restrictions. Subway maps are available in any station. Station entrances lit by green globes are open 24hr.; entrances with red globes are somehow restricted. **Buses,** often slower than subways, but relatively safer and cleaner, stop roughly every 2 blocks and run crosstown (east-west), as well as uptown and downtown (north-south). Blue signposts announce bus numbers; glass-walled shelters display bus schedules and route maps. In the outer boroughs, some buses are run by independent contractors. Be sure to grab a borough bus map. **Metro-Cards,** the dominant currency for subway and buses, have a pre-set value (every $15 gets you 1 free ride) and can make free bus and subway transfers but must be made within 2hr. The 1-day ($4), 7-day ($17), and 30-day ($63) "Unlimited Rides" MetroCards (as opposed to $1.50 "Pay-Per-Ride" cards) are good for tourists visiting many sights.

Taxis: Most people in Manhattan hail yellow (licensed) cabs on the street.

▌! **SUBWAY SAFETY.** In crowded stations (most notably those around 42nd St.), pickpockets find work; violent crimes occasionally occur in stations that are deserted. Stay alert and stick to well-lit areas; most stations have clearly marked "off-hours" waiting areas that are under observation and significantly safer. When boarding, pick a car with a number of other passengers in it, or sit near the middle of the train, in the conductor's car. *For safety reasons, try to avoid riding the subways between midnight and 7am, especially above E. 96th St. and W. 120th St., and outside Manhattan.*

▐ PRACTICAL INFORMATION

New York Convention and Visitors Bureau, 810 Seventh Ave., at 53rd St. (☎484-1222). Open M-F 8:30am-6pm, Sa-Su 9am-5pm. Other locations in Grand Central and Penn Station.

Hotlines: AIDS Hotline, ☎800-825-5448. Open daily 9am-9pm; 24hr. recording. **Crime Victims' Hotline,** ☎577-7777. **Sex Crimes Report Line,** ☎267-7273. Both 24hr.

Bi-Gay-Lesbian Concerns: Callen-Lorde Community Health Center, 356 W. 18th St., between Eighth and Ninth Ave. (☎271-7200; www.callen-lorde.org). Open M 12:30-8pm, Tu and Th-F 9am-4:30pm, W 8:30am-1pm and 3-8pm. **Gay Men's Health Crisis-Geffen Clinic,** 119 W. 24th St., between Sixth and Seventh Ave. (☎807-6655). Walk-in counseling M-F 10am-6pm. Open M-F 11am-8pm. Confidential HIV testing M-F 10am-9pm, Sa noon-3pm. **Gay and Lesbian National Hotline** (☎989-0999). Open M-F 4pm-midnight, Sa noon-5pm, 24hr. recording.

Medical Services: Doctors Walk-in Clinic, 55 E. 34th St., between Park and Madison Ave. (☎252-6001, ext. 2). Open M-Th 8am-8pm, F 8am-7pm, Sa 9am-3pm, Su 9am-2pm. Last walk-in 1hr. before closing.

Post Office: General Post Office, 421 Eighth Ave., at W. 32nd St. (☎330-3002). Open daily 24hr. General Delivery at 390 Ninth Ave., at W. 30th St. **ZIP code:** 10001.

Area codes: 212, 347, or 646 (Manhattan); 718 (other 4 boroughs); 917 (cell phones). Starting February 1, 2003, all New York City calls made within and between all five area codes must be dialed using 10-digit dialing; that is, 1 + the area code + the 7-digit telephone number. *In listings, area code is 212 except where otherwise noted.*

⌂ ACCOMMODATIONS

Accommodations in New York are very expensive. A night in a hostel averages $25; in a cheap hotel, $60-80. A mid-range hotel room can easily cost over $120.

HOSTELS

▨ **Jazz on the Park,** 36 W. 106th St./Duke Ellington Blvd. (☎932-1600), between Manhattan Ave. and Central Park West. Subway: B, C to 103rd St./Central Park W. Clean, brightly-colored hostel with funky, fun decor and 210 beds. Lockers and A/C. Enough activities that you might not actually leave the hostel: live jazz in the downstairs lounge, all-you-can-eat BBQs on the terrace on Sa in summer ($5), and Su gospel brunches. Internet access $1 per 5min. Linen, towels, and breakfast included. Check-in and check-out 11am. June-Oct. reservations required. 10- to 12-bed dorm $27; 6- to 8-bed dorm $29; 4-bed dorm $32; private room (full/bunk bed) $80. ❶

▨ **New York International Hostel (HI-AYH),** 891 Amsterdam Ave., at 103rd St. (☎932-2300). Subway: 1 to 103 St./Broadway; B, C to 103rd St./Central Park W. The largest US youth hostel, in a block-long landmark building, with 90 dorm-style rooms and 624 beds. Soft carpets, spotless bathrooms, A/C, kitchens, dining rooms, communal TV lounges, and large outdoor garden. Internet access. Linen and towels included. 28-night max. stay, in summer 7 nights max. Credit card reservations required. Check-in noon. Check-out 11am. Nov.-Apr. 10- to 12-bed dorms $29; 6- to 8-bed dorms $32; 4-bed dorms $35. Family rooms (queen and 2 bunks) available. May-Oct. dorms $2 more. Nonmembers $3 more. ❶

▨ **Central Park Hostel,** 19 W. 103rd St. (☎678-0491), between Manhattan Ave. and Central Park West. Subway: B, C to 103rd St./Central Park W. Clean rooms with A/C and a nice TV lounge. Shared bathrooms. Linen and towels provided. Lockers available. Key deposit $2. 13-night max. stay. Dorms $25; private doubles $75. ❶

▨ **Sugar Hill International House,** 722 St. Nicholas Ave., at 146th St. (☎926-7030). Subway: A, B, C, D to 145th St./St. Nicholas Ave. Must have passport ID or be US citizen. Brownstone with large and spacious rooms and a quiet family feel. Friendly staff is a living library of Harlem history and culture. No smoking. Rooms for 2-9 people. All-female room available. Free Internet access. Key deposit $10. 2-week max. stay. Check-in 9am-9pm. Check-out 11am. Reserve 1 month ahead during off-season, no reservations accepted July-Sept. Dorms $25; doubles $30 per person. ❶

■ **Big Apple Hostel,** 119 W. 45th St., (☎302-2603; www.bigapplehostel.com), between Sixth and Seventh Ave. Subway: 1, 2, 3, 7, N, Q, R, S, W to 42nd St.-Times Sq. This centrally located hostel is the budget traveler's best option. Clean rooms, kitchen with refrigerator, luggage room, big back deck with grill, common rooms, and laundry facilities. Americans accepted with out-of-state photo ID or other strong proof that they're tourists. Reception 24hr. Internet access $1 per 8min. Check-in and check-out 11am. No reservations accepted Aug.-Sept. except through website or by fax—send credit card number. No wheelchair access. Bunks with shared bath $33; singles and doubles $90. ❷

Chelsea Center Hostel, 313 W. 29th St. (☎643-0214), between Eighth and Ninth Ave. Subway: A, C, E to 34th St.-Penn Station/Eighth Ave.; 1, 2, 3 to 34th St.-Penn Station/Seventh Ave. To enter, ring the labeled buzzer at the door to this quiet residential-home-turned-hostel. Room for 15 in a spacious basement room with a summer camp feel; 5 more in a slightly cramped bedroom on the main floor. A garden adds to the charm. 2 showers. Light breakfast included. Linen provided. Check-in 8:30am-10:45pm. Check-out 11am. Flexible lockout 11am-5pm. Cash and traveler's checks only. Dorms $30. ❶

Chelsea International Hostel, 251 W. 20th St. (☎647-0010), between Seventh and Eighth Ave., in Chelsea. Subway: 1, 2 to 23rd St./Seventh Ave.; C, E to 23rd St./Eighth Ave. Congenial staff offers pizza W night. Backyard garden. Sparsely-furnished, smallish, utilitarian rooms. Kitchens, laundry room, TV rooms. Internet access 19¢ per min. Key deposit $10. Check-in 8am-6pm, passport required. Check-out 1pm. Reservations recommended. Dorms $25; private doubles $60. ❶

International Student Center, 38 W. 88th St. (☎787-7706), between Central Park West and Columbus Ave. Subway: B, C to 86th St./Central Park W. Must be age 18-30 with ID. No-frills, tolerable dorms with showers and linens. Single, mixed-sex rooms available. Large basement TV lounge with kitchen, fridge, and affable atmosphere. Key deposit $10. Max. stay June-Aug. 7 nights; Sept.-May 14 nights. Reception daily 8am-11pm. Reserve in winter only. Call after 10:30am on the day you wish to stay to check for availability. 8- to 10-bed dorm $20. Cash or travelers checks only. ❶

GUEST HOUSES & BED & BREAKFASTS

■ **Akwaaba Mansion,** 347 MacDonough St. (☎718-455-5958), in Bedford-Stuyvesant. Subway: A, C to Utica Ave. Photographers often come here to do fashion and advertising shoots. Each of the 18 rooms has its own theme; all are decorated in African cultural decor. Library, TV room, tree-shaded patio, and breakfast in an elegant dining room. Rooms comfortably accommodate 2. All include private bath and A/C. Check-in 4-7pm. Check-out 11am. F jazz and Su brunch with Southern/African cuisine ($10). Reserve at least 1 month ahead. Rooms M-F $120-135, Sa-Su $135-150. ❺

■ **Colonial House Inn,** 318 W. 22nd St. (☎243-9669 or 800-689-3779), between Eighth and Ninth Ave. Subway: C, E to 23rd St. A very comfortable B&B in a classy Chelsea brownstone. All rooms have cable TV, A/C, and phone; some have bath and fireplace. Sun deck with a "clothing optional" area. 24hr. desk and concierge. Continental breakfast included. Internet access 20¢ per min. Check-in 2pm. Check-out noon. Reservations suggested and require 2 nights' deposit 10 days in advance. Double bed room $80-99; queen-size bedroom $99-125, with private bath and fridge $125-140. ❹

Bed & Breakfast on the Park, 113 Prospect Park W. (☎718-499-6115), between 6th and 7th St., in Prospect Park. Subway: F to Seventh Ave./Ninth St., then 2 blocks east and 2 blocks north. Perfect for putting up nervous parents who doubt the city's safety (or beauty). A magnificently restored brownstone jam-packed with Victoriana, this decadent, aromatic opiate of a hotel lacks only adequate horse stables and gas lighting. Gourmet breakfast in sumptuous (not-so) common room. 8 doubles (2 with shared bath), each in a different style, $125-300. ❺

HOTELS

▨ **Gershwin Hotel,** 7 E. 27th St. (☎545-8000), between Madison and Fifth Ave. Subway: N, R to 28th St./Broadway; 6 to 28th St./Park Ave. S. This chic, pristine hotel full of modern furniture and artsy twenty-somethings offers spaces for comedy, concerts, open-mic poetry nights, and artwork. Private rooms with bathroom, cable TV, A/C, and phone. Internet $1 per 4min. Reception 24hr. Check-in 3pm. Check-out 11am. Rooms for 1-2 $99-179; 1-bedroom suite $299; triples/quads add $10 per person. $15 extra Th-Sa. 8-12 bed dorms also offered, $29-59 per bed. ❷

▨ **Carlton Arms Hotel,** 160 E. 25th St. (☎679-0680), between Third and Lexington Ave. Subway: 6 to 23rd St./Park Ave. S. 54 spacious rooms, each decorated by a different artist. 11C, the "good daughter/bad daughter" room, combines teeny-bopper and horror-movie posters. Check-in noon. Check-out 11:30am. Reserve in summer 2 months ahead; confirm 10 days ahead. Singles $60, with bath $75; doubles $80/95; triples $99/110; quads $105/117. 10% discount if you pay for 7+ nights up front. ❸

▨ **Hotel Stanford,** 43 W. 32nd St. (☎563-1500 or 800-365-1114), between Fifth Ave. and Broadway. Subway: B, D, F, N, Q, R, V, W to 34th St.-Herald Sq. This Korean District hotel's lobby has class. Impeccable rooms with bathroom, cable TV, phone, A/C, refrigerator. Continental breakfast included. Check-in 3pm. Check-out noon. Reservations recommended. Singles $120-150; doubles $150-180; suites $200-250. ❺

▨ **ThirtyThirty,** 30 E. 30th St. (☎689-1900 or 800-497-6028), between Park Ave. S and Madison Ave. Subway: N, R to 28th St./Broadway; 6 to 28th St./Park Ave. S. Sleek hotel in a prime location at relatively low price. All rooms have cable TV, A/C, and phones. Check-in 3pm. Check-out 11am. Singles $125; doubles $165; suites $245. ❺

Hudson Hotel, 356 W. 58th St. (☎554-6000), between Eighth and Ninth Ave. Subway: A, C, B, D, 1, 2 to 59th St.-Columbus Circle. Chic, swank full-service hotel featuring customized greenhouses, utopian garden courtyard, and 2 popular bars. Each decadent room has down comforters, oak walls, art exhibits, mood lighting, and an ultra-modern bathroom. Check-in 3pm. Check-out noon. Standard rooms $155-$255. ❺

Hotel Pickwick Arms, 230 E. 51st St. (☎355-0300 or 800-742-5945), between Second and Third Ave. Subway: 6 to 51st St.; E, V to 53rd St.-Lexington Ave. Business types congregate in this well-priced, mid-sized Midtown hotel. Chandelier-lit marble lobby contrasts with tiny rooms and tinier hall bathrooms. Roof garden and airport service available. A/C, cable TV, phone. Check-in 2pm. Check-out 1pm. Internet $1 per 4min. Singles $75-115; doubles with bath $140-150; studio with double bed and sofa for 2 people $215. Additional person $20. ❹

Larchmont Hotel, 27 W. 11th St. (☎989-9333), between Fifth and Sixth Ave. Subway: 4, 5, 6, L, N, Q, R, W to 14th St.-Union Sq. Spacious, clean rooms in a whitewashed brownstone on a quiet block. A/C, TV, desks, closets, and wash basins. Shared bath. Continental breakfast included. Check-in 3pm. Check-out noon. Reserve 5-6 weeks ahead. Singles $70-95; doubles $90-115. ❸

St. Mark's Hotel, 2 St. Mark's Pl., at Third Ave. (☎674-2192). Subway: 6 to Astor Pl. Pleasant rooms in exciting location. Call ahead to reserve. All rooms with private bath and cable TV. Singles $90-100, doubles $100-120. Cash and travelers checks only. ❹

Chelsea Pines Inn, 317 W. 14th St. (☎929-1023), between Eighth and Ninth Ave. Subway: A, C, E to 14th St.; L to Eighth Ave. Friendly gay-owned and operated inn with cozy rooms, vintage film posters, and many amenities. Gorgeous garden and "greenhouse" out back. A/C, cable TV, refrigerator, and showers. 3-day min. stay Sa-Su. Continental breakfast included, with fresh homemade bread. Reservations required. Rooms with private showers and shared toilet $99-169; with queen-size bed and private bath $129-$159; with queen-size suite with private bath $139-$169. $20 per extra person. ❺

Murray Hill Inn, 143 E. 30th St. (☎683-6900 or 888-996-6376), between Third and Lexington Ave. Subway: N, R to 28th St./Broadway; 6 to 28th St./Park Ave. S. Simple rooms, reasonable prices. Rooms have A/C, cable TV, and phone. 21-night max. stay. Check-in 3pm. Check-out noon. Singles $75, with bath $115; doubles $95/125. ❷

☐ FOOD

New York will dazzle you with its culinary bounty. City dining, like the population, spans the globe, ranging from sushi bars and Italian eateries to French bistros.

CHINATOWN

▨ **H.S.F. Restaurant,** 46 Bowery (☎374-1319), between Bayard and Canal St. Wonderful dim sum ($3-5) served 11am-5pm. Open daily 8:30am-midnight. 2

▨ **Vietnam,** 11-13 Doyers St. (☎693-0725), between Bowery and Pell St.; follow the steps downstairs. All of the standards—brittle spring rolls, shrimp on sugar cane, noodle soups, and then some. Open daily 11am-9:30pm. ❷

Vegetarian Dim Sum House, 24 Pell St., at Doyers St. (☎226-6572). This small eatery's soy and wheat byproducts, taro root, and mushrooms stand in for meat. 3 great dumplings for $2. Most entrees $6-10. Ice-cold lotus-seed/lychee drink $2. Open daily 11am-11pm. Cash only. ❷

Chinatown Ice Cream Factory, 65 Bayard St., at Elizabeth St. (☎608-4170). Yummy homemade ice cream in exotic flavors like lychee, taro, ginger, red bean, and green tea. 1 scoop $2.20, 2 for $4, 3 for $4.80. Open in summer M-Th 11:30am-11:30pm, F-Su 11:30am-midnight; fall-spring daily noon-11pm.

LITTLE ITALY

▨ **Lombardi's Coal Oven Pizza,** 32 Spring St. (☎941-7994), between Mott and Mulberry St. Claims to be oldest pizzeria in US (est. 1905). Large pie feeds 2 ($13.50). Open M-Th 11:30am-11pm, F-Sa 11:30am-midnight, Su 11:30am-10pm. Cash only. ❷

▨ **Rocky's Italian Restaurant,** 45 Spring St. (☎274-9756), at Mulberry St. True neighborhood joint's lunch menu offers pizza hero ($4.50) and sandwiches ($4.50-9) until 5pm. Pasta $7-13, entrees $10-19. Great chicken with garlic sauce ($14). Cheap wine (carafe $16). Open Tu-Su 11am-11pm; kitchen closes at 10:30pm. ❸

Caffè Palermo, 148 Mulberry St. (☎431-4205), between Hester and Grand St. Best of the cafes along Mulberry. Most pastries $3-5. Tasty tiramisu $5, cannoli $2.75, and cappuccino $3.25. Open Su-Th 10am-midnight, F-Sa 10am-2am.

NOLITA

Rice, 227 Mott St. (☎226-5775), between Prince and Spring St. Subway: 6 to Spring St.; F, S, V to Broadway-Lafayette St.; N, R to Prince St. Serves all kinds of rices, from basmati to Bhutanese red ($1-3.50), with wide selection of fixings (mango chutney $1, ratatouille and chicken satay $4-9.50). Open daily noon-midnight. Cash only. ❷

Cafe Gitane, 242 Mott St., at Prince St. (☎334-9552). This fashionable cafe is a prime spot to see and be seen. Salads $5.25-9, tasty grilled eggplant with goat cheese and pesto on rice pilaf $8, tiramisu $4.50. Open daily 9am-midnight. Cash only. ❷

Cafe Colonial Restaurant, 276 Elizabeth St., at Houston St. (☎274-0044). Great entree options like veggie burgers ($7.25) and soft-shell crab sandwiches ($10). Open daily 8am-11pm. ❷

LOWER EAST SIDE

▨ **El Sombrero,** 108 Stanton St., at Ludlow St. (☎254-4188). Subway: F, J, M, Z to Delancey St.-Essex St. Divine budget Mexican food with kitschy aura. Satisfying vegetable enchiladas ($8), lovely Fajitas Mexicana ($12). Small margaritas $3, beer $2-4. Hours vary; M-F 10am-approx. midnight, Sa-Su 10am-approx. 3am. Cash only. ❸

Katz's Delicatessen, 205 E. Houston St. (☎254-2246), between Orchard and Ludlow St. Subway: F, V to Lower East Side-Second Ave. A neighborhood institution since 1888, every president in the last 3 decades has proudly had a Katz salami. Orgasmic food (as Meg Ryan confirmed in *When Harry Met Sally*) includes knishes and franks $2.40, sandwiches around $10. Open Su-Tu 8am-10pm, W-Th 8am-11pm, F-Sa 8am-3am. ❸

Sentosa, 3 Allen St. (☎925-8018), between Canal and Division St. Subway: F, V, S to Broadway-Lafayette St. Really cheap Malaysian food with Chinese twist in banal part of neighborhood. Hainanese chicken rice $7, rice dishes $4. Open 9am-midnight. ❶

GREENWICH VILLAGE

▧ **Corner Bistro,** 331 W. 4th St. (☎242-9502), on the corner of Jane St., at Eighth Ave. Subway: A, C, E, L to 14th St./Eighth Ave. Unbelievable hamburgers ($4.50-5.50) and cold beer ($2-3). Open M-Sa 11:30am-4am, Su noon-4am. Cash only. ❶

▧ **Chez Brigitte,** 77 Greenwich Ave. (☎929-6736), between Seventh Ave. and Bank St. Subway: 1, 2, 3 to 14th St./Seventh Ave. Lively hole-in-the-wall French diner/bistro. Entrees $7-9. Diner-style counter service. Open daily 11am-10pm. Cash only. ❷

Moustache, 90 Bedford St. (☎229-2220), between Barrow and Grove St. Subway: 1, 2 to Christopher St. Sumptuous Middle Eastern fare includes lentil soup ($3.50), salads ($4-9.50), tabouleh ($3.50), falafel sandwich ($5.50). Open daily noon-11pm. ❶

The Grey Dog, 33 Carmine St. (☎462-0041), between Bleecker and Bedford St. Subway: A, C, E, F, V, S to W. 4th St. Hip, cheap cafe with young patrons. Medium coffee just $1, snacks $5.50-8. Open M-F 6:30am-11:30pm, Sa-Su 7am-12:30am.

EAST VILLAGE

▧ **Yakitori Taisho,** 5 St. Mark's Pl. (☎228-5086), between Second and Third Ave. Subway: 6 to Astor Pl. Look for the huge red paper lantern out front. Tiny eating space with good, cheap Japanese fare. 10 *yakitori* (tender chicken and vegetables on skewers) $12, cold ramen $4, chicken teriyaki $7. Open daily 11am-11pm. ❷

▧ **National Cafe,** 210 First Ave., at E. 13th St. (☎473-9354). Subway: L to First Ave. Mediocre decor but great garlic-heavy home cooking, Cuban style. From 10:30am-3pm, $4.60 gets you an entree of the day, rice and beans or salad, plantain, a cup of soup, and bread. Everything on menu well under $10. Open M-Sa 10:30am-10pm. ❷

Second Ave. Delicatessen, 156 Second Ave., at 10th St. (☎677-0606). Subway: 6 to Astor Pl. The Lebewohl family has maintained this definitive, strictly kosher New York deli (no outside food allowed) since 1954. Famous chopped liver ($6.50), babka ($3.25), kasha varnishkes ($4), mushroom barley ($4), and pastrami/corned beef sandwiches ($8-11). Open M-Sa 10am-8:30pm, Su 11am-7pm. ❷

CHELSEA

▧ **Blue Moon Mexican Cafe,** 150 Eighth Ave. (☎463-0560), between 17th and 18th St. Subway: A, C, E, L to 14th St./Eighth Ave. Funky hangout, popular both for Mex-Cali fusion food and the margaritas. Generous portions, vegetarian-friendly dishes. Giant burritos $9; entrees $11-13. Omelettes or french toast $8, pancakes $7. Open Su-Th noon-11pm, F-Sa 11:30am-midnight. ❷

Minar, 5 W. 31st St. (☎684-2199), between Fifth Ave. and Broadway Subway: B, D, F, N, Q, R, V, W to Herald Sq. Long, narrow Indian eatery serves spicy vegetable curries ($4.25) and regular curries ($5.25-5.50) with small salad and choice of bread or rice. South Indian fare also. Open M-F 10am-7:30pm, Sa 10am-5:30. ❷

Food Bar, 149 Eighth Ave. (☎243-2020), between W. 17th and W. 18th St. Subway: A, C, E, L to 14th St./Eighth Ave.; 1, 2 to 18th St./Seventh Ave. Popular, chic hangout with mostly male patrons. Tasty sandwiches $6-11; large-portioned dinner entrees $10-18. Open M-F 11am-4pm, daily 5pm-11:30pm. Min. $10 order at night. ❷

MID-ATLANTIC

$$$ **THE BIG SPLURGE**

SARDI'S OF BROADWAY

If you want to do Broadway your way, you might consider a stop at **Sardi's**, alongside the big spenders (and big personalities) of the theater scene. According to long-standing tradition, cast and crew gather here after opening night on Broadway to drink the hours away as they wait for dawn—and the *New York Times* review that will make or break the show. Ironically, the late, legendary *NYT* reviewer Vincent Cambi also decamped to Sardi's after performances, espresso in hand, to jot down his notes. Another tradition is an annual invitation-only Super Bowl Party that's attended by everyone from the mayor to Joe Namath. The food here is worthy of the hype: the steak tartar ($26) is a mouth-watering favorite, while the *prix-fixe* dinner ($43.50) features a multi-course meal. It's not a bad price to pay to kick off or finish up an unforgettable night on Broadway. *(234 W. 44th St., between Broadway and Eighth Ave. Subway: B, D, F, V to 42nd St./Ave. of the Americas.* ☎ *221-8440. Open Tu-Th 11:30am-11:30pm, F-Sa 11:30am-12:30am, Su noon-7:30pm.* ❺*)*

THEATER DISTRICT

Hourglass Tavern, 373 W. 46th St. (☎265-2060), between Eighth and Ninth Ave. Dark, crowded, triangular Restaurant Row joint for the fast-moving. 59min. time limit is strictly enforced when crowds are waiting. *Prix-fixe* entrees ($12-14) are always changing but regularly feature fresh fish and filet mignon. Open M-Tu 5-11:15pm, W and Sa 4:30-11:30pm, Th-F 4-11:30pm, Su 4:30-10:30pm. ❸

Original Fresco Tortillas, 536 Ninth Ave. (☎465-8898), between 39th and 40th St. Tiny 9-seater with great, cheap homemade food: fajitas/tacos $1-2, huge burritos $4-5. No artificial spices or MSG. Open M-F 11am-11pm, Sa-Su noon-10pm. ❶

Becco, 355 W. 46th St. (☎397-7597), between Eighth and Ninth Ave. Gourmet cuisine that makes you forget your budget. 70 wines priced at $20 per bottle allow for moderate splurges. $17 *prix-fixe* lunch (dinner $22) gets you a gourmet antipasto platter or Caesar salad, plus unlimited servings of the 3 pastas of the day. $16 food min. per person for dinner, $14 for lunch. Open daily noon-3pm and 5pm-midnight. ❹

UPPER EAST SIDE

▨ **Barking Dog Luncheonette,** 1678 Third Ave., at 94th St. (☎831-1800). Subway: 6 to 96th St. Big, tasty portions. "Mom's Lovin' Meatloaf" $11; salads $5-11; sandwiches $6-8. Specials (M-F 5-7pm) include soup/salad and dessert. Open daily 8am-11pm. ❷

▨ **Le Pain Quotidien,** 1131 Madison Ave. (☎327-4900), between 84th and 85th St. Subway: 4, 5, 6 to 86th St./Lexington Ave. Boutique bakery with some of NYC's freshest bread. Pick up a *baguette à l'ancienne* ($2.50), or sit for a full meal at their trademark communal wooden tables. Open M-F 7:30am-7pm, Sa-Su 8am-7pm. ❶

Saigon Grill, 1700 Second Ave., at 88th St. (☎996-4600). Subway: 4, 5, 6 to 86th St./Lexington Ave. So-so decor, fresh Vietnamese food. Entrees $8-14. Open daily 11:30am-11:30pm. 2nd location at 2381 Broadway, at W. 87th St. (☎875-9072). ❸

UPPER WEST SIDE

▨ **Big Nick's Burger Joint and Pizza Joint,** 2175 Broadway, at 77th St. (☎362-9238). Subway: 1, 2 to 79th St. Cramped but clean source of tried-and-true pizza, plate-sized burgers ($5-6.75), and breakfast dishes from a vast menu. Free delivery. Open 24hr. Another cramped location at 70 W. 71st St., at Columbus Ave. (☎799-4444). ❷

Gray's Papaya, 2090 Broadway, at 72nd St. (☎799-0243). Subway: 1, 2, 3 to 72nd St./Broadway. Cheap, lively takeout with amazing deals on hot dogs. Never-ending "recession special" sells 2 franks and 1 fruit drink (banana daiquiri, pineapple, piña colada, papaya) for a mere $2.45. Open 24hr. ❶

Zabar's, 2245 Broadway (☎787-2000), between 80th and 81st St. Subway: 1, 2 to 79th St. This Upper West Side institution sells high-class groceries (fancy cheese, smoked salmon) and bagels. Kitchen gadgets and dishware sold upstairs. Open M-F 8am-7:30pm, Sa 8am-8pm, Su 9am-6pm.

HARLEM & MORNINGSIDE HEIGHTS

▨ **Sylvia's,** 328 Lenox (Sixth) Ave., at 126th St. (☎996-0660). Subway: 3 to 125th St./ Lenox Ave. Sumptuous soul food with nearly 40 years of history. Ribs special $11; lunch special (salmon croquette, pork chop, fried chicken leg, collard greens, and candied yams) $7. Free live jazz and R&B Sa 11am-4pm. Gospel Brunch Su 11am-4pm. Open M-F 11am-10:30pm, Sa 8am-10:30pm, Su 11am-8pm. ❷

▨ **Amir's Falafel,** 2911A Broadway (☎749-7500), between 113th and 114th St. Subway: 1 to 110th St., 116th St./Broadway. Small and simple, with cheap Middle Eastern staples like *shawerma*, and *mousaka* for vegetarians and meat-lovers alike. Sandwiches $3-5, vegetarian platters $5.50. Open daily 11am-11pm. Cash only. ❶

Koronet Pizza, 2848 Broadway, at 110th St. (☎222-1566). Subway: 1 to 110th St./ Broadway. Famously mammoth slices nearly feed 2 for $2.50. Open Su-W 10am-2am, Th-Sa 10am-4am. Cash only. ❶

BROOKLYN

▨ **Caravan,** 193 Atlantic Ave. (☎718-488-7111), between Court and Clinton St., in Brooklyn Heights. Subway: 2, 3, 4, 5, M, N, R to Court St./Borough Hall. Middle Eastern/Mediterranean/French cuisine. *Prix-fixe* lunch ($10) includes entree, hummus and *baba ghanoush*, soup/salad, dessert, and coffee. Belly-dancing and live band Sa at 8pm. Reservations recommended Sa nights. Open M-F 11am-10pm, Sa-Su noon-midnight. ❷

▨ **Patois,** 225 Smith St. (☎718-855-1535), between DeGraw and Douglass St., in Carroll Gardens. Subway: F, G to Bergen St. Quaint French bistro with rather pricey entrees ($12-17) and delicious traditional starters like garlic snails, and spinach and chives (around $8). Open Tu-Th 6-10:30pm, F-Sa 6-11:30pm, Su 11am-3pm and 5-10pm. ❹

Bliss, 191 Bedford Ave. (☎718-599-2547), between 6th and 7th St., in Williamsburg. Subway: L to Bedford Ave. Almost-vegan hot spot (eggs and cheese in some non-vegan dishes). Meat-free chili *con pan.* Specialty Bliss Bowl comes with vegetables, rice, potatoes, and more ($8). BYOB. Open M-F 9am-11pm, Sa-Su 10am-11pm. Cash only. ❶

QUEENS

▨ **Flushing Noodle,** 135-42 Roosevelt Ave. (☎718-353-1166), in Flushing. Subway: 7 to Flushing-Main St. One of Flushing's finest Chinese noodle shops. Noodles $3.75-5. Lunch specials $5 between 11am-3:30pm. Open daily 9am-10pm. ❶

Jackson Diner, 37-47 74th St. (☎718-672-1232), in Jackson Heights, between 37th and 38th Ave. Subway: E, F, G, R, V to Jackson Heights/Roosevelt Ave.; 7 to 74th St.-Broadway. Delicious Indian food in colorful, almost-trendy setting. Great *saag gosht* (lamb with spinach, tomato, ginger, and cumin $11) and samosas ($3.50). Lunch specials $6-7.50. Weekend lunch buffet $9 (11:30am-4pm). Open M-F 11:30am-10pm, Sa-Su 11:30am-10:30pm. Cash only. ❷

◉ SIGHTS

THE STATUE OF LIBERTY & ELLIS ISLAND

The Statue of Liberty stands at the entrance to New York Harbor, long a symbol of hope for millions of immigrants fresh from the arduous voyage across the Atlantic. In 1886, the French government presented Frederic-Auguste Bartholdi's sculpture to the US as a sign of goodwill. The actual statue is now off-limits to tourists, but Liberty Island still offers a superb view of the monument. While the Statue embodies the American Dream, the Ellis Island museum chronicles the harsh realities of immigrant life in the New World. *(Subway: 4, 5 to Bowling Green; N, R to Whitehall St. ☎ 363-3200. Ferry Information: ☎ 269-5755. Ferries run in a loop, Battery Park-Liberty Island-Ellis Island, daily every 30min. 9am-3:50pm. Tickets for ferry, the Statue of Liberty, and Ellis Island: $10, seniors $8, ages 4-12 $4, under 4 free.*

FINANCIAL DISTRICT & CIVIC CENTER

The southern tip of Manhattan is a financial powerhouse: the Wall St. area, less than ½ mi. long, has one of the highest concentrations of skyscrapers in the world. Crooked streets retain NY's original Dutch layout; lower Manhattan was the first part of the island to be settled. *(Subway: 1, 2, to Wall St./William St.; 4, 5 to Bowling Green, Wall St./Broadway; N, R to Rector St., Whitehall St.; 1, 2, 4, 5, A, C, J, M, Z to Fulton St./Broadway-Nassau St.; J, M, Z to Broad St.)*

FINANCIAL DISTRICT. Once the northern border of the New Amsterdam settlement, Wall St. is named for the wall built in 1653 to shield the Dutch colony from British invasion. By the early 19th century, the area was the financial capital of the US. On the southwest corner of Wall and Broad St. stands the **New York Stock Exchange.** This 1903 temple to capitalism sees billions of dollars change hands daily. The exchange, founded in 1792 at 68 Wall St., is now off-limits to tourists.

WALL STREET. Around the corner, at the end of Wall St., stands the seemingly ancient **Trinity Church,** with its delicately crafted steeple towering anomalously amid the Financial District's canyons. Alexander Hamilton is buried here. *(74 Trinity Place. ☎ 602-0800.)* **Bowling Green,** the city's first park, lies at the intersection of Battery Pl., Broadway, and Whitehall St. The site of the city's first mugging, it's also where Peter Minuit purchased Manhattan for the equivalent of $24 in trade goods. The Beaux Arts **U.S. Custom House,** 1 Bowling Green, overlooks the park. *(1 Bowling Green St. ☎ 668-6624.)*

WORLD TRADE CENTER MEMORIAL SITE (GROUND ZERO). Once the city's tallest buildings, the WTC's Twin Towers were destroyed by terrorism on September 11, 2001. A fitting memorial to the over 2800 victims has not yet been built.

CIVIC CENTER. Fittingly, the city's center of government is located immediately north of its financial district, as the city tries to keep tabs on any unscrupulous dealings perhaps the finest piece of architecture in the city is **City Hall.** This elegant Neoclassical structure where New York's mayor keeps his offices is also the neighborhood's center; around it revolve myriad courthouses, civic buildings, and federal buildings. The building's interior is closed indefinitely to the public. *(Broadway at Murray St., off Park Row.)* The **Woolworth Building,** a sumptuous, 1913 Neo-Gothic skyscraper built for $15.5 million to house F.W. Woolworth's five-and-dime store empire, looms south of City Hall. Arches and mosaics adorn the resplendent lobby of this "Cathedral of Commerce." *(233 Broadway, between Barclay St. and Park Pl.)* A block and a half south on Broadway lies **St. Paul's Chapel;** Manhattan's oldest public building in continuous use hasn't missed a day since George Washington prayed here on his inauguration day. *(Between Vesey and Fulton St. Open M-F 9am-3pm, Su 7am-3pm. Su Eucharist 8am. ☎ 602-0747.)*

SOUTH STREET SEAPORT. The shipping industry thrived at the **South Street Seaport** for most of the 19th century, when New York was the most important port city in the US. During the 20th century, bars, brothels, and crime flourished. Now a 12-block "museum without walls," South Street Seaport features old schooners, sailboats, and houses. Visit the Seaport Museum Visitors Center for info on attractions. *(Between FDR Dr. and Water St., and between Beekman and John St. Subway: 1, 2, 4, 5, A, C, J, M, Z to Fulton St./Broadway-Nassau St. Visitors Center: 12 Fulton St. ☎ 748-8600. Open Apr.-Sept. W-M 10am-6pm; Oct.-Mar. W-M 10am-5pm. Admission to ships, shops and tours $5, under 12 free. Walking around the museum is free.)* The **Fulton Fish Market,** the largest fresh-fish mart in the country (and a notorious former mafia stronghold), lies on South St., on the other side of the overpass. *(☎ 748-8786. Market opens at 4am. Market tours May-Oct. 1st and 3rd W of each month, 6am. $12. Reservations required, call around 1 week in advance. Walking around the fish market free.)*

CHINATOWN & LITTLE ITALY

Mott and **Pell St.,** the unofficial centers of Chinatown, brim with Chinese restaurants and commercial activity. Chinese-style baby jackets, bamboo hats, and miniature Buddhas crowd the storefronts. **Canal St.** abounds in low-priced, creatively labeled merchandise (those are *not* Rolexes). **Mulberry St.** remains the heart of the Little Italy, which has been largely taken over by Chinatown in recent decades. *(Subway to Chinatown: J, M, Z to Canal St./Centre St.; N, Q, R, W to Canal St./Broadway; 4, 6 to Canal St./ Lafayette St. Subway to Little Italy: 6 to Spring St./Lafayette St.; J, M, Z to Canal St./ Centre St.; N, Q, R, W to Canal St./ Broadway; 4, 6 to Canal St./Lafayette St.; S to Grand St.; F to E. Broadway; F, V, S to Broadway-Lafayette St.)*

LOWER EAST SIDE

The Lower East Side was once the most densely settled area in New York. The Irish came in the mid-1800s, Eastern Europeans in the 50 years preceding WWI, African-Americans and Puerto Ricans post-WWII, and Latin Americans and Asians in the 1980s and 90s. Main thoroughfares like E. Broadway reflect the area's multicultural roots. Orchard St., an historic shopping area that fills up on Sundays, still has traces of the Jewish ghetto. *(Subway: F, V to Lower East Side-Second Ave.; F to E. Broadway; F, J, M, Z to Delancey St.-Essex St.)*

LOWER EAST SIDE SITES. The **Lower East Side Visitors Center** is a source of maps and brochures, and also organizes a free area shopping tour. *(261 Broome St., between Orchard and Allen St. ☎ 226-9010. Open daily 10am-4pm.)* At the **Lower East Side Tenement Museum,** tours lead through three meticulously restored apartments of immigrant families: the Gumpertzes in 1870, the Rogarshevskys in 1918, and the Baldizzis in 1939. *(90 Orchard St. ☎ 431-0233. Call for info on tours of tenements and neighborhood. Admission: $8-9, students and seniors $6-7.)* The **Eldridge Street Synagogue** *(12 Eldridge St. ☎ 219-0888)* and **Congregation Anshe Chesed** *(172-176 Norfolk St., at Stanton St. ☎ 865-0600)* are two splendid old synagogues.

SOHO

The architecture in the area **South of Houston**—with Canal St. on the south, Broadway on the west, and Crosby St. on the east—is American Industrial, notable for its cast-iron facades. Inhabited by New York's prospering *artistes*, SoHo is filled with galleries (see **Galleries,** p. 229), chic boutiques, and very expensive shopping. *(Subway: C, E to Spring St./Ave. of the Americas; 6 to Spring St./Lafayette St.; N, R to Prince St.; 1, 2 to W. Houston St.; F, S, V to Broadway-Lafayette St.)*

MID-ATLANTIC

THE HIDDEN DEAL

GREEN GUERILLAS

In 1973, Liz Christy and the "green Guerrillas" began planting neighborhood window boxes and tree pits and throwing water balloons filled with seeds into the East Village and Alphabet City's abandoned lots. By 1986 they had transformed the northeast corner of Bowery and Houston into a flowering oasis named the **Liz Christy Bowery-Houston Garden,** 110 E. Houston St., between Bowery and Second Ave. (Open Sa noon-4pm; May-Sept. also open Tu 6pm-dusk.) The trend caught on, and community gardens blossomed across the East Village—a manifestation of residents' combined love for nature and for social activism.

One example is the **De Colores Community Yard and Garden,** E. 8th St., between Ave. B and C. Work on De Colores began in May of 1996. The group of East Village and Lower East Side community members decided to clear out a rubble-filled, city-owned lot and create a garden. This was partially a response to the city's destruction of a large, longstanding garden across the street in order to create a residence for the elderly. The community members, left to their own devices by the city, cut down trees, cleared building rubble, and even removed junkies' needles in order to create the De Colores garden. Once the lot was cleared, garden plots with wood and rocks were created along the perimeter and grass seed planted in the center.

(continued on next page)

TRIBECA

TriBeCa, or Triangle Below Canal St., has been anointed (by resident Robert DeNiro and others) as one of the hottest neighborhoods in the city. Hidden inside the industrial warehouses are SoHo-trendy lofts, restaurants, bars, and galleries—without the upscale airs. Admire the cast-iron edifices lining White St., Thomas St., and Broadway, the 19th-century Federal-style buildings on Harrison St., and the shops, galleries, and bars on Church and Reade St. *(Subway: 1, 2 to Canal St./Varick St., Franklin St., Chambers St./W. Broadway; C, E to Canal St./Ave. of the Americas; A, C to Chambers St./ Church St.)*

GREENWICH VILLAGE

Once a staid high-society playground in the mid-19th century, the Village (west of Broadway, between Houston and 14th St.) has undergone a relentless process of cultural ferment that layered grime, activism, and artistry atop its quaint, meandering streets. The last 40 years brought the Beat movement, the homosexual community around Christopher St., and the punk scene; the gentrification process of the 1980s and 90s has made the Village a fashionable and comfortable settlement for wealthier New Yorkers with a bit more spunk than their uptown counterparts. *(Subway: A, C, E, F, V, S to W. 4th St.; A, C, E, L to 14th St./Eighth Ave.; 1, 2, 3 to 14th St./Seventh Ave.; F, L, V to 14th St./Ave. of the Americas (Sixth Ave.); 4, 5, 6, L, N, Q, R, W to 14th St.-Union Sq.; 1, 2 to Houston St., Christopher St.; N, R to 8th St.-NYU; L to Sixth Ave., Eighth Ave.; 6 to Bleecker St.)*

WASHINGTON SQUARE. Washington Square Park has a rich history. By the beginning of the 20th century, it had already served as a potter's field for the burial of the poor and unknown (around 15,000 bodies lie buried here); a hanging-grounds during the Revolutionary War; a park and parade ground; and the center of New York's elite social scene during the mid-1800s. On the north side of the park is **The Row,** a stretch of 1830s stately brick residences that were soon populated by writers, dandies, and professionals. At the north end of the Park stands the **Washington Memorial Arch,** built in 1889 to commemorate the centennial of George Washington's inauguration. Until 1964, Fifth Ave. actually ran through the arch; residents, however, complained of the noisy traffic and the city altered the esteemed avenue. **New York University,** the country's largest private university, has some of the Village's least appealing contemporary architecture. On the park's southeast side, where Washington Sq. S meets LaGuardia Pl., NYU's **Loeb Student Center** sports pieces of scrap metal representing birds in flight.

WEST VILLAGE. The area of Greenwich Village west of 6th Ave. boasts eclectic summer street life and excellent nightlife. A visible gay community thrives around **Sheridan Sq.**, at the intersection of Seventh Ave., W. 4th St., and Christopher St. The 1969 Stonewall Riot, arguably the beginning of the modern gay rights movement, started here. The neighborhood is a magnet for literary pilgrimages. **Chumley's,** a former speakeasy, was a hangout for such authors as Ernest Hemingway and John Dos Passos. *(86 Bedford St., between Grove and Barrow St. ☎ 675-4449. Open Su-Th 5pm-midnight, F-Sa 5pm-2am.)* Off 10th St. and Sixth Ave. you'll see an iron gate and street sign marking **Patchin Place.** e.e. cummings, Theodore Dreiser, and Djuna Barnes lived in the 145-year-old buildings that line this path. The Village's narrowest building, **75½ Bedford St.**, only 9½ ft. in width, housed writer Edna St. Vincent Millay in the 1920s, when she founded the nearby **Cherry Lane Theater** at 38 Commerce St. Actors Lionel Barrymore and Cary Grant also appreciated the cramped quarters.

EAST VILLAGE & ALPHABET CITY

The East Village—north of Houston St., east of Broadway, and south of 14th St.—was carved out of the Bowery and the Lower East Side in the early 1960s, when artists and writers moved here to escape high rents in Greenwich Village. Today East Village's wide-ranging population includes punks, hippies, ravers, rastas, guppies, goths, and beatniks. The tensions of gentrification have forged the East Village into one of the city's most politicized neighborhoods. *(Subway: 6 to Astor Pl., Bleecker St.; L to First Ave., Third Ave.; F, V to Lower East Side-Second Ave.)*

EAST VILLAGE. Full of pot-smoking flower children and musicians in the 1960s, **St. Mark's Place** hosted the punk scene's teens in the late 1970s. Nowadays, those youths still line the street—in their "old-tattooed-geezer" incarnations. The present-day St. Mark's Pl. is a drag full of tiny ethnic eateries, street level shops, sidewalk vendors selling trinkets of all kinds, and tattoo shops. Simmering with street life, **Astor Place,** at the intersection of Lafayette, E. 8th St., and Fourth Ave., is distinguished by a large black cube balanced on its corner.

ALPHABET CITY. East of First Ave. and south of 14th St., the avenues run out of numbers and adopt letters. During the area's heyday in the 1960s, Jimi Hendrix played open-air shows here to bright-eyed love children. The area was once ravaged by drug-related crime, but locals have done an admirable job of making the neighborhood livable again, starting a number

(continued from previous page)

People design their own plots, and the common plots and grass are tended to communally. De Colores flowers have brightened this formerly dark and dangerous place. A flea market takes place every Saturday at 10am near the spacious garden.

Another notable community garden is the **6th Street and Avenue B Garden.** The mother of all community gardens, this fantasy jungle contains a towering sculpture by Edward Boros. (Open in summer daily 8am-8pm; other times Sa-Su 1-6pm.) The **Campos Plaza,** E. 12th St., between Ave. B and C, contains a plethora of fruits and veggies. (Open Mar.-Oct. Su 3-5pm and intermittently during the week.) For more about garden activists, visit www.greenguerillas.org.

Other spectacular East Village community gardens include:

El Sol Brillante, E. 12th St., between Ave. A and B.

Gilbert's Sculpture Garden, E. 8th St., between Ave. C and D.

Miracle Garden, E. 3rd St., at Ave. B. (entrance on E. 2nd St.). Small but tall and lush.

of community gardens. Alphabet City's extremist Boho activism has made the neighborhood chronically ungovernable; police officers in 1988 set off a riot when they attempted to evict a band of the homeless and their supporters in **Tompkins Sq. Park.** *(E. Seventh St. and Ave. A.)*

LOWER MIDTOWN

UNION SQUARE. At the intersection of Fourth Ave. and Broadway, Union Square and the surrounding area sizzled with high society before the Civil War. Today, the park hosts the ▒**Union Square Greenmarket,** a pleasant farmers market. *(Between Broadway and Park Ave., and 14th and 17th St. Subway: 4, 5, 6, L, N, Q, R, W to 14th St.-Union Sq.)* The very photogenic **Flat Iron Building** is the world's first skyscraper. Originally named the Fuller Building, was nicknamed after its dramatic wedge shape (imposed by the intersection of Broadway, Fifth Ave., 22nd St., and 23rd St.).

CHELSEA. Home to some of the most fashionable clubs, bars, and restaurants in the city, Chelsea (west of Fifth Ave., between 14th and 30th St.) boasts a large gay and lesbian community, an increasing artsy-yuppie population, and innovative **art galleries** (see **Museums and Galleries,** p. 226) fleeing high SoHo rents. *(Subway: 1, 2, 3 to 14th St./Seventh Ave.; A, C, E, L to 14th St./Eighth Ave.; C, E to 23rd St./Eighth Ave.; 1, 2 to 23rd St./Seventh Ave.; 1 to 28th St./Seventh Ave.)* The historic **Hotel Chelsea,** between Seventh and Eighth Ave., has sheltered such artists as Sid Vicious of the Sex Pistols and Edie Sedgwick (he torched the place with a cigarette between Warhol films). Countless writers spent their days searching for inspiration here, including Arthur Miller, Vladimir Nabokov, and Dylan Thomas. *(222 W. 23rd St., between Seventh and Eighth Ave. ☎ 243-3700.)*

HERALD SQUARE AREA. Herald Square is located between 34th and 35th St., between Broadway and Sixth Ave. The area is a center for shopping. *(Subway: B, D, F, N, Q, R, W to Herald Sq.)* This **Empire State Building,** now the city's tallest building after the WTC tragedy, dominates postcards, movies, and the city's skyline. The limestone and granite structure, stretches 1454 ft. into the sky, and its 73 elevators run through 2 mi. of shafts. The nighttime view from the top is spectacular. *(350 Fifth Ave., at 34th St. Observatory: ☎ 736-3100. Open daily 9:30am-midnight; last elevator up at 11:30pm. $9; seniors $7, under 12 $4. Skyride: ☎ 279-9777. Open daily 10am-10pm. $11.50, seniors and ages 4-12 $8.50.)* East on 34th St. stands **Macy's.** This Goliath of department stores sponsors the **Macy's Thanksgiving Day Parade,** a NYC tradition buoyed by ten-story Snoopys, marching bands, and floats. *(Between 7th Ave. and Broadway, in Herald Sq.)* The **Garment District,** surrounding Macy's, but selling cheaper clothing, was once a red-light district, and purportedly contained the world's largest concentration of apparel workers during the 1930s. *(Between Broadway and Eighth Ave.)*

MIDTOWN

East of Eighth Ave., from about 42nd St. to 59th St., lie Midtown's mammoth office buildings, posh hotels, and high-brow stores. *(Subway: 4, 5, 6, 7, S to 42nd St.-Grand Central; E, V, 6 to 51st St.; 4, 5, 6, N, R, W to 59th St.-Lexington Ave.; F to Lexington Ave./ 63rd St.; B, D, F, V, 7 to 42nd St.-Bryant Park; B, D, F, V to 47th-50th St.-Rockefeller Center; 1, 2, 3, 7, N, Q, R, S, W to 42nd St.-Times Square; A, C, E to 42nd St.-Port Authority; E, V to Fifth Ave./53rd St.; 1, 2 to 50th St./Broadway.)*

FIFTH AVENUE. A monumental research library in the style of a classical temple, this main branch of the **New York Public Library,** between 40th and 42nd St., contains world's seventh largest research library and an immense reading room. *(42nd St. and Fifth Ave. ☎ 869-8089.)* The pleasant **Bryant Park** behind the library features free, extremely popular summertime cultural events, like classic film screenings, jazz concerts, and live comedy. *(☎ 484-1222 for events schedule. Open 7am-9pm.)* Designed by James Renwick, the twin spires of **St. Patrick's Cathedral** stretch 330 ft. into the air. New York's most famous church is actually the largest Catholic cathedral in the US. *(51st. St. ☎ 753-2261.)* On 59th St., at the southeast corner of Central Park, sits the legendary **Plaza Hotel**, constructed in 1907 at an astronomical cost. Its 18-story, 800-room French Renaissance interior flaunts five marble staircases, countless ludicrously named suites, and a two-story Grand Ballroom.

ROCKEFELLER CENTER. The main entrance to Rockefeller Center is on Fifth Ave. between 49th and 50th St. **The Channel Gardens**, so named because they sit between the **Maison Française** on the left and the **British Empire Building** on the right, usher the pedestrian toward **Tower Plaza**. This sunken space, topped by the gold-leafed statue of Prometheus, is surrounded by the flags of over 100 countries. During spring and summer an **ice-skating rink** lies dormant beneath an overpriced cafe. The rink, which is better for people-watching than for skating, reopens in winter in time for the **annual Christmas tree lighting**, one of New York's greatest traditions. **Tours of Rockefeller Center** are available through NBC. *(Tours meet at 30 Rockefeller Plaza, at W. 49th St. between Fifth and Sixth Ave. ☎ 664-3700. 1¼hr. Every hr. M-Sa 9am-4pm, Su 10am-4pm. No children under 6. $10, seniors and ages 6-16 $8, groups over 3 $8.)*

Behind Tower Plaza is the **General Electric Building**, a 70-story skyscraper. NBC, which makes its home here, offers an hour-long tour that traces the history of the network, from their first radio broadcast in 1926 through the heyday of TV programming in the 1950s and 60s to today's sitcoms. The tour visits six studios including the infamous 8H studio, home of Saturday Night Live. *(30 Rockefeller Plaza. ☎ 664-3700 for tours. Every 30min. M-Sa 8:30am-5pm, Su 9:30am-4:30pm. No children under 6. $17.50, seniors and ages 6-16 $15, groups over 3 $15.)* A block north is **Radio City Music Hall**. Narrowly escaping demolition in 1979, this Art Deco landmark received a complete interior restoration shortly thereafter. Radio City's main attraction is the Rockettes, a high-stepping long-legged troupe of dancers. Tours of the Music Hall take the visitor through The Great Stage and various rehearsal halls. *(50th St. at Sixth Ave. ☎ 247-4777. $17, under 12 $10, group discounts available.)*

PARK AVENUE. A luxurious boulevard with greenery running down its center, **Park Avenue** from 45th St. to 59th St. is lined with office buildings and hotels. Completed in 1913, the **Grand Central Terminal** has a richly classical main facade on 42nd St.; on top stands a beautiful sculpture of Mercury, Roman god of transportation. An info booth sits in the middle of the commuter-filled Concourse. *(Between 42nd and 45th St.)* Several blocks uptown is the *crème de la crème* of Park Avenue hotels, the **Waldorf-Astoria**. *(Between 49th and 50th St.)* The **Seagram Building**, Ludwig Mies Van der Rohe's dark, gracious modern monument, stands a few blocks uptown. *(375 Park Ave., between 52nd and 53rd St.)*

UNITED NATIONS AREA. The **United Nations**, a "center for harmonizing the actions of nations" founded in 1945 in the aftermath of World War II, is located in international territory along what would be First Ave. The UN complex consists of the Secretariat Building (the skyscraper), the General Assembly Building, the Hammarskjöld Library, and the Conference Building. The only way into the General Assembly Building is by guided tour. *(First Ave., between 42nd and 48th St. ☎ 963-4475. 1hr. tours depart every 15min. from the UN visitor's entrance at First Ave. and 46th St. M-F 9:15am-4:45pm, Sa-Su 9:30am-4:45pm. $8.50, students $6, over 62 $7, ages 4-14 $5; disabled 20% discount. Under 4 not admitted.)* At the **Chrysler Building**, a spire influenced by radiator grille design tops this Art Deco palace. *(On 42nd St. and Lexington Ave.)*

TIMES SQUARE & THEATER DISTRICT. At 42nd St., Seventh Ave., and Broadway, the city offers up one of the largest electronic extravaganzas in the world. Times Square, a onetime dark metropolis covered with strip clubs, neon, and filth, is now at least partially cleaned up. Madame Tussaud's and AMC united to rebuild three

MID-ATLANTIC

major theaters into a wax museum and 29-screen movie megaplex. Some theaters have been converted into movie houses or simply left to rot as the cost of Broadway productions has skyrocketed, but approximately 37 theaters remain active, most of them grouped around 45th St. One highlight of the Theater District is **Shubert Alley,** a half-block west of Broadway between 44th and 45th St. Originally built as a fire exit between the Booth and Shubert Theaters, the alley now serves as a private street for pedestrians.

57TH ST. AND CENTRAL PARK SOUTH. Several luxury hotels, including the **Essex House,** the **St. Moritz,** and **the Plaza** overlook Central Park from their perch on Central Park S, between Fifth and Eighth Ave., where 59th St. should be. Amid 57th St.'s galleries and stores is New York's musical center, **Carnegie Hall** (see p. 237). A $60 million restoration program has returned the 1891 building to its earlier splendor. *(881 Seventh Ave., at W. 57th St. ☎ 247-7800 or 903-9765. Tours M–F 11:30am, 2, and 3pm. 1hr. Tickets sold at box office on tour days. $6, students and seniors $5, under 12 $3.)*

CENTRAL PARK

> ❗ Central Park is fairly safe during the day, but less so at night. Don't be afraid to go to events in the Park at night, but take large paths and go with someone. Do not wander the darker paths at night, especially if you are a woman. In an **emergency,** use one of the call-boxes located throughout the park. **24hr. Police Line, ☎** 570-4820.

Once an 843-acre squatting-place for the very poor, Central Park was founded in the mid-18th century, when some wealthy New Yorkers—longing for their own European-style playground—advocated the creation of a public space to ameliorate social ills. Frederick Law Olmsted collaborated with Calvert Vaux to design the park in 1858. Their Greensward plan took 15 years and 20,000 workers to implement, and the result is a beautiful park very well-used by New Yorkers.

Expansive fields such as the **Sheep Meadow,** from 66th to 69th St., and the **Great Lawn,** from 80th to 85th St., complement developed spaces such as the **Mall,** between 66th and 71st St.; the **Shakespeare Garden,** at 80th St.; and the **Imagine Mosaic,** commemorating the music and dreams of John Lennon on the western side of the park at 72nd St. Don't miss the park's free summertime performances at Central Park Summerstage and Shakespeare in the Park. *(☎ 360-3444; parks and recreation info 360-8111, M–F 9am-5pm. Free park maps at Belvedere Castle, located mid-park at 79th St.; the Charles A. Dana Discovery Center, at 110th St. near 5th Ave.; the North Meadow Recreation Center, mid-park at 97th St.; and the Dairy, mid-park near 65th St.)*

UPPER EAST SIDE

Since the late 19th and early 20th centuries, when some of New York's wealthiest citizens built elaborate mansions along **Fifth Avenue,** the Upper East Side has been home to the city's richest residents. Today, some of these park side mansions have been turned into museums, such as the Frick Collection and the Cooper-Hewitt Museum. They are just two of the world-famous museums that line **Museum Mile,** from 82nd to 104th St. on Fifth Ave. (see p. 226). **Park Avenue** from 59th to 96th St. is lined with dignified apartment buildings. Lexington and Third Ave. are commercial, but as you go east, the neighborhood becomes more and more residential. *(Subway: N, R, W to Fifth Ave./59th St. 4, 5, 6, N, R, W to 59th St.-Lexington Ave.; F to Lexington Ave./63rd St.; 6 to 68th St., 77th St., 96th St.; 4, 5, 6 to 86th St./Lexington Ave.)*

UPPER WEST SIDE

While Central Park West and Riverside Dr. flank the Upper West Side with residential quietude, Columbus Ave., Amsterdam Ave., and Broadway buzz with action. Organic fruit and progressive politics dominate the area between 59th and 110th St., west of Central Park. *(Subway: 1, 2, A, B, C, D to 59th St.-Columbus Circle; 1, 2 to 66th St., 79th St., 86th St./Broadway; 1, 2, 3 to 72nd St., 96th St./Broadway; B, C to 72nd St./Central Park W, 81st St.; B, C to 86th St., 96th St./Central Park W.)*

LINCOLN CENTER. Broadway intersects Columbus Ave. at Lincoln Center, the cultural hub of the city (see p. 236). The airy architecture reinterprets the public plazas of Rome and Venice, but the Center's performance spaces for opera, ballet, and classical music take center stage. *(Between 62nd and 66th St.)*

THE DAKOTA APARTMENTS. Far away from the city in 1894 and surrounded by open land and shanties, the complex got its name when someone remarked that "It might as well be in the Dakota Territory." John Lennon was shot outside the building in 1980; *Rosemary's Baby* was filmed there. *(1 W. 72nd St.)*

MORNINGSIDE HEIGHTS. Above 110th St. and below 125th St., between Amsterdam Ave. and the Hudson River, Morningside Heights finds itself caught between the chaos of Harlem and the bourgeois glamour of the Upper West Side. *(Subway: 1 to Cathedral Pkwy. (110th St.), 116th St.-Columbia University, 125th St./Broadway.)* The centerpiece of **Columbia University's** urban campus is the majestic Roman Classical Low Library, which looms over College Walk, the school's central promenade that bustles with academics, students, and quacks. *(Morningside Dr. and Broadway, from 114th to 120th St.)* The still-unfinished cathedral of **St. John the Divine,** under construction since 1892, is the largest in the world. It features altars and bays dedicated both to the sufferings of Christ and to the experiences of immigrants, victims of genocide, and AIDS patients. *(1047 Amsterdam Ave., between 110th and 113th St. ☎316-7540; tours ☎932-7347. Open M-Sa 7:30am-6pm, Su 7:30am-6pm. Suggested donation $2, students and seniors $1. Tours Tu-Sa 11am, Su 1pm. $5.)* **Riverside Church,** near Columbia has an observation deck in the tower with an amazing view. Concerts make use of the world's largest carillon (74 bells), a gift of John D. Rockefeller, Jr. *(490 Riverside Dr., at 120th St. ☎212-870-6792. Open M-F 9am-4:30pm. Bell tower hours: Open Tu-Sa 10:30am-5pm, Su 9:45-10:45am and noon-4pm. Admission to observation deck: Tu-Sa $2, students and seniors $1. Call for free tours.)* **Grant's Tomb,** a huge presidential grave commemorating the onetime Civil War general for the Union side, lies at 122nd St. and Riverside Dr. *(Open 9am-5pm.)*

HARLEM

Over the years Harlem has entered the popular psyche as the archetype of America's frayed edges. Manhattan's largest neighborhood extends from 110th Street to the 150s, between the Hudson and East Rivers. Harlem began its transformation into a black neighborhood between 1910-1920. The 1920s brought prosperity and the artistic/literary Harlem Renaissance movement; Civil Rights and radical Black Power activism came in the 1960s. Today, thanks to the community activism and economic boom of recent decades, pockets of Harlem are thriving again after a period of economic decline. *(Subway: 6 to 103rd St., Central Park N (110th St.), 116th St. at Lexington Ave.; 4, 5, 6 to 125th St./Lexington Ave.; 2, 3 to Central Park N (110th St.), 116th St., 125th St., 135th St. at Lenox (Sixth) Ave.; 3 to 145th St./Lenox (Sixth) Ave., 148th St.; B, C to Cathedral Pkwy. (110th St.), 116th St., 135th St. at Central Park W; A, B, C, D to 125th St., 145th St./Central Park W; A, B, C, D to 145th St./St. Nicholas Ave.; 1 to 137th St., 145th St. at Broadway.)*

MID-ATLANTIC

STRIVER'S ROW. Perhaps Harlem's most prized possessions are its historic buildings, especially its beautiful brownstones. Originally envisioned as a "model housing project" for middle-class whites, Striver's Row reputedly acquired its nickname from lower-class Harlemites who felt their neighbors were striving to attain uppity middle-class status. The beautiful tan-bricked buildings, ranging in style from neocolonial to Italian Renaissance, sport wrought-iron railings and inviting stoops. (*138th and 139th St., between Powell and Frederick Douglass Blvd.*)

WASHINGTON HEIGHTS

North of 155th St., Washington Heights affords a taste of urban life with an ethnic flavor. You can eat a Greek dinner, buy Armenian pastries and vegetables from a South African, and discuss the Talmud with a **Yeshiva University** student. Fort Tryon Park is home to **The Cloisters,** a museum specializing in medieval art (see p. 227). *Subway: C to 155th St./St. Nicholas Ave., 163rd St.; 1, A, C to 168th St.-Broadway; A to 175th St., 181st St., 190th St.; 1, to 181st St./St. Nicholas Ave., 191st St.*

BROOKLYN

Part of NYC since 1898, Brooklyn is now the most populous borough. In the coverage below, neighborhoods are arranged from north to south.

WILLIAMSBURG & GREENPOINT. Having become home to a growing number of artists in the last decade, Williamsburg's galleries match its artsy population (see **Galleries,** p. 229). **Greenpoint,** bounded by Java St. to the north, Meserole St. to the south, and Franklin St. to the west, is Brooklyn's northernmost border with Queens and home to a large Polish population. The birthplace of Mae West and the Union's Civil War ironclad the USS *Monitor*, Greenpoint features charming Italianate and Grecian houses built during the 1850s shipbuilding boom. *(Subway: L to Bedford Ave.; G to Nassau Ave.)*

FULTON LANDING. Fulton Landing hearkens back to days when the ferry—not the subway or the car—was the primary means of transportation between Brooklyn and Manhattan. Completed in 1883, the nearby ▓**Brooklyn Bridge**—spanning the gap between lower Manhattan and Brooklyn—is the product of elegant calculation, careful design, and human exertion. A walk across the bridge at sunrise or sunset is one of the most exhilarating strolls New York City has to offer. *(From Brooklyn: entrance at the end of Adams St., at Tillary St. Subway: A, C to High St./Cadman Plaza E. From Manhattan: entrance at Park Row. Subway: J, M, Z, 4, 5, 6 to Brooklyn Bridge-City Hall.)*

DOWNTOWN. Brooklyn Heights, a well-preserved 19th-century residential area, sprang up with the development of steamboat transportation between Brooklyn and Manhattan in 1814. Rows of posh Greek Revival and Italianate houses in this area essentially created New York's first suburb. **Montague Street,** the main drag, has the stores, cafes, and mid-priced restaurants of a cute college town. **Downtown** is the location of Brooklyn's Civic Center, and holds several grand municipal buildings. *(Subway: M, N, R, 1, 2, 4, 5 to Court St.-Borough Hall.)*

PROSPECT PARK. Park Slope is a residential neighborhood with charming brownstones. Neighboring **Prospect Park** is the borough's answer to Manhattan's Central Park (Frederick Law Olmsted and Calvert Vaux designed the park in the mid-1800s). It has a zoo, an ice skating rink, a children's museum, and plenty of wide open spaces. In the middle of Grand Army Plaza, the 80-foot-high **Memorial Arch,** built in the 1890s to commemorate the North's Civil War victory, marks one of the park's entrances. *(Bounded by Prospect Park W, Flatbush Ave., Ocean Ave., Parkside Ave., and Prospect Park SW. Subway: 1, 2 to Grand Army Plaza; F to 15 St.-Prospect Park; Q, S to Prospect Park. ☎ 718-965-8951; events hotline ☎ 718-965-8999.)*

BROOKLYN BOTANIC GARDEN. Adjacent to the park, this 52-acre fairyland features the **Fragrance Garden for the Blind** (with mint, lemon, violet, and other appetizing aromas) and the more formal **Cranford Rose Garden.** *(1000 Washington Ave.; other entrances on Eastern Pkwy. and on Flatbush Ave. ☎ 718-623-7000. Open Apr.-Sept. Tu-F 8am-6pm, Sa-Su 10am-6pm; Oct.-Mar. Tu-F 8am-4:30pm, Sa-Su 10am-4:30pm. $3, students and seniors $1.50, under 16 free; free Tu all day and Sa 10am-noon; seniors free every F.)*

CONEY ISLAND. Once an elite resort (until the subway made it accessible to the masses), legendary Coney Island is now fading. The **Boardwalk** squeaks nostalgically as tourists are jostled by roughnecks. The **Cyclone,** 834 Surf Ave., built in 1927, was once the most terrifying roller coaster ride in the world. Meet walruses, sharks, or other marine beasties at the **New York Aquarium.** *(Surf Ave. and W. 8th St. Subway: F, Q, W to Coney Island-Stillwell Ave.; F, Q to W. 8th St.-NY Aquarium; Q to Ocean Pkwy., Brighton Beach. ☎ 718-372-5159. Open mid-June to Sept. daily noon-midnight; late March to mid-June F-Su noon-midnight. $5.)*

QUEENS

ASTORIA & LONG ISLAND CITY
In the northwest corner of Queens lies Astoria, where Greek-, Italian-, and Spanish-speaking communities mingle amid lively shopping districts and cultural attractions. Long Island City is just south, across the river from the Upper East Side. The **Isamu Noguchi Garden Museum,** the **Museum for African Art,** and the juggernaut **MoMa** (see **Museums,** p. 226) have all temporarily relocated to Long Island City. *(Astoria is located in the northwestern corner of Queens, across the river from Manhattan. Long Island City is located southwest of Astoria. Subway: All N and W stops between 36th Ave. and Astoria Ditmars Blvd. G, R, V to 36th St. or Steinway St.)*

SOCRATES SCULPTURE PARK. Led by sculptor Mark di Suvero, artists transformed this onetime abandoned landfill into an artistic exhibition space with thirty-five stunning day-glo and rusted metal abstractions. *(At the end of Broadway, across the Vernon Blvd. intersection. ☎ 718-956-1819. Park open daily 10am-dusk.)*

FLUSHING & FLUSHING MEADOWS PARK
Flushing boasts colonial neighborhood landmarks, a bustling downtown, and a huge Asian immigrant population. Nearby **Flushing Meadows-Corona Park** was the site of the 1939 and 1964 World's Fair, and now holds **Shea Stadium** (home of the Mets), the **USTA National Tennis Center** (where the US Open is played), and the simple yet interesting **New York Hall of Science.** *(47-01 111th St. at 48th Ave. ☎ 718-699-0005. Open July-Aug. M-W 9:30am-2pm, Th-F 9:30am-5pm, Sa-Su 10:30-6pm; Sept.-June Tu-W 9:30am-2pm, Th-Su 9:30am-5pm. $7.50; students, seniors, and ages 5-17 $5. Parking $6.)* The **Unisphere,** a 380-ton steel globe in front of the New York City Building, is the retro-futuristic structure featured in the 1997 *Men In Black.* *(Subway to Flushing: 7 to Main St.-Flushing. Subway to Flushing Park: 7 to 111th St. or Willets Point-Shea Stadium.)*

THE BRONX
The relentless stream of immigration, once Italian and Irish but now mostly Hispanic and Russian, has created many vibrant ethnic neighborhoods in Brooklyn, including a Little Italy that puts its Manhattan counterpart to shame.

YANKEE STADIUM. In 1923, Babe Ruth's success as a hitter inspired the construction of the Yankees' own ballpark. The Yankees played the first night game here in 1946, and the country's first message scoreboard tallied runs here in 1954. Inside the 11.6-acre park (the field itself measures only 3½ acres), monuments honor Yankee greats like Lou Gehrig, Joe DiMaggio, and Babe Ruth. The Yankees offer tours of the Stadium, but games are better. *(E. 161st St., at River Ave. Subway: 4, B, D to 161st St. ☎ 718-293-6000. Tours daily at noon. $10, seniors and under 15 $5.)*

THE BRONX ZOO. The most popular reason to come to the Bronx is the **Bronx Zoo/Wildlife Conservation Park.** The largest urban zoo in the US, it houses over 4000 animals. Soar into the air on the **Skyfari** aerial tramway ($2) that runs between Wild Asia and the **Children's Zoo.** *(Subway: 2, 5 to West Farms Sq.-E. Tremont Ave. Follow Boston Rd. for 3 blocks until the Bronx Park S. gate. Bus: Bx9, Bx12, Bx19, Bx22, and Q44 pass various entrances to the zoo. ☎ 718-367-1010; for disabled access info ☎ 718-220-5188. Open M-F 10am-5pm, Sa-Su 10am-5:30pm. $11, seniors $7, ages 2-12 $6; W free, donation suggested.)*

NEW YORK BOTANICAL GARDEN. Located adjacent to the Zoo, the city's most extensive botanical garden (250 acres) includes a 40-acre **hemlock forest,** kept in its natural state. Although it costs an extra few dollars to enter, the different ecosystems in the gorgeous domed greenhouse **Conservatory** are worth a visit. *(Bronx River Pkwy. Exit 7W and Fordham Rd. Subway: 4 to Bedford Park Blvd.-Lehman College; B, D to Bedford Park Blvd. Walk 8 blocks east or take the Bx26 bus. Bus: Bx19 or Bx26. Train: Metro-North Harlem line goes from Grand Central Terminal to Botanical Garden station. ☎ 718-817-8700. Open Apr.-Oct. Tu-Su 10am-6pm; Nov.-Mar. Tu-Su 10am-4pm. $3, students and seniors $2, children 2-12 $1; W all day and Sa 10am-noon free. Call for tours.)*

BELMONT

Arthur Ave. is the center of this uptown Little Italy, which is home to wonderful homestyle southern Italian cooking. To get a concentrated sense of the area, stop into **Arthur Avenue Retail Market,** 2334 Arthur Ave., between 186th and Crescent St. The recent Kosovar influx has put Kosovar flags in the fronts of many stores and eateries. *(Centering on Arthur Ave. and E. 187th St., near the Southern Blvd. entrance to the Bronx Zoo. Subway: B, D to Fordham Rd./Grand Concourse; then walk 11 blocks east to Arthur Ave. and head south.)*

STATEN ISLAND

It's probably more trouble to get to Staten Island than it's worth, although the 30 minute ferry ride from Manhattan's Battery Park to Staten Island lets you cruise by the Statue of Liberty for free. Because of the distances (and some dangerous neighborhoods in between), it's a bad idea to walk from one site to the next. Plan excursions with the bus schedule in mind. The beautiful 19th-century **Snug Harbor Cultural Center** houses the **Newhouse Center for Contemporary Art,** a small art gallery with a summer sculpture show, and the **Staten Island Botanical Gardens.** *(1000 Richmond Terrace. Bus S40. ☎ 718-448-2500. Free tours of the grounds Apr.-Nov. Sa-Su 2pm, starting at the Visitors Center. Botanical Garden: ☎ 718-273-8200. Open daily dawn-dusk.)*

🏛 MUSEUMS

For listings of upcoming exhibits consult *Time Out: New York*, *The New Yorker*, *New York* magazine and Friday's *The New York Times* (Weekend section). Most museums are closed on Monday and are jam-packed on weekends. Many museums request a "donation" in place of an admission fee—don't be embarrassed to give as little as a dollar. Most are free one weeknight.

UPPER WEST SIDE

▨ **American Museum of Natural History,** Central Park West (☎ 769-5100), between 77th and 81st St. Subway: B, C to 81st St. You're never too old for the Natural History Museum, one of the world's largest museums devoted to science. The main draw is the 4th fl. dinosaur halls, which display real fossils in 85 percent of the exhibits, (most museums use fossil casts). Perhaps the most impressive part of the museum is the sparkling Hayden Planetarium within the Rose Center for Earth and Space. Wheelchair accessible. Open daily 10am-5:45pm; Rose Center also open F until 8:45pm. Suggested donation $10, students and seniors $7.50, children $6.

New York Historical Society, 2 W. 77th St., at Central Park West (☎873-3400). Subway: 1, 2 to 79th; B, C to 72nd St./Central Park W, 81st St. Founded in 1804, this is New York's oldest continuously operated museum. The Neoclassical building houses both a library and museum. Wheelchair accessible. Open Memorial Day-Labor Day Tu-Su 11am-6pm, Labor Day-Memorial Day Tu-Su 11am-5pm. $6, students and seniors $4, children free.

WASHINGTON HEIGHTS

■ **The Cloisters** (☎923-3700), at Fort Tryon Park. Subway: A to 190th St.; then follow Margaret Corbin Dr. 5 blocks north. Crowning a hilltop at the northern tip of Manhattan, this tranquil branch of the Metropolitan Museum of Art incorporates pieces of 12th- and 13th-century French monasteries into its own medieval design. The tremendous collection includes the Unicorn Tapestries; the Treasury, where the museum's most fragile offerings are found; and the Robert Campin's altarpiece, one of the first known oil paintings. Open Mar.-Oct. Tu-Su 9:30am-5:15pm; Nov.-Feb. Tu-Su 9:30am-4:45pm. Suggested donation $10, students and seniors $5.

UPPER EAST SIDE

■ **Metropolitan Museum of Art,** 1000 Fifth Ave., at 82nd St. (☎535-7710, concerts and lectures 570-3949). Subway: 4, 5, 6 to 86th St./Lexington Ave. The largest in the Western Hemisphere, the Met's art collection includes over 2 million works spanning 5000 years of world history. Highlights include the Egyptian Art holdings (including the completely reconstructed Temple of Dendur), the awesome European paintings collection, and extensive exhibits of American art. Also of note is the Costume Institute, which houses over 75,000 costumes and accessories from five continents from the 17th century to the present, as well as the recently overhauled collection of Greek and Roman art. Call ☎535-7710 for wheelchair info. Open Su and Tu-Th 9:30am-5:15pm, F-Sa 9:30am-8:45pm. Suggested donation $10, seniors and students $5.

■ **Frick Collection,** 1 E. 70th St., at Fifth Ave. (☎288-0700). Subway: 6 to 68th St. Henry Clay Frick left his house and art collection to the city, and the museum retains the elegance of his chateau. The Living Hall displays 17th-century furniture, Persian rugs, Holbein portraits, and paintings by El Greco, Rembrandt, Velázquez, and Titian. The courtyard is inhabited by elegant statues surrounding the garden pool and fountain. Wheelchair accessible. Open Tu-Sa 10am-6pm, Su 1-6pm. $10, students and seniors $5. Under 10 not allowed, under 16 must be accompanied by an adult.

Museum of the City of New York, 1220 Fifth Ave., at 103rd St. (☎534-1672). Subway: 6 to 103rd St./Lexington Ave. This fascinating museum details the history of the Big Apple, from the construction of the Empire State Building to the history of Broadway theater. Cultural history of all varieties is on parade—don't miss the model ships, NYC paintings, hot pants, and Yankees World Series trophies. Open W-Sa 10am-5pm, Su noon-5pm. Suggested donation $7; students, seniors, and children $4.

The Jewish Museum, 1109 Fifth Ave., at 92nd St. (☎423-3200). Subway: 6 to 96th St. The gallery's permanent collection details the Jewish experience throughout history using ancient Biblical artifacts and ceremonial objects, as well as contemporary masterpieces by Marc Chagall, Frank Stella, and George Segal. Open M-W 11am-5:45pm, Th 11am-9pm, F 11am-3pm, Su 10am-5:45pm. $8, students and seniors $5.50, members and under 12 free; Th 5-9pm pay what you wish.

Whitney Museum of American Art, 945 Madison Ave., at 75th St. (☎570-3676). Subway: 6 to 77th St. The only museum with a historical mandate to champion the works of living American artists has assembled the largest collection of 20th- and 21st-century American art in the world. Even the modern-art skeptic will be thoroughly impressed by Jasper Johns's *Three Flags* and Frank Stella's *Brooklyn Bridge*. Open Tu-Th 11am-6pm, F 1-9pm, Sa-Su 11am-6pm. $10, students and seniors $8, under 12 free; F 6-9pm pay-what-you-wish.

MID-ATLANTIC

IN RECENT NEWS

TALKING OF MICHELANGELO

The entire art world is abuzz over a recently discovered rare, unsigned drawing by legendary Italian Renaissance painter, sculptor, draftsman, architect, and poet Michelangelo Buonarroti (commonly known, like must superstars from any time period, by his first name alone). The drawing of a seven-branched candelabrum in the form of a menorah, 43 by 25.4cm in size and done in black chalk and brown ink wash on lined cream paper, is in startlingly pristine condition—even after nearly five centuries. And it was found in the collection of New York's own Cooper-Hewitt National Design Museum.

The work, valued at $10-12 million, was purchased by the museum in 1942 for $60, as part of a larger collection. It languished in storage for decades before visiting curator Sir Timothy Clifford discovered it in a box containing light fixture designs by unknown artists. The drawing, which numerous experts agree is the work of the Renaissance master, is slated to be unveiled to the public in 2003, in conjunction with the Cooper-Hewitt's new Nancy and Edwin Marks Collections Gallery.

Museum of American Illustration, 128 E. 63rd St. (☎ 838-2560), between Lexington and Park Ave. Established in 1981 by the Society of Illustrators, this treasure of a museum owns over 1500 works by such legendary artists as Rockwell, Pyle, and Wyeth. Open Tu 10am-8pm, W-F 10am-5pm, Sa noon-4pm. Free.

Cooper-Hewitt National Design Museum, 2 E. 91st St., at Fifth Ave. (☎ 849-8400). Subway: 4, 5, 6 to 86th St./Lexington Ave.; 6 to 96th St./Lexington Ave. Occupying the splendid Carnegie Mansion since 1967, the Cooper-Hewitt holds a collection of over 250,000 objects—one of the largest collections of design in the world. Unfortunately, the vast majority of this permanent collection is never on display to the public. Make an appointment to see more. Wheelchair accessible. Open Tu 10am-9pm, W-Sa 10am-5pm, Su noon-5pm. $8, students and seniors $5, under 12 free; Tu 5-9pm free.

MIDTOWN

Museum of Television and Radio, 25 W. 52nd St. (☎ 621-6600), between Fifth and Sixth Ave. Subway: B, D, F, V to 47th-50th St.-Rockefeller Center/Sixth Ave. or E, V to Fifth Ave./53rd St. More archive than museum, this shrine to modern media contains over 100,000 easily accessible TV and radio programs. The museum also hosts a number of film screenings that focus on topics of social, historical, or artistic interest. Open Tu-W and F-Su noon-6pm, Th noon-8pm; F until 9pm for theaters only. Suggested donation $6, students and seniors $4, under 13 $3.

Pierpont Morgan Library, 29 E. 36th St., at Madison Ave. (☎ 685-0610). J.P. Morgan and son left a stunning collection of rare books, sculptures, and paintings, including hand-written sheet music by Beethoven and Mozart, Thoreau's journal, a Gutenberg Bible, and a 12th-century triptych believed to contain fragments of the Holy Cross. Open Tu-Th 10:30am-5pm, F 10:30am-8pm, Sa 10:30am-6pm, Su noon-6pm. $8, students and seniors $6, under 12 free.

DOWNTOWN

New Museum of Contemporary Art, 583 Broadway (☎ 219-1222), between Princeton and W. Houston St. Subway: N, R to Prince St.; C, E to Spring St./Ave. of the Americas (Sixth Ave.); 6 to Spring St./Lafayette St.; F, S, V to Broadway-Lafayette St. One of the world's premier museums of modern art, with the newest (and, usually, the most controversial) in contemporary art. Open Tu-W and F-Su noon-6pm, Th noon-8pm. $6, students and seniors $3, under 18 free; Th 6-8pm $3.

BROOKLYN

Brooklyn Museum of Art, 200 Eastern Pkwy., at Washington Ave. (☎718-638-5000). Subway: 1, 2 to Eastern Pkwy.-Brooklyn Museum. The museum's enormous Oceanic and New World art collection takes up the central 2-story space on the first floor. You'll find outstanding Ancient Greek, Roman, Middle Eastern, and Egyptian galleries on the 3rd fl. Open W-F 10am-5pm, Sa-Su 11am-6pm. Open 1st Sa of month 11am-11pm. Suggested donation $6, students and seniors $3, under 12 free; free on 1st Sa of month.

QUEENS

Museum for African Art, 36-01 43rd Ave. (☎966-1313), Long Island City. Subway: 7 to 33rd St./Queens Blvd. Features two major exhibits a year, along with several smaller exhibitions of stunning African and African-American art on such themes as storytelling, magic, religion, and mask-making. Objects on display span centuries, from ancient to contemporary, and come from all over Africa. Many hands-on, family-oriented workshops on traditional African activities (e.g. weaving and drumming) also offered. Open Tu-F 10:30am-5:30pm, Sa-Su noon-6pm. $5, students and seniors $2.50; Su free.

Museum of Modern Art (MoMa), 45-20 33rd St. (☎708-9400), at Queens Blvd., in Long Island City. Subway: 7 to 33rd St./Queens Blvd. Relocated to Queens until its Manhattan location at 11 W. 53rd St. finishes renovations in early 2005, the MoMa still boasts one of the world's most impressive collections of post-Impressionist, late 19th-century, and 20th-century art. Some of the collection's most renowned works are Picasso's *Les Demoiselles d'Avignon;* Rodin's *John the Baptist;* and van Gogh's *The Starry Night.* Open Sa-M and Th 10am-5pm, F 10am-7:45pm. $12, students and seniors $8.50, under 16 free; pay what you wish F 4-7:45pm.

◪ GALLERIES

New York's galleries provide a riveting—and free—introduction to the contemporary art world. To get started, pick up a free copy of *The Gallery Guide* at any major museum or gallery. Published every two to three months, it lists the addresses, phone numbers, and hours of nearly every showplace in the city. Most galleries are open Tuesday to Saturday, from 10 or 11am to 5 or 6pm. Galleries are usually only open on weekend afternoons in the summer, and many are closed from late July to early September.

SOHO

Many galleries cluster between Broadway and W. Broadway south of Houston St.

Artists Space, 38 Greene St., 3rd fl., at Grand St. (☎226-3970). Subway: 1, 2 to Canal St./Varick St.; A, C, E to Canal St./Ave. of the Americas (Sixth Ave.). Nonprofit gallery open since 1972. Its space is usually divided into several small exhibits by emerging artists. Slide file of unaffiliated artists gives those without backing a chance to shine. Open Tu-Sa 11am-6pm. Slide file open by appointment F-Sa.

The Drawing Center, 35 Wooster St. (☎219-2166), between Grand and Broome St. Subway: 1, 2 to Canal St./Varick St.; A, C, E to Canal St./Ave. of the Americas (Sixth Ave.). Specializing in original works on paper, this nonprofit space sets up high-quality exhibits. Historical and contemporary works—everything from Picasso to Kara Walker—on rotation. Open Tu-F 10am-6pm, Sa 11am-6pm; closed Aug. Suggested donation $3.

Exit Art, 548 Broadway, 2nd fl. (☎966-7745), between Prince and Spring St. Subway: 6 to Spring St./Lafayette St.; C, E to Spring St./Ave. of the Americas (Sixth Ave.). Fun, friendly, and happening "transcultural" and "transmedia" non-profit space, featuring experiments in the presentation of visual art, theater, film, and video. Open Tu-F 10am-6pm, Sa 11am-6pm. Suggested contribution $5.

CHELSEA

Many of the galleries originally in SoHo have been lured by cheaper rents to Chelsea's warehouses west of Ninth Ave., between 17th and 26th St.

Dia Center for the Arts, 548 W. 22nd St. (☎989-5566), between Tenth and Eleventh Ave. Subway: C, E to 23rd St./Eighth Ave. 4 floors of longer-term (3-9 mo.) exhibits cover a balanced range of media and styles. The roof holds an ongoing video installation piece, *Rooftop Urban Park Project,* as well as a cafe with a decent view of Chelsea. Open W-Su noon-6pm; closed mid-June to mid-Sept. $6, students and seniors $3.

The Museum at the Fashion Institute of Technology, Seventh Ave., at 27th St. (☎217-5800). Subway: 1, 2 to 18th St./Seventh Ave. Changing exhibits pertain to all things sartorial, from photography to mannequin displays. Open Tu-F noon-8pm, Sa 10am-5pm. Free.

Sonnabend, 536 W. 22nd St. (☎627-0489), between Tenth and Eleventh Ave. Subway: C, E to 23rd St./Eighth Ave. Originally from SoHo, this famous gallery has shown works by well-known US and European artists for 40 years. Open Tu-Sa 10am-6pm; closed Aug.

UPPER EAST SIDE

The upper east side is a ritzy neighborhood with chi-chi showplaces to match. The **Fuller Building,** 41 E. 57th St., between Park and Madison Ave., harbors 12 floors of galleries. (Most open M-Sa 10am-5:30pm; Oct.-May most closed M.)

Pace Gallery, 32 E. 57th St. (Pace Prints and Primitive ☎421-3237, Pace-MacGill ☎759-7999, Pace Wildenstein ☎421-3292), between Park and Madison Ave. Subway: N, R to Fifth Ave./59th St.; 4, 5, 6 to 59th St./Lexington Ave. 4 floors dedicated to the promotion of widely disparate forms of art. Open Oct.-May Tu-Sa 9:30am-6pm; June-Sept. M-Th 9:30am-6pm, F 9:30am-4pm.

Sotheby's, 1334 York Ave., at 72nd St. (☎606-7000, ticket office 606-7171). Subway: 6 to 68th St. One of the city's most respected auction houses, offering everything from Degas to Disney. Auctions open to anyone, but the more popular require a ticket (first come, first served). They also have several galleries for works soon to be auctioned off. Open Labor Day-late June M-Sa 10am-5pm, Su 1-5pm; late June-Labor Day closed Sa-Su.

Leo Castelli, 59 E. 79th St., between Park and Madison Ave. (☎249-4470). Subway: 6 to 77th St. Showing a selection of contemporary artists such as Jasper Johns and Ed Ruscha. Open mid-Aug. to late June Tu-Sa 10am-6pm; late June to mid-Aug. Tu-F 11am-5pm. Occasionally closed between exhibitions; call ahead.

WILLIAMSBURG

The Bohemian pilgrims who moved into Brooklyn's Williamsburg in the 1980s have helped transformed it into one of NYC's artistic centers.

Lunar Base, 197 Grand St. (☎718-599-2905), between Bedford St. and Driggs Ave. Subway: L to Bedford Ave. Amid many other nearby galleries, this new gallery boasts bold abstract and contemporary works from international artists. Open Th-Su 1-7pm.

Pierogi, 177 N. 9th St. (☎718-599-2144), between Bedford and Driggs Ave. Subway: L to Bedford Ave. Hosts 2 big-name solo shows a month, but the front files still display hundreds of affordable works by emerging artists. Open F-M noon-6pm.

The Williamsburg Art and Historical Center, 135 Broadway, 2nd fl. (☎ 718-486-7372), between Bedford and Driggs Ave. Subway: J, M, Z to Marcy Ave.; L to Bedford Ave. The epicenter of the Williamsburg arts scene, this historic building's beautiful 2nd-floor gallery exhibits the work of local and international artists. A monthly musical performance and biannual international show keep this Center bustling with artists from all backgrounds. Theater and music events also featured. Open Sa-Su noon-6pm.

LONG ISLAND CITY
Long Island City is the center of the Queens arts scene.

New York Center for Media Arts, 45-12 Davis St. (☎ 718-472-9414), off Jackson Ave., in Long Island City. Subway: E, V to 23rd St.-Ely Ave.; G to 21st St.; 7 to 45th Rd.-Courthouse Sq. Spacious converted warehouse featuring rotating installations of multimedia artwork. Exhibits rotate every few months. Open Th-Su noon-6pm.

P.S.1 Contemporary Art Center, 22-25 Jackson Ave. (☎ 718-784-2084), at 46th Ave., in Long Island City. Subway: 7 to 45th Rd.-Courthouse Sq.; E, V to 23rd St.-Ely Ave.; G to 21st St./Jackson Ave. P.S.1, the first public school in then-independent Long Island City, has been converted into a cutting-edge art space with rotating exhibits. Wheelchair accessible. Open W-Su noon-6pm. Suggested donation $5, students and seniors $2.

🗂 SHOPPING

There is no easier place to blow your dough than NYC—stores run the gamut from the world's (second) largest department store to sidewalk stands peddling bootleg Top 40 selections. Here's a quick, style-conscious walking tour of the city.

The best place to start is downtown on the **Lower East Side,** where hip, new designers sell their uneven hemlines and poly-nylon-rubber-day-glo shirts on Orchard, Stanton, and Ludlow St. Next stop is **Chinatown,** where you can pick up a (fake) Kate Spade from any of the million vendors along Canal St. Not to worry: they'll stick the label on for you. Pick up other imitation items right off the sidewalk, from CDs to Polo shirts. Walk up to **SoHo** to spend some major cash, this time on hip but established designers. Wooster, Prince, and West Broadway are home to the likes of Rowley and Sui, but Broadway is cheaper, with the NYC staple Canal Jeans Co. between Spring and Prince St. **Greenwich Village** has a mishmash of offerings, from the city's largest comic book store (Forbidden Planet) to Cheap Jack's Vintage Clothing, to city's best used bookstore, the Strand, 828 Broadway, at 12th St. Just east of Broadway is the more risqué **East Village,** a den of tattoo parlors, silver trinkets, sex shops, and cheap CD stores centered on St. Mark's Pl. Find some more fashionable enclaves on 9th St. farther east, and a number of good vintage stores all over. In **Herald Square** you'll find department stores like Macy's. Designer flagships line **Fifth Ave.** between 42nd and 59th St.; peruse them for a look at the really unattainable—Chanel, Armani, Prada, Louis Vuitton, Tiffany's, etc. alongside elite department stores like Bergdorf, Saks, and Bloomingdale's. To keep the kids quiet while you shop at Versace, try F.A.O. Schwarz on 5th Ave. at 58th St. **Uptown** has everything, from cute boutiques along **Columbus Ave.** on the West Side to the cheapest kicks and FuBu gear on 125th St. in **Harlem.** The outer boroughs are a mixed bag, and are too far away for most short-term visitors, although **Brooklyn** has the hippest vintage warehouse: Domsey's in Williamsburg.

🎭 ENTERTAINMENT

Publications with noteworthy entertainment and nightlife sections are the *Village Voice, Time Out: New York, New York* magazine, and the Sunday edition of *The New York Times. The New Yorker* has the most comprehensive theater survey.

WALKING TOUR

TIME: Twenty minute walking time, not including local diversions.

DISTANCE: One mile

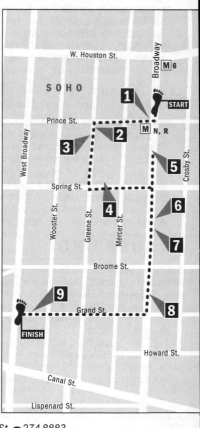

Window-shop and check out the hip, happening scenes in SoHo and TriBeCa.

1 PRADA. This breathtaking two-floor store/ public space, which opened in December 2001, contains a vast, glass cylindrical elevator and a 200-seat auditorium for events. Dressing rooms have automatic sliding doors that you close by stepping on a big black rubber button on the floor. You then step on another button and the clear glass doors mist over (so that no one can see you cramming yourself into clothing made for people so thin that they're two-dimensional). Don't look too carefully at those shoes; they cost $300-400. *575 Broadway.* ☎ *334-8888.*

2 LOUIS VUITTON. Swing by this luxury bag, and now clothing, store to check out the latest in handbags (steamer trunks are a steal at $30,000). The exorbitant prices aren't just due to hype, though: this stuff lasts forever, and the smaller bags are a bit more affordable. *116 Greene St.* ☎ *274-9090.*

3 ANNA SUI. Take a walk on the wild side of haute couture: Anna's funky designs and accessories are a perfect fit for the hip SoHo scene. *113 Greene St.* ☎ *941-8406.*

4 PENANG. Take a break from shopping to savor an exotic Ice Kacang (shaved ice with ice cream and other surprising goodies). *109 Spring St.* ☎ *274-8883.*

5 EXIT ART. Marvel at the sensory overload in this large SoHo gallery filled with experimental art in every medium imaginable. See p. 230 for more details. *548 Broadway. 966-7745.*

6 CANAL JEAN. Outfit yourself with all the urban wear your heart desires at this multi-level jeans and clothing store. A bit more mainstream and affordable than other SoHo clothiers, it's a great place to pick-up a comfy sweatshirt or funky kicks. *504 Broadway.* ☎ *226-1130.*

7 HAUGHWOUT BUILDING. Take a moment to appreciate another kind of beauty besides couture. No, not the models roaming the streets: *architecture.* This beautiful building with the Corinthian columns (and, alas, the Staples store) will have you wishing you lived there. *488 Broadway.*

8 MIRO CAFE. Tired from a long day of shopping? Grab a seat, recharge your batteries, and chow down on a heaping sandwich made with scrumptious bread. *474 Broadway.* ☎ *431-9391.*

9 LUCKY STRIKE. Unwind with an ice-cold beer at Lucky Strike. The mix between a Parisian cafe and Western saloon is ultra-cool. Grab a stool at the copper-covered bar; wish you spoke French and had a pair of cowboy boots. Au revoir, partner. *59 Grand St.* ☎ *941-0479.*

CHEAP SEATS To The budget traveler, the Great White Way's major theatrical draws may seem locked away in gilded Broadway cages. Never fear, however, *Let's Go* is here! Er, that is to say, you can find cheap tickets, compadre. Should Ticketmaster and TKTS fail, other avenues remain open to you.

Rush Tickets: Some theaters distribute them on the morning of the performance; others make student rush tickets available 30min. before showtime. Lines can be extremely long, so get there *early*. Call the theater before to find out their policy.

Cancellation Line: No rush luck? Some theaters redistribute returned or unclaimed tickets several hours before showtime. You might have to sacrifice your afternoon—but, come on, Dame Edna is worth it! Once again, call ahead.

Hit Show Club: 630 9th Ave. (☎581-4211), between 44th and 45th St. This free service distributes coupons redeemable at the box office for 30% or more off regular ticket prices. Call for coupons via mail or pick them up them up at the club office.

Standing-room Only: Sold on the day of show, these tend to be around $15 or $20. Call first, as some theaters can't accommodate standing room.

THEATER

Broadway tickets usually start from $50, but many money-saving schemes exist (see **Cheap Seats**, p. 233). **TKTS,** Duffy Square, at 47th St. and Broadway, sells tickets for many Broadway and some larger off-Broadway shows at a 25-50% discount on the day of the performance. The lines begin to form an hour or so before the booths open, but they move fairly quickly. More tickets become available as showtime approaches, so you may find fewer possibilities if you go too early. (☎768-1818. Tickets sold M-Sa 3-8pm for evening performances, W and Sa 10am-2pm for matinees, and Su 11am-7pm for matinees and evening performances.)

The **Theatre Development Fund** (☎221-0885) offers discount vouchers for off- and off-off-Broadway productions, as well as for other events sponsored by small, independent production companies. Those eligible—students, teachers, performing-arts professionals, retirees, union and armed forces members, and clergy—must first join the TDF mailing list by paying $20. Once you are a member, which may take 6-8 weeks after you mail in the application, you can purchase 4 vouchers for $28. These are redeemable at the box office of any participating production.

You may reserve full-price tickets over the phone and pay by credit card using **Tele-Charge** (☎239-6200 or outside NYC 800-432-7250) for Broadway shows; **Ticket Central** (☎279-4200) for off-Broadway shows; and **Ticketmaster** (☎307-4100 or outside NYC 800-755-4000) for all types of shows. All three services have a per-ticket service charge, so ask before purchasing. You can avoid these fees if you buy tickets directly from the box office.

Shakespeare in the Park (☎539-8750) is a New York summer tradition. From June through August, two plays are presented at the **Delacorte Theater** in Central Park, near the 81st St. entrance on the Upper West Side, just north of the main road. Tickets are free, but lines form extremely early.

EXPERIMENTAL/PERFORMANCE SPACES

▨ **Knitting Factory,** 74 Leonard St. (☎219-3006), between Broadway and Church St. Subway: 1, 2 to Franklin St. This multi-level performance space features several shows nightly, from avant-garde and indie rock to jazz and hip-hop. Summertime jazz festival. Cover $5-25. Box office open M-F 10am-2am, Sa noon-2am, Su 2pm-2am. Tickets available by phone M-F 10am-4pm, Sa noon-4am, Su 2pm-4am. Bar open 6pm-4am.

■ **The Kitchen,** 512 W. 19th St. (☎255-5793; www.thekitchen.org), between Tenth and Eleventh Ave. Subway: C, E to 23rd St./Eighth Ave. Features experimental and avant-garde film and video, as well as concerts, dance performances, and poetry readings in unassuming spot. Ticket prices vary by event; box office open M-F 10am-5pm.

Collective Unconscious, 145 Ludlow St. (☎254-5277), between Rivington and Stanton St. Subway: F, J, M, Z to Delancey St.-Essex St. Popular off-off-Broadway performance space debuts performances from the downtown artistic community. Rev. Jen's Anti-Slam Comedy Act (W) brings in a big crowd. BYOB. Cover varies, usually $5-10. 1-1½hr. shows Th-Sa 8, 10pm, midnight; call for other events.

JAZZ JOINTS

The **JVC Jazz Festival** puts on all-star performances from June to July. Tickets go on sale in early May, but many events are outdoors and free. Check the newspaper or call 501-1390. Annual festivals sponsored by major corporations draw local talent and industry giants. The concerts take place throughout the city (some free), but center at TriBeCa's **Knitting Factory** (see above).

■ **Small's,** 183 W. 10th St., at Seventh Ave. (☎929-7565). Subway: 1, 9 to Christopher St. Small's serves no alcohol, and thus is allowed to stay open all night. It's a splendid after-hours spot and a late, late night showcase for musicians who still have chops left after performances at other clubs. Cover $10; free show Sa 6:30-9pm; call ahead for early bird specials (no cover). Open Su-Th 10pm-8am, F-Sa 6:30pm-8am.

Smoke, 2751 Broadway (☎864-6662), between 105th and 106th St. This sultry cocktail lounge jumps with excellent jazz seven nights a week. Although slightly congested, the intimate space swells with music and an animated atmosphere. Jam sessions M at 10pm and Th at midnight. W funk, Su Latin jazz. Happy hour daily 5-8pm. Cover Th-Sa $10-20. $10 drink min. Open daily 5pm-4am.

Detour, 349 E. 13th St. (☎533-6212), between First and Second Ave. Subway: L to First Ave. Great nightly jazz and no cover—a perfect mix. One-drink minimum. Happy hour (2-for-1 drinks) M-F 4-7pm. Mixed drinks $6, bottled beer $4. Open M-Th 3pm-2am, F-Su 3pm-4am. Wheelchair accessible.

Apollo Theatre, 253 W. 125th St. (☎ 749-5838; box office 531-5305) between Frederick Douglass and Adam Clayton Powell Blvd. Subway: A, B, C, D to 125th St. This Harlem landmark has heard Duke Ellington, Count Basie, Ella Fitzgerald, and Billie Holliday. A young Malcolm X shined shoes here. W Amateur Night ($13-30) is legendary. Order tickets through Ticketmaster (☎307-7171) or at the box office. Open M-Tu and Th-F 10am-6pm, W 10am-8:30pm, Sa noon-6pm.

ROCK, POP, PUNK, FUNK

New York City has a long history of producing bands on the vanguard of popular music and performance, from the Velvet Underground to Sonic Youth. **Music festivals** provide the opportunity to see tons of bands at a (relatively) low price. The **CMJ Music Marathon** (☎877-633-7848) runs for four nights in late October or early November, including over 400 bands and workshops on the alternative music scene. **The Digital Club Festival** (☎677-3530), a newly reconfigured indie-fest, visits New York in late July. The **Macintosh New York Music Festival** presents over 350 bands over a week-long period in July.

■ **Mercury Lounge,** 217 E. Houston St. (☎260-4700), between Essex and Ludlow St. This converted gravestone parlor has attracted an amazing number and range of big-name acts, from folk to pop to noise, to its fairly small-time room. Past standouts include spoken-word artist Maggie Estep, Morphine, and Mary Lou Lord. Great sound system. Cover varies. Box office open M-Sa noon-7pm. Cash only.

SPEAKING THE WORD
Almost 60 years after *Howl*, poetry readings still flourish in NYC

Ever since Allen Ginsberg and his fellow beats took to howling their poetry and prose in coffeeshops and bars across the US, the spoken word and the written word have been irrevocably linked. Literary readings are now a staple of the publishing world, a chance for writers to hawk their wares and audiences to listen. Readings have become the standard—not only for the famous up-and-coming novelist or poet, but for the would-be writer at the beginning of his or her career.

One flight up a dimly lit staircase, directly above a small off-off-off Broadway theater, tucked into the front corner of an old four-story house in the East Village, sits the **KGB Bar,** 85 E. 4th St., at Second Ave. (☎ 505-3360). True to its name, KGB is draped in red paint and cloth that covers the ceiling and floor in a self-consciously over-the-top parody of Soviet propaganda. Photos and relics of the old Soviet regime, including a hammer and sickle and a portrait of Lenin above the bar, hang on the walls. The entire place is the size of a large living room, with space for about 40 of your closest friends. On a Sunday night, especially when a big-name author is on the bill, the crowd squeezes in so tightly that there is hardly room to lift a drink to your mouth.

The KGB readings have taken on their own place in New York's literary history. They have their own dedicated following, and several anthologies of poetry and prose to match. The roster of writers who have performed here reads like a *New Yorker's* "Best Young Writers" list, without the glossy photos and six-figure book deals. The Sunday night series is one of the most famous and well regarded, known among New York's venerable literati as the best place to have a drink, listen, and have another drink. Writers, more often than not, are young, talented, and in the opening stages of their careers—which is precisely what makes the KGB series the most attractive in the city. The idea of the hot young writer is brought into full play from the moment the crowd spills through the door: the writer approaches the podium with a drink in hand. A few witty remarks are exchanged between writer and audience. A tuft of cigarette smoke streams through the air; the reading begins with a small clamor of applause.

Readings, of course, are not just for the celebrated and the published. Before that first book deal, many writers often step up to the podium at some of the smaller and lesser-known readings held throughout Manhattan and Brooklyn. In the absence of a finished manuscript or *New York Times* book review, a public reading held at a small bar or cafe is the best chance writers have to share their work with someone other than their mother. The East Village's **Telephone Bar,** 149 Second Ave. (☎ 529-5000), at E. 9th St., and the West Village's **Cornelia Street Cafe,** 29 Cornelia St. (☎ 989-9319), between Sixth Ave. and Bleecker St. both host readings aimed at drawing the first-time novelist or poet into the temporary limelight of a crowded bar. Cornelia Street's readings date back over two decades and range from an Italian-American writers night to an evening of graduate student poetry. **Halcyon** (p. 243), in Brooklyn, has inaugurated a Wordsmith reading series with both political and aesthetic themes.

The writers at these smaller series may be right off the streets, MFA writing students, or invited guests. As with the publishing world, the range of talent varies dramatically, and there can often be more bad writing than good. Performance becomes essential, and not only to maintain an audience's interest: there is often the quiet hope that sitting somewhere in the audience is the literary agent or editor, with contract or book deal in hand, ready to make someone's career. This world presents writing as showcase or cabaret. Almost every writer, regardless of status, will at some point stand before an audience and thank them for coming. The famous author or poet and the unknown struggling writer share at least this one common page. As for the crowd that attends, they are there too, with drink or cigarette in hand, affirming the necessity of our spoken word.

Dinaw Mengestu has lived in New York for the past two years. He has written for the Princeton Review and SparkNotes, and is in the process of writing a novel for his master's thesis.

Arlene Grocery and Butcher Bar, 95 Stanton St. (☎358-1633), between Ludlow and Orchard St. Subway: F, V to Lower East Side-Second Ave. Hosts at least 3 bands back-to-back every night. Mostly local indie acts, but big names like Sheryl Crow have also played in this intimate space. Bob Dylan once stopped by, but only to use the bathroom. Stop by next door at the Butcher Bar—a leg of the "grocery"—where drafts cost $5. M has free Punk Rock Karaoke. 21+. Cover $5. Shows start at 7pm.

CBGB/OMFUG (CBGB's), 315 Bowery, at Bleecker St. (☎982-4052). Subway: F, V to Lower East Side-Second Ave.; 6 to Bleecker St. Initials have stood for "country, blue-grass, blues, and other music for uplifting gourmandizers," but the New York Dolls, the Ramones, Patti Smith, and Talking Heads rendered this venue (est. 1973) synonymous with punk. Music still loud, raw, hungry. 16+. Cover $3-10. Shows nightly around 8pm. Next door, **CB's Gallery,** 313 Bowery (☎677-0455), has softer live music.

FILMS

Many films open in New York weeks before they're distributed elsewhere, and the response of Manhattan audiences and critics can shape a film's success or failure. Big-screen fanatics should check out the cavernous **Ziegfeld,** 141 W. 54th St., one of the largest screens left in America. (☎765-7600. Subway: 1, 9 to 51st St. Tickets $9.50, seniors and children $6.) Eight screens project art-house cinema at the **Angelika Film Center,** 18 W. Houston St., at Mercer St. (☎995-2000). Subway: 6 to Bleecker St.; F, V, S to Broadway-Lafayette St. **Anthology Film Archives,** 32 Second Ave., at E. 2nd St. (☎505-5181), is a forum for independent filmmaking. Subway: F, V to Lower East Side-Second Ave.

OPERA & DANCE

You can do it all at ■**Lincoln Center,** as the world's largest cultural complex, many of the city's best opera, dance, and performance groups reside here. (Between 62nd and 66th St., between Ninth and Tenth Ave. ☎875-5456. Subway: 1, 2 to 66th St.) Check *The New York Times* listings. The **Metropolitan Opera Company's** premier outfit performs on a Lincoln Center stage as big as a football field. You can stand in the orchestra for $16 or all the way back in the Family Circle for $12. (☎362-6000. Season runs Sept.-May M-Sa. Box office open M-Sa 10am-8pm, Su noon-6pm. Regular tickets run over $195; upper balcony around $65. The cheapest seats have an obstructed view.)

Alongside the Met, the **New York City Opera** has come into its own. "City" has a split season (Sept.-Nov. and Mar.-Apr.) and keeps its ticket prices low. (☎870-5630. Box office open M 10am-7:30pm, Tu-Sa 10am-8:30pm, Su 11:30am-7:30pm. Tickets $25-92; $10 student and senior rush tickets the morning of the performance.) **Dicapo Opera Theatre,** 184 E. 76th St., between Third and Lexington Ave., is a small company that garners standing ovations after *every* performance. (☎288-9438. Subway: N, R to 23rd St./Broadway. Tickets around $40.)

The **New York State Theater** in Lincoln Center is home to the late George Balanchine's ■**New York City Ballet.** Tickets for the *Nutcracker* in December sell out almost immediately. (☎870-5570. Season Nov.-Mar. Tickets $16-88.) The **American Ballet Theater** dances at the Metropolitan Opera House. (☎212-477-3030, box office 212-362-6000. Tickets $17-75.) **City Center,** 131 W. 55th St. (☎581-1212), has some of the city's best dance, from modern to ballet, including the ■**Alvin Ailey American Dance Theater.** The dance company **De La Guarda** (think disco in a rainforest with an air show overhead) performs at 20 Union Sq. E. (☎239-6200. Standing-room only. $45-50, some $20 tickets sold 2hr. before show. Box office open Tu-Th 1-8:15pm, F 1-10:30pm, Sa 1-10pm, Su 1-7:15pm.) Other venues for dance include **Dance Theater Workshop,** 219 W. 19th St. (☎924-0077), between Seventh and Eighth

Ave.; **Joyce Theater,** 175 Eighth Ave. (☎242-0800), between 18th and 19th St.; and **Thalia Spanish Theater,** 41-17 Greenpoint Ave. (☎718-729-3880), between 41st and 42nd St. in Sunnyside, Queens.

CLASSICAL MUSIC

Lincoln Center has the most selection in its halls. The **Great Performers Series,** featuring famous and foreign musicians, packs the Avery Fisher and Alice Tully Halls and the Walter Reade Theater from October until May (see above for contact info; tickets from $10). **Avery Fisher Hall** presents the annual **Mostly Mozart Festival.** Show up early; there are usually recitals 1hr. before the main concert that are free to ticketholders. (☎875-5766. July-Aug. Tickets $25-50.) The **New York Philharmonic** begins its regular season in mid-September. Students and seniors can sometimes get $10 tickets day of; call ahead. Check about seeing morning rehearsals. (☎875-5656. Tickets $10-60.) For a few weeks in late June, the Philharmonic holds **free concerts** on the Great Lawn in Central Park, at Prospect Park in Brooklyn, at Van Cortlandt Park in the Bronx, and elsewhere (☎875-5709). Free outdoor events at Lincoln Center occur all summer (☎875-5928).

Carnegie Hall, on Seventh Ave., at 57th St., sometimes offers rush tickets (☎247-7800. Box office M-Sa 11am-6pm, Su noon-6pm. Tickets $10-60.) A good, cheap way to absorb New York musical culture is to visit a music school. Except for opera and ballet productions ($5-12), concerts are usually free and frequent. The best options are the **Juilliard School of Music,** Lincoln Center (☎769-7406), the **Mannes College of Music,** 150 W. 85th St. (☎580-0210), and the **Manhattan School of Music,** 120 Claremont Ave. (☎749-2802).

SPORTS

Most cities are content to have one major-league team in each big-time sport. New York opts for the Noah's Ark approach: two baseball teams, two hockey teams, NBA and WNBA basketball teams, two football teams... and one lonely soccer squad. The **Mets** bat at **Shea Stadium** in Queens. (Subway: 7 to Willets Point-Shea Stadium. ☎718-507-6387. $13-30.) The legendary **Yankees** play ball at **Yankee Stadium** in the Bronx. (Subway: 4, B, D to 161st St. ☎718-293-4300. $8-65.) Both the **Giants** and the **Jets** play football across the river at **Giants Stadium** in East Rutherford, NJ (☎201-507-8900; tickets from $25), and the **New York/New Jersey Metrostars** play soccer in the same venue. The **Knickerbockers** (that's the Knicks to you), as well as the WNBA's **Liberty,** play basketball at **Madison Square Garden** (☎465-5800; from $22 and $8, respectively), and the **Rangers** play hockey there (from $25). The **Islanders** hit the ice at the **Nassau Veterans Memorial Coliseum** in Uniondale. (☎516-794-9300. Tickets $27-70.) New York also hosts a number of other world-class events. Get tickets three months in advance for the prestigious **U.S. Open,** held in late August and early September at the USTA Tennis Center in Flushing Meadows, Queens. (☎888-673-6849. $33-69.) On the first Sunday in November, 2 million spectators witness the 22,000 runners of the **New York City Marathon.** The race begins on the Verrazano Bridge and ends at Central Park's Tavern on the Green; call 212-860-4455 for more info.

⛵ NIGHTLIFE

The city is awash with nightlife options: see performance art, hear live hip-hop, sip a highball, work it at a drag show, learn to salsa. Whether you prefer Times Square's blinding lights or a Harlem jazz club, a smoky Brooklyn bar or a Lower East Side be-seen-ery, allow yourself to succumb to the Gotham's dark side.

THE LOCAL STORY

SEBASTIAN JUNGER: WRITER/BAR OWNER

Sebastian Junger is the bestselling author of both The Perfect Storm *and* Fire. *When his books aren't being made into blockbuster movies, he does travel journalism for several major magazines, although he still calls NYC home. Lets Go caught up with him in August 2003 at Chelsea's* **Half King** *(p. 240), a bar he part-owns.*

Q: You just got back from a trip. Where were you?
A: L.A. movie business. I haven't been on assignment since last fall in Afghanistan. I was there for 1½ months with the Northern Alliance. I saw the fall of Kabul.

Q: What do you like about coming home to New York?
A: Some of my closest friends are here. I don't think it's a coincidence. I think the city draws really dynamic people. More generally, New York just has an energy and a velocity to it that I just love.

Q: How did this new bar of yours get started?
A: A friend and another well-known journalist, Scott Anderson, he and I decided we wanted to start a bar. His girlfriend is a documentary filmmaker and a contractor who was also in the movie business. The four of us got together two years ago. We wanted to build a place that would attract people in those businesses: film, documentary film, journalism, publishing. We have author readings Monday nights and photojournalism exhibits.

(continued on next page)

BARS

LOWER EAST SIDE

▓ **bOb Bar,** 235 Eldridge St. (☎777-0588), between E. Houston and Stanton St. Subway: F, V to Lower East Side-Second Ave. Small and laid-back, with a hip-hop crowd and graffiti paintings on the walls. Happy hour F 7-10pm, $3 beers. Tu alternates between Latin, reggae, and hip-hop; Th-Sa strictly hip-hop. Cover Th-Sa $5 after 10pm; $3 for women. Anti-thugwear dress code in effect (no sports apparel or hats). Open daily 7pm-4am.

▓ **Idlewild,** 145 E. Houston St. (☎477-5005), between Forsyth and Eldridge St. Subway: F, V to Lower East Side-Second Ave. Using the former name of JFK Airport has lifted eclectic theme bar to new heights. Venue shaped like an airplane, replete with a fuselage-shaped interior, reclining seats with tray tables, and boarding ramp. Beer $4-5. Martinis $9. Open Su, Tu, W 8pm-3am; Th-Sa 8pm-4am.

Orchard Bar, 200 Orchard St. (☎673-5350), between E. Houston and Stanton St. Subway: F, V to Lower East Side-Second Ave. Long, narrow haunt frequented by hip LES scene-sters. It's too cool for a sign, so keep your eyes open. Beer $4-5. Other drinks $5-6. DJ after 10pm on some weekend nights. F is house with one of NY's best DJs, Rob Salmon. Open W-Su 6pm-4am.

SOHO & TRIBECA

▓ **Naked Lunch Bar and Lounge,** 17 Thompson St., at Grand St. (☎-343-0828). Subway: 1, 2, A, C, E to Canal St. Adorned with the roach-and-typewriter theme found in the William S. Burroughs book of the same name. Uninhibited after-work crowd has no qualms about dancing in the aisle alongside the bar. Unbeatable martinis like the Tanqueray tea $8. Occasional $7 cover F-Sa after 10pm. Happy hour Tu-F 5-9pm, $2 off all drinks. Open Tu-Sa 5pm-4am.

▓ **Milady's,** 160 Prince St., at Thompson St. (☎226-9069). Subway: C, E to Spring St./Ave. of the Americas (Sixth Ave.). A rough in the overbearing SoHo diamond mine. Down-to-earth neighborhood haunt with a cast of affable regulars and, supposedly, SoHo's only pool table. Everything under $6. Good, inexpensive food served M-Th 11am-midnight, F-Sa 11am-1am, Su 11am-11pm. Bar open daily until 4am.

Cafe Noir, 32 Grand St., at Thompson St. (☎431-7910). Subway: 1, 2 to Canal St./Varick St.; C, E to Canal St./Ave. of the Americas (Sixth Ave.). Cool in so many ways. The patrons, the bartenders, and the street-front windows all provide this small bar/lounge/restaurant with a classy but unaffected feel. Draft beers $5-6. Entrees $12-20. Open daily noon-4am.

Lucky Strike, 59 Grand St., at W. Broadway (☎941-0772). Subway: 1, 2 to Canal St./Varick St.; C, E to Canal St./Ave. of the Americas (Sixth Ave.). Don't let the beautiful people stop you. They're too secure to be pretentious, so all are welcome. Lovely food and divine drinks from $5. Vanilla shanti ($8.50) is a carnival in a martini glass. Open Su-Th noon-2am, F-Sa noon-4am.

GREENWICH VILLAGE

▨ **The Whitehorse Tavern,** 567 Hudson St., at W. 11th St. (☎243-9260). Subway: 1, 2 to Christopher St. Dylan Thomas drank himself to death here, pouring 18 straight whiskeys through an already tattered liver. Boisterous students and locals squeeze into one of New York's oldest bars to pay the poet homage by tattering their own livers. Outdoor patio. Beer $3.50-5. Open Su-Th 11am-2am, F-Sa 11am-4am.

The Village Idiot, 355 W. 14th St. (☎989-7334), between Eighth and Ninth Ave. Subway: A, C, E, L to 14th St./Eighth Ave. Honky-tonk, New York style. Cheap beer ($1.50 mugs of MGD), loud country music, and a vibe as close to a roadhouse as this city gets. As if the customers' drunken antics or the bras hanging from the bar weren't enough, the (female) staff occasionally dances on the bar. Open daily noon-4am.

EAST VILLAGE

▨ **Tribe,** 132 First Ave., at St. Mark's Pl. (☎979-8965). Subway: 6 to Astor Pl. Behind the frosted glass windows lies a chic, friendly bar with colorful but subtle back lighting. Comfortable lounging areas. Beer $5, cocktails $5-10. DJ nightly with M live music. Open daily 5pm-4am.

▨ **Izzy Bar,** 166 First Ave., at E. 10th St. (☎228-0444). Subway: L to First Ave. Wooden-decor-laden, votive-lit hangout. Also one of the East Village's best music spots, with DJs spinning house or hip-hop Tu and Th, plus live jazz Su. Corona $5. Cover M-F $5, F-Sa $10. Open daily 7pm-4am.

d.b.a., 41 First Ave., between E. 2nd and 3rd St. (☎475-5097). Subway: F, V to Lower East Side-Second Ave. With 19 premium beers on tap (around $5), well over 100 bottled imports and microbrews, classy bourbons and whiskeys ($6), and 45 different tequilas, this extremely friendly space lives up to its motto— "drink good stuff." Mellow jazz, sassy crowd. Popular outdoor beer garden open until 10pm. Open daily 1pm-4am.

Beauty Bar, 231 E. 14th St., between Second and Third Ave. (☎539-1389). Subway: L to Third Ave. Unless you knew this was a bar, it would be easy enough to walk by "Thomas Hair Salon." Both exterior and interior retain the look of an old beauty parlor, and customers

(continued from previous page)

Q: What's your favorite neighborhood in New York?
A: I live in the Lower East Side. Rivington St. That neighborhood, even in the last two years, seems to have become much more trendy. So I don't know if I could call it my favorite neighborhood. What I like about it is that it's the old Jewish neighborhood from a hundred years ago, and then the blacks and Hispanics moved in, and then trendy artsy people moved in. And no one got pushed out, it's just layers. In that way it could be the most New York neighborhood. I think I'm gonna move to some place quieter though, it's pretty noisy. Maybe Brooklyn.

Q: Any advice for travelers in NYC for the first time?
A: Don't be scared. Crime is really low. You can have an amazing time in the old neighborhoods. It's the human experience, not the churches and museums, that you can get in NY like you can't get anywhere else. You'll never be insulated from the people around you here.

are well primped in slightly punk East Village style. Crowded all week, with patrons drawn in by cheap cocktails (Amaretto sour $4). Beer $3-4.50. Happy hour M-F 5-8pm, all drinks $1 off. Open Su-Th 5pm-4am, F-Sa 7pm-4am.

Remote Lounge, 327 Bowery (☎228-0228), between 2nd and 3rd St. Subway: F, V to Lower East Side-Second Ave.; N, R to 8th St.-NYU, Prince St.; 6 to Bleecker St. Over 60 video cameras cover every square foot of the space from multiple angles. Snag your own Cocktail Console, zoom in on the other patrons, and message them if you like what you see. Beer $5, mixed drinks $6, martinis up to $11. Call ahead for theme nights and performers. Cover around $4. Open daily 6pm-4am.

CHELSEA & UNION SQUARE

Billiard Club, 220 W. 19th St. (☎206-7665), between Seventh and Eighth Ave. Subway: 1, 2 to 23rd St./Seventh Ave. This pool hall's red felt tables await both the hustlin' type and those who just enjoy a game of eight-ball. Low-lying lounge ottomans and a 10 ft. square TV screen greet the rest. $13 per hour before 6pm, $14 after. You must be over 21 to play after 6pm. (If you look like you're in high school, they won't let you in until 2pm.) Open M-Th 1pm-2am, F-Sa 1pm-4am, Su 2pm-2am.

The Half King, 505 W. 23rd St., at Tenth Ave. (☎462-4300). Subway: C, E to 23rd St./Eighth Ave. Named after a mysterious and brutal Seneca Chief, this restaurant/bar has quickly become the hot spot for journalists, writers, and filmmakers on the West Side. Rotating photojournalism exhibits, weekly reading series, and a secluded patio keep everyone happy whether they're dining on a filet of salmon with asparagus ($13) or downing a pint of beer ($4.50). Open Su-Th 9am-noon, F-Sa 9am-4am.

UPPER EAST SIDE

▧ **The Big Easy,** 1768 Second Ave., at 92nd St. (☎348-0879). Subway: 6 to 96th St./Lexington. A post-grad hangout for those who miss their college glory years. With 2 beirut (a.k.a beer pong) tables in back, "Power Hour" of $1 Bud drafts nightly 11pm-midnight, and well drinks 11pm-midnight, this place can get "sloppy" in the best sense of the word. Open daily 5pm-4am.

American Spirits, 1744 Second Ave. (☎289-7510), between 90th and 91st St. Subway: 4, 5, 6 to 86th St./Lexington Ave. Cozy sports bar. Beer $4-5, mixed drinks $7-8. Karaoke Tu and Th; live music every 3rd Sa of the month. Happy hour M-F 4-8pm with $2 drafts and $3 well drinks. Open daily 3pm-4am.

Ship of Fools, 1590 Second Ave. (☎570-2651), between 82nd and 83rd St. Subway: 4, 5, 6 to 86th St./Lexington Ave. This sports bar's 35 TV screens will let you catch everything from baseball to rugby. Happy hour M-F 3-7pm. Ladies night Th 3-9pm. Open M-Th 3pm-4am, F-Su noon-4am.

UPPER WEST SIDE

▧ **The Evelyn Lounge,** 380 Columbus Ave., at 78th St. (☎724-2363). Subway: B, C to 81st St. A somewhat upscale bar for the after-work set, with fireplaces and settees creating a homey setting. Drinks ($9 martinis) are a bit pricey, but comfy couches and classy hipsters make them worthwhile. Enticing bar menu $7-14. Downstairs features a DJ W-Sa, spinning hip-hop F-Sa. Open M-Th 6pm-4am, F-Su 5pm-4am.

Potion Lounge, 370 Columbus Ave. (☎721-4386), between 77th and 78th St. Subway: 1 to 79th; B, C to 81st St. A silvery-blue lounge complete with local art on the walls, bubbles rising through pipes in the windows, and velvety sofas. The lounge takes its name from the colorful layered drinks ("potions" $10) it serves. Draft beers $5-6, martinis $9. DJs on weekends. Open Tu-Sa 6pm-4am.

BROOKLYN

▨ Galapagos, 70 N. 6th St. (☎ 718-782-5188), between Kent and Wythe St. Subway: L to Bedford Ave. *A bit deserted at night; go with a friend.* Once a mayonnaise factory, this is now one of the hipper cultural spots in the city. Great bar in an interesting futuristic decor, complete with an enormous reflecting pool, Vaudeville performances on M, and weekly film series (Su 7 and 9:30pm, M 8:30pm; $5 cover). DJs every Tu-Sa. Occasional $5 cover. Happy hour M-Sa 6pm-8pm. Open Su-Th 6pm-2am, F-Sa 6pm-4am.

Montero's Bar & Grill, 73 Atlantic Ave., at Hicks St. (☎ 718-624-9799). Subway: 2, 3, 4, 5, M, N, R to Court St./Borough Hall. Loaded with nautical paraphernalia, this friendly dive still looks like the longshoremen's bar it once was. Beer $3. Open M-Sa 10am-4am, Su noon-4pm.

Waterfront Ale House, 155 Atlantic Ave. (☎ 718-522-3794), between Henry and Clinton St. Subway: 2, 3, 4, 5, M, N, R to Court St./Borough Hall. A friendly neighborhood joint, and a great spot to go for beer and burgers. The 15 beers on tap change seasonally; try to get a pint of Brooklyn Brown. Specials like mussels in a *weiss* beer broth broaden the definition of pub grub. Mugs $3.50, pints $4.50. Live jazz Sa 11pm-2am. Happy hour (pints $3) M-F 4-7pm. Open daily noon-11pm; bar open until 3 or 4am.

DANCE CLUBS

Club scenes are about carefree crowds, unlimited fun, and huge pocketbook damage. It can pay to call ahead to put your name on the guest list. Come after 11pm unless you crave solitude, but the real party starts around 1 or 2am. A few after-hours clubs keep at it until 5-6am, or even later.

▨ Centrofly, 45 W. 21st St. (☎ 627-7770), between Fifth and Sixth Ave. Subway: 1, 2 to 23rd St./Seventh Ave.; 6 to 23rd St./Park Ave. S; F, V to 23rd St./Ave. of the Americas (Sixth Ave.); N, R to 23rd St./Broadway. Where the beautiful people and music aficionados come to dance to the latest house and techno, often by big-name DJs. All seating, except for champagne room, is waitress service. Cover $10-20. Mixed drinks $8-10. Open M-Sa 10pm-5am.

▨ Filter 14, 432 W. 14th St., at Washington St. (☎ 366-5680). Subway: A, C, E, L to 14th St./Eighth Ave.; 1, 2, 3 to 14th St./Seventh Ave. Leave the pretension behind: everyone here is all about the music. Intimate, no-frills club with some of the best house—from progressive to experimental to soul—in the city. Funky crowd, but dress code not strictly in effect. Cover $5-12. Open Tu-Sa 10pm-4am.

Nell's, 246 W. 14th St. (☎ 675-1567), between Seventh and Eighth Ave. Subway: A, C, E, L to 14th St./Eighth Ave.; 1, 2, 3 to 14th St./Seventh Ave. With various themes from Cuban Salsa to Comedy, this bar/club packs in a diverse crowd. Mingle upstairs, dance downstairs. Leather couches and dark wood recall a 1930s bar. Metal detector policy in effect. No sneakers, jeans, or work boots. Hours and cover vary daily.

Spa, 76 E. 13th St. (☎ 388-1060), between Broadway and Fourth Ave. Subway: 4, 5, 6, L, N, Q, R, W to 14th St.-Union Sq. Don't be intimidated by the doorperson's earpiece or the Herculean-sized bouncers. Dress funky and walk in with attitude. Booths around large, lit-up dance floor; waterfall behind one of the bars. Lots of Plexiglass. Tu is a popular night. Cover Su and Tu-Th $20, F-Sa $25. Open Tu-Sa 10pm-4am.

Webster Hall, 125 E. 11th St. (☎ 353-1600), between Third and Fourth Ave. Subway: 4, 5, 6, L, N, Q, R, W to 14th St.-Union Sq. This popular (if somewhat mainstream) club offers 4 floors dedicated to R&B/hip-hop, 70s and 80s/Top 40, house/techno/trance, and Latin. Sports bar and coffee bar to boot. One of the only 19+ clubs in the city. Cover Th $20 for men, free for women; F-Sa $30. www.websterhall.com has guest passes that get you $10-15 off. Open Th-Sa 10pm-6am.

Go, 73 Eighth Ave. (☎496-1200), between 13th and 14th St. Subway: 1, 2, 3, to 14th St./Seventh Ave.; A, C, E, L to 14th St./Eighth Ave. Smaller club with beautiful people. All-white decor makes a perfect canvas for the "light DJ" to work his magic with the computer operated LED lighting system. Rumored to be the favorite NYC nightspot of pop princess Britney Spears. Cover $20. Open Th-Su 10pm-4am.

GAY & LESBIAN NIGHTLIFE

Gay nightlife in New York is centered in **Chelsea**, especially along Eighth Ave. in the 20s, and in the **West Village**, on Christopher St. **Park Slope** in Brooklyn is home to a growing lesbian community.

GREENWICH VILLAGE

▨ **Bar d'O,** 29 Bedford St., at Downing St. (☎627-1580). Subway: 1, 2 to Christopher St. Mixed, cozy, dimly-lit bar/lounge. Go early for the atmosphere, around midnight for the shows. Don't leave in the middle of a show, or you'll be in for a nasty tongue-lashing. Superb performances by drag divas Raven O and Joey Arias Tu and Sa-Su at 11pm. M night is "Pleasure" for lesbians. Cover $5-7. Open Sa-Su 6pm-4am, M-F 6pm-3am.

▨ **Stonewall Inn,** 53 Christopher St., at Seventh Ave. S (☎463-0950). Subway: 1, 2 to Christopher St. Heroic bar of the 1969 Stonewall Riots. Join the diverse crowd in this renovated bar to toast the brave drag queens who fought back. 3 bars. 2-for-1 Happy hour M-F 3-9pm. Sa-Su $4 Cosmos. Cover for special shows. Open daily 3pm-4am.

▨ **Henrietta Hudson,** 438 Hudson St. (☎243-9079), between Morton and Barrow St. Subway: 1, 2 to Christopher St. A young, clean-cut lesbian crowd presides at this neighborhood bar. Also gay male and straight friendly. 2-for-1 Happy hour M-F 4-7pm. M Karaoke, W-Sa DJ, Su Tea dance. Cover $5 Su-F after 9pm, Sa after 7pm. Open M-F 4pm-4am, Sa 1pm-4am, Su 3pm-4am.

EAST VILLAGE

The Cock, 188 Ave. A, at E. 12th St. (☎946-1871). Subway: L to First Ave. A crowded boy bar with a full offering of nightly gay-oriented diversions. Call for the always changing entertainment fare. Computerized lights and "X-rated go-go boys." M drinks $3. Open Tu-Su 10pm-4am, M 9pm-4am.

Boiler Room, 86 E. 4th St. (☎254-7536), between First and Second Ave. Subway: F, V to Lower East Side-Second Ave. Popular locale catering to alluring alternative types, NYU college students, and eager refugees from the sometimes stifling Chelsea clone scene. Formerly predominantly gay male bar, now more mixed crowd. Terrific jukebox and pool table give the evening a democratic spin. Open daily 4pm-4am.

Wonder Bar, 505 E. 6th St. (☎777-9105), between Ave. A and B. Subway: L to First Ave.; 6 to Astor Pl. or Bleecker St. "Mostly gay" bar with mostly college crowd. 80% male, but women welcome. 2-for-1 happy hour daily 6-8pm. Open daily 6pm-4am.

CHELSEA

▨ **SBNY,** 50 W. 17th St. (☎691-0073), between Fifth and Sixth Ave. Subway: 1, 2 to 18th St./Seventh Ave.; F, V to 23rd St./Ave. of the Americas (Sixth Ave.). One of the most popular gay mega-bars, the newly-renamed Splash Bar New York (formerly known simply as Splash) has an enormous 2-floor complex. Cool, almost sci-fi decor provides a sleek backdrop for a very crowded scene. Drinks $4-7. Cover varies, peaking at $7. Open Su-Th 4pm-4am, F-Sa 4pm-5am.

g, 223 W. 19th St. (☎929-1085), between Seventh and Eighth Ave. Subway: 1, 2 to 18th St./Seventh Ave. Glitzy, popular bar shaped like an oval racetrack. Famous frozen Cosmos satisfy the thirst of those logging their miles. Open daily 4pm-4am.

MID-ATLANTIC

La Nueva Escuelita, 301 W. 39th St., at Eighth Ave. (☎ 631-0588). Subway: A, C, E to 42nd St.-Port Authority. Drag Latin dance club with merengue, salsa, soul, hip-hop, and arguably the best drag shows in New York. Largely, but not entirely, gay Latin crowd. F, starting at 10pm, is Her/She Bar, with go-go gals, performances, and special events. Cover Th $5; F $12; Sa $15; Su 7-10pm $8, after 10pm $10. Her/She ☎ 631-1093; $8 before midnight, $10 after. Open Th-Sa 10pm-5am, Su 7pm-4am.

MISCELLANEOUS HIPSTER HANGOUTS

Some New York institutions defy characterization. Here's a short list.

ABC No Rio, 156 Rivington St. (☎ 254-3697), between Clinton and Suffolk St. Subway: F, J, M, Z to Delancey St.-Essex St. Nonprofit, community-run art space with a vibrant mural marking its entrance. Center is open to the public and hosts many community events, from art exhibitions featuring local teenagers to hard-core and punk shows. No alcohol or beverages served. Cover $2-5.

Halcyon, 227 Smith St. (☎ 718-260-9299), between Butler and Douglass St. Get there by taxi to avoid walking south of Atlantic Ave. after dark. The hippest Brooklyn hangout south of Flatbush Ave., Halcyon combines record store, cafe, and lounge (and even furniture store). Laid-back atmosphere allows you to soak in the sounds of the DJ while playing old board games like Twixt or smoking in the back garden. BYOB. Open Su and Tu-Th 8pm-midnight, F-Sa 9pm-2am.

The Anyway Cafe, 34 E. 2nd St., at Second Ave. (☎ 533-3412). Subway: F, V to Lower East Side-Second Ave.; 6 to Bleecker St. Sample Russian-American culture at this dark, relaxed, leopard-spotted hangout. Literary readings M-F, as well as jazz F-Sa nights. Music nightly from 9pm. Friendly and free of pretension. Great place to kick back with homemade sangria and gourmet Russian food ($8-12). Open M-Th 5pm-2am, F-Sa 5pm-4am, Su noon-1am.

Nuyorican Poets Cafe, 236 E. 3rd St. (☎ 505-8183), between Ave. B and C. Subway: F, V to Lower East Side-Second Ave. NYC's leading joint for poetry slams (check out F night slam at 10pm) and spoken-word performances; several regulars have been featured on MTV. Mixed bag of doggerel and occasional gems. If you don't like the poets, don't worry—there's likely to be a heckler in the house. Cover $5-12. Open Tu-Su 7:30pm-midnight, F-Sa 7:30pm-2:30am.

LONG ISLAND ☎ 631

Long Island, a sprawling suburbia stretching 120 mi. east of Manhattan, is both a home to over 2.7 million New Yorkers (excluding those who live in the Queens and Brooklyn) and a sleepy summertime resort for wealthy Manhattanites. It is both expensive and difficult to navigate without a car.

⊠ PRACTICAL INFORMATION. Long Island Railroad (LIRR) services the island from Penn Station in Manhattan (34th St. at Seventh Ave.; subway: 1, 2, 3 to 34th St.-Penn Station/Seventh Ave.; A, C, E to 34th St.-Penn Station/Eighth Ave.) and stops in Jamaica, Queens (subway: E, J, Z) before proceeding to "points east." (☎ 718-217-5477. $4.75-15.25; lower in off-peak hours.) To reach **Fire Island,** take the LIRR to Sayville, Bayshore, or Patchogue. The **Sayville ferry** serves Cherry Grove, the Pines, and Sailor's Haven. (☎ 589-0810. Round-trip $9-11, under 12 $5.) The **Bay Shore ferry** sails to Fair Harbor, Ocean Beach, Ocean Bay Park, Saltaire, and Kismet. (☎ 516-665-3600. Round-trip $11.50, under 12 $5.50.) The **Patchogue ferry** shuttles to Davis Park and Watch Hill. (☎ 516-475-1665. Round-trip $11, under 12 $4.25.)

The Hamptons are accessible by LIRR or by car. Take the Long Island Expwy. to Exit 70, go south to Rte. 27 (Sunset Hwy. or Montauk Hwy.), and head east to Montauk (approx. 50 mi. on Rte. 27). Towns are located either directly off, or on, the highway. **Long Island Convention and Visitors Bureau** has four locations throughout the island. Call 951-2423 or 877-386-6654 for locations and hours. **Area code:** 631 and 516. In listings, 631 unless otherwise noted.

FIRE ISLAND

A gay hot spot and extraordinarily well-preserved site off Long Island's shores, Fire Island is a 32 mile long barrier island buffering the South Shore from the roaring waters of the Atlantic. Cars are allowed only on the easternmost and westernmost tips of the island; there are no streets, only "walks." A hip countercultural enclave during the 1960s and home to the disco scene of the 1970s, the island's communities, both gay and straight, still party loud.

Two prominent Fire Island resort hamlets, **Cherry Grove** and Fire Island Pines (called **"the Pines"**), host largely gay communities—and parties that rage late into the night. Crowded "streets," or wooden pathways, border spectacular Atlantic Ocean beaches. Weekdays provide an opportunity to enjoy the island's beauty and charm in a low-key setting, Thursdays and Sundays offer an ideal balance of sanity and scene, while Fridays and Saturday see mounting crowds and prices.

Gay nightlife on Fire Island has a very established rhythm that may be confusing to newcomers. Since neither Cherry Grove nor the Pines are very big, it's best just to ask around, either at your hotel or restaurant. More commercial than the Pines, the roadless Grove is lined with narrow, raised boardwalks leading to the small, uniformly shingled houses overflowing with men. Lesbian couples, however, make up the majority of the town's population. A night in Cherry Grove usually begins at the **Ice Palace,** attached to the **Cherry Grove Beach Hotel,** where you can disco until dawn. (☎597-6600. Open Sept.-June daily noon-10pm; July-Aug. daily noon-4am). Most go to the Pines for late-night partying; you can catch a water taxi from the docks at Cherry Grove, or walk 10min. up the beach. The Pines has traditionally looked down its nose at its uninhibited neighbor. Houses here are spacious and often stunningly modern. Unfortunately, the Pines' active and upscale nighttime scene has a bit of a secret club feel to it—you need to be in the know or somehow be able to look like you are. **Tea Dance** (a.k.a. "Low Tea"), from 5-8pm, takes place inside and around the Yacht Club bar/club beside the Botel hotel (☎597-6500). Move on to disco **High Tea** at 8pm in the **Pavilion** (☎597-6131), the premier disco in Cherry Grove, but make sure you have somewhere to disappear to during "disco naptime" (after 10pm). You can unabashedly dance until dawn at the **Island Club and Bistro** (☎597-6001), better known as the Sip-and-Twirl. The Pavilion becomes hot again late-night on weekends, including Sundays during the summer.

THE HAMPTONS AND MONTAUK

West Hampton, Southampton, Bridgehampton, and East Hampton make up the entity known as **the Hamptons,** where the upper crust of society roam the sidewalks before heading to the beach for the afternoon. As a result of the clientele, the prices are high here. Try going to Montauk, at the eastern tip of Long Island, for slightly cheaper accommodations. While lodging anywhere on the South Fork requires some research and often reservations, clean rooms can be had at **Tipperary Inn ⑤,** 432 West Lake Ln. (☎668-2010), accessible via the S-94 bus to Montauk Dock. The Inn provides A/C, TV, phone, and fridge. (☎668-2010. Rooms for 2-6 people in summer $125-160, off-season $75-95.

Many beaches in the Hamptons require a permit to park, but anyone can walk on for free. Sights include the **Montauk Point Lighthouse and Museum,** off Rte. 27 at the far eastern tip of the island, which was built in 1796 by special order of President

George Washington. (☎668-2544. Open June-Sept. M-F and Su 10:30am-6pm, Sa 10:30am-7:30pm; other months call for info. $6, seniors $5, under 12 $3.) Whaling buffs shouldn't miss the **Sag Harbor Whaling Museum,** at the corner of Main and Garden St. in Sag Harbor. (☎725-0770. Open May-Sept. M-Sa 10am-5pm, Su 1-5pm. $3, seniors $2, ages 6-13 $1. Tours by appointment $2.)

> If you're going to see the state of New York outside the city, camping is an option worth considering. **Visitors Centers** line I-87, in the heart of the Adirondacks and Catskills, and provide free maps of New York State and information about camping. It is wise to make **reservations;** many sites fill quickly. (☎800-456-2267, customer service ☎800-777-9644; www.ReserveAmerica.com. Reservation fee $8.50, more for cabins. The fee for camping without reservations is only $2.75 per site. Reservations can be made 2 days to 11 months in advance. Credit card or check payment only.)

THE CATSKILLS   ☎845

According to the legend, the Catskills cradled Rip Van Winkle during his century-long repose, and according to those who were there, they rocked the world in 1969 during the famed Woodstock rock festival. Today the region's best attractions are the miles of pristine hiking and skiing trails, the diminutive villages, and the crystal-clear fishing streams of the state-managed **Catskill Forest Preserve.**

⚡ PRACTICAL INFORMATION. Traveling from I-87, follow **Rte. 28 W** for the easiest way to explore the region. **Adirondack/Pine Hill Trailways** provides excellent service through the Catskills. The main stop is in **Kingston,** 400 Washington Ave., on the corner of Front St. (☎331-0744 or 800-858-8555. Ticket office open M-F 5:45am-11pm, Sa-Su 6:45am-11pm.) Buses run to **New York City** (2hr.; 13 per day; $19, Tu-Th same-day round-trip $26.25). Other stops in the area include **Hunter, Pine Hill,** and **Woodstock;** each connects with **Albany, New York City,** and **Utica.** Four stationary **tourist cabooses** dispense info, including the extremely useful *Ulster County: Catskills Region Travel Guide;* cabooses are located at the traffic circle in Kingston, on Rte. 28 in Shandaken, on Rte. 209 in Ellenville, and on Rte. 9 W in Milton. (Open May-Oct. daily 9am-5pm, but hours vary depending on volunteer availability.) **Area code:** 845, unless otherwise noted.

CATSKILL FOREST PRESERVE

The 250,000 acre **Catskill Forest Preserve** contains many small towns and outdoor adventure opportunities. Ranger stations distribute free permits for **backcountry camping,** which are necessary for stays over three days. Most of the **campgrounds** sit at gorgeous trailheads that mark great day-long jaunts. Reservations are vital in summer, especially on weekends. The **Office of Parks** (☎518-474-0456) distributes brochures on the campgrounds. Required permits for **fishing** (out-of-state residents $20 for five days) are available in sporting goods stores and at many campgrounds. **Ski season** runs from November to mid-March, with slopes down numerous mountainsides along Rte. 28 and Rte. 23A. Although hiking trails are maintained, some lean-tos are dilapidated and crowded. For more info, call the **Dept. of Environmental Conservation** (☎256-3000).

MT. TREMPER

▓**Kaleidoworld,** one of the buildings in Catskill Corners on Rte. 28, comes a close second to Mother Nature in the contest for most spectacular attraction in the Catskills. The two largest kaleidoscopes in the world are displayed here; the largest, at 56 ft., leaves ex-flower children muttering, "I can see the music!" (☎ 688-5800. Open Su-Th 10am-7pm, F-Sa 10am-5pm. $10, seniors and under 4½ ft. $8.) The **Kenneth L. Wilson Campsites ❶** on Wittenburg Rd. (Rte. 40), 3¾ mi. from Rte. 212, have wooded spots with showers and a quiet atmosphere. Make a hard right onto Wittenburg Rd., then turn right at the next intersection. The view from the beach features a gorgeous panorama of mountains surrounding the small lake. Canoe and kayak rentals, fishing, and hiking round out the options. (☎ 679-7020. Registration 8am-9pm. Reservations recommended for the weekend. Sites $16. Day use $5 per car, $1 on foot or bike; seniors free M-F. Canoes and kayaks $10 per 4 hr.)

PHOENICIA

Phoenicia is a central, small town in the Catskills. The **Esopus Creek**, to the west, has great trout fishing, and **The Town Tinker,** 10 Bridge St., rents inner tubes for river-riding. (☎ 688-5553. Inner-tubes $7 per day, with seat $10. Driver's license or $15-50 deposit required. Tube taxi transportation $3. Life jackets $2. Open mid-May to Sept. daily 9am-6pm; last rental 4:30pm.) A drier alternative to seeing the countryside is the wheezing, 100-year-old **Catskill Mountain Railroad,** which follows Esopus Creek for three scenic miles from Bridge Street to Mt. Pleasant. (☎ 688-7400. 40min. Runs Sa-Su and holidays, 1 per hr. May-Sept. 11am-5pm; Sa-Su and holidays, 1 per hr. Sept.-Oct. noon-4pm. $4, round-trip $7; ages 4-11 any ride $4; under 4 free.) At the 65 ft. high **Sundance Rappel Tower,** off Rte. 214, visitors lower themselves back to earth under their own steam power. (☎ 688-5640. 4 levels of lessons; beginner 3-4hr., $22. Must be at least group of 8 for a lesson. Reservations required 1 week in advance.) A 9¾ mi. hike to the 4204 ft. summit of **Slide Mt.** lends a view of New Jersey, Pennsylvania, and the Hudson Highlands; for a trip to the peak, head to Woodland Valley campground. Nestled in the woods, the **Zen Mountain Monastery,** off Rte. 40 north of Rte. 28, has about 35-40 Buddhists living and working together. (☎ 688-2228. Office open Tu 2-5pm, W-Sa 8:30am-5pm. Meditation training sessions W 7pm and Su 8:45am. Free, but $5 suggested donation on Su because dinner is provided.)

With 72 sites, the somewhat primitive **Woodland Valley campground ❶**, on Woodland Valley Road off High St., 7 mi. southeast of Phoenicia, has flush toilets, showers, and access to many hiking trails. (☎ 688-7647. Office open Su-Th 8am-4:30pm, F-Sa 8am-9pm. Open late May-early Oct. Sites $14.) Surrounded by mountains, the **Cobblestone Motel ❸**, on Rte. 214, has friendly managers, an outdoor pool, and newly renovated rooms. (☎ 688-7871. Doubles $49; large doubles $60, with kitchenette $69; 1-bedroom cottages $80; 3-room cottages with kitchen $99.)

PINE HILL

Pine Hill sits near **Belleayre Mt.,** which offers hiking trails as well as both downhill and cross-country ski slopes. (☎ 254-5600 or 800-942-6904. Lift tickets M-F $32, Sa-Su $41; ages 13-22 and 62+ $29/$33. Equipment rental $20.) **Belleayre Music Festival** hosts a series of classical, jazz, and folk concerts in July and August. (☎ 800-942-6904. Lawn tickets $10, occasional free concerts.) Having undergone major renovations recently, **Belleayre Hostel ❶** is a lodging bargain. Follow Rte. 28 past Big Indian, make a left at the "Pine Hill" sign onto Main St., then turn left at the small blue "hostel" sign. Bunks and private rooms sit on a small hill. Amenities include a recreational room, kitchen access, a picnic area, Internet access, grill, and sporting equipment. (☎ 254-4200. Laundry $2. Check-in 2-11pm. Check-out 11am. Reservations recommended. Bunks $15, under 17 accompanied by adult $7.50; private rooms $40; cabins for up to 6 $60-$75; 6 brand-new cabins for up to 8 $120-160.)

ALBANY   ☎518

While Albany—the capital of New York State and the oldest continuous European settlement in the original 13 colonies—proclaims itself "the most livable city in America," it is hardly a booming tourist town. On weekdays, downtown shops and restaurants thrive on the purses of politicians, but weekends find the plaza and capitol buildings deserted.

🔁 PRACTICAL INFORMATION. Amtrak, 555 East St., across the Hudson from downtown Albany (☎462-5710; station open M-F 4:30am-midnight, Sa-Su 5:30am-midnight; ticket counter M-F 4:30am-9:30pm, Sa-Su 5:30am-9:30pm), has service to Buffalo (5hr., 4 per day, $50-79) and New York City (2½hr., 12-13 per day, $43-50). **Greyhound,** 34 Hamilton St. (☎434-8461 or ☎800-231-2222; station open 24hr.), runs buses to Buffalo (5-6hr., $58), New York City (3hr, $37), Rochester (4½hr., $44), Syracuse (3hr., $38); and Utica (1½-2hr., $19-28). *Be careful here at night.* From the same station, **Adirondack Trailways** (☎436-9651) connects to Kingston (1hr., 6 per day, $10), Lake George (1¾hr., 4 per day, $12), and Lake Placid (4½hr., 1 per day, $27). For local travel, the **Capital District Transportation Authority (CDTA;** ☎482-8822) serves Albany ($1), Schenectady ($1.35), and Troy ($1.25). Schedules are available at the Amtrak and Trailways stations. The **Albany Visitors Center,** 25 Quackenbush Sq., at Clinton Ave. and Broadway, runs trolley tours of downtown and Albany's historic homes. (☎434-0405; www.albany.org. Open M-F 9am-4pm, Sa-Su 10am-4pm. Trolley tours of downtown: late June-late Sept. F 11am and Sa 10:30am; arrive 20min. early. Tours of historic homes: July-Aug. W 10am. $10, seniors $9, under 15 $5.) **Post Office:** 45 Hudson Ave. (☎462-1359. Open M-F 8am-5:30pm.) **ZIP code:** 12207. **Area code:** 518.

🏠🏚 ACCOMMODATIONS & FOOD. Pine Haven Bed & Breakfast ❸, 531 Western Ave., stands at the convergence of Madison and Western Ave.; parking is in the rear. The large Victorian house offers gorgeous rooms with phone, TV, and A/C in an inviting setting. (☎482-1574. Breakfast included. Reservations required. Rooms $59-89.) **Red Carpet Inn ❸,** 500 Northern Blvd., provides laundry facilities and clean rooms with A/C and cable TV in a downtown location near the airport. (☎462-5562. Rooms $55.) **Thompson's Lake State Park ❶,** on Rte. 157 north of East Berne, 18 mi. southwest of Albany, offers the closest camping, with 140 primitive sites, fishing, hiking, and a swimming beach. Follow I-85 out of Albany, turn right on Rte. 157, and look for signs. (☎872-1674. Sites $13.)

Two areas have good concentrations of restaurants. Lark St. is full of ethnic eats and coffeeshops in a young, college-town atmosphere, while S. Pearl St. has traditional American food. In downtown Albany, the best eating option involves doing time at the **Big House Brewing Company ❷,** 90 N. Pearl St., at Sheridan St. The Big House serves pizzas, sandwiches, and burgers alongside Al Capone Amber Ale. (☎445-2739. Entrees $6-7. Happy Hour 5-7pm. Live bands F. Kitchen open Tu-W 4-9pm, Th-Sa 4-10:30pm. Bar open Tu-W until 1am, Th-Sa until 3am; later depending on crowds.) At **Stone Soup Deli ❶,** 484 Central Ave., inside Honest Weight Food Co-op, wash down a sandwich and salad ($4.75) with one of a variety of organic shakes ($2-3). Bring your favorite tunes along; there's a tape deck for your listening pleasure. (☎482-2667. Open M-F 9am-8pm, Sa 9am-6pm, Su 10am-6pm.)

📷🎭 SIGHTS & ENTERTAINMENT. Albany's sights are centered around the **Rockefeller Empire State Plaza,** between State and Madison St., a $1.9 billion, towering, modernist Stonehenge. The plaza houses state offices, stores, a bus terminal, a post office, and a food court. (Free parking M-F after 2pm.) The huge flying saucer at one end of the Plaza is the **Empire Center for the Performing Arts,** also known as "The Egg," a venue for professional theater, dance, and concerts. (☎473-1845. Box office open in summer M-F 10am-4pm; off-season M-F 10am-5pm, Sa noon-3pm. $15-30.) Across the street, the **New York State Museum** has in-depth exhibits on the state's history, people, and wildlife. (☎474-5877. Open daily 9:30am-5pm. Free.) The **Capitol Repertory Theatre,** 111 N. Pearl St., stages some of Albany's best theatre. (☎445-7469. Box office open M-Sa 10am-5pm. $30-38.) The magnificent **New York State Capitol,** adjacent to the Plaza, has provided New York politicians with luxury quarters since 1899. Tours leave from the Senate staircase on the 1st floor; no backpacks allowed on tour. (☎474-2418. Tours begin daily at 10am, noon, 2, and 3pm. Free.)

Bounded by State St. and Madison Ave. north of downtown, **Washington Park** has tennis courts, paddle boats, and plenty of room for celebrations and performances. The **Park Playhouse** stages free musical theater from July to mid-Aug. (☎434-2035. Open Tu-Su 8pm.) Folks come **Alive at Five** to free concerts at the **Tricentennial Plaza,** across from Fleet Bank on Broadway. (☎434-2032. Concerts June-July Th. 5-8pm.) The biggest summer event, the annual **Tulip Festival** (☎434-2032), mid-May in Washington Park, celebrates the town's Dutch heritage and the blooming of the tulips with entertainment, arts and crafts, a Tulip Queen crowning, and food vendors. For events, call the **Albany Alive Line** (☎434-1217).

Biking aficionados traverse the **Mohawk-Hudson Bikeway** (☎386-2225), which passes along old railroad grades and canal towpaths as it weaves through the capital area. Maps available at the Visitors Center. For rentals, check out the **Down Tube Cycle Shop,** 466 Madison Ave. (☎434-1711. Open M-F 11am-7pm, Sa 10am-5pm. Full-day $25, 2 days $35.)

COOPERSTOWN ☎607

For earlier generations, Cooperstown recalled images of Leatherstocking, the frontiersman hero of novelist James Fenimore Cooper, who roamed the woods around Lake Otsego. Tiny Cooperstown now evokes a different source of American legend—baseball. Tourists file through the Baseball Hall of Fame, eat in baseball-themed restaurants, and sleep in baseball-themed motels. Visitors in the spring and fall score reduced motel and guest house rates.

▌ PRACTICAL INFORMATION. Cooperstown is accessible from **I-90** and **I-88** via **Rte. 28. Main St.** is the main drag in town and is chock full of restaurants and baseball memorabilia shops. Street parking is rare in Cooperstown; park in the three free lots just outside of town on Rte. 28, on Glen Ave. at Maple St., or adjacent to the Fenimore House. From these lots, it's an easy 5-15min. walk to Main St. (Rte. 31). **Trolleys** also leave from the lots, dropping riders off at major stops in town, including the **Hall of Fame,** the **Farmer** and **Fenimore museums, Doubleday Field,** and the **Chamber of Commerce.** (Trolleys run late June to mid-Sept. daily 8:30am-9pm; early June and late Sept. Sa-Su 8:30am-6pm. All-day pass $2, children $1.) **Pine Hall Trailways** (☎800-858-8555) picks up visitors at Clancy's Deli on Rte. 28 and travels to **Kingston** (3¼hr., 1-2 per day, $21) and **New York City** (6 hr., 2 per day, $41). **Cooperstown Area Chamber of Commerce and Visitor Information Center,** 31 Chestnut St., on Rte. 28 near Main St., has a helpful staff willing to talk about the sights and the history of the town. (☎547-9571; www.cooperstownchamber.org. Generally open daily 9am-5pm; hours vary.) **Post Office:** 40 Main St. (☎547-2311; open M-F 8:30am-5pm, Sa 8:30am-noon). **ZIP code:** 13326. **Area code:** 607.

MID-ATLANTIC

░ ACCOMMODATIONS. Peak summertime lodging (late June to mid-Sept.) is expensive, and many accommodation seekers strike out. The cheapest options are to camp, or to travel in the off-season when many motels and guest houses slash rates $20-30. The **Mohican Motel ❹**, 90 Chestnut St., offers large beds, cable TV, and A/C at relatively affordable prices. (☎547-5101. Late June-early Sept. Su-F 2- to 6-person rooms range from $78-122 Su-F, Sa $118-162; mid-Sept. to mid-June Su-F $52-77, Sa $72-97.) **Glimmerglass State Park ❶**, 8 mi. north of Cooperstown on Rte. 31 on the north shore of Lake Otsego, has 43 campsites, including 4 handicapped sites, in a rolling 600-acre lakeside park. Daytime visitors can swim, fish, bike, and boat. (☎547-8662. Park open 8am-7pm. Showers, dumping station; no hookups. Beach opens at 11am. Registration daily 11am-9pm. $6 per vehicle. $8 service charge for reservations. Sites $13.) Close to the Hall of Fame, **Cooperstown Beaver Valley Campground ❶**, off Rte. 28 10min. south of Cooperstown, has wooded sites, pool, recreation area, small pond, baseball diamond, and boat rentals. (☎293-8131 or 800-726-7314. Sites $28, with hookup $31.)

❑ FOOD. The **Doubleday Cafe ❶**, 93 Main St., serves up a tasty bowl of chili ($3) amid eye-catching memorabilia of the Babe and other baseball greats. (☎547-5468. Burgers $3-5. Open daily 7am-10pm or 11pm, depending on crowd; bar closes after kitchen.) For elegant but affordable dining, **hoffman lane bistro ❸**, 2 Hoffman Ln., off Main St. across from the Hall of Fame, has airy rooms with checkered black-and-white tablecloths. Their crabcakes ($8) leave customers rooting for more. (☎547-7055. Entrees around $12. Clams over linguine $6. Kitchen open Tu-Sa 11:30am-3pm and 5-10pm; bar open until 2am. Late-night menu served until midnight.) A Cooperstown institution, **Schneider's Bakery**, 157 Main St., has been creating delicious 40¢ "old-fashioneds"—doughnuts less greasy and a tad smaller than their commercial cousins—since 1887. (☎547-9631. Open M-Sa 6:30am-5:30pm.)

◙ SIGHTS. With a daily turnstile count in the summer that exceeds the town population, the ▨**National Baseball Hall of Fame and Museum**, on Main St., is an enormous, glowing monument to America's national pastime. The building is home to priceless memorabilia—everything from the bat with which Babe Ruth hit his famous "called shot" home run in the 1932 World Series to the infamous jersey worn by 3 ft. 7in. St. Louis Brown Eddie Gaedel. The museum also features a multimedia tribute to the sport, a candid display on African-American ballplayers' experiences in the Negro Leagues, and exhibits tracing the myth-making game to ancient Egyptian rituals. (☎547-7200 or 888-425-5633. Open Apr.-Oct. daily 9am-9pm; Oct.-Apr. 9am-5pm. $9.50, seniors $8, ages 7-12 $4.)

The **Hall of Fame Induction Weekend** for new inductees takes place on either the last weekend of July or the first weekend of August; ceremonies take place on the field adjacent to the **Clark Sports Center** on Susquehanna Ave., a 10min. walk south from the Hall. Admission to the event is free; the autographs of the Hall of Famers who line Main St. are not. The annual **Hall of Fame Game** between two rotating Major League teams concludes the festival on Monday at 2pm in the delightfully intimate Doubleday Field. Plan accordingly—over 40,000 visitors are expected. Rooms must be reserved months in advance.

Overlooking a pristine lawn and Lake Otsego, **Fenimore Art Museum**, on Lake Rd./ Rte. 80 about one mile from Main St., houses a collection of American folk art, Hudson River School paintings, James Fenimore Cooper memorabilia, and an impressive array of Native American art. (☎547-1400 or 888-547-1450. Open June-Oct. daily 10am-5pm; Apr.-May and Oct.-Dec. Tu-Su 10am-4pm. $9, seniors $8, ages 7-12 $4.) Nine miles north of Cooperstown on Lake Rd./Rte. 80, the **Glimmerglass Opera** stages summer performances. (☎547-2255. $24-94.)

MID-ATLANTIC

ITHACA & THE FINGER LAKES ☎ 607

According to Iroquois legend, the Great Spirit laid his hand upon the earth, and the impression of his fingers resulted in the Finger Lakes: Canandaigua, Cayuga, Seneca, and eight others. Whether it was the Great Spirit or mere Ice Age glaciers, the results are spectacular. Students from Ithaca College and Cornell University tote bookbags amongst the waterfalls of Ithaca's ruggedly carved gorges, while north of Ithaca, a divine nectar flows—the rich wine of the area's acclaimed vineyards.

7 PRACTICAL INFORMATION. Ithaca Commons, in downtown Ithaca, is a pedestrian area lined with shops and restaurants. Atop a steep hill, **Collegetown** is an area of hole-in-the-wall bars and diners adjacent to Cornell's campus. **Ithaca Bus Terminal,** 710 W. State St., at Rte. 13 (☎272-7930; open daily 6:30am-6pm), houses **Short Line** (☎277-8800) and **Greyhound** (☎272-7930), with service to: Buffalo (4hr., 5 per day, $27); New York City (5hr., 12 per day, $37); and Philadelphia (7hr., 2 per day, $52). **Tompkins Consolidated Area Transit (T-CAT;** ☎277-7433) is the only choice for getting to Cayuga Lake without a car. Buses stop at Ithaca Commons; westbound buses also stop on Seneca St. and eastbound buses stop on Green. (Buses run daily; times vary by route. 75¢-$2, students and seniors 50¢.) The **Ithaca/Tompkins County Convention and Visitors Bureau,** 904 E. Shore Dr., has the best map of the area ($2.50), hotel and B&B listings, and brochures. (☎272-1313 or 800-284-8422. Open late May-early Sept. M-F 8am-5pm, Sa 10am-5pm, Su 10am-4pm; mid-Sept. to late May M-F 8am-5pm.) **Post Office:** 213 N. Tioga St., at E. Buffalo. (☎272-5455. Open M-F 7am-6pm, Sa 7am-1pm.) **ZIP code:** 14850. **Area code:** 607.

⛺ ACCOMMODATIONS. Ithaca is filled with cheap roadside motels, but for a better bargain, camp in one of the nearby state parks or negotiate a good price at a bed & breakfast. For information and brochures on camping and B&Bs, contact the Visitor's Bureau. **◼Elmshade Guest House ❷,** 402 S. Albany St., at Center St. three blocks from Ithaca Commons, offers impeccably clean and well-decorated rooms with shared bath, cable TV, and an unbelievably tasty continental breakfast. This B&B is by far the best budget option in Ithaca. From the bus station, walk up State St. and turn right onto Albany St. (☎273-1707. Reservations recommended. Singles $45; doubles $60-65.) There are three nearby state parks with camping. **Taughannock Falls ❶,** north on Rte. 89, is taller than Niagara and simply breathtaking. (☎387-6739. Sites $15. Cabins for 4 people $122-239.) The huge waterfall commands the entrance to the campsite at **Buttermilk Falls ❶,** on Rte. 13 south of Ithaca. The closest park to Ithaca, Buttermilk has 46 sites and miles of trails following Buttermilk Creek through the woods. (☎273-5761. Sites $13.) **Robert H. Treman ❶,** on Rte. 327, off Rte. 13 south of Ithaca only 5 mi. out of town, has 72 sites with a few miles of trails along a gorge. (☎273-3440. Sites $13.)

◻ FOOD. Restaurants in Ithaca center on Ithaca Commons and Collegetown. **Moosewood Restaurant ❷,** 215 N. Cayuga, at Seneca St. in the Dewitt Mall, features an amazing selection of wonderfully fresh and creative vegetarian options. (☎273-9610. Lunch $6.50; dinner $10-13. Open daily 11:30am-4pm and 6-9pm.) Tasting is the theme at **Just a Taste ❸,** 116 N. Aurora St., near Ithaca Commons. Wines are served as quarter glasses in groups of 4-6 wines known as a flight ($6-11). A smorgasbord of tempting *tapas* ($5-7 each), desserts, and beers rounds out the menu. (☎277-9463. Open Su-Th 11:30am-3:30pm and 5:30-10pm, F-Sa 11am-3:30pm and 5:30-11pm.) The **Lost Dog cafe/coffeehouse ❹,** 106-122 S. Cayuga St., at Ithaca Commons, has appetizing lunches and dinners in a sleek setting. Vegetarian/vegan options and a selection of wine and beer are served. (☎277-9143. Sandwiches $8. Dinner entrees $13-16. Open Tu-Sa 11:30am-10pm, Su 11:30am-9pm.)

◙ SIGHTS. Cornell University, youngest of the Ivy League schools, sits on a steep hill in Ithaca between two tremendous gorges. The suspension bridge above Fall Creek provides a heart-pounding walk above one gorge, while the **Central Avenue Stone Arch Bridge** above Cascadilla Creek has a brilliant sunset view. The **Information and Referral Center,** in the Day Hall Lobby, has info on campus sights and activities. (☎254-4636. Open M-F 8am-5pm; telephone staffed Sa 8am-5pm and Su noon-1pm. Tours Apr.-Nov. M-F 9, 11am, 1, and 3pm; Sa 9am and 1pm; Su 1pm. Dec.-Mar. daily 1pm.) The boxy, yet strangely pleasing cement edifice rising from the top of the hill houses Cornell's **Herbert F. Johnson Museum of Art,** at the corner of University Ave. and Central Ave. The small collection of European and American paintings and sculpture includes works by Giacometti, Matisse, O'Keeffe, de Kooning, and Hopper; the rooftop sculpture garden yields an amazing view. (☎255-6464. Open Tu-Su 10am-5pm. Free.) At **Cornell Plantations,** a series of botanical gardens and an arboretum lay serenely in the northeast corner of campus. A short hike to the lookout point provides a view of campus and the surrounding area. (☎255-3020. Open daily sunrise to sunset. Free.) The free *Passport to the Trails of Tompkins County,* available from the Visitors Bureau, is a comprehensive guide to navigating the landscape. Adventurous hikes into the Cornell gorge include the worthwhile 1½ mi. **Founder's Loop.** Among the booths at the **Ithaca Farmer's Market,** 3rd St. off Rt. 13, are local and Cambodian food stalls, fresh produce, cider tastings, and hand-crafted furniture. (☎273-7109. Open Apr.-Dec. Sa 9am-2pm; June-Oct. Su 10am-2pm.)

The fertile soil of the Finger Lakes area has made it the heart of New York's wine industry. Three designated **wine trails** provide opportunities for wine tasting and vineyard touring—locals say that the fall harvest is the best time to visit. (For more information ☎800-684-5217.) The ten vineyards closest to Ithaca lie on the **Cayuga Trail,** with most located along Rte. 89 between Seneca Falls and Ithaca. Other wineries are found on the **Seneca Lake Trail,** with 21 wineries on the east side (Rte. 414) and west side (Rte. 14) of the lake, and the **Keuka Trail,** with seven wineries along Rte. 54 and Rte. 76. Some wineries offer free picnic facilities and tours. All give free tastings; some require purchase of a glass ($2).

◪ NIGHTLIFE. Collegetown, centering on College Ave., harbors student hangouts and access to a romantic path along the gorge. Split down the middle, **Stella's,** 403 College Ave., has two entrances—one leads to a smoky, red-walled cafe and the other heads to a blue-walled jazz bar. (☎277-8731. Happy Hour daily 6-7pm. Food served daily 11am-12:30am. Coffeeshop open in summer M-F 8am-1am, Sa-Su 10am-1am. Jazz bar open daily 11am-1am.) The **Rongovian Embassy to the USA ("The Rongo"),** on Rte. 96 in Trumansburg about 10 mi. from Ithaca, is a music club worth the drive. A huge wall map allows travelers to plot a trip to "Nearvarna" or other fictitious destinations in the nation of Rongovia. (☎387-3334. Beer $2.50. Cover F-Sa $5-6. Open Tu-Su 5pm-1am.) High-minded moviegoers head to the **Cornell Cinema,** 104 Willard Straight Hall on the Cornell campus, a traditional arthouse theater showing old films, new indies, and the occasional blockbuster. (☎255-3522. $6, undergraduates and seniors $5, graduate students and under 13 $4.) The **Hangar Theatre,** 2 mi. from downtown at the Rte. 89 N. Treman Marina entrance, puts together a professional array of musicals and plays. (☎273-4497. Shows Tu-Su 7:30 or 8pm; matinees Sa-Su 3pm. $12-26.) A local student favorite, **Ruloff's,** 411 College St., exudes a classic college bar atmosphere. At half past midnight, the bartender spins the "wheel of fortune" to pick the night's drink special. (☎272-6067. Open M-Sa 11:30am-1am, Su 10am-1am.) For a night on the town, the free *Ithaca Times,* available at most stores and restaurants, has complete listings of entertainment options.

MID-ATLANTIC

BUFFALO

☎ 716

Buffalo loves its underdogs. Her less-than-glorious sports teams aren't the only fiercely defended competitors; even the last stragglers of the marathon draw enthusiastic cheers. The combination of small-town warmth and big-city perks (including a top-notch cafe-and-theater district) makes Buffalo a soothing place to spend a day. From the downtown skyline to the small-scale pastel charm of historic Allentown, Buffalo trades urbanity for honest, modern Americana.

⑦ PRACTICAL INFORMATION. Amtrak, 75 Exchange St., at Washington St. (☎856-2075; office open M-F 7am-3:30pm) leaves for **New York** (8hr., 3 per day, $59) and **Toronto** (4hr., 1 per day, $16). **Greyhound,** 181 Ellicott St., at N. Division St. (☎855-7533 or 800-231-2222; station open 24hr.), in the Buffalo Transportation Center sends buses to: **New York** (8½hr., 15 per day, $65); **Boston** (11½hr., 10 per day, $57); **Niagara Falls, ON** (1hr., 11 per day, $4); and **Toronto** (2½hr., 12 per day, $16). The **Niagara Frontier Transit Authority** (NFTA; ☎855-7211 or 283-9319) offers bus and rail service in the city ($1.25-1.85; seniors, children, and disabled riders 55¢-85¢) with additional buses to **Niagara Falls, NY** (see **Buffalo Transportation Center,** p. 253) and free rides on the Main St. Metrorail. **Taxi:** Cheektowaga Taxi (☎822-1738). **Visitors Center:** 617 Main St., in the Theater District. (☎852-2356 or 800-283-3256. Open M-F 10am-2pm. Tour $5.) **Post Office:** 701 Washington St. (☎856-4604. Open M-F 8:30am-5:30pm, Sa 8:30am-1pm.) **ZIP code:** 14203. **Area code:** 716.

⌐ ACCOMMODATIONS. Budget lodgings are a rarity in Buffalo, but chain motels can be found near the airport and **I-90,** 8-10mi. northeast of downtown. **Hostelling International Buffalo (HI-AYH) ①,** 667 Main St., houses 50 beds and spotless floors in a centrally-located neighborhood. Friendly staff lead frequent outings and make travelers feel at home. (☎852-5222. Free linen, access to microwave, pool table, and laundry facilities. Reception May-Sept. daily 8-11am and 4-11pm; Oct.-Apr. 8-11am and 5-10pm. Dorms $19, nonmembers $22.) The **Hotel Lenox ③,** 140 North St., take bus #7 to North St. and Irving Ave., offers travelers cozy, slightly retro rooms in a pleasant residential neighborhood. (☎884-1700. Cable TV, kitchens available. Reservations strongly suggested in summer. Single rooms from $59; doubles from $69.) See **Niagara Falls** (p. 254) for campsites in the area.

◘⚏ FOOD & NIGHTLIFE. Despite its initially Gothic facade, **Gabriel's Gate ②,** 145 Allen St., creates a casual environment for people-watching. Enjoy the garden *souvlaki* ($7) or taco salad ($6) from the comfy shaded patio. (☎886-0602. Open M-Th 11:30am-1am, F-Sa 11:30am-2am, Su noon-1am.) **Frank and Teressa's Anchor Bar ②,** 1047 Main St., serves up the original Buffalo Wing, invented here in 1964. (☎886-8920. Ten wings $6, 20 wings $10. Open M-Th 11am-11pm, F-Sa 11am-1am, Su noon-11pm.) The city's surprisingly lively nightlife centers on **Chippewa Street, Franklin Street,** and **Elmwood Avenue;** pick up a copy of the *Art Voice* for event listings. With its hip atmosphere and great deals, **Quote,** 263 Delaware Ave., at Chippewa St., has grabbed Buffalo's attention. (☎854-2853. Sa cover $3. Open W-F 3:30pm-4am, Sa-Su 6pm-4am.) Next door, **City SPoT** is the place to go for a wide array of cheap coffee and tea concoctions. (☎856-2739. Open 24hr.) **The Calumet Arts Cafe,** 56 W. Chippewa St., plays live jazz and blues on the weekends. (☎855-2220. Open M-W 5:30-10pm, Th-Sa 5:30pm-4am.)

◙⚏ SIGHTS & ENTERTAINMENT. The **Albright-Knox Art Gallery,** 1285 Elmwood Ave., take bus #32 "Niagara," houses a jaw-dropping collection of over 6000 modern pieces, including works by Piccasso and Rothko. (☎882-8700. Open Tu-Sa 11am-5pm, Su noon-5pm. $5, seniors and students $4, families $10; free Sa 11am-

1pm.) The Allentown Village Society organizes the popular **Outdoor Arts Festival** (☎881-4269), a two-day celebration of local artists in early June. At the **Naval and Military Park** on Lake Erie, at the foot of Pearl and Main St., visitors can climb aboard a guided missile cruiser, a destroyer, and a WWII submarine. (☎847-1773. Open Apr.-Oct. daily 10am-5pm, Nov. Sa-Su 10am-4pm. $6, seniors and ages 6-16 $3.50.) In winter, **Ralph Wilson Stadium** (☎649-0015), in Orchard Park, hosts the NFL's **Buffalo Bills,** while hockey's **Buffalo Sabres** slap the puck at the **HSBC Arena,** 1 Seymour H. Knox III Plaza (☎855-4000).

NIAGARA FALLS ☎716

One of the seven natural wonders, Niagara Falls also claims the title of one of the world's largest sources of hydroelectric power—not to mention daredevil risk-takers. Since 1901, when 63-year-old schoolteacher Annie Taylor was the first to survive the beer-barrel plunge, the Falls have attracted many thrill-seekers. Modern-day Taylors beware—heavy fines and possible death await the daring. For those of a sounder mind, outlet shopping and neon lights cram the streets.

▐ TRANSPORTATION

Trains: Amtrak, at 27th and Lockport St. (☎285-4224), 1 block east of Hyde Park Blvd. Take bus #52 to Falls/Downtown. To **New York City** ($60) and **Toronto** ($16). Open M and Th-Su 7am-11pm, Tu-W 7am-3pm.

Buses: Niagara Falls Bus Terminal, at 4th and Niagara St. (☎282-1331), sells **Greyhound** tickets for use in Buffalo. Open M-F 9am-4pm, Sa-Su 9am-noon. To get a bus in Buffalo, take bus #40 "Grand Island" from the Niagara Falls bus terminal to the **Buffalo Transportation Center,** 181 Ellicott St. (1 hr., 13 per day).

Public Transit: Niagara Frontier Metro Transit System, 343 4th St. (☎285-9319), provides local city transit ($1.25). **ITA Buffalo Shuttle** (☎800-551-9369) has service from Niagara Falls info center and major hotels to Buffalo Airport ($22).

Taxis: Blue United Cab, ☎285-9331. **Niagara Falls Taxi,** ☎905-357-4000, in Canada.

▟▐ ORIENTATION & PRACTICAL INFORMATION

Niagara Falls spans the US-Canadian border (addresses given here are in NY, unless noted). Take **U.S. 190** to the Robert Moses Pkwy., or skirt the tolls (but suffer traffic) by taking Exit 3 to Rte. 62. In town, **Niagara Street** is the main east-west artery, ending in the west at **Rainbow Bridge,** which crosses to Canada (pedestrian crossings 50¢, cars $2.50; tolls only charged going into Canada). North-south streets are numbered, increasing toward the east. Stores, restaurants, and motels line **Route 62 (Niagara Falls Blvd.)** outside of town. Customs procedures, while still casual in tone, are taken extremely seriously since September 11th. Many businesses in the Niagara area accept both American and Canadian currency.

Visitor info: Orin Lehman Visitors Center (☎278-1796), in front of the Falls' observation deck; the entrance is marked by a garden. Open May-Sept. daily 8am-6:15pm; Oct. to mid-Nov. 8am-8pm; mid-Nov. to Dec. 8am-10pm; Jan.-Apr. 8am-6:15pm. An **Info center** (☎284-2000) adjoins the bus station on 4th and Niagara St., a 10min. walk from the Falls. Open mid-May to mid-Sept. daily 8:30am-7:30pm; mid-Sept. to mid-May 9am-5pm. **Niagara Falls Tourism,** 5515 Stanley Ave., ON (☎905-356-6061; www.discoverniagara.com), has info on the Canadian side. Open daily 8am-8pm; off-season 8am-6pm. On the Canadian side, tune in to 105.1FM for tourist info.

Post Office: 615 Main St. (☎285-7561). Open M-F 7:30am-5pm, Sa 8:30am-2pm. **ZIP code:** 14302. **Area code:** 716 (NY), 905 (ON). In text, 716 unless otherwise noted.

ACCOMMODATIONS

Many newlyweds spend part of their honeymoon by the awesome beauty of the Falls, which are especially romantic at night. Cheap motels (from $25) advertising free wedding certificates line **Lundy's Lane** on the Canadian side and **Route 62** on the American side, while many moderately priced B&Bs overlook the gorge on **River Road** between the Rainbow Bridge and the Whirlpool Bridge on the Canadian side. Reservations are always recommended.

Hostelling International Niagara Falls (HI-C), 4549 Cataract Ave., Niagara Falls, ON (☎905-357-0770 or 888-749-0058), just off Bridge St., about 2 blocks from the bus station and VIA Rail. Once a brothel, this hostel is still a free-spirited atmosphere; a cheerful staff of self-described "hippies" settles customers into comfortable, convivial lodgings behind rainbow-colored doors. Organized activities include pub crawls, nature hikes, and barbecues. Family rooms, laundry facilities, and Internet access. Linen CDN$2. Reception 24hr. Check-out 10:30am. CDN$18, nonmembers CDN$22. ❶

Hostelling International Niagara Falls (HI-AYH), 1101 Ferry Ave. (☎282-3700). From the bus station, walk east on Niagara St., then turn left onto Memorial Pkwy.; the hostel is at the corner of Ferry Ave. *Avoid walking alone on Ferry Ave. at night.* 44 beds in a friendly old house. Kitchen, TV lounge, and limited parking. Family rooms available. Linen $1.50. Open Feb. to mid-Dec. Check-in 7:30-9:30am and 4-11pm. Lockout 9:30am-4pm. Curfew 11:30pm; lights out midnight. Dorms $14, nonmembers $17. ❶

All Tucked Inn, 574 3rd St. (☎282-0919 or 800-797-0919). Clean, attractive rooms with shared baths. Common TV room. Continental breakfast included in summer. In summer, singles from $39; doubles from $59. Off-season $27/$49. Discounts for *Let's Go* toters. ❷

Niagara Glen-View Tent & Trailer Park, 3950 Victoria Ave., Niagara Falls, ON (☎800-263-2570), close to the Falls. Hiking trail across the street. Ice, showers, laundry facilities, and pool. Shuttle from driveway to the foot of Clifton Hill in summer every 30min. 8:45am-2am. Office open daily 8am-11pm. Park open May to mid-Oct. June-Sept. sites CDN$35, with hookup CDN$42; May-Oct. $28/35. ❷

FOOD

Backpackers and locals alike flock to **The Press Box Restaurant ❶,** 324 Niagara St., for enormous meals at microscopic prices. On Mondays, feast on buffalo wings for only 15¢ apiece. (☎284-5447. Open daily 9am-11pm.) **Sardar Sahib ❷,** 626 Niagara St., serves mouth-watering, authentic Indian food with a wide array of vegetarian selections. (☎282-0444. Daily specials $7. Open daily 11:30am-midnight.) On the Canadian side, the restaurants on **Victoria Avenue** by Clifton Hill are touristy but inexpensive. Located one block from the hostel, **Simon's Restaurant ❷,** 4116 Bridge St., ON, serves huge breakfasts (CDN$6.50), giant homemade muffins (CDN69¢), and homestyle dinners. (☎905-356-5310. Open M-Sa 5:30am-8pm, Su 5:30am-2pm.) Across from the bus station, **The Peninsula Bakery and Restaurant ❷,** 4568 Erie Ave., ON, has authentic Pan-Asian food. Look for the sign that says "Chinese Food." (☎905-374-8176. Malaysian stir-fried noodles CDN$7.50. Open M 10:30am-7pm, W-Su 10:30am-10pm.)

🅖 SIGHTS

While the most popular attraction is (of course) the Falls, entrepreneur and tourist offices on both sides of the border have made sure to provide plenty of competition. For three days in February the Niagara area enjoys winter revels during the **Ice Festival** (☎ 800-338-7890). The rest of the year, a wide range of sights and events ensures that there's always plenty to see and do.

AMERICAN SIDE. For over 150 years, the **Maid of the Mist** boat tour has thrilled, entertained, and soaked visitors by shuttling them to the foot of both falls. (☎ 284-8897. Open daily 10am-6pm. Tours leave in summer M-Th every 30min. $8.50, ages 6-12 $4.80. 50¢ elevator fee.) The **Caves of the Wind Tour** lends out yellow raincoats for an exciting body-soaking hike to the base of the Bridal Veil Falls, including an optional walk to Hurricane Deck where gale-force waves slam down from above. (☎ 278-1730. Open May to mid-Oct.; hours vary depending on season and weather conditions. Trips leave every 15min. Must be at least 42 in. $6, ages 6-12 $5.50.)

The **Master Pass,** available at the park's Visitors Center, covers admission to the theater, Maid of the Mist, Caves of the Wind, **Schoellkopf's Geological Museum** in Prospect Park, the **Aquarium,** and the **Niagara Scenic Trolley**—a tram-guided tour of the park. (Master Pass $24, ages 6-12 $17. Museum: ☎ 278-1780. Open May-Sept. daily 9am-7pm, Apr.-May and Sept.-Oct. 9am-5pm. $1. Dramatic film every 30min. Aquarium: 701 Whirlpool St. ☎ 285-3575. Open daily 9am-7pm. $7, ages 4-12 $5. Trolley: ☎ 278-1730. Hours vary; call ahead. Runs daily every 15min. $4.50, children $3.50.)

Continuing north, the **Niagara Power Project** features hands-on exhibits, displays, and videos on energy, hydropower, and local history. While there, you can visit the newly renovated Visitors Center or catch salmon, trout, or bass from the fishing platform. (5777 Lewiston Rd. ☎ 286-6661. Open daily 9am-5pm. Call ahead to arrange a guided tour. Free.) Farther north in **Lewiston, NY,** the 200-acre state **Artpark,** at the foot of 4th St., focuses on visual and performing arts, offering opera, pops concerts, and rock shows. (☎ 800-659-7275. Shows May-Dec.; call for schedule. Box office open M-F 9am-5pm, later on event days. $15-33.) **Old Fort Niagara** was built for French troops in 1726, but now plays host to a cast of historical reenactors highlighting aspects of 18th-century life. (Follow Robert Moses Pkwy. north from Niagara Falls. ☎ 745-7611. Open June-Aug. daily 9am-5:30pm; off-season hours vary. $7, seniors $6, ages 6-12 $4.)

CANADIAN SIDE. On the Canadian side of Niagara Falls (across Rainbow Bridge), **Queen Victoria Park** provides the best view of **Horseshoe Falls.** Starting 1hr. after sunset, the Falls are illuminated for 3hr. every night. Parking in Queen Victoria is expensive (CDN$9.75). **Park 'N' Ride** is a better deal, offering parking at Rapids View, across from Marineland at the south end of Niagara Pkwy. **People Movers** efficiently and comfortably take you through the 30km area on the Canadian side of the Falls, stopping at attractions along the way. (☎ 357-9340. Mid-June to early Sept. daily 9am-11pm; off-season hours vary. CDN$5.50, children CDN$3.) Bikers, in-line skaters, and walkers enjoy the 32km **Niagara River Recreation Trail,** which runs from Fort Erie to Fort George and passes many interesting historical sights.

High above the crowds and excitement, **Skylon Tower** has the highest view (on a clear day all the way to Toronto) of the Falls at 236m. Far above the swarms of tourists, the 159m **Observation Deck** offers a calming, unhindered view of the Falls. (5200 Robinson St. ☎ 356-2651. Open in summer daily 8am-11:30pm; in winter hours change monthly. CDN$9, seniors CDN$8, children CDN$4.50.) The **Discovery Pass** includes passage to: **Journey Behind the Falls,** a tour behind Horseshoe Falls; **Great Gorge Adventure,** a long boardwalk next to the famous Niagara River Rapids (haunted by many lucky and not-so-lucky daredevils over the years); and the **Spanish Aero Car,** an aerial cable ride over the whirlpool waters. (Pass: CDN$32, children CDN$17. Journey: ☎ 354-

1551. CDN$7, children CDN$3.50. Great Gorge: ☎374-1221. Open mid-June to early Sept. daily 9am-8:30pm; off-season hours fluctuate. CDN$6, children CDN$3. Aero Car: ☎354-5711. Open year-round but hours vary; in winter operation often closed due to inclement weather. CDN$6, children CDN$3.)

Meanwhile, commercialism can be as much of a wonder as any natural sight. The Canadian side of the Falls offers the delightfully tasteless **Clifton Hill**, a collection of wax museums, funhouses, and overpriced shows. **Ripley's Believe It or Not Museum** displays wax model wonders and a selection of medieval torture devices. Unfortunately, the authentic New Guinea Penis Guard, used for protection from hungry mosquitoes, is not for sale. *(4960 Clifton Hill. ☎356-2238. Open in summer daily 9am-2am; off-season hours vary. CDN$8.50, seniors CDN$6.50, ages 6-12 CDN$4.)*

NORTHERN NEW YORK

THE ADIRONDACKS   ☎518

Demonstrating uncommon foresight, the New York State legislature established the **Adirondack Park** in 1892, preserving a six million-acre swath of terrain. The largest US park outside Alaska, it is one of the few places in the Northeast where hikers can still spend days without seeing another soul. Thousands of miles of ruggedly scenic trails carve through the park and around more than 2000 glittering lakes and ponds.

🚹 **PRACTICAL INFORMATION. Adirondacks Trailways** (☎800-858-8555) services the region. From Albany, buses set out for Lake Placid and Lake George. From the Lake George bus stop at Lake George Hardware, 35 Montcalm St., buses go to Albany (4 per day, $11.65), Lake Placid (1 per day, $15.30), and New York City (5 per day, $49). The **Adirondack Mountain Club (ADK)** is the best source of info on outdoor activities in the region. Offices are located at 814 Goggins Rd., Lake George 12845 (☎668-4447; open May-Sept. M-Sa 8:30am-5pm; Jan.-Apr. M-F 8:30am-4:30pm), and at Adirondack Loj Rd., P.O. Box 867, Lake Placid 12946 (☎523-3441; open Sa-Th 8am-8pm, F 8am-10pm). The Lake Placid ADK has the scoop on outdoor skills classes such as canoeing, rock climbing, whitewater kayaking, and wilderness medicine. For the latest backcountry info, visit ADK's **High Peaks Information Center,** 3 mi. east of Lake Placid on Rte. 73, then 5 mi. down Adirondack Loj Rd. The center also has washrooms and sells basic outdoor equipment, trail snacks, and a variety of extremely helpful guides to the mountains for $11-25. (☎523-3441. Open M-Th 8am-5pm, F 8am-10pm, Sa-Su 8am-8pm.) The ADK and the Mountaineer (see **Sights and Activities,** p. 257) provide basic info on the conditions and concerns of backwoods travel. **Area code:** 518.

🛏🍴 **ACCOMMODATIONS & FOOD.** The ADK also runs two lodges near Lake Placid. The ▓**Adirondack Loj ❷**, at the end of Adirondack Loj Rd., off Rte. 73, lures hikers off the trails with its cozy atmosphere. Situated on Heart Lake, the log cabin has 38 bunks and a den decorated with deer and moose trophies, warmed by an imposing fieldstone fireplace. In summer, guests swim, fish, and canoe on the premises (canoe or kayak rental 7am-7pm; $5 per hr., guests $3). In colder weather, guests can explore the wilderness trails by renting snowshoes or cross-country skis. (☎523-3441. Breakfast included; lunch $5.50, dinner $14. Reservations highly recommended. Bunks $36, off-season $31; private room $55/48 per person. Lean-tos $26; campsites $23; 4-person cabins $104, 16-person $230. Snowshoes $10 per day, cross-country skis $20 per day.) Two mi. east of Tupper Lake, **Northwood Cabins ❸**, 92 Tupper-Sara Hwy., rents nine antique, heated cabins. (☎359-9606 or 800-727-5756. Open mid-May to mid-Oct. Cabins $42-$68.) For a more rustic experience, hike 3½ mi. from the closest trailhead to the **John's Brook Lodge ❷**, in Keene Valley. From Lake Placid, follow Rte. 73 15 mi. through Keene to Keene Valley, and turn right at the Ausable Inn. The hike runs slightly uphill, but the meal waiting at the end rewards the effort. John's Brook is no secret—beds fill completely on weekends. Make reservations one day in advance for dinner, earlier for a weekend, and bring sheets or a sleeping bag. (Call the Adirondack Loj for reservations, ☎523-3441. Dinner $14. July-early Sept. bunks from $30.) The **White Birch Cafe ❷**, 2 Demars Blvd., in Tupper Lake, serves up good, fresh food at reasonable prices. (☎359-8044. Fish sandwich $5.50. Open M and W-Su 11am-8pm.)

Camping is free anywhere on public land in the backcountry as long as it is at least 150 ft. away from a trail, road, water source, or campground, and below 4000 ft. in altitude. Inquire about the location of free trailside shelters before planning a hike in the forest. The State Office of Parks and Recreation (see New York **Practical Information,** p. 203) has more details.

🔲 **SIGHTS.** Of the six million acres in the Adirondacks Park, 40% are open to the public, offering a slew of outdoor activities. The other 60% is privately owned by logging companies, residents, and outdoors clubs. The winding trails that pass through the forest provide spectacular mountain scenery for hikers, snowshoers, and cross-country skiers. Meanwhile, the rivers and streams that cross the mountains offer kayakers, canoers, and whitewater rafters seasonal rapids amid the breathtaking landscape. The hard-core outdoor enthusiast should consider conquering **Mt. Marcy,** the state's highest peak (5344 ft.), or taking advantage of a dozen other well-known alpine centers. For those who prefer spectator sports, the town of Lake Placid (see below) frequently hosts national and international competitions. Tupper Lake and Lake George have carnivals every January and February. In mid-July, Tupper hosts the **Tin Man Triathlon.** Meanwhile, the **Great Outdoor Games** (☎523-2685) take over Mirror Lake and Lake Placid for four days in mid-July, pitting the best of logrollers, sporting dogs, archers, and wood-choppers against each other.

Rock climbers should consult the experienced staff at the **Mountaineer,** in Keene Valley, between I-87 and Lake Placid on Rte. 73. The Mountaineer reels in alpine enthusiasts as it hosts the **Adirondaok International Mountalnfest** on the weekend of Martin Luther King Day. (☎576-2281. Open in summer Su-Th 9am-5:30pm, F 9am-7pm, Sa 8am-7pm; off-season M-F 9am-5:30pm, Sa 8am-5:30pm, Su 9am-5:30pm. Snowshoes $16 per day, ice-climbing boots and crampons $20, rock shoes $12.) The 🔲**Adirondack Museum,** off Rte. 30 in Blue Mountain Lake, showcases the history of the Adirondacks, from 19th century miners to the outdoorsmen of today. Twenty-one exhibits overlook the gorgeous Blue Mountain Lake. (☎352-7311. Open late May to mid-Oct. daily 9:30am-5:30pm. $10; seniors $9; students, military, and ages 7-17 $5; under 6 free.)

LAKE PLACID   ☎ 518

Tucked away beneath the High Peaks Mountains, Lake Placid lives and breathes winter sports. Host to the Olympic Winter Games in both 1932 and 1980, this modest town has seen thousands of pilgrims and, aside from the manifold motels, has remained charmingly untainted by its popularity. World-class athletes train year-round in the town's extensive facilities, lending an international flavor which distinguishes Lake Placid from its Adirondack neighbors.

🔃 PRACTICAL INFORMATION. Lake Placid sits at the intersection of Rte. 86 and Rte. 73. **Adirondack Trailways** (☎ 800-225-6815) stops at Lake Placid Video, 324 Main St., and has extensive service in the area. Destinations include Lake George ($15) and New York City ($62). The town's Olympic past defines the Lake Placid of today. The **Olympic Regional Development Authority,** 216 Main St., Olympic Center, operates the sporting facilities. (☎ 523-1655 or 800-462-6236. Open M-F 8:30am-5pm.) Find info on food, lodging, and area attractions at the **Lake Placid-Essex County Visitors Bureau,** also in the Olympic Center. (☎ 523-2445; www.lakeplacid.com. Open daily 9am-5pm; in winter closed Su.) **Weather Info:** ☎ 523-1363. **Internet access: Lake Placid Public Library,** 67 Main St. (☎ 523-3200. Open M-F 11am-5pm, Sa 11am-4pm. No email.) **Post Office:** 201 Main St. (☎ 523-3071. Open M-F 8:30am-5pm, Sa 8am-noon.) **ZIP code:** 12946. **Area code:** 518.

🏠 ACCOMMODATIONS. If you avoid the resorts on the west end of town, both lodgings and food can be had cheaply in Lake Placid. The **White Sled ❶,** 3½ mi. east of town on Rte. 73, has a standard bunkhouse with 38 beds, three bathrooms, kitchen and barbecue facilities, and cable TV. For a little more money, sleep in one of 15 motel rooms or rent the ten-bed cottage. (☎ 523-9314. Bunks $20, motel rooms $45-55.) If you prefer to stay right in town, the **High Peaks Hostel ❶** offers slightly more crowded living quarters. Located at 337½ Main St., across from the bowling alley and just a few blocks from Olympic Center, the hostel has kitchen facilities, a TV, a common room, and 14 bunks. (☎ 523-4951. Bunks $20.)

🏕 CAMPING. Meadowbrook State Park ❶, 5 mi. west of town on Rte. 86 in Ray Brook, and **Wilmington Notch State Campground ❶,** about 8 mi. east of Lake Placid on Rte. 86, are the region's best camping areas, although the crowded sites may disappoint those who anticipate pristine Adirondack splendor. Both offer shady, wooded sites that accommodate two tents without hookups. (Meadowbrook: ☎ 891-4351. Sites $10. Wilmington Notch: ☎ 946-7172. Sites $10-$12.) One of the state's most beautiful campgrounds, **Ausable Point ❶,** is situated right on Lake Champlain, an hour from Lake Placid, 12 mi. south of Plattsburgh on Rte. 9. (☎ 561-7080. Make reservations for weekends and holidays. $14, with electricity $17.)

🍴📷 FOOD & NIGHTLIFE. Lake Placid Village, concentrated primarily along Main St., has a number of reasonably priced dining establishments. The **Hilton Hotel's ❶** lunch buffet, 1 Mirror Lake Drive, serves sandwiches, soups, salads, and a hot entree for only $7.50. (☎ 523-4411. Buffet daily noon-2pm.) The **Brown Dog Deli and Wine Bar ❹,** 3 Main St., builds tasty sandwiches with meats and cheeses on their homemade bread. (☎ 523-3036. Sandwiches $7. Entrees $15-18. Open daily 11am-9pm.) The **Black Bear Restaurant ❷,** 157 Main St., across from the municipal parking lot, dishes out meals from the grill as well as a few vegetarian/vegan options and smoothies. (☎ 523-9886. Daily specials $15. Breakfast $3-6. Lunch $8. Open daily 6am-9pm.) **The Cottage ❷,** 5 Mirror Lake Dr., offers a spectacular view of Mirror Lake, where you can sometimes catch the US national canoeing or kayaking teams at practice. The awesome sandwiches and salads are all under $9. (☎ 523-9845. Kitchen open daily 11:30am-10pm; bar open until midnight or 1am, depending on the crowd.) **Mud Puddles,** 3 School St., is one of Lake Placid's few late-night hot spots. (☎ 523-4446. No cover M-F, Sa-Su $3. Open daily 8am-3am.)

🌅 SIGHTS. The **Olympic Center** (www.orda.org) in downtown Lake Placid houses the 1932 and 1980 hockey arenas, as well as the petite, memorabilia-stuffed **Winter Sports Museum.** The museum features an 8min. intro video to Lake Placid and its Olympic history. (☎ 523-1655, ext. 226. Open daily 10am-5pm. $4, seniors $3, under age 6 $2. Public skating 8-9:30pm. $5, children $4; skate rental $3.) Purchase tickets for a guided tour of the **Olympic Ski Jumps,** which is part of the **Olympic Jumping Complex,** just east of town on Rte. 73. On summer mornings, take a chairlift and elevator ride to the top and watch jumpers soaring off the AstroTurf-covered Olympic ramp into a swimming pool. (☎523-2202. Open 9am-4pm. $5, with chairlift $8; seniors and children $3/5.) About 5 mi. east of town on Rte. 73, the **Olympic Sports Complex** at Mt. Van Hoevenberg offers bobsled rides down the actual Olympic track, no matter the season. In colder weather, the bobsleds run on ice and will set you back a chilly $30 per ride. In warmer weather, the sleds grow wheels but cost the same. (☎523-4436. Open W-Su 10am-12:30pm and 1:30-4pm. Winter runs Dec.-Mar.; summer Apr.-Nov. Must be at least 48 in. tall; under 18 need a parent.) While at the complex, consider whipping yourself into shape Olympian-style by taking a **mountain bike** run down one of the several cross-country ski paths. Bike rentals are available inside the complex. (☎523-1176. Open mid-June to early Sept. daily 10am-5pm; early Sept.-early Oct. Sa-Su 10am-5pm. Bikes $10-50 per day; trail fee $6 per day, $10 per 2 days; required helmet $3 per day.)

For those planning to visit Lake Placid's Olympic attractions, the **Olympic Sites Passport** is the best bargain. For $19 per person, the pass includes entrance to the Olympic Jumping Complex (including chairlift and elevator ride), the Olympic Sports Complex at Mt. Van Hoevenberg, the Winter Sports Museum, and choice of either the **Scenic Gondola Ride** to the top of Little Whiteface or access to the **Veterans Memorial Highway** that climbs Whiteface Mountain. Purchase a passport at any Olympic venue or at the **Olympic Center Box Office** (☎523-1655 or 800-462-6236; www.lakeplacid.com).

Popular tour boat cruises at **Lake Placid Marina** travel 16 narrated miles across Lake Placid on turn-of-the-century watercrafts. Passengers glimpse impressive estates, accessible by vehicles only in the winter, when the lake partially recedes and locals drive across. (☎523-9704. Cruises depart M-F 10:30am and 2:30pm; Sa-Su 10:30am, 2:30, and 4pm. $7.25, seniors $6.25, children $5.25.) For a bird's eye view, drive up Whiteface Mountain on the **Veterans Memorial Highway,** 11 mi. east of Lake Placid on Rte. 86. The alpine-style tollbooth at the bottom of the hill has info about the highway and is the starting point for a self-guided nature walk. Stop at one or two of the many parking areas on the way up for spectacular mountain vistas before reaching the observatory at the summit. (☎946-7175. Open July-Aug. daily 9am-4pm; mid-May to June and Sept.-early Oct. 8:30am-5pm, longer if weather permits. Car and driver $8; motorcycle and driver $5; $4 per passenger.) The tasting room of Finger Lake-based **Swedish Hill Winery,** 1 mi. east of downtown on Rte. 73, pours up selections of award-winning wine. (☎523-2498. Open M-Sa 10am-6pm, Su noon-6pm. 8 tastes and a wineglass $3.)

THOUSAND ISLAND SEAWAY ☎315

Spanning 100 miles from the mouth of Lake Ontario to the first of the many locks on the St. Lawrence River, the Thousand Island region of the St. Lawrence Seaway forms a natural US-Canadian border. Surveys conducted by the US and Canadian governments determined that there are over 1700 islands in the Seaway, with requirements being that at least one square foot of land must sit above water year-round and one tree should grow on it. Not only is the Thousand Island region a fisherman's paradise, with some of the world's best bass and muskie catches, it's also the only area in the nation with a salad dressing named after it.

◪ PRACTICAL INFORMATION. The Thousand Island region hugs the St. Lawrence River just two hours from Syracuse by way of **I-81 N.** From south to north, **Cape Vincent, Clayton,** and **Alexandria Bay** ("Alex Bay" to locals) are the main towns in the area. Cape Vincent and Clayton are quieter than the more touristy Alex Bay. For Wellesley Island, Alexandria Bay, and the eastern 500 islands, stay on I-81 until you reach Rte. 12 E. For Clayton and points west, take Exit 47 and follow Rte. 12 until you reach Rte. 12 E. **Greyhound,** 540 State St., in Watertown (☎ 788-8110; open M-F 9:15am-1pm, 3-4pm, and 6:10-6:30pm; Sa-Su only at departure times), runs to Albany (5hr., 2 per day, $36), New York City (7½hr., 2 per day, $47.50), and Syracuse (1¾hr., 2 per day, $8.50). **Thousand Islands Bus Lines** (☎ 287-2782) leaves from the same station for Alexandria Bay ($5.60) and Clayton ($3.55), with departures for both M-F 1pm. Return trips leave Clayton from the Nutshell Florist, 234 James St. (☎ 686-5791; departs daily 8:45am), and Alexandria from the Dockside Cafe, 17 Market St. (☎ 482-9849; departs daily 8:30am).

The **Clayton Chamber of Commerce,** 510 Riverside Dr., hands out the free *Clayton Vacation Guide* and *Thousand Islands Seaway Region Travel Guide.* (☎ 686-3771. Open mid-June to mid-Sept. daily 9am-4pm; mid-Sept. to mid-June M-F 9am-4pm.) The **Alexandria Bay Chamber of Commerce,** 11 Market St., is just off James St. (☎ 482-9531. Open May-Sept. M-F 8am-6pm, Sa 10am-5pm.) The **Cape Vincent Chamber of Commerce** welcomes visitors at 175 James St., by the ferry landing. (☎ 654-2481. Open May-Oct. Tu-Sa 9am-5pm; late May-early Sept. Su-M 10am-4pm.) **Internet access: Cape Vincent Community Library,** at the corner of Broadway and Real St. (☎ 654-2132. Open Tu and Th 9am-8pm, Sa-Su 9am-1pm.) **Clayton Post Office:** 236 John St. (☎ 686-3311. Open M-F 9am-5pm, Sa 9am-noon.) **ZIP code:** 13624. **Alexandria Bay Post Office:** 13 Bethune St. (☎ 482-9521. Open M-F 8:30am-5:30pm, Sa 8:30am-1pm.) **ZIP code:** 13607. **Cape Vincent Post Office:** 362 Broadway St., across from the village green. (☎ 654-2424. Open M-F 8:30am-1pm and 2-5:30pm, Sa 8:30-11:30am.) **ZIP code:** 13618. **Area code:** 315.

📕 ACCOMMODATIONS. The **Tibbetts Point Lighthouse Hostel (HI-AYH) ❶,** 33439 County Rte. 6, along the western edge of the Seaway on Cape Vincent, stands near where Lake Ontario meets the St. Lawrence River. Take Rte. 12 E into town, turn left onto Broadway, and follow the river until the road ends. The lighthouse is still active, and the hypnotic rhythm of the waves lulls visitors to sleep at night. (☎ 654-3450. Full kitchen with microwave. Linen $1. Check-in 5-10pm. Reservations strongly recommended in July and August. Open mid-May to Oct. Dorms $12, non-members $15.) There are several state and private campgrounds in the area, especially along Rte 12 E. Sites, however, are quite close together and fill up well in advance on weekends. **Burnham Point State Park ❶,** on Rte. 12 E, 4 mi. east of Cape Vincent and 11 mi. west of Clayton, sports 52 campsites and three picnic areas. Without a beach, it tends to be less crowded than other camping options. (☎ 654-2324. Showers. Wheelchair accessible. Open late May-early Sept. daily 8am-10pm. Sites $13-19, with electricity $16-20. Boat dockage for the day $6, overnight $13. $2.50 surcharge for each registration.) **Wellesley Island ❶,** across the $2 toll bridge on I-81 N before Canada, boasts 2,600 acres of marshes and woodland. (☎ 482-2722. 430 sites plus cabins. Showers, beach, marina, museum, and hiking. Sites $13-19, with electricity $16, full hookup $20.)

⬕ EXPLORING THE SEAWAY. Any of the small towns that pepper Rte. 12 serve as a fine base for exploring the region, although Clayton and Cape Vincent tend to be less expensive than Alexandria Bay. With fact-packed live narrations, **Uncle Sam Boat Tours,** 604 Riverside Dr., in Clayton (☎ 686-3511), and 45 James St., in Alex Bay (☎ 482-2611 or 800-253-9229), delivers the best views of the islands and of the plush estates that call them home. A variety of tours highlight the Seaway, including **Heart Island** and its famous **Boldt Castle** (see below), but they do not cover the price of admission to the castle. (Tours leave late Apr.-Oct. daily $13.75-27.75, ages 4-12 $6.75-19.50; prices vary with type of tour. Lunch and dinner cruises must be reserved in advance.) Endorsed by maniacal boaters, the **Antique Boat Museum,** 750 Mary St., in Clayton, houses practically every make and model of hardwood, fresh-water, and recreational boat ever conceived. (☎686-4104. Open mid-May to mid-Oct. daily 9am-5pm. $6, students $2, seniors $5, under 5 free.) **French Creek Marina,** 250 Wahl St. (☎686-3621), off Strawberry Lane just south of the junction of Rte. 12 and Rte. 12 E, rents 14 ft. fishing boats ($50 per day) and launches ($5), and also provides overnight docking ($20). **Fishing licenses** are available at sporting goods stores or at the **Town Clerk's Office,** 405 Riverside Dr., in Clayton. (☎686-3512. Open M-F 9am-noon and 1-4pm. $11 per day, $20 per 5 days, $35 per season.) No local store rents equipment; bring rods or plan to buy.

NEW JERSEY

Travelers who refuse to get off the interstates envision New Jersey as a conglom-eration of belching chemical plants and ocean beaches strewn with garbage and gamblers. This false impression belies the quieter delights of the state. The interior blooms with fields of corn, tomatoes, and peaches, and placid sandy beaches out-line the southern tip of the state. The state shelters quiet hamlets, the Pine Barrens forest, and two world-class universities—Rutgers and Princeton—that clashed in the first ever intercollegiate football game. And if nothing else, Bruce Springsteen calls it home.

🛈 PRACTICAL INFORMATION

Capital: Trenton.

Visitor info: State Division of Tourism, 20 W. State St., P.O. Box 826, Trenton 08625 (☎609-292-2470; www.state.nj.us/travel). **New Jersey Dept. of Environmental Pro-tection and Energy,** 401 E. State St., Trenton 08625 (☎609-292-2797).

Postal Abbreviation: NJ. **Sales Tax:** 6%; no tax on clothing.

ATLANTIC CITY   ☎609

For over 50 years, board-gaming strategists have been wheeling and dealing with Atlantic City geography, passing "Go" to collect their $200 and buying properties in an effort to control this coastal city as reincarnated on the *Monopoly* board. Meanwhile the opulence of Boardwalk and Park Place have gradually faded into neglect and then into mega-dollar tackiness. Casinos rose from the rubble of the boardwalk in the 1970s, and nowadays Atlantic City's status is defined by the waves of urban professionals looking for a fast buck and quick tan...and maybe even a loose romance.

▐ TRANSPORTATION

Atlantic City lies halfway down New Jersey's eastern seashore, accessible via the **Garden State Pkwy.** and the **Atlantic City Expwy.,** and easily reached by train from Philadelphia or New York.

Airport: Atlantic City International (☎645-7895 or 800-892-0354). Located just west of Atlantic City in Pamona. Served by Spirit, USAirways, and Continental.

Trains: Amtrak, at Kirkman Blvd., near Michigan Ave. Follow Kirkman to its end, bear right, and follow the signs. Open daily 6am-10:15pm. To **New York** (5½hr., 5 per day, $54) and **Philadelphia** (2½hr., 6 per day, $8).

Buses: Greyhound (☎609-340-2000). Buses travel every 30min. between **New York** Port Authority and most major casinos (2½hr., $26 round-trip). Many casinos, in addition to round-trip discounts, give gamblers $15-20 in coins upon arrival. Greyhound also has service from casinos to **Philadelphia** (18 per day, $12 round-trip). **New Jersey Transit** (☎215-569-3752 or 800-582-5946) offers hourly service from the station on Atlantic Ave. between Michigan and Ohio St. to **New York** ($25, seniors $23). **Gray Line Tours** (☎800-669-0051; terminal open 24hr.) offers daytrips from **New York** (3hr., $27). Your receipt is redeemable for cash, chips, or food from casinos upon arrival. The bus drops riders at the casino and picks them up later the same day. Call for nearest NYC bus pickup locations.

✈🛈 ORIENTATION & PRACTICAL INFORMATION

Attractions cluster on and around the **Boardwalk,** which runs east-west along the Atlantic Ocean. Running parallel to the Boardwalk, **Pacific** and **Atlantic Ave.** offer cheap restaurants, hotels, and convenience stores. *Atlantic Ave. can be dangerous after dark, and any street farther out can be dangerous even by day.* Getting around is easy on foot on the Boardwalk. **Parking** at the Sands Hotel is free but "for patrons only." Lots near the boards run $3-7.

Visitor info: Atlantic City Convention Center and Visitors Bureau, 2314 Pacific Ave. (☎888-228-4748). Open daily 9am-5pm. Another Visitors Center is on the Atlantic Expwy. (☎449-7130), 1 mi. after the Pleasantville Toll Plaza. Open daily 9am-5pm.

Medical Services: Atlantic City Medical Center (☎344-4081), at Michigan and Pacific Ave.

Hotlines: Rape and Abuse Hotline, ☎646-6767. **Gambling Abuse,** ☎800-426-2537. Both 24hr. **AIDS Hotline,** ☎800-281-2437.

Post Office: 1701 Pacific Ave., at Illinois Ave. (☎345-4212). Open M-F 8:30am-6pm, Sa 8:30am-12:30pm. **ZIP code:** 08401. **Area code:** 609.

▐ ACCOMMODATIONS

Large, red-carpeted, and overpriced beachfront hotels have bumped smaller operators a few streets back. Smaller, privately owned hotels along **Pacific Ave.,** one block from the Boardwalk, charge about $60-95 in the summer, when the local population surges to 250,000. Reserve ahead, especially on weekends, or else spend your hard-earned blackjack money on mediocre lodging. Many hotels lower their rates mid-week and during winter, when water temperature and gambling fervor drop. Exit 40 from the Garden State Pkwy. leads to Rte. 30 and cheap rooms in **Absecon,** about 8 mi. from Atlantic City.

Inn of the Irish Pub, 164 St. James Pl. (☎344-9063), near the Ramada Tower, just off the Boardwalk, has spacious, clean rooms with floral wall designs. The best budget accommodation in town has a porch equipped with relaxing rocking chairs and a refreshing Atlantic breeze. The downstairs bar offers lively entertainment and a friendly atmosphere. Key deposit $5. Doubles with shared bath $45-52, with private bath $75-90; quad with shared bath $85-99. Rates drop on weekends. ❷

Comfort Inn, 154 South Kentucky Ave. (☎348-4000 or 888-247-5337), near the Sands (see p. 263). Basic rooms with king-size or 2 queen-size beds and—true to Atlantic City swank—a jacuzzi. Breakfast, free parking, and a heated pool. Rooms with ocean views $20 extra, but come with fridge, microwave, and a bigger jacuzzi. Reserve well in advance for Sa-Su and holidays. Sept.-May $59-69; June-Aug. $89-109. ❹

Red Carpet Motel, 1630 Albany Ave. (☎348-3171). A bit out of the way, off the Atlantic Expwy. on the way into town, the Red Carpet provides standard, comfortable, uninspiring rooms and free shuttles to the boardwalk and casinos. Cable TV/HBO, restaurant in lobby. Doubles $39-59; quads $55-79; all with private bath. Prices can jump to $130 on summer weekends. *Be careful in the surrounding neighborhood after dark.* ❷

Shady Pines Campground, 443 S. 6th Ave. (☎652-1516), in Absecon, 6 mi. from Atlantic City. Take Exit 12 from the Expwy. This leafy, 140-site campground sports a pool, playground, laundry, firewood service, and new showers and restrooms. Call ahead for summer weekend reservations. Open Mar.-Nov. Sites with water and electricity $31. ❷

🄵 FOOD

Although not recommended by nutritionists, 75¢ hot dogs and $1.50 pizza slices are all over the Boardwalk. Some of the best deals in town await at the casinos, where all-you-can-eat lunch ($7) and dinner ($11) buffets abound. Tastier, less tacky food can be found a little farther from the seashore. For the scoop on local dining, pick up a free copy of *Shorecast Insider's Guide at the Shore* or *Whoot.*

Inn of the Irish Pub, 164 St. James Pl. (☎345-9613), may not serve the healthiest food, but it tastes damn good. Start off with a 20th St. Sampler (buffalo wings, fried mozzarella, potato skins, and chicken thumbs, $7). The lunch special (M-F 11:30am-2pm) includes a pre-selected sandwich and a cup of soup for $2. All-you-can-eat Su brunch $7. Domestic drafts $1. Open 24hr. Cash only. ❷

White House Sub Shop, 2301 Arctic Ave. (☎345-1564). Sinatra was rumored to have had these immense subs ($4-9) flown to him while he was on tour. Pictures of White House sub-lovers Joe DiMaggio, Wayne Newton, and Mr. T adorn the walls. Italian subs and cheesesteaks $6. Open M-Th 10am-midnight, F-Sa 10am-1am, Su 11am-11pm. ❷

Tony's Baltimore Grille, 2800 Atlantic Ave. (☎345-5766), at Iowa Ave. Tourists can't resist the old-time Italian atmosphere with personal jukeboxes, not to mention the $3-6 pasta and pizza. Seafood platter $12. Open daily 11am-3am. Bar open 24hr. ❷

Custard and Snack House (☎345-5151), between South Carolina and Ocean Ave. on the boardwalk, makes 37 flavors of ice cream and yogurt, ranging from peach to double chocolate mint. If it's too chilly for dessert, try the coffee, tea, or hot cocoa—each only $1. One scoop $2.25. Open Su-Th 10am-midnight, F-Sa 10am-3am. ❶

Tun Tavern, 2 Ocean Way (☎347-7800). For a little fine dining in a casual atmosphere, check out the Tun, where locals and tourists alike enjoy nightly live music. Order the $22 filet mignon with freshly steamed vegetables, or opt for the less costly but equally satisfying $6 big bowl of corn and crab chowder. W $5 pitchers and 25¢ chicken wings after 10pm. Th karaoke 9pm. F dance floor opens 5:30pm for R&B performances. Open daily 11:30am-2am. ❹

🄲 CAINO, THE BOARDWALK, & BEACHES

All casinos on the Boardwalk fall within a dice toss of one another. The farthest south is the elegant **Hilton** (☎347-7111), between Providence and Boston Ave., and the farthest north is the gaudy **Showboat** (☎343-4000), at Delaware Ave. and Boardwalk. Donald Trump's glittering **Taj Mahal,** 1000 Boardwalk (☎449-1000), is too ostentatious to be missed; neglected payments on this tasteless tallboy cast the financier into his billion dollar tailspin. You, too, can board a magic carpet ride to bankruptcy! Speaking of *Monopoly*, Trump owns three other hotel casinos in the city: the recently remodeled **Trump Plaza** (☎ 441-6000); **Trump World's Fair** (☎ 800-473-7829), on the Boardwalk; and **Trump Castle** (☎ 441-2000), at the Marina. In summer, energetic partiers go to "rock the dock" at Trump Castle's indoor/outdoor bar/restaurant, **The Deck** (☎ 877-477-4697). Many a die is cast at **Caesar's Boardwalk Resort and Casino** (☎ 348-4411), at Arkansas Ave. The **Sands** (☎ 441-4000), at Indiana Ave., stands tall and flashy with its seashell motif. All are open 24hr.

There's something for everyone in Atlantic City—thanks to the Boardwalk. Those under 21 (or those tired of losing cash) **gamble for prizes** at one of the many arcades that line the Boardwalk. It feels like real gambling, but the teddy bear in the window is easier to win than the convertible on display at Caesar's. The **Steel Pier**, an extension in front of the Taj Mahal, juts into the coastal waters with a ferris wheel that spins riders over·the Atlantic. It also offers the rest of the usual amusement park suspects: roller coaster, carousel, and many a game of "skill." (Open daily noon-midnight; call the Taj Mahal for winter hours. Rides $2-5 each.) When and if you tire of spending money, check out the historic **Atlantic City beach.** Just west of Atlantic City, **Ventnor City** offers more tranquil shores.

CAPE MAY   ☎ 609

At the southern extreme of New Jersey's coastline, Cape May is the oldest seashore resort in the US, and the money here is no younger. Once the summer playground of Upper Eastside New Yorkers, the town still demonstrates the signs of affluent infiltration in the elegant restaurants of Beach Ave. but is no longer characterized by it. Meanwhile, the resort's main attraction continues to be the sparkling white beaches which shun the commercialism of more modern beach towns. At night, candles in the windows of 19th-century B&Bs infuse the streets with Victorian romance.

■ 🚹 ORIENTATION & PRACTICAL INFORMATION. Despite its geographic isolation, Cape May is easily accessible by car or bus. Start digging for loose change (most tolls 35¢) as you follow the tollbooth-laden Garden State Pkwy. as far south as it goes. Watch for signs to Center City until on Lafayette St. Alternately, take the slower, scenic Ocean Dr. 40 mi. south along the shore from Atlantic City. Rte. 55 brings beachgoers from Philadelphia. **NJ Transit** (☎ 215-569-3752 or 800-582-5946) makes a stop at the bus depot on the corner of Lafayette and Ocean St. It runs to: Atlantic City (2hr., 18 per day, $3.45); New York City (4½hr., 3 per day, $30); and Philadelphia (3hr., 18 per day, $15). **Cape Area Transit (CAT)** runs buses on Pittsburgh Ave., Beach Dr., Lafayette St., and Ocean Ave. (☎ 889-0925 or 800-966-3758. Operates July-Aug. daily 10am-10pm; late May-June and Sept.-Oct. F 4-10pm, Sa 10am-10pm, Su 10am-4pm. $2 per ride, $6 unlimited rides all day; exact change.) **Cape May Seashore Lines** runs four old-fashioned trains per day to attractions along the 26 mi. stretch to Tuckahoe. (☎ 884-2675. $8, children $5.) Bike the beach with the help of **Shields' Bike Rentals,** 11 Gurney St. (☎ 830-2453. Open daily 7am-7pm. $4 per hr., $9 per day; tandems $10/30; surreys $24 per hr.) Other services include: **Welcome Center:** 405 Lafayette St. (☎ 884-9562. Open daily 9am-4:30pm.) **Chamber of Commerce:** 513 Washington St. Mall (☎ 465-7181; open M-F 9am-5pm, Sa-Su 10am-6pm) and in the **historic kiosk** at south of the mall. **Post Office:** 700 Washington St. (☎ 884-3578. Open M-F 9am-5pm, Sa 8:30am-12:30pm.) **ZIP code:** 08204. **Area code:** 609.

⚄ ACCOMMODATIONS. Sleeping does not come cheaply in Cape May. Luxurious hotels and Victorian B&Bs along the beach run $85-250 per night. Farther from the shore, prices drop. Although the **Hotel Clinton ❷**, 202 Perry St., may lack Presidential suites and A/C, the Italian family-owned establishment offers 16 breezy rooms, the most affordable rates in town, and priceless warmth and welcome from the charismatic proprietors. (☎ 884-3993. Open mid-June to Sept. Singles $35; doubles $45. Reservations recommended.) Next door, the **Parris Inn ❷**, 204 Perry St., rents a variety of spacious, comfortable rooms and apartments (some much nicer than others), most with private baths, A/C, and TV. (☎ 884-8015. Open mid-Apr. to Dec. Singles in summer $45-65; doubles $65-125; lower rates off-season.) Campgrounds line U.S. 9 just north of Cape May. In a prime seashore location, **Cape Island Campground ❷**, 709 Rte. 9, is connected to Cape May by the Seashore Line (see above). The fully equipped campground features mini-golf, two pools, a playground, a store, and laundry facilities. (☎ 800-437-7443. Sites $35, full hookup $37.) More primitive, but only 10 blocks from Cape May, **Depot Travel Park ❶**, 800 Broadway, 2 mi. north on Rte. 626 (Seashore Rd.), off Rte. 9, is convenient for beach seekers. (☎ 884-2533. Open May-late Sept. Sites with water and electricity $24, full hookup $25. A/C $1.25 extra per night.)

❒❒ FOOD & NIGHTLIFE. Cape May's cheapest food is the generic pizza and burger fare along **Beach Ave.** Shell out a few more clams for a more substantial meal at one of the posh beachside restaurants. Crawling with pedestrians hunting for the most heavenly fudge and saltwater taffy, the **Washington St. Mall** supports several popular food stores and eateries. Start the morning off right with a gourmet breakfast on the porch of the **Mad Batter ❺**, 19 Jackson St. Try a stack of maple walnut pancakes with warm syrup ($9), or chose from a variety of steak and seafood options ($14-25) for lunch or dinner. (☎ 884-9619. Open daily 8am-10pm.) A meal at the pub-like **Ugly Mug ❷**, 426 Washington St. Mall, is worth battling through the initially suffocating smokescreen. Fresh air can be had on the patio as patrons inhale a New England cup o' chowder for $2.25 or the ever-popular "oceanburger" for $5.75. (☎ 884-3459. Free pizza Su 10pm-2am. Open M-Sa 11am-2am, Su noon-2am; hot food served until 11pm.) At **Gecko's ❷**, in the Carpenter St. Mall, Mexican chefs prepare southwestern-style seafood for $8 with Taco La Playa—two corn tortillas filled with grilled shrimp, lettuce, tomato, and black beans. (☎ 898-7750. Open daily 10:30am-10pm.)

The rock scene collects around **Carney's,** on Beach Ave., with nightly entertainment in the summer beginning at 10pm. Themed parties include "Island Tropics" and "Animal House." (☎ 884-4424. Su jams 4-9pm. Open daily 11:30am-2am.) A chic crowd congregates at **Cabana's,** at the corner of Decatur St. and Beach Ave. across from the beach. You'll have to find a lot of sand dollars if you want an entree, but there is no cover for the nightly blues or jazz. (☎ 884-8400. Acoustic sessions Sa 4-6:30pm. Open daily noon-2am.)

◀ HITTING THE BEACH. Cape May's sands actually sparkle, studded with the famous Cape May "diamonds" (actually quartz pebbles). A **beach tag** is required for beachgoers over 11. Tags are available from roaming vendors or from the **Beach Tag Office,** located at Grant and Beach Dr. (☎ 884-9522. Open 9:30am-5:30pm. Tags required June-Sept. daily 9:30am-4pm. $4, 3-day $8, weekly $11, seasonal $17.) Those in search of exercise and a spectacular view of the seashore can ascend the 199 steps to the beacon of the 1859 **Cape May Lighthouse** in **Cape May Point State Park,** west of town at the end of the point. (☎ 884-5404. Park open 8am-dusk. Lighthouse open Apr.-Nov. daily 9am-8pm; Dec.-Mar. Sa-Su 8am-dusk. $4, ages 3-12 $1.) The behemoth bunker next to the lighthouse is a WWII gun emplacement, used to

MID-ATLANTIC

scan the shore for German U-boats. In summer, several shuttles run the 5 mi. from the bus depot on Lafayette St. to the lighthouse ($5, ages 3-12 $4). Even migratory birds flock to Cape May for a break from the long, southbound flight. Sneak a peak at more than 300 types of feathered vacationers at the **Cape May Bird Observatory,** 701 E. Lake Dr., on Cape May Point, a birdwatcher's paradise. Bird maps, field trips, and workshops are all available here. (☎884-2736. Open Tu-Su 10am-5pm.) For a look at some larger creatures, including dolphins and whales, take an action-packed cruise with **Cape May Whale Watch and Research Center.** (☎888-531-0055. $17-22, ages 7-12 $8-12.) **Faria's,** 311 Beach Ave., rents beach necessities. (☎898-0988. Open Apr.-Sept. daily 9am-4pm. Surfboard $16-20.) For those thinking of doing a little wave jumping, rent boats, waverunners, and kayaks from **Cape May Watersports,** 1286 Wilson Dr. (☎884-8646. Open daily 8am-sunset. Boats $50-60 per 4hr., waverunners $50 per hr., kayaks $15 per hr.)

PENNSYLVANIA

Established as a colony to protect Quakers from persecution, Pennsylvania has clung to the ideals of freedom from the drafting of the Declaration of Independence in Philadelphia to the present. In 1976, Philadelphia groomed its historic shrines for the nation's bicentennial, and today the colonial monuments serve as the centerpiece of the city's ambitious renewal. Pittsburgh, the steel city with a raw image, was once dirty enough to fool streetlights into burning during the day but has recently began a cultural renaissance. Removed from the noise of its urban areas, Pennsylvania's landscape has retained much of the rustic beauty first discovered by colonists centuries ago, from the farms of Lancaster County to the gorges of the Allegheny Plateau.

⚡ PRACTICAL INFORMATION

Capital: Harrisburg.

Visitor Info: Pennsylvania Travel and Tourism, 453 Forum Bldg., Harrisburg 17120 (☎800-847-4872; www.state.pa.us). **Bureau of State Parks,** Rachel Carson State Office Bldg., 400 Market St., Harrisburg 17108 (☎888-727-2757). Open M-F 8am-4:30pm.

Postal Abbreviation: PA. **Sales Tax:** 6%.

PHILADELPHIA   ☎ 215

With his band of Quakers, William Penn founded the City of Brotherly Love in 1682. But it was Ben, not Penn, that transformed the town into the urban metropolis it is today. Benjamin Franklin, ingenious American ambassador, inventor, and womanizer, almost singlehandedly built Philadelphia into an American colonial capital. Sightseers will eat up Philly's historic attractions, world-class museums, and architectural accomplishments—not to mention the native cheesesteaks (a staple here) and the endless culinary choices of the city's ethnic neighborhoods.

✈ INTERCITY TRANSPORTATION

Airport: Philadelphia International (☎937-6800), 8 mi. southwest of Center City on I-76. The 20min. **SEPTA Airport Rail Line** runs from Center City to the airport. Trains leave 30th St., Suburban, and Market East Stations daily every 30min. 5:25am-

11:25pm. $5 at window, $7 on train. Last train from airport 12:10am. **Airport Limelight Limousine** (☎ 782-8818) will deliver travelers to a hotel or specific address downtown; $8 per person. Taxi to downtown $25.

Trains: Amtrak, 30th St. Station (☎ 824-1600), at Market St. in University City. Station open 24hr. To: **Baltimore** (2hr., 10 per day, $43); **Boston** (7hr., 10 per day, $74); **New York** (2hr.; 30-40 per day; $48, express trains $90); **Pittsburgh** (8hr., 2 per day, $51); and **Washington, D.C.** (2hr., 33 per day, $45). Office open M-F 5:10am-10:45pm, Sa-Su 6:10am-10:45pm.

Buses: Greyhound, 1001 Filbert St. (☎ 931-4075 or 800-231-2222), at 10th and Filbert in downtown Philadelphia, 1 block north of Market near the 10th and Market St. subway/commuter rail stop. Station open daily 24hr. To: **Atlantic City** (2hr., 12 per day, $8.50); **Baltimore** (2hr., 12 per day, $19); **Boston** (7hr., 24 per day, $55); **New York** (2hr., 32 per day, $21); **Pittsburgh** (7hr., 8 per day, $38); and **Washington, D.C.** (3hr., 12 per day, $22). **New Jersey Transit** (☎ 569-3752) is in the same station. To: **Atlantic City** (1hr., daily every 30min, $9); **Ocean City** (2hr., $40); and other points on the New Jersey shore.

■ ORIENTATION

Penn planned his city as a logical and easily accessible grid, though the prevalence of one-way streets can cause a migraine behind the wheel. As an incentive for visitors to walk, Philadelphia has done well to help pedestrians maneuver through its busy streets. Almost every corner features a map with the handy-dandy "you are here" star, along with arrows indicating directions to specific destinations. The north-south streets ascend numerically from the **Delaware River,** flowing from **Penn's Landing** and **Independence Hall** on the east side to the **Schuylkill River** (SKOO-kill) on the west. The first street is **Front;** the others follow consecutively from 2 to 69 across the Schuylkill River. This **Center City** area is distinguished from poorer South and Northeast Philly and affluent Northwest Philly. The intersection of **Broad (14th)** and **Market St.** is the focal point of Center City, marked by the ornate City Hall. This framework sounds simple, but Penn omitted the alleys in his system. Some can accommodate cars while others are too narrow, but street addresses often refer to alleys not pictured on standard maps of the city. The **SEPTA transportation map,** available free from the tourist office, is probably the most complete map of the city.

Due to the proliferation of one-way streets and horrendous traffic, driving is not a great way to get around town. However, parking near the historic sights is about $10 per day, and lower-priced options scatter at farther but walkable distances. Meterless 2hr. parking spaces can sometimes be found in the Washington Sq. district or on the cobblestones of Dock St. Day-long deals require vehicles to be in by 10am and out by 6pm. At 10th between Race and Vine St., a large lot discounts on weekends and evenings ($4 Sa-Su and after 3pm). Park outside the city and ride Philly's **buses** and **subway** to most major downtown destinations. *Public transportation can be unsafe after dark.*

NEIGHBORHOODS

The **Historic District** stretches from Front to 6th St. and from Race to South St. The hip **Washington Square District** runs from 6th to Broad St. and Market to South St. The affluent **Rittenhouse Square District** lies directly to the west. **Chinatown** comprises the blocks around 10th and Arch St., while the **Museums District** takes up the northwest quadrant bordered by Market and Broad St. Across the Schuylkill River, **University City** includes the sprawling campuses of the **University of Pennsylvania** and **Drexel University.**

MID-ATLANTIC

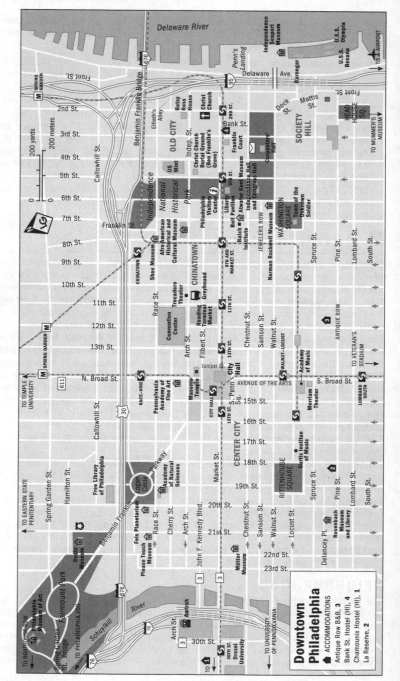

Downtown Philadelphia

ACCOMMODATIONS
Antique Row B&B, **3**
Bank St. Hostel (HI), **4**
Chamounix Hostel (HI), **1**
La Reserve, **2**

▣ LOCAL TRANSPORTATION

Public Transit: Southeastern Pennsylvania Transportation Authority (SEPTA), 1234 Market St. (☎580-7800). Extensive bus and rail service to the suburbs. Buses serve the 5-county area. Most operate 5am-2am, some 24hr. 2 major subway routes: the blue east-west **Market St. line** (including 30th St. Station and the historic area) and the orange north-south **Broad St. line** (including the stadium complex in south Philadelphia). *The subway is unsafe after dark;* buses are usually safer. Subway connects with commuter rails—the R5 main line local runs through the western suburb of Paoli ($3.75-4.25). The R7 runs north to **Trenton, NJ** ($5). Pick up a free SEPTA system map at any subway stop. $1.60, transfers 40¢. Unlimited all-day pass for both $5. In the tourist area, convenient, purple **Phlash** buses come by every 10min. and hit all major sights. $1.50, day-pass $3. **Philadelphia Sight-Seeing Tours** operates similarly to Phlash but also provides informative headsets and a knowledgeable trolley driver. ($20 per day, children $15; extra day $6.)

Taxis: Yellow Cab, ☎922-8400. **Liberty Cab,** ☎389-2000.

Car Rental: Budget (☎492-9400), downtown at 21st and Market St., or in the 30th St. Station, is reliable and easy to find but relatively expensive. Rates start at $35 per day with unlimited miles; $25 per day surcharge for under 25. Major credit card required.

Bike Rental: Frankenstein Bike Work, 1529 Spruce St. (☎893-4467). Flexible owner allows bikes to be kept overnight, if necessary. Open May-Sept. Tu-Su 10:30am-6:30pm. Call ahead for M service. Cruisers $12 for 4hr., $20 per day.

▧ PRACTICAL INFORMATION

Visitor info: The **City Visitor Center** and the **National Park Service Visitors Center** (☎597-8974, 627-1776 for a recording) are both in one convenient location at 5th St., between Market St. and Chesnut St. They offer maps, schedules, and brochures on all city attractions. Open in summer daily 9am-6pm; in winter 9am-5pm.

Hotlines: Suicide and Crisis Intervention, ☎686-4420. **Youth Crisis Line,** ☎787-0633. **Women Against Abuse,** ☎386-7777. All 24hr.

Bi-Gay-Lesbian Resources: Gay and Lesbian Counseling Services, ☎732-8255. Operates M-F 6-9pm, Su 5-8pm. **William Way Lesbian, Gay, and Bisexual Community Center** (☎732-2220) has info about gay events and activities. Open M-F noon-10pm, Sa 10am-5pm, Su 10:30am-8:30pm.

Internet access: The Free Library of Philadelphia (see p. 276).

Post Office: 2970 Market St., at 30th St., across from the Amtrak station. (☎387-1318. Open M-F 7am-5:45pm.) **ZIP code:** 19104. **Area code:** 215.

▨ ACCOMMODATIONS

Aside from its two hostels, inexpensive lodging in Philadelphia is uncommon, but if arrangements are made a few days in advance, comfortable rooms close to Center City can be had for around $60. The motels near the airport at Exit 9A on I-95 sacrifice location for the most affordable rates in the area. The personable proprietors at **Antique Row Bed and Breakfast** and **La Reserve** (see below) will recommend rooms if they're full. **Bed and Breakfast Connections/Bed and Breakfast of Philadelphia,** in Devon, PA, books rooms in Philadelphia and southeastern Pennsylvania, but requires 20% payment. (☎610-687-3565. Open 9am-7pm. Reserve at least a week in advance. Singles $60-90; doubles $75-250.)

■ **Chamounix Mansion International Youth Hostel (HI-AYH),** (☎878-3676 or 800-379-0017), in West Fairmount Park. Take bus #38 from lower Market St. to Ford and Cranston Rd.; take Ford Rd., turn left on Chamounix Dr., and follow to hostel. A young, energetic staff maintains uncommonly lavish hosteling in a converted mansion. Showers, kitchen, laundry, TV/VCR, piano, and bikes. Free parking, discounted bus tokens, and free summer orchestra passes. Internet access $1 per 5min. Linen $2. Check-in 8-11am and 4:30pm-midnight. Lockout 11am-4:30pm. Curfew midnight. Dorms $13, nonmembers $16. ❶

■ **Bank Street Hostel (HI-AYH),** 32 S. Bank St. (☎922-0222 or 800-392-4678). From the bus station, walk down Market St.; it's in an alleyway between 2nd and 3rd St. Subway: 2nd St. This very social hostel rests in a prime location in the historic district, near the waterfront and South St. Travelers convene nightly to watch movies on the lounge's big screen TV. A/C, free coffee and tea, laundry facilities, kitchen, and pool table. 70 beds. Internet access $5 per 30min. Linen $2. Lockout 10am-4:30pm. Curfew M-F 12:30am, Sa-Su 1am. Cannot reserve rooms via phone; must mail payment in advance—call for details. Dorms $18, nonmembers $21. ❶

Antique Row Bed and Breakfast, 341 S. 12th St. (☎592-7802). Enchanting traditional B&B at the heart of colonial rowhouses. The engaging owner offers her guests expert restaurant referrals and serves her own hearty breakfast. Four apartments geared toward longer visits with TV, utilities, and laundry. Free local calls. $65-100, depending on size of suite; reduced rate for longer stays. ❸

La Reserve (a.k.a. **Bed and Breakfast Center City**), 1804 Pine St. (☎735-1137). Entertains guests with an extravagant dining room that is often the site of lively dinner parties and visits from local musicians. Personable owner is a reliable source of Philadelphia advice and sidesplitting humor. Full breakfast. Plush doubles $80-130. ❹

Timberline Campground, 117 Timber Ln., (☎609-423-6677), 15 mi. from Center City, across the Delaware River, in New Jersey. Take U.S. 295 S to Exit 18B (Clarksboro), follow straight through the traffic light ½ mi. and turn right on Friendship Rd. Timber Ln. is one block on the right. Sites $18, full hookup $24. ❶

◻ FOOD

Street vendors are at the forefront of Philly specialties, hawking cheesesteaks, hoagies, cashews, and soft pretzels. Ethnic eateries gather in several specific areas: hip **South St.,** between Front and 7th St.; **18th St.** around Sansom St.; and **2nd St.,** between Chestnut and Market St. **Chinatown,** bounded by 11th, 8th, Arch, and Vine St., offers well-priced vegetarian restaurants. For the carnivorous, no Philly visit is complete without a cheesesteak. The quintessential Philly cheesesteak rivalry squares off at 9th and Passyunk Ave., in South Philadelphia; **Pat's King of Steaks ❷** (☎468-1546), the legendary founder of the cheesesteak, faces the larger, more neon **Geno's Steaks ❷** (☎389-0659). Both offer cheesesteaks for $5-6 and stay open 24hr. Whichever establishment you choose to visit, ordering a cheesesteak and the subsequent consumption will be an adventure. Prepare to order quickly and convincingly or risk being tossed to the back of the line, "No cheesesteak for you!" Grab a fistful of napkins to stay the grease that pours from the sandwich.

Fresh fruit and other foodstuffs pack the mobbed streets of the immense **Italian Market,** which spans the area around 9th St. below Christian St. Philadelphia's original farmer's market (since 1893), the **Reading Terminal Market,** at 12th and Arch St., stocks globally diverse food under one roof and is fabulous for lunch. Check the pamphlet available at vendors for events. (☎922-2317. Open M-Sa 8am-6pm; Amish merchants W-Sa.)

HISTORIC DISTRICT

Famous 4th St. Delicatessen, 700 S. 4th St. (☎922-3274), at Bainbridge St. Some say Philadelphia lacks a good Jewish deli, but this one comes close to even New York's finest. A Philadelphia landmark since 1923, the Delicatessen has earned its stellar reputation by faithfully serving favorites, like hot corned beef sandwiches ($7.50), in its antique dining room. Open M-Sa 7:30am-6pm, Su 7:30am-4pm. ❷

Jim's Steaks, 400 South St. (☎928-1911). Though the place looks a little run-down on the outside, the inside bustles with activity. Customers arrive in droves for the authentic Philly hoagie ($3.50-5) and fries ($1.25), and pass the time in line by inspecting the impressive wall of fame. Open M-Th 10am-1am, F-Sa 10am-3am, Su noon-10pm. ❶

Pink Rose Pastry Shop, 630 S. 4th St. (☎592-0565), at Bainbridge St., across from the Delicatessen. Friendly students serve up the widest selection of homemade delicacies at intimate tables graced with freshly-cut flowers. The sour cream apple pie ($4.50) is unforgettable, while white chocolate raspberry mousse cake ($5.50) with a latte ($2.75) leaves diners crooning for more. Open Tu-Th 10am-10:30pm, F 10am-11:30pm, Sa 9am-11:30pm, Su 9am-8:30pm. ❶

South Street Souvlaki, 507 South St. (☎925-3026), serves up great Greek specialties. Lunch sandwiches are reasonably priced, but the dinner menu is pricier. The fine food and friendly service is worth the extra money. Marinated beef in pita with sauteed vegetables and feta $5. Greek-style shrimp in white wine and garlic sauce with fresh pasta $15. Open daily 11am-10pm. Closed during some summer months; call ahead. ❸

CHINATOWN

▨ **Singapore,** 1006 Race St. (☎922-3288). Health-conscious Chinese food fanatics flock to this restaurant for options like the vegetarian roast duck ($8) or celery with bean curd ($7). Open M-Th 11:30am-10:30pm, F 11:30am-11pm, Sa-Su noon-11pm. ❷

▨ **Rangoon,** 112 9th St. (☎829-8939). Simple pink and plastic decor belies the complex, spicy scents of Burmese cuisine wafting onto the sidewalk. The crisp lentil fritters ($9) and tasty mint kebab ($9) earn this place its reputation as the best Chinese in Chinatown. Open daily 11:30am-9:30pm. ❸

Sang Kee Duck House, 238 9th St. (☎925-7532). Locals of all types pack the large, new dining room for a taste of the extensive menu. Shrimp seaweed soup $5. Entrees $6-10. Open Su-Th 11am-11pm, F-Sa 11am-midnight. ❷

CENTER CITY

▨ **Jamaican Jerk Hut,** 1436 South St. (☎545-8644). This tropical paradise brightens an otherwise bleak block. While chefs jerk Negril garlic shrimp ($10) to perfection, Bob Marley tunes jam in the backyard veranda. BYOB. Live music F-Sa 7pm; entertainment charge $2. Open Su-Th 11am-10pm, F-Sa 11am-11pm. ❸

Lombardi's, 132 S. 18th St. (☎564-5000), makes some of the best pizza this side of Italy. Established in 1905, this hometown favorite uses a coal oven to cook its crusts to perfection. Original pizza with fresh mozzarella, basil, and homemade meatballs $15.50. White pizza topped with green leaf spinach $17. Fresh salads $6-8. Pastas $7-11. Open daily 11:30am-11pm. ❹

The Philadelphia Cafe, 123 S. 18th St. (☎563-4424). A quiet cafe serving up creamy creations amid the bustle of downtown. Features 3 diverse ice cream brands including Philly's famed Bassett's ($3) and Colombo's surprisingly good, fat-free, sugar-free soft frozen yogurt ($2.50). Open M-Th 11:30am-10pm, F-Su 11:30am-11pm. ❶

Brasserie Perrier, 215 Walnut St., (☎568-3000). From the kitchen of Georges Brasserie, one of the nation's most well-respected chefs, come artistic creations that taste as good as they look. Three-course lunches with choice of lobster, steak, or special entree ($26) are more than worth their price tag. Large bar, upstairs dining room, and patio seating. Open M-Th 11:30am-2:30pm and 5:30-10pm, F-Sa 11:30am-2:30pm and 5:30-10:30pm, Su 5-9:30pm. ❺

Samson St. Oyster House, 1516 Sansom St. (☎567-7683). Businesspeople and professionals seek seafood delight in the nautically-bedecked dining room. Known for having one of the best raw bars in town, oysters top the menu ($7.25 for a half-dozen), but broiled bluefish ($7.50) and the popcorn shrimp po' boy ($6.25) are also great catches. Open daily 11am-1pm and 4-10pm. ❸

UNIVERSITY CITY

🎖**Tandoor India Restaurant,** 106 S. 40th St. (☎222-7122). Every college has a good, cheap Indian restaurant nearby, and this is one of them. Northern Indian cuisine with bread fresh from the clay oven (ask to see it). Lunch ($6) and dinner ($9) buffets. 20% student discount with valid ID. Open daily 11:30am-10:30pm. ❷

Smokey Joe's, 210 S. 40th St. (☎222-0770), between Locust and Walnut St. Hearty meals at student-friendly prices make it the most popular UPenn bar and restaurant. All-you-can-eat pasta, broiled salmon, or BBQ baby ribs $8. Lighter eaters can opt for the Palestra deal (salad, healthy sub, and drink $7). Local groups occasionally perform Su-Tu 10pm. Open daily 11am-2am; closed mid-June to mid-Aug. ❷

Abner's Cheesesteaks, 3813 Chestnut St. (☎662-0100), at 38th St. Local fast food attracts tipsy UPenn students deep into the night, and a more professional set for lunch. Friendly steak-makers cook up onion-laden cheesesteak, large soda, and fries for $6. Open Su-Th 11am-midnight, F-Sa 11am-3am. ❷

❻ SIGHTS

INDEPENDENCE MALL

REVOLUTIONARY SIGHTS. The **Independence National Historical Park,** a small green bounded by Market, Walnut, 2nd, and 6th St., is comprised of a rash of historical buildings. At night, the **Lights of Liberty Show** illuminates the American Revolution in a breathtaking way. A 1hr. guided tour through the Park narrates the happenings of the Revolution while an impressive laser light show illuminates five key sites in the downtown area. *(Park: ☎597-8974. Open June-Aug. daily 9am-6pm; Sept.-May 9am-5pm. Lights Show: ☎877-462-1776. Shows Tu-Sa.)* Instead of wandering blindly through the Park, begin your trip down American history memory lane at the newly renovated and rather impressive **Visitors Center** (see **Practical Information,** p. 269), at Market St. between 5th and 6th St. They dispense detailed maps and brochures, offer a small exhibit detailing each historical site, and provide electronic trip-planners that cater to the desires of each individual visitor. One of the most popular of Philadelphia's historic landmarks, **Independence Hall** abounds with revolutionary tourism. After Jefferson elegantly drafted the Declaration of Independence, the delegates signed the document here in 1776 and reconvened in 1787 to ink their names onto the US Constitution. Today, knowledgeable park rangers take visitors on a brief but informative tour through the nation's first capitol building. *(Between 5th and 6th St. on Chestnut St. Open daily 9am-5pm; arrive early in summer to avoid a long line. Free guided tours every 15min. Tickets distributed exclusively at the Visitors Center.)* The US Congress first assembled in nearby **Congress Hall.** While soaking up the history, guests can take a reclining rest in one of the plush Senate chairs. *(At Chest-*

nut and 6th St. Open daily 9am-5pm.) The predecessor to the US Congress, the First Continental Congress united against the British in **Carpenters' Hall,** which is now a mini-museum heralding the carpenters responsible for such architectural achievements as Old City Hall and the Pennsylvania State House. *(320 Chesnut St., in the block bounded by 3rd, 4th, Walnut, and Chestnut St. ☎ 925-0167. Open Tu-Su 10am-4pm.)* The **Portrait Gallery in the Second Bank** features portraits of the historical figures who are remembered today as the founders of this country. From Thomas Jefferson to Martha Washington to Noah Webster, the facial expressions are moving and the colors rich. *(At the corner of 3rd and Arch St. Open daily 10am-3pm. $3, under 17 free.)* North of Independence Hall, in its own pavilion, rests the country's most revered bell. While freedom may still ring at the **Liberty Bell Pavilion,** the (cracked) Liberty Bell does not. *(On Market St., between 5th and 6th St. ☎ 597-8974. Open 9am-5pm. Free.)* The **National Constitution Center,** set to open in July 4, 2003, promises visitors an in-depth look at the history and significance of the American Constitution. *(525 Arch St. In Independence Historical National Park, between 5th and 6th St. ☎ 923-0004, general information ☎ 866-917-1787. $5, seniors and under 12 $4.)*

OTHER SIGHTS. The rest of the park preserves residential and commercial buildings of the Revolutionary era. On the northern edge of the Mall, a replica of Ben Franklin's home presides over **Franklin Court.** The original abode was unsentimentally razed by the statesman's heirs in 1812 in order to erect an apartment complex. The home contains an underground museum, a 20min. movie, and a replica of Franklin's printing office. *(318 Market St., between 3rd and 4th St. Open daily 10am-6pm. Free.)* On a more somber note, a statue of the first American president and army general presides over the **Tomb of the Unknown Soldier,** in Washington Sq., where an eternal flame commemorates the fallen heroes of the Revolutionary War.

Adjacent to the house where Jefferson drafted the Declaration of Independence, the **Balch Institute for Ethnic Studies** is an academic glimpse into America's social history, including the plight of the African immigrant and of Japanese Americans during World War II. *(18 S. 7th St. ☎ 925-8090. Open M-Sa 10am-4pm. $3; students, seniors, and under 12 $1.50; Sa 10am-noon free.)* Across the street, the **Atwater Kent Museum** offers rare Pennsylvania artifacts such as the wampum belt received by William Penn from the Lenni Lenape at Shakamaxon in 1682, and, of course, still more Franklin exhibits. *(15 S. 7th St. ☎ 685-4830. Open M and W-Su 10am-5pm. $5, seniors and ages 13-17 $3, under 13 free).*

OUTSIDE INDEPENDENCE MALL

COLONIAL MADNESS. A penniless Ben Franklin arrived in Philadelphia in 1723 and strolled by the colorful and clustered rowhouses that line the narrow **Elfreth's Alley,** near 2nd and Arch St. The vigorous neighborhood—the oldest continuously inhabited street in America—now provides a shaded retreat from today's blaring horns and a window into the daily lives of Philadelphia's patriots. A museum gives visitors some of the alley's history. *(126 Elfreth's Alley. ☎ 574-0560. Open Feb.-Dec. Tu-Sa 1am-4pm, Su noon-4pm; Jan. Sa 10am-4pm, Su noon-4pm. $2, ages 5-18 $1.)* The **Betsy Ross House**—home of one of the most celebrated female patriots—conveys, through child-oriented placards, the skills that led seamstress Betsy Ross to sew America's first flag in 1777. *(239 Arch St. ☎ 686-1252. Open Apr.-Sept. daily 10am-5pm; Oct.-Mar. Tu-Su 10am-5pm. Suggested donation $2, children $1.)*

OTHER SIGHTS. For those who like to get off on the right foot, the Temple University School of Podiatric Medicine houses the **Shoe Museum.** The 6th fl. collection features footwear from the famous feet of Reggie Jackson, Lady Bird Johnson, Dr. J, Nancy Reagan, and others. *(On the corner of 8th and Race St., 6th fl. ☎ 625-5243. Tours W and F 9am-noon; tours are limited, call for appointments.)* The powder-blue **Benjamin Franklin Bridge,** off Race and 5th St., connects Philadelphia to New Jersey, and provides an expansive view of the city for those not afraid of heights. The bridge adds a touch of urban art after dark as its sweeping expanse is highlighted by hundreds of color-changing lights.

SOCIETY HILL & THE WATERFRONT

Society Hill proper begins on Walnut St., between Front and 7th St., east of Independence Mall. Though Independence Mall may end at Walnut St., its history continues to preside over 200-year-old townhouses and cobblestone walks illuminated by electric "gaslights."

HISTORICAL SIGHTS. Flames don't have a chance in **Head House Square,** at 2nd and Pine St., which holds the distinction of being America's oldest firehouse and marketplace, now housing restaurants and boutiques. Bargain hunters can test their haggling skills at an outdoor fine arts and craft fair. (☎ 790-0782. Open June-Aug. Sa noon-11pm, Su noon-6pm. Free workshops held Su 1-3pm.) Each January, sequin- and feather-clad participants join in a rowdy New Year's Day Mummer's parade; south of Head House Sq., the **Mummer's Museum** swells with the glamour of old costumes. (1100 S. 2nd St., at Washington Ave. ☎ 336-3050. String band concerts Tu evenings, free. Open Tu-Sa 9:30am-5pm, Su noon-5pm; July-Aug. closed Su. $2.50; students, seniors, and under 12 $2.)

ON THE WATERFRONT. A looming, neon sign at the easternmost end of Market St. welcomes visitors to **Penn's Landing,** the largest freshwater port in the world. Philadelphian shipbuilding, cargo, and immigration unfold at the **Independence Seaport Museum.** Kids can get their sea legs at the "Boats Float" exhibit, which welcomes junior sailors aboard ships. Near the museum a host of old ships bobs at the dock, including the USS *Olympia,* the oldest steel warship still afloat, and the USS *Becuna,* a WWII submarine. (☎ 925-5439. Open daily 10am-5pm. Museum and ships $8, seniors $6.50, children $5.) Finish the waterfront day in relaxing fashion at a free **waterfront concert.** (☎ 629-3257. Apr.-Oct. Big bands Th nights. Children's theater Su.)

CENTER CITY

As the financial and commercial hub of Philly, Center City barely has enough room to accommodate the professionals who cram into the area bounded by 12th, 23rd, Vine, and Pine St. Although rife with business activity during the daytime, the region retires early at night.

ART & ARCHITECTURE. The country's first art museum and school, the **Pennsylvania Academy of Fine Art's** permanent displays include artwork by Winslow Homer and Mary Cassatt, while current students show their theses and accomplished alumni get their own exhibits each May. (118 N. Broad St., at Cherry St. ☎ 972-7600. Open Tu-Sa 10am-5pm, Su 11am-5pm. Tours available by reservation. $5, students with ID and seniors $4, ages 5-18 $3. Special exhibits $8/7/5.) Presiding over Center City, the granite and marble **City Hall** remains the nation's largest working municipal building. Until 1908, it reigned as the tallest building in the US, aided by the 37 ft. statue of William Penn stretching toward the heavens. A historic statute prohibited building anything higher than the apex of Penn's hat until entrepreneurs overturned the law in the mid-1980s, launching historical Philadelphia into the modernism of the skyscraper era. A commanding view of the city still awaits visitors in the building's tower. (At Broad and Market St. ☎ 686-2840. Open M-F 9:30am-4:30pm. Tour daily 12:30pm. Suggested donation $1.)

RITTENHOUSE SQUARE

Masons of a different ilk left their mark in the brick-laden **Rittenhouse Square District**, a ritzy neighborhood southeast of Center City. This part of town cradles the musical and dramatic pulse of the city, housing several performing arts centers.

RITTENHOUSE MUSEUMS. Not short on other means of tourist entertainment, Rittenhouse Sq. offers visitors two distinctly dissimilar museum options. For the best results, completely digest lunch before viewing the bizarre and often gory medical abnormalities displayed at the highly intriguing **Mütter Museum.** Among the potentially unsettling fascinations are a wall of skulls and human horns. The museum also contains an exhibit on infectious diseases such as the Black Death and AIDS. The exhibit displays a Level 4 biohazard suit worn by scientists who work with the most deadly diseases of our time. *(19 S. 22nd St. ☎ 563-3737. Open daily 10am-5pm. $8; seniors, students with ID, and ages 6-18 $5.)* Just south of the square, the more benign **Rosenbach Museum and Library** permanently displays the original manuscript of James Joyce's *Ulysses* and the collected illustrations of Maurice Sendak among rotating exhibits. The museum will reopen in Spring 2003 after renovations are completed. *(2010 Delancey St. ☎ 732-1600. Open Sept.-July Tu-Su 11am-4pm. Guided 1¼hr. tours $5, students and seniors $3.)*

PARKWAY/MUSEUM DISTRICT

Once nicknamed "America's Champs-Elysées," the **Benjamin Franklin Pkwy.** has seen better days. While it sports an international flag row cutting through Philadelphia's streets, the surrounding areas suffer from a lack of upkeep. Nevertheless, the Parkway supports some of Philly's finest cultural attractions.

SCIENCE. A modern assemblage of everything scientific, the highly-interactive **Franklin Institute** would make the old inventor proud. The newly installed skybike allows kids and adults to explore scientific theories while pedaling across a tightrope suspended nearly four stories high. The "Secrets of Aging" exhibit shows why our bodies change for better and worse. *(At 20th and Ben Franklin Pkwy. ☎ 448-1200. Open daily 9:30am-5pm. $12, over 62 and ages 4-11 $9. IMAX Theater ☎ 448-1111. Advance tickets recommended, $8. Museum and IMAX $16, children $13.)* Part of the Institute, the newly renovated **Fels Planetarium** boasts an advanced computer-driven system projecting a scientific spectacle of light. Lively laser shows flash on Friday and Saturday nights. *(222 N. 20th St. ☎ 448-1388. $6, seniors and ages 4-11 $5. Exhibits and laser show $12.75/10.50. Exhibits and both shows $14.75/12.50.)* Opposite Fels, the **Academy of Natural Sciences,** the world's leader in natural discovery, allows budding archaeologists to try their hand at digging dinosaur fossils. *(1900 Ben Franklin Pkwy., at 19th St. ☎ 299-1000. Open M-F 10am-4:30pm, Sa-Su 10am-5pm. $9, seniors and military $8.25, ages 3-12 $8. Wheelchair accessible.)* For a little family fun, visit the **Please Touch Museum,** where kids can romp around in the Alice In Wonderland Funhouse, play miniature golf in the Science Park, or hone their broadcasting skills in the Me On TV workshop. *(210 N. 21st St. ☎ 963-0667. Open July-Aug. daily 9am-6pm; Sept.-June 9am-4:30pm. $9; Su 9-10am free.)*

ART. Sylvester Stallone may have etched the sight of the **Philadelphia Museum of Art** into the minds of movie buffs everywhere when he bolted up its stately front stairs in *Rocky*, but it is the artwork that has solidified the museum's fine reputation. A world-class collection includes Cezanne's *Large Bathers* and Toulouse-Lautrec's *At the Moulin Rouge*, as well as extensive Asian, Egyptian, and decorative art collections. *(Benjamin Franklin Pkwy. and 26th St. ☎ 763-8100. Open Tu, Th, and Sa-Su 10am-5pm; W and F 10am-8:45pm. Tours daily 10am-3pm. Live jazz, fine wine, and light fare*

F 5:30-8:30pm. $9; students, seniors, and ages 5-18 $7; Su before 1pm free.) A casting of *The Gates of Hell* outside the **Rodin Museum** guards the portal of human passion, anguish, and anger in the most extensive collection of the prolific sculptor's works this side of the Seine. *(At Benjamin Franklin Pkwy. and 22nd St. ☎ 763-8100. Open Tu-Su 10am-5pm. $3 suggested donation.)*

BOOKS AND INMATES. The Free Library of Philadelphia scores with a library of orchestral music and one of the nation's largest rare book collections. The user-friendly library is conveniently divided into subject rooms. Philadelphia art students frequently seek sketching subjects and inspiration amid the classical architecture of the building. *(At 20th and Vine St. ☎ 686-5322. Open Oct.-May M-W 9am-9pm, Th-F 9am-6pm, Sa 9am-5pm, Su 1-5pm; June-Sept. closed Su.)* In a reversal of convention, guests pay to get into prison at the castle-like **Eastern State Penitentiary.** Once a ground-breaking institution of criminal rehabilitation, tours twist through the smoldering dimness Al Capone once called home. Fascinating stories tell of daring inmates and their attempted escapes from behind these very bars. *(Fairmount Ave. at 22nd St. ☎ 236-3300. Open May and Sept.-Oct. Sa-Su 10am-5pm; June-Aug. W-Sa 10am-5pm. Tours every hr. 10am-4pm. $7, students and seniors $5, ages 7-12 $3, under 7 not permitted.)*

UNIVERSITY CITY

The **University of Pennsylvania (UPenn)** and **Drexel University,** across the Schuylkill from Center City, are in west Philly within easy walking distance of the 30th St. subway station. The Penn campus, a thriving assemblage of luscious green lawns and red brick quadrangles, contrasts sharply with the dilapidated buildings surrounding it. Ritzy shops and hip cafes spice up 36th St. A statue of the omnipresent Benjamin Franklin, who founded the university in 1740, greets visitors at the entrance to the Penn campus on 34th and Walnut St. *Much of the area surrounding University City is unsafe at night.*

U-CITY SIGHTS. The **University Museum of Archaeology and Anthropology** journeys through three floors of the world's major cultures under a beautiful stone and glass rotunda. *(At 33rd and Spruce St. ☎ 898-4001. Open Tu-Sa 10am-4:30pm, Su 1-5pm. $5, students and over 62 $2.50.)* In 1965, Andy Warhol had his first one-man show at the **Institute of Contemporary Art,** which has always stayed on the cutting edge of art and technology. *(At 36th and Sansom St. ☎ 898-7108. Open during academic terms W-F noon-8pm, Sa-Su 11am-5pm. $3; students, seniors, and artists $2; Su 11am-1pm free.)* North of the University area, the **Philadelphia Zoo,** the oldest zoo in the country, houses more than 2000 animals, including lowland gorillas, bearded pigs, and giant anteaters. The zoo also has wild, kid-friendly exhibits like the new walk-through the Galapagos. *(At 34th and Girard St. ☎ 243-1100. Open Feb.-Nov. daily 9:30am-5pm; Dec.-Jan. 11am-4pm. $13, seniors and ages 2-11 $10. Parking $5.)*

🎵 ENTERTAINMENT

Modeled after Milan's La Scala, the **Academy of Music,** at Broad and Locust St., houses the **Philadelphia Orchestra.** The orchestra performs from September to May. (☎ 893-1930. $15-90. $5 general admission tickets go on sale at the Locust St. entrance 45min. before F-Sa concerts. $8 student rush tickets Tu and Th 30min. before show.) The theater also hosts the six yearly productions of the **Pennsylvania Ballet.** (☎ 551-7000. $20-85.)

With 5000 seats under cover and 10,000 on outdoor benches and lawns, the **Mann Music Center,** on George's Hill near 52nd and Parkside Ave. in Fairmount Park, hosts big name entertainers like Tony Bennett, Willie Nelson, and the Philadelphia Orchestra, as well as a variety of jazz and rock concerts. Tickets are available from the Academy of Music box office on Broad and Locust St. From June through August free lawn tickets for the Orchestra are available from the Visitors Center, at 16th and JFK Blvd., on the day of a performance. (☎567-0707. Pavilion seats $10-32.) **The Trocadero,** 1003 Arch St., at 10th St., is now 120 years old. This oldest operating Victorian theater in the US hosts local as well as big-name bands. The upstairs balcony bar is sometimes open on non-show nights. (☎922-5486. Cover $6-16. Advance tickets through Ticketmaster. Box office open M-F noon-6pm, Sa noon-5pm.) The **Robin Hood Dell East** (☎685-9560), on Ridge Ave. near 33rd St. in Fairmount Park, brings in top names in pop, jazz, gospel, and ethnic dance in July and August. As many as 30,000 people gather on the lawn when the Philadelphia Orchestra holds free performances here in summer.

Many of Philadelphia's most appealing cultural events take a leave of absence in summer. During the school year, however, theatrical entertainment bustles. The students of the world-renowned **Curtis Institute of Music,** 1726 Locust St., give free concerts. (Mid-Oct. to Apr. M, W, and F at 8pm.) **Merriam Theater,** 250 S. Broad St. in Center City, stages performances ranging from student works to Broadway hits; past performers include Katherine Hepburn, Laurence Olivier, and Sammy Davis Jr. (☎732-5446. Box office open M-Sa 10am-5:30pm.) The **Old City,** from Chestnut to Vine and Front to 4th St., comes alive for the **First Friday** (☎800-555-5191) celebration on the first Friday of every month from October to June. The streets fill with live music and many art galleries, museums, and restaurants open their doors to entice visitors with free food and sparkling wine.

Philly gets physical with plenty of sports venues, and four professional teams play just a short ride away on the Broad St. subway line. Baseball's **Phillies** (☎463-1000) and football's **Eagles** (☎463-5500) play at **Veterans Stadium,** at Broad St. and Pattison Ave. Across the street, fans fill the **First Union Center** (☎336-3600) on winter nights to watch the NBA's **76ers** (☎339-7676) and the NHL's **Flyers** (☎755-9700). General admission tickets for baseball and hockey start at $10; football and basketball tickets go for $15-50.

⊠ NIGHTLIFE

Check the Friday *Philadelphia Inquirer* for entertainment listings. The free Thursday *City Paper* and the Wednesday *Philadelphia Weekly* have weekly listings of city events. A diverse club crowd jams to the sounds of live music on weekends along **South St.** toward the river. Many pubs line **2nd St.** near Chestnut St., close to the Bank St. hostel. Continuing south to Society Hill, especially near **Head House Sq.,** a slightly older crowd fills dozens of streetside bars and cafes. **Delaware Ave.,** or **Columbus Blvd.,** running along Penn's Landing, has recently become a trendy local hot spot full of nightclubs and restaurants that attract droves of yuppies and students. Gay and lesbian weeklies *Au Courant* (free) and *PGN* (75¢) list events taking place throughout the Delaware Valley region. Most bars and clubs that cater to a gay clientele congregate along **Camac, S. 12th,** and **S. 13th St.**

⊠ **Kat Man Du,** Pier 25 (☎629-1724), at N. Columbus Blvd. Hawaiian-shirt-clad partiers take refuge in the shadows of the Ben Franklin Bridge. Rock and hip-hop boom over the palm trees and open-air deck at Philly's hottest summer venue, where yuppies go to see and be seen. Talented DJs nightly; live music most weekends. Th $1 bottled beer and mixed drinks beginning at 10pm. Cover M-Th after 8:30pm $5; F-Sa $8; Su before 5pm $2, after 5pm $5. Open daily noon-2am.

The Khyber, 56 S. 2nd St. (☎238-5888). A speakeasy during the days of Prohibition, The Khyber now legally gathers a young crowd to listen to a range of punk, metal, and hip-hop music. The ornate wooden bar was shipped over from England in 1876. Vegetarian sandwiches $3. Happy Hour M-F 5-7pm. Live music daily at 10pm. Cover $5-15. Open daily 11am-2am.

Warmdaddy's (☎627-8400), at Front and Market St. Though entrees tend to be pricey, Bayou dreamers will eat up this Cajun club renowned for its blues and diversity. Special musical guests and reduced-price entrees Su 3pm. $5 cover on Th grants entrance into a midnight Happy Hour. Live music in summer at 7pm; in winter 8:30pm. Cover F-Sa $10; varies during the week. Open Tu-Sa 5pm-2am, Su noon-2am.

The Five Spot, 1 S. Bank St. (☎574-0070), is where the hip crowd goes to enjoy an old-time hang-out and good live bands. The classically designed lounge encourages cool cats to drink heartily, while the cramped dance floor upstairs hosts swingers of all levels and abilities. Th Latin dancing with free lessons. F-Sa DJ spins modern, rap, and R&B. 21+. Cover $5. Open daily 9pm-2am.

Moriarty's, 1116 Walnut St. (☎627-7676). Tucked near the office buildings of downtown, this Irish pub draws a healthy crowd late into the night. Pictures and Philly memorabilia adorn the walls in a quiet, comfortable bar scene. Over 20 beers on tap, ESPN on the TV, and private booths galore. Open Su-Th 11am-1am, F-Sa 11am-2am; extensive menu served until 1am.

Woody's, 202 S. 13th St. (☎545-1893). An outgoing gay crowd frequents this lively club, which features a cyber bar, coffee bar, dining room, and dance floor. Happy Hour daily 5-7pm, with 25¢ off all drinks. M karaoke. Tu Big Gay Divas night. Lunch daily noon-3:30pm; bar open M-Sa 11am-2am, Su noon-2am.

◪ OUTDOOR ACTIVITIES

Philly's finest outdoor opportunities can be found in the resplendent **Fairmount Park.** Larger than any other city park and covered with bike trails and picnic areas, the park offers city-weary vacationers the adventure of the great outdoors and stirring vistas of the Schuylkill River, all within a stone's throw of urban museums. The Grecian ruins by the waterfall immediately behind the Art Museum are the abandoned **Waterworks,** built between 1819 and 1822. Free tours of the Waterworks' romantic architecture, technology, and social history meet on Aquarium Dr., behind the Art Museum. (☎685-4935. Open Sa-Su 1-3:30pm.) Farther down the river, Philly's place in the rowing world is evidenced by line of crew clubs forming the historic **Boathouse Row.** The Museum of Art hosts $3 guided tours of Boathouse Row on Wednesday and Sunday, and trolley tours to some of the mansions in Fairmount Park. The area near Boathouse Row is also Philly's most popular in-line skating spot, and many joggers seeking recreation and a refreshing river breeze also crowd the local paths. In the northern arm of Fairmount Park, trails follow the secluded Wissahickon Creek for 5 mi., as the concrete city fades to a distant memory. The **Japanese House and Garden,** off Montgomery Dr. near Belmont Ave., is designed in the style of a 17th-century *shoin;* the authentic garden offers the utmost in tranquility. (☎878-5097. Open May to early Sept. Tu-Su 10am-4pm; mid-Sept. to Oct. Sa-Su 10am-4pm. $2.50, students and seniors $2.) *Some neighborhoods surrounding the park are not safe, and the park is not safe at night.*

⊠ DAYTRIP FROM PHILADELPHIA

VALLEY FORGE

In 1777-78, it was the frigid winter, not the British military, that almost crushed the Continental Army. When George Washington selected Valley Forge as the winter camp for his 12,000 troops after a defeat at Germantown in October, the General could not have predicted the fate that would befall his troops. Three arduous months of starvation, bitter cold, and disease nearly halved his forces. It was not until Baron Friedrich von Steuben arrived with fresh troops and supplies that recovery seemed possible. Renewed, the Continental Army left Valley Forge and its harrowing memory on June 19, 1778 to win the Battle of Monmouth.

The hills that once tormented the frost-bitten soldiers now roll through **Valley Forge National Historical Park.** Visitors can explore the park in one of three ways: by car, foot, or bus. The 10 mi. self-guided **auto tour** (audio tapes $9, tape players $15), begins at the Visitors Center. Also beginning at the Visitors Center is the ¼ mi. guided **walking tour,** led by a knowledgeable park ranger. (Daily 10:50am and 1:50pm. Free.) The **bus tour** allows visitors to explore sites at their own pace (7-10 sites; pick-up every ½hr. $6, children $5.) The **Visitors Center,** 600 W. Germantown Pike, also features a small museum and an 18min. film. (☎834-1550. Open daily 9am-5pm. Film every 20min. 9am-4:30pm.) All tours pass Washington's headquarters, reconstructed soldier huts and fortifications, and the Grand Parade Ground where the Continental Army drilled. The park has three picnic areas but no camping; those seeking to pitch a tent can obtain information at the Visitors Center. Joggers can take a revolutionary trip down a paved 6 mi. trail through deer-populated forests. (☎610-783-1077. Park open daily sunrise-sunset. Free.)

Valley Forge lies 30min. from Philadelphia by car. To get there, take I-76 west from Philly for about 12 mi. Get off at the Valley Forge exit (Exit 24), then take Rte. 202 S for 1 mi. and Rte. 422 W for 1½ mi. to another Valley Forge exit. **SEPTA** runs buses to the Visitors Center daily; catch #125 at 16th and JFK ($3.50).

LANCASTER COUNTY ☎717

Lancaster County produces 30 eggs, six gallons of milk, and three pounds of pork per second. Nevertheless, Lancaster's chief industry is not agricultural, but rather stems from the county's unusual composite of residents—the Amish, the Mennonites, and the Brethren. The simplicity of the undeveloped, unassuming Amish lifestyle fascinates a technologically dependent society. Thousands of visitors flock to this pastoral area every year to observe a modest way of life that eschews modern conveniences like motorized vehicles, television, and cellular phones. Point, but don't shoot—many Amish have religious objections to being photographed.

■ **ⅶ ORIENTATION & PRACTICAL INFORMATION.** Lancaster County covers an area almost the size of Rhode Island. County seat Lancaster City, in the heart of Dutch country, has red brick row houses huddled around historic **Penn Sq.** The rural areas are mostly accessible by car (or horse and buggy), but it is easy to see the tourist sites with a bike or to walk the mile or two between public transportation drop-offs. Travelers beware: on the country roads of Lancaster, **Intercourse** suspiciously leads to **Paradise.** From Paradise, **U.S. 30 W** plots a straight course into **Fertility.** Visitors should be aware that the area is heavily Mennonite, so most businesses and all major attractions close on Sunday. **Amtrak,** 53 McGovern Ave. (☎291-5080; ticket office open daily 5:30am-10pm), in Lancaster City, runs to Philadelphia (1hr., 8-10 per day, $16) and Pittsburgh (6½hr., 2 per day, $48). **Capital Trailways** (☎397-4861; open daily 8am-10pm), in the same location, buses to Philadelphia (3hr., 1 per day, $16) and Pittsburgh (6hr., 3 per day, $44). **Red Rose Transit,** 45 Erick Rd., serves Lancaster and some areas in the surrounding countryside. (☎397-4246. Buses run daily approximately 5am-6pm, but routes and times vary. Base fare $1.15, over 65 free.) The **Pennsylvania Dutch Visitors Bureau,** 501 Greenfield Rd., on the east side of Lancaster City off Rte. 30, dispenses info on the region, including excellent maps and walking tours. A 15min. slide show makes Lancaster look a little more exciting than it actually is. (☎299-8901 or 800-735-2629. Open June-Aug. daily 8am-6pm; Sept.-May 8:30am-5pm.) **Post Office:** 1400 Harrisburg Pike. (☎396-6925. Open M-F 7:30am-7pm, Sa 9am-2pm.) **ZIP code:** 17604. **Area code:** 717.

⌐i ACCOMMODATIONS. Hundreds of hotels and B&Bs cluster in this area, as do several working farms with guest houses; Visitors Centers can provide room information. As part of a religious outreach mission, the amicable staff at the **Mennonite Information Center** (see **Sights**, p. 280) will try to find a Mennonite-run guest house for about the same price. Camping can be found very easily. Hear the hooves and neighs of the Amish horses from dawn until the wee hours at the **Kendig Tourist Home ❶**, 105 N. Ronks Rd., left off Rte. 30 E, just past Flory's Campgrounds. The spotless rooms come with TV and A/C; some have private bath. (☎393-5358. Singles $26-36.) The **Pennsylvania Dutch Motel ❸**, 2275 N. Reading Rd., at Exit 21 off the Pennsylvania Turnpike, has spacious, clean rooms with cable TV and A/C. The helpful hostess eagerly distributes written directions to major sights. (☎336-5559. Singles $50, doubles $60; prices lower in winter.) Jacuzzis, fireplaces, and a candlelit gourmet breakfast make for a lovely setting inside the Victorian-style **Intercourse Village Bed and Breakfast ❹**, Rte. 340 Main St. (☎768-2626. Rooms $85-160, depending on size and season. Ha! Intercourse prices depend on size.) The wilderness setting at the **Sickman's Mill Campground ❶**, 671 Sand Hill Rd., off State Rd. 272, 6 mi. south of Lancaster, keeps things quiet. Amenities include hot showers, clean toilets, a playground, and firewood. Recreational activities include freshwater creek fishing, tours of the 19th-century mill, and river tubing. (☎872-5951. Office open daily 10:30am-9pm. Sites $15. Tours $4. Inner tube rental $6.)

◖ FOOD. Amish food, wholesome and generous in portion, is characterized by a heavy emphasis on potatoes and vegetables. Palatable alternatives to high-priced "family-style" restaurants are the **Farmers Markets** and the **produce stands** that dot the roadway. ▨**The Central Market,** in downtown Lancaster City at the northwest corner of Penn Sq., has been doing business since the 1730s. Nowadays, simply dressed Pennsylvania Dutch invade the city to sell affordable fresh fruit, meats, cheeses, vegetables, sandwiches, and desserts alongside more conventionally dressed vendors. (Open Tu and F 6am-4pm, Sa 6am-2pm.) Lancaster restaurants surround the market. Though a chain, **Isaac's Restaurant and Deli ❷**, 44 N. Queen St., in Central Mall is a culinary option worth considering. Personal pizzas with roasted red pepper and portabella mushroom aim to please ($7-9), as does the Salty Eagle sandwich (grilled ham and swiss with honey dijon mustard, $5.25). (☎394-5544. Open M-Th 10am-9pm, F-Sa 10am-10pm, Su 11am-9pm.) Across the street, **My Place ❶**, 12 N. Queen St., provides a slice of Italy in Amish country. The place looks like a dive, but the food makes up for what the ambiance lacks. (☎393-6405. Pizza slice $1.30, filling cheesesteak hoagie $4, generous salads $2-3. Open M-Th 10:30am-10pm, F-Sa 10:30am-11pm.) At the **Amish Barn ❸**, 3029 Old Philadelphia Pike, quilts surround the tables where patrons feed on Amish specialties like $2 chicken corn soup and $3.50 Amish apple dumpling. (☎768-8886. Entrees around $10. Open June-Aug. M-Sa 7:30am-9pm; spring and fall M-Sa 8am-8pm; call for winter hours.) For big spenders with a voracious appetite, the **Stockard Inn Restaurant ❺**, 1147 Lititz Pike, serves sumptuous steak ($14-22) and shrimp entrees ($14-18) in a 1750 farmhouse that was once owned by President James Buchanan. Cocktails and an extensive wine list are available. (☎394-7975. Open Tu-Th 11:30am-9pm, F 11:30am-9:30pm, Sa 4-9:30pm, Su 11:30am-8pm.)

◖ SIGHTS. To develop an understanding and appreciation of Amish culture, visit the informative **People's Place**, 3513 Old Philadelphia Pike, on Main St./Rte. 340, 11 mi. east of Lancaster City in Intercourse. The complex encompasses most of the block, with bookstores, craft shops, and a quilt museum, and an exhibit called **20Q**, for the 20 most-asked questions about the Amish, detailing the nuances of their unique lifestyle. The film, *Who Are the Amish?*, takes care of any lingering doubts. (☎768-7171. Open June-Aug. M-Sa 9:30am-7pm; Sept.-May M-Sa 9:30am-5pm. Film shown every 30min. 9:30am-5pm. $5, seniors $4, under 12 $2.50. Film and 20Q $8/7/4.) To get the story from the people who live it, stop in the **Mennonite Information Center** (☎299-0954), on Millstream Rd., off Rte. 30 east of Lancaster. The Mennonites, unlike the Amish, believe in outreach and established this center to help tourists distinguish between the two faiths. Exceptionally cordial hostesses offer to guide guests through a Mennonite Tabernacle reproduction.

For the most authentic exploration of Amish country available in a car, wind through the verdant fields off U.S. 340, near Bird-in-the-Hand. Cyclists can capture the simplistic spirit on the **Lancaster County Heritage Bike Tour,** a 46 mi., reasonably flat route past covered bridges and historic sites, run out of the Visitors Center. A visit to Lancaster is not complete without using the preferred mode of local transportation, the horse and buggy. **Ed's Buggy Rides,** 253 Hartman Bridge Rd., on Rte. 896, 1½ mi. south of U.S. 30 W in Strasburg, bumps along 3 mi. of scenic backwoods, covered bridges, and countryside. (☎687-0360. Open daily 9am-5pm. $7, under 11 $3.50.) **Amish Country Tours** offers 1½hr. trips that include visits to one-room schools, Amish cottage industries, breathtaking farmland vistas, and roadside stands. (☎786-3600. Tours given June-Oct. daily 10:30am and 1:30pm; May and Nov. Sa-Su 10:30am and 1:30pm. $15, ages 4-12 $7.) Old country crafts and food can be found in early July at the **Pennsylvania Dutch Folk Festival,** at Exit 31 off I-81 S, which offers an unusual combination of polka bands, pot pies, and petting zoos. (☎610-683-8707. $10, ages 5-12 $5.)

Lancaster also attracts visitors with its many outlet malls, located along Rt. 30 E, where smart shoppers find the best deals on designer goods. For nighttime entertainment, the **Dutch Apple Dinner Theater,** 510 Centerville Rd., has hosted such recent performances as *Grease, Annie Get Your Gun, Pinnochio,* and *The Jungle Book.* (☎898-1900. Shows run Tu-Su evenings, with selected matinee dates. $20, under 19 $15.)

GETTYSBURG ☎717

During perhaps the most memorable dates of the US Civil War, the three sweltering days of July 1-3, 1863 buckled with the clash of Union and Confederate forces at Gettysburg. The Union forces ultimately prevailed, though at a high price of over 50,000 casualties between North and South. President Lincoln arrived in Gettysburg four months later to dedicate the Gettysburg National Cemetery, where 979 unidentified Union soldiers still rest. Today, the National Soldier's Monument towers where Lincoln once delivered his legendary Gettysburg Address. Each year, thousands of visitors visit these fields and are reminded of the President's declaration "that these dead shall not have died in vain."

HERSHEY'S CANDYLAND Around the turn of the century, Milton S. Hershey, a Mennonite resident of eastern Pennsylvania, discovered how to mass market a rare and expensive luxury—chocolate. Today, the company that bears his name operates the world's largest chocolate factory, in Hershey, about 45min. from Lancaster. East of town at the amusement park **Hersheypark,** the **Chocolate World Visitors Center** presents a free, automated tour through a simulated chocolate factory. After the tour, visitors emerge into a pavilion full of chocolate cookies, discounted chocolate candy, and fashionable Hershey sportswear. *(Theme Park:* ☎534-3900. *Open June M-F 10am-10pm; July-Aug. M-F 10am-10pm, Sa-Su 10am-11pm; May to early June and Sept. call for hours. $30, seniors and ages 3-8 $17; after 5pm $16. Visitors Center:* ☎800-437-7439. *Opens with park and closes 2hr. earlier. Free; parking $5.)*

MID-ATLANTIC

⑦ PRACTICAL INFORMATION. Inaccessible by Greyhound or Amtrak, Gettysburg is in south-central Pennsylvania, off U.S. 15, about 30 mi. south of Harrisburg. **Towne Trolley** makes in-town trips, but doesn't serve the battlefield. (Runs Apr.-Oct. $1.) The **Gettysburg Convention and Visitor's Bureau,** 31 Carlisle St., has walls of helpful maps and brochures, and provides the *Gettysburg Visitors Guide,* which is full of important facts and phone numbers. (☎334-6274; www.gettysburg.com. Open daily 8:30am-5pm.) **Post Office:** 115 Buford Ave. (☎337-3781. Open M-F 8am-4:30pm, Sa 9am-noon.) **ZIP code:** 17325. **Area code:** 717.

⌂⎕ ACCOMMODATIONS & FOOD. Follow Rte. 34 N to Rte. 233 to reach the closest hostel, **Ironmasters Mansion Hostel (HI-AYH) ❶,** 20 mi. from Gettysburg, within the entrance of Pine Grove Furnace State Park. Unusually large and luxurious, the building holds 46 beds in a tranquil, idyllic area. Spacious porches, an ornate dining room, and a decadent jacuzzi make this hostel seem more like a Club Med resort. (☎486-7575. Linen $2. Laundry. Internet access $3 per 15min. Reception 7:30-9:30am and 5-10pm. By reservation only Dec.-Feb. Dorms $14, nonmembers $17.) Multiple motels line Steinwehr Rd. near the battlefield, but finding summer rates below $100 is difficult anywhere in the downtown area. For those willing to sacrifice proximity to restaurants, stores, and attractions, the **Red Carpet Inn ❸,** 2450 Emmitsburg Rd., 4 mi. south of Military Park has comfortable rooms with heat and A/C, large beds, and a pool. (☎334-1345 or 800-336-1345. Rooms $60-80.) **Artillery Ridge ❶,** 610 Taneytown Rd., 1 mi. south of the Military Park Visitors Center, maintains over 200 sites with access to showers, stables, laundry, a pool, nightly movies, a pond, and bike rentals. (☎334-1288. Open Apr.-Nov. Sites $17.50, with hookup $22; each additional person $4, children $2.)

In addition to the scenic beauty of its battlefields, Gettysburg features an adorable downtown area complete with quaint shops and lively restaurants. Hefty rations persist in the town's square and just beyond the entrance to the battlefield. In Gettysburg's first building (ca. 1776), now the **Dobbin House Tavern ❹,** 89 Steinwehr Rd., guests can create their own grilled burger ($6) under the candlelight and view an Underground Railroad shelter. For finer dining, the House also serves fresh cut steaks, seafood, lamb, veal, and other elegant entrees for $14-22. (☎334-2100. Jazz each month on the 1st W 7:30pm. Open Su-Th 9am-10pm, F-Sa 10am-11:30pm; fine dining begins at 5pm.) Near the battlefield, **General Pickett's Restaurant ❸,** 571 Steinwehr Rd., charges $7-11 for a Southern-style, all-you-can-eat buffet. (☎334-7580. Open M-Sa 11am-3:15pm and 4:30-8pm, Su 11am-8pm.)

◻ SIGHTS. Visitors can explore Gettysburg in many ways. A sensible start is the **National Military Park Visitors Information Center,** 97 Taneytown Rd., which distributes free maps for an 18 mi. self-guided driving tour. (☎334-1124, ext. 431. Visitors Center open June-Aug. daily 8am-6pm; Sept.-May 8am-5pm. Park open daily 6am-10pm. $3, seniors $2.50, under 15 $2.) General admission to the battlefield is free, but prepare to spare a penny or two for a more in-depth look at the historic grounds. **Park rangers** squeeze into the family wagon to personally guide visitors through the monuments and landmarks. (2hr. tour 1-5 people $40, 6-12 people $60. Arrive by 9am to ensure a time slot.) If uncomfortable with inviting a ranger into the car, follow the free walking tour or purchase an audio tape driving tour ($3).

The chilling sights and sounds of battle surround the audience at the **Cyclorama Center,** next to the Visitors Center. The center shows a 20min. film on the battle every hour, and a 30min. light show spins around a 9500 sq. ft. mural of the battle. (☎334-1124, ext. 499. Open daily 9am-5pm. $3, seniors $2.50, ages 6-16 $2.) Artillery Ridge Campgrounds (see **Accommodations,** above) rents **bikes** and conducts **horseback tours** by reservation. (Bikes $30 per day. 1hr. horseback tour $27.50, 2hr.

MID-ATLANTIC

horseback and history tour $50. No one under age 8 or over 240lbs.) Adjacent to the campground office is a meticulously detailed diorama of the Gettysburg battle, along with other exhibits. ($4.50, seniors and children $3.50.) **Historic Tours** trundles visitors around the battlefield in classic 1930 Yellowstone Park buses. (☎334-8000. 2hr. tours $17, children $11.) Based on the chilling tales told by author Mark Nesbitt, candlelit **ghost walks**, leaving from 55 Steinwehr Ave., reawaken the war-ridden dead. (☎337-0445. Walks at 8, 8:15, and 9:45pm. $6, under 8 free.)

The grim **Jennie Wade House,** 528 Baltimore St., preserves the kitchen where Miss Wade, the only civilian killed in the battle of Gettysburg, was mortally wounded by a stray bullet. The hole in the wall, through which the fatal bullet traveled, is still visible today. Legend has it that unmarried women who pass their finger through the fatal bullet hole will be engaged within a year. (☎334-4100. Open May-Aug. daily 9am-9pm; Sept.-Apr. 9am-5pm. $6, ages 6-11 $3.50.) Perhaps as frightening as the prospect of marriage are the uncomfortably lifelike Civil War scenes on display at the **National Civil War Wax Museum,** 297 Steinwehr Ave., across from the Military Park entrance. (☎334-6245. Open daily 9am-8:15pm. Adults $5.50, ages 13-17 $3, ages 6-12 $2, under 6 free). The most impressive example of Civil War reenactment can be seen at the **Annual Civil War Battle Reenactments,** a week-long event that features six main battles and a living history village. (☎338-1525 for tickets and information. Times, dates, and locations vary each summer.)

PITTSBURGH   ☎412

Those who come to the City of Steel expecting sprawling industry and hordes of soot-encrusted American Joes are bound to be disappointed. The decline of the steel industry has meant cleaner air and rivers, and a recent economical renaissance has produced a brighter urban landscape. City officials are desperate to provide Pittsburgh with a new image, going so far as to propose a theme park filled with robotic dinosaurs. Throughout renewals, Pittsburgh's neighborhoods have maintained strong and diverse identities—some ethnic, some intellectual, and some based in the counter culture. Admittedly, some of the old, sooty Pittsburgh survives in the suburbs, but one need only ride up the Duquesne Incline and view downtown from atop Mt. Washington to see how thoroughly Pittsburgh has entered a new age.

▛ TRANSPORTATION

Airport: Pittsburgh International (☎472-5526), 18 mi. west of downtown, by I-279 and Rte. 60 N in Findlay Township. The Port Authority's **28x Airport Flyer** bus serves downtown and Oakland from the airport. Operates daily every 30min. 6am-midnight. $2. **Airline Transportation Company** (☎321-4990 or 471-8900) runs to downtown M-F every hr. 7am-11:30pm, reduced service Sa. $14. Taxi to downtown $30.

Trains: Amtrak, 1100 Liberty Ave. (☎471-6170), at Grant St. on the northern edge of downtown, next to Greyhound and the post office. Generally safe inside, *but be careful walking from here to the city center at night.* Station open daily 6am-midnight. To: **Chicago** (9½-10hr., 3 per day, $57-106); **New York** (10-13hr., 2 per day, $65-121); and **Philadelphia** (8½-11½hr., 2 per day, $48-89).

Buses: Greyhound, 55 11th St. (☎392-6526), at Liberty Ave. Open 24hr. To **Chicago** (8-12hr., 9 per day, $56) and **Philadelphia** (7hr., 9 per day, $40).

Public Transit: Port Authority of Allegheny County (PAT) (☎442-2000). Within downtown, bus free until 7pm; subway between the 3 downtown stops free. Beyond downtown, bus $1.60, transfers 25¢, all-day weekend pass $4; subway $1.60. Ages 6-11 half-price for bus and subway. Schedules and maps at most subway stations.

Taxi: Yellow Cab, ☎665-8100.

MID-ATLANTIC

◄⧖ 🔃 ORIENTATION & PRACTICAL INFORMATION

Pittsburgh's downtown, the **Golden Triangle**, is shaped by two rivers—the **Allegheny** to the north and the **Monongahela** to the south—which flow together to form a third river, the **Ohio**. Streets in the Triangle that run parallel to the Monongahela are numbered one through seven. The **University of Pittsburgh** and **Carnegie Mellon University** lie east of the Triangle in Oakland. The **Wayfinder system** helps tourists and locals alike navigate the often confusing streets of the city. The 1500 color-coded signs point the way to major points of interest, business areas, and universities. Don't venture into one of Pittsburgh's many tight-knit neighborhoods without getting directions first—the city's streets and 40-odd bridges are notoriously difficult to navigate. Be careful in the area north of PNC Park where some museums reside, and in Allentown where the hostel is located. To stay oriented, pick up the detailed *Pittsburgh StreetMap* ($4) in any convenience store.

Visitor info: Pittsburgh Convention and Visitors Bureau, 425 Sixth Ave., 30th fl. (☎281-7711 or 800-359-0758; www.pittsburgh-cvb.org). Open M-F 9am-5pm. There are two **Visitors Centers,** one downtown on Liberty Ave. (open M-F 9am-5pm, Sa 9am-3pm) and one at the airport.

Hotlines: Rape Action Hotline, ☎765-2731. Operates 24hr. **Gay, Lesbian, Bisexual Center,** ☎422-0114. Operates M-F 6:30-9:30pm, Sa 3-6pm.

Post Office: 700 Grant St. (☎642-4472). Open M-F 7am-6pm, Sa 7am-2:30pm. **ZIP code:** 15219. **Area code:** 412.

🏠 ACCOMMODATIONS

▨ **Pittsburgh Hostel (HI-AYH),** 830 E. Warrington Ave. (☎431-1267), across the river and up a steep hill in Allentown, 1 mi. south of downtown. Take bus #52, "Allentown." Sparkling clean, grade-A hostel living with spacious rooms, laundry, kitchen, A/C, free parking, a great common room, and an elevator in a vault. Friendly, knowledgeable staff point visitors to their favorite 'Burgh spots. *Be careful walking around the nearby area at night.* Linen $1, towels 50¢. Check-in 8-10am and 5pm-midnight. Lockout 10am-5pm. Dorms $19, nonmembers $22, under 18 $9.50. Private rooms for 2 $43-48/ $49-54. Wheelchair accessible. ❶

Motel 6, 211 Beecham Dr. (☎922-9400), off I-79 at Exit 60A, 10 mi. from downtown. Standard lodging with TV and A/C. Reservations suggested for summer weekends. Singles $39, doubles $45; $3 per extra person. ❷

Pittsburgh North Campground, 6610 Mars Rd. (☎724-776-1150), in Cranberry Township, 20min. north of downtown; take I-79 to the Cranberry/Mars exit. The closest camping near Pittsburgh. 110 campsites, showers, swimming. Office open daily 8am-9pm. Tent sites for 2 $20, with hookup $27.50; each additional adult $3, children $2. ❶

🍴 FOOD

Aside from the pizza joints and bars downtown, **Oakland** is the best place to find a good inexpensive meal. Collegiate watering holes and cafes pack **Forbes Ave.** around the University of Pittsburgh, and colorful eateries and shops line **Walnut St.** in Shadyside and **E. Carson St.** in South Side. The **Strip District** on Penn Ave. between 16th and 22nd St. (north of downtown along the Allegheny) bustles with Italian, Greek, and Asian cuisine. The Saturday morning **Farmers Market** sells an abundance of fresh produce and fish.

■ **Spice Island Tea House,** 253 Atwood St. (☎687-8821), in Oakland. Escape to this taste-filled island with lots of vegetarian and vegan options. Cool off with a thai iced tea or heat things up with one of the spicy salads in this tiny, dark cafe. Entrees from $5. Open daily 11am-11pm. ❷

La Fiesta, 346 Atwood St. (☎687-8424), in Oakland, serves fresh Mexican fare in a multi-colored, sombrero-filled setting. The lunch buffet is a great deal for $7 and the half-priced, late-night menu will cure any travelers' munchies without emptying their wallets. Open M-F 11:30am-10:30pm, Sa 11:30am-1am, Su 11:30am-10pm. ❷

Dave & Andy's, 207 Atwood St. (☎681-9906). The possibilities are endless at this ice cream shop with its huge inventory of flavors made on site. Try one of the homemade waffle cones (from $1.86) and find an M&M surprise at the end. Open M-F 11:30am-10pm, Sa-Su noon-10pm. ❶

Zenith Tea Room, 86 S. 26th St. (☎481-4833), at Sarah St., in the South Side. Attached to a gallery cluttered with antiques and artwork for sale, the tea room treats patrons to a creative selection of vegetarian entrees ($9), sandwiches ($5), and home-brewed iced teas. Menu changes every week. Open Th-Sa 11:30am-9pm, Su 11:30am-3pm. ❷

The Original Oyster House, 20 Market Sq. (☎566-7925). Pittsburgh's oldest and per-haps cheapest restaurant and bar. Serves seafood platters ($4-6) and fresh fish sand-wiches ($3-5) in a smoky marble and wrought-iron bar, decorated with photos of sports heroes and panoramic shots of Miss America pageants. Open M-Sa 9am-11pm. ❶

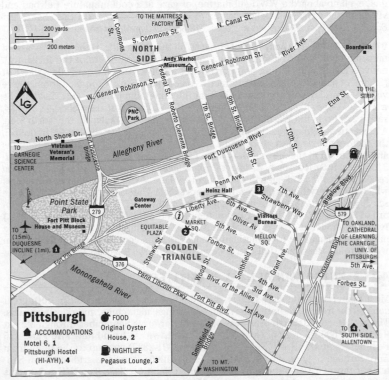

MID-ATLANTIC

◉ SIGHTS

GOLDEN TRIANGLE. The **Golden Triangle** is home to **Point State Park** and its famous 200 ft. fountain. A ride up the **Duquesne Incline,** in the South Side, grants a spectacular view of the city. *(1220 Grandview Ave. ☎381-1665. Open M-Sa 5:30am-12:45am, Su 7am-12:45am. Round-trip $3.60.)* Founded in 1787, the **University of Pittsburgh** stands in the shadow of the 42-story **Cathedral of Learning,** at Bigelow Blvd. between Forbes and 5th Ave. in Oakland. The Cathedral, built in part thanks to the dimes of Depression-era Pittsburgh schoolchildren, features 25 "nationality classrooms" decorated by artisans from the city's many ethnic traditions, from austere 16th Century English to elaborate 18th century African styles. In December, the rooms are decorated in various traditional holiday styles. *(☎624-6000. Cassette-guided tours M-F 9am-2:30pm, Sa 9:30am-2:30pm, Su 11am-3pm. $3, seniors $2, ages 8-18 50¢.)*

CARNEGIE. When Pittsburgh was a bustling steel metropolis, Andrew Carnegie was its biggest robber baron—and its biggest benefactor. Carnegie's most spectacular gift, **The Carnegie,** across the street from the Cathedral of Learning, holds two museums. The **Natural History Museum** houses models of all seven continents under one roof, and robotic tour guides dispense information. After exploring the history of the earth, visitors can enter the **Art Museum** to see an impressive collection of artwork through the ages. *(4400 Forbes Ave. ☎622-3289. Open Tu-Sa 10am-5pm, Su 1-5pm; July-Aug. also M 10am-5pm. $6, students and ages 3-18 $4, seniors $5.)* Feel an earthquake, climb aboard a WWII submarine, or gaze at a cool miniature railroad and village at the **Carnegie Science Center.** *(1 Allegheny Ave. ☎237-3400. Open Su-F 10am-6pm, Sa 10am-9pm. $10, seniors and ages 3-18 $8; with OmniMax or planetarium $14/10.)*

OTHER SIGHTS. The **Andy Warhol Museum,** on the North Side, is the world's largest museum dedicated to a single artist. It supports seven floors of the Pittsburgh native's material, including pop portraits of Marilyn, screenings of films like *Eat* (39min. of a man eating), and interactive pieces like *Silver Clouds*, a room where visitors can play among floating helium filled metallic pillows. *(117 Sandusky St. ☎237-8300. Open Tu-Th and Sa-Su 10am-5pm, F 10am-10pm. $8, students and ages 3-18 $4, seniors $7.)* From the Warhol, walk 20min. to **The Mattress Factory** in the North Side. A museum recognized as the best facility of site-specific installation art in the US, the factory allows guests to literally walk into artwork. Call ahead for directions and be careful in the surrounding area. *(505 Jacksonia Way, off East Commons. ☎231-3169. Open Tu-Sa 10am-5pm, Su 1-5pm. Open Sa until 7pm through Apr. 30. $6, students and seniors $4. Free Th.)* Take a trip down memory lane at **Groovy Pop Culture Emporium,** which sells everything from Pez dispensers to Star Wars action figures. *(1304 E. Carson St. ☎381-8010. Open M-Sa noon-7pm.)* East of town in Penn Hills, an eastern suburb of Pittsburgh, lies the first Hindu temple in the US. The **Sri Venkateswara (S.V.) Temple** is modeled after a temple in Andhra Pradesh, India, and has become a major pilgrimage site for American Hindus since its completion. Non-Hindus can walk through the Great Hall and observe prayer. *(1230 S. McCully Dr. ☎373-3380.)*

🎵 🍸 ENTERTAINMENT & NIGHTLIFE

Most restaurants and shops carry the weekly *City Paper* and *Pulp*, both great sources for free, up-to-date entertainment listings, nightclubs, and racy personals. The acclaimed **Pittsburgh Symphony Orchestra** performs September through May at **Heinz Hall,** 600 Penn Ave. (☎392-4900), downtown. At brand new **PNC Park,** 115 Federal St., on the North Side, the **Pirates** (☎321-2827) step up to the plate from April through September. The **Steelers** (☎323-1200) storm the gridiron from September through December down the road at **Heinz Stadium.** The NHL's **Penguins** (☎800-642-7367) rock the winter ice at Mellon Arena.

For nightlife, the **Strip** downtown is still relatively dense with revelers, especially for a town that closes down at 5pm. The hip crowd fills **E. Carson St.** on the South Side, which overflows on weekend nights.

Metropol and the more intimate **Rosebud,** 1600 Smallman St. (☎261-4512), in the Strip District, fill a spacious warehouse with two dance floors of steely partygoers. Cover $5. Doors open 8pm.

Nick's Fat City, 1601-1605 E. Carson St. (☎481-6880), in the South Side, features popular local and regional rock 'n' roll bands and $3 draughts of Yuengling (a favorite PA brew) in a memorabilia-laden bar. Cover varies. Open Tu-Sa 11am-2am.

Jack's, 1117 E. Carson St. (☎431-3644), at S. 12th St., in the South Side. The only bar in the 'Burgh open 365 days a year packs in a rowdy but friendly crowd. M hot dogs 25¢. W wings 10¢. M-W $1 beers. 21+. Open M-Sa 7am-2am, Su 11am-2am.

K&M Pub, 200 Mount Oliver St. (☎431-9655), near the hostel. Serves up local beers to local characters and blares tunes from the best jukebox in the city. *Be careful in the surrounding area at night.* Opens daily at 11am-2am.

Pegasus Lounge, 818 Liberty Ave. (☎281-2131), downtown, plays house and drag shows for the gay and lesbian community. Open Tu-Sa 9pm-2am.

◪ DAYTRIPS FROM PITTSBURGH

OHIOPYLE STATE PARK

Throngs come each year to raft Ohiopyle's 8 mi. class III rapids. Some of the best whitewater rafting in the East, the rapids take about 5hr. to conquer. For novices, class I and II rapids ease rafts down sections of the river. Four outfitters front Rte. 381 in "downtown" Ohiopyle: **White Water Adventurers** (☎800-992-7238), **Wilderness Voyageurs** (☎800-272-4141), **Laurel Highlands River Tours** (☎800-472-3846), and **Mountain Streams** (☎800-723-8669). Trip prices on the Youghhiogheny River ("The Yock" to locals) vary dramatically ($35-60 per person per day), depending on the season, day of the week, and difficulty. (Rentals: Rafts about $12-15 per person; canoes $20; inflatable kayaks about $20-26.) In order to float anything, you need a **launch permit** from the park office. (M-F free, Sa-Su $2.50. Call at least 30 days in advance for Sa permits.) Rental companies provide free permits.) For guided trips, park in the lot on Dinnerbell Rd. across the street from the park office. At the end of the trip, a shuttle takes adventurers back to their car.

The **Visitors Center,** off Rte. 381 on Dinnerbell Rd. offers information on the park and surrounding areas. (☎329-8591. Open May-Oct. daily 10am-4:30pm.) **ZIP code:** 15470. **Area code:** 724.

FALLINGWATER

Fallingwater, 8 mi. north of Ohiopyle on Rte. 381, is a masterpiece by the king of modern architecture, Frank Lloyd Wright. Designed in 1935 for Pittsburgh's wealthy Kaufmann family, "the most famous private residence ever built" blends into the surrounding terrain, and original boulders are part of its architecture. The house appears as though it will cascade over the waterfall it hangs over, and the water's gentle roar can be heard in every room. (☎329-8501. Open Apr.-Oct. Tu-Su 10am-4pm; Mar. and Nov.-Dec. Sa-Su 10am-4pm. Reservations required. Tours Tu-F $10, ages 6-18 $7; Sa-Su $15/8. Children under 6 must be left in child care, $2 per hr.) For a more intimate, quainter Frank Lloyd Wright home, head to the nearby **Kentuck Knob,** on Kentuck Rd., 6 mi. north of U.S. 40, where a guided tour exhibits the grounds, rustic home, and greenhouse. (☎329-1901. Open Tu-Su 10am-4pm.)

DELAWARE

Tiny Delaware is a sanctuary from the sprawling cities of the Boston, New York, and Washington, D.C. Delaware was first to ratify the US Constitution on Dec. 7, 1787, and proudly totes its tag as the "First State." The history of Delaware has been dominated by the wealthy DuPont clan, whose gunpowder mills became one of the world's biggest chemical companies. Tax-free shopping, scenic beach towns, and convenient location lure visitors to Delaware from all along the nation's eastern shores.

▨ PRACTICAL INFORMATION

Capital: Dover.

Visitor Info: Delaware State Visitors Center, Duke of York and Federal St., Dover 19903 (☎302-739-4266 or 800-292-9507; www.state.de.us). Open M-F 8am-4:30pm. **Delaware State Chamber of Commerce,** 1201 N. Orange St., Wilmington 19899 (☎800-422-1181).

Postal Abbreviation: DE. **Sales Tax:** 8% on accommodations.

LEWES   ☎302

Explored by Henry Hudson and founded in 1613 by the Dutch, Lewes was the first town in the first state and over the years has attracted colonists, pirates, hardy fishermen, and now summer renters. Nevertheless, Lewes (pronounced Lewis) hasn't changed much with the times, still featuring untouched Victorian houses, quiet streets, and a genuine lack of tourist culture. The town has plotted out a walking tour of its colonial attractions, but the main draw remains the beautiful beach, which draws an older and wealthier vacationing set away from the bustling boardwalk of nearby Rehoboth Beach.

◼▨ ORIENTATION & PRACTICAL INFORMATION. Unless you own a private chopper, automobile is the only sensible way to reach Lewes. From points north, Rte. 1 S brings you directly to Lewes and Savannah Rd., which bisects the town. From the west, begin traveling east on Rte. 404, then take Rte. 9 E at Georgetown. This will land you at Rte. 1; continue south until Savannah Rd. The best public transportation option is the **Delaware Resort Transit** (☎800-553-3278) shuttle bus, which runs from the ferry terminal through Lewes to Rehoboth and Dewey Beach. (Operates every 30min. late May to early Sept. daily 7am-3am. $1 per ride, seniors and disabled 40¢; day pass $2.) **Seaport Taxis** (☎645-6800) will take you door-to-door anywhere in Lewes for a small fee. Note that the beach is not in town—a bridge separates the two, and it's a long walk to the beach without a car. Thankfully, the beach has abundant parking. The **Post Office** is at 116 Front St. (☎645-6548. Open M-F 8:30am-5pm, Sa 8am-noon.)

The **Lewes Chamber of Commerce,** 20 King's Hwy., operates out of the Fisher-Martin House (c. 1730) and offers useful Lewes info and a free walking tour of founders' houses, old meeting places, and buildings that saw action during the War of 1812. (☎645-8073. Open in summer M-F 10am-4pm, Sa 9am-3pm, Su 10am-2pm; off-season M-F 10am-4pm.)

▎◖ ACCOMMODATIONS & FOOD. A charming, kid-friendly B&B with a lavish vegetarian breakfast and seven rooms, the **Savannah Inn ❸,** 330 Savannah Rd., tops other Lewes accommodations in price and earth-friendly philosophy. Don't be fooled by the hints of peeling paint; this building is well-maintained and clean. (☎645-5592. No A/C. June-Sept. breakfast. Oct.-May $10 off room rates. Single rooms with shared bath $50; doubles $70; rooms for 3-4 $75-80.) **An Inn by the Bay** ❺, 205 Savannah Rd., offers a delightful stay in a Victorian-style home. The pricey master suite is an entire wing of the upstairs. (☎833-2565; www.aninnbythe-bay.com. TV, VCR, A/C, refrigerators, and breakfast buffet. Rooms in summer $140-240; less off-season.) To reach **Cape State Park** ❶ from the north, bypass Savannah Rd. and continue on Rte. 1 until signs direct you to take a left that leads to the park. These popular sites feature new restrooms and visitors' facilities and are a short hike to the beach. (☎645-2103. Campground open Apr.-Nov. Park open year-round 7am-11pm. Sites $25, with water hookup $27. Price for 4, each additional person $2.)

The few restaurants in Lewes cluster primarily on 2nd St. **Rosa Negra** ❸, 128 2nd St., offers huge plates of Italian classics. (☎645-1980. Seafood-filled ravioli $15. Early bird special M-Th 25% off all entrees. Open daily 6-11pm.) Sniff the rich aroma of brews like "Linzer torte" and "coconut kiss" at **Oby Lee Coffee Roasters** ❶, 124 2nd St. Tiptoe around the bags of coffee piled on the floor to order sandwiches ($4-6), fruit smoothies ($3), and the $1.50 "Opposite of Hot Cocoa," Vanilla Dream. (☎645-0733. Open daily 7am-10pm.) Locals go to the wood-paneled **Rose and Crown Restaurant and Pub** ❷, 108 2nd St., to eat great burgers ($4-7) and jam to live blues, rock, and karaoke on weekends. (☎645-2373. Happy hour daily 4-6pm, $1 discounts on drafts. Open daily 11am-1am.)

◪ **SIGHTS.** While the towns on the Eastern Shore pride themselves on their independence from the tourism industry, Lewes is struggling to turn itself into a vacationer's historical playground. Unfortunately, Lewes has few notable historical sites. The town has gathered some historic buildings into the **Historical Society Complex**, on Shipcarpenter St. near 2nd St. (☎645-7670. Open June-Aug. M and W-F 10am-4pm, Sa 10:30am-noon. $6.) Secluded among sand dunes and scrub pines 1 mi. east of Lewes on the Atlantic Ocean is the 4000-acre **Cape Henlopen State Park.** The family-oriented beach caters to youngsters frolicking in the waves under the watchful eyes of lifeguards, and parents and young couples soaking up the rays from their lawn chairs. The **Seaside Nature Center,** the park's museum on beach and ocean life, holds weekly talks on local animals and leads hikes. (☎645-6852. Open daily 9am-4pm.) The park is home to sparkling white "walking dunes," a 2 mi. paved trail ideal for biking or skating, a well-preserved WWII observation tower, and an expansive beach with a bathhouse. (Path open daily 8am to sunset. $5 per car.)

REHOBOTH BEACH ☎302

While Ocean City attracts rowdy underage high-schoolers, Rehoboth balances its discount-boardwalk fun with an antique beach cottage ambience. The rambling patios of Rehoboth's bed and breakfasts still outnumber those of its strip motels. Well-heeled Washington families and a burgeoning gay population constitute the summer crowd, supplemented by daytrippers seeking relaxation away from their more touristy stops.

▣▮ **ORIENTATION & PRACTICAL INFORMATION.** To reach the town from Rte. 1, take Rte. 1B to Rehoboth Ave. and follow it to the water. If using metered parking, don't press your luck—Rehoboth meter monitors are on the prowl. **Greyhound/Trailways,** 251 Rehoboth Ave. (☎800-231-2222 or 227-7223), stops next to the Rehoboth Beach Chamber of Commerce. Buses go to and from Baltimore (3½hr., 1 per day, one-way $32), Philadelphia (4hr., 2 per day, one-way $34), and Washington, D.C. (3½hr., 3 per day, one-way $36). The **ferry** to Cape May is the best option for island-hopping. (☎800-642-2777 or 644-6030. Office open daily 8:30am-4:30pm. 8 per day. $25 per vehicle, $8 per passenger.) The **Rehoboth Beach Chamber of Commerce,** 501 Rehoboth Ave., a recycled railroad depot next to an imitation lighthouse, doles out Delaware info, free maps, and coupons. (☎800-441-1329 or 227-2233; www.beach-fun.com. Open M-F 9am-5pm, Sa-Su 9am-noon.) The **Post Office** is at Rehoboth Ave. and 2nd St. (☎227-8406. Open M-F 9am-5pm, Sa 8:30-12:30am.) **Zip Code:** 19971.

🏠🍴 ACCOMMODATIONS & FOOD. Inexpensive lodgings abound in Rehoboth, and culinary offerings range from classic beach pizza parlors to high-end brasseries. **The Abbey Inn ❸,** 31 Maryland Ave., is just a street away from the noise of Rehoboth Ave. and always has a conversation waiting on the porch. (☎227-7023. Min. stay 2 days. Open late May to early Sept. Singles and doubles with shared bath from $48; triples and quads with shared bath $61; suite with private bath $105; 15% surcharge on weekends.) **The Beach View Motel ❹,** 6 Wilmington Ave. 50 yards from the boardwalk, has the feel of a hotel but the structure of a motel. Clean, nicely decorated rooms come with refrigerator, telephone, microwave, continental breakfast, and helpful desk attendants. (☎227-2999. In summer $80-180; off-season $45-80. Prices change week to week.) **Big Oaks Family Campground ❶,** 1 mi. off Rte. 1 on Rd. 270, offers a rugged alternative to town lodging. (☎645-6838. Sites $32.)

Cafe Papillon ❶, 42 Rehoboth Ave., in the Penny Lane Mall, is an authentic European twist to a very American scene. French cooks speaking the international language of good food serve up fresh crêpes ($2.75-7), croissants ($2-3.50), and stuffed baguette sandwiches for $5-7. (☎227-7568. Open May-Oct. daily 8am-11pm.) **Eden ❺,** 122 Rehoboth Ave., is *the* haute cuisine destination in Rehoboth. Pastel interior with wall paintings as beautiful as the beach. Though there is no jacket-and-tie formality be prepared to spend more than you did on all meals combined since coming to town. (☎227-3330. Lobster pot pie with mushrooms, asparagus, potatoes, chives, and vanilla $22. Open daily from 6pm.) At **Nicola's Pizza ❶,** 8 1st St., customers of all kinds are drawn by the aroma of an Italian kitchen and indulge in pasta dishes for $4-7. (☎227-6211. Open daily 11am until "the wee hours of the morning.") **Royal Treat ❶,** 4 Wilmington Ave., flips up a stack of pancakes and bacon for just $5.50. (☎227-6277. Breakfast 8-11:30am; ice cream 1-11:30pm.)

🌙 NIGHTLIFE. The congestion on the sparkling **beach** thins to the north of the boardwalk. Party-goers head out early to maximize their time before the 1am last calls. **The Blue Moon,** 35 Baltimore Ave., an established hot spot, rocks to the sounds of techno music for a predominantly gay crowd. (☎227-6515. Happy hour M-F 4-6pm. Su brunch with Bloody Mary bar $17. Open daily 4pm-1am.) **Cloud 9,** 234 Rehoboth Ave., is the heart of the gay scene in Rehoboth. (☎226-1999. Happy hour daily 4-7pm. M half-price pasta. Th buy-one-get-one-free entrees. DJ F-M. Open Apr.-Oct. daily 4pm-1am; Nov.-Mar. Th-M 4pm-1am.) Look for live weekend music at **Dogfish Head Brewings & Eats,** 320 Rehoboth Ave. Weekdays, the crowd is less diverse and more laid-back. (☎226-2739. Happy hour with $2 pints M-F 4-7pm. Open M-F 4pm-1am, Sa-Su noon-1am.) **The Summer House Saloon,** 228 Rehoboth Ave., across from City Hall, is one of Rehoboth's favorite spots to flirt. (☎227-3895. Su half-price daiquiris. M half-price burgers. F half-price Hurricanes.)

MARYLAND

Once upon a time, folks on Maryland's rural eastern shore captured crabs, raised tobacco, and ruled the state. Meanwhile, across the bay in Baltimore, workers loaded ships and ran factories. Then the federal government expanded, industry shrank, and Maryland had a new focal point: the Baltimore-Washington Pkwy. As a result, suburbs grew, Baltimore revitalized, and the "Old Line State" acquired a new, liberal urbanity. As D.C.'s generic suburbs continue to swell beyond the limits of Maryland's Montgomery and Prince George counties, Baltimore revels in its immensity, while Annapolis—the state capital—remains a small town of sailors. The mountains of the state's western panhandle remain relatively untouched.

⓿ PRACTICAL INFORMATION

Capital: Annapolis.

Visitor Info: Office of Tourism, 217 E. Redwood St., Baltimore 21202 (☎800-543-1036; www.mdisfun.org). **Dept. of Natural Resources,** 580 Taylor Ave., Annapolis 21401 (☎410-260-8186). Open M-F 8am-4:30pm.

Postal Abbreviation: MD. **Sales Tax:** 5%.

BALTIMORE ☎410

Nicknamed "Charm City" for its mix of small-town hospitality and big-city flair, Baltimore still manages to capture the hearts of visitors with its lively restaurant and bar scene, first-class museums, and loving attention to historical sights. The true pulse of the city lies beyond the glimmering Inner Harbor, in Baltimore's over-stuffed markets, coffee shops, and diverse city folk. Baltimore's southern heritage is visible in its many neighborhoods. In Roland Park, for instance, every house has a front porch and everyone greets you in a friendly "Bawlmer" accent. Birthplace of the *Star-Spangled Banner*, Baltimore lies just north of the nation's capital and is now home to two major sports teams that provide year-round spectacle—win or lose—for its proud residents.

▐ TRANSPORTATION

Airport: Baltimore-Washington International (BWI; ☎859-7111), on I-195 off the Baltimore-Washington Parkway (I-295), about 10 mi. south of the city. Take MTA bus #17 to the Nursery Rd. Light Rail station. Shuttles to hotels (☎859-0800) run daily every 30min. 5:45am-11:30pm. $11 to downtown Baltimore, round-trip $17). Shuttles leave for D.C. daily every hr. 5:45am-11:30pm. $26-34. Amtrak trains from BWI run to Baltimore ($5) and D.C. ($12). MARC commuter trains are cheaper, slower and run M-F. To: **Baltimore** $3.25 and **D.C.** $5.

Trains: Penn Station, 1500 N. Charles St. (☎800-872-7245), at Mt. Royal Ave. Easily accessible by bus #3 or 11 from Charles Station. Amtrak trains run every 30min.-1hr. To: **New York** (from $70); **Philadelphia** (from $40); **Washington, D.C.** (from $26). On weekdays, 2 **MARC commuter lines** (☎800-325-7245 in MD) connect Baltimore to D.C.'s Union Station (☎859-7400 or 291-4268) via **Penn Station** (with stops at BWI) or **Camden Station** (☎613-5342), at Howard and Camden St. Open daily 5:30am-9:30pm; self-serve open 24hr. (credit card only). Both $5.75, round-trip $10.25.

Buses: Greyhound (☎800-231-2222) has 2 locations: downtown at 210 W. Fayette St. (☎752-7682), near N. Howard St.; and 5625 O'Donnell St. (☎752-0908), 3 mi. east of downtown near I-95. Connections to: **New York** ($37, round-trip $69); **Washington, D.C.** ($11/22); and **Philadelphia** ($19/30). **Public Transit: Mass Transit Administration (MTA),** 300 W. Lexington St. (☎800-543-9809 or 539-5000 for bus and Metro schedule info; operator available M-F 6am-9pm), near N. Howard St. Bus, Metro, and Light Rail service to most major sights in the city. Bus #17 runs from the Nursery Rd. Light Rail stop to BWI Airport. Some buses 24hr. Metro operates M-F 5am-midnight, Sa 6am-midnight. Light Rail operates M-F 6am-11pm, Sa 8am-11pm, Su 11am-7pm. One-way fare for each $1.35, higher depending on distance traveled.

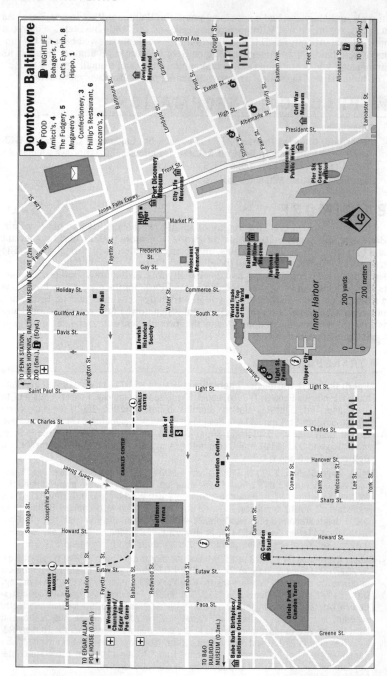

Downtown Baltimore

● FOOD
Amicci's, **4**
The Fudgery, **5**
Mugavero's
Confectionery, **3**
Phillip's Restaurant, **6**
Vaccaro's, **2**

■ NIGHTLIFE
Bohager's, **7**
Cat's Eye Pub, **8**
Hippo, **1**

Ferries: Harbor Boating, Inc., 1615 Thames St. (☎800-658-8947 or 563-3901). Main stop at Inner Harbor; other stops at the harbor museums, Harborplace, Fells Point, Little Italy, and more. An easy way to travel to 40 of Baltimore's main sights, especially in summer. Service every 8-18min. May-Aug. daily 9am-midnight; Apr. and Sept.-Oct. 9am-9pm; every 40min. Nov.-Mar. 9am-6pm. 1-day unlimited rides $5, ages 10 and under $3. Ticket includes coupons for Baltimore attractions.

Taxis: Checker Cab, ☎685-1212. **Royal Cab,** ☎327-0330. City fares start at $1.50 and accrue $1.20 per mi., 30¢ every cross-county mile.

⊕ 🛈 ORIENTATION & PRACTICAL INFORMATION

Baltimore lies 35 mi. north of D.C. and about 150 mi. from the Atlantic Ocean. The southern end of the **Jones Falls Expressway (I-83)** bisects Baltimore near the Inner Harbor, and the **Baltimore Beltway (I-695)** circles the city. **I-95** cuts across the southwest corner of the city as a shortcut to the wide arc of the Beltway. During rush hour, traffic slows to a crawl. The city is divided into quarters by **Baltimore St.** (east-west) and **Charles St.** (north-south). Directional prefixes indicate every other street's relation to these main streets. Baltimore, has no free parking. Either come fisting shiny quarters or expect to pay garages about $9 per day. Meters and garages away from the harbor are less expensive.

Inner Harbor, near the corner of Pratt and Charles St., is a scenic tourist trap and home to historic ships, a shopping mall, and an aquarium. The museum-laden **Mount Vernon** neighborhood—served by city buses #3, 9, and 11—occupies N. Charles St. around Monument St. and Centre Ave. Ethnic **Little Italy** sits a few blocks east of the Inner Harbor past the Jones Falls Expressway. Continuing past Little Italy, a short walk to the southeast brings you past Broadway to bar-happy **Fells Point.** Old-fashioned **Federal Hill** preserves Baltimore history, while the area east of **Camden Yards** has recently been renewed.

Visitor Info: Baltimore Area Visitors Center, 451 Light St. (☎837-7024). Located in a red-trimmed white trailer, the user-friendly center provides dozens of maps, brochures with discounts for sights and restaurants, and the helpful *Quickguide.* Open M-Sa 9am-5pm. **Traveler's Aid,** has 2 desks at BWI Airport and direct-line telephones at the Penn Station and Greyhound terminals. Open M-F 9am-9pm, Su 1-9pm.

Hotlines: Suicide, ☎531-6677. **Sexual Assault and Domestic Violence,** ☎828-6390. Both 24hr. **Gay and Lesbian,** ☎837-8888. Operators daily 7pm-midnight, recording all other times.

Post Office: 900 E. Fayette St. (☎800-275-8777). Open M-Sa 6am-11pm. **ZIP Code:** 21233.

⌐ ACCOMMODATIONS

Expensive chain hotels dominate the Inner Harbor, and reputable inexpensive hotels are hard to find. For a convenient way to reserve B&Bs, call **Amanda's Bed and Breakfast Reservation Service,** 1428 Park Ave. (☎225-0001 or 800-899-7533. Open M-F 8:30am-5:30pm, Sa 8:30am-noon. Rates from $50.)

Capitol KOA, 768 Cecil Ave. (☎800-562-0248 or 923-2771, from Baltimore ☎987-7477), in Millersville. Take Rte. 50E to Rte. 3N, bear right after 8 mi. onto Veterans Hwy.; turn left under the highway onto Hog Farm Rd., and follow blue camping signs. Mostly RVs, some cabins, and a small wooded area for tents. Free shuttles to MARC commuter train, New Carrollton Metro, and Union Station. Max. stay 2 weeks. Open late Mar. to Oct. Tent site for 2 $30; RV water and electricity $34, full hookup $39. 1-room cabin $49; 2-room cabin $59. Each additional adult $5, children $3. ❶

GOT THAT, HON? As *The Baltimore Sun* puts it, **hon** is a "provincial term of affection" in Baltimore. In 1994, the **"Hon Man,"** a mysterious vandal led a campaign to add "Hon" to the "Welcome to Baltimore" sign Parkway. For two years, he repeatedly stuck placards saying "Hon" to the sign only to have highway workers remove them. When state troopers caught him in the act, they extracted his promise never to hang a "Hon" sign again. With one relapse, he's kept his word.

Duke's Motel, 7905 Pulaski Hwy. (☎686-0400), in Rosedale off the Beltway, 30 min. drive from the Inner Harbor. The bulletproof glass in the front office is nothing to worry about—all the neighborhood motels have it. The area is actually safer than most parts of downtown Baltimore. Clean and efficiently run. Simple, dark rooms have A/C and cable TV. Key deposit $5. ID required. Singles from $45; doubles from $50. ❷

Quality Inn Inner Harbor, 1701 Russell St. (☎800-221-2222 or 727-3400), near the Beltway in South Baltimore, about 1 mi. from Inner Harbor. Standard rooms, cable TV, data ports, outdoor pool, and complimentary continental breakfast. Some rooms with fridges and microwaves. *Be careful at night.* Singles M-F $80, Sa-Su $90; doubles $85/95. AARP/AAA and military 10% discount. ❹

🍴 FOOD

🍽 **Mugavero's Confectionery,** 300 S. Exeter St. (☎539-9798). This menu-less deli has been a fixture for 54 years thanks to the unwavering service of the friendly proprietor. Patrons can invent their own sandwich ($4) or entrust it to the owner-operator's creative imagination. Open daily 10am-9pm, sometimes later. Cash only. ❶

Amicci's, 231 S. High St. (☎528-1096). Mediterranean zest and the Italian movie decor is apparent on the menu. *Ziti la rosa* (ziti in tomato pesto served with shrimp in marsala sauce, $13) is a standout. Live large with the renowned *pane rotundo*, jumbo shrimp stuffed into a round loaf of soft Italian bread ($6). Pasta dishes under $10. Open M-Th noon-10pm, F-Sa noon-11pm, Su noon-9pm. ❸

The Fudgery, 301 Light St. (☎539-5260), on the 1st. fl. in the Light St. Pavilion. Nirvana for chocolate cravers. A musically inclined staff sings while preparing heavenly fudge. $6 per half-pound slice. Open M-Th 9am-10pm, F-Sa 9am-11:30pm, Su 9am-9pm. ❶

Vaccaro's, 222 Albemarle St. (☎685-4905). Specializing in traditional Italian desserts and coffees, this pastry shop rises above the rest. Freshly made cannoli ($1-3), peanut to and fudge gelato ($3) or hot mochaccino ($4), delight taste buds at this family-run spot in the heart of Little Italy. Open Su-Th 9am-11pm, F-Sa 9am-1am. ❶

Phillip's Restaurant, 301 Light St. (☎800-782-2722), on the 1st fl. in the Light St. Pavilion. Loyal fans and families flock to the Inner Harbor's seafood hot spot for magnificent marine dishes. Try Phillip's Seafood Market right next door for inexpensive takeout. Sandwiches $6-13. Entrees from $12. Tykes under 5 eat free. Open M-F 9am-10pm, Sa 9am-11pm, Su 9am-8pm. ❸

👁 SIGHTS

Baltimore's gray harbor ends with a colorful bang in the Harborplace, a five-square-block body of water bounded on three sides by an aquarium, shopping malls, science museum, and bevy of boardable ships. The nation's first pier-pavilion, the Harborplace Mall is Baltimore's most imitated building. Crowds flock to Harborplace's Pratt and Light St. Pavilions for shopping and air-conditioned bliss. (☎332-4191. Open M-Sa 10am-9pm, Su 10am-6pm.)

THE NATIONAL AQUARIUM. The **National Aquarium** is perhaps that one magical attraction that sets Baltimore apart from all other major American cities. The aquarium's ever-changing exhibits give returning visitors an opportunity to always take a fresh look into the mysterious world of water. Of course, new visitors are unfailingly impressed by the awesome layout—which includes a gigantic deep sea tank and a lively tropical rainforest. Though a visit to the outdoor sea pool to watch slaphappy seals play is free to the general public, it is worth the time and money to venture inside. On ground level, an enclosed bridge leads to the **Marine Mammal Pavilion,** which has dolphins, whales, and an amphitheater with performances every hour on the half-hour. *(Pier 3, 501 E. Pratt St. ☎ 576-3800; www.aqua.org. July-Aug. daily 9am-8pm; Mar.-June and Sept.-Oct. M-Th and Sa-Su 9am-5pm, F 9am-8pm; Nov.-Feb. M-Th and Sa-Su 10am-5pm, F 10am-8pm. Remains open 2hr. after last entrance time. $17.50, seniors $14.50, ages 3-11 $9.50, 3 and under free. $5 discount in winter F after 5pm.)*

PORT DISCOVERY. Baltimore's newest children's museum, **Port Discovery** provides children with the ultimate educational playhouse. The creativity and imagination displayed in the museum's various programs and exhibits is invigorating for adults and inspiring to kids; the overall energy of the place is contagious. Constantly buzzing with goofy sounds and colorful sights, the self-proclaimed "kid powered" museum is just that. Well, more precisely, at this museum, the show goes on only with the help of eager young participants. *(35 Market Pl. In Power Plant Live. ☎ 727-8120. Open Sept.-May Tu-Sa 10am-5pm, Su noon-5pm; June daily 10am-5pm; July-Aug. daily 10am-6pm. F Fun Nights 10am-8pm. $11, children $8.50, 3 and under free.)*

BALTIMORE MARITIME MUSEUM. Several ships grace the harbor by the aquarium, most of which belong to the **Baltimore Maritime Museum.** Visitors may clamber through the interior of USS *Torsk,* the intricately-painted submarine that sank the last WWII Japanese combat ships. Covered under the same entrance fee are the lightship *Chesapeake* and the Coast Guard cutter *Roger B. Taney,* one of the survivors of the Pearl Harbor attack. The fee also allows access to the octagonal lighthouse on Pier 5. Other historic boats moored behind the lighthouse include *Lady Maryland,* a replica 18th-century schooner, and *Mildred Belle,* a 20th-century motorboat. For all this and more, purchase the **Seaport Day Pass,** which grants access to not just the Maritime Museum, but also the Museum of Industry, the monuments at Fort McHenry, the view of the city from high inside Baltimore's World Trade Center, and time aboard USS *Constellation*—the last all-sail warship built by the US Navy. *(Piers 3 and 4. ☎ 396-3453. Spring to fall M-Th and Su 10am-5:30pm, F-Sa 10am-6:30pm; winter F-Su 10:30am-5pm. Boats stay open 1hr. later than ticket stand. $6, seniors $5, ages 5-13 $3. Day Pass $24/20/13.)*

WALTERS ART GALLERY. Spanning 50 centuries through three buildings, the **Walters Art Gallery,** Baltimore's premier art museum, houses one of the largest private art collections in the world. The Ancient Art collection on the second level features sculpture, jewelry, and metalwork from Egypt, Greece, and Rome and is the museum's pride and joy. Paintings on the third and fourth floors reflect every European style between the 12th and 19th centuries, highlighting the later periods. At the **Hackerman House,** in an exquisite townhouse/mansion attached to the gallery, rooms filled with dark wood furniture, patterned rugs, and velvet curtains display art from China, Korea, Japan, and India. *(600 N. Charles St. Take bus #3 or 11. ☎ 547-9000. Tu-Su 10am-5pm, first Th every month until 8pm. Tours W noon and Su 1:30pm. $8, students with ID $5, seniors $6, 18 and under free. Admission to collection free Sa 10am-1pm and all day on the first Th of every month. Wheelchair accessible through the Hackerman House.)*

BALTIMORE ZOO. The **Baltimore Zoo** occupies a corner of the rolling hills of Druid Hill Park, the nation's second largest city park after New York's Central Park. The park has a spectacular palm tree Conservatory in a soaring Victorian greenhouse and a lake surrounded by lush greenery. In the zoo, small enclosures bring visitors almost within touching distance of some of the animals. *(Off I-83 at Exit 7; bear right off ramp onto Druid Hill Park. June-Aug. Sa-Su shuttle bus from Woodberry Light Rail stop.* ☎ *366-5466. Zoo: Open in summer M-F 10am-4pm, Sa-Su 10am-6pm; in winter daily 10am-4pm. Live jazz, country, and oldies June-Aug. Sa 4-8pm. $10, seniors, $8, 16 and under $6. Conservatory Th-Su 10am-4pm. Free.)*

🎵 ENTERTAINMENT

Vacationing in the city can be expensive, but fortunately for the budget traveler, much of Baltimore's finest entertainment can be enjoyed free of charge. At Harborplace, daytime street performers entertain tourists with magic acts, juggling, and clowning around during the day. At night, dance, dip, and dream to the sounds of anything from country to calypso to oldies (occasional Th-Sa nights).

MUSIC

The offers free summer jazz concerts in its sculpture garden. **Jazzline** (☎ 466-0600) lists jazz shows from September to May; call for schedules and information. Big-name musicians, however, usually come with a price. They can be found performing several times a week from May to October at the canvas-topped **Pier 6 Concert Pavilion.** (☎ 625-3100, TicketMaster ☎ 625-1400 or 481-7328. Open noon-6pm. Tickets $15-30. For a more private performance from local artists and some big names, **Fletcher's** (see **Bars and Clubs,** below) features everything from rock to rap to blues. Zydeco enthusiasts gather at **Harry's,** 1200 N. Charles, a Vegas-style bar and performance space. (☎ 685-2828. Shows F-Sa. Cover $3-10. Open F 11am-2am, Sa 2pm-2am.) The **Baltimore Symphony Orchestra** plays at Meyerhoff Symphony Hall, 1212 Cathedral St., from September to May and during their month-long Summerfest. (☎ 783-8000. Box office open M-F 10am-6pm, Sa-Su noon-5pm, and 1hr. before performances. Tickets $15-52. Groups of 20 or more 20% off; discounts also available for tickets 1hr. before concerts. Call for dates of Summerfest.)

THEATER

The **Lyric Opera House,** 110 W. Mt. Royal Ave., near Maryland Ave., hosts the **Baltimore Opera Company** from October to April. (☎ 727-6000. Box office open M-F 10am-5pm. Tickets $24-109.) Broadway shows are performed all year at the **Mechanic Theater,** 25 Hopkins Plaza, at Baltimore and N. Charles St. (☎ 800-638-2444. Box office open 9am-5pm. Tickets $27-60.) The **Theater Project,** 45 W. Preston St., near Maryland St., experiments with theater, poetry, music, and dance. (☎ 752-8558. Box office open 1hr. before shows; call to charge tickets. Shows Th-Sa 8pm, Su 3pm. $15, seniors $10.) The **Arena Players,** the first black theater group in the country, performs comedies, drama, and dance at 801 McCullough St., at Martin Luther King, Jr. Blvd. (☎ 728-6500. Tickets start at $15. Box office open M-F 10am-2pm.) From June through September, the **Showcase of Nations Ethnic Festivals** celebrate Baltimore's ethnic neighborhoods with a different culture featured each week. The festivals take place all over the city; call the Baltimore Visitors Bureau (☎ 800-282-6632) for info.

SPORTS

The beloved **Baltimore Orioles** play at **Camden Yards,** just a few blocks from the Inner Harbor at the corner of Russell and Camden St. (Tickets standing in outfield promenade $7; field-level boxes from $50.) The main attraction in Baltimore sports, though, is the rough-and-ready **Ravens** (☎ 481-7328) football team. The expansion-team Ravens, successors to the defunct Baltimore Colts, matured fast enough to win the 2001 Super Bowl. They play in **Ravens Stadium,** adjacent to Cam-

TROUBLED WATERS While Baltimore proudly claims a history of fine music, dance, and theater, the undisputed king of Charm City arts is director **John Waters,** master of the high-camp cult movie. Born in Baltimore, Waters grew up fascinated with sex, violence, and every other topic his Catholic-school education warned him against. By his teens he was making 8mm films and drawing fervent audiences to midnight showings. He rocketed to national prominence in 1973 with *Pink Flamingos*, in which the lead actress consumes dog feces on screen. Waters, who claims to pride himself on his works' lack of common decency and over-the-top visual appeal, has since made several toned-down mainstream comedies. Vestiges of his trademark obsessions remain, though, and as commercial as he may have become, he still shoots all his films in Baltimore.

den Yards. Just outside of Baltimore, head off to the races at **Laurel** (☎ 792-7775) on MD-216 off I-95 and **Pimlico Race Tracks** (☎ 542-9400), on MD-129. The two tracks alternately hold thoroughbred horse races for much of the spring, summer, and fall. **The Preakness Stakes** (☎ 542-9400, ext. 4484 for tickets), leg two of the Triple Crown, is run annually at Pimlico on the third Saturday in May.

◪ NIGHTLIFE

Last call in Baltimore is at 2am; hearty partiers should plan to start their evenings early. After 2am, check out Fells Point and its throng of revellers.

Bohager's, 701 S. Eden St. (☎ 563-7220), in Fells Point. Patrons jive to the sounds of live island and house mixes under a retractable dome. Without a doubt, the most dependably debauched club in Baltimore. Th college night reduced cover. F-Sa $15 open bar. Open M-F 11:30am-2am, Sa-Su 3pm-2am.

Cat's Eye Pub, 1730 Thames St. (☎ 276-9866), in Fells Point. An older crowd of regulars packs in one of the city's oldest buildings every weeknight for live blues, jazz, folk, or traditional Irish music. Occasional cover for national musical acts. Over 25 different drafts and 60 bottled beers $3.25-4.50. Numerous flags drape the walls, lending this Irish bar an odd international flair. Happy hour $2 off pints M-F 4-7pm. Su live blues 4-8pm. Music M-Th 9pm, F-Sa 4pm. Open daily noon-2am.

Fletcher's, 701 S. Bond St. (☎ 558-1889), at the intersection of Bond and Aliceanna St. This popular rock club/bar combination is laid-back, except on show nights when the upstairs rocks into the wee hours. Bar thrives on a jukebox, pool, and foosball (50¢). Beer specials vary nightly. Happy hour M-F 4:30-7pm. Cover for 18+. Concert venue upstairs $5-20. Open M-Th 4pm-2am, F-Su 11am-2pm.

Hippo, 1 W. Eager St. (☎ 547-0069), across the street from Central Station. Baltimore's largest gay bar provides pool tables, a piano bar, and a packed dance floor in an industrial setting. Ladies' Tea is one of the largest lesbian events this side of the Mississippi, first Su of every month 6-10pm. $1 off all drinks daily 4-8pm. Tu $1 domestic drafts. Cover Th-F $3, Sa $6. Saloon open daily 4pm-2am; dance bar Th-Sa 10pm-2am.

ANNAPOLIS   ☎ 410

Settled in 1649, Annapolis became the capital of Maryland in 1694. After its 1783 stint as temporary capital of the US (hot on the heels of Philadelphia, New York, and Trenton, NJ), Annapolis has walked the tightrope between a residential port town and a naval garrison dominated by its world-famous Naval Academy. With its brick-paved sidewalks and narrow streets, the historic waterfront district retains its 18th-century appeal despite the presence of ritzy boutiques.

⚙️🛈 ORIENTATION & PRACTICAL INFORMATION. Annapolis lies southeast of U.S. 50, 30 mi. east of D.C. and 30 mi. south of Baltimore. The city extends south and east from two landmarks: **Church Circle** and **State Circle. School St.**, in a blatantly unconstitutional move, connects Church and State. **East St.** runs from the State House to the Naval Academy. **Main St.**, where food and entertainment congregate, starts at Church Circle and ends at the docks. Compact and walkable, the downtown area of Annapolis, besides being a vibrant town center, is also very safe. Finding a parking space—unless in an expensive lot or the public garage ($7-11 per day)—can be tricky. Parking at the **Visitors Center** is the best bet. ($1 per hr., $8 max. weekdays, $4 max. for the weekend.) There is also free weekend parking in State Lots A and B at the corner of Rowe Blvd. and Calvert St.

Greyhound (☎800-231-2222) buses stop at the local Mass Transit Administration bus stop in the football field parking lot at Rowe Blvd. and Taylor St. Tickets are available from the bus driver; cash only. To: Baltimore (1hr.; 5 per day; $10, round-trip $18); Philadelphia (4hr.; 2 per day; $20, round-trip $33); and Washington, D.C. (1-2hr.; 4 per day; $14, round-trip $28). **Annapolis Dept. of Public Transportation** operates a web of city buses connecting the historic district with the rest of town. (☎263-7964. Buses M-Sa 5:30am-10pm, Su 8am-7pm. 75¢, over 60 or disabled 35¢.) Services include: **Taxis: Annapolis Cab Co.**, ☎268-0022. **Checker Cab**, ☎268-3737. **Annapolis and Anne Arundel County Conference and Visitors Bureau,** 26 West St., has free maps and brochures. (☎280-0445; www.visit-annapolis.org. Open daily 9am-5pm.) **Post Office:** 1 Church Circle (☎263-9292. Open M-F 8:30am-5pm.) **ZIP code:** 21401. **Area code:** 410.

🛏 ACCOMMODATIONS. The heart of Annapolis lacks cheap motels in favor of elegant bed and breakfasts, a better choice than the hotels scattered about western Annapolis far from central attractions. Rooms should be reserved in advance, especially for weekends, spring graduations, and the busy summer months, when accommodations frequently sell out. **Bed and Breakfasts of Maryland** is a good resource. (☎800-736-4667, ext. 15. Open M-F 9am-5pm, Sa 10am-3pm.)

True to its name, six flags wave from the porch of the breezy Victorian **📖Flag House Inn ❹**, 26 Randall St., next to the Naval Academy. Each of the five rooms room has TV, A/C, and private bath. The inn also provides a comfortable library, large front porch downstairs, free off-street parking, and a full breakfast. (☎800-437-4825 or 280-2721. Reserve 2-4 weeks in advance. Rooms from $95; 2-person suites $145; 4-person suites $230.) **Gibson's Lodgings ❹**, 110 Prince George St., one block from City Dock on Randall St., offers a patio and spacious common parlors among its three ivy-covered brick buildings. (☎268-5555. A/C, free continental breakfast, and courtyard parking. Min. stay 2 nights. Singles and doubles $99-179; additional cot $25. Off-season $10 discount. One wheelchair-accessible room.)

🍴 FOOD. Most restaurants in the area cluster around **City Dock,** an area packed with people in summertime, especially Wednesday nights at 7:30pm, when the spinnaker races finish at the dock. Luckily, the brisk business has yet to drive up the prices. The best place to find cheap eats is the **Market House** food court at the center of City Dock, where a hearty meal costs under $5. An acclaimed menu, extensive wine list, and simple-chic design make **Aqua Terra ❹**, 164 Main St., a worthwhile splurge. The entrees range from the less expensive items like Vietnamese noodles with jumbo shrimp and bok choy ($9) to $24 spring lamb loin with summer squash, eggplant, and goat cheese. (☎263-1895. Open Tu-Th noon-2:30pm and 5:30-10pm, F-Sa noon-2:30pm and 5:30-11pm, Su noon-2:30pm and 5-9pm.) Numerous newspaper clippings adorn the walls of **Chick & Ruth's Delly ❶**, 165 Main St., paying homage to this pre-war Annapolis institution. Dishes are named for

FREUDIAN SLIPPING Like a pubescent rite of passage, first year "plebes" at the Naval Academy must shimmy up the **Herndon Monument,** a large, imposing obelisk in front of the chapel. At the starting gun's shot, the mob of plebes sprints toward the shaft. The hilariously humiliating event ends only when a hat is snatched off the top of the structure. Sounds easy, right? But it's not just wham, bam, thank you ma'am: the midshipmen lubricate the massive shaft with over 200 lb. of lard to prolong the event. The climactic grasping of the hat is never a quickie—one year, the spectacle lasted over three hours—a record for the Navy.

local and national politicians, like the George Bush smoked turkey sandwich. Delivery is available. (☎ 269-6737. Omelettes $3-7. Corned beef sandwich $5. Malted milkshake $2.75. Ice cream happy hour M-F 2-5:30pm. Open M-Tu 6:30am-4pm, W-Th and Su 6:30am-10pm, F-Sa 6:30am-11pm.) A cool, calm coffeehouse with a view of dock concerts, **City Dock Cafe ❶,** 18 Market Space, at Pinkney St. adds sophistication to Annapolis with its Frank Lloyd Wright-esque appearance and great espresso drinks ($1-3). Bright seascape paintings enliven an otherwise dull interior. (☎ 269-0969. Quiche $5. Fresh fruit salads $3. Scrabble, dominoes, and checker boards available. Open Su-Th 6:30am-10pm, F-Sa 6:30am-midnight.)

◙ SIGHTS. In many senses the **US Naval Academy,** 52 King George St., is Annapolis, and Annapolis is the Academy. The legendary military school, known in many circles simply as "Navy," turns harried, short-haired "plebes" (first-year students) into Naval-officer "middies" (midshipmen) through rigorous drilling and hazing. President Jimmy Carter and billionaire H. Ross Perot are among the academy's celebrity alumni. (☎ 263-6933. Tours every 30min. Apr.-Nov. M-F 10am-3pm, Sa 9:30am-3pm, Su 12:30-3pm; Dec.-Mar. M-Sa 10am-2:30pm, Su 12:30-2:30pm. $6, seniors $5, 18 and under $4.) Once at the Academy, the first stop should be the **Leftwich Visitors Center,** in the Halsey Field House, which doubles and triples as a food court and hockey rink. **King Hall,** the world's largest dining facility, turns into a madhouse at lunchtime, serving the entire student populace in under 20 frenzied minutes. On summer Saturdays, alumni weddings (as many as 1 per hr.) take place in the Academy's **chapel.** Underneath the chapel is the final resting place of **John Paul Jones,** father of the United States Navy, who uttered the famous words, "I have not yet begun to fight!" as he rammed his sinking ship into a British vessel. (Chapel open M-Sa 9am-4pm, Su 1-4pm. Often closed in summer Sa for weddings.)

An elegant 1774 building designed by Colonial architect William Buckland, the historic **Hammond-Harwood House,** 19 Maryland Ave., at King George St., retains period decor right down to the candlesticks. The house is most renowned for its impeccably preserved colonial doorway. The **William Paca House,** 186 Prince George St., was the first Georgian-style home built in Annapolis. Paca, an early governor of Maryland, was one of the original signers of the Declaration of Independence. The elegant house overlooks two acres of lush vegetation, and the garden hides shaded benches with a view of trellises, water lilies, and gazebos. Both houses have historical exhibits on life in the late 1700s. (Both houses: ☎ 263-4683. Tours on the hr. Mar.-Dec. M-Sa 10am-4pm, Su noon-4pm; Jan.-Feb. F-Sa 10am-4pm, Su noon-4pm; last tour 1hr. before closing. Hammond-Harwood: $6, students $5. William Paca: garden $5, house and garden $8. Both houses: $10.)

Built from 1772 to 1779, the Corinthian-columned **State House,** 90 State Circle, in the center of State Circle, is the oldest working capitol building in the nation. It was the US Capitol building from 1783 to 1784, and the Treaty of Paris was signed inside on January 14, 1784. The State House is perfect for a romp through Maryland's history. Visitors can explore the historical exhibits and silver collection or watch the state legislature bicker in two exquisite marble halls. On nice days, the manicured grounds surrounding the building provide an ideal setting for sunbathing and picnics. (☎974-3400. Open daily 9am-5pm; grounds 6am-11pm. Tours daily 11am and 3pm. State legislature mid-Jan. to mid-Apr. Free.)

🚹🎵 **ENTERTAINMENT & NIGHTLIFE.** Locals and tourists generally engage in one of two activities: wandering along City Dock or schmoozing 'n' boozing at upscale pubs. The bars and taverns that line downtown Annapolis draw crowds every night. If you want more culture than drink can provide, Annapolis also has performance options. Theatergoers can check out **The Colonial Players, Inc.,** 108 East St., for innovative and often unknown works. (☎268-7373. Performances Th 8pm, Su 2:30 and 8pm. Tickets $7, students and seniors $5; F-Sa $10.) During the summer, the **Annapolis Summer Garden Theater,** 143 Compromise St., offers musical "theater under the stars" in an open courtyard theater near the City Dock. (Tickets $10, students and seniors $8.)

The Irish **McGarvey's,** 8 Market Space, packs in a variety of locals and officers under naval pilot-donated helmets and a two-story tree growing through the bar. Saddle up to the bar for Aviator Lager, the manliest-sounding beer in town or the less manly $5 fish taco. (☎263-5700. Happy hour M and W 10pm-2am. Th 6pm-1am house beer $1.50. Open M-Sa 11:30am-2am, Su 10am-2am.) As close as you can get to the water without falling in, **Pusser's Landing,** 80 Compromise St., is a working pier with seats. Crowds are mixed during the day, but it attracts a more mature clientele at night. (☎626-0004. Beers $2-4. Open daily 10:30am-2am.) **Ram's Head Tavern,** 33 West St., attracts beer connoisseurs, midshipmen, and tourists who enjoy 135 different ales, lagers, and stouts, including international microbrews. Free live music fills the back patio many evenings. (☎268-4545. Thick steaks $16-22. Happy hour M-F 4-7pm and daily after midnight. Open M-Sa 11am-2am, Su 10am-2am.) The owners of **Sean Donlon Pub,** 37 West St., worked off the floor plans of Irish originals in Dublin to make the pub as "authentic" as American Irish-pub takeoffs can get. Soda bread, fireplaces, and nightly live Gaelic music—as well as the Guinness and Harp ($3.50) served behind the bar—complete the atmosphere. Weekend brunch has a varied menu, from Eggs Benedict with Irish bacon to Limerick cockles and mussels in a white wine sauce. (☎263-1993. Brunch entrees $7. Brunch Sa-Su 11am-4pm. Open daily 11am-2am.)

ASSATEAGUE & CHINCOTEAGUE ☎ 757

Crashing waves, windswept dunes, wild ponies galloping free—if it sounds like the stuff of a childhood fantasy, that's because it is. Local legend has it that ponies first came to Assateague Island by swimming ashore from a sinking Spanish galleon. A less romantic and more likely theory is that miserly colonial farmers put their horses out to graze on Assateague to avoid mainland taxes. Whatever their origins, the famous ponies now roam free across the unspoiled beaches and forests of the picturesque island.

🛄🎵 **ORIENTATION & PRACTICAL INFORMATION.** Telling the two islands apart, especially since their names are sometimes used interchangeably, can often leave visitors bewildered. Assateague Island is the longer barrier island facing the ocean, while Chincoteague Island is nestled between Assateague and mainland Eastern Shore. Maryland and Virginia share Assateague Island, which is divided into three distinct parts. The best way to get to Assateague Island is by car. From Rte. 50, take Rte. 611 south. If traveling from points south, use Rte. 113 N to Rte. 376 E in Berlin, MD. Follow Rte. 376 to access Rte. 611 and continue to the island. To reach Chincoteague and the Chincoteague Wildlife Refuge (which is actually on Assateague Island) from Rte. 50, take U.S. 13 south at Salisbury and turn east onto State Rd. 175. To reach the island by bus, take a **Greyhound** (☎800-752-4841) to Ocean City, via daily routes from Greyhound stations in Baltimore (4hr., 2 per day, $30) or Washington, D.C. (5hr., 3 per day, $40). **Trailways** (☎824-5935) runs buses from **Salisbury, MD** ($12.75) and **Norfolk, VA** ($22.25), stopping at T's Corner Store on U.S. 13, 11 mi. from Chincoteague. From Ocean City, take a **taxi** to the island (☎410-208-2828. About $30.) **Visitor info:** Available at the **Chincoteague Chamber of Commerce,** 6733 Maddox Blvd., in Chincoteague. (☎336-6161; www.chincoteague-chamber.com. Open M-Sa 9am-4:30pm.) **ZIP code:** 23336. **Area code:** 757.

⌐⌐ ACCOMMODATIONS & FOOD. Due to Assateague's lack of civilization, visitors eat and sleep on **Chincoteague Island,** across an inlet from southern Assateague. Motels line the sides of **Maddox Blvd.** near the Chincoteague-Assateague Causeway. Midway down this motel mile, the **Mariner ❸,** 6273 Maddox Blvd., offers spotless rooms with wide, comfortable beds. (☎336-6565 or 800-221-7490. Outdoor pool and continental breakfast. Reservations suggested in summer. Economy rooms in summer $63, off-season $52; doubles from $81/67.) Across from the Mariner, the clean and quiet **Sea Hawk Motel ❸,** 6250 Maddox Blvd., has slightly smaller rooms with cable TV and pool. (☎336-6527. Rooms in summer $75-80; off-season $45-55; 2 rooms with 1 double bed $65/39.) **Maddox Family Campground ❶,** off to the right immediately before the causeway, has 250 sites, many with shade. (☎336-3111. Pool and playground. Open Mar.-Nov. Sites $28.)

For fresh, absurdly cheap seafood takeout (no seats), head to **Melvin's Seafood ❷,** 3117 Ridge Rd., situated in a family backyard on the south side of the island; follow signs from Main St. Don't be bashful, just drive right into their driveway where the owner family sells crab cakes for $2.50, a dozen steamed crabs for $12, and oyster sandwiches for $3.50. (☎336-3003. Open daily 9am-7pm.) Locals swear by the all-you-can-eat steamed crabs ($22) and patriotic decor at **Wright's Seafood Restaurant ❺,** Wright Rd. From southbound Rte. 175, turn left on Atlantic Rd., go straight for 1½ mi., and turn left on Wright Rd. (☎824-4012. Entrees $13-24. Open Tu-Sa 4-9pm, Su noon-9pm.) Chincoteague's most beloved dessert, nighttime snack, or breakfast treat is a Belgian waffle topped with ice cream and fruit ($6) from **Muller's Old Fashioned Ice Cream Parlor,** 4034 Main St. The **Hot Stuff** hot sauce store is attached. (☎336-5894. Single scoops $1.80; double $3. Open summer noon-11pm; off-season hours vary.)

⌐⌐ OUTDOOR ACTIVITIES. The **Assateague State Park ❶,** Rte. 611 in southeast Maryland, is a 2 mi. stretch of picnic areas, beaches, bathhouses, and campsites. Fishing without a license is permitted; supply your own equipment. (☎410-641-2120, for reservations ☎888-432-2267. Open daily 9am-sunset. $2 per person, seniors free. Campsite registration open late Mar. to Sept. 8am-8pm. Sa-Su min. stay 2 night. Reservations available June-Sept. Sites $20, with hookup $30.)

The **Assateague Island National Seashore** claims most of the long sandbar north and south of the park and has its own campground and beaches, most of which are inaccessible by car. The ranger station distributes back-country camping permits. (Distribution noon-5pm, arrive early. $5.) The **Barrier Island Visitors Center,** on Rte. 611, provides maps, an introduction to the park, and films on the park's natural treasures. (☎410-641-1441. Open daily 9am-5pm.) Secluded beachcombing to the north of the state park provides unguided and adventurous opportunities to unlock the park's natural treasures. Three meandering, half-mile nature trails give visitors a closer look at the island's flora and fauna. The **Forest Trail** offers the best viewing tower, but the **Marsh Trail** has fewer mosquitoes. Notorious gnats pester visitors all over the island, so bring plenty of repellent. (Reservations ☎800-365-2267. Water, cold showers, chemical toilets, grill. No hookups. Reservations needed May-Oct. Campsites May-Oct. $16; Nov. to Apr. $12.)

The **Chincoteague National Wildlife Refuge** stretches across the Virginia side of the island. Avid bird-watchers flock here to see rare species such as peregrine falcons, snowy egrets, and black-crowned night herons. The wild pony roundup, held the last consecutive Wednesday and Thursday in July, brings hordes of tourists to Assateague. During slack tide, local firemen herd the ponies together and swim them from Assateague to Chincoteague Island, where the fire department auctions off the foals the following day. The adults swim back to Assateague and reproduce, providing next year's crop. Ponies can be seen almost every day along the refuge's trails, especially the Wildlife Loop Rd., which begins at the Visitors Center. (Open May-Sept. 5am-10pm; Nov.-Mar. 6am-6pm; Apr. and Oct. 6am-8pm.) If you are lucky enough to spot one of the awesome creatures, be careful to gawk from a safe distance—the ponies may appear harmless, but they can strike at random. For more info, visit the **Chincoteague Refuge Visitor Contact Station.** (☎ 757-336-6122. Open daily 9am-5pm. $5 fee per car per week.)

OCEAN CITY   ☎ 410

Ocean City is a lot like a kiddie pool—it's shallow and plastic, but can be a lot of fun if you're the right age, or just in the right mood. This 10 mi. strip of prime Atlantic beach packs endless bars, all-you-can-eat buffets, hotels, mini-golf courses, boardwalks, flashing neon, and sun-seeking tourists into a thin region between the ocean and the Assawoman Bay. Tourism is the town's only industry, and Ocean City is not afraid to shake its money-maker. The siren call of senior week beckons droves of recent high school and college graduates to alcohol- and hormone-driven fun, turning O.C. into a city-wide block party in June. July and August cater more to families and professional singles looking for easily available and inexpensive fun in the sun.

◼◪ ORIENTATION & PRACTICAL INFORMATION. Driving is the most sensible mode of transportation to reach the ocean resort. From the north, simply follow Rte. 1, which becomes Coastal Highway (Philadelphia Ave.). From the west, Rte. 50 also leads directly to Ocean City. If you're trekking to Ocean City from points south, take Rte. 113 to Rte. 50 and follow that into town. Ocean City runs north-south, with numbered streets linking the ocean to the bay. Most hotels are in the lower numbered streets toward the ocean; most clubs and bars are uptown toward the bay. **Trailways** (☎ 289-9307), at 2nd St. and Philadelphia Ave., sends buses to Baltimore (3½ hr., 3 per day, $30) and Washington, D.C. (5hr., 4 per day, $40). In town, **public buses** (☎ 723-1607) run the length of the strip and are the best way to get around town. (Operates 24hr. $1 per day for unlimited rides.) The **Ocean City Visitors Center,** 4001 Coastal Hwy., at 40th St. in the Convention Center, gives out discount coupons. (☎ 800-626-2326. Open June-Aug. M-Th 8:30am-5pm, F-Sa 8:30am-6pm, Su 9am-5pm; Sept.-May daily 8:30am-5pm.) **Byte Size,** 4100 Coastal Hwy., offers Internet access to electronically deprived beachgoers. (☎ 723-2702. Open M-F 9am-7pm, Sa 10am-6pm. $5 per 30min.) The **Post Office** is at 4th St. and Coastal Hwy. (☎ 289-7819. Open M-F 8am-4:30pm, Sa 8am-noon.) **Zip Code:** 21842.

◤ ACCOMMODATIONS. Atlantic House Bed and Breakfast ❹, 501 N. Baltimore Ave., offers free bike rentals, full breakfast buffet, great location, and a wholesome change of pace from the Ocean City motel trend. (☎ 289-2333. A/C, cable TV, hot tub, and parking. Rooms in summer with shared baths from $75, with private baths $140; lower off-season.) **Cabana Motel ❹**, 1900 Coastal Hwy., caters primarily to families. Small, comfortable rooms are outfitted with A/C and TV. (☎289-9131. Outdoor pool. Open May-Oct. Singles and doubles June $75-80; July-Aug. $85-90; lower off-season.) **Ocean City International Student Services ❶**, 304 Baltimore Ave., in the south end of town, provides a cheap summer boarding house for students. Private rooms and dorms, both without A/C, have access to kitchen, TV, living room, deck, hammock, and grill. (☎289-0350. Reservations required. Open Apr.-Oct. Cost averages $90 per week.) Sporting a dark wood interior and copious amenities, **Sea Spray Motel ❹**, 12 35th St., 50 yards from the beach, has rooms with kitchen, porch, cable TV, and A/C. (☎800-678-5702 or 289-6648. Gas grill access and laundry facilities. Rooms in summer from $90.) The only in town campground is **Ocean City Travel Park ❶**, 105 70th St. (☎524-7601. Tents $25-38; RVs $25-53.)

🄲 FOOD. Ocean City's cuisine is all about being plentiful and cheap; don't expect gourmet quality because you won't find any such food. With freshly caught food and a friendly atmosphere, **The Embers ❺**, 24th St. and Coastal Hwy., has the biggest seafood buffet in town. All the clams, oysters, crab, prime rib, and steak you can eat is $23. (☎888-436-2377 or 289-3322. Happy hour 4-7pm. Open daily 3-10pm.) When craving cheap eats better than anything you'll find on the boardwalk, **Fat Daddy's Sub Shop ❶**, 216 S. Baltimore Ave., cuts to the chase with satisfying deli sandwiches ($2.50-4.50) and subs ($4-6) until the early morning. (☎289-4040. Free delivery. Open daily 11am-4am.) Enjoy healthier and trendier food at **Coral Reef Cafe ❷** on the boardwalk at 17th St. Crab dip with toasted focaccia ($7) and the New Orleans chicken wrap with mozzarella and homemade spicy cream cheese ($9) are just a couple of the specialities. (☎289-6388. Open daily 10am-8pm.) No word of warning is sufficient for the sheer amount of food served at **Paul Revere's Smorgasbord ❸** between 2nd and 3rd St. on the boardwalk. Patrons can add inches to their waistline with as much lasagna, roast beef, seafood, vegetables, cake, and pie than they can possibly eat. (☎524-1776. 15% off 4-5pm. Open daily 4-9pm. $9, ages 9-12 $6, 8-5 $4, under 4 free).

🄴🄼 ENTERTAINMENT & NIGHTLIFE. Ocean City's star attraction is its beach. The wide stretch of surf and sand runs the entire 10 mi. of town and can be accessed by taking a left onto any of the numerous side streets off Philadelphia and Baltimore Ave. The breaking waves know no time constraints, but beach-goers are technically limited to 6am-10pm. When the sun goes down, hard-earned tans glow under the glaring lights of Ocean City's bars and nightclubs. Professional party-goers will no doubt be impressed by **Seacrets**, on 49th St., a virtual entertainment mecca and amusement park for adults. (☎524-4900. Cover $3-5. Open M-Sa 11am-2am, Su noon-2am.) The elder statesman of the bayside clubs, **Fager's Island**, 60th St., in the bay, attracts hordes to walk the plank to its island location. Live rock, R&B, jazz and reggae play accompaniment nightly to the 100+ beers. No one seems to know the source of the classical music tradition, but the 1812 Overture booms at every sunset. (☎524-5500. M night deck party cover $7. Happy hour Tu-F half-price drinks and appetizers. Open daily 11am-2am.) Saunter up to the seaside **Brass Balls Saloon**, between 11th and 12th St. on the boardwalk. Known for its $1 jello shots, their motto is "Drink Hearty, Eat Healthy." (☎289-0069. Open Mar-Oct. daily 8:30am-2am.) A new addition to the Ocean City scene is the huge **Party Block complex,** 17th St. and Coastal Hwy. Patrons pay one cover to flirt between four different clubs from the laid-back Oasis Bar to the flashy Rush Club.

WASHINGTON, D.C.   ☎202

The United States chose the location of its capital after years of moving and heated debate. Both North and South wanted the capital on their turf. The final location—100 square miles donated by Virginia and Maryland—was a compromise, an undeveloped swamp wedged between the two sides. Congress commissioned French engineer Pierre L'Enfant to design the city. The city had hardly begun to expand when the British torched it in 1814; a post-war vote to give up and move the capital failed in Congress. Today, D.C. consists of two distinct worlds: an inner circle of government buildings and an outer area of residential neighborhoods. Federal Washington, the town of press conferences, power lunches, and presidential intrigue, is what most visitors come to see. The other part of Washington, the "second city," consists of a variety of communities, some prosperous and others overcome by drugs and crime. For more about Washington, D.C., check out ▨*Let's Go: Washington, D.C. 2003*.

✖ INTERCITY TRANSPORTATION

Airports: Ronald Reagan National Airport (☎703-417-8000). Metro: National Airport. It's best to fly here from within the US; National is on the Metro and closer to the city. Taxi from downtown $10-15. The **Super Shuttle** (☎800-258-3826) runs between National and downtown M-F every 30min. **Dulles International Airport** (☎703-369-1600) is much farther from the city. Taxis from downtown cost $40+. The **Washington Flyer Dulles Express Bus** (☎888-927-4359) hits the West Falls Church Metro every 30min. 6-10am and 6-10:30pm, every 20min. 10am-2pm, every 15min. 2-6pm. $8. **Buses**, 15th and K St. NW, to downtown take 45min. Depart M-F every 30min. 5:20am-10:20pm, Sa-Su every hr. 5:20am-12:20pm, every 30min. 12:50-10:20pm. $16; groups of 3 or more $13 each.

Trains: Amtrak operates from Union Station, 50 Massachusetts Ave. NE (☎484-7540). To: **Baltimore** (40min., $21); **Boston** (8½hr., $68); **New York** (3½hr.; reserved $67, metroliner $118); **Philadelphia** (2hr., $50). Maryland's commuter train, **MARC** (☎410-859-7400, 24hr.), departs from Union to Baltimore ($5.75) and the suburbs.

✖ ORIENTATION

Diamond-shaped D.C. stretches its tips in the four cardinal directions. The **Potomac River** forms the jagged southwest border, its waters flowing between the district and Arlington, VA. **North Capitol, East Capitol,** and **South Capitol St.** slice up the city into four quadrants: NW, NE, SE, and SW. The **Mall** stretches west of the Capitol. The suffixes of the quadrants distinguish otherwise identical addresses (e.g. 800 G St. NW and 800 G St. NE).

Washington's streets lie in a simple grid. Streets that run east-to-west are labeled alphabetically in relation to North Capitol/South Capitol St., which runs through the Capitol. Since the street plan follows the Roman alphabet, in which "I" and "J" are the same letter, there is no J St. After W St., east-west streets take on two-syllable names, then three-syllable names, then the names of trees and flowers. The names run in alphabetical order, but sometimes repeat or skip a letter. Streets running north-south are numbered all the way to 52nd St. NW and 63rd St. NE. Addresses on lettered streets indicate the number of the cross street. For instance, 1100 D St. SE is on the corner of D and 11th.

Major roads include **Pennsylvania Ave., Connecticut Ave., Wisconsin Ave., 16th St. NW, K St. NW, Massachusetts Ave., New York Ave.,** and **North Capitol St.** Washington, D.C. is ringed by the **Capital Beltway/I-495** (except where it's part of I-95). The Beltway is bisected by **U.S. 1** and meets **I-395** from Virginia. The high-speed **Baltimore-Washington Pkwy.** connects Washington, D.C. to Baltimore. **I-595** trickles off the Capital Beltway east to Annapolis, and **I-66** heads west into Virginia.

NEIGHBORHOODS

Postcard-perfect and pristine white, **Capitol Hill** symbolizes the democratic dream with the Capitol building, Supreme Court, and the Library of Congress. The **Mall** is flanked by the Smithsonian Museums and the National Gallery of Art, and monuments and memorials fill its west end. Cherry trees bud and blossom along the brink of the Tidal Basin. **Foggy Bottom** has evolved from undeveloped swampland to the stomping grounds of the State Dept. and the blockbuster White House at 1600 Pennsylvania Ave. The **Federal Triangle** area is home to a growing commercial and banking district. The International Trade Center and the Ronald Reagan Building share the wide avenues with federal agencies like the FBI. It's a wonderful (corporate) life in glass-walled **Farragut,** where government agencies, lobbying firms, and lawyers make their home.

There's more to D.C. than politics; the neighborhoods comprising up the **Second City** bustle with sights, shops, and eateries. **Adams-Morgan** is a hub of nightlife and good food. **Chinatown,** more of a block than a neighborhood, offers fairly authentic Chinese cuisine. Fashionable and picturesque **Georgetown** has the feel of a college town with Georgetown University nearby and enough nightlife to keep college students dazed and happy. Ever-trendy **Dupont Circle** hosts eateries, art sophisticates, and diplomats. *Use caution in this area at night.* The **Upper Northwest,** an upper-class residential neighborhood, is home to American University and the National Zoo. A historically African-American area, the **U District** now parties nightly—and deafens passersby—as its clubs blast trance and techno until the sun rises. *Be careful in the area at night.*

▛ LOCAL TRANSPORTATION

Public Transit: Metrorail and Metrobus (METRO), 600 5th St. NW (☎637-7000) is relatively safe. Office open M-F 6am-10:30pm, Sa-Su 8am-10:30pm. $1.10-3.25, depending on time and distance traveled; 1-day Metro pass $5. **Flash Pass** ($20) allows unlimited bus rides for 2 weeks. Trains run M-F 5:30am-midnight, Sa-Su 8am-2am. For bus transfers, get a pass on the platform *before* boarding the train. The **Metrobus** system serves Georgetown, downtown, and the suburbs. $1.10.

Taxis: Yellow Cab, ☎544-1212.

Car Rental: Bargain Buggies Rent-a-Car, 3140 N. Washington Blvd. (☎703-841-0000), in Arlington. Open M-F 8am-7pm, Sa 9am-3pm, Su 9am-noon. $23 per day, $150 per week; 100 free mi. per day, 20¢ each additional mi. Must be 18 with major credit card or $250 cash deposit.

Bike Rental: Big Wheel Bikes, 315 7th St. SE (☎543-1600). Metro: Eastern Market. Open Tu-F 11am-7pm, Sa 10am-6pm, Su noon-5pm. Mountain bikes $5 per hr., min. 3hr.; $25 per business day; $32 per 24hr. Major credit card required for deposit.

▟ PRACTICAL INFORMATION

Visitor Info: Washington, D.C. Convention and Visitors Association (WCVA), 1212 New York Ave. NW, #600 (☎789-7000; www.washington.org). Open M-F 9am-5pm. **D.C. Committee to Promote Washington,** 1212 New York Ave. NW, #200 (☎347-2873 or 800-422-8644). **Meridian International Center,** 1630 Crescent Pl. NW (☎667-6800). Metro: Dupont Circle. Open M-F 9am-5pm.

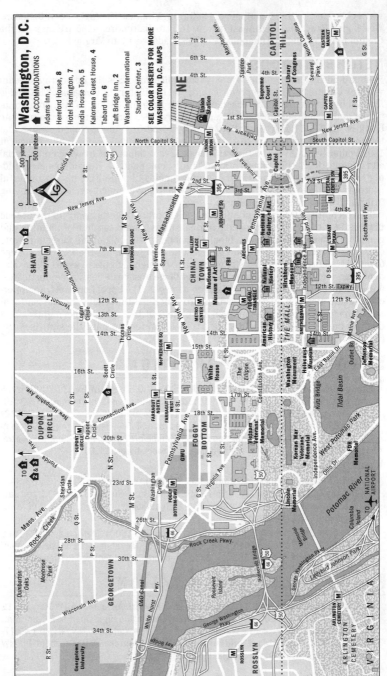

Washington, D.C.

♦ ACCOMMODATIONS

Adams Inn, 1
Hereford House, 8
Hotel Harrington, 7
India House Too, 5
Kalorama Guest House, 4
Tabard Inn, 6
Taft Bridge Inn, 2
Washington International
   Student Center, 3

SEE COLOR INSERTS FOR MORE
WASHINGTON, D.C. MAPS

Hotlines: Rape Crisis Center, ☎333-7273. 24hr. **Gay and Lesbian Hotline,** ☎833-3234. Operates 7-11pm. **Traveler's Aid Society,** ☎546-3120. Offices at Union Station, National and Dulles Airports, and downtown at 512 C St. NE. Hours vary.

Medical Services: Children's National Medical Center, 111 Michigan Ave. NW (☎884-5000). **Georgetown University Medical Center,** 3800 Reservoir Rd. NW (☎687-2000). **Whitman-Walker Clinic** (☎797-3500) provides AIDS and STD counseling. **Planned Parenthood,** 1108 16th St. NW (☎347-8500).

Internet access: Atomic Grounds, 1555 Wilson Blvd. #105, (☎703-524-2157), in Arlington. Open M-F 6:30am-6:30pm, Sa-Su 8am-6:30pm.

Post Office: 900 Brentwood Rd. NE (☎636-1532). Indescribably inconvenient location. Open M-F 8am-8pm, Sa 8am-6pm, Su noon-6pm. **ZIP code:** 20066. **Area code:** 202.

ACCOMMODATIONS

In D.C., even the tiniest hotel rooms fetch big-ticket prices. The best escape from these ridiculous rates is staying outside the city or visiting in the off season. Hostels also offer unbeatable rates and the chance to mingle with an international crowd. Don't forget that D.C. adds a 14.5% occupancy tax to your bill.

HOSTELS & STUDENT CENTERS

India House Too, 300 Carroll St. (☎291-1195), on the border of D.C. and Takoma Park. Metro: Takoma. Hostelers are encouraged to make the house their own. They can come and go as they please, smoke and drink in certain areas, or fire up a BBQ in the backyard. Free linens and use of kitchen. A/C in some rooms. Reservations preferred. Dorms with 2-3 bunk beds $16 per person; private rooms with shared path $36. ❶

Hostelling International-Washington DC (HI-AYH), 1009 11 St. NW (☎737-2333), 3 blocks north of Metro on 11th St. Metro: Metro Center (11th St. exit). The prime location, friendly staff, and reasonable rates make the hostel an appealing choice for any D.C. visitor. In the heart of D.C., 5 blocks from the White House and a 20min. walk from the National Mall. *Use caution in this area at night.* Wheelchair accessible (give advance notice). $26, nonmembers $29. Credit card required for reservation. ❶

Washington International Student Center, 2451 18th St. NW (☎800-567-4150 or 667-7681), in Adams Morgan. Metro: Woodley Park-Zoo. This hidden hostel barely squeezes itself into the neighborhood. It's dirt-cheap and perhaps the most central to the heartbeat of Adams Morgan, but visitors will have to crash on triple-decker bunks. Unkept rooms and kitchen. Check-in 8am-11pm. Check-out noon. Beds $18 per night. ❶

HOTELS

Taft Bridge Inn, 2007 Wyoming Ave. (☎387-2007), at the intersection of 20th and Wyoming. A short walk from Dupont Circle and Woodley Park Metro stops. Warm fireplace for winters; relaxing porch and garden for summers. All rooms have modem hookup, phones, voicemail, and A/C; cable TV in rooms with private bath. Laundry facilities available. Full breakfast included. Wheelchair accessible. Singles in summer $99-119; off-season $59-79; additional person $15. Parking $10 per day. ❹

Hotel Harrington, (☎800-424-8532 or 628-8140), 11th and E St. Metro: Metro Center or Federal Triangle. On the verge of turning 90, this hotel has a long tradition of clean rooms and a great location. Next door to the newly built ESPN Zone and 3 blocks from the Smithsonian. Tours can be arranged through the gift shop. Cable TV, A/C, and laundry. Singles $89-95; doubles $99-119. 10% discount for students and AAA members. Children under 16 stay free. Special group rates available. Parking $8.50 per day. ❹

Hereford House, 604 S. Carolina Ave. SE (☎543-0102), at 6th St., 1 block from the Eastern Market Metro. No sign marks this 4-room, 6-bed, British-style B&B in a townhouse run by a friendly English hostess. Shared baths, laundry, A/C, refrigerator, living room, home-cooked breakfast, and garden patio. No smoking. 50% due for reservation, balance due on arrival. Singles $58-72; doubles $74-82. No credit cards. ❸

GUEST HOUSES

Kalorama Guest House at Kalorama Park, 1854 Mintwood Pl. NW (☎667-6369), off Columbia Rd. a block south of 18th St. Continental breakfast included. Parking behind guest house by reservation, $7 per night. Reception M-Tu 8am-8pm, W-Su 8am-10pm. Reservations with credit card required, payment due upon arrival. Rooms with shared bath $45-70 for 1 person, $50-75 for 2; with private baths $65-95/70-100. Two-room suites start at $100. ❷

Adams Inn, 1744 Lanier Pl. NW (☎800-578-6807 or 745-3600), 2 blocks north of the center of Adams Morgan. Free continental breakfast, coffee and tea, cable TV, 2 pay phones, and coin laundry facilities. Rooms vary in size and style, but all have A/C and private sinks. Internet access in office. Reception M-Sa 8am-9pm, Su 1-9pm. Reservations require first night deposit. Singles $65, with private bath $75; additional person $10. ISIC 10% discount. Limited parking $7 per night. ❸

Tabard Inn, 1739 N St. NW (☎785-1277), between 17th and 18th St., just south of the Circle. Individually decorated rooms in 3 townhouses connected by a maze of passages, stairways, and lounges. Rooms have nice hardwood floors and stone-tile bathrooms as well as A/C, phone, and data port. Patio, bar, and lounges. Breakfast and passes to the YMCA included. Dinner at the Tabard Inn restaurant is highly recommended. Reception 24hr. Singles $72-105, with private bath $105-175; doubles $95-120/120-190. $20 each additional person. ❹

◘ FOOD

How do you feast like a senator on an intern's slim budget? Savvy natives go grubbing at Happy Hours. Bars often leave out free appetizer platters to bait early evening clients (see **Nightlife**). As for budget eateries, **Adams Morgan** and **Dupont Circle** are home to the *crème de la crème* of succulent ethnic delights. Suburban **Bethesda, MD** features over 100 different restaurants within a four-block radius.

ADAMS-MORGAN

▨ **The Grill from Ipanema,** 1858 Columbia Rd. (☎986-0757). Perennially chosen by local newspapers as one of the best places to eat, this Brazilian restaurant is a bit of a splurge. The atmosphere shifts to a lively bar scene after dinner hours with Latin music and a lively crowd. Mixed meat platter *Carne de Sol* $19. Open M-F 5-11pm, Sa-Su noon-midnight. ❺

▨ **Mixtec,** 1792 Columbia Rd. NW (☎332-1011), near 18th St. Voted the Very Best Bargain Restaurant by the *Washingtonian* from 1997 to 2000 for good reason. The small taqueria's specialties include *tacos al carbón* (two small tortillas filled with beef; $7), tacos and Mexican subs ($6.50), and nachos ($6.50). Try the various fruit drinks for a refreshing treat ($1.75). Some vegetarian options. Appetizers $3-6.50. Entrees $6.50-13. Sangria $2.50 per glass. Open M-Th 8am-10:30pm, F 8am-11pm, Sa 9am-11pm, Su 9am-10:30pm. ❷

Julia's Empanadas, 2452 18th St. NW (☎328-6232), near Columbia Rd. Other locations: 1000 Vermont Ave. NW (☎789-1878); 1221 Connecticut Ave. (☎861-8828); and 1410 U St. (☎387-4100). Not many restaurants in D.C. can claim the most expensive item on their menu is $3. Despite its fast-food feel, the empanadas are "Made by Hand, Baked with Love." The delicious meat- or vegetable-filled dough shells are best described as Spanish calzones. Options include *chorizo* (Spanish sausage), spinach, vegetarian, and more ($3). Open Su-Th 10am-10:30pm, F-Sa 10am-4am. Cash only. ❶

So's Your Mom, 1831 Columbia Rd. NW (☎462-3666). This busy sandwich shop offers first-rate sandwich ingredients (such as imported meats and cheeses), portions as big as your mom, and unexpected sandwich choices (sliced beef tongue $6). Fresh pasta and salads also available. Sandwiches $3.50-6.45. Freshly baked goods $1.25-2. Takeout only. Open M-F 7am-8pm, Sa 8am-7pm, Su 8am-3pm. Cash only. ❶

BETHESDA

▨ **Bacchus,** 7945 Norfolk Ave. (☎301-657-1722). Bacchus manages to create a highly elegant and authentic atmosphere without being intimidating. The menu features over 50 varieties of appetizers, cold and hot, all in the vicinity of $5. The *schwarma* is highly recommended. Copious outdoor seating. Open M-Th noon-2:30pm and 6-10pm, F noon-2:30pm and 6-10:30pm, Sa 6-10:30pm. ❷

▨ **Cafe Deluxe,** 4910 Elm St. (☎301-656-3131). This airy, bustling bistro has low-lit booths inside and white-draped tables outside on the sidewalk. It may be a chain, but Cafe Deluxe delivers solid American and Italian cooking at mid-range prices. Most entrees $8-15. Reservations recommended. Open M-Th 11:30am-10:30pm, F-Sa 11:30am-11pm, Su 11am-10pm. ❸

Oodles Noodles, 4907 Cordell Ave. (☎301-986-8833). The pleasant interior and good service make this a popular lunch spot. 18 mouth-watering varieties of noodle dishes ($7-9) from all reaches of East Asia are the staple. Grill dishes $7-10. Lunch M-Sa 11:30am-3pm; dinner Su-Th 5-10pm, F-Sa 5-10:30pm. ❷

Philadelphia Mike's, 7732 Wisconsin Ave. (☎301-656-0103), near Middleton Ave. Mike's successfully replicates the gooey taste of an authentic Philly cheesesteak ($4-8) served over the counter in a modest, pizza shop setting. Burgers and deli sandwiches $4-8. Breakfast subs under $3. Lunch specials $3. Delivery min. for lunch $12, for dinner $10. Open M-F 8am-9pm, Sa 9am-9pm, Su 9am-4pm. ❶

Grapeseed, 4865 Cordell Ave. (☎301-986-9592). Determined to make connoisseurs of us all, Grapeseed provides an unpretentious environment for experimentation in the intimidating field of wine tasting. Serves dishes in both *tapas*-sized ($4-12) and entree-sized portions ($17-23) with accompanying wine recommendations. Open for lunch M-F 11:30am-2pm; dinner M-Th 5-10pm, F-Sa 5-11pm. ❺

CHINATOWN

▨ **Hunan Chinatown,** 624 H St. NW (☎783-5858). Upscale restaurant serving standard Chinese food; locals say the cuisine is well worth the added expense. Kung Pao chicken $6.75. Tea-smoked duck $15. Hunan lamb (thin slices of lamb sautéed over broccoli) $14. Open M-Th and Su 11am-10pm, F-Sa 11am-11pm. ❸

Tony Cheng's Seafood Restaurant, 619 H St. NW (☎371-8669), on the 2nd fl. of a garishly decorated building. Lunch specials $7-11. Full dim sum brunch daily 11am-3pm. In **Tony Cheng's Mongolian Restaurant** downstairs, patrons choose from a buffet of meat and vegetables, which are then stir-fried. Lunch: one serving $8.50; all-you-can-eat

THE BIG SPLURGE

PRIME TIME

In a city suffering from perhaps an appalling steakhouse glut, it's hard for one high-end, meat-and-potato vendor to distinguish itself from another. However, the **Prime Rib** manages to surpass venerable chains, political hangouts, and gourmet beeferies. Its biggest advantage: A little touch of the old world.

Walk through the monogrammed glass doors and prepare for a step back in time. If you're male and not wearing a jacket and tie, the tuxedoed staff will outfit you with one; this is the only restaurant in town with such a strict written dress code. Add dark leather, mahogany bars, a little pleasant tinkling on a baby grand, and leopard carpet. Combine with a charismatic owner, C. Peter "Buzz" Beler, who once chased and caught a group of Eurotrash tab-jumpers across town, and there you have it: A D.C. legend.

The signature dish sets the tone for the food: top-quality ingredients simply and perfectly prepared. Nothing exotic here, just the best in beef, seafood, and shellfish with an equally impressive and extensive California wine list. *(2020 K St. NW. ☎ 466-8811. Entrees $25-40.* ❺ *)*

$15. Open M-Th and Su 11am-11pm, F-Sa 11am-midnight. ❸

Szechuan Gallery, 617 H St. NW (☎ 898-1180). Renowned for dishes like *congee,* a mouthwatering rice soup ($5). Lunch specials $5-8. Dinner entrees $9-14. Open M-Th and Su 11am-10pm, F-Sa 11am-11pm. ❷

DUPONT CIRCLE

▨ **Lauriol Plaza,** 1865 18th St. NW (☎ 387-0035). More of a complex than a restaurant, Lauriol occupies half the block with 3 magnificent floors of Mexican dining. Appetizers $2.50-7. Copious entrees $10-17. Su brunch 11am-3pm $6-9. No reservations. Open M-Th and Su 11:30am-11pm, F-Sa and holidays 11:30am-midnight. Free parking. ❶

▨ **Raku,** 1900 Q St. NW (☎ 265-7258, delivery ☎ 232-8646), off Connecticut Ave. Taking its name from the Japanese word for "pleasure," this upscale restaurant serves a standard noodle selection ($8-12), salads ($5-11), sushi ($4-13), and "pan-Asian *tapas"* (a variety of dumplings, rolls, and skewers; $3-8). In summer, sample specialty cocktails on the covered patio. Open Su-Th 11:30am-10pm, F-Sa 11:30am-11pm. ❷

Pizzeria Paradiso, 2029 P St. NW (☎ 223-1245), near 21st St. A modest awning hides the open and breezy restaurant. The smell of freshly baked pizza in their wood-burning oven will make your mouth water as soon as you walk through the door. This very refined pizza place serves fresh olives before you order. 8 in. $7-10; 12 in. $12-16; toppings 75¢-$1.75. Sandwiches $5-7. Salads $3-5. Open daily M-Th 11:30am-11pm, F 11:30am-midnight, Sa 11am-midnight, Su noon-10pm. ❷

Cafe Luna, 1633 P St. NW (☎ 387-4005), near 17th St. Truly a neighborhood joint, this popular basement restaurant, serves mostly vegetarian and low-fat fare for the health-conscious. Many dishes can be prepared fat-free upon request. Local artists reserve 6 months in advance to display their works on the walls. All-day breakfast $1-5. Huge sandwiches $4-6. Pasta $6-9. Brunch Sa-Su 10am-3pm $5-7. Takeout available. Open M-Th 8am-11pm, F 8am-1am, Sa 10am-1am, Su 10am-11pm. ❶

Firehook Coffee Shop and Bakery, 1909 Q St. NW (☎ 588-9296), off Connecticut Ave. Firehook sells a variety of coffees ($1.10), cappuccinos ($1.65), and frozen coffee drinks ($3.25). Their unique twist on the run-of-the-mill coffee shop is baking a daily batch of organic bread ($4.50), massive muffins ($1.43) that disappear quickly in the morning, and sumptuous cakes (small $15-19, large $28-30). Open M-F 7am-9pm, Sa-Su 8am-9pm. ❶

GEORGETOWN

■ **Cafe La Ruche,** 1039 31st St. NW (☎965-2684, takeout ☎965-2591), 2 blocks south of M St. "La Ruche" means "the beehive," and this place gets buzzing late at night when romantics move in for dessert and coffee. La Ruche serves up French fare, including soups ($4), salads ($4-9), quiche ($8), and sandwiches ($7-9). Enjoy a full meal or skip right to the chocolate mousse ($5.50). Outdoor seating available. Open M-Th 11:30am-11:30pm, F 11:30am-1am, Sa 10am-1am, Su 10am-10:30pm. ❷

■ **Thomas Sweet,** 3214 P St. NW (☎337-0616), at Wisconsin Ave. A local ice cream parlor that makes cheap bagel sandwich breakfasts ($1-3), sandwiches ($4-6), and over 30 flavors of homemade ice cream and frozen yogurt (1 scoop $2). Open M-Th 8am-midnight, F-Sa 8am-1am, Su 9am-midnight. Cash only.

■ **Aditi,** 3299 M St. NW (☎625-6825), at the corner of M and 33rd St. Famous for its skillfully prepared Indian food. Elegant dining room with a carved wooden ceiling. Weekday lunch specials $6. Appetizers $2-6. Entrees $8-16. Lunch M-Sa 11:30am-2:30pm, Su noon-2:30pm; dinner M-Th and Su 5:30-10pm, F-Sa 5:30-10:30pm. ❷

Moby Dick House of Kabob, 1070 31st St. NW (☎333-4400), near the corner of M and 31st St. Traditional Iranian dishes with lean, marinated meats. Try the *kubideh* and *chenjeh* combo with rice and clay-oven pita bread ($9.25) or one of Moby's famous sandwiches ($4-5). Open M-Th and Su 11am-10pm, F-Sa 11am-4am. Cash only. ❶

Au Pied de Cochon, 1335 Wisconsin Ave. NW (☎337-6400), at the corner of Wisconsin and Dumbarton St. French specialties like *coq au vin* ($10.50) or *bouillabaisse*, which incudes shrimp, scallop, clams, mussels, salmon, and lobster in a saffron-flavored seafood stock ($17), along with sandwiches and burgers ($6-7). "Early bird special" daily 3-8pm includes appetizer, entree, dessert, and coffee or tea for $10. Open 24hr. ❸

UPPER NORTHWEST

■ **Jandara,** 2606 Connecticut Ave. NW (☎387-8876). Celestial decorations and heavenly blues and purples create an out-of-this-world atmosphere. The food is equally stunning with Thai standards and specialty dishes like *gaeng ped yang* (slices of roasted duck simmered in a red curry sauce with pineapple; $9). Lunch menu $5-10. Takeout and delivery; outdoor seating available. Open M-Th and Su 11:30am-10:30pm, F-Sa 11:30am-11pm. ❷

■ **49 Twelve Thai Cuisine,** 4912 Wisconsin Ave. NW (☎966-4696). Metro: Friendship Heights or Tenleytown-AU. With some of the best Thai food in the D.C. area, this inconspicuous and unassuming restaurant is worth the time you'll spend deciding which Metro stop to use. *Pad thai* $7. Drunken noodles and curry dishes $7-9. Delivery 5:30-9:30pm. Open M-Th and Su 11:30am-10pm, F-Sa 11:30am-11pm. ❷

Yanni's, 3500 Connecticut Ave. NW (☎362-8871). Bright, airy neighborhood restaurant with extra-friendly service and homestyle Greek cooking (e.g. fresh herbs and a whole lot of olive oil). Outdoor seating available. Try charbroiled octopus, crunchy on the outside and delicately tender within, served with rice and vegetables ($13). Appetizers $5-8. Entrees $7-16. Open daily 11:30am-11pm. ❸

Armand's Chicago Pizzeria, 4231 Wisconsin Ave. NW (☎686-9450), between Yuma and Van Ness St. Metro: Tenleytown-AU. A casual 2 room pizzeria with bar. Buffet lunch $6.50. Lunch M-F 11:30am-2pm; Sa-Su 11:30am-3pm. Dinner M-Th and SU 2pm-10pm, F-Sa 3pm-11pm. ❷

Cactus Cantina, 3300 Wisconsin Ave. NW (☎686-7222), at Macomb St. near the Cathedral. Metro: Tenleytown-AU and any 30-series bus toward Georgetown. Cantina is a popular and enormous restaurant that offers great Tex-Mex. Fajitas ($12-15); lunch specials like enchilada platters (M-F until 3pm; $6-7). Salsa, chips, and tortillas made on the spot. No reservations; be prepared to wait on weekends. M-Th and Su 11:30am-11pm, F-Sa 11:30am-midnight. ❸

Rocklands, 2418 Wisconsin Ave. NW (☎333-2558). The sweet smell of barbecue emanating from Rocklands attracts long lines at lunch and dinner; snack on free peanuts while you wait. No gas or electricity in the BBQ pit—just red oak, hickory, and charcoal. Very limited seating at the weathered mahogany counters, but you can take out a quarter-rack of pork ribs ($5) or a half chicken ($5). Sandwiches $4-6.25. Salads $1.60. Open M-Sa 11:30am-10pm, Su 11am-9pm. ❶

◉ SIGHTS

CAPITOL HILL

THE CAPITOL. The ◧US Capitol may be an endless font of cynicism, but it still evokes the glory of the republican ideal. The **East Front** faces the Supreme Court. From the times of frontiersman Andrew Jackson (1829) to peanut-farmin' Jimmy Carter (1977), presidents were inaugurated here. The East Front entrance brings visitors into the 180 ft. high rotunda, where soldiers slept during the Civil War. From the lower-level crypt, visitors can climb to the second floor for a view of the House or Senate visitors chambers. Americans may obtain a free gallery pass from the office of their representative or senator in the House or Senate office buildings near the Capitol. Foreigners may get one-day passes by presenting identification at the "appointments desks" in the crypt. *(Metro: Capitol South. ☎225-6827. Open daily Mar.-Aug. 9am-8pm; Sept.-Feb. 9am-4:30pm. Tours Mar.-Aug. M-F 9am-7pm, Sa 9am-4pm; Sept.-Feb. M-Sa 9am-4pm. Free.)* The real business of Congress, however, is conducted in committee hearings. Most are open to the public; check the *Washington Post's* "Today in Congress" box for times and locations. The free **Capitol subway** (the "Capitol Choo-Choo") shuttles between the basement of the Capitol and the House and Senate office buildings; a buzzer and flashing light signal an imminent vote.

SUPREME COURT. In 1935, the justices of the **Supreme Court** decided it was time to take the nation's separation of powers literally and moved from their makeshift offices in the Capitol into a new Greek Revival courthouse across the street. Oral arguments are open to the public; show up early to be seated or walk through the standing gallery to hear 5min. of the argument. *(1 1st St. Metro: Capitol South. ☎479-3000. In session Oct.-June M-W 10am-noon and open 1-3pm for 2 weeks every month; courtroom open when Justices are on vacation. Court open M-F 9am-4:30pm. Seating before 8:30am. Free.)*

LIBRARY OF CONGRESS. The ◧Library of Congress, between East Capitol and Independence Ave., is the world's largest library with 113,026,742 objects stored on 532 mi. of shelves, including a copy of *Old King Cole* written on a grain of rice. The collection was torched by the British in 1814 and then restarted from Thomas Jefferson's personal stocks. The collection is open to anyone of college age or older with a legitimate research purpose—a tour of the facilities and exhibits is available for tourists. The **Jefferson Building's** green copper dome and gold-leafed flame tops a spectacular octagonal reading room. *(1st St. SE. ☎707-5000. Great Hall pen M-Sa 8:30am-5:30pm. Visitors Center and galleries open 10am-5:30am. Free.)*

UNION STATION. Trains converge at **Union Station,** two blocks north of the Capitol. Colonnades, archways, and domed ceilings hark back to imperial Rome—if Rome was filled with stores and a food court. *(50 Massachusetts Ave. NE. Metro: Union Station. ☎371-9441. Retail shops open M-Sa 10am-9pm, Su 10am-6pm.)*

MONUMENTS

WASHINGTON MONUMENT. With a $9.4 million restoration project completed a year ago, this shrine to America's first president is even more impressive. The ▓Washington Monument was once nicknamed the "the Beef Depot monument" after the cattle that grazed here during the Civil War. The rock used to build the monument came from multiple quarries, which explains the stones' multiple colors. The **Reflecting Pool** mirrors Washington's obelisk. *(Metro: Smithsonian. Admission to the monument by timed ticket. Apr.-Aug. Monument: open Apr.-Aug. daily 8am-midnight; Sept.-Mar. 9am-5pm. Ticket kiosk: open Apr.-Aug. daily 7:30am until all tickets distributed; Sept.-Mar. 8:30am until all tickets distributed. Free. No tickets needed after 8pm Apr.-Aug.)*

VIETNAM VETERANS MEMORIAL. Maya Ying Lin, who designed the ▓Vietnam Veterans Memorial, received a "B" when she submitted her memorial concept for a grade as a Yale senior. She went on to beat her professor in the public memorial design competition. In her words, the monument is "a rift in the earth—a long, polished black stone wall, emerging from and receding into the earth." The wall contains the names of the 58,132 Americans who died in Vietnam, indexed in books at both ends. *(Constitution Ave. at 22nd St. NW. Metro: Foggy Bottom/GWU. ☎ 634-1568.)*

LINCOLN MEMORIAL. The ▓Lincoln Memorial, at the west end of the Mall, recalls the rectangular grandeur of Athens' Parthenon. A seated Lincoln presides over the memorial and everything that takes place below it. From these steps, Martin Luther King, Jr. gave his "I Have a Dream" speech during the 1963 March on Washington. Climbing the 19 ft. president is a federal offense; a camera will catch you if the rangers don't. *(Metro: Smithsonian or Foggy Bottom/GWU. ☎ 426-6895. Open 24hr.)*

KOREAN WAR MEMORIAL. The 19 colossal polished steel statues of the **Korean War Memorial** trudge up a hill, rifles in hand, an eternal expression of weariness mixed with fear frozen upon their faces. The statue is accompanied by a black granite wall with over 2000 sandblasted photographic images from this war, in which 54,000 Americans lost their lives. *(At the west end of the Mall, near Lincoln. Metro: Smithsonian or Foggy Bottom/GWU. ☎ 632-1002.)*

FRANKLIN DELANO ROOSEVELT MEMORIAL. Occupying a stretch of West Potomac Park (the peninsula between the Tidal Basin and the Potomac River) just a short walk from the Jefferson or Lincoln Memorials, the ▓Franklin Delano Roosevelt Memorial is more of a stone garden than a monument. Whether or not to display the disabled Roosevelt in his wheelchair was hotly debated when the memorial was being planned; as a compromise, Roosevelt is seated, a position based on a famous picture taken at Yalta. The memorial is laid out in four "rooms" of red granite, each representing a phase of FDR's presidency. *(Metro: Smithsonian. ☎ 376-6704.)*

JEFFERSON MEMORIAL & TIDAL BASIN. A 19 ft. bronze Thomas Jefferson stands in the domed rotunda of the **Jefferson Memorial,** designed to resemble Jefferson's own Monticello. The memorial overlooks the Tidal Basin. Quotes from the Declaration of Independence, the Virginia Statute of Religious Freedom, *Notes on Virginia*, and an 1815 letter adorn the walls. *(Metro: L'Enfant Plaza. ☎ 426-6821.)*

SOUTH OF THE MALL

US HOLOCAUST MEMORIAL MUSEUM. A block off the mall lies the ▓US Holocaust Memorial Museum, where displays chronicle the rise of Nazism, the events leading up to the war in Europe, and the history of anti-Semitism. Films show troops liberating concentration camps, shocked by the mass graves and emaciated prisoners they encountered. An eternal flame burns in the "Hall of Remembrance."

A HALF-ASS JOB It seemed like such a good idea to have local artists paint statues of the "Party Animals," 4 ft. high elephants and donkeys, and put them up all over D.C. But these political beasts have caused dissension across the city. First, there was the embarrassing revelation that the donkeys were not anatomically correct; the statues' horse-like tails are actually found on the donkey's sterile offspring, the mule. Zoologists add that the body structure of the artists' works were more like that of a mule than that of the Democratic party's mascot. More controversy started when certain neighborhoods complained that the animals were unevenly distributed around the city, thereby denying some businesses of added tourist traffic.

(100 Raoul Wallenberg Pl. SW. Metro: Smithsonian. ☎ 488-0400. Open in summer daily 10am-8pm; in winter 10am-5:30pm. Free. Get in line early for tickets.)

BUREAU OF ENGRAVING & PRINTING. Also known as "the Mint," the Bureau offers tours of the presses that annually print over $20 billion worth of money. The love of money has made this the area's longest line; expect to grow old while you wait. *(At 14th and C St. SW. Metro: Smithsonian. ☎ 847-2808. Open M-F 9am-2pm. Free.)*

FEDERAL TRIANGLE

NATIONAL BUILDING MUSEUM. Montgomery Meigs's Italian-inspired edifice remains one of Washington's most striking sights. *(F St. NW, between 4th and 5th St. Metro: Judiciary Sq. ☎ 272-2448. Open in summer M-Sa 10am-5pm, Su noon-5pm; off-season M-Sa 10am-4pm, Su noon-4pm. Suggested donation $3, students and seniors $2.)*

NATIONAL ARCHIVES. Visitors line up at the ▧**National Archives** to view the original Declaration of Independence, US Constitution, and Bill of Rights. *(8th St. and Constitution Ave. NW. Metro: Archives-Navy Memorial. ☎ 501-5000. Open Apr.-Aug. daily 10am-9pm; Sept.-Mar. 10am-5:30pm. Free.)*

FEDERAL BUREAU OF INVESTIGATION. The ▧**Federal Bureau of Investigation** is one of the city's best tours. Lines form on the outdoor plaza of the J. Edgar Hoover Building. *(☎ 324-3447. Open M-F 8:45am-4:15pm. Free.)*

FORD'S THEATRE. John Wilkes Booth shot President Abraham Lincoln during a performance at the preserved **Ford Theater**. National Park Rangers describe the events with animated gusto during a 20min. talk. *(511 10th St. NW. Metro: Metro Center. ☎ 426-6924. Open daily 9am-5pm. Free.)*

OLD POST OFFICE. A classical masterpiece, the **Old Post Office** building rebukes its contemporary neighbors with arched windows, conical turrets, and a clock tower—all sheathing a shopping mall. *(Pennsylvania Ave. and 12th St. NW. Metro: Federal Triangle. ☎ 289-4224. Tower open mid-Apr. to mid-Sept. daily 8am-10:45pm; off-season 10am-6pm. Shops open M-Sa 10am-8pm, Su noon-6pm.)*

WOMEN IN THE ARTS. In a former Masonic Temple, the **National Museum of Women in the Arts** tours works by the likes of Mary Cassatt, Georgia O'Keeffe, and Frida Kahlo. *(1250 New York Ave. NW. Metro: Metro Center. ☎ 783-5000. Open M-Sa 10am-5pm, Su noon-5pm. Free.)*

WHITE HOUSE & FOGGY BOTTOM

WHITE HOUSE. With its simple columns and expansive lawns, the ▧**White House** seems a compromise between patrician lavishness and democratic simplicity. Thomas Jefferson proposed a design of the building, but his entry lost to that of amateur architect James Hoban. Today's Presidential staff works in the West Wing, while the First Lady's cohorts occupy the East Wing. Staff who cannot fit in the White House work in the nearby **Old Executive Office Building.** The President's official office is the **Oval Office,** site of many televised speeches. *(1600 Pennsylvania Ave. NW. ☎ 456-7041. Currently no tours are available to the public.)*

LAFAYETTE PARK. Historic homes surround **Lafayette Park** north of the White House. These homes include the Smithsonian-owned **Renwick Gallery** craft museum, which has some remarkable 1980s sculptures. *(17th St. and Pennsylvania Ave. NW. Metro: Farragut West. ☎ 357-2700. Open daily 10am-5:30pm. Free.)* Once housed in the Renwick's mansion, the **Corcoran Gallery** now boasts larger quarters and displays American artists. *(17th St. between E St. and New York Ave. NW. ☎ 639-1700. Open M, W, and F-Su 10am-5pm, Th 10am-9pm. Suggested donation $3, students and seniors $1, families $5.)* Nearby, the **Octagon,** a curious building designed by Capitol architect William Thornton, is reputedly filled with ghosts. Tour guides explain its history. *(Open Tu-Su 10am-4pm. $5, seniors and students $3.)*

KENNEDY CENTER. A few blocks above Rock Creek Pkwy., the **John F. Kennedy Center for the Performing Arts** rises like a marble sarcophagus. The Washington Monument could fit in the gargantuan **Grand Foyer,** were it not for the 18 Swedish chandeliers shaped like grape clusters. *(25th St. and New Hampshire Ave. NW. Metro: Foggy Bottom-GWU. ☎ 467-4600. Open daily 10am-midnight. Free tours every hr. M-F 10am-5pm, Sa-Su 10am-1pm.)* Across the street is Tricky Dick Nixon's **Watergate Complex.**

GEORGETOWN

Georgetown's quiet, narrow, tree-lined streets are sprinkled with trendy boutiques and points of historic interest that make for an enjoyable walking tour. Retired from commercial use since the 1800s, the **Chesapeake & Ohio Canal** extends 185 mi. from Georgetown to Cumberland, MD. Today, the towpath where trusty mules once pulled barges on the canal belongs to the National Park Service.

DUMBARTON OAKS MANSION. The former home of John Calhoun, ▧**Dumbarton Oaks Mansion** holds a beautiful collection of Byzantine and pre-Columbian art, and was the site of the 1944 Dumbarton Oaks Conference that helped write the United Nations charter. *(1703 32nd St. NW. ☎ 339-6401. Art gallery open Tu-Su 2-5pm. Suggested donation $1. Gardens open Apr.-Oct. daily 2-6pm; Nov.-Mar. 2-5pm. $5, seniors and children $3.)*

GEORGETOWN UNIVERSITY. Founded in 1789 by Archbishop John Carroll when he learned where the new capital would be built, **Georgetown** was the first Catholic institution of higher learning in the US. *(37th and O St.)*

UPPER NORTHWEST

WASHINGTON NATIONAL ZOOLOGICAL PARK. A preeminent zoo, ▧**Washington National Zoological Park** added two important animals in January 2001—Mei Xiang and Tian Tian, two giant pandas, now live in the zoo's newly refurbished panda habitat. The zoo's orangutans are allowed to swing through the park via a series of 40 ft. high towers. The Valley Trail (marked with blue bird tracks) connects the bird and sealife exhibits, while the Olmsted Walk (marked with red elephant feet) links land-animal houses. *(3001 Connecticut Ave. Metro: Woodley Park-Zoo. ☎ 673-4800. Grounds open May to mid-Sept. daily 6am-8pm; mid-Sept. to Apr. 6am-6pm. Buildings open in summer daily 10am-6pm; off-season 10am-4:30pm. Free.)*

WASHINGTON NATIONAL CATHEDRAL. This church, the sixth-largest in the world, was built from 1907 to 1909. Rev. Martin Luther King, Jr. preached his last

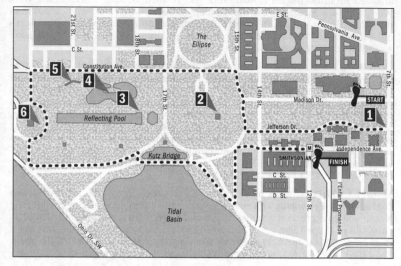

1 HIRSHHORN SCULPTURE GARDEN. At this hour, the Garden won't be open, but you can make out the glistening edges of Maillol and Matisse figures. Pick the least and most lifelike shapes and then try to name the sculptors.

2 WASHINGTON MONUMENT. The great American phallus is doubly impressive at night, illuminated from above by the moon and below by massive spotlights. Fifty

TIME: One hour.

LENGTH: One mile.

TIME OF DAY: Whenever the moon is out.

START: Capitol Hill, Foggy Bottom, or the Smithsonian.

FINISH: Smithsonian Metro.

American flags fly in a circle at its base. Be sure to turn northward for a stunning view of the White House, the South Lawn, and the Ellipse. The massive fountain and towering columns are often impressive enough to make visitors forget that the White House is still a residence, not just a figurehead or museum.

3 REFLECTING POOL. The mirror of all the nation's glory is calm at night. Admire the glimmering image of the Washington Monument, or if you're bold enough, dip your toes for a midwalk refresher. Full-on (Forrest Gump style) runs down the length of the pool are discouraged, except for steeplechase champions who don't fear the mounted park police.

4 CONSTITUTION GARDENS. Beside a perfectly placid pond, this is the ultimate lovers' trysting ground. Look for slumbering ducklings and play hide-and-go-seek among the trees, or steal off for a kiss in the shaded island before heading west again.

5 VIETNAM VETERANS MEMORIAL. A wall of marble testifies to the losses in a divisive time. Admire the reflections off the smooth, black surface and run your hands over the almost countless names for a reminder of the nation's loss. If you have a paper and a pencil, make a rubbing of any resonating names.

6 LINCOLN MEMORIAL. Perhaps the most classically beautiful of all the monuments, Abraham Lincoln sits proudly atop this marble pedestal overlooking the Potomac. Lincoln's most famous quotes line the walls, inspiring recollections of high school history classes and thoughts of bygone eras when presidents wrote their own speeches. Breathe in the midnight air and survey the land before returning to the Metro and heading home.

Sunday sermon from the pulpit. The elevator rises to the Pilgrim Observation Gallery, revealing D.C. from the highest vantage point in the city. At the **Medieval Workshop,** children can carve stone, learn how a stained-glass window is created, or mold a gargoyle out of clay for $2. *(Massachusetts and Wisconsin Ave. NW. Metro: Tenleytown, then take the #30, 32, 34, or 36 bus toward Georgetown; or walk up Cathedral Ave. from Metro: Woodley Park-Zoo. ☎537-6200 or 364-6616. Cathedral open May-Aug. M-F 10am-9pm, Sa 10am-4:30pm, Su 12:30-4:30pm; Sept.-Apr. M-Sa 10am-5pm, Su 12:30-4pm. Suggested donation for tour $3, under 12 $1.)*

DUPONT CIRCLE

Once one of Washington's swankier neighborhoods, Dupont Circle attracted embassies because of its stately townhouses and large tracts of land. Today, it is a haven for an international, artsy, and gay crowd; this mix of business, politics, and pleasure make it one of the city's most exciting parts. *(Metro: Dupont Circle.)*

ART GALLERY DISTRICT. A triangle of creativity, the **Art Gallery District** contains over two dozen galleries displaying everything from contemporary photographs to tribal crafts. *(Bounded by Connecticut Ave., Florida Ave., and Q St. Information ☎232-3610.)*

PHILLIPS COLLECTION. ◪**Phillips Collection,** a well-endowed house of contemporary work, was the first museum of modern art in the US. Visitors gape at Renoir's masterpiece, *Luncheon of the Boating Party*, as well as works by Delacroix, Miró, and Turner that line the Annex. *(Q St. NW at 1600 21st St. ☎387-2151. Open Tu-Sa 10am-5pm, Su noon-7pm. $7.50, students and seniors $4, under 12 free.)*

EMBASSY ROW. The stretch of Massachusetts Ave. between Dupont Circle and Observatory Circle is also called **Embassy Row.** Before the 1930s, Washington socialites lined the avenue with extravagant edifices, and status-conscious diplomats found the mansions perfect for their purposes. Flags line the entrance to the **Islamic Center,** a brilliant white building where stunning designs stretch to the tips of spired ceilings. *(2551 Massachusetts Ave. NW. ☎332-8343. No shorts allowed; women must cover their heads, arms, and legs. Open daily 10am-5pm; prayers held 5 times per day.)*

🏛 MUSEUMS

The Smithsonian Museums on the Mall constitute the world's largest museum complex. The **Smithsonian Castle,** on the south side of the mall, Metro: Smithsonian or Federal Triangle, has an introduction to and info on the Smithsonian buildings. (☎357-2700. All Smithsonian museums open daily 10am-5:30pm, extended summer hours determined annually. Free. Wheelchair accessible.)

- ◪ **National Air and Space Museum,** on the south side of the Mall across from the National Gallery, is the world's most popular museum with 7.5 million visitors per year. Airplanes and space vehicles dangle from the ceilings; the Wright brothers' original biplane hangs in the entrance gallery. Walk through the Skylab space station, the Apollo XI command module, and a DC-7.
- ◪ **National Gallery of Art** (☎737-4215), east of Natural History, is not technically a part of the Smithsonian, but a close cousin due to its location on the mall. The West Wing houses its pre-1900 art in a domed temple in the Western Tradition. Artists include El Greco, Raphael, Rembrandt, Vermeer, and Monet. Leonardo da Vinci's earliest surviving portrait, *Ginevra de' Benci,* the only one of his works in the US, hangs among a fine collection of Italian Renaissance Art. The East Building holds the museum's 20th-century collection, including works by Picasso, Matisse, Pollock, Warhol, and Rothko. The building also contains the museum's temporary exhibits. The National Gallery recently unveiled an outdoor sculpture garden. Open M-Sa 10am-5pm, Su 11am-6pm.

▨ **Hirshhorn Museum and Sculpture Garden,** on the south side of the mall west of Air and Space. The 4-story, slide-carousel-shaped brown building has outraged traditionalists since 1966. Each floor consists of 2 concentric circles: an outer ring of rooms with modern, postmodern, and post-postmodern paintings and an inner corridor of sculptures. The museum claims a comprehensive set of 19th- and 20th-century Western sculpture.

▨ **Freer Gallery of Art** (☎357-4880) just west of the Hirshhorn, displays American and Asian art. The static American collection consists of the holdings of Charles L. Freer, the museum's benefactor, and focuses on works by James McNeill Whistler. The rotating Asian collections include bronzes, manuscripts, and jade.

National Museum of American History, on the north side of the Mall, closest to the Washington Monument, houses several centuries' worth of machines, photographs, vehicles, harmonicas, and US detritus. When the Smithsonian inherits quirky artifacts of popular history, like Dorothy's slippers from *The Wizard of Oz,* they end up here. Hands-on exhibits are geared toward children.

Museum of Natural History, east toward the Capitol from American History, ruminates on the earth and its life in 3 big, crowded floors. Objects on display in the spectacular golden-domed, Neoclassical buildings include dinosaur skeletons, the largest African elephant ever captured, and an insect zoo with live creepy-crawlies. Visitors still line up to see the cursed Hope Diamond.

National Museum of African Art and the **Arthur M. Sackler Gallery** hide together underground in the newest museum facility on the Mall, to the west of the Hirshhorn. The Museum of African Art displays artifacts from sub-Saharan Africa such as masks, textiles, ceremonial figures, and musical instruments. The Sackler Gallery showcases an extensive collection of art from China, South and Southeast Asia, and Persia. Exhibits include illuminated manuscripts, Chinese and Japanese painting, jade miniatures, and friezes from Egypt, Phoenicia, and Sumeria.

◢ ENTERTAINMENT

MUSIC

The D.C. rock and trance scenes are among the nation's most lively. The biggest rock events take place at the sports arenas: **RFK Stadium** in the summer and **MCI Center** year-round. Tickets are usually available from **Protix** (☎410-481-6500, 703-218-6500, or 800-955-5566) or **Ticketmaster** (☎432-7328). The **U District,** D.C.'s ear-blasting epicenter, has sent the D.C. punk and rock scene off the Richter scale for decades. On weekends in summer, shows from jazz and R&B to the **National Symphony Orchestra** occupy the outdoor, 4200-seat **Carter Barron Amphitheater,** set into Rock Creek Park at 16th St. and Colorado Ave. (☎426-6837. Tickets under $20.)

THEATER & DANCE

Arena Stage, 6th St. and Maine Ave. SW, is often called the best regional theater company in America. (☎488-4377. Metro: Waterfront. Box office open M-Sa 10am-8pm, Su noon-8pm. Tickets $25-45, lower for smaller stages; students 35% off; seniors 20% off; half-price rush usually available 1½hr. before show.) The **Kennedy Center,** at 25th St. and New Hampshire Ave., offers scores of ballet, opera and dramatic productions, most of them expensive. Most productions offer half-price tickets the day of performance to students, seniors, military, and the disabled. (☎416-8000, for rush tickets info ☎467-4600. $10-75.) The **Millennium Stage** presents free performances in the Grand Foyer of the Kennedy Center. The prestigious **Shakespeare Theater,** at the Lansburgh, 450 7th St. NW at Pennsylvania Ave., offers a Bard-heavy repertoire. (☎547-1122, TTY ☎638-3863. Metro: Archives-Navy Memorial. $10. Standing-room tickets 2hr. before curtain.) In the **14th St. theater district,** tiny repertory companies explore and experiment with enjoyable results (check *CityPaper* for listings). **Woolly Mammoth,** 1401 Church St. NW (☎393-3939), Metro: Dupont Circle; **Studio Theater,** 1333 P St. NW (☎332-3300), at 14th St., Metro: Dupont Circle; and **The Source Theater,** 1835 14th St. NW (☎462-1073), between S and T St., Metro: U St.-Cardozo, are all fine theaters in the neighborhood near Dupont Circle. Tickets for all three run $25.

SPORTS

The 20,000-seat **MCI Center,** 601 F St. NW, in Chinatown, is D.C.'s premier sports arena. (☎628-3200: Metro: Gallery Pl.-Chinatown.) The NBA's **Washington Wizards** continue their struggle against dismal play and a lame mascot. (Tickets $19-85.) The **Washington Capitals** skate from October through April. (Tickets $20-75.) Three-time Superbowl champions the **Washington Redskins** draw crowds to **Fed-Ex Stadium,** Raljon Dr., in Raljon, MD, from September through December. (☎301-276-6050. Tickets $40-60.) At **Robert F. Kennedy Stadium,** the **D.C. United** play soccer mid-April through October. (☎608-1119. Tickets $12-40.)

◪ NIGHTLIFE

BARS & CLUBS

Talk about leading a double life. D.C. denizens who crawl through red tape by day paint the town red by night. If you find yourself taking Jell-O body shots off a beautiful stranger at an all-you-can-drink-fest, just don't say we didn't warn you. If you ache for a pint of amber ale, swing by the Irish pub-laden **Capitol Hill.** If you like girls (or boys) who wear Abercrombie & Fitch, hit up **Georgetown,** where youthful prepsters go to get happy. **Dupont Circle** is home to glam gay and lesbian nightlife, while **Adams-Morgan** plays host to an international crowd. To party with rock stars, head to none other than **U District** for the best live rock 'n' roll in all of Dixieland.

DUPONT & SHAW

◪ **Dragonfly,** 1215 Connecticut Ave. NW (☎331-1775). Beauty may be fleeting, but there is no better place to revel in it than amidst the chic clientele of Dragonfly. Ice-white interior, pod-like chairs, techno music, and video projections. Drinks are expensive, but good sushi is served all night at reasonable prices. DJs every night. No cover. Open M-Th 5:30pm-1am, F 5:30pm-2am, Sa 6pm-2am, Su 6pm-1am.

◪ **State of the Union,** 1357 U St. NW (☎588-8810), near 14th St. Throbbing hip-hop, techno, and other jazzy genres keep the crowd bouncing on a small dance floor under murals and busts of famous commies. Happy hour (daily until 8:30pm) means half-price drinks, with specialty twists on Russian faves—Starburst vodka, comrade? The back room has a moveable wall for summer patio action. 21+. Occasional $7 drink min. Open M-Th 5pm-2am, F-Sa 5pm-3am, Su 7pm-3am.

◪ **Eighteenth Street Lounge,** 1212 18th St. NW (☎466-3922). Now 7 years old and still the mod-est of the mod, this progenitor of the now-swelling D.C. lounge scene draws musical tourists from around the globe to hear its top-shelf DJs and bask in its coolness. The main attraction here is the DJs, most of whom are signed to ESL's own independent record label. Dress to impress. Cover generally $10-20. Open Tu-W 9:30pm-2am, Th 5:30pm-2am, F 5:30pm-3am, Sa 9:30pm-3am.

The Big Hunt, 1345 Connecticut Ave. NW (☎785-2333). Leopard-print couches and jungle-themed paraphernalia adorn the 3 floors and upstairs patio of this bar, where the casual khaki and flip-flops crowd hunts for potential mates. Notorious as a pickup joint among college kids and Hill workers pretending they're still in college. Happy hour M-F 4-7pm. Open Su-Th 4pm-2am, F-Sa 4pm-3am.

IN RECENT NEWS

FAKING IT

While underage drinking in Georgetown and Foggy Bottom used to be a collegiate way of life and even the most preposterous fake IDs worked flawlessly, times have changed in D.C....drastically.

The year 2000 brought a string of major fake ID crackdowns and sting operations in Georgetown, forcing even lax bars to tighten their policies. Hundreds of students with a variety of D.C. and out-of-state IDs spent a night in jail, faced judges at court dates, and paid hefty fines. Some even lost their actual driver's licenses for six months or more. But no bad experience with the D.C. police can compare to the oft-repeated story of one young Georgetown freshman. After narrowly escaping arrest at one bar on a crackdown night, the young lad sad down at yet another bar and ordered yet another illegal drink, smiling smugly. He then looked up at the TV to see the local news broadcasting live images of police bursting through the door of a Georgetown bar not unlike the one he was in—and approaching a man who looked not unlike himself—and before he knew what was happening, he too had been hauled off to jail.

The moral of the story? Fake IDs in D.C., especially in Georgetown, are a risky proposition. Anticipate strict carding and be aware of the harsh penalties that await offenders.

Chi Cha Lounge, 1624 U St. NW (☎234-8400). A swanky well-dressed crowd frequents this mellow, 2-room lounge. The coffeehouse crowd sips liquor instead of java on the various couches, chairs, and tables. Andean food and Arabic tobacco are also served. Fruit-flavored *sheesha* water pipes available Su-Tu. Live Latin music Su-W 9pm. Open Su-Th 5:30pm-1:30am, F-Sa 5:30pm-3am.

ADAMS MORGAN

⬛ Blue Room, 2123 18th St. NW (☎332-0800). Chic *tapas* restaurant by day, alluring lounge and dance club by night. Trendy clientele gravitates to this stylish, blue world of polished chrome. Beers $4-9; cocktails $5-8. Live music Tu. Down tempo Th-Sa. Cover F-Sa $5-10. Proper attire required (no jeans, athletic gear, or sneakers). Open 11:30pm-3am.

Brass Monkey, 2317 18th St. NW (☎667-7800). The funky inside has a wooden floor and outdoor patio that fills with a fashionable preppy college crowd partying to rock and hip-hop. A pool table is at the center of a raised, couch-strewn section. Drafts $3.50, bottles $4; generic liquors $4-5. No cover. Open daily M-Th and Su 1pm-2am, F-Sa 1pm-3am.

Tryst, 2459 18th St. NW (☎232-5500). Coffee bar with an atmosphere that combines that of an art gallery and rec room—huge sofas, pastiche paintings, board games, books, and caffeine addicts. Tryst's after-hours spiked coffees and hyper-hip ambience draw a huge crowd. F-Sa after 9pm 21+. Open M-Th 7am to last call (around 12:30am), F-Sa 7am-3am, Su 8am-midnight.

CAPITOL HILL

⬛ Platinum, 915 F St. NW (☎393-3555). Metro: Gallery Place-Chinatown. Snoop Dogg and Allen Iverson have been sighted at this posh club known for its top-shelf liquors (Cristal anyone?) and faux-flame chandeliers. Chill in the 3rd floor VIP section (reservations required) or watch 30-somethings dance from your perch on the 2nd and 3rd floor balconies. Beer and cocktails $5-6. Th-F 18+; Sa ladies 18+, gentlemen 21+. F ladies free before midnight. Cover $10. Open Th-Su 10pm-3am.

Zanzibar on the Waterfront, 700 Water St. SW (☎544-1900). Metro: Waterfront. Neon abstract elegance, shimmering waterfront views, and big-name acts have made Zanzibar the premier D.C. destination for affluent black thirty-somethings. W salsa and merengue. Th international jazz and oldies. F-Sa international music. Open some Su for special shows. Cover W and F after 7pm, Sa after 9pm $10. Arrive early or purchase tickets in advance for live acts (around $30). Open W-Th 5pm-1am, F 5pm-3am, Sa 9pm-4am.

GAY NIGHTLIFE

The *Washington Blade* is the best source of gay news and club listings; published every Friday, it's available in virtually every storefront in Dupont Circle.

▨ **J.R.'s,** 1519 17th St. NW (☎328-0090). D.C.'s busiest bar: beautiful bartenders, bar hoppers, and interior. Packed every night with "guppies" (gay yuppies). M Show-tune Sing-a-Long. W South Park. Happy hour M-F 5-8pm. Th happy hour $7 all-you-can-drink. Open M-Th 11:30am-2am, F-Sa 11:30am-3am, Su noon-2am.

▨ **Club Chaos,** 1603 17th St. NW (☎232-4141), at Q St. Metro: Dupont Circle. Lives up to its name; so many shows, deals, and games going on, it's hard to have a bad time. "Performances" start around 10pm and entail just about anything. Happy hour Tu-F 5-8pm. Tu Drag Queen bingo. W ladies night. Th Latin night. The best drag show in town F-Sa 10pm. Start your Sunday with the Hollywood Drag Brunch 11am-3pm. Cover $3-5 buys a drink ticket of equal value. Open Tu-Th 4pm-1am, F-Sa 4pm-3am, Su 11am-3pm and nightly special events.

Badlands, 1415 22nd St. NW (☎296-0505), near P St. Stark exterior and limited hours prove that Badlands was built with a singular purpose: to host packed wild gay dance parties. The Annex upstairs is home to a mellower video bar with pool table, but most come for drag karaoke F-Sa. Tu and Th are under 21 nights. Th no cover with a college ID. Cover F-Sa 9-10pm $4, after 10pm $8. Open Th-Sa 9pm to very late, Su 9pm-2am.

The Fireplace, 2161 P St. NW (☎293-1293). Video bar on 2 floors caters mostly to older professional males and the men who love them. Look for the "outdoor" fireplace, complementing the gentlemen's club brick exterior. Weekends and evenings can get pretty packed. Happy hour M-F 1-8pm. No cover. Open Su-Th 1pm-2am, F-Sa 1pm-3am.

⊠ DAYTRIPS FROM D.C.

ARLINGTON, VA

The silence of the 612-acre **Arlington National Cemetery** honors those who sacrificed their lives in war. The Kennedy Gravesites hold the remains of President John F. Kennedy, his brother Robert F. Kennedy, and his wife Jacqueline Kennedy Onassis. The Eternal Flame flickers above JFK's simple memorial stone. The **Tomb of the Unknowns** honors all who died fighting for the US and is guarded by soldiers from the Army's Third Infantry. (Changing of the guard Apr.-Set. every 30min.; Oct.-Mar. every hr.) Pierre L'Enfant, originally buried within the District, was reinterred at Arlington along with soldiers from the Revolutionary War and the War of 1812. His distinctive grave on the hillside in front of **Arlington House** overlooks the city he designed. Farther down the hill among the plain headstones lies General of the Armies John J. Pershing, commander of US forces during WWI, who asked to be buried among his men. Arlington also holds the bodies Arctic explorers Robert E. Peary and Richard Byrd and legendary populist attorney and presidential candidate William Jennings Bryan. Robert E. Lee's home, Arlington House, overlooks the cemetery; tours are self-guided. (☎703-697-2131. Metro: Arlington Cemetery. Cemetery open Apr.-Sept. daily 8am-7pm; Oct.-May 8am-5pm. Free.) Head down Custis

Walk in front of Arlington House, exit the cemetery through Weitzel Gate, and walk for 20min. to get to the **Iwo Jima Memorial,** based on Joe Rosenthal's Pulitzer Prize-winning photo of Marines straining to raise the US flag on Mt. Suribachi. The statistics on **the Pentagon,** the world's largest office building, are mind-boggling: five concentric and ten radial hallways totalling 17.5 mi., 7754 windows, 131 stairways, and four ZIP codes of its own. Although the Pentagon no longer offers tours, even a look around the grounds can give visitors an idea of the damage a plane-turned-terrorist bomb inflicted on September 11, 2001.

ALEXANDRIA, VA

Alexandria didn't become a tourist attraction until the 1980s, when city residents backed away from proposed high-rises and decided to revitalize Old Town. Capital-izing on original 18th-century architecture and the legacy of historical all-stars like George Washington and Robert E. Lee, the town re-cobbled the streets, rebricked the sidewalks, installed gardens, restored over 1000 original facades, and invited tall ships and contemporary shops. As a result, today, the area is packed with tourists. **Old Town Alexandria,** has cobblestone streets, brick sidewalks, tall ships, and quaint shops, and sights cluster along Washington and King St. (Metro: King St.) George Washington and Robert E. Lee used to pray at **Christ Church,** 118 N. Washington St. (☎703-549-1450), at Cameron St., a red brick Colonial building with a domed stee-ple. Both slept in **Robert E. Lee's Boyhood Home,** 607 Oronoco St. (☎703-548-8454), near Asaph St. Thirty-seven different Lees inhabited the **Lee-Fendall House,** 614 Oronoco St. (☎703-549-1789). The **Ramsay House Visitors Center,** 221 King St., cor-dially offers free maps, literature, and directions to everything in town. The house, a 1724 building shipped upriver from Dumfries, VA, to Alexandria, was originally the home of Scottish merchant and Lord Mayor William Ramsay. (☎703-838-4200; www.funside.com. Open daily 9am-5pm.)

MT. VERNON

George Washington's fabulous estate **Mt. Vernon** is easily accessible in Fairfax County, VA. Visitors can see Washington's bedroom and tomb and the estate's fields, where slaves once grew corn, wheat, and tobacco. Even during his days as president, Washington found time to dedicate his leisure time to beautifying the mansion's interior and administering the corps of slaves that ran the farm. The estate maintains 30-40% of Washington's original furnishings, which are now on display. To get there, take the Fairfax Connector 101 bus from the Huntington Metro stop, or take I-395 S to George Washington Pkwy. S, which becomes Mt. Vernon Hwy.; use the Mt. Vernon exit. (☎703-780-2000. Open Apr.-Aug. daily 8am-5pm; Sept.-Oct. and Mar. 9am-5pm; Nov.-Feb. 9am-4pm. $9, seniors $8, ages 5-11 $4, under 5 free.)

VIRGINIA

If Virginia is obsessed with its past, it has good reason. Many of America's forma-tive experiences—the English settlement of North America, the boom in the slave trade, the final establishment of American independence, and much of the Civil War—took place in Virginia. More recently, the state has begun to abandon its Old South lifestyle in search of a cosmopolitan image. The western portion of the state, with its towering forests and fascinating underground caverns, provides a welcome respite from nostalgia and relentless Southern heat.

🔟 PRACTICAL INFORMATION

Capital: Richmond.

Visitor info: Virginia Division of Tourism, 901 E. Byrd St., 19th fl., Richmond 23219 (☎804-786-4484 or 800-847-4882; www.virginia.org). Open M-F 8am-5pm. **Dept. of Conservation and Recreation,** 203 Governor St., Richmond 23219 (☎804-786-1712). Open daily 8am-5pm.

Postal Abbreviation: VA. **Sales Tax:** 4.5%.

RICHMOND ☎804

The Civil War is still being waged in this capital city, once known as the "Cradle of the Confederacy." As recently as four years ago, residents vehemently lobbied against the inclusion of black tennis great Arthur Ashe's statue alongside those of secessionist heroes like Jefferson Davis and Stonewall Jackson. At the same time, the city honors the rich African-American heritage of Jackson Ward, an area that once rivaled Harlem as a center of black thought and culture. Aside from its history, Richmond offers a diverse range of festivals, sports, and hip nightlife.

▐ TRANSPORTATION

Trains: Amtrak, 7519 Staple Mills Rd. (☎264-9194 or 800-872-7245). Open 24hr. To: **Baltimore** (3½hr., 8 per day, $48); **New York City** (6hr., 8 per day, $111); **Philadelphia** (4¾hr., 8 per day, $71); **Virginia Beach** (3¼hr., 2 per day, $27); **Washington, D.C.** (2¼hr., 8 per day, $24); **Williamsburg** (1¼hr., 2 per day, $19).

Buses: Greyhound, 2910 N. Blvd. (☎254-5910 or 800-231-2222), 2 blocks from downtown. Take GRTC bus #24 north. To: **Baltimore** (3hr., 25 per day, $22); **Charlottesville** (1½hr., 4 per day, $17.50); **New York City** (6½hr., 25 per day, $56); **Norfolk** (2½hr., 9 per day, $19.50); **Philadelphia** (6hr., 15 per day, $35); **Washington, D.C.** (2hr., 17 per day, $19); **Williamsburg** (1hr., 8 per day, $8.50).

Public Transit: Greater Richmond Transit Co., 101 S. Davis Ave. (☎358-4782). Maps available in the basement of City Hall at 900 E. Broad St., the 6th St. Marketplace Commuter Station, and in the Yellow Pages. Most buses leave from stops along Broad St. downtown. $1.25, seniors 50¢; transfers 15¢.

Taxis: $2.50 plus 30¢ per one-fifth mile. **Veterans Cab,** ☎276-8990. **Yellow Cab,** ☎222-7300. **Star Cab** ☎754-8556.

➕🔟 ORIENTATION & PRACTICAL INFORMATION

Broad St. is the city's central artery, and the streets that cross it are numbered from west to east. Most parallel streets to Broad St., including **Main St.** and **Cary St.,** run one-way. Both I-95, leading north to Washington, D.C., and I-295 encircle the urban section of the city. The **Court End** and **Church Hill** districts, on Richmond's eastern edges, comprise the city's historic center. Further southeast, **Shockoe Slip** and **Shockoe Bottom** overflow with after-dark partiers. **Jackson Ward,** in the heart of downtown (bounded by Belvedere, Leigh, Broad, and 5th St.) recently underwent major construction to revamp its City Center. *Be careful in this area at night.* **The Fan,** named for its shape, is bounded by the Boulevard, I-95, the walk of statues along **Monument Ave.,** and **Virginia Commonwealth University.** *The Fan is notoriously dangerous at night; exercise caution.* The pleasant bistros and boutiques of **Carytown,** past the Fan on Cary St., and the tightly knit working community of **Oregon Hill** add texture to the cityscape. *Be careful here at night.*

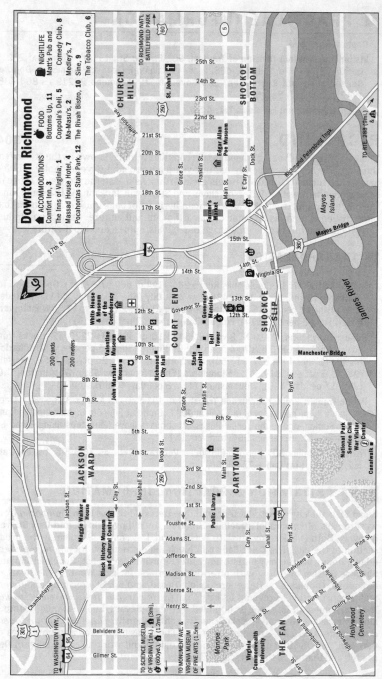

Downtown Richmond

▲ ACCOMMODATIONS
Comfort Inn, 3
The Inns of Virginia, 1
Massad House Hotel, 4
Pocahontas State Park, 12

● FOOD
Bottoms Up, 11
Coppola's Deli, 5
Ma-Masu's, 2
The Rivah Bistro, 10

📔 NIGHTLIFE
Matt's Pub and
Comedy Club, 8
Medley's, 7
Sine, 9
The Tobacco Club, 6

Visitor info: Richmond Metropolitan Visitor's Bureau, 405 N. 3rd St. (☎783-7450; www.richmondva.org), in the Richmond Convention Center; Exit 95 S onto 3rd St. and follow signs. Helpful 9min. video introduces the city's attractions. Bus/van tours and maps of downtown and the metro region available. Open daily 9am-6pm.

Hotlines: Rape Crisis, ☎643-0888. **AIDS/HIV,** ☎800-533-4148. M-F 8am-5pm. **Women's Health Clinic,** ☎800-254-4479. M-F 8am-5pm, Sa 7am-noon. **ROSMY (Richmond Organization for Sexual Minority Youth),** ☎353-2077.

Post Office: 1801 Brook Rd. (☎775-6133). Open M-F 7am-6pm, Sa 9am-2pm. **ZIP code:** 23219.

ACCOMMODATIONS

Budget motels in Richmond cluster on **Williamsburg Rd.,** at the edge of town, and along **Midlothian Turnpike,** south of the James River. Public transportation to these areas is unreliable. As usual, the farther you stay from downtown, the less you pay. The Visitors Center can reserve accommodations, often at $20-35 discounts.

Comfort Inn, 3200 W. Broad St. (☎359-4061), 2 mi. from town. Recently renovated, this 7-story hotel now strikes the city's best balance between desirable accommodation and affordable prices. Cable TV, A/C, coffee makers, high-speed Internet, pool, and access to a nearby gym. Free deluxe continental breakfast. 2-room suites available. Singles $69, with Visitors Center discount $49; suites $139. ❸

The Inns of Virginia, 5215 W. Broad St. (☎288-2800), 3 mi. from town; use bus #6. This motel, with modest but clean rooms and a lavish lobby, borders a large shopping center. A/C, cable TV, and an outdoor pool. Rooms $49-89; $200 per week. ❸

Massad House Hotel, 11 N. 4th St. (☎648-2893), 5 blocks from downtown. Surround yourself with antique furnishings and oil paintings, in a European atmosphere. A/C and cable TV. Singles $59; doubles $69; students and seniors 10% off. ❸

Pocahontas State Park, 10301 State Park Rd. (☎796-4255); for reservations, ☎800-933-7275 or 225-3867). From Richmond, take I-95 S to Rte. 288 and connect to Rte. 10. The park is 10 mi. south on Rte. 10 at the cross of Rte. 655 in Chesterfield. Showers, biking, boating, picnic areas, and the 2nd largest pool in Virginia. Canoe or paddleboat $5 per hr. Open year-round. Sites with water and electricity $18. ❶

FOOD

College students strapped for cash dominate the downtown Richmond cuisine scene—which ranges from greasy spoons to inexpensive Southern and ethnic foods. Brimming with farm fruits, veggies, and homemade delicacies, the outdoor **Farmers Market,** N. 17th and E. Main St., brings the freshest country crops into the city. Surrounding the market in **Shockoe Bottom,** pizza and deli food top the menu. The self-proclaimed "artsy" crowd of Virginia Commonwealth University convenes in hip coffeehouses and restaurants.

Bottoms Up, 1700 Dock St. (☎644-4400), at 17th and Cary St. Named "Richmond's Best Pizza" 5 years in a row. Take a choose-your-own-pizza adventure, or go with signatures like the Jo-Jo (tomatoes, feta, and shrimp) or the Chesapeake (spicy crab meat). $3-5.25 per slice. Drafts $3.25-4.25, bottles $2.75-4.50. Delivery available. Open Su-W 11:30am-11pm, Th 11am-midnight, F-Sa 11am-2am. ❶

The Rivah Bistro, 1417 E. Cary St. (☎344-8222), is where the stars dine when they come to town. Delicacies include lobster ravioli ($19) and chicken Dijon with asparagus ($15). Regulars never pass up dessert. Vanilla creme brulée ($6) and freshly made sorbet in a dark chocolate shell ($4) are sure to please. Open M-Th 11:30am-10pm, F-Sa 11:30am-11pm, Su 10:30am-9pm. ❺

MID-ATLANTIC

Coppola's Deli, 1116 E. Main St. (☎255-0454). One of the best-kept secrets of downtown Richmond—with a very plain exterior and dark windows, the place almost looks closed down from the outside—has a sandwich to suit every personality and culinary persuasion ($7). Local favorites include the Acropolis (feta, black olives, and tomato; $5.25) and the cheese tortellini ($2). Open M-Sa 10am-pm. ❷

Ma-Masu's, 2043 W. Broad St. (☎355-8063). Ma-Masu, "Spiritual Mother" extraordinaire, introduces her guests to Liberian culture with a mural that reads: "It's okay to lick your fingers here." *Keli-willy* (fried plantains with spices and onions) and *toywah* beans ($6), collard greens ($2.50), coconut juice ($2). Delivery available. Open Tu-F noon-9pm, Sa 6-11pm. ❷

ⓢ SIGHTS

AROUND ST. JOHN'S CHURCH. St. John's Church is the site of Patrick Henry's famed 1775 "Give me liberty or give me death" speech. The church still serves as an active house of worship. *(2401 E. Broad St. ☎648-5015. 25min. tours M-Sa 10am-3:30pm, Su 10am-1pm. Services Su 8:30 and 11am. Speech recreation Su 2pm, organ recital 1:30pm. Admission $5, seniors $4, 16 and under $3.)* Nearby is the **Edgar Allan Poe Museum,** in Richmond's oldest standing house, where visitors try to unravel the mysterious death of the morbid author. Inspect a coffin fragment and a lock of hair to draw your own conclusions, then bristle with fear as Poe's bust glares from a spooky archway in the garden. *(1914 E. Main St. ☎888-648-5523. Tours every hr. Tu-Sa 10am-5pm, Su 11am-5pm.; last tour 4pm. Tours $6; students, seniors, and AAA $5; under 9 free.)*

COURT END DISTRICT. Richmond's most important sites can be found in the **Court End** district. The Neoclassical **State Capitol** was designed by Thomas Jefferson, and the building served as the seat of the Confederate government during the Civil War. Meet the real George Washington at the imposing Houdon statue, the only one for which he actually posed. *(At 9th and Grace St. ☎698-1788. Open daily 9am-5pm.)*

CONFEDERATE SOUTH. The Civil War South is celebrated at the **Museum of the Confederacy.** The poignant painting "Last Meeting of Lee and Jackson" and the collection of artifacts and documents detailing gruesome Confederate medical treatments are intriguing. Next door, the museum runs tours through the White House of the Confederacy, where a South-shall-rise-again attitude permeates the air. *(1201 E. Clay St. ☎649-1861; www.moc.org. Open M-Sa 10am-5pm, Su noon-5pm. 45min. tours every ½hr. M, W, F-Sa 10:30am-4:30pm; Tu and Th 11:30am-4:30pm. Admission $9.50, seniors $9, ages 7-18 $5, under 7 free.)* There are no cupids or candy hearts in The Valentine Museum, just the South's largest collection of costumes. Here, ruffles abound—and that's just the men's clothing. Old playbills, diaries, photographs, and letters fascinate visitors. Admission includes a tour through the **Wickham House,** an architectural masterpiece by Alexander Parris—the architect of both the Virginia Governor's Mansion and Boston's Faneuil Hall. *(1015 E. Clay St. ☎649-0711; www.richmondhistorycenter.com. Open Tu-Sa 10am-5pm, Su noon-5pm. House tours every hr. Tu-Sa 11am-4pm, Su 1-4pm. Admission $5, students and seniors $4, ages 7-12 $3.)*

SHOCKOE SLIP. South of Court End, the **Shockoe Slip** district features fancy shops in restored warehouses, but few bargains. *(Runs from Main, Canal, and Cary St. between 10th and 14th St.)* This upscale financial district acquired its unusual name from the creek that used to flow through it, "Shacoquochan"—the Native American word for a large, flat stone at the end of a river. The **Shockoe Bottoms Arts Center** crams in the cutting-edge creations of 120 artists. *(2001 E. Grace St. ☎643-7959. Open Tu-Sa 10am-5pm. Free.)* Also in the Slip, the **Canalwalk,** linking the **Kanawha Canal** next to the James River, has gorgeous vistas and stylish eateries.

JACKSON WARD. Considered the birthplace of African-American capitalism, **Jackson Ward** was recently listed by the National Trust for Historic Preservation as one of the 11 most endangered sites in the country. The **Black History Museum and Cultural Center of Virginia** has rotating exhibits on African-American history, including African wall hangings and a Woolworth's counter. *(00 Clay St. ☎ 780-9093. Open Tu-Sa 10am-5pm, Su 11am-5pm. $4, students and seniors $3, under 12 $2. Wheelchair-accessible.)*

THE FAN. This old-world section of Richmond is home of the country's largest and best preserved Victorian neighborhood. Stroll down **Monument Ave.**, a boulevard lined with gracious old houses and towering statues of Virginia heroes. The statue of Robert E. Lee faces south, while Stonewall Jackson faces north so that he can perpetually scowl at the Yankees. The statue of African-American tennis hero Arthur Ashe, who died of AIDS, created a storm of controversy when built at the end of the avenue.

CARYTOWN. Located past the Fan near the VCU campus, this nine-block stretch of **Cary St.** is full of little boutiques, charming restaurants, and culture. At dinnertime, Carytown welcomes an interesting mix of restaurant-goers from the wealthy to starving students.

VIRGINIA MUSEUM OF FINE ARTS. The **Virginia Museum of Fine Arts**—the South's largest art museum—features a collection by some of the world's most renowned painters: Monet, Renoir, Picasso, and Warhol, as well as treasures from ancient Rome, Egypt, and Asia. *(2800 Grove Ave. ☎ 340-1400. Open Tu-W and Th-Su 11am-5pm, Th 11am-8pm. Free highlight tour 2:30, 6, and 7pm. Suggested donation $5. Tickets $10.)*

🎵 🎭 ENTERTAINMENT & NIGHTLIFE

One of Richmond's most entertaining and delightful diversions is the marvelous old **Byrd Theatre,** 2908 W. Cary St. Movie buffs buy tickets from a tuxedoed agent and are treated on weekends to a pre-movie Wurlitzer organ concert. (☎ 353-9911. All shows $2; Sa balcony seating $3.) Free concerts abound downtown and at the **Nina Abody Festival Park,** near the bottom of 17th St. *Style Weekly,* a free magazine available at the Visitors Center, and its younger counterpart, *Punchline,* found in most hangouts, both list concert lineups. Cheer on the **Richmond Braves,** Richmond's AAA minor-league baseball team, on Boulevard St. for a fraction of major-league prices. (☎ 359-4444. Boxes $8; general $5, youth and seniors $3.)

Matt's Pub and Comedy Club, 109 S. 12th St. (☎ 643-5653), pours out a bit of Brit wit within dark wooden walls. Tex-Mex and pub cuisine $3-7; microbrews and drafts $2.75-$3.60; cocktails $3.25. Stand-up comedy F 8 and 10:30pm, Sa 8 and 11pm. Cover around $8.50. Reservations recommended. Open F-Sa 11:30am-2am.

Medley's, 1701 E. Main St. (☎ 648-2313). A place where your level of coolness increases as soon as you step through the door. Live blues and French-Cajun food. Po' boy sandwiches $5.50-9; gumbo $8. Cover F-Sa $3-5. Open W-Sa 6pm-2am.

Sine, 1327 E. Cary St. (☎ 649-7767). With its revamped menu and always-entertaining crowd of drinkers, this pub stays lively all day. Patty melt with chips $6. Beers $2-4. Live music Tu-Sa. No cover. Open daily 11:30am-2am.

The Tobacco Company Club, 1201 E. Cary St. (☎ 782-9555). At this pricey bar, an older crowd drinks martinis, smokes cigars, and discusses the joys of oppressing the lower classes. Drink specials Th-Sa 8-9pm. Th Ladies Night. Cover $3. Open Th-Sa 8pm-2am.

MID-ATLANTIC

FREDERICKSBURG ☎ 540

Fredericksburg sits almost exactly halfway between the Union capital at Washington, D.C., and the old Confederate capital at Richmond. A foothold in Fredericksburg during the Civil War meant control of the road between the capitals and a distinct military advantage. As a result, Fredericksburg experienced a near-river of bloodshed as men battled for control of the city. Years before the battle of Fredericksburg shattered the silent landscape with gunshots, the colonial post was an important tobacco port on the banks of the Rappahanock River. After the Civil War dust cleared in 1865, Fredericksburg lay stained with carnage, but the town has recovered, mixing gorgeous city plantations and somber battlefields with cafes and elegant boutiques.

■▐ ORIENTATION & PRACTICAL INFORMATION. Fredericksburg's position on I-95 between Washington and Richmond makes it an easily accessible and pleasant destination en route to either capital. By car, take Exit 130A off I-95 and onto Rte. 3 to access the city. The city is divided into two parts by **Lafayette Blvd.**, with personal residences to the south. The **Historic Downtown** crams museums, historical sites, and chic cafes into a network of one-ways that is easily traversed by foot. **William Street** (Rte. 3) runs northeast over the Rappahanock River into Falmouth. One-way **Caroline Street** is the main historic and commercial route.

Amtrak (☎800-872-7245 or 872-7245) runs trains to Fredericksburg twice daily as a stop on the Maine-Florida line. **Virginia Railway Express** or **VRE** (☎800-743-3873 or 703-684-1001) makes several trips daily to Union Station in D.C. Both companies use the same station, 200 Lafayette Blvd., near Caroline St. (Open M-F 7am-7pm. No ticket office; call for reservations.) **Greyhound/Trailways** (☎800-231-2222 or 373-2103) buses arrive at 1400 Jefferson Davis Hwy. from: Baltimore (65min., $26.25); Richmond (1hr., $14.25); and Washington, D.C. (70min., $10.25). **Fredericksburg Regional Transit,** the public transportation system, offers extended bus service around the city with Caroline and Princess Anne St. as main thoroughfares. (☎372-1222. 25¢ per ride.) **Taxis: Yellow Cab,** ☎371-7075. **Virginia Cab Service,** ☎373-5111.

The **Fredericksburg Visitors Center,** 706 Caroline St., at the corner of Charlotte St., sells a pass that provides reduced admission to sites ($24, ages 6-18 $8) and arranges carriage ($5-10) and trolley tours ($5-12.50). It also offers extensive info on Historic Fredericksburg and guides bike and walking tours. (☎800-678-4748 or 373-1776. Open May-Sept. daily 9am-7pm; Oct.-Apr. 9am-5pm.) **Post Office:** Princess Anne St., between Charlotte St. and Lafayette Blvd. (☎800-275-8777. Open M-F 8:30am-5pm, Sa 9am-2:30pm.) **ZIP Code:** 22401. **Area Code:** 540.

▐ ACCOMMODATIONS. Chain motels rule the areas around Exits 118, 126, 130, and 133 off I-95. To reach the **Best Western ❸,** 2205 William St., take Exit 130A off I-95 and turn left at the 2nd light. A 10min. drive from the historic downtown area, the hotel has free continental breakfast, spotless rooms, an outdoor pool, and a very friendly staff. (☎371-5050. Singles $62; doubles $75. AARP/AAA 10% discount.) The **Econo Lodge ❷,** 2802 Plank Rd., has some of the cheapest rates in Fredericksburg. Take Exit 130B off I-95 and turn left at the first light. Desks, A/C, cable TV, and rosy interiors make for a comfortable stay. (☎786-8374. Free doughnuts, coffee, and juice. Singles $49; doubles $59. AAA and military 10% discount. Pets allowed with $25 deposit.) The **Fredericksburg Colonial Inn ❸,** 1707 Princess Anne St., has walls exquisitely decorated with Civil War nostalgia and antiques. Suites include bedroom, sitting room, parlor, and beautifully tiled bath. (☎371-5666. TV, refrigerators, and A/C. Complimentary breakfast. Singles and doubles $70; suites $90.)

◘ FOOD. Nearly every fast-food and restaurant chain known to man accompanies the motel mania off Exits 130A and 130B. The locals head to **Caroline Street** for a barrage of healthy options and less congested dining. **Goolrick's Pharmacy ❶**, 901 Caroline St., is home to the oldest continuously operating soda fountain in America. Patrons enjoy cheap chicken salad ($2.50), thick milkshakes ($3) and freshly squeezed lemonade ($1.35) in this 1950s time warp. (☎373-3411. Open M-F 9am-7pm, Sa 9am-5pm.) **Sammy T's ❷**, 801 Caroline St., a block from the Visitors Center, has a comprehensive menu that pleases poultry cravers and animal lovers, as well as unique daily specials. (☎373-2008. Chicken parmesan $9.25. Vegan sandwich $7. Open M-Th 11am-10pm, F-Sa 11am-10:30pm.) At **La Familia Castiglia's ❸**, 324 William St., the effervescent family staff offers a broad menu, including enormous calzones ($4.50), sumptuous veal marsala ($10), and *zuppa di cozze antipasto* (mussels in wine sauce) for $6.50. (☎373-6650. Open Su-Th 11am-10pm, F-Sa 11am-11pm.) **Lee's Ice Cream ❶**, 821 Caroline St., scoops over 100 flavors of ice cream. Try Kahlua fudge, amaretto cappuccino brickle, or Arbuckle's, finely ground Swiss cocoa mixed into vanilla ice cream. (☎370-4390. Single scoop $2; double $3. Open M-Th 11am-11pm, F-Sa 11am-midnight, Su 11am-10pm.)

◙ SIGHTS. Mansions, medicine, and Monroe (James, not Marilyn) take center stage in Fredericksburg's **Historic District. Kenmore Plantation,** 1201 Washington Ave., was built in 1775 for Fielding Lewis and his wife, George Washington's sister, Betty. After being dazzled by the elegant dining room, gawk at the garden, which is so pristine it looks artificial. (☎373-4255. Open Mar.-Dec. M-Sa 10am-5pm, Su noon-4pm. $6, ages 6-17 $3. Grounds free.) Since George was a bit busy founding a nation, he wanted his aging mother to be near his sister Betty. The result is the **Mary Washington House,** 1200 Charles St., packed with 18th-century trinkets. (☎373-1569. Open Mar.-Nov. daily 9am-5pm; Dec.-Feb. 10am-4pm. $4, children $1.50.) Learn why leeches purify the blood at the **Hugh Mercer Apothecary Shop,** 1020 Caroline St., which offers fascinating insights into old-fashioned medical practices. (☎373-3362. Open Mar.-Nov. daily 9am-5pm; Dec.-Feb. 10am-4pm. $4, ages 6-18 $1.50.) Originally Monroe's law office, the **James Monroe Museum,** 908 Charles St., is a repository of memorabilia. Parisian-purchased, Louis XVI-influenced furniture includes the desk where James drafted his famous doctrine. (☎654-1043. Open Mar.-Oct. daily 9am-5pm; Nov.-Feb. 10am-4pm. $4, seniors $3.20, children $1.)

◙◙ ENTERTAINMENT & NIGHTLIFE. In the olden times, sundown meant bedtime. Well, not much has changed in Fredericksburg. However, the town does have a few nocturnal pleasures. The **Colonial Theatre,** 907 Caroline St. (contact the Visitors Center at 800-678-4748), showcases symphonic performances and the occasional play. At the **Klein Theater,** College and Thornton Ave., the **Fredericksburg Theatre Co.** performs in the summer. (☎654-1124. $18-20.) The folk music at **Orbits,** 406 Lafayette Blvd., attracts a local crowd to the only consistently hopping nightspot in town. (☎371-2003. Monthly reggae performances. Drafts $3. M open-mic night. W acoustic showcase 7:30pm. F-Sa variety of shows. Cover F-Su $5. Open M-Th 11am-1:30am, F-Sa 11:30am-1:30am.) **Santa Fe Grille and Saloon,** 216 William St., has a new flavor of music every day of the week, as well as $6 pitchers and complimentary nachos. (☎371-0500. M Goth night. Tu hip-hop. W open-mic night. Th-Sa live bluegrass and rock. Open Su-Th 11am-2am, F-Sa 11:30am-2am.) **Spirits,** 816 Caroline St., is a cool place to listen to music and grab a drink with friends. Great pizza, pasta, and subs make this restaurant and lounge a hometown favorite. (☎371-9595. Happy hour with free pizza and appetizers daily 4pm-7pm. Restaurant open Su-Th 11am-9pm, F-Sa 11am-10pm; upstairs lounge open daily 4pm-2am.)

MID-ATLANTIC

NEAR FREDERICKSBURG: NATIONAL BATTLEFIELD PARKS

What today is a serene green expanse witnessed bloody decimation between December 1862 and May 1864. Under the leadership of Confederate Generals Robert E. Lee and Stonewall Jackson and Union Generals Ambrose E. Burnside, Joseph Hooker, and Ulysses S. Grant, four devastating Civil War battles were contested in the 20 sq. mi. around the town. Today, a 76 mi. driving tour winds through the battlefields of **Fredericksburg, Chancellorsville**, the **Wilderness**, and **Spotsylvania**.

Three walking tours—the **Sunken Road Walking Tour**, following the entrenchment line at Fredericksburg; the **Chancellorsville History Trail**; and the **Spotsylvania History Trail**—encircle the battlefields and provide strategic viewpoints of all major sights of battle, including the Bloody Angle at Spotsylvania. A captivating and comprehensive journey into the Civil War, the battlefields enliven the nation's history. Stop by the **Visitors Center**, 1013 Lafayette Blvd., for info. (☎373-6122. Open in summer daily 8:30am-6:30pm; in winter 9am-5pm. $4, under 17 free.)

WILLIAMSBURG ☎757

After its prosperous colonial era, Williamsburg fell upon hard economic times until philanthropist John D. Rockefeller, Jr., restored a large chunk of the historic district in the 1920s. In present-day Colonial Williamsburg, a fife-and-drum corps marches down the streets, and costumed wheelwrights, bookbinders, and blacksmiths go about their tasks using 200-year-old methods. Travelers who visit in late fall or early spring will avoid the crowds and humidity of summer, but miss the extensive array of special summer programs.

⌐ TRANSPORTATION

Airport: Newport News and Williamsburg International Airport, 20min. away in Newport News, has frequent connections to Dulles Airport by United Express and USAir. Take state road 199 W to I-64 S.

Trains: Amtrak (☎800-872-7245 or 229-8750) shares the transportation center with Greyhound at 408 N. Boundary St. Open daily 7:30am-10pm. From: **Baltimore** (5hr., 2 per day, $48); **New York** (7½-8hr., 2 per day, $90); **Philadelphia** (6hr., 2 per day, $65); **Richmond** (1hr., 2 per day, $22); **Washington, D.C.** (3½hr., 2 per day, $41).

Buses: Greyhound (☎800-231-2222 or 229-1460) in the Amtrak building. Ticket office open M-F 8am-5pm, Sa 8am-2pm, Su 8am-noon. From: **Baltimore** (via D.C.; 6-7hr., 8 per day, $47.50); **Norfolk** (1-2hr., 9 per day, $12); **Richmond** (1hr., 8 per day, $8); **Virginia Beach** (2½hr., 4 per day, $16); **Washington, D.C.** (3-4hr., 8 per day, $30).

Public Transit: James City County Transit or **JCCT** (☎259-4093). Bus service along Rte. 60, from Merchants Sq. west to Williamsburg Pottery or east past Busch Gardens. Operates M-Sa 6:30am-6:20pm. $1 plus 25¢ per zone change. **Williamsburg Shuttle** (R&R; ☎220-1621) provides service between Colonial Williamsburg, Water Country USA, and Busch Gardens every 30min. Operates late May to early Sept. daily 9am-10pm. All-day pass $2.

Taxis Yellow Cab, ☎245-7777. 24hr. 1st mi. $2.75; $1 each additional mi. **Williamsburg Limousine Service,** ☎877-0279. Call 8:30am-midnight for pickup.

◼ ⚡ ORIENTATION & PRACTICAL INFORMATION

Williamsburg lies 50 mi. southeast of Richmond between Jamestown (10 mi. away) and Yorktown (14 mi. away). **The Colonial Pkwy.**, which connects the three towns, has no buildings and is a beautiful route between historic destinations.

Visitor info: Williamsburg Area Convention And Visitors Bureau, 201 Penniman Rd. (☎253-0192), ½ mi. northwest of the transportation center. Provides the free *Visitor's Guide to Virginia's Historic Triangle.* Open M-F 8:30am-5pm. Colonial Williamsburg Visitors Center, 100 Visitors Center Dr. (☎800-447-8679 or 229-1000), 1 mi. northeast of the transportation center.

Post Office: 425 N. Boundary St. (☎229-0838). Open M-F 8am-5pm, Sa 9am-2pm. ZIP Codes: 23185 (Williamsburg), 23690 (Yorktown), and 23081 (Jamestown).

ACCOMMODATIONS

The hotels operated by the **Colonial Williamsburg Foundation** are generally more expensive than other lodgings in the area. **Rte. 60 W** and **Rte. 31 S** are packed with budget motels, which grow cheaper farther from the historic district.

▨ **Bryant Guest House,** 702 College Terr. (☎229-3320). From Scotland Rd., turn right onto Richmond Rd., then left onto Dillard St. 4 rooms with private baths, TV, and limited kitchen facilities in a stately, exquisitely landscaped brick home. Singles $35; doubles $45; 5-person suite $75. ❷

▨ **The Williamsburg Hospitality House,** 415 Richmond Rd. (☎800-932-9192; www.williamsburghosphouse.com), across from the College of William and Mary and within walking distance of Colonial Williamsburg. Elegant rooms and suites at comparatively affordable prices, in an old brick mansion with colorful gardens and a lovely seating area around the pool. Gym access included. Rooms $79-180; suites $140-200, depending on the season. ❹

Lewis Guest House, 809 Lafayette St. (☎229-6116), a 10min. walk from the historic district. 2 comfortable rooms, including an upstairs unit with private entrance, kitchen, partial A/C, and shared bath. Undoubtedly the most homey lodging in the area. The ageless proprietor, Mrs. Lewis, eagerly reminisces about 1930s Williamsburg while her adorable dog, Brandy, clips at your heels. Rooms $25-35. ❶

Jamestown Beach Campsites, 2217 Jamestown Rd. (☎229-7609), immediately adjacent to the Jamestown Settlement. One of the area's largest campgrounds. Frolic by the pool or in the James River. Quiet hours 11pm-8am. 2-person sites $22, with water and electricity $27.50, full hookup $31; $1.50 for each extra person up to 6. ❶

FOOD

Most of the authentic-looking "taverns" in Colonial Williamsburg are packed with sweaty tourists and overpriced grub (lunch $5-10; dinner from $18). Jumping back into the 21st century for food proves the most price-savvy option.

▨ **Berret's,** 199 S. Boundary St. (☎253-1847), at Merchants Sq. in Colonial Williamsburg's shopping district. 2 restaurants in one: the less expensive, more casual **Tap House Grill** and the pricey, more formal **Berret's Restaurant and Bar.** Tap House open daily from 4pm. Restaurant and bar open daily 11:30am-3pm and 5:30-10pm. ❹

▨ **Green Leafe Cafe,** 765 Scotland St. (☎220-3405). William and Mary students and locals attest that the substantial sandwiches ($6-7), like the grilled steak wrap, make a great light supper. Coveted Virginia microbrews are among the 30 on tap ($2.75-4). Different drink specials each night. Tu $1 drafts. Open daily 11am-2am. ❶

The Cheese Shop, 424 Prince George St. (☎220-0298). At this gourmet shop and deli, the local Virginia ham sandwich ($4.25) is balanced with the international flavor of the

Braunschweiger ($3.75). Impressive selection of domestics and Belgian imports. Outdoor seating only. Open M-Sa 10am-6pm, Su 11am-5pm. ●

Chowning's Tavern (☎ 220-7012), on Duke of Gloucester St. within the grounds of Colonial Williamsburg. Quasi-historical dishes like "Ploughman's Pastie" (roasted turkey and melted cheddar cheese in a flaky pastry with tavern slaw; $7.25) will have you chowing down like George Washington. For dessert, the Cider Cake is worth the caloric overload. Cover $3. Open daily 11am-midnight. ●

◉ SIGHTS

COLONIAL WILLIAMSBURG. Every day is a historical reenactment at Colonial Williamsburg. Though the site prides itself on its authenticity, the pristine paint on the houses and spotless garb on the "natives" gives the place more of an amusement park feel. Immersing yourself in the colonists' world doesn't require a ticket—visitors can enjoy the gorgeous gardens, march behind the fife-and-drum corps, lock themselves in the stocks, interact with the locals, and use the restrooms without ever doling out a dollar—the pay area is only a small part of the overall attraction. Two of the historic buildings—the **Wren Building** and the **Bruton Parish Church**—are free. The *Visitor's Companion* newsletter, printed on Mondays, lists free events, evening programs, and complete hours. (☎ 800-447-8679; www.colonialwilliamsburg.org. Visitors Center open daily 8:30am-9pm. Most sights open 9:30am-5pm. Day pass $33, ages 6-12 $16.50; 2 consecutive days $39/19.50; under 6 free.)

COLLEGE OF WILLIAM & MARY. Spreading west from the corner of Richmond and Jamestown Rd., the **College of William and Mary**, founded in 1693, is the second-oldest college in the US (after Harvard, see p. 121) and has educated luminaries such as presidents Jefferson, Monroe, and Tyler. Whereas most top colleges cost an arm, a leg, and many other important body parts, the still public William and Mary is a relative bargain for a first-rate college education. The **Office of Admissions,** in Blow Hall, offers free tours throughout the year, but take the free self-guided walking tour for a bit more history. **Old Campus** starts behind the concrete roads surrounding the campus, where the lawn opens up and beckons romance with a delicate picket fence. Keep an eye out for the celebrated **Crim Dell Bridge,** overflowing with thriving greenery and chirping birds. During the 1760s, Jefferson and other intellectual students formed a society to gather at pubs and chat about politics. Disbanded in 1762 and reinstituted in 1776, Jefferson's brainchild became America's first fraternity—**Phi Beta Kappa.** (☎ 221-4223. Tours M-F 10am and 2:30pm, most Sa 10am. Free.)

▚ DAYTRIPS FROM WILLIAMSBURG

JAMESTOWN & YORKTOWN

The **"Historic Triangle"** brims with US history. More authentic and less crowded than the Colonial Williamsburg empire, Jamestown and Yorktown show visitors where it all *really* began. At the **Colonial National Park,** southwest of Williamsburg on Rte. 31, you'll see the remains of the first permanent English settlement in America (1607), as well as exhibits explaining colonial life. The **Visitors Center** offers a hokey film, a free 30min. "living history" walking tour, and a 45min. audio tape tour ($2) for the five-mile **Island Loop Route.** The **Old Church Tower,** built in 1639, is the only 17th-century structure still standing; also featured is a statue of **Pocahontas.** In the remains of the settlement itself, archaeologists have uncovered the original site of **Jamestown Fort.** (☎ 229-1733. Open in summer daily 9am-5pm; off-season 9am-4:30pm. Visitors Center closes 30min. after park. $5.)

The nearby **Jamestown Settlement** is a commemorative museum with changing exhibits, a reconstruction of James Fort, a Native American village, and full-scale replicas of the three ships that brought the original settlers to Jamestown in 1607. The 20min. dramatic film details the settlement's history, including a discussion of settler relations with the indigenous Powhatan tribe. (☎229-1607. Open daily 9am-5pm. $10.75, ages 6-12 $5.25.)

The British defeat at **Yorktown** in 1781 signaled the end of the Revolutionary War. The Yorktown branch of **Colonial National Park** vividly recreates the significant last battle with an engaging film and an electric map. The **Visitors Center** rents cassettes and players ($2) for driving the battlefield's seven-mile car route. (☎898-3400. Visitors Center open daily 8:30am-5pm; last tape rental 3:30pm. $4, under 17 free.) Brush up on your high school history as you listen to the rallying cries of revolutionary figures such as Benjamin Franklin and Patrick Henry foretelling the independence won at Yorktown. The **Yorktown Victory Center,** one block from Rte. 17 on Rte. 238, boasts an intriguing "living history" exhibit—in an encampment in front, soldiers from the 1781 Continental Army take a break from combat. (☎887-1776. Open daily 9am-5pm. $8, seniors $6.75, ages 6-12 $4.)

BEER & ROLLER COASTERS

At **Busch Gardens,** proceed with caution: an arduous journey fraught with dangerous dragons, monsters, and angry gods awaits in "17th-Century Europe." Visitors over 21 can indulge in a home-brewed Anheuser-Busch beer, but consume in moderation lest your stomach churn after a pulsating 70 mph scream on the **Apollo's Chariot** roller coaster. (☎253-3350. Open late June to Aug. Su-F 10am-10pm, Sa 10am-11pm; Sept.-Oct. M and F 10am-6pm, Sa-Su 10am-7pm; call for winter and spring hours. $42, seniors $38, ages 3-6 $35; after 5pm $19.)

A three-day ticket ($50) is good for both Busch Gardens and **Water Country USA,** two mi. away. Thirty-five water rides, slides, and attractions laced with a 1950s surfing theme keep barefooted water babies splashing with delight. (Open late May to mid-June Sa-Su 10am-6pm; mid-June to mid-Aug. daily 10am-8pm; Sept. Sa-Su 10am-7pm. Hours vary; call ahead. $31, ages 3-6 $21; after 3pm $21 for all.)

VIRGINIA BEACH ☎757

Virginia's largest city, once the capital of the drunken collegiate crowd, is now gradually shedding its playground image and maturing into a family-oriented vacation spot. As with its nearby neighbors Norfolk, Newport News, and Hampton, the streets of this former Spring Break mecca now welcome parents and their baby carriages alongside tipsy twenty-somethings. Fast-food joints, motels, and cheap discount stores still abound, but culture now penetrates the plastic veneer.

⌐ TRANSPORTATION

Trains: Amtrak (☎800-872-7245 or 245-3589). The nearest train station, in Newport News, runs 45min. bus service to and from the corner of 19th and Pacific St. Call ahead to reserve a train ticket. To Newport News from: **Baltimore** (5½hr., $55); **New York City** (8hr., $81); **Philadelphia** (7hr., $64); **Richmond** (2hr., $25); **Washington, D.C.** (4½hr., $47); **Williamsburg** (45min., $28).

Buses: Greyhound, 1017 Laskin Rd. (☎800-231-2222 or 422-2998), ½ mi. from the oceanfront area. Connects with Maryland via the Bridge-Tunnel. From: **Richmond** (3½hr., $15); **Washington, D.C.** (6½hr., $30); **Williamsburg** (2½hr., $16).

MID-ATLANTIC

Public Transit: Virginia Beach Transit/Trolley Information Center (☎437-4768), Atlantic Ave. and 24th St. Info on area transportation and tours, including trolleys, buses, and ferries. Trolleys transport riders to major points in Virginia Beach. The Atlantic Avenue Trolley runs from Rudee Inlet to 42nd St. Other trolleys run along the boardwalk, the North Seashore, and to Lynnhaven Mall. May-Sept. daily noon-midnight. 50¢, seniors and disabled 25¢; 3-day passes $3.50. **Hampton Roads Regional Transit (HRT),** (☎222-6100), in the Silverleaf Commuter Center at Holland Rd. and Independence Blvd., runs buses connecting Virginia Beach with Norfolk, Portsmouth, and Newport News. $1.50, seniors and disabled 75¢, 17 and under $1, children under 38 in. free.

Taxis: Yellow Cab, ☎460-0605. $1.75 plus $1.60 per mi. 24hr. **Beach Taxi,** ☎486-4304. **Action Taxi & Sedan Service,** ☎460-2034. **James Taxi Service,** ☎437-2123.

Bike Rental: RK's Surf Shop, 305 16th St. (☎428-7363). Rents aquatic equipment bikes. Open daily June-Sept. 9am-10pm; Oct.-May 11am-6pm; bikes must be returned 2hr. before closing. $4 per hr., $16 per day.

➕🛈 ORIENTATION & PRACTICAL INFORMATION

In Virginia Beach, east-west streets are numbered and the north-south avenues, running parallel to the beach, have ocean names. Prepare to feel like a thimble on a Monopoly board: **Atlantic** and **Pacific Ave.** comprise the main drag. **Arctic, Baltic,** and **Mediterranean Ave.** are farther inland.

Visitor Info: Virginia Beach Visitors Center, 2100 Parks Ave. (☎800-822-3224 or 491-7866), at 22nd St. Info on budget accommodations and area sights. Helpful, knowledgeable tour guides. Open daily May-Sept. 9am-8pm; Sept.-May 9am-5pm.

Internet access: WebCity Cybercafe, 116 S. Independence Blvd. (☎490-8690), Exit 17B off I-264. Open M-Sa 10am-11pm, Su noon-9pm. $5 per 30min.

Post Office: 2400 Atlantic Ave. (☎800-275-8777), at 24th St. and Atlantic Ave. Open M-F 8am-4:30pm. **ZIP Code:** 23458. **Area Code:** 707

▐ ACCOMMODATIONS

As could be expected with an ocean resort, a string of endless motels lines the waterfront in Virginia Beach. Oceanside, Atlantic, and Pacific Ave. buzz with activity during the summer and boast the most desirable hotels. If reserved in advance, rates are as low as $45 in winter and $65 on weekdays in summer.

▧ **Angie's Guest Cottage, Bed and Breakfast,** and **HI-AYH Hostel,** 302 24th St. (☎428-4690), only 1 block from the oceanfront. Barbara "Angie" Yates and her personable staff welcome predominantly young international and domestic guests with discounted trolley tokens and great advice about the beach scene. Co-ed dorm rooms. Kitchen and lockers; no A/C. Linen $2. Min. stay for private rooms 2 days. Check-in 10am-9pm. No lockout. Reservations helpful. Open Apr.-Sept. 4- to 9-person dorms $16, nonmembers $19; off-season $11.50/13. Singles $35, with 2 people $48; much less off-season. ❶

The Castle Motel, 2700 Pacific Ave. (☎425-9330), 2 blocks from the beach. Quite possibly the best bang for your buck as far as motels go. Spacious, clean rooms come with cable TV, refrigerator, shower and bath, desk, and 2 full beds. Check-out 11am. Must be 21 to check in. Rates M-F from $49, Sa-Su $79. ❸

The Virginian Motel, 310 24th St. (☎428-2999), a couple doors down from Angie's hostel, lacks oceanfront glamour but is well-run and features sizeable rooms, an outdoor pool, and reasonable rates. Cable TV, A/C, kitchens. Weekdays $89, weekends $99. ❹

First Landings, 2500 Shore Dr. (☎800-933-7275 or 412-2300), about 8 mi. north of town on Rte. 60., in the state park bearing the same name. Take the North Seashore Trolley. With its desirable location amid sand dunes and cypress trees, the park is very popular. Private swimming area on a sprawling beach, a bathhouse, and boat launching areas. Cabin rates June-Aug. $85-95; Apr.-May and Sept.-Nov. $65-75 per night. ❸

◘ FOOD

Prepare for more $6 all-you-can-eat breakfast specials than you have ever previously encountered. Alternatively, fish for a restaurant on **Atlantic Ave.**, where each block is a virtual buffet of fried, fatty, sweet, and creamy dining options.

▨ **Giovanni's Pasta Pizza Palace,** 2006 Atlantic Ave. (☎425-1575). Speedy service, scrumptious rolls, and bargain prices make Giovanni's a must on the boardwalk. Their pizzas ($8-18) are the best on the beach. Inexpensive pastas, stromboli ($6-11), and a fabulous veggiboli ($6) also await. Open daily noon-11pm. ❸

Cuisine and Co., 3004 Pacific Ave. (☎428-6700). This sophisticated escape serves up gourmet lunches and rich desserts, including tuna melts ($5), chunky chicken salad ($5.25), and decadent cookies ($7.50 per lb.). Open M-Sa 9am-8pm, Su 9am-6pm. ❶

Ellington's Restaurant, 2901 Atlantic Ave. (☎428-4585), inside the Oceanfront Inn on the boardwalk. Patrons gaze over the ocean while enjoying some of the most overlooked food in the city. Ridiculously cheap lunch specials ($5) range from meatloaf to fish and chips; each comes with a side salad or cup of soup. Huge salads $7. Dinner entrees $8-17. Open daily 7am-10pm. ❷

Happy Crab's, 550 Laskin Rd. (☎437-9200). Massive crab carving on the wall and hanging fishing nets. Early-bird specials (daily 5-6:30pm) offer unbeatable 2-person seafood platters ($13) and 1-person servings big enough to split, like sumptuous ribs ($15). All-you-can-eat crab buffet daily 5pm $25. Open in summer M-Th 11am-10pm, F-Su 11am-11pm; in winter M-F 5-10pm, Sa-Su 11am-10pm. ❹

The Jewish Mother, 3108 Pacific Ave. (☎422-5430). Let Mom fill your belly with deli in this popular Virginia chain restaurant. The newspaper format menu includes humongous sandwiches with a scoop of potato salad ($4.50-6.75), a $10 prime rib, and overwhelming desserts ($3.50-4.50). Transforms into a local barfly's delight after 11pm with live music. Cover $3. Open M-F 8am-1am, Sa 8am-3am, Su 7am-2am. ❶

♫ ▧ ENTERTAINMENT & NIGHTLIFE

On summer nights, the Virginia Beach boardwalk becomes a haunt for lovers and teenagers, and **Atlantic Ave.**, a.k.a. "Beach Street, USA," hums with travelling shows and street performers. Rousing jazz and classic rock performances can be heard every other block. Larger outdoor venues at 7th, 17th, and 24th St. draw bigger names and crowds. Schedules for the main events are posted along the street. (☎440-6628 for more info. Free.) Each June for nearly 50 years, the **Virginia Beach Boardwalk Arts Festival** has been a summer highlight.

▨ **Chicho's,** 2112 Atlantic Ave. (☎422-6011), on "The Block" of closet-sized college bars clustered between 21st and 22nd St. One of the hottest spots on the strip features gooey pizza ($2.25-3.25 per slice) dished out from the front window and tropical mixed drinks ($5-7). M live rock music. Open M-F 11am-2am, Sa-Su 11am-2am.

Harpoon Larry's, 216 24th St. (☎422-6000), at Pacific Ave. 1 block from the HI-AYH hostel. The amicable bartender and manager welcome customers into an everybody-knows-your-name atmosphere. Nightly drink specials make it easy to drink lots and spend little. Specials include crab cakes for $7. Happy hour M-F 7-9 pm. Tu rum runners $2. W $1.25 Coronas with 25¢ jalapeño poppers. Open daily noon-2am.

Mahi Mah's, 615 Atlantic Ave. (☎437-8030), at 7th St. inside the Ramada Hotel. Sushi, tiki parties, and oceanfront views. Wine "flights" W 5-9pm: 4 tastes $2 each. Mouth-watering sushi ($6 rolls). 11am-5pm, bigger menu after 5pm. Outdoor band nightly. Well-dressed crowd. Open daily 7am-1am.

Peabody's, 209 21st St. (☎422-6212). A young, scantily clad crowd bops to Top 40 hits. "Hammertime" breaks it down daily 7-9pm with drinks for $1.50. All-you-can-eat fresh crab legs and shrimp $15. Th Ladies night. F College Night (free admission with college ID). Sa Bash at the Beach (karaoke and a laser light dance party). Cover $5; pool $1. Open Th-Sa 7pm-2am.

CHARLOTTESVILLE   ☎434

Thomas Jefferson, composer of the Declaration of Independence and colonial Renaissance man, built his dream house, Monticello, high atop his "little mountain" just southeast of Charlottesville. Around his personal paradise, Jefferson endeavored to create the ideal community. In an effort to breed further intellect and keep him busy in his old age, Jefferson humbly created the University of Virginia (UVA). Jefferson would be proud to know his time was not wasted—today the college sustains Charlottesville economically, geographically, and culturally.

▐ TRANSPORTATION

Airport: Charlottesville-Albemarle Airport (☎973-8342), 8 mi. north of Charlottesville, 1 mi. west of Rte. 29 on Airport Rd. Served by USAir, United, and Delta. Fares and destinations vary; call for information. Hertz, Avis, and National rental cars available.

Trains: Amtrak, 810 W. Main St. (☎296-4559). Open daily 6am-9:30pm. To: **Baltimore** (3½hr., 1 per day, $67); **New York City** (7hr., 1 per day, $130); **Philadelphia** (5½hr., 1 per day, $100); **Washington, D.C.** (2¾hr., 1 per day, $41).

Buses: Greyhound/Trailways, 310 W. Main St. (☎295-5131), within 3 blocks of downtown. Open daily 6:15am-10pm. To: **Baltimore** (6hr., 4 per day, $44.50); **Norfolk** (5½hr., 4 per day, $37.50); **Philadelphia** (10¼hr., 4 per day, $56); **Richmond** (1¼hr., 4 per day, $18.25); **Washington, D.C.** (4hr., 7 per day, $21).

Public Transit: Charlottesville Transit Service (☎296-7433). Bus service within city limits. Maps available at info centers and on the buses. Buses M-Sa 6:30am-midnight. 75¢, seniors and disabled 35¢, under 6 free. The more frequent UVA buses technically require UVA student ID, but a studious look usually suffices.

Taxis: Yellow Cab, ☎295-4131.

◼✴ ▐ ORIENTATION & PRACTICAL INFORMATION

Charlottesville streets are numbered from east to west, using compass directions; 5th St. NW is 10 blocks from (and parallel to) 5th St. NE. There are two downtowns: **The Corner,** on the west side across from the university, is home to student-run delis and coffeeshops. **Historic Downtown,** about a mile east, is a tad higher on the price scale. The two are connected by east-west **University Ave.,** which starts as Ivy Rd. and becomes Main St. after the end of the bridge in The Corner district.

Visitor info: Chamber of Commerce, 415 E. Market St. (☎295-3141), at 5th St. Within walking distance of Amtrak, Greyhound, and downtown. Maps, guides, and info about special events available. Open M-F 9am-5pm. **Charlottesville-Albemarle County Convention and Visitors Bureau** (☎977-1783), off I-64 on Rte. 20. Arranges discount lodgings and travel packages to Jeffersonian sights and shows a free 30min. film, "The Pursuit of Liberty," about Jefferson's life. Also features a free exhibit with 400 original Jeffersonian objects. Open daily Mar.-Oct. 9am-5:30pm; Nov.-Feb. 9am-5pm. **University of Virginia Information Center** (☎924-7969), at the Rotunda in the center of campus, offers brochures, a university map, and tour information. Open daily 9am-4:45pm. Film in summer every hr.; off-season 11am and 2pm.

Police: Campus Police, ☎4-7166 on a UVA campus phone, otherwise ☎924-7166. Exit 120A off U.S. 250 W.

Hotlines: Region 10 Community Services, ☎972-1800. **Sexual Assault Crisis Center,** ☎977-7273. Both 24hr. **Mental Health,** ☎977-4673. Open M-F 9am-6pm. For emergencies, call Region 10. **Women's Health Clinic** (in Richmond), ☎800-254-4479. Open M-Sa 8am-5pm.

Post Office: 513 E. Main St. (☎963-2661). Open M-F 8:30am-5pm, Sa 10am-1pm. **ZIP code:** 22902. **Area code:** 434.

■ ACCOMMODATIONS

Emmet St. (U.S. 29) is home to generic hotels and motels ($40-60) that fill up during summer weekends and big UVA events. **The Budget Inn ❷,** 140 Emmet St., is the closest motel to the university and offers 36 big rooms with lots of sunlight and cable TV. (☎293-5141. Rooms $42-58; each additional person $5.) Equally attractive to the budget traveler are the 60 rooms of the **Econo Lodge ❷,** 400 Emmet St. (☎296-2104. Pool, cable TV, and continental breakfast. Rooms $42-62.) **Charlottesville KOA Campground ❶,** Rte. 708, 10 mi. outside Charlottesville; take U.S. 20 S to Rte. 708 W. Shaded campsites keep guests cool. (☎296-9881 or 800-562-1743. Laundry facilities, recreation hall, pool, and volleyball court. Fishing and pets allowed. Open Mar.-Oct. Sites $20, with water and electricity $24, full hookup $27.)

■ FOOD

Students and tourists dictate the menus in Charlottesville. Intellectual crowds dine at **The Corner,** on University Ave. across from the university, where good, cheap food is plentiful. For a glitzier culinary experience, a stroll down the cobblestone streets by the **Downtown Mall** unveils romantic, unique eateries, most with outdoor dining in summer.

The Hardware Store, 316 E. Main St. (☎977-1518 or 800-426-6001), in the Downtown Mall. It requires a handyman's dexterity to go bottoms-up on the half-meter and meter beer tubes (half $5; full $7). The Store sends patrons to the head of the class with the *summa cum laude* sandwich (smoked salmon and swiss on pumpernickel; $8.75). Other sandwiches from $6. Open M-Th 11am-9pm, F-Sa 11am-10pm.

Southern Culture, 633 W. Main St. (☎979-1990). Delve into Cajun culture with the pasta jambalaya ($14) or the more affordable Cajun burger ($6) served up by an amicable staff. M Down-Home night. Open M-Sa 5-10pm, Su 11am-2:30pm and 5-10pm.

Littlejohn's, 1427 University Ave. (☎977-0588). During lunch hours, this deli becomes as overstuffed as its sandwiches. In the wee, wee hours of the morning, barflies trickle into Littlejohn's to kick back and relax with the Easy Rider (baked ham, mozzarella, and coleslaw; $3.75). Many, many beers ($2-3). Open 24hr.

MID-ATLANTIC

◎ SIGHTS

MONTICELLO. Jefferson oversaw every stage of the development of his beloved **Monticello,** a home that truly reflects the personality of its brilliant creator. The house is a quasi-Palladian jewel filled with fascinating innovations, such as a fireplace dumbwaiter to the wine cellar and a mechanical copier (all compiled or conceived by Jefferson). The grounds include orchards and flower gardens that afford magnificent views. *(1184 Monticello Loop. ☎984-9822. Open daily Mar.-Oct. 8am-5pm; Nov.-Feb. 9am-4:30pm. $11, ages 6-11 $6.)* The partially reconstructed **Michie Tavern** has an operating grist mill and a general store. *(Just west of Monticello on the Thomas Jefferson Pkwy. ☎977-1234. Open daily 9am-5pm; last tour 4:20pm. $8, seniors and AAA $7, ages 6-11 $3.)* **Ash Lawn-Highland** was the 535-acre plantation home of President James Monroe. Although less distinctive than Monticello, Ash Lawn reveals more about family life in the early 19th century and hosts living history exhibitions. Kids are mesmerized by the colorful peacocks in the backyard. *(1000 James Monroe Pkwy. Off Rte. 792 2½ mi. east of Monticello. ☎293-9539. Open daily Mar.-Oct. 9am-6pm; Nov.-Feb. 10am-5pm. Tour $8, seniors and AAA discount $7.50, ages 6-11 $5. Wheelchair accessible.)*

UVA. Most activity on the grounds of the **University of Virginia** clusters around the **Lawn** and fraternity-lined **Rugby Rd.** Monticello is visible from the lawn, a terraced green carpet that is one of the prettiest spots in American academia. Professors live in the Lawn's pavilions; Jefferson designed each one in a different architectural style. Privileged Fourth Years (never called seniors) are chosen each year for the small Lawn singles. Room 13 is dedicated to ne'er-do-well **Edgar Allen Poe,** who was kicked out for gambling. The early morning clanging of the bell that used to hang in the **Rotunda** provoked one incensed student to shoot at the building. *(☎924-7969. Tours meet at Rotunda entrance facing the Lawn. Tours daily 10, 11am, 2, 3, and 4pm; no tours on Thanksgiving, mid-Dec. to mid-Jan., and early to mid-May.)* The **Bayley Art Museum** features changing exhibits and a small permanent collection that includes a cast of Rodin's *The Kiss. (155 Rugby Rd. ☎924-3592. Open Tu-Su 1-5pm. Free.)*

🎵🎭 ENTERTAINMENT & NIGHTLIFE

This preppy college town is full of jazz, rock, and pubs. A kiosk near the fountain in the center of the Downtown Mall has posters with club schedules; the free *Weekly C-ville* can tell you who's playing when. English-language opera and musical theater highlight the **Summer Festival of the Arts,** in the Box Gardens behind Ash Lawn. *(☎293-4500. Most shows 8pm. Some earlier kids programs. Open June-Aug. M-F 9am-5pm. "Music at Twilight" series W 8pm. Series $10, students $8, seniors $9.)* There's daily skating at the **Charlottesville Ice Park,** 230 W. Main St. *(☎817-1423),* at the end of the Downtown Mall; call ahead for times and prices.

> **Buddhist Biker Bar and Grille,** 20 Elliewood Ave. *(☎971-9181).* UVA students and local twenty-somethings flock to this bar for its huge lawn and drink specials. The food ain't bad either—try the spinach dip ($5) or stuffed mushrooms ($3.75). Beers $2.50-4. M $1 beers. W $2 cocktails. Th Live bluegrass. Open M-Sa 3:30pm-2am.

> **Orbit,** 102 14th St. NW *(☎984-5707).* The hottest new bar and restaurant among C-ville locals. The recently opened downstairs has a *2001: A Space Odyssey* theme, and the garage-door windows open on those hot summer nights. Upstairs has 8 pool tables and another bar with extensive taps, including many imports ($2.50-4.50). Tu ladies shoot pool for free. Th $2 drafts. Su live acoustic music occasionally. Open daily 5pm-2am.

> **Baja Bean,** 1327 W. Main St. *(☎293-4507).* Cheap burritos, tamales, and *chimichangas* go down smooth for under $8 at this Mexican bar and restaurant. Every 5th of the

month is the Cinco Celebration, a fiesta highlighted by $3 Coronas. W 9pm-midnight dance parties with lasers and DJ-fueled music. Open daily 11am-2am.

SHENANDOAH NATIONAL PARK ☎540

Shenandoah's amazing multicolored mountains—covered with lush, green foliage in the summer and streaked with brilliant reds, oranges, and yellows in the fall—offer relaxation and recreation throughout the year. As America's first great nature reclamation project, Shenandoah National Park had humble beginnings, starting out as a 280-acre tract of over-logged, over-hunted land that Congress authorized Virginia to purchase in 1926. In 1936, a decree from Franklin Roosevelt sought to improve the land and foster new life upon the slowly rejuvenating soil by experimenting with trappers. Today, the national park spans 196,000 acres with 500 miles of trails and more plant species than all of Europe. Despite pollution problems, visitors can see miles of ridges and treetops on a clear day.

🌲🦌 ORIENTATION & PRACTICAL INFORMATION

The park runs nearly 75 mi. along the famous **Skyline Drive,** which extends from Front Royal in the north to Rockfish Gap in the south before evolving into the **Blue Ridge Parkway.** Skyline Drive closes during (and following) bad weather. Mile markers are measured north to south and denote the location of trails and stops. Three major highways divide the park into sections: the **North Section** runs from Rte. 340 to Rte. 211; the **Central Section** from Rte. 211 to Rte. 33; and the **South Section** from Rte. 33 to I-64. A park pass is valid for seven days and is necessary for re-admittance. (Most facilities hibernate in winter; call ahead. Entrance fee $10 per vehicle; $5 per hiker, biker, or bus passenger; disabled persons free.) **Greyhound** sends two buses a day to Waynesboro, near the park's southern entrance, from Charlottesville ($9), Richmond ($30), and Washington, D.C. ($50). No bus or train serves Front Royal, near the park's northern entrance.

The **Dickey Ridge Visitors Center,** at Mi. 4.6, and the **Byrd Visitors Center,** at Mi. 51, answer questions and maintain small exhibits about the park, including a 12min. introductory slide show. (Dickey Ridge: ☎635-3566. Byrd: ☎999-3283. Both open Apr.-Dec. daily 8:30am-5pm; additional hours July-Sept. F-Sa, 8:30am-6pm.) The station's rangers conduct informative presentations on local wildlife, guide short walks among the flora, and wax romantic during outdoor, lantern-lit evening discussions. Pick up a free *Shenandoah Overlook* visitor newsletter for a complete listing of programs. Comprehensive and newly updated, the *Guide to Shenandoah National Park and Skyline Drive* ($7.50 and worth every penny) is available at both Visitors Centers. (General park info ☎999-2297, recorded message ☎999-3500. Operates daily 8am-4:30pm.) Send **mail** to: Superintendent, Park Headquarters, Shenandoah National Park, Rte. 4, P.O. Box 348, Luray, VA 22835. (For emergencies call ☎800-732-0911.) **Area code:** 540.

🏠 ACCOMMODATIONS

In a miniature stone castle, **The Bear's Den (HI-AYH) ❶,** 18393 Blue Ridge Mountain Rd., 35 mi. north of Shenandoah on Rte. 601, can hold 20 mountain-weary travelers within its two standard dorm rooms. Take Rte. 340 N to Rte. 7 E and follow it for 10 mi. to 601 N; travel ½ mi. on 601 and turn right at the gate. Aside from the more standard amenities, the hostel also offers access to simple, straightforward hiking trails geared towards inexperienced woodsy folk. A convenience store spares travelers the 9 mi. trek to the nearest supermarket. (☎554-8708. Max. stay 5 days.

Reception 7:30-9:30am and 5-10pm. Check-out 9:30am. Front gate locked and quiet hours begin at 10pm. 24hr. access to hikers' basement room. Beds $12, nonmembers $15; private room for 2 $30/$36, each additional person $12/$15. Camping $3 per person, with use of hostel facilities $6-$7.) The park also maintains three affordable "lodges"—essentially motels with nature-friendly exteriors. Reservations (☎800-999-4714) can be made up to six months in advance and are necessary at all lodges. **Skyland ❸,** Mile 42 on Skyline Drive, offers wood-furnished cabins and more upscale motel rooms. (☎999-2211. Cabins: Open Apr.-Oct. $65. Motel rooms: Open Mar.-Nov. $97-155.) **Big Meadows ❸,** Mile 51, has similar services, with a historic lodge and cabins. (☎999-2221. Open late Apr.-Nov. Cabins $55-85; lodges $55-150.) **Lewis Mountain ❷,** Mile 57, operates regular cabins and tent cabins. (☎999-2255. Cabins $45-67; tent cabins $17-22.)

⛺ CAMPING

The park service (☎800-365-2267) maintains four major campgrounds: **Mathews Arm ❶,** Mi. 22 ($14); **Big Meadows ❶,** Mi. 51 ($17); **Lewis Mountain ❶,** Mi. 58 ($14); and **Loft Mountain ❶,** Mile 80 ($14). The latter three have stores, laundry, and showers, but no hookups. Heavily wooded and uncluttered by RVs, Mathews Arm and Lewis Mountain are best. Reservations are possible only at Big Meadows.

The **Appalachian Trail (AT)** runs the length of the park. Twelve three-sided shelters are strewn at eight- to ten-mile intervals along the AT. Unwritten trail etiquette usually reserves the cabins for those hiking large stretches of the trail. **Backcountry camping** is free, but you must obtain a permit at park entrances, Visitors Centers, or ranger stations. Camping without a permit or above 2800 ft. is illegal and unsafe. The **Potomac Appalachian Trail Club (PATC) ❶,** 118 Park St. SE, in Vienna, a volunteer organization, maintains six cabins in backcountry areas of the park. Bring lanterns and food; the primitive cabins contain only bunk beds, blankets, and stoves. (☎703-242-0693. Headquarters open M-W 7-9pm, Th noon-2pm and 7-9pm, F noon-2pm. One group member must be 21+. Reservations required. Su-Th $15 per group, F-Sa $25.) Trail maps and the PATC guide can be obtained at the Visitors Center. The PATC puts out three topographical maps ($5 each).

⚡ OUTDOOR ACTIVITIES

HIKING

The trails off Skyline Dr. are heavily used and safe for cautious day-hikers with maps, appropriate footwear, and water. The middle section of the park, from **Thorton Gap,** Mile 32, to **South River,** Mile 63, bursts with photo opportunities and stellar views, although it also tends to be crowded with tourists. Rangers recommend purchasing *Hiking Shenandoah Park* ($13), a guide detailing the distance, difficulty, elevation, and history of 59 hikes.

Whiteoak Canyon Trail (Mi. 42.6; 4.6 mi., 4hr.) is a strenuous hike that opens upon the 2nd highest waterfall in the park (plunging an impressive 86 ft.), rewarding those who ascend the 1040 ft. of trail with views of the ancient Limberlost hemlocks.

Limberlost Trail (Mi. 43; 1.3 mi., 1hr.) slithers into a hemlock forest. Weaving through orchards, passing over a footbridge, and remaining relatively level, it is recommended for all ages and activity levels. No pets allowed. Wheelchair accessible loop.

Old Rag Mountain Trail (Mi. 45; 8.8 mi., 6-8hr.) starts outside the park. From U.S. 211, turn right on Rte. 522, then right on Rte. 231. Trail scrambles up 3291 ft. to triumphant views of the valley below. Be careful in damp weather, rocks can get slippery. Hikers 16 and older who have not paid Shenandoah admission must pay $3.

Stony Man Nature Trail (Mi. 41.7; 1.6 mi., 1½hr.) is a self-guided trail that offers independent hikers the opportunity to gain altitude, gradually climbing to the park's second-highest peak. The surrounding forests contain a vast variety of trees. No pets allowed.

OTHER ACTIVITIES

There are two other ways to explore Shenandoah: by boat and by beast. **Downriver Canoe Co.** in Bentonville offers canoe, kayak, raft, and tube trips. From Skyline Dr. Mi. 20, follow U.S. 211 W for 8 mi., then take U.S. 340 N 14 mi. to Bentonville; turn right onto Rte. 613 and go 1 mi. (☎635-5526 or 800-338-1963. Open M-F 9am-6pm, Sa-Su 7am-7pm.) Guided **horseback rides** are available at the Skyland Lodge, Mi. 42. (☎999-2210. Riders must be 4 ft. 10 in. Open Mar.-Oct. $20 per 1hr. ride.)

🔖 DAYTRIPS FROM SHENANDOAH

LURAY CAVERNS

In 1878, three young boys discovered 64 acres of underground craftsmanship, now known as the **Luray Caverns,** at U.S. 211 off I-81 Exit 264. View mineral formations in the shape of fried eggs, shaggy dogs, and ice cream cones on the 1hr. guided tour through moist, 57°F tunnels. Access to the automobile museum and an outdoor garden maze are included in the admission. (☎743-6551. Open mid-June to Aug. daily 9am-7pm; mid-Mar. to mid-June and Sept.-Oct. 9am-6pm; Nov. to mid-Mar. M-F 9am-4pm, Sa-Su 9am-5pm. $16, seniors $14, ages 7-13 $8.)

ENDLESS CAVERNS

Escape the tourist congestion of Luray Caverns to discover the beauty of infinity at **Endless Caverns,** 1800 Endless Caverns Rd. Follow signs from the intersection of U.S. 11 and U.S. 211 in New Market. The caverns are considered "endless" because they encompass over 5 mi. of mapped cave passages with no visible end. Cave temperature is cool, and the tour is relatively physical; wear a jacket and sturdy shoes. (☎896-2283. Open June-Aug. daily 9am-7pm; Sept.-Nov. and Mar.-June 9am-5pm; Nov.-Mar. 9am-4pm. $12, AAA and AARP $11, ages 3-12 $6.)

SKYLINE CAVERNS

Smaller than Endless and Luray Caverns, **Skyline Caverns,** on U.S. 340, 1 mi. from the junction of Rte. 340 and Skyline Drive, contains an orchid-like garden of white rock spikes. Respect the formation! Only one grows every 7000 years. Most remarkable are the anthodites, a type of crystal only found in a few other places in the world. Notable tour stops include The Capitol Dome, The Wishing Well, Cathedral Hall, and Rainbow Falls—pouring 37 ft. from one of the three cavern streams. (☎635-4545 or 800-296-4545. Open mid-Mar. to mid-June M-F 9am-5pm, Sa-Su 9am-6pm; mid-June-Sept. M-F 9am-6:30pm, Sa-Su 9am-6pm; mid-Nov. to mid-Mar. daily 9am-4pm. $12; seniors, AAA, and military $10; ages 7-13 $6.)

NEW RIVER GORGE   ☎304

The New River Gorge is an electrifying testament to the raw beauty and power of nature. One of the oldest rivers in the world, the **New River** carves a narrow gorge through the **Appalachian Mountains,** creating precipitous valley walls that tower an average of 1000 ft. above the white waters. These steep slopes remained virtually untouched until 1873, when industrialists drained the region to uncover coal and timber. With the coal mines now defunct, the gorge has come full circle, reverting to a natural marvel burgeoning with wildlife.

MID-ATLANTIC

The beauty of unrestrained wilderness does not end at the southern gates of Shenandoah National Park. Jaws will continue to drop as travelers weave through the world's longest scenic drive—the 469 mi. Blue Ridge Parkway. Merging with Skyline Dr., the parkway winds through Virginia and North Carolina, connecting Shenandoah National Park (p. 339) in Virginia to the Great Smoky Mountains (p. 367) in Tennessee, and offering an endless array of stunning vistas along the way. Administered by the National Park Service, the parkway sprouts hiking trails, campsites, and picnic grounds with humbling mountain views. While still accessible in the winter, the Parkway lacks maintenance or park service from November to April. *The steep bending roads can be treacherous, exercise caution, especially during inclement weather.*

For general information, call the park service in Roanoke, VA (☎857-2490), or write to **Blue Ridge Parkway Superintendent**, 199 Hemphill Knob Rd., Asheville, NC 28801 (☎828-298-0398). Twelve **Visitors Centers** line the Parkway at Mi. 6, 64, 86, 169, 218, 294, 305, 316, 365, and 382, located at entry points where highways intersect the Blue Ridge. (Most open daily 9am-5pm.) **Area code:** 540, except where otherwise noted.

1 GEORGE WASHINGTON NATIONAL FOREST. From Shenandoah National Park, the Blue Ridge trails south from Waynesboro to Roanoke south through Virginia's 1.8 million acre George Washington National Forest. A **Visitors Center** (☎291-1806), 12 mi. off the Parkway at Mi. 70, at the intersection of Rte. 130 and Rte. 11 in Natural Bridge, distributes information on hiking, camping, canoeing, and swimming at **Sherando Lake ❶**, 4½ mi. off the Parkway at Mi. 16. In addition to its 65 campsites, the lake has some excellent fishing. (Site with hook-up $15; recreational user fee $8.)

2 HUMPBACK ROCKS. Excellent hiking trails along the parkway vary in difficulty and duration, offering naturalists of all ages and abilities a chance to explore the peaks and valleys of the Blue Ridge. Whether moseying along easy trails through the scenic backdrop or scrambling up the more strenuous climbs through the Humpback Mountains, there is something for everyone. One of the less demanding trails, **Humpback Rocks** (Mi. 5.8), a formation of green volcanic rock, is a quick hike near the namesake Emerald Mounds. The **Mountain Farm Trail** (Mi. 5.9) is an easy 20min. hike that leads to a reconstructed homestead.

BLUE RIDGE PARKWAY

3 LEXINGTON. At the intersections of I-81 and I-64, the college town of Lexington drips with Confederate pride. Check out the Lee Chapel and Museum, at the center of the **Washington and Lee** campus, which holds Confederate General (and college namesake) Robert E. Lee's crypt along with the remains of his trusty horse Traveler. (☎463-8768. Open Apr.-Oct. 9am-5pm, Su 1-5pm; Nov.-Mar. M-Sa 9am-4pm, Su 1-4pm. Free.) For accommodations and further attractions, contact the **Lexington Visitors Center,** 106 E. Washington St. (☎463-3777). Other cities and towns along the Parkway also offer accommodations, primarily motels for around $35-55.

DISTANCE: 469 mi.

SEASON: Spring, summer, and fall

STATES INCLUDED: Virginia, North Carolina, Tennessee

4 NATURAL BRIDGE. Across from the Visitors Center in George Washington National Forest, a water-carved **Arc de Triomphe** towers 215 ft. above green-lined falls and an underground river. One of the seven natural wonders of the world, the 100 million-year-old **Natural Bridge** still bears the initials carved into the side by a vandalous George Washington. The nightly "Drama of Creation" light and sound show chronicles the biblical seven days of creation. (☎291-2121 or 800-533-1410. Bridge open daily 8am-dark. Drama show Su-F 9pm, Sa 9 and 10pm. $10; students, seniors, AAA, and military $8; ages 6-15 $5. Wheelchair accessible.)

5 PEAKS OF OTTER. Three- to five-mile hiking trails start from Peaks of Otter (Mi. 86), where visitors can hike among peaks as high as 4500 ft. The **Sharp Top** (3.2 mi.; 3875 ft.), beginning at the Visitors Center, climbs to the to the peak of Sharp Top Mountain for an amazing panoramic view of the surrounding Blue Ridge Mountains. Other trails ascend **Flat Top Mountain** (5.7 mi.; 4004 ft.) and **Harkening Hill** (4.2 mi.; 3364 ft.), providing a chance to drive through some well-forested terrain.

6 LINN COVE VIADUCT. The majority of the Blue Ridge Parkway was completed by 1967, but a small stretch that remained as the "missing link" for 20 years. The completion of the parkway was inhibited by the existence of the imposing **Grandfather Mountain.** In order to finish the parkway without damaging the mountain, a lengthy construction process was undertaken. The trail was built from the top down as a sweeping S shape to minimize disturbance to the national environment. The nearly $10 million project was completed in 1983, creating a 1243 ft. expanse of concrete curving around the boulders at **Linn Cove.** For wheelchair accessible outdoor activities, try the ¼ mi. **Linn Cove Viaduct Access Trail** (Mi. 304.4 in North Carolina).

7 MOSES H. CONE MEMORIAL PARK. The sprawling estate at **Moses H. Cone Memorial Park** (Mi. 294) features a Visitors Center and craft store, and rents canoes on **Price Lake** at Mi. 291. (☎295-3782. Open June-Aug. daily 8:30am-6pm; May and Sept.-Oct. Sa-Su 10am-6pm. Canoes $4 for 1hr., $3 each additional hr.) The Park Service hosts a variety of ranger-led activities, including historical talks, campfire circles, guided nature walks, slide shows, and musical demonstrations; information is available at the Blue Ridge Visitors Centers.

⌘ PRACTICAL INFORMATION. Amtrak runs through the heart of the gorge, stopping on Rte. 41 N in Prince and Hinton. (☎ 253-6651. Trains Su, W, and F. Open Su, W, and F 10:30am-7pm; Th and Sa 7am-2:30pm.) **Greyhound** stops at 105 Third Ave. in Beckley. (☎ 253-8333. Open M-F 7am-noon and 1-8:30pm, Sa 7am-noon and 3-8:30pm, Su 7-9am and 4-8:30pm.) Bike tours, rentals, and repairs are available at **Ridge Rider Mountain Bikes,** 103 Keller Ave., off U.S. 19 in Fayetteville. (☎ 574-2453 or 800-890-2453. Open daily 9am-6pm. Half-day $25, full-day $35.)

The park operates four **Visitors Centers.** Off Rte. 19 near Fayetteville at the northern extreme of the park, **Canyon Rim** has information on all park activities. (☎ 574-2115. Open June-Aug. daily 9am-8pm; Sept.-May 9am-5pm.) **Grandview,** on Rte. 9 near Beckley, attracts visitors in May when the rhododendrons are in bloom. (☎ 763-3145. Open May-Sept. daily 10am-8pm; Sept.-May 9am-5pm.) The other Visitors Centers are **Hinton,** on Rte. 20, and **Thurmond,** on Rte. 25 off I-19. (Hinton: ☎ 466-1597. Thurmond: ☎ 465-8550. Both open June-Aug. daily 9am-5pm; Sept.-May Sa-Su 9am-5pm.) Area information is also available at the **Fayetteville County Chamber of Commerce,** 310 Oyler Ave., in Oak Hill. (☎ 465-5617. Open daily 9am-5pm.) **Area code:** 304.

⌘ ACCOMMODATIONS. Budget motels can be found off **I-77** in Beckley ($45-60), while smaller lodges and guest houses are scattered throughout Fayetteville (accommodations info ☎ 800-225-5982). The **Whitewater Inn ❷,** on the corner of Appalachian Dr. off U.S. 19, features small but clean rooms at affordable rates. (☎ 574-2998. No in-room phones. Rooms $35-45.) **Canyon Rim Ranch ❶,** off Gatewood Rd. next to Cunard Access, offers bunkhouses and tidy cabins for six with A/C and shared bath. For the bunkhouses, visitors must supply their own linens, blankets, and towels. (☎ 574-3111. Bunkhouses $15 per person; cabins $89 per night.) Many raft companies operate private campgrounds, while four public campgrounds stake a claim in the area. The most central public campground, **Babcock State Park ❶,** on Rte. 41 south of U.S. 60, 15 mi. west of Rainelle, is the largest public campground in the Gorge and has 26 shaded sites and a range of cabins. Recreational activities include swimming, horseback riding, basketball, and tennis. (☎ 438-3004 or 800-225-5982. Sites $13, with electricity $17. Cabins $55-100.) On Ames Heights Rd., ½ mi. north of the New River Gorge Bridge, **Mountain State Campground ❶** has tent sites with platforms (by request) and cabins. (☎ 574-0947 or 800-252-7784. Open Apr.-Oct. Sites $7-8. Primitive cabins for 3 $75, for 10 $170.)

◪ SIGHTS. Where Rte. 19 crosses the river at the park's northern end, the man-made grandeur of the **New River Gorge Bridge,** the second highest bridge in the US, overlooks the Canyon Rim cut out of the gorge. Towering 876 ft. above New River, the bridge claims the world's largest single steel arch span. The Visitors Center at this site offers a decent vista, but for something more adventurous, descend the stairs to the lower level lookout. On **Bridge Day** (☎ 800-927-0263), the third Saturday in October, thousands of extreme sports enthusiasts leap off the bridge by bungee or parachute as on-lookers enjoy the festival's food and crafts. (To register: ☎ 707-793-2273; www.newrivercvb.com. $60 fee. Limited to 300 jumpers.) For more stable flying, charter planes offer **scenic plane rides** ($10) at the Fayetteville airstrip, 2 mi. south of town. Retired coal miners lead tours down a mine shaft at the **Beckley Exhibition Coal Mine,** on Ewart Ave. in Beckley at New River Park. Explore the mining industry by riding behind a 1930s engine through 150 ft. of underground passages. A jacket is suggested, as the tunnels are chilly. (☎ 256-1747. Open Apr.-Oct. daily 10am-5:30pm. $9, seniors $8, ages 4-12 $6, under 4 free.)

⌘ OUTDOOR ACTIVITIES. The **New River Gorge National River** runs north from Hinton to Fayetteville, falling over 750 ft. in 50 mi. As a way to conserve its magnificent natural, scenic, and historic value, the New River Gorge has been protected by the park service since 1958. The park service oversees all outdoor activities in the gorge. Whitewater rapids range from the family-friendly class I to the panic-inducing class V. A state information service (☎800-225-5982) connects you to some of nearly 20 outfitters on the New River and the rowdier Gauley River. Brochures are at the **Fayetteville County Chamber of Commerce** (see **Practical Information,** above). **USA Raft,** at the intersection of Rte. 16 and Rte. 19 in Fayetteville, runs cheap express trips. (☎800-346-7238. New River: Su-F $48, Sa $58. Gauley River: upper portion $55/$65, lower portion $66/$76.)

Though the renowned rapids draw the most tourists, the park's numerous trails provide hikers with an appreciation for the river and its coal industry. The most rewarding trails are the 2 mi. **Kaymoor Trail** and the 6.4 mi. **Thurmond Minden Trail** (only 2.5 mile round-trip to main overlook). Kaymoor starts at the bridge on Fayette Station Rd. and runs past the abandoned coke ovens of Kaymoor, a coal mining community that shut down in 1962. Thurmond Minden, left off Rte. 25 before Thurmond, has vistas of the New River, Dunloup Creek, and the historic community of Thurmond.

Horseback riding trips are another way to explore the gorge. **New River Trail Rides, Inc.** leads 2hr. rides, sunset trips, and overnight adventures year-round. (☎888-742-3982. Rides start at $39.) All levels of experience can take advantage of the Gorge's spectacular rock climbing with **New River Mountain Guides** (☎574-3872 or 800-732-5462), at Wiseman and Court St. in downtown Fayetteville. For a vertical challenge, climb the **Endless Wall,** which runs southeast along the New River and offers great river views from a height of 1000 ft. The wall is accessible from a trail off the parking lot at Canyon Rim Visitors Center (see **Practical Information,** above).

WEST VIRGINIA

With 80% of the state cloaked in untamed forests, hope of commercial expansion and economic prosperity once seemed a distant dream for West Virginia. When the coal mines—formerly West Virginia's primary source of revenue—became exhausted, the state appeared doomed, until government officials decided to capitalize on the area's evergreen expanses, tranquil trails, and raging rivers. Today, thousands of tourists forge paths into West Virginia's breathtaking landscape.

🔁 PRACTICAL INFORMATION

Capital: Charleston.

Visitor Info: Dept. of Tourism, 2101 Washington St. E., Bldg. #17, Charleston 25305; P.O. Box 30312 (☎800-225-5982; www.callwva.com). **US Forest Service,** 200 Sycamore St., Elkins 26241 (☎304-636-1800). Open M-F 8am-4:45pm.

Postal Abbreviation: WV. **Sales Tax:** 6%.

HARPERS FERRY   ☎304

A bucolic hillside town overlooking the Shenandoah and Potomac rivers, Harpers Ferry earned its fame when a band of abolitionists led by John Brown raided the US Armory in 1859. Although Brown was captured and executed, the raid brought the disagreements over slavery into the national spotlight. Brown's adamant belief in violence as the only means to overcome the problem of slavery soon gained credence, and the town became a major theater of conflict, changing hands eight times during the Civil War. Today, Harpers Ferry attracts more mild-mannered guests, as outdoor enthusiasts come to enjoy the town's surrounding wilderness.

⚡🔒 ORIENTATION & PRACTICAL INFORMATION. Harper's Ferry is on West Virginia's border with Maryland. **Amtrak** (☎535-6406), on Potomac St., has one train per day to Washington, D.C. (1¾hr., $17); reservations are required, as no tickets are sold at the station. The same depot serves **MARC**, the **Maryland Rail Commuter** (☎800-325-7245; open M-F 5:30am-8:15pm), offering a cheaper and more frequent service to Washington, D.C. (M-F 2 per day, $7.25). The **Appalachian Trail Conference (ATC**, see **Outdoor Activities**, p. 347) runs buses to Charles Town ($2). **The Outfitter**, 111 High St. (☎535-2087), about halfway along the Appalachian Trail, rents bikes ($20 per day), sells outdoor apparel, and conducts informative hiking tours. The **Visitors Center** is just inside the Harpers Ferry National Historic Park entrance, off Rte. 340. (☎535-6298. Open daily 8am-5pm. 3-day admission $5 per car, $3 per hiker or bicyclist. Shuttles leave the parking lot for town every 10min.) **Post Office:** 1010 Washington St., on the corner of Washington and Franklin St. (☎535-2479. Open M-F 8am-4pm, Sa 9am-noon.) **ZIP code:** 25425. **Area code:** 304.

🔒 ACCOMMODATIONS. Ragged hikers find a warm welcome and a roof over their heads at the social and spacious **Harpers Ferry Hostel (HI-AYH) ❶**, 19123 Sandy Hook Rd., at Keep Tryst Rd. off Rte. 340 in Knoxville, MD. This renovated auction house, complete with a backyard trail to Potomac overlooks, welcomes guests into four rooms with 37 well-cushioned beds. (☎301-834-7654. Check-in 7-9am and 6-11pm. Laundry, limited parking. 3-night max. stay. Open mid-Mar. to mid-Nov. Beds $15, nonmembers $17. Camping $6/9, includes use of hostel kitchen and bathrooms. Primitive campsites $3/4.50.) For private quarters, the **Hillside Motel ❷**, 19105 Keep Tryst Rd., 3 mi. from town in Knoxville, MD, has 19 clean, adequate rooms inside a sweet-looking stone motel. Unfortunately, hitting the nearby local restaurant and liquor store may be the wildest activity on a Saturday night. (☎301-834-8144. Singles $36; doubles $45; winter rates lower.) For a quainter stay, the charming **Harpers Ferry Guest House ❹**, 800 Washington St., is ideally located in the center of the historic district. (☎535-6955. M-Th $75, F-Su $95.) Camp along the **C&O Canal ❶**, where free camping sites lie 5 mi. apart, or in one of the five Maryland state park campgrounds within 30 mi. of Harpers Ferry. (Ranger station ☎301-739-4200.) **Greenbrier State Park ❶**, on Rte. 40 E off Rte. 66, has 165 campsites and outdoor recreation revolving around a lake. (☎301-791-4767 or 888-432-2267. Open May-Oct. Sites $20, with hookup $25.)

🔲 FOOD. Harpers Ferry has sparse offerings for hungry hikers on a budget. Most restaurants in town are pricey dining rooms in hotels and B&Bs. **Rte. 340** welcomes fast food fanatics with various chain restaurants. Across the street from the Hillside Motel, the **Cindy Dee Restaurant ❶**, 19112 Keep Tryst Rd., at Rte. 340, fries enough chicken ($5) to clog all your arteries, and their homemade apple dumplings ($2.50) are delectable. (☎301-695-8181. Open daily 7am-9pm.) The historic area, especially High St. and Potomac St., caters to the luncher with either burgers and fries or salads and steaks, but vacates for dinner. For nightlife and varied cuisine, the tiny **Shepherdstown**, 11 mi. north of Harpers Ferry, is practically a bustling culinary metropolis in these quiet parts. From the Ferry, take Rte. 340 S for 2 mi. to Rte. 230 N or bike 13 mi. along the C&O towpath. Amid the colonial architecture of E. German St., the **Mecklinburg Inn**, 128 E. German St., provides alliterative entertainment: rock 'n' roll and Rolling Rock for $1.75 on open mic night every Tuesday from 9pm to midnight. (☎876-2126. Happy Hour M-F 4:30-6:30pm. 21+ after 5pm. Open M-Th 3pm-12:30am, F 3pm-1:30am, Sa 1pm-2am, Su 1pm-12:30am.)

◻ SIGHTS. Parking in historic Lower Town is nonexistent; it's necessary to park at the Visitors Center and board the free, frequently-running bus to town, or walk about 20min. The bus stops at **Shenandoah St.**, where a barrage of replicated 19th-century shops greet visitors; for example, the **Dry Goods Store** displays clothes, hardware, liquor, and groceries that would have been sold over one hundred years ago. The **Harpers Ferry Industrial Museum**, on Shenandoah St., describes the methods used to harness the powers of the Shenandoah and Potomac rivers, and details the town's status as the endpoint of the nation's first successful rail line. The unsung stories of the Ferry captivate visitors at **Black Voices from Harpers Ferry**, on the corner of High and Shenandoah St., where well-trained actors play fettered slaves expressing their opinions of John Brown and his raid. Next door on High St., the plight of Harpers Ferry's slaves is further elaborated in the **Civil War Story**. Informative displays detail the importance of Harpers Ferry's strategic location to both the Union and Confederate armies. A ticket is required to enter some of the exhibits. The **Harpers Ferry National Historic Park** puts out the *Lower Town Trail Guide* to facilitate historical exploration. In addition, the park offers occasional battlefield demonstrations, parades, and other reenactments of Harpers Ferry's history. (☎ 535-6298. ¾-1hr. ranger tours in summer daily 10:30am-4pm. Free.)

The **John Brown Museum**, on Shenandoah St., just beyond High St., is the town's most captivating historical site. A 30min. video chronicles Brown's raid of the armory with a special focus on the moral and political implications of his actions. A daunting, steep staircase hewn into the hillside off High St. follows the **Appalachian Trail** to **Upper Harpers Ferry**, which has fewer sights but is laced with interesting historical tales. Allow 45min. to ascend past **Harper's House**, the restored home of town founder Robert Harper, and **St. Peter's Church**, where a pastor flew the Union Jack during the Civil War to protect the church.

◪ OUTDOOR ACTIVITIES. After digesting the historical significance of Harpers Ferry, many choose to soak up the town's outdoors. Go to the park's Visitors Center for trail maps galore. The **Maryland Heights Trail**, the town's most popular trail, located across the railroad bridge in the Lower Town of Harpers Ferry, wanders 4 mi. through steep Blue Ridge Mountains that include precipitous cliffs and glimpses of crumbling Civil War-era forts. The more wooded 7.5 mi. **Loudon Heights Trail** starts in Lower Town off the Appalachian Trail and leads to Civil War infantry trenches and scenic overlooks. For more moderate hiking, the 2.5 mi. **Camp Hill Trail** passes by the Harper Cemetery and ends at the former Stoner College. History dominates the **Bolivar Heights Trail**, starting at the northern end of Whitman Ave. Along the trail, exhibits and a three-gun battery frame the site where Stonewall Jackson and his Confederate troops once prevailed in battle. Stonewall's horse didn't fail him and neither should your feet on the easy 1.25 mi. loop.

The **Chesapeake & Ohio Canal** towpath, off the end of Shenandoah St. and over the railroad bridge, serves as a lasting reminder of the town's industrial roots and is the point of departure for a day's bike ride to Washington, D.C. The **Appalachian Trail Conference**, 799 Washington St., at Washington and Jackson St., offers catalogs with deals on hiking books and trail info, and provides a maildrop for hikers. (☎ 535-6331. Open late May-Oct. M-F 9am-5pm, Sa-Su 9am-4pm; Nov. to mid-May M-F 9am-5pm. Membership $30, seniors and students $25.)

River & Trail Outfitters, 604 Valley Rd., 2 mi. out of Harpers Ferry off Rte. 340, in Knoxville, MD, rents canoes, kayaks, inner tubes, and rafts. They also organize everything from scenic daytrips to placid rides down the Shenandoah River ($15) to wild overnights. (☎ 301-695-5177. Canoes $55 per day. Raft trips $55-60 per person, children $40. Tubing $32 per day.) At **Butt's Tubes, Inc.**, on Rte. 671 off Rte. 340, adventurers can buy a tube for the day and sell it back later. (☎ 800-836-9911. Open M-F 10:30am-3pm, last pickup at 5pm; Sa-Su 10am-4pm, last pickup at 6pm. $5-20.) Horse activities in the area include a variety of recreational trips offered through **Elk Mountain Trails** (☎ 301-834-8882).

MONONGAHELA NATIONAL FOREST   ☎304

Mammoth Monongahela National Forest sprawls across the Eastern portion of the state, sustaining wildlife (including nine endangered species), limestone caverns, weekend canoers, fly fisherman, spelunkers, and skiers. Over 500 campsites and 600 mi. of wilderness hiking trails lure adventurers to this outdoor haven. Surrounded by a luscious green thicket, Monongahela's roads are indisputably scenic, and the beauty of **Rte. 39** from Marlinton down to Goshen, VA, past Virginia's swimmable Maury River, is unsurpassed. (Rte. 150) The **Highland Scenic Hwy.** (Rte. 150) runs near the Nature Center and stretches 43 mi. from Richwood to U.S. 219, 7 mi. north of Marlinton. Tempting as it is to gaze at the forest's splendor, driving through the tortuous and often foggy roads can be treacherous—focus on the road.

Aside from displaying an informative wildlife exhibit that includes hissing rattlesnakes and carnivorous plants, the **Cranberry Mountain Nature Center** (see below) conducts free weekend tours of the **Cranberry Glades** June through August at 2pm. Wrapping 6 mi. around the glades is the **Cow Pasture Trail**, which passes a WWII German prison camp and beaver dams. Two popular short hikes in the area are the panoramic **High Rocks Trail**, leading off of the Highland Scenic Hwy., and the awesome 2 mi. **Falls of Hills Creek**, off Rte. 39/55 south of Cranberry Mountain Nature Center, with three falls ranging in height from 25-63 ft. *Remove valuables from vehicles, as thieves are common in this area.*

Those with several days might choose to hike, bike, or cross-country ski a part of the **Greenbrier River Trail,** a 75 mi., 1° grade track from Cass to North Caldwell; the trailhead is on Rte. 38 off U.S. 60. Lined with numerous access points and campgrounds, the trail offers multiple vistas and arguably the highest concentration of butterflies in West Virginia. **Watoga State Park** (☎799-4087), in Marlinton, has maps. For downhill delights, head over to **Canaan Valley** and the 54 trails at **Snowshoe resort,** just outside the National Forest. (☎572-1000. Open Nov.-Apr. daily 8:30am-10pm. M-F lift tickets $38, students and seniors $30; Sa-Su $44. Ski rental $26, children $18. Prices subject to change.) In summer, **mountain biking** is the outdoor activity of choice, though the abundant trout that flow through the Williams and Cranberry rivers make for great **fishing.** For all types of gear, try **Elk River ❸,** off Rte. 219 in Slatyfork. Trails to the National Forest begin right outside the door, and the outfitter gives year-round fly fishing tours while running a rustic B&B. (☎572-3771. $45-105 per night.)

Each of Monongahela's six districts has a campground and a recreation area, with ranger stations off Rte. 39 east of Marlinton and in the towns of Bartow and Potomack. (Open M-F 8am-4:30pm.) The forest **Supervisor's Office,** 200 Sycamore St., in Elkins, distributes a full list of sites and fees, and provides info about fishing and hunting. (☎636-1800. Open M-F 8am-4:45pm.) Established sites are $5; backcountry camping is free, but register at the **Cranberry Mountain Nature Center,** near the Highland Scenic Hwy. at the junction of Rte. 150 and Rte. 39/55. (☎653-4826. Open Apr.-Nov. daily 9am-5pm.) **Cranberry Campground ❶,** in the Gauley district, 13 mi. from Ridgewood on Forest Rd. 76, has hiking trails through cranberry bogs and campsites ($8). Most public transportation in the forest area goes to White Sulphur Springs at the forest's southern tip. **Amtrak,** 315 W. Main St. (☎800-872-7245 for reservations), across from the Greenbrier resort, runs trains Sunday, Wednesday, and Friday to Washington, D.C. from Charlottesville ($23), Hinton ($55), and White Sulphur Springs ($50). If you request it, an extra stop may be made in downtown Alderson. **Greyhound** (☎800-231-2222) will drop passengers off along Rte. 60 but does not run outbound from the forest. **Area code: 304.**

THE SOUTH

The American consciousness has become much more homogeneous since the 1860s, when regional differences ignited the bloodiest conflict in the nation's history. Yet differences persist between North and South, as much in memory as in practice: what's known as "the Civil War" up North is here rather defiantly referred to as "The War Between the States." And outside the area's commercial capitals—Atlanta, Nashville, Charlotte, and New Orleans—Southerners continue to live slower-paced and friendlier lives than their northern cousins.

Perhaps the greatest unifying characteristic of the South is its legacy of extreme racial division: slavery continues to place a nearly unbearable burden on Southern history, and the Civil Rights movement of the 1950s and 1960s remains too recent to be comfortably relegated to textbook study. At the same time, racial tensions and interactions have inspired many strands of American culture rooted in the South, from the novels of William Faulkner to nearly *all* American music: gospel, blues, jazz, country, R&B, and rock 'n' roll. Although much of the South remains relatively poor, the area maintains a rich cultural heritage; its architecture, cuisine, and language all borrow from Native American, English, African, French, and Spanish influences. Landscapes are equally varied—nature blessed the region with mountains, marshlands, sparkling beaches, and fertile soil.

HIGHLIGHTS OF THE SOUTH

FOOD. Some of the best Southern barbecue is at Dreamland in Mobile, AL (p. 430). New Orleans, LA (p. 439) has spicy and delicious Cajun cuisine. Southern "soul food" completes the spirit—Nita's Place, Savannah, GA (p. 418) will take you higher.

MUSIC. Make time for Tennessee—Nashville (p. 359) is the country music hot spot, but if you're a believer, you'll be heading to Graceland (p. 372).

CIVIL RIGHTS MEMORIALS. The Martin Luther King Center in Atlanta, GA (p. 401) and the Birmingham Civil Rights Institute, AL (p. 428) will move you to tears.

OLD SOUTH. Charm and Elegance. Nowhere is the antebellum way of life so well-kept as in stately Charleston, SC (p. 391) or Savannah, GA (p. 418).

KENTUCKY

Legendary for the duels, feuds, and stubborn spirit of its earlier inhabitants (such as the infamous Daniel Boone), Kentucky invites travelers to kick back, take a shot of local bourbon, grab a plate of burgoo (a spicy meat stew), and relax amid rolling hills and bluegrass. Today, the spirit of Kentucky can be boiled down into one pastime: going fast. Finding speed by horse and car, Kentucky is home to the Kentucky Derby and to the only American sports car, the Corvette. Louisville ignores its vibrant cultural scene and active nightlife at Derby time, and Lexington devotes much of its most beautiful farmland to breeding champion racehorses.

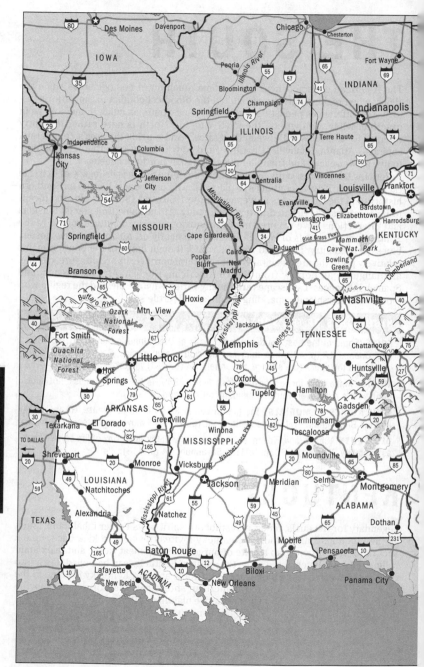

The South

🔼 PRACTICAL INFORMATION

Capital: Frankfort.

Visitor Info: Kentucky Dept. of Travel, 500 Mero St., Suite 2200, Frankfort 40601 (☎502-564-4930 or 800-225-8747; www.kentuckytourism.com). **Kentucky State Parks,** 500 Mero St., Suite 1100, Frankfort 40601 (☎800-255-7275; www.kystateparks.com).

Postal Abbreviation: KY. **Sales Tax:** 6%.

LOUISVILLE ☎502

Louisville (pronounced "Lua-Vul" by locals) is caught between two pasts. One past left a legacy of smokestacks, stockyards, and crumbling structure; the other shines with beautiful Victorian neighborhoods, ornate buildings, and the elegant, twin-spired Churchill Downs. Louisville's premier attraction, however, remains the Kentucky Derby. This extravagant event, the nation's most prestigious horse race, will pack the city with visitors May 3, 2003.

🔳 🔼 ORIENTATION & PRACTICAL INFORMATION. Interstates through the city include **I-65** (north-south expressway), **I-71,** and **I-64.** The easily accessible **Watterson Expwy. (I-264)** rings the city, while the **Gene Snyder Fwy. (I-265)** circles farther out. In central downtown, **Main St.** and **Broadway** run east-west, and **Preston Hwy.** and **19th St.** run north-south. The **West End,** beyond 20th St., is a rough area. The **Louisville International Airport** (☎368-6524) is 15min. south of downtown on I-65; take bus #2 into the city. A taxi downtown is $13-15. **Greyhound,** 720 W. Muhammad Ali Blvd. (☎561-28051; open 24hr.), at 7th St., runs to Chicago (5hr., 7 per day, $38); Cincinnati (2hr., 10 per day, $19.50); and Indianapolis (1¼hr., 9 per day, $17.50). **Transit Authority River City's (TARC)** extensive bus system serves most of the metro area. (☎585-1234. Runs daily 5am-11:30pm. 75¢, M-F 6:30-8:30am and 3:30-5:30pm $1.) Two free trolley routes service Main St. and 4th St. downtown. Operates daily 8am-5pm. **Taxis: Yellow Cab,** ☎636-5511. **Bike rental: Highland Cycle,** 1737 Bardstown Rd. (☎458-7832. Open M-F 9am-5:30pm, Sa 9am-4:30pm. Bikes from $3.25 per hr., $12 per day.) **Visitor info: Louisville Convention and Visitors Bureau,** 3rd and Market St. (☎584-2121. Open M-Sa 8:30am-5pm, Su noon-4pm.) **Hotlines: Rape Hotline** (☎581-7273) and **Crisis Center** (☎589-4313) both operate 24hr.; **Gay/Lesbian Hotline** (☎457-7613. Operates daily 6-10pm.) **Post Office:** 1420 Gardner Ln. (☎454-1766. Open M-F 7:30am-7pm, Sa 7:30am-3pm.) **ZIP code:** 40213. **Area code:** 502.

🔽 HITCHIN' POSTS. Lodging in downtown Louisville is easy to find but pricey. Budget motels are on **I-65** near the airport or across the river in **Jeffersonville. Newburg Rd.,** 6 mi. south, is also a budget haven. To get Derby Week lodging, make reservations six to 12 months in advance and be prepared to spend big. Starting mid-March, the Visitors Bureau helps travelers arrange rooms for the event.

Super 8 ❸, 927 S. 2nd St., has basic rooms, and an airport shuttle can be secured by appointment. (☎584-8888. Singles $53; doubles $58. Some wheelchair accessible rooms.) For those that are truly on a budget, **Emily Boone Guest House ❶,** 102 Pope St., off Frankfort St., rents space in a safe neighborhood near several restaurants and a bus stop. It's literally a foam mattress on a basement floor, but it's only 10 bucks a night. (☎585-3430. Be sure to call ahead.) The local franchise of the **KOA ❶** regime, 900 Marriot Dr., has paved camping convenient to downtown. Follow I-65 N across the bridge and take Exit 1. (☎282-4474. Grocery, playground, free pool access, mini golf, and fishing lake. Sites for 2 $23, with hookup $28; $4 per extra person, under 18 $2.50. Kabins for 2 $35. Rates drop mid-Nov. to mid-Mar.)

◘ OATS & HAY. Louisville's food is varied, but good budget fare can be hard to find in the heart of downtown. **Bardstown Rd.** is lined with cafes, budget eateries, and local and global cuisine, while **Frankfort Rd.** is rapidly catching up to Bardstown with restaurants and chi-chi cafes of its own. Downtown, **Theater Sq.**, at Broadway and 4th St., has several restaurants that serve various lunch options. **▓Twice Told ❶**, 1604 Bardstown Rd., was the first coffeehouse in Louisville, and it's still hot after all these years. Poetry readings, comedy, punk, jazz, and blues entertain at the stage in the back. (☎456-0507. Portabella melt $5.75. Tu open stage. Shows M-Sa at 9pm. Cover under $10; some shows free. Open M-Th noon-midnight, F noon-1am, Sa 9am-1am.) **Mark's Feed Store ❷**, 1514 Bardstown Rd., serves award-winning barbecue in a dining room decorated with metal animal feed ads. (☎459-6275. Sandwiches $4-5. BBQ dinners under $8. M free dessert after 4pm. Open Su-Th 11am-10pm, F-Sa 11am-11pm.) **Molly Malloy's Irish Pub and Restaurant ❷**, 933 Baxter Ave., is perfect for a quick bite to eat. Fantastic pub fare and salads (under $10) are served up on a lovely patio. (☎473-1222. Open daily 11am-11pm.)

◙ NOT JUST A ONE-HORSE TOWN. The **Highlands** strip, buses #17 and 23, runs along Baxter/Bardstown and is bounded by Broadway and Trevilian Way on the south. This "anti-mall" of unfranchised cafes, pizza pubs, antique shops, and record stores is worth a gander. Nearby, the **American Printing House for the Blind,** 1839 Frankfort Ave., has a small but fascinating museum on the development of Braille and other lesser-known systems for aiding the blind. (☎895-2405. Open M-F 9am-4:30pm; guided tours 10am and 2pm. Free.) Farther south, the impressive galleries of the **J.B. Speed Art Museum,** 2035 S. 3rd St., bus #2 or 4, have a dynamic collection that ranges from early Southern furniture to works by classic French Impressionists like Cézanne. (☎634-2700. Open Tu-W and F 10:30am-4pm, Th 10:30am-8pm, Sa 10:30am-5pm, Su noon-5pm. Free; parking $1.50 per hr.)

The **Belle of Louisville**, an authentic paddle-wheel craft built in 1914, docks at 4th St. and River Rd. (☎574-2355. 2hr. cruises depart from Riverfront Plaza early June to early Sept.; call for schedule and prices.) Nearby, the world's tallest baseball bat (120 ft.) leans against the **Hillerich and Bradsby Co. (Louisville Slugger Factory and Museum),** 800 W. Main. Inside a film about the history of the illustrious baseball bat and a tour of the museum show how Sluggers are made. At the tour's end, visitors receive a free miniature bat. (☎588-7228. Open Dec.-Mar. M-Sa 9am-5pm; Apr.-Nov. M-Sa 9am-4pm, Su noon-5pm. $6, seniors $5, children $3.50.)

▨ WIN, PLACE, OR SHOW. The **Kentucky Derby Festival** kicks off with 64 tons of fireworks at **Thunder Over Louisville,** the largest fireworks show in North America, and continues for two weeks with balloon and steamboat races, concerts, and a parade. All of this is a mere prelude to the climactic 80,000 mint juleps consumed on the first Saturday in May at the nation's most prestigious horse race, the **Kentucky Derby,** also referred to as the **Run for the Roses.** The rollicking, week-long extravaganza leading up to the big day corrals over 500,000 visitors. When the horses leave the gate, the stands are mesmerized by "the most exciting two minutes in sports;" after all, $15 million ride on each Derby Day. A one- to ten-year waiting list stands between you and a ticket for the Derby, but never fear—on Derby morning, tickets are sold for standing-room-only spots in the infield ($35). No one is turned away, but these seats do not afford a very good view of the track. They will, however, give an idea of the spectacle surrounding the race, a sneak peek at the famous hats worn by female spectators, and a chance to size up the horses as the jockeys lead them to the gate. Even if you miss the Derby, be sure to visit **Churchill Downs,** 700 Central Ave., 3 mi. south of downtown. Take bus #4 to Central Ave. No bets are necessary to admire the twin spires, the colonial columns, the gardens,

THE SOUTH

THE VINE THAT ATE THE SOUTH So some refer to the leafy kudzu plant, which seems to cover everything in the Deep South that stands still: trees, telephone poles, abandoned buildings, occasionally entire hillsides. Local legend has it that nervous Southern mothers often keep watch over their children on summer nights, for fear that the vine—capable of growing a foot daily—will choke their sleeping infants. Defined as a "weed" and a "pest plant" for its tendency to obliterate native vegetation, kudzu is nonetheless admired for its ability to enshroud ordinary landscape in surreal, biomorphic abstraction. Aesthetics aside, however: it's still best to close the window before turning out the light...

and the sheer scale of the track. (☎636-4400. Races late Apr.-Nov.; schedules and prices vary. Tours available through the Kentucky Derby Museum. $2, seniors $1, under 13 free.) The **Kentucky Derby Museum,** at Gate One at Churchill Downs, offers a short film on a 360° screen, a simulated horse race for betting practice, tips on exactly what makes a horse a "sure thing," a chance to see a thoroughbred and talk with its trainer, and tours of the Downs every day. (☎637-1111. Open M-Sa 9am-5pm, Su noon-5pm; last tour at 4:15pm. $7, seniors $6, ages 5-12 $3, under 5 free.)

🏛🎭 **HORSIN' AROUND.** The free weekly arts and entertainment newspaper, *Leo,* is available at most downtown restaurants and at the Visitors Center. All's well that ends well at the **Kentucky Shakespeare Festival,** at the zoo and in Central Park, during June and July. (☎583-8738. Performances 8pm. Free.) **The Louisville Palace,** 625 S. 4th Ave. (☎583-4555), is one of only 15 remaining "atmospheric theaters." Go to see the Broadway shows, comedy acts, and big-name music acts that play in the lavish Spanish Baroque interior.

Clubs cluster on Baxter Ave. near Broadway. **Phoenix Hill Tavern,** 644 Baxter Ave., cranks out blues, rock, and reggae on four stages, including a deck and roof garden. (☎589-4957. Cover $2-5. Open W-Th and Sa 8pm-3:30am, F 5pm-3:30am.) For gay nightlife, make **The Connection,** 120 Floyd St. This black-and-white-and-mirrored-all-over club combines four venues under one roof. The different bars have different theme nights and varying hours, but Monday through Saturday at least two are open after 10pm. (☎585-5752. Cover $4-5. Open M-W 5pm-2am and Th 5pm-4am; Dance Bar Th-Sa 10pm-4am; showroom F-Sa 10:30pm-3:30am.)

NEAR LOUISVILLE

BARDSTOWN. Kentucky's second-oldest city, 17 mi. east on Rte. 245 from I-65 Exit 112, is proudly known as the "Bourbon Capital of the World." In 1791, Kentucky Baptist Reverend Elijah Craig left a fire unattended while heating oak boards to make a barrel for his aging whiskey. The boards were charred, but Rev. Craig carried on, and bourbon was born in that first charred wood barrel. Today, 90% of the nation's bourbon hails from Kentucky, and 60% of that is distilled in Nelson and Bullitt Counties. **Jim Beam's American Outpost,** 15 mi. west of Bardstown in Clermont off Rte. 245, features the "master distiller emeritus" himself; Jim Beam's grandson, Booker Noe, narrates a film about bourbon. Jim Beam's has free sampling (M-Sa), as well as complimentary lemonade, coffee, and bourbon candies. (☎543-9877. Open M-Sa 9am-4:30pm, Su 1-4pm. Free.) Those who want an up close and personal introduction to the way bourbon is made should visit **Maker's Mark**

Distillery, 19 mi. southeast of Bardstown, follow signs from downtown, on Rte. 52 E in Loretto. Any day but Sunday, buy a bottle of bourbon in the gift shop, and you can hand-dip it yourself in the label's famous trademark red wax. (☎865-2099. Tours every hr. M-Sa 10:30am-3:30pm, Su 1:30-3:30pm. Free.) The **Oscar Getz Museum of Whiskey History,** 114 N. 5th St., in Spalding Hall, examines Kentucky's favorite beverage along with the state's other contribution to alcohol history—rabid Prohibitionist Carry Nation. (☎348-2999. Open May-Oct. M-Sa 9am-5pm, Su 1-5pm; Nov.-Apr. Tu-Sa 10am-4pm, Su 1-4pm.) **Visitor info: Bardstown Visitors Center,** 107 E. Stephen Foster Ave. (☎348-4877 or 800-638-4877. Open Apr.-Sept. M-F 8am-6pm, Sa 9am-6pm, Su 11am-3pm; Oct.-Mar. M-Sa 8am-5pm.)

BOWLING GREEN. Auto enthusiasts inevitably pay their respects to the home of the classic American sports car, the Corvette. The extensive **National Corvette Museum,** 350 Corvette Dr., off I-65 Exit 28, displays 'Vettes from the original chrome-and-steel '53 to futuristic concept cars; the display rotates constantly. (☎800-538-3883. Open daily 8am-5pm. $8, seniors $5, ages 6-16 $4.50.) To see their production in action, visit the **General Motors Corvette Assembly Plant,** Exit 28 off I-65. If you're lucky, you may even get a chance to test-start one of the mint condition products. (☎270-745-8419. Tours M-F 9am and 1pm. Free.) **Time zone:** Central.

MAMMOTH CAVE ☎859

Hundreds of enormous caves and narrow passageways cut through **Mammoth Cave National Park,** 80 mi. south of Louisville off I-65, then west on Rte. 70. Mammoth Cave comprises the world's longest network of cavern corridors—over 365 mi. in length. The mine produced most of the gunpowder used in the War of 1812. After the war, the mine continued its profitable history by opening its doors to the public, giving tourists a little bang for their buck. The first tours ran in 1816, and the original tour guides were slaves who worked the cave's saltpeter mining operation; nowadays tours are guided by park rangers. The caves are a chilly 54°F; be sure to bring a jacket. There are a wide range of tours available. The **Historic Tour** takes approximately 2hr. and covers 2 mi. of caves. A basic tour, it gives visitors a feeling for the caves and a chance to see most of the historic sights that lie within their walls. (In summer every hr. 8:15am-3:15pm; in winter tour times vary. $9, seniors and children $5.) The **Discovery Tour** consumes a bit less time and money. The ½hr. self-guided tour leads straight to one of the largest rooms in the cave. (Visitors admitted 10am-2:15pm. $4, seniors and children $2.) For the truly adventurous, the **Wild Cave Tour** is not to be missed. Twists, turns, and tight spaces lie in store for spelunkers on this 6hr. excursion—bring hiking boots. (Must be 16 or older. One tour daily at 10am. $45, seniors $23.) Above ground, the park also features numerous walking, biking, and horseback riding trails. (Visitors Center: ☎758-2328 or 800-967-2283. Reservations recommended. Open daily 7:30am-7pm; off-season 8am-6pm.) Camping with toilets is available at the **Headquarters campground ❶,** near the Visitors Center. (☎800-967-2283. Reservations recommended. Sites $14.) For RV sites, check out **Maple Springs Campground ❶,** across the river from the Visitors Center by ferry, or by a 35 mi. detour. (☎800-967-2283. Reservations required. $25.) **Backcountry camping** permits can be obtained for free at the Visitors Center. For those who choose not to camp, charming rooms await at the **Mammoth Cave Hotel ❸,** next to the Visitors Center. (☎758-2225. Cabins without A/C $52. Singles from $62; doubles from $68.) **Greyhound** travels to Cave City, just east of I-65 on Rte. 70. **Time zone:** Central.

THE SOUTH

LEXINGTON   ☎ 859

In the early 1800s, Lexington's wealth from tobacco and hemp farms helped fund one of the most active cultural scenes west of the Appalachians, leaving a legacy of historic mansions near downtown. These days Lexington's most high-profile money comes from horse farming. Farms that have raised some of the most famous racehorses in the world ring the city in the scenic "bluegrass country" for which eastern Kentucky is famous.

▄ TRANSPORTATION

Airport: Blue Grass, 4000 Versailles Rd. (☎255-7218), southwest of downtown. Ritzy downtown hotels run shuttles, but there is no public transportation. Taxi to downtown about $20.

Buses: Greyhound, 477 New Circle Rd. NW (☎299-0428). Open M-F 7:30am-11pm, Sa-Su 7:30am-6pm. To: **Cincinnati** (1½hr., 6 per day, $20-25); **Knoxville** (4hr., 4 per day, $41-44); **Louisville** (2hr., 4 per day, $16-17).

Public Transit: LexTran, 109 W. Louden Ave. (☎253-4636). Buses leave from the Transit Center, 220 E. Vine St., on a long block between Limestone and Rose St., generally 15min. before and after the hour. Serves the university and city outskirts. Most routes run 6am-midnight. $1, seniors and disabled 50¢, ages 6-18 80¢; transfers free. On racing days, LexTran runs a $1 shuttle to Keeneland.

Taxis: Lexington Yellow Cab, ☎231-8294.

▄▄ ORIENTATION & PRACTICAL INFORMATION

New Circle Rd. (Rte. 4/U.S. 60 bypass) loops the city, intersecting with many roads that connect the downtown district to the surrounding towns. **High, Vine,** and **Main St.,** running east-west, and **Limestone** and **Broadway St.,** running north-south, provide the best routes through downtown. Beware of the many curving one-way streets downtown and near the **University of Kentucky (UK).**

Visitor info: Lexington Convention and Visitors Bureau, 301 E. Vine St. (☎233-7299 or 800-845-3959; www.visitlex.com), at Rose St. Open in summer M-F 8:30am-5pm, Sa 10am-5pm, Su noon-5pm; off-season closed Su.

Hotlines: Crisis Intervention, ☎253-2737 or 800-928-8000. **Rape Crisis,** ☎253-2511 or 800-656-4673. Both 24hr.

Medical Services: St. Joseph East Hospital, 150 N. Eagle Creek Dr. (☎268-4800). **Lexington Women's Diagnostic Center,** 1701 Bobolink Dr. (☎277-8485).

Internet access: Lexington Public Library, 140 E. Main St. (☎231-5500), at Limestone St. Open M-Th 9am-9pm, Su 1-5pm.

Post Office: 1088 Nandino Blvd. (☎254-6156). Open M-F 8am-5pm, Sa 9am-1pm. **ZIP code:** 40507. **Area code:** 859.

▄ ACCOMMODATIONS

A concentration of horse-related wealth raises accommodation prices; the cheapest places are outside the city on New Circle Rd. or near I-75. The Visitors Bureau (see above) can help find lodging.

Microtel, 2240 Buena Vista Dr. (☎299-9600), off I-75 at the Winchester Rd. (Rte. 60) exit. Take bus #7. Pleasant motel rooms with window seats. A/C and cable TV. Wheelchair-accessible rooms available. Singles Su-Th $45, F-Sa $52; doubles $52/56. ❸

Comfort Suites, 5531 Athens Boonesboro Rd. (☎263-0777), Exit 104 off of I-75, has large, comfortable rooms with microwave and fridge. A great deal, even though it is about 20min. from the city center. Singles from $39. ❷

Kentucky Horse Park Campground, 4089 Ironworks Pike (☎259-4257 or 800-370-6416), 10 mi. north of downtown off I-75 at Exit 120. Groomed camping plus laundry, showers, basketball courts, and swimming pool. Tent sites are wide open, while RV sites nicely mix shade and lawn. Max. stay 2 weeks. Apr.-Oct. $13, with hookup $18, seniors $15.50. Nov.-Mar. $11/14/12. ❶

🝆🝎 FOOD & NIGHTLIFE

🝂**Atomic Cafe: Caribbean Restaurant and Bar ❸,** 465 N. Limestone St., in Lexington, excites the taste buds, and the ears as well. Gourmands will enjoy jerk chicken or spicy fish entrees ($10-15) while toes tap to live reggae music. (☎254-1969. Open Tu-Sa 4pm-10:30pm; drinks until 1am.) With a menu of international and veggie/vegan meals that change nightly, **Alfalfa Restaurant ❸,** 557 S. Limestone St. near UK, serves up great, affordable food. Dinners with filling soups and salads range in price from $7-14. (☎253-0014. Live jazz, folk, and other music Tu-Sa 8-10pm. No cover. Open M 11am-2pm, Tu-Th 11am-2pm and 5:30-9pm, F-Sa 10am-2pm and 5:30-10pm, Su 10am-2pm.) At the **Parkette Drive-In ❶,** 1230 E. New Circle Rd. between Liberty and Winchester Rd., bargain food comes in a classic 50s setting. Booths inside let carless folks wax nostalgic. (☎254-8723. Burgers, chicken strips, and hot dogs $1-5. Open Su 11am-11pm, M-Th 10am-11:30pm, F-Sa 10am-12:30am.)

In general, those looking for a good time after dark hit the area around Main St. west of Limestone St. and the eastern fringes of UK. For current info, read the "Weekender" section of the Friday *Herald-Leader*. **The Bar,** 224 E. Main St., a popular disco cabaret/lounge complex, caters to gays and lesbians. (☎255-1551. Cover F $4, Sa $5. Lounge open M-Sa 4pm-1am; club Tu-Th 11pm-1am, F 10pm-1am, Sa 10pm-3:30am.) **Lynagh's Pub,** in University Plaza at Woodland and Euclid St., is a casual, buzzing neighborhood bar near UK that has been a Lexington staple for years. (☎255-1292. Cover $3-15. Open M-Sa 11am-1am, Su noon-11pm.)

🜚 SIGHTS

CITY ATTRACTIONS. A few blocks northeast of the town center, in the **Gratz Park** area near the old Public Library, a tiny haven of fantastically beautiful houses stands as a throwback to a time when plantation owners escaped the suffocating heat of the South in milder Lexington. Wrap-around porches, stone foundations, and rose-covered trellises distinguish these old estates, all of which are situated around the small park, from newer homes. The **Hunt Morgan House** stands at the end of the park across from the Carnegie Literacy Center. Built in 1814 by John Wesley Hunt—the first millionaire west of the Alleghenies—the house was called home by many notable characters, including Nobel laureate Thomas Hunt and the colorful Confederate General John Hunt Morgan, the "Thunderbolt of the Confederacy." As legend has it, Hunt Morgan, while being pursued by Union troops, rode his horse up the front steps and into the house, leaned down to kiss his mother, and rode out the back door. In the week before Halloween, Gratz Park "ghost tours" begin here in the evenings—brief tours of the area that focus on the neighborhood's many other-worldly inhabitants. *(201 N. Mill St. At W. 2nd St. ☎233-3290. Tours 15min. past the hr. Tu-Sa 10am-4pm, Su 2-5pm. $5, students $3.)* Another famous home near Gratz Park is the **Mary Todd Lincoln House.** The childhood home of President Abraham Lincoln's wife, the house was the first existing monument to a First Lady. Visitors can experience a bit of Mary's childhood and even grasp the banister that Lincoln used when he climbed the stairs. How's that for walking in Honest Abe's footsteps? *(578 W. Main St.* ☎ *233-9999. Open mid-March to mid-Nov. M-Sa 10am-4pm. $7, children $6.)* Hollywood jeweler George W. Headley's creations are shown at the **Headley-Whitney Museum.** Included on the museum grounds is the "Shell Grotto," a former carriage house that Headly studded with thousands of seashells. *(4435 Old Frankfort Pike.* ☎ *255-6653. Open Feb.-Dec. Tu-F 10am-5pm, Sa-Su noon-5pm. $6, students $4, seniors $5.)*

HORSE ATTRACTIONS. Lexington horse farms are gorgeous places to visit; the Visitors Bureau can help arrange tours of open farms. **Kentucky Horse Park** has extensive equine facilities, a museum tracing the history, science, and pageantry of horses, and many live examples. The last weekend in April, the horse park hosts the annual Rolex tournament qualifier for the US equestrian team. *(4089 Ironworks Pkwy. Off Ironworks Pike, Exit 120 from I-75.* ☎ *233-4303. Open mid-Mar. to Oct. daily 9am-5pm; Nov. to mid-Mar. W-Su 9am-5pm. Apr.-Oct. $12, ages 7-12 $6; Nov.-Mar. $9/5.50; live horse shows and horse-drawn vehicle tours included. 45min. horse ride and tour additional $13; pony rides $4. Parking $2. Wheelchair accessible.)* Every April, the **Keeneland Race Track** holds the final prep race for the Kentucky Derby. It also has impressive grounds worth exploring while waiting for the races. A $4 cafeteria-style breakfast and the chance to chat with a jockey or horse owner may make the track kitchen the best breakfast deal in town. *(4201 Versailles Rd. West across U.S. 60 across from the airport.* ☎ *254-3412 or 800-456-3412. Races Oct. and Apr.; post time 1pm. $2.50. Workouts free and open to the public mid-Mar. to Nov. 6-10am. Free. Breakfast mid-Feb. to Jan. daily 5:30-11am.)*

🏇 DAYTRIP FROM LEXINGTON

WHITE HALL

At Exit 95 off I-75, the elegant Georgian-Italianate mansion **White Hall** was home to abolitionist (not boxer) Cassius M. Clay, cousin of Senator Henry Clay. Cassius Clay was known not only for his views on abolition, but also for firing a cannon at tax collectors. In addition, he wrote a book on the finer points of knife-fighting, a field of personal expertise (he killed an intruder in his home at the age of 87). The house may be as unique, though thankfully not as threatening to strangers, as Clay himself. Though the original house still stands in the interior, Clay built a grander home around it, complete with an innovative plumbing system that collected water from the roof and siphoned it through the taps of sinks, bathtubs, and toilets. (☎ 623-9178. 45min. guided tours only. Open Apr.-Aug. daily 9am-5:30pm, last tour at 4:30pm; Sept.-Oct. W-Su 9am-5:30pm. $5, under 13 $2.50, under 6 free.)

> ## WHISKEY BUSINESS
> All bourbon is whiskey, but not all whiskey is bourbon. So what makes bourbon so special? It's all in the making, codified by the US government. For alcohol to be bourbon, it must fulfill these six requirements:
>
> 1. It must be aged in a new white oak barrel, flame-charred on the inside. (Scotch, alternatively, must be aged in used barrels.)
> 2. It must age at least 2 years in that barrel.
> 3. It must be at least 51% corn.
> 4. It cannot be distilled over 160 proof (80% alcohol).
> 5. It cannot go into the barrel over 125 proof.
> 6. It can have no additives or preservatives.

TENNESSEE

In the east, Tennessee explodes out of the Appalachian Mountains in Great Smoky National Park. While in the west, the terrain settles out into the wide Mississippi River. But the varied terrain of the Volunteer State has one unifying factor: music. From the twang of eastern bluegrass to the woes of Nashville country and from the roguish jazz and gut-wrenching blues of Memphis, music is the soul of the state. Similarly, some might argue that the heart of the state bursts out of Jack Daniels Tennessee Whiskey, while spirit is bottled back up and redeemed by Tennessee's Bible-producing business, the largest in the world.

◪ PRACTICAL INFORMATION

Capital: Nashville.

Visitor info: Tennessee Dept. of Tourist Development, 320 6th Ave., Nashville 37243 (☎ 615-741-2159; www.tourism.state.tn.us). Open M-F 8am-4:30pm. **Tennessee State Parks Information,** 401 Church St., Nashville (☎ 800-421-6683).

Postal Abbreviation: TN. **Sales Tax:** 6-8%.

NASHVILLE   ☎ 615

Long-forgotten Francis Nash is one of only four Revolutionary War heroes honored with US city names (Washington, Wayne, and Knox are the others), but his tenuous foothold in history pales in comparison to Nashville's notoriety as the banjo-pickin', foot-stompin' capital of country music. Be prepared to have a rollicking good time in a city where live music and beer are available 24 hours a day. Nicknamed "the Athens of the South," Nashville's architecture is one of a kind, and its support for higher education is evidenced by the presence of the prestigious Vanderbilt and Fisk Universities. Home to the Southern Baptists, the city wears the moniker of the "buckle of the bible belt."

▐ TRANSPORTATION

Airport: Metropolitan (☎ 275-1675), 8 mi. south of downtown. An airport **shuttle** (☎ 275-1180) operates out of major downtown hotels. $11, round-trip $17. The bus system is complicated and does not run very frequently. Bus fare downtown $1.55, includes a transfer. Taxi to downtown $20.

Buses: Greyhound, 200 8th Ave. S. (☎ 255-3556), at Broadway downtown. Borders on a rough neighborhood, but the station is well-lit. Station open 24hr. To: **Birmingham** (3½hr., 7 per day, $26-28); **Chattanooga** (2½hr., 5 per day, $18-19); **Knoxville** (3½hr., 7 per day, $22-24); **Memphis** (4hr., 6 per day, $27-29).

Public Transit: Metropolitan Transit Authority, or **MTA,** (☎ 862-5950). Buses operate on limited routes, usually once per hr. Times vary route to route, but none run M-F before 5:30am or after 11:15pm; Sa-Su less frequent service. $1.45, transfers 10¢.

Taxis: Nashville Cab, ☎ 242-7070. **Music City Taxi,** ☎ 262-0451.

Car Rental: Thrifty, 414 11th Ave. N. (☎ 248-8888), downtown. $33 per day. Must be over 25 with a major credit card.

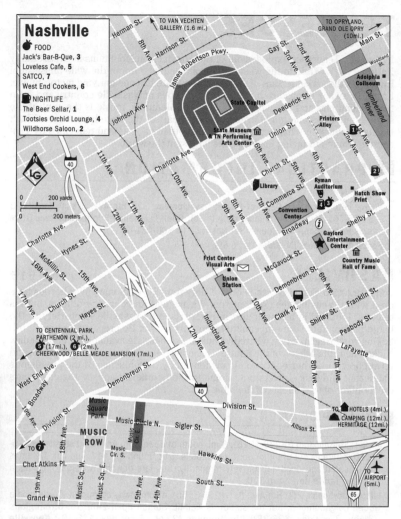

Nashville

🍎 FOOD
Jack's Bar-B-Que, **3**
Loveless Cafe, **5**
SATCO, **7**
West End Cookers, **6**

🍸 NIGHTLIFE
The Beer Sellar, **1**
Tootsies Orchid Lounge, **4**
Wildhorse Saloon, **2**

✦❷ ORIENTATION & PRACTICAL INFORMATION

Nashville's streets are fickle, often interrupted by curving parkways and one-way streets. Names change constantly and without warning. **Broadway,** the main east-west thoroughfare, melts into **West End Ave.** just outside downtown at Vanderbilt St. and I-40. In downtown, numbered avenues run north-south, parallel to the Cumberland River. The curve of **James Robertson Pkwy.** encloses the north end, becoming **Main St.** on the other side of the river (later **Gallatin Pike**) and **McGavock St.** at the south end. Be careful where you park, and mind the parking meters; it's easy to get a ticket. *The area south of Broadway between 2nd and 7th Ave. and the region north of James Robertson Pkwy. are both unsafe at night.*

Visitor info: Nashville Visitors Bureau, 501 Broadway (☎259-4747), in the Gaylord Entertainment Center (previously the Nashville Arena), off I-65 at Exit 84, James Robertson Pkwy. Open daily 8:30am-7pm; off-season 8:30am-5:30pm.

Hotlines: Crisis Line, ☎244-7444. **Rape Hotline,** ☎256-8526. Both 24hr. **Gay and Lesbian Switchboard,** ☎297-0008. Operates nightly 6-9pm.

Medical Services: Metro General Hospital, 1818 Albion St. (☎341-4000).

Internet access: Nashville Public Library, 615 Church St. (☎862-5800), between 6th and 7th Ave. Open M-Th 9am-8pm, F 9am-6pm, Sa 9am-5pm, Su 2-5pm.

Post Office: 901 Broadway (☎255-3613), next to Union Station. Open M-F 7:30am-6pm, Sa 9am-2pm. **ZIP code:** 37202. **Area code:** 615.

⛏ ACCOMMODATIONS

Finding a room in Nashville can be expensive, especially in summer. There are several deals on motel rooms, and coupons are available at the Visitors Center. Budget motels concentrate around **W. Trinity Ln.** and **Brick Church Pike,** off I-65. Dirtcheap hotels inhabit the area around **Dickerson Rd.** and **Murfreesboro,** but the neighborhood is seedy at best. Closer to downtown (but still sketchy), several motels huddle on **Interstate Dr.** just over the Woodland St. Bridge.

Ramada Inn at the Stadium, 303 Interstate Dr. (☎244-6690), next to the stadium and just blocks from downtown. For those who don't mind spending a little more, the Ramada has fantastic rooms with A/C, HBO, and cable TV. Laundry, deluxe continental breakfast, and a guitar-shaped pool. Rooms from $49. ❸

The Cumberland Inn, 150 W. Trinity Ln. (☎226-1600 or 800-704-1028), at Exit 87A off I-65 N, has cheerful rooms, many with a fridge. A/C, HBO, laundry, and continental breakfast. Singles $25; doubles $33. ❶

Knights Inn, 1360 Brick Church Pike (☎226-4500 or 800-843-5644), at Exit 87B on I-65, has nice clean rooms at a great price, despite the shabby outer appearance. A/C, cable TV, coffee and donuts. Singles M-F $25, Sa-Su $30; doubles $32/37. ❶

Nashville Holiday Travel Park, 2572 Music Valley Dr. (☎889-4226 or 800-547-4480), near Opryland USA, has a wooded area for tenting and crowded RV sites. Sites for 2 $21, water and electricity $33, full hookup $41; each additional person over 11 $4. ❶

Opryland KOA, 2626 Music Valley Dr. (☎889-0286), has a pool and, true to its name, live summer music. Sites $23, with hookup $36. 1-room kabins with A/C and electricity $40, 2-room kabins $49. ❶

🍴 FOOD

In Nashville, music influences even the local delicacies. **Goo-Goo Clusters** (peanuts, pecans, chocolate, caramel, and marshmallow), sold most places, bear the initials of the Grand Ole Opry. Nashville's other finger-lickin' traditions, barbecue or fried chicken followed by pecan pie, are no less sinful. Restaurants for collegiate tastes and budgets cram **21st Ave., West End Ave.,** and **Elliston Pl.,** near Vanderbilt.

Loveless Cafe, 8400 Rte. 100 (☎646-9700 or 800-889-2432). A Nashville tradition. Feast on nationally renowned biscuits made from scratch with homemade preserves, country ham ($10), fried chicken ($11), and good ol' Southern hospitality. Reservations recommended. Open M-F 8am-2pm and 5-9pm, Sa-Su 8am-9pm. ❸

SATCO (San Antonio Taco Company), 416 21st Ave. S. (☎327-4322), is the home of both great Mexican food and great deals. The student hangout has fajitas for $1.50 and tacos for $1. Large combo platter $5. Single beers $2; bucket of 6 $10. Open in summer Su-W 11am-midnight, Th-Sa 11am-1am. ❶

Jack's Bar-B-Que, 416 Broadway (☎254-5715), is a bit of a legend—both for the flashing neon-winged pigs above the door and the succulent, tender pork. Sandwiches $3-4. Plates $7-11. Open M-Th 10:30am-8pm, F-Sa 10:30am-10pm, Su noon-8pm; off-season M-W 10:30am-3pm, Th 10:30am-8pm, F-Sa 10:30am-10pm. ❷

West End Cookers, 2609 West End Ave. (☎327-2925), has a large menu stuffed with a variety of old-fashioned American grub. The salads are fantastic ($8), and the walls are lined with pictures of Nashville, creating a cozy atmosphere. Open daily 11am-10pm. ❷

👁 SIGHTS

GOO(D) OLE COUNTRY LOVIN'. Country music doesn't just find its home in Nashville; country is the driving force behind the whole city. The first stop of any visitor—country fan or not—needs to be the **Country Music Hall of Fame.** Leave plenty of time to wander through the history of the music, listen to samples from greats like Johnny Cash and Patsy Cline, and watch films of modern artists discussing life as a star. *(222 5th Ave. S. ☎416-2001. Open June-Aug. F-W 10am-6pm, Th 10am-10pm; Sept.-May daily 10am-6pm. $15, ages 6-15 $8, under 6 free.)* After sampling the country music scene, two-step over to the **Ryman Auditorium,** the site of the legendary Grand Ole Opry for over 30 years. The Opry eventually had to move to a bigger venue to accommodate the growing crowd of fans, but the Ryman continues to host fantastic shows every weekend. There is also a museum that outlines the fascinating history of the building. *(116 5th Ave. ☎889-3060. Open for self-guided tours 9am-4pm. $8, ages 4-11 $4. Showtimes and prices vary.)* Finally, there is the main country venue in the city, and in the nation, the **Grand Ole Opry (GOO).** Visitors can enjoy musical performances, tour the backstage areas, or visit the free museum detailing the history of the Opry. Performers are listed in *The Tennessean*. *(2804 Opryland Dr. Exit 11, off Hwy. 155, accessible from both I-40 and I-65. ☎889-6611. Museum open M-Th 10am-5pm, F 10am-8pm, Sa 10am-10pm. Free. Tours F-Sa 10:30am-2:30pm. $8.65, ages 4-11 $4. Reservations suggested. Live music F 7:30, Sa 6:30 and 9:30pm. $25.)*

MUSEUMS AND MORE. Nashville's pride and joy awaits in **Centennial Park,** a 15min. walk west along West End Ave. from Music Row. The "Athens of the South" boasts a full-scale replica of the **Parthenon.** Built as a temporary exhibit for the Tennessee Centennial in 1897, the Parthenon was rebuilt to last and now regally sits atop a hill in Centennial Park. In its first floor gallery, the building also houses the **Cowan Collection of American Paintings,** a selection of 19th- and early 20th-century American art. *(☎862-8431. Open Nov.-Mar. Tu-Sa 9am-4:30pm, Su 12:30-4:30pm; Apr.-Oct. closed Su. $3.50, seniors and ages 4-17 $2. Wheelchair accessible.)* Right in the heart of downtown, the **Frist Center for the Visual Arts** inspires young and old with an interesting array of rotating exhibits and a hands-on learning center that allows visitors to make prints, draw figures, and take photographs. *(919 Broadway St. ☎244-3340. Open M-W and F-Sa 10am-5:30pm, Th 10am-8pm, Su 1-5pm. $6.50, students and seniors $4.50, children free.)* **Fisk University's Carl Van Vechten Gallery** consists of a portion of the private collection of Alfred Steiglitz and Georgia O'Keeffe. The Gallery is tiny, but anyone who enjoys contemporary art should view the outstanding Steiglitz photographs hanging among works by Picasso and Renoir. *(At Jackson St. and D.B. Todd Blvd., off Jefferson St. ☎329-8543. Open in summer Tu-F 10am-5pm, Sa 1-5pm; in winter Tu-F 10am-5pm, Sa-Su 1-5pm. Free, but donations accepted. Wheelchair accessible.)*

CHEEKWOOD MUSEUM AND BELLE MEADE MANSION. If you tire of the downtown area, rest at the **Cheekwood Botanical Garden and Museum of Art.** The well-kept gardens are a respite from the flashiness of downtown and complement the museum's 19th-century art perfectly. *(8 mi. southwest of town on Forrest Park Dr. between Rte. 100 and Belle Meade Blvd. Bus #3 "West End/Belle Meade" from downtown to Belle Meade*

THE SOUTH

Blvd. and Page Rd. ☎ *356-8000. Open Tu-Sa 9:30am-4:30pm, Su 11am-4:30pm. $10, students and ages 6-17 $5, seniors $8.)* After losing yourself in the winding paths and extensive array of gardens at Cheekwood, follow the experience by wandering over to the **Belle Meade Mansion.** "The Queen of Tennessee Plantations," this lavish 1853 plantation was the site of the nation's first thoroughbred breeding farm. It was also host to seven US presidents, including the 380 lb. William Howard Taft, who spent some time lodged in the mansion's bathtub. Prior to Taft's second visit, his hosts installed a rather amply proportioned shower. *(5025 Harding Rd.* ☎ *356-0501 or 800-270-3991. Open M-Sa 9am-5pm, Su 11am-5pm. 2 guided tours per hr.; last tour 4pm. $10, seniors $8.50, ages 6-12 $4. Partially wheelchair accessible.)*

OTHER SIGHTS. A comely Greek Revival structure atop a hill on Charlotte Ave. next to downtown, the **Capitol** leads tours of the tomb of former President James K. Polk. *(On Charlotte Ave. next to downtown.* ☎ *741-1621. Open daily 9am-4pm. Tours every hr. M-F 9-11am and 1-3pm. Free. Wheelchair accessible.)* The impressive array of the original furnishings in Andrew Jackson's graceful manor, the **Hermitage,** encourages breaking away from the sociable squeeze of downtown for a couple of hours. Admission includes a 16min. film, access to the house and grounds, and a visit to the nearby **Tulip Grove Mansion and Church.** *(4580 Rachel's Ln. Exit 221A off I-40.* ☎ *889-2941. Open daily 9am-5pm. $10, students and seniors $9, ages 6-12 $5; families $30. Wheelchair accessible, except for the nature trail and the 2nd floor of the mansion.)*

🎵 ENTERTAINMENT

The hordes of visitors that converge upon Nashville have turned the **Grand Ole Opry** (see above) into a grand American institution. However, there are other great forms of entertainment in the capital city as well. The **Tennessee Performing Arts Center,** Deaderick and 6th Ave. N. (☎ 782-4000, or ☎ 255-2787 for tickets), hosts the Nashville Symphony, opera, ballet, and other non-country entertainment. Listings for the area's music and events fill the free publications *Nashville Scene* and *Rage,* available at most area establishments. The Visitors Center hands out a list of gay and lesbian establishments.

Two major-league franchises dominate the Nashville sports scene. The National Football League's **Tennessee Titans** play at **Adelphia Coliseum,** 460 Great Circle Rd., across the river from downtown. (☎ 565-4000. Tickets $12-52.) The **Nashville Predators,** a new National Hockey League team, face-off at the **Gaylord Entertainment Center,** 501 Broadway. (☎ 770-200 for info, ☎ 770-2040 for tickets. $10-95.)

📍 NIGHTLIFE

Nightlife downtown centers on Broadway and 2nd Ave., where bars and tourist attractions draw large crowds. Parking can sometimes be difficult on summer evenings, especially when something is going on at the Gaylord Entertainment Center. Near Vanderbilt, **Elliston Pl.** hops with a wealth of college-oriented music venues.

Bluebird Cafe, 4104 Hillsboro Rd. (☎ 383-1461), in the strip mall in Green Hills. The place where Garth Brooks got his start, this famous bird sings country, blues, and folk. $7 per person food/drink minimum if sitting at a table. Cover after 9:30pm $4-10; no cover Su. Open daily 5:30pm until the singing stops (usually between 11pm and 1am). Early show 7pm. Reservations recommended Tu-Sa.

Wildhorse Saloon, 120 2nd Ave. N (☎ 902-8211). Bring your cowboy boots and hat, and two-step through the night in this huge country dance hall—the birthplace of the TNN dance show. Dance lessons M-F 6-9pm, Sa-Su 2-9pm. Live music Tu-Sa. Cover after 7pm $4-6. Open Su-Th 11am-1am, F-Sa 11am-3am.

THE GREAT PRIMATE DEBATE
The Scopes Monkey Trial

On March 21, 1925, the governor of Tennessee signed into law "an act prohibiting the teaching of the Evolution Theory in all the Universities, Normals, and all other public schools" in the state. The American Civil Liberties Union quickly offered to defend anyone accused of violating the statute, and it wasn't long before George Rappalyea convinced his friend John Thomas Scopes, a 24-year-old school teacher from Dayton, to provide the test case.

Rappalyea was a curious figure, both an opponent of the Christian fundamentalism sweeping rural America at the time and a booster of Dayton, a town that had been shrinking precipitously since the 19th century. Hoping that the case would both bring new life to the town and heap the nation's scorn upon the resolute ignorance of the fundamentalist movement, he originally hoped science fiction writer H.G. Wells would come to Tennessee to lead the defense.

Scopes was duly charged with the crime of teaching evolution, but Wells never came. Nevertheless, the trial quickly grew from a simple publicity stunt to a debate about the soul of America. Clarence Darrow, a masterful orator and an evangelical agnostic, was the point man for the defense. William Jennings Bryan, a three-time candidate for the US Presidency and an ardent fundamentalist, joined the prosecution, ready to fight what he called a "battle-royal between unbelief that attempts to speak through so-called science and the defenders of the Christian faith."

The battle-royal that both sides sought moved beyond any question about Scopes' guilt (the teacher received a $100 fine, which was thrown out on appeal by the Tennessee Supreme Court on technical grounds). H.L. Mencken, a renowned American journalist covering the trial for a Baltimore newspaper, observed that the trial "serves notice on the country that Neanderthal man is organizing in these forlorn backwaters of the land, led by a fanatic who is rid of sense and devoid of conscience." Bryan complained that "man used to be content to slaughter his fellow men on a single plane," but that science, as exemplified by evolutionary theory, allowed them to kill in the sky and below the sea. Darrow, calling Bryan to the witness stand, compelled the man known as the Great Commoner to admit that he did not believe the Bible to be literally correct. Bryan could not take it—he died less than a week after the trial. Mencken commented on the tragedy of seeing a man "begin life as a hero and end it as a buffoon." This trial was about grander things than a fine.

Looking back on the trial in 1965, John Scopes said that "the Dayton trial had some part in bringing to birth [a] new era," in which free men, religious and not, could "address one another in an atmosphere of mutual respect and of a common quest for truth." The trial was about how one could live, although no court could ever settle that question. Bryan feared evolutionary theory would rob the "human ship" of its moral rudder and compass, as many still do today, and refused to believe that life is worth living without some old-time religion to fend off the modern age. On the other side, Darrow fought to prevent "the setting of man against man and creed against creed until with flying banners and beating drums we are marching backward to the glorious ages of the 16th century when bigots lighted fagot to burn the men who dared to bring any intelligence and enlightenment and culture to the human mind."

T.J. Kelleher was the editor of Let's Go: USA 2000, *an Associate Editor for* USA 1999, *and a Researcher-Writer for* Let's Go: Australia 2001. *He is now a magazine editor for the American Museum of Natural History.*

The Beer Sellar, 107 Church St. (☎254-9464). Enjoy a laid-back atmosphere and over 50 different drafts ($2.50-4.50) and 135 bottled beers. Happy hour M-F 2-7pm. Open daily 2pm-3am.

Tootsies Orchid Lounge, 422 Broadway (☎726-0463). The unique purple color of this bar is almost as colorful as its past. One of the oldest bars on Broadway, it was the Orchid Lounge that launched several famous careers, including Willie Nelson's. Supposedly Tootsie had a soft spot in her heart for struggling musicians and used to slip $5 and $10 bills in their back pockets at the end of the night. Open daily 10am-2am.

KNOXVILLE   ☎865

Knoxville was settled after the Revolutionary War and named for Washington's Secretary of War, Henry Knox. Once the capital of Tennessee, the city hosted the 1982 World's Fair, which attracted 10 million visitors, and is still home to the 26,000 students of the University of Tennessee (UT). Shaded by the stunning Great Smoky Mountains and hemmed in by vast lakes created by the Tennessee Valley Authority, Knoxville somehow provides a friendly urban air.

🚩 **PRACTICAL INFORMATION.** Downtown stretches north from the **Tennessee River,** bordered by **Henley St.** and **World's Fair Park** to the west. **Greyhound,** 100 E. Magnolia Ave. (☎522-5144; open 24hr.), at Central St., buses to Chattanooga (2hr., 3 per day, $14-15), Lexington (4hr., 6 per day, $39-41), and Nashville (3hr., 6 per day, $22-24). *Avoid this area at night.* **Public transit: KAT** buses cover the city. (☎637-3000. M-F 6:15am-6:15pm, some later depending on the route; Sa-Su reduced service. $1, transfers 20¢.) Two free **trolley** lines run throughout the city: Blue goes downtown and eastward, while Orange heads downtown and westward to the park and UT. (Blue line: 6am-6:20pm; Orange line: 7am-6pm.) **Gateway Regional Visitors Center,** 900 Volunteer Landing, along the river on the southeast side of downtown, hosts a small museum. (☎971-4440. Apr.-Oct. M-Sa 9am-6pm, Su 1-5pm; Nov.-Mar. M-Sa 9am-5pm.) **Internet access: Lawson McGhee Library,** 500 W. Church Ave. (☎215-8750. Open June-Aug. M-Th 9am-8:30pm, F 9am-5:30pm, Su 1-5pm; Sept.-May M-Th 9am-8:30pm, F 9am-5:30pm, Sa-Su 1-5pm.) **Post Office:** 501 W. Main Ave. (☎521-1070. Open M-F 7:30am-5:30pm.) **ZIP code:** 37902. **Area code:** 865.

🚩 **ACCOMMODATIONS.** Many not-quite-budget motels sit along **I-75** and **I-40,** just outside the city. **The Knoxville Hostel (HI-AYH) ❶,** 404 E. 4th Ave., features not only clean rooms, a kitchen, and a comfortable common room, but also has free Internet access and continental breakfast. Friendly, helpful management foster a community feel among the guests. *Be cautious around this neighborhood at night. If you arrive at the Greyhound station, call the hostel and they will pick you up.* (☎546-8090. Free local calls. Laundry. No lockout. Office open 7:30-11:30am and 4-8pm. $12, nonmembers $15.) Women should consider staying in the transit room at the **YWCA ❶,** 420 W. Clinch St., downtown at Walnut St. The pleasing room is located right in the heart of downtown within walking distance of many of Knoxville's attractions. (☎523-6126. Call ahead M-F 9am-5pm. Single with shared bath $12 per night, $40 per week.) **Scottish Inns ❶,** 301 Callahan Dr., at Exit 110 off I-75, keeps inviting rooms equipped with A/C and cable TV. (☎689-7777. Free local calls and outdoor pool. Singles Su-Th $30, F-Sa $34; doubles $35/39.) **Volunteer Park Campground ❶,** 9514 Diggs Gap Rd., at Exit 117 off I-75, is closer to the city than most other campgrounds. (☎938-6600 or 800-238-9644. Pool, clubhouse, restaurant, and laundry. Sites with water and electricity $18, full hookup $25.)

⬛ FOOD. Part of Cumberland Ave. along campus proper, **The Strip** is lined with student hangouts, bars, and restaurants. **Market Sq.**, a popular plaza to the east of World's Fair Park, presents restaurants, fountains, and shade, but shuts down at night. The other center for chowing, browsing, and carousing, **Old City,** spreads north up Central and Jackson St. and stays active later than Market Sq. **The Tomato Head ❶,** 12 Market Sq., whips up gourmet pizzas (9 in. $6-18.25) and sandwiches ($4.25-6), with vegetarian/vegan options galore. (☎637-4067. Open M 11am-3pm, Tu-Th 11am-10pm, F-Sa 11am-11pm.) The **Crescent Moon Cafe ❷,** 705 Market St., in an alley between Church Ave. and Cumberland Ave., is a slice of gourmet, budget- and health-friendly heaven. (☎637-9700. Lunch specials and sandwiches with a side $6.25. Open M-F 8-10am and 11am-2:15pm.) **The Lunch Box ❷,** 1 Tennessee Plaza, in the First Tennessee building, makes lunch food ($5-7) and desserts ($3.50) just the way your mother used to. (☎525-7421. Open M-F 11am-2pm.) For a unique collegiate atmosphere, the **11th St. Espresso House ❶,** 1016 Laurel Ave., near UT in an old Victorian house, has innovative food to match the ambience. (☎546-3003. Lemon Basil Tuna $4.75. W poetry readings. Th live music. Open M-Sa 9am-midnight, Su noon-7pm.)

◼ SIGHTS. The must-see ⬛**Museum of Appalachia,** 16 mi. north of Knoxville at I-75 Exit 122 in Norris, a smattering of buildings—the cabin where Samuel Langhorne Clemens (Mark Twain) was conceived—cradles one-of-a-kind artifacts and exudes true Appalachian charm. Full of personal anecdotes and the tools and household items of everyday Appalachian living, the museum is a stylish testament to the region's unique culture. (☎494-7680. Open daily 8am-5pm. Live music Apr.-Dec. 9:30am-5pm. $10, seniors and AAA $8, ages 6-15 $5; families $24.)

The self-guided **Cradle of Country Music Tour** ambles through the eastern end of downtown, lingering at scraps of hallowed ground where county triumphs and heartaches left their mark. Sights include the theater where Roy Acuff made his first public performance and the hotel where Hank Williams spent the last night of his life. Maps and information are available at the Visitors Center.

World's Fair Park recently underwent major reconstruction, adding a new swath of greenery stretching to the river, and expanding the Convention Center. The distinctive golden "sunsphere" still stands, easily recognizable as it towers 266 ft. over the Park. The **Knoxville Museum of Art,** 1050 World's Fair Park Dr., houses high-caliber changing exhibits and an interesting permanent collection. (☎525-6101. Open Tu-Th and Sa 10am-5pm, F 10am-9pm, Su noon-5pm. $10, seniors $9, ages 12-17 $7, under 12 free.)

The ⬛**Women's Basketball Hall of Fame,** 700 Hall of Fame Dr., traces the involvement of women in the sport since its conception and generates excitement for generations of ballplayers yet to come. (☎633-9000. Open M-Sa 10am-7pm, Su 1-6pm. $8, seniors and ages 6-15 $6, under 6 free. Wheelchair accessible.) Nearby, the **James White Fort,** 205 E. Hill Ave., preserves portions of the original stockade built in 1786 by the founder of Knoxville, while giving the scoop on 18th century life in Knoxville. (☎525-6514. Open Mar.-Dec. M-Sa 9:30am-4:30pm; Jan.-Feb. M-F 10am-4pm. Continuous tours until 3:30pm. $5, seniors and AAA $4.25, ages 5-12 $2.) Providing further information on the original inhabitants of Knoxville, **Blount Mansion,** 200 W. Hill Ave., home to Tennessee's first Governor, William Blount, is a cozy house on the banks of the Tennessee River. Tours include a short video. (☎525-2375. Tours Apr.-Dec. M-Sa every hr. 9:30am-5pm; Jan.-Mar. closed Sa. $5, ages 6-12 $2.50.)

⬛⬛ ENTERTAINMENT & NIGHTLIFE. Knoxville is a great place to visit for college sports fans; UT's **football** and **women's basketball** consistently impress fans (☎974-2491 for tickets). From April to September, the **Tennessee Smokies,** an AA baseball team, hit the field. (☎637-9494. $6-9.) If sports aren't your thing, the **Dog-**

wood **Arts Festival** is all about food, folks, fun, and a lot of trees. (☎ 637-4561. April 11-17, 2003.) The **Tennessee Theatre**, 604 S. Gay St. (☎ 522-1174), plays classic movies and hosts major bands.

The Old City has several hot nightclubs to choose from. **Fiction,** 214 W. Jackson Ave., spins a web of lights and music into a dizzying dance club experience. (☎ 329-0039. 18+. Cover $3-8. W Gothic night. Open W and F-Sa 10pm-3am.) The **Rainbow Club West,** 7211 Kingston Pike, is an upscale gay bar and restaurant in west Knoxville. (☎ 212-9655. Th karaoke, F-Sa drag shows. Happy Hour daily 5-8pm. Cover on weekends. Open daily 5pm-3am.) For goings-on around the town, pick up a free copy of *Metro Pulse.*

GREAT SMOKY MOUNTAINS   ☎ 865

The largest wilderness area in the eastern US, Great Smoky Mountains National Park encompasses 500,000 acres of gray-green Appalachian peaks bounded by the misty North Carolina and Tennessee valleys. Black bears, wild hogs, groundhogs, wild turkeys, and a handful of red wolves root through the area, not to mention more than 1500 species of flowering plants. Whispering conifer forests line the mountain ridges at elevations of over 6000 feet. Spring sets the mountains ablaze with wildflowers and azaleas, and in June and July, rhododendrons burst into their full glory. By mid-October, the mountains are a vibrant quilt of autumnal color. Unfortunately, the area has not remained untouched by human presence. Fifty years ago, a visitor at Newfound Gap could see 93 mi.; today, poorer air quality has cut visibility to only 15 mi.

🛈 PRACTICAL INFORMATION

Rte. 441, known as the Newfound Gap Rd., is the only road connecting the Tennessee and North Carolina sides of the park. The invaluable *Smokies Guide* (25¢) details the park's tours, lectures, activities, and changing natural graces.

Visitors Centers: Sugarlands (☎ 436-1291), on Newfound Gap Rd. 2 mi. south of Gatlinburg, TN, next to the park's headquarters, shows an interesting 20min. film on the history of the park and contains an exhibit on regional plants and animals. Open June-Aug. daily 8am-7pm; Apr.-May and Sept. 8am-6pm; Mar. and Oct. 8am-5pm; Nov.-Feb. 8am-4:30pm. On the North Carolina side of the park, **Oconaluftee** (☎ 828-497-1900), 4 mi. north of Cherokee, shares its grounds with an outdoor Mountain Farm Museum made up of historic buildings relocated from throughout the park and preserved in the 1950s. Open daily 8am-7pm; off-season hours vary.

Buses: East Tennessee Human Resource Agency (ETHRA), 298 Blair Bend Rd., (☎ 800-232-1565), in Loudon, offers transportation from Knoxville and other towns in the vicinity. Operates M-F 8am-4:30pm. Call at least 48hr. in advance to schedule a trip. $2 and up.

Info line, ☎ 436-1200. Operates daily 8:30am-4:30pm. **Area code:** 865.

🏠 ACCOMMODATIONS

Motels, lining Rte. 441 and Rte. 321, decrease in price with distance from the park. Small motels cluster in both Cherokee and Gatlinburg. In general, Cherokee motels are cheaper (from $35) and Gatlinburg motels are nicer (from $45). Prices soar on weekends. Visitors can gamble on motels, but in general it is better to splurge on a Bed and Breakfast or stay in hostel-style accommodations near the park. Beautiful B&Bs and some good restaurants can be found in Bryson City, NC, about 15min.

from the main entrance to the park. Ten **campgrounds** lie scattered throughout the park, each with tent sites, limited trailer space, water, and bathrooms. There are no showers or hookups. **Smokemont, Elkmont,** and **Cades Cove** accept reservations from mid-May to late October. (Sites $17. Cancellation fee $10.) The rest are first come, first served. (Sites $12-14.) In summer, reserve spots near main roads at least eight weeks in advance. (☎800-365-2267, park code GRE. Open 10am-10pm.) **Backcountry camping** is by reservation only; **permits** are free at ranger stations and Visitors Centers. (☎436-1231. Office open daily 8am-6pm.)

> **Folkestone Inn,** 101 Folkestone Rd., (☎828-488-2730), in Bryson City, runs right up to the park with gorgeous rooms and a spectacular landscape. Total relaxation in this remote hide-away is inescapable, especially after starting the day with a belly full of a fantastic breakfast. Check-in 3pm. Be sure to call ahead. Rooms from $88. ❹

> **Charleston Inn,** 208 Arlington Ave. (☎828-488-4644). Within walking distance to the shops and restaurants of Bryson City, this gorgeous B&B is about 15min. from the park. Welcoming innkeepers, full breakfast. Check-in 3-10pm; call if arriving later. Check-out 11am. Rooms from $75. ❹

> **Nantahala Outdoor Center (NOC),** 13077 U.S. 19 W. (☎888-662-1662), 13 mi. southwest of Bryson City, just south of the National Park, beckons with cheap beds and three restaurants. They also have trips into the great outdoors and bike rentals. Showers, kitchen, and laundry facilities. Call ahead. Bunks in simple cabins $15. ❶

> **Bell's Wa-Floy Retreat (HI-AYH),** 3610 East Pkwy. (☎436-5575), 10 mi. east of Gatlinburg on Rte. 321. This Christian retreat (though it welcomes those of other faiths) was the dream of Mrs. Bell, a retired teacher and amateur poet who longed to share the solace of the mountain with others. The community includes a pool, tennis courts, and meditation area as well as a hostel. Check-in before 10pm. Reservations required. 2-night min. stay. First night $15, thereafter $12; nonmembers $25/25. ❶

◖ FOOD

> 🐾 **Mountain Perks,** 9 Depot St. (☎828-488-9561), in the heart of Bryson City, across from the train station. Live music gets the crowds going weekends at 8pm. Orgasmic desserts, scrumptious oversized wraps, and amazing salads $5 or less. ❶

> **Smokin' Joe's Bar-B-Que,** 8303 Rte. 73, (☎448-3212), in Townsend. Authentic Tennessee cookin' is the order of business here. With succulent, slow-cooked meats and homemade side dishes like BBQ beans, Joe's smokes the competition. Dinners come with 2 sides, meat, bread, and choice of sauce. Sandwiches $2.50-4.50. Open in summer Su-Th 8am-9pm, F-Sa 8am-10pm; off-season hours vary. ❷

> **Anthony's Pizzeria,** 103 Depot St. (☎828-488-8898), in Bryson City, serves up authentic New York-style pizza at a fraction of the price (large $6.50). Open M-Th and Su 11am-9pm, F-Sa 11am-10pm. ❶

> **Hearth and Kettle,** 7767 E Lamar Alexander Pkwy. (☎448-6059), in Townsend, serves up $9-15 entrees and a host of $4-8 sandwiches. Open daily 7am-9:30pm. ❸

◣ OUTDOOR ACTIVITIES

HIKING

Over 900 mi. of hiking trails and 170 mi. of road meander through the park. Rangers at the Visitors Centers will help devise a trip appropriate for your ability. Great Smoky Mountains National Park is known for phenomenal **waterfalls,** and many of the park's most popular hikes culminate in stunning cascade views. Less crowded areas not accessible from Rte. 441 include **Cosby** and **Cataloochee,** both on the eastern edge of the park. Cataloochee is also a biking hot spot. A backcountry camping **permit,** free from the Visitors Centers, is required to hike unmarked trails. *Wherever you go, bring water and don't feed the bears.*

Rainbow Falls (5.5 mi., 4hr.) is a moderate to strenuous hike that reveals the Smokies' highest single-plunge waterfall. The park's most popular hike.

Laurel Falls (2.5 mi., 2hr.) is one of the easier hikes on the Tennessee side of the park, following a paved trail through a series of cascades before reaching the 60 ft. falls.

Ramsay Cascades (8 mi., 5hr.) is a strenuous hike. The trailhead is in the Greenbrier area, and the cascades fall 100 ft. down the mountainside.

Chimney Tops (4 mi., 2hr.) is a steep scramble leading up to two 4755 ft. rock spires, where breathtaking views await.

Andrews Bald (3.6 mi., 2hr.), a fairly easy-going hike, heads downslope to a bald hilltop overlooking the southern section of the park.

Charlies Bunion (8 mi., 4hr.), a difficult hike tracing the Appalachian Trail and the state-line ridge, has splendid views worth the extra effort.

BIKING

Biking is permitted along most roads within the park, with the exception of the Roaring Fork Motor Nature Trail. The best opportunities for cyclists are in the **Foothills Parkway, Cades Cove,** and **Cataloochee.** While the Smokies boast no mountain biking trails, a few gravel trails in the park, including the **Gatlinburg Trail** and the **Oconaluftee River Trail,** allow bicycles. Bike rental is available at **Cades Cove Campground Store and Bicycle Rental.** (☎448-9034. Open June-Aug. M and W 7am-7pm, Tu and Th-Su 9am-7pm; no rental after 4:30pm. May and Sept. daily 9am-5pm; no rental after 2:30pm. $4 per hr., $20 per day.)

FISHING

Forty species of fish swim in the park's rivers and streams. The Smokies permit fishing in open waters year-round from 30min. before sunrise to 30min. after sunset, though the brook trout (native only to the Smokies) is off-limits due to extensive habitat restoration programs. All anglers over 12 (over 15 in North Carolina) must possess a valid Tennessee or North Carolina **fishing license.** The park itself does not sell licenses; check with local Chambers of Commerce, sports shops, and hardware stores for purchasing information.

RIDING

Over 500 mi. of the park's trails are open to horses. Five **horse camps** are located within the park: **Anthony Creek, Big Creek, Cataloochee, Roundbottom,** and **Towstring.** (☎800-362-2267; http://reservations.nps.gov. Reservations required.) **Cades Cove Riding Stables,** at the entrance to Cades Cove Loop, across from the ranger station, provides one-hour guided rides, scenic hayrides, and frequent carriage rides. (☎448-6286. Open daily 9am-5pm. 1hr. rides $20; 25-30min. carriage rides every 30min., $7.50. Mar.-Oct. 1½-2hr. hayrides every 2hr., $6 per person; nighttime hayrides M-W and F-Sa 6:30pm, $8.)

NEAR SMOKY MOUNTAINS: CHEROKEE RESERVATION

The **Cherokee Indian Reservation,** on the southeast border of the national park, features a number of museums, shops, attractions, and—most notably—an all-electric, dry casino. Three historical attractions stand in marked contrast to miles and miles of rampant commercialism. From May to October, the reservation offers a tour of the **Oconaluftee Indian Village,** a recreated Native American village throwing back to the mid-18th century. (☎828-497-2315. Open mid-May to late Oct. daily 9am-5:30pm. $12, ages 6-13 $5.) For an in-depth look at the history and traditions of the Cherokee people, visit the **Museum of the Cherokee Indian,** on Drama Rd. off Rte. 441. (☎828-497-3481. Open M-Sa 9am-8pm, Su 9am-5pm. $8, ages 6-13 $5; AAA and AARP discounts.) **"Unto these Hills,"** a moving impressive outdoor drama, retells the story of the Cherokees and the Trail of Tears. (☎828-497-2111. Show mid-June to Aug. 8:30pm, pre-show 7:45pm.) For less somber entertainment, roll the dice at **Harrah's Cherokee Casino,** 777 Casino Dr. (☎877-811-0777. 21+. Open 24hr.)

The **Nantahala Outdoor Center** (☎888-662-1662) facilitates many types of activities. **Whitewater rafting expeditions** are pricey, but with some amount of rafting competency, you can rent your own raft for a trip down the Nantahala River. (Rafts Su-F $20, Sa $25. 1- or 2-person inflatable "ducks" Su-F $31/24, Sa $37/29. Rafters must be at least 60 lb. Higher prices July-Aug. weekends. Prices include transportation to site and all necessary equipment.) The center also runs biking trips and is a wealth of knowledge for outdoor enthusiasts. (☎800-232-7238 for general information. Mountain bike rentals from $30, including helmets and car racks.) The **Appalachian Trail** and **Cades Cove Loop** also cut through the reservation. The **Cherokee Visitors Center,** 498 Tsali Blvd., provides information; follow signs from Rte. 441 or Rte. 19. (☎800-438-1601. Open M-F 7:45am-4:30pm, Sa-Su 8:45am-5pm.)

CHATTANOOGA   ☎423

Chattanooga was made famous by the legendary railroad that once drove through the fertile river valley: the Chattanooga Choo-Choo. Since then, it has been home to a major Civil War battle, the first ever tow truck, and the original Coca-Cola bottling factory. Since the conception of Ruby Falls and Lookout Mountain tourists have been a common sight in the town. Downtown, Lookout Mountain, and the River Bluff Arts District are the three distinct parts of the town, each with their own character. They share, however, the common bond of old-fashioned Southern charm.

🛈 **PRACTICAL INFORMATION.** Chattanooga straddles the Tennessee/Georgia border at the junction of I-24, I-59, and I-75. **Greyhound,** 960 Airport Rd. (☎892-1277; open daily 6:30am-9:30pm), buses to Atlanta (2hr., 8 per day, $18-19); Knoxville (2hr., 4 per day, $14-15); and Nashville (3½hr., 5 per day, $18-19). **Chattanooga Area Transportation Authority (CARTA)** runs local buses. (☎629-1473. Buses 5am-11pm. $1, children 50¢; transfers 20¢/10¢.) **Visitors Center:** 2 Broad St., next to the aquarium. (☎756-8687 or 800-322-3344. Open daily 8:30am-5:30pm.) **Internet access: Public Library,** 1001 Broad St., at 10th St. (☎757-5310. Open June-Aug. M-Th 9am-9pm, F-Sa 9am-6pm; Sept.-May M-Th 9am-9pm, F-Sa 9am-6pm, Su 2-6pm.) **Post Office:** 900 Georgia Ave., between Martin Luther King Blvd. and 10th St. (☎267-1609. Open M-F 7:30am-5:30pm.) **ZIP code:** 37402. **Area code:** 423.

🛏 **ACCOMMODATIONS.** The most affordable, up-scale places are off I-24 west of the city. The cheaper, more run-down hotels are east on I-24/I-75. There are a few budget accommodations on **Broad St. Ramada Inn Stadium ❸,** 100 W. 21st St., Exit 178 off I-24, has clean, cozy rooms in a fantastic location. The friendly staff is very helpful in orienting visitors. (☎265-3151. A/C, cable TV, HBO, and pool. Rooms from $49.) Though a bit on the expensive side, **Chanticleer Inn ❹,** 1300 Mockingbird Ln., just down the street from Lookout Mountain, is worth every penny. Guests are treated to sincere hospitality, gorgeous scenery, and a scrumptious full breakfast. Each room is housed in its own stone cabin, some with fire places. (☎706-820-2015. A/C, cable TV, and pool. Rooms from $89; AAA discount.) **Best Holiday Trav-L-Park ❶,** 1709 Mack Smith Rd., in Rossville ½ mi. off I-75 at the East Ridge exit, enlivens tent and RV sites with a Civil War theme. (☎706-891-9766 or 800-695-2877. Laundry and pool available. 2-person site $17, with water and electricity $21, full hookup $23; cabins $36.) **Chickamauga** and **Nickajack** lakes also have campgrounds.

◖ **FOOD.** The ▨**Pickle Barrel ❶**, 1012 Market St., downtown, moves beyond cucumbers to scrumptious sandwiches. The open-air deck upstairs is a must in nice weather. (☎266-1103. Spicy black bean burger $5.25. 21+ after 9pm, except families. Open M-Sa 11am-3am, Su noon-3am.) **Jacks Back Alley** houses several places to eat, including **Sticky Fingers ❷**, 420 Broad St., the best place in town for ribs. Enjoy a heaping mound of BBQ ($8) or a simple salad for $2. (☎265-7427. Open daily 11am-10pm.) In the Bluff View River district, **Rembrant Cafe ❶**, 204 High St., is the perfect place for a light meal or a good cup of coffee. Sample their scrumptious pastries (under $4) on the lovely stone patio, complete with fountain. (☎265-5033, ext. 3. Sandwiches and salads around $4.50. Open daily M-Th 7am-10pm, F 7am-11:30pm, Sa 8am-11:30pm, Su 8am-10pm.)

◪ ♫ **SIGHTS & ENTERTAINMENT. Downtown Chattanooga,** a small area between 10th St. and the river, is full of attractions, shops, and restaurants. The biggest catch in town is the **Tennessee Aquarium,** 1 Broad St., on Ross's Landing, with the largest turtle collection in the world, as well as 7000 other animals, an IMAX screen, and several hands-on exhibits. (☎800-322-3344. Open May-Sept. M-Th 9am-6pm, F-Su 9am-8pm; Oct.-Apr. daily 10am-6pm. $13, ages 3-12 $7; IMAX $7.25/5; both $17/10.) Almost as fascinating, the **International Towing and Recovery Hall of Fame and Museum,** 401 Broad St., chronicles the creation and life of the tow truck. Even if you're not interested in cars, this museum is a testament to human ingenuity. (☎267-3132. Open M-F 10am-4:30pm, Sa-Su 11am-5pm. $4, seniors and ages 5-18 $3, under 6 free.) The **Chattanooga Regional History Museum,** 400 Chestnut St., charts the city's history from a small farm town to the present. (☎265-3247. Open M-F 10am-4:30pm, Sa-Su 11am-4:30pm. $4, seniors $3.50, ages 5-13 $3.) A **riverwalk pathway** runs between downtown, the aquarium, and the Bluff View Art District.

The **Bluff View Arts District** is a small neighborhood of upscale shops and cafes, anchored by the **Hunter Museum of Art,** 10 Bluff View. The museum has the South's most complete American art collection. There is a well-done contemporary section and a fantastic display of classical American painting in the grand mansion. (☎267-0968. Open Tu-Sa 10am-4:30pm, Su 1-4:30pm. $5, students $3, seniors $4, ages 3-11 $2.50. Wheelchair accessible.) Across the street is the ▨**Houston Museum,** 201 High St. This amazing collection is the life work of Anna Houston, a bit of a nut who was called "Antique Annie" because she lived in a barn with all of her precious possesions. She bequeathed her collection—including music boxes and an amazing glass collection—to a committee that started a museum in this picturesque house on the banks of the river. (☎267-7176. Open in summer M-Sa 9:30am-4pm, Su noon-4pm; off-season closed Su. $6, ages 13-18 $3.50.)

One of the most popular sights in Chattanooga is **Lookout Mountain.** Take S. Broad St. and follow signs or hop on bus #15 or 31. The **Incline Railway** takes passengers up an insane 72.7% grade to an observation deck (also accessible by car). From the top, the expansive view encompasses six states on a clear day. (☎629-1411. Open June-Aug. daily 8:30am-9:15pm; Sept.-May 9am-5:15pm. $9, ages 3-12 $4.50. Wheelchair accessible.) The nature trail **Rock City Gardens** combines the natural spectacle of scenic outlooks and narrow rock passages with decidedly less organic additives: the trail has been outfitted with strategically placed shops and finishes at a cave decked out with colorful elves and fairy tale dioramas. (☎706-820-2531. Open June-Aug. daily 8:30am-8pm; Sept.-May 8:30am-6pm. $12, ages 3-12 $6.50.) One thousand feet inside the mountain, the **Ruby Falls** cavern formations and a 145 ft. waterfall—complete with colored lights and sound effects—add Disney-style pizzazz to a day of sightseeing. (☎821-2544. Open daily 8am-8pm. 1hr. tour $11.50, ages 3-12 $5.50.)

THE SOUTH

MOUNTAINS OF FUN A mythical American village created by Dolly Parton in the Tennessee hills, **Dollywood** dominates Pigeon Forge. The park celebrates the cultural legacy of the east Tennessee mountains and the country songmistress herself, famous for some mountainous topography of her own. In Dolly's world, craftspeople demonstrate their skills and sell their wares, 30 rides offer thrills and chills, and country favorites perform. While Dolly asserts that she wants to preserve the culture of the Tennessee mountains, she also seems to want you to pay to come again—Dollywood's motto is "Create Memories Worth Repeating." *(1020 Dollywood Ln. ☎ 865-428-9488. Park open Apr.-Dec. Open mid–June to mid-Aug. daily, most days 9am-8pm, but hrs. vary. $34, seniors $30, ages 4-11 $25; enter after 3pm during the summer and get in free the next day. Discount coupons available at tourist centers, restaurants, and motels.)*

■ **ENTERTAINMENT.** The riverfront completely shuts down for nine nights in mid-June for the live music of the **Riverbend Festival.** (☎ 265-4112. $23-30.) For regular entertainment listings, check the free weekly *Outlook*, available at many restaurants and shops. Most of the nightlife revolves around the downtown area, especially **Jack's Back Alley,** right in the heart of downtown. There are several bars off of the commercialized alley, but **Taco Mac's,** 423 Market St., offers the best selection with over 50 beers on tap. (☎ 267-8226. Open M-F 11am-3am, Sa-Su noon-3am.) The **Chattanooga Lookouts,** a minor league baseball farm team for the Reds, play at the new **BellSouth Park,** at 2nd and Chestnut St. (☎ 267-2208 or 800-852-7572. Tickets $4-8, seniors and under 12 $2.)

MEMPHIS
☎ **901**

Music makes this city run. The streets of Memphis, particularly Beale St., have seen the creation of jazz, blues, soul, and rock 'n' roll over the last century. Ever since musical greats like John Coltrane played in the bars, Memphis has been much more than just a place to get terrific barbecue. Today, the musical tradition is still alive and well. Most visitors make the Memphis pilgrimage to see Graceland, the former home of Elvis Presley and one of the most deliciously tacky spots in the US. The King may be dead, but his legend most certainly lives on in the city's attractions.

■ **TRANSPORATION**

Airport: Memphis International, 2491 Winchester Rd. (☎ 922-8000), south of the southern loop of I-240. Taxi fare to the city around $22—negotiate in advance. Operated by MATA, **DASH** runs buses frequently from the airport for $1.25.

Trains: Amtrak, 545 S. Main St. (☎ 526-0052), at Calhoun on the southern edge of downtown. *The surrounding area can be unsafe.* The Main St. Trolley line runs to the station. To: **Chicago** (10½hr., 1 per day, $84-150); **Jackson** (4½hr., 1 per day, $30-59); **New Orleans** (8½hr., 1 per day, $44-86).

Buses: Greyhound, 203 Union Ave. (☎ 523-1184), at 4th St. downtown. *The area can be unsafe at night.* Open 24hr. To: **Chattanooga** (9hr., 4 per day, $37-39); **Jackson** (4-5hr., 7 per day, $29-31); **Nashville** (4hr., 13 per day, $27-29).

Public Transit: Memphis Area Transit Authority, or **MATA,** (☎ 274-6282), corner of Auction Ave. and Main St. Bus routes cover most suburbs but run infrequently. Major downtown stops are at the intersection of Front and Jefferson St., and 2nd St. and Madison Ave. Major routes run on Front, 2nd, and 3rd St. Buses run M-F from 5:30am, Sa-Su from

6am and stop between 6pm and midnight, depending on the route. $1.25, transfers 10¢. Refurbished 19th-century **trolley cars** cruise Main St. and the Riverfront. Main St.: M-Th 6am-midnight, F 6am-1am, Sa 9:30am-1am, Su 10am-6pm. Riverfront: M-Th 6:30am-midnight, F 6:30am-1am, Sa 9:30am-1am, Su 10am-6pm. 60¢; seniors 30¢, M-F 11am-1:30pm 25¢; under 5 free. 1-day pass $2, 3-day $5.

Taxis: City Wide, ☎324-4202. In taxi-deprived Memphis, expect a long wait.

✈🛈 ORIENTATION & PRACTICAL INFORMATION

Downtown, named avenues run east-west and numbered ones run north-south. **Madison Ave.** divides north and south addresses. Two main thoroughfares, **Poplar** and **Union Ave.** are east-west; **2nd** and **3rd St.** are the major north-south routes downtown. **I-240** and **I-55** encircle the city. **Bellevue** becomes **Elvis Presley Blvd.** and leads south straight to Graceland. **Midtown** lies east of downtown.

Visitor info: Tennessee Welcome Center, 119 Riverside Dr. (☎543-6757), at Jefferson St. Open 24hr. The uniformed **blue suede brigade** roaming the city will happily give directions or answer questions—just stay off of their shoes.

Hotlines: Crisis Line, ☎274-7477. 24hr. **Gay/Lesbian Switchboard,** ☎324-4297. Operates daily 7:30-11pm.

Internet access: Cossitt-Goodwin Public Library, 33 S. Front St. (☎526-1712), at Monroe. Open M-F 10am-5pm.

Post Office: 555 S. 3rd St. (☎521-2559). Open M-F 8:30am-5:30pm, Sa 10am-2pm. **ZIP code:** 38101. **Area code:** 901.

🛏 SINCE M'BABY LEFT ME, I GOT A NEW PLACE T'DWELL

A few downtown motels have prices in the budget range; more lodgings are available near Graceland at **Elvis Presley Blvd.** and **Brooks Rd.** For the celebrations of Elvis's historic birth (Jan. 8) and death (Aug. 16), as well as for the Memphis in May festival, book rooms six months to one year in advance.

Homestead Village Guest Studios, 6500 Poplar Dr. (☎767-5522). Though a bit distant, the impeccably clean rooms come with a full kitchen. Visitors will feel like they are living in their own apartment, complete with laundry room. The surrounding area also offers plenty of dining options. Singles $49, when staying the whole week $39 per night. ❸

American Inn, 3265 Elvis Presley Blvd. (☎345-8444), Exit 5B off I-55. You can't help falling in love with the large rooms and even larger Elvis-themed mural in the lobby. Cable TV, A/C, and continental breakfast. Singles $34; doubles $46. ❷

Memphis Hostel, 340 W. Illinois St. (☎942-3111), Exit 12C off I-55. Located in the Days Inn Riverbluff, the hostel consists of hotel rooms furnished with bunk beds. The hostel is cheap and close to downtown, but the rooms are co-ed and the area is not very safe. Dorms $15. ❶

Memphis/Graceland RV Park, 3691 Elvis Presley Blvd. (☎396-7125), right next door to Graceland. No privacy, but the location is great. Pool, laundry, and free shuttle to Beale St. Sites $22, with water and electricity $31, full hookup $34; cabins with A/C $38; each additional person $4. ❶

Memphis South Campground, 460 Byhalia Rd. (☎662-429-1818), Coldwater, MS, 20 mi. south of Memphis, at Exit 280 off I-55. A relaxing, green spot with a pool and laundry. Office open daily 8-10am and 4-8pm. Sites $12, with water and electricity $15, full hookup $17; each additional person $2. ❶

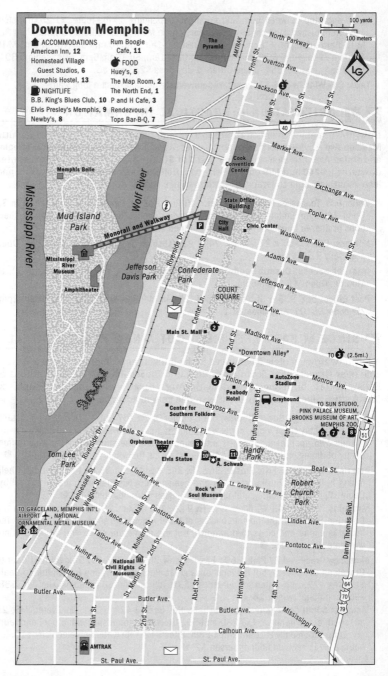

Downtown Memphis

🏠 ACCOMMODATIONS
American Inn, **12**
Homestead Village
  Guest Studios, **6**
Memphis Hostel, **13**

📷 NIGHTLIFE
B.B. King's Blues Club, **10**
Elvis Presley's Memphis, **9**
Newby's, **8**

Rum Boogie
  Cafe, **11**

🍎 FOOD
Huey's, **5**
The Map Room, **2**
The North End, **1**
P and H Cafe, **3**
Rendezvous, **4**
Tops Bar-B-Q, **7**

THE SOUTH

☆ MEALS FIT FOR THE KING

In Memphis, barbecue is as common as rhinestone-studded jumpsuits; the city even hosts the **World Championship Barbecue Cooking Contest** in May. Don't fret if gnawing on ribs isn't your thing—Memphis has plenty of other Southern restaurants with down-home favorites like fried chicken, catfish, chitlins, and grits.

Rendezvous, 52 2nd St. (☎523-2746), around back on "Downtown Alley." A Memphis legend, serving large portions of ribs ($12-15) and cheaper sandwiches ($3-6); look for the long line up. Open Tu-Th 4:30-11pm, F-Sa 11:30am-11:30pm. ❸

Tops Bar-B-Q ❶, 1286 Union Ave. (☎725-7527). If you'd prefer not to wait so long, Tops dishes up old-fashioned Memphis BBQ without any frills. Sandwich and two sides $4.25. Open daily 8:30am-11:45pm. ❷

The North End, 346 N. Main St. (☎526-0319), at Jackson St., downtown. The spicy food and extensive beer list contribute to the hoppin' atmosphere. Specialties are tamales, wild rice, stuffed potatoes, and Creole dishes ($3-12). The orgasmic hot fudge pie is known as "sex on a plate" ($3.75). Happy hour daily 4-7pm. Live music F-Sa 10pm. Open daily 11am-3am.

The Map Room, 2 S. Main St. (☎543-8686). Business folk, travelers, and neo-hippies lounge together on sofas to read loaned books and sip "lateas." Sandwiches like pimento-and-cheese ($3.50) are a respite from Memphis's otherwise meaty options. Live music daily. Open 24hr. ❶

Huey's, 77 S. 2nd St. (☎527-2700), downtown. Voted best burgers ($4) in Memphis since 1984. Patrons show their appreciation by launching toothpicks into the ceiling with straw-blowguns. Live music Su 4pm. Open M-Sa 11am-3am, Su noon-3am. ❶

P and H Cafe, 1532 Madison Ave. (☎726-0906). The initials aptly stand for Poor and Hungry. The "beer joint of your dreams" grills food for budgeteers. The waitresses and kitschy decor are the real draw. During Death Week in Aug., P and H hosts the infamous "Dead Elvis Ball." Sandwiches around $5. Open M-F 11am-3am, Sa 5pm-3am. ❶

☆ MEMPHIS MUSIC & MARVELS

GRACELAND. Bow down before **Graceland,** Elvis Presley's home and a paragon of Americana that every Memphis visitor must see. Surrender yourself to the crush of tourists swarming in a delightful orgy of gaudiness at the tackiest mansion in the US. You'll never forget the faux-fur furnishings, mirrored ceilings, carpeted walls, and yellow-and-orange decor of Elvis's 1974 renovations. A blinding sheen of hundreds of gold and platinum records illuminates the **Trophy Building.** The King and his court are buried next door in the **Meditation Gardens.** (3763 Elvis Presley Blvd. Take I-55 S to Exit 5B or bus #13 "Lauderdale." ☎332-3322 or 800-238-2000. Ticket office open M-Sa 9am-5pm, Su 10am-4pm; Nov.-Feb. closed Tu. Attractions remain open 2hr. after ticket office closes. $16, students and seniors $14.60, ages 7-12 $6.)

MORE ELVIS. If you love him tender, love him true then visit the peripheral Elvis attractions across the street from the mansion. The **Elvis Presley Automobile Museum** houses a fleet of **Elvis-mobiles** including pink and purple Cadillacs and a battalion of golf carts and motorized toys. ($7, students and seniors $6.30, children $3.) Walk a Mile in My Shoes, a free 20min. film screened every 30min., contrasts the early (slim) years with the later (fat) ones. **Elvis Airplanes** showcases the two Elvis planes: the Lisa Marie, complete with blue suede bed and gold-plated seatbelt, and the tiny Hound Dog II Jetstar. ($6, seniors $5.40, children $3.) The **Sincerely Elvis** exhibit glimpses into Elvis's private side; see the books he read, the pajamas he wore, and the TVs he shot. *($5, seniors $4.50, children $2.50.)* The **Platinum Tour Package** discounts admission to the mansion and all attractions. *($25, students and seniors $22.50, ages 7-12 $12.)* All have wheelchair access except the airplanes.

Every year on the week of August 16 (the date of Elvis's death), millions of the King's cortege get all shook up for **Elvis Week,** an extended celebration that includes a pilgrimage to his junior high school and a candlelight vigil. The days surrounding his birthday, January 8, also see some Kingly activities.

MUSIC: THE MEMPHIS HEARTBEAT. Long before Sam Phillips and Sun Studio produced Elvis, Jerry Lee Lewis, U2, and Bonnie Raitt, historic **Beale St.** saw the invention of the blues and the soul hits of the Stax label. For an idea of how all these different elements influenced each other and American culture at large, head over to the must-see ◪**Rock 'n' Soul Museum.** Numerous artifacts are on display, including B.B. King's famous guitar, "Lucille." Best of all, the audio tour contains a hundred complete songs, from early blues classics to Isaac Hayes's *Shaft* theme song. *(145 Lt. George W. Lee Ave. One block south of Beale St.* ☎ *543-0800. Open daily 10am-6pm. $8.50, seniors $7.50, ages 5-17 $5. Wheelchair accessible.)* No visit to Memphis is complete without a visit to ◪**Sun Studio,** where rock 'n' roll was conceived. In this legendary one-room recording studio, Elvis was discovered, Johnny Cash walked the line, Jerry Lee Lewis was consumed by great balls of fire, and Carl Perkins warned everyone to stay off his blue suede shoes. *(706 Union Ave.* ☎ *521-0664. 30min. tours every hr. on the ½hr. Open daily 10am-6pm. $8.50, under 12 free; AAA discount. some memorabilia is on display at the gift shop for free. Wheelchair accessible.)*

OVERTON PARK. The four seamlessly connected buildings of the **Brooks Museum of Art,** in the southwest corner of Overton Park east of downtown, showcase artwork as diverse as their architecture. *(1934 Poplar Ave.* ☎ *544-6200. Open Tu-F 10am-4pm, Sa 10am-5pm, Su 11:30am-5pm, first W of each month 10am-8pm. $5, students $2, seniors $4; W free. Wheelchair accessible.)* Also in the park is the impressive, but small, **Memphis Zoo.** The cat park is a roar and the China section takes visitors to another world. *(200 Prentis Place.* ☎ *276-9453. Open daily 9am-5pm. $10, seniors $9, ages 2-11 $6.)*

UNIQUE MUSEUMS. The powerful ◪**National Civil Rights Museum** is housed at the site of Martin Luther King Jr.'s assassination in the **Lorraine Motel** at Calhoun St. Relive the horrific struggle of the Civil Rights movement through photographs, videos, and interviews in this moving exhibit. *(450 Mulberry St., at Calhoun St.* ☎ *521-9699. Open June-Aug. M-Sa 9am-6pm, Su 1-6pm; Sept.-May 9am-6pm, Su 1-5pm. $8.50, students with ID and seniors $7.50, ages 4-17 $6.50.)* South of downtown, the ◪**National Ornamental Metal Museum,** the only such institution in the US, displays fine metalwork from contemporary artists. Get a better idea of how the art is made at the working blacksmith shop behind the museum, alongside a sculpture garden overlooking the Mississippi River. Check out the front gate as you walk in. *(374 Metal Museum Dr. Exit 12C from I-55.* ☎ *774-6380. Open Tu-Sa 10am-5pm, Su noon-5pm. $4, students $2, seniors $3.)* The **Pink Palace Museum and Planetarium** is a child-oriented museum housed in an impressive old mansion. Visitors are treated to a bit of Memphis history, an IMAX theater, and some funky exhibits like a collection of shrunken heads. The museum itself is a pink marble mansion originally built to house Piggly-Wiggly founder Clarence Saunders, who relinquished the house after losing his fortune on Wall Street. *(3050 Central Ave.* ☎ *320-6362. Open M-Th 9am-4pm, F-Sa 9am-9pm, Su noon-6pm. $7, seniors $6.50, ages 3-12 $4.50; IMAX film $6.50/6/5; planetarium show $3.50/3/3. Package deals available. Wheelchair accessible.)* **A. Schwab,** a small, family-run department store (circa 1876), still offers old-fashioned bargains. The mezzanine houses a "museum" of never-sold relics, including an array of voodoo potions. Elvis bought some of his ensembles here. *(163 Beale St.* ☎ *523-9782. Open M-Sa 9am-5pm. Free tours upon request.)*

AQUAMMODATIONS William Faulkner once said that "the Delta meets in the lobby of the **Peabody Hotel.**" Every day at 11am the hotel rolls out the red carpet, and the ducks that live in their own luxury suites on the top floor ride down the elevator, with the help of a personal attendant, and waddle over to a large fountain in the center of the floor to the tune John Phillip Sousa's *Stars and Stripes Forever* or *King Cotton March.* The procession is repeated, in reverse, when the ducks retire at the start of cocktail hour at 5pm. *(149 Union Ave. Downtown. ☎529-4000.)*

MUD ISLAND. A quick monorail ride over the Mississippi to **Mud Island** allows you to explore the renowned World War II B-17 *Memphis Belle* and to stroll and splash along a 1½ mi. scale model of the Mississippi River. **Free tours** of the River-walk and Memphis Belle run several times daily. Also on the island, the **Mississippi River Museum** charts the history and culture of the river over the past 10,000 years with artifacts, videos, and life-sized replicas of steamboats and ironclads. *(Monorail leaves from 125 Front St. ☎576-7241 or 800-507-6507. Tours June-Aug. daily 10am-7:15pm; Sept.-May Tu-Su 9am-4:15pm. Museum $8, seniors $6. Wheelchair accessible.)*

PARKS & GARDENS. Memphis has almost as many parks as museums, each offering a slightly different natural setting. The 96-acre **Memphis Botanical Gardens** are the perfect place to take a long stroll; relish the fantastic rose garden with 57 varieties of the flower, and the Japanese sensory garden. *(750 Cherry Rd. In Audubon Park off Park Ave. ☎685-1566. Open Mar.-Oct. M-Sa 9am-6pm, Su 11am-6pm; Nov.-Feb. M-Sa 9am-4:30pm, Su 11am-4:30pm. $4, students and seniors $3, ages 6-17 $2. Free every Tu after noon.)* Across the street, the **Dixon Galleries and Garden** flaunts an impeccable garden accented with an impressive range of sculptures, and a collection of European art with works by Renoir, Degas, and Monet. *(4339 Park Ave. ☎761-2409. Open Tu-Sa 10am-5pm, Su 1-5pm. $5, seniors $4, students free. On M, only the gardens are open; admission is half-price. Seniors free on Tu.)*

🎵 🎬 ARE YOU LONESOME TONIGHT?

W.C. Handy's 1917 "Beale St. Blues" claims that "You'll find that business never closes 'til somebody gets killed." Beale St. has changed a lot since Handy's day; today's visitors are more likely to encounter the Hard Rock Cafe and all the mega-commercialism that comes with it than the rough and tumble juke joints of old. Despite all the change, the strip between 2nd and 4th St. is still the place visitors come for live music. Few clubs have set closing times. On Friday nights, a $10 wristband lets you wander in and out of any club on the strip. You can save a few bucks by buying a drink at one of the many outdoor stands and soaking up the blues and acrobatics of street performers as you meander from show to show. Hot blues joints change frequently; ask the folks at the **Center for Southern Folklore,** 119 S. Main St. (☎525-3655. Open Su-Th 11am-7pm, F-Sa 11am-11pm.) The free *Memphis Flyer* and the "Playbook" section of the Friday morning *Memphis Commercial Appeal* can also tell you what's goin' down in town.

BEALE ST. BLUES

B.B. King's Blues Club, 143 Beale St. (☎524-5464 or 800-443-0972). The laid-back atmosphere combined with succulent ribs make this place a popular joint for locals, visitors, and celebrities alike. B.B himself still shows up for some meals, and occasionally plays a show. Entrees $7-18. Beer $3.25. Cover $3-7, when B.B. plays $35-100. Open M-F 4:30pm-1am, Sa-Su 11am-12:30am.

Elvis Presley's Memphis, 126 Beale St. (☎527-6900). Graceland-sponsored. Serves Elvis grub like fried peanut butter and banana sandwiches ($5.75). Su gospel brunch. Shows begin 8:30-9:30pm. Open Su-Th 11am-midnight, F-Sa 11am-1am.

THE SOUTH

Rum Boogie Cafe, 182 Beale St. (☎528-0150). One of the first clubs on Beale St., Rum Boogies still rocks with honest homegrown blues and a friendly ambience. Check out the celebrity guitars hanging from the ceiling and the original Stax Records sign. Music 9:30pm. Open Su-Th 8:30am-12:20am, F-Sa 9:30am-1:30am.

NIGHTLIFE OFF BEALE ST.
For a collegiate atmosphere, try the **Highland St.** strip near **Memphis State University.**

Wild Bill's, 1580 Vollintine Rd. (☎726-5473), a more off-the-beaten-track club, capitalizes on the juke joint/hole-in-the-wall tradition; it's best to arrive after 11pm. Live music F-Su. Cover F-Su $5. Open M-Th 7am-11pm, F-Su 7am until late.)

J-Wag's Lounge, 1268 Madison (☎725-1909), the city's hot gay bar, was featured in the movie *The People vs. Larry Flynt.* F-Sa DJ. Open 24hr.

Newby's, 539 S. Highland St. (☎452-8408), is a hopping college bar. Happy hour 4-7pm. Live music W-Sa around 10:30pm. Cover $3-10. Open daily 3pm-3am.

ENTERTAINMENT
The majestic **Orpheum Theater,** 203 S. Main St., shows classic movies with an organ prelude and a cartoon. (In summer F 7:15pm.) The grand old theater, with 15 ft. high chandeliers, has occasional live music and Broadway shows. (☎525-3000. Box office open M-F 9am-5pm and before shows. Movies $6, students and seniors $5. Music and shows $15-45.) **Memphis in May** (☎525-4611) celebrates throughout the month with concerts, art exhibits, food contests, and sporting events.

◪ DAYTRIPS FROM MEMPHIS

THE MISSISSIPPI DELTA
South of Memphis, U.S. 61 runs to Vicksburg through the swamps and flatlands of the Mississippi Delta region, where cotton was king and the blues were born. Times are still hard in **Clarksdale, MS,** 70 mi. south of Memphis in the heart of the Delta, where some of the most famous musicians were born and are now glorified at festivals and in museums. The **Delta Blues Museum,** 1 Blues Alley, at the intersection of John Lee Hooker Ln., off 3rd. St., displays photographs and rare artifacts, including harmonicas owned by Sonny Boy Williamson, and a guitar fashioned by ZZ Top from a log cabin Muddy Waters once lived in. (☎662-627-6820. Open Mar.-Oct. M-Sa 9am-5pm; Nov.-Feb. M-Sa 10am-5pm. $6, ages 6-12 $3.) Twenty miles north on U.S. 49, across the river in Arkansas, lies **Helena.** The legendary King Biscuit Time radio show was first broadcast here in 1941, featuring live music from Sonny Boy Williamson. The first weekend of October, the town hosts the **King Biscuit Blues Festival,** the largest free blues festival in the South. The **Delta Cultural Center,** 141 Cherry St., displays exhibits on the rich land and poor people that figure so prominently in regional culture. (☎870-338-4350 or 800-358-0972. Open M-Sa 10am-5pm, Su 1-5pm. Free.)

NORTH CAROLINA

From whitewater rafting and downhill skiing in the west to the cultural activities of the Research Triangle, North Carolina has a lot to offer. In the east, the pace of life slows almost to a halt among the beach culture of the Outer Banks, where great surfing and fresh fish come in equal parts. Despite the marked diversity across the state, one thing can be said for the whole of the "Old North State"—natural beauty and gentle hospitality are the rule.

🛈 PRACTICAL INFORMATION

Capital: Raleigh.

Visitor info: Dept. of Commerce, Travel and Tourism, 301 N. Wilmington St., Raleigh 27601 (☎919-733-4171 or 800-847-4862; www.visitnc.com). **Dept. of Natural Resources and Community Development,** Division of Parks and Recreation, 1615 Mail Service Ctr., Raleigh 27699 (☎919-733-4181).

Postal Abbreviation: NC. **Sales Tax:** 6%.

THE RESEARCH TRIANGLE   ☎919

A trio of towns—Raleigh, Durham, and Chapel Hill—sporting large universities and top-notch scientists, "the Triangle" was born in the 1950's with the creation of the spectacularly successful Research Triangle Park. As a result, the area is alive with students, scholars, and things to do. **Raleigh,** the state capital and home to North Carolina State University (NC State), is a historic town that has recently revamped its tourist attractions. **Durham,** formerly a major tobacco producer, now supports Duke University and multiple hospitals and medical research projects devoted to finding cancer cures (now that's irony, isn't it?). The University of North Carolina (UNC), chartered in 1789 as the nation's first state university, is located just 20 miles down the road in **Chapel Hill.** College culture infuses the area with a hip music scene and a plethora of stores.

🚍 TRANSPORTATION

Airport: Raleigh-Durham International (☎840-2123; www.rdu.com), 10 mi. from both downtown Raleigh and Durham, on U.S. 70. A taxi to downtown Raleigh or Durham costs about $27.

Trains: Amtrak, 320 W. Cabarrus St., Raleigh (☎833-7594), 4 blocks west of the Civic Ctr. Open 24hr. To **Richmond** (3½hr., 2 per day, $28-50) and **Washington D.C.** (6hr., 2 per day, $43-78).

Buses: Greyhound has a station in both Raleigh and Durham. **Raleigh:** 314 W. Jones St. (☎834-8275). Open 24hr. To: **Chapel Hill** (80min., 4 per day, $10); **Charleston** (7½hr., 2 per day, $59); and **Durham** (40min., 9 per day, $6.50). **Durham:** 820 W. Morgan St. (☎687-4800), 1 block off Chapel Hill St. downtown, 2½ mi. northeast of Duke. Open daily 7:30am-9:30pm. To **Chapel Hill** (25min., 4 per day, $8) and **Washington D.C.** (6hr., 6 per day, $50).

Public Transit: Capital Area Transit, Raleigh (☎828-7228). Buses run M-Sa. 75¢; transfers free. **Durham Area Transit Authority (DATA),** Durham (☎683-3282). Most routes start downtown at Main and Morgan St. on the loop. Operates daily; hours vary by route; fewer on Su. 75¢; seniors, under 18, and disabled 35¢; children under 43 in. free; transfers free. **Chapel Hill Transit,** Chapel Hill (☎968-2769). Office open M-F 4:45am-10pm. Buses run 5:40am-8pm. 75¢. There is also a **free shuttle** on the UNC campus. Public transportation between the cities is available through **Triangle Transit Authority** (☎549-9999; www.ridetta.org). Buses run approximately 6am-11pm. $1.50.

Taxis: Cardinal Cab, ☎828-3228.

🛈 PRACTICAL INFORMATION

Visitor info: Raleigh Visitors Center, 301 N. Blount St. (☎733-3456). Open M-F 8am-5pm, Sa 10am-5pm, Su 1-5pm. **Durham Convention Center & Visitors Bureau,** 101 E. Morgan St. (☎800-446-8604). Open M-F 8:30am-5pm, Sa 10am-2pm. **Visitor Info Center & Chapel Hill Chamber of Commerce,** 104 S. Estes Dr. (☎967-7075). Open M-F 9am-5pm.

THE SOUTH

Hotline: Rape Crisis, ☎919-403-6562. 24hr.

Post Office: Raleigh: 311 New Bern Ave. (☎828-5902). Open M-F 8am-5:30pm, Sa 8am-noon. **ZIP code:** 27611. **Durham:** 323 E. Chapel Hill St. (☎683-1976). Open M-F 8:30am-5pm. **ZIP code:** 27701. **Chapel Hill:** 125 S. Estes St. (☎967-6297). Open M-F 8:30am-5:30pm, Sa 8:30am-noon. **ZIP code:** 27514.

Area code: 919.

ACCOMMODATIONS

Raleigh's budget lodging can be found on Capital Blvd., in the Crabtree area, about 2½ mi. northeast of town, a mile or so inside the I-440 beltline. Reasonably priced accommodations are slightly harder to come by in Chapel Hill.

Homestead Suites, 4810 Bluestone Dr. (☎510-8551), in Raleigh, has new, comfortable rooms with kitchenettes, A/C, cable TV, free local calls, and Internet access. Rooms from $39. ❷

Carolina-Duke Motor Inn (☎286-0771 or 800-438-1158 for reservations), on Guess Rd. exit off I-85, provides travelers with clean, budget-priced rooms, laundry facilities, and a shuttle to both the Duke and V.A. hospitals. Pool, A/C, cable TV, free local calls, and continental breakfast included. DATA access across the street. Wheelchair accessible. Singles $40; doubles $48; additional person $3. 10% AARP/AAA discount. ❷

Red Roof Inn, 5623 Chapel Hill Blvd. (☎489-9421), at the intersection of U.S. 15-501 and I-40, offers standard rooms. A/C, disabled access, free local calls, and cable TV. Singles $47-53; doubles $54-59; $4 each additional person. ❸

Falls Lake State Recreation Area (☎676-1027), about 12 mi. north of Raleigh, off Rte. 98. Reservations taken with 7-14 days notice for stays of more than 7 days. $12, with hookup $17.) ❶

FOOD

Each of the area's major universities has spawned a region of affordable and interesting eateries; Raleigh's **Hillsborough St.** and **Capital Blvd.,** Durham's **9th St.,** and Chapel Hill's **Franklin St.** all cater to a college (and thus budget-oriented) crowd.

Skylight Exchange, 405½ W. Rosemary St. (☎933-5550), entrance in an alley off of Rosemary, a block over from Franklin. Doubles as a cafe and used book/music store. The Exchange is home to a vast array of sandwiches ($3-8) and the legendary 50¢ cup of coffee. Live music M-Sa 9pm. Open daily 11am-11pm. ❶

Ramshead Rathskellar, 157½ E. Franklin St. (☎942-5158), has been a local legend since 1948. The uniquely decorated interior of "the Rat" has seen more than 50 years of Tarheels come and go. Sandwiches under $8. Meals $6-17. Open M-W 11am-2:30pm and 5-9pm, Th 11am-2:30pm and 5-9:30pm, F 11am-2:30pm and 5-10pm, Sa 11:30am-10:30pm, Su 11:30am-9pm. ❸

Elmo's Diner, 776 and 9th St. (☎416-3823), in Durham, is the local favorite and serves breakfast all day for about $5. Open Su-Th 6:30am-10pm, F-Sa 6:30am-11pm. ❶

Francesca's, 706 9th St. (☎286-4177), farther down 9th St., dishes up delectable desserts for around $3. Be sure to sample some of the homemade gelato for $2.50. Open M-Th 11am-11pm, F-Sa 11am-midnight, Su 11am-10pm. ❶

Cosmic Cantina, 1920½ Perry St. (☎286-1875), at the end of the shops on 9th St. A great stop for authentic, cheap, and quick Mexican fare ($3-5). Upstairs is a student hotspot. Open Su-Th 11am-midnight, F-Sa 11am-3am. ❶

🔘 SIGHTS

RALEIGH. Raleigh has grown rapidly in recent years, but its downtown area still retains much of the character of an old North Carolina town—with added gleaming tourist attractions. Across from the capitol building are two first-rate museums. The **North Carolina Museum of History** looks back through the North Carolina timeline via an ever-changing array of special exhibits. The **Museum of Natural Sciences** is home to "Willo, the dinosaur with a heart," a rare dinosaur fossil with an iron concretion within the ribcage. The museum also contains a tropical forest and enough live animals to legally be recognized as a zoo. *(Museum of History: 5 E. Edenton St. ☎ 715-0200. Open Tu-Sa 9am-5pm, Su noon-5pm. Free. Museum of Natural Sciences: 11 W. Jones St. ☎ 733-7450. Open M-Sa 9am-5pm, Su noon-5pm. Free.)* The area around **Moore Square**, a few blocks southeast of the capitol, is a small district of youthful arts. Adjacent to the Square is a collection of shops, cafes, and bars known as **City Market.**

CHAPEL HILL. Chapel Hill and neighboring Carrboro are virtually inseparable from the **University of North Carolina at Chapel Hill.** The university's **Dean Dome** hosts sporting events and concerts (tickets available through Ticketmaster). Until 1975, NASA astronauts trained at UNC's **Morehead Planetarium,** which now projects several different shows per year and houses a small museum. *(250 E. Franklin St. ☎ 549-6863. Open M-Sa 10am-5pm and 7-9:45pm, Su 12:30-5pm and 7-9:45pm. $4.50; students, seniors, and children $3.50. Exhibits free.)*

DURHAM. Durham's main attractions center around the Duke family and their principle legacy, **Duke University,** which is divided into East and West Campuses. The neo-gothic **Duke Chapel,** completed in the early 1930s, looms grandly at the center of West Campus. Over a million pieces of stained glass and a host of statues depicting both Christian and Southern figures grace the chapel. *(☎ 684-2572. Open Sept.-May daily 8am-10pm; June-Aug. 8am-8pm. Free. Self-guided tour available.)* Nearby on Anderson St. the 55-acre **Sarah P. Duke Gardens** showcase both native and non-native plants in a lush, shaded setting complete with ponds and a vine-draped gazebo. *(☎ 684-3698. Open daily 8am-dusk. Free.)* At the other end of Durham, the **Duke Homestead and Tobacco Museum** champions the history of both the Duke family and the tobacco industry. The museum provides a rare opportunity to watch old TV ads for cigarettes and learn about tobacco farming. *(2828 Duke Homestead Rd., off Guess Rd. ☎ 477-5498. Open Apr.-Oct. M-Sa 9am-5pm, Su 1-5pm; Nov.-Mar. Tu-Sa 10am-4pm, Su 1-4pm. Free. Call to schedule Homestead tours.)* The 1988 movie *Bull Durham* was filmed in the **Durham Bulls'** ballpark. The AAA farm team for the Tampa Bay Devil Rays still plays here, minus Kevin Costner. *(Take "Durham Bulls Stadium" exit right off of I-40. ☎ 687-6500; www.durhambulls.com.)*

🎵 🖼 ENTERTAINMENT & NIGHTLIFE

Pick up a free copy of the weekly *Spectator* and *Independent* magazines, available at most restaurants, bookstores, and hotels, for listings of Triangle news and events. Chapel Hill offers the best nightlife, especially in terms of music. A number of live music clubs congregate near the western end of Franklin St., where it becomes Main St. in the neighboring town of Carrboro. **Cat's Cradle,** 300 E. Main St., in Carrboro, is the area's main venue, hosting a wide variety of local and national acts. Recent performers include John Mayer and Dispatch. *(☎ 967-9053. Cover and show times vary based on performer.)* Another nearby club, **Local 506,**

506 W. Franklin St., focuses on indie and rock 'n' roll. (☎942-5506. 21+. Cover around $5.) In Raleigh, **Greenshields**, 214 E. Martin St., at Blount St. in City Market, brews their own beer in a fun, relaxed environment. (☎829-0214. Open Su-Th 11:30am-midnight, F-Sa 11:30am-1am.) While in City Market, check out **Flying Saucer**, 328 W. Morgan St., which boasts over 150 beers on tap. (☎821-7468. Open M and Th-Sa 11am-2am, Tu-W 11am-1am, Su noon-midnight.)

WINSTON-SALEM ☎336

Winston-Salem was, as its name suggests, originally two different towns. Salem was the religious center of the Moravian movement, while Winston was the urban center of tobacco farming. Salem abounded with crafts and traditional religious beliefs, while Winston was home to one of the biggest tobacco companies in the South—R.J. Reynolds's. Both Reynolds and his wife were fond of the arts and fine architecture, and they nurtured these dueling loves in the then-tiny town by funding **Wake Forest University**. When the two cities merged, it created a unique blend of cultural diversity that still exists today.

🛈 PRACTICAL INFORMATION. Visitors Center: 601 N. Cherry St. (☎800-331-7018, www.visitwinstonsalem.com.) **Winston-Salem Transit Authority** has a main depot right in the city on 4th St. (☎727-2000. Fare $1.) **Post Office:** 1500 Patterson Ave. (☎721-1749. Open M-F 8:30am-5pm.) **Zip code:** 27101. **Area code:** 336.

🖪🖸 ACCOMMODATIONS & FOOD. There are scores of motels that are perfect for the budget traveler at Exit 184 off I-40, on the way into town. On the northern side of the city, budget motels center around Hwy. 52, just past Patterson Ave. Most rooms run $39-69. For luxury accommodations at a fraction of the price, stay at ▧**Lady Anne's Victorian Bed and Breakfast ❸**, 610 Summit Ave., 6 blocks from the center of town. The gorgeous Victorian home has a cozy veranda perfect for sitting and relaxing, delicious breakfasts, and good old-fashioned Southern charm. (☎724-1074. A/C, cable TV, refrigerator, data ports. Rooms around $55.)

Winston-Salem is alive with good food. In the heart of the Old Salem Village, the **Old Salem Tavern ❺**, 36 Main St., will delight both taste buds and imaginations with fantastic fare such as Grilled Citrus barbecued Salmon, served by waiters and waitresses in traditional Moravian garb. (☎748-8585. Entrees around $17. Open daily 11am-2pm and 5-10pm.) **The West End Cafe ❶**, 926 W. 4th St., is a local favorite with something for everyone, including unique entrees that change nightly. (☎723-7602. Good ol' hamburgers $4.50. Open M-F 10am-10pm, Sa noon-10pm.) In the center of town, **Bistro 420 ❸**, 420 4th St., adds a gourmet twist to Southern favorites with dishes like potato-crusted catfish ($16). (☎721-1336. Shrimp and grits $8.25. Open M-F 11am-2pm and W-Sa 5:30-10:30pm.)

◙ SIGHTS. There are two main attractions in Winston-Salem, each of which could easily take more than a day to visit. **Old Salem Village** takes visitors back in time to a working Moravian village. The Moravians, an early Protestant group, came to North Carolina from the present-day Czech Republic in order to live in political and religious harmony. Today the village, occupying the entire southern part of Winston-Salem, outlines their fascinating history and traditions. (☎888-653-7253. Open M-Sa 9am-5pm, Su 12:30-5pm.) Delicious baked goods can be found in the Old Salem Museum at **Winkler Bakery** which still cooks the same way the Moravians did 100 years ago—in a large, wood-burning brick ovens. Strong believers in the education of women, the Moravians founded the first school of higher learning for women in the United States, **Salem College**, here. The village also includes the **Museum of Early Southern Decorative Art (MESDA)**. The museum is "ropes free," meaning the rooms are reconstructed to look and feel the same as the rooms in famous historical Southern homes. Tours allow visitors to walk among the very artifacts and decorative art removed from homes before they were destroyed.

Reynolda House, on the other side of town, is perhaps one of the South's most famous houses. (☎725-5325. Open Tu-Sa 9:30am-4:30pm, Su 1:30-4:30pm. $6, students and children free, seniors $5.) Now owned by Wake Forest University, the house is credited to the vision of Katherine Smith, the wife of tobacco giant R.J. Reynolds. In its heyday, the household was completely self-sufficient, with a working "village" on the grounds. Although home to a large collection of American art, including works by Thomas Cole, the beauty of the manor is outshone by the two acres of gardens that surround it. The **Reynolda Gardens** were created for the enjoyment of the Reynolds family and the public, and they remain one of the most aesthetic attractions in Winston-Salem. (☎758-5593. Open dawn to dusk. Free.)

CHARLOTTE   ☎704

Charlotte is aptly named the "Queen City." The second-largest financial center in the nation and the largest city of the Carolinas, Charlotte's gleaming "uptown" region bustles with well-funded charm and vigor, attracting visitors with its topnotch science museum, ritzy clubs and bars, and successful sports teams.

◪ PRACTICAL INFORMATION. Amtrak, 1914 N. Tryon St. (☎376-4416), and **Greyhound,** 601 W. Trade St. (☎372-0456), stop in Charlotte. Both stations are open 24hr. **Charlotte Transit,** 901 N. Davidson St., operates local buses. (☎336-3366. $1, $1.40 for outlying areas; free transfers.) Within the uptown area, **Gold Rush** (☎332-2227) runs free shuttles that resemble old-fashioned cable cars. **Visitors Center:** 122 E. Stonewall St. (☎800-722-1994. Open M-F 8:30am-5pm, Sa 10am-4pm, Su 1-4pm.) **Hotlines: Rape Crisis,** ☎375-9900. **Suicide Line,** ☎358-2800. Both 24hr. **Gay/Lesbian Hotline,** ☎535-6277. Operates Su-Th 6:30-10pm. **Post Office:** 201 N. McDowell (☎333-5135). Open M-F 7:30am-6pm, Sa 9am-1pm. **ZIP code:** 28204. **Area code:** 704.

◪◩ ACCOMMODATIONS & FOOD. There are several clusters of budget motels in the Charlotte area: on Independence Blvd. off the John Belk Freeway; off I-85 at Sugar Creek Rd., Exit 41; off I-85 at Exit 33 near the airport; and off I-77 at Clanton St., Exit 7. The **Continental Inn ❷,** 1100 W. Sugar Creek Rd., has immaculate, inviting rooms. (☎597-8100. A/C, cable TV. M-Th singles $36, F-Sa $40; doubles $40/45.) **Suite Carolina ❷,** 5820 Monroe Rd., offers clean, quiet rooms with kitchenettes and is conveniently located on the main bus line. (☎319-1900. Cable TV, A/C, data ports, and free local calls. Rooms $45.)

Two areas outside of uptown offer attractive dining options. North Davidson ("NoDa"), around 36th St., is home to a small artistic community inhabiting a set of historic buildings. South from city center, the **Dilworth** neighborhood, along East and South Blvd., is lined with restaurants serving everything from ethnic cuisine to pizza and pub fare. In NoDa, **Fat City Deli ❷,** 3027 N. Davidson St., offers a bizarre twist of the South and the indie rock scene. During the day it is a perfect place to enjoy a sandwich ($5-7) outside, while in the evenings patrons can listen to live music. (☎343-0240. Open M-F 11:30am-2am, Sa-Su noon-2am; kitchen closes Su-Th at 11pm, F-Sa at midnight.) **Smelly Cat Coffeehouse,** 514 36th St., in NoDa, serves up delectable drinks in a fun, youthful atmosphere. (☎374-9656. S'mores mocha with marshmallows and caramel $2.75. Open M-Th 7am-9pm, F-Sa 7am-11pm.) Organic health food is the name of the game at **Talley's Green Grocery and Cafe ❶,** 1408-C East Blvd., an upscale grocery with a deli counter. (☎334-9200. Sandwiches under $6. Open M-Sa 7:30am-9pm, Su 10am-7pm.) East of downtown, the colorful **Antony's Caribbean Cafe ❸,** 2001 E. 7th St., spices up life with cheerful decor and deli-

THE SOUTH

cious food. (☎342-0749. Entrees $6-11. Open M-F 11:30am-2:30pm; also M-Sa 5:30-10pm.) For a slightly pricier option in town, **Cosmos Cafe ❺**, 300 N. College St., at E. 6th St., is a hip splurge but becomes a popular yuppie bar at 10pm. Swing by Wednesday nights for superb gourmet martinis at half price. (☎372-3553. Banana quesadilla $6. Dinners around $18. Open M-F 11am-2am, Sa 5pm-2am.)

◙ **SIGHTS.** Most of Charlotte's museums are clustered around the center of the city, at the intersection of Tryon and Trade St. The largest and most publicized of these is **The Discovery Place**, 301 N. Tryon St., a hands-on science museum. (☎372-6261 or 800-935-0553. Open in summer M-Sa 9am-6pm, Su 1-6pm; off season M-Sa 9am-5pm, Su 1-5pm. Museum $7.50, seniors $6.50, ages 6-12 $6, ages 3-5 $5. Museum and OmniMax Theater $12/11/10/8.) The well-curated **Mint Museum of Craft and Design,** 220 N. Tryon St., features an eclectic array of exhibits, from furniture to pottery to technology. Included in the Craft and Design admission, the **Mint Museum of Art**, 2730 Randolph Rd., across town, displays American decorative and visual arts. (Both museums: ☎337-2000. Craft and Design open Tu-Sa 10am-5pm, Su noon-5pm; art museum Tu 10am-10pm, W-Sa 10am-5pm, Su noon-5pm. $6, students and seniors $5, ages 6-17 $3.) The ◙**Levine Museum of the New South,** 200 E. 7th St., is a fantastic new hands-on museum that explores the history of the Charlotte and Carolina Piedmont area. (☎333-1887 Open Tu-Sa 10am-5pm, Su noon-5pm. $6; students, seniors, and ages 6-18 $5; under 6 free.)

◪◫ **ENTERTAINMENT & NIGHTLIFE.** Charlotte is a big sports town. Basketball's **Sting** (women) play in the **Coliseum** (☎357-4700), and the NFL's **Panthers** play in Ericsson Stadium (☎358-7538), near the Visitor's Center. The Charlotte **Knights** play AAA minor league baseball at Knights Castle, off I-77 S at Exit 88 in South Carolina. (☎364-6637. $5, seniors and children $3.50.)

For nightlife, arts, and entertainment listings, grab a free *Creative Loafing* in one of Charlotte's shops or restaurants, or check the E&T section of the F *Charlotte Observer*. **Amos' Southend,** 1423 S. Tryon St., beckons with live music most nights alongside pool and foosball tables. (☎377-6874. Cover $3-35. Open Th-Tu 9pm-2am.) Several clubs are clustered in uptown Charlotte at the corner of 6th St. and College St. **Bar Charlotte,** 300 N. College St., is packed with young people searching for a good time. (☎342-2545. Th ladies night. Cover $5 21+, under 21 $10. Open Th 9pm-2am, F-Sa 8pm-2am.)

CAROLINA MOUNTAINS

The aptly named High Country includes the territory between Boone and Asheville, 100 mi. to the southwest, and fills the upper regions of the Blue Ridge Mountains. The central attraction of the mountains is the Blue Ridge Parkway (see p. 343), a national parkway that snakes through the mountains from northern Virginia to southern North Carolina. Views from many of the Parkway's scenic overlooks are staggering, particularly on rainy days when the peaks are wreathed in mist. Southwards lies the Great Smoky Mountains National Park (see p. 367). The sharp ridges and rolling slopes of the southern Appalachian range create some of the most spectacular scenery in the Southeast.

ASHEVILLE   ☎828

Hazy blue mountains, deep valleys, and spectacular waterfalls all supply a splendid backdrop to this small city. Once a coveted layover for the nation's well-to-do, Asheville housed enough Carnegies, Vanderbilts, and Mellons to fill a 1920s edition of *Who's Who on the Atlantic Seaboard.* The population these days tends more toward dreadlocks, batik, and vegetarianism, providing funky nightlife and festivals all year. In contrast to the laid-back locals, Asheville's sights are fanatically maintained and its downtown meticulously preserved, making for a pleasant respite from the Carolina wilderness.

7 PRACTICAL INFORMATION. Greyhound, 2 Tunnel Rd. (☎253-8451; open daily 8am-9pm), 2 mi. east of downtown near the Beaucatcher Tunnel, sends buses to: Atlanta (6¾hr., 1 per day, $32-34); Charlotte (2½-5hr.; 5 per day; M-Th $26, F-Su $28); Knoxville (2hr., 5 per day, $25-27); and Raleigh (8-12hr., 5 per day, $49-52). The **Asheville Transit System,** 360 W. Haywood St. (☎253-5691), handles bus service within city limits. Pick up a copy of bus schedules and routes from the Visitors Center or visit the **Asheville Transit Center,** 49 Coxe Ave., across from the Post Office. (75¢, transfers 10¢; short trips in downtown free. Discounts for seniors, disabled, and multi-fare tickets.) The **Chamber of Commerce and Visitor Center,** 151 Haywood St., Exit 4C off I-240, on the northwest end of downtown, dispenses a wealth of knowledge to visitors. (General info ☎800-257-1300; Chamber of Commerce ☎258-6101; www.exploreasheville.com. Open M-F 8:30am-5:30pm, Sa-Su 9am-5pm.) **Post Office:** 33 Coxe Ave., off Patton Ave. (☎271-6429. Open M-F 7:30am-5:30pm, Sa 9am-1pm.) **ZIP code:** 28802. **Area code:** 828.

⻔ ACCOMMODATIONS. The cheapest lodgings are on **Tunnel Rd.,** east of downtown. Slightly more expensive (and fewer) options can be found on **Merrimon Ave.,** just north of downtown. The ritziest of the budget circle hover around the Biltmore Estate on **Hendersonville Ave.,** south of downtown. The **Log Cabin Motor Court ❷,** 330 Weaverville Hwy., 10min. north of downtown, provides immaculate, inviting cabins with cable TV and laundry. Some also have fireplaces and kitchenettes, though none have A/C. (☎645-6546. Singles from $32; doubles from $53; each additional person $5.) **Econo Lodge East ❷,** 1430 Tunnel Rd., has comfortable, clean rooms for a fantastic price. (☎298-5519. A/C, cable TV, and pool. Rooms in summer $45-95; off-season from $31.) **Powhatan ❶,** on Wesley Branch Rd. 12 mi. southwest of Asheville off Rte. 191, is the closest campsite in the Pisgah National Forest. Wooded sites on a ten-acre trout lake mean opportunities for fishing, swimming, and hiking. (☎877-444-6777. No hookups. Gates close 11pm. Open Apr.-Oct. Sites $14.) **Bear Creek RV Park and Campground ❶,** 81 S. Bear Creek Rd., follow signs from I-40 Exit 47, features "luxury" camping with a pool, laundry facilities, groceries, and a game room. (☎800-833-0798. Sites $20, with water and electricity $22; RV sites with hookup $27-32.)

🗋 FOOD. For a delicious dinner before a night on the town, hit the strip of restaurants along **Broadway St.** You'll find the greasy links of most fast-food chains on **Tunnel Rd.** and **Biltmore Ave.** The **Western North Carolina Farmers Market,** at the intersection of I-40 and Rte. 191, sells fresh produce and crafts. (☎253-1691. Open Apr.-Oct. daily 8am-6pm; Nov.-Mar. 8am-5pm.) For those with a sweet tooth, ▧**Old Europe,** 18 Battery Park Ave., near Wall St., sell pastries handmade by the Hungarian owners. (☎252-0001. Cookies under $1; pastries under $4. Beer $3. Open in summer daily 9am-midnight; in winter 9am-10 or 11pm.) Even more goodies are found at **Sweet Heaven Ice Cream and Music Cafe,** 35 Montford Ave., where visitors are treated to scrumptious, huge portions of ice cream with names like "mud puppy." (☎259-9848. Live music in the evenings. Open Su-M and W-Th noon-10pm, F-Sa noon-11pm.) The **Laughing Seed Cafe ❷,** 40 Wall St., behind Patton Ave., caters to vegetarian and vegan fantasies with sumptuous dishes and reasonable prices. Sunday brunch draws a bustling crowd—and never disappoints. (☎252-3445. Salads $2.50-8. Sandwiches $4-7. Open M and W-Th 11:30am-9pm, F-Sa 11:30am-

10pm, Su 10am-9pm.) If you're looking for a bite to eat without the hassle, try **Bean-streets ❶**, 3 Broadway St., which serves coffee, sandwiches, and omelettes (under $5.50) in a quirky, laid-back environment. (☎ 255-8180. Open M-W 7:30am-6pm, Th-F 7:30am-midnight, Sa 7:30am-midnight, Su 9am-4pm.)

◙ SIGHTS. George Vanderbilt's palatial **Biltmore Estate**, 1 North Pack Sq., three blocks north of I-40 Exit 50, was built in the 1890s. Modeled on the chateaux of the Loire valley, the Biltmore is the largest private home in America. A tour can take all day; try to arrive early. Tours of the surrounding gardens and the Biltmore winery are included in the admission price. (☎ 225-1333 or 800-543-2961. Open daily 8:30am-5pm. Jan.-Oct. $34, ages 10-15 $25.50, disabled $24; Nov.-Dec. $2-3 more. Winery open M-Sa 11am-7pm, Su noon-7pm. Wine tasting for those 21+.) Meanwhile, free scenery blooms at the **Botanical Gardens**, 151 Weaver Blvd. (☎ 252-5190), as well as the **North Carolina Arboretum**, Exit 2 on I-26 or Exit 47 on I-40, (☎ 665-2492). Both attractions are open dawn to dusk.

Four museums huddle at **Pack Place** downtown: the Asheville Art Museum, the YMI Culture Center, Health Adventure, and the Colburn Gem and Mineral Museum. Tickets for all four can be purchased inside Pack Place. The **Asheville Art Museum** displays 20th-century American artwork. (☎ 253-3227. Open Tu-Th and Sa 10am-5pm, F 10am-8pm, Su 1-5pm. $6; students, seniors, and ages 4-15 $5.) The **YMI Culture Center** focuses solely on African-American art. (☎ 252-4614. Open Tu-Sa 10am-5pm. $4/3.) **Health Adventure** lets you become one with your body, but is geared more toward children. (☎ 254-6373. Open Tu-Sa 10am-5pm, Su 1-5pm. $5/4.) The **Colburn Gem and Mineral Museum** showcases all that glitters. (☎ 254-7162. Open Nov.-May Tu-Sa 10am-5pm; June-Oct. Tu-Sa 10am-5pm, Su 1-5pm. $4/3.)

The **Thomas Wolfe Memorial**, between Woodfin and Walnut St., celebrates one of the early 20th century's most influential American authors. The Visitors Center houses an exhibit on Wolfe's life and his impact on other authors, and shows a compelling biographical film. Though the inside of the novelist's boyhood home is closed due to fire, tours of the exterior are available. (☎ 253-8304. Tours every hr. on the half-hr. Apr.-Oct. M-Sa 9am-5pm; Nov.-Mar. Tu-Sa 10am-4pm. $1, students 50¢.) The scenic setting for *Last of the Mohicans* rises up almost ½ mi. in **Chimney Rock Park**, 25 mi. southeast of Asheville on Rte. 74A. After driving to the base of the Chimney, take the 26-story elevator to the top or walk up for a 75 mi. view. (☎ 800-277-9611. Ticket office open in summer daily 8:30am-5:30pm; in winter 8:30am-4:30pm. Park open 1½hr. after office closes. In summer $12, ages 4-12 $5.50; in winter $8/4.50.)

◪ ENTERTAINMENT. The downtown area, especially the southeast end around the intersection of Broadway and College St., offers music, munchies, and movies. Every Sunday night from June to September, **The New Ebony Bar & Grill**, 19 Eagle St., takes the party to the streets, closing Eagle St. to traffic to accommodate rollicking live music, dancing, and rows of folding chairs. (☎ 645-0305. Open daily 5pm-late.) Indie and artsy flicks play at the **Fine Arts Theater**, 36 Biltmore Ave. (☎ 232-0257. $6.50, matinees and seniors $5.) A popular bar, **Barley's Taproom**, 42 Biltmore Ave., hops with locals, $3 beers from 42 taps, and pool tables upstairs. (☎ 255-0504. Live music Tu, Th, and Su. Open M-Sa 11:30am-2am, Su noon-midnight.)

Summer shouldn't be anyone's season of discontent, not with free **Shakespeare in Montford Park,** at Hazel Robinson Amphitheater. (☎ 254-4540. Performances June-early Aug. F-Su 7:30pm.) During the last weekend in July, let your feet loose on the street, along with thousands of others, at North Carolina's largest free street fair, **Bele Chere Festival** (☎ 259-5800). The free weekly paper, *Mountain Express*, and *Community Connections*, a free gay publication, have entertainment listings.

NORTH CAROLINA COAST

Lined with barrier islands that shield inlanders from Atlantic squalls, the Carolina Coast has a history as stormy as the hurricanes that pummel its beaches. England's first attempt to colonize North America ended in 1590 with the peculiar disappearance of the Roanoke Island settlement. Later in its history, the coast earned the title "The Graveyard of the Atlantic"—over 600 ships have foundered on the Outer Banks' southern shores. But the same wind that sank ships lifted the world's first powered flight in 1903, thanks to some assistance from the Wright brothers. Flying now forms the basis of much of the area's recreational activity: hang-gliding, paragliding, windsurfing, and good ol' kite-flying.

OUTER BANKS   ☎ 252

The Outer Banks explode in the north with a burst of insistent glitz that tapers into an endearing tranquility in the south. On the northern half of Bodie Island, the three contiguous towns of Kitty Hawk, Kill Devil Hills, and Nags Head, like many other well-touristed beach areas on the East Coast, are heavily trafficked and dense with stores. Farther south on Rte. 12, though, the pristine beaches remain fairly uncrowded, and Ocracoke Island, despite its growing popularity with visitors, retains the feel of a small community.

ORIENTATION

The Outer Banks consist of four narrow islands strung along half the length of the North Carolina coast. **Bodie Island,** the northernmost island, is joined to the mainland by U.S. 158 and serves as most travelers' point of entry. For much of Bodie Island, Rte. 12 (known as the Beach Road) and U.S. 158 (called the Bypass) run parallel. At the northern edge of the **Cape Hatteras National Seashore,** Rte. 12 continues south through the park to the great sandy elbow that is **Hatteras Island,** connected by a bridge to Bodie. **Ocracoke Island,** the southernmost island, is linked by ferry to Hatteras Island and towns on the mainland. Both Hatteras and Ocracoke are almost entirely park land. **Roanoke Island.** Directions to locations on Bodie Island are usually given in terms of distances in miles (marked as MP for Mile Post) from the Wright Memorial Bridge. There is **no public transit** on the Outer Banks. The flat terrain makes hiking and biking pleasant, but ferocious traffic calls for extra caution and travel time.

PRACTICAL INFORMATION

Ferries: Free ferries run between **Hatteras** and **Ocracoke** (40 min., daily 5am-midnight). Toll ferries run to **Ocracoke** (☎800-345-1665) from **Cedar Island** (☎800-856-0343; 2¼hr.), east of New Bern on Rte. 12, off U.S. 70, and from **Swan Quarter** (☎800-773-1094; 2½hr.), on U.S. 264. Call ahead for schedules and reservations. $1 per pedestrian, $2 per cyclist, $10 per car.

Taxis: Beach Cab (☎441-2500), for Bodie Island and Manteo.

Bike Rental: Pony Island Motel (☎928-4411), on Ocracoke Island. Open daily 8am-10pm. $2 per hr., $10 per day.

Visitor Info: Outer Banks Visitors Bureau, 704 S. Rte. 64 (☎473-2138 or 800-446-6262; www.outerbanks.com), in Manteo; info for all the islands except Ocracoke. Open M-F 8am-6pm, Sa-Su noon-4pm. **Cape Hatteras National Seashore Information Centers: Whalebone Junction** (☎441-6644), on Rte. 12 at the north entrance to the park.

Open Apr.-Nov. daily 9am-5pm. **Bodie Island** (☎441-5711), on Rte. 12 at Bodie Island Lighthouse. Open June-Aug. daily 9am-6pm; Sept.-May 9am-5pm. **Ocracoke Island** (☎928-4531), next to the ferry terminal at the south end of the island. Open Apr.-Nov. daily 9am-6pm; Sept.-May 9am-5pm. **Hatteras Island** (☎995-4474), on Rte. 12 at the Cape Hatteras Lighthouse. Open summer daily 9am-6pm; off-season 9am-5pm.

Internet access: Dare County Library, 400 Mustian St. (☎441-4331), in Kill Devil Hills, on U.S. 158. Open M and Th-F 9am-5:30pm, Tu-W 10am-7pm, Sa 10am-4pm.

Post Office: 3841 N. Croatan Hwy. (☎261-2211), in Kitty Hawk, MP 4 on the 158 Bypass. Open M-F 9am-4:30pm, Sa 10am-noon. **ZIP code:** 27949. **Area code:** 252.

■ ◗ ACCOMMODATIONS & FOOD

Most motels line **Rte. 12** on crowded Bodie Island. For more privacy, go farther south; **Ocracoke** is the most secluded. On all three islands, rooming rates are highest from late May to early September. Reservations are needed seven to ten days ahead for weeknights and up to a month in advance for weekends. For campers, long tent spikes, tents with fine screens, and strong insect repellent are all recommended. Sleeping on the beach may result in fines, but there are several lovely campsites owned by the National Park Service that are practically on the shore.

BODIE ISLAND

Outer Banks International Hostel (HI-AYH) ❶, 1004 W. Kitty Hawk Rd., is the best deal in the northern islands. From U.S. 158, turn south onto The Woods Rd. (2nd traffic light after the Wright Memorial Bridge), continue until the end of the road, then turn right onto Kitty Hawk Rd. This clean and friendly hostel has 40 beds, two kitchens, A/C, volleyball, shuffleboard, and a variety of fascinating people. (☎261-2294. Members $15, nonmembers $18; private singles $30/$35; doubles $40/$50. Camping spot on the grounds $12, $6 each additional person; tent rental $6.) The **Nettlewood Motel ❸,** MP 7 Beach Rd., offers clean and cheery rooms with private access to a sandy, uncluttered strip of beach. (☎441-5039. TV, A/C, heat, refrigerators, and pool. Doubles are equipped with a kitchenette. Mid-June to late Aug. singles $50, doubles $72; late May to mid-June and late Aug. to late Sept. $41/52; Jan. to late May and Oct.-Dec. $33/38.)

Tortuga's Lie ❸, MP 11 Beach Rd., serves Caribbean-influenced seafood and grill items in a straight-up casual setting. Try an order of Jamaican Jerk Chicken with beans and rice for $9, or catch the daily fresh fish specials. Desserts baked fresh by "a little local lady." (☎441-7299. W sushi night. Open Su-Th 11:30am-midnight, F-Sa 11:30am-1am. No reservations, usually a wait for dinner.) For a more stylized take on casual cuisine, stop by the **Flying Fish Cafe ❹,** MP 10 U.S. 158, and experience American and Mediterranean cuisine in a dining area breezy with unassuming class. Early bird specials before 6pm are all priced under $10. (☎441-6894. Entrees $12-20. Open daily 5-10pm.)

HATTERAS & OCRACOKE

The bright rooms at the **Sand Dollar Motel ❹,** off Rte. 12 in Ocracoke, exude a beach-cabin allure. Turn right at the Pirate's Chest gift shop, right again at the Back Porch restaurant, and left at the Edwards Motel. (☎928-5571. Open Apr.-late Nov. Refrigerators, A/C, heat, pool, and breakfast. Queen bed $70, 2 double beds $75; off-season rates vary.) For a lodging experience complete with wood paneling, a game room, and quilt-covered beds, **Blackbeard's ❹,** 111 Back Rd., is sure to satisfy. Turn right off of Rte. 12 just before the boat filled with sea shells. (☎928-3421. A/C, cable TV, and pool. Rooms from $75.) Although slightly more expensive, **The Cove Bed and Breakfast ❹,** 21 Loop Rd., drips with hospitality and has gorgeous rooms with views of the sound and the lighthouse. (☎928-4192. Rooms from $85.)

Sea lovers can sail on over to **Jolly Roger ❷,** on Silver Lake Harbor off of Rte. 12, for the only waterfront dining in Ocracoke. Inhale the sea breeze along with locally caught fresh fish specials (market price) and sandwiches for $4-8. (☎928-3703. Open Apr.-Nov. daily 11am-10pm.) Occupying a counter along the back wall of Styron's General Store (est. 1920) at the corner of Lighthouse and Creek Rd. in Ocracoke, the **Cat Ridge Deli ❷** specializes in Thai-influenced cuisine. (☎928-3354. Wraps around $6. Open M-Sa 11am-7pm, Su 11am-5pm.) Patrons at **sMacNally's ❷,** at the Anchorage Marina, enjoy the outdoor atmosphere while eating fresh fish specials ($9) and a variety of hamburgers ($6-9). sMacNally's advertises "Food So Good It'll Make You Wanna Smack Yo' Mamma!" How can you argue with that logic? (☎928-9999. Open 11am-11pm, depending on the weather.)

◉ SIGHTS

The **Wright Brothers National Memorial,** MP 8 on U.S. 158, marks the spot where Orville and Wilbur Wright took to the skies in history's first powered flight. Exhibits and reproductions of the Wright gliders are on display in the Visitors Center. (☎441-7430. Open June-Aug. daily 9am-6pm; Sept.-May 9am-5pm. $3 per person, $5 per car.) At the nearby **Jockey's Ridge State Park,** MP 12 on U.S. 158, **Kitty Hawk Kites** (☎441-4124 or 877-359-8447) takes aspiring hang-gliding pilots under its wing. Beginner lessons including flights start at $65. Those preferring to explore things at ground level can shuffle through the 6 million truckloads of sand that make up the tallest dunes on the east coast. (Park ☎441-7132. Open in summer daily 8am-8:45pm; off-season hours vary. Free.)

Roanoke Island is a locus of historical and cultural draws. Facing the Manteo Waterfront, **Roanoke Festival Park** (follow signs from the highway), staffed largely by actors in 16th-century garb, is centered around its fun, interactive, kid-friendly museum and the sailing ship *Elizabeth II*, a replica of a 16th-century English merchant ship. (☎475-1500. Park open daily 10am-7pm; ship open Apr.-Oct. daily 10am-6pm, Nov.-Mar. 10am-5pm. $8, students $5.) In summer, students from the North Carolina School for the Arts perform at the Park's outside pavilion (suggested donation $5, students and seniors $3). The **Fort Raleigh National Historic Site,** off U.S. 64, offers several attractions. The **Lost Colony,** the longest-running outdoor drama in the US, has been performed here since 1937, commemorating the first English colony in America, which mysteriously disappeared in 1590. (☎473-3414 or 800-488-5012. Shows June-Aug. M-Sa 8:30pm. $16, seniors $15, under 11 $8.)

Verdant paths unfold into a sculpted array of flowers, antique statues, and fountains in the **Elizabethan Gardens.** This lovely garden shines with southern flair. (☎473-3234. Open in summer daily 9am-8pm; off-season hours vary. $5, seniors $4.50, ages 6-18 $1, under 5 free with adult.) Located 1 mi. west of U.S. 64 on Airport Rd., 3 mi. north of Manteo, the **North Carolina Aquarium** displays the underwater scene from the coastal plain to the Gulf Stream. (☎473-3493. Open June-Aug. daily 9am-7pm; off-season 9am-5pm. $4, seniors and military $3, ages 6-17 $2. Combo pass for aquarium, gardens, and Festival Park available at each location $14, ages 6-18 $6; with Lost Colony ticket $28/14.)

SCENIC DRIVE: CAPE HATTERAS NATIONAL SEASHORE

Get two shores for the price of one along the 70 mi. expanse of the Cape Hatteras National Seashore: one faces out to the Atlantic Ocean and another looks across the Pamlico Sound to North Carolina's mainland. Dotted with dunes, stunted trees, and occasional stretches of marshland, the park's main appeal is this unique landscape. Driving south from Hatteras to Ocracoke, the water reaches out to the horizon on either side with magnificent, largely empty beaches on both coasts.

THE SOUTH

Rte. 12 is the main artery of the park, running all the way from the northern entrance of the park at the Whalebone Junction information center to the town of Ocracoke, except for a 40min. stretch from Hatteras to Ocracoke that is covered by a free ferry. For its entire length, Rte. 12 is a paved two-lane road. Total transport time from Whalebone to Ocracoke is about 2½hr.

All of the major attractions of the park are accessible and clearly marked from Rte. 12. The chief of these are the Outer Banks' three **lighthouses** on Bodie, Hatteras, and Ocracoke Islands. The tallest lighthouse in North America is the 257-step Cape Hatteras lighthouse, built in 1870. The lighthouse has been closed for climbing while structural repairs are made to the staircase, but it is scheduled to reopen for the summer of 2003.

Another set of attractions along Rte. 12 serves to remind visitors that lighthouses have a value apart from the picturesque—various **shipwrecks** are visible from spots on the shore. The schooner *A. Barnes* can be seen from Coquina Beach on Bodie Island, across from the lighthouse. For a schedule of the various daily programs run at the Visitors Centers located at each lighthouse, pick up a copy of the free paper *In The Park.*

The seashore's rich wildlife is on display at the **Pea Island National Wildlife Refuge** on the northern tip of Hatteras Island. Adjoining the **Visitors Center** is the marsh-country **Charles Kuralt Nature Trail,** which affords trekkers a chance to glimpse grackles, pelicans, and the Carolina salt marsh snake. (Visitors Center usually open in summer daily 9am-4pm; off-season Sa-Su only. Beaches in the Refuge are open only during daylight.) Farther south, the **Pony Pasture,** on Rte. 12 in Ocracoke, acts as the stomping ground for a herd of horses peculiar to the island.

Three oceanside **campgrounds ❶,** off Rte. 12 along the Cape Hatteras National Seashore, are open mid-April to early October: **Oregon Inlet,** on the southern tip of Bodie Island; **Frisco,** near the elbow of Hatteras Island; and **Ocracoke,** in the middle of Ocracoke Island. **Cape Point,** in Buxton, is open late May to early September. All four have sites that include water, restrooms, cold-water showers, and grills. Ocracoke is closest to the ocean, with its campsites clustered near the water. Frisco, with its winding roads and scalloped hills, takes the prize for most interesting terrain. Ocracoke sites can be reserved from mid-May to early September. (☎800-365-2267; http://reservations.nps.gov. Sites $17.) All other sites are rented on a first-come, first-served basis. Listings of open sites at all four campgrounds are posted at Whalebone Junction. Contact **Cape Hatteras National Seashore** (☎473-2111) for any and all park concerns.

SOUTH CAROLINA

South Carolina's pride in the Palmetto State may seem extreme. Inspired by the state flag, the palmetto tree logo decorates hats, bottles and bumper stickers across the landscape. To some, pride lies in the unrivaled beaches of the Grand Strand; others revel in the stately elegance of Charleston. Columbia offers an impressive art and cultural experience without the smog and traffic that plague other cities of the New South. Tamed for tourists and merchandising, the Confederate legacy of the first state to secede from the Union is groomed as a cash cow. In recent years, South Carolina has been in the national news for its refusal to remove the controversial Confederate flag from the statehouse. In July 2000, state legislators approved moving the flag from the Statehouse dome to the lawn. However, the NAACP plans to boycott the state until it is removed entirely.

⚑ PRACTICAL INFORMATION

Capital: Columbia.

Visitor info: Dept. of Parks, Recreation, and Tourism, Edgar A. Brown Bldg., 1205 Pendleton St., #106, Columbia 29201 (www.travelsc.com). **South Carolina Forestry Commission,** 5500 Broad River Rd., Columbia 29212 (☎803-896-8800).

Postal Abbreviation: SC. **Sales Tax:** 5-7%.

CHARLESTON   ☎843

Built on rice and cotton, Charleston's antebellum plantation system yielded vast riches now seen in its numerous museums, historic homes, and ornate architecture. An accumulated cultural capital of 300 years flows like the long, distinctive drawl of the natives. Several of the south's most renowned plantations dot the city, while two venerable institutions, the **College of Charleston** and **the Citadel,** add a youthful eccentricity. Horse-drawn carriages, cobblestone streets, pre-Civil War homes, beautiful beaches, and some of the best restaurants in the Southeast explain why Charleston often heads the list of the nation's top destinations.

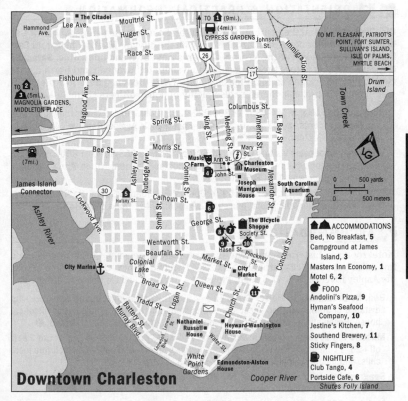

THE SOUTH

Downtown Charleston

⚓⚓ ACCOMMODATIONS
Bed, No Breakfast, **5**
Campground at James Island, **3**
Masters Inn Economy, **1**
Motel 6, **2**

◗ FOOD
Andolini's Pizza, **9**
Hyman's Seafood Company, **10**
Jestine's Kitchen, **7**
Southend Brewery, **11**
Sticky Fingers, **8**

▮ NIGHTLIFE
Club Tango, **4**
Portside Cafe, **6**

Shutes Folly Island

⌐ TRANSPORTATION

Trains: Amtrak, 4565 Gaynor Ave. (☎744-8264), 8 mi. west of downtown. Open daily 6am-10pm. To: **Richmond** (6¾hr., 2 per day, $129); **Savannah** (1¾hr., 2 per day, $38); **Washington, D.C.** (9½hr., 2 per day, $171.)

Buses: Greyhound, 3610 Dorchester Rd. (☎747-5341 or 800-231-2222 for schedules and fares), in N. Charleston. *Avoid this area at night.* Station open daily 8am-9:30pm. To: **Charlotte** (5-9 hr.; 3 per day; M-Th $41, F-Su $43); **Myrtle Beach** (2½hr., 2 per day, $23/25); **Savannah** (2¾hr., 2 per day, $24/26). **CARTA's** "Dorchester/Waylyn" bus goes into town from the station area; return "Navy Yard: 5 Mile Dorchester Rd." bus.

Public Transit: CARTA, 36 John St. (☎724-7420). $1, seniors 50¢, disabled 25¢; 1-day pass $3, 3-day $7. CARTA's **Downtown Area Shuttle (DASH)** is made up of trolley routes that circle downtown daily 8am-11pm; same fares apply. Visitors Center has schedules.

Taxis: Yellow Cab, ☎577-6565.

Bike Rental: The Bicycle Shoppe, 280 Meeting St. (☎722-8168), between George and Society St. Open M-Sa 9am-7pm, Su 1-5pm. $5 per hr., $20 per day.

■✦☑ ORIENTATION & PRACTICAL INFORMATION

Old Charleston lies at the southernmost point of the mile-wide peninsula below **Calhoun St.** The major north-south routes through the city are **Meeting, King,** and **East Bay St.** The area north of the Visitors Center is run-down and uninviting. **Savannah Hwy./U.S. 17** cuts across the peninsula going south to Savannah and north across two towering bridges to Mt. Pleasant and Myrtle Beach. There are plenty of metered parking spaces; there are also plenty of police officers giving tickets.

Hotlines: Crisis Line, ☎744-4357 or 800-922-2283. 24hr. general counseling and referral. **Teen concerns,** ☎747-8336. M-F 4pm-8pm. **People Against Rape,** ☎745-0144 or 800-241-7273. 24hr.

Visitor Info: Charleston Visitors Center, 375 Meeting St. (☎853-8000 or 800-868-8118; www.charlestoncvb.com), across from Charleston Museum. Open Apr.-Oct. daily 8:30am-5:30pm; Nov.-Mar. 8:30am-5pm.

Post Office: 83 Broad St. (☎577-0690). Open M-F 8:30am-5:30pm, Sa 9:30am-2pm. Also houses a cute little postal museum. **ZIP code:** 29402. **Area code:** 843.

⌐ ACCOMMODATIONS

Motel rooms in historic downtown Charleston are expensive. Cheap motels are a few miles out of the city, around Exits 209-11 on I-26 W in N. Charleston, or across the Ashley River on U.S. 17 S in Mt. Pleasant—not practical for those without cars.

Bed, No Breakfast, 16 Halsey St. (☎723-4450). The only budget option within walking distance of downtown. Two guest rooms with shared bath are available in this historical house. Reservations recommended. Rooms $60-95. No credit cards accepted. ❸

Masters Inn Economy, 6100 Rivers Ave. (☎744-3530 or 800-633-3434), at Exit 211B off I-26, 11 mi. from downtown. Spacious rooms with A/C and cable TV. Pool, free local calls, and laundry. Singles Su-Th $39, F-Sa $43; $43/49. ❷

Seagrass Inn, 2355 Aviation Ave. (☎744-4900), behind Waffle House. Clean, comfortable rooms with cable TV, pool, A/C. Singles from $44. ❷

Motel 6, 2058 Savannah Hwy. (☎556-5144), 5 mi. south of town. Pleasant, but far from downtown and often full. Rooms Su-Th $44, F-Sa $54; $6 each extra person. ❸

Campground at James Island County Park (☎ 795-4386 or 800-743-7275). Take U.S. 17 S to Rte. 171 and follow the signs. Spacious, unwooded sites. The spectacular park feature 16 acres of lakes, bicycle and walking trails, and a small water park. Bike and boat rental. Primitive sites $13; tent sites $19, hookup $26. Seniors 10% discount. ❶

🔲 FOOD

Charleston has some of the best food in the country. While most restaurants cater to big-spending tourists, there are plenty of budget-friendly opportunities to sample the Southern cooking, barbecue, and fresh seafood that has made the low country famous. Alluring options await on nearly every street.

Hyman's Seafood Company, 215 Meeting St. (☎ 723-6000). Since 1890, this casual restaurant has offered 15-25 different kinds of fresh fish daily ($7-15), served in any one of 8 styles—broiled, fried, Cajun, Cajun light, sauteed, jerk, scampi, or steamed. No reservations; expect long waits. Open daily 11am-11pm. ❹

Southend Brewery, 161 E. Bay St. (☎ 853-4677). Outstanding ribs ($13-20), eclectic pizzas ($8-10), and home-brewed beers ($3.50) entice many to frequent this 3-story brewhouse—not to mention the opportunity to color on the paper tablecloths with crayons. Happy hour daily 4-7pm. Open Su-W 11:30am-10pm, Th-Sa 11:30am-11pm; bar open daily until 1am. ❸

Jestine's Kitchen, 251 Meeting St. (☎ 722-7224). If you had a Southern country grandma and this grandma had a restaurant, it would probably be something like Jestine's. Excellent crispy fried chicken with 2 fresh veggies $8. Open Tu-Th 11am-9:30pm, F-Sa 11am-10pm, Su 11am-9pm. ❷

Andolini's Pizza, 82 Wentworth St. (☎ 722-7437), at King St. Reputedly the best New York-style pizza place in the South, Andolini's makes all items from scratch. Large thin-crust cheese pie $11. Calzones from $5. Open M-Th 11am-11pm, F-Sa 11am-midnight, Su noon-10pm. ❷

Sticky Fingers, 235 Meeting St. (☎ 853-7427). Voted the best barbecue in town on numerous occasions. Pulled pork sandwich $6. Ribs $12-26. Open M-Sa 11am-11pm, Su 11am-10pm. ❹

👁 SIGHTS

Charleston's ancient homes, historical monuments, churches, galleries, and gardens can be seen by foot, car, bus, boat, trolley, or horse-drawn carriage—or on one of the *nine* ghost tours. **City Market,** downtown at Meeting St., stays abuzz in its newly restored 19th-century building. (Open daily from about 9am-5pm.)

PLANTATIONS AND GARDENS. The 300-year-old **Magnolia Plantation and Gardens** is by far the most majestic of Charleston's plantations, not to mention the oldest major public garden in the country. Visitors can enjoy the Drayton family's staggering wealth by exploring their 50 acres of gorgeous gardens with 900 varieties of camelia and 250 varieties of azalea. Other attractions include a hedge maze, bike and canoe rental, swamp, and bird sanctuary. *(On Rte. 61, 10 mi. out of town off U.S. 17. ☎ 571-1266 or 800-367-3517. Open Feb.-Nov. daily 8am-5:30pm; call for winter hours. Gardens $12, seniors $11, ages 13-19 $9, ages 6-12 $6; with house admission $19/18/16/13; with nature trail $18/17/15/10; with swamp garden $17/16/13/9. Canoes or bikes $5 per 3hr.)* A bit farther down the road, **Middleton Place** is a more manicured plantation with working stables, gardens, house, restaurant, and inn. *(On Rte. 61, 14 mi. northwest of downtown. ☎ 556-6020 or 800-782-3608. Open daily 9am-5pm. Gardens $20, seniors $19, under 16 $12; house tour additional $10. AAA discount.)* Even farther out, but well worth the trip, **Cypress Gardens** lets visitors paddle their own boats out onto the eerie, gator-filled swamps. *(3030 Cypress Gardens Rd. Off Rte. 52. ☎ 553-0515; www.cypressgardens.org. Open daily 9am-5pm. $9, ages 6-12 $3.)*

CHARLESTON MUSEUM & HISTORIC HOMES. Across the street from the Visitors Center stands the **Charleston Museum,** the country's oldest museum. Learn about the Low Country through artifacts, from fossils to fashion and skeletons to silver. *(360 Meeting St. ☎ 722-2996. Open M-Sa 9am-5pm, Su 1-5pm. $8, children $4.)* Although a combo ticket is available for the museum and two historic homes—the 1722 **Heyward-Washington House** and 1803 **Joseph Manigault House**—just pick one house and save the money. *(Heyward-Washington House: 87 Church St. ☎ 722-0354. Joseph Manigault House: 350 Meeting St. ☎ 723-2926. Both homes open M-Sa 10am-5pm, Su 1-5pm. One house $8, ages 3-12 $4; museum and 1 home $12; museum and 2 homes $18.)* The **Nathaniel Russell House** and **Edmondston-Alston House** are both examples of the late Federal style of architecture, with the former boasting a "free-flying" staircase and the latter overlooking the Charleston Harbor. *(Nathaniel Russell: 51 Meeting St. ☎ 724-8481. Open M-Sa 10am-5pm, Su 2-5pm. $7, under 6 free. Edmondston-Alston: 21 E. Battery. ☎ 722-7171 or 800-782-3608. Open Su-M 1:30-4:30pm, Tu-Sa 10am-4:30pm. $10.)*

PATRIOT'S POINT & FORT SUMTER. Climb aboard four Naval ships, including a submarine and the giant aircraft carrier *Yorktown,* in **Patriot's Point Naval and Maritime Museum,** the world's largest naval museum. *(40 Patriots Point Rd. Across the Cooper River in Mt. Pleasant. ☎ 884-2727. Open Apr.-Sept. daily 9am-6pm, ships close at 7:30pm; Oct.-Mar. 9am-5pm, ships close at 5:30pm. $12.50, seniors and military $11, ages 6-11 $6, under 6 free.)* From Patriots Point in Mt. Pleasant, **Fort Sumter Tours** has boat excursions to the National Historic Site where the Civil War began in 1861. There is a dock at Liberty Square next to the South Carolina Aquarium in Charleston. *(Tours: ☎ 881-7337. Fort Sumter: ☎ 883-3123; www.nps.gov/fosu. 2¼hr. total tour, 1hr. is at the Fort. 1-3 tours per day from each location. $12, seniors $11, ages 6-11 $6, under 6 free.)*

BEACHES. **Folly Beach** is popular with local students from the Citadel, College of Charleston, and USC. *(☎ 588-2426. Over the James Bridge and U.S. 171, about 20 mi. southeast of Charleston.)* The more wide open **Isle of Palms** extends for miles down toward the less-crowded **Sullivan's Island.** *(Isle of Palms: ☎ 886-3863. Across the Cooper Bridge, drive 10mi. down Hwy. 17 N, and turn right onto the Isle of Palms Connector.)*

SOUTH CAROLINA AQUARIUM. This well-executed and extremely interesting aquarium has quickly become Charleston's biggest attraction. Although a bit overpriced, exhibits showcase aquatic life from the region's swamps, marshes, and oceans. Stare down the fishies at the 330,000-gallon Great Ocean Tank, which boasts the nation's tallest viewing window. *(At the end of Calhoun St. on the Cooper River, overlooking the harbor. ☎ 720-1990; www.scaquarium.org. Open mid-June to mid-Aug. daily 9am-6pm; mid-Aug. to mid-June 9am-5pm. $14, seniors $12, ages 3-11 $7.)*

BULL ISLAND. To get away from human civilization, take a ferry to Bull Island, a 5000-acre island off the coast of Charleston. The boat is often greeted by dolphins swimming in some of the cleanest water on the planet. Once on the island there are 278 different species of bird and 16 mi. of hiking trails. *(☎ 881-4582. ½hr. ferries depart from Moore's Landing, off Seewee Rd., 16 mi. north of Charleston off U.S. 17. Departs Mar.-Nov. Tu and Th-Sa 9am and 12:30pm; returns Tu and Th-Sa noon and 4pm; departs Dec.-Feb. Sa 10am; returns 3pm. Round-trip $30, under 12 $15.)*

🎵 🎭 ENTERTAINMENT & NIGHTLIFE

With nearby colleges and a constant tourist presence, Charleston's nightlife beats strong. Free copies of *City Paper,* in stores and restaurants, list concerts and other events. Big-name bands take center stage nightly at the **Music Farm,** 32 Ann St. (☎ 853-3276. Tickets $5-25.) Nearby, **Club Tango,** 39 John St., lures hot-steppers to the alley between John and Hutson St. as night falls. (☎ 577-2822. Cover $5, under 21

$10. Open Th-F 9pm-3:30am, Sa 9pm-3am.) The more relaxed scene at **Portside Cafe,** 462 King St., combines an outdoor patio, an excellent blend of nouveau American and Southern food, and nightly live music. (☎722-0409. Sandwiches under $7. Barbecue from $8. Open M-F 6:30pm-4am, Sa 6:30pm-2am.) The city will explode with music, theater, dance, and opera, as well as literary and visual arts events, when Charleston hosts the 27th **Spoleto Festival USA,** the nation's most comprehensive arts festival. Founded in 1977 and dedicated to young artists, the celebration is the American counterpart to the Festival of Two Worlds in Spoleto, Italy. (☎722-2764; www.spoletousa.org. May 23-June 8, 2003. $10-75.)

▐ DAYTRIP FROM CHARLESTON: BEAUFORT

Listen closely, and you will hear a musical language spoken in the coastal islands of southeastern South Carolina. During the slave trade, numerous African cultures merged with the European cultures of slave traders to produce **Gullah,** a unique blend of language, food, arts, and religion. After the Civil War, Gullah largely faded across the South, except in the geographically isolated South Carolina lowcountry. Today, bridges allow easy access to the area and exploration of this culture. St. Helena is considered the center of Gullah, largely due to the preservation efforts of the **Penn Center** (☎838-2432), about 1 mi. down Martin Luther King Jr. Dr. off U.S. 21, the first school for freed slaves in the South. King wrote his "I Have a Dream" speech on retreat at the center. The area's unique heritage is preserved in the **York W. Bailey Museum.** (☎838-2432. Open M-Sa 11am-4pm. $4, students $2.)

The best way to truly experience Gullah is on the **Gullah 'n' Geechie Mahn Tours,** led by community activist, historian, scholar, and all-around expert Kitty Greene. Adding substance to the leisurely drive, Greene carefully conveys the Gullah culture by examining its language, religion, art, and food. Included is a trip to the "praise house," the 300-year-old religious center for plantation slaves. Two-hour tours leave from 847 Sea Island Parkway, in St. Helena. (☎838-7516. Tours M-F 9:45am and 1:45pm, Sa by arrangement. $17, under 11 $15. Reservations required.)

One of the Palmetto State's strangest sites is the **Kingdom of Oyotunji,** a Yoruba African village in Sheldon, 10 mi. north of Beaufort on Rte. 17. The 30-year-old sanctuary for African priests is led by a self-proclaimed African king and his several wives. Make an appointment before the heartfelt, yet bizarre, tour to speak with the king. (☎846-8900. Open 10am-dusk. Tours $5.) Stately Beaufort hosts the lively **Gullah Festival** (www.gullahfestival.com) every May and chows at the packed **Shrimp Festival** every October.

Beaufort is 60 mi. from both Savannah and Charleston, on Rte. 21, 15 mi. south of I-95 Exit 33. **Greyhound,** 1307 Boundary St. (☎524-4646), runs to Savannah (1hr.; 4 per day; M-Th $11.25, F-Su $12.25). From the **Greater Beaufort Visitors Center and Chamber of Commerce,** 1106 Carteret St., travel 5 mi. south on Rte. 210 to St. Helena. (☎524-3163. Open daily 9am-5:30pm.) **Area code:** 843.

COLUMBIA   ☎803

Much ado is made over Columbia's Civil War heritage, and understandably so, as Old South nostalgia brings in big tourist dollars. However, locals point out that more antebellum buildings have been lost to developers in the last century than were burned by Sherman and his rowdy troops. Still, the town is the heart of the nation's "rebel" child, and a defiant spirit is cultivated in Columbia's bars, businesses, and citizens. The **University of South Carolina (USC)** complements the city with its wide, green spaces and museums.

THE SOUTH

IN RECENT NEWS

THE STARS & BARS

When it comes to the **Confederate flag**, there exists a fine line between Southern pride and racism, and nowhere has that been more strongly felt than in South Carolina. The State House in Columbia began flying the ensign in 1962, in celebration of the Civil War Centennial. In recent years, though, many have questioned the flag's appropriateness, and emotions reached a climax during the political campaigns of 2000. The NAACP pressured the government to remove the Confederate flag from Capitol grounds, arguing that the banner represented slavery and secession. They also implemented a tourism boycott that cost state businesses $20 million. Within a few months, the government relented, and the flag was removed from the dome and placed instead at a monument to Confederate soldiers, elsewhere on the State House grounds. The commotion died down, though the NAACP still expressed dissatisfaction.

However, in April 2002, a man wearing a black Santa Claus suit was caught atop the Capitol's flagpole, setting fire to the infamous flag. As police at the scene tried to coax the man down, a white man was heard shouting from a passing car, "String him up right there!," while a crowd of black onlookers applauded the Santa's efforts. When asked by reporters if this incident would rekindle the flag debate, House Minority Leader Doug Jennings replied, "I don't know that the debate ever really ended."

■◆🛈 **ORIENTATION & PRACTICAL INFORMATION.** The city is laid out in a square, bordered by Huger and Harden St. running north-south and Blossom and Calhoun St. east-west. **Assembly St.** is the main drag, running north-south through the heart of the city, and **Gervais St.** is its east-west equivalent. The Congaree River marks the city's western edge.

Columbia Metropolitan Airport, 3000 Aviation Way (☎822-5000), is in West Columbia. A taxi to downtown costs about $13-15. **Amtrak,** 850 Pulaski St. (☎252-8246; open daily 10pm-5:30am), sends one train per day to Miami (15hr., $142); Savannah (2½hr., $41); and Washington D.C. (10hr., $117). **Greyhound,** 2015 Gervais St. (☎256-6465), at Harden St., buses to Atlanta (5hr., 7 per day, $49.50); Charleston (2½ hr., 2 per day, $26.25); and Charlotte (2hr., 3-4 per day, M-Th $16, F-Su $18). **Connex TCT** runs transit through Columbia from 5:30am to midnight. Most main routes depart from pickup/transfer depots at Sumter and Laurel St. and at Assembly and Taylor St. (☎217-9019. Runs daily 5:30am-midnight; call for schedules. 75¢; seniors and disabled, except 3-6pm, 25¢; under 6 free. Free transfers.) **Columbia Metropolitan Convention and Visitors Bureau,** 801 Lady St., has maps and info. (☎254-0479. Open M-F 9am-5pm, Sa 10am-4pm.) For info on USC, try the **University of South Carolina Visitors Center,** 937 Assembly St. (☎777-0169 or 800-922-9755. Open M-F 8:30am-5pm, Sa 9:30am-12:30pm. Free parking pass.) **Post office:** 1601 Assembly St. (☎733-4643. Open M-F 7:30am-6pm.) **ZIP code:** 29201. **Area code:** 803.

🛏 **ACCOMMODATIONS.** Generally, the cheapest digs lie farthest from the city center. One convenient option a short drive from downtown is the **Masters Inn ❷,** 613 Knox Abbott Dr.; take Blossom St. across the Congaree River, where it becomes Knox Abbott Dr. The inn offers free local calls, morning coffee, a pool, and cable TV. (☎796-4300. Singles $33-36; doubles $35-38.) Inexpensive motels also line the three interstates (I-26, I-77, and I-20) that circle the city. **Knights Inn ❷,** 1987 Airport Blvd., Exit 133 off I-26, has lots of amenities for a low price. Rooms have refrigerators, microwaves, cable TV, A/C, free local calls, and pool access. (☎794-0222. Singles and doubles Su-Th $35, F-Sa $39; 10% senior discount.) Or try **Royal Inn ❶,** 1323 Garner Lane. From I-20, take Exit 65 then take a slight right on to Garner. (☎750-5060. Cable TV, HBO, and continental breakfast. Singles $30; doubles $35.) The 1400 acres **Sesquicentennial State Park ❶** include swimming and fishing, a nature center, hiking trails, and 87 wooded sites with electricity and water. Public transportation does not serve the park; take I-20 to the Two Notch Rd./U.S. 1, Exit 17, and head northeast for 3 mi. (☎788-2706. Gate open Apr.-Oct. daily 7am-9pm; Nov.-Mar. 8am-6pm. Campsites $16. Entrance $1.50 per person.)

◻ **FOOD.** It's little wonder that **Maurice's Piggie Park ❶**, 800 Elmwood Ave., 1600 Charleston Hwy., and nine other SC locations, holds the world record for "Most BBQ sold in one day." Maurice's cash "pig" is his exquisite, mustard-based sauce that covers the $4.50 Big Joe pork BBQ sandwich. (☎256-4377. Open M-Sa 10am-10pm.) **Groucho's ❷**, 611 Harden St., has received high marx from the collegiate crowd for 60 years, thus proving the allure of "dipper" sandwiches ($5.69) served with one of Groucho's special sauces. (☎799-5708. Open M-Sa 11am-4pm.) For healthy, organic temptations, **Rosewood Market ❶**, 2803 Rosewood Dr., has a grocery store and a deli-style counter. (☎765-1083 or 888-203-5950. Smoked tofu and chipolte wrap $5.25. Macrobiotic carrot raisin muffin $1.75. Open M-Sa 9am-9pm, Su 10am-6pm. Lunch daily 11:30am-2:30pm; dinner 5-7:30pm.) The **Columbia State Farmers Market**, 1001 Bluff Rd., across from the football stadium, is a chance to experience the Palmetto State's produce in all its raw, unadulterated glory. (☎737-4664. Open M-Sa 6am-9pm, Su 1-6pm.)

◙ **SIGHTS.** One of the top ten zoos in the country, **Riverbanks Zoo and Garden**, on I-126 at Greystone Blvd., northwest of downtown, recreates natural habitats to house over 2000 species. In addition to a fish and reptile kingdom, desert, interactive Southern farm, and bird pavilion, gorillas and koalas will soon join the zoo. (☎779-8717. Open M-F 9am-5pm, Sa-Su 9am-6pm. $7.75, students $6.50, seniors $6.25.)

Bronze stars mark the impact of Sherman's cannonballs on the **Statehouse**, an Italian Renaissance high-rise. Lawmakers spent $70 million to restore Columbia's dominant structure to its turn-of-the-century glory. (On Sumter, Assembly, and Gervais St. ☎734-2430. Open M-F 9am-5pm, Sa 10am-5pm; 1st Su each month 1-5pm. Free tours available.) Across Sumter St. from the Statehouse is the central green of the USC campus—the **Horseshoe.** Here, students play frisbee, sunbathe, study, and nap beneath a canopy of shade trees. At the head of the green, sitting at the intersection of Bull and Pendleton St., **McKissick Museum** explores the folklife of South Carolina and the Southeast through history, art, and science. (☎777-7251. Open May-Aug. M-F 9am-4pm, Sa-Su 1-5pm; Sept.-Apr. Tu-W and F 9am-4pm, Th 9am-7pm, Su 1-5pm. Free.) The **South Carolina Confederate Relic Room and Museum**, 301 Gervais St., houses an impressive and well-maintained collection of Civil War artifacts. (☎737-8095. Call for hours. Free.) Two 19th-century mansions, the **Robert Mills Historic House and Park** and the **Hampton-Preston Mansion**, 1616 Blanding St., two blocks east of Bull St., elegantly compete as examples of antebellum opulence and survivors of Sherman's Civil War rampage. Both have been lovingly restored with period fineries. (☎252-1770. Tours every hr. Tu-Sa 10am-3pm, Su 1-4pm. Tours $5, students, military, and AAA $4, under 5 free. Buy tickets at Mills House Museum Shop.) For a broader experience of 19th-century life, stop by the **Manns-Simons Cottage,** owned by a former slave, and the **Woodrow Wilson Boyhood Home**, 1705 Hampton St. (Open Tu-Sa 10am-4pm, Su 1-4pm. Tickets at the Mills House Museum Shop.)

◪ **NIGHTLIFE.** Columbia's nightlife centers around the collegiate **Five Points District,** at Harden and Devine St., and the blossoming, slightly more mature **Vista area,** on Gervais St. before the Congaree River. **Group Therapy**, 2107 Greene St., is good for what "ales" you. The oldest bar in Columbia is "in session" until everyone "is cured." Try the Mullet ($6.50): warm gentleman Jack with cold Bud spells "business in the front, party in the back." (☎256-1203. Open daily 4:30pm to late.)

THE SOUTH

Across the street at **Big Al's,** 749 Saluda Ave., locals shoot pool and liquor in the dark smoky den. (☎758-0700. Open M-F 5pm until late, Sa 5pm-2am, Su 9pm-2am.) In the Vista, the **Art Bar,** 1211 Park St., attracts a funky crowd to match its ambience. Glow paint, Christmas lights, kitschy 1950s bar stools, and a troop of life-size plastic robots are complemented by an eclectic music line-up from 80s theme night to "sin-dustrial" rock. (☎929-0198. Open M-F 8pm to late, Sa-Su 8pm-2am.) The weekly publication *Free Times* gives details on Columbia's club and nightlife scene. *In Unison* is a weekly paper listing gay-friendly nightspots.

MYRTLE BEACH & THE GRAND STRAND   ☎843

Each summer, millions of Harley-riding, RV-driving Southerners make Myrtle Beach the second-most-popular summer tourist destination in the country. During spring break and early June, Myrtle Beach is thronged with rambunctious students on the lookout for a good time. The rest of the year, families, golfers, shoppers, and others partake in the unapologetic tackiness of the town's theme restaurants, amusement parks, and shops. The pace slows significantly on the rest of the 60 mi. Grand Strand. South of Myrtle Beach, Murrell's Inlet is the place to go for good seafood, Pawley's Island is lined with beach cottages and beautiful private homes, and Georgetown, once a critical Southern port city, showcases its white-pillared 18th-century-style rice and indigo plantation homes.

⊞🛈 ORIENTATION & PRACTICAL INFORMATION. Most attractions are on **Rte. 17/Kings Hwy.,** which splits into a Business Route and a Bypass 4 mi. south of Myrtle Beach. **Ocean Blvd.** runs along the ocean, flanked on either side by cheap pastel motels. Avenue numbers repeat themselves after reaching 1st Ave. in the middle of town; note whether the Ave. is "north" or "south." Also, take care not to confuse north **Myrtle Beach** with the town **North Myrtle Beach,** which has an almost identical street layout. **Rte. 501** runs west toward Conway, **I-95,** and—most importantly—the factory outlet stores. Unless otherwise stated, addresses on the Grand Strand are for Myrtle Beach. **Greyhound,** 511 7th Ave. N (☎448-2471; open daily 9am-1:45pm and 3-6:45pm), runs to Charleston (2½hr.; 2 per day; M-Th $24, F-Su $25). **The Waccamaw Regional Transportation Authority,** 1418 Third Ave., provides minimal busing; pick up a copy of schedules and routes from the Chamber of Commerce or from area businesses. (☎488-0865. Runs daily 5am-2am. Local fares 75¢-$2.) They also operate the **Ocean Boulevard Lymo,** a bus service that shuttles tourists up and down the main drag. (☎488-0865. Runs daily 8am-midnight. Unlimited day pass $2.50.) Rent bikes at **The Bike Shoppe,** 715 Broadway, at Main St. (☎448-5335. Open M-F 9am-6pm, Sa 9am-5pm. Beach cruisers $5 per half-day, $10 per day; mountain bikes $10/15.) **Visitor info: Myrtle Beach Chamber of Commerce,** 1200 N. Oak St., parallel to Kings Hwy., at 12th N. (☎626-7444 or 800-356-3016. Open daily 8:30am-5pm.) **Mini Golf:** absolutely everywhere. **Post Office:** 505 N. Kings Hwy., at 5th Ave. N. (☎626-9533. Open M-F 8:30am-5pm, Sa 9am-1pm.) **ZIP code:** 29577. **Area code:** 843.

▐ ACCOMMODATIONS. There are hundreds of motels lining Ocean Blvd., with those on the ocean side fetching higher prices than those across the street. Cheap motels also dot Rte. 17. October through March, prices plummet as low as $20-30 a night for one of the luxurious hotels right on the beach. Call the **Myrtle Beach Lodging Reservation Service,** 1551 21st Ave. N., #20, for free help with reservations. (☎626-9970 or 800-626-7477. Open M-F 8:30am-5pm.) The family-owned **Sea Banks Motor Inn ❷,** 2200 S. Ocean Blvd., across the street from the ocean, has rooms with large windows, mini-fridges, cable TV, laundry, and pool and beach access. (☎448-2434 or 800-523-0603. Mid-Mar. to mid Sept. singles $45; doubles $75; mid-Sept. to mid-Mar. $22/28.) The **Hurl Rock Motel ❷,** 2010 S. Ocean Blvd., has big, clean rooms with access to a pool and hot tub. (☎626-3531 or 888-487-5762. Must be 25+ to rent a single. Singles $45; doubles $54-89; off-season as low as $25/28.) **David's Landing ❸**, 2708 S. Ocean Blvd., features large, modern 1- and 2-room apartments, all with ocean views and private balconies. (☎626-8845 or 800-561-3504. Must be 25+ to rent. Mid-June to mid-Aug. $50-65; mid-Apr. to mid-June and mid-Aug. to Sept. $35-50; Oct. to mid-Apr. $25-35.) **Huntington Beach State Park Campground ❶**, 3 mi. south of Murrell's Inlet on U.S. 17, is located in a diverse environment including lagoons, salt marshes, and a beach. Gators come within yards of the sites. (☎237-4440. Open Apr.-Oct. daily 6am-10pm; Nov.-Mar. 6am-6pm. Tent sites Apr.-Oct. $12, water and electricity $25, full hookup $27; Nov.-Mar. $10/21/23. Day use $4.) **Myrtle Beach State Park Campground ❶**, 3 mi. south of town off U.S. 17, is more crowded and less attractive than Huntington, but its 347 sites come with access to a beach, fishing pier, pool, and nature trail. (☎238-5325. Showers and laundry. Office open daily 8am-5pm. Sites $23. Cabins for 4-8 people available for weekly rental; call ahead. Day use $2.)

◖ FOOD. The Grand Strand tempts hungry motorists to leave the highway with over 1800 restaurants serving every type of food in every type of setting imaginable. Massive family-style, all-you-can-eat joints beckon from beneath the glow of every traffic light. **Rte. 17** offers countless steakhouses, seafood buffets, and fast food restaurants. Seafood, however, is best on **Murrell's Inlet.** With license plates adorning the walls and discarded peanut shells crunching underfoot, the **River City Cafe ❶**, 404 21st Ave. N., celebrates a brand of American informality bordering on delinquency. Peruse the enthusiastic signatures of patrons on tables and walls as you polish off a burger ($3-6) or knock back a beer. (☎448-1990. Open daily 11am-10pm.) While most of the restaurants in Broadway at the Beach seem to sacrifice food quality for elaborate decor, **Benito's ❸**, in the "Caribbean Village" part of the complex, puts together $5-15 fancy brick oven pizzas, $6-7 calzones, and $9-12 pasta dishes. (☎444-0006. Open daily 11am-10:30pm.) Split your belly with one of the monstrous sandwiches ($4-8) at **Dagwood's Deli ❷**, 400 11th. Ave. N. Beach bums and businessmen come together to enjoy a "Shag" (ham, turkey, and swiss cheese) or a "Beachboy" (salami, pepperoni, and provolone cheese). Be prepared to wait. (☎448-0100. Open M-Sa 11am-9pm.)

◉▣ SIGHTS & NIGHTLIFE. The boulevard and the beach are both "the strand," and while you're on it, the rule is see or be seen. Fashionable teens strut their stuff, low riders cruise the streets, and older ambivalent beachgoers showcase their fresh sunburns. Coupons are everywhere—never pay full price for any attraction in Myrtle Beach. Pick up a copy of the *Monster Coupon Book, Sunny Day Guide, Myrtle Beach Guide,* or *Strand Magazine* at any tourist info center or hotel.

The colossal **Broadway at the Beach,** Rte. 17 Bypass and 21st Ave. N. (☎444-3200 or 800-386-4662), is a sprawling 350-acre complex determined to stimulate and entertain with theaters, a water park, mini golf, 20 restaurants, nightclubs, 100 shops, and other attractions. Within Broadway the **Butterfly Pavilion,** the first facility of its kind in the nation, showcases over 40 species of butterflies in free flight. (☎839-4444. Open daily 10am-11pm. $11, seniors $10, ages 3-12 $8.) South Carolina's most visited attraction is Broadway's **Ripley's Aquarium,** featuring sharks and sting rays swimming overhead and an exhibit on the mysteries of the Bermuda Triangle. (☎916-0888 or 800-734-8888. Open daily 9am-11pm. $15, ages 5-11 $9, ages 2-4 $3.) The reptile capital of the world is the amazing ▣**Alligator Adventure,** Rte. 17 in North Myrtle Beach at Barefoot Landing. Mesmerized children and Animal Planet gurus crowd the boardwalk to see the hourly gator feedings and marvel at the expansive collection of exotic snakes, lizards, and frogs. Don't miss the park's 20ft., 3000lb. resident, Utan, the largest reptile in the world. (☎361-0789. Open daily 9am-10pm. $13, seniors $11, ages 4-12 $9.)

A PIG PRIMER Southerners have always found unique ways to prepare all parts of the pig. Chitlins, a tasty (but smelly) fall treat, are pig intestines cleaned, boiled, fried, and then seasoned. Hogmau is boiled and seasoned pig stomach. Throughout the South, pickled pig's feet soak in pool hall countertop jars. And those in a hurry can always grab a pig's ear sandwich.

Most visitors to Myrtle Beach putter over to one of the many elaborately themed **mini golf** courses on Kings Hwy. The **NASCAR Speedpark,** across from Broadway at the Beach on the Rte. 17 Bypass, provides 7 different tracks of varying difficulty levels, catering to the need for speed. (☎918-8725. Open daily 10am-11pm. Unlimited rides $25, under 13 $15.) The 9100-acre **Brookgreen Gardens,** Rte. 17 opposite Huntington Beach State Park south of Murrell's Inlet, provide relief from downtown's frenzied antics in their large collection of American sculpture on display beneath massive oaks. Guided tours of the gardens and wildlife trail are offered in addition to summer drama, music, and food programs. (☎235-6000. Open daily 9:30am-5pm. 7-day pass $12, seniors and ages 13-18 $10, 12 and under free.)

For a night on the town, the New Orleans-style nightclub district of **Celebrity Square,** at Broadway at the Beach, facilitates stepping out in any style with ten nightclubs, from classic rock to Latin themed. Elsewhere, **Club Millennium 2000,** 1012 S. Kings Hwy. (☎445-9630), and **2001,** 920 Lake Arrowhead Rd. (☎449-9434), bring clubbers a hot-steppin' odyssey.

GEORGIA

Georgia presents two faces: the rural southern region contrasts starkly with the sprawling commercialism of the north. But the state somehow manages to balance its many different identities. Cosmopolitan Atlanta boasts of Coca-Cola and Ted Turner's CNN, both of which have networked the globe, while Savannah fosters a different sort of life stubbornly preserving its distinctive antebellum atmosphere. And while collegiate Athens breeds "big" bands, Georgia's Gold Coast mellows in slow-paced seaside existence. This state of countless contradictions was called home by two former presidents as well: Jimmy Carter's hometown of Plains and Franklin D. Roosevelt's summer home in Warm Springs both stand on red Georgia clay. No matter where you go in Georgia, however, one thing remains constant—the peachy Southern hospitality.

⚑ PRACTICAL INFORMATION

Capital: Atlanta.

Visitor info: Dept. of Industry and Trade, Tourist Division, 285 Peachtree Center Ave., Atlanta 30303 (☎404-656-3590 or 800-847-4842; www.georgia.org), in the Marriot Marquis 2 Tower, 10th fl. Open M-F 8am-5pm. **Dept. of Natural Resources,** 205 Butler St. SE #1352, Atlanta 30334 (☎404-656-3530 or 800-864-7275). **U.S. Forest Service,** 1800 NE Expwy., Atlanta 30329 (☎404-248-9142). Open W-Su 11am-7:30pm.

Postal Abbreviation: GA. **Sales Tax:** 4-7%, depending on county.

ATLANTA

☎404

An increasingly popular destination for those just out of college and craving urban life but weary of more manic cities, Atlanta strives to be cosmopolitan with a smile. Northerners, Californians, the third-largest gay population in the US, and a host of ethnicities have diversified this unofficial capital of the South while giving it a distinctly un-Southern feel. A national economic powerhouse, Atlanta holds offices for 400 of the Fortune 500 companies, including the headquarters of Coca-Cola, Delta Airlines, the United Parcel Service, and CNN. Nineteen colleges, including Georgia Tech, Morehouse College, Spelman College, and Emory University, also call "Hotlanta" home. The city is just as blessed with subtle gems; getting lost on Atlanta's streets reveals a seemingly endless number of trendy restaurants and beautiful old houses.

✈ INTERCITY TRANSPORTATION

Flights: Hartsfield International Airport (☎ 530-2081; www.atlanta-airport.com), south of the city. MARTA (see **Public Transit**) is the easiest way to get downtown, with rides departing from the Airport Station (15min., every 8min. daily 5am-1am, $1.75). **Atlanta Airport Shuttle** (☎ 524-3400) runs vans from the airport to over 100 locations in the metropolis and outlying area (every 15min. daily 7am-11pm, shuttle downtown $14). Taxi to downtown $20.

Train: Amtrak, 1688 Peachtree St. NW (☎ 881-3062), 3 mi. north of downtown at I-85, or 1 mi. north of Ponce de Leon on Peachtree St. Take bus #23 from "Arts Center" MARTA station. To **New Orleans** (10½hr., 1 per day, $52-119) and **New York** (19hr., 1 per day, $111-273). Open daily 7am-9:30pm.

Buses: Greyhound, 232 Forsyth St. SW (☎ 584-1728), across from "Garnett" MARTA station. To: **New York** (18-23hr., 14 per day, $91); **Savannah** (5hr., 6 per day, $45); **Washington, D.C.** (15hr., 12 per day, $75-79). Open 24hr.

⊞ ORIENTATION

Atlanta sprawls across ten counties in the northwest quadrant of the state at the junctures of I-75, I-85 (the city "thru-way"), and I-20. **I-285** (the "Perimeter") circumscribes the city. Maneuvering around Atlanta's main thoroughfares, arranged much like the spokes of a wheel, challenges even the most experienced native. **Peachtree St.** (one of over 100 streets bearing that name in Atlanta), is a major north-south road; **Spring St.** and **Piedmont Ave.** run parallel to Peachtree. On the eastern edge **Moreland Ave.** traverses the length of the city, through Virginia Highland, Little Five Points (L5P), and East Atlanta. Major east-west roads include **Ponce de Leon Ave.** and **North Ave.** Navigating Atlanta requires a full arsenal of transportation strategies, from walking to public transportation to driving. The city is more a conglomeration of several distinct neighborhoods than a single metropolis. The outlying areas of Buckhead, Virginia Highlands and Little Five Points are easiest to get to by car, but once you've arrived, the restaurant- and bar-lined streets encourage walking. Atlanta's most popular attractions, centered in downtown and midtown, are best explored using MARTA.

THE SOUTH

NEIGHBORHOODS

Sprouting out of downtown Atlanta, the **Peachtree Center** and **Five Points MARTA** stations deliver hordes of tourists to shopping and dining at **Peachtree Center Mall** and **Underground Atlanta,** respectively. Downtown is also home to **Centennial Olympic Park** as well as Atlanta's major sports and concert venues. Directly southwest of downtown, the **West End,** an African-American neighborhood, is the city's oldest historic quarter. From Five Points, head northeast to **Midtown,** from Ponce de Leon Ave. to 17th St., for museums and **Piedmont Park.** East of Five Points at Euclid and Moreland Ave., the **Little Five Points (L5P)** district is a local haven for artists and youth subculture. North of L5P, **Virginia Highland,** a trendy neighborhood east of Midtown and Piedmont Park, attracts yuppies and college kids. **Buckhead,** a swanky area north of Midtown on Peachtree St., (MARTA: Buckhead), houses designer shops and dance clubs.

⊑ LOCAL TRANSPORTATION

Public Transit: Metropolitan Atlanta Rapid Transit Authority, or **MARTA** (☎848-4711; schedule info M-F 6am-11pm, Sa-Su 8am-10pm). Clean, uncrowded trains and buses provide hassle-free transportation to Atlanta's major attractions. Rail operates M-F 5am-1am, Sa-Su and holidays 6am-12:30am in most areas. Bus hours vary. $1.75, exact change or a token from a station machine needed; transfers free. Unlimited weekly pass $13. Pick up a system map at the **MARTA Ride Store,** Five Points Station downtown, or at the airport, Lindbergh, or Lenox stations. The majority of trains, rail stations, and buses are wheelchair accessible.

Taxis: Atlanta Yellow Cab, ☎521-0200. **Checker Cab,** ☎351-1111.

Car Rental: Atlanta Rent-a-Car, 3185 Camp Creek Pkwy. (☎763-1110), just inside I-285 2½ mi. east of the airport. Ten other locations in the area including 2800 Campelton Rd. (☎344-1060) and 3129 Piedmont Rd. (☎231-4898). $25 per day, 100 free mi. per day, 24¢ each additional mi. Must be over 21 with major credit card.

⊉ PRACTICAL INFORMATION

Visitor Info: Atlanta Convention and Visitors Bureau, 233 Peachtree St. NE, Peachtree Center #100 (☎521-6600 or ☎800-285-2682; www.atlanta.net), downtown. Open M-F 8:30am-5:30pm. Automated **information service** ☎222-6688. For maps, stop in at the **Visitors Center,** 65 Upper Alabama St. (☎521-6688), on the upper level of Underground Atlanta MARTA: Five Points. Open M-Sa 10am-6pm, Su noon-6pm.

Bi-Gay-Lesbian Resources: The Atlanta Gay and Lesbian Center, 159 Ralph McGill Blvd., #600 (☎523-7500; www.aglc.org). **Gay Yellow Pages,** ☎892-6454.

Hotline: Rape Crisis Counseling, ☎616-4861. 24hr.

Post Office: Phoenix Station (☎521-2963), at the corner of Forsyth and Marietta St., one block from MARTA: Five Points. Open M-F 9am-5pm. **ZIP code:** 30301. **Area code:** 404 inside the I-285 perimeter, 770 outside. In text, 404 unless otherwise noted. 10-digit dialing required.

⌐ ACCOMMODATIONS

▓ **Guests Atlanta,** 811 Piedmont Ave. NE (☎872-5846 or 800-724-4387). Nestled on a shaded lane in the center of Atlanta. 3 houses offer charming, recently renovated rooms that are a pleasing mix between modern and old Victorian styles. Laundry. Reservations recommended in summer. Singles $79; doubles $99. ❹

Atlanta Hostel, 223 Ponce de Leon Ave. (☎875-9449), in Midtown. From MARTA: North Ave., exit onto Ponce de Leon and walk about 3½ blocks east to Myrtle St., or take bus #2. Clean, dorm-style rooms in a cozy home that resembles a B&B. Enjoy complimentary breakfast on the lovely patio. No sleeping bags allowed, but free blankets are distributed. Laundry facilities, pool table, kitchen, and Internet. Luggage storage $1. Linen $1. Free lockers. Dorms $18; private rooms $39-49. ❶

Masters Inn Economy, 3092 Presidential Pkwy. (☎770-454-8373 or 800-633-3434), off Chamblee Tucker Rd. in Doraville; Exit 94 off I-85. Clean, large rooms with king-size beds, local calls, cable TV, and pool. Singles M-Th and Su $40, F-Sa $44; doubles $44/49. ❷

Motel 6, 2820 Chamblee Tucker Rd. (☎770-458-6626), Exit 94 off I-85 in Doraville. Spacious and immaculate rooms. Free local calls, morning coffee, and A/C. Under 18 stay free with parents. Singles $43. ❷

Stone Mountain Family Campground (☎770-498-5710), on U.S. 78. Gorgeous sites, many on the lake. Bike rentals, free laser show, and Internet access. Max. stay 2 weeks. Sites $20-28, full hookup $32-37. Entrance fee $6 per car. ❶

◘ FOOD

From Vietnamese to Italian, and from fried to fricasseed, Atlanta cooks up ample options for any craving. "Soul food," designed to nurture the spiritual as well as the physical, nourishes the city. Have a taste of the South and dip cornbread into "pot likker," water used to cook greens. For a sweet treat, you can't beat the Atlanta-based **Krispy Kreme Doughnuts,** whose glazed delights (60¢) are a Southern institution. The factory store, 295 Ponce de Leon Ave. NE (☎876-7307), continuously bakes their wares. (Open Su-Th 5:30am-midnight, F-Sa 24hr.; drive-through daily 24hr.) A depot for Soul food's raw materials since 1923, the **Sweet Auburn Curb Market,** 209 Edgewood Ave., has more substantial fare, from cow's feet to ox tails. (☎659-1665. Open M-Sa 8am-6pm.)

BUCKHEAD

▨ **Fellini's Pizza,** 2809 Peachtree Rd. NE (☎266-0082), welcomes hungry customers with its bright yellow awnings, spacious deck (complete with fountain), and yummy pizza. Four other Atlanta locations, including 909 Ponce de Leon (☎873-3088). Slices $1.45, toppings 40¢; pies $8.50-12.50. Open M-Sa 11:30am-2am, Su 12:30pm-midnight. ❷

East Village Grille, 248 Buckhead Ave. NE (☎233-3345). Located in the middle of the Buckhead nightlife scene, this trusty diner serves up late-night munchies. Breakfast specials $3. Kitchen open M-F 11am-midnight, Sa-Su 11am-2am; bar daily until 4am. ❶

Buckhead Diner, 3073 Piedmont Rd. (☎262-3336). Frequented by celebrities, this is probably the only diner with valet parking. A place to see and be seen. Though the menu is a bit expensive, it's an Atlanta institution well worth the few extra bucks. Sandwiches $8-13. Lunch $10-17. Open M-Sa 11am-midnight, Su 10am-10pm. ❹

BUFORD HIGHWAY

Little Szechuan, 5091-C Buford Hwy. (☎770-451-0192), at I-285, Exit 25. In the heart of the ethnically diverse Buford Hwy. area. Lunch specials ($6) come in not-so-little doses. Open W-M 11:30am-2:30pm and 5-9:30pm. ❷

Pho Hoa, 5150-C Buford Hwy., (☎770-455-8729), at I-285, Exit 25. *Pho*, Vietnamese noodle soup, provides a healthy one-dish alternative for any meal. Soups $3-4. Meals $7-8. Open daily 10am-10pm. ❷

MIDTOWN

Tortillas, 774 Ponce de Leon Ave. (☎892-0193). The student crowd munches dirt-cheap, tasty Mexican food. Try the patio for open-air eating. Soft chicken tacos $1.75. Large variety of burritos from $3. Open Su-Th 11am-10pm, F-Sa 11am-11pm. ❶

The Varsity, 61 North Ave. NW (☎881-1707), at Spring St. MARTA: North Ave. Originator of the assembly-line school of food preparation, the world's largest drive-in is best known for the greatest onion rings in the South and the 2 mi. of hot dogs sold daily. Most items around $2. Open Su-Th 9am-11:30pm, F-Sa 9am-12:30am. ❶

Mary Mac's Tea Room, 224 Ponce de Leon Ave. (☎876-1800), at Myrtle; take the "Georgia Tech" bus north. Mary Mac's provides a 1940s atmosphere, amazing cinnamon rolls ($3.75 per dozen after 5pm), and delicious Southern-style cobbler. Entree and side $9. Open M-Sa 11am-8:30pm, Su 11am-3pm. Cash only. ❸

10TH ST.

Zocalo's, 187 10th St. (☎249-7576), is gourmet Mexican for the frugal-minded. Gorgeously fresh, authentic dinners start at $8.75. Open M-Th 11:30am-2:30pm and 5:30-11pm, F-Sa 11:30am-midnight, Su 8:30am-10pm. ❸

Nickiemoto's, 990 Piedmont Ave. (☎253-2010). The plates of sushi delight both the taste buds and the eyes. Combo plates from $10.50. Open M-Th 11:30am-11pm, F 11:30am-midnight, Sa noon-midnight, Su 2-11pm. ❸

Outwrite Bookstore & Coffeehouse, 991 Piedmont Ave. (☎607-0082). With rainbow-wigged mannequin heads gracing the windows, specialty coffees and sandwiches ($6) in the back corner, and inviting furniture on the deck, this gay and lesbian establishment has a relaxed, stylish air. Open daily 9am-11pm. ❶

The Flying Biscuit, 1001 Piedmont Ave. (☎874-8887). As expected, biscuits are the forte here. Breakfast-lovers will gobble up the orange-scented French toast ($6) in the hip joint often frequented by such celebrities as Reese Witherspoon and hubby Ryan Phillipe. Breakfast is served all day, but other options abound. Open daily 7am-11pm. ❷

VIRGINIA HIGHLAND

Cheap, fantastic food and young, fresh faces come with a side of attitude in Virginia Highland. There are several clusters of restaurants on N. Highland St—if you don't find what you want right away, keep walking and you're bound to be pleased.

▨ **Doc Chey's,** 1424 N. Highland Ave. (☎888-0777), serves up heaping mounds of noodles at fantastic prices ($6-8). The pan-Asian restaurant is ultra-popular among young Atlanta locals. Though there are 2 locations, the original is in Virginia Highlands. Try the unique spicy tomato ginger noodle bowl ($8), one of Doc's originals. Open Su-Th 11:30am-10pm, F-Sa 11:30am-11pm. ❷

Fontaine's Oyster House, 1026½ N. Highland Ave. (☎872-0869). Oysters are the name of the game at Fontaine's; have them on the half-shell (6 for $5) or eat them roasted in 1 of 8 ways ($8-15). Oysters are not all they have—sink your teeth into some juicy alligator. Open M and W-F 10:30am-4am, Tu 4pm-4am, Su 10:30am-midnight; kitchen closes M-Sa midnight, Su 11:30pm. ❸

Everybody's, 1040 N. Highland Ave. (☎873-4545), has received high accolades for selling Atlanta's best pizza. Their inventive pizza salads, a colossal mound of greens and chicken on a pizza bed ($11.25), use the freshest of ingredients. Open M-Th 11:30am-11pm, F-Sa 11:30am-1am, Su noon-10:30pm. ❸

Majestic Food Shop, 1031 Ponce de Leon Ave. (☎875-0276), at Cleburne. Perfect for those late-night cravings, this place is packed into the wee hours of the morning with people on their way home from the clubs. Burgers $2. Grits $1.15. Open 24hr. ❶

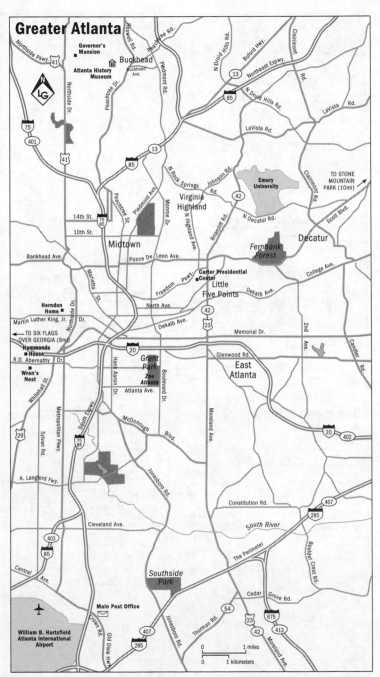

Greater Atlanta

Atlanta Area

MARTA System

NORTH LINE
NORTHEAST LINE
WEST LINE
EAST LINE
SOUTH LINE

AREA OF MAIN MAP

N11
N10
N9
N8
NE10/Doraville
NE9/Chamblee
N7/Buckhead
NE8
NE7
N6
N5
N4
N3
N2
N1
E7/Avondale
E8/Decatur
E9
P4
W3 W2 W1 S1 Five Points E1 E2 E3 E4 E5
W5 W4
S2/West End
S3
S4
S5
S6
S7/Airport

Downtown Atlanta

🏠 **ACCOMMODATIONS**
Atlanta Hostel, **15**
Guests Atlanta, **12**
Masters Inn Economy, **1**
Motel 6, **2**
Stone Mountain Family Campground, **3**

🍴 **FOOD**
The Flying Biscuit, **7**
Mary Mac's Tea Room, **13**
Nickiemoto's, **6**
Outwrite, **9**
The Varsity, **14**
Zocalo's, **5**

🌙 **NIGHTLIFE**
Après Diem, **10**
Backstreet, **11**
Blake's, **8**
Burkhardt's, **4**

0   1000 yards
0   1 kilometer

THE SOUTH

Manuel's Tavern, 602 N. Highland Ave. (☎525-3447). Occupying a prime spot between L5P and the Highland, this casual bar and grill is a longtime hangout of Atlanta's Democrats; Jimmy Carter is known to swing by for a burger ($5.50) and a beer. Open M-Sa 11am-2am, Su 11am-midnight. ❶

LITTLE FIVE POINTS

La Fonda Latina, 1150 Euclid Ave. (☎577-8317). Lounge under the glow of palm leaves fashioned from neon lights amid the vibrantly decorated walls, while savoring a terrific Cuban sandwich ($6.25-7). Open M-Th 11:30am-11pm, F-Sa 11:30am-midnight, Su 12:30-11pm. ❷

◙ SIGHTS

SWEET AUBURN DISTRICT

MARTIN LUTHER KING, JR. Some of the most powerful sights in the city run along Auburn Ave. in Sweet Auburn. Reverend Martin Luther King, Jr.'s birthplace, church, and grave are all part of the 23-acre ▨**Martin Luther King, Jr. National Historic Site.** The **Visitors Center** houses poignant displays of photographs, videos, and quotations oriented around King's life and the struggle for Civil Rights. *(450 Auburn Ave. NE. MARTA: King Memorial. ☎331-5190. Open June-Aug. daily 9am-6pm; Sept.-May 9am-5pm. Free.)* The Visitors Center administers tours of the **Birthplace of MLK.** *(501 Auburn Ave. Arrive early to sign up; advance reservations not accepted.)* Across the street from the Visitors Center stands **Ebenezer Baptist Church,** where King gave his first sermon at age 17 and co-pastored with his father from 1960 to 1968. *(407 Auburn Ave. ☎688-7263. Open June-Aug. daily 9am-6pm; Sept.-May 9am-5pm.)* King's **grave** and reflecting pool are next door at the **Martin Luther King, Jr. Center for Nonviolent Social Exchange.** The center holds a collection of King's personal articles, an overview of his role model, Gandhi, and an exhibit on Rosa Parks. *(449 Auburn Ave. NE. ☎331-5190. Open June-Aug. daily 9am-6pm; Sept.-May 9am-5pm. Free.)* Plaques lining Sweet Auburn point out the architecture and prominent past residents of this historically black neighborhood.

DOWNTOWN & AROUND

From March to November, the **Atlanta Preservation Center** offers walking tours of six popular areas, including Druid Hills, the setting of *Driving Miss Daisy.* *(537 Peachtree St. NE. ☎876-2041. $5, students and seniors $4.)*

GRANT PARK. In Grant Park, directly south of Oakland Cemetery and Cherokee Ave., the world's largest painting (48 ft. tall and 348 ft. in circumference), the 116-year-old **Cyclorama** takes visitors back in time, revolving them on a huge platform in the middle of the "1864 Battle of Atlanta." *(800 Cherokee Ave. SE. Take bus #31 or 97 from Five Points. ☎624-1071. Open June-Sept. daily 9:30am-5:30pm; Oct.-May 9:30am-4:30pm. $5, seniors $4, ages 6-12 $3.)*

ZOO ATLANTA. Next door to the park, the zoo delights visitors young and old with a spectacular array of animals. Komodo dragons, an artist-elephant, Allen the orangutan, a petting zoo, two giant pandas of Chengdu, a silverback gorilla, and a Sumatran tiger are just a few of the specimens waiting here. *(800 Cherokee Ave. SE. Take bus #31 or 97 from Five Points. ☎624-5600. Open Apr.-Oct. M-F 9:30am-4:30pm, Sa-Su 9:30am-5:30pm; Nov.-Mar. daily 9:30am-4:30pm. $15, seniors $11, ages 3-11 $10.)*

WORLD OF COCA-COLA (WOC). Two blocks from the capitol, the World of Coca-Cola details the rise of "the real thing" from its humble beginnings in Atlanta to its position of world domination. A replica soda fountain, complete with a "jerk" demonstrating the art of cola concocting, informs and entertains. The whole experience ends with a bang—rather than a fizzle—in the sampling room, where guests enthusiastically partake of 46 different soft drinks from around the world. *(55 Martin Luther King, Jr. Dr. ☎676-5151. Open June-Aug. M-Sa 9am-6pm, Su 11am-6pm; Sept.-May M-Sa 9am-5pm, Su noon-6pm. $6, seniors $4, ages 6-12 $3.)*

UNDERGROUND ATLANTA. Adjacent to the WOC, this redeveloped part of Atlanta gets down with six subterranean blocks of mall and over 120 chain restaurants, shops, and night spots. Once a hot spot for alternative music, the underground resembles a cross between a mall and a carnival these days. *(Descend at the entrance beside the Five Points subway station. ☎523-2311. Shops open June-Sept. M-Sa 10am-9:30pm, Su 11am-7pm; Oct.-May M-Sa 10am-9pm, Su noon-6pm. Bars and restaurants close later.)*

CNN. High-tech Atlanta's multinational business powerhouses reign from the **Five Points District. Turner Broadcasting System** offers a behind-the-scenes peek with its **Cable News Network (CNN) Studio Tour.** Witness anchors broadcasting live and get the inside scoop on production techniques and special effects. *(At Techwood Dr. and Marietta St. MARTA: Omni/Dome/GWCC Station at W1. ☎827-2300. 45min. tours every 10-15min. daily 9am-6pm. $8, seniors $6, ages 5-12 $5.)*

OLYMPIC PARK. Across the street from CNN, the **Centennial Olympic Park** unfolds, celebrating the 1996 Olympic games, which were held in Atlanta. Despite the tragic bombing that occurred here, the park is a great place to relax or cool off. On hot days the **Fountain of Rings** fills with children splashing about. *(20min. shows daily 12:30, 3:30, 6:30, and 9pm.)*

CARTER PRESIDENTIAL CENTER. This charming museum, north of Little Five Points, traces Georgia peanut farmer Jimmy Carter's political career through interesting, and at times humorous, exhibits and films. Attached to the museum, the **Jimmy Carter Library,** one of only eleven Presidential libraries in the country, serves as an archival depository for historical materials from the Carter Administration. *(441 Freedom Pkwy. Take bus #16 to Cleburne Ave. ☎331-0296. Museum open M-Sa 9am-4:45pm, Su noon-4:45pm; grounds open to the public daily 6am-9pm. $5, seniors $4, under 16 free.)*

WEST END

AFRICAN-AMERICAN HISTORY. Dating from 1835, the West End is Atlanta's oldest neighborhood. Experience several eccentric twists on the "historic home" tradition at the **Wren's Nest.** Home to author Joel Chandler Harris, who popularized the African folktale trickster Brer Rabbit, the Wren's Nest offers a glimpse into middle-class life as it was at the beginning of the century. The house sparks further interest with a look into Harris's bedroom, left untouched since his death. Energetic professional storytellers continue the author's legacy. *(1050 R.D. Abernathy Blvd. Take bus #71 from West End Station/S2. ☎753-7735. Open Tu-Sa 10am-2:30pm. Tours every hr. on the ½hr. $7, seniors and ages 13-19 $5, ages 4-12 $4.)* The **Hammonds House** displays unique contemporary and historic works in Georgia's only collection dedicated entirely to African-American and Haitian art. *(503 Peeples St. SW. ☎752-8730. Open Tu-F 10am-6pm, Sa-Su 1-5pm. $2, students and seniors $1.)* Originally born to slaves, Alonzo F. Herndon, a prominent barber and founder of Atlanta Life Insurance Co., became Atlanta's wealthiest African-American in the 1900s. A Beaux-Arts Classical mansion, the **Herndon Home** was built in 1910. *(587 University Pl. NW. Take bus #3 from Five Points station to the corner of Martin Luther King, Jr. Dr. and Maple, walk 1 block west, turn right on Walnut, and walk 1 block. ☎581-9813. Tours every hr. $5, students $3. Open Tu-Sa 10am-4pm. W Community Day: donations accepted.)*

MIDTOWN

SCITREK. Near Piedmont Park, **SciTrek (Science and Technology Museum of Atlanta)**, with over 150 interactive exhibits for all ages, is one of the nation's top science centers. *(395 Piedmont Ave. NE. MARTA: Civic Center. Walk 3 blocks east on Ralph McGill Blvd., and turn left on Piedmont. ☎522-5500. Open M-Sa 10am-5pm, Su noon-5pm. $7.50; students, seniors, military, and ages 3-17 $6.)*

MARGARET MITCHELL. Reopened in 1997 after two arson-related fires, the **Margaret Mitchell House** and **Gone With the Wind Movie Museum** showcase the apartment where Mitchell wrote *Gone With the Wind*, as well as her typewriter and autographed copies of the novel. The Movie Museum includes the door to "Tara," the portrait of Scarlet at which Clark Gable hurled a cocktail onscreen (complete with stain), and other original props from the movie set. If you weren't already in love with the classic novel, you'll be inspired to reconsider after a visit here. *(990 Peachtree St., at 10th and Peachtree St. adjacent to MARTA: Midtown. ☎249-7015. Open daily 9:30am-5pm. 1hr. tours every 10min. $12, students and seniors $9, ages 6-17 $5.)*

WOODRUFF ARTS CENTER. Culture vultures, the **Woodruff Arts Center (WAC)** and the **High Museum of Art** is your place. To the west of Piedmont Park, Richard Meier's award-winning buildings of glass, steel, and white porcelain, are matched only by the treasures they contain. The museum's permanent collection contains one of Andy Warhol's Marilyn Monroe paintings. *(1280 Peachtree St. NE. MARTA: Arts Center and exit Lombardy Way. WAC: ☎733-4200. High Museum of Art: ☎733-4400. Open Tu-Sa 10am-5pm, Su noon-5pm. $8, students with ID and seniors $6, ages 6-17 $4.)* The **Folk Art & Photography Galleries,** part of the High Museum, house additional exhibits. *(30 John Wesley Dobbs Ave. NE. 1 block south of MARTA: Peachtree Center. ☎577-6940. Open M-Sa 10am-5pm, and the first Th of every month 10am-8pm. Free.)*

WILLIAM BREMAN JEWISH HERITAGE MUSEUM. The **William Breman Jewish Heritage Museum,** the largest Jewish museum in the Southeast, features a powerful, gripping Holocaust exhibit and a gallery tracing the history of the Atlanta Jewish community from 1845 to the present. *(1440 Spring St. NW. From MARTA: Peachtree Center Station, walk 3 blocks north to 18th St. and Spring St. ☎873-1661. Open M-Th 10am-5pm, F 10am-3pm, Su 1-5pm. $5, students and seniors $3, under 7 free.)*

CENTER FOR PUPPETRY ARTS. Across the street from the Jewish Heritage Museum, the **Center for Puppetry Arts** enthralls all ages. The Center stages live shows, has puppet-making workshops, and holds a museum of puppet history and culture throughout the world. A few of Jim Henson's Muppets, as well as traditional Punch and Judy figures, can be found in the collection. *(1404 Spring St. NW., at 18th St. ☎873-3391. Open Tu-Sa 9am-5pm, Su 11am-5pm. $8, students and seniors $7. Puppet workshop ages 5 and over $5.)*

FERNBANK MUSEUM OF NATURAL HISTORY. The **Fernbank Museum of Natural History** sports dinosaurs, an IMAX theater, discovery centers, and fossils embedded in the limestone floor tiles. *(767 Clifton Rd. NE. Off Ponce de Leon Ave.; take bus #2 from North Ave. or Avondale Station. ☎929-6300. Open M-Sa 10am-5pm, Su noon-5pm. Museum $12, students and seniors $11, ages 3-12 $10; IMAX film $10/9/8; both attractions $17/15/13.)* The adjacent **R.L. Staton Rose Garden** awakens with gorgeous blooms from spring until December. *(Corner of Ponce de Leon Ave. and Clifton Rd.)*

BUCKHEAD

A drive through **Buckhead,** north of Midtown and Piedmont Park, off Peachtree St. near W. Paces Ferry Rd., uncovers Atlanta's Beverly Hills—the sprawling mansions of Coca-Cola bigwigs and other specimens of high culture. This area is very conducive to wining and dining; the area around W. Paces Ferry and Peachtree St. is strung with dance clubs and restaurants frequented by Atlanta's 20-somethings.

BUCKHEAD ATTRACTIONS. One of the most exquisite residences in the Southeast, the Greek Revival **Governor's Mansion** has elaborate gardens and one of the finest collections of furniture from the Federal Period. *(391 W. Paces Ferry Rd. ☎ 261-1776. Tours Tu-Th 10-11:30am. Free.)* In the same neighborhood, the **Atlanta History Museum** traces Atlanta's development from a rural area to an international cityscape. Its Civil War Gallery spotlights the stories of both Confederate and Union soldiers, while the Folklife Gallery expounds on Southern culture from grits to banjos. Also on the grounds are the **Swan House,** a lavish Anglo-Palladian Revival home built in 1928, and the **Tullie Smith Farm,** an 1845 Yeoman farmhouse. *(130 W. Paces Ferry Rd. NW. ☎ 814-4000. Open M-Sa 10am-5:30pm, Su noon-5:30pm. $10, students and seniors $8, ages 6-17 $5; tours of the houses each an additional $1.)*

🎭 ENTERTAINMENT

For hassle-free fun, buy a MARTA pass (see **Practical Information,** p. 400) and pick up the city's free publications on music and events. *Creative Loafing, Music Atlanta,* the *Hudspeth Report,* or "Leisure" in the Friday edition of the *Atlanta Journal and Constitution* give visitors the latest info. Check for free summer concerts in Atlanta's parks.

The **Woodruff Arts Center** (see **Midtown,** p. 409) houses the Atlanta Symphony, the Alliance Theater Company, the Atlanta College of Art, and the High Museum of Art. **Atlantix,** 65 Upper Alabama St., MARTA: Five Points, sets you up with half-price rush tickets to dance, theater, music, and other attractions throughout the city. (☎ 678-318-1400. Walk-up service only. Tu 11am-3pm, W-Sa 11am-6pm, Su noon-3pm.) The **Philips Arena,** 100 Techwood Dr. (☎ 878-3000 or 800-326-4000), hosts concerts, the **Atlanta Hawks** basketball team, and the **Atlanta Thrashers** hockey team. In 2003 Atlanta will host the NCAA Women's Final Four Basketball Tournament. The National League's **Atlanta Braves** play at **Turner Field,** 755 Hank Aaron Dr., MARTA: West End or bus #105, where a Coke bottle over left field erupts with fireworks after home runs. (☎ 522-7630; Ticketmaster 800-326-4000. $5-15, $1 skyline seats available game day.) One-hour tours of Turner Field include views of the diamond from the $200,000 skyboxes. (☎ 614-2311. Open non-game days M-Sa 9:30am-3pm, Su 1-3pm; evening-game days M-Sa 9:30am-noon; no tours afternoon-game days; off-season M-Sa 10am-2pm. $8, under 13 $4.) See the **Atlanta Falcons** play football at the **Georgia Dome,** MARTA: Omni/Dome/World Congress Center, the world's largest cable-supported dome. Public tours are available by appointment. (☎ 223-8687. Open daily 10am-4pm. $2; students, seniors, and ages 3-12 $1.)

Six Flags Over Georgia, 275 Riverside Pkwy., at I-20 W, is one of the largest amusement parks in the nation. Take bus #201 "Six Flags" from Hamilton Homes. Check out the 54 mph "Georgia Scorcher" roller coaster and the new "Superman" roller coaster, with a pretzel-shaped inverted loop. (☎ 770-948-9290. Open mid-May to Aug. M-F 10am-9pm, Sa 10am-10pm; off-season hours vary. $40, seniors and under 4 ft. $25. Parking $10-12.)

⊠ NIGHTLIFE

Atlanta's rich nightlife lacks a true focal point. Fortunately, it also lacks any limits; young people can be found partying until the wee hours and beyond. Scores of bars and clubs along Peachtree Rd. and Buckhead Ave. in **Buckhead** cater to a very young crowd. Pricier **Midtown** greets the glitzy and the glamorous. Alternative **Little Five Points** plays hosts to bikers and goths, while **Virginia Highland** and up-and-coming **East Atlanta** feature an eclectic mix of all of types imaginable.

BARS & PUBS

Lu Lu's Bait Shack, 3057 Peachtree Rd. NE (☎262-5220). Cool off with a 96 oz. fishbowl in the heart of Buckhead's popular, young nightlife scene. Open Tu-F 7pm-4am, Sa 5pm-3am.

Apres Diem, 931 Monroe Dr. (☎872-3333), in Midtown, blends stylishly presented food, 12 kinds of coffee drinks, and a hip night scene with an international, gay-friendly crowd. Located in a strip mall, it's easy to miss—don't, you'll regret it. Open Su-Th 11:30am-midnight, F-Sa 11:30am-2am.

Masquerade, 695 North Ave. NE (☎577-8178, concert info 577-2007), occupies an original turn-of-the-century mill. The bar has 3 different levels: "heaven," with live music from touring bands; "purgatory," a more laid-back pub and pool house; and "hell," a dance club with everything from techno to 1940s big band jazz. An outside space provides dancing under the stars, while the 4000-seat amphitheater caters to metal and punk tastes. 18+. Cover $3-8 and up. Open W-Su 8pm-4am.

Blind Willie's, 828 N. Highland Ave. NE (☎873-2583), in Virginia Highland. Feel your way over here for a dazzling line-up of live blues, zydeco, and folk acts. A bit of a hole-in-the-wall from the outside, it's still an Atlanta legend. Live music starts around 10pm. Cover $5-10. Open Su-Th 8pm-2am, F 8pm-3am, Sa 8pm-2:30am.

The Vortex, 438 Moreland Ave. (☎688-1828), in L5P. Many bikers park their choppers here—the home of Atlanta's best burger—for a drink at their favorite watering hole. Open M-Sa 11am-2am, Su 11am-midnight.

Flatiron, 520 Flat Shoals Ave. (☎688-8864), is anchoring the growing East Atlanta scene. With the catchphrase, "If you love this country, you'll love this bar," how can you go wrong? Open Su-Th 11am-2am, F-Sa 11am-3pm.

Fountainhead Lounge, 485 Flat Shoals Ave. SE (☎522-7841). If the streets of East Atlanta seem uncrowded, it's because everyone is packed into this suave hideout. Couches near the bar and tables in the small upstairs offer rest for the weary, but be prepared to stand with the rest of the trendsetters. DJ spins F-Sa. Open M-Sa 7pm-3am.

Steamhouse, 3041 Bolling Way (☎233-7980). For those who like raw oysters with their beer, Steamhouse has plenty of both. A great place for a hot evening—the party often spills out onto the patio. Open daily 11:30am-2am.

DANCE CLUBS

Chaos, 3067 Peachtree Rd. NE (☎995-0064). One of the largest and newest clubs in Buckhead, Chaos manages to avoid the cheesy commercialism of some of its neighbors. M hip-hop; other nights Top 40 and techno. Cover $10 for men, women free. Open M-F 9pm-4am, Sa 9pm-3am.

Tongue & Groove, 3055 Peachtree Rd. NE (☎261-2325). An international crowd frequents this hangout, Buckhead's answer to some of Atlanta's swankier establishments. W Latin night. Th house. F hip-hop. Sa Euro night. Cover: men W and F $5, Sa $10; women W $5, Sa $10 after midnight. Open W-Sa 9pm-4am, Su 11:30am-2am.

The Riviera, 1055 Peachtree St. NE (☎607-8050). Like the Midtown crowd it serves, the Riv is fun, flashy, and full of itself. Shoot pool and/or kamikazes while cooling off from the dance floor. Frequent live music shows. Cover $15. Open daily 10pm-6am.

GAY & LESBIAN NIGHTLIFE

Most of Atlanta's gay culture centers around **Midtown** and several blocks north in **Ansley Sq.,** near Piedmont and Monroe. In Atlanta, straight and gay often party together, and some of the city's best all-around joints are rainbow-colored. For information on gay happenings and special events in Hotlanta, check out the free *Southern Voice* newspaper, available everywhere.

Backstreet, 845 Peachtree St. NE (☎873-1986), is Atlanta's most popular gay club and *the* hangout for all the city's late-night partiers. One of the oldest clubs in the area, the behemoth Backstreet still rocks out with a vast dance floor, several balconies and 3 full bars. Required quarterly "membership" $10. Cover F-Sa $5. Open 24hr.

Blake's, 227 10th St. (☎892-5786). Midtown males flock to this friendly bar, where see-and-be-seen is a way of life. Also a popular destination for the young lesbian crowd. Open daily 3pm-2am.

Burkhart's, 1492 Piedmont Ave. NE (☎872-4403), in Ansley Sq. Slightly less pretentious than Blake's, this bar is Atlanta's other gay mainstay. Su tea dances with free food. Open M-Sa 4pm-4am, Su 2pm-midnight.

◪ OUTDOOR ACTIVITIES

In the heart of Midtown, **Piedmont Park** is a hotbed of fun, free activities. Look for the **Dogwood Festival,** an art festival, in the spring and the **Jazz Festival** in May. In June, the park celebrates with the **Gay Pride Festival,** and on July 4th, Atlanta draws 55,000 people to the world's largest 10K race. Every summer Turner Broadcasting and HBO present "Screen on the Green," a series of free films projected once a week in the meadow behind the Visitors Center. To the north, a vast park sprawls around the 60-acre **Atlanta Botanical Garden,** 1345 Piedmont Ave. NE. Take bus #36 frp, MARTA: Arts Center Station; on Su, bus #31 Lindburgh from Five Points. Stroll through 15 acres of landscaped gardens, a hardwood forest with trails, and an interactive children's garden focusing on health and wellness. (☎876-5859. Open Apr.-Sept. Tu-Su 9am-7pm; Oct.-Mar. Tu-Su 9am-6pm. $10, students $5, seniors $7; Th free after 3pm.) The Garden's **Dorothy Chapman Fuqua Conservatory** contains hundreds of species of endangered plants. (Opens at 10am.)

Sixteen miles east of the city on U.S. 78, **Stone Mountain Park** provides a respite from the city with a dose of nature and a fabulous **Confederate Memorial** carved into the world's largest mass of granite. The "Mt. Rushmore of the South" profiles Jefferson Davis, Robert E. Lee, and Stonewall Jackson and rises 825 ft. The hike up the **Confederate Hall Trail** (1½ mi.) is rewarded with a spectacular view of Atlanta. The mountain is surrounded by a 3200-acre historic park. A dazzling laser show illuminates the side of the mountain on summer nights. Take bus #120 "Stone Mountain" from MARTA: Avondale. (☎770-498-5600 or 800-317-2006. Park gates open daily 6am-midnight. Attractions open in summer daily 10am-8pm; off-season 10am-5pm. $19, ages 3-11 $15. Laser show daily 9:30pm. Free.)

ATHENS
☎ 706

In the grand Southern tradition of naming college towns after great classical cultural centers, Athens is perhaps the most successful at living up to its namesake. Of course, the only Greeks around here live in the University of Georgia's (UGA) frat houses, and the city is better known for its production of rock stars than philosophers or mathematicians. Residents will tell you Athens is Georgia's best city, as vibrant as Atlanta without the traffic, smog, or pretension. Athens's music scene is especially vibrant; the university and surrounding bars have been the spawning ground for hundreds of popular bands, including R.E.M. and the B-52s. Residents of all ages and walks of life make Athens more of a miniature city than a college town.

🛈 **PRACTICAL INFORMATION.** Situated 70 mi. northeast of Atlanta, Athens can be reached from I-85 via U.S. 316, which runs into U.S. 29. Although there is a commuter airport (☎ 549-5783), it's easier to fly into Atlanta and take a **commuter shuttle** (☎ 800-354-7874) to various points in and around Athens ($30). **Southeastern Stages**, 220 W. Broad St. buses to Atlanta and Augusta. (☎ 549-2255. Call for schedules. Open M-F 7:15am-7:15pm, Sa-Su 7:15am-2:30pm.) The **Athens Transit System** runs "The Bus" every 30min. on loops around downtown, UGA, and surrounding residential areas. Well-marked stops line the sidewalks. Schedules and info are available at the Transit Information Center, in front of City Hall on Washington St. (☎ 613-3430. Buses M-F 6:15am-7:15pm, Sa 7:30am-7pm. $1, seniors 50¢, ages 6-18 75¢; transfers free.) UGA's **Campus Transit System** runs everywhere on campus and to some stops downtown. (☎ 369-6220. Free.) **Taxis: Alfa Taxi,** ☎ 583-8882. Two blocks north of the UGA campus are the **Athens Welcome Center,** 280 E. Dougherty St., in the Church-Waddel-Brumby House. (☎ 353-1820. Open M-Sa 10am-6pm, Su noon-6pm.) The **UGA Visitors Center,** at the intersection of College Station and River Rd. on campus, provides info on UGA attractions. (☎ 542-0842. Open M-F 8am-5pm, Sa 9am-5pm, Su 1-5pm.) **Medical Services: Athens Regional Medical Center,** 1199 Prince Ave. (☎ 549-9977.) **Hotlines: Crisis Line,** ☎ 353-1912. **Helpline Georgia,** ☎ 800-338-6745. **Community Connection,** ☎ 353-1313. **Post Office:** 575 Olympic Dr. (☎ 800-275-8777. Open M-F 8:30am-4:30pm.) **ZIP code:** 30601. **Area code:** 706.

🛏 **ACCOMMODATIONS.** Accommodations are usually reasonably priced, but rates rise for football weekends. The **Perimeter Inn ❷,** 3791 Atlanta Hwy., 5 mi. from downtown, is a reasonably priced, comfortable, independently-owned motel with a Spanish flair. (☎ 548-3000 or 800-934-2963. Singles $38; doubles $44.) Within walking distance of the campus and downtown, the posh **Magnolia Terrace Guest House ❹,** 277 Hill St., between Milledge Ave. and Prince St., is a simple B&B with seven luxurious rooms and a full breakfast in the morning. (☎ 548-3860. Rooms M-F $95, Sa-Su up to $150.) **Watson Mill Bridge State Park ❶,** 650 Watson Mill Rd., 21 mi. east of Athens, is the best place in the area to camp. The park boasts the longest original-site covered bridge in Georgia, as well as a mill pond with an old grist mill, horse and hiking trails, canoe and boat rentals, and plenty of fishing. From Athens, take Hwy. 72 east to the town of Comer, turn right onto Hwy. 22, go south for 3 mi., and then turn left onto Watson Mill Rd. (☎ 783-5349 or 800-864-7275. Park open daily 7am-10pm; office 8am-5pm. Sites $15, with water and electricity $17; secluded primitive sites $20.)

❑ FOOD. The ▨**Last Resort Grill ❸**, 174 and 184 W. Clayton St., at the corner of Hull St., is an eclectic lunch-and-dinner restaurant with a gourmet atmosphere and reasonable prices. Order a fried green tomato sandwich ($4.75) and receive a delicious, artful presentation on a gigantic white plate, or indulge in desserts that are widely considered the best in Athens. (☎549-0810. Lunches $5-10. Dinners $10-20. Open Su-Th 11am-3pm and 5-10pm, F-Sa 5-11pm; bar until 2am.) R.E.M. fans that wonder what "automatic for the people" means should ask Dexter Weaver, the owner of **Weaver D's Fine Foods ❶**, 1016 E. Broad St., to whom the phrase originally belongs. Weaver D's is a tiny restaurant that serves pork chop sandwiches ($4.25) and soul-food lunches ($5-6) out of a small roadside house. R.E.M. was one of Weaver's biggest fans and repaid him for the use of his phrase as their 1992 album title by inviting him to the Grammy Awards. (☎353-7797. Open M-F 11am-6pm.) **The Grill ❷**, 171 College St., is Athens's version of the all-night burger-and-malt joint that is vital to the life of every college town. In addition to the standard megaburger platter ($7) and luscious malts ($3.25), the Grill has a mean vegetarian side. (☎543-4770. Open 24hr.) **The Grit ❶**, 199 Prince Ave., is Athens at its crunchiest and coolest, serving up scrumptious, healthy meals, including a great weekend brunch. International dishes from Mexico, the Middle East, and Italy give the menu a foreign flair. (☎543-6592. Vegetable samosas two for $6. Entrees $3-7. Open M-W 11am-10pm, Th-F 11am-10:30pm, Sa-Su 10am-3pm and 5-10pm.)

◙ SIGHTS. The **University of Georgia,** chartered in 1785 as the first land-grant college in the US, is the very reason Athens exists and tops its list of tourist attractions. The campus **Visitors Center,** at the corner of College Station and River Rd. in south campus, has self-guided tours, maps, and helpful answers. (☎542-0842. Open M-F 8am-5pm, Sa 9am-5pm, Su 1-5pm.) The campus begins downtown on Broad St., where **The Arch** guards the official entrance to the institution. The home turf of UGA's "Dawgs," **Sanford Stadium,** in the white English bulldogs that served as the school's mascot. **Butts-Mehre Heritage Hall,** on the corner of Pinecrest Dr. and Rutherford St., houses the school's athletic offices and the **Heritage Museum,** which celebrates generations of UGA athletes—and white English bulldogs. (☎542-9094. Open M-F 8am-5pm, Sa-Su 2-5pm.) Also on campus, the **Georgia Museum of Art,** 90 Carlton St., in the Performing and Visual Arts Complex off East Campus Dr., is an impressive state-funded collection of over 7000 works of art. (☎542-4662. Open Tu and Th-Sa 10am-5pm, W 10am-9pm, Su 1-5pm. Free, $1 suggested donation.)

Beyond the university, Athens boasts a wealth of historic sites, homes, and artifacts chronicling the town's genteel and wealthy history. The many lush gardens and arboretums encourage long walks and picnics. Maps and tours of the city's historic areas and green spaces are available at the Athens Welcome Center (see **Practical Information,** p. 413), the oldest residence in town. The **U.S. Navy Supply Corps School and Museum,** 1425 Prince Ave., was originally a teacher's college, then a Carnegie library, and is now one of only 11 official U.S. Navy Museums. Exhibits of ship models, uniforms, and all manner of Navy flotsam are on display. (☎354-7349. Open M-F 9am-5:15pm, Sa-Su noon-4pm. Free.) The city's most elaborate garden, the **State Botanical Garden of Georgia,** 2450 S. Milledge Ave., houses 313 acres of trails, a tropical conservatory, and a Day Chapel. (☎542-1244. Open daily 8am-sunset; Visitors Center Tu-Sa 9am-4:30pm, Su 11:30am-4:30pm. Free.)

If you hesitate to bequeath your property to undeserving offspring, consider making your favorite plant an heir. Professor William H. Jackson set the legal precedent when he willed to a beloved oak tree all the land within eight feet of its trunk. Today, **The Tree That Owns Itself,** a successor to the original tree that was downed in a storm in 1942, flourishes at the intersection of Finley and Dearing St., near Broad St. downtown. By far Athens's best Civil War relic, **The Double-Barreled**

Cannon was a great idea that failed spectacularly in testing. On the grounds of City Hall, at Washington and College St., the two barrels face northward threateningly, though the two cannonballs chained together will never fly out of them.

🎵 🎸 **ENTERTAINMENT & NIGHTLIFE.** Known for its music scene, Athens has cradled hundreds of fledging bands in all styles of music over the years. R.E.M. is arguably Athens's most well-known homegrown band, but those plugged into the music world will know that most musicians show up in Athens at one point or another to play in a true-blue music mecca. It would take a week to visit the scores of clubs and bars that stuff the downtown area—there's always something going on. To see the hot night spots of Yore, pick up *Flagpole Magazine's* **Walking Tour of Athens Music History**, available at the Visitors Center. All this musical energy reaches its peak in late June, when **Athfest** takes over the town. (☎ 548-2516. 1 day $10, both days $15.) Take a look at Athens's free weekly newspaper, *Flagpole Magazine*, available everywhere downtown, to find out which bands are playing where. If you're broke, tune in to **WUOG 90.5,** one of the nation's last bastions of real college radio. The students who run the station play tons of local music, and liven it with unscripted, unplanned, and often incoherent commentary.

R.E.M. got their start at **The 40 Watt Club,** 285 W.Washington St., a real Athens institution. Born in 1979 as a raucous Halloween party lit by a single 40 watt bulb, the club has had numerous incarnations and locations, but currently kicks with live music most nights. (☎ 549-7871. Cover $5-15. Open daily 10pm-3am.) If you want to do something other than listen to music, Athens lives up to its name theatrically as well as academically. **The Classic Center,** 300 N. Thomas St., hosts Broadway productions, all sorts of entertainers and concerts, and the Athens Symphony. (☎ 357-4444. Call for schedules and ticket prices.) **The Morton Theater,** 195 W. Washington St., was built in 1910 as a Vaudeville Theater and was entirely African-American owned and operated. Today it is a fully restored, high-tech performing arts center home to all sorts of theater and music. (☎ 613-3770. Call for schedules and ticket prices.) **Jittery Joe's,** 1210 S. Millege Rd., offers a posh, classy coffeeshop atmosphere. (☎ 208-1979. Open M-Th 6:30am-midnight, F 6:30am-1am, Sa 8:30am-1am, Su 8:30am-midnight.)

MACON ☎ 478

Before Macon was officially established in 1823, the area along the banks of the Ocmulgee River was the heart of the Creek Native American territory before President Andrew Jackson forced them to move to Oklahoma to make way for white settlers in the "Trail of Tears." White men turned the sacred ground into a port city that became one of Georgia's cultural centers. In the 20th century, Macon developed into a magnet for many of Georgia's top musicians, most of whom performed at the Douglass Theater, one of the greatest venues for black performers in the country. Today, Macon is a strange mix of small-town south and big-city ambition.

🏛 📍 **ORIENTATION & PRACTICAL INFORMATION.** Macon sits at the intersection of I-75 and I-16, about 75 mi. southwest of Atlanta. **I-475** makes a large arc west of downtown, branching off of I-75. Downtown is a grid with numbered streets running east-west and named streets running north-south. The town is actually set at a 45° angle, so north means northwest, and south means southeast. **Riverside Dr.** is a main artery parallel to I-75 and the river. **Martin Luther King Blvd. (MLK)** runs east-west through the heart of downtown. Shops, bars, and restaurants cluster on **Cherry St.,** the main north-south thoroughfare. West of downtown, MLK Blvd. becomes Houston (HOUSE-ston) Ave., which feeds onto Eisenhower Pkwy. North of town along Riverside Dr. lie more shopping centers and pricier hotels.

Greyhound, 65 Spring St. (☎743-2868; open daily 4:30am-midnight), runs to Athens (8hr., 2 per day, $68); Atlanta (1½hr., 12 per day, $15.25); and Birmingham (5-6hr., 7 per day, $50). **Macon-Bibb County Transit Authority (MTA-MAC),** 1000 Terminal Dr., is "Macon a way for the community" with 20 buses throughout the downtown area and **MITSI,** a trolley that stops downtown and shuttles passengers from attraction to attraction. (☎746-1387. Operates M-Sa 5:30am-11pm. 75¢, students 50¢, seniors 35¢; transfers 25¢. Trolley 25¢.) Services include: **Hotlines: Crisis Line,** ☎745-9292. **Medical Services: Medical Center of Central Georgia,** 777 Hemlock St. (☎633-1000), downtown. **Internet access: Washington Memorial Library,** 1180 Washington St., at the corner of College St. (☎744-0800. Open M-Th 9am-9pm, F-Sa 9am-6pm, Su 1:30-5pm.) **Visitors info: Macon-Bibb Country Convention and Visitors Bureau,** 200 Cherry St., at the southern tip of downtown. (☎743-3401 or 800-768-3401; www.maconga.org. Open M-Sa 9am-5pm. Free parking.) **Post Office:** 451 College St. (☎752-8432. Open M-F 8am-6pm, Sa 9am-2pm.) **ZIP code:** 31213. **Area code:** 478.

⌂ ACCOMMODATIONS. Macon has many hotels, but forces you to make a tough choice: surrender to the chain motels, pay outrageous prices, or gamble with questionable safety. The chains are plentiful along I-75 north of town and on Eisenhower Pkwy. west of town near I-475. The cheap prices, quality amenities, and safe atmosphere at **Masters Inn ❶,** Exit 160 off I-75 at Pio Nono Ave., make it a good bet in a convenient location. (☎788-8910 or 800-633-3434. Free local calls, continental breakfast, and pool. Singles $27; doubles $29.) Perched amidst mansions overlooking the city, the **1842 Inn ❺,** 353 College St., is as much museum as lodging. Huge white columns encase a large balcony, while period furniture, complimentary hors d'ouevres, a private health club, canopied four-poster beds, optional breakfast in bed, and many more perks bathe guests in luxury. (☎741-1842 or 800-336-1842. Reservations recommended. Singles from $125; doubles from $195; in summer weekend rates $170-230.)

◻ FOOD. 🍴**Jeneane's Cafe ❶,** 524 Mulberry St., serves lightning-fast lunch to the noontime crowd in the most personal, efficient, sweetie-eat-your-vegetables way imaginable. Desserts are concocted daily by a retired pastry chef, and the teal plastic cafeteria seats have an ambiance all their own. (☎743-5267. Meat-and-vegetable lunch plate $4.95. Open M-F 6:30am-2:30pm.) **Len Berg's Restaurant ❶,** 240 Post Office Alley, walk south down Walnut St.; a big sign points to an unassuming one-story building. A 1908 sit-down lunch counter with such a loyal local clientele that there's often a 30min. wait for a table. The food is classic Southern lunch counter: grilled liver and onions with boiled potatoes and snap beans or shrimp creole on rice with carrot and raisin salad and broccoli casserole. (☎742-9255. All meals under $7. Open M-F 11am-2:30pm.) An old neighborhood bar and earthy restaurant, **The Rookery ❷,** 543 Cherry St., caters to aging hippies and sells burgers ($5-7), steaks, lasagna, and other dishes. At night, a variety of live bands play to the local crowd. (☎746-8658. Cover F-Sa $5, W free. Bands W and F-Sa 9:30pm-1:30am. Kitchen open daily 11am-10pm.)

◙ SIGHTS. Macon is a tour-planner's dream—the entire downtown is compact and walkable, and the major museums are all within one block of each other. The 🎵**Georgia Music Hall of Fame,** 200 MLK Blvd, at the end of Mulberry St., will overwhelm us with its mind-boggling collection of inductees, including Ray Charles, The Allman Brothers, Gladys Knight, James Brown, and the Indigo Girls. From some of Little Richard's wacky suits to Lynyrd Skynyrd's keyboard and cassette case, the Hall of Fame has priceless treasures and memorabilia. The exhibits are divided into themed areas, including a model chapel that celebrates great Georgian gospel singers and a wonderful interactive area for kids. (☎750-0350. Open M-Sa

9am-5pm, Su 1-5pm. $8; students with ID, seniors, and AAA $6; ages 4-16 $3.50.) The **Georgia Sports Hall of Fame**, 301 Cherry St., is another lavishly designed showcase of Georgia talent. It includes relics from the life of Hank Aaron and a basketball court that visitors can play on in between ooh-ing at exhibits. (☎752-1585. Open M-Sa 9am-5pm, Su 1-5pm. $6; students, seniors, and military $5; ages 6-16 $3.50.)

The **Tubman African American Museum**, 340 Walnut Ave., is the South's largest museum that is exclusively devoted to African-American art, history, and culture. Beginning in ancient Africa, the museum traces the ancestry and legacy of African-Americans by showcasing art, music, and great historical figures from every era of history. In 2003, the museum may move to a new location on Cherry St., directly across from the Georgia Sports Hall of Fame. (☎743-8544. Open M-Sa 9am-5pm, Su 2-5pm. $3, under 12 $2.) An impressive National Park, the **Ocmulgee National Monument**, 1207 Emery Hwy., across the river from downtown, protects some of the gigantic mounds, prehistoric trenches, and village sites of the five distinct Indian groups that inhabited it for over 12,000 years. The largest of the mounds rises 45 ft. above the trees and presents an amazing view of Macon and the countryside beyond. The Visitors Center houses a small museum where pottery and artifacts are displayed. (☎752-8257. Park and Visitors Center open daily 9am-5pm. Free.)

Macon has many historical houses, including **Cannonball House**, 856 Mulberry St., the city's only casualty of the Civil War. (☎745-5982. Open M-Sa 10am-5pm. $3, children $2.) **Hay House**, 934 Georgia Ave., near downtown, is the most opulent of all the city's magnificent dwellings. The gigantic Italian Renaissance Revival mansion was built in 1860 and boasts wide marble hallways, crystal chandeliers, and plenty of pomp and grandiosity to awe visitors. (☎742-8155. Open M-Sa 10am-4:30pm, Su 1-4:30pm. $8, students $4, seniors and AAA $7.) A beautiful place to walk in the afternoon, the **Rose Hill Cemetery**, 1091 Riverside Dr., northeast of town, is the final resting place of Duane Allman and Berry Oakley of the Allman Brothers Band. It was a favorite hangout of the Allman Brothers in life as well; after dark they often had a drink or smoke among the headstones. (☎751-9119. Open sunrise to sunset. Free.)

🔲🔳 **ENTERTAINMENT & NIGHTLIFE.** The biggest event of Macon's year is the annual **Cherry Blossom Festival**, March 20-31, 2003. The city hosts thousands of visitors, who come to admire the 265,000 Yoshino Cherry trees blooming in every backyard and on every street. With its median of cherry trees, 3rd St. is the center of the celebration. Over 500 mostly free events—like concerts, tours, and parades—keep the masses tickled pink. After the blossoms fade, there are still plenty of amusements. The **Macon Little Theater**, 4220 Forsyth Rd., puts on musicals and plays ranging from serious to ridiculous year-round. (☎471-7529. Box office open M-Sa 10am-5pm. Most shows $16, seniors $14, under 23 $11.) Formerly the stage for Georgia's black talent in the 20th century, **The Douglass Theater**, 355 Martin Luther King Blvd., is now a multicultural arts center featuring films and live theatrical performances. (☎742-2000. Prices and schedules vary; call for details.)

Macon has more bars and nightclubs than you'd expect from a small southern town—but hey, this *is* where Little Richard grew up. Entertainment clusters along Cherry St. downtown. The Visitors Center has a list of the area nightspots, and the free *Synergy Magazine*, available outside stores and in newsstands downtown, has entertainment listings for Southeast Georgia. **The Rookery** (see above) is a good bet for a variety of live bands. Gay-friendly and open to all, **Club Synergy**, 425 Cherry St., has 2 dance floors, DJs from all over, a full bar, and a willingness to occasionally flood itself for the odd beach party theme. (☎755-9383. Cover $5-7. Open W-Sa 8pm until late.) **River Front Bluez**, 550 Riverside Dr., in a shack by the side of the road, is a great place to hear gritty, down-and-out blues. (☎741-9970. Live bands W-Sa around 9pm.) If upscale plush clubbing is your thing, go to **Déa**,

420 Martin Luther King Blvd. This swank outfit's dress code is a small price to pay for feeling like a movie star as you strut into the dark interior. (☎755-1620. Cover varies, but can be quite high. Open W-Sa 8pm-2am.)

ANDERSONVILLE   ☎229

Fifty-five miles south of Macon and 10 mi. northeast of Americus on Rte. 49, the **Andersonville National Historic Site** preserves the location where 45,000 Union soldiers were confined in a primitive prison pen without food, water, or shelter in 1864 near the end of the Civil War. Nearly 13,000 men died horrible deaths within the camp's wooden walls due to the barbaric conditions and severe overcrowding—at one point more than 32,000 men were confined in a space intended to hold 10,000. One of Andersonville's enduring legacies is the term "deadline," which was the name of a literal line 19ft. from the prison wall beyond which a prisoner would be immediately shot. Today the prison is an empty field with a few markers and model shanties recalling the deadly environment. On the grounds, the excellent **National Prisoner of War Museum,** 496 Cemetery Rd., memorializes the experience of American POWs with artifacts, interactive video testimonials, recordings, photographs, and journals. The museum is extraordinarily sobering as you pass actual rations that kept men alive for days, view myriad portrayals of horrible suffering and amazing strength, and finally exit into a small memorial in the sunlight. Also on the grounds, the **Andersonville National Cemetery** is a fitting place to end the visit. (☎924-0343, ext. 201. Park open daily 8am-5pm; museum 8:30am-5pm. Special talks daily 11am and 2pm. Museum audio tours $1.)

Directly across Rte. 49 from the park exit is the tiny town of Andersonville. The **Welcome Center,** 114 Main St., doubles as a dusty little museum stuffed with bric-a-brac. To the left of the monument in the middle of town and up the street a quarter mile on the left, the **Andersonville Restaurant ❶** (it's the only one in town) serves an unpretentious buffet lunch for $5.50 and chatty conversation for free. (☎928-8480. Open M-Sa 11am-2pm and 5pm-9pm, Su 11am-2pm.)

SAVANNAH   ☎912

In February 1733, General James Oglethorpe and a ragtag band of 120 vagabonds founded the city of Savannah and the state of Georgia. General Sherman later spared the city during his famous rampage through the South. Some say he found Savannah too pretty to burn—presenting it instead to President Lincoln as a Christmas gift. Today, the general's reaction is still believable to anyone who sees Savannah's stately old trees and Federalist and English Regency houses interwoven with spring blossoms.

■ ⁊ ORIENTATION & PRACTICAL INFORMATION. Savannah rests on the coast of Georgia at the mouth of the **Savannah River,** which runs north of the city along the border with South Carolina. The city stretches south from bluffs overlooking the river. The restored 2½ sq. mi. **downtown historic district,** bordered by East Broad St., Martin Luther King Jr. Blvd., Gwinnett St., and the river, is best explored on foot. *Do not stray south of Gwinnett St.; the historic district quickly deteriorates into an unsafe area.* A parking pass ($8) allows 2-day unlimited use of all metered parking, city lots, and garages. **Tybee Island,** Savannah's beach, 18 mi. east on U.S. 80 and Rte. 26, makes a fine daytrip. **Amtrak,** 2611 Seaboard Coastline Dr. (☎234-2611; open Sa-Th 4:30am-12:15pm and 5pm-12:45am, F 4:30am-12:45am), chugs to Charleston (1½hr., 1 per day, $38). **Greyhound,** 610 W. Oglethorpe Ave. (☎232-2135; open 24hr.), at Fahm St., sends buses to Atlanta (6hr.; 5 per day; M-Th $36, F-Su $38); Charleston (3hr., 2 per day, $24/26); and Jacksonville (2½hr., 13 per day, $19/20). **Chatham Area Transit (CAT),** 124 Bull St.

BETTER HOMES & GARDENS A notorious and sophisticated antique dealer, a scandalous and flamboyant drag queen, and the prim and proper members of the Married Women's Card: these are a few of the characters that landed John Berendt's *Midnight in the Garden of Good and Evil* on the *New York Times* best-seller list. The plot revolves around a highly publicized fatal shooting at Mercer House, a venerable and elegant old home on Monterey Sq. Although the social elite about town have denounced "The Book's" exposure of their secrets in indignant whispers, tourism has skyrocketed by 46% since it was published. A fan club, midnight tours, a Hollywood adaptation, and **"The Book" Gift Shop**, 127 E. Gordon St., at Calhoun Sq., all attest to the interest that "The Book" has generated. (☎ 233-3867. Open M-Sa 10:30am-5pm, Su 12:30-4pm.)

(☎ 233-5767), in the Chatham County Court House, runs city buses and a free shuttle through the historic area. (Open daily 7am-11pm. Shuttle M-Sa 7am-9pm, Su 9:40am-5pm. 75¢, seniors 37¢; no transfers. Weekly pass $12.) The **Savannah Visitors Center**, 301 Martin Luther King Jr. Blvd., at Liberty St. in a lavish former train station, offers a reservation service for local inns and hostels. (☎ 944-0455, reservation service ☎ 877-728-2662. Open M-F 8:30am-5pm, Sa-Su 9am-5pm.) **Post Office:** 2 N. Fahm St., at Bay St. (☎ 235-4610. Open M-F 7am-6pm, Sa 9am-3pm.) **ZIP code:** 31402. **Area code:** 912.

⌂ ACCOMMODATIONS. Downtown motels cluster near the historic area, Visitors Center, and Greyhound station. For those with cars, **Ogeechee Rd. (U.S. 17)** has several budget options. **Savannah International Youth Hostel (HI-AYH) ❶**, 304 E. Hall St., is located in a restored Victorian mansion in the historic district. (☎ 236-7744. Internet access. Linen $1. Bike rental $10. Check-in 7-10am and 5-11pm; call for late-night check-in. Lockout 10am-5pm. Max. stay 3 night. Open Mar.-Oct. Dorms $18; private rooms $35.) **Thunderbird Inn ❷**, 611 W. Oglethorpe Ave., has the least expensive rooms downtown. The modest exterior belies the pleasant furnishings within. (☎ 232-2661. Singles Su-Th $40, F-Sa $50. 5% off with mention of *Let's Go*.) **Skidaway Island State Park ❶** is 6 mi. southeast of downtown off Diamond Causeway; follow Liberty St. east from downtown until it becomes Wheaton St., turn right on Waters Ave., and follow it to the Diamond Causeway. (☎ 598-2300 or 800-864-7275. Bathrooms, heated showers, electricity, and water. Open daily 7am-10pm. Check-in before 10pm. Sites $18, with hookup $20.) **Fort McAllister State Park ❶**, Exit 90 off I-95, has wooded sites with water and electricity, some with a water view, on an island. (☎ 727-2339 or 800-864-7275. Office open daily 8am-5pm; campground 7am-10pm. Check-in before 10pm. Sites $15, with hookup $17. Parking $2.)

◻ FOOD. Nita's Place ❸, 129 E. Broughton St., gives reason enough to come to Savannah. You can read enthusiastic letters from satisfied customers pressed beneath the glass tabletops while you experience the uplifting power of soul food. The dessert-like squash casserole, a delight beyond description, will make you a believer. (☎ 238-8233. Entrees $10-13. Open M-Th 11:30am-3pm, F-Sa 11:30am-3pm and 5-8pm.) **Wall's BBQ ❶**, 515 E. York Ln., in an alley between York and Oglethorpe, is a tiny, no-nonsense restaurant consisting of a counter, a few tables, and amazing BBQ sandwiches and ribs. (☎ 232-9754. Sandwiches and ribs $4.50-12. Baked deviled crabs $3. Open Th-Sa 11am-9pm.) **Mrs. Wilkes Boarding House ❸**, 107 W. Jones St., is a Southern institution where friendly strangers gather around large tables for homestyle atmosphere and food. Fried chicken, butter beans, and superb biscuits are favorites, but don't leave before dessert! (☎ 232-5997. All-you-can-eat $12. Open M-F 8-9am and 11am-3pm.) **Clary's Cafe ❶**, 404 Abercorn St., has

THE HIDDEN DEAL

CUMBERLAND ISLAND

About 50 miles east of Okefenokee Swamp, 17½ miles of salt marsh, live oak forest, and sand dunes laced with trails and a few decaying mansions, make **Cumberland Island National Seashore** the gem of the Georgia Coast Isles.

The Park Service allows only 300 visitors per day to the island, meaning that a jaunt to the secluded playground of the Carnegies is rewarded with enchanted solitude. You can walk all day on the hard-packed beaches without seeing another human, but keep an eye peeled for wild horses. Phone reservations are necessary for entry into the parks. (☎ 912-882-4335 or 888-817-3421. Open M-F 10am-4pm.) The **ferry**, the only way to access the island, leaves from St. Mary's at the end of Rte. 40. (45min. Mar.-Nov. Su-Tu 2 per day, W-Sa 3 per day; Dec.-Feb. Th-M 2 per day. $16, under 12 $11.)

Nearby **St. Mary's**, voted the best small town in America by *Money* magazine, provides overnight stays near Cumberland. About 3 mi. outside downtown, **Cumberland Kings Bay Lodges**, 603 Sand Bar Dr., provides comfortable mini-suites with fridge, stove, and microwave. (☎ 912-882-8900 or 800-831-6664. Breakfast included. Pool and laundry access. Singles $35; doubles $40; weekly rates from $160. Discounts for seniors and military.)

been family-owned since 1903. The famous weekend brunch thrives on $4 malted waffles. (☎ 233-0402. Open M-Tu and Th-F 7am-4pm, W 7am-5pm, Sa-Su 8am-4:30pm.) The **Voo-Doo Cafe ❷**, 321 Habersham St., is open for breakfast and lunch with wraps, salads, and pasta. Tables outside look onto Troup Sq. (☎ 447-1999. Entrees under $10. Open M-F 10:30am-3:30pm; Sa-Su brunch 8:30am-3:30pm.)

🅖 **SIGHTS.** Most of Savannah's 21 squares contain some distinctive centerpiece. Elegant antebellum houses and drooping vine-wound trees often cluster around the squares, adding to the classic Southern aura. Bus, van, and horse carriage **tours** leave from the Visitors Center, but walking can be more rewarding. (Tours every 10-15min. $13-15.) Two of Savannah's best-known historic homes are the **Davenport House**, 324 E. State St., on Columbia Sq., and the **Owens-Thomas House**, 124 Abercom St., one block away on Oglethorpe Sq. The Davenport House showcases a cantilevered staircase, as well as exemplary plasterwork and woodwork. The carriage house at the Owens-Thomas is free, housing artifacts and relating stories about slave life. (Davenport: ☎ 236-8097. Open M-Sa 10am-4pm, Su 1-4pm. $7, under 18 $3.50, under 7 free. Owens-Thomas: ☎ 233-9743. Open M noon-5pm, Tu-Sa 10am-5pm, Su 1-5pm; last tour 4:30pm. $8, students $4, seniors $7, ages 6-12 $2.) The **Green Meldrim House**, 1 W. Macon St., on Madison Sq., is a Gothic Revival mansion that served as one of General Sherman's headquarters during the Civil War. (☎ 232-1251. Open Tu and Th-F 10am-4pm, Sa 10am-1pm. Tours every 30min. $5, students $2.)

Girl Scouts past and present explore their heritage with a pilgrimage to the **Juliette Gordon Low Birthplace**, 10 E. Oglethorpe Ave., near Wright Sq. The Girl Scouts' founder was born here on Halloween in 1860, which might explain the Girl Scouts' door-to-door treat technique. The house contains an interesting collection of Girl Scout memorabilia, but sorry, no cookies. (☎ 233-4501. Open M-Tu and Th-Sa 10am-4pm, Su 12:30-4:30pm. $8, students $6.) Savannah's four forts once protected the city's port from Spanish, British, and other invaders. The most intriguing, **Fort Pulaski National Monument**, 15 mi. east of Savannah on U.S. 80 E. and Rte. 26, marks the Civil War battle where rifled cannons first pummeled walls. (☎ 786-5787. Open in summer daily 9am-7pm; off-season 9am-5pm. $3, under 16 free.)

Special events in Savannah include the **Annual NOGS Tour of the Hidden Gardens of Historic Savannah** (☎ 238-0248), in late April, when private walled gardens are opened to the public who can partake of a special Southern teatime. Green is the theme of the **St.**

Patrick's Day Celebration on the River, a five-day, beer- and fun-filled party that packs the streets and warms celebrants up for the **Annual St. Patrick's Day Parade,** the second-largest in the US. (Celebration: ☎234-0295. Parade: ☎233-4804. Mar. 17, 2003. Begins 10:15am.) **First Friday for the Arts** (☎232-4903) occurs on the first Friday of every month in City Market, when visitors meet with residents of a local art colony. **First Saturday on the River** (☎234-0295) brings arts, crafts, entertainment, and food to historic River St. each month. A free paper, *Connect Savannah*, found in restaurants and stores, has the latest in news and entertainment.

🌙 **NIGHTLIFE.** The waterfront area (River St.) brims with endless oceanfront dining opportunities, street performers, and a friendly pub ambience. **Kevin Barry's Irish Pub,** 117 W. River St., jigs with live Irish folk music. (☎233-9626. Music W-Sa after 8:30pm. Cover $2. Open M-F 2pm-3am, Sa 11:30am-3am, Su 12:30pm-2am.) **The Warehouse Bar and Grill,** 18 E. River St., boasts the "coldest, cheapest beer in town." (☎234-6003. Draft beers from $1.50. Open M-Sa 11am-3am, Su noon-2am.) If sugary drinks are your pleasure, head to **Wet Willies,** 101 E. River St., for its casual dining and irresistible frozen daiquiris. (☎233-5650. Drinks $4-6. Open Su-Th 11am-1am, F-Sa 11am-2am.) Local college students eat, drink, and shop at **City Market.** Delivering better than the rest, **Malone's Bar and Grill,** 27 W. Barnard St., serves up dancing, drinks, and live music. The lower floor opens up to a game room, while techno and rap beat upstairs Friday and Saturday night. (☎234-3059. Happy hour 4-8pm. F-Sa top level 18+. Open M-Sa 11am-3am, Su noon-2am; kitchen closes at 1am.) Hustlers will enjoy the ten pool tables and more than 80 beers at **B&B Billiards,** 411 W. Congress St. (☎233-7116. Free pool Tu and Th. Open M-Sa 4pm-3am.) For the best alternative scene and a gay- and lesbian-friendly atmosphere check out **Club One,** 1 Jefferson St. near Bay St, where the Lady Chablis, a character featured in *Midnight in the Garden of Good and Evil* (see p. 359), performs regularly. (☎232-0200. Cover $3-10. Open M-Sa 5pm-3am, Su 5pm-2am.) **The Velvet Elvis,** 127 W. Congress St., is in costume with a giant crown in the front window and a smattering of Elvis paraphernalia decking the walls. (☎236-0665. Live music W-Sa. Cover $3-5. Open M-Sa 6:30pm-3am.)

ALABAMA

The "Heart of Dixie" and the "Cradle of the Confederacy" is often remembered for its controversial role in the Civil Rights movement of the 1960s, when Governor George Wallace fought a vicious campaign opposing integration. Once a stalwart defender of segregation, today the state strives to de-emphasize this past and broaden its image. While pierced with monuments and homages to the tumult of the Civil Rights movement, testaments to many of Alabama's less contentious legacies also shine through. Its rich colonial past, Native American heritage, legacy of immigration, interesting environmental location, and Southern take on life have combined with ethnically inspired cuisine, local festivities, and nationally acclaimed gardens to create the 'Bama of today.

PRACTICAL INFORMATION

Capital: Montgomery.

Visitor info: Alabama Bureau of Tourism and Travel, 401 Adams Ave., Montgomery 36104 (☎334-242-4169 or 800-252-2262; www.touralabama.org). Open M-F 8am-5pm. **Division of Parks,** 64 N. Union St., Montgomery 36104 (☎800-252-7275). Open daily 8am-5pm.

Postal Abbreviation: AL. **Sales Tax:** 4%, plus county tax.

IN RECENT NEWS

WHERE CAN I CATCH THE BUS?

Montgomery is famous for being the birthplace of Civil Rights, where Rosa Parks took her courageous stand—or rather sit—on a city bus, igniting the movement for racial integration in the United States. What's happened to Montgomery's buses since is an ironic footnote to the city's Civil Rights history and an ominous indicator of what modern Montgomery has become—a city trapped in time. After the bus boycott won the battle for integrated ridership on Montgomery buses in 1956, white ridership gradually began to decline. Nowadays, a white face on a Montgomery bus is extremely rare, and over the years bus service has gotten slower and more decrepit.

The bus system is representative of a larger trend in Montgomery. Urban flight, de facto segregation, and rising crime rates are coupled with a legacy of racial discord that is still seen today in the form of mansions abutting slums. Many natives express dismay and worry over the city's future. As well they should. It is a city where white and black live in isolated spheres, with their interactions always marked by extreme, wary politeness, where a white woman can expect a black man to give her a wide, respectful berth when she walks past, where the favorite local restaurants are the ones that best recapture the atmosphere of pre-integration 1950s, and where buses don't run like they used to. Montgomery is a city living in its past, masking its scars with a Southern politeness that is as tragic as it is hospitable.

MONTGOMERY ☎334

Today, Montgomery stands still and quiet, in sharp contrast to its turbulent past as the first capital of the Confederacy and the birthplace of America's Civil Rights movement. Montgomery's role in the movement took off in 1955, when local authorities arrested Rosa Parks, a black seamstress, because she refused to give up her seat to a white man on a city bus. The success of the ensuing bus boycott, organized by local minister Dr. Martin Luther King, Jr., encouraged nationwide reform. Montgomery now relies on its prominent past to overcome a nondescript present—Civil Rights movement battlegrounds are the main attractions.

⊞⚡ ORIENTATION & PRACTICAL INFORMATION. Downtown follows a grid pattern. Major east-west routes are Madison Ave. downtown and Vaughn Rd. south of I-65; main north-south roads are Perry St. and Decatur St., which becomes Norman Bridge Rd. farther south. Dexter Ave. is Montgomery's main street, running east-west up an imposing hill to the Capitol. West of downtown, **I-65** runs north-south and intersects **I-85,** which forms downtown's southern border. A ring road, varyingly called East, South, West, and North Boulevard, encircles both downtown and the outlying residential neighborhoods. **Greyhound,** 950 W. South Blvd. (☎286-0658; open 24hr.), at Exit 168 on I-65 and a right onto South Blvd., runs to: Atlanta (3hr., 9 per day, $27); Birmingham (2hr., 7 per day, $36); Mobile (3hr., 8 per day, $29); Selma (55min., 5 per day, $25 round-trip); and Tuskegee (45min., 9 per day, $19 round-trip). **Montgomery Area Transit System** runs local buses. (M-F 5:30am-6pm. "Fixed route" bus $1; no transfers.) Call one day in advance to schedule a pick-up and **Demand and Response Transit (DART)** service will send a bus to your exact location. (☎262-7321. $2.) **The Lightning Route Trolley** arrives every 20min. at well-marked stops near downtown attractions (M-Sa 9am-6pm. 25¢, seniors and disabled with MAP card 10¢; day pass $1/50¢. **Taxis: Yellow Cab,** ☎262-5225; **New Deal Cab,** ☎262-4747. **Visitors Center:** 300 Water St., in Union Station. (☎262-0013. Open M-Sa 8:30am-5pm, Su noon-4pm.) **Hotlines: Council Against Rape,** ☎286-5987. Operates 24hr. **Post Office:** 135 Catoma St. (☎263-4974. Open M-F 7:30am-5:30pm, Sa 8am-noon.) **ZIP code:** 36104. **Area code:** 334.

🛏 ACCOMMODATIONS. For those with a car, South Blvd., Exit 168 off I-65, overflows with inexpensive beds, while most exits off I-85 lead to standard, more expensive chains. Beware the cheapest of the cheap can be fairly seedy. Kind, enthusiastic owners set the tone at the **Red Bluff Cottage ❹**, 551 Clay St., a B&B experience worth the expensive price tag. Atop a high hill, the breezy front porch has an amazing view of the Capitol and downtown. Themed rooms, full baths, Internet, TV, bathrobes, and flowers add to the cottage's allure. (☎264-0056 or 888-551-2529. Walk-ins allowed. Singles $80; doubles $90. $25 deposit required.) Downtown, with walking distance of most points of interest, rooms at the comfortable **Town Plaza ❷**, 743 Madison Ave., at N. Ripley St., come with all the perks: A/C, TV, free local calls, and fridges. (☎269-1561. Singles $33; doubles $37.) Easily visible from I-65 Exit 168 and two right turns away, **The Inn South ❷**, 4243 Inn South Ave., greets travelers with an unusually dramatic lobby for a budget motel. (☎288-7999 or 800-642-0890. Continental breakfast, free local calls, cable TV, and laundry. Wheelchair accessible. Singles $35; doubles $38; each additional person $2. Weekly rate $135.) The site of a 1763 French stronghold, **Fort Toulouse Jackson Park ❶**, 12 mi. north of Montgomery on Ft. Toulouse Rd., off U.S. 231, has 39 sites with water and electricity under hanging Spanish moss in beautiful woods. (☎567-3002. Registration daily 8am-5pm. In spring and fall, reservations are recommended at least 2 weeks in advance. Sites $11, with hookup $14; seniors $8/11.)

▣ FOOD. In a tiny pink house filed with charming paintings and Baptist posters, **▨Martha's Place ❶**, 458 Sayre St., is a true Bible Belt gem. Fried chicken, pork chops, collard greens, and black-eyed peas are all included in Martha's gigantic, authentic lunch. Don't miss the pound cake! (☎263-9135. Traditional lunch $5.50, 4-vegetable plate $4. Open M-F 11am-3pm.) Eat with the old guard of Montgomery high society at **Sahara Restaurant ❹**, 511 East Edgemont Ave. Amid oil paintings of Alabama, tuxedoed waiters serve $20 dinners of whole grilled fish and filet mignon. (☎262-1215. Blue-plate southern lunch with veggies, beverage, and dessert $6-9. Open M-Sa 11am-10pm.) The unofficial heart of the historic Cloverdale neighborhood, **Derek's Filet and Vine ❶**, 431 Cloverdale Rd., on the corner of Decatur/Northman Bridge Rd., houses a full deli and hot bar, racks of liquor, and a small produce market with European cheeses. (☎267-8463. Down-home sandwiches and veggie wraps ("for the ladies") $2-6. Hot food $3-6. Open M-Sa 7am-7pm; hot food bar M-F 11am-3pm.) **El Rey ❷**, 1031 E. Fairview, provides gigantic veggie and non-veggie burrito, taco, and quesadilla options ($5.50-9.50) in a funky, collegiate setting. (☎832-9688. Open M-Th and Sa 11am-10pm, F 11am-11pm.) Even though the center of Montgomery life has moved from Dexter Ave., **Chris' Hot Dogs ❶**, 138 Dexter Ave., the oldest restaurant (and combination magazine stand) in town, has continued to make hot dogs like nobody else. (☎265-6850. Open M-Th and Sa 10am-7pm, F 10am-8pm.)

◰ SIGHTS. The **State Capitol**, at Bainbridge St. and Dexter Ave., is, as any self-respecting state capitol should be, an imposing Greek Revival structure sporting marble floors, cantilevered staircases, and neat echo chambers. On the front steps, a bronze star commemorates the spot where Jefferson Davis took the oath of office as president of the Confederacy. (☎242-3935. Open M-F 9am-5pm, Sa 9am-4pm. Guided tours available. Free.) Only two football fields away is the 112-year-old **King Memorial Baptist Church**, 454 Dexter Ave., where Martin Luther King was pastor for six years. (☎263-3970. Open Sa 1:30-2pm for walkthrough. Guided tours M-Th 10am and 2pm; Sa 10:30, 11:15am, noon, 12:45pm.) Maya Lin, the architect who designed the Vietnam Veterans Memorial in Washington D.C. (p. 313), also designed Montgomery's newest sight—the **Civil Rights Memorial**, 400 Washington Ave., in front of the Southern Poverty Law Center. The outdoor monument, over which water continuously flows, pays tribute to activists who died fighting for civil rights. (☎264-0286. Open 24hr. Free. Wheelchair accessible.) The **Rosa Parks Library and Museum**, 252 Montgomery St., was dedicated 45 years after Rosa Parks refused to give up her seat on December 1, 1955. The museum uses video, artifacts, audio, and an actual 1955 Montgomery bus to recreate that fateful day and the subsequent events that rocked the city and the nation. (☎241-8661. Open M-F 9am-5pm, Sa 9am-3pm. $5, under 12 $3.) The **Hank Williams Museum,** 118 Commerce St., features the Montgomery native's outfits, memorabilia, and the '52 Cadillac in which he died. January 1, 2003 marks the 50th anniversary of Williams's death. The museum will feature special events to celebrate the quintessential, prolific country hero who released 225 songs in five years before dying at age 29. (☎262-3600. Open M-Sa 9am-6pm, Su 1-4pm. $5.50, under 12 $1.25.)

Old Alabama Town, 301 Columbus St., at Hull St., reconstructs 19th-century Alabama with over 40 period buildings, including a pioneer homestead, an 1892 grocery, and an early African-American church. (☎240-4500. Tickets sold M-Sa 9am-3pm; grounds open until 4:30pm. $7, seniors $6.30, ages 6-18 $3.) A modest exterior hides the quirky **F. Scott and Zelda Fitzgerald Museum,** 919 Felder Ave., off Carter Hill Rd. at Dunbar. The curator will be happy to show you photographs, Zelda's paintings, and some of Scott's original manuscripts, not to mention evidence of the couple's stormy marriage and many love letters. (☎264-4222. Open W-F 10am-2pm, Sa-Su 1-5pm. Free.) The **Montgomery Museum of Fine Arts,** 1 Museum Dr., part of the Blount Cultural Park (for directions see Shakespeare Festival, below), houses a collection of 19th- and 20th-century American paintings along with "Artworks," a hands-on gallery and art studio for kids. (☎244-5700. Open Tu-W and F-Sa 10am-5pm, Th 10am-9pm, Su noon-5pm. Free, but donations appreciated.)

🎭🎵 **ENTERTAINMENT & NIGHTLIFE.** The **Alabama Shakespeare Festival** is staged at the **Carolyn Blount Theater** on the grounds of the 300-acre private estate, **Wynton M. Blount Cultural Park;** take East Blvd. 15min. southeast of downtown to Vaughn Rd., or Exit 6 off I-85, onto Woodmere Blvd. The theater also hosts contemporary plays; the 2003 season includes *Brighton Beach Memoirs, Arcadia, Noises Off, Othello,* and *Two Gentlemen of Verona.* (☎271-5353 or 800-841-4273. Box office open M-Sa 10am-6pm, Su noon-4pm; performance nights until 9pm. $12-40, under 25 with ID $10, seniors half-price 1hr. prior to show.) **Gator's Blues Bayou,** 5040 Vaughn Rd., at Vaughn Plaza, does delta, acoustic, blues, and rock in its cafe and nightclub. (☎274-0330. Live music Tu-Sa, usually 8pm until late. Kitchen open M-F 11am-2pm and 5-10pm, Sa 5-10pm, Su 11am-2pm.) For artsy films, try the **Capri Theater,** 1045 E. Fairview (☎262-4858), Montgomery's only independent movie theater. Of course, on a lonely night, many locals enjoy their greyhound racing. Montgomery's dog track is **Victoryland** at I-85 Exit 22 in Tuskegee. (☎269-6087. 19+. Open M-Sa; call for race times.) The Thursday *Montgomery Advertiser* lists other entertainment options.

NEAR MONTGOMERY

TUSKEGEE

After Reconstruction, "emancipated" blacks in the South remained segregated and disenfranchised. **Booker T. Washington,** a former slave, believed that blacks could best improve their situation through hard work and learning a trade. The curriculum at the college Washington founded in 1881, the Tuskegee Institute, consequently revolved around such practical endeavors as agriculture and carpentry, with students constructing almost all of the campus buildings. Today, a more academically-oriented **Tuskegee University** (☎727-8347 for tours) fills 160 buildings on 5000 acres, while the buildings of Washington's original institute comprise a national historical site. On campus, the **George Washington Carver Museum** has exhibits and informative films on both Washington and Carver. Artist, teacher, scientist, and head of the Tuskegee Agricultural Dept., Carver improved the daily lives of Macon County's poor by discovering hundreds of practical uses for common, inexpensive products like the peanut. (☎727-3200. Open daily 9am-4:30pm. Free.) Across the street from the campus on Montgomery Rd. lies **The Oaks,** a restoration of Washington's home. The building—right down to the bricks themselves—was built by students in just one year from 1899-1900 and was the first home with electricity in Macon County. (Tours available daily every 2hr. 10am-4pm; call to schedule.)

To get to Tuskegee, take I-85 toward Atlanta, get off at Exit 32, and follow the signs. Alternatively, exit at Rte. 81 S. and turn right at the intersection with Old Montgomery Rd. onto Rte. 126. **Greyhound** (☎727-1290) runs from Montgomery (45min., 6 per day, $8-9). **Area code:** 334.

SELMA

Selma is more infamous than famous, though this really shouldn't be the case. The small, historic Southern town was shaped by two momentous events that took place 100 years apart. As a stronghold for the Confederate armies (Selma's arsenal produced two-thirds of the South's ammunition during the last years of the war), its fall in 1865 marked a decisive victory for the North. A century later, Selma gained notoriety during the Voting Rights movement. In the Selma of 1964, only 1% of eligible blacks had the right to vote due to state-imposed restrictions. In 1965, to protest these conditions, civil rights activists organized an ill-fated march on the state capitol that was quashed by billy club-swinging troops. Their spirits battered but not destroyed, the marchers tried again, and again. A third try resulted in a 54 mi. trek from Selma to Montgomery that Dr. King declared the "greatest march ever made on a state capitol in the South." Six months later, Congress passed the Voting Rights Act, which prohibited states from using prerequisites to disqualify voters on the basis of color.

Nowadays, though, the city has a lot more to it than these bloody conflicts. Selma has the largest historic district in Alabama, with over 1200 historic structures, and calls itself home to one of America's most interesting festivals, the **Tale Tellin' Festival.** Storytellers and yarn-spinners from across the South converge on Selma during the second Friday and Saturday in October. The **National Voting Rights Museum & Institute,** 1012 Water Ave., houses memorabilia relating to the Voting Rights Act of 1965 and continues to disseminate information about voting rights and responsibilities. (☎418-0800. Open Tu-F 9am-5pm, Sa by appointment. Donations suggested.) The **Brown Chapel AME Church and King Monument,** 410 Martin Luther King St., served as the headquarters for many civil rights meetings during the Movement and was the starting point for the march to Montgomery. (☎874-7897. Tours available by appointment M-Sa 10am-4pm, Su 1-4pm.) A map available from the Visitors Center directs you to other Civil Rights points of interest in Selma. **The Old Depot Museum,** 4 Martin Luther King St., explores the history of Selma with artifacts of past and present, some dating back thousands of years to the area's original inhabitants. (☎874-2197. Open M-Sa 10am-4pm, Su by appointment. $4, students $2, seniors $3.)

Downtown Selma is bordered by **Jeff Davis Ave.** to the north and the **Alabama River** to the south. **U.S. 80,** which becomes **Broad St.,** runs straight through town. **Greyhound,** 434 Broad St. (☎874-4503; open daily 7am-9pm), runs to Montgomery (1hr., 6 per day, $12). **Visitors Center:** 2207 Broad St. (☎875-7485; www.selmashowcase.com. Open daily 8am-8pm.) **Post Office:** 1301 Alabama Ave. (☎874-4678. Open M-F 8am-4:40pm, Sa 8am-noon.) **Zip code:** 36703. **Area code:** 334.

FROM THE ROAD

THE DOC IS IN

I walked into the Alabama Jazz Hall of Fame when I soon met a tall, white-haired black man with large-framed glasses and a mustache, wearing a grandfatherly vest. He brightly welcomed me and asked where I was from. When I told him, he launched into a reverie about his days at Howard, telling me stories about his old English professor, the troubles he'd had with math, and fun he'd had playing with his band. "Oh, so he's a musician," I thought. "Isn't it nice that he works here at the Jazz Hall of Fame and plays jazz himself."

He talked so much and chuckled at himself so hard that there was no opening for me to do my research, and soon he said to me, "Let me show you around the place." And then he ushered me into the exhibits, talking in great detail about everything on display. As he spoke of what it was like to be taught by one of the greatest jazz teachers of all time, I noticed that he spoke in the first person, as if he had been there. I thought, "That's unique; describing it as a memory is a nice way to make a tourist really feel the history."

My guide then drew me in front of a large mural of Alabama jazz greats. As I looked at the painted figures I realized that one of them looked very familiar. It was a tall, white-haired black man with large-framed glasses and a mustache playing a saxophone.

(continued on next page)

BIRMINGHAM ☎ 205

For most people, Birmingham recalls the struggle for black Civil Rights in the 1960s. Leaders like Martin Luther King, Jr. and Fred Shuttleworth faced some of their toughest fights in what was labeled "Bombingham" after dozens of bombs rocked the city in the early 1960s. Despite adversity, black culture thrived around neighborhood churches, movie theaters, and restaurants. Today's Birmingham, Alabama's largest city, has turned the corner and focused its efforts on building a substantial medical research community. The city does not shy from its stormy past, however. Some of the most powerful and moving civil rights monuments in the South are located downtown.

▐ TRANSPORTATION

Airport: Birmingham International Airport (☎595-0533).

Trains: Amtrak, 1819 Morris Ave. (☎324-3033), just south of 1st Ave N at 19th St. Open daily 8:30am-5pm. One train per day to **Atlanta** (5hr., $27) and **New Orleans** (7hr., $32).

Buses: Greyhound, 618 19th St. N (☎252-7190). Open 24hr. To: **Atlanta** (3hr., 12 per day, $22); **Mobile** (5½-8hr., 6 per day, $41); **Montgomery** (2hr., 6 per day, $20); **Nashville** (3½-5½hr., 6 per day, $26).

Public Transit: Metropolitan Area Express (MAX) and **Downtown Area Rapid Transit (DART).** MAX: M-F most routes 6am-6pm. $1, students 60¢; transfers free. DART trolley runs to downtown tourist destinations. Most routes daily 10am-midnight. 50¢, some routes free. (☎521-0101).

Taxi: Yellow Cab, ☎252-1131.

▟ ORIENTATION

Downtown Birmingham is a regular grid, with numbered avenues running east-west and numbered streets running north-south. Richard Arrington, Jr. Blvd. is the one exception, running along what would have been called 21st St. Downtown is divided by railroad tracks running east-west through the center of the city—thus, avenues and streets are designated "N" or "S." Avenue numbers decrease as they near the railroad tracks (with 1st Ave. N and S running alongside them), while street numbers grow from 11th St. at the western edge of downtown to 26th St. at the east. **20th St.** is the main north-south thoroughfare. **I-65** to the west, **I-20/59** to the north, and **Rte. 31** to the east form a U around downtown, leaving the southern side exposed. Five Points, the center of youthful nightlife, is at the intersection of 20th St. S and 11 Ave. S, while the **University of Alabama-Birmingham** is just to the northeast, between 6th Ave S. and 10th Ave. S., west of 20th St. S. While most of the city is pancake-flat, the southeastern edge climbs up suddenly into the bluffs, and the streets curl, wind, and become both very confusing and very beautiful. Birmingham's three interstates are readily accessible; I-20 approaches from Atlanta to the east; I-65 runs north to Nashville and south to Mobile; and I-59 runs northeast from New Orleans into the heart of the city.

Visitor Info: Greater Birmingham Convention and Visitors Center, 2200 9th Ave., N, 1st fl. (☎458-8000 or 800-458-8050; www.bcvb.org), will answer your questions and try to sell you Birmingham tote bags. Open M-F 8:30am-5pm.

Hotlines: Crisis Center, ☎323-7777. **Rape Response,** ☎323-7273. Both 24hr. **Gay Info line,** ☎326-8600.

Internet Access: Birmingham Public Library, 2100 Park Place (☎226-3610), at the corner of Richard Arrington Jr. Blvd near the Visitors Center. Tell them you're from out-of-town to get a sign-on code. Open M-Tu 9am-8pm, W-Sa 9am-6pm, Su 2-6pm.

Post Office: 351 24th St. N (☎521-0302). Open M-F 6am-11pm. **ZIP code:** 35203. **Area code:** 205.

ACCOMMODATIONS

Relatively cheap hotels and motels dot the Greater Birmingham area along the various interstates. The closer to downtown, the more expensive the room.

The Hospitality Inn, 2127 7th Ave. S (☎322-0691), four blocks north of Five Points and near the University, is a pleasant option in the city. This is one of the best deals in the city with clean, wood-paneled rooms, a convenient location, and a pleasant staff. Singles or two twin beds $41; two double beds $50. Wheelchair accessible. ❷

Delux Inn and Suites, 7905 Crestwood Blvd. (☎956-4440 or 800-338-9275), Exit 132 off I-20, then left on Crestwood, in the eastern section of town. Comfortable rooms with A/C, cable TV, continental breakfast, and a pool make this motel one of the better deals for its price. Rooms for 1-4 people $55-59. ❸

Oak Mountain State Park (☎620-2527 or 800-252-7275), 15 mi. south, off I-65 in Pelham at Exit 246. Alabama's largest state park, with 10,000 acres of horseback rides, golf, and hiking, and an 85-acre lake with a beach and fishing. Sites $10.75, with water and electricity $14.50, full hookup $16.75. Parking $2. ❶

(continued from previous page)

It was just starting to dawn on me when he pointed at the image and said with a chuckle, "And this is me, Frank Adams, but most people call me 'Doc' Adams," he said. "I play most everything that blows...In fact, I'll play you a little something right now." He vanished for a moment behind a door while I registered that an important jazz musician was about to serenade me.

He came back, clarinet in hand, and began to play. Two feet in front of me, this man, who I realized must have been at least 80 years old, swayed and bent to a soft, lilting tune, his fingers liquid on the instrument, the sound clear and haunting between the quiet display cases. He finished, and then asked me my name. "Well now, I'm going to make up a song, and only play it this one time and never again, a song just for you," he said. "Because that's improvisation what jazz really is. So here's Julia's song." Again the perfectly clear blue notes, ripply and jumping, climbing up a scale and sliding down again. He put down the clarinet and smiled, ushering me upstairs to look at Ella Fitzgerald's ball gown and Sun Ra's album covers.

Doc Adams played in Duke Ellington's band, and was a staple of the jazz scene in most of the South. Later, he helped found the Alabama Jazz Hall of Fame. Occasionally, he comes down and leads tour groups through the Hall, plays a little clarinet or sax, and chats with young visitors who have no clue who they're talking to. I think that's the way he likes it.

—Julia Reischel

MOUNDVILLE When white settlers first came across **Moundville**, 60 mi. southwest of Birmingham on I-59/20, they believed they had come across the city of some lost classical race. Archaeologists eventually placed the two dozen flat-topped earthen mounds, the highest at 58 ft., as the work of the same Mississippian civilization that built **Effigy Mounds** in Iowa (see p. 626). From 1000-1500 AD, the site was the ceremonial capital of the Mississippian people. The exact purposes of the mounds and the causes of their builders' disappearance are unknown. In addition to the mounds, the park contains the **Jones Archeological Museum**, where exhibits and artifacts from the mounds are on display, and a model **Indian Village** features life-size dioramas on the daily life of the Moundville Indians. Every year during the first full week of October, the **Moundville Native American Festival** is held on the grounds and features Native American dances, crafts, storytelling, and celebration.

🍴 FOOD

An old streetcar suburb near the University of Alabama-Birmingham, **Five Points South**, at the intersection of 20th St. S. and 11th Ave. S., is the best place to eat cheap and meet young people.

■ **Bahama Wing,** 321 17th St. N (☎324-9464), in downtown. A hole-in-the-wall that's so local, you'll be the only diner who doesn't live two doors down. It is *the* place for tasty and cheap wings, from 2 pieces served with a slice of toasted white bread and fries ($1.75) to 15 pieces ($10.50). These aren't your usual wings; they come in dozens of flavors ranging from Spicy Jerk to Bahama Breeze. Catfish dinner $7.25. Open M-W 11am-6pm, Th-Sa 11am-10pm. ❷

Fish Market Restaurant, 611 Richard Arrington Jr. Blvd. S (☎322-3330). Birmingham's oldest seafood wholesaler doubles as a no-frills joint with cheap catches. Fish entrees $8-9. Open M-Th 10am-9pm, F-Sa 10am-10pm. ❷

Jim 'N Nick's Barbecue, 744 29th St. S (☎323-7082), near the corner of Clairmont Ave. and University Blvd., roasts chicken, pork, and beef BBQ sandwiches ($3.50) on a hickory wood fire in a brick pit out back. Get a big dinner BBQ platter for $9, and finish it off with a tasty piece of homemade pie. Open in summer M-Th and Sa 10:30am-9pm, F 10:30am-10pm, Su 11am-9pm; in winter M-Sa 10:30am-9pm, Su 11am-8pm. ❷

👁 SIGHTS

CIVIL RIGHTS. Birmingham's efforts to reconcile itself with its ugly past have culminated in the **Birmingham Civil Rights District,** a nine-block tribute to the battles and bombings that took place there. The district is centered around **Kelly Ingram Park,** the sight of numerous Civil Rights protests. Commemorative statues and sculptures now grace the green lawns. *(At 5th and 6th Ave. N between 16th and 17th St. Park open daily 6am-10pm.)* The **Sixteenth St. Baptist Church** served as the center of Birmingham's Civil Rights movement and weathered many a mob siege while speakers like Martin Luther King Jr. spoke to supporters packed inside. Four young black girls died in the church in a September 1963 bombing by white segregationists, spurring protests in the nearby park. A small exhibit in the church's basement chronicles its past. *(1530 6th Ave. N. ☎251-9402. Open Tu-F 10am-4pm, Sa by appointment. $2 suggested donation.)* Across the street from the church, the powerful ■**Birmingham Civil Rights Institute** traces the nation's Civil Rights struggle through the lens of Alabama's own segregation battle. Traditional displays and documentary footage balance the imaginative exhibits and disturbing artifacts from the Jim Crow era, like the actual burnt-out shell of a torched Greyhound bus. The institute also highlights contemporary human rights issues across the globe and serves as a public research facility. *(520 16th St. N. ☎328-9696. Open Tu-Sa 10am-5pm, Su 1-5pm. $8, students $4, seniors $5, under 18 free; Su free.)*

4TH AVENUE. In the heart of the old historic black neighborhood, now known as the **4th Avenue District** is the **⊠Alabama Jazz Hall of Fame.** Jazz greats from Erskine Hawkins to Sun Ra and his Intergalactic Arkestra to the magnificent Ella Fitzgerald each get a small display on their life work. *(1631 4th Ave. N, in the Carver Theater 1 block south of Kelly Ingram Park. ☎254-2731. Open Tu-Sa 10am-5pm, Su 1-5pm. Free.)* Bama's sports greats, from Willie "The Say Hey Kid" Mays to runner Carl Lewis, are immortalized in the **Alabama Sports Hall of Fame.** *(2150 Civic Center Blvd., at the corner of 22nd St. N. ☎323-6665. Open M-Sa 9am-5pm, Su 1-5pm. $5, students $3, seniors $4.)* Two blocks away, the **Birmingham Museum of Art** is the largest municipal art museum in the South, containing over 18,000 works and a sculpture garden. The extensive galleries include impressive exhibits from artists around the world. *(2000 8th Ave. N. ☎254-2565. Open Tu-Sa 10am-5pm, Su noon-5pm. Free, donations appreciated.)*

SMELTING. Birmingham remembers its days as the "Pittsburgh of the South" at the **Sloss Furnaces National Historic Landmark.** Although the blast furnaces closed 20 years ago, they stand as the only preserved example of 20th-century iron-smelting in the world. Ballet, drama, and music concerts are held in a renovated furnace shed next to the stacks. *(10 32nd St. N. Adjacent to the 1st Ave. N overpass off 32nd through 34th St. downtown. ☎324-1911. Open Tu-Sa 10am-4pm, Su noon-4pm. Tours Sa-Su 1, 2, 3pm. Free.)* Another towering emblem of the industrial age is the gigantic statue of **Vulcan.** This likeness of the Roman god of the forge is the tallest cast-iron statue in the world and stands in its own beautiful park on Red Mountain overlooking the heart of the city. *(20th St. S and Valley Ave. ☎328-6198. Park open dawn to dusk. Free.)*

OTHER SIGHTS. For a breather from the heavy-duty ironworks, revel in the marvelously sculpted grounds of the **Birmingham Botanical Gardens.** Spectacular floral displays, an elegant Japanese garden, and an enormous greenhouse vegetate on 67 acres. *(2612 Lane Park Rd. Off U.S. 31. ☎414-3900. Garden Center open daily 8am-5pm; gardens dawn to dusk. Free.)* If you prefer cogs and grease to petals and pollen, the **Mercedes-Benz U.S. International Visitors Center** is a 24,000 sq. ft. museum that spares no technological expense while celebrating the history of all things Mercedes. You can tag along on a tour of the nearby factory. *(I-20/59 off Exit 89 on Mercedes Dr. at Vance St. ☎507-2266 or 888-286-8768. Open M-F 9am-5pm, Sa 10am-5pm. $4, seniors and children $3. Under 12 not allowed on factory tour.)*

🎵 🎭 ENTERTAINMENT & NIGHTLIFE

Opened in 1927, the **Historic Alabama Theater,** 1817 3rd Ave. N, is booked 300 nights of the year with films, concerts, and live performances. Their organ, the "Mighty Wurlitzer," entertains the audience pre-show. (☎251-0418. Order tickets at the box office 1hr. prior to show. Open to the public M-F 9am-4pm. Free. Showtimes generally 7pm; Su 2pm. Films $6, seniors and under 12 $5. Organ plays ½hr. before the official show time.) Those lucky enough to visit Birmingham on May 16-18, 2003 can hear everything from country to gospel to big name rock groups at **City Stages.** The three-day festival, held on multiple stages in the blocked-off streets of downtown, is the biggest event all year and includes food, crafts, and children's activities. (☎251-1272 or 800-277-1700; www.citystages.org. $20, weekend pass $30.)

Nightlife centers around **Five Points South,** at 20th St. S and 11th Ave. S. On spring and summer nights, many grab outdoor tables, loiter by the fountain until late, or rock in one of the many lively nightclubs nearby. The hippest people jam at **The**

Nick, 2514 10th Ave. S, at the corner of 24th St., which locals call "the place." The poster-covered exterior says it clearly and proudly: "The Nick...rocks." (☎252-3831. Happy hour M-F 3-9pm. Live music most nights. Cover $5-10; usually free M. Open M-F 3pm to late, Sa 8pm-6am.) Live bands, from reggae to alternative, entertain a collegiate crowd at **The Hippodrum,** 2007 Highland Ave. (☎933-6565. Live music Tu-Sa. Hours and cost vary.) For more info on bands and times, the free *Birmingham Weekly* and the biweekly *black & white* are available in many stores and shops downtown.

HUNTSVILLE   ☎256

Huntsville, 80 mi. north of Birmingham, was the first English-speaking settlement in Alabama and the location of the state's Constitutional Convention in 1819. Far more momentous, however, was the 1950 decision to locate the nation's rocket program here, as initially proposed by Wernher von Braun. The 363 ft. replica of a Saturn V rocket at the **US Space and Rocket Center,** Exit 15 off I-565, is easily recognizable for miles. This self-proclaimed "fun center of the universe" features space-flight simulators, an IMAX theater, and tours of the Marshall Space Flight Center. (☎837-3400. Open early spring to late fall daily 9am-6pm; late fall to early spring 9am-5pm. $17, ages 3-12 $12. Discounts available at the Visitors Center.)

Miles of budget motels and chain restaurants cluster on **University Dr.,** northwest of downtown. To peruse possible lodgings, get off I-565 at Exit 19 and head northwest to University Dr. Another option is the **Southland Inn ❷,** 3808 Governors Dr., off I-565 between Exits 15 and 17. Extremely convenient, yet out of the way of the crush and bustle of University Dr., these simple but functional rooms and the small outdoor pool and continental breakfast make it a good deal. (☎539-9391. Singles $33; doubles $38.) **Wild Rose Cafe ❷,** 121 N Side Sq., a traditional lunch counter serving up quality meat-and-three (vegetables, that is) platters on Styrofoam plates for $7. (☎539-3658. Open M-F 7-9:30am and 11am-2:30pm.)

Greyhound, 601 Monroe St. (☎534-1681; open daily 7:30am-11:45pm), runs buses to Birmingham (2¼hr., 5 per day, $15); Memphis (7hr., 5 per day, $50); and Nashville (2hr., 6 per day, $15). A very convenient **tourist shuttle** runs between downtown, museums, points on University Dr., and the Space and Rocket Center. The trolley can also make hotel pickup stops by reservation. (Every hr. M-F 6:40am-6:40pm, Sa 8:40am-7:10pm. $1, all-day pass $2. Wheelchair accessible.) **Huntsville Shuttle** also runs 11 routes. (☎532-7433 for info on both shuttles. Runs M-F 6am to 6pm. $1; students, seniors, and children under 7 50¢; transfers free.) **Visitors Center:** 700 Monroe St., in the Von Braun Center. (551-2230. Open M-Sa 9am-5pm, Sun noon-5pm.) **Area code:** 256.

MOBILE   ☎251

Although Bob Dylan lamented being stuck here, Mobile (*mo-BEEL*) has had plenty of fans in its time—French, Spanish, English, Sovereign Alabama, Confederate, and American flags have each flown over the city since its founding in 1702. This historical diversity is revealed in local architecture as well as in the local population: antebellum mansions, Italianate dwellings, Spanish and French forts, and Victorian homes line azalea-edged streets. Today, Mobile offers an untour, ed version of New Orleans. The site of the very first Mardi Gras, the city still holds a thrilling three-week long Fat Tuesday celebration—without the hordes that plague its Cajun counterpart.

🖿 🛈 ORIENTATION & PRACTICAL INFORMATION. The downtown district borders the Mobile River. **Dauphin St.,** which is one-way downtown, and **Government Blvd. (U.S. 90),** which becomes **Government St.** downtown, are the major east-west routes. **Airport Blvd., Springhill Rd.,** and **Old Shell Rd.** are secondary east-west roads.

Royal St. and **Broad St.** are major north-south byways. **Water St.** runs along the river downtown, becoming the **I-10 causeway.** A road variously called **I-65 East/West Access Rd., Frontage Rd.,** and the **Beltline** lies west of downtown.

Amtrak, 11 Government St., (☎432-4052), next to the convention center, is scheduled to be replaced by a new Gulf-Mobile-Ohio (GMO) station in October 2002. GMO plans to run trains to many major cities in the US; call the Visitors Center (see below) for details. Amtrak currently sends passengers to Atlanta (see above) via Motorcoach, a Greyhound bus that honors Amtrak tickets. **Greyhound,** 2545 Government Blvd., at Pinehill St. west of downtown, near the Foodworld, runs buses to: Atlanta (6-9hr., 2 per day, $46); Birmingham (6hr., 5 per day, $43); Montgomery (3hr., 7 per day, $30); and New Orleans (3hr., 8 per day, $26). **Mobile Transit Authority (MTA)** has major depots at Bienville Sq. and the Royal St. parking garage, near the Adams Mark Hotel. (☎344-5656. Runs every hr. M-F 6am-6pm; reduced service on Sa. $1.25, seniors and disabled 60¢; transfers 10¢.) **Moda!** runs free, electric **trolleys** with A/C to most of the sights downtown, including the Visitors Center. (☎208-7540. Operates M-F 7am-6pm.) Services include: **Taxis: Yellow Cab,** ☎476-7711; **Cab Service Inc.,** ☎342-0024. **Visitor info: Fort Condé Info Center,** 150 S. Royal St., in a reconstructed French fort near Government St., is an island oasis in the stormy sea of traveling. (☎208-7658. Open daily 8am-5pm.) **Hotlines: Rape Crisis,** ☎473-7273. **United Way Helpline,** ☎431-5111. Both 24hr. **Medical Services: Mobile Infirmary Medical Center,** ☎431-2400. **Post Office:** 250 St. Joseph St. (☎694-5936. Open M-F 7am-5pm, Sa 9am-noon.) **ZIP code:** 36601. **Area code:** 251.

▟ ACCOMMODATIONS. A slew of affordable motels lines I-65 on Beltline, from Exit 5A (Spring Hill Rd.) to Exit 1 (Government Blvd.), and Rte. 90 west of downtown. You'll pass several cheap motels on Government Blvd. before finding ▓**Olsson's Motel ❷,** 4137 Government Blvd., Exit 1B off I-65, two miles west on the left-hand side. Though farther from downtown than many lodgings, Olsson's has some fun, quirky perks that make it worthwhile: recliners and mini-fridges, wooden furniture and four-poster beds, a homey layout, and exceptional cleanliness. (☎661-5331. Singles $33-37; doubles $37-40.) **Family Inn ❷,** 980 S. Beltline Rd., Exit 3 off I-65 at Airport Blvd., then left onto the southern branch of the W. I-65 Access Rd., is the best of the chain lodgings. (☎344-5500. Firm beds, free local calls, continental breakfast, and cable TV. Singles $32-33; doubles $38. AAA and AARP discounts.) **Mobile's I-10 Kampground ❶,** 6430 Theodore Dawes Rd., lies 7½ mi. west on I-10, south off Exit 13. This is a great place...if you like RVs. (☎653-9816 or 800-272-1263. 150 mostly shady sites, pool, and laundry facilities. Tent sites $14, RV hookup $21; each additional person $1.)

▛▜ FOOD & NIGHTLIFE. Mobile's Gulf location means fresh seafood (surf) and Southern cookin' (turf). ▓**Wintzell's Oyster House ❸,** 605 Dauphin St., is a longtime local favorite that offers oysters "fried, stewed, or nude" in rooms covered with thousands of signs. Beat the 1 hr. oyster-eating record of 21½ dozen and the meal is on them. (☎432-4605. Happy Hour specials M-F 4pm-7pm with 25¢ raw oysters. Meals $8-14. Open M-Sa 11am-10pm, Su noon-8pm.) For turf, follow the cloud of wood smoke to ▓**Dreamland ❷,** 3314 Old Shell Rd. Their ribs, cooked over the open fire in the dining room, will put you in a blissful food coma; wake up with a tall glass of iced tea, the house drink of choice. (☎479-9898. Half-slab $9. Half-chicken $6.50. Open M-Sa 10am-10pm, Su 11am-9pm.) **The Little Kitchen ❶,** 102 Dauphin St., at the corner of Royale St., is an unbeatable deal. A no-frills, cafeteria-style dive, it serves huge portions of Southern breakfast and lunch (that's grits 'n' smothered chicken) for $3-5. (☎334-438-6927. Cheap-as-hell sandwiches go for $2.25. Open M-F 7am-2pm.) Mobile has a lengthy and proud Greek heritage. To taste some of it, go to **Roussos ❸,** 166 S. Royale St., next to the Welcome Center. A family-run seafood place right by the banks of the river, Roussos serves all sorts of

THE SOUTH

seafood dinners for $8-14. Ask them to prepare food "Greek style" with olive oil and lemon juice. (☎433-3322. Open M-Sa 11am-10pm.) Mobile's late-night scene is a bit one-dimensional—pool is the name of the game. The **Lower Dauphin St. Entertainment District** is a fancy name for the downtown block of bars, each of which on any given night has a couple of pool tables, 20 or more youngish locals, and drinks for under $5. Most places close around 2 or 3am. For those still feisty after 3am, trek out to **Solomon's,** 5753 Old Shell Rd., at University Rd., which is open 24hr. The warehouse-sized space, with 18 pool tables, darts, video games, and great burgers, gets pretty empty in the wee hours. (☎344-0380. Happy Hour daily 11am-7pm.)

🔲 **SIGHTS.** Mobile's attractions lie scattered inland, around downtown, and near the bay. The **Museum of Mobile,** 111 S. Royal St., is a new attraction that celebrates and documents "Mobilian" history in all its glory. Exhibits cover "The Founding of Mobile" and the fate of the slave ship Clotilda alongside the private hoards of prominent Mobile families. (☎208-7569. Open M-Sa 9am-6pm, Su 1-5pm. $5, students $3, seniors $4, families $20.) **Bienville Square,** at the intersection of Dauphin and Conception St., is the central park downtown and a main hangout for locals. Eight separate historic districts display the evidence of the city's varied architectural and cultural influences. In particular, the buildings of the **Church St. East Historic District** showcase Federal, Greek Revival, and Victorian architecture. The staff at the Fort Condé Visitors Center gives several ready-made walking and driving tours of these neighborhoods and will design one especially for you.

Several spectacular mansions and houses have been converted into museums. In the **DeTonti Historical District,** north of downtown, brick townhouses with wrought-iron balconies surround the restored **Richards-DAR House Museum,** 256 North Joachim St. The house's ornate iron lace is some of the most elaborate of its era. (☎208-7320. Open M-F 11am-3:30pm, Sa 11am-4pm, Su 1-4pm. Tours $5, children $2. Free tea and cookies.) **Oakleigh Historical Complex,** 350 Oakleigh Pl., 2½ blocks south of Government St. at George St., contains the grandiose **Oakleigh House Museum,** the working-class **Cox-Deasy House Museum,** and the **Mardi Gras Cottage Museum.** The houses attempt to portray the everyday and festival lives of various classes of Mobilians in the 1800s. (☎432-1281. Open M-Sa 10am-4pm. Tours every 30min.; last tour 3:30pm. $5, seniors and AAA $4.50, ages 6-11 $2.) The **Bragg-Mitchell Mansion,** 1906 Springhill Ave., is the most plantation-like of Mobile's old homes. (☎471-6364. Open for tours Tu-F 10am-3:30pm. $5.)

The 🔲**USS Alabama,** moored 2½ mi. east of town at Battleship Park (accessible from I-10 and Government St.'s Bankhead Tunnel), earned nine stars from battles fought in WWII. Open passageways let landlubbers explore the ship's depths. The park also houses a collection of airplanes and the USS Drum, a submarine that visitors can walk through. (☎433-2703. Open daily Apr.-Sept. coupon available at Fort Condé Visitors Center, $2 AAA discount. Parking $2.) **Bellingrath Gardens,** 12401 Bellingrath Gardens Rd., Exit 15A off I-10, was voted one of America's top five formal garden displays for its lush rose and oriental gardens, bayou boardwalk, and 900-acre setting. You can also tour the Bellingrath Museum Home or take the *Southern Belle* river tour. (☎800-247-8420. Open daily 8am-dusk; ticket office closes at 5pm. Gardens $9, ages 5-11 $6.)

Early spring is the time to be in Mobile. Azaleas bloom and a pink line beginning at the Visitors Center appears on the city streets marking the 27 mi. **Azalea Trail,** twisting through the city. In February, Mobile's **Mardi Gras,** the oldest one in the country and the precursor to the debauchery that is New Orleans, erupts with parades, costumes, an Out-of-Towners ball, and the crowning of the Mardi Gras King and Queen. To add more fuel to the Fat Tuesday fire, in 2003 the **Mardi Gras Museum** will open in Mobile; call the Visitors Center for details. The *Mobile Traveler,* available at Fort Condé Visitors Center, has an updated list of all Mobile attractions.

MISSISSIPPI

The "Deep South" bottoms out in Mississippi. The legacy of extravagant cotton plantations, a dependence upon slavery, and subsequent racial strife and economic ruin are more visible here than in any other state. In the 1850s, Natchez and Vicksburg were two of the most prosperous cities in the nation, but during the Civil War, the state was devastated. Hatred and injustice drowned Mississippi in the 1960s, as blacks protested against continuing segregation and many whites reacted with campaigns of terror, government-sanctioned beatings, and murder. Despite its tribulations, though, Mississippi has had a number of remarkable triumphs. Ironically, one of the least literate states in the nation has produced some of the nation's greatest literary giants: William Faulkner, Eudora Welty, and Tennessee Williams. Musicians Bessie Smith, W.C. Handy, and B.B. King grew out of the Mississippi Delta (see Clarksdale, p. 378) to bring their riffs to Memphis, Chicago, and the world.

🛈 PRACTICAL INFORMATION

Capital: Jackson.

Visitor Info: Division of Tourism, P.O. Box 1705, Ocean Springs 39566 (☎800-927-6378; www.visitmississippi.org). **Department of Parks,** P.O. Box 451, Jackson 39205 (☎800-467-2757).

Postal Abbreviation: MS. **Sales Tax:** 7%.

JACKSON   ☎601

Jackson makes a concerted effort to overcome Mississippi's troubled, bloody past and lingering backwater image. Some impressive museums and sights line Pascagoula and State St. downtown, but their sleek, well-endowed facades stand in stark contrast to much of the city and its surrounding neighborhoods. Nonetheless, as the state's political and cultural capital, Jackson strives to bring the world to its people. North Jackson's lush homes and plush country clubs epitomize wealthy Southern living, while shaded campsites, cool reservoirs, and national forests invite outdoor exploration. Just don't arrive on a Sunday—true to its deep Southern roots, Jackson will be completely closed.

🖥🛈 ORIENTATION & PRACTICAL INFORMATION. West of I-55 and north of I-20, downtown is bordered on the north by **High St.,** on the south by **South St.,** and on the west by **Lamar St.** North-south **State St.** bisects the city. **Jackson International Airport,** 100 International Dr. (☎939-5631), lies east of downtown off I-20. **Amtrak,** 300 W. Capitol St. (☎355-6350; open daily 10:15am-5:15pm), runs to Memphis (4½hr., 7 per week, $33) and New Orleans (4hr., 7 per week, $21). **Greyhound,** 201 S. Jefferson St. (☎353-6342; open 24hr.), sends buses to Memphis (5hr.; 5 per day; M-Th $30.25, F-Su $32.25), Montgomery (5hr., 7 per day, $49.50/52.50), and New Orleans (4½hr., 4 per day, $27.25/29.25). **Avoid this area at night. Jackson Transit System (JATRAN)** provides limited public transportation. Maps are posted at most bus stops and available at JATRAN headquarters, 1025 Terry Rd. (☎948-3840. Open M-F 8am-5pm. Transit runs at least every 30min. M-F 5am-6pm; every hr. Sa 5:30am-6pm. $1, transfers free.) Services include: **Taxis: City Cab,** ☎355-8319. **Visitor info: Jackson Convention & Visitors Bureau,** 921 N. President St., downtown (☎960-1891 or 800-354-7695. Open M-F 8am-5pm.) **Hotlines: Rape,** ☎982-7273. 24hr. **Post Office:** 401 E. South St. (☎351-7096. Open M-F 7am-6pm, Sa 8am-noon.) **ZIP code:** 39205. **Area code:** 601.

THE SOUTH

█ ACCOMMODATIONS. If you have a car, head for the motels along **I-20** and **I-55**, where the interstate is crawling with the standard mid-range chains. If you're up for some cheap but rather seedy digs, search near **Terry Rd.** and **Hwy. 80**, south of town and north of I-20. **Parkside Inn ❶**, 3720 I-55 N, at Exit 98B off the access road, is the area's cheap and surprisingly clean motel where savvy travelers go to beat the high prices of more obvious chains. (☎982-1122. Pool, cable TV, and free local calls. Singles $22; doubles with microwave and fridge $35-49.) The **Tarrymore Motel ❶**, 1651 Terry Rd., at the intersection of Hwy. 80, is no cottage in the country, but it's a great deal for the budget-conscious. Don't stay here if you don't have a car; *the neighborhood between the motel and downtown isn't safe to walk through.* (☎355-0753. Kitchenettes and king-sized beds available. Singles $28; doubles $38.) For camping, head to **Timberlake Campgrounds ❶**. Take I-55 N to Lakeland East (Exit 98B), turn left after 6 mi. onto Old Fannin Rd. and go 4 mi.; it's just inside the Barnett Reservoir. (☎992-9100. Pool, video games, tennis and basketball courts, playground. Office open daily 8am-5pm. Tent sites $14, seniors $12. Full hookup May-Sept. $19/16; Oct.-Apr. $13/10.)

█▨ FOOD & NIGHTLIFE. Franchised grease palaces can be found north between I-55 and I-220, on County Line Rd., dubbed "restaurant alley" by natives. For the real Jackson scene, the ▨**George St. Grocery ❷**, 416 George St., off of West St., is the place to be. Packed with state politicians by day and students by night, George's serves up some of the best Southern food around. (☎969-3573. All-you-can-eat Southern lunch buffet $8. Orgasmic red beans and rice $7. Live music Th-Sa 9pm-2am. Restaurant open M-Th 11am-9pm, F 11am-10pm, Sa 5-10pm.) **Keifer's ❶**, 705 Poplar St., off State St., 1½ mi. north of downtown, serves gyros and other tasty pita wraps ($4.50-6) with a funky college flair. (☎355-6825. Open Su-Th 11am-10pm, F-Sa 11am-11pm.) **Hal & Mal's Restaurant and Brew Bar,** 200 S. Commerce St., near the corner of State and Pascagoula, stages live music in an old warehouse. (☎948-0888. Cover F-Sa under $5. Restaurant open M 11am-3pm, Tu-F 11am-10:30pm, Sa 5-10:30pm. Bar open M-Th until 11pm, F-Sa until 1am.) On Thursday, pick up the *Clarion-Ledger* for a list of weekend events.

◙ SIGHTS. A museum absolutely unique to Jackson—the only one of its kind in the US—is the newly established ▨**International Museum of Muslim Cultures (IMMC),** 117 E. Pascagoula St. Created initially as a temporary satellite to an exhibit at the Mississippi Art Museum, the IMMC has become a permanent museum in response to overwhelming community enthusiasm. New exhibits in 2003 will explore Muslim influence in western life and highlight the lives of Muslim-Americans. (☎960-0440. Open M-Th and Sa 9:30am-5pm, F 9:30am-12:30pm. $7; students, seniors, children, and disabled $4.) The **Mississippi Museum of Art (MMA),** 201 E. Pascagoula St., at Lamar St., will amaze you with its lovely and spacious galleries that display over 3100 works of art, from regional and local to regularly rotating national and international exhibits. An extremely sophisticated museum, it is one of Jackson's gems. (☎960-1515. Open M and W-Sa 10am-5pm, Tu 10am-8pm, Su noon-5pm. $5, students $3, seniors $4, ages 6-17 $2. Prices may vary; call ahead.) Adjacent to the MMA, the out-of-this-world **Russell C. Davis Planetarium** shows both large format movies and astronomical sky shows accompanied by music and lasers. (☎960-1550. Shows daily. Times vary; call ahead. $5.50, students $3, seniors and under 12 $4.)

The **Old Capitol Museum,** at the intersection of Capitol and State St., houses an excellent, Smithsonian-caliber collection documenting Mississippi's turbulent history. Make sure to visit the Civil Rights room, arguably the most important (and well-done) of the museum's offerings. (☎359-6920. Open M-F 8am-5pm, Sa 9:30am-4:30pm, Su 12:30-4:30pm. Free.) The **New State Capitol,** 400 High St., between West and President St., was completed in 1903, and a recent restoration project preserved the

Beaux Arts grandeur of the building. (☎359-3114. Self-guided tours M-F 8am-5pm. Free.) Tour the grandiose **Governor's Mansion,** 300 E. Capitol St., one of only two inhabited governor's mansions in the country. (☎359-6421. Tours every 30min. Tu-F 9:30-11am. Free.) From King Cotton to logging to crop dusting, the **Mississippi Agriculture and Forestry Museum,** 1150 Lakeland Dr., ½ mi. east of I-55 Exit 98B, is a fascinating historical account of the changing practices of agriculture and land use in the state. Actual crop dusting aircraft are on site in the **National Agricultural Aviation Museum,** as well as many restored buildings and farm implements. (☎713-3365 or 800-844-8687. Open M-Sa 9am-5pm. $4, seniors $3, ages 6-18 $2, ages 3-5 50¢.)

VICKSBURG   ☎601

Vicksburg's verdant hills and prime location on the Mississippi River were host to one of the major battles of the Civil War. President Lincoln called the town the "key" and maintained that the war "can never be brought to a close until that key is in our pocket." After a 47-day siege, the Confederacy surrendered to Ulysses S. Grant's army on July 4, 1863. The city held quite a grudge—it refused to celebrate the Fourth of July until the late 1940s. Today, the battlefield is the sleepy town's main attraction—though it has a surprisingly quirky, only-in-America underbelly that is easily overlooked. Lush green parks atop high bluffs on the riverbanks yield breathtaking views, the thriving riverfront casinos give the town a slight Vegas feel, and the "downtown" strip along Washington St. has a weird mix of Confederate pride stores and wacky avant-garde art galleries.

🔃 PRACTICAL INFORMATION. A car is necessary in Vicksburg. The bus station, the Visitors Center, downtown, and the far end of the sprawling military park mark the city's extremes; no public transportation runs between them. **Greyhound** (☎638-8389; open daily 7am-8:30pm) pulls out at 1295 S. Frontage Rd. for Jackson (1hr., 6 per day, $11.25). The **Tourist Information Center,** on Clay St., across from the military park entrance, west off I-20, has an extremely helpful map of sights, accommodations, and restaurants. (☎636-9421 or 800-221-3536. Open in summer daily 8am-5:30pm; in winter Sa-Su 8am-5pm.) **Post Office:** 3415 Pemberton Blvd., is off U.S. 61 S. (636-1022. Open M-F 8:30am-5pm, Sa 9am-noon.) **ZIP code:** 39180. **Area code:** 601.

🔃 ACCOMMODATIONS. Vicksburg is a Bed and Breakfast town. **The Corners ❹,** 601 Klein St., off Washington St., is a gorgeous B&B high on a tall bluff with a spectacular view across the river. Both the beautiful garden in back and the historic building are permeated with the smell of flowers and furnished with antiques. A full plantation breakfast is served in the mansion's dining room. (☎636-7421 or 800-444-7421. Singles $80-120; doubles $90-130. Rates lower in winter; call for details.) Inexpensive lodging comes easy in Vicksburg. The **Hillcrest Motel ❶,** 40 Rte. 80 E, ¼ mi. east from I-20 Exit 4, has well-worn but nonetheless homey and spacious rooms with a pool. (☎638-1491. Singles $26; doubles $30.) Rooms at the **Beechwood Motel ❶,** 4449 E. Clay St., a block west of the Hillcrest, include cable TV, microwave, and fridge. (☎636-2271. Singles $32; doubles $36.) Most hotels cluster near the park; one of the few cheap downtown options is the **Relax Inn Downtown ❷,** 1313 Walnut St., at the corner of Clay St. (☎631-0097. Microwave and fridge. Laundry. Singles $32; doubles $35.) **Magnolia RV Park ❶,** 211 Miller St., Exit 1B off Hwy. 61, has 66 full RV hookups, a pool, game room, and playground. From downtown, head south on Washington to I-20 Exit 1A, and take a left on Rifle Range Rd. to Miller St. (☎631-0388. Office open M-Sa 8:30am-7:30pm. Sites $18.) Closer to the military park, with a free shuttle to all the casinos, is **Battlefield Kampground ❶,** 4407 I-20 Frontage Rd., off Exit 4B. (☎636-2025. Pool, playground, and laundry. Tent sites $12, with water and electricity $15, full hookup $18. Motel rooms $25.)

THE SOUTH

FROM THE ROAD

SOUTHERN "HOSPITALITY"

You can never be quite sure of the reactions you'll get when you're a short-haired girl traveling alone though the Deep South. Wandering around a submarine/museum in Alabama, I heard a boy's voice behind me: "Wow, that kid just climbed up that ladder. Let's follow him!"

I realized that *I* had just climbed a ladder, and that I was the only one at the top. Figuring it was time to get out before any more theories on gender were explored, I moved to climb down the ladder. One boy hit the other and said, "Move it, let her get by." The second boy looked at the first condescendingly and said, "That's not a girl—that's a kid." The first said curiously, "I don't think so...I think it's a girl." Unable to take it anymore, I yelled "I'M A GIRL!" They both gasped and looked stricken, then started apologizing profusely.

Later in New Orleans—wearing the same clothes, my hair the same mere two inches long—I again heard a male voice behind me. "G'morning," said a man carrying a cup as he left his house, "How are you?"

"Great," I said. "A little hungry."

"Here!" he said, "have my soup!" He put the cup in my hands, took my face in his hands, and kissed me lingeringly on the cheek. "Enjoy it, beautiful," he said.

The South will treat you with its full range of politeness and ignorance, hospitality and bigotry, and frequently mixed-up combinations of them all. Roll with it. Assert your own identity (and gender!) when necessary. And always, always accept soup.

—Julia Reischel

FOOD & NIGHTLIFE. At ▨Walnut Hills ❸, 1214 Adams St., just north of Clay St., noontime is "dinnertime." All-you-can-eat round table dinners of catfish, ribs, okra, snap peas, biscuits, and iced tea cost $12. The apple crisp is absolutely divine. Blue plate specials of the same delicious food are available for $7, and the a la carte menu is served all night. (☎ 638-4910. Round table dinners Su-F 11am-2pm. Open M-F 11am-9pm, Su 11am-2pm.) While downtown, indulge in home-cooked meals at **Burger Village ❶**, 1220 Washington St. Old fashioned burgers are nothing but 100% all-American beef. (☎ 638-0202. Meals $4.25-5.25. Open M-Sa 9am-6pm.) **The Biscuit Company Cafe ❸**, 1100 Washington St., is the town's big nightspot for music, especially blues. Jimbo Mathis, Squirrel Nut Zippers, and the North Mississippi Allstars are a few of the names that regularly rock the large, wood-paneled, warehouse-sized joint. (☎ 631-0099. Po' boys $7. Pasta $12-14. Pizza $11. Surf 'n' turf entrees $12-18. W "Biscuits and Jam" night, open mic. Live music F-Sa begins around 10pm. Cover $3-7, more for big-name bands. Open M-Th 11am-10pm; F-Sa 11am-4am, sometimes later. Kitchen open daily 11am-10pm.) Wannabe high-rollers, who are tired of jamming, can get lost in one of the four **casinos** that line the river.

SIGHTS. Vicksburg is a mecca for thousands of touring schoolchildren, Civil War buffs, and Confederate and Union army descendents. Memorials and combat site markers riddle the grassy 1700-acre **Vicksburg National Military Park,** lending the grounds a sacred air. The park sits on the eastern and northern edges of the city with its Visitors Center on Clay St., about ½ mi. west of I-20 Exit 4B. Driving along the 16 mi. path, there are three options: taking a self-guided tour with a free map available at the entrance, using an informative audio tour, or hiring a guide to narrate the sights. (☎ 636-2199. Park center open daily 8am-6pm. Grounds open in summer daily 7am-7pm; in winter 7am-5pm. $5 per car. Tape $6, CD $11, live guide $25.) Within the park, the sunk and saved Union **USS Cairo Museum** contains artifacts salvaged in the early 1960s from the old ironclad. (☎ 636-2199. Usually open daily Apr.-Oct. 9:30am-6pm; Nov.-Mar. 8:30am-5pm. Free with park fee.) The **Old Courthouse Museum,** 1008 Cherry St., is an excellent Civil War museum. During the siege of Vicksburg in 1863, Confederate troops used the cupola as a signal station and held Union prisoners in the courtroom. It now houses a collection of Jefferson Davis memorabilia and a completely restored courtroom. (☎ 636-0741. Open Apr.-Sept. M-Sa 8:30am-5pm, Su 1:30-5pm; Oct.-Mar. M-Sa 8:30-4:30pm, Su 1:30-5pm. $3, seniors $2.50, under 18 $2.)

Vicksburg also has a bunch of attractions not related to the war. Most can be found on **Washington St.**, running along the river as the town's tiny commercial main street. The █**Corner Drug Store,** 1123 Washington St., is a fully operating modern pharmacy—on one half of the floor. On the other half, the owner has created a very elaborate 1800s drug store museum, displaying the store as it was set up a century ago, complete with archaic drugs like cocaine, arsenic, opium, and "haschissh." All sorts of old implements adorn the walls, and a small collection of Civil War battle paraphernalia and old moonshine jugs sit in one corner. (☎363-2756. Open M-Sa 8am-6pm, Su 9:30-11:30am. Free.) Down the street, the **Bieden-harn Museum of Coca-Cola Memorabilia,** 1107 Washington St., is a good place to grab an ice cream cone. Standing in a reconstructed 1900 soda fountain, learn everything there is to know about the bottling of "the ideal brain tonic"—Coca-Cola. (☎638-6514. Open M-Sa 9am-5pm, Su 1:30-4:30pm. $2.25, age 6-12 $1.75. AAA discount.) The **Attic Gallery,** 1101 Washington St., has a collection of Southern contemporary art and an eclectic display of glassware, pottery, books, and jewelry. (☎638-9221. Open M-Sa 10am-5pm. Free.)

OXFORD   ☎662

When westward explorers first came to this quaint town in northern Mississippi, they decided to name it "Oxford" in hopes of getting the state government to open a university here. The plan worked brilliantly, eventually landing Oxford the **University of Mississippi (Ole Miss).** The school gained notoriety in the early 1960s, when James Meredith attempted to be the first black student to enroll. Mississippi Governor Ross Burnett openly defied federal law, banning Meredith until the National Guard arrived. Underneath its rough past, Oxford is the "little postage stamp of native soil" that William Faulkner decided "was worth writing about." Outside of Ole Miss and Faulkner, Oxford remains a classic little college town with cozy independent bookstores, funky coffeeshops, and eclectic shopping, most of which clusters around Courthouse Sq. in the middle of town.

█▐ **ORIENTATION & PRACTICAL INFORMATION.** Oxford is 30 mi. east of I-55 on Rte. 6 (Exit 243), 55 mi. south of Memphis, and 140 mi. north of Jackson. Main east-west roads are **Jackson Ave.** and **University Ave.,** while **Lamar Blvd.** runs north-south. The center of town is **Courthouse Sq.,** at the intersection of Jackson Ave. and Lamar St., and bordered by Van Buren Ave. **Oxford Tourism Info Center,** 111 Courthouse Sq., offers free audio walking tours and loads of info on Faulkner. (☎234-4680 or 800-758-9177. Open M-F 9am-5pm. The little house next door is open Sa-Su 10am-2pm.) **Greyhound,** 2625a W. Oxford Loop (☎234-0094; open M-F 8:30am-5pm, Sa 8:30am-noon), runs to Memphis (2hr., 1 per day, $20); Nashville (9hr., 1 per day, $60); and New Orleans (14 hr., 2 per day, $79). **Internet access: Public Library,** 401 Bramlett Blvd., at Jackson Ave. (☎234-5751. Open M-Th 9:30am-8pm, F-Sa 9:30am-5:30pm, Su 2-5pm.) **Post Office:** 401 McElroy Dr. (☎234-5615. Open M-F 9am-5pm, Sa 9:30am-12:30pm.) **ZIP code:** 38655. **Area code:** 662.

▌ **ACCOMMODATIONS.** Spend a night in Southern comfort at the **Oliver-Britt House Inn ❹,** 512 Van Buren Ave., an unpretentious B&B. Five comfortable but small rooms fit in this turn-of-the-century house. (☎234-8043. Breakfast on weekends. Rooms Su-Th $79-105, F-Sa $89-115; football weekends $20 more.) The town's best independently-owned cheap hotel is **Johnson's Inn ❷,** 2305 W. Jackson Ave., west of town off Hwy. 6. It sports spacious, relatively new rooms with microwaves and fridges, cable TV, and free local calls. (☎234-3611. Singles $38; doubles $42-50.) **Wall Doxy State Park ❶,** 23 mi. north of town on Rte. 7, is a scenic spot with an expansive lake. (☎252-4231 or 800-467-2757. Sites with water and electricity $9; RV sites with dump stations $13. Cabins $52-58 per night. Min. stay for cabins 3 nights. Entrance fee $2 per car.)

🄲🗗 **FOOD & ENTERTAINMENT.** Food is best found in **Courthouse Sq.**, at Jackson Ave. and Lamar Blvd. It's hip to be at ▨**Square Books ❶**, 160 Courthouse Sq. The heart of this literary college town, true to its heritage, stocks an extensive Faulkner section. Read his tangled narratives while sampling coffee drinks ($2) and pastries ($1-2) on a balcony overlooking the downtown area. (☎ 236-2262. Open M-Th 9am-9pm, F-Sa 9am-10pm, Su 10am-6pm.) **Ajax Diner ❷**, 118 Courthouse Sq., cooks excellent, down-home meat-and-vegetable platters ($7) accompanied by jalapeño cornbread. (☎ 232-8880. Traditional po' boy sandwiches $6. Open M-Sa 11:30am-10pm.) The **Bottletree Bakery ❸**, 923 Van Buren Ave., serves large deli sandwiches ($7-8) and fresh pastries in a funky atmosphere with brightly painted walls and junkyard furniture. (☎ 236-5000. Open Tu-F 7am-4pm, Sa 9am-4pm, Su 9am-2pm.) At night, live music rolls from **Proud Larry's ❸**, 211 S. Lamar Blvd., while hand-tossed pizzas are served up piping hot. (☎ 236-0050. Dinners $8-10. Cover $5-7. Music M-W and Su 10pm-midnight, F-Sa 10pm-1am. Kitchen open M-Sa 11am-10pm, Su 11:30am-3pm.) For local listings, check the free weekly *Oxford Town*.

🄶 **SIGHTS.** Faulkner remains the South's favorite son, and his home, **Rowan Oak,** just south of downtown on Old Taylor Rd., off S. Lamar Blvd., is Oxford's biggest attraction. Entranced by the home's history (it had belonged to a Confederate general), Faulkner bought the place in 1930 and named the property after the Rowan tree, a symbol of peace and security. True to form, the pastoral and tree-covered location meant little sound and less fury, and gave Faulkner peace of mind to work. The plot outline of his 1954 novel *A Fable* is scribbled in pencil on the walls of the study. (☎ 234-3284. The house is currently closed for renovations. Regular hours: Tu-F 10am-noon and 2-4pm, Sa 10am-4pm, Su noon-4pm. Grounds open sunrise to sunset. Free self-guided tours.)

Outside of Faulkner, Oxford's sights are all affiliated with another symbol of Southern intellectualism—Ole Miss. The town's covered sidewalks and tall cedar trees make it a fitting home for the **Center for the Study of Southern Culture,** a University department in the old Barnard Observatory on the Grove Loop near the Student Union at Ole Miss. Here, visitors can pick up pamphlets or attend conferences, including the ever-popular annual **Faulkner & Yoknapatawpha Conference** (July 20-25, 2003). Other conferences and festivals sponsored by the center include **The Oxford Conference on the Book,** in April, which celebrates a different important author each year, and the **Southern Foodways Symposium,** which brings people together in late October to discuss weighty academic subjects, like barbecue and other Southern food traditions. (☎ 915-5993. Center open M-F 8am-5pm. Free.) The big project for 2003 is the construction of the **Civil Rights Memorial** that will "commemorate equality in education" on the grounds of the Ole Miss Campus. As the 40th anniversary of the famous integration of Ole Miss, 2003 promises year-long events, conferences, and lectures to mark the occasion, all culminating in the Memorial's installation and opening in the spring of 2003.

Blues buffs will revel in the **Ole Miss Blues Archive,** on the 2nd fl. of the main campus library on University Circle, which has one of the largest collections of blues memorabilia, sheet music, and records (over 40,000) in the world. The collection is a part of Ole Miss's vast archive library, which also houses a substantial collection of 20th century cinema materials, Faulkner detritus, and many fragile historical wonders. There are two small exhibit areas in the lobby of the archives which visitors are welcome to look at, but you must request permission to go into the closed stacks and listening stations. (☎ 915-7408. Open M-F 9am-5pm. Free.) The **University Museums,** at 5th St. and University Ave., contain four main collections ranging from classical Greek pottery to 19th-century scientific instruments, as well as a small but impressive collection of Southern folk and "outsider" art. (☎ 915-7073. Open Tu-Sa 10am-4:30pm, Su 1-4pm. Free.)

THE SOUTH

LOUISIANA

After exploring the Mississippi River valley in 1682, Frenchman René-Robert Cavalier proclaimed the land "Louisiane," in honor of Louis XIV. The name has endured three centuries, though French ownership of the vast region clearly has not. The territory was tossed between France, England, and Spain before Thomas Jefferson and the US snagged it in the Louisiana Purchase of 1803. Nine years later, a smaller, redefined Louisiana was admitted to the Union. Each successive government lured a new mix of settlers to the bayous: Spaniards from the Canary Islands, French Acadians from Nova Scotia, Americans from the East, and free blacks from the West Indies. Louisiana's multinational history, Creole culture, Catholic governmental structure (under which counties are called "parishes"), and Napoleonic legal system are unlike anything found in the 49 other states.

◪ PRACTICAL INFORMATION

Capital: Baton Rouge.

Visitor info: Office of Tourism, P.O. Box 94291, Baton Rouge 70804 (☎225-342-8100 or 800-261-9144; www.louisianatravel.com). Open M-F 8am-4:30pm. **Office of State Parks,** P.O. Box 44426, Baton Rouge 70804 (☎225-342-8111 or 888-677-1400; www.lastateparks.com). Open M-F 9am-5pm.

Postal Abbreviation: LA. **Sales Tax:** 8%.

NEW ORLEANS ☎504

First explored by the French, *La Nouvelle Orléans* was secretly ceded to the Spanish in 1762; the citizens didn't find out until 1766. Spain returned the city to France just in time for the United States to grab it in the Louisiana Purchase of 1803. Centuries of cultural cross-pollination have resulted in a vast melange of Spanish courtyards, Victorian verandas, Cajun jambalaya, Creole gumbo, and French *beignets*. The city's nickname, "the Big Easy," reflects the carefree attitude characteristic of this fun-loving place where food and music are the two ruling passions. New Orleans has its own style of cooking, a distinct accent, and way of making music—at the start of the 20th century, its musicians invented the musical style that came to be known as jazz. While New York may claim to be "the city that never sleeps," N'awlins holds the title for "the city that won't stop partying." The only thing that stifles this vivacity is the heavy, humid air that slows folks to a near standstill during the summer. But when the day's heat retreats into the night, the city jumps with drinking and dancing into the early morning. Come late February, there's no escaping the month-long celebration of Mardi Gras, the peak of the city's already festive mood.

◪ INTERCITY TRANSPORTATION

Airport: Louis Armstrong New Orleans International Airport, 900 Airline Dr. (☎465-2303), 15 mi. west of the city. Cab fare to the Quarter is set at $24 for 1-2 people; $10 each additional person. The **Louisiana Transit Authority,** 118 David Dr. (☎818-1077), runs buses from the airport to Elk St. downtown M-Sa every 15-30min. 5:30am-5:40pm. After 5:40pm, buses go to Tulane Ave. and Carollton Ave. (mid-city) until 11:30pm. Station open M-F 8am-4pm. $1.50; exact change needed. Pick-up on the upper level, near the exit ramp.

Trains: Amtrak, 1001 Loyola Ave. (☎ 800-872-7245), in the Union Passenger Terminal, a 10min. walk to Canal St. via Elk. Station open daily 6am-10pm. Ticket office open M, W, and F-Sa 6:15am-8:30pm; Tu, Th, and Su 6:15am-11pm. To: **Atlanta** (12hr., 7 per week, $50-89); **Houston** (9hr., 3 per week, $50-89); and **Jackson** (4hr., 7 per week, $18-36).

Buses: Greyhound, 1001 Loyola Ave. (☎ 524-7571 or 800-231-2222), in the Union Passenger Terminal. Open 24hr. To: **Atlanta** (12-14hr., 7 per day, $67); **Austin** (12-15hr., 6 per day, $91); and **Baton Rouge** (2hr., 9 per day, $11).

◪ ORIENTATION

Most sights in New Orleans are located within a central area. The city's main streets follow the curve of the **Mississippi River,** hence the nickname "the Crescent City." Directions from locals reflect watery influences—lakeside means north, referring to **Lake Ponchartrain,** and "riverside" means south. Uptown lies west, up river; downtown is down river. The city is concentrated on the east bank of the Mississippi, but **"The East"** refers only to the easternmost part of the city. **Parking** in New Orleans is relatively easy (☎ 299-3700 for parking info). Throughout the French Quarter (and in most other residential neighborhoods), signs along the streets designate "2-hour parking residential" areas. Many streets throughout the city have meters, which become free M-F after 6pm and on weekends and holidays. Parking lots sell day-long spaces $5-12. Of course, during Mardi Gras, most of the free spots will be taken. As a general rule, avoid parking on deserted streets at night. After sunset, it's often best to take a cab or the St. Charles Streetcar.

NEIGHBORHOODS

Less populated regions of the city, like **Algiers Point,** are on **the West Bank** across the river. Tourists flock to the small **French Quarter (Vieux Carré),** bounded by the Mississippi River, **Canal St., Rampart St.,** and **Esplanade Ave.** Streets in the Quarter follow a grid pattern, making foot travel easy. Just northeast of the Quarter across Esplanade Ave., **Faubourg Marigny** is a residential neighborhood that has recently developed a crop of trendy nightclubs, bars, and cafes attracting as many locals as tourists. Northwest of the Quarter across Rampart St., the little-publicized black neighborhood of **Tremé** has a storied history, but has been ruined somewhat by the encroaching highway overpass and the housing projects lining its Canal St. border. *Be careful in Tremé at night.* Uptown, the residential **Garden District,** bordered by **St. Charles Ave.** to the north and **Magazine St.** to the south, is distinguished by its elegant homes. The scenic **St. Charles Streetcar route,** easily picked up at Canal St. and Carondelet St., passes through parts of the **Central Business District** ("CBD" or "downtown"), the Garden District via St. Charles Ave., and the **Uptown** and **Carrollton** neighborhoods along **S. Carollton Ave.** and past **Tulane** and **Loyola Universities.** For a detailed guide to all of the city's neighborhoods, pick up *Historic Neighborhoods of New Orleans,* a pamphlet available at the Jackson Sq. Visitors Center.

◪ LOCAL TRANSPORTATION

Public Transit: Regional Transit Authority (RTA), 6700 Plaza Dr. (☎ 248-3900). Open M-F 8am-5pm. Most buses pass Canal St., at the edge of the French Quarter. Major buses and streetcars run 24hr., but are notoriously irregular and often don't come at all after midnight. Most buses and streetcars $1.25 in exact change. Express buses and the Riverfront Streetcar $1.50, seniors and disabled passengers 40¢; transfers 25¢. 1-day pass $5, 3-day pass $12; passes sold at major hotels in the Canal St. area. Office has bus schedules and maps.

Taxis: United Cabs, ☎522-0629 or 800-232-3303. **Checker Yellow Cabs,** ☎943-2411.

Bikes: French Quarter Bicycles, 522 Dumaine St. (☎529-3136), between Decatur and Chartres St. $5 per hr. $20 per day, $87.50 per week; includes lock, helmet, and map. Also rents wheelchairs and baby joggers. Credit card or $200 cash deposit required. Open M-F 11am-7pm, Sa-Su 10am-6pm.

🔢 PRACTICAL INFORMATION

Visitor info: Metropolitan Convention and Visitors Bureau, 529 St. Ann St. (☎568-5661 or 800-672-6124; www.neworleanscvb.com), by Jackson Sq. in the French Quarter. Open daily 9am-5pm. Beware of the many false Visitors Centers in the Quarter--condominium dealers post "visitor information" signs in their doors to attract business, but they are just trying to sell something. The Jackson Sq. center is the only official center in the French Quarter.

Hotlines: Cope Line, ☎523-2673, for crises. **Rape Crisis Hotline,** ☎482-9922. **Domestic Violence Hotline,** ☎800-672-6124. All 24hr.

Medical Services: Charity Hospital, 1532 Tulane Ave. (☎568-2311). **LSU Medical Center,** 433 Bolivar St. (☎568-4806).

Internet access: New Orleans Public Library, 219 Loyola Ave. (☎529-7323), 1½ blocks west of Canal St. Open M-Th 10am-6pm, F-Sa 10am-5pm. **The Contemporary Arts Center,** 900 Camp Rd., and **Royal Blend,** 621 Royal St., also have Internet access.

Post Office: 701 Loyola Ave. (☎589-1714), near the bus station. Open M-F 7am-8pm, Sa 8am-5pm, Su noon-5pm. **ZIP code:** 70113. **Area code:** 504.

New Orleans

THE SOUTH

🍎 FOOD
Cafe Atchafalaya, 14
Camellia Grill, 7
Dunbar's, 10
Frankie & Johnny's, 17
Juan's Flying Burrito, 12
Magazine Po' Boy and
  Sandwich Shop, 13
Tee Eva's, 15
Tremé Corner Cafe, 2

🍸 NIGHTLIFE
Carrollton Station, 5
Jimmy's, 4
Tipitina's, 16

⚓ ACCOMMODATIONS
India House, 3
Jude Travel Park, 1
House of the Rising Sun B&B, 6
Longpre House and St.
  Charles Guest House, 11
Marquette House (HI-AYH), 9
St. Charles Guest House, 8

▭▭▭ St. Charles Streetcar
- - - - Ferry

> **❗ SAFETY IN NEW ORLEANS.** New Orleans is not as dangerous as it
> used to be. The city has increased its police force and made an effort to keep
> tourists safe. But New Orleans still has high crime rates, and many areas should
> be avoided. Many neighborhoods change character very quickly, with danger
> sometimes lurking one block from a tourist attraction. The tenement areas
> directly north of the French Quarter and northwest of Lee Circle pose particular
> threats to personal safety. At night, stick to busy, well-lit roads. Never walk alone
> after dark. Make some attempt to downplay the tourist image (e.g., don't wear a
> t-shirt that has the words "New Orleans" anywhere on it) and have a good idea
> of where you want to go. Avoid parks, cemeteries, and housing projects at night.

⌂ ACCOMMODATIONS

Finding inexpensive yet decent rooms in the **French Quarter** can be as difficult as
staying sober during Mardi Gras. Luckily, other parts of the city compensate for
the absence of cheap lodging downtown. Several **hostels** cater to the young and
almost penniless, as do guest houses near the **Garden District.** Accommodations for
Mardi Gras and the Jazz Festival get booked up to a year in advance. During peak
times, proprietors will rent out any extra space—be sure you know what you're
paying for. Rates tend to sink in the off-season (June to early Sept.) when business
is slow, and negotiation can pay off. Campers will discover oodles of campsites,
but even those get pricey during Mardi Gras. Pick up a copy of the *Louisiana
Official Tour Guide* at the Jackson Sq. Visitors Center; it has the most comprehensive, unbiased campsite listings available.

HOSTELS

▨ **India House,** 124 S. Lopez St. (☎821-1904), at Canal St. What this bohemian haunt
lacks in tidiness it makes up for in character. Hand-painted murals and pictures of past
guests fight for space on the walls. Communal eating (and, on busier nights, sleeping),
comfy couches, and backyard patio complete the setting of this beautiful house that
used to be a full-time brothel. Kitchen, pool, turtle pond out back, laundry, Internet, A/
C, and lounge areas. No key deposit—hell, no keys; the doors don't lock. Linen deposit
$5. Dorms $15, peak times $18; weekly $90. Private rooms $35, with A/C $40. ❶

Marquette House New Orleans International Hostel (HI-AYH), 2249 Carondelet St.
(☎523-3014), in the Garden District. A wonderful hostelling experience, especially for
hostel virgins, due to its no-alcohol policy, cleanliness, and modicum of strictness.
Extremely large, semi-rustic private rooms are also available at reasonable prices. 162
beds, A/C, kitchen (no stove), study rooms, Internet access 10¢ per minute, basic food
supplies for cheap. Very quiet. Wheelchair accessible. Linen $2.50. No lockout or cur-
few. Key deposit $5. Dorms $17, nonmembers $20. Private rooms with queen-sized
bed and pull-out sofa $50/53. Each additional person after 2 people $10. Weekly
rates available. ❶

HOTELS & GUEST HOUSES

▨ **St. Charles Guest House,** 1748 Prytania St. (☎523-6556). This is that unique little
boarding house experience many dream of. Located in one of New Orleans's prettiest
neighborhoods, nice rooms come complete with a large courtyard, beautiful pool, and
continental breakfast. Down-to-earth enough to completely avoid the standard hotel
experience (no phones or TVs, large antique signs hang haphazardly in the hallway, and
the staff lives out back). Cabin-style single rooms $25, with A/C $45. Rooms with 1
queen-sized bed or 2 twins $55-95, depending on season. ❶

■ **House of the Rising Sun Bed and Breakfast,** 335 Pelican Ave. (☎888-842-2747), across the river. Located in quaint Algiers Point only minutes away from the French Quarter and downtown via ferry, the river effectively hides this house and its historic neighborhood away from the touristy atmosphere and mad hijinks of Bourbon St. Run by two enthusiastic hosts, one English, and Cajun, offering "cajun and cockney hospitality." Quiet, homey, and off the beaten path. Rooms Sept.-May $95, June-Aug. $75; up to $150 around Mardi Gras. ❹

Lamont House Hotel, 622 Esplanade Ave. (☎947-1161 or 800-367-5858), is a truly imposing 1839 pink townhouse-turned-hotel across the street from the French Quarter. 20 rooms feature antique furniture, cable TV, phones, A/C, and full bathrooms. Continental breakfast is served in the house's marvelous dining room, and the large pool is the perfect place to enjoy the complimentary afternoon sherry. Rooms May-Sept. and Dec. $79; Oct.-Nov. and Jan.-Apr. $129. ❺ Behind the big pink building is the smaller Marigny Guest house, 621 Esplanade Ave. (☎944-9700), built in 1890 with simpler rooms starting at $59. ❸

Longpre House, 1726 Prytania St. (☎581-4540), is in the midst of remodeling. The 145-year-old house, complete with 20 ft. ceilings, will be reborn in 2003. One block south of St. Charles, Longpre is a rather sketchy 25min. walk from the Quarter; to be safe, take the St. Charles streetcar. For better or worse, it lacks the strong personality present at many other glasshouses in town. Kitchen and Internet available. Singles with shared bath Sept.-May $80; June-Aug. Su-Th $35, F-Sa $40, during special events $50. ❹

Depot House at Mme. Julia's, 748 O'Keefe Ave. (☎529-2952), a ½ mi. walk from the Quarter through the CBD. This B&B has plain, comfortable rooms for 1 or 2 people. Shared bathrooms. Continental breakfast. Reservations required. Rooms $65-75. ❸

CAMPING

Jude Travel Park and Guest House, 7400 Chef Menteur Hwy./U.S. 90 (☎241-0632 or 800-523-2196), just east of the eastern junction of I-10 and U.S. 90, Exit 240B. Bus #98 "Broad" drives past the front gate to #55 "Elysian Fields," which heads downtown. Pool and hot tub, showers, laundry, 24hr. security, and shuttle bus to French Quarter. 46 tent/RV sites $20. 5-room guest house available $75-120 per person per night. ❶

St. Bernard State Park, 501 St. Bernard Pkwy. (☎682-2101), 18 mi. southeast of New Orleans; take I-10 Exit 246A, turn left onto Rte. 46, travel for 7 mi., then turn right on Rte. 39 S. for 1 mi. 51 sites with water and electricity, as well as swimming pools and walking trails. Office open daily 7am-9pm. Sites $12. ❶

◘ FOOD

If the eats in the Quarter prove too trendy, touristy, or tough on the budget, there are plenty of other options, most notably on **Magazine St.** and in the Tulane area. The French Market, between Decatur and N. Peters St., on the east side of the French Quarter, sells pricey fresh vegetables.

FRENCH QUARTER

■ **Coop's Place,** 1109 Decatur St. (☎525-9053), near the corner of Ursuline St., has some of the Quarter's best Southern cooking. Their gumbo is thick and spicy ($4.35 per bowl), their beer-battered alligator bits ($8) have won awards, and their jambalaya ($8) has a unique flavor found nowhere else. A cozy neighborhood bar to boot, it's a great place to get a glimpse of what N'awlins is really like. Open daily 11am-2am. ❷

CREOLE SOUL(FOOD) New Orleans offers a long list of regional specialties that have evolved from the mixing of Acadian, Spanish, Italian, African, French, and Native American cuisines. Creole cuisine (a mixture of Spanish, French, and Caribbean) is famous for red beans and rice, po' boys (French bread sandwiches filled with sliced meat or seafood and vegetables; "dressed" means with mayo, lettuce, tomatoes, pickles, etc.), and shrimp or crawfish *étouffée*. Jambalaya (a Cajun jumble of rice, shrimp, oysters, sausage, and ham or chicken mixed with spices) and gumbo (chicken or seafood stew over rice) grace practically every menu in the city. A Southern breakfast of grits, eggs, bacon, and buttermilk biscuits satisfies even the most ardent eater. Laura's Candies, 331 Chartres St., between Conti and Bienville St., has some of the best Creole pralines. (☎525-3880. *Pralines $1.25. Open daily 10am-6pm.*)

Johnny's Po' boys, 511 St. Louis St. (☎524-8129), near the Decatur St. corner. This French Quarter institution, with 40 varieties of the famous sandwich, is the place to try a po' boy ($4-7.50). Decent Creole fare is also on the menu. Jambalaya $4.25. Gumbo $6.25. Open M-F 8am-4:30pm, Sa-Su 9am-4pm. ❷

Acme Oyster House, 724 Iberville St. (☎522-5973). At the bar, patrons slurp fresh oysters (6 for $4, 12 for $6.50) shucked before their eyes by Hollywood, the senior shucker. Acme must be responsible for Bourbon St. debauchery; their motto is "eat Louisiana oysters, love longer." Open Su-Th 11am-10pm, F-Sa 11am-11pm. ❶

Croissant d'Or, 617 Ursulines St. (☎524-4663). Fair-priced and delicious French pastries, sandwiches, and quiches are served to the local crowd that comes here to read the morning paper. Croissants $1.60. Chocolatey delights $2. Open M-Sa 7am-5pm. ❶

Mama Rosa's, 616 N. Rampart St. (☎523-5546). Locals adore this Italian *ristorante*, and with good reason. Served in a cozy neighborhood setting, Mama Rosa's pizza is some of the best you'll ever eat. 14 in. cheese pie $9. The "outrageous *muffuletta*" $6.50 for a half. Open Su-Th 11am-10pm, F-Sa 11am-11pm. ❷

Central Grocery, 923 Decatur St. (☎523-1620), between Dumaine and St. Philip St. Try an authentic *muffuletta* (deli meats, cheeses, and olive salad on Italian bread) at the place that invented them. A half ($5) serves 1, while a whole ($9) is best split between 2. Open M-Sa 8am-5:30pm, Su 9am-5:30pm. ❷

Magazine Po' Boy and Sandwich Shop, 2368 Magazine St. (☎522-3107), on the corner of 1st and Magazine St. in the Garden District. Delicious new spins on *muffulettas*. Open M-F 7am-6:30pm, Sa 10am-6:30pm. ❷

Royal Blend, 621 Royal St. (☎523-2716). The quiet garden setting provides an escape from the hustle of Royal St. and the ubiquitous chain coffee stores in the Quarter. Over 20 hot and iced coffees available, as well as a mighty fine selection of teas. Light meals (croissant sandwiches, quiches, and salads) $5-6. Pastries $1-2. Internet cafe upstairs $3 for 15min. Open M-Th 9am-8pm, F-Sa 9am-midnight, Su 9am-6pm. ❶

Café du Monde, 813 Decatur St. (☎587-0833 or 800-772-2927), at the tip of the French Market. The consummate people-watching paradise since 1862 really only does 2 things: hot *café au lait* and scrumptious *beignets* (each $1.25). Today, it's a tourist mob, but it's worth doing the cliché thing when the cliché thing is covered in powdered sugar and found nowhere else. Open 24hr. ❶

Clover Grill, 900 Bourbon St. (☎598-1010). The Clover has been open 'round the clock since 1950, serving greasy and delicious burgers ($4 and up) grilled under an American-made hubcap as well as breakfast any time for $2-3. The only place in New Orleans where bacon comes with a side of sexual innuendo—"You can beat our prices, but you can't beat our meat." Open 24hr. ❶

OUTSIDE THE QUARTER

☒ Tremé Corner Cafe, 1500 Governor Nicholls St. (☎566-7172). A youth-run neighborhood restaurant in Tremé, the Cafe sells home-cooked Creole-Caribbean food at dirtcheap prices. You'll be glad you got off the beaten-to-death path of the Quarter and into this local store. Sandwiches $6. Specials, like jerk chicken or jambalaya, $7. Open M-Sa 10:30am-3pm. ❷

☒ Juan's Flying Burrito, 2018 Magazine St. (☎569-0000), makes some of the best burritos on the planet—they're somehow crunchy, tastier than any you've ever had. For $5.75, get the "gutter punk" burrito, a meal the size of your head, and wash it down with some Mexican beers ($2.50) from their full-service bar. Open M-Sa 11am-11pm, Su noon-10pm. ❶

☒ Franky and Johnny's, 321 Arabella St. (☎899-9146), southwest of downtown toward Tulane on the corner of Tchoupitoulas St. A noisy and popular local hangout where you can sample alligator soup ($3 a cup) or crawfish pie ($4). Feb.-June oiled crawfish $6-11 for 2 lbs. Open Su-Th 11am-10pm, F-Sa 11am till the cows come home. ❷

The Marigny Brasserie, 640 Frenchmen St. (945-4472), at Royal St. in Marigny. Upscale eats in an architecturally-chic setting. Experience the sophisticated side of raucous N'awlins and dine surrounded by women in gorgeous dresses and waiters with inscrutable foreign accents. Some of the city's famous favorite dishes are expanded here; mushroom-crusted salmon ($18) is a swanky version of the classic cajun blackened redfish. Open Su-Th 5:30-11pm, F-Sa 5:30pm-1am, Su brunch 10:30am-3:30pm. ❺

Dunbar's, 4927 Freret St. (☎899-0734), on the corner of Robert St. Take St. Charles Ave. west to Jackson St., turn right on Jackson and then left onto Freret. Residents call it the best place to get mama-just-cooked-it soul food—better, they'll tell you, than anyplace in the Quarter. Gumbo meal $5.50. Specials, like the seafood platter, $15. Open M-Sa 7am-9pm. ❸

Camellia Grill, 626 S. Carrollton Ave. (☎866-9573). Take the St. Charles Streetcar to the Tulane area; Camellia is across the tracks. Classic, counter-service diner where cooks don't mind telling the whole restaurant about their marital problems. Big drippin' plates, crowds, and excellent service. Chef's special omelette $7. "Whole meal" sandwiches $6-7. Open M-Th 9am-1am, F-Sa 8am-3am, Su 8am-1am. ❷

Tee Eva's, 4430 Magazine St. (☎899-8350). Eva sells bayou cooking from her bright yellow storefront window. Soul food ($4-6) lunches change daily. Creole pralines $2, 9 oz. snow balls (flavored shaved ice) for $1.50. Crawfish pie $3. Sweet potato and pecan pie $2. Open daily 11am-7pm. ❷

Cafe Atchafalaya, 901 Louisiana Ave. (☎891-5271), at Laurel St. Take the #11 bus "Magazine St." This cozy cottage serves mouth-watering traditional Southern cuisine. Simple dishes like red beans and rice with salad ($6.50) and an appetizer of fried green tomatoes ($3.50) are exquisite. Open for lunch Tu-Su 11:30am-2pm; dinner Tu-Sa 5:30-9:30pm. ❷

Mother's Restaurant, 401 Poydras St. (☎523-9656), at the corner of Tchoupitoulas St., 4 blocks southwest of Bourbon St. It claims to serve the "world's best baked ham," and the long line outside at lunch seems to testify. Their signature baked ham po' boy is $8. Jambalaya bowl $10, cup $5. Open M-Sa 6:30am-10pm, Su 7am-10pm. ❷

⊚ SIGHTS

FRENCH QUARTER

Allow *at least* a full day in the Quarter. The oldest section of the city is famous for its ornate wrought-iron balconies—French, Spanish, and uniquely New Orleans

THE SOUTH

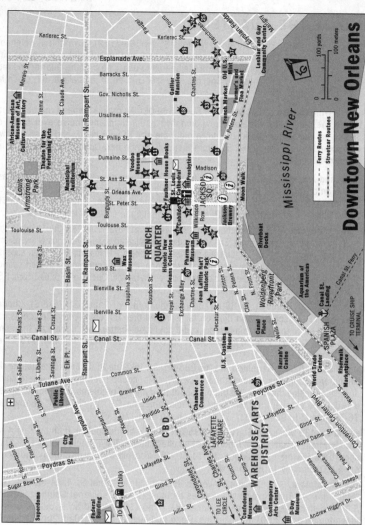

Downtown New Orleans

Mississippi River

FRENCH QUARTER

CBD

WAREHOUSE/ARTS DISTRICT

Louis Armstrong Park

Jackson Sq.

- - - Ferry Routes
— Streetcar Routes

0   100 yards
0   100 meters

TO LEE CIRCLE

TO CRUISE SHIP TERMINAL

◆ ACCOMMODATIONS
Depot House at Mme. Julia's, **12**
Lamont House Hotel, **19**

● FOOD AND DRINKS
Acme Oyster House, **13**
Café du Monde, **30**
Central Grocery, **31**
Clover Grill, **11**
Coop's Place, **33**
Croissant d'Or, **18**
Johnny's Po' boys, **26**
Laura's Candies, **20**
Mama Rosa's, **1**
The Marigny Brasserie, **25**
Mother's Restaurant, **39**
Royal Blend, **14**

★ ENTERTAINMENT/NIGHTLIFE
735 Nightclub and Bar, **5**
Bourbon Pub and Parade Disco, **6**
Café Brasil, **22**
Cafe Lafitte in Exile, **7**
Checkpoint Charlie's, **36**
Crescent City Brewhouse, **29**
d.b.a, **23**
Donna's, **3**
Dragon's Den, **37**
El Matador, **35**
Funky Butt, **2**
Good Friends, **4**
House of Blues, **28**
Lafitte's Blacksmith Shop, **8**
Le Petit Théâtre du Vieux Carré, **21**
Molly's at the Market, **32**
O'Flaherty's Irish Channel Pub, **27**
Oz, **10**
Pat O'Briens, **15**
Pirate's Alley, **17**
Preservation Hall, **9**
Shim Sham Club, **16**
Snug Harbor, **24**
Whirling Dervish, **34**

architecture—and raucous atmosphere. Known as the **Vieux Carré** (view ca-RAY), or Old Square, the historic district of New Orleans offers dusty used book stores, voodoo shops, museums, art galleries, bars, and tourist traps. **Bourbon St.** is packed with touristy bars, strip clubs, and pan-handlers disguised as clowns. **Decatur St.** has more mellow coffeeshops and bars.

ROYAL STREET. A streetcar named "Desire" once rolled down Royal St. now one of the French Quarter's most aesthetically pleasing avenues, packed with historic structures. Pick up the *French Quarter Self-Guided Walking Tour* from the Visitors Center on St. Ann St. to begin an informed jaunt past balconies of wrought-iron oak leaves and acorns, as well as Louisiana's oldest commercial and government buildings. Highlights of Royal St. are the **Maison LeMonnier**, known as the "first skyscraper," a towering three stories high, and the **LaLaurie House**, rumored to be haunted by the souls of the slaves abused by the LaLaurie family. *(LeMonnier: 640 Royal St. LaLaurie: 1140 Royal St.)*

JACKSON SQUARE. During the day, much activity in the French Quarter centers on Jackson Sq., a park dedicated to Gen. Andrew Jackson, victor of the Battle of New Orleans. The square swarms with artists, mimes, musicians, psychics, magicians, and con artists. Catch a horse-drawn tour of the Quarter for $10; wait on the Decatur St. side. The oldest Catholic cathedral in the US, **St. Louis Cathedral** possesses a simple beauty. Fully operational since 1718, services are still performed. *(615 Pere Antoine Alley. ☎525-9585. Tours daily every 15-20min. 9am-5pm; cathedral open daily 6:30am-6:30pm. Free.)* Behind the cathedral lies **Cathedral Garden**, also known as **St. Anthony's Garden**, bordered by **Pirate's Alley** and **Père Antoine's Alley**. Legend has it that the former was the site of covert meetings between pirate Jean Lafitte and Andrew Jackson as they conspired to plan the Battle of New Orleans. In reality, the alley wasn't even built until 16 years later. Pirate's Alley is also home to **Faulkner House Books**, where the late American author wrote his first novel, *Soldier's Pay*. Upholding the literary tradition, the bookshop is a treasure-trove of Faulkner's essays and books, and Southern literature in general. *(624 Pirate's Alley. ☎524-2940. Open daily 10am-6pm.)*

FRENCH MARKET. The historic French Market takes up several city blocks just east of Jackson Sq., toward the water along N. Peters St. *(☎522-2621. Shops open daily 9am-8pm.)* The market begins at the famous **Café du Monde** (see p. 443) and for the first block or two is a normal strip mall of touristy shops housed in a historic building. Down by Gov. Nicholls St., the market becomes the outdoor **Farmer's Market**, which never closes (though they're only really active from dawn to dusk) and has been selling "most anything that grows" since 1791. Beyond the Farmer's Market is the **Flea Market**, where vendors sell everything from feather boas to woodcarvings. For a map of the whole strip, stop at the **Visitors Center**. *(700 Decatur St., Under Washington Artillery Park. ☎596-3424. Open daily 8:30am-5pm. Flea Market open daily 8:30am-5pm.)*

OTHER ATTRACTIONS. The **Jean Lafitte National Historical Park and Preserve Visitors Center** conducts free walking tours through the Quarter. *(419 Decatur St. ☎589-2636. 1½hr. tour daily 9:30am. Come early; only the first 25 people are taken. Daily presentations on regional topics 3pm. Office open daily 9am-5pm.)* It's always a great night to stroll the **Moon Walk**, a promenade stretching alongside the "Mighty" Mississippi. The walk offers a fantastic riverside view and a chance for Michael Jackson jokes. *Don't go alone at night.* At the southwest corner of the Quarter, the **Aquarium of the Americas** houses an amazing collection of sea life and birds. Among the 500 species are black-footed penguins, endangered sea turtles, and extremely rare white alligators. *(1 Canal St. ☎565-3033. Open May-Aug. daily 9:30am-7pm; Sept.-Apr. 9:30am-6pm. $13.50, seniors $10, ages 2-12 $6.50.)* The steamboat **Natchez** breezes down the Mississippi on 2hr. cruises with live jazz and narration on riverside sights. An Audubon Adventure Passport includes a steamboat ride from the Aquarium and the Audubon Zoo upriver, a ticket to the IMAX theater, and a Grey Line daytime tour or cemetery and ghost walking tour. *(Departs near the Aquarium and across from Jackson Brewery. ☎ 586-8777 or 800-233-2628. Departs 11:30am and 2:30pm. $55 per person.)*

OUTSIDE THE QUARTER

WATERFRONT. The **Riverwalk,** a multimillion-dollar conglomeration of overpriced shops overlooking the port, stretches along the Mississippi. *(☎ 522-1555. Open M-Sa 10am-9pm, Su 11am-7pm.)* Take a chance on the newly opened **Harrah's New Orleans Casino,** at Canal and the river. An endless Mardi Gras of slot machines suck down not-so-endless buckets of quarters. *(☎ 800-427-7247. 21+. Open 24hr.)* For an up-close view of the Mississippi River and a unique New Orleans district, take the free **Canal St. Ferry** to Algiers Point. The Algiers of old was home to many of New Orleans's African Americans and was the birthplace of many of the city's famous jazz museums. Once called "the Brooklyn of the South," it is now a quiet, beautiful neighborhood to explore by foot. Stop at the **Dry Dock Cafe,** just off the ferry landing, to pick up a map of the area. At night, the ferry's outdoor observation deck affords a panoramic view of the city's sights. *(Departs daily every 30min. 5:45am-midnight, from the end of Canal St. Cars $1 round-trip.)*

WAREHOUSE ARTS DISTRICT. Relatively new to the downtown area, the **Warehouse Arts District,** centered roughly at the intersection of Julia and Camp St., contains several revitalized warehouse buildings turned contemporary art galleries, as well as many of the city's museums. The galleries feature widely attended exhibition openings the first Saturday of every month. On **White Linen Night,** the first Saturday in August, thousands take to the streets donning their fanciest white finery. *(☎ 522-1999; www.neworleansartsdistrictassociation.com for Arts District info.)* In an old brick building with a modern glass-and-chrome facade, the **Contemporary Arts Center** mounts exhibits ranging from puzzling to positively cryptic. *(900 Camp St. ☎ 528-3805. Internet access. Open Tu-Su 11am-5pm. Exhibits $5, students and seniors $3, under 12 free. Th free.)* In the rear studio of the **New Orleans School of Glassworks and Printmaking Studio,** observe students and instructors transform blobs of molten glass into vases and sculptures. *(727 Magazine St. ☎ 529-7277. Open in summer M-F 11am-5pm; in winter M-Sa 11am-5pm. Free.)* The **Jonathan Ferrara Gallery** hosts an annual "No Dead Artists: A Juried Exhibition of New Orleans Art Today" every April. Ferrara was nationally recognized for his involvement in "Guns in the Hands of Artists," a 1996 program in which people turned in guns that were then made into works of art. His gallery hosts all sorts of local and regional artists. *(841 Carondelet St. ☎ 522-5471. Open Tu-Sa noon-6pm. Free.)* Just west of the Warehouse District, the **Zeitgeist Multi-Disciplinary Arts Center** offers films, theatrical and musical performances, and art exhibitions. Alternative, experimental, and provocative, their mission is "something for and against everyone!" *(1724 Oretha Castle Haley Blvd., 4 blocks north of St. Charles St. ☎ 525-2767. $6, students and seniors $5.)* A few blocks farther west on St. Charles St., in **Lee Circle,** stands a bronze Confederate Gen. Robert E. Lee, continuing to stare down the Yankees: he faces due North.

ST. CHARLES STREETCAR. Much of the Crescent City's fame derives from the **Vieux Carré,** but areas uptown have their fair share of beauty and action. The **St. Charles Streetcar** still runs west of the French Quarter, passing some of the city's finest buildings, including the 19th-century homes along **St. Charles Ave.** *Gone With the Wind-*o-philes will recognize the whitewashed bricks and elegant doorway of the house on the far right corner of Arabella St.—it's a replica of Tara.

BEFORE YOU DIE, READ THIS: Being dead in New Orleans has always been a problem. Because the city lies 4-6 ft. below sea level, a 6 ft. hole in the earth fills up with 5 ft. of water. At one time coffins literally floated in the graves, while cemetery workers pushed them down with long wooden poles. One early solution was to bore holes in the coffins allowing them to sink. Unfortunately, the sight of a drowning coffin coupled with the awful gargling sound of its immersion proved too much for the families of the departed. Burial soon became passé, and stiffs were laid to rest in beautiful raised stone tombs. Miles and miles of creepy, cool marble tombs now fill the city's graveyards and ghost stories.

Frankly, my dear, it's not open to the public. For more views of fancy living, get off the streetcar in the **Garden District,** an opulent neighborhood around Jackson and Louisiana Ave. French, Italian, Spanish, and American architectural legacies create an extraordinary combination of colors, ironwork, and gardens.

CITY PARK. Stuffed with golf courses, ponds, statues, Greek Revival gazebos, softball fields, a stadium, and **Storyland,** a theme park for kids, City Park is a huge green wonderland of non-alcoholic activities. The **New Orleans Botanical Garden** is also found here. (1 Palm Dr., at the Northern end of Esplanade Ave. ☎ 482-4888. Maps at Jackson Sq. Visitors Center.)

HISTORIC HOMES & PLANTATIONS

Called the "Great Showplace of New Orleans," **Longue Vue House and Gardens** epitomizes the grand Southern estate with lavish furnishings, opulent decor, and sculpted gardens that were inspired by the Spanish Alhambra. (7 Bamboo Rd., off Metairie Rd. ☎ 488-5488. Tours every hr. M-Sa 10am-4:30pm, Su 1-5pm. $10, students $5, seniors $9, under 5 free. Tours available in English, French, German, Spanish, Italian, and Japanese.) On the way to Longue Vue, pause for a peek at the 85 ft. tall monument among the raised tombs in the **Metairie Cemetery,** where country/rock legend Gram Parsons is buried in the Garden of Memories. Across from downtown New Orleans, **River Rd.** curves along the Mississippi River accessing several plantations preserved from the 19th century. *Great River Road Plantation Parade: A River of Riches*, available at the New Orleans or Baton Rouge Visitors Centers, contains a good map and descriptions of the houses. Pick carefully, since a tour of all the privately owned plantations is quite expensive. Those below are listed in order from New Orleans to Baton Rouge.

HERMANN-GRIMM HISTORIC HOUSE. Built in 1831, the house exemplifies French style, replete with a large central hall, guillotine windows, a fan-lit entrance, and the original parterre beds. On Thursdays from October to May, trained volunteers demonstrate period cooking in an 1830s Creole kitchen. (820 St. Louis St. ☎ 525-5661. Tours every hr. M-F 10am-4pm; last tour 3:30pm. $6, ages 8-18 $5.)

GALLIER HOUSE MUSEUM. The elegantly restored residence of James Gallier, Jr., the city's most famous architect, displays the taste and lifestyle of the wealthy in the 1860s. (1118-1132 Royal St. ☎ 525-5661. Open M-F 10am-4pm; last tour 3:30pm. $6; students, seniors, and ages 8-18 $5; under 8 free.)

SAN FRANCISCO PLANTATION HOUSE. Beautifully maintained since 1856, the San Francisco is an example of Creole style with a bright blue, peach, and green exterior. (Rte. 44, 2 mi. northwest of Reserve, 42 mi. from New Orleans on the east bank of the Mississippi. Exit 206 off I-10. ☎ 535-2341 or 888-322-1756. Tours Mar.-Oct. daily 10am-4:30pm; Nov.-Feb. 10am-4pm. $8, ages 12-17 $4, ages 6-11 $3.)

LAURA: A CREOLE PLANTATION. ▓**Laura,** unlike the others on the riverbank, was owned and operated by slave-owning Creoles who lived a life entirely apart from that of white antebellum planters. Br'er Rabbit hopped into his first briar patch here, the site of the first recorded "Compair Lapin" West African stories. A valuable, entirely unique look at plantation life in the south. *(2247 Hwy. 18/River Rd., at the intersection of Rte. 20 in Vacherie.* ☎ *225-265-7690 or 888-799-7690. Tours based on the "memories" of the old plantation home daily 9:30am-4pm. $8.)*

OAK ALLEY. The name Oak Alley refers to the magnificent lawn-alley bordered by 28 evenly spaced oaks corresponding to the 28 columns surrounding the Greek Revival house. The Greeks wouldn't have approved, though: the mansion is bright pink. *(3645 Rte. 18., between St. James and Vacherie St.* ☎ *800-442-5539. Tours Mar.-Oct. daily every 30min. 9am-5:30pm; Nov.-Feb. 9am-5pm. $10, ages 13-18 $6, ages 6-12 $4.)*

HOUMAS HOUSE. This plantation served as the setting for the movie *Hush, Hush, Sweet Charlotte,* starring Bette Davis and Olivia de Havilland. Huge, moss-draped oaks shade the spacious grounds and scenic gardens. "Southern Belle" guides lead tours in authentic antebellum attire. *(40136 Rte. 942, in Burnside just over halfway to Baton Rouge.* ☎ *225-473-7841 or 888-323-8314. Tours every 30min. daily 10am-5pm; Nov.-Jan. 10am-4pm. $8, ages 13-17 $6, ages 6-12 $3.)*

NOTTOWAY. The largest plantation home in the South, Nottoway is often called the "White Castle of Louisiana." A 64-room mansion with 22 columns, a large ballroom, and a three story stairway, it was the first choice for filming *Gone with the Wind,* but the owners wouldn't allow it. *(30970 Hwy. Rte. 405., between Bayou Goula and White Castle, 18 mi. south of Baton Rouge on the southern bank of the Mississippi.* ☎ *225-545-2730 or 888-323-8314. Open daily 9am-5pm. Admission and 1hr. tour $10, under 12 $4.)*

🏛 MUSEUMS

▓ **National D-Day Museum,** 945 Magazine St. (☎527-6012), in the Historic Warehouse District on the corner of Magazine and Andrew Higgins Dr. Founded by renowned historian Stephen Ambrose and dedicated in 2000 by the likes of Tom Hanks and Stephen Spielberg, this museum lives up to its hype. An engaging, exhaustive, and moving study of World War II in its entirety is a rare find, but one that confronts the lesser-known, gruesome Pacific battles and the prickly, ugly issues of race and propaganda is remarkable—especially when done with such unbiased scrutiny. Open daily 9am-5pm. $10; students, seniors, and military with ID $6; ages 5-17 $5; military in uniform free.

▓ **New Orleans Pharmacy Museum,** 514 Chartres St. (☎565-8027), between St. Louis and Toulouse St. This apothecary shop was built by America's first licensed pharmacist in 1823. On display in the old house are 19th-century "miracle drugs" like cocaine and opium, voodoo powders, a collection of old spectacles, the still-fertile botanical garden, and live leeches. Open Tu-Su 10am-5pm. $2, students and seniors $1, under 12 free.

African-American Museum of Art, Culture, and History, 1418 Governor Nicholls St. (☎565-7497), 4 blocks north of Rampart St. in Tremé. In an 1829 Creole-style villa rescued from blight in 1991, this museum displays a wide variety of changing and permanent exhibits showcasing local and national African-American artists, along with important historical themes. Slightly off the beaten path and well worth the trek, the museum reveals a different New Orleans from the showy one of the French Quarter. Open M-F 10am-5pm, Sa 10am-2pm. $5, seniors $3, ages 4-17 $2.

Louisiana State Museum, P.O. Box 2448, New Orleans 70176 (☎800-568-6968; lsm.crt.state.la.us). The "State Museum" really oversees 8 separate museums, 6 of which are in New Orleans. The **Cabildo,** 701 Chartres St., portrays the history of Louisiana from Indian times to the present, and holds Napoleon's death mask. The **Arsenal,** 615 St. Peter (enter through the Cabildo), studies the history of the Mississippi River and New Orleans as a port city. The **Presbytère,** 751 Chartres St., features a gigantic and very interactive exhibit about the history of Mardi Gras. The **1850 House,** 523 St. Ann St., on Jackson Sq., is—you guessed it—a recreated house from the time period. **Mme. John's Legacy,** 632 Dumaine St., showcases a rare example of Creole architecture as well as an exhibit on contemporary self-taught Louisiana artists. The **Old US Mint,** 400 Esplanade, focuses not only on currency, but on the history of jazz in an exhibit that includes Satchmo's first horn. All open Tu-Su 9am-5pm. Old US Mint, Cabildo, Presbytère: $5; students, seniors, and active military $4. 1850 House, Mme. John's Legacy: $3/2. Under 12 free for all museums. 20% discount on tickets to 2 or more museums.

New Orleans Museum of Art, or NOMA (☎488-2631), in City Park, at the City Park/Metairie exit off I-10. Take the Esplanade bus from Canal St. or the Carollton Ave. bus. This magnificent museum houses art from North and South America, one of the 5 best glass collections in existence, opulent works by the jeweler Fabergé, a strong collection of French paintings, and some of the best African and Japanese cultural collections in the country. In 2003, the museum's new sculpture garden will open and host several special exhibits celebrating the Louisiana Purchase Bicentennial. Open Tu-Su 10am-5pm. $6, seniors $5, ages 3-17 $3. Free tours available; call for schedule.

The Voodoo Museum, 724 Dumaine St. (☎523-7685), in the Quarter. Learn why all those dusty shops are in the Quarter selling *gris-gris* and alligator parts at this quirky haunt. A priest or a priestess will be glad to do a reading or a ritual for a fee, or visitors can just walk through the rooms full of portraits and artifacts for the basic entrance fee. $7; students, seniors and military $5.50; high school $4.50; 12 and under $3.50.

Musée Conti Wax Museum, 917 Conti St. (☎525-2605 or 800-233-5405), between Burgundy and Dauphine St. A great mix of the historically important, sensationally infamous, and just plain kitschy history of New Orleans in 31 tableaux. Perennial favorites include a voodoo scene, Napoleon in the bathtub, and a mock-up of Madame LaLaurie's torture attic. Open M-Sa 10am-5:30pm, Su noon-5:30pm. $6.75, seniors $6.25, under 17 $5.75.

Confederate Museum, 929 Camp St. (☎523-4522), in a brownstone building called Memorial Hall, just south of Lee Circle at Howard St. and the I-10 Camp St. exit. The state's oldest museum is a wood-beamed, ancient hall lined with Confederate uniforms and flags, as well as a lot of Jefferson Davis memorabilia. Open M-Sa 10am-4pm. $5, students and seniors $4, under 12 $2.

Louisiana Children's Museum, 420 Julia St. (☎523-1357), between Magazine and Tchoupitoulas St. This place invites kids to play and learn as they star in their own news shows, run their own cafe, or shop in a re-created mini-mart. Toddlers have their own specially designed playscape. Open Apr.-Aug. M-Sa 9:30am-4:30pm, Su noon-4:30pm; Sept.-May closed M. $6.

Louisiana Nature and Science Center (☎246-5672), Joe Brown Memorial Park. Go east on I-10 and take Exit 244; the park is off Read Blvd. Trail walks, exhibits, planetarium, laser shows, and 86 acres of natural wildlife preserve. From Basin St., take bus #64 "Lake Forest Express" ($1.25) to reach this wonderful escape. Open Tu-F 9am-5pm, Sa 10am-5pm, Su noon-5pm. $5, seniors $4, ages 3-12 $3.

GIRLS GONE WILD French quarter shops sell beads for $1-5, but why buy them when you can *earn* them? The best bead bartering locations are strung along the 700th block of Bourbon St., especially near the balconies above the Cat's Meow and Tricou House. Women (and even men) who flash body parts on the street are compensated with beads. Only in New Orleans is exposing oneself so colorfully rewarded.

⬛ ENTERTAINMENT

THEATER & MUSIC

Le Petit Théâtre du Vieux Carré, 616 St. Peters St., is one of the city's most beloved and historical theaters. The oldest continuously operating community theater in the US, the 1789 building replicates the early 18th-century abode of Joseph de Pontalba, Louisiana's last Spanish governor. About five musicals and plays go up each year, as well as three fun productions in the "Children's Corner." (☎ 522-9958. Box office open M-Sa 10:30am-5:30pm, Su noon-5pm. $20 for plays, $26 for musicals.)

Uptown tends to house authentic Cajun dance halls and popular university hang-outs, while the **Marigny** is home to New Orleans's alternative/local music scene. Check out *Off Beat*, free in many local restaurants, or the Friday *Times-Picayune* to find out who's playing where. Born at the turn of the century in **Armstrong Park,** traditional New Orleans jazz still wails nightly at the tiny, dim, historic **Preservation Hall,** 726 St. Peters St. Jazz is in its most fundamental element here. With only two small ceiling fans trying to move the air around, most people can only stay for one set, meaning you can usually expect to find a place. (Daytime ☎ 522-2841 or 800-785-5772; after 8pm ☎ 523-8939. No food or drink allowed. Cover $5. Doors open at 8pm; music 8:30pm-midnight.) Keep your ears open for **Cajun** and **zydeco** bands, which use accordions, washboards, triangles, and drums to perform hot dance tunes (true locals two-step expertly) and saccharine waltzes. Anyone who thinks couple-dancing went out in the 50s should try a *fais-do-do,* a lengthy, wonderfully energetic traditional dance that got its name from the custom parents had of putting their children to sleep and then running off to dance the night away (*fais-do-do* is Cajun baby talk for "to make sleep").

FESTIVALS

New Orleans's **Mardi Gras** celebration is the biggest party of the year, a world-renowned, epic bout of lascivious debauchery that fills the three weeks leading up to Ash Wednesday—the beginning of Lent and a time of penance and deprivation in the Catholic tradition. Mardi Gras, which literally means "Fat Tuesday," is a sort of all-out hedonistic pleasure-fest before 40 days of purity. Parades, gala, balls, and general revelry take to the streets as tourists pour in by the plane-full (flights into the city and hotel rooms fill up months in advance). In 2003, Mardi Gras falls on March 4th, and the biggest parades and bulk of the partying will take place the two weeks prior to that. The ever-expanding **New Orleans Jazz and Heritage Festival** attracts 7000 musicians from around the country to the city's fairgrounds. The likes of Aretha Franklin, Bob Dylan, Patti LaBelle, and Wynton Marsalis have graced this festival. Less drunken and more serious than its Mardi Gras counterpart, music plays simultaneously on twelve stages in the midst of a huge food and crafts festival; the biggest names perform evening riverboat concerts. The festival grows bigger and, unfortunately, more commercialized each year. (☎ 522-4786; Apr. 25-May 4, 2003.)

The year 2003 also marks 200 years since Napoleon signed over almost half of the American continent to the United States. The **Louisiana Purchase Bicentennial** (☎ 225-342-9149; www.louisianapurchase2003.com) promises to be a substantial celebration, complete with exhibits and festivals throughout the entire year and across the state.

☑ NIGHTLIFE

Life in New Orleans is and always will be a party. On any night of the week, at any time of the year, the masses converge on **Bourbon St.** to drift in and out of bars and strip joints. Ask any local what to do on a weekend, and they'll probably tell you to avoid Bourbon at all costs; the street has become increasingly touristy of late. Where tons of independent, hole-in-the-wall bars, music clubs, and "gentlemen's clubs" used to create an air of classy sin, now chain bars repeat themselves over and over down the strip. Much of the titillating underground nudity and dancing has been ousted by crass porno chains like Hustler. To experience what the Quarter was like before the tourist traps took over, get off Bourbon and explore the less-traveled side streets. Go up around **Rampart St.** or northeast toward **Esplanade Ave.** and poke your head into quieter corners--you will be rewarded by hidden bars, wacky nightclubs, and dank dungeons. Of course, don't do this alone at night. **Marigny,** an up-and-coming nightclub district northeast of the Quarter, offers some swank bars and clubs, particularly on Frenchmen St. **Decatur St.,** near the French market, is a quieter, slightly touristy nightlife area.

While the Quarter offers countless bars and jazz, blues, and brass venues, be assured that there's more to New Orleans entertainment. Head uptown toward the bars and clubs of **Tulane University** to sample the collegiate culture.

Bars in New Orleans stay open late, and few keep a strict schedule; in general, they open around 11am and close around 3am, but many go all night when there's a crowd or a party. Most blocks feature at least one establishment with cheap draft beer and Hurricanes (sweet juice-and-rum drinks). All establishments are 21+ unless otherwise noted.

BARS

FRENCH QUARTER

☒ **Lafitte's Blacksmith Shop,** 941 Bourbon St. (☎522-9377), at Phillip St. Appropriately, one of New Orleans's oldest standing structures is a bar—one of the oldest bars in the US. Built in the 1730s, the building is still lit by candlelight after sunset. Named for the scheming hero of the Battle of New Orleans, it offers shaded relief from the elements of the city and a dim hiding place for celebrities. Live piano 8pm until late. Beers $4-5. Open daily 10 or 11am to 4 or 5am.

☒ **Funky Butt,** 714 N. Rampart St., (☎558-0872), is an awesome hideout to hear some late live jazz and marvel at the wonder of the *derrière*. Walk in to face a gigantic, languorous nude painting and hear the strains of a live band 5 ft. from the door. Stay to sip a funkybuttjuice ($6) and sit with only a score of people in the tiny space alongside the band. 7pm house band. Sets nightly 10pm and midnight. Cover $5-10. Open daily 7pm-2am.

Pat O'Brien's, 718 St. Peters St. (☎525-4823). Housed in the first Spanish theater in the US, this busy bar, one of the most famous in the French Quarter, bursts with happy (read: drunk) patrons who carouse in a courtyard lined with plants and flowers. Home of the original Hurricane; purchase your first in a souvenir glass ($8, without glass $6). Open Su-Th 10am-4am, F-Sa 10am-5am.

Pirate's Alley, 628 Pirate's Alley (☎586-0468), down the alley on your left when facing the front of St. Louis Cathedral. Alley cats will rub your ankles as you sip a white russian ($6) outside this cool dive of a bar. Its location on a side street in the Quarter, coupled with its plain wooden walls and awnings, make this bar feel like a genuine local hangout. Open daily 10am-4am.

Molly's at the Market, 1107 Decatur St. (☎525-5169). A vibrant late night retreat from the touristy frenzy of the Quarter, Molly's offers tasty and widely acclaimed frozen Irish coffee ($4.50), as well as a hang-out space for eclectic locals, old and young. Open daily 10am-6am.

Crescent City Brewhouse, 527 Decatur St. (☎522-0571). This classy brewpub sells its own blends, with names like "Black Forest" and "Red Stallion." "Drink and stroll" at their to-go bar in the doorway, or try some classy, expensive Southern fare (entrees $16-23) that come with tailored drink recommendations. Glass walls and balcony make for good people-watching, a wonderful activity when set to live jazz (nightly 6-9pm). 12 oz. $4, 20 oz. $5, or sample 5 different brews for $7. Open Su-Th 11am-10pm, F-Sa 11am-midnight.

O'Flaherty's Irish Channel Pub, 514 Toulouse St. (☎529-1317). O'Flaherty's bills itself as the meeting point of disparate Celtic nations, and it's not kidding. "The closest thing to a Gaelic embassy in town" is not a bad description. In addition to the bar, O'Flaherty's has a concert room, a lounge, and a courtyard. They also host annual festivals like the Celtic Festival (the first weekend in Sept.). Proudly serves *meade* and *potcheen* (Irish moonshine), drinks you'll be hard-pressed to find anywhere else in America. Eavesdrop on Gaelic conversation while listening to Scottish bagpipes, watching Irish dances, eating Irish food (shepherd's pie $9), and/or singing along to Irish tunes. Music Sept.-May Su-Th 8pm, F-Sa 9pm; June-Aug. W-Su 8pm. Special Irish breakfast Su 8am, $8. Cover $3-10. Open daily noon until usually 1:30 or 2am.

OUTSIDE THE QUARTER

Snug Harbor, 626 Frenchmen St. (☎949-0696), near Decatur St. Regulars include big names in modern jazz like Charmaine Neville and Ellis Marsalis. Cover is steep ($12-18), but the music and its fans are authentic. All ages. Shows nightly 9 and 11pm. Restaurant open Su-Th 5-11pm, F-Sa 5pm-midnight; bar until 1am.

Checkpoint Charlie's, 501 Esplanade (☎947-0979), is a combination bar, laundromat, and restaurant that feels like a cozy neighborhood coffeeshop or a wild nightclub, depending on where you're standing. In one night here you can drink while you wash your clothes, listen to a poetry slam over jazz, buy a used book, or have a greasy burger while shooting a game of pool. Live music nightly, usually starting around 10pm. Beer $2-3, pitchers $7.50. Burgers $5-7. No cover. Food served 24hr.

Donna's, 800 N. Rampart St. (☎596-6914). As one fan says, this is "the place where you can sit and watch New Orleans roll by." On the edge of the French Quarter, right where the gay bars face the projects, the extremes of the city swirl together in front of Donna's. Brass bands play inside, and the smell of ribs and chicken wafts out as customers sit on the sidewalk and take it all in. Open M and F-Su 6:30pm until 1:30am.

Carrollton Station, 8140 Willow St. (☎865-9190), at Dublin St. A cozy neighborhood club with live music, antique bar games, and friendly folks. As one of the regulars says, "a place with character full of characters." 12 beers on tap ($2-5) and nearly 40 varieties of rum. Music Th-Su at 10pm. Cover varies. Open daily 3pm-6am.

d.b.a., 618 Frenchmen St. (☎942-3731), next to Snug Harbor. Try one of the beers in their wood-paneled bar. Live music most nights at 10pm. Monthly beer and tequila tastings. Open M-F 4pm-4am, Sa-Su 4pm-5am.

Jimmy's, 8200 Willow (☎861-8200). When school is in session, this is where the college crowd goes wild—a huge dance floor and long-as-hell bar can accommodate tons of tightly packed twenty-somethings. Live music most weekends. Daily drink specials. 18+ for women, 19+ for men. Cover around $5. Open daily 9pm until late.

Dragon's Den, 435 Esplanade (☎949-1750), upstairs from Siam Cafe. This opium den-like establishment bills itself as a "social aid and pleasure club." Live music daily 10:30pm, Thursday poetry slam and open mic 8pm. Monday 2-for-1 hot *sake*. No cover M-Th, F-Sa $6. Open daily 6pm until dawn; food served until 1am.

DANCE CLUBS

FRENCH QUARTER

735 Nightclub and Bar, 735 Bourbon St. (☎581-6740). Great music and a hip mixed crowd keep this dance club energized well into the night. Techno, progressive house, and trance play downstairs, with 80s music on the 2nd fl. 18+. Cover $5, under 21 $10. Open W-Su 10pm-3am.

Shim Sham Club, 615 Toulouse St. (☎565-5400). Sophisticated cocktails and red leather booths downstairs, wild bands of most genres from rap to zydeco in the large hall in back, a cozy mini-bar with a hell motif upstairs—everything happens here. Sa night "Glitter glam rock 'n' roll" shows and 25¢ beers. Th night history of Alternative Rock 'n Roll lecture/performance and even the occasional theatrical play in the concert-hall-turned-theater. No cover before 11pm; varies after 11pm. Open daily 2pm-6am.

El Matador, 504 Esplanade Ave. (☎569-8361). A mix of patrons and a wide range of musical styles make this nightclub a good place to relax and start the night. Usually no cover, but it varies according to the fame of the band. Live flamenco show Sa 7:30pm. Open M-Th 9pm until late, F-Su 4pm until late.

House of Blues, 225 Decatur St. (☎529-2624). A sprawling complex with a large music/dance hall (capacity over 1000) and a balcony and bar overlooking the action. Concerts nightly 9:15pm. 18+. Cover usually $5-10, big names up to $30. Restaurant open Su-Th 11am-11pm, F-Sa 11am-midnight.

OUTSIDE THE QUARTER

▩ **Tipitina's,** 501 Napoleon Ave. (☎558-0204). The best local bands and some big national names—such as the Neville Brothers, John Goodman, and Harry Connick, Jr.—play so close you can almost touch them. Su 5-9pm feature Cajun *fais-do-dos*. 18+. Cover $4-25. Music usually W-Su at 10:30pm; call ahead for times and prices.

▩ **Mid City Lanes Rock 'n' Bowl,** 4133 S. Carrollton Ave. (☎482-3133), in the mini-mall at Tulane Ave. Uncut N'awlins that attracts tons of locals and celebrities in the know. The "home of Rock 'n' Bowl" is a bowling alley by day and dance club by night (you can bowl at night, too). Lanes $12 per hr. plus $1 for shoes. Drinks are $2.50-3.50. Live music Tu-W 8:30pm, Th 9:30pm, F-Sa 10pm. Th 9:30pm local zydeco. 18+ at night when the bar gets hopping. Cover $5-7. Open daily 12pm to around 1 or 2am.

The Red Room, 2040 S. Charles St. (☎528-9759). Latin beats and R&B mark this swanky throwback to the opulent, jazzy 1930s. One of the mellowest, classiest clubs in the Big Easy. Dress up lest you look drab against the posh red decor. W tango night. 18+. Cover $5-10. Open Su-F 7pm-2am, Sa 7pm-late; music starts at 9pm.

Maple Leaf, 8316 Oak St. (☎866-9359). The best local dance bar, with zydeco, brass band, and Cajun music, has everyone doing the two-step. Large, pleasant covered patio. Poetry readings Su 3pm, free. Cover $7. Music and dancing start M-Sa 10:30pm, Su 9pm. Open daily 3pm until late.

THE LOCAL STORY

GENDER JAMBALAYA

Crystal, 60, is a leading member of the New Orleans gay community. A transsexual, she says she was one of the first to bring about public awareness that there are transgendered people—"common, everyday people"—other than drag artists in the community. She is active in many organizations serving the BGLT community.

Q: Would you say that New Orleans is the most gay-friendly city in the US?
A: Yes, most definitely. New Orleans has always been a melting pot, because it was a port, and so much of the world came in. Everyone in a neighborhood had to live and work together, and you had to learn to accept those who were different.

Q: How does gay life in New Orleans differ from other cities?
A: The New Orleans community is unique—the whole community works very well together. Those who are just cross-dressers often don't have a ton of places to go. But you'll notice we don't have any "segregated" bars, that is, between men and women, leather and trans, etc. I used to work at one of the biggest women's bars in New Orleans, and I'd be at the door and we'd have people from New York and San Fran who were amazed that there were men, women, everybody else in the bar. "Oh, we don't do this at home." Well, that's your problem. That's what we do here.

Q: How has the city changed?
A: New Orleans doesn't change. Buildings change, but the atmosphere doesn't. There's just something that's always been here.

Whirling Dervish, 1135 Decatur St., (☎568-1111). This bar/Daniels/gathering place has known many names through the years, and its latest incarnation continues to attract the secret, underground elements of the city, from romantics and vampire-lovers to mystics and goths. Open daily 10pm-6am.
Cafe Brasil, 2100 Chartres St. (☎949-0851), at Frenchmen St. Unassuming by day, Brasil is full on weekend nights with locals who come to see a wide variety of New Orleans talent. All ages. Cover F-Sa after 11am $6-10. Open daily 7pm-late.

☑ GAY & LESBIAN ACTIVITIES

New Orleans also has a vibrant gay scene, rivalling and perhaps surpassing that of San Francisco, according to locals. Gay establishments cluster toward the northeast end of Bourbon St., and St. Ann St. is known to some as the **"Lavender Line."** The oldest bar in the city was gay-friendly farther back than any one can remember—meaning that, yes, one of the first structures used as a bar on American soil was a de facto gay bar.

Facts like this only skim the surface of gay history in New Orleans. Luckily, someone is keeping track: Robert Batson, "history laureate" of New Orleans, leads the **Gay Heritage Tour**—a walking tour through the French Quarter—leaving from Alternatives, 909 Bourbon St. It lasts for 2½hr. and is perhaps the best possible introduction to New Orleans for anyone, gay or straight. (☎945-6789. W and Sa 2pm. $20 per person. Reservations required.)

As for gay nightlife, to find the real lowdown, get a copy of *The Whiz Magazine*, a locally produced guide to BGLT nightlife; there's always a copy on top of the radiator in Cafe Lafitte in Exile. *Ambush* and *Eclipse* are more impersonal, mass-produced gay entertainment mags that can be found at many French Quarter businesses. For info and tailored entertainment and community fact sheets, go to the **Lesbian and Gay Community Center of New Orleans,** 2114 Decatur St., in Marigny. (☎945-1103. Open M-W 2-8pm, Th-F noon-8pm, Sa 11am-6pm, Su noon-6pm. Report hate crimes to 944-HEAL.)

NIGHTLIFE

Cafe Lafitte in Exile, 901 Bourbon St. (☎522-8397). This is where it all started. Exiled from Laffite's Blacksmith Shop in 1953 when Lafitte's came under new management, the ousted gay patrons trooped up the street to found this haven. On the opening night, surrounded by patrons dressed as their favorite exile, Cafe Lafitte in Exile lit an "eternal flame" (it still burns today) that aptly represents the soul of the gay community in New Orleans. Today, though Cafe Lafitte has video screens, occasional live music, pageants, and shows, it's still the same old neighborhood gathering place at heart. Open 24hr.

Kim's 940, 940 Elysian Fields Ave. (☎944-4888, for guest house info ☎258-2224). If you're a girl, go here. This new bar/dance club/guest house has quickly become the center of the New Orleans lesbian circuit, which is much smaller than the male-oriented nightlife. Dancing, drinking, and flirting mesh alongside the official BGLT Pride events and gatherings Kim's often hosts. All are welcome. Live DJ Th-Sa. Cover F $3, Sa $5. Open daily 4pm until everyone goes home.

Good Friends, 740 Dauphine St. (☎566-7191). This is a gay Cheers episode. A cozy, friendly neighborhood bar full of locals who are all too happy to welcome in a refugee from Bourbon St. They host the occasional pool tournament, drink specials, and "hot buns" contest, but usually things are pretty calm. Open 24hr.

Oz, 800 Bourbon St., (☎593-9491), hosts *Glitz,* a professional female impersonation extravaganza Th nights at 9pm, and bingo and professional dancers on the weekends. With a huge dance floor, video screens, a well-staffed bar, and an enormous sound system, the only flaw is the somewhat canned and unoriginal dance music. Open 24hr.

Cowpokes, 2240 St. Claude Ave. (☎947-0505), 1 block off Elysian Fields in Marigny. Line dancing, country-western games, ten-gallon hats, and spurs can be as wholesome as you want to make them. Cowgirls and pardners welcome. Th ladies' night, country line dancing lessons and 2-for-1 drinks 8-11pm. Open Su-Th 4pm-1am, F-Sa 4pm-2am.

Bourbon Pub & Parade, 801 Bourbon St. (☎529-2107), is directly opposite Oz, but more dance-oriented and less show-oriented. The Parade disco is upstairs nightly after 10pm. Two bars, video screens, and live dancers get the crowd going. Because it's farther up Bourbon St. than most gay bars, unwitting tourists and the curious drift in relatively frequently. As a result, the crowd is a mixture of soccer moms, drunken frat boys, gay and lesbian tourists, and natives. Open 24hr.

◪ OUTDOOR ACTIVITIES

The St. Charles Streetcar eventually makes its way to **Audubon Park,** near **Tulane University.** Audubon contains lagoons, statues, stables, and the award-winning ◪**Audubon Zoo,** where white alligators swim in a re-created Louisiana swamp. Tigers, elephants, rhinos, sea lions, and all the standard zoo residents are grouped into exhibit areas that highlight historical and natural regions of the globe, while peacocks roam the walkways freely. Free museum shuttle between park entrance and zoo every 15min. (☎581-4629. Zoo open in winter daily 9:30am-5pm; in summer M-F 9:30am-5pm, Sa-Su 9:30am-6pm. $9, seniors $5.75, ages 2-12 $4.75.)

One of the most unique sights in the New Orleans area, the coastal wetlands along Lake Salvador make up a segment of the **Jean Lafitte National Historical Park** called the **Barataria Preserve,** 7400 Barataria Blvd. South of New Orleans, take Business 90 to Rte. 45. (☎589-2330. Daily park-sponsored foot tour through the swamp 11am. Open daily 7am-5pm; extended summer hours. Visitors Center open daily 9am-5pm. Free.) Many commercial boat tours operate around the park; **Cypress Swamp Tours** will pick you up from your hotel for free, but the tour itself is damn expensive. (☎581-4501 or 800-633-0503. 2hr. tours 9:30, 11:30am, 1:30, and 3:30pm. $22, ages 6-12 $12. Call for reservations.)

BATON ROUGE ☎225

Once the site of a tall cypress tree marking the boundary between rival Native American tribes, Baton Rouge ("red stick") has blossomed into Louisiana's capital and second largest city. State politics have shaped this town—it was once the home of notorious governor, senator, and populist demagogue "Kingfish" Huey P. Long. The presence of **Louisiana State University (LSU)** adds an element of youth and rabid Tigertown loyalty. Baton Rouge has a simple meat-and-potatoes flavor, albeit spiced with a history of political corruption, that contrasts the flamboyant sauciness of New Orleans.

🔢 PRACTICAL INFORMATION. Close to downtown, **Greyhound,** 1253 Florida Blvd. (☎383-3811 or 800-231-2222; open 24hr.), at 13th St., sends buses to Lafayette (1hr., 12 per day, $12.25) and New Orleans (2hr., 8 per day, $11). *The area is unsafe at night.* **Buses: Capitol Transportation,** ☎336-0821. **Taxis: Yellow Cab,** ☎926-6400. **Visitor info: State Capitol Visitors Center,** on the 1st fl. of the State Capitol. (☎342-7317. Open daily 8am-4:30pm.) **Baton Rouge Convention and Visitors Bureau,** 730 North Blvd. (☎383-1825 or 800-527-6843. Open M-F 8am-5pm.) For community information, including weather, call **Community Connection** (☎267-4221). **Post Office:** 750 Florida Blvd., off River Rd. (☎800-275-8777. Open M-F 7:30am-5pm, Sa 8am-12:30pm.) **Hotlines: 24hr. Crisis line,** ☎924-1231. **Internet access: State Library of Louisiana,** 701 N. Fourth St., a beautiful library that most residents don't go to regularly, making it a quiet oasis of free, fast Internet access—most often without a wait. (☎342-4915. Open daily 8am-4:30pm.) **ZIP code:** 70821. **Area code:** 225.

🏨 ACCOMMODATIONS. Though Baton Rouge has mostly overpriced chain hotels squatting along the highway, there are some cheap accommodations in town. The city's cheapest deal is **Allround Suites ❶,** 2045 N. 3rd St., but make sure you get there before 8pm to check in on weekdays, when they lock the gates. All rooms have fridge, stove, satellite TV, pool, and laundry. (☎344-6000. Reception M-F 8am-8pm, Sa 9am-9pm, Su 9am-8pm. Singles $27-37; doubles $43. Credit card or $25 cash deposit required. Wheelchair accessible.) One of the best of the chains is **Highland Inn ❷,** 2605 S. Range Ave., at I-12 Exit 10 in Denham Springs, 15min. from downtown. Only one year old, the building still gleams. (☎225-667-7177. Cable TV, continental breakfast, free local calls, and pool. Singles $40; doubles $45.) **KOA Campground ❶,** 7628 Vincent Rd., 1 mi. off I-12 at the Denham Springs exit, keeps 110 well-maintained sites, clean facilities, and a big pool. (☎664-7281 or 800-562-5673. Sites $19; full RV hookup $27, 50 amp $29. Kabins $35.)

🍴 FOOD. Downtown, sandwich shops and cafes line 3rd St. Head to LSU at the intersection of Highland Rd. and Chimes St., off I-10, for cheaper chow and an abundance of bars and smoothie shops. **Louie's Cafe ❷,** 209 W. State St., grills up fabulous omelettes ($5.25-11) and some great veggie fare in a cross between college hangout and mama's kitchen. (☎346-8221. Veggie po' boy $6.75. Open 24hr.) When you want a good sit-down meal, check out **The Chimes ❸,** 3357 Highland Rd., at (surprise) Chimes St. A big restaurant and bar where you can sample a brew from almost every country, they stock 120 different beers with 30 on tap. Start the meal with an appetizer of Louisiana alligator (farm-raised, marinated, fried, and served with Dijon mustard sauce) for $7.50, then dig into some $8 crawfish *étouffée.* (☎383-1754. Seafood and steak entrees $8-14. Open M-Sa 11am-2am, Su 11am-11:45pm.)

◙ SIGHTS. In a move reminiscent of Ramses II, Huey Long ordered the construction of the unique **Louisiana State Capitol,** a magnificent, modern, and somewhat startling skyscraper, to be completed over a mere 14 months in 1931 and 1932.

Called "the house that Huey built," the building was meant to raise Louisiana's image and prestige and pave Long's path to the presidency of the US. It's ironic, then, that Long was assassinated inside it three years later; toward the back of the 1st floor a display marks the exact spot of the shooting. The **observation deck,** on the 27th fl., provides a fantastic view of the surrounding area. (☎342-7317. Open daily 8am-4pm. Free.) The **Old State Capitol,** 100 North Blvd., resembles a cathedral with a fantastic cast-iron spiral staircase and domed stained glass. Inside are interactive political displays urging voter responsibility alongside exhibits about Huey Long and Louisiana's tumultuous (and often corrupt) political history. (☎800-488-2968. Open Tu-Sa 10am-4pm, Su noon-4pm. $4, students $2, seniors $3.)

The **Old Governor's Mansion,** 502 North Blvd., may look a little familiar—the venerable Huey Long insisted that his governor's residence resemble his ultimate goal— the White House. The building is now home to the **Foundation for Historical Louisiana.** Inside, a museum displays many of Long's personal belongings including a book he wrote, somewhat prematurely, called *My First Days in the White House.* (☎387-2464. Open Tu-F 10am-4pm, but hours may vary. $5, students $3, seniors $4.)

The **Louisiana Art and Science Museum (LASM),** 100 S. River Rd., is a large, expanding complex and a strange combination of art gallery and hands-on science museum that will have a new planetarium in 2003. From October 2003 to January 2004, LASM will host *The Riches and Splendor of Josephine Bonaparte,* an exhibit of Josephine artifacts lent from the Malmaison in France in honor of the statewide Louisiana Purchase celebration. (☎344-5272. Open Tu-F 10am-3pm, Sa 10am-4pm, Su 1-4pm. $4; students, seniors, and children $3. First Su of every month free.) At the **USS Kidd and Nautical Center,** 305 S. River Rd., at Government St. and the Mississippi River, you can check out the *Destroyer Kidd,* which was hit directly by a kamikaze during its career and has been restored to its WWII glory. Visitors can explore most of the nooks and crannies of its hull. The nautical museum features a huge model ship collection and a full-size mock-up of the gun deck of "Old Ironsides." (☎342-1942. Open daily 9am-5pm. $6, children $3.50.)

The **⬛LSU Rural Life Museum,** 4560 Essen Ln., just off I-10 at Exit 160, depicts the life of 18th- and 19th-century Creoles and working-class Louisianans through their original furnished shops, cabins, and storage houses. Fifteen 19th-century structures were physically moved from their original sites by Steele Burden, the founder of the museum, who installed them on the museum's 10 acres. The museum also has a prodigious collection of daily life artifacts, ranging from dolls to farm implements to a horsedrawn, glass-windowed hearse. If you're polite, the museum's staff might let you feed the resident oxen some cucumbers. The museum is adjacent to the lakes, winding paths, and flowers of the **Windrush Gardens.** (☎765-2437. Both open daily 8:30am-5pm. $7, seniors $6, ages 5-12 $4.)

NATCHITOCHES ☎318

Be careful not to say it how it's spelled; pronounced *NAK-ah-tish,* the oldest city in Louisiana was founded in 1714 by the French to facilitate trade with the Spanish in Mexico. The town was named after the original Native American inhabitants of the region. With its strategic location along the banks of the Red River, Natchitoches should have become a major port city, much like New Orleans. A big logjam, however, changed the course of the city's history, redirecting the Red River and leaving the town high and dry, with only a 36 mi. long lake running along historic downtown. More recently, the town was the setting for the 1988 movie *Steel Magnolias,* which cast most of the townspeople as extras. Ask locals about *Steel Magnolias,* and they'll likely tell you that they went to school with one of the characters depicted—if you're going to visit Natchitoches, see the movie first.

⁷ PRACTICAL INFORMATION. Downtown Natchitoches is tiny. **Hwy. 6** enters town from the west off I-49 and becomes **Front St.**, the main drag, where it follows the **Cane River**, running north until it becomes Hwy. 6 again. **2nd St.** runs parallel to Front St., and the town stems out across the lake from those two streets. Historic homes highlight the town, while the plantations lie from 7 to 18 mi. south of town, off **Rte. 1 S.** Both the plantations and Rte. 1 follow the Cane River. **Greyhound,** 331 Cane River Shopping Center (☎352-8341; open M-F 8am-5pm), sends buses to: Dallas (6hr., 3 per day, $55); Houston (8-10hr., 2 per day, $59); and New Orleans (6½hr., 3 per day, $49). Visitor info is at **Natchitoches Convention and Visitors Bureau,** 781 Front St. (☎352-8072 or 800-259-1714; www.natchitoches.net. Open M-F 8am-6pm, Sa 9am-5pm, Su 10am-4pm.) The **post Office** is at 240 Saint Denis St. (☎352-2161. Open M-F 8am-4:30pm, Sa 9-11am.) **ZIP code:** 71457. **Area code:** 318.

Γ₁ ACCOMMODATIONS. Don't say we didn't warn you: Natchitoches isn't a cheap town. As the "B&B Capital" of Louisiana, Natchitoches abounds with cozy rooms in historic homes, and the ambiance comes with a high price. Beware of Christmas time; during the annual **Festival of Lights** (see below), room rates as much as triple, and reservations are booked months in advance. Happily, the B&Bs are usually worth the money. The **Natchitoches Convention and Visitors Bureau** has a handy listing of all the B&Bs in town.

One of the best deals is the **Fleur de Lis Bed and Breakfast ❸,** 336 Second St., near the southern end of town. The Fleur de Lis is an adorable, gingerbready Victorian with a whimsical pastel exterior and an aromatic herb garden. It's set apart from the city's other B&Bs (almost 40 total) in that it's not too large or hotel-like, it's close to downtown, and it has a quirky flavor all its own. (☎352-6621 or 800-489-6621. Rooms Jan.-Nov. $65-85, Dec. $100. Inquire about children under 12.) To experience the lifestyle of artistic reverie, book a stay at a real log cabin built in 1934 and designed to house artists and fan their creative flames, **The Log Cabin Guest House ❺,** 614 Williams Ave., just left of the bridge on the east bank of the Cane River Lake, gives you the chance to flirt with artistic reverie. The cabin is directly on the water and is fully equipped with 21st-century amenities, though the steep walk down to its door and its low-slung, rustic air still smacks of Bohemian spirit. (☎357-0520. Check-in 3pm. Check-out 11am. Cabin for 4 $110-150.)

West of town, where I-49 meets **Rte. 6,** sit chain motels that aren't much cheaper than the B&B's. One of the nicest is the well-furnished **Microtel Inn ❸,** 5335 Rte. 6 W. (☎214-0700 or 888-771-7171. A/C, cable TV, fridges, pool access, and continental breakfast. Singles $49; doubles $56. 10% AAA discount.) The 600,000-acre **Kisatchie National Forest ❶** offers basic outdoor living with trails and scenic overlooks, but getting to that pristine beauty is a trek. The park is about 25 mi. south of the Rte. 6 Ranger Station near Natchitoches, and many of its sites, though equipped with bathhouses, are primitive. The **Kisatchie Ranger District,** 106 Rte. 6 W, ¼ mi. past the Microtel Inn, has maps, camping information, and park conditions, and provides help finding the well-hidden sites. (☎352-2568. Open M-F 8am-4:30pm. Sites $2-3. No hookups.)

⊡⊠ FOOD & NIGHTLIFE. Lasyone's ❷, 622 2nd St., is the place to go for downhome cooking. Their specialty is meat pie ($2.75; with salad bar and veggies $7.25), and travelers can get an eyeful of the 5 ft. model in the window before enjoying a more manageable size. (☎352-3353. Lunch specials $6. Open M-Sa 7am-7pm.) **Mama's Oyster House ❸,** 606 Front St., is a downtown staple, cooking up lunch gumbo for $9 a bowl and oyster po' boys for $7. For dinner, fried crawfish ($12) complements the live entertainment on the first and third Friday of each month. (☎356-7874. Open M-Sa 10am-11pm.) Drink with a friendly, local crowd at **Pioneer**

Pub, 812 Washington St., opposite the Visitors Center. (☎ 352-4884. Live music Th-Sa at 9pm. Open daily 11am-2am, or until the crowd leaves.) For those who want to go jukin', seek out **Roque's Grocery,** 237 Carver St. (don't bother looking for the number; it fell off long ago). A throwback to the old Southern tradition of juke joints—usually grocery stores or gas stations that locals flocked to at night to listen to bands and dance the night away—Roque's is only open a couple of Friday nights a month. When it's open, bands from all over come to play old-school style. Largely unadvertised, ask around to find out if a show is in town. To get there, cross the river from Front St., turn right on Williams, then left onto Carver. Home to **Northwestern State University,** located along Rte. 6 on the western side of town, Natchitoches also has its share of rowdy college bars.

◙ ⬛ SIGHTS & ENTERTAINMENT. Much of Natchitoches's charm lies on the Cane River Lake along **Front St.,** where coffeeshops, little restaurants, and antique stores fill the storefronts of historic buildings that date back to the mid-19th century. To see Natchitoches' landmarks from the comfort of a large, green trolley, including many of the *Steel Magnolias* filming sites, take a 1hr. ride with the **Natchitoches Transit Company,** 100 Rue Beau Port, next to the tourist center just off Front St. (☎ 356-8687. Call for departure times. $8, seniors $7, ages 3-12 $5.)

Many of the popular tourist destinations are outside the city limits in the **Cane River National Heritage Area,** the plantation-dotted and Creole-influenced countryside around Natchitoches. The Visitors Center has tons of information about all the plantations and a free tourist newspaper, *Historic Natchitoches,* which lists all the points of interest in the area. To see the next generation of handbags and belts, drive out to ▨**Bayou Pierre Gator Park & Show,** 8 mi. north of Natchitoches off Rte. 1 N (look for the big school bus in the shape of a gator off Rte. 1). Originally a conservation project for the scaly beasts, the park now entertains visitors with regular feeding shows, a snake house, an aviary, and a nutria exhibit (nutria are Louisiana swamp rats the size of small dogs). In addition to alligators, the management collects knives; check out the "world's largest folding pocketknife" in the gift shop. (☎ 354-0001 or 877-354-7001. Open daily mid-Apr. to Oct. 10am-6pm; call for winter hours, when the alligators are hibernating. $6, ages 3-12 $4.50.)

A string of plantation homes line the Cane River, south of downtown along Rte. 1. The **Melrose** plantation, 14 mi. south on Rte. 1, then left on Rte. 493, is unique in origin—its female founder was an ex-slave. The African House, one of the outhouses, is the oldest structure of Congo-like architecture on the North American continent. William Faulkner, John Steinbeck, and Sherwood Anderson all stayed on the plantation, as did the painter Clementine Hunter, Louisiana's most celebrated primitive artist. (☎ 379-0055. Open daily noon-4pm. $6, ages 13-17 $4, ages 6-12 $3.)

While Natchitoches may not see a white Christmas, she'll most definitely see a light Christmas. The town's residents spend months putting up some 300,000 Christmas bulbs, only to be greeted in turn by 150,000 camera-toting tourists flocking like moths to the **City of Lights** display, held during the **Christmas Festival of Lights.** The month-long exhibition peaks the first weekend in December when a carnival-like atmosphere—complete with a fair, fireworks, and parade—fills the air. (☎ 800-259-1714; www.christmasfestival.com. Dec. 2, 2002 to Jan 3, 2003.)

ACADIANA

Throughout the early 18th century, the English government in Nova Scotia became increasingly jealous of the prosperity of French settlers *(Acadians)* and deeply offended by their refusal to kneel before the British Crown. During the war with France in 1755, the British rounded up the Acadians and deported them by the

FOWL PLAY
Cockfighting in Louisiana

"Do you know where I can see any cockfights around here?" I never thought I'd be asking this, especially to a delicate old lady at the Lafayette Visitors Center, but my editors had discovered that Louisiana was one of three states in the US that allows cockfighting and demanded that I "go find out about it." To my surprise, the woman smiled and leaned toward me, not at all perturbed. She had a friend, "a retired school-teacher," who could help me. And so I went out to Edith Lanphier's house, walking past large, brightly-plumed chickens to talk about raising prize-winning gamecocks. Edith began on the defensive, "what some people forget is this is just a chicken, good for frying and baking and in gumbo." But once she saw that I wasn't judging her and just wanted to hear her story, she opened up.

Cockfighting, according to Edith, is a centuries-old sport that is found across the US, from California to Philadelphia, both in cities and out in the country. It has been traced back to Egyptian times, and in Spanish churches, cockfighting pits are built near the altars. Even in the US, look around for the distinctive triangular tin huts lining backyards or fields—the mark of a trainer or breeder. Raising, breeding, and fighting chickens is a full-time job, and three different magazines are dedicated to the subject. Cockfighting is a winter sport, though small "derbies" are held year-round in the backs of stores, in fields, and in homes. The major derbies, one of the biggest of which is in Sunset, LA, attract cocks and their trainers from around the world for large, 5-cock death duels that award thousands of dollars.

Edith took me outside and walked me by the wooden pens of hens and their chicks. She showed me the cages built to hold the immature males, which take two years to reach adulthood, when their spurs—the pointy built-in weapons all gamecocks have on their legs—harden. We walked past rows and rows of mature roosters with beautiful feathers, each tied by the leg with a cord to his own little triangular shelter, his own territory. "Territorial," she explains. "That's why they fight—their instinct is to protect their territory. It's not anything we do to them. It's instinct." She picked up one of the roosters and shows me how it flies when she throws it, to exercise the wings, and tells me that manure is dumped in the pens to make the chickens scratch and walk, to exercise their legs.

Edith glances slyly at me. "Do you want to see them fight?" I quickly say, "well, I don't want any to get hurt..." but Edith picks up the rooster and brings it near another. When they get within five feet of each other, both birds transform from ordinary chickens into a huge, aggressive flash of feathers. They caw at each other, challenging. Edith drops her rooster, and immediately, they are a whirl of feathers, darting, flying, jumping, turning. They jab and feint at each other like fencers, their plumage on end. They are gorgeous. This isn't a bloodbath—it's a dance. Edith picks the rooster up again deftly—"they can't do too much damage in a short time," she says—and that's the end of it. Both cocks deflate, ordinary and docile once more.

I left Edith with a new, decidedly positive opinion on cockfighting. Yes, these animals kill each other in a blood sport that they are raised for. Yes, gamblers stake their wins and losses on fast deaths. But what I saw was not a depraved breeding ground for manipulated animals, but rather a race of birds that live, in immaculate conditions, for the fight of their lives. "They would do this anyway," Edith says. She is right—the only thing humans add to instinct is a forum, an organization. Compared to chickens that Americans eat everyday, fighting cocks have long, comfortable lives, and die doing what they do with honor. Compared to being raised for food in a tiny cage with no exercise before being slaughtered slowly and painfully, I would choose the life of a fighting cock any day—and I think I may become a vegetarian.

Julia Reischel is a researcher-writer for Let's Go: USA 2003. *Originally from Washington, D.C., she is pursuing a degree in the History and Literature of Latin America and America at Harvard University. She still wants to be a gamecock when she grows up.*

shipload in what came to be called *le grand dérangement*, "the Great Upheaval." The "Cajuns" (as they are known today) of St. Martin, Lafayette, New Iberia, and St. Mary parishes are descendants of these settlers. Since the relocation, several factors have threatened Acadian culture. In the 1920s, Louisiana passed laws forcing Acadian schools to teach in English. Later, during the oil boom of the 1970s and 1980s, oil executives and developers envisioned the Acadian center of Lafayette as the Houston of Louisiana and threatened to flood the area with mass culture. The proud people of southern Louisiana have resisted homogenization—the state is officially bilingual.

LAFAYETTE ☎337

The center of Acadiana, Lafayette is the perfect place to savor boiled crawfish or two-step to a fiddle and accordion. Get beyond the highway's chains and into downtown on Jefferson St., and there is no question that Cajuns rule the roost. Cajun music and Creole zydeco heats up dance floors every night of the week, and locals continue to answer their phones with a proud *bonjour*.

ORIENTATION & PRACTICAL INFORMATION. Lafayette stands at a crossroads. **I-10** leads east to New Orleans and west to Lake Charles; **U.S. 90** heads south to New Iberia and the Atchafalaya Basin and north to Alexandria and Shreveport; **U.S. 167** runs north into central Louisiana. Most of the city is west of the **Evangeline Thwy. (U.S. 49/U.S. 90),** which runs north-south. **Jefferson Blvd.** intersects Evangeline Thwy. and is the main street through town. **Johnston St.** delineates the east border of downtown with many fast-food restaurants. **Amtrak,** 133 E. Grant St. (☎800-872-7245), sends three trains per week to Houston (5½hr., $35), New Orleans (4hr., $21), and San Antonio (10hr., $55). **Greyhound,** 315 Lee Ave. (☎235-1541; open 24hr.), buses to Baton Rouge (1hr., 12 per day, $12.25), New Iberia (30min., 2 per day, $7.75), and New Orleans (3½hr., 10 per day, $16.25). Amtrak and Greyhound will move to a new, central terminal in 2003; call for details. The **Lafayette Bus System,** 1515 E. University St., is centered at Lee and Garfield St. (☎291-8570. Infrequent service M-Sa 6:30am-6:30pm; service until 11pm on some routes. Buses approximately every 30min. 75¢, seniors and disabled 35¢, ages 5-12 50¢.) Services include: **Taxis: Yellow/Checker Cab Inc.,** ☎234-2111. **Visitor info: Lafayette Parish Convention and Visitors Commission,** 1400 N. Evangeline Thwy. (☎232-3808. Open M-F 8:30am-5pm, Sa-Su 9am-5pm.) **Medical Services:** Lafayette General Medical Center, 1214 Coolidge Ave. (☎289-7991). **Post Office:** 1105 Moss St. (☎269-7111. Open M-F 8am-5:30pm, Sa 8am-noon.) **ZIP code:** 70501. **Area code:** 337.

ACCOMMODATIONS & FOOD. Inexpensive hotels line the Evangeline Thwy. **Travel Host Inn South ❷,** 1314 N. Evangeline Thwy., rents out clean rooms with cable TV, microwaves, fridges, continental breakfast, and an outdoor pool. (☎233-2090. Singles $30; doubles $35.) Close to the center of Lafayette, **Acadiana Park Campground ❶,** 1201 E. Alexander, off Louisiana Ave., has 75 sites with access to tennis courts and a soccer field. (☎291-8388. Office open Sa-Th 8am-5pm, F 8am-8pm. Full hookup $9.) The lakeside **KOA Lafayette ❶,** 5 mi. west of town on I-10 at Exit 97, has over 200 sites and offers a store, mini-golf course, and two pools. (☎235-2739. Office open daily 7:30am-8:30pm. Sites $19, with water and electricity $24.50, full hookup $26.)

It's not hard to find reasonably priced Cajun and Creole cuisine in Lafayette, a city that prides itself on its food. Of course, it also prides itself on music, which can be found live in most of those same restaurants at night. Since 1927, **Dwyer's Cafe ❶,** 323 Jefferson St., a diner with stained glass and murals on the walls, has been the best place in town to get breakfast or lunch. They serve a bang-up break-

THE HIDDEN DEAL

I SAW YOU STANDING ALONE

For one of the best lodging experiences in the South, travelers of all stripes should head straight downtown to the ⌂ **Blue Moon Guest House.** As you walk in, take a gander at the bottle tree in the backyard, check out the walkway paved with (fake) doubloons, or immerse yourself in the local art showcased on the surrounding walls. Chat with the hosts about their world travels in French, or let them tell about the music scene in Lafayette. The Blue Moon offers spacious common areas, a deck, backyard, and an attached "saloon" where local and out-of-town bands whoop it up Thursday through Saturday. (Of course, they're done by 11pm to give sleepy guests and neighbors some shut-eye.) Kitchen, Internet access ($3 per day), beautiful baths, large, air-conditioned dorms, and spacious, comfy private rooms are a steal. **The Blue Moon Saloon,** in the backyard of the hostel, is quickly making a name for itself as a nice place to have a beer and watch some local or out-of-town bands at close range. *(215 E. Convent St. Take Exit 103A from I-10, turn south on Johnston and left on Convent. ☎ 234-3442. Check-in 8am-noon and 5-10pm. Check-out 11am. Lockout 10am-5pm. Dorms $15; private rooms $40-55, on festival weekends $70.* ❶*)*

fast (grits, eggs, ham, biscuits, juice, and coffee) for $4. At lunch locals saunter in from the heat to eat a plate lunch (different everyday) of gigantic proportions for $7. (☎ 235-9364. Open M-F 5am-4pm, Sa-Su 5am-2pm.) In central Lafayette, **Chris' Po' boys ❷,** 631 Jefferson St., offers seafood platters ($7-10) and—whaddya know—po' boys for under $6. (☎ 234-1696. F night live blues and Cajun. Open M-Th 10:30am-8:30pm, F 10:30am-9pm.) **The Filling Station ❶,** 900 Jefferson St., lives up to name by occupying the shell of an old gas station while serving gigantic burritos and burgers for scandalously low prices. A popular, relaxing local hangout with outdoor tables, their full bar will fill your tank nicely, too. (☎ 291-9625. Burritos $2.95. Margaritas $4.50. Kitchen open M-F 11am-9pm; bar open until people empty out.) **The Judice Inn ❶,** 3134 Johnston St., serves up great burgers in a roadside time-warp the old-fashioned way—without fries. (☎ 984-5614. Cheeseburgers $2. Open M-Sa 10am-10pm.)

◪ **SIGHTS.** Driving through south-central Louisiana means driving over America's largest swamp, the Atchafalaya Basin. The **Atchafalaya Fwy.** (I-10 between Lafayette and Baton Rouge) crosses 32 mi. of swamp and cypress trees. To get down and dirty dancing on the levee and possibly see some gators, exit at Henderson (Exit 115), turn right, then immediately left; drive 5 mi. on Rte. 352, until the road hits a large earthen wall. This is the border of the swamp itself, which has many "landings" at its edge. Follow signs to **McGee's Landing,** 1337 Henderson Rd., which sends three 1½hr. **boat tours** into the Basin each day. (☎ 228-2384 or 800-445-6681. Tours daily 10am, 1, and 3pm. Spring and fall sunset tour 5pm. $12, seniors and under 12 $10, under 2 free.) The **Acadian Cultural Center,** 501 Fisher Rd. (take Johnston St. to Surrey, then follow the signs) is a unit of the **Jean Lafitte National Historical Park and Preserve** that runs throughout the delta region of Louisiana. The Acadian Center has a dramatic 40min. documentary chronicling the arrival of the Acadians in Louisiana, as well as terrific bilingual exhibits on Cajun history and culture. (☎ 232-0789. Open daily 8am-5pm. Shows every hr. 9am-4pm. Free.) Next door, a "living museum" re-creates the Acadian settlement of **Vermilionville,** 1600 Surrey St., with music, crafts, food, actors in costume, and dancing on the Bayou Vermilion banks. (☎ 233-4077 or 800-992-2968. Live bands Su 1-4pm. Cajun cooking lessons daily 10:30am, 12:30, and 1:30pm. Open Tu-Su 10am-4pm. $8, seniors $6.50, ages 6-18 $5.) **Acadian Village,** 200 Greenleaf Rd., features authentic 19th-century Cajun homes with a fascinating array of artifacts and displays. Take Johnston (U.S. 167 S) to Ridge

Rd., then left on Broussard, and follow the signs. While at the village, view a small collection of Native American artifacts at the **Native American Museum,** or see the collection of 19th-century medical paraphernalia at the **Doctor's House.** (☎981-2489 or 800-962-9133. Both open daily 10am-5pm. $7, seniors $6, ages 6-14 $4.) Next to the cathedral, the 400-year-old **St. John's Cathedral Oak,** 914 St. John St., shades an entire lawn with spidery branches reaching from a trunk with a 19 ft. circumference. The largest branch weighs an astonishing 72 *tons.*

🎭🎵 **ENTERTAINMENT & NIGHTLIFE.** While in Lafayette, be sure to take advantage of the many local festivals and music performances, though be warned that hotel rates rise sharply with the noise level. Lafayette kicks off **Downtown Alive!,** a 12-week annual concert series held at the 700 block of Jefferson St., playing everything from New Wave to Cajun and zydeco. (☎291-5566. Apr.-June and Sept.-Nov. F 5:30pm, music 6-8:30pm.) The **Festival International de Louisiane** is the largest outdoor free francophone festival in the US, transforming Lafayette into a gigantic, French-speaking fairground for a wild weekend in April. Book a hotel or campground well in advance; prices will likely double. (☎232-8086. April 23-April 27, 2003.) The **Breaux Bridge Crawfish Festival** in nearby Breaux Bridge, 10 mi. east on I-10, stages crawfish races, live music, dance contests, cook-offs, and a crawfish-eating contest. (☎332-6655. May 2-4, 2003.)

To find the best zydeco in town, pick up a copy of *The Times,* free at restaurants and gas stations. On Sunday afternoons, the place to be is **Angelle's Whiskey River Landing,** 1365 Henderson Levee Rd., in Breaux Bridge, where live cajun music heats up the dance floor on the very lip of the levee looking out over the swamp. (☎228-8567. Live music Sa 9pm-1am, Su 1-4pm.) **Hamilton's Zydeco Club,** 1808 Verot School Rd., is just one of the many places to cut loose at night with live Cajun bands and wild dancing. (☎991-0783. Open daily 5pm to whenever the crowd dies down.) **Grant St. Dance Hall,** 113 Grant St., features bands playing everything from zydeco to metal. (☎237-8513. 18+. Cover usually $5-10. Only open days of shows; call ahead.) **Randol's,** 2320 Kaliste Saloom Rd., romps with live Cajun and zydeco music nightly and doubles as a restaurant. (☎981-7080. Open Su-Th 5-10pm, F-Sa 5-11pm.) At **El Sid O's Blues and Zydeco,** 1523 Martin Luther King Dr., you might glimpse the legendary Buckwheat Zydeco. (☎318-235-0647. Open F-Su 7pm-2am.)

ARKANSAS

Encompassing the Ozark and Ouachita mountains, the clear waters of Hot Springs, and miles of lush pine forests, "the Natural State" lives up to its nickname. The state's subcultures are as varied as its geography. The bluesy Mississippi Delta region seeps into southeast Arkansas, while the northern Ozark mountains support a close-knit, no-pretenses community with a rich heritage all its own. All across Arkansas, however, one thing remains constant—travelers are easily accepted into the friendly family.

🧭 **PRACTICAL INFORMATION**

Capital: Little Rock.

Visitor info: Arkansas Dept. of Parks and Tourism, One Capitol Mall, Little Rock 72201 (☎501-682-7777 or 800-628-8725; www.arkansas.com). Open M-F 8am-5pm.

Postal Abbreviation: AR. **Sales Tax:** 6%.

LITTLE ROCK
☎ **501**

Located squarely in the middle of the state along the Arkansas River, Little Rock became a major trading city in the 19th century. A small rock just a few feet high served as an important landmark for boats pushing their way upstream, and, lo and behold, Little Rock was born. The capital was the focus of a nationwide civil rights controversy in 1957, when Governor Orval Faubus and local white segregationists violently resisted nine black students who entered Central High School under the shields of the National Guard. Fortunately, Little Rock has since become a more integrated community and a cosmopolitan center for the state with outdoor markets and a thriving downtown.

■ **PRACTICAL INFORMATION.** Little Rock is at the intersection of **I-40** and **I-30**, 140 mi. west of Memphis. Downtown, numbered streets run east-west, while named streets run north-south. Major streets are **Main** and **Martin Luther King Jr. St.** Near the river, Markham is 1st St. and Capitol is 5th St. The east side of Markham St. is now President Clinton Ave. and moves through the hopping Riverwalk district. North Little Rock is essentially a separate city across the river from Little Rock proper. **Greyhound,** 118 E. Washington St. (☎372-3007), at Poplar St., is in North Little Rock; take bus #7 or 18. Buses run to: Memphis (2½hr., 8 per day, $26); New Orleans (12½hr., 4 per day, $83); and St. Louis (8½hr., 1 per day, $51). **Amtrak,** 1400 W. Markham St., at Victory St. (☎372-6841; open Sa-Tu 11pm-7:30am, W-F 11pm, 8am), runs from Union Station Square; take bus #1 or 8. Trains run to Dallas (6½hr., $60); Malvern, near Hot Springs (1hr., $10); and St. Louis (7hr., $53). **Central Arkansas Transit (CAT)** operates an extensive and tourist-friendly bus system through downtown and the surrounding towns. Go to the **River Cities Travel Center,** 310 E. Capitol St., to catch buses and trolleys and get detailed route and schedule info. (☎375-1163. Buses run M-Sa every 30-40min. 6am-6pm, some routes until 10pm; Su 9am-4pm. $1, seniors 55¢; transfers 10¢.) CAT also runs **free trolleys** from the business district to River Market. (M-F 7am-7:30pm.) Take the 6th or 9th St. exit off I-30 and follow the signs to **Little Rock Visitor Information Center,** 615 E. Capitol Ave., in the newly renovated Curran Hall. (☎370-3290 or 877-220-2568; www.littlerock.com. Open daily 8am-6pm.) **Internet access** is available at the **Main Library,** 100 Rock St., near River Market. (☎918-3000. Open M-Th 9am-8pm, F-Sa 9am-6pm, Su 1-5pm. Free.) **Post Office:** 600 E. Capitol St. (☎375-5155. Open M-F 7am-5:30pm.) **ZIP code:** 72701. **Area code:** 501.

■ **ACCOMMODATIONS.** Budget motels are particularly dense on I-30 southwest of town and at the intersection of I-30 and I-40 in North Little Rock. The **Master's Inn ❷,** 707 I-30, off Exit 140 at 6th St. and 9th St., adores pineapple imagery. Three blocks from the heart of downtown with spacious rooms, it offers a pool and complimentary breakfast. (☎372-4392 or 800-633-3434. Singles $30-42; doubles $47; each additional adult $4. Under 16 free with parent.) The **Cimarron Motel ❶,** 10200 I-30, off Exit 130, has basic rooms and a pool. (☎565-1171. Key deposit $5. Singles $30; doubles $35.) If saving money is your only objective, **King Motel ❶,** 10420 I-30, near the Cimarron, has relatively comfortable, cheap rooms without frills. (☎565-1501. Key deposit $5. Singles $25; doubles $30.) **Maumell Park ❶,** 9009 Pinnacle Valley Rd., on the Arkansas River, has 129 sites near the beautiful Pinnacle Mountain State Park. From I-430, take Rte. 10 (Exit 9) west 3 mi., turn right on the Pinnacle Valley Rd., and continue for 3 mi. (☎868-9477. Sites with water and electricity $15. Boat launch $2; free for campers.)

▣☑ FOOD & NIGHTLIFE. The city is obviously pouring money into the downtown **River Market**, 400 President Clinton Ave., and people are responding. The downtown lunch crowd heads there for a wide selection of food shops, coffee stands, delis, and an outdoor **Farmers Market.** (☎375-2552. Market hall open M-Sa 7am-6pm; many shops only open for lunch. Farmer's Market Tu and Sa 7am-3pm.) Throughout the year, River Market sponsors a wide variety of events from ice cream tastings to antique car shows; call for details. Near Market Hall, **◪The Flying Fish ❷**, 511 President Clinton Ave. (look for the outboard motors on the outside wall), has quickly become downtown's favorite fishy hangout. Hungry patrons clamor for catfish baskets (2 fillets $5.50), po' boy sandwiches (oyster and catfish po' boys $6.50), and on-tap brewskies. (☎375-3474. Open daily 11am-10pm.) **Vino's ❶**, 923 W. 7th St., at Chester St., is Little Rock's original microbrewery/nightclub with tasty Italian fare and a clientele ranging from lunchtime's corporate businessmen to midnight's pierced and dyed punks. (☎375-8466. Cheese pizza slices $1.15. Calzones from $5.50. Live music Th-Sa. Cover $5-12. Open M-W 11am-10pm, Th 11am-11pm, F 11am-midnight, Sa 11:30am-midnight, Su 1-9pm.) **Sticky Fingerz ❶**, 107 Commerce St., at President Clinton Ave., is one of the River Market District's hopping nightspots. A restaurant and lounge covered with bright murals and junkyard art inside and out, it hosts live music almost every night. Their "famous chicken fingerz" are only $5 for a platter. (☎372-7707. Open M-Sa 11am-2pm and 4:30pm until the band gets tired.) **Juanita's ❸**, 1300 S. Main St., is a local favorite, serving $7 Mexican lunches, while the adjoining bar hosts all sorts of live music most nights. (☎372-1228. Dinner $8-12. Cover up to $10. Open M 11am-2:30pm and 5:30-9pm, Tu-Th 11am-2:30pm and 5:30-10pm, F 11am-2:30pm and 5:30-10:30pm, Sa 11am-10:30pm.) For more nightlife information, pick up a free copy of *La Presse Libre*, Little Rock's monthly entertainment paper with a bohemian twist.

◪ SIGHTS. Tourists can visit **"Le Petite Roche,"** the actual little rock of Little Rock, at Riverfront Park at the north end of Rock St. From underneath the railroad bridge at the north end of Louisiana St., look straight down, the rock is part of the embankment. Little Rock's most important attraction lies at the corner of Daisy L. Gatson Bates Dr. (formerly 14th St.) and Park St. **Central High School** remains a fully functional (and fully integrated) school; it's therefore closed to visitors. But in a restored Mobil station across the street, a **◪Visitors Center**, 2125 Daisy L. Gatson Bates Dr., contains an excellent exhibit on the "Little Rock Nine." (☎374-1957. Open M-Sa 10am-4pm, Su 1-4pm. Free.) The **MacArthur Museum of Arkansas Military History**, 503 E. 9th St., on the grounds of the Arkansas Arts Center, is a little gem. Located in the birthplace of Gen. Douglass MacArthur, it contains a small but very in-depth exhibit of military paraphernalia. (☎376-4602. Open M and Th-Sa 10am-4pm, Su 1-4pm. Free.) The **Arkansas Art Center**, 501 East 9th St., is a huge complex that'll keep your aesthetic senses tingling for hours. This is not your ordinary, boring selection of landscapes and still lifes; one of the most prominent sculptures, **Heavy Dog Kiss**, has a huge human head kissing a huge dog head on the lips. (☎372-4000. Open Tu-Sa 10am-5pm, Su 11am-5pm. Suggested donation $5.)

In the middle of downtown, the **Arkansas Territorial Restoration**, 200 E. Third St., displays life in 19th-century Little Rock as period actors show off old-time tricks of Arkansas frontier living. (☎324-9351. Open M-Sa 9am-5pm, Su 1-5pm. $2.50, seniors $1.50, under 18 $1.) The **State Capitol**, at the west end of Capitol St., isn't an exact replica of the US Capitol, but there's definitely a family resemblance. When the Legislature is not in session, visitors can freely explore the building and its chambers. (☎682-5080. Open M-F 7am-5pm, Sa-Su 10am-5pm.) Construction of the **Clinton Presidential Library** (☎370-8000 for information) is slated to finish sometime in 2004. Next to the River Market district, the Library will update the old Little Rock skyline.

FLORIDA

Ponce de León landed in St. Augustine on the Florida coast in 1513, in search of the elusive Fountain of Youth. Although the multitudes who flock to Florida today aren't seeking fountains, many find their youth restored in the Sunshine State—whether they're dazzled by Disney World or bronzed by the sun on the state's seductive beaches. Droves of senior citizens also migrate to Florida, where the sun-warmed air is just as therapeutic as de León's fabled magical elixir. Florida's recent population boom has strained the state's natural resources; commercial strips and tremendous development have turned many pristine beaches into tourist traps. Still, it is possible to find a deserted spot on the peninsula on which to plop down with a paperback and get some sand in your toes.

HIGHLIGHTS OF FLORIDA

BEACHES. White sand, lots of sun, clear blue water. Pensacola (p. 515) and St. Petersburg (p. 509) win our thumbs-up for the best of the best.

DISNEY WORLD. Orlando's cash cow...er, mouse (p. 479). What else is there to say?

EVERGLADES. The prime Florida haunt for fishermen, hikers, canoers, bikers, and wildlife watchers (p. 499). Check out the unique mangrove swamps.

KEY LIME PIE. This famous dessert hails from the Florida Keys (p. 502).

⌨ PRACTICAL INFORMATION

Capital: Tallahassee.

Visitor info: Florida Division of Tourism, 126 W. Van Buren St., Tallahassee 32301 (☎888-735-2872; www.flausa.com). **Division of Recreation and Parks,** 3900 Commonwealth Blvd., #536, Tallahassee 32399 (☎850-488-9872).

Postal Abbreviation: FL. **Sales Tax:** 6%. **Accommodations Tax:** 11%.

JACKSONVILLE ☎904

At almost 1000 square miles, Jacksonville is geographically the largest city in the continental US. Without theme parks, star-studded beaches, or tropical environs, Jacksonville struggles to shine through the cluttered tourist offerings of southern Florida. The city, however, still draws visitors with its family-oriented attractions, and its downtown is undergoing a massive makeover to prepare for the 2005 Super Bowl. Tourists can anticipate a more accessible and exciting Jacksonville in the near future, but for now, expect the construction to bring that about.

◪⌨ ORIENTATION & PRACTICAL INFORMATION. Three highways intersect in Jacksonville, making driving around the city relatively easy. **I-95** runs north-south, while **I-10** starts in the downtown area and heads west. **I-295** forms a giant "C" on the western half of the city, and **Arlington Expressway** becomes **Atlantic Blvd. (Rte. 10)** heading to the beach. The St. Johns River snakes throughout the city. **Airport: Jacksonville International,** 2400 Yankee Clipper Dr. (☎741-4902), 18 mi. north of the city on I-95, Exit 127B. **Amtrak,** 3570 Clifford Ln. (☎766-5110; open 24hr.), off I-95 exit 20th St. W, sends coaches to Orlando (3½hr., 2 per day, $34). Take Northside 4 Moncreif Bus A to get to the terminal. **Greyhound,** 10 N. Pearl St. (☎356-9976, open 24hr.), at Central Station Skyrail stop downtown, buses to Atlanta (6-8hr.; 8

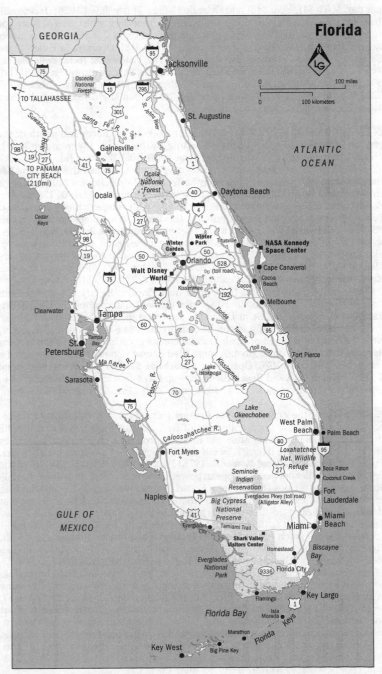

Florida

GEORGIA

95

Jacksonville

Osceola
National
Forest

10   295

TO TALLAHASSEE

St. Augustine

Santa Fe R.

301

Suwannee River

Gainesville

98
19
27

TO PANAMA
CITY BEACH
(210mi)

41   75

Ocala

Ocala
National
Forest

40   Daytona Beach

Cedar
Keys

4

27

98
19

Winter
Park   Titusville   NASA Kennedy
Space Center

Winter
Garden

50   50   Cape Canaveral

Orlando   528
(toll road)   Cocoa
Beach

Walt Disney
World   Cocoa

4   Kissimmee   192

Florida

Melbourne

Clearwater   Tampa   60   Turnpike
(toll road)

St.   Tampa
Petersburg   Bay

Manatee R.   27   Lake
Istokpoga   Kissimmee R.   95   1

Sarasota   Peace R.   70   710   Fort Pierce

75

Lake
Okeechobee

Caloosahatchee R.   West Palm
Beach   Palm Beach

Fort Myers   80   95

Loxahatchee
Nat. Wildlife
Refuge   27   Boca Raton

Semanole
Indian
Reservation   Coconut Creek

Naples   75   Everglades Pkwy (toll road)
(Alligator Alley)   Fort
Lauderdale

Big Cypress
National
Preserve   Miami
Beach

41   Tamiami Trail

Everglades   Miami

GULF OF
MEXICO   Everglades
City   Shark Valley
Visitors Center   Homestead   Biscayne
Bay

Everglades
National
Park   9336   Florida City

Flamingo   Key Largo

Florida Bay   Isla
Morada

Marathon   Florida Keys

Key West   Big Pine Key   1

ATLANTIC
OCEAN

0   100 miles
0   100 kilometers

per day; M-Th $41, F-Su $43) and Orlando (3-5hr.; 11 per day; $24/26). **Jacksonville Transportation Authority** runs throughout the city from the main station at State and Union downtown. (☎630-3181. Operates daily 5am-10pm. 75¢.) The **Skyway** monorail is the best way to maneuver downtown. (☎630-3181. Operates M-F 6am-11pm, Sa 10am-11pm. 35¢.) **Taxis: Yellow Cab,** ☎260-1111. **Visitor Info: Jacksonville and the Beaches Convention and Visitors Bureau,** 201 E. Adams St., downtown. (☎798-9111 or 800-733-2668; www.jaxcvb.com. Open M-F 8am-5pm.) **Hotlines: Rape Crisis,** ☎355-7273. **Post Office:** 311 W. Monroe St. (☎353-3445. Open M-F 8:30am-5pm, Sa 9am-1pm.) **Zip Code:** 32202. **Area code:** 904.

█▐█ ACCOMMODATIONS & FOOD. Along I-95 to the north and south of the city and on the Arlington Expwy. heading to the ocean, inexpensive hotels abound. Bare-bones but clean, the **Best Value Inn ❷,** 1057 Broward Rd., off I-95 Exit 124B north of the city, has large rooms with TV and A/C, while the adjoining **Red Hare Restaurant ❷** provides a $6 Sunday buffet. (☎757-0990. Rooms $40.) Just steps from the sands of Jacksonville Beach, **Fig Tree Inn Bed and Breakfast ❹,** 185 4th Ave. S, offers five differently themed rooms brimming with antiques. Enjoy your breakfast or afternoon tea on the front porch of this beach-style shingle cottage. (☎246-8855 or 877-217-9830. Rooms from $75.) **Kathryn Abbey Hanna Park ❶,** 500 Wonderwood Dr., in Mayport, has 293 wooded sites near the beach, all with full hookup, along with 4 cabins with A/C. Twenty mi. of bike paths and a water playground are also on sight. (☎249-4700. Cabins min. stay 2 nights. Reception open 8am-9pm. Reservations recommended for cabins. Tent sites $13.50; RVs $18; cabins $34.)

Closer in the culinary spirit to Georgia than Florida, the city has an excellent taste of the three fundamentals: BBQ, fried chicken, and seafood. **Jenkins' Quality Bar-B-Que ❶,** 830 N. Pearl St. at Union St., serves up spicy barbecue with a hint of mustard. (☎353-6833. Beef and chicken sandwiches $4-6. Open M-Sa 11am-2am.) Near the beach, the smell of fresh biscuits constantly fills the air at **Famous Amos Restaurant ❷,** 375 Atlantic Blvd. A huge fried chicken dinner with veggies and a salad costs $6. (☎249-3025. Open 24hr.) **Beachside Seafood Market and Restaurant ❷,** 120 N. 3rd St./A1A and Beach Blvd., fries up fish sandwiches and baskets ($4-6) using its own fresh catches. (☎241-4880. Open M-Sa 11am-6:30pm, Su 11am-5pm.)

◙ SIGHTS. At the **Anheuser-Busch Brewery Tour,** 111 Busch Dr., off I-95 10min. north of downtown, a video collection of Bud's greatest ads amuses, while the Brew Hall peeks into the century-old brewing process. Complimentary samples are available for those over 21. (☎696-8373. Open M-Sa 9am-4pm, hourly tours. Free.) **Fort Caroline National Memorial,** 12713 Fort Caroline Rd., was the site of the first armed conflict between European powers over new world settlement. In 1565 Spanish forces overtook the fort from French Huguenots, who had established the first North American Protestant colony there. Today visitors can try their hand at storming a replica of the fort; the less aggressive can peruse the museum's Native American and French artifacts. (☎641-7155. Open daily 9am-5pm. Free.) The fort occupies a small patch of the **Timucuan Ecological and Historic Preserve,** 13165 Mt. Pleasant Rd., where 46,000 serene acres of saltwater marshes and tidal creeks teem with fish, dolphins, and eagles. (☎641-7155. Open daily 8am to dusk. Free.)

The **Museum of Science and History (MOSH),** 1025 Museum Circle, highlights northeast Florida's natural history and entertains visitors with a multimedia show in its planetarium. (☎396-7062. Open M-F 10am-5pm, Sa 10am-6pm, Su 1-6pm. $7, seniors $5.50, ages 3-12 $5.) The beautiful grounds of the **Cummer Museum of Art and Gardens,** 829 Riverside Ave., line the St. Johns River south of downtown. Indoors there are numerous Renaissance and Baroque paintings and an exciting hands-on art education center for children. (☎356-6857. Open Tu and Th 10am-9pm, W and F-Sa 10am-5pm, Su noon-5pm. $6, students $3, seniors $4. Free Tu 4-9pm; college students with ID free Tu-F after 1:30pm.)

🎭🎬 ENTERTAINMENT & NIGHTLIFE. Acts ranging from Ringo Starr to the Dixie Chicks to Gilbert and Sullivan theater have performed at the historic **Florida Theatre**, 128 E. Forsyth St. (☎355-2787), built in 1927. The theater hosts more than 300 performances a year; check out www.floridatheatre.com for upcoming shows. A different kind of popular culture thrives at the **Alltel Stadium** (☎633-2000), East Duval St. and Haines St., home to the NFL's Jaguars. Much of Jacksonville's nightlife centers around **Jacksonville Landing**, Main St. and Independent Dr., a riverfront area packed with restaurants, bars, shopping, and live entertainment. (☎353-1188. Open M-Th 10am-8pm, F-Sa 10am-9pm, Su noon-5:30pm.) At the Landing, **Bourbon Street Raw Bar and Grille** draws a crowd for weekday specials. (☎632-0062. Happy hour M-F 3-7pm with 2-for-1 domestic drafts and 25¢ wings. Open M-Sa 11am-1am, Su 1-10pm.) Next door, wolf down some Not 'cho Average Nachos ($8) while taking in the game at **Legends Sports Bar.** During Monday Night Football you can chase your chips down with $4 pitchers of beer. (☎353-4577. Open daily 11am-2am.)

🏖 BEACHES. Miles of uncrowded white sands can be found at **Jacksonville Beach**, as well as neighboring **Atlantic Beach**, **Neptune Beach**, and **Ponte Vedra Beach.** To reach the Atlantic take Rte. 90/Beach Blvd. or Rte. 10/Atlantic Blvd. east from downtown for about 30min. Fishermen stake out spots on the Jacksonville Beach Pier, while golfers take advantage of the more than 20 area golf courses. The Boardwalk is abuzz with activity, from musical festivals to sand-castle building contests. Surfing and volleyball tournaments take place in May. Staple Florida attractions are nearby, including a dog track, mini golf, go-karts, and a water park.

ST. AUGUSTINE   ☎904

Spanish adventurer Pedro Menéndez de Aviles founded St. Augustine in 1565, making it the first European colony in North America, and the oldest continuous settlement in the United States. Thanks to preservation efforts, much of St. Augustine's Spanish flavor remains intact. This city's pride lies in its provincial cobblestone streets, *coquina* rock walls, and antique shops rather than in its token beaches. Forget L.A.'s high-priced plastic surgeons—eternal youth costs just $5.75 around here, in the form of admission to the famed Fountain of Youth.

✴🛈 ORIENTATION & PRACTICAL INFORMATION

Most of St. Augustine's sights conveniently lie within a 10-15min. walk from the hostel, motels, and bus station. Narrow streets, one-ways, and abundant parking meters can make driving unpleasant. Parking is available at the Visitors Center all day for just $3. The city's major east-west routes, **King St.** and **Cathedral Place**, run through downtown and become the Bridge of Lions that leads to the beaches. **San Marco Ave.**, or **Avenida Menendez**, runs north-south. **Castillo Dr.** grows out of San Marco Ave. near the center of town. **Saint George St.**, a north-south pedestrian route, contains most of the shops and many of the sights in town. **Greyhound**, 100 Malaga St. (☎829-6401; open daily 7:30am-8:30pm), has service to Daytona Beach (1¼hr.; 6 per day; M-Th $12.75, F-Su $13.75) and Jacksonville (1hr.; 6 per day; $9.25/10.25). If the station is closed, the driver accepts cash. **Public Transit: Public Street Corner,** offers bus service; expect a bus every ½hr. at the Greyhound station, where all routes converge. (☎823-4816 for schedules and info. Operates daily 6am-5pm. $1.) **Sightseeing Trains,** 170 San Marco Ave., shuttle travelers on a red trolley that hits all the major attractions on their 20 stops. (☎829-6545 or 800-226-6545. Operates every 15-20min. 8:30am-5pm. $12, ages 6-12 $5. Ticket good for 3 consecutive days.) **Taxis: Ancient City Taxi, ☎**824-8161. **Visitors Center:** 10 Castillo Dr., at San Marco Ave. From the bus station, walk three blocks north on Riberia St., then right on Orange St. (☎825-1000. Open daily 8:30am-5:30pm.) **Post Office:** 99 King St. (☎829-8716. Open M-F 8:30am-5pm, Sa 9am-1pm.) **ZIP code:** 32084. **Area code:** 904.

FLORIDA

⌐ ACCOMMODATIONS

◪ **Pirate Haus Inn and Hostel,** 32 Treasury St. (☎808-1999 or 877-466-3864), just off Saint George St., is the place to stay with spacious dorms, beautiful private rooms, helpful management, and a great location. From Rte. 16 E, make a left on King St. and then left on Charlotte St.; parking is available. Weary travelers are pampered by a lively common room, big lockers, Internet access, and a tasty pancake breakfast. A/C and free lockers. Key/linen deposit $5. Office hours 8-10am and 6-10pm, no lockout for registered guests. Dorms $15, nonmembers $17; private rooms $46. Under 13 free. ❶

Sunrise Inn, 512 Anastasia Blvd. (☎829-3888), is the best option among the many motels along Rte. A1A. A/C, cable TV, phones, and pool. Check-in/check-out 10am. Singles Su-Th $28, F-Sa $38; doubles $33/43. ❷

Seabreeze Motel, 208 Anastasia Blvd. (☎829-8122), has clean rooms with refrigerators and pool access. A/C, cable TV, and free local calls. Kitchenette available. Singles M-F $40, Sa-Su $45; doubles $45/50. ❷

Anastasia State Recreation Area, on Rte. A1A, 4 mi. south of the historic district. From town, cross the Bridge of Lions and turn left past the Alligator Farm. Nearby, Salt Run and the Atlantic Ocean provide opportunities for great windsurfing, fishing, swimming, and hiking. (☎461-2033. Office open daily 8am-dusk. Reservations recommended F-Sa. Sites $18, with electricity $20. Vehicle entrance fee $3.25, pedestrians $1. ❶

◨◪ FOOD & NIGHTLIFE

The bustle of daytime tourists and the abundance of budget eateries make lunch in St. Augustine's historic district a delight, especially among the cafes and bars of **Saint George St.** At the **Bunnery Bakery and Cafe ❶,** 121 Saint George St., delectable sandwiches, *panini*, salads, and hearty breakfasts draw locals and tourists alike. The inventive and filling chicken walnut sandwich is $5. (☎829-6166. Open 8am-6pm. No credit cards.) An excellent healthy option, the **Manatee Cafe ❶,** 179 San Marco Ave., just past the Fountain of Youth, prepares cuisine with pure filtered water and certified organically-grown produce. Tasty grilled hummus pita reuben ($5.25) gets points for originality. (☎826-0210. Open Th-Tu 8am-3pm.) As God is your witness, never go hungry again at **Scarlett O'Hara's ❷,** 70 Hypolita St. at Cordova St., where monster "Big Rhett" burgers run $6. Live music, usually rock or reggae, entertains nightly. (☎824-6535. Happy hour M-F 4-7pm. Occasional $2 cover. Open daily 11am-12:30am.)

St. Augustine supports a variety of bars, many on S. A1A and Saint George St. *Folio Weekly* contains event listings. Local string musicians play on the two stages in the **Milltop,** 19½ Saint George St., a tiny bar above an old mill in the restored district. (☎829-2329. Music daily 1pm until closing. Cover varies. Open M-Sa 11am-1am, Su 11am-10pm.) Throw back a Dolphin's Breath Lager at the **Oasis Deck and Restaurant,** 4000 Rte. A1A S. at Ocean Trace Rd. (☎471-3424. Sample gator tail $6. Seafood sandwich $3-7. Happy hour 4-7pm. Live rock or reggae M-Sa 8pm-12:30am, Su 7-11:30pm. Open daily 6am-1am.) Cheap flicks and bargain eats await at **Pot Belly's,** 36 Granada St. This combination pub, deli, and cinema serves a range of junk food to tables in the theater and screens mainly new releases—the ice cream drinks are divine. (☎829-3101. Movie tickets $4.75. Shows 6:30 and 8:45pm.)

◙ SIGHTS

FOUNTAIN OF YOUTH. No trip to St. Augustine would be complete without a trek down beautiful Magnolia Dr. to the **Fountain of Youth,** the infamous legend that sparked Ponce de León's voyage to the New World. A guided tour goes through hundreds of years of Spanish conquistador history in minutes. To fully capture the historical significance of the place, take a swig of the sulfury libation and try to ignore the fact that the water now runs through a pipe. *(11 Magnolia Ave. Go right on Williams St. from San Marco Ave. and continue until it dead-ends into Magnolia Ave. ☎829-3168 or 800-356-8222. Open daily 9am-5pm. $5.75, seniors $4.75, ages 6-12 $2.75.)*

SPANISH HERITAGE. The oldest masonry fortress in the continental US, **Castillo de San Marcos National Monument** has 14 ft. thick walls built of *coquina*, the local shell-rock. The fort, a four-pointed star complete with drawbridge and moat, contains a museum, a large courtyard surrounded by livery quarters for the garrison, a jail, a chapel, and the original cannon brought overseas by the Spanish. *(1 Castillo Dr. Off San Marco Ave. ☎829-6506. Open daily 8:45am-5:15pm, last admission at 4:45pm. $6, ages 6-16 $2. Occasional tours; call ahead.)* Tucked away from the hustle and bustle of the historic district **La Leche Shrine and Mission of Nombre de Dios** is the birthplace of American Catholicism; the first Mass in the US was held here over 400 years ago. A 208 ft. cross commemorates the city's founding, and the shaded lawns make for a peaceful stroll. *(27 Ocean St. Off San Marco Ave. ☎824-2809. Open M-F 8am-5pm, Sa 9am-5pm, Su 9:30am-5pm. Mass M-F 8:30am, Sa 6pm, Su 8am. Free, donation suggested.)*

HISTORICAL SIGHTS. Not surprisingly, the oldest continuous settlement in the US holds some of the nation's oldest stuff. The **Gonzalez-Alvarez House** is the oldest house on the National Registry of Historic Places. Many passed through its doors between its construction in the 1600s and 1918 when it became a museum. *(14 Saint Francis St. ☎824-2872. Open daily 9am-5pm, last admission 4:30pm. $5, students $3, seniors $4.50; families $12.)* Step into the past at the **Oldest Store Museum,** a former general store showcasing over 100,000 turn-of-the-century items, from a high-wheel bicycle to a Model T. *(4 Artillery Ln. ☎829-9729. Open M-Sa 10am-4pm, Su noon-4pm. $5, ages 6-12 $1.50.)* Climb 219 stairs to a dazzling view of the coast at the **St. Augustine Lighthouse and Museum,** one of only six lighthouses in the state open to the public. Tour the 19th-century tower and keeper's house to learn about marine archaeological studies in the surrounding waters. *(81 Lighthouse Ave. Off A1A across from the Alligator Farm. ☎829-0745. Open daily 9am-6pm. Tower, grounds, and house $6.50, seniors $5.50, ages 7-11 $4. House and grounds $4/3/2.)*

RESTORED HOTELS. Take a student-guided tour through **Flagler College,** a small liberal arts institution housed in the restored Spanish Renaissance-style **Ponce de Leon Hotel.** Constructed by railroad and Standard Oil tycoon Henry Flagler in 1888, Thomas Edison outfitted the hotel with electricity. The stained glass windows in the large banquet room were designed by Tiffany himself before he became famous. *(☎823-3378; www.flagler.edu. Tours mid-May to mid-Aug. daily on the hr. 10am-4pm. $4, under 12 $1.)* In 1947, Chicago publisher and art lover Otto Lightner converted the Alcazar Hotel into the **Lightner Museum** to hold an impressive collection of cut, blown, and burnished glass, as well as old clothing and oddities like nun and monk beer steins. *(75 King St. ☎824-2874. Open daily 9am-5pm. 18th-century musical instruments play daily 11am-2pm. Admission $6, students and ages 12-18 $2.)*

JUST FOR FUN. Across the Bridge of Lions, the ⊠**St. Augustine Alligator Farm** allows visitors to get up close and personal with some of nature's finest reptiles. This century-old park is the only place in the world where all 23 known crocodilian species live. *(On Rte. A1A S. ☎824-3337. Open daily 9am-8pm. Presentations every hr. Feeding daily 1:30pm. Admissions $14.25, ages 5-11 $8.50. Discounts available for AAA/CAA, military, and seniors.)* A mouth-watering adventure of a different sort awaits at **Whetstone Chocolates.** Tour the only chocolate factory in Florida, learn the intricate production process, and enjoy a free sample of their product—just don't drool on the glass. *(2 Coke Rd. Just east of State Rd. 312 and U.S. 1. ☎825-1700. Open M-Sa 10am-5:30pm. Free.)* Relax at **Summer Concerts in the Plaza,** when local musicians bring jazz, blues, pop, and classical tunes to visitors at Downtown Plaza. *(Between Cathedral and King Streets off Saint George St. ☎825-1010. June-Aug. Th 7-9pm. Free.)*

FLORIDA

DAYTONA BEACH ☎ 386

When locals first started auto-racing on the hard-packed sands along the ocean in Daytona Beach more than 60 years ago, they were combining two aspects of life that would come to define the town's entire mentality: speed and sand. Daytona played an essential role in the founding of the **National Association of Stock Car Auto Racing (NASCAR)** in 1947, and the mammoth Daytona International Speedway still hosts several big races each year. While the hard-packed sands no longer host races, 23 mi. of Atlantic beaches still pump the lifeblood of the community.

■ **ORIENTATION.** Daytona Beach lies 53 mi. northeast of Orlando and 90 mi. south of Jacksonville. **I-95** parallels the coast and the barrier island. **Atlantic Ave. (Rte. A1A)** is the main drag along the shore, and a scenic drive up A1A goes to St. Augustine and Jacksonville. **International Speedway Blvd. (U.S. 92)** runs east-west, from the ocean, through the downtown area, and to the racetrack and airport. Daytona Beach is a collection of smaller towns; many street numbers are not consecutive and navigation can be difficult. To avoid the gridlock on the beach, arrive early (8am) and leave early (around 3pm). Visitors must pay $5 to drive onto the beach, and police strictly enforce the 10 mph speed limit. Free parking is plentiful during most of the year but sparse during spring break (usually mid-Feb. to Apr.), Speedweeks, Bike Week, Biketoberfest, and the Pepsi 400.

■ **PRACTICAL INFORMATION. Amtrak,** 2491 Old New York Ave. (☎734-2322; open daily 8:30am-7pm), in DeLand, 24 mi. west on Rte. 92, tracks to Miami (7hr., 1 per day, $97). **Greyhound,** 138 S. Ridgewood Ave. (☎255-7076; open daily 6:30am-10:30pm), 4 mi. west of the beach, goes to Jacksonville (2hr.; 11 per day; M-Th $16, F-Su $17) and Orlando (1½hr.; 7 per day; $10/11). **Volusia County Transit Co. (VOTRAN),** 950 Big Tree Rd., operates local buses and a trolley that covers Rte. A1A between Granada Blvd. and Dunlawton Ave. All buses have bike racks. On beach areas where driving is prohibited, free beach trams transport beachgoers. (☎761-7700. Service M-Sa 6am-8pm, Su 7am-6:30pm; trolley M-Sa noon-midnight. $1, seniors and ages 6-17 50¢. Free maps available at hotels.) **Taxis: Yellow Cab,** ☎255-5555. **Visitor Info: Daytona Beach Area Convention and Visitors Bureau,** 126 E. Orange Ave., on City Island. (☎255-0415 or 800-544-0415; www.daytonabeachcvb.org. Open M-F 9am-5pm.) **Rape Crisis Line,** ☎255-2102. **Post Office:** 220 N. Beach St. (☎226-2618. Open M-F 8am-5pm, Sa 9am-noon.) **ZIP code:** 32115. **Area code:** 386.

■ **ACCOMMODATIONS.** Almost all of Daytona's accommodations front **Atlantic Ave. (Rte. A1A),** either on the beach or across the street; those off the beach offer the best deals. Daytona has peak and off-season rates. Spring break and race events drive prices to absurdly high levels, but off-season rates are more motel-like. Almost all the motels facing the beach cost $35 for an off-season single; on the other side of the street it's $25. The **Camellia Motel ❷,** 1055 N. Atlantic Ave. (Rte. A1A), across the street from the beach, is an especially welcoming retreat with cozy, bright rooms, free local calls, cable TV, and A/C. (☎252-9963. Reserve early. Singles $30; doubles $35. During spring break, singles $100; each additional person $10. Kitchens additional $10.) The **Streamline Hotel ❶,** 140 S. Atlantic Ave. (A1A), one block north of E. International Speedway Blvd., stands out amid low level motels. Great location near the boardwalk, but rooms are not as luxurious. (☎258-6937. Key deposit $5. Singles $23; doubles $29; during special events $150-200.) For a truly unique sleeping experience, try the **Travelers Inn ❶,** 735 N. Atlantic Ave. Each of the 22 rooms has a different theme from Jimi Hendrix to Star Wars to NASCAR. (☎253-3501 or 800-417-6466. Singles $29-49; doubles $39-59; each additional person $10. With kitchens $10 more. Prices triple during special events.) **Tomoka State Park ❶,** 2099 N. Beach St., 8 mi. north of Daytona in Ormond Beach, has 100 sites under a tropical canopy. Enjoy salt-water fishing, nature trails, and a sculpture museum. (☎676-4050, for reservations ☎800-326-3521. Open daily 8am-dusk. Sites May-Oct. $11, with electricity $13; Nov.-Apr. $17/19; seniors 50% discount. $3.25 entrance fee for vehicles, $1 for pedestrians and bicyclists.)

◘ FOOD. One of the most famous (and popular) seafood restaurants in the area is **Aunt Catfish's ❷**, 4009 Halifax Dr., at Dunlawton Ave. next to the Port Orange Bridge. Lunch and earlybird specials include a hot bar. Salads ring in under $9. (☎767-4768. Open M-Sa 11:30am-9:30pm, Su 9am-9:30pm.) **Sweetwater's ❺**, 3633 Halifax Dr., in Port Orange, has been a long-time local favorite, voted everything from Best Seafood to Best Early Bird Special to Best Waterfront View. Feast upon the $18 Hungry Seaman dinner, a marine cornucopia of fish, shrimp, scallops, and lobster scampi. (☎761-6724. Open daily 11:30am-10pm.) "If it swims…we have it," boasts **B&B Fisheries ❷**, 715 E. International Speedway Blvd. Take out, or sit in, with fresh fish, just $5.50. (☎252-6542. Open M-F 11am-8:30pm, Sa 4-8:30pm.)

⚑ START YOUR ENGINES. The center of the racing world, the **Daytona International Speedway** hosts NASCAR's Super Bowl: the Daytona 500 (Feb. 16, 2003). **Speedweek** (Feb. 1-16, 2003) precedes the Daytona 500, while the **Pepsi 400** (for those who think young) heats up the track July 3-5, 2003. Next door, **Daytona USA**, 1801 W. International Speedway Blvd., includes a new simulation ride, an IMAX film on the history of Daytona, and a fun teaching program on NASCAR commentating. The breathtaking **Speedway Tour** is a unique chance to see the garages, grandstands, and famous 31° banked turns up close. The **Richard Petty Driving Experience** puts fans in a stock car for a ride-along at 150 mph. (☎947-6800, NASCAR tickets 253-1223. Open daily 9am-7pm. $16, seniors $13, ages 6-12 $8. Tours every ½hr. daily 9:30am-5:30pm, $7. Richard Petty: ☎800-237-3889. 16+. $106.) **Bike Week** draws biker mamas for various motorcycle duels, and **Biketoberfest** brings them back for more. (Bikeweek: Feb. 28-Mar. 9, 2003; www.bikeweek.com. Biketoberfest: Oct. 16-19, 2003; www.biketoberfest.com.)

⚑ NIGHTLIFE. When spring break hits, concerts, hotel-sponsored parties, and other events answer the call of students. News about these travels fastest by word of mouth, but the *Calendar of Events* and *SEE Daytona Beach* make good starting points. On mellow nights, head to the boardwalk to play volleyball or shake your groove-thing at the **Oceanfront Bandshell**, an open-air amphitheater constructed entirely of *coquina* rock. Dance clubs thump along Seabreeze Blvd. near the corner of N. Atlantic Ave. **Razzle's**, 611 Seabreeze Blvd., caters to the Spring Break crowd with its high energy dance floors, flashy light shows, and nightly drink specials. (☎257-6326. Cover around $5. Open daily 7pm-3am.) **Ocean Deck**, 127 S. Ocean Ave., stands out among the clubs with its live music on the beach. Reggae, jazz, and calypso every night except Sunday, when a rock band takes over. (☎253-5224. Music nightly 9:30pm-2:30am. 21+ after 9pm. Open daily 11am-3am; kitchen until 2am.) **The Oyster ❷**, 555 Seabreeze Blvd., promises great food and great action for sports fans, with 34 TVs and a pool and game room. (☎255-6348. Sandwiches $4-8. Oyster dishes from $6. Open daily 11:30am-3am.)

ORLANDO ☎407

When Walt Disney was flying over the small towns of Central Florida in search of a place to put his Florida operation, he marveled at the endless number of lakes and streams that dominate the Orlando area. Amidst this beautiful setting, he foresaw a world full of thrill-packed amusement rides and life-sized, cartoonish figures. While Orlando is older than Disney World, most of the city's resources are dedicated to servicing the tourism industry that is the lifeblood of the economy. Theme parks, hotels, diners, and other kitschy treats line every major street; even downtown Orlando, 20 mi. from Disney, overflows with tourists.

FLORIDA

⌐ TRANSPORTATION

Airport: Orlando International, 1 Airport Blvd. (☎825-2001), from the airport take Rte. 436 N, exit to Rte. 528 W/Bee Line Expwy, then head east on I-4 for downtown, and west on I-4 to the attractions, including Disney and Universal. City bus #42 or 51 make the trip for $1. **Mears Motor Shuttle** (☎423-5566), has booths at the airport for transportation to most hotels (price varies depending on destination, about $15 per person). No shuttle reservations are necessary from the airport; for return, call 1 day in advance.

Trains: Amtrak, 1400 Sligh Blvd. (☎843-7611), 3 blocks east of I-4. Take S. Orange Ave., head west on Columbia, then take a right on Sligh. Station open daily 7:30am-7pm. To **Jacksonville** (3-4hr.; 3 per day; $34).

Buses: Greyhound, 555 N. John Young Pkwy. (☎292-3440), just south of W. Colonial Dr. (Rte. 50). Open 24hr. To **Jacksonville** (2½-4hr.; 9 per day; M-Th $25, F-Su $27) and **Kissimmee** (40min.; 8 per day; $7/8).

Public Transit: LYNX, 445 W. Amelia St., Suite 800 (☎841-2279 or 800-344-5969). Downtown terminal between Central and Pine St., 1 block west of Orange Ave. and 1 block east of I-4. Buses operate daily 6am-9pm, hours vary with route. $1, seniors and under 18 25¢; transfers 10¢. Weekly pass $10. Look for signposts with a colored paw. Serves the airport, downtown, and all major parks.

Taxis: Yellow Cab, ☎ 699-9999.

◼◪ ORIENTATION & PRACTICAL INFORMATION

Orlando lies at the center of hundreds of small lakes, toll highways, and amusement parks. **Orange Blossom Trail (Rte. 17/92 and 441)** runs north-south and **Colonial Dr. (Rte. 50)** east-west. The **Bee Line Expwy. (Rte. 528)** and the **East-West Expwy. (Rte. 408)** exact several tolls for their convenience. The major artery is **I-4**, which actually runs north-south through the center of town, despite being labeled an east-west highway. The parks—**Disney World, Universal Studios,** and **Sea World**—await 15-20 mi. southwest of downtown on I-4 W; Winter Park is 3-4 mi. northeast.

Visitor Info: Orlando Official Visitor Center, 8723 International Dr., #101 (☎363-5872; www.orlandoinfo.com), southwest of downtown; take bus #8. Get the free "Magic Card" for discounts at sites, restaurants, and hotels. Open daily 8am-7pm. Tickets sold 8am-6pm.

Hotlines: Rape Hotline, ☎740-5408. **Crisis Hotline,** ☎843-4357.

Post Office: 46 E. Robinson St., downtown (☎425-6464). Open M-F 7am-5pm. **ZIP code:** 32801. **Area code:** 407. 10-digit dialing required.

⌐ ACCOMMODATIONS

With more than 110,000 hotel rooms to choose from, there are plenty of options for all tastes and wallet sizes. Prices rise as you approach Disney World. **U.S. 192** (Irlo Bronson Memorial Highway) runs from Disney World to downtown Kissimmee, and is probably the best place to find a deal. Public transportation goes from Kissimmee to the major parks. **International Drive (I-Drive),** a north-south thoroughfare that parallels the interstate, is the center of Orlando's lodging world. Most accommodations provide free transportation to nearby Universal and Disney.

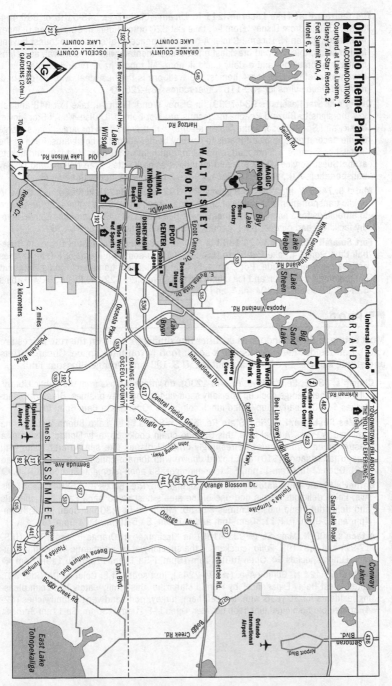

Orlando Theme Parks

ACCOMMODATIONS
Courtyard at Lake Lucerne, 1
Disney's All-Star Resorts, 2
Fort Summit KOA, 4
Motel 6, 3

LAKE COUNTY
OSCEOLA COUNTY
LAKE COUNTY
ORANGE COUNTY
LAKE COUNTY

TO CYPRESS
GARDENS (20mi.)

TO 4
(5mi.)

N

LG

27

192

192

546

Hartzog Rd.

Seidel Rd.

W. Irlo Bronson Memorial Hwy.

Lake
Wilson

Old Lake Wilson Rd.

Reedy Cr.

4

WALT DISNEY WORLD

MAGIC
KINGDOM

ANIMAL
KINGDOM

Blizzard
Beach

DISNEY-MGM
STUDIOS

Wide World
of Sports

EPCOT
CENTER

Typhoon
Lagoon

World Dr.

Epcot Center Dr.

Bay
Lake

River
Country

Lake
Mabel

Winter Garden-Vineland Rd.

Lake
Sheen

Downtown
Disney

E. Buena Vista Dr.

Apopka-Vineland Rd.

Lake
Bryan

536

535

535

192

192

2

3

4

0   2 miles
0   2 kilometers

Poinciana Blvd.

Osceola Pkwy.

535

530

17
92

Kissimmee
Municipal
Airport

Vine St.

Bermuda Ave.

KISSIMMEE

527

531

525

441

192

Simpson
Rd.

Florida's
Turnpike

Buena Ventura Blvd.

Orange Ave.

Dart Blvd.

Boggy Creek Rd.

Boggy Creek Rd.

East Lake
Tohopekaliga

Shingle Cr.

John Young Pkwy.

Central Florida Greenway

417

ORANGE COUNTY
OSCEOLA COUNTY

International Dr.

Discovery
Cove

Sea World
Adventure
Park

Central Florida Pkwy.

Bee Line Expwy (Toll Road)

423

482

Kirman Rd.

Orlando Official
Visitors Center

ORLANDO

Universal Orlando

TO DOWNTOWN ORLANDO AND
THE HOLY LAND EXPERIENCE,
(5mi.)

Big
Sand
Lake

44
192
11

Orange Blossom Dr.

Florida's Turnpike

527

528

Wetherbee Rd.

531

Sand Lake Road

Orlando
International
Airport

Airport Blvd.

Semoran Blvd.

Conway
Lakes

436

FLORIDA

The Courtyard at Lake Lucerne, 211 N. Lucerne Circle E (☎648-5188 or 800-444-5289), 30min. from Disney. From I-4, take Exit 82C onto Anderson St., right on Delaney Ave., and right on N. Lucerne Circle. A beautiful, peaceful alternative to tourist havens further south, this bed and breakfast offers complimentary wine upon arrival, as well as continental breakfast and a daily cocktail hour. All rooms have TV and phone, and 6 have whirlpool tubs. Of the 4 homes, the Wellborn is the best deal, with 15 one-bedroom Art Deco suites for $89-115. Other rooms $89-225. ❹

Disney's All-Star Resorts (☎934-7639), in Disney World. From I-4, take Exit 64B and follow the signs to Blizzard Beach—the resorts are just behind it. Disney's All Star Movie, Music, and Sports Resorts, the "value resorts," are a great deal for large groups. Large theme decorations, from surfboards to cowboy boots, adorn the courtyards. Each of the hotels has 2 pools, a food court, a pool bar, and laundry facilities. Get info and tickets at the Guest Services Desk to avoid long lines at park gates. Free parking and Disney transportation. A/C, phone, TV. Rooms $77-124; under 18 free with adult. ❹

Motel 6, 7455 W. Irlo Bronson Highway/Rte. 192 (☎396-6422), in Kissimmee. Close to public transportation and a slew of chain restaurants, Motel 6 also offers shuttle service to attractions for a nominal fee. Rooms have free local calls, HBO, morning coffee, laundry facilities, and outdoor pool. Rooms $30, each additional person $4. ❶

Fort Summit KOA (☎863-424-1880 or 800-424-1800), 11mi. west of Disney in Baseball City. From I-4, take Exit 55 to U.S. 27; then go south on Frontage Rd. Palm trees and oaks provide shade. Pool, hot tub, Internet access, horseback riding, frequent bingo games, cookouts, and ice cream socials. Tent sites $22-27; RVs $30-34; kabins $39-46. Discounts for KOA, AAA, and AARP. ❶

🍴 FOOD

Most eating in the Orlando area is either fine dining or done on-the-run. Prices are exorbitant inside theme parks; pack some food if you have space. Cheap buffets and ethnic eateries line International Dr., U.S. 192, and Orange Blossom Trail.

Champ's, 132 E. Central Blvd. (☎649-1230), downtown across from the Public Library. Lilia and Chef George cook up specialty sandwiches and tasty pastries. Breakfast sandwiches $1.50. Hearty soup/salad lunch combo $4. Open M-Sa 6am-6pm. ❶

Pebbles Restaurant, 12551 State Rd. 535 (☎827-1111), Lake Buena Vista, in the Crossroads Plaza. A local fave, this Orlando chain cooks up tasty Florida cuisine in a casual green atmosphere. Refreshingly original dishes like seared crab cake with mango tartar sauce ($10) and baked chèvre with tomato concasse and garlic bread ($6). Open M-Th 11am-11pm, F 11am-midnight, Sa noon-midnight, Su noon-11pm. ❷

Barney's Steak and Seafood, 1615 E. Colonial Dr./Rte. 50 (☎896-6864), near Mills Ave. Enjoy delicious steaks and one of the area's best salad bars. Early bird specials and delightful piano music. Entrees $11-30. Music Su-Tu 5:30pm. Open M 11:30am-4pm and 5-9pm, Tu-F 11:30am-4pm and 5-10pm, Sa 5-10pm, Su 4-9pm. ❺

Azteca's, 809 N. Main St. (☎933-8155), in Kissimmee at Orange Blossom Trail (U.S. 17-92) and U.S. 192. Pollo (chicken) is the specialty at this authentic Mexican restaurant. Lunch specials $4. Open Tu-Th 11am-10pm, F-Sa 11am-11pm, Su 11am-9pm. ❶

Beefy King, 424 N. Bumby Ave. (☎894-2241), just south of E. Colonial Dr. (Rte. 50). Voted "Best Beefy Experience" by Florida Magazine, this family eatery has been pleasing residents for 30 years with its beef, ham, turkey, pork, and veggie sandwiches ($2-4) at their old-fashioned luncheon counter. Open M-F 10am-5:30pm, Sa 11am-3pm. ❶

🎵 🎭 ENTERTAINMENT & NIGHTLIFE

Check the Calendar section Friday's *Orlando Sentinel* for happenings around town; the free *Orlando Weekly* is another source for cool entertainment. Relatively inexpensive bars line **N. Orange Ave.**, the city's main drag. For more family- and tourist-oriented attractions, head to the bright lights and neon of **International Drive**, where mini-golf, Ripley's Believe It or Not, the world's largest McDonald's, and Wonderworks (a science funhouse in an upside-down building) await.

■ **SAK Comedy Lab**, 380 W. Amelia St. (☎648-0001), at Hughey Ave. Audience participation and clean humor are the trademarks of this intimate club, where comedy shows will split your sides. Shows Tu and W 9pm; Th-F 8 and 10pm; Sa 8, 10pm, midnight. $5-13.

Tabu, 46 N. Orange Ave. (☎648-8363), provides a safe haven for twenty-somethings in search of the South Beach scene. Tu college night. Th women get in and drink free all night. Usually 18+. Cover $5-10. Stylish dress required. Open Tu-Sa 10pm-3am.

Jax 5th Ave. Deli and Ale House, 11 S. Court Ave. (☎841-5322), downtown, stocks a smashing 250 brands of beer. A friendly and knowledgeable staff will help you choose from the dazzling displays. Deli and pub food $5-10. Live jazz Sa nights. Open M-Th 11am-1am, F 11am-2am, Sa noon-2am.

Back Booth, 37 W. Pine St. (☎999-2570). Catch up-and-coming local bands ranging from jazzy funk to ska punk. Cover $3-10. Shows usually 9 or 10pm; call for schedule.

WALT DISNEY WORLD ☎407

Disney World is the Rome of central Florida: all roads lead to it. The name is more apt than one might imagine, as Disney indeed creates a "world" of its own among the lakes, forests, hills, and streams. Within this Neverland, theme parks, resorts, golf courses, theater, restaurants, and nightclubs all work together to make fun the buzzword. Of course, the only setback is that magical amusement comes with a price—everything in Walt Disney's World costs almost thrice as much as in the real world. In the end the corporate empire that is Disney leaves no one unhappy or bored, and despite the expense, WDW wins the prize of best park in the US.

🛈 PRACTICAL INFORMATION

Disney dominates **Lake Buena Vista**, 20 mi. west of Orlando via I-4. (☎824-4321 or 939-4636; www.disneyworld.com.) The one-day entrance fee ($51, ages 3-9 $40) admits visitors to one of the four parks, allowing them to leave and return to the same park later in the day. A better option, the **Park-Hopper Pass** buys admission to all four parks for several days. (4-day $204, ages 3-9 $161; 5-day $230/182.) The **Park Hopper Plus** includes a set number of days of admission plus free access to other Disney attractions. (5-day with 2 extras $262/209; 6-day with 3 extras $294/235; 7-day with four extras $325/262.) The Hopper passes need not be used on consecutive days, never expire, and allow for unlimited transportation between attractions on the Disney monorail, boats, buses, and trains. Attractions that charge separate admissions include **Typhoon Lagoon** ($30/24), **Pleasure Island** ($21, 18+ unless with adult), **Blizzard Beach** ($30/24), and **Disney's Wide World of Sports Complex** ($10/8). For descriptions, see **Other Disney Attractions** (p. 482). *Never pay full gate fare for a Disney park.* Official Tourist Info Centers and the like all sell Park Hopper passes for an average $10-15 less.

FLORIDA

THE LOCAL STORY

A DAY IN THE PARK

Janet Cannon is a Walt Disney World cast member of 14 years and has been at Disney-MGM Studios since its opening in 1989. She's a server at the Hollywood Brown Derby, an intimate and classy restaurant serving California cuisine.

Q: What are the perks of working at Disney World?
A: One of the best perks is that I get to interact with guests one-on-one, probably for a longer period of time than any of the other cast members. Serving food to them is such a personal kind of experience.

Q: What's your favorite Disney attraction?
A: Currently, my favorite is Test Track at EPCOT Center. At the end of it, you go really fast; you just start laughing and can't stop.

Q: Any insider's tips?
A: Don't make your stay too structured; allow for a little bit of rest time where you can actually sit down, relax, and enjoy yourself.

Q: Have you had any magical moments lately?
A: Magical moments happen nearly every day. Last night I had guests from the UK. They had two sons; one was probably around eight or ten. He was so adorable; he thought everything was "lovely." During the meal, he looked up at me and said, "You know, before I came to Disney World, I didn't believe in magic, and now I do." I said, "That's why we're all so happy here; we all believe in magic."

Disney World opens its gates 365 days a year, but hours fluctuate by season. Expect the parks to open at 9am and close between 7 and 11pm, but call beforehand—the schedule is set a month in advance. Prepare for crowds (and afternoon thunderstorms) in summer, but the enormously crowded peak times are Christmas, Thanksgiving, and the month around Easter. The parks are least crowded in January, after New Years. The **FASTPASS** option at all of the theme parks allows you to bypass long lines on popular rides. Simply insert your park entrance ticket into a FASTPASS station, and you will receive a ticket telling you when to return, usually 30min. to 2hr. later.

THE PARKS

MAGIC KINGDOM
Seven lands comprise the Magic Kingdom: **Main Street, USA; Tomorrowland; Fantasyland; Liberty Square; Frontierland; Adventureland;** and **Mickey's Toontown Fair.** More than any of the other Disney parks, this is geared toward children.

MAIN STREET, USA. As the entrance to the "Most Magical Place on Earth," Main Street captures the spirit and bustle of early 20th-century America, with vendors peddling their wares and a daily parade. The aroma of freshly baked cookies and cakes beckons from **Main Street Bakery,** and the **Emporium** is a one-stop shop for Magic Kingdom souvenirs. A horse-drawn trolley carries visitors up Main St. to **Cinderella's Castle,** Disney's own Statue of Liberty, where there are frequent dancing and singing shows by your favorite Disney characters.

TOMORROWLAND. In the 1990s, Tomorrowland received a neon facelift that skyrocketed it out of the space-race days of the 1960s and into a futuristic intergalactic nation. The indoor roller coaster **Space Mountain** dominates the landscape, providing chills and thrills in the blackness of outer space. **Buzz Lightyear's Space Ranger Spin** equips *Toy Story* fans with laser cannons to fight the Evil Emperor Zurg. A science experiment gone wrong, the frightening **ExtraTERRORestrial Alien Encounter** has an angry alien breathing down your neck.

MICKEY'S TOONTOWN & FANTASYLAND. Meet all your favorite characters at the **Hall of Fame** and **Mickey's Country House.** Bring an autograph book and camera to the **Judge's Tent** to meet Mickey, but expect a long line of fans. **Fantasyland** brings some of Disney's all-time favorite animated films to life. Soar above London and Neverland in a pirate ship sprinkled with pixie dust at **Peter Pan's Flight,** then dance with dwarves at **Snow White's Scary Adventures** (watch out for the Wicked Witch). For some saccharine but heartwarming melodies, meet mechanical children from around the world on the classic boat ride **"It's a small world."**

LIBERTY SQUARE & FRONTIERLAND. Welcome to Disney-style Americana. Liberty Sq. introduces visitors to the educational and political aspects of American history; Frontierland showcases the America of cowboys and Indians. **The Hall of Presidents** is a fun exhibit on US heads of state, from George Washington to George Bush. Next door, the spooky **Haunted Mansion** houses 999 happy haunts. In Frontierland, take a lazy raft ride over to **Tom Sawyer Island** and explore as Tom did, or take on the two thrill rides—**Splash Mountain** and **Big Thunder Mountain Railroad.**

ADVENTURELAND. Sail on the classic **Pirates of the Caribbean** and uncover hidden treasures, or fly on the new **Magic Carpets of Aladdin** for an aerial view of the park. One of the original rides from the park's opening, **The Jungle Cruise** provides a tongue-in-cheek take on exploration, riding through the world's amazing rivers to supply good wet fun and lots of bad puns.

EPCOT CENTER

In 1966, Walt dreamed up an "Experimental Prototype Community Of Tomorrow" (EPCOT), which would evolve constantly to incorporate new ideas from US technology—eventually becoming a self-sufficient, futuristic utopia. At present, Epcot splits into **Future World** and the expansive **World Showcase.** After a day of walking around the world, it's no wonder that some joke that the true acronym is "Every Person Comes Out Tired."

The trademark 180 ft. high geosphere (or "golfball") at the entrance to Future World houses the **Spaceship Earth** attraction, where visitors board a "time machine" for a tour through the evolution of communications. **Body Wars** takes visitors on a tour of the human body (with the help of a simulator), while at nearby **Test Track** riders become crash test dummies on one of Disney's fastest and longest rides. The immensely popular **Honey, I Shrunk the Audience** boasts stellar 3D effects.

At the World Showcase, architectural styles, monuments, and typical food and crafts represent 11 countries from around the world, while people in traditional dress perform various forms of cultural entertainment. **Maelstrom** is an amusing and thrilling boat ride through Norway, complete with Vikings and trolls. The best cultural film, **Impressions de France** has gorgeous panoramic views of the country accompanied by captivating classical music of French composers. Every night at 9pm, Epcot presents a magnificent mega-show called **IllumiNations** with music, dancing fountains, laser lights, and fireworks. World Showcase also specializes in regional cuisine. The all-you-can-eat meat, seafood, and salad buffet ($19) at **Restaurant Akershus,** in the Norway Pavilion, is actually a Disney dining bargain. Watch a dexterous chef prepare your meal at your table in Japan's **Mitsukoshi Teppanyaki Dining Room,** a moderately priced theatrical dining experience.

DISNEY-MGM STUDIOS

Disney-MGM Studios sets out to create a "living movie set." Restaurants resemble their Hollywood counterparts, and movie characters stroll the grounds signing autographs. MGM is built around several stunt shows and mini-theatricals; plan your day according to the ones you want to see. Enter the greatest scenes in movie history at the **Great Movie Ride,** inside a replica of Mann's Chinese Theater. **The Twilight Zone Tower Of Terror** drops guests 13 stories in a runaway elevator. The thrilling, twisting, "limo" ride that is **Rock 'n' Roller Coaster** will take you from zero to sixty mph in less than three seconds; it's also the only Disney attraction to take you upside down. Based on the hit TV game show, **Who Wants to Be a Millionaire?**

Play It! replicates the real show, save affable host Regis Philbin. The **Indiana Jones Epic Stunt Spectacular** shows off some of the greatest scenes from the trilogy in live action. **The Magic of Disney Animation,** a tour that introduces you to actual Disney animators, teaches you how they create Disney animated films and offers a sneak peak at the sketches of upcoming Disney classics.

DISNEY'S ANIMAL KINGDOM

If fake plastic characters and make-believe are getting to be too much, the Animal Kingdom is a heavy dose of reality. **Kilimanjaro Safaris** depart for the exotic Harambe preserve where elephants, hippos, giraffes, and other creatures of the African savannah roam. A **Maharajah Jungle Trek** drops riders among tigers, tapirs, and bats. Animal Kingdom is not all about immersion in foreign lands. Like any Disney park, shows and rides make up a large part of the attraction (the park's catchphrase is NAHTAZU: "not a zoo"). **DINOSAUR** puts travelers in the middle of the early Cretaceous, while the new coaster **Primeval Whirl** puts you in a dinosaur's jaws. Another 3-D spectacular, **It's Tough to be a Bug!** put on by the cast of the animated flick *A Bug's Life*, is sure to entertain all ages and species.

OTHER DISNEY ATTRACTIONS

Besides the four main parks, Disney offers several other draws with different themes and separate admissions. **Blizzard Beach** is a water park built on the premise of a melting mountain. Ride a ski lift to the fastest water-slide in the world, plummeting down a 120 ft. descent. **Typhoon Lagoon,** a 50-acre water park, centers on the nation's largest wave-making pool and the seven-foot waves it creates. Beyond eight water slides, the lagoon has a creek for inner-tube rides and a saltwater coral reef stocked with tropical fish and harmless sharks. Water parks fill up early on hot days; late arrivals might get turned away. With more than nine sports venues for over 30 sports, **Disney's Wide World Of Sports Complex** is a hubbub of athletic activity. Catch the Atlanta Braves in spring training, or test your skills at punting and passing at the **NFL Experience.** The larger-than-life **Downtown Disney** is a neon conglomeration of theme restaurants, nightlife, and shopping encompassing the **Marketplace, Pleasure Island,** and the **West Side.** In the Marketplace at the **LEGO Imagination Center,** you can take a photo with large LEGO sculptures or try creating your own. In the West Side, **Cirque Du Soleil** presents La Nouba, a breathtaking blend of circus acrobatics and theater—with a pricetag ($71) that will also take your breath away. Next door, the high-tech interactive games of **Disney Quest** guarantee a "virtually" exciting time. *($31, ages 3-9 $25.)* **Pleasure Island** is hedonistic Disney with an attitude. Party at eight nightclubs—from comedy to jazz to 80s pop. *(Open daily 8pm-2am. 18+ unless accompanied by parent. Admission $21.)*

LIFE BEYOND DISNEY   ☎407

The big non-Disney theme parks band together in competition with Mickey. "Flex-Tickets," combine admission prices to various parks at a discount. A four-park ticket ($170, ages 3-9 $135) covers Sea World, both Universal Studios parks, and Wet 'n Wild, and allows 14 consecutive days of visiting with free transportation. The five-park ticket ($203/165) adds Busch Gardens in Tampa (see p. 509) and also lasts 14 consecutive days. Universal City Travel (☎800-224-3838) sells tickets.

◉ THE PARKS

SEA WORLD

One of the largest marine parks in the US, **Sea World Adventure Park** makes a splash with marine-themed shows, rides, and exhibits. In recent years, it has reinvented itself from a repository of cutting-edge marine technology to a full-fledged park emphasizing the mystery and dark side of sea creatures. Eels, barracudas, sharks, and other beasties lick their chops in **Terrors of the Deep,** the world's largest collection of dangerous sea creatures. **The Shamu Adventure** thrills with amazing aquatic acrobatics executed smartly by a family of Orcas and their trainers. Whale belly flops send waves of 52°F salt water into the cheering "soak zone." The park's first thrill ride, **Journey to Atlantis,** gets rave reviews, as does **Kraken,** a floorless roller coaster billed as the highest, fastest, and longest coaster in Orlando. *(12 mi. southwest of Orlando off I-4 at Rte. 528/Beeline Expwy. Take bus #8. ☎351-3600. Open daily 9am-7pm; extended hours in summer. $53, ages 3-9 $43. Parking $7.)* Orlando's newest vacation destination is the adjacent **Discovery Cove.** Swim with dolphins, snorkel among tropical fish, and frolic in an aviary with more than 200 birds. *(☎877-434-7268. Open daily 9am-5:30pm. $119-399. Reservations required.)*

CYPRESS GARDENS

The botanical gardens of **Cypress Gardens** feature over 8000 varieties of plants and flowers with winding walkways and electric boat rides for touring. Hoop-skirted Southern Belles patrol the grounds. Despite all the pretty flowers, the **water-ski shows** attract the biggest crowds and the loudest applause. *(Southwest of Orlando in Winter Haven; take I-4 southwest to Rte. 27 S, then Rte. 540 W. ☎863-324-2111. Open daily 9:30am-5pm. $35, ages 6-12 $20.)*

UNIVERSAL ORLANDO

A less cartoonish alternative to Disney World is Universal: nothing magical, just movie rides that thrill, spin, and make you squeal. With its two parks **(Universal Studios Florida** and **Islands of Adventure),** three resort hotels, and an entertainment complex called **CityWalk,** Universal is no longer an afterthought to the "other park." *(I-4 Exit 74B or 75A. ☎363-8000. Open daily 9am, closing times vary. CityWalk open until 2am. Each park $53, ages 3-9 $43. CityWalk is ungated and free. Parking $7.)*

UNIVERSAL STUDIOS FLORIDA. The original park to "ride the movies" showcases a mix of rides and behind-the-scenes extravaganzas. Rid the world of invading aliens on **Men In Black: Alien Attack,** the park's newest attraction. **Back to the Future...The Ride,** a staple of any Universal visit, utilizes seven-story OmniMax surround screens and spectacular special effects. A studio tour of **Nickelodeon** offers an interactive look at the sets, stages, and slime.

ISLANDS OF ADVENTURE. This park encompasses 110 acres of the most technologically sophisticated rides in the world and typically has short wait times. Five islands portray different themes, ranging from cartoons to Jurassic Park to Marvel Superheroes. **The Amazing Adventures of Spider Man** is the crown jewel; new technology and several patents sprung from its conception. A fast-moving car whizzes around a 3-D video system as you and Peter Parker find the stolen Statue of Liberty. The most entertaining island is **Seuss Landing,** home of the **Green Eggs & Ham Cafe** (green eggs and ham-wich $5.60). **The Cat in the Hat** turns the classic into a ride on a wild couch that loops its way through the story. If that's too tame, the **Dueling Dragons** is the world's first inverted, dueling roller coaster.

CITYWALK. The free CityWalk greets the eager tourist upon entering Universal Studios. A mix of unique restaurants, a few clubs, and free evening parking make it an appealing alternative to Pleasure Island. The **NASCAR Cafe, Jimmy Buffet's Margaritaville,** and **Emeril's** are a few of the pricey theme restaurants that line the main street. Clubs on the walk include **Bob Marley's** and **The Groove.** (21+. Cover $4-5.)

THE HOLY LAND EXPERIENCE

Step back in time at this small, controversial park billed as a "living biblical museum." Take in the architecture and sights of ancient Jerusalem, and watch as costumed performers reenact biblical scenes. The **Scriptorium** is a one-of-a-kind museum displaying valuable artifacts, scrolls, and manuscripts relating to the Bible. *(655 Vineland Rd. I-4 Exit 78. ☎872-2272. Open M-Th 10am-5pm, F-Sa 10am-6pm, Su noon-6pm. $22, ages 4-12 $17.)*

COCOA BEACH & CAPE CANAVERAL   ☎321

Cape Canaveral and the surrounding "Space Coast" were a hot spot during the Cold War. Once the great Space Race began heating up, the area took off—it became the base of operations for every major space exploration, from the Apollo moon landings to the current International Space Station effort. The towns of Cocoa Beach and nearby Melbourne, however, provide typical beach atmosphere, including the surfer's Mecca, **▧Ron Jon's Surf Shop.** Beware during summer launch dates; tourists pack the area and hotel prices follow NASA into the stratosphere.

▧ ▨ ORIENTATION & PRACTICAL INFORMATION. The Cocoa Beach area, 50 mi. east of Orlando, consists of mainland towns Cocoa and Rockledge, oceanfront towns Cocoa Beach and Cape Canaveral, and Merritt Island in between. Both **I-95** and **U.S. 1** run north-south on the mainland, while **Rte. A1A** (North Atlantic Ave.) is the beach's main drag, cutting through Cocoa Beach and Cape Canaveral. **Greyhound,** 302 E. Main St. (☎636-6531; station open daily 7am-5:30pm), in Cocoa, 8 mi. inland, runs to Daytona (1¾hr.; 4 per day; M-Th $15, F-Su $16) and Orlando (1hr.; 5 per day; $10/11). **Space Coast Area Transit (SCAT)** has North Beach and South Beach routes and stops at every town in Brevard County. Surfboards are allowed inside buses. (☎633-1878. Operates M-F 6am-6:45pm, weekend service on some routes. $1; students, seniors, and disabled 50¢; transfers free.) **Blue Dolphin Shuttle** connects Cocoa Beach with the Orlando Airport; call in advance. (☎433-0011. $60.) **Taxis: Checker Taxi,** ☎777-9339. **Visitor Info: Cocoa Beach Chamber of Commerce,** 400 Fortenberry Rd., on Merritt Island. (☎459-2200; www.cocoabeachchamber.com. Open M-F 8:30am-5pm.) **Space Coast Office of Tourism,** 8810 Astronaut Blvd. (A1A), #102. (☎407-868-1126 or 800-936-2326. Open M-F 8am-5pm.) **Post Office:** 500 N. Brevard Ave., Cocoa Beach. (☎783-4800. Open M-F 8:30am-5pm, Sa 8:30am-noon.) **ZIP code:** 32931. **Area code:** 321. 10-digit dialing required.

▧ ▣ ACCOMMODATIONS & FOOD. Across from the beach, **Motel 6 ❷,** 3701 N. Atlantic Ave. (A1A), beats the rates of most accommodations in Cocoa Beach. (☎783-3103. A/C, TV, pool, laundry, and shuffleboard. Singles $43; F-Sa $6 each additional person.) Behind the bus station and the water tower, the **Dixie Motel ❷,** 301 Forrest Ave., is a family-owned establishment with clean rooms, floor-to-ceiling windows, A/C, cable TV, and a swimming pool. (☎632-1600. Laundry available. Rooms May-Oct. from $40; Nov.-Apr. from $55.) Pitch your tent at scenic **Jetty Park Campgrounds ❶,** 400 E. Jetty Rd., at the northern tip of Cape Canaveral. (☎783-7111. Reserve 3 months ahead, especially before shuttle launches. Jan.-Apr. primitive sites $19, with water and electricity $23, full hookup $26; May-Dec. $17/21/24.)

Bikini contests, live music, karaoke, delicious drink specials, and tasty seafood make **Coconut's on the Beach ❸,** 2 Minutemen Causeway at A1A, a popular hangout. Try the classic crab cake for lunch ($7) or the coconut-crusted mahi-mahi for dinner ($15), while chilling on the deck and ogling surfers. Call for monthly events schedule. (☎784-1422. Open M-Sa 11am-1:30am, Su 10am-1:30am.) Lines awaiting "famous" New York-style pizza stream out the door of **Bizzarro ❶,** #4 1st Ave., off A1A in Indialantic. (☎724-4799. Sicilian slice $1.50. Open M-Th 11am-9pm, F-Sa 11am-11pm, Su noon-9pm.) The **Tea Room ❶,** 6211 N. Atlantic Ave. (A1A), combines home cookin' and a little TLC to start your engine. (☎783-5527. Daily breakfast specials around $3. Pastries 50¢-$1.25. Open M-F 7am-2pm, Sa-Su 8am-2pm.)

THE FINAL FRONTIER. All of **NASA's** shuttle flights take off from the **Kennedy Space Center,** 18 mi. north of Cocoa Beach on Rte. 3, accessible by car via Rte. 405E off I-95, or Rte. 528E from the Beeline Expwy. From Cocoa Beach, take Rte. A1A until it turns west onto Rte. 528, then follow Rte. 3 N. The recently renovated **Kennedy Space Center Visitors Complex (KSC)** provides a huge welcoming center for visitors, complete with two 3-D IMAX theaters, a Rocket Garden, and continuously updated exhibits on the latest in-space exploration. KSC offers two tours of their 220 sq. mi. grounds. The **Kennedy Space Center Tour** hits the three main attractions: the LC 39 Observation Gantry, Apollo/Saturn V Center, and the International Space Station Center. (Departs regularly 9am-2:15pm.) Meet a real space pioneer face-to-face at the daily **Astronaut Encounter,** when astronauts past and present discuss their otherworldly experiences. The **NASA Up Close Tour** provides access to facilities that are restricted on the standard tour. Check out the shuttle launch pad, the gigantic VAB building (where the shuttle is put together), and the Crawler Transporter. With NASA's ambitious **launch schedule,** you may have a chance to watch the space shuttles *Endeavor*, *Columbia*, *Atlantis*, or *Discovery* thunder off into the blue yonder above the Cape. A combo package will get you admission to the Visitors Complex and transportation to a viewing area to watch the fiery ascension. (☎452-2121; 449-4444 for launch info; www.kennedyspacecenter.com. Open daily 9am-5:30pm. Standard KSC grounds tours $26, ages 3-11 $16; Up Close tour additional $20. Launch combo $17.)

Surrounding the NASA complex, the **Merritt Island National Wildlife Refuge** stirs with sea turtles, manatees, wild hogs, otters, and over 300 species of birds, including several endangered ones. Exit 80 off I-95, east on Garden St. to SR 402. (☎861-0667. Open daily dawn to dusk. Visitors Center open M-F 8am-4:30pm, Sa-Su 9am-5pm.) **Canaveral National Seashore,** on the northeastern shore of the wildlife refuge, covers 67,000 acres of undeveloped beach and dunes. Take Rte. 406 E off U.S. 1 in Titusville. (☎407-867-0677. Open Apr.-Oct. daily 6am-8pm; Nov.-Mar 6am-6pm. Closed 3 days before and 1 day after NASA launches. $5 per car, $1 per pedestrian/bicyclist.)

PALM BEACH & WEST PALM BEACH ☎561

Nowhere else in Florida is the line between the "haves" and the "have-nots" as visible as at the intracoastal waterway dividing aristocratic vacationers on Palm Beach Island from blue-collar residents of West Palm Beach. Five-star resorts and guarded mansions reign over the "Gold Coast" island, while auto repair shops and fast food restaurants characterize the mainland. Budget travel may be difficult here, but the region still offers some unique museums and stunning houses.

ORIENTATION & PRACTICAL INFORMATION. Palm Beach is located along the southeast coast of Florida, approximately 60 mi. north of Miami and 150 mi. southeast of Orlando. In Florida, north-south **I-95** runs from St. Augustine to Daytona Beach, through the center of West Palm Beach, then continues south to Fort Lauderdale and Miami. The more scenic coastal highway, **A1A,** also travels north-south, crossing over Lake Worth at the Flagler Memorial Bridge to Palm Beach. Large highways cut through urban areas and residential neighborhoods; finding your way around can be a bit confusing. Stick to the major roads like north-south **Hwy. 1** (which turns into S. Dixie Hwy.) **A1A,** east-west **Palm Beach Lakes Blvd.,** and **Belvedere Rd.** The heart of downtown West Palm Beach is **Clematis St.,** across from the Flagler Memorial Bridge, and **City Place,** 222 Lakeview Ave. (☎835-0862); both contain affordable restaurants and nightclubs.

Palm Beach International Airport (☎471-7420), at Belvedere and Australian Ave., Exit 51 from I-95 N, is 2½ mi. east of downtown West Palm Beach. The Tri-Rail stops at the airport, as does bus #44 from downtown West Palm Beach Quadrille.

Amtrak, 201 S. Tamarind Ave., is east of I-95 in the downtown West Palm Beach Quadrille. (☎832-6169. Open daily 7:30am-8:45pm.) **Public Transit: Palm Tran,** 3201 Electronics Way, has 35 routes from North Palm Beach Gardens to Boca Raton, with #41 and #42 traveling through the Palm Beach area. The major hub is at the intersection of Quadrille Blvd. and Clematis St. in downtown West Palm Beach. Schedules available on all buses, at the main office, or at any public library. (☎841-4200 or 877-870-9489. $1.25; students under 21, seniors, and disabled 60¢; 1 day pass $3/2.) **Tri-Rail** connects West Palm Beach to Fort Lauderdale and Miami. (☎954-788-7936 or 800-874-7245. Hours vary by route: generally M-F 4am-10pm, Sa-Su 7am-5pm. $2-6; students, seniors, and disabled half-price; under 4 free.) **Taxis: Yellow Cab** ☎689-2222. **Visitor Info: Palm Beach County Convention and Visitors Bureau,** 1555 Palm Beach Lakes Blvd. (☎471-3995. Open M-F 8:30-5:30.) **Internet access: Clematis St. News Stand,** 206 Clematis St. (☎832-2302. Open Su-W 7:30am-10pm, Th-Sa 7:30am-midnight. $8 per hr.) **Post Office:** 640 Clematis St., in West Palm Beach. (☎833-0929. Open M-F 8:30am-5pm.) **Zip code:** 33401. **Area code:** 561.

⌐ ACCOMMODATIONS. Catering to the rich and famous (with an emphasis on *rich*) who flock to Palm Beach during the winter months, extravagant resorts and hotels are arguably the most notable attraction lining the Gold Coast. While the idea of mingling with royalty might sound like a fairytale come true, the words "budget" and "hostel" will only receive blank stares from receptionists. Many reasonably priced B&Bs are booked far in advance; reserve a room before you arrive. West Palm Beach is the best bet for an affordable room near the action, but the absolute cheapest options are the chain hotels near the highway. Built in 1922 by a former Palm Beach mayor and elegantly restored in 1990, ▨**Hibiscus House Bed & Breakfast ❹,** 501 30th St., in West Palm Beach at the corner of Spruce St. west of Flagler Dr., is affordable without sacrificing luxury. Sleep in one of nine antique decorated bedrooms and wake up to a two-course gourmet breakfast served on Waterford crystal. Each room has a terrace, TV, phone, and A/C. (☎863-5633 or 800-203-4927. Call ahead for reservations. Rooms Apr.-Nov. $75-135; Dec.-Mar. $100-270.) **Hotel Biba ❹,** 32 Belvedere Rd., in West Palm Beach, bus #44, is fun, funky, and eclectic. This newly renovated Art Deco hotel is quickly becoming a hot spot for trendy travelers. Beautiful bodies lounge on the pool deck and gather in the garden bar for drinks in the evening. (☎832-0094. Breakfast included. Rooms Apr.-Nov. $79-109; Dec.-Mar. $109-129.) **Heart of Palm Beach Hotel ❺,** 160 Royal Palm Way, in Palm Beach, bus #41, welcomes visitors with cool pinks and greens. Palm Beach's most inexpensive hotel is a favorite of travelers who enjoy staying close to Worth Ave.'s ritzy shopping/dining district. (☎655-5600. Internet access, refrigerators, TV, heated pool, free parking. Call ahead for reservations. Rooms Apr.-Nov. $99-169; Dec.-Mar. $199-399; under 18 stays free with parents.)

◨▨ FOOD & NIGHTLIFE. Clematis St. in downtown West Palm Beach offers a lively option for travelers on the cheap. A mixture of pool hall, sports bar, concert venue, and meat market, ▨**Spanky's ❷,** 500 Clematis St., features busty barmaids serving up inexpensive bar food and cold beer (pitchers $5). Every night is a different theme and drink special, like Island Tuesdays with 75¢ Coronas and $2 Rum Runners. (☎659-5669. Beer-battered onion rings $4. Hot wings 12 for $8. Open M-F at 11:30am, Sa noon, Su 1pm; closes when the place empties out.) Voted "Best Burger" and "People's Choice" in a recent cook-off, **O'Shea's Irish Pub and Restaurant ❷,** 531½ Clematis St., at Rosemary St., will modify any dish to fit vegetarian needs. Locals flock here for the live nightly music, usually Irish rock or folk, and Mrs. O'Shea's $7.50 savory chicken pie. (☎833-3865. Open Su-Tu 11am-10pm, W-Th 11am-midnight, F-Sa 11am-1am.) **Dax Bar & Grill,** 300 Clematis St., a restaurant with a longer daiquiri list than menu, touts "tropical latitudes, tropical attitudes," but somehow is always filled with families. (☎ 833-0449. "Banana Banshee" $4.25. Open M-W 11:30am-midnight, Th-Sa 11:30am-3am, Su noon-10pm.)

Known for exclusive dinner parties and black tie galas, nightlife on Palm Beach is an invitation-only affair. You won't find a disco or "local bar" anywhere along the ritzy downtown area. You will, however, find **Sprinkles Ice Cream & Sandwich Shop ❶**, 279 Royal Poinciana Way, the best bargain for a hungry stomach. Customers line up for a scoop of homemade ice cream ($3.75) in a hand-dipped cone. (☎ 659-1140. French bread pizza $5.50. Open Su-Th 10am-10pm, F-Sa 10am-11pm.)

◙ SIGHTS. Perhaps one of West Palm Beach's greatest treasures is the **Norton Museum of Art**, 1451 S. Olive Ave. Well-known for its collection of European, American, contemporary, and Chinese art, as well as photography, the museum boasts works by Gauguin, Matisse, O'Keeffe, and Pollock. (☎ 832-5196. Open May-Sept. Tu-Sa 10am-5pm, Su 1-5pm; Nov.-Apr. M-Sa 10am-5pm, Su 1-5pm. $6, ages 13-21 $2, under 13 free. Tours M-Su 2-3pm; lectures M-F 12:30-1pm. Free. Self-guided audio tour $4.) If you're visiting in early spring, catch the training season of the **Montreal Expos** and **Atlanta Braves**, who make their winter home at **Municipal Stadium**, 1610 Palm Beach Lakes Blvd. (☎ 683-6012. Call ahead for times and schedules.)

In Palm Beach, just walking around can be one of the most enjoyable (and affordable) activities. Shopping is ritzy on **Worth Ave.**, between S. Ocean Blvd. and Coconut Row. Known as the "Rodeo Drive of the South," boutiques on the avenue outfit wealthy Palm Beach residents in Gucci, Chanel, and Armani. Walk or drive along **Ocean Blvd.** to check out the spectacular, enormous mansions owned by celebrities and millionaires. One particularly remarkable complex is **The Breakers**, 1 S. County Rd., a sizable Italian Renaissance resort. Even if you can't afford the bare-minimum $270 price tag for a night of luxury, live vicariously though a guided tour. (☎ 888-273-2537. Tour W 3pm. $10.)

Of course, a trip to Palm Beach County is incomplete without relaxing on one of its picturesque beaches. Although most of the beachfront property in Palm Beach is private, more public beaches can be found in West Palm Beach. Good options on Palm Beach include the popular **Mid-town Beach**, 400 S. Ocean Blvd., and **Phipps Ocean Park**, 2185 S. Ocean Blvd. (☎ 585-9203).

FORT LAUDERDALE ☎ 954

City streets and highways may be fine for most city's transportation needs, but Fort Lauderdale adds a third option: canals. Intricate waterways connect ritzy homes with the intracoastal river—owning a yacht (over 40,000 in town) is both practical and stylish. "The Venice of America" also boasts 23 miles of beach, making Fort Lauderdale fun even for those who can't afford a yacht. For the aquaphobic, trendy Las Olas Blvd. has some of the best shopping in south Florida.

▛ TRANSPORTATION

Airport: Fort Lauderdale/Hollywood International, 1400 Lee Wagoner Blvd. (☎ 359-6100), 3½ mi. south of downtown on U.S. 1. Or take I-595 E from I-95 to Exit 12B. Buses to and from the airport go through Broward Transit Central Terminal (☎ 367-8400). Take bus #11 south to the airport, and #1 when leaving the airport.

Trains: Amtrak, 200 SW 21st Terr. (☎ 587-6692), just west of I-95, ¼ mi. south of Broward Blvd. Take bus #22 from downtown. Open daily 7:15am-9:15pm. To **Orlando** (4¾hr., 2 per day, $29-56).

FLORIDA

Fort Lauderdale

🏠 ACCOMMODATIONS
Floyd's Hostel/Crew House, **3**
Fort Lauderdale Beach Hostel, **1**
Tropic-Cay, **4**
Tropi-Rock, **5**

🍴 FOOD
The Floridian, **2**
Ocean Drive Cafe, **6**

🍸 NIGHTLIFE
Elbo Room, **7**

Buses: Greyhound, 515 NE 3rd St. (☎764-6551), 3 blocks north of Broward Blvd. down-town. *Be careful in this area, especially at night.* Open 24hr. To: **Daytona Beach** (7hr., 4 per day, $35.50); **Miami** (1hr., 17 per day, $5); **Orlando** (5½hr., 6 per day, $33.50).

Public Transit: Broward County Transit (BCT); ☎357-8400. Central Terminal located at NW 1st Ave. and Broward Ave. downtown. Buses #11 and 36 run north-south on A1A through the beaches. Operates daily 6am-11pm. $1; seniors, under 18, and disabled 50¢; trans-fer 15¢. One-day passes ($2.50), 7-day passes ($9), 10-ride passes ($8), and sched-ules available at hotels, libraries, and the central terminal. **City Cruiser** (☎761-3543) loops through downtown and the beach strip between Sunrise Blvd. and Las Olas Blvd. F-Sa every 30min. 6pm-1am. Free. **Tri-Rail** (☎728-8445 or 800-874-7245) connects West Palm Beach, Fort Lauderdale, and Miami. Trains run M-F 4am-10pm, Sa-Su 7am-5pm. Schedules available at airport, motels, or Tri-Rail stops. $2-6; children, disabled, stu-dents and seniors with Tri-Rail ID 50% discount.

Taxis: Yellow Cab ☎777-7777. **Public Service Taxi** ☎587-9090.

Bike Rental: Mike's Cyclery, 5429 N. Federal Hwy. (☎493-5277). Open M-F 10am-7pm, Sa 10am-5pm. A variety of bicycles $20 per day, $50 per week; racing bikes slightly more. Credit card deposit required.

✳ ORIENTATION

North-south I-95 connects West Palm Beach, Fort Lauderdale, and Miami. Rte. 84/I-75 (Alligator Alley) slithers 100 mi. west from Fort Lauderdale across the Everglades to small cities on Florida's Gulf Coast. Florida's Turnpike runs parallel to I-95. Fort Lauderdale is bigger than it looks. The city extends westward from its 23 mi. of beach to encompass nearly 450 sq. mi. Streets and boulevards are east-west and avenues are north-south. All are labeled NW, NE, SW, or SE according to a quadrant. The two major roads in Fort Lauderdale are **Broward Blvd.**, running east-west, and **Andrews Ave.**, running north-south. The brick-and-mortar downtown centers around Federal Hwy. (U.S. 1) and Las Olas Blvd., about 2 mi. west of the oceanfront. Between downtown and the waterfront, yachts fill the ritzy inlets of the **Intracoastal Waterway. The Strip** (a.k.a. Rte. A1A, Fort Lauderdale Beach Blvd., 17th St. Causeway, Ocean Blvd., or Seabreeze Blvd.) runs 4 mi. along the beach between Oakland Park Blvd. to the north and Las Olas Blvd. to the south.

ⓘ PRACTICAL INFORMATION

Visitor Info: Greater Fort Lauderdale Convention and Visitors Bureau, 1850 Eller Dr. #303 (☎765-4466, for published info 800-227-8669, 24hr. phone line for travel directions and hotel info 527-5600), in the Port Everglades, has the useful *Superior Small Lodgings,* a comprehensive and detailed list of low-priced accommodations. Open M-F 8:30am-5pm. **Chamber of Commerce,** 512 NE 3rd Ave. (☎462-6000), 3 blocks off Federal Hwy. at 5th St. Open M-F 8am-5pm.

Hotlines: First Call for Help, ☎467-6333. **Sexual Assault and Treatment Center,** ☎761-7273. Both 24hr.

Post Office: 1900 W. Oakland Park Blvd. (☎527-2028). Open M-F 7:30am-7pm, Sa 8:30am-2pm. **ZIP code:** 33310. **Area code:** 954.

▮ ACCOMMODATIONS

Thank decades of spring breakers for the abundance of hotels lining the beachfront. Generally, you can easily find an available room at any time of the year, depending on how much you are willing to pay. High season runs from mid-February to early April. Motels just north of the strip and a block west of A1A are the cheapest. Many hotels offer off-season deals for under $35. The **Greater Fort Lauderdale Lodging and Hospitality Association,** 1412 E. Broward Blvd., provides a free directory of area hotels (☎567-0766; open M-F 9am-5pm). The *Fort Lauderdale News* and the *Miami Herald* occasionally sport listings by local residents who rent rooms to tourists in spring. Sleeping on the well-patrolled beaches is illegal and virtually impossible between 9pm and sunrise. Instead, check out one of the outstanding hostels in the area that provide cheap and plentiful housing options.

▧ **Fort Lauderdale Beach Hostel,** 2115 N. Ocean Blvd./A1A (☎567-7275). On A1A N between Sunrise and Oakland Park Blvd. Take bus #11 from the central terminal. After a long day of tanning and swimming at the adjacent beach, backpackers mingle in the large tropical courtyard and the well-stocked kitchen. A/C, ping-pong, grill, free Internet access, and local phone calls make this a traveler's paradise. Call ahead for free daytime pickup from anywhere in Fort Lauderdale. Breakfast included. Free lockers. Linen deposit $10. Dorms $16-18. Reservations suggested Dec.-Jun. ❶

THE HIDDEN DEAL

MONKEY BUSINESS

Four decades ago the entertainers at the Monkey Bar got a "bee in their bonnet" and escaped the nightclub for a more peaceful hangout. Today, their 35 descendants are still swinging in the lofty canopy of the **Bonnet House**. Lively chatter from these Brazilian squirrel monkeys, along with two swans, a few raccoons, and many birds, entertain visitors along the 30min. trail through 35 acres of mangrove swamp, desert garden, and tropical fruit grove.

Originally part of the property Hugh Taylor Birch purchased in 1863 when there were only six other residents of Ft. Lauderdale, the land was given as a wedding gift in 1919 to his daughter, artist Fredrica Bartlett. The southern plantation, named by Mrs. Evelyn Bartlett after she saw the alligators bobbing in her pond wearing water lilies on their heads, contains architectural whimsies such as a Chickee hut built by Seminole Indians, a thatched Island Theater, and a Shell Museum complex. *(900 N. Birch Rd., across from Birch Park on A1A. ☎ 563-5393. Open weather permitting Dec.-Apr. W-Sa 10am-4pm, Su noon-4pm; May-Nov. W-F 10am-3pm, Sa 10am-4pm, Su noon-4pm. Tours every 30min. until 2:30pm. Grounds and home $10, students $8, seniors $9; grounds only $6. Wheelchair accessible.)*

Floyd's Hostel/Crew House, 445 SE 16th St. (☎ 462-0631). From downtown take bus #1 or 40 and get off at 17th St. Call ahead for free pick-up in the Fort Lauderdale area. Floyd's is a homey hostel catering to international travelers and boat crews. The owners got engaged thanks to *Let's Go: USA 1995* (ask them for details). Free food consists of pasta, beans, and cereal. Cable TV, linen, lockers, laundry, and Internet access. Check-in by midnight or call for special arrangement. Passport or American driver's license required. 4-bed dorms $16, $115 per week; international workers get 5th day free in the summer. Private rooms in summer $40; in winter $55. ❶

Tropic-Cay Beach Hotel, 529 N. Ft. Lauderdale Beach Blvd./A1A (☎ 564-5900 or 800-463-2333), directly across from the beach; take bus #11 or 44. Don't be fooled by the lackluster exterior; during spring break Tropic-Cay is one of the most crowded party spots on the beach. Super-clean rooms, outdoor patio bar, cable TV, and heated pool. Free parking. Kitchens available. During spring break, you must be 21+ to rent. Key deposit $10. Doubles May-Sept. $35-59; Sept.-May $59-99; $10 per extra person. ❸

Tropi-Rock Resort, 2900 Belmar St. (☎ 564-0523 or 800-987-9385), 2 blocks west of A1A at Birch Rd.; take bus #11 or 44. A few blocks inland from the beach, you would miss this new hotel if it weren't painted orange and yellow. The lush hibiscus garden with caged birds surrounding the pool and Tiki bar sings with a little more privacy and luxury than neighboring motels. Gym, Internet access, tennis courts, free local calls, and refrigerators. Rooms Apr. to mid-Dec. $65-105; mid-Dec. to Apr. $85-160. ❹

FOOD

Though clubs along the strip offer massive quantities of free happy hour grub—wieners, chips, and hors d'oeuvres come on surfboard-sized platters—most bars have hefty cover charges (from $5) and drink minimums (from $3).

The Floridian, 1410 E. Las Olas Blvd. (☎ 463-4041), is a local favorite, serving up heaping portions of french toast ($4.75), cheeseburgers ($5), and veggie burger platters ($7). For some, the $3.75 milkshakes are only slightly less delicious than the posters of cheerleaders, swimsuit models, and pop singers adorning the walls. Open 24hr. ❶

Ocean Drive Cafe, 401 Ft. Lauderdale Beach Blvd./A1A (☎ 779-3351), is one affordable option along the strip providing both savory dishes and a vantage point for people-watching. Calzones $7. Veggie burger $6.50. Open daily 8:30am-midnight. ❷

Squiggy's N.Y. Style Pizza, 207 SW 2nd St. (☎522-6655). When hitting the bars of Fort Lauderdale, stop by Squiggy's for after-hours munchies. Gooey slices of Sicilian pie ($2, after 8pm $2.50) will certainly please you and the honey you met grooving under the strobe lights. Open M 11am-11:30pm, Tu-W 11am-3am, Th-Su 11am-4am. ●

👁 SIGHTS

Most visitors flock to Fort Lauderdale to lounge on the sunny beaches. When floating in the crystal-clear waves of the Atlantic, it's easy to forget the city's other notable attractions. Cruising down the palm-lined shore of A1A: Beachfront Ave., biking through a nature preserve, or boating through the winding intracoastal canals reveals the less sandy side of Fort Lauderdale.

ON THE WATERFRONT. Fort Lauderdale Beach doesn't have a dull spot on it, but most of the action is between Las Olas Blvd. and Sunrise Blvd. The latest on-the-beach mall, **Los Olas Waterfront,** boasts clubs, restaurants, and bars. (2 SW 2nd St.) The **Water Taxi** offers a breezy way to maneuver through town. The friendly captains will drive right up to any Las Olas restaurant or drop you off anywhere along the Intracoastal Waterway of New River. Alternatively, ride through the entire route for an intimate viewing of the fabulous, colossal houses along the canal. (651 Seabreeze Blvd./A1A. ☎467-6677. Call 30min. before pick-up. Open 9am-midnight. $4, seniors and under 12 $2; 1-day unlimited pass $5, 3-day pass $7.) If traveling with a family or young children, take a relaxing tour aboard the **Jungle Queen.** The captain's commentary acquaints you with the changing scenery as the 550-passenger riverboat cruises up the New River. (801 Seabreeze Blvd. At the Bahia Mar Yacht Center, on Rte. A1A 3 blocks south of Las Olas Blvd. ☎462-5596. 3hr. tours daily 10am, 2, and 7pm. $13.75, ages 2-10 $9.25; 7pm tour $30/17, dinner included.) On the beach, **Water Sports Unlimited** rents water-sports equipment, including wave runners. (301 Seabreeze Blvd./Rte. A1A. ☎467-1316. Open daily 9am-5pm. Parasailing trips $60-70.)

ON DRY LAND. Get lost in an oasis of subtropical trees and animals in the middle of urban Fort Lauderdale at **Hugh Taylor Birch State Park.** Bike, jog, canoe, or drive through the 3½ mi. stretch of mangroves and royal palms, or relax by the fresh lagoon filled with herons, gopher, tortoises, and marsh rabbits. For a real treat, bring lunch and relax at one of the picnic tables as butterflies gather around you. (3109 E. Sunrise Blvd., west off A1A. ☎564-4521. Open 8am-dusk. $1 entrance fee. Canoes $5.30 per hr. Cabins and primitive sites available by reservations; call ahead.) Anointed by Guinness as the "fastest game in the world," Jai Alai still remains mostly unknown to Americans outside the state of Florida. Take a break from the beach heat and watch a match at **Dania Jai-Alai,** which sports one of the largest frontons (courts) in the state. (301 E. Dania Beach Blvd. Off U.S. 1, 10min. south of Fort Lauderdale. ☎927-2841. Games Tu and Sa noon and 7:15pm, W-F 7:15pm, Su 1pm. General admission $1.50, reserved seats from $2.50.) Learn to fly-fish and reel in the virtual "big one" at the **International Game Fishing Association's Fishing Hall of Fame & Museum.** For the true fish fetishist, check out the large wooden replicas of world-record catches adorning the museum's ceiling and the film Journeys in the big screen theater. (300 Gulf Stream Way. Off I-95 at Griffin Rd., Exit 26. ☎922-4212. Open daily 10am-6pm. $5, seniors $4.50, children $4. IGFA members free.)

🏠 NIGHTLIFE

Ask any waiter or local that works along the strip and they'll tell you that the real action is in **Old Town.** Two blocks northwest of Las Olas on 2nd St. near the **Riverwalk** district, the 100 yards of Old Town are packed with raucous bars, steamy clubs, cheap eats, and a stylish crowd. Considerably more expensive, and geared specifically toward tourists, the **Strip** houses several popular nightspots across from the beach.

FLORIDA

■ **Tarpon Bend,** 200 SW 2nd St. (☎523-3233). Always the busiest place on the block. Starched shirts from the office converge with flirty black tube tops around the icy beer tubs of "the Bends." Bottle beers $3-4; "draft of the month" $1. W Ladies drink free until 11pm. Open daily 11:30am-1am, sometimes later.

The Voodoo Lounge, 111 SW 2nd St. (☎522-0733). A well-dressed and well-known party in lush red VIP rooms. The pretentious bouncers and velvet rope may seem out of character for the beach crowd, but this club has something for everyone. Su Drag shows, W Ladies night. F-Sa 21+. Cover F-Sa $10. Open W and F-M 10pm-4am.

Rush Street, 220 SW 2nd St. (☎524-1818), attracts a younger crowd of tight-miniskirt, Diesel-jeans-wearing partiers. It's hard to imagine that the cavernous dance floor could ever be filled, but the neon lights, blaring music, and lack of cover might explain the sea of dancers every Friday night. Lunch M-F 11am-2pm. Open M-Th 5:30-10pm, F-Sa 5:30-11pm, Su 4:30-9pm.

Elbo Room (☎463-4615), on prime real estate at the corner of A1A and Las Olas Blvd. The booming sidewalk bar, chock full of scantily clad beach beauties, is one of the most visible and packed scenes on the strip. Live music nightly. Open M-Th 11am-2am, F-Sa 11am-3am, Su noon-2am.

Club Atlantis, 219 S. Ft. Lauderdale Beach Blvd. (☎779-2544), is a popular hangout for hormone-raging teens. Mud wrestling and scandalous grinding fill the dance floors. 18+. Cover varies. Open daily 9pm-4am.

MIAMI & MIAMI BEACH ☎305

Miami's Latin heart pulses to the beat of the largest Cuban population this side of Havana—speaking Spanish is very useful. Beautiful buildings and beautiful people have established the city as a tourist haven. When it's cold in New York or smoggy in Los Angeles, Miami Beach seems to be the preferred hangout for an inordinate number of celebrities, and the hopping nightclub scene lets the average Joe enjoy a lifestyle along with them. But it's not all bikinis and sand—Miami is the starting point for one of America's greatest natural habitats, the Everglades, as well as the gateway to the Florida Keys and the Caribbean.

▐ TRANSPORTATION

Airport: Miami International (☎876-7000), at Le Jeune Rd. and NW 36th Ave., 7 mi. northwest of downtown. Bus #7 runs downtown; many others make downtown stops. From downtown, take bus "C" or "K" to South Beach. Taxi to Miami Beach $24.

Trains: Amtrak, 8303 NW 37th Ave. (☎835-1223), near the Northside Metrorail station. Bus "L" goes directly to Lincoln Rd. Mall in South Beach. Open daily 6:30am-10pm. To: **Charleston** (13-14hr., 2 per day, $64-149); **New Orleans** (24hr., 3 per week, $206-387); **Orlando** (5hr., 2 per day, $33-64).

Buses: Greyhound, Miami Station, 4111 NW 27th St. (☎871-1810). To: **Atlanta** (17-19hr., 13 per day, $85.50); **Fort Lauderdale** (1hr., every hr., $5); **Key West** (5hr., 4 per day, $30.25); **Orlando** (5-9hr., 10 per day, $36). Open 24hr.

Public Transit: Metro Dade Transportation (☎770-3131; info M-F 6am-10pm, Sa-Su 9am-5pm). The extensive **Metrobus** network converges downtown, where most long trips transfer. Over 100 routes, but the major, lettered bus routes A, C, D, G, H, J, K, L, R, S, and T serve Miami Beach. After dark, some stops are patrolled (indicated with a sign). Buses run M-F 4am-2:30am. $1.25, transfers 25¢; students, seniors, and disabled 60¢/10¢. Call for weekend schedule. Exact change only. The **Metrorail** services downtown's major business and cultural areas. Rail runs daily 5am-midnight. $1.25, rail-to-bus transfers 50¢. The **Metromover** loop downtown is linked to the Metrorail stations.

Miami

SEE SOUTH BEACH MAP P. 495

FLORIDA

Runs daily 5am-midnight. 25¢, seniors 10¢, free transfers from Metrorail. **Tri-Rail** (☎ 800-874-7245) connects Miami, Fort Lauderdale, and West Palm Beach. Trains run M-Sa 4am-8pm, Su 7am-8pm. M-F $6.75, Sa-Su $4; students, seniors, and ages 5-12 50% off. The **Electrowave** (☎ 843-9283) offers shuttles along Washington Ave. from S. Pointe to 17th St. Pick up a brochure or just hop on in South Beach. Runs M-W 8am-2am, Th-Sa 8am-4am, Su and holidays 10am-2am. 25¢.

Taxis: Metro, ☎ 888-8888. **Central Cab,** ☎ 532-5555. 1st mi. $3, $2 per mi. thereafter.

Bike Rental: Miami Beach Bicycle Center, 601 5th St. (☎ 531-4161), at the corner of Washington Ave., Miami Beach. Open M-Sa 10am-7pm, Su 10am-5pm. $5 per hr., $20 per day, $70 per week. Credit card or $200 cash deposit required.

ORIENTATION

Three highways crisscross the Miami area. **I-95,** the most direct north-south route, merges into **U.S. 1 (Dixie Hwy.)** just south of downtown. U.S. 1 runs to the Everglades entrance at Florida City and then continues as the Overseas Hwy. to Key West. **Rte. 836 (Dolphin Expwy.),** a major east-west artery through town, connects I-95 to **Florida's Turnpike,** passing the airport in between.

When looking for street addresses, pay careful attention to the systematic street layout; it's easy to confuse North Miami Beach, West Miami, Miami Beach, and Miami addresses. Streets in Miami run east-west, avenues north-south; both are numbered. Miami divides into NE, NW, SE, and SW quadrants; the dividing lines downtown are **Flagler St.** (east-west) and **Miami Ave.** (north-south). Some numbered roads also have names. Get a map that lists both numbers and names.

Several causeways connect Miami to **Miami Beach.** The most useful is **MacArthur Causeway,** which becomes 5th St. Numbered streets run east-west across the island, increasing as you go north. In South Beach, **Collins Ave. (A1A)** is the main north-south drag; parallel are the club-filled **Washington Ave.** and the beachfront **Ocean Ave.** The commercial district sits between 6th and 23rd St. One-way streets, traffic jams, and limited parking make driving around **South Beach (SoBe)** frustrating. Tie on your most stylish sneakers and enjoy the small island at your leisure. It only takes about 20min. to walk up Collins Ave. from 6th to 16th St., not counting all the time you spend checking out the funky fashion stores and restaurants.

Back in Miami, the heart of **Little Havana** lies between SW 12th and SW 27th Ave.; take bus #8, 11, 17, or 37. One block north of **Calle Ocho** (SW 8th St.), **W. Flagler St.** is a hub of Cuban business. **Coconut Grove,** south of Little Havana, centers on the shopping and entertainment district on **Grand Ave.** and **Virginia St. Coral Gables,** an upscale residential area, rests around the intersection of **Coral Way (SW 24th St.)** and **Le Jeune Rd.,** also known as **SW 42nd Ave.** Though public transportation is reliable and safe, a car can be useful to get around the city and its suburbs. Posted signs indicate different parking zones; cars in residential areas will be towed.

PRACTICAL INFORMATION

Visitor Info: Miami Beach Visitors Center, 420 Lincoln Rd. (☎ 672-1270). Open M-F 9am-6pm, Sa-Su 10am-4pm. **Info booth,** 401 Biscayne Blvd. (☎ 539-2980), downtown outside of Bayside Marketplace. Open daily 10am-6:30pm. In South Beach, **The Art Deco Welcome Center,** 1001 Ocean Dr. (☎ 531-3484) offers 1½hr. guided walking tours of the area's most notable architecture. Open M-F 11am-6pm, Sa 10am-10pm, Su 11am-10pm. Tours Th 6:30pm and Sa 10:30am ($15). **Coconut Grove Chamber of Commerce,** 2820 McFarlane Ave. (☎ 444-7270). Open M-F 9am-5pm. **Greater Miami Convention and Visitors Bureau,** 701 Brickell Ave. (☎ 539-3000 or 800-283-2707), 27th fl. of Barnett Bank Bldg. downtown. Open M-F 9am-5pm.

Hotlines: Crisis Line, ☎358-4357. 24hr. **Gay Hotline,** ☎759-5210. **Abuse Hotline,** ☎800-342-9152.

Medical Services: Mt. Sinai Medical Center, 1300 Alton Rd. (☎674-2121). **Rape Treatment Center and Hotline** (☎585-7273), at Jackson Memorial Hospital, 1611 NW 12th Ave. Open 24hr.

Internet access: Miami Public Library, 101 W. Flagler St. (☎375-2665), across from the Museum of Art. Open M-W and F-Sa 9am-6pm, Th 9am-9pm, Su 1-5pm. 45min. free. **Kafka's Cafe,** 1464 Washington Ave. (☎673-9669), in Miami Beach. Open daily 8am-midnight. 8am-noon and 8pm-midnight $3 per hr., noon-8pm $6 per hr.

Post Office: 500 NW 2nd Ave. (☎639-4284), in downtown Miami. Open M-F 8am-5pm, Sa 9am-1:30pm. **ZIP code:** 33101. **Area code:** 305.

🏨 ACCOMMODATIONS

Cheap rooms abound in South Beach, and choosing a place to stay is all about attitude. Hostels in Miami Beach are the cheapest option for people traveling alone. If young bohemian isn't your thing, cruise farther down Collins Ave. to the funky, hot-pink Art Deco hotels. Get a discount when you stay more than two nights in one of the trendy **South Beach Group Hotels,** including Whitelaw, Mercury, Shelly, Chelsea, Chesterfield, and Lily. In general, high season for Miami Beach runs late December through mid-March; during the off-season, hotel clerks are often quick to bargain. The **Greater Miami and the Beaches Hotel Association,** 407 Lincoln Rd. #10G, can help you find a place to crash. (☎531-3553. Open M-F 9am-5pm.) The Miami Beach Visitors Center (see **Practical Information,** above) can get you the cheapest rates. **Camping** is not allowed on Miami Beach.

■ **Banana Bungalow,** 2360 Collins Ave. (☎538-1951), at 23rd St. along the northern edge of the Art Deco district.

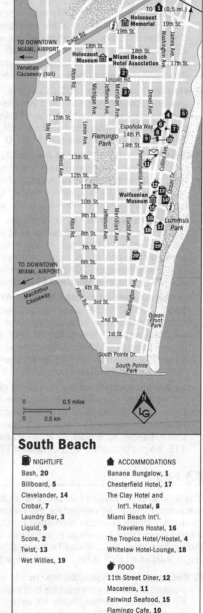

South Beach

🌙 NIGHTLIFE
Bash, **20**
Billboard, **5**
Clevelander, **14**
Crobar, **7**
Laundry Bar, **3**
Liquid, **9**
Score, **2**
Twist, **13**
Wet Willies, **19**

🏨 ACCOMMODATIONS
Banana Bungalow, **1**
Chesterfield Hotel, **17**
The Clay Hotel and
    Int'l. Hostel, **8**
Miami Beach Int'l.
    Travelers Hostel, **16**
The Tropics Hotel/Hostel, **4**
Whitelaw Hotel-Lounge, **18**

🍴 FOOD
11th Street Diner, **12**
Macarena, **11**
Fairwind Seafood, **15**
Flamingo Cafe, **10**
Taystee Bakery, **6**

Banana Bungalow is known as "party central"—the festive atmosphere around its pool/ bar area hops all year long. The activity desk provides opportunities for canoeing, kayaking, and clubbing as well as free guest passes for the club *du jour*. All rooms have A/ C and cable TV, though not all the fixtures work. Free coffee, tea, and toast in the well-equipped communal kitchen. Full bar with grill poolside. Free lockers in dorms. Key/ linen deposit $20. Internet access 20¢ per min. Dorms $17-19; private rooms $75-84, depending on season. Limited, free, guarded parking. ●

■ **Whitelaw Hotel-Lounge,** 808 Collins Ave. (☎398-7000). From 7-9pm, bright white leather and chrome greet beautiful party people lured into to the hotel's lobby by complimentary cocktails. Plush down comforters, continental breakfast, TV, A/C, refrigerator, free Internet access, free airport shuttle, and VIP guest passes to any club in SoBe. Doubles Apr.-Dec. $70; Jan.-Mar. $125. ●

Chesterfield Hotel, 855 Collins Ave. (☎531-5831). Deep house music pumps through the chic retreat, where the motto is "our rooms were made for sharing." Fabulous amenities, great location, and a surprisingly helpful "hipper-than-thou" staff. Continental breakfast, TV, A/C, free Internet access, free airport shuttle, bar, cafe, and free VIP passes to any area club. Rooms Apr.-Nov. $85, 3rd night is free; Dec.-Mar $125. ●

The Tropics Hotel/Hostel, 1550 Collins Ave. (☎531-0361), across the street from the beach. From the airport, take bus "J" to 41st St., transfer to bus "C" to Lincoln Rd., walk 1 block south on Collins, and its next to the parking garage. Quiet, large rooms, A/C, private baths, pool access, and an outdoor kitchen. Lockers at front desk; none in rooms. Internet access 20¢ per min. Free linen. Laundry. Key deposit $10. 4- to 8-bed dorms $18; singles or doubles $50. ISIC discount. ●

The Clay Hotel and International Hostel (HI-AYH), 1438 Washington Ave. (☎534-2988 or 800-379-2529), in the heart of the Art Deco district; take bus "C" from downtown. This historic Mediterranean-style building, once the center of Al Capone's Miami gambling syndicate, was often featured on the TV series *Miami Vice*. International crowd. Kitchen, laundry facilities, and A/C. Dorms come with phone and fridges; some have TV. Lockers $1 per day. Internet access $6 per hr. Linen/key deposit $10. 4- to 8-bed dorms $16, nonmembers $17; private rooms $43-79. ●

Miami Beach International Travelers Hostel (9th St. Hostel), 236 9th St. (☎534-0268 or 800-978-6787), at Washington Ave. From the airport, take bus "J" to 41st and Indian Creek, then transfer to bus "C" or "K." Central location, but difficult parking. Lively international atmosphere near the beach. Laundry and common room with TV and movie library. Internet access $8 per hr. 4-bed dorms with A/C and bath $13, nonmembers $15. Singles or doubles $55; off-season $36. ●

◐ FOOD

The food in Miami is just like the people: fun, exciting, and very diverse. Four-star restaurants owned by celebrities and renowned chefs are just as prevalent as four-choice sandwich counters renowned for their affordability. The South Beach strip along Ocean Drive houses an eclectic mix of tourist traps like **Hard Rock Café**, stargazing favorites like **Joia** and **Tantra,** and booty-shaking pseudo-clubs like **Mango.** Go at least one block inland from the beach to find more wallet-pleasing prices.

■ **Macarena,** 1334 Washington Ave. (☎531-3440), in Miami Beach. Dance your way to wonderful food in an atmosphere that's intimate and festive. This place is a favorite of hip-swirling Euro-hotties. *Paella* big enough for two ($14, lunch $7) and the best rice pudding ever ($5.50) make for the perfect Spanish treat. Wine comes from their own vineyards. W and F Flamenco dancing. Th ladies night. Sa live salsa. Lunch daily 12:30-3:30pm; dinner Su-Tu 7pm-1am, W-Th 7pm-1:30am, F-Sa 7pm-5am. ●

SALSA Miami's rich ethnic diversity has also made it a haven for top-notch Latin cuisine. Cuban specialties include medianoche sandwiches (a club sandwich on a heated and compressed roll); bright red mamey-flavored ice cream and shakes; hearty *frijoles negros* (black beans); and *picadillo* (shredded beef and peas in tomato sauce, served with white rice). For sweets, seek out a *dulcería* (sweetshop), or sample thimble-sized shots of sweet *café cubano* (around 35¢). For other treats, try plátanos, large starchy bananas fried or caramelized, or mojitos—rum, lime and mint spritzers.

▨ **Fairwind Seafood,** 1000 Collins Ave (☎538-6663), across from the Essex House. Treat yourself to some of the best food on the beach at surprisingly low prices. Try the superb *sashimi* tuna salad with mango salsa ($9.50), seafood pasta ($10.50), and Key Lime Creme Brulée ($4). Open daily 7am-6am. ❸

11th St. Diner, 1065 Washington Ave. (☎534-6373), at 11th St. in Miami Beach. Classic diner with the requisite soda fountain and ancient Coca-Cola clock. Originally built and operated in Wilkes-Barre, PA, the diner (the actual train car) was moved down to the Art Deco district and reopened in 1992. A popular spot after a long night of revelry. 24hr. breakfast $3-7. Sandwiches $4-7. Best shakes in Miami $4. Open 24hr. ❶

King's Ice Cream, 1831 SW 8th St./Calle Ocho (☎643-1842), in Miami. Tropical fruit *helado* (ice cream) flavors include a regal coconut (served in its own shell), *mamey,* and mango ($1 for a small cup). Open M-Sa 10am-11pm, Su 1-11pm.

Flamingo Cafe, 1454 Washington Ave. (☎673-4302), near the Clay Hostel in Miami Beach. Small counter with friendly service, all of which is in Spanish. Breakfast plate (eggs, toast, and meat) $2. Beef tacos and salad $2.75. *Frijoles con queso* $2.75. Lunch specials $5-7. Open M-Sa 7am-9:30pm. ❶

Taystee Bakery, 1450 Washington Ave. (☎538-4793). A unique Cuban bakery that uses only kosher products, Taystee also has a large selection of super-cheap, no sugar/ no salt baked goods. Guava pastries $1. *Empanadas* $1. Open M-Sa 6:30am-7:30pm.

◎ SIGHTS

SOUTH BEACH. South Beach is the reason to come to Miami. The liberal atmosphere, hot bodies, Art Deco design, and excellent sand make these 17 blocks seem like their own little world. *(Between 6th and 23rd St.)* Going topless is illegal, but the law is rarely enforced. **Ocean Dr.** is America's ultimate see-and-be-seen strip, lined with many bars or cafes for dodging the sun. The **Art Deco Welcome Center** (see **Practical Information,** above) gives out free info pamphlets and maps on the area's most notable buildings. Walking tours start at the **Oceanfront Auditorium.** *(1001 Ocean Dr., at 10th St. ☎672-2014. 1½hr. tours Th 6:30pm and Sa 10:30am; $10. 1¼hr. self-guided tours daily 11am-4pm; $5.)* The **Holocaust Memorial** commemorates the 6 million Jews who fell victim to genocide in WWII. Marvel at the 42 ft. bronze arm protruding from the ground with sculptured people attempting to climb it to freedom. *(1933-45 Meridian Ave. ☎538-1663. Open daily 9am-9pm. Free.)* **The Wolfsonian** examines the art of advertising design from 1885 to 1945, exhibiting over 70,000 objects. The exhibits include Russian propaganda, London subway signs, and a rather funny "plastics" room. *(1001 Washington Ave. ☎531-1001. Open M-Tu and F-Sa 11am-6pm, Th 11am-9pm, Su noon-5pm. $5, students and seniors $3.50. Free Th 6-9pm.)*

COCONUT GROVE. A stroll through the lazy streets of **Coconut Grove** uncovers an unlikely combination of haute boutiques and tacky tourist traps. People-watching abounds at the open-air mall, CocoWalk, along Grand Ave. On the bayfront between the Grove and downtown stands the **Vizcaya Museum and Gardens.** Euro-

FLORIDA

THE INSIDER'S CITY

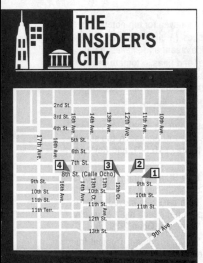

ANDANDO POR CALLE OCHO

Explore the sights, smells, tastes, and sounds of Little Havana on *Calle Ocho* (8th St.) for an inexpensive, fun, and cultural afternoon. Drive or take the bus (#8, 11, 37) to 8th St. and 11th Ave.

1 In **La Gloria Cubana,** 1106 SW 8th St., you can take a free tour to see how those famous Cuban stogies are rolled.

2 Head west on 8th St. to explore the many small record and clothing *bodegas* lining the street.

3 Stop for lunch at any of the small cafeterias. **Salon Tropical,** 1226 8th St., serves huge portions of beans and rice. Lunch here is remarkably cheap; for $5 you can eat an enormous amount of food: try a Cuban sandwich ($2), a cup of black beans ($1), a side of *plantinos* ($1.50), and a pineapple soda (50¢). The staff only speaks Spanish, but you can just point to the steaming plates of black beans, pulled pork, and chicken quarters.

4 Work off your feast with a leisurely stroll to **Maximo Gomez Park,** at the corner of 15th Ave., and jump into a lively domino tournament.

pean antiques, tapestries, and art fill this 70-room Italianate mansion, surrounded by ten acres of lush gardens. *(3251 S. Miami Ave. ☎ 250-9133. Open daily 9:30am-5pm; last entry 4:30pm. $10, ages 6-12 $5 ISIC discount. Gardens free.)*

BAYSIDE. On the waterfront downtown, Miami's sleek **Bayside** shopping center hops nightly with talented street performers. Stores and restaurants cater mostly to cruise ship guests and tourists with money to burn. *(Open M-Th 10am-10pm, F-Sa 10am-11pm, Su 11am-9pm.)* The **American Police Hall of Fame and Museum** is a quirky celebration of America's "men in blue," including a memorial engraved with names of officers who have died in the line of duty. Some exhibits feature grisly execution equipment, including a gas chamber and "Old Sparky," Florida's infamous electric chair. *(3801 Biscayne Blvd. ☎ 573-0070. Open daily 10am-5:30pm. $6, seniors $4, ages 6-12 $3, police officers free; discounts at Visitors Center.)*

CORAL GABLES. Scenic **Coral Gables** boasts one of the most beautiful planned communities in the region and houses the **University of Miami.** Nearby, the family-friendly **Venetian Pool,** founded in 1923, once drew Hollywood stars like Esther Williams and Johnny Weissmuller. Waterfalls and Spanish architecture dress up this swimming hole, which is always crowded on hot summer weekends. *(2701 DeSoto Blvd. ☎ 460-5356. Open in summer M-F 11am-7:30pm, Sa-Su 10am-4:30pm; hours vary off-season. $8.50, under 12 $4.50; Nov.-Mar. $5/2. Children under 3 years or 38 in. not admitted.)*

🎵 🎬 ENTERTAINMENT & NIGHTLIFE

For the latest on Miami entertainment, check out the "Living Today," "Lively Arts," and Friday "Weekend" sections of the *Miami Herald.* Weekly *Oceandrive*, the *New Times*, *Street*, and the *Sun Post* list local happenings. *TWN* and *Miamigo*, the major gay papers, are available free in paperboxes along Ocean Dr. **Performing Arts and Community Education (PACE)** manages more than 400 concerts each year (jazz, rock, soul, dixieland, reggae, salsa, and bluegrass); most are free. **Carnaval Miami,** the nation's largest Hispanic festival, fills 23 blocks of Calle Ocho in early Mar. with salsa, music, and the world's longest conga line.

Nightlife in the Art Deco district of South Miami Beach starts late (usually after midnight) and continues until well after sunrise. Gawk at models, stars, and beach bunnies while eating dinner at one of Ocean Blvd.'s open cafes or bars, then head down to **Washington Ave.,** between 6th and 18th St., for some serious fun. Miami Beach's club scene is transient;

what's there one week may not be there the next. Many clubs don't demand covers until after midnight, and often the $20+ door charge includes an open bar. Most clubs have dress codes and everyone dresses to the nines, even on so-called "casual" nights. If discos aren't your thing, pull up a stool at one of the frat-boy party bars along the beach.

■ **Crobar,** 1445 Washington Ave. (☎531-8225). Crawling with clean-shaven backpackers and easy-going local hipsters, Crobar's always-packed dance floor is stylish without unnecessary pretension. Su gay night. 21+. Reduced cover until 11:30pm. Open daily 10pm-5am, sometimes later.

Wet Willies, 760 Ocean Dr. (☎532-5650), pours a constant stream of strong, cheap daiquiris. If you're 21+, check out the outdoor bar upstairs, a great people-watching place. No cover. Open daily noon-2am.

Clevelander, 1020 Ocean Dr. (☎531-3485). A staple of backpackers and college tourists, the Clevelander combines a super-long bar with a moat-like pool—can you say wet T-shirt contest? No cover. Open daily 11am-3am.

Bash, 655 Washington Ave. (☎538-2274). The large indoor dance floor grooves to house and progressive while the courtyard in back jams to worldbeat. Th fashion shows. F Brazilian parties. 21+. Cover Th $10, F-Su $20. Open Th-Su 10pm-5am.

Liquid, 1439 Washington Ave. (☎532-9154). The beautiful and famous go to this ultra-chic club, owned by Madonna's brother Michael Ciccone and her chum Ingrid Casares. 21+. Cover $20. Open 10pm-5am.

Billboard (☎538-2251), 15th St. and Ocean Dr. Shake that healthy butt at SoBe's hip hop palace. Look for special appearances by stars like Ginuwine, Usher, and the Neptunes. Ladies free until 11pm. Open daily 10pm until late.

BETTER THAN BOOTYLICIOUS: GAY & LESBIAN NIGHTLIFE

South Beach's vibrant gay scene takes to the street at night in search of the new "it club." Gay and mixed clubs in the area have bragging rights as the most trendy, amorphous hot spots, attracting a large crowd of both gay and straight partiers.

Twist, 1057 Washington Ave. (☎538-9478), is a 2-story club with an outdoor lounge and a rockin' dance floor. One of the most popular bars on SoBe; you're apt to find straight couples at the bar as well. Cover varies. Open daily 1pm-5am.

Laundry Bar, 721 Lincoln Lane (☎531-7700). Soak your jockeys (and then dry and fold) in this most unusual nightclub. A DJ spins the latest in house music while the mixed crowd sips cocktails while doing their wash. No cover. Open 7am-5am.

Score, 727 Lincoln Rd. Mall (☎535-1111). Clientele is mixed, and there are frequent theme nights and lots of hookin' up. Bring your hot body, but leave your conscience at home. 21+. No cover. Open daily M-Sa 3pm-5am, Su 3pm-2am.

EVERGLADES ☎305

Encompassing the entire tip of Florida and spearing into Florida Bay, Everglades National Park spans 1.6 million acres of one of the world's most unique and fragile ecosystems. Vast prairies of sawgrass spike through broad expanses of shallow water, creating the famed "river of grass," while tangled mazes of mangrove swamps wind up the western coast. To the south, delicate coral reefs lie below the shimmering blue waters of the bay. A host of species found nowhere else in the world inhabits these lands and waters: American alligators, dolphins, sea turtles, and various birds and fishes, as well as the endangered Florida panther, Florida manatee, and American crocodile. Unfortunately, the mosquito is the most prevalent and noticeable Everglades species.

FLORIDA

▓ ORIENTATION & PRACTICAL INFORMATION

The main entrance to the park, the **Ernest Coe Visitors Center**, 40001 Rte. 9366, sits just inside the eastern edge of the Everglades. (☎242-7700. Open daily 8am-5pm.) Rte. 9366 cuts 40 mi. through the park past campgrounds, trailheads, and canoe waterways to the **Flamingo Visitors Center** (☎695-2945; open daily in summer 8am-5pm, in winter 7:30am-5pm) and the heavily developed Flamingo Outpost Resort. At the northern end of the park off U.S. 41 (Tamiami Trail), the **Shark Valley Visitors Center** provides access to a 15 mi. loop through a sawgrass swamp that can be accessed by foot, bike, or a 2hr. tram. **Shark Valley** is an ideal site for those who want a taste of the freshwater ecosystem but can't venture too deep into the park. (☎221-8776. Open daily 8:30am-6pm. Tram tours May-Nov. daily 9:30, 11am, 1, and 3pm; Dec.-Apr. every hr. 9am-4pm; $10, seniors $9, under 12 $5.50. Reservations recommended. Wheelchair accessible with reservations. Bike rental daily 8:30am-3pm. $4.25 per hr., including helmets.) The **Gulf Coast Visitors Center**, 800 Copeland Ave. S, in Everglades City in the northwestern end of the park, provides access to the western coastline and the vast river network throughout the park. (☎695-3311. Open in summer daily 8:30am-5pm; extended hours in winter.) **Entrance fees** vary, depending on the area of the park. (Ernest Coe $10 per day, $5 per pedestrian or bike. Shark Valley $8/4. Gulf Coast free.) For other area information on lodgings and local discounts, check out the **Tropical Everglades Visitors Center**, on U.S. 1 in Florida City. (☎245-9180 or 800-388-9669. Open daily 9am-5pm.) **Emergency: Park headquarters,** ☎247-7272. **Area code:** 305.

Summer visitors can expect to get eaten alive by swarming mosquitoes. Stay away from swampy areas during sunrise and sunset. The best time to visit is winter or spring when heat, humidity, storms, and bugs are at a minimum and wildlife congregate in shrinking pools of evaporating water. *Wear long-sleeve clothing and bring insect repellent at all times.*

▐ ▐ ACCOMMODATIONS & FOOD

Outside the eastern entrance to the park, **Florida City** offers some cheap motels along U.S. 1. The ▓**Everglades International Hostel (HI-AYH)** ❶, 20 SW 2nd Ave., off Rte. 9336, presents a far better option. The owners have created a home away from home. Hang out with fellow travelers in the gazebo, the gardens, or the kitchen house, which has a large-screen TV with a free video collection. (☎248-1122 or 800-372-3874. Internet access. Bike rental $5. Canoe rental $20. Linen $2. Dorms $13, with A/C $14; nonmembers $17/18. Private rooms $33/35, nonmembers $36/38.) The only option for lodging inside the park, **Flamingo Lodge** ❸, 1 Flamingo Lodge Hwy., has large rooms with A/C, TV, private baths, and a great view of the Florida Bay. (☎800-600-3813. Continental breakfast included in summer. Reservations recommended. Singles and doubles May-Oct. $65; Nov.-Dec. and Apr. $79; Jan.-Mar. $95.) A few **campgrounds** line Rte. 9336. All sites have drinking water, grills, dump sites, and restrooms, but none have hookups. (☎800-365-2267. Reservations required Nov.-Apr. Sites in summer free; in winter $14.) **Backcountry camping** inside the park is accessible primarily by boat (see **Sights,** below). Required **permits** are available on a first come, first served basis at the Flamingo and Gulf Coast Visitors Centers. (Applications must be made in person at least 24hr. in advance. Dec.-Apr. $10 for 1-6 people; May-Nov. free.)

Near the northwest entrance, motels, RV parks, and campgrounds scatter around Everglades City. The **Barron River Villa, Marina, and RV Park** ❶ offers 67 RV sites, 29 on the river, and tiny motel rooms with TV and A/C. (☎800-535-4961. RV sites May-Sept. full hookup $18, on the river $20; Oct.-Apr. $28/34. Motel rooms May-Aug. $41; Sept.-Dec. $49; Jan.-Apr. $57.)

Right across the street from the hostel, **Rosita's ❶**, 199 Palm Dr., has the best Mexican food in the area. Breakfast eggs ($4) can get you ready for a long day of exploring the park. Come back to relax with some great *chiles rellenos* or cheese enchiladas for $5. (☎246-3114. Open daily 8:30am-9pm.) Up Rte. 997 in Homestead, the **Main St. Cafe ❷**, 128 N. Krome Ave., guarantees a good time when the community comes together for open mic nights. Try a gourmet smoothies ($2-4) or the all-you-can-eat soup and salad bar ($8). They have lots of vegetarian and vegan options. (☎245-7575. Th teen open mic 8-11pm; F open mic 7pm-midnight. Sa folk and acoustic rock 7pm-midnight. Open M-W 10am-5pm, Th-Sa 10am-midnight.)

🔼 OUTDOOR ACTIVITIES

The park is swamped with fishing, hiking, canoeing, biking, and wildlife-watching opportunities. Forget swimming; alligators, sharks, and barracuda patrol the waters. From November through April, the park sponsors amphitheater programs, canoe trips, and ranger-guided Slough Slogs (swamp tours).

HIKING

Visitors to the Everglades can walk the well-developed short trails to explore the wildlife without exerting too much energy. Two of the best start at the **Royal Palm Visitors Center,** 4 mi. inside the park from the main entrance. The famous **Anhinga Trail** has the best opportunities, especially from December to March, to see alligators, anhinga birds, turtles, and giant crickets. For a spectacular view from horizon to horizon, the **Pa-hay-okee overlook,** on the main road, is worth the half-mile trip.

BOATING

If you really want to experience the Everglades, start paddling. The 99 mi. **Wilderness Waterway** winds its way from the northwest entrance to the Flamingo station in the far south. Adventurous camping spots along the journey include chickees (wooden platforms elevated above mangrove swamps), beaches, and groundsites. (In summer free; in winter $10.) **Everglades National Park Boat Tours,** at the Gulf Coast Visitors Center, rents canoes and offers two boat tours into the park. (☎695-2591 or 800-445-7724. Canoes $20 per day.) Shorter canoe trails wind from Rte. 9336; the **Hell's Bay Canoe Trail** threads through mangrove swamps past primitive campsites like Pearl Bay. Canoes are also available at the **Flamingo Marina,** but faint-of-heart beware—the low-gliding canoes often find themselves face-to-face with swimming gators. (☎800-600-3813. $22 per 4hr., $32 per day. $40 deposit.) Naturalists on the **Ten Thousand Island Cruise** lead the relaxing 1½hr. jaunt through the heart of the coastal "Ten Thousand Islands" and into the Gulf of Mexico with the occasional manatee, bottle-nosed dolphin, and bald eagle sighting.

GARDENS & GATORS

For a truly bizarre time, head up U.S. 1 to the **Coral Castle,** 28655 South Dixie Hwy., in Homestead. Over 20 years, Latvian immigrant Ed Leedskalnin turned hundreds of tons of dense coral rock into a garden of magnificent sculptures. The incredible sight has since been studied by anthropologists who thought it might explain how humans built the Egyptian pyramids. (☎248-6344. Open M-Th 9am-6pm, F-Su 9am-7pm. Guided tours daily. $7.75, seniors $6.50, ages 7-12 $5. Discounts at Visitors Center) View gators, crocs, and snakes at the **Everglades Alligator Farm,** 40351 SW 192 Ave., 4 mi. south of Palm Dr. Although it's ultra-touristy, it is the best place to see thousands of gators, from little hatchlings clambering for the sun to 18-footers clambering for...um...you. (☎247-2628 or 800-644-9711. Open May-Sept. daily 9am-6pm. $9, ages 4-10 $5. Wildlife shows $8. Discounts at Visitors Center.)

FLORIDA KEYS

Intense popularity has transformed this long-time haven for pirates, smugglers, and treasure hunters into supreme beach vacationland. Whether smothered in tourists or outcasts, the Keys retain an "anything goes" mentality. When former Key West mayor Tony Tarracino arrived here decades ago, he did a quick inventory of bars and strip clubs, and concluded that he'd reached heaven (see p. 506). If this sounds more like hell, take a dive. Gardens of coral 6 mi. off the coast enchant scuba divers and snorkelers, surrounding them with millions of colorful fish along the 100-yard wide barrier reef between Key Largo and Key West. Don't believe the hype; sharks are scarce here.

🛈 PRACTICAL INFORMATION

The **Overseas Hwy. (U.S. 1)** bridges the divide between the Keys and the southern tip of Florida, stitching the islands together. Mile markers section the highway and replace street addresses. The first marker, Mi. 126 in Florida City, begins the long countdown to zero in Key West. **Greyhound** runs to the Keys from Miami ($32), stopping in Homestead, Key Largo, Marathon, Big Pine Key, and Key West. Most bus drivers are willing to stop at mile markers along the side of the road. Tiny Greyhound signs along the highway indicate bus stops (usually hotels), where you can buy tickets or call the **info line** on the red phones provided. **Biking** along U.S. 1 is treacherous due to fast cars and narrow shoulders; instead of riding, bring your bike on the bus. Beer flows freely in the Keys, and drunk driving has become a problem recently—stay alert when on the roads. *Drunk driving is illegal and extremely stupid; don't even think about doing it.*

KEY LARGO ☎ 305

Over half a century ago, Hollywood stars Humphrey Bogart and Lauren Bacall immortalized the name "Key Largo" in their hit movie. Quick-thinking locals of Rock Harbor, where some of the scenes were shot, soon changed the name of their town to Key Largo to attract tourists. It worked. Key Largo is now the gateway to the rest of the enchanting, laid-back islands. While some (older) visitors still come to see the relics of the moviemaking past, more are drawn to Key Largo's greatest natural assets: the coral reefs and the incredible fishing. Pennekamp State Park was the country's first completely *underwater* park, and divers of all abilities flock to the isle for the chance to glimpse at the reef ecosystem and the numerous shipwrecks.

🛈 **PRACTICAL INFORMATION.** Greyhound (☎871-1810; open daily 8am-6pm), Mi. 102 at the Howard Johnson, goes to Key West (3 hr., 4 per day, $26-29) and Miami (1¾hr., 3 per day, $12.50-14.50). **Taxis: Mom's Taxi,** ☎852-6000. **Visitor info: Key Largo Chamber of Commerce/Florida Keys Visitors Center,** 106000 U.S. 1, Mi. 106 (☎451-1414 or 800-822-1088. Open daily 9am-6pm). **Post Office:** 100100 U.S. 1, Mi. 100. (☎451-3155. Open M-F 8am-4:30pm.) **ZIP code:** 33037. **Area code:** 305.

🛏 **ACCOMMODATIONS. Ed and Ellen's Lodgings ❸,** 103365 U.S. 1, Mi. 103.4, has clean, large rooms with cable TV, A/C, and kitchenettes. They also help with diving or snorkeling reservations. (☎451-9949 or 888-333-5536. Doubles $49-79; off-season $39-49; rates increase on weekends, holidays, and lobster season. Each additional person $10.) A few lodgings near downtown Key Largo boast reasonable rates. The **Bay Cove Motel ❸,** 99446 Overseas Hwy, Mi. 99.5, borders a small beach on the bay side of the island. Rooms have cable TV, A/C, and mini-fridges. (☎451-1686. Doubles $50-80, depending on season.) The waterside **Hungry Pelican ❸**, Mi. 99.5, boasts bougainvillea vines, tropical birds in the trees, and cozy rooms with double beds, fridges, and cable TV. Free use of paddle boats, canoes, and hammocks. (☎451-3576. Continental breakfast. Rooms $50-115; each additional person $10.) Reservations are necessary for the popular **John Pennekamp State Park Campground ❶** (see **Sights**, below). The 47 sites are clean, convenient, and well worth the effort required to obtain them. One-half are available through advance registration, and the others are given out first come, first served. Pets are not allowed. (☎451-1202. Bathrooms and showers. Max. stay 14 days. Open 8am-dusk. $24; with electricity $26.)

◻ **FOOD.** Seafood restaurants of varying price, quality, specialty, and view litter the Overseas Hwy. Try ▨**Islamorada Fish Company ❷**, Mi. 81.5, along the Bayside. If you can't catch the fish yourself, pull your boat into the docks for the freshest fins in all the Keys. The grouper or Mahi sandwich ($7) will melt in your mouth, and the conch gazpacho ($4) is a spicy favorite. When you finish, be sure to pick up a piece of frozen chocolate-covered Key Lime Pie ($3.25) in the neighboring **Islamorada Fish Shop**. (☎664-9271 or 800-258-2559. Open daily 11am-9pm, sometimes later.) Follow your meal from the boat to the plate at **Calypso's ❷**, 1 Seagate Dr., near Mi. 99 on the marina across from Key Largo Fisheries. The coconut shrimp ($6) is a sweet, fried delight, and the tangy white wine sangria ($3.50) will definitely go to your head. (☎451-0600. Open M and W-Th noon-10pm, F-Sa noon-11pm.) **Alabama Jack's ❷**, 5800 Card Sound Rd., between Homestead and Key Largo, east of Overseas Highway, rocks the southern Florida wetlands with live country music. It is probably the southernmost place to enjoy "hoppin' john" ($6), a southern dish of black-eyed peas, rice, and ham. (☎248-8741. Live music Sa 2-5pm, Su 2-7pm. Open M-F 11am-7pm, Sa-Su 11am-7:30pm.)

◪ **SIGHTS.** Key Largo is the self-proclaimed "Dive Capital of the World" and many diving instructors offer their services via highway billboards. The best place to go is the nation's first underwater sanctuary, **John Pennekamp State Park**, Mi. 102.5, 60 mi. from Miami. The park extends 3 mi. into the Atlantic Ocean, safeguarding a part of the coral reef that runs the length of the Keys. (☎451-1202. $2.50 per vehicle with 1 occupant, 2 occupants $5; each additional person 50¢. Walk- or bike-in $1.50.) Stop by the **Visitors Center** for complimentary maps, boat and snorkeling tour info, and hourly films on the park. To see the reefs, visitors must take their own boat or rent. (☎451-9570, for reservations 451-6325. Deposit required. Open daily 8am-5pm. 19 ft. motor boat $28 per hr. Canoes $10 per hr.) **Scuba trips** depart from the Visitors Center. (☎451-6322. 9:30am and 1:30pm. $37 per person for a two-tank dive. Deposit required.) A **snorkeling tour** also allows you to partake of the underwater quiet. (☎451-1621. 2½hr. total, 1½hr. water time. Tours 9am, noon, and 3pm. $26, under 18 $20; equipment $5. Deposit required.) Head to any of the local marinas to charter a spot on a **fishing boat**. To avoid paying activity promoters' commission, hang out on the docks and ask one of the friendly captains yourself. A relatively new addition, **Glass Bottom Boat Tours**, provides a crystal clear view of the reefs without wetting your feet. (☎451-1621. 2½hr. Tours 9:15am, 12:15, and 3pm. $18, under 12 $10.)

KEY WEST ☎305

The small "last island" of the Florida Keys, Key West has always drawn a cast of colorful characters. Henry Flagler, Ernest Hemingway, Tennessee Williams, Truman Capote, and Jimmy Buffett have all called the quasi-independent "Conch Republic" home. Today thousands of tourists hop on the Overseas Highway to

FLORIDA

glimpse the past, visit the over 300 bars, and kick back under the sun. The crowd is as diverse as Key West's past: families spend a week enjoying the water; twenty-somethings come to party and work; and a swinging gay population finds a haven of clubs and resorts oriented exclusively to them. Key West is as far south as you can get in the continental US. This is the end of the road—enjoy it.

▮ TRANSPORTATION

Buses: Greyhound, 3535 S. Roosevelt Blvd. (☎296-9072), at the airport. Open daily 8am-6pm. To **Miami** (4½hr., 3 per day, $32-36).

Public Transit: Key West Port and Transit Authority (☎292-8161), at City Hall, has clockwise ("Old Town") and counterclockwise ("Mallory Sq. Rte.") routes. Service daily every 1½hr. 7am-10:30pm. 75¢, students and seniors 35¢.

Bike rental: The Bicycle Center and Keys Moped & Scooter, 523 Truman Ave. (☎294-4724), rents wheeled adventures. Open daily 9am-6pm. Bikes $4 per half-day, $30 per week. Mopeds $18 per day, $23 per 24hr. Electric cars $29 per hr.

Taxis: Keys Taxi, ☎296-6666.

◼◢◪ ORIENTATION & PRACTICAL INFORMATION

Key West lies at the end of U.S. 1, 155 mi. southwest of Miami (3-3½hr.). Divided into two sectors, the eastern part of the island (known as **New Town**) harbors tract houses, chain motels, shopping malls, and the airport. Beautiful old conch houses fill **Old Town,** west of White St. **Duval St.** is the main north-south thoroughfare in Old Town; Truman Ave. (U.S. 1) is a major east-west route. A car is the easiest way to get to Key West, though driving in town is neither easy nor necessary. *Do not park overnight on the bridges.*

Visitor info: Key West Welcome Center, 3840 N. Roosevelt Blvd. (☎296-4444 or 800-284-4482), just north of the intersection of U.S. 1 and Roosevelt Blvd., is a private reservation service. Open M-Sa 9am-7:30pm, Su 9am-6pm. **Key West Chamber of Commerce,** 402 Wall St. (☎294-2587 or 800-527-8539), in old Mallory Sq. Open M-F 8:30am-6:30pm, Sa-Su 8:30am-6pm.

Bi-Gay-Lesbian Resources: The Key West Business Guild Gay and Lesbian Information Center, 728 Duval St. (☎294-4603), is helpful for locating exclusively gay guest-houses. Open M-F 9am-5pm.

Hotlines: Help Line, ☎296-4357. Operates 24hr.

Internet access: Internet Isle Cafe, 118 Duval St. (☎293-1199). $8 per hr. Open daily 8am–11pm.

Post Office: 400 Whitehead St. (☎294-2557), 1 block west of Duval St. at Eaton. Open M-F 8:30am-5pm, Sa 9:30am-noon. **ZIP code:** 33040. **Area code:** 305.

▮ ACCOMMODATIONS

Key West is packed virtually year-round, particularly from January through March, so reserve rooms far in advance. In Old Town the multi-colored 19th-century clapboard houses capture the charming flavor of the Keys. B&Bs dominate, and "reasonably priced" means over $50. Some of the guest houses in Old Town are for gay men exclusively.

▨ **Casablanca Hotel,** 900 Duval St. (☎296-0815), in the center of the main drag. This charming B&B once hosted Humphrey Bogart and James Joyce. Pool, A/C, cable TV, breakfast, and large bathrooms. Call ahead for reservations during Fantasy Fest. June-Nov. $59-99; Dec.-May $89-200. ❸

Key West Hostel (HI-AYH), 718 South St. (☎296-5719), offers basic rooms with shared bath, as well as a common room with TV. Internet access $8 per hr. No alcohol allowed. Free parking. Lockers $1. Linen free. Key deposit $5. Reception 24hr. Bike rentals $8 per 24hr. Reservations essential Dec.-Mar. Call for late arrival. 6- to 12-bed dorms $19.50, nonmembers $22.50. ❶

Caribbean House, 226 Petronia St. (☎296-1600 or 800-543-4518), has festive Caribbean-style rooms with A/C, cable TV, free local calls, fridge and comfy double beds. Continental breakfast. Reservations not accepted for cottages. Rooms in summer from $49; in winter $69. Cottages $69/89. ❸

Wicker Guesthouse, 913 Duval St. (☎296-4275 or 800-880-4275), on the main drag, has a pastel decor, private baths, A/C, and cable TV. Most rooms have kitchenettes. No phones. Kitchen, pool access, free parking, and breakfast included. Reservations recommended; ask for summer specials. Rooms June to late Dec. $89-105; late Dec. to May $130-150. ❹

Eden House, 1015 Fleming St. (☎296-6868 or 800-533-5397), just 5 short blocks from downtown, is a brightly painted, Art Deco hotel with a hostel-like atmosphere. Clean rooms with private or shared bath. Pool, jacuzzi, hammock area, and kitchens. Bike rentals $10 per day. Free happy hour daily 4-5pm. Rooms with shared bath in summer $105; off-season $80. ❺

Boyd's Campground, 6401 Maloney Ave. (☎294-1465), sprawls over 12 oceanside acres and provides full facilities, including showers. Take a left off U.S. 1 onto Macdonald Ave., which becomes Maloney. Sites for 2 in summer $42-60, with water and electricity $52-70, full hookup $57-75; in winter $45-70/55-80/60-85; each additional person $8. Waterfront sites additional $6-14. ❷

🍴 FOOD

Expensive and trendy restaurants line festive **Duval St.** Side streets offer lower prices and fewer crowds. **Blue Heaven** ❸, 729 Thomas St., one block from the Caribbean House has the best grub in town in a laid-back, hippie atmosphere. This menu covers a wide range: healthy breakfasts with fresh banana bread ($2-9); Caribbean or Mexican lunches ($2.50-10); and heavenly dinners ($9-19) that include plantains, corn bread, and fresh veggies. (☎296-8666. Open M-Sa 8am-3pm and 6-10:30pm, Su 8am-1pm and 6-10:30pm.) The best Cuban fare can be found at **El Siboney** ❷, 900 Catherine St., where $7 buys a ton of beans, rice, and meat. (☎296-4184. Open M-Sa 11am-9:30pm.)

👁 SIGHTS

ON LAND. Because of limited parking, traversing Key West by bike or moped is more convenient and comfortable than driving. For those inclined towards riding, the **Conch Tour Train** is a fascinating 1½hr. narrated ride through Old Town. *(Leaves from Mallory Sq. at 3840 N or from Roosevelt Blvd., next to the Quality Inn. ☎294-5161. Runs daily 9am-4:30pm. $18, ages 4-12 $9.)* **Old Town Trolley** runs a similar narrated tour, and you can get on and off throughout the day at nine stops. *(☎296-6688. Tours 9am-5:30pm. Full tour 1½hr. $18, ages 4-12 $9.)* No one can leave Key West without a visit to the ■**Ernest Hemingway Home**, where "Papa" wrote *For Whom the Bell Tolls* and *The Snows of Kilimanjaro*. Take a tour with hilarious guides as hilarious who'll teach you about Hemingway and Key West history, then traipse through on your own among 50 descendants of Hemingway's cat, half of which have extra toes. *(907 Whitehead St. ☎294-1136. Open daily 9am-5pm. $9, ages 6-12 $5.)* A tour of the **Harry S. Truman Little White House Museum** provides a fascinating view of one of America's greatest leaders. *(111 Front St. ☎294-9911. Open daily 9am-5pm. $10, children $5;*

> # "BRAINS DON'T MEAN SHIT" This brief profundity
> sums up the philosophy of Captain Tony Tarracino, gun runner, mercenary, casino
> owner, and one-time mayor of Key West. "All you need in this life is a tremendous sex
> drive and a great ego," proclaimed the Captain, who escaped to Key West over 40
> years ago while evading the New Jersey bookies he cheated. Tarracino arrived to find
> an island populated by bar-hoppers, petty criminals, and other deviants. In this setting,
> he thrived. Tony attempted to organize his local popularity into a political campaign,
> and after four unsuccessful bids, he was finally voted mayor in 1989. Though he wasn't
> re-elected, Tony T. isn't going anywhere soon—he even mocks his own mortality. "I
> know every stripper in this town," he boasts. "When I'm dead, I've asked them all to
> come to my casket and stand over it. If I don't wake up then, put me in the ground."

includes tour.) The **Audubon House** shelters fine antiques and a collection of original engravings by naturalist John James Audubon. *(205 Whitehead St. ☎294-2116. Open daily 9:30am-5pm. $8, students $7.50, seniors $5, ages 6-12 $3.50.)*

ON WATER. The **glass-bottomed boat** *Fireball* cruises to the reefs and back. *(☎296-6293. 2-2½hr. cruises daily noon, 2, and 6pm. Tickets $20, at sunset $25; ages 5-12 $10/12.50.)* The **Mel Fisher Maritime Heritage Society Museum** showcases the amazing discovery of the Spanish galleon *Atocha*, which sank off the Keys in the 17th century with hundreds of millions in gold and silver. An illuminating film is included in the entrance fee. *(200 Greene St. ☎294-2633. Open daily 9:30am-5pm; last film 4:30pm. $6.75, students $5.50, ages 6-12 $3.50.)* Down Whitehead St., past the Hemingway House, you'll come to the southernmost point in the continental US at the fittingly named **Southernmost Beach.** A small, conical monument marks the spot: "90 miles to Cuba." Locals and tourists alike take part in the daily tradition of watching the sun go down. At the **Mallory Sq. Dock,** street entertainers (including Tomas the incredible living statue) and kitsch-hawkers work the crowd, while boats parade in revue during the **Sunset Celebration.** After the sun finally disappears, it's time to drink.

📺 NIGHTLIFE

The free *Island News*, found in local restaurants and bars, lists dining spots, music, and clubs; *Celebrate!* covers the gay and lesbian community. Nightlife in Key West revs up at 11pm and winds down in the wee daylight hours. The action centers around upper **Duval St.** Key West nightlife reaches its annual exultant high the third week of October during **Fantasy Fest** (☎296-1817), when decadent floats filled with drag queens, pirates, and wild locals take over Duval St.

Capt. Tony's Saloon, 428 Greene St. (☎294-1838), the oldest bar in Key West and reputedly one of Tennessee Williams's preferred watering holes, has been serving since the early 1930s. Bras and business cards festoon the ceiling. Tony Tarracino, the 84-year-old owner and former mayor of Key West (see graybox), enters through a secret door on weekends. Live entertainment daily. Open M-Sa 10am-2am, Su noon-2am.

Rick's, 202 Duval St. (☎296-4890). An unabashed meat market, Rick's boasts well-placed body shots and a hot clientele. Happy hour, with $2 longneck Buds, daily 3-6pm. W and Th $7 all-you-can-drink nights. Open M-Sa 11am-4am, Su noon-4am.

Sloppy Joe's, 201 Duval St. (☎294-5717). For a real party, with both tourists and locals, stop by Hemingway's favorite hangout. Grab the *Sloppy Joe's News* to learn the latest on upcoming entertainment. 21+. Open M-Sa 9am-4am, Su noon-4am.

Margaritaville (☎296-3070), on Duval St. Search for your lost shaker of salt in this Jimmy Buffet-inspired bar that specializes in, that's right, margaritas. True Parrotheads may not appreciate the infestation of squawking tourists. Open daily 11am-2am.

GAY & LESBIAN NIGHTLIFE

Known for its wild, outspoken gay community, Key West hosts more than a dozen fabulous drag lounges, night clubs, and private bars for the gay man's enjoyment. Most clubs also welcome straight couples and lesbians, but check with the bouncer before entering. Most gay clubs line Duval St. south of Fleming Ave.

> **KWEST, 711 Duval St.** (☎ 292-8500), is the newest drag club in Key West. You're likely to see many wide-eyed tourists checking out the singing beauties. Next door, **KWEST MEN** is a sweaty, scandalous dance club, where boys in G-strings gyrate on the dance floor. No cover. 21+. Drag show nightly 10pm. Tu amateur night. Open 4pm-4am.

> **The Bourbon Street Pub, 724 Duval St.** (☎ 296-1992). This strip dance club is so hot, you'll soon find yourself shirtless, too. No cover. Open 4pm-4am. Its sister club, **801 Bourbon, 801 Duval St.** (☎ 294-4737), is also very popular. Open daily 11am-4am.

GULF COAST

TAMPA
☎ **813**

Even with beautiful weather and perfect beaches, Tampa has managed to avoid the plastic pink flamingos that plague its Atlantic Coast counterparts. While most tourists wait on line at Busch Gardens, Tampa's main theme park, the rest of the bay city provides a less commercial vacation spot. Ybor City, Tampa's Cuban district, is a rejuvenated hotbed of culture, where sun-bleached tourists can find many of Tampa's good restaurants, bars, and clubs. Downtown is not very inviting, but a few gems proudly display the city's charm.

🗐 🔁 ORIENTATION & PRACTICAL INFORMATION. Tampa wraps around Hillsborough Bay and sprawls northward. **Nebraska Ave.** and **Dale Mabry Rd.** parallel **I-275** as the main north-south routes; **Kennedy Blvd., Columbus St.,** and **Busch Blvd.** are the main east-west arteries. With some exceptions, numbered streets run north-south and numbered avenues run east-west. **Ybor City,** Tampa's nocturnal playland, is bounded roughly by Nuccio Pkwy. on the north, 22nd St. on the south, Palm St. on the east, and 5th St. on the west. *Be careful not to stray outside these boundaries; the area can be dangerous.*

Tampa International Airport (☎ 870-8770) is 5 mi. west of downtown, Exit 39 off I-275. HARTline bus #30 runs between the airport and downtown Tampa. **Amtrak,** 601 Nebraska Ave. (☎ 221-7600; open daily 6am-10:30pm), at the end of Zack St., 2 blocks north of Kennedy St., runs to Miami (5hr., 1 per day, $49). **Greyhound,** 610 E. Polk St. (☎ 229-2174; open daily 5am-midnight), buses to Atlanta (11-14hr.; 9 per day; M-Th $61, F-Su $65); Miami (7-10hr.; 10 per day; $36/38); and Orlando (2-3hr.; 7 per day; $15/16). **Hillsborough Area Regional Transit (HARTline)** provides public transportation. Buses #3, 8, and 46 run to Ybor City from downtown. (☎ 254-4278. $1.25, seniors and ages 5-17 60¢; exact change required.) The **Tampa Town Ferry** (☎ 223-1522) runs between many attractions along the Alaia and Hillsborough Rivers, including the Florida Aquarium and Lowry Park Zoo. The free Tampa-Ybor Trolley runs during lunchtime between the two areas; schedules are available at the Visitors Center. **Visitor Info: Tampa Bay Convention and Visitors Bureau,** 400 N. Tampa St., Suite 2800. (☎ 223-1111 or 800-448-2672; www.visittampabay.com. Open M-F 8:30am-5:30pm.) **Hotlines: Crisis Hotline,** ☎ 234-1234. **Helpline,** ☎ 251-4000. **Post Office:** 401. S Florida Ave. (☎ 223-4332. Open M-F 8:30am-4:30pm.) **ZIP code:** 33601. **Area code:** 813.

◪ ACCOMMODATIONS. Dedicated to the art of staying young at heart, owner Mark Holland started the Gram Parsons Foundation as a way to memorialize the late 1970s singer-songwriter. That dedication has turned into a top-notch bed and breakfast. **Gram's Place Bed & Breakfast/Hostel ❶**, 3109 N. Ola Ave., in a refurbished train car always has music playing, and the outdoor jacuzzi, patio and BYOB bar add to the bohemian, eclectic attitude. From I-275, take Martin Luther King Blvd. west to Ola Ave., then left on Ola. (☎221-0596. Dorms June-Nov. $17; Dec.-May $25. B&B theme rooms $65/80, with private bath $80/95.) **Villager Lodge ❷**, 3110 W. Hillsborough Ave., 5 mi. from the airport at Exit 30 off I-275, has 33 small rooms with A/C, cable TV, and pool access. (☎876-8673. Singles $40; doubles $55; each additional person $5.) **Super 8 Motel ❸**, 321 E. Fletcher Ave., 3 mi. from Busch Gardens in northwest Tampa, offers clean rooms with cable TV, pool access, and breakfast; some rooms have a fridge and stove. (☎933-4545. Coffee and doughnuts. Singles M-F $47, Sa-Su $52; doubles $54/58. Students with ID 10% discount.) The rooms at the **Garden View Motel ❷**, 2500 E. Busch Blvd., have cable TV, A/C, and pool. Discount tickets to Busch Gardens are available at the front desk. (☎933-3958. Singles $40-45; doubles $45-50. Students with ID 10% discount.)

▢ FOOD. Tampa is blessed with many inexpensive restaurants. Heading that list is **Skipper's Smokehouse ❷**, 910 Skipper Rd., off Nebraska Ave., a giant complex of thatched huts, wreckage, and wood planks on the northern outskirts of town. Skipper's also has a separate oyster bar and "Skipper Dome," where guests groove to blues, zydeco, reggae and worldbeat tunes. (☎971-0666. Tender fried alligator tail sandwich $5. Cover varies. Happy hour Th-F 4-8pm. Restaurant and bar open Tu 11am-10pm, W-F 11am-11pm, Sa noon-11pm, Su 1-10pm.) The original hand-rubbed marinade behind **Kojak's House of Ribs ❸**, 2808 Gandy Blvd., reminds you that this is still the South. (☎837-3774. Ribs with 2 sides $8.50. Open Tu-Th 11am-10pm, F-Sa 11am-10:30pm, Su 4-9:30pm.) Tampa's gulf shore heritage is evident at **Cafe Creole ❸**, 1330 E. 9th Ave., an Ybor City joint known for oysters and jambalaya. (☎247-6283. Entrees $6-18. Live jazz nightly. Happy hour Tu-F 4-7pm. Open Tu-Th 11:30am-10:30pm, F 11:30am-11:30pm, Sa 5-11:30pm.)

◪ SIGHTS. Tampa blossomed only after the success of Ybor City, a planned community once known as the cigar capital of the world. Early 20th-century stogie manufacturer Vincent Martínez Ybor employed a wide array of immigrants, thus marking the area with a rich and varied ethnic heritage. The **Ybor City State Museum**, 1818 9th Ave., details the rise and fall of the neighborhood's tobacco empire and the workers behind it. Photographs examine the art and culture of the hand-rolled cigar. (☎247-6323. Open daily 9am-5pm. $2, under 6 free. Neighborhood walking tours Sa 10:30. $4.)

The **Florida Aquarium**, 701 Channelside Dr., invites you to mash your face to the glass for a *tête-à-tête* with fish from Florida's various lagoons. Snakes, tarantulas, and scorpions star in the wildly creepy "Frights of the Forest" exhibit, while wild dolphins stage a meet 'n' greet on DolphinQuest Eco-Tours of Tampa Bay. (☎273-4000. Open daily 9:30am-5pm. $15, seniors $12, ages 3-12 $10. Eco-Tours M-F 2pm; Sa-Su noon, 2, and 4pm. $18/17/13. Combo tickets available.) A former resort hotel and Spanish-American war headquarters, the **Henry B. Plant Museum**, 401 W. Kennedy Blvd., in a wing of the University of Tampa's Plant Hall, is now a college administration building that showcases 19th-century railroad tycoon Henry Plant's lavish collection of European sculptures, paintings, and knick-knacks. (☎254-1891. Open Tu-Sa 10am-4pm, Su noon-4pm. Free; suggested donation $5.) Downtown, the **Tampa Museum of Art**, 600 N. Ashley Dr., houses a noted collection of ancient Greek and Roman works as well as a series of changing, family-oriented exhibits. (☎274-8130.

Open Tu-W and F-Sa 10am-5pm, Th 10am-8pm, Su 1-5pm. Tours Th 5-8pm, Sa 10am-noon. $5, seniors $4, ages 6-18 $3. Free Sa 10am-noon and Th 5-8pm.)

It's never Miller time at **Busch Gardens**, 3000 E. Busch Blvd., Anheuser Busch's addition to the world of Floridian theme parks. Thrill-seekers head for the park's famous rollercoasters Kumba, Montu, and Gwazi, while those without stomachs of steel watch 2500 animals roam, fly, slither, and swim through the African-themed zoo areas. The "Edge of Africa" safari experience remains among the park's most popular attractions. (☎987-5082. Hours vary, call ahead; usually open daily 9:30am-7pm. $50, ages 3-9 $41. Parking $7.) The nearby **Adventure Island**, 10001 Malcolm McKinley Dr., serves as Busch Garden's water park. (☎987-5660. Open June-Aug. daily; Sept.-Oct. Sa-Su. Hours vary, usually M-Th 9am-7pm, F-Su 9am-8pm. $28, ages 3-9 $26. Parking $5. Busch Gardens/Adventure Island combo ticket $60, ages 3-9 $50.)

🎭📷 **ENTERTAINMENT & NIGHTLIFE.** Brief yourself on city entertainment with the free *Tampa Weekend* or *Weekly Planet*, found in local restaurants, bars, and street corners. Gay travelers should check out the free *Stonewall*. Every year in the first week of February, the **Jose Gasparilla** (☎876-1747), a fully rigged pirate ship loaded with hundreds of exuberant "pirates," invades Tampa, kicking off a month of parades and festivals. The **Gasparilla Festival of the Arts** (☎876-1747), draws worldwide talent Mar. 1-2, 2003. Thousands pack Ybor City every October for **"Guavaween"** (☎621-7121), a Latin-style Halloween celebration.

With over 35 clubs and bars in a condensed area, **Ybor City** really does offer it all. Most nighttime hangouts are located on the well-lit 7th and 9th Ave. *Use caution when walking down side streets.* During the week, many restaurants close at 8pm, and clubs don't open until 10pm. Tampa's trendy congregate at **Velvet**, 1430 E. 7th St. The swanky bar serves up a mean martini, the erudite puff on cigars while perched on sleek couches, and the DJ spins "lounge funk." (☎247-2711. 21+. Open F-Sa 9pm-3am.) **The Castle**, 2004 N. 16th St., at 9th St., caters to the goth scene, but is open to all who want to enter the friendly sanctum. (☎247-7547. M 80s night, Th music video night, F-Sa goth nights. 18+. Cover $3-5. Open M and Th-Sa 9:30pm-3am.) Latin and high-energy dance have swept aside country line-dancing at **Spurs**, 1915 7th Ave. (☎247-7787. Open Th-Sa and Su 7:30pm-3am.)

ST. PETERSBURG & CLEARWATER ☎727

Across the bay, 22 mi. southwest of Tampa, St. Petersburg caters to a relaxed community of retirees and young singles. The town enjoys 28 mil. of soft white beaches, emerald-colored water, and about 361 days of sunshine per year. The St. Petersburg-to-Clearwater stretch caters to beach bums and city strollers alike. While the outdoor scenery draws the crowds, indoor activities are equally captivating—museum exhibits on Salvador Dalí and JFK rival even the nicest sunset.

🔲🔢 **ORIENTATION & PRACTICAL INFORMATION.** In St. Petersburg, **Central Ave.** parallels numbered avenues, running east-west in the downtown area. **34th St. (U.S. 19), I-275,** and **4th St.** are major north-south thoroughfares. The beaches line a strip of barrier islands on the far west side of town facing the Gulf. Several causeways, including the **Clearwater Memorial Causeway (Rte. 60),** access the beaches from St. Pete. Clearwater sits at the far north of the strip. **Gulf Blvd.** runs down the coastline, through Belleair Shores, Indian Rocks Beach, Indian Shores, Redington Shores, Madeira Beach, Treasure Island, and St. Pete Beach. The stretch of beach past the huge pink Don Cesar Hotel, in St. Pete Beach, and Pass-a-Grille Beach have the best sand, and less pedestrian and motor traffic. **St. Petersburg Clearwater International Airport** (☎453-7800), off Roosevelt Blvd. sits across the bay from Tampa. **Airport Super Shuttle** runs shuttles. (☎572-1111. $19.) **Greyhound,**

FLORIDA

180 9th St. N at 2nd Ave. N in St. Pete (☎822-1497; open daily 4:30am-11:30pm), buses to Clearwater (½hr.; 7 per day; M-Th $8, F-Su $9) and Orlando (3-4hr.; 5 per day; $15/16). The Clearwater station is at 2811 Gulf-to-Bay Blvd. (☎796-7315. Open daily 6am-9pm.) **Pinellas Suncoast Transit Authority (PSTA),** handles public transit; most routes depart from Williams Park at 1st Ave. N and 3rd St. N. (☎530-9911. $1.25, students 75¢, seniors 60¢. 1-day unlimited pass $3.) To reach Tampa, take express bus #100X M-F from the Gateway Mall ($1.50). A beach trolley runs up and down the Pier. (Daily every 20-30min. 5am-10pm $1.25. A 1-day unlimited bus pass is $3.) **Visitor Info: St. Petersburg Area Chamber of Commerce,** 100 2nd Ave. N. (☎821-4069; www.stpete.com. Open M-F 8am-5pm, Sa 10am-5pm, Su noon-5pm.) **The Pier Information Center,** 800 2nd Ave. NE. (☎821-6443. Open M-Sa 10am-8pm, Su 11am-6pm.) Several downtown kiosks also provide maps. **Hotlines: Rape Crisis,** ☎530-7233. **Helpline,** ☎344-5555. Both 24hr. **Post Office:** 3135 1st Ave. N, at 31st St. (☎322-6696. Open M-F 8am-6pm, Sa 8am-12:30pm.) **ZIP code:** 37370. **Area code:** 727.

⌂ ACCOMMODATIONS. St. Petersburg and Clearwater offer two hostels, and many cheap motels line **4th St. N** and **U.S. 19** in St. Pete. Some establishments advertise singles for as little as $25, but these tend to be very worn- down. To avoid the worst neighborhoods, stay on the north end of 4th St. and the south end of U.S. 19. Several inexpensive motels cluster on the beaches along Gulf Blvd. The **Clearwater Beach International Hostel (HI-AYH) ❶**, 606 Bay Esplanade Ave., off Mandalay Ave. at the Sands Motel in Clearwater Beach features a common room with TV and a pool, in addition to nearby volleyball, tennis, and shuffleboard courts. (☎443-1211. Internet access $1 per 8min. Linen and key deposit $5. Office hours 9am-noon and 5-9pm. Dorms $13, nonmembers $14; private rooms $30-40. Surcharge for credit card payments.) In downtown St. Pete at the Kelly Hotel, the **St. Petersburg Youth Hostel ❶**, 326 1st Ave. N, consists of one four-person room with private bath in a large historic hotel. (☎822-4141. Common room, TV and A/C. Youth hostel card or student ID required. Bunks $20. Hotel rooms $43.) The **Treasure Island Motel ❷**, 10315 Gulf Blvd., across the street from the beach, has big rooms with A/C, fridge, color TV, pull-out couch, and use of a beautiful pool. Catch dinner off a pier in back. (☎367-3055. Singles and doubles from $40.) The **Grant Motel ❷**, 9046 4th St. N, is 4 mi. north of St. Pete on U.S. 92. All rooms have A/C, fridge, and pronounced country decor, including straw hats and lacy curtains. The beautifully landscaped grounds have an outdoor pool. (☎576-1369. Reservations strongly recommended. Singles $39; doubles $42.) **Fort De Soto County Park ❶**, 3500 Pinellas Bayway S, composed of 5 islands, has the best camping around, and ranks among the best state parks in Florida. The small island centers around the Spanish Fort De Soto, which can be explored by day. Reservations must be made in person either at the park office, 501 1st Ave. N, #A116, or at the Parks Dept., 631 Chestnut St. in Clearwater. (☎582-2267. Min. stay 2 nights. Max. stay 14 days. Front gate locked 9pm. Curfew 10pm. Aug.-Dec. $23; Jan.-July $33. Park office: ☎582-7738. Open daily 8am-4:30pm. Parks Dept.: ☎464-3347. Open daily 8am-5pm.)

🍴 FOOD. St. Petersburg's cheap, health-conscious restaurants cater to its retired population, and generally close by 8 or 9pm. **Dockside Dave's ❷**, 13203 Gulf Blvd. S, in Madeira Beach, is one of the best-kept secrets on the islands. The half-pound grouper sandwich (market price, around $8) is simply sublime. (☎392-9399. Open M-Sa 11am-10pm, Su noon-10pm.) City polls have repeatedly ranked **Tangelo's Bar and Grille ❷**, 226 1st Ave. N, as a top Cuban restaurant, and the polls never lie. Their imported sauce accents the $5.50 Oaxacan *mole negro* chicken breast sandwich. (☎894-1695. Open M-Sa 11am-7pm, Su seasonally.) Also in St. Pete is the **Fourth Street Shrimp Store ❷**, 1006 4th St. N—a purveyor of all things shrimp. (☎822-0325. Filling shrimp taco salad $7. Open Su-Th 11am-9pm, F-Sa 11am-

9:30pm.) A traditional local favorite in Clearwater Beach is **Frenchy's Cafe ❸**, 41 Baymont St. The house specialty, boiled shrimp, comes dusted in their secret seasonings for $13. Alternatively, go for the original grouper burger ($7). (☎446-3607. Open M-Th 11:30am-11pm, F-Sa 11:30am-midnight, Su noon-11pm.)

◙ SIGHTS. Grab a copy of *See St. Pete* or the *St. Petersburg Official Visitor's Guide* for the lowdown on area events, discounts, and useful maps. Downtown St. Pete is cluttered with museums and galleries that make it worth the effort to leave the beach. Relive the 1960s at the ▨**Florida International Museum**, 100 2nd St. N. The exhibit **Cuban Missile Crisis: When the Cold War Got Hot** takes visitors through a day in the life in the atomic age. **John F. Kennedy: The Exhibition** provides a comprehensive look at JFK's personal and political life through hundreds of personal artifacts. (☎822-3693 or 800-777-9882. Open M-Sa 10am-5pm, Su noon-5pm; ticket office closes 4pm. $12, students $6, seniors $11.) Melting clocks and phallic symbols mark the exhaustive ▨**Salvador Dalí Museum**, 1000 3rd St. S, the largest private collection of the Surrealist's work in the world. Guided tours provide some intriguing explanations of the great master's puzzling works. (☎823-3767 or 800-442-3254. Open M-W and F-Sa 9:30am-5:30pm, Th 9:30am-8pm, Su noon-5:30pm. $10, students $5, seniors $7, under 10 free.) The **Florida Holocaust Museum**, 55 5th St. S, covers pre-war Europe to the birth of Israel in one of the largest museums of its kind in the country. (☎820-0110 or 800-960-7448. Open M-F 10am-5pm, Sa-Su noon-5pm. $8, students and seniors $7, under 19 $3.)

Beaches are the most worthwhile—but not the only—attraction along the coastline. The nicest beach may be **Pass-a-Grille Beach**, but its parking meters eat quarters for breakfast. Check out **Clearwater Beach**, at the northern end of the Gulf Blvd. strand, where mainstream beach culture is the norm in a decidedly fantastic white sand beach setting. The **Sunsets at Pier 60 Festival** brings arts and entertainment to Clearwater Beach, but the sunsets are what draw the crowds. (☎449-1036; www.sunsetsatpier60.com. Daily 2hr. before sundown until 2hr. after.)

▧ NIGHTLIFE. St. Pete caters to those who want to end the night by 9 or 10pm; most visitors and locals looking for nightlife either head to Tampa or to the beach. Clearwater hotels, restaurants, and parks often host free concerts. Free copies of *Weekly Planet* or *Tampa Tonight/Pinellas Tonight* grace local restaurants and bars. A smattering of establishments hit the bull's-eye for those looking for a night on the town. **Beach Nutts**, 9600 W. Gulf Blvd., Treasure Island, has fresh grouper ($10) and decent burgers ($6), while the porch has a spectacular view of the beach, and bands play nightly. (☎367-7427. Open daily 11am-2am.) Locals wind down with a beer and a game of pool at the **Beach Bar**, 454 Mandalay Ave. If not in the mood for darts on the weekend, then walk around the corner to groove on the dance floor. (☎446-8866. Dancing F-Sa 9pm-2am. 21+. Bar open daily 10am-2am.) The younger crowd likes to make a dash for the mainland and party at **Liquid Blue**, 22 North Ft. Harrison St., Clearwater's premier nightspot for techno and weekly drink specials. (☎446-4000. 18+. Cover varies. Open Tu-Sa 9pm-2am.)

GAINESVILLE ☎352

Break from the beach-and-theme-park monotony at Gainesville, Florida's version of a university town. The University of Florida (UF) lends the town a notably attractive population and an air of high culture mixed with equal parts bohemian, frat house, and Old South. From the dizzying clubs to drag racing to professional theater, Gainesville has a little of something for everyone. Located in lush North Central Florida, Gainesville and surrounding Alachua County also provide ample opportunities for the nature lover.

⚅⚄ ORIENTATION & PRACTICAL INFORMATION. Gainesville is accessible primarily by I-75. **Main St.** divides the town east and west, while **University Avenue** (referred to locally as "The Avenue") divides it north-south. The city follows a grid system: streets run north-south and avenues east-west. The University of Florida is located on the west side of town at the intersection of University Ave. and **SW 13th St. (U.S. 441). Greyhound,** 516 SW 4th Ave. (☎376-5252; open M-Sa 7am-10:30pm, Su 10am-10:30pm) heads to Miami (9hr.; 10 per day; M-Th $49, F-Su $52); Orlando (2½hr.; 10 per day; $21/23); and Tampa (3-5hr., 8 per day, $19/20). **Regional Transit System** runs trains and buses around the city. (☎334-2600. Operates M-F 6am-7pm, Sa-Su 7am-7pm. $1; students, seniors, and disabled 50¢. 1-day unlimited pass $2.) **Taxis: Gator Cab Co.,** ☎375-0313. **Visitor info: The Alachua County Visitors and Convention Bureau,** 30 E. University Ave., downtown (☎374-5231; www.visitgainesville.net. Open M-F 8:30am-5pm.) **Post Office:** 401 SE 1st Ave. (☎377-4038. Open M-F 8:30am-5pm, Sa 9am-noon.) **ZIP code:** 32601. **Area code:** 352 or 904. In text, 352 unless otherwise noted.

⚄⚅ ACCOMMODATIONS & FOOD. Plenty of motels are located right off I-75 or on 13th St., increasing in price as you approach the University of Florida. On football weekends in September through November or on Gatornationals race weekend in mid-March, rates are at least double for any place you can squeeze into. The **Gainesville Lodge ❷,** 413 W. University Rd., is a downtown steal and a short stumble from the nightclubs. (☎376-1224. TV, A/C, and pool. Singles $40; doubles $50.) The **Classic Inn ❷,** 3820 SW 13th St., features clean rooms just minutes from UF. (☎371-2500. Cable TV, pool, and continental breakfast. Singles $40; doubles $48.) An expensive and luxurious treat, the **Magnolia Plantation ❹,** 309 SE 7th St., downtown, is one of Florida's best B&Bs. (☎375-6653 or 800-201-2379. Rooms $90-105; cottages $150-300.) Sleep amid Floridian flora and fauna at **Paynes Prairie State Reserve** (see **Sights,** below), 10 mi. south on U.S. 441 at Exit 73 off I-75 in Micanopy. There are plenty of opportunities for fishing, boating, skating, bicycling, and hiking, but swimming is not allowed. (☎466-3397. 15 tent and 35 RV sites with water $11, with electricity $13.)

Gainesville's diverse university population seems to have one taste they agree on—cheap food. University Ave. and 13th St. hold the standard college eateries: pizza, burger, and taco joints. **Farah's on the Avenue ❸,** 1120 W. University Ave., doles out delectable Mediterranean cuisine. The *dolmathes* (rolled grape leaves stuffed with rice and meat) are unique specialties and come as either a $3.50 appetizer (6 leaves) or a $9 meal platter. (☎378-5179. Live jazz Sa 8pm. Open M-Tu 11am-10pm, W-Sa 11am-11pm.) **Leonardo's By the Slice ❶,** 1245 W. University Ave., offers basic pastas ($4-6) and pizzas (slices $2-4). A cafe sells breakfasts and treats throughout the day. (☎375-2007. Open M-Th 9am-10pm, F-Sa 9am-11pm, Su 10am-10pm.) To see where frantic UF students get their caffeine fix, check out **Maude's Classic Cafe ❶,** 101 SE 2nd Pl. Imagine the "John Lennon," a large piece of lemon poppyseed cake with whipped cream for only $2.75. (☎336-9646. Open Su-W 10am-midnight, Th-Sa 10am-2am.)

◼ SIGHTS. As the town's lifeblood, the **University of Florida** provides most of the area's culture and happenings. The UF Cultural Complex, at Hull Rd. and SW 34th St., holds two free museums. The **Samuel P. Harn Museum of Art** displays 19th- and 20th-century painting and sculpture, mostly American and Caribbean. (☎392-9826. Open Tu-F 11am-5pm, Sa 10am-5pm, Su 1-5pm. Free.) Next door, the **Florida Museum of Natural History** has one of the largest collections of natural history artifacts in the Southeast. (☎846-2000. Open M-Sa 10am-5pm, Su 1-5pm. Free.) Down Museum Rd. lies the **Bathouse,** where locals traditionally gather at sunset, turning their backs to the alligators in Lake Alice to watch the bats fly from their abode.

Ben Hill Griffin Memorial Stadium, more commonly known as "The Swamp," hosts the highly successful "Fightin' Gators" football team. When UF scientists helped develop a new sports drink, they named it Gatorade after the famous gridders. Gator tickets (☎384-3261 or 877-428-6742) sell out as soon as they go on sale, so make your pigskin plans well in advance.

North Central Florida's natural beauty also surrounds Gainesville. Teeming with gators, wild horses, and herds of buffalo, the 21,000 acres of **Paynes Prairie State Reserve** lie 10 mi. south on U.S. 441. On the reserve the "Great Alachua Savannah" was the site of many battles during the 18th-century Seminole Wars. More than 20 mi. of trails are open to hiking; in the winter, park rangers lead overnight expeditions through the basin. (☎466-4100 for reservations. Open daily 8am to sunset. $3.25 per car.) A big hole in the ground may not sound like interesting sightseeing but the **Devil's Millhopper State Geological Site,** 4732 NW 53rd Ave., is an anomaly worth checking out. The 120 ft. deep, 500 ft. wide natural sinkhole was named for its funnel-like shape and the discovery of fossilized bones and teeth at its bottom—legend claims bodies were once fed to the devil here. (☎955-2008. Open daily 9am-5pm. Parking $2.) **Silver Springs,** 5656 E. Silver Springs Blvd., 30 mi. south of Gainesville near Ocala, has been offering its famous glass-bottom boat tours since 1878. Marvel at this unique view of Central Florida's pure spring waters and frolic with the animals in the 350-acre nature theme park. Call for a schedule of the park's year-round concerts and festivals. (☎236-2121. Open daily 10am-5pm. $33, seniors $30, ages 3-10 $24.)

🎭🎨 **ENTERTAINMENT & NIGHTLIFE.** The annual **Downtown Festival & Art Show** displays the work of more than 250 artists and the talents of the local music scene; Tom Petty and Sister Hazel among others hail from Gainesville. The weekend festival features 50 bands. (☎334-5064. Nov. 15-16, 2003.) At the outdoor **Gainesville Community Plaza,** E. University Ave. and SE 1st St., expect live music or movie screenings every Friday night from April to October. (☎334-2787. Shows 8pm. Free.) The *Gator Times* and UF's daily *Alligator* list local events and nightlife info; look for them at Gainesville restaurants and street corners. In mid-March, drag racing fans flock to Gainesville for the annual **Mac Tools Gatornationals,** a series of NHRA-sponsored competitions. See all the action at the **Gainesville Raceway,** 11211 N. County Rd. 225 (☎377-0046).

Clubs dot the intersection of W. University Ave. and 2nd St. downtown. With three floors of dancing, a cigar lounge, and nightly drink specials, **Orbit Lounge,** 238 W. University Ave., is the place in town for hip hop and techno. (☎335-9800. 18+. Cover $5. Open Th-Sa 10pm-2am.) Follow your ears to the wickedly hip **Soulhouse,** 15 SW 2nd Pl. and 1st St., a local secret known for its notorious beanbag room. (☎377-7685. Cover $5. Open M-Th 10pm-2am, F-Sa 10am-3am.) Every Thursday an oyster bar turns into *the* place for live local bands at **Purple Porpoise,** 1728 W. University Ave. (☎376-1667. Happy hour M-F 4-7pm. Open daily 11am-2am.)

PANAMA CITY BEACH ☎850

Panama City Beach is the place to find everything touristy, beachy, and kitschy that America has produced crammed into a 27 mi. long, yards-wide strip running along the Gulf of Mexico. Billed as "the world's greatest beaches," views of PCB's sands are often obscured by thousands of tourists. Regardless of whether you're in college or not, the PCB experience is the essence of a collegiate spring-break rampage. As the heart of the "Redneck Riviera," there is no pretension or high culture here—just miles and miles of parties and loud, thumping bass in high season. Warm-as-a-bath turquoise water, roller coasters, surf shops, and water parks round out the entertainment possibilities.

FLORIDA

⛶ 🔁 ORIENTATION & PRACTICAL INFORMATION. After crossing Hathaway Bridge from the east, **Thomas Dr.** and **Front Beach Rd.** (marked as Alt. U.S. 98) fork off from U.S. 98 and run along the gulf. This becomes that glorious tourist trap-crammed beachfront that is also known as the "Miracle Strip," the main drag of PCB. Beware the sunset and late-night rush; this two-late road grinds to a standstill at busy times. From the west, cross the Phillips Inlet Bridge and turn right onto Front Beach Rd. to access the strip. Regular Rte. 98 becomes **Panama Beach Pkwy.** and runs parallel to Front Beach Rd. and Thomas Dr. inland, and is the less-trafficked "express route" around the strip. **Greyhound,** 917 Harrison Ave. (☎785-6111; open M-Sa 7am-9pm, Su 7am-2pm and 5-9pm), stops at the junction of U.S. 98 and U.S. 79 and continues on to Atlanta (9hr., 1 per day, $47-51) and Orlando (8-11hr., 6 per day, $62-65). **Bay Town Trolley,** 1021 Massalina Dr., shuttles along the beach. (☎769-0557. M-F 6am-6pm. 50¢, students and seniors 25¢; $1 to cross bridge.) Services include: **Taxis: Yellow Cab,** ☎763-4691. **Panama City Beach Convention and Visitors Bureau,** 17001 Panama City Beach Pkwy., at the corner of U.S. 98 (PCB Pkwy.) and U.S. 79, has a free Internet kiosk. (☎800-722-3224; www.pcbeach.com. Open daily 8am-5pm.) **Hotlines: Domestic Violence and Rape Crisis,** ☎763-0706. **Crisis and Mental Health Emergency,** ☎769-9481. Both 24hr. **Post Office:** 420 Churchwell Dr. (☎800-275-8777. Open M-F 8:30am-5pm, Sa 9am-12:30pm.) **ZIP code:** 32401. **Area code:** 850.

⛶ ACCOMMODATIONS. Depending on the Strip location and the time of year, rates range from outrageous to extremely outrageous. High season runs from the end of April until early September and typically means $100+ rooms; rates drop in fall and winter. Call well in advance for summer reservations. While rates generally correspond to distance from the beach, far-inland motels are still quite expensive in summer and around holidays. The **⛶South Pacific Motel ❷,** 16701 Front Beach Rd., is far and away the best deal on the beach, thanks to a secret treasure: two motel rooms that are 20 paces away from the surf and go for $45 in peak season. The rest of the rooms at South Pacific are also relatively cheap, even in summer, and the family-owned ambience makes it a nice contrast to the impersonal, touristy gaudiness of the rest of the strip. (☎234-2703 or 800-966-9439. Pool, private beach, and cable TV. In summer 2 of the rooms $45; doubles $75; 2-bedroom apartments $95.) **Travelodge ❷,** 9424 Front Beach Rd., ½ mi. from the beach, has clean, spacious rooms with two double beds, free cable TV, and coffee. (☎235-1122 or 800-523-4369. Singles or doubles $45-79.) Camp on the beach at **St. Andrews State Recreation Area ❶,** 4607 State Park Ln., at the east end of Thomas Dr. Call up to 11 months in advance for reservations at this extremely popular campground. All 176 sites are beneath the pines and on or close to the water. (☎233-5140, for reservations ☎800-326-3521. Sites $17, with electricity or waterside $19; in winter $10/12. $2 each additional person, $3 per additional car.)

⛶ FOOD & NIGHTLIFE. Buffets stuff the Strip and Thomas Dr. "Early bird" specials, usually offered 4-6pm, get you the same food at about half the price. While much food on the strip is of low quality, **Scampy's ❸,** 4933 Thomas Dr., is a notable exception. Offering seafare in a smaller, less harried atmosphere than the mega-troughs. This place is obviously the local favorite and might be the only place in town that seems to actually cook, rather than reheat, scoop, or squirt. (☎235-4209. 18 different lunch specials $4-7.50. Seafood salad $9. Dinner entrees $11-20. Open Su-Th 11am-10pm, F-Sa 11am-11pm.) At night, many of the restaurants on the Strip turn into bars and clubs, and most have live bands. Cool off at **Sharky's,** 15201 Front Beach Rd., with a Hurricane or a Sharkbite specialty drink ($5.25). More adventurous spirits will savor their signature appetizer, "shark bites" (fried shark cubes; $7). Raw oysters go for $2 per dozen daily 4-6pm. (☎235-2420. Live performers on the beach deck most nights. Cover $8. Kitchen open daily 11:30am-11pm; club open until 2am.)

The back patio bar at **Harpoon Harry's,** 12627 Front Beach Rd., overlooks the beach. Build a midnight sandcastle after having one of their signature drinks. (☎234-6060. Open daily 11am-2am.) The largest club in the US (capacity 8000) and MTV's former Spring Break headquarters, **Club LaVela,** 8813 Thomas Dr., has eight clubs and 48 bar stations under one jammin' roof. Live bands work the Rock Pavilion every night. Wet T-shirt, bikini, and male hard body contests fill the weekends and every night during Spring Break. (☎234-3866. 18+. No daytime cover; nightly cover varies. Open daily 10am-4am.) Next door, **Spinnaker,** 8795 Thomas Dr., contains a restaurant, a pool deck, and a playground for kids. This enormous beach clubhouse hosts live bands throughout the week. (☎234-7882. Fresh seafood $8-20. Live music Th-Su starting at 10:30pm. Happy Hour 9-11pm. 21+, 18+ during spring break. Cover $5-15. Restaurant open daily 11am-10pm; club 10pm-4am.)

◙◪ SIGHTS & ENTERTAINMENT. Over 1000 acres of gators, nature trails, and beaches make up the **St. Andrews State Recreation Area** (see **Accommodations,** above; open daily 8am-sunset; $4 per car). **The Glass Bottom Boat** takes visitors on a dolphin-watching excursion and sails to Shell Island from **Treasure Island Marina,** 3605 Thomas Dr. (☎234-8944. 3hr. trips at 9am, 1, and 4:30pm. $15, seniors $14, under 12 $8.) Also in the Marina, the world's largest speed boat, the **Sea Screamer,** 3601 Thomas Dr., cruises the Grand Lagoon. (☎233-9107. In summer 4 cruises per day; spring and fall departures vary, call for times. $14, ages 4-12 $8.) Sister to the Screamer is the **Sea Dragon,** an authentic pirate ship that takes swashbucklers on Pirate Cruises. (☎234-7400. 2hr. cruises in daytime, evening, and sunset; call ahead for times. $16, seniors $14, ages 3-14 $11, under 2 $5.) An assortment of dolphin shows, parasailing outfits, and amusement parks lines **Front Beach Rd. Miracle Strip Amusement Park** and **Shipwreck Island Water Park,** 12000 Front Beach Rd., both have a number of thrill rides and shows for those who've had enough of the beach. (Amusement park: ☎234-5810. Open in summer Su-F 6-11pm, Sa 1-11:30pm; spring and fall hours vary. $17, seniors $11, under 35 in. free. Water park: ☎234-0368. Open in summer daily 10:30am-5:30pm; spring and fall hours vary. $22.50, seniors $12.75. Admission to both parks $31.50.)

PENSACOLA   ☎850

Pensacola's military-infused population and reputation for conservatism have been a part of the city's make-up since before the Civil War, when three forts on the shores of Pensacola formed a triangular defense to guard the deep-water ports. Most visitors, however, will be drawn to the area for its sugar-white beaches and the secluded, emerald waters along the **Gulf Island National Seashore.**

For those seeking solace from sunburn, the **National Museum of US Naval Aviation,** inside the Naval Air Station, at Exit 2 off I-10 (follow the signs), provides ample diversion. The excitement of more than 130 planes of past and present, dangling from the ceiling or parked within arm's reach, will have pilot wanna-bes soaring on natural highs. (☎452-3604. Open daily 9am-5pm. 1½hr. tours daily at 9:30, 11am, 1, and 2:30pm. Free.) For fun that doesn't involve winged killing machines, head across the 3mi. Pensacola Bay Bridge and past the chintzy motels to the **Naval Live Oaks Area,** 1801 Gulf Breeze Pkwy. Relaxing paths meander through a forest that John Quincy Adams established as the first and only naval tree reservation in the US. Its live oaks were used to make warships. (☎934-2600. Open daily 8am-5:30pm.) Pay $1 to cross the Pensacola Beach Bridge to **Santa Rosa Island** for some of the best beaches around. A hodgepodge of military bunkers from different wars, ◪**Fort**

FLORIDA

Pickens, where Apache leader Geronimo was once imprisoned in the late 1800s, commands the western part of Santa Rosa. An $8 fee lets visitors explore the ruins and sunbathe on the secluded seashore. (Park open daily 7am-10pm. Visitors Center open Mar.-Oct. 9:30am-5pm; Nov.-Feb. 8:30am-4pm.)

Hotels along the beach cost at least $65 and get more expensive in summer. The **Five Flags Inn ❹,** 299 Fort Pickens Rd., is one of the better beachfront deals, offering free local calls, gulfside rooms, beach patio and pool, and coffee. (☎932-3586. Rooms May-Aug. $95; Sept.-Feb. $55; Mar.-Apr. $75.) Cheaper options lie inland, north of downtown at the exits of I-10 and I-110, a 15min. drive from the beach. Clean and well-furnished, the **Civic Inn ❷,** 200 N. Palafox St., is near downtown and budget friendly. (☎432-3441. A/C, TV. Singles Su-Th $40, F-Sa $48; doubles $48/58. Senior and military discounts.) At the western edge of Santa Rosa Island, the **Fort Pickens Campground** on the Gulf Islands National Seashore offers sites within walking distance of gorgeous beaches. (☎934-2622 for camping info, ☎800-326-2622 for reservations. Sites $15, with electricity $21.) ⌘**Hopkins House ❷,** 900 Spring St., has incredibly popular, all-you-can-eat family-style dinners ($8) on Tuesday and Friday evenings, as well as regular lunch and breakfast specials such as biscuits, grits, and any omelette for only $3.50. (☎438-3979. Open Tu-Su 7-9:30am and 11:15am-2pm. Open for dinner Tu and F 5:15-7:30pm.) **Tre Fratelli ❸,** 304 Alcaniz St., a Sicilian restaurant and pizzeria, concocts fantastic pasta sauces and makes them fresh when you order. While waiting for your pasta, watch the locals relax in Seville Square, across the street. (☎438-3663. Pasta $8-13. Pizza $10-15. Open M-Sa 11am-3pm and 5-10pm.) The owner of **King's BBQ,** 2120 N. Palafox St., built the drive-up stand (with picnic tables for those who want to sit down) with his own hands. (☎433-4479. Rib sandwiches $5.50. Dinner with coleslaw, potato salad, baked beans, and bread $8.50. Open M-F 10:30am-6:30pm, Sa 10:30am-3pm.)

The city buttresses Pensacola Bay. **Palafox St.,** which becomes one-way near the bay, and **I-110** are the main north-south byways. **Government, Gregory,** and **Main St.** run east-west. Main St. becomes **Bayfront Pkwy.** along the edge of the bay and runs over the **Pensacola Bay Bridge.** On the other side, **Pensacola Beach Rd.** leads to Santa Rosa Island and Pensacola Beach, while **Gulf Breeze Parkway** trails along the coast. **Amtrak,** 980 E. Heinburg St. (☎433-4966 or 800-872-7245; open M, W, and F midnight-1pm; Tu and Th 5:30am-1pm; Sa 5:30am-8:30am), stops by on its east-west route between New Orleans (7hr., 3 per week, $30-65) and Orlando (13hr., 3 per week, $50-108). **Greyhound,** 505 W. Burgess Rd. (☎476-4800; open 24hr.), heads to: Atlanta (9-14hr., 5 per day, $51); New Orleans (4-7hr., 2 per day, $31); and Orlando (9hr., 7 per day, $62). A **trolley** runs two lines through downtown, complete with tours. Stops line Palafox St. (M-F 9am-3pm; 25¢). During the summer, two free Tiki Trolley shuttles run along the beach. (F-Sa 10am-3am, Su 10am-10pm.) Services include: **Taxis: Yellow Cab,** ☎433-3333. **Visitor info: Pensacola Convention and Visitors Bureau,** 1401 E. Gregory St., near the Pensacola Bay Bridge. (☎800-874-1234. Open daily 8am-5pm.) **Post Office:** 101 S. Palafox St. (☎439-0169. Open M-F 8am-5pm.) **ZIP code:** 32501. **Area code:** 850.

GREAT LAKES

Though the region's alternate name--the Midwest--evokes a bland image of corn-fields and small-town, white-picket-fence America, the states that hug the five Great Lakes encompass a variety of personalities. The world's largest freshwater lake, Lake Superior and its unpopulated, scenic coast cradle some of the most stunning natural features in the region—from the dense forests in northern Wisconsin to the waterfalls of the Upper Peninsula in Michigan. Along the Michigan, Indiana, and Illinois coast, Lake Michigan hosts sand dunes and a paradise of swimming, sailing, and deep-water fishing. Minneapolis and St. Paul have the panache of any coastal metropolis, while Chicago dazzles with a stunning skyline, incredible culinary offerings, and world-class museums.

HIGHLIGHTS OF THE GREAT LAKES

FOOD. Wisconsin cheese, Chicago pizza (p. 559), "pasties" in Michigan's Upper Peninsula (p. 550), and Door County's fishboils (p. 584) are some regional specialties.

RECREATIONAL ACTIVITIES. Canoeing and kayaking are popular in the northern reaches of the Great Lakes; Grand Traverse Bay (p. 546) is an recreation hot spot.

SCENIC VISTAS. Reach the top of the Log Slide in MN (p. 552) or the Dune Climb in MI (p. 546), and you'll never want to come down.

SCENIC DRIVES. In MI, see the Lake Michigan shore on U.S. 31 and Rte. 119 (p. 549); Brockway Mountain Dr. (p. 553); or the dirt roads of Pictured Rocks State Park (p. 551). In MN, drive Rte. 61 N from Duluth along the Lake Superior shore (p. 601).

OHIO

Of all the Great Lake states, Ohio probably most closely resembles the traditional definition of "Middle America." The state's perfect farmland is a patchwork of cornfields and soybean plants, and three cities—Cincinnati, Cleveland, and Columbus—are home to millions of Ohioans. Away from the big cities, small towns cultivate a friendly, Midwest atmosphere. Flat landscape in the northern part of the state contrasts the endless rolling wooded hills of the southern half.

▨ PRACTICAL INFORMATION

Capital: Columbus.

Visitor info: State Office of Travel and Tourism, 77 S. High St., 29th fl., Columbus 43215 (☎614-466-8844; www.ohiotourism.com). Open M-F 8am-5pm. **Ohio Tourism Line** (☎800-282-5393). **Ohio Department of Natural Resource,** in Fountain Sq., Columbus 43224 (☎614-265-7000).

Postal Abbreviation: OH. **Sales Tax:** 5.75%.

CLEVELAND

☎ **216**

The city formerly known as the "Mistake on the Lake" has undergone an extensive facelift in recent years in an attempt to correct its beleaguered image. The arrival of the Rock and Roll Hall of Fame and three sports stadiums has brightened the previously bleak visage of abandoned urbanity and created a stunning skyline against the waterfront. Modern sculptures and flower-lined streets give the downtown a sense of vitality, and **Case Western Reserve University** complements the downtown with interesting modern architecture, sculptures, and museums.

⌐ TRANSPORTATION

Airport: Cleveland Hopkins International (☎ 265-6030), 10 mi. southwest of downtown in Brook Park. RTA line #66X "Red Line" to Terminal Tower. Taxi to downtown $20.

Trains: Amtrak, 200 Cleveland Memorial Shoreway NE (☎ 696-5115), across from Brown Stadium east of City Hall. Open daily midnight-7am and noon-7:30pm. To **Chicago** (7hr., 4 per day, $75-92) and **Pittsburgh** (3hr., 2 per day, $33-40).

Buses: Greyhound, 1465 Chester Ave. (☎ 781-1841), at E. 14th St., 7 blocks from Terminal Tower. Near RTA bus lines. To: **Chicago** (7-7½hr., 4per day, $40); **Cincinnati** (4½-6½hr., 6 per day, $33.50); **New York City** (9hr., 3 per day, $75); **Pittsburgh** (2½-4½ hr., 4 per day, $20). Most eastbound buses stop over in Pittsburgh.

Public Transit: Regional Transit Authority (RTA), 315 Euclid Ave. (☎621-9500). Open M-F 6:30am-6:30pm. Bus lines, connecting with Rapid Transit trains, travel from downtown to most of the metropolitan area. Service daily 5am-midnight; call for info on "owl" (after-midnight) service. Train $1.50. Bus $1.25, express $1.50, downtown loop 50¢, 1-day pass $4; ask the driver for free transfers. Travelers with cars staying outside of the downtown area can park for free at one of the many park and rides and take the train to Terminal Square for $1.50. The **Waterfront Line** serves the Science Center, Rock and Roll Hall of Fame, and the Flats.

Taxis: Americab, ☎429-1111.

ORIENTATION & PRACTICAL INFORMATION

Terminal Tower, in **Public Sq.,** at the intersection of Detroit Ave. and Ontario St., forms the center of downtown and separates the city into east and west. Many street numbers correspond to the distance of the street from Terminal Tower; e.g., E. 18th St. is 18 blocks east of the Tower. To reach Public Sq. from **I-90** or **I-71,** take the Ontario Ave./Broadway exit. From **I-77,** take the 9th St. exit to Euclid Ave., which runs into Public Sq. While the downtown area and **University Circle** are relatively safe, the area between the two around 55th St. can be rough. **The Flats,** along both banks of the Cuyahoga River, and **Coventry Rd.,** in Cleveland Heights, are the happening spots for food and nightlife.

Visitor Info: Cleveland Convention and Visitors Bureau, 3100 Tower City Ctr. (☎621-4110 or 800-321-1001), 1st fl. of Terminal Tower at Public Sq. Open M-F 10am-4pm.

Hotline: Rape Crisis Line, ☎619-6192 or 619-6194. Operates 24hr.

Internet access: Cleveland Public Library, 525 Superior Ave (☎623-2904). 15min. limit if crowded. Open M-Sa 9am-6pm, Su 1-5pm; closed Su in summer.

Post Office: 2400 Orange Ave. (☎443-4494, after 5pm ☎443-4096.) Open M-F 7am-8:30pm, Sa 8:30am-3:30pm. **ZIP code:** 44101. **Area code:** 216; 440 or 330 in suburbs. In text, 216 unless noted otherwise.

ACCOMMODATIONS

With hotel taxes (not included in the prices listed below) as high as 14.5%, cheap lodging is hard to find in Cleveland. So-called "budget" motels tend to run at least $60. **Cleveland Private Lodgings,** P.O. Box 18557, Cleveland 44118, will place you in a home around the city for as little as $45. (☎321-3213; my.en.com/~privlodg/. Call M-F 9am-noon or 3-5pm. Allow 2-3 weeks for a letter of confirmation; for faster response, correspond by email.) Those with cars might consider staying in the suburbs or near the airport, where prices tend to be lower, or heading south to the **Cuyahoga Valley National Park** (see p. 523), where hostels and camping are options.

Motel 6 ❸, 7219 Engle Rd. (☎440-234-0990), off Exit 235 on I-71, 15 mi. southwest of the city, has comfy rooms with cable TV and A/C. Located near restaurants, stores, and a park and ride lot. Singles Su-Th $46, F-Sa $56; doubles $52/62.

Knights Inn ❷, 22115 Brookpark Rd. (☎440-734-4500), close to the airport at Exit 9 off I-480; take the first 2 rights after the freeway. Standard motel rooms, free local phone calls, continental breakfast, free shuttle to airport, and a restaurant. Must be 21+. Singles $40, doubles $45; weekly rate $175.

GREAT LAKES

🍴 FOOD

The delis downtown satiate most hot corned beef cravings, but Cleveland has more to offer elsewhere. A hip, young crowd of vegetarians, musicians, and artists head to **Coventry Rd.,** in **Cleveland Heights,** for innovative vegetarian food and a colorful neighborhood. The sound of Italian crooners and outdoor displays fill the sidewalks of **Little Italy,** around **Mayfield Rd.,** where visitors can shop in the tiny stores before settling down to a delicious Italian lunch or dinner. Seafood and standard pub fare are abundant in **the Flats.** Over 100 vendors hawk produce, meat, and cheese at the old-world style **West Side Market,** 1979 W. 25th St., at Lorain Ave. (☎771-8885. Open M and W 7am-4pm, F-Sa 7am-6pm.)

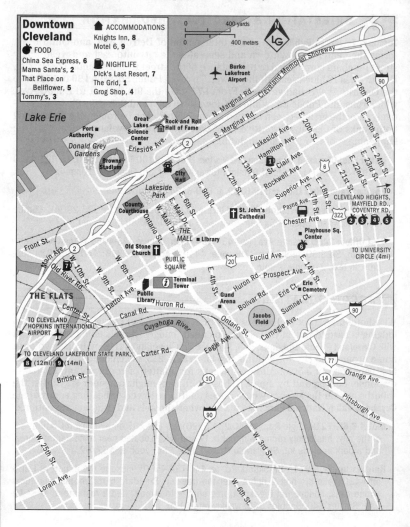

Downtown Cleveland

🍴 FOOD
China Sea Express, **6**
Mama Santa's, **2**
That Place on Bellflower, **5**
Tommy's, **3**

🏠 ACCOMMODATIONS
Knights Inn, **8**
Motel 6, **9**

🍸 NIGHTLIFE
Dick's Last Resort, **7**
The Grid, **1**
Grog Shop, **4**

Tommy's, 1824 Coventry Rd. (☎321-7757), in Cleveland Heights, up the hill from University Circle. Take bus #9X east to Mayfield and Coventry Rd. Tommy's whips up tantalizing veggie cuisine, like falafel with veggies or cheese pie. The extensive menu offers non-vegetarian options as well. Entrees around $5. Open M-Th 7:30am-10pm, F-Sa 7:30am-11pm, Su 9am-10pm. ❶

Mama Santa's, 12305 Mayfield Rd. (☎231-9567), in Little Italy just east of University Circle, serves sumptuous Sicilian pizzas along with authentic pasta dishes in a no-frills setting. Lasagna and *cavatelli* with meatballs both $7. Pizzas $5.25-6.25. Open M-Th 11am-10:30pm, F-Sa 11am-11:30pm; closed most of Aug. ❷

That Place on Bellflower, 11401 Bellflower Rd. (☎231-4469), in University Circle, serves up those huge, juicy hamburgers ($6) in the artsy bar and restaurant. Open M 11:30am-2:30pm, Tu-Th and Su 11:30am-10pm, F-Sa 11:30am-11pm. ❷

China Sea Express, 1507 Euclid Ave (☎861-0188), downtown, has Chinese food worth more than its price. A delicious all-you-can-eat lunch buffet is $5.75 and includes soup, salad, and all of the expected Chinese staples. Open Su-Th 11am-9pm, F-Sa 11am-10pm. ❷

☉ SIGHTS

DOWNTOWN. The aspirations of a new Cleveland are revealed in the made-over downtown—a self-declared "Remake on the Lake." Mega-hits blaring from outdoor speakers welcome travelers to the **Rock and Roll Hall of Fame,** a dizzying exploration of the rock music world. Though many visitors flock to the museum to view Elvis's jumpsuits and Mick Jagger's bellbottoms, the hall also takes a fascinating audio tour through the roots of rock 'n' roll. *(1 Key Plaza. ☎ 781-7625. Open daily 10am-5:30pm; also June-Aug. Sa 10am-9pm. $17, students with ID $15, seniors $13, ages 9-11 $11. W after 6pm $5.)* Next door, the **Great Lakes Science Center** educates with hands-on exhibits and demonstrations. Stretch your voice with computers and explore Saturn in a makeshift NASA ground control. *(601 Erieside Ave. ☎694-2000. Open Su-Th 9:30am-5:30pm, Sa 9:30am-6:45pm. Science center or IMAX $8, seniors $7, ages 3-17 $6; both $11/10/8. Parking for Hall of Fame and Science Center $7.)* **Cleveland Lakefront State Park** is a 14 mi. park near downtown with beaches and great picnic areas. *(Accessible via Lake Ave., Cleveland Memorial Shoreway, or Lakeshore Blvd. ☎881-8141. Open daily 6am-11pm; Everett Beach closes at dusk.)*

UNIVERSITY CIRCLE. Seventy-five cultural institutions cluster in **University Circle,** a part of Case Western University's campus, 4 mi. east of the city. The **Cleveland Museum of Art** boasts a hall of armor—part Medieval, part Asian—along with a survey of art from the Renaissance to the present. Exceptional collections of Impressionist and modern art. *(11150 East Blvd. ☎421-7340. Open Tu, Th, and Sa 10am-6pm; W and F 10am-9pm, Su 10am-5pm. Free.)* Nearby, the **Cleveland Museum of Natural History** sends visitors to the stars in the planetarium, while those dreaming of a different kind of sparkle can explore the new gallery of gems and jewels. *(1 Wade Oval Dr. ☎231-4600. Open Sept.-May M-Tu and Th-Sa 10am-5pm, W 10am-10pm, Su noon-5pm; Oct.-Apr. M-Sa 10am-5pm, Su noon-5pm. $6.50; students, seniors, and ages 7-18 $4.50; ages 3-6 $3.50.)* The **Cleveland Botanical Garden** provides a peaceful respite from urban life, with traditional Victorian and Japanese gardens, streams, and shaded pathways. *(11030 East Blvd. ☎721-1600. Open Apr.-Oct. M-Sa 9am-dusk, Su noon-dusk. Free.)*

GREAT LAKES

🎵 🎭 ENTERTAINMENT & NIGHTLIFE

Baseball's **Cleveland Indians** (☎420-4200) hammer the hardball at **Jacobs Field**, 2401 Ontario St. Tickets are difficult to get; the best way to see the field is on a 1hr. **stadium tour.** (☎241-8888 for tickets. Tours May-Sept. every 30min. M-Sa 10am-2pm; June-Aug. Su noon-2:30pm when there's no game. $6, seniors and under 15 $4.) The **Cleveland Cavaliers** (☎420-2000) hoop it up from November to April at **Gund Arena**, 1 Center Ct.; from June through August, the WNBA's **Cleveland Rockers** (☎263-7625) take over.

The **Cleveland Orchestra**, one of the nation's best, performs at **Severance Hall**, 11001 Euclid Ave. (☎231-7300. Box office open Sept.-May M-F 9am-6pm, Sa 10am-6pm. From $25.) **Playhouse Square Center**, 1519 Euclid Ave. (☎771-4444), a 10min. walk east of Terminal Tower, is the second-largest performing arts center in the US. Inside, the **State Theater** hosts the **Cleveland Opera** (☎575-0900) and the renowned **Cleveland Ballet** (☎426-2500) from October to June. The **Cleveland Cinematheque** (☎421-7450), at the Institute of Art, screens arthouse films for $6.

Most of Cleveland's nightlife is centered in **the Flats**. For info on clubs and bands, pick up a copy of *Scene* or the *Free Times*. The *Gay People's Chronicle* and *OUTlines* are available at gay clubs, cafes, and bookstores.

Dick's Last Resort, 1096 Old River Rd. (☎241-1234), serves dinner with an attitude, and the stage hosts cover bands that rock the crowds with hits from the 1950s, 60s, 70s, and 80s. Live music Th-Su. Su swing band. Open M-Th 11am-1am, F-Sa 11am-2am, Su 10am-11pm.

Grog Shop, 1765 Coventry Rd. (☎321-5588), in Cleveland Heights, has regional and national acts. Indie rock, pop, punk, and counterculture bands jam in the industrial setting. Open M-F 7pm-2:30am, Sa-Su 1pm-2:30am.

The Grid, 1437 St. Claire Ave. (☎623-0113), recently relocated to a larger space, entertains a predominantly gay crowd with a space-aged dance floor, four bars, and male strippers on select nights. 18+. Free parking. Open M-Sa 5pm-2:30am, Su 4pm-2:30am; dance floor open F-Sa until 4am.

🔎 DAYTRIPS FROM CLEVELAND

CUYAHOGA VALLEY NATIONAL PARK

Just 10 mi. south of Cleveland lies the northern edge of the surprisingly scenic **Cuyahoga Valley National Park.** The **Cuyahoga River,** an oasis near the city, winds 22 mi. through the dense forests and open farmland of the park, passing stables, aqueducts, and mills along the way. The best way to see the soothing natural beauty of the park is by hiking or biking its long trails. The **Ohio & Erie Canal Towpath Trail** runs through shaded forests and past the numerous locks used in the canal during its heyday. For wheels, go to **Century Cycles**, 1621 Main St. in Peninsula, which rents bikes. (☎330-657-2209. Open M-Th 10am-8pm, F-Sa 10am-6pm, Su 10am-5pm. $5 per hr.) To see the park by rail, hop on the **Cuyahoga Valley Scenic Railroad,** which runs several excursions along the river's banks from Peninsula, Independence, and Akron. (☎330-657-2000. Open Feb.-Dec. $11-20, seniors $10-18, children $7-12. Call ahead for reservations.) The park also has a few seasonal attractions. In the summer, the **Cleveland Orchestra** performs evening concerts at the **Blossom Music Center**, 1145 W. Steels Corners Rd., in Cuyahoga Falls, a few mi. south of the park. (☎33-920-8040. Lawn seating $22-70.) In winter, **Boston Mills/ Brandywine Ski Resorts** boasts 16 lifts, snow tubing, and night skiing on both sides of the Cuyahoga. (☎330-467-2242. Boston Mills: 7100 Riverview Rd., in Peninsula. Brandywine: 1146 W Highland Rd., in Sagamore Hills. 8hr. lift ticket $39, seniors and ages 5-12 $34.)

GREAT LAKES

CEDAR POINT AMUSEMENT PARK

Consistently ranked the "best amusement park in the world" by *Amusement Today* and other industry magazines, **Cedar Point Amusement Park,** off U.S. 6, 65 mi. west of Cleveland in Sandusky, earns its superlatives. Many of the world's highest and fastest roller coasters are born here, and the enormous new **Millennium Force** (310 ft., 90 mph) offers a grand old adrenaline rush for all. (☎419-627-2350 or 800-237-8386. Patriotic laser light shows in summer nightly at 10pm. Open June-Aug. daily 10am-11pm; Sept.-early Oct. hours vary. Parking $7. $39, seniors $23, children under 4 or shorter than 4 ft. $15.)

FOOTBALL HALL OF FAME

The **Pro Football Hall of Fame,** 2121 George Halas Dr. NW, in Canton, 60 mi. south of Cleveland, Exit 107A from I-77, honors the pigskin greats. Bronze busts of football luminaries line the Hall of Heroes, while interactive exhibits test sports fans' knowledge of the game. O.J. Simpson's jersey and helmet are displayed, but not his glove. (☎330-456-8207. Open June-Aug. daily 9am-8pm; early Sept.-late May 9am-5pm. $12, seniors $8, ages 6-14 $6.)

COLUMBUS ☎614

Rapid growth, a huge suburban sprawl, and some gerrymandering have nudged Columbus's population beyond that of Cincinnati or Cleveland. Columbus, however, is still America without any glitz, fame, pretentiousness, or smog—a clean, wholesome land of farmers and hardworking, everyday folk. Friendly neighborhoods and down-to-earth people make Columbus a pleasant stop for any traveler heading across the United States.

◼◪ ORIENTATION & PRACTICAL INFORMATION. Columbus, a planned capital city, is laid out in an easy grid. **High St.,** running north-south, and **Broad St.,** running east-west, are the main thoroughfares, dividing the city into quadrants. High St. heads north from the towering office complexes of downtown to the lively galleries in the Short North. It ends in the collegiate cool of **Ohio State University (OSU),** America's largest university, with over 60,000 students. South of downtown, schnitzel is king at historic **German Village. Greyhound,** 111 E. Town St. (☎221-2389 or 800-231-2222), offers service from downtown to Chicago (7-11hr., 6 per day, $51), Cincinnati (2-3½hr., 10 per day, $17), and Cleveland (2-4½hr., 11 per day, $20-25). The **Central Ohio Transit Authority (COTA),** 177 S. High St., runs local transportation until 11pm or midnight, depending on the route. (☎228-1776. Office open M-F 8:30am-5:30pm. $1.10, express $1.50.) **Taxis: Yellow Cab,** ☎444-4444. **Greater Columbus Visitors Center,** 111 S. 3rd St., on the 2nd fl. of City Center Mall. (☎221-6623 or 800-345-2657. Open M-Su 11am-6pm.) **Post Office:** 850 Twin Rivers Dr. (☎469-4521. Open M-F 7am-8pm, Sa 8am-2pm.) **ZIP code:** 43215. **Area code:** 614.

▛◨ ACCOMMODATIONS & FOOD. Travelers under the age of 21 will have a hard time finding accommodations in Columbus; a city ordinance prevents hotels from renting to underaged visitors. Head to one of the nearby suburbs, like Hilliard, for a room. **Motel 6 ❷,** 5910 Scarborough Dr., 20min. from downtown off I-70 at Exit 110A, has what you'd expect from a standard chain. (☎755-2250. Singles $37-45; $6 per each additional adult.)

High St. features a variety of tasty budget restaurants. The **J&G Diner ❶,** 733 N. High St., in the Short North District, serves filling Belgian waffles ($4) and "hippie" or "rabbi" omelettes ($7) amid provocative paintings of a green-clad Cinderella figure. (☎294-1850. Open M-F 10:30am-10pm, Sa 9am-10pm, Su 9am-9pm.) College kids gather at **Brenen's Cafe ❶,** 1864 N. High St., for huge sandwich baskets ($4.50) and baked goods like triple chocolate muffins. (☎291-7751. Open M-Th 7am-11pm, F 7am-10pm, Sa 8am-10pm, Su 8am-11pm. Summer hours vary.) **Bernie's Bagels and Deli ❶**, 1896 N. High St., has healthy sandwiches ($3-5) and an all-day breakfast in a no-frills deli and bar. (☎291-3448. Open daily 11am-2:30am.) **La Bamba ❶**, 1980 N. High St., is the colorful home of the $5.65 burrito that's "Bigger Than Your Head." The proof is on the wall—in a mural of the OSU football team, each player sports a burrito for a head. (☎294-5004. Open Tu-W 11am-2:30am, Th-Sa 11am-3:30am, Su-M 11am-midnight.)

◙ **SIGHTS. Ohio State University (OSU)** rests 2 mi. north of downtown. **The Wexner Center for the Arts**, 1871 N. High St., by 15th Ave., was the first public building by controversial modernist architect Peter Eisenman. Though the four galleries are being renovated over the next 18 months, the display of avant-garde art in all media will still be housed in some of the rooms, as well as in satellite locations around the city. Performance spaces host dance, music, and theater productions. (☎292-3535. Exhibits open Feb.-June Tu-W and F-Sa 10am-6pm, Th 10am-9pm, Su noon-6pm. $3, students and seniors $2. Free Th 5-9pm. Call for info on satellite locations. Wheelchair accessible.) The **Columbus Museum of Art**, 480 E. Broad St., hosts a growing collection of contemporary American art and Impressionist works in an intimate setting. (☎221-6801. Open Tu-W and F-Su 10am-5:30pm, Th 10am-8:30pm. $6, students and seniors $4. Free Th. Parking $3.) Fire, water, explosions, nylon mittens, uranium, and kids add up to some good ol' fun at the **Center of Science and Industry (COSI)**, 333 W. Broad St. (☎288-2674. Open daily 10am-5pm. $12, seniors $10, ages 2-12 $7. Wheelchair accessible.) Nearby, James Thurber's childhood home, the **Thurber House**, 77 Jefferson Ave., off E. Broad St., one block west of I-71, guides visitors through the major events of the famous *New Yorker* writer's life. It also serves as an impressive literary center with book events and a writer-in-residence. (☎464-1032. Open daily noon-4pm. Free. Tours Su $2.50, students and seniors $2.)

For some good Germanica, march down to the **German Village**, south of Capitol Sq. This area, first settled in 1843, is now the largest privately funded historical restoration in the US, full of stately homes and beer halls. At **Schmidt's Sausage Haus**, 240 E. Kossuth St., traditional German oompah bands Schnickel-Fritz, Schnapps, and Squeezin' 'n' Wheezin' lead polkas. Between dances, *lederhosen*-clad servers bring out $8.50 plates of homemade sausage. (☎444-6808. Polkas in summer W-Th 7pm and F-Sa 8pm; no W show in winter. Open Su-M 11am-9pm, Tu-Th 11am-10pm, F-Sa 11am-11pm.) One block west, **Schmidt's Fudge Haus**, 220 E. Kossuth St., mixes up savory fudge and chocolate concoctions named for local celebrities. (☎444-2222. M-Th noon-7pm, F-Sa noon-9pm, Su noon-4pm.) The **German Village Society Meeting Haus**, 588 S. 3rd St., provides info on the happenings around the village. (☎221-8888. Open M-F 9am-4pm, Sa 10am-2pm; shorter hours in winter.) Ask about **Oktoberfest**, inexplicably held in early September.

🎭📺 **ENTERTAINMENT & NIGHTLIFE.** Four free weekly papers available in shops and restaurants—*The Other Paper*, *Columbus Alive*, *The Guardian*, and *Moo*—list arts and entertainment options. Columbus' brand-new NHL hockey team, the **Blue Jackets** (☎246-3350), plays winter games in Nationwide Arena. The **Clippers**, a minor league affiliate of the NY Yankees, swing away from April to early September. (☎462-5250. Tickets $5-8.) The eccentric **Gallery V**, 694 N. High St., exhibits contemporary paintings and sculptures along with handcrafted jewelry from all over the US. (☎228-8955. Open Tu-Sa 11am-5pm. Free.)

If you're feeling bored, Columbus has a sure cure: rock 'n' roll. Bar bands are a Columbus mainstay, and it's hard to find a bar that doesn't have live music on the weekend. Bigger national acts stop at the **Newport,** 1722 N. High St. (☎228-3580. Tickets $5-40.) Famed chocolate martinis ($6) and TV-covered walls highlight the **Union Station Video Cafe,** 630 N. High St., which entertains a primarily gay crowd. (☎228-3740. Beers $2.50-3.50. Show tunes Su 6-11pm. Open daily 11am-2:30am.) South from Union Station is the **Brewery District,** where barley and hops have replaced the coal and iron of the once industrial area.

NEAR COLUMBUS

One hour south of Columbus, the area around **Chillicothe** (*CHILL-i-caw-thy*) features several American Indian cultural sites. The **Hopewell Culture National Historical Park,** 16062 Rte. 104, swells with 23 Hopewell burial mounds spread over 13 acres that serve as one of the few keys to a 2000-year-old culture. A museum provides theories about the mounds and their origin. (☎740-774-1126. Museum open Sept.-May daily 8:30am-5pm; June-Aug. extended hours. Grounds open dawn to dusk. $5 per car, $3 per pedestrian.) For a more lively presentation of Native American life, head to the **Sugarloaf Mountain Amphitheater,** on the north end of Chillicothe off Rte. 23. Between mid-June and early September the theater presents *Tecumseh,* a drama reenacting the life and death of the Shawnee leader. A behind-the-scenes tour answers questions about how the stuntmen dive headfirst off the 21 ft. cliff. (☎775-0700 or 866-775-0700. Shows M-Sa 8pm. Su-Th $14, F-Sa $16; under 10 $6.) After seeing the local sights, travelers can get back to nature at **Scioto Trail State Park ❶,** 10 mi. south of Chillicothe off U.S. 23, with walk-in **camping** across from Stuart Lake. (☎740-663-2125. Sites $9, with electricity $13.)

CINCINNATI ☎513

Founded by German pig salesmen, Cincinnati has earned the nickname of "Porkopolis," although Longfellow gave it the more regal title "Queen City of the West." Located just across the Ohio River from Kentucky, Cincinnati has the feel—and sometimes the accent—of a Southern city. Unfortunately, recent racial tensions also allude to a Southern past. Nevertheless, its stellar ballet, world-class zoo, and one-of-a-kind chili make Cincinnati a highlight of the region.

▐ TRANSPORTATION

Airport: Greater Cincinnati International (☎859-767-3151), in Kentucky, 12 mi. south of Cincinnati and accessible by I-75, I-71, and I-74. **Jetport Express** shuttles to downtown (☎859-767-3702. $12, $16 round-trip.) The **Transit Authority of Northern Kentucky,** or **TANK** (☎859-331-8265), also offers shuttle services.

Trains: Amtrak, 1301 Western Ave. (☎651-3337), in Union Terminal. Open M-F 9:30am-5pm and Tu-Su 11pm-6:30am. To **Chicago** (8-9hr., 1 per day, $19-36) and **Indianapolis** (4hr., 1 per day, $19-35). *Avoid the area to the north, especially Liberty St.*

Buses: Greyhound, 1005 Gilbert Ave. (☎352-6012), past the intersection of E. Court and Broadway. Open 24hr. To: **Cleveland** (4-6hr., 10 per day, $40); **Columbus** (2hr., 11 per day, $17); **Louisville, KY** (2hr., 10 per day, $21).

Public Transit: Cincinnati Metro and **TANK,** both in the bus stop in the Mercantile Center, 115 E. 5th St. (☎621-9450). Open M-F 8am-5pm. Most buses run out of Government Sq., at 5th and Main St., to outlying communities. In summer 50¢; in winter 65¢, winter rush-hour 80¢; extra to suburbs. Office has schedules and info.

Taxi: Yellow Cab, ☎241-2100.

IN RECENT NEWS

CINCINNATI'S RED

On election night in 2000, most of the country had its eye turned to the tight presidential race, but in Cincinnati, a tense race war was about to erupt. That night, 29-year-old African-American Robert Owensby died while in the custody of Cincinnati police, raising questions about **police brutality** and **racial profiling** in the city. While the white police officers involved were being investigated, the ACLU, the Black United Front, and some local businessmen filed a lawsuit against the police for several years of mistreatment of blacks. As black community leaders called on celebrities and tourists to boycott Cincinnati in the hopes of crippling the tourism industry, tensions mounted. On April 7, three days of riots erupted after the shooting of 19-year-old Timothy Thomas by a police officer.

The ACLU lawsuit was eventually settled, and the police department agreed to sweeping reforms. The trial in the Owensby case resulted in a mistrial, and the announcement that the county prosecutor would not retry the officers. Although an internal investigation was supposed to be released on the Owensby case, the report has still not been released 20 months after his death. Today, the police department continues to introduce new reform measures, such as complaint cards that citizens can file against the police. But protestors still flock to the downtown streets to fight what they see as racial injustice.

⚜ PRACTICAL INFORMATION

The downtown business district is a simple grid centered around **Fountain Sq.**, at **5th** and **Vine St.** Cross streets are numbered and designated E. or W. by their relation to Vine St. **Downtown** is bounded by Central Pkwy. on the north, Broadway on the east, 3rd on the south, and Central Ave. on the west. The **University of Cincinnati** spreads out from the Clifton area north of the city. **Cinergy Field,** the **Serpentine Wall,** and the **Riverwalk,** all to the south, border the Ohio River. *Be careful outside of the downtown area at night, especially north of Central Pkwy.*

> **Visitor Info: Cincinnati Convention and Visitors Bureau,** 300 W. 6th St. (☎621-2142 or 800-246-2987). Open M-F 9am-5pm. **Visitor Center at Fifth Third Center,** 511 Walnut St., on Fountain Sq., offers brochures on sights all over the area. Staff can also help find discounted tickets to shows and various sights. Free Internet access. Open M-Sa 10am-5pm, Su noon-5pm.

> **Hotlines: Rape Crisis Center,** 216 E. 9th St., downtown (☎872-9259). **Gay/Lesbian Community Switchboard,** ☎591-0222. Both 24hr.

> **Internet access: Public Library,** 800 Vine St. (☎369-6900). Open M-F 9am-9pm, Sa 9am-6pm, Su 1-5pm.

> **Post Office:** 525 Vine St., on the Skywalk. (☎684-5667. Open M-F 8am-5pm, Sa 8am-1pm.) **ZIP code:** 45202. **Area codes:** 513; Kentucky suburbs 859. In text, 513 unless noted otherwise.

⌂ ACCOMMODATIONS

Few cheap hotels can be found in downtown Cincinnati. About 30 mi. north of Cincinnati, in **Sharonville,** budget motels cluster along **Chester Rd.** Just 12 mi. south of the city, inexpensive accommodations line I-75 at Exit 184. The motels at **Central Pkwy.** and **Hopple St.** offer good, mid-priced lodging.

> **Knights Inn-Cincinnati/South,** 8048 Dream St., in Florence, KY (☎859-371-9711), just off I-75 at Exit 180, has homey rooms. Cable TV, A/C, and pool. Must be 21+ to rent. Singles $36-40, doubles $40-45. ❷

> **Budget Host Town Center Inn,** 3356 Central Pkwy. (☎283-4678 or 800-283-4678), Exit 3 off I-75, 10min. from downtown. Near public transportation, the rooms of this smallish motel are faded. What visitors save in money, they might lose in sleep, due to the rowdy bar on-site. Pool, A/C, and satellite TV. Must be 21+ to rent. Singles $45-60, doubles $50-65. ❷

> **Stonelick State Park** (☎625-6593), 25 mi. east of the city, outside the I-275 loop. 115 campsites provide welcome relief from Cincinnati's pricey lodgings. Sites $11, with electricity $15. ❶

🅒 FOOD

Cincinnati's greatest culinary innovation is its chili; it consists of noodles topped with meat, cheese, onions, and kidney beans—and a distinctive secret ingredient.

Skyline Chili, everywhere. Locations all over Cincinnati, including 643 Vine St. (☎241-2020), at 7th St., dish up the best beans in town. The secret ingredient has been debated for years—some say chocolate, but curry is more likely. 5-way large chili $5.70. Cheese coney dog $1.30. Open M-F 10:30am-8pm, Sa 11am-4pm. ❶

Graeter's, 41 E. 4th St. (☎381-0653), between Walnut and Vine St. downtown, as well as 14 other locations. Since 1870, Graeter's has blended their specialty giant chocolate chips into dozens of different ice cream flavors. Sandwiches and baked goods also served. Single cone $1.85. Open M-F 7am-6pm, Sa 7am-5pm.

Roly Poly, 2502 W. Clifton Ave (☎861-1666), in Clifton. One of three locations. Over fifty rolled sandwich options satisfy any craving from standard turkey or tuna to a chocolate cheese cake wrap. Sandwiches served half (from $3.25) or whole (from $5). Open M-Sa 10am-9pm. ❶

House of Sun, 35 E. 7th St. (☎721-3600), between Vine and Walnut St. Plentiful, cheap Chinese cuisine makes this a favorite among locals. Try the lunch special, which includes soup, entree, and fried rice for $5.25. Open M-Sa 11am-9:30pm. ❶

👁 SIGHTS

DOWNTOWN. Downtown Cincinnati orbits around the **Tyler Davidson Fountain,** at 5th and Vine St., a florid 19th-century masterpiece and ideal people-watching spot. To the east, the expansive garden at **Procter and Gamble Plaza** is just one mark that the giant company has left on its hometown. Around **Fountain Sq.,** business complexes and great shops are connected by a series of 2nd-floor skywalks. The observation deck at the top of **Carew Tower** provides the best view in the city. Close to Fountain Sq., the **Contemporary Arts Center** houses temporary modern exhibits. The Center will be moving in the summer of 2003 to a new building, complete with six floors of exhibition space. *(115 E. 5th St., 2nd fl. of the Mercantile Center. New location: 6th and Walnut St.; call for info on exhibits and building space. ☎345-8400. Open M-Sa 10am-6pm, Su noon-5pm. $3.50, students and seniors $2; M free. Wheelchair accessible.)* When it reopens in the spring of 2003, the **Taft Museum** will have a large educational space to complement its extensive collection of classical masters, including Rembrandts and Whistlers. Until the reopening, a small portion of the collection is displayed at the Cincinnati Art Museum. *(316 Pike St., at the east end of 4th St. ☎241-0343. Open M-Sa 10am-5pm, Su 1-5pm. $4, students and seniors $2, under 18 free; W and Su free.)*

EDEN PARK. Eden Park provides a nearby respite from the city with rolling hills, a pond, and cultural centers. *(Northeast of downtown and Mt. Adams. Take bus #49 to Eden Park Dr. Open daily 6am-10pm.)* The collections at the **Cincinnati Art Museum,** inside the park, span 5000 years, including Near Eastern artifacts, Chagall and Cassatt's impressionism, and Andy Warhol's rendition of infamous Cincinnati baseball great Pete Rose. *(953 Eden Park Dr. ☎721-5204. Open Tu and Th-Sa 10am-5pm, W 10am-9pm, Su noon-6pm. $5, students and seniors $4, under 18 free; Sa by donation. Special exhibits cost extra.)* The nearby **Krohn Conservatory** is one of the largest public greenhouses in the world, boasting a lush rainforest and a butterfly garden. *(☎421-5707. Open daily 10am-5pm. Free; donations accepted. Wheelchair accessible.)* For more outdoor fun, head to the famous **Cincinnati Zoo,** where standard inhabitants like elephants and gorillas are neighbors to rare species like manatees. *(3400 Vine St. ☎281-4700. Call for seasonal schedules. $11.50, children $9. Parking $6.50.)*

🎵 ENTERTAINMENT

The free newspapers *City Beat, Everybody's News,* and *Downtowner* list the happenings around town. The community of **Mt. Adams** supports a thriving arts and entertainment district. Perched on its own wooded hill in Eden Park, the **Playhouse in the Park,** 962 Mt. Adams Circle, performs theater in the round. (☎ 421-3888. Performances mid-Sept. to June Tu-Su. $26-40; senior rush tickets 2hr. before show, student 15min. before show. All rush tickets $13.50.)

The **Music Hall,** 1243 Elm St. (☎ 721-8222), hosts the **Cincinnati Symphony Orchestra** and the **Cincinnati Pops Orchestra** from September through May. (☎ 381-3300. $16.50-63.) The **Cincinnati Opera** also sings here. (☎ 888-533-7149. $12-90.) For updates on these and more, call **Dial the Arts** (☎ 621-4744). The symphony's summer season (June-July) tunes up at **Riverbend,** near Coney Island. The **Cincinnati Ballet Company** (☎ 621-5219) is at the **Aronoff Center for the Arts,** 650 Walnut St., which also hosts a Broadway series. (☎ 241-7469. Ballet performances Oct.-May. $12-47, matinees $9-40; musicals $15-65. Wheelchair accessible.)

In Mason, 24 mi. north of Cincinnati, off I-71 at Exit 24, the amusement park **Paramount's King Island** cages **The Beast,** the world's longest wooden roller coaster, which spreads its tentacles over 35 acres and 2 ZIP codes. (☎ 573-5800 or 800-288-0808. Open late May-late Aug. Su-F 9am-10pm, Sa 9am-11pm. $42, seniors and ages 3-6 $22. Parking $8. Wheelchair accessible.) Sports fans watch baseball's **Reds** (☎ 421-7337; $5-28) at **Cinergy Field,** 201 E. Pete Rose Way, and football's **Bengals** (☎ 621-3550; $35-50) at **Paul Brown Stadium** five blocks west.

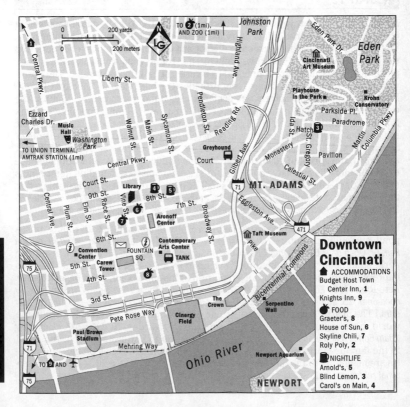

■ NIGHTLIFE

Overlooking downtown from the east, the winding streets of **Mt. Adams** have spawned some off-beat bars and late-night coffeeshops, creating a relaxed environment removed from the bustling city below.

Blind Lemon, 936 Hatch St. (☎241-3885), at St. Gregory St. Live blues, folk and acoustic rock fill the stage where Jimmy Buffet started out. Draft $2. Live music M-Sa 9:30pm, Su 8pm. 21+. Open M-Th 5pm-2:30am, F 4pm-2:30am, Sa-Su 3pm-2:30am.

Arnold's, 210 E. 8th St. (☎421-6234), between Main and Sycamore St. This wood-paneled mainstay, Cincinnati's oldest tavern, provides good domestic beer ($2.50-3.75). After 9pm, Arnold's does live ragtime, bluegrass, swing, and more in the courtyard. Pasta and sandwiches $4-20. All ages. Open M-F 11am-1am, Sa 4pm-1am.

Carol's On Main, 825 Main St. (☎651-2667), inserts funk and style into downtown Cincinnati. Drawing theater groups and thirtysomething yuppies, this restaurant/bar is known for great food and late hours. Cock-a-Noodle-Do salad $9. Kitchen open M-Tu 11:30am-11pm, W-F 11:30am-1am, Sa-Su 4pm-1am; bar closes M-Tu at 1:30am, W-Su at 2:30am.

Plush, 825 Main St. (☎651-2667), a cabaret upstairs from Carol's, thumps to drum and bass music on Tu and shakes things up with local Latin stylings on Th. Open nightly; see Carol's bar for hours.

INDIANA

The cornfields of southern Indiana's Appalachian foothills give way to expansive plains in the industrialized north, where Gary's smokestacks spew black clouds over the waters of Lake Michigan, and urban travel hubs string along the interstates. Despite its official motto—"The Crossroads of America"—Indiana is a modest, slow-paced state, where farms roll on and on, big cities are a rarity, and countless Hoosier school kids grow up dreaming of becoming the next Larry Bird.

⍰ PRACTICAL INFORMATION

Capital: Indianapolis.

Visitor info: Indiana Division of Tourism, 1 N. Capitol Ave., #700, Indianapolis 46204 (☎800-289-6646; www.state.in.us/tourism). **Division of State Parks,** 402 W. Washington, #W-298, Indianapolis 46204 (☎317-232-4125).

Postal Abbreviation: IN. Sales Tax: 5%.

Time zone: Eastern Standard Time. *With the exception of a few counties in the northwest and southwest corners, most of Indiana does not observe Daylight Savings Time;* this means it is on "Central time" during the summer and "Eastern time" in the winter.

INDIANAPOLIS   ☎317

Surrounded by flat farmland, Indianapolis feels like a model Midwestern city. Folks shop and work all day among downtown's skyscrapers, then drive home to sprawling suburbs in the evening. Life ambles here—until May, that is, when 350,000 spectators overrun the city and the road warriors of the Indianapolis 500 speed into the spotlight.

GREAT LAKES

530 ■ INDIANA

■ ⁊ ORIENTATION & PRACTICAL INFORMATION. The city is laid out in concentric circles, with a dense central cluster of skyscrapers and low-lying outskirts. The very center of Indianapolis is just south of **Monument Circle,** at the intersection of **Washington St. (U.S. 40)** and **Meridian St.** Washington St. divides the city north-south; Meridian St. divides it east-west. **I-465** circles the city and provides access to downtown. **I-70** cuts through the city east-west. Meter parking is abundant along the edge of the downtown area and near the Circle Centre Mall, so driving is easy in the city.

Indianapolis International Aiport (☎ 487-7243) is located 7 mi. southwest of downtown off I-465, Exit 11B; take bus #8 "West Washington." Taxi to downtown around $17. **Amtrak,** 350 S. Illinois St. (☎ 263-0550; open daily 7am-2:30pm and 11pm-6:30am), behind Union Station, rolls to Chicago (5hr., 1 per day, $18-34) and from Cincinnati (3hr., 1 per day, $19-34); trains travel east to west only. **Greyhound,** 350 S. Illinois St. (☎ 267-3071; open 24hr.), buses to Bloomington (1hr., 2 per day, $16); Chicago (4hr., 12 per day, $33); and Cincinnati (3-7hr., 4 per day, $21). **Indy Go,** 209 N. Delaware St., handles public transportation. (☎ 635-3344. Office open M-F 8am-6pm, Sa 9am-4pm. $1, under 6 free.) **Taxis: Yellow Cab,** ☎ 487-7777. **Visitor Info: Indianapolis City Center (Visit Indy),** on the first floor of Circle Centre Mall, has a helpful 3-D model of the city. (☎ 237-5200 or 800-323-4639. Free Internet access. Open M-F 10am-5:30pm, Sa 10am-5pm, Su noon-5pm.) **Hotlines: Rape Crisis Line,** ☎ 800-221-6311; 24hr.; **Gay/Lesbian Switchboard,** ☎ 251-7955; operates daily 7-11pm. **Post Office:** 125 W. South St., across from Amtrak. (☎ 464-6376. Open M-W and F 7am-5:30pm, Th 7am-6pm.) **ZIP code:** 46204. **Area code:** 317.

⌂ PIT STOP. Budget motels line the I-465 beltway, 5 mi. from downtown. Make reservations a year in advance for the Indy 500, which drives rates up in May. Head to **Motel 6 ❷,** 6330 Debonair Ln., at Exit 16A off I-465, for clean, pleasant rooms with A/C and cable TV. (☎ 293-3220. Singles $35-40; doubles $41-46.) Though occasionally hard to come by, the rooms at the **Methodist Tower Inn ❸,** 1633 N. Capitol Ave., are the cheapest ones close to downtown. A short walk from Monument Circle, the inn provides large rooms with TV and A/C. (☎ 925-9831. Rooms $70; $5 each additional person.) Live in the lap of luxury in the elegant **Renaissance Tower Historic Inn ❹,** 230 E. 9th St., for longer stays in the area. Rooms have stately canopy beds and a sitting area. (☎ 261-2652 or 800-676-7786. Rooms $75-95; call for availability.) Especially busy during the state fair, the **Indiana State Fairgrounds Campgrounds ❶,** 1202 E. 38th St., bus #4 or 39 from downtown, has 170 sod-and-gravel sites, mostly packed by RVs. To get close to nature, go elsewhere. (☎ 927-7520. Sites $16, full hookup $19.)

❏ HIGH-OCTANE FUEL. Ethnic food stands, produce markets, and knick-knack vendors fill the spacious **City Market,** 222 E. Market St., a renovated 19th-century building. (☎ 630-4107. Open M-W and F 6am-6pm, Th 6am-8pm, Sa 6am-4pm.) Chains and moderately priced restaurants cluster in Indianapolis's newly constructed **Circle Centre,** 49 West Maryland St. (☎ 681-8000). Massachusetts Ave. houses some of the liveliest restaurants and bars in the city; in the summer, crowded outdoor patios seat diners every night. **Bazbeaux Pizza ❷,** 334 Massachusetts Ave. (☎ 636-7662) and 832 E. Westfields Blvd. (☎ 255-5711), serves Indianapolis's favorite pizza. The Tchoupitoulas pizza, topped with a spicy concoction of shrimp, is a Cajun masterpiece (serves 2; $12). Construct your own culinary wonder ($5.75) from a choice of 53 toppings. (Both locations open M-Th 11am-10pm, F-Sa 11am-11pm, Su 4:30-10pm.) **The Abbey ❷,** 771 Massachusetts Ave. (☎ 269-8426) and 923 Indiana Ave. (☎ 917-0367), is a popular coffee shop, offering a full menu of wraps, salads, and sandwiches ($6-7). Sip cappuccinos in overstuffed velvet chairs for $2.25. (Both locations open M-Th 8am-midnight, F 8am-1am, Sa 11am-1am, Su 11am-midnight.) After the clubs close, make a run for **Paco's Cantina ❶,** 723 Broad Ripple Ave. (☎ 251-6200. Tacos $2.50. Burritos $4.50. Open 24hr.)

⊙ **SUNDAY DRIVE.** The newly restored canal at **White River State Park,** near downtown, entices locals to stroll, bike, or nap on the banks. Pedal boats are available for rent at **Central Canal Rental** (☎ 634-1824). Near the park entrance, the **Eiteljorg Museum of American Indians and Western Art,** 500 W. Washington St., features an impressive collection of art from the settlers of the Old West, along with interactive exhibits on Native American crafts. (☎ 636-9378. Open Tu-Sa 10am-5pm, Su noon-5pm; also May-Sept. M 10am-5pm. Tours daily at 1pm. $7, students with ID and ages 5-17 $4, seniors $6.) It may be far from downtown, but the **Indianapolis Museum of Art,** 1200 W. 38th St., is worth a visit. The museum's beautiful 152 acres offer nature trails, art pavilions, a botanical garden, a greenhouse, and a theater. (☎ 923-1331. Open Tu-W and F-Sa 10am-5pm, Th 10am-8:30pm, Su noon-5pm. Free; special exhibits $5.)

A majestic stained-glass dome graces the marbled interior of the **State House,** 200 W. Washington St., between Capitol and Senate St. (☎ 233-5293. Open M-F 8am-4:00pm. 1hr. guided tours, 2-4 per day. Free.) Animal lovers should check out the seemingly cageless **Indianapolis Zoo,** 1200 W. Washington St., which holds large whale and dolphin pavilions. (☎ 630-2001. Open June-Aug. daily 9am-5pm; Sept.-May 9am-4pm. $9.75, seniors $7, ages 3-12 $6. Parking $3.) Travel the world, explore outer space, and delve into history in the hands-on exhibits at the **Indianapolis Children's Museum,** 3000 N. Meridian St., in a brightly decorated brick building. (☎ 334-3322. Open Mar.-Aug. daily 10am-5pm; Sept.-Feb. Tu-Su 10am-5pm. $9.50, seniors $8, children $4.)

🏎 **DAYS OF THUNDER.** The country's passion for fast cars reaches fever pitch during the **500 Festival** (☎ 636-4556), an entire month of parades and hoopla leading up to race day at the **Indianapolis Motor Speedway,** 4790 W. 16th St., off I-465 at the Speedway Exit, bus #25. The festivities begin with time trials in mid-May and culminate with the "Gentlemen, start your engines" of the **Indianapolis 500** the Sunday before Memorial Day. When the track lies dormant, buses full of tourists drive around the 2½ mi. track. (☎ 481-8500. Track tours daily 8am-4pm. $3, ages 6-15 $1.) The **Speedway Museum,** at the south end of the infield, houses **Indy's Hall of Fame.** (☎ 484-6747. Open daily 9am-5pm. $3, ages 6-15 $1.) Tickets for the race go on sale the day after the previous year's race and usually sell out within a week. NASCAR's **Brickyard 400** sends stock cars zooming down the speedway in early August. (☎ 800-822-4639 for ticket order forms for any event.)

📷🎭 **IN THE FAST LANE.** The **Walker Theatre,** 617 Indiana Ave., a 15min. walk northwest of downtown, used to house the headquarters of African-American entrepreneur Madame C.J. Walker's beauty enterprise. Today the national historic landmark hosts various arts programs, including the biweekly **Jazz on the Avenue.** (☎ 236-2099. Tours M-F 9am-5pm. Jazz F 6-10pm. $5.)

A somewhat bland area by day, the **Broad Ripple** area, 6 mi. north of downtown at College Ave. and 62nd St., transforms into a center for nightlife after dark. Partyers fill the clubs and bars and spill out onto the sidewalks off Broad Ripple Ave. until about 1am on weekdays and 3am on weekends. The **Jazz Cooker,** 925 E. Westfield Blvd., heats up when the Steve Ball Trio or Johnny Dial Trio begin jamming. Attached to the Jazz Cooker, **Monkey's Tale** is a relaxed bar where a great jukebox spins tunes. (☎ 253-2883. Music F-Sa 7-10pm. Bar open M-Sa until 3am, Su 12:30am.) **Average Joe's Sports Pub,** 814 Broad Ripple Ave., is a standard bar offering five pool tables and $2.75 beers. (☎ 253-5844. Open M-Sa 5pm-3am, Su 5pm-12:30am.) If you need some laughs, head to the **Crackers Comedy Club,** 6281 N. College Ave., at Broad Ripple Ave. (☎ 255-4211. Tu amateur night. Shows Tu-Th 8:30pm, F-Sa 8 and 10:30pm, Su 8pm. $8-15.)

BLOOMINGTON ☎ 812

The region's rolling hills create an exquisite backdrop for Bloomington's most prominent institution, **Indiana University (IU)**. The college town atmosphere, nightlife hot spots, and die-hard fans of Hoosier basketball help Bloomington compete with its northern neighbor, Indianapolis.

⊞ ⚇ ORIENTATION & PRACTICAL INFORMATION. Bloomington lies south of Indianapolis on Rte. 37. **N. Walnut** and **College St.** are the main north-south thoroughfares. **Greyhound,** 219 W. 6th St. (☎332-1522; station open M-F 9am-5pm, Sa-Su noon-4pm), connects Bloomington to Chicago (5hr., 2 per day, $52) and Indianapolis (1hr., 2 per day, $16). **Bloomington Transit** sends buses on seven routes through both the town and the IU campus. Service is infrequent; call ahead. (☎332-5688. 75¢, seniors and ages 5-17 35¢.) The campus also has its own shuttle (75¢). **Taxis: Yellow Cab** (☎336-4100) charges by zone. The **Visitors Center,** 2855 N. Walnut St., offers free local calls and a helpful staff. (☎334-8900 or 800-800-0037. Open May-Oct. M-F 8:30am-5pm, Sa 9am-4pm; Nov.-Apr. M-F 8:30am-5pm, Sa 10am-3pm. Brochure area open 24hr.) **Internet access: Monroe County Public Library,** 303 E. Kirkwood Ave. (☎349-3050. Open M-Th 9am-9pm, F 9am-6pm, Sa 9am-5pm, Su 1-5pm.) **Post Office:** 206 E. 4th St., two blocks east of Walnut St. (☎334-4030. Open M and F 8am-6pm, Tu-Th 8am-5:30pm, Sa 8am-1pm.) **ZIP code:** 47404. **Area code:** 812.

⚆ ACCOMMODATIONS. Budget hotels are located around the intersection of N. Walnut St. and Rte. 46. **College Motor Inn ❸,** 509 N. College Ave., close to the university, has a classy exterior and plush rooms with cable TV and comfortable furniture. (☎336-6881. Reservations recommended. Singles from $55, doubles from $60. Prices rise for weekends and special events.) Usually rooms at the **Scholar's Bed & Breakfast ❹,** 801 N. College Ave., run for over $100, but good deals can be found on weekdays, when the lush rooms with TV/VCR, A/C, and private baths drop in price. (☎332-1892. Check-in 4-6pm. Call for room availability. Rooms from $89.) **Paynetown State Recreation Area ❶,** 10 mi. southeast of downtown on Rte. 446, has open field campsites in a well-endowed park on Lake Monroe with access to hiking trails. Boat rental available. (☎837-9490. Primitive sites $7, with shower $12, with electricity $15. Vehicle registration $5, IN residents $3.)

⚆ FOOD. Downtown Sq. hosts a wealth of veggie-heavy restaurants, bookstores, and cute clothing shops in a four-block stretch on Kirkwood Ave., near College Ave. and Walnut St. **⚈Snow Lion ❷,** 113 S. Grant St. just off Kirkwood Ave., owned by the Dalai Lama's nephew, is one of only a few Tibetan restaurants in the country. Spicy dishes and authentic decor transport diners to Tibet. (☎336-0835. *Momo* dinner $8. Tibetan Butter Tea $1.50. Open daily 11am-10pm.) **The Laughing Planet Cafe ❶,** 322 E. Kirkwood Ave., in the Kenwood Manor Building, serves up burritos ($4) and other organic delights made from local produce in a colorful cafe setting. (☎323-2233. Open daily 11am-9pm.) For tasty sandwiches with a French twist, the **Bakehouse ❶,** 125 N. College Ave., delivers fresh ingredients and generous samples of their fudgy brownies. (☎331-6029. Pastries $2-3, sandwiches $5-10. Open M-Sa 7:30am-9pm, Su 9am-6pm.)

⚆ SIGHTS. The **Tibetan Cultural Center,** 3655 Snoddy Rd., offers meditation and info on Tibetan culture. (☎334-7046. Grounds open Sa-Su noon-4pm. Center open Su noon-3pm.) IU's architecturally striking **Art Museum,** E. 7th St., on campus, maintains an excellent collection of Oriental and African artwork along with a mixture of European art from Medieval to modern times. (☎855-5445. Open Tu-Sa 10am-5pm, Su noon-5pm. Free.) Nearby, the **Mathers Museum of World Cultures,** 416 N. Indiana St., near E. 8th St., takes visitors on an alphabetical anthropological tour of technologies and traditional dress from around the world. (☎855-6873. Open Tu-F 9am-4:30pm, Sa-Su 1-4:30pm.) **Oliver Winery,** 8024 N. State Rd. 37, not only has flow-ery, fountain-filled grounds, but also offers free tastings of its 20 wines, including blackberry wine, the local favorite. (☎876-5800 or 800-258-2783. Open M-Sa 10am-6pm, Su noon-6pm.)

■ **NIGHTLIFE.** Bloomington's nightlife scene is just what you'd expect from a Midwestern college town in Middle America: it's all about beer and rock. **The Crazy Horse,** 214 W. Kirkwood Ave., drafts an alcohol army of 80 beers. (☎336-8877. Open M-W 11am-1am, Th-Sa 11am-2am, Su noon-midnight.) **Nick's,** 423 E. Kirkwood Ave., looks like a quaint English pub outside, but inside IU students guzzle beer and cheer on their favorite sports teams. (☎332-4040. Beers from $2. Open M-Sa 11am-2am, Su noon-midnight.) **Bluebird,** 216 N. Walnut St., showcases local musi-cal talent. (☎336-2473. Open in winter M-Sa 9pm-3am; in summer Tu-Sa 9pm-3am.) The doors at **Rhino's,** 325½ S. Walnut St., are open to those under 21 for dancing and performances. (☎333-3430. Live music F-Sa 8pm.) **Bullwinkle's,** 201 S. College Ave., caters to a gay crowd with drag shows, but a mixed clientele grooves on the dance floor. (☎334-3232. Drag shows M and W 11pm and 1am. Open M and W-Th 9pm-3am, F-Sa 8pm-3am.)

MICHIGAN

Pressing up against four of the Great Lakes, two peninsulas present visitors with two distinct Michigans. The sparsely populated Upper Peninsula hangs over Lake Michigan, housing moose, wolves, and stunning waterfalls in the Hiawatha National Forest. Campers and hikers have recently begun discovering the U.P., and the resplendent forests now entertain backpackers and families alike. In the Lower Peninsula, beach bums hang out in the many quaint communities along the western coast of the state, sunning and boating along some of Michigan's 3000 miles of coastline. Those craving an urban environment head to Ann Arbor, the intellectual center of the state, or to industrial Detroit, for world class museums.

◪ PRACTICAL INFORMATION

Capital: Lansing.

Visitor info: Michigan Travel Bureau, 333 S. Capitol St., Ste. F, Lansing 48909 (☎888-784-7328; www.michigan.org). **Dept. of Parks and Recreation,** Information Services Ctr., P.O. Box 30257, Lansing 48909 (☎517-373-9900). Entry to all state parks requires a motor vehicle permit; $4 per day, $20 annually. Call ☎800-447-2757 for reservations at any state park campground.

Postal Abbreviation: MI. **Sales Tax:** 6%.

DETROIT   ☎313

Long the ugly step-sister of America's big cities, Detroit has nowhere to go but up. Violent race riots in the 1960s caused a massive flight to the suburbs; the popula-tion has more than halved since 1967, turning neighborhoods into ghost towns. The decline of the auto industry in the late 1970s added unemployment to the city's ills, beleaguering an already depressed area. Today, the five gleaming towers of the riverside Renaissance Center symbolize the hope of a city-wide renewal

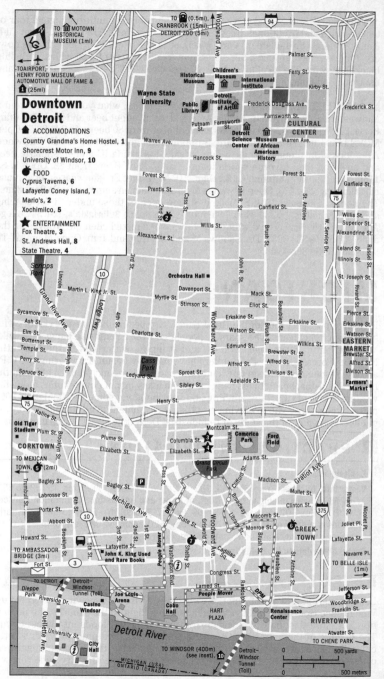

TO MOTOWN HISTORICAL MUSEUM (1mi)

TO AIRPORT, HENRY FORD MUSEUM, AUTOMOTIVE HALL OF FAME & (25mi)

TO CRANBROOK (15mi), DETROIT ZOO (5mi) (0.5mi)

Woodward Ave.

94

Palmer St.

Ferry St.

Kirby St.

Frederick St.

Wayne State University

Historical Museum

Children's Museum

International Institute

Public Library

Detroit Institute of Art

Frederick Douglass Ave.

Farnsworth St.

Putnam Farnsworth St.

Detroit Science Center

Museum of African American History

CULTURAL CENTER

Warren Ave.

Warren Ave.

Hancock St.

Forest St.

Forest St.

Forest St.

Garfield St.

Prentis St.

Cass St.

John R. St.

St. Antoine

75

Canfield St.

2nd St.

Willis St.

Willis St.

Superior St.

Alexandrine St.

John R. St.

Brush St.

Alexandrine St.

Leland St.

Illinois St.

Russel St.

St. Joseph St.

Downtown Detroit

🏠 ACCOMMODATIONS
Country Grandma's Home Hostel, 1
Shorecrest Motor Inn, 9
University of Windsor, 10

🍎 FOOD
Cyprus Taverna, 6
Lafayette Coney Island, 7
Mario's, 2
Xochimilco, 5

⭐ ENTERTAINMENT
Fox Theatre, 3
St. Andrews Hall, 8
State Theatre, 4

Scripps Park

Grand River Ave.

Lincoln St.

10

Martin L. King Jr. St.

Lodge Fwy.

3rd St.

Orchestra Hall ■

Davenport St.

Rivard St.

Pierce St.

Sycamore St.
Ash St.
Elm St.
Butternut St.
Temple St.
Perry St.
Spruce St.

4th St.

Myrtle St.
Stimson St.

Mack St.

Eliot St.

Beaubien St.

Erskine St.

Erskine St.

Watson St.

Brooklyn St.

Charlotte St.

Erskine St.
Watson St.
Edmund St.

Brush St.

Wilkins St.

EASTERN MARKET

Brewster St.

Cass Park

Alfred St.

Alfred St.

St. Antoine

Alfred St.

Pine St.

Ledyard St.

Sproat St.

Divison St.

Divison St.

Sibley St.

Adelaide St.

Farmers' Market

75

Kaline St.

Henry St.

Old Tiger Stadium ■

Plum St.

Brooklyn St.

Montcalm St.

Whiterell

Comerica Park

Ford Field

CORKTOWN

Plume St.

Columbia St.

Cass St.

TO MEXICAN TOWN, 6 (2mi)

Elizabeth St.

Elizabeth St.

Adams St.

Grand Circus Park

Gratiot Ave.

Bagley St.

Bagley St.

Clifford St.

Broadway

Madison St.

Mullet St.

375

Labrosse St.

Michigan Ave.

State St.

Clinton St.

Trumbull St.

6th St.

Porter St.

Abbott St.

Abbott St.

3rd St.

2nd St.

1st St.

DPM

Griswold St.

Library St.

Macomb St.

Monroe St.

6 GREEK-TOWN

Rivard St.

Nicolet Pl.

Joliet Pl.

Howard St.

10

Brooklyn St.

5th St.

Lafayette St.

John K. King Used and Rare Books

Washington Blvd.

Shelby St.

Woodward Ave.

Cadillac Sq.

Beaubien St.

St. Antoine St.

Lafayette St.

Navarre Pl.

TO BELLE ISLE (1mi)

TO AMBASSADOR BRIDGE (3mi)

Fort St.

3

Congress St.

8

Lamed St.

Randolph St.

DPM

TO DETROIT

Dieppe Park

Riverside Dr.

Detroit–Windsor Tunnel (Toll)

Casino Windsor

Joe Louis Arena

Cobo Hall

People Mover

HART PLAZA

Renaissance Center

Jefferson St.

Woodbridge St.

Franklin St.

RIVERTOWN

TO CHENE PARK

Ouellette Ave.

University St.

City Hall

Detroit River

TO WINDSOR (400m) (see inset)

10

Detroit–Windsor Tunnel (Toll)

Atwater St.

0   500 yards

0   500 meters

MICHIGAN (USA)
ONTARIO (CANADA)

GREAT LAKES

effort to revitalize downtown Detroit. Despite the real poverty and violence that plague Detroit, the aggressive tourism industry focuses on the city's jewels. Top-notch museums cluster in the cultural center of the city, while professional sports and a music scene descendent from Motown entertain both locals and travelers.

▐ TRANSPORTATION

Airport: Detroit Metropolitan (☎734-247-7678), 2 mi. west of downtown, off I-94 at Merriman Rd. in Romulus. **Checkered Sedan** (☎800-351-5466) offers taxi service to downtown for $42.

Trains: Amtrak, 11 W. Baltimore St. (☎873-3442), at Woodward St. Open daily 5:45am-11:30pm. To **Chicago** (6hr., 3 per day, $19-50) and **New York** (16hr., 1 per day, $72-135). For Canadian destinations, take **VIA Rail,** 298 Walker Rd., Windsor ON (☎519-256-5511 or 800-561-3949). To **Toronto** (4hr., 5 per day, CDN$7; 40% discount with ISIC card).

Buses: Greyhound, 1001 Howard St. (☎961-8011). Station open 24hr.; ticket office open daily 6am-12:30am. To: **Ann Arbor** (1hr., 5 per day, $7); **Chicago** (5½hr., 8 per day, $24); and **Cleveland** (4hr., 9 per day, $20). *At night, the area is unsafe.*

Public Transit: Detroit Dept. of Transportation (DOT), 1301 E. Warren St. (☎933-1300). Serves downtown, with limited service to the suburbs. Many buses stop service at midnight. $1.25, some short routes 50¢; transfers 25¢. **DOT Attractions Shuttle** delivers tourists to the metro area's most popular sights 10am-5:45pm. All-day ticket $5. An ultramodern elevated tramway, **People Mover,** 150 Michigan Ave., circles the Central Business District on a 2.7 mi. loop; worth a ride just for the view of the riverfront and downtown architecture. (☎962-7245 or 800-541-7245. Runs M-Th 7am-11pm, F 7am-midnight, Sa 9am-midnight, Su noon-8pm. 50¢.) **Southeastern Michigan Area Regional Transit (SMART),** 600 Woodward Ave. (☎962-5515), runs bus service to the suburbs 4am-midnight. Times vary depending on route. $1.50, transfers 25¢.

Taxis: Checker Cab, ☎963-7000.

◢★▐ ORIENTATION & PRACTICAL INFORMATION

Detroit lies on the Detroit River, which connects Lake Erie and Lake St. Clair. Across the river to the south, the town of **Windsor, ON,** can be reached by tunnel just west of the Renaissance Center (toll $2.50), or by the Ambassador Bridge. Detroit can be a dangerous town, but is typically safe during the day. The **People Mover** surrounds the downtown area where businesses and sports venues cluster; the area it encircles is safe during business hours. Driving is the best way to negotiate this sprawling city, where good and bad neighborhoods alternate on a whim. Though streets tend to end suddenly and reappear several blocks later, driving avoids the inefficient and potentially less safe public transportation.

Detroit's streets form a grid. The **Mile Roads** run east-west as major arteries. **Eight Mile Rd.** is the city's northern boundary and the beginning of the suburbs. **Woodward Ave.** heads northwest from downtown, dividing city and suburbs into "east side" and "west side." **Gratiot Ave.** flares out northeast from downtown, while **Grand River Ave.** shoots west. **I-94** and **I-75** pass through downtown. For a particularly helpful map, check the pull-out in *Visit Detroit*, available at the Visitors Bureau.

Visitor Info: Convention and Visitors Bureau, 211 W. Fort St., 10th fl. (☎202-1800 or 800-338-7648). Open M-F 9am-5pm.

Hotlines: Crisis Hotline, ☎224-7000. **Sexual Abuse Helpline,** ☎876-4180. Both 24hr.

Bi-Gay-Lesbian Organizations: Triangle Foundation of Detroit, ☎537-3323. **Between the Lines,** ☎248-615-7003. **Affirmations,** 195 W. 9 Mile Rd. (☎248-398-7105), in Ferndale, has a large library and info on gay nightlife.

Post Office: 1401 W. Fort St. (☎226-8304. Open 24hr.). **ZIP code:** 48233. **Area codes:** 313 (Detroit); 810, 248, and 734 (suburbs). In text, 313 unless noted otherwise.

⌂ ACCOMMODATIONS

Detroit's suburbs harbor loads of chain motels. Ones near the airport in **Romulus** tend to be overpriced, and others along **E. Jefferson,** near downtown, can be skanky. For a mix of convenience and affordability, look along **Telegraph Rd.** off I-94, west of the city. If the exchange rate is favorable, good deals can be found across the border in **Windsor.** *Visit Detroit* lists accommodations by area and includes price ranges.

Country Grandma's Home Hostel (HI-AYH), 22330 Bell Rd. (☎734-753-4901), in New Boston, 6 mi. south of I-94 off I-275, between Detroit and Ann Arbor. Take Exit 11B, turn right, and then make an immediate right onto Bell Rd. Though it's inaccessible by public transportation, the comfort, hospitality, and respite from urban Detroit make it worth the trip. 6 beds, kitchen, and free parking. Bring your own linen. Reservations required; call ahead. Dorms $15, nonmembers $18. Wheelchair accessible. ❶

Shorecrest Motor Inn, 1316 E. Jefferson Ave. (☎568-3000 or 800-992-9616), as close to downtown as the budget traveler can get. Rooms include A/C, fridges, and computer data ports. Key deposit $20 when paying by cash. Reservations recommended. Clean, comfortable singles $69; doubles $89. Free parking. Wheelchair accessible. ❸

University of Windsor, 401 Sunset Ave. (☎519-973-7074), in Windsor, rents rooms from early May-late Aug. Free use of university facilities. Singles CDN$32, students with college ID CDN$19; doubles CDN$40. Wheelchair accessible. ❶

Pontiac Lake Recreation Area, 7800 Gale Rd. (☎248-666-1020), in Waterford, 45min. northwest of downtown; take I-75 to Rte. 59 W, turn right on Will Lake northbound, and left onto Gale Rd. Huge wooded sites in rolling hills, just 4 mi. from the lake. 176 sites with electricity $11. Vehicle permit $4. ❶

◖ FOOD

Although many restaurants have migrated to the suburbs, there are still some budget dining options in town. The downtown area doesn't offer much after 5pm, but ethnic neighborhoods provide interesting choices. At the **Greektown** People Mover stop, Greek restaurants and excellent bakeries line one block of Monroe St., near Beaubien St. To snag a *pierogi,* cruise Joseph Campau Ave. in **Hamtramck** (*Ham-TRAM-eck*), a Polish neighborhood northeast of Detroit. No traveler should miss the **Eastern Market,** at Gratiot Ave. and Russell St., an 11-acre produce-and-goodie festival. (☎833-1560. Open Sa 4am-5pm.)

Cyprus Taverna, 579 Monroe St. (☎961-1550). A local favorite for Greek cuisine. In the heart of Greektown, large portions of *mousaka* and *spanakopita* are served in a quiet atmosphere. Lunch specials from $5.25. Dinner entrees $9-13. Open Su-Th 11am-1:30am, F-Sa 11am-4am. ❸

Mario's, 4222 2nd Ave. (☎832-6464), downtown. All meals include antipasto platters, salad, and soup. If the whole table can agree on one of the 5 specialty dinners, the meal will be prepared tableside by one of the capable chefs. Live bands and ballroom dancing shake the place up on the weekends, and free shuttle service takes customers to and from major sporting and theater events. Entrees from $18. Open M-Th 11:30am-11pm, F 11:30am-midnight, Sa 4pm-midnight, Su 2pm-10pm. ❺

Lafayette Coney Island, 118 W. Lafayette St. (☎964-8198). Detroit's most famous culinary establishment, Lafayette doles out its coney dogs ($2.10) and chili cheese fries ($2.85). Brusque service—and the antacids you'll need after the meal—is worth it for a near-perfect dog. Open M-Th 7:30am-4am, F-Sa 7:30am-5am, Su 9:30am-4am. ❶

Xochimilco, 3409 Bagley St. (☎843-0129). Say *so-she-Mo-ko* and no one will know you're an out-of-towner. Large dining areas with muraled walls create a festive atmosphere. Enjoy cheap, delicious specialties like enchiladas and burrito platters ($5-8). Open daily 11am-2am. ❷

📷 SIGHTS

Sections of Detroit and the surrounding area allow visitors a chance to explore everything from books to wildlife while enjoying the public parks in the city. For wandering book lovers, **John K. King Used and Rare Books,** 901 W. Lafayette St., is a four-floor maze of over a million books on every topic imaginable. Friendly and knowledgeable staff help guide new customers through the impressive warehouse. (☎961-0622. Open M-Sa 9:30am-5:30pm.)

DETROIT ZOO. Lions and tigers and bears...and red pandas and amphibians and monkeys...roam the suburban grounds of the **Detroit Zoological Park.** The park features the National Amphibian Conservation Center, while the all-new Arctic Ring of Life exhibit stars polar bears and includes a trek through the Tundra. *(8450 W. Ten Mile Rd., just off the Woodward exit off Rte. 696 in Royal Oak. ☎248-398-0900. Open mid-May to late June M-Sa 10am-5pm, Su 10am-6pm; late June to Aug. M-Tu and Th-Sa 10am-5pm, W 10am-8pm, Su 10am-6pm; Apr. to mid-May and Sept.-Oct. daily 10am-5pm; Nov.-Mar 10am-4pm. $8, seniors and ages 2-18 $6, under 2 free. Parking $4.)*

ONE HELL OF A PREP SCHOOL. Fifteen mi. north of Detroit in posh Bloomfield Hills, **Cranbrook's** scholarly campus holds public gardens, several museums, and an art academy. Far and away the best of the lot is the **Cranbrook Institute of Science,** 39221 N. Woodward Ave., with rotating exhibits emphasizing educational fun. *(☎248-645-3209 or 877-462-7262. Open M-Th and Sa-Su 10am-5pm, F 10am-10pm. $7, seniors and ages 2-12 $4.)*

BELLE ISLE. The best escape from Detroit's hectic pace is **Belle Isle,** where a conservatory, nature center, aquarium, maritime museum, and small zoo allow animal lovers to drift from site to site. *(3 mi. from downtown via the MacArthur Bridge. ☎852-4078. Isle accessible daily 6am-10pm; attractions 10am-5pm. $2 per site, ages 2-12 $1; zoo $3/1.)*

🏛 MUSEUMS

🎵 **Motown Historical Museum,** 2648 W. Grand Blvd. (☎875-2264). Take Woodward St. north and turn left on Grand. "Dexter Avenue" bus. Upstairs, an impressive collection of memorabilia includes the piano used by all the legendary Motown artists. Downstairs, Studio A—where the Jackson 5, Marvin Gaye, Smokey Robinson, and Diana Ross recorded—has been meticulously preserved, right down to the sheet music, vending machine, and telephones. Open in summer Su-M noon-6pm, Tu-Sa 10am-6pm; in winter Su-M noon-5pm, Tu-Sa 10am-5pm. $7, under 12 $4.

🎨 **Detroit Institute of Arts,** 5200 Woodward Ave. (☎833-7900). Under construction until 2007, the majority of the museum's large collection of American art is on tour until 2003 while the museum undergoes renovations. However, there is an extensive collection of traditional Dutch and Flemish art in an elaborate setting. Another highlight, Diego Rivera's mural "Detroit Industry," pays homage to the city and its industrial past. Open W-Th 10am-4pm, F 10am-9pm, Sa-Su 10am-5pm; first F of each month 11am-9pm. Suggested donation $4, students and children $1.

Henry Ford Museum, 20900 Oakwood Blvd. (☎271-1620), off I-94 in Dearborn. Take SMART bus #200 or 250. More than just a tribute to planes, trains, and automobiles, the museum takes visitors on a fascinating automotive tour of the major cultural changes in American history—from drive-ins and fast food to the protection of the President. The premises boast the limousine in which President Kennedy was assassinated and the chair in which Lincoln was shot. Next door, experience a microcosm of America at **Greenfield Village,** where over 80 historic edifices salute American ingenuity. Visit the workshop of the Wright Brothers or the factory where Thomas Edison researched. Museum and village open M-Sa 9am-5pm, Su 11am-5pm; village closed Jan.-Mar. Museum $13.50, seniors $12.50, ages 5-12 $8.50. Village $16/15/10. Combination pass $20/19/14.

Museum of African American History, 315 E. Warren Rd. (☎494-5800), features a moving core exhibit addressing the slave trade in the United States and ending in a bittersweet display of present day African-American culture. Fantastic special exhibits add to the main collection. Open W-Sa 9:30am-5pm, Su 1-5pm. $5, under 17 $3.

Detroit Science Center, 5020 John R St. (☎577-8400). Children of all ages can learn about waves while strumming a harp or discover new worlds looking under microscopes. Open mid-Sept. to early June M-F 9:30am-3pm, Sa-Su 10:30am-6pm; mid-June to early Sept. open M-F 9:30am-5pm, Sa-Su 10:30am-6pm. $7, seniors and ages 2-12 $6; IMAX additional $4.

🎵 ENTERTAINMENT

Music has always filled the streets of Detroit, with the city's sidewalk performers carrying on the Motown legacy. Though Motown has come and gone, a vibrant music scene still dominates the Motor City. The **Detroit Symphony Orchestra** performs at **Orchestra Hall,** 3711 Woodward Ave., at Parsons St. (☎962-1000, box office ☎576-5111. Open M-F 9am-5pm. Half-price student and senior rush tickets 1½hr. prior to show.)

You'll be impressed with the dramatic work performed in the newly renovated and restored **theater district,** clustered around Woodward Ave. and Columbia St. The **Fox Theatre,** 2211 Woodward Ave., near Grand Circus Park, features high-profile dramas, comedies, and musicals in a 5000 seat movie theater that occasionally shows epic films. (☎983-3200. Box office open M-F 10am-6pm. $25-100; movies under $10.) The **State Theater,** 2115 Woodward Ave. (☎961-5450, for event info ☎810-932-3643), brings a variety of popular concerts to the city.

Sports fans won't be disappointed in Detroit. During the dog days of summer, baseball's **Tigers** round the bases in the newly built **Comerica Park,** 2100 Woodward Ave. (☎471-2255. $8-35.) Football's **Lions** hit the gridiron for the first time at **Ford Field,** 200 Brush St., in the 2002-03 season. (☎800-616-7627. $15-35.) Inside the **Joe Louis Arena,** 600 Civic Center Dr., the 2002 Stanley Cup champion **Red Wings** play hockey. (☎645-6666. $20-40.) Thirty minutes outside Detroit in Auburn Hills, basketball's **Pistons** hoop it up at **The Palace at Auburn Hills,** 2 Championship Dr. (☎377-0100. $10-60.)

🎉 📍 FESTIVALS & NIGHTLIFE

Detroit's numerous **festivals** draw millions of visitors. Most outdoor events take place at **Hart Plaza,** a downtown oasis that hugs a scenic expanse of the Detroit River. A new and rousingly successful downtown tradition, the ▓**Detroit Electronic Music Festival** (☎393-9200; www.demf.org) has lured over one million ravers to Hart Plaza on Memorial Day weekend. Jazz fans jet to the riverbank during Labor Day weekend for the four-day **Ford Detroit International Jazz Festival** (☎963-7622), which features more than 70 acts on three stages and mountains of international food at the World Food Court. A week-long extravaganza in late June, the international **Freedom Festival** (☎923-7400), celebrates the friendship between the US and Canada. The continent's largest fireworks display ignites the festivities on both sides of the border. On the Detroit side, food and a bandstand dominate the festival, while Windsor provides a carnival complete with rides and cotton candy. **Detroit's African World Festival** (☎ 494-5853) brings over a million people to Hart Plaza on the third weekend in August for free reggae, jazz, and gospel concerts. The nation's oldest state fair, the **Michigan State Fair** (☎ 369-8250), at Eight Mile Rd. and Woodward Ave., beckons with bake-offs, art, and livestock birth exhibits during the two weeks before Labor Day.

For info on the trendiest nightspots, pick up a free copy of *Orbit* in record stores and restaurants. The *Metro Times* also contains complete entertainment listings. *Between the Lines*, also free, has bi-gay-lesbian entertainment info. Head to **Harmony Park,** near Orchestra Hall, for some of Detroit's best jazz. Alternative fans should check out **St. Andrews Hall,** 431 E. Congress St., which hosts local and national alternative acts. **Shelter,** the dance club downstairs in St. Andrews Hall, draws young, hip crowds on non-concert nights. (☎ 961-6358. St. Andrews 18+; Shelter 21+. Shows F-Su. Advance tickets through Ticketmaster $7-10.) Saturdays, the State Theater houses **Ignition,** a giant party that enlists DJs from a local radio station to play alternative dance music. (2115 Woodward Ave. Cover starts at $5. 18+. Sa 9pm-2am.) The bars and clubs along **Ouellette Ave.** in Windsor (see below) attract young party kids looking to take advantage of Ontario's lower drinking age.

NEAR DETROIT: WINDSOR, ON ☎ 519

Combining cultural highlights, natural attractions, and a vibrant nightlife, Windsor offers tourists an alternative to the industrial city across the river. Outdoor cafes, tree-filled streets, and lively shopping give Windsor a pleasant European feel. The many bars, favorable exchange rates, and drinking age (19) lure Detroiters of all ages across the river, creating a cosmopolitan mix on the crowded streets.

For a small industrial city, Windsor scores big with its collection of contemporary art. Stroll through the "museum without walls" at the **Odette Sculpture Garden,** part of a 6 mi. long riverfront green area between the Ambassador Bridge and Curry Ave. Visitors are enchanted by native totem poles next to unusual modern sculptures. (☎ 253-2300. Open daily dawn to dusk. Free.) The city's other major exhibit space, **The Art Gallery of Windsor,** 401 Riverside Dr. W, provides a showcase for a rotating cast of Canada's best modern artists. (☎ 977-0013. Open Tu-Th 11am-7pm, F 11am-9pm, Sa-Su 11am-5pm. Free.) Beauty of the natural type is on display at **Point Pelee National Park of Canada,** 407 Robson St., Leamington, ON, 45 mi. southeast of downtown. Visitors look for the butterflies flying through the park's tall grass. (☎ 322-2365. Open Apr. and June to mid-Oct. daily 6am-9:30pm; mid-Oct. to Mar. 7am-6:30pm; May 5am-9:30pm. CDN$3.25, students CDN$1.60, seniors CDN$2.40; family CDN$8.55. Guided butterfly tours in Sept. $20; includes T-shirt.)

Locals come from miles around to dine at the ▨**Tunnel Bar-B-Q ❸**, 58 Park St. E, across from the tunnel exit. (☎ 258-3663. Great half-strip rib dinner CDN$14. Open Su-Th 8am-2am, F-Sa 8am-4am.) The rest of Windsor's culinary and nightlife activity is centered along Ouellette (OH-let) Ave. downtown. Family-run **Aar-D-Vark Blues Cafe,** 89 University Ave. W, offers a Canadian take on a traditional Chicago blues joint. Pink aardvarks lead customers into the graffittied bar. (☎ 977-6422. Live music Tu-Su. Open M-F noon-2am, Sa 4pm-2am, Su 7pm-2am.) The **Amsterdam,** 26 Pelissier St., attracts trendy party-goers with drum and bass music. An international line-up of DJs entertains on Fridays. (☎ 977-7232. Cover F-Sa after 12:30am CDN$5. Open daily 6pm-2am.) For the traveler who prefers the clank of quarters to the beat of drums, the **Casino Windsor,** 377 Riverside Dr., offers three floors of gambling in a glimmering new building. Test Lady Luck 24hr. a day. (For reservations ☎ 800-991-8888, for info ☎ 800-991-7777. 19+.)

GREAT LAKES

Canada's national rail service, **VIA Rail,** 298 Walker Rd. (☎256-5511 or 800-561-3949; ticket window open M-Sa 5:15am-9pm, Su 6am-9pm), provides service to Toronto (4hr.; 5 per day; CDN$79, 40% discount with ISIC card). **Transit Windsor,** 3700 North Service Rd. E, sends buses throughout the city. (☎944-4111. CDN$2.15, students CDN$1.50.) **Taxi: Veteran's Cab,** ☎256-2621. **Visitor info: The Convention and Visitors Bureau of Windsor, Essex County, and Pelee Island,** 333 Riverside Dr. W, #103. (☎255-6530 or 800-265-3633; www.city.windsor.on.ca/cvb. Open M-F 8:30am-4:30pm.) The **Ontario Travel Center,** 110 Park St., offers brochures, maps, and help from a knowledgeable staff. (☎973-1338. Open daily 8am-8pm.) **Post Office:** City Centre, corner of Park St. and Ouellette Ave. (☎253-1252. Open M-F 8am-5pm.) **Postal code:** N9A 4K0. **Area code:** 519.

ANN ARBOR   ☎734

Ann Arbor's namesakes, Ann Rumsey and Ann Allen—the wives of two of the area's early pioneers—supposedly enjoyed sitting under grape arbors. The town has managed to prosper without losing its relaxed charm, despite being tucked between several major industrial hubs. Meanwhile, the huge and well-respected University of Michigan adds a hip collage of young liberal Middle Americans.

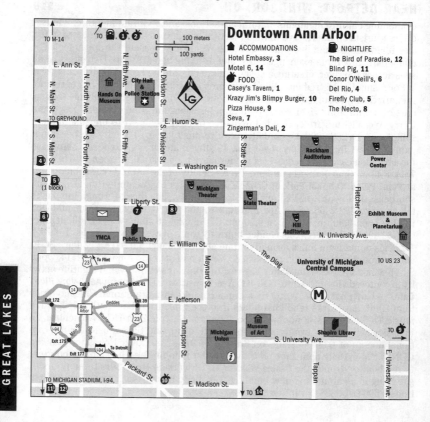

Downtown Ann Arbor

🏠 ACCOMMODATIONS
Hotel Embassy, **3**
Motel 6, **14**

🍴 FOOD
Casey's Tavern, **1**
Krazy Jim's Blimpy Burger, **10**
Pizza House, **9**
Seva, **7**
Zingerman's Deli, **2**

🎭 NIGHTLIFE
The Bird of Paradise, **12**
Blind Pig, **11**
Conor O'Neill's, **6**
Del Rio, **4**
Firefly Club, **5**
The Necto, **8**

🔌🔢 ORIENTATION & PRACTICAL INFORMATION. Ann Arbor's streets lie in a grid, but watch out for the *slant* of Packard St. and Detroit St. **Main St.** divides the town east-west, and **Huron St.** cuts it north-south. The central campus of the **University of Michigan (U of M)** lies four blocks east of Main St. and south of E. Huron, a 5min. walk from downtown. Although street meter parking is plentiful, authorities ticket ruthlessly. Downtown Ann Arbor is very walkable, and a car is generally unnecessary. One-way streets and frequent dead-ends also make driving near campus stressful.

Amtrak, 325 Depot St. (☎994-4906; ticket window open daily 7:15am-11:30pm), sends trains to Chicago (5hr., 2-3 per day, $31-57) and Detroit (1hr., 2-3 per day, $12-21). **Greyhound,** 116 W. Huron St. (☎662-5511; open M-Sa 8am-6:30pm, Su 8-9am and noon-6:30pm), sends buses to Chicago (6hr., 5 per day, $29-31); Detroit (1-1½hr., 4 per day, $9-10); and Grand Rapids (2-4hr., 3 per day, $19). **Ann Arbor Transportation Authority (AATA),** 331 S. 4th Ave., provides public transit service in Ann Arbor and a few neighboring towns. (☎996-0400. Station open M-F 7:30am-9pm. Buses run M-F 6am-11pm, Sa-Su 8am-6pm. 75¢, $1 if boarding outside Ann Arbor.) AATA's **Nightride** provides safe door-to-door transportation. (☎663-3888 to reserve; the wait is 5-45min. Runs M-F 11pm-6am, Sa-Su 7pm-6am. $2.) **Checker Sedan** moves travelers between Ann Arbor and the Detroit Metro Airport. (☎800-351-5466. One-way $46. Reserve in advance.)

Visitor info: Ann Arbor Area Convention and Visitors Bureau, 120 W. Huron St., at Ashley. (☎995-7281 or 800-888-9487. Open M-F 8:30am-5pm.) **Hotlines: Sexual Assault Crisis Line,** ☎483-7273. **U. Michigan Sexual Assault Line,** ☎936-3333. **S.O.S. Crisis Line,** ☎485-3222. All 24hr. **U. Michigan Gay/Lesbian Referrals,** ☎763-4186. Operates M-F 9am-5pm. **Internet access: Ann Arbor Public Library,** 343 S. Fifth Ave. (☎324-4200. Open M 10am-9pm, Tu-F 9am-9pm, Sa 9am-6pm, Su 1-5pm.) **Post Office:** 2075 W. Stadium Blvd. (☎665-1100. Open M-F 7:30am-5pm.) **ZIP code:** 48103. **Area code:** 734.

🏠 ACCOMMODATIONS. Expensive hotels, motels, and B&Bs cater to the many business travelers and college sports fans who flock to Ann Arbor throughout the year. Reservations are always advisable, especially during the school year. Reasonable rates exist at discount chains farther out of town or in Ypsilanti, 5 mi. southeast along I-94. The **Hotel Embassy ❸,** 200 E. Huron St., at 4th Ave., a short walk from campus, offers the best deal in the heart of the town with tidy, well-appointed rooms that include a microwave and small refrigerator. (☎662-7100. Key deposit $5. Singles $59.) Just south of I-94 on the outskirts of Ann Arbor, good ol' **Motel 6 ❸,** 3764 S. State St., rents well-kept, standard rooms. (☎665-9900. Singles $46-56; doubles $52-62.) Seven campgrounds lie within a 20 mi. radius of Ann Arbor, including the **Pinckney Recreation Area ❶,** 8555 Silver Hill, in Pinckney, and the **Waterloo Recreation Area ❶,** 16345 McClure Rd., in Chelsea. (Pinckney ☎426-4913. Waterloo ☎475-8307. Both campgrounds: primitive sites $6, with water and electricity $14; $4 vehicle permit.)

🍴 FOOD. Where there are students, there are cheap eats. The cheapest cram the sidewalks of **State St.** and **S. University St.,** while the more upscale line **Main St.** At **Zingerman's Deli ❸,** 422 Detroit St., 40 varieties of huge sandwiches ($6-12) satisfy any taste, while Zingerman's Next Door scoops up gelato and baked goods. (☎663-3354. Open daily 7am-10pm.) Enjoy meatless delights at Ann Arbor's long-established veggie haven **Seva ❸,** 314 E. Liberty St. Its earthy decor complements a menu that has Mexican, stir-fry, goat cheese ravioli, and all points in between. (☎662-1111. Open M-Th 10am-9pm, F 10:30am-10pm, Sa 9am-10pm, Su 10am-9pm. Entrees $8-13.) The truly hungry should head to **Casey's Tavern ❷,** 304 Depot St., across from the train station, for gigantic portions. The Caesar Steak Sandwich ($8) has locals and transients alike raving. (☎665-6775. Open M-Th 11am-11pm, F-Sa 11am-midnight.) In the birthplace of Domino's, **Pizza House ❸**, 618 Church St., reigns supreme with the best pies in town. (☎995-5095. Pizzas $7-22. Open daily 10:30am-4:30am.) **Krazy Jim's Blimpy Burger ❶**, 551 S. Division St., near campus, is a favorite of college kids for their great, self-proclaimed $1.70 "cheaper than food" burgers ($1.70). Make sure to read *all* the instructions before ordering. (☎663-4590. Open daily 11am-10pm.)

◙ ♫ SIGHTS & ENTERTAINMENT. Most of Ann Arbor's attractions stem from its identity as the home of a major university. The **University of Michigan Museum of Art (UMMA)**, 525 S. State St., at the corner of S. University St., packs a collection of African artifacts, early European painting, and pieces of American interior design into a small but stately building. Two pieces by Picasso highlight the museum's cache. (☎763-8662. Open Tu-W and F-Sa 10am-5pm, Th 10am-9pm, Su noon-5pm. Free.) The **University of Michigan Exhibit Museum of Natural History**, 1109 Geddes Ave., at Washtenaw, displays T-rex and Mastodon skeletons along with other exhibits on zoology, astronomy, and geology. The planetarium offers indoor stargazing on weekends. (☎764-0478. Open M-Sa 9am-5pm, Su noon-5pm. Museum free; planetarium $3.) Outside the university, the **Ann Arbor Hands-On Museum**, 220 E. Ann St., presents a tactile wonderland of exhibits on everything from the mechanics of springs to sandcastles to TV shows. Prepare to get your hands dirty with displays designed to be felt, turned, touched, pushed, and plucked by children of all ages. (☎995-5437. Open M-Sa 10am-5pm, Su noon-5pm. $7; students, seniors, and ages 2-17 $5.)

Artists and chefs peddle handmade paper, unique clothing. and gourmet food in a trio of historic brick buildings at the **Kerrytown shops,** on Detroit St. Browsing never hurts, even if the prices are a little high. (☎662-5008. M-F 8am-7pm, Sa 7am-6pm, Su 9am-5pm.) In front of the shops, growers haul their crops, baked goods, and perennials to the popular **Farmers Market,** 315 Detroit St. (☎994-3276. Open May-Dec. W and Sa 7am-3pm; Jan.-Apr. Sa 8am-2pm.) Paintings and pottery take over the market space on Sundays, when numerous local artists display their creations at the **Artisans Market.** (Open May-Dec. Su 11am-4pm.) Book lovers should scour the many **bookshops** along S. Main St. for unusual or inexpensive finds.

It's nigh-impossible to get tickets for a Wolverine football game at U of M's 115,000 capacity stadium, but fans can give it a shot by calling the athletics office (☎764-0247). As tens of thousands of students depart for the summer, locals indulge in a little celebration. In late July, thousands pack the city to view the work of nearly 600 artists at the **Ann Arbor Summer Art Fair** (☎995-7281). The **Ann Arbor Summer Festival** (☎647-2278) draws crowds from mid-June to early July for a collection of national and local comedy, dance, and theater productions, as well as musical performances including jazz, country, and classical. The festival includes nightly outdoor performances followed by movies at **Top of the Park,** on top of the Fletcher St. parking structure, next to the Health Services Building. The **County Events Hotline** (☎930-6300) has more info, and the Visitor Center has schedules. Classical music lovers should contact the **University Musical Society,** in the Burton Memorial Clock Tower at N. University and Thouper, for info on area performances. (☎764-2538 or 800-221-1229. Open M-F 10am-5pm. $12-67.)

◪ NIGHTLIFE. Free in restaurants, music stores, and elsewhere, the monthly *Current, Agenda, Weekender Entertainment,* and the weekly *Metrotimes* print up-to-date nightlife and entertainment listings. For gay and lesbian info pick up a copy of *OutPost* or *Between the Lines.* The hottest spot in town for live music, the **Blind Pig,** 208 S. First St., feels its way through the night with rock 'n' roll, reggae, blues, and swing. (☎996-8555. 19+. Cover $5-10. Open daily 3pm-2am.) The **Firefly Club,** 207 S. Ashley St., offers an intimate setting for all varieties of jazz from traditional big band to modern avant garde. (☎665-9090. Blues every Th. M and W-Su 21+, Tu 18+. Cover $5-20. Open M-W and Sa 7pm-2am, Th-F and Su 5pm-2am.) Tucked away under the Zydeco Cajun Restaurant, **The Bird of Paradise,** 312 S. Main St., straightens up and flies right with live jazz every night. (☎662-8310. Cover $3-25. Music starts at 9pm.) **The Necto,** 516 E. Liberty St., lights up the dance floor with neon-filled theme nights while an international collection of DJs spins tunes from around the world. Renovations planned for the summer of 2003. (☎994-5436. Tu and F gay nights. 18+. Cover $3-20. Open Tu-Sa 9pm-2am.) Mingle with locals and students at **Conor O'Neill's,** 318 S. Main St., Ann Arbor's "Best Pick-Up Joint," where the food and beer is as authentically Celtic as the bartenders. (☎665-2968. Open daily 11am-2am.) On weekends, locals hang out at **Del Rio,** 122 W. Washington St., at Ashley, for burgers, Mexican food, and vegetarian options. (☎761-2530. Free jazz Su 5:30-9pm, Tu 5-7pm. Open Su-F 4:30pm-2am, Sa 1pm-2am. Cash only.)

GRAND RAPIDS ☎616

From its humble beginning as one of many fur trading posts, Grand Rapids worked hard to distinguish itself from its neighbors. While many towns opted for tourist chic and quaint, old-fashioned looks, Grand Rapids plowed ahead to become a city of concrete and tall buildings. In recent years, Grand Rapids has experienced a renaissance, with a growing nightlife scene and fine museums. Close to both Chicago and Detroit, the city acts as a hub for travelers.

🔃 PRACTICAL INFORMATION. Most of Grand Rapids' streets are neatly gridded. The town is quartered by the north-south Division St. and the east-west Fulton St. **Amtrak,** 507 Wealthy St., at Market, has service to the south and west, including Chicago (4hr.; 1 per day; $32-46, round-trip $58). The station only opens when trains pass through. Tickets can be purchased at the station by credit card or on the train. **Greyhound,** 190 Wealthy St. (☎456-1709; station open daily 6:45am-10pm), connects to Ann Arbor (3hr., 1 per day, $18-21); Chicago (4½hr., 4 per day, $27-29); and Detroit (3½hr., 5per day, $23-27). **Grand Rapids Transit Authority (GRATA),** 333 Wealthy St. SW, sends buses throughout the city and suburbs. (☎776-1100. Runs M-F 5:45am-11:15pm, Sa 6:30am-9:30pm, Su 8am-7:45am. $1.25, seniors 60¢; 10-ride pass $9.) **Taxi: Veterans Taxi,** ☎459-4646. The **Grand Rapids/Kent County Convention and Visitors Bureau,** 140 Monroe Center St. (☎459-8287 or 800-678-9859; open M-F 9am-5pm) and the **West Michigan Tourist Association,** 1253 Front Ave. NW (☎456-8557 or 800-442-2084; open M-Th 8:30am-5pm, F 8:30am-6pm, Sa 9am-1pm), furnish general area info. **Hotline: Suicide, Drug, Alcohol, and Crisis Line,** ☎336-3535. Operates 24hr. **Internet access: Grand Rapids Public Library,** 1100 Hynes SW, Ste. B (☎988-5400. Open in summer M-Th 9am-9pm, F-Sa 9am-5:30pm, Su 1-5pm; off-season M-Th 9am-9pm, F-Sa 9am-5:30pm.) **Post Office:** 2929 Michael St. (☎532-2109. Open M-F 9am-5:30pm, Sa 9am-12:30pm.) **ZIP code:** 49503. **Area code:** 616.

🛏 ACCOMMODATIONS. Those under 21 should note that there is a city ordinance against renting hotel rooms to people under this age. Most of the cheaper motels and restaurants are south of the city along Division and 28th St. **The Grand Rapids Inn ❷,** 250 28th St. SW, offers serviceable rooms at rock-bottom prices. The location is a bit out of the way and the area can be noisy, but it's still one of the best deals in the city. (☎452-2131. Singles from $33, doubles from $40.) Just 12 mi. northeast of downtown, **Grand Rogue Campgrounds ❶,** 6400 W. River Dr., has wooded, riverside sites. Take Rte. 131 north to Comstock Park Exit 91, then head left on W. River Dr. for 4 mi. (☎361-1053. Sites $20, with hookup $26.)

🏠🖰 **FOOD & NIGHTLIFE.** Throngs of locals pack the **Beltline Bar and Café ❷**, 16 28th St. SE, for Grand Rapids' most popular Mexican food. Wet burritos, the house specialty, start at $5. (☎245-0494. Open M-Tu 7am-midnight, W-Sa 7am-1am, Su noon-10:30pm.) The **Four Friends Coffeehouse ❶**, 136 Monroe Ctr., has excellent coffee concoctions (from $1), fresh muffins ($1.25), and delicious sandwiches ($3) in a trendy atmosphere. (☎456-5356. Live music F-Sa during the school year. Open June-Aug. M-Th 7am-10pm, F 7am-midnight, Sa 8am-midnight.) The **Grand Rapids Brewing Company ❷**, 3689 28th St. SE, makes tasty burgers ($6) and steaks. (☎285-5970. Handcrafted beer $3.50. Open M-Th 11am-midnight, F-Sa 11am-1am, Su 11am-11pm; kitchen closes Su-Th at 10pm, F-Sa at 11pm.)

Detailed listings on events and nightlife in Grand Rapids can be found in *On the Town* or *In the City*; both are available in most shops, restaurants, and kiosks. The artsy **Eastown District** once housed the bulk of the local music scene, but now much of the nightlife has moved into the downtown area. The focal point of the nightlife is a set of chic bars and restaurants housed in the **B.O.B** (Big Old Building), a spacious brick structure downtown at the intersection of Ottawa and Louis, with a balcony and plenty of bar space. Live performances go on every night in one or more of the spaces. The wild **Diversions**, 10 Fountain St. NW, is *the* place to show off stylin' moves. (☎451-3800. Karaoke W and Sa 10pm. Ages 18-20 cover usually $5, 21+ free. Open daily 8pm-2am; dance floor opens at 10pm.)

🔲 **SIGHTS.** The largest sculpture garden in the Midwest, the 🔲**Frederik Meijer Gardens and Sculpture Park,** 1000 E. Beltline NE, keeps over 100 sculptures, from classical to modern abstract, among numerous tropical plants on 70 acres. Smaller gardens include a Victorian courtyard, a mock rainforest, and a display of carnivorous plants. Collection highlights are a $12.8 million addition and a three-story replica of a Da Vinci horse sculpture. (☎957-1580. Open June-Aug. M-W and F-Sa 9am-5pm, Th 9am-9pm, Su noon-5pm; Sept.-May M-Sa 9am-5pm, Su noon-5pm. $7, seniors $6, students and ages 5-13 $3.50.) The brightly colored **Public Museum of Grand Rapids,** 272 Pearl St. NW, showcases everything from automobiles to the history of housewifery, and includes such marvels as a 76 ft. whale skeleton, a large antique carousel, and a planetarium. (☎456-3977. Open M-Sa 9am-5pm, Su noon-5pm. $6, seniors $5, ages 3-17 $2.50. Carousel $1. Planetarium $2.) Across the street, **The Ford Museum,** 303 Pearl St. NW, pays homage to former US President Gerald Ford in his hometown. The museum focuses on the volatility of American culture during his presidency. Among the museum's interesting artifacts are the original tools used in the Watergate break-in. (☎451-9263. Open daily 9am-5pm. $4, seniors $3, under 16 free.) Architecture enthusiasts shouldn't miss the **Meyer May House,** 450 Madison Ave. SE, designed by Frank Lloyd Wright in his famous multi-tiered style. (☎246-4821. Open Tu and Th 10am-2pm, usually Su 1-5pm. Free.)

LAKE MICHIGAN SHORE

The freighters that once powered the rise of Chicago still steam along the coast of Lake Michigan, but have long since been supplanted by pleasure boats. Valleys of sand cushion sunbathers, while hikers trek through the forested cliffs of Michigan's state parks. When autumn comes, the weather forbids swimming, but inland, nature takes over with a vibrant display of fruit harvests—from cherries in July to apples in September. Almost every town holds a festival celebrating a local fruit or blossom. Snow covers much of the coastal beauty in winter, drawing snowmobile, skiing, and ice skating enthusiasts. The coastline stretches 350 miles north from the Indiana border to the Mackinac Bridge; its southern end is a scant two hours from downtown Chicago.

🛈 PRACTICAL INFORMATION

Many of the region's attractions lie in the small coastal towns that cluster around **Grand Traverse Bay** in the north. **Traverse City**, at the southern tip of the bay, is famous as the "cherry capital of the world." Fishing is best in the Au Sable and Manistee Rivers. The main north-south route along the coast is U.S. 31. Numerous green "Lake Michigan Circle Tour" signs lead closer to the shoreline, providing an excellent view of the coast. Coastal accommodations can be quite expensive; for cheaper lodging, head inland. Determined travelers can occasionally find a good deal lakeside, and numerous camping options exist during the summer months. Based in Grand Rapids, the **West Michigan Tourist Association,** 1253 Front Ave. NW, hands out info on the area. (☎456-8557 or 800-442-2084. Open M-Th 8:30am-5pm, F 8:30am-6pm, Sa 9am-1pm.) **Area code:** 616 and 231.

SOUTHERN MICHIGAN SHORE

GRAND HAVEN   ☎616

Thirty-five mi. west of Grand Rapids, off I-96, Grand Haven is one of the area's best beach communities. The town offers a relaxed, resort-like atmosphere and lots of sand—so pure that auto manufacturers use it to make cores and molds for engine parts. The small downtown area attracts visitors to its sunny boardwalk, where bikers and walkers can watch the action on the lake while soaking up some rays. In the heart of downtown, **Washington St.** is lined with shops, restaurants, and laid-back people. The **Musical Fountain,** on the island, pulses with water and light to the beat of different music each night. Shows can be viewed from the end of Washington St. (☎842-4910. Shows June-Aug. around 9:30pm.)

The **⬛Khardomah Lodge ❸,** 1365 Lake Ave., has charmingly decorated rooms and enormous common areas, and the white picket fence, library, and piano to match. Its distinctly American character, warm service, and convenient location to the beach make it one of the best budget lodgings on all of Michigan's lakeshore. (☎842-2990. Kitchen, shared bath. Reservations strongly recommended a few weeks in advance.) Doubles $58, each additional person $10.) Campers will love the picturesque **Grand Haven State Park ❶,** 1001 Harbor Dr. (☎847-1309; 800-447-2757 for reservations. Open early Apr.-Oct. Sites with electricity $20; permit $4. Reservations strongly recommended, up to 6 months in advance.) **Grand Haven Area Visitors Bureau:** 1 S. Harbor Dr., at Washington St. (☎842-4499 or 800-303-4096. Open in summer M 9:30am-5pm, Tu-F 8:30am-5pm, Sa 10am-2pm.)

CENTRAL MICHIGAN SHORE

SLEEPING BEAR DUNES   ☎231

The Sleeping Bear Dunes lie along the western shores of the Leelanau Peninsula, 20 mi. west of Traverse City on Rte. 72. The town of **Empire**, while not the metropolis its name implies, serves as the gateway to the **Sleeping Bear Dunes National Lakeshore,** an expanse including both the Manitou Islands and 25 mi. of lakeshore on the mainland. Near the historic Fishtown shops, **Manitou Island Transit,** in Leland, makes daily trips to South Manitou. (☎256-9061. Check-in 9:15am. July to late Aug. daily trips to North Manitou; mid-June to July and late Aug. to Sept. 5 per week; call ahead for May-June and Sept.-Nov. schedule. Round-trip $23, under 12 $13.) **Camping** is available on both islands with the purchase of a **permit** ($5), though there is an entrance fee ($7 for 7 days; available at the Visitors Center). The

Manitou Islands do not allow any wheeled vehicles, including cars and bikes. Hardcore **backpackers** looking for an adventure can camp on both Manitou islands. On South Manitou, a small village near the dock provides shopping and a rest area for day hikers. North Manitou Island travelers should come prepared; once the daily boat leaves for the day, hikers are cut off from the modern world until the next morning. *In bad weather, the ferry won't venture to the island until the weather clears, even if that is several days later.*

Willing climbers can be king of the sandhill at **Dune Climb**, 5 mi. north of Empire on Rte. 109. From there, a 2½ mi. hike over sandy hills leads to Lake Michigan. If you'd rather let your car do the climbing, drive to an overlook along the 7 mi. **Pierce Stocking Scenic Drive**, off Rte. 109 just north of Empire, where a 450 ft. sand cliff descends to the cool water below. (Open mid-May to mid-Oct. daily 9am-10pm.) For maps and info on the numerous cross-country skiing, hiking, and mountain biking trails in the lakeshore area, stop by the **National Parks Service Visitors Center**, 9922 Front St., in Empire. (☎326-5134. Open June to late Oct. M-F 9am-6pm, Sa 9am-5pm, Su 11am-3pm; Nov.-May M-F 9am-5pm, Sa 9am-3pm.)

The Sleeping Bear Dunes have four **campgrounds: DH Day ❶** (☎334-4634), in Glen Arbor, with 83 primitive sites ($10); **Platte River ❶** (☎325-5881 or 800-365-2267), off the southern shore, with 179 sites and showers ($14, with electricity $19); and two backcountry campsites, **Whitepine ❶** and **Valley View ❶**, accessible by 1½ mi. trails (no reservations; $7 permit required, available at Visitors Center or at any campground). The Platte River, at the southern end of the lakeshore, and the Crystal River, at the northern end, are ideal for canoeing or lazy floating. **Crystal River Outfitters**, 6249 Western Ave. (Rte. 22), near Glen Arbor, offers 1-4hr. kayak excursions. (☎231-334-4420 or 888-554-7773. From $15 per person.) **Riverside Canoes**, 5042 Scenic Hwy. (Rte. 22), at Platte River Bridge, lets less adventurous types play with water toys. (☎325-5622. Open May-early Oct. daily 8am-9pm. Inner tubes $6-$5 for 1hr., $13-15 for 2hr.; canoes $25-29; kayaks $16. Includes shuttle to river.)

TRAVERSE CITY ☎231

Traverse City offers the summer vacationer a slew of sandy beaches and picturesque orchards—half of the nation's cherries are produced in the surrounding area. Swimming, boating, and scuba diving interests focus on Grand Traverse Bay, and the scenic waterfront makes for excellent biking. The **TART** bike trail runs 8 mi. along E. and W. Grand Traverse Bay, while the 30 mi. loop around Old Mission Peninsula, north of the city, provides great views of the Bay. **McLain Cycle and Fitness**, 750 E. 8th St. and 2786 Garfield Rd. N, rents bikes and other outdoor equipment and dispenses biking info. (☎941-7161. Open in summer M-F 9am-6pm, Sa 9am-5pm, Su 11am-4pm; off-season closed Su. $15 per day, $30 for a weekend.)

Many attractions in Traverse City focus on the area's fruit. The annual **National Cherry Festival** (☎947-4230), held the first full week in July, is a rousing tribute to the annual cherry harvest, with concerts, parties, and lots of cherry pie. The National Cherry Queen presides over the festivities. In early to mid-July, five orchards near Traverse City let visitors pick their own cherries, including **Amon Orchards**, 10 mi. north on U.S. 31. (☎938-9160. Open daily 9am-6pm. $1.25 per lb.; free if you pick 'em.) More sophisticated fruit connoisseurs can indulge their taste buds at one of the area's many well-respected wineries. The scenic **Château Grand Traverse**, 12239 Center Rd., 8 mi. north of Traverse City on Rte. 37, has free tours and tastings. (☎223-7355 or 800-283-0247. Open June-Aug. M-Sa 10am-7pm, Su noon-6pm; May and Sep.-Oct. M-Sa 10am-6pm, Su noon-6pm; Nov.-Apr. M-Sa 10am-5pm, Su noon-5pm. Tours in summer every hr. noon-4pm.)

East Front St. (U.S. 31) is lined with motels, but it is nearly impossible to find a room for under $50 in the busy summer months. **Northwestern Michigan College ❷**, 1701 E. Front St., West and East Halls, has some of the cheapest beds in the city. Rooms are small, with free local calls and all the comfort of college life. (☎995-1409. Linen $8. Reserve several weeks in advance. Open early June to Aug. Singles $35, doubles $45, suite with bathroom $55.) For those who prefer to commune with nature—or at least with 300 other campers—**Traverse City State Park ❶**, 1132 U.S. 31 N, 2 mi. east of town, has 344 wooded sites across the street from the beach. (☎922-5270 or 800-447-2757. Sites with hookup $15; $4 vehicle permit fee.) Front St. downtown offers a range of appealing food options. **Poppycock's ❷**, 128 E. Front St., doles out $5-7 gourmet sandwiches—vegetarian and otherwise. (☎941-7632. Open in summer M-Th 11am-10pm, F-Sa 11am-10:30pm, Su noon-9pm; off-season M-Th 11am-9pm, F-Sa 11am-10pm.) The smell of freshly baked goods tempts the hungry into **The Omelette Shoppe ❷**, 124 Cass St., for 18 varieties of omelettes (around $6.50) and other breakfast foods. (☎946-0912. Pancakes $4-5, sandwiches $6. Open M-F 6:30am-2:30pm, Sa-Su 7am-3pm.) For all things cherry, from cherry pie to cherry salsa, head to the **Cherry Stop**, 211 E. Front St. (☎929-3990 or 800-286-7209. Open M-Sa 10am-6pm, Su 11am-4pm.) The **U & I Lounge**, 214 E. Front St., is the hottest bar in town, thanks in part to the tasty local beer. (☎946-8932. Open M-Sa 11am-2am, kitchen closes 1:35am; Su noon-2am, kitchen closes 1:15am.) For more entertainment info, pick up the weekly *Northern Express* at corner kiosks around the city.

Indian Trails and **Greyhound**, 3233 Cass Rd. (☎946-5180), run to Detroit (9hr., 3 per day, $37-41) and to the Upper Peninsula via St. Ignace (3hr., 1 per day, $18). Call the **Bay Area Transportation Authority** and they'll pick you up; a 24hr. notice is preferred. (☎941-2324. Available M-Sa 6am-1:30am, Su 8am-1:30am. $2, seniors $1.) **Traverse City Convention and Visitors Bureau:** 101 West Grandview Pkwy./U.S. 31 N. (☎947-1120 or 800-872-8377. Open daily 9am-6pm.) **Post Office:** 202 S. Union St. (☎946-9616. Open June to mid-Oct. M-F 9am-6pm, Sa 9am-5pm, Su 11am-3pm; mid-Oct. to May M-F 9am-5pm, Sa 9am-3pm.) **ZIP code:** 49684. **Area code:** 231.

NORTHERN MICHIGAN SHORE

STRAITS OF MACKINAC ☎231

Mackinac is pronounced *mack-i-NAW*; only fur'ners say *"mack-i-NACK."* The five-mile **Mackinac Bridge** ("Mighty Mac"), connecting **Mackinaw City** to St. Ignace in the Upper Peninsula, is the third longest suspension bridge in the US and the tenth longest in the world. A local tradition not to be missed is the annual **Labor Day Bridge Walk**, where Michigan's governor leads thousands of Michiganders across the bridge from Mackinaw City to St. Ignace. Near the bridge in Mackinaw City, **Colonial Michilimackinac Fort** still guards the straits between Lake Michigan and Lake Huron. (☎436-4100. Open early May to mid-Oct. daily 9am-5pm; mid-July to late Aug. 9am-6pm. $8.25, ages 6-17 $5.25.) **Historic Mill Creek** is located 3½ mi. south of Mackinaw City on Rte. 23. (☎436-4100. Open early May to mid-Oct. daily 9am-5pm; mid-July to late Aug. 9am-6pm. $7, ages 6-17 $4.25.) Historic Mill Creek, Fort Michilimackinac, and **Fort Mackinac** (on Mackinac Island, see p. 548) form a trio of State Historic Parks in the area. Fort enthusiasts should buy a **Combination Pack,** good for seven days from date of purchase, for unlimited daily admission to all three. ($17.50, ages 6-17 $10. Available at all 3 forts.)

GREAT LAKES

Lakeshore options abound on Rte. 23, south of the city. The best lodging deals in the area lie across the Mackinac Bridge and away from the lakeshore on the **I-75 Business Loop** in St. Ignace. 5min. from the docks, the lakeside **Harbor Light Motel ❷**, 1449 State St., on I-75, rents newly refurbished rooms with cable TV. Join other travelers for a late-night bonfire on the beach. (☎906-643-9439. In summer singles $45, doubles $47; off-season $30/32.) Mackinaw City offers many motel and hotel options. **Motel 6 ❸**, 206 N. Nicolet St., located two blocks from the main shopping streets and transportation to the island, provides clean, spacious rooms with cable TV, A/C, and free local phone service. (☎436-7317. Rooms from $52.) For an outdoor escape, campers can crash at one of the 600 sites of **Mackinac Mill Creek Campground ❶**, 3 mi. south of town on Rte. 23. Located near the lake, the grounds provide beach access, fishing, and biking trails. (☎436-5584. Sites $15, full hookup $17.50; cabins $40.) Sites at the **Wilderness State Park ❶**, 11 mi. west of the city on Wilderness Park Dr., offer a peaceful, rustic experience but also provide showers and electricity. (☎436-5381. Sites $15, 4- to 8-person cabins $40, 20-person bunkhouse $55. $4 permit required.)

Family-oriented restaurants cluster around Central St., near Shepler's Dock in St. Ignace. **Cunningham's ❸**, 312 E. Central St., serves homemade pasties and fresh fish in a relaxed atmosphere. (☎436-8821. Dinner specials $8.50. Open May to mid-Oct. In spring daily 8am-8pm; in summer 8am-10pm; in fall 8am-9pm.) At **Audie's ❷**, 314 N. Nicolet St., in Mackinaw City, huge sandwiches at affordable prices keep visitors happy. For fine dining, try their Chippewa Room. (☎436-5744. Lunch $7-8. Open daily 7:30am-10pm.)

For transportation outside the city, **Indian Trails** (☎517-725-5105 or 800-292-3831) has a flag stop at the Big Boy restaurant on Nicolet Ave. One bus runs north and one south each day; buy tickets at the next station. The **Michigan Dept. of Transportation Welcome and Travel Information Center,** on Nicolet St. off I-75 at Exit 338, has loads of helpful info on lodging, food, and area attractions. (☎436-5566. Open mid-June to Aug. daily 8am-6pm; Sept. to mid-June 9am-5pm. Free reservation service.)

MACKINAC ISLAND   ☎231

Mackinac Island, a 16min. ferry ride from the mainland, has long been considered one of Michigan's greatest treasures. Victorian homes and the prohibition of cars on the heavily touristed island—and the resulting proliferation of horse-drawn carriages—give Mackinac an aristocratic air with a decidedly equine aroma. Travelers flock to the island for its stunning parks, museums, and coastal, old-world charm. Escape the touristy Main St. for a quiet look at what made the island popular in the first place—its beautiful fauna and rolling hills.

Fort Mackinac is one of the island's main draws. (☎436-4100. Open early May to mid-Oct. daily 9am-6pm; mid-July to late Aug. 9am-7pm. $8.25, ages 6-17 $5.25, under 6 free.) Tickets to the Fort also allow access to four museums of island history that are housed in refurbished Victorian mansions. Travelers with a sweet tooth will immediately recognize the island as the birthplace of Mackinac Fudge (½ lb. $5.50), sold in shops all over the island and along the entire Michigan coastline. **Horse-drawn carriages** cart guests on tours all over the island, showcasing architectural wonders such as the ritzy Grand Hotel. (Carriage tours ☎906-847-3325. Open daily 9am-5pm. $15.50, ages 4-11 $7.50. Saddle horses $30 1st hr., $25 each additional hr.) Bicycles are the best way to see the peaceful beaches and forests of the island. Rentals line Main St. by the ferry docks ($5 per hr.). Encompassing 80% of the island, **Mackinac Island State Park** features a circular 8.2 mi. shoreline road for biking and hiking.

Hotels rates on the island are exorbitantly high; the mainland is the place to stay. For food, **Mighty Mac ❶** cooks it cheap, with huge ¼ lb. burgers for under $4. (☎ 847-8039. Open daily 8am-8pm.) The **Pink Pony ❸** serves handmade pastas, fresh salads, and fish dishes under the watchful eye of the pink-colored horses on the wall. (☎ 906-847-3341. Entrees from $10. Open daily 8am-10pm.)

Transportation to the island via ferry is quick and pleasant, providing terrific views of the Mackinac Bridge. Three ferry lines leave Mackinaw City (in summer every 30min. 8am-11pm) and St. Ignace with overlapping schedules, though service from St. Ignace is less frequent. **Shepler's** (☎ 800-828-6157) offers the fastest service. Catamarans operated by **Arnold Transit Co.** are also a fun way to jet to the island. (☎ 847-3351 or 800-542-8528. Check at the ticket counter for exact times. Round-trip $16, under 16 $8; bikes $6.50.) The invaluable *Mackinac Island Locator Map* ($1) and the *Discover Mackinac Island* book ($2) can be found at the **Mackinac Island Chamber of Commerce and Visitors Center,** on Main St. (☎ 906-847-3783. Open June-Sept. daily 8am-6pm; Oct.-May 9am-5pm.)

SCENIC DRIVE: NORTHERN MICHIGAN SHORE DRIVE

Cherry trees, tranquil lake shores, and intimate resort villages dot the Northern Michigan Shore. Once used by Native Americans and French traders to peddle goods, the route now guides visitors through the diversity of Michigan's natural beauty. Heading north, the drive begins in Michigan's coastal beach communities before moving through lush forest.

U.S. 31 winds its way 65 mi. north from Traverse City to Petoskey, where the tortuous Rte. 119 takes over and completes the 31 mi. journey to Cross Village. It takes about 3hr. to do justice to the drive, stopping along the way to admire both the natural and fabricated wonders that line the route. Although the roads are generally well maintained, drivers should exercise special caution on the spectacular 27 mi. stretch of Rte. 119 between Cross Village and Harbor Springs, known as the **Tunnel of Trees.** This patch of road is extremely narrow and twists through many sharp curves, necessitating slow speeds and care in passing.

North of Traverse City, tiny towns form the center of picturesque orchard communities. Twelve mi. outside of the city, lush cherry orchards line the road around **Acme.** Twenty mi. north of Acme, then west on Barnes Park Road, the village of **Torch Lake** harbors pristine, isolated beaches on **Grand Traverse Bay** at **Barnes County Park.** More cherry trees line the route north of **Atwood,** one of the most prolific areas of the cherry harvest. Though many towns along the route are easily missed, they are worth the stop; many have small antique and unique clothing shops.

Rolling hills and increasingly elaborate homes mark the entrance into **Charlevoix** (*SHAR-le-voy*), a resort village that inhabits the narrow strip of land between Lake Michigan and Lake Charlevoix. The resort community that once served as the setting for Ernest Hemingway's Nick Adams stories now inspires yachting and sunbathing. The **Charlevoix Area Chamber of Commerce,** 408 Bridge St., dispenses info on golfing, boating, and shopping in the area. (☎ 547-2101. Open M-F 9am-5pm.) Lodging rarely comes cheap in this coastal resort town, but the **Colonial Motel ❷,** 6822 U.S. 31 S, is better than the rest with cable TV, use of grill and picnic area, and easy access to the state park. (☎ 547-6637. Open May-Oct. Singles Su-Th $30-35, F-Sa $60-75; off-season rates lower. Special rates for longer stays.) Campers who don't mind doing without showers and electricity can bask in 90 sites on the shores of Lake Michigan at **Fisherman's Island State Park ❶,** on Bells Bay Rd., 5 mi. south of Charlevoix on U.S. 31. The park rewards patient hikers who trek through the forest with a spectacular beach. (☎ 547-6641 or 800-447-2757. Rustic sites $6; vehicle permit

$4.) Charlevoix also serves as the gateway to **Beaver Island**, the Great Lakes' most remote inhabited island. Hiking, boating, biking, and swimming abound on the island's 53 sq. mi., a 2hr. ferry trip from shore. **Ferries** depart from 102 Bridge St., in Charlevoix. (☎547-2311 or 888-446-4095. 1-3 per day. Round-trip $33, ages 5-12 $17; bikes $16.) **Beaver Island Chamber of Commerce:** ☎448-2505.

PETOSKEY   ☎231

Eighteen mi. north of Charlevoix on the mainland, the slightly larger resort town of Petoskey is best known for its Petoskey Stones—fossilized coral from an ancient sea that remain strewn about the area's beaches. Another vacation haunt of Hemingway, the town honors him with a dedication at the **Little Traverse History Museum**, 100 Depot Ct., on the waterfront downtown. (☎347-2620. Open in summer M-F 10am-4pm, Sa-Su 1-4pm. $1.) Nearby, off northbound U.S. 31, the gazebo and grassy areas of **Sunset Park Scenic Overlook** are unbeatable places to watch the sun sink below the horizon.

The cheapest rooms in town are at the homey **North Central Michigan College ❶**, 1515 Howard St., which rents single beds and rooms within a suite; every room has two beds. (☎348-6611, or reservations 348-6612. Linen provided. $15 per person. Reservations recommended. Cash or check only.) If dorm life isn't your thing, the major chains clump around the junction of U.S. 31 and U.S. 131. Petoskey's **Gaslight District**, just off U.S. 31 downtown, features local crafts and foods in period shops. In the heart of the district, a colorful outdoor collage of coffee cups lures the hungry into the **Roast and Toast Cafe ❶**, 309 E. Lake St., for large sandwiches ($5), freshly baked cookies, and a cup o' joe. (☎347-7767. Open in summer daily 7am-9:30pm; in winter 7am-8pm.) The **City Park Grill ❷**, 432 E. Lake St., sells sandwiches ($6-8) in an elegant 1910 setting befitting the quaint town. (☎347-0101. Live entertainment W-Sa 10pm. Cover $3 Th-Sa. Open Su-Th 11:30am-10pm, F-Sa 11:30am-11pm; bar open later.)

Although it lies 20 mi. east of Petoskey in a remote woodland just outside Indian River, the **Cross in the Woods**, 7078 Rte. 68 (☎238-8973), is worth seeing. A 31 ft. bronze Jesus, cleaved onto a 55 ft. tall wooden cross, presides over an outdoor sanctuary and forms a monument to both the religious fervor of Middle America and the country's obsession with size.

UPPER PENINSULA

A multi-million-acre forestland bordered by three of the world's largest lakes, Michigan's Upper Peninsula (U.P.) is among the most scenic, unspoiled stretches of land in the world. Vacationers in the Upper Peninsula escape hectic urban life in a region of the country where cell phones don't work and locals laugh if you ask where the nearest computer with Internet access is located. Dominated by the **Hiawatha National Forest**, the U.P. is a wonderland of hiking, biking, hunting, and kayaking. Those who are less adventurous can enjoy the waterfalls and sand dunes from outlooks in the park. Natural deposits of copper have colored the cliffs with a tapestry of colors that draw visitors from all over the state.

Only 24,000 people live in the U.P.'s largest town, **Marquette**. Here hikers enjoy numerous treks, including Michigan's section of the **North Country Trail**, a national scenic trail extending from New York to North Dakota. The **North Country Trail Association**, 49 Monroe Ctr. NW, Ste. 200B, Grand Rapids, MI 49503 (☎616-454-5506), provides details on the path. A vibrant spectrum of foliage makes autumn a beautiful time to hike; in the winter, skiers and snowmobilers replace hikers as layers of snow blanket the trails. After the ice thaws, dozens of pristine rivers beckon canoers. Those who heed the call of the water should contact the **Michigan Association of Paddlesport Providers**, P.O. Box 270, Wellston, MI 49689 (☎616-862-3227), for canoeing tips.

Outside the major tourist towns, motel rooms in the U.P. generally start around $24. The peninsula has 200 **campgrounds** (☎ 800-447-2757 for reservations). Bring extra blankets—temperatures in these parts drop to 50°F, even in July. For regional cuisine, indulge in the Friday night **fish-fry:** all-you-can-eat whitefish, perch, or walleye buffets served in most restaurants. The local ethnic specialty is a **pasty** (*PASS-tee*), a meat pie imported by Cornish miners in the 19th century.

⌚ PRACTICAL INFORMATION

Helpful **Welcome Centers** guard the U.P. at its six main entry points: **Ironwood,** 801 W. Cloverland Dr. (☎ 932-3330; open June-Sept. daily 8am-6pm; Oct.-May 8am-4pm); **Iron Mountain,** 618 S. Stephenson Ave. (☎ 774-4201; open June-Sept. daily 7am-5pm; Oct.-May 8am-4pm); **Menominee,** 1343 10th Ave. (☎ 863-6496; open June-Sept. daily 8am-5pm; Oct.-May 8am-4pm); **Marquette,** 2201 U.S. 41 S (☎ 249-9066; open daily 9am-6pm); **Sault Ste. Marie,** 943 Portage Ave. W (☎ 632-8242; open June-Sept. daily 8am-6pm; Oct.-May daily 9am-5pm); and **St. Ignace,** on I-75 N just north of the Mackinac Bridge (☎ 643-6979; open June-Aug. daily 8am-6pm; Sept.-May daily 9am-5pm). The **Upper Peninsula Travel and Recreation Association** (☎ 800-562-7134; info line staffed M-F 8am-4:30pm) publishes the invaluable *Upper Peninsula Travel Planner.* For additional help planning a trip into the wilderness, write or call the **U.S. Forestry Service** at the **Hiawatha National Forest,** 2727 N. Lincoln Rd., Escanaba 49829 (☎ 786-4062). **Area code:** 906.

SAULT STE. MARIE & THE EASTERN U.P.   ☎ 906

The shipping industry rules in gritty Sault ("Soo") Ste. Marie, where "the locks" are the primary attraction for both tourists and prospective residents. Back in the day, St. Mary's River dropped 21 vertical feet over one mile in this area, rendering the river impassable by boat. In 1855, entrepreneurs built the first lock here, opening up industrial opportunities that led the region to relative economic prosperity. Now the busiest in the world, the city's four locks float over 12,000 ships annually, gradually lowering them through successive, emptying chambers.

On the American side of the bridge, a 2hr. **Soo Locks Boat Tour,** leaves from both 1157 and 515 E. Portage Ave., and introduces travelers to the mechanics of the locks' operation. (☎ 632-6301 or 800-432-6301 for departure times. Open mid-May to mid-Oct. $17.50, ages 13-18 $15.50, ages 4-12 $8, under 4 free. Call ahead for specific dock.) For landlubbers, the **Locks Park Historic Walkway** runs parallel to the water for 1 mi., allowing visitors a close-up view of the 1000 ft. long supertankers that use the locks. On the waterfront, at the end of Johnston St., lies the **Museum Ship Valley Camp,** a 1917 steam-powered freighter turned tribute to the U.P. sailing industry. A theater and the **Marine Hall of Fame** highlight the museum. (☎ 632-3658. Open July-Aug. daily 9am-9pm; mid-May to June and Sept. to mid-Oct. 10am-6pm. $8, ages 6-16 $4.)

MIDDLE OF THE PENINSULA   ☎ 906

The western branch of the **Hiawatha National Forest ❶** dominates the middle of the Peninsula, offering limitless wilderness activities and many rustic **campsites.** (Pit toilets, no showers; first come, first served. $7-11.) **Rapid River,** on Rte. 2, is home to the southern office of the west branch. Those looking for some comic relief should stop by **Da Yooper's Tourist Trap,** 490 N. Steel St., 12 mi. west of Marquette on U.S. 41. This little roadside theme park is the ultimate attraction for anyone looking for tacky Americana. Out front, the lawn hosts the world's largest operational chainsaw and the world's biggest rifle, while the backyard pays homage to infamous Yoopers (U.P. residents) of the past. (☎ 800-628-9978. Open M-Th and Sa 9am-8pm, F 9am-9pm, Su 9am-7pm.) In the north, **Munising,** on Rte. 28, accesses the forest and the not-to-be-missed **Pictured Rocks National Lakeshore,** where water

GREAT LAKES

saturated with copper, manganese, and iron oxide paints the cliffs with multicolored bands. Various car- and foot-accessible overlooks within the park offer spectacular glimpses of the rocks, but the **Pictured Rocks Boat Cruise**, at the city dock in Munising, gives the best view. (☎387-2379. 3hr. tour $25, ages 6-13 $10, under 6 free; rates subject to change.) The forest and lakeshore share a **Visitors Center** at the intersection of M-28 and Rte. 58 in Munising. (☎387-3700. Open mid-May to mid-Oct. daily 8am-6pm; mid-Oct. to mid-May M-Sa 9am-4:30pm.) From Munising, Rte. 58—a bumpy, partially unpaved gem of a road—weaves along the lakeshore past numerous trailheads and campsites. Ask about road conditions at the Visitors Center before driving there. For a paved (but less scenic) alternative from Munising to Grand Marais, go east on Rte. 28, then north on Rte. 77.

Within the park, **Miner's Falls**, 10 mi. east of Munising off Rte. 58, rewards visitors with a rocky, staggering waterfall. Two mi. farther up the road, **Miner's Castle Overlook** allows trekkers to walk up to the edge of the cliffs and see the colorful rocks across the deep blue water of the lake. Twenty mi. east of Miner's Castle off Rte. 58, visitors can stroll, birdwatch, or collect smooth stones along the shore at **Twelve Mile Beach** (self-registered campsites $10; running water only). From atop the sandy **⛰Log Slide**, 5 mi. west of Grand Marais on Rte. 58, hikers are rewarded with a magnificent view of Lake Superior. Thick state forests are to the left, while expansive sand dunes are on the right. In the winter months, "polar bears" (read: fat guys with balls of steel) plunge into the icy water.

As an alternative to the developed campsites at Twelve Mile Beach, **backcountry camping permits ❶** for 1-6 people ($15) are available from the **Munising** or **Grand Sable Visitors Center,** 2 mi. west of Grand Marais on Rte. 58. (☎494-2660. Open mid-May to early Oct. daily 9am-7pm.) For non-campers, the **Poplar Bluff Cabins ❷,** Star Rte. Box 3118, 12 mi. east of Munising on Rte. 28, then 6 mi. south from Shingleton on Rte. 94, have lakeview rooms with kitchens. (☎452-6271. Cottages $40-50 per night, from $200 per week. Free use of boats on lake.)

West of the city, the uncrowded eastern branch of the Hiawatha offers stunning natural attractions. At **Tahquamenon Falls State Park** (☎492-3415), on Rte. 123, the Upper and Lower Falls cascade down copper tinted cliffs. Amateur voyageurs can explore the Lower Falls via **canoe** ($10 per half-day) or **rowboat** ($12 per person). The less daring can gawk at the spectacular 50 ft. Upper Falls. North of Tahquamenon, over **300 shipwrecks** protected in an Underwater Preserve lie off **Whitefish Point,** affording divers an unbeatable opportunity to search for sunken treasure. The town of **Paradise,** at the eastern border of the Hiawatha, lies south of Whitefish Point and serves as the entrance point to the museum, lighthouse, and beaches.

KEWEENAW PENINSULA ☎906

As the northern-most part of Michigan, the Keweenaw (KEE-wa-naw) Peninsula—with its lush forests, low mountains, and smooth stone beaches—doesn't seem like part of the Midwest. The peninsula once basked in the glory of a copper mining boom, but when mining petered out, the land was left barren and exploited. Now, with the help of reforestation efforts, Keweenaw has become a beacon for outdoor enthusiasts. Towering pines shade hiking trails while state parks provide beaches and camping grounds for those looking to get back to nature. In the winter, visitors don skis and snowshoes to trek across the mountains.

The **Visitors Center,** near the junction of Rte. 107 and South Boundary Rd. inside the park, provides required **permits** good for all Michigan state parks. (☎885-5208. Open in summer daily 10am-6pm.) The **Porcupine Mountain Wilderness State Park ❶,** affectionately known as "The Porkies," hugs Lake Superior at the base of the peninsula. (☎885-5275. Reservations required for cabins. Rustic sites $9; with toilets, showers, and electricity at the Union $19; 2- to 8-person rustic cabins $45-55.) Eight miles inside the park on Rte. 107, **Lake of the Clouds** outlook leads visitors to the top of a cliff where woods give way to a spectacular view of the lake etching out a path between rugged cliffs and mountains in the Big Carp River valley. From the park, paths lead into the **Old Growth Forest,** the largest tract of uncut forest between the Rockies and the Adirondacks.

The twin towns of **Houghton** and **Hancock** link the Porkies to the rest of Keweenaw. Eight miles north of Hancock on Rte. 203, **McLain State Park ❶** is home to some of the area's best camping. The campground rests along a 2 mi. agate beach and harbors an impressive lighthouse. (☎482-0278. Sites with electricity $19; required vehicle permit $4 per day.) From the state park, U.S. 41 winds north through the Keweenaw. Drivers and bikers can take Rte 26, off Rte. 41, to access the most scenic path to the tip of the peninsula. Rising 1337 ft. above sea level, the breathtaking **Brockway Mountain Dr.** (6 mi.), between Eagle Harbor and Copper Harbor, offers a panoramic view of the extensive pine-covered peaks and lake-filled valleys of the Upper Peninsula. In **Copper Harbor,** the northernmost town in Michigan, the **Keweenaw Adventure Company,** 145 Gratiot St., provides kayaks and bikes to those who wish to explore the wild side of Keweenaw. (☎289-4303. 2½hr. intro paddle $29; bike rentals $27 for ½ day, $40 per day.)

ILLINOIS

Illinois can best be characterized as a state of dual personalities. In the northern part of the state, Chicago gleams as a Midwestern metropolis with top-notch museums, stunning architecture, and suburban sprawl stretching into two neighboring states. Once removed from that sprawl, a second Illinois—the "Land of Lincoln"—reaches outward with endless corn and soybean fields and small towns. Illinois, in its politics and its culture, is a compromise between these two contrasting characters, mixing together an urban sophistication and rural family values.

▣ PRACTICAL INFORMATION

Capital: Springfield.

Visitor info: Illinois Office of Tourism (☎800-226-6632; www.enjoyillinois.com), 310 S. Michigan Ave., Ste. 108, Chicago 60616. **Springfield Office of Tourism,** 109 N. 7th St., Springfield 62701 (☎800-545-7300).

Postal Abbreviation: IL. **Sales Tax:** 6.25-8.75%, depending on the city.

CHICAGO ☎312

From the renowned museums and shopping that dot the downtown lakefront to the varied and vibrant music and comedy scenes, Chicago's charms please almost any visitor. Retaining some of the flavor of its industrial legacy, Chicago today is both a contemporary city, and a city with strong historical roots. In the mid-1800s, machine politics flourished and blurred the line between organized government and organized crime. Thus, the "Windy City" was named for its politicians' hot air rather than the city's cold, fierce gusts. Today, Chicago is a city of many voices, diverse neighborhoods, and spectacular food and entertainment offerings.

GREAT LAKES

✈ INTERCITY TRANSPORTATION

Airports: O'Hare International (☎ 773-686-2200), off I-90. Depending on traffic, a trip between downtown and O'Hare can take up to 2hr. The Blue Line **Rapid Train** runs between the Airport El station and downtown (40min.-1hr., $1.50). **Midway Airport** (☎ 773-767-0500), on the western edge of the South Side, often offers less expensive but less frequent flights. To get downtown, take the El Orange Line from the Midway stop. **Airport Express** (☎ 888-284-3826) connects to downtown hotels from O'Hare (45min.-1hr.; every 5-10min. 6am-11:30pm; $20) and Midway (30-45min.; every 10-15min. M-F 6am-10:30pm, Sa-Su 6am-11pm; $15).

Trains: Amtrak, Union Station, 225 S. Canal St. (☎ 558-1075), at Adams St. just west of the Loop. Amtrak's nationwide hub. Getting there by bus is easiest; buses #1, 60, 125, 151, and 156 all stop at the station. Otherwise, take the El to State and Adams St., then walk 7 blocks west on Adams. Luggage storage at desk $1.50 per day. Station open 6:30am-9:30pm; tickets sold daily 6am-9pm. To: **Detroit** (8hr., 3 per day, $31-57); **Milwaukee** (1½hr., 6 per day, $20); and **New York** (20hr., 2 per day, $90-165).

Buses: Greyhound, 630 W. Harrison St. (☎ 408-5980), at Jefferson and Desplaines Ave. Take the El to Linton, or buses #60, 125, 156, or 157 to the terminal. Open 24hr. To: **Detroit** (6-7hr., 6 per day, $27-29); **Indianapolis** (3½-4½hr., 9 per day, $29-31); **Milwaukee** (2hr., 13 per day, $14); **St. Louis** (5-7hr., 9 per day, $33).

◪ ORIENTATION

It is a good idea to stay within the boundaries made apparent by tourist maps. Aside from small pockets such as Hyde Park and the U. of Chicago, areas south of the loop and west of the little ethnic enclaves are mostly industrial or residential and pose a safety threat to the unwary tourist. Cabrini Green (bounded by W. Armitage Ave. on the north, W. Chicago Ave. on the south., Sedgwick St. on the east, and Halsted St. on the west), an infamously dangerous public housing development, sits within tourist map borders—other unsafe neighborhoods are usually outside them.

Chicago has overtaken the entire northeastern corner of Illinois, running north-south along 29 mi. of the southwest Lake Michigan shorefront. The city sits at the center of a web of interstates, rail lines, and airplane routes; most cross-country traffic swings through the city. A good map is essential for navigating Chicago; pick up a free one at the tourist office or any CTA station.

The flat, sprawling city's grids usually make sense. Navigation is pretty straight-forward, whether by car or by public transportation. At the city's center is the **Loop** (p. 562), Chicago's downtown business district and the public transportation system's hub. The block numbering system starts from the intersection of State and Madison, increasing by about 800 per mi. The Loop is bounded loosely by the Chicago River to the north and west, Wabash Ave. to the east, and Congress Pkwy. to the south. Directions in *Let's Go* are usually from downtown. South of the Loop, east-west street numbers increase towards the south. Many ethnic neighborhoods lie in this area (see **Neighborhoods,** below), but farther south, avoid the struggling South Side. Most of the city's best spots for food and nightlife jam the first few mi. north of the Loop. Beware the 45mph speed limit on **Lake Shore Dr.,** a scenic freeway hugging Lake Michigan that offers express north-south connections.

To avoid driving and parking in the city, daytrippers can leave their cars in one of the suburban park-and-ride lots ($1.75); call CTA (see above) for info. Parking downtown costs around $8-15 per day. Check out the lots west of the South Loop and across the canal from the **Sears Tower** (p. 562), for the best deals.

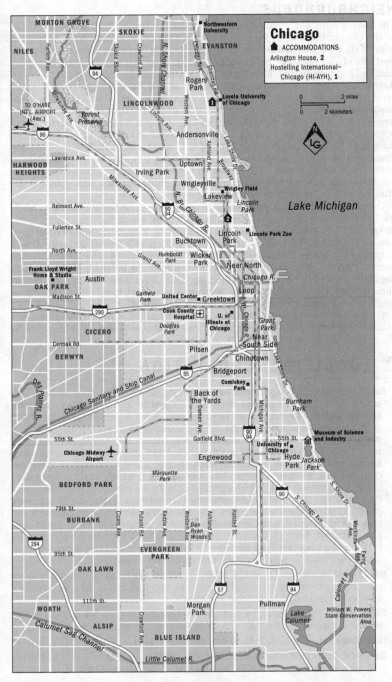

Chicago

⌂ ACCOMMODATIONS
Arlington House, **2**
Hostelling International–
Chicago (HI-AYH), **1**

0 — 2 miles
0 — 2 kilometers

MORTON GROVE

SKOKIE

NILES

EVANSTON

■ Northwestern University

Harlem Ave.

Crawford Ave.

Skokie Blvd.

N. Shore Channel

Chicago Ave.

Sheridan Rd.

Rogers Park

TO O'HARE INT'L. AIRPORT (4mi.)

Milwaukee Ave.

Forest Preserve

LINCOLNWOOD

Lincoln Ave.

Western Ave.

⌂ Loyola University of Chicago

Lake Shore Dr.

Broadway

Lake Michigan

Lawrence Ave.

HARWOOD HEIGHTS

Andersonville

Ashland Ave.

Uptown

Irving Park

Milwaukee Ave.

Wrigleyville

■ Wrigley Field

Belmont Ave.

N. Br. Chicago R.

Lakeview

Lincoln Park

Fullerton St.

2

Bucktown

Lincoln Park ■ Lincoln Park Zoo

Frank Lloyd Wright Home & Studio

Grand Ave.

Humboldt Park

Wicker Park

Near North

North Ave.

Austin

OAK PARK

Madison St.

Garfield Park

United Center ■ ● Greektown

Chicago R.

Loop

Cook County Hospital ✚

U. of Illinois at Chicago

St. Chicago R.

Grant Park

Douglas Park

CICERO

Cermak Rd.

Near South Side

BERWYN

Pilsen

Chinatown

Lake Shore Dr.

Des Plaines R.

Chicago Sanitary and Ship Canal

Bridgeport

Comiskey Park ■

Michigan Ave.

Burnham Park

Back of the Yards

Damen Ave.

55th St.

Garfield Blvd.

55th St.

University of Chicago

■ Museum of Science and Industry 🏛

Chicago Midway Airport ✈

Englewood

Hyde Park

Jackson Park

S. Shore Dr.

Marquette Park

BEDFORD PARK

S. Chicago Ave.

MacKinaw Ave.

BURBANK

79th St.

Cicero Ave.

Pulaski Rd.

Kedzie Ave.

Western Ave.

Ashland Ave.

Dan Ryan Woods

Halsted St.

Ewing Ave.

294

95th St.

EVERGREEN PARK

OAK LAWN

111th St.

WORTH

Crawford Ave.

Morgan Park

Pullman

Lake Calumet

Calumet R.

William W. Powers State Conservation Area

ALSIP

Calumet Sag Channel

BLUE ISLAND

Little Calumet R.

NEIGHBORHOODS

The diverse array of communities that compose the Windy City justifies its title as a "city of neighborhoods." North of the Loop, LaSalle Dr. loosely defines the west edge of the posh **Near North** area; here, most activity is centered along the **Magnificent Mile** of Michigan Ave. between the Chicago River and Oak St. A trendy restaurant and nightlife district, **River North** lines N. Clark St., just north of the Loop and west of Michigan Ave. The primarily residential **Gold Coast** shimmers on N. Lakeshore Dr. between Oak St. and North Ave. Northwest of the Gold Coast, the **Bucktown/Wicker Park** area—at the intersection of North, Damen, and Milwaukee Ave.—is the place to be for artsy, cutting-edge cafes and nightlife. **Lincoln Park,** a hotbed of activity, revolves around the junction of N. Clark St., Lincoln Ave., and Halsted St. To the north, near the 3000s of N. Clark St. and N. Halsted St., sits **Lakeview,** a gay-friendly area teeming with food and nightlife that becomes **Wrigleyville** in the 4000s. **Andersonville,** 5 mi. farther up N. Clark St. north of Foster Ave., is the historic center of the Swedish community, though immigrants from Asia and the Middle East have recently settled here.

The near south and west sides are filled with other vibrant ethnic districts. While the German community has scattered, the beer halls, restaurants, and shops in the 3000s and 4000s of N. Lincoln Ave. remain. The former residents of **Greektown** have also moved, but S. Halsted St., just west of the Loop, still houses authentic Greek restaurants. The area is bustling and safe until the restaurants close, at which point tourists clear out. Nearby, **Little Italy** has fallen prey to the **University of Illinois at Chicago (UIC),** and little of the once-bustling district remains. Jewish and Indian enclaves center on Devon Ave., from Western Ave. to the Chicago River. The **Pilsen** neighborhood, southwest of the loop, around 18th St., offers a slice of Mexico and a developing art community. Chicago's Polish population is the largest of any city outside of Warsaw; those seeking Polish cuisine should go near Bucktown to N. Milwaukee Ave. between blocks 2800 and 3100.

▛ LOCAL TRANSPORTATION

Public Transit: The **Chicago Transit Authority (CTA),** 350 N. Wells, 7th fl. (☎836-7000 or 888-968-7282), runs efficient trains, subways, and buses. The **elevated rapid transit train system,** called the **El,** encircles the Loop. Some downtown routes run underground but are still referred to as the El. The El operates 24hr., but *late-night service is infrequent and unsafe in many areas.* Some buses do not run all night; call the CTA for schedules and routes. Many routes are "express," and different routes may run along the same track. Extremely helpful CTA maps are available at many stations and at the Chicago Visitor Information Center. Train and bus fare is $1.50; add 25¢ for express routes. Get a transfer (30¢), which allows for up to 2 more rides on different routes during the following 2hr., from bus drivers or when you enter the El stop. Buy **transit cards** ($1.50-$1.90) for fares and transfers at all CTA stations and some supermarkets and museums. CTA also offers consecutive-day passes for tourists, available at airports and Amtrak stations: 1-day $5, 2-day $9, 3-day $12, and 5-day $18. On Sa from early May to late Oct., a **Loop Tour Train** departs on a free 40min. elevated tour of the downtown area (tickets must be picked up at the **Chicago Cultural Center;** see p. 558).

METRA, 547 W. Jackson St. (☎836-7000), distributes free maps and schedules for its extensive commuter rail network of 11 rail lines and 4 downtown stations. Open M-F 8am-5pm. Fare $2-6.60, depending on distance.

PACE (☎836-7000) operates the suburban bus system. Numerous free or cheap shuttle services run throughout the loop, with schedules available most places.

Taxis: Yellow Cab, ☎829-4222. **Flash Cab,** ☎773-561-1444.

Car Rental: Dollar Rent-a-Car (☎800-800-4000), at O'Hare and Midway St. Call for specific price information; must be 21 to rent; under 25 surcharge $18 per day.

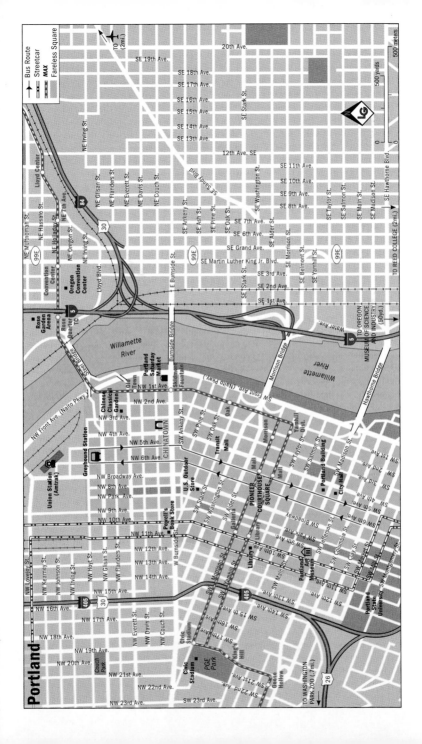

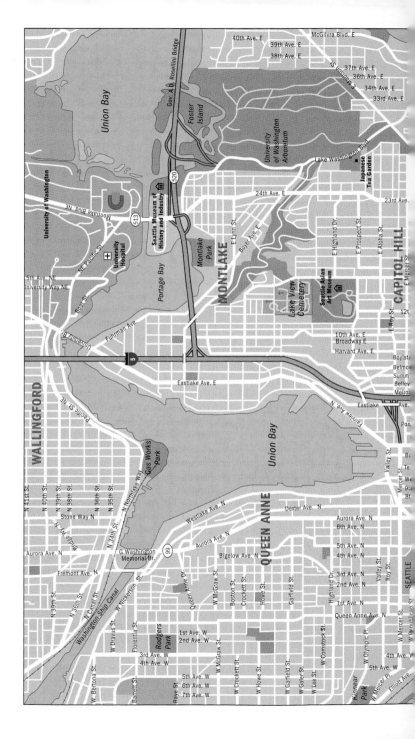

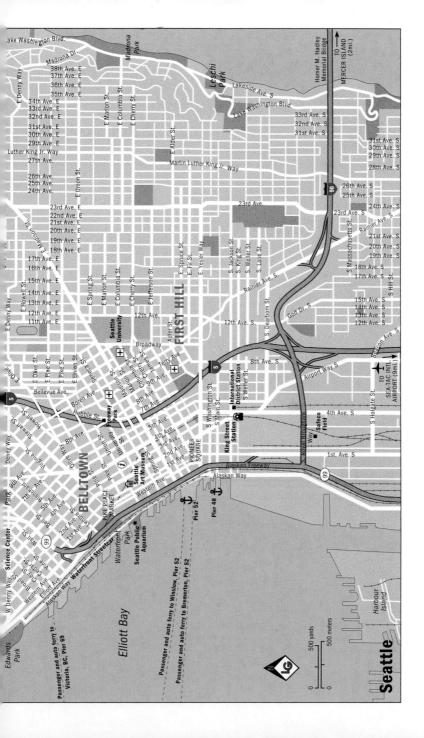

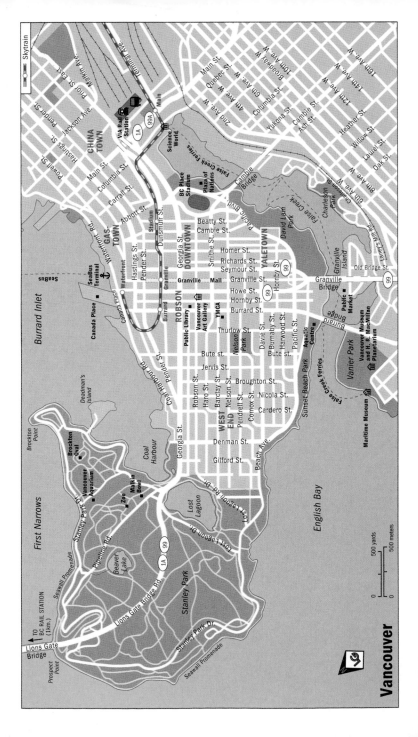

Vancouver

Skytrain

Burrard Inlet

First Narrows

Prospect Point

Deadman's Island

Brockton Point

Lions Gate Bridge

TO BC RAIL STATION (1km.)

Stanley Park

Seawall Promenade

Pipeline Rd.

Beaver Lake

Lost Lagoon Dr.

Lost Lagoon

Stanley Park Dr.

Seawall Promenade

Stanley Park Dr.

Brockton Oval

Vancouver Aquarium

Zoo

Malkin Bowl

Coal Harbour

Georgia St.

Lions Gate Bridge Rd.

99

1A

Coal Harbour Rd.

Pender St.

Waterfront Rd.

Seabus

SeaBus Terminal

Canada Place

Burrard

Granville

Dunsmuir St.

Stadium

Hastings St.

Pender St.

Columbia St.

Carrall St.

Abbott St.

Main St.

GAS TOWN

CHINA TOWN

Powell St.

Hastings St.

Jackson Ave.

Pender St.

Main St.

VIA Rail Station

1A

99A

Main

Pilot St. East

Terminal Ave.

Malkin Ave.

Main St.

Waterfront

Canada Place

Burrard Inlet

West End

Denman St.

Gilford St.

Beach Ave.

Georgia St.

Robson St.

Haro St.

Barclay St.

Nelson St.

Pendrell St.

Comox St.

Broughton St.

Nicola St.

Cardero St.

Bute St.

Jervis St.

Thurlow St.

Burrard St.

Hornby St.

Howe St.

Granville St.

Seymour St.

Richards St.

Homer St.

Smithe St.

Cambie St.

Beatty St.

Georgia St.

DOWNTOWN

ROBSON

Public Library

Vancouver Art Gallery

YMCA

Granville Mall

Davie St.

Burnaby St.

Harwood St.

Pacific St.

Bute st.

Nelson Park

Sunset Beach Park

Aquatic Centre

Vanier Park

Maritime Museum

Vancouver Museum and H. R. MacMillan Planetarium

English Bay

False Creek Ferries

Burrard Bridge

Public Market

Granville Island

Granville Bridge

YALETOWN

99

David Lam Park

Pacific Blvd.

False Creek

Cambie Bridge

Charleston Park

Old Bridge St.

99

BC Place Stadium

Plaza of Nations

False Creek Ferries

Science World

Main St.

Quebec St.

Columbia St.

Yukona St.

Ash St.

Cambie St.

Heather St.

Willow St.

Laurel St.

Oak St.

2nd Ave. W

4th Ave. W

6th Ave. W

Broadway W

10TH Ave. W

12th Ave. W

14th Ave. W

16th Ave. W

8th Ave. W

Christian St.

Fir St.

Granville St.

500 yards

500 meters

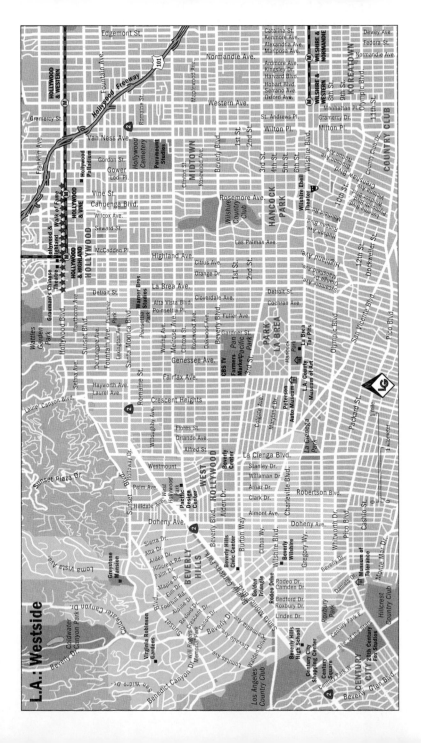

L.A.: Westside

Metropolitan
Los Angeles

○ *Metro Green Line*
○ *Metro Blue Line*
○ *Metro Red Line*

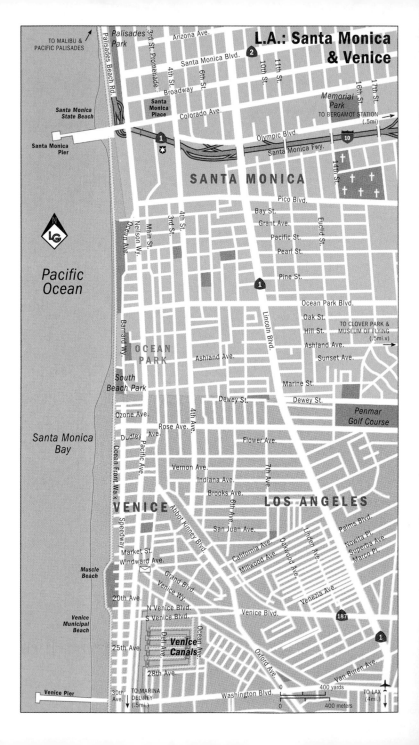

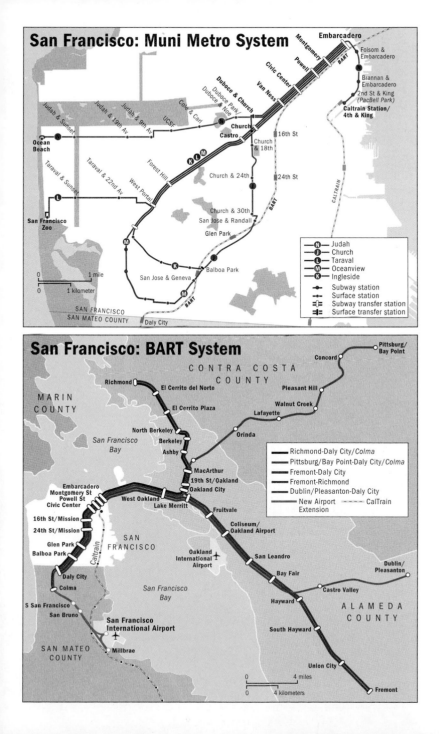

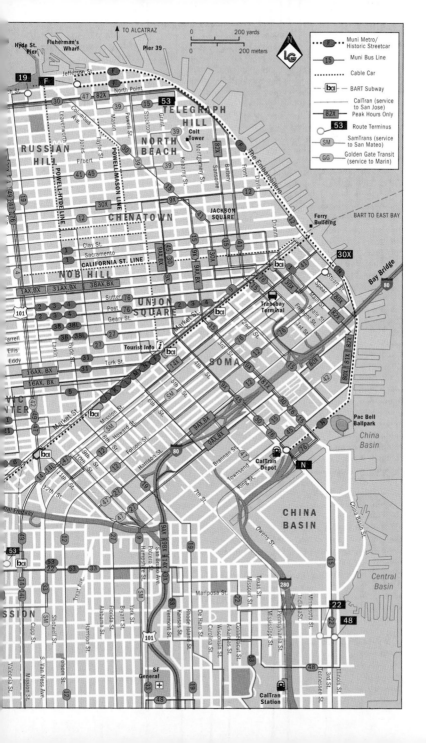

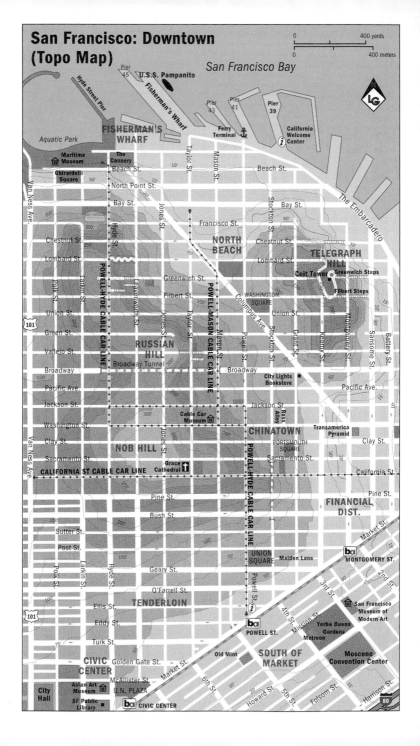

San Francisco: Downtown (Topo Map)

0 — 400 yards
0 — 400 meters

San Francisco Bay

LG

Pier 45
U.S.S. Pampanito
Fisherman's Wharf
Pier 43
Pier 41
Pier 39
Hyde Street Pier
Ferry Terminal
California Welcome Center

Aquatic Park
FISHERMAN'S WHARF

Maritime Museum
The Cannery
Ghirardelli Square
Beach St.
North Point St.
Bay St.

Beach St.
Bay St.

The Embarcadero

Van Ness Ave.

10'
50'
15'
20'

Taylor St.
Mason St.
Stockton St.

Francisco St.
50'

Chestnut St.
Lombard St.

NORTH BEACH
Chestnut St.
Lombard St.

TELEGRAPH HILL
Coit Tower
Greenwich Steps
Filbert Steps

100'
200'
250'

Hyde St.
Larkin St.
Leavenworth St.
Jones St.
Taylor St.

Greenwich St.
Filbert St.

WASHINGTON SQUARE
Union St.

Columbus Ave.

Polk St.

POWELL-HYDE CABLE CAR LINE
POWELL-MASON CABLE CAR LINE

101
Union St.
Green St.
Vallejo St.
Broadway

RUSSIAN HILL
Broadway Tunnel

Mason St.
Powell St.
Stockton St.
Grant Ave.
Kearny St.
Montgomery St.
Sansome St.
Battery St.

Broadway
City Lights Bookstore
Pacific Ave.

Pacific Ave.
Jackson St.
Washington St.
Clay St.

Jackson St.
Ross Alley

CHINATOWN
Transamerica Pyramid
Clay St.

Cable Car Museum

PORTSMOUTH SQUARE
Sacramento St.

NOB HILL
Jones St.

Sacramento St.
CALIFORNIA ST CABLE CAR LINE
Grace Cathedral
California St.

POWELL-HYDE CABLE CAR LINE

Pine St.

FINANCIAL DIST.
Pine St.

150'
200'

Bush St.
Sutter St.
Post St.

Market St.

100'

ba
MONTGOMERY ST.

Polk St.
Larkin St.
Hyde St.

150'

UNION SQUARE
Malden Lane

2nd St.
3rd St.

Geary St.

Powell St.

O'Farrell St.

TENDERLOIN
Ellis St.

San Francisco Museum of Modern Art

ba
POWELL ST.

Yerba Buena Gardens
Metreon

Eddy St.
Turk St.

4th St.
Mission St.

SOUTH OF MARKET

Moscone Convention Center

CIVIC CENTER
Golden Gate St.
Old Mint

75'

City Hall
Asian Art Museum
McAllister St.
U.N. PLAZA
Market St.
6th St.
5th St.
Howard St.
Folsom St.
Harrison St.

SF Public Library
ba CIVIC CENTER

30'

80

Boston MBTA

LEGEND

Transit lines & stop

Commuter rail & station

Terminal station

Free interchange with other lines

Accessible Station

Parking

*Chinatown: Accessible July 2002
*State: Not accessible by Blue line inbound.

Boston Harbor Ferry Services

1. Lovejoy Wharf to Charlestown Navy Yard
2. Lovejoy Wharf to U.S. Courthouse to World Trade Center
3. Long Wharf to Charlestown Navy Yard
4. Hingham Ship Yard to Rowes Wharf, Boston
5. Quincy Shipyard and Pemberton Point, Hull to Long Wharf, Boston

For schedule & fare information, call (617) 222-3200 or visit our website at www.mbta.com

© MBTA 2002

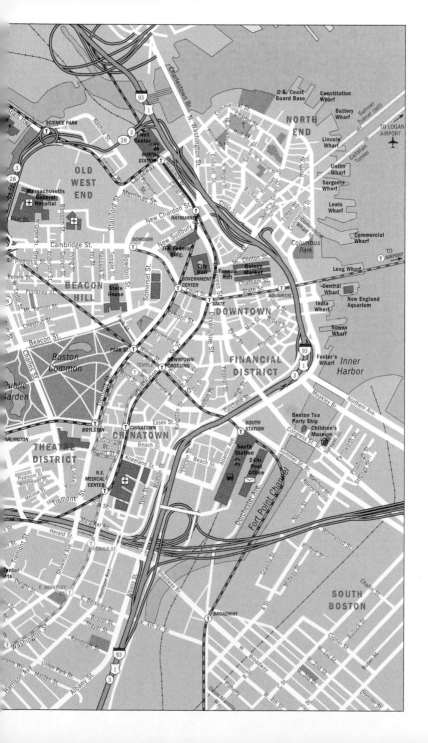

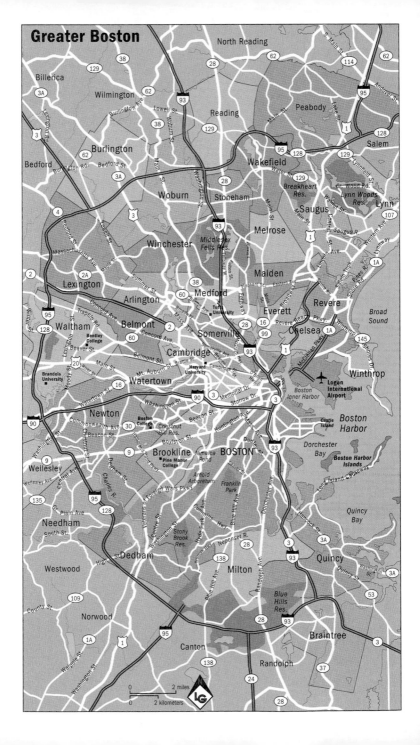

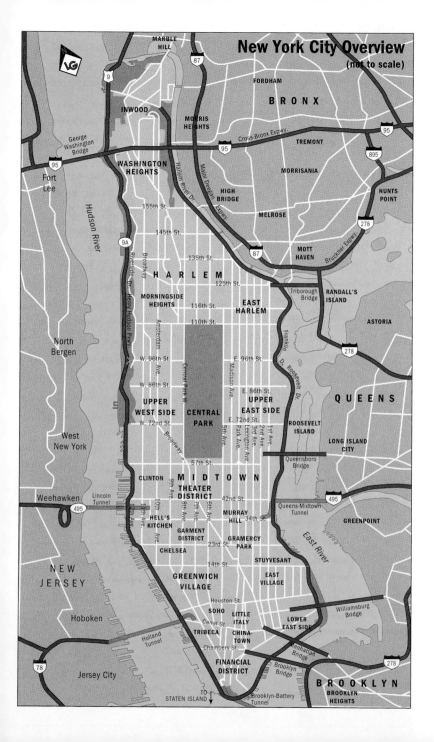

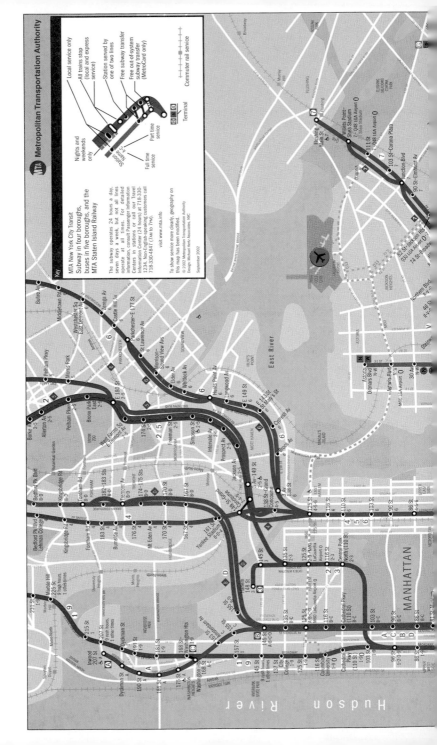

MTA New York City Subway

New York City: Downtown

W. 60th St.

W. 59th St.

St. Paul the Apostle ✝

W. 58th St.

W. 57th St.

COLUMBUS CIRCLE

A,B,C,D 1,2

Central Pa

W. 56th St.

W. 55th St.

W. 54th St.

W. 53rd St.

W. 52nd St.

W. 51st St.

W. 50th St.

W. 49th St.

W. 48th St.

W. 47th St.

W. 46th St.

W. 45th St.

W. 44th St.

W. 43rd St.

W. 42nd St.

W. 41st St.

NYC & Company
Convention & Visitors Bureau

Twelfth Ave.

Eleventh Ave.

Tenth Ave.

Ninth Ave.

Eighth Ave.

Intrepid Sea-Air-Space Museum

Schubert Theater

New York Times Building

1,2,3 N,Q,R,S

TIMES SQUARE

A,C,E

7

C,E

Ca

Port Authority Bus Terminal

Lincoln Tunnel

W. 39th St.

Jacob K. Javits Convention Center

HELL'S KITCHEN

Tenth Ave.

Dyer Ave.

Ninth Ave.

Eighth Ave.

GARM
DISTR

W. 34th St.

A,C,E

Hudson River

Joe Dimaggio Hwy.

Twelfth Ave.

General Post Office

Madison Square Garden

1,2,3

P
S

W. 31st St.

W. 30th St.

W. 29th St.

W. 28th St.

W. 27th St.

W. 23rd St.

General Theological Seminary

Tenth Ave.

Ninth Ave.

Eighth Ave.

Chelsea Hotel

Seventh Ave.

Cushman Row

CHELSEA

C,E

1

0   500 yards

0   500 meters

New York City: Midtown

W. 14th St.

A,C,E,L

1

Grand
Army Plaza

E. 60th St.

**Roosevelt
Island Tramway**

N,R,W

Queensboro Bridge

N,R,W

E. 59th St.

4,5,6

Bloomingdale's

Plaza Hotel

**F.A.O.
Schwarz**

E. 58th St.

**Madison-Lexington
Venture Building**

E. 57th St.

Second Ave.

First Ave.

F

E. 56th St.

**Marborough
Gallery**

**Trump
Tower**

**IBM
Building**

E. 55th St.

E. 54th St.

**Museum of
Modern Art**

**St.
Thomas**

**Museum of
Television &
Radio**

**Central
Synagogue**

**Citicorp
Center**

🏛

🏛

✡

St. Peter's

E. 53rd St.

**Seagram
Building**

E

E

**CBS
Building**

E

E. 52nd St.

6

**Radio City
Music Hall**

**St. Patrick's
Cathedral**

E. 51st St.

**Rockefeller
Center**

✝

St. Batholemew's

E. 50th St.

**TURTLE
BAY**

**Sak's Fifth
Avenue**

**Waldorf-Astoria
Hotel**

E. 49th St.

E. 48th St.

Fifth Ave.

Madison Ave.

Park Ave.

Lexington Ave.

E. 47th St.

**United
Nations**

E. 46th St.

**Met Life
Building**

E. 45th St.

E. 44th St.

**Algonquin
Hotel**

**Grand Central
Terminal**

4,5,6,S

**Chrysler
Building**

E. 43rd St.

**Ford
Foundation**

B,D,F,V

7

7

E. 42nd St.

**Daily News
Building**

**Bryant
Park**

**New York
Public
Library**

**Whitney
Museum
Branch**

🏛

E. 41st St.

Queens-Midtown Tunnel

W. 40th St

E. 40th St.

FDR Dr.

**American Standard
Building**

E. 39th St.

W. 38th St.

MURRAY

E. 38th St.

**East
River**

W. 37th St.

HILL

Third Ave.

E. 37th St.

W. 36th St.

**Pierpont
Morgan
Library**

🏛

E. 36th St.

W. 35th St.

E. 35th St.

HERALD
SQUARE

**Empire State
Building**

E. 34th St.

B,D,F,N,
Q,R,V,W

6

E. 33rd St.

W. 33rd St.

**International
Student Hospice**

E. 32nd St.

Lexington Ave.

Second Ave.

First Ave.

W. 32nd St.

E. 31st St.

E. 30th St.

N,R

E. 29th St.

Madison Ave.

Park Ave.

6

E. 28th St.

E. 27th St.

W. 26th St.

**Madison
Square
Park**

E. 26th St.

W. 25th St.

E. 25th St.

W. 24th St.

**Metropolitan
Life Insurance
Buildings**

E. 24th St.

E. 23rd St.

F

N,R

6

Flatiron Building

E. 22nd St.

Peter Cooper Rd.

W. 22nd St.

W. 21st St.

**Gramercy
Park**

E. 21st St.

W. 20th St.

E. 20th St.

GRAMERCY

Avenue of the Americas

16th Ave

Broadway

Fifth Ave.

W. 19th St.

**Theodore
Roosevelt
Birthplace**

E. 19th St.

Irving Pl.

PARK

W. 18th St.

E. 18th St.

W. 17th St.

E. 17th St.

First Ave.

Third Ave.

W. 16th St.

**Union
Square
Park**

E. 16th St.

**STUYVESANT
SQUARE**

V

W. 15th St.

E. 15th St.

L

Ave. A

Ave. B

Ave. C

W. 14th St.

N,R,Q,W

L,4,5,6

L

E. 14th St.

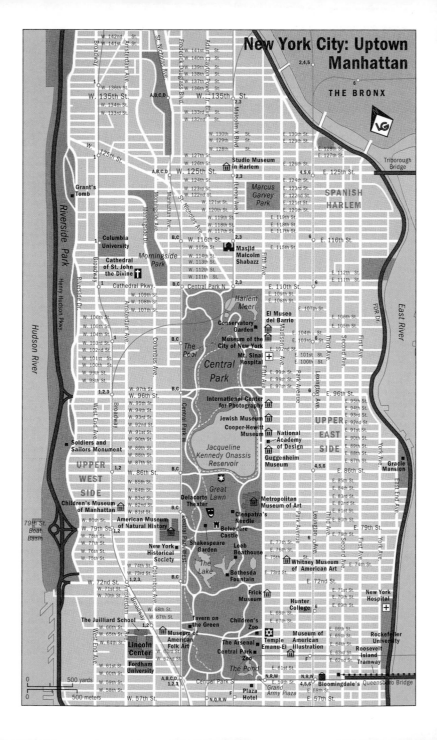

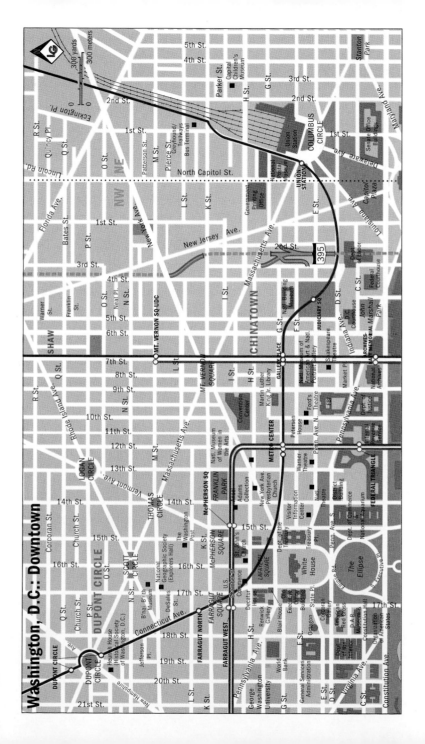

Washington, D.C.: Downtown

Central
Washington, D.C.

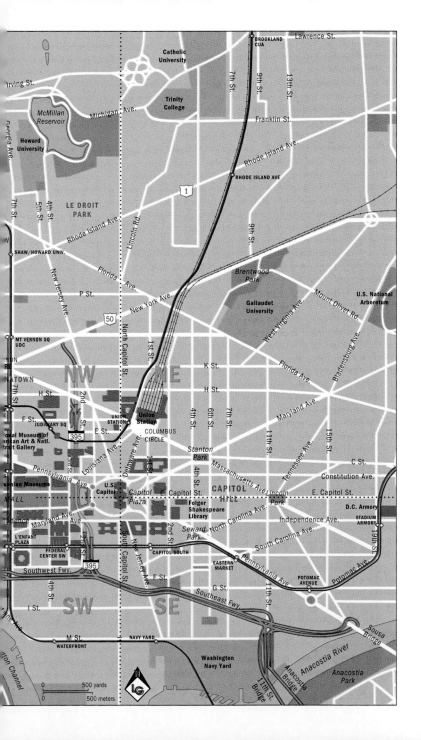

Washington, D.C.: The Mall Area

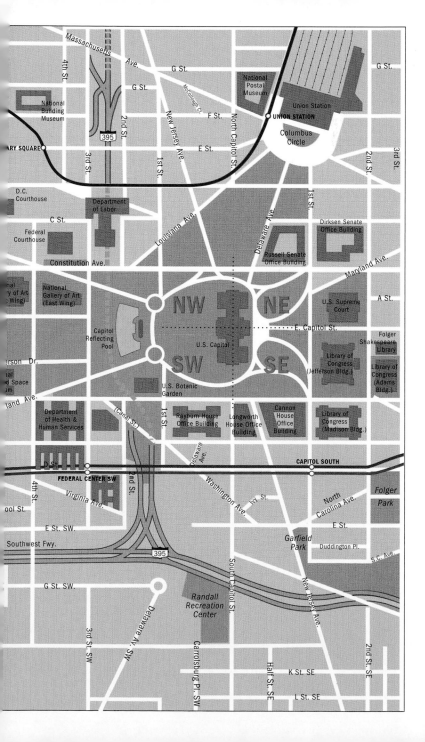

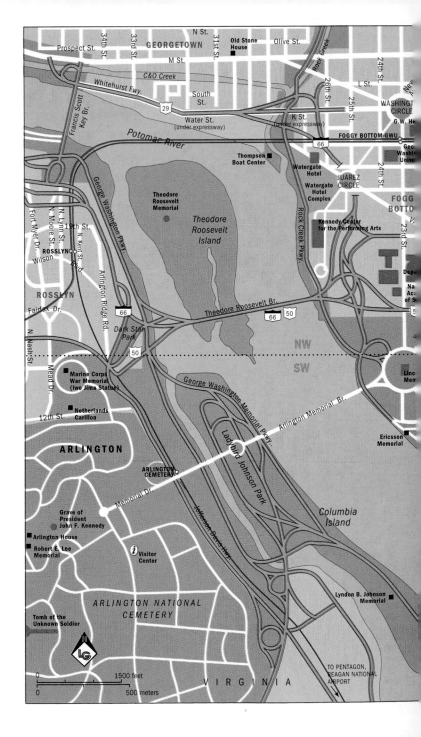

Washington, D.C.:
White House Area, Foggy Bottom,
and Nearby Arlington

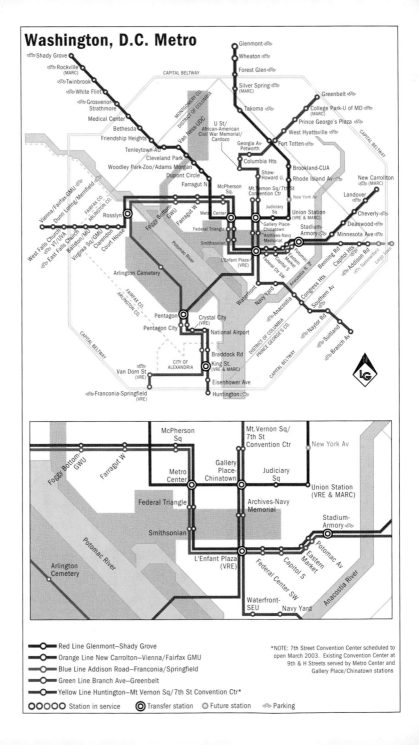

Washington, D.C. Metro

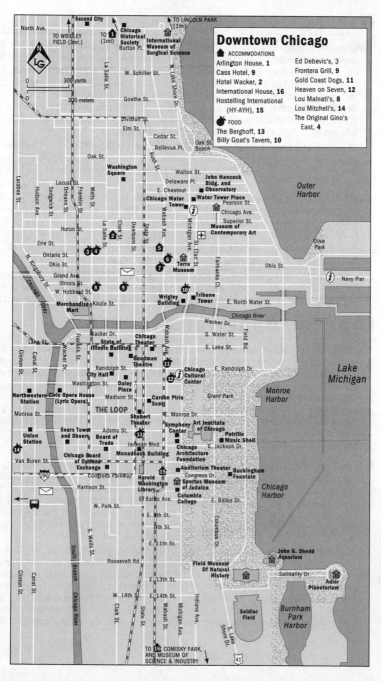

Downtown Chicago

▲ ACCOMMODATIONS

Arlington House, **1**
Cass Hotel, **9**
Hotel Wacker, **2**
International House, **16**
Hostelling International
(HY-AYH), **15**

🍴 FOOD
The Berghoff, **13**
Billy Goat's Tavern, **10**

Ed Debevic's, **3**
Frontera Grill, **9**
Gold Coast Dogs, **11**
Heaven on Seven, **12**
Lou Malnati's, **8**
Lou Mitchell's, **14**
The Original Gino's
East, **4**

⊠ PRACTICAL INFORMATION

Visitor Info: Chicago has 3 Visitor Centers, each located in a well-known landmark. **Chicago Cultural Center,** 77 E. Randolph St., at Michigan Ave., has map and tour information. Open M-F 10am-6pm, Sa 10am-5pm, Su 11am-5pm. **Water Works Visitor Center,** 163 E. Pearson St. (☎744-2400), at Michigan Ave., is located in the Water Tower Pumping Station. Open M-F 9:30am-7pm, Sa 10am-7pm, Su 11am-6pm. On the lake sits the **Navy Pier Info Center,** 700 E. Grand Ave. (☎595-7437). Open Su-Th 10am-10pm, F-Sa 10am-noon. The **International Visitors Center,** 520 N. Michigan Ave. (☎645-1836), aids foreign visitors with their itineraries. Call for assistance.

Bi-Gay-Lesbian Resources: Gay and Lesbian Hotline, (☎773-929-4357). Operates 6-10pm. For current info on events and nightlife, pick up a copy of the *Windy City Times* or *Gay Chicago* at Lakeview's **Unabridged Books,** 3251 N. Broadway (☎773-883-9119).

Medical Services: Northwestern Memorial Hospital, 251 E. Huron St. (☎908-2000), near Michigan Ave.; **emergency division** at 250 E. Erie St. (☎926-5188). Open 24hr. **Cook County Hospital,** 1835 W. Harrison St. (☎633-6000). Take the Congress A train to the Medical Center Stop. Open 24hr.

Internet access: Free at the **Chicago Public Library.** Main branch at 400 S. State St., at Congress. Open M-Th 9am-7pm, F-Sa 9am-5pm, Su 1-5pm.

Post Office: 433 W. Harrison St. (☎800-275-8777), at the Chicago River. Free parking. Open 24hr. **ZIP code:** 60607. **Area code:** 312 (downtown) or 773 (elsewhere in Chicago); 708, 630, or 847 (outside the city limits). In text, 312 unless otherwise noted.

⊡ ACCOMMODATIONS

Find a cheap, convenient place to rest your head at one of Chicago's many hostels. If you have a car, the motels on **Lincoln Ave.** in Lincoln Park are accessible and moderately priced. Motel chains off the interstates, about 1hr. from downtown, are out of the way and more expensive (from $35), but are an option for late-night arrivals. **Bed and Breakfast Chicago** (☎800-375-7084) offers a reservation and referral service for many downtown B&Bs. Most have a two-night minimum stay, and rooms average around $120. Chicago has a 15% tax on most accommodation rates.

HOSTELS

▩ **Hostelling International–Chicago (HI-AYH),** 24 E. Congress Pkwy. (☎360-0300), off Wabash St. in the Loop. Take the El Orange Line to State and Van Buren, walk 1 block east to Wabash St., turn right, walk 1 block to Congress. The location offers easy access to the major museums during the day, but *be careful on the deserted streets of the Loop at night.* Student center, library, kitchen, and organized activities give the hostel a lively social atmosphere. Laundry and Internet access. All rooms with A/C. Reservations recommended. Dorms $29, nonmembers $32. ❶

Arlington House, 616 W. Arlington Pl. (☎773-929-5380 or 800-467-8355), off Clark St. just north of Fullerton in Lincoln Park. The social atmosphere and brilliant location ensure a lively stay in this enormous hostel. Newly renovated dorms are tidy and pleasant with clean bathrooms. The private rooms and shared baths, however, are sometimes poorly kept and not worth the price. Safe, central neighborhood near food and nightlife. Kitchen, TV room, and laundry. Linen and deposit $10. Reservations recommended. Dorms $22; private singles with shared bath $50, with private bath $51. ❶

HOTELS & GUEST HOUSES

Cass Hotel, 640 N. Wabash Ave. (☎787-4030 or 800-227-7850), just north of the Loop. Take the El to State St. Reasonable rates and a convenient location near the Magnificent Mile make this newly renovated hotel a favorite find of the budget-conscious. The $2 breakfast downstairs at the coffeeshop is a great deal. Parking available ($26 per day). Laundry room. Key deposit $5 if paying cash. Singles from $79, doubles from $84. Reservations recommended. Wheelchair accessible. ❹

International House, 1414 E. 59th St. (☎773-753-2270), in Hyde Park, off Lake Shore Dr. Take the Illinois Central Railroad from the Michigan Ave. station (20min.) or METRA South Shore Line to 59th St. and walk a half-block west. On the grounds of the University of Chicago; *don't wander off-campus at night*. Common areas and an outdoor courtyard filled with the activity of an international collection of students augment neat, spacious singles with shared bath. Linen provided. Laundry, tennis courts, game room, weight room, and cafeteria. Reservations with credit card required. Rooms $50. ❸

Hotel Wacker, 111 W. Huron St. (☎787-1386), at N. Clark St. A green, formerly neon sign on the corner makes this place easy to find. Small, well-appointed rooms have reasonable prices. Wheelchair accessible. TV, A/C, phone. Key and linen deposit $5. Check-in 24hr. Singles $50, doubles $65. ❸

◖ FOOD

Chicago's many culinary delights, from pizza to po' boy sandwiches, are among its main attractions. One of the best guides to city dining is the monthly *Chicago* magazine, which includes an extensive restaurant section, indexed by price, cuisine, and quality. It can be found at tourist offices and newsstands everywhere.

PIZZA

No trip to Chicago would be complete without sampling the city's deep-dish pizza. Try either standard-style with the cheese on top, or be bold and order with toppings under the tomato sauce.

▩ Pizzeria Uno, 29 E. Ohio St. (☎321-1000), and younger sister **Due,** 619 N. Wabash Ave. (☎943-2400). It may look like any other Uno's, but this is where the legacy of deep-dish began. Lines are long, and pizza takes 45min. to prepare, but the pizza has a made-from-scratch taste worth the wait. Individual-sized pies ($5) only take 25min. Same short menu at Due (right up the street), with a terrace and more room than Uno's. Uno open M-F 11:30am-1am, Sa 11:30am-2am, Su 11:30am-11:30pm. Due open Su-Th 11am-1:30am, F-Sa 11am-2am. ❶

Lou Malnati's, 439 N. Wells St. (☎828-9800), at Hubbard downtown. A Chicago mainstay for 30 years, Lou's is a local sports memorabilia-themed chain with bubbling deep-dish masterpieces. There are seven other branches throughout the city and suburbs. Pizzas $5-20. Open M-Th 11am-11pm, F-Sa 11am-midnight, Su noon-10pm. ❸

The Original Gino's East, 633 N. Wells St. (☎266-5421), at Ontario downtown. Stake your claim on the customer-decorated walls of this legendary deep-dish joint. Pizza $9-23. Mini-pizza weekday lunch special $4. Open daily 11am-11pm. ❹

'ROUND THE LOOP

Many of Chicago's best restaurants, from ragin' Cajun to tried-and-true German, inhabit the streets of the Loop.

▨ **Lou Mitchell's,** 565 W. Jackson Blvd. (☎939-3111), 2 blocks west of the Sears Tower. Recently inducted into the restaurant hall of fame, this retro diner has been stuffing faithful customers for over 75 years. Start the day with "meltaway pancakes" that take up the whole plate ($6) and the "world's finest cup of coffee" ($1.50). Lines are long but move fast. Female customers (and persistent men) get a free box of Milk Duds and fresh donut holes while they wait. Cash only. Open M-Sa 5:30am-3pm, Su 7am-3pm. ❷

Heaven on Seven, 111 N. Wabash Ave. (☎263-6443), 7th fl. of the Garland Bldg. This is heaven Cajun-style, from the Mardi Gras and voodoo decor to the endless hot sauce and spicy cuisine. The line is long, but hell, the jambalaya is fantastic. Open M-F 8:30am-5pm, Sa 10am-3pm. ❸

Billy Goat's Tavern, 430 N. Michigan Ave. (☎222-1525), underground on lower Michigan Ave. Gruff service is part of this bar/diner's charm. Delicious cheeseburgers $2.50. "Butt in anytime" M-F 6am-2am, Sa 10am-3am, Su 11am-2am. ❶

Gold Coast Dogs (☎527-1222), at Wabash and Randolph St. Hot dogs are sacred in Chicago, but only when they're topped Second City-style with a veritable salad of relish, onions, pickles, tomatoes, and more. Locals rank Gold Coast among the best. Hot dogs from $2. Open M-F 7am-10pm, Sa-Su 11am-8pm. ❶

The Berghoff, 17 W. Adams St. (☎427-3170). Take the El to Adams. This dim, cavernous German restaurant filled with lunching traders has been a Chicago institution for over 100 years. Bratwurst $4.50. Stein of Berghoff's own beer $3. Open M-Th 11am-9pm, F 11am-9:30pm, Sa 11am-10pm. ❶

RIVER NORTH

River North houses some of the trendiest eateries in town, as well as Chicago's pizza institutions (see **Pizza,** above).

▨ **Ed Debevic's,** 640 N. Wells St. (☎664-1707), at Ontario across from Gino's East Pizza. Don't be surprised when your waiter sits down at the table with you to take your order. This faux 1950s diner trades heavily in kitsch—the aquamarine interior and poodle skirt waitresses come with the great burgers ($7) and shakes ($4). Hang out in a booth or at the counter while the staff dances and a DJ spins classic tunes. Open mid-June to Aug. Su-Th 11am-10pm, F-Sa 11am-midnight; Sept.-June Su-Th 11am-9pm, F-Sa 11am-11pm. ❷

Frontera Grill, 455 N. Clark St. (☎661-1434), between Illinois and Hubbard St. Take El Red Line to Grand/State. A delightful departure from chain tacos and burritos, Frontera delivers what many claim is the best authentic Mexican cuisine in the region. Entrees ($7-22) change every month but are always superb. The usual 2hr. wait is bearable if you snag a bar seat and order appetizers (from $3). Lunch: Tu-Th 11:30am-2:30pm, Sa 10:30am-2:30pm. Dinner: Tu 5:20-10pm, W-Th 5-10pm, F-Sa 5-11pm. Reservations accepted for parties of 5 or more. ❹

SOUL FOOD

Head to the **South Side** for good, cheap American-style soul food like ribs, fried chicken, and greens. *Be very careful south of the Loop,* though, especially after dark. **Wicker Park,** to the north, is another option for satisfying soul food.

▨ **Army & Lou's,** 422 E. 75th St. (☎773-483-6550), on the South Side. Locals come here for some of the best southern fare around, served in a surprisingly upscale setting. Fried chicken and 2 sides $9; mixed greens and ham $8. Open M and W-Su 9am-10pm. ❸

Dixie Kitchen & Bait Shop, 5225 S. Harper St. (☎773-363-4943). Tucked back in a parking lot on 52nd St. in Hyde Park, this new place is fast becoming a local hot spot. Fried green tomatoes ($4) and oyster po' boy sandwiches ($8) are among Dixie's southern highlights. Fried catfish $10. Blackened Voodoo beer $2. Open Su-Th 11am-10pm, F-Sa 11am-11pm. ❷

The Smokedaddy, 1804 W. Division St. (☎773-772-6656), north of the Loop in Wicker Park. Fantastic ribs ($8), vegetarian BBQ sandwiches ($6), and pulled pork sandwiches ($6) merit the "WOW" proclamation of the neon sign out front. Live blues nightly. Open M and F-Sa 11:30am-1am, Tu-Th 5pm-1am, Su 11:30am-1am. ❷

GREEKTOWN

▨ **The Parthenon,** 314 S. Halsted St. (☎726-2407). Look in the window around dinner time and you will see meat slowly roasting on a spit. The staff converses in Greek, the murals transport you to the Mediterranean, and the food wins top awards. The tasty Greek Feast family-style dinner ($16) includes everything from *saganaki* (flaming goat cheese) to baklava. Open daily 11am-1am. ❸

Rodity's, 222 S. Halsted St. (☎454-0800), between Adams St. and Jackson Blvd. With slightly cheaper fare than the other Greektown options (daily specials under $9), Rodity's prepares more than generous portions of *spanakopita* ($8) and other delectable Greek treats. Open Su-Th 11am-midnight, F-Sa 11am-1am. ❷

LINCOLN PARK

▨ **Cafe Ba-Ba-Reeba!,** 2024 N. Halsted St. (☎935-5000), just north of Armitage. Well-marked by the colorful, glowing facade, the sprawling Ba-Ba-Reeba pleases with unbeatable *tapas* ($3-8) and hearty Spanish *paellas* ($10-15 per person). During the summer sip sangria ($3.50) on the outdoor terrace. Lunch: Sa-Su noon-5pm. Dinner: Su-Th 5-10pm, F-Sa 5pm-midnight. Reservations recommended. ❸

▨ **Potbelly Sandwich Works,** 2264 N. Lincoln Ave. (☎773-528-1405), between Belden and Webster. This laid-back deli, appropriately decorated with a potbelly stove and player piano, offers delicious subs ($4). Yogurt smoothies $2. Open daily 11am-11pm. Call for additional locations. ❶

Penny's Noodle Shop, 950 W. Diversey Ave. (☎773-281-8448), at Sheffield Ave. One of the best budget options in town, Penny's delivers generous portions of Asian noodles (all under $6) to scores of locals who pack the place at all hours. Try one of the noodle soups for a change of pace. No reservations; sit at the counter or prepare to wait. Open Tu-Th and Su 11am-10pm, F-Sa 11am-10:30pm. ❷

Crêpe de Paris, 2433 N. Clark St. (☎773-404-1300). The crepes are perfect for a late breakfast. Travelers with a sweet tooth can bite into scrumptious crepes oozing with Nutella ($5-7), or drop in for the lunch special ($6). Vegetarian options are plentiful. Open Su-Th 10am-10pm, F-Sa 10am-11pm. ❷

ANDERSONVILLE

Kopi, A Traveller's Cafe, 5317 N. Clark St. (☎773-989-5674), near Foster St., a 10min. walk from the Berwyn El, 4 blocks west on Berwyn. Sip on well-brewed coffee while browsing the cafe's extensive travel library. Espresso $1.50. Music M and Th nights. Open M-Th 8am-11pm, F 8am-midnight, Sa 9am-midnight, Su 10am-11pm.

Ann Sather, 5207 N. Clark St. (☎773-271-6677). The last authentic Swedish diner left in the neighborhood delights locals with their wildly popular, addictive, gooey cinnamon rolls ($4). Open Su-Th 7am-10pm, F-Sa 7am-11pm. Call for other locations. ❶

BUCKTOWN/WICKER PARK

Kitsch'n on Roscoe, 2005 W. Roscoe St. (☎773-248-7372), at Damen Ave. in nearby Roscoe Village. Kitsch abounds at this breakfast and lunch spot, which serves a surprisingly good "Kitsch-n Sink Omelette." Enjoy "Jonny's Lunch Box" (soup, sandwich, fruit, and a snack cake served in a lunch box) on campy theme tables. Star Trek, anyone? Meals $3-12. Breakfast and lunch: Tu-F 7:30am-2pm, Sa-Su 9am-3pm. Dinner: Tu-F and Su 5-9pm, Sa 5-10pm. ❷

GREAT LAKES

Earwax Cafe, 1565 N. Milwaukee Ave. (☎773-772-4019). It's hard to miss the purple, yellow, and green store front of this primarily vegetarian sandwich shop. The murals on the walls and funky light fixtures give the cafe, which has a video rental store in the back, an artsy feel to match the neighborhood. Open M-Th 11am-midnight. ❷

Zoom Kitchen, 1646 N. Damen Ave. (☎773-278-7000). Visit this space-age diner for fresh sandwiches ($4-6) prepared just as you like them. The friendly staff will top your meal with handfuls of veggies picked from giant piles behind the counter. Open M-Sa 11am-10pm, Su 10am-8pm. ❶

◉ SIGHTS

Only a fraction of Chicago's eclectic sights are revealed by tourist brochures, bus tours, and strolls through the downtown area. Sights range from well-publicized museums to undiscovered back streets, from beaches and parks to towering skyscrapers. To see it all requires some off-the-beaten path exploring.

THE LOOP

When the **Great Fire of 1871** burned Chicago's downtown, the city rebuilt itself with a vengeance. As a result, the functional became the fabulous, and one of the most concentrated clusters of architectural treasures in the world was created.

TOURS. Visitors can explore an architectural street museum via **walking tours** organized by the **Chicago Architectural Foundation.** One tour of early skyscrapers and another of modern architecture start at the foundation's gift shop and last 2hr. Highlights include Louis Sullivan's arch, classic Chicago windows, and Mies van der Rohe's revolutionary skyscrapers. *(224 S. Michigan Ave. ☎922-8687. $12 for 1 tour, $18 for both.)*

SEARS TOWER. A few blocks west on Jackson, the **Sears Tower** is undoubtedly Chicago's most immediately recognizable architectural landmark. The Tower is the second-tallest building in the world (first, in the minds of staunch Chicagoans). The impressive structure stands 1454 ft. tall, and on a clear day, visitors to the 103rd fl. Skydeck can see three bordering states. *(233 S. Wacker Dr.; enter on Jackson. ☎875-9696. Open May-Sept. daily 10am-10pm; Oct.-Apr. 10am-8pm. $9.50, seniors $7.75, youth $6.75. Lines are long, usually at least 1hr.)*

THE PLAZA. The **Bank One Building and Plaza** is one of the world's largest bank buildings. It leads gazes skyward with its diamond-shaped, diagonal slope. Back on the ground, Marc Chagall's vivid mosaic, *The Four Seasons*, lines the block and sets off a public space often used for concerts and lunchtime entertainment. The mural is a fabulous sight at night, when it is lit by various colored bulbs. Two blocks north, the Methodist **Chicago Temple,** the world's tallest church, sends its Babel-esque steeples heavenward. *(77 W. Washington St., at the corner of Clark and Washington St. ☎236-4548. Tours M-F 2pm, Sa-Su 9:30am and noon.)*

STATE STREET. State and Madison St., the most famous intersection of "State Street, that great street," form the focal point of the Chicago street grid as well as another architectural haven. Here, Louis Sullivan's beloved **Carson Pirie Scott** store is adorned with exquisite ironwork and the famous extra-large Chicago window. Sullivan's other masterpiece, the **Auditorium Building,** sits several blocks south at the corner of Congress St. and Michigan Ave. Intricate design and flawless acoustics highlight this Chicago landmark.

OTHER ARCHITECTURAL WONDERS. Burnham and Root's **Monadnock Building,** deserves a glance for its serene, alternating bays of purple and brown rock. *(53 W. Jackson.)* Just to the southeast, the **Sony Fine Arts Theatre** screens current artistic and foreign films in the grandeur of the **Fine Arts Building.** *(418 S. Michigan Ave. ☎939-2119.)*

Open M-Th. $8.25; students $6; seniors, children, and matinees $5.) The $144 million **Harold Washington Library Center** is a researcher's dream, as well as a postmodern architectural delight. *(400 S. State St. ☎ 747-4300. Open M-Th 9am-7pm, F-Sa 9am-5pm, Su 1-5pm. Tours M-Sa noon and 2pm, Su 2pm.)* On the north side of the Loop, at Clark and Randolph, the **State of Illinois Building** is a postmodern town square. The elevator ride to the top gives a thrilling (and free) view of its sloping atrium, circular floors, and hundreds of employees.

SCULPTURE. In addition to its architectural masterpieces, Chicago is decorated with one of the country's premier collections of outdoor sculpture. Large, abstract designs punctuate many downtown corners, making a walking tour of Loop outdoor sculpture a terrific way to spend an afternoon. The Chicago Cultural Center sells the *Loop Sculpture Guide* for $4 (see p. 558). The piece known simply as "The Picasso," at the foot of the **Daley Center Plaza**, is an unofficial symbol of Chicago. *(Intersection of Washington and Dearborn St. ☎ 443-3054.)* Directly across Washington St. rests surrealist Joan Miró's *Chicago*, the artist's voluptuous gift to the city. *(69 W. Washington St.)* Three blocks south on Dearborn at Adams, Alexander Calder's *Flamingo*, a stark red structure that is half-statue, half-mobile, stands in front of the Federal Center Plaza. Calder's other Chicago masterpiece, *The Universe*, swirls in the lobby of the Sears Tower.

NEAR NORTH

TRIBUNE TOWER. North of the Loop along the lake, just past the Michigan Ave. Bridge, lies the city's ritziest district. The Tribune Tower, a Gothic skyscraper just north of the bridge, overlooks this stretch. The result of an international design competition in the 1920s, the tower is now home to Chicago's largest newspaper, *The Chicago Tribune. (435 N. Michigan Ave.)*

THE MART. Over 8 mi. of corridors fill the nearby Merchandise Mart. As one of the largest commercial buildings in the world (25 stories high and 2 blocks long), it even has its own ZIP code. The first two floors house a mediocre public mall, while the remainder contains private showrooms where design professionals converge to choose home and office furnishings. **Tours at the Mart** guides visitors through the building. *(Entrance on N. Wells or Kinzie St., north of the river. Bus #114. ☎ 644-4664. 2hr. tours Th and F 1:30pm. $12, seniors $10, students $9.)*

NAVY PIER. Big, bright, and always festive, Navy Pier captures the carnival spirit 365 days a year. No small jetty, the mile-long pier has it all: a concert pavilion, dining options, nightspots, sightseeing boats, a spectacular ferris wheel, a crystal garden with palm trees, and an Omnimax theater. Now *that's* America. From here, explorers can rent **bicycles** to navigate the Windy City's streets. *(600 E. Grand Ave. Take El Red Line to Grand/State and transfer to a free pier trolley bus. Bike rental open June-Sept. daily 8am-11pm; May 8am-8pm; Apr. and Oct. 10am-7pm. $9 per hr., $36 per day.)*

MAGNIFICENT MILE. Chicago's showy row of glitzy shops along N. Michigan Ave. between the Chicago River and Oak St. can magnificently drain the wallet. Several of these retail stores were designed by some of the country's foremost architects and merit a look. The area is also home to one of the country's few **Virgin Megastores,** a music store palace full of popular American and British albums. The relatively plain **Chicago Water Tower** and **Pumping Station** stick out among the ritzy stores at the corner of Michigan and Pearson Ave. Built in 1867, these structures were the only ones in the area to survive the Great Chicago Fire. The pumping station houses the multimedia show *Here's Chicago* and a comprehensive tourist center (see p. 558). Across Pearson St., expensive, trendy stores pack **Water Tower Place,** the first urban shopping mall in the US. One block north, the **John Hancock Building** rockets toward the sky in black steel and glass.

OLD TOWN. The bells of the pre-fire **St. Michael's Church** ring 1 mi. north of the Magnificent Mile in **Old Town,** a neighborhood where eclectic shops and nightspots fill revitalized streets. Architecture buffs should explore the W. Menomonee and W. Eugenie St. area. In early June, the **Old Town Art Fair** attracts artists and craftsmen nationwide. *(Take bus #151 to Lincoln Park and walk south down Clark or Wells St.)*

NORTH SIDE

LINCOLN PARK. Urban renewal has made **Lincoln Park** a popular choice for wealthy residents. Bounded by Armitage to the south and Diversey Ave. to the north, Lincoln Park offers a lakeside community of splendid harbors and parks. Cafes, bookstores, and nightspots pack its tree-lined streets. For some of Chicago's liveliest clubs and restaurants, check out the area around N. Clark St., Lincoln Ave., and N. Halsted St.

LAKEVIEW. North of Diversey Ave. on N. Clark St., the streets of Lincoln Park become increasingly diverse as they melt into the community of Lakeview around the 3000s block. In this self-proclaimed "gay capital of Chicago," supermarket shopping plazas alternate with tiny markets and vintage clothing stores, while apartment towers and hotels spring up between aging two-story houses. The **Blue Man Group** performs in the nearby Briar Theater, and Lakeview dance clubs form a center of Chicago nightlife. Polish diners share blocks with Korean restaurants, and Mongolian eateries face Mexican bars in this ethnic potpourri.

WRIGLEYVILLE. Around the 4000s block of N. Clark, Lakeview shifts into **Wrigleyville.** Even though the **Chicago Cubs** (p. 569) haven't won a World Series since 1908, Wrigleyville residents remain fiercely loyal to their hometown team. Tiny, ivy-covered **Wrigley Field,** 1060 W. Addison, just east of the junction of Graceland and N. Clark, is the North Side's most famous institution. A pilgrimage here is a must for the serious or curious baseball aficionado interested in seeing the country's most patient fans. Tours of the historic park are available when the Cubs are away *(☎ 773-404-2827.)*

NEAR WEST SIDE

The Near West Side, bounded by the Chicago River to the east and Ogden Ave. to the west, assembles a cornucopia of vibrant ethnic enclaves.

HULL HOUSE. Aside from great food options, the primary attraction on the Near West Side lies a few blocks north on Halsted, where activist Jane Addams devoted her life to the historic Hull House. This settlement house bears witness to Chicago's (and Addams's) role in turn-of-the-century reform. Although the house no longer offers social services, it has been painstakingly restored as a small museum. *(800 S. Halsted St. Take El Blue Line to Halsted/U of I or bus #8 "Halsted." ☎ 413-5353. Open M-F 10am-4pm, Su noon-5pm. Free.)*

SOUTH OF THE LOOP

HYDE PARK & THE UNIVERSITY OF CHICAGO. Seven miles south of the Loop along the lake, the scenic campus of the **University of Chicago** dominates the **Hyde Park** neighborhood. The university's efforts at revitalizing the area have resulted in a community of scholars and a lively campus life amidst the degenerating neighborhoods surrounding it. University police patrol the area bounded by 51st St. to the north, Lakeshore Dr. to the east, 61st St. to the south, and Cottage Grove to the west—but *don't test these boundaries, even during the day.* Lakeside Burnham Park, east of campus, is *fairly safe during the day, but not at night.* The impressive **Oriental Institute, Museum of Science and Industry** (see **Museums,** p. 565), and **DuSable Museum of African-American History** are all in or near Hyde Park. *(From the Loop, take bus #6 "Jefferson Express" or the METRA Electric Line from the Randolph St. Station south to 59th St.)*

ROBIE HOUSE. On campus, Frank Lloyd Wright's famous **Robie House,** designed to resemble a hanging flower basket, is the seminal example of his Prairie-style house. Now in the midst of a ten-year restoration project, Robie House is being restored to its original 1910 state. The house will remain open to visitors during all stages of renovation. *(5757 S. Woodlawn, at the corner of 58th St. ☎ 773-834-1847. Tours M-F 11am-3pm, Sa-Su 11am-3:30pm. $9, seniors and ages 7-18 $7.)*

WEST OF THE LOOP

OAK PARK. Gunning for the title of the most fantastic suburb in the US, Oak Park sprouts off of Harlem St. *(10 mi. west of downtown, I-290 W to Harlem St.)* Frank Lloyd Wright endowed the downtown area with 25 of his spectacular homes and buildings, all of which dot the Oak Park Historic District. His one-time home and workplace, the ⊠**Frank Lloyd Wright House and Studio,** offers an unbeatable look at his interior and exterior stylings. *(951 Chicago Ave. ☎ 708-848-1976. Open daily 10am-5pm. 45min. tours of the house M-F 11am, 1, and 3pm; Sa-Su every 20min. 11am-3:30pm. 1hr. self-guided tours of Wright's other Oak Park homes, with a map and audio cassette, available daily 10am-3:30pm. Guided tours Mar.-Nov. Sa-Su every hr. 11am-4pm; Dec.-Feb. Sa-Su every hr. noon-2pm. $9, seniors and under 18 $7; combination interior/exterior tour tickets $14/$10.)* Visitors should also stop by the former home of Ernest Hemingway. Throughout the year, fans flock to the **Ernest Hemingway Birthplace and Museum** to take part in the many events honoring this legendary master of the novel. *(Birthplace: 339 N. Oak Ave. Museum: 200 N. Oak Park Ave. ☎ 708-848-2222. House and museum pen Th-F and Su 1-5pm; Sa 10am-5pm. $6 combined ticket, seniors and under 18 $4.50.)* Swing by the **Visitors Center** for maps, guidebooks, tours, and local history. *(158 Forest Ave. ☎ 708-848-1500 or 888-625-7275. El Green Line to Harlem.)*

🏛 MUSEUMS

Chicago's museums range from some of the largest collections in the world to one room galleries. The first five listings (known as the **Big Five**) provide a diverse array of exhibits, while a handful of smaller collections target specific interests. Lake Shore Drive has been diverted around Grant Park, linking the Field Museum, Adler, and Shedd. This compound, known as **Museum Campus,** offers a free shuttle between museums. Visitors who plan on seeing all five, plus the Hancock Observatory, can save money by purchasing a **CityPass** that grants admission to the sights and provides discount coupons for food and shopping ($39, ages 3-11 $29; available at each attraction).

⊠ **Art Institute of Chicago,** 111 S. Michigan Ave. (☎443-3600), at Adams St. in Grant Park; take the El Green, Brown, Purple, or Orange Lines to Adams. It's easy to feel overwhelmed in this expansive museum, whose collections span four millennia of art from Asia, Africa, Europe, and beyond. Make sure to see Chagall's stunning *America Windows*—the artist's blue stained glass tribute to the country's bicentennial—between visits to Wood's *American Gothic* and Monet's haystacks. Open M and W-F 10:30am-4:30pm, Tu 10:30am-8pm, Sa-Su 10am-5pm. $10, students and children $6, under 6 free; Tu free.

⊠ **Field Museum of Natural History,** 1400 S. Lake Shore Dr. (☎922-9410), at Roosevelt Rd. in Grant Park; take bus #146 from State St. Sue, the largest *T. rex* skeleton ever unearthed towers over excellent geology, anthropology, botany, and zoology exhibits. Other highlights include Egyptian mummies, Native American halls, and a dirt exhibit. Open daily 9am-5pm. $8; students, seniors, and ages 3-11 $4; under 3 free.

⚽ **Shedd Aquarium,** 1200 S. Lake Shore Dr. (☎939-2438), in Grant Park. The world's largest indoor aquarium has over 6600 species of fish in 206 tanks. The Oceanarium features beluga whales, dolphins, seals, and other marine mammals in a giant pool that appears to flow into Lake Michigan. See piranhas and tropical fish of the rainforest in the *Amazon Rising* exhibit or get a rare glimpse of seahorses in the oceanarium exhibit *Seahorse Symphony.* Open June-Aug. M-W and F-Su 9am-6pm, Th 9am-10pm (Oceanarium and *Seahorse Symphony* 9am-8pm); Sept.-May M-F 9am-5pm, Sa-Su 9am-6pm. Feedings M-F 11am, 2, and 3pm. Combined admission to Oceanarium and Aquarium $15, seniors and ages 3-11 $11. Tour of Oceanarium $3.

Museum of Science and Industry, 5700 S. Lake Shore Dr. (☎773-684-1414), at 57th St. in Hyde Park. Take bus #6 "Jeffrey Express," the #10 "Museum of Science and Industry" bus (runs daily in summer, Sa-Su and holidays rest of year), or METRA South Shore line to 57th St. The Museum features the *Apollo 8* command module, a full-sized replica of a coal mine, and a host of interactive exhibits on topics from DNA to the Internet. Stop by the *Yesterday's Main Street* exhibit for a scoop at the 1920s-style ice cream parlor. Open Sept.-May daily 9:30am-4:30pm; June-Aug. 9:30am-5:30pm. Call for a schedule of Omnimax shows. Admission $9, seniors $7.50, ages 3-11 $5; with Omnimax $15/$12.50/$10. Parking $7 per day.

Adler Planetarium, 1300 S. Lake Shore Dr. (☎922-7827), on Museum Campus in Grant Park. Aspiring astronauts can discover their weight on Mars, read the news from space, and examine astronomy tools. Open daily 9:30am-4:30pm. Admission and choice of sky show $13, seniors $12, ages 4-17 $11. Some exhibits $5 extra. Sky show daily on the hr. $5.

Museum of Contemporary Art, 220 E. Chicago Ave. (☎280-2660), 1 block east of Michigan Ave.; take #66 "Chicago Ave." bus. The beautiful view of Lake Michigan is the only unchanging feature in the MCA's ultra-modern exhibition space. Pieces from the outstanding permanent collection rotate periodically. Call to see what is on display—their extensive collection includes works by Calder, Warhol, Javer, and Nauman. Open Tu 10am-8pm, W-Su 10am-5pm. $8, students and seniors $6, under 12 free; free Tu.

Terra Museum of American Art, 664 N. Michigan Ave. (☎664-3939), between Huron and Erie St. Wedged between the posh shops on N. Michigan, this is one of few galleries to exclusively showcase American art from colonial times to the present. Open Tu 10am-8pm, W-Sa 10am-6pm, Su noon-5pm. $7; seniors $3.50; students, teachers with ID, and under 12 free. Free on Tu, Th, and first Su of month. Free tours Tu-F noon and 6pm, Sa-Su noon and 2pm.

Museum of Holography, 1134 W. Washington Blvd. (☎226-1007), just west of the Loop. This unconventional museum explores the wild world of holograms, including fantastic hologram pictures of famous people. Open W-Su 12:30-4:30pm. $5, children under 12 $3.

Spertus Institute of Jewish Studies, 618 S. Michigan Ave. (☎322-1747), near Harrison St. downtown; take El Red Line to Harrison. A diminutive but moving Holocaust Memorial is the only permanent exhibit at this small museum that features Jewish art and history. Open Mar.-Dec. Su-W 10am-5pm, Th 10am-8pm, F 10am-3pm. Artifact center open Su-Th 1-4:30pm. $5; students, seniors, and children $3; free F.

International Museum of Surgical Science, 1524 N. Lake Shore Dr. (☎642-6502), at North Ave. A sculpture of a surgeon holding his wounded patient marks the entrance to this unique museum, a harrowing journey through the history of surgery. Highlights, if they can be so called, include a fascinating collection of gallstones and bladderstones. Open Tu-Su 10am-4pm. $6, students and seniors $3; free Tu.

🎵 ENTERTAINMENT

The free weeklies *Chicago Reader* and *New City*, available in many bars, record stores, and restaurants, list the latest events. The *Reader* reviews all major shows with times and ticket prices. *Chicago* magazine includes theater reviews alongside exhaustive club, music, dance, and opera listings. *The Chicago Tribune* includes an entertainment section every Friday. *Gay Chicago* provides info on social activities as well as other news for the area's gay community.

THEATER

One of the foremost theater centers of North America, Chicago's more than 150 theaters feature everything from blockbuster musicals to off-color parodies. Downtown, the recently formed Theater District centers around State St. and Randolph, and includes the larger venues in the city. Smaller, community-based theaters are scattered throughout Chicago. Most tickets are expensive. Half-price tickets are sold on the day of performance at **Hot Tix Booths**, 108 N. State St., and on the 6th fl. of 700 N. Michigan Ave. Purchases must be made in person. (☎ 977-1755. Open M-F 10am-7pm, Sa 10am-6pm, Su noon-5pm.) **Ticketmaster** (☎ 559-1212) supplies tickets for many theaters; ask about student, senior, and child discounts at all Chicago shows. The "Off-Loop" theaters on the North Side specialize in original productions, with tickets usually under $18.

Steppenwolf Theater, 1650 N. Halsted St. (☎ 335-1888), where Gary Sinise and the eerie John Malkovich got their start and still stop by. Tickets Su-Th $40, F-Sa $45; half-price Tu-F after 5pm, Sa-Su after noon. Box office open Su-M 11am-5pm, Tu-F 11am-8pm, Sa 11am-9pm.

Goodman Theatre, 170 N. Dearborn (☎ 443-3800), which recently moved into its brand new building with two stages, presents consistently solid original works. Tickets around $18-40; half-price after 6pm or after noon for matinees. Box office open M-F 10am-5pm; 10am-8pm show nights, usually Sa-Su.

Shubert Theater, 22 W. Monroe St. (☎ 977-1700), presents big-name Broadway touring productions and occasionally plays host to shows before they hit New York. Tickets $15-70. Box office open M-Sa 10am-6pm.

Victory Gardens Theater, 2257 N. Lincoln Ave. (☎ 773-549-5788), in Lincoln Park. The mainstage presents new works by the company's troupe of playwrights, while three smaller stages host other Chicago performance groups. Tickets $20-33; student rush 1hr. before curtain $15. Box office open M-F 10am-6pm.

Bailiwick Repertory, 1225 W. Belmont Ave. (☎ 773-327-5252), in the Theatre Bldg. A mainstage and experimental studio space. Tickets from $10. Box office open W noon-6pm, Th-Su noon-showtime.

COMEDY

Chicago boasts a plethora of comedy clubs. The most famous, **Second City**, 1616 N. Wells St. (☎ 642-8189), at North Ave. in Old Town, spoofs Chicago life and politics. Second City alums include Bill Murray and late greats John Candy, John Belushi, and Gilda Radner, among others. Most nights a free improv session follows the show. **Second City Etc.**, a group of up-and-coming mainstagers offers more comedy next door at 1608 N. Wells. (☎ 642-6514. Tickets $18. Shows for both M-Th 8:30pm, F-Sa 8 and 11pm, Su 8pm. Box office open daily 10:30am-10pm. Reservations recommended for weekend shows.) Watch comedians compete to bust your gut at **Comedy Sportz**, 2851 N. Halsted. (☎ 773-549-8080. Shows F-Sa 8 and 10:30pm.)

SELF IMPROV-MENT
The Chicago Improv Comedy Scene

On any given evening in the city of Chicago, a small miracle occurs. In theaters all over the city, from the big to the black box, scores of temp workers shed their administrative assistant personas and become actors. Very, very, funny actors. Is there something in the water?

Maybe. Chicago was, and is, the breeding ground for most of the 20th and 21st century's greatest American, (and, let's be fair, Canadian) comics. Theaters like **The Second City** and the **Improv Olympic** have produced alumni like Mike Meyers, John Belushi, Chris Farley, Tina Fey, and Gilda Radner. And judging from the numbers that flock to Chicago for training, they will produce a lot more.

The heart of Chicago comedy is improvisation, more frequently just called "improv." The premise of improv is this: everything done on stage is made up on the spot—no scripts, no whispering in the wings. But from that point on definitions differ. Each Chicago improv theater has a different take on the art, much like the way traditional theaters follow different theories of acting or production. The Second City, Chicago's oldest and perhaps most prestigious theater, uses improvisation to create scenes that will be performed in a scripted revue. The Improv Olympic, founded by the late eccentric genius Del Close, performs fully improvised shows that last about an hour in a kind of improv known as "long form." Both theaters will tickle your funny bone. What's more, once you enter their doors, you're not just walking into any old theater—the improv community in Chicago is simultaneously a grass-roots movement and a national phenomenon.

What happens in Chicago is national because people in the entertainment industry know Chicago makes a good comic. What makes the town even more interesting is that you'll *never* see some of the most talented people outside of Chicago, simply because they love improv so much, and because Chicago—formerly the king of meat-packing—is now the undisputed capital of improv. Sitting down with any Chicago improvisor, or just having a beer in the theater bar, will draw you into a discussion of "long form" versus "short form," of ensembles, of styles, and of who's doing what, and where.

Chicago's comedy scene does not end with the two titans mentioned above. In recent years, other theaters have cropped up to examine the dramatic side of improvisational theater, or simply to serve as an additional performance space for the crowded and eclectic improv scene.

Visiting one of these theaters will allow even the most brazen, fanny-pack laden tourist a glimpse into a genuine slice of Chicago life. The list below will guide you to the best, and the cheapest, show in Chicago. Be careful, though. Many an innocent audience member becomes so inspired that he or she decides to drop everything and move to Chicago to give it a shot. You wouldn't be the first.

To see the best of Chicago's comedy, for the least money, check out the following **free** shows:

Second City, 1616 N. Wells St. (877-778-4704; www.secondcity.com), in Piper's Alley, offers free improv sets after its W-Sa shows. The sets begin roughly 10:30pm W-Th and 1am F-Sa. To see a bona fide Second City review will cost you $17.

Improv Olympic, 3541 N. Clark St. (☎773-880-0199; www.improvolympic.com), is free on W nights. **Carl and the Passions,** a veteran ensemble, is a must-see act. Most other shows are less than $10, and the lineup is constantly changing.

The Playground, 3341 N. Lincoln Ave. (☎773-871-3793), presents a mélange of styles. See the stars of the day-after-tomorrow. Most shows $8, with coupon $5.

Sarah Haskins was a Researcher-Writer for Let's Go: Ireland 2001. She now lives in Chicago, supporting her improv habit by writing commercials.

DANCE, CLASSICAL MUSIC, & OPERA

Ballet, comedy, live theater, and musicals are performed at **Auditorium Theatre,** 50 E. Congress Pkwy. (☎922-2110. Box office open M-F 10am-6pm.) From October through May, the sounds of the **Chicago Symphony Orchestra,** conducted by Daniel Barenboim, resonate throughout **Symphony Center,** 220 S. Michigan Ave. (☎294-3333). **Ballet Chicago** pirouettes throughout theaters in Chicago. (☎251-8838. Tickets $12-45.) The acclaimed **Lyric Opera of Chicago** performs from September through March at the **Civic Opera House,** 20 N. Wacker Dr. (☎332-2244). While other places may suck your wallet dry, the **Grant Park Music Festival** affords a taste of the classical for free. From mid-June through late August, the acclaimed **Grant Park Symphony Orchestra** plays a few free evening concerts per week at the Grant Park **Petrillo Music Shell.** (☎552-8500. Usually W-Su; schedule varies.)

FESTIVALS

The city celebrates summer on a grand scale. The **Taste of Chicago** festival cooks for eight days through July 4th. Seventy restaurants set up booths with endless samples in Grant Park, while crowds chomp to the blast of big name bands. The Taste's fireworks are the city's biggest and most popular. (Free entry, food tickets 50¢ each.) The first week in June, the **Blues Festival** celebrates the city's soulful music. The **Chicago Gospel Festival** hums and hollers in mid-June, and Nashville moves north for the **Country Music Festival** at the end of June. The ¡**Viva Chicago!** Latin music festival steams up in late August, while the **Chicago Jazz Festival** scats over Labor Day weekend. All festivals center at the Grant Park Petrillo Music Shell. The Mayor's Office's **Special Events Hotline** (☎744-3370) has more info on all six free events.

The regionally famous **Ravinia Festival** (☎847-266-5100), in the northern suburb of Highland Park, runs from late June to early September. During the festival's 14-week season, the Chicago Symphony Orchestra, ballet troupes, folk and jazz musicians, and comedians perform. On certain nights, the Orchestra allows students free lawn admission with student ID. (Lawn seats $10-15, other $20-75. Shows 8pm, occasionally 4:30 and 7pm. Call ahead. Round-trip on the METRA costs about $7; the festival runs 1½hr. Charter buses $12.)

SPORTS

The National League's **Cubs** step up to bat at **Wrigley Field,** 1060 W. Addison St., at N. Clark St., one of the few ballparks in America to retain the early grace and intimate feel of the game. (☎773-404-2827; www.cubs.com. $10-22.) The **White Sox,** Chicago's American League team, swing on the South Side at new **Comiskey Park,** 333 W. 35th St. (☎674-1000. $12-24.) The **Bears** (☎888-792-3277) of the NFL will be playing at the University of Illinois at Urbana-Champaign while the **Soldier Field Stadium** undergoes a two-year renovation project. The **Bulls** have won three NBA championships at the **United Center,** 1901 W. Madison, just west of the Loop. (☎943-5800. $30-450.) Hockey's **Blackhawks** skate onto United Center ice when the Bulls aren't hooping it up. (☎455-4500. $25-100.) **Sports Information** (☎976-4242) has up-to-the-minute info on local sports events. For tickets to all games, call **Ticketmaster** (Bulls and Blackhawks ☎559-1212; White Sox ☎831-1769).

◪ NIGHTLIFE

"Sweet home Chicago" takes pride in the innumerable blues performers who have played here. Jazz, folk, reggae, and punk clubs throb all over the **North Side.** The **Bucktown/Wicker Park** area, west of Halsted St. in Northwest Chicago, stays open late with bucking bars and dance clubs. Aspiring pickup artists swing over to **Rush** and

Division St. Full of bars, cafes, and bistros, **Lincoln Park** is frequented by singles and young couples, both gay and straight. The vibrant center of gay culture is between 3000 and 4500 **N. Halsted St.**; many of the more festive and colorful clubs and bars line this area. For more upscale raging, raving, and discoing, there are plenty of clubs near **River North,** in Riverwest, and on Fulton St.

BARS & BLUES JOINTS

■ The Green Mill, 4802 N. Broadway Ave. (☎ 773-878-5552). El Red Line: Lawrence. Founded as a Prohibition-era speakeasy, Mafiosi-in-training can park themselves in Al Capone's old seat. An authentic jazz club, this hot spot draws late-night crowds after other clubs shut down. The cover-free jam sessions on weekends after the main acts finish are reason enough to chill until the wee hours. Cover $5-8. Open daily noon-4am.

The Hideout, 1354 W. Wabansia Ave. (☎ 773-227-4433). El Brown Line: Clybourn and North, West Town. Nestled in a municipal truck parking lot, this creative joint is the insider's indie rock club. Some weekends, the lot fills with special "kid's shows" geared toward families who still like to rock. Arrangements with a top record company have established the club as one of the nation's best places to catch rising alt-country acts. Tu-F cover $5-10. Open M 8pm-2am, Tu-F 4pm-2am, Sa 7pm-3am.

B.L.U.E.S., 2519 N. Halsted St. (☎ 773-528-1012). El to Fullerton, then take the eastbound "Fullerton" bus. Crowded and intimate with unbeatable music. Success here led to the larger **B.L.U.E.S. etc.,** 1124 W. Belmont Ave. (☎ 773-525-8989). El to Belmont, then 3 blocks west on Belmont. *The* place for huge names: Albert King, Bo Diddley, Dr. John, and Wolfman Washington have played here. Live music every night 9pm-1:30am. 21+. Cover for both clubs M-Th $6-8, F-Sa $8-10.

Metro, 3730 N. Clark St. (☎ 773-549-0203), between Addison and Roscoe St., in Wrigleyville. El: Addison. At this outstanding live alternative and pop music venue, local bands are showcased every Su. 18+; occasionally, all ages are welcome. Cover $5-12, more for big bands.

Wild Hare & Singing Armadillo Frog Sanctuary, 3530 N. Clark St. (☎ 773-327-4273), in Wrigleyville. Live Roots Reggae acts perform in front of both dreadlocked hipsters and yuppies. W ladies free. No cover before 9:30pm. Cover W-Su $5-8. Open Su-F 7pm-2am, Sa 7pm-3am.

Checkerboard Lounge, 423 E. 43rd St. (☎ 773-624-3240), at King Dr. The true blues bar experience, the Checkerboard is the most authentic, intimate joint in town. The spirit of this down-and-out neighborhood seeps into the music, but *be careful.* Cover $5-7. Open M-F 1pm-2am.

DANCE CLUBS

■ Berlin, 954 W. Belmont Ave. (☎ 773-327-7711). El Red or Brown line: Belmont, in Lakeview. Anything and everything goes at Berlin, a mainstay of Chicago's gay nightlife scene. Crowds pulsate to house/dance music amid drag contests, disco nights, The Artist Formerly Known As Prince night, and other theme parties. W ladies night. 21+. Cover F-Sa after midnight $5. Open M-F 4pm-4am, Sa 2pm-5am, Su 4pm-2am.

Funky Buddha Lounge, 728 W. Grand Ave. (☎ 666-1695). El Blue Line: Chicago, just west of River North. Extremely trendy, eclectic dance club and lounge where hip-hop and funk blend with crazy leopard, velvet, and Buddha decor. Su gay night. Cover $10-20. Open M-W 10pm-2am, Th-F 9pm-2am, Sa 9pm-3am, Su 6pm-2am.

Smart Bar, 3730 N. Clark St. (☎ 773-549-4140), downstairs from the Metro. Resident DJ spins punk, techno, hip-hop and house. 21+. Cover $5-9; Metro (see above) concertgoers free. Opening times vary (around 10pm); closes around 4am on weekends.

Crobar Night Club, 1543 N. Kingsbury St. (☎413-7000). El Red Line: North and Clybourn. Cavernous, candle-strewn dance club where a young, leather-clad crowd slithers to house beats in cages and on the floor. Gay night Su. Cover $5-20. Open W, F, and Su 10pm-4am; Sa 10pm-5am.

◪ OUTDOOR ACTIVITIES

A string of lakefront parks fringe the area between Chicago proper and Lake Michigan. On sunny afternoons dog walkers, in-line skaters, and skateboarders storm the shore. Close to downtown, the two major parks are Lincoln and Grant. ◪**Lincoln Park** extends across 5 mi. of lakefront on the north side with winding paths, natural groves of trees, and asymmetrical open spaces. The **Lincoln Park Zoo** is usually filled with children fascinated by the zoo's caged gorillas and lions. (Open daily 10am-5pm; in summer M-F 10am-5pm, Sa-Su 10am-7pm. Free.) Next door, the **Lincoln Park Conservatory** provides a veritable glass palace of plants from varied ecosystems. (☎742-7736. Open daily 9am-5pm. Free.)

Grant Park, covering 14 lakefront blocks east of Michigan Ave., follows the 19th-century French park style: symmetrical and ordered with corners, a fountain, and wide promenades. The Grant Park Concert Society hosts free summer concerts in the **Petrillo Music Shell,** 520 S. Michigan Ave. (☎742-4763). Colored lights illuminate **Buckingham Fountain** from 9-11pm. On the north side, Lake Michigan lures swimmers and sun-bathers to **Lincoln Park Beach** and **Oak St. Beach.** Beware, though: the rock ledges are restricted areas, and swimming from them is illegal. Although the beaches are patrolled 9am-9:30pm, they can be unsafe after dark. The **Chicago Parks District** (☎747-7529) has further info.

Starting from the Hyde Park area in the south, **Lake Shore Drive** offers sparkling views of Lake Michigan all the way past the city and one of the best views of the downtown skyline. At its end, Lake Shore becomes **Sheridan Rd.,** which twists and turns its way through the picturesque northern suburbs. Just north of Chicago is **Evanston,** a lively, affluent college town (home to **Northwestern University**) with an array of parks and nightclubs. Ten minutes farther north is upscale **Wilmette,** home to the ornate and striking **Baha'i House of Worship,** 100 Linden Ave., at Sheridan Rd. This architectual wonder is topped by a stunning nine-sided dome. (☎847-853-2300. Open June-Sept. daily 10am-10pm; Oct.-May 10am-5pm. Services M-Sa 12:15pm, Su 1:15pm).

The ◪**Indiana Dunes State Park** and **National Lakeshore** lie 45min. east of Chicago on I-90. The State Park's gorgeous dune beaches on Lake Michigan provide hikes through dunes, woods, and marshes. The beaches are packed on summer weekends, when Chicagoans flee the frantic pace of the city for swimming and sunning. Info about the State Park is available at their office, 1600 N. 25 E. in Chesterton, IN (☎219-926-1952). Obtain Lakeshore details at their **Visitors Center,** 1100 N. Mineral Springs Rd., in Porter, IN (☎219-926-7561).

SPRINGFIELD   ☎217

Springfield, "the town that Lincoln loved," owes much to its most distinguished former resident. A hotbed of political activity during the increasingly fractured antebellum years, the small town attracted the attention of the entire nation when it hosted the heated Lincoln-Douglass debates of 1858. Although Springfield has declined from national prominence into near obscurity, the town welcomes tourists to learn everything there is to know about Honest Abe.

🛮 PRACTICAL INFORMATION. Amtrak, (☎753-2013; station open daily 6am-9:30pm) at 3rd and Washington St., near downtown, runs trains to Chicago (3½hr., 3 per day, $21-44) and St. Louis (2hr., 3 per day, $19-31). **Greyhound,** 2351 S. Dirksen Pkwy. (☎800-231-2222; depot open M-F 8am-noon and 2-8pm, Sa-Su 8am-noon and 2-4pm), on the eastern edge of town, rolls to: Bloomington (1hr., 1 per day, $57); Chicago (5hr., 6 per day, $40); Indianapolis (7hr., 2 per day, $49); and St. Louis (2hr., 4 per day, $26). For local transportation, try **Springfield Mass Transit District,** 928 S. 9th St. Pick up maps at transit headquarters, most banks, or the Illinois State Museum. (☎522-5531. Buses operate M-Sa 6am-6pm. 75¢, seniors 35¢; transfers free.) The **downtown trolley** system is designed to take tourists to eight designated places of historic interest. (☎528-4100. Trolleys run W-Su 9am-4pm; call ahead to confirm hours. Hop-on/off $10, seniors $9, ages 5-12 $5; circuit $5.) **Taxis: Lincoln Yellow Cab,** ☎523-4545. **Visitors info: Springfield Convention and Visitors Bureau,** 109 N. 7th St. (☎789-2360 or 800-545-7300. Open M-F 8am-5pm.) **Internet access: Lincoln Public Library,** 326 S. 7th St. (☎753-4900. Open June-Aug. M-Th 9am-9pm, F 9am-6pm, Sa 9am-5pm; Sept.-May M-Th 9am-9pm, F 9am-6pm, Su noon-5pm.) **Post Office:** 411 E. Monroe, at Wheeler St. (☎788-7470. Open M-F 8am-4:30pm.) **ZIP code:** 62701. **Area code:** 217.

🛏🍴 ACCOMMODATIONS & FOOD. Bus service to the cheap lodgings off I-55 and U.S. 36 on Dirksen Pkwy. is limited. Downtown hotels may be booked solid on weekdays when the legislature is in session, but ask the Visitors Center about weekend packages. Rooms should be reserved early for holiday weekends and the **State Fair** in mid-August. For a comfortable stay without a hefty price, head to the **Pear Tree Inn ❸,** 3190 S. Dirksen Pkwy. (☎529-9100. Breakfast included. Cable TV, free local calls. Rooms from $46.) **Mister Lincoln's Campground ❶,** 3045 Stanton Ave., off Stevenson Dr., has free showers. Take bus #10. (☎529-8206. Reception in summer daily 8am-8pm; in winter 8am-6pm. Sites $16, with hookup $21. Cabins with A/C $25.) Interesting cuisine is sparse in Springfield. Still, you can get some kicks on historic Rte. 66 at the **Cozy Drive-In ❶,** 2935 S. 6th St., a family-owned diner devoted to roadside memorabilia and great greasy food. (☎525-1992. Cozy Dog $1.50. Open M-Sa 8am-8pm.) Let's Go to the well-named **Andiamo ❷,** 206 S. 6th St., near the Old State Capitol, a classy and versatile cafe serving both daily lunch specials ($5) and authentic Italian dinners. (☎523-3262. Open M-Sa 11am-10pm.)

🌅 SIGHTS. Springfield zealously recreates Lincoln's life. Walking from sight to sight allows you to retrace the steps of the monumental man himself. Happily, many Lincoln sights are free. (Info line ☎800-545-7300.) The **Lincoln Home Visitors Center,** 426 S. 7th St., screens a 19min. film on "Mr. Lincoln's Springfield" and doles out free tickets to see the **Lincoln Home,** at 8th and Jackson St. The only house Abe ever owned, and Springfield's main draw, the National Historic Site sits in a restored 19th-century neighborhood complete with hoops-playing girls and rickety boardwalks. (☎492-4241. Open Apr.-Sept. daily 8am-6pm. 10min. tours every 5-10min. from the front of the house. Arrive early to avoid the crowds.) The magnificent limestone **Old State Capitol,** where Lincoln delivered his stirring and prophetic "House Divided" speech in 1858, also witnessed the epic Lincoln-Douglass debates. (☎785-7961. Open Mar.-Oct. daily 9am-5pm, Nov.-Feb. 9am-4pm. Last tour 1hr. before closing. Donation suggested.) Lincoln, his wife Mary Todd, and three of their sons rest at the massive **Lincoln Tomb,** 1500 Monument Ave., at Oak Ridge Cemetery. (☎782-2717. Open Mar.-Oct. daily 9am-5pm, Nov.-Feb. 9am-4pm.)

For a break from Lincolnland walk, to the **🏠Dana-Thomas House,** 301 E. Lawrence Ave., six blocks south of the Old State Capitol. Built in 1902, the stunning and well-preserved home was one of Frank Lloyd Wright's early experiments in Prairie Style and still features Wright's original fixtures. Tour guides give an in-depth explanation of the house and of the eccentric millionaire who lived there. (☎782-6776. Open W-Su 9am-4pm. 1hr. tours every 15-20min. Suggested donation $3.) Rte. 66, that fabled American highway of yesteryear, is remembered in Springfield by **Shea's**, 2075 Peoria Rd., a truck shop with masses of memorabilia, including gas pumps, signs, and license plates. (☎522-0475. Open Tu-F 7am-4pm, Sa 7am-noon.)

WISCONSIN

Hospitality is served up with every beer and every piece of Wisconsin cheddar sold in the Great Lakes' most wholesome party state. Deer, rabbits, and birds make themselves at home in the thick woods of Wisconsin's extensive park system, while the state's favorite animal—the cow—grazes near highways. Along the shoreline, fishermen haul in fresh perch, and on rolling hills farmers grow barley for beer. Visitors to "America's Dairyland" encounter cheese-filled country stores en route to the ocean-like vistas of Door County, as well as the ethnic *fêtes* (not to mention other, less refined beer bashes) of Madison and Milwaukee.

◪ PRACTICAL INFORMATION

Capital: Madison.

Visitor Info: Division of Tourism, 123 W. Washington St., P.O. Box 7976, Madison 53707 (☎608-266-2161 or 800-432-8747; www.tourism.state.wi.us).

Postal Abbreviation: WI. **Sales Tax:** 5-5.5%, depending on county.

MILWAUKEE   ☎414

Home to beer and countless festivals, Milwaukee is a city with a reputation for *gemütlichkeit* (hospitality). Ethnic communities take turns throwing rollicking, city-wide parties each summer weekend, from the traditional Oktoberfest to the brightly colored Asian Moon festival. When the weather turns cold, the city celebrates with the International Arts Festival Milwaukee, when galleries and museums extend their hours in honor of Milwaukee's extensive art community. Milwaukee's 1500 bars and taverns fuel the revelry with as much beer as anyone could ever need—or stomach. Aside from merrymaking, the city boasts top-notch museums, German-inspired architecture, and a long expanse of scenic lakeshore.

▛ TRANSPORTATION

Airport: General Mitchell International Airport, 5300 S. Howell Ave. (☎747-5300). Take bus #80 from 6th St. downtown (30min.). **Limousine Service,** ☎769-9100 or 800-236-5450. 24hr. pickup and dropoff from most downtown hotels. $10, round-trip $18. Reservations required.

Trains: Amtrak, 433 W. St. Paul Ave. (☎271-0840), at 5th St. downtown. In a fairly safe area, but less so at night. To **Chicago** (1½hr., 6 per day, $20) and **St. Paul** (6½hr., 1 per day, $45-98). Open M-Sa 5:30am-10pm, Su 7am-10pm.

Buses: Greyhound, 606 N. 7th St. (☎272-2156), off W. Michigan St., 3 blocks from the train station. To **Chicago** (2-3hr., 16 per day, $14) and **Minneapolis** (7-9hr., 6 per day, $49). Station open 24hr.; office open daily 6:30am-11:30pm. **Coach USA Milwaukee** (☎262-544-6503), in the same terminal, covers southeastern Wisconsin. **Badger Bus,** 635 N. James Lovell St. (☎276-7490 or 608-255-1511), across the street, burrows to **Madison** (1½hr., 6 per day, $10). Open daily 6:30am-10pm. *Be cautious at night.*

Public Transit: Milwaukee County Transit System, 1942 N. 17th St. (☎344-6711). Efficient metro area service. Most lines run 5am-12:30am. $1.50, seniors and children 75¢; weekly pass $11. Fare includes a transfer that can be used 1-2 hrs. after first ride. Free maps at the library, hotels, or at Grand Ave. Mall. Call for schedules. The **Trolley** (☎344-6711) runs downtown, to festivals and Brewers games. 50¢, seniors 25¢. Open June-Aug. M-Th 6:30am-10pm, F 6:30am-midnight, Sa 10am-midnight, Su 10am-6pm; Sept.-May M-Th 6:30am-6:30pm, F 6:30am-midnight, Sa 10am-midnight.

Taxis: Veteran, ☎291-8080. **Yellow Taxi,** ☎271-6630.

✈ ⑦ ORIENTATION & PRACTICAL INFORMATION

Most of Milwaukee's action is centered on the east side of downtown, which lies between **Lake Michigan** and **10th St.** Address numbers increase north and south from **Wisconsin Ave.,** the center of east-west travel. Most north-south streets are numbered, increasing from Lake Michigan toward the west. The **interstate system** forms a loop around Milwaukee: **I-43 S** runs to Beloit; **I-43 N** runs to Green Bay; **I-94 E** is a straight shot to Chicago; **I-94 W** goes to Madison and then Minneapolis/St. Paul; **I-794** cuts through the heart of downtown Milwaukee; and **I-894** (the downtown bypass) connects with the airport.

Visitor Info: Greater Milwaukee Convention and Visitors Bureau, 400 W. Wisconsin Ave. (☎273-7222 or 800-554-1448), located in the Midwest Express Center lobby. Open year-round M-F 9am-5pm; summer also Sa 9am-2pm, Su 11am-3pm.

Hotlines: Crisis Intervention, ☎257-7222. **Rape Crisis Line,** ☎542-3828. Both operate 24hr. **Gay People's Union Hotline,** ☎562-7010. Operates daily 7-10pm.

Post Office: 345 W. St. Paul Ave. (☎270-2308), south along 4th Ave. from downtown, by the Amtrak station. Open M-F 7:30am-8pm. **ZIP code:** 53201. **Area code:** 414.

🏠 ACCOMMODATIONS

Downtown lodging options tend to be expensive; travelers with cars should head out to the city's two hostels. **Bed and Breakfast of Milwaukee** (☎277-8066) finds rooms in picturesque B&Bs from $55 around the area.

Milwaukee Summer Hostel (HI), 1530 W. Wisconsin Ave. (☎288-1685), in McCormick Hall on Marquette University's campus. Take bus #10 or 30 down Wisconsin to 16th St. This hostel offers small, sparsely furnished rooms, but the central location and low prices make it a good summer option. Laundry facilities, free Internet access, and parking nearby (Su-Th $3.50, F-Sa free). Check-in 5-10pm, check-out 8-11am. Open June to mid-Aug. Dorm beds $17, nonmembers $20. Private rooms $34/40. ●

University of Wisconsin at Milwaukee (UWM), Sandburg Hall, 3400 N. Maryland Ave. (☎229-4065 or 299-6123). Take bus #30 north to Hartford St. Close to East Side restaurants and bars, the UWM sports spotless, dorm suites, divided into singles and doubles. Laundry facilities, cafeteria, and free local calls. 2-day advance reservations required. Open June to mid-Aug. Singles with shared bath $36; doubles $60. ❷

Wellspring Hostel (HI-AYH), 4382 Hickory Rd. (☎262-675-6755), in Newburg. Take I-43 N to Rte. 33 W to Newburg and exit on Main St.; Hickory Rd. intersects Newburg's Main St. just northwest of the Milwaukee River. The idyllic setting, far from downtown on a riverside farm, is worth the 45min. drive for those looking to get back to nature. Well-kept with 10 beds, kitchen, and nature trails. Linens $1 each. Office open daily 8am-8pm. Dorms $15. ● **Wellspring B&B,** in the same location, provides a pricier option. Reservations required. Private room $50. ❸

Inn Towne Hotel, 710 N. Old Third St. (☎224-8400 or 800-528-1234), downtown. This centrally located Best Western offers spacious rooms with complimentary continental breakfast, exercise facilities, cable TV, and A/C. A new restaurant and bar adds a lively social atmosphere. Parking $10 per day. Rooms from $79. ❹

🅰 FOOD

From *wurst* to *bier*, Milwaukee is best known for its German traditions. Restaurants are scattered along nearly every street in the city, particularly downtown, where most adopt continental attitudes and hefty prices to match their 100 years of experience. In addition to its German influences, the city takes advantage of its location and diverse population. Nearby Lake Michigan provides the main ingredient to a local favorite called the **Friday night fish fry.** Polish and Serbian influences dominate the **South Side,** and good Mexican food prevails in **Walker's Point,** at National and 5th St. **East Side** eateries are cosmopolitan and quirky, with a mix of ethnic flavors. Downtown, the Riverwalk project has revitalized the **Water St. Entertainment District,** which boasts hot new restaurants for a range of palates. On the north end of the Riverwalk, **Old World Third St.** is home to the city's best brew-pubs. For those who prefer to skip straight to the sweet stuff, the Dairy State's special treat—extra-creamy ice cream known as **frozen custard**—is the way to go.

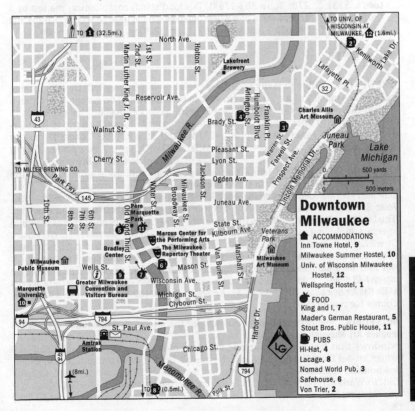

Downtown Milwaukee

🅰 ACCOMMODATIONS
Inn Towne Hotel, **9**
Milwaukee Summer Hostel, **10**
Univ. of Wisconsin Milwaukee Hostel, **12**
Wellspring Hostel, **1**

🅵 FOOD
King and I, **7**
Mader's German Restaurant, **5**
Stout Bros. Public House, **11**

🅿 PUBS
Hi-Hat, **4**
Lacage, **8**
Nomad World Pub, **3**
Safehouse, **6**
Von Trier, **2**

GREAT LAKES

Mader's German Restaurant, 1037 N. Old World Third St. (☎271-3377), downtown. Mader's is a local favorite with *schnitzels* and *schaumtorte* well worth the steep prices. Suits of armor, steins, and guns along the halls conjure up images of old Bavaria. Entrees from $12. Open M-Th 11:30am-9pm, F-Sa 11:30am-10pm, Su 10:30am-9pm. Reservations recommended. ❹

La Fuente, 734 S. 5th St. (☎271-8595), on the South Side. Locals flock here for authentic Mexican food and the best margaritas in town. Murals and a patio add to the laid-back atmosphere. Lunches from $4, entrees $6-11. Open daily 10am-10pm. ❷

Stout Bros. Public House, 777 N. Water St. (☎273-2337), downtown. One of Milwaukee's many brew pubs, this restaurant serves up hearty sandwiches ($6-8) and homemade beers in a historic building. Try "The Yank," their flagship ale ($3.25). Open M 11am-10pm, Tu-Sa 11am-11pm, Su 11am-3pm. ❷

King and I, 823 N. 2nd St. (☎276-4181). The bountiful lunch buffet ($7) is a favorite at this very authentic Thai place. Entrees $10-15. Open M-F 11:30am-10pm, Sa 5-11pm, Su 4-9pm. ❸

Casablanca, 730 W. Mitchell St. (☎383-2363), on the South Side. Vegetarians delight in the falafel and tabouli at the unbeatable all-you-can-eat lunch buffet ($5) in this serene Middle Eastern storefront. *Be careful in surrounding areas after dark.* Entrees $5-10. Lunch buffet Tu-F 11am-3:30pm. Open Tu-Sa 11am-9pm, Su noon-6pm. ❷

Leon's, 3131 S. 27th St. (☎383-1784). This food stand, conspicuously marked by a huge neon sign, scoops some of the best frozen custard in town (2 scoops, $1.25). Hot dogs $1.10. Open Su-Th 11am-midnight, F 11am-12:30am, Sa 11am-1am. ❶

◉ SIGHTS

BREWERIES. Although many of Milwaukee's breweries have left, the city's name still evokes images of a cold one. No visit to the city would be complete without a look at the yeast in action. The ▨**Miller Brewery,** a corporate giant that produces 43 million barrels of beer annually, leads a free 1hr. tour followed by a trip to the biergarten for three generous samples. *(4251 W. State St. ☎931-2337. Under 18 must be accompanied by an adult. ID required. Open M-Sa 10:30am-3:30pm; 2 tours per hr., 3 during busy days; call for winter schedule.)* For a taste of Milwaukee's microbreweries, take a three-hour **Riverwalk Boat Tour.** The tour's pontoon boat, appropriately titled the *Brew City Queen,* travels to three breweries along the Milwaukee River. *(Tours start from Père Marquette Park on Old World Third St. between State and Kilbourn. ☎283-9999. Tours Sa-Su, call for times. $12.)* Some microbreweries offer their own tours as well. The **Lakefront Brewery** produces five popular year-round beers and several seasonal specials, including pumpkin beer and cherry lager. *(1872 N. Commerce St., off Pleasant St. ☎372-8800. Tours F 5:30pm; Sa 1:30, 2:30, and 3:30pm. $3 for plastic cup, $5 for souvenir mug.)* One of the state's most renowned microbreweries, **Sprecher Brewing,** doles out four beer samples following a one-hour tour. *(701 W. Glendale, 5 mi. north of the city on I-43, then east on Port Washington St. ☎964-2739. Tours F-Sa; Jun.-Aug. additional tours M-Th. Call for tour times. $2, under 21 $1. Reservations required.)* Most breweries offer discounts for non-drinkers.

MUSEUMS. Several excellent museums dot the shores of Milwaukee. The ▨**Milwaukee Art Museum** is a sculpture in and of itself with its cylindrical elevators and windows that frame a spectacular view of Lake Michigan. Moveable, sail-like wings jut out from the building, which controls the light and temperature in galleries housing Haitian folk art, 19th-century German art, and American works from folk to Warhol. *(700 N. Art Museum Dr., on the lakefront downtown. ☎224-3200. Open Tu-W and Sa 10am-5pm; Th noon-9pm; F 10am-9pm. $6, students and seniors $4, under 12 free.)*

The intimate **Charles Allis Art Museum** combines East Asian artifacts with Classical antiques in a stately, refurbished 1910 mansion. *(1801 N. Prospect Ave. at E. Royal Pl., 1 block north of Brady. Take bus #30, 31, or River Rte. Trolley. ☎278-8295. Open W 1-9pm, Th-Su 1-5pm. $5, students and seniors $3, children free.)* Visitors can wander through the streets of Old Milwaukee or venture into a replica of a Costa Rican rainforest at the **Milwaukee Public Museum.** *(800 W. Wells St., at N. 8th St. ☎278-2732. Open M-Sa 9:30am-8:30pm, Su 10:30am-4pm. $6.75, children $5.75, under 3 free. Free M. IMAX Theater $4. Parking available.)*

PARKS. Better known as "The Domes," the **Mitchell Park Horticultural Conservatory** recreates a desert and a rainforest and mounts seasonal floral displays in a series of seven-story conical glass greenhouses. *(524 S. Layton Ave., at 27th St. Take bus #10 west to 27th St., then #27 south to Layton. ☎649-9830. Open daily 9am-5pm. $4, seniors and ages 6-17 $2.50, under 6 free.)* The **Boerner Botanical Gardens** cultivate billions of gorgeous blossoms and host open-air concerts on Thursday nights. *(5879 S. 92nd St., in Whitnall Park between Grange and Rawsen St. ☎425-1130. Open mid-Apr. to Oct. daily 8am-7pm. Parking $3.50.)* For an escape from the city, visit one of the many county parks along the waterfront (parks are marked on most maps of the city).

OTHER SIGHTS. A road warrior's nirvana, locally headquartered **Harley-Davidson** gives 1hr. tours of its engine plant that will enthrall the aficionado. *(11700 W. Capitol Dr. ☎342-4680. Tours June-Aug. M-F 9:30, 11am, 1pm; Sept.-Dec. M, W, and F 9:30, 11am, and 1pm. Call ahead; the plant sometimes shuts down in summer. Reservations required for groups larger than 5. Closed shoes must be worn.)* For a brush with Olympic glory, amateur ice skaters should head to daily open skates at the **Pettit National Ice Center.** Home to the US Speedskating team, the Pettit includes several hockey and figure-skating rinks. *(500 S. 84th St., at I-94, next to the state fairgrounds. ☎266-0100. Call for open skating schedules. $5, seniors and children $4. Skate rental $2.50.)*

🎵 ENTERTAINMENT

Music comes in almost as many varieties as beer in Milwaukee. The modern **Marcus Center for the Performing Arts,** 929 N. Water St., across the Milwaukee River from Père Marquette Park, is the area's major arts venue. Throughout the summer the center's Peck Pavilion hosts **Rainbow Summer,** a series of free lunchtime concerts ranging from country to jazz to new age, performed by both professional and local bands (☎273-7121. Concerts M-F noon-1:15pm. Call for additional evening performances). The music moves indoors to the center during the winter with the **Milwaukee Symphony Orchestra,** the **Milwaukee Ballet,** and the **Florentine Opera Company.** (☎273-7121. Symphony $17-52, ballet $13-62, opera $15-80. Ballet and symphony offer half-price student and senior rush tickets.) From September through May the **Milwaukee Repertory Theater,** 108 East Wells St., stages innovative shows alongside the classics. (☎224-1761. $8-30; half-price student and senior rush tickets available 30min. before shows.)

The **Milwaukee Brewers** baseball team steps up to bat under the retractable ceiling of **Miller Park,** at the interchange of I-94 and Rte. 41 (☎902-4000 or 800-933-7890; tours available, call for schedule), while the **Milwaukee Bucks** hoop it up at the **Bradley Center,** 1001 N. 4th St., downtown (☎227-0500).

🎪 FESTIVALS

Summertime livens up Milwaukee's scene with countless free festivals and live music events. On any given night, a free concert is happening; call the **Visitors Bureau** (☎273-7222) to find out where. On Thursdays in summer, **Cathedral Park Jazz** (☎272-0993) jams for free in **Cathedral Square Park,** at N. Jackson St. between

Wells and Kilbourn St. In Père Marquette Park, between State and Kilbourn St., **River Flicks** (☎270-3560) screens free movies at dusk Thursdays in August.

Locals line the streets in mid-July for ⬛**The Great Circus Parade** (☎608-356-8341), a recreation of turn-of-the-century processions, complete with trained animals, daredevils, costumed performers, and 65 original wagons. Thirteen soundstages fill with big name musicians for 11 days during **Summerfest**, the largest and most lavish of Milwaukee's festivals. Daily life halts as a potpourri of big-name musical acts, culinary specialties, and an arts and crafts bazaar take over. (☎273-3378 or 800-273-3378. Tickets M-Th $9, F-Su $10.) In early August, the **Wisconsin State Fair** rolls into the fairgrounds toting 12 stages along with exhibits, contests, rides, fireworks, and a pie-baking contest. (☎266-7000 or 800-884-3247. $7, seniors $5, ages 7-11 $3.) Ethnic festivals also abound during festival season. The most popular are: **Polish Fest** (☎529-2140) and **Asian Moon** (☎821-9829), both in mid-June; **Festa Italiana** (☎223-2193) in mid-July; **Bastille Days** (☎271-7400) around Bastille Day (July 14); **German Fest** (☎464-9444) in late July; **Irish Fest** (☎476-3378) in mid-August; **Mexican Fiesta** (☎383-7066) in late August; **Indian Summer Fest** (☎774-7119) in early September; and **Arabian Fest** (☎384-4441) in mid-September. (Most festivals $7, under 12 free; some free plus price of food.) Pick up a copy of the free weekly *Downtown Edition* or call ☎800-554-1448 for more information on festivals.

🎵 NIGHTLIFE

Milwaukee never lacks something to do after sundown. The downtown business district becomes desolate at night, but the area along **Water St.** between Juneau and Highland Ave. offers hip, lively bars and clubs. Nightspots that draw a college crowd cluster around the intersection of **North Ave.** and **N. Farwell St.**, near the UW campus. Running east-west between Farwell St. and the Milwaukee River, **Brady St.** is lined with the hottest bars and coffeehouses. **S. 2nd St.** is a fairgrounds for eclectic, ultra-trendy nightclubs, including dance clubs, sports bars, lounges, and the city's best gay bars.

⬛ Safehouse, 779 N. Front St. (☎271-2007), across from the Pabst Theater downtown. A brass plate labeled "International Exports, Ltd." welcomes guests to this bizarre world of spy hideouts, secret passwords, and drinks with names like "The Under Cover Girl." A briefing with "Moneypenny" in the foyer is just the beginning of the intrigue. Draft beer $2.75; 24 oz. specialty drinks from $5. Cover $1-3. Open M-Th 11:30am-1:30am, F-Sa 11:30am-2am, Su 4pm-midnight.

Von Trier, 2235 N. Farwell Ave. (☎272-1775), at North Ave. Flower boxes and a brick facade invite customers into this German-style biergarten. The intricate wood carvings, big oak bar, and stein-lined walls create a laid-back atmosphere for enjoying some serious beer. A house special is German beer topped with German gin ($5). Open Su-Th 4pm-2am, F-Sa 4pm-2:30am.

Hi-Hat, 1701 Arlington St. (☎225-9330), at Brady St. Jazz be-bops from speakers above the cavernous, candlelit bar. The restaurant above occasionally plays host to live music. The Su brunch is a local favorite. M-W swing and jazz. Open daily 4pm-2am, Su brunch 10am-3pm.

Nomad World Pub, 1401 E. Brady St. (☎224-8111), down the street from Hi-Hat. The TV here features two programs: Packers games and cricket. Daily, imported specials and a new menu every month keep the barflies content before and after the games. Open M-Th 1pm-2am, F 1pm-2:30am, Sa noon-2:30am, Su noon-2am.

Lacage, 801 S. 2nd Ave. (☎383-8330). The largest pub in town attracts a mostly twenty- and thirty-something gay clientele. Lacage considers themselves "straight-friendly," and crowds are often mixed due to the welcoming atmosphere. DJs spin to keep 2 large floors grooving. F-Sa the bar splits: dancing on one side and drag shows on the other. Cover W $2, Th $3, F-Sa $5. Open Su-Th 9pm-2am, F-Sa 9pm-2:30am.

MADISON ☎608

Locals in Madison refer to their city as "The Isthmus." For those who have forgotten their seventh-grade geography, that's a narrow strip of land that connects two larger landmasses. In other words, it's a rather awkward place to build a city. As a result, the Capitol and the University of Wisconsin-Madison share very close living quarters. The odd coupling, though, has proven fruitful as Madison's peculiar flavor is a fine blend of the mature stateliness and youthful vigor.

✦ ORIENTATION

Madison's main attractions are centered around the Capitol and the University of Wisconsin-Madison. **State St.**, which is reserved for pedestrians, bikers, and buses, connects the two and serves as the city's hub for eclectic food, shops, and nightlife. The northeast and southwest ends of the isthmus are joined by **Washington Ave./US 151,** the city's main thoroughfare, and house malls, chain restaurants, and chain motels. **I-90** and **I-94** are joined through the city, but separate on either side of it. I-94 E goes to Milwaukee, then Chicago; I-94 W goes to Minneapolis/St. Paul; I-90 E goes direct to Chicago through Rockford, IL; I-90 W goes to Albert Lea, MN.

◪ PRACTICAL INFORMATION

Greyhound, 2 S. Bedford St. (☎257-3050), has buses to **Chicago** (3-4hr.; 8 per day; M-Th $21, F-Su $23) and **Minneapolis** (5-6hr.; 6 per day; M-Th $37, F-Su $39). **Badger Bus** (☎255-6771) departs to **Milwaukee** from the same address throughout the day. **Madison Metro Transit System,** 1101 E. Washington Ave. (☎266-4466), serves downtown, campus, and environs ($1.50). **Greater Madison Convention and Visitors Bureau:** 615 E. Washington Ave. (☎255-2537 or 800-373-6376; open M-F 8am-5pm). **Internet access: Madison Public Library,** 201 W. Mifflin St. (☎266-6300; open M-W 8:30am-9pm, Th-F 8:30am-6pm, Sa 9am-5pm; Oct.-Apr. also open Su 1-5pm). **Taxi: Union Cab,** (☎242-2000). **Post Office:** 3902 Milwaukee St., at Rte. 51 (☎246-1228; open M-F 8am-6pm, Sa 9am-2pm). **ZIP code:** 53714. **Area code:** 608.

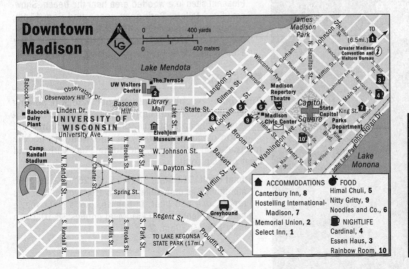

Downtown Madison

Lake Mendota

James Madison Park

Greater Madison Convention and Visitors Bureau

UW Visitors Center

The Terrace

Observatory Hill Dr.

Bascom Hill

Library Mall

State St.

Madison Repertory Theatre

Capitol

State Capitol

King St.

State Capitol Square

Babcock Dairy Plant

Linden Dr.

UNIVERSITY OF WISCONSIN

University Ave.

Madison Civic Center

Elvehjem Museum of Art

Parks Department

Camp Randall Stadium

W. Johnson St.

W. Dayton St.

Lake Monona

Spring St.

W. Mifflin St.

Regent St.

Greyhound

TO LAKE KEGONSA STATE PARK (17mi.)

⌂ ACCOMMODATIONS	🍴 FOOD
Canterbury Inn, 8	Himal Chuli, 5
Hostelling International-Madison, 7	Nitty Gritty, 9
Memorial Union, 2	Noodles and Co., 6
Select Inn, 1	🍸 NIGHTLIFE
	Cardinal, 4
	Essen Haus, 3
	Rainbow Room, 10

GREAT LAKES

THE BIG SPLURGE

CANTERBURY INN

Well-read travelers should make a pilgrimage to the **Canterbury Inn**, with its six lavish rooms named for characters from Chaucer's *Canterbury Tales*. Lounge in front of the medieval murals in your room, or head over to the Canterbury Bookstore and Café, located on the first floor, to peruse the shelves and sip coffee. If you don't share the Wife of Bath's aversion to bathing, take a soak in the whirlpool tubs found in each suite. Alas and Alack! In the absence of the Miller's relentless punning, modern day travelers will have to entertain themselves with TV, VCR, and CD player. Start the day off in style with the fresh baked goods served for breakfast, then make merry with wine and cheese each afternoon. *(315 W. Gorham St., at State St. ☎ 258-8899; www.madison-canterbury.com. Su-Th $130-245, F-Sa $185-315. ❺)*

ACCOMMODATIONS

For motels stretching along Washington Ave. (U.S. 151) near the intersection with I-90, rooms start at $40 per weeknight and rise dramatically on weekends. From the Capitol, bus routes #6 and 7 shuttle the 5 mi. between the Washington Ave. motels and downtown. Prices steepen downtown, starting around $60.

Hostelling International—Madison (HI-AYH), 141 S. Butler St. (☎441-0144; www.madisonhostel.org), near State St. This new, ideally located hostel is a good bet for social, nightlife-loving travelers. Cheerful, homey setting and spotless rooms. 31 beds, kitchen, laundry, Internet access. Office hours 7:45am-10pm. $16, nonmembers $19; private rooms $35/$38. ❶

Memorial Union, 800 Langdon St. (☎262-1583), on the UW campus. Large, elegant rooms with excellent lake and city views. Cable TV, A/C, and free parking. Call ahead; the 6 rooms fill up—especially on football weekends—up to a year in advance. No-frills **college cafeterias** here dole out the quickest, cheapest food in town, with meals from $5-8. Rooms from $62. ❸

Select Inn, 4845 Hayes Rd. (☎249-1815), near the junction of I-94 and U.S. 151. Large rooms with cable TV, A/C, and whirlpool. Continental breakfast included. Summer singles from $46; doubles from $57. Winter $39/$46. ❸

Lake Kegonsa State Park, 2405 Door Creek Rd. (☎873-9695), 20min. south on I-90 in Stoughton. Pleasant sites in a wooded area near the beach. Showers, flush toilets. Park open year-round 6am-11pm; campground open May 1-Oct. 31. Sites $9, WI residents $7; $11/$9 on weekends. Parking permits $10/ $5 per day. ❶

FOOD

Fine dining establishments pepper Madison, spicing up the university and Capitol areas. **State St.** hosts a variety of cheap restaurants, including chains and Madison originals; at its west end, vendors peddle international delicacies, including Thai, Cuban, and East African treats.

Himal Chuli, 318 State St. (☎251-9225). This State St. storefront stirs up excellent Nepalese favorites, such as *tarkari, dal,* and *bhat.* In English, that's great veggie meals and lentil soup ($3). Meat entrees $8-10. Open daily 11am-9:30pm. ❸

Nitty Gritty, 223 N. Frances St. (☎251-2521), at Johnston St. A popular college hangout and the self-proclaimed official birthday bar of the city, this laid-back grill celebrates a gazillion birthdays each day with balloons and free beer (for the birthday person only). Just don't wear your birthday suit. Entrees $3-9. Open M-Th 11am-2am, F-Sa 11am-2:30am, Su 5pm-midnight. ❷

Noodles and Co., 232 State St. (☎257-6393), at Johnson St. This corner shop features a global array of tasty noodle dishes. Generous portions of pan-fried noodles and *pad thai* share counter space with Stroganoff and Wisconsin-style macaroni and cheese. Entrees $3-6. Open M-Th 11am-9pm, F-Sa 11am-10pm, Su noon-8pm. ❶

🅖 SIGHTS

INSIDE MADISON

With its double nature as a seat of government and home to a thriving college scene, there's lots to see on the isthmus. The imposing, Roman Renaissance-style **State Capitol,** in Capitol Square at the center of downtown, boasts beautiful ceiling frescoes and mosaics. (☎266-0382. Open daily 6am-8pm. Free tours from the ground fl. info desk M-F on the hr. 9-11am and 1-4pm, Sa 9-11am and 1-3pm, Su 1-3pm.) Every Saturday and Wednesday morning from late April to early November, visitors swarm the Capitol grounds for the **Farmers Market,** an attraction full of farmers selling their crops and Madison radicals advocating animal rights. (☎800-373-6376. W 8:30am-1:30pm, Sa 6am-2pm.) The **University of Wisconsin–Madison (UW)** itself has a few noteworthy museums. One of the state's most acclaimed art museums, the **Elvehjem Museum of Art** (*EL-vee-hem*) boasts an astounding collection of Ancient Greek coins and vases, several galleries of American and European painting, and decorative arts dating from 2300 BC. (800 University Ave. ☎263-2246; www.lvm.wisc.edu. Open Tu-F 9am-5pm, Sa-Su 11am-5pm. Free.) UW produces its own brand of ice cream at the **Babcock Dairy Plant,** 1605 Linden Dr., at Babcock Dr. An observation deck allows visitors to watch their favorite flavor being made. (☎262-3045. Store open M-F 9am-5:30pm, Sa 10am-1:30pm.) Also part of UW, the outdoor **Olbrich Botanical Gardens** and indoor **Bolz Conservatory** house a plethora of plant life. The Gardens showcase floral settings, from butterfly-attracting plants to an English herb garden, and an exquisite, recently gifted Thai Pavilion—the only one of its kind in the continental USA—constructed entirely without nails. Free-flying birds, waterfalls, and tropical plants grace the inside of the conservatory dome. (3330 Atwood Ave. ☎246-4550. Gardens: open Apr.-Sept. daily 8am-8pm; Oct.-Mar. 9am-4pm. Free. Conservatory: open M-Sa 10am-4pm, Su 10am-5pm. $1, under 5 free; free W and Sa 10am-noon.) Aspiring botanists can trek along the 20 mi. of trails amongst the 1260 acres of trees at the **University Arboretum,** 1207 Seminole Hwy., off Beltline Hwy. (☎263-7760. Grounds open daily 7am-10pm; Visitors Center open M-F 9:30am-4pm, Sa-Su 12:30-4pm.) For more info visit the **UW Visitors Center,** 716 Langdon St., on the west side of the Memorial Union (☎263-2400.).

OUTSIDE MADISON

Some of Madison's most unique sights are far from the isthmus. Forty-five minutes west of Madison off U.S. 14, **House on the Rock,** 5754 Rte. 23, in Spring Green, is an unparalleled multilevel house built into a chimney of rock. The 40-acre complex of gardens, fantastic architecture, kitsch, and collections features wall-to-wall-to-ceiling shag carpeting, a 200-foot fiberglass whale engaged in an epic struggle with an octopus, and the world's largest carousel—of its 269 animals, not one is a horse. (☎935-3639. Open Mar.-Oct. daily 9am-7pm. $19.50, ages 7-12 $11.50, ages 4-6

$5.50.) Nine miles north of the House on the Rock, Frank Lloyd Wright's famed **Taliesin** home and school hugs the hills and valley that inspired his style of organic architecture. (On rte. 23 at Rte. C in Spring Green. ☎588-7900. Open May-Oct. daily 8:30am-5:30pm. Shuttle tours offered in Apr. and Nov. Sa-Su 10am-4pm. Four 1-4 hr. walking tours per day $10-70. Call the Visitors Center for exact rates and schedules.)

♫ ENTERTAINMENT

20,000 music-lovers flood the Square on Wednesday nights in June and July when the Wisconsin Chamber Orchestra performs **Concerts on the Square.** (☎257-0638. 7pm.) Leading out from the Capitol, Madison's pedestrian-only **State St.** exudes a lively college atmosphere, sporting many offbeat clothing stores and record shops. The **Madison Civic Center,** 211 State St. (☎266-9055; www.madcivic.org) is undergoing extensive remodeling and expansion and will be completed in 2005 as the state-of-the-art Overture Center. The Civic Center remains open during construction and continues to stage frequent arts and entertainment performances in the Oscar Mayer Theatre, and hosts the **Madison Symphony Orchestra.** (☎257-3734; www.madisonsymphony.org. Office open M-F 11am-5:30pm, Sa 11am-2pm. Season runs late Aug. to May. Tickets from $20.) The building is also home to the rotating contemporary exhibits and permanent modern collection of the **Madison Art Center.** (☎257-0158. Open Tu-Th 11am-5pm, F 11am-9pm, Sa 10am-9pm, Su 1-5pm. Free.) The **Madison Repertory Theatre,** also located in the Civic Center, performs classic and contemporary works. (☎266-9055; www.madisonrep.org. Showtimes vary; tickets $6.50-22.) Students and locals pass their days and nights hanging out at the southwest end of State St. at the **University of Wisconsin—Madison's,** gorgeous, lakeside **Union Terrace.** (800 Langdon St. ☎265-3000.) The terrace is home to free weekend concerts year-round, which take place on the lakeshore in the summer, and move indoors in the winter.

▼ NIGHTLIFE

Fueled by the 40,000-plus students who pack the reputed "party school," Madison's nightlife scene is active and eclectic. Clubs and bars are scattered throughout the isthmus, particularly along **State St.** and **U.S. 151.**

Essen Haus, 514 E. Wilson St. (☎255-4674), off U.S. 151. This lively German bar and grill plays host to live polka bands, semi-rowdy crowds, and ten-gallon hats. Incredible beer selection (from $1.50). Open Tu-Th 4pm-2am, F-Sa 4pm-2:30am, Su 3-11pm.

Cardinal, 418 E. Wilson St. (☎251-0080). Renowned for its quirky, mixed crowds, Cardinal provides a wide array of themed dance nights every day of the week, from goth industrial and electronic underground to Latin jazz and 80s hits. Cover $3-5. Open Su-Th 8pm-2am, F-Sa 8pm-2:30am.

Rainbow Room, 131 W. Main St. (☎251-5838), near the Capitol. Male strippers on Th nights and karaoke on F draw oglers and divas of all sorts, and welcome a diverse, mixed crowd. Live DJ Th-Sa. No cover. Open Su-Th 12pm-2am, F-Sa 10am-2:30am.

◩ OUTDOOR ACTIVITIES

Madison's many parks and lakeshores offer endless recreational activities and opportunities for more personal contact with nature. There are 10 gorgeous public **beaches** for swimming or strolling along the two lakes (☎266-4711 for more info). Back on dry land, **bicycling** is possibly the best way to explore the isthmus and surrounding park lands. Madison, in fact, is the bike capital of the Midwest, with more bikes than cars traversing the landscape. **Budget Bicycle Center,** 1230 Regent St.

BARABOO'S BIZARRE The Greatest Show on Earth is in Baraboo, Wisconsin—permanently. Twenty miles northwest of Madison along the Baraboo River, a swath of bank has been set aside by the State Historical Society to honor the one-time winter home of the world-famous **Ringling Brothers** circus. The **Circus World Museum** packs a full line-up of events from big-top performances to street parades. *(426 Water St. ☎356-8341; www.circusworldmuseum.com. Open in summer daily from 9am-6pm. Big top shows at 11am and 3:30. $15, seniors $13, ages 5-11 $8.)* Baraboo, however, has more to offer than plumed horse parades. The **fantastical sculpture garden of Dr. Evermor** lies just south of Baraboo on Rte. 12. Here, Tom Every, a self-taught artist and welder since the 1960s, transforms industrial scrap metal into whimsical creatures—including a full orchestra of musical birds made from old instruments—with some help from his wife, son, and blow torch. The centerpiece is a massive palace/rocketship structure, *Forevertron*, which has been recognized by *Guinness* as the largest junk sculpture in the world. *(For more info, call Eleanor Every at ☎592-4735 or 219-7830. Open daily 10:30am-5:30pm. Free.)*

(☎251-8413), loans out all types of two-wheel transportation ($7 per day, $21 per week, tandems $10-30 day). Hikers and picnickers should head to **Picnic Point** on Lake Mendota. A bit of a hike off University Bay Dr., this spot provides great views of the college. For other city parks, the **Parks Department,** 215 Martin Luther King Jr. Blvd., in the Madison Municipal Building, can help with specific park info. (☎266-4711. Office open M-F 8am-4:15pm; park open daily 4am-dusk. Admission to Madison parks is free.)

DOOR COUNTY   ☎920

Jutting out like a thumb from the Wisconsin mainland between Green Bay and Lake Michigan, the Door Peninsula exudes a coastal spirit unlike any other in the nation's heartland. The rocky coastline, azure waters, and towering pines resemble a northeastern fishing village more than a Midwestern getaway. Door County beckons to both campers and vacationers with miles of bike paths, national and state parks, beaches, and quaint country inns. Despite its undeniable popularity as a tourist destination, the Door has managed to carefully avoid fast-paced, neon-lit commercialism. Its 12 villages swing open on a summer-oriented schedule; visitors are advised to make reservations for accommodations and campsites if they plan to be on the peninsula during a weekend in either July or August.

⬛🟧 ORIENTATION & PRACTICAL INFORMATION. Door County begins north of **Sturgeon Bay,** where Rte. 42 and Rte. 57 converge and then split again. Rte. 57 hugs the eastern coast of the peninsula; Rte. 42 runs up the west. The peninsula's west coast, which borders Green Bay, tends to be more artsy and expensive. The colder, calmer east coast contains most of the peninsula's park area. From south to north along Rte. 42, **Egg Harbor, Fish Creek, Ephraim, Sister Bay,** and **Ellison Bay** are the largest towns. During the summer, the days are warm, but temperatures can dip to 40°F at night, even in July. Public transportation only comes as close as **Green Bay,** 50 mi. southwest of Sturgeon Bay, where **Greyhound** has a station at 800 Cedar St. (☎432-4883. Open M-F 6:30am-5pm; Sa-Su 6:30-6:50am, 10am-noon, and 3:30-5:10pm.) and runs to **Milwaukee** (3 per day, $20). Reserve tickets at least a day in advance. **Door County Chamber of Commerce:** 6443 Green Bay Rd., on Rte. 42/57 entering Sturgeon Bay. (☎743-4456 or 800-527-3529. Open Apr.-Oct. M-F 8:30am-5pm, Sa-Su 10am-4pm; Nov.-Mar. M-F 8:30am-4:30pm.) **Post Office:** 359 Louisiana, at 4th St. in Sturgeon Bay. (☎743-2681. Open M-F 8:30am-5pm, Sa 9:30am-noon.) **ZIP code:** 54235. **Area code:** 920.

ⓘ ACCOMMODATIONS. Unique, country-style lodgings crowd Rte. 42 and Rte. 57; reservations for July and August should be made far in advance. The **⧄Century Farm Motel ❸**, 10068 Rte. 57, 3 mi. south of Sister Bay on Rte. 57, rents intimate, carefully maintained two-room cottages hand-built by the owner's grandfather in the 1920s. The motel, situated on a chicken and buffalo farm, is removed from the tourist activity of the Door's towns and offers fantastic peak season prices. (☎854-4069. A/C, TV, private bath, and fridge. Open mid-May to mid-Oct. $45-60.) Relaxed and convenient, the **Lull-Abi Motel ❸**, 7928 Egg Harbor Rd./Rte. 42 in Egg Harbor, soothes visitors with spacious rooms, a patio, an indoor whirlpool, and free coffee. (☎868-3135. Open May-late Oct. Doubles $50-84, depending on season. Suites with wet bar and refrigerator $62-99.)

☗ CAMPING. Except for **Whitefish Dunes**, the area's **state parks ❶** offer outstanding camping ($10, WI residents $8; F-Sa $12/$10). All state parks require a **motor vehicle permit** ($3 per hour; $7/$5 per day; $25/$18 per year). **Peninsula State Park,** just past Fish Creek village on Rte. 42, contains 20 mi. of shoreline and 17 mi. of trails alongside the largest of the state park campgrounds. (☎868-3258. 469 sites with showers and toilets. Make reservations far in advance, or come in person to put your name on the waiting list for one of 70 walk-in sites.) The relatively uncrowded **Potawatomi State Park,** 3740 Park Dr., sits just outside Sturgeon Bay off Rte. 42/57, south of the bridge. (☎746-2890. 125 campsites, 19 open to walk-ins.) Highlighted by hidden coves, **Newport State Park,** 7 mi. from Ellison Bay off Rte. 42, is a shaded wildlife preserve at the tip of the peninsula. Vehicles are permitted, but sites are accessible by hiking only. (☎854-2500. 16 sites, 3 open to walk-ins.) The untamed **Rock Island State Park** offers 40 remote sites on Washington Island. (☎847-2235. Open mid-Apr. to mid-Nov.)

◖ FOOD. Food from the lake and Scandinavian customs dominate Door County fare. Many people visit the region just for **fishboils**, a Scandinavian lumberjack tradition, in which cooks toss potatoes, spices, and whitefish into a large kettle over a wood fire. To remove the fish oil from the top of the water, the boilmaster throws kerosene into the fire, producing a massive fireball; the cauldron boils over, signaling chow time. Door County's best-known fishboils bubble up at **The Viking Grill ❹**, in Ellison Bay. (☎854-2998. Open daily 6am-8pm, fishboils mid-May to Oct. 4:30-8pm. $13.25, under 12 $10.25.) Door cooks up much more than just fishboils. Drop in on **Al Johnson's Swedish Restaurant,** 700-710 Bayshore Dr., in the middle of Sister Bay on Rte. 42, for Swedish pancakes, a crepe-like breakfast served with lingonberries. The restaurant is hard to miss; just look for the goats grazing atop the sod covered roof. (☎854-2626. Open daily 6am-9pm; in winter 7am-8pm.) At the **⧄Bayside Tavern ❶**, on Rte. 42 in Fish Creek, Bob cooks up his spicy, Cincinnati-style chili ($4). At night, Bayside becomes a lively bar, with local music on Monday and Saturday and open-mic on Thursday. (☎868-3441. Sa cover $6. Open Su-Th 11am-2am, F-Sa 11am-2:30am.) Just across the street, local favorite **Sister Bay Bowl and Supper Club ❷** rolls out generous portions of chicken, fish, and sandwiches along with a six-lane bowling alley. (☎854-2841. Open daily 11:30am-2pm and 5-10pm; in winter 11:30am-2pm and 5-9pm. Entrees from $5, bowling from $3.)

◉ SIGHTS. Most of Door County's sights are located on the more populated West Side. At the base of the peninsula, Sturgeon Bay houses the intriguing **Door County Maritime Museum,** at 120 N. Madison St., downtown. The museum offers insight into the area's ship-building and water-charting history with antique boats and interactive, hands-on exhibits. (☎743-5958. Open May-Oct. daily 9am-6pm;

Nov.-Apr. 10am-5pm. $3.) **Door Peninsula Winery,** 5806 Rte. 42, in Sturgeon Bay, invites vine-lovers into a former school house that now produces 30 different flavors of award-winning fruit wine. (☎743-7431 or 800-551-5049. 15-20min. tours and tastings in summer 9am-6pm; off-season 9am-5pm. $1.50.) One of the few drive-ins left in the USA, the ◪**Skyway Drive-In,** on Rte. 42 between Fish Creek and Ephraim, screens double features at great prices. (☎854-9938. Current release double feature $6, ages 6-11 $3. Call for schedules.) Just south of the Skyway, Peninsula State Park houses the outdoor **American Folklore Theatre,** where a local troupe performs original, Wisconsin-themed shows like the Door County hit *Lumberjacks in Love.* (☎869-2329. $12, ages 13-19 $6.50, ages 6-12 $3.50.)

The shipping town of **Green Bay,** 50 mi. south of Sturgeon Bay at the foot of the Door peninsula, is best known as home to the Green Bay Packers. Chances of snagging a ticket to a Packer's game are slim, but the appropriately green and yellow **Lambeau Field** is worth a look. (☎496-5719. $32-39.) The **Packer Hall of Fame,** 855 Lombardi Ave., across from the stadium, has a cathedral-like feel as thousands come here to worship their gridiron heroes. (☎499-4281. Open daily 9am-5pm. 1½hr. tours June-Aug. $8, under 15 $5.50.)

◪ OUTDOOR ACTIVITIES. Biking is the best way to take in the largely untouched lighthouses, rocks, and white-sand beaches of the Door's rugged eastern coastline. Village tourist offices have free bike maps. **Whitefish Dunes State Park,** off Rte. 57, glimmers with Wisconsin's most extensive sand dunes, hiking/biking/skiing trails, and a well-kept wildlife preserve. (Open daily 8am-8pm. $7 vehicle permit required.) Just north of the Dunes off Rte. 57 on Cave Point Rd., the rugged **Cave Point County Park** has some of the best views on the peninsula. (Open daily 6am-9pm. Free.) In **Baileys Harbor,** 3 mi. north of Lakeside, waves and wind have carved miles of swirling sand ridges along the coastline. **Ridges Sanctuary,** north of Baileys Harbor off Rte. Q, has trails meandering through over 30 of the ridges, as well as birdwatching and a boreal forest at **Toft's Point.** (☎839-2802. Nature center open daily 9am-4pm. $2.) **Baileys Harbor Ridges Beach,** a usually uncrowded stretch of sand that allows for secluded swimming, adjoins the sanctuary on Ridges Rd. Reached from Cana Island Rd. off Rte. Q, **Cana Island Lighthouse** juts out from the lake, compelling visitors to cross the sandpath (at low tide) or wade through the frigid waters (at high tide) to reach its oft-photographed shores. There is no access to the lighthouse itself but the island provides an expansive view of the bay. (No phone. No facilities. Open daily 10am-5pm. $3, children $1.)

The West Side's recreational offerings are fewer than the East Side's, but they are no less exciting. **Peninsula State Park,** in Fish Creek, is a popular spot for tourists. Visitors rent boats and ride bicycles along 20 mi. of shoreline road. More crowded than east coast beach options, **Nicolet Beach** (inside the park) attracts sunbathers from all over the peninsula. One mile and 110 steps up from the beach, **Eagle Tower** offers the highest view of the shore. On a clear day, the tower allows a glimpse of Michigan's shores across the waters of Green Bay. (Open daily 6am-11pm. Vehicle permit required. $3 per hr.) Directly across from the Fish Creek entrance, **Nor Door Sport and Cyclery,** 4007 Rte. 42, rents out bikes and winter equipment. (☎868-2275. From $5 per hr., $20 per day. Cross-country skis $9 per day.)

APOSTLE ISLANDS   ☎715

The National Lakeshore protects 21 of the breathtaking islands off the coast of Wisconsin, as well as a 12 mi. stretch of mainland shore. Bayfield, a tiny mainland town, serves as the access point to the islands. Tourism is focused on the mainland and Madeline Island where coastal inns draw families looking for a back-to-nature weekend. The smaller islands are still dominated by campers and outdoor sportsmen. Backpackers pour into town on their way to and from hikes, kayakers explore island caves, and sailers delight in the clear waters. Adventure companies allow summer tourists with all levels of outdoor experience to enjoy the kayaking, hiking, spelunking, and camping among the unspoiled sandstone bluffs.

⑦ PRACTICAL INFORMATION. Most excursions begin in the sleepy mainland town of **Bayfield** (pop. 686), in northwest Wisconsin on the Lake Superior coast. The **Bay Area Rural Transit (BART),** 300 Industrial Park Rd., 21 mi. south on Rte. 13 in Ashland, offers a shuttle to Bayfield. (☎682-9664. 4 per day M-F 7am-5pm. $1.80, students $1.50, seniors $1.10.) **Bayfield Chamber of Commerce,** 42 S. Broad St. (☎779-3335 or 800-447-4094. Open M-Sa 8am-5pm, Su 10am-2pm). **National Lakeshore Headquarters Visitors Center,** 410 Washington Ave., distributes hiking info and **camping permits.** (☎779-3398. Open mid-May to mid-Sept. daily 8am-6pm; mid-Sept. to mid-May W-Su 8am-4:30pm. Permits for up to 14 consecutive days $15.) For **short-term work** picking apples, contact the **Bayfield Apple Company,** on County J near the intersection of Betzold Rd. (☎779-5700 or 800-363-4526. Open May-Jan. daily 9am-6pm.) **Post Office:** 22 S. Broad St., Bayfield. (☎779-5636. Open M-F 9am-4:30pm, Sa 9am-11am.) **ZIP code:** 54814. **Area code:** 715.

⛺ ACCOMMODATIONS. In summer months, the budget pickings are slim in Bayfield. Weekends in July and August are particularly busy; rooms should be booked weeks in advance. The best deal in town is the **Seagull Bay Motel ❸,** off Rte. 13 at S. 7th St., offering spacious, smoke-free rooms with cable TV and a lake view. (☎779-5558. Mid-May to mid-Oct. from $65; mid-Oct. to mid-May $35.) Just south on Rte. 13, **Lakeside Lodging ❹** has rooms with a patio, private entrance and bath, and continental breakfast. (☎779-5690. Open mid-May to mid-Oct. In summer, reservations recommended 1 month in advance. Rooms $79.) For a more rustic Bayfield experience, **Dalrymple Park ❶,** ¼ mi. north of town on Rte. 13, has 30 campsites in a grand setting under tall pines on the lake. (No showers; self-regulated; no reservations. Sites $12.) **Apostle Islands Area Campground ❶,** ½ mi. south of Bayfield on County Rd. J off Rte. 13, has 60 camp sites buried in the woods of Bayfield. (☎779-5524. July-Aug. reservations recommended 1 month in advance. Sites $15, with hookup $17, with full sewer and cable $27.) The Chamber of Commerce has info on **guest houses** (from $35).

◖ FOOD. The bright pink exterior is just the beginning at **Maggie's ❷,** 257 Manypenny Ave., where satisfying burgers ($6) and the best fajitas on the islands have as much flavor as the Mardi Gras interior and flamingo decor. (☎779-5641. Open Su-Th 11am-10pm, F-Sa 11am-11pm.) One of the oldest establishments in Bayfield, **Greunke's Restaurant ❸,** 17 Rittenhouse Ave., at 1st St., specializes in huge breakfasts by day ($4-6) and famous fishboils by night. While waiting for a hearty meal, check out photos of celebrities who have graced Gruenke's door step. (☎779-5480. Fishboils W-Su 6:30-8pm. $11, children $6. Open M-Sa 6am-10pm, F-Su 7am-9:30pm.) **Egg Toss Cafe ❷,** 41 Manypenny Ave., serves a variety of breakfasts and sandwiches ($5-7) in a patio setting. (☎779-5181. Open daily 6am-3pm.) With lots of vegetarian options, **Wild By Nature Market ❶,** 100 Rittenhouse Ave., sells organic goodies (perfect for pre-hike nourishment) and delicious wraps ($4-5) for pick up. (☎779-5075. Open daily 9am-6pm.) The **Gourmet Garage ❷,** just south of Bayfield on Rte. 13, provides exactly what it's name and sign say—lots of fresh, homemade pies ($7-10) sold out of a converted garage. (☎779-5365. Open in summer M-Sa 8am-5pm, Su 8am-4pm; Oct.-May Sa-Su, call for hours.)

◙ ⚠ SIGHTS & OUTDOOR ACTIVITIES. Though often overshadowed by Bayfield and Madeline Island (see below), the other 21 islands have their own subtle charms. The sandstone quarries of Basswood and Hermit Islands and the abandoned logging and fishing camps on some of the other islands serve as silent reminders of a more prosperous era. The restored **lighthouses** on Sand, Raspberry, Long, Michigan, Outer, and Devil's Islands offer spectacular views of the surrounding country. **Sea caves,** carved out by thousands of years of wind and water, create a spectacular sight on several islands. The **Apostle Islands Cruise Service** runs narrated 3hr. tours for a less exorbitant fee than most companies. From late June to early September, the cruise service runs an inter-island shuttle that delivers campers and lighthouse lovers to their destinations. (☎ 779-3925 or 800-323-7619. Tours of the archipelago depart the Bayfield City Dock mid-May to mid-Oct. daily 10am. Call for additional tours and departure times. $25, children $14.) The best beach on the mainland is **Bay View Beach,** just south of Bayfield along Rte. 13, near Sioux Flats. Look carefully for the hard-to-find dirt road marked Bayview Park Road to enter this serene beach. **Trek and Trail,** at First and Washington St., rents bikes and kayaks. (☎ 800-354-8735. Bikes $5 per hr., $20 per day. 4hr. kayak rental $20, all equipment included, but renters must complete $50 kayaking safety course.)

Bayfield's apples attract visitors after the summer hikers leave. The population swells to 40,000 during the **Apple Festival** in the first full weekend of October, when natives and tourists alike gather for the street fairs. The **Bayfield Apple Company** has fresh-picked fruit and tasty jam (see p. 586).

MADELINE ISLAND ☎ 715

Several hundred years ago, the Ojibwe tribe came to Madeline Island from the Atlantic in search of the megis shell, a light in the sky purported to bring prosperity and health. The island maintains its allure by housing a colorful colony of artists alongside relaxing beaches frequented by thousands of summer visitors. ·

The **Madeline Island Motel ❹,** on Col. Woods Ave. across from the ferry landing, has private patios as well as clean rooms named for local historical figures. (☎ 747-3000. Mid-June to Oct. doubles $95; Oct.-May $60.) Rooms in the area fill during the summer; call ahead for reservations. Madeline Island has two campgrounds. **Big Bay Town Park ❶,** 6½ mi. from La Pointe off Big Bay Rd., sits next to tranquil Big Bay Lagoon. (☎ 747-6913. Sites $10, with electricity $13. No reservations accepted.) Across the lagoon, **Big Bay State Park ❶** rents 55 primitive sites. (☎ 747-6425, for reservations ☎ 888-475-3386. Reservations $4. Sites $10-12. Daily vehicle permit $7, WI residents $5.) **Tom's Burned Down Cafe ❷,** 1 Middle Rd., may look like a garage sale with bizarre sculptures out front, but the lively bar serves healthy food, including many vegan options, and hosts the islands' artist community (☎ 747-6100. Open daily 10am-2pm. Sandwiches $7, pizzas $9.)

With roughly five streets, Madeline Island is easy to navigate. **Visitor Info: Madeline Island Chamber of Commerce,** on Middle Rd. (☎ 747-2801 or 888-475-3386. Open M-Sa 8am-4pm.) For pamphlets about the island, visit the chamber's booth near the ferry landing in Bayfield. **Madeline Island Ferry Line** shuttles between Bayfield and La Pointe on Madeline Island. (☎ 747-2051. June-Sept. daily every 30min. 9:30am-6pm, every hr. 6:30-9:30am and 6-11pm. One-way $4, ages 6-11 $2; bikes $1.75; cars $9.25. Mar.-June and Sept.-Dec. ferries run less frequently and prices drop.) In winter, the state highway department builds a road across the ice. During transition periods, the ferry service runs **windsleds** between the island and the mainland. At **Motion to Go,** 102 Lake View Pl., on Middle Rd., about one block from the ferry, "Moped Dave" rents scooters and bikes to those who want to avoid automobiles on the island. (☎747-6585. Open July-Aug. daily 8am-8pm; May-June 8:30am-7pm; Sept. to mid-Oct. 9am-7pm. Mopeds $17.50 per hr., $65 per day; mountain bikes $7/$26.) **Post Office** is just off the dock on Madeline Island in La Pointe. (☎747-3712. Open M-F 9am-4:20pm, Sa 9:30am-12:50pm.) **ZIP code:** 54850.

MINNESOTA

In the 19th century, floods of German and Scandinavian settlers forced native tribes out of the rich lands now known as Minnesota, a name derived from a Dakota word meaning "sky-tinted waters." Minnesota's white pioneers transformed the southern half of the state into a stronghold of commercial activity; however, the north has remained largely untouched, an expanse of wilderness quilted with over 15,000 lakes. Attempts at preserving this rugged frontier have helped raise awareness about Minnesota's natural resources and the culture of the Ojibwe, the state's Native American antecedents.

▇ PRACTICAL INFORMATION

Capital: St. Paul.

Visitor info: Minnesota Office of Tourism, 100 Metro Sq., 121 7th Pl. E., St. Paul 55101 (☎800-657-3700; www.exploreminnesota.com). Open M-F 8am-5pm.

Postal Abbreviation: MN. **Sales Tax:** 6.5%.

MINNEAPOLIS & ST. PAUL   ☎612

Native son Garrison Keillor wrote that the "difference between St. Paul and Minneapolis is the difference between pumpernickel and Wonder bread." St. Paul is characterized as an old Irish Catholic, conservative town, and Minneapolis has a reputation as a young, fast-paced metropolis of the future. Minneapolis's theaters and clubs rival those of New York, while the traditional capitol and the cathedral reside in St. Paul. In both cities, consumer culture, the bohemian youth world, corporate America, and an international community thrive together.

▐ TRANSPORTATION

Airport: Minneapolis-St. Paul International (☎726-5555; www.msairport.com), 15min. south of the cities on Rte. 5, off I-494 in Bloomington. From the airport, take bus #7 to Washington Ave. in Minneapolis or bus #54 to St. Paul. **Airport Express** (☎827-7777) shuttles to both downtowns and to some hotels roughly every 30min. Operates 4:30am-11pm. To **Minneapolis** ($13) and **St. Paul** ($11).

Trains: Amtrak, 730 Transfer Rd. (☎651-644-1127 or 800-872-7245), on the east bank off University Ave. SE, between the Twin Cities. City bus #7 runs from the station to St. Paul, and #16 connects to both downtowns. Open daily 6:30am-11:30pm. To **Chicago** (8hr., 1 per day, $87-105) and **Milwaukee** (6hr., 1 per day, $81-97).

Buses: Greyhound, 29 9th St. N. (☎371-3325; open daily 5:30am-1am), in Minneapolis downtown. In St. Paul, 166 W. University Ave. (☎651-222-0507; open daily 6:15am-9pm), 2 blocks west of the capitol. To **Chicago** (9-12hr.; 9 per day; M-Th $54, F-Su $58) and **Milwaukee** (7-9 hr.; 7 per day; M-Th $49, F-Su $52); both routes depart from Minneapolis and St. Paul stations.

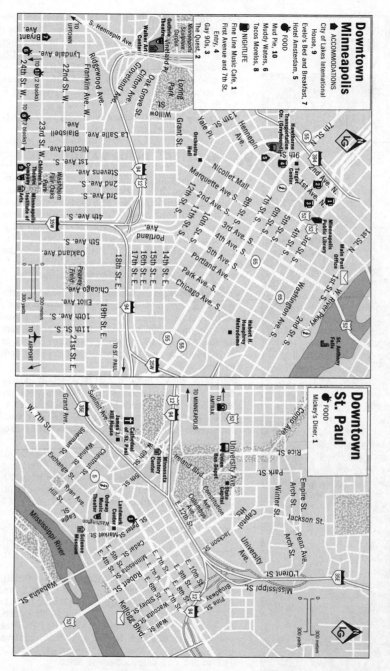

Downtown Minneapolis

♦ ACCOMMODATIONS

City of Lakes International House, **9**
Evelo's Bed and Breakfast, **7**
Hotel Amsterdam, **5**

♠ FOOD

Mud Pie, **10**
Muddy Waters, **6**
Tacos Morelos, **8**

♦ NIGHTLIFE

Fine Line Music Cafe, **1**
First Avenue and 7th St. Entry, **4**
Gay 90s, **3**
The Quest, **2**

Downtown St. Paul

♠ FOOD

Mickey's Diner, **1**

IN RECENT NEWS

MOVERS & SHAKERS

Minneapolis-St. Paul is second only to Atlanta in congestion growth, and the Twin Cities' overcrowded highways—especially I-494 and I-35 W—testify to this statistic. The estimated time citizens waste in congested traffic is 38hr. per person per year. Beginning with a $49.5 million dollar appropriation by the U.S. Secretary of Transportation, the Minnesota State Government began to approach their congestion problem. Government officials and business leaders came together in Bloomington for the Congestion Solutions Summit. From this summit, a new era in public transportation was born—the **Hiawatha Light Rail.** To alleviate commuter headaches, the state is spending more than $675 million to build the Light Rail. When completed, the Hiawatha Light Rail will be an 11.6-mile corridor that connects downtown Minneapolis, the airport, and the Mall of America. Service is expected to begin in the winter of 2003, with construction completed by the following fall. Planners predict that workers, students, travelers, and shoppers alike will benefit, whisked to their destinations at speeds of up to 55mph at the same price it would cost to ride the city bus. Leaders also foresee the creation of new housing developments and more job opportunities as a result of the Light Rail project. For the time being, the Twin Cities suffer from the side-effect of all great transportation projects—traffic.

Public Transit: Metropolitan Transit Commission, 560 6th Ave. N (☎373-3333; www.metrotransit.org), serves both cities. Most major lines end service by 12:45am; some buses operate 24hr. $1.25; seniors, ages 6-12, and disabled 75¢. Peak fare (M-F 6-9am and 3:30-6:30pm) $1.75/1.25. Express lines $2.25/1.75. Bus #16 connects the 2 downtowns 24hr. (50min.); bus # 94 (b, c, or d) takes 30min.

Taxis: Yellow Taxi, ☎824-4444 in Minneapolis; ☎651-222-4433 in St. Paul.

🛈 PRACTICAL INFORMATION

Curves and one-way streets tangle both of the downtown areas; even the numbered grids in the cities are skewed, making north-south and east-west designations tricky without a map. Downtown Minneapolis lies about 10 mi. west of downtown St. Paul via **I-94. I-35** splits in the Twin Cities, with **I-35 W** serving Minneapolis and **I-35 E** serving St. Paul. **I-494** runs to the airport and the Mall of America, while **I-394** heads to downtown Minneapolis from the western suburbs.

Visitor info: Minneapolis Convention and Visitors Association, 40 S. 7th St. (☎661-4700), near Hennepin Ave., on the 1st. fl. of the City Center. Open M-Sa 10am-6pm, Su noon-5pm. **St. Paul Convention and Visitors Bureau,** 175 W. Kellogg, #502 (☎800-627-6101 or 651-265-4900; www.stpaulcvb.org), in the River Centre. Open M-F 8am-4:30pm.

Short-Term Work: Contact a local **Minnesota Workforce Center** for year-round opportunities in Northern Minneapolis (☎520-3500), Southern Minneapolis (☎821-4000), Northern St. Paul (☎651-450-2667), or Western St. Paul (☎651-552-5000). **Job Bank** (☎651-296-8400) can also be of assistance.

Hotlines: Crime Victim Center Crisis Line, ☎340-5400. **Rape/Sexual Assault Line,** ☎825-4357. Both open 24hr. **Gay-Lesbian Helpline,** ☎822-8661 or 800-800-0907. Open M-F noon-midnight, Sa 4pm-midnight. **Gay-Lesbian Information Line,** ☎822-0127. Open M-F 2-10pm, Sa 4-10pm.

Internet access: Minneapolis Public Library, 300 Nicollet Mall (☎630-6000). Open M-Th 9am-9pm, F 9am-6pm, Sa 10am-6pm. **St. Paul Public Library,** 90 W. 4th St. (☎651-266-7000). Call for hours.

Post Office: 100 S. 1st St., Minneapolis (☎349-0359), at Marquette Ave. on the river. Open M-F 7am-11pm, Sa 9am-1pm. 180 E. Kellogg Blvd., St. Paul (☎651-293-3268). Open M-F 8:30am-5:30pm, Sa 9am-noon. **ZIP code:** Minneapolis 55401, St. Paul 55101. **Area codes:** Minneapolis 612, St. Paul and eastern suburbs 651, southwestern suburbs 952, northwestern suburbs 763. In text, 612 unless otherwise noted.

▐ ACCOMMODATIONS

The Twin Cities are filled with unpretentious, inexpensive accommodations. The Visitors Centers have lists of **B&Bs**, while the **University of Minnesota Housing Office** (☎624-2994; www.umn.edu/housing/offcampus.htm) keeps a list of local rooms ($15-60) that rent on a daily or weekly basis. The section of I-494 at Rte. 77, near the Mall of America, is lined with budget chain motels from $40. The nearest private campgrounds are about 15 mi. outside the city; the closest state park camping is in the **Hennepin Park** system, 25 mi. away. **Minnesota State Parks** (☎651-296-6157 or 888-646-6367) and **Minnesota Alliance of Campground Operators** (☎651-778-2400) have more camping information.

▓ **City of Lakes International House and Hostel,** 2400 Stevens Ave. S (☎871-3210), Minneapolis, south of downtown by the Institute of Arts. Take bus #17 or 18 from Nicollet Mall to 24th St. and walk 2 blocks east to Stevens. Visitors from around the country and the world lend this clean hostel a strong community atmosphere. Kitchen, TV, lockers, on-site parking, Internet access, and bikes. Linen $2, towel $1. Key deposit $20. Check-in daily 9am-10pm. Check-out 11am. Call for reservations. Beds $20, students and foreign travelers $18; 2 singles $38. ❶

Select Inn, 7851 Normandale Blvd. (☎952-835-7400), in Bloomington, at the intersection of Hwy. 100 and I-494. A 10-minute drive from downtown Minneapolis, Select Inn boasts spacious, well-kept rooms, an indoor pool, continental breakfast, HBO, and shuttle service to the airport. Singles from $73; doubles from $80. ❹

Evelo's Bed and Breakfast, 2301 Bryant Ave. (☎374-9656), in south Minneapolis, just off Hennepin Ave. Take bus #17 from downtown to Bryant Ave. 15min. walk from downtown. Kind owners rent out 3 lovingly tended rooms in a house with fine Victorian artifacts. Reservations and deposit required. Singles $55; doubles $70. ❸

Hotel Amsterdam, 828 Hennepin Ave. (☎288-0459), in downtown Minneapolis, between 8th and 9th St. Located above the Saloon nightclub, this warm hotel offers visitors comfortable rooms, shared showers, and easy access to downtown action and attractions. A 24hr. lounge, Internet access, coffee, and complimentary condoms also provided. "The inn that's out" is geared toward the BGLT community, but all are welcome. Reservations recommended. Singles $44; doubles $50-65. ❷

▐ FOOD

The Twin Cities' cosmopolitan, cultured vibe is reflected in the culinary choices. Posh restaurants share the streets with intimate cafes. **Uptown** Minneapolis, around the intersection of Lake St. and Hennepin Ave., offers plenty of funky restaurants and bars with reasonable prices. In downtown Minneapolis, the **Warehouse District,** on 1st Ave. N between 8th St. and Washington Ave., and **Nicollet Mall,** a 12-block pedestrian stretch of Nicollet Ave., attract locals and tourists with trendy shops and cafes. While grabbing a bite to eat, check out the new statue of the girl who turned the whole world on with her smile, **Mary Tyler Moore,** at Nicollet and 7th St. In St. Paul, the upscale **Grand Ave.,** between Lexington and Dale, is lined with laid-back restaurants and bars. South of downtown, Nicollet turns into **Eat Street,** a 17-block stretch of international cuisine. In downtown St. Paul, **Lowertown,** along Sibley St. near 6th St., is a popular nighttime hot spot. Near the University of Minnesota (U of M) campus between the downtowns, **Dinkytown,** on the east bank of the river, and the **Seven Corners** area of the **West Bank,** on Cedar Ave. across the river, cater to student appetites. To get to either one, follow the signs off of I-94 for East Bank or West Bank. In the Twin Cities, many forego restaurants for the plentiful **cafes** (see p. 592). For do-it-yourselfers, pick up fresh produce at the **St. Paul Farmers Market,** on Wall St., between E. 4th and 5th St. downtown. (☎651-227-6856. Open late Apr. to mid-Nov. Sa 6am-1pm.)

GREAT LAKES

MINNEAPOLIS

🗹 **Chino Latino,** 2916 Hennepin Ave. (☎824-7878), at Lake St., Uptown. A curtain of gold sequins dances above the outside entrance, but beware: "no iron gut, no service" at this Latin-Asian fusion. The trendiest restaurant in town packs in the young, hipper-than-thou crowds with its *satay* bar ($7-9) and pu pu platter ($28; serves an army). Open M-Sa 4:30pm-1am, Su 11am-1am. Reservations strongly recommended. ❸

Figlio, 3001 Hennepin Ave. (☎822-1688), at W. Lake St. in Calhoun Sq., Uptown. Dishing up Italian with flare, Figlio has been awarded the honor of "Best Late Night Dining" by Twin City residents for many years for its scrumptious sandwiches (from $8), pastas and pizzas (from $10), and seafood (from $15). When the end (of your meal) is near, be sure to indulge in the "Death By Chocolate" dessert ($6). Open Su-Th 11:30am-1am, F-Sa 11:30am-2am. ❸

Bryant-Lake Bowl, 810 W. Lake St. (☎825-3737), at Bryant St. near Uptown. Built in the 1930s, this funky bowling alley-*cum*-bar-*cum*-cabaret is also—surprise—a really good, inexpensive restaurant. The "BLB Scramble" (a breakfast dish of eggs and vegetables, $5.25), ravioli, soups, and sandwiches ensure that the stylish patrons throw strikes with pleasantly full stomachs. Bowling $3. Entrees from $5. Open daily 8am-1am. ❷

Tacos Morelos, 14 26th St. W (☎870-0053), at Nicollet Ave. Hispanophiles can practice their Spanish at this authentic Mexican establishment. Try the 3 amigos enchiladas (one enchilada with each of 3 sauces, $10), or gorge on their famous tacos ($2 each). Entrees from $6. Open daily 10am-10pm. ❷

Mud Pie, 2549 Lyndale Ave. S (☎872-9435), at 26th St., Uptown. Mud Pie has won so many "Best Vegetarian" awards, they "don't know where to put them all." Try the delicious veggie burger ($7). Open in summer M-Th 11am-10:30pm, F 11am-11:30pm, Sa 10am-11:30pm, Su 10am-10:30pm; in winter all closing times 1hr. earlier. Brunch Sa-Su 10am-2pm. ❷

ST. PAUL

🗹 **Cafe Latte,** 850 Grand Ave. (☎651-224-5687), at Victoria St. More gourmet than its prices and cafeteria-style setup would suggest, meals at this cafe/bakery/pizza wine bar are consistently wonderful, and desserts are to die for. Chicken-salsa chili ($5) and turtle cake ($4) fill the 2 floors with chic, hungry locals. Open M-Th 9am-11pm, F-Sa 9am-midnight, Su 9am-10pm. ❶

Mickey's Diner, 36 W. 7th St. (☎651-222-5633), at St. Peter St. A 1939 diner on the National Register of Historic Places, Mickey's offers food that outshines its bright history and chrome-and-vinyl decor. Take a spin at a counter stool, or groove to some oldies on the juke box at each booth. Steak and eggs from $6. Pancakes $3.75. Open 24hr. ❶

◖ CAFES

Cafes are an integral part of the Twin Cities' nightlife. Particularly in Uptown Minneapolis, quirky coffeehouses caffeinate the masses and draw crowds as large as any bar. Come hungry, since most complement their java with some of the cheapest food in town.

🗹 **Uncommon Grounds,** 2809 Hennepin Ave. S. (☎872-4811), at 28th St., Uptown. The self-described "BMW of coffeeshops" uses only the most secret ingredients to make the tastiest coffees and teas around. With velour booths and relaxing music in a smoke-free interior, this coffeeshop lives up to its name. Open M-F 5pm-1am, Sa-Su 10am-1am.

Pandora's Cup and Gallery, 2516 Hennepin Ave. (☎381-0700), at 25th St., Uptown. One of the newest coffee spots in town, Pandora's is also the most lively. Hordes of twenty-somethings pack the shop's 2 stories. The tragically hip sip their espresso ($1.35-2) and munch on peanut butter and jelly "sammiches" ($2) and free ginger snaps. $1 minimum. Open daily 7am-1am.

Plan B Coffeehouse, 2717 Hennepin Ave. (☎872-1419), between 27th and 28th St. Plan B is first-rate. The desk toward the back may be littered with boring dictionaries, but the animated conversation, artwork, and mismatched furniture tell a different story. Try the "tripper's revenge" ($3.75). Open Su-Th 9am-midnight, F-Sa 9am-1am.

Muddy Waters, 2401 Lyndale Ave. S (☎872-2232), at 24th St., Uptown. The linoleum tables and vinyl chairs of this self-proclaimed "caffeine canteen" recall a smoky 1950s diner, but the music, stylish mosaic, outstanding coffee, and pierced staff keep it on the cutting edge. Mochas, cereal and milk, and Spaghetti-o's (with half a bagel, $4) are just the beginning of the eclectic menu. Open M-F 7am-1am, Sa-Su 8am-1am.

🅖 SIGHTS

MINNEAPOLIS

LAKES & RIVERS. In the land of 10,000 lakes, Minneapolis boasts many of its own; the city contains 22 lakes, 150 parks, and 100 golf courses. **Lake Calhoun,** on the west end of Lake St., Uptown, is the largest of the bunch and a recreational paradise. Scores of in-line skaters, bicyclists, and runners loop the lake on all but the coldest days. Ringed by stately mansions, the serene **Lake of the Isles** is an excellent place to commune with Canadian geese. Just southeast of Lake Calhoun on Sheridan St., **Lake Harriet** lures the locals with tiny paddleboats and a bandshell with nightly free concerts in summer. The city maintains 28 mi. of lakeside trails around the three lakes for strolling and biking. **Calhoun Cycle Center,** three blocks east of Lake Calhoun, rents out bikes for exploring the paths. *(1622 W. Lake St. ☎827-8231. Open M-Th 10am-8pm, F-Su 9am-9pm. $15-25 per ½ day, $24-40 per day. Must have credit card and driver's license.)* At the northeast corner of Lake Calhoun, the **Minneapolis Park & Recreation Board** handles canoe and rowboat rentals. *(2710 W. Lake St. ☎370-4964. Open daily 10am-8pm. Canoes $6 per hr.; rowboats $11 for 4hr. $10 deposit.)*

Get a good look at the Mighty Mississippi from several points in town. Off Portland Ave. downtown, **Stone Arch Bridge** offers pedestrians and bikers a scenic view of **St. Anthony Falls.** The Visitors Center at the **Upper St. Anthony Lock and Dam,** at Portland Ave. and West River Pkwy., provides a sweeping view of the falls and a helpful explanation of the locks that allow big boats access to the city. *(☎ 651-333-5336. Observation tower open mid-Mar. to mid-Dec. daily 10am-6pm.)* Several miles downstream, **Minnehaha Park** allows a gander at the more impressive **Minnehaha Falls,** immortalized in Longfellow's *Song of Hiawatha. (Park is near the airport; take bus #7 from Hennepin Ave. downtown. Falls are off Minnehaha Ave. at Minnehaha Pkwy.)*

MUSEUMS. The lakes are only the beginning of Minneapolis's appeal—locals and visitors have plenty to do during the (at least) six months of frigid winter. The **Minneapolis Institute of Arts,** south of downtown, boasts more than 100,000 art objects spanning 5,000 years, including Rembrandt's *Lucretia* and the world-famous *Doryphoros,* Polykleitos's perfectly proportioned man. The collection of 19th- and 20th-century European and American paintings is also commendable, with pieces by Degas, Picasso, Matisse, Mondrian, and Dali. *(2400 3rd Ave. S ☎870-3131; www.artsmia.org. Open Tu-W and Sa 9am-5pm, Th-F 9am-9pm, Su noon-5pm. Free.)* A few blocks southwest of downtown, the world-renowned ▓**Walker Art Center** counts daring exhibits by Lichtenstein, Rothko, and Warhol among its amazing galleries of contemporary art. *(725 Vineland Pl. at Lyndale Ave. ☎ 375-7622; www.walkerart.org. Open Tu-W and F-Sa 10am-8pm, Th 10am-9pm, Su 11am-5pm. $6; students, seniors, and ages 12-18 $4. Free Th and 1st Sa of the month.)* Next to the Walker lies the **Minneapolis Sculpture Garden**, the largest urban sculpture garden in the US. The tongue-in-cheek, post-card-friendly **Spoonbridge and Cherry** is the highlight of the worthwhile gardens. The adjacent **Cowles Conservatory** houses an array of plants and a Gehry fish sculpture. *(Gardens open daily 6am-midnight; conservatory open Tu-Sa 10am-8pm, Su 10am-5pm. Both free.)* Frank Gehry also holds the honor of having designed the Cities' most unique and controversial structure: the **Weisman Art Museum**, on the East Bank of the U of M campus. The undulating metallic pseudo-building was the rough draft for his famous Guggenheim Bilbao and hosts an inspired collection of modern art, including works by O'Keeffe and Hartley. Check out the walk-through apartment replica, by Edward and Nancy Reddin Kienholz, that engages all the senses by asking viewers to eavesdrop at each door. *(333 E. River Rd. ☎ 625-9494. Open Tu-W and F 10am-5pm, Th 10am-8pm, Sa-Su 11am-5pm. Free.)*

ST. PAUL

ARCHITECTURE. St. Paul's history and architecture are among its greatest assets. Nowhere is this more evident than along ■**Summit Ave.**, the nation's longest continuous stretch of Victorian houses, including a former home of novelist **F. Scott Fitzgerald** and the Minnesota **Governor's Mansion.** *(Fitzgerald: 599 Summit Ave. Currently a private residence. Governor's Mansion: 1006 Summit Ave. ☎ 651-297-8177. Tours May-Oct. F 1-3pm. Reservations required. Free.)* Also on Summit, the magnificent home of railroad magnate **James J. Hill**—the largest and most expensive home in the state when it was completed in 1891—offers 1¼-hr. tours every 30minutes. *(240 Summit Ave. ☎ 651-297-2555. Open W-Sa 10am-3:30pm. Reservations preferred. $6, seniors $5, ages 6-15 $4.)* **Walking Tours of Summit Ave.**, lasting 90min., depart from the Hill House and explore the architectural and social history of the area. *(☎ 651-297-2555. Sa 11am and 2pm. $4-6.)* Golden horses top the ornate **State Capitol**, the world's largest unsupported marble dome. *(75 Constitution Ave. ☎ 651-296-2881. Open M-F 9am-5pm, Sa 10am-4pm, Su 1-4pm. Tours on the hr. Free.)* A scaled-down version of St. Peter's in Rome, the **Cathedral of St. Paul**, at the end of Summit Ave, overlooks the capitol. St. Paul's is undergoing a $35 million renovation to replace the original copper roof. *(239 Selby Ave. ☎ 651-228-1766. Open daily 7:30am-5:30pm. Mass M-Th 7:30am and 5:15pm; F 7:30am; Sa 8am and 7pm; Su 8, 10am, noon, and 5pm. Tours M, W and F 1pm. Free.)*

HISTORICAL SIGHTS. Along the river, the innovative and exciting ■**Minnesota History Center** houses ten interactive, hands-on exhibit galleries on Minnesota history. Learn how Minnesotans cope with their extreme seasons in "Weather Permitting," or admire Prince's "Purple Rain" attire in "Sounds Good to Me: Music in Minnesota." *(345 Kellogg Blvd. W. ☎ 651-296-6126; www.mnhs.org. Open Sept.-May W-Sa 10am-5pm, Tu 10am-8pm, Su noon-5pm; July-Aug. M and W-Sa 10am-5pm, Tu 10am-8pm, Su noon-5pm. Free.)* Downtown's **Landmark Center** is a grandly restored 1894 Federal Court building replete with towers and turrets, a collection of pianos, a concert hall, and four courtrooms. *(75 W. 5th St. ☎ 651-292-3225. Open M-W and F 8am-5pm, Th 8am-8pm, Sa 10am-5pm, Su 1-5pm. Free tours Th 11am, Su 1pm.)* Out front, **Rice Park,** the oldest park in Minnesota, is an ideal place for a stroll or a picnic.

AMUSEMENTS. Out in suburban Apple Valley, the **Minnesota Zoo** houses local and exotic animals in their natural habitats, including 15 endangered and threatened species and a new Tiger Lair exhibit. *(13000 Zoo Blvd. Take Rte. 77 S to zoo exit and follow signs. ☎ 952-431-9500 or 800-366-7811. Open June-Aug. daily 9am-6pm; Sept. and May M-F 9am-4pm, Sa-Su 9am-6pm; Oct.-Apr. daily 9am-4pm. $10, seniors $6.25, children*

SHOP 'TIL YOU DROP Welcome to the largest mall in America— the **Mall of America.** Boasting an indoor roller coaster, ferris wheel, mini-golf course, and 2 mi. of stores, the Mall of America is the consummation of an American love affair with all that is obscenely gargantuan. With 520 specialty stores, 60 restaurants and nightclubs, a movie megaplex, an amusement park, and an aquarium alongside traditional stores and multiple food courts, the Mall is a great idea for a day of mind-numbing entertainment or a good old-fashioned shopping spree. *(60 E. Broadway. From St. Paul, take I-35 E south to I-494 W to the 24th Ave. exit. ☎ 883-8800; www.mallofamerica.com. Open M-Sa 10am-9:30pm, Su 11am-7pm.)*

$5, 2 and under free.) In Shakopee, even the most daring thrill-seekers can get their jollies at **Valleyfair,** a quality amusement park with five coasters and the heart-stopping Power Tower, which drops over ten stories. *(1 Valleyfair Dr. Take Rte. 169 south to Rte 101 W. ☎ 800-386-7433; www.valleyfair.com. Open June-Aug. daily; May and Sept. select days. Call for hours, usually 10am-10pm. $32, ages over 60 and under 48 in. $16, under 3 free. Parking $7.)*

ENTERTAINMENT

Second only to New York in number of theaters per capita, the Twin Cities are always full of drama and music. Most parks feature free evening concerts in the summer, and the thriving alternative, pop, while classical music scenes fill out the wide range of cultural options. For more info, read the free *City Pages* (www.citypages.com), available at libraries, most cafes, and newsstands around town.

THEATER
The renowned repertory **⬛Guthrie Theater,** 725 Vineland Pl., Minneapolis, adjacent to the Walker Art Center just off Hennepin Ave., draws praise for its mix of daring and classical productions. (☎ 377-2224; www.guthrietheater.org. Season Aug.-June. Box office open M-F 9am-8pm, Sa 10am-8pm, Su hours vary. $16-44, students and seniors $5 discount. Rush tickets 15min. before show $12.50; line starts 1-1½hr. before show.) Touring Broadway shows take the stage at either the historic **State Theatre,** 805 Hennepin Ave., in downtown Minneapolis, or across the street at the **Orpheum Theatre,** 910 Hennepin Ave. N (both box offices ☎ 339-7007; www.state-orpheum.com). For family-oriented productions, the **Children's Theater Company,** 2400 3rd Ave. S., next to the Minneapolis Institute of Arts, comes through with first-rate plays. (☎ 874-0400. Season Sept.-June. Box office open in season M-Sa 9am-5pm; in summer M-F 9am-4pm. $15-28; students, seniors, and children $9-22. Rush tickets 15min. before show $11.) The ingenious **Théâtre de la Jeune Lune,** 105 1st St. N, stages critically acclaimed, off-the-beaten- path productions in an old warehouse. (☎ 332-3968; box office ☎ 333-6200. Open M-F 10am-6pm. $10-26.) **Brave New Workshop,** 3001 Hennepin Ave., in Uptown, stages satirical comedy shows and improv in an intimate club. (☎ 332-6620; www.bravenewworkshop.com. Box office open M-W 9:30am-5pm, Th-F 9:30am-9pm, Sa 10am-11pm. $15-22.)

MUSIC
The Twin Cities' vibrant music scene offers everything from opera and polka to hip-hop and alternative. **Sommerfest,** a month-long celebration of Viennese music put on by the **Minnesota Orchestra,** is the best of the cities' classical options during July and August. **Orchestra Hall,** 1111 Nicollet Mall, downtown Minneapolis, hosts the event. (☎ 371-5656 or 800-292-4141; www.minnesotaorchestra.org. Box office open M-Sa 10am-6pm. $15-65. Student rush tickets 30min. before show $10.)

Nearby, **Peavey Plaza**, on Nicollet Mall, holds free nightly concerts and occasional film screenings. The **St. Paul Chamber Orchestra**, the **Schubert Club**, and the **Minnesota Opera Company** all perform at St. Paul's glass-and-brick **Ordway Center For The Performing Arts**, 345 Washington St., which also hosts touring Broadway productions. (☎651-224-4222; www.ordway.org. Box office open M-F 9am-6pm, Sa 11am-5pm, Su 11am-4pm. $15-85.) Bands from all over gravitate to the studio complex of the artist Prince formerly and currently known as **Paisley Park**, located just outside the city in Chanhassen.

SPORTS

The puffy **Hubert H. Humphrey Metrodome**, 900 S. 5th St., in downtown Minneapolis, houses baseball's **Minnesota Twins** (☎375-7454) and football's **Minnesota Vikings** (☎338-4537). Basketball's **Timberwolves** (☎337-3865) howl at the **Target Center**, 601 1st Ave. (☎673-0900), between 6th and 7th St. in downtown Minneapolis. The expansion NHL team, the **Wild**, takes to the ice at St. Paul's **RiverCentre** (☎651-222-9453). The soccer craze hits the Midwest with the minor-league **Thunder**, at the **National Sports Center** (☎763-785-5600) in suburban Blaine.

FESTIVALS

Both to liven up the dreary cold days and to celebrate the coming of summer, the Twin Cities celebrate countless festivals. In late January to early February, the ten-day **St. Paul Winter Carnival**, near the state capitol, cures cabin fever with ice sculptures, ice fishing, and skating contests. In July, the 12-day **Fringe Festival** for the performing arts stages edgy plays around town. (www.fringefestival.org. $4-5.) On the 4th of July, St. Paul celebrates the **Taste of Minnesota** with fireworks, concerts, and regional and ethnic cuisine from hordes of local vendors. On its coattails rides the ten-day **Minneapolis Aquatennial**, with concerts and art exhibits glorifying the regional lakes. The first weekend in August, the excellent **Uptown Art Fair** takes over the junction of Hennepin and Lake and draws thousands of people. In the two weeks prior to Labor Day, everyone in town heads to the nation's largest state fair, the **Minnesota State Fair**, at Snelling and Como St. in St. Paul. With cheese curds and walleye-on-a-stick, the fair provides a sampling of the area's flavor. (☎651-642-2200; www.mnstatefair.org. $8, seniors and ages 5-12 $7, under 5 free.)

🎵 NIGHTLIFE

Minneapolis's vibrant youth culture feeds the Twin Cities' nightlife. The post-punk scene thrives in the Land of 10,000 Aches: Soul Asylum, Hüsker Dü, and The Replacements all rocked here before they went big (or bad). A cross-section of the diverse nightlife options can be found in the downtown **Warehouse District** on Hennepin Ave.; in **Dinkytown**, by the U of M, and across the river on the **West Bank** (bounded on the west by I-35 W. and to the south by I-94), especially on **Cedar Ave.** The Twin Cities card hard, even for cigarettes.. The top floor of the **Mall of America** (see **Shop 'til You Drop**, p. 595) invites bar-hopping until the wee hours.

The Quest, 110 5th St. (☎338-3383), between 1st Ave. N and 2nd Ave. N in the Warehouse District. Once owned by Prince, this poppin' dance club pays homage to his purple highness with purple windows and lots of funk. Live salsa on M and house music draw in a young, cosmopolitan crowd. Cover $5-10. Hours vary, so call ahead.

Ground Zero, 15 4th St. NE (☎378-5115), off Hennepin Ave., just north of the river, has cages for dancing and wild theme nights for adventurous clubgoers. Bondage A Go-Go on Th and Sa. Open Th-Sa 9pm-1am.

First Avenue and 7th St. Entry, 701 1st Ave. N (☎332-1775), downtown Minneapolis, rocks with the area's best live music several nights a week, including concerts with the hottest rock bands in the nation. First Ave. is where cutting-edge twenty-somethings go to dance and be seen. Music from grunge to hip-hop to world beat. Cover $6-10, for concerts $6-30. Usually open M-Th 8pm-2am, F-Sa 9pm-3am, Su 7pm-2am.

Fine Line Music Cafe, 318 1st Ave. N (☎338-8100), in the Warehouse District. Even musicians love to sit in the audience at the Fine Line, where a range of local and national folk, blues, rock, and jazz acts induce enthusiastic toe-tapping. Live band karaoke Tu. Cover $6-15. Nightly shows at 9pm. Open daily 8pm-1am.

The Gay 90s, 408 Hennepin Ave. (☎333-7755), at 4th St., claims the seventh highest liquor consumption rate of all clubs in the nation. This superplex hosts thousands of gay and lesbian partiers in its many bars and showrooms, though the straight crowd is sizeable. Tu-Su drag shows upstairs. W-Th and Su 18+, M-Tu and F-Sa 21+. Cover after 9pm $3-5. Open M-Sa 8am-1am, Su 10am-1am.

DULUTH
☎218

If cities were sold at auctions, Duluth would fetch a high price: the people are nice, the parks are clean, the streets are safe, and the location is amazing. Bidders on a vacation here can expect to eat well, find relatively inexpensive lodging, and watch some serious shipping action. As the largest freshwater port in the world, Duluth harbors huge ships from over 60 different countries. The recently restored area of Canal Park, along Lake St., as well as the newly built **Lois M. Paulucci Music Pavilion** on the Bayfront have tempted microbreweries, restaurants, theaters, and museums to occupy the old factories and depots down on the wharf, turning a once-overlooked tourist destination into a hot spot of northern activity.

🔃 PRACTICAL INFORMATION. Greyhound, 4426 Grand Ave. (☎722-5591; bus tickets daily 6:30am-5:30pm), stops 3 mi. west of downtown; take bus #1 "Grand Ave. Zoo" from downtown. Buses run only to Minneapolis (3½hr.; 3 per day; M-Th $20, F-Su $21). The **Duluth Transit Authority,** 2402 W. Michigan St., buses within the city (☎722-7283. Peak fare M-F 7-9am and 2:30-6pm $1, students 75¢; off-peak 50¢.) The **Port Town Trolley** moves tourists around. (☎722-7283. Runs June-Aug. daily 11am-7pm. 25¢.) **Convention and Visitors Bureau:** 100 Lake Place Dr., at Endion Station in Canal Park. (☎722-4011 or 800-438-5884; www.visitduluth.com. Open M-F 8:30am-5pm.) **Short Term Work: Duluth Workforce Center,** 332 City Hall (☎723-3771). **Crisis Line:** ☎723-0099. **Duluth Public Library:** 520 W. Superior St. (☎723-3836. Open May-Sept. M-Th 10am-8:30pm, F 10am-5:30pm; Oct.-Apr. M-Th 10am-8:30pm, F 10am-5:30pm, Sa 10am-4pm.) **Post Office:** 2800 W. Michigan St. (☎723-2555. Open M-F 8am-5pm, Sa 9am-1pm.) **ZIP code:** 55806. **Area code:** 218.

🔃 ACCOMMODATIONS. Motel rates rise and rooms fill during the warm months. The **Chalet Motel ❸,** 1801 London Rd., 2 mi. west of downtown, offers decent rooms near scenic Leif Erickson Park, which overlooks Lake Superior. (☎728-4238 or 800-235-2957. Apr.-Sept. M-F singles $45; doubles $58; Sa-Su $55/68. Prices lower in winter.) A few mi. south of town, the warm **Duluth Motel ❷,** 4415 Grand Ave., houses visitors in affordable, well-kept rooms. (☎628-1008. In summer $40-60; in winter $10-50.) With a decidedly less urban feel, the rocky **Jay Cooke State Park ❶,** southwest of Duluth on I-35 Exit 242, draws in families and travelers with hiking, snowmobiling, cross-country skiing, and 80 campsites among the tall trees of the St. Louis River Valley. (☎384-4610 or 800-246-2267. Open daily 9am-9pm; park gates open until 10pm. Office open daily 9am-4pm. Reservations recommended; $8.50 reservation fee. Backpack sites $7, sites with showers $12, with electricity $15; vehicle permit $4 per day.)

⊠ **FOOD & NIGHTLIFE.** Upscale **Fitger's Brewery Complex,** 600 E. Superior St., and the **Canal Park** region, south from downtown along Lake Ave., feature plenty of pleasant eateries. The **Brewhouse ❷,** in Fitger's Brewery Complex, has beer and pub food ($5-8), including Big Boat Oatmeal Stout from $2.75. (☎726-1392. Live entertainment F-Sa. Open daily 11am-1am; grill closes 10pm.) The **DeWitt-Seitz Marketplace,** in the middle of Canal Park Dr., has slightly pricier restaurants. The friendly staff at the **Blue Note Cafe ❷,** 357 Canal Park Dr., serves delicious sandwiches ($5-8) and desserts ($2-4) in a coffeehouse setting. (☎727-6549. Live music F-Sa. Open May-Sept. M-Th 9:30am-9pm, F-Sa 9:30am-10pm, Su 9:30am-8pm; call for winter hours.) Located in an old pipe-fitting factory in Canal Park, **Grandma's Sports Garden,** 425 S. Lake Ave., has dining, a bar, and a huge dance floor. (☎722-4724. Club open daily 9pm-1am. Dancing W and F-Sa. Restaurant open June-Aug. daily 11am-10pm; Sept.-May daily 11:30am-10pm.)

◨ **SIGHTS & ENTERTAINMENT.** Duluth's proximity to majestic **Lake Superior** is its biggest draw. At nearly 400 mi. across, it is the largest body of fresh water in the world. Many visitors head down to **Canal Park** to watch the big ships go by at the ▨**Aerial Lift Bridge.** Accompanied by deafening horn blasts, this unique bridge climbs 138 ft. in 1min. to allow vessels to pass; late afternoon is prime viewing time. Ships load at the **Ore Docks Observation Platform,** 35th Ave. W. and Superior St. downtown and are tracked by the **Boatwatcher's Hotline** (☎722-6489). The **Duluth Shipping News** (☎722-3119; www.duluthshippingnews.com) is published daily, usually available by 3pm at the **Lake Superior Maritime Visitors Center,** by the Aerial Lift Bridge at Canal Park. The Visitors Center prepares extensive displays on commercial shipping in Lake Superior. (☎727-2497. Open daily 10am-9pm.) Canal Park also serves as the beginning and end of the looped **Duluth Lakewalk,** a beautiful four-mile promenade.

A 39-room neo-Jacobean mansion built on iron-shipping wealth, **Glensheen Historical Sites,** 3300 London Rd., lies on the eastern outskirts of town and provides visitors with a glimpse of Duluth's most prosperous period. (☎726-8910 or 888-454-4536. Open May-Oct. daily 9:30am-4pm; Nov.-Apr. F-Su 11am-2pm. $9.50, seniors and ages 12-15 $7.50, ages 6-11 $4.50. Reservations recommended.) Waterfront tours aboard the giant steamer **William A. Irvin** reveal more of Duluth's shipping past. (☎722-5573. Open May and Sept. to mid-Oct. Su-W 10am-4pm, Th-Sa 10am-6pm; June-Aug. Su-W 9am-6pm, Th-Sa 9am-8pm. $6.75, students and seniors $5.75, ages 3-12 $4.50.) Across the Aerial Lift Bridge, **Park Point** has excellent but cold swimming areas (Lake Superior's water averages 39°F), parks, and sandy beaches. The scenic **Willard Munger State Trail** links West Duluth to Jay Cooke State Park, providing 14 mi. of paved path perfect for bikes and skates; the **Willard Munger Inn,** 7408 Grand Ave., rents both. (☎624-4814 or 800-982-2453. Bikes and inline skates $15 for 2hr.; $20 for 4hr.)

Featuring fascinating exhibitions on animal life in Lake Superior and loads of hands-on displays, the new ▨**Great Lakes Aquarium and Freshwater Discovery Center,** 353 Harbor Dr., is America's first and only all-freshwater aquarium. (☎740-3474; www.glaquarium.org. Open Memorial Day to Sept. Su-W 9am-6pm, Th-Sa 9am-8pm; call for off-season hours. $11, seniors $9, children 4-17 $6, under 4 free.) History buffs should stop by the outstanding **Karpeles Manuscript Library Museum,** 902 E. 1st St., which houses original drafts of the Bill of Rights, Handel's Messiah, and the Emancipation Proclamation. (☎728-0630. Open June-Aug. daily noon-4pm; Sept.-May Tu-Su noon-4pm. Free.) **The Depot,** 506 W. Michigan St., a former railroad station, features five performing arts groups and four museums. (☎727-8025. All museums and a trolley ride, ages 6-13 $5.25, families $23.50. Open June-Aug. daily 9:30am-6pm; Sept.-May M-Sa 10am-5pm, Su 1-5pm. $8.50.)

CHIPPEWA NATIONAL FOREST   ☎218

Gleaming white strands of birch lace the Norway pine forests of the Chippewa National Forest, home to the highest density of breeding bald eagles in the continental US. The national forest shares territory with the **Leech Lake Indian Reservation,** land of 3725 Ojibwe tribespeople. The Ojibwe, mistakenly called Chippewa, migrated from the Atlantic coast in the 18th century and, in the mid-19th century, were forced onto reservations such as Leech Lake by the US government.

Cheap, plentiful, and available in varying degrees of modernity, **camping** is the way to stay in the forest. The Forest Office (see below) has info on 23 campgrounds and more than 400 free primitive recreation sites. Billboards for private campgrounds string the edges of Rte. 71 along the western border of the forest. For those who prefer more permanent forms of shelter, **Stony Point Resort ❺**, 8724 Stoney Point Camp Trail NW, 7 mi. east of Walker off Rte. 200 then 4 mi. north on Onigum Rd., rents modern lakeside cabins. (☎547-1665 or 800-338-9303. Open May-Sept. Rates for 4 or 6 from $115; $20 for each additional person.) Next door, the **National Forest Campground ❶** provides a budget-friendly alternative. (☎877-444-6777. Self-regulated sites $18.)

For the northbound traveler, **Walker,** a small town in the southwest corner of the park and reservation, is an ideal gateway to the forest. Known as the "Fishing Capital of Minnesota," it draws thousands of tourists each summer. **Leech Lake Area Chamber of Commerce** is on Rte. 371 downtown. (☎547-1313 or 800-833-1118; www.leech-lake.com. Open May-Sept. M-F 9am-5pm, Sa 10am-1pm; Oct.-Apr. M-F 9am-5pm.) The **Forest Office,** just east of town on Rte. 371, has the dirt on outdoor activities. (☎547-1044. Open M-F 7:30am-4:30pm.) **Greyhound** runs from Minneapolis to Walker (4½hr., daily 12:20pm, $42.50); buy tickets from the driver. **Post Office:** 515 Michigan Ave. (☎547-1123. Open M-F 9am-4pm, Sa 9-11:30am.) **ZIP code:** 56484. **Area code:** 218.

IRON RANGE   ☎218

It was the cry of *"Gold!"* that brought a flood of miners to join loggers and trappers already in the area, but it was the staying power of iron that kept settlers in the Iron Range. With 120 mi. of wilderness and small towns along Minnesota Rte. 169, the Range produces over 50% of the country's steel. Although taconite mining techniques have undermined the profitability of underground mines, Iron Rangers continue to celebrate their heritage with exhibitions of past industrial glory.

EVELETH

The Iron Range could also be named the Hockey Player Range after its other major export. The town of Eveleth, 10 mi. east of Chisolm on Rte. 53, has produced more elite hockey players than any other city of its size in the country. As such, it is the home of the **US Hockey Hall of Fame,** 801 Hat Trick Ave. Focusing on collegiate and Olympic success, the Hall honors American-born players of this the hardest hitting sport. (☎744-5167 or 800-443-7825; www.ushockeyhall.com. Open M-Sa 9am-5pm, Su 10am-3pm. $6, seniors and ages 13-17 $5, ages 6-12 $4, under 6 free.) Further proof that they take their hockey seriously in Eveleth: the 107 ft. long **World's Largest Hockey Stick**, at Grant and Monroe St. Follow the signs marked "Big Stick."

SOUDAN

For those who feel the need to dig deeper, the town of Soudan, 50 mi. northeast of Chisolm on Rte. 169, features an unforgettable journey ½ mi. underground in a high-speed elevator (or "cage") at the ◼**Soudan Underground Mine State Park,** off Rte. 1. The oldest and deepest iron ore mine in the state, the "Cadillac of Underground Mines" offers fascinating tours given by retired miners and their families.

GREAT LAKES

Visitors go by train almost a mile into the underground maze to experience the dark, difficult lives of ore workers in the Iron Range. Bring sturdy shoes and a jacket—it's always a chilly 50°F underground. (☎753-2245. Park open June-Sept. daily 9am-6pm; tours every 30min. 10am-4pm. $7, ages 5-12 $5, under 5 free; $4 state park vehicle permit required.) Next door, the **McKinley Park Campground ❶**, overlooking Lake Vermilion, rents semi-private campsites, with restrooms, showers, laundry facilities, bait and tackle, and firewood. (☎753-5921. Open May-Oct. Sites $15, with hookup $20.)

ELY

The charming town of Ely serves as a launching pad into both the **Boundary Waters Canoe Area Wilderness** (**BWCAW**; see **Boundary Waters**, p. 602) and the Iron Range, and thus supports its share of wilderness outfitters and attractions. The **International Wolf Center,** just north of downtown at 1396 Rte. 169, houses five gray wolves, offers BWCAW permits, and has displays on *Canis lupus.* (☎365-4695 or 800-359-9653. Open July-Aug. daily 9am-7pm; May-June and Sept.-Oct. 9am-5pm; Nov.-Apr. Sa-Su 10am-5pm. $6.50, seniors $6, ages 6-12 $3.25. Call for wolf presentation times.) **Stony Ridge Resort ❶**, 60 W. Lakeview Pl., off Shagawa Rd., has some RV or tent campsites and cabins. (☎365-6757. RV and tent sites $15 with water, electricity, and showers. 1-bedroom cabins from $75. Canoe rental $20 per day.)

VOYAGEURS NATIONAL PARK   ☎218

Voyageurs National Park sits on Minnesota's boundary with Ontario, accessible almost solely by boat. Named for the French Canadian fur traders who once traversed the area, the park invites today's voyagers to leave the auto-dominated world and push off into the longest inland lake waterway on the continent. As the traders did, today's travelers can also canoe to reach these northern woods. Preservation efforts have kept the area much as it was in the late 18th century, with wolves, bear, deer, and moose roaming freely. Summer visitors explore the seven hiking trails the park offers, while winter visitors bundle up to cross-country ski and snowmobile. *The dangers of undeveloped wilderness still remain. Water should be boiled for at least 10min.; some fish contain mercury. Ticks bearing Lyme disease have been found as well. Visitors should take precautions* (see **Preventing Disease**, p. 40).

Many of the campsites in the park are accessible only by water. Several car-accessible sites lie outside Voyageurs in the state forest, including **Woodenfrog ❶**, about 4 mi. from Kabetogama Lake Visitors Center on Rte. 122, and **Ash River ❶**, 3 mi. from the Visitors Center on Rte. 129. (☎875-2602. Primitive sites $9.) The **Ash Trail Lodge ❺**, 10 mi. east of Rte. 53 on Rte. 129, is a good option for the wilderness-challenged, offering roomy cabins, a restaurant/bar, and lots of socializing in a wooded environment. (☎374-3131 or 800-777-4513. 10 cabins available; min. stay 3 nights. 3 nights $300-1200.) **International Falls,** the inspiration for Rocky and Bullwinkle's hometown of Frostbite Falls, has other lodging options and a few attractions outside Voyageurs. For traditional indoor accommodations, Rte. 53 is loaded with motels. The **Tee Pee Motel ❷**, 1501 2nd Ave., at Rte. 53, features homey rooms with cable TV, fridge, and A/C. (☎283-8494. Singles $40; doubles $50.) **International Voyageurs RV Campground ❶**, 5min. south of town on Rte. 53 at City Rd. 24, offers decent camping with showers and laundry. (☎283-4679. RV sites for 1-2 people with full hookup $18; tent sites for 1-2 people $12; additional person $2.)

The **International Falls Convention and Visitors Bureau**, 301 2nd Ave. in downtown, hands out travel info on the area. (☎800-325-5766. Open M-F 8am-5pm.) The park can be accessed through **Crane Lake, Ash River, Kabetogama Lake,** or **Rainy Lake** (all east of Rte. 53) or through **International Falls,** at the northern tip of Rte. 53, just

FOLLOW THE YELLOW BRICK ROAD Best remembered as gingham-checked Dorothy in the cinematic classic "The Wizard of Oz," Judy Garland was born "Frances Gumm" somewhere over the rainbow in Grand Rapids, MN, 40 mi. southwest of Chisolm. Today, the white house and garden are preserved as the **Judy Garland Birthplace and Museum.** Tour the premises, or drop by in June to mingle with Munchkins at the annual **Judy Garland Festival.** To get there, click your heels three times, or travel south on Hwy. 169 in Grand Rapids. (☎ *800-664-5839; www.judygarlandmuseum.com. Open mid-May to mid-Oct. daily 10am-5pm. $3.)*

below Ft. Frances, ON. There are three Visitors Centers in the park: **Rainy Lake,** at the end of Rte. 11, 12 mi. east of International Falls (☎ 286-5258; open mid-May to Sept. daily 9am-5pm; Oct. to mid-May W-Su 9am-4:30pm); **Ash River,** 8 mi. east of Rte. 53 on Rte. 129, then 3 mi. north (☎ 374-3221; open mid-May to Sept. daily 9am-5pm); and **Kabetogama Lake,** 1 mi. north of Rte. 122 marked with signs to follow (☎ 875-2111; open mid-May to Sept. daily 9am-5pm). Voyageurs offers many ranger-led hikes and boat cruises; call any Visitors Center for info.

SCENIC DRIVE: NORTH SHORE DRIVE

Vast and mysterious, Lake Superior shapes the landscape of Northeastern Minnesota with its jagged, glacier-carved edges and seemingly limitless surface. Scenic overlooks on the lake's North Shore provide harrowing views of the crashing waves below. Inland, the **Sawtooth Mountains** hover over the lake with stunning rock formations and tall, sweeping birch trees.

The true Lake Superior North Shore extends 646 mi. from Duluth, MN to Sault Ste. Marie, ON; but **Rte. 61,** winding 150 mi. along the coast from Duluth to Grand Portage, gives travelers an abbreviated version of the spectacular journey. Most of the small, touristy fishing towns along the shore maintain Visitors Centers. The **R.J. Houle Visitor Information Center,** 21 mi. from Duluth up Rte. 61 in picturesque **Two Harbors,** has lodging guides and information for each town along the Minnesota stretch of the North Shore. (☎ 834-4005 or 800-554-2116. Open June to mid-Oct. M-Sa 9am-5pm, Su 9am-3pm; mid-Oct. to May W-Sa 9am-1pm.) Rte. 61 is often congested with boat-towing pickup trucks and family-filled campers on summer weekends. Accommodations flanking the roadside fill up fast in summer; make reservations early. Remember to bring warm clothes—temperatures can drop as low as 40°F, even on summer nights.

Striking views of the jagged cliffs that descend to the massive lake are the greatest appeal of Rte. 61. State parks scattered along the route not only afford more in-depth looks at the shore but also boast stunning attractions of their own. Camping at **Gooseberry Falls State Park ❶** is an appealing lodging option. (☎ 834-3855. Park open daily 8am-10pm; Visitors Center open 9am-7pm. Primitive sites with shower $12; vehicle permit $4 per day.) Twenty miles northeast of the Visitors Center, **Gooseberry Falls** crashes down to the lake with five rugged waterfalls and scenic overlooks. The adventuresome can climb on the middle or lower falls for a head-on view, or hike ½ mi. to the spectacular rocky shore.

Eight miles down the road, the **Split Rock Lighthouse** takes visitors back to the lake's industrial heyday and elevates them to a birds-eye view atop a 130 ft. cliff. (☎ 226-6372. Open mid-May to mid-Oct. daily 9am-6pm; call for winter hours. $6, seniors $5, ages 6-12 $4.) Rte. 61 becomes more convoluted as it enters the **Lake Superior National Forest** and passes over countless winding rivers and creeks toward Tofte, where the 1526 ft. **Carlton Peak** dominates the landscape. The pine-paneled **Cobblestone Cabins ❶,** off Rte. 61, 2 mi. north of Tofte, provide the road-weary eight cabins to stay in and access to a cobblestone beach, canoes, a wood-burning sauna, and kitchenettes. (☎ 633-7957. Open May-Oct. Cabins $30-80.)

GRAND MARAIS   ☎218

Near the north end of the 150 mi. scenic drive, this fishing resort village and former artists' colony is a popular tourist spot and a good place to sleep and eat. **The Grand Marais Visitor Information Center** can be found at N. Broadway off Rte. 61. (☎387-2524 or 888-922-5000. Open M-Sa 10am-4pm.) **Nelson's Traveler's Rest ❷,** on Rte. 61, ½ mi. west of town, provides fully-equipped cabins with a lake view. (☎387-1464 or 800-249-1285. Open mid-May to mid-Oct. Call in advance. Single cabins from $35; doubles from $49.) **Grand Marais Recreation Area RV Park-Campground ❶,** off Rte. 61, has wooded and mostly private primitive sites by the lake. (☎387-1712 or 800-998-0959. Office open daily 6am-10pm. Reservations recommended. Open May to mid-Oct. Primitive sites May-June and Sept.-Oct. $16, July-Aug. $21; with water and electricity $20/25; discounted use of municipal pool.)

Cheap and popular with locals and fishermen, **South of the Border Cafe ❶,** 4 W. Rte. 61, specializes in huge breakfasts (served all day) and satisfying diner food. The bluefin herring sandwich (fried, of course) costs $3.25. (☎387-1505. Breakfast under $7. Open daily 5am-2pm.) No sweet tooth can accuse **World's Best Doughnuts ❶,** at the intersection of Wisconsin and Broadway St., of false advertising. (☎387-1345. Open late May to mid-Oct. daily 7:30am until sold out, usually around 4pm. Doughnuts from 55¢.)

🏕 **BOUNDARY WATERS.** Grand Marais also serves as a gateway to the **Boundary Waters Canoe Area Wilderness (BWCAW),** a designated wilderness area comprising 1.2 million acres of lakes, streams, and forests. The BWCAW is understandably finicky about when, where, and how many people it will allow to enter; phoning ahead is essential. One mile south of Grand Marais, the **Gunflint Ranger Station** distributes permits. (☎387-1750. Open June-Sept. daily 6am-8pm; Oct.-Apr. M-F 8am-4:30pm; May 6am-6pm.) Make reservations with National Recreation Reservation Service. (☎877-444-6777; www.reserveusa.com. Day permits free, camping permits $10 per person per trip.) Running northwest from town, the 60 mi. paved **Gunflint Trail** (County Rd. 12) is the only developed road offering access to the wilderness from Rte. 61. Both resorts and outfitters gather on this lone strip of civilization. **Bear Track Outfitting Co.,** 2011 W. Rte. 61, across from the Gunflint Ranger Station, rents boats and sells camping necessities. (☎387-1162 or 800-795-8068. 1-2 day canoe rental including accessories from $24. 1-2 day kayak rental from $32.)

GREAT PLAINS

In 1803, the Louisiana Purchase doubled America's size, adding French territory west of the Mississippi at the bargain price of 4¢ per acre. Over time, the plains spawned legends of pioneers and cowboys and of Native Americans struggling to defend their homelands. The arrival of railroad transportation and liberal land policies spurred an economic boom, until a drought during the Great Depression transformed the region into a dust bowl. Since the 1930s, the region has been struggling to settle on an effective course of development. Modern agriculture has reclaimed the soil, and the heartland of the United States now thrives on the trade of farm commodities. The Plains are also a vast land of prairies, where open sky stretches from horizon to horizon, broken only by long, thin lines of trees. Grasses and grains paint the land green and gold. The land rules here, as its inhabitants know. While signs of humanity are unmistakable—checkerboard farms, Army posts, and railroad corridors—the region's most staggering sights are the work of nature, from the Badlands and the Black Hills to the mighty Missouri and Mississippi Rivers.

HIGHLIGHTS OF THE GREAT PLAINS

NATIONAL PARKS AND MONUMENTS. Discover the uncrowded gems of Theodore Roosevelt National Park, ND (p. 608), and the Badlands, SD (p. 612), or join the crowds in the Black Hills around Mt. Rushmore (p. 615).

HISTORICAL SITES. Scotts Bluff National Monument, NE (p. 633), and Chimney Rock, NE (p. 633) will fascinate anyone interested in the pioneers.

NORTH DAKOTA

An early visitor to Fargo declared, "It's a beautiful land, but I doubt that human beings will ever live here." Posterity begs to differ. The stark, haunting lands that intimidated early settlers eventually found willing tenants, and the territory became a state along with South Dakota on Nov. 2, 1889. The inaugural event was not without confusion—Benjamin Harrison concealed the names when he signed the two bills, so both Dakotas claim to be the 39th state. North Dakota lies just a bit too far north to attract throngs of summer tourists, but awe-inspiring natural beauty greets those who do visit.

🛈 PRACTICAL INFORMATION

Capital: Bismarck.

Visitor info: Tourism Dept., 400 E. Broadway, #50, Bismarck 58501 (☎800-435-5663; www.ndtourism.com). **Parks and Recreation Dept.,** 1835 Bismarck Expwy., Bismarck 58504 (☎328-5357; www.ndparks.com). **Game and Fish Dept.,** 100 N. Bismarck Expwy., Bismarck 58501 (☎328-6300). All state offices open M-F 8am-5pm.

Postal Abbreviation: ND. **Sales Tax:** 7%.

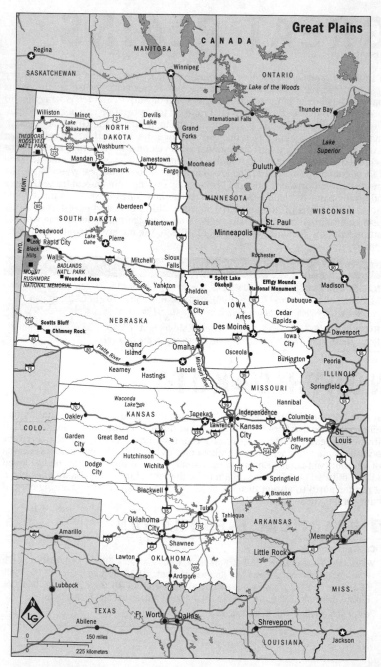

Great Plains

FARGO ☎ 701

Although it is North Dakota's largest city, Fargo languished in anonymity until the Oscar-winning 1996 film *Fargo* brought its name recognition. Very little of the movie was filmed in the town, however, and its parodied accents are more northern Minnesota than North Dakota. All the same, Fargo and its sister city, Moorhead, MN, are home to 20,000 students who pack lectures at **North Dakota State University (NDSU), Moorhead State,** and **Concordia College.** Amid this youthful vigor, the region's northern European cultural heritage flourishes.

🔃 PRACTICAL INFORMATION. Fargo and Moorhead flank the **Red River of the North** on the west and east, respectively. Numbered streets running north-south and numbered avenues running east-west connect the cities. **Main Ave.** is the central east-west thoroughfare and intersects **I-29. Hector International Airport** is at 2801 32nd Ave. NW (☎ 241-8168), off N. 19th Ave. in northern Fargo. **Amtrak** is at 420 N. 4th St. (☎ 232-2197). **Greyhound** is at 402 Northern Pacific (N.P.) Ave. (☎ 293-1222. Open daily 6am-6pm and 10pm-1:30am.) **Metro Area Transit,** 502 North Pacific Ave., runs buses across the city. (☎ 232-7500. Operates M-Sa.) Sort out your visit at the **Fargo-Moorhead Convention and Visitors Bureau,** 2001 44th St. SW, off 45th St. Follow the blue signs from I-29 Exit 63B. (☎ 800-235-7654; www.fargomoorhead.org. Open May-Aug. M-F 7:30am-7pm, Sa 9am-6pm; Sept.-Apr. M-F 8am-5pm, Sa 9am-6pm.) **Public Library:** 102 N. 3rd St. (☎ 241-1491; open Sept.-May M-Th 9am-9pm, F 11am-6pm, Sa 9am-6pm, Su 1-6pm; June-Aug. M-Th 9am-9pm, F-Sa 9am-6pm.) **Crisis Line:** ☎ 235-7335. Operates 24hr. **Post Office:** 657 N. 2nd Ave. (Open M-F 7:30am-5:30pm, Sa 8am-2pm.) **ZIP code:** 58102. **Area code:** 701.

🖪🖸 ACCOMMODATIONS & FOOD. Cheap chain motels abound at I-29 and 13th Ave.; take Exit 64 off I-29. **The Sunset Motel ❶,** 731 W. Main, in West Fargo about 3 mi. west off I-29 Exit 65, offers clean rooms, free local calls, continental breakfast, and an indoor pool with a snazzy two-story waterslide. (☎ 800-252-2207. Call early on weekends. Singles $29-40, with kitchenette $34-45; doubles from $49/54.) The best bed and breakfast deal in town is at **Chez Susanne ❸,** 1100 S. 3rd Ave., at S. 11th St. A beautifully restored 1899 Victorian home on the National Historic Register, Chez Susanne beckons guests with a library, office, exercise equipment, and freshly baked goods. (☎ 866-787-2663. Make reservations early in summer. One 2-room suite $85; two 3-room suites $100.) Follow signs from I-94, Exit 351, to **Lindenwood Park ❶,** at 17th Ave. and S. 5th St. The campground offers sites close to the peaceful Red River of the North. The park also has extensive trails ideal for mountain biking. (☎ 232-3987. Restrooms and showers available. Tent sites $10, RV sites with water and electricity $17.)

Erbert & Gerbert's ❶, 68 Broadway, puts together great club sandwiches and subs on freshly baked bread. Vegetarians will be delighted with the "Jacob Bluefinger" ($3.75). There are plenty of meat options as well. (☎ 235-3445. Open M-Th and Su 10:30am-11pm, F-Sa 10:30am-2am.) **Cafe Aladdin ❷,** 530 N. 6th Ave., is popular for its scrumptious Greek and Middle Eastern food. (☎ 298-0880. Sweet, flaky baklava $1.65. Entrees $4-7.50. Open M-Sa 10:30am-8pm.) Named for a small zoo that once sat by the edge of the Red River, the **Red Bear Grill and Tavern ❸,** 700 N. 1st Ave., in Moorhead, serves mouth-watering burgers ($5-7) and prime rib ($12-14) in a historic building. (☎ 218-287-0080. Open M-Sa 11am-1am, Su 10:30am-midnight.)

🖼🖾 SIGHTS & ENTERTAINMENT. The **Heritage Hjemkomst Center,** 202 1st Ave. N, in Moorhead, pays a moving tribute to the area's Norwegian roots. Inside looms the Hjemkomst (*YEM-komst*), a 76 ft. Viking ship replica built by Moorhead native Robert Asp that sailed the 6100 mi. from Duluth, MN to Bergen, Norway in 1982.

Outside, a 72 ft. stave church replica, built by Moorhead native Guy Paulson, greets visitors. (☎218-299-5511. Open M and W-Sa 9am-5pm, Tu 9am-9pm, Su noon-5pm. $4.50, seniors and college students $4, ages 5-17 $3.) The **Scandinavian Hjemkomst Festival** is a big draw, complete with cultural exhibits, music and dance shows, and food. (☎218-299-5452. June 27-29, 2003.) From June to August, **Troll-wood Park Weekends** (☎241-8160) feature similar events.

NDSU students tend to frequent the bars along Broadway near Northern Pacific Ave. The newest and most frequented dance club in the city is **Old Broadway**, 22 Broadway, with two levels of dance floors and plenty of people-watching spots. (☎237-6161. Cover F-Sa $2. Open M-Sa 4pm-1am.) If you're craving culture, head to the **Historic Fargo Theatre**, 314 Broadway. Restored to its 1937 Art Deco Period, the theater now shows art flicks and hosts the **Fargo Film Festival** every spring. (Box office ☎235-4152; www.fargotheatre.org. Tickets $7.)

BISMARCK ☎701

Bismarck is extremely clean, the people are open and friendly, and the scenery is spectacular. Even with only 55,000 residents, it still has the look and feel of a large town. Bismarck is the most comfortable North Dakotan city to relax, enjoy the scenery, and learn about pioneer culture. The city was founded on land that defies the notion that all prairies are flat: seas of yellow wildflowers, grids of green farmland, and fields of golden wheat blend with surprising harmony. Meanwhile, the city lures travelers back indoors with upscale restaurants and lively nightspots.

■ ■ **ORIENTATION & PRACTICAL INFORMATION.** Bismarck is on I-94, halfway between Fargo and Theodore Roosevelt National Park. The **Missouri River** separates Bismarck from Mandan, its neighbor to the west. **Washington** and **9th St.** are the main north-south thoroughfares and are intersected by Main, Divide, and Interstate Ave. The **Bismarck Municipal Airport** (☎222-6502), is on Airport Rd., 2 mi. southeast of the city. **Greyhound**, 3750 E. Rosser Ave. (☎223-6576; open daily 9am-1pm and 5-8pm), runs buses to Fargo (4hr.; 3 per day; M-Th $33, F-Su $35) and Billings (7½hr.; 3 per day; M-Th $67, F-Su $71). **Taxis: Taxi 9000** (☎223-9000). **Short-Term Work:** Job Service North Dakota, 216 N. 2nd St. (☎800-247-0981). **Internet access** is free for 1hr. at the **Bismarck Public Library**, 515 N. 5th St. (☎222-6410), but email costs 50¢ per 30min. (Open June-Aug. M-Th 9am-9pm, F 9am-6pm, Sa 9am-5pm, Su 1-5pm; Sept.-May M-F 9am-9pm, Sa 9am-5pm, Su 1-5pm.) The **Bismarck-Mandan Visitors Center**, 1600 Burnt Boat Dr., Exit 157 off I-94, has the *Bismarck-Mandan Visitors Guide*. (☎800-767-3555; www.bismarck-mandancvb.org. Open June-Aug. M-F 7:30am-7pm, Sa 8am-6pm, Su 10am-5pm; Sept.-May M-F 8am-5pm.) **Post Office:** 220 E. Rosser Ave. (☎221-6501. Open M-F 7:45am-5:50pm, Sa 10am-noon.) **ZIP code:** 58501. **Area code:** 701.

■ ■ **ACCOMMODATIONS & FOOD.** Budget motels abound at I-94 at Exit 159. The best value around is the **Select Inn ❷**, 1505 Interchange Ave., Exit 159 off I-94, with clean and spacious rooms, laundry access, and continental breakfast. (☎800-641-1000. Coupons in the *Bismarck-Mandan Visitors Guide*. Singles $45; doubles $52. AAA discount.) The **Bismarck Motor Hotel ❷**, 2301 E. Main Ave., offers decent rooms, each with a microwave and fridge. (☎223-2474. Singles $32.50; doubles $42.50.) Camping is relaxing in the beautiful **Fort Abraham Lincoln State Park ❶** (see **Sights**, below), 7 mi. south on Rte. 1806 in Mandan. Tent sites line the banks of the Missouri River and have an amazing view of the surrounding prairie. (☎663-9571. $7, with electricity $12.; vehicle fee $4.)

YOU ARE NOW ONLY FIVE PAGES FROM WALL DRUG.

With an enormous menu of pasta, chicken, seafood, and sandwiches ($5-10), the ◼Walrus ❷, 1136 N. 3rd. St., in Arrowhead Plaza, is a local favorite. The Italian sausage pizziola ($6.50) is a house specialty. (☎250-0020. Open M-Sa 10:30am-1am.) **Peacock Alley Bar and Grill ❷**, 422 E. Main Ave., delivers scrumptious salads ($5-7), sandwiches ($6-8), and pastas ($8) among peacock blue decor in the old Patterson Hotel—the tallest building in the state when it was built in 1910. (☎255-7917. Open for brunch Sa 10am-12:30pm and Su 9am-1pm; lunch M-F 11am-2pm; and dinner M 5:30-9pm and Tu-Sa 5:30-10pm.) What **Happy Joe's ❶**, 2921 N. 11th St., in the Amoco Station near State St. and Century Ave., lacks in atmosphere, it makes up for with fantastic pizza. Lunch specials with beverage are $3.15, and whole pizzas cost $10-15. (☎355-1146. Open M-Th and Su 7am-10pm, F-Sa 7am-11pm.) Housed in the old Northern Pacific train depot, **Fiesta Villa ❷**, 411 E. Main Ave., serves quesadillas, tacos, and other Mexican fare with homemade sauces. Enjoy your selection inside the historic building or soak up the atmosphere on the open-air patio. (☎222-8075. Entrees $6-9. Open M-Sa 11am-11pm; patio open until 1am on busy evenings.)

◪ **SIGHTS.** The **North Dakota State Capitol,** 600 E. Boulevard Ave, the efficient 19-story office-style building was built between 1932 and 1934 for only $2 million. Inside, visitors view examples of Art Deco architecture in the beautiful Memorial Hall. The observation deck on the 19th floor is a great place to see the prairie and the Capitol's 130 acres of well-manicured grounds. (☎328-2580. Open M-F 7am-5:30pm. 30-45min. tours leave Sept.-May M-F every hour 8-11am and 1-4pm; June-Aug. M-F 8-11am and 1-4pm, Sa 9-11am and 1-4pm, Su 1-4pm. Free.) Right next door to the Capitol is the **North Dakota Heritage Center,** 612 E. Boulevard Ave., an excellent historical museum with exhibits ranging from triceratops to traders to tractors. (☎328-2666. Open M-F 8am-5pm, Sa 9am-5pm, Su 11am-5pm. Free.) On Rte. 1806 in Mandan, **Fort Abraham Lincoln State Park** houses an "On-a-Slant" Mandan Indian village as well as replicas of the cavalry post and Victorian-style home of Lt. Col. George Armstrong Custer. (☎663-3069. Open June-Aug. Buildings open daily 9am-7pm; park 9am-9:30pm. $4, students $2; vehicle fee $4.)

A daytrip from Bismarck satisfies the curiosity of those interested in the Corps of Discovery, the expedition led by Captains Meriwether Lewis and William Clark. The **Lewis and Clark Interpretive Center,** 38 mi. north of Bismarck at the junction of Rte. 83 and Rte. 200A, presents an overview of the explorer's wilderness journey. Visitors can don buffalo robes and a cradle board, just like the one young Sakajawea once wore, or simulate trading with the Indians using an interactive computer program. Two miles away at **Fort Mandan,** modern-day trailblazers can enter a replica of the rugged riverside lodgings that sheltered the expedition during the winter of 1804. (☎462-8535 or 877-462-8535. Center open June-Aug. daily 9am-7pm; Sept.-May 9am-5pm. Fort open daily 8:30am-sunset. Admission to both attractions $5, students $3.)

🎭🎬 **ENTERTAINMENT & NIGHTLIFE.** The **Bismarck Symphony** (☎258-8345) plays in the magnificent **Belle Mehus Auditorium,** 201 N. 6th St. The symphony celebrates holidays in style—8000 people turn up for their Fourth of July concert on the Capitol steps. From October to April, musical programs can be heard on select Sunday afternoons. Locals agree that the coolest place to be in Bismarck these days is **Borrowed Buck's Roadhouse,** 118 S. 3rd St. Decorated like an old service station, Buck's has a full dance floor and a live DJ every night. Rock music is the

THE LOCAL STORY

SPEAK SOFTLY...

For the past six years, Ray Anderson has donned spectacles, sported a moustache, and adopted a hearty belly laugh to portray US President Theodore Roosevelt in the one-man show Bully *and guest star in the* Medora Musical.

Q: How did you come to portray the character of Teddy Roosevelt?

A: In 1997, I answered an ad in the paper in Minneapolis, went to an audition, and got the job. It had never occurred to me that I would look like Teddy Roosevelt or could act like him. So I started studying Teddy Roosevelt and discovered that I really liked the guy, and then I discovered that I really could look like him, too.

Q: What makes TR so likable?

A: For one thing, he was the most totally honest politician who ever existed, and he would not take orders from anyone.

Q: What's your favorite Roosevelt phrase or quote?

A: BULLY!..."Far better it is to dare mighty things, to win glorious triumphs, even though checkered by failure, than to take rank with those poor spirits who neither enjoy much nor suffer much because they live in the gray twilight that knows not victory nor defeat." It's one of my favorite things about Roosevelt—he believed in taking chances. Marvelous man, absolutely marvelous man.

Q: Do you have any teddy bears of your own?

A: I've got about 30, and I give them away all the time. Kids love 'em.

focus, but on Wednesday the venue changes to country for the "Dance Ranch." Live bands take the stage once or twice a month, and the performances are well-advertised around the city. (☎224-1545. 21+. Open M-F 4pm-1am, Sa noon-1am.) If only one night of country a week isn't enough, look no farther than **Lonesome Dove**, 3929 Memorial Hwy. on the border of Mandan. The *real* country joint in Bismarck, Lonesome Dove has a large dance floor and live, toe-tappin' country music W-Su. (☎663-2793. Open daily noon-1am.)

THEODORE ROOSEVELT NATIONAL PARK ☎701

After his mother and wife died on the same day, pre-White House Theodore Roosevelt moved to his ranch in the Badlands for spiritual renewal. He was so influenced by the red and brown hued buttes and gorges, horseback riding, big-game hunting, and cattle ranching in this "place of grim beauty" that he later claimed, "I never would have been President if it weren't for my experiences in North Dakota." Inspired by his wilderness days, Roosevelt established numerous national parks, monuments, and bird refuges. Roosevelt National Park was created in 1947 as a monument to his conservationist efforts.

🔌🔁 ORIENTATION & PRACTICAL INFORMATION. The park is split into **south** and **north units** and is bisected by the border separating **Mountain** and **Central Time Zones.** The entrance to the more-developed south unit is just north of I-94 in **Medora**, a revamped tourist haven with many an ice cream parlor and gift "shoppe." **Greyhound** serves Medora from Western Edge Books at the corner of Broadway and Fourth St., with buses to Bismarck (3½hr., 3 per day, $25-27) and Billings (6hr., 2 per day, $52-55). There is no ticket office in Medora; buy your ticket during the **Dickinson** layover. **Dakota Cyclery**, 275 3rd Ave., rents bikes. (☎623-4808. Open daily 9am-6pm. $20-30 per half-day; full-day $30-45.) The Cyclery also leads bike tours by reservation of the plains and badlands. Off-road biking is not allowed in either unit of Theodore Roosevelt National Park. The park entrance fee ($5 per person, under 17 free; $10 max. per vehicle) covers admission to both units of the park for seven days. The **South Unit's Visitors Center**, in Medora, maintains a mini-museum displaying Roosevelt's guns, spurs, and old letters, as well as a beautiful 13min. film detailing his relationship with the land. (☎623-4466. Open late June to Sept. daily 8am-8pm; Sept. to mid-June 8am-4:30pm.) The **North Unit's Visitors Center** has an interesting exhibit on the nature and wildlife in the park. (☎842-2333. Open year-round daily 9am-5:30pm.) For more info, write to **Theodore Roosevelt National Park**, P.O. Box 7, Medora 58645, call the Visitors Center, or check out their website (www.nps.gov/thro).

Medora lacks a real pharmacy and grocery store. However, both the **Ferris Store**, 251 Main St. (☎623-4447; open daily 8am-8pm), and **Medora Convenience and Liquor**, on Pacific Ave. at Main St. (☎623-4479; open daily 7am-10pm), sell basic pharmaceutical goods, food, and cooking items. There is a 24hr. **Walmart** (☎225-8504) in Dickinson, 30 mi. east on I-94. **South unit time zone:** Mountain (2hr. behind Eastern). **North unit time zone:** Central (1hr. behind Eastern). **Post Office:** 355 3rd Ave., in Medora. (☎623-4385. Open M-Sa 8am-7pm; window service M-F 8am-noon and 12:30-4:30pm, Sa 8:15am-9:45am.) **ZIP code:** 58645. **Area code:** 701.

ⁿⁿ ACCOMMODATIONS & FOOD. Free backcountry camping permits are available from the Visitors Centers. **Cottonwood Campgrounds ❶** lies just inside the south entrance. In the north, **Juniper Campground ❶,** 5 mi. west of the north unit entrance, is in a beautiful valley. The campground is a popular buffalo nightspot all year, so beware. Both campgrounds have toilets and running water in the summer, but only pit toilets in the winter. (Sites $10; during winter $5.) It's not easy to find cheap lodging in Medora without camping. The **Medora Motel ❸,** 400 E. River Rd. South, offers some of the cheapest rates and has A/C, cable TV, and an outdoor heated swimming pool. (☎800-633-6721. Register at the Badlands Motel on Pacific Ave. Open Memorial Day-Labor Day. Singles $57; doubles $64; family units $85. Children free.) Teddy Roosevelt was known to bunk down at the **Rough Riders Hotel ❹,** 301 3rd Ave. The hotel's room rates are a little high, but the restaurant serves reasonable breakfasts and lunches ($4-7) and dinner ($12-20) in an upscale atmosphere. (☎623-4444, ext. 497. Open daily 7am-9pm. In winter, B&B only. Singles $73-83.) The **Iron Horse Saloon ❸,** 160 Pacific Ave., offers great American standards year-round. (☎623-9894. Breakfast and lunch $4-7. Dinner $7-15. Open June-Sept. daily 6am-1am; Oct.-May 10:30am-1am.)

⬛ ENTERTAINMENT. The popular **Medora Musical** is a comical singing, dancing, and theatrical experience, attracting hordes nightly with a celebration of the glory of the West and Teddy Roosevelt himself. The show, held in the open-air **Burning Hills Amphitheatre** west of town, incorporates the magnificent natural landscape into the performance and includes various outside talent acts, ranging from magicians to comedians to Argentine Gauchos. ($20-22, students $11.50-12.50. Show early June to early Sept. daily 8:30-10:30pm.) Before the show, cast members from the musical serenade the audience as they clog their arteries at the **Pitchfork Fondue ❺.** The "chef" puts ten steaks on a pitchfork and dips them into a vat of boiling oil for five minutes. ($20, under 18 $11.50; includes buffet. Daily at 6:30pm. Reservations required.) Tickets for both the musical and the fondue are available at the Burning Hills Amphitheatre, 335 4th St., at the **Harold Schafer Heritage Center** (☎800-633-6721; www.medora.com. Open daily 10am-6pm.)

⬛ OUTDOOR ACTIVITIES. The **south unit** is busier and more crowded than the north unit and includes a 36 mi. **scenic automobile loop,** from which all sights and trails are accessible. **Painted Canyon Overlook,** 7 mi. east of Medora off I-94, has its own **Visitors Center** with picnic tables and a breathtaking panoramic view of the Badlands, while the occasional buffalo roams through the parking lot. The **Painted Canyon Trail** is a worthwhile 1 mi. hiking loop that undulates gently through shady wooded areas and scorching buttes. (☎575-4020. Open June-Aug. daily 8am-6pm; mid-Apr. to late May and early Sept. to mid-Nov. 8:30am-4:30pm. Free.) **Peaceful Valley Ranch,** 7 mi. into the park, offers horseback excursions. (☎623-4568. 1½hr. trail rides leave in summer daily 8:30am-2pm; evening ride 6pm. 8-9 per day. $20.)

SINGING IN THE PLAIN. The seclusion of Theodore Roosevelt Park provides ample opportunity for wildlife contact, but be careful not to surprise the buffalo; one ranger advises singing while hiking so they can hear you coming. Also beware of rattlesnakes and black widow spiders living in prairie dog burrows. ⚐Prairie dogs have bites more menacing than their barks.

The **Ridgeline Trail** is a self-guided 0.6 mi. hiking trail. Signs along the way describe the ecology and geology of the terrain. The 0.8 mi. **Coal Vein Trail** traces a seam of lignite coal that ignited and burned from 1951 to 1977; the searing heat of the blaze served as a natural kiln, baking the adjacent clay and sand. **Buck Hill** is accessible by car, but a short climb up a steep paved path yields a full view of the Badlands landscape. Constant winds continue to morph the soft sands of **Wind Canyon,** and a short dirt path leads along the bluffs giving a closer look at the canyon walls and the river below. The third largest **petrified forest** in the US is a day's hike into the park; if you prefer to drive, ask the ranger for directions and expect to walk about ¾ mi. For more info on hiking, pick up a copy of the *Backcountry Guide* ($2) at one of the Visitors Centers. Tours leave periodically from the South Unit's Visitors Center for TR's **Maltese Cabin,** circa 1883. (Tours in summer 8:45am-4:15pm.)

The less-visited **north unit** of the park is 70 mi. from the south unit on U.S. 85. Equally as scenic as the south unit, it is infinitely more conducive to hiking and exploring. Most of the land is wilderness, resulting in unlimited **backcountry hiking** possibilities. For those eager to escape the crowds, but reluctant to leave the car, the north unit boasts a **14 mi. scenic drive.** The drive connects the entrance and Visitors Center to **Oxbow Overlook** and is as unsullied as possible. The 1 mi. **Little Mo Trail** weaves through woodlands and badlands, and ¾ of the 1 mi. trail is wheelchair accessible. The 11 mi. **Buckhorn Trail** is a long but relatively easy walk that includes a visit to a prairie dog town. The 1.6 mi. (round-trip) **Caprock Coulee Trail** connects with the Buckhorn Trail and journeys on fairly level ground through prairie and dry-water gulches. Seasoned hikers and adventurers will thrive on the challenging 16 mi. **Achenbach Trail** that features vertical drops and uphill climbs as it winds around the Little Missouri River, visible from the **River Bend Outlook.**

SOUTH DAKOTA

With fewer than ten people per square mile, South Dakota has the highest ratio of sights to people in all of the Great Plains. Colossal carvings such as Mt. Rushmore and the Crazy Horse Memorial and stunning natural spectacles like the Black Hills and the Badlands make tourism the state's largest industry. Buffalo roam parts of the state as do adventure-seeking tourists. Small and patient, down-to-earth and friendly, South Dakota is the highlight of the Plains.

�🛈 PRACTICAL INFORMATION

Capital: Pierre.

Visitor Info: Department of Tourism, 711 E. Wells Ave., Pierre, SD 57501 (☎605-773-3301 or 800-732-5682; www.travelsd.com). Open M-F 7am-7pm. **US Forest Service,** 330 Mt. Rushmore Rd., Custer 57730 (☎605-673-4853). Open M-F 7:30am-4:30pm. **Game, Fish, and Parks Dept.,** 523 E. Capitol Ave., Foss Bldg., Pierre 57501 (☎605-773-3391, for campground reservations ☎800-710-2267), has info on state parks and campgrounds. Open M-F 8am–5pm.

Postal Abbreviation: SD. **Sales Tax:** 4%.

SIOUX FALLS ☎ **605**

South Dakota's eastern gateway, Sioux Falls, is your typical "nice guy"—quiet, friendly, clean-cut, and a little boring—more of a place to catch your breath than a destination in itself. The city's namesake rapids are at Falls Park, north of downtown. The **Sioux River Greenway Recreation Trail** circles the city from Falls Park in the northeast to the Elmwood golf course in the northwest. At **Buffalo Ridge,** 5 mi. west of Sioux Falls at Exit 390 on I-90, you can visit a dilapidated yet endearing ghost town with over 50 educational exhibits portraying life in the Old West. Catch a glimpse of the ghost of Comanche, Custer's horse, and witness the mechanized murder of Bill Hickock in the saloon. A herd of over 50 buffalo also makes appearances near the town from time to time. (☎528-3931. Open early Apr.-Oct. sunrise to sunset. $4, children 5-12 $3.) The **Corn Palace,** 604 N. Main St., in Mitchell, 70 mi. west of Sioux Falls on I-90, poses as a regal testament to the "a-maize-ing" power of corn. Dating back to 1892, the structure is refurbished with a new mural every year using 600,000 pieces of corn in nine colors and 3,000 bushels of grains and grasses. (☎996-5031 or 800-257-2676. Open June-Aug. daily 8am-10pm; May and Sept. 8am-5pm; Oct.-Apr. M-F 8am-5pm. Free.) During summer, the **Wells Fargo Falls Park Light and Sound Show,** at the Visitors Center, enhances the natural beauty of Sioux Falls with a little help from modern technology. (Memorial Day to Labor Day nightly starting ½hr. after sunset. Free.) **Great Bear Ski Valley,** 5901 E. Rice St., has skiing, snowboarding, and snowshoeing. (☎367-4309. Call after Dec. 1 for lift ticket and rental prices.)

Budget motels flank 41st St. at Exit 77 off I-29. The **Select Inn ❷,** 3500 Gateway Blvd., is a particularly good value. (☎361-1864. Continental breakfast included. Singles $42; doubles $50; AAA discounts.) There are a number of state parks nearby. **Split Rock City Park ❶,** 20 mi. northeast in Garretson, has the cheapest camping. From I-90 E, take Exit 406, Rte. 11 N. (Corson), and drive 10 mi. to Garretson; turn right at the sign for Devil's Gulch; the park will be on your left before the tracks. (☎594-6721. Pit toilets and drinking water. Sites $6.) **Soda Falls ❶,** at the **Zandbroz Variety Store,** 209 S. Phillips Ave., has everything from fantastic sandwiches ($2-4) and sundaes ($3-4) to free gift-wrapping of purchases. The lunch counter was built in the 1920s from some of the first marble used in the Dakotas. (☎331-5137. Open M-Sa 9am-8pm, Su noon-5pm.)

A tucked-away spot with big-name comedy acts, **The Funny Bone,** 431 N. Phillips Ave., showcases local talent along with Hollywood imports. (☎339-4816. Cover $8-10. Box office opens W-F 6pm, Sa 3pm, Su 5pm. Club office open Tu-F 10am-6pm.) Dance the night away at South Dakota's best dance club, the **ACME,** 305 N. Main Ave., where clubbers spill from the dance floor onto the back patio. (☎339-1131. W 18+, Th-Sa 21+. Cover W $5, Th-Sa no cover. Open W 9pm-1am, Th-Sa 8pm-2am.)

Jack Rabbit Buses, 301 N. Dakota Ave. (☎336-0885; open daily 7:30am-5pm), hop to Minneapolis (6hr., 3 per day, $50); Omaha (4hr., 3 per day, $37); and Rapid City (9hr., 1 per day, $86). **Sioux Falls Transit** buses run throughout the city. (☎367-7183. Buses operate M-Sa 5:40am-6:55pm. $1; free transfers.) **Taxis: Yellow Cab, ☎**336-1616. **Visitors Center:** in Falls Park, between Main Ave. and Weber Ave. on Falls Park Dr. (☎367-7430. Open mid-Apr. to Sept. daily 9am-9pm; Oct. to mid-Apr. Sa-Su 9am-5pm.) The free climb up the Visitors Center's observation tower has an aerial view of the falls. **Internet access: Sioux Falls Public Library,** 201 N. Main Ave., at 8th St. (☎367-7081. Open June-Aug. M-Th 9:30am-9pm, F 9:30am-6pm, Sa 9:30am-5pm; Sept.-May M-Th 9:30am-9pm, F 9:30am-6pm, Sa 9:30am-5pm, Su 1-5pm.) **Post Office:** 320 S. 2nd Ave. (☎357-5001. Open M-F 7:30am-5:30pm, Sa 8am-1pm.) **ZIP code:** 57104. **Area code:** 605.

THE LOCAL STORY

THE WRITING IS ON THE WALL

*Ted Hustead is the third-generation president of **Wall Drug**, 510 Main St. (☎605-279-2175), the world's largest drug store. With nearly 200 enticing billboards stretching across the state and countless others across the world, Wall Drug, with its western memorabilia, clothing, and artwork, has become a major attraction for tourists in western South Dakota.*

In 1936, my grandmother came up with an idea on a hot day in the middle of summer... She said, "Ted, we've got to let the people know that we have a business here, the people that are going past Wall on their way to Mt. Rushmore and Yellowstone on dusty, dirty highway 14... Let's put up a sign and advertise our business. Let's advertise free ice water; it's 110 degrees today." My grandpa thought it was a little corny, but he was up for trying anything. He hired a couple local people and made a series of signs and put them on the edge of town: "Slow down the ol' hack—Wall Drug, just across the railroad track. Free ice water." That summer, they had to hire nine ladies here in town just to wait on all the customers that started pouring into this business as soon as they started advertising on the highway... There is a moral to this story: If Ted and Dorothy Hustead could come out here in western South Dakota during the 1930s with the unemployment rate at 26% and be successful, there is no part of the country that's godforsaken...On a busy day in the summertime, we can wait on 10,000-15,000 people...People love this place...It has become an institution.

THE BADLANDS ☎605

Early explorers, when faced with the mountainous rock formations that suddenly appear out of the prairie, were less than enthusiastic. General Alfred Sully called these arid and treacherous formations "Hell with the fires out," and the French translated the Sioux name for the area, *mako sica*, as *les mauvaises terres:* "bad lands." Late spring and fall in the Badlands offer pleasant weather that can be a relief from the extreme temperatures of mid-summer and winter; no matter how "bad" it gets, though, it is always well worth a visit. Deposits of iron oxide lend layers of marvelous red and brown hues to the present land, and the colorful moods of the Badlands change with the time, season, and weather. According to geologists, the Badlands erode about 2 in. every year. At that rate they will disappear in 500,000 years—hurry and visit before it's too late.

🛈 PRACTICAL INFORMATION

Badlands National Park lies about 50 mi. east of Rapid City on I-90. The **entrance fee** comes with a free copy of *The Prairie Preamble* with trail map. ($10 per car, $5 per person on bike, foot, or motorcycle.) **Driving tours** of the park can start at either end of Rte. 240, which winds through wilderness in a 32 mi. detour off I-90 Exit 110 or 131. The **Ben Reifel Visitors Center,** 5 mi. inside the park's northeastern entrance, serves as the Park Headquarters. (☎433-5361. Open mid-Apr. to May daily 8am-5pm; June to mid-Aug. 7am-8pm; mid-Aug. to mid-Sept. 8am-6pm; mid-Sept. to mid-Oct. 8am-5pm; mid-Oct. to Apr. 9am-4pm.) Another ranger station, the **White River Visitors Center,** is located 55 mi. to the southwest, off Rte. 27, in the park's less-visited southern section. (☎455-2878. Open June-Aug. daily 10am-4pm.) Both Visitors Centers have potable water. The **National Grasslands Visitors Center (Buffalo Gap),** 708 Main St., in Wall, has films and an exhibit on the complex ecosystem of the surrounding area. (☎279-2125. Open June-Aug. daily 7am-8pm; Sept.-May 8am-4:30pm.) For info, write to Badlands National Park, P.O. Box 6, Interior, SD 57750 (www.nps.gov/badl). **Area code:** 605.

🏠 ACCOMMODATIONS

In addition to standard lodging and camping, **backcountry camping** (½ mi. from the road and out of sight) allows an intimate introduction to this austere landscape, but water must be brought along. *You are strongly urged to contact one of the rangers at the Visitors Center before heading out. Wherever you sleep, don't cozy up to bison; they are dangerous.*

Badlands Inn (☎433-5401 or 800-341-8000), south of the Ben Reifel Visitors Center in Interior on Rte. 44, just outside the park. The Inn offers comfortable rooms with free local calls and great sunrise views. Open mid-May to mid-Sept. Singles $32-40, with 2 people $37-50; doubles $40-57. ❷

The Homestead, 113 6th Ave. (☎279-2303), along the main tourist drag in Wall, offers equally comfortable rooms with cable TV and A/C. All rooms $46. ❸

Cedar Pass Lodge, 1 Cedar St. (☎433-5460), next to the Ben Reifel Visitors Center inside the park, rents cabins with A/C and showers. Reservations recommended. Open mid-Mar. to mid-Oct. 1 person $48, each additional person $4. ❸

Cedar Pass Campground, just south of the Ben Reifel Visitors Center. In the summer, it's best to get there early, since it sometimes fills up by late afternoon. Sites with water and restrooms $10. ❶

Sage Creek Campground, 13 mi. from the Pinnacles entrance south of Wall, take Sage Creek Rim Rd. off Rte. 240. You sleep in an open field where there are pit toilets, no water, and fires are not allowed—but hey, it's free. ❶

🍴 FOOD

Cedar Pass Lodge Restaurant (☎433-5460) is the only one in the park. Only brave diners try the $3.65 buffalo burger. Open mid-May to late Oct. daily 7am-8:30pm. ❶

Cuny Table Cafe (☎455-2957), in Buffalo Gap, 8 mi. west of the White River Visitor Center on Rte. 2, only a short detour from Wounded Knee, provides your stomach with more loving fare. It's worth the drive to try the area's best Indian Tacos ($5)—home-cooked fry bread piled with veggies, beans, and beef. Open daily 5am-5pm. ❶

A&M Cafe (☎433-5340), just 2 mi. south of the Ben Reifel Visitors Center on Rte. 44 in Interior, has generous breakfasts and ample sandwich platters for $3-6. Open daily 6:30am-9:30pm. ❶

🏔 OUTDOOR ACTIVITIES

The 244,000-acre park protects large tracts of prairie and stark rock formations. The Ben Reifel Visitors Center has an 18-minute video on the Badlands as well as a wealth of info on nearby activities and camping. Park rangers offer free talks and daily excursions in summer. Check the handy *Prairie Preamble* for schedules.

HIKING
Hiking is permitted throughout the entire park, although climbing on the formations is discouraged. Rangers encourage hikers to explore the backcountry and offer guidance in planning routes. For backcountry hikers, it's a good idea to bring a compass, a map, and lots of water. Despite the burning heat in summer, long pants are advisable to protect from poison ivy, stinging and biting insects, and the park's one venomous snake—the prairie rattlesnake. Five hiking trails begin off Loop Rd. near the Ben Reifel Visitor Center.

Door Trail (¾ mi., 20min.) is wheelchair accessible for the first 100m. The rest of the trail cuts through buttes and crevices for spectacular views of the surrounding countryside. Self-guide brochure (50¢) available at the start of the trail.

Window Trail (¼ mi., 20min.), more of a scenic overlook than an actual hike, consists of a wheelchair accessible ramp with a splendid view.

Cliff Shelf Nature Trail (½ mi., 30min.) also has self-guide brochures (50¢). Half of the trail is wooded and unpaved, and wooden steps connect this less-traveled, tranquil half to the more trodden path.

Notch Trail (1½ mi., 1½-2hr.) demands surefootedness and a willingness to climb a shaky ladder at a 45° angle. Not for the faint of heart, the trail blazes around narrow ledges before making its way to the grand finale: an unbelievable view of the Cliff Shelf and White River Valley. **Saddle Pass Trail** (¼ mi., ½-1hr.), for more experienced hikers, involves a quick scramble up the Badlands Wall before connecting with the longer and more level **Castle** and **Medicine Root Trails.**

DRIVING

A scenic drive along **Rte. 240/Loop Rd.** serves as an excellent introduction to the entire northern portion of the park. The road makes its way through rainbow-colored bluffs and around hairpin turns, while providing views of many distinct types of Badlands terrain. The gravel **Sage Creek Rim Rd.**, west of Rte. 240, has fewer people and more animals. Highlights are the Roberts Prairie Dog Town and the park's herds of bison and antelope; across the river from the Sage Creek campground lies another prairie dog town and some popular bison territory.

RIDING

Travelers interested in exploring the area on horseback can check out **Badlands Trail Rides,** 1.5 mi. south of the Ben Reifel Visitors Center on Rte. 377. While the trails do not lead into the park, they do cover territory on the park's immediate outskirts. All levels are welcome, and a full introduction is given before the ride. (☎433-5453. Open in summer daily 8am-7pm. $15 for 30min. ride; $20 for 1hr. ride.)

RAPID CITY   ☎605

Rapid City's location makes it a convenient base from which to explore the Black Hills and the Badlands. The area welcomes three million tourists each summer, over 60 times the city's permanent population. Be sure to pick up a map of the **Rapid City Star Tour** at the Civic Center or any motel. The route leads to twelve free attractions, including a jaunt up Skyline Drive for a bird's-eye view of the city and the seven concrete dinosaurs of **Dinosaur Park.** Also on the tour is a magical trip to **Storybook Island,** a kids' amusement park inhabited by the Gingerbread Man, the Three Little Pigs, Winnie the Pooh, and other childhood pals. Runners, walkers, and bikers traverse the eight-mile **Rapid City Riverwalk** along Rapid Creek.

Rapid City accommodations are more expensive during the summer. Make reservations, as motels often fill weeks in advance, especially during the first two weeks in August when nearby Sturgis hosts its annual **motorcycle rally** (see p. 615). Winter travelers are in luck because of an abundance of off-season bargains from September to May. Large billboards guide the way to **Big Sky Motel ❸,** 4080 Tower Rd., just south of town on a service road off Mt. Rushmore Rd. The rooms are super clean and many have great views. (☎348-3200 or 800-318-3208. No phones. Singles $48; doubles $64. AAA discounts. Lower off-season; call for rates.) **Camping** is available at **Badlands National Park** (see p. 612), **Black Hills National Forest** (see p. 615), and **Custer State Park** (see p. 618).

The **Millstone Family Restaurant ❷,** 2010 W. Main St., at Mountain View Rd., cooks up large, hot portions of chicken ($6.25-7.65), spaghetti and meatballs ($7.85), and pork ribs ($8.50). Try the steak and salad bar combo for $7.65. (☎343-5824. Open daily 6am-11pm.) The cosmopolitan **Once Upon a Vine ❷,** 507 6th St., has the city's best wine selection. The chef puts together delectable sandwiches ($6.50-7.75) and gourmet pizzas ($7.75) for discerning taste buds. (☎343-7802. Cafe open Tu-Th 11:30am-2pm and 5-8pm, F 11:30am-2pm and 5-10pm, Sa 5-10pm. Wine bar open Tu-Th 11:30am-9pm, F 11:30am-11pm, Sa 5-11pm.) Nightlife options line **Main St.** between 6th St. and Mt. Rushmore Rd. For a beer as black as the Hills, toss back a Smokejumper Stout ($3) at the **Firehouse Brewing Co.,** 610 Main St., *the* bar in Rapid

City. Located in a restored 1915 firehouse, the company brews five beers in-house and serves sandwiches, burgers, and salads for $6-10. (☎348-1915. Open M-Th 11am-10pm, F-Sa 11am-11pm, Su 4-9pm.) After dinner at the firehouse, head upstairs to **Fat Boys Saloon** for pool, foosball, music, and more beer. (☎348-1915. Open M-Sa 7pm-1am.)

Driving in Rapid City is easy; roads are laid out in a sensible grid pattern. **St. Joseph St.** and **Main St.** are the main east-west thoroughfares, and **Mt. Rushmore Rd./Rte. 16** is the main north-south route. Many north-south roads are numbered, and numbers increase from east to west, beginning at **East Blvd.** Take a flight from **Rapid City Regional Airport** (☎393-9924), off Rte. 44, 8½ mi. east of the city. **Jack Rabbit Lines** scurries east from the Milo Barber Transportation Center, 333 6th St. (☎348-3300), downtown, with one bus daily to Omaha (12hr., $106); Pierre (4hr.; M-Th $34, F-Su $36); and Sioux Falls (10hr., $96). **Powder River Lines**, also in the Center, runs once daily to Billings (8hr., $61) and Cheyenne (8hr., $70). Station open M-F 8am-5pm, Sa-Su 10am-noon and 2-5pm. **Rapid Ride** runs city buses. Pick up a schedule at the terminal in the Milo Barber Transportation Center. (☎394-6631. Operates M-F 6:25am-5:30pm. $1, seniors 50¢.) **Visitor info: Rapid City Chamber of Commerce and Visitors Information Center,** 444 Mt. Rushmore Rd., in the Civic Center. (☎343-1744. Open M-F 8am-5pm.) **Short-Term Work Opportunities: Rapid City Human Resources,** 300 6th St. (☎394-4136. 24hr. Jobline ☎394-5329). **Internet access: Rapid City Public Library,** 610 Quincy St., at 6th St. (☎394-4171. Open June-Aug. M-Th 9am-9pm, F-Sa 9am-5:30pm; Sept.-May M-Th 9am-9pm, F-Sa 9am-5:30pm, Su 1-5pm. 1hr. per day. Free.) **Post Office:** 500 East Blvd., several blocks east of downtown. (☎394-8600. Open M-F 8am-5:30pm, Sa 8:30am-12:30pm.) **ZIP code:** 57701. **Area code:** 605.

BLACK HILLS REGION

The Black Hills, so-called for the dark hue that the green, pine-covered hills take on when viewed from a distance, have long been considered sacred by the Sioux. The Treaty of 1868 gave the Black Hills and the rest of South Dakota west of the Missouri River to the tribe. But when gold was discovered in the 1870s, the US government snatched back the land. The dueling monuments of Mt. Rushmore (a national memorial, see p. 616) and Crazy Horse (an independent project, see p. 617) strikingly illustrate the clash of the two cultures that reside among these hills. Today, the area attracts millions of visitors annually with a trove of natural treasures, including Custer State Park, Wind Cave National Park, and Jewel Cave National Monument.

BLACK HILLS NATIONAL FOREST   ☎605

Most of the land in the Black Hills is part of the Black Hills National Forest and exercises the "multiple use" principle—mining, logging, ranching, and recreation all take place in close proximity. Attractions like reptile farms and even a Flintstones theme park lurk around every bend of the sinuous roads. The forest itself provides opportunities for backcountry hiking and camping, as do park-run campgrounds and private tent sites. In the hills, the **Visitors Center,** on I-385 at Pactola Lake, has details on backcountry camping and $7 waterproof maps. (☎343-8755. Open Memorial Day-Labor Day daily 8:30am-6pm.) **Backcountry camping** in the national forest is free. Camping is allowed 1 mi. away from any campground or Visitors Center and at least 200 ft. off the side of the road (leave your car in a parking lot or pull off). Open fires are prohibited, but controlled fires in provided grates are allowed. Good campgrounds include **Pactola ❶**, on the Pactola Reservoir just south of the junction of Rte. 44 and U.S. 385; **Sheridan Lake ❶**, 5 mi. northeast of Hill City on U.S. 385 (north entrance for group sites, south entrance for individuals); and **Roubaix Lake ❶**, 14 mi. south of Lead on U.S. 385. (Sites 3 $17-19.) All National Forest campgrounds (☎877-444-6777; www.reserveusa.com for reservations) are quiet and wooded, offering fishing, swimming, and pit toilets. No hookups are provided. The national forest extends into Wyoming, and a **ranger station** can be found in Sundance. (☎307-283-1361. Open M-F 7:30am-5pm, Sa 9am-3pm.) The Wyoming side of the forest permits campfires, allows horses, and draws fewer visitors. The hostel in **Deadwood** (see p. 619) is the cheapest indoor accommodation in these parts.

I-90 skirts the northern border of the Black Hills from Spearfish in the west to Rapid City in the east. **U.S. 385** twists from Hot Springs in the south to Deadwood in the north. The road is certainly beautiful, but don't expect to get anywhere fast. These winding routes hold drivers to half the speed of the interstate. Unless astride a flashy piece of chrome and steel, steer clear of the Hills in early August, when over 12,000 motorcyclists converge on the area for the **Sturgis Rally** (☎605-347-9190; Aug. 4-10, 2003). Winter in the Black Hills offers stellar skiing and snowmobiling. Unfortunately many attractions close or have limited hours, and most resorts and campgrounds are closed altogether in winter. The **Black Hills Visitor Information Center** is at Exit 61 off I-90 in Rapid City. (☎355-3700. Open in summer daily 7am-8pm; off-season 8am-5pm; hours subject to change.)

MOUNT RUSHMORE   ☎605

Mt. Rushmore National Memorial boasts the faces that launched a thousand minivans. Historian Doane Robinson originally conceived of this "shrine of democracy" in 1923 as a memorial for local Western heroes; sculptor Gutzon Borglum chose four presidents instead. Borglum initially encountered opposition from those who felt the work of God could not be improved, but the tenacious sculptor defended the project's size, insisting that "there is not a monument in this country as big as a snuff box." In 1941, the 60 ft. heads of Washington, Jefferson, Theodore Roosevelt, and Abraham Lincoln were finished. The 465 ft. tall bodies were never completed, as work ceased when US funds were diverted to WWII. The disembodiment doesn't seem to perturb the millions of visitors who come here every year.

From Rapid City, take U.S. 16 and 16A to Keystone, and Rte. 244 up to the mountain. Remote parking is free, but the lot fills early. There is an $8 per car "annual parking permit" for the lot adjacent to the entrance. The **info center** details the monument's history and has ranger tours. A state-of-the-art **Visitors Center** chronicles the monument's history and the lives of the featured presidents in addition to showing a film that explains how the carving was accomplished—about 90% of the sculpting was done with dynamite. (Info center ☎574-3198. Visitors Center ☎574-3165. Both open in summer daily 8am-10pm; winter usually 8am-5pm.)

From the Visitors Center, it is ½mi. along the **Presidential Trail** to **Borglum's Studio**. After taking over 300 steps down a planked wooden trail, visitors can stare at Borglum's full-bodied plaster model of the carving as well as tools and designs for Mt. Rushmore. (Open in summer daily 9am-6pm.) During the summer, the **Mt. Rushmore Memorial Amphitheater** hosts a monument-lighting program. (☎574-2523; www.nps.gov/moru. Patriotic speech and film 9pm, light floods the monument 9:30-10:30pm. Trail lights extinguished 11pm.)

Horsethief Campground ❶ lies 2 mi. west of Mt. Rushmore on Rte. 244 in the Black Hills National Forest. Former President George Bush fished here in 1993; rumor has it that the lake was overstocked with fish to guarantee his success. (☎877-444-6777; www.reserveusa.com. Water and flush toilets in the woods. Reservations recommended on weekends. Sites $19, lakeside sites $21.) The rather commercialized **Mt. Rushmore KOA/Palmer Gulch Lodge ❶**, 7 mi. west of Mt. Rushmore on Rte. 244, has campsites for two and kabins with showers, stoves, pool, spa, laundry, nightly movies, and free shuttle service to Mt. Rushmore. (☎574-2525 or 800-562-8503. Make reservations early, up to 2 months in advance for kabins. Open May-Oct. Sites June-Aug. $26, with water and electricity $33, kabins $47-54; May and Sept.-Oct. $23/30/42-49.)

CRAZY HORSE MEMORIAL ☎605

In 1947, Lakota Chief Henry Standing Bear commissioned sculptor Korczak Ziolkowski to sculpt a memorial to Crazy Horse as a reminder to whites that Native Americans have their own heroes. A famed warrior who garnered respect by refusing to sign treaties or live on a government reservation, Crazy Horse was treacherously stabbed by a white soldier in 1877. The Crazy Horse Memorial, which at its completion will be the world's largest sculpture, will stand as a spectacular tribute to the revered Native American leader.

To no one's surprise, the project didn't receive any initial government funding. The sculptor went solo for years, twice refusing later offers of $10 million in federal funding. Today, his wife Ruth and seven of their ten children carry on the work. Crazy Horse's completed face (all four of the Rushmore heads could fit inside it) was unveiled in June 1998. Part of his arm is now visible, and eventually, his entire torso and head, as well as part of his horse, will be carved into the mountain. The memorial, 17 mi. southwest of Mt. Rushmore on U.S. 385/U.S. 16, includes the Indian Museum of North America, the Sculptor's Studio-Home, and the Native American Educational and Cultural Center, where native crafts are displayed and sold. The orientation center shows a moving 17min. video entitled "Dynamite and Dreams." (☎673-4681; www.crazyhorse.org. Open May-Sept. daily 7am-dark; Oct.-Apr. 8am-dark. Monument lit nightly about 10min. after sunset for 1hr. $9, $19 per carload; with a senior $7/17; under 6 free.)

WIND CAVE & JEWEL CAVE ☎605

In the cavern-riddled Black Hills, the subterranean scenery often rivals the above-ground sites. Local entrepreneurs may attempt to lure you into the holes in their backyards, but the government owns the area's prime underground real estate: **Wind Cave National Park** (☎745-4600), adjacent to Custer State Park (p. 618) on U.S. 385, and **Jewel Cave National Monument** (☎673-2288, tour reservations ☎800-967-2283), 13 mi. west of the U.S. 385/U.S. 16 junction, in Custer. There is no public transportation to the caves. Bring a sweater on all tours—Wind Cave remains a constant 53°F, while Jewel Cave is 49°F.

WIND CAVE. Wind Cave was discovered by Tom Bingham in 1881 when he heard the sound of air rushing out of the cave's only natural entrance. The wind was so strong, in fact, that it knocked his hat off. When Tom returned to show his friends the cave, his hat got sucked in. Air forcefully gusts in and out of the cave due to changes in outside pressure. Scientists estimate that only 5% of a potential 2000 mi. of passageways have been discovered. Currently, within the 100 mi. that have been explored geologists have found a lake over 200 ft. long in the cave's deepest depths. Wind Cave is known for its "boxwork," a honeycomb-like lattice of calcite covering its walls. Five **tours** cover a range of caving experience. (☎745-4600. Tours June-Aug. daily 8:40am-6pm; less frequently in winter.) The **Garden of Eden Tour** (1hr., ¼ mi., 5 per day, 150 stairs) is the least strenuous. ($6, seniors and ages 6-16 $3.) The **Natural Entrance Tour** (1¼hr., ½ mi., 11 per day, 300 stairs) and the **Fairgrounds Tour** (1½hr., ½ mi., 8 per day, 450 stairs) are both moderately strenuous, and one of the two leaves about every 30min. ($8, seniors and ages 6-16 $4.) Light your own way on the more rigorous **Candlelight Tour.** (Limited to 10 people. 2hr. June-Aug. 10:30am and 1:30pm. $9, seniors and children $4.50. Under 8 not admitted. "Non-slip" soles on shoes required.) The rather difficult **Wild Cave Tour,** an intro to basic caving, is limited to ten people ages 16 and over who can fit through a 10 in. high passageway. (Parental consent required for under 18. 4hr. tour daily 1pm. $20, seniors $10. Reservations required.) In the afternoon, all tours fill up about 1hr. ahead of time, so buy tickets in advance. **Wind Cave National Park Visitors Center** at RR1, P.O. Box 190, Hot Springs, can provide more info. (☎745-4600. Open June to mid-Aug. daily 8am-7:30pm; winter hours vary. Parts of some tours are wheelchair accessible.) The **Elk Mountain Campground ❶**, part of Wind Cave National Park, is an excellent site in the woods that rarely fills up during the summer. (Potable water and restrooms. Sites mid-May to mid-Sept. $10; mid-Sept. to late Oct. and Apr. to mid-May $5.)

JEWEL CAVE. Distinguishing itself from nearby Wind Cave's boxwork, the walls of Jewel Cave are covered with a layer of calcite crystal. The **Scenic Tour** (1¼hr., ½ mi. 723 stairs.) includes a peek at a 27 ft. cave formation that bears a striking resemblance to a strip of bacon. (Leaves in summer roughly every 20min. 8:30am-6pm; in winter call ahead. $8, ages 6-16 $4.) The **Candlelight Tour** is a rather illuminating journey lasting 1¾hr. (In summer every hour 9am-5pm; in winter call ahead. $8, ages 6-16 $4.) Reservations, pants, a long-sleeve shirt, knee-pads, sturdy boots, and a willingness to get down and dirty are required for the 3-4hr. **Spelunking Tour,** limited to five people over age 16. (June-Aug. daily at noon. $27. Must be able to fit through an 8½ in. by 2 ft. opening.) The **Visitors Center** has more info. (☎673-2288. Open mid-May to mid-Oct. daily 8am-7:30pm; mid-Oct. to mid-May 8am-4:30pm.) Behind the Visitors Center, Jewel Cave offers visitors two alluring hiking trails. The **Roof Trail** is short, but provides a memorable introduction to the Black Hills' beauty. The bucolic 3½ mi. **Canyons Trail** winds through small canyons and fields and up forested hills before returning to the Visitors Center.

CUSTER STATE PARK   ☎605

Peter Norbeck, governor of South Dakota in the late 1910s, loved to hike among the thin, towering rock formations that haunt the area south of Sylvan Lake and Mt. Rushmore. In order to preserve the land, he created Custer State Park. The spectacular **Needles Hwy. (Rte. 87)** within the park follows his favorite hiking route. Norbeck designed this road to be especially narrow and winding so that newcomers could experience the pleasures of discovery. **Iron Mountain Road (U.S. 16A)** from Mt. Rushmore to near the Norbeck Visitors Center (see below) takes drivers through a series of tunnels, "pigtail" curves, and switchbacks. The park's **Wildlife Loop Road** twists past prairie dog towns, popular bison wallows, and wilderness areas near prime hiking and camping territory. If "lucky," one of Custer's **1500 bison** will come up to your car. Don't get out—they are dangerous.

The park requires an **entrance fee.** (7 day pass May-Oct. $5 per person, $12 per carload; Nov.-Apr. $2.50/6.) The **Peter Norbeck Visitors Center,** on U.S. 16A, ½ mi. west of the State Game Lodge, serves as the park's info center. (☎255-4464; www.custerstatepark.info. Open Apr.-May and mid-Oct. to Nov. daily 9am-5pm; June-Aug. 8am-8pm; Sept. to mid.-Oct. 8am-6pm.) The Visitors Center can also give information about **primitive camping,** which is available for $2 per night in the **French Creek Natural Area ❶**. Eight **campgrounds ❶** have sites with showers and restrooms. No hookups are provided. (☎800-710-2267 daily 7am-9pm. Over 200 of the 400+ sites are reserveable; the entire park fills in summer by 3pm. Sites $13-18. $5 non-resident users fee.) The Elk Mountain Campground in Wind Cave National Park is an excellent alternative, and rarely fills up. Motels in the surrounding area include the convenient **Chalet Motel ❷**, 933 Mt. Rushmore Rd./16A, just west of the Stockade Lake entrance to the park. One, two, or three bedroom units with kitchenettes, are available; no phones are installed. (☎673-2393 or 800-649-9088. Reservations recommended. Rooms from $42.) Food is available at all park lodges, but the general stores in Custer, Hermosa, and Keystone are usually cheaper. **The Bank**

Coffee House ❶, 548 Mt. Rushmore Rd., serves $3-5 sandwiches (until 2pm) and $3 pie. (☎673-5698. Open June-Aug. daily 7am-10pm; Sept.-May M-Sa 6am-9pm.)

At 7242 ft., **Harney Peak** is the highest point east of the Rockies and west of the Pyrenees. Waiting at the top are a few mountain goats and a great view of the Black Hills. Bring water and food, wear good shoes, and leave as early in the morning as possible. For less extreme hikers, the park provides 30 lower-altitude trails. You can also hike, fish, paddle boat, or canoe at popular **Sylvan Lake,** on Needles Hwy. (☎574-2561. Kayaks $4 per person per 30min.) One hour horse rides are available at **Blue Bell Lodge,** on Rte. 87 about 8 mi. from the south entrance. (☎255-4531, stable ☎255-4571. $18, under 12 $15.) Mountain bikes can be rented at the **Legion Lake Resort,** on U.S. 16A, 6 mi. west of the Visitors Center. (☎255-4521. $10 per hour, $25 per half-day, $40 per day.) All lakes and streams permit fishing with a daily license, which, along with equipment, are available at area lodges. ($7, non-residents $12; 3-day non-resident license $30.) The strong granite of the Needles makes for great rock climbing. For more info contact **Granite Sports/Sylvan Rocks,** at the corner of Elm and Main St. in Hill City. (☎574-2121. Open in summer daily 10am-8:30pm; off-season hours vary.)

DEADWOOD   ☎605

Mosey down Main St. from Lead for 3 mi., and you'll find yourself in Deadwood. Gunslingers **Wild Bill Hickock** and **Calamity Jane** sauntered into this town during the height of the Gold Rush. Bill stayed just long enough—two months—to spend eternity here. Jane and Bill now lie side-by-side in the **Mt. Moriah Cemetery,** just south of downtown. ($1, ages 5-12 50¢—is nothing sacred?) On Cemetery St. off Rte. 85, follow the signs. **Saloon #10,** 657 Main St., was forever immortalized by the murder of Wild Bill Hickock. Hickock was shot holding black aces and eights, thereafter infamous to poker players as a "dead man's hand." Every summer, the shooting is reenacted on location. (☎578-3346 or 800-952-9398. Saloon open daily 8am-2am. Reenactments daily 1, 3, 5, and 7pm.) Assassin Jack McCall is apprehended by authorities outside of Saloon #10. (Tu-Su 7:45pm.) Those willing to pay $8 can follow the angry mob to a comical reenactment of **McCall's trial** in the **Old Town Hall,** 12 Lee St. (☎578-3583 for ticket reservations. Pick up reserved tickets at the Old Town Hall.) There are also **random shootouts** along Main St. at 2, 4, and 6pm—listen for gunshots and the sound of Calamity Jane's whip. **Alkali Ike Tours** offers 1hr. narrated bus tours of the Deadwood region. Tickets are sold at the booth on Main St., just outside Saloon #10. (☎578-3147. July-Aug. 5 tours per day. $6.50, ages 7-13 $3, under 7 free.)

If Lead is where the gold is found, then Deadwood is where the gold is lost. Gambling takes center stage in Deadwood—brazen casinos line **Main St.,** and many innocent-looking establishments have slot machines waiting in the wings. Children are allowed in the casinos until 8pm. There's live music outside the Stockade and 24hr. gambling at the **Buffalo Saloon,** 658 Main St. (☎578-1300). For the fun of gambling without the high stakes, many casinos offer nickel slot machines. Even those who lose most of their money at the gambling tables can afford to stay at ▨**Hostelling International Black Hills at the Penny Motel (HI-AYH) ❶,** 818 Upper Main St.; look for the Penny Motel sign. A great kitchen, comfortable beds, and super clean rooms await visitors. (☎578-1842 or 877-565-8140. Dorms $13, nonmembers $16. One private room $36. Motel rooms: singles $49; doubles $59.) The **Whistlers Gulch Campground ❶,** off U.S. 85, has a pool, laundry facilities, and showers. (☎578-2092 or 800-704-7139. Sites $20, full hookup $30.) Casinos monopolize the food and dining market; for help finding a wholesome meal, try the **Deadwood History and Information Center,** 3 Siever St. (☎578-2507 or 800-999-1876. Open in summer daily 8am-8pm; in winter 9am-5pm.) **Free parking** is available in the Sherman St. parking lot on Rte. 85 heading towards Lead. **Area code:** 605.

IOWA

Named for the Ioway Native Americans who farmed along the state's many river banks, Iowa contains one fourth of all US Grade A farmland. Farming *is* the way of life in Iowa, a land where men are measured by the size of their John Deere tractors. Fertile and beautiful, the state ripples with gentle hills. Created by wind-blown quartz silt, the striking Loess Hills in the west are a geological rarity found only in Iowa and China. The Mississippi River Valley in Eastern Iowa offers amazing views of the Mighty Miss from limestone bluffs. Despite its distinctly American landscape, Iowa preserves its European heritage in small towns that maintain their German, Dutch, and Scandinavian traditions.

■ PRACTICAL INFORMATION

Capital: Des Moines.

Visitor Info: Iowa Dept. of Economic Development, 200 E. Grand Ave., Des Moines, 50309 (☎800-345-4692 or 515-242-4705; www.traveliowa.com).

Postal Abbreviation: IA. **Sales Tax:** 5%; some towns add an additional 1-2%.

DES MOINES ☎515

Like many American cities, Des Moines has experienced a rebound of late; the Skywalk, a second-floor maze of passageways connecting buildings downtown, is without equal in the Midwest. A beautiful system of interconnecting parks traces the area's rivers and presents a welcome contrast to the now-bustling downtown area. From the "BarbeQlossal" World Pork Expo (June 5-7, 2003) to world-class art, Des Moines' offerings run the gamut from kitsch to class.

■ TRANSPORTATION

I-80 and U.S. 65 encircle Des Moines; I-235 bisects the circle.

Airport: Des Moines International, 5800 Fleur Dr. (☎256-5195; www.dsmairport.com), at Army Post Rd. 5 mi. southwest of downtown; M-F take bus #8 "Havens". Taxi to downtown $11-15.

Buses: Greyhound, 1107 Keo Way (☎243-1773 or 800-231-2222), at 12th St., just northwest of downtown; take bus #4 "Urbandale." To: **Iowa City** (2hr.; 7 per day; $22), **Omaha** (2hr.; 8 per day; M-Th $23, F-Su $25); **Chicago** (8hr.; 10 per day; M-Th $38, F-Su $40); and **St. Louis** (10hr.; 5 per day; M-Th $67, F-Su $71). Station open 24hr.

Public Transit: Metropolitan Transit Authority (MTA), 1100 MTA Lane (☎283-8100; www.dmmta.com), south of the 9th St. viaduct. Open M-F 8am-5pm. Buses run M-F approximately 6am-11pm, Sa 6:45am-5:50pm. $1, seniors (except M-F 3-6pm) and disabled persons 50¢ with MTA ID card; transfers 10¢. Routes converge at 6th and Walnut St. Maps at the MTA office and website as well as the public library.

Taxis: Yellow Cab, ☎243-1111.

Car Rental: Enterprise, 5601 Fleur Dr. (☎285-2525), just outside the airport, with speedy airport pickup. $42 with 150 mi. per day, 30¢ each additional mi. Weekend special: F-M $10 per day with 150 in-state mi. per day. Must be 21+ with major credit card. No surcharge for under 25. Open M-F 7:30am-6pm, Sa 9am-1pm.

✈ 🏃 ORIENTATION & PRACTICAL INFORMATION

Numbered streets run north-south, named streets east-west. Addresses begin with zero downtown at the **Des Moines River** and increase as you move east or west; **Grand Ave.** divides addresses north-south. Other east-west thoroughfares, moving northward, are **Locust St., University Ave.** (home to Drake University), and **Hickman Rd.** Note that Des Moines and West Des Moines are different places, and the numbered streets within each are not the same.

Visitor info: Greater Des Moines Convention and Visitors Bureau, 405 6th Ave. (☎286-4960 or 800-451-2625; www.seedesmoines.com), along Locust in the Skywalk (Ste. 201). Open M-F 8:30am-5pm. Up a few blocks is the **Chamber of Commerce,** 700 Locust St. (☎286-4950). Open M 9am-5pm, Tu-Th 8am-5pm, F 8am-4pm.

Internet access: Des Moines Public Library, 100 Locust St. (☎283-4152), and all other branches. Free 1hr. per day with the option of signing up a day in advance. Open M-W 10am-9pm, Th-F 10am-6pm, Sa 10am-5pm. Also open Oct.-Apr. Su 10am-5pm.

Post Office: 1165 2nd Ave. (☎283-7585), downtown, just north of I-235. Open M-F 7:30am-5:30pm. **ZIP code:** 50318. **Area code:** 515.

🏠 ACCOMMODATIONS

Finding cheap accommodations in Des Moines is usually no problem, though you should make reservations a few months in advance for visits during the **State Fair** in August and at least one month in advance during the high school sports tournament season in March. Beware of the 7% hotel tax. Several campgrounds can be found west of the city off I-80, and cheap motels are sprinkled along I-80 and Merle Hay Rd., 5 mi. northwest of downtown. Take bus #4 "Urbandale" or #6 "West 9th" from downtown.

⬛ The Carter House Inn, 640 20th St. (☎288-7850), at Woodland St. in historic Sherman Hill. The Nelson family has converted this old Victorian home into a beautifully furnished and immaculately clean B&B. A large home-cooked breakfast is served on fine china, by candlelight, to classical music. Only 4 rooms available; call ahead. Rooms $70-100. Student discounts around 15% can be arranged if extra rooms are available. ❹

Motel 6, 4817 Fleur Dr. (☎287-6364), 10min. south of downtown at the airport. Clean, secure rooms with free local calls and HBO. Singles $45; doubles $52. AARP discount available. Two wheelchair-accessible rooms. ❷

Iowa State Fairgrounds Campgrounds, E. 30th St. (☎261-0678) at Grand Ave. Take bus #1 "Fairgrounds" to the Grand Ave. gate and follow East Grand Ave. straight east through the park. 1800 campsites on 160 acres. No fires. Check-in until 10pm. Reservations accepted only during the State Fair in Aug. Open mid-Apr. to Oct. Sites with water and electricity $18; full hookup $20. Fee collected in the morning. ❶

🍴 FOOD

Good eating places tend to cluster on **Court Ave.** downtown. West Des Moines also boasts an assortment of budget eateries along Grand Ave. and in the antique-filled **Historic Valley Jct.** The **Farmers Market** (☎243-6625) sells loads of fresh fruit and vegetables, baked goods, and ethnic food on Saturday mornings (mid-May to Oct. 7am-noon), and Court Ave. between 1st and 4th St. is blocked off for the extravaganza.

⬛ Big Daddy's Bar-B-Q, 1000 E. 14th St. (☎262-0352), just north of I-235, sends several people to the hospital every year with its killer sauces, which, according to locals, are "just that damn hot." The adventurous—or insane—are encouraged to try the "Last Supper," "ER," or "Code Blue" sauces; the "Final Answer" is reserved for only the highest pain thresholds. Rib platters for 2 $9; beef, pork, or ham sandwiches $4; cornbread 75¢ per slice. Open Tu-Sa 11am-5pm; takeout Tu-Th 11am-6pm, F-Sa 11am-7pm. ❷

Stella's Blue Sky Diner, 400 Locust St. (☎246-1953), #235 at the Skywalk level in Capital Sq. Mall. At this old-school diner, you can slide into a vinyl booth and enjoy classic food along with pure 1950s tack. Be brave and ask for a milkshake ($3) "on the head;" when the waiter brings your shake, balance an empty glass on your forehead and he will pour it—without making a mess—while standing above you on a chair. Breakfast $3-5; 10 different hamburgers all under $6. Open M-Th 6:30am-6pm, Sa 8am-6pm. ❶

Noah's Ark Ristorante, 2400 Ingersoll Ave. (☎288-2246). One day in 1946, restaurant owner Noah Lacona was repairing the roof of his establishment when a friend passed by and teased, "Are you working on Noah's Ark?" The name stuck, and since then, Noah has been serving up Italian cuisine. Savor pastas ($8-10), steaks ($13-24), seafood ($13-17), or Noah's famous Neopolitan pizzas ($7-9) in a dining area as dark, cozy, and eclectic as a family den. Open M-Th 11am-11pm, F-Sa 11am-1am. ❹

Bauder's Pharmacy and Fountain, 3802 Ingersoll Ave. (☎255-1124), at 38th St. With old-fashioned ice cream, an authentic lunch counter, and a soda fountain, Bauder's makes a convincing stab at nostalgia. Ice cream $1.25 per scoop; shakes, floats, and malts $2.50. Bauder's also sells simple sandwiches for $2-3. Open M-F 8:30am-7pm, Sa 9am-5pm, Su 10am-3pm. ❶

👁 SIGHTS

Though currently undergoing renovations, the inspiring gold-domed **State Capitol,** E. 9th St. and Grand Ave., offers a clear view of the Des Moines skyline. (☎281-5591. Open M-F 7am-5pm, Sa 9am-4pm. Free tours of the Capitol daily; call for exact times.) Located at the base of the Capitol complex parking lot, the **Iowa Historical Building,** 600 E. Locust St., addresses such topics such as Native American culture and conservation, and the exhibit "A Few of Our Favorite Things," which showcases 100 creations from the past century that have changed the way Iowans live, from jazz to Jell-O. (☎281-5111. Open Sept.-May Tu-Sa 9am-4:30pm, Su noon-4:30pm; June-Aug. also open M 9am-4:30pm. Free.) Built on urban renewal land east of the Des Moines River, the geodesic greenhouse and outdoor gardens of the **Botanical Center,** 909 E. River Dr., house exotic flora and fauna. (☎323-8900. Open M-Th 10am-5pm, F 10am-9pm, Sa-Su 10am-5pm. $1.50, students 50¢, seniors 75¢.)

Most cultural sights cluster west of downtown on Grand Ave. The phenomenal ◙**Des Moines Art Center,** 4700 Grand Ave., is composed of three buildings designed by world-renowned architects Eliel Saarinen, I.M. Pei, and Richard Meier. In addition to a collection of African tribal arts, the museum houses modern masterpieces by Monet, Matisse, and Picasso, along with an expansive collection of Pop, Minimalist, and contemporary paintings and sculptures by Andy Warhol, Eva Hesse, and Jeff Koons. (☎277-4405. Open Tu-W and F-Sa 11am-4pm, Th and 1st F of the month 11am-9pm, Su noon-4pm. Free.) Behind the Art Center lie the immaculately groomed **Rose Garden** and **Greenwood Pond**—a small, still-water lagoon where you can relax in the sun (or ice skate in the winter). Across from Greenwood Pond, the **Science Center of Iowa,** 4500 Grand Ave., has exhibits for kids, dazzling laser shows set to popular music, and planetarium spectacles. (☎274-4138. Open M-Sa 10am-5pm, Su noon-5pm. $3.50, seniors and ages 2-12 $2.)

🎵🎭 ENTERTAINMENT & NIGHTLIFE

The **Civic Center,** 221 Walnut St. (☎246-2300), sponsors theater and concerts; call for info. On Thursday, the Des Moines *Register* publishes "The Datebook," a helpful listing of concerts, sporting events, and movies. *Cityview,* a free local weekly, lists free events and is available at the Civic Center box office and most supermarkets. The **Iowa State Fair,** one of the nation's largest, captivates Des Moines for eleven days in mid-August with prize cows, crafts, cakes, and corn. (☎800-545-4692; www.iowastatefair.org. Runs Aug. 7-17, 2003, with the theme "One in a Million." Call for prices and to purchase tickets in advance.) Tickets for **Iowa Cubs** baseball games are a steal; Chicago's farm team plays at **Sec Taylor Stadium,** 350 SW 1st St. Call for game dates and times. (☎243-6111. General admission $5.50, children $3.50; reserved grandstand $8, children $5.50.) **Jazz in July** (☎280-3222; www.metroarts.org) presents free concerts throughout the city every day of the month; pick up a schedule at restaurants, Wells Fargo banks, or the Visitors Bureau. **Music Under the Stars** presents free concerts on the steps of the State Capitol (☎283-4294; June-July Su 7-9pm.)

Court Ave., in the southeast corner of downtown, serves as the focal point for much of Des Moines's nightlife scene. **Java Joe's,** 214 4th St., a hip, mellow coffeehouse with Internet access ($1 per 10min.), sells exotic coffee blends and beer ($2.50-3). Vegetarians will delight in the creative array of sandwiches, all for $3-5. Call for schedule of live music and open mic nights. (☎288-5282. Open M-Th 7:30am-11:30pm, F-Sa 7:30am-1am, Su 9am-11pm.)

▐ DAYTRIPS FROM DES MOINES

PELLA

Forty-one miles east of Des Moines on Hwy. 163, Pella blooms in May with its annual **Tulip Time** festival, a time of Dutch dancing, a parade, concerts, and glockenspiel performances. (☎888-746-3882. May 1-3, 2003.) For a dose of Dutch culinary culture, visit the **Jaarsma Bakery,** 727 Franklin St. (☎641-628-2940. Pecan rolls 2 for $1.60. Almond poppyseed cakes 4 for $1.39. Open M-Sa 6am-6pm.) Also open year-round, the **Pella Historical Village,** 507 Franklin St., is the site of America's tallest working windmill. (☎641-628-2409. Open June-Aug. M-Sa 9am-5pm; Sept.-May M-F 9am-5pm. $7, students $1.)

PRAIRIE CITY

Twenty miles east of Des Moines on Hwy. 163 at Hwy. 117, the **Neal Smith National Wildlife Refuge,** a veritable time machine, transports visitors to Iowa's prairie days of 150 years ago, when nearly 31 million acres of tallgrass prairie graced the Iowa plains. Today, only one-tenth of one percent of that remains. The Neal Smith National Wildlife Refuge restores 8600 acres of this endangered landscape. The refuge is home to 37 bison, 12 elk, and a learning center that is particularly kid-friendly. In August, the big bluestem grass grows up to 6 ft. (☎994-3400; Learning Center open M-Sa 9am-4pm, Su noon-5pm. Trails and auto tour open daily sunrise to sunset. Free.)

MADISON COUNTY

Twenty miles south of Des Moines lies Madison County, immortalized in the novel and movie *The Bridges of Madison County.* **Winterset,** the county seat, welcomed American tough guy John Wayne into the world in 1907 when he was christened Marrion Robert Morrison. The **John Wayne Birthplace,** 216 S. 2nd St., has been converted to a museum featuring two rooms of memorabilia and two rooms authentically furnished in turn-of-the-century style. (☎462-1044. Open daily 10am-4:30pm. $2.50, seniors $2.25, children $1.) For information on the county's famous **covered bridges,** visit the **Madison County Chamber of Commerce,** 73 Jefferson St. (☎462-1185 or 800-298-6119. Open M-F 9am-5pm, Sa 9am-4pm, Su 11am-4pm.)

IOWA CITY ☎319

Home to the **University of Iowa**, Iowa City exudes youthful exuberance and energy. Don't come expecting pitchfork-toting farmers: the town is better known for college football, shopping, inexpensive restaurants, and an active nightlife. In the summer, cultural activities abound, from the Iowa Arts Festival in June (☎337-7944) to the Iowa City Jazz Festival in July (☎358-9346).

🔢 🎫 ORIENTATION & PRACTICAL INFORMATION. Iowa City is off I-80, 112 mi. east of Des Moines. North-south **Madison** and **Gilbert St.** and east-west **Market** and **Burlington St.** mark off downtown. **Greyhound** and **Burlington Trailways** are both located at 404 E. College St. (☎337-2127. Station open M-F 6:30am-8pm, Sa-Su 10am-8pm.) Buses travel to: **Des Moines** (2-4hr.; 7 per day; M-Th $21, F-Su $22); **Chicago** (6hr.; 8 per day; M-Th $40, F-Su $42); **St. Louis** (10-11hr.; 2 per day; M-Th $65, F-Su $69); and **Minneapolis** (8-12hr.; 5 per day; M-Th $58, F-Su $62). The **Cambus** runs daily all over campus and downtown and is free. (☎335-8633. Operates M-F 5am-midnight, Sa-Su noon-midnight; summer M-F 6:30am-6pm, Sa-Su noon-6pm.) **Iowa City Transit** runs a free downtown shuttle daily from 7:30am-6:30pm as well as other routes. (☎356-5151. Operates M-F 6:30am-10:30pm, Sa 6:30am-7pm. 75¢; children 5-12 50¢; seniors with pass 35¢ 9am-3:30pm, after 6:30pm, and Sa.)

The **Convention and Visitors Bureau,** 408 1st Ave., sits across the river in Coralville off U.S. 6. (☎337-6592 or 800-283-6592; www.icccvb.org. Open M-F 8am-5pm, Sa-Su 10am-4pm.) More area info is available at the University of Iowa's **Campus Information Center,** in the **Iowa Memorial Union** at Madison and Jefferson St. (☎335-3055. Open Sept.-May M-F 8am-8pm, Sa 10am-8pm, Su noon-4pm; June-Aug. M-F 8am-5pm.) **Internet access: Iowa City Public Library,** 123 S. Linn St. (☎356-5200; open M-Th 10am-9pm, F-Sa 10am-6pm, Su 1-5pm). Iowa City's neo-futuristic lounge, **Serendipity Laundry Cafe,** 702 S. Gilbert St., also offers Internet access (10¢ per minute), as well as laundry facilities, tanning beds, copiers, scanners, fax machines, pool tables, drinks, and sandwiches. (☎354-4575. Open daily 10am-2am; summer hours 10am-midnight.) **Post Office:** 400 S. Clinton St. (☎354-1560; open M-F 8:30am-5pm, Sa 9:30am-1pm). **ZIP code:** 52240. **Area code:** 319.

🔢 ❑ ACCOMMODATIONS & FOOD. Six blocks from downtown is **Haverkamp's Linn Street Homestay ❷,** 619 N. Linn St. An unbeatable value, this 1907 bed and breakfast contains three reasonably priced rooms; call ahead for reservations. (☎337-4636. Rooms $35-50.) Cheap motels line U.S. 6 in **Coralville,** 2 mi. west of downtown, and **1st Ave.** at Exit 242 off I-80. The cheapest of the bunch is the **Big Ten Inn ❷,** 707 1st Ave., off U.S. 6. (☎351-6131. Singles $38; doubles $50.) Nearby is the **Capri Motor Lodge ❷,** 705 2nd St., which offers morning coffee, as well as a microwave, fridge, foldout couch, and cable TV in each room. (☎354-5100. Singles $43; doubles $51.) **Kent Park Campgrounds ❶,** 15 mi. west on U.S. 6, has 86 secluded sites near a lake with fishing, boating, and swimming. (☎645-2315. Check-in by 10:30pm. $10, with electricity $15.)

Downtown boasts cheerful, moderately-priced restaurants and bars. At the open-air **Pedestrian Mall,** on College and Dubuque St., the melodies of street musicians drift through the eateries and shops, and vendors sell food until 3am if demand is strong. Dine at the city's oldest family-owned restaurant, **Hamburg Inn #2 Inc. ❷,** 214 N. Linn St. "The Burg," as it is known to locals, serves huge portions of breakfast staples, burgers, and desserts. Nearly everything on the menu is under $7. (☎337-5512. Open daily 6am-11pm.) North one block, **Pagliai's Pizza ❸,** 302 Bloomington St., tosses up crusty, crumbly thin-crust pizzas for $7-13. (☎351-5073. Open M-Sa 4pm-midnight, Su 4-11pm.) **Masala ❷,** 9 S. Dubuque St., Iowa City's award-winning vegetarian Indian restaurant, has a $6.25 lunch buffet and a $5

Winding roads, sheer limestone cliffs, and breathtaking views of the Mississippi River characterize the **Great River Road.**

TIME: 2-3hr.

DISTANCE: 120 mi.

1 SABULA. This island community of 750 is held in place by the extensive lock and dam system on the Mississippi.

2 DUBUQUE. From Sabula, a 45 mi. drive on Rte. 52 N brings you to the industrial city Dubuque, Iowa's oldest city. Though not particularly glamourous, Dubuque provide travelers an opportunity to fill their tanks and stomachs before continuing down the road.

3 BALLTOWN RD. A stretch of road extending off of Rte. 52 N, Balltown Rd. traces the high bluffs overlooking the mighty Mississippi.

4 GUTTENBERG. This historical river town is the home to **Lock and Dam No. 10**—the path to the river from Rte. 52 is marked by signs. Hungry travelers can find gourmet sandwiches ($3.75-5.25) at the **Guttenberg Bakery and Cafe,** 422 S. River Park Dr., where the "food is so good the owners eat here." (☎319-252-2225. Open Tu-Sa 6am-2pm, Su 7am-1pm.

5 MCGREGOR. To finish the drive, pick up Rte. 340 north and pass through McGregor. The quiet town features a small-town commercial strip, a fine example of the quintessential American downtown.

6 EFFIGY MOUNDS NATIONAL PARK. Though the drive officially ends 3 mi. from McGregor, travelers can opt to continue on to the intriguing Effigy Mounds.

Monday dinner special. Student discounts are given. (☎338-6199. Open daily 11am-2:30pm and 5-10pm.) Iowa City's only Greek restaurant is **The Parthenon ❹**, 320 E. Burington St., where columns emerge from the cool, blue walls and Grecian urns and sculptures are sprinkled throughout. Savor the warm pita bread, and sup upon *mousaka* (the national dish of Greece, $11), classic salads ($6-9), steaks ($15-20), or seafood ($13-40). Vegetarian dishes are also served. (☎358-7777. Open for lunch M-Sa 11:30am-2pm; dinner M-Th 4:30-9pm, F-Sa 4:30-10pm, Su 4-8pm.)

◙ **SIGHTS.** The University of Iowa's **Museum of Natural History**, at Jefferson and Clinton St., details the ecology, geology, and Native American culture of Iowa, including whimsical but informative dioramas and a large collection of stuffed mammals and birds. Don't miss the reproduction of the giant ground sloth that roamed Iowa's woods many centuries ago. (☎335-0482. Open M-Sa 9:30am-4:30pm, Su 12:30-4:30pm. Free.) A short drive from downtown lies the **Plum Grove Historic Home**, 1030 Carroll St. Explore the 1844 home and garden of the first governor of the Iowa Territory. (☎351-5738. Open Memorial Day-Oct. W-Su 1-5pm. Free.) In West Branch, 15 minutes northeast of the city (Exit 254 on I-80; follow signs), lies the **Herbert Hoover National Historic Site**. Over 100 acres beautifully recreate the feel of an 1870s American town. Take a walking tour of the 31st President's birthplace cottage, his father's blacksmith shop, and the schoolhouse and Quaker meetinghouse he attended. A ½ mi. trail through "restored" prairie is also situated next to the **Herbert Hoover Presidential Library-Museum**. (☎643-2541. Open daily 9am-5pm. $3, seniors $1, under 16 free. Wheelchair accessible.)

🌙 **NIGHTLIFE.** Ever the college town, Iowa City is loaded with places to...well, get loaded. Many bars double as dance clubs, and loud music seems to be the common denominator downtown. **The Union Bar,** 121 E. College St., brags that it's the "biggest damn bar in college football's 'Big Ten.'" (☎339-7713. 18+ with college ID. Cover usually $5. Open Tu-Sa 8pm-2am.) **Et Cetera,** 118 S. Dubuque St., attracts a young, impeccably dressed crowd. (☎341-8382. Cover F-Su $5. Open daily 8pm-2am.) Complete with proudly mounted bull horns, the more traditional **Deadwood,** 6 S. Dubuque St., is often lauded as the city's best bar, touting live bluegrass, classic rock, and folk acts. (☎351-9417. Open M-F 10am-2am, Sa 10:30am-2am, Su 12pm-2am.) Local musicians play Thursday to Saturday at 9:30pm (only Friday and Saturday in the summer) in **The Sanctuary,** 405 S. Gilbert St. Escape into a restaurant and bar with 120 beers and comfortable sofas. (☎351-5692. Cover varies. Bar open M-Sa 4pm-2am; restaurant open M-Tu 4-11pm, W-Sa 4pm-midnight.) In summer, the **Friday Night Concert Series** (☎354-0863; 6:30-9:30pm) offers everything from jazz to salsa to blues, while **Just Jazz Saturdays** (6:30-9:30pm) features exactly what it advertises.

EFFIGY MOUNDS

Mysterious and striking, the Effigy Mounds were built by Native Americans as early as 1000 BC. The enigmatic effigies are low-lying mounds of piled earth formed into distinct geometric and animal shapes. Though they once covered much of the Midwest, farmers' plows have ensured that only a scattering of them remain, mostly in western Wisconsin and eastern Iowa. One of the largest concentrations of intact mounds composes the **Effigy Mounds National Monument**, 151 Rte. 76, 100 mi. west of Madison in Marquette, Iowa. Offering striking views of the Mississippi from high, rocky bluffs, the trails winding through the park explore the lives of these indigenous people and the social and spiritual meanings the mounds had for them. Take Rte. 18 W from Madison. (☎319-873-3491. Visitors Center open June-early Sept. daily 8am-6pm; closes earlier in the fall. Guided tours are available June-early Sept.; call ahead for times.) **Wyalusing State Park ❶,** just across the Mississippi and

10 mi. south of Prairie du Chien in Wisconsin, offers more than 110 campsites overlooking the stunning confluence of the Wisconsin River and the mighty Mississippi
as well as its own assortment of mounds and trails. (☎ 608-996-2261. Campsites $10;
summer weekends $12. Electricity an additional $3 per night.)

SPIRIT LAKE & OKOBOJI ☎ 712

In attempts to rival its neighbors, Iowa boasts its own Great Lakes. **Spirit Lake,
West Okoboji Lake,** and **East Okoboji Lake** are all popular vacation destinations. West
Okoboji Lake ranks with Switzerland's Lake Geneva and Canada's Lake Louise as
one of the world's blue-water lakes, carved out by a glacier 10,000 years ago and
continuously replenished with spring water.

It's hard to miss the **amusement park** in Arnold's Park, off Rte. 71, with its roller
coaster, kiddie rides, and ice cream shops. (☎ 332-2183 or 800-599-6995. Hours
vary, usually 11am-10pm. $16, children 3-4 ft. tall and seniors $12, under 3 ft. free.
Individual ride tickets $1.50-4.50.) The park's **Roof Garden** hosts open air concerts,
including an annual **Blues and Zydeco Festival** each June (call the park for info). One
block west of the amusement park, **Abbie Gardner Historic Log Cabin** is a museum that
presents a 13-minute video explaining the unfurling of the dispute between
encroaching settlers and members of the Sioux that eventually led to the Spirit
Lake Massacre of March 1857. (☎ 332-7248. Open June-Aug. M-F noon-4pm, Sa-Su
9am-4pm. Free, but donation suggested.) Theater buffs can catch productions by
the **Stephens College Okoboji Summer Theater.** (☎ 332-7773. Box office open M 10am-
6pm, Tu-Sa 10am-9pm, Su 1-7pm. $11-13.) For a dose of the outdoors, hike, skate,
or bike **The Spine,** a 14½ mi. trail that runs through the area. Rent bikes at **Okoboji
Bikes,** on Rte. 71 in Fox Plaza just south of the amusement park. (☎ 332-5274. Open
M-F 10am-6pm, Sa 10am-5pm, Su noon-5pm. Half-day $15, full day $25.)

Budget accommodations in the immediate lake area are scarce, especially in
summer. Cheap motels line U.S. 71 in Spencer, about 15 mi. south of Okoboji. **The
Northland Inn ❸,** at the junction of Rte. 9 and Rte. 86, just north of West Okoboji
Lake, offers wood-paneled rooms and a continental breakfast. (☎ 336-1450. May-
Sept. 1 bed $50, 2 beds $60; Oct.-Apr. 1 bed $23-28, 2 beds $38.) Pitch your tent year-
round at tranquil **Marble Beach Campground ❶** (☎ 336-4437, in winter ☎ 337-3211), in
the state park on the shores of Spirit Lake. Other camping options include **Emerson
Bay ❶** and **Gull's Point ❶,** both off Rte. 86 on West Okoboji Lake. (Sites at all 3 campgrounds $11, with electricity $16.) The **Koffee Kup Kafe ❶,** off U.S. 71 in Arnold's
Park, serves up an all-day power breakfast (eggs, bacon, pancakes, hash browns,
and juice) for $5.75. Those craving more simplicity can try a variety of tasty pan-
cakes ($1-3), also served all day. (☎ 332-7657. Open daily 6am-2pm.) A local lunch
spot, **Tweeter's ❷,** off U.S. 71 in Okoboji, grills burgers ($6-10), tosses salads ($5-7),
and melts sandwiches. (☎ 332-9421. Open Apr.-Oct. daily 10am-midnight; Nov.-Mar.
10am-11pm.) The **Iowa Great Lakes Chamber of Commerce,** at the **Iowa Welcome Center,** through the gate to the amusement park, overflows with info. (☎ 322-2107 or
800-839-9987. Open 9am until 1hr. before park closes.) **Area code:** 712.

NEBRASKA

Nebraska often has it rough—imagine having to deal with persistent accusations
of being "boring," "endless," or "the Great American Desert." Nebraska's landscape is, in actuality, its greatest attraction. Central Nebraska features the San-
dhills, a breathtakingly huge windblown dune region with cattle, ranches,
windmills, and tiny towns. The Panhandle offers Western-style mountains and

canyons, historical trails, and National Monuments. For the more urbane traveler, Omaha and Lincoln feature quality sports, fine music, and some of the best Grade A meat in America. While the urge might be to speed through the Cornhusker State, patient travelers will be rewarded with a true Great Plains experience.

⑦ PRACTICAL INFORMATION

Capital: Lincoln.

Visitor Info: Nebraska Tourism Office, 700 S. 16th St., Lincoln, NE 68509 (☎402-471-3796 or 800-228-4307; www.visitnebraska.org). Open M-F 8am-5pm. **Nebraska Game and Parks Commission,** 1212 Deer Park Blvd., Omaha, NE 68108 (☎402-595-2144). Open M-F 8am-5pm.

State Soft Drink: Kool-Aid. **Postal Abbreviation:** NE. **Sales Tax:** 5-6.5%, depends on city.

OMAHA ☎402

Omaha is a city of seemingly endless sprawl, spreading over miles and miles of the Nebraska prairie. The heart of the city, however, is refreshingly compact. Omaha's museums, world-renowned zoo, and sports complex are the envy of other medium-sized cities. The Old Market in downtown lures visitors with a surprisingly large concentration of quiet cafes, breweries, and nightclubs. Overall, the town seems to settle comfortably into its role as a gateway to the West.

✦⑦ ORIENTATION & PRACTICAL INFORMATION. Omaha rests on the west bank of the **Missouri River,** brushing up against Iowa's border. While it wears a facade of geometric order, Omaha is actually an imprecise grid of numbered streets (north-south) and named streets (east-west). **Dodge St.** (Rte. 6) divides the city east-west. **I-480/Rte. 75** (the Kennedy Expwy.) intersects with **I-80,** which runs across the southern half of town. *At night, avoid N. 24th St., Ames Ave., and the area north of I-480.* **Amtrak,** 1003 S. 9th St. (☎342-1501; open 10:30pm-8am), at Pacific St., chugs to Chicago (10hr., 1 per day, $72) and Denver (9hr., 1 per day, $75). **Greyhound,** 1601 Jackson St. (☎341-1906; open 24hr.), runs to Des Moines (2-2½hr.; 10 per day; M-Th $24, F-Su $26); Lincoln (1hr., 7 per day, $10/11); and St. Louis (9hr., 3 per day, $75/79). **Metro Area Transit (MAT),** 2222 Cumming St., handles local transportation. Get schedules at 16th and Douglas St. near the Greyhound station, Park Fair Mall, and the library. (☎341-0800. Open M-F 8am-4:30pm. $1.25, transfers 5¢.) The **Greater Omaha Convention and Visitors Bureau,** 6800 Mercy Rd., #202, at the Ak-Sar-Ben complex off S. 72nd St. north of I-80, has tourist info. (☎444-4660 or 866-937-7624; www.visitomaha.com. Open M-F 8am-4:30pm.) **Hotlines: Rape Crisis,** ☎345-7273. 24hr. **First Call for Help,** ☎330-1907. M-F 8am-5pm. **Internet access: Omaha Library,** 215 S. 15th St., between Douglas and Farnham. (☎444-4800. Open M-Th 9am-9pm, F-Sa 9am-5:30pm, Su 1-5pm.) **Post Office:** 1124 Pacific St. (☎348-2543. Open M-F 7:30am-6pm, Sa 7:30am-noon.) **ZIP code:** 68108. **Area code:** 402.

♖ ACCOMMODATIONS. Motels in Omaha are not particularly budget-friendly. For better deals, head to the outskirts; start around L St. and 60th and head west from there. The **Satellite Motel ❷,** 6006 L St., south of I-80 Exit 450 (60th St.), is a round two-story building with lots of personality. Clean, wedge-shaped rooms come equipped with fridge, microwave, coffee-maker, and cable TV. (☎733-7373. Singles $40; doubles $46.) For a taste of the countryside, go to the first B&B in Nebraska, **Bundy's Bed and Breakfast ❶,** 16906 S. 255th St., 20 miles southwest of Omaha in Gretna. Take Exit 432 off I-80, follow Hwy. 6 west for 4 mi., and take a right on 255th St. before the Linoma Lighthouse. (☎332-3616. No smoking, drinking, or children. Singles $25; doubles $45.) Outdoorsfolk should set up camp at the **Haworth Park Campground** ❶, in Bellevue on Payne St. at the end of Mission Ave. Take the exit for Rte. 370 E off Rte. 75, turn right onto Galvin Rd., left onto Mission Ave., and right onto Payne St. before the toll bridge. Tent sites are separate from the RV area but not entirely out of view. (☎291-3379. Showers, toilets, and shelters. Open daily 6am-10pm, but stragglers can enter after hours. Check-out 3pm. Tent sites $7, with hookup $9; RV sites $15.)

▢ FOOD. It's no fun being a chicken, cow, or vegetarian in Omaha, where there is a fried chicken joint on every block and a steakhouse in every district. Once a warehouse area, the brick streets of the **Old Market**, on Jackson, Howard, and Harney St. between 10th and 13th, now feature popular shops, restaurants, and bars. The **Farmers Market** (☎345-5401) is located at 11th and Jackson St. (mid-July to mid-Aug. W 4-8pm, Sa 8am-12:30pm; mid-May to mid-Oct. Sa 8am-12:30pm.) If you want to find out what all the hubbub's about, sink your teeth into some USDA prime grade beef at **Omaha Prime** ❸, 415 S. 11th St., in the Old Market. Their steak and chops will cost you $25-40, but when that bill comes, remember that only 5% of all beef holds the honor of being "prime." (☎341-7040. Open M-Sa 5-9pm.) **Upstream Brewing** ❷, 514 S. 11th St., at Jackson St., dishes out creative entrees ($9-18) that can be wolfed down inside, out on the patio, or up on the rooftop deck. (☎344-0200. Pizza and burgers $6-8. Home-brewed beers $3. Open daily 11am-1am.) **Délice European Cafe** ❶, 1206 Howard St., at 12th St. in the Old Market, sells scrumptious pastries and deli fare ($2-6) in a bright, spacious setting. They also serve wine and beer ($2.50-6.50), making the meal appropriately European, and the patio affords shaded views of the Court St. area. (☎342-2276. Open M-Th 7:30am-9pm, F-Sa 7:30am-11pm, Su 7:30am-6pm.) **McFoster's Natural Kind Cafe** ❸, 302 S. 38th St., at Farnam St., sells healthy dishes ($5-14), including free-range chicken, vegan eggplant parmesan, and artichoke specialties. (☎345-7477. Live music nightly. Open M-Th 11am-10pm, F-Sa 11am-11pm, Su 10am-3pm.) **The Diner** ❷, 409 S. 12 St., is as plain as its name suggests, serving up heaping portions in no time. (☎341-9870. Pancakes run $3-4. Everything under $7. Open M-Sa 6am-4pm.)

◪ SIGHTS. With the world's largest desert dome and indoor rainforest and North America's largest cat complex, **Henry Doorly Zoo,** 3701 S. 10th St. (reached by exiting I-80 at 13th St., at Bert Murphy Blvd.), is the number one tourist attraction in Nebraska. Bring your NightVision goggles to the largest nocturnal exhibit in the world, opening in the spring of 2003. (☎733-8401; www.omahazoo.com. Open daily 9:30am-5pm. $8.50, over 62 $7, ages 5-11 $4.75.) Just down the road at the **Simmons Wildlife Safari Park,** drive your all-terrain vehicle (or beat-up Chevette) 4½ mi. through a nature preserve inhabited by bison, pronghorns, moose, wolves, and other beasts. (☎944-9453. Open Apr.-Oct. daily 9:30am-5pm. $10 per car. Sa-Su guided tram tours an additional $1.)

The **Durham Western Heritage Museum,** 801 S. 10th St., occupies the former Union Train Station, an impressive Art Deco structure. Climb aboard an old steam engine or lounge car on the Track Level, learn about Omaha's neighborhoods in the historical galleries, or indulge in a malted milkshake at the authentic soda fountain. (☎444-5071. Open Tu-Sa 10am-5pm, Su 1-5pm. $5, seniors $4, ages 3-12 $3.50.) Nebraska's largest art museum is Omaha's **Joslyn Art Museum,** 2200 Dodge St., which displays a surprising collection of 19th- and 20th-century American and European art. Dance for joy around the original plaster cast of Degas's famous sculpture 'Little Dancer,' complete with an authentic billowing tutu. (☎342-3300. "Jazz on the Green" mid-July to mid-Aug. Th 7-9pm. Open Tu-Sa 10am-4pm, Su noon-4pm. $6, students and seniors $4, ages 5-17 $3.50; Sa 10am-noon. Free.) See the gargantuan remnants of US airpower from the last half-century in the equally

GREAT PLAINS

ARE WE GONNA DO STONEHENGE TOMORROW?

Everything looks the same as you drive through the plains and farmlands of western Nebraska until, suddenly, a preternatural power sweeps the horizon and the ultimate shrine to bizarre Americana springs into view—**Carhenge.** Consisting of 36 old white-washed cars, this oddly engaging sculpture, built in celebration of the 1987 summer solstice, has the same orientation and dimensions as Stonehenge in England. When asked why he built it, the artisan Jim Reinders replied, *"Plane, loqui deprehendi,"* or, "Clearly, I spoke to be understood." *(Alliance, NE, 60 mi. northeast of Scotts Bluff. From Rte. 385, take Rte. 2 east in Alliance, then follow Rte. 87 north for 3½ mi. ☎ 800-738-0648. Open daily 24hr.)*

enormous **Strategic Air and Space Museum,** Exit 426 off I-80 in Ashland. The museum displays military aircraft, including a B-52 bomber, as well as exhibits on military history. Bunker down in a 1950s bomb shelter, or practice your duck-and-cover technique in a 1960s classroom. (☎ 827-3100 or 800-358-5029. Open daily 9am-5pm. $7, seniors and military $6, ages 5-12 $3.)

🎭 🎵 **ENTERTAINMENT & NIGHTLIFE.** At **Rosenblatt Stadium,** across from the zoo on 13th St., you can watch the **Omaha Royals** round the bases from April to early September (☎ 738-5100. General admission $4; reserved seat $6; box seat $8. Wheelchair accessible.) The stadium has also hosted the NCAA College Baseball World Series every June since 1950. In late June and early July, **Shakespeare on the Green** stages free performances in Elmwood Park, on 60th and Dodge St. (☎ 280-2391. Th-Su 8pm.)

Punk and progressive folk have found a niche at the several area universities; check the window of the **Antiquarian Bookstore,** 1215 Harney St., in the Old Market, for the scoop on shows. Several good bars await nearby. **The Dubliner,** 1205 Harney St., below street level, stages live traditional Irish music on Friday and Saturday evenings. (☎ 342-5887. Cover $2-3. Open M-Sa 11am-1am, Su 1pm-1am.) The **13th Street Coffee Company,** 519 S. 13th St., keeps more than 20 types of beans on hand and brews three different varieties every day. The hopelessly romantic, or just plain hopeless, can imbibe Love Poison—white chocolate mocha with hot cinnamon. (☎ 345-2883. Live music most weekends; call ahead for details. Free Internet access. Open M-Th 6:30am-11pm, F 6:30am-midnight, Sa 8am-midnight, Su 9am-11pm.) **The Max,** 1417 Jackson St., is one of the most popular gay bars in the state. With five bars, a disco dance floor, DJ, fountains, and patio, the Max is Omaha's gay haven. (☎ 346-4110. Happy Hour 4-9pm. 21+. Cover F-Sa $5, Su $3. Open daily 4pm-1am.) For country tunes and line dancing, head to **Guitars and Cadillacs,** 10865 W. Dodge Rd., near the junction of I-680. Follow the signs for Old Mill Rd. (☎ 333-5500. F-Sa 1-3am after-hours dancing for those 18+. Open Th 8pm-1am, F 6pm-3am, Sa 7pm-3am, and Su 6pm-midnight.)

LINCOLN   ☎ 402

The spirit of Lincoln rises and falls with the success of its world-famous college football team, the Nebraska Cornhuskers. Many youngsters spend their childhoods running wind sprints, weightlifting, and practicing, all for the dream of stepping onto the cornhusker's field. Life does go on off the field, however. Lincoln houses the Nebraska state legislature, the only one-house legislature in the Union, as well as quality restaurants and scenic parks.

⑦ PRACTICAL INFORMATION. Lincoln's grid makes sense—numbered streets increase as you go east, and lettered streets progress through the alphabet as you go north. **O St.** is the main east-west drag. It becomes Hwy. 6 west of the city, and Rte. 34 east. **R St.** runs along the south side of the **University of Nebraska-Lincoln (UNL).** Most downtown sights lie between 7th and 16th St. and M and R St. **Lincoln Airport** (☎458-2480) is located 5 mi. northwest of downtown on Cornhusker Hwy.; take Exit 399 off I-80. **Amtrak,** 201 N. 7th St. (☎476-1295; open Su-Th 11:30pm-7am), runs once daily to: Chicago (12hr., $94), Denver (7hr., $89), and Omaha (1hr., $16). Prices vary with availability. **Greyhound,** 940 P St. (☎474-1071; ticket window open M-F 7:30am-6pm, Sa 9:30am-3pm), sends buses to Chicago (12hr.; 5 per day; M-Th $54, F-Su $58); Denver (9-18hr., 5 per day, $77/81); Kansas City (6-10hr., 3 per day, $52/56); and Omaha (1 hr., 3 per day, $10/11). **Star Tran,** 710 J St., handles public transportation. Schedules are available on the bus, at the office on J St., and at many locations downtown. (☎476-1234. Buses run M-F 5am-7pm, Sa 6:30am-7pm. $1, seniors and ages 5-18 50¢.) **Visitors Center:** 201 N. 7th St., in the Haymarket district. (☎434-5348 or 800-423-8212; www.lincoln.org. Open May-Sept. M-F 9am-8pm, Sa 4am-4pm, Su noon-4pm; Oct.-Apr. M-F 9am-6pm, Sa 8am-4pm, Su noon-4pm.) **Internet access: Lincoln Public Library,** 136 S. 14th St., at N St. (☎441-8500. Open M-Th 9am-9pm, F-Sa 9am-6pm, Su 1:30-5:30pm.) **Post Office:** 700 R St. (☎458-1844. Open M-F 7:30am-6pm, Sa 9am-1pm.) **ZIP code:** 68501. **Area code:** 402.

⬤ ACCOMMODATIONS. There are few inexpensive motels downtown. Cheaper places are farther east around the 5600 block of Cornhusker Hwy. (U.S. 6). The **Cornerstone Hostel (HI-AYH) ❶,** 640 N. 16th St., at U St. just south of Vine St., on frat row, is conveniently located in a church basement in the university's downtown campus. It rarely fills up, and while the basement can get stuffy in summer, the sounds of the organ drifting from upstairs will take your mind off the heat. (☎476-0926. Two single-sex rooms; 5 beds for women, 3 for men. Full kitchen and laundry facilities. Free parking and linen. Curfew 11pm. Dorms $10, nonmembers $13.) **The Great Plains Budget Host Inn ❷,** 2732 O St., at 27th St., has large rooms with fridges and coffee makers. Take bus #9 "O St. Shuttle." (☎476-3253 or 800-288-8499. Free parking and kitchenettes available. Singles $42; doubles $48; 10% AAA discount.) Experience the elegance of the **Atwood House Bed and Breakfast ❸,** 740 S. 17th St., at G St., two blocks from the Capitol. With antiques nestled in every corner and whirlpool baths awaiting in most suites, this 1894 mansion will surely provide a relaxing respite for the weary traveler. (☎438-4567 or 800-884-6554. Suites $115-179.) The 199 sites at the **Nebraska State Fair Park Campground ❶,** 2400 N. 14th St., at Cornhusker Hwy., are centrally located, but next to a highway and train tracks. Take bus #7 "Belmont." (☎473-4287. Fills up early in Aug., but no reservations accepted. Open Apr.-Oct. Sites for 2 $15, full hookup $18; each additional person $1.) To get to the pleasant **Camp-A-Way ❶,** 200 Ogden Rd., near 1st and Superior St., take Exit 401 or 401a from I-80, then Exit 1 on I-180/Rte. 34. Though next to a highway, the 81 sites are peaceful and shaded. (☎476-2282 or 866-719-2267. Showers, laundry, pool, and convenience store. Reservations recommended during fair time in Aug. Sites $15, with water and electricity $20, full hookup $26.)

⬛⬛ FOOD & NIGHTLIFE. Historic Haymarket, 7th to 9th St. and O to R St., is a renovated warehouse district near the train tracks with cafes, bars, restaurants, and a **farmers market.** (☎435-7496. Open mid-May to mid-Oct. Sa 8am-noon.) All downtown buses connect at 11th and O St., two blocks east of Historic Haymarket. Get breakfast all day at **Kuhl's ❶,** 1038 O St., at 11th St. The Lincoln special—

two eggs; toast; hash browns; and ham, bacon, or sausage—sets the local standard at $5.75. (☎476-1311. Breakfasts $3-6. Open M-F 6am-7pm, Sa 6am-4pm, Su 7am-3pm.) **Maggie's Bakery and Vegetarian Vittles ❶**, 311 N. 8th St., sustains Lincoln's vegetarians and vegans with $1.50-2 pastries, $4-6 wraps, and $6 lunch specials. (☎477-3959. Open M-F 8am-3pm.) **Valentino's ❷**, 232 N. 13th St., at Q St., is a regional chain with roots in Lincoln. (☎475-1501. Pasta dishes $5-7. F-Sa 8-11pm all-you-can-eat pizza buffet $3-5. Open Su-Th 11am-10pm, F-Sa 11am-11pm.) **Lazlo's Brewery and Grill ❸**, 710 P St., prides itself on fresh fish ($10-20), ground beef, and freshly brewed beers ($4). The servers, luckily, are not fresh. (☎434-5636. Burgers $5-7. Steak and chops $15-21. Open Su-Th 11am-10pm, F-Sa 11am-11pm.)

Nightspots abound in Lincoln, particularly those of the sports bar variety. For the biggest names in Lincoln's live music scene, try the suitably dark and smoky **Zoo Bar**, 136 N. 14th St., where blues is king six nights a week. (☎435-8754. Cover $2-10. Open M-Sa 3pm-1am.) **Q**, 226 S. 9th St., between M and N St., is a great gay and lesbian bar with a large dance floor. Come the first Thursday of the month for amateur strip night, and expect Saturday night drag shows monthly. (☎475-2269. Tu 19+. Cover usually $3. Open Tu-Su 8pm-1am.) For the best of the college sports bar genre, head to **Iguana's**, 1426 O St. (☎476-8850. Open M-Sa 7pm-1am.)

◙ SIGHTS. The "Tower on the Plains," the 400 ft. **Nebraska State Capitol Building,** at 15th and K St., wows with its streamlined exterior and detailed interior, highlighted by a beautiful mosaic floor. Although exterior renovations continue, the inside remains untouched and remarkably beautiful. The 19 ft. statue "The Sower" sits atop the building. (☎471-0448. Open M-F 8am-5pm, Sa 10am-5pm, Su 1-5pm. Free 30min. tours every hr. except noon.) The **Museum of Nebraska History,** on Centennial Mall, a renamed portion of 15th St., has a phenomenal collection of headdresses, moccasins, jewelry, and other artifacts in its permanent exhibit on Plains Indians. (☎471-4754. Open M-F 9am-4:30pm, Sa-Su 1-4:30pm. Free.) The **University of Nebraska State Museum,** 14th and U St., in Morrill Hall, boasts an amazing fossil collection that includes Archie, the largest mounted mammoth of any American museum. (☎472-2642. Open M-Sa 9:30am-4:30pm, Su 1:30-4:30pm. $4, ages 5-18 $2, under 5 free.) In the same building, the **Mueller Planetarium** lights up the ceiling with several daily shows. (☎472-2641. Laser shows F-Sa. Planetarium $6, under 19 $4; laser shows $5/4.) For a wheel-y good time, coast on over to the **National Museum of Roller Skating,** 4730 South St., at 48th St., to learn the history of the sport. (☎483-7551, ext. 16. Open M-F 9am-5pm. Free, but donations appreciated.)

Come August, in addition to livestock, crafts, and fitter family contests, the **Nebraska State Fair** offers car races, tractor pulls, and plenty of rides to please all. (☎474-5371; www.statefair.org. Aug. 23 to Sept. 2, 2002. $6, ages 6-12 $2.) **Pioneers Park,** 3201 S. Coddington Ave., ¼ mi. south of W. Van Dorn, is a sylvan paradise perfect for a prairie picnic. The **Pioneers Park Nature Center** has bison and elk within its sanctuary and is also the starting point for 6 mi. of trails. (☎441-7895. Park open sunrise to sunset. Nature Center open June-Aug. M-Sa 8:30am-8:30pm, Su noon-8:30pm; Sept.-May M-Sa 8:30am-5pm, Su noon-5pm. Free. Wheelchair accessible.)

SCOTTS BLUFF ☎308

Known to the Plains Indians as *Me-a-pa-te* ("hill that is hard to go around"), the imposing clay and sandstone highlands of **Scotts Bluff National Monument** were landmarks for people traveling the Mormon and Oregon Trails in the 1840s. For some time the bluff was too dangerous to cross, but in the 1850s a single-file wagon trail was opened just south of the bluff through narrow **Mitchell's Pass,** where traffic wore deep marks in the sandstone. Today, a half-mile stretch of the original **Oregon**

Trail is preserved at the pass, complete with a pair of covered wagons. Tourists can gaze at the distant horizons to the east and west as pioneers once did. The **Visitors Center**, at the entrance on Rte. 92, relates the multiple and contradictory accounts of the mysterious death of Hiram Scott, the fur trader who gave the Bluffs their name. Don't miss the twelve-minute slide show about life on the Oregon Trail. (☎436-4340. Open in summer daily 8am-7pm; in winter 8am-5pm. $5 per carload, $2 per motorcycle.) To get to the top of the bluffs, hike the challenging **Saddle Rock Trail** (1½ mi. each way) or motor up **Summit Dr.** At the top, you'll find two short **nature trails.** Guide books (50¢) are available at the trailheads and the Visitors Center. The **North Overlook** is a ½ mi. paved walk with a view of the North Platte River Valley. The **South Overlook** is ¼ mi. and provides a spectacular view of Scotts Bluff.

Take U.S. 26 to Rte. 71 to Rte. 92, and the Monument is on Rte. 92 about 2 mi. west of **Gering** (*not* in the town of Scotts Bluff). A 1.2 mi. bike trail links Gering with the base of the bluffs. From July 10-13, 2003, expect the 82nd annual **Oregon Trail Days Festival** to pack the towns near Scotts Bluff with festive folk. Twenty miles east on Rte. 92, just south of Bayard, the 475 ft. spire of **Chimney Rock,** visible from more than 30 mi. away, served as another landmark that inspired travelers on the Oregon Trail. Unfortunately, there is no path up to the base of the rock due to the rough terrain and rattlesnakes. The Nebraska State Historical Society operates a **Visitors Center.** (☎586-2581. Open in summer daily 9am-6pm; in winter 9am-5pm. $3, under 18 free.) For an extra historical delight, continue down the road past the Visitors Center, take a right onto Chimney Rock Rd., and follow the gravel road ½ mi. to its end. Here you will find the first graveyard of settlers on the Oregon Trail and a closer view of the rock itself. **Area code:** 308. **Time Zone:** Mountain.

KANSAS

In 1935, a University of Chicago professor conducted a study and determined that respondents would cut off their little toe for $100, but would only move to Kansas if given $10,000. Thankfully, enthusiasm for Kansas has picked up since then. The state continues to serve as an important stopover for cross-country travelers, and its inhabitants are quick to sing the praises of the Sunflower State. Grueling feuds over Kansas's status as a slave state before the Civil War gave rise to the term "Bleeding Kansas." The wound has since healed, and Kansas now presents a serene blend of small-town charm and miles of farmland. Highway signs subtly remind that "every Kansas farmer feeds 101 people—and *you.*"

⚡ PRACTICAL INFORMATION

Capital: Topeka.

Visitor info: Division of Travel and Tourism: 1000 SW Jackson #1300, Topeka 66414 (☎785-296-2009 or 800-252-6727; www.travelks.com). Open daily 8am-5pm. **Kansas Wildlife and Parks,** 512 SE 25th Ave., Pratt 67124 (☎620-672-5911; www.kdwp.state.ks.us). Open M-F 8am-5pm.

Postal Abbreviation: KS. **Sales Tax:** 5.3% or higher, depending on city.

STUCK IN THE MIDDLE Have you ever wanted to be at the center of the action? Go 2 mi. northwest of Lebanon, KS. Sit by the stone monument and feel special—you are the geographic center of the United States.

FROM THE ROAD

THE OPEN ROAD

As someone who grew up in a city and spent his entire life in fairly big cities, it was at first bewildering for me to drive through hundreds of miles of empty land. Of course, it is not *really* empty; there are trees, and cows, and even a few people, and signs with messages like, "The Largest Hand-Dug Well in the World: 50 Miles," but it sure felt empty to me as I passed down Highway 154 from Dodge City, Kansas to Wichita. First, the fears bubbled to the surface. What if my car breaks down? What if I run out of gas? What if something even worse happens (as scenes from *Deliverance* flash through my mind)? But once those were dismissed, a new feeling came—one of incredible serenity. There is something inexplicably satisfying about rolling through acres of wheatfields and cow pastures, with a slight breeze coming through the window, country music on the radio, and an unending blue sky in front of you. Of course, there is also the tedium, and after a while I began to think to myself, "How much longer until the largest hand-dug well in the world?" in a desperate effort to break the monotony. Finally it came, but as I peered down into the vast depth of the well, I became anxious to get back on the road. I returned to the car, took a right back onto the highway, and happily headed off once again on a warm Kansas day through land that isn't empty after all.

—Aaron Haas

WICHITA
☎ 316

Coronado came to the site of present-day Wichita in 1541 searching for the mythical, gold-laden city of Quivira. Upon arriving, he was so disappointed that he had his guide strangled for misleading him. Despite this unpromising beginning, Wichita survived the 19th century by fending off cattle thieves and bringing frontier justice to the Wild West. In the 20th century, Wichita's economy took off as a center of aviation manufacturing and an agricultural commodities hub for the southern and central Plains. Downtown gives off a suburban vibe, but as the Old Town area gets revamped, yuppies party deeper into the Kansas night.

🛈 **PRACTICAL INFORMATION.** Wichita lies on I-35, 170 mi. north of Oklahoma City and about 200 mi. southwest of Kansas City. A small and quiet downtown makes for easy walking or parking. **Broadway St.** is the major north-south artery. **Douglas Ave.** separates the numbered east-west streets to the north from the named east-west streets that run to the south. Running east-west, **Kellogg Ave. (U.S. 54)** serves as an expressway through downtown, and as a main commercial strip. The closest **Amtrak** station, 414 N. Main St. (☎283-7533; open M-F midnight-8am), 30 mi. north of Wichita in the town of Newton, sends one very early train west to Dodge City (2½hr., $70-120) and another northeast to Kansas City (5hr., $88-152). **Greyhound,** 312 S. Broadway St., two blocks east of Main St. (☎265-7711; open daily 3am-noon), services Denver (12hr., 2 per day, $75); Kansas City (4hr., 3 per day, $32.25); and Oklahoma City (4hr., 3 per day, $32.25). **Wichita Transit,** 214 S. Topeka St., runs 18 bus routes in town. (☎265-7221. Open M-F 6am-6pm, Sa 7am-5pm. Buses run M-F 5:45am-6:45pm, Sa 6:45am-5:45pm. $1, seniors and disabled 50¢, ages 6-17 75¢; transfers 10¢.) **Visitor info: Convention and Visitors Bureau,** 100 S. Main St., at Douglas Ave. (☎265-2800 or 800-288-9424. Open M-F 8am-5pm.) **Internet access: Public Library,** 223 S. Main St. (☎261-8500. Open M-Th 10am-9pm, F-Sa 10am-5:30pm, Su 1-5pm.) **Post Office:** 330 W. 2nd St. N, at N. Waco St. (☎267-7710. Open M-F 7am-5:30pm, Sa 9am-1pm.) **ZIP code:** 67202. **Area code:** 316.

📠 ACCOMMODATIONS. Wichita offers a bounty of cheap hotels. S. Broadway St. has plenty of mom-and-pop places, *but be wary of the surrounding areas.* The chains line **E. and W. Kellogg Ave.** 5 to 8 mi. from downtown. Only 10 blocks from downtown, the **Mark 8 Inn ❶**, 1130 N. Broadway, has small, comfortable rooms with free local calls, cable TV, A/C, fridge, and laundry facilities. (☎265-4679 or 888-830-7268. Singles $30; doubles $33.) The **English Village Inn ❷**, 6727 E. Kellogg Dr., is, in fact, American, urban, and a motel, but it does keep large rooms with aging furnishings in tidy repair for very reasonable rates. (☎683-5613 or 800-365-8455. Cable TV and HBO in the rooms, popcorn in the lobby. Singles from $32; doubles from $36.) **USI Campgrounds ❶**, 2920 E. 33rd St., right off Hillside Rd., is the most convenient of Wichita's hitchin' posts with laundry, showers, playground, and storm shelter—in case there's a twister a-comin'. (☎838-0435. No tents. RV sites $22.50.)

📩 FOOD. Beef is what's for dinner in Wichita. If you eat only one slab here, get it from **Doc's Steakhouse ❸**, 1515 N. Broadway St., bus #13 "N. Broadway," where the most expensive entree—a 17 oz. T-bone with salad, potato, and bread—is only $10. (☎264-4735. Open M-Th 11:30am-9:30pm, F 11:30am-10pm, Sa 4-10pm.) The **Old Town** area is a good choice for lunch. Several restaurants offer $5 buffets and other specials. The **River City Brewing Company ❷**, 150 N. Mosley St., is one of the newest dining spots in the neighborhood. (☎263-2739. Hearty entrees $6-10. Open daily 11am-10pm.) Go to **N. Broadway,** around 10th St., for authentic Asian food, mostly Vietnamese. Large paper umbrellas hang from the ceiling of **Pho 99 ❶**, 1015 N. Broadway St., which ladles 32 kinds of hot *pho* (noodles) and vermicelli dishes ($4-6). Only in Kansas would Vietnamese noodles be accompanied by strips of rib-eye steak. (☎267-8188. Open daily 10am-8:30pm.)

◪ SIGHTS. The four **Museums on the River** are within a few blocks of each other; take the trolley or bus #12 to "Riverside." Walk through the rough and tumble cattle days of the 1870s in the **Old Cowtown**, 1871 Sim Park Dr., lined with many original buildings. (☎264-6398. Open Apr.-Oct. M-Sa 10am-5pm, Su noon-5pm; Nov.-Mar. Sa 10am-5pm, Su noon-5pm. $7, seniors $6.50, ages 12-18 $5, ages 5-11 $3.50, under 5 free; seniors 2-for-1 Tu and W. Call for special events info.) The **Mid-America All-Indian Center and Museum,** 650 N. Seneca St., displays Native American artifacts. The late Blackbear Bosin's awe-inspiring sculpture *Keeper of the Plains* stands guard over the confluence of the Arkansas and Little Arkansas Rivers. The center also holds the **Mid-America All-Indian Intertribal Powwow** in late July with traditional dancing, foods, arts, and crafts. (☎262-5221. Open Apr.-Dec. M-Sa 10am-5pm, Su 1-5pm; Jan.-Mar. closed M. $2, ages 6-12 $1.)

Wichita's newest and most impressive piece of riverfront architecture houses the city's interactive museum, **Exploration Place**, 300 N. McLean Blvd. Come learn how to shoot air out of a cannon or see how tornadoes and steam currents propagate. (☎263-3373 or 877-904-1444. Open M noon-6pm, Tu-Th and Su 9am-6pm, F-Sa 9am-9pm. $7, seniors $6.50, ages 5-15 $5, ages 2-4 $2.) **Botanica,** 701 N. Amindon St., the Wichita botanical gardens, contains a wide collection of flora from the Americas and Asia. Large indoor exhibits afford a chance to beat the heat, while the outdoor exhibits are spellbinding. (☎264-0448. Open M-Sa 9am-5pm, Su 1-5pm. $4.50, students $2, seniors $4.)

LAWRENCE   ☎ 785

Lawrence was founded in 1854 by anti-slavery advocates to ensure Kansas became a free state. Nowadays, Lawrence, home to the flagship **University of Kansas (UK)**, offers numerous first-rate artistic, architectural, historical, cultural, and social activities. The UK's **Watkins Community Museum of History**, 1047 Massachusetts St., whets the appetites of Kansas history buffs. (☎ 841-4109. Open Tu-Sa 10am-4pm, Su 1:30-4pm. Free.) The main attractions, however, are two tours through downtown Lawrence. A 1½hr. driving tour beginning at 1111 E. 19th St., **Quantrill's Raid: The Lawrence Massacre,** traces the events leading up to the murder of over 200 men by pro-slavery vigilantes on August 21, 1863. The second tour, **House Styles of Old West Lawrence,** provides a look at gorgeous 19th-century homes. There is a walking (45min.) and driving (25min.) tour. Maps are at the Visitors Center, Chamber of Commerce, and library.

Inexpensive motels are hard to come by in Lawrence. The best place to look is around Iowa and 6th St., just west of campus. The town also offers several B&B options. Three blocks from downtown, the **Halcyon House Bed and Breakfast ❸**, 1000 Ohio St., is extremely close to local attractions and good parking. (☎ 841-0314. Breakfast included. Rooms $49.) The traditional **Westminster Inn and Suites ❸**, 2525 W. 6th St., offers several amenities to make stays more comfortable, including a pool and free day passes to the nearby health club. (☎ 841-8410. Breakfast included. Singles M-Th $54, F-Su $64; doubles $64/74. $5 AAA discount. 2 wheelchair accessible rooms.)

Downtown Lawrence features both traditional barbecue joints and more health-conscious offerings. The **Wheatfields Bakery and Cafe ❷**, 904 Vermont St., serves up large sandwiches ($5-6.50) on French bread, freshly baked rye, or focaccia. Plenty of vegetarian options are available. (☎ 841-5553. Open M-Sa 6:30am-8pm, Su 7:30am-4pm.) **Cafe Nova ❶**, 745 New Hampshire St., percolates several varieties of coffee each day; sweeteners range from maple syrup to sweet cream. (☎ 841-3282. Internet access $6 per hr. Sandwiches $3-4. Open M-W 7am-midnight, Th-Sa 7am-2am, Su 7am-1am.) The **Free State Brewing Company ❷**, 636 Massachusetts St., the first legal brewery in Kansas and a popular local hangout, ferments over 50 beers yearly and always has at least five on tap. (☎ 843-4555. Beers $2.50 Sandwiches $6. Pasta dishes $8-10. M $1.25 beers. Open M-Sa 11am-midnight, Su noon-11pm.) For live music and a neighborhood bar atmosphere, head down to the well-equipped **Jazzhaus**, 926½ Massachusetts St. Performers range from local groups to the occasional regional act. (☎ 749-3320. Cover after 9pm $2-8, depending on show; Tu $1.50, but no live music. Open daily 4pm-2am; music begins at 9pm.)

Lawrence lies just south of I-70 in northeastern Kansas. There is an unstaffed **Amtrak** station at 413 E. 7th St.; trains chug to Chicago (11hr., 1 per day, $74-110). **Greyhound**, 2447 W. 6th St. (☎ 843-5622; ticket window open M-F 7:30am-4pm, Sa 7:30am-noon), runs buses to Dallas (13-15hr., 5 per day, $76-84); Denver (11-12hr., 2 per day, $66-74); and Kansas City, MO (1hr., 3 per day, $12-14). The **Lawrence Transit System (the "T")**, 930 E. 30th St., has schedules at the office, the library or on any bus. (☎ 832-3465. Open M-F 6am-8pm, Sa 7am-8pm. 50¢, seniors and disabled 25¢.) **Visitors Center:** 400 N. 2nd St., at Locust St. (☎ 865-4499 or 888-529-5267. Open Oct.-Mar. M-Sa 9am-5pm, Su 1-5pm; Apr.-Sept. M-F 8:30am-5:30pm, Su 1-5pm.) **Lawrence Chamber of Commerce:** 734 Vermont St. #101. (☎ 865-4411. Open M-F 8am-5pm.) **Internet access: Public Library**, 707 Vermont Ave. (843-3833. Open M-F 9am-9pm, Sa 9am-6pm, Su 2-6pm.) **Post Office:** 645 Vermont St. (☎ 843-1681. Open M-F 8am-5:30pm, Sa 9am-noon.) **ZIP code:** 66045. **Area code:** 785.

BOOZE, BOOTS, & BOVINES In its heyday in the 1870s, Dodge City, KS ("the wickedest little city in America") was a haven for gunfighters, prostitutes, and other lawless types. At one time, the main drag had one saloon for every 50 citizens. Disputes were settled man to man, with a duel, and the slower draw ended up in Boot Hill Cemetery, so named for the boot-clad corpses buried there. Legendary lawmen Wyatt Earp and Bat Masterson earned their fame cleaning up the streets of Dodge. Today, the town's most conspicuous residents, about 50,000 cows, reside on the feedlots on the east part of town. Hold your nose and whoop it up during the **Dodge City Days,** complete with rodeo, carnival, and lots of steak. You'll know when you're getting close. (☎620-227-3119. July 25-Aug. 3, 2003.)

MISSOURI

Nestled in the middle of the country, Missouri serves as the gateway to the west while hugging the Midwest and South, blending the three identities into a state that still defies regional stereotyping. Its large cities are defined by wide avenues, long and lazy rivers, numerous parks, humid summers, and blues and jazz wailing into the night. In the countryside, Bible factory outlets stand amid fireworks stands and barbecue pits. Missouri's patchwork geography further complicates its characterization. In the north, near Iowa, amber waves of grain undulate. Along the Mississippi, towering bluffs inscribed with Native American pictographs evoke western canyonlands, while in Hannibal, spelunkers enjoy the winding limestone caves that inspired Mark Twain.

🛈 PRACTICAL INFORMATION

Capital: Jefferson City.

Visitor Info: Missouri Division of Tourism, P.O. Box 1055, Jefferson City 65102 (☎573-751-4133 or 800-877-1234; www.visitmo.org). Open M-F 8am-5pm; toll-free number operates 24hr. **Dept. of Natural Resources,** Division of State Parks, P.O. Box 176, Jefferson City 65102 (☎573-751-2479 or 800-334-6946). Open M-F 8am-5pm.

Postal Abbreviation: MO. **Sales Tax:** 6-7% depending on the county.

ST. LOUIS   ☎314

Directly south of the junction of three rivers—the Mississippi, Missouri, and Illinois—St. Louis marks the transition between Midwest and West. The silvery Gateway Arch pays homage to American expansion, while another great US tradition, baseball, thrives at Busch Stadium. Innovative musicians crowd bars and cafes, influenced by great St. Louis blues and ragtime players of the past. Sprawling and diverse, St. Louis offers visitors both high-paced life in a city and lazy days spent floating on the Mississippi.

▣ TRANSPORTATION

Airport: Lambert-St. Louis International (☎426-8000), 12 mi. northwest of the city on I-70. MetroLink and Bi-state bus #66 "Maplewood-Airport" provide access to downtown ($1.25). Taxis to downtown $20. A few westbound Greyhound buses stop at the airport.

Trains: Amtrak, 550 S. 16th St. (☎331-3000). Office open daily 6am-1am. To **Chicago** (6hr., 3 per day, $27-58) and **Kansas City** (5½hr., 2 per day, $26-52).

Buses: Greyhound, 1450 N. 13th St. (☎231-4485), at Cass Ave. From downtown, take Bi-State bus #30, less than 10min. away. *Be cautious at night.* To **Chicago** (6½hr., 11 per day, $31) and **Kansas City** (5hr., 5 per day, $28).

Public Transit: Bi-State (☎231-2345) runs local buses. Info and schedules available at the **Metroride Service Center,** in the St. Louis Center. (☎982-1485. Open M-F 6am-8pm, Sa-Su 8am-5pm.) **MetroLink,** the light-rail system, runs from 5th St. and Missouri Ave., in East St. Louis, to Lambert Airport. Operates M-Sa 5am-midnight and Su 6am-11pm. Travel for free in the "Ride Free Zone" (from Laclede's Landing to Union Station) M-F 11:30am-1pm. Bi-State or MetroLink $1.25, transfers 10¢; seniors and ages 5-12 50¢/5¢. Day pass $4, available at MetroLink stations. **Shuttle Bugs,** small buses painted like ladybugs, cruise around Forest Park and the Central West End. Operates M-F 6:45am-6pm, Sa-Su 10am-6pm. $1.25. The **Shuttle Bee** buzzes around Forest Park, Clayton, Brentwood, and the Galleria. Operates M-F 6am-11:30pm, Sa 7:30am-10:30pm, Su 9:30am-6:30pm. $1.25.

Taxis: Yellow Cab, ☎361-2345.

⚔🔃 ORIENTATION & PRACTICAL INFORMATION

U.S. 40/I-64 runs east-west through the entire metropolitan area. Downtown is defined as the area east of Tucker between **Martin Luther King** and **Market St.,** which divides the city running north-south. Numbered streets parallel the Mississippi River, increasing to the west. The historic **Soulard** district borders the river south of downtown. **Forest Park** and **University City,** home to **Washington University** and old, stately homes, lie west of downtown; the Italian neighborhood called **The Hill** rests south of these. St. Louis is a driving town: parking comes easy, wide streets allow for lots of meters, and private lots are usually cheap (from $2 per day).

Visitor Info: St. Louis Visitors Center, 308 Washington Ave. (☎241-1764). Open daily 9:30am-4:30pm. The *Official St. Louis Visitors Guide* and the monthly magazine *Where: St. Louis,* both free, contain helpful info and decent maps. A second **information center** is inside the America's Convention Center. Open M-F 9am-5pm, Sa 9am-2pm.

Hotlines: Rape Hotline, ☎531-2003. **Suicide Hotline,** ☎647-4357. **Kids Under 21 Crisis,** ☎644-5886. All 24hr. **Gay and Lesbian Hotline,** ☎367-0084. Operates M-Sa 6-10pm.

Medical Services: Barnes-Jewish Hospital, 216 S. Kingshighway Blvd. (☎747-3000). **Metro South Women's Health Center,** 2415 N. Kingshighway Blvd. (☎772-1749).

Post Office: 1720 Market St. (☎436-4114. Open M-F 8am-8pm, Sa 8am-1pm.) **ZIP code:** 63101. **Area code:** 314 (in St. Louis), 636 (in St. Charles), 618 (in IL); in text, 314 unless noted otherwise.

🏠 ACCOMMODATIONS

Most budget lodging is far from downtown. For chain motels, try Lindbergh Blvd. (Rte. 67) near the airport, or the area north of the I-70/I-270 junction in Bridgeton, 5 mi. beyond the airport. Watson Rd. near Chippewa is littered with cheap motels; take bus #11 "Chippewa-Sunset Hills" or #20 "Cherokee."

Huckleberry Finn Youth Hostel (HI-AYH), 1908 S. 12th St. (☎241-0076), at Tucker Blvd., 2 blocks north of Russell Blvd. in the Soulard District. Take bus #73 "Carondelet." A full kitchen, free parking, friendly staff, and unbeatable prices make the cramped dorms tolerable. Ask about work opportunities; occasionally the owner hires hostelers to do odd jobs on the grounds. Linen $2. Key deposit $5. Reception daily 8-10am and 6-10pm. Check-out 9:30am. Dorm-style rooms $15, nonmembers $18. ❶

Royal Budget Inn, 6061 Collinsville Rd., Fairmont City, IL (☎618-874-4451), 20min. east of the city off I-55/I-70 Exit 6. Clean, one-bed purple-lit rooms with an aqua-green, Taj Mahal flavor make for an unusual budget option. Rooms Su-Th $35, F-Sa $38. ❷

The Brick House, 2220 S. 11th St. (☎772-7693 or 877-927-6233). A choice of three different rooms at this elegant B&B awaits travelers. A gourmet breakfast and private bath are included. Reservations recommended. Rooms from $72-82. ❹

The Mayfair, 806 St. Charles St. (☎421-2500). Constructed at the height of the Jazz Age, the Mayfair has hosted famous musicians and politicians. Standard rooms are spacious with marble-topped sinks and soft queen-sized beds. Suites have a sitting room in addition to bedrooms. Rooms from $109, suites from $120. ❺

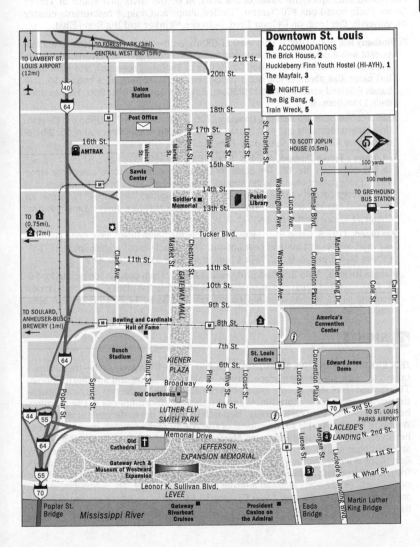

Downtown St. Louis

♦ ACCOMMODATIONS
The Brick House, 2
Huckleberry Finn Youth Hostel (HI-AYH), 1
The Mayfair, 3

■ NIGHTLIFE
The Big Bang, 4
Train Wreck, 5

◖ FOOD

In St. Louis, the difference of a few blocks can mean vastly different cuisine. The area surrounding **Union Station**, at 18th and Market St. downtown, is being revamped with hip restaurants and bars. The **Central West End** offers coffeehouses and outdoor cafes. A slew of impressive restaurants waits just north of Lindell Blvd. along **Euclid Ave.** (Take the MetroLink to "Central West End" and walk north, or catch the Shuttle Bug.) St. Louis's historic Italian neighborhood, **The Hill**, southwest of downtown and just northwest of Tower Grove Park, produces plenty of inexpensive pasta; take bus #99 "Lafayette." Cheap Thai, Philippine, and Vietnamese restaurants spice the **South Grand** area, at Grand Blvd. just south of Tower Grove Park; board bus #70 "Grand." Coffee shops and unique restaurants cluster on **University City Loop**, on Delmar Blvd. between Skinker and Big Bend Blvd.

■ **Blueberry Hill**, 6504 Delmar Blvd. (☎727-0880), on the Loop. Eclectic rock 'n' roll restaurant with 9 different rooms including the "Duck Room" and the "Elvis Room." Walls decked with record covers, Howdy Doody toys, a *Simpsons* collection, and giant baseball cards. Call ahead to find out if Chuck Berry is playing. Big, juicy burgers $5. Live bands F-Sa and some weeknights 9:30pm. Cover $4-15. 21+ after 9pm. Kitchen open daily 11am-9pm. ❷

Kaldi's Coffeehouse and Roasting Company, 700 De Mun Ave. (☎727-9955), in Clayton. University students dig into freshly baked brownies and sandwiches. Panini $5. Wholewheat pizza $3 per slice. Open daily 7am-11pm. ❶

Ted Drewe's Frozen Custard, 4224 S. Grand Blvd. (☎352-7376) and 6726 Chippewa (☎481-2652), on Rte. 66. *The* place for the summertime St. Louis experience since 1929. Those patient enough to get through the line are rewarded by the "chocolate chip cookie dough concrete shake," whose blended toppings are thick enough to hang in an overturned cup ($1.60-3.60). Both locations open May-Aug. daily 11am-midnight; Chippewa St. site Sept.-Dec. and Feb.-May 11am-11pm. ❶

Pho Grand, 3195 S. Grand Blvd. (☎664-7435), in the South Grand area. Good Vietnamese food, with vegetarian and beef options. *Pho* (noodle soup) is their specialty ($4). Entrees $4-6. Open Su-M and W-Th 11am-10pm, F-Sa 11am-11pm. ❶

Mangia Italiano, 3145 S. Grand Blvd. (☎664-8585). Fresh pasta made on site for $5-9. A handpainted mural and mismatched tables add to the place's character. Jazz on weekend nights. Kitchen open M-F noon-10pm and Sa-Su 12:30-10:30pm; bar open until 1:30am. ❷

◖ SIGHTS

JEFFERSON EXPANSION MEMORIAL. At 630 ft., the ■**Gateway Arch**—the nation's tallest monument—towers gracefully over all of St. Louis and southern Illinois. The ground-level view is impressive, but the 4min. ride to the top in quasi-futuristic elevator modules is more fun. Waits are shorter after dinner or in the morning, but are uniformly long on Saturday. Beneath the arch, the underground **Museum of Westward Expansion** adds to the appeal of the grassy park complex known comprehensively as the **Jefferson Expansion Memorial**. The museum celebrates the Louisiana Purchase and its exploration. (☎982-1410. Museum and arch open in summer daily 8am-10pm; in winter 9am-6pm. Tram $8, ages 13-16 $5, ages 3-12 $3.) Scope out the city from the water with **Gateway Riverboat Cruises;** tours leave from the docks in front of the arch. (☎621-4040, arch and riverboat line ☎800-878-7411. 1hr. riverboat tours daily; call for departure times. $9, ages 13-16 $9, ages 3-12 $4. Discounts on combination arch/riverboat tickets. Limited wheelchair access.) Across the street but still part of the Memorial, the magnificently ornate **Old Courthouse,** where the Dred Scott case began, has been restored as a museum detailing the history of the building and its role in St. Louis. *(11 N. 4th St. ☎ 655-1600. Open daily 8am-4:30pm. Tours in summer usually every hr.; in winter less frequently. Free. Limited wheelchair access.)*

ST. LOUIS HISTORY. It's a strike either way at the **International Bowling Museum and Hall of Fame** and the **St. Louis Cardinals Hall of Fame Museum,** across from Busch Stadium. The amusing bowling museum features little-known facts about bowling, while the baseball museum exhibits memorabilia from the glory days of St. Louis hardball. *(111 Stadium Plaza. ☎ 231-6340. Open Apr.-Sept. daily 9am-5pm, game days until 6:30pm; Oct.-Mar. Tu-Su 11am-4pm. $6, ages 5-12 $4. Includes 4 frames of bowling downstairs. Wheelchair accessible.)* Historic **Union Station,** 1 mi. west of downtown, houses a shopping mall, food court, and entertainment center in a magnificent structure that was once the nation's busiest railroad terminal. *(At 18th and Market St. Metrolink to Union Station. ☎ 421-6655.)* "The Entertainer" lives on at the **Scott Joplin House,** just west of downtown near Jefferson St., where the ragtime legend tickled the ivories and penned classics from 1901 to 1903. The 45min. tour delves into Joplin's long-lasting influence on American music. *(2658 Delmar Blvd. ☎ 340-5790. Apr.-Oct. M-Sa tours every 30min. 10am-4pm, Su noon-5pm.; Nov.-Mar. M-Sa 10am-3pm, Su noon-4pm. $2, ages 6-12 $1.50. Wheelchair accessible.)*

SOUTH & SOUTHWEST OF DOWNTOWN. Soulard is bounded by I-55 and Seventh St. In the early 1970s, the city proclaimed this area a historic district because it once housed German and East European immigrants, many of whom worked in the breweries. The district surrounds the bustling **Soulard Farmers Market,** where fresh, inexpensive produce abounds. *(730 Carroll St. From downtown travel south on Broadway or 7th St. to Lafayette. Take bus #73 "Carondelet." ☎ 622-4180. Open W-Sa 7am-7pm; hours vary among merchants.)* The end of 12th St. features the largest brewery in the world, the **Anheuser-Busch Brewery.** The 1½hr. tour is markedly less thrilling than sampling the beer at the end. *(1127 Pestalozzi St., at 12th and Lynch St. Take bus #40 "Broadway" south from downtown. ☎ 577-2626. Tours June-Aug. M-Sa 9am-5:30pm, Su 11:30am-6:30pm; Sept.-May Su closes at 5:30pm. When busy, free tickets required from the office. Wheelchair accessible.)*

The internationally acclaimed 79-acre **Missouri Botanical Garden** thrives north of Tower Grove Park on grounds left by entrepreneur Henry Shaw. The Japanese Garden is guaranteed to soothe the weary traveler. *(4344 Shaw Blvd. From downtown, take I-44 west by car or ride MetroLink to "Central West End" and take bus #13 "Union-Missouri Botanical Gardens" to the main entrance. ☎ 800-642-8842. Open M 9am-8pm, Tu-Su 9am-5pm. $7, seniors $5, under 12 free. Guided tours daily at 1pm. Wheelchair accessible.)* **Grant's Farm,** the former home of President Ulysses S. Grant, is now a wildlife preserve. The tram-ride tour crosses terrain inhabited by over 1000 free-roaming animals. *(3400 Grant St. Take I-55 west to Reavis Barracks Rd. and turn left onto Gravois. ☎ 843-1700. Open May-Aug. Tu-Sa 9:30am-4pm, Su 10am-5pm.; call for Apr. and Sept. hours. Free. Parking $5.)*

FOREST PARK. Forest Park contains three museums, a zoo, a planetarium, a 12,000-seat amphitheater, a grand canal, and countless picnic areas, pathways, and flying golf balls. *(Take MetroLink to Forest Park and catch the Shuttle Bug. All Forest Park sites are wheelchair accessible.)* Marlin Perkins, the late host of TV's *Wild Kingdom,* turned the **St. Louis Zoo** into a world-class institution, complete with frisbee-playing sea lions and an impressive children's zoo. *(☎ 781-0900. Open late May-early Sept. M and W-Su 9am-5pm, Tu 9am-dusk; Sept.-May daily 9am-5pm. Free.)* Atop **Art Hill,** a statue of France's Louis IX, the city's namesake, raises his sword in front of the **St. Louis Art Museum,** which contains masterpieces of Asian, Renaissance, and Impressionist art. *(☎ 721-0072. Open Tu-Su 10am-5pm. Main museum free; special exhibits usually $10, students and seniors $8, ages 6-12 $6; F free.)*

CENTRAL WEST END. From Forest Park, head east a few blocks to gawk at the Tudor homes of the **Central West End.** The vast **Cathedral Basilica of St. Louis** is a unique amalgam of architectural styles; visitors are enchanted by the intricate ceilings and mosaics depicting Missouri church history. *(4431 Lindell Blvd. MetroLink stop "Central West End" or bus #93 "Lindell" from downtown. ☎ 533-0544. Open in summer daily 6am-7pm; off-season 6am-5pm. Tours M-F 10am-3pm, Su after noon Mass. Call to confirm hours. Wheelchair accessible.)* At a shrine of a different sort, monster truck enthusiasts pay homage to **Bigfoot,** the "Original Monster Truck," who lives with his descendants near the airport. *(6311 N. Lindbergh St. ☎ 731-2822. Open M-F 9am-6pm, Sa 9am-3pm. Free.)* Northwest of the Central West End, the sidewalks of the **Loop** are studded with gold stars on the **St. Louis Walk of Fame.** *(6504 Delmar Blvd. ☎ 727-7827.)*

🎵 ENTERTAINMENT

Founded in 1880, the **St. Louis Symphony Orchestra** is one of the country's finest. **Powell Hall,** 718 N. Grand Blvd., holds the 101-member orchestra in acoustic and visual splendor. (☎ 534-1700. Performances Sept.-May Th-Sa 8pm, Su 3pm. Box office open late May to mid-Aug. M-F 9am-5pm; mid-Aug. to late May M-Sa 9am-5pm; and before performances. Tickets from $10; rush tickets often available for half-price on day of show.)

St. Louis offers theatergoers many choices. The outdoor **Municipal Opera,** the "Muny," presents hit musicals on summer nights in Forest Park. (☎ 361-1900. Box office open June to mid-Aug. daily 9am-9pm. Tickets $8-43.) Productions are also regularly staged by the **St. Louis Black Repertory,** 634 N. Grand Blvd. (☎ 534-3807), and by the **Repertory Theatre of St. Louis,** 130 Edgar Rd. (☎ 968-4925). The **Fox Theatre,** 537 N. Grand, was originally a 1930s movie palace, but now hosts Broadway shows, classic films, and Las Vegas, country, and rock stars. (☎ 534-1111. Open M-Sa 10am-6pm, Su noon-4pm. Tours Tu, Th, Sa 10:30am. Tu $5, Th and Sa $8; under 12 $3. Call for reservations.) **Metrotix** has tickets to most area events. (☎ 534-1111. Open daily 9am-9pm.)

A recent St. Louis ordinance permits gambling on the river for those over 21. The **President Casino on the Admiral** floats below the Arch on the Missouri side. (☎ 622-1111 or 800-772-3647. Open Su-Th 8am-4am, F-Sa 24hr. Entry tax $2.) On the Illinois side, the **Casino Queen** claims "the loosest slots in town." (☎ 618-874-5000 or 800-777-0777. Open daily 9am-7am.) Parking for both is free, and both are wheelchair accessible.

Six Flags St. Louis, 30min. southwest of St. Louis on I-44 at Exit 261, reigns supreme in the kingdom of amusement parks. The vaunted "Boss" wooden roller coaster features a 570° helix. (☎ 636-938-4800. Hours vary by season. $39, seniors and under 48 in. $24.) The **St. Louis Cardinals** play ball April through early October at **Busch Stadium.** (☎ 421-3060. $10-38.) The 2000 Super Bowl champion **Rams,** formerly of L.A., have brought football back to St. Louis in shining fashion at the **Edward Jones Dome.** (☎ 425-8830. $39.) The **Blues** hockey team slices ice at the **Savvis Center** at 14th St. and Clark Ave. (☎ 843-1700. Tickets from $15.)

🌃 NIGHTLIFE

Music rules the night in St. Louis. The *Riverfront Times* (free at many bars and clubs) and the *Get Out* section of the *Post-Dispatch* list weekly entertainment. The *St. Louis Magazine*, published annually, lists seasonal events. For beer and live music, often without a cover charge, St. Louis offers **Laclede's Landing,** a collection of restaurants, bars, and dance clubs housed in 19th-century industrial buildings north of the Arch on the riverfront. In the summer, bars take turns sponsoring "block parties," with food, drink, music, and dancing in the streets. (☎ 241-

5875. 21+. Generally open 9pm-3am, with some places open for lunch and dinner.) Other nightlife hot spots include the bohemian **Loop** along Delmar Blvd., **Union Station** and its environs, and the less touristy and quite gay-friendly **Soulard** district.

Brandt's Market & Cafe, 6525 Delmar Blvd. (☎ 727-3663), a Loop mainstay, offers live jazz, along with beer, wine, espresso, and a varied menu. During the summer, specials are served outside, while musicians jam in the dark interior. Open daily 11am-midnight.

The Pageant, 6161 Delmar Blvd. (☎ 726-6161). Line up early for a spot in the fantastic 33,000 sq. ft. nightclub, which hosts national acts. Call for ticket and cover prices. 18+. Doors usually open 7pm.

The Big Bang, 807 N. 2nd St., at Laclede's Landing. Dueling pianists lead the crowd in a rock 'n' roll sing-along show. Open daily until 3am.

Train Wreck, 720 N. 1st St. (☎ 436-1006), at Laclede's Landing, features a multi-level entertainment center with a nightclub, restaurant, and sports bar. Alternative cover bands F-Sa nights. Cover $3. Open Su-Th 11am-10pm, F-Sa 11am-3am.

Clementine's, 2001 Menard St. (☎ 664-7869), in Soulard, contains a crowded restaurant and St. Louis's oldest gay bar (established in 1978). Open M-F 10am-1:30am, Sa 8am-1:30am, Su 11am-midnight.

HANNIBAL   ☎ 573

Hannibal anchors itself on the Mississippi River 100 mi. west of Springfield and 100 mi. northwest of St. Louis. Stopping along the bluffs while driving towards town allows for a stunning view of the Mississippi River and a glimpse of what Missouri would have looked like before tourists arrived. Founded in 1819, Hannibal slept in obscurity until Mark Twain used his boyhood home as the setting of *The Adventures of Tom Sawyer.* Tourists now flock to Hannibal to imagine Tom, Huck, and Becky romping around the quaint streets and nearby caves. Despite all the tourist traps, Hannibal retains its small-town hospitality and charm.

Start the Mark Twain tour at the annex of the **Mark Twain Boyhood Home and Museum,** 208 Hill St. (☎ 221-9010), which has been restored with an assortment of memorabilia to commemorate the events of the witty wordsmith's life. Across the street sit the **Pilaster House** and **Clemens Law Office,** where a young Twain awoke one night to find a murdered man lying on the floor next to him. Further down Main St., the **New Mark Twain Museum** takes visitors on an interactive tour through Twain's novels. Upstairs, the highlight of the museum is the collection of Norman Rockwell illustrations entitled *Tom and Hucks.* The impressive display contains paintings, original sketches, and Rockwell's anecdotes about the drawings. (☎ 221-9010. Open June-Aug. daily 8am-6pm; off-season hours vary dramatically. $6 covers all sites.) The **Mark Twain Riverboat,** at Center St. Landing, steams down the Mississippi for a one-hour sightseeing cruise that is part history, part folklore, and part advertisement for the land attractions. (☎ 221-3222. Late May-early Sept. 3 per day; May and Sept.-Oct. 1 per day. $9.50, ages 5-12 $6.50; dinner cruises 6:30pm $27/18.) The **Mark Twain Cave,** 1 mi. south of Hannibal on Rte. 79, winds visitors through the complex series of caverns Twain explored as a boy, while guides point to the author's favorite spots. Graffiti from as early as the 1830s, including Jesse James's signature, still mark the walls. The cave tour includes the only section of the cave christened by Twain, **Aladdin's Castle,** the picturesque spot where Tom and Becky were "married." (☎ 221-1656. Open June-Aug. daily 8am-8pm; Apr.-May and Sept.-Oct. 9am-6pm; Nov.-Mar. 9am-4pm. 1hr. tour $12, ages 5-12 $6.) From June to August, nearby **Cameron Cave,** Hwy. 79 S, provides a slightly longer and far spookier lantern tour. (Tickets available at Mark Twain Cave. $14, ages 5-12 $7.) Every 4th of July weekend, 100,000 fans converge on Hannibal for the fence-painting, frog-jumping fun of the **Tom Sawyer Days** festival (☎ 221-2477).

As befits a state bordering the Deep South, Hannibal is home to some tasty barbecue establishments. Even though catfish is the specialty at ⊠**Bubba's** ❶, 101 Church St., a former warehouse that dishes out good food and Southern hospitality, the pit-smoked BBQ pork and beef sandwiches are not to be missed. Sandwiches with home-style vegetable sides like cole slaw and jambalaya $5.50. (☎221-5552. Open daily 11am-9pm.) Cool down with an ice cream ($1.50) at the **Main St. Soda Fountain,** 207 S. Main St., home to a one hundred-year-old soda fountain. (☎248-1295. Open Tu-Su 11am to late evening.)

The **Hannibal Convention and Visitors Bureau,** 505 N. 3rd St., offers free local calls and information. (☎221-2477. Open M-F 8am-6pm, Sa 9am-6pm, Su 9:30am-4:30pm.) **Post Office:** 801 Broadway. (☎221-0957. Open M-F 8:30am-5pm, Sa 8:30am-noon.) **ZIP code:** 63401. **Area code:** 573.

KANSAS CITY   ☎816

With over 200 public fountains and more miles of boulevard than Paris, Kansas City looks and acts more European than one might expect from the "Barbecue Capital of the World." But make no mistake, KC has a strong tradition of booze and good music. When Prohibition stifled most of the country's fun in the 1920s, Mayor Pendergast let the good times continue to roll. The Kansas City of today maintains its big bad blues-and-jazz reputation in a metropolis spanning two states: the highly suburbanized and mostly bland half in Kansas (KCKS) and the quicker-paced commercial half in Missouri (KCMO).

▐▀ TRANSPORTATION

Airport: Kansas City International (☎243-5237), 18 mi. northwest of KC off I-29. Take bus #29. **KCI Shuttle** (☎243-5000 or 800-243-6383) services downtown, Westport, Crown Center, and Plaza in KCMO and Overland Park, Mission, and Lenexa in KCKS. Departs daily every 30min. 4:30am-10pm. $14. Taxi to downtown $30-40.

Trains: Amtrak, 2200 Main St. (☎421-3622), at Pershing Rd., next to the renovated old Union Station. Take bus #27. Open daily 7am-midnight. To **Chicago** (8hr., 2 per day, $50-133) and **St. Louis** (5-6½hr., 2 per day, $27-41).

Buses: Greyhound, 1101 N. Troost (☎221-2835). Take bus #25. *Stay alert—the terminal is in an unsafe area.* Open daily 5:30am-midnight. To **Chicago** (12-18hr., 5-6 per day, $46.50-49.50) and **St. Louis** (6hr., 3 per day, $29.25-31.25).

Public Transit: Kansas City Area Transportation Authority (Metro), 1200 E. 18th St. (☎221-0660), near Troost St. Excellent downtown coverage. Buses run 4am-1am. $1, seniors and disabled 50¢; free transfers. $1.20 to Independence, MO. **Downtowner Shuttles** run north-south on Main St. and east-west on 11th St. M-F every 10min. 6am-6:30pm. 25¢.

Taxis: Yellow Cab, ☎471-5000.

▐▛ ▐▌ ORIENTATION & PRACTICAL INFORMATION

The KC metropolitan area sprawls almost interminably, making travel difficult without a car. Most sights worth visiting lie south of downtown on the Missouri side or in the 18th and Vine Historic District. *All listings are for KCMO, unless otherwise indicated.* Although parking around town is not easy during the daytime, there are many lots that charge $5 or less per day. **I-70** cuts east-west through the city, and **I-435** circles the two-state metro area. KCMO is laid out on a grid with numbered streets running east-west from the Missouri River well out into suburbs, and named streets running north-south. **Main St.** divides the city east-west.

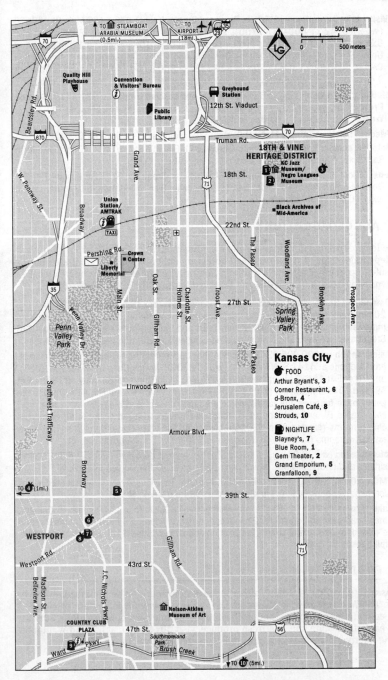

Kansas City

🍎 FOOD
Arthur Bryant's, **3**
Corner Restaurant, **6**
d-Bronx, **4**
Jerusalem Café, **8**
Strouds, **10**

🏠 NIGHTLIFE
Blayney's, **7**
Blue Room, **1**
Gem Theater, **2**
Grand Emporium, **5**
Granfalloon, **9**

Visitor Info: Convention and Visitors Bureau of Greater Kansas City, 1100 Main St., #2550 (☎221-5242 or 800-767-7700), 25th fl. of the City Center Sq. Bldg. Open M-F 8:30am-5pm. Other locations in the Plaza (open M-Sa 10am-6pm, Su 11am-5pm) and Union Station (open M-Sa 10am-10pm, Su noon-5pm). **Missouri Tourist Information Center,** 4010 Blue Ridge Cut-Off (☎889-3330 or 800-877-1234); follow signs from Exit 9 off I-70. Open daily 8am-5pm, except on days when the Chiefs are playing at home.

Hotlines: Rape Crisis Line, ☎531-0233. **Gay and Lesbian Hotline,** ☎931-4470. **Suicide Prevention,** ☎889-3939 or 800-784-2433. **Troubled Youth Line,** ☎741-1477. **Women and Children's Center,** ☎452-8535. All 24hr.

Medical Services: Truman Medical Center, 2301 Holmes St. (☎556-3000).

Internet access: Kansas City Public Library, 311 E. 12th St. (☎701-3400). Open M-Th 9am-9pm, F-Sa 9am-5pm, Su 1-5pm.

Post Office: 315 W. Pershing Rd. (☎374-9361), at Broadway St.; take bus #40 or 51. Open M-F 8am-5pm. **ZIP code:** 64108. **Area code:** 816 in Missouri, 913 in Kansas; in text 816 unless noted otherwise.

⚡ ACCOMMODATIONS

The least expensive lodgings are near the interstates, especially I-70, and toward Independence, MO. Downtown most hotels are either expensive, uninhabitable, or unsafe—sometimes all three. For help finding a bed in an inn or a home closer to downtown (from $50), call **Bed and Breakfast Kansas City** (☎913-888-3636).

⊠ Serendipity Bed and Breakfast, 116 S. Pleasant St. (☎833-4719 or 800-203-4299), 20min. from downtown KC in Independence, MO. A Victorian mansion with all the trimmings and an ample breakfast. Historic tours and train pickups are available in a 1926 Studebaker, weather and time permitting. Singles $30-80; doubles $45-100. ❷

American Inn (☎800-905-6343), a chain that dominates the KC budget motel market, has locations at 4141 S. Noland Rd. (☎373-8300); Woods Chapel Rd. (☎228-1080), off I-70 at Exit 18; 1211 Armour Rd. (☎471-3451), in North Kansas City off I-35 at Exit 6B; and 7949 Splitlog Rd. (☎913-299-2999), in KCKS off I-70 at Exit 414. Despite the gaudy neon facades, the rooms inside are large, cheap, and pleasant. A/C, free local calls, cable TV, and outdoor pools. Rates are subject to a rather annoying game: the cheap rooms (singles from $30; doubles from $45) sell immediately, leaving more expensive rooms (singles $46-56; doubles $50-60). 10% AAA discount. ❷

Interstate Inn (☎229-6311), off I-70 at Exit 18. A great deal if you get one of the walk-in singles and doubles ($35), which can't be reserved. Other singles $44-79. ❷

YMCA, 900 N. 8th St. (☎913-371-4400) in KCKS. Take bus #1 or 4. A variety of rooms for men. Key deposit $10. No nightly rates; $84 per week. ❶

Lake Jacomo (☎795-8200), 22 mi. southeast of KCMO. Take I-470 south to Colbern, then head east on Colbern for 2 mi. Lots of water activities, 33 forested campsites, and a nifty dam across the street. Reservations accepted. Sites $10, with electricity $15, full hookup $22. ❶

❐ FOOD

Kansas City rustles up a herd of barbecue restaurants that serve unusually tangy ribs. The **Westport** area, at Westport Rd. and Broadway St. just south of 40th St., has eclectic menus, cafes, and coffeehouses. Ethnic fare clusters along **39th St.** just east of the state line. For fresh produce, visit **City Market,** at 5th and Walnut St. along the river. (☎842-1271. Open Su-F 9am-4pm, Sa 6am-4pm.)

▨ **Arthur Bryant's,** 1727 Brooklyn Ave. (☎231-1123). Take the Brooklyn exit off I-70 or bus #110 from downtown. A KC tradition, this restaurant is a perennial candidate for best barbecue in the country. "Sandwiches"—little wimpy triangles of bread drowning in a mass of perfectly-cooked meat—are $7. Vegetarians should probably head elsewhere. Open M-Th 10am-9:30pm, F-Sa 10am-10pm, Su 11am-8:30pm. ❷

Strouds, 1015 E. 85th St. (☎333-2132), at Troost Ave., 2 mi. north of the Holmes exit off I-435. All-you-can-eat portions of vegetables and potatoes are served along with entrees. The chicken-fried steak ($11) is well-endowed in size and taste; save room for homemade cinnamon rolls (usually included in the price). Open M-Th 4-10pm, F 11am-11pm, Sa 2-11pm, Su 11am-10pm. ❸

d-Bronx, 3904 Bell St. (☎531-0550), on the 39th St. restaurant row. A New York deli transplanted to Middle America, d-Bronx has 35 kinds of subs (half-sub $3-6, whole $6-10) and brownies ($1.50). Open M-Th 10:30am-10:30pm, F-Sa 10:30am-midnight. ❶

Jerusalem Cafe, 431 Westport Rd. (☎756-2770). Vegetarians can breathe a sigh of relief at this healthy (and tasty) sanctuary. Sandwiches with rice and salad $5-7. Entrees $9-11. Open M-Sa 11am-10pm, Su noon-8pm. ❷

Corner Restaurant, 4059 Broadway St. (☎931-6630), in the heart of Westport. Large breakfast specials. Plate-sized pancakes $2-3. Biscuits and gravy $4. Lunch specials $6. Open M-F 7am-3pm. ❶

🄶 SIGHTS

18TH & VINE. Jazz once flourished in the recently designated **18th and Vine Historic District.** (☎474-8463.) The **Kansas City Jazz Museum** brings back the era with classy displays, music listening stations, neon dance hall signs, and everything from Ella Fitzgerald's eyeglasses to Louis Armstrong's lip salve. Swinging in the same building, the **Negro Leagues Baseball Museum** recalls the segregated era of America's pastime with photographs, interactive exhibits, and bittersweet nostalgia. *(1616 E. 18th St. Take bus #108 "Indiana." Jazz museum: ☎474-8463. Baseball museum: ☎221-1920. Both open Tu-Sa 9am-6pm, Su noon-6pm. One museum $6, under 12 $2.50; both museums $8/4.)* Nearby, the **Black Archives of Mid-America** holds a large collection of paintings and sculpture by African-American artists and focuses on local black history. *(2033 Vine St. ☎483-1300. Open M-F 9am-4:30pm; tours 10am. $2, under 17 50¢.)*

OTHER MUSEUMS. A taste of KC's masterpieces, the **Nelson-Atkins Museum of Art** contains one of the best East Asian art collections in the world and a sculpture park with 13 Henry Moores. Renovations scheduled to be completed in 2003 may cause exhibit closings—call ahead. Admission is free while the construction is going on, except for special exhibits. *(4525 Oak St. 3 blocks northeast of Country Club Plaza. Take bus #147, 155, 156, or 157. ☎561-4000. Open Tu-Th 10am-4pm, F 10am-9pm, Sa 10am-5pm, Su noon-5pm. Jazz F 5:30-8:30pm. $5, students $2, ages 6-18 $1; F free. Free walking tours Sa 11am-2pm, Su 1:30-3pm.)* The *Arabia* sank in the Missouri River and was quickly buried in the silt-filled banks. 150 years later, the course of the river shifted, and the excavations along the banks yielded 200 tons of treasure. Bottles of bourbon, plates, stationery, clothing, and most of the original logs from the ship now find rest at the **Steamboat Arabia Museum.** *(400 Grand Blvd. ☎471-1856. Open M-Sa 10am-6pm, Su noon-5pm. $9.75, seniors $9.25, ages 4-12 $4.75.)*

THE PLAZA & CROWN CENTER. A few blocks to the west of the Nelson-Atkins Museum, at 47th St. and Southwest Trafficway, **Country Club Plaza,** known as "the Plaza," is the oldest and perhaps most picturesque shopping center in the US. Modeled after buildings in Seville, Spain, the Plaza boasts fountains, sculptures, hand-painted tiles, and reliefs of grinning gargoyles. (☎ 753-0100. Take buses #139, 140, 147, 151, 155, 156, or 157. Free concerts June-Aug. F-Sa.) **Crown Center,** headquarters of Hallmark Cards, houses a maze of restaurants and shops and the children's **Coterie Theatre.** In the winter, the **Ice Terrace** is KC's only public outdoor ice-skating rink. On the third level of the center, see how cards and accessories are made at the **Hallmark Visitors Center.** (2450 Grand Ave. 2 mi. north of the Plaza near Pershing Rd. Take bus #140, 156, 157, or any trolley. Crown Center: ☎ 274-8444. Coterie: ☎ 474-6785. $8, under 18 $6. Ice Terrace: ☎ 274-8412. Rink open Nov.-Dec. Su-Th 10am-9pm, F-Sa 10am-11pm; Jan.-Mar. daily 10am-9pm. $5, under 13 $4; rentals $1.50. Visitors Center: ☎ 274-3613, 274-5672 for a recording. Open M-F 9am-5pm, Sa 9:30am-4:30pm.)

🎭 ENTERTAINMENT

The **Missouri Repertory Theatre,** 50th and Oak St., stages American classics. (☎ 235-2700. Season Sept.-May. Box office open M-F 10am-5pm; call for weekend hours. Tickets from $25, students and seniors $3 off.) **Quality Hill Playhouse,** 303 W. 10th St., produces off-Broadway plays and revues year-round. (☎ 235-2700. Tickets around $20, students and seniors $2 off.) Late June to mid-July, the **Heart of America Shakespeare Festival** in Southmoreland Park, 47th and Oak St., puts on free shows. (☎ 531-7728. Most nights 8pm. In Shawnee Mission, KS, the **New Theatre Restaurant,** 9229 Foster St., stages dinner theater productions of classic comedies and romances and attracts nationally recognized actors. Take Metcalf Ave. and turn into the Regency Park Center between 91st and 95th St. (☎ 913-649-7469. Box office open M-Sa 9am-6pm, Su 11am-3pm. Tickets $22-44, buffet meal included.)

Sports fans stampede to **Arrowhead Stadium,** at I-70 and Blue Ridge Cutoff, home to football's **Chiefs** (☎ 920-9400 or 800-676-5488; tickets from $30) and soccer's **Wizards** (☎ 472-4625; tickets $10-15). Next door, a water-fountained wonder, **Kauffman Stadium** houses the **Royals,** Kansas City's baseball team (☎ 921-8000 or 800-676-9257. Tickets $7-17; M and Th most seats half-price.) A stadium express bus runs from downtown and Country Club Plaza on game days.

🌃 NIGHTLIFE

In the 1920s, jazz musician Count Basie and his "Kansas City Sound" reigned at the River City bars. Twenty years later, saxophonist Charlie "Bird" Parker spread his wings and soared. The Crown Center still rocks annually with the **Kansas City International Jazz Festival,** held the last weekend in June. (☎ 888-337-8111. Tickets from $12.) The restored **Gem Theater,** 1615 E. 18th St., stages old-time blues and jazz. (☎ 842-1414. Box office open M-F 10am-4pm.) Across the street, the **Blue Room,** 1600 E. 18th St., cooks four nights a week with some of the smoothest acts in town. (☎ 474-2929. Cover F-Sa $5. Bar open M and Th 5-11pm, F 5pm-1am, Sa 7pm-1am.) The **Grand Emporium,** 3832 Main St., twice voted the best blues club in the US, has live music five nights a week. (☎ 531-1504. Live music M and W-Sa. Cover $5-15. Open daily noon-3am.) For something besides jazz, bars and dancing hot spots cluster in the Westport area.

Granfalloon, 608 Ward Pkwy. (☎ 753-7850), in the Plaza area. During the daytime, this noisy hot spot serves up sandwiches ($5-6.50) and salads ($4-6). The young and beautiful strut their stuff at night, when $1.50 domestic beer specials are on tap. Open daily 9am-2:30am.

Blayney's, 415 Westport Rd. (☎ 561-3747). Intense R&B pours onto a newly built deck. Cover $2-7. Open Tu-Th 8pm-3am, F-Sa 6pm-3am.

GIVE 'EM HELL The buck stops at Independence, MO, the hometown of former President Harry Truman and a 15min. drive east of KC on I-70 or U.S. 24. The **Harry S. Truman Library and Museum,** 500 W. U.S. 24, at Delaware St., has a replica of the Oval Office and exhibits about the man, the times, and the presidency. (☎833-1400 or 800-833-1225. Open M-W and F-Sa 9am-5pm, Th 9am-9pm, Su noon-5pm. $5, seniors $4.50, ages 6-18 $3.) Just down the street, the **Harry S. Truman Home,** 219 N. Delaware St., known as the "Summer White House," provides a glimpse into the ex-President's home life. Get tickets to tour the Victorian mansion at the **Truman Home Ticket and Info Center,** 223 Main St. (☎254-9929. Open daily 8:30am-5pm. $3, under 17 free.)

Kiki's Bon-Ton Maison, 1515 Westport Rd. (931-9417). The music ranges from reggae to hard rock, while the Cajun cookin' clears your sinuses. Open M-Th 11am-10pm, F-Sa 11am-11pm, Su 11am-8pm.

America's Pub, 510 Westport Rd. (☎531-1313). "Retro" and "disco" are the key words here. An oh-so-young crowd gyrates on the packed dance floor, while elevated barstools provide a chance to relax. Cover $6. Open W-Sa 8pm-3am.

The Hurricane, 4048 Broadway St. (☎752-0884), caters to both young and old with different local acts each night. Beers $3. Cover $5. Open daily 8pm-3am.

BRANSON
☎417

Back in 1967, the Presley family had no idea the impact the tiny theater they opened on **West Rte. 76,** a little road nestled in the gorgeous Missouri end of the Ozark mountains, would have. Now, more than 30 years later, over 7 million tourists, mostly retirees, clog Branson's strip amid the rolling hills each year to visit the "live country music capital of the Universe." Billboards, motels, and giant showplaces call to the masses that visit Branson to embrace a collage of all things plastic, franchised, and "wholesome." Branson boasts over 30 indoor theaters and a few outdoor ones as well, all housing family variety shows, magic acts, comedians, plays, and straight-up music. Many of them have two shows a day, one in the afternoon and one around 8pm, though some theaters specialize in morning shows. Box office prices for most shows run $20-50, depending on who's playing. Some acts change monthly, while others, like the Presley's, have been here for decades. Never pay full price for a show or attraction in Branson—coupon books, including the *Sunny Day Guide* and the *Best Read Guide*, offer dozens of discounts as well as helpful maps, schedules, and info.

Big-name country acts, such as Loretta Lynn and Billy Ray Cyrus, play the **Grand Palace,** 2700 W. Rte. 76. (☎336-1220 or 800-884-4536. Feb.-Dec. $35-50, children $12-15.) Performed at the Shepherd of the Hills outdoor theater on Rte. 76 West, one of Branson's more unique shows is **The Shepherd of the Hills,** an a outdoor drama that serves dinner as it tells the story of a preacher stranded in the Ozark mountains and his growing relationship with the simple people of those hills. A flock of sheep, children, and many cast members bring the story to life. (☎334-4191 or 800-653-6288. Apr.-Oct. $32, under 17 $16. Price includes dinner, show, and tour of complex and its viewing tower.)

Competition is fierce among accommodations, and consumers win out most of the time. Motels along Rte. 76 generally start around $25, but prices often increase from July to September. Less tacky inexpensive motels line Rte. 265, 4 mi. west of the strip, and Gretna Rd. at the west end of the strip. **Budget Inn ❶,** 315 N. Gretna Rd., has slightly dim but spacious rooms very close to the action. (☎334-0292. A/C, free local calls, cable TV, and pool access. Rooms from $25.) Branson's location along Lake Taneycomo and Table Rock Lake makes it a popular camping area as well. Over 15 campgrounds and RV parks lie within a 10 mi. radius. **Indian Point ❶**, at the end of Indian Point Rd., south of Rte. 76 and west of town, has lakeside sites with swimming and a boat launch. (☎338-2121 or 888-444-6777. Reception daily 9am-7pm. Sites $12, with electricity $16.)

Branson is impossible without a car, but infuriating with one. With no public transportation and no Amtrak or Greyhound, a tourist without a car has a hard time getting around. In a car, especially on weekends, there endless traffic jams clog Hwy. 76, the two-lane road that runs by all the attractions. Avoid peak tourist times, like Saturday nights. **Jefferson Shuttle**, 155 Industrial Park Dr. (☎339-2550), in Hollister, across the river from Branson, behind Lowe's Home Improvement Center, runs once daily to Kansas City ($39) via Springfield, MO ($11). Branson's off-season runs from January to March, when many attractions close. Beware of fake "tourist information centers." Though they probably will have useful information, they are also trying to sell you something. The real tourist info center is the **Branson Chamber of Commerce and Convention and Visitors Bureau Welcome Center,** 269 Rte. 248, just west of the Rte. 248/65 junction. In early 2003, the welcome center will move to a new location at the junction of Hwy. 65 and Hwy. 160. (☎334-4139 or 800-961-1221; www.explorebranson.com. Open M-Sa 8am-5pm, Su 10am-4pm; extended hours in summer.) **Area code:** 417.

OKLAHOMA

Oklahoma is a state that remembers its distinctive, though not always glamorous, history. In 1838-39, President Andrew Jackson forced the relocation of "The Five Civilized Tribes" from the southeastern states to the designated Oklahoma Indian Territory in a tragic march that came to be known as "The Trail of Tears." In 1889, the tribes were forced onto reservations even further west when Oklahoma was opened up to settlers, called Sooners. Today, Oklahoma celebrates its Indian heritage through museums, artwork, and cultural events. Oklahoma is also a state rich with African-American heritage, as blacks settled here in large numbers during the 19th century and played a substantial role in the Civil War. In 1995, Oklahoma City was hit with the second worst terrorist attack on American soil. The former site of the Federal Building is now home to a striking and beautiful memorial.

🔁 PRACTICAL INFORMATION

Capital: Oklahoma City.

Visitor Info: Oklahoma Tourism and Recreation Dept., 15 N. Robinson Ave., #801, Oklahoma City 73152 (☎405-2406 or 800-652-6552; www.travelok.com), in the Concord Bldg. at Sheridan St. Open M-F 8am-5pm.

Postal Abbreviation: OK. **Sales Tax:** 8%. **Tolls:** Oklahoma is fond of toll-booths, so keep a wad of bills (and a roll of coins for unattended booths) handy.

TULSA   ☎918

Though Tulsa is not Oklahoma's political capital, it is in many ways the center of the state. First settled by Creek Native Americans arriving on the Trail of Tears, Tulsa's location on the banks of the Arkansas River made it a logical trading outpost. Contemporary Tulsa's Art Deco skyscrapers, French villas, Georgian mansions, and distinctively large Native American population reflect its varied heritage. Rough-riding motorcyclists and slick oilmen, seeking the good life on the Great Plains, have recently joined the city's cultural melange.

■ 🛛 **ORIENTATION & PRACTICAL INFORMATION.** Tulsa is divided neatly into one-square-mile quadrants. Downtown surrounds the intersection of **Main St.** (north-south) and **Admiral Blvd.** (east-west). Numbered streets lie in ascending order north or south from Admiral. Named streets run north-south in alphabetical order; those named after western cities are west of Main St., while eastern cities lie to the east. **Tulsa International Airport** (☎ 838-5000; call M-F 8am-5pm), just northeast of downtown, is accessible by I-244 or U.S. 169. **Greyhound,** 317 S. Detroit Ave. (☎ 584-4428; open 24hr.), departs for Dallas (7hr., 7 per day, $44.50-49); Kansas City (6½hr., 1 per day, $55.50-61.50); Oklahoma City (2hr., 4 per day, $15); and St. Louis (8-10hr., 5 per day, $76.25-80.50). **Metropolitan Tulsa Transit Authority,** 510 S. Rockford Ave., runs local buses. (☎ 582-2100. Call center open M-Sa 4:30am-9pm, Su 9am-5pm. Buses operate daily 5am-12:30am. $1, seniors and disabled 50¢, ages 5-17 75¢, under 5 free; transfers 5¢.) **Taxis: Checker Cab,** ☎ 582-6161. **Medical Services: Hillcrest Medical Center,** 1120 S. Utica Ave. (☎ 579-1000). **Center for Women's Health,** 1822 E. 15th St. (☎ 749-4444). **Visitor info: Tulsa Convention and Visitors Bureau:** 616 S. Boston Ave., Suite 100. (☎ 585-1201 or 800-558-3311. Open M-F 8am-5pm.) **Internet access: Tulsa Public Library,** 400 Civic Center (☎ 596-7977. Open June-Aug. M-Th 9am-9pm, F-Sa 9am-5pm, Su 1-5pm; Sept.-May M-Th 9am-9pm, F-Sa 9am-5pm.) **Post Office:** 333 W. 4th St. (☎ 732-6651. Open M-F 7:30am-5pm.) **ZIP code:** 74103. **Area code:** 918.

📍 **ACCOMMODATIONS.** Decent budget accommodations are scarce downtown. The best deal can be found at the **YMCA ❶,** 515 S. Denver Ave., which has six rooms for women. (☎ 583-6201. Pool, track, weight rooms, and racquetball courts. Deposit $20. Rooms $20 per day.) Also close to downtown, the **Village Inn ❷,** 114 E. Skelly Dr., offers rooms with free local calls, cable TV, fridge, and whirlpool. (☎ 743-2009. Check-out 11am. Singles Su-Th $35, F-Sa $42; doubles $46/48.) You can also try the budget motels around the junction of **I-44** and **I-244** (Exit 222 off I-44); take bus #17 "Southwest Blvd." **Georgetown Plaza Motel ❶,** 8502 E. 27th St., off I-44 at 31st and Memorial St., rents clean, frayed, rooms with free local calls and cable TV. (☎ 622-6616. Singles $28-31; doubles $34.) The **Gateway Motor Hotel ❷,** 5600 W. Skelly Dr., at Exit 222C, has adequate rooms decorated in pea-green and timber fashion. (☎ 446-6611. Check-out 11am. Singles $29-35; doubles $35.) The 250-site **Mingo RV Park ❶,** 801 N. Mingo Rd., at the northeast corner of the I-244 and Mingo Rd. intersection, provides laundry and showers in a semi-urban setting. (☎ 832-8824 or 800-932-8824. Reception daily 8:30am-8pm. Full hookup $25.)

📷 🍴 **FOOD & NIGHTLIFE.** Most downtown restaurants cater to lunching businesspeople, closing at 2pm on weekdays and altogether on weekends. **Nelson's Buffeteria ❶,** 514 S. Boston Ave., is an old-fashioned diner that has served their blue plate special (two scrambled eggs, hash browns, biscuit and gravy $2.50) and famous chicken-fried steak ($6) since 1929. (☎ 584-9969. Open M-F 6am-2pm.) After lunch, S. Peoria Ave. is the place to go. Located in a converted movie theater, **The Brook Restaurant ❷,** 3401 S. Peoria, has classic Art Deco appeal. A traditional menu of chicken, burgers, and salads ($6-8) is complemented by an extensive list of signature martinis for $4.50-5.25. (☎ 748-9977. Open M-Sa 11am-2am, Su 11am-11pm.) For really extended hours, try **Mama Lou's Restaurant ❶,** 5688 W. Skelly Dr., where breakfast—including two eggs, three pancakes, hash browns, and bacon for $4.35—happens all day long. (☎ 445-1700. Open 24hr.)

Read the free *Urban Tulsa*, at local restaurants, and *The Spot* in the Friday *Tulsa World* for up-to-date specs on arts and entertainment. Good bars line an area known as **Brookside,** in the 3000s along S. Peoria Ave., and 15th St. east of Peoria. Let the party animal inside escape at **ID Bar,** 3340 S. Peoria Ave. With a posh interior and quality DJs, this dance club has a strong cosmopolitan feel. (☎ 743-

0600. Live music W. 21+. Cover F-Sa $5-7. Open W-Su 9pm-2am.) Catering to the young adult crowd, 18th and Boston Ave. raises a ruckus at night. College kids flock to the blues-happy **Steamroller,** 1738 Boston Ave., commonly billed as the "snob-free, dork-free, band-and-brewski place to be." (☎583-9520. Local bands Th-Sa 10pm. Cover $5. Open M-W 11am-10pm, Th-F 11am-2am, Sa 5pm-2am.)

🖼 🎵 **SIGHTS & ENTERTAINMENT.** Perched atop an Osage foothill 2 mi. northwest of downtown, the **Thomas Gilcrease Museum,** 1400 Gilcrease Museum Rd., houses the world's largest collection of Western American art, as well as 250,000 Native American artifacts. Take the Gilcrease exit off Rte. 412 or bus #47. (☎596-2700 or 888-655-2278. Open mid-May to mid-Sept. M-Sa 9am-5pm, Su 11am-5pm; mid-Sept. to mid-May closed M. $3 requested donation.) The **Philbrook Museum of Art,** 2727 S. Rockford Rd., bus #5 "Peoria," presents tastefully selected works of Native American and international art in a renovated Italian Renaissance villa, complete with a grassy sculpture garden. (☎749-7941 or 800-324-7941. Open Tu-W and F-Sa 10am-5pm, Th 10am-8pm, Su 11am-5pm. $5, students and seniors $3, under 13 free.) The ultra-modern, gold-mirrored architecture of **Oral Roberts University,** 7777 S. Lewis Ave., rises out of an Oklahoma plain about 6 mi. south of downtown between Lewis and Harvard Ave.; take bus #12. In 1964, Oral had a dream in which God commanded him to "Build Me a University," and thus Tulsa's biggest tourist attraction was born. The **Visitors Center,** in the Prayer Tower, has free tours. (☎495-6807. Open June-Aug. M-Sa 9am-5pm, Su 1-5pm; Sept.-May M-Sa 10am-5pm, Su 1-5pm. Tours every 15min.)

Tulsa thrives during the **International Mayfest** (☎582-6435) in mid-May. In mid-June, the city hosts the **Oklahoma Jazz Hall of Fame** ceremonies and concerts at Greenwood Park, 300 N. Greenwood Dr. Come mid-August the **Intertribal Powwow,** at the Tulsa Fairgrounds Pavilion (Expo Sq.), attracts Native Americans and thousands of onlookers for a three-day festival of food, crafts, and nightly dance contests. (☎744-1113. $5 per person, $16 per "family" of four.)

NEAR TULSA: TAHLEQUAH

The Cherokees, suffering from the loss of nearly one-quarter of their population along the Trail of Tears, began anew by placing their capital in Tahlequah, 66 mi. southeast of Tulsa on Rte. 51. In the center of town, on Cherokee Sq., stands the capitol building of the **Cherokee Nation,** 101 S. Muskogee Ave. (Rte. 51/62/82). Built in 1870, the building, along with other tribal government buildings like the Supreme Court building and the Cherokee National Prison, formed the highest authority in Oklahoma until the state was admitted to the Union in 1907.

The **Cherokee Heritage Center,** 4 mi. south of town on Rte. 82, reminds visitors of the injustice perpetrated against Native Americans. In the Center's **Ancient Village,** local Cherokees recreate a 16th-century settlement with ongoing demonstrations of skills like bow-making and basket-weaving. Next door, the well-executed **Cherokee National Museum** presents a wealth of information on the Trail of Tears using artifacts and personal histories. (☎456-6007 or 888-999-6007. Village and Museum open May-Oct. daily 10am-5pm; Feb.-Apr. M-Sa 10am-5pm; Nov.-Dec. M-Sa 10am-5pm, Su 1-5pm. $8.50, under 13 $4.25; 10% AAA discount.) Across from the northeast corner of Cherokee Sq., the **Visitors Center,** 123 E. Delaware St., offers free maps of the major sites downtown. (☎456-3742. Open M-F 9am-5pm.)

OKLAHOMA CITY ☎405

Oklahoma City serves as a crossroads, both north-south and east-west. In the late 1800s it was a major transit point on cattle drives from Texas to the north, and today its Stockyards are a fascinating window into a world not often seen by outsiders. Lying along the Santa Fe Railroad, the city was swarmed by over 100,000 homesteaders when Oklahoma was opened to settlement in 1889, and it continues to celebrate American Westward expansion at one of the largest museums devoted to the West in the country. Casting a shadow over all this is the haunting memorial to the almost 200 victims of the bombing of the Federal Building in 1995.

⚄♫ ORIENTATION & PRACTICAL INFORMATION. Oklahoma City is constructed as a nearly perfect grid. **Santa Fe Ave.** divides the city east-west, and **Reno Ave.** slices it north-south. Cheap and plentiful parking makes driving the best way to go. **Will Rogers World Airport** (☎680-3200), is on I-44 southwest of downtown, Exit 116B. **Amtrak** has an unattended station at 100 S. Ek Gaylord Blvd., and rumbles to Fort Worth (4½ hr., 1 per day, $26). To get to the **Greyhound** station, 427 W. Sheridan Ave. (☎235-4083; open 24hr.), at Walker St., take city bus #4, 5, 6, 8, or 10. *Be careful at night.* Buses run to Fort Worth (6-11hr., 9 per day, $34.50-36.50); Kansas City, MO (6-10hr., 3 per day, $73.25-77.50); and Tulsa (2-3hr., 5 per day, $15). **Oklahoma Metro Transit** has bus service; all routes radiate from the station at 200 N. Shartel St. Their office, 300 SW 7th St., distributes free schedules. (☎235-7433. Open M-F 8am-5pm. Buses M-Sa 6am-6pm. $1.10, seniors and ages 6-17 55¢. Trolley 25¢.) Look for the **Oklahoma Spirit** trolley downtown and in Bricktown. **Taxis: Yellow Cab,** ☎232-6161. The **Oklahoma City Convention and Visitors Bureau,** 189 W. Sheridan Ave., at Robinson St., has city info. (☎297-8912 or 800-225-5652. Open M-F 8:30am-5pm.) **Internet access: Oklahoma City Public Library,** 131 Dean McGee Ave. (☎231-8650. Open M and W-F 9am-6pm, Tu 9am-9pm, Sa 9am-5pm.) **Post Office:** 320 SW 5th St. (☎800-275-8777. Open M-F 6am-10pm, Sa 8am-5pm.) **ZIP code:** 73102. **Area code:** 405.

▟ ACCOMMODATIONS. Ten minutes from downtown and 5min. from a huge mall and plenty of eateries, **Flora's Bed and Breakfast ❸,** 2312 NW 46th St., has two traditional rooms available. (☎840-3157. Singles $60; doubles $65.) Other cheap lodging lies along the interstate highways, particularly on I-35 north of the I-44 junction. **The Royal Inn ❶,** 2800 S. I-35, south of the junction with I-40, treats you to free local calls, HBO, and adequate rooms. (☎672-0899. Singles $28.50; doubles $34.) Behind a strip mall, the 172 sites of **Abe's RV Park ❶,** 12115 I-35 Service Rd., have a pool, laundry, and showers. Take southbound Frontage Rd. off Exit 137; it's ¼ mi. to the red-and-white "RV" sign. (☎478-0278. Open in summer daily 8am-8pm; off-season 8am-6pm. Sites $19.) A more scenic option, **Lake Thunderbird State Park ❶** offers campsites near a beautiful lake fit for swimming or fishing. Take I-40 east to Choctaw Rd. (Exit 166), go south 10 mi. until the road ends, then make a left, and drive another mile. (☎360-3572. Showers available. Office open M-F 8am-5pm, with a host for late or weekend arrivals. Sites $8-10, with water and electricity $16-21; huts $45.)

◨▤ FOOD & NIGHTLIFE. Oklahoma City contains the largest cattle market in the US, and beef tops most menus. Most downtown eateries close early in the afternoon after they've served business lunchers. Restaurants with longer hours lie east of town on Sheridan Ave. in the Bricktown district and north of downtown along Classen Blvd. and Western Ave. Asian restaurants congregate around the intersection of Classen and NW 23rd St. **Pho Pasteur ❷,** 2800 N. Classen Blvd., Suite #108, has Vietnamese and Chinese food in a classy setting. (☎524-2233. Beef noodle soups $5. Open Su-Th 8:30am-9pm, F-Sa 8:30am-10pm.) Everyone's fighting for the rights to the late Leo's recipes at **Leo's Original BBQ ❶,** 3631 N. Kelley St., a classic hickory-smoking outfit in the northwest reaches of town. (☎424-5367. Beef sandwich and baked potato $4.20. Open M 11am-2pm, Tu-Sa 11am-7pm.) Unfortunately, hot nightlife here is almost as rare as the elusive jackalope, but at least the Bricktown district has restaurants with live music. The **Bricktown Brewery,** 1 N.

Oklahoma St., at Sheridan Ave., brews five beers daily. (☎232-2739. Live music Tu and F-Sa 9pm. Upstairs 21+. Cover $5 during live music. Open Su-M 11am-10pm, Tu-Th 11am-midnight, F-Sa 11am-1:30am.) **Studio 54 at Bricktown,** 15 E. California Ave., a crowded dance club, provides great views of Oklahoma City and the dressed-to-impress clientele. (☎235-3533. Tu Ladies night. Open Tu-Su 8pm-2am.)

◙ ♫ **SIGHTS & ENTERTAINMENT.** Monday morning is the time to visit the **Oklahoma City Stockyards,** 2500 Exchange Ave. (☎235-8675), the busiest in the world. Take bus #12 from the terminal to Agnew and Exchange Ave. Cattle auctions (M-Tu) begin at 8am and may last into the night. Visitors enter free of charge via a catwalk that soars over cow pens and cattle herds from the parking lot northeast of the auction house. The auction is as Old West as it gets; only those with a wide-brim cowboy hat, blue jeans, boots, and faded dress shirt fit in.

Plant lovers should make a bee-line for **Myriad Gardens,** 301 W. Reno Ave., where a 70 ft. diameter glass cylinder, called the Crystal Bridge, perches above a large pond. The gardens include both a desert and a rainforest. (☎297-3995. Glass Cylinder: Open M-Sa 9am-6pm, Su noon-6pm. $4, students and seniors $3, ages 4-12 $2. Gardens: Open daily 7am-11pm. Free.) The **National Cowboy and Western Heritage Museum,** 1700 NE 63rd St., features an extensive collection of Western art and exhibits on rodeo, Native Americans, and frontier towns. (☎478-2250. Open daily 9am-5pm. $8.50, seniors $7, ages 6-12 $4, under 6 free.)

The **Oklahoma City National Memorial,** at 5th and Harvey St. downtown, is a powerful tribute to the victims of the 1995 bombing of the Murrah Federal Building. It has two parts: an outdoor memorial and a museum. The memorial consists of a Field of Empty Chairs (one for each of the 168 victims), a stone gate at each end, and a reflecting pool. It is especially dramatic at night, when each of the chairs is lit. The Museum tells the story of the bombing through photographs, videos, and testimonials. (☎235-3313. Museum open M-Sa 9am-6pm, Su 1-6pm. $7, students $5, seniors $6, under 6 free.) The **Red Earth Festival** is the country's largest celebration of Native American culture; the **Myriad Convention Center** hosts art fairs and dance competitions. (☎427-5228. June 6-8, 2003. $7.) Fall visitors should check out the **Deep Deuce Jazz Festival,** at NE 2nd and Walnut St. (☎424-2552; Oct. 4-5, 2003) and the **World Championship Quarter Horse Show** (☎948-6800) in mid-November.

TEXAS

Covering an area as long as the stretch from North Carolina to Key West, Texas has more the brawn of a country than a state. The fervently proud, independent citizens of the "Lone Star State" seem to prefer it that way: where else do you see "Don't Mess With Texas" on official road signs and "No firearms allowed" at restaurants and museums? After revolting against the Spanish in 1821 and splitting from Mexico in 1836, the Republic of Texas stood alone until 1845, when it entered the Union as the 28th state. The state's unofficial motto proclaims that "everything is bigger in Texas." This truth is evident in prolific wide-brimmed hats, styled and sculpted ladies' coifs, boat-sized American autos, giant ranch spreads, countless steel skyscrapers, and oil refineries the size of small towns.

HIGHLIGHTS OF TEXAS

FOOD. Drippin' barbecue and colossal steaks reign supreme in the state where beef is king and vegetables are for the cows. Some of the best beef awaits in Austin (p. 670) and Amarillo (p. 686).

SAN ANTONIO. Remember the Alamo! A city rich with Spanish heritage (p. 686).

RODEOS/COWBOYS. The ol' West lives on in Fort Worth (p. 675) and at the Mesquite Rodeo in Dallas (p. 674), with the finest rope-riders in the land.

PRACTICAL INFORMATION

Capital: Austin.

Visitor info: Texas Travel Information Centers (☎800-452-9292; www.tourtexas.com), near state lines on all major highways into Texas. Call 8am-6pm (centers open daily 8am-5pm) for a free guidebook. **Texas Division of Tourism,** P.O. Box 12728, Austin 78711 (☎512-462-9191 or 800-888-8839). **Texas Parks and Wildlife Dept.,** Austin Headquarters Complex, 4200 Smith School Rd., Austin 78744 (☎512-389-4800 or 800-792-1112).

Postal Abbreviation: TX. **Sales Tax:** 6-8.25%.

SAN ANTONIO ☎210

Though best known as the home of the Alamo—the symbol of Texas's break from Mexico—San Antonio today is more defined by its integration of Anglo and Hispanic cultures. The early Spanish influence can be seen in missions originally built to convert Indians to Catholicism, and in La Villita, once a village for the city's original settlers that is now a workshop for local artisans. Mexican culture is on display in Market Square, where mariachi bands and fajita stands entertain weekend revelers. Still, there are enough barbecue joints and ten-gallon hats to remind travelers that they are in Lone Star country. The blend of cultures comes together at the Riverwalk, where natives from all walks of life enjoy the restaurants, clubs, and shops in a vibrant and enchanting setting.

TRANSPORTATION

Airport: San Antonio International Airport, 9800 Airport Blvd. (☎207-3411), north of town. Accessible by I-410 and U.S. 281. Bus #2 ("Airport") connects the airport to downtown at Market and Alamo. Taxi to downtown $14-15.

Trains: Amtrak, 350 Hoefgen St. (☎223-3226), facing the northern side of the Alamodome. To: **Dallas** (9hr., 1 per day, $28); **Houston** (5hr., 3 per week, $30); and **Los Angeles** (27hr., 4 per week, $135). Open daily 10am-4pm.

Buses: Greyhound, 500 N. Saint Mary's St. (☎270-5824). To: **Dallas** (5-6hr., 15 per day, $34) and **Houston** (4hr., 9 per day, $21). Open 24hr.

Public Transit: VIA Metropolitan Transit, 800 W. Myrtle (☎362-2020). Buses operate daily 5am-midnight; many routes stop at 6pm. Infrequent service to outlying areas. 80¢, transfers 15¢. One-day "day tripper" passes $2, available at 260 E. Houston St.

Taxis: Yellow Cab, ☎226-4242.

PRACTICAL INFORMATION

Visitor info: 317 Alamo Plaza (☎207-6748), downtown across from the Alamo. Open daily 8:30am-6pm. Free maps and brochures.

Hotlines: Rape Crisis, ☎349-7273. Operates 24hr. **Supportive Services for the Elderly and Disabled,** ☎337-3550. Referrals and transportation.

Medical Services: Metropolitan Methodist Hospital, 1310 McCullough Ave. (☎208-2200).

Internet access: San Antonio Public Library, 600 Soledad St. (☎207-2534). Open M-Th 9am-9pm, F-Sa 9am-5pm, Su 11am-5pm.

Post Office: 615 E. Houston (☎800-275-8777), 1 block from the Alamo. Open M-F 8:30am-5:30pm. **ZIP code:** 78205. **Area code:** 210.

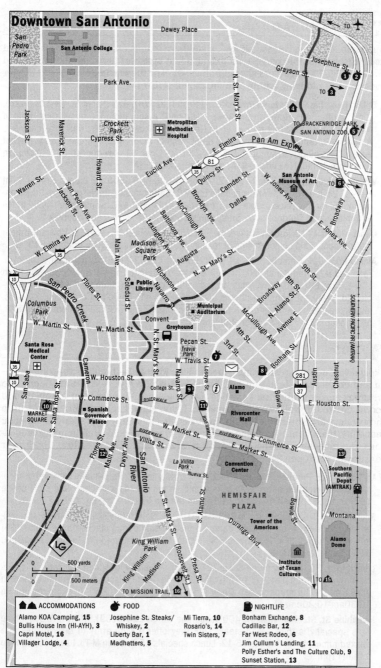

Downtown San Antonio

ACCOMMODATIONS
Alamo KOA Camping, **15**
Bullis House Inn (HI-AYH), **3**
Capri Motel, **16**
Villager Lodge, **4**

FOOD
Josephine St. Steaks/ Whiskey, **2**
Liberty Bar, **1**
Madhatters, **5**
Mi Tierra, **10**
Rosario's, **14**
Twin Sisters, **7**

NIGHTLIFE
Bonham Exchange, **8**
Cadillac Bar, **12**
Far West Rodeo, **6**
Jim Cullum's Landing, **11**
Polly Esther's and The Culture Club, **9**
Sunset Station, **13**

⌐ ACCOMMODATIONS

For cheap motels, try **Roosevelt Ave.**, a southern extension of Saint Mary's St., and **Fredericksburg Rd.** Inexpensive motels also line **Broadway** between downtown and Brackenridge Park. Drivers should follow **I-35 N** or the **Austin Hwy.** to find cheaper and often safer lodging within a 15 mi. radius of town.

Bullis House Inn San Antonio International Hostel (HI-AYH), 621 Pierce St. (☎223-9426), 2 mi. north of downtown on Broadway, right on Grayson. From the bus station, walk to Navarro St. and take bus #11 or 15 to Grayson and New Braunfels; walk 2 blocks west. A spacious, ranch-style hostel in a quiet neighborhood. Pool, kitchen, and Internet access. Fills quickly in summer. Breakfast $4.50. Linen $2. Key deposit $10. Reception daily 8am-10pm. No curfew. $18, nonmembers $21. ❶

Villager Lodge, 1126 E. Elmira (☎222-9463 or 800-584-0800), 3 blocks east of Saint Mary's, 1 mi. north of downtown. Take bus #8. Caring management provides the cleanest rooms for this price. Cable TV, 5 free local calls, and A/C. Some rooms have fridge and microwave. Outdoor pool. Small singles $27; large singles and doubles $34. ❶

Capri Motel, 1718 Roosevelt Ave. (☎533-2583), about 2 mi. south of downtown near the missions. Fairly clean rooms at reasonable prices. Singles $35; doubles $40. ❷

Alamo KOA, 602 Gembler Rd. (☎224-9296 or 800-833-7785), 6 mi. from downtown. Take bus #24 "Industrial Park" from the corner of Houston and Alamo downtown. From I-10 E, take Exit 580/W.W. White Rd., drive 2 blocks north, then take a left onto Gembler Rd. Well-kept grounds with lots of shade. Each site has a grill and patio. Showers, laundry facilities, pool, and free movies. Reception daily 7:30am-9:30pm. Sites $28, full hookup $31; each additional person $4. ❶

⌐ FOOD

Expensive cafes and restaurants surround the **Riverwalk**—breakfast beyond a muffin and coffee can clean you out. North of town, Asian restaurants open onto **Broadway** across from Brackenridge. On weekends, hundreds of carnival food booths crowd the walkways of **Market Sq.** If you come late in the day, prices drop and vendors are willing to haggle. (☎207-8600. Open May-Sept. daily 10am-8pm; Sept.-May 10am-6pm.) **Pig Stand** diners offer cheap, decent grub in multiple locations; the branches at 801 S. Presa, off S. Alamo, and 1508 Broadway (both near downtown) stay open 24hr.

▨ Mi Tierra, 218 Produce Row (☎225-1262), in Market Sq. Perpetually smiling *mariachi* musicians serenade patrons. Delicious chicken enchiladas with chocolate mole sauce $8.50. Lunch specials $7. Grab dessert on the run from the bakery. Open 24hr. ❸

Rosario's, 910 S. Alamo St. (☎223-1806), at S. Saint Mary's St., is widely acknowledged by locals to be the best eatery in town. Scrumptious chicken quesadillas ($6) uphold the reputation. Live music F-Sa nights. Open M 11am-3pm, Tu-Th 11am-10pm, F-Sa 11am-12:30am. ❷

Liberty Bar, 328 E. Josephine St (☎227-1187). A friendly local hangout with daily specials and sandwich plates ($7-9). Try the Karkade (iced hibiscus and mint tea with fresh ginger and white grape juice). Open M-Th 11am-10:30pm, F-Sa 11am-midnight, Su 10:30am-10:30pm. ❷

Josephine St. Steaks/Whiskey, 400 Josephine St. (☎224-6169), at Ave. A. Josephine St.'s specialty is thick Texan steaks, but they offer a wide array of tasty dishes in a relaxed atmosphere. Entrees $5-12. Lunch specials $5-7. Open M-Th 11am-10pm, F-Sa 11am-11pm. ❸

Twin Sisters, 124 Broadway and 6322 N. New Braunfels (☎354-1559). Some of the best vegetarian eats around. Try the Caesar with eggless tofu salad ($8) or the tofu quesadillas ($6). Open M-F 9am-3pm. ❷

Madhatters, 36036 Ave. B (☎821-6555), at Brackenridge Park, just off Broadway at Mulberry. Features over 50 teas and a famous Sunday brunch in a casual, fun space. M-F Breakfast specials $5. Open M-F 7:30am-10pm, Sa 9am-10pm, Su 9am-3pm. ❶

🄶 SIGHTS

Much of historic San Antonio lies in the present-day downtown and surrounding areas. The city may seem diffuse, but almost every major site or park is within a few miles of downtown and is accessible by public transportation.

DOWNTOWN

THE ALAMO. Though built as a Spanish mission during the colonization of the New World, **The Alamo** has come to signify the bravery of those who fought for Texas's independence and to serve as a touchstone of Lone Star pride. For 12 days in 1836 Texan defenders of the Alamo, outnumbered 20 to 1, held their ground against Mexican attackers. The morning of the 13th day saw the end of the defiant stand as the strains of the infamous *deguello* (literally "throat-cutting" in Spanish, the *deguello* is military music that had come to signify annihilation of the enemy in Spanish history) were heard. All 189 men were killed. The massacre served to unite Texans behind the independence movement, and "Remember the Alamo!" became the rallying cry for Sam Houston's ultimately victorious forces. After languishing for decades (including use as an arms depot during the Civil War), the site is presently under the care of the Daughters of the Republic of Texas and the locus of the city's downtown. *(At the center of Alamo Plaza near Houston and Alamo St. ☎225-1391. Open M-Sa 9am-5:30pm, Su 10am-6:30pm. Free.)*

OTHER MISSIONS. The San Antonio Missions National Historical Park preserves the five missions along the river that once formed the soul of San Antonio. To reach the missions, follow the brown and white "Mission Trail" signs beginning on S. Saint Mary's St. downtown. **Mission San José** (a.k.a. the "Queen of the Missions") has remnants of its own irrigation system, a gorgeous sculpted rose window, and numerous restored buildings. As the largest of San Antonio's missions, it best conveys the self-sufficiency of these institutions. **Mission Concepción** is the oldest unrestored stone church in North America, and traces of the once-colorful frescoes are still visible. **Mission San Juan Capistrano** and **Mission San Francisco de la Espada,** smaller and simpler than the others, evoke the isolation of such outposts. Between them lies the Espada Aqueduct, the only remaining waterway built by the Spanish. *(Bus #42 stops within walking distance of Mission Concepción and right in front of Mission San José. The main Visitors Center is located at Mission San José. ☎534-8833 for info on all missions. San José: 6701 San José Dr., off Roosevelt Ave. ☎922-0543. 4 Catholic masses held each Su 7:45, 9, 10:30am, and a noon "Mariachi Mass." Concepción: 807 Mission Rd., 4 mi. south of the Alamo off E. Mitchell St. ☎534-1540. San Juan: 9101 Graf St. ☎534-0749. San Francisco: 10040 Espada Rd. ☎627-2021. All missions open daily 9am-5pm. Free.)*

SECULAR SAN ANTONIO

DISTRICTS. Southwest of the Alamo, black signs indicate access points to the 2½ mi. **Paseo del Río (Riverwalk),** a series of shaded stone pathways that follow a winding canal built by the WPA in the 1930s. Lined with picturesque gardens, shops, and cafes, the Riverwalk connects most of the major downtown sights and is the hub of San Antonio's nightlife. To ride the river, try **Yanaguana Cruise Services.** Buy tickets at the Rivercenter Mall or at any of the hotels along the walk; board almost anywhere along the river. *(315 E. Commerce St.* ☎ *244-5700 or 800-417-4139. Open daily 9am-10pm. $5.25, seniors $3.65.)* A few blocks south, the recreated artisans' village, **La Villita**, contains restaurants, craft shops, and art studios. *(418 Villita.* ☎ *207-8610. Shops open daily 10am-6pm; restaurant hours vary.)* On weekends, **Market Sq.** features the upbeat tunes of *Tejano* bands and the omnipresent buzzing of frozen margarita machines. *(Between San Saba and Santa Rosa St.* ☎ *207-8600. Open May-Sept. daily 10am-8pm; Sept.-May 10am-6pm.)*

HEMISFAIR PLAZA. The site of the 1968 World's Fair, **HemisFair Plaza**, on S. Alamo, draws tourists with nearby restaurants, museums, and historic houses. The observation deck of the **Tower of the Americas** rises 750 ft. above the Texas Hill Country—the view is best at night. *(600 HemisFair Park.* ☎ *207-8617. Open Su-Th 9am-10pm, F-Sa 9am-11pm. $3, seniors $2, ages 4-11 $1.)* Inside the park, the **Institute of Texan Cultures** showcases 27 ethnic and cultural groups and their contributions to the history of Texas. *(*☎ *458-2300. Open Tu-Su 9am-5pm.)*

OTHER ATTRACTIONS. Home to the San Antonio Spurs, the **Alamodome** resembles a Mississippi riverboat. *(100 Montana St., at Hoefgen St. Take bus #24 or 26.* ☎ *207-3600. Tours Tu and F 11am and 1pm, except during scheduled events. $4, seniors and ages 4-12 $3.)* The **San Antonio Museum of Art,** housed in the former Lone Star Brewery just north of the city center, showcases an extensive collection of Latin American folk art, as well as Texan furniture and an impressive variety of pre-Columbian, Egyptian, Oceanic, Asian, and Islamic art. *(200 W. Jones Ave.* ☎ *978-8100. Open Tu 10am-9pm, W-Sa 10am-5pm, and Su noon-5pm. $5, seniors and students with ID $4, ages 4-11 $1.75; free Tu 3-9pm. Free parking.)*

OUTSIDE CITY CENTER

BRACKENRIDGE PARK. To escape San Antonio's urban congestion, amble down to **Brackenridge Park**. The 343-acre show ground includes playgrounds, a miniature train, and a driving range. The main attraction of the park is a lush, perfumed Japanese tea garden with pathways weaving in and out of a pagoda and around a goldfish pond. *(3910 N. Saint Mary's St., 5 mi. north of the Alamo. Take bus #8.* ☎ *223-9534. Open daily 5am-11pm. Train daily 9am-6:30pm. $2.25, children $1.75.)* Directly across the street, the **San Antonio Zoo**, one of the country's largest, keeps over 3500 animals from 800 species in reproductions of their natural settings, including an extensive African mammal exhibit. *(3903 N. Saint Mary's St.* ☎ *734-7184. Open June-Aug. daily 9am-6pm; Sept.-May 9am-5pm. $7, seniors and ages 3-11 $5.)*

A LITTLE SOMETHING DIFFERENT. The 140 million-year-old stalactites and stalagmites of **Natural Bridge Caverns** change continuously; some grow as much as an inch every hundred years. *(26495 Natural Bridge Caverns Rd. Take I-35 N to Exit 175 and follow the signs.* ☎ *651-6101. Open June-Aug. daily 9am-6pm; Sept.-May 9am-4pm. $12, ages 4-12 $7. 1¼hr. tours every 30min.)* Next door, the **Natural Bridge Wildlife Ranch** offers "Texas safaris," where animals from all over the world—including giraffes, zebras, rhinos, jaguars, and ostriches—roam freely and will approach your car for food. *(Open June-Aug. daily 9am-6:30pm; offseason 9am-5pm. $11 per adult, $6 per child 3-11. Free animal feed.)* If you have an itchy trigger finger, **A Place to Shoot** is—well, just that. *(13250 Pleasanton Rd. Exit 46 off I-410 S.* ☎ *628-1888. Open M-F 10am-7pm, Sa-Su 9am-7pm. $7 per person; $5 per 25 clays. Earplug rental 50¢.)* For cowboy paraphernalia, the **Texas Pioneer, Trail Driver, and Texas Ranger's Museum** contains a splendid collection of artifacts, old guns, documents, and portraits. *(3805 Broadway.* ☎ *822-9011. Open May-Aug. M-Sa 10am-5pm, Su noon-5pm. $3, seniors $2, ages 6-12 $1.)*

🎵 📺 ENTERTAINMENT & NIGHTLIFE

In late April, **Fiesta San Antonio** (☎227-5191) ushers in spring with concerts, parades, and plenty of Tex-Mex celebrations to commemorate the victory at San Jacinto and to pay homage to the heroes of the Alamo. The first Friday of every month is a fiesta in San Antonio: the art galleries along S. Alamo St. put on a huge event called **Artswalk** (for info ☎207-6748), with free food and drink. For excitement after dark any time, any season, stroll down the Riverwalk. The **Theatre District,** just north of the Riverwalk downtown, puts on concerts, opera, and theatre in three restored 1950s movie houses. *The Friday Express* or weekly *Current* (available at the tourist office) are guides to concerts and entertainment.

Sam's Burger Joint, 330 E. Grayson St. (☎223-2830), hosts the **Puro Poetry Slam** every Tuesday night at 10pm ($2). Sam's also features live music and the "Big Monster Burger," a pound of beef for $7. For authentic **Tejano music,** a Mexican and country amalgam, head to the **Cadillac Bar,** 212 S. Flores St., where every weeknight a different band whips the huge crowd (anywhere from 500-1000 people) into a cheering and dancing frenzy. (☎223-5533. 21+. Open M-Sa 11am-2am.) Right around the corner from the Alamo, San Antonio's biggest gay dance club, the **Bonham Exchange,** 411 Bonham St., plays high-energy music with some house and techno on the side. A younger, more mixed crowd files in on Wednesdays for college night. (☎271-3811. Cover for 21+ $3-5, for 18-20 up to $10. Open M-Th 4pm-2am, F 4pm-3am, Sa 8pm-3am.) Some of the best traditional jazz anywhere goes down at **Jim Cullum's Landing,** 123 Losoya St., in the Hyatt downtown, including the legendary Cullum and his jazz band and the improv jazz quintet Small World. (☎223-7266. Small World performs Su nights. Tidy dress recommended. All ages. Cover M-Th $3.50, F-Sa $6.50; Su no cover. Open M-Sa 4:30pm-1am, Su noon-1am; Cullum band performs M-Sa 8:30pm-1am.) Also along the Riverwalk, **Polly Esthers** and **The Culture Club,** 212 College St., pump up the crowd with 1970s disco on the 2nd floor and 1980s retro on the 3rd floor, respectively. (☎220-1972. 21+. Cover $3-7. Open Su-W 8pm-2am, Th 8pm-3am, F-Sa 8pm-4am.) **Far West Rodeo,** 3030 Rte. 410 NE, plays two types of music—country *and* Western. With an indoor rodeo on Friday and Saturday nights, a mechanical bull, and two dance floors, you best bring your ten-gallon hat to enjoy the fun. (☎646-9378. 18+. Cover $3-6. Open W-Th 7pm-2am, F-Sa 8pm-2am.) **Sunset Station,** 1174 E. Commerce St. (222-2017), across from the Amtrak Station, houses concerts and clubs in a restored train depot.

AUSTIN ☎512

If the "Lone Star State" still inspires images of rough-and-tumble cattle ranchers riding horses across the plains, then Austin attempts to put the final nails in the coffin of that stereotype. In recent years, 17,000 new millionaires have made their fortune in Austin and big industry has become increasingly prominent, with Fortune 500 companies and Internet startups seeking to redefine the city's essence. With booming growth, the population has skyrocketed, and driving in and around Austin has become quite an ordeal. Austin's reputation for musical innovation as the "Live Music Capital of the World," plus the 50,000 college students at the **University of Texas,** make it a vibrant city. A liberal, alternative oasis in a traditional state, Austin should be the first stop on any traveler's Texas itinerary.

ROADTRIP

Parts of the **Texas Hill Country** are as country as they come. Longhorns graze in rolling expanses of scraggly brush interrupted by jagged hills, while rusty pickup trucks driven by big men in big hats dominate the roads. But the Texas Hill Country is more than ranches and cattle: the limestone-rich soil is well-suited for wine-making and peach-growing. There is a noticeable German influence in the area, dating back to 1846 and the founding of **Fredericksburg**—stop off at a biergarten to sample some German cuisine. Finally, a series of well-maintained parks links San Antonio and Austin while offering campers and day visitors alike the chance to experience the natural beauty of Texas firsthand. Although not the most direct route between these two cities, unique diversions and beautiful scenery make up for the few extra miles.

TIME: 2 days (at a very leisurely pace)

DISTANCE: 220 mi.

1 NEW BRAUNFELS. The entire economy of New Braunfels, TX, depends on the inner tube. Almost 2 million visitors per year come to this town hoping to spend a day floating along the spring-fed Comal River. **Rockin' "R" River Rides** will send you off with a life jacket and tube before picking you up downstream 2½hr. later. (193 S. Liberty. ☎830-620-6262. Open May-Sept. daily 9am-7pm. Tube rentals $9, bottomless floats $7. Car keys, proper ID, or $25 deposit required for rental.) If the Comal doesn't float your boat, head for the chlorinated waters of **Schlitterbahn**, a 65-acre waterpark extravaganza with 17 waterslides, nine tube chutes, and five gigantic hot tubs. The park has recently added the planet's only uphill watercoaster, the Master Blaster. To find both attractions, take I-35 to Exit 189, turn left, and follow the signs for Schlitterbahn. (400 N. Liberty. ☎830-625-2351. Call for hours; generally around 10am-8pm. Open May-Sept. Full-day passes $27.50, ages 3-11 $22.75.) From New Braunfels, take Rte. 46 west for 6½ mi., then turn left on Herbelin Rd. Here you'll find **Dry Comal Creek Vineyards,** 1741 Herbelin Rd., beckoning with free tastings and tours of the small vineyard. (☎830-885-4121. Open W-Su noon-5pm.) Yes, Texas makes wine—in fact, the state is currently fifth in the nation in wine production.

2 GUADALUPE RIVER STATE PARK. Twenty-five miles west of Dry Comal Creek along Rte. 46 you can swim in the cliff-lined river or camp on the nearby sites of **Guadalupe River State Park ●.** (☎830-438-2656, for reservations 512-389-8900. Open M-F 8am-8pm, Sa 8am-10pm. Day entrance $4 per person, under 12 free; $15 for water and electricity, $12 for water only. Additional charge of $3 per person, under 12 free.)

3 BOERNE. Farther down Rte. 46 is Boerne (pronounced BUR-nee), an antique lover's paradise where a string of converted barns and old farmhouses sell a wide array of odds and ends.

4 BANDERA. After 12 mi. of twists through a series of low hills along the way to Bandera, Rte. 46 intersects with Rte. 16; take Rte. 16 north. Bandera's central street passes through a row of ramshackle buildings that look like backdrops to old cowboy movies. Consistent with the image, Bandera is home to the █ **Frontier Times Museum,** 510 13th St., a haven for cowboy memorabilia and odd knick-knacks like Peruvian shrunken heads. (☎830-796-3864. Open M-Sa 10am-4:30pm, Su 1-4:30pm. $2, ages 6-18 25¢.)

5 MEDINA. Continuing down 15 mi. of zig-zag roads through dramatic countryside, Rte. 16 N then brings you to the town of Medina, the "apple capital of Texas." Stop off at **Love Creek Orchards** (☎800-449-0882), on Rte. 16 on the north side of town, to buy some fresh cider ($5 per ½ gallon) for the trip. Leaving Medina on Rte. 16 N, the next 35 miles wind through some of the most breathtaking Texas country. *Be especially cautious driving this leg of the trip; hairpin turns and steep inclines can be treacherous.* Safety aside, the real reason to proceed slowly is to enjoy the scenery.

6 KERRVILLE. The **Cowboy Artists of America Museum,** 1550 Bandera Hwy., take Rte. 173 S from Rte. 16 N, showcases action-packed scenes of the Wild West that demonstrate the creative side of America's gun-toting heroes. (☎830-896-2553. Open June-Aug. M-Sa 9am-5pm, Su 1-5pm; Sept.-May Tu-Sa 9am-5pm, Su 1-5pm. $5, ages 6-18 $1, seniors $3.50.)

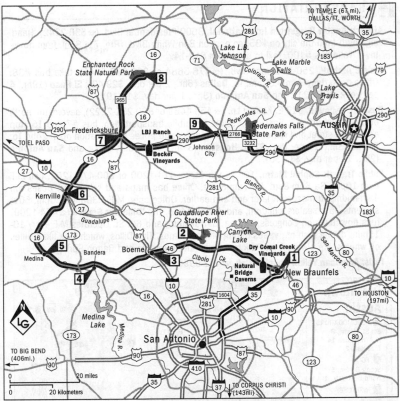

7 FREDERICKSBURG. Twenty-two miles along Rte. 16 from Kerrville sits historic Freder-icks-burg, a German-rooted town of biergartens, wineries, and sausage, and the heart of the Hill Country. **The Fredericksburg Convention and Visitors Bureau,** 106 N. Adams (☎888-997-3600), has maps and information. (Open M-F 9am-5pm.) Fredericksburg's **Admiral Nimitz Museum,** 340 E. Main St., contains an excellent exhibit on the Pacific theater of World War II. (☎830-997-4379. Open daily 10am-5pm. $5, students $3.)

8 ENCHANTED ROCK STATE NATURAL PARK. With the double allure of being both a natural wonder (a tree-less, 440 ft. dome of pink granite) as well as a place to pitch a tent, **Enchanted Rock State Natural Park ❶,** 18 miles north of Fredericksburg on Rte. 965, offers hiking—a relatively easy scramble to the top—and rock-climbing for the experienced. (☎800-792-1112. Open daily 8am-5pm. Entrance fee $5, under 12 free. 46 regular tent sites available with shower, water, and grill $9; 60 primitive sites $7. No RVs or trailers permitted. Reservations strongly recommended.)

9 JOHNSON CITY. Ten miles east of Fredericksburg on U.S. 290, **Becker Vineyards,** on Jenschke Ln., offers tastings as well as free tours of the winery. (☎830-644-2681. Open daily 10am-5pm.) Farther down U.S. 290, is Johnson City, the **birthplace of 36th President Lyndon Baines Johnson.** Nine miles east of Johnson City off Rte. 2766 is **Pedernales Falls State Park ❶.** Waterfalls, extensive hiking trails, tent sites, and swimming/tubing areas make the park a favorite getaway from Austin. (☎800-792-1112. Park open daily 8am-10pm; office open M-Th 8am-7pm, F 8am-10pm, Sa-Su 8am-8pm. Entrance fee $4 per person, under 12 free. Sites with water and electricity $16, primitive sites $7.)

TRANSPORTATION

Airport: Austin Bergstrom International, 3600 Presidential Blvd. (☎530-2242). Heading south from the city on I-35, go east on Ben White Blvd. (Rte. 71) 8 mi. from downtown. Take bus #100. Taxi to downtown $12-14.

Trains: Amtrak, 250 N. Lamar Blvd. (☎476-5684 or 800-872-7245); take bus #38. Office open daily 7am-9:30pm. To: **Dallas** (6hr., 2 per day, $29-42); **El Paso** (19hr., 4 per week, $98-121); and **San Antonio** (3hr., 1 per day, $12-19).

Buses: Greyhound, 916 E. Koenig Ln. (☎458-4463 or 800-231-2222), several mi. north of downtown off I-35. Easily accessible by public transportation, bus #7 and 15 stop across the street and run downtown. Schedules and prices vary. Station open 24hr. To: **Dallas** (3hr., 11 per day, $25); **Houston** (3½hr., 7 per day, $17); and **San Antonio** (2hr., 13 per day, $13.50).

Public Transit: Capitol Metro, 106 E. 8th St. (☎474-1200 or 800-474-1201; call M-F 6am-10pm, Sa 6am-8pm, Su 7am-6pm). Office has maps and schedules. Buses run 4am-midnight; most start later and end earlier. Office open M-F 7:30am-5:30pm. 50¢; students 25¢; seniors, children, and disabled free. The **'Dillo Bus Service** (☎474-1200) runs downtown on Congress, Lavaca, San Jacinto, and 6th St. Operates M-F every 10-15min. during rush hr.; varies during off-peak times. The 'Dillos, which look like trollies on wheels, are always free. Park free in the lot at Bouldin and Barton Springs.

Taxis: American Yellow Checker Cab, ☎452-9999.

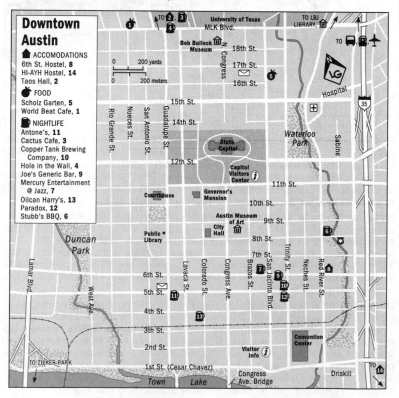

Downtown Austin

▲ ACCOMODATIONS
6th St. Hostel, **8**
HI-AYH Hostel, **14**
Taos Hall, **2**

● FOOD
Scholz Garten, **5**
World Beat Cafe, **1**

◗ NIGHTLIFE
Antone's, **11**
Cactus Cafe, **3**
Copper Tank Brewing Company, **10**
Hole in the Wall, **4**
Joe's Generic Bar, **9**
Mercury Entertainment @ Jazz, **7**
Oilcan Harry's, **13**
Paradox, **12**
Stubb's BBQ, **6**

Bike Rental: Completely yellow bicycles are free rides—compliments of the city. If used, though, make sure to leave the bike in a conspicuous spot for the next person to use. Most buses have bicycle racks. **Waterloo Cycles,** 2815 Fruth St. (☎472-9253), offers rentals. Open M-W and F-Sa 10am-7pm, Th 10am-8pm, Su noon-5pm. $15 per day, $20 on weekends; fee includes helmet. Lock rental $5. Delivery available.

■* 🔋 ORIENTATION & PRACTICAL INFORMATION

The majority of Austin lies between **Mopac Expwy./Rte. 1** and **I-35,** both running north-south and parallel to one another. UT students inhabit central **Guadalupe St.** (**"The Drag"**), where plentiful music stores and cheap restaurants thrive. The state capitol governs the area a few blocks to the southeast. South of the capitol dome, **Congress Ave.** has upscale eateries and classy shops. The many bars and clubs of **6th St.** hop and clop at night, though some nightlife has moved to the growing **Warehouse District,** around 4th St., west of Congress. Away from the urban gridiron, **Town Lake** offers a haven for the town's joggers, rowers, and cyclists.

Visitor info: Austin Convention and Visitors Bureau/Visitors Information Center, 201 E. 2nd St. (☎478-0098 or 800-926-2282). Open M-F 8:30am-5pm, Sa-Su 9am-5pm.

Medical Services: St. David's Medical Center, 919 E. 32nd St. (☎476-7111). Off I-35, close to downtown. Open 24hr.

Hotlines: Crisis Intervention Hotline, ☎472-4357. **Austin Rape Crisis Center Hotline,** ☎440-7273. Both operate 24hr. **Outyouth Gay/Lesbian Helpline,** ☎800-969-6884; www.outyouth.org. Open W, F, and Su 5:30-9:30pm.

Internet access: Austin Public Library, 800 Guadalupe St. (☎974-7599). Open M-Th 10am-9pm, F-Sa 10am-6pm, Su noon-6pm.

Post Office: 510 Guadalupe (☎800-275-8777 or 494-2210), at 6th St. Open M-F 7am-6:30pm, Sa 8am-3pm. **ZIP code:** 78701. **Area code:** 512.

📍 ACCOMMODATIONS

Chain motels lie along **I-35,** running north and south of Austin. This funkified city, however, is a great place to find cheap options with character. In town, **co-ops** run by college houses at UT peddle rooms and meals to hostelers. Guests have access to all co-op facilities, including fully stocked kitchens. (☎476-5678, though it may be difficult to reach someone over the phone. Reservations recommended. Open May-Aug.) For those interested in camping, only a 10-20min. drive separates Austin and the nearest campgrounds.

📨 **Hostelling International-Austin (HI-AYH),** 2200 S. Lakeshore Blvd. (☎444-2294 or 800-725-2331), about 3 mi. from downtown. From the Greyhound station, take bus #7 "Duval" to Burton, then walk 3 blocks north. From I-35, exit at Riverside, head east, and turn left at Lakeshore Blvd. Beautifully situated, quiet hostel with a 24hr. common room overlooking Town Lake. Features live music by local acts M-Sa. 40 dorm-style beds, single-sex rooms. Rents bikes, kayaks, and canoes ($10 each). Linen provided; no sleeping bags allowed. No curfew. No alcohol. Reception daily 8-11am and 5-10pm; arrivals after 10pm must call ahead to check in. $16, nonmembers $19. ❶

📨 **6th St. Hostel,** 604 6th St. (☎495-9772 or 866-467-8356). Stay here to be where the action is, and leave peace and quiet behind. Advertises "free earplugs (for those who sleep)." Free coffee and tea. Call ahead for free pickup/drop-off from airport, train, or bus station. Small kitchen and game room with pool table. Purchase a hostel wrist band for $5 and get discounts, including free cover at over 20 6th St. hot spots. Linen provided; no sleeping bags allowed. 24hr. reception. Dorms $18, private rooms $63. ❶

Taos Hall, 2612 Guadalupe St. (☎476-5678), at 27th St. The UT co-op where you're most likely to get a private room. Those staying a week or more or drafted into the chore corps. Office open M-F 10am-6pm. Open June-Aug. Three meals and a bed $20. ❶

21st St. Co-op, 707 W. 21st St. (☎476-5678). Take bus #39 on Airport Blvd. to Koenig and Burnet, transfer to the #3 S, and ride to Nueces St.; walk 2 blocks west. Treehouse-style building arrangement and hanging plants have residents calling the co-op the "Ewok Village." A bit grungy, but only from all the fun. Suites with A/C, and common room on each floor. Office open M-F 10am-6pm. $15 per person includes 3 meals and kitchen access. ❶

McKinney Falls State Park, 5808 McKinney Falls Pkwy. (☎243-1643, reservations ☎389-8900), southeast of the city. Turn right on Burleson off Rte. 71 E, then right on McKinney Falls Pkwy. Caters to RV and tent campers. Swimming permitted in the stream; 7 mi. of hiking trails. Open Su-Th 8am-5pm, F 8am-8pm, Sa 8am-7pm. Primitive sites (accessible only by foot) $9; with water and electricity $12. Daily park usage fee $2 per person, under 13 free. ❶

Austin Lonestar RV Resort (☎444-6322 or 800-284-0206), 6 mi. south of the city; Exit 227 off I-35 and continue on the northbound service road. Offers pool, clean bathrooms, game room, laundry facilities, grocery store, and playground. Open 8am-9pm. RV and tent sites with water and electricity $41-43; 3rd night free if on a weekday. 4-person cabins $45; 6-person $56. 10% off with AAA. ❷

◖ FOOD

Scores of fast-food joints line the west side of the UT campus on **Guadalupe St.** Patrons can often enjoy drink specials and free hors d'oeuvres around **6th St.,** south of the capitol, where the battle for happy hour business rages with unique intensity. Although a bit removed from downtown, **Barton Springs Rd.** offers a diverse selection of inexpensive restaurants, including Mexican and Texas-style barbecue joints. The **Warehouse District** has more expensive seafood and Italian eateries. Prepare your own meals from groceries purchased at the **Wheatsville Food Co-op,** 3101 Guadalupe. The only food co-op in Texas, Wheatsville features organic foods and is a community gathering place. (☎478-2667. Open daily 9am-11pm).

▣ **Ruby's BBQ,** 512 W. 29th St. (☎477-1651). Ruby's barbecue is good enough to be served on silver platters, but that just wouldn't seem right in this cow-skulls and butcher-paper establishment. The owners only order meat from farm-raised, grass-fed cows. Scrumptious brisket sandwich $4.25. Open daily 11am-midnight. ❶

▣ **World Beat Cafe,** 600 Martin Luther King Jr. Blvd. (☎236-0197). This eclectic cafe has African specialties such as okra vegetable soup ($5) and yam *fu fu* with *egusi*, as well as terrific burger and fries specials ($2.75) on Tu, Th, and Su. Open M-Sa 11am-9pm, Su noon-7pm. ❶

Madam Mam's, 2514 Guadalupe St. (☎472-8306). This new Thai restaurant serves up a wide variety of innovative soups and noodle dishes. Pad thai $6. Open M-F 11am-9pm, Sa-Su noon-9pm. ❷

The Kerbey Lane Cafe, 3704 Kerbey Ln. (☎451-1436), is an Austin institution. Locations throughout town, including one near UT. For dinner, try their fajitas ($7.25); for breakfast, order their *migas,* a corn tortilla soufflé ($5.25). Open 24 hr. ❷

Magnolia Cafe, 1920 S. Congress Ave. (☎455-0000); another location at 2304 Lake Austin Blvd. (☎478-8645). A colorful, lively place with a variety of healthy, tasty dishes. Try 2 "Tropical Turkey" tacos for $6.50. Open 24hr. ❷

Guero's, 1412 S. Congress Ave. (☎447-7688), across the river from downtown. This wholesome Mexican restaurant is very popular with locals. Lunch specials $6-8. Combo plates $8.50-12.50. Open M-F 11am-11pm, Sa-Su 8am-11pm. ❸

Trudy's Texas Star, 409 W. 30th St. (☎477-2935); another location at 8800 Burnet Rd. (☎454-1474). Fine Tex-Mex dinner entrees ($5.25-8) and a fantastic array of margaritas. Famous *migas* ($5.25). Happy hour all-day M. Open M-Th 2am-midnight, F 7am-2am, Sa 8am-2am, Su 8am-midnight; bar open M-Th 2pm-2am, F-Su noon-2am. ❷

Threadgill's, 301 W. Riverside Dr. (☎472-9304); another location at 6416 N. Lamar Blvd. (☎451-5440). A legend in Austin since 1933, Threadgill's serves up terrific Southern soul food, such as fried chicken ($8), among creaky wooden floors, slow-moving ceiling fans, and antique beer signs. Surprisingly large variety of vegetarian and non-dairy options. Live music Th at 7pm. Open M-Sa 11am-10pm, Su 10am-9:30pm. ❷

Scholz Garten, 1607 San Jacinto Blvd. (☎474-1958), near the capitol. UT students and state politicians alike gather at this Austin landmark, recognized by the legislature for "epitomizing the finest traditions of the German heritage of our state." Popular chicken-fried steak dinners ($7.30) and sausage and bratwurst po' boys ($5.30). Open M-W 11am-10pm, Th-Sa 11am-11pm. ❷

Casa De Luz, 1701 Toomey Rd. (☎476-2535). Those familiar with macrobiotic cooking (essentially vegetarian) will enjoy the lovingly prepared meals served in a tranquil, communal setting. Lovers of furry, fishy, or feathered fare might find themselves asking "Where's the beef?" Most meals $9. Brunch $11. Open M-F 11:30am-2pm and 6-8pm; brunch Sa-Su 11:30am-2pm. ❸

🅖 SIGHTS

GOVERNMENT. Not to be outdone, Texans built their **state capitol,** 7 ft. higher than the national one. *(At Congress Ave. and 11th St. ☎463-0063. Open M-F 7am-10pm, Sa-Su 9am-8pm. 45min. tours every 15min. Free.)* The **Capitol Visitors Center** is located in the southeast corner of the capitol grounds. *(112 E. 11th St. ☎305-8400. Open daily 9am-5pm. Parking: 12th and San Jacinto St. 2hr. garage.)* Near the capitol, **Governor's Mansion** is open for tours. *(1010 Colorado St. ☎463-5516. Free tours M-F every 20min. 10-11:40am.)* The **Austin Convention and Visitors Bureau** sponsors free walking tours of the area from March to November. *(☎454-1545. Tours Th-F 9am; Sa-Su 9, 11am, and 2pm. Tour starts at the capitol steps.)*

MUSEUMS. The first floor of the **Lyndon B. Johnson Library and Museum** focuses on Texas-native LBJ and the history of the American presidency, while the 8th floor features a model of the Oval Office. *(2313 Red River St. Take bus #20. ☎916-5137. Open daily 9am-5pm. Free.)* If you've ever wondered about "The Story of Texas," the **Bob Bullock Texas State History Museum** is waiting to tell it to you in three floors of exhibits and two IMAX theaters. The museum traces the history of the state from its Native American legacy and Spanish colonization to statehood and the 20th century oil boom. *(1800 N. Congress Ave. ☎936-8746. Open M-Sa 9am-6pm, Su 1-6pm. Exhibits $5, seniors $4.25, under 19 free; IMAX $6.50, seniors $5.50, under 19 $4.50; cheaper combination tickets available.)*

The downtown **Austin Museum of Art** features American and European masters and an Asian collection. *(At the corner of Congress Ave. and 8th St. ☎458-8191. Grounds open Tu-Sa 10am-5pm, Su noon-5pm. Free.)* A second branch, at 3809 W. 35th St., is housed in a Mediterranean-style villa in a beautiful country setting. The **Mexic-Arte Museum** features a permanent collection of Mexican masks and photos, as well as revolving exhibits. *(419 S. Congress Ave. ☎480-9373. Open M-Sa 10am-6pm.)*

WHERE HAVE ALL THE HIPPIES GONE? About

15 mi. northeast of downtown Austin lies **Hippie Hollow**. Free spirits go *au naturel* in the waters of the lovely Lake Travis in Texas's only public nude swimming and sunbathing haven. Take Mopac (Rte. 1) north to the exit for F.M. 2222. Follow 2222 west and turn left at the I-620 intersection; Comanche Rd. will be on your right. *(7000 Comanche Trail. ☎ 473-9437. 18+ only. Open daily 8am-9pm, no entry after 8:30pm. $5 per car, pedestrians $2.)*

PARKS. Mt. Bonnell Park offers a sweeping view of Lake Austin and Westlake Hills from the highest point in the city. *(3800 Mt. Bonnell Rd., off W. 35th St.)* On hot afternoons, Austinites come in droves to riverside **Zilker Park,** just south of the Colorado River. *(2201 Barton Springs Rd. Take bus #30. ☎ 477-7273. Open daily 5am-10pm. Free.)* Flanked by walnut and pecan trees, **Barton Springs Pool,** a spring-fed swimming hole in the park, stretches 1000 ft. long and 200 ft. wide. The pool's temperature hovers around 68°F. *(☎ 499-6710. Pool open M-W and F-Su 5am-10pm, Th 5-9am and 7-10pm. M-F $2.50, Sa-Su $2.75; ages 12-17 $1, under 12 50¢. Free daily 5-8am and 9-10pm.)* The **Barton Springs Greenbelt** offers challenging hiking and biking trails.

OTHER SIGHTS. The **University of Texas at Austin (UT)** is both the wealthiest public university in the country, with an annual budget of almost a billion dollars, and America's largest, with over 50,000 students. UT forms the backbone of city cultural life. Just before dusk, head underneath the south side of the **Congress Ave. Bridge,** near the Austin American-Statesman parking lot, and watch the massive swarm of ■**Mexican free-tail bats** emerge from their roosts to feed on the night's mosquitoes. When the bridge was reconstructed in 1980, the engineers unintentionally created crevices which formed ideal homes for the migrating bat colony. The city began exterminating the night-flying creatures until **Bat Conservation International** moved to Austin to educate people about the bats' harmless behavior and the benefits of their presence—the bats eat up to 3000 lbs. of insects each night. Today, the bats are among the biggest tourist attractions in Austin. The colony, seen from mid-March to November, peaks in July, when a fresh crop of pups increases the population to around 1.5 million. *(For flight times, call the bat hotline ☎ 416-5700, ext. 3636; Commissioner Gordon mans the bat signal, ext. POW!)*

🎵 📷 ENTERTAINMENT & NIGHTLIFE

Beverly Sheffield Zilker Hillside Theater (☎ 397-1463 for events schedule), across from the Barton Springs pool, hosts free outdoor bands, ballets, plays, musicals, and symphony concerts every weekend from May to October. In mid-March, the **South by Southwest Music, Media, and Film Festival** draws entertainment industry's giants and thousands of eager fans (☎ 467-7979). The Austin Arts Guild sponsors an **arts and crafts festival** the first week of April (☎ 494-9224, ext. 300 for info). Austin's smaller events calendar is a mixed bag. The **Spamarama,** in early April, gathers Spam fans from all walks of life pay homage to...this, er, product...with food, sports, and live music at the **Spam Jam.**

Austin has replaced Seattle as the nation's underground music hot spot, so keep an eye out for rising indie stars, as well as old blues, folk, country, and rock favorites. On weekends, nighttime swingers seek out dancing on **6th St.,** an area bespeckled with warehouse nightclubs and fancy bars. More mellow, cigar-smoking night owls gather at the **4th St. Warehouse District.** Still another area for night-life in Austin is along **Red River St.**, with a series of bars and clubs that have all of the grit of 6th St., but less of the glamour. A more low-key alternative to the bars and clubs is the Austin coffeehouse scene. The weekly *Austin Chronicle* and *XL-ent* provide details on current music performances, shows, and movies. The *Gay Yellow Pages* is free at stands along Guadalupe St.

■ **Mojo's Daily Grind,** 2714 Guadalupe St. (☎477-6656), is simply "the hub of subculture in Austin." DJs spin music Th-Sa nights. Open 24hr.

■ **Antone's,** 213 W. 5th St. (☎474-5314). This blues paradise has attracted the likes of B.B. King and Muddy Waters and was the starting point for Stevie Ray Vaughn. All ages. Shows at 10pm. Cover $5-25. Open daily 9pm-2am.

■ **Mercury Entertainment @ Jazz,** 214 E. 6th St. (☎478-6372). Represents the new side of Austin that has moved away from the usual country music and classic rock and caters to hip twenty-somethings looking for the latest in jazz, funk, and hip-hop. Cover ages 18-20 $9 and up, 21+ $6 and up. Open daily 9:30pm-2am.

Spider House, 2908 Froth St. (☎480-9562), just off Guadalupe St. Large booths in a dark interior along with patio seating. Open daily 8am-2am.

Stubb's BBQ, 801 Red River St. (☎480-8341). Don't miss Stubb's fabulous (but pricey) Sunday gospel brunch—all-you-can-eat buffet plus live gospel for $15 (reservations recommended, sittings at 11am and 1pm). Otherwise, the 18+ club downstairs hosts nightly acts. Swing by earlier for some scrumptious, inexpensive grub like beef brisket with 2 side dishes for $7.25. All ages welcome for amphitheater shows. Cover $5-25. Shows at 10:30pm. Open Tu-W 11am-10pm, Th-Sa 11am-11pm, Su 11am-9pm; nightclub open Tu-Sa 11am-2am.

Oilcan Harry's, 211 W. 4th St. (☎320-8823). One of the biggest and best gay bars in Austin. Tu and Su strip shows 10:30pm-1:30am. 21+. M-Tu and Th-Su no cover; W cover ages 18-20 $12, 21+ $7. Open Su-Th 2pm-2am, F-Sa 8pm-4am.

Copper Tank Brewing Company, 504 Trinity St. (☎478-8444). Probably the city's best microbrewery, its namesake copper tanks dispense beers right behind the bar. W $1 beers, Th $1 any drink, F $2 any drink. 21+. Open Tu-F 5pm-2am, Sa 8pm-2am.

Hole in the Wall, 2538 Guadalupe St. (☎472-5599), at 26th St. Its self-effacing name belies the popularity of this renowned music spot, which features a mix of punk/alternative and country-western bands. Music nightly. 21+. Su-M no cover, Tu-Sa $3-5. Open M-F 11am-2am, Sa-Su noon-2am.

Cactus Cafe, at 24th and Guadalupe St. (☎475-6515), in the Texas Union. Features adventurous acoustic music every night. Specializing in folk-rock and Austin's own "New Country" sound, the Cactus gave Lyle Lovett his start. No smoking permitted. All ages welcome. Cover $2-15. Music starts 9pm. Open M-F 8pm-1am, Sa 8pm-2am.

Joe's Generic Bar, 315 E. 6th St. (☎480-0171). Find your way here for some raunchy Texas-style blues that are anything but generic. 21+. No cover. Open daily 7pm-2am.

Broken Spoke, 3201 S. Lamar Blvd. (☎442-6189). For some honky-tonk, good old-fashioned country twang, put on your spiffiest Western dress and make tracks for the Broken Spoke. The restaurant serves the world's best chicken-fried steak dinner for $8.25. All ages. Cover $5-8. Music starts nightly at 8pm, closing time varies. Open Su-Th 11am-10:30pm, F-Sa 11am-11:30pm.

Paradox, 311 E. 5th St. (☎469-7615), at Trinity St. In a city hurting for dance clubs, this 12,000 sq. ft. warehouse-style dance club plays alternative, hip-hop, and high energy dance music. Cover $5-10. Open W-Su 9pm-4am.

DALLAS

☎214

Despite being the nation's largest inland city, Dallas is still overlooked by many travelers. Though its image is one of oilers and cowboys, Dallas has quietly become a cosmopolitan center, housing one of the finest Asian art museums in the country and more restaurants per capita than any other city in the U.S.—four times that of New York. The mix of oil and conservative politics is part of the intrigue surrounding the assassination of President Kennedy, whose death haunts the city to this day. But beyond this dark legacy lies a vibrant city waiting to be discovered.

▐ TRANSPORTATION

Airport: Dallas-Ft. Worth International (☎972-574-8888), 17 mi. northwest of downtown; take bus #202 ($2). For door-to-gate service, take the **Super Shuttle,** 729 E. Dallas Rd. (☎800-258-3826). 24hr. service. 1st passenger $16; each additional passenger $6. Taxi to downtown $38.

Trains: Amtrak, 400 S. Houston St. (☎653-1101), in Union Station. Open daily 9am-6:30pm. To: **Los Angeles** (42hr., 4 per week, $138); **Austin** (6½hr., 1 per day, $22); and **Little Rock** (7½hr., 1 per day, $53).

Buses: Greyhound, 205 S. Lamar St. (☎655-7727), 3 blocks east of Union Station. Open 24hr. To: **New Orleans** (13hr., 11 per day, $78); **Houston** (4hr., 11 per day, $34); and **Austin** (4hr., 15 per day, $28).

Public Transit: Dallas Area Rapid Transit (DART), 1401 Pacific Ave. (☎979-1111). Open M-F 5am-10pm, Sa-Su 8am-6pm. Buses radiate from 2 downtown transfer centers, East and West, and serve most suburbs. Darts daily 5:30am-9:30pm, to suburbs 5:30am-8pm. Fare $1, suburban park-and-ride stops $2; transfers free. Maps at Elm and Ervay St. office (open M-F 7am-6pm). **DART Light Rail** runs north-south through downtown. Operates daily 5:30am-12:30am. Fare $1.

Taxis: Yellow Cab Co., ☎426-6262 or 800-749-9422.

✴❼ ORIENTATION & PRACTICAL INFORMATION

Most of Dallas lies within the **I-635** loop, which is bisected north-south by **I-35 E (Stemmons Fwy.)** and **U.S. 75 (Central Expwy.)** and east-west by **I-30.** The suburbs stretch along the northern reaches of Central Expwy. and the **Dallas North Toll Rd.,** northwest of downtown. Many of downtown Dallas's shops and restaurants lie underground in a maze of tunnels accessible from any major office building. Navigating the freeways can be confusing, and parking in downtown Dallas is a pain—many parking meters are in effect until 10pm every day of the week. If parking for more than an hour, relatively cheap lots can be found along **Ross Ave.**

Visitor Info: Dallas Convention and Visitors Bureau, 100 S. Houston St. (☎571-1000, 24hr. events hotline ☎571-1301), at Main St., in the Old Red Courthouse. Open M-F 8am-5pm, Sa-Su 9am-5pm.

Hotlines: Suicide and Crisis Center, ☎828-1000. **Contact Counseling,** ☎972-233-2233, for general counseling. Both operate 24hr.

Dallas Gay and Lesbian Community Center: 2701 Reagan St. (☎528-9254).

Internet access: Dallas Public Library, 1515 Young St. at Ervay St. (☎670-1400). Open M-Th 9am-9pm, F-Sa 9am-5pm, Su 1-5pm. Be careful around this area at night.

Post Office: 401 Dallas-Ft. Worth Tpk. (☎760-4526). Take Sylvan exit. Open daily 24hr. **Downtown branch** is located in the Federal Building on Main St. Open M-F 9am-5pm. **General Delivery** is at 1500 Dragon St. Go north on Lamar St., which turns into Continental; take the first right after I-35. Open M-F 9am-12pm. **ZIP code:** 75201; for General Delivery 75221. **Area codes:** 214, 817, and 972. In text, 214 unless otherwise noted.

TEXAS

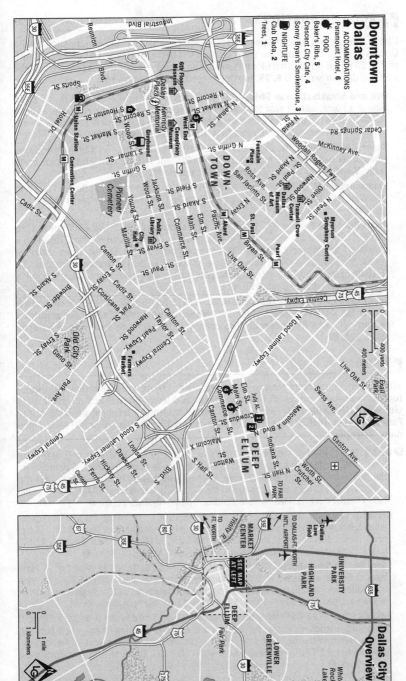

Downtown Dallas

➤ ACCOMMODATIONS
Paramount Hotel, 6

☞ FOOD
Baker's Ribs, 5
Crescent City Cafe, 4
Sonny Bryan's Smokehouse, 3

🎵 NIGHTLIFE
Club Dada, 2
Trees, 1

(Downtown Dallas map labels) 6th Floor Museum, Dealey Plaza, Kennedy Memorial, West End, Conspiracy Museum, Greyhound, Pioneer Cemetery, City Hall, Public Library, Farmers Market, Old City Park, Fountain Place, Ross Ave., San Jacinto St., Dallas Museum of Art, Trammell Crow, Myerson Symphony Center, DEEP ELLUM, Crowdus St.

Streets: Industrial Blvd., Reunion Blvd., Sports St., Hotel Dr., Union Station, Convention Center, N Record St., N Houston St., S Market St., S Wood St., S Lamar St., S Griffin St., Jackson St., Wood St., Field St., Akard St., Main St., Elm St., Commerce St., Pacific Ave., St. Paul St., Bryan St., Live Oak St., N Market St., N Lamar St., N Griffin St., DOWNTOWN, Harwood St., Olive St., N Pearl St., N St. Paul St., N Akard St., N Field St., Woodall Rodgers Fwy., McKinney Ave., Cedar Springs Rd., Cadiz St., Canton St., Young St., Marilla St., Ervay St., St. Paul St., Cadiz St., S Ervay St., S Corsicana St., Park St., Taylor St., Harwood St., Central Expwy., Browder St., S Marid St., S Ervay St., Gano St., Park Ave., Central Expwy., Canton St., S Good Latimer Expwy., Louise St., Hickory St., Dawson St., Ferris St., Corinth St., S Hall St., Walton St., Malcolm X Blvd., Indiana St., N Hall St., Swiss Ave., Gaston Ave., Crutcher St., Worth St., Elm St., Main St., Commerce St., Malcolm X Blvd., July Al., N Good Latimer Expwy., Live Oak St., Exall Park, TO FAIR PARK

Scale: 0 — 400 yards / 0 — 400 meters

Dallas City Overview

Map labels: MARKET CENTER, TO FT. WORTH, Trinity R., TO DALLAS–FT. WORTH INTL. AIRPORT, Dallas Love Field, UNIVERSITY PARK, HIGHLAND PARK, DEEP ELLUM, Fair Park, LOWER GREENVILLE, White Rock Lake, SEE MAP AT LEFT

Highways: 30, 67, 35E, 80, 635, 75, 45, 175, 35E

Scale: 0 — 1 mile / 0 — 1 kilometers

ACCOMMODATIONS

Cheap lodging in Dallas is nearly impossible to come by; big events such as the Cotton Bowl (Jan. 1) and the state fair in October exacerbate the problem. Look within 10 mi. of downtown along three of the major roads for inexpensive motels: north of downtown on **U.S. 75,** north along **I-35,** and east on **I-30.**

Bed and Breakfast Texas Style, 4224 W. Red Bird Ln. (☎972-298-8586), will place you in a home, usually near town, with friendly residents anxious to make y'all as comfortable as possible. It's an especially good deal for two people. Call a few days ahead. Open M-F 8:30am-4:30pm. Singles from $55; doubles from $65. ❸

Super 7 Motel Mesquite, 3629 U.S. 80 E (☎972-613-9989), lies 15min. from downtown; after bearing right onto U.S. 80 from I-30, exit at Town East Blvd. Rooms come with TV and free local calls. Singles $30.50; doubles $35. ❶

Paramount Hotel, 302 S. Houston St. (☎761-9090), downtown near Dealey Plaza and the West End, stands 2½ blocks from the Light Rail and CBD West transfer center. Singles $69; doubles $79. ❸

Cedar Hill State Park (☎972-291-3900, for reservations ☎512-389-8900), near Lake Joe Pool 20-30min. southwest of the city, provides 355 tent and RV sites. Take I-35 E to Rte. 67 and turn right onto FM 1382; the park is on the left. Swimming area, marina, jet-ski rental, and 3 walking trails. Reserve at least 2 weeks in advance. Office open M-F 10am-5pm, Sa-Su 10am-10pm; 24hr. gate access with reservations. Sites $15, primitive $7; each additional adult $5. ❶

Sandy Lake RV Park, 1915 Sandy Lake Rd. (☎972-242-6808). Take I-35 E north of the city to Exit 444, then go left under the highway about a mile. Sandy Lake provides a worthy option for RV campers. Office open M-F 8am-8pm, Sa 8am-7pm, Su 1-6pm. Sites $25. ❶

FOOD

While many restaurants tend to be rather pricey, there are a few that offer great food at reasonable prices. For the lowdown on dining options, pick up the "Friday Guide" of the *Dallas Morning News.* Stock up on the freshest produce at the **Farmers Market,** 1010 S. Pearl, next to International Marketplace. (☎939-2808. Open daily 7am-6pm.)

EatZi's, 3403 Oaklawn Ave. (☎526-1515), at Lemmon Ave., 1 mi. east of Oaklawn exit from I-35E, north of downtown. Take the #2 or 51 bus from downtown. A paradise for the frugal gourmet, this grocery, cafe, kitchen, and bakery forms a culinary delight. Sounds of Vivaldi surround heapings of focaccia ($3), sandwiches ($4-7), and a multitude of other delights. Free sample platters. Open daily 7am-10pm. ❶

Crescent City Cafe, 2615 Commerce St. (☎745-1900). One of the city's most popular lunch spots, the cafe serves up New Orleans cooking in the heart of Deep Ellum. 3 *beignets* (rumored to be better than those of the Cafe du Monde in New Orleans) $1.50. Half a *muffaletta* (an Italian sandwich) $6.25. Open M-Sa 8am-3pm. ❷

Sonny Bryan's Smokehouse, 302 N. Market St. (☎744-1610), in the West End. A landmark of Dallas, although a little more commercialized than the average BBQ joint. Try a beef sandwich ($4.25) or combine 3 smokehouse delicacies ($13). Vegetarian options available. Open M-Th 11am-10pm, F-Sa 11am-11pm, Su noon-9pm. ❸

Baker's Ribs, 2724 Commerce St. (☎748-5433), east of downtown in Deep Ellum. If good BBQ is what you're craving, Baker's is the answer—serving hearty meals between walls covered in banjos, washpans, cowboy pictures, and other pieces of Texan glory. Sandwiches $3.75. Combination plates $7.25-9.50. Open M-Th 11am-7pm, F-Su 11am-9pm. ❷

◎ SIGHTS

Oil-flushed Dallas is packed with showy displays of 20th-century architecture and sculpture. Located in the heart of downtown, "historic Dallas" can easily be seen on a walking tour. Dallas, however, is more notorious for its recent history—JFK's assassination during a campaign parade in 1963 is permanently preserved in various museums and landmarks.

JFK SIGHTS. At the **6th Floor Museum,** stand on the sixth floor and look out the window through which Lee Harvey Oswald allegedly fired the shot that killed President John F. Kennedy on Nov. 22, 1963. Nowadays this fascinating museum is devoted to the Kennedy legacy, tracing the dramatic and macabre moments of the assassination through various media. *(411 Elm St., at Houston St., in the former Texas School Book Depository building. ☎747-6660. Open daily 9am-6pm. $10; seniors, students, and ages 6-18 $9. Audio cassette rental $3.)* To the south of the depository, Elm St. runs through **Dealy Plaza,** a national landmark beside the infamous grassy knoll. Philip Johnson's **Memorial** to Kennedy looms nearby at Market and Main. The cenotaph (open tomb), a symbol of the freedom of JFK's spirit, is most striking when viewed at night. The **Conspiracy Museum** unravels the shadowy conspiracies behind the assassinations of four U.S. presidents and Martin Luther King Jr. Their conspiracy collection includes the Zapruder film that captured JFK's killing. *(110 Market St., across the street from the Memorial. ☎741-3040. Open daily 10am-6pm. $7, students and seniors $6, children $3.)*

ART & ARCHITECTURE. The architecture of the **Dallas Museum of Art** is as graceful and beautiful as its impressive collections of Egyptian, African, Early American, Impressionist, modern, and decorative art. *(1717 N. Harwood St. ☎922-1200. Open Tu-W and F 11am-5pm, Th 11am-9pm, Sa-Su 11am-5pm. Free. Special exhibits $5-8. Parking $2 first hr., $1 each additional hr.)* Directly across Harwood St., the ◙**Trammel Crow Center** has a must-see collection of Asian art, and its beautiful sculpture garden has works by Rodin, Maillol, and Bourdelle. *(2010 Flora St., at Hardwood and Olive St. ☎979-6430. Open Tu-W and F-Su 11am-6pm, Th 11am-9pm. Free.)* The ubiquitous **I.M. Pei** designed many downtown Dallas buildings. One of his creations, the spectacular **Fountain Place** at the Wells Fargo Bldg., is on Ross St. just past Field St. The **Morton H. Meyerson Symphony Center,** 2301 Flora St., a few blocks east, and the imposing **Dallas City Hall** were also designed by Pei. Free tours of the Symphony Center are sometimes available. *(100 Marilla St., off Young St. ☎670-3600. Tours on selected M, W, and F-Sa 1pm.)*

ATTRACTIONS. At the **Dallas World Aquarium** admission is steep, but the multilevel rainforest exhibit with caged bats, swimming penguins, sleepy crocodiles, and wildly flying birds make this aquarium worth the plunge. *(1801 N. Griffin St. Northeast of the West End, 1 block north of Ross Ave. ☎720-2224. Open daily 10am-5pm. $11.85, seniors and children $6.50.)* Resplendent flowers and trees fill the 66-acre **Dallas Arboretum.** On the east shore of White Rock Lake, the arboretum also provides a haven for walkers, bikers, and in-line skaters. *(8617 Garland Rd. Take bus #19 from downtown. ☎327-8263. Open June-Aug. M-Th 10am-9pm, F-Su 10am-5pm; Sept.-May. daily 10am-5pm. $6, seniors $5, ages 6-12 $3. Parking $3.)*

FAIR PARK. Home to the state fair since 1886, **Fair Park** earned national landmark status for its Art Deco architecture. During the fair, **Big Tex**—a 52 ft. smiling cowboy float—towers over the land, and only the **Texas Star,** a huge ferris wheel, looms taller. The 277-acre park also hosts the **Cotton Bowl** on January 1. In association with the Smithsonian Institute, **The Woman's Museum: An Institute for the Future** features a timeline of US women's history from 1500 to the present along with exhibits on famous American women. *(3800 Parry Ave. ☎915-0860. Open Tu-Sa 10am-5pm, Su noon-5pm. $5, seniors and ages 13-18 $4, ages 5-12 $3.)*

HISTORIC DALLAS. Thirty-five late 19th-century buildings around Dallas (including a dentist's office, a bank, and a farmstead that still raises animals) have been restored and moved to **Old City Park,** the city's oldest and most popular recreation and lunch spot. *(1717 Gano St., 9 blocks south of City Hall at Ervay St. ☎421-5141. Open daily 9am-6pm. Exhibit buildings open Tu-Sa 10am-4pm, Su noon-4pm. $7, seniors $5, children $3.)* The **West End Historic District and Marketplace,** full of broad sidewalks, shops, and restaurants, lies north of Union Station. *(Most stores open M-Sa 11am-10pm, Su noon-6pm.)* Dallas's **mansions** are in the **Swiss Avenue Historic District** and along the streets of the **Highland Park** area, between Preston Rd. and Hillcrest Ave. south of Mockingbird Ln.

🎵 ENTERTAINMENT

The Observer, a free weekly found in stands across the city, has unrivaled entertainment coverage. For the scoop on Dallas's **gay scene,** pick up copies of the *Dallas Voice* and *Texas Triangle* in **Oak Lawn** shops and restaurants.

Prospero works his magic at the **Shakespeare in the Park** festival, at Samuel-Grand Park just northeast of Fair Park. During June and July (no performances the last week of June), two free plays run six nights per week. (☎559-2778. Performances Tu-Su 8:15pm. Gates open 7:30; arrive early. $4 optional donation.) At Fair Park, the **Music Hall** showcases **Dallas Summer Musicals.** (☎421-0662, 373-8000 for tickets; 696-4253 for half-price tickets on show days. Shows run June-Oct. $9-70.) The **Dallas Symphony Orchestra** plays in the Symphony Center, at Pearl and Flora St. in the arts district. (☎692-0203. Sept.-May. Box office open M-F 10am-6pm. $12-87.) In the summer, free outdoor jazz concerts are held every Thursday night at 9pm in front of the Museum of Art.

If you come to Dallas looking for cowboys, the **Mesquite Championship Rodeo,** 1818 Rodeo Dr., is the place to find them. Take I-30 east to I-635 S to Exit 4 and stay on the service road. Nationally televised, the rodeo is one of the most competitive in the country. (☎972-285-8777 or 800-833-9339. Shows Apr. to early Oct. F-Sa 8pm. Gates open at 6:30pm. $10, seniors $5, children 3-12 $5. Dinner $9.50, children $6.50. Parking $3.)

Six Flags Over Texas, 20 mi. from downtown off I-30 at Rte. 360 in Arlington, between Dallas and Fort Worth, boasts 38 rides, including the speedy, looping roller coasters "Batman: The Ride" and "Mr. Freeze." (☎817-640-8900. Open June to early Aug. daily from 10am; late Aug.-Dec. and Mar.-May Sa-Su from 10am. Park sometimes opens at 11am and closing times vary from 7-10pm. $40, over 55 or under 4 ft. $25. Parking $9.) Across the highway lies the mammoth 47-acre waterpark, **Hurricane Harbor.** Shoot down superspeed water flumes or experience simulated seasickness in the one million gallon wave pool. (☎817-265-3356. Open late May to mid-Aug. daily 10:30am-8pm. $28, over 55 and under 4 ft. $18, parking $7.) Find coupons for both parks on soda cans and at Dallas or Ft. Worth tourist information offices.

In Dallas, the moral order is God, country, and the **Cowboys.** Football fanatics flock to **Cowboys Stadium** at the junction of Rte. 12 and Rte. 183, west of Dallas in Irving. (☎972-785-5000. Sept.-Jan. Ticket office open M-F 9am-5pm. From $36.) **The Ballpark in Arlington,** 1000 Ballpark Way, plays host to the **Texas Rangers.** (☎817-273-5100. Apr.-Sept. Ticket office open M-F 9am-6pm, Sa 10am-4pm, Su noon-4pm. $4-30.) Experience the mystique of the game with a 1 hr. tour of the locker room, dugout, and the press box on the **ballpark tour.** (☎817-273-5098. Non-game days tours M-Sa 9am-4pm, Su noon-4pm every hr.; hours vary for game days. $5, students and seniors $4, ages 4-18 $3.)

■ NIGHTLIFE

For nightlife, head to **Deep Ellum,** east of downtown. In the 1920s, the area was a blues haven for legends Blind Lemon Jefferson, Lightnin' Hopkins, and Robert Johnson; in the 1980s, Bohemians revitalized the area. The first Friday of every month is **Deep Friday,** when a $7 wrist band gets you into 9 Deep Ellum clubs featuring local rock acts. Other nightlife epicenters include **Lower Greenville Ave.; Yale Blvd.,** near Southern Methodist University's fraternity row; and **Dallas Alley** (☎ 720-0170; $3-6), an amalgam of seven differently themed clubs located in the touristy **West End.** Many gay clubs rock just a bit north of downtown in **Oak Lawn.**

Trees, 2709 Elm St. (☎ 748-5009), rated the best live music venue in the city by the *Dallas Morning News,* occupies a converted warehouse with a loft full of pool tables and tree trunks in the middle of the club. Bands tend to play alternative rock music. 17+. Cover $2-10. Open W-Sa 9pm-2am.

Club Dada, 2720 Elm St. (☎ 744-3232). A former haunt of Edie Brickell and the New Bohemians, this hoppin' club boasts an eclectic clientele. Live local acts and a recently added outdoor patio add to the fun. 21+. Cover W-Sa $3-5. Open W-Th 7pm-2am, F-Sa 5pm-2am, Su 8pm-2am.

Poor David's Pub, 1924 Greenville Ave. (☎ 821-9891), stages live music ranging from Irish folk tunes to reggae. Tickets available after 6pm at the door; cash only. Cover $1-20. Open Tu-Sa 7pm-2am; closed nights when no performance is scheduled.

Green Elephant, 5612 Yale Blvd. (☎ 750-6625). Full of pseudo-1960s psychedelica, the Green Elephant is the watering hole of choice near SMU. Open M-Sa 11am-2am, Su 6pm-2am.

Roundup, 3912 Cedar Springs Rd. (☎ 522-9611), at Throckmorton St. A huge, cover-free country-western bar that packs a large, mixed crowd on weekends. Free dance lessons Th 8:30pm. Open Tu-Th 3pm-2am, F–Sa noon-2am.

FORT WORTH   ☎817

If Dallas is the last Eastern city, Fort Worth is undoubtedly the first Western one. Dallas's less famous neighbor lies less than 40min. west on I-30, providing a worthwhile daytrip and some raw Texan entertainment. Fort Worth is divided into three districts, each marked by red brick streets: the **Stockyards Historic District, Sundance Square,** and the **Cultural District.**

The Stockyards Historic District, located along East Exchange Ave., 10min. north of downtown on Main St., attracts a throng of felt-hat and leather-boot hipsters. A walk along Exchange Ave., the main drag, provides a window into the Wild West, offering a slew of saloons, restaurants, shows, and gambling parlors. There is a **cattle drive** down Exchange Ave. daily at 11:30am and 4pm. With live country music every night, brass footrails, and a prodigious collection of cowboy hats, the **White Elephant Saloon,** 106 Exchange Ave., is a local favorite. (☎ 624-1887. Cover F-Sa $8. Open Su-Th noon-midnight, F-Sa noon-2am.)

Just down the road at 121 Exchange Ave., the **Cowtown Coliseum** (☎ 625-1025 or 888-269-8696) hosts two weekly events: **rodeos** (F and Sa 8pm; $8.50, seniors $7, children $5) and **Pawnee Bill's Wild West Show,** complete with sharp-shooting, trick-roping, and a bullwhip act every Saturday and Sunday at 2:30 and 4:30pm. ($7.50, seniors $6, ages 3-12 $4.) To uncover the mystery of cattle raising, visit the **Cattle Raisers Museum,** 1301 7th St., between the Stockyards and Cultural Districts. (☎ 332-8551. Open M-Sa 10am-5pm, Su 1-5pm. $3, seniors and 13-18 $2, 4-12 $1.)

TEXAS

IN RECENT NEWS

WISHIN' FOR DEMOLITION

Fort Worth could have the world's largest eyesore. A tornado ripped through downtown on March 28th, 2000, and devastated the 37-story **Bank One Tower**. Engineers determined that the building had to be torn down. Because the owners did not have enough money to do so, it could not be razed until sold to another investor, who planned to tear it down and turn it into a parking lot. The high-rise would have become one of the tallest buildings ever to be imploded. However, city officials then discovered that the tower was full of asbestos and could not be razed without spreading the dangerous substance throughout the area. Currently, city officials and the owners are working out an arrangement to clean out the building and either tear it down or convert it to be used for something else. Meanwhile, until its fate is determined, the condemned building still stands empty, with cardboard covering the outside where the windows were blown out. Everyone in town considers it an eyesore, but no one quite knows what to do with it. Some people are already saying that the best solution is probably for another tornado to come along, one that will finish the job this time.

In mid-June, the **Chisholm Trail Round-Up** (☎ 624-4741), a three-day jamboree in the Stockyards, preserves the heritage of the cowhands who led cattle drives to Kansas 150 years ago. The **Armadillo Races** are a Round-Up must-see; children and visitors are allowed to try their hand at making the critters move. For more on the stockyards, pick up a copy of the *Stockyards Gazette* at the **Visitors Center**, 130 E. Exchange Ave.

The world's largest honky-tonk, **Billy Bob's Texas**, 2520 Rodeo Plaza, ropes in the crowds for some night clubbing with big names in country music. The 100,000 sq. ft. of floor space includes a restaurant, pool tables, and 42 bar stations. (☎ 624-7117. Free dance lessons Th 7pm. Professional bull-riding F-Sa 9 and 10pm. Under 18 must be accompanied by parent. Cover before 6pm $1; after 6pm Su-M $3, Tu-Th $4, F-Sa $6.50-11, depending on performers. Open M-Sa 11am-2am, Su noon-2am.)

Downtown, Sundance Sq., a pedestrian-friendly area, offers quality shops, museums, and restaurants. Parking is free in lots and garages on weekends and after 5pm on weekdays. In the square, the **Sid Richardson Collection**, 309 Main St., displays an impressive 55 paintings by Western artists Remington and Russell. (☎ 332-6554. Open Tu-W 10am-5pm, Th-F 10am-8pm, Sa 11am-8pm, Su 1-5pm. Free.)

A few minutes west of downtown along 7th St., the Cultural District offers an array of intimate collections and exhibitions. The **Kimbell Museum**, 3333 Camp Bowie Blvd., touted as "America's best small museum," displays masterpieces from Caravaggio to Cézanne. (☎ 332-8451. Open Tu-Th and Sa 10am-5pm, F noon-8pm, Su noon-5pm. Free; special exhibits $10, students and seniors $8, ages 3-18 $6.) To see the newest art in the oldest art museum in Texas, visit the **Modern Art Museum**, 1309 Montgomery St., near the Kimbell. (☎ 738-9215. Open Tu-F 10am-5pm, Sa 11am-5pm, Su noon-5pm. Free.) **Ft. Worth Visitor's Bureau:** ☎ 336-8791. **Zip code:** 76102. **Area code:** 817.

HOUSTON ☎ 713

Though often overshadowed by its more famous counterparts, Houston has quietly become America's fourth-largest city, creating a cosmopolitan atmosphere with distinctive Texan style. From its birth in 1836, when New York brothers Augustus and John Allen came slicing through the weeds of the Buffalo Bayou to market America's next great shipping port, Houston has been a city fueled by commerce. Today, that fuel is oil, and the headquarters of energy conglomerates dominate the impressive skyline. Beyond the glass-and-steel skyscrapers lies a city with a surprising array of world-class restaurants, museums,

SNAKE, RATTLE, & ROLL Charming Sweetwater, about 40 miles west of Abilene, is most famous for its **Rattlesnake Round-Up,** held every second weekend in March (March 7-9, 2003). Begun in 1958 as a modest effort by farmers and ranchers to get rid of the rattlesnakes that were plaguing them and their livestock, the "world's largest" Rattlesnake Round-Up has become an international phenomenon, doubling the population of this sleepy town every spring. Since its inception, over 250,000 pounds of rattlesnakes have been killed. The 30,000 annual visitors enjoy a weekend full of events, ranging from snake milking lessons to a cook-off (and a rattlesnake meat eating contest) to the Miss Snake Charmer beauty pageant. *For this year's schedule of events, contact the Chamber of Commerce. 810 E. Broadway. ☎915-235-5488 or 800-658-6757; www.rattlesnakeroundup.com. Open M-F 8:30am-5pm.*

and performing arts companies. New sports arenas, a recently-built $88 million performing arts center, and a light rail system (set to be completed in 2004) supplement Houston's rapid growth. With its Southern hospitality and unpretentious air, Houston is waiting to be discovered as America's next great city.

⌐ TRANSPORTATION

Flights: Bush Intercontinental Airport (☎281-230-3000), 25 mi. north of downtown. Get to city center via **Express Shuttle** (☎523-8888); buses daily every 30min. to 1hr., depending on the destination. Runs 5am-11:30pm. $19-20, ages 12-18 $6, under 12 free. **Hobby Airport,** 7800 Airport Blvd. (☎640-3000), lies about 10 mi. south of downtown and specializes in regional travel.

Trains: Amtrak, 902 Washington Ave. (☎224-1577), *in a rough neighborhood.* From downtown, during the day, catch a bus west on Washington Ave. to Houston Ave.; at night, call a cab. To **San Antonio** (5hr., 3 per week, $31-56) and **New Orleans** (9hr., 3 per week, $50-89). Open M-Tu, Th, and Sa 7am-9pm; Su, W, and F 7am-midnight.

Buses: Greyhound, 2121 Main St. (☎759-6565). *At night call a cab—this is an unsafe area.* Open 24hr. To: **Dallas** (4-5hr., 10 per day, $32); **San Antonio** (3½hr., 11 per day, $22); **Santa Fe** (24hr., 5 per day, $119).

Public Transit: Metropolitan Transit Authority (☎635-4000). Offers reliable service anywhere between NASA (15 mi. southeast of town) and Katy (25 mi. west of town). Operates M-F 6am-9pm, Sa-Su 8am-8pm; less frequently on weekends. The METRO operates a free trolley throughout downtown. Free maps available at the **Houston Public Library** (see **Internet access,** below) or at Metro stores. Open M-F 9am-9pm, Sa 9am-6pm, Su 2-6pm. $1, seniors 40¢, ages 5-11 25¢; day pass $2.

Taxis: United Cab, ☎699-0000.

◢◪ ORIENTATION & PRACTICAL INFORMATION

Though the flat Texan terrain supports several mini-downtowns, the true downtown Houston, a squarish grid of interlocking one-way streets, borders the **Buffalo Bayou** at the intersection of I-10 and I-45. **The Loop (I-610)** encircles the city center with a radius of 6 mi. Anything inside the Loop is easily accessible by car or bus. *Be careful in some areas of south and east Houston, as they may be unsafe.* The shopping district of **Westheimer Boulevard,** in uptown Houston, grows ritzier to the west. Nearby, restaurants and shops line **Kirby Drive** and **Richmond Avenue;** the upper portion of Kirby Dr. winds past spectacular mansions. The downside to Houston's booming economy is the ongoing roadwork—look out for detours.

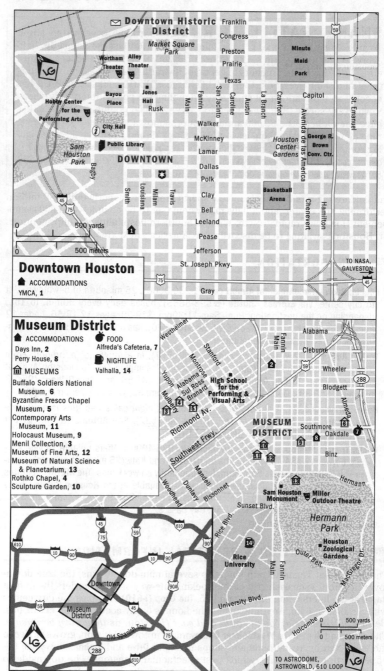

Downtown Houston

♦ ACCOMMODATIONS
YMCA, **1**

Museum District

♦ ACCOMMODATIONS
Days Inn, **2**
Perry House, **8**

🏛 MUSEUMS
Buffalo Soldiers National
 Museum, **6**
Byzantine Fresco Chapel
 Museum, **5**
Contemporary Arts
 Museum, **11**
Holocaust Museum, **9**
Menil Collection, **3**
Museum of Fine Arts, **12**
Museum of Natural Science
 & Planetarium, **13**
Rothko Chapel, **4**
Sculpture Garden, **10**

🍴 FOOD
Alfreda's Cafeteria, **7**

🍸 NIGHTLIFE
Valhalla, **14**

Visitor Info: Greater Houston Convention and Visitors Bureau (☎437-5200 or 800-446-8786), in City Hall, at the corner of Walker and Bagby St. Open daily 9am-4pm.

Hotlines: Crisis Center, ☎228-1505. **Rape Crisis,** ☎528-7273. **Women's Center,** ☎528-6798. **Gay and Lesbian Switchboard of Houston** (☎529-3211; www.gayswitchboard-houston.org) has entertainment info. All operate 24hr.

Medical Services: Bellaire Medical Center, 5314 Dashwood (☎512-1200), has a 24hr. emergency room. **Woman's Hospital of Texas,** 7600 Fannin (☎790-1234).

Internet access: Houston Public Library, 500 McKinney (☎236-1313), at Bagby St.

Post Office: 701 San Jacinto St. (☎800-275-8777). Open M-F 8am-5pm. **ZIP code:** 77052. **Area codes:** 713, 281, and 832 (in text 713, unless indicated).

ACCOMMODATIONS

A few cheap motels dot the **Katy Freeway (I-10W)** and **South 59th Street.** Budget accommodations along **South Main Street** are more convenient, but *not all are safe.* (Bus #8 goes down S. Main St.) Prices start at $30 for a single. Most campgrounds in the Houston area lie a considerable distance from the city center.

Perry House, Houston International Hostel, 5302 Crawford St. (☎523-1009), at Oakdale St., in the museum district near Hermann Park. From the Greyhound station, take bus #8 or #15 south to Southmore St.; walk 6 blocks east to Crawford St. and 1 block south to Oakdale St. 30 beds in 6 spacious rooms. Internet ($3 per hr.) and well-equipped kitchen. Free use of bicycles with a $20 deposit (check out the bicycle store next door). Reception 7-9am and 5-9pm. Lockout 10am-5pm; common area open all day. Dorms $15; some minor chores may be required. ❶

YMCA, 1600 Louisiana Ave. (☎659-8501), between Pease and Leeland St. Downtown location features small, spartan rooms—all singles—with daily maid service. Some have private baths. Towel deposit $2.50. Key deposit $10. Singles $25-35. **Another branch,** located at 7903 South Loop East (☎643-2804), off the Broadway exit from I-610, near I-45, is farther out but less expensive. Take bus #50 to Broadway. Key deposit $10. Singles $22. ❶

Red Carpet Inn, 6868 Hornwood Dr. (☎981-8686 or 800-251-1962), near the Bellaire exit off U.S. 59 S/SW Fwy. Plain but well-kept rooms. Free coffee and continental breakfast. Singles $35; doubles $42. ❷

Days Inn, 4640 Main St. (☎523-3777), Take bus #8 from downtown. Clean, comfortable rooms. Swimming pool and continental breakfast included. Singles $54; doubles $59. ❸

KOA Houston Central, 1620 Peachleaf St. (☎281-442-3700 or 800-562-2132). From I-45 N, go east on Aldine-Bender Rd., then turn right on Aldine-Westfield Rd., and right again on Peachleaf. Sites with pool and shower access. Sites for 2 $18, with hookup $24; each additional adult $5. 1-room cabins $30, 2-room $40. ❶

FOOD

Houston's port has witnessed the arrival of many immigrants, and its restaurants reflect this diversity. The city's cuisine features Mexican, Greek, Cajun, Asian, BBQ, and Southern soul food. Search for reasonably priced restaurants along the chain-laden streets of **Westheimer** and **Richmond Avenue,** especially where they intersect with **Fountainview.** Houston has two **Chinatowns:** a district south of the George R. Brown Convention Center along Main St. and a newer area on **Bellaire Boulevard** called **DiHo.** Many small Mexican restaurants line the strip malls outside of the downtown region and are usually a good value for an empty stomach. For authentic Mexican fare, try Houston's East End.

SLICK BUSINESS

The oil business has always been one of booms and busts—tremendous windfalls and spectacular downfalls, but few companies in history can match the rise and fall of **Enron**. The Houston-based energy trading company went from being the sixth-largest corporation in America to being the largest bankruptcy in US history.

Enron used alleged sham transactions and deceptive accounting, along with political clout to sustain a mythic image of a company using cutting-edge techniques in the energy trade. When questions began to arise about its dealings, Enron's inflated stock price started to decline. As the downward spiral accelerated and new revelations came to light, the stock price collapsed, leaving employee pensions in ruins.

Once people realized the magnitude of Enron's alleged deception, and of the flaws in the system that allowed it to go on for so long, political questions arose. The fact that Enron and its employees were hefty political contributors during the **2000 Presidential Campaign** and could have been affected by changes in energy regulations only made people more suspicious. Before long, a federal criminal investigation was underway, and congressional hearings were scheduled.

Houston, meanwhile, lost its biggest corporation and one of its most generous civic contributors. Though Enron Field, the home of baseball's Houston Astros, will be renamed, ordinary Houstonians have gone on without flinching—for it is only a matter of time before the next oil company strikes it rich.

◙ **Goode Company BBQ,** 5109 Kirby Dr. (☎522-2530), near Bissonnet St. The mesquite-smoked brisket, ribs, and sausage links (all smothered in homemade sauce) will make your mouth water. Sandwiches from $3.75; one meat with two veggies $7-10. Open daily 11am-10pm. ❷

One's A Meal, 607 W. Gray St. (☎523-0425), at Stanford St. This family-owned, Greek-American institution serves everything from chili 'n' eggs ($6) to a gyro with fries ($6). Try the 4 varieties of Greek pizza (6 in. $6) or the colossal breakfast special (you guessed it—$6). Open 24hr. ❷

Ragin' Cajun, 4302 Richmond Ave. (☎623-6321). A local favorite that specializes in Cajun-style fish. Indoor picnic tables, creole music, and a casual atmosphere. Po' boys $6-9. Cup of gumbo $4. Longneck beers $2.75. Open M-Th 11am-10pm, F-Sa 11am-11pm. ❷

Alfreda's Cafeteria, 5101 Almeda Rd. (☎523-6462), close to Perry House. Alfreda's serves cheap soul food. The special of the day includes meat and two vegetables for only $4. Open daily 6am-8pm. ❶

Taco Cabana, 11079 Westheimer St. (☎278-8526). Fast-food Mexican that is better than Taco Bell. Locations throughout Houston. Two tacos and chips con queso $3. Open daily 9am-11pm. ❶

◎ SIGHTS

JOHNSON SPACE CENTER. The city's most popular attraction, **Space Center Houston** is technically not even in Houston but 20 mi. from downtown in Clear Lake, TX. The Mission Control Center is still operational. When today's astronauts say, "Houston, we have a problem," these are the people that answer. Admission includes tours of the mission control center and other astronaut training facilities. Among the attractions are out-of-this-world harnesses; strap in and bounce around like a real spaceman. The complex also houses models of Gemini, Apollo, and Mercury crafts. *(1601 NASA Rd. 1. Take I-45 south to NASA Rd. exit, then head east 3 mi.; or take bus #246. ☎281-244-2100 or 800-972-0369. Open June-Aug. daily 9am-7pm; Sept.-May M-F 10am-5pm, Sa-Su 10am-7pm. $16, seniors $15, ages 4-11 $12. Parking $3.)*

SAN JACINTO. The **San Jacinto Battleground State Historical Park** is the most important monument to Lone Star independence. On this battleground in 1836, Sam Houston's outnumbered Texan Army defeated Santa Anna's Mexican forces, thereby gaining Texas's independence from Mexico. When the US annexed Texas ten years later, it set off the Mexican-American War. The **San Jacinto Monument,** the world's tallest memorial tower, honors all those who fought for Texas's independence. Riding to the top of the 50-story tower yields a stunning view of the area. The **museum** inside the monument celebrates Texas history with remnants like the *Battleship Texas*, the only surviving naval vessel to have served in both World Wars, and the last remaining dreadnought. *(Monument: 21 mi. east on Rte. 225 and 3 mi. north on Rte. 134. ☎281-479-2421. Open daily 9am-6pm. $3, seniors $2.50, under 12 $2. Museum: ☎281-479-2431. Open daily 9am-6pm. Free. 40min. projector, multimedia slide show daily every hr. 10am-5pm. $3.50/ $3/$2.50. Combo tickets with elevator ride $6/$5/$4. Battleship: Right next to the monument. ☎281-479-2431. Open daily 10am-5pm. $5, seniors $4, ages 6-18 $3, under 6 free.)*

HERMANN PARK. The 388 acres of beautifully landscaped grounds of **Hermann Park,** by Rice University and the Texas Medical Center, encompass the Miller Outdoor Theater (see **Entertainment,** below), a children's zoo, golf course, sports facilities, a kiddie train, and a Japanese garden. Near the northern entrance of the park, the **Houston Museum of Natural Science** offers a six-story glass butterfly center, some formidable looking dinosaurs (all dead), a splendid display of gems and minerals, a planetarium, an IMAX theatre, and a hands-on gallery geared towards children. At the southern end of the park, crowds flock to see more animated attractions—such as gorillas, hippos, and reptiles—in the **Houston Zoological Gardens.** The park grounds also encompass the Miller Outdoor Theater (see p. 682), a children's zoo, a golf course, sports facilities, a kiddie train, and a Japanese garden. *(Museum of Natural Science: 1 Hermann Circle Dr. ☎639-4629. Exhibits open M-Sa 9am-6pm, Su 11am-6pm. Museum $6, seniors and under 12 $3.50; IMAX $7/$4.50; planetarium $5/$3.50; butterfly center $5/$3.50. Japanese tea garden: Open daily 10am-6pm. Free. Zoo: 1513 N. MacGregor. ☎523-5888. Open daily 10am-6pm. $2.50, seniors $2, ages 3-12 50¢.)*

ART ATTRACTIONS. The **Museum of Fine Arts** features paintings of the American West by artists such as Frederic Remington and the largest collection of African gold pieces outside the African continent. Its two large buildings also host Impressionist and post-Impressionist art as well as works from Asia, Africa, and Latin America. The museum's **Sculpture Garden** includes pieces by Matisse and Rodin. *(1001 Bissonet. ☎639-7300. Open Tu-W 10am-5pm, Th 10am-9pm, F-Sa 10am-7pm, Su 12:15-7pm. $5, students and seniors $2.50; Th free. Garden: 5101 Montrose St. Open daily 9am-10pm. Free.)* Across the street, the **Contemporary Arts Museum** frequently rotates exhibits. *(5216 Montrose St. ☎284-8250. Open Tu-W and F-Sa 10am-5pm, Th 10am-9pm, Su noon-5pm. Suggested donation $3.)*

The Menil Foundation exhibits an array of artwork in four buildings grouped within a block of each other. The **Menil Collection** showcases an eclectic assortment of Surrealist paintings and sculptures alongside Byzantine and medieval artifacts and European, American, and African art. *(1515 Sul Ross. ☎525-9400. Open W-Su 11am-7pm; chapel closes at 6pm. Free.)* A block away, the **Rothko Chapel** houses 14 of the artist's paintings in a non-denominational sanctuary. Worshipping fans of modern art will delight in Rothko's ultra-simplicity; others will wonder where the paintings are. The **Byzantine Fresco Chapel Museum** displays the ornate dome and apse from a 13th-century Byzantine chapel in Cyprus that was rescued in 1983 from antiquity thieves before they were sold on the black market. *(3900 Yupon. ☎524-9839. Open daily 10am-6pm. Free. Byzantine: 4011 Yupon. ☎521-3990. Open W-Su 11am-6pm. Free.)*

OTHER MUSEUMS. Between the end of the Civil War in 1866 and the integration of the armed forces in 1944, the US Army had several all-black units. During the Indian Wars of the late 1800's, the Cheyenne soldiers nicknamed these troops "Buffalo Soldiers," both because of their naturally curly hair and as a sign of respect for their fighting spirit. Learn the history of the Buffalo Soldiers and African-Americans in the military from the Revolutionary War to the present at the

🏛Buffalo Soldiers National Museum. *(1834 Southmore.* ☎ *942-8920. Open M-F 10am-5pm, Sa 10am-3pm. Free.)* The **Holocaust Museum** features a chilling architectural style that recalls the concentration camps. The museum also has a rotating art gallery and two films about the Holocaust. *(5401 Caroline St.* ☎ *942-8000. Open M-F 9am-5pm, Sa-Su noon-5pm. Free.)*

BAYOU BEND. The American decorative art from 1620 to 1870 at **Bayou Bend Collection and Gardens** in **Memorial Park** is an antique-lover's dream. The collection, housed in the mansion of millionaire Ima Hogg (sticks and stones...), daughter of former Gov. Jim "Boss" Hogg, includes John Singleton Copley portraits. *(1 Westcott St.* ☎ *639-7750, ext. 7750. Collection open Tu-Sa 10am-5pm, Su 1-5pm. $10, seniors and students $8.50, ages 10-18 $5, under 10 not admitted. Gardens open Tu-Sa 10am-5pm, Su 1-5pm. 1½hr. garden tours by reservation. $3, under 10 free.)*

JUST FOR FUN. In downtown, earthly pleasures can be found underground. Hundreds of shops and restaurants line the 18 mi. **Houston Tunnel System,** which connects all the major buildings, extending from the Civic Center to the Tenneco Building and the Hyatt Regency. Duck into the air-conditioned passageways via any major building or hotel. Most entries are closed Saturday and Sunday.

Many a Bacchanalian feast must have preceded the construction of the **Beer Can House.** Adorned with 50,000 beer cans, strings of beer-can tops, and a beer-can fence, the house was built by the late John Mikovisch, an upholsterer from the Southern Pacific Railroad. At 5¢ a can, the tin abode has a market price of $2500 just for the decorations. *(222 Malone St., off Washington Ave.)*

🎭 ENTERTAINMENT

From April to October, symphony, opera, and ballet companies and various professional theaters stage free performances at the **Miller Outdoor Theatre** (☎ 284-8352), in Hermann Park. The annual **Shakespeare Festival** struts and frets upon the stage from late July to early August. The downtown **Alley Theatre,** 615 Texas Ave., puts on Broadway-caliber productions at moderate prices. (☎ 228-8421. Tickets $32-44; Su-Th $12 student rush tickets 1hr. before the show.) For downtown entertainment, **Bayou Place,** 500 Texas Ave., holds a pool hall and a live music venue. Inside the Bayou the **Angelika Film Center and Café,** 510 Texas Ave., plays foreign, independent, and classic American films. (☎ 225-5232. $7-10.) The new **Hobby Center for the Performing Arts,** 800 Bagby St. (☎ 227-2001), slated to be finished in 2003, features a dome ceiling with a fiberoptic display of the Texas night sky and hosts **Theatre Under the Stars** and the **Houston Broadway Series. Jones Hall,** 615 Louisiana Blvd. (☎ 227-3974), stages more of Houston's highbrow entertainment. The **Houston Symphony Orchestra** performs in Jones September through May. (☎ 227-2787. $20-70.) Between October and May, the **Houston Grand Opera** produces six operas in the nearby **Wortham Center,** 500 Texas Ave. (☎ 546-0200. $35-200. 50% student discount at noon on the day of some shows; $20-70 off tickets bought 1hr. before show.) The **Houston Ballet** also performs in the Wortham Center from September to June. (☎ 523-6300. $41-101.)

The **Astros** play ball at **Astros Field** (☎ 295-8000), located at the intersections of Texas, Crawford, and Congress St. near Union Station downtown. From February to mid-March, there's plenty of space in the Astrodome to house the **Houston Livestock Show and Rodeo** (☎ 629-3700). Houston's basketball team, the **Rockets,** hoop it up at a new arena at the corner of Polk and Crawford St. south of the Convention Center, while the brand-new **Houston Texans** play football at **Reliant Stadium,** 8400 Kirby Dr. (☎ 336-7700).

☑ NIGHTLIFE

Most of Houston's nightlife, however, happens west of downtown around Richmond and Westheimer Ave. Several gay clubs cluster on lower Westheimer, while enormous, warehouse-style dancehalls line the upper reaches of Richmond. A growing number of upscale bars, restaurants, and clubs surround **Market Square.** **Main Street** also boasts a growing club scene.

City Streets, 5078 Richmond Ave. (☎ 840-8555), is a complex with 6 different clubs offering everything from country and live R&B to disco and a pool hall. Cover $2-5, good for all 6 clubs. Open W-F 5pm-2am, Sa 7:30pm-2am.

Sam's Boat/Sam's Place, 5720 Richmond Ave. (☎ 781-2628). Good-natured drinkers gather on the patio to chat and hear live music. Cover up to $3. Open daily 11am-2am; live music Tu 5pm-2am, F 8pm-2am, Sa 6pm-2am.

Valhalla (☎ 348-3258), in the center of the Rice campus across from the library. Stop by for "gods, heroes, mythical beings, and cheap beer" (75¢). Open M-F 4pm-2am, Su 7pm-2am.

Rich's, 2401 San Jacinto (☎ 759-9606). The 2-story gay dance club pumps with an awesome sound system. Cover $5. Open Su-Th 9pm-2am, F-Sa 9pm-4am.

▶ DAYTRIP FROM HOUSTON

GALVESTON ISLAND

In the 19th century, Galveston was the "Queen of the Gulf" as the most prominent port and wealthiest city in Texas—before the glamour came to an abrupt end on September 8, 1900, when a devastating hurricane ripped through the city, claiming 6000 lives. The Galveston hurricane still ranks as one of the worst natural disasters in US history. **Seawall Boulevard** follows the southern coastline, and Broadway runs between Seawall and the historic Strand district. **Strand Street,** near the northern coastline, between 20th and 25th St., is a national landmark restored with authentic gas lights and brick-paved walkways, along with many Victorian buildings, cafes, restaurants, and shops. The elegant **Moody Mansion,** 2618 Broadway, features handcarved wood and stunning stained glass. (☎ 762-7688. Open M-Sa 10am-4pm, Su noon-4pm. $6, seniors $5, ages 6-18 $3.) Turn onto 81st from Seawall and find the fabulous and pricey attractions of **Moody Gardens.** The shop- and restaurant-packed area makes room for three glass pyramids housing interactive space exhibits, and IMAX ride-film theaters, a tropical rainforest, 2000 exotic species of flora and fauna, and an aquarium. The newest attraction is Palm Beach, an artificial white sand beach. (☎ 683-4200 or 800-582-4673. Open in summer daily 10am-9pm; in winter Su-Th 10am-6pm, F-Sa 10am-9pm. Aquarium $13, seniors $10, ages 4-12 $7. Rainforest $9/7/6. IMAX $9/7/6. Ridefilm $8/7/6. Day pass to all attractions $30, everything half price after 6pm.)

The only beach in Galveston which permits alcoholic beverages is **Apffel Park,** on the far eastern edge of the island (known as East Beach). On the west end of the island, east of Pirates Beach, **#3 Beach Pocket Park** (numbers 1 and 2 were destroyed by the ocean) has bathrooms, showers, playgrounds, and a concession stand. (Open daily 9am-9pm; some open later. Car entry for beaches generally $5.) At Ferry Rd. (off the far eastern end of Seawall, across from the Sandpiper Motel), catch a ferry to **Bolivar Island,** where bathing suit restrictions are rumored to be much less stringent.

The oldest restaurant on the island, **The Original Mexican Cafe ❷**, 1401 Market St., cooks up great Tex-Mex meals with homemade flour tortillas. Lunch specials run $6-8. (☎762-6001. Open M-Th 11am-9:30pm, F 11am-10pm, Sa-Su 8am-10pm.) **Benno's ❶**, 1200 Seawall Rd., serves tasty Cajun seafood. (☎762-4621. Po' boys $5.25. Fish, fries, and hush puppy lunch specials $5.25. Open Su-Th 11am-10pm, F-Sa 11am-11pm.)

CORPUS CHRISTI
☎361

Corpus Christi's economy depends almost entirely on its shore-side location. While local refineries are fed by the crude oil found offshore in the Gulf, year-round warm beaches bring the tourists in droves. Vacationers crowd the beaches in the summer, only to be replaced in the cooler months by "winter Texans," many of them elderly mobile home owners fleeing the chill of the northern states. Corpus Christi is defined by its pricey knick-knacks, cheap gas, natural stretches of sand, and the encroaching waste that floats in from the Gulf.

▐ TRANSPORTATION. Greyhound, 702 N. Chaparral (☎882-9206; open daily 8am-2:30am). To: Austin (5-7½hr., 4 per day, $25); Dallas (9-10hr., 7 per day, $42); Houston (5hr., 9 per day, $21-22). **Regional Transit Authority** (☎289-2600), also known as the "B," buses within Corpus Christi. Pick up maps and schedules at the Visitors Center or at **The B Headquarters**, 1806 S. Alameda (☎883-2287; open M-F 8am-5pm). City Hall, Port Ayers, Six Points, and the Staples St. stations serve as central transfer points. (Runs M-Sa 5:30am-9:30pm, Su 11am-6:30pm. Fare 50¢; students, seniors, and children 25¢; Sa 25¢; transfers free.) The **Harbor Ferry** follows the shoreline and stops at the aquarium (runs daily 10:30am-6:30pm; each way $1). On the north side of Harbor Bridge, the free **Beach Shuttle** also travels to the beach, the Aquarium, and other attractions (runs May-Sept. 10:30am-6:30pm). **Taxis: Yellow Cab**, ☎884-3211.

▐ PRACTICAL INFORMATION. Corpus Christi's tourist district follows **Shoreline Drive**, which borders the Gulf Coast, 1 mi. east of the downtown business district. **Convention and Visitors Bureau**, 1823 Chaparral, 6 blocks north of I-37 and 1 block from the water. (☎561-2000 or 800-766-2322. Open daily 9am-5pm.) **Medical Care: Spohn Hospital Shoreline**, 600 Elizabeth St. (☎881-3000). **Hotlines: Hope Line** (☎855-4673) and **Battered Women and Rape Victims Shelter** (☎881-8888); both operate 24hr. **Internet access:** Corpus Christi Public Library, 805 Comanche. (☎880-7000. Open M-Th 9am-9pm, F-Sa 9am-6pm, Su 2pm-6pm.) **Post Office:** 809 Nueces Bay Blvd. (☎800-275-8777. Open M-F 7:30am-5:30pm, Sa 8am-1pm.) **ZIP code:** 78469. **Area code:** 361.

▐ ACCOMMODATIONS. Cheap accommodations are scarce downtown, and posh hotels and motels take up much of the shoreline. The best motel bargains lie several miles south on Leopard St. (take bus #27) or I-37 at Navigation Blvd. The best option is **Days Inn ❷**, 901 Navigation Blvd., which provides clean, comfortable rooms at reasonable prices (☎888-8599. Singles $35, doubles $40.) Campers should head to **Padre Island National Seashore** (p. 685). Nueces River **City Park** (☎241-1464), off I-37 N from Exit 16 and approximately 18 mi. from downtown Corpus, has free tent sites but only pit toilets and no showers. Camping permits available from the ranger station on the way into the park.

▐▐ FOOD & NIGHTLIFE. The mixed population and seaside locale of Corpus Christi have resulted in a wide range of cuisines. Non-chain restaurants can be found on the south side of the city, around Staples St. and S. Padre Island Dr. **BJ's**

❷, 6335 S. Padre Island Dr., serves four-topping, crispy-crust pizzas (8 in. $5), while patrons shoot pool and drink one of 300 varieties of beer. (☎992-6671. Open M-Sa 11am-10:30pm, Su noon-9:30pm.) **Pier 99 ❷**, 2822 N. Shoreline Dr., specializes in fried fresh fish, including shrimp or oyster baskets ($7). (☎887-0764. Open daily 11am-10pm.)

Get your groove on at **Stinger's** and **Dead Eye Dick's,** both at 301 N. Chaparral St. Stomp to country and rock music at Stinger's, then shake it to traditional dance tunes at Dick's. (☎887-0029. Cover W-Th $5, F-Sa $8. Open W-Sa 11am-2am.)

🄶 **SIGHTS.** Corpus Christi's most significant sight is the shoreline, bordered by miles of rocky seawall and wide sidewalks with graduated steps down to the water. Overpriced seaside restaurants, sail and shrimp boats, and aggressive, hungry seagulls overrun the piers. The best beach is Port Aransas, reachable by ferry (on Rte. 361). To find beaches that allow swimming (some lie along Ocean Dr. and north of Harbor Bridge), just follow the signs. On the north side of Harbor Bridge, the **Texas State Aquarium,** 2710 N. Shoreline Blvd., showcases sharks and rays roaming, in true Texas fashion, beneath an oil platform (☎881-1200 or 800-477-4853. Open June-Aug. M-Sa 9am-6pm, Su 10am-6pm; early Sept. to late May M-Sa 9am-5pm, Su 10am-5pm. $9, seniors $7.50, ages 4-12 $5.25.)

Just offshore floats the aircraft carrier **USS Lexington,** a World War II relic now open to the public. In her day, the "Blue Ghost" set more records than any carrier in the history of naval aviation. Be sure to check out the crews' quarters—you won't complain about small hostel rooms ever again. (☎888-4873 or 800-523-9539. Open June-Aug. daily 9am-6pm; early Sept. to late May 9am-5pm. $10, seniors $8, ages 4-12 $5.) Pick up $1 off coupons to both the aquarium and ship at the Visitors Center. Lay down a few clams on your favorite pooch at the **Corpus Christi Greyhound Race Track,** I-37 at Navation exit. (☎289-9333 or 800-580-7223. $1.)

PADRE ISLAND ☎361

With over 80 miles of painstakingly preserved beaches, dunes, and wildlife refuge land, the **Padre Island National Seashore (PINS)** is a priceless (though debris-flawed) gem, sandwiched between the condos of North Padre Island and the spring-break hordes of South Padre Island. The seashore provides excellent opportunities for windsurfing, swimming, or surf fishing. Driving is permitted at most places on the beach, though four-wheel-drive is recommended. Padre Island is divided into several areas; gain entrance to each area through the access roads. Access 1a is at the far northern tip of the island near Port Aransas, while Access 6 is closest to PINS. Motorists enter the PINS via the JFK Causeway, from the Flour Bluff area of Corpus Christi. PINS can only be reached by car. For up-to-date info on prices and activities within PINS, call or visit the **Malaquite Visitors Center.** (☎949-8068. Open in summer daily 8:30am-6pm; in winter 8:30am-4:30pm.) Garbage from nearby ships frequently litters the sands, but a lucky few may spot one of the endangered Kemp's Ridley sea turtles nurtured by PINS. A yearly pass into PINS costs $20 for cars, or buy a weekly pass for $10. Windsurfing or launching a boat from the Bird Basin will cost you an extra $10 for a yearly pass or $5 for a daily pass. Many beachcombers avoid these fees by going to the free **North Beach.** Cast your own line or just take a look at what others are catchin' at **Bob Hall Pier,** Access 4, the main fishing pier on the island. (☎949-0999. Open daily 24hr. $1.)

Five miles south of the entrance station, **Malaquite Beach** makes your day on the sand as easy as possible with restrooms and rental picnic tables. In summer, the rental station is set up on the beachfront. (Inner tubes $2 per hr., chairs $1 per hr., body boards $2.50 per hr.) The Malaquite Visitors Center (see above) has free maps and exhibits about the island.

Loose sands prevent most vehicles from venturing far onto the beach. Visitors with four-wheel-drive and a taste for solitude should make the 60 mi. trek to the **Mansfield Cut,** the most remote and untraveled area of the seashore. Call the **Malaquite Ranger Station** (☎949-8173), 3½ mi. south of the park entrance, for emergency assistance. No wheels? Hike the **Grasslands Nature Trail,** a ¾ mi. loop through sand dunes and grasslands. Guide pamphlets are available at the trailhead.

The **PINS Campground ❶,** less than 1 mi. north of the Visitors Center, consists of an asphalt area for RVs, restrooms, and cold-rinse showers—no soap is permitted on PINS. (Sites $8.) Outside of this area—excluding the 5 mi. pedestrian-only beach—camping is free wherever vehicles can go. For camping with amenities, the **Padre Balli County Park ❶,** Access 5 on Park Rd. 22, 3½ mi. from the JFK Causeway, near the National Seashore, provides running water, electricity, laundry, and hot showers for campers. (☎949-8121. $5 water key deposit. Sites with water and hookup $15. Beach tent sites $6. 3-day max. stay.) **Area code:** 361.

WEST TEXAS

Hundreds of miles from Dallas's Trinity River and even farther from the rolling hills and bright lights of Austin, West Texas offers a look at the unpolished side of the Lone Star State. Populated by prickly-pears and yuccas, rattlesnakes and mountain lions, the desert plains and jagged mountains of West Texas remain untamed. Moreover, the region is a summertime pressure cooker with temperatures reaching and occasionally exceeding 110°F.

The outdoors of West Texas are a playground for savvy enthusiasts and novices alike. Big Bend National Park is a haven for bikers and backpackers, while the Guadalupe Mountains draw climbers from across the country. In the northern portion of the region (the Panhandle), visitors are treated to a complex American flavor that offers something for most every traveler.

AMARILLO   ☎806

Named for the yellow clay of a nearby lake (*amarillo* is Spanish for "yellow"), Amarillo opened for business as a railroad construction camp in 1887. Within a decade it had become one of the nation's largest cattle-shipping markets. For years, the economy depended largely on the meat industry, but the discovery of oil gave Amarillo a kick in the 1920s. Amarillo is now the prime overnight stop for motorists en route from Dallas, Houston, or Oklahoma City to Denver and other Western destinations. It's little more than a one-day city—but what a grand, shiny truck stop it is.

The outstanding **Panhandle-Plains Historical Museum,** 2401 4th Ave., I-27 S to Rte. 87 in nearby Canyon, has fossils, local history and geology exhibits, and a collection of Southwestern art. (☎651-2244. Open in summer M-Sa 9am-6pm, Su 1-6pm; off-season M-Sa 9am-5pm, Su 1-6pm. $4, seniors $3, ages 4-12 $1.) The **American Quarter Horse Heritage Center and Museum,** 2601 I-40 E, at Exit 72B, presents the heroic story of "America's horse." (☎376-5181 or 888-209-8322. Open M-Sa 9am-5pm, Su noon-5pm. $4, seniors $3.50, ages 6-18 $2.50.) At **Cadillac Ranch,** Stanley Marsh III planted 10 Cadillacs—model years 1948 to 1963, representing the golden era of cars—at the same angle as the Great Pyramids. Get off I-40 at the Hope Rd. exit, 9 mi. west of Amarillo, cross to the south side of I-40, turn right at the end of the bridge, and drive ½ mi. down the highway access road to the west.

Amarillo is a popular place for travelers to hang up their Stetson for the evening. Budget motels proliferate along the entire stretch of I-40, I-27, and U.S. 287/87 near town. Prices rise near downtown. One of the best non-chain options is the **Big Texan Motel ❸,** 7701 I-40 E, near the Big Texan Steak Ranch. (☎372-5000. Restaurant and swimming pool. Breakfast included. Rooms under $50; rates vary.) **KOA Kampground ❶**, 1100 Folsom Rd., has a pool in summer. Take I-40 to Exit 75, head north to Rte. 60, then east 1 mi. (☎335-1792. Laundry and coffee. Reception June-Aug. daily 8am-9:30pm; Sept.-May 8am-8pm. Sites $20, with water and power $25, full hookup $26.) In the Old San Jacinto district along historic Route 66, **Adam's Ribs ❷**, 2917 W. 6th, has excellent ribs ($7) and more. (☎371-8777. Open daily 11am-10pm.) Dine amid fountains and Mexican murals at **Abuelo's ❸**, 3501 45th St. (☎354-8294. *Cena mexicana* $10. Open Su-Th 11am-10pm, F-Sa 11am-11pm.)

Amarillo sprawls at the intersection of I-27, I-40, and U.S. 287/87. To explore you need a car. Rte. 335 (the Loop) encircles the city. Amarillo Blvd. (historic Rte. 66) runs east-west, parallel to I-40. **Greyhound**, 700 S. Tyler (☎374-5371; open 24hr.), buses to Dallas (8hr., 4 per day, $59.50-63.50) and Santa Fe (6-10hr., 4 per day, $59-63). **Amarillo City Transit**, 801 SE 23rd, operates eight bus routes departing from 5th and Pierce St. Maps are at the office. (☎342-9143. Buses run every 30min. M-Sa 6:30am-6:30pm. 75¢.) The **Texas Travel Info Center**, 9400 I-40E, at Exit 76, has state info. (☎335-1441. Open daily 8am-6pm.) **Amarillo Convention and Visitors Bureau,** 1000 S. Polk, at 10th St., dishes the local scoop. (☎374-1497 or 800-692-1338. Open M-F 8am-5pm.) **Internet access: Public Library,** at the corner of Buchanan and 7th Ave. (Open M-F 9am-9pm, Sa noon-9pm, Su 1-5pm.) **Post Office:** 505 E. 9th Ave., at Buchanan St. (☎379-2148. Open M-F 7:30am-5pm.) **ZIP code:** 79105. **Area code:** 806.

NEAR AMARILLO: PALO DURO CANYON STATE PARK

23 mi. south of Amarillo, take I-27 to Exit 106 and head east on Rte. 217, Palo Duro Canyon, known as the "Grand Canyon of Texas," covers 16,000 acres of jaw-dropping beauty. The beautiful 16 mi. **scenic drive** through the park begins at the headquarters. Rangers allow backcountry **hiking**, but the majority of visitors stick to the marked trails. Most hikers can manage the **Sunflower Trail** (3 mi.), the **Juniper Trail** (2 mi.), or the **Paseo del Río Trail** (2 mi.), but only experienced hikers should consider the rugged **Running Trail** (9 mi.). Avid bikers enjoy the **Capitol Peak Mountain Bike Trail** (4 mi.). The **Lighthouse Trail** (4½ mi.) leads to magnificent geological formations. (Park open daily 7am-10pm; in winter 8am-10pm. $3, under 12 free.) *Temperatures in the canyon frequently climb to 100°F; bring at least 2 quarts of water.* The park headquarters, just inside the park, has maps of hiking trails and info on park activities. (☎488-2227. Open daily 7am-10pm; in winter 8am-5pm.) The official play of Texas, the musical ▓**Texas,** performed in Pioneer Amphitheater, 1514 5th Ave., is a must-see. The performance covers the state's early days against the backdrop of the canyon's scenery. (☎655-2181. In summer Th-Tu 8:30pm. $10-23, under 12 $5-23.)**Old West Stables,** ¼ mi. farther along, rents horses and saddles. (☎488-2180. Rides offered Apr.-Oct. 10am, noon, 2, and 4pm; June-Aug. 10am, noon, 2, 4, and 6pm. $20 per hr., wagon rides for groups of 6-8 $5. Reservations recommended.) A ½ mi. past the HQ, the **Visitors Center** displays exhibits on the canyon's history (open M-Sa 9am-5pm, Su 1-5pm).

GUADALUPE MOUNTAINS NATIONAL PARK   ☎915

Rising austerely above the parched west Texas desert, these peaks form the highest and most remote of the west Texas ranges. Mescalero Apaches hunted and camped on these lands, until they were driven out by the US army. Before being forced out, Apache chief Geronimo claimed that the greatest gold mines in the world were hidden in the peaks. Despite the country's craze for gold, few settlers bought the prophecy; by the late 1800s, only a handful of miners inhabited the rugged region. Today, Guadalupe Mountains National Park encompasses 86,000 acres of desert, caves, canyons, and highlands. Drivers can glimpse the park's most dramatic sights from U.S. 62/180: **El Capitán**, a 2000 ft. limestone cliff, and **Guadalupe Peak,** the highest point in Texas (8749 ft.). The mountains promise over 80 mi. of

BLUE DAYS, BLACK NIGHTS The fiery youth, meteoric rise to fame, and tragic death of Buddy Holly, perhaps more than of any other legend of the 1950s captured the hearts and imaginations of a generation of music enthusiasts eager to embrace the risk, bravado, and poignancy of rock 'n' roll as a channel for their emerging souls. Every one from Waylon Jennings to John Lennon, and Mick Jagger to Linda Ronstadt was influenced by Holly's unassuming charm and earnest musicality. Since his early death in 1959, fans have remembered Buddy Holly in Lubbock, TX, his hometown. Today the **Buddy Holly Center**, 1801 Ave. G, houses a gallery of memorabilia, including Holly's Fender Strat and signature horn-rimmed glasses, an art gallery, and the Texas Musicians Hall of Fame. (☎806-767-2686. Open Tu-F 10am-6pm, Sa 11am-6pm.) Pay your respects at the **Buddy Holly Statue and Walk of Fame** on Ave. G at the intersection with 7th, and at **Buddy Holly's Grave** at E. 34th St. and Martin Luther King Jr. Blvd.

challenging desert trails to those willing to explore the area. Entrance to the park is currently free, though a fee is planned for 2002. **Carlsbad, NM** (see p. 849), 55 mi. northeast, makes a good base, with cheap motels, campgrounds, and restaurants.

The major park trailhead is at Pine Springs Campground, near the headquarters (see below). From this starting point, imposing **Guadalupe Peak** can be scaled in a difficult but rewarding full-day hike (5-6hr., 8.4 mi.). A shorter trek (2-3hr., 4.2 mi.) traces the sheltered streambed of **Devil's Hall.** A full-day hike (9 mi., 6-7hr.) leads from the campground to the **Bowl,** a high-country forest of Douglas Fir and Ponderosa Pines. The **Spring Trail** (1-2hr., 2.3 mi.) leads from the **Frijole Ranch,** about 1 mi. north of the Visitors Center, to a mountain spring frequented by park wildlife. Beginning at the **McKittrick Visitors Center,** several mi. northeast of the main Visitors Center, a trail leads up scenic McKittrick Canyon to the historic **Pratt Cabin.**

The park's lack of development is attractive to backpackers, but it creates some inconveniences. The nearest gas and food spot is the **Nickel Creek Cafe,** 5 mi. north of Pine Springs. (☎828-3295. Open M-Sa 7am-2pm and 6-9pm. Burgers $4. Cash only.) The park's two simple campgrounds, **Pine Springs,** just past park headquarters, and **Dog Canyon,** south of the New Mexico border at the north end of the park, have water and restrooms but no hookups or showers. (☎828-3251. Reservations for groups only. Sites $8.) Dog Canyon is accessible only via Rte. 137 from Carlsbad, NM (72 mi.), or by a full-day hike from the **Main Visitors Center** at Pine Springs, off U.S. 62/180. (☎828-3251. Open June-Aug. daily 8am-6pm; Sept.-May 8am-4:30pm. After hours, info is posted on the outside bulletin board.) Free **backcountry camping** permits are available at the Visitors Center.

Guadalupe Park lies 110 mi. east of El Paso. For additional info, contact the Visitors Center or write to **Guadalupe Mountains National Park,** HC 60, Box 400, Salt Flat 79847. **TNM&O Coaches** (☎505-887-1108) runs along U.S. 62/180 between Carlsbad, NM, and El Paso and will make a flag stop at the Pine Springs Visitors Center if you call ahead (from Carlsbad 2½hr., $26). **Area code: 915.**

EL PASO   ☎915

The largest of the US border towns, El Paso boomed in the 17th century as a stopover on an important east-west wagon route that followed the Río Grande through "the pass" (*el paso*) between the Rocky Mountains and the Sierra Madre. Today, the El Paso-Ciudad Juárez metropolitan area has nearly three million inhabitants, a number that keeps growing due to an increase in the cross-border enterprises fueled by NAFTA. Nearly everyone in El Paso speaks Spanish, and the majority of denizens are of Mexican ancestry. After dark, activity leaves the center of town, migrating toward the suburbs and south of the border to raucous Ciudad Juárez.

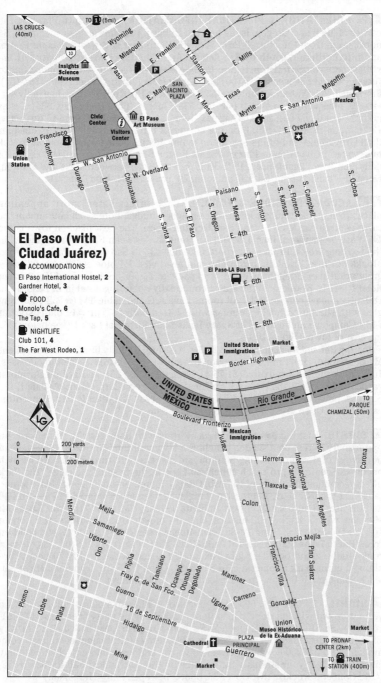

TEXAS

El Paso (with Ciudad Juárez)

🏠 ACCOMMODATIONS
El Paso International Hostel, 2
Gardner Hotel, 3

🍴 FOOD
Monolo's Cafe, 6
The Tap, 5

🎵 NIGHTLIFE
Club 101, 4
The Far West Rodeo, 1

■ ☎ ORIENTATION & PRACTICAL INFORMATION. San Jacinto Plaza, at the corner of Main and Oregon, is the heart of El Paso. **I-10** runs east-west and **U.S. 54** north-south from the city. El Paso is divided into east and west by **Santa Fe Ave.** and into north and south by **San Antonio Ave.** *Tourists should be wary of the streets between San Antonio and the border late at night.* **Amtrak** runs trains to **Tucson** (6hr., 3 per week, $57-100) and **San Antonio** (12½hr., 3 per week, $86-151). **Greyhound,** 200 W. San Antonio, (☎532-2365) near the Civic Center, has daily service to: **Albuquerque** (5½hr., 3 per day, $38); **Tucson** (6hr., 6 per day, $35); **Dallas** (12hr., 7 per day, $60); and **Los Angeles** (16hr., 6 per day, $45). **El Paso-LA Bus Lines,** 720 Oregon St. (☎532-4061), on the corner of 6th Ave, is significantly cheaper than Greyhound and offers service to major destinations in the Southwest. **Visitors Center:** 1 Civic Center Plaza, at Santa Fe and San Francisco. (☎544-0062. Open daily 8am-5pm.) **Post Office:** 219 E. Mills (☎532-8824), between Mesa and Stanton. Open M-F 8:30am-5pm, Sa 8:30am-noon. **ZIP code:** 79901. **Area Code:** 915

⌂ ☐ ACCOMMODATIONS & FOOD. El Paso offers safer, more appealing places to stay than Ciudad Juárez. Several good budget hotels can be found in the town center near Main St. and San Jacinto Square. The best place in town is the ■**El Paso International Hostel ❶,** 311 E. Franklin, between Stanton and Kansas in the Gardner Hotel. From the airport, take bus #33 to San Jacinto Park, walk two blocks north to Franklin, turn right, and head east 1½ blocks. The hostel takes great pride in meeting the needs of backpackers. (☎532-3661. Dorms $15.) **Gardner Hotel 1,** 311 E. Franklin, is the oldest continually operating hotel in El Paso. John Dillinger stayed here in 1934. All rooms have A/C and cable TV. (☎532-3661. Singles with shared bath $25; doubles with shared bath $37; private baths start at $48.) Camping can be found at **Hueco Tanks State Historical Park 1** (see below), 32 mi. east of town. (Sites $10.)

The Tap Bar and Restaurant 1, 408 E. San Antonio, is dimly lit but it has excellent Mexican food. Don't mind the mirrored walls or the waitresses' skimpy dresses. Just enjoy the tasty burritos ($1.75-4), enchiladas ($4.25), and grilled shrimp in garlic for $9. (☎532-1848 Open M-Sa 7am-2am, Su noon-2am.) **Manolo's Cafe 1,** 122 S. Mesa, between Overland and San Antonio, serves $2 *menudo* and $1 burritos. (☎532-7661. Open M-Sa 7am-5pm, Su 7:30am-3pm.)

◙ SIGHTS. Historic **San Jacinto Plaza** swarms with daily activity and affords an opportunity to rest on a shaded bench. For a view of the Río Grande Valley, head northwest of downtown along Stanton and make a right turn on Rim Rd. (which becomes Scenic Dr.) to reach **Murchison Park,** at the base of the ridge. The Park offers a commanding vista of El Paso, Ciudad Juárez, and the Sierra Madre Mountains that is particularly impressive at night. Sixteen miles west of El Paso off I-10 and on Rte. 28, at a small airport in Santa Teresa, NM stands the **War Eagles Air Museum,** which displays 29 historic aircraft, mostly from WWII and the Korean War. (☎505-589-2000. Open Tu-Su 10am-4pm. $5, seniors $4, students and children free.) **Hueco Tanks State Historical Park,** 32 mi. east of town off U.S. 62, has the best rock climbing and bouldering in Texas. Call ahead because only 70 people are allowed in the park at one time. (☎849-6684. Open Oct.-Apr. 8am-6pm; May-Sept. M-Th 8am-6pm, F-Su 7am-7pm. Park admission $4, children free.)

▟ NIGHTLIFE. Club 101, 500 San Francisco, is El Paso's oldest club, drawing a vibrant crowd with its three dance floors and changing party scene. (☎544-2101. W-F 18+, Sa 21+. Cover $5. Open W-Sa 9pm-3am.) **Far West Rodeo,** 1225 Airway Blvd., the largest nightclub in El Paso, is a Western entertainment complex accommodating up to 6000 cowboys, urban cowboys, and just plain city slickers at any given time. Test your strength and balance on the mechanical bull for $2. (☎772-9378. Concerts weekly. 18+. Cover $5. Sports bar open daily 11am-2am.)

BIG BEND
☎ 915

Roadrunners, coyotes, wild pigs, mountain lions, and a few black bears make their home in Big Bend National Park, an 800,000-acre tract (about the size of Rhode Island) cradled by the mighty meander of the Río Grande. Spectacular canyons, vast stretches of the Chihuahua Desert, and the airy Chisos Mountains occupy this literally and figuratively "far-out" spot. The high season for visitation is in the early spring—during the summer, the predominantly desert park is excruciatingly hot.

⊑ TRANSPORTATION. There is no transportation service into or around the park. **Amtrak** offers trains to Alpine TX, 103 mi. north of the park entrance. **Car rentals** are also available there. Three roads lead south from U.S. 90 into the park: from Marfa, U.S. 67 to Rte. 170; from Alpine, Rte. 118; from Marathon, U.S. 385. The fastest route to the park headquarters is via U.S. 385. There are two **gas stations** within the park, one at **Panther Junction** (☎477-2294; open Sept.-Mar. daily 7am-7pm; Apr.-Aug. 8am-6pm; 24 hr. credit card service), next to the park headquarters, and one at **Río Grande Village** (☎477-2293; open Mar.-May daily 9am-8pm; June-Feb. 9am-6pm). The **Study Butte Store** also sells gas. (Open 24hr. Credit cards only.)

⊞⊡ ORIENTATION & PRACTICAL INFORMATION. Park headquarters is at **Panther Junction,** 26 mi. inside the park. (☎477-2251. Open daily 8am-6pm; vehicle pass $10 per week, pedestrians and bikers $5. National park passes accepted.) For info, write the Superintendent, Big Bend National Park, Box 129, 79834. **Ranger stations** are located at Río Grande Village, Persimmon Gap, Castolon, and Chisos Basin. (Persimmon open daily 8am-5pm; Chisos open daily 9am-4:30pm; others closed June-Oct.). The Río Grande Village Store has **public showers** (75¢). **Emergency:** ☎477-2251 until 5pm; afterwards, call 911. **Post Office:** Main office (☎477-2238) in Panther Junction, next to Park Headquarters. Open M-F 8am-4pm. Chisos Basin office is inside the grocery store. Open M-Sa 9am-5pm. Post Office accepts general delivery mail addressed to visitor's name, Big Bend National Park, TX. There is another Post Office in Study Butte next to the bank. **ZIP code:** 79834. **Area code:** 915.

⊓⊡ ACCOMMODATIONS & FOOD. The expensive **Chisos Mountains Lodge ❹,** in the Chisos Basin, 10 mi. from park headquarters, offers the only motel-style shelter within the park. Reservations are a must for high season; the lodge is often booked a year in advance. (☎477-2291. Singles $78; doubles $84; additional person $10.) The lodge contains the only **restaurant ❷** in the park, serving three square meals a day. (Open daily 7-10am, 11:30am-4pm, and 5:30-8pm. Breakfast buffet $6.75, lunch sandwiches $4-8, dinner entrees $6-15.) The closest budget motel to the park, the **Chisos Mining Co. Motel ❷,** on Rte. 170, ¾ mi. west of the junction with Rte. 118, provides clean rooms with A/C. Life at this gateway to Big Bend is welcoming enough to skip staying in the Basin. (☎371-2254. Singles $37; doubles $47; 5-6 person cabins with kitchenettes $60.)

The three developed campsites within the park do not take reservations and are run on a first-come, first-served basis. During Thanksgiving, Christmas, March, and April the campgrounds fill early; call park headquarters (☎477-2251) to inquire about availability. The **Chisos Basin Campground ❶,** at 5400 ft., has 65 sites with running water and flush toilets and stays cooler than the other campgrounds in the summer. The **Río Grande Village Campground ❶** has 100 sites near the only showers in the park. Flush toilets and water are also available. The **RV park ❶** at Río Grande Village has 25 full hookups ($14.50 for up to two people; $1 per additional person). **Backcountry camping ❶** in the park is free but requires a permit from one of the area's Visitors Centers.

TEXAS

Restaurants are scarce in the Big Bend area, though there are some options near Terlingua and Lajitas. **Ms. Tracy's Cafe ❷**, on Rte. 118 just south of the intersection with Rte. 170, has outdoor seating and decorative cacti. Ms. Tracy serves eggs, hamburgers, and burritos and a number of vegetarian entrees. (☎371-2888. Open Oct.-May 7am-9:30pm; June 7am-2pm; July-Sept. 7am-5pm.) Off Rte. 170 in Terlingua, 7 mi. from the park entrance, the lively **Starlight Theater Bar and Grill ❷** has healthy portions of Tex-Mex ($3-9) and live music. (☎371-2326. Food served daily 5:30-10pm; bar open Su-F 5pm-midnight, Sa 5pm-1am. Indoor pool: no joke.)

⚲ OUTDOOR ACTIVITIES.

Big Bend encompasses several hundred miles of hiking trails, ranging from 30min. nature walks to backpacking trips several days long. *Always carry at least one gallon of water per person per day in the desert.* The 43 miS. **scenic drive** to Santa Eleña Canyon is handy for those short on time. Many of the park's roads can **flood** during the "rainy" late summer months.

Park rangers at the Visitors Centers are happy to suggest hikes and sights. Pick up the *Hiker's Guide to Big Bend* pamphlet ($2), available at Panther Junction. The **Lost Mine Trail** (3-4hr., 4.8 mi.) leads to an amazing view of the desert and the Sierra de Carmen in Mexico. Also in the Chisos, the **Emory Peak** (5-8hr. one way. 4.5 mi.) requires an intense hike. An easier walk (1½hr., 1.7 mi.) ambles through the **Santa Eleña Canyon** along the Río Grande. Canyon walls rise as high as 1000 ft. over the riverbank.

Though upstream damming has markedly decreased the river's flow, rafting is still big fun on the Río Grande. Free permits and info are available at the Visitors Center. Several companies offer **river trips** down the 118 mi. of designated Río Grande Wild and Scenic River within park boundaries. **Far-Flung Adventures,** next door to the Starlight Theater Bar and Grill in Terlingua, organizes one to seven-day trips. (☎371-2633 or 800-839-7238; www.farflung.com/tx.) In Terlingua off Hwy. 170, **Big Bend River Tours** (☎371-3033 or 800-545-4240; www.bigbendrivertours.com) rents canoes ($45 per day) and inflatable kayaks ($35 per day). Guided trips available. (Half-day $62, full day $130.) Both offer **shuttle services** to pick people up downriver.

ROCKY MOUNTAINS

Created by immense tectonic forces some 65 million years ago, the Rockies mark a vast wrinkle in the North American continent. Sculpted by wind, water, and glaciers over eons, their weathered peaks extend 3000 miles from northern Alberta to New Mexico and soar to altitudes exceeding two vertical miles. Cars overheat and humans gulp thin alpine air as they ascend into grizzly bear country. Dominated by rock and ice, the highest peaks of the Rockies are accessible only to veteran mountain climbers and wildlife adapted for survival in scant air and deep snow.

Although the whole of the Rocky Mountain area supports less than 5% of the US population, each year millions flock to its spectacular national parks, forests, and ski resorts, while hikers follow the Continental Divide along the spine of the Rockies. Nestled in valleys or appearing out of nowhere on the surrounding plains, the region's mountain villages and cowboy towns welcome travelers year-round.

HIGHLIGHTS OF THE ROCKY MOUNTAINS

HIKING. Memorable trails include the Gunnison Rte. in the Black Canyon, CO (p. 761); lake, geyser and canyon trails in Yellowstone National park (p. 715); and just about anything in the Grand Tetons (p. 724).

SKIING. The Rockies are filled with hot spots, but try Sawtooth, ID (p. 698); Vail, CO (p. 753); or Jackson Hole, WY (p. 729).

SCENIC DRIVES. Going-to-the-Sun Rd. in Glacier National Park (p. 712) is unforgettable, as is phenomenally high San Juan Skyway in Colorado (p. 764). The Chief Joseph Scenic Hwy. (p. 724) explores the rugged Wyoming wilderness.

ALPINE TOWNS. Aspen, CO (p. 756), and Stanley, ID (p. 698): two of the loveliest.

IDAHO

Idaho is a land of tremendous geographic diversity. The Rocky Mountains divide the state into three distinct regions, each with its own natural aesthetic. Northern Idaho possesses the greatest concentration of lakes in the western US, interspersed by lush green valleys and rugged mountain peaks. In Central Idaho, plentiful ski slopes, hiking trails, and hot springs span across the semi-arid landscape. To the southeast, world-famous potatoes are cultivated in valleys rich with volcanic sediment. With miles of untouched National Forest and wilderness, has seen little change since 1805, when Lewis and Clark first laid eyes on the state.

⚠ PRACTICAL INFORMATION

Capital: Boise.

Visitor info: Idaho Department of Commerce, 700 W. State St., P.O. Box 83720, Boise 83720 (☎208-334-2470 or 800-842-5858). **Idaho Information Line,** ☎800-847-4843; www.visitid.org. **State Parks and Recreation Dept.,** 5657 Warm Springs Ave., Boise

83712 (☎334-4199). **Idaho Outfitters and Guide Association,** 711 N. 5th St., Boise 83702 (☎800-494-3246; www.ioga.org). Open in summer M-F 8:30am-4pm.

Postal Abbreviation: ID. **Sales Tax:** 5%. **Area code:** 208.

BOISE   ☎208

Built along the banks of the Boise River, Idaho's surprisingly cosmopolitan capital straddles the boundary between desert and mountains. A network of parks protects the natural landscape of the river banks, creating a greenbelt perfect for walking, biking, or skating. Most of the city's sights cluster in the ten-block area between the Capitol and the River, making Boise supremely navigable. A revitalized downtown offers a vast array of ethnic cuisine as well as a thriving nightlife.

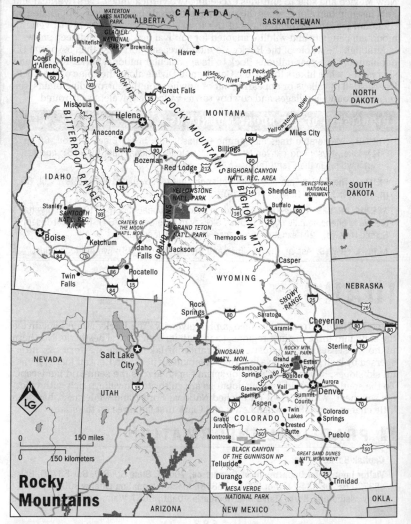

🛈 PRACTICAL INFORMATION. The pedestrian-friendly Grove is a brick walkway between Main and Front St. **Greyhound,** 1212 W. Bannock (☎343-3681; station open 5:30am-9pm and 11pm-2:30am), a few blocks west of downtown, runs to Portland (11hr., 3 per day, $47); Salt Lake City (7hr., 3 per day, $45); and Seattle (14hr., 3 per day, $47). **Boise Urban Stages** (the **BUS,** very clever) has several routes throughout the city. (☎336-1010. Maps available at the Visitors Center. Buses operate M-F 5:15am-7:40pm, Sa 7:45am-6:10pm. M-F 75¢, seniors 35¢, ages 6-18 50¢; Sa all fares 35¢.) **McU's Sports,** 822 W. Jefferson St., rents a good selection of outdoor gear and offers hiking tips. (☎342-7734. M-Sa 9:30am-6pm, Su 11am-5pm. In-line skates $10 for 3hr., $15 for 8hr. Mountain bikes $15 per half-day, $25 per day.) McU's also has a **ski shop** at 2314 Bogus Basin Rd. (☎336-2300. Ski equipment $16 per day, children $13.) **Visitors Center:** 245 8th St., at Boise Centre on the Grove. (☎344-5338. Open M-F 10am-4pm, Sa 10am-2pm.) **Internet access: Boise Public Library,** 715 S. Capitol Blvd. (☎384-4076. Open M-Th 10am-9pm, F 10am-6pm, Sa 10am-5pm.) **Post Office:** 750 W. Bannock St. (☎331-0037. Open M-F 8:30am-5pm.) **ZIP code:** 83702. **Area code:** 208.

🛏 ACCOMMODATIONS. A recent addition to the town of Nampa, 📷**Hostel Boise (HI-AYH) ❶,** 17322 Can-Ada Rd., is 15-20min. from downtown Boise. Take Exit 38 off I-84 W and turn right onto Garrity Blvd., which turns into Can-Ada Rd. This country-style home has mountain views and evening campfires. (☎467-6858. Internet access $1 per 15min. Max. stay 3 nights. Dorm-style beds $17.50.) Inexpensive motels bunch around Exit 53 of I-84, near the airport. The newly renovated **University Inn ❸,** 2360 University Dr., next to Boise State University, has free local calls, cable TV and HBO, pool and jacuzzi, and a shuttle to the airport. (☎345-7170 or 800-345-7170. Singles $50-58; doubles $55-65.) The **Cabana Inn ❷,** 1600 Main St., in downtown Boise, has basic rooms in a Spanish-style villa, containing TV, A/C, fridges, and microwaves. (☎343-6000. Reservations recommended. Singles $43; doubles $52; 8-person suite $75.) The **Boise National Forest Office/Bureau of Land Management,** 1387 S. Vinnell Way, provides info about Boise's RV-oriented campgrounds. (☎373-4007. Open M-F 7:45am-4:30pm.) It's always a party at **Fiesta RV Park ❶,** 11101 Fairview Ave. (☎375-8207. Pool. Reception Oct.-May daily 8am-6pm; June-Sept. 8am-8pm. Sites $21, partial hookup $23, full hookup $24.)

🍴📷 FOOD & NIGHTLIFE. You may be surprised to discover that Boise offers much more than just baked potatoes and french fries. Besides its fine selection of potato wedges, there are also 80 restaurants of varying cuisines. The downtown area, centered around **8th** and **Main St.,** bustles with lunchtime delis, coffeeshops, ethnic cuisine, and several stylish bistros. For amazingly fresh and creative vegetarian food, try **Kulture Klatsch ❷,** 409 S. 8th. This hip and multicultural eatery has an extensive veggie menu, including numerous vegan options, and hosts live music five nights a week. (☎345-0452. Lunch specials $5. Breakfasts $3-8. Dinners $7-9. Open M 7am-3pm, Tu-Th 7am-10pm, F 7am-11pm, Sa 8am-11pm, Su 8am-3pm.) For breakfast, head to **Moon's Kitchen ❶,** 815 W. Bannock St., a vintage 1950s diner that has blended malts since 1955. (☎385-0472. Shakes $4. Breakfast $4.50-7. Open M-F 6:30am-3pm, Sa 8am-3pm, Su 9am-2pm.) The casual yet trendy **Bittercreek Alehouse ❷,** 246 N. 8th St., in downtown Boise, has burgers and pita sandwiches for $6-9. (☎345-1813. 21+ after 10pm. Open daily 11am-late.)

Musicians regularly perform on Main St., while vendors from nearby restaurants hawk food and beer. Cheap beer and live music draw the locals to **Blues Bouquet,** 1010 Main St., downtown's only Western saloon. (☎345-6605. 21+. Open M-F 1pm-2am, Sa-Su 8pm-2am.) At **The Balcony,** 150 N. 8th St., #226, one block from the Grove Center, DJs spin nightly. All kinds of people gather at this gay-friendly bar to dance and play pool. (☎336-1313. Happy hour daily 2-7pm. 21+. Open 2pm-2am.)

◙ **SIGHTS.** The logical starting point for exploring Boise is the beautiful **Julia Davis Park.** Free parking is available along Capitol Blvd. near the museums. The **Boise Tour Train** covers approximately 75 city sights in 1¼hr. Tours begin and end in the parking lot at Julia Davis Park. (☎342-4796. Tours June-early Sept. M-Sa 10am-3pm, Su noon-3:45pm; in fall W-F noon and 1:30pm, Sa 10:30am-3pm, Su noon-3pm. $7, seniors $6, ages 4-12 $4.50.) To learn about Idaho and the Old West at your own pace, stroll through the **Historical Museum,** 610 Julia Davis Dr., which showcases a replica 19th-century bar complete with a display of a two-headed calf. Other notable exhibits include Native American artifacts and a timeline of Ernest Hemingway's life. (☎334-2120. Open in summer M-Sa 9am-5pm, Su 1-5pm; in winter closed M. $2, students $1.) The **Boise Art Museum,** 670 Julia Davis Dr., displays an impressive selection of contemporary international and local works while offering educational programs, lectures, and tours. (☎345-8330. Open June-Aug. M-F 10am-5pm, Sa-Su noon-5pm; Sept.-May closed M. $4, students and seniors $2, ages 6-18 $1; free the 1st Th of every month.) Raptors perch and dive at the **World Center for Birds of Prey,** 566 W. Flying Hawk Ln. From I-84, take Exit 50 and go south on S. Cole; turn right onto W. Flying Hawk Ln. (☎362-8687. Open Mar.-Oct. daily 9am-5pm; Nov.-Feb. 10am-4pm. $4, seniors $3, children $2, under 4 free.) Basque culture is preserved at the **Basque Museum and Cultural Center,** at the corner of Grove St. and Capital Blvd. This fascinating museum includes a gallery of Basque art and a replica of a Basque herder's house. (☎343-2671. Open Tu-F 10am-4pm, Sa 11am-3pm. Free, donations accepted.)

At the 22 mi. **Boise River Greenbelt,** visitors can go tubing in the river in summer. The ever-growing **Boise Shakespeare Festival** (☎336-9221) hits town from June to September. Every year in late June, Boise hosts a **River Festival,** featuring hot-air balloons, a carnival, live music, fireworks, and sporting events. (☎338-8887; June 27-29, 2003.) Upcoming events are showcased in Thursday's *The Boise Weekly.*

KETCHUM & SUN VALLEY ☎208

In 1935, Union Pacific heir Averill Harriman sent Austrian Count Felix Schaff-gotsch to scour the western US for a site to develop into a ski resort that would rival Europe's best. The Count finally settled on the small mining and sheep-herding town of Ketchum in Idaho's Wood River Valley. Sun Valley was quickly recognized as a world-class ski resort, fulfilling Harriman's dream. While Ketchum's permanent population is only 5300, traffic extends for miles in each direction during peak months. Skiing reigns supreme in winter, while in summer the days are long and the nights are even longer, as those who come for the biking, hiking, and fishing sample the industrial-sized nightlife.

◪ **PRACTICAL INFORMATION.** The best time for fun in the Sun is winter and summer. The town does its best to shut down during "slack" times (Oct.-Nov., May-early June), but during these periods accommodations offer lower rates while the natural beauty stays the same. **Sun Valley Express** runs one bus daily to the Boise airport. (☎877-622-8267. Leaves Ketchum 8:30am, leaves Boise 2:45pm. Summer $57-62; winter $59-64. Reservations recommended.) **KART,** Ketchum's bus service, tours the city and its surrounding areas. Maps are available at the Chamber of Commerce. (☎726-7576. Runs daily 7:20am-midnight. Free.) **Chamber of Commerce/Visitors Center:** 4th and Main St. in Ketchum. (☎726-3423 or 800-634-3347; www.visitsunvalley.com. Open in peak season daily 9am-6pm; hours vary during spring and fall.) **Internet access: Community Library,** 415 Spruce Ave. (☎726-3493. Open M and Sa 9am-6pm, Tu and Th noon-9pm, W 9am-9pm, F 1-6pm. Free.) **Post Office:** 151 W. 4th St. (☎726-5161. Open M-F 8:30am-5:30pm, Sa 11am-2pm.) **ZIP code:** 83340. **Area code:** 208.

ⓘ ACCOMMODATIONS. From early June to mid-October, camping is the best option for cheap sleep in the Sun Valley area. Check with the **Ketchum Ranger Station,** 206 Sun Valley Rd., just outside of Ketchum on the way to Sun Valley. (☎ 622-5371. Open daily 8:30am-noon and 1-5pm.) **Boundary Campground ❶,** 3 mi. northeast of town on Trail Creek Rd. past the Sun Valley resort, is closest to town and has nine wooded sites near a creek. (Restrooms, water, picnic area. Sites $11.) There are also free primitive dispersed campsites farther along Trail Creek. Up Rte. 75 into the SNRA lie several scenic camping spots; the cheapest ($10) are **Murdock ❶** (11 sites) and **Caribou ❶** (7 sites). They are, respectively, 2 and 3 mi. up the unpaved North Fork Rd., which begins as a paved road to the right of the Visitors Center. The **North Fork ❶** (29 sites; $11) and **Wood River** (30 sites) are 8 mi. north of Ketchum, along Rte. 75. For North Fork, take the first campground road north of SNRA headquarters; Wood River is 2 mi. north. Enjoy great views and prices about as low as can be found in Ketchum at the **Lift Tower Lodge ❸,** 703 S. Main St. (☎ 726-5163 or 800-462-8646. Rooms $66-90.)

◨◪ FOOD & NIGHTLIFE. Ketchum's small confines bulge with over 80 restaurants catering to the gourmet tastes of resort visitors, but relatively cheap eats can still be found. Only the brave (or hungover) dare try the Spam sub at **Johnny G's Subshack ❶,** 371 Main St. Delicious alternatives to that notorious sub include the Club Tahiti and the Middle School Madness—a toasted stack of turkey, bacon, and cheddar. (☎ 725-7827. Subs under $5. Open M-F 11am-4pm, Sa noon-3pm.) Beer cans of all shapes and sizes grace the walls of **Grumpy's,** 860 Warm Springs Rd., a flavorful local hangout. (No phone. PBR cans $1. 32oz. goblet of beer $3.25. Open 11am-10pm.) Head downstairs to the **Cellar Pub,** 400 Sun Valley Rd. near Leadville Ave., for a lively young crowd, excellent burgers and bangers, and a plethora of inventive pints like the "straight jacket." (☎ 622-3832. Open daily 5pm-2am.) Chase back some stiff drinks for 100 pennies on Sunday and Tuesday at **Whiskey Jacques,** 251 Main St. (☎ 726-5297. Live music most nights 9:30pm-2am. Cover $3-5. Open daily 4pm-2am.)

▨ OUTDOOR ACTIVITIES. The **Wood River and Sun Valley trail system,** follow Rte. 75 south of town, consists of over 20 mi. of paved trails. The trail begins in Bellevue and continues through Ketchum and Sun Valley, passing by ski slopes and historic sites. The *Wood River Trails* pamphlet, available at the Visitors Center, has more info. Visible for miles, **Bald Mountain,** or "Baldy," is a beacon for serious skiers. Two plazas serve Baldy, River Run on the north side of town and Warm Springs on the south side. Whereas mostly advanced skiers are on Bald Mountain, the gentle slopes of **Dollar Mountain** are perfect for beginners. (☎ 800-786-8259, ski conditions ☎ 800-635-4150. Full-day lift ticket $59, under 12 $32.)

The Sawtooth area is nationally renowned for its stunning mountain bike trails, which traverse the gorgeous canyons and mountain passes of the SNRA. *Beware: trails might be snowbound or flooded well into July.* Take a high-speed quad to the top of Bald Mountain and ride down on a mountain bike during summer months. (☎ 622-2231. Open in summer daily 9am-3:45pm. $15 per ride, $20 per day.) Inquire about trail conditions and rent gear at **Formula Sports,** 460 N. Main St. (☎ 726-3194. Bikes from $12 per 4hr., $18 per day; tandems $20/30. Skis $18-40.) **The Elephant's Perch,** 280 East Ave., at Sun Valley Rd., has a complete stock of outdoor gear. (☎ 726-3497. Open daily 9am-6pm. Bikes $12 per 4hr., $20 per day. Backpack $15 per day, sleeping bag $25 per day, tents $20 per day. Nordic and telemark ski packages $15-30 per day.) Inquire about biking trails at the Chamber of Commerce or the SNRA Headquarters.

THE SUN VALLEY ALSO RISES Ernest Hemingway's love affair with both rugged outdoor sports and wealthy celebrities fits Ketchum's dualistic spirit. After spending many vacations hunting and fishing in the Sawtooth Range, the author built a cabin in Sun Valley where he died from a self-inflicted gun-shot wound on July 2, 1961. While Hemingway's house is off-limits, there are a number of sites in town that commemorate the author. His grave is located in the Ketchum Cemetery, just north of town on Rte. 75. The **Ketchum-Sun Valley Heritage and Ski Museum** displays exhibits on Hemingway's life. *(180 1st St. E, at Washington Ave.* ☎ *726-8118. Open M-F 11am-5pm, Sa 1-4pm. Times vary in winter.)* A bust of Hemingway is tucked away in a shady spot along the river at the **Hemingway Memorial**, about 1 mi. outside of Sun Valley on the way to Boundary Campground (see **Accommodations**, above). Each year on Hemingway's birthday, July 21, the community library hosts a lecture. *(*☎ *726-3493.)*

After a hard day of biking or hiking, Ketchum locals soak their weary legs in one of several hot springs. Hidden in the hills and canyons of Ketchum, the hot springs are no longer a well-kept secret. Melting snow and rain can bury the springs underwater, rendering them inaccessible in spring and early summer. The springs are safe for swimming once the current subsides in July. The Chamber of Commerce has suggestions on which pools are safe and accessible. One of the more accessible, non-commercial springs is **Warfield Hot Springs,** on Warm Springs Rd., 11 mi. west of Ketchum. An alternative to these pools can be found at **Easley Hot Springs,** 12 mi. north of Ketchum on Rte. 75. (☎ 726-7522. Open Tu and Th-Sa 11am-7pm, W 11am-5pm, Su noon-5pm. $5.50, seniors $4, children $4.50.) For the best info on **fishing,** including equipment rentals, stop by **Silver Creek Outfitters,** 500 N. Main St. (☎ 726-5282. Open M-Sa 9am-6pm, Su noon-5pm; hours vary in peak season. Fly rods, waders, and boots $15 per day.

SAWTOOTH NATIONAL RECREATION AREA (SNRA) ☎ 208

Established by Congress in 1972, the **Sawtooth National Recreation Area (SNRA)** sprawls over 756,000 acres of National Forest, including 217,000 acres of untouched wilderness. The park is home to four mountain ranges with more than 40 peaks over 10,000 feet. The Sawtooth and White Cloud Mountains tower above the surrounding landscape in the north, while the Smokey and Boulder Mountains dominate the southern horizon. Over 300 mountain lakes and the headwaters of four of Idaho's major rivers are interspersed throughout the park's dense forest.

◪ **PRACTICAL INFORMATION.** The tiny (pop. 69), frontier-style town of **Stanley,** located 60 mi. north of Ketchum at the intersection of Rte. 21 and 75, serves as a northern base for exploring Sawtooth. The small business district is located one block south of Rte. 21, along Ace of Diamonds St. The **Stanley Ranger Station,** 3 mi. south of Stanley on Rte. 75, offers maps, SNRA passes, and sage outdoor advice. (☎ 774-3000. Open in summer M-Sa 8am-4:30pm; in winter M-F 8:30am-4:30pm.) At the entrance to Redfish Lake, 5 mi. south of Stanley and 55 mi. north of Ketchum on Rte. 75, an **Info booth** dispenses a wide range of info about hiking, camping, and outdoor sports. (☎ 774-3536. Sporadic hours; the booth is usually staffed during sunny, busy weekends.) The **Redfish Lake Visitors Center** can provide additional information about the park, including educational programs about wildlife and geology. (☎ 774-3376. Open mid-June to early Sept. daily 9am-5pm; late May to mid-June Sa-Su 9am-

5pm.) **Sawtooth National Recreation Area (SNRA) Headquarters,** 6 mi. north of Ketchum off Rte. 75, stocks detailed info on the hot springs and area forests and trails. SNRA maps are $6-7 and local hiker Margaret Fuller's excellent trail guides are $14-18. (☎727-5013 or 800-260-5970. Open in summer 8am-5pm; in winter 9am-3:30pm.) **Chamber of Commerce:** Rte. 21, P.O. Box 8. (☎774-3411 or 800-878-7950.) **Post Office:** Ace of Diamonds St., Stanley. (☎774-2230. Open M-F 8-11am and noon-5pm.) **ZIP code:** 83278. **Area code:** 208.

ⅠⅠ ACCOMMODATIONS. The SNRA boasts 33 campgrounds scattered throughout the park; consult a ranger for help in selecting (and locating) a campsite. **Alturas Lake ❶,** 21 mi. south of Stanley on Rte. 75 (the turn-off is marked about 10 mi. north of Galena Pass), has three campgrounds with fishing and swimming. (Vault toilets and water. 55 sites $11-13.) The area around **Redfish Lake ❶,** 5 mi. south of Stanley off Rte. 75, is a scenic but sometimes overcrowded spot. The eight campgrounds in the area are conveniently close to Stanley and many trailheads. (Sites $11-13.) East on Rte. 75, past the town of Stanley, numerous sites are available alongside the wild and scenic **Salmon River ❶.** (Water available; no hookup. First come, first served. Sites $11.) One of the best campgrounds is **Mormon Bend,** 8 mi. east of Stanley on Rte. 75, with 15 sites close to whitewater rafting. Other scenic and inviting spots are **Casino Creek,** 8 mi. east of Stanley on Rte. 75; the **Salmon River Campground,** 9 mi. east of Stanley on Rte. 75; and **Upper and Lower O'Brien,** 2 mi. past Sunbeam Dam. In most areas, a trailhead pass, available at the Stanley Ranger Station, is required for parking.

For a real bed, Stanley provides more scenic and more reasonable lodging than Ketchum. At **Danner's Log Cabin Motel ❸,** on Rte. 21, ex-mayor and Stanley history buff Bunny Danner rents historic cabins built by goldminers in 1939. The office, built in 1906, was the first building in town and originally served as the ranger station. (☎774-3539. Cabins in summer $55-125; spring and fall $42-80.)

ⅭⅯ FOOD & NIGHTLIFE. Dining options are rather limited in Stanley. Before exploring the SNRA, stock up on food and gas, as well as fishing licenses, at **Jerry's Country Store and Motel,** on Rte. 75 in Lower Stanley. (☎774-3566 or 800-972-4627. Open M-Sa 8:30am-9pm, Su 9am-7pm.) Locals rave about the $5 deli sandwiches at **Papa Brunee's ❷,** Ace of Diamonds St., downtown. (☎774-2536. Pizza $4-20. Open daily 11am-10pm.) The local watering hole is the **Rod and Gun Club Bar,** on Ace of Diamonds St. This authentic western bar has pool tables, a dance floor, and live weekend music. (☎774-9920. 21+. Open daily 8pm-2am.)

ⅠⅠ OUTDOOR ACTIVITIES. The rugged backcountry of the SNRA is perfect for hiking, boating, fishing, and mountain biking. Pick up a free map of the area and inquire about trail conditions at SNRA headquarters before heading into the park, particularly in early summer, when trails may be flooded. Much of the backcountry stays buried in snow well into the summer. Watch out for black bears; ranger stations have information about necessary precautions. The Sawtooth Scenic Byway (Rte. 75) spans 60 miles of National Forest land between Ketchum and Stanley, crossing the Galena Pass at 8701 ft. Pause at the **Galena Overlook,** 31 mi. north of Ketchum, for a spectacular view of the park.

Redfish Lake is the source of many trails. Some popular, leisurely hikes include those to **Fishhook Creek** (excellent for children), **Bench Lakes,** and the **Hell Roaring trail.** The long, gentle loop around **Yellow Belly, Toxaway,** and **Petit Lakes** is a moderate overnight trip suitable for novices. Two miles northwest of Stanley on Rte. 21, the 3 mi. Iron Creek Rd. leads to the trailhead of the 5½ mi. **Sawtooth Lake Hike.** Bionic hikers can try the steep 4 mi. hike to **Casino Lakes,** which begins at the Broadway Creek trailhead southeast of Stanley.

ROCKY MOUNTAINS

The Sawtooths have miles of mountain biking, but check a map first; riding is allowed in National Forest areas but prohibited in the Sawtooth Wilderness. **River-wear,** on Rte. 21 in Stanley, rents bikes. (☎774-3592. Open daily 7am-10pm. Bikes from $17 per day.) The 18 mi. **Fischer/Williams Creek Loop** is the most popular biking trail, ascending to an elevation of 8280 ft. Beginners will enjoy riding the dirt road that accesses the North Fork campgrounds from the Visitors Center. This gorgeous passage parallels the North Fork of the Wood River for 5 mi. before branching off into other narrower and steeper trails for more advanced riders. These trails can be combined into loops; consult the trail map or the ranger station. The steep **Boulder Basin Rd.,** 5 mi. from SNRA headquarters, leads to pristine Boulder Lake and an old mining camp. Topographical maps ($4) and various trail books ($6-20) are available at **McCoy's Tackle and Gift Shop,** on Ace of Diamonds St. McCoy's also sells sporting goods, fishing tackle, and licenses. (☎774-3377. Open June-Sept. daily 8am-8pm; off-season hours vary.) **Sawtooth Adventure Rentals,** on Rte. 75 in Lower Stanley, rents kayaks and rafts. (☎866-774-4644. Open May-Sept. Kayaks $25-50. Rafts $75 for 8 people.) For boat tours of the lake, head for **Redfish Lake Lodge Marina.** (☎774-3536. Open in summer daily 7am-8:30pm. 1hr. tours $8, ages 6-12 $5; $32 minimum. Paddleboats $5 per 30min. Canoes $10 per hr., $32 per half-day, $50 per day. Outboards $15 per hr., $50 for half-day, $80 per day.) The most inexpensive way to enjoy the SNRA waters is to visit the **hot springs** just east of Stanley. **Sunbeam Hot Springs,** 10 mi. east of Lower Stanley on Rte. 75, triumphs over the rest, though high water can wash out the hot springs temporarily.

CRATERS OF THE MOON ☎208

The otherworldly landscape at **Craters of the Moon National Monument** first drew national attention in the 1920s. An early visitor to the landscape claimed it was "the strangest 75 square miles on the North American continent." The same geological hot spot responsible for the thermal activity in Yellowstone National Park created the Monument's twisted lava formations. Located 70 mi. southeast of Sun Valley at the junction of Rte. 20 and 26/93, the park's unusual craters and rock formations make for an interesting visit. ($5 per car, $3 per person.)

There are 52 **sites** scattered throughout the monument's single campground, located just past the entrance station. (Water and restrooms. No hookups. $10.) Wood fires are prohibited, but charcoal fires are permitted in the grills. Camping at unmarked sites in the dry lava wilderness of the park is permitted with a free **back-country permit,** available at the **Visitors Center,** off Rte. 93 and 20/26 between Arco and Carey. (☎527-3257. Open in summer daily 8am-6pm; off-season 8am-4:30pm.) **Echo Crater,** a short four-mile hike from the Tree Molds parking lot, is one of the most popular backcountry campsites.

The Visitors Center has videos, displays, and printed guides outlining the area's geological past. A seven-mile drive winds through much of the monument, guiding tourists to the major sights. Several short trails lead to more unusual rock formations and a variety of caves; the Visitors Center has guides. Don't forget sturdy shoes, water, sunscreen, and hats; the black rocks absorb heat and there are no trees for miles.

The town of **Arco,** 18 mi. east of the Craters of the Moon on Rte. 20, claims to be the "first city in the world lighted by atomic energy." Arco is also the closest source of services and lodgings for travelers visiting the monument. Cheap rooms with telephones and cable TV are available at the **D-K Motel ❷,** 316 S. Front St. (☎527-8282 or 800-231-0134. Singles $32; doubles $40-47.) The **Arco Deli Sandwich Shop ❷,** on Rte. 20/26/93, at Grand Ave. and Idaho St., serves fresh deli sandwiches. (☎527-3757. Foot-long sandwiches $7.50. Open M-Sa 8am-8pm.) The **Chamber of Commerce** (☎527-8977), 159 N. Idaho, has info on local attractions. If traveling from Arco to Sun Valley (see p. 698), you can also pick up a free cassette tour of the Central Idaho Rockies.

MONTANA

If any part of the scenery dominates the Montana landscape more than the pristine mountain peaks and shimmering glacial lakes, it's the sky—welcome to Big Sky country. With 25 million acres of national forest and public lands, Montana's grizzly bears, mountain lions, and pronghorn antelope outnumber the people. Small towns, set against unadulterated mountain vistas, offer a true taste of the Old West. Copious fishing lakes, 500 species of wildlife (not including millions of insect species), and beautiful rivers combine with hot springs and thousands of ski trails to make Montana an American paradise.

🖬 PRACTICAL INFORMATION

Capital: Helena.

Visitor info: Travel Montana, P.O. Box 7549, Missoula 59807 (☎800-847-4868; www.visitmt.com). **National Forest Information,** Northern Region, Federal Bldg., 200 E. Broadway, Box 7669, Missoula 59807 (☎406-329-3511).

Postal Abbreviation: MT. **Sales Tax:** None.

HELENA ☎406

As Montana's capital city, Helena has successfully modernized while still retaining the historical feel of the Old West. A product of the 1864 Gold Rush at Last Chance Gulch, Helena has transformed itself from a humble mining camp into a sophisticated city equipped with a symphony, several theaters, and an outdoor walking mall downtown. Halfway between Glacier and Yellowstone National Parks, Helena provides a pleasant stopover for travelers tackling the two, but is an outdoors destination in its own right with hiking, boating, and fishing opportunities.

🖬 PRACTICAL INFORMATION. I-15, U.S. 12, and **U.S. 287** intersect in Helena. **Rimrock Trailways,** 3100 U.S. 12 E (☎442-5860), behind the High Country Travel Plaza Truck stop, departs daily at 8:15am and 6:45pm and sends separate buses to Billings ($36); Bozeman ($17); and Missoula ($21.50). **Greyhound** connects in all three cities to further points. **Helena Area Chamber of Commerce,** 225 Cruse Ave., has visitor information. (☎442-4120. Open M-F 8am-5pm.) **Post Office:** 2300 N. Harris (☎443-3304). **ZIP code:** 59601. **Area code:** 406.

🖪🖸 ACCOMMODATIONS & FOOD. There aren't that many cheap places in Helena to hang your hat, but **Budget Inn Express ❷,** 524 N. Last Chance Gulch, has an attractive downtown location and large, tidy rooms. (☎442-0600 or 800-862-1334. Laundry, cable TV, and kitchenettes. Singles in summer $37; in winter $34. Doubles $47/44.) The **Helena Campground and RV Park ❶,** 5820 N. Montana Ave., north of Helena just west of I-15, has grassy, shaded tent sites. (☎458-4714. Laundry and showers. Sites $22, full hookup $23; cabins $38.) Just to the southeast of Helena, public campgrounds line **Canyon Ferry Reservoir;** take either Canyon Ferry Rd. or Rte. 284 from U.S. 12. (Sites under $12.) The free **Fish Hawk Campground ❶,** on West Shore Drive, is reserved for tents and has toilets but no drinking water. The **BOR Canyon Ferry Office,** 7661 Canyon Ferry Rd. (☎475-3310), has more info.

Rub elbows with state legislators and officials at the **Windbag Saloon and Grill ❷,** 19 S. Last Chance Gulch, in the walking mall, and enjoy Montana-sized burgers for $6-7. (☎443-9669. Open M-Sa 11am-midnight.) For a taste of regional sesame flavor, head over to **Bert & Ernie's ❷,** 361 N. Last Chance Gulch, and sink your teeth into a juicy half-pound burger ($6-7). Sandwiches ($7) and heart-healthy entrees satisfy burger-phobes. (☎443-5680. Open M-Sa 11am-9pm.)

◙ 瓜 **SIGHTS & OUTDOOR ACTIVITIES.** A strategic point from which to begin an exploration of Helena, the **Montana Historical Society Museum,** 225 N. Roberts St., runs several tours of the city. (☎444-2694. Open June-Aug. M-F 8am-6pm, Sa-Su 9am-5pm; Sept.-May M-F 8am-5pm, Sa 9am-5pm. $3, children $1.) Among the historical society's tours is the popular hour-long **Last Chance Tour Train.** (☎442-1023. Tours May and Sept. M-Sa 3 per day; June M-Sa 5 per day; July-Aug. M-Sa 7 per day. $5.50, seniors, ages 4-12 $4.50.) The **State Capitol** building, 1301 6th Ave. at Montana Ave., has several pieces of notable artwork, including C.M. Russell's *Lewis and Clark Meeting the Flathead Indians at Ross' Hole* and a statue of Jeannette Rankin, the first woman elected to the US Congress. (☎444-4789. Self-guided tours M-F 6am-5pm, Sa 8am-5pm, Su noon-5pm; in summer guided tours every hr. M-Sa 9am-4pm, Su noon-4pm. Free.) The gold vanished from **Last Chance Gulch** long ago, but today this walking mall offers restaurants, shops, and public artwork. Housed in the old jail, the **Myrna Loy Center,** 15 N. Ewing St. (☎443-0287), presents foreign film, dance, music, and performance art.

Take in all of Helena and the surrounding area from the top of **Mt. Helena** (elevation 5460 ft.); the trail begins from the Adams St. Trailhead, just west of Reeders Alley. Observe the Missouri River just as Lewis and Clark did by taking a boat tour of the **Gates of the Mountains,** 18 mi. north of Helena, just off I-15. The boat stops near Mann Gulch, where a 1949 forest fire killed 13 smokejumpers. (☎458-5241. June-Sept., usually 2-4 per day. Call for times. $9.50, seniors $8.50, ages 4-17 $6.)

LITTLE BIG HORN

Little Big Horn National Monument, 60 mi. southeast of Billings, off I-90 on the Crow Reservation, marks the site of one of the most dramatic episodes in the conflict between Native Americans and the US government. Here, on June 25, 1876, Sioux and Cheyenne warriors, led by Sioux chiefs Sitting Bull and Crazy Horse, retaliated against years of genocide by annihilating five companies of the US Seventh Cavalry under the command of Lt. Colonel George Armstrong Custer. White stone graves mark where the US soldiers fell. The exact Native American casualties are not known, since their families and fellow warriors removed the bodies from the battlefield almost immediately. The renaming of the monument, formerly known as the Custer Battlefield Monument, signifies the government's admission that Custer's brutal acts against Native Americans merit no glorification. Congress also prescribed that a memorial be built in honor of the Native Americans killed at the battle. This memorial, which the Cheyenne have been working toward since 1925, was finally completed in September 2002.

The **Visitors Center** has a small movie theater and an electronic map of the battlefield. (☎638-2621, ext. 124. Monument open late May to early Sept. daily 8am-9pm; Visitors Center open daily 8am-7:30pm. Both open in fall daily 8am-6pm; in winter 8am-4:30pm. Entrance $10 per car, $5 per person.) Rangers here offer thorough explanatory talks daily during the summer, every hour 9am-6pm. Visitors can also ride through the monument guided by an audio tour, narrating the battle's progression. ($15.) A one-hour **bus tour** leaves from the Visitors Center at 9, 10:30am, noon, 2, and 3:30pm. ($10, seniors $8, under 12 $5.)

BOZEMAN ☎406

Surrounded by world-class hiking, skiing, and fishing, Bozeman has recently become a magnet for outdoor enthusiasts. To Montanans, however, Bozeman remains "that boisterous college town." Cowboy hats and pickup trucks are still popular among students at **Montana State University (MSU),** but the increasing diversity of the student body reflects the cultural vigor of this thriving community.

🖪 PRACTICAL INFORMATION. Greyhound and **RimRock Stages,** 1205 E. Main St. (☎587-3110; open M-F 7:30am-5pm and 7pm-midnight; Sa-Su 7:30am-noon, 3:30-5pm, and 7pm-midnight), both send buses to: Billings (3hr., 4 per day, $23); Butte (2hr., 3 per day, $16); Helena (2hr., 1 per day, $16); and Missoula (5hr., 4 per day, $37.50). **Car Rental: Budget Rent-a-Car,** at the airport. (☎388-4091. Open daily 7:30am-11pm, or until last flight. Rental $50 per day, 100 free mi., 25¢ per additional mi. Ages 21-24 $15 per day surcharge. Credit card required.) **Visitor info: Bozeman Area Chamber of Commerce,** 2000 Commerce Way, at the corner of 19th Ave. and Baxter Ln. (☎586-5421 or 800-228-4224; www.bozemanchamber.com. Open M 9am-5pm, Tu-F 8am-5pm.) **Internet access: Bozeman Public Library,** 220 E. Lamme St. (☎582-2400. Open in winter M-Th 10am-8pm, F-Sa 10am-5pm, Su 1-5pm; in summer closed Su.) **Post Office:** 32 E. Babcock St. (☎586-2373. Open M-F 9am-5pm.) **ZIP code:** 59715. **Area code:** 406.

🛏 ACCOMMODATIONS. A number of budget motels line Main St. and 7th Ave. north of Main. **Alpine Lodge ❷,** 1017 E. Main St., has reasonable prices and spacious rooms with breakfast included. (☎586-0356 or 888-922-5746. Reservations recommended. Rooms $40-98.) Across the street, the **Blue Sky Motel ❷,** 1010 E. Main St., offers comfortable rooms off an enclosed front porch that runs the length of the motel. (☎587-2311. Singles $45; doubles $54.) The **Bear Canyon Campground ❶,** 4 mi. east of Bozeman, south of I-90 at Exit 313, has great views of the surrounding countryside. (☎587-1575 or 800-438-1575. Laundry, showers, and pool. Sites $15, with water and electricity $20, full hookup $25; each additional person $2.) **Spire Rock Campground ❶,** 26 mi. south of Bozeman on U.S. 191, is one of several national forest campgrounds that line the highway. (☎522-2520. $7 per night.)

🍴🌙 FOOD & NIGHTLIFE. Thrifty eateries aimed at the college crowd line W. College near the university. Now a popular chain throughout Montana, the original **Pickle Barrel ❶** resides at 809 W. College. Enormous sandwiches with fresh ingredients and free pickles have drawn MSU students for years. (☎587-2411. Hefty half-sandwiches $4.65-5.40. Open in summer daily 10:30am-10pm; in winter 11am-10:30pm.) **Sweet Pea Bakery and Cafe ❷,** 19 S. Wilson St., cooks up a gourmet lunch and brunch, like mango chicken salad, for around $8. Pastries and lattes square off in a battle for morning supremacy. (☎587-2411. Open in summer M-Tu 7am-3pm, W-Su 7am-9:30pm; in winter Tu 7am-3pm, W-Su 7am-9:30pm.) **The Burrito Shop ❷,** 207 N. 7th Ave., is not afraid to smother its burritos with love, along with more traditional toppings like green chili, sour cream, and cheese. (☎586-1422. Burrito happy hour 2:30-4pm. Burritos with chips and salad $6.75. Open M-Sa 11am-9pm.) Locals and travelers thirsty for good beer and great live music head over to the **🎷Zebra Cocktail Lounge,** in the basement at the corner of Rouse Ave. and Main St. The large selection of beers and the hipster atmosphere always draw a young, cool crowd. (☎585-8851. W-Sa DJ or bands. Open daily 8pm-2am.) Sample some of Montana's best beer at the **Spanish Peaks Brewery,** 14 N. Church Ave. (☎585-2296. Open Su-F 11:30am-10pm, Sa 5-10pm.) Get the lowdown on music and nightlife from the weekly *Tributary* or *The BoZone.*

📷🏞 SIGHTS & OUTDOOR ACTIVITIES. Get up close and personal with dinosaurs and other artifacts of Rocky Mountain history at the **Museum of the Rockies,** 600 West Kagy Blvd., near the university. Dr. Jack Horner (the basis for the main character in *Jurassic Park*) and other paleontologists make this their base for excavating prehistoric remains throughout the West. While there, check out the exhibit on Native American culture. (☎994-3466. Open in summer daily 8am-8pm; in winter M-Sa 9am-5pm, Su 12:30-5pm. $7, ages 5-18 $4, under 5 free.)

ROCKY MOUNTAINS

Surrounded by three renowned trout fishing rivers—Yellowstone, Madison, and Gardiner—the small town of **Livingston**, about 25 mi. east of Bozeman off I-90, is an angler's heaven. This is gorgeous country; the film *A River Runs Through It* was shot in Bozeman and Livingston. Livingston's Main St. features a strip of early 20th century buildings housing bars (with gambling), restaurants, fishing outfitters, and a few modern businesses. If fishing's your thing, **Dan Bailey's**, 209 W. Park St., sells licenses and rents gear. (☎ 222-1673 or 800-356-4052. Open in summer M-Sa 8am-7pm; in winter M-Sa 8am-6pm. Fishing license 2-day $22, season $67. Rod and reel $10; waders and boots $10.)

Bozeman provides its share of downhill thrills. The world-class ski area, **Big Sky**, 45 mi. south of town on U.S. 191, has over 120 trails and short lift lines. The Lone Peak trams reach an altitude of 11,166 ft. for extreme skiing options. (☎ 800-548-4486. Open mid-Nov. to mid-Apr. Full-day ticket $56, college students with ID and ages 11-17 $44, under 10 free. Ski rentals $26-40, juniors $19; snowboard $34.) More intimate and less expensive than Big Sky, **Bridger Bowl Ski Area**, 15795 Bridger Canyon Rd., 16 mi. northeast of town on Hwy. 86, has trails for a variety of abilities. (☎ 586-1518 or 800-223-9609. Open early Dec. to early Apr. Full-day ticket $34, seniors $28, ages 6-12 $13, under 6 free. Rentals: skis $20, junior skis $10; snowboard $30.) In summer, scenic **lift rides** soar up Big Sky. (Open June to early Oct. daily 9:45am-5pm. $13, under 10 free.) Equestrian types gallop at nearby **Big Sky Stables**, on the spur road off U.S. 191, about 2 mi. before Big Sky's entrance. (☎ 995-2972. Open June-Sept. $30 for 1hr., $50 for 2hr. 1-day notice required.) **Yellowstone Raft Co.** shoots the rapids of the Gallatin River, 7 mi. north of the Big Sky area on U.S. 191. Trips meet at the Yellowstone Raft Co. office, between mileposts 55 and 56 on U.S. 191. (☎ 995-4613 or 800-348-4376. Half-day $39, children $30.)

RED LODGE ☎ 406

The small historic mining town of Red Lodge (pop. 2000) is nestled in the foothills of the Beartooth Mountains. The Absaroka (Crow) Indians are the region's original inhabitants, and legend has it that the name "Red Lodge" derives from the red clay adhering to Absaroka tepees. Today, Red Lodge offers a plethora of outdoor activities and entertainment, from renowned rodeos to skiing at Red Lodge Mountain.

◪ PRACTICAL INFORMATION. The closest bus stop is in Billings (60 mi. northeast), but the **Red Lodge Shuttle** offers transportation between Billings and Red Lodge during the summer (☎ 446-2257 or 888-446-2191; call for schedules and prices). The folks at the **Visitors Center**, 601 N. Broadway, on the north side of town, can help you occupy your time. (☎ 446-1718. Open in summer daily 8am-7pm; in winter M-F 9am-5pm.) **Medical Services: Beartooth Hospital and Health Clinic**, 600 W. 21st St. (☎ 446-2345). **Internet access: Red Lodge Carnegie Library**, 3 W. 8th St. (☎ 446-1905. Free. Open M-F 9am-6pm.) **Post Office:** 119 S. Hauser (☎ 446-2629. Open M-F 8am-4:30pm, Sa 9am-1pm.) **ZIP code:** 59068. **Area code:** 406.

⌂◪ ACCOMMODATIONS & FOOD. Most accommodations in Red Lodge are expensive. **The Eagles Nest ❷**, 702 S. Broadway, has affordable rates and a location adjacent to Rock Creek and close to downtown. (☎ 446-2312 or 800-746-2312. Phone and cable TV. Singles in summer $40, in winter $36; doubles $60/52. Skihouse for 8 with kitchen $125.) Four miles north of Red Lodge on Rte. 212, the **Red Lodge KOA ❶** has 75 sites on Rock Creek. (☎ 446-2364 or 800-562-7540. Open late May to mid-Sept. Sites with water and electricity $28, full hookup $30. Kabins from $45.) A number of free and inexpensive campsites lie south of Red Lodge on U.S. 212, along Rock Creek. The ranger station (☎ 446-2103) has more info.

Stop by the sophisticated **Bridge Creek Backcountry Kitchen & Wine Bar ❷**, 116 S. Broadway, downtown, for lunch; dinner is more pricey. (☎446-9900. Lunch combinations $6. Open daily 11am-9pm.) **Bogart's,** 11 S. Broadway, downtown, a Western-style pizza/Mexican joint, dices up homemade salsa good enough to be served at the *Cafe Americano.* (☎446-1784. Burgers $5-7. Mexican food $8-10. Open daily 11am-9pm.) Gossip comes free with a counter breakfast at **Hank's Place,** 407 S. Broadway. (☎446-1250. Open daily 6am-2pm.) Wallpapered with personalized license plates and irreverent bumper stickers, the raucous ▨**Snow Creek Saloon** provides a haven for scandalous dances on the tables. (☎446-2542. Live music F-Sa. Open daily 2pm-2am.)

◨ ♫ **SIGHTS & OUTDOOR ACTIVITIES.** Red Lodge Mountain offers 69 runs and over 1600 newly expanded acres of skiable terrain. The mountain's 2400 ft. vertical drop provides some of the finest downhill skiing and snowboarding in the region. A variety of cross-country skiing options are also available. (☎446-2610 or 800-444-8977. Open early Nov. to mid-Apr. $36, ages 13-18 $33, under 12 $14. Ski rentals $17; snowboards $30.) The **Red Lodge Nordic Center** (☎446-9191), 2 mi. west of Red Lodge on Rte. 78, has over 9 mi. of groomed cross-country trails that cover a wide range of difficulties. The roads along Rock Creek south of town are good for beginners. Mountain bikers converge at Red Lodge each year in late July for the **Fat Tire Frenzy,** an off-road and slalom competition. The **Meeteetse Trail,** off U.S. 212 south of Red Lodge, and the **Silver Run Trails,** near the West Fork of Rock Creek, are popular among mountain bikers.

A number of other festivals and special events attract visitors to Red Lodge in winter and fall. The first weekend in March, the town and ski area jointly host **Winter Carnival** (☎446-2610) which makes good use of abundant snow with ice sculptures, sledding, and music. The 4th of July **Home of Champions Rodeo** (☎877-733-5634) celebrates a local infatuation with the cowboy sport. Red Lodge's first settlers were miners from all over Europe, and the town celebrates this multicultural heritage with the week-long **Festival of Nations** each August. **Bear Creek Downs,** 7 mi. east of Red Lodge on Rte. 308, features wildly popular (and curious) pig races. The races are sponsored by the **Bear Creek Saloon,** where you can get a healthy portion of beef, but no pork. (☎446-3481. Burgers $5. Open Th-Su 2pm-2am. Pig races in summer F-Su 7pm.) For the past six years, Harley enthusiasts have gathered in Red Lodge in mid-July for the celebratory **Iron Horse Rodeo** (☎877-733-5634). Riders stop at five locales along the Beartooth and Chief Joseph Hwy., picking up a playing card at each; the rider with the best poker hand at the end picks up $1000. Other events include a street dance, live music, and the motorcycle decathlon.

MISSOULA ☎406

A liberal haven in a largely conservative state, Missoula attracts new residents every day with its revitalized downtown and bountiful outdoors opportunities. Home to the **University of Montana,** downtown Missoula is lined with bars and coffeehouses spawned by the large student population. Four different mountain ranges and five major rivers surround Missoula, supporting skiing during the winter and fly fishing, hiking, and biking during the summer.

▨ **PRACTICAL INFORMATION.** Flights stream into the **Missoula International Airport,** 5225 Hwy. 10 W (☎728-4381), 6 mi. west of town. Follow Broadway, which turns into Hwy. 10/200. **Greyhound,** 1660 W. Broadway (☎549-2339), has buses to Bozeman (4½-5½hr., 3 per day, $33.50) and Spokane (4hr., 3 per day, $34.50-36.50). From the same terminal, **RimRock Stages** serves Whitefish via St. Ignatius and Kalispell (3½hr.; 1 per day; M-Th $23, F-Su $25) and Helena (2½hr., 1 per day, M-Th $19/21). Catch a ride on the reliable **Mountain Line City Buses** from the Transfer Center, at the corner of Ryman and Pine St., or at a curbside around town. (☎721-3333. Buses operate M-F 6:45am-8:15pm, Sa 9:45am-5:15pm. Fare 85¢.) **Taxis: Yellow Cab,** ☎543-6644. **Rent-A-Wreck,** 1905 W. Broadway, provides free transportation to and from the airport and great prices on rentals. (☎721-3838. 25+. $29-45 per day; 150 free mi., 25¢ each additional mi.) **Visitor Info: Missoula Chamber of Commerce,** 825 E. Front St. at Van Buren. (☎543-6623; www.exploremissoula.com. Open late May to early Sept. M-F 8am-7pm, Sa 10am-6pm; early Sept. to late May M-F 8am-5pm.) **Internet access: Missoula Public Library,** 301 E. Main St. (☎721-2665. Open M-Th 10am-9pm, F-Sa 10am-6pm. Free.) **Post Office:** 200 E. Broadway St. (☎329-2222. Open M-F 8am-5:30pm.) **ZIP code:** 59801. **Area code:** 406.

ⓕ ACCOMMODATIONS. There are no hostels in Missoula, but there are plenty of inexpensive alternatives along **Broadway.** Rooms at the **City Center Motel ❷,** 338 E. Broadway, have cable TV, fridges, and microwaves. (☎543-3193. May-Sept. singles $45; doubles $48-52. Sept.-Dec. $35/42.) To reach the **Aspen Motel ❷,** 3720 Rte. 200 E, in East Missoula, get off I-90 at Exit 107 and travel ½ mi. east. (☎721-9758. Clean rooms, cable TV, and A/C. Singles $40; 1-bed doubles $46, 2-bed $57.) The **Missoula/El-Mar KOA Kampground ❶,** 3450 Tina Ave., just south of Broadway off Reserve St., is one of the best KOAs around, providing shaded tent sites apart from RVs. (☎549-0881 or 800-562-5366. Pool, hot tub, mini-golf courses, and 24hr. laundry facilities. Sites for two $21, with water and electricity $25, full hookup $31; kabins $38-43; each additional person $3.)

ⓕⓜ FOOD & NIGHTLIFE. Missoula, the culinary capital of Montana, boasts a number of innovative, delicious, and thrifty eating establishments. Head downtown, north of the Clark Fork River along Higgins Ave., and check out the array of restaurants and coffeehouses that line the road. ▓**Worden's ❶,** 451 N. Higgins Ave., is a popular local deli, serving a wide variety of world-class sandwiches in three sizes: 4 in. roll ($4.25), 7 in. ($5.75), and 14 in. ($10.75). You can also pick up groceries while munching. (☎549-1293. Open in summer M-Th 8am-10pm, F-Sa 8am-11pm, Su 9am-10pm; in winter M-Th 8am-9pm, F-Sa 8am-10pm, Su 9am-10pm.) **Eat to Live ❶,** 1916 Brooks St., prides itself on serving healthy, low-fat meals reminiscent of Mom's home cooking. (☎721-2510. All meals $3 or less. Open M-F 11:30am-3pm.) **Tipu's ❷,** 115½ S. 4th St. W, functions as one of the only all-veggie establishments and the lone Indian restaurant in Montana. (☎542-0622. All-you-can-eat lunch buffet $7. Open daily 11:30am-9:30pm.) At **Tacos del Sol ❶,** 422 N. Higgins Ave., get a Mission Burrito for under $4. (☎327-8929. Open M-F 11am-7pm.)

College students swarm the downtown bar area around Front St. and Higgins Ave. during the school year. Bars have a more relaxed atmosphere in summer. **Charlie B's,** 420 N. Higgins Ave., where seeing is believing, draws an eclectic clientele of bikers, farmers, students, and hippies. Framed photos of longtime regulars blot out the walls—park at the bar for 10 or 20 years and join them. Hungry boozers can weave their way to the **Dinosaur Cafe** at the back of the room for Creole culinary delights. (☎549-3589. Open daily 8am-2am.) The popular **Iron Horse Brew Pub,** 501 N. Higgins Ave., always packs a crowd; the large patio fills up during the summer months. (☎728-8866. Open daily 11am-2am.) Follow the advice of the "beer coaches" at **The Kettle House Brewing Co.,** 602 Myrtle, one block west of Higgins between 4th and 5th, and "support your local brewery." The Kettle House serves a delectable assortment of beers, including their aptly named hemp beer—Bongwater Stout. (Open M-Th 3-9pm, F-Sa noon-9pm; no beer served after 8pm. 2

free samples; then $2.75 per pint.) The *Independent* and *Lively Times*, available at newsstands and cafes, offer the lowdown on the Missoula music scene, while the *Entertainer*, in the Friday *Missoulian*, has movie and event schedules.

■ **SIGHTS.** Missoula's hottest sight is the **Smokejumper Center,** 5765 Rte. 10, just past the airport, 7 mi. west of town on Broadway. It's the nation's largest training base for smokejumpers, aerial firefighters who parachute into flaming, remote forests. (☎ 329-4934. Open daily 8:30am-5pm. Tours May-Sept. every hr. 10-11am and 2-4pm. Free.) The **Carousel,** in Caras Riverfront Park, is one of the oldest hand-carved carousels in America. (☎ 549-8382. Open June-Aug. daily 11am-7pm; Sept.-May 11am-5:30pm. $1, seniors and under 19 50¢.) **Out to Lunch,** also in Caras Riverfront Park, offers free performances in the summer; call the Missoula Downtown Association for more info. (☎ 543-4238. W 11am-1:30pm.) The **Western Montana Fair and Rodeo,** held the beginning of August, has live music, a carnival, fireworks, and commercial concession booths. (☎ 721-3247. Open 10am-10pm.) You can soak your weary feet at the **Lolo Hot Springs,** 35 mi. southwest of Missoula on Hwy 12. The 103°-105°F springs served as an ancient meeting place for local Native Americans and were frequented by Lewis and Clark in 1806. (☎ 273-2290 or 800-273-2290. $6, under 13 $4.) If you're willing to brave the Lolo Pass, farther along Rte. 12 into Idaho there are two free natural **hot springs,** Jerry Johnson and Weir, which are well worth the extra miles.

⚡ OUTDOOR ACTIVITIES. Nearby parks, recreation areas, and surrounding wilderness areas make Missoula an outdoor enthusiast's dream. Bicycle-friendly Missoula is located along both the Trans-America and the Great Parks bicycle routes, and all major streets have designated bike lanes. **Open Road Bicycles and Nordic Equipment,** 517 S. Orange St., has bike rentals. (☎ 549-2453. Open M-F 9am-6pm, Sa 10am-5pm, Su 11am-3pm. $3.50 per hr., $17.50 per day.) The national **Adventure Cycling,** 150 E. Pine St., is the place to go for info about local trails, including the Trans-America and Great Parks routes. (☎ 721-1776 or 800-755-2453. Open M-F 8am-5pm.) The **Rattlesnake Wilderness National Recreation Area,** 11 mi. northeast of town off the Van Buren St. exit on I-90, and the **Pattee Canyon Recreation Area,** 3½ mi. east of Higgins on Pattee Canyon Dr., are highly recommended for their biking trails. **Missoulians on Bicycle,** P.O. Box 8903, Missoula 59807, is a local organization that hosts rides and events for cyclists (www.missoulabike.org.).

Alpine and Nordic **skiing** keep Missoulians busy during winter. **Pattee Canyon** has groomed trails that are conveniently close to town, and **Marshall Mountain** is a great place to learn how to downhill ski, with night skiing and free shuttles from downtown. (☎ 258-6000. $19 per day.) Experienced skiers should check out the extreme **Montana Snowbowl,** 12 mi. northwest of Missoula, with a vertical drop of 2600 ft. and over 35 trails. (☎ 549-9777 or 800-728-2695. Open Nov.-Apr. daily 9:30am-4pm. Full-day $29, children $13, under 5 free.)

Floating on rafts and tubes is a favorite activity for locals on weekends. The Blackfoot River, along Rte. 200 east of Bonner, makes a good afternoon float. Call the **Montana State Regional Parks and Wildlife Office,** 3201 Spurgin Rd., for information about rafting locations. (☎ 542-5500. Open M-F 8am-5pm.) Rent tubes or rafts from the **Army and Navy Economy Store,** 322 N. Higgins. (☎ 721-1315. Open M-F 9am-7:30pm, Sa 9am-5:30pm, Su 10am-5:30pm. Tubes $3 per day. Rafts $40 per day, credit card required; $20 deposit.) **Hiking** opportunities also abound in the Missoula area. The relatively easy ½ hour hike to the "M" (for the U of M, not Missoula) on Mount Sentinel, has a tremendous view of Missoula and the surrounding mountains. The **Rattlesnake Wilderness National Recreation Area,** named after the shape of the river (there are no rattlers for miles), is 11 mi. northeast of town, off the Van Buren St. exit from I-90, and makes for a great day of hiking. Other popular areas include **Pattee Canyon** and **Blue Mountain,** located south of town. Maps ($6) and information on longer hikes in the Bitterroot and Bob Marshall areas are at the **US Forest Service Information Office,** 200 E. Broadway; the entrance is at 200 Pine St. (☎329-3511. Open M-F 7:30am-4pm.) For equipment rentals, stop by **Trailhead,** 110 E. Pine St., at Higgins St. (☎543-6966. Open M-F 9:30am-8pm, Sa 9am-6pm, Su 11am-6pm. Tents M-F $10-14, Sa-Su $18; backpacks $9; sleeping bags $5.)

Western Montana is **fly fishing** country, and Missoula is at the heart of it all. Fishing licenses are required and can be purchased from the **Department of Fish, Wildlife, and Parks,** 3201 Spurgin Rd. (☎542-5500), or from local sporting goods stores. **Kingfisher,** 926 E. Broadway, offers licenses ($22-67) and pricey guided fishing trips. (☎721-6141. Open in summer daily 7am-8pm; off-season 9am-5pm.)

FROM MISSOULA TO GLACIER

St. Ignatius Campground and Hostel, off U.S. 93 in **St. Ignatius** (look for the camping sign), offers lodging in its recently renovated "earthship," an eco-friendly structure built into a hillside and made from recycled tires and aluminum cans. Faux cave paintings decorate the plaster walls. The hostel rents skiing equipment and new mountain bikes for $10 and is a convenient blasting-off point for exploring the backcountry. (☎745-3959. Showers, laundry, and kitchen. Beds $13. Campsites for 1 $10, for 2 $12.) **RimRock Stages** (☎745-3501) makes a stop ½ mi. away in St. Ignatius, at the Malt Shop on Blaine St.

The **National Bison Range** was established in 1908 in an effort to save the dwindling number of bison from extinction. At one time 30-70 million roamed the plains, but after years of over-hunting the population dropped to less than 1000. The Range is home to 350-500 buffalo as well as deer, pronghorn, elk, bighorn sheep, and mountain goats. The two-hour Red Sleep Mountain self-guided tour offers a spectacular view of the Flathead Valley and the best chance for wildlife observation. To access the range, travel 40 mi. north of Missoula off U.S. 93, then 5 mi. west on Rte. 200, and 5 mi. north on Rte. 212. (☎644-2211. Visitors Center open Nov. to mid-May M-F 8am-4:30pm; mid-May to Oct. daily 8am-6pm. Red Sleep Mountain drive open mid-May to mid-Oct. daily 7am-dusk. $4 per vehicle.) With large displays of old posters, uniforms, motorcycles, and weapons, the ■**Miracle of America Museum,** 58176 U.S. 93, at the southern end of Polson, houses one of the country's greatest collections of Americana. A general store, saddlery shop, barber shop, soda fountain, and gas station sit among the classic memorabilia. The museum celebrates Live History Day the third weekend in July. (☎883-6804. Open June-Sept. daily 8am-8pm; Oct.-May M-Sa 8am-5pm, Su 2-6pm. $3, ages 3-12 $1.) Fresh fruit stands line **Flathead Lake,** the largest natural lake west of the Mississippi. Renowned for its fresh cherries and fresher fish, the lake is located along U.S. 93 between Polson and Kalispell.

WATERTON-GLACIER PEACE PARK

Waterton-Glacier transcends international boundaries to encompass one of the most strikingly beautiful portions of the Rockies. Both established in 1932, the two parks are connected by a natural unity of landscape and wildlife. The massive Rocky Mountain peaks span both parks, providing sanctuary for many endangered bears, bighorn sheep, moose, mountain goats, and gray wolves. Perched high in the Northern Rockies, Glacier is sometimes called the "Crown of the Continent," and the high alpine lakes and glaciers shine like jewels.

7 PRACTICAL INFORMATION

Technically one park, Waterton-Glacier is actually two distinct areas: the small **Waterton Lakes National Park** in Alberta, and the enormous **Glacier National Park** in Montana. There are several **border crossings** nearby: **Piegan/Carway,** at U.S. 89 (open daily 7am-11pm); **Roosville,** on U.S. 93 (open 24hr.); and **Chief Mountain,** at Rte. 17 (open mid- to late May and Sept. daily 9am-6pm; June-Aug. 7am-10pm). The fastest way to Waterton is to head north along the east side of Glacier, entering Canada through Chief Mountain. Since snow can be unpredictable, the parks are usually in full operation only from late May to early September—check conditions in advance. The *Waterton Glacier Guide,* provided at any park entrance, has dates and times of trail, campground, and border crossing openings. To find out which park areas, hotels, and campsites will be open when you visit, contact the **Park Headquarters,** Waterton Lakes National Park, Waterton Park, AB T0K 2M0 (☎ 403-859-2224), or **Glacier National Park,** West Glacier, MT 59936 (☎ 406-888-7800). Mace and firewood are not allowed into Canada.

GLACIER NATIONAL PARK ☎ 406

F TRANSPORTATION

Amtrak (☎ 226-4452) traces a dramatic route along the southern edge of the park. The station in West Glacier is staffed mid-May to September, but the train still stops at the station in the winter. Trains chug daily to East Glacier (1½hr., $12-24); Seattle (14hr., $78-164); Spokane (6hr., $39-80); and Whitefish (30min., $12-24). Amtrak also runs from East Glacier to Chicago (32hr., $132-280) and Minneapolis (23hr., $114-241). **RimRock Stages** (☎ 800-255-7655), the only bus line that nears the park, stops in Kalispell at the Kalispell Bus Terminal, 3794 U.S. 2 E, and goes to Missoula (M-Th $19, F-Su $20) or Billings ($62/66). As in most of the Rockies, a car is the most convenient mode of transport, particularly within the park. **Glacier Park, Inc.'s** famous red jammer buses run tours on Going-to-the-Sun Rd. (½ day tours $20.75, ¾ day $31.75; children half price.) **Sun Tours** offers additional tours of the park, leaving from East Glacier and St. Mary. (☎ 226-9220 or 800-786-9220. $45 for all-day tour.) Shuttles for hikers ($8-17; under 12 50% off) roam the length of Going-to-the-Sun Rd. from early July to early September; schedules are available at Visitors Centers (see **Practical Information,** below).

💥 ORIENTATION

There are few roads in Glacier, and the locals like it that way. Glacier's main thoroughfare is the **Going-to-the-Sun Rd.,** which connects the two primary points of entry, West Glacier and St. Mary. **U.S. 2** skirts the southern border of the park and is the fastest route from Browning and East Glacier to West Glacier. At the "Goat Lick," about halfway between East and West Glacier, mountain goats traverse steep cliffs to lap up the natural salt deposits. **Rte. 89** heads north along the eastern edge of the park past St. Mary. Anyone interested in visiting the northwestern section of the park must brave the unpaved and pothole-ridden **Outside North Fork Rd.** While most of Glacier is primitive backcountry, a number of villages provide lodging, gas, and food: St. Mary, Many Glacier, and East Glacier in the east, and West Glacier, Apgar, and Polebridge in the west.

ROCKY MOUNTAINS

ROCKY MOUNTAINS

7 PRACTICAL INFORMATION

Before entering the park, visitors must pay **admission:** $10 per week per car, $5 for pedestrians and cyclists; yearly passes $20. The accessible and knowledgeable rangers at each of the three **Visitors Centers** give the inside scoop on campsites, day hikes, weather, flora, and fauna. **St. Mary** guards the east entrance of the park. (☎ 732-7750. Open May and Sept. to mid-Oct. daily 8am-5pm; June 8am-6pm; July-Aug. 8am-9pm.) **Apgar** is located at the west entrance. (☎ 888-7939. Open May-June and Sept.-Oct. daily 8am-4:30pm; late June-Aug. 8am-8pm.) A third Visitors Center graces **Logan Pass,** on the Going-to-the-Sun Rd. (Open June daily 9am-4:30pm; July-Aug. 9am-7pm; Sept. 10am-4:30pm; Oct. 10am-4pm.) The **Many Glacier** ranger station can answer important questions. (Open May-June and Sept. daily 8am-4:30pm; July-Aug. 8am-6pm.)

Visitors planning overnight backpacking trips must obtain the necessary **backcountry permits.** With the exception of the **Nyack/Coal Creek** camping zone, all backcountry camping must be done at designated campsites equipped with pit toilets, tent sites, food preparation areas, and food hanging devices. (June-Sept. overnight camping fee $4 per person per night, ages 9-16 $2; Oct.-May no fees. Reservations available beginning in mid-Apr. for a $20 fee. and at least 24hr. in advance.) Reservations (www.nps.gov/glac/home.htm) can be made in person at the Apgar Permit Center and other park offices and Visitors Centers, or by writing to Backcountry Reservation Office, Glacier National Park, West Glacier, MT 59936. The free *Backcountry Camping Guide* is indispensable and available at Visitors Centers and permit stations. The **Backcountry Permit Center,** next to the Visitors Center in Apgar, is valuable for those seeking to explore Glacier's less-traveled areas. (Open May-June and mid-Sept.-Oct. daily 8am-4pm; July to mid-Sept. 7am-4pm.) **Medical Services: Kalispell Regional Medical Center,** 310 Sunny View Ln. (☎ 752-5111), north of Kalispell off Rte. 93. **Post Office:** 110 Going-to-the-Sun Rd., in West Glacier. (☎ 888-5591. Open M-F 8:30am-12:30pm and 1:30-4:45pm.) **ZIP code:** 59936. **Area code:** 406.

ACCOMMODATIONS

Staying indoors within Glacier is expensive, but several affordable options lie just outside the park boundaries. On the west side of the park, the small town of **Polebridge** provides access to Glacier's remote and pristine northwest corner. From Apgar, take Camas Rd. north, and take a right onto the poorly-marked gravel Outside North Fork Rd., just past a bridge over the North Fork of the Flathead River. (Avoid Inner North Fork Rd.—your shocks will thank you.) From Columbia Falls, take Rte. 486 north. To the east, inexpensive lodging is just across the park border in **East Glacier.** The distant offices of **Glacier Park, Inc.** (☎ 756-2444; www.glacierparkinc.com) handle reservations for all in-park lodging.

Brownies Grocery (HI-AYH), 1020 Rte. 49 (☎ 226-4426), in East Glacier Park. Check in at the grocery counter and head upstairs to the spacious hostel on the second floor, feasting your eyes on a stunning view of the Rockies from the porch. Travelers can also refuel with a thick huckleberry shake ($4) or a vegan sandwich ($5). Kitchen, showers, linens, and laundry provided. Check-in by 9pm; call ahead for late arrivals. Key deposit $5. Check out 10am. Reservations recommended. Open May-Sept., weather permitting. Dorms $14, nonmembers $17. Private singles $18/21; doubles $26/29; family room for 4-6 $38/41. Tent sites $10. Extra bed $5. Credit card required. ❶

North Fork Hostel, 80 Beaver Dr. (☎888-5241), in Polebridge; follow the signs through town. The wooden walls and kerosene lamps are reminiscent of a deep woods hunting retreat. Showers, but no flush toilets. During the winter, old-fashioned wood stoves warm frozen fingers and toes after skiing or snowshoeing. Call ahead for a pickup from the West Glacier Amtrak station ($30-35). Light chores. Nominal rent for canoes, mountain bikes, snowshoes, and nordic ski equipment. Showers $4 for non-lodgers. Linen $2. Check-in by 10pm. Check-out noon. Call ahead, especially in winter. Dorms $15, $12 after 2 nights; cabins $30; log homes $65. ❶

Backpacker's Inn Hostel, 29 Dawson Ave. (☎226-9392), just east of the East Glacier Amtrak station and behind Serrano's Mexican Restaurant, has 14 clean beds in co-ed rooms. Hot showers. Sleeping bags $1. Open May-Sept. Rooms $10 per night. Private room with queen-sized bed and full linen: $20 for 1 person, $30 for 2. ❶

Swiftcurrent Motor Inn, (☎732-5531), in Many Glacier Valley, is one of the few budget motels in the area. No toilets. Open early June to early Sept. 1-bedroom cabins $43, 2-bedroom $53. ❷

🔅 FOOD

Polebridge Mercantile Store (☎888-5105), on Polebridge Loop Rd. ¼mi. east of N. Fork Rd., has homemade pastries ($1-3) that are as splendid as the surrounding peaks. Gas, gifts, and pay phones are also available. ❶

Northern Lights Saloon (☎888-5669), right next to the Mercantile, serves fabulous $5.50 cheeseburgers and $3 cold pints in a one-room log cabin with slices of tree trunk for barstools. Kitchen open June-Sept. daily 4-9pm; bar open until midnight. ❶

Whistle Stop Restaurant, (☎226-9292), in East Glacier next to Brownies Grocery. Sample homemade Montanan delicacies at this restaurant best known for its huckleberry french toast and omelettes ($6-7). Open daily 7am-9pm. ❷

Park Cafe, (☎732-4482), in St. Mary on Rte. 89, just north of the park entrance, provides sustenance to those who dare to cross the Going-to-the-Sun Rd. Incredible homemade pies $2.75 per slice. "Hungry Hiker" special (2 eggs with hash browns and toast) $3.50. Vegetarian Caribbean Burrito $4.75. Open May-Sept. daily 7:30am-10pm. ❶

🥾 HIKING

Most of Glacier's spectacular scenery lies off the main roads and is accessible only by foot. An extensive trail system has something for everyone, from short, easy day hikes to rigorous backcountry expeditions. Stop by one of the Visitors Centers for maps with day hikes. *Beware of bears and mountain lions. Familiarize yourself with the precautions necessary to avoid an encounter, and ask the rangers about wildlife activity in the area in which you plan to hike.*

Avalanche Lake (4 mi., 3hr.) is a breathtaking trail and by far the most popular day hike in the park.

Trail of the Cedars (0.7 mi., 20min.) begins at the same trailhead, north of Lake McDonald on the Going-to-the-Sun Rd. Also offers a shorter, wheelchair accessible hike.

Numa Ridge Lookout (12 mi., 9hr.) starts from the Bowman Lake Campground, near Polebridge. After climbing 2930 ft., the hike ends with sweeping vistas of Glacier's rugged northeast corner.

Grinnell Glacier Trail (11 mi., 7hr.) passes within close proximity of several glaciers. Trailhead at the Many Glacier Picnic Area.

Scenic Point (6.3 mi, 5hr.) allows, on a clear day, a view all the way to Sweetgrass Hills, nearly 100 mi. away. The trailhead is ¼ mi. east of the Two Medicine Ranger Station.

ROCKY MOUNTAINS

ROADTRIP

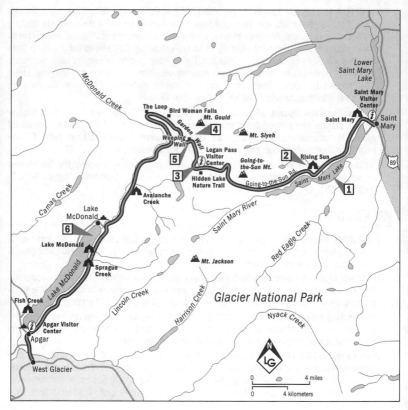

Glacier National Park

Carving its way through the mountains from St. Mary to West Glacier, the Going-to-the-Sun Rd. tantalizes visitors with expansive valleys and gushing waterfalls. Drivers, however, should keep their eyes on the road. Vehicles over 21 ft. in length or 8 ft. in width are prohibited.

TIME: 2-3hr.

DISTANCE: 50 mi.

SEASON: Spring to fall.

1 ST. MARY LAKE. Passing through **Two Dog Flats,** a wind-swept plain, the drive follows the blue-green of St. Mary Lake.

2 RISING SUN. Campgrounds and a full-service boat dock are available at Rising Sun, just before the road turns to offer a stunning view of **Wild Goose Island.** The looming snow-capped peaks have graced many a postcard.

3 LOGAN PASS. Going-to-the-Sun Mountain and Mount Siyeh appear to the right as the road ascends toward Logan Pass. The **Logan Pass Visitor Center** has information on wildlife.

4 GARDEN WALL. The road begins its descent below the treeline along the Garden Wall. From **Bird Women Falls Overlook,** cascading waterfalls on distant mountains are visible.

5 WEEPING WALL. Slow down as you pass the Weeping Wall, where water rushes down the cliffs onto the road below, spraying the windshields of unexpecting drivers.

6 LAKE MCDONALD. After **The Loop,** a giant hairpin turn, the road goes back into the trees and follows McDonald Creek until it reaches Lake McDonald.

Hidden Lake Nature Trail (3 mi., 460 ft. elevation gain, approx. 2hr.), beginning at the Logan Pass Visitor Center, is a chance to stretch your legs while winding along the Going-to-the-Sun Rd.

OTHER OUTDOOR ACTIVITIES

BIKING & HORSEBACK RIDING

Opportunities for bicycling are limited and confined to roadways and designated bike paths; cycling on trails is strictly prohibited. Although the Going-to-the-Sun Rd. is a popular **bike route**, only experienced cyclists with appropriate gear and legs of titanium should attempt this grueling ride; the sometimes nonexistent shoulder of the road can create hazardous situations. From mid-June to August, bike traffic is prohibited 11am-4pm from the Apgar campground to Sprague Creek and eastbound (uphill) from Logan Creek to Logan Pass. The Inner Fork Rd., which runs from Kintla Lake to Fish Creek on the west side of the park, is good for **mountain biking**, as are the old logging roads in the Flathead National Forest. Ask at a Visitors Center for more details. **Equestrian** explorers should check to make sure trails are open; there are steep fines for riding on closed trails. **Trail rides** from **Mule Shoe Outfitters** ($45 for 2hr.) are available at Many Glacier (☎732-4203) and Lake McDonald (☎888-5121).

BOATING

The **Glacier Park Boat Co.** (☎888-5727) provides **boat tours** that explore all of Glacier's large lakes. Tours leave from **Lake McDonald** (☎888-5727; 1hr., 4 per day, $10); **Two Medicine** (☎226-4467; 45min., 5 per day, $10); **Rising Sun,** at St. Mary Lake (☎732-4430; 1½hr., 5 per day, $11); and **Many Glacier** (☎732-4480; 1¼hr., $12). Children ride for half price. The tours from Two Medicine, Rising Sun, and Many Glacier provide access to Glacier's backcountry, and there are sunset cruises from Rising Sun and Lake McDonald. **Glacier Raft Co.,** in West Glacier, leads trips down the middle fork of the Flathead River. (☎888-5454 or 800-235-6781. Half-day $41, under 13 $31; full-day trip with lunch $65, under 13 $48.) You can rent **rowboats** ($10 per hr.) at Lake McDonald, Many Glacier, Two Medicine, and Apgar; **canoes** ($10 per hr.) at Many Glacier, Two Medicine, and Apgar; **kayaks** ($10 per hr.) at Apgar and Many Glacier; and **outboards** ($17 per hr.) at Lake McDonald and Two Medicine. Call Glacier Boat Co. for more details.

FISHING

No permit is needed to **fish** in the park, and limits are generally high. Some areas, however, are restricted, and certain species may be catch-and-release. Pick up *Fishing Regulations*, available at Visitors Centers for info. Lake Ellen Wilson, Gunsight Lake, and Lake Elizabeth are good places to sink a line. Outside the park, on Blackfeet Indian land, a special permit is needed, and everywhere else in Montana a state permit is required.

NEAR GLACIER ☎406

BROWNING

The center of the **Blackfeet Indian Reservation,** Browning, 12 mi. east of East Glacier, provides a glimpse into the past and present of Native American life. The **Museum of the Plains Indian,** at the junction of U.S. 2 and U.S. 89, displays traditional Native American clothing, artifacts, and crafts. (☎338-2230. Open June-Sept. daily 9am-5pm; Oct.-May M-F 10am-4:30pm. $4, ages 6-12 $1; Oct.-May free.) During **North American Indian Days** (2nd weekend in July), Native Americans from the surrounding Blackfeet Reservation and elsewhere gather for a celebration that includes tribal dancing, a rodeo, and a fantastic parade (Sa 11am). Call **Blackfeet Planning** (☎338-7406) for more details.

ROCKY MOUNTAINS

WATERTON LAKES NATIONAL PARK, AB ☎403

Only a fraction of the size of its Montana neighbor, Waterton Lakes National Park offers spectacular scenery and activities without the crowds that plague Glacier during July and August. The town of Waterton is a genuine alpine town, complete with a Swiss-style chalet. Bighorn sheep and mule deer frequently wander down the surrounding slopes into town, causing unexpected traffic delays.

🔃 PRACTICAL INFORMATION. Admission to the park in summer is CDN$4 per day, CDN$8 for groups of two to seven people; admission is free in winter. The only road from Waterton's park entrance leads 8½km south to **Waterton Park.** En route, stop at the **Waterton Visitors Center,** 8km inside the park on Rte. 5, for a schedule of events and hikes. (☎859-5133. Open mid-June to Aug. daily 8am-6pm; mid-May to mid-June and Sept.-Oct. 9am-6pm, although hours may vary depending on weather.) In the off-season, pick up info at **Park Administration,** 215 Mt. View Rd. (☎859-2224. Open M-F 8am-4pm.) US dollars can be exchanged for Canadian at the **Tamarack Village Sq.** on Mt. View Rd. (☎859-2378. Open July-Aug. daily 8am- 8pm; May-June and Sept.-Oct. usually 10am-5pm.) **Pat's Gas and Cycle Rental,** Mt. View Rd., Waterton, rents bikes. (☎859-2266. Mountain bikes CDN$6 per hr., CDN$30 per day.) **Medical Services: Ambulance,** ☎859-2636. **Post Office:** in Waterton on Fountain Ave. at Windflower Ave. (Open M, W and F 8:30am-4:30pm; Tu and Th 8:30am-4pm.) **Postal code:** T0K 2M0. **Area code:** 403.

🏠🍴 ACCOMMODATIONS & FOOD. The park's three campgrounds are very affordable. **Belly River ❶,** on Chief Mountain Hwy. outside the park entrance, has scenic and uncrowded primitive sites. (Sites CDN$12.) **Crandell ❶,** on Red Rock Canyon Rd., is situated in a forest area. (Sites CDN$14.) Camp with 200 of your best RV pals at **Townsite ❶** in Waterton Park, which has showers and a lakeside vista, but no privacy. The walk-in sites are satisfactory and are generally the last to fill. (Sites CDN$18, walk-in sites CDN$16, full hookup CDN$24.) **Backcountry camping** requires a permit from the Visitors Center. Campsites are rarely full, and several, including **Crandell Lake ❶,** are less than one hour's hike from the trailhead. (☎859-5133. Permit CDN$6. Reservable up to 90 days in advance for CDN$10.)

Travelers preferring to stay indoors should reserve one of the 21 comfy beds with thick mattresses at the **Waterton International Hostel (HI) ❶,** in the Waterton Lakes Lodge. (☎859-2151, ext. 2016. Health club and pool next door. Laundry and kitchen. CDN$21, nonmembers CDN$25; family room CDN$28/32 per person, ages 6-17 CDN$11/15.) The **Country Bakery and Lunch Counter ❶,** 303 Windflower Ave., across the street from the Waterton Lakes Lodge, cooks up meat pies and waffles for CDN$2.75-5.50. (☎859-2181. Open M-Sa May-Sept. 8am-9pm, Su 9am-7pm.)

🏔 OUTDOOR ACTIVITIES. Waterton Lakes include 120 mi. of trails of varying difficulty. In addition to exploring the snow-capped peaks of Waterton Lakes, many of these trails link up with the trail network of Glacier National Park. **Waterton-Glacier International Peace Park Hike,** a free guided hike, takes off from the Bertha Trailhead, just south of the Waterton townsite, and crosses the border into the US. (Hikes late June-late Aug. Sa 10am. Only US citizens can cross the border into the US.) After 8.5 mi. of moderately easy hiking, participants can take a boat back from the Goat Haunt Ranger Station. The **Carthew-Alderson Trail** starts from Cameron Lake and leads through 18km of incredible views on its way back into town. (11.8 mi. one-way, 1440 ft. elevation gain, 6-7hr.) A shorter day hike follows the shore of Cameron Lake. (2.3 mi., 1hr.) The **Hiker Shuttle** runs from Tamarack Village Sq., in town, to Cameron Lake and other trailheads. (☎859-2378. Reservations strongly recommended. CDN$7.50.) The popular **Crypt Lake Trail** trickles past waterfalls in a narrow canyon, through a 20m natural tunnel, and, after 6km, arrives at icy, green Crypt Lake, straddling the international border. (10½ mi., 2100 ft. elevation gain, 5-6hr.) To get to the Crypt trailhead, take the **water taxi** run by **Waterton Shoreline Cruises,** in Waterton Park. The marina also runs a 2hr. boat tour of Upper Waterton Lake. (☎859-2362. Open mid-May to mid-Sept. Water taxi: 4 per day; CDN$14, ages 4-12 CDN$6. Tour: CDN$24, ages 13-17 CDN$12, ages 4-12 CDN$8.) Gear is available at **Waterton Outdoor Adventures,** in the Tamarack Village Sq., which also sponsors guided hiking tours. (☎859-2378. Open daily 8am-8pm.) Horses are allowed on many trails. **Alpine Stables,** 1km north of the townsite, conducts trail rides. (☎859-2462. Open May-Sept. 1hr. ride CDN$20, 4hr. CDN$65.)

Fishing in Waterton requires a **license** (CDN$6 per week, CDN$13 per season), available from the park offices, campgrounds, warden stations, and service stations in the area. Lake trout cruise the depths of **Cameron** and **Waterton Lakes,** while pike prowl the weedy channels of **Maskinonge Lake.** Most of the backcountry lakes and creeks support rainbow and brook trout. There are many fish in the creeks that spill from Cameron Lake, about 200m to the east of the parking lot, and Crandell Lake, a 1.5km hike. Rent **rowboats, paddleboats,** or **canoes** at Cameron Lake. (CDN$18 first hr. for 2 people, CDN$14 each additional hr.; CDN$22/17 for 4.)

WYOMING

The ninth-largest state in the Union, Wyoming is also the least populated. This is a place where men don cowboy hats and boots, and livestock outnumbers citizens. It is also a land of unique firsts: it was the first state to grant women the right to vote without later repealing it, and was the first to have a national monument (Devils Tower, p. 734) and a national park (Yellowstone, p. 731) within its borders. Those expecting true Western flavor will not be disappointed; Wyoming boasts the "Rodeo Capital of the World" in Cody (p. 731), where cowboys and cowgirls thrill audiences with a genuine taste of the Old West.

⚡ PRACTICAL INFORMATION

Capital: Cheyenne.

Visitor info: Wyoming Business Council Tourism Office, I-25 at College Dr., Cheyenne 82002 (☎307-777-7777 or 800-225-5996; www.wyomingtourism.org). Info center open daily 7:30am-6pm. **Dept. of Commerce, State Parks, and Historic Sites Division,** 122 W. 25th St., Herschler Bldg., 1st fl. E., Cheyenne 82002 (☎307-777-6323; www.wyobest.org). Open M-F 8am-5pm. **Game and Fish Dept.,** 5400 Bishop Blvd., Cheyenne 82006 (☎307-777-4600; http://gf.state.wy.us). Open M-F 8am-5pm.

Postal Abbreviation: WY. **Sales Tax:** 5%.

YELLOWSTONE NATIONAL PARK   ☎307

Yellowstone National Park holds the distinction of being the largest park in the contiguous US, and the first national park in the world. Yellowstone also happens to be one of the largest active volcanoes in the world, with over 300 geysers and thousands of thermal fissures spewing steam and boiling water from beneath the earth's crust. The park's hot springs are popular among local wildlife; bison and elk gather around the thermal basins for warmth during the winter months.

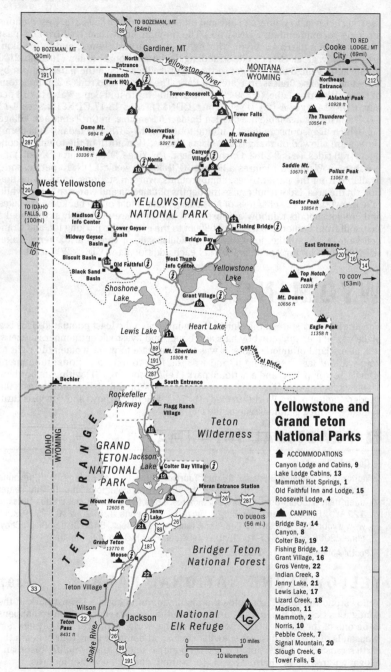

ROCKY MOUNTAINS

TO BOZEMAN, MT
(84mi)
89

TO BOZEMAN, MT
(90mi)

Gardiner, MT

Cooke
City

TO RED
LODGE, MT
(69mi)

North
Entrance

Yellowstone River

191

287

Mammoth
(Park HQ)
2 1

Tower-Roosevelt

MONTANA
WYOMING

212

3

4

5 Tower Falls

6

Northeast
Entrance

7 *Ablathar Peak*
10928 ft

Dome Mt.
9894 ft

*Observation
Peak
9397 ft*

Mt. Washington
10243 ft

The Thunderer
10554 ft

Mt. Holmes
10336 ft

Norris

Canyon
Village

9

8

*Saddle Mt.
10670 ft*

*Pollux Peak
11067 ft*

10

*Castor Peak
10854 ft*

West Yellowstone

20

**YELLOWSTONE
NATIONAL PARK**

TO IDAHO
FALLS, ID
(100mi)

11

Madison
Info Center

12 Fishing Bridge

*Top Notch
Peak
10238 ft*

East Entrance

20 16

14

TO CODY
(53mi)

MT
ID

Lower Geyser
Basin

13

Midway Geyser
Basin

Bridge Bay

14

Biscuit Basin

15 Old Faithful

West Thumb
Info Center

Yellowstone
Lake

*Mt. Doane
10656 ft*

Black Sand
Basin

Shoshone
Lake

Grant Village

16

*Eagle Peak
11358 ft*

Lewis Lake

Heart Lake

17

*Mt. Sheridan
10308 ft*

89

191

Continental Divide

287

Bechler

South Entrance

Rockefeller
Parkway

Flagg Ranch
Village

*Teton
Wilderness*

18

IDAHO
WYOMING

**GRAND
TETON
NATIONAL
PARK**

Jackson
Lake

Colter Bay Village

19

Moran Entrance Station

20

26 287

*Mount Moran
12605 ft*

Jenny
Lake

26

TO DUBOIS
(56 mi.)

21

*Grand Teton
13770 ft*

89

187

Moose

*Bridger Teton
National Forest*

22

Teton Village

33

Wilson

*Teton
Pass
8431 ft*

22

26

Jackson

*National
Elk Refuge*

N

LG

Snake River

89

191

0   10 miles

0   10 kilometers

Yellowstone and Grand Teton National Parks

⌂ ACCOMMODATIONS

Canyon Lodge and Cabins, **9**
Lake Lodge Cabins, **13**
Mammoth Hot Springs, **1**
Old Faithful Inn and Lodge, **15**
Roosevelt Lodge, **4**

▲ CAMPING

Bridge Bay, **14**
Canyon, **8**
Colter Bay, **19**
Fishing Bridge, **12**
Grant Village, **16**
Gros Ventre, **22**
Indian Creek, **3**
Jenny Lake, **21**
Lewis Lake, **17**
Lizard Creek, **18**
Madison, **11**
Mammoth, **2**
Norris, **10**
Pebble Creek, **7**
Signal Mountain, **20**
Slough Creek, **6**
Tower Falls, **5**

Today, Yellowstone is still recovering from devastating forest fires that burned over a third of the park in 1988. The destruction is especially evident in the western half of the park, where charred tree stumps line the roads. Despite the fires, Yellowstone has retained its rugged beauty, and the park's roads are clogged with RVs and tourists eagerly snapping photos of geysers and wildlife. With the reintroduction of wolves in 1995, all of the animals that lived in the Yellowstone area before the arrival of Europeans still roam the landscape, with the exception of the black-footed ferret.

⌐ TRANSPORTATION

The bulk of Yellowstone National Park lies in the northwest corner of Wyoming with slivers in Montana and Idaho. **West Yellowstone, MT,** and **Gardiner, MT** are the most developed and expensive entrance points to the park. **Cooke City, MT** the northeast entrance to the park, is a small rustic town nestled in the mountains. From Cooke City, you can pick up the **Beartooth Hwy.** (U.S. 212; open only in summer) and ascend the surrounding slopes for a breathtaking view of eastern Yellowstone. **Cody** (see p. 731) lies to the east of the park along Rte. 14/16/20. The southern entrance to the park is bordered by **Grand Teton National Park** (see p. 724). Payment of the park's **entrance fee** is good for one week at both Yellowstone and Grand Teton. (Cars $20, pedestrians $10, motorcycles $15.)

> **Buses: Greyhound,** West Yellowstone Office Services, 132 Electric St., West Yellowstone (☎ 646-0001). To: **Boise** (18hr., 1 per day, $107); **Bozeman** (2hr., 1 per day, $18); **Salt Lake City** (9hr., 1 per day, $53). **Powder River Transportation** departs from Cody (see p. 731).

> **Car Rental: Big Sky Car Rental,** 415 Yellowstone Ave. (☎ 646-9564 or 800-426-7669), West Yellowstone, MT. Open May to mid-Oct. daily 8am-5pm. $45 per day, 10% discount for 7 days or more, unlimited mi. Must be 21 with a credit card.

> **Bike Rental: Yellowstone Bicycle and Video,** 132 Madison Ave. (☎ 646-7815), West Yellowstone, MT. Open May-Oct. daily 8:30am-8:30pm; Nov.-Apr. 11am-7pm. Mountain bikes with helmet and water $3.50 per hr., $12.50 per half-day, $19.50 per day.

◾ ORIENTATION

Yellowstone is huge; both Rhode Island and Delaware could fit within its boundaries. Yellowstone's roads are designed in a figure-eight configuration, with side roads leading to park entrances and some of the lesser-known attractions. The natural wonders that make the park famous (e.g. Old Faithful) are scattered along the Upper and Lower Loops. Construction and renovation of roads is continually ongoing; call ahead (☎ 344-7381; www.nps.gov/yell) or consult *Yellowstone Today*, available at the entrance, to find out which sections will be closed during your visit. Travel through the park can be arduously slow regardless of construction. The speed limit is 45 mph, and steep grades, tight curves, and frequent animal crossings increase driving delays.

▨ PRACTICAL INFORMATION

The park's high season extends roughly from mid-June to mid-September. If you visit during this period, expect large crowds, clogged roads, and filled-to-capacity motels and campsites. Most of the park shuts down from November to mid-April, then gradually reopens as the snow melts.

> **!** Yellowstone can be a dangerous place. While roadside wildlife may look tame, these large beasts are unpredictable and easily startled. Stay at least 75 ft. from any animal, 300 ft. from bears. Both black bears and grizzly bears inhabit Yellowstone; consult a ranger about proper precautions before entering the backcountry. If you should encounter a bear, inform a ranger for the safety of others. Bison, regarded by many as mere overgrown cows, can actually travel at speeds of up to 30 mph; visitors are gored every year. Finally, watch for "widow makers," dead trees that can fall over at any time, especially during high winds.

Over 95% of Yellowstone, almost 2 million acres, is backcountry. To venture overnight into the wilds of Yellowstone requires a free **backcountry permit** from a ranger station or Visitors Centers. There is almost always space available in the backcountry, although the more popular areas fill up in July and August. You can reserve a permit in person between one to two days in advance. To reserve a permit ahead of time ($20), write to the **Central Backcountry Office**, P.O. Box 168, Yellowstone National Park 82190, to receive a **trip planning worksheet.** (☎344-2160. Open daily 8am-5pm.) Before heading into the backcountry, visitors must watch a short film outlining safety regulations. No firearms, pets, or mountain bikes are permitted in the backcountry. In many backcountry areas campfires are not permitted; plan on bringing a stove and related cooking gear. Consult a ranger before embarking on a trail; they can offer tips on how to avoid bears, ice, and other natural hindrances.

Fishing and **boating** are both allowed within the park, provided you follow a number of regulations. Permits, available at ranger stations and Visitors Centers, are required for fishing, and some areas may be closed due to feeding patterns of bears. The park's three native species are catch-and-release only. (Permits age 16 and older $10 for 10-day pass, $20 for season.) In addition to the lake, popular fishing spots include the Madison and Firehole rivers; the Firehole is available for fly fishing only. To go boating or even floating on the lake, you'll need a **boating permit,** available at backcountry offices (check *Yellowstone Today*), Bridge Bay marina, a few park entrances, and the Lewis Lake campground. (Motorized vessels $10 for 10-day pass, $20 for season. Motor-free boats $5 for 10-day pass, $10 for season.) **Xanterra** rents row boats, outboards, and dockslips at Bridge Bay Marina. (☎344-7311. Mid-June to early September. Rowboats $7 per hr., outboards $30 per hr.; dockslips $12-18 per night.) Parts of Yellowstone Lake and some other lakes are limited to non-motorized boating; inquire at the Lake Village or Grant Village ranger stations for more advice.

Visitor info: Most regions of the park have their own central station. All centers offer general info and backcountry permits, but each has distinct hiking and camping regulations, and features special **regional exhibits.** All stations are usually open late May to early Sept. daily 8am-7pm. Albright and Old Faithful are open through the winter.

Albright Visitors Center (☎344-2263), at Mammoth Hot Springs: History of Yellowstone Park and the Beginnings of the National Park Idea.

Grant Village (☎242-2650): Wilderness and the 1988 Fire.

Fishing Bridge (☎242-2450): Wildlife and Yellowstone Lake.

Canyon (☎242-2550): Bison; **Old Faithful** (☎545-2750): Geysers; **Norris** (☎344-2812): Geothermic Features of the Park.

Madison (☎344-2821) and **West Thumb** (☎242-2652), on the southern edge of the Lake. Open 9am-5pm.

West Yellowstone Chamber of Commerce, 30 Yellowstone Ave. (☎406-646-7701), West Yellowstone, MT, 2 blocks west of the park entrance. Open late May to early Sept. daily 8am-8pm; early Sept. to late May M-F 8am-5pm.

General Park Information: ☎344-7381. **Weather:** ☎344-2113. **Radio information:** Park information 1610AM.

Medical Services: Lake Clinic, Pharmacy, and Hospital (☎242-7241), across the road from the Lake Yellowstone Hotel. Clinic open late May to mid-Sept. daily 8:30am-8:30pm. Emergency room open May-Sept. 24hr. **Old Faithful Clinic** (☎545-7325), near the Old Faithful Inn. Open early May to mid-Oct. daily 8:30am-1pm and 2-5pm. **Mammoth Hot Springs Clinic** (☎344-7965). Open in summer daily 8:30am-1pm and 2-5pm; in winter M-F 8:30am-1pm and 2-5pm. The **Clinic at West Yellowstone,** 236 Yellowstone Ave. (☎406-646-0200), in West Yellowstone. Open late May to early Sept. M-F 8am-noon and 1-5pm; early Sept. to late May hours vary.

Disabled Services: All entrances, Visitors Centers, and ranger stations offer the *Visitor Guide to Accessible Features.* Fishing Bridge RV Park, Madison, Bridge Bay, Canyon, and Grant campgrounds have accessible sites and restrooms; Lewis Lake and Slough Creek each have accessible sites. Write the **Park Accessibility Coordinator,** P.O. Box 168, Yellowstone National Park, WY, 82190. For more info visit www.nps.gov/yell.

Post Office: There are 5 post offices in the park at **Lake, Old Faithful, Canyon, Grant,** and **Mammoth Hot Springs** (☎344-7764). All open M-F 8:30am-5pm. Specify which station at Yellowstone National Park when addressing mail. **ZIP code:** 82190. In **West Yellowstone, MT:** 209 Grizzly Ave. (☎406-646-7704). Open M-F 8:30am-5pm, Sa 8-10am. **ZIP code:** 59758.

Area codes: 307 (in the park), 406 (in West Yellowstone, Cooke City, and Gardiner, MT). In text, 307 unless noted otherwise.

▌ ACCOMMODATIONS

Camping is cheap, but affordable indoor lodging can be found with advanced preparation. Lodging within the park can be hard to come by on short notice but is often a better deal than the motels along the outskirts of the park. During peak months, the cost of a motel room can skyrocket to $100, while in-park lodging remains relatively inexpensive. Without reservations, affordable lodgings within the park are scarce, and nearby motels fill early in the afternoon.

IN THE PARK

Xanterra (☎344-7311; www.travelyellowstone.com) controls all accommodations within the park, employing a unique code to distinguish between cabins: "Roughrider" means no bath, no facilities; "Budget" offers a sink; "Pioneer" offers a shower, toilet, and sink; "Frontier" is bigger, more plush; and "Western" is the biggest and most plush. Facilities are located close to cabins without private bath. Rates are based on two adults; $10 for each additional adult; under 12 free. Reserve cabins well in advance of the June to September tourist season.

Roosevelt Lodge, 19 mi. north of Canyon. A favorite of Teddy Roosevelt, who seems to have frequented every motel and saloon west of the Mississippi. Provides cheap and scenic accommodations, located in a relatively isolated section of the park. Roughrider cabins with wood-burning stoves $54. Frontier cabins with full bath $97. ❸

Mammoth Hot Springs, 18 mi. west of Roosevelt area, near the north entrance, makes a good base for early-morning wildlife sighting excursions. Lattice-sided Budget cabins $62. Frontier cabins (some with porches) from $97. Hotel room without bath $74. ❸

Old Faithful Inn and Lodge, 30 mi. southwest of the west Yellowstone entrance, is a sea awash with ice cream-toting tourists and RVs, but is conveniently located. Pleasant Budget cabins $45. Frontier cabins $72-75. Well-appointed hotel rooms without bath from $76, with private bath $102-137. ❷

ROCKY MOUNTAINS

Lake Lodge Cabins, 4 mi. south of Fishing Bridge, is a cluster of cabins from the 1920s and 1950s, all just a stone's throw from Yellowstone Lake. Pioneer cabins $57. Larger Western cabins $125. Next door, **Lake Yellowstone Hotel and Cabins** has yellow Frontier cabins with no lake view for $92. ❸

Canyon Lodge and Cabins, 15 mi. north of Fishing Bridge, overlook the "Grand Canyon" of Yellowstone. Less authentic and more expensive than Roosevelt Lodge's cabins, but centrally located and more popular among tourists. Pioneer cabins $64. Frontier cabins $90. Western cabins $128. ❸

WEST YELLOWSTONE, MT

Guarding the west entrance of the park, West Yellowstone capitalizes on the hordes of tourists who pass through en route to the park. The closest of the border towns to popular park attractions, West Yellowstone has numerous budget motels, with more reasonable prices than Gardiner.

West Yellowstone International Hostel, 139 Yellowstone Ave. (☎406-646-7745 or 800-838-7745), at the **Madison Hotel,** provides the best indoor budget accommodations around the park. The friendly staff and welcoming lobby make travelers feel at home. Kitchen only has microwave and hot water. Internet access $5 per hr. Open late May to mid-Oct. Dorms $19; private singles and doubles $26-36. ❶

Lazy G Motel, 123 Hayden St. (☎406-646-7586), has an affable staff and spacious 1970s-style rooms featuring queen-sized beds, refrigerators, and TVs. Open May-March. Singles $43; doubles $53, with kitchenette $53-63. ❷

GARDINER, MT

The Town Cafe and Motel (☎406-848-7322), on Park St. across from the park's northern entrance. These wood-paneled, carpeted rooms are one of the best deals in town. TVs but no phones. Singles June-Sept. $45; Oct.-May $25. Doubles $55/30-35. ❷

Jim Bridger Court Modern Cabins (☎406-848-7371), on U.S. 89, has clean, no-frills cabins with a sheltered front stoop and a terrific view. TVs but no phones. 1 queen bed $60, 2 queen beds $70. ❸

Hillcrest Cottages (☎406-848-7353 or 800-970-7353), on U.S. 89 across from the Exxon, rents out deluxe cabins with kitchenettes. Open May to early Sept. Singles $64; doubles $76; $6 per additional adult, $2 per additional child under 18. ❸

COOKE CITY, MT

Cooke City is located at the northeast corner of the park. The Nez Percé slipped right by the US cavalry here, Lewis and Clark deemed the area impassable, and few people visit this rugged little town. Nonetheless, Cooke City is a great location for exploring the remote backcountry of Yellowstone and is conveniently situated between the park and the junction of two scenic drives: the **Chief Joseph Scenic Hwy. (Rte. 296)** and the **Beartooth Hwy (Rte. 212).**

Antler's Lodge (☎406-838-2432). Built in 1936, each cabin has its own personality and a great mountain view. Ernest Hemingway spent several nights editing *For Whom the Bell Tolls* here. Singles $47; doubles $50-60. ❸

◤ CAMPING

Campsites fill quickly during the summer months; be prepared to make alternate arrangements. Call **Park Headquarters** (☎344-7381) for info on campsite vacancies. **Xanterra,** P.O. Box 165, Yellowstone National Park 82190, runs five of the 12 developed campgrounds within the park: **Canyon, Grant Village, Madison, Bridge Bay** (all $15), and **Fishing Bridge RV** ($33; RVs only). Xanterra accepts advance (☎344-7311) and same-day reservations (☎344-7901). Reservations are accepted up to two years in advance. During peak summer months (especially on weekends and holidays) all available sites may be reserved beforehand. The two largest Xanterra campgrounds, **Grant Village** (425 sites) and **Bridge Bay** (430 sites), are the best bet for last-minute reservations.

The seven National Park campgrounds do not accept advance reservations. During the summer, these smaller campgrounds generally fill by 10am, and finding a site can be frustrating. Check-out time is 10am, and the best window for claiming a campsite is between 8 and 10am. Two of the most beautiful campgrounds are **Slough Creek Campground ❶**, 10 mi. northeast of Tower Jct. (29 sites; open late May to Oct.; $10) and **Pebble Creek Campground ❶** (32 sites; no RVs; open mid-June to early Sept.; $10). Both are located in the northeast corner of the park, between Tower Falls and the Northeast Entrance (generally the least congested area), and both offer relatively isolated sites and good fishing. You can also try **Lewis Lake ❶** (85 sites; $10), halfway between West Thumb and the South Entrance, or **Tower Falls ❶** (32 sites; $10), between the Northeast entrance and Mammoth Hot Springs. **Norris ❶** (116 sites; open late May-late Sept.; $12); **Indian Creek ❶**, between the Norris Geyser Basin and Mammoth Hot Springs (75 sites; open mid-June to mid-Sept.; $10); and **Mammoth ❶** (85 sites; open year-round; $12) are less scenic but still great places to camp. Campgrounds at Grant Village, Fishing Bridge, and Canyon have coin laundries ($1.25 wash, $1 dry) and pay showers ($3). The lodges at Mammoth and Old Faithful have showers for $3 (towels and shampoo included) but no laundry facilities.

◗ FOOD

Buying food at the restaurants, snack bars, and cafeterias in the park can be expensive; stick to the **general stores** at each lodging location. The stores at Fishing Bridge, Lake, Grant Village, and Canyon sell lunch-counter style food. (Open daily 7:30am-9pm, but times may vary.) Stockpile provisions at the **Food Round-Up Grocery Store,** 107 Dunraven St., in West Yellowstone (☎406-646-7501. Open in summer daily 7am-10pm; in winter 7am-9pm.) Marking the original entrance to the park, Gardiner is smaller and less touristy than West Yellowstone; it is also significantly more pricey. **Food Farm,** on U.S. 89 in Gardiner across from the Super 8, has cheap food. (☎406-848-7524. Open M-Sa 7am-9pm, Su 8am-8pm.)

> **Running Bear Pancake House** (☎406-646-7703), at the corner of Madison and Hayden in West Yellowstone, has inexpensive breakfast and lunch. Meals $5-6. Open daily 7am-2pm. ❶
>
> **Timberline Cafe,** 135 Yellowstone Ave. (☎646-9349), in West Yellowstone, prepares travelers for a day at the park with homemade pies. Burgers $6-7.50. Sandwiches and omelettes $6-8. Open daily 6:30am-10pm. ❷
>
> **Helen's Corral Drive-In,** a few blocks west on U.S. 89 in Gardiner, rounds up killer ½ lb. burgers ($4-7). Open in summer daily 11am-11pm. ❷
>
> **Grizzly Pad Grill and Cabins** (☎406-838-2161), on Rte. 212 on the eastern side of Cooke City, dishes out the Grizzly Pad Special—an incredible milkshake, fries, and a large cheeseburger ($7). Open in summer daily 7am-9pm; off-season hours vary. Closed mid-Oct. to late Dec. and mid-Apr. to late May. ❷
>
> **The Miner's Saloon** (☎406-838-2214), on Rte. 212 in downtown Cooke City, is the best place to go for a buffalo burger ($6.50) and a frosty Moose Drool beer. Open daily noon-2am. ❷

> ⚠ Beware: the crust around many of Yellowstone's thermal basins, geysers, and hot springs is thin, and boiling, acidic water lies just beneath the surface. Stay on the marked paths and boardwalks at all times. In the backcountry, keep a good distance from hot springs and fumaroles.

⚙ SIGHTS

Xanterra (☎ 344-7311) organizes tours, horseback rides, and chuckwagon dinners. However, these outdoor activities are expensive, and, given enough time, Yellowstone is best explored on foot. Visitors Centers give out informative self-guiding tour pamphlets with maps for each of the park's main attractions (25¢; Old Faithful, Mammoth Hot Springs, and Canyon 50¢). Trails to these sights are accessible from the road via walkways, usually extending ¼ to 1½ mi. into the various natural environments.

Yellowstone is set apart from other National Parks and Forests in the Rockies by its **geothermal features**—the park protects the largest geothermic area in the world. The bulk of these geothermal wonders can be found on the western side of the park between Mammoth Hot Springs in the north and Old Faithful in the south. The most dramatic thermal fissures are the **geysers.** Hot liquid magma close to the surface of the earth superheats water until it boils and bubbles, eventually builds up enough pressure to burst through the cracks with steamy force. The extremely volatile nature of this area means that attractions may change, appear, or disappear due to forces beyond human control.

While bison-jams and bear-gridlock may make wildlife seem more of a nuisance than an attraction, they afford a unique opportunity to see a number of native species co-existing in their natural environment. The best times for viewing are early morning and just before dark, as most animals nap in the shade during the hot midday. The road between Tower-Roosevelt and the northeast entrance, in the Lamar Valley, is one of the best places to see wolves and grizzlies (among other species). Consult a ranger for more specific advice.

OLD FAITHFUL AREA

Yellowstone's trademark attraction, Old Faithful, is the most predictable of the large geysers and has consistently pleased audiences since its discovery in 1870. Eruptions typically occur every 45min. to 2hr. (average 90min.) and are usually 120 ft. to 140 ft. in height. Eruptions last anywhere from 5min. to 1½hrs. Predictions for the next eruption, usually accurate to within 10min., are posted at the Old Faithful Visitors Center. Old Faithful lies in the **Upper Geyser Basin,** 16 mi. south of the Madison area and 20 mi. west of Grant Village. Numerous other geysers and hot springs flow in this area and trails connect them all. The spectacular **Morning Glory Pool** is an easy 1½ mi. from Old Faithful, and provides an interesting diversion between eruptions.

FIREHOLE RIVER

Between Old Faithful and Madison, along the Firehole River, lie the **Midway Geyser Basin** and the **Lower Geyser Basin.** Many of these geysers are visible from the side of the road, although stopping for a closer look is highly recommended. The **Excelsior Geyser Crater,** a large, steaming lake created by a powerful geyser blast, and the **Grand Prismatic Spring,** the largest hot spring in the park, sit about 5 mi. north of Old Faithful and are well worth the trip. Eight miles north of Old Faithful gurgles the **Fountain Paint Pot,** a bubbling pool of hot milky mud. Four types of geothermal activity present in Yellowstone (geysers, mudpots, hot springs, and fumaroles) are found along the trails of the Firehole River. There is a strong temptation to wash off the grime of camping in the hot water, but swimming in the hot springs is prohibited. You can swim in the **Firehole River,** near Firehole Canyon Dr., just south of Madison Jct., but prepare for a chill; the name of the river is quite deceiving. Call park info (☎ 344-7381) to make sure the river is open.

NORRIS GEYSER BASIN

Fourteen mi. north of Madison and 21 mi. south of Mammoth, the colorful **Norris Geyser Basin** is both the oldest and the hottest active thermal zone in the park. The geyser has been erupting hot water at temperatures of up to 459°F for over 115,000 years. **Echinus,** in the Black Basin, is the largest known acid-water geyser, erupting 40-60 ft. every 35-90min. Its neighbor, **Steamboat,** is the tallest active geyser in the world, erupting over 300 ft. for anywhere from 3-40min. Steamboat's eruptions, however, are entirely unpredictable; the last eruption occurred April 26, 2002 after 2 years of inactivity.

MAMMOTH HOT SPRINGS

Shifting water sources, malleable limestone deposits, and temperature-sensitive, multicolored bacterial growth create the most rapidly changing natural structure in the park. The hot spring terraces resemble huge wedding cakes at **Mammoth Hot Springs,** 21 mi. to the north of the Norris Basin and 19 mi. west of Tower. When visiting, ask a local ranger where to find the most active springs. Also ask about area trails, that provide some of the park's best wildlife viewing. Xanterra offers **horse rides** just south of the Hot Springs. (☎ 344-7311; call at least 1 day ahead. Late May to early Sept. $23.50 per hr., $35.50 per 2hr.) **Swimming** is permitted in the **Boiling River,** 2½ mi. north. Check with a ranger to make sure that this area is open.

GRAND CANYON

The east side's featured attraction, the **Grand Canyon of the Yellowstone,** wears rusty red and orange hues created by hot water acting on the volcanic rock. The canyon is 800-1200 ft. deep and 1500-4000 ft. wide. For a close-up view of the mighty **Lower Falls** (308 ft.), hike down the short but steep **Uncle Tom's Trail** (over 300 steps). **Artist Point,** on the southern rim, and **Lookout Point,** on the northern rim, offer broader canyon vistas and are accessible from the road between Canyon and Fishing Bridge. Keep an eye out for bighorn sheep along the canyon's rim. Xanterra also runs **horse rides** at Canyon, as well as in the Tower-Roosevelt area 19 mi. north, and **Stagecoach rides** ($6.75, ages 2-11 $5.50) are available early June to early Sept. at Roosevelt Lodge.

YELLOWSTONE LAKE AREA

Situated in the southeast corner of the park, **Yellowstone Lake** is the largest high-altitude lake in North America and serves as a protective area for the cutthroat trout. While the surface of the lake may appear calm, geologists have found evidence of geothermal features at the bottom. **AmFac** offers lake cruises that leave from the marina at Bridge Bay. (☎ 344-7311. Open early June to mid-Sept. 5-7 per day. $9, ages 2-11 $5.) Geysers and hot springs in **West Thumb** dump an average of 3100 gallons of water into the lake per day. Notwithstanding this thermal boost, the temperature of the lake remains quite cold, averaging 45°F during the summer. Visitors to the park once cooked freshly-caught trout in the boiling water of the **Fishing Cone,** but this is no longer permitted. Due to efforts to help the endangered cutthroat population, fishing off the **Fishing Bridge** is now forbidden. The sulphurous odors of **Mud Volcano** can be distinguished from miles away, but these unique turbulent mudpots are worth the assault on your nose. Located 6 mi. north of Fishing Bridge and 10 mi. south of Canyon Jct., the unusual geothermal features have descriptive names such as **Dragon's Mouth, Sour Lake,** and **Black Dragon's Cauldron.**

OFF THE (EXTREMELY WELL) BEATEN PATH

Most visitors to Yellowstone never get out of their cars, and therefore miss out on over 1200 mi. of trails in the park. Options for exploring Yellowstone's more pristine areas range from short day hikes to long backcountry trips. When planning a hike, pick up a topographical trail map ($9-10) at any Visitors Center and ask a ranger to describe the network of trails. Some trails are poorly marked; allow extra time (at least 1hr.) in case you get lost. The 1988 fires scarred over a third of the park; hikers should consult rangers and maps on which areas are burned. Burned areas have less shade, so hikers should equip themselves with hats, extra water, and sunscreen.

In addition to the self-guiding trails at major attractions, many worthwhile sights are only a few miles off the main road. The **Fairy Falls Trail**, near Old Faithful, provides a unique perspective on the Midway Geyser Basin. The 5¼ mi. round-trip trail begins in the parking lot marked Fairy Falls just south of Midway Geyser Basin. The trail to the top of **Mt. Washburn** is enhanced by an enclosed observation area with sweeping views of the park. This trail begins at Chittenden Rd. or Dunraven Pass parking areas and totals about 6 mi. round-trip. The free *Backcountry Trip Planner* and rangers can help plan more extended trips.

SCENIC DRIVE: NORTH FORK DRIVE

Linking Yellowstone National Park with Cody, WY, the **Buffalo Bill Cody** scenic byway, also known as U.S. 14/16/20, bridges the majestic peaks of the Absaroka Mountains (*ab-SOR-ka*) with the sagebrush lands of the Wyoming plains. This 52 mi. drive winds through the canyon created by the North Fork of the Shoshone River and is a spectacular departure from Yellowstone. The high granite walls and sedimentary formations of the **Shoshone Canyon** are noticeable from the road, as is the smell of sulfur from the DeMaris springs located in the Shoshone River. Once the world's tallest dam, the **Buffalo Bill Dam Visitors Center and Reservoir** celebrates man's ability to control the flow of water to fit human needs. Built between 1904 and 1910, the Buffalo Bill Dam measures 350 ft. in height. (☎ 527-6076. Visitors Center open June-Aug. 8am-8pm; May and Sept. daily 8am-6pm.) West of the dam, **strange rock formations,** created millions of years ago by volcanic eruptions in the Absarokas, dot the dusty hillsides. Sagebrush and small juniper trees gradually lead into the thick pine cover of the **Shoshone National Forest,** the country's first national forest. This area, known as the **Wapiti Valley,** is home to over 18 dude ranches. The **East Entrance** to Yellowstone National Park guards the west end of the scenic byway and is closed in winter.

The **Chief Joseph Scenic Hwy. (Rte. 296)** connects Cooke City, MT, to Cody, WY, and passes through rugged, sagebrush-covered mountains across the summit of **Dead Indian Hill.** This scenic byway traces the route traveled by the Nez Percé Indians as they skillfully evaded the US army in the summer of 1877. From Cody, follow the Buffalo Bill Cody scenic byway back into eastern Yellowstone, completing a spectacular drive through the western half of Wyoming.

GRAND TETON NATIONAL PARK ☎ 307

One of the most impressive skylines in the Rockies, twelve Teton peaks tower over 12,000 feet. The Grand Tetons are the youngest mountains in the entire Rocky Mountain system, their jagged peaks sculpted by glaciers more than 3000 feet thick. When French trappers from the Hudson Bay Company first observed the three most prominent peaks—South Teton, Grand Teton, and Mt. Teewinot—they dubbed the mountains *"Les trois tetons,"* meaning "the three breasts." Later discovering that the three nipples were surrounded by numerous smaller peaks, the erstwhile Frenchmen renamed the range *"Les grands tetons."* Grand Teton National Park, officially established in 1929, continues to delight hikers with miles of strenuous trails and steep rock cliffs along the range's eastern face.

✈ ℹ ORIENTATION & PRACTICAL INFORMATION

Scenic Teton vistas are accessible from **Rte. 89,** which runs the length of the park, connecting Yellowstone to Jackson. Teton Park Rd. gives a closer look at the peaks between Jackson Lake Jct. and Moose Jct. and provides access to Jackson Lake. There are two entrance stations to the park, at Moose and Moran Jct. The stretch of Rte. 89 between Moran Jct. and Jackson does not pass through either entrance and offers excellent, free views of the Tetons. Those who elect to enter the park pay an **entrance fee.** ($20 per car, $10 per pedestrian or bicycle, $15 per motorcycle. Pass good for 7 days in Tetons and Yellowstone.)

To **backcountry camp** in a mountain canyon or on the shores of a lake in summer, make reservations early. No reservations required for winter camping, but be sure to check in at a Ranger station. To make a reservation, contact the **Moose Visitor Center.** (☎ 739-3309. $15.) After May 15, two-thirds of all backcountry spots are available first come, first served; get a free permit up to 24hr. in advance at one of the Visitors Centers. The staff can help plan routes and find campsites. Wood fires are only permitted within existing fire grates, so check with rangers before singing 'round the campfire. At high elevations, snow often remains into July, and the weather can become severe or even deadly any time of the year. Severe weather gear is strongly advised.

Public Transit: Grand Teton Lodge Co. (☎ 800-628-9988) runs in summer from Colter Bay to Jackson Lake Lodge. $7. Shuttles also run to the **Jackson Hole** airport (9 per day, $25) and **Jackson** (5 per day, $25).

Visitor info: Visitors Centers and campgrounds have free copies of the *Teewinot* newspaper which has info on special programs, hiking, camping, and news. For general info and a visitor's packet, or to make backcountry camping reservations, contact **Park Headquarters** (☎ 739-3600) or write the **Superintendent,** Grand Teton National Park, P.O. Drawer 170, Moose WY 83012.

Moose Visitors Center (☎ 739-3399), Teton Park Rd., at the southern tip of the park, ½ mi. west of Moose Jct. Open early June to early Sept. daily 8am-7pm; early Sept. to mid-May 8am-5pm.

Jenny Lake Visitors Center (☎ 739-3392), next to the Jenny Lake Campground. Open early June to early Sept. daily 8am-7pm; Sept. 8am-5pm.

Colter Bay Visitors Center (☎ 739-3594), on Jackson Lake in the northern part of the park. Open late May to early Sept. daily 8am-7pm; early May to mid-May and Sept. 8am-5pm.

Info lines: Weather, ☎ 739-3611. **Wyoming Hwy. Info Center,** ☎ 733-1731. **Wyoming Dept. of Transportation,** ☎ 888-996-7623. **Road Report,** ☎ 739-3614.

Emergency: Sheriff's office, ☎ 733-2331. **Park dispatch,** ☎ 739-3300.

Medical Services: Grand Teton Medical Clinic, Jackson Lake Lodge (☎ 543-2514, after hours ☎ 733-8002). Open late May to mid-Oct. daily 10am-6pm. **St. John's Hospital,** 625 E. Broadway (☎ 733-3636), in Jackson.

Post Office: In Moose (☎ 733-3336), across from the Park HQ. Open M-F 9am-1pm and 1:30-5pm, Sa limited hours. **ZIP code:** 83102. **Area code:** 307.

🏠 🍴 ACCOMMODATIONS & FOOD

The Grand Teton Lodge Co. runs all indoor accommodations in the park. (Reservations ☎ 800-628-9988; or write **Reservations Manager,** Grand Teton Lodge Co., P.O. Box 240, Moran 83013. Deposits are required.) Most lodges are pricey, but there are two options for affordable, rustic cabins at Colter Bay that are open late May to early October. **Colter Bay Tent Cabins ❷** is the cheaper option, but provides less shelter from the elements. The cabins are charming but primitive log and canvas shelters with dusty floors, tables, wood-burning stoves, and bunks. Sleeping bags, cots, and blankets are available for rent. (☎800-628-9988. Office open early June to early Sept. 24hr. Restrooms and $3 showers nearby. Tent cabins for 2 $34; each additional person $4.) **Colter Bay Log Cabins ❷** maintains 208 quaint log cabins near Jackson Lake. The cabins with shared baths are probably the best deal in the entire Jackson Hole area; book early. Ask the staff about hikes and excursions. (☎543-2828. Open late May to late Sept. 2-person cabins with semi-private bath from $34, 1-room with private bath $69-104; 2-room with private bath $109-129.)

The best way to eat in the Tetons is to bring your own food. Non-perishables are available at **Dornan's General Store** in Moose. (☎733-2415. Open daily 8am-8pm.) Jackson has an **Albertson's** supermarket, 105 Buffalo Way, at the intersection of W. Broadway and Rte. 22. (☎733-5950. Open daily 6am-midnight.) The **Chuck Wagon Restaurant,** in Colter Bay, serves breakfast, lunch, and dinner. (☎543-1077. Open daily 7am-9pm.) Across the street, **Dornan's Deli ❶** has affordable sandwiches. (Sandwiches $4-6. Open daily 8am-7pm.)

🏕 CAMPING

To stay in the Tetons without emptying your wallet, find a tent and pitch it. The park service maintains five campgrounds, all first come, first served. (☎739-3603 for info. Sites generally open mid-May to late Sept.) All sites have restrooms, cold water, fire rings, dump stations, and picnic tables. There is a maximum of six people and one vehicle per site, but Colter Bay and Gros Ventre accept larger groups.

Jenny Lake has 49 sites that are among the most beautifully developed in the US. Mt. Teewinot towers 6000 ft. above tents pitched at the edge of the lake. Sites usually fill before 8am; get there early. No RVs. Max. stay 7 days. Vehicle sites $12, bicycle sites $3 per person. ❶

Lizard Creek, closer to Yellowstone than the Tetons, has 60 spacious, secluded sites along the northern shore of Jackson Lake. The campsites fill up by about 2pm. Max. stay 14 days. Vehicle sites $12, bicycle sites $3 per person. ❶

Colter Bay is not exactly a wilderness experience—with its 350 crowded sites, tenters should stay away. Grocery store, laundromat, and two restaurants. Showers $3. Sites with full hookup $31. ❷

Signal Mountain, along the southern shore of Jackson Lake. The 86 sites are roomier and more secluded than at Colter Bay. The campground is usually full by 10am.

Gros Ventre (☎739-3516; Jan.-May ☎739-3473), along the edge of the Gros Ventre River, close to Jackson, is the biggest campground with 360 sites and 5 group sites. However, the Tetons are hidden from view by Blacktail Butte. The campsite rarely fills and is the best bet for late arrivals.

🧗 OUTDOOR ACTIVITIES

While Yellowstone wows visitors with geysers and mudpots, the Grand Tetons boast some of the most scenic mountains in the US, if not the world. Only 2-3 million years old, the Tetons range between 10,000-13,770 ft. in elevation. The absence of foothills creates spectacular mountain vistas that accentuate the range's steep rock faces. These dramatic rocks draw scores of climbers, but less seasoned hikers can still experience the beauty of the Teton's backcountry.

HIKING

All Visitors Centers provide pamphlets about day hikes and sell numerous guides and maps ($3-10). Rangers also lead informative hikes; check the *Teewinot* or the Visitors Centers for more info. Before hitting the trail or planning extended hikes, be sure to check in at the ranger station; trails at higher elevations may still be snow-covered. During years with heavy snowfall, prime hiking season does not begin until well into July.

The Cascade Canyon Trail (14 mi. with boat ride, 18 mi. without boat ride; 6-8hr.) begins on the far side of tranquil Jenny Lake and follows Cascade Creek through U-shaped valleys carved by glaciers. The **Hidden Falls Waterfall** is located ½ mi. up; views of Teewinot, Mt. Owen, and Grand Teton are visible to the south. Hikers with more stamina can continue another ½ mi. upwards towards **Inspiration Point,** but only the lonely can trek 6¾ mi. further to **Lake Solitude** (9035 ft.). Guides for Cascade Canyon are available (for a small fee) at Visitors Centers. Hikers can reach the Cascade Canyon Trial by following part of the 6.6 mi. trail around Jenny Lake or by taking one of the shuttles offered by **Jenny Lake Boating.** (☎ 733-2703. Boats leave from Jenny Lake Visitors Center every 20min. 8am-6pm. One-way $5, ages 7-12 $4; round-trip $7/5.)

Taggert Lake (3.2 mi., 2hr.) is another self-guided hike. This moderate trail winds through a broad spectrum of plant life, including the remains of a 1985 forest fire, and emerges for spectacular views of the mountains at the lake. The trail begins in the Taggert Lake parking area, 3 mi. north of Moose.

Hermitage Point (8.8 mi., 4hr.) beginning at Colter Bay, is a unique perspective on Jackson Lake and a prime spot for observing wildlife.

The Amphitheater Lake Trail (9.8 mi., 8hr.), originating just south of Jenny Lake at the Lupine Meadows parking lot, treks to one of the park's glacial lakes. Lupines, the purple flowers visible all along the roads in the park, bloom from June to July along the trail.

Static Peak Divide (15.6 mi., 10hr.) is a loop trail up 4020 ft. from the Death Canyon trailhead, 4.5 mi. south of Moose Visitors Center. With some of the best vistas in the park, the Death Canyon area is prime for longer two- to three-day hikes.

The Cunningham Cabin Trail (0.8 mi., 1hr.) relives the history of cattle ranching in the valley. Trailhead lies 6 mi. south of Moran.

CLIMBING

Two climbing guide companies offer more extreme backcountry adventures, including four-day packages that let beginners work their way up to the famed Grand Teton. **Jackson Hole Mountain Guides and Climbing School,** 165 N. Glenwood St., in Jackson, has a one-day beginner course for $90; more advanced (and more expensive) programs are also available. (☎ 733-4979 or 800-239-7642. Reservations necessary.) **Exum Mountain Guides** offer similar classes and rates. (☎ 733-2297. 1-day beginner rock-climbing course $95. Guided 1- to 2-day climbs $120-385. Reservations necessary.)

BOATING, FISHING, & BIKING

Boating and hand-powered crafts are permitted on a number of lakes; Jackson, Jenny, and Phelps Lakes allow motorboats. Permits for boating can be obtained at the Moose or Colter Bay Visitors Centers. (Motorized boats $10 per 7 days, $20 annual; non-motorized craft $5/10.) **Grand Tetons Lodge Company** rents boats at Colter Bay and Jenny Lake and has scenic cruises of Jackson Lake, leaving from Colter Bay. (Colter Bay Marina ☎ 543-2811; Jenny Lake ☎ 733-2703. Cruises $15, ages 3-11 $7. Canoes $9 per hr.; motor boats $18 per hr.; 2hr. min.) **Fishing** is permitted within the park with a Wyoming license, available at Moose Village Store, Signal Mountain Lodge, Colter Bay Marina, and Flagg Ranch Village. ($10 Wyoming Conservation stamp required with all fishing licenses. WY residents $3 per day; $15 per season, ages 14-18 $3. Non-residents $10 per day; $65/15 per season.) The Grand Teton Lodge Company offers float trips on the Snake River. (☎ 800-628-9988. $39.50, ages 6-11 $20.) **Mountain biking** is a popular activity on roads in the park, but is strictly forbidden on hiking trails.

Outdoor equipment rentals can be found in Jackson and at Moose Village. **Adventure Sports,** a division of Dornan's in Moose, rents bikes and provides advice on where to trek. (☎ 733-3307. Open in summer daily 9am-6pm; off-season hours vary. Mountain bikes from $8 per hr., $18 per half-day. Credit card or deposit required.) **Snake River Angler,** next to Dornan's, rents rods. (☎ 733-3699. Open daily 8am-8pm, off-season 9am-5pm. Rods $15-25 per day.) Next door, **Moosely Seconds** rents a variety of outdoor equipment. (☎ 733-7176. Open in summer daily 8am-9pm; winter hours vary. Climbing shoes $6, crampons $10, ice axes $6, trekking poles $4.)

WINTER ACTIVITIES

In the winter, all hiking trails and the unploughed sections of Teton Park Rd. are open to **cross-country skiers.** Pick up winter info at Moose Visitors Center. Guides lead free **snowshoe hikes** from the Moose Visitors Center. (☎ 739-3399. Jan.-Mar. Th-Tu 1pm.) **Snow Creek Nordic & Snowshoe Center,** in Jackson, keeps over 9 mi. of groomed skiing trails, and guides cross-country and snowshoe tours of the Tetons. (☎ 733-8833 or 800-443-6139. Trail fee $8 per day, seniors and children $5. Ski tours $45 per half-day, $70 per day. Snowshoe tours $30 per half-day.) **Snowmobiling** is only allowed on the continental divide snowmobile trail; pick up a $15 permit at Moose Visitors Center and a map and guide at the Jackson Chamber of Commerce. **Grand Teton Park Snowmobile Rental,** near Moran Jct., rents snowmobiles (☎ 733-1980 or 800-563-6469. $79 per ½ day, $119 per day; includes clothing, helmet, and boots.) The Colter Bay and Moose parking lots are available for parking in the winter. All **campgrounds** close in winter, but **backcountry snow camping** (only for those who know what they're doing) is allowed with a permit purchased from the Moose Visitors Center. Before making plans, consider that temperatures regularly drop below -25°F. Be sure to carry extreme weather clothing and check with a ranger station for current weather conditions and avalanche danger.

SCENIC DRIVE: CENTENNIAL SCENIC DRIVE

Passing through some of the most beautiful country on earth, this all-day drive is like a vacation unto itself. For 162 mi., the Centennial Scenic Byway passes by the high peaks, roaring whitewater rivers, and broad windswept plains of western Wyoming. The drive is open year-round but may occasionally close due to snow.

The drive begins in the small frontier town of **Dubois,** home of the **National Bighorn Sheep Interpretive Center,** 907 W. Ramshorn St., a fascinating and bizarre museum that educates visitors about the furry creatures. (☎ 455-3429. Open in summer 9am-8pm; in winter 8am-5pm. $2, family $5.) Leaving town on Rte. 26, the crumbly breccia of the volcanic Absaroka mountains becomes visible to the north; the 11,920 ft. high towering mountain is **Ramshorn Peak.** Gently rising through a conifer forest, the road eventually reaches **Togwotee Pass,** elevation 9544 ft.

As the road begins to descend, the famed panorama of the Teton mountain range becomes visible. The highest peak is the Grand Teton (13,770 ft.); the exhibit at the Teton Range Overlook labels each visible peak in the skyline. After entering **Grand Teton National Park** (see p. 724), the road winds through the flat plain of the **Buffalo Fork River,** a striking contrast to the high peaks and mountain forests. This floodplain is the beginning of the wide, long valley known as Jackson Hole (early trappers referred to any high mountain valley as a hole).

Once in the park, the road follows the legendary **Snake River,** renowned for its whitewater rafting and kayaking. Nearing Jackson (see p. 729), the **National Elk Refuge** is visible to the east and is the winter home of 6000-7000 elk. To bypass Jackson, take U.S. 189/191 south. As the Tetons fade out of sight, the **Wind River Range** appears on the horizon, and soon the highest peak in Wyoming, **Gannet Peak** (13,804 ft.), appears against the horizon. The drive ends in the tiny, authentically Western town of **Pinedale.** In Pinedale, the **Museum of the Mountain Man** chronicles the history of the Plains Indians, the fur trade, and the white settlement of western Wyoming. (☎877-686-6266. Open early May to late Sept. daily 10am-5pm. $4, seniors $3, children $2.)

JACKSON ☎307

Jackson Hole, the valley that separates the Teton and Gros Ventre mountain ranges, is renowned for its world-class skiing, but that is not the area's only attraction. In recent years, the small town of Jackson (pop. 5000) has exploded into a cosmopolitan epicenter. Downtown is lined with chic restaurants, faux-Western bars, and expensive lodgings. The area's true beauty, however, can only be appreciated by exploring the nearby Tetons or navigating the winding Snake River.

■ ▶ ORIENTATION & PRACTICAL INFORMATION. Downtown Jackson is centered around the intersection of Broadway and Cache St. and marked by the **Town Sq. Park.** The majority of shops and restaurants are within a four-block radius of this intersection. South of town, at the intersection with Rte. 22, W. Broadway becomes U.S. 191/89/26. To get to **Teton Village,** take Rte. 22 to Rte. 390 (Teton Village Rd.) just before the town of Wilson. Winding backroads, unpaved at times, connect Teton Village to Moose and the southern entrance of the National Park. North of Jackson, Cache St. turns into Rte. 89, leading directly into the park.

Jackson Hole Express (☎733-1719 or 800-652-9510) runs to the Salt Lake City airport (5½hr., 2 per day, $54) and the Idaho Falls airport (2hr., 2 per day, $31). Reservations are required. **Jackson START** runs buses within the region. (☎733-4521. Late May to mid-Sept. 6am-10:30pm; early Dec. to early Apr. 6am-11pm. In town free, on village roads $1, to Teton Village $2; under 9 free.) **Leisure Sports,** 1075 Rte. 89, has boating equipment and the best deals on camping and backpacking rentals. (☎733-3040. Open in summer and winter daily 8am-6pm, in fall and spring 8am-5pm. Tents $6-15, sleeping bags $6, backpacks $3. Canoes and kayaks $35-45 per day, rafts $90-115 per day.) **Visitor info: Jackson Hole and Greater Yellowstone Information Center,** 532 N. Cache St. (Open early June to early Sept. daily 8am-7pm; in early Sept. to early June M-F 8am-5pm.) **Internet access: Jackson Library,** 125 Virginian Ln. (☎733-2164. Open M-Th 10am-9pm, F 10am-5:30pm, Sa 10am-5pm, Su 1-5pm.) **Post Office:** 1070 Maple Way, at Powderhorn Ln. (☎733-3650. Open M-F 8:30am-5pm, Sa 10am-1pm.) **ZIP code:** 83002. **Area code:** 307.

▌ ACCOMMODATIONS. Jackson draws hordes of visitors year-round, making rooms expensive and hard to find without reservations. ◪**The Hostel X (HI-AYH) ❸,** 12 mi. northwest of Jackson in Teton Village, lets skiers and others stay close to the slopes for cheap. The hostel has a lounge with TVs and games, a ski-waxing room, and is a close stumble from the Mangy Moose (see **Nightlife,** below). 4 beds in dorm rooms; 20 rooms with king-size beds. Private bath and maid service. (☎733-3415. Open in summer and winter. 1-2 people $50; 3-4 $63.) Rooms are costly during peak months, but **The Pioneer ❹,** 325 N. Cache St., is a bargain during the spring. Lovely rooms come with microwaves, refrigerators, free local calls, and handcrafted quilts. (☎733-3673. Dec.-Mar. rooms $45-65 for 1-2 people; June-Sept.

ROCKY MOUNTAINS

$75-95.) For those on a serious budget, **The Bunkhouse ❶**, 215 N. Cache St., in the basement of the Anvil Motel, is a viable option. (☎733-3668. Showers, coin laundry, and ski storage. Beds $22.)

For those willing to rough it, the primitive campgrounds in Grand Teton National Park and the **Bridger-Teton National Forest** are the cheapest accommodations in the area. **Gros Ventre** campground (see p. 726) is only a 10min. drive from Jackson. There are 45 **developed campgrounds** in the Bridger-Teton National Forest, including several along U.S. 26 west of Jackson. (Some have water, no showers. $5-15.) The publication *The Bridge* is available at the Visitors Center in Jackson; the National Forest offices have additional info. Dispersed camping is free within the National Forest; campers must stay at least 200 ft. from water and 100 ft. from roads or trails. Consult with a ranger beforehand, as some areas may be restricted.

◘ FOOD. Jackson has dozens of restaurants, but few are suited to the budget traveler. **The Bunnery ❷**, 130 N. Cache St., attracts both locals and tourists with its special O.S.M. (oats, sunflower, and millet) bread and classic club. (☎733-5474. Classic club $7.50. Sandwiches $6-8. Omelettes $7.50 Open in summer daily 7am-9pm; in winter 7am-2pm.) For a homeopathic remedy, or just a healthy bite to eat, the **Harvest Bakery and Cafe ❷**, 130 W. Broadway, is a New Age jack-of-all-trades. (☎733-5418. Smoothies $3-4.50. Fresh pastries $2. Soup and salad $6. Breakfast under $6. Open M-F 7am-8pm, Sa 7am-7pm, Su 8am-4pm; in winter M-Sa 8am-7pm, Su 8am-3:30pm.) A popular family restaurant, **Bubba's ❸**, 515 W. Broadway, serves generous portions of ribs and sides. (☎733-2288. Spare ribs $8.75. Open in summer daily 7am-10pm; in winter 7am-9pm.) **LeJay's 24 Hour Sportsmen Cafe ❷**, at the corner of Glenwood and Pearl, draws an eclectic crowd hungry for authentic Western cooking after the bars close. (☎733-3110. Ribs, steaks, burgers, sandwiches, and breakfast around $5-10. Open 24hr.) At **Mountain High Pizza Pie ❸**, 120 W. Broadway, build your own pizza or choose from a large selection of pies. (☎733-3646. Pizza $7-20. Subs $6. Open in summer daily 11am-midnight; in winter 11am-10pm.)

▣ ▨ FESTIVALS & NIGHTLIFE. When the sun goes down on a long day of skiing, hiking, or rafting, Jackson has bars, concerts, and festivals to suit all tastes. Catch cowboy fever at the **JH Rodeo**, held at the fairgrounds, two blocks west of the Snow King ski area. (☎733-2805. Late May to early Sept. W and Sa 8pm. $9, ages 4-12 $7; reserved tickets $11; families $28.) Over Memorial Day weekend, the town's population explodes as tourists, locals, and nearby Native American tribes pour in for the dances and parades of **Old West Days**; for info call the Chamber of Commerce (☎733-3316). World-class musicians roll into Teton Village each summer for the **Grand Teton Music Festival.** (☎733-1128. Early July to late Aug. Festival orchestra concerts F-Sa 8pm. $30, students $15. Spotlight concerts Th 8pm. $25/12.50. Chamber music concerts Tu-W 8pm. $15/7.50. Open rehearsal F 9:30am. $5/2.50.) In mid-September, the **Jackson Hole Fall Arts Festival** (☎733-3316) showcases artists, musicians, and dancers in a week-long celebration.

Head straight from the slopes to **The Mangy Moose,** in Teton Village at the base of Jackson Hole Ski Resort, a quintessential *après-ski* bar. The atmosphere is more sedate during the summer, but in winter, this is the place to be. The entertainment lineup has headlined everyone from Blues Traveler to Dr. Timothy Leary. (☎733-4913. Cover $3-15, big names $20-25. Kitchen open daily 5:30-10pm; bar open 11:30am-2am.) Slither on down to the award-winning **Snake River Brewery**, 265 S. Millward St., for the award-winning "Zonkers Stout." (☎739-2337. Pints $3.50, pitchers $11. Open daily noon-1am; food served until 11pm.) Live music and good beer make the **Stagecoach Bar,** 7 mi. west of Jackson on Rte. 22 in Wilson, a popular nightspot, especially on Thursday Disco Night. (☎733-4407. Happy hour 4-6pm. Live music Su. Bar open Su-Th 11am-12:30am, F-Sa 11am-1am.)

🎿 **OUTDOOR ACTIVITIES.** Jackson puts on a good show, but the feature presentation is the quality of outdoor adventure. World-class skiing and climbing lie within minutes of Jackson, and **whitewater rafting** on the legendary Snake River is an adrenaline rush. **Barker-Ewing,** 45 W. Broadway, provides tours of varying lengths and difficulty levels. (☎733-1000 or 800-448-4202. 8 mi. tour $38-43, ages 6-12 $30-35; 16 mi. tour $68/50; overnight 16 mi. adventure $120/90.) **Mad River,** 1255 S. Rte. 89, 2 mi. south of Town Sq., offers similar trips with a promise of "small boats, big action." (☎733-6203 or 800-458-7238. 8 mi. trip $39, under 13 $29; scenic/whitewater combo $69/49.) During winter months, skiing enthusiasts flock to Jackson to experience pure Wyoming powder. **Jackson Hole Mountain Resort,** 12 mi. north of Jackson in Teton Village, has some of the best runs in the US, including the jaw-droppingly steep Corbet's Couloir. (☎733-2292. Open early Dec. to Apr. Lift tickets $58, seniors and under 14 $36.) Even after the snow melts, the **aerial tram** whisks tourists to the top of Rendezvous Mountain (elevation 10,450 ft.) for a panoramic view of the valley. (☎733-2292. Open late May to late Sept. daily 9am-5pm. $15, seniors $13, ages 6-12 $5.) Located in the town of Jackson, **Snow King** presents less expensive and more relaxed skiing. (☎733-5200. Lift tickets: half-day $20, full-day $32, night $15; seniors and children $14/22/10. $8 per hr.) Snow King also has summer rides to the summit for views of the Tetons. ($8 round-trip.) Jackson Hole is a prime locale for **cross-country skiing. Skinny Skis,** 65 W. Delorney, in downtown Jackson, points nordics in the right direction. (☎733-6094. Rentals with skis, boots, and poles half-day $10; full-day $15.)

CODY   ☎307

To this day, as numerous billboards proclaim, Cody *is* Rodeo—a visit to this cowboy town is your best chance to catch the sport. Praised also for its breathtaking scenery and Western charm, Cody is home to the longest-running rodeo in the US. For 63 straight years, the **Cody Nite Rodeo** has thrilled audiences every night in summer. (☎587-5855. June-Aug. 8:30pm. $12-14, ages 7-12 $6-8.) Over 4th of July weekend the town attracts the country's most prestigious cowboys when the **Buffalo Bill Cody Stampede,** voted by the cowboys themselves as the best "large outdoor rodeo" in the world, rough-rides into town. (☎587-5155 or 800-207-0744. $15. Reserve ahead.) The **Cody Trolley Tour** offers a one-hour tour of the city, visiting frontier sites and portraying the historical Old West. (☎527-7043. $12, over 62 $9, ages 6-12 $6.) **Rafting** trips on the Shoshone provide more energetic diversions. To make arrangements, call **Wyoming River Trips,** 1701 Sheridan Ave., at Rte. 120 and 14. (☎587-6661 or 800-586-6661. Open May-Sept. Easy 2hr. trip $22, half-day trip $54.) **Powder River Tours** offers guided daytrips through Yellowstone National Park and departs from several locations in town. (☎527-3677 or 800-442-3682, ext. 114. $60, seniors $54, under 16 $30. Reservations recommended.) For equine adventures, try **Cedar Mountain Trail Rides.** (☎527-4966. $20 for 1hr., $33 for 2hr., $64 for 4hr., $100 full-day.)

Rates go up in the summertime, but reasonable motels line **W. Yellowstone Ave.** Just a block from downtown, the **Pawnee Hotel ❶,** 1032 12th St., has 18 unique rooms. (☎587-2239. Rooms $22-38.) The **Rainbow Park Motel ❸,** 1136 17th St., is a bargain in the winter, but prices jump during the more popular summer months. Carpeted, wood-paneled rooms have phone, HBO, and A/C. (☎587-6251. Singles in summer $75, in winter $34; doubles $82/43.) **Buffalo Bill State Park** offers two campgrounds on the Buffalo Bill Reservoir with incredible views. One, the **North Shore Bay Campground,** is located 9 mi. west of town on U.S. 14/16/20. (☎527-6274. Sites $12.) **Peter's Cafe and Bakery ❶,** at 12th St. and Sheridan Ave., a popular local establishment, serves cheap breakfasts (3 buttermilk pancakes $3) and stacks thick subs, including vegetarian options, from $3. (☎527-5040. Open M-F 6:45am-8pm, Su 6:45am-4:15pm.) Celebrate the women of the Wild West at **Annie Oakley's Cowgirl**

ROCKY MOUNTAINS

THE HIDDEN DEAL

ROUGH RIDIN' LEGEND "BUFFALO BILL"

Cody's namesake, Col. William F. "Buffalo Bill" Cody, was an authentic Western hero who rode for the Pony Express, fought during the Civil War with the Kansas Jayhawkers (a Union guerilla group), and later helped the first transcontinental railroad come to fruition by hunting to supply meat for the men laying down the tracks. For his services, Cody was affectionately named "Buffalo Bill." Cody catapulted the image of the cowboy across the world with his outdoor extravaganza, Buffalo Bill's Wild West Show. The Wild West Show toured both the United States and Europe, attracting the attention of royalty and statesmen. The **Buffalo Bill Historical Center,** 720 Sheridan Ave., keeps Cody's legacy alive with five museums under one roof: the **Buffalo Bill Museum,** exploring the life of the legend; the **Whitney Gallery of Western Art,** featuring works by Remington, Moran, and others; the **Plains Indians Museum,** interpreting the lives of the Sioux, Crow, Shoshone, and other tribes; the **Draper Museum of Natural History,** a brand new museum "integrating humanities with natural sciences;" and the **Cody Firearms Museum,** featuring an impressive collection of Winchester firearms. (☎587-4771. Open Apr. daily 10am-5pm; May daily 8am-8pm; June to mid-Sept. daily 7am-8pm; mid-Sept. to Oct. daily 8am-5pm; Nov.-Mar. Tu-Su 10am-3pm. $15, students $6, seniors $13, ages 6-17 $4. Tickets good for 2 consecutive days.)

Cafe ❷, 1244 Sheridan Ave., downtown. The $10 Rocky Mountain Oysters appeal to the adventurous traveler. (☎587-1011. Burgers $5-8. Sandwiches $5-6. Wraps $5-6. Open in summer daily 11am-10pm; winter hours vary.)

Cody is only 54 mi. from Yellowstone National Park along the Buffalo Bill Cody Scenic Byway, at the junction of Rte. 120, 14A, and 14/16/20. The town's main street is **Sheridan Ave.,** which turns into **Yellowstone Ave.** west of town. **Powder River Transportation** (☎800-442-3682) runs buses from the Cody Chamber of Commerce to Billings, MT (3hr., 1 per day, $27); Cheyenne (9hr., 1 per day, $68); and Denver, CO(14hr., 1 per day, $78). **Visitor info: Chamber of Commerce Visitors Center,** 836 Sheridan Ave. (☎587-2297. Open in summer M-Sa 8am-6pm, Su 10am-3pm; off-season M-F 8am-5pm.) **Internet access: Cody Public Library,** 1157 Sheridan Ave. (☎527-8820. Open in summer M-F 10am-5:30pm, Sa 10am-1pm; winter hours vary.) **Post Office:** 1301 Stampede Ave., 1 mi. south of downtown on 13th St. (☎527-7161. Open M-F 8am-5:30pm, Sa 9am-noon.) **ZIP code:** 82414. **Area code:** 307.

SHERIDAN ☎307

The hub of northeast Wyoming and southern Montana, Sheridan offers stunning views of the surrounding prairie and mountain range along with authentic Western atmosphere. **King's Saddlery and Cowboy Museum,** 184 N. Main St., in the building behind the main store, ropes 'em in with over 550 remarkably crafted, award-winning saddles on display. Watch as ropes and saddles are made in the warehouse. The most elaborate saddles can take up to four months to complete and can cost as much as $10,000. (☎672-2702 or 800-443-8919. Open M-Sa 8am-5pm. Free.) The **Trail End State Historic Site,** 400 Clarendon Ave., showcases the impressive mansion and gardens of John B. Kendrick—rags-to-riches cattle baron, former Wyoming governor, and US senator. (☎674-4589. Open June-Aug. daily 9am-6pm; Apr.-May and Sept. to mid-Dec. 1-4pm. $2, residents $1; under 18 free.)

Built in 1892 and now a National Landmark, the **Sheridan Inn,** 856 Broadway, at 5th St., saw scores of colorful characters in its day; Buffalo Bill Cody used the porch to audition cowpokes for his *Wild West Show.* (☎674-5440. Guided tours on the hr. M 10am-1pm and Tu-F 9am-1pm. Tours also available by appointment. $5, seniors $3, under 12 free. Museum free.) Area men and women flock to town several days a week for polo games at the **Big Horn Polo Club.** (☎674-8687; www.bighornpoloclub.com. Games mid-May to Aug.) The **Sheridan WYO Rodeo** also ropes in the summer crowds. (☎672-9084. July 10-12, 2003. $9-14.) There are motels aplenty along Main St. and Coffeen Ave. The **Aspen Inn ❷**, 1744 N. Main St., offers the best deal. (☎672-9064. Singles $33; doubles $46.) Camp at the **Sheridan KOA ❶** with the typical KOA amenities: laundry, showers, water, pool, restaurant, and mini golf course. Go south off Exit 20 on I-90, turn right at the Port of Entry, take an immediate right on Rte. 338, and go about ¾ mi. (☎674-8766. Sites for 2 $18, with water and electricity $24, full hookup $26; each additional person $2.50. Kabins $35.) Camping is more rustic at **Connor Battlefield Campground ❶**, in Ranchester, 15 mi. north of Sheridan; take Rte. 14 west at Exit 9 off I-90, turn left on to Gillette St. and follow the signs to the battlefield/campground. (☎684-7629. Pit toilets, water, and fishing. Sites $9 for non-residents.) Find good, hearty meals at the **Sheridan Palace Restaurant ❷**, 138 N. Main St., not far from King's Saddlery. The menu features delicious burgers and sandwiches ($5-6) with a good selection of freshly made pies ($2 per slice, $3 a la mode) for dessert. (☎672-2391. Open M-Th 6am-2pm, F-Sa 6am-9pm.) The **Mint Bar**, 151 N. Main St., has served beer and whiskey to cowboys, ranchers, and dudes of all sorts since 1907. (☎674-9696. Open M-Sa 8am-2am.)

Powder River buses leave from their terminal, at 588 E. 5th St. (☎674-6188; 24hr.), twice daily for Billings (2hr., $28) and Cheyenne (8hr., $54). The **Sheridan Chamber of Commerce** sits just off I-90 at Exit 23. (☎672-2485 or 800-453-3650. Open in summer M-F 8am-7pm, Sa-Su 8am-5pm; in winter M-F 8am-5pm.) The Sheridan **Ranger Station**, 2013 Eastside 2nd St., is located off I-90 Exit 23. (☎674-2600. Open M-F 8am-4:30pm.) **Post Office:** 101 E. Loucks St. (☎672-0713. Open M-F 7:30am-5:30pm, Sa 8am-noon.) **ZIP code:** 82801. **Area code:** 307.

BIGHORN MOUNTAINS ☎307

Relatively uncrowded, the **Bighorn National Forest**, with more than 1 million acres of grasslands, meadows, canyons, and deserts, may be one of the best kept secrets in the Rocky Mountains. The Bighorns erupt from the hilly pasture land of northern Wyoming, providing a dramatic backdrop for grazing cattle, sprawling ranch houses, and valleys full of wildflowers. Visitors can hike through the woods or follow **scenic highways U.S. 14/14A** in the north and **U.S. 16** in the south to waterfalls, layers of prehistoric rock, and views above the clouds. The **Medicine Wheel**, a 3 mi. round-trip hike from the end of the dirt road off U.S. 14A, is a mysterious 75 ft. wide stone formation at 10,000 ft. that dates from around 500 BC. This site is sacred to 89 Native American tribes, and several people pray there each day. **Cloud Peak Wilderness** offers sheer solitude, and registration at major trailheads is required to enter the Cloud Peak area. The most convenient access to the wilderness area is from the trailheads off U.S. 16, around 20 miles west of Buffalo. From the **Hunter Corrals Trailhead**, move to beautiful **Seven Brothers Lake**, 3 mi. off U.S. 16 on Rd. 19, 13 mi. west of Buffalo, an ideal base for day-hikes into the high peaks beyond. Visitors can also enter the wilderness area on U.S. 14/14A to the north. To get to the top of 13,175 ft. Cloud Peak, most hikers enter at **West Tensleep Trailhead**, accessible from the town of **Tensleep** on the western slope, 55 mi. west of Buffalo on U.S. 16. Tensleep was so named because it took the Sioux ten sleeps to travel from there to their main winter camps. Ask a forest office to find out about more out-of-the-way treks, and always check on local conditions with a ranger before any hike. A listing of all of Bighorn's attractions, a map of the area, and other helpful info can be found in *Bighorn Bits and Pieces*, free at all Visitors Centers.

Thirty-five campgrounds (☎877-444-6777; www.reserve.com) fill the forest. **Doyle Campground ❶**, near a fish-filled creek, has 19 sites with toilets and water. Drive 26 mi. west of Buffalo on U.S. 16, then south 6 mi. on Hazelton Rd./County Rd. 3—it's a rough ride. (☎684-7981. Sites $9.) There is no fee to camp at the uncrowded **Elgin Park Trailhead**, 16 mi. west of Buffalo off U.S. 16, which promises

ROCKY MOUNTAINS

DEALING WITH THE DEVIL Devils Tower is considered one of the best technical rock climbing sites in North America, and scaling the monument's 1267 ft. is indeed a feat. Native Americans, however, consider the tower a sacred site and would rather rock climbing be banned. A partial compromise reached in 1995 calls for a voluntary refrain from climbing during the month of June, the most sacred time of the year due to the solstice.

good fishing along with parking and toilets. Off U.S. 14, about 27 mi. in from I-90 in the east, the **Sibley Lake Campground ❶** offers 25 sites at 7900 ft. ($10, with electricity $13. Wheelchair accessible.) If Sibley is crowded, **Tie Flume ❶** and **Dead Swede ❶**, off Rte. 14 about 10 mi. south of the Burgess Jct. Visitors Center, are great campground sites ($9). Many other campgrounds line U.S. 14 and 16; the map in *Bighorn Bits and Pieces* will guide the way. Campgrounds rarely fill up in the Bighorns, but if they do free **backcountry camping** (☎674-2600) is permitted at least 100 yd. from the road.

US Forest Service **ranger stations** are in **Buffalo, Lovell** at 604 E. Main St. (☎548-6541; open M-F 8am-4:30pm), **Sheridan** (see p. 733), and **Worland** at 101 S. 23rd St. (☎347-5105; open M-F 8am-4:30pm), as well as within the park. The **Burgess Junction Visitor Center,** off U.S. 14 about halfway into the area, houses lots of great info and several films on the surroundings. (Open mid-May through Sept. daily 8am-5:30pm.) The **Bighorn Canyon Visitors Center,** on Rte. 14A in Lovell, shows movies on the Medicine Wheel and can also offer assistance. (☎548-2251. Open in summer daily 8am-6pm; off-season 8:30am-5pm.) **Area code:** 307.

DEVILS TOWER NATIONAL MONUMENT   ☎307

A Native American legend tells of seven sisters who were playing with their little brother when the boy turned into a bear and began to chase them. Terrified, the girls ran to a tree stump and prayed for help. The stump grew high into the sky, becoming today's Devils Tower, and the girls became the stars of the Big Dipper. Others tell of a core of fiery magma that shot up without breaking the surface 60 million years ago; centuries of wind, rain, and snow reputedly eroded the surrounding sandstone, leaving a stunning spire. Still others, not of this world, have used the stone obelisk as a landing strip *(Close Encounters of the Third Kind)*. The massive column that figures so prominently in the myths of Native Americans, geologists, and space aliens is the centerpiece of **Devils Tower National Monument** in northeastern Wyoming, the nation's first national monument. (One-week pass $8 per car; $3 per person on bike, foot, or motorcycle. Free map on entry.)

To reach the monument from I-90, take U.S. 14 for 25 mi. north to Rte. 24. Read about the rock and register to climb at the **Visitors Center,** 3 mi. from the entrance. (☎467-5283, ext. 20. Open late May-Sept. daily 8am-8pm; Mar.-late May and Oct.-Nov. usually 8am-5pm.) Cool **climbing demos** are given outside the Visitors Center. (July-Aug.; call for times.) For more horizontally-oriented adventurers, there are several **hiking trails.** The most popular, the paved **Tower Trail** (1.3 mi.), loops the monument and provides great views of the multi-faceted columns of the tower, each with its own personality depending on the angle, time of day, and weather conditions. The **Red Beds Trail,** a 3 mi. loop, takes hikers up and around the bright red banks of the Belle Fourche River. Hikers can opt for a longer hike by connecting with the shorter **Valley View Trail** (0.6 mi.) for a flat walk through the prairie dog town and the **South Side Trail** (0.6 mi.), which climbs back to the bluffs of the Red Beds Trail. Ask a ranger to identify leafy spurge and poison ivy, which abound near the monument. The park maintains a **campground ❶** near the red banks of the Belle

Fourche River. (☎467-5283. Water, bathrooms, grills, picnic tables, and lots of noisy prairie dogs; no showers. Open roughly Apr.-Oct.; call ahead. Sites $12.) The best camping deal around is at the **Devils Tower View Store Campground ❶**, on Rte. 24, a few miles before the monument. Though not much shade, there is a great view of the monument and an inexpensive restaurant next door. (Water and nice port-o-potties. Open June-Sept. Sites $9.) **Area code:** 307.

CASPER ☎307

From 1841 to 1866, some 350,000 pioneers passed through Casper on the famed Oregon, Mormon, California, and Bozeman Trails, earning Casper the moniker "Crossroads of the West." Casper continues this tradition today, hosting hordes of tourists en route to Yellowstone, the Black Hills, and elsewhere. Stalwartly midwestern in atmosphere, Casper has managed to escape the touristy brand of Western commercialism that overruns much of the area.

Relive the pioneer experience at **Fort Caspar,** 4001 Fort Caspar Rd., a former trading post, stage stop, mail stop, and telegraph office, as well as a temporary home for cavalrymen protecting the North Platte River area from Indian raids. The fort sponsors reenactments each June and periodically throughout the rest of the year. (☎235-8462. Reconstructed buildings and museum open in summer M-Sa 8am-7pm, Su noon-7pm; museum open in winter M-F 8am-5pm, Su 1-4pm. $2, students $1.) The **Nicolayson Art Museum and Discovery Center,** 400 E. Collins Dr., exhibits Wyoming and world artwork and houses a children's art discovery center. (☎235-5247. Open Tu-W and F-Sa 10am-5pm, Th 10am-8pm, Su noon-4pm. Free.) For hands-on fun, visit the **Wyoming Science Adventure Center,** on the third floor of the same building. (Open Tu-F noon-5pm, Sa 1-5pm. $2, ages 2-12 $1.) The **Central Wyoming Fair and Rodeo,** 1700 Fairgrounds Rd., gets everyone excited about livestock. (☎235-5775. July 8-12, 2003.)

Near the interstate, the **Showboat National 9 Inn ❷**, 100 W. F St., has spacious rooms, cable TV, free local calls, and continental breakfast. (☎235-2711 or 800-524-9999. Singles $39; doubles $50.) **Fort Caspar Campground ❶**, 4205 Ft. Caspar Rd., is a friendly RV community, but tent sites are also available. (☎234-3260. Free showers and laundry. Reception 8am-8pm. RV sites with full hookup $20-22; $111-122 per week. Tent sites $14; $76 per week. 10% AAA discount.) Locals love **Johnny J's Diner ❶**, 1705 E. 2nd St., for breakfast ($3-6), burgers ($6), and shakes ($3). Dinner specials are a good bargain. (☎234-4204. Chicken dinners $4-6. Open Su-Th 6:30am-9pm, F-Sa 6:30am-10pm.)

Powder River Transportation Services (☎266-1904 or 800-433-2093; open daily 5:30am-6pm), at I-25 and Center St. in the Parkway Plaza Motel, buses to Cheyenne (4hr., 2 per day, $37) and Denver (7hr., 2 per day, $51). **Casper Area Chamber of Commerce:** 500 N. Center St. (☎234-5311. Open Memorial Day-Labor Day M-F 8am-6pm, Sa-Su 10am-6pm; Labor Day-Memorial Day M-F 8am-5pm.) **Post Office:** 150 E. B St. (☎266-4034. Open M-F 8am-6pm, Sa 9am-noon.) **ZIP code:** 82601. **Area code:** 307.

CHEYENNE ☎307

"Cheyenne," the name of the Native American tribe that originally inhabited the region, was considered a prime candidate for the name of the whole Wyoming Territory. The moniker was struck down by notoriously priggish Senator Sherman, who pointed out that the pronunciation of Cheyenne closely resembled that of the French word *chienne,* meaning "bitch." One of the fastest growing frontier towns, Cheyenne may have slowed down significantly, but its historical downtown area still exhibits traditional Western charm, complete with simulated gunfights.

ROCKY MOUNTAINS

⁊ PRACTICAL INFORMATION. Greyhound, 222 Deming Dr. (☎634-7744; open 24hr.), off I-80, makes trips to Chicago (19hr., 3 per day, $12); Denver (3-5hr., 5 per day, $19); Laramie (1hr., 3 per day, $13); Rock Springs (5hr., 3 per day, $53); and Salt Lake City (8hr., 3 per day, $71). **Powder River Transportation** (☎634-7744), in the Greyhound terminal, honors Greyhound passes and sends buses daily to Billings (11½hr., 2 per day, $75); Casper (4hr., 2 per day, $37); and Rapid City (10hr., 1 per day, $72). For local travel, flag down one of the shuttle buses provided by the **Cheyenne Transit Program.** (☎637-6253. Buses run M-F 6:30am-6:30pm. $1.) **Visitors Info: Cheyenne Area Convention and Visitors Bureau,** 309 W. Lincolnway (☎778-3133 or 800-426-5009), just west of Capitol Ave. **Hotlines: Domestic Violence and Sexual Assault Line,** ☎637-7233. 24hr. **Internet access: Laramie County Public Library,** 2800 Central Ave., has 30min. first come, first served slots available. (☎634-3561. Open mid-May to mid-Sept. M-Th 10am-9pm, F-Sa 10am-6pm; mid-Sept. to mid-May also Su 1-5pm.) **Post Office:** 4800 Converse Ave. (☎800-275-8777. Open M-F 7:30am-5:30pm, Sa 7am-1pm.) **ZIP code:** 82009. **Area code:** 307.

ᴦ ACCOMMODATIONS. It's easy to land a cheap room here among the plains and pioneers, unless your visit coincides with **Frontier Days,** the last full week of July, when rates skyrocket and vacancies disappear. Budget motels line Lincolnway (U.S. 30/16th St.). **Plains Hotel ❷,** 1600 Central Ave., across from the I-180 on-ramp, one block away from downtown, rents cavernous hotel rooms with marble sinks and cable TV. (☎638-3311. Singles $35; doubles $43; each additional person $5.) The **Frontier Motel ❷,** 1400 W. Lincolnway, provides singles with a living room, large bathroom, free cable TV, and A/C. (☎634-7961. Singles from $35.) The aging **Pioneer Hotel ❶,** 208 W. 17th St., provides the cheapest lodgings in the downtown area. (☎634-3010. Cable TV. Singles $17.) **Curt Gowdy State Park ❶,** 1319 Hynds Lodge Rd., 24 mi. west of Cheyenne on Rte. 210/Happy Jack Rd. provides year-round camping centered around two lakes with excellent fishing, horseback riding (bring your own horse), and archery. (☎638-7066. Sites $12.)

◻ FOOD. Cheyenne has only a smattering of non-chain restaurants with reasonably-priced cuisine. The walls at the popular **Sanford's Grub and Pub ❷,** 115 E. 17th St., are littered with every type of kitschy decor imaginable. The giant menu includes burgers, sandwiches, and salads ($6-7). Fifty-five beers on tap, 99 bottles of beer on the wall, and 132 different liquors. While waiting for food, check out the game room downstairs. (☎634-3381. Open M-Sa 11am-midnight, Su 11am-10pm.) For a dirt-cheap breakfast or lunch, the **Driftwood Cafe ❶,** 200 E. 18th St. at Warren St., has a mom-and-pop atmosphere to complement the homestyle cooking. (☎634-5304. Burgers $3-6. Cinnamon rolls $1.45. Slice of pie $2. Open M-F 7am-3pm.) **Lexie's Cafe ❷,** a historic brick building at 216 E. 17th St., has cheerful, cottage-style decor featuring wicker chairs and flowers. (☎638-8712. Filling breakfast combos $4-7. Burgers $6. Open M-Th 7:30am-8pm, F-Sa 7am-10pm.)

◧ ☒ SIGHTS & NIGHTLIFE. During the last week in July, make every effort to attend the one-of-a-kind **Cheyenne Frontier Days,** 10 days of non-stop Western hoopla. The town doubles in size when anyone who's anyone in the West comes to see the world's largest outdoor rodeo competition and partake of the free pancake breakfasts, parades, big-name country music concerts, and square dancing. (☎778-7222 or 800-227-6336. July 18-27, 2003. Rodeo $10-22.) During June and July, a "gunfight is always possible," as the entertaining **Cheyenne Gunslingers,** W. 16th and Carey, shoot each other. (☎653-1028. M-F 6pm, Sa high noon.) The **Wyoming State Capitol Building,** at the base of Capitol Ave. on 24th St., has beautiful stained glass windows and a gorgeous rotunda under the gold-leaf dome; self-guide brochures are available. (☎777-7220. Open M-F 8:30am-4:30pm. Free.) The **Old West Museum,** 4610 N. Carey Ave., in Frontier Park, houses a collection of Western memorabilia, including the biggest carriage collection in the world. (☎778-7290 or 800-266-2696. Open in summer M-F 9am-6pm, Sa-Su 10am-6pm; in winter M-F 9am-5pm, Sa-Su 10am-5pm. $5 donation requested, under 12 free.)

Twang with the locals at the popular **Cowboy Restaurant and Bar,** 312 S. Greeley Hwy., and test your skill as a cowboy on the mechanical bull ($3 per ride). The live music and large dance floor always draw a crowd. (☎637-3800. Open M-Sa 11am-2am, Su 11am-10pm.) Shoot pool upstairs or descend underground to dance at the **Crown Bar,** 222 W. 16th St. at the corner of Carey St. (☎778-9202. Open M-Sa 11am-2am, Su 11am-10pm.)

THE SNOWY RANGE ☎307

Local residents call the forested granite mountains to the east of the Platte Valley the Snowy Mountain Range because snow falls nearly year-round on the higher peaks. Even when the snow melts, quartz outcroppings reflect the sun, creating the illusion of a snowy peak. The Snowy Range is part of the **Medicine Bow National Forest,** spread over much of southeastern Wyoming. Cross-country skiing is popular in the winter; campsites and hiking trails usually don't open until May. On the west side of the Snowy Range along Rte. 130, chase the cold away with the geothermal stylings of **Saratoga's hot springs,** at the end of E. Walnut St., behind the public pool. Running between 104° and 120°F, the Hobo Pool's soothing waters are especially popular during the early morning and evening hours. (Free. Open 24hr.) A few feet from the springs, the **North Platte River** offers excellent fishing. Fishing permits ($10) are available at the **Country Store** Gas Station (☎326-5638) on Rte. 130. **Hack's Tackle Outfitters,** 407 N. 1st St., also sells hunting and fishing licenses. The store's knowledgeable owner offers both fishing advice and guided trips. (☎326-9823. Fishing tours for 2 $235 per half-day, $350 per day. Canoes $35 per day, rafts $95 per day; $100 per boat deposit required.)

At **Snowy Range Ski and Recreation Area,** enjoy 25 downhill trails, cross-country trails, and a snowboard halfpipe. Take Exit 311 off I-80 to Rte. 130 W. (☎745-5750 or 800-462-7669. Open mid-Dec. to Easter. Lift ticket $31, ages 6-12 $17.) From late May to November, the **Snowy Range Scenic Byway (Rte. 130)** is cleared of snow, and cars can drive 27 mi. through seas of pine trees and around treeless mountains and picture-perfect crystal lakes to elevations of two vertical miles. Along the Byway, the **Libby Flats Observation Point** features a very short wildflower nature walk and an awe-inspiring view of the surrounding land. The challenging 4.5 mi. **Medicine Bow Trail** has trailheads at both **Lake Marie** and **Lewis Lake** and climbs to **Medicine Bow Peak** (12,013 ft.), the highest point in the forest. Nearby, **Silver Lake ❶** offers 17 first come, first served wooded camp sites ($10). A little west of the Centennial entrance, **Nash Fork ❶** is another serene and untrammeled campground with 27 well-shaded sites ($10). All 16 of the park's developed campgrounds are only open in summer and have toilets and water, but no hookups or showers. Reservations for some campgrounds are available through the National Recreation Reservation Service. (☎877-444-6777; www.reserveusa.com. Reservation fee $9.) A drive up **Kennaday Peak** (10,810 ft.), Rte 130 to Rte. 100 and 215, at the end of Rte. 215, leads to an impressive view.

Mountain biking is generally prohibited on high country trails because of the frail alpine plants and rocky terrain. However, biking and driving are permitted on designated trails in the high country and on trails below 10,000 ft. The 7 mi. **Corner Mountain Loop,** just west of Centennial Visitors Center, is an exhilarating roller coaster ride through forests and small meadows. During the winter, the mountain biking and hiking trails are used for cross-country skiing.

ROCKY MOUNTAINS

Brush Creek Visitors Center is located at the west entrance. (☎326-5562. Open mid-May to Oct. daily 8am-5pm.) **Centennial Visitors Center,** 1 mi. west of Centennial, guards the east entrance. (☎742-6023. Open late May to early Sept. Tu-Su 9am-4pm; early Sept. to late May Sa-Su 9am-4pm.) Rent cross-country equipment at the **Cross Country Connection,** 222 S. 2nd St. in Laramie. (☎721-2851. Open M-F 10am-6pm, Sa 9am-5pm, Su noon-4pm. $10 per day.) Downhill ski and snowboard rentals can be found at **The Fine Edge,** 1660E N. 4th St. (☎745-4499. Open in winter M-Th 8am-6pm, F-Sa 7am-6:30pm, Su 7:30am-5pm; in summer M-Sa 9am-6pm, Su 11am-5pm. Skis $16 per full-day, children $12. Snowboards $22/17; boots $9. $300 credit card or check deposit required for snowboards.) **Area code:** 307.

LARAMIE   ☎307

Laramie, home of the **University of Wyoming (UW),** the state's only four-year college, is a comfortable stop-over for those traveling across the Cowboy State. The university infuses cultural diversity and urban sophistication into a town otherwise defined by a thriving ranching economy. Laramie does its darndest to bring its rough and rugged 19th-century history back to life at the **Wyoming Territorial Park,** 975 Snowy Range Rd., a reconstructed frontier town where, you can have a friend or relative arrested by the town marshal for $5. The **National US Marshals Museum** presents the history of the marshals and their interactions with Native Americans and Western outlaws. (☎745-6161 or 800-845-2287. Open early June to late Aug. daily 10am-5pm; open May and Sept. 9am-6pm. $10-12. Under 13 free.) In early July, don't miss the chance to attend a rodeo at Laramie's **Jubilee Days** festival. (☎745-7339 or 866-876-1012. Tickets $9-15, under 12 $4-10.)

Lined with hotels and fast food, **3rd St.** leads south into the heart of town, crossing Ivinson and Grand St., both of which burst with student hangouts. The rooms are large and comfortable at the sprawling **Motel 8 ❷,** 501 Boswell St., down the street from the Caboose, on the outskirts of town. (☎745-4856 or 888-745-4800. Singles in summer from $45; in winter $39. Doubles $55/46.) Within walking distance of numerous restaurants and bars, **Ranger Motel ❶,** 453 N. 3rd St., patrols downtown. (☎742-6677. HBO, fridge, and microwave. Singles $37; doubles $46.) A local favorite, **Jeffrey's Restaurant ❷,** 123 Ivinson St., at 2nd. St., doles out homemade bread and hot healthy sandwiches for $5-9. (☎742-7046. Open M-Sa 11am-9pm.) **Altitude,** 320 South 2nd St., serves up their own brews and brewpub food. Try the "Backcountry Bitter," or order a "growler" (half-gallon of beer, $8) to go. (☎721-4031. Open Su-Th 11am-10pm, F-Sa 11am-2am.) Both beat-up student cars and Harleys steer their way into the **Buckhorn Bar,** 114 Ivinson St., a neighborhood saloon with busy pool tables and live weekend music. (☎742-3554. Open M-Sa 8am-2am, Su 10am-midnight.) UW students can honestly tell their parents that they spent the weekend in the **Library,** 1622 Grand Ave. Pull up a table in their "stacks" for a salad ($4-7), steak ($11-14), or daily special ($5-6). Next door, the Library's oft-frequented bar has $2-3 beers on tap. (☎742-3900. Restaurant open Su-W 11am-9pm, Th-Sa 11am-10pm. Bar open M-Sa 11am-2am, Su 11am-midnight.) Laramie's **Chamber of Commerce** is at 800 S. 3rd. St., Exit 313 off I-80. (☎745-7339; www.laramie.org. Open M-F 8am-5pm.) **Post Office:** 152 N. 5th St. (☎755-5510. Open M-F 8am-5:15pm, Sa 9am-1pm.) **ZIP code:** 82070. **Area code:** 307.

COLORADO

In the high, thin air of Colorado, golf balls fly farther, eggs take longer to cook, and visitors tend to lose their breath just getting out of bed. Hikers, skiers, and climbers worship Colorado for its peaks and mountain enclaves. Denver—the country's highest capital—has long since shed its cow-town image and matured into the cultural center of the Rocky Mountains. Colorado's extraordinary heights are matched by its equally spectacular depths. Over millions of years, the Gunnison and Colorado Rivers have etched the natural wonders of the Black Canyon and the Colorado National Monument. Silver and gold attracted early settlers to Colorado, but it is Mother Nature that has continued to appeal to travelers.

🔢 PRACTICAL INFORMATION

Capital: Denver.

Visitor Info: Colorado Travel and Tourism Authority, CTTA, 1127 Pennsylvania St., Denver 80203 (☎303-832-6171; for info packet ☎800-265-6723; www.colorado.com). **US Forest Service,** Rocky Mountain Region, 740 Sims St., Golden, 80401 or P.O. Box 25127, Lakewood 80225 (☎303-275-5350). Open M-F 7:30am-4:30pm. **Ski Country USA,** 1560 Broadway, #2000, Denver 80202 provides info on all Colorado ski resorts. (☎303-837-0793; ☎ski report 825-7660.) Open M-F 8:30am-5:30pm. **National Park Service,** 12795 W. Alameda Pkwy., P.O. Box 25287, Lakewood 80225 (☎303-969-2000; park reservations ☎800-365-2267). **Colorado State Parks,** 1313 Sherman St., #618, Denver 80203 (☎303-866-3437; state park reservations ☎303-470-1144). Open for calls M-F 7am-4:45pm. There is a $7 reservation fee; reservations must be made at least 3 days in advance.

Postal Abbreviation: CO. **Sales Tax:** 7.4%.

DENVER   ☎303

In 1858, the discovery of gold in the Rocky Mountains brought a rush of eager miners to northern Colorado. After an excruciating trek through the plains, the desperados set up camp for a breather and a stiff shot of whiskey before heading west into "them thar hills." Overnight, Denver was transformed into a flourishing frontier town. The Mile High City is a bona fide melting pot of cultures and peoples, not to mention a city of surprises. Recently named the number one sports town in America, Denver also boasts the nation's largest city park system, brews the most beer of any metropolitan area, and has the highest number of high school and college graduates per capita. However, the city's greatest characteristic is its vibrant atmosphere—a unique combination of urban sophistication and Western grit.

▣ TRANSPORTATION

Airport: Denver International, or **DIA** (☎342-2000), 23 mi. northeast of downtown off I-70. Shuttles run from the airport to downtown and ski resorts in the area. The **RTD Sky Ride** (☎299-6000) runs buses every hour from the Market St. station downtown to the airport. Office hours M-F 6am-8pm, Sa-Su 8am-8pm. Buses operate 5am-10:30pm. $8, seniors and disabled $3. From the main terminal, **Supershuttle** (☎370-1300 or 800-525-3177) runs to downtown hotels (1hr., $18). A **taxi** to downtown costs about $50.

Trains: Amtrak, Union Station, 1701 Wynkoop St. (☎534-2812 for arrivals/departures, ☎825-2583 for ticket office), at 17th St. Office open daily 6am-9pm. To: **Chicago** (20hr., 1 per day, from $107); **Salt Lake City** (15hr., 1 per day, from $73); and **San Francisco** (35hr., 1 per day, from $109). **Río Grande Ski Train** (☎296-4754), housed in the same building, chugs 2¼hr. through the Rockies, stopping in **Winter Park** within walking distance of the lifts. Free ground transport to town provided. Lift discounts included. Reservations required. Runs Jan. Sa-Su; Feb. to mid-June F-Su; mid-June to mid-Aug. Sa. Round-trip $45, under 14 $25.

ROCKY MOUNTAINS

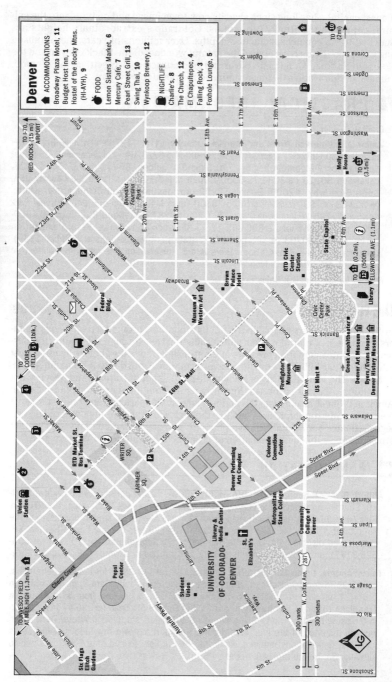

Denver

▲ ACCOMMODATIONS
Broadway Plaza Motel, **11**
Budget Host Inn, **1**
Hostel of the Rocky Mtns.
(HI-AYH), **9**

● FOOD
Lemon Sisters Market, **6**
Mercury Cafe, **7**
Pearl Street Grill, **13**
Swing Thai, **10**
Wynkoop Brewery, **12**

■ NIGHTLIFE
Charlie's, **8**
The Church, **12**
El Chapultepec, **4**
Falling Rock, **3**
Foxhole Lounge, **5**

Buses: Greyhound, 1055 19th St. (☎293-6555). Office open daily 6am-11:45pm. To: **Chicago** (20-22hr., 6 per day, $86); **Colorado Springs** (1½hr., 7 per day, $14); **Salt Lake City** (10-13hr., 3 per day, $46); **Santa Fe** (7½-9hr., 4 per day, $61).

Public Transit: Regional Transportation District (RTD), 1600 Blake St. (☎299-6000 or 800-366-7433). Serves Denver, as well as Longmont, Evergreen, Golden, and suburbs. Route hours vary; many lines shut down by 9pm. 75¢, seniors and disabled 25¢; peak hours $1.25. Exact change required. Major terminals are at Market and 16th St. and at Colfax and Broadway. The free 16th St. **mall shuttle** covers 14 blocks downtown. Runs daily 5:45am-1am. **Light Rail** services the perimeter of the city and suburbs, from I-25 and Broadway north to 30th and Downing.

Taxis: Yellow Cab, ☎777-7777. **Metro Taxi,** ☎444-8888.

Car Rental: Enterprise, 7720 Calawaba Ct. (☎800-720-7222), at the airport. Open daily 7am-10pm. Prices fluctuate but usually start around $50 per day; extra $15 per day for ages 21-24. Security deposit of $250 or a major credit card required.

■✴🛈 ORIENTATION & PRACTICAL INFORMATION

Running north-south, **Broadway** slices Denver in half. East of Broadway, **Colorado Blvd.** is also a major north-south thoroughfare. **Colfax Ave.,** running east-west, is the main north-south dividing line. Both named and numbered streets run diagonally in the downtown area. In the rest of the city, numbered avenues run east-west and increase as you head north. Named streets run north-south. Many of the avenues on the eastern side of the city become numbered streets downtown. The **16th St. Mall** is the hub of Denver's downtown and could easily be called the social, dining, and entertainment center of the city. *At night, avoid the west end (Colfax Ave., Federal Blvd., S. Santa Fe Blvd.), the Capitol Hill area (on the east side of town beyond the Capitol), and 25th-34th St. on the west side of the Barrio.*

Visitor info: Denver Visitors Bureau, 1668 Larimer St. (☎892-1112 or 800-645-3446; www.denver.org), just north of the 16th St. Mall. Open M-F 8am-5pm, Sa 9am-1pm.

Hotlines: Rape Crisis Hotline, ☎322-7273.

Bi-Gay-Lesbian Organizations: The Gay, Lesbian and Bisexual Community Services Center of Colorado, ☎733-7743. Open M-F 10am-6pm.

Internet access: Public Library, 10 W. 14th Ave. (☎865-1363). Open M-W 10am-9pm, Th-Sa 10am-5:30pm, Su 1-5pm.

Post Office: 951 20th St. (☎800-275-8777). Open M-F 7am-6pm, Sa 9am-1pm. **ZIP code:** 80202. **Area code:** 303. 10-digit dialing required.

🛏 ACCOMMODATIONS

Hostel of the Rocky Mountains (HI-AYH), 1530 Downing St. (☎861-7777), just off E. Colfax Ave. The hostel is 10 blocks from the Capitol, next to 2 major bus routes and a trolley stop, and the best value in Denver. Laundry facilities, library, kitchens. Internet access $1 per 10min. Free pickup from the Greyhound depot or Union Station. Airport drops $17. Breakfast free. Linen $2. Key deposit $5. Reception daily 7am-11pm. Reservations recommended. Dorms $19; private rooms $40. ❶ The affiliated **B&B of the Rocky Mountains,** next door to the hostel, shares the same address and phone number. Classier and decidedly quieter than the hostel, the rooms here are clean and spacious with shared baths. Guests can enjoy free breakfast next door at the hostel or use the kitchen facilities to fend for themselves. Rooms $40-55. ❷

Broadway Plaza Motel, 1111 Broadway (☎893-0303), 3 blocks south of the Capitol building. Spacious, clean rooms within walking distance of downtown Denver. Free HBO. Singles $45-55; doubles $55-65. ❸

Budget Host Inn, 2747 Wyandot St. (☎458-5454), has clean, comfortable rooms conveniently located near Six Flags Elitch Gardens. Great discounts on Six Flags tickets. Singles from $46; doubles from $56. ❸

Cherry Creek State Park, 4201 S. Parker Rd., in Aurora, is conveniently located in an urban area. Take I-25 to Exit 200, then head north for about 3 mi. on I-225 and take the Parker Rd. exit. A few groves of pine trees provide limited shade. Arrive early; the park often fills up. Open Apr.-Oct. Sites $10, with electricity $16. Daily entrance fee $7. ❶

⬭ FOOD

Downtown Denver offers a full range of cuisines, from Russian to traditional Southwestern. Al fresco dining in warm weather and people-watching are both available along the **16th St. Mall.** Gourmet eateries are located southwest of the Mall on Larimer St., in **Larimer Sq.** Sports bars and trendy restaurants occupy **LoDo,** the neighborhood extending from Wynkoop St. to Larimer Sq., between Speer Blvd. and 20th St. Outside of downtown, **Colorado Blvd.** and **6th Ave.** also have their share of posh restaurants. **E. Colfax Ave.** offers a number of reasonably priced ethnic restaurants, including Greek and Ethiopian cuisine. You may wonder what sort of delicacies **"Rocky Mountain oysters"** are, especially given Denver's distance from the ocean. Never fear; these salty-sweet bison testicles, sold at the **Buckhorn Exchange,** 1000 Osage St. (☎534-9505), do not actually hail from the sea.

▧ Mercury Cafe, 2199 California St., (☎294-9281), at 22nd St. Decorated with a new-age flair, the Merc specializes in home-baked wheat bread and a slew of reasonably priced soups ($2-3), salads ($6-9), enchiladas ($5.50-7), and vegetarian specials. Live bands provide music in the dining room and upstairs dance area. Usually all ages. Open Tu-F 5:30-11pm, Sa-Su 9am-3pm and 5:30-11pm; dancing F-Sa until 2am, Tu-Th and Su 1am. ❷

Spicy Pickle Sub Shop, 745 Colorado Blvd. (☎321-8353), serves up fresh grilled foccacia sandwiches ($6) with—what else—a spicy pickle. Open daily 10:30am-9pm. ❷

Pearl Street Grill, 1477 S. Pearl St. (☎778-6475), in the trendy and laid-back Washington Park area. Gourmet food at prices that won't break the bank. Enjoy your food and the night on the patio. "PSG Favorites" $7-12. Brunch served 11am-3pm. Open M-Sa 11am-2am, Su 11am-midnight. ❸

Benny's Restaurant and Cantina, 301 E. 7th (☎894-0788), remains a local favorite for cheap, tasty Mexican food. Burritos $6.25. Open M-F 8am-11pm, Sa-Su 9am-11pm. ❷

Wynkoop Brewery, 1634 18th St. (☎297-2700), at Wynkoop St. across from Union Station in LoDo. Colorado's 1st brewpub serves beer (20 oz. $2.50), homemade root beer, lunch, and dinner. Features pool tables upstairs and an independent improv comedy troupe downstairs (☎297-2111). Pints $2. Burgers from $6. Happy hour M-F 3-6pm. Kitchen open M-Th 11am-11pm, F-Sa 11am-midnight, Su 11am-10pm. Bar open M-Sa until 2am, Su until midnight. Free brewery tour Sa 1-5pm. ❷

Swing Thai, 845 Colorado Blvd. (☎777-1777), is an understandably popular restaurant with a wide assortment of high-quality food at cheap prices. Those sick of pizza and burgers can indulge on specialties such as the *hot* Jungle Curry ($6.50) or Pineapple Fried Rice ($5.50). Huge wok specials from $6.50. Open daily 11am-10pm. ❷

Lemon Sisters Market, 1530 Blake St. (☎825-4133), is a hidden treasure of tasty breakfast burritos ($2.50-3), hearty soups, and a variety of daily specials ($3-5). Sesame noodles, *baba ganoush,* and hummus satisfy those with less Western cravings. Deli sandwiches $5.50. Open M-Th 7am-9pm, F 7am-7pm, Sa-Su 10am-6pm. ❶

👁 SIGHTS

CULTURAL CONNECTION TROLLEY. One of the best tour deals around, the trolley visits over 20 of the city's main attractions. The easiest place to begin a tour is along the 16th St. Mall, near the Mall Ride stops, but the tour can be joined at many local attractions; look for the trolley symbol sign. (*☎ 289-2841. Buses depart every hr. 8:30am-4:30pm. $16, under 13 $8.)*

COLORADO STATE CAPITOL. Many of the best sights in Denver center around downtown, which makes touring on foot easy. The **Capitol Building** is a sensible place to start a visit to the Mile High City—marked by a small engraving, the 15th step leading to the building's entrance sits exactly 1 mile above sea level. (*☎ 866-2604. 45min. tours every 30min. M-F 7am-5:30pm, Sa 9:30am-2:30pm.)*

DENVER ART MUSEUM. Just a few blocks west of the Capitol stands the **Denver Art Museum (DAM)**, a unique seven-story "vertical" museum. The DAM houses a world-class collection of Native American art and pre-Colombian artifacts. The gallery's impressive holdings warrant several hours of exploration. (*100 W. 14th Ave. Pkwy. ☎ 865-5000. Open Tu and Th-Sa 10am-5pm, W 10am-9pm, Su noon-5pm. Tours July-Aug. Tu-Sa 11am and 1:30pm, Su 1:30pm; Sept.-June Su-F 1:30pm, Sa 11:30am and 1:30pm. $4.50; students, seniors, and children $2.50; under 5 free.)*

SIX FLAGS. Make a splash at the Island Kingdom water park at **Six Flags Elitch Gardens,** across the freeway from Mile High Stadium. The Boomerang, Mind Eraser, Tower of Doom, and the new Flying Coaster keep thrill seekers content. (*At Elitch Circle and Speer Blvd. ☎ 595-4386. Open June-Aug. daily 10am-10pm; spring and early fall Sa-Su; call for exact hrs. $33, seniors and under 4 ft. $20. Look for money-saving coupons in the Elitch Gardens brochures. AAA discounts available.)*

OCEAN JOURNEY. Denver's brand new aquarium guides visitors through two spectacular underwater exhibitions: the **Colorado River Journey,** descending from the Continental divide to the Sea of Cortez in Mexico, and the **Indonesian River Journey,** emptying from the volcanic Barisan Mountains in Sumatra into the South China Sea. The aquarium also houses over 15,000 exotic marine creatures, including several species of sharks, sea otters, and the magnificent Napoleon wrasse. (*700 Water St. ☎ 561-4450 or 888-561-4450. Open in summer daily 10am-6pm; call to confirm winter hours. $15, seniors and ages 13-17 $13, ages 4-12 $7.)*

DENVER MUSEUM OF NATURE AND SCIENCE. This gigantic museum hosts a variety of interesting exhibits under its roof. You won't want to miss the Hall of Life or the Prehistoric Journey room. (*2001 Colorado Blvd., at Colorado and Montview St. ☎ 322-7009 or 800-925-2250. Open daily 9am-5pm. $8; students, seniors, and ages 3-12 $5.50. IMAX and museum $12/8. Call for IMAX shows and times.)*

COORS BREWERY. Located in nearby Golden, this is the world's largest one-sight brewery. Interestingly, the brewery also has one of the nicest wellness centers in the corporate world. All 42,000 workers are allowed two free beers after every shift, and can work them off in the company workout center. Interesting 40min. walking tours take visitors through the entire Coors brewing process from start to finish. Coors samples available after the tour. (*Take I-70 W to Exit 264; head west on 32nd Ave. for 4½ mi., then turn left on East St. and follow the signs. A shuttle bus runs from the parking lot to the brewery, but not before a very short historical tour of Golden. ☎ 303-277-2337. 1½ hr. tours every 30min. M-Sa 10am-4pm.)*

ROCKY MOUNTAINS

🎵 🎭 ENTERTAINMENT & OUTDOOR ACTIVITIES

Life in Denver is never boring for sports fans. Denver's baseball team, the **Colorado Rockies**, plays at **Coors Field**, 20th and Blake St. (☎800-388-7625. Tickets $4-37. $4 "Rockpile" bleacher tickets available day of game.) Football's **Denver Broncos** have moved to **Invesco Field at Mile High** (☎720-258-3333), which is used by soccer's **Colorado Rapids** (☎299-1570) during the spring and summer. The NBA **Nuggets** and the NHL **Colorado Avalanche** share the state-of-the-art **Pepsi Center**, 1000 Chopper Cir. (☎405-1100 for info on both teams).

Denver has more public parks per square mile than any other city, providing prime space for bicycling, walking, or lolling. **Cheesman Park**, 8th Ave. and Humboldt St., offers picnic areas and a view of the snow-capped peaks of the Rockies. **Confluence Park**, at Cherry Creek and the South Platte River, lures bikers and hikers with paved paths along the river. Live music for a broad range of musical tastes is the name of the game at **Confluence Concerts** (☎455-7192), along the banks of the South Platte (Th in the late July-early Aug.). **City Park** (☎697-4545) houses a museum, zoo, running paths, and golf course. **Colorado State Parks** has the lowdown on nearby state parks. (☎866-3437. Open M-F 8am-5pm.) At **Roxborough State Park**, visitors can hike and ski among red rock formations. Take U.S. 85 S, turn right on Titan Rd., and follow it 3½ mi. to the park. (Open year-round dawn-dusk.)

The mammoth **Red Rocks Amphitheater and Park** (Ticketmaster ☎830-8497), 12 mi. southwest of Denver, on I-70 at the Morrison exit, is carved into red sandstone. As the sun sets over the city, performers such as R.E.M., U2, and the Denver Symphony Orchestra compete with the view behind them. The actual Red Rocks Park contains more than 600 acres and features numerous hiking trails. Forty miles west of Denver, the road to the top of **Mt. Evans** (14,264 ft.) is the highest paved road in North America. Take I-70 W to Rte. 103 in Idaho Springs. (☎567-2901. Open late May to early Sept.)

⬤ FESTIVALS

Every January, Denver hosts the nation's largest livestock show and one of the biggest rodeos, the **National Western Stock Show**, 4655 Humboldt St. (☎295-1660. January 12-26, 2003.) Here, cowboys compete for prize money while over 10,000 head of cattle compete for "Best of Breed." **Cinco de Mayo** (☎534-8342, ext. 106) attracts 250,000 visitors per year in celebration of Mexico's victory over the French in 1862. The **Capitol Hill People's Fair** (☎830-1651), the first full week of June, is a large outdoor celebration with food vendors and local bands at **Civic Center Park**, near the capitol. The Bluebird Theater, 3317 E. Colfax Ave. (☎322-2308), is an old theater-turned-music venue that hosts local and occasional national acts. In the town of Larkspur, the **Renaissance Festival** takes guests back in time with jousting, music, and plenty of free spirits in medieval garb. (☎688-6010. June-July Sa-Su.) **The Festival of Mountain and Plain: A Taste of Colorado** (☎295-6330) packs Civic Center Park on Labor Day weekend for one last summer shebang. Food, crafts, free entertainment, and carnival rides are all part of the fun.

🎤 NIGHTLIFE

Downtown Denver, in and around the 16th St. Mall, is an attraction in itself. With ample shopping, dining, and people-watching opportunities, there's something for everyone. Many restaurants host live bands on a regular basis, and concerts are never lacking in the Civic Center Park area. Local restaurants and bars cater to a college-age and slightly older singles crowd. A copy of the weekly *Westword* gives the lowdown on LoDo.

El Chapultepec, 1962 Market St. (☎295-9126), at 20th St., is a be-boppin' jazz holdover from Denver's Beat era of the 50s. No cover. 1-drink min. per set. Open daily 8am-2am. No credit cards.

The Church, 1160 Lincoln Ave. (☎832-3528). In a remodeled chapel, The Church offers 4 full bars, a cigar lounge, and a weekend sushi bar. On weekends, the congregation swells with 3 floors of dancing. F Ladies night. Cover after 10pm $5-15. Th 18+, F-Su 21+. Open Th and Su 9pm-2am, F-Sa 8pm-2am.

Falling Rock, 1919 Blake St. (☎293-8338). With 75 beers on tap ($3.75) and a web site called www.nocrapontap.com, it is the place to sample a variety of microbrews from the impressive beer menu. Open daily 11am-2am.

Foxhole Lounge, 2936 Fox St. (☎298-7378). A popular gay club, this is the place to be on Su nights, so get there early or expect a long wait. Th house. Sa hip-hop. No cover. Open Th-F 8am-2am, Sa-Su 2pm-2am.

Charlie's, 900 E. Colfax Ave. (☎839-8890), at Emerson, is a well-known gay bar with a big dance floor and a Western-style atmosphere. Open daily 11am-2am.

MOUNTAIN RESORTS ON I-70   ☎970

WINTER PARK
Nestled among delicious-smelling mountain pines in the upper Fraser River Valley, 67 mi. from Denver, the popular **Winter Park Resort** is the closest ski and summer resort to Denver. **Winter Park Mary Jane Ski Area** (☎726-5514 or 800-453-2525) boasts a 3060 ft. vertical drop, the most snow in Colorado, and 22 lifts. Though affiliated, Winter Park caters to families, while Mary Jane serves the expert crowd. (Single-day lift ticket $56, multiday tickets $42-46.) Winter Park is also on the vanguard of summer fun, with mountain scooters, a maze, climbing walls, and a zip-line. (Summer activities pass M-F $40, Sa-Su $45.) **Viking Ski Shop,** on Hwy. 40, under the Viking Lodge, rents ski packages in winter and bikes in summer. (☎800-421-4013. Open daily in winter 8am-9pm. Ski packages from $13 per day; kids rent skis free with adult rental. Bikes from $15 per day.) In the summer, mountain biking and hiking trails climb the mountains of the Continental Divide. The **Zephyr Express** chairlift blows to the summit of Winter Park Mountain, allowing mountain bikers to reach the peak and then ride down on 50 mi. of single-track trails. (Open mid-June to early Sept. daily 10am-5pm. Full-day chair pass $21. Mountain bike rentals from $14 per hr., $33 per day. 2hr. clinic $20.) Spend an hour tubing at the **Fraser Tubing Hill,** half a mile off Rte. 40, behind the Alco complex in Fraser. (☎726-5954. $12 per hr., children $10 per hr.) **Mad Adventures,** a popular **whitewater rafting** company, provides the opportunity to ride the rapids. (☎726-5290 or 800-451-4844. Half-day $37, full-day $56.) The **High Country Stampede Rodeo** bucks at the John Work Arena, west of Fraser on County Rd. 73. (☎726-4118 or 800-903-7275 for info. July-Aug. 7:30pm. $10, seniors $8, ages 6-13 $6.)

 MUDSLIDE. During mud season, typically May, October, and November, many places close or shorten their hours, and lodging prices are generally lower. For those traveling during mud season, be sure to call ahead.

ROCKY MOUNTAINS

The **Viking Lodge ❷**, on Rte. 40 in Winter Park, next to the shuttle stop for the lifts, offers tiny rooms with phones and color TVs. Lodgings include access to the hot tub and sauna, and a 10% discount on rentals at the adjacent store. (☎726-8885 or 800-421-4013. Reception 8am-9pm. Singles $35; doubles $34. In winter $40-65/45-70.) Perhaps the best family lodging deal in the Fraser Valley is the **Snow Mountain Ranch YMCA ❶**, 12 mi. past the town of Winter Park; take I-70 W to U.S. 40 W. The ranch features a host of recreational activities, including nordic skiing. (☎887-2152, ext. 4110. Quad with private bath $69. Campsites $20-25.) Deliciously healthy breakfasts and lunches ($5-8) are served on the patio at **Carver's Bakery Cafe ❷**, at the end of the Cooper Creek Mall off U.S. 40. (☎726-8202. Massive cinnamon rolls $2.25. Turkey Philly $7. Open daily 7am-2pm, until 3pm during winter.) Herbivores and carnivores alike will love the sandwiches at **Rudi's Deli ❶**, at the Park Plaza Center off U.S. 40. Don't be afraid of Chaz's Nut Burger, only $5.75. (☎726-8955. Open daily 10am-8pm.)

To reach Winter Park from Denver, take I-70 W to U.S. 40. The Chamber of Commerce (see below) also serves as the **Greyhound** depot with service to Denver (1¾hr., 1 per day, $15-16). **Home James Transportation Services** runs door-to-door shuttles to and from Fraser or Winter Park and the Denver airport. (☎726-5060 or 800-359-7536. Office open daily 8am-6pm. Reservations required. $39.) The **Río Grande Ski Train** (☎303-296-4754; Dec.-Mar. Sa-Su; mid-June to Aug. Sa) leaves Denver's Union Station for Winter Park (see p. 739). **Visitor info: Winter Park-Fraser Valley Chamber of Commerce**, 78841 Rte. 40. (☎726-4118 or 800-903-7275. Open daily 8am-5pm.) **Snow conditions:** ☎303-572-7669 or 800-729-5813. **Area code:** 970.

SUMMIT COUNTY

Skiers, hikers, and mountain bikers can tap into a sportsman's paradise in the highest county in the US, about 70 mi. west of Denver. **Copper Mountain** features a 2601 ft. drop and 125 trails. (☎968-2882 or 800-458-8386; snow conditions ☎800-789-7609. Lift ticket $57.) **Keystone** (☎800-427-8308), has a 2900 ft. drop and 116 trails, including 17 available for night skiing. (☎800-427-8308. $59 per day.) **Arapahoe Basin** has some of the most challenging terrain and lacks the creature comforts that many skiers have come to expect, which is a good thing for those who come to ski rather than shop. (☎468-0718 or 888-272-7246. Lift tickets $46.) All three resorts are alternatives to the more expensive resorts of Aspen and Vail.

The **Alpen Hütte ❶**, 471 Rainbow Dr., in Silverthorne, has welcoming hosts, a familial atmosphere, clean rooms with beautiful mountain views, and year-round outdoor activities including fly fishing on the Blue River behind the hostel. Summit Stage stops outside the door. (☎468-6336. Laundry, free ski storage, and parking. Linen and towels $1.50. Lockers $5 deposit. Reception daily 7-11am and 4pm-midnight. Midnight curfew. Reserve for winter 1-2 months in advance. Dorms in summer $18, in winter $29.) There are several Forest Service campgrounds in the nearby **White River National Forest;** the **Dillon Ranger District Office**, 680 Blue River Pkwy., can provide more info. (☎468-5400, reservations ☎877-444-6777. Open M-F 8am-5pm.) Free **Summit Stage** (☎668-0999) buses connect the resorts with Frisco, Dillon, and Silverthorne. **Visitor info: Summit County Chamber of Commerce**, 916 N. Summit Blvd., in Frisco. (☎668-2051. Open daily 9am-5pm.) **Silverthorne-Dillon Info Center**, 246 Rainbow Drive, ¼ mi. south of I-70 on Rte. 6. (☎262-0817. Open M-Sa 9am-5pm.) **Area code:** 970.

BRECKENRIDGE

Fashionable Breckenridge lies west of Silverthorne on I-70, 9 mi. south of Frisco. The most popular ski resort in the country, **Breckenridge** (☎453-5000 or 800-789-7669; snow conditions ☎453-6118), has a 3398 ft. vertical drop, 139 trails, the best halfpipe in North America, and 2043 acres of skiable terrain made accessible by 25 lifts. Summer activities in this scenic town include a scenic **chairlift** ride (single ride $5, seniors and ages 7-12 $3), a superslide ($8/7), Colorado's largest human maze ($5, ages 5-12 $4), and a climbing wall ($5 per climb). The **Breckenridge Mountain Bike Park** offers a variety of biking trails (chairlift $8, children $6). More sophisticated alternatives include the **Breckenridge Music Festival,** providing a wide selection of musical performances, including the Breckenridge Music Institute Orchestra and the National Repertory Orchestra. (☎547-3100. Box office open Tu-Su 11am-5pm. $15-25, students $5, seniors $13-23.)

Despite the many expensive restaurants and stores in town, you can still find reasonably priced, smoke-free accommodations at the ⬛**Fireside Inn (HI-AYH) ❷,** 114 N. French St., two blocks east of Main St. on the corner of Wellington Rd. The indoor hot tub is great for *après-ski*. (☎453-6456. Breakfast $3-6. Office open daily 8am-9pm. Dorms in summer $25; in winter $35. Private rooms $65/105.) Start your day at the **Cool River Coffeehouse ❶,** 325 S. Main St., with an espresso drink and a sandwich ($5-5.25). The purple-tinted Stacy's Chunky Chicken Salad sandwich ($5) is a local favorite. (☎453-1736. Open Su-Th 7am-5pm, F-Sa 7am-8pm, sometimes later.) Fly down to **Angel's Hollow ❸,** 113 S. Ridge St., for happy hour with colorful locals and $8-9 "Big as Yer Head" Burritos. (☎453-8585. Happy hour daily 4:30-6:30pm. Open daily 11am-10pm.) **Breckenridge Activities Center:** 137 S. Main St, at Washington St. (☎453-5579. Open daily 9am-5pm.) **Ski Conditions and Weather:** ☎453-6118. **Area code:** 970.

BOULDER   ☎303

The 1960s have been slow to fade in Boulder. A liberal haven in an otherwise conservative region of the country, the city is brimming with fashionable coffeeshops, teahouses, and organic juice bars. Boulder is home to both the central branch of the University of Colorado (CU) and Naropa University, the only accredited Buddhist university in the United States. Seek spiritual enlightenment through meditation and healing workshops at Naropa, or pursue a physical awakening through Boulder's incredible local outdoor activities, including biking, hiking, and rafting along Boulder Creek.

⬛🗾 **ORIENTATION & PRACTICAL INFORMATION.** Boulder is a small, manageable city, easily accessible from Estes Park and Denver by Rte. 36. The most developed area lies between **Broadway (Rte. 93)** and **28th St. (Rte. 36),** two busy streets running north-south through the city. Broadway, 28th St., and **Baseline Rd.** border the **University of Colorado (CU)** campus. The area around the school is known as **the Hill.** The pedestrian-only **Pearl St. Mall,** between 9th and 15th St., is lined with cafes, restaurants, and posh shops. **Greyhound,** at 30th and Diagonal Hwy. (☎800-231-2222; open 24hr.), rolls to Denver (1hr., 2 per day, $6); Glenwood Springs (6-7hr., 2 per day, $35-37); and Vail (5-5½hr., 2 per day, $28-30). Boulder's extensive yet confusing **public transit** system is run by **RTD,** at 14th and Walnut St., in the center of town. (☎299-6000 or 800-366-7433. Open M-F 6am-8pm, Sa-Su 8am-8pm. Call for schedules and fares.) **Taxis: Boulder Yellow Cab** ☎442-2277. **Bike Rental: University Bicycles,** 839 Pearl St., downtown, rents mountain bikes with helmet and lock. (☎444-4196. Open M-F 10am-7pm, Sa 10am-6pm, Su 10am-5pm. $25 per 24hr., kids' bikes $20 per 24hr. Snowshoes $10 per 24hr.) **Visitor Info: Boulder Chamber of Commerce/Visitors Service,** 2440 Pearl St., has info and free Internet access. (☎442-1044. Open M-Th 8:30am-5pm, F 8:30am-4pm.) **Internet access: Boulder Public Library,** 11th and Arapahoe. (☎441-3100. Open M-Th 9am-9pm, F-Sa 9am-6pm, Su noon-6pm.) **University of Colorado Information,** 2nd fl. of the University Memorial Center (UMC) student union, has both Internet access and free local calls. (☎492-

6161. Open in summer M-Th 7am-11pm, F-Sa 7am-midnight, Su 11am-11pm; term-time M-Th 7am-midnight, F-Sa 7am-1am, Su 11am-midnight.) **Post Office:** 1905 15th St., at Walnut St. (☎938-3704. Open M-F 7:30am-5:30pm, Sa 10am-2pm.) **ZIP code:** 80302. **Area code:** 303. 10-digit dialing required.

ACCOMMODATIONS. Budget accommodations are few and far between, but some bargains can be found. **Boulder International Hostel ❶**, 1107 12th St., at College Ave., is the best deal in town. Youthful travelers fill the spacious downstairs lobby to watch cable TV and surf the Internet ($2 per 30min.). The front door is locked after 11pm, but guests are given a code to enter after hours. (☎442-0522. Kitchen, laundry. Linen $4. Key deposit $10. Max. stay 3 days. Lockout 10am-5pm. Dorms $17; singles $39 per night, $205 per week; doubles $40/235. Prices lower in winter.) **Lazy L Motel ❹**, 1000 28th St., on Frontage Rd., has standard, clean rooms and is conveniently located near busy Rte. 36. (☎442-7525. Singles in summer $75; in winter $45; doubles $85/55.) **Chautauqua Association ❸**, off Baseline Rd. at the foot of the Flatirons, has lodge rooms as well as private cottages. To get there, turn at the Chautauqua Park sign and take Kinnikinic to Morning Glory Dr. or take RTD bus #203. (☎442-3282, ext. 11. Office open in summer M-F 8:30am-7pm, Sa-Su 9am-5pm; in winter M-F 8:30am-7pm. Reserve months in advance. Min. stay 4 nights. In summer lodge rooms $57-98; 1-bedroom suites $70-98; 2-bedroom cottages $95-190, 3-bedroom $130-136. In winter, limited number of cottages $81-190.)

Camping info for **Arapahoe/Roosevelt National Forest** is available from the **Boulder Ranger District**, 2140 Yarmouth Ave., just off of Rte. 36 to the north of town. (☎541-2500, reservations 800-444-6777. Open in summer M-Th 8am-4:30pm, F 8am-6pm, Sa 8am-2:30pm; in winter M-F 8am-4:30pm. Campsites open mid-May to Oct. $12 per night unless otherwise noted.) The 46 sites of **Kelly Dahl ❶** lie among pine trees and picnic tables 3 mi. south of Nederland on Rte. 119. To reach **Rainbow Lakes ❶**, 6.5 mi. north of Nederland, turn at the Mountain Research Station (CR 119) and follow the dirt road for 5 mi. The 16 sites are first come, first served. (No water. $6 per night.) The two gems of the forest are **Peaceful Valley ❶**, with 17 sites, and **Camp Dick ❶**, with 41 sites; both lie north on Rte. 72. (Reservations recommended, especially on weekends.)

FOOD & NIGHTLIFE. The streets on the **Hill**, surrounding CU and along the **Pearl St. Mall**, burst with good eateries, natural foods markets, and colorful bars. Boulder almost has more options for vegetarians than meat-eaters. **Johnny McGuire's ❶**, 1220 Pennsylvania Ave., is a local favorite for its specialty deli subs and sandwiches (6 in. $5.25, 8 in. $6.25, 1 ft. $10). The walls are covered with pictures, postcards, and headlines from around the globe. (☎413-9254. Open Sept.-May daily 11am-8pm; June-Aug. daily 11am-3:30pm.) **Illegal Pete's ❶**, 1320 College Ave. and 1447 Pearl St., on the Mall, creates scrumptious burritos for $4.85. (☎444-3055. Open Sept.-May daily 11am-8pm; June-Aug. daily 11am-3:30pm.) A supermarket specializing in organic foods, **Wild Oates**, 1651 Broadway, is a good place to buy provisions. (☎442-0909. Open daily 7am-11pm.)

Boulder overflows with nightlife hot spots, each with its own unique spin. For bluegrass, funk, and the best brews in Boulder (try the "kind crippler"), head to **Mountain Sun Pub and Brewery**, 1535 Pearl St. (☎546-0886. Su acoustic performances 10pm-1am. Open M-Sa 11:30am-1am, Su noon-1am.) The **Bookend Cafe**, 1115 Pearl St., attached to the famous **Boulder Bookstore**, is an established local favorite where people go to see and be seen. Signs beseech "Be nice or leave." Treat yourself to a muffin, burrito, or piece of pie while observing the vibrant activity along the Mall from the outdoor patio. (☎440-6699. Open M-F 6:45am-10pm, Sa-Su 8am-10pm.) A Boulder classic, **The Sink ❷,** 1165 13th St., still awaits the return of its one-time janitor, Robert Redford, who quit his job and headed to California in the late 1950s. The Sink serves surprisingly upscale new cuisine and great pizzas amid wild graffiti, low ceilings, and pipes. Students fill the Sink for late-night drinking. (☎444-7465. Burgers $6-8. Open M-Sa 11am-2am, Su noon-2am; food served until 10pm.) The **West End Tavern,** 926 Pearl St., has a rooftop bar with quite the view of downtown. (☎444-3535. Draft beers $3-4. Kitchen open M-Sa 11am-11pm, Su 11:30am-11pm; bar open until 1:30am.) For house and trance, head over to **Soma,** 1915 Broadway. If the music doesn't get to you, the red-lighted interior and dizzyingly large dance floor will make your brave new world spin. (☎402-1690. Open daily 8pm-2am.)

◪ 环! **SIGHTS & OUTDOOR ACTIVITIES.** Due to its proximity to the mountains, Boulder's location supports many outdoor activities. **Boulder Creek,** at the foot of the mountains, is prime hiking and biking territory, as is **Scott Carpenter Park. Chautauqua Park** has a number of trails varying in length and difficulty that climb up and around the **Flatirons.** The self-guided **Enchanted Mesa/McClintock Trail** is a self-guided nature trail that is partially wheelchair-accessible. Before heading out into the wilderness, learn how to protect yourself against mountain lions, and grab a trail map at the entrance to Chautauqua Park.

The tiny **Boulder Museum of Contemporary Art,** 1750 13th St., has rotating exhibits. (☎443-2122. Open in summer W-F noon-8pm, Su noon-5pm; in winter Tu-Sa 10am-6pm, Su noon-5pm. $4, students and seniors $3, children free.) Next to the museum, the ◪**Dushanbe Teahouse,** 1770 13th St., was built by artists in Tajikistan, and then was piece-mailed from Boulder's sister city of Dushanbe. The building is now owned by the city and leased to a private restauranteur, who lays out a scrumptious spread. (☎442-4993. Tea $2-4. Lunch from $5.50. Dinner from $7. Open M-Th 8am-5pm, F 8am-10pm, Sa 5-10pm, Su 5-9pm.) The intimate **Leanin' Tree Museum,** 6055 Longbow Dr., presents 200 paintings and 80 bronze sculptures depicting Western themes. (☎530-1442 ext. 299. Open M-F 8am-4:30pm, Sa-Su 10am-4pm. Free.) Minutes away, **The Celestial Seasonings Tea Company,** 4600 Sleepytime Dr., lures visitors with tea samples and free tours of the factory, including the infamous Peppermint Room. (☎530-5300. Open M-F 9am-6pm, Sa 9am-5pm, Su 11am-4pm. Tours M-Su every hr.) The **Rockies Brewing Company,** 2880 Wilderness Pl., off Valmont, offers tours and free beer. (☎444-8448. Pub open in summer M-F 11am-10pm, Sa noon-8pm; in winter M-Tu 11am-8pm, W-F 11am-9pm. 25min. tours M-Sa 2pm. Free.)

🎭 **ENTERTAINMENT.** An exciting street scene pounds through both the Mall and the Hill; the university's kiosks have the lowdown on downtown happenings. The **University Memorial Center,** 1609 Euclid (16th St. becomes Euclid on campus), hosts many events (☎492-6161). On the 3rd fl., the Cultural Events Board (☎492-3221) has the latest word on all CU-sponsored activities. From late June to early August, the **Colorado Shakespeare Festival** draws over 50,000 people, making it the third-largest festival of its kind. (☎492-0554. Tickets $10-46, previews $5-23. $5 student and senior discount.) The **Colorado Music Festival** performs July through August. (☎449-2413. Lawn seats $5; other prices vary.) The local indie music scene is on display at the popular **Fox Theater and Cafe,** 1135 13th St. (☎447-0095). Twice a week from April through October, Boulder shuts down 13th St. between Canyon and Arapahoe for a **Farmers Market.** (Open Apr.-Oct. W 10am-2pm, Sa 8am-2pm.)

ROCKY MOUNTAINS

ROCKY MOUNTAIN NATIONAL PARK ☎970

Of all the US national parks, Rocky Mountain National Park is closest to heaven, with over 60 peaks exceeding 12,000 feet. A third of the park lies above the treeline, and Longs Peak pierces the sky at 14,255 ft. Here among the clouds, the alpine tundra ecosystem supports bighorn sheep, elk, dwarf wildflowers, and arctic shrubs interspersed among granite boulders and crystalline lakes. The city of **Estes Park,** immediately east of the park, hosts the vast majority of would-be mountaineers and alpinists who crowd the shopping areas in the summer. To the west of the park, the town of **Grand Lake,** on the edges of two glacial lakes, is a more tranquil base from which to explore Rocky Mountain National Park's less traversed but equally stunning western side.

■✈🅭 ORIENTATION & PRACTICAL INFORMATION

You can reach the national park from Boulder via U.S. 36 or scenic Rte. 7. From the northeast, the national park can be accessed up the Big Thompson Canyon via U.S. 34, but beware of flash floods. **Trail Ridge Rd./U.S. 34** runs 48 mi. through the park from Grand Lake to Estes Park.

Visitor Info: Park Headquarters and Visitors Center (☎586-1206), 2½ mi. west of Estes Park on Rte. 36, at the Beaver Meadows entrance to the park. Open mid-June to late Aug. daily 8am-9pm; Sept. to mid-June 8am-5pm. Educational programs in summer daily 7:30pm; year-round Sa 7pm. 8:30am-4pm. **Kawuneeche Visitors Center** (☎627-3471), just outside the park's western entrance and 1¼ mi. north of Grand Lake, offers similar info. Open mid-May to late Aug. daily 8am-6pm; Sept. 8am-5pm; Oct. to mid-May 8am-4:30pm. Educational programs in summer Sa 7pm; call for winter program. The high-altitude **Alpine Visitors Center,** at the crest of Trail Ridge Rd., has a great view of the tundra. Open mid-June to late Aug. daily 9am-5pm; late May to mid-June and late Aug. to mid-Oct. 10am-4:30pm. **Lily Lake Visitors Center,** 6 mi. south of Park Headquarters on Rte. 7 is open in summer daily 9am-4:30pm. Park **entrance fee** $15 per vehicle, $5 per cyclist or pedestrian; valid for 7 days.

Weather: Park Weather and Road Conditions, ☎586-1333.

Medical Services: Estes Park Medical Center, ☎586-2317. **Park Emergency,** ☎586-1399.

Internet access: Estes Park Public Library, 335 E. Elkhorn (☎586-8116). Open in summer M-Th 9am-8pm, F-Sa 9am-5pm, Su 1-5pm; in winter M-Th 10am-9pm, F-Sa 10am-5pm, Su 1-5pm.

Post Offices: Grand Lake, 520 Center Dr. (☎627-3340). Open M-F 8:30am-5pm. **ZIP code:** 80447. **Estes Park,** 215 W. Riverside Dr. (☎586-0170). Open M-F 9am-5pm, Sa 10am-2:30pm. **ZIP code:** 80517. **Area code:** 970.

🅖 ACCOMMODATIONS

ESTES PARK

Although Estes Park has an abundance of expensive lodges and motels, there are a few good deals on indoor beds near the national park, especially in winter, when temperatures drop and tourists leave.

The Colorado Mountain School, 341 Moraine Ave. (☎586-5758). Tidy, dorm-style accommodations are open to travelers unless already booked by mountain-climbing students. Wood bunks with comfortable mattresses, linen, and showers. 16 beds. Reservations recommended 1 week in advance. $25 per person. ❶

Estes Park Center YMCA, 2515 Tunnel Rd. (☎586-3341, ext. 1010), 2 mi. from the park entrance. Follow Rte. 36 to Rte. 66. Extensive facilities on the 860-acre complex include mini-golf and a pool, as well as horseback rides and daily hikes for guests. Call ahead; reservations for summer accepted starting May 1st. 4-person cabin with kitchen and bath from $71; 5-person cabins $135; 7-person cabins $171. 1-day "guest membership" required: $3, families $5. ❹

GRAND LAKE

Grand Lake is the "snowmobile capital of Colorado" and offers spectacular cross-country routes. Boating and swimming are popular summertime activities.

🏠 **Shadowcliff Hostel (HI-AYH),** 405 Summerland Park Rd. (☎627-9220). From the western entrance, veer left to Grand Lake, then take the left fork ½ mi. into town on W. Portal Rd. In downtown Grand Lake, take a left at Garfield, and turn right onto W. Portal. The handbuilt pine lodge perches on a cliff overlooking Grand Lake, Shadow Mountain Lake, and the Rockies. Hiking trails, kitchen, showers, and a wood burning stove. Linen $1. Min. stay 6 days. Make cabin reservations as far as a year in advance. Open June to Sept. Dorms $12, nonmembers $14. Private singles $40; doubles $40; each additional person $10. 6-8 person cabins $80-90 ❶

Sunset Motel, 505 Grand Ave. (☎627-3318). Stands out against the mountains with its yellow front and baby blue trim. Friendly owners, cozy rooms, and the only heated indoor pool in Grand Lake. Singles $60; doubles $90. In winter $40/60. ❸

Bluebird Motel, 30 River Dr. (☎627-9314), on Rte. 34 west of Grand Lake, overlooks Shadow Mountain Lake and the snowcapped Continental Divide. Variety is the key word here. Some rooms have couches, many have fridges, others have complete kitchenettes. Singles $40-60; doubles $50-75. ❷

📷 CAMPING

You can camp a total of seven days anywhere within the park. In the backcountry, the maximum stay increases to 14 days. All national park campgrounds are $16 in the summer; winter sites are $10, unless otherwise noted. None have water in the winter. A backcountry camping **permit** ($15) is required in the summer. On the eastern slope, permits are available inside the park from the **Backcountry Permits and Trip Planning Building,** a 2min. walk from the park headquarters. (☎586-1242. Open in summer daily 7am-7pm; in winter 8am-4:30pm.) In the west, see the folks at the **Kawuneeche Visitors Center.** (Open daily 8am-6pm.)

GRAND LAKE

The cheapest camping in the National Park is in the surrounding national forests. **Stillwater Campground,** west of Grand Lake on the shores of the hot boating spot Lake Granby, has 127 tranquil sites ($15-18). **Green Ridge Campground,** on the south end of Shadow Mountain Lake, is also a good bet with 78 sites ($12). Both campgrounds have toilets, water, and boat ramps. Some sites available on a first come, first served basis. (Both sites: reservations ☎877-444-6777; www.reserveusa.com. Reserve at least 8 days in advance. Open late May to early Sept.) **Timber Creek,** 10 mi. north of Grand Lake, is the only national park campground on the western side of the park. Open year-round, it offers 100 woodsy sites on a first come, first served basis.

EAST SIDE OF THE PARK

Moraine Park, 3 mi. west of Beaver Meadows Park Headquarters on Bear Lake Rd., is open year-round and has 247 sites on open, sunny spots. Open only in summer, **Glacier Basin,** 9 mi. from Estes, south of Moraine Park, provides 150 secluded sites with a spectacular view of the mountains. Both Moraine Park and Glacier Basin require reservations in summer (☎800-365-2267; http://reservations.nps.gov). **Aspenglen,** 5 mi. west of Estes Park near the Fall River entrance, has 54 first come, first served sites late May to September. **Longs Peak Campground** has 26 year-round sites, in a prime location to begin climbing Longs Peak. There is a three-night maximum stay, and no water in winter.

ⓕ FOOD

ESTES PARK
🍴 **The Notchtop Pub,** 459 E. Wonderview, #44 (☎586-0272), in the upper Stanley Village Shopping Plaza, east of downtown off Rte. 34. Locals flock here for homemade "natural foods and brews." Breads, pastries, and pies baked fresh every morning. Soups $3. Salads $4-7. Sandwiches from $6. Open M-Th 7am-10pm, F-Su 7am-11pm. ❷

Local's Grill, 153 E. Elkhorn Ave. (☎586-6900), in the heart of downtown, is a self-proclaimed "world-famous gathering place." Customers crowd the front patio for gourmet sandwiches ($5-8) and pizza ($5-11). Open M-Th 11am-9pm, F-Su 11am-10pm. ❷

GRAND LAKE
Pancho and Lefty's, 1120 Grand Ave. (☎627-8773). The price is right, as are the portions. Try the deliciously spicy tamales ($6.25) or crunchy *chimichangas* ($7.25), and wash it all down with a margarita ($4). Open in summer M-F 11am-8pm, Sa-Su 11am-9pm; in winter W-M 6am-8pm. ❷

E.G.'s Garden Grille, 1000 Grand Ave. (☎627-8404). Patrons cool off on the shaded patio while enjoying a drink from the bar. Dinner is rather pricey, but lunchtime sandwiches, subs, and burgers are affordable ($6-7). Lunch specials $5.50. Open daily 11am-9pm. ❷

🏔 OUTDOOR ACTIVITIES

SCENIC DRIVES
The star of the park is **Trail Ridge Rd.** (U.S. 34), a 48 mi. stretch that rises 12,183 ft. above sea level into frigid tundra. The round-trip drive takes roughly 3hr. by car; beware of slow-moving tour buses and people who stop without warning to ogle wildlife. The road is sometimes closed or inaccessible, especially from October to May, for weather reasons. Many sights within the park are accessible from Trail Ridge Rd. Heading west, **Rainbow Curve** and then the **Forest Canyon Overlook** offer impressive views of the vast tree-carpeted landscape. The interesting 30min. **Tundra Communities Trail** provides a once-in-a-lifetime-look at the fragile alpine tundra. Signposts along the paved trail explain the geology and wildlife of the tundra. The **Lava Cliffs** attract large crowds, but are worth the hassle. The **Alpine Visitors Center** lies just beyond the Lava Cliffs to the west. Beyond the Alpine Visitors Center, the traffic and congestion become noticeably thinner.

A wilder alternative to Trail Ridge Rd. is **Old Fall River Rd.** Entering Rocky Mountain National Park from the east side on Rte. 34, you'll pass **Sheep Lakes,** a popular crossing for Bighorn Sheep. After Sheep Lakes, veer right toward the **Alluvial Fan** and Old Fall River Rd. Starting at **Endovalley** picnic area, Old Fall River Rd. is a 9 mi. unpaved, one-way uphill road with spectacular mountain views. Drivers will notice the destruction caused by flooding. The road intersects Trail Ridge Rd. behind the Alpine Visitors Center.

Bear Lake Rd., south of Trail Ridge Rd., leads to the most popular hiking trails within the park. **Moraine Park Museum**, off of Bear Lake Rd. 1½ mi. from the Beaver Meadows entrance, has exhibits on the park's geology and ecosystem, as well as comfortable rocking chairs with a view of the mountains. (☎586-1206. Open in summer daily 9am-5pm.)

SCENIC HIKES

Numerous trailheads lie in the western half of the park, including the Continental Divide and its accompanying hiking trail. Trail Ridge Rd. ends in **Grand Lake**, a small town with ample outdoor opportunities. An overnight trek from Grand Lake into the scenic and remote **North** or **East Inlets** leaves the crowds behind.

Lake Nanita (11 mi., 5½hr.), leaving from North Inlet, ascends 2240 ft. through pristine wilderness to a fantastic view of the lake.

Lake Verna (7 mi., 3½hr.), departs from East Inlet and gains a total of 1800 ft. in elevation as it passes mountain streams before re-entering the alpine forest. The culmination of the hike is an overlook of the fjord-like lake.

Mt. Chapin (1.5 mi., 1hr.), accessible from Old Fall River Rd., lies mostly above the timberline. Start early to avoid unpredictable weather. You can climb Mt. Chapin or hike around it to the saddle, a great place to picnic. From here, the adventurous can continue on to **Mt. Chiquita** and **Ypsilon Mt.** (combined time 5-6hr.; 10 mi.), but watch for storms and plan accordingly—the tundra offers little protection.

Mill Creek (1.5 mi., 40min.), beginning at Hollowell Park. This easy trail crosses an open meadow and then empties out into a serene field of aspen, providing a look at the significant beaver activity along the creek.

Bear Lake Hikes. The park's most popular trails are all accessible from the Bear Lake Trailhead. Bear Lake serves as the hub for snowshoeing and cross-country skiing. In the summer, the Bear Lake parking lot fills up by 9am, and the Glacier Gorge parking lot even earlier. For the slow to rise, the **Bear Lake Shuttle Bus** provides convenient transportation between the Shuttle Bus parking area and Bear Lake, also stopping at Glacier Gorge. (Buses every 8-10min. 9am-5pm; every 20min. 7-9am and 5-7pm.)

Flattop Mt. (4.4 mi., 3hr.), the most challenging and picturesque of the Bear Lake hikes, climbs 2800 ft. to a vantage point along the Continental Divide.

Nymph (0.5 mi., 15min); **Dream** (1.1 mi., 30min.); and **Emerald Lakes** (1.8 mi., 1hr.) are a series of 3 glacial pools offering inspiring glimpses of the surrounding peaks. Although the first 2 legs of the hike are relatively easy, the Emerald Lake portion is steep and rocky at points.

Lake Haiyaha (2.3 mi., 1¼hr.), forking left from the trail, is more intimate, with superb views of the mountains. A scramble over the rocks at the end of the trail earns you a peek at hidden (and sometimes difficult to find) Lake Haiyaha, arguably the most astounding of the 4 lakes.

VAIL ☎970

The largest one-mountain ski resort in all of North America, trendy Vail has its fair share of ritzy hotels, swank saloons, and sexy boutiques, but it's the mountain that wows skiers with its prime snow and back bowls (try the new Blue Sky Basin). Discovered by Lord Gore in 1854, Vail and its surrounding valley were invaded by miners during the Rockies gold rush in the 1870s. According to local folklore, the Ute Indians adored the area's rich supply of game, but they became so upset with the white settlers that they set fire to the forest, creating the resort's open terrain.

ROCKY MOUNTAINS

⚠ PRACTICAL INFORMATION. Vail Village and Lionshead Village form the entity known as Vail. They are pedestrian only; visitors must park in garages off **Frontage Rd.**, but parking is free during the summer. Free **Vail Transit** buses link the two villages; stops are marked by signs. **Greyhound,** in the Transportation Building next to the main Visitors Center, (☎476-5137; ticket office open daily 8am-6:30pm) buses eager skiers out of its depot to Denver (2hr., 5 per day, $12.50); Glenwood Springs (1½hr., 4 per day, $15.50); and Grand Junction (3½hr., 4 per day, $15.50). **EcoTransit** runs bus routes between Vail and its surrounding areas, including Eagle and Edwards. (☎328-3520. Office open daily 6:30am-10pm. $2-3.) Free bus service (☎477-3456 for schedule info) covers the area around Vail Village, Lionshead, and East and West Vail. Vail's two **Visitors Centers** are each at the top of the parking structures on S. Frontage Rd. at either end of the village. The larger one is at the **Vail Transportation Center** (☎479-1394 or 800-525-3875; open daily 8am-6pm), and the smaller is in **Lionshead Village** (☎800-525-3875; open in summer daily 9am-5pm; in winter 8am-5pm). **Weather: Road report,** ☎476-2226. **Snow report,** ☎476-8888. **Internet access: Vail Public Library,** 292 W. Meadow Dr. (☎479-2184. Open M-Th 10am-8pm, F 10am-6pm, Sa-Su 11am-6pm.) **Post Office:** 1300 N. Frontage Rd. W. (☎476-5217. Open M-F 8:30am-5pm, Sa 8:30am-noon.) **ZIP code:** 81657. **Area code:** 970.

⚕ ACCOMMODATIONS. The phrase "cheap lodging" is not part of Vail's vocabulary. Rooms in the resort town rarely dip below $175 per night in winter, and summer lodging is often equally pricey. The **Roost Lodge ❹,** 1783 N. Frontage Rd., in West Vail, provides affordable lodging in a convenient location. The small rooms are impressively clean and come with cable TV, fridge, microwave, and access to a jacuzzi, sauna, and pool. (☎476-5451 or 800-873-3065. Continental breakfast in winter. Singles in summer from $49; in winter from $89.) Located in Eagle, about 30 mi. west of Vail, **The Prairie Moon ❸,** 738 Grand Ave., offers some of the cheapest lodging near the resort. EcoTransit shuttles visitors daily between Eagle and Vail (see **Practical Information,** above). The large, clean rooms have fridges and microwaves. (☎328-6680. Singles from $55; doubles from $68.) The **Holy Cross Ranger District,** right off I-70 at Exit 171 (follow signs), provides info on the six summer campgrounds near Vail. (☎827-5715. Open June-Aug. M-F 8am-5pm, Sa-Su 8am-4:30pm; Sept.-May M-F 8am-5pm.) With 25 sites, **Gore Creek ❶** is the closest and most popular campground. Well-situated among birch trees, wild flowers, and mountains just outside East Vail, Gore Creek is within hiking distance of the free East Vail Express bus route. (Max. stay 10 days. Sites with water $12.)

⬛ FOOD. The original place for *après-ski* at Vail, the **Red Lion ❷,** 304 Bridge St., has served award-winning chili ($4-5.50) and delicious sandwiches ($8-9) since 1962. (☎476-7676. Live music daily 4-6pm and 9-11pm. Open daily 11am-2am; kitchen open until 10pm.) **Garfinkel's ❸,** 536 E. Lionshead Circle, a hidden hangout accessible by foot in Vail's Lionshead Village (directly across from the gondola) calls out "Ski hard, party harder" with daily specials on food and booze. Enjoy your meal on a porch that practically merges with the ski slope. (☎476-3789. Meals $8-10. Restaurant open daily 11am-10pm; bar open until 2am.)

◧ SIGHTS. The **Ski Hall of Fame** is housed in the **Colorado Ski Museum,** in the Transportation Building in Vail Village, and captures both the history of the sport and of Vail. (☎476-1876. Open June-Sept. and Nov.-Apr. Tu-Su 10am-5pm. $1, under 12 free.) In the summer, the **Gerald R. Ford Amphitheater** presents a number of outdoor concerts, dance festivals, and theater productions on its grounds. (☎476-2918. Box office open Tu-Sa 3-6pm. Lawn seats $5; Tu free.) The **Vilar Center for the Arts** (☎845-8497 or 888-920-2787), at Beaver Creek, hosts world-renowned musicians, actors, and dancers.

ROCKY MOUNTAINS

▓ OUTDOOR ACTIVITIES. Before slaloming, the unequipped visit **Ski Base,** 675 W. Lionshead Circle, for equipment. (☎476-5799. Open in winter daily 8am-7pm. Skis, poles, and boots from $14 per day; snowboard and boots from $20 per day.) The store transforms into the **Wheel Base Bike Shop** in the summer. (Open daily 9am-6pm. Path bikes $15 per 8hr.; mountain bikes from $23 per 8hr.)

Vail caters to sun worshippers in the summer, when the ski runs turn into hiking **and biking trails.** The **Eagle Bahn Gondola** at Lionshead and the **Vista Bahn chairlift,** part of the Vail Resort, whisk hikers, bikers, and sightseers to the top of the mountains for breathtaking views. (☎476-9090. Office open 8:30am-4:30pm. Eagle Bahn open in summer Su-W 10am-4pm, Th-Sa 10am-9pm; in winter F-Su 10am-4pm. Vista Bahn open mid-July to early Sept. F-Su 10am-4pm. All-day summer pass on the Eagle Bahn $16, ages 65-69 and under 13 $10, 70 and over $5; includes hauling fees.) During the summer months, enjoy the **Eagle Bahn Gondola Twilight Ride.** (F and Sa 5-9pm. Free.) Rental **bikes** are available atop Vail Mountain. (☎479-4380. $15 per hr., $35 per 4hr., $45 per day.) The **Holy Cross Ranger District** (see above) provides maps and information on the many snowmobile, X-C skiing, and hiking routes near Vail Pass. The **Gore Creek Fly Fisherman,** 183-7 Gore Creek Dr., reels in the daily catch and has river info. (☎476-3296 or 800-369-3044. Open July-Aug. daily 7am-10pm; mid-May to June and Sept. to mid-Oct. Su-Th 8am-8pm. Rod rentals $15 per day, with boots and waders $25.)

STEAMBOAT SPRINGS ☎970

West of RMNP and north of the slopes of Vail, the somewhat isolated resort town of Steamboat Springs boasts great outdoor activities and a gong-show nightlife, be it January or July. **Steamboat Resort** boasts the best snow in Colorado; their trademark "Champagne Powder" is light, fluffy, and near-perfect for skiing. Ski between trees and exploit all of the area's astonishing 3600 ft. vertical drop. (☎871-5252. Open Dec. to mid-Apr.) In summer, Steamboat turns into a center for everything from mountain biking to kayaking. Perhaps the best commercial hot springs in the West, the **Strawberry Hot Springs** has various rock-lined pools nestled in the crook of a roaring cold-water creek. Seven miles north of town, turn east on 7th St. and follow the "Hot Springs" signs. Local rumors purport that clothing becomes optional as the night progresses. (☎879-0342. Open daily 10am-10:30pm. M-F before 5pm $5, children $3; M-F after 5pm and Sa-Su $10/5.)

Though Steamboat does not head the list of cheap places to stay, a few motels offer low rates and nice rooms. The relatively inexpensive pine-paneled rooms at the **Nite's Rest Motel ❸,** 601 Lincoln St., provide a cozy place to sleep. (☎839-8890. Singles $50-70; doubles $55-80.) The **Nordic Lodge ❸,** 1036 Lincoln Ave., has an indoor hot tub. (☎879-0531. Office open daily 8am-11pm. Singles from $52; doubles from $62.) Not known for its cheap eats, Steamboat has a few places with reasonable prices. **Backcountry Provisions ❷,** 635 Lincoln Ave., packs up sandwiches like the Sherpa ($6) and the Pilgrim ($6.50) for trips into the bush. (☎879-3617. Open daily 7am-5pm.) Adding some heat to any trip, **Double Z's Bar and Bar-B-Q ❷,** 1124 Yampa St., has filling, saucy BBQ sandwiches for $6.25. (☎879-3617. Open daily 11am-10pm.) Rock out at the **Tugboat,** 1860 Ski Time Sq., at the base of the mountain, with live music most nights. (☎879-7070. Cover $3-10. Open daily 11:30am-1:30am.) If on the hunt for dance floor prey, the **Wolf Den,** 703 Church St., is the place to be. (☎871-0008. Th Ladies night. Open in winter daily 5pm-1:30am; in summer closed Su. No credit cards.)

For visitor info head to the **Chamber of Commerce,** 1255 S. Lincoln Ave. (☎879-0882, ext. 202. Open in winter M-F 8am-5pm, Sa 10am-4pm; off-season closed Sa.) **Post Office:** 200 Lincoln St. (Open M-F 8:30am-5pm, Sa 9am-noon.) **ZIP code:** 80487. **Area code:** 970.

ASPEN ☎970

Aspen was founded as a silver mining camp, but the silver ran out quickly and by 1940 the town was almost gone. Wealthy visionaries took one look at the location of the floundering village and transformed it into a winter playground. Today, Aspen's skiing, scenery, and festivals are matched only by the prices in the exclusive boutiques downtown. To catch Aspen on the semi-cheap, stay in Glenwood Springs (see p. 757), 40 miles north on Rte. 82, and visit the aspen groves in the nearby national forest.

◪ PRACTICAL INFORMATION. Visitors Centers: 320 Hyman Ave., in the Wheeler Opera House (☎920-7148; open daily 10am-6pm); and 425 Rio Grand Pl. (☎925-1940 or 888-290-1324; open M-F 8am-5pm). **The Aspen Ranger District,** 806 W. Hallam, provides info on hikes and camping within 15 mi. of Aspen. (☎925-3445. Open June-Aug. M-Sa 8am-5pm; Sept.-May M-F 8am-4:30pm. Topographic maps $4.) **Roads and Weather:** ☎877-315-7623. **Snow Report:** ☎925-1221 or 888-277-3676. **Post Office:** 235 Puppy Smith Rd. (☎925-7523. Open M-F 8:30am-5pm, Sa 9am-noon.) **ZIP code:** 81611. **Area code:** 970.

◨ ACCOMMODATIONS. Staying in Aspen means biting the bullet and reaching deep into your pockets. The last sound deal in town, **St. Moritz Lodge ②,** 344 W. Hyman Ave., charms ski bums with a pool, steam room, and hot tub. (☎925-3220 or 800-817-2069. Dorm beds $26-39, depending on season. Hotel rooms $55-159.) Unless 6 ft. of snow covers the ground, **camping ❶** is available in one of the seven National Forest campgrounds that lie within 5 mi. of Aspen. Sites scatter just west of town on Maroon Creek Rd. and southeast on Rte. 82. (☎877-444-6777. 5-day max. stay throughout the district. Open June to mid-Sept. Reservations recommended; sites fill before noon. Some first come, first served sites available. Sites $9-14 per night.) Camping requires a $3 Colorado Hiking Certificate (search-and-rescue insurance fee) that can be paid at the ranger station or local sporting goods stores.

◖ FOOD. Fast, cheap, and easy, **The Big Wrap ②,** 520 E. Durant Ave., rolls up gourmet wraps, like the tasty "to thai for." (☎544-1700. Fresh salads $6. Smoothies $4. Open M-Sa 10am-6pm.) Always packed, the **Hickory House ❸,** 730 W. Main St., smokes up award-winning BBQ favorites. (☎925-2313. Lunches from $6; dinners $10-20. Open daily 6am-10pm.) Try the famed beef stew at **Little Annie's Eating House ❸,** 517 E. Hyman Ave., a longtime Aspen staple for booze and burgers. (☎925-1098. Burgers $8.25. Veggie lasagna $10. Open daily 11:30am-10pm; bar until 2am.) **Main Street Bakery ②,** 201 E. Main St., serves gourmet soups ($5), homemade granola with fruit ($6), and vegetarian sandwiches ($7). Their patio is a prime people-watching spot. (☎925-6446. Open daily 7am-9:30pm.) The **Cooper St. Pier ②,** 508 E. Cooper St., is one of the best deals in town, especially the lunchtime hamburger special (burger with fries and a soda or beer) for only $6.50. (☎925-7758. Open daily 11am-10pm; bar open until 2am. No credit cards.)

◩ ENTERTAINMENT. Entering its 53rd season, the internationally acclaimed **Aspen Music Festival** features jazz, opera, and classical music late June through August. A variety of shows are held every night in many venues around town. A free **Music Shuttle** bus transports listeners from Rubey Park to the music tent every 30min. prior to the concert. (☎925-9042. Many concerts free.) **Aspen Theatre in the Park** presents a variety of shows each night from mid-June to late August. (☎925-9313, box office ☎920-5770. $25-30.)

⛷ **SKIING.** Skiing is the main attraction in Aspen. The surrounding hills contain four ski areas: Aspen Mountain, Aspen Highlands, Buttermilk Mountain, and Snowmass, known collectively as **Aspen/Snowmass.** Interchangeable lift tickets enable the four areas to operate as a single extended resort; for the best deal, buy multiday passes at least two weeks in advance. (☎925-1220 or 800-525-6200. Day passes from $60, ages 13-27 $45, ages 7-12 $37, ages 65-69 $55, over 70 and under 7 free; prices vary by season.) Each of the mountains offers unique skiing opportunities of varying difficulty. **Buttermilk's** gentle slopes are perfect for beginners interested in lessons (and snowplowing their way down the mountain). The **Highlands** now includes the steep cliffs of Highland Bowl and offers a large and diverse selection for advanced and expert skiers. **Aspen Mountain,** though smaller than the Highlands, also caters to expert skiers; there are no easy trails in this terrain. The granddaddy of the Aspen ski areas, **Snowmass,** with its 20 lifts and countless runs, remains the most family-friendly of the mountains. All but the most timid of beginners will find something to enjoy here. Snowmass is also popular among snowboarders, with its half-pipes and terrain parks.

📷 **OUTDOOR ACTIVITIES.** In summer, the **Silver Queen Gondola** heads to the 11,212 ft. summit of Aspen Mountain, providing an unparalleled panorama. (☎925-1220 or 800-525-6200. Open mid-June to early Sept. daily 10am-4pm. $15 per day, $29 per week.) At **Snowmass Mountain,** you can take a chairlift to the top and ride your mountain bike down. (Open in summer Th-M 10am-4pm. $10.) Hikers can explore the **Maroon Bells** on the unforgettable 1.8 mi. trek to **Crater Lake.** Maroon Creek Rd. is closed to traffic from 8:30am to 5pm daily in an effort to preserve the surrounding wilderness. To avoid paying $5 for a slow RFTA tour bus that departs every 30min. from **Rubey Park,** plan either an early morning or a sunset hike. In Aspen proper, the steep but short **Ute Trail** departs from Ute Ave. and weaves its way to the top of a rock ledge, a spectacular sunset-watching spot. The gentler **Hunter Trail** wanders through town and is a popular place for jogging and biking.

GLENWOOD SPRINGS
☎970

Next door to Aspen, Glenwood Springs allows budget travelers to stay near the famed slopes at refreshingly affordable prices. But Glenwood Springs is more than just Aspen's little brother. The hot springs are a popular year-round destination, and the spectacular Fairy Caves are considered one of the region's wonders.

Glenwood Hot Springs Lodge and Pool, 401 N. River Rd., is a huge resort complex containing the world's largest outdoor hot springs pool, a waterslide, and spas at various water temperatures. (☎945-6571 or 800-537-7946. Open daily 7:30am-10pm. Day pass $9.50, after 9pm $6.25; ages 3-12 $6.25/5.75.) Sweat out the stress of travel in 125°F natural steam caves, then relax in the Solarium at **Yampah Spa and Vapor Caves,** 709 E. 6th St. (☎945-0667. Open daily 9am-9pm. $8.75, Glenwood Springs Hostelers $4.75 with hostel pass/receipt.) While most skiers head to Aspen's fab four, Glenwood Spring's **Sunlight,** 10901 County Rd. 117, 10 mi. west of town, has relaxed family-style skiing. (☎945-7491 or 800-445-7931. $32 per day, ages 5-13 $21; hosteler discount.) Dubbed the eighth wonder of the world in 1896, the **Fairy Caves** were recently reopened to the public. **Glenwood Caverns,** 508 Pine St., explores the caves with both family-oriented and advanced tours. (☎945-4228 or 800-530-1635. Open mid-Apr. to Oct. 2hr. tours depart every hr. 9am-4pm. Family tours $12, ages 3-12 $7. Wild tours $50; 50% discount at Glenwood Springs Hostel.)

Within walking distance of the springs and downtown, the 📷**Glenwood Springs Hostel (HI-AYH) ❶,** 1021 Grand Ave., consists of a spacious Victorian house and a newer building next door. The hostel offers a wide variety of trips and tours in the area, and offers discounts on skiing at Aspen. Amenities include two kitchens, the owner's amazing vinyl collection, a backyard patio, and a lounge with murals covering the walls. (☎945-8545 or 800-946-7835. Linen $2. Lockout 10am-4pm. Internet access. Max. stay 4 nights. Dorms $12, 4 nights $39; private singles $19; private doubles $26.) One of the least expensive motels in town, the **Frontier Lodge ❸**, 2834 Glen Ave., provides clean, spacious rooms with cable TV, A/C, fridge, microwave, and access to a hot tub. (☎945-5496 or 888-606-0602. June-Aug. singles $50-80, doubles $50-100; Sept.-May $30-50/40-60. AAA discount.) The **Daily Bread Cafe and Bakery ❷**, 729 Grand Ave., attracts locals with fresh, wholesome breakfasts and lunches. The quiche of the day ($7) is a favorite and usually sells out by early afternoon. (☎945-6253. Open M-F 7am-2pm, Sa 8am-2pm, Su 8am-noon.) Shoot some pool as you digest at **Doc Holliday's Saloon ❷**, 724 Grand Ave., the best place for burgers ($6-8). (☎945-9050. Open daily 10am-2am; kitchen 11am-11pm.)

Amtrak, 413 7th St. (☎945-9563; open daily 9:30am-4:30pm) runs to Denver (6¾hr., $48-72) and Salt Lake City (8¼hr., $59-101). **Greyhound** (☎945-8501; open M-F 8am-4:30pm) sends buses to Denver (3½hr., 5 per day, $31-33), as well as Durango (5hr., 1 per day, $33-37) and Salt Lake City (6hr., 1 per day, $50-55) via Grand Junction (2hr., 4 per day, $14.25). The **Roaring Fork Transit Agency** or **RFTA** (☎925-8484; open M-F 9am-5pm), has several stops in Glenwood Springs and runs to Aspen (1½hr.; 14 per day; $6, ages 6-16 $5). The **White River National Forest Headquarters**, 9th and Grand Ave., has outdoor info. (☎945-2521. Open M-F 8am-5pm.) **Visitor Info: Glenwood Springs Chamber Resort Association**, 1102 Grand Ave. (☎945-6589. Open June-Aug. M-F 9am-5pm, Sa-Su 10am-3pm; Sept.-May Sa-Su 10am-5pm. Brochure area open 24hr.) **Post Office:** 113 9th St. (☎945-5611. Open M-F 8am-6pm, Sa 9am-1pm.) **ZIP code:** 81601. **Area code:** 970.

COLORADO SPRINGS ☎719

Once a resort town only frequented by the elite, Colorado Springs has grown to be the second most visited city in Colorado. When early Colorado gold seekers found bizarre red rock formations here, they named the region Garden of the Gods, partly because of a Ute legend that the rocks were petrified bodies of enemies hurled down by the gods. Here the US Olympic Team continues the quest for gold, while jets from the US Air Force Academy roar overhead.

◨ ⁊ ORIENTATION & PRACTICAL INFORMATION. Colorado Springs is laid out in a grid of broad thoroughfares. **Nevada Ave.** is the main north-south strip, just east of I-25. **Colorado Ave.** and **Pikes Peak Ave.** run east-west across the city. Numbered streets west of Nevada ascend moving westward. **I-25** from Denver cuts through downtown, separating Old Colorado City from the eastern sector of the town. East of Nevada Ave. remains largely residential. **Greyhound,** 120 S. Weber St. (☎635-1505; tickets sold M-Sa 5:15am-10pm, Su 7:15am-9pm), runs buses to Albuquerque (8hr., 4 per day, $61); Denver (1½-2hr., 7 per day, $14); and Pueblo (1hr., 6 per day, $8). **City Bus Service,** 127 E. Kiowa St. (☎385-7423), at Nevada St., serves the Garden of the Gods, Manitou Springs, and Widefield. Pick up a schedule at the Kiowa bus terminal. ($1.25, seniors and ages 5-11 60¢, under 6 free; to Ft. Carson, Widefield, Fountain, Manitou Springs, and Peterson AFB 35¢ extra.) **Pikes Peak Tours,** 3704 Colorado Ave. (☎633-1181 or 800-345-8197; open daily 8am-5pm), offers whitewater rafting trips on the Arkansas River (7hr.; $70, under 13 $45; includes lunch). **Taxis: Yellow Cab,** ☎634-5000. **Visitor Info: Visitors Bureau,** 515 S. Cascade Ave. (☎635-7506 or 800-888-4748. Open daily 8:30am-5pm.) **Post Office:** 201 E. Pikes Peak Ave., at Nevada Ave. (☎570-5336. Open M-F 7:30am-5:30pm, Sa 8am-1pm.) **ZIP code:** 80903. **Area code:** 719.

⚡ ACCOMMODATIONS. Campgrounds and lodgings along **W. Pikes Peak Ave.** and **W. Colorado Ave.** provide more favorable accommodations than the shabby motels along **Nevada Ave.** The **Apache Court Motel ❷**, 3401 W. Pikes Peak Ave., at 34th St., has pink adobe rooms with A/C, cable TV, refrigerator, and a common hot tub. (☎471-9440. Rooms $32-65.) The rooms at the **Maverick Motel ❷**, 3620 W. Colorado Ave., are an explosion of pastels, and come fully equipped with cable TV, fridge, and microwaves. (☎634-2852 or 800-214-0264. Singles $35-59; off-season $30. 2-room unit $85, call to reserve.) The dark, simple rooms at the **Amarillo Motel ❷**, 2801 W. Colorado Ave., include kitchens equipped with fridge and microwave. (☎635-8539 or 800-216-8539. TV and laundry facilities. Singles in summer $40; in winter $28. Doubles $45/30-40.)

Several **Pikes National Forest ❶** campgrounds lie in the mountains flanking Pikes Peak, about 30min. from Colorado Springs. No local transportation serves this area. Campgrounds clutter Rte. 67, 5-10 mi. north of **Woodland Park,** 18 mi. northwest of the Springs on U.S. 24. Try **Colorado, Painted Rocks,** or **South Meadows,** near Manitou Park; others border U.S. 24 near the town of Lake George, 50 mi. west of the Springs. (Generally open May-Sept. Sites $12-14.) Farther afield, visitors may camp on Lake George reservoir, at the **Eleven Mile State Recreation Area ❶**, off a spur road from U.S. 24. (☎748-3401, for reservations ☎800-678-2267. Reservations 7am-4:45pm. Pay showers and laundry. Sites $10, with electricity $14; vehicle fee $5.) Unless otherwise posted, you can camp on national forest property for free if you are at least 500 ft. from a road or stream. The **Pikes Peak Ranger District Office,** 601 S. Weber St., has maps of the area. (☎636-1602. Open M-F 8am-4:30pm.)

⚡🍴 FOOD & NIGHTLIFE. Students and the young-at-heart perch among outdoor tables in front of the cafes and restaurants lining **Tejon Ave.,** a few blocks east of downtown. **Old Colorado City** is home to a number of fine eateries. During the summer months, there are several **Farmers Markets** scattered throughout the city. **Poor Richard's Restaurant ❷**, 324½ N. Tejon Ave., is a popular local hangout with great pizza (cheese slices $3; pies $12), sandwiches ($6), and salads. (☎632-7721. Tu live folk music, W bluegrass, Th Celtic. Open in summer daily 11am-10pm; in winter 11am-9pm.) The oldest Mexican restaurant in town, **Henri's ❷**, 2427 W. Colorado Ave., has served up *chimichangas* ($6.50) and a wide variety of *cervezas* on the cheap for over 50 years. (☎634-9031. Open Tu-Th 11am-8pm, F 11am-9pm, Sa 9am-9pm, Su 9am-8pm.) **Meadow Muffins ❷**, 2432 Colorado Ave., is a virtual museum of old movie props. The two buckboard wagons hanging from the ceiling were used in the filming of *Gone With The Wind,* and the windmill-style fan installed above the bar was originally cast in *Casablanca.* (☎633-0583. Drafts $3.50. Burgers $6-7. Open daily 11am-2am.) The giant seating area at **Rum Bay,** 20 N. Tejon St., is dwarfed only by the gargantuan main bar, where a library ladder provides the only means of reaching the top two shelves. (☎634-3522. Specialty rum drinks $6-7. Th-Sa live music or DJs. Open daily 11am-2am.)

⚡ SIGHTS. Olympic hopefuls train with some of the world's most high-tech sports equipment at the **US Olympic Complex,** 750 E. Boulder St., on the corner of Union St. The complex has free 1hr. tours. (☎578-4644 or 888-659-8687. Open M-Sa 9am-5pm, Su 10am-5pm. Tours every ½-1hr.) Slightly earlier quests for gold are recorded at the **Pioneers' Museum,** 215 S. Tejon St., which recounts the settling of Colorado Springs. (☎385-5990. Open in summer Tu-Sa 10am-5pm, Su 1-5pm; in winter closed Su. Free.) More information and souvenirs can be found at the **Barry Goldwater Visitors Center.** (☎333-2025. Open mid-May to early Sept. daily 9am-6pm; early Sept. to mid-May 9am-5pm.)

⚡ OUTDOOR ACTIVITIES. Between Rte. 24 (Colorado Ave.) and 30th St. in northwest Colorado Springs, the red rock towers and spires of the **Garden of the Gods** rise strikingly against a mountainous backdrop. (Open May-Oct. daily 5am-11pm; Nov.-Apr. 5am-9pm.) **Climbers** are lured by the large red faces and over 400 permanent routes. Climbers must register at the Visitors Center; $500 fines greet those who climb without permit or proper gear. A number of exciting **mountain biking** trails cross the Garden as well. The park's hiking trails, many of which are paved wheelchair accessible routes, have great views of the rock formations and can easily be completed in one day. A map is available from the park's **Visitors Center**, 1805 N. 30th St., at Gateway Rd. (☎634-6666. Open June-Aug. daily 8am-8pm; Sept.-June 9am-5pm. Walking tours depart in summer 10, 11am, 1, and 2pm; in winter 10am and 2pm.) *Lock valuables in your trunk; thefts are common.*

From any part of town, one can't help but notice the 14,110 ft. summit of **Pikes Peak** on the horizon. Ambitious climbers can ascend the peak along the strenuous, well-maintained **Barr Trail** (26 mi. round-trip). The trailhead is in Manitou Springs by the "Manitou Incline" sign on Ruxton Ave. Don't despair if you don't reach the top—explorer Zebulon Pike never reached it, either. Nowadays you can pay to drive up the gorgeous 19 mi. **Pikes Peak Hwy.**, a well-maintained dirt road. (☎385-7325 or 800-318-9505. Open mid-Sept. to Apr. daily 9am-3pm; May to mid-Sept., weather permitting, 7am-7pm. $35 per car; $10 per person.) Five miles west in Manitou Springs, visitors can hop on the **Pikes Peak Cog Railway**, 515 Ruxton Ave., operating since 1891, which takes visitors to the summit every 80min. From the summit, the Sangre de Cristo Mountains, the Continental Divide, and the state of Kansas unfold in a lofty view that inspired Kathy Lee Bates to write "America the Beautiful." (☎685-5401. Open late Apr. to early Nov. daily; call for hours. Round-trip $25.50, children $13.50. Reservations recommended.)

For adventurous hiking through subterranean passages, head to the contorted caverns of the **Cave of the Winds,** on Rte. 24, 6 mi. west of Exit 141 off I-25. The lantern tour goes into the raw area of the cave. (☎685-5444. Guided tours late May-Aug. daily every 15min. 9am-9pm; Sept. to late May 10am-5pm. $15, ages 6-15 $8. Adventure tour $18/9. Laser light show in summer daily 9pm; $6/3.) Just above Manitou Springs on Rte. 24, the **Cliff Dwellings Museum** contains replicas of ancestral Puebloan dwellings dating from AD 1100-1300. (☎685-5242 or 800-354-9971. Open June-Aug. daily 9am-8pm; Sept.-May 10am-5pm. $8, seniors $7, ages 7-11 $6.) The **Seven Falls**, 10min. west of downtown on Cheyenne Blvd., are lit up on summer nights. (☎632-0765. Before 5pm $7, ages 6-15 $4.50; after 5pm $8.50/5.50.)

SAN JUAN MOUNTAINS

Ask Coloradans about their favorite mountain retreats, and they'll most likely name a peak, lake, stream, or town in the San Juan Range of southwestern Colorado. Four **national forests**—the **Uncompahgre** (un-cum-PAH-gray), the **Gunnison,** the **San Juan,** and the **Río Grande**—encircle this sprawling range. **Durango** is an ideal base camp for forays into these mountains. Northeast of Durango, the **Weminuche Wilderness** tempts the hardy backpacker with a vast expanse of rugged terrain where wide, sweeping vistas stretch for miles. Get maps and hiking info from the **USFS headquarters** at 15 Burnett Ct., Durango. (☎247-4874. Open Apr. to mid-Dec. daily 8am-5pm; mid-Dec. to Mar. 8am-4:30pm.)

The San Juan Mountains are easily accessible via U.S. 50, which is traveled by hundreds of thousands of tourists each summer. **Greyhound** serves the area, but very poorly; traveling by car is the best option in this region. On a happier note, the San Juans are loaded with HI-AYH hostels and campgrounds, making them one of the most economical places to visit in Colorado.

BLACK CANYON OF THE GUNNISON NATIONAL PARK ☎970

Native American parents used to tell their children that the light-colored strands of rock streaking through the walls of the Black Canyon were the hair of a blond woman—and that if they got too close to the edge they would get tangled in it and fall. The edge of **Black Canyon of the Gunnison National Park** is a staggering place, literally—watch for those trembling knees. The Gunnison River slowly gouged out the 53-mile long canyon, crafting a steep 2500-foot gorge that is, in some places, deeper than it is wide. The Empire State Building, if placed at the bottom of the river, would reach barely halfway up the canyon walls.

The Black Canyon lies 15 mi. east of the town of **Montrose**. The **South Rim** is easily accessible via a 6 mi. drive off U.S. 50 ($7 per car, $4 walk-in or motorcycle); the wilder **North Rim** can only be reached by an 80 mi. detour around the canyon followed by a gravel road from Crawford off Rte. 92. The road is closed in winter. The spectacular 8 mi. South Rim Drive traces the edge of the canyon, and boasts jaw-dropping vistas including the spectacular **Chasm View,** where you can peer 2300 ft. down the highest cliff in Colorado at the Gunnison River and the "painted" wall. *Don't throw stones;* you might kill a defenseless hiker in the canyon below. On the South Rim, the moderate 2 mi. round-trip **Oak Flat Loop Trail** and the North Rim's 7 mi. round-trip **North Vista Trail** both give a good sense of the terrain below. From the South Rim, you can scramble down the **Gunnison Route,** which drops 1800 ft. over a 1 mi. span. Or, tackle the much more difficult **Tomichi** or **Warner Routes,** which can make good overnight hikes. Not surprisingly, the sheer walls of the Black Canyon make for a climbing paradise; register at the South Rim Visitors Center. Between the **Painted Wall** and **Cedar Point Overlooks,** a well-worn path leads to **Marmot Rocks,** which offer great bouldering for those not ready for the big walls.

At the canyon, the **South Rim Campground ❶** has 102 well-designed sites with pit toilets, charcoal grills, water, and some with paved wheelchair access ($10). The **North Rim Campground ❶** offers more space, rarely fills, and is popular with climbers (water and toilets; $10). Many inexpensive motels line Main St./U.S. 50 in downtown Montrose, including the **Western Motel ❷,** 1200 E. Main St. (☎249-3481 or 800-445-7301. Singles in summer from $45, in winter from $35.), and the **Traveler's B&B Inn ❷,** 502 S. 1st St. (☎249-3472. Singles $32, with private bath $34-36; doubles $42.) **Nav-Mex Tacos ❶,** 475 W. Main St., serves up the best Mexican cuisine around. (Open M-F 11am-9pm, Sa-Su 9am-9pm. Tacos $1.25; tostadas $3.) For tasty sandwiches ($4.50) and omelettes ($5.50), head for the **Daily Bread Bakery and Cafe ❶,** 346 Main St. (☎249-8444. Open M-Sa 6am-3pm.)

Greyhound (☎249-6673) shuttles once a day between Montrose and the **Gunnison County Airport,** 711 Río Grande (☎641-0060), and will drop you off on U.S. 50, 6 mi. from the canyon ($12). **Gisdho Shuttles** conducts tours of the Black Canyon and Grand Mesa from Grand Junction. (☎800-430-4555. 10-11hr. May-Oct. W and Sa. $39.) A **Visitors Center** sits on the South Rim. (☎249-1914, ext. 23. Open May-Oct. daily 8am-6pm; Nov.-Apr. 8:30am-4pm.) **Post Office:** 321 S. 1st St. (☎249-6654. Open M-F 8am-5pm, Sa 10am-noon.) **ZIP code:** 81401. **Area code:** 970.

CRESTED BUTTE ☎970

Crested Butte, 27 miles north of Gunnison on Rte. 135, was first settled by miners in the 1870s. The coal was exhausted in the 1950s, but a few years later the steep powder fields on the Butte began attracting skiers. Thanks to strict zoning rules, the historic downtown district is a throwback to those early mining days. Three miles north of town, **Crested Butte Mt. Resort,** 12 Snowmass Rd., takes skiers to "the extreme limits" and offers over 800 acres of bowl skiing. Many of the other 85 runs are less spine-tingling, but the panoramic views are equally inspiring. (☎800-544-8448. Open mid-Dec. to mid-Apr. Prices vary. Day passes around $50; ages 65-69 half-price; over 70 free; children 5-16 pay the numerical value of their age.)

ROCKY MOUNTAINS

Come summertime, Crested Butte becomes the mountain biking capital of Colorado. During the last week of June, the town hosts the **Fat Tire Bike Festival,** four days of mountain biking, racing, and fraternizing. In 1976, a group of cyclists rode from Crested Butte to Aspen, starting the oldest mountain biking event in the world. Every September, experienced bikers repeat the trek over the 12,705 ft. pass to Aspen and back during the **Pearl Pass Tour,** organized by the **Mountain Biking Hall of Fame,** 200 Sopris St. (☎349-1880). Biking trail maps are available at bike shops and **The Alpineer,** 419 6th St. (☎349-5210. Open June to mid-Sept. and Dec. to mid-Apr. 9am-6pm; otherwise 10am-5pm.) Trails begin at the base of Mt. Crested Butte and extend into the exquisite Gothic area. **Trail 401** is a demanding and famous 24 mi. round-trip loop with an excellent view.

Finding budget accommodations in the winter is about as easy as striking a vein of gold, but there are a few possibilities. ◙**Crested Butte International Hostel and Lodge ❶,** 615 Teocalli Ave. (☎349-0588 or 888-389-0588; hostel@crested-butte.net), two blocks north of the four-way stop, treats travellers to a tidy stay in gorgeous modern facilities. Its huge kitchen and bright common area make it an ideal base for exploring the area. (No curfew or lockout. Showers for non-guests $5. Coin-op laundry. Rates rise during ski season. Group discounts. Roomy 4-6 bed dorms $22, $20 for multiple-night guests; doubles $55-65. Spacious 3rd-fl. apartment sleeps up to 6; $115-160.) **Gunnison National Forest Office,** 216 N. Colorado, 30 mi. south in Gunnison, has info on area **campgrounds.** (☎641-0471. Open M-F 7:30am-4:30pm.)

Pitas in Paradise ❶, 214 Elk Ave., a self-proclaimed "Mediterranean Cafe with Soul," wows diners with its delicious $5 gyros, $3.75 salads, and $3 smoothies. Watch your meal being made at the counter or sit down to wait for it in the backyard. (☎349-0897. Open daily 7-11am and 11am-10pm.) **The Secret Stash ❺,** 21 Elk Ave., all the way at the west end of town, operates one of the highest coffee roasters in the world. With a menu ranging from eclectic pizzas ($8-17) to salads and wraps ($3.50-8) to grilled wings (10 for $7), this hip joint aims to please, and succeeds. Sip a soy latte in the side garden or on the vast second floor, where one might mistake the cushy couches, mood lighting, wall tapestries, and acoustic guitar for a hippie's living room. Happy hour runs 4:20-6:20pm, featuring $1.50 beers and slices and $4 forties. (☎349-6245. Open M-Sa 11am-11pm.) The **Crested Butte Chamber of Commerce:** 601 Elk Ave. (☎800-215-2226. Open daily 9am-5pm.) A free **shuttle** to the mountain leaves from the chamber. (☎349-5616. Every 40min. 7:20am-10:20am and 8pm-midnight, every 20min. 10:20am-8pm.) **Post Office:** 215 Elk Ave. (☎349-5568. Open M-F 7:30am-4:30pm, Sa 10am-1pm). **ZIP code:** 81224. **Area code:** 970.

TELLURIDE   ☎970

Site of the first bank Butch Cassidy ever robbed (the San Miguel), Telluride was very much a town of the Old West. Locals believe that their city's name derives from a contraction of "to hell you ride," a likely warning given to travelers to the once hell-bent city. Things have quieted down a bit in the last few years; outlaw celebrities have been replaced with film celebrities, and six-shooter guns with cinnamon buns. Skiers, hikers, and vacationers come to Telluride to pump gold and silver *into* the mountains, and the town also claims the most festivals per capita of any ZIP code in the US. During the summer and fall, Telluride is inundated every few weeks, a schedule that allows just enough time for the community to catch its breath before the next onslaught. Still, a small-town feeling prevails—rocking chairs sit outside brightly painted houses, and dogs lounge on storefront porches.

🏵 PRACTICAL INFORMATION. Telluride sits on a short spur of Rte. 145, 127 mi. southeast of Grand Junction. The public **bus** line, **Galloping Geese**, runs the length of town on a regular basis. (☎728-5700. May-Nov. every 20min. 7:30am-6pm; Dec.-Apr. every 10min. 7am-midnight. Town loop free, outlying towns $1-2.) A **gondola** runs from downtown to Mountain Village. (☎728-8888. Runs 7am-midnight. Free.) **Taxi** service from **Mountain Limo** serves the western slope. (☎728-9606 or 888-546-6894. Airport fare $8.) The **Visitors Center** is upstairs from **Rose's Grocery Store**, 666 W. Colorado Ave., near the entrance to town. (☎728-4431 or 888-288-7360. Open in summer M-Sa 9am-7pm, Su noon-5pm.) Other services include: **Police,** ☎728-3818; **Rape Crisis Hotline,** ☎728-5660. **Telluride Medical Center,** 500 W. Pacific (☎728-3848); and free **Internet access** at the **Wilkinson Public Library,** 100 W. Pacific St. (☎728-4519; open M-Th 10am-8pm, F-Sa 10am-6pm, Su noon-5pm). **Post Office:** 150 S. Willow St. (☎728-3900. Open M-F 9am-5pm, Sa 10am-noon.) **ZIP code:** 81435. **Area code:** 970.

🛏 ACCOMMODATIONS. If you're visiting Telluride during a festival, bring a sleeping bag; the cost of a bed is outrageous. The **Oak Street Inn ❷,** 134 N. Oak St., offers cozy rooms. (☎728-3383. Singles $42, with private bath $66; doubles $58/$66; rooms around $20 more during festivals.) William Jennings Bryan delivered his "Cross of Gold" speech from the front balcony of the **New Sheridan Hotel ❹,** 231 W. Colorado Ave., and if you can afford it, the luxurious rooms make it worth your while. (☎728-4351 or 800-200-1891. Rooms with shared bath from $90.) The 🖾**Telluride Town Park Campground ❶,** east of downtown, offers particularly nice sites along the San Miguel River. (☎728-2173. Water, full bathrooms. 7-night max. stay. Mid-May to mid-Oct. $12 per vehicle; primitive sites $10.) During festival times, you can crash anywhere; hot showers ($2) are available at the high school.

🍴 FOOD. 🖾**Baked in Telluride ❷,** 127 S. Fir St., has enough rich coffee, delicious pastries, pizza, sandwiches, and 60¢ bagels to get you through a festival weekend. The apple fritters ($2) are rightly famous, and the enormous calzones ($5-7) might be the best deal in town. (☎728-4775. Open daily 5:30am-10pm.) The subterranean locale at **Deli Downstairs ❶,** 217 W. Colorado St., feels more like a food stand at a Grateful Dead show than a sedentary establishment, and the sandwiches ($3-8) will keep you boogying for hours. (Open daily 10am-midnight. Cash only.) The wooden benches and long tables at **Fat Alley Barbeque ❸,** 122 S. Oak St., are reminiscent of the sawdust saloons of yore, but Telluride's miners never ate barbecue ($5-17) like this. (Open daily 11am-10pm.)

📷🎭 FESTIVALS & NIGHTLIFE. Given that only 1900 people live in Telluride, the sheer number of festivals in the town seems staggering. For general festival info, contact the **Telluride Visitors Center** (☎728-4431 or 888-288-7360). Gala events occur throughout the summer and fall, from the quirky **Mushroom Festival** (late Aug.), to the multi-sport challenge of the **360° Adventure** (mid-July) and the renowned **Bluegrass Festival.** (☎800-624-2422; www.planetbluegrass.com. 3rd weekend in June. $55 per day, 4-day pass $155.) One weekend in July is actually designated "Nothing Festival" to give locals a break from the onslaught of visitors and special events. The **Telluride International Film Festival** premiers some of the hippest independent flicks; *The Crying Game* and *The Piano* were both unveiled here. (☎728-4401. 1st weekend in Sept.) Telluride also hosts a **Jazz Celebration** during the first weekend of August (☎728-7009) and a **Blues & Brews Festival** (☎728-8037) during the third weekend in September. For some festivals, volunteering to usher or perform other tasks can result in free admission. Throughout the year a number of concerts and performances go up at the **Sheridan Opera House,** 110 N. Oak St. (☎728-6363).

Telluride may have a new-age air by day, but its bars still rollick with old-fashioned fun by night. Telluride's freshest musical talent jives at **Fly Me to the Moon Saloon**, 132 E. Colorado Ave., which thrills groovers with its spring-loaded dance floor. Jam bands like Leftover Salmon and The String Cheese Incident have played many a free show here. (☎728-6666. $1-5 cover. Open daily 9pm-2:30am. Cash only.) The lively **Last Dollar Saloon**, 100 E. Colorado Ave., is a favorite among locals, who affectionately refer to it as "the buck." With the juke box blaring and darts flying, it's not hard to see why. (☎728-4800. Open daily 11:30am-2am. Beer $2.75-3.75. Cash only.) The **New Sheridan Bar**, 231 W. Colorado Ave., (☎728-3911; open daily 3pm-2am), and the **Roma Bar & Cafe**, 133 E. Colorado Ave. (☎728-3669; open daily 11:30am-3pm and 5pm-2am; dinner until 10pm), are great for ending the evening.

▟ OUTDOOR ACTIVITIES. Biking, hiking, and backpacking opportunities are endless; ghost towns and lakes are tucked behind almost every mountain crag. The tourist office has a list of suggestions for hikes in the area. The most popular trek (about 2hr.) is up the jeep road to **Bridal Veil Falls**, the waterfall visible from almost anywhere in Telluride. The trailhead is at the end of Rte. 145. Continuing another 2.5 mi. from the top of the falls will lead to **Silver Lake**, a steep but rewarding and serene climb. For more Rocky Mountain highs, ride the free gondola to the top of the mountain. A number of hiking and biking trails run from the St. Sophia station.

In winter, even avowed atheists can be spied praying before hitting the "Spiral Stairs" and the "Plunge," two of the Rockies' most gut-wrenching ski runs. For more info, contact the **Telluride Ski Resort**, P.O. Box 11155, Telluride 81435. (☎728-3856. Regular season lift tickets: full-day $65, half-day $58; children $36/$28.) A free year-round gondola connects the mountain village with the rest of the town and runs from 7am-11pm. **Paragon Ski and Sport**, 213 W. Colorado Ave., rents bikes in summer and skis in winter. (☎728-4525. Open daily 9am-8pm; in ski season 8:30am-9pm. Bikes from $16 per half-day/$28 per day; skis and boots $20 per day.)

SCENIC DRIVE: SAN JUAN SKYWAY

More a runway to the mountains and clouds than a terrestrial highway, the San Juan Skyway soars across the rooftop of the Rockies. Winding its way through San Juan and Uncompahgre National Forests, Old West mountain towns, and Native American ruins, the byway passes a remarkably wide range of southwestern Colorado's splendors. Reaching altitudes up to 11,000 feet, with breathtaking views of snowy peaks and verdant valleys, the San Juan Skyway is widely considered one of America's most beautiful drives. Travelers in this area inevitably drive at least parts of it as they head to destinations like Telluride, Durango, and Mesa Verde. Call the San Juan (☎970-247-4874) or Uncompahgre (☎970-874-6600) National Forests to check road conditions or to inquire about driving the skyway. A loop road, piggy-backing on Rte. 550, 62, 145, and 160, the skyway voyage can be started from anywhere along the loop, at towns like Durango, Ridgeway, or Cortez. Beginning in Durango, the skyway heads north along Rte. **550 N (Million Dollar Highway)**, climbing into the San Juan Mountains, and paralleling the Animas River.

Twenty-seven miles north of Durango, the road passes **Durango Mountain Resort** as it ascends. At Mile 64 on Rte. 550, the road peaks at Molas Point, a whopping 10,910 ft. above sea level. (☎800-979-9742. Annual snowfall 260 in. Open late Nov.-early Apr. 9am-4pm. $34-48, under 12 $17-29.). **Molas Lake** (☎970-749-9254 or 800-846-2172) offers visitors an oasis with tent and RV sites ($14), cabins ($25), canoe rentals ($5 per hr.), horseback riding ($20 per hr.), and picnic tables. Descending to a mere 9000 ft., the skyway arrives in the easy-going Silverton. A mining town until the early 90s, **Silverton** is a subdued mountain village that boasts some of Colorado's best ice climbing. The **Visitors Center** sits close to the entrance to town on Rte. 550. (☎387-5654 or 800-752-4494; www.silverton.org. Open June-Sept. daily 9am-6pm; Oct.-May 10am-4pm.) Hiking, mountain biking, and skiing at Kendall Mountain ($6 lift tickets) await those who can still catch their breath.

From Silverton, the San Juan Skyway climbs higher until it reaches 11,018 ft. at Mile 80 on Rte. 550. Known as **Red Mountain Pass,** this scenic point has some hiking and more than a few Kodak moments. Continuing north, the drive from Silverton to Ouray showcases stellar 14,000 ft. mountain peaks and defunct mines. In 1991, the Reclamation Act shut down most of the mines, leaving only remnants of the past. The skyway next arrives in **Ouray,** a yodeler's delight. With fabulous mountain views and hedonistic hot springs, this heavily Swiss-influenced town is a relaxing stop for the weary. Beyond Ouray, the skyway returns to Earth. Traversing mesas, Rte. 550 junctions with Rte. 62 in Ridgeway. Rte. 62 assumes the reigns of the skyway and leads travelers to Placerville, where the skyway connects with Rte. 145.

Telluride next awaits travelers along Rte. 145. Past the Mountain Village, the dubiously named **Lizard's Pass** offers a tranquil 6 mi. hike reaching over 12,000 ft. From the pass, the skyway glides down along the Taylor Mesa through the quiet towns of Rico, Stoner, and Dolores. Rte. 145 connects with Rte. 160 just east of Cortez and west of **Mesa Verde National Park.** Moving east along Rte. 160, the skyway cuts through **Mancos** and finally returns to Durango.

DURANGO
☎970

In its heyday, Durango was one of the main railroad junctions in the Southwest. Walking down the town's main thoroughfare today, it is easy to see that Durango remains a crossroads. Dreadlocked, hemp-clad youths share the sidewalks with weathered ranchers in ten-gallon hats and stiff Wranglers, and toned, brazen mountain bikers rub shoulders in the bars with camera-toting tourists. These folks are brought together by their experiences in the great expanses of wilderness that engulf the town: enjoying the flora, roping dogies at the rodeo, biking the San Juans, or riding the narrow gauge railroad.

◨ PRACTICAL INFORMATION. Durango is at the intersection of U.S. 160 and U.S. 550. Streets run perpendicular to avenues, but everyone calls Main Ave. "Main St." **Greyhound,** 275 E. 8th Ave. (☎259-2755; open M-F 7:30am-noon and 3:30-5pm, Sa 7:30am-noon, Su and holidays 7:30-10am), runs once per day to: Grand Junction (5hr., $35-37); Denver (11½hr., $60-64); and Albuquerque (5hr., $42-45). The **Durango Lift** provides trolley service up and down Main Ave. every 20min. (☎259-5438. Runs Memorial Day-Labor Day daily 6am-10pm. 50¢.) **Taxi: Durango Transportation,** ☎259-4818. The **Durango Area Chamber Resort Association,** 111 S. Camino del Río, on the southeast side of town, offers info on sights and hiking. (☎247-0312 or 800-525-8855. Open M-Sa 8am-5:30pm, Su 10am-4pm.) **Road Conditions:** ☎264-5555. **Police:** 990 E. 2nd Ave. (☎385-2900). **Internet access:** free at **Durango Public Library,** 1188 E. 2nd Ave. (☎385-2970. Open M-W 9am-9pm, Th-Su 9am-5:30pm). **Post Office:** 222 W. 8th St. (☎247-3434. Open M-F 8am-5:30pm, Sa 9am-1pm). **ZIP code:** 81301. **Area code:** 970.

▮❒ ACCOMMODATIONS & FOOD. The **Durango Hostel ❶,** 543 E. 2nd Ave., one block from downtown, maintains clean, simple bunks in a large converted house. Located near the heart of downtown, this hostel serves as a focal point for Durango's young backpacking crowd. While the men's dorm room is barracks-style, the women enjoy more comfortable accommodations. (☎247-9905. Check-in 7-10am and 5-10pm. No lockout. Check-out 10am. Dorms $20.) Located right by the lift to downtown, the **Alpine Motel ❷,** 3515 Main Ave., is one of the best places to stay in Durango for a reasonable price. (☎247-0402 or 800-818-4042. Reception

8am-10pm. June-Aug. singles $42-68; doubles $58-84. Sept.-May $28-32/38-42.) Find great camping at **Junction Creek Campground ❶**, on Forest Rd. 171. From Main Ave., turn west on 25th St., which becomes Forest Rd. 171 after 4 mi.; the turn-off is 1 mi. past the national forest entrance. (14-night max. stay. $12 per vehicle, each additional person $6.)

Back in Durango, "dill-icious" pickles and subs abound at **Johnny McGuire's Deli ❶**, 552 Main Ave., where you can choose between more than 25 sandwiches ($5) with names like the Free Iron Willy and the 4:20 Vegan. (☎259-8816. Open M-Sa 7am-7:30pm, Su 7am-6pm. Cash only.) Locals eat at **Carver's Bakery and Brewpub ❷**, 1022 Main Ave., where breakfast specials ($2-7) and pitchers of home-brewed beer ($8) are favorites. (☎259-2545. Open M-F 6:30am-10pm, Su 6:30am-1pm.) The best vegetarian place in town, **Skinny's Grill ❸**, 1017 Main Ave., offers great food in a low key atmosphere. (☎382-2500. Open Su-Th 11:30am-9pm, F-Sa 11:30am-10pm.) The ski-lodge atmosphere and frequent live music at **The Summit**, 600 Main Ave., near the train station, attracts the college crowd for good rowdy fun. (☎247-2324. Open daily 4pm-2am.)

◎ ▣ SIGHTS & ENTERTAINMENT. More of a tourist attraction than a means of transportation, the **Durango and Silverton Narrow Gauge Train,** 479 Main St., runs up the Animas River Valley to the historic mining town of Silverton. Old-fashioned, 100% coal-fed locomotives wheeze through the San Juans, making a 2hr. stop in Silverton before returning to Durango. It may be cheaper and more comfortable to drive the route yourself, but you'll miss out on a piece of living history that has been in continuous operation since 1881. The train also offers excellent access to the Weminuche Wilderness, dropping off and picking up backpackers at various scenic points; call for more info on this service and on monthly special events. (☎247-2733; www.durangotrain.com. Office open June to mid-Aug. daily 6am-8pm; mid-Aug. to Oct. 7am-7pm; Nov.-Apr. 8am-5pm; May 7am-7pm. Morning trains from Durango and afternoon trains from Silverton; 9hr. including stop, layover day optional. Mid-June to mid-Aug. $60; Sept.-early Oct. $55; ages 5-11 $30/27.50.)

The **Durango Pro Rodeo Series,** at the LaPlata County Fairgrounds at 25th St. and Main Ave., moseys into town every summer. Saddling up on Tuesday and Wednesday nights, the action starts at 7:30pm with a barbecue at 6pm. (☎247-2790. Mid-June to Aug. $12, under 12 $6.) On U.S. 550 at the northern edge of town, **Trimble Hot Springs** allow visitors to soak in two hot pools and one regular one with a great view of Missionary Ridge (of 2002 fire fame) for $8.

◩ OUTDOOR ACTIVITIES. Unlike most Colorado towns that thrive on tourism, Durango's busiest season is summer, though winter is no stranger to strangers. **Durango Mountain Resort,** 27 mi. north on U.S. 550, hosts skiers of all levels (see p. 764). Bikes are available at **Hassle Free Sports,** 2615 Main St. (☎259-3874 or 800-835-3800. Open summer M-Sa 9:30am-6pm, Su 9am-5pm; winter daily 7:30am-7pm; spring and fall M-Sa 8:30am-6pm. Half-day $16, full-day $25. Full suspension $24/35. Ski rental packages $16-27 per day.) **Southwest Adventures,** 1205 Camino del Río, offers mountain bikes, climbing gear, and backpacking gear. (☎259-0370. Open daily 8am-6pm.) The entire Durango area is engulfed by the **San Juan National Forest.** Call the Forest Headquarters for info on hiking and camping in the forest, especially if you're planning a trip into the massive **Weminuche Wilderness,** northeast of Durango. (☎247-4874. Open Apr. to mid Dec. daily 8am-5pm; mid-Dec. to Mar. 8am-4:30pm.) The **Animas River** offers everything from placid Class II rapids to intense Class V battles. The largest area outfitter is **Mild to Wild Rafting,** 701 Main Ave. (☎247-4789 or 800-567-6745. Open daily 8am-8pm. Half-day mild trips $41, full-day mild trips $65; children $32/55. Full-day intense trips $105. Reservations recommended.)

PAGOSA SPRINGS ☎970

The Ute people—the first to discover the waters of Pagosa—believed that the springs were a gift of the Great Spirit, and the Chamber of Commerce would be hard-pressed not to think so too. Pagosa Springs, some of the hottest and largest in the world, bubble from the San Juan Mountains 60 mi. east of Durango on Rte. 160, and draw visitors from around the globe. Follow the sulfur smell to **The Springs,** 157 Hot Springs Blvd., right beside the Chamber of Commerce, where 15 different outdoor pools ranging from 89° to 114°F are available "to relax the body and refresh the spirit." (☎264-2284 or 800-225-0934. Open daily 7am-1am. $12 per person.) **Chimney Rock Archaeological Area,** 17 mi. west of Pagosa Springs on U.S. 160 and Rte. 151 S, is a national Historical Site containing the ruins of a high-mesa Ancestral Puebloan village, where over 200 undisturbed structures have been found in a 6 sq. mi. area. (☎883-5359; www.chimneyrockco.org. Open daily mid-May to late Sept. 9am-4pm. 2½hr. tours leave at 9:30, 10:30am, 1, and 2pm. $5, ages 5-11 $2.) **Wolf Creek Ski Area,** 20 mi. east of Pagosa, claims to have the most snow in Colorado, and offers access to glades and bowls. Six lifts service over 1500 acres and 1600 ft. of vertical drop. (☎264-5639 or 800-754-9653; www.wolfcreekski.com. Adult full day lift ticket $42, rental $13.)

The **Mountain Express** bus line provides transportation in and around town. (☎264-2250. M-F about every 1½hr. 6:30am-7:50pm. 50¢.) The **Pagosa Springs Chamber of Commerce,** 402 San Juan St., offers info on accommodations, food, and sights. (☎264-2360 or 800-252-2204; www.pagosaspringschamber.com. Open M-F 8am-6pm, Sa-Su 9am-5pm May-Oct.; Nov.-Apr. Sa-Su 10am-2pm.) **Pinewood Inn ❸,** 157 Pagosa St., four blocks from downtown, rents 25 wood-paneled rooms with cable TV and phones, several with kitchens. (☎264-5715 or 888-655-7463. Reception 7:30am-11pm. Check-in 2pm. Check-out 11am. Singles $35-48; doubles $55-80.) **East Fork Campground ❶,** on East Fork Rd., is a quiet little spot 11 mi. east of Pagosa Springs offering many shaded, rarely crowded sites with toilets and water faucets. (☎264-2268. 14-night max. stay. $8 per vehicle. Open May-Sept.) **Daylight Donuts & Cafe ❶,** 2151 W. Rte. 160, dishes out big portions of classic breakfast and lunch fare for just $3-5.50. (☎731-4050. Open daily 6am-2pm.) **Harmony Works ❶,** 145 Hot Springs Blvd., sells organic food and serves some interesting vegetarian and vegan options ($1-5) for breakfast, lunch and dinner. (☎264-6633. Open May-Sept. M-Th 8am-9pm, F-Sa 8am-10pm, Su 8am-8pm; Oct.-Apr. M-Th 8am-8pm, F-Sa 8am-9pm, Su 8am-7pm.) **Area code:** 970.

MESA VERDE ☎970

Mesa Verde ("Green Table" in Spanish) rises from the deserts of southwestern Colorado, the southern-tilting slopes of its top noticeably friendlier to vegetation than the dry lands below. The landscape is not, however, the main attraction—some of the most elaborate Pueblo dwellings found today draw the largest crowds. Fourteen hundred years ago, Native American tribes began to cultivate the valleys of the area, and in the centuries that followed the Ancestral Puebloans constructed a series of cliff dwellings beneath the overhanging sandstone shelves surrounding the mesa. Around AD 1275, the Pueblo people abruptly left behind their eerie and starkly beautiful dwellings. Established in 1906, Mesa Verde National Park is the only national park set aside exclusively for archaeological remains. Mesa Verde is not for the snap-a-shot-and-go tourist; the best sites require a bit of a physical effort to reach and are too extraordinary to let the camera do all the marveling.

FOUR CORNERS   New Mexico, Arizona, Utah, and Colorado meet at an unnaturally neat intersection about 40 mi. northwest of **Shiprock, NM**, on the Navajo Reservation. **Four Corners** epitomizes American ideas about land; these state borders were drawn along scientifically determined lines of longitude and latitude, disregarding natural boundaries. There's little to see; nonetheless, a large number of people veer off the highway to marvel at the geographic anomaly. At the very least, getting down on all fours to put a limb in each state is a good story for a cocktail party. *(Open in summer daily 7am-8pm; in winter 8am-5pm. $2.)*

PRACTICAL INFORMATION. The park's sole entrance is off U.S. 160, 36 mi. from **Durango** and 8 mi. from **Mancos**. The entrance fee is $10 for vehicles, $5 for pedestrians and bikers. The **Far View Visitors Center** is 15 mi. from the entrance on the main road. (☎529-5036. Open mid-Apr. to mid-Oct. daily 8am-5pm.) When it is closed, head to the museum (see **Sights**, below) or the **Colorado Welcome Center/ Cortez Chamber of Commerce**, 928 E. Main St., in Cortez. (☎565-3414. Open daily 8am-6pm late May-early Sept.; mid-Sept. to mid-May 8am-5pm.) Sights here are up to 40 mi. apart; a car is essential. **Area code:** 970.

ACCOMMODATIONS. Lodging in the park is pricey. Rooms at Mesa Verde's only motel-style accommodation, the **Far View Lodge ❺**, are costly and not particularly interesting. (☎592-4422 or 800-449-2288. June-Aug. $100+, Apr.-May and Sept.-Oct. $80.) The **Ute Mountain Motel ❶**, 531 S. Broadway (☎565-8507. Reception 8am-11pm. Check-out 11am. Singles $26-32; doubles $30-42.), or the **Sand Canyon Inn ❷**, 301 W. Main St. (☎565-8562. Reception open 24hr. Check-out 11am. Singles $36-51; doubles $44-65.), both in Cortez, are other options. Mesa Verde's **Morfield Campground** is expensive but beautiful, and its 452 sites never fills up. (☎564-1675 or 800-449-2288. Reception 7am-9pm. Check-out 11am. Open Apr. to mid-Oct. Tent sites $20, RVs $26.)

SIGHTS. A good starting point, the **Far View Visitors Center** is a long 15 mi. drive from the entrance gate along Rte. 160. At the Visitors Center, the park divides into **Chapin Mesa**, featuring the largest number of cliff dwellings, and the smaller and quieter **Wetherill Mesa**. The **Chapin Mesa Archaeological Museum**, along the first loop of the Chapin branch (before the dwellings), can give you an overview of the Ancestral Puebloan lifestyle and is a good place to start before exploring the mesa. (☎529-4631. Open daily 8am-6:30pm; Oct.-May 8am-5pm. Rangers lead **tours** of the cliff dwellings at Cliff Palace and Balcony House, each lasting about 1hr., departing every 30min. $2.25 tickets must be purchased at Visitors Center.) Tours of the spectacular **Cliff Palace** (Apr.-Oct. daily 9am-6:30pm) explore the largest cliff dwelling in North America, with over 200 preserved rooms. The impressive **Balcony House** is a 40-room dwelling 600 ft. above the floor of Soda Canyon; entrance requires climbing several ladders and squeezing through a tunnel. (Open mid-May to mid-Oct. daily 9am-5:30pm. Tickets required.) A few self-guided tours of sites are accessible from Chapin Mesa. **Spruce Tree House** is Mesa Verde's third-largest cliff dwelling and features a reconstructed *kiva* that you can explore. This is the only dwelling open in winter, when it is part of a tour leaving from the museum. (Trail 0.5 mi. Open daily 9am-6:30pm.) About ½ mi. north of the museum, the **Cedar Tree Tower** and **Farming Terraces Trail** give a sense of what work was like on the mesa top. (0.5 mi. Open daily 8am-sunset.) Three miles farther down the road and 2 mi. from the Visitors Center, the **Far View Sites** are comprised of five mesa-top villages. (Trail 0.8 mi. Open daily 8am-sunset.) A more low-key approach to the Chapin Mesa is the self-guided **Mesa Top Loop Rd.**, passing ruins from the 6th through the 13th century. (6 mi. Open daily 8am-sunset.)

THE SOUTHWEST

The Ancestral Puebloans (formerly Anasazi) of the 10th and 11th centuries were the first to discover that the Southwest's arid lands could support an advanced agrarian civilization. Years later, in 1803, the US claimed parts of the Southwest with the Louisiana Purchase. The idealistic hope for a Western "empire of liberty," where Americans could live the virtuous farm life, both motivated further expansion and inspired the region's individualist psychology.

Today, Southwestern desert's vastness—from the dramatically colored canvas of Arizona's red rock, sandstone, scrub brush, and pale sky, to the breathtaking vistas from Utah's mountains—invites contemplation, awe, and photo-ops. The area's rich potential for mild and extreme outdoor adventures (whether hiking in Canyonlands, biking around Moab, rafting on the Colorado, backpacking in the remote Gila Wilderness, or skiing the slopes of northern Utah) is as unparalleled as its intriguingly kaleidoscopic mix of cultures. True to the land's eccentric spirit, hippies, cowboys, New Age spiritualists, Native Americans, Mexican-Americans, government scientists, conservatives, liberal outdoor junkies, and droves of tourists seeking real American desert have all called the Southwest home.

HIGHLIGHTS OF THE SOUTHWEST

MEXICAN FOOD. You can't get away from it, and in the satisfying eateries of New Mexico's Albuquerque (p. 839) and Santa Fe (p. 831), you may not want to.

NATIONAL PARKS. Utah's "Fab Five" (p. 787) and Arizona's Grand Canyon (p. 795) reveal a stunning landscape of bizarre rock formations and brilliant colors.

SKIING. In a region famous for its blistering sun, the Wasatch Mountains (p. 782) near Salt Lake City, UT get some of the nation's choicest powder in winter.

LAS VEGAS. Attractions include casinos, casinos, and casinos (p. 771).

NEVADA

Nevada once walked the straight and narrow. Explored by Spanish missionaries and settled by Mormons, the Nevada Territory's scorched expanses seemed a perfect place for ascetics to strive for moral uplift. However, with the discovery of gold in 1850 and silver in 1859, the state was won over permanently to the worship of filthy lucre. When the precious metals ran out, gambling and marriage-licensing became big industries. The final moral cataclysms came when the state legalized prostitution on a county-by-county basis and spawned lounge idol Wayne Newton. But there *is* another side to Nevada. Lake Mead National Recreation Area, only 25 mi. from Las Vegas, is an oasis in stunning desert surroundings, and the forested slopes of Lake Tahoe provide serene resorts for an escape from the cities.

⚡ PRACTICAL INFORMATION

Capital: Carson City.

Visitor info: Nevada Commission on Tourism, Capitol Complex, Carson City 89701 (☎800-638-2328; line staffed 24hr.). **Nevada Division of State Parks,** 1300 S. Curry St., Carson City 89703-5202 (☎702-687-4384). Open M-F 8am-5pm.

Postal Abbreviation: NV. **Sales Tax:** 6.75-7%; 9% room tax in some counties.

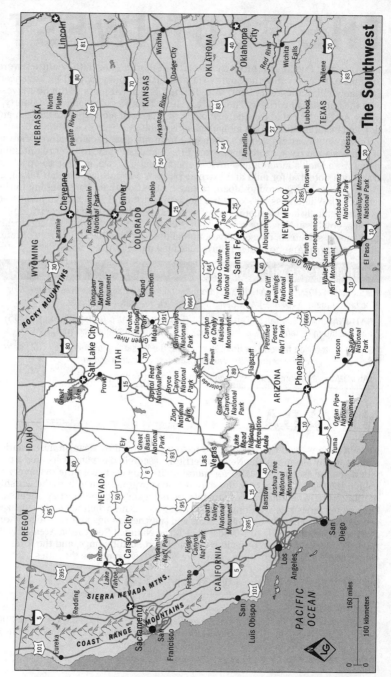

LAS VEGAS

☎ 702

Las Vegas is a shimmering tribute to excess, an oasis of vice and greed, and one very, very good time for those who embrace it. Nowhere else in America do so many shed their inhibitions and indulge otherwise dormant appetites. Vegas is about money and sex—but mostly money. The opulent mega-casinos that dominate Vegas are stupendously successful at snatching dollars, but the entertainment is outstanding and cheap deals are everywhere.

▐ TRANSPORTATION

Airport: McCarran International (☎261-5211), at the southwestern end of the Strip. Main terminal on Paradise Rd. Vans to the Strip and downtown $4-5; taxi $10-15.

Buses: Greyhound, 200 S. Main St. (☎384-9561 or 800-231-2222), downtown at Carson Ave. To: **Flagstaff** (5-7hr., 3 per day, $46.50) and **L.A.** (5-7hr., 10 per day, $34).

Public Transit: Citizens Area Transit or **CAT** (☎228-7433). Buses #117, 301, and 302 serve downtown and the Strip. Buses #108 and 109 serve the airport. All wheelchair accessible. Buses run daily 5:30am-1:30am (24hr. on the Strip). Routes on the Strip $2, residential routes $1.25, seniors and ages 6-17 60¢. **Las Vegas Strip Trolleys** (☎382-1404) cruise the Strip every 15min. daily 9:30am-1:30am. $1.65; use exact change.

Taxis: Yellow, Checker, Star (☎873-2000).

Car Rental: Sav-Mor Rent-A-Car, 5101 Rent-A-Car Rd. (☎736-1234 or 800-634-6779), at the airport. From $35 per day, $149 per week; 150 mi. per day included, each additional mi. 20¢. Must be 21+, under-25 surcharge $8 per day. Discounts can be found in tourist publications. Open daily 5:30am-1am; airport window opens at 7am.

◀▐ ORIENTATION & PRACTICAL INFORMATION

Driving to Vegas from L.A. is a straight, 300 mi. shot on I-15 N (4½hr.). From Arizona, take I-40 W to Kingman and then U.S. 93 N. Las Vegas has two major casino areas. The **downtown** area, around 2nd and Fremont St., has been converted into a pedestrian promenade. The other main area is the **Strip,** a collection of mammoth hotel-casinos along **Las Vegas Blvd.** Parallel to the east side of the Strip and in its shadow is **Paradise Rd.,** also strewn with casinos. Some areas of Las Vegas are unsafe. *The neighborhoods just north of Stewart St. and west of Main St. in the downtown vicinity are especially demanding of caution.*

Despite, or perhaps as a result of, its reputation for debauchery, Las Vegas has a **curfew.** Those under 18 are not allowed unaccompanied in most public places Sunday through Thursday from 10pm to 5am and Friday through Saturday from midnight to 5am. On the Strip no one under 18 is allowed unless accompanied by an adult from 9pm to 5am Monday through Friday and 6pm to 5am on the weekends.

Visitor Info: Las Vegas Convention and Visitors Authority, 3150 Paradise Rd. (☎892-0711), 4 blocks from the Strip in the big pink convention center by the Hilton. Up-to-date info on headliners, conventions, shows, hotel bargains, and buffets. Open daily 8am-5pm.

Tours: Coach USA, 4020 E. Lone Mountain Rd. (☎384-1234 or 800-634-6579). Guided "neon and lights" night tour (3½hr., 1 per day, $39). Bus tours from Las Vegas to **Hoover Dam/Lake Mead** (4 hr., 2 per day, $39) and the **Grand Canyon's South Rim** (full-day, includes breakfast, box lunch, and tours; $149). Discounts with coupons in tourist publications and for ages 3-11. Reserve at least 24hr. in advance.

THE SOUTHWEST

FROM THE ROAD

GETTING THE KING'S BLESSING

When my wife and I decided it was high time we got married, we had little trouble deciding how. Some people may want a grand to-do with cake and clergy, others a justice of the peace. We chose The King.

We arrived at the Luxor Hotel/Casino the day before the big event. Having lived briefly in Las Vegas as a kid, I thought I knew what to expect from our accommodations, but the age of the gargantuan theme hotels has long since replaced the classic 1950s-era fare I remembered. Both Megan and I were delightfully overwhelmed by the pyramid construction and un-self-conscious "Ancient Egypt" decor of our surroundings. That evening we tossed away a few quarters in Paris, jetted back to Merry England at Excalibur, and took a spin through New York's pre-fab skyline in a rollercoaster that looked and felt like a real Gotham cab—the main difference being that you know you're safe and you can't get lost.

Like any amusement park, Vegas combines fun with industrial efficiency, and this goes for weddings as well. The morning of the big day, we went to the County Clerk's Marriage Bureau and stood in line with every kind of bride and groom: young and old, rich and poor, rented and mail-order. In Nevada getting a marriage license requires no further ado than an ID, fifty bucks, and a smile. About an hour before showtime, Megan and I, along with our few guests, piled into the improbably long limousine to the Viva Las Vegas Wedding Chapel had

(continued on next page)

Marriage License Bureau, 200 S. 3rd St. (☎455-4415), in the courthouse. 18+ (16 with parental consent). Licenses $35; cash only. No waiting period or blood test required. Open M-Th 8am-midnight, F-Su 24hr. Also see **Getting the King's Blessing,** at left.

Compulsive Gamblers Hotline, ☎800-567-8238. **Gamblers Anonymous,** ☎385-7732. **Rape Crisis Hotline,** ☎366-1640. **Suicide Prevention,** ☎731-2990.

Post Office: 301 E. Stewart Ave. (☎800-275-8777), downtown. Open M-F 8:30am-5pm. General Delivery M-F 9am-2pm. **ZIP code:** 89101. **Area code:** 702.

ACCOMMODATIONS

Even though Vegas has over 100,000 rooms, most hotels fill up on weekend nights. If you get stuck, call the **Room Reservations Hotline** (☎800-332-5333). The earlier you reserve, the better chance you have of snagging a special rate. Room rates at most hotels in Vegas fluctuate all the time, and many hotels have different rate ranges for weekdays and weekends. A room that costs $30 during a promotion can cost hundreds during conventions. There is a cluster of inexpensive motels north of the Strip (1200-1400 S. Las Vegas Blvd.), but these are far from the action in a sketchy part of town. *The 9% state hotel tax is not included in room rates listed below.*

■ **Silverton,** 3333 Blue Diamond Rd. (☎800-588-7711). Cheaper because it's off the Strip, this spooky ghost town-themed gambling den has a free Las Vegas Blvd. shuttle for guests until 10pm. Singles Su-Th from $29, F-Sa $49; doubles $39/$69. RV park also available (hookups $27). ❶

■ **San Remo,** 115 E. Tropicana Ave. (☎800-522-7366). Just off the Strip, this is a smaller, friendlier version of the major player casinos, without the gimmicks, crowds, and high prices. Live entertainment every night. Rooms may go as low as $29 during slow periods, but are usually Su-Th $42, F-Sa $70. ❷

■ **Whiskey Pete's** (☎800-248-8453), in Primm Valley, NV, 45 mi. south of Vegas on I-15, just before the California border. Whiskey Pete's is the cheapest of 3 Western-themed casinos right in the middle of the desert. Cheap as fool's gold and home to the wildest roller coaster in Nevada ($6). Su-Th $19, F-Sa $50; prices vary with availability. ❷

USA Hostels Las Vegas, 1322 Fremont St. (☎385-1150 or 800-550-8958). Though it is far from the Strip and in an unattractive neighborhood, its rooms are clean. Private and dorm rooms are available, along with a pool, jacuzzi, laundry, kitchen and billiard room. Shared bathrooms. Offers free pickup from Greyhound station. Su-Th dorms $14-19, F-Sa $17-23; suites $40-42/49-51. *Must have international passport, proof of international travel, or student ID.* ❶

Lake Mead National Recreation Area (☎293-8906), 25 mi. south of town on Rte. 93/95. Numerous campsites available throughout. Showers only at Calville and Overton Beach. Sites with flush toilets $10. ❶

Circusland RV Park, 500 Circus Circus Dr. (☎734-0410). Pool, jacuzzi, convenience store, showers. Open 6am-midnight. Hookups Su-Th $19, F-Sa $21. ❶

🍴 FOOD

Sloshed and insatiable gamblers gorge themselves day and night at Las Vegas's gigantic buffets. For the bottomless gullet, there is no better value than the caloric intensity of these gut-busting eateries. Beyond the buffets, Vegas has some of the best restaurants in the world, though there's little for the true budget adventurer.

▩ Carnival World Buffet at the Rio, 3700 W. Flamingo Rd. (☎252-7777). Hands down the greatest buffet in Vegas. Enjoy truly delicious food from any of the 11 stations, each reflecting a different theme. Breakfast $8 (8-10:30am), lunch $11 (11am-3:30pm), dinner $15 (3:30-11pm). ❸

The Plaza Diner, 1 Main St. (☎386-2110), near the entrance to Jackie Gaughan's Plaza Hotel/Casino. Cheap prime rib dinner $6 (noon-midnight). Open 24hr. $1 beers. ❷

Rincon Criollo, 1145 S. Las Vegas Blvd. (☎388-1906), across from Las Vegas International Hostel. Dine on filling Cuban food beneath a wall-sized photograph of palm trees. Daily special including rice and black beans $6.50. Hot sandwiches $3.50-4.50. Open Tu-Su 11am-9:30pm. ❶

🏛 🍸 CASINO-HOPPING & NIGHTLIFE

The quintessentially Vegas themes of cheap buffets, booze, and entertainment were enough; now casinos spend millions of dollars to fool guests into thinking they are somewhere else. "Exact" images of Venice, New York, Rio, Paris, Cairo (complete with Pyramids), and Monte Carlo already thrive on the Strip. Remember: *gambling is illegal for those under 21.* If you are of age, look for casino *funbooks* that allow gamblers to buy $50 in chips for only $15. *Never bring more money than you're prepared to lose cheerfully.* Keep your wallet in your front pocket, and beware of thieves trying to nab winnings from newly rich jubilants.

(continued from previous page)

sent for us and made our way across town to the place where a singing Elvis impersonator would soon pronounce us husband and wife.

Megan and I wanted a wedding that would be, in a sense, entirely for us. We giggled over every detail at the chapel, especially the release that would allow our nuptials to be broadcast live over the Internet (it was), and the disclaimer that should we allow the images to be archived on their website, the chapel could not be held responsible for what computer-savvy teenagers might do with them. After a short delay—on busy days, this particular chapel may perform up to thirty weddings—we were ushered into the main room. Once we were through with the snarls, swaggers, I-do's, and the inevitable "Thank you very much," I crushed a glass under my foot in a traditional Jewish "mazel tov," with which our Elvis seemed pleasantly familiar.

The following day Meg and I rented a car and drove our to Red Rock Canyon, where wild burros wander leisurely around the desert and it is impossible to imagine that there is civilization, so to speak, over the ridge. Strolling along the trails, we reminisced about our glorious wedding, which lasted about three minutes according to the videotape The King presented us afterward. We still watch it with immodest frequency.

–Benjamin Paloff was a Researcher-Writer for Let's Go: Eastern Europe 1998, *the editor of* Eastern Europe 1999, *and a Managing Editor in 2000.*

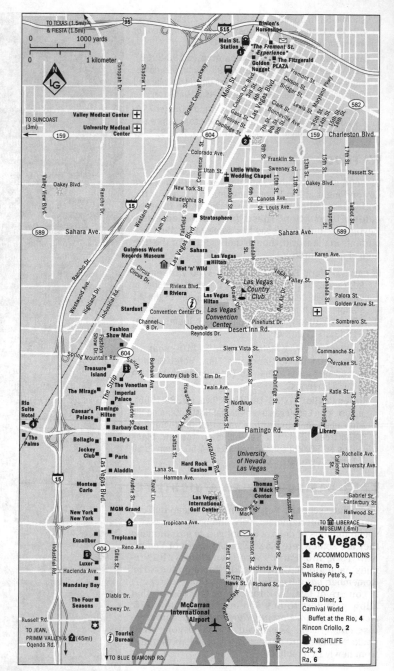

TO TEXAS (1.5mi)
& FIESTA (1.5mi)

0   1000 yards

0   1 kilometer

N
LG

TO SUNCOAST
(3mi)
159

Binion's
Horseshoe

Main St.
Station

"The Fremont St.
Experience"

The Fitzgerald
PLAZA

Golden
Nugget

Valley Medical Center
University Medical
Center

Charleston Blvd.

Colorado Ave.

Commerce St.

Little White
Wedding Chapel

Franklin St.
Sweeney St.

Hassett St.

Oakey Blvd.

New York St.

Oakey Blvd.

Philadelphia St.

Canosa Ave.
St. Louis Ave.

Chapman

Talbot St.

Stratosphere

Sahara Ave.

Sahara Ave.

Guinness World
Records Museum

Sahara

Las Vegas
Hilton

Karen Ave.

Wet 'n' Wild

Circus
Circus Dr.

Riviera Blvd.

La Canada St.

Riviera

Las Vegas
Hilton

Las Vegas
Country
Club

Palora St.
Golden Arrow St.

Stardust

Las Vegas
Convention
Center

Sombrero St.

Channel
8 Dr.

Debbie
Reynolds Dr.

Pinehurst Dr.

Desert Inn Rd.

Fashion
Show Mall

Sierra Vista St.

Commanche St.

Spring Mountain Rd.

Dumont St.

Cherokee St.

Treasure
Island

The Strip

Elm Dr.

Katie St.

The Mirage

The Venetian
Imperial
Palace

Twain Ave.

Spencer St.

Rio
Suite
Hotel

Caesar's
Palace

Flamingo
Hilton

Barbary Coast

Flamingo Rd.

Library

The
Palms

Bellagio

Jockey
Club

Bally's

Paris

Rochelle Ave.

University Ave.

Aladdin

Hard Rock
Casino

University
of Nevada
Las Vegas

Monte
Carlo

Harmon Ave.

Gabriel St.
Canterbury St.
Hallwood St.

New York
New York

MGM Grand

Las Vegas
International
Golf Center

Thomas
& Mack
Center

TO 🏛 LIBERACE
MUSEUM (.6mi)

Tropicana Ave.

Excalibur

Tropicana

Reno Ave.

La$ Vega$

🏠 ACCOMMODATIONS

Luxor

Hacienda Ave.

San Remo, **5**
Whiskey Pete's, **7**

Mandalay Bay

🍴 FOOD

The Four
Seasons

Russell Rd.

TO JEAN,
PRIMM VALLEY & 🚗(45mi)
Ogendo Rd.

McCarran
International
Airport

Tourist
Bureau

TO BLUE DIAMOND RD.

Plaza Diner, **1**
Carnival World
Buffet at the Rio, **4**
Rincon Criollo, **2**

🎵 NIGHTLIFE

C2K, **3**
Ra, **6**

THE SOUTHWEST

Casinos, nightclubs, and some wedding chapels are open 24hr. There are far more casinos and far more attractions within them than can be listed here; use the following as a compendium of the best, but explore the Strip for yourself. Check with the Visitors Center for more casino listings. A huge bronze lion (and some live ones inside) guard the **MGM Grand**, 3799 S. Las Vegas Blvd. (☎891-7979). In addition to more than 5000 rooms, MGM also contains the Grand Adventures Amusement Park. Legendary **Caesar's Palace** is at 3570 S. Las Vegas Blvd. (☎731-7110). You can roll through the mean streets of New York aboard the muscular Manhattan Express Roller Coaster, a fast and acrobatic thrill.

Nightlife in Vegas gets rolling around midnight and keeps going until everyone drops. **C2K** at the **Venetian**, 2800 S. Las Vegas Blvd., is the newest resort-casino's palatial showroom, transformed nightly into a mind-shattering *über*-club. (☎933-4255. Open W-Su 10:30pm-6am.) **Ra**, 3900 S. Las Vegas Blvd., is a super-hot Egyptian-themed nightclub at the **Luxor**. (☎262-4000. Open W-Sa 10pm-6am.)

LEAVING LAS VEGAS

HOOVER DAM

Built to subdue the Colorado River, the Hoover Dam took 5000 men five years of seven-day weeks to construct. When their sweat dried, over 6.6 million tons of concrete had been crafted into a 726 ft. colossus that now shelters precious agricultural land, pumps big voltage to Vegas and L.A., and furnishes jet-skiers with azure waters to churn. The excellent tours and interpretive center explore the dam's history, though in a varnished and self-congratulatory way. This is a prize artifact from America's "think-big" era of ambitious landscaping and culturally-transforming public works projects. The Visitors Center leads tours to the generators at the structure's bottom. (☎294-3510. Open daily 9am-5pm. Self-guided tours with short presentation $10, seniors $8, ages 6-16 $4.)

LAKE MEAD

A multi-tiered program of flood control, irrigation, and water storage is fulfilled by Lake Mead—turquoise spot in the arid wasteland between Arizona and Nevada. Dubbed "the jewel of the desert" by its residents, the lake and its environs offer more than the social planning and deficit spending that created it. Lake Mead is really sustained by the multitude of Californians driving pickup trucks with jet skis in tow. Boats and other watercraft can be rented at concessionaires along the shores. **Boulder Beach** is accessible by Lakeshore Dr., off U.S. 93. (☎800-752-9669. Jet skis $50 per hr., $270 per day; fishing boats $55 per 4hr., $100 per day.)

Alongside the Park Service **campsites ❶** ($10), concessionaires usually operate RV parks (most of which have become mobile home villages), marinas, restaurants, and occasionally motels. More remote concessionaires, including **Echo Bay Resort ❶**, offer motel and camping options. (☎800-752-9669. Singles overlooking lake $85; doubles $100; hookups $18.) Its restaurant, **Tale of the Whale**, is decorated in nautical motifs, features a stunning view of Lake Mead, and cooks up $6 burgers. The resort rents jetskis ($50 per hr., $270 per day) and fishing boats ($30 for 2hr., $75 per day).

RENO ☎775

Reno, with its decadent casinos cradled by snowcapped mountains, captures both the natural splendor and capitalist frenzy of the West. The hub of northern Nevada's tourist cluster, which includes Lake Tahoe and Pyramid Lake, the self-proclaimed "biggest little city in the world" does a decent job of compressing Las Vegas-style gambling, entertainment, and dining experience into a few city blocks.

THE SOUTHWEST

🔢 PRACTICAL INFORMATION. Amtrak is at 135 E. Commercial Row. (☎800-872-7245. Open daily 8:30am-4:45pm.) **Greyhound,** 155 Stevenson St. (☎800-231-2222), a half-block from W. 2nd St., rolls to **Las Vegas** (1 per day, $72) and to **San Francisco** (17 per day, $30-33). **Reno-Sparks Convention and Visitors Center,** 100 N. Virginia St., is on the 2nd fl. of the Cal-Neva Building. (☎800-367-7366; www.playreno.com or www.renolaketahoe.com. Open daily 9am-5pm.) **Post Office:** 50 S. Virginia St., at Mill St. (Open M-F 8:30am-5pm, Sa 10am-2pm.) **ZIP code:** 89501. **Area code:** 775.

📷 ACCOMMODATIONS. While weekend prices at casinos are usually on the high side, gambler's specials, weekday rates, and winter discounts provide some great, cheap rooms. Prices fluctuate, so call ahead. **Harrah's Reno ❹,** 219 N. Center St. (☎800-427-7247); **Atlantis ❸,** 3800 S. Virginia St. (☎825-4700); and **Fitzgerald's Casino/Hotel ❸,** 255 N. Virginia St. (☎800-535-5825), have been known to offer some good deals to go along with their central locations and massive facilities. (Rates can get as low as $32, but they generally hover around $60 for a single.) Be advised—heterosexual prostitution is legal in most of Nevada (though not in Reno itself), and certain motels are therefore cheap but lacking a particularly wholesome feel. Travelers of the same sex sharing a hotel room may be required to book a room with two beds. Southwestern downtown has the cheapest lodging. *The prices below don't include Reno's 12% hotel tax.*

Circus Circus ❺, 500 N. Sierra St., is deemed the family casino of Little Sin City, with over 1800 newly renovated rooms, acres of casinos, restaurants, activities, health club, a kitschy monorail-trolley, and a real live big top. Rooms are large, posh, and quiet. (☎329-0711 or 800-648-5010. M-Th from $60, F-Su from $109.) **Motel 6 ❷** has 3 clean, comfortable, cheap locations in Reno: 866 N. Wells Ave. (☎786-9852), north on I-80 Exit 14; 1901 S. Virginia St. (☎827-0255), 1½ mi. down Virginia St. at Plumb Ln.; and 1400 Stardust St. (☎747-7390), north on I-80 Keystone Exit and west onto Stardust St. (Reserve 2 weeks in advance. Singles June-Sept. Su-Th $40; F-Sa $50; Oct.-May $36/45.) **El Cortez Hotel ❷,** 239 W. 2nd St., is a 116-room downtown hotel, with A/C, cable TV, exposed pipes, and thin walls. (☎322-9161. Singles Su-Th $29, F-Sa $38; doubles $43/49.)

🍴 FOOD. Eating in Reno is cheap. In order to entice gamblers and prevent them from wandering out in search of food, casinos offer a wide range of all-you-can-eat buffets and 99¢ breakfasts. Buffet fare, admittedly, can be greasy and overcooked, and Reno's other inexpensive eateries offer better food. The large Basque population cooks up spicy, hearty cuisine locals enthusiastically recommend. Locals swear by the tangy Basque cuisine at **Santa Fe Restaurant ❹,** 235 Lake St., in the Santa Fe Hotel in the heart of downtown. (☎323-1891. Open daily 11am-2pm and 6-9pm. Lunch $7-9. 7-course dinner $14.) **Miguel's Fine Mexican Food ❷,** 1415 S. Virginia St., has received both local and critical acclaim. (☎322-2722. Open daily 11am-9pm. Entrees $5-10.)

🎭 ENTERTAINMENT. Almost all casinos offer live nighttime entertainment, but most shows are not worth the steep admission prices. **Harrah's,** however, is an exception, carrying on a dying tradition with its **dinner shows** in Sammy's Showroom. Starting at $32.50, Harrah's offers dinner and a performance by headlining impersonator Gordie Browne, named "Entertainer of the Year" by the *Sacramento Bee.* At **Circus Circus** (see above), 500 N. Sierra (☎329-0711), a small circus above the casino performs "big top" shows every ½ hr. These shows and others are listed in the weekly *Showtime,* while *Best Bets* and *Fun & Gaming* has listings of discounted local events and shows. The *Nevada Events & Shows* section of the Nevada visitors' guide lists sights, museums, and seasonal events. More info is in the *Reno Gazette-Journal* and *News & Review*.

NEAR RENO: PYRAMID LAKE

Thirty miles north of Reno on Rte. 445, on the Paiute Indian Reservation, lies emerald green Pyramid Lake, one of the most heart-achingly beautiful bodies of water in the US. The pristine tides of Pyramid Lake are set against the backdrop of a barren desert, making it a soothing respite from neon Reno. **Camping** is allowed anywhere on the lake shore, but only designated areas have toilet facilities. A $5 permit is required for use of the park, and the area is carefully patrolled by the Paiute tribe. Permits are available at the **Ranger Station** (☎476-1155), which is located on the western side of the lake. **Boat rental** (☎476-1156) is available daily at the marina near the Ranger Station; call for reservations. **Area code:** 775.

UTAH

Beginning in 1848, persecuted members of the Church of Jesus Christ of Latter-Day Saints (colloquially called Mormons) settled on the land that is now Utah, intending to establish and govern their own theocratic state. President James Buchanan struggled to quash their efforts in 1858, as many others had tried before. The Mormons eventually gave up their dreams of theocracy and their rights to polygamy, and statehood was finally granted on January 4, 1896. Today the state's population is 70% Mormon—a religious presence that creates a haven for family values. Utah's citizens dwell primarily in the 100-mile corridor along I-15, stretching from Ogden to Provo. Outside this area, Utah's natural beauty dominates, intoxicating visitors in a way that Utah's watered-down 3.2% beer never could. Just east of Salt Lake City, the Wasatch range beckons skiers in the winter and bikers in the summer. Southern Utah is like no other place on Earth; red canyons, river gorges, and crenelated cliffs attest to the creative powers of wind and water.

THE SOUTHWEST

⚆ PRACTICAL INFORMATION

Capital: Salt Lake City.

Visitor Info: Utah Travel Council, 300 N. State St., Salt Lake City 84114 (☎801-538-1030 or 800-200-1160; www.utah.com), across from the capitol building. Distributes the *Utah Vacation Planner's* lists of motels, national parks, and campgrounds, as well as brochures on statewide biking, rafting, and skiing. **Utah Parks and Recreation,** 1594 W. North Temple, Salt Lake City 84116 (☎801-538-7220). Open M-F 8am-5pm.

Controlled Substances: Mormons abstain from "strong drinks" (coffee and tea), nicotine, alcohol, and, of course, illegal drugs. While you probably won't have trouble getting a pack of cigarettes or a cup of coffee, alcohol is another matter. State liquor stores are sprinkled sparsely about the state and have inconvenient hours. Grocery and convenience stores only sell beer. While most upscale restaurants serve wine, licensing laws can split a room, and drinkers may have to move to the bar to get a mixed drink. Law requires that waiters not offer drink menus; diners wanting a list must request one. Establishments that sell hard alcohol are required to be "members only;" tourists can either find a "sponsor"—i.e., an entering patron—or get a short-term membership.

Postal Abbreviation: UT. **Sales Tax:** 5.75-7.75%.

Salt Lake City

ACCOMMODATIONS
Armstrong Mansion B&B, 3
City Creek, 2
Ute Hostel, 5

FOOD
Red Iguana, 1
Sage's Cafe, 4

SALT LAKE CITY   ☎801

Tired from five gruelling months of travel, Brigham Young looked out across the
Great Salt Lake and proclaimed: "This is the place." He believed that in this desolate valley his band of Mormon pioneers had finally found a haven where they
could practice their religion freely, away from the persecution they had faced in
the East. To this day, Salt Lake City remains dominated by Mormon influence. The
Church of Jesus Christ of Latter-Day Saints (LDS) owns the tallest office building
downtown and welcomes visitors to Temple Square, the spiritual epicenter of the
Mormon religion. Despite its commitment to preserving tradition, Salt Lake is rapidly attracting high-tech firms, as well as droves of outdoor enthusiasts drawn by
world-class ski resorts, rock climbing, and mountain trails. The city, for all its
homogeneity, supports a surprising variety of culturally diverse communities.

▐▛ TRANSPORTATION

Airport: Salt Lake City International, 776 N. Terminal Dr. (☎575-2400), 6 mi. west of
Temple Sq. UTA buses #50 and 150 run between the terminal and downtown for
$1.25; buses leave hourly M-Sa 7-11pm, service ends at 6pm on Su. Taxi to Temple Sq.
costs about $15.

Trains: Amtrak, 340 S. 600 W (☎322-3510). *The station is in an unsafe area of town.* To **Denver** (15hr., 1 per day, $75-112) and **San Francisco** (19hr., 1 per day, $77-115). Station open daily 10:30pm-6am.

Buses: Greyhound, 160 W. South Temple (☎355-9579), near Temple Sq. To: **Denver** (7-10hr., 5 per day, $54); **Las Vegas** (12-13hr., 2 per day, $49); and **Los Angeles** (15-18hr., 2 per day, $93). Open daily 6:30am-11:30pm, summer 6:30am-2:30am, ticket window until 10:30pm.

Public Transit: Utah Transit Authority, or **UTA** (☎743-3882). Frequent service to University of Utah campus. Buses to Ogden (#70/72/73 express), suburbs, airport, mountain canyons. The #11 express runs to Provo ($2.25). New trax light rail follows Main St. from downtown to Sandy and the University of Utah. Buses every 20min.-1hr. M-Sa 6am-11pm. $1-2, senior discounts, under 5 free. Maps available at libraries and the Visitors Center. Buses and trains traveling downtown near major sites are free.

Taxis: Ute Cab, ☎359-7788. **Yellow Cab,** ☎521-2100. **City Cab,** ☎363-5550.

■ ORIENTATION & PRACTICAL INFORMATION

Salt Lake City's grid system may seem confusing, but once you get the hang of it, it makes navigation easy. Brigham Young designated **Temple Sq.** as the heart of downtown. Street names increase in increments of 100 and indicate how many blocks east, west, north, or south they lie from Temple Sq.; the "0" points are **Main St.** (north-south) and **South Temple** (east-west). State St., West Temple, and North Temple are 100 level streets. Occasionally, streets are referred to as 13th S or 17th N, which are the same as 1300 S or 1700 N. Local address listings often include two numerical cross streets, acting as a type of coordinate system (no maps needed!). A building on 13th S (1300 S) might be listed as 825 E. 1300 S, meaning the cross street is 800 E (8th E). Smaller streets and those that do not fit the grid pattern sometimes have non-numeric names.

Visitor info: Salt Palace Convention Center and Salt Lake City Visitors Bureau, 90 S. West Temple (☎534-4902). Located in Salt Palace Convention Center, 1 block south of Temple Sq. Open daily 9am-5pm.

Hotlines: Rape Crisis, ☎467-7273. **Suicide Prevention,** ☎483-5444. Both 24hr.

Gay/Lesbian Information: The Little Lavender Book (☎323-0727), distributed twice yearly, presents a directory of gay-friendly Salt Lake City services.

Internet access: Salt Lake Public Library, 209 E. 500 S (☎524-8200). Free Internet access. Open M-Th 9am-9pm; F-Sa 9am-6pm; Su 1-5pm. Free Internet access is also available at the **Family Search Center** on Temple Sq. Open M-Sa 9am-9pm.

Post Office: 230 W. 200 S, 1 block south and 1 block west of Visitors Center. Open M-F 8am-5pm, Sa 9am-2pm. **ZIP code:** 84101. **Area code:** 801.

▟ ACCOMMODATIONS

Affordable chain motels cluster at the southern end of downtown, around 200 W and 600 S, and on North Temple.

▓ **Base Camp Park City,** 268 Historic Main St. (☎655-7244 or 888-980-7244), 30 mi. east of Salt Lake City on I-80 and south on Rte. 224. This brand new, state-of-the-art, dazzling, and friendly hostel offers 70 affordable beds in an exorbitant town. Free Internet, free parking, discounts on selected Main St. restaurants, spectacular movie/DVD theater, and free transportation to Deer Valley, The Canyons, and Park City. Taxis/shuttles from Salt Lake City airport available. Winter dorms $35, summer $25; private room (sleeps up to 4) $120/80. Make reservations as far in advance, as possible during ski season, the hostel tends to fill up rapidly. ❷

Ute Hostel (AAIH/Rucksackers), 21 E. Kelsey Ave. (☎ 595-1645 or 888-255-1192), near the intersection of 1300 S and Main St. Located 2 blocks from the new UTA trax line for easy downtown/ski-shuttle access. Young international crowd. Free pick-up can be arranged from airport, Amtrak, Greyhound, or the Visitors Center. Kitchen, no curfew, free tea and coffee, parking, linen. Check-in 24hr. 14 dorm beds, $15 each. 2 private rooms; single-occupancy $25; double-occupancy $35. Reservations accepted only with pre-payment, recommended from July-Sept. and Jan.-Mar. No credit cards. ❶

City Creek Inn, 230 W. North Temple (☎ 533-9100), a stone's throw from Temple Sq. Offers 33 tastefully decorated, immaculate ranch-style rooms for cheaper rates than any of its downtown competitors. Singles $53; doubles $64. ❸

Armstrong Mansion Bed and Breakfast, 667 E. 100 S (☎ 531-1333 or 800-708-1333). This over-the-top romantic getaway features 15 sumptuously decorated Victorian rooms, many with jacuzzis only a few feet from the bed. Rates range from $119 for a basic room with king to $229 for the honeymoon suite in the tower. ❺

Tanners Flat and Albion Basin, in Little Cottonwood Canyon. Take I-215 to Rte. 210 E. Brown recreation signs point the way to both campsites, about 30 mi. from downtown Salt Lake, are two of the closest campgrounds for summer camping. (Tanners Flat: open early July to late Sept.; 39 sites; $12. Albion Basin: higher altitude; open early July to late Sept.; 26 sites; $12). Arrive early on weekends to ensure a space; for summer weekends, call in advance. The **Salt Lake Ranger District** (☎ 943-1794) fields calls for camping reservations and more info.

⌂ MORAL FIBER

Good, cheap restaurants are sprinkled around the city and its suburbs. Despite its white bread reputation, Salt Lake hosts a number of ethnic cuisines. If you're in a hurry downtown, **ZCMI Mall** and **Crossroads Mall,** both across from Temple Sq., have standard food courts.

Sage's Cafe, 473 E. 300 S (☎ 322-3790). This organic, vegan cafe is a nexus of culinary and political revolution. Describing themselves as "culinary astronauts," talented chefs produce a surprising variety of delectable dishes. Weekday lunch buffet $6.75. Try a refreshing soy milkshake ($4) or sample from their smoothie selection (also $4). Open W-Th 11am-10pm, F 11am-11pm, Sa 9am-11pm, Su 9am-10pm. ❷

Red Iguana, 736 W. North Temple (☎ 322-4834), across the bridge from downtown in the bright orange building. This popular eatery serves up authentic pre-Columbian Mexican food. A la carte burritos, enchiladas, tacos ($5-7), and combo plates ($10-12). Open M-Th 11am-10pm, F 11am-11pm, Sa noon-10pm, Su noon-9pm. ❸

◉ SIGHTS

LATTER-DAY SIGHTS. The majority of Salt Lake City's sights are sacred to the Church of Jesus Christ of Latter-Day Saints, and are free. The seat of the highest Mormon authority, and the central temple, **Temple Sq.** is the symbolic center of the Mormon religion. The square has two **Visitors Centers,** north and south. Visitors can wander the flowery 10-acre square, but the sacred temple is off-limits to non-Mormons. (☎ 800-537-9703, an automated visitor info line providing up-to-date hours and tour info. 45min. tours leave from the flagpole every 15min.) The Testaments, a film detailing the coming of Jesus Christ to the Americas (as related by the Book of Mormon), is screened at the **Joseph Smith Memorial Building.** (☎ 240-4383 for film show times, 240-1266 to arrange a tour. Open M-Sa 9am-9pm. Free.) Temple Sq. is also home to the **Mormon Tabernacle** and its famed choir. Weekly rehearsals and performances are free. (Organ recitals M-Sa noon-12:30pm, Su 2-2:30pm; in summer also M-Sa 2-2:30pm. Choir *rehearsals Th 8-9:30pm; choir broadcasts Su 9:30-10am, must be seated by 9:15am.)* In the summer, there are free concerts at **Assembly Hall** next door. *(☎800-537-9703.)*

The **Church of Jesus Christ of Latter Day Saints Office Building** is the tallest skyscraper in town. The elevator to the 26th floor grants a view of the Great Salt Lake to the west opposite the Wasatch Range. *(40 E. North Temple. ☎240-3789. Observation deck open M-F 9am-5pm.)* The LDS church's collection of genealogical materials is accessible and free at the **Family Search Center**, 15 E. South Temple St., in the Joseph Smith Memorial Building. The Center has computers and staff to aid in your search. The actual collection is housed in the **Family History Library.** *(35 N. West Temple. ☎240-2331. Center: Open M-Sa 9am-9pm. Library: Open M 7:30am-5pm, Tu-Sa 7:30am-10pm.)*

CAPITOL HILL. At the northernmost end of State St., Utah's **State Capitol** features beautiful grounds, including a garden that changes daily. *(☎538-3000. Open M-F 8am-5pm. Tours M-F 9am-4pm.)* Down State St., the **Hansen Planetarium** has free exhibits and laser shows set to music. *(15 S. State St. ☎531-4925. Open M-Th 9am-9pm, F-Sa 9:30am-midnight, Su 1-5pm. Laser show $6; planetarium science show $4.50.)*

MUSEUMS. At the **Children's Museum,** you can build houses with enormous Legos or work in the "color factory." *(840 N. 300 W. ☎322-5268. Take bus #70. Open M-Th and Sa 10am-6pm, F 10am-8pm. $3.75, under 1 free.)* Visiting exhibits and a permanent collection of world art wow enthusiasts at the newly expanded **Utah Museum of Fine Arts,** on the University of Utah campus. *(☎581-7332. Open M-F 10am-5pm, Sa-Su noon-5pm. Free.)* Also on campus, the **Museum of Natural History** focuses its display space on the history of the Wasatch Front. *(☎581-6927. Open M-Sa 9:30am-5:30pm, Su noon-5pm. $4, ages 3-12 $2.50, under 3 free.)* The **Salt Lake Art Center** displays an impressive array of contemporary art and documentary films. *(20 S. West Temple. ☎328-4201. Open Tu-Th and Sa 10am-5pm, F 10am-9pm, Su 1-5pm. Suggested donation $2.)*

THE GREAT SALT LAKE. The Great Salt Lake, administered by Great Salt Lake State Marina, is a remnant of primordial Lake Bonneville and is so salty that only blue-green algae and brine shrimp can survive in it. The salt content varies between 5-27%, providing unusual buoyancy. No one has ever drowned in the Great Salt Lake—a fact attributable to the Lake's chemical make-up. Decaying organic material on the lake shore gives the lake its pungent odor, a stench that locals prefer not to discuss. **Antelope Island State Park ❶,** in the middle of the lake, has beaches, hiking trails, camping, picnic spots, and buffalo. *(☎625-1630. To get to the south shore of the lake, take I-80 17 mi. west of Salt Lake City to Exit 104. To get to the island, take Exit 335 from I-15 and follow signs to the causeway. Open daily 7am-10pm; in winter dawn to dusk. Day use: vehicles $8, bicycles and pedestrians $4. Camping $10 per vehicle for first night, $8 each additional night. Reservations recommended; call ☎800-322-3770.)*

🎵 📺 ENTERTAINMENT & NIGHTLIFE

Concerts abound in the sweltering summer months. At 7:30pm every Tuesday and Friday, the **Temple Sq. Concert Series** *(☎240-2534, call for a schedule)* presents a free outdoor concert in Brigham Young Historic Park, with music ranging from string quartet to unplugged guitar. The **Utah Symphony Orchestra** performs in **Abravanel Hall,** 123 W. South Temple. *(☎533-6683. Office open M-F 10am-6pm. Sept. to early May $15-40. Limited summer season: call 1 week in advance.)* The University of Utah's **Red Butte Garden,** 300 Wakara Way *(☎587-9939; www.redbuttegarden.org),* offers an outdoor summer concert series with quality national acts. The **Utah Jazz** *(Oct.-Apr. $10-83)* play at **Delta Center,** 301 W. South Temple *(☎325-7328).*

The free *City Weekly* (available from bars, clubs, and restaurants) lists events. Famous teetotalers, the early Mormon theocrats instated laws making it illegal to serve alcohol in a public place. Hence, all liquor-dispensing institutions fall under the "private club" rubric, serving only members and their "sponsored" guests. In order to get around this cumbersome law, most bars and clubs charge a "temporary membership fee," essentially the same as a cover charge. The result of all this is a surprisingly active nightlife, centered on S. West Temple and the run-down blocks near the railroad tracks. To meet throngs of sweaty locals pulsating to heavy beats in cramped quarters, check out either **Club Axis**, 108 S. 500 W (☎519-2947), or the **Bricks**, 200 S. 600 W. Both clubs cater to a trendy crowd and have separate 18+ and 21+ areas. Cover $5-7. The **Dead Goat Saloon**, 165 S. West Temple, showcases local jazz and blues acts in a relaxed atmosphere with pool, darts, and a grill. (☎328-4628. Open M-Sa 6pm-2am, Su 6pm-midnight.) **The Zephyr**, 301 S. West Temple, features live music and attracts national acts. (☎355-2582. Call for events schedule. Hours vary.) A diverse mix of the Salt Lake gay and lesbian crowd flocks to video-bar/dance-club **Zipperz**, 155 W. 200 S. (☎521-8200. W 80s night.) Classic movies ($4) are accompanied by microbrews ($3) at **Brewvies**, 667 S. 200 W (☎355-5500), a movie theater-*cum*-brewpub.

⛷ SKIING

Utah sells itself to tourists with pictures of intrepid skiers on pristine powder, hailed by many as "the greatest snow on earth." Seven major ski areas lie within 45min. of downtown Salt Lake, making Utah's capital a good, inexpensive base camp from which to explore the winter vacation paradise of the Wasatch Mountains. Nearby **Park City** is the quintessential ski town with the excellent but lonely ▓**Base Camp Park City** (see p. 779) as its only budget option. Call, or check ski area web sites for deals before purchasing lift tickets. Besides being a good source of fun, the Utah ski hills are also an excellent source of employment. If you are interested in working while you ski, check the employment section on each hill's website or call Snowbird's job hotline (☎947-8240). Most slopes are open in the summer for hiking, mountain biking and horseback riding.

Alta (☎359-1078; www.alta.com), 25 mi. southeast of Salt Lake City in Little Cottonwood Canyon. Cheap tickets; magnificent skiing. In business since 1938, this funky, no-frills resort continues to eschew both opulence and snowboarding. Skiing daily from 9:15am-4:30pm. Lift tickets: half-day $29, full day $38; day pass for beginner lifts only $22. Offers a joint ticket with nearby Snowbird for $68. 4 rental shops in Alta ski village offer competitive rates.

Brighton (☎800-873-5512; www.skibrighton.com), south of Salt Lake in Big Cottonwood Canyon. Open early Nov. to late Apr. daily 9am-4pm and M-Sa until 9pm for night skiing. Lift tickets: half-day $34, full-day $39, night $24; children under 10 free. Rentals: adult ski/board package $26 per day; child ski/board package $18; high performance ski/board package $32.

The Canyons (☎435-649-5400; www.thecanyons.com), in Park City. Features 8 mountain peaks and over 3500 skiable acres. Open Nov.-Apr. daily M-F 9am-4pm, Sa-Su 8:30am-4pm. Lift tickets: half-day $45, full day $62; children and seniors $31/24. Rentals: adult ski/board package $34 per day, child ski package $24, child board package $27, high performance ski package $40. Free season pass in exchange for 1 day of work at the resort per week. Call ahead for more info.

Deer Valley (☎435-649-1000; www.deervalley.com), in Park City. Hosted the slalom, mogul, and aerial events of the 2002 Winter Olympics. No snowboards. Skiing Dec.-Apr. daily 9am-4:15pm. Lift tickets: half-day $46, full-day $67; children $36/28; senior $46/30. Rentals: adult ski package $39 per day, child ski package $28, high performance ski package $49.

Park City (☎435-649-8111; www.parkcitymountain.com). Its exceptional facilities earned it the Olympic snowboarding events. Open mid-Nov. to mid-Apr. daily 9am-4pm; night skiing until 9pm after Dec. 25. Lift tickets vary by season; high season half-day $42, full-day $60+; ages 65-69 $30; over 69 free. Rentals: ski package $20 per day, child ski package $17, snowboard packages $32, high performance ski package $37.

▓ DAYTRIP FROM SALT LAKE CITY: TIMPANOGOS CAVE

Legend has it that a set of mountain lion tracks first led Martin Hansen to the mouth of the cave that today bears his name. **Hansen's Cave** forms but one-third of the cave system of American Fork Canyon, collectively called Timpanogos Cave. Situated in a rich alpine environment, Timpanogos is a true gem for speleologists (cave nuts) and tourists alike. Though early miners shipped boxcar loads of stalactites and other mineral wonders back east to sell to universities and museums, enough remain to bedazzle guests along the 1hr. walk through the depths. Today, the cave is open to visitors only via ranger-led tours.

Timpanogos Cave National Monument is solely accessible via Rte. 92 (20 mi. south of Salt Lake City off I-15, Exit 287; Rte. 92 also connects with Rte. 189 northeast of Provo). The **Visitors Center** dispenses tour tickets and info on the caves. Summer tours tend to sell out by early afternoon; reservations for busy summer weekends should be made as early as 30 days in advance; during less busy times they are available up to the day before the tour. Bring water and warm layers: the rigorous hike to the cave climbs 1065 ft. over 1.5 mi., but the temperature remains a constant 45°F inside. (☎756-5238. Open mid-May to late Oct. daily 7am-5:30pm. 3hr. hikes depart daily 7am-4:30pm every 15min. $6, ages 6-15 $5, Golden Age Passport and ages 3-5 $3, age 2 and under free.)

The National Monument is dwarfed by the surrounding **Uinta National Forest,** which blankets the mountains of the Wasatch Range. The **Alpine Scenic Drive (Rte. 92)** provides excellent views of Mt. Timpanogos and other snowcapped peaks. The loopy 20 mi. trip takes almost 1hr. in one direction. The Forest Service charges $2 for recreation along the road. The **Timpooneke Trail** (16.2 mi.) leads to the sheer summit of **Mt. Timpanogos** (11,749 ft.), beginning at the Aspen Grove Trailhead (6860 ft.) and meeting the summit trail at Emerald Lake.

The **Pleasant Grove Ranger District** has info on the campgrounds in the area (☎800-280-2267 for reservations. Sites $11-13.) **Backcountry camping ❶** throughout the forest requires no permit or fee as long as you respect minimum-impact guidelines. While the National Park Service forbids camping within the national monument itself, **Little Mill Campground ❶,** on Rte. 92 past the monument provides an excellent jumping-off point from which to beat the Timpanogos Cave crowds. (Open early May to late Sept. $11.) Rte. 89 in nearby Pleasant Grove and Orem has gas stations, supermarkets, and fast food.

DINOSAUR NATIONAL MONUMENT & VERNAL   ☎435

Dinosaur National Monument was created in 1915, seven years after paleontologist Earl Douglass happened upon an array of fossilized dinosaur bones here. The rugged landscape that today includes the beautiful Green and Yampa rivers was once home to legions of dinosaurs that eventually left their remains for tourists to ogle. The monument's main attraction is the dinosaur quarry, but adventurous types may find more distractions in the less-explored parts of the area. The town of Vernal, west of Dinosaur on U.S. 40, is a popular base for exploring the monument, Flaming Gorge, and the Uinta Mountains.

THE SOUTHWEST

█↔ 7 **ORIENTATION & PRACTICAL INFORMATION.** The national monument collects an entrance fee of $10 per car, and $5 per cyclist, pedestrian, or tour-bus passenger. The national monument's western entrance lies 20 mi. east of Vernal on Rte. 149, which splits from U.S. 40 southwest of the park in Jenson, UT. Once inside the park, pay a visit to the **Dinosaur Quarry Visitors Center**, a remarkable Bauhaus building that houses exhibits, a bookstore, and an exposed river bank brimming with dinosaur bones. During summer, a **shuttle** whisks passengers ½ mi. to the Visitors Center; between Labor Day and Memorial Day cars can drive directly to the Center. (☎781-7700. Open June-Aug. 8am-7pm, Sept.-May 8am-4:30pm.) **Monument Headquarters** is 45 mi. along Rte. 40 from the Rte. 149 turnoff in Dinosaur, CO. (☎970-374-3000. Open June-Aug. daily 8am-6pm; Sept.-May M-F 8am-4:30pm.) **Gas** is available in Vernal, Jenson, and Dinosaur, CO.

Greyhound runs buses to **Denver** (8hr., 2 per day, $56) and **Salt Lake City** (4½hr., 2 per day, $35) from Frontier Travel, 72 S. 100 W. (☎789-0404. Open M-F 8:30am-5:30pm). Jensen is a flag stop, as is Monument Headquarters, 2 mi. west of Dinosaur, CO. **The Northeast Utah Visitors Center**, 235 E. Main St., provides info on regional recreational activities. (☎789-7894. Open daily 8am-9pm). The **Ashley National Forest Service Office**, 355 N. Vernal Ave., has info about hiking, biking, and camping in the Ashley and Uinta National Forests. Mail kitschy dino postcards from the **Post Office**, 67 N. 600 W. **ZIP code:** 84078. **Area code:** 435.

▐ ⬭ **ACCOMMODATIONS & FOOD.** The most easily accessible site during summer months, **Green River ❶**, lies along Cub Creek Rd. about 5 mi. from the entrance fee station. (88 sites. Flush toilets and water. $12.) Nearby **Split Mountain** hosts only groups during summer, but is free and open to all during winter. **Echo Park ❶**, 13 mi. along Echo Park Rd. from Harper's Corner Drive (four-wheel-drive road and impassable when wet), provides the perfect location for an evening under the stars. (9 sites. Vault toilets and water. $6.) Free **backcountry camping ❶** permits are available from Monument Headquarters or the Quarry Visitors Center.

For those inclined to rough it, Vernal is civilization's beacon. The comfortable **Sage Motel ❸**, 54 W. Main St., has standard rooms, A/C, satellite TV, and free local calls. (☎789-1442 or 800-760-1442. Singles in winter $45, in summer $50; doubles $55/60.) On the outskirts of town toward the National Monument, **Split Mountain Motel ❷**, 1015 E. U.S. 40, has clean rooms with A/C, microwave, and minifridge. (☎789-9020. Singles in winter $40, in summer $45; doubles $50/55.)

The **7-11 Ranch Restaurant ❶**, 77 E. Main, in Vernal, packs in locals and tourists for monster breakfasts ($5) and fresh java. (☎789-1170. Open M-Sa 6am-11pm; breakfast served until noon.) Imported to the **Weston Inn** from nearby LaPointe, **Stockman's ❶**, 1684 W. U.S. 40, lures hordes of hungry Vernalites for an exciting menu of Southwest cuisine, steak, and seafood. Burgers ($5-7) and gargantuan decadent desserts ($5-6) are highlights. (☎781-3030. Open Tu-F 10am-11pm, Sa 11:30am-11pm.)

◪ **SIGHTS.** Some 350 million tons of dinosaur remains have been carted away from this Jurassic cemetery, but over 1600 fossils remain exposed in the **Quarry Visitors Center** (see **Practical Information,** above). Scenic drives and hikes are the best way to appreciate the unique beauty and history of the area. Stop by the Visitors Center in Vernal to pick up free guides to auto tours in the area. These pamphlets direct motorists to historical sights and beautiful vistas. **Harper's Corner,** at the confluence of the Green and Yampa Rivers (take the Harper's Corner Rd. from the monument headquarters) has one of the best views around. At the end of the road, an easy 2 mi. round-trip hike leads to the view.

Don Hatch River Expeditions, 221 N. 400 E. in Vernal, is descended from one of the nation's earliest commercial rafting enterprises. Well-respected Hatch Expeditions floats through the monument and the nearby Flaming Gorge. Be sure to request a paddle trip if you're interested in helping steer the raft. (☎789-4316 or 800-342-8243; www.hatchriver.com. Open M-F 9am-5pm. One-day trip $66, age 6-12 $56; seniors 10% off. Advance reservations recommended.)

FLAMING GORGE NATIONAL RECREATION AREA   ☎435

Seen at sunset, the contrast between the red canyons and the aquamarine water of the Green River, the landscape appears to glow, hence the moniker "Flaming Gorge." Apparently not everyone was satisfied with this natural beauty; legislation was passed in 1963 to dam the Green River. The resulting body of water is now home to the Flaming Gorge National Recreation Area. Boating and fishing enthusiasts descend into the gorge every summer to take advantage of the water.

The Green River below the dam teems with trout, allowing for top-notch **fishing.** To fish, obtain a **permit,** available at Flaming Gorge Lodge, Dutch John Recreation Services, and stores in Manila. For more info, call the **Utah Division of Wildlife Resources,** 1594 W. North Temple, in Salt Lake City. (☎800-538-4700. Open M-F 7:30am-6pm.) Several establishments rent the requisite gear for reservoir recreation. **Cedar Springs Marina,** 3 mi. before the dam, rents boats and accessories. (☎889-3795. Open daily 8am-6pm. 10-person pontoon boats from $120 for 3hr., $200 per day. 6-person ski boats $130/220; skis $15 per day. 6-person fishing boats $50/90.) Nearby, **Flaming Gorge Lodge** rents fishing rods. (☎889-3773; www.fglodge.com. Open daily 6:30am-8pm. $15 per day.)

Hikers and bikers will delight in the area's trails, some of which snake along dangerous cliff edges. The **Canyon Rim Trail** (2.7 mi. one-way or 5 mi. loop) has access points at Red Canyon Visitors Center and several campgrounds. Another hike (6-7hr., 10 mi.) begins at **Dowd Mountain,** off Rte. 44 west of Manila, and travels up Hideout Canyon. All trails in the area allow bikes. The strenuous **Elk Park Loop** (20 mi.) departs Rte. 44 at Deep Creek Rd., follows it to Forest Rd. 221 and Forest Rd. 105, skirts Browne Lake, and runs single-track along **Old Carter and South Elk Park Trails.** For cars, the **Sheep Creek Geologic Loop,** an 11 mi. scenic drive off Rte. 44 south of Manila, passes towering, sculpted strata and desert wildlife.

Camping in the area is scenic and accessible. With over 30 campgrounds spread around the lake, the **Visitors Center** offers sound advice for reserving sites. (☎888-444-6777; call 5 days ahead.) The 18 secluded sites at **Dripping Springs ❶,** just past Dutch John on Rte. 191, sport a prime fishing location. (Sites $13. Reservations accepted. Open year-round.) **Canyon Rim ❶,** on the road to the Red Canyon Visitors Center, offers a feeling of high-country camping with nearby views of the red-walled gorge ($13). For a roof and four walls, the **Red Canyon Lodge ❸,** 2 mi. south of the Visitors Center on Rte. 44, offers great location, views, and activities in line with a luxury resort, but at budget prices. (☎889-3759. Private lake, restaurant. 2-person cabins with restrooms $55, 4-person $65; each additional adult $6, under 12 $2; rollaway beds $6 per night.) In **Manila,** the **Steinnaker Motel ❷,** at Rte. 43 and 44, offers cramped but clean rooms. (☎784-3104. Check-in at the Chevron station. Singles $36; doubles $44; tax included.)

From Vernal, follow U.S. 191 north to the recreation area. The reservoir extends as far north as Green River, WY, and is also accessible from I-80. A recreation pass ($2 per day, $5 per 16 days) can be obtained at the **Flaming Gorge Visitors Center,** on U.S. 191 atop the Flaming Gorge Dam, or at most stores surrounding the Gorge. The Visitors Center also offers free tours of the dam.(☎885-3135. Open daily 8am-

6pm; off-season 10am-4pm.) A few miles off U.S. 191 and 3 mi. off Rte. 44 to Manila, the **Red Canyon Visitors Center** hangs 1360 ft. above the reservoir, offering staggering views into the canyon. (☎889-3713. Open late May-Aug. daily 10am-5pm.) Gas and other services cluster around the dam and the towns of Manila and Dutch John. **Post Office:** 4 South Blvd., in Dutch John. (☎885-3351. Open M-F 7:30am-3:30pm, Sa 8:30am-11am and 1:45-3:15pm.) **ZIP code: 84023. Area code: 435.**

MOAB   ☎435

Moab first flourished in the 1950s, when uranium miners rushed to the area and transformed the town from a quiet hamlet into a gritty desert outpost. Today, the mountain bike has replaced the Geiger counter, as tourists rush into the town eager to bike the red slickrock, raft whitewater rapids, and explore the surrounding Arches and Canyonlands National Parks. The town itself has changed to accommodate the new visitors and athletes; microbreweries and t-shirt shops now fill the rooms of the old uranium building on Main St.

⚡🔢 ORIENTATION & PRACTICAL INFORMATION. Moab sits 30 mi. south of I-70 on U.S. 191, just south of the junction with Rte. 128. The town center lies 5 mi. south of the entrance to Arches National Park and 38 mi. north of the turnoff to the Needles section of Canyonlands National Park. U.S. 191 becomes Main for 5 mi. through downtown. The closest **Amtrak** and **Greyhound** stations are in Green River, 52 mi. northwest of town. Some hotels and hostels will pick guests up from the train or bus for a fee. In addition, **Bighorn Express** (☎888-655-7433) makes a daily trip to and from the Salt Lake City airport, with stops in Green River and Price along the way. Shuttles leave from the Ramada Inn, 182 S. Main. (Departs Salt Lake City airport at 2pm, departs Moab at 7:30am. 4½ hr. trip. $49 each way. Reservations recommended.) **Roadrunner Shuttle** (☎259-9402) and **Coyote Shuttle** (☎259-8656) take you where you want to go on- or off-road in the Moab area. **Moab Information Center**, 3 Center St., at the intersection of Center and Main. (☎259-8825 or 800-635-6622.) This umbrella organization for the **Chamber of Commerce**, the **National Park Service**, the **US Forest Service**, and the **BLM**, doles out copious information on the city and the surrounding outdoors. (Open Mar.-Apr. daily 8am-7pm; May 8am-8pm; June to mid-Oct. 8am-9pm; Nov.-Feb. 9am-5pm.) **Post Office:** 50 E. 100 N. (☎259-7427. Open M-F 8:30am-5:30pm, Sa 8:30am-1pm.) **ZIP code:** 84532. **Area code:** 435.

🎒 ACCOMMODATIONS. Chain motels clutter Main, but Moab is not cheap, and fills up fast from April to October, especially on weekends. **Lazy Lizard International Hostel ❶**, 1213 S. U.S. 191, is near the "A1 Self Storage" sign 1 mi. south of Moab on U.S. 191. The owners of this well-maintained hostel will give you the lowdown on Moab. The kitchen, VCR, laundry, and hot tub draw a mix of college students, backpackers, and aging hippies. (Reception 8am-11pm, but late arrivals can be arranged. Check-out 11am. No curfew. Reservations recommended for weekends in the spring and fall. Dorms $8; private rooms for 1 or 2 from $20; cabins sleeping up to 6 $25-44; tent sites $6.) **Hotel Off Center ❶**, 96 E. Center St., a block off Main, the gracious owners offer eclectically lavish rooms accented by such items as a miner's hat, a Victrola, and fishing nets. (☎259-4244. Open Mar.-Nov. Dorms $12; singles $39; doubles $49.) The small **Silver Sage Inn ❷**, 840 S. Main St., offers the best rates in town, with simple rooms in a somewhat institutional building. (☎259-4420. Apr.-Oct. singles $40, doubles $45. Nov.-Mar. $25/$30.)

One thousand campsites inhabit the Moab area, so finding a place to sleep under the stars shouldn't be much of a problem. **Goose Island, Hal Canyon, Oak Grove, Negro Bill**, and **Big Bend Campgrounds ❶**, all on Rte. 128, sit on the banks of the Colorado River three to nine mi. northeast of downtown Moab. Many of the sites are shaded, and the locations couldn't be better. (☎259-2100. Fire pits but no hookups or showers. Water is available at Matrimony Spring and Negro Bill at the intersection of U.S. 191 and Rte. 128. Sites $10.) The shaded, secluded **Up the Creek Campground ❶**, 210 E. 300 S, is just a walk away from downtown and caters solely to tent camping. (☎259-6995. 20 sites. Showers. Open Mar.-Oct. $10 per person.)

◻ FOOD. Retro booths at the ▨**Moab Diner and Ice Cream Shoppe ❷**, 189 S. Main, might take you back to the 1950s, but with veggie specials and tasty green chili ($4-10), the food won't. (☎259-4006. Open Su-Th 6am-10pm, F-Sa 6am-10:30pm.) ▨**EklectiCafe ❶**, 352 N. Main St., dishes out a wide array of ambrosial pastries, coffee drinks (all made with organic, fair-trade beans), breakfasts ($3-7), and lunch options ($4-8). Locals perform live roots music on Sunday mornings to an audience crunchier than the brunch food. (☎259-6896. Open M-Sa 7:30am-2:30pm, Su 7:30am-1pm.) **Desert Bistro ❺**, 92 E. Center St., is a fine-dining option bringing together big-city haute cuisine and Moab attitude. (☎259-0756. Open daily from 5:30pm. Entrees $18-25, salads $6-8.) The **Peace Tree Juice Cafe ❶**, 20 S. Main, will cool you off with a smoothie or fresh juice ($2.50-5) the perfect antidote to a hot day in the desert. (☎259-6333. Open Su-Th 9am-5pm, F-Sa 9am-9pm.)

▧ OUTDOOR ACTIVITIES. Mountain biking and **rafting**, along with nearby national parks, are the big draws in Moab. The well-known **Slickrock Trail** (10 mi.) rolls up and down the slickrock outside of Moab. The trail has no big vertical gain, but it's technically difficult and temperatures often reach 100°F. **Rim Cyclery**, 94 W. 1st St., rents bikes and distributes info about the slickrock trails. (☎259-5333. Open Su-Th 9am-6pm, F-Sa 8am-6pm. $32-50 per day; includes helmet.)

Countless raft companies are based in Moab. ▨**OARS/North American River Expeditions**, 543 N. Main St., offers the best guides on the river. (☎259-5865 or 800-342-5938. Half-day $36, ages 5-17 $27; includes snacks and a natural history lesson.) **Western River Expeditions** offers good deals as well. (☎259-7019 or 800-453-7450. Half-day $34, children $27; full-day $47/34; includes lunch.) Various outfitters arrange horseback, motorboat, canoe, jeep, and helicopter rides.

UTAH'S NATURAL WONDERS

Arches, Canyonlands, Bryce Canyon, Zion, and Capitol Reef National Parks lie in a northeast-to-southwest-oriented line running through the southern portion of Utah, connected by a well-traveled series of scenic highways. These popular parks are geographically dwarfed by Grand Staircase-Escalante National Monument, the new kid on the block, sprawling south and east of Bryce Canyon and west of Capitol Reef. The spectacular arches, canyons, amphitheaters, plateaus, and vibrant redrock of these public lands make them one of the densest collections of geological and panoramic brilliance the entire nation has to offer.

From Moab in the northeast, take U.S. 191 N 5 mi. to **Arches.** Continue 60 mi. north on U.S. 191 to Rte. 313 S and the Islands in the Sky area of **Canyonlands.** Or, take U.S. 191 south from Moab to Rte. 211 W to reach the Needles area of Canyonlands (87 mi.). To reach **Capitol Reef,** continue driving north on U.S. 191 and then west on I-70; leave I-70 at Exit 147, and follow Rte. 24 S to Hanksville; then west to the park (81 mi. from I-70). Rte. 24 W runs to Torrey, where scenic Rte. 12 branches south and west through the Dixie National Forest to **Bryce Canyon.** For **Zion,** stay on Rte. 12 W to U.S. 89 S through Mt. Carmel Jct., and pick up Rte. 9 W. The 122mi. stretch of **Rte. 95** between Blanding and Hanksville, known as the Bicentennial Highway because it was built in 1976, is one of the most scenic in the lower 48 and highlights a diverse cross-section of southern Utah.

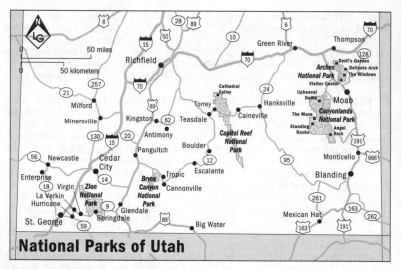

National Parks of Utah

The two national forests in Southern Utah are divided into districts, some of which lie near the national parks and serve as excellent places to stay on a cross-country jaunt. **Manti-La Sal National Forest** has two sections near Arches and the Needles area of Canyonlands. **Dixie National Forest** stretches from Capitol Reef through Bryce all the way to the western side of Zion NP.

ARCHES   ☎435

"This is the most beautiful place on earth," novelist Edward Abbey wrote of Arches National Park. Thousands of sandstone arches, spires, pinnacles, and fins tower above the desert in overwhelming grandeur. Some arches are so perfect in form that early explorers believed they were constructed by a lost civilization. Deep red sandstone, green piñon pines and juniper bushes, and a strikingly blue sky combine in an unforgettable palette of colors best explored on foot.

◼️🔢 ORIENTATION & PRACTICAL INFORMATION. The park entrance is on U.S. 191, 5 mi. north of Moab. Although no public transportation serves the park, shuttle bus companies travel to both the national park and Moab from surrounding towns and cities. While most visitors come in the summer, 100°F temperatures make hiking difficult; bring at least one gallon of water per person per day. The weather is best in the spring and fall when temperate days and nights combine to make a comfortable stay. In the winter, white snow provides a brilliant contrast to the red arches. The **Visitors Center,** to the right of the entrance station, distributes free park service maps. (☎719-2299. Open daily 8am-4:30pm; extended hours approximately Mar.-Sept.) An **entrance pass** ($10 per carload, $5 per pedestrian or biker) covers admission for a week. Write the Superintendent, Arches National Park, P.O. Box 907, Moab 84532. **Area code:** 435.

🔢 CAMPING. The park's only campground, **Devil's Garden ❶,** has 52 excellent campsites nestled amid piñons and giant red sandstone formations. The campsite is within walking distance of the Devil's Garden and Broken Arch trailheads; however, it is a long 18 mi. from the Visitors Center. Because Devil's Garden doesn't take reservations, sites go quickly. (No wood-gathering. Running water mid-Mar. to Oct.; 1-week max. stay. Sites $10; in winter $5.)

If the heat becomes unbearable at Arches, the aspen forests of the **Manti-La Sal National Forest** offer a respite. Take Rte. 128 along the Colorado River and turn right at Castle Valley, or go south from Moab on U.S. 191 and turn to the left at the Shell Station. There are a number of campgrounds here including **Warner Lake ❶**, where beautiful sites sit 4000 ft. above the national park and are invariably several degrees cooler. (Sites $10; Oowah Lake sites free.) **Oowah**, a three-mile hike from the Geyser Pass Rd., is a rainbow trout haven. Fishing permits are available at stores in Moab and at the Forest Service Office, 62 E. 100 N, for $5 per day. Contact the Manti-La Sal National Forest (☎259-7155).

◪ **HIKING.** While the striking red slickrock around Arches may seem like attraction enough, the real points of interest here lie off the paved road. Load up on water and sunscreen and seek out the park's thousands of natural arches, each one pinpointed on the free map and guide that is passed out at the fee collection booth. For more detailed maps and info on hiking, especially desert precautions, stop at the Visitors Center. Hiking in the park is unparalleled, especially in the cool days of spring and fall. Stay on trails; the land may look barren but the soil actually contains cryptobiotic life forms that are easily destroyed by footsteps. The most popular hike in the park leads to the oft-photographed **Delicate Arch**. The trail (2½hr., 3 mi.) leaves from the Wolfe Ranch parking area and climbs 480 ft; be sure to bring lots of water. To view the spectacular Delicate Arch without the 3 mi. hike, take the **Delicate Arch Viewpoint "Trail"** which begins in the Viewpoint parking area. This 300 ft. trail takes around 15min. and is wheelchair accessible. The loop through **Devils Garden** (3-5hr., 7.2 mi.) requires some scrambling over rocks, but hearty travelers will be rewarded by the eight arches visible from this trail. The trek is not recommended in wet or snowy conditions. **Tower Arch** (2-3hr., 3.4 mi.) can be accessed from the trailhead at the Klondike Bluffs parking area via Salt Valley Rd. This moderate hike explores one of the remote regions of the park, and is a good way to escape crowds. The trail ascends a steep, short rock wall before meandering through sandstone fins and sand dunes. Salt Valley Rd. is often washed out—check at the Visitors Center before departing.

CAPITOL REEF ☎435

What do you get when you cross rock formations that strangely resemble the capitol dome of the State House in Washington with precipitous rock cliffs? A strangely inappropriate name for Utah's stunning, youngest national park. The hundred-mile Waterpocket Fold is a geologist's fantasy and the park's feature attraction. With its rocky peaks and pinnacles, the Fold bisects Capitol Reef's 378 sq. mi., presenting visitors with millions of years of stratified natural history.

■◪ **ORIENTATION & PRACTICAL INFORMATION.** The middle link in the Fab Five chain, east of Zion and Bryce Canyon and west of Arches and Canyonlands, Capitol Reef is unreachable by major bus lines. The closest **Greyhound** stop is in Green River. For a fee, **Wild Hare Expeditions** (see **Sights and Outdoor Activities,** below) will provide shuttle service between Richfield and the park. **Entrance** to the park is free except for the scenic drive that costs $4 per vehicle. The **Visitors Center,** on Rte. 24, supplies travelers with waterproof topo maps, regular maps, free brochures on trails, and info on daily activities such as ranger-led jaunts. (☎425-3791. Open June-Aug. daily 8am-6pm; Sept.-May 8am-4:30pm.) The free park newspaper, *The Cliffline,* lists a schedule of park activities. *When hiking, keep in mind that summer temperatures average 95°F. After rain, beware of flash floods.* Contact the Superintendent, Capitol Reef National Park, HC 70 Box 15, Torrey 84775 (☎425-3791). **Post Office:** 222 E. Main St., in Fruita. (☎425-3488. Open M-F 8am-1pm, Sa 7:30-11am.) **ZIP code:** 84775. **Area code:** 435.

▚▐ ACCOMMODATIONS & FOOD. The park's campgrounds offer sites on a first come, first served basis. The main campground, **Fruita ❶**, 1¼ mi. south of the Visitors Center off Rte. 24, contains 71 sites with water and toilets but no showers. The campground nestles between orchards, and visitors can eat all the fruit they want (sites $10). **Cedar Mesa Campground ❶**, on the Notom-Bullfrog Rd., and **Cathedral Valley ❶**, in the north (accessible by four-wheel-drive vehicle or on foot), have only five sites each; neither has water, but they're free. Both areas and all backcountry camping require a free **backcountry permit**, available at the Visitors Center. **Torrey**, a sleepy town 11 mi. west of the Visitors Center on Rte. 24, is home to the nearest lodging and restaurants to Capitol Reef. The friendly ▨**Sandcreek Hostel ❶**, 54 Rte. 24, features an espresso and smoothie bar, organic produce, local crafts, and remarkably inexpensive accommodations. A single dorm room houses eight comfy beds, a minifridge, and a microwave. There are also 12 tent sites, 12 hookups, and two rustic cabins that can sleep up to four people. (☎425-3577. Showers for non-guests $3. Linens $2. Reception 7:30am-8pm. Check-out 11am. Open Apr. to mid-Oct. Dorms $10, tent sites $10, hookups $15-18, cabins $28-34.) Down the road, the **Capitol Reef Inn and Cafe ❷**, 360 W. Main St., puts up guests with flair in Southwestern themed rooms with handmade furniture, plus access to a jacuzzi and one of the best restaurants in town. (☎425-3271. Reception 7am-10pm. Check-out 11am. Open Apr.-Oct. Rooms $40, each additional person $4.)
Capitol Reef Inn and Cafe ❸, 360 W. Main St., dishes up local rainbow trout (smoked or grilled) and other fresh, natural ingredients in a dining room that looks out on the russet hills. Don't miss the $7.75 grilled trout sandwich served on a bagel with cream cheese or one of their $8-11 lush salads. (☎425-3271. Open Apr.-Oct. daily 7am-9pm.) Greasier offerings await at **Brink's Burgers ❶**, 163 E. Main St. (☎425-3710. Open daily 11am-9pm. Take-out available. Entrees $2-5. Cash only.)

◉▟ SIGHTS & OUTDOOR ACTIVITIES. The Reef's haunting landforms can be explored from the seat of your car on the 25 mi. scenic drive, a 1½hr. round-trip jaunt next to the cliffs along paved and improved dirt roads. Along Rte. 24, you can ponder the bathroom-sized **Fruita Schoolhouse** built by Mormon settlers, 1000-year-old **petroglyphs** etched on the stone walls, and **Panorama Point. Chimney Rock** and the **Castle** are two striking sandstone formations along the route. **Wild Hare Expeditions**, 2600 E. Rte. 24, in the Best Western Capitol Reef Resort, embarks on a variety of backpacking and hiking tours. (☎425-3999 or 888-304-4273. Hours vary. $40-50 per half-day, children $35; full-day $60-75/50.)
For a change of scenery check out the bucolic **orchards**, which lie within the park in the Fruita region. Eat as much fruit as you like while in the orchards, but you must pay to take some home. In the northern and southern sections of the park, all hikes are considered backcountry travel. Be sure to get a **free backcountry permit** for all overnight trips. More reasonable and plebeian day hikes depart from trailheads along Rte. 24. Check at the Visitors Center for more info on hikes.

BRYCE CANYON ☎435

If Nature enjoys painting with a big brush in the Southwest, she discarded her usual coarse tools for finer instruments when creating Bryce Canyon. The canyon brims with slender, fantastically shaped rock spires called hoodoos. What it lacks in Grand Canyon-esque magnitude, Bryce makes up for in intricate beauty. Early in the morning or late in the evening the sun's rays bring the hoodoos to life, transforming them into color-changing stone chameleons. The first sight of the canyon can be breathtaking: as Ebenezer Bryce, a Mormon carpenter with a gift for understatement, put it, the canyon is "one hell of a place to lose a cow."

⚡🗺 ORIENTATION & PRACTICAL INFORMATION. Approaching from the west, Bryce Canyon lies 1½hr. east of Cedar City; take Rte. 14 to U.S. 89. From the east, take I-70 to U.S. 89, turn east on Rte. 12 at Bryce Jct. (7 mi. south of Panguitch), and drive 14 mi. to the Rte. 63 junction; head south 4 mi. to the park entrance. There is no public transportation to Bryce Canyon. The park's entrance fee is $20 per car, $10 per pedestrian. The **Visitors Center** is just inside the park. (☎834-5322. Open June-Aug. 8am-8pm; Apr.-May and Sept.-Oct. 8am-6pm; Nov.-Mar. 8am-4:30pm.) To assuage the park's traffic problem, the Park Service has implemented a **shuttle system,** serving all destinations via three routes. Private vehicles can travel park roads, but the Park Service offers a $5 admission discount to those who park at the junction of Rte. 12 and 63 and ride the shuttle into the park. **Post Office** is in Bryce Lodge. (☎834-5361. Open M-F 8am-noon and 1-5pm, Sa 8am-noon.) **ZIP code:** 84717. **Area code:** 435.

📷🏠 ACCOMMODATIONS & FOOD. North and **Sunset Campgrounds ❶,** both within 3 mi. of the Visitors Center, offer toilets, picnic tables, potable water, and 210 sites on a first come, first served basis. (Sites $10; arrive early to claim the best spots.) **Backcountry camping permits** are free from the ranger at the Visitors Center. Two campgrounds lie just west of Bryce on scenic Rte. 12, in Dixie National Forest. The **King Creek Campground ❶,** 11 mi. from Bryce on a dirt road off Rte. 12 (look for signs to Tropic Reservoir), features lakeside sites. (☎800-280-2267. $10.) At 7400 ft., the **Red Canyon Campground ❶** has 36 sites ($11) on a first come, first served basis amid the glory of the red rocks.

Sleeping inside the park requires either a tent and sleeping bag or a fat wallet. The historic **Bryce Canyon Lodge ❺,** the only in-park hotel, offers motel-style rooms and cabins. (☎834-5361. Open Apr.-Oct. Rooms for 2 people $100; cabins for 2 people $111; each additional person $5.) Away from the park, rates drop; better deals line Rte. 12 in Tropic, and Panguitch, 23 mi. west of the park on U.S. 89, has more than 15 inexpensive, independent motels. For most area accommodations, room rates fluctuate with the season and tourist flow. Winter rates are much, much lower, and in slow summers, bargain walk-in rates abound. ✪**Bybee's Steppingstone Motel ❷,** 21 S. Main St., in Tropic, offers clean, bright, spacious and inexpensive rooms minutes from the park entrance, but far away from the tourist bustle. (☎679-8998. Singles in summer $40; doubles $45.) In Panguitch, the ✪**Marianna Inn ❷,** 699 N. Main St., boasts large, immaculate, newly remodeled rooms and amenities such as a large outdoor pergola for relaxing on hot summer days and a hot tub for warming up on chilly fall afternoons. (☎676-8844. Singles in summer $35, in winter $30; doubles $45/40.)

Inside and immediately surrounding the national park, feeding options are scarce. A quick slice of pizza or a microwave burrito await at the **Bryce Canyon General Store.** For a sit-down lunch inside the park, try the $5-6 burgers and sandwiches at **Bryce Canyon Lodge Dining Room ❷.** With a little driving, more affordable and varied alternatives multiply. Thick, golden brown pancakes ($2) await starving passersby at the **Hungry Coyote ❶,** on N. Main St. in Tropic. (☎679-8811. Open Apr.-Oct. daily 6:30-10:30am and 5-10pm.) Several miles west of the park on Rte. 12, the **Bryce Pines Restaurant ❸** serves delicious home-cooked meals. (☎834-5441. Open in summer daily 6:30am-9:30pm. Sandwiches $4-6; dinner entrees $10-14.)

📷🥾 SIGHTS & OUTDOOR ACTIVITIES. Bryce's 18 mi. main road winds past spectacular lookouts such as **Sunrise Point, Sunset Point, Inspiration Point,** and **Rainbow Point,** but a range of hiking trails makes it a crime not to leave your car. A word to the wise: the air is thin—if you start to feel giddy or short of breath, take a rest. Very sturdy shoes or hiking boots are a must for hiking into the canyon. One oft-missed viewpoint is **Fairlyland Point,** at the north end of the park, 1 mi. off the main road, with some of the best sights in the canyons. The **Rim Trail** (4-6hr., 11 mi.) parallels the Amphitheater and offers views over longer than a 100 mi; between sunrise Point and Sunset Point is wheelchair accessible, and a good way to peer onto the sea of hoodoos. The loop of the **Navajo** and **Queen's Garden Trails** (2-3hr., 3.1 mi.) leads into the canyon past some natural bridges. More challenging options include **Peek-A-Boo Loop** (3-4hr., 3.5 mi.), winding in and out through hoodoos, and the **Trail to the Hat Shop** (4 mi.), an extremely steep trail (tough both ways). **Canyon Trail Rides** arranges guided horseback rides. (☎ 679-8665. $27-40 per person.)

GRAND STAIRCASE-ESCALANTE NAT'L MONUMENT ☎ 435

The last virgin corner of American wilderness to be captured by a cartographer's pen, Grand Staircase-Escalante National Monument remains remote, rugged, pristine, and beautiful. The 1.9 million acre expanse of painted sandstone, high alpine plateau, treacherous canyons, and raging rivers shelters diverse areas of geological, biological, and historical interest.

Travelers just passing through the Escalante area en route to national parks east and west have a variety of options for getting a brief glimpse of the Monument's wild beauty. Scenic **Rte. 12,** tracing picturesque slickrock hills 28 mi. between Boulder and Escalante, is arguably one of the Southwest's most spectacular stretches of highway. While cresting and plunging between colored sandstone, Rte. 12 feels like driving through a miniature Zion. Just before descending into the farming community of Boulder, the highway threads a narrow flat between dramatic drops, the vehicular equivalent to a titillating summit-ridge hike.

A **free backcountry permit** is required for all multi-day trips into the monument. The most popular destination for backpacking trips are the **Canyons of Escalante,** in the eastern portion of the monument. Cutting through the slickrock towards Lake Powell, the Escalante and its feeder drainages create a series of canyons ripe for exploration. Many routes require technical canyoneering skills. Primary access to the canyons of Escalante comes via the **Hole-in-the-Rock Rd.,** heading south from Rte. 12 east of Escalante. One of the most challenging routes in the area, this 30 mi. trek through Death Hollow Wilderness navigates narrow slot canyons north of town and earns its ominous name with lethal flash floods. The hike involves technical climbing and long stretches of swimming with a heavy pack through pools. Two campgrounds reside in the Escalante area. The 13 shaded sites at **Calf Creek Campground ❶,** 15 mi. east of Escalante, offer access to the Calf Creek Trail. (Toilets and water. Sites $7.) Six miles north of Boulder on Rte. 12, there are primitive sites at **Deer Creek ❶** (7 sites; toilets, no water; $4). **Bestway Groceries,** 9 W. Main St., stocks Escalante's only selection of grocery items. (☎ 826-4226. Open M-Sa 8am-8pm.)

Nearly two million acres is a lot of space, probably more than an entire lifetime's worth of walking could cover. Being so large, several communities serve as gateways to different portions of the monument. In the south, **Rte. 89** between Kanab and **Lake Powell** cuts into the monument and provides access to the popular **Cottonwood Canyon Rd.** At the far eastern limit of the monument, many Glen Canyon recreationalists park their boats for day hikes in the lower canyons of the Escalante drainage. Visitor information is available at the **Escalante Interagency Visitors Center,** 755 W. Main (☎ 826-5499), in Escalante. Helpful and friendly staff steer eager hikers to appropriate routes. The official monument headquarters is at **Kanab Field Office,** 318 N. 100 E., in Kanab. (☎ 644-2672. Open M-F 8am-4:30pm.)

ZION NATIONAL PARK ☎435

Russet sandstone mountains loom over the puny cars and hikers that flock to Zion National Park in search of the promised land, and rarely does Zion disappoint. In the 1860s, Mormon settlers came to the area and enthusiastically proclaimed that they had found Zion, the promised land. Brigham Young disagreed, however, and declared that the place was awfully nice, but "not Zion." The name "not Zion" stuck for years until a new wave of entranced explorers dropped the "not," giving the park its present name. The park might very well be the fulfillment of Biblical prophecy for outdoor recreationalists. With hiking trails nonpareil and challenging and mysterious slot canyons set against a tableau of sublime sandstone, visiting Zion is a spiritual event.

▓▓ **ORIENTATION & PRACTICAL INFORMATION.** The main entrance to Zion is in **Springdale**, on Rte. 9, which borders the park to the south along the Virgin River. Approaching Zion from the west, take Rte. 9 from I-15 at Hurricane. In the east, pick up Rte. 9 from U.S. 89 at Mt. Carmel Jct. **Greyhound**, 43 mi. southwest of the park on I-15 in St. George (☎673-2937) depart from a McDonald's (1235 S. Bluff St., at St. George Blvd). The brand new, ecologically harmonious **Zion Canyon Visitors Center,** just inside the south entrance, houses an info center, bookstore, and backcountry permit station. At the west entrance to the park, the **Kolob Canyons Visitors Center** offers info on the Kolob Canyon Scenic Drive and the surrounding trail system, as well as books and maps. (☎772-3256. Both centers open in summer daily 8am-7pm; in winter reduced hours.) The park's entrance fee is $20 per car, $10 per pedestrian. **Emergency:** ☎772-3322. The **Post Office** is located inside the Zion Canyon Lodge. **ZIP code:** 84767. **Area code:** 435.

▐ **ACCOMMODATIONS.** The closest hostel is the ▓**Dixie Hostel (HI-AYH),** 73 S. Main St., 20 mi. west of Zion in Hurricane. Fresh-smelling, pink-hued, and without a speck of dust, the hostel is a comfortable stay and only 2hr. from Las Vegas, Lake Powell, the North Rim, and Bryce Canyon. (☎635-8202. Linen, laundry, kitchen, and continental breakfast. Internet access $1 per hr. Dorms $15; singles $35.) Springdale's least expensive lodging, the family-owned **El Río Lodge ❸,** 995 Zion Park Blvd., welcomes guests with clean rooms, friendly service, and dazzling views of the Watchman Face. (☎772-3205 or 888-772-3205. Singles $47; doubles $52; winter rates dip to around $35.) Across the street, the **Terrace Brook Lodge ❸,** 990 Zion Park Blvd., offers clean and reasonably inexpensive rooms. (☎800-342-6779. Singles $55, with 2 beds $71; $10 less in winter. AAA discounts.)

More than 300 sites are available at the **South** and **Watchman Campgrounds ❶,** near the brand new Visitors Center. Campgrounds fill quickly in summer; arrive before noon to ensure a spot. **Watchman Campground** takes reservations, but **South** is first come, first served. (☎800-365-2267 for Watchman reservations. Water, toilets, and sanitary disposal station. Both $14. Open year-round.) Avoid the crowds at the six free primitive sites at **Lava Point ❶,** a nearly 1hr. drive from the Visitors Center, in close proximity to the panoramic Lava Point overlook and the Western Rim Trailhead. (Open June-Nov.) **Zion Canyon Campground ❶,** 479 Zion Park Blvd., refreshes the weary, hungry, and filthy with a convenience store, pizzeria, grocery store, showers ($3 for non-guests), and coin-op laundry. (☎772-3237. Office open daily 8am-9pm. Store open daily 8am-9pm; off-season 8am-5pm. Sites for 2 $18, full hookups $22; $3.50 per additional adult, $2 per additional child under 15.) **Zion Frontier Campground ❶,** ¼ mi. outside the east entrance, is 1000 ft. higher and about

THE SOUTHWEST

10°F cooler than the sites inside the park, and offers a laundromat, showers, restaurant, and gas station. (☎648-2154. Office open 24hr. 60 tent sites $12; 19 hookups $20; tepees and a hogon $20; cabins $25.)

🏔 OUTDOOR ACTIVITIES. Zion seems to have been made for hiking; unlike in the foreboding canyons that surround it, most of the trails won't have you praying for a stray mule to show up. However, a number of trails spiral around cliffs with narrow trails and long drop-offs. Hiking boots are recommended on trails like Angel's Landing of Hidden Canyons. The trails are serviced by a prompt shuttle bus system that delivers bright-eyed hikers to and from trailheads (runs 6:30am-11:15pm). Shuttle maps are available at the Visitors Center.

The **Riverside Walk** (1-2hr., 2 mi.), paved and wheelchair accessible with assistance, begins at the Temple of Sinawava at the north end of Zion Canyon Dr. Running alongside the Virgin River and some beautiful wildflower displays, Riverside is Zion's most popular and easiest trail. The **Emerald Pools Trail** (1-3hr., 1.2-3.1 mi.) has wheelchair access along its lower loop, but the middle and upper loops are steep and narrow. Swimming is not allowed in any of the pools. The challenging **Angel's Landing Trail** (4hr., 5 mi.) begins at the Grotto picnic area, and rises 1488 ft. above the canyon; the last terrifying stretch climbs a narrow ridge with guide chains blasted into the rock. A shorter, but equally harrowing trail is **Hidden Canyon Trail** (2-3hr., 2 mi.), rewarding hikers with impressive valley views. The difficult **Observation Point Trail** (5hr., 8 mi.) leads through **Echo Canyon,** a spectacular kaleidoscope of sandstone, where steep switchbacks explore the unusually gouged canyon. Overnight hikers can spend days on the 13 mi. course of the **West Rim Trail.**

One of the best ways to take in Zion's splendor is to ride the shuttle bus loop. Called the **Zion Canyon Scenic Loop,** this 1½ hr. narrated ride gives great views of the rocks from below. Another motorized way to take in the scenery is the 10 mi. **Zion-Mt. Carmel Highway,** connecting the east and south entrances. Spiraling around the Canyon, the highway gives excellent views of the valley, as well as a fun trip through an 80 year-old mountain tunnel.

When visiting the **Kolob Canyons,** check out **Zion Canyon.** The 7 mi. dead-end road on the canyon floor rambles past the giant **Sentinel, Mountain of the Sun,** and the symbol of Zion, the **Great White Throne.** A shuttle from the Lodge runs this route every hour on the hour. (During summer daily 9am-5pm. $3.)

Despite being overshadowed by the boastful Moab, the Zion area has a loyal **mountain biking** following and trails to compete with the big boy to the north. **Gooseberry Mesa,** about 15 mi. from Springdale, has some great singletrack and novice trails. **Bike Zion,** 1458 Zion Park Blvd., can hook you up with wheels and trail advice. (☎772-2453. Open daily 8am-6pm. Rigid bike full-day $23, half-day $17; front suspension $29/22; full suspension $35/27.)

NEAR ZION: CEDAR BREAKS NATIONAL MONUMENT ☎435

Shaped like a gigantic amphitheater, the semicircle of canyons that makes up Cedar Breaks National Monument measures more than 3 mi. in diameter and 2000 ft. in depth. A gallery of sandstone spires decorate the red, orange, and yellow surface of the bowl. To reach this marvel of geology, take Rte. 14 east from Cedar City and turn north on Rte. 148. A 28-site **campground ❶** perched at 10,200 ft. (open June to mid-Sept.; water, flush toilets; sites $12) and the **Visitors Center** (☎586-0787; open May-Sept. daily 8am-6pm) await at **Point Supreme.** There are no services inside the monument; the nearest gas, food, and lodging are found either in Cedar City or Brian Head. (☎586-9451. Entrance $3; under 17 free.)

Tourists travel to the Monument nearly exclusively for the view, most easily reached by parking at the Visitors Center and walking to Point Supreme, or by stopping at one of several vistas along the 5 mi. stretch of scenic Rte. 143. The Monument has two established trails that provide for a more extended visit. Originating at the **Chessman Ridge Overlook** (10,467 ft., roughly 2 mi. north of the Visitors Center), the popular 2 mi. round-trip **Alpine Pond Trail** follows the rim to a spring-fed alpine lake whose waters trickle into the breaks, winding toward slow evaporation in the Great Basin. The hike takes 1-2hr. and is accompanied by an instructive trail guide available at the Visitors Center or trailhead ($1). The 4 mi. round-trip **Ramparts Trail** departs from the Visitors Center at 10,300 ft. and traces the edge of the amphitheater through a Bristlecone grove to a 9950 ft. point, providing spectacular views of the terrain below. Though reaching the monument during the winter proves difficult on snowy roads, cross-country skiers cherish the rolling meadows and serene winter scenery.

ARIZONA

Populated primarily by Native Americans until the end of the 19th century, Arizona has been hit in the past hundred years by waves of settlers—from the speculators and miners of the late 1800s, to the soldiers who trained here during World War II and returned after the war, to the more recent immigrants from Mexico. Traces of lost Native American civilization remain at Canyon de Chelly, Navajo National Monument, and Wupatki and Walnut Canyons, while deserted ghost towns are scattered throughout the state. The descendents of area tribes now occupy reservations on one-half of the state's land, making up one-seventh of the US Native American population, while urban Phoenix sprawls wider and wider. Arizona is a state always in flux, yet the majesty of the land is perhaps the one constant. No manmade structures can overshadow Arizona's natural masterpieces—the Grand Canyon, Monument Valley, and the gorgeous landscapes viewed from the state's highways.

🛈 PRACTICAL INFORMATION

Capital: Phoenix.

Visitor info: Arizona Tourism, 2702 N. 3rd St., #4015, Phoenix 85004 (☎ 602-230-7733 or 888-520-3434; www.arizonaguide.com). Open M-F 8am-5pm. **Arizona State Parks,** 1300 W. Washington St., Phoenix 85007 (☎ 602-542-4174 or 800-285-3703). Open M-F 8am-5pm.

Postal Abbreviation: AZ. **Sales Tax:** variable 5%.

Time Zone: Mountain Standard Time. *With the exception of the Navajo reservation, Arizona does not observe Daylight Savings Time.*

GRAND CANYON

Long before its designation as a national park in 1919, the Grand Canyon captured the imagination of each person who strolled to its edge and beheld it. Every summer, millions of visitors travel from across the globe to witness this natural wonder which, in one panorama, captures the themes that make the Southwest so captivating. First, there's the space: 277 miles long and over one mile deep, the

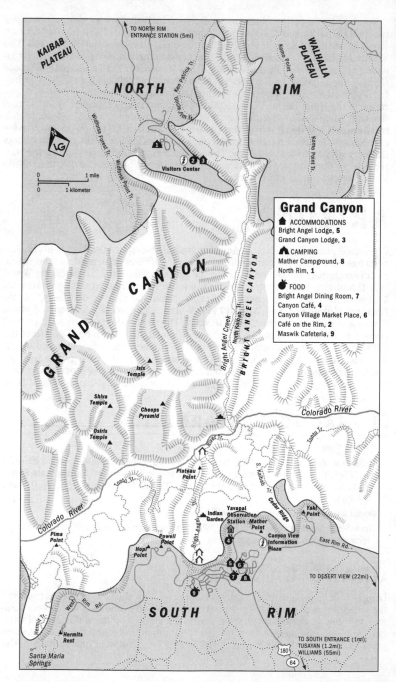

Grand Canyon

♦ ACCOMMODATIONS
Bright Angel Lodge, **5**
Grand Canyon Lodge, **3**

🏕 CAMPING
Mather Campground, **8**
North Rim, **1**

🍎 FOOD
Bright Angel Dining Room, **7**
Canyon Café, **4**
Canyon Village Market Place, **6**
Café on the Rim, **2**
Maswik Cafeteria, **9**

Canyon overwhelms the human capacity for perception. Then, there's the color: a panoply of hues demarcate billions of years of geologic history. Finally, there's the river: the chaotically creative force behind most of the Southwest's beautifully artful landforms is on full display. For some visitors, seeing the Canyon is a spiritual experience. For others, the Canyon demonstrates the ancient history of our earth. In all cases, the Canyon elicits reflection as deep as the Canyon itself.

The Grand Canyon extends from Lee's Ferry, AZ to Lake Mead, NV. In the north, the Glen Canyon Dam backs up the Colorado into mammoth Lake Powell. To the west, the Hoover Dam traps the remaining outflow from Glen Canyon to form Lake Mead. Grand Canyon National Park is divided into three sections: the most popular South Rim; the more serene North Rim; and the canyon gorge itself. Traveling between rims takes approximately five hours, either via a 13-mile hike or a long drive to the bridge in Lee's Ferry. Sandwiched between the national park and Lake Mead, the Hualapai and Havasupai Reservations abut the river.

SOUTH RIM ☎928

During the summer, everything on two legs or four wheels converges on this side of the Grand Canyon. If you plan to visit during the mobfest, make reservations well in advance for lodging, campsites, and/or mules, and prepare to battle the crowds. A friendly Park Service staff, well-run facilities, and beautiful scenery help ease crowd anxiety. Fewer tourists brave the Canyon's winter weather; hotels and facilities often close during the off season.

▐ TRANSPORTATION

There are two park entrances: the main **south entrance** is about 6 mi. from the Visitors Center, while the eastern **Desert View** entrance is 27 mi. away. Both are accessed via Rte. 64. From Las Vegas, the fastest route to the South Rim is U.S. 93 S to I-40 E, and then Rte. 64 N. From Flagstaff, head north on U.S. 180 to Rte. 64.

Trains: The **Grand Canyon Railway** (☎800-843-8724) runs an authentically restored train from Williams, AZ to the Grand Canyon (2¼hr.; leaves 10am, returns 3:30pm; $68, children $27). Guided tours of the rim area run $25-35.

Buses: North Arizona Shuttle and Tours (☎866-870-8687) departs its Flagstaff depot, 1300 S. Milton St., for the Grand Canyon daily (2hr.; leaves 7:30am and 2:30pm, returns to Flagstaff 10am and 4:30pm; $20 each way). Fares don't include $6 entrance fee. Shuttles also head to Sedona twice a day ($25).

Public Transit: Free shuttle buses run the West Rim Loop (daily 1hr. before sunrise to sunset) and the Village Loop (daily 1hr. before sunrise to 11pm) every 10-30min. A free **hiker's shuttle** runs every 30min. between the info center and the South Kaibab Trailhead, on the East Rim near Yaki Point. Early buses run at 4, 5, and 6am.

Taxis: ☎638-2822.

Auto Repairs: Grand Canyon Garage (☎638-2631), east of the Visitors Center on the main road, just before the rim lodges. Open daily 8am-5pm. 24hr. emergency service.

▐ ORIENTATION & PRACTICAL INFORMATION

Posted maps and signs in the park make it easy to orient oneself. Lodges and services concentrate in **Grand Canyon Village**, at the end of Park Entrance Rd. The east half of the village contains the Visitors Center and the general store, while most of the lodges and the challenging **Bright Angel Trail** lie in the west section. The shorter but more difficult **South Kaibab Trail** is off East Rim Dr., east of the village. Free shuttle buses to eight rim overlooks run along **West Rim Dr.** (closed to private vehicles during the summer). Avoid walking on the drive; the rim trails are safer and more scenic. The **entrance pass** is $20 per car and $10 for travelers using other modes of transportation, including bus passengers. The pass lasts for one week. For most services in the Park, call the main switchboard number at 638-2631.

Visitor Info: The new **Canyon View Information Plaza,** across from Mather Point just after the entrance to the park, is the one-stop center for Grand Canyon info. The Visitors Center stocks copies of *The Guide* (an essential), and assorted other pamphlets. To get there, park at Mather Pt., then get out and hoof it for ½ mi. to the info plaza. The Park Service, through the Grand Canyon Association, sells a variety of informational books and packets (☎800-858-2808; www.grandcanyon.com, or check out www.nps.gov/grca). The **transportation info desks** in **Bright Angel Lodge** and **Maswik Lodge** (☎638-2631) handle reservations for mule rides, bus tours, plane tours, Phantom Ranch, taxis, and more. Open daily 6am-8pm.

Equipment Rental: In the General Store. Comfy hiking boots, socks included ($8 1st day, $5 per additional day); sleeping bags ($9/5); tents (2 person $15/9, 4 person $16/9); day packs ($6 large, $4 small); and other camping gear (stoves $5). Deposits required; major credit cards accepted. Open daily 7am-8:30pm.

Weather and Road Conditions: ☎638-7888.

Medical Services: Grand Canyon Clinic (☎638-2551). Turn left at the first stoplight after the South Rim entrance. Open M-F 7am-7pm, Sa 10am-4pm. 24hr. emergency aid.

Post Office: 100 Mather Business Ctr. (☎638-2512), in Market Plaza, next to the General Store. Open M-F 9am-4:30pm, Sa 10am-5pm. **ZIP code: 86023. Area code: 928.**

♖ ACCOMMODATIONS

Compared to the six million years it took the Colorado River to carve the Grand Canyon, the year it will take you to get indoor lodging near the South Rim is nothing. Summer rooms should be reserved eleven months in advance. That said, there are frequent cancellations; if you arrive unprepared, check for vacancies or call the operator (☎638-2631) and ask to be connected with the proper lodge.

Maswik Lodge (☎638-2631), in Grand Canyon Village near the rim and several restaurants. Small, clean cabins with showers but no heat are $66. Motel rooms with queen beds and ceiling fans are also available. Singles $79; doubles $121. $7-9 each additional person. ❺

Bright Angel Lodge (☎638-2631), in Grand Canyon Village. The cheapest indoor lodging in the park, located in a historic building right on the rim. Very convenient to Bright Angel Trail and shuttle buses. "Rustic" lodge singles and doubles with shared bath $53, with private bath $71. "Historic" cabins, some of which have fireplaces, are available for 1 or 2 people $84-107. $7 per additional person in rooms and cabins. ❷

Phantom Ranch (☎638-2631), on the canyon floor, a day's hike down the Kaibab Trail or Bright Angel Trail. Male and female dorms $28; seldom-available cabins for 1 or 2 people $71.50; $10.50 per additional person. Don't show up without reservations, which can be made up to 23 months in advance. Breakfast $17; box lunch $8.50; stew dinner $20; steak dinner $29; vegetarian option $20. If you're dying to sleep on the canyon floor but don't have a reservation, show up at the Bright Angel transportation desk at 6am on the day prior to your planned stay, and take a shot at the waiting list. ❶

⛺ CAMPING

The campsites listed here usually fill up early in the day. In the **Kaibab National Forest,** along the south border of the park, you can pull off a dirt road and camp for free. No camping is allowed within ¼ mi. of U.S. 64. Convenient **dispersed camping** can be had along N. Long Jim Loop Rd. For quieter and more remote sites, follow signs for the Arizona Trail into the national forest between Mile 252 and 253 on U.S. 64. Sleeping in cars is *not* permitted within the park, but it is allowed in the Kaibab Forest (although *Let's Go* does not recommend it). For more info, contact the **Tusayan Ranger Station**, Kaibab National Forest, P.O. Box 3088, Grand Canyon, AZ 86023 (☎ 638-2443). Reservations for some campgrounds can be made through **SPHERICS** (☎ 800-365-2267).

Mather Campground (☎ 800-365-2267), in Grand Canyon Village, 1 mi. south of the Canyon Village Marketplace; follow signs from Yavapai Lodge. 320 shady, relatively isolated sites with no hookups. Check at the office even if the sign says the campground is full. 7-night max. stay. For Mar.-Nov., reserve up to 3 months in advance; Dec.-Feb. first come, first served. Sept.-May $12; June-Aug. $15. ❶

Desert View Campground (☎ 638-7888), 25 mi. east of Grand Canyon Village. Short on shade and far from the hub of the South Rim, but a perfect place to avoid the crowd. 50 sites with phone and restroom access, but no hookups or campfires. Open mid-May to Oct. No reservations; usually full by early afternoon. Sites $10. ❶

Camper Village (☎ 638-2887), in Tusayan, 1 mi. south of the park entrance behind the general store. Showers and flush toilets. First come, first served tent sites; reservations required for RVs. 2-person hookups and tent sites $18-26; $2 per additional adult. ❷

▶ FOOD

The **Canyon Village Market Place** ❶, at the Market Plaza 1 mi. west of Mather Point on the main road, has a deli counter with the cheapest eats in the park, a wide selection of groceries, a camping supplies department, and enough Grand Canyon apparel to clothe each member of your extended family with a commemorative gift. (☎ 638-2262. Open daily in summer 7am-8:30pm; deli open 7am-6pm. Sandwiches $2-4.) The well-stocked **Canyon Cafe** ❶, across from the General Store, offers a wider variety of food than the deli. (Open daily 6:30am-9pm; hamburgers $3, pizza $3.50-5, dinners $5-7.) **Maswik Cafeteria** ❶, in Maswik Lodge, serves a variety of grilled food, country favorites, Mexican specialties, and healthy alternatives in a wood-paneled cafeteria atmosphere. (Open daily 6am-10pm. Hot entrees $6-7, sandwiches $3-5.) **Bright Angel Dining Room** ❷, in Bright Angel Lodge, serves hot sandwiches for $7-9. Breakfasts run $6-7 and pricey dinner entrees range $10-15. (☎ 638-2631. Open daily 6:30am-10pm.) Just out the door of the dining room, the **Soda Fountain** ❶ at Bright Angel Lodge chills eight flavors of ice cream and stocks a variety of snack-bar sandwiches. (Open daily 8am-8pm. 1 scoop $2.)

▶ HIKING

Hikes in and around the Grand Canyon can be broken down into two categories: day hikes and overnight hikes. Confusing an overnight hike for a day hike can lead to disaster, and permanent residency in the canyon. Hiking to the Colorado River is reserved for overnight trips. All overnight trips require permits obtained through the Backcountry Office. In determining what is an appropriate day hike, remember that the Canyon does not have any loop hikes. Be prepared to retrace every single footstep uphill on the way back. Begin before 7am for day hikes, and consult a ranger before heading out. Park Service rangers also present a variety of free, informative talks and guided hikes; times and details are listed in *The Guide*.

The **Rim, Bright Angel, South Kaibab,** and **River** trails are the only South Rim trails regularly maintained and patrolled by the park service. There are a number of other trails and paths into and around the Canyon, such as **South Bass, Grandview,** and **Tonto**. These trails are only for the experienced hiker, and may contain steep chutes and technical terrain. Consult a ranger and *The Guide* before heading out.

Rim Trail (4-6hr., 11 mi. one-way). The Rim Trail is excellent for hikers seeking a tame way to see the Canyon. The trail follows the shuttle bus routes along Hermit Rd. past the Grand Canyon Village to Mather Point. Near the Grand Canyon Village, the Rim Trail resembles a city street crammed with people, but toward the eastern and western ends, hikers have a bit more elbow room. Hopi Point is a great place to watch the sunset with its panoramic canyon views—*The Guide* list times for sunsets and sunrises.

Bright Angel Trail (up to 18 mi. round-trip, 1-2 days). Bright Angel's frequent switchbacks and refreshing water stations make it the into-the-canyon choice of moderate hikers. The trail departs from the Rim Trail near the western edge of the Grand Canyon Village, and the first 1-2 mi. of the trail generally attract droves of day hikers. Rest houses are stationed 1.5 and 3 mi. from the rim, each with water between May and Sept. **Indian Gardens**, 4.5 mi. down, offers restrooms, picnic tables, and shade. From rim to river, the trail drops 4420 ft. The 18mi. round-trip is too strenuous for a day hike. With the compulsory permit, overnighters can camp at Indian Gardens or Bright Angel Campground, while day hikers are advised to go no farther than Plateau Point (12.2 mi. round-trip) or Indian Gardens (9.2 mi. round-trip). The **River Trail** (1.7 mi.) connects the Bright Angel Trail with the South Kaibab Trail.

South Kaibab Trail (7 mi. one-way to Phantom Ranch, 4-5hr. descent). Beginning at Yaki Pt. (7260 ft.), the trickier and steeper Kaibab lacks shade or water, but it rewards the intrepid with a better view of the canyon. Day hikes to Cedar Ridge (3 mi. round-trip; toilet facilities available) and **Skeleton Point** (6 mi. round-trip) are reasonable only for experienced hikers. For overnight hikes, Kaibab meets up with Bright Angel at the Colorado. Fewer switchbacks and a more rapid descent make the South Kaibab Trail 1.7 mi. shorter than the Bright Angel to this point. Guests staying at the Phantom Ranch or Bright Angel Campground use the Bright Angel or South Kaibab to reach the ranch.

⚄ OTHER OUTDOOR ACTIVITIES

Beyond using your feet, there are others ways to conquer the canyon. **Mule trips** from the South Rim are expensive and booked up to one year in advance, although cancellations do occur. (☎303-297-2757. Day trip to Plateau Point 6 mi. down the Bright Angel Trail $127; overnight including lodging at Phantom Ranch and all meals: $343 per person.) Mule trips from the North Rim are cheaper and more readily available (☎435-679-8665). **Whitewater rafting** trips through the canyon vary in length and book well in advance. The *Trip Planner* lists 16 commercial guides licensed to offer trips in the canyon; check the park website for info.

❗ From your first glimpse of the canyon, you may feel a compelling desire to see it from the inside, an enterprise that is harder than it looks. Even the young at heart and body should remember that an easy downhill hike can become a nightmarish 50° incline on the return journey. Also, keep in mind that the lower you go, the hotter it gets; when it's 85°F on the rim, it's around 100°F at Indian Gardens and around 110°F at Phantom Ranch. Heat stroke, the greatest threat to any hiker, is marked by a monstrous headache and red, sweatless skin. *For a day hike, you must take at least a gallon of water per person; drink at least a quart per hour hiking upwards under the hot sun.* Footwear with excellent tread is also necessary—the trails are steep, and every year several careless hikers take what locals morbidly call "the 12-second tour." Safety tips can be found in *The Guide,* but speak with a ranger before embarking on a hike. Parents should think twice about bringing children more than 1 mi. down any trail.

NORTH RIM ☎928

If you're coming from Utah or Nevada, or want to avoid the crowds at the South Rim, the park's North Rim is wilder, cooler, and more serene—all with a view almost as spectacular as that from the South Rim. Unfortunately, it's hard to reach by public transportation, and by car it's a long drive. From October 15 to December 1, the North Rim is open for day use only; from December 1 to May 15, it is closed entirely. Any visit to the North Rim centers on the North Rim Lodge, an elegant structure overlooking the canyon.

■✚ 🛈 ORIENTATION & PRACTICAL INFORMATION

To reach the North Rim from the South Rim, take Rte. 64 E. to U.S. 89 N, which runs into Alt. 89; from Alt. 89, follow Rte. 67 S to the edge. Altogether, the beautiful drive is over 200 mi. From Utah, take Alt. 89 S from Fredonia. From Page, take U.S. 89 S to Alt. 89 to Rte. 67 S. Snow closes Rte. 67 from mid-October through mid-May, and park visitor facilities (including the lodge) close for the winter. The visitor **parking** lot lies near the end of Rte. 67, closer to the Visitors Center and lodge.

Buses: Transcanyon, P.O. Box 348, Grand Canyon 86023 (☎638-2820). Buses run to the South Rim (late May to Oct. 5hr. 7am from the North Rim Lodge; 1:30pm from the Bright Angel Lodge at the South Rim; $65, round-trip $110). Reservations required.

Public Transit: A **hikers' shuttle** runs from the Lodge to the North Kaibab Trailhead late May to Oct. (5:20am, 7:20am; $5, $2 per additional person). Tickets must be purchased in advance at the Lodge.

Gas and Car Repairs: Chevron, on the campground road just off Rte. 67. The station does not service cars, but can arrange a tow to Kanab for repairs. 7am-7pm daily.

Visitor info: North Rim Visitors Center (☎638-7864), on Rte. 67 just before the Lodge. Open daily 8am-6pm. **Kaibab Plateau Visitors Center** (☎643-7298), at Jacob Lake, next to the Inn. Interpretive displays provide details on the creation of the canyon and its ecosystem. Backcountry permits are issued here. Open daily 8am-5pm.

Weather Conditions: (☎638-7888). Updated at 7am daily.

Post Office: Grand Canyon Lodge (☎638-2611). Open M-F 8am-11am and 11:30am-4pm, Sa 8am-1pm. **ZIP code:** 86052. **Area code:** 928.

⌂ ACCOMMODATIONS

The North Rim has one campground, creatively named "North Rim Campground," and it generally fills entirely by reservation during the summer. **SPHERICS** (☎800-365-2267) handles reservations. If you can't get in-park lodgings, head for the **Kaibab National Forest,** which runs from north of Jacob Lake to the park entrance. You can camp for free, as long as you're ¼ mi. from the road, water, or official campgrounds, and 1 mi. from any commercial facility. Less expensive accommodations may be found in **Kanab, UT,** 80 mi. north.

Grand Canyon Lodge (reservations ☎303-297-2757; front desk ☎303-297-2757), on the edge of the rim. Open mid-May to Oct. Singles or doubles in frontier cabins or hotel rooms $88; 4-person pioneer cabins $100. ❹

Jacob Lake Inn (☎643-7232), 32 mi. north of the North Rim entrance at Jacob Lake. Reception daily 6:30am-9:30pm. Charming lodge, gift shop, cafe, and bakery. 2-person cabins $72-83, 3-person $86-88, 4-person $90-92; motel units $91-106. ❹

North Rim Campground (☎800-365-2267), on Rte. 67 near the rim, the only park campground on this side of the chasm. 83 sites. Open mid-May to mid-Oct. 7-night max. stay. Sites $15, 4 "premier sites" with canyon views $20. ❶

DeMotte Park Campground, about 16 mi. north of North Rim in Kaibab National Forest. Be an early bird to avoid disappointment; 23 woodsy sites are first come, first served and generally fill by noon. No hookups. $10 per vehicle per night. ❶

☐ FOOD

Grand Canyon Lodge (☎ 638-2612, ext. 160) monopolizes in-park eating options, which tend toward the pricey side. The lodge's dining room, treating guests to sweeping canyon views and *haute cuisine*, serves breakfast for $5-8, lunch for $6.50-8.50, and dinner for $13 and up. Open daily 6:30-10am, 11:30am-2:30pm, and 5-9:30pm. Reservations required for dinner. ❸

Cafe on the Rim dishes out standard salads from $4-6, and cheese pizza by the slice goes for $2.50. Breakfasts range $3-5. Open daily 7am-9pm. ❷

Jacob Lake Inn is a superb alternative to the North Rim establishments. The intimate diner counter, a fine-dining restaurant, and amiably staffed bakery combine to offer a pleasing variety of options. Pick up a gravity-defying milkshake to make the remaining miles to the rim a bit more enjoyable. Sandwiches $6, amazing milkshakes $3, breakfasts $5-6, dinners $12-15. ❸

⚠ OUTDOOR ACTIVITIES

Hiking in the leafy North Rim seems like a trip to the mountains. This mountain, however, is upside-down—the hike back up comes after the legs are already a little weary from hiking down. All precautions for hiking at the South Rim are even more important at the North Rim, where the elevations are higher and the air is thinner. In-depth info on trails can be found in the North Rim's version of *The Guide*. Several day hikes of variable lengths beckon the active North Rim visitor. Pick up the indispensable of the *Official Guide to Hiking the Grand Canyon*, available in all Visitors Centers and gift shops. Overnight hikers must get permits from the **Backcountry Office** in the ranger station. (Open daily 8am-noon and 1-5pm.) Write to the **Backcountry Office**, P.O. Box 129, Grand Canyon, AZ 86023; it may take a few days to get a permit in person.

Bright Angel Point Trail (0.5 mi.) begins near the Visitors Center and winds around behind the Lodge, ending with a seraphic view of the Canyon. The **Uncle Jim Trail** (5 mi. round-trip) follows the **Ken Patrick Trail** along Roaring Spring Canyon, then completes a circle on a plateau that juts out between the Roaring Springs and Bright Angel Canyons, offering superior views of both. Combining Canyon views with alpine forest greenery, the **Widforss Trail** (10 mi. round-trip) is perfect for a casual, if long, day's saunter. The popular and well-maintained **North Kaibab Trail** (14.2 mi. one-way) descends the Roaring Spring Canyon to the Bright Angel Canyon and eventually to the Colorado. Day hikers are advised not to proceed beyond the spring, located 4.7 mi. into the hike. Some of the most scenic and least-traveled backpacking in the park is made available via the **Thunder River Trail** (15 mi. one-way), which descends steep cliffs, follows the Esplanade to Surprise Valley, and then follows Thunder River to the Colorado. The alternative **Deer Creek** route travels west from Surprise Valley through Deer Creek Valley to the Colorado.

Park Rangers run nature walks, lectures, and evening programs at the North Rim Campground and Lodge. Check the info desk or campground bulletin boards for schedules. One-hour ($20), half-day ($45), and full-day ($95) **mule trips** through **Canyon Trail Rides** circle the rim or descend into the canyon. (☎435-679-8665. Open daily 7am-7pm. No credit cards.) Reservations are recommended but walk-ins can be accommodated more frequently than on the South Rim.

HAVASUPAI RESERVATION   ☎928

To the west of the hustle and bustle of the South Rim lies the tranquility of the Havasupai Reservation. Meaning "people of the blue-green water," the Havasupai live in a protected enclave, bordered by the national park. Ringed by dramatic sandstone faces, their village, Supai, rests on the verdant shores of the Havasu River. Just beyond town, this rushing wonder of crystal-clear water cascades over a series of spectacular falls. Such beauty attracts thousands of visitors yearly, but luckily, a grueling 10 mi. hike separates the falls from any vehicle-accessible surface and prevents the Disney-fication of the reservation. For most, blistered feet or a saddle-sore rump make bathing in the cool waters even sweeter.

Supai and the campground can only be reached by a trail originating on the rim at the Hualapai Hilltop. To reach the trailhead, take I-40 E until Rte. 66 at Seligman; follow Rte. 66 for 30 mi. until it meets with Indian Rd. 18, which ends at the Hilltop after 60 mi. No roads lead to Supai, although mules and helicopters can be hired to carry bags or people. For mule reservations, contact **Havasupai Tourist Enterprise**. (☎448-2141. $75 one-way; includes 4 pieces of luggage.) The hike is not to be underestimated. The well-marked trail is a grueling, exposed 8 mi. to Supai and then an additional 2 mi. to the campground. *Do not hike down without a reservation*—you may have to turn around and walk right back to the trailhead.

Reservations for the campground, lodge, and mules can be made by calling the **Havasupai Tourist Enterprise**. Visitors must first check-in at the **Tourist Office** in Supai before heading onto the campground. In the village, there's a Post Office, a general store, and cafe. Prices are high, because everything must be brought in by mule or helicopter. Bringing your own food to the campground is advised. All trash must be packed-out. No **gas** or **water** is available past Rte. 66; stock up beforehand.

The Havasupai tribe operates two accommodations: the ▨**Havasupai Campground** and the **Havasupai Lodge**, both on the canyon floor. The friendly campground, 2 mi. beyond Supai, lies between Havasu and Mooney Falls. Many campers consider the campsites heaven-on-earth—they border the blue-green water of the Havasu River and are near to swimmer-friendly lagoons. The Tribe charges a one-time entry fee ($20 per visitor and $10 per night) at the campground. There are no showers, and the non-flush toilets tend to smell up the sites. A spring provides fresh water, and the falls are just a quick jaunt away. The **Havasupai Lodge ❹**, in Supai, offers basic accommodation ($75-95 for up to 6 people, plus the entrance fee).

The trail from Supai to the campground extends to **Mooney Falls** (1 mi. from campground), **Beaver Falls** (4 mi.), and the **Colorado** (7 mi.). The vertiginous hike down to Mooney Falls may turn your stomach. Extreme caution should be exercised—shoes with good tread are a must. Swimming and frolicking are both permitted and encouraged in the lush lagoons at the bottom of the falls.

FLAGSTAFF   ☎928

Born on the 4th of July, Flagstaff began as a rest stop along the transcontinental railroad; its mountain springs provided precious aqueous refreshment along the long haul to the Pacific. The past 100 years have echoed with the logging industry's innumerable cries of "timber!," seen a scientist in search of canal-digging Martians, witnessed an emerging milieu of diverse cultures and ideologies, and felt the unrelenting onslaught of backpackers and fannypackers alike. One thing hasn't changed, though: Flagstaff is still a major rest stop on the way to Southwestern must-sees. Trains plow through town 72 times a day, while travelers pass through on their way to the Grand Canyon, Sedona, and the Petrified Forest—all within day-trip distance. The energetic citizens welcome travelers to their rock formations by day and their breweries by night; many have wandered into town with camera in hand and ended up settling down. Retired cowboys, earthy Volvo owners, New Agers, and serious rock climbers comprise much of the population.

THE SOUTHWEST

THE BIG SPLURGE

INN THE MONEY

Although Flagstaff is home to one of the best hostel scenes in the Southwest, it also knows how to live large. For those who want to take a break from nickel-and-diming their vacation, or for those who just can't abide without room service, *Let's Go* can make a few recommendations.

🛏 **Inn at 410,** 410 N. Leroux St. (☎774-0088 or 800-774-2088), the best place to stay in Flagstaff and one of the Southwest's premier B&Bs. Situated in a beautiful 1894 craftsman home, the Inn boasts nine distinctive rooms, some with oversized jacuzzi and fireplace decorated in classic Southwestern, Victorian, or arts and crafts styles. Rooms $135-190. ❺

Birch Tree Inn, 824 W. Birch Ave. (☎744-1042 or 888-774-1042), offers five comfortable, themed rooms in a restored 1915 Victorian home. Decor ranges from Southwestern to antique. Rooms $69-109. ❹

Inn at NAU, on S. San Francisco St. on the Northern Arizona University campus (523-1616). The Inn is operated by NAU's School of Hotel Management and is staffed entirely by NAU students. Its unassuming interior conceals 19 spacious and well-appointed rooms. Complimentary breakfast; all rooms have refrigerators, some have computers. With the exception of the presidential suite, all rooms $89. ❹

⎚ TRANSPORTATION

Flagstaff sits 138 mi. north of Phoenix (take I-17), 26 mi. north of Sedona (take U.S. 89A), and 81 mi. south of the Grand Canyon's south rim (take U.S. 180).

Trains: Amtrak, 1 E. Rte. 66 (☎774-8679). Two trains leave daily. Eastbound train leaves at 5:11am, heading to **Kansas City, MO** and **Chicago** via **Winslow** (1hr., $14-23), **Gallup, NM** (2½hr., $35-61), and **Albuquerque** (5hr., $63-110). Westbound train leaves at 9:25pm, heading to **Los Angeles** (12hr., $68-119). Occasional discount offers and specials may reduce rates considerably. Station open daily 4:45pm-7:30am.

Buses: Four separate bus lines provide service to regional destinations.

Greyhound: 399 S. Malpais Ln. (☎774-4573), across from NAU campus, 3 blocks southwest of the train station on U.S. 89A. Turn off 89A by Dairy Queen. To: **Albuquerque** (6½hr., 5 per day, $41); **Las Vegas** (5-6hr., 3 per day, $47); **Los Angeles** (10-12hr., 8 per day, $49); and **Phoenix,** including airport (3hr., 5 per day, $22). Terminal open 24hr.

Sedona Shuttle Service: Coconino/Yavapai Shuttle Service (☎775-8929 or 888-440-8929) offers daily trips from Flagstaff to **Sedona.** The 1hr. trip leaves from Flagstaff M-F at 8am and 4pm, and returns from Sedona at 2:30pm. On Sa, Flagstaff-Sedona leg leaves at 10am with no return trip. No Su service. One-way $18, round-trip $36.

Grand Canyon Coaches (☎638-0821 or 866-746-8439) offers shuttle service to the **Grand Canyon.** Shuttles depart from the Flagstaff Visitors Center daily at 9am and 6:40pm and return from Maswik Lodge at the Canyon at 7am and 4:40pm. One-way $20, round-trip $40.

Northern Arizona Shuttle and Tours (☎773-4337 or 866-870-8687) provides transportation between **Phoenix** and Flagstaff. Three daily departures from the Flagstaff Visitors Center and various locations in Phoenix. One-way $30, prepaid round-trip $55. Call for departure times.

Public Transit: Mountain Line (☎779-6624). Routes cover most of town. Buses run once per hr.; route map and schedule available at Visitors Center in Amtrak station. One-way 75¢, seniors and disabled 35¢, children 60¢; book of 20 passes $13.

Taxis: Friendly Cab, ☎214-9000.

🛈 PRACTICAL INFORMATION

The downtown area revolves around the intersection of **Beaver St.** and **Rte. 66** (formerly Santa Fe Ave.). **S. San Francisco St.,** two blocks east of Beaver St., marks the eastern edge of downtown. Split by Rte. 66, the northern area is more swank and upscale, while the area south of the tracks is more down to earth, housing hostels and vegetarian eateries.

Visitor info: Flagstaff Visitors Center, 1 E. Rte. 66 (☎774-9541 or 800-842-7293), in the Amtrak station. Open M-Sa 8am-6pm, Su 8am-5pm.

Police: 911 Sawmill Rd. (☎556-2316 general info; ☎774-1414 non-emergencies).

Medical Services: Flagstaff Medical Center, 1200 North Beaver St. (☎779-3366), provides medical services in the area, including 24hr. emergency service.

Internet access: Free access at NAU's **Cline Library** (☎523-2171). Open M-Th 7:30am-10pm, F 7:30am-6pm, Sa 9am-6pm, Su noon-10pm. Free public access also available at the **Flagstaff Public Library,** 300 W. Aspen Ave. (☎774-4000). Open M-Th 10am-9pm, F 10am-7pm, Sa 10am-6pm, Su 11am-6pm.

Post Office: 2400 N. Postal Blvd. (☎714-9302), for general delivery. Open M-F 9am-5pm, Sa 9am-1pm. **Downtown** at 104 N. Agassiz St. 86001 (☎779-2371). Open M-F 9am-5pm, Sa 9am-1pm. **ZIP code:** 86004. **Area code:** 928.

⌐ ACCOMMODATIONS

When swarms of summer tourists descend on Flagstaff, accommodation prices shoot up. Historic **Rte. 66** is home to many cheap motels, although the private rooms at the hostels and hotels listed below rival them both in price and in quality. *The Flagstaff Accommodations Guide,* available at the Visitors Center, lists all area accommodations.

The Weatherford Hotel, 23 N. Leroux St. (☎779-1919), on the other side of the tracks 1 block west of San Francisco St. The oldest hotel in Flagstaff, dating to 1897, the Weatherford has spacious rooms with amazing balconies and bay windows. Equipped with elegant furnishings and located in the middle of downtown Flagstaff. Reservations recommended. Rooms $55. ❸

Hotel Monte Vista, 100 N. San Francisco St. (☎779-6971 or 800-545-3068), downtown. Feels like a classy hotel, with quirky decor, a bar that occasionally hosts hardcore and punk bands, and pool tables and video games downstairs. Chock-full of colorful history, the staff swears the hotel is chock-full of ghosts, too. Private rooms named after movie stars who slept there start at $70. ❹

⌐ CAMPING

Free backcountry camping is available around Flagstaff in specifically designated wilderness areas. Pick up a map from the **Peaks Ranger Station,** 5075 N. 89A (☎526-0866), to find out where. All backcountry campsites must be located at least 200 ft. away from trails, waterways, wet meadows, and lakes. There is a 14-night limit for stays in the Coconino National Forest. For info on campgrounds and backcountry camping, call the **Coconino Forest Service.** (☎527-3600. Open M-F 7:30am-4:30pm.) An alternative to backcountry camping is staying at one of the numerous maintained campsites in the forest. Many of these campsites flank the idyllic lakes to the south of Flagstaff.

Lakeview Campground, on the side of Upper Lake Mary, 11½ mi. south on Lake Mary Road (off I-17 south of Flagstaff), is surrounded by a pine forest that supports an alpine ecosystem. Open May-Oct.; no reservations. Drinking water, pit toilets. $10 per vehicle per night. ❶

Pinegrove Campground, (☎877-444-6777), 5 mi. south of Lakeview at the other end of Upper Lake Mary, is set in a similarly charming locale. Open May-Oct. Reservations available. Drinking water and flush toilets. $12 per vehicle. ❶

Ashurst/Forked Pine Campground flanks both sides of Ashurst lake, a smaller, secluded lake on Forest Rd. 82 E (turn left off of Lake Mary Rd., across from Pine Grove Campground). Water and flush toilets are on-site, and the fishing is stupendous. 64 sites are available on a first come, first served basis. $10 per vehicle. ❶

🍴 FOOD

All the deep-fat-frying chains are readily available outside of downtown, but the creative and off-beat rule near the heart of Flagstaff. The downtown core brims with pubs, restaurants, and cafes with a variety of cuisines to suit all tastes.

Macy's, 14 S. Beaver St. (☎ 774-2243), behind Motel Du Beau, is a cheery student hangout serving only vegetarian food (and excellent vegan selections) in an earthy atmosphere. $4-7 specials change daily. Get there early and start the day with a bowl of granola ($4) and one of their fresh roasted coffees ($1-3.50). Open Su-W 6am-8pm, Th-Sa 6am-midnight. Food served until 1hr. before closing. Cash only. ❶

Pasto, 19 E. Aspen (☎ 779-1937). Delicious Italian cuisine in a high-class atmosphere. Entrees range from seafood, chicken, and veal to more traditional pasta dishes ($10-18). Reservations recommended. Open Su-Th 5pm-9pm, F-Sa 5pm-9:30pm. ❹

The Black Bean, 12 E. Rte. 66 (☎ 779-9905), is a great place for on-the-go burritos ($3-5). They come with your choice of fixin's, and make a hefty meal. Creative specialty wraps $5. Open M-Sa 11am-9pm, Su noon-8pm. ❶

🔆 SIGHTS

In 1894, Percival Lowell chose Flagstaff as the site for an astronomical observatory, and then spent the rest of his life here, devoting himself to the study of heavenly bodies, and culling data to support his theory that life exists on Mars. The **Lowell Observatory,** 1400 W. Mars Hill Rd., 1 mi. west of downtown off Rte. 66, where he discovered the planet Pluto, doubles as both a general tribute to his genius and as a high-powered research center sporting five super-duper telescopes. During the daytime, admission includes tours of the telescopes, as well as a museum with hands-on astronomy exhibits. If you have stars in your eyes, come back at night for an excellent program about the night sky and the constellations. (☎ 774-3358; www.lowell.edu. Open in winter daily noon-5pm, in summer 9am-5pm. Evening programs W and F-Sa 7:30pm; in summer M-Sa 8:00pm. $4, ages 5-17 $2.)

The more down-to-earth **Museum of Northern Arizona,** off U.S. 180, a few mi. north of town, features exhibits on the Native peoples of the area. Galleries house expansive collections of Native American art and an intimidating dinosaur skeleton. (☎ 774-5213. Open daily 9am-5pm. $5, students $3, seniors $4, ages 7-17 $2.)

🎵 📷 ENTERTAINMENT & NIGHTLIFE

North of town near the museum, the **Coconino Center for the Arts** (☎ 779-7258 or 774-6272) houses exhibits, festivals, performers, and even a children's museum. In the middle of June, the annual **Flagstaff Rodeo** (☎ 800-638-4253) comes to town. Competitions and events go on all weekend at the Coconino County Fair Grounds. The town's birthday, the **4th of July,** is a foot-stomping good time with festivals and fireworks. At the end of the summer, the **Coconino Country Fair** digs its heals into Flagstaff with rides, animal competitions, and carnival games. **Theatrikos,** 11 W. Cherry Ave. (☎ 774-1662), stages plays year-round in their own playhouse.

Charly's, 23 N. Leroux St., plays live jazz and blues in one of the classiest buildings in town. (☎ 779-1919. Happy hour 5-7pm. Open daily 11am-10pm. Bar open daily 11am-1am.) **Joe's Place,** on the corner of San Francisco and Rte. 66, hosts indie bands weekend nights. (☎ 774-6281. Happy hour 4-7pm. Open 11am-1am.) **The Alley** plays to a similar crowd as Joe's, and sees many out-of-towners. (☎ 774-7929. Happy hour M-Sa 3-7pm, Su free nacho bar. Open 3pm-1am.) If country is your thang, the **Museum Club,** 3404 E. Rte. 66, a.k.a. the **Zoo,** is the premier spot for honky-tonk action. (☎ 526-9434. Cover $3-5. Open daily 11am-3am.)

OUTDOOR ACTIVITIES

With the northern **San Francisco Peaks** and the surrounding **Coconino National Forest,** Flagstaff offers numerous options for the rugged outdoorsman or those simply interested in walking off last night's fun. Nature's playground provides skiing, hiking, biking, and general awe-struckedness. Due to the 7000 ft. plus altitudes, bring plenty of water, regardless of the season or activity. In late spring and summer, National and State Park Rangers may close trails if the potential for fire gets too high. The mountains occupy national forest land, so backcountry camping is free.

SKIING

The **Arizona Snow Bowl,** open from mid-December to April, operates four chairlifts and maintains 32 trails. The majestic **Humphrey's Peak,** standing a whopping 12,670 ft., is the backdrop for the Snow Bowl, as well as the Hopi's sacred home of the Kachina spirits. With an average snowfall of 260 in. and 2300 ft. of vertical drop, the Snow Bowl rivals the big-boy ski resorts of the Rockies. (☎ 779-1951. Open daily 9am-4pm. Lift tickets $37.) To reach the Snow Bowl, take U.S. 180 about 7 mi. north to the Fairfield Snow Bowl turn-off. Cross-country skiing is available at the **Flagstaff Nordic Center** (☎ 779-1951), 8 mi. north of Snow Bowl Rd. on U.S. 180. The vista at the top of the **Snow Bowl's Skyride** is stunning. When the air is clear, the North Rim of the Grand Canyon, the Painted Desert, and countless square miles of the southwest can be seen from the peak. (30min. Runs daily late May-early Sept. 10am-4pm; early Sept. to mid-Oct. F-Su 10am-4pm. $9, seniors $6.50, ages 6-12 $5.)

HIKING

In the summer, these peaks attract different species: hikers and bikers. The Coconino National Forest has many trails for hikers of all abilities. Consult the **Peaks Ranger Station,** 5075 N. 89A (☎ 526-0866), for trail descriptions and possible closures. For the more energetic hiker, the **Elden Lookout Trail** is ideal for jaw-dropping mountain-top views. Only 6 mi. in length (round-trip), the trail climbs 2400 ft.; it is demanding, but worth the view. The trail begins at the Peaks Ranger station. The most popular trail in the area is the hike to Humphrey's Peak, Arizona's highest mountain. This 9 mi. round-trip begins in the first parking lot at the Snow Bowl ski area. For a longer hike, the moderate to strenuous 17.4 mi. round-trip Weatherford Trail offers excellent opportunities for bird- and animal-spotting. The trailhead can be found next to Schultz Tank, about 7 mi. from Flagstaff.

MOUNTAIN BIKING

Flagstaff also offers excellent mountain biking. The **Dry Lake Hills** and the **Elden Mountains** are two great areas, both north of Flagstaff, to tear it up on two wheels. Popular routes include the easy **Rocky Ridge Trail** (4.4 mi. round-trip), which begins close to the intersection of Forest Rd. 557 and 420, and can be combined with lesser trails to lengthen the trip. Bike rentals are available at **Absolute Bikes,** 18 N. San Francisco St. (☎ 779-5969), starting at $25 per day. **Sinagua Cycles,** 113 S. San Francisco St. (☎ 779-9969), leads free bike rides Monday to Friday at 4:30pm.

DAYTRIPS FROM FLAGSTAFF

WALNUT CANYON NATIONAL MONUMENT

The remnants of more than 300 rooms in 13th-century Sinaguan dwellings make up Walnut Canyon National Monument. A glassed-in observation deck in the **Visitors Center,** 10 mi. east of Flagstaff, at Exit 204 off I-40, overlooks the whole canyon. (☎ 526-3367. Open daily 8am-6pm; off-season 9am-5pm. $3, under 17 free.) The

THE SOUTHWEST

IN RECENT NEWS

PROTOTYPE OF A CITY

The planned city of **Arcosanti**, off I-17 at Exit 262, embodies Italian architect Paolo Soleri's concept of "arcology," or architecture and ecology. Arcology's main tenet is treating human habitation as an ecological, as well as a structural problem; the goal is to create a living environment that optimally fuses with the surrounding natural environment. Every facet of Arcosanti is engineered to meld together residents' needs with the desert's resources.

Every bit of space is maximized and used ingeniously. The heating vents harness the excess heat generated by the bronze foundry, and a waterfall-on-demand flows through the community theater. When complete, the city will be extremely efficient, supplying food, power, and all other resources. Arcosanti has been under construction since 1970 and is expected to be finished by 2010.

A great alternative to merely viewing the innovative factory is to partake in its construction. Anyone with an interest in "arcology" may participate in either the one-week ($450) or five-week ($950) program (prices include room and board). The first week is a seminar led by Soleri, while the last four weeks of the longer program are spent either building the town's structures, gardening the surprisingly fertile desert land, or both. Eco-conscious participants learn a respect for finding a reasonable median between human need and want, and what the earth can provide. (☎632-7135; www.arcosanti.org. Visitors Center open daily 9am-5pm. Tours daily every hr. 10am-4pm. $8 donation requested.)

steep, self-guided **Island Trail** snakes down from the Visitors Center past 25 cliff dwellings. The **Rim Trail** (0.75 mi.) offers views of the canyon and passes rimtop sites. Every Saturday morning from 10am-1pm, rangers lead groups of five on 2 mi. hikes into Walnut Canyon to the original Ranger Cabin and more remote cliff dwellings. Reservations are required for these challenging 2½hr. hikes. There is a trailhead for the Mexico-to-Utah portion of the Arizona trail.

SUNSET CRATER VOLCANO NATIONAL MONUMENT

The crater encompassed by Sunset Crater Volcano National Monument appeared in AD 1065. Over the next 200 years, a 1000 ft. high cinder cone took shape as a result of eruptions. The self-guided **Lava Flow Nature Trail** wanders 1 mi. through the surreal landscape surrounding the cone, 1½ mi. east of the Visitors Center, where gnarled trees lie uprooted amid the rocky black terrain. Hiking up Sunset Crater itself is not permitted. The **Visitors Center**, 12 mi. north of Flagstaff on U.S. 89, has more info. (☎526-0502. Open daily 8am-6pm; off-season 8am-5pm. $3, under 16 free; includes admission to Wupatki.)

WUPATKI NATIONAL MONUMENT

Wupatki possesses some of the Southwest's most scenic Pueblo sites, situated 18 mi. northeast of Sunset Crater, along a stunning road with views of the Painted Desert. The Sinagua moved here in the 11th century, after the Sunset Crater eruption forced them to evacuate the land to the south. Archeologists speculate that in less than 200 years, droughts, disease, and over-farming led the Sinagua to abandon these stone houses. Five empty pueblos face the 14 mi. road from U.S. 89 to the Visitors Center. Another road to the ruins begins on U.S. 89, 30 mi. north of Flagstaff. The largest and most accessible, **Wupatki**, on a 0.5 mi. round-trip loop from the Visitors Center, rises three stories. The spectacular **Doney Mountain Trail** rises ½ mi. from the picnic area to the summit. Get info and trail guide brochures at the **Visitors Center.** Backcountry hiking is not permitted. (☎679-2365. Monument and Visitors Center open daily 8am-5pm.)

SEDONA   ☎928

Being that Sedona is a UFO sighting hot spot, one wonders if the Martians are simply mistaking its deep red-rock towers for home. The scores of tourists who descend upon the town year-round (Sedona rivals the Grand Canyon for tourist mass) certainly aren't; they come for sights that put Newton's theories to shame. Dramatic copper-toned behemoths dotted with pines tower over Sedona, rising from the earth with such flair and crowd appeal that they seem like manufactured tourist attractions. Some folks in town will tell you that they were manmade, perhaps by the Egyptians—Sedona is also the New Age capital of the US. Though the downtown is overrun with overpriced shops, the rocks are worth a visit.

■ ⁊ ORIENTATION & PRACTICAL INFORMATION.

Sedona lies 120 mi. north of Phoenix (take I-17 north to Rte. 179) and 30 mi. south of Flagstaff (take I-17 south to Rte. 179). The **Sedona-Phoenix Shuttle** (☎282-2066) runs six trips daily ($40). The **Sedona Chamber of Commerce**, at Forest Rd. and U.S. 89A, provides info on accommodations and local attractions. (☎282-7722. Open M-Sa 8:30am-5pm, Su 9am-3pm.) **Post Office:** 190 W. U.S. 89A. (☎282-3511. Open M-F 9am-5pm.) **ZIP code:** 86336. **Area code:** 928.

⁊ ACCOMMODATIONS.

Lodging in town is a bit pricey, but a few deals can be had. Just the same, it's not a bad idea to make Sedona a daytrip from Flagstaff or Cottonwood. **White House Inn ❸**, 2986 W. U.S. 89A (☎282-6680), is the second cheapest option, with singles and doubles, some with kitchenettes, for $48-64. A popular alternative to commercial lodging is renting a room in a private residence. Check the local papers or bulletin boards at New Age shops for opportunities. In addition, cheaper options can be found in Cottonwood, 15 mi. away, where a number of budget motels line U.S. 89. The **Willow Tree Inn ❷**, off I-17 in Cottonwood, offers classy, comfortable rooms. (☎634-3678. Singles Nov.-Apr. $40-42; Mar.-Oct. $44-48; doubles $44-48/$50-59.)

Most of the campsites in the area are clustered around U.S. 89A as it heads north along Oak Creek Canyon on its way to Flagstaff. There are private campgrounds aplenty, but most cater to the RV crowd rather than to backpackers. The **US Forest Service campsites ❶** along 89A provide the best, cheapest option for tent-toters. North of Sedona, between nine and 20 mi. from the town, four separate campgrounds—**Manzanita, Bootlegger, Cave Springs, and Pine Flat (east and west)**—maintain over 150 campsites. They all have similar facilities, with picnic tables, toilets, drinking water (except at Bootlegger), and trash containers located at every campground. (☎527-3600 for local info; ☎877-444-6777 national reservation service number. 7-night max. stay. Tent sites $12.)

◖ FOOD.

Like many things in Sedona, restaurants can be expensive. However, there are a few good deals to be had. **Casa Rincon ❸**, 2620 U.S. 89A, attracts patrons with a daily happy hour (3-6pm; $3 margaritas), mouth-watering combination platters ($10-13), and almost daily live entertainment. Bring your appetite and check your troubles at the door. (☎282-4849. Open daily 11:30am-9pm.) **The Coffee Pot Restaurant ❶**, 2050 W. U.S. 89A, a local favorite, serves 101 varieties of omelettes ($5-8) and 3 kinds of tacos for $4. (☎282-6626. Open daily 6am-9pm.) **The Red Planet Diner ❷**, 1665 W. U.S. 89A, beams patrons in with a flying saucer and extraterrestrial allure. Martian milkshakes ($4) and Universal noodle bowls ($6-9) are "out-of-this-world." (☎282-6070. Open daily 11am-11pm.)

◙ SIGHTS.

The incredible formations at **Red Rock State Park** (☎282-6907) invite strolling or just contemplation. Located 15 mi. southwest of Sedona, the Park entrance can be found along the Red Rock Loop Road off U.S. 89A. Rangers lead daily nature hikes into the nearby rock formations and are happy to give trail recommendations. The **Chapel of the Holy Cross,** on Chapel Rd., lies just outside a 1000 ft. rock wall in the middle of red sandstone. The view from the parking lot is a religious experience itself. (☎282-4069. Open daily 9am-5pm.)

Montezuma Castle National Monument, 10 mi. south of Sedona on I-17, is a 20-room cliff dwelling built by the Sinagua tribe in the 12th century. Unfortunately, you can't get very close to the ruins, but the view from the paved path below is excellent and wheelchair accessible. (☎567-3322. Open daily 8am-7pm; off-season 8am-5pm. $2, under 17 free.) A beautiful lake formed by the collapse of an underground cavern, **Montezuma Well,** off I-17 11 mi. north of the castle, once served as a source of water for the Sinagua who lived here. (Open daily 8am-7pm. Free.) Take U.S. 89A to Rte. 279 and continue through Cottonwood to reach **Tuzigoot National Monument,** 20mi. southwest of Sedona, a dramatic Sinaguan ruin over the Verde Valley. (☎634-5564. Open daily 8am-7pm; in winter 8am-5pm. $2, under 17 free.)

🏔 OUTDOOR ACTIVITIES. In terms of hiking, it's nearly impossible to go wrong with any of the well-maintained and well-marked trails in and around Sedona. Most trailheads are located on the forest service roads that snake from the highways into the hills and canyons around Sedona. Highlights include the **Wilson Mountain Loop** (4.5 mi.), ascending Wilson Mountain, and the **Huckaby Trail** (5.2 mi. round-trip), traversing fantastic red rocks. Biking offers similar wonders. Considered a rival to Moab, UT by those in the mountain-biking know, Sedona has some of the best tracks in the world. Tamer trails can be found along the **Bell Rock Pathway,** which lies south of town. Bike rentals (starting at $25 per day) and good trail information can be found at **Mountain Bike Heaven,** 1695 W U.S. 89A. They also lead occasional free bike trips (call for dates and times) and do repairs for devilish spills. (☎282-1312. Open M-F 9am-6pm, Sa 8am-5pm, Su 9am-5pm.)

Scenic driving is nearly as plentiful as the red rocks. The Chamber of Commerce is very helpful in suggesting routes. The **Red Rock Loop** (20 mi., 1hr.) provides a little dirt road adventure and views of mind-blowing rock formations. Dry Creek and Airport Rd. are also good drives. For those hoping to see Sedona's wild off-road side, jeep tours are available from a number of companies. Generally, trips are $35-75 and 2-4hr. in length. **Sedona Adventures,** 276 N. U.S. 89A (☎282-3500 or 800-888-9494), offers some of the least expensive trips in the area.

NAVAJO RESERVATION

Although anthropologists believe the Navajo are descended from groups of Athabascan people who migrated to the Southwest from Northern Canada in the 14th and 15th centuries, the Navajo themselves view their existence as the culmination of a journey through three other worlds to this life, the "Glittering World." Four sacred mountains bound Navajoland—Mt. Blanca to the east, Mt. Taylor to the south, San Francisco Peak to the west, and Mt. Hesperus to the north. The land is holy to the Navajo and this is apparent in their reverence for it.

During the second half of the 19th century, Indian reservations evolved out of the US government's *ad hoc* attempts to prevent fighting between Native Americans and Anglos while facilitating white settlement on native lands. Initially, the reservation system imposed a kind of wardship over the Native Americans, which lasted for over a century, until a series of Supreme Court decisions beginning in the 1960s reasserted the tribes' legal standing as semi-sovereign nations. Today, the **Navajo Nation** is the largest reservation in America and covers more than 27,000 sq. mi. of northeastern Arizona, southeastern Utah, and northwestern New Mexico. Home to over 180,000 Navajo, or Dineh ("the People") as they call themselves, the reservation comprises one-tenth of the US Native American population. Within the Navajo borders, the smaller **Hopi Reservation** is home to around 10,000 Hopi ("Peaceable People").

For visitors to the reservation, cultural sensitivity takes on a new importance; despite the many state and interstate roads that traverse the reservation, the land is legally and culturally distinct. Superficially, much of the Navajo Nation and other reservations resemble the rest of the US. In reality, deep rifts exist between Native American and "Anglo" culture—the term used to refer to the non-reservation US society. The reservation has its own police force and laws. Driving or hiking off designated trails and established routes is considered trespassing unless accompanied by a guide. Possession and consumption of alcohol are prohibited on the reservation. General photography is allowed unless otherwise stated, but photographing the Navajo people requires their permission (a gratuity is usually expected). Tourist photography is not permitted among the Hopi. As always, the best remedy for cultural friction is simple respect.

Lively reservation politics are written up in the local *Navajo-Hopi Observer* and *Navajo Times*. For a taste of the Navajo language and Native American ritual songs, tune your **radio** to 660AM, "The Voice of the Navajo." Remember to advance your watch 1hr. during the summer; the Navajo Nation runs on **Mountain Daylight Time,** while the rest of Arizona, including the Hopi Reservation, does not observe daylight savings, and thus operates on Pacific Time during the warmer months and Mountain Standard Time during the cooler months. The **area code** for the reservation is 928 in Arizona, 505 in New Mexico, 435 in Utah.

Monument Valley, Canyon de Chelly, Navajo National Monument, Rainbow Bridge, Antelope Canyon, and the roads and trails that access these sights all lie on Navajo land. Those planning to hike through Navajo territory should head to one of the many **parks and recreation departments** for a backcountry permit, or mail a request along with a money order or certified check to P.O. Box 9000, Window Rock, AZ 86515 ($5 per person). The "border towns" of **Gallup, NM** (see p. 844) and **Flagstaff, AZ** (see p. 803) are good gateways to the reservations, with car rental agencies, inexpensive accommodations, and frequent Greyhound service on I-40. Budget travelers can camp at the National Monuments or Navajo campgrounds, or stay in one of the student-run motels in high schools around the reservation.

MONUMENT VALLEY ☎ 435

The red sandstone towers of Monument Valley are one of the southwest's most otherworldly sights. Paradoxically, they're also one of the most familiar, since countless Westerns have used the butte-laden plain as their backdrop. Long before the days of John Wayne, Ancestral Puebloans managed to sustain small communities here, despite the arid climate. The park's looping 17 mi. **Valley Drive** winds around 11 of the most spectacular formations, including the famous pair of **Mittens** and the slender **Totem Pole.** However, the gaping ditches, large rocks, and mudholes on this road can be jarring to both you and your car—drive at your own risk and observe the 15 mph speed limit. The drive takes at least 1½hr. Other, less-touristed parts of the valley can be reached only by four-wheel-drive vehicle, horse, or foot. *Leaving the main road without a guide is forbidden.* The Visitors Center parking lot is crowded with booths selling jeep, horseback, and hiking tours. (1½hr. jeep tour about $25 per person, full-day $100; horseback tours $30/120.) In winter, snow laces the rocky towers. Call the Visitors Center for road conditions.

The park entrance lies on U.S. 163 just across the Utah border, 24 mi. north of **Kayenta,** at the intersection of U.S. 163 and U.S. 160. The **Visitors Center** has info. (☎ 727-3353. Park and Visitors Center open May-Sept. $3, under 7 free.) There are few accommodations in the area. **Mitten View Campground,** ¼ mi. southwest of the Visitors Center, has showers but no hookups. (Sites $10; in winter $5. Register at the Visitors Center.) Cheap motels are in **Mexican Hat, UT** and **Bluff, UT.**

IN RECENT NEWS

RESERVATIONS & CONCERNS

There is a very standard narrative of Anglo expansion into the Native American lands in and around the Southwest: settlers arrive to cultivate the land, and Natives, through warfare, disease, and social marginalization, disappear from the scene.

Yet Native Americans themselves refuse to be ignored on the land they once ruled. The Navajo Nation has taken an all-American approach to defending its interests: it has filed a lawsuit. At issue is whether then Interior Secretary David Hodel, as the Navajo Nation alleges, conspired with Peabody Coal Co. to undermine the tribe's contract negotiations with Peabody in the 1980s. The Navajo Nation is seeking over half a billion dollars in damages.

Unfortunately, the lawsuit is only the least of the Nation's worries. To wit, the Navajos are beset by a host of problems, including a lack of infrastructure, poorly paved roads, a shortage of electricity and water, high unemployment, chronic alcoholism, and limited police and fire protection. With the recent exposure given to the Navajo Nation through the aforementioned lawsuit, as well as the recent release of *Windtalkers*, chronicling the Navajo's successful contribution to the American military effort in WWII, perhaps the public will realize that the Native American is not yet vanished.

NAVAJO NATIONAL MONUMENT ☎ 520

Until the late 1200s, a small population of the ancestors of the modern Hopi inhabited the region, though hard times left the villages vacant by 1300. Today, the site contains three cliff dwellings. **Inscription House** has been closed to visitors since the 1960s due to its fragile condition; the other two admit a very limited number of visitors. The stunning **Keet Seel** (open late May to early Sept.) can be reached only via a challenging 17 mi. round-trip hike. Hikers can stay overnight in a free campground nearby (no facilities or drinking water). Reservations for permits to visit Keet Seel must be made up to two months in advance through the Visitors Center (see below). Ranger-led tours to **Betatakin**, a 135-room complex, are limited to 25 people. (Open May to late Sept. 1 per day at 8:15am; first come, first served the morning of the tour.) If you're not up for the trek to the ruins, the paved, 1 mi. round-trip **Sandal Trail** lets you gaze down on Betatakin from the top of the canyon. The **Aspen Forest Overlook Trail,** another 1 mi. hike, overlooks canyons and aspens, but no ruins. To get to the monument, take Rte. 564 from U.S. 160, 20 mi. southwest of Kayent. The **Visitors Center** lies 9 mi. along this road. (☎ 672-2700. Open daily 8am-5pm.) The free **campground,** next to the Visitors Center, has 30 sites.

HOPI RESERVATION ☎ 520

An island of coal-rich ore amid a sea of Navajo Nation grassland, Black Mesa and its three constitutive spurs, First Mesa, Second Mesa, and Third Mesa, have harbored the Hopi people and its traditions for over a millennium. The villages on **First Mesa** are the only places in the reservation really geared toward visitors. The **Ponsi Hall Community Center** serves as a general info center and a starting point for **guided tours.** (☎ 737-2262. Open June-Aug. daily 9am-6pm; Sept.-May 9:30am-5pm. Tours $5.) The villages on the **Second** and **Third Mesas** are less developed for tourism. However, on Second Mesa, the **Hopi Cultural Center,** 5 mi. west of the intersection of Rte. 264 and 87, serves as a Visitors Center and contains the reservation's only museum, displaying Hopi baskets, jewelry, pottery, and info about the tribe's history. (☎ 734-6650. Open M-F 8am-5pm, Sa-Su 9am-3pm. $3, under 14 $1.) **Free camping** is allowed at ten primitive sites next to the Cultural Center.

Visitors are welcome to attend a few Hopi **village dances** throughout the year. Often announced only a few days in advance, these religious ceremonies usually occur on weekends and last from sunrise to sundown. The dances are formal occasions; do not wear shorts, tank tops, or other casual wear. Photos, recordings, and sketches are strictly forbidden. Often several villages will hold dances on the same day, giving tourists the opportunity to village-hop. The **Harvest Dance,** in mid-September at the Second Mesa Village, is a spectacular ceremony with tribes from all over the US. Inquire at the cultural center, or the **Hopi Cultural Preservation Office** (☎ 734-2214), Box 123, Kykotsmovi 86039, for the dates and sites of all traditional dances.

PETRIFIED FOREST NATIONAL PARK ☎ 520

Spreading over 60,000 acres, the Petrified Forest National Park looks like the aftermath of some prehistoric Grateful Dead concert—an enormous tie-dye littered with rainbow-colored trees. Some 225 million years ago, when Arizona's desert was a swampland, volcanic ash covered the logs, slowing their decay. When silica-rich water seeped through the wood, the silica crystallized into quartz, producing rainbow hues. Layers of colorful sediment were also laid down in this floodplain, creating the stunning colors that stripe its rock formations.

■♂ **ORIENTATION & PRACTICAL INFORMATION.** Roughly speaking, the park can be divided into two parts: the northern Painted Desert and the southern Petrified Forest. An entrance station and Visitors Center welcomes guests at each end and a 28 mi. road connects the two sections. With lookout points and trails strategically located along the road, driving from one end of the park to the other is a good way to take in the full spectrum of colors and landscapes.

You can enter the park either from the north or the south. (Open June-Aug. daily 7am-7pm; Sept.-May 8am-5pm. Entrance fee $10 per vehicle, $5 per pedestrian; $5 motorcycle.) There is no public transportation to either part of the park. To access the southern section of the park, from St. Johns take U.S. 180 36 mi. west or from Holbrook 19 mi. east. The **Rainbow Forest Museum** provides a look at petrified logs up close and serves as a **Visitors Center.** (☎ 524-6822. Open June-Aug. daily 7am-7pm; Sept.-May 8am-5pm. Free.) To reach the northern Painted Desert section of the park, take I-40 to Exit 311, 107 mi. east of Flagstaff and 65 mi. west of Gallup, NM. The **Painted Desert Visitors Center** is less than 1 mi. from the exit. (☎ 524-6228. Open June-Aug. daily 7am-7pm; Sept.-May 8am-5pm.) **Water** is available at both Visitors Centers and the Painted Desert Inn. There is also **gas** at the Painted Desert Visitors Center. In case of **emergency,** call the ranger dispatch (☎ 524-9726).

There are no established campgrounds in the park, but **backcountry camping** is allowed in the fantastical Painted Desert Wilderness with a free permit. Backpackers must park their cars at Kachina Point and enter the wilderness via the 1 mi. access trail. No fires are allowed. Budget accommodations and roadside diners abound on Rte. 66. To get a real taste of the road, stay at the **Wigwam Motel ❷,** 811 W. Hopi Dr., where 19 concrete tepees await travelers. (☎ 524-3048. Reception 4-9pm. Check-out 11am. Singles $35; doubles $41.) **Gallup** and **Flagstaff** offer more lodging and eating options.

◙ **SIGHTS.** Most travelers opt to drive the 27 mi. park road from north to south. From the north, the first stop is **Tiponi Point.** From the next stop at **Tawa Point,** the **Painted Desert Rim Trail** (½ mi. one-way) skirts the mesa edge above the Lithodendron Wash and the Black Forest before ending at **Kachina Point.** The panoramas from Kachina Point are among the best in the park, and the point provides access for travel into the **Painted Desert Wilderness,** the park's designated region for backcountry hiking and camping. As the road crosses I-40, it enters the Petrified Forest portion of the park. The next stop is the 100-room **Puerco Pueblo.** A short trail through the pueblo offers viewpoints of nearby petroglyphs. Many more petroglyphs may be seen at **Newspaper Rock,** but at a a distance. The road then wanders through the eerie moonscape of **The Tepees,** before arriving at the 3 mi. **Blue Mesa** vehicle loop. The **Long Logs** and **Giant Logs Trails,** near the southern Visitors Center, are littered with fragments of petrified wood. Both trails are less than 1 mi. and fairly flat but travel through the densest concentration of petrified wood in the world. Picking up fragments of the wood is illegal and traditionally unlucky.

LAKE POWELL & PAGE   ☎428

The decision to curb the Colorado River's steady procession to the Pacific was made in 1956, and ten years and ten million tons of concrete later, Glen Canyon Dam, the second-largest dam in the country, was completed. Stopped in its tracks in northern Arizona, the mighty river backed-up into the once remote Glen Canyon. The monolith spawned a vacation destination that draws visitors to the crown jewel of a national recreation area, and contains hydroelectric machinery that creates energy for much of the region. Lake Powell, the pelagic expanse formed by the dam, has 1960 ft. of shoreline, exceeding the amount of beach lining continental America's Pacific coast.

Page (pop. 6800) lies just southeast of the dam and features numerous businesses, all competing fiercely for the summertime dollar. The town originally housed dam workers during the dam's construction, which lasted into the mid-1960s. As a launchpad from which visitors can explore the "Grand Circle" of lakes, cliffs, and canyons, Page has a healthy tourist infrastructure of motels and cheap eats, but little else. Besides the brilliant blue spread of Lake Powell, other natural wonders surround the area. Just east of Page, narrow Antelope Canyon wows visitors with sculpted sandstone and spectacular lighting. Farther east lies the Rainbow Bridge National Monument, the world's tallest natural bridge, and across the lake stretch the wild reaches of Grand Staircase-Escalante National Monument.

◄▮ ORIENTATION & PRACTICAL INFORMATION

All tourist services available inside the recreation area operate under **ARAMARK,** the concessionaire contracted by the Park's Service. The company operates four major marinas: **Wahweap** on U.S. 89 in the south near the dam, **Bullfrog** and **Halls Crossing,** across the reservoir from each other, on Rte. 276 and connected by daily ferry service, and **Hite,** hidden in Lake Powell's northernmost reaches on Rte. 95. A single info line (☎800-528-6154) handles all questions and reservations for ARAMARK facilities. Although Park Service monitoring keeps the monopoly mostly in check, services inside the recreation area are pricier than those outside.

Page continues to serve a transient crowd and has much better bargains than inside the recreation area. Motels, unspectacular restaurants, and a litany of churches line Lake Powell Blvd., a wide, U-shaped road connecting with **U.S. 89** both north and south of town. Page's economy relies almost entirely on the tourist industry, and, as such, is highly seasonal. Expect price mark-downs at those few businesses that do remain open through the winter.

Visitor Info: Carl Hayden Visitors Center (☎608-6404), just across the bridge from Page on U.S. 89 N. Open May-Sept. daily 8am-7pm; Oct.-Apr. 8am-6pm. At the **Bullfrog Marina,** 45 mi. northeast of the dam, a Visitors Center welcomes tourists entering the recreation area from Rte. 276 in Utah. Open Apr.-Oct. daily 8am-5pm. In Page, the **Chamber of Commerce,** 644 N. Navajo Dr. (☎888-261-7243), in the Dam Plaza. Carries info on local services and rentals for watersports. Open daily 9am-6pm; in winter M-F 9am-5pm. In a pinch, info kiosks at several corners of Lake Powell Blvd. have helpful info to get you through the night.

Bike Rentals: Lakeside Bicycles, 118 6th Ave. (☎645-2266). Hard trail bikes with helmet $25 per day. Open M-F 9am-6pm, Sa 8am-noon.

Laundromat: Sunshine Laundry and Dry Cleaners, 131 S. Lake Powell Blvd. (☎645-9703). Open daily 7am-9pm. Wahweap and Bullfrog Marinas also offer machines. At Wahweap, atop the hill at the RV park.

Showers: At Wahweap RV Park. Guests free, campers and walk-ins $2. Free outdoor beach-type showers at Lone Rock Campground.

Medical Care: Page Hospital, 501 N. Navajo Dr. (☎645-2424). 24hr. emergency care.

Internet access: Page Public Library, 479 S. Lake Powell Blvd. (☎645-4270. Open M-Th 10am-8pm, F-Sa 10am-5pm. Free Internet.)

Post Office: 44 6th Ave. (☎645-2571. Open 8:30am-5pm M-F.) **ZIP code:** 86040. **Area code:** 428.

ACCOMMODATIONS

Although the main drag through Page grows increasingly populated with high-end chain hotels, a few gems of an earlier, more affordable era remain. A cluster of quality budget accommodations resides on 8th Ave. between S. Navajo and Elm St. (from either direction on Lake Powell Blvd., head north on S. Navajo and make a left onto 8th Ave.). Pegged as "Page's Old Quarter," this "Avenue of Little Motels" shelters an idiosyncratic cluster of converted dam worker apartments. For the price of one night in the **Wahweap Lodge,** you could buy yourself a decent tent, and camping on the lake is beautiful and inexpensive. Visitors with boats can camp nearly anywhere along the endless lakeshore, so long as they have a **portable toilet.** The lake's marinas rent them. Don't get caught without one—the rangers are vigilant, and besides, no one wants to swim in your sewage.

Away from the dam area, tent sites and hookups are readily available at the **Bullfrog ❶, Halls Crossing ❶,** and **Hite Marinas ❶.** Call **ARAMARK** (☎800-528-6154) for camping info. Sites $6.

Lake Powell International Hostel & Pension, 141 8th Ave. (☎645-3898). After a hiatus, this comfortable hostel with a European clientele has reopened. Sand volleyball in the yard, basketball hoop, free shuttles to the lake and airport. Free linen. Friendly owners oversee dozens of bunks ($12-15), private bedrooms with shared bathrooms ($30), with kitchens, cable TV, VCRs, and living room ($40 and up) and full apartments. ❶

K.C.'s Motel, 126 8th Ave. (☎645-2947). Named for the owner's affectionate Yorkie, K.C.'s offers spacious, recently renovated suites with cable TV and multiple bedrooms at discount prices. Rooms start at $39, but rates drop in winter. ❸

Wahweap Campground/RV Park (☎800-528-6154), at Wahweap Marina. Near lake swimming areas, boat rentals, and ramps. Shuttles to the lodge, showers, laundry, general store, and Page. Tent sites $15, hookups $27. ❷

Lone Rock Campground, on Lone Rock Rd. just on the Utah side of the border. Camp anywhere on the beach to enjoy the water, the sunsets, the constant purring of RV generators, and the drone of ATVs operated by campers too lazy to walk 200 yards to the pit toilets. Water, showers, and boat ramp available. Sites $6. ❶

◘ FOOD

Despite the fact that Page transforms into a bustling, cosmopolitan center for half the year, dining options in town barely escape the hum-drum steak, potatoes, and Mexican cuisine so pervasive in the area. Most eateries lie on Lake Powell Blvd., though some gather along N. Navajo Dr. There are two important bonuses to the over-abundance of Western cooking: hearty "cowboy appetite" portions at bargain "ranch-hand" prices. If the meager choices have got you down, plan your own meal at **Safeway,** 650 Elm St. (☎645-8155).

> **Ranch House Grill,** 819 N. Navajo Dr. (☎645-1420). Try their breakfasts. The owner picked the name to evoke generous helpings of food, and his restaurant delivers. Bulging 3-egg omelettes ($4-6) come with hash browns and toast, biscuits and gravy, or two pancakes. Open daily 6am-3pm; breakfast served all day. ❶

> **Dos Amigos Restaurant and Cantina,** 287 N. Lake Powell Blvd. (☎645-9394) in the Quality Inn. Prepares delectable Mexican fare and furnishes a stunning view and patio. Deals include a bargain list of lunch specials ($5-6) and an a la carte menu (tacos begin at $2.50) that fits even the tightest of budgets. Dinners start at $11, but include a soup/salad bar. Restaurant open 7am-11pm; cantina 10am-midnight. ❸

◉ ⚑ SIGHTS & OUTDOOR ACTIVITIES

Jaded with the thrills of cigarette boats and jet skis, many visitors to Lake Powell seek out slightly more sedate, but equally enthralling ways to spend a day. Both the **Rainbow Bridge National Monument** and **Antelope Canyon** draw countless visitors to revel in the artistry of water at work on sandstone canvas. The damming of Lake Powell created easy access to Rainbow Bridge, an originally remote wonder of the natural world. Despite its current tourist-attraction status, the arch remains sacred to area native cultures. Out of respect, visitors are asked not to approach, climb on, or pass through this breathtaking lesson in erosional art. Hiking to Rainbow Bridge on Navajo land requires a **hiking permit,** obtainable by writing Navajo Nation Parks and Recreation Department, Box 9000, Window Rock 86515. Most visitors, however, come by boat. A courtesy dock floats about ½ mi. from the bridge, and is accessible after 4hr. ride from either the Wahweap, Halls Crossing, or Bullfrog Marinas. Only the park concessionaire, **ARAMARK,** has permission to offer tours. (☎800-528-6154. 7hr. full-day tours with lunch $114, children $74; 5hr. half-day tours $86/58.)

Over the course of millions of years, raging torrents and swirling eddies have lifted particles of sand from the base and walls of Antelope Canyon. This ceaseless erosion has sculpted a canyon of exceptional variety and beauty. For ages, Native Americans have approached this canyon, called *Tse bighanilini* ("the place where water runs through rocks") in Navajo, with profound respect and spiritual reverence. Antelope Canyon is divided by Rte. 98 into two parts: upper and lower. **Upper Antelope,** the most frequently visited, is most accessible and arguably the easier to appreciate. Descending **Lower Antelope** requires climbing ladders and slipping through extremely narrow gaps. ($5 Navajo use fee; shuttle to upper canyon or guide services in lower canyon $12.50.)

For a truly low-key and highly informational afternoon, visit the **John Wesley Powell Museum,** 6 N. Lake Powell Blvd. (☎645-9496. Open in summer M-Sa 9am-6pm. $7.) The **Carl Hayden Visitors Center,** adjacent to the dam on U.S. 89, guides visitors into the bowels of the concrete behemoth. (☎608-6404. Tours in summer every 30min. 8:30am-4:30pm; off-season every hr. Visitors Center open May-Sept. daily 8am-6pm; off-season 8am-5pm.)

PHOENIX ☎602

The name Phoenix was chosen for a small farming community in the Sonoran desert by Anglo settlers who believed that their oasis had risen from the ashes of ancient Native American settlements like the legendary phoenix of Greek mythology. The 20th century has seen this unlikely metropolis live up to its name; the expansion of water resources, the proliferation of railroad transportation, and the introduction of air-conditioning have fueled Phoenix's ascent to its standing among America's leading cities. Shiny high-rises now crowd the business district, while a vast web of six-lane highways and strip malls surrounds the downtown area. Phoenix's rise has not been without turmoil, though: its greatest asset, the sun, is also its greatest nemesis. During the balmy winter months, tourists, golfers, and business travelers flock to the resort-perfect temperatures. In the summer, the city crawls into its air-conditioned shell as temperatures climb to an average of 100°F and lodging prices plummet.

▐ TRANSPORTATION

Airport: Sky Harbor International (☎273-3300; www.phxskyharbor.com), just southeast of downtown. Take the Valley Metro Red Line bus into the city (5:45am-10pm, $1.25). The largest city in the Southwest, Phoenix is a major airline hub and tends to be an affordable and convenient destination.

Buses: Greyhound, 2115 E. Buckeye Rd. (☎389-4200). To: **El Paso** (8hr., 13 per day, $35); **Los Angeles** (7hr., 12 per day, $35); **San Diego** (8hr.; 6 per day; M-Th $47.50, F-Su $49); and **Tucson** (2hr., 13 per day, $14). Open 24hr. There is no direct rail service to Phoenix, but **Amtrak** (☎800-USA-RAIL, www.amtrak.com) operates connector buses to and from rail stations in Tucson and Flagstaff for those interested in train travel. The Greyhound bus station is their busiest connecting Thruway motorcoach service location.

Public Transit, Downtown Phoenix: Valley Metro (☎253-5000). Most lines run to and from Central Station, at Central and Van Buren St. Routes tend to operate M-F 5am-8pm with reduced service on Sa. $1.25; disabled, seniors, and children 60¢. All-day pass $3.60, 10-ride pass $12. Bus passes and system maps at the Terminal. In Tempe, the **City of Tempe Transit Store,** 502 S. College Ave., Ste. 101, serves as public transit headquarters. The red line runs to and from Phoenix, and the last few stops of the yellow line are also in Tempe. The red line also extends beyond Tempe to service Mesa. Bus passes and system maps at the Terminal. Loloma Station, just south of Indian School and Scottsdale Rd., is Scottsdale's main hub for local traffic. The green line runs along Thomas St. to Phoenix.

Taxis: Yellow Cab, ☎252-5252. **Discount Taxi,** ☎254-1999.

Car Rental: Enterprise Rent-a-car, 1402 N. Central St. (☎257-4177; www.enterprise.com), with other offices throughout the city. Compact cars at around $45 per day, with lower weekly and monthly rates. No surcharge for drivers over 21 (call ahead if under 21, as there are different requirements). A valid credit card and driver's license are required. N. Central St. office open M-F 7:30am-6pm, Sa 9am-noon; other offices' hours vary.

▟ ▐ ORIENTATION & PRACTICAL INFORMATION

The intersection of **Central Ave.** and **Washington St.** marks the heart of downtown. Central Ave. runs north-south, Washington St. east-west. One of Phoenix's peculiarities is that numbered avenues and streets both run north-south; avenues are numbered sequentially west from Central, while streets are numbered east. Greater Phoenix includes a number of smaller municipalities. **Tempe,** east of Phoenix, is dominated by students from Arizona State University. **Mesa,** east of Tempe, handles much of Tempe's overflow. **Scottsdale,** north of Tempe, is a swank district brimming with adobe palaces, shopping centers, and interesting sights.

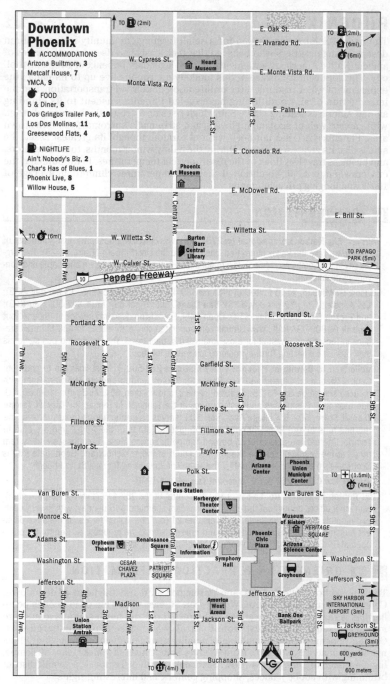

Downtown Phoenix

ACCOMMODATIONS
Arizona Builtmore, **3**
Metcalf House, **7**
YMCA, **9**

FOOD
5 & Diner, **6**
Dos Gringos Trailer Park, **10**
Los Dos Molinas, **11**
Greesewood Flats, **4**

NIGHTLIFE
Ain't Nobody's Biz, **2**
Char's Has of Blues, **1**
Phoenix Live, **8**
Willow House, **5**

TO ① (2mi)

E. Oak St.
E. Alvarado Rd.

TO ② (2mi),
③ (6mi),
④ (6mi)

W. Cypress St.

Heard Museum

E. Monte Vista Rd.

Monte Vista Rd.

1st St.

N. 3rd St.

E. Palm Ln.

E. Coronado Rd.

Phoenix Art Museum

E. McDowell Rd.

E. Brill St.

⑤

N. Central Ave.

E. Willetta St.

TO ⑥ (6mi)

W. Willetta St.

Burton Barr Central Library

TO PAPAGO PARK (5mi)

N. 7th Ave.

N. 5th Ave.

W. Culver St.

⑩ Papago Freeway

E. Portland St.

Portland St.

1st St.

Roosevelt St.

Roosevelt St.

⑦

7th Ave.

5th Ave.

3rd Ave.

1st Ave.

Central Ave.

Garfield St.

McKinley St.

McKinley St.

3rd St.

5th St.

7th St.

N. 9th St.

Pierce St.

Fillmore St.

Fillmore St.

Taylor St.

Taylor St.

⑧ Arizona Center

Phoenix Union Municipal Center

TO ✚ (1.5mi),
⑩ (4mi)

⑨

Polk St.

Central Bus Station

Herberger Theater Center

Van Buren St.

S. 9th St.

Van Buren St.

Monroe St.

Museum of History

HERITAGE SQUARE

Adams St.

Orpheum Theater

Renaissance Square

Visitor Information ⓘ

Phoenix Civic Plaza

Arizona Science Center

Washington St.

CESAR CHAVEZ PLAZA

PATRIOT'S SQUARE

Symphony Hall

E. Washington St.

Jefferson St.

Greyhound

Jefferson St.

Jefferson St.

TO SKY HARBOR INTERNATIONAL AIRPORT (3mi)

7th Ave.

6th Ave.

5th Ave.

4th Ave.

Madison

3rd Ave.

2nd Ave.

1st Ave.

1st St.

America West Arena

Jackson St.

3rd St.

Bank One Ballpark

7th St.

E. Jackson St.

TO GREYHOUND (3mi)

Union Station Amtrak

N

LG

Buchanan St.

TO ⑪ (4mi)

0   600 yards
0   600 meters

Visitor Info: Phoenix and Valley of the Sun Convention and Visitors Center (☎254-6500 or 877-225-5749, recorded info and events calendar ☎252-5588; www.phoenixcvb.com). Downtown location: 2nd and Adams St. Open M-F 8am-5pm. Free Internet (5min. limit). Biltmore Fashion Park location: 24th St. and East Camelback. Open daily 8am-5pm. Camping and outdoors information available at the **Bureau of Land Management Office,** 222 N. Central (☎417-9200).

Hotlines: Crisis Hotline, ☎254-4357. 24hr. **Gay Hotline,** ☎234-2752. Daily 10am-10pm.

Internet access: Burton Barr Central Library, 1221 N. Central Ave. (☎262-4636). Open M-Th 9am-9pm, F-Sa 9am-6pm, Su 1-5pm. Sign-up required, but computers usually available.

Post Office: 1441 E. Buckeye Rd. (☎407-2051). Open M-F 7:30am-5pm. **ZIP code:** 85026. **Area codes:** 602, 623 or 480. In text, 602 unless otherwise noted.

ACCOMMODATIONS

Budget travelers should consider visiting Phoenix during July and August when motels slash their prices by as much as 70%. In the winter, when temperatures drop and vacancies are few, prices go up; make reservations if possible. The reservationless should cruise the rows of motels on **Van Buren St.** east of downtown, toward the airport. Parts of this area can be unsafe; *guests should examine a motel thoroughly before checking in.* Although they are more distant, the areas around Papago Fwy. and Black Canyon Hwy. are loaded with motels and may present some safer options. **Mi Casa Su Casa/Old Pueblo Homestays Bed and Breakfast,** P.O. Box 950, Tempe 85280, arranges stays in B&Bs throughout Arizona, New Mexico, southern Utah, southern Nevada, and southern California. (☎800-456-0682. Open M-F 9am-5pm, Sa 9am-noon. $45 and up.)

▨ **Arizona Biltmore,** (☎800-950-0086) at 24th and Missouri St. Designed by Frank Lloyd Wright, this lavish hotel has everything a vacationer could hope for, and the price tag to back it up. Whether you prefer golfing, hiking, biking, relaxing at the spa, or any combination thereof, it can all be found at this centrally located bastion of comfort. Prices from late May to Sept. are significantly lower than during the cooler months, though still steep, start at $175 per night. ❺

Metcalf House (HI-AYH), 1026 N. 9th St. (☎254-9803), a few blocks northeast of downtown. Look for the house with lots of foliage out front. From Central Station, take bus #10 down 7th St. to Roosevelt St., walk 2 blocks east to 9th St., and turn left—the hostel is ½ block north in a shady and quiet residential area. Last bus leaves at 8:30pm. The neighborhood has seen better days—the coin lockers available in the dorms are probably a good idea. Evening gab sessions common on the front porch. Dorm-style rooms with wooden bunks adjoin a kitchen and common room. Bikes for rent, and discounts to some city sights included in the price. Check-in 7-10am and 5-10pm. Chores required. $15. ❶

YMCA Downtown Phoenix, 350 N. 1st Ave. (☎253-6181). Another option in the downtown area, the YMCA provides small, single-occupancy rooms and shared bathrooms. Various athletic facilities. A small supply of women's rooms available. Ask at the desk about storing valuables. Open daily 9am-10pm. 18+. Daily $30; weekly $119. ❷

FOOD

While much of the Phoenix food scene seems to revolve around shopping mall food courts and expensive restaurants, rest assured that hidden jewels can be found. Downtowners feed mainly at small coffeehouses, most of which close on weekends. **McDowell** and **Camelback Rd.** offer a (small) variety of Asian restaurants. The **Arizona Center,** an open-air shopping gallery at 3rd St. and Van Buren, boasts food venues, fountains, and palm trees. Sports bars and grilles hover around the America West Arena and Bank One Ballpark. The *New Times* (☎271-4000) makes restaurant recommendations.

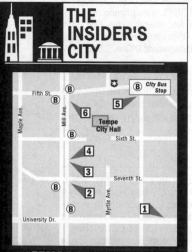

THE INSIDER'S CITY

TEMPE PUB CRAWL

Near Phoenix, and home of Arizona State University, Tempe has more watering holes than you can shake a dead armadillo at. When you're done crawling and ready to head home, you can grab a green line bus at any of the stops below.

1 Start the evening at **Dos Gringos Trailer Park.** Sip a seemingly bottomless margarita for $4.

2 Get Arizona's finest chicken wings (try the suicide wings) at **Long Wong's**—but don't choke on a bone.

3 Rack 'em up at the **Mill Cue Club,** and prepare to get schooled by the ASU kids.

4 Nurse your bruised ego back to health on sweet sweet micro brews at the **Mill Ave. Beer Co.**

5 Stagger down to the last real tavern in Tempe, the **Bandersnatch Brew Pub.** Enjoy your brew the traditional way or, for the more adventurous, try it topically through the "Beer in your Face Club."

6 Stumble into **Beeloe's Cafe & Underground Bar** for live music and a hip ASU crowd.

Los Dos Molinos, 8646 S. Central Ave. (☎243-9113). From downtown, head south on Central Ave. Go very far, and once you're sure you've gone too far, go farther. Once you leave the barrio, it comes up suddenly on your right. One look and you'll know why you've made the trip; Los Dos Molinos is lively, colorful, and fun. Locals throng here on weekends, filling the indoor restaurant and the colorful courtyard, and spilling onto the street. Come early; they don't take reservations. Enchiladas $3.50, burritos $5.25-7. Open Tu-F 11am-2:30pm and 5-9pm, Sa 11am-9pm. ●

5 & Diner, 5220 N. 16th St. (☎264-5220), with branches dotting the greater metro area. 24hr. service and all the sock-hop music that one can stand. Vinyl booths, smiley service, and juke boxes teach you what the fifties *could* have been. Burgers go for $6-7 and sandwiches are $5-7. You can get the best milkshakes in town for only $3-4. Afternoon blue plate specials change daily, but are always your money's worth (M-F 11am-4pm, $3-6). Outdoor seating with view of scenic N. 16th St. available. ●

Dos Gringos Trailer Park, 216 E. University (☎480-968-7879), in Tempe. The best atmosphere in Tempe, bar-none. Dos, as it's affectionately known, draws people of all walks of life with its open, laid-back feel and its inexpensive yet tasty Mexican food. Deals include a Hangover Special ($5.25) that helps one recuperate from the night before, and countless meals for under $6. Open M-Sa 10am-1am, Su noon-1am. ●

Greasewoods Flats, 27500 N. Alma School Rd. (☎480-585-9430), in Scottsdale. With the most eclectic mix of patrons in Scottsdale, Greasewoods Flats dishes out classic American cuisine at reasonable prices, including succulent hamburgers ($6-8). Rub elbows with hippies, bikers, yuppies, bobos, and everything in between. Open M-F 10am-11pm, Sa 10am-midnight, Su 10am-10pm. ❷

◉ SIGHTS

DOWNTOWN. Downtown Phoenix offers a few museums and mounting evidence of America's growing consumer culture. The price of most downtown attractions hovers around $7; fortunately, the majority are worth it. The **Heard Museum** is renowned for its presentation of ancient Native American art, and features exhibits focusing on contemporary Native Americans. (2301 N. Central Ave., 4 blocks north of McDowell Rd. ☎ 252-8840, recorded info ☎ 252-8848. Open daily 9:30am-5pm. Free tours at noon, 1:30, and 3pm. $7, seniors $6, ages 4-12 $3, Native Americans with status cards free.) Three blocks south, the **Phoenix Art Museum** exhibits art of the American West, including paintings from the Taos and Santa Fe art colonies. There are also impressive collections of 19th-century European and American works. *(1625 N. Central Ave., at McDowell Rd. ☎ 257-1880. Open Tu-Su 10am-5pm, Th 10am-9pm. $7, students and seniors $5, ages 6-18 $2. Free on Th and after 4:15pm.)*

PAPAGO PARK & FARTHER EAST. The **Desert Botanical Garden,** in Papago Park, 5 mi. east of downtown, grows a colorful collection of cacti and other desert plants. The park's trails make a pleasant stroll, and many of the desert flowers are hard to find in the wild. *(1201 N. Galvin Pkwy. ☎ 941-1225, recorded info ☎ 481-8134. Open daily May-Sept. 7am-8pm; Oct.-Apr. 8am-8pm. $7.50, students with ID $4, seniors $6.50, ages 5-12 $3.50.)* Take bus #3 east to **Papago Park,** on the eastern outskirts of the city. The park has spectacular views of the desert along its hiking, biking, and driving trails. If you spot an orangutan strolling around the cacti, it's either a mirage or you're in the **Phoenix Zoo,** located within the park and boasting a formidable collection of South American, African, and Southwestern critters. *(455 N. Galvin Pkwy. ☎ 273-1341. Open Sept.-May daily 9am-5pm. $12, seniors $9, children $5; June-Aug. 7am-9pm; $9, seniors $7, children $5.)* Still farther east of the city, in Mesa, flows the **Salt River,** one of the last remaining desert rivers in the US. **Salt River Recreation** arranges tubing trips. *(☎ 984-3305. Open May-Sept. daily 9am-4pm. Tube rental $9.)*

SCOTTSDALE SIGHTS. Taliesin West was originally built as the winter camp of Frank Lloyd Wright's Taliesin architectural collective; in his later years he lived there full-time. Now it serves as a campus for an architectural college run by his foundation. *(At the corner of Frank Lloyd Wright Blvd. and Cactus St. ☎ 860-8810. Open Sept.-June daily 9am-4pm; July-Aug. M and Th-Su 9am-4pm. 1hr. or 1½hr. guided tours required. $10-14, students and seniors $8-12, ages 4-12 $3-8.)* Wright also designed the **Arizona Biltmore** hotel. *(24th St. and Missouri. ☎ 955-6600.)* One of the last buildings designed by Wright, the **Gammage Memorial Auditorium** wears the pink-and-beige earth tones of the surrounding environment. *(Mill Ave. and Apache Blvd., on the Arizona State University campus in Tempe. Take bus #60, or #22 on weekends. ☎ 965-3434. 20min. tours daily in winter.)* One of Wright's students liked Scottsdale so much he decided to stay. **Cosanti** is a working studio and bell foundry designed by the architect and sculptor Paolo Soleri. The buildings here fuse with the natural landscape even more strikingly than those at Taliesin West. *(6433 Doubletree Rd., in Scottsdale. With I-10 behind you turn right off of Scottsdale Rd.; it will be on your right in about 5 blocks. ☎ 480-948-6145. Open M-Sa 9am-5pm, Su 11am-5pm, $1 donation suggested.)*

🎵 🎭 ENTERTAINMENT & NIGHTLIFE

Phoenix offers many options for the sports lover. NBA basketball action rises with the **Phoenix Suns** (☎ 379-7867) at the **America West Arena,** while the **Arizona Cardinals** (☎ 379-0101) provide American football excitement. The 2002 World Series Champions **Arizona Diamondbacks** (☎ 514-8400) play at the state-of-the-art **Bank One Ballpark,** complete with a retractable roof, an outfield swimming pool, and "beer gardens." (☎ 462-6799. Tickets start at $6. Special $1 tickets available 2hr. before games, first come, first served. Tours of the stadium; proceeds go to charity.)

The free *New Times Weekly*, available on local magazine racks, lists club schedules for Phoenix's after-hours scene. The *Cultural Calendar of Events* covers area entertainment in three-month intervals. *The Western Front*, found in bars and clubs, covers gay and lesbian nightlife.

Char's Has the Blues, 4631 N. 7th Ave., houses local jazz acts. On Friday night, come early for the BBQ. (☎ 230-0205. For shows, doors open 7pm. Cover F-Sa $7. Hours vary.) **Phoenix Live,** 455 N. 3rd St. (☎ 252-2502), at the Arizona Center, houses three bars and a restaurant. **America's Original Sports Bar** is the largest of the three, with a DJ spinning Top 40. The dance floor at **Decades,** a retro club playing 1960s-

THE SOUTHWEST

80s hits, is much larger and busier. For those who don't feel like sweating to the oldies, **Ltl Ditty's** features dueling baby grand pianos in a lounge atmosphere. ($5 weekend cover buys access to it all. Open Su-Th 4pm-midnight, F-Sa 4pm-1am.) **The Willow House,** 149 W. McDowell Rd., is a self-proclaimed "artist's cove," combining a chic coffee house, a New York deli, and a quirky musicians' hangout. (☎252-0272. No alcohol. 2-for-1 coffee happy hour M-F 4-7pm. Live music Sa starting at 8pm. Open M-Th 7am-midnight, F 7am-1am, Sa 8am-1am, Su 8am-midnight.) A large lesbian bar, **Ain't Nobody's Biz,** 3031 E. Indian School Rd. #7, has more space devoted to pool tables than to the dance floor. (☎224-9977. No regular cover, but occasional guest vocalists and charges. Open M-F 4pm-1am, Sa-Su 2pm-1am.) **Boom,** 1724 E. McDowell Rd., *the* place for young gay men in Phoenix, is popular with throngs of gyrating Adonis-featured youth who like to party untill the wee hours. (☎254-0231. 18+ after 10pm. Open Th-F 4pm-3am, Sa 4pm-6am.)

SCENIC DRIVE: APACHE TRAIL

Steep, gray, and haunting, the **Superstition Mountains** derive their name from Pima Native American legends. Although the Native Americans were kicked out by the Anglo gold prospectors who settled the region, the curse stayed. In the 1840s, a Mexican explorer found gold in these hills, but was killed before he could reveal the location of the mine. More famous is the case of Jacob Waltz, known as "Dutchman" despite having come from Germany. During the 1880s, he brought out about $250,000 worth of high-quality gold ore from somewhere in the mountains. Upon his death in 1891, he left only a few clues to the whereabouts of the mine. Strangely, many who have come looking for it have died violent deaths—one prospector burned to death in his own campfire, while another was found decapitated in an *arroyo*. Needless to say, the mine has never been found.

Rte. 88, a.k.a. **Apache Trail,** winds from **Apache Junction,** a small mining town 40 mi. east of Phoenix, through the mountains. Although the road is only about 50 mi. long one-way, trips require at least 3hr. behind the wheel because it's only partially paved. The car-less can leave the driving to **Apache Trail Tours,** which offers on- and off-road Jeep tours. (☎480-982-7661. 2-4hr. tours $60 per person. Reserve at least 1 day in advance.) For more info, head to the **Apache Junction Chamber of Commerce,** 112 E. 2nd Ave. (☎480-982-3141. Open M-F 8am-5pm.)

The scenery is the Trail's greatest attraction; the dramatic views of the arid landscape make it one of the most beautiful driving routes in the nation. The deep blue waters of the manmade **Lake Canyon, Lake Apache,** and **Lake Roosevelt** contrast sharply with the red and beige-hued rock formations surrounding them. **Goldfield Ghost Town Mine Tours,** 5 mi. north of the U.S. 60 junction on Rte. 88, offers tours of the nearby mines and gold-panning in a resurrected ghost town. (☎480-983-0333. Open daily 10am-5pm. Mine tours $5, ages 6-12 $3; gold-panning $4.) "Where the hell am I?" said Jacob Waltz when he came upon **Lost Dutchman State Park ❶,** 1 mi. farther north on Rte. 88. At the base of the Superstitions, the park offers nature trails, picnic sites, and campsites with showers but no hookups. (☎480-982-4485. Entrance $5 per vehicle. First come, first served sites $10.) Grab a saddle for a barstool at **Tortilla Flat,** another refurbished ghost town 18 mi. farther on Rte. 88. The town keeps its spirits up and tourists nourished with a restaurant, ice cream shop, and saloon. (☎480-984-1776. Restaurant open M-F 9am-6pm, Sa-Su 8am-7pm.) **Tonto National Monument,** 5 mi. east of Lake Roosevelt on Rte. 88, preserves 800-year-old masonry and pueblo ruins built by Ancestral Puebloans. (Open daily 8am-4pm. $4 per car.) **Tonto National Forest ❶** offers nearby camping. (☎602-225-5200. Sites $4-11.) The trail ends at the **Theodore Roosevelt Dam** (completed in 1911), the last dam constructed by hand in the US. For those who complete the Trail, Rte. 60 is a scenic trip back to Phoenix; the increased moisture and decreased temperatures of the higher elevations give rise to lush greenery (by Arizona standards).

TUCSON
☎ 520

A little bit country, a little bit rock 'n' roll, Tucson is a city that carries its own tune and a bundle of contradictions. Mexican property until the Gadsden Purchase, the city retains many of its south-of-the-border influences and shares its Mexican heritage with such disparate elements as the University of Arizona, the Davis-Monthan Airforce Base, and McDonald's. Boasting mountainous flora beside desert cacti and art museums next to the war machines of the Pima Air and Space museum, the city nearly defies categorization. In the last several years, a re-energized downtown core has attracted artists and hipsters, while families and retirees populate the sprawling suburbs. With arguably better tourist attractions and more bustle and vitality than almost any other Southwestern city, Tucson offers the conveniences of a metropolis without the nasty aftertaste.

▐ TRANSPORTATION

Airport: Tucson International Airport (☎ 573-8000; www.tucsonairport.org), on Valencia Rd., south of downtown. Bus #25 runs every hr. to the Laos Transit Center; from there, bus #16 goes downtown. **Arizona Stagecoach** (☎ 889-1000) goes downtown for around $14 per person; $3 each additional person. 24hr. Reservations recommended.

Trains: Amtrak, 400 E. Toole Ave. (☎ 623-4442), at 5th Ave., 1 block north of the Greyhound station. To: **Albuquerque** via El Paso (4 per week, $99); **Las Vegas** via L.A. (3 per week, $124); **Los Angeles** (3 per week, $72); and **San Francisco** via L.A. (3 per week, $130). Book 2 weeks ahead or rates are substantially higher. Open Sa-M 6:15am-1:45pm and 4:15-11:30pm, Tu-W 6:15am-1:45pm, Th-F 4:15-11:30pm.

Buses: Greyhound, 2 S. 4th Ave. (☎ 792-3475), between Congress St. and Broadway. To: **Albuquerque** (12-14hr., 5 per day, $88); **El Paso** (6hr., 12 per day, $35); **Los Angeles** (9-10hr., 4 per day, $40); and **Phoenix** (2hr., 16 per day, $15). Open 24hr.

Public Transit: Sun-Tran (☎ 792-9222). Buses run from the Ronstadt terminal downtown at Congress and 6th St. 85¢, under 19 60¢, seniors and disabled 35¢, day pass $2. Service roughly M-F 5:30am-10pm, Sa-Su 8am-7pm; times vary by route.

Taxis: Yellow Cab, ☎ 624-6611.

Bike Rental: Fairwheels Bicycles, 1110 E. 6th St. (☎ 884-9018), at Fremont. $20 first day, $10 each additional day. Credit card deposit required. Open M-F 9am-6pm, Sa 9am-5:30pm, Su noon-4pm.

▐▐ ORIENTATION & PRACTICAL INFORMATION

Just east of I-10, Tucson's downtown area surrounds the intersection of **Broadway Blvd.** and **Stone Ave.,** two blocks from the train and bus terminals. The **University of Arizona** lies 1 mi. northeast of downtown at the intersection of **Park** and **Speedway Blvd.** "Avenues" run north-south, "streets" east-west; because some of each are numbered, intersections such as "6th and 6th" are possible. Speedway, Broadway, and **Grant Rd.** are the quickest east-west routes through town. To go north-south, follow **Oracle Rd.** through the heart of the city, **Campbell Ave.** east of downtown, or **Swan Rd.** farther east. The hip, young crowd swings on **4th Ave.** and on **Congress St.,** both with small shops, quirky restaurants, and a slew of bars.

Visitor info: Tucson Convention and Visitors Bureau, 130 S. Scott Ave. (☎ 624-1817 or 800-638-8350), near Broadway. Open M-F 8am-5pm, Sa-Su 9am-4pm.

Bi-Gay-Lesbian Organization: Gay, Lesbian, and Bisexual Community Center, 300 E. 6th St. (☎ 624-1779). Open M-Sa 11am-7pm.

Hotlines: Rape Crisis, ☎ 624-7273. **Suicide Prevention,** ☎ 323-9373. Both 24hr.

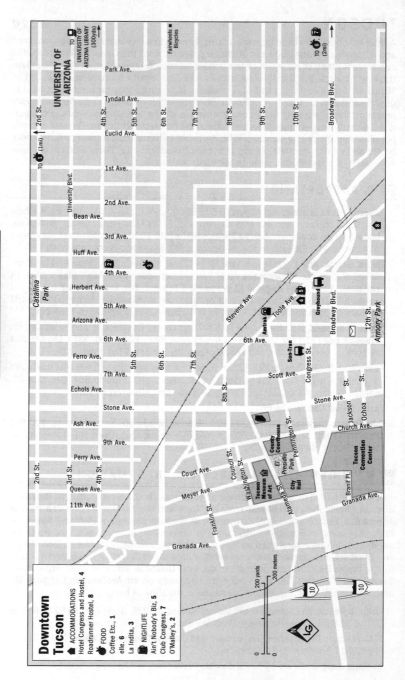

THE SOUTHWEST

Downtown Tucson

ACCOMMODATIONS
Hotel Congress and Hostel, **4**
Roadrunner Hostel, **8**

FOOD
Coffee Etc., **1**
elle. **6**
La Indita, **3**

NIGHTLIFE
Ain't Nobody's Biz, **5**
Club Congress, **7**
O'Malley's, **2**

UNIVERSITY OF ARIZONA

Catalina Park

Park Ave.
Tyndall Ave.
Euclid Ave.
1st Ave.
2nd Ave.
Bean Ave.
3rd Ave.
Huff Ave.
4th Ave.
Herbert Ave.
5th Ave.
Arizona Ave.
6th Ave.
Ferro Ave.
7th Ave.
Echols Ave.
Stone Ave.
Ash Ave.
9th Ave.
Perry Ave.
Queen Ave.
11th Ave.

University Blvd.

2nd St.
4th St.
5th St.
6th St.
7th St.
8th St.
9th St.
10th St.

Broadway Blvd.

Stevens Ave.
Toole Ave.
6th Ave.
Scott Ave.
Congress St.
Stone Ave.
Church Ave.
Jackson
Ochoa
Granada Ave.

5th St.
6th St.
7th St.
8th St.

Court Ave.
Council St.
Washington St.
Alameda St.
Franklin St.
Meyer Ave.
Granada Ave.

Amtrak
Sun-Tran
Greyhound
Broadway Blvd.
12th St.
Armory Park

Tucson Museum of Art
El Presidio Park
County Courthouse
City Hall
Pennington St.
Branif Pl.
Tucson Convention Center

TO UNIVERSITY OF ARIZONA LIBRARY (300yds)
Fairwheels Bicycles
TO (2mi)
TO (1mi)

200 yards
200 meters

N

Medical Services: University Medical Center, 1501 N. Campbell Ave. (☎694-0111).

Internet access: Free at the **University of Arizona main library,** 1510 E. University Blvd. Open Sept.-May M-Th 7:30am-1am, F 7:30am-9pm, Sa 10am-9pm, Su 11am-1am; June-Aug. M-Th 7:30am-11pm, F 7:30am-6pm, Sa 9am-6pm, Su 11am-11pm.

Post Office: 1501 S. Cherry Bell (☎388-5129). Open M-F 8:30am-8pm, Sa 9am-1pm. **ZIP code:** 85726. **Area code:** 520.

ACCOMMODATIONS

There's a direct correlation between the temperature in Tucson and the warmth of its lodging industry to budget travelers: expect the best deals in summer, when rain-cooled evenings and summer bargains are consolation for the midday scorch. **The Tucson Gem and Mineral Show,** the largest of its kind in North America, is an added hazard for budget travelers. The mammoth show fills up most of the city's accommodations, and drives prices up considerably during its two-week run at the end of January and the beginning of February.

▨ **Roadrunner Hostel,** 346 E. 12th St. (☎628-4709). Wows guests with unparalleled amenities such as a giant 52 in. TV, a formidable movie collection, free high-speed Internet access, purified water, free coffee and tea, and swamp cooling. Located in a pleasant house a few blocks from downtown, the hostel is exceptionally clean and friendly. No curfew and no chores are required; they'll even pick you up at the Greyhound or Amtrak terminal. Apr.-Sept. international guests get 2 free additional nights when they pay for the first 2. Free linen, towels, lockers, and laundry soap. Kitchen and laundry. Dorms $18; private doubles $35. ❶

▨ **Loews Ventana Canyon Resort,** 7000 N. Resort Dr. (☎299-2020). A quintessential 5-star hotel 5 mi. north of downtown off Oracle Rd. At the base of an 80 ft. waterfall, the incredible Ventana delivers on every level—from its relaxing spa to its championship golf course to the beautiful surrounding Catalina Mountain foothills. Singles start at $95. ❹

Hotel Congress and Hostel, 311 E. Congress (☎622-8848). Conveniently located across from the bus and train stations. Superb lodging for night-owl hostelers. Downstairs, Club Congress booms until 1am on weekends, making it rough on early birds. Private rooms come with bath, phone, vintage radio, and ceiling fans. The cafe downstairs serves great salads and omelettes. Dorms $17. Singles June-Aug. $29; Sept.-Nov. and May $49; Dec.-Apr. $68. Doubles June-Aug. $38; Sept.-Nov. and May $53; Jan.-Apr. $82. 10% discount for students, military, and local artists. ❶

In addition to the backcountry camping available in **Saguaro Park** and **Coronado Forest,** there are a variety of other camping options. **Gilbert Ray Campground** ❶ (☎883-4200), just outside Saguaro West, offers $7 campsites with toilets and drinking water. A variety of camping areas flank **Sky Island Scenic Byway** at Mt. Lemmon. All campgrounds charge a $5 road access fee in addition to the camping costs. **Spencer Canyon** ❶ (sites $12) and **Rose Canyon** ❶ ($15) have water and toilets, while **Molino Basin** and **General Hitchcock** ❶ have toilets but no potable water (both $5). Call the Santa Catalina Ranger District for more info (☎749-8700).

FOOD

Tucson, as any good college town should, brims with inexpensive, tasty eateries. Cheap Mexican dominates the scene, but every style of cooking is represented.

▨ **Elle,** 3048 E. Broadway Blvd. (☎327-0500), brings out the gastronome in all who are fortunate enough to sample its succulent menu. Cool classical jazz resonates through this stylish eatery, as mouth-watering chicken penne ($12 is enjoyed in elle's *über*-elegant, yet welcoming, surroundings. Open M-F 11:30am-10pm, Sa 4:30pm-10pm. ❸

THE SOUTHWEST

La Indita, 622 N. 4th Ave. (☎ 792-0523), delights customers with traditional Mexican cuisine ($3-9) served on tasty tortillas. The food is still prepared by *la indita* herself, and as a result, the food has a bit of added kick. Open M-Th 11am-9pm, F 11am-6pm, Sa 6-9pm, Su 9am-9pm. ❶

Coffee Etc., 2830 N. Campbell Ave. (☎ 881-8070) a Tex-Mex coffeeshop, offers sandwiches and light meals ($5-10) and has unbeatable hours. Open 24hr. daily. ❷

⊙ SIGHTS

UNIVERSITY OF ARIZONA. Lined with cafes, restaurants, galleries, and vintage clothing shops, **4th Ave.** is an alternative magnet and a great place to take a stroll. Between Speedway and Broadway Blvd., the street becomes a historical shopping district with increasingly touristy shops. Lovely for its varied and elaborately irrigated vegetation, the **University of Arizona's** mall sits where E. 3rd St. should be, just east of 4th Ave. The **Center for Creative Photography,** on campus, houses various changing exhibits, including the archives of Ansel Adams and Richard Avedon. *(☎ 621-7968. Open M-F 9am-5pm, Sa-Su noon-5pm. Archives available to the public, but only through print-viewing appointments. Free.)* The **Flandrau Science Center,** on Cherry Ave. at the campus mall, dazzles visitors with a public observatory and a laser light show. *(☎ 621-7827. Open M-Tu 9am-5pm, W-Sa 9am-5pm and 7-9pm, Su noon-5pm. $3, under 14 $2. Shows $5/$4, seniors and students $4.50.)* The **University of Arizona Museum of Art** offers visitors a free glimpse of modern American and 18th-century Latin American art, as well as the singularly muscular sculpture of Jacques Lipchitz. The best student art is exhibited here too. *(1031 N. Olive. ☎ 621-7567. Open M-F 10am-3pm, Su noon-4pm.)*

TUCSON MUSEUM OF ART. This major attraction presents impressive traveling exhibits in all media, in addition to its permanent collection of varied American, Mexican, and European art. Historic houses in the surrounding and affiliated Presidio Historic Block boast an impressive collection of Pre-Columbian and Mexican folk art, as well as art of the American West. *(140 N. Main Ave. ☎ 624-2333. Open M-Sa 10am-4pm, Su noon-4pm. Closed M between Memorial Day and Labor Day. $5, seniors $4, students $3, under 13 free. Su free.)*

SIGHTS ON WEST SPEEDWAY. As Speedway Blvd. winds its way west from Tucson's city center, it passes by a variety of sights. The left fork leads to **Old Tucson Studios,** an elaborate Old West-style town constructed for the 1938 movie *Arizona* and used as a backdrop for Westerns ever since, including many John Wayne films and the 1999 Will Smith vehicle *Wild Wild West.* It's open year-round to tourists, who can stroll around in the Old West mock up, view gun fight reenactments and other tourist shows, and, if fortunate, watch the filming of a current Western. *(☎ 883-0100. Open daily 10am-6pm, sometimes closed on M in winter. Call ahead as occasionally Old Tucson is closed for group functions. $15, seniors $13.45, ages 4-11 $9.45.)* Those opting to take the right fork will eschew the Wild Wild West for the merely wild West; less than 2 mi. from the fork lies the **Arizona-Sonora Desert Museum,** a first-rate zoo and nature preserve. The living museum recreates a range of desert habitats and features over 300 kinds of animals. A visit requires at least 2hr., preferably in the morning before the animals take their afternoon siestas. *(2021 N. Kinney Rd. ☎ 883-2702. Follow Speedway Blvd. west of the city as it becomes Gates Pass Rd., then Kinney Rd. Open Mar.-Sept. daily 7:30am-5pm; Oct.-Feb. 8:30am-5pm; June-Sept. Sa 7:30am-10pm. $9; Nov.-Apr. $10; ages 6-12 $1.75.)*

CAVES. Caves are all the rage in Tucson. The recently opened **Kartchner Caverns State Park** is enormously popular, filled with magnificent rock formations and home to over 1000 bats. This is a "living" cave, which contains water and is still experiencing the growth of its formations; the damp conditions cause the formations to shine and glisten in the light. Taking a tour is the only way to enter the cave. *(Located 8 mi. off I-10 at Exit 302. ☎ 586-4100. Open daily 7:30am-6pm. 1hr. tours run every 30min. 8:30am-4:30pm. Entrance fee $10 per vehicle, tour $14, ages 7-13 $6. Reservations strongly recommended.)* Near **Saguaro National Park East** (see p. 827), **Colossal Cave** is one of the only dormant (no water or new formations) caves in the US. A variety of tours are offered; in addition to 1hr. walking tours that occur throughout the day, a special ladder tour through otherwise sealed-off tunnels, crawlspaces, and corridors can be arranged. *(☎ 647-7275. Open mid-Mar. to mid-Sept. M-Sa 8am-6pm, Su 8am-7pm; mid-Sept. to mid-Mar. M-Sa 9am-5pm, Su 9am-6pm. $7, ages 6-12 $4. Ladder tour: Sa 5:30-8pm; $35, includes meal and equipment rental. Reservations required.)*

PIMA AIR AND SPACE MUSEUM. This impressive museum follows aviation history from the days of the Wright brothers to its modern military incarnations. While exhibits on female and African-American aviators are interesting, but the main draw is a fleet of decommissioned warplanes. *(☎ 574-0462. Open M-F 7am-3pm, Sa-Su 7am-5pm; in summer daily 9am-5pm. $7.50, seniors $6.50.)* Tours of the **Davis-Monthan Air Force Base** are also offered. *(M-F 5 tours per day. $5, ages 6-12 $3.)*

🔼 OUTDOOR ACTIVITIES

SAGUARO NATIONAL PARK

North of the desert museum, the western half of Saguaro National Park (Tucson Mountain District) has hiking trails and an auto loop. The **Bajada Loop Drive** runs less than 9 mi., but passes through some of the most striking desert scenery the park has to offer. The paved nature walk near the **Visitors Center** passes some of the best specimens of Saguaro cactus in the Tucson area. *(☎ 733-5158. Park open 24hr.; Visitors Center daily 8:30am-5pm; auto loop 7am-sunset. Free.)*

There are a variety of hiking trails through Saguaro West; **Sendero Esperanza Trail,** beginning at the Ez-kim-in-zin picnic area, is the mildest approach to the summit of **Wasson Peak,** the highest in the Tucson Mountain Range (4687 ft.). The **Hugh Norris Trail** is a slightly longer, more strenuous climb to the top of Wasson Peak.

Mountain biking is permitted only around the **Cactus Forest Loop Drive** and **Cactus Forest Trail,** at the western end of the park near the Visitors Center. The trails in Saguaro East are much longer than those in the western segment of the park. One of the only trails that can easily be completed in a single day is the Cactus Forest.

🎵📺 ENTERTAINMENT & NIGHTLIFE

The free *Tucson Weekly* is the local authority on nightlife, while the weekend sections of the *Star* or the *Citizen* also provide good coverage. Throughout the year, the city of the sun presents **Music Under the Stars,** a series of sunset concerts performed by the **Tucson Symphony Orchestra** (☎ 792-9155). For **Downtown Saturday Nights,** on the first and third Saturday of each month, Congress St. is blockaded for a celebration of the arts with outdoor singers, crafts, and galleries. Every Thursday, the **Thursday Night Art Walk** lets you mosey through downtown galleries and studios. For more info, call **Tucson Arts District** (☎ 624-9977). UA students rock 'n' roll on **Speedway Blvd.,** while others do the two-step along **N. Oracle.** Young locals hang out on **4th Ave.,** where most bars have live music and low cover charges.

Club Congress, 311 E. Congress St. (☎ 622-8848), has DJs during the week and live bands on weekends. The friendly hotel staff and a cast of regulars make it an especially good time. The venue for most of the indie music coming through town. M 80s night with 80¢ drinks. Cover $3-5. Open daily 9pm-1am.

THE SOUTHWEST

O'Malley's, 247 N. 4th Ave. (☎623-8600), is a good spot with decent bar food, pool tables, and pinball. As its name implies, this is a better place to nurse your pint of Guinness than it is to get your groove on. Cover Th-Sa varies. Open daily 11am-1am.

Ain't Nobody's Biz, 2900 E. Broadway Blvd. (☎318-4838), in a shopping plaza, is the little sister of its Phoenix namesake, and is the big mama of the Tucson lesbian scene. A large bar, "Biz" attracts crowds of all backgrounds and has some of the best dancing in Tucson. Open daily 11am-1am.

▶ DAYTRIPS FROM TUCSON

BIOSPHERE 2. Ninety-one feet high, with an area of more than three acres, Biosphere 2 is sealed off from Earth—"Biosphere 1"—by 500 tons of stainless steel. In 1991, eight research scientists locked themselves inside this giant greenhouse to cultivate their own food and knit their own socks as they monitored the behavior of five man-made ecosystems: savanna, rainforest, marsh, ocean, and desert. After two years, they began having oxygen problems and difficulty with food production. No one lives in Biosphere 2 now, but it's still used as a research facility. The Biosphere is 30min. north of Tucson; take I-10 west to the "Miracle Mile" exit, follow the miracles to Oracle Rd., then travel north until it becomes Rte. 77 N. From Phoenix, take I-10 to Exit 185, follow Rte. 387 to Rte. 79 (Florence Hwy.), and proceed to Oracle Junction and Rte. 77. Guided 2hr. tours include two short films, a walk through the laboratory's research and development models for the Biosphere 2 ecosystems, and a stroll around Biosphere 2 itself, including the crew's living quarters. Walking around unchaperoned is also permitted. *(The Biosphere is 30min. north of Tucson; take I-10 west to the "Miracle Mile" exit, follow the miracles to Oracle Rd., then travel north until it becomes Rte. 77 N. From Phoenix, take I-10 to Exit 185, follow Rte. 387 to Rte. 79, and proceed to Oracle Junction and Rte. 77. ☎896-6200 or 800-838-2462. Tours daily 9am-4:30pm. Grounds open 8:30am-5:30pm; last admission at 5pm. $13, students and seniors $11.50, ages 13-17 $9, ages 6-12 $6.)*

MISSION SAN XAVIER DE BAC. Built by the Franciscan brothers in the late 1700s, this is the northernmost Spanish Baroque church in the Americas, and the only such church in the US. The Tohono O'odham Indian Reservation lacked the funds to restore it until the late 20th century. In the early 1990s, a local group gathered money in order to preserve and protect this singular church; since then, the mortar has been restored, the frescoes have been retouched and preserved, and the statuary cleaned of centuries of soot and desert sand. The result is a dazzling house of God, well-earning its nickname "white dove of the desert." *(South of Tucson off of I-19 to Nogales, take the San Xavier exit and follow the signs. ☎294-2624. Open for viewing 8am-6pm; masses held daily. Admission is free both to the church and to the small adjoining museum, although donations are accepted.)*

TOMBSTONE ☎520

Long past the glory days when it was the largest city between the Pacific and the Mississippi, Tombstone has sanitized itself from an authentic, debauched, and dangerous Western town into a Cowboy Disneyland. In Tombstone you can get anything you want—as long as it's a shot of rot-gut or a gunfight reenactment.

By inviting visitors to view the barnyard where Wyatt Earp and his brothers kicked some serious butt, Tombstone has turned the **shootout at the O.K. Corral,** on Allen St. next to City Park, into a year-round tourist industry. (☎457-3456. Open daily 9am-5pm. $2.50.) The voice of Vincent Price narrates the town's history next door to the O.K. Corral in the **Tombstone Historama,** while a plastic mountain revolves onstage and a dramatization of the gunfight is shown on a movie screen.

(☎457-3456. Shows daily every hr. 9am-4pm. $2.50.) Site of the longest poker game in Western history (8 years, 5 months, and 3 days), the **Bird Cage Theater,** at 6th and Allen, was named for the suspended cages that once housed prostitutes. (☎457-3421. Open daily 8am-6pm.) John Slaughter battled outlaws at the **Tombstone Courthouse,** at 3rd and Toughnut St. The courthouse is now a museum. (☎457-3311. Open daily 8am-5pm. $2.50, ages 7-13 $1.) The **tombstones** of Tombstone, largely the result of all that gunplay, stand in Boothill Cemetery on Rte. 80 just north of town. (☎457-3421 or 800-457-3423. Open daily 7:30am-6pm. Free.) For something different, the **Rose Tree Museum,** at 4th and Toughnut St., shelters the largest rose tree in the world. (☎457-3326. Open daily 9am-5pm. $2, under 14 free.)

A good idea is to stay in Benson and commute out for a day in Tombstone. If you want to stay in town, the **Larian Motel ❷,** on the corner of Fremont and 5th, is clean, nicely furnished, roomy, and within easy walking distance of all sights. (☎457-2272. Singles $40-45, doubles $45-59.)

Nellie Cashman's Restaurant ❷, named after the "angel of the mining camps" who devoted her life to clean living and public service, is a little less Old West and a bit more down-home. Delicious ½ lb. hamburgers start at $5.50. (☎457-2212. Open daily 7:30am-9pm.) For a bit of moonshine and country music, smell your way to **Big Nose Kate's Saloon,** on Allen St., named for "the girl who loved Doc Holliday and everyone else too." (☎457-3107. Open daily 10am-midnight.)

To get to Tombstone, head to the Benson Exit off I-10, then go south on Rte. 80. The nearest **Greyhound** station is in **Benson** (see above). The **Douglas Shuttle** (☎364-9442) has service to Tucson ($10), Bisbee ($5), and Benson ($5). The **Tombstone Visitors Center** provides info and maps, although Tombstone is so small that nothing is hard to find. (☎457-3929. Open M-F 9am-4pm, Sa-Su 10am-4pm.) The Tombstone **Marshal's Office** (☎457-2244) is just behind City Hall. **Internet access** is available at **Desert Gold Web Services** on Freemont. (☎457-3250. Open 7am-6pm. 15¢ per min.) The **Post Office** is at 516 E. Allen St. **ZIP code:** 85638. **Area code:** 520.

BISBEE ☎520

One hundred miles southeast of Tucson and 20 mi. south of Tombstone, mellow Bisbee, a former mining town, is known throughout the Southwest as a laid-back artists' colony. Visitors revel in the town's proximity to Mexico, picture-perfect weather, and excellent, relatively inexpensive accommodations.

Queen Mines, on the Rte. 80 interchange entering Old Bisbee, ceased mining in 1943 but continues to give educational 1¼hr. tours. (☎432-2071. Tours at 9, 10:30am, noon, 2, and 3:30pm. $10, ages 7-15 $3.50, ages 3-6 $2.) The Smithsonian-affiliated **Mining and Historical Museum,** 5 Copper Queen, highlights the discovery of Bisbee's copper surplus and the lives of the fortune-seekers who extracted it. (☎432-7071. Open daily 10am-4pm. $4, seniors $3.50, under 16 free.) For a less earthly and more heavenly experience, visit the **Chihuahua Hill Shrines.** A 25min. hike over rocky ground leads to a Buddhist, and then a Mexican-Catholic shrine.

About 18 mi. west of Bisbee along Rte. 92, along the Mexican border, **Coronado National Memorial** marks the place where Francisco Coronado and his expedition first entered American territory. **Coronado Cave,** a small, relatively dry cave, is ¾ mi. from the Visitors Center along a short, steep path. A free permit is required to explore the cave, and can be picked up at the Visitors Center as long as each spelunker has a flashlight. (☎366-5515. Park open daily dawn to dusk. Visitors Center open daily 8am-5pm. **Ramsey Canyon Preserve,** 5 mi. farther down the road, attracts nearly as many bird-watchers as birds. In the middle of migratory routes for many North American birds, thousands of hummingbirds throng here in the late summer. (Open daily 8am-5pm. $5, under 16 free; first Sa of every month free.)

THE SOUTHWEST

About a 10min. walk from downtown, the **Jonquil Inn** ❷, 317 Tombstone Canyon, offers clean and smoke-free rooms. (☎432-7371. Singles $40-45; doubles $50-60; in winter about $10 more.) On Tombstone Canyon Rd., at the south end of town, the **School House Inn** ❸ houses guests in a remodeled 1918 school house. Rooms are all themed and vary in size; the Principal's Office is palatial, while the numbered classrooms have a cozier sort of charm. (☎432-2966 or 800-537-4333. All rooms have private bath. Full breakfast included, TV in common room. Ironically, no children under 14. Single bed $55; double/queen/king $60-80; 2-bed suite $90.) **Old Tymers** ❷ serve steak ($11) and hamburger ($5) any way you like, from bleeding to burnt. (☎432-7364. Open Su-Th 11am-9pm, F-Sa 11am-10pm.)

The **Chamber of Commerce**, 31 Subway St., provides maps that will help you navigate the labyrinthine streets of Bisbee. (☎432-5421. Open M-F 9am-5pm, Sa-Su 10am-4pm.) The **Post Office**, on Main St., is one block south of the highway exit. (☎432-2052. Open M-F 8:30am-4:30pm.) **ZIP code:** 85603. **Area code:** 520.

CHIRICAHUA NATIONAL MONUMENT   ☎520

A cross between Zion and Bryce Canyon, Chiricahua was aptly called the "Land of the Standing-Up Rocks" by Apaches and the "Wonderland of Rocks" by pioneers. And while Chiricahua nearly equals the natural splendor of Bryce and Zion, it happily falls short of their popularity, indulging in peace and tranquility.

Chiricahua is located 40 mi. off I-10, and 70 mi. from Bisbee; take Rte. 80 E to Rte. 191 N to 181 N. The **Visitors Center** is just beyond the entrance station. (☎824-3560, ext. 104. Open daily 8am-5:30pm. Entrance fee for vehicles $6, pedestrians $3.) Most of the park is federally designated wilderness; no backcountry camping, bicycles, or climbing allowed. Overnight backcountry camping is not permitted. The **Bonita Creek Campground** ❶ within the park offers 24 sites with toilets and running water, but no showers (sites $8). There is a bountiful selection of day hikes in the monument. A detailed **trail map** can be purchased for 25¢.

NEW MEXICO

Sometimes overshadowed by its more extreme neighbors, New Mexico is nevertheless a dreamscape of varied terrains and peoples. Going back to the days when Spaniards arrived with delusions of golden riches, this expansive land of high deserts, mountain vistas, and roadrunners has always been a place where people come to fulfill their fantasies. Today, most explorers arrive in search of natural beauty, adobe architecture, and cultural treasures rather than gold. It makes sense that New Mexico is a haven for hikers, backpackers, cyclists, mountain-climbers, and skiers. And with its mix of Spanish, Mexican, Native American, and Anglo heritage, New Mexico is as culturally varied as it is geographically diverse.

◪ PRACTICAL INFORMATION

Capital: Santa Fe.

Visitor info: New Mexico Dept. of Tourism, 491 Old Santa Fe Trail, Santa Fe 87501 (☎800-545-2040; www.newmexico.org). Open M-F 8am-5pm. **Park and Recreation Division,** 2040 S. Pacheco, Santa Fe 87505 (☎505-827-7173). Open M-F 8am-5pm. **US Forest Service,** 517 Gold Ave. SW, Albuquerque 87102 (☎505-842-3292). Open M-F 8am-4:30pm.

Postal Abbreviation: NM. **Sales Tax:** 6.25%.

Santa Fe

▲ ACCOMMODATIONS
Hyde State Park, **1**
Silver Saddle Motel, **12**
Thunderbird Inn, **11**

🍴 FOOD
Cafe Oasis, **10**
Tia Sophia's, **7**
The Shed, **5**

🍸 NIGHTLIFE
Cowgirl Hall of Fame, **8**
Paramount, **9**

🏛 MUSEUMS
Georgia O'Keeffe, **2**
Institute of American
   Indian Arts, **6**
Museum of Fine Arts, **3**
Musuem of Indian Arts &
   Culture, **14**
Museum of International
   Folk Art, **13**
Palace of the Governors, **4**

SANTA FE   ☎505

You're much more likely to encounter khaki-clad tourists than conquistadors in Santa Fe today; nonetheless, it is still possible to find places with character and authenticity in the cracks. Traditional adobe buildings adorn narrow streets, and, unlike in any other city in the Southwest, walking is still a viable means of transportation. Founded by the Spanish in 1608, Santa Fe is the second-oldest city in the US and the only state capital to serve under the administrations of three countries. These days, art is the trade of choice, with Native Americans, native New Mexicans, and exiled New Yorkers all hawking their wares on the streets and in the galleries surrounding the Central Plaza. In recent years, Santa Fe's popularity has skyrocketed, leading to an influx of gated communities, ritzy restaurants, and Californian millionaires. The city can be expensive, but the fabulous art museums, churches, and mountain trails make it a worthwhile stop.

▐ TRANSPORTATION

Buses: Greyhound, 858 St. Michael's Dr. (☎471-0008). To: **Albuquerque** (1½hr., 4 per day, $12.60); **Denver** (8-10hr., 4 per day, $59); and **Taos** (1½hr., 2 per day, $15.75). Open M-F 7am-5:30pm and 7:30-9:45pm; Sa-Su 7-9am, 12:30-1:30pm, 3:30-5pm, and 7:30-9:30pm.

Trains: Amtrak's nearest station is in Lamy (☎466-4511), 18 mi. south on U.S. 285. 1 train daily to: **Albuquerque** (1hr., $20); **Flagstaff** (7hr., $63-113); **Kansas City** (17hr., $108-192); and **Los Angeles** (18½hr., $71-127). Call 982-8829 in advance for a shuttle to Santa Fe ($14). Open daily 9:30am-6:30pm.

Public Transit: Santa Fe Trails (☎955-2001) runs 9 downtown bus routes (M-F 6am-10pm, Sa 8am-8pm). Most bus routes start at the downtown Sheridan Transit Center, 1 block from the plaza between Marcy St. and Palace Ave. Buses #21-24 go down Cerrillos Rd., #10 goes to the museums on Camino Lejo, #5 goes to the Greyhound station. 50¢, ages 6-12 25¢; day pass $1. **Sandía Shuttle Express** (☎474-5696 or 888-775-5696) runs to the Albuquerque airport (10 per day, $23) from downtown hotels. Reserve at least 1 day in advance. Open M-F 7am-6pm, Sa-Su 7am-5pm.

Taxis: Capital City Taxi, ☎438-0000.

✴ ⓝ ORIENTATION & PRACTICAL INFORMATION

Except for the museums southeast of the city center, most upscale restaurants and sights in Santa Fe cluster within a few blocks of the **downtown plaza** and inside the loop formed by the **Paseo de Peralta.** Narrow streets make driving troublesome; park your car and pound the pavement. You'll find **parking lots** behind Santa Fe Village, near Sena Plaza, and one block east of the Federal Courthouse near the plaza. Metered spaces (max. 2hr.) line the streets south of the plaza. Parking is also available along the streets near the galleries on Canyon Rd.

Visitor info: Visitors Information Center, 491 Old Santa Fe Trail (☎875-7400 or 800-545-2040). Open daily 8am-6:30pm; off-season 8am-5pm. **Santa Fe Convention and Visitors Bureau,** 201 W. Marcy St. (☎800-777-2489 or 955-6200). Open M-F 8am-5pm. **Info booth,** at the northwest corner of the plaza, next to the First National Bank. Open mid-May to Aug. daily 9:30am-4:30pm.

Equipment Rental: Wild Mountain Outfitters, 541 W. Cordova Rd. (☎986-1152), has a large selection of outdoor gear. Open M-Sa 9am-8pm, Su 10am-5pm.

Rape Abuse Hotline, ☎986-9111. 24hr.

Police: 2515 Camino Entrada (☎955-5033).

Hospital: St. Vincent Hospital, 455 St. Michael's Dr. (☎983-3361).

Internet access: Santa Fe Public Library, 145 Washington Ave. (☎955-6781), 1 block northeast of the Plaza. Open M-Th 10am-9pm, F-Sa 10am-6pm, Su 1-5pm.

Post Office: 120 S. Federal Pl., next to the courthouse. (☎988-6351. Open M-F 7:30am-5:45pm, Sa 9am-1pm.) **ZIP code:** 87501. **Area Code:** 505.

▟ ACCOMMODATIONS

Hotels in Santa Fe tend toward the expensive side. As early as May, they become swamped with requests for rooms during **Indian Market** (3rd week of Aug.) and **Fiesta de Santa Fe** (2nd weekend of Sept.). Make reservations early or plan to sleep in your car, which *Let's Go* does not recommend. In general, the motels along **Cerrillos Rd.** have the best prices, but even these places run $40-60 per night. Two popular sites for free primitive camping are **Big Tesuque ❶** and **Ski Basin Campgrounds ❶** on national forest land. These campgrounds are both off Rte. 475 toward the Ski Basin, and have pit toilets.

Thunderbird Inn, 1821 Cerrillos Rd. (☎983-4397). A bit out of the way, but an excellent value. Large rooms, some with fridge and microwave, all with A/C and cable TV. Reception 24hr. Summer singles $50-55, doubles $55-60; winter $39-44/44-49. ❸

Silver Saddle Motel, 2810 Cerrillos Rd. (☎471-7663). Beautiful adobe motel rooms decorated with cowboy paraphenalia have A/C and cable TV. Reception 6am-11:30pm. Summer singles $67; winter $45. Doubles $72/50. ❸

Hyde State Park Campground (☎983-7175), 8 mi. from Santa Fe on Rte. 475, has over 50 sites in the forest with water, pit toilets, fire rings, and shelters. No reservations for tent sites. Tent sites $10, hookups $14. ❶

⬚ FOOD

Meals can be expensive in Santa Fe, but there are deals to be had. **Albertson's,** 199 Paseo de Paralta, ½ mi. northwest of the plaza in the De Vargas Mall, is the closest supermarket to downtown. (☎988-2804. Open daily 6am-midnight.) The **Santa Fe Farmers Market** (☎983-4098), at the Railyard near the intersection of Guadalupe St. and Paseo de Peralta, has fresh fruits and vegetables. (Open late Apr.-early Nov. Tu, Sa 7am-noon. Call to inquire about indoor winter location and hours.)

▧ **Tia Sophia's,** 210 W. San Francisco St. (☎983-9880). It looks and feels like a diner (the servers are quick and curt), but the food is exceptional. The most popular item is the Atrisco plate ($6)—chile stew, cheese enchilada, beans, *posole,* and a *sopapilla.* Arrive before noon for the fastest service. Open M-Sa 7am-2pm. ❷

▧ **Cafe Oasis,** 526 Galisteo St. (☎983-9599), at Paseo de Peralta. All the food is organic at this laid-back restaurant that feels like a hippie commune. The collection of dining rooms includes the Tahitian Tea Room, the Mystic Room, the Victorian Room, the Mushroom, and an outdoor patio garden lit with torches and lanterns at night. Creative dishes range from veggie enchiladas ($10) to *Samari* stir-fry ($13). Breakfast served all the time. Live music nightly. Open M-W 10am-midnight, Th-F 10am-2am, Sa 9am-2am, Su 9am-midnight. ❸

The Shed, 113½ E. Palace Ave. (☎982-9030), up the street from the plaza, feels like an open garden, even in the enclosed section. Lots of vegetarian dishes including quesadillas ($6) and excellent blue corn burritos ($8.50). Meat-eaters will enjoy the amazing chicken *enchilada verde* ($9). Lunch M-Sa 11am-2:30pm, dinner M-Sa 5:30-9pm. ❷

◉ ♫ SIGHTS & ENTERTAINMENT

The grassy **Plaza de Santa Fe** is a good starting point for exploring the museums, sanctuaries, and galleries of the city. Since 1609, the plaza has been the site of religious ceremonies, military gatherings, markets, cockfights, and public punishments—now it holds ritzy shops and loitering tourists. Historic **walking tours** leave from the blue doors of the Palace of the Governors on Lincoln St. (May-Oct., M-Sa 10:15am. $10.) **Fiesta Tours** offers 75min. open-air van tours from the corner of Lincoln St. and Palace Ave. (☎983-1570. 3-6 per day. $7, children $4.)

MNM MUSEUMS. Sante Fe is home to six world-class, imaginative museums. Four are run by **The Museum of New Mexico.** They all hold the same hours and charge the same admission. A worthwhile four-day pass ($15) includes admission to all four museums; it can be purchased at any of the four. *(☎827-6463. Open Tu-Su 10am-5pm; single visit $7, under 17 free. The 2 downtown museums—Fine Arts and Palace of the Governors—are both free on F 5-8pm.)* Inhabiting a large adobe building on the northwest corner of the plaza the **Museum of Fine Arts** dazzles visitors with the works of major Southwestern artists, as well as contemporary exhibits of often controversial American art. *(107 W. Palace Ave. ☎476-5072. Open daily 10am-5pm)* The **Palace of the Governors,** on the north side of the plaza, is the oldest public building in the US and was the seat of seven successive governments after its construction in 1610. The *haciendas* palace is now a museum with exhibits on Native American, Southwestern, and New Mexican history, with an interesting exhibit on Jewish Pioneers.

THE SOUTHWEST

(107 W. Palace Ave. ☎ 476-5100.) The most unique museums in town are 2½ mi. south of the Plaza on Old Santa Fe Trail. The fascinating **Museum of International Folk Art,** houses the Girard Collection, which includes over 10,000 handmade dolls, doll houses, and other toys from around the world. The miniature village scenes are straight out of a fairy tale. Other galleries hold changing ethnographic exhibits. *(706 Camino Lejo. ☎ 476-1200.)* Next door, the **Museum of American Indian Arts and Culture** displays Native American photos and artifacts. *(710 Camino Lejo. ☎ 476-1250.)*

OTHER PLAZA MUSEUMS. While the two other Sante Fe museums have no affiliation with the Museum of New Mexico, they are just as worthwhile. The popular **Georgia O'Keeffe Museum** attracts the masses with O'Keeffe's famous—and famously suggestive—flower paintings, as well as some of her more abstract works. Spanning her entire life, the museum's collection demonstrates the artist's versatility. *(217 Johnson St. ☎ 946-1017. Open daily 10am-5pm. $8, under 17 and students with ID free; F 5-8pm free. Audio tour $5.)* The **Institute of American Indian Arts Museum,** downtown, houses an extensive collection of contemporary Indian art with an intense political edge. *(108 Cathedral Place. ☎ 983-8900. Open M-Sa 9am-5pm, Su noon-5pm. $4, students and seniors $2, under 16 free.)* The round **New Mexico State Capitol** was built in 1966 in the form of the Zia sun symbol. The House and Senate galleries are open to the public, and the building also contains an impressive art collection. *(5 blocks south of the Plaza on Old Santa Fe Rd. ☎ 986-4589. Open M-F 7am-7pm; June-Aug. Sa 8am-5pm. Free tours M-F 10am and 2pm.)*

CHURCHES. Santa Fe's Catholic roots are evident in the Romanesque **St. Francis Cathedral,** built from 1869 to 1886 under the direction of Archbishop Lamy (the central figure of Willa Cather's *Death Comes to the Archbishop*), to bring Catholicism to the "ungodly" westerners. The cathedral's architecture is especially striking against the New Mexican desert. *(One block east of the Plaza on San Francisco St. 213 Cathedral Pl. ☎ 982-5619. Open daily 7:30am-5:30pm.)* The **Loretto Chapel** was the first Gothic building west of the Mississippi River. The church is famous for its "miraculous" spiral staircase. *(207 Old Santa Fe Trail. 2 blocks south of the Cathedral. ☎ 982-0092. Open M-Sa 9am-6pm, Su 10:30am-5pm. $2.50, seniors and children $2.)* About five blocks southeast of the plaza lies the **San Miguel Mission,** at DeVargas St. and the Old Santa Fe Trail. Built in 1610 by the Tlaxcalan Indians, the mission is the oldest functioning church in the US. Also in the church is the San Jose Bell, made in Spain in 1356 and the oldest bell in the US. *(☎ 983-3974. Open M-Sa 9am-5pm, Su 10am-4pm; may close earlier in winter. $1.)*

GALLERIES. Santa Fe's most successful artists live and sell their work along Canyon Rd. To reach their galleries, depart the Plaza on San Francisco Dr., take a left on Alameda St., a right on Paseo de Peralta, and a left on Canyon Rd. Extending for about 1 mi., the road is lined on both sides by galleries displaying all types of art, as well a number of indoor/outdoor cafes. Most galleries are open from 10am until 5pm. At the **Hahn Ross Gallery,** the art is hip, enjoyable, and way out of your price range. *(409 Canyon Rd. ☎ 984-8434. Open daily 10am-5pm.)* **Off the Wall** vends offbeat jewelry, pottery, clocks, and sculpture, with a coffee bar out back. *(616 Canyon Rd. ☎ 983-8337. Open daily 10am-5pm.)*

A BIT OF CLASS. Strange verse and distinguished acting invade the city each summer when **Shakespeare in Sante Fe** raises its curtain. The festival shows plays in an open-air theater on the St. John's College campus from late June to late August. *(Shows run F-Su 7:30pm. Number of shows per week varies; call to check the schedule. Reserved seating tickets $15-32; lawn seating is free, though a $5 donation is requested. Tickets available at show, or call 982-2910.)* The **Santa Fe Opera,** on Opera Dr. 7 mi. north of Santa Fe on Rte. 84/285, performs outdoors against a mountain backdrop. Nights are cool; bring a blanket. *(☎ 800-280-4654 or 877-999-7499. July W and F; Aug. M-Sa. Per-*

formances begin 8-9pm. $20-200, rush standing-room tickets $8-15; 50% student discount on same-day reserved seats. The box office is at the opera house; call or drop by the day of the show for specific prices and availability.) The **Santa Fe Chamber Music Festival** celebrates the works of great Baroque, Classical, Romantic, and 20th-century composers in the **St. Francis Auditorium of the Museum of Fine Arts** and the **Lensic Theater.** *(Info ☎983-2075, tickets ☎982-1890. Mid-July to mid-Aug. $16-40, students $10.)*

FESTIVALS. Santa Fe is home to two of the US's largest festivals. In August, the nation's largest and most impressive **Indian Market** floods the plaza (Aug. 23-24, 2003). The **Southwestern Association for Indian Arts** (☎983-5220) has more info. Don Diego de Vargas's peaceful reconquest of New Mexico in 1692 marked the end of the 12-year Pueblo Rebellion, now celebrated in the three-day **Fiesta de Santa Fe** (☎988-7575). Held in early September, festivities begin with the burning of the *Zozobra* and include street dancing, processions, and political satires. The *New Mexican* publishes a guide and a schedule of the fiesta's events.

◪ NIGHTLIFE

Only in Santa Fe can you walk into a bar and sit between a Wall Street investment banker and a world-famous sculptor. Here, nightlife tends to be more mellow than in Albuquerque. The ▨**Cowgirl Hall of Fame,** 319 S. Guadalupe St., has live music hoe-downs that range from bluegrass to country. BBQ, Mexican food, and burgers are served up all evening, with midnight food specials and 12 microbrews on tap. (☎982-2565. Sa-Su ranch breakfast. Happy hour 3-6pm and midnight-1am; Cowgirl Margaritas $3.50. 21+ after midnight. Cover varies but is never more than $3. Open M-F 11am-2am, Sa 8:30am-2am, Su 8:30am-midnight.) **Paramount,** 331 Sandoval St., is the only dance club in Santa Fe. Everyone in town shows up for trash disco Wednesdays. (☎982-8999. Live music Tu, Th and Su. Sa dance. 21+. Cover $5-7, Sa $5-20. Open M-Sa 9pm-2am, Su 9pm-midnight.) **Bar B** has a futuristic setting and live music. (☎982-8999. Cover $2-7. Open M-Sa 5pm-2am, Su 5pm-midnight.)

◪ OUTDOOR ACTIVITIES

The nearby **Sangre de Cristo Mountains,** which reach heights of over 12,000 ft., and **Pecos** and **Río Grande** rivers offer countless opportunities for outdoor enthusiasts. Before heading out, stop by the **Public Lands Information Center,** 1474 Rodeo Rd., near the intersection of St. Francis Rd. and I-25, to pick up maps and get friendly advice. (☎438-7542. Open M-F 8am-5pm.) The Sierra Club Guide to *Day Hikes in the Santa Fe Area* and the Falcon Guide to *Best Easy Day Hikes in Santa Fe* are good purchases for those planning to spend a few days hiking in the area.

The closest **hiking** trails to downtown Santa Fe are along Rte. 475 on the way to the Santa Fe Ski Area. On this road, 10 mi. northeast of town, the **Tesuque Creek Trail** (2hr., 4 mi.) leads through the forest to a flowing stream. Near the end of Rte. 475 and the Santa Fe Ski Area, trailheads venture into the 223,000 acre **Pecos Wilderness.** A variety of extended backpacking trips can be had throughout this swath of pristine alpine forests. For a rewarding day hike 14 mi. northeast of Santa Fe on Rte. 475, the strenuous full-day climb to the top of 12,622 ft. **Santa Fe Baldy** (8-9hr., 14 mi.) affords an amazing vista of the Pecos Wilderness to the north and east.

Located in the towering Sangre De Cristo Mountains on Rte. 475, **Ski Santa Fe** operates six lifts, including four chairs and two surface lifts, servicing 43 trails (20% beginner; 40% intermediate; 40% advanced) on 600 acres of terrain with a 1650 ft. vertical drop. (☎982-4429. Snowboards welcome. Annual snowfall 225 in. Open late Nov.-early Apr. 9am-4pm. Lift tickets: full-day $43, teens $36, children and seniors $28. Rental packages start at $18.)

▓ DAYTRIPS FROM SANTA FE

LOS ALAMOS. Known only as the mysterious P.O. Box 1663 during the heyday of the Manhattan Project, Los Alamos is no longer the nation's biggest secret. With the infamous distinction of being the birthplace of the atomic bomb, Los Alamos now attracts visitors with its natural beauty and outdoor activities. Overlooking the Río Grande Valley, Los Alamos hovers above the Pueblo and Bayo Canyons on thin finger-like mesas, 35 mi. to the northeast of Sante Fe. In town, the **Bradbury Science Museum,** corner of 15th St. and Central, explains the history of the Los Alamos National Laboratory and its endeavors with excellent videos and hands-on exhibits. (☎ 667-4444. Open Tu-F 9am-5pm, Sa-M 1-5pm. Free.) Not to be missed in Los Alamos is the ▓**Black Hole,** 4015 Arkansas St., which sells the junk the laboratory doesn't want anymore, including 50-year-old calculators, flow gauges, timemark generators, optical comparators, and other technological flotsam. Leave with your very own $2 atomic bomb detonator cable. (☎ 662-5053. Open M-Sa 10am-5pm.) Outdoors, the town brims with great activities. The **Sante Fe National Forest** provides countless trails for hiking and biking in and along the town's many canyons. The **Valles Caldera,** an expansive and lush volcanic crater, has just recently become a National Preserve. It's 15 mi. to the east on Rte. 4 along the scenic Jemez Mountain Trail. **Los Alamos Visitors Center** is on Central Ave. just west of 15th St. (☎ 662-8105. Open M-F 9am-5pm, Sa 9am-4pm, Su 10am-3pm.)

BANDELIER NATIONAL MONUMENT. Bandelier, 40 mi. northwest of Santa Fe (take U.S. 285 to 502 W, then follow the signs), features some amazing pueblos and cliff dwellings, as well as 50 sq. mi. of dramatic mesas, ancient ruins, and spectacular views of surrounding canyons. The **Visitors Center,** 3 mi. into the park at the bottom of **Frijoles Canyon,** has an archaeological museum and shows a short video. (☎ 672-3861, ext. 517. Open June-Aug. daily 8am-6pm; Sept. to late Oct. daily 9am-5:30pm; late Oct.-late Mar. 8am-4:30pm; late Mar.-May 9am-5:30pm.) All visitors to the park should start by hiking the 1.4 mi. **Main Loop Trail** to see the **cliff dwellings** and the ruins of the Tyuonyi Pueblo. Those with more time should continue 0.5 mi. further to the **Ceremonial Cave,** a *kiva* carved into a natural alcove, high above the canyon floor. The **Frijoles Falls Trail** (3hr., 5 mi.), begins at the Visitors Center parking lot and follows the Frijoles Creek downstream 2.5 mi. to the Río Grande. Upper Frijoles Falls, dropping 80 ft., is 1.5 mi. from the trailhead. A strenuous two-day, 22 mi. hike leads from the Visitors Center to **Painted Cave,** decorated with over 50 Ancestral Puebloan pictographs. Free permits are required for backcountry hiking and camping; topographical maps ($10) are sold at the Visitors Center. Just past the main entrance, **Juniper Campground ❶** offers the only developed camping in the park, with water and toilets (sites $10). The park entrance fee is $10 per vehicle and $5 per pedestrian; National Park passes are accepted.

TAOS ☎ 505

Before 1955, Taos was a remote artist colony in the Sangre de Cristo Mountains. When the ski valley opened and the thrill-seekers trickled in, they soon realized that the area also boasted the best whitewater rafting in New Mexico, as well as some excellent hiking, mountain biking, and rock climbing. By the 1970s, Taos had become a paradise for New-Age hippies, struggling artists, and extreme athletes, and the deluge of tourists wasn't far behind. Today, Taos has managed to balance a ski resort culture with a Bohemian pace and lifestyle without losing any of its sunflower charm.

⊞ ⋈ ORIENTATION & PRACTICAL INFORMATION. Once in town, **Rte. 68** becomes Paseo del Pueblo (Sur and Norte). Drivers should park on Camino de la Placita, a block west of the plaza, or at the meters scattered on side streets. **Greyhound,** 1213A Gusdorf St. (☎758-1144), sends two buses daily to Albuquerque (3hr., $23), Denver (7½hr., $60), and Santa Fe (1½hr., $17). The local bus service, the **Chile Line,** runs every 15-30min. along Paseo del Pueblo from Ranchos de Taos, south of town, to and from the pueblo. In ski season, a bus runs from the center of Taos to the Ski Valley every 2½hr. (☎751-4459. Daily 7am-7pm. 50¢, ski shuttle $5.) **Taxi** service is offered by **Faust's Transportation** (☎758-3410) daily until 8:30pm. Visitor info is available at the **Chamber of Commerce,** 1139 Paseo del Pueblo Sur, 2 mi. south of town at the junction of Rte. 68 and Paseo del Cañon. (☎758-3873 or 800-732-8267. Open daily 9am-5pm.) The **Carson National Forest Office,** 208 Cruz Alta Rd., has free info on camping and hiking. (☎758-6200. Open M-F 8am-4:30pm.) Services include: **Internet access** ($1 per 30min.) at the **public library,** 402 Camino de la Placita (☎758-3063; open M noon-6pm, Tu-Th 10am-7pm, F 10am-6pm, Sa 10am-5pm); **Post Office,** 318 Paseo Del Pueblo Norte, ¼ mi. north of the plaza (☎758-2081; open M-F 8am-5pm). **ZIP code:** 87571.

⋒ ACCOMMODATIONS. The **Abominable Snowmansion Hostel (HI-AYH),** 9 mi. north of Taos in the village of Arroyo Seco, is a snowbird's delight with spacious dorm rooms and a pool table adorning the common room. A hostel by summer, ski lodge by winter, the Snowmansion is only 9 mi. west of the ski valley. Teepees and camping are available in the warmer months. (☎776-8298. Reception 8am-noon and 4-10pm. Reservations recommended. Breakfast included. Mid-Apr. to mid-Nov. dorms $15, nonmembers $17; dorm tepees $15/17; private doubles $38-42; tent sites $12. Mid-Nov. to mid-Apr. dorms $22, weekly $120; private rooms $40-52.) The **Budget Host Motel,** 1798 Paseo del Pueblo Sur, 3¼ mi. south of the Plaza, is the least expensive motel in Taos, with spacious rooms. (☎758-2524 or 800-323-6009. Singles $43-54; doubles $49-61. 10% AAA discount.)

Camping around Taos is easy with a car. The **Kit Carson National Forest** has three campgrounds to the east of Taos on Rte. 64. Tent sites are adjacent to a stream and are surrounded by tall pines. The closest, **Las Petacas,** is 4 mi. east of Taos and has vault toilets but no drinking water. **Capulin Campground,** 7 mi. east of Taos, and **La Sombra,** 1 mi. further, both have drinking water and vault toilets. For more info about these campgrounds, contact the Carson National Forest Office in Taos (☎758-6200; sites $12.50). Campgrounds on the road to Taos Ski Valley are free, but have no facilities. **Backcountry camping** doesn't require a permit. Dispersed camping is popular along Rte. 518 south of Taos and Forest Rd. 437. Park on the side of the road and pitch your tent a few hundred feet inside the forest.

◖ FOOD. Restaurants cluster around Taos Plaza and Bent St. but cheaper options can be found north of town along Paseo Del Pueblo. **▨Island Coffees and Hawaiian Grill ❷,** 1032 Paseo del Pueblo Sur, just might get you lei-ed at a reasonable price, in a grass hut to boot. Popular Polynesian and southeast Asian dishes include mango coconut chicken ($6) and *lomi lomi* vegetables ($8). Many of the dishes are vegetarian. (☎758-7777. Open M-Sa 10am-9pm.) **Casa Vaca Cafe ❶,** 6 mi. north of Taos in Arroyo Seco, feels like it was plucked right out of New York's East Village. Have a cappuccino ($1.50) and green chile omelette ($5) for breakfast. (☎776-5640. Open daily 7am-6pm.)

◪ SIGHTS. For such a small town, Taos has a surprising number of high-quality art museums. The **Harwood Museum,** 238 Ledoux St., houses works by early and mid-20th-century local artists, including a gallery of minimalist painter Agnes Martin, as well as a large collection of Hispanic Art including a striking *Día de los Muertos* piece. (☎758-9826. Open Tu-Sa 10am-5pm, Su noon-5pm. $5.) The **Millicent Rogers Museum,** 4 mi. north of the Plaza on Rte. 64, turn left at the sign, has an extravagant collection of Indian jewelry, textiles, pottery, and Apache baskets once belonging to Millicent Rogers, a glamour queen and socialite. (☎758-2462. Open Apr.-Oct. daily 10am-5pm; Nov.-Mar. Tu-Su 10am-5pm.)

The ◪**Martinez Hacienda,** 2 mi. southwest of the plaza on Ranchitos Rd., is one of the few surviving Spanish Colonial mansions in the United States. Built in 1804, this fortress-like adobe structure was home to the prosperous Martinez family and served as the headquarters of a large farming and ranching operation. The restored 21-room hacienda features excellent exhibits on life in the northernmost reaches of the Spanish Empire. (☎758-1000. Open Apr.-Oct. daily 9am-5pm; Nov.-Mar. 10am-4pm. $5, children $3.)

Taos ranks second only to Santa Fe as a center of Southwestern Art. Galleries clustered around the Plaza and Kit Carson Rd. include the **Lumina Gallery and Sculpture Garden,** which is more captivating than any art museum in town. Set in a stunning adobe home with five acres of rolling grassy lawn, gardens, and fountains, the cutting-edge contemporary paintings and sculptures here are captivating.

The five-story adobe homes of the **Taos Pueblo** are between 700 and 1000 years old, making it the oldest continuously inhabited settlement in the US. Taos Pueblo was named a UNESCO world heritage site in 1992, and is the only pueblo in Northern New Mexico where the inhabitants still live traditionally, without electricity or running water. Guided tours are offered daily May through September, and visitors can take self-guided tours all day. The Pueblo includes the **San Geronimo Church,** the ruins of the old church and cemetery, the adobe houses, and the *kivas*.

◪ OUTDOOR ACTIVITIES. Hailed as one of the best ski resorts in the country, **Taos Ski Valley,** about 15 mi. northeast of town on Rte. 150, offers powder conditions in bowl sections and short but steep downhill runs that rival Colorado's. With 72 trails and 12 lifts, Ski Valley boasts over 2500 ft. of vertical drop and over 300 in. of annual snowfall. (☎776-2291, lodging info ☎800-992-7669, ski conditions ☎776-2916. Lift tickets $37-47; equipment rental from $19 per day.) Reserve a room well in advance if you plan to come during the winter holiday season. There are also two smaller, more family-oriented ski areas near Taos: **Angel Fire** (☎377-6401; lift tickets $43, teenagers $35) and **Red River** (☎800-494-9117; lift tickets $43). Money-saving multi-day passes are available for use at all three resorts (from $36 per day). In summer, the nearly deserted ski valley and the nearby **Wheeler Peak Wilderness** become a hiker's paradise (most trails begin off Rte. 150). Due to the town's prime location near the state's wildest stretch of the Río Grande, **river rafting** is very popular in Taos. **Los Ríos River Runners** (☎776-8854 or 800-544-1181), **Far Flung Adventures** (☎758-2628 or 800-359-2627), and **Native Sons Adventures** (☎758-9342 or 800-753-7559) all offer a range of guided half-day ($40-50) and full-day ($80-110) rafting trips. For bike rentals, visit **Gearing Up,** 129 Paseo del Pueblo Sur. (☎751-0365. Open daily 9:30am-6pm. Bikes $35 per day, $90 per 5 days.)

Albuquerque

▲ ACCOMMODATIONS   🍴 FOOD
Rte. 66 Youth Hostel, **1**   Java Joe's, **2**
Sandía Mountain   Kanome, **4**
  Hostel, **7**   El Norteño, **6**

🍷 NIGHTLIFE
Banana Joe's Island
  Party, **3**
O'Neil's Pub, **5**

ALBUQUERQUE ☎ 505

As the crossroads of the Southwest, anyone traveling north to Denver, south to Mexico, east to Texas, or west to California passes through this commercial hub. But Albuquerque is also a place full of history and culture, with many ethnic restaurants and offbeat cafes, and raging nightclubs. Most residents still refer to Central Avenue as Route 66, and visitors can feel the energy flowing from this mythic highway. The University of New Mexico is responsible for the town's young demographic, while the Hispanic, Native American, and gay and lesbian communities chip in cultural vibrancy and diversity. From historic Old Town to modern museums, ancient petroglyphs to towering mountains, travelers will be surprised at how much there is to see and do in New Mexico's largest city.

▐▀ TRANSPORTATION

Airport: Albuquerque International, 2200 Sunport Blvd. SE (☎842-4366), south of downtown. Take bus #50 from 5th St. and Central Ave., or pick it up along Yale Blvd. **Airport Shuttle** (☎765-1234) shuttles to the city ($12, 2nd person $5). Open 24hr.

Trains: Amtrak, 214 1st St. SW (☎842-9650). 1 train per day to: **Flagstaff** (5hr., $59-106); **Kansas City** (17hr., $116-207); **Los Angeles** (16hr., $67-120); and **Santa Fe** (1hr. to Lamy, $16. 20min. shuttle to Santa Fe $14. Reservations required. Open daily 10am-5:30pm.

Buses: Greyhound (☎243-4435) and **TNM&O Coaches,** 300 2nd St. Both run buses from 3 blocks south of Central Ave. to: **Denver** (10hr., 5 per day, $64); **Flagstaff** (6hr., 5 per day, $41); **Los Angeles** (18hr., 7 per day, $76); **Phoenix** (10hr., 5 per day, $43); and **Santa Fe** (1½hr., 4 per day, $12.60). Station open 24hr.

Public Transit: Sun-Tran Transit, 601 Yale Blvd. SE (☎843-9200; office open M-F 8am-6pm, Sa 8am-noon). Pick up maps at Visitors Centers, the transit office, or the main library. Most buses run M-Sa 6:30am-8:30pm and leave from Central Ave. and 5th St. Bus #66 runs the length of Central Ave. 75¢, seniors and ages 5-18 25¢. Request free transfers from driver.

Taxis: Albuquerque Cab, ☎883-4888.

◀✦ ▞ ORIENTATION & PRACTICAL INFORMATION

Central Ave. (Rte. 66) is still the main thoroughfare of Albuquerque, running through all the city's major neighborhoods. Central Ave. (east-west) and **I-25** (north-south) divide Albuquerque into four quadrants. All downtown addresses come with a quadrant designation: NE, NW, SE, or SW. The adobe campus of the **University of New Mexico (UNM)** spreads along Central Ave. from University Ave. to Carlisle St. **Nob Hill,** the area of Central Ave. around Carlisle St., features coffee shops, bookstores, used CD stores, and art galleries. The revitalized **downtown** lies on Central Ave. between 10th St. and Broadway. Historic **Old Town Plaza** sits between San Felipe, North Plaza, South Plaza, and Romero, off Central Ave.

Visitor info: Albuquerque Visitors Center, 401 2nd St. NW (☎842-9918 or 800-284-2282), 3 blocks north of Central Ave. in the Convention Center. Open M-F 9am-5pm. Recorded info 24hr. **Old Town Visitors Center,** 303 Romano St. NW (☎243-3215), in the shopping plaza west of the church. Open Apr.-Oct. daily 9am-5pm; Nov.-Mar. 9:30am-4:30pm. Airport **info booth** open Su-F 9:30am-8pm, Sa 9:30am-4:30pm.

Police: 5408 2nd St. NW (☎761-8800), at Montano.

Hotlines: Rape Crisis Center, 1025 Hermosa SE (☎266-7711). Center open M-F 8am-noon and 1-5pm, hotline 24hr. **Gay and Lesbian Information Line,** ☎891-3647. 24hr.

Hospital: Presbyterian Hospital, 1100 Central Ave. SE (☎841-1234), just east of I-25.

Post Office: 1135 Broadway NE (☎346-8044, at Mountain St.). Open M-F 7:30am-6pm. **ZIP code:** 87101. **Area code:** 505.

▐ ACCOMMODATIONS

Cheap motels line **Central Ave.,** even near downtown. Though many of them are worth their price, be sure to evaluate the motel before paying. During the October **balloon festival** (see **Sights,** p. 841), rooms are scarce; call ahead for reservations.

▩ **Route 66 Youth Hostel,** 1012 Central Ave. SW (☎247-1813), at 10th St. Located between downtown and Old Town, it offers a down-home feel. Dorm and private rooms are simple but clean. Key deposit $5. Reception daily 7:30-10:30am and 4-11pm. Check-out 10:30am. Chores required. Dorms $14; singles with shared bath $20; doubles $25; 2-bed doubles with private bath $30. ❶

▩ **Sandía Mountain Hostel,** 12234 Rte. 14 N (☎281-4117), in nearby Cedar Crest. Take I-40 E to Exit 175 and go 4 mi. north on Rte. 14. Only 10 mi. from the Sandía Ski Area. Comfortable living room with fireplace, kitchen, and a family of resident donkeys. Sandía hiking and mountain biking trails are just across the street. Linen $1. Coin-op laundry. Wheelchair accessible. Dorms $12; private cabins $30. ❶

Coronado Campground (☎980-8256), about 15 mi. north of Albuquerque. Take I-25 to Exit 242 and follow the signs. Located on the Río Grande. Adobe shelters offer a respite from the heat. Toilets, showers, and water available. Office open daily 8am-5pm; see host to check in after hours. Tent sites $8, with water and electricity $18. Remote shelters $11. Open M and W-Su 8:30am-5pm. ❶

🖸 FOOD

A diverse ethnic community, a lot of hungry interstate travelers, and one big load of green chiles render Albuquerque surprisingly tasty. The area around **UNM** is the best bet for inexpensive eateries. A bit farther east, the hip neighborhood of **Nob Hill** is a haven for yuppie fare, including avocado sandwiches and iced cappuccino.

▩ **Java Joe's,** 906 Park Ave. SW (☎765-1514), 1 block south of Central Ave., and 2 blocks from the Rte. 66 Hostel. This lively restaurant with a laid-back atmosphere has hearty wraps ($5), sandwiches ($5.50), salads ($4-5), and great breakfast burritos ($3). Lots of vegetarian dishes and occasional live music. Open daily 6:30am-3:30pm. ❶

El Norteño, 6416 Zuni (☎256-1431), at California, is family-run and renowned as the most authentic and varied Mexican food in town. Shrimp roasted with garlic is a treat, and their extensive repertoire runs from chicken *mole* ($8) to *caldo de res* (a beef stew) to beef tongue ($7-9). Open daily 8:30am-9pm. ❷

Kanome, 3128 Central Ave. SE (☎265-7773), defies all conventional food logic. No visitor should miss this unique pan-Asian Tex-Mex fusion restaurant: the Ginger shrimp with scallion pancakes ($14) and the won ton nachos with slivered duck ($8) are good enough to get you arrested. Open Tu-Th 5pm-10pm, F-Sa 5pm-11pm, Su 5pm-10pm. ❸

🖸 SIGHTS

OLD TOWN. When the railroad cut through Albuquerque in the 19th century, it missed Old Town by almost 2 mi. As downtown grew around the railroad, Old Town remained untouched until the 1950s, when the city realized that it had a tourist magnet right under its nose. Just north of Central Ave. and east of Río Grande Blvd., the adobe plaza today looks remarkably as it did over 100 years ago, save for ubiquitous restaurants, gift shops, and jewelry vendors. Old Town is an architectural marvel and a stroll through it is worthwhile. **Walking tours** of Old Town meet at the Museum of Albuquerque. *(1hr. Tu-Su 11am. Free with admission.)* On the north side of the plaza, the **San Felipe de Neri Church,** dating back to 1793, has stood the test of time. *(Open daily 9am-5pm; accompanying museum open M-Sa 10am-4pm; Su mass in English 7 and 10:15am, in Spanish 8:30am.)* A posse of museums and attractions surrounds the plaza. To the northeast, the **Albuquerque Museum** showcases

New Mexican art and history. The comprehensive exhibit on the Conquistadors and Spanish colonial rule is a must-see for anyone interested in history. *(2000 Mountain Rd. NW. ☎ 243-7255. Open Tu-Su 9am-5pm. $3, seniors and children $1. Wheelchair accessible.)* Tours of the Sculpture Garden are available. *(Tu-F at 10am: free with admission. The museum also offers tours of the historic Casa San Ysidro in Corrales, NM. ☎ 898-3915 for reservations.)* Across the street from the museum, Spike and Alberta, two statuesque dinosaurs, greet tourists outside the kid-friendly **New Mexico Museum of Natural History and Science.** Inside, interactive exhibits take visitors through the history of life on earth. The museum features a five-story dynatheater, planetarium, and simulated ride through outer space. *(1801 Mountain Rd. NW. ☎ 841-2802. Open daily 9am-5pm; closed M in Sept. $5, seniors $4, children $2; combination Dynamax theater ticket $10/8/4.)* No visit to Old Town would be complete without seeing the **Rattlesnake Museum,** which lies just south of the plaza. With over 30 species from the deadly mojave to the tiny pygmy, this is the largest collection of live rattlesnakes in the world. *(202 San Felipe NW. ☎ 242-6569. Open M-Sa 10am-6pm, Su 1-5pm. $2.50, seniors $2, 17 and under $1.50.)*

UNIVERSITY MUSEUMS. The University of New Mexico has a couple of museums on campus that are worth a quick visit. The **University Art Museum** features changing exhibits focusing on 20th-century New Mexican paintings and photography. *(☎ 277-4001. Near the corner of Central Ave. and Cornel St. Open Tu-F 9am-4pm. Free.)* **The Maxwell Museum of Anthropology** has excellent exhibits on the culture and ancient history of Native American settlement in the Southwest. *(On University Blvd., just north of MLK Blvd. ☎ 277-5963. Open Tu-F 9am-4pm, Sa 10am-4pm. Free.)*

CULTURAL ATTRACTIONS. The **Indian Pueblo Cultural Center** provides a good introduction to the history and culture of the 19 Indian Pueblos of New Mexico. The center includes a museum, store, and restaurant. *(2401 12th St. NW. ☎ 843-7270. Take bus #36 from downtown. Museum open daily 9am-4:30pm. Art demonstrations Sa-Su 10am-3pm, Native American dances Sa-Su 11am and 2pm. $4, seniors $3, students $1.)* The **Hispanic Cultural Center** has an excellent art museum with exhibits exploring folk-art and representations of Hispanic social and cultural life in America. *(1701 4th St. SW, on the corner of Bridge St. Open Tu-Su 10am-5pm. $3, seniors $2, under 16 free.)*

🎦 NIGHTLIFE

If you're looking for a change from honky-tonk bars, Albuquerque is an oasis of interesting bars, jamming nightclubs, art film houses, and a large university. Check flyers posted around the university area for live music shows or pick up a copy of *Alibi,* the free local weekly. During the first week of October, hundreds of aeronauts take flight in colorful hot-air balloons during the **balloon festival.** Even the most grounded of souls will enjoy the week's barbecues and musical events.

Most nightlife huddles on and near Central Ave., downtown and near the university; Nob Hill establishments tend to be the most gay-friendly. The offbeat **Guild Cinema,** 3405 Central Ave. NE, runs independent and foreign films. *(☎ 255-1848. M-Th at 4:30 and 7pm, F-Su at 2, 4:30, and 7pm.)*

Banana Joe's Island Party, 610 Central Ave. SW *(☎ 244-0024)*, is the largest club in Albuquerque. With 6 bars, a tropical outdoor patio, a performance hall, and 1 big dance floor, Banana Joe's delivers nightlife to the masses. Nightly live music ranges from reggae to flamenco. DJ downstairs Th-Sa. Happy hour daily 5-8pm. 21+. Cover Th-Sa $5. Open Tu-Su 5pm-2am.

O'Neil's Pub, 3211 Central Ave. NE *(☎ 256-0564)*, in Nob Hill. This friendly neighborhood pub has 16 beers on tap, Guinness included, as well as the famous Parrot Rum Punch ($4.25, happy hour $2.75). The pub also serves great hamburgers and sandwiches to its loyal crowd. Live music Sa 10pm-1am, Celtic tunes Su 5-8pm. 21+ unless accompanied by parent. No cover. Open M-Sa 11am-2am, Su 11am-midnight. Happy hour daily 4-7pm and 10pm-1am.

🏕 OUTDOOR ACTIVITIES

Rising a mile above Albuquerque to the northeast, the sunset-pink crest of the **Sandía Mountains** gives the mountains their name—watermelon in Spanish. The crest beacons to New Mexicans, drawing thousands to hike and explore. One of the most popular trails in New Mexico, **La Luz Trail** (7.5 mi. one-way) climbs the Sandía Crest, beginning at the Juan Tabo Picnic Area. From Exit 167 on I-40, drive north on Tramway Blvd. 9.8 mi. to Forest Rd. 333. Follow Trail 137 for 7 mi. and take 84 to the top. To eliminate one leg of the journey, hikers can drive or take the tram. The Sandía Mountains have excellent mountain biking trails. Warm up on the moderately easy **Foothills Trail** (7 mi.), which skirts along the bottom of the mountains, just east of the city. The trail starts at the Elena Gallegos Picnic Area, off Tramway Blvd. The most popular place for biking is at the **Sandía Peak Ski Area,** 6 mi. up Rte. 536 on the way to Sandía Crest. Bikers can take their bikes up the chairlift and then ride down on 35 mi. of mountain trails and rollers, covering all skill levels. (☎242-9133. Chairlifts run June-Aug. Sa-Su 10am-4pm. Full-day lift ticket $14, single ride $8. Bike rentals at the summit $38 per day. Helmets required.)

Sandía Peak Ski Area, only 30min. from downtown, is a serviceable ski area for those who can't escape north to Taos or south to Ruidoso. Six lifts service 25 short trails (35% beginner; 55% intermediate; 10% advanced) on 200 skiable acres. The summit (10,378 ft.) tops a vertical drop of 1700 ft. (☎242-9133. Snowboards allowed. Annual snowfall 125 in. Open mid-Dec. to mid-Mar. daily 9am-4pm. Full-day $39, half-day $28, ages 13-20 $32, under 13 and seniors $28.) There are also excellent cross-country skiing trails in the **Cibola National Forest.** The North Crest and 10-K trails are popular with skiers.

🔁 DAYTRIPS FROM ALBUQUERQUE

PETROGLYPH NATIONAL MONUMENT
Located on Albuquerque's west side, this national monument features more than 20,000 images etched into lava rocks between 1300 and 1680 by Pueblo Indians and Spanish settlers. The park encompasses much of the 17 mi. West Mesa, a ridge of black basalt boulders that formed as a result of volcanic activity 130,000 years ago. The most easily accessible petroglyphs can be found via three short trails at **Boca Negra Canyon,** 2 mi. north of the Visitors Center. The **Rinconada Canyon Trail,** 1 mi. south of the Visitors Center, has more intricate rock art and is an easy 2.5 mi. desert hike along the base of the West Mesa. To see the nearby volcanoes, take Exit 149 off I-40 and follow Paseo del Volcán to a dirt road. The volcanoes are 4.8 mi. north of the exit. To reach the park itself, take I-40 to Unser Blvd. (Exit 154) and follow signs for the park. (☎899-0205. Park open daily 8am-5pm. Admission to Boca Negra Canyon M-F $1, Sa-Su $2; National Parks passes accepted.)

ACOMA PUEBLO
Perched on a sheer mesa with a spectacular view, this "Sky City" is one of the longest continuously inhabited sites in the US. Today, Acoma Pueblo is a vibrant community—just as it was 900 years ago. About 30 of the Acoma people live here year-round, and on holidays hundreds drive to the mesa from the surrounding reservation for traditional celebrations and dancing. Acoma, at the end of Rte. 32, is 13 mi.

south of Exit 96 off I-40, and 11 mi. south of Exit 102 off I-40. Both routes are well-marked. Visitors can only experience the pueblo through a guided tour. Video cameras are forbidden, and permits are required for still cameras. (☎800-747-0181. Open Nov.-Mar. daily 8am-4:30pm; Apr.-Oct. 8am-7pm. No tours July 10-13 and the 1st and 2nd weekends of Oct. Last tours depart 1hr. before closing. $9, seniors $8, children $6; camera permit $10.)

GALLUP ☎505

Gallup's proximity to the Petrified Forest National Park (see p. 813), the Navajo Reservation (see p. 810), Chaco Culture National Historic Park (see p. 844), and the El Morro National Monument (see p. 845) redeems it for many travelers. It's also a good base for exploring the Four Corners region.

Old Rte. 66, which runs parallel to I-40 through downtown, is lined with dirt-cheap motels, often with the emphasis on the dirt. The best place to stay in town, hands down, is **El Rancho Hotel and Motel ❷**, 1000 E. Rte. 66, which is a step up in price from most other options, but a leap in quality. (☎863-9311. Reception 24hr. Check-in 2pm. Check-out noon. Singles $47; doubles $55.) You can pitch a tent in the shadow of red sandstone cliffs at **Red Rock State Park Campground ❶**, on Rte. 566, which offers access to hiking 5 mi. east of town off Rte. 66. (☎863-1329. 142 sites with showers and hookups. Tent sites $10, hookups $14.) In addition to the usual fast-food suspects, a number of diners and cafes line both sides of I-40. **Earl's Restaurant ❷**, 1400 E. Rte. 66, has been around since 1947, and the food and prices show why. (☎863-4201. Open M-Sa 6am-9:30pm, Su 7am-9pm. Entrees $4-10.) **The Ranch Kitchen ❸**, 3001 W. Rte 66, has filling breakfasts, sandwiches and burgers ($5-7), and steaks. (Open in summer 7am-10pm; in winter 7am-9pm).

You can visit the **Gallup Visitors Center,** 701 Montoya Blvd., just off Rte. 66, for info on all of New Mexico. (☎863-4909 or 800-242-4282; www.gallupnm.org. Open daily 8am-5pm, June-Aug. 8am-6pm.) For mail, check out the **Post Office:** 950 W. Aztec. (☎722-5265. Open M-F 8:30am-5pm, Sa 10am-1:30pm.) **ZIP code:** 87301. **Greyhound,** 201 E. Rte. 66 (☎863-3761), runs buses to **Albuquerque** (2½hr., 4 per day, $21) and **Flagstaff** (4hr., 4 per day, $38).

CHACO CULTURE NATIONAL HISTORICAL PARK ☎505

Sun-scorched Chaco Canyon served as the first great settlement of the Ancestral Puebloans. The ruins here, which date from the 9th century, are among the most well-preserved in the Southwest. Evidence of inhabitance thousands of years older than even the oldest Ancestral Pueblo dwellings enriches the landscape, though the societies that flourished during the turn of the first millennium make the site truly remarkable. The Chaco societies demonstrated superior scientific knowledge and designed their buildings in accordance with solar patterns. One such structure, **Pueblo Bonito,** is the canyon's largest pueblo; it was once four stories high and housed more than 600 rooms. Nearby **Chetro Ketl** houses one of the Southwest's largest *kivas*. The largest pueblos are accessible from the main road, but **backcountry hiking trails** lead to many others; snag a free **backcountry permit** from the Visitors Center before heading off.

Chaco Canyon lies 92 mi. northeast of Gallup. From the north, take Rte. 44/550 to County Rd. 7900 (3 mi. east of **Nageezi** and 50 mi. west of **Cuba**), and follow the road for 21 mi., 16 of which are unpaved. From the south, take Rte. 9 from **Crownpoint** (home of the nearest ATM and grocery stores to the park) 36 mi. east to the marked park turn-off in Pueblo Pintado; turn north onto unpaved Rte. 46 for 10 mi.; turn left on County Rd. 7900 for 7 mi.; turn left onto unpaved County Rd. 7950 and follow it 16 mi. to the park entrance. *There is no gas in the park, and gas stations en route are few and far between.* Call the park in advance (☎988-6727) to inquire about road conditions, which may deteriorate in bad weather.

The **Visitors Center,** at the east end of the park, has an excellent museum exhibiting Ancestral Puebloan art and architecture and includes an enlightening film. All the ruins have interpretive brochures at their sites that can be purchased for 50-75¢. (☎786-7014. Open June-Aug. daily 8am-6pm; Sept.-May 8am-5pm. $8 per vehicle.). Offering a closer look at the ruins, the **Wijiji Trail** (1½hr., 3 mi.) starts at the Wijiji parking area 1 mi. east of the Visitors Center and explores Wijiji, a great house built around AD 1100.

No food is available at the park. The **Gallo Campground ❶,** a little more than 1 mi. from the Visitors Center, offers serene desert camping for $10 per site; register at the campground. The 48 sites have access to tables, fireplaces, and central toilets. The most accessible inexpensive lodging is in Farmington, 75 mi. north.

EL MORRO NATIONAL MONUMENT   ☎505

Drawn by a nearby spring while traveling through what is now New Mexico, Native Americans, Spanish explorers, and Anglo pioneers left their inscriptions on a giant sandstone bluff. **Inscription Rock,** its signatures dating back to 1605, has been the center piece of El Morro National Monument since its founding in 1906. The monument is located just west of the Continental Divide on Rte. 53, 42 mi. west of Grants and 56 mi. southeast of Gallup. The **Visitors Center** includes a small museum and warnings against emulating the graffiti of old. (☎783-4226. Open June-Aug. daily 8am-7pm; off-season 9am-5pm. $3, under 17 free.) The small, tranquil **El Morro Campground ❶** has running water, primitive toilets, and is rarely full. (9 sites, 1 wheelchair accessible. $5 per site.)

TRUTH OR CONSEQUENCES   ☎505

In 1950, the popular radio game show, *Truth or Consequences,* celebrated its 10th anniversary by renaming a small town, formerly Hot Springs, NM, in its honor. As its maiden name suggests, T or C was a tourist attraction prior to the publicity stunt. The mineral baths infuse the town with fountain-of-youth effects and a funky down-home spirit. Maybe there's something in the water.

■▐ ORIENTATION & PRACTICAL INFORMATION. T or C sits about 150 mi. south of Albuquerque on I-25. The **Chamber of Commerce,** 201 S. Foch St., has free maps and brochures about area attractions. (☎894-3536. Open M-F 9am-5:30pm, Sa 9am-1pm.) **Post Office:** 300 Main St., in the middle of town. (open M-F 9am-3pm) or 1507 N. Date St. (open 8:30am-5pm). **ZIP code:** 87901. **Area code:** 505.

▐ ACCOMMODATIONS. ▓**Riverbend Hot Springs Hostel (HI-AYH) ❶,** 100 Austin St., can be reached from I-25. Take Exit 79, turn right, and continue 1½ mi. to a traffic light. Turn left at the light, then immediately turn right onto Cedar St. and follow it down to the river and the blue building at the road's bend. Riverbend is reason enough to stop in T or C—many travelers plan to spend a night and end up staying a week. Use of on-site mineral baths and a meditation cove are free for guests. (☎894-6183. Kitchen and laundry. Reception open 8am-10pm, call ahead for late-night arrivals. Tepees or dorms $14, nonmembers $16; private rooms $30-48; tent site $10, nonmembers $12.) The **Charles Motel and Spa ❷,** 601 Broadway, offers simple and clean accommodations. The large rooms have kitchenettes, A/C, and cable TV. There are also mineral baths on the premises. (☎894-7154 or 800-317-4518. Singles $30, with kitchenette $35; doubles $39; rooftop suites $45.) **Campsites** at the nearby **Elephant Butte Lake State Park ❶** have access to restrooms and cold showers. (Primitive sites $8; developed sites with showers $10; with electricity $14.)

◘ FOOD. Nearly all of T or C's restaurants are as easy on the wallet as the baths are on the body. For groceries, try **Bullock's**, at the corner of Broadway and Post. (☎894-6622. Open M-Sa 7:30am-8pm, Su 8am-7pm.) **La Hacienda ❷**, 1615 S. Broadway, is well worth the drive out of the center of town. *Arroz con pollo* ($7) and breakfast *chorizo con huevos* ($5) make this the best Mexican food around. (Open Tu-Sa 11-9pm, Su 11-8pm.) The popular **La Cocina ❷**, 1 Lake Way Dr. (look for the "Hot Stuff" sign above N. Date St.), pleases with huge portions of Mexican and New Mexican food, including *chimichangas* ($7). A Carrizozo cherry cider ($1.50) will slake your thirst. (☎894-6499. Open daily 10:30am-10pm.) **Hot Springs Bakery Cafe ❷**, 313 Broadway, located in a stucco turquoise building, has an outdoor patio and cactus garden. Pizzas go for $7-14. (☎894-5555. Open Tu-Sa 8am-3pm.) **Bar-B-Que on Broadway ❷**, 308 Broadway, serves plentiful breakfast specials (starting at $2.50) and hearty lunch entrees ($5-8) as well as local buzz. (☎894-7047. Open M-Sa 7am-4pm.)

◙ ♨ SIGHTS & OUTDOOR ACTIVITIES. T or C's **mineral baths** are the town's main attraction; locals claim that they heal virtually everything. The only outdoor tubs are located at the **Riverbend Hostel**, where four co-ed tubs (bathing suits must be worn) abut the Río Grande. Access to the baths is $6 per hr. for the public (10am-7pm), but complimentary for hostel guests. (Open 7am-10am and 7pm-10pm.)

Five miles north of T or C (take Date St. north until the sign for Elephant Butte; turn right onto 181 and follow the signs), **Elephant Butte Lake State Park** is home to New Mexico's largest lake. A public works project dammed up the Río Grande in 1916 after the resolution of a major water rights dispute between the US and Mexico. The resulting lake is named after the elephantine rock formation at its southern end. The park offers sandy beaches for swimming and a marina for boating. (Cars $4, bikes and pedestrians free.) **Sports Adventure**, on the lake at the end of Long Point Rd., rents jet skis. (☎744-5557 or 888-736-8420. Rentals start at $35 per 30min.) The marina at the **Dam Site** rents motorized boats of all kinds. (☎894-2041. Must be 18+ and have a valid driver's license to rent. Motorboats $20 per hr., pontoon boats $30 per hr., ski boats $45 per hr.) There is a **Visitors Center** at the entrance to the park with a small museum on the natural history of the area. (☎877-664-7787. Open M-F 7:30am-4pm, Sa-Su 7:30am-10pm.) An easy 1.6 mi. nature trail begins in the parking lot just past the Visitors Center.

GILA CLIFF DWELLINGS & NATIONAL FOREST ☎505

The mysterious Gila Cliff Dwellings National Monument preserves over 40 stone and timber rooms carved into the cliff's natural caves by the Mogollon tribe during the late 1200s. Around a dozen families lived here for about 20 years, farming on the mesa top and along the river. During the early 1300s, however, the Mogollon abandoned their homes for reasons unknown, leaving the ruins as their only trace.

From Silver City, the Cliff Dwellings are 44 mi. down **Forest Rd. 15** through Piños Altos. From San Lorenzo, **Rte. 35** leads 26 mi. and ends 19 mi. south of the monument at an intersection with Forest Rd. 15. Though both roads are narrow and winding, Forest Rd. 15 is somewhat steeper and more difficult. Both roads require 2hr. for safe passage. Road conditions can be impassable in winter; pay close attention to the weather and the road surface.

The **Visitors Center,** at the end of Rte. 15, shows an informative film and sells various maps of the Gila National Forest. (☎536-9461. Open daily 8am-6pm, off-season 8am-4:30pm.) The picturesque 1 mi. round-trip **hike** to the dwellings begins past the Upper Scorpion Campground, and rangers occasionally give short interpretive tours through the cliffs. A trail guide (50¢) can be purchased at the trailhead or Visitors Center. (Dwellings open daily 8am-6pm; off-season 9am-4pm. Entrance fee $3, under 12 free.)

The nearest accommodations can be found at the comfy **Grey Feathers Lodge** ❸, 20 mi. south at the intersection of Forest Rd. 15 and Rte. 35. Drawing as many as 4000 hummingbirds on certain summer weekends, the lodge is a perfect place to relax and bird-watch. (☎536-3206. Singles $45; doubles $50.) The adjoining **cafe** ❶ outfits travelers with sandwiches ($3-7) and ice cream ($1.25 per scoop).

WHITE SANDS NAT'L MONUMENT   ☎505

The giant sandbox of White Sands evokes nostalgia for playground days. Situated in the Tularosa Basin between the Sacramento and San Andres Mountains, the world's largest dunes formed as rainwater flushed gypsum from the nearby peaks and into Lake Lucero. As desert heat evaporated the lake, the gypsum crystals were left behind and now form the blindingly white sand dunes. These drifts of fine sand create an arctic tundra look, but don't be fooled: the midday sun assaults the shadeless with a light and heat that can be unbearable. Trekking or rolling through the dunes provides hours of mindless fun or mindful soul-searching; the sand is particularly awe-inspiring at sunset.

■◪ **ORIENTATION & PRACTICAL INFORMATION.** White Sands lies on Rte. 70, 15 mi. southwest of Alamogordo and 52 mi. northeast of Las Cruces. Rte. 70 is prone to closures due to missile testing at the nearby military base. Delays can run up to 1hr.; call 479-9199 to check the status of Rte. 70 closures. The **Visitors Center** has a small museum with an introductory video and a gift shop. (☎479-6124. Park open June-Aug. daily 7am-10pm, last entrance 9pm; Sept.-May 7am-sunset. Visitors Center open June-Aug. daily 8am-7pm; Sept.-May 8am-5pm. Park admission $3, under 16 free.) The nearest **grocery store, ATM, Post Office, hospital,** and **Internet access** are in Alamogordo. In an **emergency,** call 479-9199. For more info visit the park web site (www.nps.gov/whsa) or write to the Superintendent, White Sands National Monument, P.O. Box 1086, Holloman AFB, NM 88330.

▟ **CAMPING.** The only way to spend the night inside the park is to camp at one of the **backcountry campsites** ❶. The ten sites ($3 per person in addition to the park entry fee) are available on a first come, first served basis and have no water or toilet facilities; they are not accessible by road and require up to a 2 mi. hike through the sand dunes. Campers must register in person at the Visitors Center and be in their sites before dark. Campfires are prohibited, but stoves are allowed. Sleeping amid the white dunes can be an rewarding experience, but plan ahead, because sites fill up early on full-moon nights. Occasionally, the sites are closed due to Missile Range launches (900 per year).

▨✘ **SIGHTS & OUTDOOR ACTIVITIES.** The 8 mi. **Dunes Drive** is a good way to begin a visit to White Sands. To really experience the uniqueness of the monument, though, you must get out of your car and take a walk across the dunes. Off-trail hiking is permitted anywhere in the eastern section of the park. Anyone considering a backcountry hike should bring a compass and map; it is quite easy to get lost in the vast sea of seemingly uniform gypsum dunes.

The best hike in the park is the **Alkali Flat Trail,** a moderately strenuous 4.6 mi. loop through the dunes to the parched, salty lakebed of Lake Otero. The trail is marked by white posts with reflective tape. *Do not hike the trail in strong winds, when blowing sand reduces visibility and makes it very easy to lose the trail. Bring lots of water and protect yourself from the intense sunlight.*

There is a free guided **sunset stroll** every evening (call ahead), and on summer nights, a park ranger gives an **evening talk** on various topics (June-Aug. 8:30pm). On **full moon nights** in the summer, the park stays open late (until 11pm, last entrance 10pm), and a guest speaker offers his two cents. A **star talk** takes place most Fridays during the summer at 8:30pm. During the **Perseid Meteor Shower** (usually the 2nd week of Aug.), the park remains open until midnight.

ROSWELL   ☎ 505

With giant inflatable Martians advertising used cars, streetlights donning painted-on pointy eyes, and flying saucers adorning fast-food signs, one thing is certain: aliens *have* invaded Roswell. The fascination began in July 1947, when an alien spacecraft reportedly plummeted to the earth near the dusty town. The official press release reported that the military had recovered pieces of a "flying saucer," but a retraction arrived the next day—the wreckage, the government claimed, was actually a harmless weather balloon. Many people weren't convinced.

Both believers and skeptics will find the alien side of Roswell entertaining, if not enlightening. During the first week of July, the **UFO Festival** commemorates the anniversary of the alleged encounter, drawing thousands for live music, an alien costume contest, and a 5km "Alien Chase" race. With a plastic flying saucer above its storefront, the popular **International UFO Museum and Research Center,** 114 N. Main St., recounts what happened near Roswell in 1947. Exhibits feature testimonials and newspaper clippings about the incident, as well as features on alien sightings worldwide. (☎625-9495. Open daily 9am-5pm. Free. Audio tour $1.) Long-time Roswell resident **Bruce Roads** (☎622-0628) gives private tours of the crash site in his four-wheel-drive Suburban. Take a tour to the Ragsdale impact site (3½hr.; $75) or the Corona debris site (6hr.; $150). 24hr. notice is required for tours.

Fast-food restaurants are as prevalent in Roswell as allusions to alien life, and they are concentrated along N. Main St. and W. 2nd St. Side streets are home to less commercial budget eateries. **Albertson's Supermarket** is at 1110 S. Main St. (☎623-9300). Just around the corner from the UFO Museum, the **Crash Down Diner** ❷, 106 W. 1st St., is an out-of-this-world-themed restaurant. Try a Starchild burrito creation ($5.75), a "hungry alien" sub ($3-5), or an "unidentified" burger ($4). A giant alien mural covers the wall, and even the salt and pepper shakers are shaped like aliens. (☎627-5533. Open M-Sa 8am-6pm, Su 8am-6pm.) **Martin's Capitol Cafe** ❶, 110 W. 4th St., delights with tasty Mexican dishes at down-to-earth prices. The gigantic burritos, with red or green salsa, (starting at $3.50) scream "take me to your stomach." (☎624-2111. Open M-Sa 6am-8:30pm.) **Peppers Bar and Grill** ❷, 500 N. Main St., serves American and Mexican food indoors and on an outdoor patio. (☎623-1700. Live music Apr.-Oct. F-Sa, DJ spinning on the patio W. Dining room open M-Sa 11am-10pm; bar open 11am-midnight.)

Aside from its extraterrestrial peculiarities, Roswell is a fairly normal town. The intersection of 2nd St. (Rte. 70/380) and Main St. (Rte. 285) is the sun around which the Roswell solar system orbits. To reach Roswell from Albuquerque, head 89 mi. south on I-25 to San Antonio, then 153 mi. east on U.S. 380. **Greyhound,** 1100 N. Virginia Ave. (☎622-2510), in conjunction with TNM&O, runs buses to Albuquerque (4hr.; Tu-Sa 2 per day, Su 1 per day; $33) and El Paso (4½hr.; 3 per day; M-Th $41, F-Su $43). The cheery and helpful **Visitors Center** is at 426 N. Main St. (☎624-0889 or 623-5695. Open M-F 8:30am-5:30pm, Sa-Su 10am-3pm.) The **public library,** 301 N. Pennsylvania Ave., has **free Internet access.** (Open M-Tu 9am-9pm, W-Sa 9am-6pm, Su 2pm-6pm.) The **Post Office** is on 415 N. Pennsylvania Ave. (☎623-7232. Open M-F 7:30am-5:30pm, Sa 8am-noon.) **ZIP code:** 88202. **Area code:** 505.

CARLSBAD CAVERNS ☎505

Imagine the surprise of European wanderers in southeastern New Mexico at the turn of the century when 250,000 bats appeared at dusk, seemingly out of nowhere. This swarm led to the discovery of the Carlsbad Caverns. By 1923, colonies of tourists clung to the walls of this desolate attraction. Carlsbad Caverns National Park marks one of the world's largest and oldest cave systems; even the most jaded spelunker will be struck by its unusual geological formations. (Natural entrance open June to mid-Aug. daily 8:30am-3:30pm; mid-Aug. to May 8:30am-2pm. Big room open June to mid-Aug. daily 8:30am-5pm; mid-Aug. to May 8:30am-3:30pm. $6, age 6-15 $3. Audio tour $3.) The **King's Palace Tour,** guided by a ranger, passes through four of the cave's lowest rooms and some of the most awesome anomalies. (1½hr. tours every hr. 9-11am and 1-3pm. $8, Golden Age Passport holders and ages 6-15 $4. Advance reservations required.) Other guided tours in the Big Room include a lantern tour though the **Left Hand Tunnel** (daily; $7) and a climbing tour of the **Lower Cave** (M-F; $20). Plan your visit for late afternoon to catch the magnificent **bat flight.** The ritual, during which hungry bats storm out of the cave at a rate of 6000 per min., is preceded by a ranger talk. (May-Oct. daily just before sunset.) **Backcountry hiking** is permitted above ground, but a permit, a map, and massive quantities of water are required.

Tours of the undeveloped **Slaughter Canyon Cave** offer a more rugged spelunking experience. A reliable car is required to get there; there's no public transportation, and the parking lot is 23 mi. down Rte. 418, an unpaved road, several miles south of the main entrance to the park on U.S. 62/180. The cave entrance is a steep, strenuous 0.5 mi. from the lot. Ranger-led tours (bring a flashlight) traverse difficult and slippery terrain; there are no paved trails or handrails. (2hr. tours; June-Aug. 2 per day, Sept.-May Sa-Su only. $15, Golden Age Passport holders and ages 6-15 $7.50. Call the Visitors Center at least 2 days ahead to reserve.) Tours of **Hall of the White Giant** and **Spider Cave** require crawling and climbing through tight passages. *Let's Go* does not recommend these tours for claustrophobes. (☎800-967-2283. Tours 4hr. 1 per week. $20. Call at least a month in advance to reserve.)

The **Stage Coach Inn ❷,** 1819 S. Canal St., is the nicest of the lot with an outdoor pool, indoor jacuzzi, and laundry. Comfortable, clean rooms have A/C, cable TV, and refrigerators. (☎887-1148. Singles $40; doubles $47. 15% AAA and AARP discount.) The **Carlsbad RV Park and Campground ❶,** 4301 National Parks Hwy. (☎888-885-6333), 4 mi. south of town, has two wooden camping cabins with a full-size bed, two bunk beds, and A/C ($30; linen not provided). Tepees ($22) and low-privacy tent camping ($14.50) are available. Showers and swimming pool offered.

The closest town to the park is **White's City,** on U.S. 62/180, 20 mi. southwest of Carlsbad, 6 mi. from the park Visitors Center. Flash floods occasionally close the roads; call the park for road conditions. **El Paso, TX** (see p. 688) is the nearest major city, 150 mi. west past **Guadalupe Mountains National Park** (see p. 687). **Greyhound,** in cooperation with **TNM&O Coaches** (☎887-1108), runs two buses per day between El Paso ($32), and will make a flag stop at White's City. **Carlsbad Caverns Visitors Center** has trail maps and tour info. (☎785-2232. Open daily 8am-7pm; late Aug. to May 8am-5:30pm. Entrance fee $6.) Make reservations by phone through the **Guided Tour Reservation Hotline** (☎800-967-2283) or on the web (www.reservations.nps.gov). White's City's **Post Office,** 23 Carlsbad Caverns Hwy., resides next to the Best Western gift shop. (☎785-2220. Open M-F 8am-noon and 12:30-4:30pm, Sa 8am-noon.) **ZIP code:** 88268. **Area code:** 505.

THE SOUTHWEST

CALIFORNIA

California is a place to freak out—to redefine boundaries, identities, and attitudes. It is a land that rubs away the past to experiment with the new and unexplored, anticipating the constant changes in mass culture and channeling them into the trends of the future. Gold miners frenzied here in the 1840s, flower children went wild in the 1960s, and hungry young actors and ambitious dot-com moguls leap for the good life today. Folks dig deep for richness in California's hype, commerce, industry, art, and insanity, then stamp it on the collective brain of the world.

Glaring movie spotlights, clanging San Francisco trolleys, *barrio* bustle, vanilla-scented Jeffrey pines, alpine lakes, and ghostly, shimmering desert landscapes all thrive in California. It is the edge of the West, the testing ground of extremes, the drawing board for the American dream. There's so much going on you'd need a whole book (like ▦*Let's Go: California 2003*) to describe it.

HIGHLIGHTS OF CALIFORNIA

LOS ANGELES. Follow your star to the place where media legends carouse, Ice Age fossils calcify, and boardwalk freaks commune (p. 850).

SAN FRANCISCO. Drive through the Golden Gate Bridge to the City by the Bay, where bluesmen, iconoclasts, students, and old hippies all congregate (p. 896).

SCENIC DRIVES. Along the coast, Rte. 1 and U.S. 101 breeze past earthy beach towns and along soaring cliffs, passing Santa Barbara (p. 888), Hearst Castle (p. 893), and Redwood National Park (p. 933).

NATIONAL PARKS. Hike among the granite peaks of Yosemite (p. 941), or climb a boulder and view the sunset at Joshua Tree (p. 885).

▉ PRACTICAL INFORMATION

Capital: Sacramento.

Visitor Info: California Office of Tourism, 801 K St., #1600, Sacramento 95814. (☎800-862-2543; www.visitcalifornia.com). **California State Parks Department,** P.O. Box 942896, Sacramento 94296. ☎800-777-0369.

Postal Abbreviation: CA. **Sales Tax:** 7-8%, depending on county.

LOS ANGELES   ☎213

The greater L.A. area (pop. 9.9 million; 4753 sq. mi.), stretching from Antelope Valley in the north to Catalina Island in the south, with a desert basin center, two mountain ranges, and 76 mi. of dazzling coastline, is the epicenter of the "California Dream." In a city where nothing seems to be more than 30 years old, the latest trends get more respect than the venerable. Many come here to erase the past and make (or re-make) themselves, and what better place? Angelenos are free to indulge in what they choose, and the resulting atmosphere is delicious with potential. Some savor L.A.'s image-bound culture, while others may be appalled by its excess. Either way, it's one hell of a show.

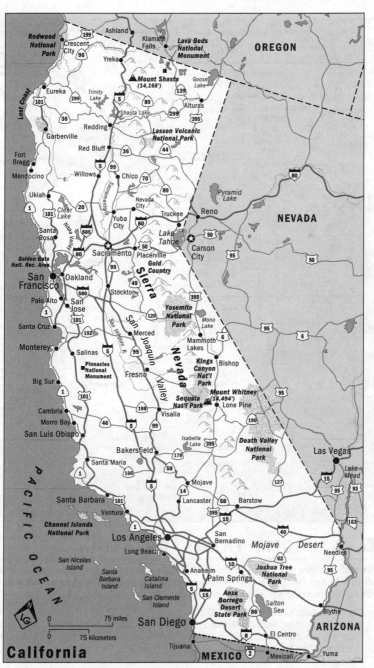

Redwood National Park
Crescent City
Ashland
Klamath Falls
Lava Beds National Monument
OREGON
199
96
Yreka
Lost Coast
Eureka
Trinity Lake
Mount Shasta (14,168')
Goose Lake
139
299
5
89
Alturas
299
Shasta Lake
36
Redding
Garberville
Lassen Volcanic National Park
395
Red Bluff
36
44
Fort Bragg
5
99
Willows
Chico
70
Mendocino
Sacramento R.
89
Ukiah
Nevada City
Truckee
Reno
Pyramid Lake
NEVADA
1
20
Clear Lake
Yuba City
80
Lake Tahoe
101
Napa Valley
505
50
Carson City
50
Santa Rosa
80
Sacramento
Placerville
95
Golden Gate Natl. Rec. Area
Gold Country
50
San Francisco
Oakland
99
Sierra
49
San
Stockton
Palo Alto
580
395
Jose
101
120
Yosemite National Park
Santa Cruz
San Joaquin R.
Mono Lake
95
6
Monterey
152
Merced
99
6
Salinas
5
Mammoth Lakes
Pinnacles National Monument
Joaquin
Big Sur
Fresno
San
Valley
Kings Canyon Nat'l Park
Bishop
1
101
Nevada
95
Cambria
198
Mount Whitney (14,494')
Lone Pine
Morro Bay
Visalia
Sequoia Nat'l Park
San Luis Obispo
46
5
99
190
Isabella Lake
395
Death Valley National Park
Bakersfield
Las Vegas
Santa Maria
178
Lake Mead
1
166
58
15
Mojave
95
93
5
14
127
Santa Barbara
Lancaster
58
Barstow
101
Ventura
395
15
163
1
Channel Islands National Park
Los Angeles
San Bernadino
40
Mojave Desert
Needles
San Nicolas Island
Long Beach
95
Santa Barbara Island
Catalina Island
Anaheim
10
62
Joshua Tree National Park
San Clemente Island
5
Palm Springs
15
Anza Borrego Desert State Park
Salton Sea
86
Blythe
75 miles
San Diego
El Centro
ARIZONA
75 kilometers
8
California
Tijuana
MEXICO
2
Mexicali
Yuma

CALIFORNIA

PACIFIC OCEAN

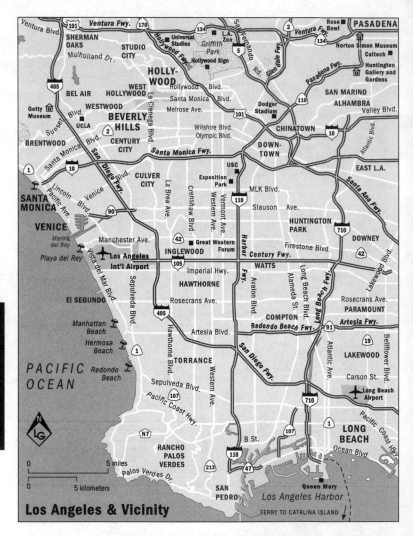

Los Angeles & Vicinity

FERRY TO CATALINA ISLAND

✈ INTERCITY TRANSPORTATION

Six main arteries pump into Greater L.A. Three of them run north from the city: the **I-5 (Santa Ana Fwy.), U.S. 101 (Ventura Fwy.),** and **Hwy. 1 (Pacific Coast Hwy.),** or "PCH." Santa Ana Fwy. also runs south, and **I-10** and **I-15** run east.

> **Airport: Los Angeles International (LAX)** (☎ 310-646-5252), in Westchester, 15 mi. south-west of downtown. Take the **Green Line Metro Rail shuttle,** leaving every 10-15min., from any terminal to the Green Line Metro Rail Aviation station. (Open daily 4:30am-11:30pm.) Taxi to Hollywood $40; to Santa Monica $25.

Trains: Amtrak rolls into Union Station, 800 N. Alameda St. (☎213-683-6729 or 800-872-7245), at the west edge of Downtown. To: **Albuquerque** (18hr., 1 per day, $100); **Las Vegas** (5½hr., 6 per day, $35-45); and **Seattle** (10½hr., 1 per day, $100-160).

Buses: Greyhound (☎213-629-8401), has a downtown station, 1716 E. 7th St. at Alameda St. (☎213-629-8536), which is in an extremely rough neighborhood. If you must get off in downtown *be very careful near 7th and Alameda St.*, 1 block southwest of the station, where you can catch MTA bus #60 traveling north to the Gateway Transit Plaza at Union Station. The new terminal in Hollywood, 1715 N. Cahuenga Blvd. (☎323-466-1249), is in a great location and close to many hotels, restaurants, and sights. To: **Las Vegas** (5-7hr., 22 per day, $33); **San Diego** (2½-3½hr., 11 per day, $13); **San Francisco** (8-11hr., 8 per day, $42); and **Tijuana**, Mexico (4hr., $15).

ORIENTATION

The City of Angels spreads its wings across the flatland basin between the coast of Southern California and the inland San Gabriel Mountains. You can still be "in" L.A. even if you're 50 mi. from downtown. Greater L.A. is like a club to which the surrounding burgs try to belong, a vast conceptual conglomeration of over 80 cities, including those in Orange, Riverside, San Bernardino, and Ventura counties.

NEIGHBORHOODS

The primarily Latino section of L.A. known as **East L.A.** begins east of downtown's Western Ave. South of downtown are the **University of Southern California (USC), Exposition Park,** and the predominantly African-American districts of **Inglewood** and **Compton.** The area south of downtown, known as **South Central,** suffered the brunt of the fires and looting that erupted in 1992. South Central and East L.A. are considered crime-ridden and offer little to attract tourists.

Northwest of downtown is **Hollywood.** Running from downtown to the ocean, east-west Sunset Blvd. presents a cross-section: beach communities, lavish wealth, famous nightclubs, and sleazy motels. East-west Hollywood Blvd. runs just beneath the celebrity-ridden **Hollywood Hills.** West of Hollywood, the **Westside** encompasses West Hollywood, Westwood, Century City, Culver City, Bel Air, Brentwood, and the independent city of **Beverly Hills.** The affluent Westside is also home to the **University of California at Los Angeles (UCLA)** and some trendy, off-beat Melrose Ave. hangouts. The area west of downtown is known as the **Wilshire District** after its main boulevard. **Hancock Park,** an affluent residential area, covers the northeast portion of the district and intersects with **Fairfax,** a Jewish community.

The Valley spreads north of the Hollywood Hills and the Santa Monica Mountains. For most people, *the* valley, is, like, the **San Fernando Valley,** where almost two million people wander among malls and TV studios. The Valley also contains the suburb of **Burbank** and the city of **Pasadena.** The basin is bounded to the north and west by the Santa Susanna Mountains and Rte. 118 (Ronald Reagan Fwy.), to the south by Rte. 134 (Ventura Blvd.), and to the east by I-5 (Golden State Fwy.).

Eighty miles of beach line L.A.'s **Coastal Region. Zuma** is northernmost, followed by **Malibu,** which lies 15 mi. up the coast from **Santa Monica.** Just a bit farther south is the funky beach community of **Venice.** The beach towns south of Santa Monica, comprising the **South Bay,** are **Marina del Rey, Manhattan, Hermosa,** and **Redondo Beach.** South across the **Palos Verdes Peninsula** is **Long Beach.** Farthest south are the **Orange County** beach cities, including **Newport Beach** and **Laguna Beach.**

⊑ LOCAL TRANSPORTATION

Nowhere is the god *Automobile* revered more than in L.A., often making the City of Angels a transportation hell. Sometimes it seems like all 3.5 million residents are out crowding the freeways at once, leaving little room for clean air, patience, or sanity. A little reminder: no matter how crowded the freeway is, it's almost always quicker and safer than taking city streets. Public transit can be confusing, slow, and even useless in L.A. Those looking to sightsee should get behind the wheel of a car. While driving in L.A. isn't much fun, it's usually the best way to get around. For freeway info, call **CalTrans** (☎897-3693). *If you hitchhike, you will probably die.* It is uncommon and exceptionally dangerous in L.A., and anyone who picks up a hitchhiker probably has ulterior motives. Don't even think about it.

Public Transit: 6 **Metropolitan Transit Authority (MTA)** Metro Customer Centers are available to point mass transit users in the right direction. They have MTA schedules, route maps, and a friendly staff to help plan your trip. **Downtown:** Arco Plaza, 515 S. Flower St., Level "C" (open M-F 7:30am-3:30pm); Gateway Transit Center, Union Station E. Portal (open M-F 6am-6:30pm). **East L.A.:** 4501-B Whittier Blvd. (open Tu-Sa 10am-6pm). **San Fernando Valley:** 14435 Sherman Way, Van Nuys (open M-F 10am-6pm). Centers are also located in Baldwin Hills and Wilshire. The local **DASH shuttle** (25¢), designed for short-distance neighborhood hops, serves major tourist destinations in many communities, including downtown, Hollywood, Fairfax, Midtown, Crenshaw, and Van Nuys/Studio City, as well as Venice in the summer. (☎213-808-2273; www.ladottransit.com. Open M-F 9am-5pm, Sa 10am-2pm.)

Taxis: Independent (☎213-385-8294 or 800- 521-8294), **L.A. Taxi/Yellow Cab Co.** (☎800-711-8294), or **Bell Cab** (☎888-235-5222).

Car Rental: Avon, 7080 Santa Monica Blvd. (☎323-850-0826), at La Brea Blvd. Cars $29 per day with 150 mi. free, $175 per week with 750 mi. free, or $600 per month with 1000 mi. free. Collision Damage Waiver $9 per day. No under-25 surcharge. Open M-F 6am-7pm, Sa-Su 7am-5pm. **Thrifty** (☎310-645-1880 or 800-367-2277), at L.A. airport. Prices vary daily, but drop as low as $25 per day with unlimited mileage in CA, NV, and AZ. CDW $9 per day. Under-25 surcharge $20 per day. Open 24hr.

⊉ PRACTICAL INFORMATION

Visitor Info: Los Angeles Convention and Visitor Bureau, 685 S. Figueroa St. (☎213-689-8822; www.visitlanow.com), between Wilshire Blvd. and 7th St. in the Financial District. Hundreds of brochures. Staff speaks English, French, Spanish, and Japanese. Detailed bus map of L.A. available. California road map $3. Distributes *LA Now*, a free booklet with tourist and lodging info. Open M-F 8am-5:30pm.

Hotlines: Rape Crisis: ☎310-392-8381. 24hr.

Medical Services: Cedars-Sinai Medical Center, 8700 Beverly Blvd. (☎310-855-5000, emergency 423-8644). **Good Samaritan Hospital,** 616 S. Witmer St. (☎213-977-2121, emergency 977-2420). **UCLA Medical Center,** 10833 Le Conte Ave. (☎310-825-9111, emergency 825-2111).

Post Office: Central branch at 7101 S. Central Ave. (☎800-275-8777). Open M-F 7am-7pm, Sa 7am-3pm. **ZIP Code:** 90001.

⊓ ACCOMMODATIONS

In choosing where to stay, the first consideration should be location. If you don't have wheels, you would be wise to decide which element of L.A. appeals to you the most. Those visiting for beach culture would do well to choose lodgings in

> **L.A. COUNTY AREA CODES. 213** covers Downtown L.A. **323** covers Hollywood, Vernon, Huntington Park, Montebello, and West Hollywood. **310** covers Santa Monica, Malibu, and Westside. **310** and **562** cover southern and eastern L.A. County. **626** covers the San Gabriel Valley and Pasadena. **818** covers Burbank, Glendale, San Fernando Valley, Van Nuys, and La Cañada. **909** covers the eastern border of L.A. County.

Venice or Santa Monica. Avid sightseers will probably be better off in Hollywood or the more expensive (but cleaner and nicer) Westside. Downtown has numerous public transportation connections, but is unsafe after dark; even those with cars should choose accommodations proximate to their interests to keep car-bound time to a minimum. **Listed prices do not include L.A.'s 14% hotel tax.**

HOLLYWOOD

Hollywood Bungalows International Youth Hostel, 2775 W. Cahuenga Blvd. (☎888-259-9990), just north of the Hollywood Bowl. Passport and international airline ticket or college ID required. Newly renovated hostel cultivates a summer camp atmosphere, with nightly jam sessions. Pool, weight room, TV, and mini-diner. Cable TV and VCR in all rooms. Internet access. Lockers 25¢. Linen and parking included. Laundry. 6- to 10-bed co-ed dorms with bathroom $15-19; private doubles for up to 4 people $59. ❶

USAHostels Hollywood, 1624 Schrader Blvd. (☎323-462-3777 or 800-524-6783), south of Hollywood Blvd., west of Cahuenga Blvd. Passport or proof of travel required. This lime-green and blue-dotted chain hostel is packed with young people looking to have some fun. Free beach shuttles run Tu, Th, and Su. All-you-can-eat pancakes, linen, and parking included. Dinner $5. 6-8 beds dorms with private bath $17; private rooms for 2-4 people $38-46. ❶

Liberty Hotel, 1770 Orchid Ave. (☎323-962-1788), south of Franklin Ave. Small hotel located on a quiet and clean residential street only 1 block north of Hollywood Blvd. Free coffee and parking; coin laundry. Add $5 for microwave and fridge, or just use the ones in the lobby. Reception 8am-11pm. Check-out 11am. Some rooms have A/C. King bed or 2 full-size beds $45-60 for 1-4 persons. ❸

SANTA MONICA & VENICE

🔳 **Los Angeles/Santa Monica (HI-AYH),** 1436 2nd St. (☎310-393-9913), Santa Monica. Take MTA #33 from Union Station to 2nd St. and Broadway, BBBus #3 from LAX to 4th St. and Broadway, or BBBus #10 from Union Station. No alcohol. Quiet hours 10pm-8am. Newly renovated kitchen, 2 nightly movies, library, central courtyard. Breakfast served 7:30-10:30am ($2-4). Safe deposit boxes and lockers. Laundry. 24hr. security and check-in. 10 consecutive day max. stay. In summer, reserve well in advance. 4- to 10-bed dorms $25-27, nonmembers $28-30; private doubles $67-73. ❶

Cadillac Hotel, 8 Dudley Ave., (☎310-399-8876), directly off the Ocean Front Walk, in Venice. Sauna, rooftop sundeck with great view, and well-equipped gym. TVs and private baths. Internet access $1 per 10min. Laundry. Reservations recommended. 4-person dorms $25. Work in exchange for night stay. Standard room $89, with queen and bunk $99. Requires 2 out of 3: valid driver's license, credit card, or passport. ❶

Hotel California, 1670 Ocean Ave. (☎310-393-2363 or 866-571-0000). Steps from the ocean, this newly renovated hotel is a great deal for its beachfront location. All rooms include satellite TV, mini-fridge, and surfboard shaped carpets. Suites with kitchenettes, dining tables, pull-out bed, stereo, and balcony available. Private beach access. Standard room with queen or 2 doubles in summer $169; 20% off if staying 7+ nights. Credit card required. ❺

WESTSIDE: BEVERLY HILLS & WESTWOOD

■ **Orbit Hotel and Hostel,** 7950 Melrose Ave. (☎323-655-1510), west of Fairfax Ave. in West Hollywood. Orbit deserves top honors for location and livability. Fashionable furniture and large room fans. Spacious kitchen, big-screen TV, courtyard, party room. Free breakfast. Internet access. 6-bed dorms $17; 4-bed dorms $20; private rooms with TV and bath $45. Dorms for US citizens and international students with passport only. ❶

Hotel Claremont, 1044 Tiverton Ave. (☎310-208-5957 or 800-266-5957), in Westwood Village, near UCLA. Pleasant and inexpensive. Owned and operated by the same family that built the hotel over 60 years ago. Clean rooms with antique dressers, ceiling fans, private baths, and phones. Victorian-style TV lounge. Reservations recommended, especially in June. Singles $45; doubles $51; 2 full-size beds for 4 $60. ❷

The Little Inn, 10604 Little Santa Monica Blvd. (☎310-475-4422). Classic old-school motel off a little dirt road. Clean, color-coordinated rooms. A/C, cable TV, and fridges. Parking included. Check-out 11am. 1 bed $50; 2 beds $55; $5 each additional person. About $10 more in summer. *Let's Go* readers get special rates Sept. 20-July 1 (excluding major holiday periods). ❸

◘ FOOD

HOLLYWOOD

Hollywood offers the best budget dining in L.A. **Melrose** is full of chic cafes, many with outdoor patios.

■ **Duke's Coffee Shop,** 8909 Sunset Blvd. (☎310-652-3100), in West Hollywood. The legendary Duke's is the best place to see hung-over rockers looking for breakfast. If the seats don't testify to it, the walls will—they are plastered with autographed album covers. Communal, canteen-style tables are a regular meeting place. Try "Sandy's Favorite" (with green peppers, cubed potatoes, and scrambled eggs) for $7.25. Entrees $5-11. Open M-F 7:30am-8:30pm, Sa-Su 8am-3:30pm. ❷

■ **Roscoe's House of Chicken and Waffles,** 1514 Gower St. (☎323-466-7453). The downhome feel and all-day menu makes this dive a popular spot for regular folk and celebs alike. Try "1 succulent chicken breast and 1 delicious waffle" ($6.90). Be prepared to wait on weekends. Open Su-Th 8:30am-12am, F-Sa 8:30am-4am. ❷

Chin Chin, 8618 Sunset Blvd. (☎310-652-1818), in West Hollywood. Other locations in Brentwood, Beverly Hills, Studio City, Marina del Rey, and Encino. Sunglassed celebrities lounge on the patio. Extremely popular with lunchtime crowds for its handmade "dim sum and then sum" ($10.75). Chinese chicken salad ($8) is the sort of Chinese-Californian cuisine befitting a restaurant whose name means "to your health." Open Su-Th 11am-11pm, F-Sa 11am-1am. ❸

SANTA MONICA

Giant table umbrellas along the 3rd St. Promenade and Ocean Ave. herald Santa Monica's upscale eating scene. Most menus have organic and vegetarian choices.

■ **Fritto Misto,** 601 Colorado Ave. (☎310-458-2829), at 6th St. This "Neighborhood Italian Cafe" lets you create your own pasta from $6. Made-to-order menu ($10-14) and cheery waitstaff. Vegetarian entrees $8-11. Daily hot pasta specials $8. Weekend lunch special (all-you-can-eat calamari and salad) $10. Omelettes Su 11:30am-4pm ($7-8). Open M-Th 11:30am-10pm, F-Sa 11:30am-10:30pm, Su 11:30am-9:30pm. ❸

Big Dean's "Muscle-In" Cafe, 1615 Ocean Front Walk (☎310-393-2666), a few steps from the Santa Monica Pier. Sun, sand, sauerkraut, and *cervezas!* Home of what they call the "burger that made Santa Monica famous" ($5.75). Veggie burgers $4.75. Happy hour M-F 4-8pm with $2 domestic beers. Open M-F 10am and Sa-Su 10:30am until dark, or until the regulars empty it out. ❶

Toppers Restaurant and Cantina, 1111 2nd St. (☎310-393-8080), sits atop the landmark Radisson Huntley Hotel. Ride the glass elevator, just inside and to the right of the 2nd St. entrance, up to "R" (for Restaurant) for some drinks and a long look out the window. You can't top this deal: it's short on cost and long on coast. Happy hour daily 4:30-7:30pm is a great bargain: buy 1 drink (sodas $1.50; half-pitcher of margarita $5.75) and get $2 Mexican appetizers. For a full meal after happy hour, the mostly Mexican entrees run from $12-17. Open daily 6:30am-1am. ❹

VENICE & MARINA DEL REY

Venetian cuisine runs the gamut from greasy to ultra-healthy, as befits its beachy-hippie crowd. The boardwalk offers cheap grub in fast food fashion.

▧ **Rose Cafe and Market,** 220 Rose Ave. (☎310-399-0711), at Main St. Gigantic rose painted walls, local art, industrial architecture, and a gift shop might make you think this is a museum, but the colorful cuisine is the main display. Healthy deli specials, including sandwiches ($6-8) and salads ($4-7) available from 11:30am. Limited menu after 3pm. Open M-F 7am-7pm, Sa 8am-7pm, Su 8am-5pm. ❷

▧ **Aunt Kizzy's Back Porch,** 4325 Glencoe Ave. (☎310-578-1005), in Marina Del Rey. In a vast strip mall at Glencoe Ave. and Mindanao Way. Done up to look like a back porch, Aunt Kizzy's is a little slice of Southern heaven. Specialties like Cousin Willie Mae's smothered pork chops come with cornbread and fresh veggies. Save room for $3 sweet potato pie. Dinner $12-13. Brunch $8. All-you-can-eat brunch buffet $13 (Su 11am-3pm). Open M-Th 11am-9pm, F-Sa 11am-11pm, Su 11am-10pm. ❸

Big Daddy's, 1425 Ocean Front Walk (☎310-396-4146), near Market Ave. With surfboard tables and the Beach Boys blaring, this is the ultimate beach food shack. These grillmasters will serve up anything the heart desires but can't quite handle. $1 menu includes hot dogs, pizza, vanilla ice cream, and more. Burgers from $4. Fried everything (zucchini $4; calamari $6). Churros $2. Open M-F 11am-9pm, Sa-Su 8am-10pm. ❶

BEVERLY HILLS

Yes, there is budget dining in Beverly Hills—it just takes a little looking to find it. An important tip: do not eat on Rodeo Dr. and stay south of Wilshire Blvd.

▧ **Al Gelato,** 806 S. Robertson Blvd. (☎310-659-8069), between Wilshire and Olympic St. Popular among the theater crowd, this homemade gelato spot also does large portions of pasta with a delicious basil tomato sauce. Giant meatball ($4.75) and rigatoni ($11). Stick to the gelato ($3.75-5.75) and made-to-order cannoli ($4.50) for dessert. Open Tu, Th, and Su 10am-midnight; F-Sa 10am-1am. No credit cards. ❷

Nate n' Al Delicatessen, 414 N. Beverly Dr. (☎310-274-0101). For 55 years, this delicatessen (no mere deli) has been serving up hand-pressed potato pancakes ($8.75), blintzes ($9), and reuben sandwiches ($11.50). The waitresses wear pink pinstripes and there's a bottle of Hebrew National Deli Mustard on every table. Open daily 7am-9pm. ❸

Ed Debevic's, 134 N. La Cienega Blvd. (☎310-659-1952). Jammed with 1950s memorabilia, Ed Debevic's was the inspiration for Jack Rabbit Slims of *Pulp Fiction* fame. Entrees $7-10. Full bar. Open Su-Th 11:30am-10pm, F-Sa 11:30am-midnight. ❸

WESTWOOD & UCLA

With UCLA nearby, Westwood overflows with good buys and beer.

▧ **Sandbag's Gourmet Sandwiches,** 11640 San Vicente Blvd. (☎310-207-4888), in Brentwood. Other locations in Westwood (☎310-208-1133) and Beverly Hills (☎310-786-7878). The perfect place for a healthy, cheap lunch with a complimentary chocolate cookie. Try the "Sundowner" (turkey, herb stuffing, lettuce, and cranberries). Most sandwiches $5.75. Open daily 9am-4pm. ❷

■ **Diddie Riese Cookies,** 926 Broxton Ave. (☎310-208-0448). Cookies baked from scratch every day. Popular late-night spot. Well worth the wait for a $1 ice cream sandwich. A buck also buys you 3 cookies and milk, juice, or coffee. Open M-Th 7am-midnight, F 7am-1am, Sa noon-1am, Su noon-midnight. ❶

Westwood Bistro, 1077 Broxton Ave. (☎310-824-7788). This modern and chic bistro offers superb French, Italian, and Asian cuisine. The always popular patio lends itself to a casual yet elegant dining experience. Salads $5-12. Entrees $9-15. Beer $2.50-5; wine $18 and up. Open Su-Th noon-10pm, F-Sa noon-11pm. ❸

DOWNTOWN

Financial District eateries vie for the business-person's coveted lunchtime dollar. Their formidable secret weapon is the lunch special... use it to your advantage.

■ **Philippe, The Original,** 1001 N. Alameda St. (☎213-628-3781), 2 blocks north of Union Station. The French dip sandwich was accidentally invented here in 1918 when Philippe unintentionally dropped a sliced French roll into a roasting pan filled with juice still hot from the oven. The sandwich has been the staple of Philippe's menu ever since. Choose from pork, beef, ham, turkey ($4.25) or lamb ($4.50). Top it off with a large slice of pie ($2.75) and a cup of coffee (10¢), and you've got a colossal meal at this L.A. institution. Free parking. Open daily 6am-10pm. ❶

■ **The Pantry,** 877 S. Figueroa St. (☎213-972-9279). Since 1924, it hasn't closed once—not for the earthquakes, not for the riots (when it served as a National Guard outpost), and not even when a taxicab drove through the front wall. There aren't even locks on the doors. Known for its large portions, free cole slaw, and fresh sourdough bread. Giant breakfast specials ($6). Lunch sandwiches $8. Open 24hr. No credit cards. ❷

Zucca Ristorante, 801 S. Figueroa St. (☎213-614-7800), in the financial district. This bright, classy, and perfectly located Italian restaurant is very popular among the local business set. Pizza $10-13. Pasta $14-16. Pesce $14-15. Open M-F 11:30am-2:30pm and 5-11pm, Sa 5-11pm. ❹

SAN FERNANDO VALLEY & PASADENA

Burbank is packed with eateries that are packed with stars venturing out in search of lunch. Stare all you want, but don't ask for autographs. Restaurants line **Colorado Boulevard** from Los Robles Ave. to Orange Grove Blvd. in Old Town.

■ **Miceli's,** 3655 W. Cahuenga Blvd. (☎323-851-3344), in Burbank. Would-be actors serenade dinner guests. Don't worry about losing your appetite during Broadway and cabaret numbers—waiters must pass vocal auditions. Pizza, pasta, or lasagna $10-15. Open M-Th 11:30am-11pm, F-Sa 11:30am-midnight, Su 3-11pm. ❸

■ **Fair Oaks Pharmacy and Soda Fountain,** 1516 Mission St. (☎626-799-1414), at Fair Oaks Ave. in South Pasadena. This old fashioned drug store, with soda fountain and lunch counter, has been serving travelers on Rte. 66 since 1915; now, a bit of Pasadena's upscale boutique flavor has crept into the establishment. Hand-dipped shakes and malts $4.25. Deli sandwiches $5.50. Patty melts $6. Soda fountain open M-Sa 9am-10pm, Su 11am-9pm; lunch counter open Su-F 11am-5pm, Sa 11am-8pm. ❷

Dalt's Grill, 3500 W. Olive Ave. (☎818-953-7750), in Burbank, at Riverside. Classic, classy, and cool American grill. Burgers and sandwiches $7-8. Chicken fajita caesar salad $9. Full bar. Beer $4.50-$5.75. Happy hour Sa-Th 4-8pm, F 4-10pm. Open M-Th 11am-midnight, F-Sa 11am-1am (bar open until 2am), Su 10am-midnight. ❷

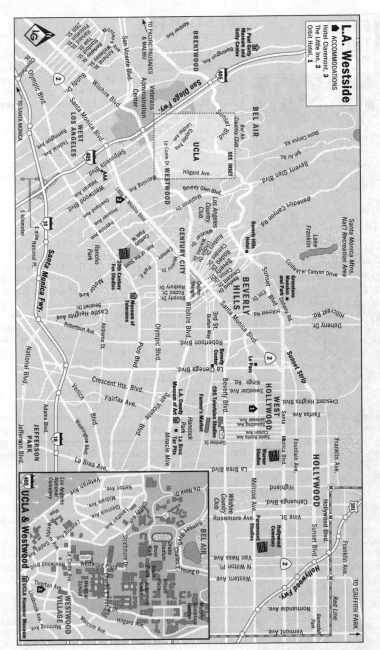

L.A. Westside

ACCOMMODATIONS

Hotel Claremont, 3
The Little Inn, 2
Orbit Hotel, 1

CALIFORNIA

FROM THE ROAD

ON LOCATION

One thing I've taken for granted as an avid TV and movie watcher is the dedication and expertise of those who we don't see on screen. Sitting at home on my sofa, I'd marvel at the beauty of the skyline caught by the camera, or the spectacular architecture of that downtown building. What I didn't realize until taking the Universal Studios and Warner Bros. behind-the-scene tours is that the beautiful skyline was painted on an enormous canvas, and the Downtown building was built with painted aluminum siding. For the next motion picture, the same skyline will be repainted by a set designer to look like a highway running through the Arizona desert, and the building will appear in hundreds of scenes, each time looking like a completely different part of the world. All the while, we will not notice.

Even on the tours, we do not notice until the tour guide points it out and shows us various scenes from different movies. Eventually the air is filled with sounds of "oh my gosh, it is, look..." and the tour guide moves on with a wide smile on his face. It would cost a studio hundreds of millions of dollars more if they had to fly to every location required for film. Instead, set designers create the location on the studio lots, and the audience never knows the difference. A successful movie requires talented actors, powerful producers, and creative directors, but the work of the designers and the manipulation of the camera is the true beauty of film making. Sometimes it takes a tour to appreciate it.

—James Kearney

◉ SIGHTS

HOLLYWOOD

Exploring the Hollywood area takes a pair of sunglasses, a camera, some cash, and a whole lot of attitude. It is best to drive through the famous Hollywood Hills and then park and explore **Hollywood Boulevard** on foot. Running east-west at the foot of the Hollywood Hills, this strip is the center of L.A.'s tourist madness. The boulevard itself, home to the Walk of Fame, famous theaters, souvenir shops, and museums, is busy day and night, especially around the intersection of Highland St. and Hollywood Blvd., then west down Hollywood Blvd.

HOLLYWOOD SIGN. The 50 ft. high, slightly erratic letters on Mt. Cahuenga north of Hollywood form a universally recognized symbol of the city. The original 1923 sign, which read HOLLYWOODLAND, was an advertisement for a new subdivision in the Hollywood Hills. You can't go frolic on the sign—there is a $500 fine if you're caught. (*To get as close to the sign as possible requires a strenuous 2.5 mi. hike. Use the Bronson Canyon entrance to Griffith Park, following Canyon Dr. to its end. Parking is free. The Brush Canyon Trail starts where Canyon Dr. becomes unpaved. At the top of the hill, follow the road to your left. For those not interested in hiking, drive north on Vine St., turn right on Franklin Ave., left on Beachwood and drive up until you are forced to drive down.*)

GRAUMAN'S CHINESE THEATER. Formerly Mann's, this theater is a garish rendition of a Chinese temple and the hottest spot for a Hollywood movie premiere. Pay homage to impressions made by movie stars in the cement, including Whoopi Goldberg's dreadlocks, Jimmy Durante's nose, and George Burns's cigar. (*6925 Hollywood Blvd., between Highland and La Brea Ave.* ☎323-461-3331.)

WALK OF FAME. Things get a little seedier all along Hollywood and Vine St., where the sidewalk is embedded with over 2000 bronze-inlaid stars, inscribed with the names of the famous, the infamous, and the downright obscure. The stars have no particular order, so don't try to find a method to the madness. To catch a glimpse of today's (or yesterday's) stars in person, call the Chamber of Commerce for info on star-unveiling ceremonies. (☎323-469-8311; www.hollywoodchamber.net.)

OTHER SIGHTS. The **Hollywood Bowl** is synonymous with picnic dining and summer entertainment in a beautiful hillside atmosphere. All are welcome to listen to the L.A. Philharmonic at rehearsals. The Bowl also hosts a summer jazz concert series. A small but cozy museum has several exhibits, as well as listening stations where you can swoon to the Beatles, Dylan, and B.B. King, all of whom played the Bowl in the 1960s. *(2301 N. Highland Ave. ☎ 323-850-2058, concert line 850-2000. Open July-Aug. Tu-Sa 10am-8:30pm; Sept.-June Tu-Sa 10am-4:30pm. Free.)* The **Capital Records Tower,** a monument to the recording industry, was designed to look like a stack of records, with fins sticking out at each floor and a needle on top that constantly blinks H-O-L-L-Y-W-O-O-D in Morse code. *(1750 Vine St., just north of Hollywood Blvd.)* The ornate **El Capitán Theatre** hosted the 1941 Hollywood premiere of *Citizen Kane.* Current Disney movies play here with interactive post-show activities. *(6838 Hollywood Blvd. ☎ 323-467-9545 or 800-347-6396. $9.50, seniors and ages 3-11 $6, matinee $6; live shows or special exhibit tickets $13-22, ages 3-11 $11-20.)*

SANTA MONICA

Santa Monica is known more for its shoreside scene than its shore. With gawkers and hawkers, the area around the carnival pier is the hub of local tourist activity.

THIRD STREET PROMENADE. The fun fair spills over into the pedestrian-only **3rd St. Promenade,** where street performers and a biweekly Farmers Market (W and Sa mornings) make for cinematic "crowd" scenes. People with clipboards often sign visitors up for **free movie passes.** Farther inland, along Main St. and beyond, a smattering of galleries, ultra-trendy design shops, and museums reveal the city's love affair with art and design.

SANTA MONICA PIER. The famed pier is the heart of the Santa Monica Beach and home of the carnivalesque family funspot Pacific Park, where the fun meets the sun and "the rides meet the tides." Roller coaster lovers and ferris wheel fanatics can have some fun among the sticky-fingered kids and sunburned parents who populate the pier. *(Off PCH on the way to Venice Beach from Santa Monica Beach. ☎ 310-656-8886. Open in summer M-Th 11am-11pm, F-Su 11am-12:30am; in winter F-Sa 11am-12:30am, Su 11am-9pm. Ticket window closes 30min. before the park closes. Tickets $1.50 each, most rides 2-3 tickets; day passes $16, children under 42 in. $9.)*

VENICE

Venice is a bustling beach town with rad politics and mad diversity. Its guitar-toting, Bukowski-quoting, wild-eyed, tie-dyed residents sculpt masterpieces in sand and compose them in graffiti, all before heading to the beach to slam a volleyball around. A stroll through in-line skating, bikini-flaunting, tattooed Venice is like an acid trip for the timid.

OCEAN FRONT WALK. Venice's main beachfront drag, the **Ocean Front Walk,** is a seaside circus of fringe culture. Bodybuilders of both sexes pump iron in skimpy spandex outfits at **Muscle Beach.** *(1800 Ocean Front Walk.)* Venice's anything-goes attitude attracts some of L.A.'s most innovative artists (and not just the guy who makes sand sculptures of Jesus). Fire-juggling cyclists, master sand sculptors, bards in Birkenstocks, and the **"skateboard grandma"** define the spirit of this playground population. Vendors selling jewelry, henna, snacks, and beach items overwhelm the boardwalk.

WEST HOLLYWOOD

Melrose Avenue, running from Santa Monica Blvd. at the edge of West Hollywood into Hollywood, lined with restaurants, art galleries, and shops, is home to the hip. The choicest stretch is between La Brea and Fairfax Ave. While much sold here is used ("vintage"), none of it is really cheap (see Shopping, p. 867). North of the Beverly Center is the **Pacific Design Center,** a sea-green glass complex nicknamed the Blue Whale and constructed in the shape of a rippin' wave. *(8687 Melrose Ave. ☎ 310-657-0800.)*

BEVERLY HILLS

Conspicuous displays of wealth can border on the vulgar in this storied center of extravagance and privilege. Residential ritz reaches its peak along the mansions that line the blocks of Beverly Dr.

RODEO DRIVE. The heart of the city, known for its flashy clothing boutiques and jewelry shops, is in the **Golden Triangle,** a wedge formed by Beverly Dr., Wilshire Blvd., and Santa Monica Blvd., centering on **Rodeo Drive.** Built like an old English manor house, Polo Ralph Lauren *(444 N. Rodeo Dr.)* stands out from the white marble of the other stores. The divine triple-whammy of Cartier *(370 N. Rodeo Dr.)*, Gucci *(347 N. Rodeo Dr.)*, and Chanel *(400 N. Rodeo Dr.)* sits on some of the area's prime real estate, where rents are as high as $40,000 per month. At the south end of Rodeo Dr. (closest to Wilshire Blvd.) is the all-pedestrian shopping complex of **2 Rodeo Drive,** or **Via Rodeo,** which contains Dior, Tiffany, and numerous salons frequented by the stars. Although it fakes European antiquity, the promenade was constructed in the last decade—cobblestone street, lampposts, and all. Across the way is the venerable **Beverly Wilshire Hotel,** whose old and new wings are connected by **El Camino Real** and its Louis XIV gates. The hotel lobby gives you a hint of just how extravagant the rooms might be. *(9500 Wilshire Blvd. ☎310-275-5200.)*

WESTWOOD & UCLA

Get a feel for mass academia UC-style at this 400-acre campus sprawling in the foothills of the Santa Monica Mountains. A prototypical California university, **UCLA** sports an abundance of grassy open spaces, dazzling sunshine, and pristine buildings. Once voted the #1 jock school in the country by *Sports Illustrated*, UCLA also boasts an illustrious film school whose graduates include James Dean, Jim Morrison, Oliver Stone, Francis Ford Coppola, and Tim Robbins. *(Take the San Diego Fwy./I-405 north to the Wilshire Blvd./Westwood exit. Take Westwood Blvd. north off Wilshire, heading straight through the center of the village and directly into the campus. By bus, take MTA route #2 along Sunset Blvd., #21 along Wilshire Blvd.; #320 from Santa Monica; #561 from the San Fernando Valley; or BBBus #1, 2, 3, 8, or 12. Parking passes $6.)*

BEL AIR, BRENTWOOD, & PACIFIC PALISADES

Most of today's stars live in these three affluent communities. Next to UCLA is **Bel Air,** home of the *Beverly Hillbillies* mansion, at 750 Bel Air Rd. A few blocks up is the former home of **Sonny and Cher,** at 364 St. Cloud. **Elizabeth Taylor** is right around the corner at 700 Nimes Rd. A few blocks away is **Nicolas Cage's** place at 363 Copa De Oro. Farther west on Sunset Blvd. is **Brentwood,** home to many a national scandal. **O.J. Simpson's** estate at 360 Rockingham Pl. was repossessed and auctioned off for a meager $2.63 million; consequently, the famous accusé no longer lives here. A one-time White House favorite herself, **Marilyn Monroe** was found dead in 1962 at her home at 12305 Fifth Helena Dr. The considerably more secluded **Pacific Palisades** brings the stars closer to the ocean and farther from the *paparazzi*. **Kurt Russell** and live-in love **Goldie Hawn** reside at 1422 Capri Dr., and **Whoopi Goldberg** is in town at 1461 Amalfi Dr. Just down the road is **Steven Spielberg,** whose house at 1513-1515 Amalfi Dr. belonged to David O. Selznick while he was producing *Gone with the Wind*. **Arnold Schwarzenegger** and **Maria Shriver,** who loved their lot so much they bought out their neighbors for $5.4 million, practice family fitness at 14205, 14209, and 14215 Sunset Blvd. **John Travolta** and **Kelly Preston** are stayin' alive at 735 Bonhill Rd.

DOWNTOWN

The **Los Angeles Conservancy** (www.laconservancy.org) offers free, printable self-guided walking tours geared toward architectural landmarks on its website as well as a variety of docent-led Saturday tours featuring Downtown's historic buildings. (☎213-623-2489. Tours $8. Make reservations at least 1 week in advance.) If driving, park in a secure lot, rather than on the streets. Parking is costly; arriving before 8am enables visitors to catch early-bird specials.

HISTORIC NORTH. The historic birthplace of L.A. lies in the northern section of downtown, bordered by Spring and Arcadia St. Where the city center once stood, **El Pueblo de Los Angeles Historical Monument** preserves a number of historically important buildings from the Spanish and Mexican eras. **Olvera St.**, one of L.A.'s original roads, resembles a small Mexican street market. The street is the site of the Cinco de Mayo and Día de los Muertos celebrations of L.A.'s Chicano population (see **Festivals**, p. 868). **Chinatown** lies north of this area, roughly bordered by Yale, Spring, Ord, and Bernard St. Pick up maps at the **Chinatown Heritage and Visitors Center.** *(411 Bernard St. DASH B.)*

CIVIC CENTRAL. The **Civic Center** is a solid wall of bureaucratic architecture sitting south of El Pueblo, bounded by the Hollywood Fwy. (U.S. 101), Grand Ave., 1st, and San Pedro St. One of the best-known buildings in the Southland, **City Hall,** 200 N. Spring St., "has starred in more movies than most actors." Tours of the three-theater complex and Music Center are offered weekdays as performance schedules permit. *(135 N. Grand Ave. ☎213-972-7211.)* The **Dorothy Chandler Pavilion,** the old site of the Academy Awards, houses the **L.A. Opera.** *(☎213-972-8001; www.laopera.org.)*

OTHER SIGHTS

GRIFFITH PARK & GLENDALE. Griffith Park stretches for 4107 acres from the hills above North Hollywood to the intersection of Rte. 134 (Ventura Fwy.) and I-5 (Golden State Fwy.). Several of the mountain roads through the park, especially the **Vista Del Valle Dr.,** offer panoramic views of downtown L.A., Hollywood, and the Westside. Unfortunately, heavy rains have made them unsafe for cars, but foot traffic is allowed on most. The five-mile hike to the top of **Mount Hollywood,** the highest peak in the park, is quite popular. For info, stop by the **Visitors Center and Ranger Headquarters.** *(4730 Crystal Spring Dr. ☎323-913-4688, emergency 323-913-7390. Park open daily 5am-10pm.)*

PLANETARIUM & OBSERVATORY. The white stucco and copper domes of the castle-like mountaintop observatory are visible from around Griffith Park, and the observatory parking lot affords a terrific view of the Hollywood sign. You may remember the planetarium from the James Dean film *Rebel Without A Cause.* Unfortunately, the observatory and planetarium are closed until 2005, when they will re-open with an additional 35,000 sq. ft. The grounds will remain open in the meantime. *(Drive to the top of Mt. Hollywood on Vermont Ave. or Hillhurst St. from Los Feliz Blvd., or take MTA #180 or 181 from Hollywood Blvd. ☎323-664-1181, recording 323-664-1191. Free parking, use Vermont St. entrance to Griffith Park. Grounds open in summer daily 12:30-10pm; in winter Tu-F 2-10pm, Sa-Su 12:30-10pm.)*

FOREST LAWN CEMETERY. A rather twisted sense of celebrity sightseeing may lead some travelers to Glendale, where they can gaze upon stars who won't run away when chased for a picture. Among the illustrious dead are Clark Gable, George Burns, and Sammy Davis, Jr. The cemetery also has reproductions of Michelangelo pieces, as well as the "largest religious painting on earth" (Jan Styka's 195 ft. by 45 ft. *Crucifixion*), transported from Europe in sections wrapped around telephone poles. Forest Lawn allegedly inspired the "Whispering Glades Cemetery" (of Evelyn Waugh's novel *The Loved One*), where death and showbiz combine to transform sorrow and spirituality into something more marketable and cliched. *(1712 Glendale Ave. ☎800-204-3131. Grounds open Mar.-Oct. daily 8am-6pm; Nov.-Feb. 8am-5pm. Mausoleum open 9am-4:30pm.)*

SAN FERNANDO VALLEY

Movie studios are the defining feature of the San Fernando Valley. Passing Burbank on Rte. 134 (the Ventura Fwy.), you will see some of the Valley's most lucrative words: **Universal, Warner Bros., NBC,** and **Disney.** To best experience the industry, attend a **free TV show taping** or take tours offered by the studios.

UNIVERSAL STUDIOS. A movie and television studio that happens to have the world's first and largest movie-themed amusement park attached, ✪**Universal Studios Hollywood** is the most popular tourist spot in Tinseltown. Located north of Hollywood in its own municipality, Universal City (complete with police and fire station), the park was born as a public tour of the studios in 1964. It has since become a full-fledged amusement park with riding attractions and live shows featuring Universal brand names. The movie itself may have bombed, but the live stunts at the *Waterworld* spectacular are impressive. Travel through time with Doc Brown in *Back to the Future: The Ride*, fly with *E.T.* on his journey across galaxies, or endure the heat of the blazing inferno in *Backdraft*. *(Take Rte. 101 to Universal Center Dr. or Landershim Blvd. Exits. MTA bus #420 west from downtown or east from the Valley. ☎818-622-3801. Open July-Aug. M-F 9am-9pm, Sa-Su 9am-10pm; Sept.-June M-F 10am-6pm, Sa-Su 9am-7pm. $45, ages 3-9 $35. Parking $8.)*

SIX FLAGS THEME PARKS. At the opposite end of the Valley, 40min. north of L.A. in Valencia, lies **Magic Mountain,** which lays claim to the scariest roller coasters in Southern California. **X,** the park's latest addition, forces riders to flip, spin, and rotate 360 degrees, creating a legitimate flying phenomenon. Next door, Six Flags' waterpark **Hurricane Harbor** features the world's tallest enclosed speed slide. *(Magic Mountain: ☎661-255-4111. Open daily Apr.-Labor Day, hours vary; open weekends and holidays Sept.-Mar. $43, seniors and under 4 ft. $27. Parking $7. Hurricane Harbor: ☎661-255-4527. Open May-Sept., hours vary. $22/15. Combo admission to both parks $53.)*

PASADENA & AROUND

With its world-class museums, graceful architecture, lively shopping district, and idyllic weather, Pasadena is a welcome change from its noisy downtown neighbor. **Old Town** Pasadena sequesters intriguing historic sights and an up-and-coming entertainment scene. The **Pasadena Freeway** (Rte. 110) is one of the nation's oldest. The city provides **free shuttles** approximately every 15min. that loop between Old Town and the downtown area around Lake Ave. *(☎626-744-4055. Shuttles run downtown M-Th 11am-7pm, F 11am-10pm, Sa-Su noon-8pm; uptown M-F 7am-6pm, Sa-Su noon-5pm.)*

HUNTINGTON LIBRARY, ART GALLERY, & BOTANICAL GARDENS. This institute was built in 1910 as the home of Henry Huntington, who made his money in railroads and California real estate. Its stunning gardens host 150 acres of plants. The library holds one of the world's most important collections of rare books, as well as British and American manuscripts, including a Gutenberg Bible, Benjamin

Franklin's handwritten autobiography, a 1410 manuscript of Chaucer's *Canterbury Tales*, and a number of Shakespeare's first folios. The art gallery is known for its 18th- and 19th-century British paintings, but also has impressive exhibits of American art, Renaissance paintings, and 18th-century French decorative art. *(1151 Oxford Rd., between Huntington Dr. and California Blvd. in San Marino. From downtown L.A., take MTA bus #79 from Union Station to San Marino Ave. and walk ½ mi. ☎626-405-2100. Open Memorial Day to Labor Day Tu-Su 10:30am-4:30pm; in winter Tu-F noon-4:30pm, Sa-Su 10:30am-4:30pm. $10, students $7, seniors $8.50, under 12 free; 1st Th of each month free.)*

▥ MUSEUMS

▨ **Los Angeles County Museum of Art (LACMA),** 5905 Wilshire Blvd. (☎323-857-6000). At the western end of Hancock Park, LACMA's renowned collection contains "more than 110,000 works from around the world, spanning the history of art from ancient times to the present." Opened in 1965, LACMA is the largest museum on the West Coast, with six main buildings around the **Times-Mirror Central Court.** The **Steve Martin Gallery,** in the Anderson Building, holds the famed benefactor's collection of Dada and Surrealist works, including R. Magritte's *Treachery of Images.* The latest addition is **LACMA West,** and its **Children's Gallery.** The museum sponsors free jazz, chamber music, film classics and documentaries, and a variety of free daily tours. Open M-Tu and Th noon-8pm, F noon-9pm, Sa-Su 11am-8pm. $7, students and seniors $5, under 18 $1; 2nd Tu of each month free. Free jazz F 5:30-8:30pm, chamber music Su 6-7pm. Film tickets $7, seniors $5.

▨ **Norton Simon Museum of Art,** 411 W. Colorado Blvd. (☎626-449-6840), at Orange Grove Blvd. The recently revamped museum features a world-class collection, chronicling Western art from Italian Gothic to 20th-century abstract, with paintings by Raphael, Botticelli, Monet, Picasso, and others. The Impressionist and Post-Impressionist hall is particularly impressive; the collection of Southeast Asian sculpture is one of the world's best. Open W-Th and Sa-Su noon-6pm, F noon-9pm. $6, seniors $3, students with ID and children under 12 free.

▨ **Armand Hammer Museum of Art and Cultural Center,** 10899 Wilshire Blvd. (☎310-443-7000), at UCLA. Houses a small collection of Western art from the 16th century to the present day. A who's who of European painters, Hammer's collection includes works by Rembrandt, Chagall, and Cézanne, but its real gem is Van Gogh's *Hospital at Saint-Rémy.* Open Tu-W and F-Sa 11am-7pm, Th 11am-9pm, Su 11am-5pm. $4.50, seniors and students $3, under 17 free with adult; Th free. Free tours of permanent collection Su 2pm, of traveling exhibits Th 6pm, Sa-Su 1pm.

▨ **J. Paul Getty Museum and Getty Center,** 1200 Getty Center Dr. (☎310-440-7330), in the Santa Monica Mountains above Bel Air. The center unites L.A.'s beloved Getty museums with its institutes on one site. The museum itself boasts the permanent Getty collection, which includes Van Gogh's *Irises,* James Ensor's *Christ's Entry into Brussels in 1889,* Impressionist paintings, and one of the nation's best Rembrandt collections. Open Tu-Th and Su 10am-6pm, F-Sa 10am-9pm. Free; headset audio guides $3.

Petersen Automotive Museum, 6060 Wilshire Blvd. (☎323-930-2277), at Fairfax. This slice of Americana showcases one of L.A.'s most recognizable symbols—the automobile. PAM is the world's largest car museum and the nation's 2nd-largest history museum (after the Smithsonian). The museum has a 1920s service station, a 50s body shop, and a 60s suburban garage. Open Tu-Su 10am-6pm; Discovery Center closes at 5pm. $7, students and seniors $5, ages 5-12 $3, under 5 free.

La Brea Tarpits, 5801 Wilshire Blvd. (☎323-857-6309). Certainly the most venerable of L.A.'s many intriguing life forms, the prehistoric critters trapped within the tarpits are worth a peek. Open M-F 9:30am-5pm, Sa-Su 10am-5pm. Grounds tours 1pm, museum tours Tu-Su 2:15pm. $6, students and seniors $3.50, ages 5-12 $2; 1st Tu of each month free.

Santa Monica Museum of Art, 2525 Michigan Ave. (☎310-586-6467), near the intersection of Olympic and Cloverfield Blvd. in the Bergamot Station Arts Center. Exhibits the work of emerging artists. Open Tu-Sa 11am-6pm, Su noon-5pm; call ahead, because it often closes for installation changes. Suggested donation $3, students and seniors $2.

Museum of Tolerance, 9786 W. Pico Blvd. (☎310-553-8043), at Roxbury St., south of Beverly Hills. This hands-on, high-tech museum has exhibits on the Holocaust, the Yugoslav genocide, the L.A. riots, and the US Civil Rights movement. Open M-Th 11:30am-4pm, F 11:30am-1pm, Su 11am-5pm. $9, seniors $7, students and ages 3-10 $5.50.

Museum of Television & Radio, 465 N. Beverly Dr. (☎310-786-1000). Complete with a radio broadcast studio and 2 theaters, this museum's biggest highlight is its library, which holds 117,000 television, radio, and commercial programs. You can request your favorite tube hits, and 5min. later the staff will have full-length episodes ready and waiting for your viewing pleasure at your own private screening station. Caricatures of television stars decorate the walls, and there is always someone watching *I Love Lucy.* Open W and F-Su noon-5pm, Th noon-9pm. Donation $6, students and seniors $4, under 13 $3.

Hollywood Heritage Museum, 2100 N. Highland Ave. (☎323-874-2276), across from the Hollywood Bowl. The museum provides a glimpse into early Hollywood filmmaking. Antique cameras, costumes worn by Douglas Fairbanks and Rudolph Valentino, props, vintage film clips, and other memorabilia fill the museum. The surrounding hills provide an ideal picnic area. Open Sa-Su 11am-3:45pm. $3, ages 3-12 $1, under 3 free.

🎬 ENTERTAINMENT

A visit to the world's entertainment capital isn't complete without some exposure to the actual business of making a movie or TV show. Fortunately, most production companies oblige. **Paramount** (☎323-956-5000), **NBC** (☎818-840-3537), and **Warner Bros.** (☎818-954-1744) offer two-hour guided walking tours, but they are made for tourists and tend to be crowded and overpriced.

TELEVISION

The best way to get a feel for the industry is to land yourself tickets to a TV taping. Tickets are free, but studios tend to overbook, so holding a ticket does not always guarantee that you'll get into the taping. Show up early.

NBC, 3000 W. Alameda Ave., at W. Olive Ave. in Burbank, is your best spur-of-the-moment bet. Show up at the ticket office on a weekday at 8am for passes to Jay Leno's **Tonight Show,** filmed at 5pm the same evening. The line to enter starts getting long at 3pm. (2 tickets per person, must be 16+.) NBC studio tours run on the hour. (☎818-840-3537. M-F 9am-3pm; $8, ages 5-12 $4.) Many of NBC's "Must-See TV" shows are taped at **Warner Bros.,** 4000 Warner Blvd. (☎818-954-6000), in Burbank. Many sitcoms are taped from August to May—call the studio at least five business days in advance to secure tickets. Call for info about the VIP tour. **Paramount** is the only major studio still in Hollywood; as a result its tours are very popular. (Every hr. M-F 9am-2pm. $15.)

A **CBS box office,** 7800 Beverly Blvd., next to the Farmers Market in West Hollywood, hands out free tickets to Bob Barker's game-show masterpiece *The Price is Right* up to one week in advance. (☎323-575-2458. Open M-Th; taping days 7:30am-5pm, non-taping days 9am-5pm.) Audience members must be over 18. You can request up to 10 tickets on a specific date by sending a self-addressed, stamped envelope to *The Price is Right* Tickets, 7800 Beverly Blvd., L.A. 90036, about four to six weeks in advance.

If all else fails, **Audiences Unlimited, Inc.,** 100 Universal City Plaza, Building 4250, Universal City 91608 (☎818-506-0067; www.tvtickets.com), is a great resource. To find out which shows are available during your visit, send in a self-addressed, stamped envelope or check the website.

SO, YOU WANNA BE IN PICTURES? Honey!

Baby! Sweetheart! You don't have to be beautiful and proportionally perfect to grace celluloid—just look at Tom Arnold or Lili Tomlin. The quickest way to get noticed is to land yourself a job as an extra—no experience necessary. One day's work will land $40-130 in your pocket and two meals in your tummy. Step One is to stop calling yourself an extra—you're an "atmosphere actor" (it's better for both your ego and your resume). Step Two is to contact a reputable casting service. **Cenex Central Casting,** 220 S. Flower St., Burbank 91506 (☎818-562-2755), is the biggest, and a good place to start. You must be at least 18 and a U.S. citizen or have a Resident Alien/ Employment Authorization card. Step Three is to show up on time; you'll need the clout of DeNiro before you can just waltz in late. Don't forget to bring $20 in cash to cover the "photo fee." Step Four is to dress the part: don't wear red or white, which bleed on film and render you unusable. Finally, after you collect three **SAG** (Screen Actors Guild; 5757 Wilshire Blvd., L.A. 90036; ☎323-937-3441) vouchers, you'll be eligible to pay the $1272 to join showbiz society. See you in the movies!

CINEMA

Countless theaters show films the way they were meant to be seen: in a big space, on a big screen, with top-quality sound. It would be a cinematic crime not to take advantage of the incredible experience that is movie-going in L.A. If you'd like to ogle the stars as they walk the red carpet into the theater for a **premiere,** call the four premiere-hounds: **Grauman's Chinese** (about 2 per month); **El Capitan** (Disney films only); **Mann's Westwood;** and the **Bruin,** 948 Broxton Ave. (☎310-248-6266), in Westwood. For info on what's playing in L.A., call ☎323-777-3456, or read the daily Calendar section of the *Los Angeles Times*.

MUSIC

L.A.'s music venues range from small clubs to massive amphitheaters. The **Wiltern Theater** (☎213-380-5005) shows alterna-rock/folk acts. The **Hollywood Palladium** (☎323-962-7600) is of comparable size, with 3500 seats. Mid-size acts head for the **Universal Amphitheater** (☎818-777-3931). Huge indoor sports arenas, such as the **Great Western Forum** (☎310-330-7300) and the newer **Staples Center** (☎213-742-7100), double as concert halls for big acts. Few dare to play at the 100,000-seat **Los Angeles Memorial Coliseum and Sports Arena**—only U2, Depeche Mode, Guns 'n' Roses, and the Warped Tour have filled the stands in past years. Call Ticketmaster ☎213-480-3232 for tickets for any of these venues. The spectacular outdoor amphitheater ▣**Hollywood Bowl,** 2301 N. Highland Ave. (☎323-850-2000), in Hollywood, is the home of the **L.A. Philharmonic.** The **Music Center,** 135 N. Grand Ave. (☎213-972-7211), at 1st St. downtown, includes the Mark Taper Forum, the Dorothy Chandler Pavilion, and the Ahmanson Theatre; in the fall of 2003, the Gehry-designed Walt Disney Concert Hall will also open. Performance spaces host the L.A. Opera, Broadway and experimental theater, and dance.

SHOPPING

In L.A., shopping isn't just a practical necessity; it's a way of life. Popular shopping areas like Santa Monica's Third Street Promenade, Pasadena's Old Town, the Westside Pavilion, and the Century City Mall are lined with identical chain boutiques with the latest cookie-cutter fashions. Nevertheless, a number of cool specialty shops with more one-of-a-kind items are tucked away from the shuffle. ▣**Book Soup,** 8818 Sunset Blvd., in West Hollywood, has a maze of new books in every category imaginable, with especially strong film, architecture, poetry, and travel sections. (☎310-659-3110. Open daily 9am-midnight.) **Moby Disc,** 2114

Wilshire Blvd., in Santa Monica, is the great white whale of used CD stores, where the odds for good finds are in your favor. (☎310-828-2887. Open daily 11am-8pm.) **Aaardvark's**, 7579 Melrose Ave., in West Hollywood, has used gear galore, from practical used Levi's ($20-25) to fabulously funky wigs. (☎323-655-6769. Open M-Th noon-8pm, F-Sa 11am-9pm, Su noon-7pm.) Cartoonist Jay Ward's old production office is now the cluttered ◪**Dudley Do-Right Emporium**, 8200 Sunset Blvd., in West Hollywood, with memorabilia based on his characters, *Rocky and Bullwinkle*, *George of the Jungle*, and *Dudley Do-Right*. (☎323-656-6550. Open Tu, Th, and Sa 11am-5pm.)

SPORTS

Exposition Park and the often dangerous city of **Inglewood**, southwest of the park, are home to many sports teams. The **USC Trojans** football team plays at the **Los Angeles Memorial Coliseum**, 3939 S. Figueroa St. (tickets ☎213-740-4672), at Martin Luther King Blvd., which seats over 100,000 spectators. It is the only stadium in the world to have the honor of hosting the Olympic Games twice. Basketball's doormat, the **Clippers** (☎213-742-7500), and the star-studded 2002 NBA Champion **Lakers** (☎310-426-6031; tickets from $23) both play at the new **Staples Center**, 1111 S. Figueroa St. (☎213-742-7100; box office 213-742-7300). They share the venue with the **Kings** hockey team (☎888-546-4752; tickets from $20) and the impressive **Sparks** women's basketball team (☎310-330-3939; tickets from $5). Tickets for these games are in high demand. For tickets, call Ticketmaster ☎213-480-3232.

Elysian Park, about 3 mi. northeast of downtown, curves around the northern part of Chavez Ravine, and is the home of **Dodger Stadium** and the popular **Dodgers** baseball team. Single-game tickets are a hot commodity during the April-October season, especially if the Dodgers are playing well. (☎323-224-1448. $6-21.)

FESTIVALS

New Year's Day is always a perfect day in Southern California, or so the **Tournament of Roses Parade and Rose Bowl** (☎626-449-7673), in Pasadena, would have it. Some of the wildest New Year's Eve parties happen along **Colorado Blvd.**, the parade route. **UCLA Mardi Gras** (☎310-825-8001), held at the athletic field, is billed as the world's largest collegiate activity. The **Chinese New Year Parade** (☎213-617-0396), in Chinatown, has fireworks and dragons to usher in this Chinese celebration. During the **Gay Pride Celebration**, L.A.'s lesbian and gay communities celebrate in full effect with art, politics, dances, and a big parade. (☎323-969-8302. Last or second-to-last weekend in June. Tickets $12.) ◪**El Día de los Muertos** is a rousing Mexican celebration for the spirits of dead ancestors revisiting the world of the living. (Nov. 1, along Olvera St., downtown.) The **Playboy Jazz Festival** (☎310-449-4070), at the Hollywood Bowl, means two days of entertainment by top-name jazz musicians of all varieties, from traditional to fusion. Sorry, no bunnies.

◪ NIGHTLIFE

L.A. clubs range from tiny danceterias and ephemeral warehouse raves to exclusive lounges catering to showbiz elite. The hub of L.A. nightlife is the **Sunset Strip** along Sunset Blvd. in West Hollywood.

LATE-NIGHT RESTAURANTS

Given the unreliability of the L.A. club scene and the short shelf-life of cafes, late-night restaurants have become reliable hangouts. The mainstay of L.A. nightlife, they're the place where underage club kids come trolling among the token celebs.

HOLLYWOOD CANTEENS
Where the famous stars boozed, binged, and blacked out

Bogart. Sinatra. Hepburn. Gable. Monroe. The greatest livers of a generation were destroyed here. Those who say L.A. has no sense of history need look no further than the bottom of their cocktail glass at these venerable (and still standing) Old Hollywood bars. Here's looking at you, kid!

Barney's Beanery, 8447 Santa Monica Blvd. (☎323-654-2287), in West Hollywood. Some like it hot—especially Marilyn Monroe. While filming the picture of the same name, she'd drop at this rough-and-tumble Rte. 66 roadhouse for chili. Janis Joplin partied here the night she died. Happy hour M-F 4-7pm. Open daily 11am-2am.

Chez Jay, 1657 Ocean Ave. (☎310-395-1741), in Santa Monica. A tiny, crusty beachside dive festooned with Christmas lights, red check tablecloths, and pictures of Sinatra. Why not? Ol' Blue Eyes dented the red vinyl here regularly in his day. Open M-F 6pm-2am, Sa-Su 5:30pm-2am.

Coach & Horses Pub, 7617 W. Sunset Blvd. (☎323-876-6900), in Hollywood. A dark, tiny ye olde hole in the wall where Richard Burton used to start his benders. If you feel like following suit, start early on a weekday. On F and Sa nights the hipsters invade, armed with apple martinis and leather pants. Open M-Sa 11am-2am, Su 5pm-2am.

The Gallery Bar at the Biltmore Hotel, 506 S. Grand Ave. (☎213-612-1532), in Downtown L.A. Glide into wood-paneled elegance, sip a martini, and wonder what really happened to the Black Dahlia. This was, after all, the last place aspiring starlet Beth Short (nicknamed for her pin-up quality black dresses) was seen alive. Back in 1947, a doorman tipped his cap to her and five days later, her severed body made her the most famous victim of an unsolved murder case in city history. Open daily 4:30pm-1:45am.

Formosa Cafe, 7156 Santa Monica Blvd. (☎323-850-9050), in Hollywood. This Suzy Wong boîte is equal parts black lacquer and 8"x10" glossies. The more than 250 star headshots plastering the walls are rumored to have been dropped off in person. Cozy up in a booth like Lana Turner used to and drink all you want, but avoid the greasy "Chinese" food. Open M-F 4pm-2am, Sa-Su 6pm-2am.

Musso & Frank Grill, 6667 Hollywood Blvd. (☎323-467-7788), in Hollywood. Where Bogie boozed, Sinatra swilled, and Bukowski blew his cash. The drinks ain't cheap, but oh, what ambience! Honeyed light, high-backed booths, and curmudgeonly red-jacketed waiters. The martini is hands-down the city's best. Raymond Chandler immortalized Musso's gin and lime juice drink in "The Long Goodbye." Open Tu-Sa 11am-10:45pm.

The Polo Lounge at the Beverly Hills Hotel, 9641 Sunset Blvd. (☎310-276-2251), in Beverly Hills. Ask to be seated in the patio section, order up a Singapore Sling, and dream about the days when Kate Hepburn and Marlene Dietrich held court here. Come F mornings and see why this place coined the term "power breakfast"—tables on the outer edge of the terrace are a classic place for movie deals to be struck. Open daily 7am-1am.

Trader Vic's at the Beverly Hilton Hotel, 9876 Wilshire Blvd. (☎310-274-7777), in Beverly Hills. A dim, linen tablecloth tiki bar that George Hamilton allegedly singled out as a great place for celebrity affairs owing to its two entrances. The house cocktails' $10 price tags are more than made up for in presentation—the pina colada comes in a whole pineapple; a gardenia graces the scorpion bowl. Open Su-Th 5pm-2am, F-Sa 5pm-1am.

Stephanie L. Smith was a researcher-writer for Let's Go: California 1997 *and* New Zealand 1998. *She worked as a freelancer for CitySearch Los Angeles, reviewing restaurants, bars, and attractions, and is now working in Hollywood as the features editor/writer for the online division of Channel One News.*

Canter's, 419 N. Fairfax Ave. (☎323-651-2030), in Fairfax. An L.A. institution, this deli has been the heart and soul of the historically Jewish Fairfax community since 1931. Grapefruit-sized matzoh ball in chicken broth is the best ever ($4.50). Giant sandwiches $8-9. Visit the Kibbitz Room nightly for live rock, blues, jazz, and cabaret-pop (from 9pm). Cheap beer ($1.50). Open 24hr.

Fred 62, 1850 N. Vermont Ave. (☎323-667-0062), in Los Feliz. "Eat now, dine later." Headrests and toasters at every booth. Hip, edgy East L.A. crowd's jukebox selections rock the house. The waffles ($4.62—all prices end in .62) are divine. Open 24hr.

The Rainbow Grill, 9015 Sunset Blvd. (☎310-278-4232), in West Hollywood, next to the Roxy. Dark red vinyl booths, dim lighting, and loud music set the scene. An insane rainbow of guests play their parts. Marilyn Monroe met Joe DiMaggio on a blind date here. Brooklyn-quality pizza $6; calamari $8; grandma's chicken soup $3.50. Open M-F 11am-2am, Sa-Su 5pm-2am.

COFFEEHOUSES

In a city where no one eats very much for fear of rounding out that bony figure, espresso, coffee, and air are vital dining options.

Un Urban Coffeehouse, 3301 Pico Blvd. (☎310-315-0056), in Santa Monica. 3 separate rooms of campy voodoo candles, Mexican wrestling masks, musty books, and leopard-print couches. Iced mocha blends $3.50, Italian sodas $2. Open mic comedy Th 7:30pm, open mic songwriters F 8pm, music showcase Sa 7pm. Sign-up for open mic ½hr. before. No cover. Open M-Th 7am-midnight, F 7am-1am, Sa 8am-1am, Su 8am-7pm.

Cow's End, 34 Washington Blvd. (☎310-574-1080), in Venice. With its asymmetrical whole-pane windows, uneven brick floor, and scantily clad beach patrons, the Cow's End is riotously popular. Sandwiches from $5.50. Smoothies from $3.75. Live music F 8pm. Open daily 6am-midnight.

COMEDY CLUBS

L.A.'s comedy clubs are the best in the world, unless you happen to chance upon an amateur night, which is generally a painful experience.

L.A. Improv, 8162 Melrose Ave. (☎213-651-2583), in West Hollywood. L.A.'s best talent, like Robin Williams and Jerry Seinfeld, have shown their faces here; Drew Carey and Ryan Stiles often join the show. Dinner at the restaurant (entrees $6-14) includes priority seating for the show. 18+. Cover $10-15. 2-drink min. Shows Su-Th 8pm, F-Sa 8:30 and 10:30pm. Bar open daily until 1:30am. Reservations recommended.

Groundling Theater, 7307 Melrose Ave. (☎323-934-9700), in Hollywood. The best improv and comedy "forum" in town. The Groundling's alums include Pee Wee Herman and many current and former *Saturday Night Live* regulars like Will Farrell, Cheri Oteri, and Chris Kattan. Don't be surprised to see *SNL* producer Lorne Michaels sitting in the back. Lisa Kudrow of *Friends* got her start here, too. Mostly polished skits. Cover $7-18.50. Shows Tu and Th 8pm, F-Sa 8 and 10pm, Su 7:30pm.

BARS

While the 1996 film *Swingers* may not have transformed every bar into The 3 of Clubs, it has had a sadly homogenizing effect on L.A.'s hipsters. Grab your retro-shirts, sunglasses, and Cadillac convertibles, 'cause if you can't beat them, you have to swing with them, daddy-o. Unless otherwise specified, bars are 21+.

Beauty Bar, 1638 Cahuenga Blvd. (☎323-464-7676), in Hollywood. A combination bar and beauty parlor. It's like getting ready for the prom all over again, except that the drinking starts before rather than after. Drinks like "Shampoo" are $5-7. Smoking room with hair-setting seats. Manicures, "up 'dos," and henna tattoos Th-Sa nights with a specialty drink ($10). DJ nightly at 10pm. Open Su-W 9pm-2am, Th-F 6pm-2am, Sa 8pm-2am.

▧ **Miyagi's,** 8225 Sunset Blvd. (☎323-656-0100), on Sunset Strip. With 3 levels, 5 sushi bars, and 7 liquor bars, this Japanese-themed restaurant, bar, and lounge is the latest Strip hot spot. *"Sake* bomb, *sake* bomb, *sake* bomb" $4.50. Open daily 5:30pm-2am.

The 3 of Clubs, 1123 N. Vine St. (☎323-462-6441), in Hollywood. In a small strip mall beneath a "Bargain Clown Mart" sign, this simple, classy, spacious, hardwood bar is famous for appearing in 1996's *Swingers.* DJ F-Sa, live bands Th. Open daily 7pm-2am.

The Room, 1626 Cahuenga St. (☎323-462-7196), in Hollywood. A speakeasy that empties into an alley, the very popular Room almost trumps The 3 of Clubs. No advertising, no sign on the door. 2nd location in Santa Monica at 14th St. and Santa Monica Blvd. Open daily 8pm-2am.

CLUBS

L.A. is famous, even infamous, for its club scene. With the highest number of bands per capita in the world, most clubs book top-notch acts night after night. These clubs can be the hottest thing in L.A. one month and extinct the next, so check the *L.A. Weekly* (free everywhere) before venturing out.

▧ **Largo,** 432 N. Fairfax Ave. (☎323-852-1073), in West Hollywood. Elegant and intimate sit-down (or, if you get there late, lean-back) club. Original rock, pop, and folk sounds along with comedy acts. Cover $2-12. Open M-Sa 8:30pm-2am.

▧ **Derby,** 4500 Los Feliz Blvd. (☎323-663-8979), in Hollywood. The concept of the Derby was conceived by Cecil B. DeMille in the 1920s. Today this joint is still jumpin' with the kings of swing. Ladies, grab your snoods, because many dress the 40s part. Choice Italian fare from Louise's Trattoria next door. Full bar. Free Lindy Hop and East Coast swing lessons Sa 7:30pm. Cover $5-10. Open daily 7pm-2am.

Roxy, 9009 Sunset Blvd. (☎310-278-9457, box office 310-276-2222), on Sunset Strip. Known as the "Sizzling Showcase," it's one of the best-known Sunset Strip clubs. Bruce Springsteen got his start here. Live rock, blues, alternative, and occasional hip-hop. Many big tour acts. All ages. Cover varies. Opens at 8pm.

Whisky A Go-Go, 8901 Sunset Blvd. (☎310-652-4205), in West Hollywood. Historically, this is the great prophet of L.A.'s music scene. It hosted progressive bands in the late 70s and early 80s, and was big in the punk explosion. The Doors, Janis Joplin, and Led Zeppelin all played here. All ages. Cover M-Th $10, F-Su $12-15. 5-6 hard rock/alternative bands play F-Su 8pm-2am. Shows begin after 8pm.

GAY & LESBIAN NIGHTLIFE

Many ostensibly straight clubs have gay nights. Check the *L.A. Weekly* for more listings or the free weekly magazine *fab!* Gay and lesbian nightlife centers around **Santa Monica Blvd.** in West Hollywood.

▧ **Abbey Cafe,** 692 N. Robertson Blvd. (☎310-289-8410), in West Hollywood, at Santa Monica Blvd. This cafe becomes a lounge, bar, and dance club as the moon rises. Impeccable service, tasteful decor. Open daily noon-2am.

Micky's, 8857 Santa Monica Blvd. (☎310-657-1176), in West Hollywood. Large, popular spot filled with delectable men. Music is mostly Top 40 dance. Serves lunch M-Sa 11am-3pm and hot go-go boys Tu-F and Su. "Cocktails with the stars" (many of them porno stars) Th 6-8:30pm. Happy hour M-F 5-9pm. Cover $3-5. Open daily 11am-2am.

Rage, 8911 Santa Monica Blvd. (☎310-652-7055), in West Hollywood. Its glory days have passed, but this institution rages on with nightly DJs till you drop. Mostly gay men; some lesbians during the day. Full lunch and dinner menu served daily noon-9pm. Happy hour (beer $2) M-F 2-8pm. Th 18+. Open daily noon-2am.

◢ BEACHES

South Bay life is beach life. **Hermosa Beach** wins both bathing suit and congeniality competitions, with a slammin' volleyball scene, gnarly waves, and killer boardwalk. The mellower **Manhattan Beach** exudes a yuppified charm, while **Redondo Beach** is by far the most commercially suburban. Ritzy **Rancho Palos Verdes** is a coast of a different breed.

Malibu's public beaches are cleaner and less crowded than any others in L.A. County, and as a whole offer better surfing. Surf's up at **Surfrider Beach,** a section of Malibu Laguna State Beach located north of the pier at 23000 PCH. You can walk onto the beach via the **Zonker Harris** access way (named after the beach-obsessed Doonesbury character), at 22700 PCH. **Malibu Ocean Sports,** 22935 PCH, across from the pier, rents surfboards ($10 per hr., $25 per day), kayaks (single $15/35; double $20/50), boogie boards ($12 per day), and wetsuits ($10 per day), and also offers surfing lessons ($100 for 2hr. lesson and full-day gear) and tours. (☎310-456-6302. Open daily 9am-7pm.)

Corral State Beach, a remote windsurfing, swimming, and scuba-diving haven, lies on the 26000 block of PCH, followed by **Point Dume State Beach,** which is larger and generally uncrowded, and has better currents for scuba diving. Along the 30000 block of PCH lies **Zuma,** L.A. County's northernmost, largest, and most user-friendly county-owned sandbox. Sections 6-8 are popular with local kids; sections 9-11 are less populated. Swimmers should only dive near lifeguard stations; because of the devastating **riptide,** rescue counts are high. Free street parking is highly coveted, so expect to park in the beach lot ($6, off-peak $2). Just south of Zuma, before Point Dume, is a clothing-optional strip nicknamed **Pirate's Cove.**

ORANGE COUNTY ☎714

Directly south of L.A. County is Orange County. It is a microcosm of Southern California: dazzling stretches of sandy shoreline, bronzed beach bums, endless strip malls, frustrating traffic snarls, and the stronghold of the late Walt Disney's cultural empire. The "Happiest Place on Earth," Disneyland is the premier inland attraction. The amazing beaches run the gamut from the budget- and party-friendly Huntington Beach to the opulent Newport Beach.

◪ PRACTICAL INFORMATION

Airport: John Wayne Orange County, 18601 Airport Way, Santa Ana (☎949-252-5006), 20min. from Anaheim. Newer, cleaner, and easier to get around than the L.A. Airport. Domestic flights only.

Trains: Amtrak. Stations (from north to south): **Fullerton,** 120 E. Santa Fe Ave. (☎714-992-0530); **Anaheim,** 2150 E. Katella Blvd. (☎714-385-1448); **Santa Ana,** 1000 E. Santa Ana Blvd. (☎714-547-8389); **Irvine,** 15215 Barranca Pkwy. (☎949-753-9713); and **San Juan Capistrano,** 26701 Verdugo St. (☎949-240-2972).

Buses: Greyhound (☎800-231-2222) has 3 stations in the area: **Anaheim,** 100 W. Winston Rd., 3 blocks south of Disneyland (☎714-999-1256; station open daily 6:30am-9pm); **Santa Ana,** 1000 E. Santa Ana Blvd. (☎714-542-2215; open daily 6am-8:30pm); and **San Clemente,** 2421 S. El Camino Real (☎949-366-2646; open daily 7am-8:30pm).

Public Transit: Orange County Transportation Authority (OCTA), 550 S. Main St., Orange. Long Beach, in L.A. County, serves as the terminus for several OCTA lines. Bus #1 travels the coast from Long Beach to San Clemente every hr. until 8pm. Buses #25, 33, and 35 travel from Fullerton to Huntington Beach; #91 goes from Laguna Hills to

Dana Point. (☎714-636-7433. $1, day pass $2.50.) **Info center** open M-F 6am-8pm, Sa-Su 8am-5pm.

Anaheim Area Visitors and Convention Bureau, 800 W. Katella Ave. (☎714-765-8888), in Anaheim Convention Ctr. Lodging and dining guides. Open M-F 8am-5pm.

Medical Services: St. Jude Medical Center, 101 E. Valencia Mesa Dr., Fullerton (☎714-871-3280). **Lestonnac Free Clinic,** 1215 E. Chapman Ave., Orange (☎714-633-4600). Open Tu-F 9am-5pm.

Post Office: 701 N. Loara St., Anaheim (☎800-275-8777), 1 block north of Anaheim Plaza. Open M-F 8:30am-5pm, Sa 9am-3pm. **ZIP Code:** 92803. **Area Code:** 714 (Anaheim, Fullerton, Fountain Valley, Santa Ana, Orange, Garden Grove), 949 (Newport, Laguna, Irvine, Misssion Viejo, San Juan Capistrano), 310 (Seal Beach). In text 714, unless otherwise noted.

▐ ACCOMMODATIONS

The Magic Kingdom is the sun around which the Anaheim solar system revolves, so budget motels and garden-variety "clean, comfortable rooms" flank it on all sides. Keep watch for family and group rates posted on marquees and seek out establishments offering the three-for-two passport (3 days of Disney for the price of 2). Orange County's beach communities have a few excellent hostels.

▨ **Huntington Beach Colonial Inn Youth Hostel,** 421 8th St. (☎536-9206), in Huntington Beach, 4 blocks inland at Pecan Ave. Take #29 or 50. International passport required; US college IDs accepted on space-available basis. This large, early 20th-century yellow and blue house was once a brothel. Things have quieted down since the neighbors moved in—quiet hours after 11pm. Common bath, large kitchen, reading/TV room, laundry, Internet access, deck, and surfboard shed. Linen and breakfast included. Key deposit $20. Americans 1-week max. stay. Check-in 7am-11pm. No lockout. Reserve 2 days in advance for summer weekends. 3-4 person dorms $22; doubles $50. ❶

Fullerton (HI-AYH), 1700 N. Harbor Blvd. (☎738-3721), in Fullerton. Shuttle from L.A. airport $21. OCTA bus #43 runs along Harbor Blvd. to Disneyland. In the woods and away from the thematic craziness of nearby Anaheim. Enthusiastic, resourceful staff. No alcohol. Kitchen, Internet access, relaxing living room, communal bathrooms. Linen $2. Free laundry. 7-night max. stay. Check-in 8-11am and 4-11pm. Reservations encouraged. Open June-Sept. Dorms $16.50, nonmembers $19.50. ❶

Balboa Inn, 105 Main St. (☎949-675-3412), on the sand at Newport. This recently renovated historical landmark offers rooms with ocean or bay views and is only a short drive from area attractions. Relax in the pool or jacuzzi. Continental breakfast and room service offered. Rooms from $119. ❺

▐ FOOD

Inexpensive ethnic restaurants in strip malls and along beaches allow escape from fast food. Many specialize in take-out or will deliver chow to your motel room.

▨ **Rutabegorz,** 211 N. Pomona Blvd. (☎738-9339), in Fullerton. This hippie-cum-hipster joint supplies a 20-page menu (printed on recycled newsprint, of course). Crepes, curries, quesadillas, and club sandwiches are all fresh and veggie-licious. Heaping salads with homemade dressings $4-9. Mexican casserole $7. Smoothies, veggie juices, and coffee drinks $1.50-4. Open M-Th 11am-10pm, F-Sa 11am-11pm, Su 4-9pm. ❷

Angelo & Vinci's Cafe Ristorante, 550 N. Harbor Blvd. (☎879-4022), in Fullerton. Prepare for opera—arias, masks, even "backstage dining." Padded red chairs, iron-rod table lamps, and indoor awnings are all part of the Sicilian motif. The food is unmistakably the stuff of family recipes (Cannelloni Vinci $10.75), with more than enough to feed the family at the lunch buffet ($6). Su champagne brunch ($9) 11am-3pm. Open Su-Th 11am-9:45pm, F-Sa 11am-11:45pm. ❸

Laguna Village Market and Cafe, 577 S. Coast Hwy. (☎949-494-6344), in Laguna Beach. Housed in an open-air gazebo, but the oceanfront terrace is the main draw. Lap up the view, along with some seafood or the house specialty Village Huevos ($9.50). Calamari plate $9. After your meal, check out local art in the surrounding gazebo. If you want a toe-ring, this is the place. Open daily 8:30am-dark. ❸

◉ SIGHTS

DISNEYLAND. Disneyland calls itself the "Happiest Place on Earth," and there is an oh-so-smiley part of every pop culture pilgrim that agrees. Stroll through Main-town, USA, visit the castle in Fantasyland, get your kicks in Adventureland, eat in New Orleans Square, take a riverboat in Frontierland, ride Splash Mountain in Critter Country, visit the gang in Mickey's Toontown, witness the future in Tomor-rowland, and visit a mini-California in **California Adventure.** Weekday and off-season visitors are rewarded with smaller crowds, but the enterprising can take advantage of the new FastPass system or wait for parades, leaving shorter lines. *Disneyland Today!* lists parade and show times. *(Main entrance on Harbor Blvd. and a smaller one on Katella Ave. ☎ 781-4565. From L.A., MTA bus #460 travels from 4th and Flower St.; service begins at 4:53am, service back to L.A. until 1:20am. Parking in the morning is easy, but leaving in the evening is not. Disneyland open Su-Th 8am-11pm. F-Sa 8am-midnight. Hours may vary; call ahead. $43, ages 3-9 $33. Under 3 free. California Adventure open Su-Th 9am-10pm, F-Sa 9am-10:30pm. $43/33. Under 3 free. Combination tickets available.)*

K(NOT)T DISNEYLAND. Buena Park offers a cavalcade of non-Disney diversions, some of which are better than others. **Knott's Berry Farm** proudly holds the title for first theme park in America; it's the birthplace of the boysenberry, too. *(8039 Beach Blvd. at La Palma Ave., 5 mi. northeast of Disneyland. From L.A., take the I-5 S to Beach Blvd.; turn right at the end of the exit ramp and proceed south 2 mi. ☎714-220-5220. Open Su-Th 9am-10pm, F-Sa 9am-midnight. Hours may vary; call ahead. $38, seniors and ages 3-11 $28, under 3 free; after 4pm all ages $17. Summer discounts available. Parking $8.)*

SPORTS. For more evidence of Disney's strong presence in Anaheim, catch a game by one of the teams they own: the major league **Anaheim Angels** play baseball from early April to October at **Edison Field.** *(☎940-2000 or 800-626-4357. General tickets $6-25.)* To check out some NHL action catch a **Mighty Ducks** hockey game at **Arrowhead Pond.** *(2965 E. Katella Ave. ☎877-945-3946.)*

◉ BEACHES

The various beach communities of Orange County have cleaner sand and better surf than their L.A. county counterparts. **Huntington Beach** was an epicenter of the legendary surfing craze that transformed California coast life in the early 1900s. **Newport Beach** is the Beverly Hills of beach towns, though the beach itself displays few signs of ostentatious wealth; it is crowded with young, rowdy hedonists cloaked in neon. Nearby **Balboa Peninsula** can be reached by Rte. 1.

Laguna Beach, 4 mi. south of Newport, is between canyons. Back in the day, Laguna was a bohemian artists' colony, but no properly starving artists can afford to live here now. The surviving galleries and art supply stores nevertheless add a unique twist to the standard SoCal beach culture that thrives on Laguna's sands. **Main Beach** and the shops nearby along Ocean Ave. are the prime parading areas, though there are less crowded spots as well. One accessible beach is **Westry Beach,**

which spreads out south of Laguna just below **Aliso Beach Park**. More tourists than swallows return each year to **Mission San Juan Capistrano**, 30min. south of Anaheim on I-5. The most beautiful of the area's missions, it is still in use today. Thousands of birds migrate between here and Central and South America each year, arriving in mid-March. (☎949-248-2048. Open daily 8:30am-5pm. $6, seniors $5, ages 3-12 $4.)

BIG BEAR   ☎909

Hibernating in the San Bernardino Mountains, Big Bear Lake draws hordes with fluffy winter skiing and stellar summer hiking, biking, and boating. Also, the consistent winds make for some of the best sailing in the state. Prices are somewhat high in Big Bear and increase when there is enough snow for skiing—usually mid-November to mid-April—so you'll have to just grin and bear it.

Hiking maps, trail descriptions, and the *Visitor's Guide to the San Bernardino National Forest* are available at **Big Bear Discovery Center** or **BBDC**, on Rte. 38 4 mi. east of Fawnskin and 1¼ mi. west of the Stanfield Cutoff. BBDC also sells the **National Forest Adventure Pass** ($5), which is required for vehicles at camping sites that charge no additional fee. (☎866-3437. Open Apr.-Sept. daily 8am-6pm; Oct.-Mar. daily 9am-5pm.) The **Woodland Trail** or the more challenging **Pineknot Trail** offer views of the lake. High altitudes here make slow climbing necessary.

Mountain biking is popular in Big Bear when the snow melts. Grab the *Ride and Trail Guide* at the Discovery Center and at **Snow Summit**, 1 mi. west of Big Bear Lake, which runs lifts in summer so that adrenaline monsters can grind serious downhill terrain. (☎866-4621. $10 per ride, day pass $20; ages 7-12 $5/10. Helmet required. Open M-F 9am-4pm, Sa 8am-5pm, Su 9am-5pm.) Those without wheels of their own can rent them from **Team Big Bear**, 476 Concklin Rd., operating out of the **Mountain Bike Shop** at the base of Snow Summit. (☎866-4565. $9 per hr., $27 for 4hr., $50 per day; helmet included. Many summer activities take place on the water. **Fishing licenses** are available at area sporting goods stores ($10 per day, $28 per season). **Boats** can be rented at any one of Big Bear's marinas, including **Holloway's Marina and RV Park**, 398 Edgemor Rd., on the south shore. (☎800-448-5335. Full day $50-175.)

When conditions are favorable, ski areas run out of lift tickets quickly. **Big Bear Resort**, 1½ mi. southeast of downtown Big Bear Lake, has 12 lifts covering 195 acres of terrain, including huge vertical drops, plus many more acres of undeveloped land for adventurous skiers. (☎585-2519. Lift tickets $39, holidays $49. Ski rentals $23, snowboards $30.)

Big Bear has few budget accommodations, especially in the winter. The best option for daytrippers is probably to stay in Redlands or San Bernardino, although the drive down Rte. 18 can be difficult at night. **Big Bear Blvd.**, the main drag on the lake's south shore, is lined with lodging possibilities. **Mountain Lodging Unlimited** arranges lodging and lift packages. (☎800-487-3168. Packages from $100 per couple. Open in ski season 7am-midnight; off-season 9am-midnight.) **Hillcrest Lodge**, 40241 Big Bear Blvd., is a favorite for honeymooners. Pine paneling and skylights give these cozy rooms a ritzy feel at a budget price. (☎800-843-4449. Jacuzzi, cable TV, and free local calls. In winter, small rooms $48-79; 4-person suites $79-139. In summer, small rooms $48-70; 4-person units with kitchen $90-140; 2-bedroom suites with hearth and kitchen $100-150.) Popular with mountain bikers, **Pineknot**, at the base of Snow Summit south of Big Bear, has 52 isolated sites with flush toilets and water. (☎877-444-6777. $18.) Groceries can be procured at **Stater Bros.**, 42171 Big Bear Blvd. (☎866-5211. Open daily 7am-11pm.)

To reach Big Bear Lake, take the San Bernardino Fwy. (I-10) to the junction of Rte. 30 and 330. Follow Rte. 330, also known as Mountain Rd., to Rte. 18, a *very* long and winding uphill road that becomes Big Bear Blvd., the main route encir-

C A L I F O R N I A

cling the lake. **Mountain Area Regional Transit Authority (MARTA)** runs two buses per day from the Greyhound station in San Bernardino to Big Bear. (☎584-1111. $5, seniors and disabled $3.75.) Buses also run the length of Big Bear Blvd. (End-to-end trip 1hr.; $1, students 75¢, seniors and disabled 50¢.) MARTA operates **Dial-A-Ride.** ($2, students $1.50, seniors $1.)

SAN DIEGO ☎619

San Diegans are fond of referring to their garden-like town as "America's Finest City." This claim is difficult to dispute—San Diego has all the virtues of other California cities without their frequently cited drawbacks. No smog fills this city's air, and no sewage spoils its silver seashores. Its zoo is the nation's best, and its city center contains a greater concentration of museums than any spot in America except Washington, D.C. The city was founded when the seafaring Spanish forayed onshore in 1769, but it didn't become a city proper until the 1940s, when it became the headquarters of the US Pacific Fleet after the Pearl Harbor attack.

▀ TRANSPORTATION

San Diego rests in the extreme southwest corner of California. **I-5** runs south from L.A. and skirts the eastern edge of downtown; **I-15** runs northeast to Nevada; and **I-8** runs east-west along downtown's northern boundary, connecting the desert with Ocean Beach. The major downtown thoroughfare, **Broadway,** also runs east-west.

Airport: San Diego International (Lindbergh Field), at the northwest edge of downtown. For info, call the Travelers Aid Society (☎231-7361) daily 8am-11pm. Take bus #2 to get downtown ($2). Taxis to downtown $8.

Trains: Amtrak, 1050 Kettner Blvd. (☎239-9021), just north of Broadway in the Santa Fe Depot. To **L.A.** (2¾hr., 10 per day, $27). Station has info on bus, trolley, car, and boat transportation. Ticket office open daily 5:15am-10:20pm.

Buses: Greyhound, 120 W. Broadway (☎239-8082), at 1st St. To **L.A.** (2½-3½hr., 30 per day, $15) and **Tijuana** (1hr., 16 per day, $5). Ticket office open 24hr.

Public Transit: San Diego Metropolitan Transit System (MTS; ☎685-4900) has info on buses, trains, and trolleys. The **Transit Store,** at 1st Ave. and Broadway, has tickets and schedules. Open M-F 8:30am-5:30pm, Sa-Su noon-4pm. The **Day Tripper** allows unlimited rides on buses, ferries, and trolleys for 1 day ($5), 2 days ($8), 3 days ($10), or 4 days ($12).

Bike Info: Rent bikes from **Action Sports,** 4000 Coronado Bay Rd. (☎424-4466), at the Marina Dock of the Loews Coronado Bay Resort. Open M-F 9am-6pm, Sa-Su 8:30am-6:30pm. Beach cruisers and mountain bikes $10 per hr., $30 per 4hr.

◼◪ ORIENTATION & PRACTICAL INFORMATION

In northeast downtown sits **Balboa Park,** home to many museums and to the justly heralded San Diego Zoo. The cosmopolitan **Hillcrest** and **University Heights** districts, both centers of the gay community, border the park to the northeast. South of downtown, between 4th and 6th St., is the **Gaslamp District,** full of nightclubs, chic restaurants, and coffeehouses. **Downtown** is situated between San Diego's two major bays: **San Diego Bay,** formed by **Coronado Island,** lies just to the south, while **Mission Bay,** formed by the **Mission Beach** spit, lies to the northwest. Up the coast from Mission Beach are **Ocean Beach, Pacific Beach,** and wealthy **La Jolla.**

Visitor info: International Visitor Information Center, 11 Horton Plaza (☎236-1212), downtown at 1st Ave. and F St. Open June-Aug. M-Sa 8:30am-5pm, Su 11am-5pm; Sept.-May M-Sa 8:30am-5pm. **San Diego Convention and Visitors Bureau,** 401 B St.,

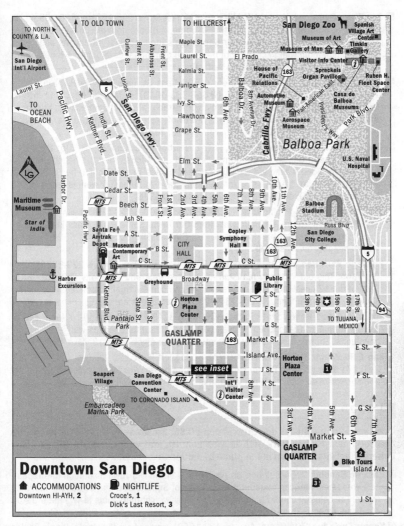

Downtown San Diego

♦ ACCOMMODATIONS
Downtown HI-AYH, **2**

🏮 NIGHTLIFE
Croce's, **1**
Dick's Last Resort, **3**

#1400, Dept. 700, San Diego 92101 (☎236-1212; www.sandiego.org). **Old Town and State Park Info,** 4002 Wallace Ave. (☎220-5422), in Old Town Sq., offers free walking tours daily noon and 2pm. Open daily 10am-5pm.

Post Office: 2535 Midway Dr. (☎800-275-8777). Take bus #6, 9, or 35. Open M 7am-5pm, Tu-F 8am-5pm, Sa 8am-4pm. **ZIP Code:** 92186. **Area Code:** 619.

🏠 ACCOMMODATIONS

San Diego offers a variety of accommodations, but rates predictably rise on weekends and during the summer season. Reservations are recommended. There is a popular cluster known as **Hotel Circle** (2-3 mi. east of **I-5** along **I-8**). Those with cars and tents can camp on the beaches outside of the city.

San Diego Downtown Hostel (HI-AYH), 521 Market St. (☎525-1531 or 800-909-4776, ext. 43), at 5th Ave., in the heart of the Gaslamp, 5 blocks from the Convention Center. Quiet, impeccably clean hostel near San Diego's most popular attractions and clubs. Airy common room with kitchen, pool table, and communal bathrooms. 4-6 bed dorms $20, nonmembers $23; doubles $45-50. ●

International House at the 2nd Floor, 4502 Cass St. (☎858-274-4325) in Pacific Beach and 3204 Mission Bay Blvd. (☎858-539-0043), in Mission Beach. Both offer excellent service, clean and bright rooms, comfortable beds, Internet access, breakfast, and great locations. 28-day max. stay. Out-of-state ID or international passport required. Dorm rooms $20, students with ID $18; $110 per week. ●

Ocean Beach International (OBI), 4961 Newport Ave. (☎223-7873 or 800-339-7263), in Ocean Beach. Clean rooms, cable TV and kitchen near the beach. Pancake breakfast included. Laundry. Free BBQ and keg parties Tu and F night; free pasta Tu in winter. 29-day max. stay. Proof of international travel in the last 6 months required. 4-6 bed dorms $18-20; doubles (some with bath) $40-43. ●

Old Town Inn, 4444 Pacific Hwy. (☎260-8024 or 800-643-3025). Clean rooms with standard amenities are a 10min. walk from Old Town. Some rooms have kitchenettes. Pool. Large continental breakfast included. Singles $50-60; doubles $50-60; prices vary depending on season. ❸

Heritage Park Bed and Breakfast Inn, 2470 Heritage Park Row (☎229-6832), near Old Town. This old Victorian mansion in Heritage Park now functions as a cozy B&B. Each of the 12 guest rooms is unique, but they all come with afternoon teas and nightly showings of vintage films. Rooms $120-250. Reservations are strongly encouraged. ❺

South Carlsbad Beach State Park (☎760-438-3143), off Carlsbad Blvd. near Leucadia, in north San Diego County. Over 100 sites. Beautiful beaches with good surfing conditions. Showers and laundry. Tent sites $12 per night; RVs $18. ●

San Elijo Beach State Park (☎760-753-5091), off Hwy. 101 south of Cardiff-by-the-Sea. 171 sites (23 with RV hookups) on seaside cliffs. Wheelchair accessible. Laundry and showers. Tent sites $12 per night; RVs $18. ●

◖ FOOD

Good restaurants cluster downtown along **C St., Broadway** and in the **Gaslamp.** The best food near Balboa Park and the Zoo is north and west in nearby **Hillcrest** and **University Heights. Old Town** is *the* place to eat Mexican cuisine.

Casa de Bandini, 2754 Calhoun St. (☎297-8211). An Old Town institution and repeatedly voted best Mexican restaurant in San Diego. Superb food and boisterous Mariachi music. The colossal combo plates ($8) and heavyweight margaritas ($4-7) are the stuff of legend. Open M-Th 11am-9:30pm, F-Sa 11am-10pm, Su 10am-9:30pm. ❷

Kono's Surf Club, 704 Garnet Ave. (☎483-1669), across from the Crystal Pier in Pacific Beach. Identifiable by the line stretching for a block out the door, Kono's is a surfer's shrine. Breakfast served all day ($3-4). Try the huge Egg Burrito #3, which includes bacon, cheese, potatoes, and sauce ($3.25). Open M-F 7am-3pm, Sa-Su 7am-4pm. ●

Berta's, 3928 Twiggs St. (☎295-2343), in Old Town. Dozens of Guatemalan, Honduran, and Costa Rican specialities $9-14. Open Tu-Su 11am-10pm. ❸

Trattoria Fantastica, 1735 India St. (☎234-1735). In the heart of Little Italy, this family-owned restaurant serves heaping portions of scrumptious Italian food. Entrees and pastas from $10. Open daily 11:30am-3pm and 5-10pm. ❸

Sushi Deli, 828 Broadway (☎231-9597). This small sushi place offers fresh sushi at amazingly low prices. Try their lunch special (teriyaki chicken, 4-piece California roll, *edamame,* rice, and salad for $6) or all-you-can-eat sushi Monday for $15. Open M-Th 11am-2pm and 5-9pm, F 11am-2pm and 5-10pm, Sa 5-10pm, Su 5-9pm. ❷

Rimel's, 1030 Torrey Pines Rd. (☎858-454-6045), In La Jolla. With a number of spits right behind the counter, this restaurant and rotisserie sends delicious smells wafting out the door and all down the block. Half chicken $9, salads and sandwiches from $6. Open daily 11:30am-9:30pm. ❷

🗗 SIGHTS

DOWNTOWN. San Diego's downtown attractions are concentrated in the corridor that includes the business, Gaslamp, and waterfront districts. **San Diego Museum of Contemporary Art** is a steel-and-glass structure that encases 20th-century works of art from the museum's permanent collection as well as visiting works. *(1001 Kettner Blvd. ☎234-1001. Open M-Tu and Th-Su 11am-5pm. Free.)* The **Gaslamp Quarter** houses antique shops, Victorian buildings, and trendy restaurants. Formerly the city's Red Light District, the area's new bars and bistros have grown popular with upscale revelers. By day, the area's charm lies in its history. The **Gaslamp Quarter Foundation** offers guided walking tours. *(William Heath Davis House, 410 Island Ave. ☎233-4692. Museum open Th-Su 11am-3pm. 2hr. tours Sa at 11am. $5; students, seniors, and ages 12-18 $3; under 12 free. Self-guided tour maps $2.)* The **Horton Grand Hotel,** like most old buildings in San Diego, is supposedly haunted. Believers may catch a glimpse of Wyatt Earp or even Babe Ruth. *(311 Island Ave. ☎544-1886. Tours W at 3pm. Free.)* The displays at the **San Diego Maritime Museum** will impress history buffs. *(1492 N. Harbor Dr. ☎234-9153. Open daily 9am-8pm. $6; seniors, military, and ages 13-17 $4; ages 6-12 $3.)*

SAN DIEGO ZOO. With over 100 acres of exquisite fenceless habitats, this zoo well deserves its reputation as one of the finest in the world. Its unique "bioclimatic" exhibits group animals and plants together by habitat. The zoo currently showcases several **pandas** and invests over a million dollars a year on panda habitat preservation in China. Young *Homo sapiens* can watch the hatching and feeding of other young species in the **children's petting zoo.** *(☎234-3153. Open late June-early Sept. daily 9am-10pm; early Sept.-late June 9am-dusk. $19.50, with 35min. bus tour $32; ages 3-11 $11.75/19.75.)*

BALBOA PARK & THE EL PRADO MUSEUMS. It would take several days to see all of Balboa Park's museums. Most of them reside within the resplendent Spanish colonial-style buildings that line **El Prado St.,** which runs west-to-east through the Park's central **Plaza de Panama.** The **Balboa Park Visitors Center** is in the House of Hospitality on El Prado St. and sells park maps (50¢) and the Balboa Park passport ($30), which allows admission into 12 of the park's museums. Passports are also available at participating museums. *(1549 El Prado. ☎239-0512. www.balboapark.org. Open in summer daily 9am-4:30pm; in winter 9am-4pm.)* Formerly a state building, the sizable **Museum of Man** anchors the west end of the park. The museum traces human evolution with exhibits on primates and early man. *(☎239-2001. Open daily 10am-4:30pm. $6, seniors $5, ages 6-17 $3; 3rd Tu of each month free. Special exhibits cost more, usually $8.)* At the east end of Balboa Park, the **Natural History Museum** displays stuffed mammals and birds. Live insects and arthropods enhance the exhibition of standard fossils. *(☎232-3821. Open Memorial Day-Labor Day daily 9:30am-5:30pm; Labor Day-Memorial Day 9:30am-4:30pm. $7, seniors $6, ages 6-17 $5; free 1st Tu of each month.)* The **Aerospace Museum** displays 24 full-scale replicas and 44 original planes, as well as aviation history exhibits. *(2001 Pan American Plaza. ☎234-8291. Open June-Aug. daily 10am-5:30pm; Sept.-May 10am-4:30pm. $8, seniors $6, ages 6-17 $3, under 6 and military in uniform free; 4th Tu of each month free.)*

CALIFORNIA

OLD TOWN. In 1769, Father Junípero Serra, supported by a brigade of Spanish infantry, established the first of 21 missions that eventually would line the California coast. Now known as Old Town, the remnants of this early settlement are one of San Diego's tourist mainstays. The most popular of the area's attractions, the **Old Town State Park,** contains museums, shops, and restaurants. **Seely Stable** gives visitor info and free tours of the stable's agricultural exhibits. (☎ 220-5422. Open daily 9am-5pm. Tours every hr. 11am-2pm.) Take a tour of the **Whaley House,** which displays an authentic Lincoln life mask and the piano used in *Gone With the Wind.* The house stands on the site of San Diego's first gallows, which might explain why it is one of two **official haunted houses** recognized by the State of California. (2482 San Diego Ave. ☎ 298-2482. Open daily 10am-4:30pm. $4, seniors $3, ages 6-12 $2.) Across the street is **Heritage Park,** a group of seven 150-year-old Victorian buildings collected from around the city. Four are open to the public. The **Serra Museum** houses exhibits detailing the settlement; outside is a *huge* flagpole marking the former location of **Fort Stockton.** (In Presidio Park. ☎ 279-3258. Open June-Aug. Tu-Su 10am-4:30pm; Sept.-May F-Su 10am-4:30pm. $5, students, seniors, and military $4, ages 6-17 $2.)

CORONADO ISLAND. Lovely Coronado Island is in fact a peninsula; a slender 7 mi. strip of sand known as the "Silver Strand" tethers it to the mainland. Famous for its elegant Hotel del Coronado, the island is perfect for strolling and browsing. Beach babes frolic in the waves that break along the southern shore, and outdoor lovers jog and bike along paved trails. Coronado has a huge military presence, and the entire northern chunk comprises the **North Island Naval Air Station,** the birthplace of American naval aviation. Among the island's many naval enterprises is the training area of the infamous SEAL (sea, air, and land) commando teams.

SEA WORLD. Though critics have long condemned the practice of training highly intelligent marine mammals to perform unnatural circus acts, most visitors find the playful goofballs irresistible. The A-list star here is the behemoth killer whale **Shamu,** whose signature move is a cannonball splash that soaks anyone in the first 20 rows (the original Shamu died long ago, but each of his 10 successors has proudly borne the moniker). The park's newest attraction is **Shipwreck Rapids,** Sea World's first-ever adventure ride. (☎ 226-3901. Open summer daily 9am-11pm. Open at 10am in winter, but closing hours vary. $43, ages 3-9 $33. Parking $7, RVs $9.)

◤ NIGHTLIFE

Nightlife in San Diego isn't centered around any one strip, but scattered in several distinct pockets of action. Upscale locals and trend-seeking tourists flock to the **Gaslamp Quarter,** while lesbian and gay clubs cluster in **University Heights** and **Hillcrest.** Away from downtown, the **beach areas** are loaded with clubs, bars, and inexpensive eateries that attract college-age revelers. Check out the free weekly *Reader,* found in shops and coffeehouses, for entertainment info.

■ **Croce's Top Hat Bar and Grille** and **Croce's Jazz Bar,** 802 5th Ave. (☎ 233-4355), at F St. in the Gaslamp. Ingrid Croce, widow of singer Jim Croce, created this rock/blues bar and classy jazz bar side-by-side. Live music nightly. Cover $5-10. Open daily 7:30am-3pm and 5pm-midnight; bar open until 2am.

Pacific Beach Bar and Grill and **Club Tremors,** 860 Garnet Ave. (☎ 858-272-1242 and 277-7228, respectively), in Pacific Beach. Live DJ packs the 2-level dance floor with a young and slinky crowd. The Bar and Grill has cheap, delicious food, more than 20 beers on tap, and live music on Su. Cover $5 if you enter through Club Tremors. Club open Th-Sa 9pm-1:30am; bar open 11am-1:30am; kitchen closes at midnight.

The Casbah, 2501 Kettner Blvd. (☎232-4355). This intimate nightspot is the best live music venue in the city. Cover varies. 21+. Call ahead for a schedule, as tickets sometimes sell out. Hours vary, usually 5pm-2am.

Dick's Last Resort, 345 4th Ave. (☎858-231-9100), in the Gaslamp. Buckets of Southern grub attract a wild bunch. Dick's stocks beers from around the globe, on top of native brews like the Dixieland Blackened Voodoo Lager. No cover for the nightly rock or blues. Lunch burgers under $4, dinner entrees $10-18. Open daily 11am-1:30am.

Cafe Lu Lu, 419 F St. (☎858-238-0114), in the Gaslamp. Coffeehouse designed by local artists. See and be seen as you sip a raspberry-mocha ($3.75). Standing room only after midnight on the weekends. Open Su-Th 9am-1am, F-Sa 9am-3am.

The Flame, 3780 Park Blvd. (☎295-4163), is a popular lesbian dance club with oodles of special events. Su Latin night, Tu Boys' Night Out, W drag king contests, Th karaoke. Call for cover. Open M-Th and Sa-Su 5pm-2am, F 4pm-2am.

Bourbon Street, 4612 Park Blvd. (☎291-0173), in University Heights, is a perennially popular piano bar with a gay following. Open M-F 2pm-2am, Sa-Su 11am-2pm.

The Brass Rail, 3796 5th Ave. (☎298-2233), in Hillcrest. San Diego's oldest gay bar. Features dancing and drag on weekends. Open daily noon-2am.

▶ DAYTRIPS FROM SAN DIEGO

LA JOLLA. Pronounced *la-HOY-a*, this affluent locality houses few budget accommodations or eateries, but its fabulous beaches are largely open to the public. The **La Jolla Cove** is popular with scuba divers, snorkelers, and brilliantly colored Garibaldi goldfish (the state saltwater fish). Surfers are especially fond of the waves at **Tourmaline Beach** and **Windansea Beach,** which can be too strong for novices. **La Jolla Shores,** next to Scripps/UCSD, has clean and gentle swells ideal for bodysurfers, boogie boarders, swimmers, and families. **Black's Beach** is not officially a nude beach, but let's just say there are plenty of wieners and buns at *this* lunchcart. *(To reach La Jolla, turn from I-5 and take a left at the Ardath exit or take buses #30 or 34 from downtown.)*

ESCONDIDO. The **San Diego Wild Animal Park** is an essential part of any trip to San Diego. Visitors gawk at the beasties from the open-air **Wgasa Bush Line Railway,** a 55min. monorail safari through four simulated habitat areas. Butterflies and birds flutter in the Hidden Jungle greenhouses. Try the 1 mi. Heart of Africa hike, the open-air Photo Caravan, or the Roar and Snore overnight camping safari, available May to September. Renting binoculars ($5-10) at the park entrance may enhance tour. *(☎747-8702. Rail tours June-Aug. 9:30am-9pm; Sept.-May 9:30am-4pm; sit on the right for best views. Park open daily 9am, closing times vary with the season. $26.50, ages 3-11 $19.50. Parking $6. Discounts often available at visitor centers and hotels.)*

TIJUANA ☎66

In the shadow of swollen, sulphur-spewing factories lies the most notorious specimen of a peculiar border subculture: Tijuana (pop. 2 million). By day, swarms of tourists cross the US border to haggle with street vendors, pour gallons of tequila down their throats, and get their picture taken with donkeys painted as zebras. By night, Revolución, the city's wide main drag, becomes a big, bad party with *mariachi* bands and exploding bottle rockets doing little to drown out the thumping dance beats blaring from the packed nightclubs. The three-ringed, duty-free extravaganza attracts more than 30 million tourists per year, most of them jaunt-

> **RUN FOR THE BORDER.** At the world's largest border crossing, north-bound lanes often have backups of more than 150 cars. To minimize the wait, cross during a weekday morning. The southbound ride is generally smoother, but weekends can be rough in both directions. If you're crossing into Tijuana for a day or so, it's easier to leave your car in a lot on the US side and join the throngs of people walking across the border. If you're in a hurry, rent a bike in Mexico, pass through the remarkably shorter bike line, and return it once across the border. You need a **tourist card** ($18) if you plan to travel farther south than Ensenada or San Felipe. Regardless of which way you are crossing, bring proper ID—ideally a driver's license or passport—and leave your bushels of fruit, truck-loads of livestock, and stashes of drugs behind.

ing across the border for a couple of hours to unload wads of cash on everything from *jai alai* gambling to slimy strip shows. In recent years, the city has made a conscious effort to clean up its act, somewhat successfully eliminating sex shops and prostitution from the center of town. Still, rife with flashy sleaze and border intrigue, it's hard to say whether it's the city's strange charm, its cheap booze, or its sprawling, unapologetic hedonism that attracts tourists to Tijuana like flies.

◼️ 🔀 ORIENTATION & PRACTICAL INFORMATION. Just south of the border, the area surrounding Revolución is known as the **Zona Centro**, the tourist hot spot. East-west *calles*, which are named and numbered, cross Revolución; perpendicular to the *calles*, *avenidas* run north-south.

The **Tourist Office** is located in a small booth on the eastern side of Revolución between Calle 3 and Calle 4. The English-speaking staff offers maps and advice for tourists. (☎ 688 05 55. Open M-Sa 8am-5pm, Su 10am-5pm.) The **Customs Office:** (☎ 683 13 90) at the border on the Mexican side, after crossing the San Ysidro bridge, is open 24hr. The **Canadian Consulate,** German Gedovius 10411, is in the Zona Río. (☎ 684 04 61, 800-706-2900 for after hours emergency assistance. Open M-F 9am-1pm.) The **UK Consulate,** Salinas 1500, is in Col. Aviación, La Mesa. (☎ 681 73 23, 686 53 20 for after-hours emergency assistance. Open M-F 9am-3pm.) The **US Consulate,** Tapachula 96, in Col. Hipódromo, is adjacent to the racetrack southeast of town. (☎ 681 74 00. Open M-F 8am-4:30pm. In an emergency, call the San Diego office ☎ 619-692-2154 and leave a message.) Banks along Constitución exchange money. **Banamex,** Constitución at Calle 4, has shorter lines (☎ 688 00 21; open M-F 9am-5pm); **Bital,** Revolución at Calle 2 (☎ 685 00 06; open M-F 8am-7pm, Sa 8am-5:30pm) is central. Both have **24hr. ATMs.** Located under billboards with exchange rates, the many *casas de cambio* offer better rates, but may charge commission and refuse to exchange traveler's checks. **Emergency:** dial ☎ 060. **Police:** Constitución at Calle 8; English is spoken (☎ 638 51 68). **Medical Services: Red Cross,** Gamboa at Silvestre; some English is spoken (☎ 621 77 87, emergency 066). **Hospital General,** Centenario 10851, in the *Zona Río.* Open 24hr. (☎ 684 02 37). **Post Office:** Negrete, at Calle 11. (☎ 684 79 50. Open M-F 8am-5pm.) **Postal Code:** 22000.

🏠 ◻️ ACCOMMODATIONS & FOOD. There's no shortage of budget hotels in Tijuana, especially on Calle 1, between Revolución and Mutalismo. Rooms tend to be roachy—ask to see them before paying. *Exercise caution when walking in this area at night.* **Hotel La Villa de Zaragoza ❷,** Madero 1120, between Calles 7a and 8a, offers fairly inexpensive rooms. Laundry, room service, and 24hr. security. (☎ 685 18 32. Singles 350 pesos; doubles 410 pesos.) Remarkably quiet for being in the middle of the chaos that is Revolución, **Hotel Lafayette ❶,** Revolución

The **LADATEL phones** that have popped up all over the country have revolutionized the way Mexico calls. To operate any LADATEL, you'll need to buy a colorful prepaid **phone card,** available at most *papelerías* (stationery stores) or *tiendas de abarrotes* (general stores)—look for the "De venta aquí LADATEL" signs posted in store windows. Cards come in 30-, 50-, and 100-peso increments. Telmex, the national phone company, has recently reconfigured the way **local calls** are made. In addition to the local number, you must dial the last digit of the area code. For example, if you are calling a hotel in Tijuana (area code 66) whose phone number is ☎ 12 34 56, dial ☎ 612 34 56. When making calls between cities, dial ☎ 0 before the area code and phone number.

325, between Calles 3a and 4a, has large rooms with color TVs, phones, fans, and private baths. (☎ 685 39 40 or 685 33 39. Singles 200 pesos; doubles 260 pesos.) **Hotel Colonial ❶,** Calle 6a 1812, between Constitución and Niños Héroes, is in a quieter neighborhood. Large, comfortable rooms have A/C and private baths. (☎ 688 16 20. Singles and doubles 260 pesos.) A huge, sparkling restaurant, **☒Restaurant Ricardo's Tortas ❶,** Madero and Calle 7, serves up the best *tortas* in town. Try the *super especial* (40 pesos), with ham, *carne asada,* cheese, avocado, tomato, and mayo. (☎ 685 40 31. Open 24hr.) **Café La Especial ❶,** Revolucion 718, is a refreshing respite from the noise of Revolución. Munch on enchiladas and tacos amidst crooning *mariachis* and local families. (☎ 685 66 54. Open daily 10am-10pm.)

◪ SIGHTS & SPORTS. Photo ops abound on Revolución, where zebra-striped donkeys and gaudily costumed cowboys vie for your attention. The multi-tiered dance clubs and curio shops that share the street are often the only sights that Tijuana tourists care to see. The beautiful and shady park, **Parque Teniente Guerrero,** on Calle 3a and 5 de Mayo, is a favorite gathering place for local families and an oasis from the noisy circus of Revolución. The **Catedral de Nuestra Señora de Guadalupe** was built in 1902 as a modest adobe chapel; modern expansions and reinforcement have made it into a huge stone cathedral checkered in adobe orange and gray and crowned with a giant image of the Virgin of Guadalupe. The cathedral's daily mass attracts a diverse congregation of devout locals and curious passersby. The grandiose baroque **Frontón Palacio,** on Revolución at Calle 7a, hosts daily competitions of **jai alai.** (☎ 685 16 12. Games M-Sa 8pm. Free.) If you're in town on the right Sunday, you can watch the graceful and savage battle of man versus bull in one of Tijuana's two bullrings. **El Toreo de Tijuana,** southeast of town just off of Agua Caliente, hosts the first round of fights (May-July, alternate Su). To get to El Toreo, catch a bus on Calle 2 west of Revolución. The seaside **Plaza Monumental** hosts the second round from August to October. Buy tickets (95-400 pesos) the Wednesday before a fight at the Mexicoach office, Revolución between Calles 6a and 7a (☎ 685 14 70), or at the stadium gate (☎ 685 15 10 or 686 12 19).

⬚ SHOPPING. As soon as tourists cross the footbridge from the US, they're bombarded with vendors peddling everything from brightly colored blankets to cheap shoes to grains of rice with the tourist's name written on it. The crazy shopping scene continues most of the way up Revolución, ending near the intersection with Calle 7a. Other spots for assorted tourist-oriented wares are the **Mercado de Artesanía,** on Calle 1a right under the pedestrian footbridge, and the vendors in **Plaza Santa Cecilia** behind the tourist office. Bargaining is a must, as quoted prices can be more than twice the bottom line. For a good selection of higher-quality *artesanía,* visit the **Bazar de México** on Revolución at Calle 7a.

CALIFORNIA

☑ NIGHTLIFE. In the 1920s, Prohibition drove US citizens south of the border to revel in the forbidden nectars of cacti, grapes, and hops, and the constant flow of American tourists eager to fill their stomachs with cheap and legal booze still remains strong. Head to **Animale**, on Revolución at Calle 4a, the biggest, glitziest, and loudest haven of them all. The huge dance floor and open balconies, as well as special drink deals (2 beers and a shot of tequila US$4, 2-for-1 mixed drinks US$6) attract kids and adults alike into the colorful lair. (Open Su-Th 10am-4am, F-Sa 10am-6am.) A sublimely wacky world of life-size plaster clowns, balloons, and various pieces of kitschy US pop culture items, **Iguanas-Ranas**, on Revolución at Calle 3a, is one of the most happening places in town. Where else do you get the opportunity to pound beers (US$2.50) in an authentic yellow school bus? (☎685 14 22. On W men pay US$1 per beer, ladies drink free. Open M-Th 10am-2am, F-Su 10am-6am.) At **Eclipse**, on Revolución at Calle 6a, prepare for a 3-tiered party. Masses of patrons come to toss back some of the cheapest booze in town: 2 beers and a shot of tequila are a mere US$3. The 3rd floor doubles as a strip club, where prices (not to mention hemlines) are much higher. (Open M-Th noon-2am, F-Su noon-4am.)

THE CALIFORNIA DESERT

Mystics and misanthropes from Native Americans to modern city slickers have long been fascinated by the austere scenery and the vast open spaces of the California desert. In winter the desert is a pleasantly warm refuge; in spring, a technicolor floral landscape; in summer, a blistering wasteland; and in fall, more of the same. A barren place of overwhelming simplicity, the desert's beauty lies in its emptiness as well as in its elusive treasures: diverse flora and fauna, staggering topographical variation, and scattered relics of the American frontier.

PALM SPRINGS ☎760

From its first known inhabitants, the Cahuilla Indians, to today's geriatric fun-lovers, the restorative oasis of Palm Springs has drawn many to its sandy bosom. With warm temperatures, celebrity residents, and more pink than a *Miami Vice* episode, this desert city provides a sunny break from everyday life.

Mt. San Jacinto State Park, Palm Springs's primary landmark, offers outdoor recreation opportunities for visitors of all fitness levels. If Mt. San Jacinto's 10,804 ft. escarpment seems too strenuous, try the **Palm Springs Aerial Tramway,** on Aerial Tramway Rd. off North Palm Canyon Dr. The observation deck has great views of the Coachella Valley. (☎325-1449. Trams run at least every 30min.; M-F 10am-8pm, Sa-Su 8am-8pm. Round-trip $21, seniors $19, ages 3-12 $14.) The **Desert Hot Springs Spa,** 10805 Palm Dr., features six naturally heated mineral pools, as well as saunas, massage professionals, and bodywraps. (☎800-808-7727. Open daily 8am-10pm. M-F $3-5, Sa-Su $6.) Prep for nearby Joshua Tree at **Uprising Rockclimbing Center,** 1500 Gene Autry Trail, a gigantic outdoor climbing structure and the only one of its kind in the US. Whether you're a beginner or a seasoned climber, you'll find a fun challenge cranking on plastic rock beneath a canopy that wards off the sun. Expert instruction available; excursions on real rock by arrangement. (☎888-254-6266. Open July-Aug. Tu-F 5-9pm, Sa-Su 9am-5pm; Sept.-June M-F 10am-8pm, Sa-Su 10am-6pm. Day pass $15, equipment rental $7. Lessons from $45 per day.)

Like most famous resort communities, Palm Springs caters mainly to those seeking a tax shelter, not a night's shelter. If you've gotta stay in town, there is a particular concentration of inexpensive motels where East Palm Canyon Dr. becomes South Palm Canyon Dr. **Orchid Tree Inn ❺,** 251 S. Belardo Rd., has large rooms with tasteful Spanish ambiance overlooking a courtyard with lush gardens and pool. (☎325-2791 or 800-733-3435. Singles or doubles July-Aug. M-Th from

$65; in winter $110-130. F-Su $15-20 more.) Palm Springs offers a kaleidoscope of sumptuous food, from the classic greasy spoon to ultra-trendy fusions of cuisines. The promise of delicious Italian food draws crowds every night of the week to █Banducci's Bit of Italy ❸, 1260 S. Palm Canyon Dr. For a rich treat, try their fettucine alfredo ($13), which comes with antipasto, minestrone soup, and buttery garlic bread. (☎325-2537. Entrees from $8-15. Open daily 5-10pm.) █Thai Smile ❷, 651 N. Palm Canyon Dr., offers authentic and inexpensive Thai cuisine. Don't miss the $5 lunch specials. (☎320-5503. Open daily 11:30am-10pm.)

Greyhound, 311 N. Indian Canyon Dr. (☎325-2053), buses to L.A. (3-4 hr., 9 per day, $17-19). **Sun Bus** connects Coachella Valley cities. (☎343-3451. Operates daily 5am-10pm. $1, transfers 50¢.) **Visitor Info: Chamber of Commerce,** 190 W. Amado Rd. (☎325-1577. Open M-F 8:30am-4:30pm.) **Post Office:** 333 E. Amado Rd. (☎322-4111. Open M-F 9am-5pm, Sa 9am-1pm.) **ZIP code:** 92262, General Delivery 92263.

JOSHUA TREE NATIONAL PARK ☎760

When devout Mormon pioneers crossed this faith-testing desert in the 19th century, they named the enigmatic tree they encountered after the Biblical prophet Joshua. The tree's crooked limbs resembled the Hebrew general, who, with his arms upraised, seemed to beckon them to the Promised Land. Even today, Joshua Tree National Park inspires reverent awe in those who happen upon it. Piles of windsculpted boulders are flanked by seemingly jubilant Joshua trees, and the park's five oases appear lushly Edenic against the desolate backdrop of the desert.

█❼ ORIENTATION & PRACTICAL INFORMATION. About 160 mi. east of L.A., Joshua Tree National Park covers 558,000 acres northeast of Palm Springs. The park is ringed by three highways: **I-10** to the south, **Rte. 62 (Twentynine Palms Hwy.)** to the west and north, and **Rte. 177** to the east. The northern entrances to the park are off Rte. 62 at the towns of **Joshua Tree** and **Twentynine Palms.** The south entrance is at **Cottonwood Spring,** off I-10 at Rte. 195, south of Palm Springs near the town of Indio. Park entrance fee $5 per person, $10 per car. Valid for seven days. **Headquarters and Oasis Visitors Center:** 74485 National Park Dr., ¼ mi. off Rte. 62 in Twentynine Palms. (☎367-5500; www.joshuatree.org. Open daily 8am-5pm. Water available.) **Post Office:** 73839 Gorgonio Dr., in Twentynine Palms. (☎369-1161. Open M-F 8:30am-5pm.) **ZIP code:** 92277.

▐ ACCOMMODATIONS. Most campgrounds in the park operate on a first come, first served basis. Reservations can be made for group sites only at Cottonwood, Sheep Pass, Indian Cove, and Black Rock Canyon through **DESTINET** (☎800-436-7275). **Backcountry camping** is also an option; ask at a ranger station for details. All campsites have fireplaces and pit toilets and are free unless otherwise noted. Campground stays are limited to 30 days in the summer and to 14 days October-May. █**Jumbo Rocks ❶,** located on Skull Rock Trail on the eastern edge of Queen Valley, is the highest and coolest campground in the park. █**Indian Cove ❶,** on the north edge of the Wonderland of Rocks, has dramatic waterfalls nearby and is a popular site for climbers. (Sites $10; group sites $20-35.) **Hidden Valley ❶,** in the center of the park off Quail Springs Rd., has secluded alcoves shaded by boulders. **Black Rock Canyon ❶,** at the end of Joshua Ln. off Rte. 62 near Yucca Valley, has wooded sites ($10) near flush toilets and running water. Indoor accommodations can be found in **Twentynine Palms.** The **29 Palms Inn ❸,** 73950 Inn Dr., is an attraction in itself, with 19 distinctly different rooms that face the Mara Oasis. (☎367-3505. Feb.-Apr. reservations required. June-Sept. doubles Su-Th $50-80, F-Sa $65-105. Oct.-May $10-20 extra.)

FROM THE ROAD

DESERT DRIVING

I've been driving in California for five years and thought I'd tackled it all: harrowing cliffs along Rte. 1, San Francisco hills with a stick-shift—this was nothing. Still, I'd never driven in the desert. What could be easier than a flat, straight road? But Death Valley threw some unexpected tricks at me.

What appears to be flat in the Valley often isn't. Rising dunes *seemed* to stretch out horizontally in front of me, but my '86 Volvo station wagon told another story. In third gear, I crawled along at 35 mph, wondering if my cell phone would work when my car quit. As the temperature gauge slowly rose, I angrily flipped off the A/C. Pressing my hand to the window told me it was still above 100°F outside. I shifted down to second, bringing me to the crest of the "flat," and I encountered the second danger of desert driving: the need for speed.

In the desert, it's very, very tempting to allow gravity to pull your car along well above the speed limit. Dips in the road become exhilarating roller coaster rides; these desert highways made driving fun again. But all this fun can have a hefty price tag. To the west of Death Valley, the whoosh of air past the car was met with another sound: sirens. My $140 speeding ticket could have paid for 20 rides on Las Vegas's fastest roller coasters.

After spending some time successfully navigating in the desert, you begin to feel invincible. The trick is to not let this feeling take over, or you'll find yourself overheated—either because the air conditioning is off, or because you're out $140.

—*Sara Clark*

◪ OUTDOOR ACTIVITIES. Over 80% of the park is designated wilderness area, safeguarded against development, and lacking paved roads, toilets, and campfires. Joshua Tree offers premium backcountry hiking and camping. There's no water in the wilderness except when a flash flood comes roaring down. The park's most temperate weather is from October to December and March to April; temperatures in other months span uncomfortable extremes.

A self-paced **driving tour** is an easy way to explore the park. All park roads are well-marked, and "Exhibit Ahead" signs point the way to unique floral and geological formations. A not-to-be-missed spot for watching the sunrise is at **Key's View,** 6 mi. off the park road just west of Ryan campground. The **Cholla Cactus Garden,** a grove of spiny succulents resembling 3-D asterisks, lies in the Pinto Basin just off the road. Four-wheel-drives can use dirt roads, such as **Geology Tour Rd.,** to climb through fascinating rock formations in the Li'l San Bernardino Mountains.

Energetic visitors are often drawn to Joshua Tree for its **rock climbing;** the world-renowned boulders at **Wonderland of Rocks** and **Hidden Valley** are especially challenging and attract thousands of climbers each year. The Visitors Center provides info on established rope routes and on wilderness areas, where the placement of new bolts is restricted.

⧯ HIKING. Hiking through the park's trails is perhaps the best way to experience Joshua Tree. Although the **Barker Dam Trail,** next to Hidden Valley, is often packed with tourists, its painted petroglyphs and eerie tranquility make it a worthwhile hike. Bring plenty of water for the strenuous, unshaded climb to the summit of **Ryan Mountain,** where the boulder formations bear an unsettling resemblance to herculean beasts of burden slouching toward a distant destination. The Visitors Center has info on the park's many other hikes, which range from the 15min. stroll to the **Oasis of Mara** to a three-day, 35 mi. trek along the **California Riding and Hiking Trail.** The ranger-led **Desert Queen Ranch Walking Tour** (Oct.-May daily 10am and 1pm; June-Aug. W and F 5:30pm; $5) covers the ranch of homesteader Bill Keys. Joshua Tree teems with flora and fauna that you're unlikely to see anywhere else in the world. Larger plants like Joshua trees, *cholla,* and the spidery *ocotillo* have adapted to the severe climate in fascinating ways, and the wildflowers that dot the desert terrain each spring attract thousands of visitors.

DEATH VALLEY NATIONAL PARK ☎760

Satan owns a lot of real estate in Death Valley National Park. Not only does he grow crops (at the Devil's Cornfield) and hit the links (at the Devil's Golf Course), but the park is also home to Hell's Gate itself. Not surprisingly, the area's astonishing topographical and climactic extremes can support just about anyone's idea of the Inferno. Winter temperatures dip well below freezing, and summer heat rivals even the hottest Hades. The second highest temperature ever recorded on Earth (134°F in the shade) was measured at the valley's Furnace Creek Ranch on July 10, 1913. It is foolish to hike to the valley floor during the summer; the average high in July is 116°F. A visit in spring lets visitors enjoy the splendor in comfort.

☎ TRANSPORTATION. There is no regularly scheduled public transportation into Death Valley; the best way to get around is by car. Of the nine park entrances, most visitors choose Rte. 190 from the east. The road is well-maintained, the pass is less steep, and you arrive more quickly at the Visitors Center. But the visitor with a trusty vehicle will be able to see more of the park by entering from the southeast (Rte. 178 west from Rte. 127 at Shoshone) or the north (direct to Scotty's Castle via Nevada Rte. 267 from U.S. 95). Unskilled mountain drivers should not attempt to enter via Titus Canyon or Emigrant Canyon Drive roads; neither has guard rails to prevent your car from sliding over precipitous cliffs.

☑ PRACTICAL INFORMATION. Visitor info: Furnace Creek Visitors Center, on Rte. 190 in the east-central section of the valley. (☎786-3200; www.nps.gov/deva. Open daily 8am-6pm.) **Ranger stations** are located at **Grapevine** (☎786-2313), at the junction of Rte. 190 and 267 near Scotty's Castle; **Stovepipe Wells** (☎786-2342), on Rte. 190; and **Shoshone** (☎832-4308), outside the southeast border of the valley at the junction of Rte. 127 and 178. (All open daily 8am-5pm.) Get gas outside Death Valley at Olancha, Shoshone, or Beatty, NV. Radiator water (*not* for drinking) is available at a few critical points on Rte. 178 and 190 and NV Rte. 374. Those who drive along the backcountry trails should carry chains, extra tires, gas, oil, radiator and drinking water, and spare parts. **Post Office:** Furnace Creek Ranch (☎786-2223; open M, W, and F 8:30am-3:30pm; Tu and Th 8:30am-5pm). **ZIP code:** 92328.

☗ ACCOMMODATIONS. During the winter months, camping out with a stock of groceries is a good way to save both money and driving time. **Stovepipe Wells Village ❸** is right in Death Valley. (☎786-2387. Doubles $50-92; each additional person $11. RV sites available; full hookup $20.) The **Panamint Springs Resort ❶,** 23 mi. east of the park's western border on Rte. 190, is remote but comfortable. The complex includes a restaurant and bar, 18 rooms, RV hookups, campsites, and gas. You can hear the thunderous roar of naval fighters as they loop and corkscrew overhead on maneuvers from China Lake Naval Weapons Station. (☎775-482-7680. Doubles from $65; RV sites $10-25; campsites $10.) The National Park Service maintains nine **campgrounds,** but only Texas Springs and Furnace Creek accept reservations. Call ahead to check availability and be prepared to battle for a space if you come during peak periods. Roadside camping is not permitted, but **backcountry camping** is free and legal, provided you check in at the Visitors Center and pitch tents at least 1 mi. from main roads, 5 mi. from any established campsite, and ¼ mi. from any water source.

HIKING. Death Valley has hiking to bemuse the gentlest wanderer and challenge the hardiest adventurer. Backpackers and day-hikers should inform the Visitors Center of their trip and take along the appropriate topographical maps. Valley-floor hikers should plan a route along roads where assistance is readily available and should not hike alone. **Artist's Dr.**, 10 mi. south of the Visitors Center on Rte. 178, is a one-way loop that twists its way through rock formations of brilliant and diverse colors. About 5 mi. south is **Devil's Golf Course,** a plane of sharp salt pinnacles made of the precipitate from the evaporation of Lake Manly, the 90 mi. long lake that once filled the lower valley. **Badwater** lies 3 mi. south of Devil's Golf Course, on I-90, a briny pool four times saltier than the ocean. The surrounding salt flat dips to the lowest point in the Western Hemisphere—282 ft. below sea level. Immortalized by Antonioni's film of the same name, **Zabriskie Point** is a marvelous place from which to view Death Valley's corrugated badlands. Perhaps the most spectacular sight in the park is the vista at **Dante's View**, reached by a 13 mi. paved road from Rte. 190.

THE CENTRAL COAST

The 400-mile stretch of coastline between Los Angeles and San Francisco embodies all that is purely Californian: surf crashing onto secluded beaches, dramatic cliffs and mountains, self-actualizing New Agers, and always a hint of the offbeat. This is the solitary magnificence that inspired Robinson Jeffers's paeans, John Steinbeck's novels, and Jack Kerouac's musings. Among the smog-free skies, sweeping shorelines, dense forests, and plunging cliffs, there is a point where inland farming communities and old seafaring towns join, beckoning citified residents to journey out to the quiet drama of the coast. The landmarks along the way—Hearst Castle, the Monterey Bay Aquarium, Carmel, and historic missions—are well worth visiting, but the real point of the Central Coast is the journey itself.

SANTA BARBARA ☎805

Santa Barbara epitomizes worry-free living. The town is an enclave of wealth and privilege, true to its soap-opera image, but in a significantly less aggressive way than its Southern Californian counterparts. Spanish Revival architecture decorates the residential hills that rise gently over a lively pedestrian district.

▐ TRANSPORTATION

Trains: Amtrak, 209 State St. (☎963-1015). *Be careful around the station after dark.* To **L.A.** (5-6hr., 2 per day, $20-25) and **San Francisco** (7hr., 3 per day, $48-68). Open daily 6:30am-9pm.

Buses: Greyhound, 34 W. Carrillo St. (☎962-2477), at Chapala St. To **L.A.** (2-3hr., 9 per day, $13) and **San Francisco** (9-10hr., 8 per day, $32). Open M-Sa 5:30am-8pm and 11pm-midnight, Su 7am-8pm and 11pm-midnight.

Santa Barbara Metropolitan Transit District (MTD), 1020 Chapala St. (☎683-3702), at Cabrillo Blvd. behind the Greyhound station. Transit center open M-F 6am-7pm, Sa 8am-6pm, Su 9am-6pm. $1, seniors and disabled 50¢, under 5 free; transfers free. MTD runs a **crosstown shuttle** from the Franklin Center on Montecito St. to Mountain and Valerio, running through the transit center. Runs M-F 7am-6:30pm; $1. The **downtown-waterfront shuttle** along State St. and Cabrillo Blvd. runs every 10min. Runs Su-Th 10:15am-6pm, F-Sa 10:15am-8pm, 25¢. Stops designated by round blue signs.

Taxis: Yellow Cab Company, ☎965-5111.

◀* 🔋 ORIENTATION & PRACTICAL INFORMATION

Santa Barbara is 96 mi. northwest of Los Angeles and 27 mi. past Ventura on the **Ventura Fwy. (U.S. 101).** Built along an east-west traverse of shoreline, the street grid is slightly skewed. The beach lies at the south end of the city, and **State St.**, the main drag, runs northwest from the waterfront. All streets are designated east and west from State St. The major east-west arteries are U.S. 101 and **Cabrillo Blvd.** Driving in Santa Barbara can be bewildering; dead-ends and one-way streets abound. Many downtown lots and streets offer 75min. of free **parking,** including two lots at Pasco Nuevo, accessible from the 700 block of Chapala St. Parking is free on Sunday. Most streets are equipped with **bike lanes.** The **Cabrillo Bikeway** runs east-west along the beach from the Bird Refuge to the City College campus.

Visitor info: Tourist Office, 1 Garden St. (☎965-3021), at Cabrillo Blvd. near the beach. Open July-Aug. M-Sa 9am-6pm, Su 10am-6pm; Sept.-Nov. and Feb.-June M-Sa 9am-5pm, Su 10am-5pm; Dec.-Jan. M-Sa 9am-4pm, Su 10am-4pm. Outdoor computer kiosk open 24hr. **Hotspots,** 36 State St. (☎564-1637 or 800-793-7666), is an espresso bar with free tourist info, hotel reservation service, and an ATM. Cafe open 24hr.; tourist info M-Sa 9am-9pm, Su 9am-4pm.

Post Office: 836 Anacapa St. (☎800-275-8777), 1 block east of State St. Open M-F 8am-6pm, Sa 9am-5pm. **ZIP Code:** 93102. **Area code:** 805.

🔋 ACCOMMODATIONS

A 10min. drive north or south on U.S. 101 rewards with cheaper lodgings than those found in Santa Barbara proper. All Santa Barbara accommodations are more expensive on the weekends.

▨ **Hotel State Street,** 121 State St. (☎966-6586), 1 block from the beach. Welcoming, comfortable, and meticulously clean European-style inn offers a good, cheap night's sleep. Common bathrooms are pristine. Cable TV, continental breakfast included. Reservations recommended. Rooms Sept.-June $50-70; July-Aug. $55-80. ❸

Santa Barbara International Tourist Hostel, 134 Chapala St. (☎963-0154). This newly-built facility has a great location for action, near the train station, the beach, and bustling State St. Bike and surfboard rentals available. Laundry. Internet $1 per 20min. Ask about 2-3 day camping trips to surrounding areas. Reservations recommended. Dorms $18-20; private singles $45-55. ❶

Carpinteria Beach State Park (☎684-2811), 12 mi. southeast of Santa Barbara along U.S. 101, has 261 developed tent sites with hot showers. Sites $12; with hookup $18; day use $2. ❶

El Capitán (☎968-1033), north of Santa Barbara off U.S. 101, has 140 well-kept sites, some with views of the Channel Islands. Sites $12. ❶

🔾 FOOD

Santa Barbara may well have more restaurants per capita than anywhere else in America, so finding a place to eat is not exactly a problem. State and Milpas St. both have many places to eat. Ice cream lovers flock to award-winning **McConnel's,** 201 W. Mission St. (☎569-2323. Open daily 10am-midnight.) **Tri-County Produce,** 335 S. Milpas St., sells fresh produce and prepared foods. (☎965-4558. Open M-Sa 9am-7:30pm, Su 9am-6pm.)

▧ **Palazzio,** 1026 State St. (☎564-1985). They say that "people don't usually leave here hungry," and you certainly shouldn't buck the trend. The depiction of the Sistine Chapel on the ceiling is nearly as impressive as the enormous pasta dishes ($11-13 for half portion, $16-18 for full) and the amazing garlic rolls. Serve-yourself wine bar. Open Su-Th 11:30am-3pm and 5:30-11pm, F-Sa 11:30am-3pm and 5:30pm-midnight. ❹

Pacific Crepes, 705 Anacapa St. (☎882-1123). Parlez-vous français? If not, you'll have to wing it. This comfortable, classy French cafe is not only filled with the delicious smells of a full menu of crepe creations, but is authentique—owned and run by a French couple qui ne parle que francais (speak French only, mon ami). The heavenly "Brittany" is topped with fresh strawberries and blueberries, fruit sauce, and ice cream ($6.25). Lunch and dinner special $15. Open Su-Tu and Th-Sa 9am-9pm. ❹

The Taj Cafe, 905 State St. (☎564-8280). Enjoy traditional village-style Indian cooking with all natural ingredients. Taj has tasty items like tandoori chicken in a sweet, tangy mango sauce ($10). Lunch specials $5.50-7.50. Many vegetarian entrees ($6.50-8). Open M-Th 11:30am-3pm and 5-10pm, F-Sa 11:30am-3pm and 5-11pm. ❷

⊙ SIGHTS

Santa Barbara is best explored in three sections—the beach and coast, swingin' State St., and the mountains. *Santa Barbara's Red Tile Tour*, a map and walking tour guide, is free at the Visitors Center.

SANTA BARBARA ZOO. The delightfully leafy habitat has low fences and such an open feel that the animals seem kept in captivity only through sheer lethargy. Attractions include a miniaturized African plain, or *veldt*, where giraffes stroll lazily, silhouetted against the Pacific. A miniature train provides a park tour. *(500 Niños Dr., off Cabrillo Blvd. from U.S. 101. Bus #14 or the downtown-waterfront shuttle. ☎962-5339. Open daily 10am-5pm. $8, seniors and ages 2-12 $6, under 2 free. Train $1.50, children $1. Parking $2.)*

BEACHES & ACTIVITIES. Santa Barbara beaches are simply breathtaking. **East** and **Leadbetter Beaches** flank the wharf on either side. **Beach Rentals** will rent beachgoers a "retro surrey": a covered-carriage, Flintstone-esque **bicycle.** You and up to eight friends can cruise along the beach paths in this stylish buggy. They also rent in-line skates. *(22 State St. ☎966-6733. Open daily 8am-8pm. Surreys $15-28 per 2hr., depending on number of riders.)* For the best **sunset** view in the area, have a drink at the bar at the Four Seasons Biltmore Hotel. This five-star lodging is a little steep, but the view is priceless. *(1260 Channel Dr., Montecito. ☎969-2261.)*

STATE STREET. Santa Barbara's monument to city planning, State St. runs a straight, tree-lined 2 mi. through the center of the city. Shops, restaurants, and cultural and historical landmarks are slathered in Spanish tile. The **Santa Barbara Museum of Art** owns an impressive 3000-year collection of classical Greek, Asian, and European works, mostly donated by wealthy local residents. *(1130 State St. ☎963-4364. Open Tu-Th and Sa 11am-5pm, F 11am-9pm, Su noon-5pm. Tours Tu-Su noon and 2pm. $6, students and ages 6-16 $3, seniors $4. Th and 1st Su of each month free.)*

MISSION SANTA BARBARA. At the so-called "Queen of Missions" there are towers containing splayed Moorish windows on either side of a Greco-Roman facade, and a Moorish fountain bubbles in front. The museum contains period rooms and a sampling of items from the mission archives. *(At the end of Las Olivas St. Bus #22. ☎682-4149. Open daily 9am-5pm. $4, under 12 free. Mass M-F 7:30am; Sa 4pm; Su 7:30, 9, 10:30am, and noon.)*

SANTA BARBARA BOTANICAL GARDEN. Though it is quite a distance from town by car, these gardens offer enjoyable hikes through 65 acres of native Californian trees, wildflowers, and cacti. *(1212 Mission Canyon Rd. ☎682-4726. Open Mar.-Oct. M-F 9am-5pm, Sa-Su 9am-6pm; Nov.-Feb. M-F 9am-4pm, Sa-Su 9am-5pm. Tours M-Th and Sa 2pm, Su-Th 10:30am; special demonstrations F and Su at 2pm, Sa at 10:30am. $5; students, seniors, and ages 13-19 $3; ages 5-12 $1; under 5 free.)*

HIKING TRAILS. The trailhead for **Seven Falls Trail** is at the junction of Tunnel and Spyglass Rd. From the end of Las Canoas Rd. off Mission Canyon Rd., you can pick up the 3.5 mi. **Rattlesnake Canyon Trail,** which features many waterfalls, pools, and secluded spots. The 7.3 mi. trek from the **Cold Springs Trail** to **Montecito Peak** is considerably more strenuous. *(From U.S. 101 S, take a left at the Hot Springs Rd. exit, and another left on Mountain Dr. to the creek crossing.)*

🎵 NIGHTLIFE

Every night of the week, the clubs on **State St.** are packed. This town is full of locals and tourists who love to eat, drink, and be mirthful. Consult the *Independent* to see who's playing on a given night. Bars on State St. charge a fairly uniform $4 for beer, so don your sleuth gear and investigate drink specials.

The Hourglass, 213 W. Cota St. (☎963-1436). With 9 spas total, pick an intimate indoor bath or watch the stars from a private outdoor tub. No alcohol allowed. Towels $1. Open 5pm-midnight. $25 per hr. for 2 people; each additional person $7. Student discount $2.

Q's Sushi A-Go-Go, 409 State St. (☎966-9177). A tri-level bar, 8 pool tables, and dancing. Stomach some sushi ($3.50-13.50) accompanied by $3.50 *sake*. Happy hour M-Sa 4-7pm, half-priced drinks and appetizers. M Brazilian night. W karaoke. Cover F-Sa after 9pm $5. Open daily 4pm-2am.

Club 634, 634 State St. (☎564-1069). Cocktails, dancing and 2 large patios. Live bands and DJs. Su and W karaoke, Th $3 Red Bull and vodkas, F 5-8pm $1.50 select beers. Occasional cover. Open M-F 2pm-2am, Sa-Su noon-2am.

SAN LUIS OBISPO   ☎805

With its sprawling green hills and its proximity to the rocky coast, San Luis Obispo (SLO) is a town where things move at a soothing, laid-back pace. Ranchers and oil-refinery employees actually make up a sizable percentage of the population, but Cal Poly State University students add a young, energetic component to the mix.

🛈 PRACTICAL INFORMATION. Greyhound, 150 South St. (☎543-2121), is open daily 7:30am-9:30pm. **Visitor Info: Chamber of Commerce,** 1039 Chorro St. (☎781-2777. Open Su-M 10am-5pm, Tu-W 8am-5pm, Th-F 8am-8pm, Sa 10am-8pm.) **State Parks Office,** 3220 S. Higuera St., #311. (☎549-3312. Open M-F 8am-5pm.) **Post Office:** 893 Marsh St. (☎543-3062. Open M-F 8:30am-5:30pm, Sa 9am-5pm.) **ZIP code:** 93405. **Area code:** 805.

🛏 ACCOMMODATIONS. Lodging rates in San Luis Obispo tend to depend on the weather, the season, and other difficult-to-predict variables. **San Luis Obispo (HI-AYH) ❶,** 1617 Santa Rosa St., has a tight-knit atmosphere. (☎544-4678. Towels 50¢, linens provided. Reception 7:30-10am and 4:30-10pm. Lockout 10am-4:30pm. Park-

THE BIG SPLURGE

PRE-MADONNA

The **Madonna Inn**, in south SLO, is probably the only hotel in the world that sells postcards of each room. Alex S. Madonna, the contractor behind the construction of much of U.S. 101 and I-5, decided in 1958 to build a Queen Anne-style hotel of 12 rooms fit for the most discerning material girl. He put his wife, Phyllis, in charge of the design. By 1962, the vision had grown into a hot-pink behemoth of 101 rooms on 2200 acres of land. The men's room is truly a work of art, featuring a giant laser-operated waterfall that doubles as a urinal. Every room has its own theme. Take a holiday in the Caveman Room, or express yourself in the Daisy Mae Room. One room even has a working waterwheel serving as a headboard. Even non-guests can cherish coffee and a bun from the Madonna's own oven or dine on steak in bubble-gum pink booths surrounding a giant gold caste tree, illuminated with flower shaped electric bulbs. You can also check out the photo album of the rooms in the reception area. At night, there's swing music from 7-11pm in the lounge to keep things hoppin'. *(100 Madonna Rd., off U.S. 101; take the Madonna Rd. exit. ☎ 543-3000. Rooms from $127-320. ❺)*

ing available. Dorms $18; private rooms for 2-4 people $50-80; nonmembers $3-5 extra. No credit cards.) The **Sunbeam Hotel ❸**, 1656 Monterey St., looks like an apartment complex, but rooms are as sunny as the staff. (☎ 543-8141. Cable TV, A/C, phones, fridges. Rooms May-Sept. M-Th $39, F-Sa $79-99; Oct.-Apr. $36-39.) **Montana de Oro State Park ❶**, on Pecho Rd. 12 mi. from SLO, south of Los Osos, offers 50 primitive sites in a gorgeous, secluded park. Outhouses and cold running water are available, but bring your own drinking water. (☎ 528-0513. Sites $10. Reserve weeks in advance during the summer.)

◨▨ FOOD & NIGHTLIFE. Monterey St. and its cross streets are lined with restaurants and cafes. The area just south of the mission along the creek is popular with lunchtime crowds. Enticing smells will lure you into the ▨**House of Bread ❶**, 858 Higuera St., which uses chemical-free Montana wheat in its delicious bread products. Raspberry pinwheels and huge cinnamon rolls run $2. (☎ 542-0255. Open M-W and F-Sa 7am-7pm, Th 7am-9pm, Su 9am-5pm.) ▨**Big Sky Cafe ❷**, 1121 Broad St., was locally voted "Best Restaurant in SLO" for delivering hearty, vegetarian-friendly food. (☎ 545-5401. Open M-Sa 7am-10pm, Su 8am-9pm.) **Grappolo's ❹**, 1040 Broad St., is a new Italian restaurant and bar with dishes ranging from $8-17; the wine list is one of the most extensive in town. (☎ 788-0260. Kitchen open Su-Th 11:30am-9pm, F-Sa 11:30am-11pm; bar open until 2am.) One half of SLO's population is under the age of 24, so the town can't help but party. It gets particularly wild after the Thursday evening **Farmers Market** along Higuera St., which is more raging block party than market. Weekdays slow down a bit while students rescue their grades. The free weekly *New Times* lists goings-on.

◙ SIGHTS. San Luis Obispo grew around the **Mission San Luis Obispo de Tolosa,** and the city continues to engage in celebrations and general lunchtime socializing around its front steps. The mission faces Mission Plaza, where Father Serra held the area's first mass. (☎ 543-6850. Open early Apr.-late Oct. daily 9am-5pm; late Oct.-early Apr. daily 9am-4pm. $2 donation requested.)

South of San Luis Obispo, **Pismo Beach** is popular and congested; the lines for the public restrooms are practically social events. Rent all kinds of beach equipment at **Beach Cycle Rentals,** 150 Hinds Ave., next to the pier. (☎ 773-5518. Open daily 9am-dusk.) **Shell Beach,** 1½ mi. from Pismo Beach, is the launching point for many a kayak. Gray whales, seals, otters, dolphins, and the occasional orca frequent **Montana de Oro State Park** (☎ 528-0513), 30min. west of SLO on Los Osos Valley Rd. The 7 mi. of shoreline remain relatively secluded. North of SLO, **Morro Bay** has dramatic coastlines formed by volcanic activity.

NEAR SAN LUIS OBISPO: HEARST CASTLE

Driving along this stretch of Rte. 1, the last thing you would expect to see is a castle that would put Xanadu to shame. Newspaper tycoon William Randolph Hearst built this palatial abode and invited wealthy elite to visit the most extravagant edifice this side of the Taj Mahal. Casually referred to by its founder as "the ranch," Hearst Castle, located on Rte. 1, 3 mi. north of San Simeon and 9 mi. north of Cambria, is a decadent conglomeration of castle, cottages, pools, gardens, and Mediterranean *esprit* perched high above the Pacific. **Tour One** covers the photogenic Neptune Pool, the opulent Casa del Sol guest house, fragrant gardens, and the main rooms of the house; this is the best bet for first-time visitors. **Tours Two, Three,** and **Four** are recommended for those already familiar with Tour One. Call weeks in advance; tours sell out. (☎ 927-2020, reservations through DESTINET ☎ 800-444-4445. Tour 1 $14, ages 6-12 $7; tours 2, 3, and 4pm $10/5 each. 2hr. evening tours feature costumed docents acting out the Castle's legendary Hollywood history; $20/10. Each tour involves 150-370 staircase steps.)

MONTEREY   ☎ 831

Whaling kept Monterey alive until 1880, when sardine fishing and packaging stepped in to take its place. In the next 50 years, the wharfside flourished like the fisherman's world immortalized by John Steinbeck in the 1940s. Monterey is now a sedate, touristed-oriented community, rich with the remnants of the past.

🛈 PRACTICAL INFORMATION. Monterey-Salinas Transit (MST), 1 Ryan Ranch Rd., runs buses. (☎ 899-2555. Call M-F 7:45am-5:15pm, Sa 10am-2:30pm.) The free *Rider's Guide,* available on buses, at motels, and at the Visitors Center, has schedules and route info. **Monterey Peninsula Visitor and Convention Bureau:** 150 Olivier St. (☎ 657-6400 or 888-221-1010; www.montereyinfo.org). **Visitors Center:** 401 Camino El Estero. (☎ 649-1770. Open May-Sept. M-F 10am-6pm, Sa-Su 10am-5pm; Oct.-Apr. daily 10am-5pm.) **Post Office:** 565 Hartnell St. (☎ 372-4003. Open M-F 8:30am-5pm, Sa 10am-2pm.) **ZIP code:** 93940. **Area code:** 831.

🖬🗋 ACCOMMODATIONS & FOOD. Reasonably priced hotels line **Lighthouse Ave.** in Pacific Grove (bus #2 and some #1 buses) and the 2000 block of **Fremont St.** in Monterey (bus #9 or 10). Others cluster along **Munras Ave.** between downtown and Rte. 1. The cheapest hotels in the area, however, are in the less-appealing towns of Seaside and Marina, just north of Monterey. **Del Monte Beach Inn ❹,** 1110 Del Monte Blvd., near downtown and across from the beach, is a Victorian-style inn with a TV room. (☎ 649-4410. Check-in 2-8pm. Reservations recommended. Rooms with shared bath Su-Th $55-66, F-Sa from $77; rooms with private bath $88-99.) The **Monterey Carpenter's Hall Hostel (HI-AYH) ❶,** 778 Hawthorne St., is located four blocks from Cannery Row. This 45-bed hostel is spacious and pristine. (☎ 649-0375. Reservations required June-Sept. Dorms $20, nonmembers $23, ages 7-17 $15.50, under 6 $11.50; private rooms from $54.) Call the **Monterey Parks** line (☎ 755-4895 or 888-588-2267) for camping info.

The sardines have left, but Monterey Bay teems with squid, crab, red snapper, and salmon. Seafood is bountiful but expensive—try an early-bird special (usually 4-6:30pm). **Fisherman's Wharf ❷** has smoked salmon sandwiches ($7) and free chowder samples. Don't despair if you loathe seafood—this is also the land of artichokes and strawberries. Free samples of fruit, cheese, and seafood are at the **Old Monterey Market Place,** on Alvarado St. (☎655-2607. Open Tu 4-8pm.) The **Old Monterey Cafe ❷,** 489 Alvarado St., has hot, hefty portions favored by locals. (☎646-1021. Lunch specials from $5.50.) **Thai Bistro II ❷,** 159 Central Ave., in Pacific Grove, has good service and a patio ringed with flowers. Lunch combos ($6) come with delicious soup. (☎372-8700. Open daily 11:30am-3pm and 5-9:30pm.)

◙ SIGHTS. The extraordinary ▨**Monterey Bay Aquarium,** 886 Cannery Row, provides visitors with a window (literally) into the most curious creatures of the Pacific. Gaze through the **world's largest window** at an enormous marine habitat containing green sea turtles, giant ocean sunfish, large sharks, and impressive yellow- and blue-fin tuna. Don't miss the oozingly graceful and mesmerizing jellyfish. Arrive with patience; the lines are as unbelievable as the exhibits themselves. (☎648-4888 or 800-756-3737. Open June-early Sept. daily 9:30am-6pm; early Sept. to May 10am-6pm. $18; students, seniors, and ages 13-17 $15; disabled and ages 3-12 $8. Audio tour in English, German, French, Japanese, and Spanish $3.)

Lying along the waterfront south of the aquarium, **Cannery Row** was once a depressed street of languishing sardine-packing plants. The ¾ mi. row has been converted into glitzy mini-malls, bars, and a pint-sized carnival complex. For a series of interpretive looks at Steinbeck's *Cannery Row,* take a peek at the **Great Cannery Row Mural;** local artists have covered 400 ft. of construction-site barrier on the 700 block with depictions of Monterey in the 1930s. The second floor bayview "Taste of Monterey" **Wine and Visitors Center,** 700 Cannery Row, offers a taste of the county's burgeoning wine industry with well-priced bottles and winery maps. The wide variety of regional wine to taste and to buy, plus the knowledgeable staff and inspiring view, makes it a great starting place for tasting tours. (☎888-646-5446. 6 tastings $5. Open daily 11am-6pm.)

Several companies on Fisherman's Wharf offer critter-spotting boat trips around Monterey Bay. The best time to go is November through March during gray whale migration season, but there are no guarantees. **Chris's Fishing Trips,** 48 Fisherman's Wharf, offers has 2-3hr. daily whale watching tours. (☎379-5951. Open daily 4am-5pm. Gray whale migration 2hr. tours May-Nov. 11am and 2pm; $25, under 13 $20. Dec.-Apr. $18/12.) **Monterey Bay Kayaks,** 693 Del Monte Ave., provides rentals, instruction, and tours. (☎373-5357 or 800-649-5357. Lessons offered. Rentals $30 per person, includes gear, wetsuit, and instruction. 3hr. beach tours given by biologist cost $55 per person. Open daily 9am-6pm; in summer F-Sa until 8pm.)

In nearby Carmel, the extraordinary 550-acre state-run ▨**Point Lobos Reserve,** on Rte. 1, is a wildlife sanctuary popular with skindivers and day hikers. Otters, sea lions, seals, brown pelicans, and gulls are visible from paths along the cliffs, so bring binoculars. Point Lobos has tide pools and marvelous vantage points for watching the whale migration, which peaks in winter but continues throughout spring. (☎624-4909. Park on Rte. 1 before the tollbooth and walk or bike in for free. MST bus #22. Open Apr.-Oct. daily 9am-7pm; Nov.-Mar. 9am-5pm. $4 per car, seniors $3; map included.)

SANTA CRUZ ☎831

One of the few places where the 1960s catch phrase "do your own thing" still applies, Santa Cruz simultaneously embraces macho surfers, aging hippies, free-thinking students, and a large lesbian, gay, and bisexual community. Along the beach and boardwalk, tourism runs rampant and surf culture reigns supreme. Nearby Pacific Ave. teems with independent bookstores and trendy cafes, providing a safe, clean hangout for locals and tourists alike. On the inland side of Mission St., the University of California at Santa Cruz sprawls luxuriously across miles of rolling forests and grasslands, filled with prime biking routes and wild students.

■ 冈 ORIENTATION & PRACTICAL INFORMATION. Santa Cruz is on the northern tip of Monterey Bay, 65 mi. south of San Francisco on Rte. 1. Passing through westside Santa Cruz, Rte. 1 becomes **Mission St.** The **University of California at Santa Cruz (UCSC)** blankets the hills inland from Mission St. Southeast of Mission St. lie the waterfront and the downtown. Down by the ocean, **Beach St.** runs roughly east-west. **Greyhound,** 425 Front St. (☎423-1800 or 800-231-2222; open daily 8:30-11:30am, 1-6:45pm, and during late bus arrivals and departures), runs to L.A. (9-11hr., 6 per day, $40); San Francisco (2½-3hr., 5 per day, $11); and San Jose (1hr., M-Th 5 per day, $6). **Santa Cruz Metropolitan Transit District (SCMTD),** 920 Pacific Ave. (☎425-8600; M-F 6am-7pm), handles local transportation. (Buses run daily 6am-11pm. $1, seniors and disabled 40¢; day pass $3/1.10. Under 46 in. free.) **Taxis: Yellow Cab,** ☎423-1234. **Bicycle Rentals: Bike Shop of Santa Cruz,** 1325 Mission St. (☎454-0909. Open daily 9am-6pm. Mountain or touring bikes $10 per hr., $40 per day. 2hr. minimum rental. HI discounts.) The **Santa Cruz County Conference and Visitor Council,** 1211 Ocean St., publishes the free *Santa Cruz County Traveler's Guide.* (☎425-1234 or 800-833-3494. Open M-Sa 9am-5pm, Su 10am-4pm.) **Post Office:** 850 Front St. (☎426-5200. Open M-F 8:30am-5pm, Sa 9am-4pm.) **ZIP code:** 95060. **Area code:** 831.

冈 ACCOMMODATIONS. Santa Cruz is solidly packed during the summer, especially on weekends; rates skyrocket, availability plummets, and price fluctuation can be outrageous. Reservations are recommended and should be made early. The **Carmelita Cottage Santa Cruz Hostel (HI-AYH) ❶,** 321 Main St., two blocks from the beach. Sporadic summer barbecues ($4) allow hungry hostelers to feed their face. (☎423-8304. 2 kitchens, common room. Chores required. Linens provided. Reception 8-10am and 5-10pm. Lockout 10am-5pm. Dorms $17, nonmembers $20, ages 12-17 $15, ages 4-11 $10, under 3 free.) The **Harbor Inn ❹,** 645 7th Ave., is a beautiful 19-room hotel well off the main drag. (☎479-9371. Check-in 2-7pm; call to arrange late check-in. Check-out 11am. Reservations recommended. Rooms Su-Th $75-115, F-Sa $75-175; off-season Su-Th $65-105/75-115.) Sleeping on the beach is strictly forbidden. **New Brighton State Beach ❶** and **Big Basin Redwoods State Park ❶,** the most scenic spots, are both accessible by public transportation. (Sites $12; day use $5 per car.)

❍ FOOD. Santa Cruz offers an astounding number of budget eateries in various locations. Without a doubt the best pre-picnic stop in town, **🏴Zoccoli's ❶,** 1534 Pacific Ave., churns out "special sandwiches" ($4-5). Daily pasta specials (about $5) come with salad, garlic bread, cheese, and a cookie. (☎423-1711. Open M-Sa 10am-6pm, Su 11am-5pm.) With excellent potatoes, freshly baked bread, and enormous omelettes, **Zachary's ❶,** 819 Pacific Ave., will fill you with reasons to laze about the beach for the rest of the day. Basic breakfast (2 eggs, oatmeal-molasses toast, and hash browns) under $5. Weekends bring crowds. (☎427-0646. Open Tu-Su 7am-2:30pm.) The **Saturn Cafe ❷,** 145 Laurel St. at Pacific Ave., serves excellent vegetarian meals (most under $6). Check it out if only for the wacky table decorations. (☎429-8505. Open 24hr.) **Malabar ❷,** 1116 Soquel Ave., at Seabright Ave. Serves healthy, vegetarian Sri Lankan cuisine like flatbread with ghee and garlic ($2.50). Entrees are reasonably priced. (☎423-7906. Open M-Th 11am-2:30pm and 5:30-9pm, F 11am-2:30pm and 5:30-10pm, Sa 5:30-10pm. No credit cards.)

◼ SIGHTS. Santa Cruz has a great beach, but the water is frigid. Without wet-suits for warmth, many casual beachgoers catch their thrills on the **Boardwalk,** a three-block-long strip of over 25 amusement park rides, guess-your-weight booths, shooting galleries, and caramel apple vendors. Try the Giant Dipper, the 1924 wooden roller coaster where Dirty Harry met his enemy in 1983's *Sudden Impact.* While the Boardwalk is relatively safe, be cautious of the surrounding area at night. (Boardwalk open daily Memorial Day-Labor Day, plus many off-season weekends and holidays. Rides $30 per 60 tickets, most rides 4 or 5 tickets; all-day pass $25 per person. Some height restrictions. Miniature golf $4.) The **Santa Cruz Wharf,** the longest car-accessible pier on the West Coast, juts off Beach St. Seafood restaurants and souvenir shops will try to distract you from the expansive views of the coast. Munch on candy from local favorite **Marini's** (☎ 423-7258) while you feed fish to the sea lions hanging out on rafters beneath the pier.

◼ NIGHTLIFE. There are weekly events listings in the free *Good Times* and *Metro Santa Cruz,* and also in the *Spotlight* section of the Friday *Sentinel.* The Boardwalk bandstand offers free summertime Friday night concerts, usually by oldies bands, around 6:30 and 8:30pm. ◼**Caffe Pergolesi,** 418A Cedar St., is a chill coffeehouse/bar perfect for reading, writing, or socializing. The cheerful color scheme and intimate tables give "Perg's" a supremely friendly atmosphere. Spe-cialties include $2.50 pints daily 7-9pm and four varieties of hot chocolate. (☎ 426-1775. Open M-Th 6:30am-11:30pm, F-Sa 7:30am-midnight, Su 7:30am-11:30pm.) The **Kuumbwa Jazz Center,** 320-322 Cedar St., offers great jazz and innovative programs. Most shows start around 8pm. (☎ 427-2227. Big acts M; local groups F. All ages. Tickets $10-20; sold through **Logos Books and Music,** 1117 Pacific Ave., open daily 10am-10pm. ☎ 427-5100.) A mega-popular gay-straight club, **Blue Lagoon,** 923 Pacific Ave., has won a plethora of local awards, from "best bartender" to "best place you can't take your parents." (☎ 423-7117. Happy hour daily 6-9pm; $3 drinks. Cover $2-5. Open daily 4pm-1:30am.) **The Catalyst,** 1011 Pacific Ave., draws national, college, and local bands. (☎ 423-1338. Shows W-Sa. Cover and age restric-tions vary widely with show; bar strictly 21+. Open M-Sa 9am-2am, Su 9am-5pm. Food served daily until 3pm; on show days until 10pm.)

◼◼ BEACHES & OUTDOOR ACTIVITIES. The **Santa Cruz Beach** (officially named Cowell Beach) is broad, reasonably clean, and packed with volleyball play-ers. Beach access points line Rte. 1; railroad tracks, farmlands, and dune vegeta-tion make several of these access points somewhat difficult, but correspondingly less crowded. To try your hand at riding the waves, contact the **Richard Schmidt Surf School,** or ask around for him at the beach. (☎ 423-0928. 1hr. private lesson $80, 2hr. group lesson $80. Includes equipment.)

Around the point at the end of W. Cliff Dr. is **Natural Bridges State Park.** While all but one of its natural bridges have collapsed, the park nevertheless offers a pris-tine beach, awe-inspiring tidepools, and tours during Monarch butterfly season from October to March. (☎ 423-4609. Open daily 8am-dusk. Parking $3.) **Parasailing** and other pricey pastimes are popular on the wharf. **Kayak Connection,** 413 Lake Ave., has ocean-going kayaks at reasonable rates. Rentals include paddle, life jacket, and a skirt or wetsuit. (☎ 479-1121. Open M-F 10am-5pm, Sa-Su 9am-6pm. Open-deck single $33 per day, closed-deck single $37. 4½hr. lessons $45.)

SAN FRANCISCO ☏415

If California is a state of mind, then San Francisco is euphoria. Welcome to the city that will take you to new highs of all kinds, leaving your head spinning, your taste buds tingling, your calves aching, and your optic nerves reeling. Though it's smaller than most "big" cities, the City by the Bay more than compensates for its size in personality. The dazzling views, huff-and-puff hills, one-of-a-kind neighborhoods, and laid-back, friendly people of SF add up to create a unique charisma. Within its mere 47 square miles, the city manages to pack an incredible amount of vitality. From its thriving art community to the bustling downtown to some of the country's most happening nightclubs, there's something for anyone who's hip.

By California standards, San Francisco is steeped in history—but it's a history of oddballs and eccentrics that resonates more today in street culture than in museums and galleries. The lineage of free spirits and troublemakers started back in the 19th century, with smugglers, pirates, and Gold Rush '49ers. In the 1950s came the brilliant, angry, young Beats, and the late 60s ushered in the most famous of SF rabble rousers—hippies and flower children, who turned on one generation and freaked out another by making love, not war. The gay community emerged in the 1970s as one of the city's most visible and powerful groups. Anti-establishment rallies and movements continue to fill the streets and newspapers. At the same time, Mexican, Central American, and Asian immigrants have made SF one of the most racially diverse cities in the United States. Like so many chameleons, San Francisco is changing with the times, but fortunately, some things stay the same: the Bay is foggy, the hills are steep, and tourists are the only ones wearing shorts. For more coverage of the City by the Bay, see ▪*Let's Go: San Francisco 2003.*

◼ INTERCITY TRANSPORTATION

San Francisco is 403 mi. north of Los Angeles and 390 mi. south of the Oregon border. The city lies at the northern tip of the peninsula separating the San Francisco Bay from the Pacific Ocean. San Francisco radiates outward from its docks, which lie on the northeast edge of the 30 mi. peninsula, just inside the lip of the Bay.

The city is 6hr. from L.A. via I-5, 8hr. via U.S. 101, or 9½hr. via Rte. 1. U.S. 101 compromises between vistas and velocity, but the stunning coastal scenery along Rte. 1 makes getting there fun. From inland California, **I-5** approaches the city from the north and south via **I-580** and **I-80**, which runs across the **Bay Bridge** (westbound toll $2). From the north, U.S. 101 and Rte. 1 come over the **Golden Gate Bridge** (southbound toll $3).

Airport: San Francisco International (☏650-821-8211), 15 mi. south of downtown via U.S. 101. Ground transportation info (☏800-736-2008). **San Mateo County Transit (SamTrans;** ☏650-817-1717) runs 2 buses to downtown. Express bus KX (35min.) runs to the Transbay Terminal. $3, seniors at off-peak times $1.25, under 17 $1.25. Bus #292 (1hr.) stops frequently along Mission St. $2.20/50¢/$1.50.

Trains: Amtrak (☏800-872-7245). connects from both Oakland and Emeryville to downtown SF ($3.50-7). To **Los Angeles** (8-12hr., 5 per day, $50). **Caltrain** (☏650-817-1717), at 4th and King St. in SoMa (operates M-F 5am-midnight, Sa 7am-midnight, Su 8am-10pm), is a regional commuter train that runs south to Palo Alto ($4, seniors and under 12 $2) and San Jose ($5.25/2.50), making many stops along the way.

Buses: Greyhound runs buses from the **Transbay Terminal,** 425 Mission St. (☎495-1575), between Fremont and 1st St. downtown. To **Los Angeles** (8-12hr., 25 per day, $45) and **Portland** (14-20hr., 7 per day, $54). **Golden Gate Transit** (Marin County, ☎923-2000), **AC Transit** (East Bay, ☎510-891-4777), and **SamTrans** (San Mateo County) also stop at the terminal.

▞ ORIENTATION

NEIGHBORHOODS

This orientation will move roughly from the tourist-laden western section of downtown San Francisco to the neighborhoods in the south, then over to the residential parts in the east. If you find that neighborhood boundaries are getting a bit confusing, don't stress—San Fran, like any living, breathing city, doesn't follow the imaginary lines that books like this one have to rely on. That said, a good map is a must.

You'll have to visit touristy **Fisherman's Wharf** at least once, and from there, move on to the posh stucco of the **Marina** and cool culture in **Fort Mason.** Just south of the Wharf, **North Beach,** a historically Italian area, overflows with restaurants and cafes in the northeastern corner of the peninsula. Food is the cornerstone of **Chinatown,** the largest Chinese community outside of Asia. To round out the northwest corner of the city, old money rises to the west on ritzy **Nob Hill,** newer money walks its dogs on **Russian Hill,** and busy **Union Square** is the retail area just north of Market St.

The majestic **Golden Gate Bridge** stretches out over the Bay from the **Presidio** in the city's northwest corner. Just south of the Presidio, **Lincoln Park** reaches westward to the ocean, while vast **Golden Gate Park** dominates the western half of the peninsula. On the opposite side of the city, the skyscrapers of the **Financial District** stretch out to the Embarcadero. City Hall, the Civic Center Public Library, and Symphony Hall crown a small but impressive collection of municipal buildings in the **Civic Center,** which lines Market St. and is bounded on the west by wide Van Ness Ave. On the other side of Van Ness Ave., newly hip **Hayes Valley** draws gallery-goers and shoppers. To the west, Union Sq. gives way to the **Tenderloin,** where—despite attempts at urban renewal—drugs, crime, and homelessness prevail. South of Market St. to the east, the **South of Market Area (SoMa)** holds large, glassy attractions near 3rd St. and scattered among industrial buildings down to 14th St.

Fillmore St. leads north to the Victorians of **Pacific Heights.** Further south, the few *udon*-filled blocks of **Japantown** offer Asian fare that rivals that found in Chinatown. West of SoMa and Hayes Valley, near Golden Gate Park, sits the former hippie haven of **Haight-Ashbury.** The diners and cafes of the **Castro,** the country's gay mecca, dazzle on Castro and Market St. northwest of the Mission. To the south of the Castro, **Noe Valley** rises up into the spectacular views of **Twin Peaks.**

The very trendy **Mission,** largely populated by Latino residents during the day and super-hip barhoppers by night, takes over south of 14th St., and **Bernal Heights** is on the rise south of the Mission. Potrero Hill, often forgotten because of Hwy. 101, offers wonderful eats. Some interesting strips of activity are sprinkled among the residential neighborhoods west of Masonic Ave., including the residential **Richmond** and **Sunset Districts.** Just east of the Sunset, **Ocean Beach** runs into the cliffs at **Fort Funston** and the shores of **Lake Merced.** And, of course, if you want to get away from it all, you can go to **Alcatraz** and **Angel Island** in the bay.

▛ LOCAL TRANSPORTATION

San Francisco Municipal Railway (MUNI; ☎673-6864) is a system of buses, cable cars, subways, and streetcars and is the cheapest and most efficient way to get around the city. Runs daily 6am-1am. $1, seniors and ages 5-17 35¢. **MUNI passports** are valid on all MUNI vehicles (1-day $6, 3-day $10, 7-day $15). Weekly Pass ($9) is valid for a single work week and requires an additional $1 to ride the cable cars. **Owl Service** runs limited routes daily 1am-5am. Wheelchair access varies among routes; all below-ground subway stations, but not all above-ground sites, are accessible.

Cable cars: Noisy, slow, and usually crammed full, but charming relics. To avoid mobs, ride in the early morning. The **Powell-Mason (PM)** line, which runs to the wharf, is the most popular. The **California (C)** line, from the Financial District up through Nob Hill, is usually the least crowded, but the **Powell-Hyde (PH)** line, with the steepest hills and the sharpest turns, may be the most fun. $2, seniors and disabled $1, under 6 free; before 7am and after 9pm $1. No transfers.

Bay Area Rapid Transit (BART; ☎989-2278) operates carpeted trains along 4 lines connecting San Francisco with the **East Bay,** including Oakland, Berkeley, Concord, and Fremont. All stations provide maps and schedules. There are 8 BART stops in San Francisco proper, but BART is not a local transportation system. Runs M-F 4am-midnight, Sa 6am-midnight, Su 8am-midnight. $1.10-6. Wheelchair accessible.

Car Rental: City, 1748 Folsom St. (☎877-861-1312), between Duboce St. and 14th St. 21+; under 25 surcharge $8 per day. From $29-35 per day, $160-170 per week. Unlimited mileage for a small fee. Open M-F 7:30am-6pm, Sa 9am-4pm. The location at 1433 Bush St., between Van Ness Ave. and Polk St., is also open Su 10am-4pm.

Taxis: Luxor Cab, ☎282-4141. **National Cab,** ☎648-4444.

◨ PRACTICAL INFORMATION

Visitor info: California Welcome Center (☎956-3493), Pier 39 at the Great San Francisco Adventure. Open M-Th 10am-6pm, F-Sa 10am-7pm.

Hotlines: Rape Crisis Center, ☎647-7273. **AIDS Hotline,** ☎800-342-2437. **Drug Crisis Line,** ☎362-3400. **Suicide Prevention,** ☎781-0500. **Crisis Line for the Handicapped,** ☎800-426-4263.

Internet access: For complete listings in SF, check **www.surfandsip.com. Chat Cafe,** 498 Sanchez St. (☎415-626-4700). $2.50 per hr., free with purchase. Open M-F 6:30am-7:30pm, Sa 8am-7:30pm, Su 8am-6:30pm.

Post Office: Union Square Station, 170 O'Farrell St. (☎415-956-0131), at Stockton St., in the basement of Macy's. Open M-Sa 10am-5:30pm, Su 11am-5pm. **ZIP Code:** 94108. **Area code:** 418, except where otherwise noted. 10-digit dialing required.

◪ ACCOMMODATIONS

Beware that some of the cheapest budget hotels may be located in areas requiring extra caution at night. Reservations are recommended at hotels.

HOSTELS

▨ **Interclub Globe Hostel,** 10 Hallam Pl. (☎431-0540), off Folsom St. between 7th and 8th St. MUNI bus #12 to 7th and Howard St. Internet access. Happening common room has pool table, TV, microwave, and fridge. All rooms have private bath. Key deposit $10. Passport required. Dorms $19; 3 nights $45; private single or double $50; off-season rates reduced. No credit cards. ❶

▨ **Adelaide Inn,** 5 Isadora Duncan (☎359-1915 or 800-359-1915), at the end of a little alley off Taylor St. between Geary and Post St. Those needing handicapped accessibility can arrange for nearby hotel accommodations at Adelaide's rates. Small shared hallway bathrooms. No curfew. Hostel offers shuttle to SFO airport each morning ($8). Reception 24hr. Reservations recommended. Check-out noon. Dorms $20; singles and doubles from $55. ❶

Green Tortoise Hostel, 494 Broadway (☎834-1000), off Columbus Ave. at Kearny St. Breakfast and kitchen access included. Storage lockers $1, small lockers free, coin laundry, free sauna, and free Internet access. Key deposit $20. Check-in noon. Check-out 11am. 10 day max. stay. Dorms $19-22; private rooms $48-56. No credit cards. ●

SF Hostel-City Center (HI-AYH), 685 Ellis St. (☎474-5721). Rooms are spare, but come with perks like cheap Internet access, nightly movie, and listings of walking tours and pub crawls. Reservations recommend. Dorms $22, nonmembers $25; doubles $66/69. ●

SF Hostel-Downtown (HI-AYH), 312 Mason St. (☎788-5604), between Geary and O'Farrell St. Internet access $1 per 10min. Weekly events list of

---

Downtown San Francisco

⬥ **ACCOMMODATIONS**
Adelaide Inn, **24**
Alisa Hotel, **21**
Ansonia Abby Hotel, **22**
Fort Mason Hostel, **3**
Green Tortoise Hostel, **10**
HI-AYH Hostel San Francisco-
  City Center, **29**
New Central Hotel & Hostel, **39**
San Remo Hotel, **4**

🍴 **FOOD**
Ananda Fuara, **38**
Basil, **42**
Bell Tower, **13**
Brandy Ho's, **12**
City View Restaurant, **20**
Dottie's True Blue Café, **23**
Grand Palace, **16**
Italian French Baking Co., **9**
Kay Cheung's Restaurant, **17**
Lori's Diner, **28**
LuLu, **33**
Pat's Café, **2**
Rico's, **7**
Zarzuela, **8**

🎵 **NIGHTLIFE/MUSIC**
The EndUp, **41**
Hotel Utah Saloon, **40**

⭐ **ENTERTAINMENT**
Biscuits & Blues, **25**
Curran Theatre, **26**
Geary Theater, **27**
Golden Gate Theater, **30**
Louise M. Davies
  Symphony Hall, **37**
Lou's Pier, **1**
The Orpheum, **36**
War Memorial Opera House, **35**
Yerba Buena Center for the
  Performing Arts, **31**

● **SIGHTS**
Asian Art Museum, **32**
Cable Car Powerhouse
  and Museum, **14**
City Lights Bookstore, **11**
"Crookedest Street in the
  World", **5**
Ross Alley, **15**
San Francisco Art Institute, **6**
San Francisco Public
  Library, **35**
Transamerica Pyramid, **18**
Waverly Place, **19**

---

free walking tours, ballgame outings, and a nightly movie. Quiet hours midnight-7am. $5 deposit for locker or key. 21-night max. stay. Wheelchair accessible. Mainly tidy and unadorned dorm-style triples and quads $22; nonmembers $25. Private rooms $60/66. Reserve by phone with credit card or show up around 8am. ●

New Central Hotel and Hostel, 1412 Market St. (☎703-9988), between Van Ness Ave. and Polk St. This conventional, no-frills hostel is dim and austere but clean. Lockers, TV room, kitchens, laundry. Linen free. Proof of travel required. Check-out 11am. Dorms $15 per night, $95 per week. Private room with shared bath $25, with private bath $45. ●

Fort Mason Hostel (HI-AYH), Bldg. #240 (☎771-7277), at the corner of Bay and Franklin St. in Fort Mason. No smoking or alcohol. Movies, walking tours, kitchen, bike storage. Usually booked weeks in advance, but a few beds are reserved for walk-ins. Minor chores expected. Lockers, laundry, parking. Check-in 2:30pm. Check-out 11am. No curfew, but lights-out at midnight. Dorms $22.50. ●

Easy Goin' Travel and California Dreamin' Guesthouse, 3145-47 Mission St. (☎552-8452), at Precita Ave. Additional location at Harrison and 7th, but check-in and booking is here, and a shuttle to Harrison and 7th St. is provided. In-room TVs, kitchen, laundry, Internet access, bike rental, and travel services. Min. 2-night stay. Check-in noon. Check-out 11am. $20 security and key deposit. Reservations recommended. Dorm beds $18-19; private rooms $40-43. ●

GUEST HOUSES

🏨 **The San Remo Hotel,** 2237 Mason St. (☎776-8688). The best value in town. Built in 1906, this non-smoking hotel has rooms that are small but elegantly furnished with antique armoires, bedposts, lamps, and complimentary (if random) backscratchers. Friendly staff will book tours, bikes, cars, and airport shuttles; they also recommend restaurants. Free modem connections. Laundry. Check-in 2pm. Check-out 11am. Reservations required. Singles $50-75; doubles $60-85; triples $75-90. ❸

Downtown San Francisco

■ **Ansonia Abby Hotel,** 711 Post St. (☎673-2670 or 800-221-6470). Free breakfast daily, dinner M-Sa, overnight storage and safety deposit, TV and fridge in every room. DSL access. Laundry. Check-out 11am. Singles $56-66; doubles $66, with bath $79. ❸

■ **The Queen Anne Hotel,** 1590 Sutter St. (☎441-2828 or 800-227-3970), at Octavia St. Each room in this beautiful mansion is uniquely and elaborately decorated with period furnishings. Breakfast, afternoon tea, and sherry served daily. Fireplaces, jacuzzis, and wheelchair accessible rooms available. All rooms include spacious private bath and TV. "Moderate" rooms from $139; deluxe from $179; suites from $199. ❺

■ **The Parker House,** 520 Church St. (☎621-3222 or 888-520-7275), near 17th St. Regularly voted best BGL B&B in the city. Cable TV and modem ports in every room. Heavenly down comforters. Spa and steam rooms. Breakfast included in a sunny porch overlooking rose gardens. 2-night min. stay on weekends. Check-in 3pm. Check-out noon. Reservations recommended. Rooms with shared bath from $119, with private bath from $139. ❺

■ **The Willows,** 710 14th St. (☎431-4770), near Church St. Handmade willow-branch furnishings, window gardens, and kimono bathrobes make for a little glen of queer happiness. Cable TV, VCR. Expanded continental breakfast, evening cocktails, pantry with microwave and fridge, sparkling hall baths, and washbasins in all 12 rooms. Reception 8am-8pm. Singles $110-140; doubles $120-150. ❺

Alisa Hotel, 447 Bush St. (☎956-3232). Small, simple hotel with clean, airy rooms. TV, telephone, private bath available. Make weekend reservations 2 weeks in advance. Single, double, and 2-bed rooms $59-159. ❹

The Red Victorian Bed, Breakfast, and Art, 1665 Haight St. (☎864-1978). Striving to create peace through tourism, guests come together at breakfast to meditate and chat. Rooms are individually decorated to honor themes like sunshine, redwoods, playground, and butterflies; even the hall bathrooms have their own motifs. Breakfast included. Reception 9am-9pm. Check-in 3-9pm or by appointment. Check-out 11am. Reservations required. Various-sized rooms $72-200; discounts for stays longer than 3 days. ❹

The Bed and Breakfast Inn, 4 Charlton Ct. (☎921-9784), off Union St. between Laguna and Buchanan St. Reception 6:30am-12:30am. Check-out noon. Beautiful rooms with twin beds and shared baths $90-125; large rooms with private baths, many with jacuzzis $175; apartment-like suites for 5-8 people $280-380. ❺

Hayes Valley Inn, 417 Gough St. (☎431-9131 or 800-930-7999). The rooms are well maintained and have cable TV, phone, and private sink and vanity. Some smoking and pet-friendly rooms. Continental breakfast. Check-in 3pm. Check-out 11am. Reservations recommended for summer and holidays. In summer singles $58; doubles $68-79; queens $78-89; queen turret $88-99. In winter $42/48-56/54-61/58-66. ❸

◘ FOOD

FISHERMAN'S WHARF & THE MARINA

■ **Pat's Café,** 2701 Leavenworth St. (☎776-8735), at N. Point St. One of a string of breakfast joints, Pat's stands out from the crowd—not just because of its bright yellow building, but for its huge, delicious, home-cooked portions. Sandwiches and big breakfast plates (most $4-7) taste just like mom's. Open daily 7:30am-2pm. No credit cards. ❷

■ **Pizza Orgasmica,** 3157 Fillmore St. (☎931-5300), at Greenwich St. "We never fake it," says the sign out front. With pizzas named "menage a trois" and "doggie style," it's hard not to get excited. Prices can get steep (pies $10-23; slices $2-3.50) so don't miss the daily all-you-can-eat special (11am-4pm; $6.50). Open Su-W 11am-midnight, Th 11am-2am, F-Sa 11am-2:30am. ❶

HAVE SOME DIM SUM
Dim Sum ("little bits of the heart") are the foods traditionally eaten at Cantonese or Southern Chinese *yum cha* ("drink tea") eateries. This heavenly dining experience involves various small dishes eaten in the morning or early afternoon, typically on Sundays, in mass quantities. Waiters and waitresses push finger-food laden carts; when they stop at your table, point to whatever looks good. The waiter will stamp a card to charge you by dish. Our favorites include:

Cha Siu Bao: Steamed BBQ pork buns.
Haar Gao: Steamed shrimp dumplings.
Dan Taat: Tiny tart shells filled with sweet egg custard.
Siu Mai: Shrimp and pork in a fancy dumpling "basket."
Walteep: The classic steamed pork dumplings.
Dou Sha Bao: Steamed rolls filled with sweet red bean paste.
Loh Bak Goh: Mashed turnip patty. Don't knock it until you've tried it.
Fun Gwor: Chicken and mushroom dumplings.
Yuebing: Flaky frosted pastry with bean paste filling.

Crepes A-Go-Go, 2165 Union St., (☎928-1919), off Fillmore St. Great crepes, sweet or savory ($2.50-6). Open M-Th 8am-10pm, F-Sa 8am-noon, Su 8am-9pm. ❶

NORTH BEACH & CHINATOWN
▨ **Brandy Ho's,** 217 Columbus Ave. (☎788-7527), at Pacific Ave., where the lines blur between Chinatown and North Beach. This Hunan food is *spicy*. Heed the chef's suggestions, like the Three Delicacies (tossed fried scallops and shrimp; $11.50), and feast in the classy dining room. Meals $10-11. Lunch specials $5-6 (M-F 11:30am-3pm). Open M-Th and Su 11:30am-11pm, F-Sa 11:30am-midnight. ❸

Italian French Baking Co., 1501 Grant Ave. (☎421-3796), at Union St. Provides nearly every restaurant in the area (as well as hungry SF civilians) with baked goods of all kinds, including breads, baguettes, and biscotti ($1-6). Oversized coconut macaroons for just $1. Although you'd never guess it from the innocent facade, the basement was the chosen locale for the murder scene in *Basic Instinct* and scenes from several mobster movies. Open M-F and Su 6am-6pm, Sa 6am-7pm. No credit cards. ❶

Grand Palace, 950 Grant Ave. (☎982-3705), between Jackson and Washington St. Chandeliers, plush red cushions, and a meticulously doting waitstaff that serves amazing entrees ($7-10) just right for a pauper's budget. Open daily 7:30am-10pm. ❷

City View Restaurant, 662 Commercial St. (☎398-2838), between Kearny and Montgomery St. City View is where Chinatown entrees meet Financial District prices. More expensive than average dim sum elsewhere ($2.30-4.20 a plate), but classier too. Open M-F 11am-2:30pm, Sa-Su 10am-2:30pm. ❷

Chef Jia, 925 Kearny St. (☎398-1626), at Pacific St., serves cheap food in a small, informal space. Tasty $4.50 lunch specials served 11:30am-4pm (try the spicy string beans with yams). Entrees $6-7. Open daily 11:30am-10pm. No credit cards. ❷

Kay Cheung's Restaurant, 615 Jackson St. (☎989-6838), at Kearny St. Patrons line up on weekends to sample some of the best dumplings Chinatown has to offer. The shrimp dumplings are a must-eat. Tasty seafood entrees "straight from the tank" ($4-7.50). Dim sum ($2.15 per plate) served 9:30am-2:30pm. Open daily 9:30am-9pm. ❷

NOB HILL & RUSSIAN HILL
▨ **Zarzuela,** 2000 Hyde St. (☎346-0800), at Union St. in Russian Hill. Authentic Spanish homestyle cooking and a festively upscale setting make $4-7 *chorizo al vino* (vegetable stew) the highlight of the evening. Full meals $10-15. Open Tu-Th 5:30-10pm, F-Sa 5:30-10:30pm. ❷

Bell Tower, 1800 Polk St. (☎567-9596), at Jackson St. A bright and casually upscale restaurant replete with sophisticated window-side tables and elegantly carved wooden bar. $6-8 appetizers like pistachio-crusted baked brie with pomegranate and $8-15 entrees to prove that exploring Californian cuisine doesn't have to be intimidating or expensive. Vegetarian friendly. Sa-Su brunch 10:30am-2pm. Open M-F 11am-2am; lunch served until 2pm; dinner starts at 5:30pm; kitchen closes at midnight. ❸

Rico's, 943 Columbus Ave. (☎928-5404), between Taylor and Lombard St. No need to pay an arm and a leg for wharf-side snacks—go to Rico's for a homemade arm-sized burrito ($3.50-6) and a cold beer ($2.50-3). Open daily 10am-10pm. ❶

UNION SQUARE & THE TENDERLOIN

▨ **Dottie's True Blue Café,** 522 Jones St. (☎885-2767), between Geary and O'Farrell St. Despite tiny portions, quirky variations like chicken-apple sausage, ceramic turtle salt shakers, and grilled eggplant with goat-cheese sandwich ($6) keep a line waiting outside during breakfast *and* lunch. Open M and Th-Su 7:30am-3pm. ❷

▨ **The California Culinary Academy,** 625 Polk St. (☎292-8229 or 800-229-2433), at Turk St. Watch and eat as Academy students prepare expert confit and sweetbreads behind the glass kitchen windows, which look into the elegant dining room. M-W features 3-course dinners ($22); Th French Buffet ($32.50); F Grande Buffet ($36). Open M-F noon-1pm and 6-8pm. ❺

Lori's Diner, 149 Powell St. (☎677-9999), at O'Farrell St. Elvis is most certainly not dead—he's working as a short-order cook at Lori's. Waitresses in period costumes careen by Gomer Pyle gas pumps with stacked burger plates and huge omelettes ($6-8). Open Su-Th 7am-10pm, F-Sa 7am-11pm. Additional locations: 336 Mason St. (☎392-8646), at Geary St. Open 24hr. 500 Sutter St. (☎891-1950), at Powell St. Open Su-Th 6am-11pm, F-Sa 6am-midnight. ❶

CIVIC CENTER & HAYES VALLEY

▨ **It's Tops Coffee Shop,** 1801 Market St. (☎715-6868), on the corner of Market and Octavia St. With a soda fountain, an old-school counter, orange booths, and a doo-wop sound track, this 1952 establishment has been around since this decor was cool. Breakfast $4.50-9; burgers $6-8; fountain drinks $2.50-5. Open M and W-F 8am-3pm and 8pm-3am, Tu 8am-3pm, Sa 8am-3am, Su 8am-11pm. ❷

▨ **Ananda Fuara,** 1298 Market St. (☎621-1994), at Larkin St. This vegetarian cafe with vegan tendencies offers creative combinations of super-fresh ingredients. Terrific smoothies ($3.25) and great sandwiches like the BBQ tofu burger ($5.50). The most popular dish and house specialty is the "neatloaf" (topped with mashed potatoes and gravy $10.25, in a sandwich $6.50.) Open M-Tu and Th-Sa 8am-8pm, W 8am-3pm. No credit cards. ❷

Moishe's Pippic, 425-A Hayes St. (☎431-2440), between Gough and Octavia St. A good old Jewish deli, with loads of hot dogs, corned beef pastrami, and chopped liver. Oy, who could forget, matzoh ball soup. Sandwiches $5.50-8. Open M-F 8am-4pm, Sa 9am-4pm. No credit cards. ❷

SOUTH OF MARKET AREA (SOMA)

▨ **LuLu,** 816 Folsom St. (☎495-5775), near 4th St. An impressive oak-burning oven fires this inventive Cali-cuisine atmosphere. Unique pizzas (from $14) and huge family-style plates of fire-roasted veggies are the best budget bets on an ever-changing menu of seasonal specialties. Reservations essential. Open M-Th and Su 11:30am-10:30pm, F-Sa 11:30am-11:30pm. Limited menu 3-5:30pm. ❹

Basil, 1175 Folsom St. (☎552-8999), near 8th St. Somberly sophisticated ambiance sets the mood for delectably classy Thai. Curries and entrees "from the grill" or "from the wok" (all $9-12) include "drunken tofu" and piquant "mussels inferno." Open M-F 11:30am-2:45pm and 5-10pm, Sa-Su 5-10:30pm. ❸

MISSION & THE CASTRO

▧ **Home,** 2100 Market St. (☎503-0333), at 14th and Church St. Inventively Californian take on meat and veggie dishes varies seasonally according to the chef's preferences. Sausalito watercress salad with jicama, peaches, and citrus vinaigrette $6. Entrees $8-13. Open M-W 5:30-10pm; Th-Sa 5:30-11pm; Su brunch 10:30am-2pm, "Flip-Flop" cocktail party 2-6pm, and dinner 5:30-10pm. ❸

▧ **Taquería El Farolito,** 2279 Mission St. (☎824-7877), at 24th St. The spot for cheap and authentic Mexican food; Taco Bell this ain't. After any kind of evening activity in Mission, El Farolito is a great late-night fix. Tacos $1.75. Open Su-Th 9am-2am, F-Sa 9am-4am. No credit cards. ❶

Nirvana, 544 Castro St. (☎861-2226), between 18th and 19th St. Heavenly Thai entrees ($7-12), a plethora of vegetarian options, and specialty drinks like the nirvana coloda ($7-8) all help you reach apotheosis in a simple, swanky setting. Open M-Th 4:30-10pm, F 4:30-10:30pm, Sa 11:30am-10:30pm, Su noon-10pm. ❷

Bissap Baobab, 2323 Mission St. (☎826-9287), just south of 19th St. Lots of vegetables, chicken, or fish. Most entrees under $10. Open Tu-Su 6-10pm. Bar open Tu-Th and Su until midnight, F-Sa until 2am. ❷

HAIGHT-ASHBURY

▧ **Squat and Gobble,** 1428 Haight St. (☎864-8484), between Ashbury St. and Masonic Ave. This popular cafe offers enormous omelettes ($5.50-6.75) and equally colossal crepes ($4.50-7.25). Lots of salads, sandwiches, and vegetarian options, too. Open 8am-10pm daily. Additional locations at 237 Fillmore St., in the Lower Haight, and 3600 16th St., in the Castro. ❷

Blue Front Café, 1430 Haight St. (☎252-5917), between Ashbury St. and Masonic Ave. This Genie-marked joint is a great place to fill your tummy with starchy goodness. Down a beer or ginseng chai (both around $2.50) to go with your sizeable wrap ($6) or Middle Eastern meal ($5-8.50). 10% discount with student ID. Open Su-Th 7:30am-10pm, F-Sa 8am-11pm. ❷

Estela's Fresh Sandwiches, 250 Fillmore St. (☎864-1850), just south of Haight St. Massive fresh sandwiches in this tiny nook. Order one pre-made ($5.50-6.75) or build your own ($6.25). Check out the "Big Sherm," filled with turkey, smoked gouda, pepperocini, and more. Open daily 10am-6pm. ❷

RICHMOND

Le Soleil, 133 Clement St. (☎668-4848), between 2nd and 3rd Ave. Serves Vietnamese food at prices so low they rival Chinatown's best. Huge vegetarian selection, and nothing on the menu cracks $8. Open M-Th 11am-10pm, F-Su 11am-11pm. ❷

Q, 225 Clement St. (☎752-2249), between 3rd and 4th Ave. Lunch entrees and salads and weekend brunch $6.50-9. Dinner gets pricey (entrees $9-11), but portions are big and good. Open M-F 11:30am-3pm and 5-11pm, Sa 10am-11pm, Su 10am-10pm. ❸

CALIFORNIA

◉ SIGHTS

GOLDEN GATE BRIDGE & THE PRESIDIO

GOLDEN GATE BRIDGE. When Captain John Fremont coined the term "Golden Gate" in 1846, he meant to name the harbor entrance to the San Francisco Bay after the Golden Horn port of Constantinople. In 1937, however, the colorful name became permanently associated with Joseph Strauss' copper-hued engineering masterpiece—the Golden Gate Bridge. Built for only $35 million, the bridge stretches across 1.2 mi. of ocean, its towers looming 65 stories above the Bay. It can sway up to 27 ft. in each direction during high winds. The views from the bridge are amazing, especially those from Vista Point in Marin County. To see the bridge itself, it's best to get a bit farther away: Fort Point and Fort Baker in the Presidio, Land's End in Lincoln Park, Mt. Livermore on Angel Island, and Hawk Hill off Conzelman Rd. in the Marin Headlands all offer spectacular views of the Golden Gate on clear days. *(MUNI bus #28 or 29.)*

PRESIDIO. When Spanish settlers forged their way up the San Francisco peninsula from Baja California in 1769, they established *presidios*, or military outposts, along the way. San Francisco's Presidio, the northernmost point of Spanish territory in North America, was dedicated in 1776. The settlement stayed in Spanish hands for 45 years, then was given to Mexico when it won independence from Spain, then was passed to the US as part of the 1848 Treaty of Guadalupe Hidalgo. Gold fever brought the expansion of the outpost and, today, the Presidio is part of the Golden Gate National Recreation Area (GGNRA), run by the National Park Service and the Presidio Trust.

FISHERMAN'S WHARF & THE BAY

Piers 39 through 45 provide access to San Francisco's most famous and touristy attractions. Easily visible from boats and the waterfront is **Alcatraz Island.**

ALCATRAZ. Mention Alcatraz, and most people think of hardened criminals and daring escapes. In its 29 years as a maximum-security federal penitentiary, Alcatraz did encounter a menacing cast of characters including Al "Scarface" Capone, George "Machine Gun" Kelly, and Robert "The Birdman" Stroud. There were 14 separate escape attempts—some desperate, defiant bolts for freedom, others carefully calculated and innovative. Only one man is known to have survived crossing the Bay; he was recaptured, while five escapees remain unaccounted for. On the rock, the cellhouse audio tour takes you back to the infamous days of Alcatraz. A **Park Ranger guided tour** can take you around the island and through its 200 years of occupation, from a hunting and fishing ground for native Americans to a civil war defensive outpost to a military prison, a federal prison and finally a birthplace of the movement for Native American civil rights. Now part of the **Golden Gate National Recreation Area**, Alcatraz is home to diverse plants and birdlife. *(To get to the island, take the Blue and Gold Fleet from Pier 41. ☎ 773-1188, tickets ☎ 705-5555. Ferries 9:30am and every 30min. between 10:15am and 4:15pm; arrive 20min. early. $9.25, seniors $7.50, ages 5-11 $6. Reservations recommended 1 day in advance, preferably 1 week. On sold-out days, the ticket counter in the basement of the DFS Galleria in Union Square offers a limited number of "extra" tickets for $2.25 extra. Tours: Audio tours daily $4, ages 5-11 $2. Park Ranger tours free. "Alcatraz after dark" $20.75, seniors and ages 12-17 $18, ages 5-11 $11.50; call for times and availability. Other boating companies run shorter boats around, but not onto, the island for about $10.)*

GHIRARDELLI SQUARE. A chocolate-lover's heaven, Ghirardelli Square houses a mall in what used to be a chocolate factory. Don't worry, you don't need a Willy Wonka golden ticket to sample the savory sweets; visit the **Ghiradelli Chocolate Manu-**

factory, with its vast selection of chocolatey goodies, or the **Ghirardelli Chocolate Shop and Caffe,** with drinks, frozen yogurt, and a smaller selection of chocolates. Both hand out **free samples** of chocolate at the door, but the Caffe is usually less crowded. *(900 North Point St. ☎ 775-5500. Mall stores open M-Sa 10am-9pm, Su 10am-6pm. Manufactory: ☎ 771-4903. Open Su-Th 10am-11pm, F-Sa 10am-midnight. Caffe: ☎ 474-1414. Open M-Th 8:30am-9pm, F 8:30am-10pm, Sa 9am-10pm, Su 9am-9pm.)* The **soda fountain,** an old-fashioned ice-cream parlor, serves up huge sundaes ($6.25) smothered with its world-famous hot fudge sauce. *(Open Su-Th 10am-11pm, F-Sa 10am-midnight.)*

MARINA & FORT MASON

PALACE OF FINE ARTS. With its open-air domed structure and curving colonnades, the ◪**Palace of Fine Arts** is one of the best picnic spots in the city. It was originally built to commemorate the opening of the Panama Canal and congratulate San Francisco's recovery from the 1906 earthquake. Shakespearean plays are often performed here during the summer. *(On Baker St., between Jefferson and Bay St. next to the Exploratorium. Open daily 6am-9pm. Free.)* The **Palace of Fine Arts Theater,** located directly behind the rotunda, also hosts various dance and theater performances and film festivals. *(☎ 563-6504. Call for shows, times, and ticket prices.)*

FORT MASON. Despite its severe facade, the Fort Mason Center is home to some of the most innovative and impressive cultural museums and resources in San Francisco. The array of outstanding attractions seem to remain unknown to most travelers and locals alike, making it a quiet waterfront counterpart to the tourist blitz of nearby Fisherman's Wharf. On the first Wednesday of every month all museums are free and open until 7pm. The grounds are also the headquarters of the **Golden Gate National Recreation Area (GGNRA).** While not nearly so spectacular as some other GGNRA lands, the manicured lawns make a swell spot for strolling and picnicking. *(The park is at the eastern portion of Fort Mason, near Gashouse Cove. ☎ 441-3400, ext. 3.)*

FINANCIAL DISTRICT

TRANSAMERICA PYRAMID. The leading lady of the city's skyline, this distinctive office building was designed to allow as much light as possible to shine on the streets below. Unless you're an employee, tight security means there is no chance of a top-floor view. The lobby is currently undergoing renovation to modernize a "virtual viewing lounge" in the Washington St. entrance so you can peer down on the masses from ground-level. Now a pillar of commerce, the location was once a site of revolutionary disgruntlement; Sun Yat-Sen scripted a dynastic overthrow in one of its 2nd-floor offices. *(600 Montgomery St., between Clay and Washington St.)*

JUSTIN HERMAN PLAZA. When not overrun by skateboarders, the Plaza is home to bands and rallyists who sometimes provide lunch-hour entertainment. U2 rock star Bono was arrested here after a concert in 1987 for spray painting "Stop the Traffic—Rock and Roll" on the fountain. Recently, the plaza has been the starting point for **Critical Mass,** a pro-bicyclist ride that takes place after 5pm on the last Friday of every month. If you happen to be around on a hot day, walk through the inviting mist of the **Vaillancourt Fountain** to cool off.

NORTH BEACH

WASHINGTON SQUARE. Washington Sq., bordered by Union, Filbert, Stockton, and Powell St., is North Beach's *piazza,* a pretty, tree-lined lawn. The wedding site of Marilyn Monroe and Joe DiMaggio, the park fills every morning with men and women from Chinatown practicing *tai chi.* By noon, sunbathers, picnickers, and bocce-ball players take over. The **Church of St. Peter and St. Paul** beckons tired sightseers to take refuge in its dark, wooden nave. *(666 Filbert St., to the north of the square.*

☎ 421-0809. Mass in English, Italian, and Cantonese.) Turn-of-the-century SF philanthropist and party-girl Lillie Hitchcock Coit donated the **Volunteer Firemen Memorial** in the middle of the square after being rescued from a fire as a young girl.

COIT TOWER. Also built by Lillie Hitchcock Coit, the **Coit Tower** stands 210 ft. high and commands a spectacular view of the city and the bay. The view from the base of the tower is by no means shabby, and paying for the elevator is not necessarily worth it. During the Great Depression, the government's Works Progress Administration employed artists to paint the colorful and surprisingly subversive murals in the lobby. *(MUNI bus #39, or climb up the Filbert Steps from the Embarcadero. ☎ 362-0808. Open daily 10am-7pm. Elevator $3.75, over 64 $2.50, ages 6-12 $1.50, under 6 free.)*

CITY LIGHTS BOOKSTORE. Drawn by low rents and cheap bars, the Beat writers came to national attention when Lawrence Ferlinghetti's **City Lights Bookstore,** opened in 1953, published Allen Ginsberg's *Howl.* First banned, then subjected to a long trial in which a judge found the poem "not obscene," the book vaulted the Beats into literary infamy. City Lights has expanded since its Beat days and now stocks fiction and poetry, but it remains committed to publishing young poets and writers under its own imprint. *(261 Columbus Ave. ☎ 362-8193. Open daily 10am-midnight.)*

CHINATOWN

WAVERLY PLACE. Find this little alley and you'll want to spend all afternoon gazing at the incredible architecture. The fire escapes are painted in bright pinks and greens and connected by railings cast in intricate Chinese patterns. Here you can visit the demure **Tien Hou Temple**—the oldest place of worship of its kind in San Fran. *(125 Waverly Pl. Open Su-W and F-Sa 9:30am-3:30pm.)*

ROSS ALLEY. **Ross Alley** was once lined with brothels and opium dens, and today still has the cramped look of old Chinatown. The narrow street has stood in for the Orient in such films as *Big Trouble in Little China, Karate Kid II,* and *Indiana Jones and the Temple of Doom.* Squeeze into a tiny doorway to watch fortune cookies being shaped by hand at the **◪Golden Gate Cookie Company.** *(56 Ross Alley. ☎ 781-3956. Open daily 10am-8pm. Bag of cookies $3, with "funny" or "sexy" fortunes $5.)*

NOB HILL & RUSSIAN HILL

THE CROOKEDEST STREET IN THE WORLD. The famous curves of **Lombard St.**— installed in the 1920s so that horse-drawn carriages could negotiate the extremely steep hill—are one-of-a-kind. From the top of Lombard St., both pedestrians and passengers enjoy the view of city and harbor. The view north along Hyde St. isn't too shabby either. *(Between Hyde and Leavenworth St. at the top of Russian Hill.)*

GRACE CATHEDRAL & HUNTINGTON PARK. The largest Gothic edifice west of the Mississippi, **Grace Cathedral** is Nob Hill's stained-glass studded crown. The castings of its portals are such exact imitations of the Baptistery in Florence that they were used to restore the originals. Inside, modern murals mix San Franciscan and national historical events with saintly scenes. The altar of the AIDS Interfaith Memorial Chapel celebrates the church's "inclusive community of love." *(1100 California St., between Jones and Taylor St. ☎ 749-6300. Services Su 7:30, 8:15, 11am, and 3:30pm; M-F 7:30, 8:30am, 12:10, and 5:15pm; Sa 9am, 3:30, and 5pm. Tour guides available M-F 1-3pm, Sa 11:30am-1:30pm, Su 1:30-2pm. Suggested donation $3.)* Outside, the building looks out onto nicely manicured **Huntington Park,** equipped with a park and playground.

UNION SQUARE & THE TENDERLOIN

MAIDEN LANE. When the Barbary Coast (now the Financial District) was down and dirty, Union Sq.'s **Morton Alley** was dirtier. Around 1900, murders on the Alley averaged one per week and prostitutes waved to their favorite customers from 2nd-story windows. After the 1906 earthquake and fires destroyed most of the flophouses, merchants moved in and renamed the area **Maiden Lane** in hopes of changing the street's image. It worked. Today, the pedestrian street that extends two blocks from Union Square's eastern side is as virtuous as they come and makes a pleasant place to stroll or sip espresso wearing newly purchased Gucci shades.

CIVIC CENTER

CIVIC CENTER. Referred to as "The Crown Jewel" of American Classical architecture, the **City Hall** reigns supreme over the Civic Center, with a dome to rival St. Paul's cathedral and an area of over 500,000 sq ft. *(1 Dr. Carlton B. Goodlett Pl., at Van Ness Ave. ☎554-4000. Open M-F 8am-8pm, Sa-Su noon-4pm.)* The seating in the $33 million glass-and-brass **Louise M. Davies Symphony Hall** was designed to give audience members a close-up view of performers. Visually, the building is a smashing success. Its **San Francisco Symphony** is equally esteemed. *(201 Van Ness Ave. ☎552-8000, tickets ☎431-5400. Open M-F 10am-6pm, Sa noon-6pm.)* The recently renovated **War Memorial Opera House** hosts the well-regarded **San Francisco Opera Company** and the **San Francisco Ballet.** *(301 Van Ness Ave., between Grove and McAllister St. Box office at 199 Grove St. ☎864-3330. Open M-Sa 10am-6pm and in Opera House 2hr. before each show.)*

MISSION

MISSION DOLORES. Founded in 1776 in the old heart of San Francisco, the Mission Dolores is thought to be the city's oldest building. Due to its proximity to the Laguna de Nuestra Señora de los Dolores (Lagoon of Our Lady of Sorrows), the mission became universally known as Misión de los Dolores. Bougainvillea, poppies, and birds-of-paradise bloom in its cemetery, which was featured in Alfred Hitchcock's 1958 film *Vertigo*. *(3321 16th St., at Dolores St. ☎621-8203. Open May-Oct. daily 9am-4:30pm; Nov.-Apr. 9am-4pm. $2, ages 5-12 $1. Mass in English M-F 7:30 and 9am; Sa 7:30, 9am, and 5pm; Su 8 and 10am. In Spanish Su noon.)*

MISSION MURALS. A walk east or west along 24th St., weaving in and out of the side streets, reveals the Mission's magnificent murals. Continuing the Mexican mural tradition made famous by Diego Rivera and Jose Orozco, the murals have been a source of pride for Chicano artists and community members since the 1980s. Standouts include the more political murals of **Balmy Alley,** off 24th St. between Harrison and Folsom St., a three-building tribute to guitar god **Carlos Santana** at 22nd St. and Van Ness Ave., the face of **St. Peter's Church** at 24th and Florida St., and the **urban living center** on 19th St. between Valencia and Guerrero St.

THE CASTRO

Stores throughout the area cater to gay-mecca pilgrims, with everything from rainbow flags and pride-wear to the latest in BGLT books, dance music, and trinkets of the more unmentionable variety. Many local shops, especially on the wildly colorful **Castro St.,** also double as novelty museums. Discover just how anatomically correct Gay Billy is at **Does Your Father Know?,** a one-stop kitsch-and-camp overdose. To read up on gay history and culture, enlighten yourself at **A Different Light Bookstore,** or head to **Getups** for vintage pizzazz.

ACID TEST In Basel, Switzerland, in 1943, Albert Hoffman synthesized a compound called lysergic acid diethylamide (LSD). The new wonder drug was said to cure psychosis and alcoholism. In the early 1950s, the CIA adopted LSD as part of Operation MK-ULTRA, a series of Cold War mind control experiments. By the end of the 60s, the drug had been tested on some 1500 military personnel in a series of shady operations. Writers Ken Kesey, Allen Ginsberg, and the Grateful Dead's Robert Hunter were first exposed to acid as subjects in these government experiments. The CIA soon abandoned the unpredictable hallucinogen, but it had been discovered by Bohemian proto-hippies in Haight-Ashbury. Amateur chemists began producing the compound, and prominent intellectuals like Timothy Leary and Aldous Huxley advocated its use as a means of expanding consciousness. In October 1966, the drug was banned in California, and Kesey's Merry Pranksters hosted their first public Acid Test. Once a secret weapon of the military-industrial complex, acid became an ingredient of the counterculture, juicing up anti-war rallies and love-ins across the Bay Area and the nation.

WALKING TOURS. For a guided tour of the Castro that includes sights other than men strolling around in cut-off shorts, check out **Cruisin' the Castro**. Trevor Hailey, a resident since 1972, is consistently recognized as one of San Fran's top tour leaders. Her 4hr. walking tours cover Castro life and history from the Gold Rush to the present. (☎ 550-8110; www.webcastro.com/castrotour. Tours Tu-Sa 10am. $40; lunch included. Reservations required.)

HAIGHT-ASHBURY

FORMER CRIBS. The former homes of several counterculture legends still attract visitors. From the corner of Haight and Ashbury St., walk just south of Waller St. to check out the house occupied by the **Grateful Dead** when they were still the Warlocks. (710 Ashbury St.) Look across the street for the **Hell's Angels** house. If you walk back to Haight St., go right three blocks, and make a left on Lyon St., you can check out **Janis Joplin's** old abode. (122 Lyon St., between Page and Oak St.) Cross the Panhandle, continue three blocks to Fulton St., turn right, and wander seven blocks toward the park to see where the Manson "family" planned murder and mayhem at the **Charles Manson** mansion. (2400 Fulton St., at Willard St.)

SAN FRANCISCO ZEN CENTER. Appropriately removed from the havoc of the Haight, the Zen Center offers a peaceful retreat. Call for information on *sutra* chanting services, or stay for a weekly program. Vegetarian meals (M-F; $7-8) Saturday meditation instruction (8:45am), lectures, and classes make this a haven for all. Visit the bookstore and the library to familiarize yourself with the Way. (300 Page St., near Laguna St. ☎ 863-3136. Bookstore open M-Th 1:30-5:30pm and 6:30-7:30pm, F 1:30-5:30pm, Sa 11am-1pm. Library open Tu-F 1:30-5pm.)

GOLDEN GATE PARK

Take your time to enjoy this park. Intriguing museums (see p. 913) and cultural events pick up where the lush flora and fauna leave off, and athletic opportunities abound. The park has a municipal golf course, an equestrian center, sports fields, tennis courts, and a stadium. On Sundays, traffic is banned from park roads, and bicycles and in-line skates come out in full force. The **Visitors Center** is located in the Beach Chalet on the western edge of the park. (☎ 751-2766. Open daily 9am-6pm.) **Surrey Bikes and Blades in Golden Gate Park** rents equipment. (50 Stow Lake Dr. ☎ 668-6699. Open daily 10am-dusk. Bikes from $6 per hr., $21 per day. Skates $7/20.)

GARDENS. The soil of Golden Gate Park is rich enough to support a wealth of flowers. The **Garden of Fragrance** is designed especially for the visually impaired; all labels are in Braille and the plants are chosen specifically for their textures and scents. Near the Music Concourse off South Dr., the **Shakespeare Garden** contains almost every flower and plant ever mentioned by the Bard. Plaques with the relevant quotations are displayed, and maps help you find your favorite hyacinths and rue. *(Open in summer daily dawn-dusk; in winter Tu-Su dawn-dusk. Free.)* The **Japanese Cherry Orchard**, at Lincoln Way and South Dr., blooms intoxicatingly the first week in April. Created for the 1894 Mid-Winter Exposition, the elegant **Japanese Tea Garden** is a serene collection of wooden buildings, small pools, graceful footbridges, carefully pruned trees, and lush plants. *(☎ 752-4227. Open daily 8:30am-6pm. $3.50, seniors and ages 6-12 $1.25; free daily 8:30-9:30am and 5-6pm.)*

LINCOLN PARK & OCEAN BEACH

TRAILS. The **Coastal Trail** loops around the interior of Lincoln Park for a scenic coastal hike. The entrance to the trail is not particularly well marked, so be careful not to mistakenly tackle a much more difficult cliffside jaunt. The path leads first into **Fort Miley**, a former army post. Near the picnic tables rests the **USS San Francisco Memorial**. The USS *SF* sustained 45 direct hits (which started 25 fires) in the battle of Guadalcanal on November 12-13, 1942. Nearly 100 men died in the clash, but the ship went on to fight in 10 more battles. *(Trail begins at Pt. Lobos and 48th Ave. Free.)*

The Coastal Trail continues for a 3 mi. hike into **Land's End**, famous for its views of both the Golden Gate Bridge and the "sunken ships" that signal treacherous waters below. Dense pine and cypress trees, colorful flowers, and a wide array of cheerful fauna line the rocky coastline. Except for the occasionally harsh winds, the trail is a few talking animals short of a Disney film paradise. Biking is permitted on the trail, although parts contain stairs and bumpy terrain better suited to mountain bikes. From Land's End, onlookers have the option to hike an extra 6 mi. into the Presidio and on to the arches of Golden Gate Bridge.

For hikers and bikers who aren't so inclined, the brisker (and flatter) walk along **El Camino Del Mar** originates close to the Coastal Trail but runs farther in from the shore. Enjoy the forrested views and a stop at the Legion of Honor before finishing "The Path of the Sea" at China Beach. In all, this makes for a pleasant 1½ mi. afternoon stroll highlighting the best of Lincoln Park. *(Begins at Pt. Lobos and Sea Rock Dr.)*

BEACHES. Swimming is allowed but dangerous at scenic **China Beach** at the end of Seacliff Ave. on the eastern edge of Lincoln Park. Adolph Sutro's 1896 **bathhouse** lies in ruins on the cliffs. Cooled by ocean water, the baths were capable of squashing in 25,000 occupants at a time, but after an enthusiastic initial opening, they very rarely did. **Ocean Beach,** the largest and most popular of San Francisco's beaches, begins south of Point Lobos and extends down the northwestern edge of the city's coastline. The strong undertow along the point is very dangerous, but die-hard surfers brave the treacherous currents and the ice-cold water anyway.

JAPANTOWN & PACIFIC HEIGHTS

SAINT DOMINIC'S ROMAN CATHOLIC CHURCH. Churchgoers and architecture buffs alike will appreciate St. Dominic's towering altar, carved in the shape of Jesus and His 12 apostles. With its imposing gray stone and gothic feel, St. Dominic's is a must see, especially its renowned shrine of **St. Jude,** skirted by candles and intricately carved oak. *(2390 Bush St., at Steiner St. Open M-Sa 6:30am-5:30pm, Su 7:30am-9pm. Mass M-F 6:30, 8am, and 5:30pm; Sa 8am and 5:30pm; Su 7:30, 9:30, 11:30am, 1:30, and 5:30pm, Su candlelight service 9pm.)*

FUJI SHIATSU & KABUKI SPRINGS & SPA. After a rigorous day hiking the city's hills, reward your weary muscles with an authentic massage at **Fuji Shiatsu.** (1721 Buchanan Mall, between Post and Sutter St. ☎346-4484. Morning $41, afternoon $44.) Alternatively, head to the bathhouse at Kabuki Hot Springs to relax in the sauna and steam-room, or enjoy the *Reiki* treatment to heal, rejuvenate and restore energy balance. *(1750 Geary Blvd. ☎922-6000. M-F before 5pm $15, after 5pm and Sa-Su $18. Open to men only Th and Sa 10am-10pm; women only Su, W, and F 10am-10pm. Co-ed with clothing required Tu 10am-10pm.)*

🏛 MUSEUMS

MARINA & FORT MASON

■ **Exploratorium,** 3601 Lyon St. (☎563-7337). The Exploratorium can hold over 4000 people, and on the 1st W of every month when admission is free, it usually does. Over 650 interactive displays, including miniature tornadoes, computer planet-managing, and giant bubble-makers, explain the wonders of the world. Inside the Exploratorium, the **Tactile Dome**—a dark maze of tunnels, slides, nooks, and crannies—helps refine your sense of touch. On the 2nd W of each month from Nov.-Mar., the Exploratorium hosts avant-garde **art cocktail nights** that feature Bay area artists, a DJ, and bar. Open June-Aug. daily 10am-6pm; Sept.-May Tu-Su 10am-5pm. Open year-round W 10am-9pm. $10, students and seniors $7.50, ages 5-17 $6. Tactile dome $14, reservations recommended.

Museum of Craft and Folk Art, Bldg. A., 1st fl. ☎775-0990. The MOCFA brings together a fascinating collection of crafts and functional art (vessels, clothing, furniture, and jewelry) from diverse cultures past and present, showcasing everything from 19th century Chinese children's hats to unwearable underwear made from Lifesaver wrappers. Open Tu-F and Su 11am-5pm, Sa 10am-5pm; 1st W of each month 11am-7pm. $3; students, seniors, and ages 12-17 $1; Sa 10am-noon and 1st W of each month free.

African-American Historical and Cultural Society Museum, Bldg. C, #165 (☎441-0640). Displays historic artifacts and artwork, modern works, and a permanent collection by local artists. Open W-Su noon-5pm. $2, seniors and children $1.

SF Museum of Modern Artists Gallery, Bldg. A., 1st fl. ☎441-4777. Over 1500 Bay Area artists show, rent, and sell their work in this space. Temporary exhibits are on display downstairs while certain pieces are sold upstairs; proceeds are split between the artist and the Museum. Rentals from $35 per month for 2-3 months. Every May, the gallery hosts a benefit sale—all works half price. Open Tu-Sa 11:30am-5:30pm. Free.

NOB HILL & RUSSIAN HILL

San Francisco Art Institute, 800 Chestnut St. (☎771-7020 or 800-345-7324). The oldest art school west of the Mississippi, the Institute is lodged in a converted mission and has produced a number of American greats including Mark Rothko, Ansel Adams, Imogen Cunningham, Dorothea Lange, and James Weeks. To the left as you enter is the **Diego Rivera Gallery,** one wall of which is covered by a huge 1931 Rivera mural. The gallery hosts weekly student exhibits with receptions Tu 5-7pm. Open during term-time daily 9am-9pm; in summer 9am-8pm. Professional exhibits are housed in the **Walter and McBean Galleries,** open Tu-Sa 11am-6pm.

Cable Car Powerhouse and Museum, 1201 Mason St. (☎474-1887). After the steep journey up Nob Hill, you'll understand what inspired the development of the vehicles celebrated here. More an educational breather than a destination in its own right, the modest building is the working center of San Fran's cable car system. Look down on 57,300 ft. of cable whizzing by or view displays about the cars, some of which date back to 1873. Open Apr.-Oct. daily 10am-6pm; Nov.-Mar. 10am-5pm. Free.

UNION SQUARE & TENDERLOIN

Martin Lawrence Gallery, 366 Geary St. (☎956-0345). A modest corner space that displays works by pop artists like Warhol and Haring, as well as some studies by Picasso and Chagall. Haring once distributed his work for free to New York commuters in the form of graffiti; it now commands upwards of $13,000 In print form. Open M-Th 9am-8pm, F-Sa 9am-9pm, Su 10am-6pm.

509 Cultural Center/Luggage Store, 1007 Market St. (☎255-5971) and 1172 Market St. (☎865-0198). Started by a group of artists and residents in the late 1980s, the centers draw on the neighborhood's rich diversity to gain a sense of community. Performing arts events, exhibitions, and arts education initiatives are presented at its 2 Tenderloin venues. With its pyromaniac nipple-clamp photographs and religious-themed BDSM paintings, the often graphic art exhibits probably won't be grandma's favorites. Regular events include comedy open mic (Tu 8pm) and improvisational music concerts. (Th 8pm. $6-10 suggested donation for each.) Next door to 509 Cultural Center, the **Cohen Alley** houses a 3rd venue for the area's creative talent; the once-abandoned alley is leased to the Luggage Store, whose vibrant murals and ornately sculpted gate have transformed the alley into an artistic showcase.

Hang Gallery, 556 Sutter St. (☎434-4264). Sleek, urban gallery housed in a cozy chrome warehouse. An annex recently opened directly across the street on the 2nd floor of 567 Sutter. Hang specializes in the rental of paintings and sculpture "by emerging artists for emerging collectors." Buyers (or renters) beware: you mess up the art, you buy the art. Open M-Sa 10am-6pm, Su noon-5pm.

SOUTH OF MARKET AREA (SOMA)

Yerba Buena Center for the Arts, 701 Mission St. (☎978-2787). The center runs an excellent theater and gallery space, with many lively programs emphasizing performance, film, viewer involvement, and local multicultural work. It is surrounded by the **Yerba Buena Rooftop Gardens,** a vast expanse of concrete, fountains, and foliage. Open Tu-Su 11am-6pm. $6, students and seniors $3.

ZEUM, 221 4th St. (☎777-2800), at Howard St. Within the Yerba Buena gardens, this recently opened "art and technology center" is aimed at children and teenagers. The best draw may be the reopened carousel, created in 1906. Open in summer Tu-Su 11am-5pm. $7, seniors and students $6, ages 5-18 $5. Carousel open Su-Th 10am-6pm, F-Sa 10am-8pm. $2 for 2 rides.

San Francisco Museum of Modern Art (SFMOMA), 151 3rd St. (☎357-4000), between Mission and Howard St. This black-and-gray marble-trimmed museum houses 5 spacious floors of art, with an emphasis on design. It houses the largest selection of 20th-century American and European art this side of New York. Free gallery tours: 4 per day. Open June-Aug. M-Tu and F-Su 10am-6pm, Th 10am-9pm; Sept.-May M-Tu and F-Su 11am-5:45pm, Th 11am-8:45pm. $10, students $6, over 62 $7, under 13 free. Half-price Th 6-8:45pm; free 1st Tu of each month.

GOLDEN GATE PARK

California Academy of Sciences, 55 Concourse Dr. (☎750-7145), on the east side of the park at 9th Ave. Houses several smaller museums specializing in different fields of science. The **Steinhart Aquarium** is home to members of over 600 aquatic species. Shark feedings M-W and F-Su 10:30am, 12:30, 2:30, and 4:30pm. Open ocean fish feedings 1:30pm. Penguin feeding daily 11:30am, 4pm. At the **Natural History Museum,** the Earthquake Theater shakes visitors. Open June-Aug. daily 9am-6pm; Sept.-May 10am-5pm. Combined admission $8.50; seniors, students, and ages 12-17 $5.50; ages 4-11 $2. Free 1st W each month (open until 8:45pm). The **Morrison Planetarium** re-creates the heavens with impressive sky shows M-F 2pm, with additional

THE HIDDEN DEAL

OAKLAND'S AVANT GARDE

Tucked away under the veneer of suburbia in gritty Oakland (east of San Francisco, just across the Bay) is an underground and emerging culture of cutting edge, experimental performance, installation, and avant garde art. Here are a couple of places in Oakland to check out:

The Black Box houses a technologically equipped theater space and art gallery and is getting increasing support from the city to perpetuate its commitment to "the spirit of experimentation, multicultural collaboration, and community building through the celebration of life, art, and the cosmos." Check the website for listings. *(1928 Telegraph Ave., just south of 20th St. ☎451-1932; www.blackboxoakland.com.)*

Oakland Metro was spawned by the Oakland Opera Theater with the vision of creating an affordable, intimate performance space. *(201 Broadway, near Jack London Sq. ☎763-1146; www.oaklandmetro.org.)*

Expressions Art Gallery offers incredible displays with a focus on installation art. *(815 Washington St., at 8th St. ☎451-6646. Open daily noon-8pm.)*

The Vulcan Lofts leads the underground revolution with Barbara's Cocktail Hour—an Internet radio show turned public party—at its Studio 56. Live broadcasts F 9pm-midnight. *(At High St. and San Leonardo Blvd. in East Oakland.)*

summer showings. $2.50; students, seniors, and ages 6-17 $1.25.

LINCOLN PARK

California Palace of the Legion of Honor (☎863-3330), in the middle of Lincoln Park. A copy of Rodin's *The Thinker* beckons visitors into the grand courtyard, where a little glass pyramid recalls another Paris treasure, the Louvre. A thorough catalogue of great masters, from the medieval to the modern, hangs inside. Other draws include a pneumatically operated 4500-pipe organ, played in free recitals weekly (Sa-Su 4pm). Just outside the Palace, a **Holocaust memorial** depicts the Holocaust through a mass of emaciated victims with a single, hopeful survivor looking out through a barbed-wire fence to the beauty of the Pacific. Open Tu-Su 9:30am-5pm. $8, seniors $6, ages 12-17 $5, under 12 free. $2 discount with MUNI transfer; Tu free.

♫ ENTERTAINMENT

MUSIC

The distinction between bars, clubs, and live music venues is hazy in San Francisco. Almost all bars will occasionally have bands, and small venues have rock and hip-hop shows. Look for the latest live music listings in *S.F. Weekly* and *The Guardian*. Hard-core audiophiles might also snag a copy of *BAM*.

■ **Café du Nord,** 2170 Market St. (☎861-5016), between Church and Sanchez St. in the Castro. Excellent live music nightly—from pop and groove to garage rock. Local favorites include vintage jazz, blues, and R&B. Special weekly events include the popular Monday Night Hoot, a showcase of local singing and songwriting talent. Happy hour 6-7:30pm; martinis, Manhattans, and cosmos $2.50. 21+. Cover after 8:30pm $5-10. Open daily 6pm-2am.

■ **Justice League,** 628 Divisadero St. (☎440-0409), at Hayes St. in the Lower Haight. Live hip-hop is hard to find in San Francisco, but the Justice League fights ever onward for a good beat. Excellent variety of artists. M reggae and dub. W soul night. 21+. Cover $5-25, usually $10-14. Usually open daily 9pm-2am.

Bottom of the Hill, 1233 17th St. (☎626-4455), between Missouri and Texas St. in Potrero Hill. Intimate rock club with tiny stage is the last best place to see up-and-comers before they move to bigger venues. Most Su afternoons feature local bands and all-you-can-eat BBQ. 21+. Cover $5-10. Open M-Th 3pm-2am, Sa 8pm-2am, Su 4-10pm.

The Fillmore, 1805 Geary Blvd. (☎346-6000), at Fillmore St. in Japantown. Bands that would pack stadiums in other cities are often eager to play at the legendary Fillmore, the foundation of San Francisco's 1960s music scene. Grand, brightly lit, and filled with anecdotal and nostalgic wall-hangings. All ages. Tickets $15-40. Call for hours.

Amoeba Music, 1855 Haight St. (☎831-1200), just east of Stanyan St. in the Upper Haight. Free concerts in the store. No, literally, in the store—you actually stand in the aisles. All types of music and some fairly well-known acts. Also features weekly in-house DJ series. Open M-Sa 10:30am-10pm, Su 11am-9pm.

THEATER

Downtown, **Mason St.** and **Geary St.** constitute **"Theater Row,"** the city's prime place for theatrical entertainment. **TIX Bay Area,** in the garage beneath Union Sq. on Geary St., is a Ticketmaster outlet with tickets for almost all shows and concerts in the city. Buy a seat in advance, or try for cash-only, half-price tickets on the day of the show. (☎433-7827; www.theaterbayarea.org. Open Tu-Th 11am-6pm, F-Sa 11am-7pm.)

Magic Theatre, Bldg. D, 3rd fl., (☎441-8822) in Fort Mason Center. The theater stages both international and American premieres. Box office open Tu-Sa noon-5pm. Shows start at 8 or 8:30pm; previews and Su matinees start at 2 or 2:30pm. W-Th $22-32, F-Su $27-37, previews and Su matinees $15. Student and senior rush tickets available 30min. before the show; $10. Call for exact times.

The Orpheum, 1192 Market St., at Hyde St. near the Civic Center. Box office at 6th and Market St. (☎512-7770). This famous San Francisco landmark hosts big Broadway shows. 2 sister theaters in the area host smaller shows: **Golden Gate Theatre,** 1 Taylor St., and **Curran Theatre,** 445 Geary St. Individual show times and ticket prices vary.

Theater Artaud, 450 Florida St. (☎437-2700; box office 621-7797), at Mariposa St. in the Mission. Shows some of the best and most diverse contemporary theater and dance in the Bay Area. Box office open Tu-Sa 1-6pm and 1hr. before each show. Ticket prices depend on the show, but students and seniors get a $2 discount. Volunteer to usher and see the show for free; call ahead.

Cobb's Comedy Club, 2801 Leavenworth St. (☎928-4320; www.cobbscomedy.com), at Beach and Hyde St. in the Cannery. This San Francisco standard provides all-professional stand-up 7 nights a week in an intimate, no-frills venue. Come for the small-time comic marathon (M-W $7) or the big-name headliners (Th-Su $10-17). 2 drink min. Purchase tickets online or at the club after 7pm.

MOVIES

▨ **Castro Theatre,** 429 Castro St. (☎621-6350), near Market St. in the Castro. Eclectic films, festivals, and double features, and live organ music before evening shows. Far from silent—a bawdy, catty, hilarious crowd turns many a movie into *The Rocky Horror Picture Show.* Highlights include the sing-along *Sound of Music,* for those who believe Julie Andrews would be much better with chest hair. $8, seniors and under 12 $5. Matinees W and Sa-Su $5. Box office opens 1hr. before 1st show. No credit cards

DANCE

▨ **Alonzo King's Lines Contemporary Ballet** (☎863-3360), in Hayes Valley. Combines elegant classical moves with wild athletic flair to the music of great living jazz, blues, and world music composers. Springtime shows are performed at the Yerba Buena Center for the Arts (p. 913). Tickets $15-25.

Oberlin Dance Company, 3153 17th St. (☎863-9834), between South Van Ness and Fulsom St. in the Mission. Mainly dance space but occasional theater, with gallery attached. 2-6 shows a week means there's always something going on. Box office open

CALIFORNIA

THE LOCAL STORY

37 PIECES OF FLAIR

Graham Kimura is Trap Door's premier "flair" bartender and is ranked one of the Top 50 in the world. Let's Go got a chance to talk with him about life behind the bar.

Flair bartending is all about showmanship, like in the movie *Cocktail.* I use every piece of equipment behind the bar: napkins, straws, garnish, glass, ice... anything to add a little style. You have to be comfortable behind the bar because you're flipping bottles in the air, trying not to spill alcohol. There is working flair and there is exhibition flair. When it's crowded and you don't have time to do much except something to catch the eye of the customer, that's working flair. You do it to make more tips and entertain the crowd. When you're out there working your ass off for 10 hours, you hate dealing with ignorant people who don't know the word "tip." If you piss off the bartender, he's going to make you a shitty drink.

Once a guy started talking shit, saying that he could out-drink me. I said, "Alright, let's do it," and made the stand-up purple hooter shots. He didn't know it, but mine had cranberry juice and a little bit of shammer. His had some 151 proof stuff and when he took a sip he threw up right on my bar. His friends just laughed and gave me tips; that pretty much shut him up for the rest of the night.

W-Sa 2-5pm. Tickets $10-20, but occasional 2-for-1 and "pay what you can" nights.

California Contemporary Dancers, 530 Moraga St. (☎ 753-6066), in the Sunset. The all-woman modern dance company brings together the best of widely diverse dance and musical traditions to create exciting, innovative performances. They play at venues throughout the city; call or check www.ccdancers.org for ticket and show information.

SPORTS

Home to the five-time Super Bowl champion **49ers** (☎ 468-2249; tickets 656-4900), **3COM Park,** also known as Candlestick Park, sits right on the ocean, resulting in trademark gusts that led to one of the lowest homerun averages in baseball back when the Giants played there. If you're driving, take U.S. 101 8 miles south to the Candlestick Park exit. MUNI buses #9X, 28X, and 47X "Ballpark Express Line" also service the stadium. The **Giants** now play at the newly built **Pacific Bell Park,** 24 Willie Mays Plaza (☎ 972-2000; tickets 510-2255 or 888-464-2468), in SoMa near the ocean off Townsend St. Take Hyde St. to 8th St., turn left on Bryant St. and right on 4th St. Via public transportation, take the Metro Ballpark Service beginning either at the Balboa Park (via M-Ocean View route) or West Portal Station.

◼ FESTIVALS

If you can't find a festival going on in San Francisco, well, you just aren't trying hard enough. Cultural, ethnic, and gay and lesbian special events are happening year-round. For two consecutive weekends in April, the Japanese **Cherry Blossom Festival** (☎ 563-2313) lights up the streets of Japantown with hundreds of performers. The oldest film festival in North America, the **San Francisco International Film Festival** shows more than 100 international films of all genres over two weeks. (☎ 561-5022. Kabuki and Castro Theaters. Most $9.) If film's your thing, you may want to check out the **San Francisco International Gay and Lesbian Film Festival** (☎ 703-8650), California's second-largest film festival and the world's largest gay and lesbian media event. The $6-15 tickets go fast. It takes place at the Roxie (at 16th and Valencia St.) and Castro Theatre (see p. 915) during the eleven days leading up to **Pride Day.** The High Holy Day of the queer calendar, Pride Day celebrates with a parade and events downtown starting at 10:30am. (☎ 864-3733. June 29, 2003.) For a similarly wild atmosphere, experience

Carnaval, San Francisco's take on Mardi Gras, featuring Latino, jazz, and samba Caribbean music. (☎920-1215. May 24-25, 2003.)

For a bit of high culture, consider the free **San Francisco Shakespeare Festival,** taking place every Saturday and Sunday in September in Golden Gate Park. (☎865-4434. Shows at 1:30pm, but get there at noon for a seat.) For more experimental theater, try the **San Francisco Fringe Festival,** featuring 63 international companies presenting shows under an hour, all for less than $8. (☎931-1094. Starts the 1st Th after Labor Day in 5 theaters downtown.) You'll find guilt-free chocolate heaven at the **Ghirardelli Square Chocolate Festival** (☎775-5500) in early September, when proceeds from sampling all the chocolate goodies go to Project Open Hand. The oldest blues festival in America, **San Francisco Blues Festival** attracts some of the biggest names in the business. (☎979-5588. 3rd weekend in Sept. in Fort Mason.) Finally, the leather-and-chains gang lets it all hang out at the **Folsom Street Fair,** Pride Day's ruder, raunchier, rowdier little brother. (☎861-3247. Sept. 28, 2003, on Folsom St. between 7th and 11th St.)

◢ NIGHTLIFE

Nightlife in San Francisco is as varied as the city's personal ads. Everyone from the "shy first-timer" to the "bearded strap daddy" can find places to go on a Saturday (or Tuesday) night. The spots listed below are divided into bars and clubs, but the lines get pretty blurred in SF after dark, and even cafes hop at night. For additional information, check out the nightlife listings in the *S.F. Weekly, S.F. Bay Guardian,* and *Metropolitan.* **Housewares,** 1322 Haight St. (☎252-1440), is a rave clothing store and a good source of flyers for parties and events.

Politics aside, nightlife alone is enough to make San Francisco a gay mecca. From the buff gym boys in nipple-tight Ts to tattooed dykes grinding to NIN, there's something for everybody. The boys hang in the **Castro** (around the intersection of Castro and Market St.), while the girls prefer the **Mission** (on and off Valencia St.); both genders frolic along **Polk St.** (several blocks north of Geary Blvd.), and in **SoMa.** Polk St. can be seedy and SoMa can be barren, so keep a watchful eye for trouble. Most clubs and bars listed below are gay-friendly. *The Sentinel* offers information on gay community events, and the free *Odyssey* and *Oblivion* are excellent guides. *Unless otherwise noted, all clubs are 21+ only.*

BARS & PUBS

▨ **Trap Door,** 3251 Scott St. (☎776-1928). House, funk, and Top 40 DJs pack the place on F and Sa nights. If anything, go just to see the only Bay Area "Flair Bartender" (see **37 Pieces of Flair,** at left). Cover around $10. Dress code. Open W-Sa 7pm-2am.

▨ **Hotel Utah Saloon,** 500 4th St. (☎546-6300). More than average bar food, including veggie options and build your own burger (from $7). Stage hosts live rock or country music nightly and one of the best open mics in the city on M (shows begin 8:30-9pm). Beer $3.75. 21+. Show cover $5-7. Open M-F 11am-2am, Sa-Su 6pm-2am.

▨ **The Bar on Castro,** 456 Castro St. (☎626-7220), between Market and 18th St. A refreshingly urbane Castro staple with dark plush couches perfect for eyeing the stylish young crowd, scoping the techno-raging dance floor, or watching *Queer as Folk.* Happy hour M-F 3-8pm, beer $2.25. Su beer $1.75. Open M-F 3pm-2am, Sa-Su noon-2am.

Café Royale, 800 Post St. (☎441-4099). "Creamsicle" *sake* cocktails and fresh sandwiches ($7.50) make this the right setting for jazz, pool, and 19th-century burgundy couch seating. DJs spin some nights for a mixed crowd. Happy hour M-F 3-7pm. Brunch

Su 11am-5pm features omelettes and chicken-apple sausage ($5-7). Open M-Th 3pm-midnight, F-Sa 3pm-2am, Su 11am-midnight.

Hush Hush, 496 14th St. (☎241-9944), at Guerrero St. You'll feel oh so hip when you find Hush Hush, since this hot spot is too cool to need a sign. Look for the blue awning with white numbers 496. Generally Latin, hip-hop, or electronica, but DJs mix it up quite a bit. MC Battle 1st Tu of every month. Smile Su with Rock DJs. Open daily 6pm-2am.

Lefty O'Doul's, 333 Geary St. (☎982-8900), between Mason and Powell St. Named after iconic baseball hero Frank "Lefty" O'Doul, this colossal Irish tavern is like 3 smaller bars in one: a piano lounge, a vast open bar with booths and sit-down tables, and a sports bar area in the back. Come for the drinks (most $4) and the nightly piano sing-along. Open daily 7am-2am; kitchen closes at midnight.

Tonga Room, 950 Mason St. (☎772-5278), in the Fairmont Hotel in Nob Hill. Go down 2 floors to level T. It "Takes Two to Mango" ($8.50), but any one can have fun at this enormous tiki (and fabulously tacky) bar featuring "bamboo" trees, muumuu-clad wait-resses, and gigantic fruity drinks ($8-11). A band performs recent covers on a floating stage in an artificial lagoon, while tropical storms roll in every 30min. with simulated thunder, lightning, and rain. During happy hour (M-F 5-7pm) drinks are $3-7 with an all-you-can-eat Polynesian buffet ($6). Open Su-Th 5-11:45pm, F-Sa 5pm-12:45am.

CLUBS

■ SF Badlands, 4121 18th St. (☎626-9320), near Castro St. Strutting past the sea of boys at the bar, the Castro's prettiest faces and bodies cruise a futuristic blue-and-chrome dance floor, where everyone can sing along to Madonna, George Michael, and Destiny's Child. Cover F-Sa $2. Open daily 2pm-2am.

Liquid, 2925 16th St. (☎431-8889), at South Van Ness Ave. Nightly mix usually includes trip-hop and hip-hop, but mainly house. Young but mature and mellow crowd fills the small space. Meet a cutie and practice those long-forgotten back seat skills; that's right, Liquid's couches are all car seats. 21+. Cover $4-5. Open daily 9pm-3am.

The Endup, 401 6th St. (☎357-0827), at Harrison St. A San Francisco institution—com-plete with outdoor garden and patio—where everyone eventually ends up. DJs spin pro-gressive house for the mostly straight KitKat Th, the pretty-boy Fag F, and the blissful hetero-homo mix during popular all-day Sa-Su parties. Sa morning "Otherwhirled" party 4am. Infamous Su "T" Dance (27 years strong) 6pm-4am. Cover $5-15. Open Th-F, and Su 10pm-4am.

Asia SF, 201 9th St. (☎255-2742), at Howard St. Expensive Cal-Asian-fusion eats served by fabulous gender-fusion trannies. Each "waitress" takes a break every half hour to perform in an audience-rousing runway show. Entrees $10-20; $25 minimum per person. Reservations required. Open daily 5-10pm for dinner and a more affordable downstairs club, club only F-Sa 10:30pm-3am with varying cover charge.

Polly Esther's, 181 Eddy St. (☎885-1977), between Taylor and Mason St. Monthly foam parties, "male revues" Sa 9-11pm, and a truly astounding girl-to-guy ratio. Down-stairs **Culture Club** spins 80s. Cover after 9pm F $10, Sa $12-15. Open Th 9pm-2am, F-Sa 8pm-4am.

Backflip, 601 Eddy St. (☎771-3547), between Larkin and Polk St. Hipsters dive into this blue and aqua urban oasis for infamously kitschy and famously cool pool-side par-ties. Plunge into open mic talent shows Tu 10pm-2am. Beer $4, cocktails $7. Open Tu-Sa 9pm-2am.

The Stud, 399 9th St. (☎252-7883), at Harrison St. This legendary bar and club (a 35-year-old stallion) recreates itself every night of the week—go Tu for the wild and wacky midnight drag and transgender shows known as "Trannyshack," Th for Reform School boy-cruising party, F for ladies' night, Sa for Sugar's free, delicious eye-candy. Crowd is

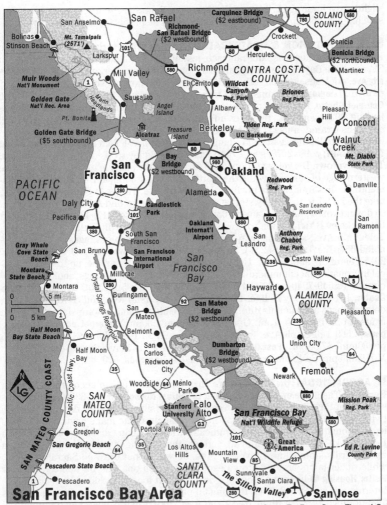

San Francisco Bay Area

mostly gay male. Cover $5-9. Open M, W, F, and Su 5pm-2am, Tu 5pm-3am, Th and Sa 5pm-4am. Cash only.

THE BAY AREA

BERKELEY   ☎510

Famous as an intellectual center and a haven for iconoclasts, Berkeley lives up to its well-founded reputation. Although the peak of its political activism occurred in the 1960s and 70s—when students attended more protests than classes—UC Berkeley continues to cultivate consciousness and brainy brawn, even if it is no longer as "Berserkeley" as it once was. The vitality of the population infuses the streets—which are strewn with hip cafes and top-notch bookstores—with a slightly psychotic vigor. Telegraph Avenue, with its street-corner soothsayers, hirsute hippies, and itinerant musicians, remains one of this town's main draws.

⊞ ⁊ ORIENTATION & PRACTICAL INFORMATION. Berkeley lies across the Bay Bridge northeast of San Francisco, just north of Oakland. If you're driving from SF, cross the Bay Bridge on **I-80** and take one of the four Berkeley exits. The **University Ave. exit** leads most directly to UC Berkeley and downtown. The magnetic heart of town, **Telegraph Ave.**, runs south from the UC Berkeley Student Union, while the **Gourmet Ghetto,** just north of campus, has some of California's finest dining. **Berkeley TRiP,** 2033 Center St., provides information on public transportation and biking, and sells extended-use transit passes and maps. (☎644-7665. Open Tu-F noon-5:30pm. Satellite office at 2543 Channing Way; open M-F 9am-2pm.) **Bay Area Rapid Transit (BART;** ☎465-2278; see p. 899) has two Berkeley stops on the **Richmond line.** The Downtown Berkeley station, 2160 Shattuck Ave., at Center St., is close to the western edge of campus, while the North Berkeley station, at Delaware and Sacramento St., lies four blocks north of University Ave. To get to Southern Berkeley, take the BART to the Ashby stop at the corner of Ashby and Adeline St. (20-30min. to downtown SF; $2.65). **Alameda County Transit** city buses #15, 43, and 51 run from the Berkeley BART station to downtown Oakland on Martin Luther King, Jr. Way, Telegraph Ave., and Broadway, respectively ($1.35; seniors, ages 5-12, and disabled 65¢; 1hr. transfers 25¢). **Visitor info: Berkeley Convention and Visitor Bureau,** 2015 Center St., at Milvia St. Helpful area maps, friendly service, up-to-date practical information, accommodation resources, the latest happenings, and tons of brochures. (☎549-7040 or 800-847-4823. Open M-F 9am-5pm.) **UC Berkeley Visitors Center,** 101 University Hall, at the corner of University Ave. and Oxford St. Clear, detailed maps and campus info. (☎642-5215. Guided campus tours depart from the center M-Sa 10am, Su 1pm. Open M-F 8:30am-4:30pm.) **Internet access: UC Computer,** 2569 Telegraph Ave. (☎649-6089. Open M-Sa 10am-6pm. $3 per 15min., $5 per 30min., $7 per hr.) **Post Office:** 2000 Allston Way, at Milvia St. (☎649-3155. Open M-F 9am-5pm, Sa 10am-2pm.) **ZIP code:** 94704. **Area code:** 510.

⌐ ACCOMMODATIONS. There are surprisingly few cheap accommodations in Berkeley. The **Berkeley-Oakland Bed and Breakfast Network** (☎547-6380) coordinates some great East Bay B&Bs with a range of rates (singles $50-150; doubles $60-150; twins $85-150). Many travelers stay in San Francisco and make daytrips to Berkeley. Although most motels are technically within walking distance of Downtown Berkeley, UC, and other prime attractions, they are much more accessible with a car. No-frills motels line University Ave. between Shattuck and Sacramento St., while ritzier joints are downtown especially on Durant Ave. **UC Berkeley Summer Visitor Housing ❸** has simple college dorms, great location, shared baths, and free Internet access. (☎642-4108. Parking $6 per day. Open June to mid-Aug. Singles $53; doubles $68; 7th night free.) **YMCA ❸,** 2001 Allston Way, has a communal kitchen, shared bath, computer room, and TV lounge. Use of pool and fitness facilities included. (☎848-6800. 10-night max. stay; special applications available for longer stays. Reception daily 8am-9:30pm. Must be 18+ with ID. Singles $46; doubles $60; triples $75.) **Capri Motel ❹,** 1512 University Ave., at Sacramento St., has clean, tasteful rooms with cable TV, A/C, and fridge. (☎845-7090. Must be 18+ with ID. Singles and doubles from $85.)

❒ FOOD. The north end of Telegraph Ave. caters to student appetites and wallets, with late-night offerings of all varieties along Durant Ave. If you'd rather talk to a cow than eat one (moo!), you're in luck; Berkeley does greens like nowhere else. A growing number of international establishments are helping to diversify the area. **Solano Ave.** to the north is great for Asian cuisine while **4th St.** is home to some more upscale (but cheaper than Gourmet Ghetto) eats. Get a huge sandwich on freshly-baked bread with salad for $5 at **Sufficient Grounds Sandwiches ❶**, 2431 Durant Ave., and wash it down with a $3.60 smoothie. (☎841-3969. Open M-F 7am-midnight, Sa-Su 8am-midnight.) North of Cedar St., **César ❸**, 1515 Shattuck Ave., is a great place for savory tapas ($3-12), *bocadillos* (a small sandwich on french bread, $5-7), desserts ($4-5), and an impressive list of spirits. (☎883-0222. Open daily 11:30am-midnight; kitchen closes Su-Th 11pm, F-Sa 11:30pm.)

◨ **SIGHTS.** In 1868, the private College of California and the public Agricultural, Mining, and Mechanical Arts College united as the **University of California.** The 178-acre university in Berkeley was the first of the nine University of California campuses, so by seniority it has sole right to the nickname "Cal." Campus is bounded on the south by Bancroft Way, on the west by Oxford St., on the north by Hearst Ave., and on the east by Tilden Park. Pass through **Sather Gate** into **Sproul Plaza,** both sites of celebrated student sit-ins and bloody confrontations with police, to enter the 160-acre Berkeley campus. Tours leave from **Sather Tower,** the tallest building on campus; you can ride to its observation level for a great view. (Open M-F 8:30am-4:30pm. $1.) ◩**Berkeley Art Museum,** 2626 Bancroft Way, is most respected for its collection of 20th-century American and Asian art. BAM is also associated with The Pacific Film Archive. (☎642-0808. Open W and F-Su 11am-5pm, Th 11am-9pm. $6; students, seniors, and ages 12-17 $4. Free Th 11am-noon and 5-9pm.) You haven't really visited Berkeley until you've been on **Telegraph Ave.,** lined with a motley assortment of cafes, bookstores, and used clothing and record stores. For some off-campus fun, check out the **Takara Sake USA Inc.,** 708 Addison St. Take bus #51 to 4th St. and walk down to Addison St. Learn the history and science of *sake* making and sample 15 different types of Japan's merciless fire-water. (☎540-8250. Open daily noon-6pm. Museum, video, and tastings all free.)

When you're ready to get out of town, Berkeley is happy to oblige. In the pine and eucalyptus forests east of the city lies the beautiful anchor of the East Bay park system—**Tilden Regional Park.** By car or bike, take Spruce St. to Grizzly Peak Blvd. to Canon Ave. Hiking, biking, running, and riding trails criss-cross the park and provide impressive views of the Bay Area. For those looking to frolic without getting sweaty, a 19th-century carousel inside the park is a fun option. (☎635-0135. Open daily dawn-dusk.) Also inside the park, **Lake Anza's** small, sandy beach is a popular swimming spot during the hottest summer days. (☎843-2137. Open in summer 11am-6pm. $3, seniors and children $2.) **Wildcat Canyon,** adjacent to Tilden, is a less developed park, but has gorgeous hiking through grassy meadows and densely wooded canyons. (Open daily dawn-dusk. No biking.)

◪◩ **ENTERTAINMENT & NIGHTLIFE.** The university offers a number of quality entertainment options. **The Underground** hides a ticket office, an arcade, bowling alleys, foosball tables, and pool tables, all run from a central blue desk at the Student Union. (☎642-3825. Open M-F noon-8pm, Sa 10am-6pm.) ◩**Caffè Strada,** 2300 College Ave., at Bancroft Way, is a glittering jewel of the caffeine-fueled intellectual scene. (☎843-5282. Open daily 6:30am-midnight.) **Jupiter,** 2181 Shattuck Ave., near the BART station, houses a huge beer garden and offers terrific pizza for $6. (☎843-8277. Open M-Th 11:30am-1am, F 11:30am-2am, Sa noon-2am, Su noon-midnight.) **924 Gilman,** 924 Gilman St., is a legendary all-ages club and a staple of California punk. (☎524-8180. Cover $5 with $2 membership card, good for 1 year.)

MARIN COUNTY ☎415

Just across the Golden Gate Bridge, the jacuzzi of the bay—Marin (muh-RIN) County—bubbles over with money-making and mantra-spouting residents who help the area strike the perfect balance between upscale chic and counterculture nostalgia. Marin's pleasure spots lend themselves nicely to roadtrippers, and a web of trails combs the string of state and national parks to welcome mountain bikers and hikers. On the eastern side of the county, Sausalito, Mill Valley, and San Rafael line U.S. 101, and San Anselemo, Fairfax, and San Jose are easily accessible as well.

▐▀ TRANSPORTATION

Buses: Golden Gate Transit (☎455-2000, in SF ☎923-2000; daily 7am-7pm), provides bus service between San Francisco and Marin County via the Golden Gate Bridge, as well as local service in Marin. Fare $2-5. **West Marin Stagecoach** (☎454-0964; 8am-5pm) provides weekday service connecting West Marin communities to the rest of the county. Stops include: Pt. Reyes Station, Samuel P. Taylor State Park, Stinson Beach, and Muir Beach. Anyone can flag the bus to pull over or drop off between scheduled stops, provided there is a safe place. Call for schedules and routes. $1.50.

Ferries: Golden Gate Ferry (☎455-2000) runs from San Francisco to the Sausalito terminal at the end of Market St. ($5.30, seniors and disabled $2.65, ages 7-18 $4), and to the Larkspur terminal (M-F $3.10/1.55/2.35; Sa-Su $5.30/2.65/4). **Blue and Gold Fleet** (☎773-1188) runs ferries from Pier 41 at Fisherman's Wharf to Sausalito and Tiburon ($6.75, under 5 free).

Taxis: Belaire Cab Co. (☎388-1234).

Bike Rental: Cycle Analysis (☎663-9164), out of a hitch-up in the empty, grassy lot at 4th and Main St. (Hwy. 1 in Point Reyes Station), rents unsuspended bikes ($30), front-suspension mountain bikes ($35), and child trailers ($25-30). Helmets included. Open F-Su 10am-5pm; weekdays by appointment.

🔼 ORIENTATION & PRACTICAL INFORMATION

The Marin peninsula lies at the northern end of the San Francisco Bay and is connected to the city by **U.S. 101** via the **Golden Gate Bridge.** U.S. 101 extends north inland to Santa Rosa and Sonoma County, while **Rte. 1** winds north along the Pacific coast. The **Richmond-San Rafael Bridge** connects Marin to the East Bay via **I-580.** Gas is scarce and expensive in West Marin, so fill up in town before you head out for the coast. Drivers should exercise caution in West Marin, where roads are narrow, sinuous, and perched on the edges of cliffs.

Visitor info: Marin County Visitors Bureau, 1013 Larkspur Landing Circle (☎499-5000; www.visitmarin.org), off the Sir Francis Drake Blvd. Exit from U.S. 101, near the ferry terminal. Open M-F 9am-5pm.

Park visitor info: Marin Headlands Visitors Center, Bldg. 948, Fort Barry (☎331-1540), at Bunker and Field Rd., has info about hiking and biking in the park, permits for free campsites, maps, and trail advice. The center is also a museum with artifacts and exhibits on the history of the Headlands. Open daily 9:30am-4:30pm. Rangers at **Point Reyes National Seashore Headquarters,** known as **Bear Valley Visitor Center (☎**464-5100; www.nps.gov/pore), on Bear Valley Rd. ½ mi. west of Olema, give out camping permits, maps, and advice on trails, tides, and weather conditions, and lead guided hikes. Open M-F 9am-5pm, Sa-Su 8am-5pm. **Pan Toll Ranger's Station,** 801 Panoramic Hwy. (☎388-2070), in Mt. Tamalpais State Park, about 2.5 mi. inland from Stinson Beach (bus #63), operates Mt. Tam's campgrounds and trails. **Muir Woods National Monument Visitors Center** (☎388-2596; www.nps.gov/muwo), near the entrance to Muir Woods. Muir Woods trail map $1. Great selection of hiking, biking, and driving maps of Marin and Mt. Tam. Open daily 9am-6pm.

Medical Services: Marin General Hospital and Community Clinic, 250 Bon Air Rd. (☎925-7000), in Greenbrae off the U.S. 101 San Anselmo exit. 24hr. emergency care.

Post Offices: 15 Calle Del Mar, at Shoreline Hwy., in Stinson Beach. Open M-F 8:30am-5pm. ZIP code: 94970. Area code: 415.

ACCOMMODATIONS

Marin Headlands Hostel (HI-AYH), Bldg. 941 on Rosenstock (☎331-2777 or 800-909-4776), up the hill from the Visitors Center. 2 spacious and immaculate Victorian houses with 100 beds, game room, kitchens, and common rooms. Internet access 10¢ per min. Linen $1; towels 50¢. Laundry $1.50. Key deposit $10. Check-in 3:30-10:30pm. Check-out 10am. Lockout 10am-3:30pm. Reservations recommended for private rooms and weekends. Dorms $15, under 17 with parent $7.50. Private doubles $45. ❶

Inverness Valley Inn, 13275 Sir Francis Drake Blvd. (☎669-7250), in Pt. Reyes. The inn is on the left immediately before Heart's Desire Beach. For bigger budgets, the Inn offers queen-sized beds, full bathrooms, gas fireplaces, 15 lush acres, 2 tennis courts, a pool and a hot tub. May-Oct. Su-Th $115 for 2 people, F-Sa $130; Nov.-Apr. $100/115. Extra bed $20. ❺

The Headlands (☎331-1540) offers 3 small walk-in campgrounds with a total of 11 primitive campsites for individual backpackers and small groups. **Haypress Backpack Camp** is in Tennessee Valley in the north end of the Headlands, ¾ mi. from the parking lot. **Hakwcamp,** the most remote site, is in Gerbode Valley, reachable by a difficult 3.5 mi. hike up the Bobcat Trail or a 3 mi. hike up the Marincello or Miwok Trails from Tennessee Valley. **Bicentennial Camp** is the most accessible, 100 yards from Battery Wallace parking lot. No fires or pets. Showers and kitchen ($2 each) at Headlands Hostel. Free outdoor cold showers at Rodeo Beach. 3-day max. per site; 9-day max. per year. For all campgrounds, individual sites are free with a permit that can be obtained at the Headlands Visitors Center (p. 922). ❶

Kirby Cove (☎800-365-2267), off Conzelman Rd. west of the Golden Gate Bridge, is in the Marin Headlands, but is not administered by the Visitors Center. 4 campsites in a grove of cypress and eucalyptus trees on the shores of the bay, with fire rings and pit toilets. Designed for larger groups. Bring your own water. No pets. 3-day max. stay. Open Apr.-Oct. Sites $25. ❶

FOOD

Marinites take their fruit juices, tofu, and double-shot cappuccinos very seriously; restauranteurs know this, and raise both the alfalfa sprouts and the prices.

Sartaj Indian Cafe, 43 Caledonia St. (☎332-7103), 1 block from Bridgeway in Sausalito. Generous portions of excellent Indian food. Low prices (curries $8, massive samosas $2, sandwiches $4) are even lower on W nights when Sartaj features live music. Open daily 6:30am-9:30pm. ❷

Cafe Reyes (☎663-9493), on Rte. 1 as you enter Point Reyes Station, just before Mesa St. Decorated like something out of a Spaghetti Western, this cafe serves burgers ($7), Mexican food, quality coffee ($1.50), beer, and wine. Open daily 11am-9pm. ❷

SIGHTS

Marin's proximity to San Francisco makes it a popular daytrip destination. Virtually everything worth seeing or doing in Marin is outdoors. An efficient visitor can hop from park to park and enjoy several short hikes along the coast and through the redwood forests in the same day, topping it off with a pleasant dinner in one of

CALIFORNIA

the small cities. Those without cars, however, may find it easier to use one of the two well-situated hostels as a base for explorations.

MOUNT TAMALPAIS & MUIR WOODS

If you make one daytrip outside of San Francisco, it should take you to beautiful **Mount Tamalpais State Park** (tam-ull-PIE-us), resting between the upscale towns of East Marin and the rocky bluffs of West Marin. The 6300-acre park, one of the oldest and most popular in the California State Park System, has miles of hilly, challenging trails on and around 2571 ft. high Mt. Tam, the highest peak in the county. The **Mountain Theater** is known throughout the area for its Mountain Play, staged every summer since 1913. The natural 3750-seat amphitheater houses many special events as well. Mt. Tam also offers an annual **Astronomy Program**, a series of free lectures held in the Mountain Theater followed by telescope observation in the Rock Spring Parking Area. On a clear day, you can gaze from Mt. Tam across all of the San Francisco shoreline. *(Take Hwy. 1 to the Panoramic Hwy. Continue for 5.3 mi. to reach the Ranger Station and Pan Toll Rd. ☎388-2070. Open in summer 8am-9pm; off-season 9am-8pm. Free. Astronomy Program: ☎455-5370.)*

TRAILS. Mt. Tam has over 50 mi. of trails, suitable for a variety of fitness levels. The bubbling waterfall on **Cataract Trail** and the **Gardner Lookout** on Mt. Tam's east peak are worthy destinations. The **Bootjack Trail** up to the Mountain Theater offers breathtaking views. The **Steep Ravine Trail** heads to the beach, and the **Matt Davis Trail** winds itself up towards the peak (connect with **Fern Creek Trail** to make it all the way to the top). The **Pan Toll Ranger Station** (see p. 922) sells maps and can offer suggestions for loops of various length and difficulty.

MUIR & STINSON BEACHES. Muir Beach is a semi-circular cove; a smidgeon farther north lies the **Muir Beach Overlook,** offering splendid parnormic coastal views. *(☎388-2596.)* Just inland from Muir Beach is the **Green Gulch Farm Zen Center,** a Buddhist community, retreat, and organic farm. Visitors are free to explore the tranquil grounds and gardens; on Sunday mornings, they offer meditation instruction and a lecture on Zen Buddhism. *(1601 Shoreline Hwy. ☎383-3134.)* On the weekends, if there's any chance of sun, hundreds of people navigate the death-defying hairpin turns along the cliffs of Hwy. 1 to **Stinson Beach,** the most popular beach town in Marin County. The tiny surfer community has only a few shops and restaurants, but through the eucalyptus trees lies a phenomenal picnic area. *The undertow can be extremely strong; swimming is only advised from May to October. (5 mi. northwest of Muir Beach or 10 mi. southeast of Olema. ☎868-0942.)* The town also hosts the popular **Shakespeare at Stinson,** an ongoing festival in which a bodacious Bard goes to the beach. *(☎868-1115. May-Aug. and Oct.-Nov. F-Sa 7pm, Su 6pm; Sept. F 7pm, Sa-Su 6pm. $23, children $16.)*

MARIN HEADLANDS

Fog-shrouded hills just west of the Golden Gate Bridge constitute the Marin Headlands. These windswept ridges, precipitous cliffs, and hidden sandy beaches offer superb hiking and biking within minutes of downtown SF. For instant gratification, drive up to any of the several look-out spots and pose for your own postcard-perfect shot of the Golden Gate Bridge and the city skyline.

POINT BONITA. The short walk down to Point Bonita is well worth a stop. The well-preserved little lighthouse at the end of the point really doesn't seem up to the job of guarding the whole San Francisco Bay, but it has done so valiantly with the same glass lens since 1855. The lens was actually lowered in 1877 in order to duck below the Bay's relentless fog. The lighthouse is accessible via a short tunnel through the rock and a miniature suspension bridge. Strong winds make Point Bonita a chilly spot; bring a jacket. *(Open M and Sa-Su 12:30-3:30pm; guided walks 12:30pm. Free.)*

PALO ALTO   ☎650

Palo Alto is 35 mi. southeast of San Francisco; from the north, take **U.S. 101 South** to the University Ave. exit, or take the Embarcadero Rd. exit directly to the Stanford campus. Alternatively, motorists from San Francisco can split off onto **Interstate 280 (Junípero Serra Highway)** for a slightly longer but more scenic route. From I-280, exit at Sand Hill Rd. and follow it to the northwest corner of Stanford University. The **Palo Alto Transit Center,** on University Ave., serves local and regional buses and trains. (☎323-6105. Open daily 5am-12:30am.) The transit center connects to points north via **San Mateo County buses** and to Stanford via the free **Marguerite Shuttle.**

Called "the World's Largest Taco Bell" by Berkeley students, **Stanford University** is the product of an academic-architectural collaboration between Jane and Leland Stanford (who wanted to build a university to honor their dead son) and Frederick Law Olmsted (who designed Manhattan's Central Park). Completed in 1885, the co-educational, secular university is built around the colonnaded **Main Quadrangle,** which is also the sight of most undergraduate activity. An **Information Booth** is across from Hoover Tower in Memorial Auditorium. Free student-led tours depart daily 11am and 3:15pm; times vary on holidays and during exam periods. (☎723-2053. Open daily 8am-5pm.)

Hidden Villa Ranch Hostel (HI-AYH) 1, 26870 Moody Rd., is about 10 mi. southwest of Palo Alto in Los Altos Hills. Dorm, family, and private rooms available. (☎949-8648. Reception 8am-noon and 4-9:30pm. Reservations required for weekends and groups. Open Sept.-May. Dorms $14, nonmembers $17, children $7. Private cabins $30-42.) **Café Borrone 3,** 1010 El Camino Real, offers great salads and entrees. (☎327-0830. Open M-Th 7am-11pm, F 7am-midnight, Sa 8am-midnight, Su 8am-5pm.) Every day is a fiesta at **Nola,** 535 Ramona St. thanks to the late-night menu and cocktails. (☎328-2722. Open daily 5:30pm-2am.)

WINE COUNTRY

NAPA VALLEY   ☎707

Napa catapulted American wine into the big leagues in 1976, when a bottle of red from Napa's Stag's Leap Vineyard beat a bottle of critically acclaimed (and unfailingly French) Château Lafitte-Rothschild in a blind taste test in Paris. While not the oldest, and not necessarily the best, the Napa Valley is certainly the best-known of America's wine-growing regions. Now firmly established as successful businesses, the big Napa wineries draw a mostly older, well-to-do crowd, but there are also a lot of young and budget-minded folks looking forward to their fill of chardonnay and a mud bath at the end of the day.

◨ ◪ ORIENTATION & PRACTICAL INFORMATION

Rte. 29 (Saint Helena Highway) runs through the Napa Valley north from **Napa** through **Yountville** and **Saint Helena** (where it's called Main St.) to **Calistoga.** Choked

CALIFORNIA

with visitors stopping at each winery, the relatively short distance makes for a surprisingly long, if scenic, drive on the weekends. The **Silverado Trail**, parallel to Rte. 29, is a less crowded route, but watch out for cyclists. Napa is 14 mi. east of Sonoma on **Rte. 12**. If you're planning a weekend trip from San Francisco, avoid Saturday mornings and Sunday afternoons; the roads are packed with like-minded people. Although harvest, in early September, is the most exciting time to visit, winter weekdays are less packed and offer more personal attention. In addition, most accommodations are less expensive in the winters. From San Francisco, take U.S. 101 over the Golden Gate Bridge, then follow Rte. 37 East, which intersects Rte. 29, which runs north to Napa.

Yountville and **Saint Helena**, which lie between the relatively busy town of Napa and the soothing spas of **Calistoga**, are well-groomed little villages that each host several small restaurants and trendy shops.

Public Transit: The nearest **Greyhound** station is in Vallejo, 1500 Lemon St. (☎643-7661 or 800-231-2222). A bus runs to Napa and Calistoga, but it's very slow—almost 3hr. from Vallejo to Calistoga—and does not stop near wineries. **Napa City Bus**, or **Valley Intercity Neighborhood Express (VINE)**, 1151 Pearl St. (☎800-696-6443), covers **Vallejo** (M-F 5:20am-8pm, Sa 6:15am-5:30pm, Su 11am-6pm; $1.50, students $1.10, seniors and disabled 75¢) and **Calistoga** (M-F 5:20am-8pm, Sa 6am-6:40pm, Su 9:30am-4:30pm; $2/1.45/1; free transfers).

Visitor Info: Napa Conference & Visitors Bureau, 1310 Town Ctr. (☎226-7459; www.napavalley.com/nvcvb.html). Free maps and info. Also sells the *Napa Valley Guidebook* ($6) with more comprehensive listings. Ask about specials and pick up coupons from local businesses. Open daily 9am-5pm.

Winery Tours: Napa Valley Holidays (☎255-1050). Afternoon tours $75 per person, $85 with round-trip transportation from San Francisco.

Bike Rental: ◙ **St. Helena Cyclery**, 1156 Main St. (☎963-7736). Open M-Sa 9:30am-5:30pm, Su 10am-5pm. Hybrid bikes $7 per hr., $25 per day; road bikes $15/45; tandem bikes $25/70. All bikes come with maps, helmet, lock, and picnic bag.

Medical Services: Queen of the Valley, 1000 Trancas St. (☎252-4411), in Napa.

Post Office: 1625 Trancas St., in Napa. (☎255-0190. Open M-F 8:30am-5pm.) **ZIP Code:** 94558. **Area code:** 707.

▛ ACCOMMODATIONS

Rooms in Napa are scarce and go fast despite high prices. Camping is a good alternative, although the heat can be intense in summer.

◙ **Golden Haven Hot Springs Spa and Resort ❹**, 1713 Lake St. (☎942-6793), a few blocks from Lincoln St. in Calistoga. More of a nice motel than a resort. Large standard-issue rooms with TVs and phones. Mineral swimming pool and hot tub access for all guests. No children under 16. Weekends 2-night min. stay, holiday weekends 3-night min. stay. Apr.-Oct. 1 queen $79; 1 king with kichenette $125; queen with private sauna $135; king with private jacuzzi $175. Nov.-Mar. $65/99/109/135.

◙ **Calistoga Inn and Brewery ❹**, 1250 Lincoln Ave. (☎942-4101), at the corner of Rte. 29 in Calistoga. 18 clean, simple rooms in the upstairs of an old Victorian house whose downstairs has turned into a microbrewery and restaurant. Shared bathrooms. Big breakfast included. Restaurant and bar open 11:30am-11pm. Rooms M-F $75, Sa-Su and holidays $100.

Bothe-Napa Valley State Park ❶, 3801 Rte. 29 (☎942-4575, reservations 800-444-7275), north of St. Helena. 50 sites near Ritchey Creek Canyon often fill up. Fairly rustic. Toilets. Pool $1, under 17 free. Hot showers 25¢. Check-in 2pm. $12, seniors $10. Picnic area day use $2. Park open for day use 8am-dusk.

🖸 FOOD

Eating in Wine Country ain't cheap, but the food is usually worth it. Picnics are an inexpensive and romantic option—supplies can be bought at the numerous delis or **Safeway** supermarkets in the area. The **Napa Farmers Market**, at Pearl and West St., offers a sampling of the valley's *other* produce. (☎252-7142. Open daily 7:30am-noon.)

First Squeeze Cafe & Juice Bar, 1126 First St. (☎224-6762), offers sandwiches, soups, salads, and smoothies. Try their most popular plate, huevos rancheros ($8), or supe-up a fresh fruit smoothie with a shot of gingko biloba or ginseng ($4). Breakfast daily until 2pm. Free downtown delivery. Open M-F 7am-3pm, Sa-Su 8am-3pm. ❷

Calistoga Natural Foods and Juice Bar, 1426 Lincoln St. (☎942-5822), in Calistoga. One of a few natural foods stores in the area. Organic juices ($3-5), smoothies ($3.50-4.50), sandwiches ($4-7.25), and bargain vegetarian specialties like the Asian veggie stir-fry or steam ($6.50) and the Yummus Hummus wrap ($6.50). Organic groceries also sold. Open M-Sa 9am-6pm, Su 10am-5pm. ❷

Armadellos, 1304 Main St. (☎963-8082), in St. Helena. Tasty vegetarian-friendly Cali-Mexican dishes (mostly $6-13). Open Su-Th 11am-9pm, F-Sa 11am-10pm. ❸

🖸 WINERIES

There are more than 250 wineries in Napa County, nearly two-thirds of which line Rte. 29 and the Silverado Trail in the Napa Valley. Wine Country's heavyweights call this valley home; vineyards include national names like Inglenook, Fetzer, and Mondavi. Style and atmosphere, from architecture down to visitor hospitality, vary from estate to estate; experiencing the larger, touristy operations coupled with the smaller vineyards adds to the fun. No matter their marketing approach, the wineries listed below do card for underage drinkers; *visitors must be 21+ to taste or purchase alcohol.*

A good way to begin your Napa Valley experience is with a tour, like the ones at **Domaine Carneros** or **Beringer**, or a free tastings class, like the one offered on Saturday mornings at **Goosecross Cellars.**

🖸 Kirkland Ranch, 1 Kirkland Ranch Rd. (☎254-9100), south of Napa off Rte. 29. Reminiscent of a ski lodge, this family-owned and operated Country Western-styled winery has windows overlooking production facilities and family pictures of cattle herding cowboys adorning the walls. Tours by appointment. Tastings $5. US military personnel and veterans receive 30% off wine purchases.

Clos Du Val Wine Company, Ltd., 5330 Silverado Trail (☎259-2225), north of Oak Knoll Rd., in Yountville. Small, stylish grounds attract lots of tourists. Tastings $5; price is applicable towards wine purchase. Free tours by appointment. Open daily 10am-5pm.

Edgewood Estate Winery, 401 St. Helena Hwy. (☎963-7293), in St. Helena. Don't let the lack of cars and crowds outside deter you—a warm, attentive staff and 5 tastes for $4 await within this small, pretty lodge. Garden patio seating for drinkers of wines by the glass. Open daily 11am-5:30pm.

Robert Mondavi Winery, 7801 Rte. 29 (☎963-9611 or 800-766-3284; www.robert-mondaviwinery.com), 8 mi. north of Napa. If you are looking to hit one massive, tourist-happy winery, this is it. Beautiful mission-style visitors complex, with 2 tasting rooms selling by the glass ($4-15) and the atmosphere of a luxury summer resort. Offers a variety of tours, differing in length and focus and with various foods. Vineyard and winery tour daily every hr. 10am-4pm. Reserve 1hr. in advance. $10, including 3 tastes and *hors d'oeuvres.* 6 other tours are each given once per week at 10 or 11am, some only seasonally, and cost $30-95 per person. Open daily 9am-5pm.

👁 🖩 SIGHTS & OUTDOOR ACTIVITIES

CALISTOGA. After a hard day of wine-tasting, the rich and relaxed converge on Calistoga, the "Hot Springs of the West," to revel in mud baths, massages, and mineral showers. A basic package consisting of a mud bath, mineral bath, eucalyptus steam, blanket wrap and 25min. massage costs around $80. Salt scrubs and facials are each about $50. Try the **Calistoga Village Inn & Spa** for quality, friendly service. (☎942-0991. *Mud bath treatment $45; 25min. massage $45; 30min. facial $49.*) **Golden Haven** is one of the less pretentious spas. (☎942-6793. *Mud bath treatment $65, 30min. massage $45, 30min. facial $45.*) Cooler water is at **Lake Berryessa** (☎966-2111), 20 mi. north of Napa off Hwy. 128, where swimming, sailing, and sunbathing are popular along the 169 mi. shoreline. If you tire of being pampered, the **Sharpsteen Museum** will educate you with exhibits detailing Calistoga's history. *(1311 Washington St.* ☎942-5911. *Open daily 11am-4pm; in winter noon-4pm. Free.)*

OLD FAITHFUL GEYSER OF CALIFORNIA. This steamy wonder should not be confused with its more famous namesake in Wyoming, although it performs similarly—it's one of only three faithful geysers in the world. The geyser regularly jets boiling water 60 ft. into the air; although it "erupts" about every 40min., weather conditions affect its cycle. The ticket vendor will tell you the estimated time of the next spurt. *(On Tubbs Ln. off Hwy. 128., 2 mi. outside Calistoga.* ☎942-6463. *Open in summer daily 9am-6pm; in winter 9am-5pm. $6, seniors $5, ages 6-12 $2.)*

BIKING. Napa's gentle terrain makes for an excellent bike tour. The area is fairly flat, although small bike lanes, speeding cars, and blistering heat can make routes more challenging, especially after several samples of wine. The 26 mi. **Silverado Trail** has a wider bike path than Rte. 29. ▨**St. Helena Cyclery,** 1156 Main St., rents bikes (see **Practical Information,** p. 926).

SEASONAL EVENTS. The annual **Napa Valley Wine Festival** takes place in November. Every weekend in February and March the **Mustard Festival** (☎259-9029; www.mustardfestival.org) lines up different musical or theatrical presentations. **Napa Valley Fairgrounds** (☎942-5111) hosts a weekend fair in August, with wine tasting, music, juggling, rides, and a rodeo. In summer, there are free afternoon concerts at **Music-in-the-Park,** downtown at the riverfront. Contact **Napa Parks and Recreation Office** (☎257-9529) for more info.

SONOMA VALLEY   ☎707

Sprawling Sonoma Valley is a quieter alternative to Napa, but home to bigger wineries than the Russian River Valley. Many wineries are on winding side roads rather than a freeway strip, creating a more intimate wine-tasting experience. Sonoma Plaza is surrounded by art galleries, novelty shops, clothing stores, and Italian restaurants. Petaluma, west of the Sonoma Valley, has more budget-friendly lodgings than the expensive wine country.

TRANSPORTATION

From San Francisco, take **U.S. 101 North** over the Golden Gate Bridge, then follow Rte. 37 East to Rte. 121 North, which crosses Rte. 12 North to Sonoma. Alternatively, follow U.S. 101 North to Petaluma, then cross over to Sonoma by Rte. 116. Allow 1-1½hr. from San Francisco. **Rte. 12** traverses the length of Sonoma Valley, from **Sonoma** through **Glen Ellen** to **Kenwood** in the north. The center of downtown Sonoma is **Sonoma Plaza**, which contains City Hall and the Visitors Center. **Broadway** comes to a dead end in front of City Hall at Napa St. The numbered streets run north-south. **Petaluma** lies to the west and is connected to Sonoma by **Rte. 116,** which becomes **Lakeville St.**

Buses: Sonoma County Transit (☎576-7433 or 800-345-7433) serves the entire county. Within Sonoma, county buses stop when flagged down at bus stops (operates M-Su 8am-4:25pm; 95¢, students 75¢, seniors and disabled 45¢). **Golden Gate Transit** (☎541-2000 from Sonoma County, 415-923-2000 from SF) runs buses frequently between San Francisco and Santa Rosa. **Volunteer Wheels** (☎800-992-1006) offers door-to-door service for people with disabilities. Call for reservations. Open daily 8am-5pm.

Bike Rental: Sonoma Valley Cyclery, 20093 Broadway (☎935-3377), in Sonoma. Bikes $6 per hr., $25 per day; includes helmet. Open M-Sa 10am-6pm, Su 10am-4pm.

PRACTICAL INFORMATION

Visitor info: Sonoma Valley Visitors Bureau, 453 E. 1st St. (☎996-1090; www.sonomavalley.com), in Sonoma Plaza. Maps $2. Open June-Oct. daily 9am-7pm; Nov.-May 9am-5pm. **Petaluma Visitors Program,** 800 Baywood Dr. (☎769-0429), at Lakeville St. Open May-Oct. M-F 9am-5:30pm, Sa-Su 10am-6pm; shorter weekend hours in the off-season. The free visitor's guide has listings of restaurants and activities.

Road Conditions: ☎817-1717.

Medical Services: Petaluma Valley, 400 N. McDowell Blvd. (☎781-1111).

Post Office: 617 Broadway (☎800-275-8777), at Patten St., in Sonoma. Open M-F 8:30am-5pm. **ZIP Code:** 95476. Also at 120 4th St., in Petaluma. Open M-F 8:30am-5pm, Sa 10am-2pm. **Postal Code:** 94952.

ACCOMMODATIONS

Pickings are pretty slim for lodging; rooms are scarce even on weekdays and generally start at $85. Less expensive motels cluster along **U.S. 101** in Santa Rosa and Petaluma. Campers with cars should try the **Russian River Valley.**

Redwood Inn, 1670 Santa Rosa Ave. (☎545-0474), in Santa Rosa. Clean, comfortable rooms and suites with kitchenettes, cable TV, phones, and bath. In summer singles $55; doubles $65. In winter $50/60. AARP and AAA discounts. ❸

Sugarloaf Ridge State Park, 2605 Adobe Canyon Rd. (☎833-5712; www.parks.ca.gov), off Rte. 12, north of Kenwood in the Mayacamas Mountains. 49 sites with tables and fire rings around a central meadow with flush toilets and running water, but no showers. In summer and fall, take advantage of the day/night sky observing at Ferguson Observatory inside the park; see www.rfo.org for details. Sites $12, seniors $10; day use $2. ❶

FROM THE ROAD

DRINK TO YOUR MIND

In my life, I had definitely consumed my fair share of assorted wine, and had even been to a wine tasting party (with a reputed expert, no less), so I felt that surely I must be prepared for wine country. However, as I wandered into the wineries around Sonoma Valley, I slowly realized how little I knew. It wasn't that I felt I was being ridiculed or ignored—quite the contrary, in fact. The staff was warm and receptive to all of my questions, no matter how elementary they were. Still, my ignorance of the language of winemaking made me a bit uncomfortable.

In the beginning, I would look over the tasting menu and choose the wine with the most awards or the highest price. Sometimes I would simply ask the server to choose. They were happy to oblige (especially when I mentioned expense level as a criterion), but I wanted to feel more instrumental in the process. My approach wasn't wrong, just weak. As I asked more questions, tasted more wines, and read more information, I began to feel like I knew a bit more about wine and what I was doing. The whole process became much less intimidating.

I discovered that a few hundred vine types exist in the world, but that most wines in California are made from about a dozen major ones, known as **varietals**. Although soil, climate, and the hand of the winemaker all play important roles in creating a wine's flavor, certain characteristics of each varietal come through in a wine no matter what. By law, at least 75% of a wine must be pressed from a very

(continued on next page)

San Francisco North/Petaluma KOA, 20 Rainsville Rd. (☎763-1492 or 800-992-2267), in Petaluma off the Penngrove Exit. Suburban camp with 300 sites plus a recreation hall with activities, a petting zoo, a pool, a store, laundry facilities, and a jacuzzi. Hot showers. Lots of folks, many families. Check-in 1pm. Check-out 11am. 1 week max. tent stay. Reservations recommended. 2-person tent sites $31-35; each additional adult $5, child $3. RVs $38-41. Kabins $55-60. ❷

🍴 FOOD

Fresh produce is seasonally available directly from area farms or at roadside stands and Farmers Markets. The **Sonoma Market,** 520 W. Napa St., in the Sonoma Valley Center, is an old-fashioned grocery store with deli sandwiches ($5-7) and fresh produce. (☎996-0563. Open daily 9am-6pm.)

🧀 **Sonoma Cheese Factory,** 2 Spain St. (☎996-1931 or 800-535-2855), in Sonoma. Forget the wine for now—take a toothpick and enjoy the free cheese samples. You can even watch the cheese-making process in the back room. Sandwiches $4.50-5.50. Open daily 9am-6pm. ❷

The Vasquez House, 414 First St. E (☎938-0510), in El Paseo de Sonoma. Inconspicuously tucked behind touristy shops, this historic house hides a library and a miniscule tea room serving coffee, tea, and lemonade (75¢) and freshly baked "indulgences" ($1). Open W-Su 1:30-4:30pm. No credit cards. ❶

Maya, 101 E. Napa St. (☎935-3500), in Sonoma. Brings a fiery Yucatan spirit to Sonoma. The festive decor, mouth-watering food, and extensive wine and tequila menu are impressive. No wonder Maya won 2002 Best New Restaurant in Sonoma County. Entrees $6-19. Live music in summer Th 9:30pm-12:30am. Open M 4-9pm, Tu-Th and Su 11:45am-9pm, F-Sa 11:45am-10pm. ❸

🍷 WINERIES

Sonoma Valley's wineries, near Sonoma and Kenwood, are less touristy but just as elegant as Napa's. As an added bonus, most of the tastings in the Sonoma Valley are complimentary. Near Sonoma, white signs will help guide you through backroads. They are difficult to read, but indicate the wineries' general directions. Bring a map along on the ride; they're all over the place and free.

■ **Gundlach-Bundschu,** 2000 Denmark St. (☎938-5277). Established in 1858, Gundlach-Bundschu is the 2nd oldest winery in Sonoma and the oldest family-owned and run winery in the country. Its unpronounceable name is offset by fragrant wines and a setting of pronounced loveliness. Outdoor events in summer, such as a Mozart series. Tours of the wine storage caves Sa-Su every hr. 11am-3pm or by appointment. Free tastings daily 11am-4:30pm and during evening events.

■ **Benziger,** 1833 London Ranch Rd. (☎935-4046 or 888-490-2379; www.benziger.com). This winery is known for its rich, buttery, accessible wines. Tourists flock here for the acclaimed 40min. tram ride ($5) through the vineyards, which runs in the summer at 11:30am, noon, 12:30, 1:30, 2, 3, and 3:30pm. Self-guided tours lead from the parking lot through the vineyards and peacock aviary. Tastings of current vintage free, limited $5, reserves $10. Open daily 10am-5pm.

Kunde, 10155 Sonoma Hwy. (☎833-5501), near Kenwood. On hot afternoons, the cave tours at Kunde offer a cool break from the California sun. Known for its Chardonnays. Free tastings. Open daily 10:30am-4pm.

⬛ SIGHTS

SONOMA STATE HISTORIC PARK. Within the park, an adobe church stands on the site of the **Mission San Francisco-Solano,** the northernmost and last of the 21 Franciscan missions. It marks the end of the El Camino Real, or the "Royal Road." Built in 1826 by Padre Jose Altimira, the mission has a fragment of the original California Republic flag, the rest of which was burned in the 1906 post-earthquake fires. *(At E. Spain and 1st St., in the northeast corner of town. ☎938-9560. Open daily 10am-5pm. $1, under 16 free. Includes Vallejo's Home, the barracks, and Petaluma Adobe.)*

JACK LONDON STATE PARK. Around the turn of the 20th century, Jack London, author of *The Call of the Wild* and *White Fang,* bought 1400 acres here, determined to create his dream home. London's hopes were frustrated when the main building, the **Wolf House,** was destroyed by arsonists in 1913. London died three years later and is buried in the park. The nearby **House of Happy Walls,** built by his widow, is now a two-story museum devoted to the writer. The park's scenic half-mile Beauty Ranch Trail passes the lake, winery ruins, and quaint cottages. *(Take Hwy. 12 4 mi. north from Sonoma to Arnold Ln. and follow signs. ☎938-5216. Park open in summer daily 9:30am-7pm; in winter 9:30am-5pm. Museum open daily 10am-5pm.)*

(continued from previous page)

specific varietal in order to list that varietal on the label. Each varietal (and its wines) has specific, distinguishing attributes. For example, the white grape **Chardonnay** produces rich, crisp, complex wines. Most are dry and full-bodied with medium acidity, and smell faintly like apples, melons, or figs. **Cabernet Sauvignon,** a red grape, can make a velvety wine. Sometimes hints of cedar, black currants, or stewed fruit are discernible. Once I knew what to expect, it became fun to compare the variations of scents and flavors within varietals and between different varietals.

After grasping the concept of varietals and memorizing their typical characteristics, I learned how soil and climate subtly affect flavor. Vineyards fall into distinct geographical regions, called **appellations.** Topography, climate, and soil define each area and impart characteristics to the grapes grown under these conditions. For a winemaker to include an appellation on the label, 85% of the wine must come from that area. Trying to detect differences in similar wines from various appellations became a game.

The most important bit of information I learned, however, was the differences in bottle sizes. Buying anything larger than a **Jeroboam** (3 liters or 4 glasses) left me far too drunk to taste what I was drinking anyway, and the 15 liter **Nebuchadnezzar** would *definitely* have to wait for larger crowds. To really compare wines and develop a critical palate, I had to restrict my desire for more. It was worth it, though, for at my next wine tasting party *I'll* be the "reputed expert."

—*Eliza Dick*

THE NORTH COAST

MENDOCINO
☎ **707**

Perched on oceanside bluffs, isolated Mendocino is a stylish coastal community of art galleries, craft shops, bakeries, and B&Bs. The town's weathered wooden shingles, sloping roofs, and clustered homes seem out of place on the West Coast; perhaps that's why Mendocino was able to masquerade for years as the fictional Maine village of Cabot Cove in the TV series *Murder, She Wrote.*

■ ⁊ ORIENTATION & PRACTICAL INFORMATION. Mendocino sits on **Rte. 1,** right on the Pacific Coast, 30 mi. west of U.S. 101 and 12 mi. south of Fort Bragg. Although driving is the best way to reach Mendocino, once there the tiny town is best explored on foot. Given Mendocino's 40-70°F weather, travelers should prepare for the chill of coastal fog.

The nearest **bus station** is 2hr. away in Ukiah. **Greyhound** runs two buses per day to Ft. Bragg. **Mendocino Stage** (☎964-0167) runs buses between Ft. Bragg and Ukiah (2 per day, $10). **Mendocino Transit Authority,** 241 Plant Rd., makes one roundtrip daily between Santa Rosa, Ukiah, Willits, Fort Bragg, and Mendocino. (☎800-696-4682. $16.) **Fort Bragg Door-to-Door Taxis** has an on-call passenger van service. (☎964-8294. Operates daily 10am-2am.) **Catcha Canoe and Bicycles, Too!,** at Rte. 1 and Comptche Rd., rents top-quality bikes, canoes, and kayaks. (☎937-0273. Open daily 9am-5:30pm.) **Lost Coast Kayaking** gives fantastic guided tours. (☎937-2434. 2hr.; $45 per person; call 24hr. in advance.) **Visitor info: Ford House,** 735 Main St. (☎937-5397. Open in summer daily 11am-4pm; winter schedule varies.) **Parks info:** ☎937-5804. **Post Office:** 10500 Ford St. (☎937-5282. Open M-F 7:30am-4:30pm.) **ZIP code:** 95460. **Area code:** 707.

⁊ ACCOMMODATIONS. It's impossible to find a hotel room in Mendocino for under $60. Fortunately, hundreds of campsites are nearby. More comfortable but less convenient, nearby Ukiah and Fort Bragg have budget motels. ▨**Jug Handle Creek Farm ❶,** 5 mi. north of Mendocino off Rte. 1 before the Caspar exit, is a beautiful old house sitting on 40 acres of gardens, campsites, and small rustic cabins. Guests have access to Jug Handle State Park, including beaches and trails. (☎964-4630. 30 beds. No linen. 1hr. of chores or $5 required per night. Dorms $20, students $14, children $9; sites $9. Cabins $28 per person. Reservations required.) **MacKerricher State Park Campground ❶,** 3 mi. north of Ft. Bragg, has excellent views of tide pool life, passing seals, sea lions, and migratory whales, as well as 9 mi. of beaches and a murky lake for trout fishing. (☎937-5804. Showers, bathrooms, and water. Sites $12; day use free. Reservations recommended.)

◖ FOOD. All of Mendocino's breads are freshly baked, all vegetables locally grown, all wheat unmilled, all coffee cappuccino, and almost everything expensive. Most restaurants close at 9pm. Picnicking on the Mendocino Headlands is the cheapest option and should be preceded by a trip to **Mendosa's Market,** 10501 Lansing St., the closest thing in Mendocino to a real supermarket. It's pricey (of course), but most items are fresh and delicious. (☎937-5879. Open daily 8am-9pm.)

Tote Fête ❶, 10450 Lansing St., has delicious tote-out food, and the crowds know it. An asiago, pesto, and artichoke heart sandwich ($4.75) hits the spot. (☎937-3383. Open M-Sa 10:30am-7pm, Su 10:30am-4pm; bakery open daily 7:30am-4pm.)

◙ **SIGHTS.** Mendocino's greatest attribute lies 900 ft. to the west, where the earth comes to a halt and falls off into the Pacific, forming the impressive fog-shrouded coastline of the ▨**Mendocino Headlands.** Beneath wildflower-laden meadows, fingers of eroded rock claw through the pounding ocean surf and seals frolic in secluded alcoves. In Fort Bragg, the **Skunk Train,** at Rte. 1 and Laurel St., offers a jolly, child-friendly diversion through deserted logging towns and a recuperating forest. (☎964-6371 or 800-777-5865. 9:30am and 2pm; off-season 10am.) A steam engine, diesel locomotive, and vintage motorcar take turns running between Fort Bragg and Willits via Northspur, with full- and half-day trips available. Schedule changes make it necessary to call ahead for reservations.

AVENUE OF THE GIANTS   ☎707

About 6 mi. north of Garberville off U.S. 101, the Avenue of the Giants winds its way through 31 mi. of the largest living creatures this side of sea level. Scattered throughout the area are several commercialized attractions like the **World Famous Tree House, Confusion Hill,** and the **Drive-Thru Tree.** There are a number of great hiking trails in the area, marked on free brochures available at the **Humboldt Redwoods State Park Visitors Center,** just south of Weott on the Avenue. (☎946-2263. Open Apr.-Oct. daily 9am-5pm; Nov.-Mar. Th-Su 10am-3pm.) The **Canoe Creek Loop Trail,** across the street from the Visitors Center, is an easy start. Uncrowded trails snake through the park's northern section around **Rockefeller Forest,** which contains the largest grove of old-growth redwoods (200 years and growing) in the world. The **Dyerville Giant,** in the redwood graveyard at Founder's Grove midway through the Avenue, deserves a respectful visit. The ½ mi. loop trail includes the **Founder's Tree** and the **Fallen Giant,** whose massive trunk stretches the length of 60 human bodies and whose three-story rootball looks like a mythical ensnarlment of evil.

With its sizable artist population, Garberville's art festivals are a big draw. **Jazz on the Lake** and the **Summer Arts Fair** begin in late June, followed by **Shakespeare at Benbow Lake** in late July. Early August brings **Reggae on the River,** a three-day music fest on the banks of the Eel River. **Visitor Info: Chamber of Commerce,** 773 Redway, in Garberville. (☎800-923-2613. Open M-F 10am-5pm.) **Area code:** 707.

REDWOOD NATIONAL & STATE PARKS   ☎707

With ferns that grow to the height of humans and redwood trees the size of skyscrapers, Redwood National Park, as John Steinbeck said, "will leave a mark or create a vision that stays with you always." The redwoods in the park are the last remaining stretch of the old-growth forest that once blanketed two million acres of Northern California and Oregon. Wildlife runs rampant here, with black bears and mountain lions in the backwoods and Roosevelt elk grazing in the meadows.

🛈 **PRACTICAL INFORMATION**

The Redwood National and State Parks are actually four: **Redwood National Park, Jedediah Smith State Park, Del Norte Coast Redwoods State Park,** and **Prairie Creek Redwoods State Park.**

> **Buses: Greyhound,** 500 E. Harding St. (☎464-2807), in Crescent City. To **San Francisco** (2 per day, $58-63) and **Portland** (2 per day, $60-65). Open M-F 7-10am and 5-7:30pm, Sa 7-8:15am and 7-7:30pm. No credit cards.

CALIFORNIA

Visitor Info: Redwood Info Center (☎464-6101, ext. 5265), on U.S. 101, 1 mi. south of Orick. Free maps. Info on trails and campsites from enthusiastic and helpful rangers. Open daily 9am-5pm.

Post Offices: 751 2nd St. (☎464-2151), in Crescent City. Open M-F 8:30am-5pm, Sa noon-2pm. **ZIP code:** 95531. **Area code:** 707.

ACCOMMODATIONS

Ravenwood, 151 Klamath Blvd. (☎482-5911 or 866-520-9875), off U.S. 101. Clean rooms with a modern decor. Conveniently located next to a market, cafe, and laundromat. Doubles $48; family unit $95. ❸

The Historic Requa Inn, 451 Requa Rd. (☎482-1425 or 866-800-8777), west off U.S. 101. This bed and breakfast has a glorious view overlooking the Klamath River. Clawfooted tubs in the bathrooms and evening dining for guests. Rooms $69-95. ❹

Camp Marigold, 16101 U.S. 101 (☎482-3585 or 800-621-8513), 3 mi. north of Klamath Bridge. Stay in a log cabin with full kitchen and cable TV. RV hookups available. 1-bed studios $48; doubles $78; 6-person lodge $195. ❸

Flint Ridge Campground (☎800-444-7245), off the end of Redwood National and State Parks Coastal Dr., has neither water nor showers, but toilets are available. Sites $12. ❶

FOOD

There are more picnic tables than restaurants in the area, so the best option for food is probably the supermarket. **Orick Market** has reasonably priced groceries. (☎488-3225. Open M-Sa 8am-7pm, Su 9am-6pm.) In Crescent City, head to the 24hr. **Safeway,** 475 M St. (☎465-3353), on U.S. 101 between 2nd and 5th St.

If cooking is not in your travel plans, there are some restaurants in the area. Hungry visitors can grab healthy fare at the ▣**Wild Rocket Juice Bar & Cafe** ❶, 309 U.S. 101, in Crescent City. The fresh vegetables in the Rocket's scrumptious wraps ($5) and salads ($4-6) are all from locally based Reese Hydro Farms. (☎464-2543. Open M-F 6am-6pm, Sa 9am-3pm.) The **Palm Cafe** ❷, on U.S. 101, is the only place to eat in Orick, and welcomes locals and visiting hikers and bikers to a mom-and-pop environment. Their homemade fruit, coconut, and chocolate pies are delicious. (☎488-3381. Open daily 5am-8pm.)

SIGHTS

In the parks, you may gather berries, but all other plants and animals are protected—even feathers dropped by birds of prey are off-limits. The national and state parks services conduct many summer activities for all ages; call the **Redwood Information Center** (☎464-6101) for info.

ORICK AREA. The Orick Area covers the southernmost section of Redwood National and State Parks. Its **Visitors Center** lies on U.S. 101, 1 mi. south of Orick and ½ mi. south of the Greyhound bus stop at Shoreline Deli. The popular **Tall Trees Grove** is accessible by car when the road is open; pick up a free permit at the Visitors Center. Allow at least 3-4hr. for the trip.

PRAIRIE CREEK AREA. The Prairie Creek Area, equipped with a **Ranger Station, Visitors Center,** and **State Park campgrounds,** is perfect for hikers, who can explore 75 mi. of trails in the park's 14,000 acres. Be sure to pick up a trail map ($1) at the ranger station before heading out; the loops of criss-crossing trails can be confusing. Starting at the Visitors Center, the **James Irvine Trail** (4.5 mi.) winds through a garden of towering old-growth redwoods of humbling height. Snaking past small waterfalls that trickle down 50 ft. fern-covered walls, the trail ends at **Fern Canyon** on **Gold Bluffs Beach,** whose sands stretch for miles upon elk-scattered miles.

KLAMATH AREA. The Klamath Area to the north consists of a thin stretch of park land connecting Prairie Creek with Del Norte State Park. The town itself consists of a few stores stretched over 4 mi., so the main attraction here is the ruggedly spectacular coastline. The **Klamath Overlook,** where Requa Rd. meets the Coastal Trail, is an excellent **whale-watching** site with a fantastic view.

CRESCENT CITY AREA. An outstanding location from which to explore the parks, Crescent City calls itself the city "where the redwoods meet the sea." The **Battery Point Lighthouse** houses a museum open only during low tide; ask guides about the resident ghost. The lighthouse is on a causeway jutting out of Front St. Turn left onto A St. at the top of Front St. (☎464-3089. Open Apr.-Sept. W-Su 10am-4pm, tide permitting. $2, children 50¢.) From June through August, the National Park offers **tide pool walks** leaving from the Enderts Beach parking lot. (☎464-6101 for schedules. Turn-off 4 mi. south of Crescent City.)

THE NORTHERN INTERIOR

In 1848, California was a rural backwater of only 15,000 people. The same year, sawmill operator James Marshall wrote in his diary: "This day some kind of mettle...found in the tailrace...looks like goald." In the next four years, some 90,000 '49ers from around the world headed for California and the 120 miles of gold-rich seams called the **Mother Lode.**

Although gold remains in them thar hills, today the towns of Gold Country make their money mining the tourist traffic. Gussied up as **"Gold Rush Towns,"** they solicit tourists traveling along the appropriately numbered **Rte. 49** through the foothills that connect dozens of small Gold Country settlements. Traffic from the coast connects with Rte. 49 via I-80 in Sacramento, which serves as a tourist hub. Wine tasting, river rafting, and spelunking are also popular, and any number of wilderness activities is available in the Cascades to the north. Most of Gold Country is about two hours from Sacramento, three hours from San Francisco.

SACRAMENTO   ☎916

Sacramento is a good place from which to explore the hills of Gold Country or head onward to the Sierra Nevada or Cascade mountain ranges. **Sacramento Hostel (HI-AYH) ❶,** 900 H St., at 9th St., in a restored Victorian mansion, has a huge modern kitchen, three large living rooms, and a library. (☎443-1691, reservations 800-909-4776 ext. 40. Chores required. Check-in 7:30-10am and 5-10pm. Check-out 9:30am. Doors lock at 11pm. Dorms $16-18, nonmembers $19-21. Wheelchair accessible.) At the **Vagabond Inn Midtown ❸,** 1319 30th St., between M and N St., rooms are comfortable and relatively inexpensive. (☎454-4400. Doubles from $50.) 🅂**The Fox and Goose,** 1001 R St., at 10th St. is a funky English pub and restaurant with open mic nights, live bands, and wizards performing magic. (☎443-8825. Open M-F 7am-2pm and 5:30pm-midnight, Sa-Su 8am-2am.) **Post Office:** 801 I St. (☎556-3415. Open M-F 8am-5pm.) **ZIP code:** 95814. **Area code:** 916.

CALAVERAS COUNTY   ☎209

The richest, southern part of the "Mother Lode," unsuspecting Calaveras County turned out to be literally sitting on a gold mine when the big rush hit. Over 550,000 pounds of gold were extracted from the county's earth. **Mark Twain** allegedly based "The Celebrated Jumping Frog of Calaveras County" on a tale he heard in Angels Camp Tavern. In response, Calaveras has held **annual frog-jumping contests** since 1928. Thousands of people gather on the third weekend of May for the festivities. **San Andreas,** at the juncture of Rte. 26 and 49, is the county hub and most densely populated area, but it isn't very big.

THE MIDAS TOUCH Dredging for gold in the Mother Lode or crevassing bedrock for hard rock mines is a notably less popular choice than it was 150 years ago, when California was populated overnight by zealous prospectors stricken with gold fever. Today, a sizable but little-known group of latter-day prospectors has emerged, many possessing the same wild determination as their predecessors. The US Geological Survey estimates that around 12% of the world's gold is located in the US, much of it in California. At current prices of about **$310 per ounce**, that adds up to about $100 billion in ore—enough to get many people excited. Joining an organization like the **Gold Prospectors Association of America** (☎ 909-699-4749) can give you access to private lands, though these have often been heavily scoured already. Just like in the days of the 49ers, if you find gold on public land, it's yours (usually); the **Bureau of Land Management** distributes claims on 20-acre parcels of unprotected public lands for an annual fee of $100. Just stake your claim, literally, with four poles, and seek out the nearest MBLM office in a hurry.

The real attractions of Calaveras County are the natural wonders. About 20 mi. east of Angels Camp on Rte. 4 lies **Calaveras Big Trees State Park.** Here the *Sequoiadendron giganteum* (Giant Sequoia) reigns as the largest living thing on land. The **North Grove Trail** (1 mi.) is wheelchair accessible, gently graded, and heavily trafficked. The less-traveled, more challenging **South Grove Trail** (4 mi.) better captures the forest's beauty and timelessness. The park also offers swimming in **Beaver Creek** and **camping,** but summertime visitors should prepare for gnats and mosquitoes. The snow comes early (sometimes in Sept.) and leaves late (mid-Apr.) at Big Trees. (☎ 795-3840. Sites $12; day use $2, seniors $1.)

Calaveras County boasts gargantuan natural wonders below ground as well as above. **Moaning Cavern** is a vast vertical cave so large that the Statue of Liberty could live there comfortably. From Angels Camp, follow Rte. 4 east for 4 mi., turn right onto Parrot's Ferry Rd., and follow signs. Descend the 236 steps or rappel 180 ft. down into the cave. (☎ 736-2708. Open in summer daily 9am-6pm; in winter M-F 10am-5pm, Sa-Su 9am-5pm. Stairs $10, ages 3-13 $5; rappelling $45.) **Mercer Caverns,** 9 mi. north of Angels Camp, off Rte. 4 on Sheep Rd. in Murphys, offers one-hour walking tours of ten internal rooms. Although smaller and less dramatic than Moaning Cavern, the caves are nearly a million years old. (☎ 728-2101. Open in summer Su-Th 9am-5pm, F-Sa 9am-6pm; in winter Su-Th 10am-4:30pm. Tours $10, ages 5-12 $6.) **California Caverns,** at Cave City, served as a naturally air-conditioned bar and dance floor during the Gold Rush, when a shot of whiskey could be purchased for a pinch of gold dust. The caverns sobered up on Sunday for church services when one stalagmite served as an altar. Walking tours and "wild cavern expedition trips" explore cramped tunnels, waist-high mud, and underground lakes. (☎ 736-2708. Tours $10, ages 3-13 $5. 2hr. expeditions $99, ages 8-16 $65.)

Calaveras County has been a producer of fine wines for nearly 150 years. Vineyards stretch along Rte. 49, and wineries abound near Plymouth. The **Stevenot Winery,** on Sheep Ranch Rd. 2 mi. north of Main St. in Murphys, is the county's largest. (☎ 728-3436. Main tasting room open daily 10am-5pm.) **Ironstone Vineyards,** on Six Mile Rd. 1½ mi. south Main St., stores wine in caverns hewn from rock. (☎ 728-1251. Free 45min. tours daily 11:30am, 1:30, and 3:30pm. Sa additional tour 2:30pm. Tasting room open daily 11am-5pm.) The **Calaveras County Information Center,** in downtown Angels Camp, is a great resource for info on sights in the area. (☎ 800-225-3764. Open M-F 9am-6pm, Sa 11am-6pm, Su 11am-4pm.) **Area code:** 209.

THE CASCADES ☎916

The Cascade Mountains interrupt an expanse of farmland to the northeast of Gold Country. In these ranges, recent volcanic activity has left behind a surreal landscape of lava beds, mountains, lakes, waterfalls, caves, and recovering forest areas. The calm serenity and haunting beauty of these mountains draw visitors in a way that the Central Valley and Gold Country cannot.

Lassen Volcanic National Park is accessible by **Rte. 36** to the south and **Rte. 44** to the north. Both roads are about 50 mi. from **Rte. 5.** In 1914, the earth radiated destruction as tremors, streams of lava, black dust, and a series of huge eruptions ravaged the land, climaxing in 1915 when Mt. Lassen belched a seven-mile-high cloud of smoke and ashes. The destructive power of this eruption is still evident in the strange, unearthly pools of boiling water and the stretches of barren moonscape. **Lassen Volcanic National Park Headquarters** are located in Mineral. (☎595-4444. Open in summer daily 8am-4:30pm.)

THE SIERRA NEVADA

The Sierra Nevada is a high, steep, and physically stunning mountain range. Thrust skyward 400 million years ago by gigantic plate collisions and shaped by erosion, glaciers, and volcanoes, this enormous hunk of granite stretches 450 miles north from the Mojave Desert to Lake Almanor near Lassen Volcanic National Park. The glistening clarity of Lake Tahoe, the heart-stopping sheerness of Yosemite's rock walls, the craggy alpine scenery of Kings Canyon and Sequoia National Parks, and the abrupt drop of the Eastern Sierra into Owens Valley are sights to behold. Temperatures in the Sierra Nevada are as diverse as the terrain. Even in the summer, overnight lows can dip below 30°F. Normally, only U.S. 50 and I-80 are kept open during the snow season. Exact dates vary from year to year, so check with a ranger station for local road conditions, especially from October to June.

LAKE TAHOE ☎530

In February of 1844, fearless explorer John C. Fremont led his expedition over the Sierra. Luckily for him, the sight of this beautiful alpine lake was enough to boost the morale of his 36 starved and weary companions. Ever since the original settlers rolled in, Lake Tahoe has been a playground for the wealthy and a year-round outdoor haven, with miles of biking, hiking, and skiing trails, long beaches, and hair-raising whitewater.

▐ TRANSPORTATION

In the northern Sierra on the California-Nevada border, Lake Tahoe is a four-hour drive from San Francisco. The two main trans-Sierra highways, **I-80** and **U.S. 50 (Lake Tahoe Blvd.),** run east-west through Tahoe, skimming the northern and southern shores of the lake, respectively. Lake Tahoe is 118 mi. northeast of Sacramento and 35 mi. southwest of Reno on I-80. From the Carson City and Owens Valley area, **U.S. 395** runs north along Tahoe's eastern shores.

> **Buses: Greyhound,** 3794 Montreal Rd. (☎530-543-1050), in the Tahoe Colony Inn at Raley's Shopping Center. To **San Francisco** (3 per day, $27-29) and **Sacramento** (3 per day, $21-23). Station open daily 8am-7pm.

Public Transit: Tahoe Casino Express (☎800-446-6128) provides shuttle service between the Reno airport and South Shore Tahoe casinos. Runs daily 6:15am-12:30am. $19, round-trip $34; up to 2 children under 12 free. **Tahoe Area Regional Transport (TART;** ☎550-1212) connects the western and northern shores from Incline Village to Tahoe City to Tahoma. Runs daily 6:30am-6pm. Buses also run to Truckee and Squaw Valley 5 times per day. $1.25, day pass $3. **South Tahoe Area Ground Express (STAGE;** ☎541-6328) operates buses around South Tahoe and connects Stateline and Emerald Bay Rd. $1.25; day pass $2; 10-ride pass $10. Most casinos operate free shuttle service along U.S. 50 to California ski resorts and motels.

◄╬► ORIENTATION & PRACTICAL INFORMATION

The lake is roughly divided into two main regions: North Shore and South Shore. The North Shore includes King's Beach, Tahoe City, and Incline Village, while the South Shore includes Emerald Bay and South Lake Tahoe City. Rte. 28 and 89 form a 75 mi. ring of asphalt around the lake; the complete loop takes nearly 3hr.

Visitor info: Lake Tahoe Visitors Center (☎573-2674), 3 mi. north of S. Lake Tahoe on Rte. 89. Detailed area maps and permits for entering the Desolation Wilderness. Open daily 8am-5pm; extended summer hours.

Internet access: South Lake Tahoe Library, 1000 Rufus Allen Blvd. (☎573-3185). Open Tu-W 10am-8pm, Th-Sa 10am-5pm. **Tahoe City Library,** 740 N. Lake Blvd. (☎583-3382). Open Tu and Th-F 10am-5pm, W noon-7pm, Sa noon-4pm. Free.

Medical Services: Barton Memorial Hospital (☎541-3420), at 3rd St. and South Ave., in S. Lake Tahoe. **Tahoe Forest Hospital** (☎587-6011), at Donner Pass Rd. and Pine Ave., Truckee.

Post Offices: Tahoe City, 950 N. Lake Blvd. #12 (☎800-275-8777), in the Lighthouse Shopping Center. Open M-F 8:30am-5pm, Sa noon-2pm. **ZIP code: 96145. South Lake Tahoe,** 212 Elk Point Rd. (☎588-5419). Open M-F 8:30am-5pm, Sa 10am-2pm. **ZIP code: 96151. Area code:** 530 in CA, 775 in NV; in text, 530 unless noted.

▐ ACCOMMODATIONS

The strip off U.S. 50 on the California side of the border supports the bulk of Tahoe's motels. Particularly glitzy and cheap in South Lake Tahoe, motels also line the quieter area along Park Ave. and Pioneer Trail. The North Shore offers more woodsy accommodations along Rte. 28.

▓ **Tahoe City Inn,** 790 N. Lake Blvd. (☎581-3333 or 800-800-8246), in Tahoe City. Deluxe rooms sporting glass block walls, jacuzzis, mini-fridges, comfy queen beds, and cable TV. Rooms with VCRs are more costly, but visitors get free access to extensive video library. Late Apr. to mid-June and late Sept.-late Nov. Su-Th $49, F-Sa $66; extra bed $10. Prices rise during peak season. ❸

▓ **Doug's Mellow Mountain Retreat,** 3787 Forest Ave. (☎544-8065), in S. Lake Tahoe. From the north turn left onto Wildwood Rd., and after 3 blocks take a left on Forest Ave.; it's the 6th house on the left. Easygoing Doug supplies a modern kitchen, BBQ, and fireplace. Internet access $5 per hr. Bedding included. No curfew. Flexible checkout times. Dorms $15 per person; private rooms available. Discounts for stays over a week. ❶

Tahoe State Recreation Area (☎583-3074), at the northeast end of Tahoe City on Rte. 28. 1 acre of land along the lake and road, with a long pier. Water, flush toilets, showers ($5). Open May-Nov. 38 sites $15-16. ❶

Sugar Pine Point State Park (☎525-7982), on the west shore, 1 mi. south of Tahoma. Popular grounds include tennis courts, cross-country ski trails, bike trails, nature center, and lakeside dock. Water, BBQ pits, and flush toilets. Hot showers 50¢. Sites $16; day use $2, seniors $1. ❶

☐ FOOD

In the south, the casinos on the Nevada side offer perpetually low-priced buffets, but there are restaurants along the lakeshore with reasonable prices, similarly large portions, and much better food. Groceries are cheaper on the California side.

Red Hut Waffles, 2749 Lake Tahoe Blvd. (☎541-9024) and 227 Kingsbury Rd. (☎588-7488). Homestyle cooking. Waffle piled with fruit and whipped cream $5.75. Bottomless coffee $1.25. Open daily 6am-2pm. No credit cards. ❶

Lakehouse Pizza, 120 Grove St. (☎583-2222), in Tahoe City. The kitchen turns out small but tasty pizzas from $9. Standard breakfast specials $3-7. California salad and sandwiches $7. Open M-Th 8am-10pm, F-Sa 8am-11pm. ❷

The Fire Sign Cafe, 1785 W. Lake Blvd. (☎583-0871), 2 mi. south of Tahoe City, 100 yd. south of TART stop. Big breakfasts served in a woodsy location. Large omelettes with home fries and a muffin $6. Daily lunch deals. Open daily 7am-3pm. ❷

Fast Eddie's Texas-Style BBQ, 690 N. Lake Blvd. (☎583-0950), in Tahoe City. The beef brisket ($15) takes 10hr. to cook—you get it in 10min. Everything is slow-cooked with oak firewood, and you can taste the difference. Open daily 11am-10pm. ❹

⚠ OUTDOOR ACTIVITIES

BEACHES

Lake Tahoe supports many beaches perfect for a day of sunning and people-watching. Parking generally costs $5; bargain hunters leave cars on the main road and walk. **Sand Harbor Beach,** south of Incline Village, has gorgeous granite boulders and clear waters that attract swimmers, sunners, and divers in droves. The parking lot ($5) is usually full by 11:30am. One mile away at Memorial Point, paved parking is free. **Hidden Beach,** also south of Incline Village, and **Kings Beach,** just across the California border on Rte. 28, come complete with waveboards and an alternative feel. Kings Beach has volleyball and basketball courts and a playground. **Pope Beach,** at the southernmost point of the lake off Rte. 89, is a wide, pine-shaded expanse of shoreline, less trafficked on its east side. **Nevada Beach,** 8 mi. north of South Lake Tahoe, is close to the casinos off U.S. 50, offering a quiet place to reflect on gambling losses while gazing up at the mountains. **Zephyr Cove Beach,** about 15 mi. north of South Lake Tahoe, is a favorite spot for the college crowd. **Meeks Bay,** 10 mi. south of Tahoe City, is family-oriented, with picnic tables, volleyball, motorboat and kayak rental, and a petite store. In the summer, the Tahoe City and South Tahoe Buses connect here. Five miles south of Meeks Bay, the **D.L. Bliss State Park** has a large beach on Rubicon Bay. Parking here ($5) is limited, so think about parking on the road and walking in.

BIKING

Lake Tahoe is a biking paradise. The excellent paved trails, logging roads, and dirt paths have not gone unnoticed; be prepared for company if you pedal around the area. The Forest Service and bike rental stores can provide advice, publications like *Bike West* magazine, maps, and trail info. No cycling is allowed in the Desolation Wilderness, or on the Pacific Crest or Tahoe Rim Trails. The staff at **Olympic Bike Shop,** 60 N. Lake Tahoe Blvd., Tahoe City, dispenses many maps. (☎581-2500. Open daily 9am-6pm. Bikes $5 per hr., $15 per 4hr., $21 per day.)

Known more for its ski trails, the North Shore is equipped with both flat lakeside jaunts and steeper woodsy rides. The **Tahoe Rim Trail,** from Kings Beach to Tahoe City, offers intermediate-level hilly biking. The trail can be accessed from Tahoe City or Brockway Summit (see below for more info). **Squaw Valley,** northwest of the lake on Rte. 89, opens its slope to hikers and mountain bikers during the summer. The cable car transports bikers and their wheels 2000 vertical ft. (1 ride $19, full-day pass $26.) The slopes are steep, but fairly easy. The South Shore boasts a variety of scenic trails for all abilities. **Fallen Leaf Lake,** just west of South Lake Tahoe, is a dazzling destination by bike or by car, but watch out for swerving drivers. The steep mountain peaks that surround the lake are breathtaking when viewed from beside Fallen Leaf's icy blue waters. Bikers looking for a challenge can try the seven-mile ring around the lake. Angora Ridge (4 mi.), accessible from Rte. 89, meanders past Fallen Leaf Lake to the Angora Lakes for a moderate challenge. The advanced 23 mi. **Flume Trail** begins at the Spooner Lake campground with the Marlette Lake Trail, a five-mile sandy road. The **West Shore Bike Path**, a 10 mi. stretch from Tahoe City to Sugar Pine Point, is a scenic way to tour the lake.

HIKING
The Visitors Center and ranger stations provide detailed info and maps for all types of hikes. Backcountry users must obtain a wilderness permit from the Forest Service for any hike into the Desolation Wilderness. The almost completed **Tahoe Rim Trail** encircles the lake, following the ridge tops of the Lake Tahoe Basin. Hiking is moderate to difficult. On the western shore, the trail is part of the Pacific Crest Trail. Current trailheads are at Spooner Summit on U.S. 50, off Rte. 89 on Fairway Dr. in Tahoe City, Brockway on Rte. 267, and Mt. Rose on Rte. 431. (Mt. Rose is a 1.3 mi. wheelchair-accessible loop.)

ROCK CLIMBING
The **Alpenglow Sport Shop,** 415 N. Lake Blvd., Tahoe City, provides free rock and ice climbing literature and rents climbing shoes. (☎583-6917. Open M-F 10am-6pm, Sa-Su 9am-6pm.) **Headwall Climbing Wall,** at Squaw Valley, offers several challenging routes in the Cable Car Building. (☎583-7673. Open daily 10am-5pm. $12 per day, indoor shoe rental $4 per day.)

DOWNHILL SKIING
With its world-class alpine slopes, knee-deep powder, and notorious California sun, Tahoe is a skier's paradise. There are approximately 20 ski resorts in the Tahoe area. The Visitors Center provides info, maps, publications like *Ski Tahoe* (free), and coupons. Lifts at most resorts operate daily 9am-4pm; arrive early for the shortest lines. Skiers on a budget should consider night skiing or half-day passes. **Squaw Valley,** off Rte. 89, was the site of the 1960 Olympic Winter Games, and its groomed bowls and tree runs make for some of the West's best skiing. The 32 ski lifts access high-elevation runs for all levels. (☎583-5585 or 800-766-9321. Day pass $56, half-day $39; seniors and ages 13-15 $28, over 75 and under 13 free.) **Alpine Meadows,** 6 mi. northwest of Tahoe City on Rte. 89, is an excellent, accessible family vacation spot with more than 2000 skiable acres. (☎583-4232 or 800-441-4423. Full-day $54, ages 65-69 $30, over 70 $8, ages 7-12 $10, under 6 $6. Basic ski rental $27, under 13 $18.) **Heavenly,** on Ski Run Blvd. off U.S. 50, is the largest and most popular resort in the area, with over 4800 skiable acres, 29 lifts, and 84 trails. Reaching over 10,000 ft., it is also Tahoe's highest ski resort. (☎775-586-7000. Full-day $57, ages 13-18 $47, seniors and ages 6-12 $29.)

CROSS-COUNTRY SKIING
One of the best ways to enjoy the solitude of Tahoe's pristine snow-covered forests is to cross-country ski at a resort. For more detachment, rent skis at an independent outlet and head onto the thick braid of trails around the lake. **Porters** has two locations: one at the Lucky-Longs Center in Truckee (☎587-1500), and one at 501 N. Lake Blvd. in Tahoe City. (☎583-2314; both open daily 8am-6pm. Skis $9-12.)

    Royal Gorge (☎426-3871), on Old Hwy. 40 below Donner Summit, is the nation's largest cross-country ski resort, with 90 trails covering 170 mi. of beginner and expert terrain. Warming huts provide a respite during your trek. **Spooner Lake,** at the junction of U.S. 50 and Rte. 28, offers 57 mi. of machine-groomed trails and incredible views. (☎775-749-5349. $15, children $3; mid-week special $11.)

YOSEMITE NATIONAL PARK ☎209

In 1868, a Scotsman named John Muir arrived by boat in San Francisco and asked for directions to "any place that is wild." Anxious to run this crazy youngster out of town, Bay Area folk directed him to the heralded lands of Yosemite. The wonders that Muir beheld there sated his wanderlust and spawned a lifetime of conservationism. His efforts won Yosemite its national park status by 1880 and Sequoia and Kings Canyon the same reward by 1890. Yosemite remains a paradise for outdoor enthusiasts; most visitors congregate in only 6% of the park (Yosemite Valley), leaving expanses of beautiful backcountry in relative peace and quiet.

⌐ TRANSPORTATION

Yosemite runs public buses connecting the park with Merced and Mariposa. **Yosemite VIA** runs buses from the station at 16th and N. St. in Merced to Yosemite. (☎384-1315 or 800-842-5463. 4 per day. $20.) VIA also runs **Yosemite Gray Line (YGL),** which meets trains arriving in Merced from San Francisco and takes passengers to Yosemite. Tickets can be purchased from the driver. (☎384-1315. Operates M-F 8am-5pm.) YGL runs buses to and from the airport, Fresno hotels, and Yosemite Valley ($20). **YARTS** (☎372-4487 or 877-989-2787) provides four daily trips to Yosemite from Merced; call ahead for fares and schedules. **Amtrak** runs a bus from Merced to Yosemite (4 per day, $10). Amtrak **trains** run to Merced from L.A. (4 per day, $28-51) and San Francisco (5 per day, $22-29). The trains connect with the waiting YGL bus. In Yosemite, a free **shuttle bus system** runs to points of interest daily every 10min. 7am-6pm, every 20min. 6-10pm.

Although the inner valley is often congested with traffic, the best way to achieve a quick overview of Yosemite is by **car.** There are no gas stations in the valley; be prepared to get ripped off in a gateway town. A more relaxing (and environmentally friendly) option is to park at one of the lodging areas and ride the free shuttle to see the valley sights, using your car only to explore sights outside of the valley. Drivers visiting the high country in spring and fall should have snow tires.

◼▢ ORIENTATION & PRACTICAL INFORMATION

General Park Information (☎372-0200). Info on weather, accommodations, and activities. Call the general line before a specific info station. All Visitors Centers have free maps and copies of *Yosemite Guide.* Listed hours are valid June-Sept. unless noted.

Yosemite Valley Visitors Center (☎372-0200), in Yosemite Village. Sign language interpreter in summer. Open daily 8am-6pm.

Wilderness Center (☎372-0308). Wilderness permit reservations are available for $5 per person up to 24 weeks in advance, or free first come, first served; call ☎372-0740 for details. Open daily 8am-5pm.

Bike Rental: Yosemite Lodge (☎372-1208) and **Curry Village** (☎372-8319). Both open daily 9am-6pm, weather permitting; restricted hours during winter. Bikes $5.25 per hr., $20 per day.

Equipment Rental: Yosemite Mountaineering School (☎372-8344), on Rte. 120 at Tuolumne Meadows. Climbing shoes rented to YMS students only. Daily rock climbing classes. Driver's license or credit card required for deposit. Open daily 9am-5pm. Sleeping bags $10 per day, backpacks $8 per day; 3rd day half-price.

CALIFORNIA

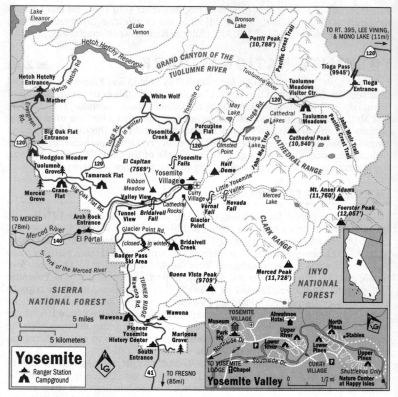

Weather and Road Conditions: ☎372-0200. 24hr.

Internet access: Yosemite Bug Hostel (☎966-6666), on Rte. 140, 30 mi. west of Yosemite in Midpines (see **Accommodations,** below). $1 per 8min.

Post Offices: Yosemite Village, 9017 Village Dr. (☎372-4475), next to the Visitors Center. Open M-F 8:30am-5pm, Sa 10am-noon. **ZIP code:** 95389. **Area code:** 209.

🏠 ACCOMMODATIONS

INSIDE THE PARK

Advance reservations are necessary and should be made up to one year in advance (☎252-4848). Rates fluctuate, but tend to be higher on weekends and during the summer. Check-in hovers around 11am. All park lodgings provide access to dining and laundry facilities, showers, and supplies.

Housekeeping Camp (☎372-8338), ¼ mi. west of Curry Village. Canvas-capped concrete "camping shelters" accommodate up to 4 people and include 2 bunk beds, a double bed, a picnic table, a firepit with grill, lights, and electrical outlets. Cottages $56. ❸

Curry Village (☎252-4848), southeast of Yosemite Village. Pool, nightly shows at the amphitheater, snack stands, and cafeteria. Ice rink Nov.-Feb. Ranger programs nearly every night. Standard motel room $112; cabin with bath $92, without bath $77; canvas tent cabin $54. ❸

Tuolumne Meadows Lodge (☎372-8413), on Tioga Pass Rd., in the northeastern corner of the park. Canvas-sided cabins, wood stoves, no electricity. Maid service $4. Cabins $59; additional adult $8.25, child $4. ❸

White Wolf Lodge (☎372-8416), on Tioga Pass Rd. in the western area of the park. Open late June-early Sept. Cabins with bath $88; tent cabins for 2 $55; each additional person $8.25. ❸

Yosemite Lodge (☎372-1274), west of Yosemite Village and directly across from Yosemite Falls. Spacious lodge rooms with private patios and A/C. Lodge rooms $120-140; standard rooms $112; each additional person $11.50. ❺

OUTSIDE THE PARK

■ **Yosemite Bug Hostel** on Rte. 140 in Midpines (☎966-6666), 25 mi. west of Yosemite. Look carefully for sign. A woodsy, spirited resort spot. International backpacking crowd lounges in hammocks. Beer on tap, kitchen, library, cafe with great food, glorious swimmin' hole with a waterfall. Dorms $16; tent sites $17; family and private rooms with shared bath $40-70; private rooms with bath $55-115. ❶

Evergreen Lodge, 33160 Evergreen Rd. (☎379-2606), 7 mi. off Rte. 120, 1 mi. before park entrance. Over 80 years old and near the quieter Hetch Hetchy region, these spacious cabins have porches, an outdoor patio and grill, and an on-site restaurant, bar, deli, and market. Standard cabins $79; family cabins $89; large family cabins $104. $10 extra during the busy season. ❹

▓ CAMPING

Yosemite is camping country; most of the valley's campgrounds are choked with tents, trailers, and RVs. Outside of the valley, campsite quality vastly improves. Reservations can be made up to five months in advance. (☎800-436-7275, outside the US 301-722-1257; www.reservations.nps.gov.) **Backcountry camping** is prohibited in the valley but is encouraged outside of it.

Sunnyside (also Camp 4), 4000 ft., at the western end of the Valley, past Yosemite Lodge. 35 sites fill up before 9am most mornings. Pervaded by a climbing culture with seasoned adventurers swapping stories of exploits on vertical rock faces. Be prepared to meet new friends, since every site is filled with 6 randomly assembled people. First come, first camp. Limited parking. $5 per person. ❶

Lower Pines, 4000 ft., in the busy eastern end of Yosemite Valley. Commercial, crowded, and plagued by the noises of cars. Next to **North Pines** campsite (4000 ft., open Apr.-Sept., 81 sites) and the **Upper Pines** campsite (4000 ft., 238 sites). Water, toilets, tables, and showers. Open Mar.-Oct. Sites $18. Reservations required. ❶

Tuolumne Meadows, 8600 ft., on Rte. 120, 55 mi. east of the Valley. Drive into the sprawling campground or escape the RVs in the 25 sites saved for walk-in hikers. 152 sites require advance reservations, 152 saved for same-day reservations. Ranger programs every night. Open July-Sept., depending on snowpack. Drive-in sites $18; backpacker sites $3 per person. ❶

▐ FOOD

Restaurants in the park are nothing special. The Yosemite Lodge and the Village Store (both open June-Sept. daily 8am-10pm; Oct.-May 8am-9pm), and stores at Wawona, Crane Flat, El Portal, and Tuolumne Meadows have slim supplies of pricey groceries. Consider buying all of your cooking supplies, marshmallows, and batteries in Merced or Fresno en route to the park.

◪ OUTDOOR ACTIVITIES

DRIVING

Although the view is better if you get out of the car, you can see a large portion of Yosemite from the bucket seat. The **Yosemite Road Guide** ($4 at every Visitors Center) is keyed to roadside markers and outlines a superb tour of the park—it's almost like having a ranger tied to the hood. Spectacular panoramas are omnipresent during the drive east along **Tioga Pass Road (Rte. 120).** The drive west from the pass brings you past **Tuolumne Meadows** with its open spaces and rippling creeks, to shimmering Tenaya Lake and its scenic views of granite slopes and canyons. No less incredible are the views afforded by the southern approach to Yosemite, **Rte. 41.** Most recognizable is the Wawona Tunnel turnout (also known as **Inspiration Point**), which most visitors will immediately recognize as the subject of many Ansel Adams photographs.

El Capitan, a gigantic granite monolith (7569 ft.), looms over awestruck crowds. If you stop and look closely (with binoculars if possible), you will see what appear to be specks of dust moving on the mountain face—they are actually world-class climbers inching toward fame. At night their flashlights shine from impromptu hammocks hung from the granite. Nearby, **Three Brothers** and misty **Bridalveil Falls** pose for hundreds of snapshots every day. A drive into the heart of the valley leads to **Yosemite Falls** (2425 ft.), **Sentinel Rock,** and mighty **Half Dome.**

DAY HIKING IN THE VALLEY

To have the full Yosemite experience, visitors must travel the outer trails on foot. A wealth of opportunities reward anyone willing to lace up a pair of boots, even if only for a daytrip. Day-use trails are very, very busy. Hiking just after sunrise is the best way to beat the crowds, but even then, trails like Half Dome are already busy. A colorful trail map with difficulty ratings and average hiking times is available at the Visitors Center (50¢). The **Mirror Lake Loop** is a level three-mile walk. **Bridalveil Falls,** another Ansel Adams favorite, is an easy ¼ mi. stroll from the nearby shuttle bus stop, and its cool spray is as close to a shower as many Yosemite campers ever get. **Upper Yosemite Falls Trail,** a back-breaking 3.5 mi. trek to the windy summit, rewards the intrepid hiker with an overview of the 2425 ft. drop. Those with energy to spare can trudge on to **Yosemite Point,** where views of the valley below rival those from more-heralded Glacier Point. The trail begins with an extremely steep, unshaded ascent. Leaving the marked trail is not a wise idea—a sign warns, "If you go over the waterfall, you will die." From the Happy Isles trailhead, the less strenuous 1.5 mi. **Mist Trail** past **Vernal Falls** to the top of **Nevada Falls.** This is perhaps the most popular day hike in the park, and with good reason—views of the falls from the trails are outstanding, and the drizzle from the nearby rocks is more than welcome during the hot summer months. From Nevada Falls, the trail continues to the base of **Half Dome,** Yosemite's most recognizable monument.

CLIMBING & RAFTING

The world's best **climbers** come to Yosemite to test themselves at angles past vertical. If you've got the courage (and the cash), you can take a lesson at the **Yosemite Mountaineering School** (see p. 941). Basic rock climbing classes (mid-Apr. to Oct.) teach simple skills on the ground such as bouldering, rappelling, and ascending an 80 ft. cliff. Reservations are useful and require advance payment, although drop-ins are accepted if space allows. (☎372-8344. Open in Curry Village daily 8:30am-noon and 1-5pm; in Tuolumne Meadows daily 9am-5pm. Classes from $70.)

Rafting is permitted on the Merced River when the water is warm and high enough, but no motorized crafts are allowed. For organized rafting trips, **All Outdoors**, 1250 Pine St. #103 (☎925-932-8993 or 800-247-2387), in Walnut Creek, leads trips on the north fork of Stanislaus River, the Merced River), the Kaweah River, and Goodwin Canyon. Call ahead to get departure locations.

WINTER IN YOSEMITE

Most folks never leave the valley, but a wilder, more isolated Yosemite awaits those who do. Topographical maps and hiking guides are especially helpful in navigating Yosemite's nether regions. **Cross-country skiing** is free, and several well-marked trails cut into the backcountry of the valley's South Rim at Badger Pass and Crane Flat. Rangers host several **snowshoe** walks, but the serene winter forests are perhaps best explored without help. Snowshoes and skis can be rented from the **Yosemite Mountaineering School** (see p. 941).

The state's oldest ski resort, **Badger Pass Ski Area,** on Glacier Point Rd. south of Yosemite Valley, is the only downhill ski area in the park. The resort's powder may not rival the soft stuff of Tahoe, but its family-fun atmosphere fosters learning and restraint. Free shuttles connect Badger Pass with Yosemite Valley. (☎372-8430. Lifts open 9am-4:30pm. 1-day lift tickets M-F $22, Sa-Su $28; under 12 daily $13. Rental packages $18 per day, under 12 $13. Some weekday discounts available through Yosemite Lodge. No snowboarding.)

MONO LAKE ☎760

Fresh water from streams and springs evaporates as it drains into this "inland sea," leaving behind a mineral-rich, 13 mi.-wide expanse Mark Twain once called "the Dead Sea of the West." The lake derives its lunar appearance from towers of calcium carbonate called tufa, which form when calcium-rich springs well up in the carbonate-filled salt water. At 1 million years old, the lake is the oldest enclosed body of water in the Western Hemisphere. The Mono Lake Committee offers **canoe tours** of the lake. (☎647-6595. Tours $17, ages 4-12 $7. Reservations required.) The unique terrain of this geological playground also makes it a great place for hikers of all levels. Trails include the 0.3 mi. **Old Marina Area Trail,** east of U.S. 395, the **Lee Vining Creek Nature Trail,** which begins behind the Mono Basin Visitors Center, and the **Panum Crater Trail,** 5 mi. south on U.S. 395.

The **El Mono Motel ❸,** at Main and 3rd St., offers a slice of modern California: faux Spanish name, white stucco exterior, espresso bar, and alternative rock in the lobby. Clean and bright rooms have cable TV but no phone. (☎647-6310. Open Apr.-Oct. Singles with shared bath $49.) None of the area's many campgrounds take reservations, but a pre-noon arrival time will almost always guarantee a spot. Most sites are clustered west of Lee Vining along Rte. 120. Try **Inyo National Forest Campgrounds ❶,** which are close to town. **Lundy** and **Lee Vining Canyons** are the best locations for lakebound travelers. (No water. Open May-Oct. Sites $7.)

In 1984, Congress set aside 57,000 acres of land surrounding Mono Lake and named it the **Mono Basin National Forest Scenic Area** (☎873-2408). For a $3 fee, investigate the **South Tufa Grove,** which harbors an awe-inspiring hoard of calcium carbonate formations. Take U.S. 395 S to Rte. 120, then go 4 mi. east and take the turn-off south to Tufa Grove. **Mono Lake Committee and Lee Vining Chamber of Commerce** (☎647-6595), at Main and 3rd St., in the orange and blue building, answers tourist questions. **Post Office:** On 4th St., Lee Vining, in the big brown building. (☎647-6371. Open M-F 9am-2pm and 3-5pm.) **ZIP code:** 93541. **Area code:** 760.

CALIFORNIA

MAMMOTH LAKES ☎ 760

Home to one of the most popular ski resorts in the US, the town of Mammoth Lakes has transformed itself into a giant year-round playground. Mammoth Mountain shifts from ski park in winter to bike park in summer, with fishing, rock climbing, and hiking to boot. Mammoth Lakes is on U.S. 395 40 mi. southeast of Yosemite's the eastern entrance. Rte. 203 runs through the town as Main St. and then veers off to the right as Minaret Summit Rd. In the winter, the roads from L.A. are jammed with weekend skiers. With 150 downhill runs, over 28 lifts, and miles of nordic skiing trails, **Mammoth** is one of the country's premier winter resorts. The season extends from mid-November to June or July. Lift tickets can be purchased at the Main Lodge on Minaret Rd. (☎934-2571. Open daily 7:30am-3pm.) A free **shuttle bus (MAS)** transports skiers between lifts, town, and the **Main Lodge.**

As with most ski resorts, lodging is much more expensive in the winter, but prices tend to be cheaper on weekdays. Condo rentals are a comfortable choice for groups of three or more, and start at $65 per night. **Mammoth Reservation Bureau** (☎800-462-5571) can make rental arrangements. For lone travelers, dorm-style motels are the cheapest option. Make reservations far in advance. One of the best views in town is from the **Davison St. Guest House ❶**, 19 Davison Rd. (☎924-2188. In summer dorms $18, singles from $35; in winter $22/53.) There are nearly 20 **Inyo Forest public campgrounds ❶** in the area, at Mammoth Lakes, Mammoth Village, Convict Lake, Red's Meadow, and June Lake. All sites have piped water, and most are near fishing and hiking. Interested parties should contact the **Mammoth Ranger District** for info. Reservations can be made for all sites, as well as at nearby Sherwin Creek. (☎924-5500 for info, 877-444-6777 for reservations. Sites $13-15.) **Schat's Bakery and Cafe,** 3305 Main St., is arguably the best bakery in town. (☎934-6055. Open daily 5:30am-6pm.)

Devil's Postpile National Monument was formed when lava flows oozed through Mammoth Pass thousands of years ago, forming 40-60 ft. basalt posts. A pleasant three-mile walk from the center of Devil's Postpile Monument is Rainbow Falls, where the middle fork of the San Joaquin River drops 101 ft. into a glistening green pool. From U.S. 395, the trailhead is 15 mi. past Minaret Summit on Rte. 203. A quick half-mile hike from the Twin Lakes turn-off culminates in spectacular views from **Panorama Dome.** Lake Mamie has a picturesque picnic area and many short hikes lead out to Lake George, where exposed granite sheets attract climbers. These trailheads and scenic spots are accessible from the **MAS shuttle.**

The stately climbing wall at **Mammoth Mountain High Adventure** stands like a modern-day shrine to extreme sports, beckoning both the inexperienced and the professional. (☎924-5683. Open daily 10am-6pm. $6 per climb, $13 per hr., $22 per day; discount for groups of 3 or more.) The **Mammoth Mountain Gondola** reaches a view miles above the rest. (☎934-2571. Open daily 8am-4pm. Round-trip $16, children $8.) Exit the gondola at the top to bike the twisted trails of **Mammoth Mountain Bike Park,** where the ride starts at 11,053 ft. and heads straight down rocky trails. (☎934-0706. Helmets required. Open 9am-6pm. Day pass $29, children $15.)

The Forest Service provides tips on the area's cross-country trails. For info, contact the **Inyo National Forest Visitors Center and Chamber of Commerce** (☎924-5500), east off U.S. 395 north of town. **Post Office:** 3330 Main St. (☎934-2205. Open M-F 8:30am-5pm.) **ZIP code:** 93546. **Area code:** 760.

PACIFIC NORTHWEST

The Pacific Northwest became the center of national attention when gold rushes and the Oregon Trail ushered masses into the region, jump-starting the political machine that had already taken over the eastern US. In the 1840s, Senator Stephen Douglas argued, sensibly, that the Cascade Range would make the perfect natural border between Oregon and Washington. Sense has little to do with politics, and the Columbia River, running perpendicular to the Cascades, became the border instead. Yet even today, the range and not the river is the region's most important cultural divide: west of the rain-trapping Cascades lies the microchip, mocha, and music meccas of Portland and Seattle; to the east sprawls farmland and an arid plateau. For more, see ■*Let's Go: Alaska & the Pacific Northwest 2003*.

HIGHLIGHTS OF THE PACIFIC NORTHWEST

SEATTLE. The offbeat neighborhoods, fine museums, ample green space, and pioneering cafes of this thriving city are not to be missed (p. 948).

NATIONAL PARKS. Oregon's Crater Lake National Park (p. 986) puts a volcanic past on display. In Washington, Olympic National Park (p. 965) has mossy grandeur and deserted beaches, and life beautifully blankets the dormant Mt. Rainier (p. 972).

SCENIC DRIVES. Rte. 20 (p. 970) winds through the emerald North Cascades, while U.S. 101 takes visitors on a spin through the Oregon Coast (p. 984).

WASHINGTON

On Washington's western shores, Pacific storms feed one of the world's only temperate rainforests in Olympic National Park. To the east, low clouds linger over Seattle, hiding the Emerald City. Visitors to Puget Sound, Washington's deep, ecologically staggering inlet, can experience everything from isolation in the San Juan Islands to cosmopolitan entertainment on the mainland. Moving west over the Cascades, the state's eastern half spreads out into fertile farmlands and grassy plains as inland fruit bowls run over.

ⓘ PRACTICAL INFORMATION

Capital: Olympia.

Visitor info: Washington State Tourism, Dept. of Community, Trade, and Economic Development, P.O. Box 42500, Olympia, WA 98504 (☎800-544-1800; www.tourism.wa.gov). **Washington State Parks and Recreation Commission,** P.O. Box 42650, Olympia, WA 98504 (☎360-902-8500 or 800-233-0321; www.parks.wa.gov).

Postal Abbreviation: WA. **Sales Tax:** 7-9.1%, depending on the county.

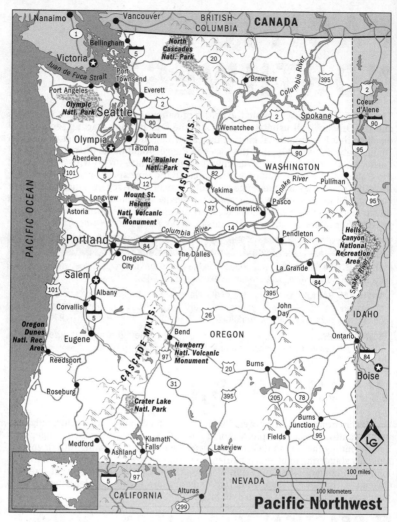

Pacific Northwest

SEATTLE

☎ **206**

Seattle's mix of mountain views, clean streets, espresso stands, and rainy weather proved to be the magic formula of the 90s, attracting transplants from across the US. The droves of newcomers provide an interesting contrast to the older residents who remember Seattle as a city-town, not a thriving metropolis bubbling over with young millionaires. Computer and coffee money have helped drive rents sky-high in some areas, but the grungy, punk-loving street culture still prevails in others. In the end, there is a nook or cranny for almost anyone in Seattle. Every hilltop offers an impressive view of Mt. Olympus, Mt. Baker, and Mt. Rainier. The city is shrouded in cloud cover 200 days a year, but when the skies clear, Seattleites rejoice that "the mountain is out" and head for the country.

▓ INTERCITY TRANSPORTATION

Airports: Seattle-Tacoma International or **Sea-Tac** (☎431-4444), on Federal Way, 15 mi. south of Seattle, right off I-5. Bus #194 departs the underground tunnel at University St. and 3rd Ave.

Trains: Amtrak (☎382-4125), King St. Station, at 3rd and Jackson St., 1 block east of Pioneer Sq. next to the stadiums. Ticket office and station open daily 6am-10:30pm. To: **Portland** (4 per day, $33-36); **Tacoma** (4 per day, $9-14); and **Vancouver** (1 per day, $23-35).

Buses: Greyhound (☎628-5526 or 800-231-2222), at 8th Ave. and Stewart St. *Try to avoid night buses, since the station can get seedy after dark.* Ticket office open daily 6:30am-2:30am. To: **Portland** (14 per day, $24); **Spokane** (6 per day, $30); **Tacoma** (9 per day, $5); and **Vancouver** (16 per day, $23). **Quick Shuttle** (☎604-940-4428 or 800-665-2122) makes 8 cross-border trips daily from Seattle (Travelodge hotel at 8th and Bell St.) and the Sea-Tac airport to the Vancouver airport and the Holiday Inn on Howe St. in downtown Vancouver (4-4½hr.; $31 from downtown, $39 from Sea-Tac).

Ferries: Washington State Ferries (☎464-6400 or 888-808-7977) has 2 terminals in Seattle. The main terminal is downtown, at Colman Dock, Pier 52. From here, service departs to: **Bainbridge Island** (35min.; $5.10, with car $10-12); **Bremerton** on the Kitsap Peninsula (1hr., passenger-only boat 40min; $5.10, with car $10-12); and **Vashon Island** (25min., passenger-only boat $7.10). The other Seattle terminal is in Fauntleroy; to reach the terminal, drive south on I-5 and take Exit 163A (West Seattle) down Fauntleroy Way. Sailings from Fauntleroy to **Southworth** on the Kitsap Peninsula (35min.; $4, with car $8.75) and **Vashon Island** (15min; $3.30, with car $13-15).

▓ ORIENTATION

Seattle stretches from north to south on an isthmus between **Puget Sound** to the west and **Lake Washington** to the east. The city is easily accessible by car via **I-5**, which runs north-south through the city, and **I-90** from the east, which ends at I-5 southeast of downtown. Get to **downtown** (including **Pioneer Sq., Pike Place Market,** and the **waterfront**) from I-5 by taking any of the exits from James St. to Stewart St. For the **Seattle Center**, take the Mercer St./Fairview Ave. exit; follow signs from there. The Denny Way exit leads to **Capitol Hill**, and, farther north, the 45th St. exit heads toward the **University District (U District)**. The less crowded **Rte. 99** (also called **Aurora Ave.** and Aurora Hwy.) runs parallel to I-5 and skirts the western side of downtown, with great views from the Alaskan Way Viaduct. Rte. 99 is often the better choice when driving downtown or to **Queen Anne, Fremont, Green Lake,** and the northwestern part of the city. For more detailed directions to these and other districts, see the individualized neighborhood listings under **Food** (p. 953), **Nightlife** (p. 959), and **Sights** (p. 955).

The **Metro ride free zone** includes most of downtown Seattle. The Metro buses cover King County east to North Bend and Carnation, south to Enumclaw, and north to Snohomish County, where bus #6 hooks up with **Community Transit**. This line runs to Everett, Stanwood, and into the Cascades. Bus #174 connects to Tacoma's Pierce County System at Federal Way. Seattle is a bicycle-friendly city. All buses have free, easy-to-use bike racks. Between 6am and 7pm, bikes may only be loaded or unloaded at stops outside the ride free zone. Check out Metro's *Bike & Ride*, available at the Visitors Center. **City of Seattle Bicycle Program** (☎684-7583) has city bike maps.

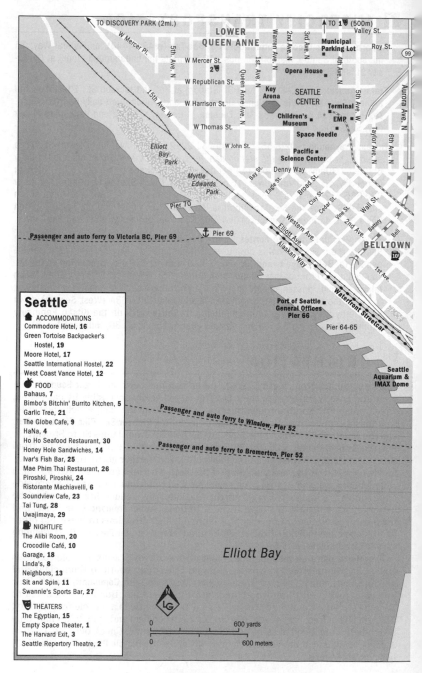

Seattle

🛏 ACCOMMODATIONS
Commodore Hotel, **16**
Green Tortoise Backpacker's
    Hostel, **19**
Moore Hotel, **17**
Seattle International Hostel, **22**
West Coast Vance Hotel, **12**

🍴 FOOD
Bahaus, **7**
Bimbo's Bitchin' Burrito Kitchen, **5**
Garlic Tree, **21**
The Globe Cafe, **9**
HaNa, **4**
Ho Ho Seafood Restaurant, **30**
Honey Hole Sandwiches, **14**
Ivar's Fish Bar, **25**
Mae Phim Thai Restaurant, **26**
Piroshki, Piroshki, **24**
Ristorante Machiavelli, **6**
Soundview Cafe, **23**
Tai Tung, **28**
Uwajimaya, **29**

🎵 NIGHTLIFE
The Alibi Room, **20**
Crocodile Café, **10**
Garage, **18**
Linda's, **8**
Neighbors, **13**
Sit and Spin, **11**
Swannie's Sports Bar, **27**

🎭 THEATERS
The Egyptian, **15**
Empty Space Theater, **1**
The Harvard Exit, **3**
Seattle Repertory Theatre, **2**

Map labels:
TO DISCOVERY PARK (2mi.)
LOWER QUEEN ANNE
TO 1 (500m)
Valley St.
Municipal Parking Lot
Roy St.
W Mercer Pl.
W Mercer St.
5th Ave. N
Warren Ave. N
2nd Ave. N
3rd Ave. N
1st Ave. N
4th Ave. N
Opera House
W Republican St.
Queen Anne Ave. N
Key Arena
SEATTLE CENTER
Terminal
5th Ave. N
W Harrison St.
Children's Museum
EMP
15th Ave. W
W Thomas St.
Space Needle
Taylor Ave. N
6th Ave. N
Elliott Bay Park
W John St.
Pacific Science Center
Myrtle Edwards Park
Denny Way
Bay St.
Eagle St.
Broad St.
Clay St.
Cedar St.
Vine St.
Wall St.
Aurora Ave. N
Pier 70
Western Ave.
2nd Ave.
Battery St.
Bell St.
Elliott Ave.
BELLTOWN
Passenger and auto ferry to Victoria BC, Pier 69
Pier 69
Alaskan Way
1st Ave.
Port of Seattle General Offices Pier 66
Waterfront Streetcar
Pier 64-65
Seattle Aquarium & IMAX Dome
Passenger and auto ferry to Winslow, Pier 52
Passenger and auto ferry to Bremerton, Pier 52
Elliott Bay
0   600 yards
0   600 meters

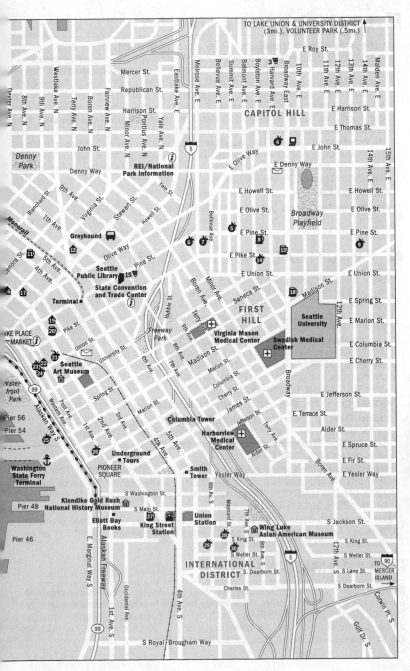

TO LAKE UNION & UNIVERSITY DISTRICT
(3mi.), VOLUNTEER PARK (.5mi.)

E Roy St.

Mercer St.

Republican St.

Harrison St.

CAPITOL HILL

John St.

E Harrison St.

E Thomas St.

Denny
Park

Denny Way

REI/National
Park Information

E John St.

E Denny Way

E Howell St.

E Olive St.

E Pine St.

E Pike St.

E Union St.

E Olive Way

E Howell St.

E Olive St.

Broadway
Playfield

E Pine St.

Greyhound

Seattle
Public Library

State Convention
and Trade Center

Terminal

E Union St.

E Spring St.

E Marion St.

FIRST
HILL

Seattle
University

E Columbia St.

E Cherry St.

Virginia Mason
Medical Center

Swedish Medical
Center

PIKE PLACE
MARKET

Seattle
Art Museum

Water
front
Park

Pier 56

Pier 54

Columbia Tower

Harborview
Medical
Center

Underground
Tours

PIONEER
SQUARE

E Jefferson St.

E. Terrace St.

Alder St.

E Spruce St.

E Fir St.

Smith
Tower

Yesler Way

Washington
State Ferry
Terminal

Pier 48

Pier 46

Klondike Gold Rush
National History Museum

Eliott Bay
Books

King Street
Station

S Washington St.

S Main St.

Union
Station

Wing Luke
Asian American Museum

S Jackson St.

S King St.

INTERNATIONAL
DISTRICT

S King St.

S Weller St.

S Lane St.

S Dearborn St.

Charles St.

S Dearborn St.

S Royal-Brougham Way

TO
MERCER
ISLAND

PACIFIC
NORTHWEST

☞ LOCAL TRANSPORTATION

Public Transit: Metro Transit, Pass Sales and Information Office, 201 S. Jackson St. (☎553-3000, 24hr. ☎800-542-7876). Open M-F 9am-5pm. The bus tunnel under Pine St. and 3rd Ave. is the heart of the downtown bus system. Fares are based on a 2-zone system. **Zone 1** includes everything within the city limits (peak hours $1.50, off-peak $1.25). **Zone 2** includes everything else (peak $2, off-peak $1.25). Ages 5-18 always $0.50. Peak hours in both zones are M-F 6-9am and 3-6pm. Exact fare required. Weekend day passes $2.50. Ride free daily 6am-7pm in the downtown **ride free area,** bordered by S Jackson on the south, 6th and I-5 on the east, Blanchard on the north, and the waterfront on the west. Free **transfers** can be used on any bus, including a return trip on the same bus within 2hr. Most buses are wheelchair accessible (info ☎684-2046). The **Monorail** runs from the Space Needle to Westlake Center. (Every 15min. daily 9am-11pm. $1.50, seniors 75¢, ages 5-12 50¢.)

Taxis: Metro Cab, ☎901-0707. **Farwest Taxi,** ☎622-1717.

Bike Rental: The Bicycle Center, 4529 Sand Point Way (☎523-8300), near the Children's Hospital. $3 per hr., 2hr. minimum; $15 per day. Open M-Th 10am-8pm, F 10am-7pm, Sa 10am-6pm, Su 10am-5pm. Credit card deposit required.

⁊ PRACTICAL INFORMATION

Visitor info: Seattle-King County Visitors Bureau (☎461-5840), at 8th and Pike St., on the 1st fl. of the Convention Center. Helpful staff doles out maps, brochures, newspapers, and Metro and ferry schedules. Open June-Oct. M-F 8:30am-5pm, Sa-Su 10am-4pm; Nov.-May M-F 8:30am-5pm. **Seattle Parks and Recreation Department,** 100 Dexter Ave. N (☎684-4075), has info and pamphlets on city parks. Open M-F 8am-5pm. **Outdoor Recreation Information Center,** 222 Yale Ave. (☎470-4060), in REI. A joint operation between the Park and Forest services, this station is able to answer any questions that might arise as you browse REI's huge collection of maps and guides. Unfortunately, the desk is not set up to sell permits. Free brochures on hiking trails. Open M-F 10:30am-7pm, Sa-Su 10am-7pm.

Hotlines: Crisis Line, ☎461-3222. **Sexual Assault Center,** ☎800-825-7273.

Medical Services: International District Emergency Center, 720 8th Ave. S, Ste. 100 (☎461-3235). Medics with multilingual assistance available. Clinic 9am-6pm, phone 24hr. **Swedish Medical Center, Providence Campus,** 500 17th Ave. (☎320-2111), for urgent care and cardiac. 24hr.

Internet access: The **Seattle Public Library,** 800 Pike St. (☎386-4636; TDD ☎386-4697), is stashed away in a temporary building near the convention center until fall 2003. One-time visitors can use Internet for free with photo ID. Open M-Th 9am-9pm, F 10:30am-6pm, Sa 9am-6pm, Su 1-5pm.

Post Office: 301 Union St. (☎748-5417 or 800-275-8777), at 3rd Ave. downtown. Open M-F 8am-5:30pm, Sa 8am-noon. General delivery window M-F 9-11:20am and noon-3pm. **Zip Code:** 98101. **Area Code:** 206.

⌂ ACCOMMODATIONS

Seattle's hostel scene is not amazing, but there are plenty of choices and establishments to fit all types of personalities. **Pacific Bed and Breakfast Association** arranges B&B singles for $50-65. (☎800-648-2932. Open M-F 8am-5pm.) For inexpensive motels farther from downtown, drive north on Rte. 99 (Aurora Ave.) or take bus #26 to the neighborhood of Fremont. Look for AAA approval ratings.

Seattle International Hostel (HI), 84 Union St. (☎622-5443 or 888-622-5443), at Western Ave., by the waterfront. Take Union St. from downtown; follow signs down the stairs under the "Pike Pub & Brewery." Great location, laundry, 199 beds, and Internet access. Max. stay in summer 7 nights. Reception 24hr. No curfew. Reservations recommended. 199 beds. $22, nonmembers $25. Private rooms for 2-3 $54/60. ❶

Green Tortoise Backpacker's Hostel, 1525 2nd Ave. (☎340-1222), between Pike and Pine St. on the #174 or 194 bus route. A young party hostel downtown. M free dinner. F free beer. Laundry, kitchen, Internet access. Key deposit $20 cash. Blanket $1 with $9 deposit. Free breakfast 7-9:30am. Reception 24hr. No curfew. Beds $18-20. ❶

Moore Hotel, 1926 2nd Ave. (☎448-4851 or 800-421-5508), at Virginia St. 1 block from Pike Place Market next to historic Moore Theater. Open lobby, cavernous halls, and attentive service. Singles $49, with bath $59; doubles $49/68. HI discount 10%. ❸

Commodore Hotel, 2013 2nd Ave. (☎448-8868), at Virginia St. Pleasant decor only a few blocks from the waterfront. Front desk open 24hr., no visitors past 8pm. Singles $59, with bath $69; double with bath $79. ❸

West Coast Vance Hotel, 620 Steward St. (☎441-8612). Built in 1926, the West Coast Vance has charming rooms from $119. The hotel is located within walking distance from Pike Place Market and the 5th Ave. shopping district. ❺

The College Inn, 4000 University Way NE (☎633-4441), at 40th St. Quiet place near UW campus and its youthful environs. Rooms are small, but turn-of-the-century bureaus and brass fixtures are so darn charming. Continental breakfast included. Singles from $45; doubles $55-75. Double with 2 beds $75-85. Credit card required. ❸

◘ FOOD

Although Seattleites appear to subsist solely on espresso and steamed milk, they do occasionally eat. When they do, they seek out healthy cuisine, especially seafood. **Puget Sound Consumer Coops (PCCs)** are local health food markets at 7504 Aurora Ave. N (☎525-3586), in Green Lake, and 6514 40th St. NE (☎526-7661), in the Ravenna District north of the university. Capitol Hill, the U District, and Fremont close main thoroughfares on summer Saturdays for **Farmers Markets.**

PIKE PLACE MARKET & DOWNTOWN

In 1907, angry citizens demanded the elimination of the middle-man and local farmers began selling produce by the waterfront, creating the Pike Place Market. Business thrived until an enormous fire burned the building in 1941. Today thousands of tourists mob the market daily. (Open M-Sa 9am-6pm, Su 11am-5pm. Produce and fish open earlier; restaurants and lounges close later.) In the **Main Arcade,** on the west side of Pike St., fishmongers compete for audiences as they hurl fish from shelves to scales.

Piroshki, Piroshki, 1908 Pike Pl. (☎441-6068). The Russian *piroshki* is a croissant-like dough baked around sausages, mushrooms, cheeses, salmon, or apples doused in cinnamon ($3-4). Watch the *piroshki* process in progress. Open daily 8am-7pm. ❶

Soundview Cafe (☎623-5700), on the mezzanine in the Pike Place Main Arcade. The sandwich-and-salad bar is a good place to brown-bag a moment of solace. Breakfast and lunch $3-6. Open M-F 8am-5pm, Sa 8am-5:30pm, Su 9am-3pm. ❶

Garlic Tree, 94 Stewart St. (☎441-5681), 1 block up from Pike Place Market. This smell will drag you in. Loads of fabulous veggie, chicken, and seafood stir-fries ($7-9). Open M-Th 11am-8pm, F-Sa 11am-10pm. ❷

THE WATERFRONT

Budget eaters, steer clear of Pioneer Sq. Instead, take a picnic to **Waterfall Garden**, on the corner of S. Main St. and 2nd Ave. S. The garden sports tables and chairs and a manmade waterfall that masks traffic outside. (Open daily 8am-6pm.)

Mae Phim Thai Restaurant, 94 Columbia St. (☎624-2979), a few blocks north of Pioneer Sq. between 1st Ave. and Alaskan Way. Slews of pad thai junkies crowd in for cheap, delicious Thai cuisine. All dishes $5.50. Open M-F 11am-7pm, Sa noon-7pm. ❷

Ivar's Fish Bar, Pier 54 (☎467-8063), north of the square. A fast-food window that serves the definitive Seattle clam chowder ($2). Clam and chips $5. Open M-Th and Su 11am–midnight, F-Sa 11am-2am. ❶

INTERNATIONAL DISTRICT

Along King and Jackson St., between 5th and 8th Ave. east of the Kingdome, Seattle's International District is packed with great eateries.

🦐 **Uwajimaya,** 600 5th Ave. S (☎624-6248). The Uwajimaya Center—the largest Japanese department store in the Northwest—is a full city block of groceries, gifts, videos, and CDs. There is even a food court, plying Korean BBQ and Taiwanese-style baked goods. Pork dumpling $7. Open M-Sa 9am-11pm. ❷

Tai Tung, 655 S. King St. (☎622-7372). Select authentic Mandarin cuisine from a comprehensive menu. Entrees $5-12. Open Su-Th 10am-11:30pm, F-Sa 10am-2am. ❷

Ho Ho Seafood Restaurant, 653 S. Weller St. (☎382-9671). Generous portions of tank-fresh seafood. Stuffed fish hang from the ceilings. Lunch $5-7. Dinner $7-12. Open Su-Th 11am-1am, F-Sa 11am-3am. ❷

CAPITOL HILL

With bronze dance-steps on the sidewalks and neon storefronts, **Broadway Ave.** is a land of espresso houses, imaginative shops, elegant clubs, and plenty of eats.

🦐 **Bimbo's Bitchin' Burrito Kitchen,** 506 E. Pine St. (☎329-9978). The name explains it, and the decorations (fake palm trees and lots of plastic) prove it. Walk right on through the door to the **Cha Cha,** a similarly-decorated bar (tequila shots $3.50). Spicy Bimbo's burrito $4.25. Open M-Th noon-11pm, F-Sa noon-2am, Su 2-10pm. ❶

Ristorante Machiavelli, 1215 Pine St. (☎621-7941), across the street from Bauhaus. A small Italian place that locals fiercely love. Pasta $8-10. Open M-Sa 5-11pm. ❸

HaNa, 219 Broadway Ave. E (☎328-1187). Packed quarters testify to the popularity of the sushi here. Lunch sushi combo platter with rice and soup $7.25. Dinner $9-10. Open M-Sa 11am-10pm, Su 4-10pm. ❷

Honey Hole Sandwiches, 703 E. Pike St. (☎709-1399). The primary colors and veggie-filled sandwiches make you feel healthy and happy. The hummus-loaded "Daytripper" is a treat ($5.50). Open M-Sa 10am-11pm, Su 10am-5pm. ❷

UNIVERSITY DISTRICT

The neighborhood around the immense **University of Washington** ("U-Dub"), north of downtown between Union and Portage Bay, supports funky shops, international restaurants, and coffeehouses. The best of each lies within a few blocks of University Way, known as "the Ave."

Flowers, 4247 University Way NE (☎633-1903). This 1920s landmark was a flower shop; now, the mirrored ceiling tastefully reflects an all-you-can-eat vegetarian buffet ($7.50). Great daily drink specials: W $2 tequila shots; Th $3 well sours; Sa $3 margaritas. Open M-Sa 11am-2am, Su 11am-midnight. ❷

Neelam's, 4735 University Way NE (☎523-5275), serves up the best authentic Indian cuisine in the University District, and the price is right. Lunch buffet $6. Lunch daily 11:30am-3pm; dinner Su-Th 5-10pm, F-Sa 5-10:30pm. ❷

Araya's Vegan Thai Cuisine, 4732 University Way NE (☎524-4332). Consistently among the top vegan restaurants in Seattle, Araya's will satisfy any meatless desire. Lunch buffet $6. Open M-Th 11:30am-9pm, F-Sa 11:30am-9:30pm, Su 5-9pm. ❷

▛ CAFES

The coffee bean is Seattle's first love. One cannot walk a single block without passing an institution of caffeination. The city's obsession with Italian-style espresso drinks even has gas stations pumping out thick, dark, soupy java.

Bauhaus, 305 E. Pine St. (☎625-1600), in Capitol Hill. The Reading Goddess, looming above the towering bookshelves, protects patrons and oversees the service of drip coffee ($1) and Kool-Aid ($1). Open M-F 6am-1am, Sa-Su 8am-1am.

The Globe Cafe, 1531 14th Ave. (☎324-8815), in Capitol Hill. Seattle's next literary renaissance is brewing as quotes overheard at the Globe are plastered on the tables. Fabulous all-vegan menu. Stir-fry tofu $5.50. Internet access $6 per hr. Open Tu-Su 7am-7:30pm.

Espresso Roma, 4201 University Way NE (☎632-6001). Pleasant patio and former warehouse interior result in spacious tables with an open air feel. The Ave.'s cheapest coffee (mocha $1.95). Open M-F 7am-10pm, Sa-Su 8am-10pm.

Ugly Mug, 1309 43rd St. (☎547-3219), off University Way. Off-beat in a 10,000 Maniacs-thrift store sort of way—eclectic chair collection is quite comfortable. Wide sandwich selection (turkey focaccia $4). Open M-F 7:30am-6pm, Sa-Su 9am-6pm.

Gingko Tea, 4343 University Way NE (☎632-7298). If you dig tea, you'll find a niche at Gingko's. Classical music and wood furniture along with 5 types of chai ($2.55). Bubble tea $2.45. Open M-Th 10:30am-11pm, F-Sa 10:30am-midnight, Su 11am-10pm.

◎ SIGHTS

It takes only three frenetic days to get a decent look at most of the city's major sights, since most are within walking distance of one another or within the Metro's ride free zone (see p. 949). Seattle taxpayers spend more per capita on the arts than any other Americans, and the investment pays off in unparalleled public art installations throughout the city (self-guided tours begin at the Visitors Center) and plentiful galleries. The investments of Seattle-based millionaires have brought startlingly new and bold architecture in the Experience Music Project and International Fountain. Outside cosmopolitan downtown, Seattle boasts over 300 areas of well-watered greenery (see **Outdoors,** p. 960).

DOWNTOWN & THE WATERFRONT

The **Pike Place Hillclimb** descends from the south end of Pike Place Market past chic shops and ethnic restaurants to the Alaskan Way and waterfront. You will not be lonely in the harbor; the waterfront is lined with vendors.

SEATTLE ART MUSEUM. Housed in a grandiose building designed by Philadelphia architect and father of postmodernism Robert Venturi, the **Seattle Art Museum (SAM)** balances special exhibits with the region's largest collection of African, Native American, and Asian art and an eclectic bunch of contemporary western painting and sculpture. Call for info on special musical shows, films, and lectures. Admission is also good for the Seattle Asian Art Museum (see p. 957) for a week.

(100 University Way, near 1st Ave. Recording ☎654-3100, person 654-3255, or TDD 654-3137. Open Tu-Su 10am-5pm. Free tours 1 and 2pm, as well as several later in the day. $10, students and seniors $7, under 12 free; first Th of the month free.)

THE SEATTLE AQUARIUM. The star attraction of the ▨Seattle Aquarium is a huge underwater dome, and the harbor seals, fur seals, otters, and plenty of fish won't disappoint. Touch tanks and costumes delight kids, while a million-dollar salmon exhibit and ladder teaches about the state's favorite fish. Feedings occur throughout the day. Next door, the **IMAX Dome** cranks out films, many focusing on natural events or habitats. *(Pier 59, near Union St. ☎386-4320, TDD ☎386-4322. Open daily 9:30am-8pm; last admission 1hr. before closing. $9.75, seniors $8.75, ages 6-18 $7, ages 3-5 $5. IMAX: Dome ☎622-1868. Films daily 10am-10pm. $7, seniors $6.50, ages 6-18 $6. Aquarium and IMAX Dome combo ticket $15.25, seniors and ages 13-18 $14.25, ages 6-13 $11.75, ages 3-5 $5.)*

THE SEATTLE CENTER

The 1962 World's Fair demanded a Seattle Center to herald the city of the future. Now the Center houses everything from carnival rides to ballet. The center is bordered by Denny Way, W. Mercer St., 1st Ave., and 5th Ave. and has eight gates, each with a model of the Center and a map of its facilities. It is accessible via a **monorail** which departs from the third floor of the Westlake Center. The anchor point is the **Center House,** which holds a food court, stage, and **Info Desk.** *(For info ☎684-8582. Monorail every 15min. M-F 7:30am-11pm, Sa-Su 9am-11pm. $1.25, seniors 75¢, ages 5-12 50¢. Info Desk open daily 11am-6pm.)*

EXPERIENCE MUSIC PROJECT (EMP). Undoubtedly the biggest and best attraction at the Seattle Center is the new, futuristic, abstract, and technologically brilliant **Experience Music Project.** The museum is the brainchild of Seattle billionaire Paul Allen, who originally wanted to create a shrine to worship his music idol Jimi Hendrix. Splash together the technological sophistication and foresight of Microsoft, dozens of ethnomusicologists and multimedia specialists, a collection of musical artifacts topping 80,000, the world-renowned architect Frank Gehry, and enough money to make the national debt appear small (fine, it was only $350 million), and you have the rock 'n' roll museum of the future. The building alone—consisting of sheet metal molded into abstract curves and then acid-dyed gold, silver, purple, light-blue, and red—is enough to make the average person gasp for breath. Walk in and strap on a personal computer guide (MEG) that allows you to interact with the exhibits. Hear clips from Hendrix's famous "Star Spangled Banner" while looking at the remnants of the guitar he smashed on a London stage. Move into the **Sound Lab** and test your own skills on guitars, drums, and keyboards linked to computer teaching devices and cushioned in state-of-the art sound rooms. When you are ready, step over to **On Stage,** a first-class karaoke-gone-haywire, and blast your tunes in front of a virtual audience. *(325 Fifth St., at Seattle Center. From I-5, take Exit 167 and follow signs to Seattle Center. Bus #3, 4, or 15. ☎367-5483 or 877-367-5483. Open in summer daily 9am-11pm; in winter Su-Th 9am-6pm, F-Sa 9am-9pm. $20, seniors and ages 13-17 $16, children $15. Free live music Tu-Sa in the lounge; national acts perform F-Sa in the Sky Church.)*

SPACE NEEDLE. Until the EMP came to town, the Space Needle appeared to be something from another time—now it matches quite well with its futuristic neighbor. On a clear day, the Needle provides a great view and an invaluable landmark for the disoriented. The elevator ride itself is a show, and operators are hired for their unique talents. The needle houses an observation tower and a high-end 360° rotating restaurant. *(☎905-2100. $12, seniors $10, ages 5-12 $5.)*

THE INTERNATIONAL DISTRICT/CHINATOWN

SEATTLE ASIAN ART MUSEUM. What do you do when you have too much good art to exhibit all at once? Open a second museum; this is just what SAM did, creating a wonderful stand-on-its-own attraction. The ▨**Seattle Asian Art Museum** collection is particularly strong in Chinese art. *(In Volunteer Park just beyond the water tower.* ☎654-3100. Open Tu-Su 10am-5pm, Th 10am-9pm. $3, under 12 free; free with SAM ticket from the previous 7 days; SAAM ticket good for $3 discount at SAM.)*

ARBORETUM. The ▨**University of Washington Arboretum** nurtures over 4000 species of trees, shrubs, and flowers, and maintains superb trails. Tours depart the **Graham Visitor Center**, at the southern end of the arboretum. *(10 blocks east of Volunteer Park. Visitors Center on Lake Washington Blvd. On Bus #11 from downtown.* ☎543-8800. Open daily sunrise to sunset; Visitors Center 10am-4pm. Free tours Sa-Su 1pm.)*

JAPANESE TEA GARDEN. The tranquil 3½ acre park is a retreat of sculpted gardens, fruit trees, a reflecting pool, and a traditional tea house. *(At the south end of the UW Arboretum, entrance on Lake Washington Blvd.* ☎684-4725. Open Mar.-Nov. daily 10am-dusk. $2.50; students, seniors, disabled, and ages 6-18 $1.50; under 6 free.)*

▣ ENTERTAINMENT

Seattle has one of the world's most notorious underground music scenes and the third-largest theater community in the US. The city supports performances in all sorts of venues, from bars to bakeries. In summer the free **Out to Lunch** series (☎623-0340) brings everything from reggae to folk dancing into parks, squares, and office buildings. Check cheeky free weekly *The Stranger* for event listings.

MUSIC

The **Seattle Opera** performs favorites from August to May. In October 2003, the Opera House will reopen after renovations. Until then all Opera House performances will be in the **Mercer Arts Arena**. Buffs should reserve well in advance, although rush tickets are sometimes available. (☎389-7676. Students and seniors can get half-price tickets 1½hr. before the performance. Open M-F 9am-5pm. Tickets from $35.) From September to June, the **Seattle Symphony** performs in the new Benaroya Hall, 200 University St. at 3rd Ave. (☎212-4700, tickets ☎215-4747. Ticket office open M-F 10am-6pm, Sa 1-6pm. Tickets from $15-39; seniors half-price; students day of show $10.)

THEATER & CINEMA

The city hosts an exciting array of first-run plays and alternative works, particularly by many talented amateur groups. Rush tickets are often available at nearly half price on the day of the show from **Ticket/Ticket**. (☎324-2744. Cash only.) ▨**The Empty Space Theatre**, 3509 Fremont Ave. N, 1½ blocks north of the Fremont Bridge, presents comedies from October to early July. (☎547-7500. Tickets $20-30. Half-price tickets 30min. before curtain.) **Seattle Repertory Theater**, 155 Mercer St., at the wonderful Bagley Wright Theater in the Seattle Center, presents contemporary and classic winter productions. (☎443-2222. Box office open on show days Tu-Su noon-5pm, on non-show days Tu-F noon-5pm. $15-45, seniors $32, under 25 $10; cheaper on weekdays. Rush tickets 30min. before curtain. Box office open Sept.-June daily noon-8pm.)

Seattle is a cinematic paradise. Most of the theaters that screen non-Hollywood films are on Capitol Hill and in the University District. On summer Saturdays, outdoor cinema in Fremont begins at dusk at 670 N. 34th St., in the U-Park lot by the bridge, behind the Red Door Alehouse. (☎767-2593. Entrance 7pm; live music 8pm. $5.) **TCI Outdoor Cinema** shows everything from classics to cartoons at the Gasworks Park. (☎694-7000. Live music 7pm to dusk. Free.) Unless otherwise specified, the theaters below charge $5 for matinees and $8 for features. **The Egyptian,** 801 E. Pine St. (☎323-4978), at Harvard Ave. on Capitol Hill, is an Art Deco art house best known for hosting the **Seattle International Film Festival** in the last week of May and first week of June. **The Harvard Exit,** 807 E. Roy St. (☎323-8986), on Capitol Hill near the north end of the Broadway business district, has quality classic and foreign films. It is a converted women's club that has its own ghost and an enormous antique projector. **Grand Illusion Cinema,** 1403 50th St. NE, in the U District at University Way, is one of the last independent theaters in Seattle and often shows old classics and hard-to-find films. (☎523-3935. $7, seniors and children $5; matinees $4.50.)

SPORTS

Recently, Seattleites cheered when the home team, the **Mariners,** moved out of the Kingdome, where in 1995 sections of the roof fell into the stands. The "M's" are now playing baseball in the half-billion dollar, hangar-like **Safeco Field,** at First Ave. S and Royal Brougham Way S, under an enormous retractable roof. (☎622-4487. From $10.) Seattle's football team, the **Seahawks,** are stuck playing in UW's Husky Stadium until construction on their new stadium is finished. (☎628-0888. From $10.) On the other side of town and at the other end of the aesthetic spectrum, the sleek **Key Arena,** in the Seattle Center, hosts Seattle's NBA basketball team, the **Supersonics.** (☎628-0888. From $9.) The **University of Washington Huskies** football team has dominated the PAC-10 for years and doesn't plan to let up. Call the Athletic Ticket Office (☎543-2200) for schedules and prices.

◼ FESTIVALS

Pick up a copy of the Visitors Center's *Calendar of Events,* published every season, for event coupons and an exact listing of area happenings. The first Thursday evening of each month, the art community sponsors **First Thursday,** a free and well-attended gallery walk. Watch for street fairs in the University District mid- to late May, at Pike Place Market over Memorial Day weekend, and in Fremont in mid-June. The International District holds its annual two-day bash in mid-July, featuring arts and crafts booths, East Asian and Pacific food booths, and presentations by a range of groups from the Radical Women/Freedom Socialist Party to the Girl Scouts. For more info, call Chinatown Discovery (☎382-1197), or write P.O. Box 3406, Seattle 98114.

Puget Sound's yachting season begins in May. **Maritime Week,** during the third week of May, and the **Shilshole Boats Afloat Show** (☎634-0911), in August, give area boaters a chance to show off their crafts. Over the 4th of July weekend, the Center for Wooden Boats sponsors the free **Wooden Boat Show** (☎382-2628), on Lake Union. Blue blazers and deck shoes are *de rigueur.* Size up the entrants (over 100 wooden boats), then watch a demonstration of boat-building skills. The year-end blow-out is the **Quick and Daring Boatbuilding Contest,** when hopefuls try to build and sail wooden boats of their own design, using a limited kit of tools and materials. Plenty of music, food, and alcohol make the sailing smooth.

☑ NIGHTLIFE

DOWNTOWN

▨ **The Alibi Room,** 85 Pike St. (☎623-3180), across from the Market Cinema in the Post Alley in Pike Place. A remarkably friendly local indie filmmaker hangout. Bar with music open daily. Downstairs dance floor F-Sa. Brunch Sa-Su. No cover. Open daily 11am-4pm and 5pm-2am.

Sit and Spin, 2219 4th Ave. (☎441-9484), between Bell and Blanchard St. Board games keep patrons busy while they wait for their clothes to dry or for bands to stop playing in the back room. Cover F-Sa $6-10. Artists cut albums in the **Bad Animal** studio down the street. Open Su-Th 9am-midnight, F-Sa 9am-2am.

Crocodile Cafe, 2200 2nd Ave. (☎448-2114), at Blanchard St. in Belltown. Cooks from scratch by day, and features live music by night (Tu-Sa). Shows usually start 9:30pm; some require advance ticket purchase. 21+ after 9pm. Cover $6-22. Open Tu-Sa 8am-2am, Su 9am-11pm.

PIONEER SQUARE

Most bars participate in a joint cover (Su-Th $5, F-Sa $10) that will let you wander from bar to bar to sample the bands. The larger venues are listed below. Two smaller venues, **Larry's Blues Cafe,** 209 1st Ave. S (☎624-7665), and **New Orleans,** 114 1st Ave. S (☎622-2563), feature great blues and jazz nightly. Most clubs close at 2am weekends and midnight weekdays.

Bohemian Cafe, 111 Yesler Way (☎447-1514). Reggae pumps every night through 3 sections—a cafe, bar, and stage—all adorned with art from Jamaica. Live shows, often national acts on weekends. Happy hour 4-7pm. No cover Tu-Th, part of the joint cover M and F-Sa. Open M-F 4pm-2am, Sa 6pm-7am.

Central Tavern, 207 1st Ave. S (☎622-0209). One of the early venues for grunge has now become a favorite for bikers. Live rock W-M 9:30pm. Tu open mic. Part of the joint cover. Open daily 11:30am-2am; kitchen closes 8pm.

Last Supper Club, 124 S. Washington St. (☎748-9975), at Occidental. 2 dance floors, DJed with everything from 70s disco (F) to funky house, drum & bass, and trance (Sa). Su nights salsa at 8:30pm. Cover F-Sa $10; W, Th, and Su $5. Open W-Su 4pm-2am.

Swannie's Sports Bar, 222 S. Main St. (☎622-9353). Share drink specials with pro ballplayers who stop by post-game. Any Seattle sports junkie will swear this is the place to be. Drink specials change daily. Open daily 11:30am-2am.

CAPITOL HILL

East off Broadway, find your atmosphere and acclimatize in a cool lounge on Pine St. West off Broadway, Pike St. has the clubs that push the limits (gay, punk, industrial, fetish, dance) and break the sound barrier.

▨ **Linda's,** 707 Pine St. E (☎325-1220). A very chill post-gig scene for Seattle rockers. On Tu night a live DJ plays jazz and old rock. Expanded menu, liquor, and breakfast on weekend. W movie night. No cover. Open M-F 2pm-2am, Sa-Su 10am-2am.

Neighbors, 1509 Broadway Ave. (☎324-5358). Enter from the alley on Pike St. A gay dance club for 20 years, Neighbors prides itself on techno slickness. W-Th and Su Midnight drag shows. M, W, and F-Sa House. Tu and Th 80s. Su Latin. Cover Su-Th $1, F-Sa $5. Open Su-W 9pm-2am, Th 9pm-3am, F-Sa 9pm-4am.

DROP THE PACK After a few months backpacking, it's no surprise that your shoulders start bruising like unrefrigerated steaks. Fortunately, there is a cure: sea kayaks. Kayaking is the perfect way to explore the nooks of Washington's labyrinthine Puget Sound, and rental boats are readily available. A truly unique resource is the **Cascadia Marine Trail,** a network of seaside campsites and launching spots maintained specifically for paddlers and sailors. The trail stretches from the San Juans south to Olympia and has over 40 places to pitch a tent along the way. Routes in the south of the Sound tend to be shorter and more protected, perfect for beginner to intermediate boaters. For information on planning a trip contact the **Washington Water Trails Association.** (4649 Sunny Side Ave. N, #305. ☎ 545-9161; www.wwta.org.)

Garage, 1130 Broadway Ave. (☎322-2296), between Union and Madison St. An automotive warehouse turned upscale pool hall that gets suave at night. Happy hour $3 microbrew 3-7pm. Su Ladies Night. Open daily 3pm-2am; kitchen M-F 4pm-midnight, Sa-Su 4pm-1am.

🏔 OUTDOOR ACTIVITIES

BIKING

Over 1000 cyclists compete in the 190 mi. **Seattle to Portland Race** in mid-July. Call the bike hotline (☎522-2453) for info. On five **Bicycle Sundays** from May to September, Lake Washington Blvd. is open exclusively to cyclists from 10am to 6pm. Call the **Citywide Sports Office** (☎684-7092) for info. The **Burke-Gilman Trail** makes for a longer ride from the University District along Montlake Blvd., then along Lake Union St. and all the way west to Chittenden Locks and Discovery Park.

WHITEWATER RAFTING

Although the rapids are hours away by car, over 50 **whitewater rafting** outfitters are based in Seattle and willing to undercut one another with merciless abandon. **Washington State Outfitters and Guides Association** (☎877-275-4964) provides advice; although their office is closed in summer, they do return phone calls and send out info. The **Northwest Outdoor Center,** 2100 Westlake Ave., on Lake Union, gives instruction in whitewater and sea kayaking. (☎281-9694. Kayak rentals $10-15 per hr. M-F 3rd and 4th hours free. Instructional programs $50-70. Make reservations.)

HIKING

4167 ft. **Mt. Si** is the most climbed mountain in the state of Washington. Just an hour from downtown Seattle, hikers can in just a few hours reach a **lookout** (1 mi. one-way) that showcases Mt. Rainier, the Olympic Mountains, and Seattle. A 4hr. hike (4 mi. one-way) brings you to **Haystack Basin,** the false summit. Don't try climbing higher unless you have rock-climbing gear. To get to Mt. Si, take I-90 E to SE Mt. Si Rd., 2 mi. from Middle Fork, and cross the Snoqualmie River Bridge to the trailhead parking lot. **Tiger Mountain** is another great day-hike near Seattle. A 4hr. hike (5½ mi. round-trip) leads to the summit of West Tiger Mountain (2522 ft.). Take I-90 to Tiger Mountain State Forest. From the Tradition Plateau trailhead, walk to Bus Road-Trail and then to West Tiger Trail. If you parked outside the gated lot, stay for sunset. For additional information, check out *55 Hikes Around Snoqualmie Pass,* by Harvey Manning. The mothership of camping supply stores, **REI,** 222 Yale Ave., near Capitol Hill., rents everything you might need, from camping gear to technical mountaineering equipment. (☎223-1944. Open M-F 10am-9pm, Sa 10am-7pm, Su 11am-6pm.)

NEAR SEATTLE: VASHON ISLAND

Only a 25min. ferry ride from Seattle, Vashon Island has remained inexplicably invisible to most Seattleites. With its forested hills and expansive sea views, this artists' colony feels like the San Juan Islands without the tourists, and budget travelers will feel well cared for in the island's hostel. Most of the island is covered in Douglas fir, rolling cherry orchards, wildflowers, and strawberry fields, and all roads lead to rocky beaches. **Point Robinson Park** is a gorgeous spot for a picnic, and free tours (☎217-6123) of the 1885 **Coast Guard lighthouse** are available. **Vashon Island Kayak Co.**, at Burton Acres Park, Jensen Point Boat Launch, runs guided tours and rents sea kayaks. (☎463-9257. Open F-Su 10am-5pm. Singles $14 per hr., $50 per day; doubles $20/65. Tours $65.) More than 500 acres of woods in the middle of the island are interlaced with mildly difficult hiking trails. The **Vashon Park District** can tell you more. (☎463-9602. Open daily 9am-5pm.)

The **Vashon Island AYH Ranch Hostel (HI-AYH) ❶**, at 12119 S.W. Cove Rd., west of Vashon Hwy., is sometimes called the "Seattle B." Resembling an old Western town, the hostel offers bunks, open-air teepees, and covered wagons. (☎463-2592. Free pancake breakfast and one-speed bikes. Sleeping bag $2. Open May-Oct. $13, nonmembers $16; bicyclists $10.) The hostel runs **The Lavender Duck B&B ❸** down the road ($60).

Vashon Island stretches between Seattle and Tacoma on its east side and between Southworth and Gig Harbor on its west side. **Washington State Ferries** (☎464-6400 or 800-843-3779) runs ferries to Vashon Island from Seattle (see **Transportation,** p. 949). The local **Thriftway**, 9740 S.W. Bank Rd., provides maps, as does the Vashon-Maury **Chamber of Commerce** (☎463-6217), 17633 S.W. Vashon Hwy.

OLYMPIA   ☎360

Inside Olympia's seemingly interminable network of suburbs, there lies a festive downtown area known for its art, antiques, liberalism, and irresistible microbrews. Evergreen State College lies a few miles from the city center, and its highly pierced tree-hugging student body spills into town in a kind of chemistry experiment that only gets weirder when Olympia politicians join in. The product of this grouping resists definition, but it is worth experiencing for yourself.

🛈 PRACTICAL INFORMATION. Olympia is at the junction of I-5 and U.S. 101. **Amtrak,** 6600 Yelm Hwy. (☎923-4602; open daily 8:15am-noon, 1:45-3:30pm, and 5:30-8:30pm), runs to Portland (2½hr., 4 per day, $15-25) and Seattle (1¾hr., 4 per day, $11-20). **Greyhound,** 107 E. 7th Ave. (☎357-5541), at Capitol Way, goes to Seattle (1¾hr.; 6-7 per day; downtown $9.25, Sea-Tac $5) and Portland (2¾hr., 6-7 per day, $22-24). **Intercity Transit (IT)** provides service almost anywhere in Thurston County and has bicycle racks. (☎786-1881 or 800-287-6348. 75¢; day passes $1.25.) The free **Capitol Shuttle** runs from the Capitol Campus to downtown or to the east side or west side. (Every 15min. 6:45am-5:45pm.) **Washington State Capitol Visitors Center** is on Capitol Way at 14th Ave., next to the State Capitol; follow the signs on I-5. (☎586-3460. Open M-F 8am-5pm.) The **Olympic National Forest Headquarters,** 1835 Black Lake Blvd. SW, provides info on land inside and outside the park. (☎956-2400. Open M-F 8am-4:30pm.) **Post Office:** 900 Jefferson SE (☎357-2289. Open M-F 7:30am-6pm, Sa 9am-4pm.) **ZIP code:** 98501. **Area code:** 360.

🛏🍴 ACCOMMODATIONS & FOOD. Motels in Olympia cater to policy-makers ($60-80), but chains in nearby Tumwater are more affordable. ▓**Grays Harbor Hostel ❶**, 6 Ginny Ln., 25 mi. west of Olympia just off Rte. 8 in Elma, is the perfect place to start a trip down the coast. (☎482-3119. Hot tub, frolf course, and a shed for bike repairs. Dorms $14; private rooms $28. Bikers camp for $10.) **Millersylvania State Park ❶**, 12245 Tilly Rd. S, 10 mi. south of Olympia, has 180 sites. Take Exit 95 off I-5 S or Exit 95 off I-5 N, then take Rte. 121 N, and follow signs to 6 mi. of trails and Deep Lake. (☎753-1519 or 800-452-5687. Showers 25¢ per 6min. Wheelchair-accessible. Sites $14, with hookup $20.) Diners, veggie eateries, and Asian quick-stops line bohemian 4th Ave. east of Columbia. The **Olympia Farmer's Market**, 700 N. Capital Way, proffers produce and fantastic fare. (☎352-9096. Open Apr.-Oct. Th-Su 10am-3pm, Nov.-Dec. Sa-Su 10am-3pm.) **The Spar Cafe & Bar ❷**, 114 E. 4th Ave., is an ancient logger haunt that moonlights as a pipe and cigar shop. (☎357-6444. Restaurant open M-Th 6am-10pm, F-Sa 6am-11pm, Su 6am-9pm. Bar open Su-Th 11am-midnight, F-Sa 11am-2am.)

◪ SIGHTS. Olympia's crowning glory is **State Capitol Campus**, a complex of state government buildings, fabulous fountains, manicured gardens, and veterans' monuments. Tours depart from just inside the front steps. (☎586-3460. Tours daily on the hr. 10am-3pm. Building open M-F 8am-5:30pm, Sa-Su 10am-4pm.) **Wolf Haven International**, 3111 Offut Lake Rd., 10 mi. south of the capitol, provides a permanent home for captive-born gray wolves reclaimed from zoos or illegal owners. (☎264-4695 or 800-448-9653. Open May-Sept. M and W-Su 10am-5pm; Oct.-Apr. 10am-4pm; Nov.-Jan. and Mar. Sa-Su 10am-4pm. 45min. tours on the hr.; last tour leaves 1hr. before closing. $6, seniors $5, ages 5-12 $4.)

◪ NIGHTLIFE. Olympia's ferocious nightlife seems to have outgrown its daylife. *The Rocket* and the daily *Olympian* list live music. At **◪Eastside Club and Tavern**, 410 E. 4th St., old men play pool, college students slam micro pints, and local bands play often. (☎357-9985. Open M-F noon-2am, Sa-Su 3pm-2am.) The **4th Ave. Alehouse & Eatery**, 210 E. 4th St., serves "slabs" of pizza ($2.25), 26 micropints ($3), and live tunes from blues to reggae. (☎956-3215. Music Th-Sa 9pm. Restaraunt open M-F 11:30am-8pm, F-Sa noon-8pm.)

SAN JUAN ISLANDS   ☎360

With hundreds of tiny islands and endless parks and coastline, the San Juan Islands are an explorer's dream. The Islands are filled with great horned owls, puffins, sea lions, and pods of orcas (killer whales) patrolling the waters. Over 1½ million visitors come ashore each year during the peak of summer. To avoid the rush and enjoy good weather, visit in late spring or early fall.

◪ PRACTICAL INFORMATION

Washington State Ferries (☎206-464-6400 or 800-843-3779), in Anacortes, serves Lopez (40min.), Shaw (30min.), Orcas (50min.), and San Juan Island (2hr.); check the schedule at the Visitors Centers in Puget Sound. To save on fares, travel to the westernmost island on your itinerary, then return: eastbound traffic travels for free. In summer, arrive 1hr. prior to departure. ($7; vehicle $17-28; bike $3. Cash only.) To reach Anacortes, take I-5 N from Seattle to Mt. Vernon, then Rte. 20 west to town; follow signs. The **Bellingham Airporter** (☎800-235-5247) shuttles between Sea-Tac and Anacortes (8 per day; $31, round-trip $56). Short hops and good roads make the islands great for biking. **Area code:** 360.

SAN JUAN ISLAND

The biggest and most popular of the islands, San Juan is the easiest to explore, with ferry docks right in town, flat roads, and a shuttle bus running throughout the island. Seattle weekenders flood the island in summer. A drive around the 35 mi. perimeter of the island takes about 2hr., and the route is good for a day's cycle. The **West Side Rd.** traverses gorgeous scenery and provides the best chance for sighting orcas offshore. Mullis Rd. merges with Cattle Point Rd. and goes straight into **American Camp,** on the south side of the island. Volunteers in period costume re-enact daily life from the time of the Pig War, a mid-19th-century squabble between the US and Britain over control of the Islands. (☎378-2902. Visitors Center open 8:30am-5pm. Camp open June-Aug. daily dawn-11pm; Sept.-May Th-Su dawn-11pm. Guided walks Sa 11:30am. Reenactments in summer Sa 12:30-3:30pm.) **British Camp,** the second half of the **San Juan National Historical Park,** lies on West Valley Rd. in the sheltered **Garrison Bay.** (Buildings open late May-early Sept. daily 8am-5pm.) **Lime Kiln Point State Park,** along West Side Rd., is renowned as the best whale-watching spot in the area. The annual **San Juan Island Jazz Festival** (☎378-5509) swings in late July.

San Juan County Park ❶, 380 Westside Rd., 10 mi. west of Friday Harbor on Small-pox and Andrews Bays, offers the chance to catch views of whales and a great sunset. (☎378-1842. Water and flush toilets; no showers or RV hookups. Park open daily 7am-10pm. Office open daily 9am-7pm. Reservations recommended. Vehicle sites $22; walk-ins $6.) **Thai Kitchen ❸,** 42 1st St., next to the Whale Museum, is a popular dinner spot with a beautiful patio for flower-sniffing or star-gazing. (☎378-1917. Entrees $8-12. Dinner M 5-9pm; lunch Tu-Sa 11:30am-2:30pm.)

San Juan Transit (☎378-8887 or 800-887-8387) circles the island every 35-55min. and will stop on request. (Fares also good on Orcas Island. Point-to-point $4; day pass $10; 2-day pass $17.) If you plan to only see San Juan Island, it may be cheaper to leave your car in Anacortes and use the shuttles. **Island Bicycles,** 380 Argyle St., up Spring St., rents bikes. (☎378-4941. Open daily 9am-6pm. $6 per hr. and $30 per day.) The **Chamber of Commerce** (☎378-5240 or 888-468-3701) is a booth on East St. up from Cannery Landing. The **San Juan National Historic Park Information Center** is at 1st and Spring St. (☎378-2240. Open in summer M-F 8:30am-4:30pm; in winter 8:30am-4pm.)

ORCAS ISLAND

Retirees, artists, and farmers dwell on Orcas Island in understated homes surrounded by green shrubs and the red bark of madrona trees. The trail to **Obstruction Pass Beach** is the best way to clamber down to the rocky shores. **Moran State Park** is unquestionably Orcas's star outdoor attraction. Over 30 mi. of hiking trails range from a one-hour jaunt around **Mountain Lake** to a day-long trek up the south face of **Mt. Constitution** (2407 ft.), the highest peak on the islands. Part-way down, **Cascade Falls** is spectacular in the spring and early summer. The **Orcas Tortas** makes a slow drive on a green bus from Eastsound to the peak. (☎376-4156. $8.) **Shearwater Adventures** runs an intense sea kayak tour of north Puget Sound and is a great resource for experienced paddlers. (☎376-4699. 3hr. tour with 30min. of dry land training $45.) **Crescent Beach Kayak,** on the highway 1 mi. east of Eastsound, rents kayaks. (☎376-2464. $10 per hr., $25 per half-day. Open daily 9am-5pm.)

Doe Bay Resort ❶, on Star Rte. 86, off Horseshoe Hwy. on Pt. Lawrence Rd., 5 mi. out of Moran State Park, includes kitchen, health food store and cafe, a treehouse, guided kayak trips, a steam sauna (bathing suits optional; coed), and a mineral bath. (☎376-2291. Reception 8am-10pm. Sauna $4 per day, non-guests $7; bathing suits optional; coed. Reservations recommended. Rooms $55; campsites $25.) **Moran State Park ❶,** on Star Rte. 22 in Eastsound, follow Horseshoe Hwy., has 12 sites and restrooms year-round. (☎376-2326 or 800-452-5687. Boats $13 per hr., $35-45 per day. Reservations recommended May-early Sept. Car sites $16, hiker/biker sites $6.) In Eastsound Sq. on N. Beach Rd., **Cafe Jama ❷** serves up a North-

PACIFIC NORTHWEST

west breakfast (specialty coffees and homemade muffins) and a variety of tasty lunch options. (☎376-4949. Soups, salads, and sandwiches $6-8.)

The ferry lands on the southwest tip of Orcas, and the main town of **Eastsound** is 9 mi. northeast. **Olga** and **Doe Bay** are an additional 8 and 11 mi. respectively down the eastern side of the horseshoe. **San Juan Transit** (☎376-8887) runs ferries to most parts of the island. To Eastsound (every 1½hr. $4). **Wildlife Cycle,** at A St. and North Beach Rd. in Eastsound, rents 21-speeds. (☎376-4708. Open M-Sa 10am-5:30pm, Su 11am-2pm. $7.50 per hr., $30 per day.)

LOPEZ ISLAND

Smaller than either Orcas or San Juan, "Slow-pez" lacks some of the tourist facilities of the larger islands. The small **Shark Reef** and **Agate Beach County Parks,** on the southwest end of the island, have tranquil and well-maintained hiking trails, and Agate's beaches are calm and deserted. Roads on the island are ideal for biking. **Lopez Village** is 4½ mi. from the ferry dock off Fisherman Bay Rd. To rent a bike or kayak, head to **Lopez Bicycle Works,** south of the village. (☎468-2847. Open July-Aug. daily 9am-9pm; Apr.-June and Sept.-Oct. 10am-5pm. Bikes $5 per hr., $25 per day. Kayaks from $10-15 per hr.) **Spencer Spit State Park ❶,** on the northeast corner of the island 3½ mi. from the ferry terminal, has primitive sites on the beach and the hill. (☎468-2251. Toilets. Open Feb.-Oct. daily until 10pm. Reservation fee $6. Sites $15; hiker/biker $6.) Ferry transport means price inflation, so it may be wise to bring a lunch. Those without lunches should munch on fresh pastries at **Holly B's ❶,** 165 Cherry Tree Ln. (☎468-2133. Open M and W-Su 7am-5pm, Su 7am-4pm.)

OLYMPIC PENINSULA

Due west of Seattle and its busy Puget Sound neighbors, the Olympic Peninsula is a remote backpacking paradise. Olympic National Park dominates much of the peninsula, and it prevents the area's ferocious timber industry from threatening the glacier-capped mountains and temperate rainforests. To the west, the Pacific Ocean stretches to a distant horizon; to the north, the Strait of Juan de Fuca separates the Olympic Peninsula from Vancouver Island; and to the east, Hood Canal and the Kitsap Peninsula isolate this sparsely inhabited wilderness from the ever-spreading sprawl of Seattle.

PORT TOWNSEND   ☎360

Unlike the salmon industry, Port Townsend's Victorian splendor has survived the progression of time and weather. Countless cafes, galleries, and bookstores line somewhat drippy streets, cheering the urbanites who move here. The **Ann Starret Mansion,** 744 Clay St., has nationally renowned Victorian architecture, frescoed ceilings, and a three-tiered spiral staircase. (☎385-3205 or 800-321-0644. Tours daily noon-3pm. $2.)

Two hostels crouch in old military haunts. The **Olympic Hostel (HI-AYH) ❶,** in Fort Worden State Park, 1½ mi. from town, has bright dorms and private rooms. (☎385-0655. Check-in 5-10pm. Dorms $14, nonmembers $17.) To reach **Fort Flagler Hostel (HI-AYH) ❶,** in Fort Flagler State Park on gorgeous Marrowstone Island, 20 mi. from Port Townsend, go south on Rte. 19, which connects to Rte. 116 E and leads directly into the park. (☎385-1288. Check-in 5-10pm. Lockout 10am-5pm. Book ahead. Dorms $14, nonmembers $17; hikers and bikers $2 off.) You can camp on the beach at the 116-site **Fort Flagler State Park ❶.** (☎385-1259. Book ahead. Tents $16; RVs $22; hiker/biker $6.)

Port Townsend sits at the terminus of Rte. 20 on the northeastern corner of the Olympic Peninsula. It can be reached by U.S. 101 on the peninsula or from the Kitsap Peninsula across the Hood Canal Bridge. **Washington State Ferries** (☎206-464-6400 or 800-808-7977) runs from Seattle to Winslow on Bainbridge Island, where a **Kitsap County Transit** bus runs to Poulsbo. From Poulsbo, **Jefferson County Transit** runs to Port Townsend. A free shuttle goes into downtown from the Park 'N' Ride lot. (☎385-4777. Most buses M-Sa, some Su. 50¢.) **Visitor info: Chamber of Commerce,** 2437 E. Sims Way, 10 blocks southwest of town on Rte. 20. (☎385-2722 or 888-365-6987. Open M-F 9am-5pm, Sa 10am-4pm, Su 11am-4pm.) **P.T. Cyclery,** 100 Tyler St., rents mountain bikes. (☎385-6470. Open M-Sa 9am-6pm. $7 per hr., $25 per day.) **Kayak P.T.,** 435 Water St., rents kayaks. (☎385-6240. Singles $25 per 4hr.; doubles $40 per 4hr. Over 84 free.) **Post Office:** 1322 Washington St. (☎385-1600. Open M-F 9am-5pm.) **ZIP code:** 98368. **Area code:** 360.

OLYMPIC NATIONAL PARK ☎360

With glacier-encrusted peaks, river valley rainforests, and jagged shores along the Pacific coast, Olympic National Park has something for everyone. Roads lead to many corners of Olympic National Park, but they only hint at the depths of its wilderness. A dive into the backcountry leaves summer tourists behind and reveals the richness and diversity of the park's many faces.

✴️📋 ORIENTATION & PRACTICAL INFORMATION

Only a few hours from Seattle, Portland, and Victoria, the wilderness of Olympic National Park is most easily and safely reached by car. U.S. 101 encircles the park in the shape of an upside-down U with Port Angeles at the top. The park's vista-filled **eastern rim** runs up to Port Angeles, from which the much-visited **northern rim** extends westward. The tiny town of **Neah Bay** and stunning **Cape Flattery** perch at the northwest tip of the peninsula. Farther south on U.S. 101, the slightly less tiny town of **Forks** is a gateway to the park's rainforested **western rim.** Separate from the rest of the park, much of the Pacific coastline comprises a gorgeous **coastal zone.** The **entrance fee,** good for seven days' access to the park, is charged during the day at ranger stations and developed entrances such as Hoh, Heart o' the Hills, Sol Duc, Staircase, and Elwha. ($10 per car; $5 per hiker/biker; backcountry users $2 extra per night. Parking $5.)

Olympic National Park Visitors Center, 3002 Mt. Angeles Rd., is off Race St. in Port Angeles. (☎565-3130. Open in summer daily 9am-5:30pm; in winter 9am-4pm.) Staff at the **Olympic National Park Wilderness Information Center** (☎565-3100), just behind the Visitors Center, helps design trips within the park.

🏠 ACCOMMODATIONS

The closest budget accommodations are at the **Rainforest Hostel ❶,** 169312 U.S. 101, 20 mi. south of Forks. Follow the signs from U.S. 101 or come by bus from North Shore Brannon's Grocery in Quinault (9am, 1, and 4:35pm; 50¢). Two family rooms, a men's dorm (5 double bunks in summer), and rooms for couples require deposits. A morning chore is required. (☎374-2270. Curfew 11pm. Wakeup 8am. Dorms $12.) Olympic National Park maintains six free campgrounds in the Hood Canal Ranger District and others within its boundaries (sites $8-12); three can be reserved (☎800-280-2267): **Seal Rock ❶, Falls View ❶,** and **Klahowga ❶.** A backcountry permit is always required. Quota limits apply to popular spots. Most drive-up camping is first come, first served. Olympic National Forest requires a trailhead pass to park at sites located off a main trail. The Washington Department of Natural Resources allows free **backcountry camping ❶** 300 ft. off any state road on DNR land, mostly near the western shore along the Hoh and Clearwater Rivers. From

July to September, most spaces are taken by 2pm. Popular sites, such as those at Hoh River, fill by noon.

⚠ OUTDOOR ACTIVITIES

EASTERN RIM

What ONP's western regions have in ocean and rainforest, the eastern rim matches with canals and grandiose views. Canyon walls rise treacherously, their jagged edges leading to mountaintops that offer glimpses of the entire peninsula and Puget Sound. Steep trails lead up **Mt. Ellinor,** 5 mi. past Staircase on Rte. 119. Once on the mountain, hikers can choose the 3 mi. path or an equally steep but shorter journey to the summit; look for signs to the Upper Trailhead along Forest Road #2419-04. Adventure-seekers who hit the mountain before late July should bring snow clothes to "mach" (as in Mach 1) down a ¼ mi. snow chute.

A 3¼ mi. hike ascends to **Lena Lake,** 14 mi. north of Hoodsport off U.S. 101; follow Forest Service Rd. 25 off U.S. 101 for 8 mi. to the trailhead. The Park Service charges a $3 trailhead pass. The **West Forks Dosewallip Trail,** a 10½ mi. trek to **Mt. Anderson Glacier,** is the shortest route to any glacier in the park. The road to **Mt. Walker Viewpoint,** 5 mi. south of Quilcene on U.S. 101, is steep, has sheer dropoffs, and should not be attempted in foul weather or a temperamental car. Yet another view of Hood Canal, Puget Sound, Mt. Rainier, and Seattle awaits intrepid travelers on top. Inquire about base camps and trails at **Hood Canal Ranger Station,** southeast of reserve lands on U.S. 101 in Hoodsport. (☎ 877-5254. Open in summer daily 8am-4:30pm; in winter M-F 8am-4:30pm.)

NORTHERN RIM

The most developed section of Olympic National Park lies along its northern rim, near Port Angeles, where glaciers, rainforests, and sunsets over the Pacific are only a drive away. Farthest east off U.S. 101 lies **Deer Park,** where trails tend to be uncrowded. Past Deer Park, the **Royal Basin Trail** meanders 6.3 mi. to the **Royal Basin Waterfall.** The road up **Hurricane Ridge** is an easy but curvy drive. Before July, walking on the ridge usually involves a bit of snow-stepping. Clear days provide splendid views of Mt. Olympus and Vancouver Island set against a foreground of snow and indigo lupine. From here, the uphill **High Ridge Trail** is a short walk from Sunset Point. On weekends from late December to late March, the Park Service organizes free guided snowshoe walks atop the ridge.

Farther west on U.S. 101, 13 mi. of paved road penetrates to the popular **Sol Duc Hot Springs Resort,** where retirees de-wrinkle in the springs and eat in the lodge. (☎ 327-3583. Open late May-Sept. daily 9am-9pm; spring and fall Th noon-6pm, F-Su 9am-6pm. $10, ages 4-12 $7.50; last 2 hours twilight $6.50. Suit, locker, or towel rental $3 each.) The **Sol Duc trailhead** is a starting point for those heading up; crowds thin dramatically above **Sol Duc Falls.** The **Eagle Ranger Station** has info and permits. (☎ 327-3534. Open in summer daily 8am-4:30pm.)

NEAH BAY & CAPE FLATTERY

At the westernmost point on the Juan de Fuca Strait and north of the park's western rim lies **Neah Bay.** The only town in the **Makah Reservation,** Neah Bay is renowned as the "Pompeii of the Pacific" and is a remarkably preserved 500-year-old village that was buried in a landslide at Cape Alava. You can reach Neah Bay and Cape Flattery by a 1hr. detour from U.S. 101. From Port Angeles, Rte. 112 leads west to Neah Bay; Rte. 113 runs north from Sappho to Rte. 112. The Makah Nation, whose recorded history goes back 2000 years, still lives, fishes, and produces artwork on this land. Just inside the reservation, the **Makah Cultural and**

Research Center, in Neah Bay on Rte. 112, beautifully presents artifacts from the archaeological site. (☎645-2711. Open June-Aug. daily 10am-5pm; Sept.-May M-F 10am-5pm. Free tours W-Su 11am. $4, students and seniors $3.) During **Makah Days,** on the last weekend of August, Native Americans from the region come for canoe races, dances, and bone games. Visitors are welcome; call the center for details. **Clallam Transit System** runs bus #14 from Oak St. in Port Angeles to Sappho, then #16 to Neah Bay. (☎452-4511. $1, seniors 50¢, ages 6-19 85¢.)

Cape Flattery, the most northwestern point in the contiguous US, is drop-dead gorgeous. Get directions at the Makah Center or just take the road through town until it turns to dirt, past the "Marine Viewing Area" sign 4 mi. to a parking area where a trailhead leads toward the cape. To the south, the reservation's **beaches** are solitary and peaceful; respectful visitors are welcome.

WESTERN RIM

In the temperate rainforests of ONP's western rim, ferns, mosses, and gigantic old growth trees blanket the earth in a sea of green. The drive along the **Hoh River Valley,** actively logged land, is alternately overgrown and barren. **Hoh Rainforest Visitors Center** sits a good 45min. drive from U.S. 101 on the park's western rim. (☎374-6925. Open mid-June to early Sept. daily 9am-6:30pm; early Sept. to mid-June 9am-4:30pm.) From the Visitors Center, take the quick ¾ mi. **Hall of Mosses Trail** for a whirlwind tour of the rainforest. With a smattering of educational panels explaining bizarre natural quirks, the slightly longer **Spruce Nature Trail** leads 1¼ mi. through lush forest and along the banks of the Hoh River. The **Hoh Rainforest Trail** is the most heavily traveled path in the area, beginning at the Visitors Center and paralleling the Hoh River for 18 mi. to **Blue Glacier** on the shoulder of Mt. Olympus.

Several other trailheads from U.S. 101 offer less crowded opportunities for exploration of the rainforest amid surrounding ridges and mountains. The **Queets River Trail** hugs its namesake east for 14 mi. from the free **Queets Campground ❶;** the road is unpaved and unsuitable for RVs or large trailers. High river waters early in the summer can thwart a trek. Hiking is best in August, but there's still a risk that water will cut off trail access. A shorter 3 mi. loop passes a broad range of rainforest, lowland river ecosystems, and the park's largest Douglas fir.

The 4 mi. **Quinault Lake Loop** or the ½ mi. **Maple Glade Trail** leave from the **Quinault Ranger Station,** 353 S. Shore Rd. (☎288-2525. Open in summer M-F 8am-4:30pm, Sa-Su 9am-4pm; in winter M-F 9am-4:30pm.) Snow-seekers flock to **Three Lakes Point,** an exquisite summit covered with powder until July. **Quinault Lake** lures anglers, rowers, and canoers. The **Lake Quinault Lodge,** next to the ranger station, rents canoes and rowboats. (☎288-2900 or 800-562-6672. Rentals from $10 per hr.)

COASTAL ZONE

Pristine coastline traces the park's slim far western region for 57 mi., separated from the rest of ONP by U.S. 101 and non-park timber land. Eerie fields of driftwood, sculptured arches, and dripping caves frame flamboyant sunsets, while the waves are punctuated by rugged sea stacks. Between the Quinault and Hoh Reservations, U.S. 101 hugs the coast for 15 mi., with parking lots just a short walk from the sand. North of where the highway meets the coast, **Beach #4** has abundant tidepools, plastered with sea stars. **Beach #6,** 3 mi. north at Mi. 160, is a favorite whale-watching spot. Near Mi. 165, sea otters and eagles hang out amid tide pools and sea stacks at **Ruby Beach.** Beach camping is only permitted north of the Hoh Reservation between **Oil City** and **Third Beach** and north of the Quileute Reservation between **Hole-in-the-Wall** and **Shi-Shi Beach.** Day hikers and backpackers adore the 9 mi. loop that begins at **Ozette Lake.** The trail is a triangle with two 3 mi. legs leading along boardwalks through the rainforest. One heads toward sea stacks at **Cape Alava,** and the other goes to a sublime beach at **Sand Point.** A 3 mi. hike down the

THE LOCAL STORY

OUT OF THE FLYING PLANE, INTO THE FIRE

Smoke jumpers—firefighters who parachute from planes to combat blazes—have one of the, um, coolest jobs on earth. Scott Wicklunc is a smoke jumper out of Winthrop, WA.

Q: A lot of people would say this is an insane job. How would you respond?
A: People would say this is an insane job because they don't realize all the safety precautions that go into it. It seems crazy because you're jumping out of a perfectly good airplane...into a forest fire! But the reality is that you've got a perfectly good parachute and you know fire behavior. So you land in a place where you're safe from any sort of fire activity and take the proper measures to control the fire.

Q: What made you decide that you wanted to do this?
A: Growing up my mom said, "Don't get that dirty; don't play with fire." I found a job that paid me to do both.

Q: Do you have a particularly scary, crazy, or weird story from your job?
A: The weirdest thing that ever happened to me? One time I landed in an 80 ft. tree, but the parachute didn't catch on the branches. I slid down the side of the tree, picking up speed until I basically knew I was going to break my leg in half a second. All of a sudden, the parachute catches on a branch and I'm hanging there a foot from the ground. Hanging there perfectly fine. Which was a great feeling.

(continued on next page)

coast links the two legs, passing ancient petroglyphs. More info is available at the **Ozette Ranger Station.** (☎963-2725. Open intermittently.) Overnighters must make permit reservations (☎565-3100) in advance; spaces fill quickly in summer.

CASCADE RANGE

Intercepting the moist Pacific air, the Cascades divide Washington into the lush, wet green of the west and the low, dry plains of the east. The Cascades are most accessible in July, August, and September. Many high mountain passes are snowed in during the rest of the year. Mt. Baker, Vernon, Glacier, Rainier, Adams, and St. Helens are accessible by four major roads. The North Cascades Hwy. (Rte. 20) is the most breathtaking and provides access to North Cascades National Park. Scenic U.S. 2 leaves Everett for Stevens Pass and descends along the Wenatchee River. Rte. 20 and U.S. 2 can be traveled in sequence as the Cascade Loop. U.S. 12 approaches Mt. Rainier through White Pass and passes north of Mt. St. Helens. I-90 sends four lanes from Seattle past the ski resorts of Snoqualmie Pass.

MOUNT ST. HELENS ☎360

In a single cataclysmic blast on May 18, 1980, the summit of Mt. St. Helens erupted, transforming what had been a perfect cone into a crater. The force of the ash-filled blast robbed the mountain of 1300 feet and razed entire forests, strewing trees like charred matchsticks. Ash from the crater rocketed 17 mi. upward, blackening the sky for days. The explosion was 27,000 times the force of the atomic bomb dropped on Hiroshima. Today, Mt. St. Helens is made up of the middle third of the **Gifford Pinchot National Forest** and the **Mount St. Helens National Volcanic Monument.** The monument is part national park, part laboratory, and encompasses most of the area affected by the explosion.

▣ ORIENTATION. Vigorous winter rains often spoil access roads; check at a ranger station for road closures before heading out. From the west, take Exit 49 off **I-5** and use the **Spirit Lake Memorial Hwy. (Rte. 504).** For most, this is the quickest and easiest daytrip to the mountain, and the main Visitors Centers line the way to the volcano. **Rte. 503** skirts the south side of the volcano until it connects with **Forest Service Rd.**

90. Though views from this side don't highlight recent destruction, green glens and remnants of age-old explosions make this the best side for hiking and camping. From the north, the towns of **Mossyrock, Morton,** and **Randle** line **U.S. 12** and offer the closest major services to the monument.

⚐ PRACTICAL INFORMATION. The monument charges an entrance fee at almost every Visitors Center, viewpoint, and cave. (One day all access $6, ages 4-15 $2. Individual monument fees $3/1.) With displays and interactive exhibits, **Mt. St. Helens Visitors Center,** across from Seaquest State Park on Rte. 504, is most visitors' first stop. (☎274-2100. Open daily 9am-5pm.) **Coldwater Ridge Visitors Center,** 38 mi. farther on Rte. 504, has an emphasis on the area's recolonization by living things through exhibits, a short film, and a ¼ mi. trail. (☎274-2131. Open daily 10am-6pm.) Overlooking the crater, **Johnston Ridge Observatory,** at the end of Rte. 504, focuses on geological exhibits and offers the best roadside view of the steaming dome and crater. (☎274-2140. Open May-Sept. daily 10am-6pm.)

Woods Creek Information Station, 6 mi. south of Randle on Rd. 25 from U.S. 12, is a drive-through info center. (Open June-Aug. daily 9am-4pm.) **Pine Creek Information Station,** 17 mi. east of Cougar on Rd. 90, shows an interpretive film of the eruption. (Open June-Sept. daily 9:30am-5:30pm.) **Apes Headquarters,** at Ape Cave on Rd. 8303 on the south side of the volcano, answers all of your lava tube questions. (Open June-Sept. daily 10am-5:30pm.) From mid-May through October, the Forest Service allows 100 people per day to hike to the crater rim (applications accepted from Feb. 1; $15). Procrastinators should head for **Jack's Restaurant and Country Store,** 13411 Louis River Rd., 5 mi. west of Cougar (I-5 Exit 21) on Rte. 503, where a lottery is held at 6pm each day to distribute the next day's 50 unreserved permits. (☎231-4276. Open daily 5:30am-9pm.)

⛺ CAMPING. Although the monument itself contains no campgrounds, a number are scattered throughout the surrounding national forest. Free dispersed camping is allowed within the monument, but finding a site takes luck. **Iron Creek Campground ❶,** just south of the Woods Creek Information Station on Rd. 25, near its junction with Rd. 76, is the closest campsite to Mt. St. Helens, with good hiking and striking views of the crater and blast zone. (☎877-444-6777. Sites with water $13-15.) Spacious **Swift**

(continued from previous page)

Q: Can you describe the feeling of crashing into a tree from the sky at 120 miles per hour?

A: You jump out of the airplane, you see the meadow below that you're supposed to be going for, and you're aiming for that; then the wind picks up, and you know you're not going to make it. At that point you start looking for some shorter trees to land, so you're not hung up too high off the ground. Then you try and cap that tree with your canopy so you're hung up well. They train you to do that, but there's still a bit of chaos. At that point you don't know exactly what's going to happen. A lot of times it's a soft landing, because you go in there and the canopy catches the tree perfectly. Other times, your feet get kicked out from underneath you, you're upside-down and falling, you're not sure that your canopy hung up, your heart's racing a million miles per hour, and then *jerk*, you're hanging.

Q: What's the injury rate like?
A: I have never been injured jumping. We might get two or three sprained ankles, maybe a blown ACL, maybe a broken femur, maybe a broken wrist every year.

Q: Would you say working here is a team effort?
A: It is every day. The first thing you do after you land is check with your partner and make sure he's okay. We always jump two at a time.

Q: Would you recommend this job to a lot of people?
A: I'd recommend it to anyone who likes having adventures but doesn't want to make a whole lot of money.

Weaving its way through the craggy peaks and lush valleys of Washington's North Cascades Range, Rte. 20 is nothing short of a blissful driving experience—the road seems to have been designed to afford drivers unadulterated pleasure. Spectacular vistas await visitors at every turn, and a string of small towns scattered along the road provides services. Rte. 20 runs east-

TIME: 2hr.

DISTANCE: 70 mi.

SEASON: Apr.-Nov.

west through northern Washington, traversing the astounding scenery of Mt. Baker Snoqualmie National Forest, North Cascades National Park, and Okanogan National Forest.

WEST OF NORTH CASCADES NATIONAL PARK

The westernmost town of note on Rte. 20 is **Sedro Woolley,** a logging town nestled in the rich farmland of the lower Skagit Valley. Sedro Woolley is home to **North Cascades National Park** and **Mt. Baker-Snoqualmie National Forest Headquarters,** at 810 State Rte. 20, near the intersection with Rte. 9. The helpful rangers and information on activities in the park can help you move out of Sedro, which should be done as quickly as possible, considering the spectacular landscape farther west. (☎856-5700. Open in summer daily 8am-4:30pm; in winter M-F 8am-4:30pm.)

Marblemount Wilderness Information Center, 1 mi. north of West Marblemount on a well-marked road, is the main attraction of **Marblemount,** 40 mi. west of Sedro Valley. The Information Center is the best resource for backcountry trip-planning in the North Cascades. It is best to explore the park on a multi-day hiking trip. The Center is also the only place to pick up backcountry **permits;** they also have updates on trails and weather. Permits must be picked up in person no earlier than the day before a trip date. (☎873-4500, ext. 39. Open July-Aug. Su-Th 7am-6pm, F-Sa 7am-8pm; off-season call ahead.) Once you leave Marblemount, there are **no major service stations** for more than 69 mi. west—you are entering the wild land of the National Park.

NORTH CASCADES NATIONAL PARK

East from Marblemount and across the Skagit River, Rte. 20 enters the wildest, most rugged park in Washington. The North Cascades National Park is unlike any other—as amazing as the views seem from the car, you can't experience this park's flavor from a vehicle. Hop out and explore; the area is rife with hiking trails.

The dramatic pinnacles rising abruptly from the park's deep glacial valleys make for the most complex and challenging moutaineering in the continental US—the region is commonly referred to as "the Alps of North America." Those determined to penetrate the park should allot a stout pair of boots and several days toward that goal. As with every national park in Washington, North Cascades is surrounded by ample national forest. Know which forest you are headed into, as different agencies, permits, and rules apply. Another source for hiking info is the **North Cascades Visitors Center and Ranger Station.** (☎386-4495. Open in summer daily 8:30am-6pm; in winter Sa-Su 9am-4:30pm.) The National Park is divided into four sections. The **North Unit** reaches up to the Canadian border and is the most remote area of the park. The few trails that do cross it mainly begin near **Mt. Baker** or **Hozemon,** a small camp accessible from British Columbia. The **Ross Lake National Recreation Area** runs along Rte. 20 and north along Ross Lake. This is the most highly used area of the park, and the one to which most confine their stay. **South Unit** is pocked by glaciers and is accessible from trails leaving Rte. 20 along its north and east sides. This portion is an inviting wilderness to explore. Finally, at the park's southernmost tip, the **Lake Chelan National Recreation Area** protects the beautiful wilderness around Stehekin and the northern tip of Lake Chelan.

The park's **Goodell Creek Campground ❶,** at Mi. 119 just west of Newhalem, is a gorgeous confined area with 21 leafy sites suitable for tents and small trailers and a launch site for white-water rafting on the Skagit River. Water is shut off after Oct., when sites are free. (Pit toilets. Sites $10.) **Newhalem Creek Campground ❶,** at Mi. 120, shares a turn-off with the Visitors Center. It is a larger facility with 111 sites ($12) geared toward RV folk.

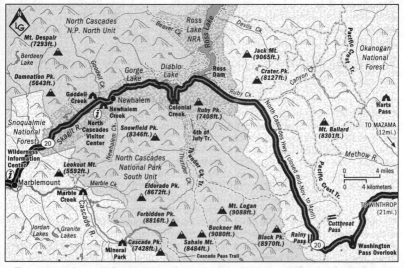

The amazing **Cascade Pass Trail** (moderate to difficult) begins 22 mi. from the bridge, and continues to Stehekin Valley Rd. The 3hr. hike gains 1700 ft. of elevation in 3½ mi. **Thunder Creek Trail** (easy) is among the most popular hikes in the area. The 1½ mi. meander through old-growth cedar and fir begins at Colonial Creek Campground, at Mi. 130 of Rte. 20. A more challenging variation is the 3¼ mi. **Fourth of July Pass Trail** (moderate to difficult). It begins 2 mi. into the Thunder Creek trail and climbs 3500 ft. toward stupendous views of glacier-draped Colonial and Snowfield peaks.

EAST OF NORTH CASCADES NATIONAL PARK

The stretch of road from **Ross Lake,** near the Eastern border of North Cascades National Park, to **Winthrop,** in the Okanogan National Forest, is the most breathtaking section of Rte. 20. The frozen creases of a mountain face stand before you—snow and granite rise on one side of the road, while sheer cliffs plummet on the other. Leaving the basin of Ross Lake, the road begins to climb, revealing the craggy peaks of the North Cascades.

The **Pacific Crest Trail** crosses Rte. 20 at **Rainy Pass** (Mi. 157) on one of the most scenic and difficult legs of its 2500 mi. course from Mexico to Canada. Near Rainy Pass, short scenic trails can be hiked in sneakers, provided the snow has melted, usually around mid-July. Just off Rte. 20, an overlook at **Washington Pass** (Mi. 162) rewards visitors with one of the state's most dramatic panoramas, an astonishing view of the red rocks exposed by **Early Winters Creek** in **Copper Basin.** The area has many well-marked trailheads off Rte. 20 that lead into the desolate wilderness. The popular 2½ mi. walk to **Blue Lake** begins half a mile east of Washington Pass—it's usually snow-free by July and provides a gentle ascent through meadows. An easier 2 mi. hike to Cutthroat Lake departs from an access road 4½ mi. east of Washington Pass. From the lake, the trail continues 4 mi. farther and almost 2000 ft. higher to **Cutthroat Pass** (6820 ft.), treating determined hikers to a view of towering, rugged peaks.

About 5 mi. east of Winthrop, the ◪ **North Cascades Smoke Jumper Base** is staffed by courageously insane smoke jumpers who give thorough and personal tours of the base, explaining the procedures and equipment they use to help them parachute into forest fires and put them out. To get there, drive east through Winthrop. At the bridge, instead of turning right to follow Hwy. 20, go straight and follow the curves of the main road; after about 5 mi., the base will be on your right. (☎997-2031. Open in summer and early fall. Daily tours 10am-5pm.)

Campground ❶ is on Rd. 90, just west of the Pine Creek Info Station. (☎503-813-6666. Sites $12.) Along Yale Lake are **Cougar Campground ❶** and **Beaver Bay ❶**, 2 and 4 mi. east of Cougar respectively. Cougar Lake has 60 sites ($15) that are more spread out and private than Beaver Bay's 78 sites ($15).

⚑ OUTDOOR ACTIVITIES. Along each approach, short interpretive trails loop into the landscape. The one-hour drive from the Mt. St. Helens Visitors Center to Johnston Ridge offers spectacular views of the crater and its resurgence of life. Another 10 mi. east, the hike along **Johnston Ridge** approaches incredibly close to the crater where geologist David Johnston died studying the eruption. On the way west along Rd. 99, **Bear Meadow** provides the first interpretive stop, an excellent view of Mt. St. Helens, and the last restrooms before Rd. 99 ends at **Windy Ridge.** The monument begins just west of Bear Meadow, where Rd. 26 and 99 meet. Rangers lead ½ mi. walks around emerald **Meta Lake;** meet at Miner's Car at the junction of Rd. 26 and 99. (Late June-Sept. daily 12:45 and 3pm.) Farther west on Rd. 99, **Independence Pass Trail #227** is a difficult 3½ mi. hike with overlooks of Spirit Lake and superb views of the crater and dome. For a serious hike, continue along this trail to its intersection with the spectacular **Norway Pass Trail,** which runs 8 mi. through the blast zone to the newly reopened **Mt. Margaret peak.** Farther west, the 2 mi. **Harmony Trail #224** provides access to Spirit Lake. From spectacular **Windy Ridge,** at the end of Rd. 99, a steep ash hill grants a magnificent view of the crater from 3½ mi. away. The **Truman Trail** leaves from Windy Ridge and meanders 7 mi. through the **Pumice Plain,** where hot flows sterilized the land.

Spelunkers should head to **Ape Cave,** 5 mi. east of Cougar just off Rd. 83. The cave is a broken 2½ mi. lava tube formed by an ancient eruption. When exploring the cave, wear a jacket and sturdy shoes, and take at least two flashlights or lanterns. Rangers lead ten free 30min. guided cave explorations per day.

MOUNT RAINIER NATIONAL PARK ☎360

At 14,411 ft., Mt. Rainier presides regally over the Cascade Range. The Klickitat native people called it Tahoma, "Mountain of God," but Rainier is simply "the Mountain" to most Washington residents. Perpetually snowcapped, this dormant volcano draws thousands of visitors from around the globe. Clouds mask the mountain 200 days each year, frustrating visitors who come solely to see its distinctive summit. Over 305 mi. of trails weave peacefully through old-growth forests, alpine meadows, rivers, and bubbling hot springs.

⬛ ORIENTATION. To reach Mt. Rainier from the west, take **I-5** to Tacoma, then go east on **Rte. 512,** south on **Rte. 7,** and east on **Rte. 706.** Rte. 706 meanders through the town of Ashford and into the park by the **Nisqually** entrance, leading to the Visitors Centers of **Paradise** and **Longmire.** Snow usually closes all other park roads from November to May. **Stevens Canyon Rd.** connects the southeast corner of the national park with Paradise, Longmire, and the Nisqually entrance, unfolding superb vistas of Rainier and the Tatoosh Range along the way.

🚩 PRACTICAL INFORMATION. Gray Line Bus Service, 4500 S. Marginal Way, runs buses from the Convention Center, at 8th and Pike in Seattle, to Mt. Rainier (depart 8am, return 6pm), allowing about 3½hr. at the mountain. (☎206-624-5208 or 800-426-7532. Runs May to mid-Sept. daily. One-day round-trip $54, under 12 $27.) **Rainier Shuttle** (☎569-2331) runs daily between Sea-Tac; Ashford (2hr., 2 per day, $40); and Paradise (3hr., 1 per day, $45).

The best place to plan a backcountry trip is at the **Longmire Wilderness Center** (☎569-4453; open Su-Th 7:30am-6:30pm, F-Sa 7am-7pm), east of the Nisqually entrance; or the **White River Ranger Station** (☎663-2273; open Su-Th 8am-4:30pm, F-

Sa 7am-7pm), off Rte. 410 on the park's east side. Both distribute **backcountry permits.** Permits are good for seven days; an **entrance fee** is required. ($10 per car, $5 per hiker. Gates open 24hr.) **Rainier Mountaineering, Inc. (RMI),** in Paradise (winter office, 535 Dock St. #209, in Tacoma; ☎253-627-6242), rents climbing gear, and expert guides lead summit climbs. (☎569-2227. Open May-Oct. daily 9am-5pm.) **Post Office:** National Park Inn, Longmire. (Open M-F 8:30am-noon and 1-5pm.) Paradise Inn, Paradise. (Open M-F 9am-noon and 12:30-5pm, Sa 8:30am-noon.) **ZIP code:** 98397 (Longmire), 98398 (Paradise). **Area code:** 360.

⌂◪ ACCOMMODATIONS & FOOD. Hotel Packwood ❷, 102 Main St., in Packwood, is a charming reminder of the Old West with a sprawled-out grizzly gracing the parlor. (☎494-5431. Shared or private bath; singles and double $32-54.) **Whittaker's Bunkhouse ❶,** 6 mi. west of the Nisqually entrance, offers spiffy rooms with firm mattresses and sparkling clean showers, as well as a homey espresso bar, but no kitchen. Bring your own sleeping bag. (☎569-2439. Reservations strongly recommended. Bunks $25; private rooms $65-90.)

Camping in the park is first come, first served from mid-June to late September. (Off-season reservations ☎800-365-2267. Sites $10-14.) National park campgrounds all have facilities for the handicapped, but no hookups or showers. Coin-operated showers are available at Jackson Memorial Visitors Center, in Paradise. **Sunshine Point** (18 sites), near the Nisqually entrance, and **Cougar Rock** (200 sites), 2¼ mi. north of Longmire, are in the southwest. The serene high canopy of **Ohanapecosh** (205 sites) is 11 mi. north of Packwood on Rte. 123, in the southeast. **White River** (112 sites) is 5 mi. west of White River on the way to Sunrise, in the northeast. **Backcountry camping** requires a **permit,** free from ranger stations and Visitors Centers. (☎569-4453. Reserve permits 2 months in advance, in person 24hr. $20 per group.) Inquire about trail closures before setting off. Hikers with a valid permit can camp at well-established trailside, alpine, and snowfield sites (most with toilets and water source). Fires are prohibited except in front-country campgrounds.

Blanton's Market, 13040 U.S. 12 in Packwood, is the closest decent supermarket and has an ATM. (☎494-6101. Open in summer daily 6am-9pm; in winter 7am-8pm.) **Highlander ❷,** in Ashford, serves standard pub fare in a single dimly-lit room with a pool table. (☎569-2953. Burgers $6-7. Open daily 7am-9pm; bar hours vary.)

⚐ OUTDOOR ACTIVITIES. Ranger-led interpretive hikes delve into everything from area history to local wildflowers. Each Visitors Center conducts hikes on its own schedule and most of the campgrounds have evening talks and campfire programs. Mt. Adams and Mt. St. Helens aren't visible from the road, but can be seen from mountain trails like **Paradise** (1.5 mi.), **Pinnacle Peak** (2.5 mi.), **Eagle Peak** (7 mi.), and **Van Trump Park** (5.5 mi.). One of the oldest stands of trees in Washington, the **Grove of Patriarchs** grows near the Ohanapecosh Visitors Center. An easy 1½ mi. walk leads to these 500- to 1000-year-old Douglas firs, cedars, and hemlocks. The **Summerland** and **Indian Bar Trails** are excellent for serious backpacking—this is where rangers go on their days off. **Carbon River Valley,** in the northwest corner of the park, is one of the only inland rainforests in the US and has access to the Wonderland Trail. Winter storms keep the road beyond the Carbon River entrance in constant disrepair. The most popular staging ground for a summit attempt, **Camp Muir** (9 mi. round-trip) is also a challenging day hike. It begins on Skyline Trail, another popular day hiking option, and heads north on Pebble Creek Trail. The latter half of the hike is covered in snow for most of the year. A segment of the **Pacific Crest Trail,** which runs from Mexico to the Canadian border, dodges in and out of the park's southeast corner. The **Wonderland Trail** winds 93 mi. up, down, and around the mountain. Hikers must get permits for the arduous but stunning trek and must complete the hike in 10 to 14 days. Call the Longmire Wilderness Center for details on both hikes. A trip to the summit of Mt. Rainier requires substantial preparation and expense. The ascent involves a vertical rise of more than 9000 ft. over a distance of 9 or more mi., usually taking two days and an overnight stay at Camp Muir on the south side (10,000 ft.) or **Camp Schurman** on the east side (9500 ft.). Permits for summit climbs cost $15 per person.

OREGON

Over a century ago, families liquidated their possessions, sank their life savings into covered wagons, corn meal, and oxen, and high-tailed it to Oregon in search of prosperity and a new way of life. Today, Oregon remains a popular destination for backpackers, cyclists, anglers, beachcrawlers, and families. The caves and cliffs of the coastline are still a siren call to tourists, Oregon's most precious non-natural resource. Inland attractions include Crater Lake National Park and Ashland's Shakespeare Festival. From microbrews to snowcapped peaks, Oregon is worth crossing the Continental Divide.

🖅 PRACTICAL INFORMATION

Capital: Salem.

Visitor Info: Oregon Tourism Commission, 775 Summer St. NE, Salem 97310 (☎800-547-7842; www.traveloregon.com). **Oregon State Parks and Recreation Dept.,** P.O. Box 500, Portland, OR 97207-0500 (☎800-551-6949; www.prd.state.or.us).

Postal Abbreviation: OR. **Sales Tax:** 0%.

PORTLAND   ☎503

With over 200 parks, the pristine Willamette River, and snowcapped Mt. Hood in the background, Portland is an oasis of natural beauty. An award-winning transit system and pedestrian-friendly streets make it feel more like a pleasantly overgrown town than a traffic-jammed, dirty metropolis. In the rainy season, Portlanders flood pubs and clubs, where musicians often strum, sing, or spin for free. Improvisational theaters are in constant production, and the brave can chime in at open-mic nights all over town. And throughout it all, America's best beer pours from the taps in the microbrewery capital of the US

🚍 TRANSPORTATION

Airport: Portland International Airport (☎460-4234) is served by almost every major airline. The airport is connected to the city center by the **MAX Red Line** (38min., every 15min. daily 5am-11:30pm, $1.55), an efficient light rail system. Taxis are also available, with flat rates to downtown.

Trains: Amtrak, 800 NW 6th Ave. (☎273-4866; reservations ☎800-872-7245), at Hoyt St. Open daily 7:45am-9pm. To **Eugene** (2½hr.; 5 per day; one-way $16-20, round-trip $38-45) and **Seattle** (4hr.; 4 per day; one-way $23-36, round-trip $56-65).

Buses: Greyhound, 550 NW 6th Ave. (☎243-2310 or 800-231-2222), at N.W. Glisan St. by Union Station. Ticket counter open daily 5am-1am. To: **Eugene** (2½-4hr., 9 per day, $14); **Seattle** (3-4½hr., 9 per day, $22); and **Spokane** (8hr., 6 per day, $40).

Public Transit: Tri-Met, 701 SW 6th Ave. (☎238-7433), in Pioneer Courthouse Sq. Open M-F 7:30am-5:30pm. **Call-A-Bus** info system ☎231-3199. Buses generally run 5am-midnight with reduced hours on weekends. $1.25-1.55, ages 7-18 95¢, over 65 or disabled persons 60¢; all-day pass $4; 10 fares $10.50. All buses and bus stops are marked with one of 7 symbols and have bike racks ($5 permit available at area bike stores). Anywhere north and east of 405, west of the river and south of Hoyt St.—the **No-Fare Zone**—all of the city's public transportation is free. **MAX** (☎228-7246), based at the Customer Service Center, is Tri-Met's light rail train running between downtown, Hillsboro in the west, and Gresham in the east. A new line serves the airport from the main line's "Gateway" stop. Transfers from buses can be used to ride MAX. Runs M-F about 4:30am-1:30am, Sa 5am-12:30am, Su 5am-11:30pm.

Taxis: Radio Cab, ☎227-1212. **Broadway Cab,** ☎227-1234.

Car Rental: Crown Rent-A-Car, 1315 N.E. Sandy Blvd. (☎230-1103). Although it has a limited selection, Crown is by far the cheapest option for anyone under 25. Ages 18-21 must have credit card and proof of insurance; 22-25 must have credit card. Transport from airport available upon request. Open M-Sa 9am-5pm or by appointment. From $20-60 per day, $110-275 per week.

▓ ▓ ORIENTATION & PRACTICAL INFORMATION

Portland lies in the northwest corner of Oregon, where the Willamette River flows into the Columbia River. **I-5** connects Portland with San Francisco and Seattle, while **I-84** follows the route of the Oregon Trail through the Columbia River Gorge, heading along the Oregon-Washington border toward Boise, ID. West of Portland, **U.S. 30** follows the Columbia downstream to Astoria, but **U.S. 26** is the fastest path to the coast. **I-405** runs just west of downtown linking I-5 with U.S. 30 and 26.

Every street name in Portland carries one of five prefixes: **N, NE, NW, SE,** or **SW,** indicating where in the city the address is to be found. **Burnside St.** divides the city into north and south, while east and west are separated by the **Willamette River.** SW Portland is known as **downtown** but also includes the southern end of Old Town and a slice of the wealthier **West Hills. Old Town,** in NW Portland, encompasses most of the city's historic sector. Some areas in the NW and SW around W. Burnside St. are best not walked alone at night, although on weekends district clubs and live music draw crowds. To the north, **Nob Hill** and **Pearl District** hold recently revitalized homes and many of the chic-est shops in the city. **Southeast** Portland contains parks, factories, local businesses, and residential areas of all income brackets. A rich array of cafes, stores, theaters, and restaurants lines **Hawthorne Blvd. Williams Ave.** frames "the North." **North** and **Northeast** Portland are chiefly residential, punctuated by a few quiet parks and the **University of Portland.**

Visitor info: Visitors Association (POVA), 701 SW Morrison St. (☎275-9750), in Pioneer Courthouse Sq. Walk between the fountains to enter. Free *Portland Book* has maps and info on local attractions. Open M-F 8:30am-5:30pm, Sa-Su 10am-4pm.

Internet access: Portland Architecture Library, 801 SW 10th Ave. (☎248-5123), between Yamhill and Taylor St., has free 1hr. access. Open Tu-Th 9am-9pm, F-Sa 9am-6pm, Su 1-5pm.

Hotline: Women's Crisis Line, ☎235-5333. 24hr.

Post Office: 715 NW Hoyt St. (☎800-275-8777). Open M-F 7am-6:30pm, Sa 8:30am-5pm. **Zip Code:** 97208.

▐ ACCOMMODATIONS

Although Marriott-esque hotels dominate downtown and smaller motels are steadily raising their prices, Portland still welcomes the budget traveler. Prices tend to drop as you leave the city center, and inexpensive motels can be found on SE Powell Blvd. and the southern end of SW 4th Ave. All accommodations in Portland fill up during the summer months, especially during the Rose Festival, so make your reservations early.

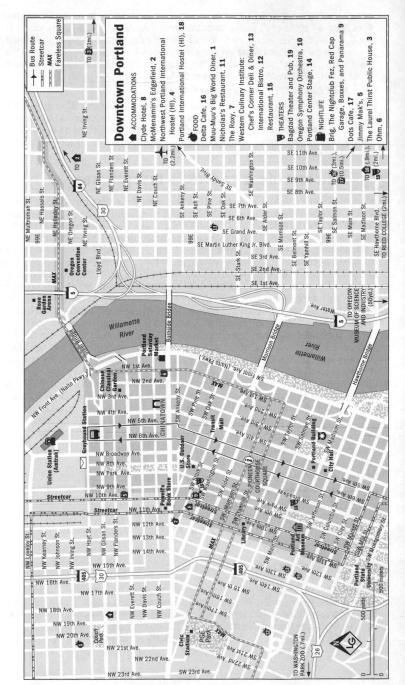

Downtown Portland

▲ **ACCOMMODATIONS**
Clyde Hotel, **8**
McMenamin's Edgefield, **2**
Northwest Portland International
   Hostel (HI), **4**
Portland International Hostel (HI), **18**

🍴 **FOOD**
Delta Cafe, **16**
Muu-Muu's Big World Diner, **1**
Nicholas's Restaurant, **11**
The Roxy, **7**
Western Culinary Institute:
   Chef's Corner Deli & Diner, **13**
   International Bistro, **12**
   Restaurant, **15**

🎭 **THEATERS**
Bagdad Theater and Pub, **19**
Oregon Symphony Orchestra, **10**
Portland Center Stage, **14**

🌙 **NIGHTLIFE**
Brig, The Nightclub Fez, Red Cap
   Garage, Boxxes, and Panarama **9**
Dots Cafe, **17**
Jimmy Mak's, **5**
The Laurel Thirst Public House, **3**
Ohm, **6**

■ **Portland International Hostel (HI)**, 3031 SE Hawthorne Blvd. (☎236-3380), at 31st Ave. across from Artichoke Music. Take bus #14 to SE 30th Ave. Lively common space and a huge porch define this laid-back hostel. Recently-installed wireless Internet access is free; "conventional" Internet is $1 per 10min. Kitchen and laundry. All-you-can-eat pancakes $1. Reception daily 8am-10pm. Check-out 11am. Fills early in summer. Dorms $15, nonmembers $18. Private rooms $41-46. ❶

Northwest Portland International Hostel (HI), 1818 NW Glisan St. (☎241-2783), at 18th Ave. between Nob Hill and the Pearl District. Take bus #17 down Glisan to corner of 19th Ave. This snug Victorian building has a kitchen, lockers, laundry, and a small espresso bar. 34 dorm beds (co-ed available). Reception daily 8am-11pm. Dorms $14-16 plus tax, nonmembers $17-19. Two private doubles $40-50. ❶

McMenamins Edgefield, 2126 SW Halsey St. (☎669-8610 or 800-669-8610), in Troutdale. Take MAX east to the Gateway Station, then Tri-Met bus #24 (Halsey) east to the main entrance. This beautiful 38-acre former farm is a posh escape that keeps two hostel rooms. On-site brewery, vineyards, 18-hole golf course, and several restaurants and pubs. 2-day rafting trips $140. Lockers included. Reception 24hr. Call ahead in summer; no reservations for the hostel. Single-sex dorm-style rooms $20 plus tax. Singles $50; doubles $95-105. ❶

The Clyde Hotel, 1022 SW Stark St. (☎517-5231), west of 10th Ave. Take MAX to SW 10th Ave. and walk towards Burnside St. Built in 1912, the charming and historic Clyde has kept all its furniture in the original style, from Victorian tubs to bureau-sized radios. Continental breakfast included. Reception daily 10am-9pm; front desk open 24hr. Reservations recommended. Rooms (double or queen) $60-110, off-season $10 less. ❸

☕ FOOD

Portland ranks high nationwide in restaurants per capita, and dining experiences are seldom dull. Downtown tends to be expensive, but restaurants and quirky cafes in the NW and SE quadrants offer great food at reasonable prices.

■ **Western Culinary Institute** (☎223-2245) would leave the Frugal Gourmet speechless. WCI has 4 eateries, each catering to a different budget niche, all of them reasonable. **Chef's Diner ❶**, 1239 SW Jefferson St., opens mornings to let cheerful students serve, taste, and discuss sandwiches, the breakfast special, or the occasional all-you-can-eat buffet ($5). Open Tu-F 7am-noon. **Chef's Corner Deli ❶**, 1239 SW Jefferson St., is good for a quick meal on-the-go. Enormous sandwiches $1.25. Open Tu-F 8am-6:30pm. Moving up the price scale, the elegant **Restaurant ❹**, 1316 SW 13th Ave., serves a classy 5-course lunch ($10) rivaled only by its superb 6-course dinner (Tu-W and F; $20). Open Tu-F 11:30am-1pm and 6-8pm. Reservations recommended. **International Bistro ❸**, 1701 SW Jefferson St., serves cuisine from a different region of the world every week, at prices that range just below those at Restaurant.

■ **The Roxy**, 1121 SW Stark St. (☎223-9160). Giant crucified Jesus with neon halo, pierced wait staff, and quirky menu. Slash (from Guns N' Roses) and other celebs have been known to stop by. Visiting the Dysha Starr Imperial Toilet seems like an important thing to do, if only because of its name. An ideal post-movie or after-bar stop. Quentin Tarantuna Melt $6.25, coffees and chai about $1-3. Open Tu-Su 24hr. ❷

■ **Muu-Muu's Big World Diner**, 612 NW 21st Ave. (☎223-8169), at Hoyt St.; bus #17. Where high and low culture smash together. Artful goofiness—the name of the restaurant was drawn from a hat—amidst red velvet curtains and gold upholstery. Brutus salad, "the one that kills a caesar" $6. 'Shroom-wich $7.50. Open M-F 11:30am-1am, Sa-Su 10am-2am. ❷

Nicholas's Restaurant, 318 SE Grand Ave. (☎235-5123), between Oak and Pine St. opposite Miller Paint; bus #6 to the Andy and Bax stop. Phenomenal Mediterranean food and atmosphere. Sandwiches $5-6. Open M-Sa 10am-9pm, Su noon-9pm. ❷

Delta Cafe, 4607 SE Woodstock Blvd. (☎771-3101). Pastoral paintings in one room, voodoo dolls and a lone, framed Chewbacca (the wookie) portrait in the other. 40 oz. Pabst Blue Ribbon comes in champagne bucket $3. Po' Boy Samwiches $4-7. Open M-F 5-10pm, Sa-Su noon-10pm. ❶

Pied Cow Coffeehouse, 3244 S.E. Belmont St. (☎230-4866). Bus #15. Sink into velvety cushions in this off-beat and friendly Victorian parlor or puff a hookah in the garden. Espresso drinks $1-3. Cakes about $4. Open M-F 4pm-1am, Sa-Su noon-1am. ❶

◎ SIGHTS

PARKS & GARDENS. Portland has more park acreage than any other American city, thanks in good measure to **Forest Park,** a 5000-acre tract of wilderness in Northwest Portland. Washington Park provides easy access by car or foot to this sprawling sea of green, where a web of trails leads through lush forests, scenic overviews, and idyllic picnic areas. Less than 2 mi. west of downtown, in the middle of the posh neighborhoods of **West Hills,** is mammoth **Washington Park,** with miles of beautiful trails and serene gardens. From there, take the MAX to the **Rose Garden,** the pride of Portland. In summer months, a sea of blooms arrests the eye, showing visitors exactly why Portland is the City of Roses. *(400 SW Kingston St. ☎823-3636.)* Across from the Rose Garden, the scenic **Japanese Gardens** are reputed to be the most authentic this side of the Pacific. *(611 SW Kingston Ave. ☎223-1321. Open Apr.-Sept. M noon-7pm, Tu-Su 10am-7pm; Oct.-Mar. M noon-4pm, Tu-Su 10am-4pm. Tours daily at 10:45am and 2:30pm. $6, students $3.50, seniors over 62 $5, under 6 free.)* The **Hoyt Arboretum,** at the crest of the hill above the other gardens, features 200 acres of trees and trails. *(4000 SW Fairview Blvd. ☎228-8733 or 823-3655. Visitors Center open M-F 9am-4pm, Sa-Su 10am-5pm.)* The largest Ming-style garden outside of China, the **Classical Chinese Gardens** occupy a city block. The large pond and ornate decorations invite a meditative stay. *(NW 3rd Ave. and Everett St. ☎228-8131. Open Apr.-Oct. daily 9am-6pm; Nov.-Mar. 10am-5pm. $6; students, seniors, and children 6-18 $5; ages 6 free.)*

MUSEUMS. The **Portland Art Museum (PAM)** sets itself apart from the rest of Portland's burgeoning arts scene on the strength of its collections, especially in Asian and Native American art. *(1219 SW Park St. At Jefferson St. on the west side of the South Block Park. Bus #6, 58, 63. ☎226-2811, ext. 4245 for info on new exhibits. Open in summer Tu-W and Sa 10am-5pm, Th-F 10am-8pm, Su noon-5pm; in winter Tu-Su 10am-5pm, Su noon-5pm. $10, students and over 55 $9, under 19 $6, under 5 free; special exhibits may be more.)* The **Oregon Museum of Science and Industry (OMSI)** keeps visitors mesmerized with science exhibits, including an earthquake simulator chamber, an Omnimax theater, and the Murdock Planetarium. *(1945 SE Water Ave., 2 blocks south of Hawthorne Blvd. next to the river. Bus #63. ☎797-4000. Open daily mid-June to Aug. 9:30am-7pm; Sept. to mid-June Tu-Sa 9:30am-5:30pm. Museum and Omnimax admission each $7, ages 3-13 and seniors $5. Omnimax: ☎797-4640. Shows on the hr. Su-Tu 11am-4pm, W-Sa 11am-7pm. Th 2-for-1 tickets after 7pm. Planetarium: ☎797-4646. Matinees daily $4; laser shows W-Su evenings $6.50. U.S.S. Blueback ☎797-4624. Open Tu-Su 10am-5pm. 40min. tour $4. Combo admission to the museum, an Omnimax film and either the planetarium or sub $16, seniors and children $12.)*

OTHER SIGHTS. The still-operational **Pioneer Courthouse,** at 5th Ave. and Morrison St., is the centerpiece of the **Square.** Since opening in 1983, it has become "Portland's Living Room." Tourists and urbanites of every ilk hang out in the brick quadrangle. *(701 SW 6th Ave. At 5th Ave. and Morrison St. along the Vintage Trolley line and the MAX light-rail. Events hotline ☎223-1613.)* Downtown on the edge of the Northwest district is the gargantuan ▉**Powell's City of Books,** a cavernous establishment with almost a million new and used volumes, more than any other bookstore in the US. *(1005 W. Burnside St. On the edge of the Northwest district. Bus #20. ☎228-4651 or 800-878-7323.*

Open daily 9am-11pm.) **The Grotto,** a 62-acre Catholic sanctuary, houses magnificent religious sculptures and gardens just minutes from downtown. *(U.S. 30 at NE 85th Ave. ☎ 254-7371. Open daily May-Oct. 9am-8:30pm; Nov.-Apr. 9am-5pm; closing times can vary.)* The **Oregon Zoo** has gained fame for its successful efforts at elephant breeding. Exhibits include a goat habitat and a marine pool as part of the zoo's "Great Northwest: A Crest to Coast Adventure" program. *(4001 SW Canyon Rd. ☎ 226-1561. Hours vary by season. $7.50, seniors $6, ages 3-11 $4.50; 2nd Tu every month free after 1pm.)*

🎵 ENTERTAINMENT

Portland's major daily newspaper, the *Oregonian*, lists upcoming events in its Friday edition, and the city's favorite free cultural reader, the Wednesday *Willamette Week*, is a reliable guide to local music, plays, and art. **Oregon Symphony Orchestra,** 923 SW Washington St., plays classics from September to June. "Monday Madness" offers $5 student tickets one week before showtime. (☎ 228-1353 or 800-228-7343. Box office open M-F 9am-5pm; in Symphony Season Sa 9am-5pm, as well. $15-60; "Symphony Sunday" afternoon concerts $10-15.) **High Noon Tunes,** at Pioneer Courthouse Sq., presents a potpourri of rock, jazz, folk, and world music. (☎ 223-1613. July-Aug. W 1pm.)

Portland Center Stage, in the Newmark Theater at SW Broadway and SW Main St., stages classics, modern adaptations, and world premiers. (☎ 274-6588. Late Sept.-Apr. Tu-Th and Su $21-38, F-Sa $21-44; youth matinee $10.) The **Bagdad Theater and Pub,** 3702 SE Hawthorne Blvd., puts out second-run films and an excellent beer menu. (☎ 288-3286. 21+. Cover $2-3.) Basketball fans can watch the **Portland Trailblazers** at the **Rose Garden Arena,** 1 Center Ct. (☎ 321-3211).

Northwest Film Center, 1219 SW Park Ave., hosts the **Portland International Film Festival** in the last two weeks of February, with 100 films from 30 nations. (☎ 221-1156. Box office opens 30min. before each show. $6.50, seniors $5.50.) Portland's premier summer event is the **Rose Festival** (☎ 227-2681) during the first three weeks of June. In early July, the outrageously good three-day 🎵**Waterfront Blues Festival** draws some of the world's finest blues artists. (☎ 282-0555 or 973-3378. Suggested donation $3-5 and two cans of food to benefit the Oregon Food Bank.) The **Oregon Brewers Festival,** on the last full weekend in July, is the continent's largest gathering of independent brewers for one incredible party at Waterfront Park. (☎ 778-5917. Mug $3; taste $1. Under 21 must be accompanied by parent.)

◤ NIGHTLIFE

Once an uncouth and rowdy frontier town, always an uncouth and rowdy frontier town. Portland's nightclubs cater to everyone from the clove-smoking college aesthete to the nipple-pierced neo-goth aesthete.

🎵 **Ohm,** 31 NW 1st Ave. (☎ 223-9919), at Couch St. under the Burnside Bridge. A venue dedicated to electronic music and unclassifiable beats. Achieve oneness dancing in the cool brick interior or mingle outside. Weekends often bring big-name live DJs. W Breakbeat and Trance. Th Spoken word. 21+. Cover $3-15. Open M-W 9pm-2:30am, Th-F 9pm-3:30am, Sa 9pm-4am, Su 9pm-3am; kitchen closes at 2am.

The Laurel Thirst Public House, 2958 NE Glisan St. (☎ 232-1504), at 30th Ave. Bus #19. Local talent makes a name for itself in 2 intimate rooms of groovin', boozin', and schmoozin'. Burgers and sandwiches $5-8. Free pool Su-Th before 7pm. Cover after 8pm $3-6. Open M noon-1:30am, Tu-Th and Su 9am-1:30am, F-Sa 9am-2am.

Jimmy Mak's, 300 NW 10th Ave. (☎ 295-6542), 3 blocks from Powell's Books at Flanders St. Jam to Portland's renowned jazz artists. Shows 9:30pm-1am. Cover $3-6. Vegetarian-friendly Greek and Middle Eastern dinners $8-17. Open Tu-Sa 11am-2am.

TO SEATTLE
(175mi.)

103

101

WASHINGTON

4

Columbia River

1

Fort Stevens
State Park

Astoria

101

26

Seaside

**Saddle Mtn.
(3283ft.)**

Ecola State
Park

2

Cannon Beach

26

Oswald West
State Park

101

Tillamook
State Forest

PACIFIC
OCEAN

Tillamook

Cape Meares
State Park

6

Cape Lookout
State Park

3

Cape Kiwanda
State Park

Siuslaw
National
Forest

101

18

18

Lincoln
City

OREGON

22

10 miles

10 kilometers

4

Newport

20

Corvallis

20

Siuslaw
National Forest

34

Yachats

Cape Perpetua
State Park

36

126

Florence

TO COOS BAY
(50mi.)

**U.S. 101
North**

From Astoria in the north to Brookings down south, U.S. 101 hugs the shore along the Oregon Coast, link-

TIME: 7hr. end-to-end

DISTANCE: 320 mi.

SEASON: Year-round

ing a string of resorts and fishing villages that cluster around the mouths of rivers that feed into the Pacific. Breathtaking ocean views spread between these towns, while parks and forests allow direct access to the big surf. Seals, sea lions, and water-fowl perch on rocks offshore.

1 ASTORIA. Victorian homes, bustling water-front, rolling hills, and persistent fog suggest Astoria as a smaller-scale San Francisco. The **Fort Clatsop National Memorial,** 5 mi. south-west of town, reconstructs Lewis and Clark's win-ter headquarters from detailed descriptions in their journals (Astoria was their last stop in 1805). The largest state park in the US, **Fort Stevens State Park ❶,** over Youngs Bay Bridge on U.S. 101 S, 10 mi. west of Astoria, has an excellent view of the Pacific Ocean, rugged and empty beaches, and bike trails. (☎861-1671, reservations ☎800-452-5687. Hot showers. Res-ervations $6. $18, with hookup $21; hiker/biker $4.25 per person; yurts $29.)

2 CANNON BEACH. Home to a veritable army of boutiques, bakeries, and galleries, Cannon Beach is a more refined alternative to some of the area's crass commercialism. The beach, how-ever, is the real draw. **Ecola Point** offers a view of hulking Haystack Rock, covered by gulls, puffins, and the occasional sea lion. (☎436-2844. Entrance fee $3.) Ecola Point also affords views of the Bay's centerpiece, the **Tillamook Light-house,** which clings to a rock like a giant barna-cle. A huge **Sand Castle Competition** transforms Cannon Beach into a fantastic menagerie on the second Saturday of June.

3 THREE CAPES LOOP. Between Tillamook and Lincoln City, U.S. 101 wanders east into wooded land, losing contact with the coast. The Three Capes Loop is a 35 mi. circle that connects a trio of spectacular promontories—**Cape Meares, Cape Lookout,** and **Cape Kiwnada State Parks.** Unless time is of the utmost impor-tance, taking the loop is a far better choice than driving straight down U.S. 101.

Cape Kiwanda State Park is the jewel of the Loop's triple crown. Home to one of the most sublime beaches on the Oregon coast, as the sheltered cape draws every kind of outdoor enthusiast.

4 NEWPORT. Newport's renovated waterfront area of pleasantly kitschy restaurants and shops are a delight. Newport's claim to fame, however, is the world-class **Oregon Coast Aquarium,** 2820 Ferry Slip Rd., at the south end of the bridge. Best known as home to Keiko the Orca from *Free Willy.* (☎867-3474. Open May-June daily 9am-6pm; July-Sept. 9am-8pm; Oct.-Apr. 10am-5pm. $10.25, seniors $9.25, ages 4-13 $6.25.) The ◨ **Mark O. Hatfield Marine Science Center,** at the south end of the bridge on Marine Science Dr., is the hub of Oregon State University's coastal research. (☎867-0100. Open in summer daily 10am-5pm; in winter M and Th-Su 10am-4pm. Admission by donation.)

5 OREGON DUNES. The **Oregon Dunes National Recreation Area** presents sand in shapes and sizes unequaled in the Northwest. Formed by millennia of wind and wave action, the dunes shift constantly and the sand sweeps over foot prints, tire marks, and—in years past—entire forests. The dunes have something for everyone, from a wild ATV ride to hikes in endless expanses of windblown sand. **Dune Buggy Adventurers,** in Winchester Bay, rents sand equipment. (☎271-6971. Open in summer 8am to last rider in; call for winter hours. ATVs $40 per hr. $150 deposit required.) For some solitude, hike the **Umpiqua Dunes Trail,** which is ATV-free and wanders through sand slopes, wind cornices, and rippled dune surfaces. Access the trailhead ¼ mi. south of Eel Creek campground.

6 BANDON-BY-THE-SEA. Despite a steady flow of summer tourists, the fishing town of Bandon-by-the-Sea has refrained from breaking out the pastels and making itself up like an amusement park. A few outdoor activities make Bandon worth a stop on a coastal tour.

7 SAMUEL H. BOARDMAN STATE PARKS. Explore 15 mi. of countless trails, some leading to beaches covered in volcanic rocks. Don't be surprised if an exploratory hike unexpectedly ends at an intimate seaside cove.

8 BROOKINGS. This is the southernmost stop on U.S. 101 before California, and one of the few towns that remains relatively tourist-free. Hardware stores are easier to find than trinket shops, and the beaches are among Oregon's least spoiled.

Brig, The Nightclub Fez, Red Cap Garage, Panorama, and **Boxxes,** 341 SW 10th St. (☎221-7262), form a network of clubs along Stark St. between 10th and 11th. On weekdays the clubs are connected, but on weekends they are often sealed off—check at the door to see what is happening where. The 23-screen video and karaoke bar is where magic happens. Cover $2-5. Open daily 9pm-2:30am; Panorama later F-Sa.

Dots Cafe, 2521 SE Clinton St. (☎235-0203). Listen to Black Sabbath, electronica, and jazz in the company of young hipsters. The usual excellent microbrews, $6 pitchers of Pabst Blue Ribbon, and a regal assemblage of kitsch memorabilia accompany Victorian paintings. Pool table 25¢ per game. Cheese fries $3.50. Open daily noon-2am.

MOUNT HOOD ☎503

Mt. Hood is by far the most prominent feature on Northwest Oregon's horizon. Fumaroles and steam vents near the top mark this as a (relatively) recently active volcano, but that's no deterrent for outdoors enthusiasts. Home to many ski resorts, the mountain satisfies Portland's skiing needs. The surrounding ridgelines and mountains are relatively mellow compared to the other mega-volcanoes to the north, Mt. Adams and Rainier, allowing for decent, non-technical hiking.

⊉ PRACTICAL INFORMATION. Mt. Hood stands near the junction of U.S. 26 and Rte. 35, 1½hr. east of Portland and 1hr. south of the Hood River. **The Mt. Hood Info Center,** 65000 E. U.S. 26, 16 mi. west of the junction of U.S. 26 and Hwy. 35 and 30 mi. east of Gresham at the entrance to the Mt. Hood village, has topo maps. (☎503-622-7674 or 888-622-4822; www.mthood.org. Open June-Oct. daily 8am-6pm; Nov.-May 8am-4:30pm.) **Hood River District Ranger Station,** 6780 Rte. 35, has more specialized info. (☎541-352-6002. Open June-Aug. daily 8am-4:30pm; Sept.-May M-F 8am-4:30pm.) **Area code:** 503.

⚐ CAMPING. Most campgrounds in **Mt. Hood National Forest** (reservations ☎877-444-6777) cluster near the junction of U.S. 26 and Rte. 35. **Lost Lake Resort ❶** provides 121 sites with water, showers, and toilets. From Rte. 35, turn east onto Woodworth Dr., right on Dee Hwy., then left on Lost Lake Rd. (Sites $15, with hookup $18.) **Trillium Lake Campground ❶,** 2 mi. east of the Timberline turn-off on U.S. 26, has trails around the crystal-clear lake and paved sites with water and toilets. Pine trees offer some privacy. (Sites $12, lakeside $14.) Just 1 mi. west of Trillium Lake, down a dirt road off U.S. 26, **Still Creek Campgrounds ❶** has a woodsier feel, unpaved sites, and a babbling brook. (Sites $12-14.) Also try **Sherwood,** 14 mi. north of U.S. 26 off Rte. 35, beside a rambling creek. (Potable water, pit toilets, no showers. Sites $10.)

⛷ SKIING. Three Mt. Hood ski areas are conveniently close to Portland. All offer night skiing and snowboard parks. **Timberline,** off U.S. 26 at Government Camp, is the largest resort in Oregon and is open year-round. (☎622-0717, snow report ☎222-2211. Open in winter daily 9am-4pm; in spring and fall 8:30am-2:30pm; in summer 7am-1:30pm. Night skiing Jan.-Feb. W-F 4-9pm, Sa-Su 4-10pm. Lift tickets $38. Rentals: ski package $21; snowboard and boots $33. Cash deposit or credit card required.) Smaller **Mt. Hood Ski Bowl,** 87000 E. U.S. 26, in Government Camp, 2 mi. west of Rte. 35, has the best night skiing and a snowboard park, though the season is limited and the vertical drop is small. (☎222-2695. Open mid-Nov. to May M-Tu 3:30-10pm, W-Th 9am-10pm, F 9am-11pm, Sa 8:30am-11pm, Su 8:30am-10pm. Lift tickets $26-30, ages 7-12 $18. $16 per night. Ski rental $19/$12. Snowboards $27.) **Mt. Hood Meadows,** 9 mi. east of Government Camp on Rte. 35, is the area's resort of choice, with varied terrain and high-speed lifts. At a medium elevation (7300 ft.),

COLUMBIA RIVER GORGE ■ 983

it often stays open through May. Mt. Hood Meadows offers discounts through local hotel. (☎337-2222, snow report ☎227-7669. Open mid-Nov. to May daily 9am-4pm. Night skiing Dec.-Mar. W-Su 4-10pm. Lift tickets $41, ages 7-12 $21; $25 through participating hotels. Night skiing $17. Ski rental package $22, ages 7-12 $15; snowboard $28/21. Beginner package with lift ticket, lesson, and rental $45.)

⚞ SUMMER ACTIVITIES. Hiking trails encircle Mt. Hood; simple maps are posted around **Government Camp.** A Northwest Forest parking pass, available at the Mt. Hood Info Center, is required at several trailheads. ($5 per day, $30 per year.) The most popular day hike is **Mirror Lake,** a 6 mi. loop that starts 1 mi. west of Government Camp, winding its way through the forest to the lake. (Open June-Oct.) Mt. Hood Ski Bowl opens its **Action Park,** which has Indy Kart racing ($5 per 5min.), helicopter rides ($20), bungee jumping ($25), and an alpine slide for $5. (☎222-2695. Open M-F 11am-6pm, Sa-Su 10am-6pm.) The Ski Bowl maintains 40 mi. of bike trails ($4 trail permit), and **Hurricane Racing** rents mountain bikes mid-June to October. ($10 per hr., half-day $25, full-day $35; trail permit included.) The Mt. Hood Visitors Center lists free hiking trails on which mountain biking is allowed. Mt. Hood is also a respectable technical alpine climb. **Timberline Mountain Guides,** based out of Timberline Lodge, guides summit climbs. (☎541-312-9242. $375.)

COLUMBIA RIVER GORGE ☎509

Stretching 75 stunning miles east from Portland, the Columbia River Gorge carries the river to the Pacific Ocean through woodlands, waterfalls, and canyons. Inland along the gorge, heavily forested peaks give way to broad, bronze cliffs and golden hills covered with tall pines. Mt. Hood and Mt. Adams loom nearby, and waterfalls plunge over steep cliffs into the river. The river widens out and the wind picks up at the town of Hood River, providing some of the world's best windsurfing.

⚐ PRACTICAL INFORMATION. To follow the gorge, which divides Oregon and Washington, take I-84 E to Exit 22. Continue east uphill on the **Columbia River Scenic Hwy. (U.S. 30),** which follows the crest of the gorge past unforgettable views. The largest town in the gorge is **Hood River,** at the junction of I-84 and Rte. 35. **Amtrak** runs trains from Portland to the foot of Walnut St. in Bingen, WA (2hr., $10-18). Station open M-Sa 8:30am-7pm and some Su afternoons. **Greyhound** buses from 600 E. Marina Way (☎541-386-1212) to Portland (1¼hr., 4 per day, $12). The **Hood River County Chamber of Commerce,** in the Expo Center north off Exit 63, has plenty of maps and helpful info. (☎541-386-2000 or 800-366-3530. Open Apr.-Oct. M-F 9am-5pm, Sa-Su 10am-5pm; Nov.-Mar. M-F 9am-5pm.) **Columbia Gorge National Scenic Area Headquarters,** 902 Wasco St., in Wyeth, offers info on hiking and a friendly earful of local lore. (☎386-2333. Open M-F 7:30am-5pm.) **Post Office:** 408 Cascade Ave., in Hood River. (☎800-275-8777. Open M-F 8:30am-5pm.) **ZIP code:** 97031. **Area codes:** 509 (WA), 541 (OR). In text, 509 unless noted otherwise.

⌂ ACCOMMODATIONS. Hotel rooms in Hood River typically start around $50 and spiral upward from there. Cheaper motels line the west end of Westcliffe Dr., north off I-84 Exit 62; they are usually full on the weekends. The **Bingen School Inn Hostel ❶,** a converted schoolhouse, is just across the Hood River Toll Bridge (75¢), 3½ blocks from the Amtrak stop in Bingen, WA. (☎493-3363. Sailboards $30 per day; lessons $65 per 3hr. Dorms $15; private rooms $35.) **Beacon Rock State Park ❶,** across the Bridge of the Gods (Exit 44) and 7 mi. west on Washington's Rte. 14, has secluded sites and easy access to hiking, mountain biking, fishing, and rock climbing. (☎427-8265. Sites $12.) **Viento State Park ❶,** 8 mi. west of Hood River off I-84, is near river hiking. (☎541-374-8811 or 800-452-5678. Tent sites $14; RV $16.) The

PACIFIC NORTHWEST

Lone Pine Motel ❶, 2429 Cascade St., in Hood River, rents comfy hostel-style rooms. (☎ 541-387-8882. $25-60 per night, $125 per week.)

🏄 WINDSURFING. Frequent 30 mph winds make Hood River a windsurfing paradise. Considered one of the best sites in the world for freestyle sailboarding (the professional term for the sport), Hood River attracts some of the best windsurfers around, and watching is as interesting as participating. Though it was once "as fast as a waterfall turned on its side" and so full of fish that the famous comedic duo of Lewis and Clark once quipped that they could walk across without getting wet, the Columbia's waters now run slower due to damming upstream. The venerated **Rhonda Smith Windsurfing Center**, in the Port Marina Sailpark, Exit 64 off I-84 under the bridge and left after the blinking red light, offers classes. (☎ 541-386-9463. $140 for two 3hr. classes, includes free evening practice.) **Big Winds**, 207 Front St., at the east end of Oak St., has cheap beginner rentals. (☎ 386-6086. $8 per hr., $15 per half-day, $25 per day.) The water near **Spring Creek Fish Hatchery**, on the Washington side, is the place to watch windsurfers. Another hub is the **Event Site**, off Exit 63 behind the Visitors Center. All-day parking costs $3.

🚵 OTHER OUTDOOR ACTIVITIES. The Gorge also has excellent mountain biking with a wide variety of trails for bikers of all skill levels. **Discover Bicycles**, 205 Oak St., rents mountain bikes, suggests routes, and sells maps. (☎ 541-386-4820. Open M-Sa 9am-7pm, Su 9am-5pm. Bikes $8-10 per hr., $50-60 per day; maps $2-5.) The 11 mi. round-trip **Hospital Hill Trail** provides views of Mt. Hood, the gorge, Hood River, and surrounding villages. To reach the unmarked trail, follow signs to the hospital, fork left to Rhine Village, and walk behind the power transformers through the livestock fence.

At **Latourell Falls**, 2½ mi. east of Crown Point, a jaunt down a paved path leads right to the base of the falls. Five miles farther east, **Wahkeena Falls** is visible from the road and hosts both a short, steep scramble and a ¼ mi. trip up a paved walk. Just a ½ mi. farther on U.S. 30, **Multnomah Falls** attracts 2 million visitors annually. The steep **Wyeth Trail,** near the hamlet of Wyeth (Exit 51), leads 4½ mi. to a wilderness boundary and 7¼ mi. to the road to Hood River and the incredible 13 mi. **Eagle Creek Trail** (Exit 44). Chiseled into cliffs high above Eagle Creek, this trail passes four waterfalls before joining the Pacific Crest Trail.

INLAND OREGON

EUGENE ☎ 541

Epicenter of the organic foods movement and a haven for hippies, Eugene has a well-deserved liberal reputation. As home to the University of Oregon, the track capital of the US due to legends such as Coach Bowerman (inventor of the artificial track) and his runner Steve Prefontaine, Eugene takes due credit for its role in the running revolution of the 1980s. Still, for all its running history, bike travel is all the rage today in Eugene, where heavy encouragement of pedal power has led to such deals as free valet bike parking at events.

🧭 ORIENTATION & PRACTICAL INFORMATION. Eugene is 111 mi. south of Portland on I-5. East-west streets are numbered beginning at Willamette St. **Hwy. 99** splits in town—**6th Ave.** runs west, and **7th Ave.** goes east. The **pedestrian mall** is downtown, on Broadway between Charnelton and Oak St. Eugene's main student drag, **13th Avenue,** leads to the **University of Oregon (U of O)** in the southeast of town. Walking the city is very time-consuming—the most convenient way to get around is by bike. Every street has at least one bike lane, and the city is quite flat. *The Whittaker area, around Blair Blvd. near 6th Ave., may be unsafe at night.* **Amtrak,** 433 Willamette St. (☎687-1383. Open daily 5:15-9pm and 11pm-midnight), at 4th Ave., treks to Seattle (6-8hr., 2 per day, $35-59) and Portland (2½-3hr., 2 per day, $16-28). **Greyhound,** 987 Pearl St. (☎344-6265. Open daily 6:15am-9:35pm), at 10th Ave., runs to Seattle (6-9hr., 9 per day, $31) and Portland (2-4hr., 10 per day, $13). **Lane Transit District (LTD)** handles public transportation. Map and timetables at the LTD Service Center, at 11th Ave. and Willamette St. (☎687-5555. Runs M-F 6am-11:40pm, Sa 7:30am-11:40pm, Su 8:30am-8:30pm. $1, seniors and under 18 50¢. Wheelchair accessible.) **Taxis: Yellow Cab,** ☎746-1234. **Visitor info:** 115 W 8th Ave., #190, door on Olive St. (☎484-5307 or 800-547-5445. Courtesy phone. Indexed map $4. Open May-Aug. M-F 8:30am-5pm, Sa-Su 10am-4pm; Sept.-Apr. M-Sa 8:30am-5pm.) **University of Oregon Switchboard,** 1244 Walnut St., in the Rainier Bldg., is a referral service for everything from rides to housing. (☎346-3111. Open M-F 7am-6pm.) **Post Office:** 520 Willamette St., at 5th Ave. (☎800-275-8777. Open M-F 8:30am-5:30pm, Sa 10am-2pm.) **ZIP code:** 97401. **Area code:** 541.

⌂❑ ACCOMMODATIONS & FOOD. The cheapest motels are on E. Broadway and W. 7th Ave. and tend toward seediness. Make reservations early; motels are packed on big football weekends. ▨**Hummingbird Eugene International Hostel ❶,** 2352 Willamette St., is a graceful neighborhood home and a wonderful escape from the city. Take bus #24 or 25 to 24th Ave. and Willamette, or park in back on Portland St. (☎349-0589. Check-in 5-10pm. Lockout 11am-5pm. Dorms $13, nonmembers $16; private rooms from $30. Cash or traveler's check only.) Tenters have been known to camp by the river, especially in the wild and woolly northeastern side near Springfield. Farther east on Rte. 58 and 126, the immense **Willamette National Forest ❶** is full of campsites ($6-16). A swamp gives the tree bark and ferns an eerie phosphorescence in the mysterious **Pine Meadows Campground ❶,** which lies alongside a reservoir and catches plenty of RV traffic. Take I-5 south to Exit 172, then head 3½ mi. south, then left on Cottage Grove Reservoir Rd., and go another 2½ mi. (☎877-444-6777. Sites $6-12.)

Eugene's downtown area specializes in gourmet food; the university hangout zone at 13th Ave. and Kincaid St. has more grab-and-go options, and natural food stores encircle the city. ▨**Keystone Cafe ❶,** 395 W. 5th St., serves creative dinners with entirely organic ingredients and many vegetarian options. Famous pancakes $3.25. (☎342-2075. Open daily 7am-5pm.) **Bene Gourmet Pizza ❸,** 225 W. Broadway Ave., serves just that. (☎284-2700. $12-19. Open M-F 11am-9pm.)

◙ SIGHTS. Take time to pay homage to the ivy-covered halls that set the scene for *National Lampoon's Animal House* at Eugene's centerpiece, the **University of Oregon.** The visitor parking and info booth is just left of the main entrance on Franklin Blvd. A few blocks away, the **Museum of Natural History,** 1680 E. 15th Ave., at Agate, shows a collection of relics from world cultures, including the oldest pair of shoes. (☎346-3024. Open W-Su noon-5pm. Suggested donation $2.)

The *Eugene Weekly* has a list of concerts and local events, as well as features on the greater Eugene community. From June 27 to July 13, 2003, during the **Oregon Bach Festival,** Baroque authority Helmut Rilling conducts performances of Bach's concerti. (☎346-5666 or 800-457-1486. Concert and lecture series $13; main events $20-45.) The vast **Oregon Country Fair,** the most exciting event of the summer, actually takes place in **Veneta,** 13 mi. west of town on Rte. 126. During the festival, 50,000 people, many still living in Haight-Ashbury happiness, drop everything to enjoy ten stages' worth of shows and 300 booths of art, clothing, crafts, herbal remedies, furniture, food, and free hugs. (☎343-4298; www.oregoncountryfair.org. Tickets F and Su $10, Sa $15; not sold on site.)

⚄ OUTDOOR ACTIVITIES. The McKenzie River has several stretches of class II-III whitewater. It is best enjoyed in June, when warm weather and high water conspire for a thrilling but comfortable ride. The Upper McKenzie is continuous for 14 mi. and can easily be paddled within 2-2½hr. **High Country Expeditions** (☎888-461-7233), on Belknap Springs Road about 5 mi. east of McKenzie Bridge, is one of the few rafting companies that floats the Upper McKenzie. (Half-day, 14 mi. trips $50; full-day, 18-19 mi. trips $75. Student and senior discounts.)

The large and popular Cougar Lake features the Terwilliger Hot Springs, known by all as **Cougar Hot Springs;** 4 mi. east of Blue River on Rte. 126, turn right onto Aufderheide Dr. (Forest Service Rd. 19), and follow the road 7¼ mi. as it winds on the right side of Cougar Reservoir ($3 day fee per person).

East from Eugene, Rte. 126 runs adjacent to the beautiful McKenzie River, and on a clear day, the mighty snowcapped Three Sisters of the Cascades are visible. Just east of the town of McKenzie Bridge, the road splits into a scenic byway loop; Rte. 242 climbs east to the vast lava fields of McKenzie Pass, while Rte. 126 turns north over Santiam Pass and meets back with Rte. 242 in Sisters. Often blocked by snow until the end of June, Rte. 242 is an exquisite drive, tunneling its narrow, tortuous way between **Mt. Washington** and the **Three Sisters Wilderness** before rising to the high plateau of McKenzie Pass.

The 26 mi. **McKenzie River Trail** starts 1½ mi. west of the ranger station (trail map $1). Parallel to Rte. 126, the trail winds through mossy forests, and leads to two of Oregon's most spectacular waterfalls—**Koosah Falls** and **Sahalie Falls.** They flank Clear Lake, a volcanic crater now filled with crystal clear waters. The entire trail is also open to mountain bikers and considered fairly difficult because of the volcanic rocks. A number of Forest Service campgrounds cluster along this stretch of Rte. 126. More ambitious hikers can sign up for overnight permits at the ranger station and head for the high country, where the hiking opportunities are endless.

⌥ NIGHTLIFE. Eugene nightlife is among the best in Oregon. In the *Animal House* tradition, the row by the university along 13th St. are often dominated by fraternity-style beer bashes. **Sam Bond's Garage,** 407 Blair Blvd., is a laid-back gem in the Whittaker neighborhood. Live entertainment every night complements an always-changing selection of local microbrews ($3 per pint). Take bus #50 or 52 or a cab at night. (☎431-6603. Open daily 3pm-1am.) **The Downtown Lounge/Diablo's,** 959 Pearl St., offers a casual dance scene with pool tables upstairs and a hip party in flame-covered walls downstairs. (☎343-2346. Cover $2-3. Open W-Sa 9pm-2:30am.) Across from 5th St. Market, **Jo Federigo's Jazz Club and Restaurant,** 259 E. 5th Ave., swings with jazz nightly. (☎343-8488. Shows start 9:30pm. Open M-F 11:30am-2pm and 5-10pm, Sa-Su 5-10pm. Jazz club daily 8:30pm-1am.)

CRATER LAKE & KLAMATH FALLS ☎541

The deepest lake in the US, the seventh deepest in the world, and one of the most beautiful anywhere, Crater Lake is one of Oregon's signature attractions. Formed about 7700 years ago in an eruption of Mt. Mazama, it began as a deep caldera and gradually filled itself with centuries worth of melted snow. The circular lake plunges from its shores to a depth of 1936 ft. Though it remains iceless in the winter, its banks, which loom as high as 2000 ft. above the 6176 ft. lake surface, are snow-covered until July. From the Visitors Center at the rim to the **Sinnott Memo-**

rial Overlook it is an easy 300 ft. walk to the park's most panoramic and accessible view. High above the lake, **Rim Dr.**, which does not open entirely until mid-July, is a 33 mi. loop around the rim of the caldera. Trails to **Watchman Peak** (¾ mi. one-way, 1hr.), on the west side of the lake, are the most spectacular. The strenuous 2½ mi. hike up **Mt. Scott,** the park's highest peak (almost 9000 ft.), begins from near the lake's eastern edge. The steep **Cleetwood Cove Trail** (2¼ mi. round-trip, 2hr.) leaves from the north edge of the lake and is the only route down to the water. It is also the home of **Wizard Island,** a cinder cone rising 760 ft. above the lake, and **Phantom Ship Rock,** a rock formation. Picnics, fishing, and swimming are allowed, but surface temperatures reach a maximum of only 50°F. Park rangers lead free tours daily in the summer and periodically in the winter (on snowshoes).

An easy base for forays to Crater Lake, Klamath Falls has several affordable hotels. The **Townhouse Motel ❶,** 5323 6th St., 3 mi. south of Main St., offers clean, comfy rooms. (☎882-0924. Cable TV, A/C, no phones. Singles $30; doubles $35.) **Mazama Campground ❶,** near the park's south entrance off Rte. 62, is swarmed by tenters and RVs from mid-June until October. (☎594-2255. Showers 75¢ per 4min. Wheelchair accessible. No reservations. Sites $15; RVs $17, electric hookup $19.) Where's **Waldo's Mongolian Grill and Tavern ❸?** It's at 610 Main St. and ready to grill your choice of veggies, meats, and sauces. (☎884-6863. Medium bowl $8.50. All-you-can-eat $10. Open M-Th 11am-11:30pm, F-Sa 11am-1am.)

Crater Lake averages over 44 ft. of snow per year, and snowbound roads can keep the northern entrance closed as late as July. Before July, enter the park from the south. The park entrance fee is $10 for cars, $5 for hikers and cyclists. The **Amtrak** Spring St. depot (☎884-2822. Open daily 7:30-11am and 8:30-10pm) is in Klamath Falls, on the east end of Main St.; turn right onto Spring St. and immediately left onto Oak St. One train per day runs to Portland ($36-60). **Greyhound,** 3817 U.S. 97 N (☎882-4616. Open M-F 8am-1am, Sa 6-9am and midnight-12:45am), rolls one per day to Bend (3hr., $20); Eugene (10hr., $40); and Redding, CA (4hr., $30). **Visitor Info: Chamber of Commerce,** 507 Main St. (☎884-0666 or 800-445-6728; www.klamath.org. Open M-F 8am-5pm.) The **William G. Steel Center,** 1 mi. from the south entrance of the park, issues free **backcountry camping** permits. (☎594-2211, ext. 402. Open daily 9am-5pm.) **Crater Lake National Park Visitors Center** is on the lake shore at Rim Village. (☎594-3100. Open June-Sept. daily 8:30am-6pm.) **Post Office:** 317 S. 7th St. in Klamath. (☎800-275-8777. Open M-F 7:30am-5:30pm, Sa 9am-noon.) **ZIP code:** 97604. **Area code:** 541.

ASHLAND ☎541

Set near the California border, Ashland mixes hip youth and British literary history to create an unlikely but intriguing stage for the world-famous **Oregon Shakespeare Festival,** P.O. Box 158, Ashland 97520 (☎482-4331; www.osfashland.org). From mid-February to October, drama devotees can choose among 11 Shakespearean and newer works performed in Ashland's three elegant theaters: the outdoor **Elizabethan Stage,** the **Angus Bowmer Theater,** and the intimate **Black Swan.** Ticket purchases are recommended six months in advance; mail-order and phone ticket sales begin in January. (In spring and fall $22-39; in summer $29-52. $5 fee per order for phone, fax, or mail orders.) At 9:30am, the **box office,** 15 S. Pioneer St., releases any unsold tickets for the day's performances and sells 20 standing room tickets for sold-out shows on the Elizabethan Stage ($11). Half-price rush tickets are sometimes available 1hr. before performances. **Backstage tours** provide a wonderful glimpse of the festival from behind the curtain. (Tu-Sa 10am. $10, ages 6-17 $7.50, under 6 not admitted.)

PACIFIC NORTHWEST

In winter, Ashland is a budget paradise; in summer, hotel and B&B rates double, while the hostel bulges. Only rogues and peasant slaves arrive without reservations. ▨**Ashland Hostel ❶**, 150 N. Main St., is well-kept and cheery with an air of elegance. (☎482-9217. Laundry and kitchen. Check-in 5-10pm. Lockout 10am-5pm. Curfew midnight. Dorms $20; private rooms $50. Cash or traveler's checks only.) The incredible food selection on N. and E. Main St. has earned the plaza a culinary reputation independent of the festival. ▨**Morning Glory ❸**, 1149 Siskiyou Blvd., deserves a medal for "most pleasant dining environment," earned either inside by the fireplace and bookcases or outside by the rose-entwined wooden porticos. (☎488-8636. Sandwiches around $9. Open daily 7am-2pm.)

Ashland is in the foothills of the Siskiyou and Cascade Ranges, 285 mi. south of Portland and 15 mi. north of the California border, near the junction of **I-5** and **Rte. 66. Greyhound** (☎482-8803) runs from the BP Station, 2073 Rte. 99 N, at the north end of town, and sends three per day to Portland (8hr., $43); Sacramento (7hr., $45); and San Francisco (11hr., $49). **Visitor Info: Chamber of Commerce,** 110 E. Main St. (☎482-3486). **Ashland District Ranger Station,** 645 Washington St., off Rte. 66 by Exit 14 on I-5, provides info on hiking, biking, and the Pacific Crest Trail. (☎482-3333. Open M-F 8am-4:30pm.) **Post Office:** 120 N. 1st St., at Lithia Way. (Open M-F 9am-5pm). **ZIP code:** 97520. **Area code:** 541.

BEND   ☎541

Defined by a dramatic landscape—volcanic features to the south, the Cascades to the west, and the Deschutes River running through its heart—Bend attracts its share of Oregon's visitors. The downtown has grown into a charming crowd-pleaser, and the outdoor opportunities are equally attractive. A few miles south of Bend, the **High Desert Museum,** 59800 S. Rte. 97, is one of the premier natural and cultural history museums in the Pacific Northwest. Stunning life-size dioramas recreate rickety cabins and cramped immigrant workshops. An indoor desertarium offers a peek at shy desert creatures. (☎382-4754. Open daily 9am-5pm. $7.75, seniors and ages 13-18 $6.75, ages 5-12 $4.)

The **Three Sisters Wilderness Area,** north and west of the Cascade Lakes Highway, is one of Oregon's largest and most popular wilderness areas. Pick up a parking permit at a ranger station or the Visitors Center ($5). Within the wilderness, the **South Sister** threads trough glaciers, making for a non-technical hike in late summer that threads between glaciers. Mountain biking is forbidden in the wilderness area, but Benders have plenty of other places to spin their wheels. Try **Deschutes River Trail** (6 mi.) for a fairly flat, forested trail ending at **Deschutes River.** To reach the trailhead, go 7½ mi. west of Bend on Century Dr. (Cascade Lakes Hwy.) until Forest Service Rd. 41, then turn left and follow the signs to Lava Island Falls.

Most of the cheapest motels line 3rd St. just outside of town, and rates are surprisingly low. To reach **Bend Cascade Hostel ❶**, 19 SW Century Dr., take Greenwood Ave. west from 3rd St. until the name changes to Newport. After ½ mi., take a left on 14th St.; the fairly safe and tidy hostel is ½ mi. up on the right side, just past the Circle K. (☎389-3813 or 800-299-3813. Foosball, laundry, kitchen, and linen. $15.) **Deschutes National Forest ❶** maintains a huge number of lakeside campgrounds along the **Cascade Lakes Hwy.,** west of town; all have toilets. (Free, with water $8-12.) **Taqueria Los Jalapeños ❶**, 601 NE Greenwood Ave., fills a simple space with locals hungry for good, cheap food, like $1.75 burritos. (☎382-1402. Open in summer M-Sa 11am-8pm, in winter 11am-7pm.)

Bend is 160 mi. southeast of Portland. **U.S. 97 (3rd St.)** bisects the town. Downtown lies to the west along the **Deschutes River; Wall** and **Bond St.** are the two main arteries. **Greyhound,** 63076 U.S. 97 N (☎382-2151; open M-F 8am-1:30pm and 2:30-5pm, Sa 8:30am-3pm, Su 8:30am-2pm), runs once a day to Eugene (2½hr., $21) and Portland (4½hr., $24). **Bend Chamber and Visitors Bureau,** 63085 U.S. 97 N, stocks free maps, coffee, and Internet access. (☎382-3221. Open M-Sa 9am-5pm.) **Deschutes National Forest Headquarters,** 1645 U.S. 20 E, has forest and wilderness info. (☎383-5300. Open M-F 7:45am-4:30pm.) **Post Office:** 2300 NE 4th St., at Webster. (Open M-F 8:30am-5:30pm, Sa 10am-1pm.) **ZIP code:** 97701. **Area code:** 541.

HELLS CANYON & WALLOWA   ☎541

With jagged granite peaks, glacier-gouged valleys, and azure lakes, the northeast corner of Oregon is the state's most rugged, remote, and arresting country. East of La Grande, the Wallowa Mountains (wa-LAH-wah) rise abruptly, looming over the plains from elevations of over 9000 ft. Thirty miles east, North America's deepest gorge plunges to the Snake River. It may take a four-wheel-drive vehicle to get off the beaten path, but those with the initiative and the horsepower will find stunning vistas and heavenly solitude in the backcountry.

⌗ PRACTICAL INFORMATION. Hells Canyon National Recreation Area and the Eagle Cap Wilderness lie on either side of the Wallowa Valley, which can be reached from Baker City, La Grande, and Clarkston, WA. Three main towns offer services within the area: **Enterprise, Joseph,** and **Halfway.** The **Wallowa Valley Stage Line** (☎569-2284) makes one round-trip Monday through Saturday from Joseph to La Grande. Pickup is at the Chevron on Rte. 82 in Joseph, the Amoco on Rte. 82 in Enterprise, and the Greyhound terminal in La Grande. One-way from La Grande to Enterprise ($10); Joseph ($11); and Wallowa Lake ($15). **Wallowa County Chamber of Commerce,** 936 W North St., is in Enterprise (☎426-4622 or 800-585-4121. Open M-F 8am-5pm). **Hells Canyon Chamber of Commerce** (☎742-4222) is in the office of Halfway Motels. **Wallowa Mountains Visitor Center,** 88401 Rte. 82, on the west side of Enterprise, has essential $4 maps. (☎426-5546. Open May-early Sept. M-Sa 8am-5pm; early Sept.-Apr. M-F 8am-5pm.)

⌂ ACCOMMODATIONS. Indian Lodge Motel ❷, 201 S. Main St., on Rte. 82 in Joseph, has elegant rooms with dark wood furniture, A/C, cable TV, and fridges. (☎432-2651 or 888-286-5484. Singles in summer $37, in winter $32; doubles $49/40.) Campgrounds here are plentiful, inexpensive, and sublime. Pick up the *Campground Information* pamphlet at the Wallowa Mountains Visitors Center for a complete listing of sites in the area. Most campgrounds are free, but not fully serviced. Check at the Visitors Center to see whether a campground has potable water. Inexplicably, the massive full-serviced **Wallowa Lake State Park campground ❶** books solid up to a year in advance. (☎432-4185 or 800-452-5687. Toilets, drinking water, and showers. Sites $17, with hookup $21.)

⚠ OUTDOOR ACTIVITIES. The canyon's endearing name comes from its legendary inaccessibility and hostility to human habitation. The walls of Hells Canyon drop over 8000 ft. to the **Snake River,** which makes it the deepest canyon in North America. Hiking is the best way to soak in the vast emptiness, and to really get into the canyon requires a trip of a few days. There are over 1000 mi. of trails, only a fraction of which are regularly maintained—bring snakebite kits, good boots, and lots of water. The dramatic 56 mi. **Snake River Trail** runs beside the river for the length of the canyon. At times, the trail is cut into the side of the rock with just enough clearance for a horse's head. Come prepared for any hazard, though outfitters and rangers patrol the river by boat at least once a day. This trail can be followed from **Dug Bar** in the north down to the Hells Canyon Dam or accessed by steep trails along the way. From north to south, **Hat Point, Freezeout,** and **P.O. Saddle** are access points. To reach Dug Bar, get a high-clearance 4-wheel drive vehicle and hit the steep, slippery Forest Rd. 4260 for 27 mi. northeast from Imnaha. The only way to get close to the canyon without taking at least a full day is to drive the **Hells Canyon National Scenic Loop Drive,** which begins and ends in Baker City, following Rte. 86, Forest Rd. 39 and 350, Rte. 82, and I-84. Even this paved route takes 6hr. to two days to drive; closures are routine. The most eye-popping views are from the 90 ft. fire lookout at **Hat Point Overlook;** go 24 mi. up the steep gravel Forest Rd. 4240 from Imnaha, turn off onto Rd. 315 and follow the signs. The easiest way to see a large portion of the canyon is on the Snake River by jet boat or raft. **Hells Canyon Adventures,** 4200 Hells Canyon Dam Rd., 1½ mi. from the Hells Canyon Dam in Oxbow, runs a wide range of jet boat and raft trips. (☎785-3352 or 800-422-3568. Jet boats 2hr. $30, 3hr. $40, full-day $105. Whitewater rafting day trip $140.)

The Wallowas often take second place to the canyon, although they are equally magnificent. Their canyons echo with the rush of rapids and their jagged peaks cover with wildflowers in spring. Over 600 mi. of hiking trails cross the **Eagle Cap Wilderness** and are usually free of snow from mid-July to October. Deep glacial valleys and high granite passes make hiking this wilderness tough going. It often takes more than a day to get into the most beautiful and remote areas. Several high alpine lakes are accessible to dayhikers. The 5 mi. hike to **Chimney Lake** from the Bowman trailhead on the Lostine River Rd. (Forest Rd. 8210) traverses fields of granite boulders sprinkled with a few small meadows. A little farther on lie the serene **Laverty, Hobo,** and **Wood Lakes,** where the path is less beaten. The **Two Pan trailhead** at the end of the Lostine River Rd. is the start of a forested 6 mi. hike to popular **Minam Lake,** which makes a good starting point for those heading to other backcountry spots like **Blue Lake,** 1 mi. above Minam. From the **Wallowa Lake trailhead,** behind the little powerhouse at the end of Rte. 82, a 6 mi. hike leads up the East Fork of the Wallowa River to Aneroid Lake. From there, hikes to Pete's Point and Aneroid Mountain deliver great views.

WESTERN CANADA

> **!** All prices in this chapter are listed in Canadian dollars unless otherwise noted.

For every urban metropolis like Vancouver in Western Canada, there's a stunning national park or outdoor area, like Banff, Jasper, and Pacific Rim (just to name a few). Hikers, mountaineers, and ice climbers will find a recreational paradise in the Canadian Rockies; the parks represent Western Canada's most consistent draw, and with good reason. They pack enough scenic punch, exhilarating thrills, and luxurious hostels to knock travelers of all ages flat. The region boasts thousands of prime fishing holes, internationally renowned fossil fields, and centers of indigenous Canadian culture.

HIGHLIGHTS OF WESTERN CANADA

THE YUKON. Flightseeing in Kluane National Park (p. 1006) and gold-panning in boomtown Dawson City (p. 1002) are both unusual and memorable.

SCENIC DRIVES. The glorious Dempster Hwy. (p. 1007) leads way up to Inuvik, NWT.

NATIONAL PARKS. Banff (p. 1009) and Jasper (p. 1011) in Alberta reign as two of the region's most beautiful. Pacific Rim National Park, BC contains the West Coast Trail (p. 1001) with its isolated beaches and old growth rainforest.

BRITISH COLUMBIA

With stunning parks and vibrant cities, British Columbia (BC) is home to the third largest movie production center in the world and a huge tourism industry. Don't worry, though; this Canadian province has room for all the; at over 900,000 sq. km, BC is more than twice as large as California and borders four US states (Washington, Idaho, Montana, and Alaska) two territories (the Yukon and Northwest) and a province (Alberta).

? PRACTICAL INFORMATION

Capital: Victoria.

Visitor Info: Tourism British Columbia, 1166 Alberni St., Ste. 600, Vancouver V6E 3Z3 (☎ 800-663-6000; www.hellobc.com). **British Columbia Parks Headquarters,** P.O. Box 9398, Stn. Prov. Govt., Victoria V8W 9M9 (☎ 250-387-5002).

Drinking Age: 19. **Postal Abbreviation:** BC. **Sales Tax:** 7% PST, plus 7% GST.

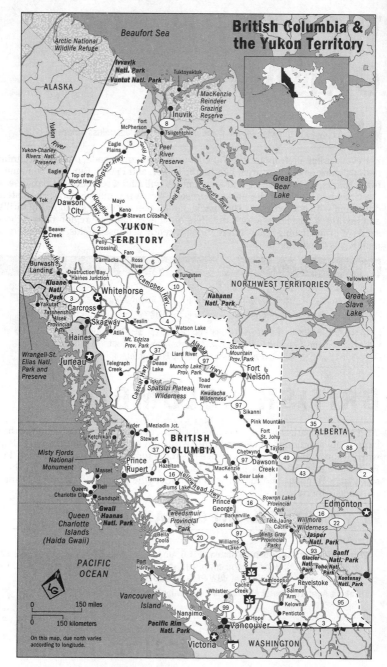

VANCOUVER ☎604

Like any self-respecting city on the west coast of North America, Vancouver boasts a thriving multicultural populace; the Cantonese influence is so strong that it is often referred to by its nickname, "Hongcouver." With the third largest Chinatown in North America and a strong showing by almost every other major culture, visitors are never hard-pressed to find exotic food or entertainment for any budget. Vancouver matches its cultural splendor with a lush, gorgeous setting and quick and easy access to outdoor adventure.

▐▘ TRANSPORTATION

Airports: Vancouver International Airport (☎207-7077), on Sea Island, 23km south of the city center. A **Visitors Center** (☎303-3601) is on level 2. Open daily 8am-11:30pm. To reach downtown, take bus #100 "New Westminster Station" to the intersection of Granville and 70th Ave. Transfer there to bus #20 "Fraser." **Airporter** (☎946-8866 or 800-668-3141) runs to downtown hotels and the bus station. (4 per hr.; 6:30am-midnight; $12, seniors $8, ages 5-12 $5.

Trains: VIA Rail, 1150 Station St. (☎800-561-8630; US ☎800-561-3949) runs eastbound trains. Open M, W-Th, and Sa 9:30am-6pm; Tu, F, and Su 9am-7pm. 3 trains per week to eastern Canada via **Edmonton** (23hr., $258) and **Jasper** (17hr., $193). **BC Rail,** 1311 W 1st St. (☎800-663-8238), in North Vancouver, runs to **Prince George** (14½hr.; Su, W, and F 7am; $247); **Whistler** (2¾hr., daily, $49); and **Williams Lake** (10hr.; W, F, and Sa 7am; $165). Open daily 8am-8pm.

Buses: Greyhound Canada, 1150 Station St. (☎482-8747 or 800-661-8747), in the VIA Rail station. Open daily 5am-12:30am. To **Banff** (14hr., 5 per day, $112); **Calgary** (15hr., 5 per day, $125); and **Jasper** (15hr., 2 per day, $106). **Pacific Coach Lines,** 1150 Station St. (☎662-8074), runs to **Victoria** every time a ferry sails (3½hr.; $29; includes ferry). **Quick Shuttle** (☎940-4428 or 800-665-2122) makes 8 trips per day from the Holiday Inn on Howe St. via the airport to **Bellingham, WA** (1½hr.; $22, students $16), **Seattle, WA** (3½hr.; $34/25), and the **Sea-Tac airport** (4hr.; $44/34). **Greyhound USA** (☎402-330-8552 or 800-229-9425) goes to **Seattle** (3-4½hr.; $20).

Ferries: BC Ferries (☎888-223-3779) arrive and leave from the **Tsawwassen Terminal,** 25km south of the city center (take Hwy. 99 to Hwy. 17). To reach downtown from Tsawwassen (1hr.), take bus #640, or take #404 "Airport" to the Ladner Exchange, then transfer to bus #601. To the **Gulf Islands, Nanaimo** (2hr.; 4-8 per day; in summer $9.50, in winter $8; cars $24-33.50), and **Victoria** (1½hr.; 8-16 per day; $9.50/8; bikes $2.50, car $24-33.50)

Public Transit: Coast Mountain Buslink (☎953-3333) covers most of the city and suburbs, with direct transport or easy connections to airport and the ferry terminals. The city is divided into 3 concentric zones for fare purposes. Riding in the **central zone,** which encompasses most of Vancouver, costs $2, seniors and ages 5-13 $1.50. During peak hours (M-F before 6:30pm), it costs $3/2 to travel between 2 zones and $4/3 for 3 zones. During off-peak hours, all zones are $2/1.50. Ask for a **free transfer** (good for 90min.) when you board buses. Day passes $8/6.

Taxis: Yellow Cab, ☎800-898-8294. **Vancouver Taxi,** ☎871-1111.

✦🛈 ORIENTATION & PRACTICAL INFORMATION

Vancouver lies in the southwestern corner of mainland British Columbia. South of the city flows the **Fraser River,** and to the west lies the **Georgia Strait,** separating the mainland from Vancouver Island. **Downtown** juts north into the Burrard Inlet from the core of the city, and **Stanley Park** goes farther north. The **Lions Gate Bridge** over Burrard Inlet links Stanley Park with North Vancouver and West Vancouver, known as **West Van.** The two collectively are known as the **North Shore.** The bridges over False Creek south of downtown link it with **Kitsilano ("Kits")** and the rest of the city. West of Burrard St. is the **West Side** or **West End. Gastown** and **Chinatown** are east of downtown. The **University of British Columbia (UBC)** lies on the west end of Kits on Point Grey, while the **airport** is on Sea Island in the Fraser River delta. The **Trans-Canada Hwy. (Hwy. 1)** enters town from the east, and **Hwy. 99** runs north-south through the city.

Visitor info: 200 Burrard St., plaza level (☎ 683-2000), near Canada Place. BC-wide info on accommodations, tours, and activities. Open daily 8am-7pm.

Bi-Gay-Lesbian Resources: The Centre, 1170 Bute St., offers counseling and info. *Xtra West* is the city's gay and lesbian biweekly, available at the Centre and around Davie St. in the West End. Open M-F 9:30am-7pm.

Hotlines: Crisis Center, ☎ 872-3311. **Rape Crisis Center,** ☎ 872-8212. Both 24hr.

Medical Services: Vancouver General Hospital, 899 W. 12th Ave. (☎ 875-4111). **UBC Hospital,** 221 Westbrook Mall (☎ 822-7121), on the UBC campus.

Internet access: Public Library, 350 W. Georgia St. (☎ 331-3600) and at 20 other branches. Open M-Th 10am-8pm, F-Sa 10am-5pm. Free.

Post Office: 349 W Georgia St. (☎ 662-5725). Open M-F 8am-5:30pm. **Postal Code:** V6B 3P7. **Area code:** 604.

Downtown Vancouver

ACCOMMODATIONS

Greater Vancouver B&Bs are a viable option for couples or small groups (singles from $45, doubles from $55). Agencies like **Town and Country Bed and Breakfast** (☎731-5942) or **Best Canadian** (☎738-7207) list options.

Vancouver Hostel Downtown (HI-C), 1114 Burnaby St. (☎684-4565 or 888-203-4302), in the West End. Sleek and clean 225-bed facility between downtown, the beach, and Stanley Park. Library, kitchen, rooftop patio. Pub crawls W and F; frequent tours of Granville Island. Reservations strongly recommended in summer. $20, nonmembers $24; private doubles $55/64. ❶

Global Village Backpackers, 1018 Granville St. (☎682-8226 or 888-844-7875), at Nelson St. Shuttle from bus/train station provided; call for details. Funky technicolor hangout in an area with great nightlife. Internet access, pool, laundry. HI, ISIC, other hosteling members $21; doubles $57, with bath $62. Nonmembers $3 more. ❶

Vancouver Hostel Jericho Beach (HI), 1515 Discovery St. (☎224-3208 or 888-203-4303), in Jericho Beach Park. Follow 4th Ave. west past Alma and bear right at the fork. Bus #4 from Granville St. downtown. Peaceful location with a great view across English Bay. Free linen, kitchens, TV room, laundry, and cafe (breakfasts around $6, dinner $7-8). Stay-and-ski package with Grouse Mountain $37. Reservations strongly recommended in summer. $17.50, nonmembers $21.50; family rooms $50-60. ❶

C&N Backpackers Hostel, 927 Main St. (☎682-2441 or 888-434-6060), 300m north on Main St. from the train station. Cheap meal deals with the **Ivanhoe Pub** ($2.50 breakfast all day) make this recently renovated hostel a bargain. Kitchen, laundry, bikes ($10 per day). May-Sept. dorms $14; single, double, or family room $35. Weekly rates available, monthly rates available in winter. ❶

Cambie International Hostel, 300 Cambie St. (☎684-6466 or 877-395-5335). Free airport pickup 9am-8pm. Easy access to the busy sights and sounds of Gastown. Common room, laundry. No kitchen, but free hot breakfast. Pool tables in the pub. June-Sept. dorms $20, singles $45; Oct.-May $17.50/40. ❶

FOOD

The diversity and quality of Vancouver's international cuisine makes the rest of BC seem provincial. Vancouver's **Chinatown** and the **Punjabi Village** (along Main and Fraser, around 49th St.) serve cheap, authentic food. The whole world, from Chinese noodle shops to Italian cafes, seems represented along **Commercial Dr.**, east of Chinatown. Produce sold along "The Drive" puts supermarkets to shame.

Restaurants downtown compete for the highest prices in the city. The **West End** caters to diners seeking a variety of ethnic cuisines, while **Gastown** lures cruise ship tourists. Many cheap and grubby establishments along Davie and Denman St. stay open 24hr. Dollar-a-slice, all-night **pizza places** pepper downtown.

Downtown Vancouver

🏠 ACCOMMODATIONS
Cambie Intl Hostel, **2**
C&N Backpackers Hostel, **10**
Global Village Backpackers, **8**
Vancouver Hostel Downtown, **7**

🍴 FOOD
Benny's Bagels, **17**
Mongolian Teriyaki, **14**
The Naam, **16**
Subeez Café, **9**

🎭 THEATRES
Arts Club Theatre, **13**
Orpheum Theatre, **5**

🍸 NIGHTLIFE
The Irish Heather, **3**
Sonar, **1**
Sugar Refinery, **11**
Wett Bar, **12**

● SIGHTS
Dr. Sun Yat-Sen Classical
  Chinese Garden, **6**
Granville Island Brewing
  Co., **15**
World's Skinniest
  Building, **4**

WESTERN CANADA

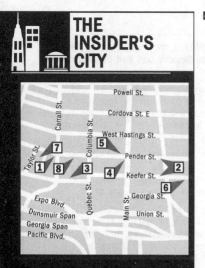

THE INSIDER'S CITY

CHINATOWN HIGHLIGHTS

Savvy tourists should take a break from downtown's slick hot spots and experience Chinatown, Vancouver at its most raw and energized.

1 Gawk at the impossibly narrow **Sam Kee Building,** said to be the narrowest in the world.

2 Barter, bicker, and haggle at the **Chinatown Night Market.** Open June-Sept. F-Su 6:30-11:30pm.

3 Let the tranquil **Dr. Sun Yat-Sen Classical Chinese Garden** (☎689-7133) ease your stress.

4 Enjoy great Chinese food on the cheap at **Kam's Garden Restaurant** (☎689-7133).

5 Recognize the trials and successes of Chinese Canadians at the **Winds of Change Mural.**

6 Choose your meal from hundreds at **Hon's Wun-Tun House** (☎688-0871).

7 Visit the huge **Western Han Dynasty Bell.**

8 Explore the permanent and changing exhibitions at the **Chinese Cultural Centre** (☎658-8865).

■ The Naam, 2724 W. 4th Ave. (☎738-7151), at MacDonald St. Bus #4 or 7 from Granville Mall. One of the most diverse vegetarian menus around, with great prices to boot. Crying Tiger Thai stir fry $9, veggie burgers under $7, *tofulati* ice cream $3.50. Live music nightly 7-10pm. Open 24hr. ❷

Subeez Cafe, 891 Homer St. (☎687-6107), at Smithe, downtown. Serves hipster kids in a cavernous, casual setting. Eclectic menu, from vegetarian gyoza ($7) to organic beef burgers ($9), complements a lengthy wine list and home-spun beats (DJs W and F-Sa 9pm-midnight). Weekly specials. Entrees $7-15. Open M-F 11:30am-1am, Sa 11am-1am, Su 11am-midnight. ❷

Mongolian Teriyaki, 1918 Commercial Dr. (☎253-5607). Diners fill a bowl with meats, veggies, sauces, and noodles, and the chefs fry everything up and serve it with miso soup, rice, and salad for only $5 (large bowl $6). Take-out menu available. Open daily 11am-10:30pm. ❶

Benny's Bagels, 2505 W. Broadway (☎731-9730). Every college student's dream. Serves the requisite beer ($3 per glass), bagels (75¢, $2.25 with cream cheese), and sandwiches and melts ($5.50-7.50). Open Su-Th 7am-1am, F-Sa 24hr. ❶

Hon's Wun-Tun House, 268 Keefer St. (☎688-0871). This award-winning Cantonese noodle-house is the place to go (bowls $3.50-6). Over 300 options make reading the menu almost as long as dinner. Attentive service. Open daily 8:30am-10pm; in summer F-Su until 11pm. Cash only. ❶

☉ SIGHTS

DOWNTOWN

■ VANCOUVER ART GALLERY. The Vancouver Art Gallery has excellent temporary exhibitions and is home to a varied collection of contemporary art. *(750 Hornby St., in Robson Sq. ☎662-4700. Open M-W and F-Su 10am-5:30pm, Th 10am-9pm; call for winter hours. $12.50, students $7, seniors $9; Th 5-9pm pay-what-you-can.)*

GARDENS

The city's temperate climate, which also includes ample rain most months of the year, allows floral growth to flourish. Locals take great pride in their private gardens, and public parks and green spaces showcase displays of plant life.

VANDUSEN BOTANICAL GARDEN. Some 55 acres of former golf course have been converted into the immense **■ VanDusen Botanical Garden,** showcasing

7500 taxa from six continents. An international **sculpture** collection is interspersed among the plants, while more than 60 species of birds can be seen in areas like Fragrance Garden, Bonsai House, Chinese Medicinal Garden, or the Elizabethan Maze, which is planted with 3000 pyramidal cedars. The **Flower & Garden Show** is the first weekend of June. *(5251 Oak St., at W 37th. Take #17 Oak bus to W. 37th and Oak. ☎878-9274. Free parking. Mostly wheelchair accessible. Open May-Aug. 10am-8pm; Sept. 10am-6pm; Oct.-Apr. 10am-4pm. Apr.-Sept. $7, over 65 and ages 13-18 $5, ages 6-12 $3.50, families $16; Oct.-Mar. up to 50% off.)*

BLOEDEL FLORAL & BIRD CONSERVATORY. Journey from tropics to desert in 100 paces inside this 43m diameter triodetic geodesic dome, constructed of plexiglass bubbles and aluminum tubing. The conservatory, maintained at a constant 18°C (65°F), is home to 500 varieties of exotic plants and 150 birds. Its elevation affords great views of downtown Vancouver. *(In the center of Queen Elizabeth Park on Cambie and 37th Ave., a few blocks east of VanDusen. ☎257-8570. Open Apr.-Sept. M-F 9am-8pm, Sa-Su 10am-9pm; Oct.-Mar. daily 10am-5pm. $3.75, over 65 $2.25, ages 13-18 $2.85, ages 6-12 $1.85, under 5 free.)*

UNIVERSITY OF BRITISH COLUMBIA (UBC)

The high point of a visit to UBC is the breathtaking ▓**Museum of Anthropology.** The high-ceilinged glass and concrete building houses totems and other massive carvings, highlighted by Bill Reid's depiction of Raven discovering the first human beings in a giant clam shell. *(6393 NW Marine Dr. Bus #4 or 10 from Granville St. Museum. ☎822-3825. Open July-Aug. M and W-Su 10am-5pm, Tu 10am-9pm; Sept.-May W-Su 11am-5pm, Tu 11am-9pm. $7, students $4, seniors $5, under 6 free; Tu after 5pm free.)* Across the street, caretakers tend to **Nitobe Memorial Garden,** the finest classical Shinto garden outside of Japan. *(☎822-6038. Open mid-Mar. to Oct. daily 10am-6pm; Nov. to mid-Mar. M-F 10am-2:30pm. $2.75, students and seniors $1.75, under 6 free.)* The **Botanical Gardens** are a collegiate Eden encompassing eight gardens in the central campus, including the largest collection of rhododendrons in North America. *(6804 SW Marine Dr. ☎822-9666. Same hours as Nitobe Garden. $4.75, students and seniors $2.50, under 6 free.)*

STANLEY PARK

Established in 1889 at the tip of the downtown peninsula, the 1000-acre **Stanley Park** is a testament to the foresight of Vancouver's urban planners. The thickly wooded park is laced with cycling and hiking trails and surrounded by a popular 10km **seawall** promenade. *(To get to the park, take bus #23, 123, 35, or 135. A free shuttle runs between major destinations throughout the park June-Sept. 10am-6pm. ☎257-8400.)*

AQUARIUM. The ▓**Vancouver Aquarium,** on the park's eastern side not far from the entrance, features exotic aquatic animals. BC, Amazonian, and other ecosystems are skillfully replicated. Dolphin and beluga whales demonstrate their advanced training and intelligence by drenching gleeful visitors. The new Wild Coast exhibit allows visitors to get a close-up view of marine life. Outside the aquarium, the **orca fountain** by sculptor Bill Reid glistens. *(☎659-3474. Open July-Aug. daily 9:30am-7pm; Sept.-June 10am-5:30pm. Shows throughout the day 10am-5:30pm. $14.75; students, seniors, and ages 13-18 $12; ages 4-12 $9; under 4 free.)*

WATER. The **Lost Lagoon,** brimming with fishies, birds, and the odd trumpeter swan, provides a utopian escape from the skyscrapers. Nature walks start from the **Nature House,** underneath the Lost Lagoon bus loop. *(☎257-8544. Open June-Aug. F-Su 11am-7pm. 2hr. walks Su 1pm. $5, under 12 free.)* The park's edges boast a few restaurants, tennis courts, a cinder running track with hot showers and a changing room, swimming beaches, and an outdoor theater, the **Malkin Bowl.** *(☎687-0174.)*

WESTERN CANADA

FALSE CREEK & GRANVILLE ISLAND

GRANVILLE ISLAND BREWING COMPANY. Canada's first micro-brewery offers daily tours of the facility, including free samples. *(Under the bridge at the southern tip of the island. ☎687-2739. Tours M-F noon, 2, and 4pm; Sa-Su hourly noon-5pm. $7, includes samples of 4 brews and a souvenir glass. Call for store hours.)*

H.R. MACMILLAN SPACE CENTRE. Housed in the same circular building as the **Vancouver Museum**, the space center runs a motion-simulator ride, planetarium, and exhibit gallery, as well as frequent laser-light rock shows. *(1100 Chestnut St. Bus #22 south on Burrard St. ☎738-7827. Open July-Aug. daily 10am-5pm; Sept.-June closed M. $12.75, students and seniors $9.75; laser-light show $9.25. Vancouver Museum ☎736-4431. $8, seniors $7, under 19 $5.50. Combined admission to both museums $17, youth $11.)*

🎵 🎤 ENTERTAINMENT & NIGHTLIFE

The **Vancouver Symphony Orchestra** (☎684-9100) plays September to May in the **Orpheum Theatre**, at the corner of Smithe and Seymour. In summer, tours of the theater are given. (☎665-3050. $5). The VSO often joins forces with other groups such as the **Vancouver Bach Choir** (☎921-8012). The **Vancouver Playhouse Theatre Co.** (☎873-3311), on Dunsmuir and Georgia St., and the **Arts Club Theatre** (☎604-687-1644), on Granville Island, stage low-key shows, often including local work. The **Ridge Theatre**, 3131 Arbutus, shows arthouse, European, and vintage film double features. (☎738-6311. $7, seniors and children $4; Tu $5/3; seniors free on M.)

🍸 **Sugar Refinery,** 1115 Granville St. (☎683-2004). Where Vancouver's arts scene goes to relax. An ever-changing program of events, music, and spoken word entertains while the tasty vegetarian meals please the stomach. Entrees $7.50-9, big sandwiches $5-7.50, tap beers served in mason jars $4.25-5.75. Open M-F 5pm-noon, Sa-Su 5pm-2am.

🍸 **Sonar,** 66 Water St. (☎683-6695). A popular beat factory. W hip-hop and reggae, F turntablist, and Sa House. Pints $3.75-5. Open M-Sa 8pm-2am, Su 9pm-midnight.

The Irish Heather, 217 Carrall St. (☎688-9779). The 2nd-highest seller of Guinness in BC, this true Irish pub and bistro serves up memories of the Emerald Isle. 20oz. draughts ($5.20), mixed beer drinks ($5.60), and a helping of bangers and mash ($14) will keep those eyes smiling. Lots of veggie dishes, too. Live music Tu-Th. Open M-Th 3-11:30pm, F-Su 11:30am-12:30pm.

Wett Bar, 1320 Richards St. (☎662-7707). Candlelit dining booths and a weekend dress code. Wields one of the most advanced stereo and light systems in Vancouver. F hip-hop, Sa top 40, W house. Open M and W-Sa 8pm-2am, Tu 9pm-1am.

The King's Head, 1618 Yew St. (☎738-6966), at 1st St., in Kitsilano. Cheap drinks, cheap food, relaxing atmosphere, and a great location near the beach. Bands play acoustic sets on a tiny stage. Daily drink specials. $3 pints. Open M-F 7am-1am, Sa 7:30am-2am, Su 7:30am-midnight.

NEAR VANCOUVER: WHISTLER ☎604

Only 125km north of Vancouver on the dangerously twisty Hwy. 99, Whistler and Blackcomb mountains provides some of North America's best skiing and snowboarding, and are popular mountain destinations in summer, too. The **"Village"** is commercialized and overpriced, but this fact can't take away from the striking beauty of the mountains or the challenge of the terrain.

Thirty-three lifts (15 of them high-speed), three glaciers, over 200 marked trails, a mile (1609m) of vertical drop, and unreal scenery make **Whistler/Blackcomb** a top destination for skiers and boarders. Whistler Creekside offers the shortest lines to park and the closest access for those coming from Vancouver. (☎932-3434 or 800-

766-0449. Lift tickets $112-141 for 3 days. Better deals for longer trips.) A **Fresh Tracks** upgrade ($15), available daily at 7am, provides a basic breakfast in the mountaintop lodge on Blackcomb and the opportunity to begin skiing as soon as the ski patrol has finished avalanche control. Most **snowboarders** prefer the younger Blackcomb for its windlips, natural quarter-pipes, and 16-acre terrain park. Endless **backcountry skiing** is accessible from resort lifts and in Garibaldi Park's **Diamond Head** area. Equipment rentals are widely available; try **Affinity Sports** next to Moguls Coffee on the Village Square (☎932-6611).

The gorgeous lakeside **Whistler Hostel (HI-C) ❶**, 5678 Alta Lake Rd., lies 5km south of Whistler Village on Hwy. 99. BC Rail stops here on request. (☎932-5492. $20; nonmembers $24.) The **Fireside Lodge ❶**, 2117 Nordic Dr., 3km south of the village, offers spacious cabins with mammoth kitchens, lounge, sauna, and a game room. (☎932-4545. Dorms late Dec.-Mar. $20; Apr. to mid-Dec. $30.)

Greyhound (☎932-5031 or 800-661-8747) runs to Vancouver from the Village Bus Loop (2½hr., 6 per day, $20). **BC Rail's** 2½hr. Cariboo Prospector (☎984-5246) departs North Vancouver for Whistler Creek at 7am and returns at 6:20pm daily ($33). **Activity and information center:** in the heart of the Village. (☎932-2394. Open daily 9am-5pm.) **Post Office:** in the Village Marketplace. (☎932-5012. Open M-F 8:30am-5:30pm, Sa 8:30am-12:30pm.) **Postal code:** V0N 1B0. **Area code:** 604.

VICTORIA   ☎250

Clean, polite, and tourist-friendly, today's Victoria is a homier alternative to cosmopolitan Vancouver. Although many tourist operations would have you believe that Victoria fell off Great Britain in a neat little chunk, its High Tea tradition began in the 1950s to draw American tourists. Double-decker buses motor past native art galleries, new-age bookstores, and countless English pubs.

🖪 PRACTICAL INFORMATION. Victoria surrounds the **Inner Harbour;** the main north-south thoroughfares downtown are **Government St.** and **Douglas St.** To the north, Douglas St. becomes Hwy. 1, which runs north to Nanaimo. **Blanshard St.,** one block to the east, becomes Hwy. 17. The **E&N Railway,** 450 Pandora St. (☎383-4324 or 800-561-8630), near the Inner Harbour at the Johnson St. Bridge, runs daily to Nanaimo (2½hr.; $23, students with ISIC $15). **Laidlaw,** 700 Douglas St. (☎385-4411 or 800-318-0818), at Belleville St., and its affiliates, **Pacific** and **Island Coach Lines,** run buses to: Nanaimo (2½hr., 6 per day, $17.50); Port Hardy (9hr., 1-2 per day, $93); and Vancouver (3½hr., 8-14 per day, $29). **BC Ferries** (☎656-5571 or 888-223-3779) depart Swartz Bay to Vancouver's Tsawwassen ferry terminal (1½hr.; 8-16 per day; $9, bikes $2.50, car and driver $24-34), and to the Gulf Islands. **Victoria Clipper** (☎382-8100 or 800-888-2535) passenger ferries travel to Seattle (2-3hr.; 4 per day May-Sept., 1 per day Oct.-Apr.; US$79-125). **Victoria Taxi,** ☎383-7111. **Visitor info: Tourism Victoria,** 812 Wharf St., at Government St. (☎953-2033. Open in summer daily 8:30am-7:30pm; in winter 9am-5pm.) **Post Office:** 621 Discovery St. (☎963-1350. Open M-F 8am-6pm.) **Postal code:** V8W 2L9. **Area code:** 250.

🖪 ACCOMMODATIONS. The colorful **🗒Ocean Island Backpackers Inn ❶**, 791 Pandora St., downtown, boasts a better lounge than most clubs, tastier food than most restaurants, and accommodations comparable to most hotels. Undoubtedly one of the finest urban hostels in North America. (☎385-1788 or 888-888-4180. 140 beds in small rooms. Free linen and towels, laundry, Internet access. Parking $5. Dorms $20, students and HI members $17.25; doubles $40-50.) To reach the **The Cat's Meow ❶**, 1316 Grant St., take bus #22 to Gernwood and Grant St. A mini-hostel with 12 quiet beds 3 blocks from downtown. It offers free parking, discounts on kayaking and whale watching, and complimentary breakfast. (☎595-8878. $19; pri-

FROM THE ROAD

A WHALE OF A TALE

I had heard that the waters around Vancouver Island had amazing wildlife, but until I got on a ship headed to Bamfield, I didn't realize just what a treat the area can be. Ryan, the captain of the ship, was known as a whale expert, so I was hoping for some long-distance sightings. Ryan said he would try to pick a few whales out of the fog for me. Within ten minutes he was successful—but at much closer range than I had anticipated. As we approached a whale surfacing in the fog, Ryan actually *recognized* the animal as a particularly friendly whale named Cookie-Cutter. Like an old friend, the whale approached the boat, completely unafraid. Cookie-Cutter rubbed up against the port side of the boat, barnacles spotting her smooth gray skin. "Lean over and pet her," Ryan instructed. I was shocked by the suggestion, but who was I to argue? I reached out and stroked the whale's skin, overwhelmed to be in such close contact with such a magnificent animal. She continued to play with the boat for almost half an hour, as all the passengers came out and enjoyed the whale's company. Ryan eventually had to tear us away from the fun to keep on schedule.

We spotted plenty more animals during the trip, but no encounter could possibly match the thrill and excitement of my up-close and personal meeting with Cookie-Cutter.

—Posy Busby

vate rooms $40-45.) **Goldstream Provincial Park ❶**, 2930 Trans-Canada Hwy., 20km northwest of Victoria, offers a forested riverside area with great hiking trails and swimming. (☎391-2300 or 800-689-9025. Flush toilets and firewood. $18.50.)

❐⛴ FOOD & NIGHTLIFE. A diversity of food can be found in Victoria, if you know where to go; ask locals, or wander through downtown. **Chinatown** extends from Fisgard and Government St. to the northwest. Coffeeshops can be found on every corner. Cook St. Village, between McKenzie and Park St., offers an eclectic mix of creative restaurants. **⛴John's Place ❷**, 723 Pandora St., is a hopping joint serving wholesome Canadian fare with a Thai twist plus a little Mediterranean flair. (☎389-0711. Entrees $5-11. Open M-F 7am-10pm, Sa 8am-4pm and 5-10pm, Su 8am-4pm and 5-9pm.) A trip to Victoria is *just not done* without a spot of tea. The Sunday High Tea ($10.25) at the **James Bay Tea Room & Restaurant ❸**, 332 Menzies St., behind the Parliament Buildings, is lower-key and significantly less expensive than the famous High Tea at the Empress Hotel. (☎382-8282. Open M-Sa 7am-8pm, Su 8am-8pm.) The free weekly *Monday Magazine* available downtown, lists venues and performers. **Steamers Public House,** 570 Yates St., attracts a young, happy dancing crowd. (☎381-4340. Open stage M, jazz night Tu. Cover $3-5 at night. Open M 11:30am-1am, Tu-Sa 11:30am-2am, Su 11:30am-midnight.)

◪⛰ SIGHTS & OUTDOOR ACTIVITIES. The very thorough **⛴Royal British Columbia Museum,** 675 Belleville St., presents excellent exhibits on the biological, geological, and cultural history of the province, from protozoans to the present. A new IMAX theater shows films that are larger than life. (☎356-7226. Open daily 9am-5pm. $9; students, seniors, and youths $6; under 6 free. IMAX $10, seniors $8.50, youth $6.50, child $3.50.) Unwind with a tour of the **Vancouver Island Brewery,** 2330 Government St., whose 1hr. tour is educational and alcoholic. (☎361-0007. Tours F-Sa 3pm. $5 for four 4 oz. samples and souvenir pint glass. 19+ to sample.)

The elaborate landscaping of the **⛴Butchart Gardens** includes a rose garden, Japanese and Italian gardens, fountains, and wheelchair-accessible paths. (Bus #75 "Central Saanich" runs from downtown. 1hr. ☎652-4422. Open July-Aug. daily 9am-10:30pm. $19.25, ages 13-17 $9.50, ages 5-12 $2, under 5 free. The Gray Line (☎388-6539) runs a package from downtown including round-trip transportation and admission to gardens. $26, youth $17.25, children $7.) Mountain bikers can tackle the **Galloping Goose,** a 100km trail beginning downtown and continuing to the west coast of the Island through towns, rainforests, and canyons. **Ocean River Sports** offers kayak rentals, tours, and lessons. (☎381-4233 or 800-909-4233. Open M-Th and Sa 9:30am-5:30pm, F 9:30am-7:30pm, and Su 11am-5pm. Single kayak $42 per day, double $50; canoe $42.) Many whale-watching outfits give discounts for hostel guests. **Ocean Explorations,** 532 Broughton St., runs 3hr. tours. (☎383-6722. Apr.-Oct. $70, hostelers and children $50; less off-season. Free pickup at hostels.)

PACIFIC RIM NATIONAL PARK ☎250

The Pacific Rim National Park stretches along a 150km sliver of Vancouver Island's remote Pacific coast. The region's frequent downpours create a lush landscape rich in both marine and terrestrial life. Hard-core hikers trek through enormous red cedar trees while long beaches on the open ocean draw beachcombers, bathers, kayakers, and surfers.

A winding, 1½hr. drive up Hwy. 14 from Hwy. 1 near Victoria lands you in **Port Renfrew.** Spread out in the trees along a peaceful ocean inlet, this isolated coastal community of 400 people is the southern gateway to the world-famous 🔳**West Coast Trail.** The other end of the trail lies 75km north, in Bamfield. The route weaves through primeval forests of giant red cedars and spruce, waterfalls, rocky slopes, and rugged beach. Exciting challenges lie at every bend, but wet weather and slippery terrain can make the trail dangerous. Hikers pay about $120 per person for access to the trail (reservation fee $25, trail-use fee $70, ferry-crossing fee $25). If you only want to spend an afternoon roughing it, visit the gorgeous **Botanical Beach Provincial Park.** Visit at low tide or don't expect to see much (Visitors Centers will have tide charts).

🔳**Whalers on the Point Guesthouse (HI-C) ❶,** 81 West St., voted the best hostel in Canada by HI, has room for 64. Free sauna, billiards, linen, and harborside views. Internet access $1 per 10min. (☎725-3443. Check-in 7am-2pm and 4-11pm. $22, nonmembers $24; private rooms $66/70.) Near Port Renfrew and adjacent to the West Coast Trail registration office lies the **Pacheedaht Campground ❶.** (☎647-5521. Tent sites $10; RV sites $16; beach campers $8.) The **Lighthouse Pub & Restaurant ❷** (☎647-5505), on Parkinson Rd., serves up tasty fish and chips.

Seek out maps, information on the area, and registration info at one of the two **Trail Information Centers,** one in **Port Renfrew** (☎647-5434), at the first right off Parkinson Rd. (Hwy. 14) once in "town"; and one at **Pachena Bay** (☎728-3234), 5km south of Bamfield. Both open daily May-Sept. 9am-5pm. **West Coast Trail Express** (☎477-8700 or 888-99-2288) runs daily from **Victoria** to **Port Renfrew** via the **Juan de Fuca** trailhead (May-Sept., 2¼hr., $35); from **Nanaimo** to **Bamfield** (3½hr., $55); from **Bamfield** to **Port Renfrew** (3hr., $50); and from **Port Renfrew** or **Banfield** to **Nitinat** (2hr., $35). Reservations are recommended, and can be made for beaches and trailheads from Victoria to Port Renfrew. The **Juan de Fuca Express** operates a water taxi between Port Renfrew and Bamfield. (☎888-755-6578. 4-7 hr., $85.)

PRINCE RUPERT ☎250

At the western end of Hwy. 16, Prince Rupert is an emerging transportation hub—a springboard for ferry travel to Alaska, the spectacular Queen Charlotte Islands, and northern Vancouver Island.

📧 TRANSPORTATION. Prince Rupert Airport is on Digby Island. (Ferry and bus to downtown $11, seniors $7, children $4; 45min.) Air Canada flies to Vancouver (2-3 per day; $401, under 25 $230). **VIA Rail** (☎627-7304 or 800-561-8630), at the BC Ferries Terminal, runs to Prince George (12hr., 3 per week, $78). A **BC Rail** (in BC ☎800-339-8752; elsewhere 800-663-8238) train continues the next morning from

WESTERN CANADA

Prince George to Vancouver (14hr., $247). **Greyhound,** on 6th St. at 2nd Ave. (☎624-5090), goes to Prince George (11 hr., 2 per day, $100) and Vancouver (24hr., 2 per day, $201). Next door, **BC Ferries** (☎624-9627 or 888-223-3779) will take you to Port Hardy (15hr.; every other day; $99, car $233) and the Queen Charlotte Islands (6-7hr.; 6 per week; $23.50, car $86.50). **Public Transit: Prince Rupert Bus Service** runs downtown, every 30min. The #52 bus runs to near the **ferry terminal.** (☎624-3343. Runs Su-Th 7am-6:45pm, F 7am-10:45pm. $1, students 75¢, seniors 60¢; day pass $2.50, students and seniors $2.)

⊞☐ ORIENTATION & PRACTICAL INFORMATION. The only major road into town is the Yellowhead Highway (Hwy. 16), leading to the ferry docks; it is known as **McBride St.** within city limits, **2nd Ave.** at the north end of downtown, and **Park Ave.** to the south. From the docks, downtown is a 30min. walk. The **Info Center,** at 1st Ave. and McBride St., is in a building modeled after a Tsimshian bighouse. (☎624-5637 or 800-667-1994. Open June-Aug. M-Sa 9am-8pm and Su 9am-5pm; Sept.-May M-Sa 10am-5pm.) **Internet access: Public Library,** 101 6th Ave. W. (☎624-8618. Open M-Th 10am-9pm, F-Sa 10am-5pm. $2 per hr.) **Post Office:** 2nd Ave. and 5th St. (☎624-2353. Open M-F 9:30am-5pm.) **Postal Code:** V8J 3P3. **Area code:** 250.

☐☐ ACCOMMODATIONS & FOOD. Nearly all of Prince Rupert's hotels are within the six-block area defined by 1st Ave., 3rd Ave., 6th St., and 9th St. **◪Andree's Bed and Breakfast ❸,** 315 4th Ave. E, in a spacious 1922 Victorian-style residence, overlooks the harbor and city. (☎624-3666. Breakfast included. Singles $50; doubles $65; twins $70; each additional person $15.) **Park Ave. Campground ❶,** 1750 Park Ave., is less than 2km east of the ferry terminal via Hwy. 16 and has well-maintained sites; some are forested, while others have a view of the bay. (☎624-5861. Laundry facilities. Sites $10.50; with hookup $18.50. Showers for non-guests $3.50.) **◪Cow Bay Cafe ❸,** 201 Cow Bay Rd., offers an ever-changing menu, including lunch specialties ($8-9) and ten smashing dessert creations for $4-5. (☎627-1212. Open Tu noon-2:30pm, W-Sa noon-2:30pm and 6-9pm.)

◪◪ SIGHTS & OUTDOOR ACTIVITIES. Prince Rupert's harbor has the highest concentration of archaeological sites in North America; **archaeological boat tours** leave from the Visitors Center daily. (2½hr. tours depart mid-June to early Sept. daily. $22, children $13, under 5 free.) The **Museum of Northern British Columbia,** in the same building as the Visitors Center, documents the history of logging, fishing, and Haida culture. (☎624-3207. Open late May to mid-Sept. M-Sa 9am-8pm, Su 9am-5pm; mid-Sept. to late May M-Sa 9am-5pm.) Tiny **Service Park,** off Fulton St., offers panoramic views of downtown and the harbor beyond. A trail winding up the side of **Mt. Oldfield,** east of town, yields an even wider vista. The trailhead is at **Oliver Lake Park,** about 6km from downtown on Hwy. 16. Contact the Visitors Center about $5 guided nature walks, May-Oct. The best time to visit Prince Rupert may be during **Seafest** (☎624-9118), an annual four-day event in early June. Surrounding towns celebrate with parades, bathtub races, and beer contests.

DAWSON CREEK   ☎250

Mile 0 of the Alaska Highway (a.k.a. the Alcan) is Dawson Creek, BC (not to be confused with Dawson City, YT, or *Dawson's Creek,* WB), first settled in 1890 as just another pipsqueak frontier village of a few hundred souls. Its later status as a railroad terminus made it a natural place to begin building the 2600km Alaska Hwy. Travelers cruising through Dawson Creek can't miss the **Mile 0 Cairn** and **Mile 0 Post,** both commemorating the birth of the Alaska Hwy., and both within a stone's throw of the Visitors Center. This town boomed during construction, literally. On February 13, 1943, 60 cases of exploding dynamite leveled the entire business district except the COOP building, now Bing's Furniture, opposite the Mile 0 post. In early August, the town plays host to the **Fall Fair & Stampede** (☎782-8911) with a carnival, fireworks, chuckwagon races, and a professional rodeo.

Those willing to rough it for bargain prices, great location, and an offbeat aura should head straight for the historic **Alaska Hotel ❸**, located above the Alaska Cafe & Pub (see **Food**, below) on 10th St., 1½ blocks from the Visitors Center. The comfortable rooms are carefully decorated, some with pictures of Marilyn Monroe and Elvis. (☎782-7998. Shared bath; no TV or phone. Singles $32; doubles $37; winter $5 less.) The newer **Voyageur Motor Inn ❸**, 801 111th Ave., facing 8th Ave., offers motoring voyagers phones, cable TV, and fridges at no extra charge in sterile boxy rooms. (☎782-1020. Singles $45; doubles $50.) The **Alaska Cafe & Pub ❷**, "55 paces south of the Mile 0 Post" on 10th St., serves excellent burgers and fries from $7. The pub offers live music nightly at 9pm (mostly country), and travelers can sing at Monday night karaoke amidst stuffed cougars, elk, and marmots. (☎782-7040. Kitchen open Su-Th 10am-10pm, F-Sa 11am-11pm; pub open daily noon-3am.) Eating too many sandwiches ($5.50) at **PotBelly Deli ❶**, 1128 102nd Ave., will give your tummy some chub too, but you won't regret it. Each night a new international cuisine inspires the chef. (☎782-5425. Open M-F 10am-7pm, Sa 10am-5pm.)

There are two ways to reach Dawson Creek from the south. From Alberta, drive northwest from Edmonton along **Hwy. 43,** through Whitecourt to Valleyview; turn left on **Hwy. 34** to Grande Prairie, and continue northwest on **Hwy. 2** to Dawson Creek for a total journey of 590km. From Prince George, drive 402km north on the John Hart section of **Hwy. 97** (see p. 1003). Both drives take the better part of a day. **Greyhound,** 1201 Alaska Ave. (☎782-3131 or 800-661-8747), runs to Edmonton (8hr., 2 per day, $78); Prince George (6½hr., 2 per day, $58); Whitehorse (20hr., June-Aug. M-Sa, $186). **Internet access: Public Library,** at 10 St. and McKellar Ave. (☎782-4661. Open Tu-Th 10am-9pm, F 10am-5:15pm, Sa-Su 1:30-5:15pm; in summer closed Su.) **Post Office:** 104th Ave. and 10th St. (☎782-9429. Open M-F 8:30am-5pm.) **Postal Code:** V1G 4E6. **Area code:** 250.

ALASKA APPROACHES

THE ALASKA HIGHWAY (HWY. 97)

Built during World War II in reaction to the Japanese bombing of Pearl Harbor and the capture of two Aleutian Islands, the Alaska Hwy. served to calm Alaskan fears of an Axis invasion. Due to the speed with which it was built, the highway stands as one of the most incredible engineering feats of the 20th century. Army troops and civilians pushed from both ends—Dawson Creek and Fairbanks—and bridged the 2451km at Mile 1202 (near Beaver Creek) in 8 months and 12 days.

While the original one lane dirt track has evolved into a "highway," the potholes that develop after the winter thaw and the patches of loose gravel give drivers a taste of the good old days. In recent years, the US Army has been replaced by an annual army of over 250,000 tourists and RV-borne senior citizens from the US and Europe. For those with the time to stop, there are countless opportunities to hike, fish, and view wildlife off the highway. If your priority is to beat the quickest path to the Yukon border, the **Cassiar Hwy.** (Hwy. 37) may be a better route for you. Another scenic option is on the far side of the Yukon border, on the **Campbell Hwy.** (Hwy. 4). **Road conditions:** ☎867-667-8215.

WESTERN CANADA

THE CASSIAR HIGHWAY (HWY. 37)

A growing number of travelers prefer the Cassiar Hwy. to the Alaska Hwy., which has become an RV institution. Built in 1972, the Cassiar slices through charred forests and snow-capped ebony peaks, passing scores of alpine lakes on its way from the Yellowhead Hwy. (Hwy. 16) in British Columbia to the Alaska Hwy. in the Yukon. Three evenly spaced provincial **campgrounds** right off the highway offer beautiful camping, and lodges in the provincial parks section in the middle provide resort-like accommodation at prices lower than highway motels on the Alaska Hwy. Any waiter or lodging owner along the Cassiar's 718km will readily list its advantages: less distance, consistently intriguing scenery, and fewer crowds. Be prepared, however, to sacrifice the frequent gas stations and hardtop pavement that come with popularity. Large sections of the road past Meziadin Junction are dirt and gravel and become slippery when wet, causing plenty of tire blowouts.

THE YUKON TERRITORY

The Yukon Territory lies at the end of a long drive along the Alaska Highway or the less-touristed Cassiar and Campbell Highways. Here the land rises into ranges that stretch for kilometers and sinks into lakes that snake toward the Arctic Ocean. The dry land's lonely beauty and its purple dusk are overwhelming.

🛈 PRACTICAL INFORMATION

Capital: Whitehorse.

Visitor Info: Tourism Yukon, P.O. Box 2703, Whitehorse Y1A 2C6 (☎867-667-5036; www.touryukon.com).

Police: ☎867-667-5555. *For emergencies outside Whitehorse, 911 may not work.*

Drinking Age: 19. **Postal Abbreviation:** YT. **Sales Tax:** 7% GST.

WHITEHORSE ☎867

Whitehorse was born during the Klondike Gold Rush, when the gold-hungry used it as a layover on their journey north. Miners en route to Dawson coined the name, claiming that whitecaps on the rapids downstream resembled galloping white stallions. With 24,000 people, Whitehorse is home to 70% of the territory's population. The most "urban" setting to be found in the Yukon, Whitehorse attracts outdoors lovers of all ages who take advantage of nearby rivers and trails.

🚌 TRANSPORTATION. Greyhound, 2191 2nd Ave. (☎667-2223), on the northeast edge of town, runs to Vancouver (41hr., $340) and Dawson Creek, BC (18hr., $187). Service is reduced from September to late June. **Alaska Direct** (☎668-4833 or 800-770-6652) runs to: Anchorage (15hr., 3 per week, US$165); Fairbanks (13hr., 3 per week, US$140); and Skagway (3hr., reservations only, US$50); in winter, one bus per week runs to the above destinations. **Whitehorse Transit's** local buses arrive and depart downtown on Ogilvie St. next to Canadian Tire. (☎668-7433. M-Th 6:15am-7:30pm, F 6:15am-10:30pm, Sa 8am-7pm. $1.50, seniors 75¢.)

🛈 PRACTICAL INFORMATION. Whitehorse is located 1500km north of Dawson Creek, BC, along the Alaska Highway and 535km south of Dawson City, YT. The **Visitors Center** is at 100 Hanson St., in the Tourism and Business Centre at 2nd Ave. (☎667-3084. Open mid-May to mid-Sept. daily 8am-8pm; mid-Sept. to mid-May M-F

9am-5pm.) The **Yukon Conservation Society**, 302 Hawkins St. (☎668-5678), offers maps and great ideas for area hikes. **Internet access: Public Library**, 2071 2nd Ave. (☎667-5239. Open M-F 10am-9pm, Sa 10am-6pm, Su 1-9pm. Free.) **Post Office:** 211 Main St. (☎667-2485. Open M-F 9am-6pm, Sa 11am-4pm). **General Delivery** is at 300 Range Rd. (☎667-2412). **Postal codes:** Y1A 3S7. **Area code:** 867.

⌐ ◖ ACCOMMODATIONS & FOOD. Interchangeable motels in town cost around $65. The **▓Hide on Jeckell Guesthouse ❷**, 410 Jeckell St., lurks between 4th Ave and 5th Ave., 1 block from Robert Service Way. Stay in the continent-themed room of your choice and pick your endangered species-labeled bed and fridge bin. Showers, coffee, kitchen, bikes, Internet access, local calls, linens, and lockers. (☎633-4933. Open year-round. $20.) **Robert Service Campground ❶**, 1km from town on South Access Rd. along the Yukon River, is a home-away-from-home for university students. (☎668-3721. Open late May to early Sept. Gates open 7am-midnight. Food trailer, firewood, playground, drinking water, toilets, showers. $14 per tent.) The 62km drive to the **Takhini Hot Springs ❶**, the Yukon's only hot springs, offers tenting plus thermal relief. Follow the Alaska Hwy. northwest from downtown, turn right onto the North Klondike Hwy., and then left to the end of Takhini Hot Springs Rd. (☎633-2706. Restaurant, showers, and laundry. $12.50, with electricity $15.) **▓Klondike Rib and Salmon Barbecue ❸**, 2116 2nd Ave., serves charred fresh salmon or halibut with homemade bread ($8) for lunch. (☎667-7554. Open mid-May to Sept. M-F 11:30am-2pm and 4-10pm, Sa-Su 5-10pm.) **▓The Talisman Cafe ❸**, 2112 2nd Ave., is elegantly decorated with local art and has the best vegetarian menu in town. (☎667-2736. Open daily 9am-8pm.)

◙ ◪ SIGHTS & OUTDOOR ACTIVITIES. The new **Yukon Beringia Interpretive Centre**, on the Alaska Hwy. 2km west of the junction with the S. Access Rd., pays homage to the forgotten continent that joined Siberia, Alaska, and the Yukon. (☎667-8855. Open mid-May to Sept. daily 8am-8pm; in winter Su 1-5pm. $6, seniors $5, children $4.) If you think you're a weary traveler, visit the **Whitehorse Fishway**, 2.4km from town, over the bridge by the S.S. Klondike, and meet the chinook salmon who swim 3000km upstream before reaching the fish ladder—designed to save them from death by dam. (☎633-5965. Open June W-Su 10am-6pm, July-Sept. daily 8:30am-9pm. Admission by donation. Wheelchair accessible.)

Grey Mountain, partly accessible by gravel road, is a somewhat rigorous day hike. Take Lewes Blvd. across the bridge by the **S.S. Klondike**, then take a left on Alsek Ave. Turn left again at the "Grey Mt. Cemetery" sign and follow the gravel road to its end. **Up North Boat and Canoe Rentals**, 86 Wickstrom Rd., lets you paddle 25km to Takhini River. (☎667-7905. 4hr. $30 includes transportation. Kayaks and canoes $25-30 per day. 8-day trip on the Teslin $200.) The **Kanoe People**, at Strickland and 1st Ave., rent outdoor gear. (☎668-4899. Open daily 9am-6pm. Mountain bikes $25 per day, canoes $25 per day, kayaks $35-45 per day. Credit card or deposit required.) The islands around **Sanfu Lake**, 1½hr. south of town on Atlin Rd., are snafu-free for kayaking.

Two Whitehorse festivals draw crowds from all over the world: the **Frostbite Music Festival** (☎668-4921) in February, and the **Yukon International Storytelling Festival** (☎633-7550) to be held May 30-June 2, 2003. The **Commissioner's Potlatch** gathers indigenous groups and visitors in June for traditional dancing, games, artistry, and a feast. Locals, transients, and native artists perform for free at noon weekdays with **Arts in Lepage Park.** (☎668-3136. At Wood St. and 3rd Ave. June to mid-Aug.) The **Yukon River** hosts the popular **Rubber Duckie Race** on Canada Day, July 1. (☎668-7979. $5 per duck. Proceeds go to charity.)

WESTERN CANADA

KLUANE NATIONAL PARK ☎ 867

The Southern Tutchone people named this area Kluane (*kloo-AH-nee*), meaning "place of many fish." They might also have mentioned that Kluane National Park is a place of many Dall sheep, eagles, glaciers, and untouched mountain landscapes. It contains Canada's highest peak, Mt. Logan (5959m), as well as the world's most massive non-polar ice fields. The ice-blanketed mountains of Kluane's interior are a haven for experienced expeditioners, but render two-thirds of the park inaccessible to humbler hikers. Fortunately, the northeast part of the park (bordering the Alaska Hwy.) offers splendid, easily accessible backpacking, canoeing, rafting, biking, fishing, and dayhiking.

⚹ PRACTICAL INFORMATION. Haines Junction, at the eastern park boundary, 158km west of Whitehorse, serves as park gateway and headquarters. **Alaska Direct** (☎668-4833 or 800-770-6652) runs from Haines Junction three times per week in the summer to Anchorage (13hr., US$145), Fairbanks (11hr., US$125), and Whitehorse (2hr., US$40). **Kluane National Park Visitor Reception Centre,** on Logan St. (Km 1635 on the Alaska Hwy.), provides wilderness permits ($5 per night, $50 per season), fishing permits ($5/35), maps ($11), and trail and weather info. (☎634-7207. Open May-Sept. daily 9am-7pm; Oct.-Apr. M-F 10am-noon and 1-5pm.) **Sheep Mountain Info Centre,** 72km north of town at Alaska Hwy. Km 1707, registers hikers headed into the park. **Emergency,** call ☎634-5555 or the **ambulance/clinic** at ☎634-4444. **Post Office:** on Haines Junction. (☎634-3802. Open M-F 10am-noon and 1-5pm.) **Postal code:** Y0B 1L0. **Area code:** 867.

⚹ ACCOMMODATIONS & FOOD. Camping by a gorgeous lake beats staying at a clean-but-forgettable highway motel or RV park any day. The idyllic **Kathleen Lake Campground ❶,** off Haines Rd. 27km south of Haines Junction, is close to hiking and fishing. (Open mid-May to mid-Sept. Toilets, fire pits, and firewood. Sites $10. Wheelchair accessible.) Popular **Pine Lake ❶,** 7km east of town, features a sandy beach. (Water, pit toilets. $8 with Yukon camping permit only.) For those who prefer a motel, the **Stardust Motel ❸,** 1km north of town on the Alaska Hwy., has spacious rooms with TVs and tubs but no phones. (☎634-2591. Shared bath. Singles $55; doubles $65.) Most Haines Junction restaurants offer standard highway cuisine, but the 🔳**Village Bakery ❷** breaks the trend, offering veggie dishes, beefy sandwiches, and tray upon tray of fudge and sweets. Substantial soups with bread ($3.50), sourdough cheese dogs ($2.25), sushi (F only; $4.50 for 5 pieces), and espresso fudge ($1.75). Make reservations to enjoy live music and salmon BBQs ($13.50) on Monday nights. (☎634-2867. Open May-Sept. daily 7am-9pm.)

⚹ OUTDOOR ACTIVITIES. A $1 pamphlet lists about 25 trails and routes ranging from 500m to 96km. Overnight visitors must register at one of the Visitors Centers ($5 per night, ages 5-16 $2.50), and use bear-resistant food canisters, which the park rents for $5 per night. The **Dezadeash River Loop** trailhead is downtown at the day-use area across from Madley's on Haines Rd. This flat, forested 5km trail makes for a nice stroll. The more challenging 15km **Auriol Loop** has a primitive campground halfway along. The trail begins 7km south of Haines Junction on Haines Rd. and cuts through boreal forest, leading to a subalpine bench (elevation gain 400m) just in front of the Auriol Range. This is a popular overnight trip, although 4-6hr. is adequate time without heavy packs. The 5km **King's Throne Rte.** is a very challenging but rewarding day hike with a 1220m elevation gain and a panoramic view. It begins at the **Kathleen Lake** day-use area at the campground.

Excellent hiking awaits near **Sheep Mountain** in the park's northern section. An easy 500m jaunt up to **Soldier's Summit** starts 1km north of the Sheep Mountain Visitors Center. The **Sheep Creek** trail, down a short gravel access road just north of the Visitors Center, is a satisfying day hike up Sheep Mountain, and one of the better bets to see Dall sheep in summer (10km roundtrip, 3-6hr., 430m elevation gain). Only experienced backpackers should attempt the trek along the **Slims River** to the magnificent **Kaskawulsh Glacier.** Two rough routes along either bank of the river are available and require three to five days to complete. One stretches 23km with an elevation gain of 910m; the other is 30km and has an elevation gain of 1340m.

The **Alsek River Valley Trail,** starting from Alcan Km 1645 and following a bumpy old mining road 14km to Sugden Creek, makes for good mountain biking. **Paddle-Wheel Adventures,** down the road from the Village Bakery in Haines Junction, arranges flightseeing over the glaciers and full-day rafting trips on the Class III and IV rapids of the **Blanchard** and **Tatshenshini Rivers.** (☎ 634-2683. $95 per person for a 30min. flight over the Kaskawulsh. Rafting $100 per person, including lunch.)

THE DEMPSTER HIGHWAY

Like no other highway in North America, the Dempster presents drivers with naked wilderness, unmolested by logging scars or advertisements. The challenge of battling the road and taking in the divine landscape makes driving the Dempster a religious experience: those who brave it across the Arctic Circle and the Continental Divide stare into the geological beginnings of the continent—and earn the right to scratch, "I did it!" in the dust coating their car. The road is not to be taken lightly. The Dempster's dirt and gravel are notorious for eating tires and cracking windshields. Parts of it are in good condition, while other sections take on the appearance of a dry river bed. While the speed limit is posted at 90kmph, the rough road will punish you for going above 50-60kmph. Services are limited to Klondike River Lodge (Km 0), Eagle Plains (Km 369), Fort McPherson (Km 550), and Inuvik (Km 734). Although a trip to Tombstone makes a pleasant overnight, the full drive takes at least 12hr. (two days each way to be fully and safely appreciated). The weather is erratic. Quick rainstorms or high winds can make portions of the route impassable (watch for flashing red lights that denote closed roads) and disrupt ferry service to Inuvik for as long as two weeks, leaving travelers stranded.

Road and Ferry Report (☎ 800-661-0752, in Inuvik 777-2678) provides up-to-date road info. The **NWT Visitor Centre** in Dawson City has free regional brochures, maps, and reports from recent drivers. A full tank of gas, dependable tires (6-ply or better), a good spare or three, extra oil and coolant, and emergency supplies (food, water, clothes, a first aid kit, and a can of gas) are necessary Dempster companions. The **Klondike River Lodge** (☎ 993-6892; open daily 7am-10:30pm, garage services limited to tire repair on Su) has full services and will rent you a gas can for $5 with a $15 deposit. If camping, bring powerful bug repellent—even 100% DEET won't thwart every skeeter bite—and some form of netting. If you lack wheels or doubt yours will survive the trip, **Dawson City Courier** (☎ 993-6688) drives up Mondays and Fridays and returns Wednesdays and Sundays for $230 each way.

ALBERTA

With its gaping prairie, oil-fired economy, and conservative politics, Alberta is the Texas of Canada. Petrol dollars have given birth to gleaming, modern cities on the plains, while the natural landscape swings from the mighty Canadian Rockies down to beautifully desolate badlands. For adventurous outdoor enthusiasts, Alberta is a year-round playground.

WESTERN CANADA

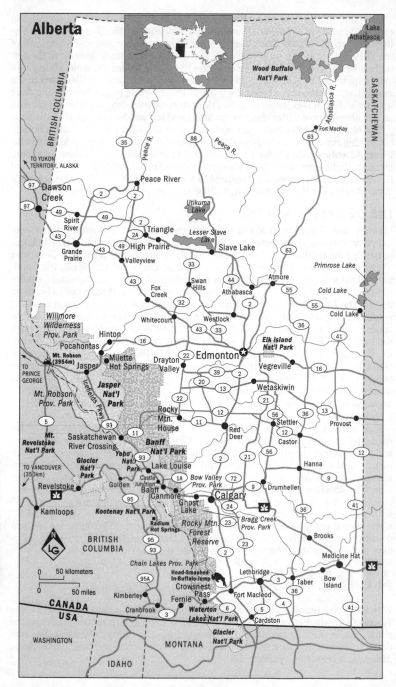

Alberta

Lake Athabasca

BRITISH COLUMBIA

SASKATCHEWAN

Wood Buffalo Nat'l Park

Athabasca R.

35

88

Peace R.

Peace R.

63

Fort MacKay

TO YUKON TERRITORY, ALASKA

97

Dawson Creek

2

Peace River

97

49

Spirit River

49

2

Triangle

Utikuma Lake

43

49

2A

High Prairie

Lesser Slave Lake

Slave Lake

63

Grande Prairie

43

49

Valleyview

33

Primrose Lake

43

Fox Creek

32

Swan Hills

44

Athabasca

2

Atmore

55

Cold Lake

Willmore Wilderness Prov. Park

Hinton

16

Whitecourt

43

33

Westlock

36

55

Cold Lake

41

Pocahontas

Milette Hot Springs

Drayton Valley

22

Edmonton

Elk Island Nat'l Park

Mt. Robson (3954m)

Jasper

TO PRINCE GEORGE

Mt. Robson Prov. Park

Jasper Nat'l Park

39

2

Vegreville

16

20

13

Wetaskiwin

5

Icefields Pkwy.

22

12

21

56

36

13

Provost

Saskatchewan River Crossing

93

11

Rocky Mtn. House

11

Red Deer

Stettler

Mt. Revelstoke Nat'l Park

Yoho Nat'l Park

93

Banff Nat'l Park

2

21

56

12

Castor

12

TO VANCOUVER (350km)

Glacier Nat'l Park

Lake Louise

Bow Valley Prov. Park

72

Hanna

9

Revelstoke

Castle Junction

1A

Calgary

Drumheller

41

Kamloops

95

Banff

Canmore

Ghost Lake

24

9

36

Kootenay Nat'l Park

Radium Hot Springs

23

Bragg Creek Prov. Park

Brooks

BRITISH COLUMBIA

Rocky Mtn. Forest Reserve

23

Medicine Hat

95

93

2

N

LG

0   50 kilometers

0   50 miles

Chain Lakes Prov. Park

Lethbridge

41

Head-Smashed-In-Buffalo-Jump

95A

Crowsnest Pass

3

Taber

Bow Island

Kimberley

Fernie

Fort Macleod

4

CANADA
USA

Cranbrook

3

Waterton Lakes Nat'l Park

6

Cardston

41

WASHINGTON

MONTANA

Glacier Nat'l Park

IDAHO

◪ PRACTICAL INFORMATION

Capital: Edmonton.

Visitor info: Travel Alberta, Commerce Pl., 10155 102 St., 3rd fl., Edmonton T5J 4G8 (☎780-427-4321 or 800-661-8888; www.discoveralberta.com). **Parks Canada,** 220 4th Ave. SE, #552, Calgary T2G 4X3 (☎403-292-4401 or 800-748-7275).

Drinking Age: 18. **Postal Abbreviation:** AB. **Sales Tax:** 7% GST.

THE ROCKIES

Every year, some five million visitors make it within sight of the Rockies' majestic peaks and stunning glacial lakes. Thankfully, much of this traffic is confined to highwayside gawkers, and only a tiny fraction of these visitors make it far into the forest. Of the big two national parks—Banff and Jasper—Jasper feels a little further removed from the crowds and offers great wildlife viewing from the road. Without a car, guided bus rides may be the easiest way to see some of the park's main attractions. **Brewster Tours** buses from Banff to Jasper. (☎403-762-6767. 9½hr.; $95.) **Bigfoot Tours** does the trip in two days. (☎888-244-6673 or 604-278-8224. $95.)

BANFF NATIONAL PARK & LAKE LOUISE ☎403

Banff is Canada's best-loved and best-known natural park, with 6641 square kilometers of peaks, forests, glaciers, and alpine valleys. Even streets littered with gift shops, clothing shops, and chocolatiers cannot mar Banff's beauty. Itinerant twenty-somethings arrive with mountain bikes, climbing gear, and skis, but a trusty pair of hiking boots remains the park's most popular outdoor equipment.

◪◪ ORIENTATION & PRACTICAL INFORMATION. The park hugs Alberta's border with BC, 129km west of Calgary. Civilization in the park centers around the towns of **Banff** and **Lake Louise,** 58km apart on Hwy. 1. All of the following info applies to Banff Townsite, unless otherwise specified. **Greyhound,** 106 Railway Ave. (☎800-661-8747; depot open daily 7:30am-9pm), runs to: Lake Louise (1hr., 4 per day, $12); Calgary (1½hr., 5 per day, $22); and Vancouver, BC (14hr., 4 per day, $105). **Brewster Transportation,** 100 Gopher St. (☎762-6767), runs buses to: Calgary (2hr., $40); Jasper (5hr., $51); and Lake Louise (1hr., $12). The **Banff Visitor Centre,** 224 Banff Ave., includes the **Banff/Lake Louise Tourism Bureau** and the **Canadian Parks Service.** (Tourism Bureau: ☎762-8421. Parks Service: ☎762-1550. Open June-Sept. daily 8am-8pm; Oct.-May 9am-5pm.) **Lake Louise Visitor Centre,** at Samson Mall in Lake Louise, shares a building with a museum. (☎522-3833. Open July-Aug. daily 8am-8pm; June and Sept. 8am-6pm; Oct.-May 9am-5pm.) **Post Office:** 204 Buffalo St. (☎762-2586. Open M-F 9am-5:30pm.) **Postal code:** T0L 0C0. **Area code:** 403.

◪◪ ACCOMMODATIONS & FOOD. HI runs a **shuttle service** connecting all the Rocky Mountain hostels and Calgary ($8-90). Beds on the wait-list become available at 6pm, and the larger hostels save some standby beds for shuttle arrivals. **☒Lake Louise International Hostel (HI-C) ❶,** 500m west of the Visitors Center in Lake Louise Townsite, on Village Rd., is more like a hotel than a hostel, with a reference library, common rooms with open, beamed ceilings, a stone fireplace, two full kitchens, ski/bike workshops, and a cafe. (☎522-2200. Dorms $26, nonmembers $30. Private rooms available. Wheelchair accessible.) **Castle Mountain Hostel (HI-C) ❶,** on Hwy. 1A, 1.5km east of the junction of Hwy. 1 and Hwy. 93, between Banff and Lake Louise. A quieter alternative, with running water, electricity, a general

FLOUR POWER Passing by the many lakes and streams in the Rockies, you may notice they have an unusual color. Looking at the swimming-pool turquoise or glowing blue color of these bodies of water, you might wonder if this is some kind of gimmick perpetuated by park wardens to bring in tourists. In fact, one visitor to Lake Louise claimed that he had solved the mystery and that the beautiful water had obviously been distilled from peacock tails. Actually, the cause of the color is **rock flour.** This fine dust is created by the pressure exerted by the glacier upon rocks trapped within the ice; the resulting ground-up rock is washed into streams and lakes in the glacial meltwater. Suspended particles trap all colors of the spectrum except for the blues and greens that are reflected back for your visual pleasure.

store, a library, and a fireplace. (☎521-8421 or 866-762-4122. Linen $1. Dorms $18, nonmembers $22). Three other rustic hostels—**Hilda Creek ❶, Rampart Creek ❶,** and **Mosquito Creek ❶**—can be booked by calling Banff International Hostel. At any of Banff's nine park **campgrounds,** sites are first come, first served ($10-24). On Hwy. 1A between Banff Townsite and Lake Louise, **Johnston Canyon ❶** and **Castle Mountain ❶** are close to hiking. The only campsite open in winter is Village 2 of **Tunnel Mountain Village ❶,** 4km from Banff Townsite, on Tunnel Mountain Rd.

The Banff and Lake Louise Hostels serve affordable meals ($3-8), but **Laggan's Deli ❶** (☎522-2017), in Samson Mall in Lake Louise, is the best thing going. A thick sandwich on whole wheat costs $4-5; a fresh-baked loaf to save for later runs $3. **Aardvark's ❸,** 304A Caribou St., does big business after the bars close. The place is skinny on seating but serves thick slices of pizza. (☎762-5500. Open daily 11am-4am. Slices $3; small pizza $6-9, large $13-21.)

🏔 OUTDOOR ACTIVITIES. Near Banff Townsite, **Fenland Trail** (2km, 1hr.) zooms through an area shared by beaver, muskrat, and waterfowl, but is closed for elk calving in late spring and early summer. Follow Mt. Norquay Rd. out of town and look for signs across the tracks on the road's left side. The summit of **Tunnel Mountain** (2.3km, 2hr.) provides a dramatic view of the **Bow Valley** and **Mt. Rundle.** Follow Wolf St. east from Banff Ave. and turn right on St. Julien Rd. to reach the head of the steep trail. At 2949m, Mt. Rundle offers a more demanding day hike (5.5km; 7-8hr.; 1600m elevation gain). **Johnston Canyon,** about 25km from Banff toward Lake Louise along the Bow Valley Pkwy. (Hwy. 1A), is a popular half-day hike that runs past waterfalls to blue-green cold-water springs known as the **Inkpots.**

The park might not exist if not for the **Cave and Basin Hot Springs,** southwest of town on Cave Ave., once rumored to have miraculous healing properties. The **Cave and Basin National Historic Site,** a refurbished resort built circa 1914, is now a museum. (☎762-1566. Open in summer daily 9am-6pm; in winter 9:30am-5pm. Tours 11am. $2.50, seniors $2, children $1.50.) For a dip in the hot water, follow the rotten-egg smell to the 40°C (104°F) springs.

The highest community in Canada, at 1530m (5018 ft.), Lake Louise and its surrounding glaciers have often passed for Swiss scenery in movies. Once at the lake, the hardest task is escaping fellow gawkers at the posh **Château Lake Louise.** Several hiking trails begin at the water; the 3.6km **Lake Agnes Trail** and the 5.5km **Plain of Six Glaciers Trail** both end at teahouses.

Fishing is legal in most of the park's bodies of water during specific seasons, but live bait and lead weights are not. Permits ($6) are available at the Visitors Center. Winter activities in the park range from world-class ice climbing to ice fishing. Those 1600km of hiking trails make for exceptional **cross-country skiing,** and three allied resorts offer a range of **skiing** and **snowboarding** opportunities from early November to mid-May. **Sunshine Mountain** has the largest snowfall (☎762-6500, snow report 760-7669; lift tickets $56); **Mt. Norquay** is smaller, closer to town, and less busy (☎762-4421; $47); but **Lake Louise**, the second-biggest ski area in Canada, has the most expert terrain (☎522-3555, snow report 762-4766; $54).

SCENIC DRIVE: ICEFIELDS PARKWAY

The 230km Icefields Parkway is one of the most beautiful routes in North America, heading north from Lake Louise to Jasper Townsite. Free maps of the Parkway are available at Visitors Centers in Jasper and Banff, or at the **Icefield Centre**, at the boundary between the two parks, 132km north of Lake Louise and 103km south of Jasper Townsite. (☎780-852-6288. Open May to mid-Oct. daily 9am-5pm.) Although the center is closed in winter, the parkway is only closed for plowing after heavy snowfalls. An extensive campground and hostel network along the Parkway makes longer trips convenient and affordable. **Cycling** the highway is also a popular option; bikes can be rented in Banff or Jasper for a one-way trip.

However you travel the Parkway, set aside time for hikes and magnificent vistas. At **Bow Summit**, the Parkway's highest point (2135m), a 10min. walk leads to a view of fluorescent aqua **Peyto Lake**, especially vivid toward the end of June. The **Athabasca Glacier,** a great white whale of an ice flow, spreads from the 325 sq. km **Columbia Icefield,** the largest accumulation of ice and snow south between the Arctic and Antarctic Circles. **Columbia Icefield Snocoach Tours** carries visitors right onto the glacier in bizarre monster buses for an 80min. trip. (☎877-423-7433. Open Apr.-Oct. daily 9am-5pm. $28, ages 6-15 $14.)

JASPER NATIONAL PARK ☎780

Northward expansion of the Canadian railway system led to the exploration of the Canadian Rockies and the creation of Jasper National Park in 1907. The largest of the four national parks in the region, Jasper encompasses herculean peaks and plummeting valleys that dwarf the battalion of motorhomes and charter buses parading through the region. In the winter, the crowds melt away, a blanket of snow descends, and a ski resort welcomes visitors to a slower, more relaxed town.

🔌 PRACTICAL INFORMATION. All of the addresses below are in **Jasper Townsite,** near the center of the park. **VIA Rail** (☎800-561-8630), on Connaught Dr., sends three trains per week to Edmonton (5hr., $142) and Vancouver (16½hr., $198). **Greyhound** (☎852-3332), in the train station, runs to Edmonton (4½hr., 3 per day, $54) and Vancouver (11½hr., 2 per day, $106). **Brewster Transportation Tours** (☎852-3332), in the station, runs daily to Calgary (7½hr., $75) via Banff (5½hr., $54). The **Park Information Centre,** 500 Connaught Dr., has trail maps. (☎852-6176. Open mid-June to early Sept. daily 8am-7pm; early Sept.-late Oct. and late Dec. to mid-June 9am-5pm.) In an **emergency,** call ☎911 or 852-4421. **Post Office:** 502 Patricia St. (☎852-3041. Open M-F 9am-5pm.) **Postal code:** T0E 1E0. **Area code:** 780.

🛏 ACCOMMODATIONS. HI runs a shuttle service connecting all the Rocky Mountain hostels and Calgary; call the Jasper Hostel for reservations. The modern **Jasper International Hostel (HI-C) ❶,** 3km up Whistlers Rd. from Hwy. 93, also known as **Whistlers Hostel,** anchors the chain of HI hostels stretching from Jasper to Calgary. Jasper International attracts gregarious backpackers and cyclists, but a "leave-your-hiking-boots-outside" rule keeps the hardwood floors and dorm rooms clean. (☎852-3215 or 877-852-0781 for all HI hostels. Curfew 2am. Dorms $18.) **Maligne Canyon Hostel (HI-C) ❶,** 11km east of town on Hwy. 16, has small cabins on the bank of the Maligne River. (Check-in 5-11pm. Oct.-Apr. $13, nonmembers $18.) **Mt. Edith Cavell Hostel (HI-C) ❶,** 12km up Edith Cavell Rd., off Hwy. 93, offers small, cozy quarters heated by wood-burning stoves. In winter, the road is

IN RECENT NEWS

THE BUSK STOPS HERE

Being a good citizen in Calgary doesn't mean giving the corner guitarist a dollar—it means turning him in to the police. **Busking,** or giving street performances, is illegal and has been since the government tightened its policy on performers in 2002. The move was innocently designed to ease major congestion problems on the city's byways, but it has infuriated supporters of Calgary's open music scene. The government responded by designating "Busk Stops," spots performers can sign up for in advance, which has eased the tension somewhat. Still, police maintain a zero-tolerance policy toward buskers who are caught anywhere that is not the south side of Olympic Plaza or the Eau Claire Market Amphitheater.

People on both sides of the issue claim that the system is imperfect and will require additional modifications. The city makes references to opening more Busk Stops, but where and when they'll do it is not entirely clear—the future of public music in Calgary hangs in the balance. For now, most of the streets of downtown Calgary lack music and life beyond the drone of the passing cars.

closed, but you can pick up keys at Jasper International Hostel and ski uphill from the highway. (Propane, pump water, solar shower, firepit. $13, nonmembers $18.)

Most of Jasper's campgrounds have primitive sites with few facilities ($13-22). They are first come, first served, and none are open in winter. Call the park Visitors Center (☎ 852-6176) for details. A 781-site behemoth, **Whistlers ❶**, on Whistlers Rd., off Hwy. 93, is closest to the townsite. (Open early May to mid-Oct. $15, full hookup $24.) The highlight of the Icefields Pkwy. campgrounds is **Columbia Icefield ❶**, 109km south of the townsite, which lies close enough to the Athabasca Glacier to intercept an icy breeze and even a rare summer night's snowfall. **Mountain Foods and Cafe ❷**, 606 Connaught Dr., offers a wide selection of sandwiches, salads, home-cooked goodies, and take-out lunches for the trail. Turkey focaccia sandwich and assorted wraps are $7.50, and a fantastic breakfast special is $5.50. (☎ 852-4050. Open daily 8am-6pm.)

⚡ OUTDOOR ACTIVITIES. The Visitors Center distributes *Day Hikes in Jasper National Park*. **Cavell Meadows Loop**, which features views of the glacier-laden peak of **Mt. Edith Cavell**, is a rewarding half-day hike. The trailhead is 30km south of the townsite; take Hwy. 93 to 93A to the end of the bumpy 15km Mt. Edith Cavell Rd. (Open June-Oct.) To scale a peak in a day, climb the **Sulpher Skyline Trail**, a challenging 4-6hr. hike with views of the limestone Miette Range and Ashlar Ridge (9.6km round-trip, 700m elevation gain). The trail leaves from the **Miette Hot Springs**, 42km north of the townsite on Hwy. 16, blending chlorinated and filtered heat therapy with panoramic views. (☎ 866-3939. Open July-Aug. 8:30am-10:30pm; late May-June and Sept.-early Oct. daily 10:30am-9pm. $6; swimsuit $1.50.)

The spectacular, if overcrowded, **Maligne Canyon** is 11km east of the townsite on Maligne Lake Rd. From the trailhead, a 4km path follows the Maligne River as it plunges through the narrow limestone gorge, across footbridges, and eventually into Medicine Lake. Brilliant turquoise **Maligne Lake,** the longest (22km) and deepest lake in the park, sprawls at the end of Maligne Lake Rd. The **Opal Hills Trail** (8.2km loop) winds through subalpine meadows and ascends 460m to views of the lake. **Maligne Tours,** 626 Connaught Dr., rents kayaks and leads fishing, canoeing, rabbiting, horseback riding, hiking, and whitewater rafting tours. (☎ 852-3370. Kayaks $70 per day.) **Rocky Mountain Unlimited** serves as a central reservation service for many local outdoor businesses. They provide prices and recommendations for rafting, fishing, horseback riding, and wildlife safaris. (☎852-4056. Open daily 9am-9pm; in winter 8am-6pm.) **Fishing permits** are available at fishing shops and the Parks Canada Visitors Center ($6 per week, $13 per year).

The **Jasper Tramway,** 4km up Whistlers Rd., climbs 1200m up Whistlers Mt., leading to a panoramic view of the park and, on a clear day, very far beyond. (☎852-3093. Open Apr.-Aug. daily 8:30am-10pm; Sept.-Oct. 9:30am-4:30pm. $19, under 14 $9.50, under 5 free.) The demanding 9km **Whistlers Trail** covers the same ground, beginning behind Jasper International's volleyball court.

CALGARY   ☎403

Mounties founded Calgary in the 1870s to control the flow of illegal whiskey, but another liquid made this city great: oil. Petroleum fuels Calgary's economy; as the city holds more corporate headquarters than any other city in Canada except Toronto. Calgary's dot on the map grew larger when it hosted the 1988 Winter Olympics; it is now Canada's second-fastest-growing city. The Calgary Stampede, the "Greatest Outdoor Show on Earth," garbs the city in cowboy duds every July.

▆▐ ORIENTATION & PRACTICAL INFORMATION. Calgary is divided into quadrants; **Centre St.** is the east-west divider, while the **Bow River** splits the north and south sections. **Avenues** run east-west, **streets** run north-south, and numbers count up from the divides. **Calgary International Airport** is about 17km northeast of the city center. **Greyhound,** 877 Greyhound Way SW (☎265-9111 or 800-661-8747), runs to: Banff (1¾hr., 4 per day, $22); Drumheller (1¾hr., 2 per day, $24); and Edmonton (3½hr., 8 per day, $43). **Brewster Tours** (☎221-8242) runs from the airport or downtown to Banff (2½hr., 4 per day, $40) and Jasper (8hr., 1 per day, $75) and offers a 10% HI discount. **Calgary Transit,** 240 7th Ave. SW, runs **C-Trains,** which are free in the downtown zone. (☎262-1000. M-F 6am-11pm, Sa-Su 6am-9:30pm. Bus fare and C-Trains outside downtown $1.75, ages 6-14 $1.10; day pass $5/3; 10 tickets $14.50/9.) **Post Office:** 207 9th Ave. SW. (☎974-2078. Open M-F 8am-5:45pm.) **Postal code:** T2P 2G8. **Area code:** 403.

▐▐ ACCOMMODATIONS & FOOD. The **Calgary International Hostel (HI-C) ❶,** 520 7th Ave. SE, is near downtown. Go east along 7th Ave. from the 3rd St. SE C-Train station; this welcoming urban hostel is on the left just past 4th St. SE. (☎269-8239. Open 24hr. Kitchen, game room, laundry, Internet access, and barbecue facilities. Linen $1. $16, nonmembers $20.) **University of Calgary ❶,** in the NW quadrant, has rooms booked through **Kananaskis Hall,** 3330 24th Ave., a 12min. walk from the University C-Train stop. (☎220-3203. Rooms available May-Aug. Shared rooms $21; singles $34, students $28; doubles $39/32. Suites with private bathrooms about $35.)

The cheapest, most satisfying food is located in Calgary's tiny Chinatown, the two square blocks at the north end of Centre St. S and 1st St. SE. Five dollars buys a feast in Vietnamese noodle-houses and Hong Kong-style cafes, many of which don't close until 3 or 4am. At ▓**Thi-Thi Submarine ❶,** 209 1st St. SE, $2.50 will buy a 10 in. "super-sub" with pork, chicken, cilantro, carrots, cucumbers, and special sauce, served hot on a fresh baguette. (☎265-5452. Open daily 10am-7pm.) **Take Ten Cafe ❷,** 304 10th St. NE, attracts clientele not for panache, but for good cuisine. All burgers are under $5.75. (☎270-7010. Open Tu-Sa 9am-6pm, Su 9am-3pm.)

◧▨ SIGHTS & NIGHTLIFE. Over a decade later, Calgary still clings to its two weeks of Olympic stardom at the **Canada Olympic Park,** 10min. west of downtown on Hwy. 1, site of the four looming ski jumps and the bobsled and luge tracks. (☎247-5452. Open daily 8am-9pm.) The **Olympic Hall of Fame,** 88 Canada Olympic Rd. SW, honors Olympic achievements with displays, films, and bobsled and ski-jumping simulators. In summer, the park opens its hills to mountain bikers. (☎247-5452. Open daily 9am-9pm. $7 includes chair lift and entrance to ski jump buildings, Hall of Fame, and icehouse. Guided tour $10, families $35. Mountain biking May-Oct. daily 10am-9pm. Hill pass $7 for cyclists. Bike rental $12 per hr., $31 per day.)

Footbridges stretch from either side of the Bow River to **Prince's Island Park,** a natural refuge near the city center. Calgary's other island park, **St. George's Island,** is accessible by the river walkway to the east and houses the **Calgary Zoo.** (☎232-9300. Parking off Memorial Dr. on the north side of the river. Open daily 9am-9pm. $12, seniors and under 17 $6; reduced winter rates. 20% AAA and 10% HI discounts.) During the first couple weekends in July, 1 million cowboys and tourists will converge on **Stampede Park,** just southeast of downtown, bordering the east side of Macleod Trail between 14th Ave. SE and the Elbow River. For ten days, the grounds are packed for the **Calgary Stampede,** with world-class steer wrestling, bareback- and bull-riding, pig racing, wild-cow-milking, and chuckwagon races. (☎269-9822 or 800-661-1767; www.calgarystampede.com. Take C-Train to the Stampede. $10, seniors and ages 7-12 $5. Rodeo and evening cost $21-55; rush tickets, when available, are $10 at the grandstand 1½hr. before showtime.)

Nightclubs in Alberta only became legal in 1990, and Calgary is making up for lost time. The best areas in town for finding pubs, clubs, and live music are the Stephen Ave. Walk (8th Ave. SW), 17th Ave. SW, and 1st and 4th St. SW. ◪**The Nightgallery Cabaret,** 1209B 1st St. SW, attracts clubbers with one large dance floor, one bar, and one diverse program. The club breaks out the best house in town at "Sunday School" and on Thursday. Reggae-Dub draws a slightly older crowd Monday. (☎269-5924. Cover $5, $1.50 highballs before 11pm. Open daily 8pm-3am.) **The Vicious Circle,** 1011 1st St. SW, draws crowds with a solid menu and keeps them happy with a selection of 140 martinis. (☎269-3951. Open daily 11am-2am.)

ALBERTA BADLANDS

In the late Cretaceous period, these were the fertile shores of an inland sea, conditions that have created one of the richest dinosaur fossil sites in the world. Once the sea dried up, wind, water, and ice cut twisting canyons down into the sandstone and shale bedrock, creating the desolate splendor of the Alberta Badlands. The ◪**Royal Tyrrell Museum of Paleontology** lies on the North Dinosaur Trail (Secondary Hwy. 838), 6km northwest of Drumheller. The museum has the world's largest display of dinosaur specimens. (☎403-823-7707 or 888-440-4240. Open late May-early Sept. daily 9am-9pm; mid-Sept. to mid-May Tu-Su 10am-5pm. $10, seniors $8, ages 7-17 $6, families $30.) The museum's popular 12-person **Day Digs** include instruction in excavation techniques and a chance to dig in a dinosaur quarry. The fee includes lunch and transportation, but all finds go to the museum. (July-Aug. daily 8:30am, returning at 4:30pm. $90, ages 10-15 $60. Reservations required.)

WESTERN CANADA

ALASKA

Alaska's beauty and intrigue are born of extremes: North America's highest mountains and broadest flatlands, windswept tundra and lush rainforests, and 15 incredible national parks cover an area roughly equal to that of England and Ireland combined. Russia, disillusioned with Alaska's dwindling fur trade, sold the region to the US for a piddling 2¢ per acre in 1867. Critics mocked "Seward's Folly," named after the Secretary of State who negotiated the deal, but just 15 years after the purchase, huge deposits of gold were unearthed in the Gastineau Channel.

Many say the Klondike gold rush of 1898 was only the first in a string, from the "liquid gold" of the oil pipeline boom to the "ocean gold" pulled up in the form of king crab pots in the Bering Sea. Boom and bust has always been the name of the game, but the one thing that has remained constant is Alaska's overwhelming scale. From the 850-square-mile Malaspina Glacier to the 2000-mile Yukon River to the 20,320-foot Denali, Alaska is a land where everything is bigger, tougher, and more exciting. For more on Alaska and its wonders, check out 🔖 *Let's Go: Alaska & the Pacific Northwest 2003*.

Alaska

HIGHLIGHTS OF ALASKA

NATURAL WONDERS. Denali National Park (p. 1020) is the state's crown jewel. Wrangell-St. Elias National Park (p. 1020) houses massive glaciers, while Glacier Bay National Park (p. 1027) basks in a symphony of sea and ice.

WILDLIFE. Cruises out of Seward into Kenai Fjords National Park (p. 1019) are stuffed with opportunities to view sea critters.

RECREATION. Southeast Alaska's grandest features include kayaking in Misty Fjords National Monument (p. 1026), climbing Deer Mountain in Ketchikan (p. 1024), and hiking the West Glacier Trail in Juneau (p. 1027).

🔃 PRACTICAL INFORMATION

Capital: Juneau. **Biggest City:** Anchorage. **Biggest Party City:** Ketchikan.

Visitor Info: Alaska Division of Tourism, P.O. Box 110809, Juneau 99811 (☎907-465-2012; www.dced.state.ak.us/tourism). **Alaska Department of Fish & Game,** P.O. Box 25526 Juneau 99802 (☎907-465-4190; www.state.ak.us/adfg/adfghome.htm).

Postal Abbreviation: AK. **Sales Tax:** 0%.

✖ TRANSPORTATION

The **Alaska Railroad Corporation (ARRC)** (☎800-544-0552) covers 470 mi. from Seward to Fairbanks, with stops in Anchorage and Whittier. The **Alaska Marine Hwy.** (☎800-642-0066) remains the most practical and enjoyable way to explore much of the Panhandle, Prince William Sound, and the Kenai Peninsula. Most of the state's major **highways** are known by their name as often as their number (e.g., George Parks Hwy. is the same as Rte. 3, which is the same as The Parks). Highways reward drivers with stunning views and access to true wilderness, but they barely scratch the surface of the massive state. (See p. 1003 for the two major highway approaches into the state from points south.) For Alaska's most remote destinations, **air travel** is an expensive necessity. Intrastate airlines and charter services, many of them based at the busy Anchorage airport, transport passengers and cargo to virtually every village in Alaska.

ANCHORAGE ☎907

Alaska's primary metropolis, Anchorage is home to 254,000 people—two-fifths of the state's population. As far north as Helsinki and almost as far west as Honolulu, the city achieved its large size (2000 square miles) by hosting three major economic projects: the Alaska Railroad, WWII military developments, and the Trans-Alaska Pipeline. Anchorage serves as a good place to get oriented and stock up on supplies before journeying into the breathtaking wilderness outside.

📧 **TRANSPORTATION.** Most Alaskan airstrips can be reached from **Anchorage International Airport** (☎266-2437) either directly or through a connection in Fairbanks. **Alaska Railroad,** 411 W. 1st Ave. (☎265-2494 or 800-544-0552; ticket window open M-F 5:30am-5pm, Sa-Su 5:30am-1pm), runs to: Denali (8hr., $125); Fairbanks (12hr., $175); and Seward (4hr., in summer only, $90). Flagstops are anywhere along the route; wave the train down with a white cloth. **Grayline Alaska** (☎800-544-2206) sends buses daily to Valdez (10hr., $71) and twice per week to Skagway ($219, overnight). **Alaska Marine Hwy.,** 605 W. 4th Ave., sells ferry tickets. (☎800-

642-0066. Open daily 7:30am-4:30pm; in winter M-F.) **People Mover Bus,** in the Transit Center on 6th Ave. between G and H St., sends local buses all over the Anchorage area. (☎343-6543. Runs M-F 6am-10pm; restricted schedule Sa-Su. $1, over 65 25¢, ages 5-18 50¢; day passes $2.50.) **Airport Car Rental,** 502 W. Northern Lights Blvd., charges $39 per day, with unlimited mileage. (☎243-3370. Open M-F 8am-8pm, Sa-Su 9am-6pm. Must be 21; under 25 surcharge $5 per day. Credit card or cash deposit required.) **Taxi: Yellow Cab,** ☎272-2422.

█ █ ORIENTATION & PRACTICAL INFORMATION. Downtown Anchorage is laid out in a grid: numbered avenues run east-west, with addresses designated east or west from **C St.** North-south streets are lettered alphabetically to the west and named alphabetically to the east of **A St.** The rest of Anchorage spreads out along major highways. The **Log Cabin Visitor Information Center,** on W. 4th Ave. at F St., sells a $3.50 bike guide. (☎274-3531. Open June-Aug. daily 7:30am-7pm; May and Sept. 8am-6pm; Oct.-Apr. 9am-4pm.) The **Alaska Public Lands Information Center,** Old Federal Building, 605 W. 4th Ave., between F and G St., combines the Park, Forest, State Parks, and Fish and Wildlife Services under one roof. (☎271-2737. Open daily 9am-5:30pm.) **Internet access: Loussac Library,** on 36th Ave. and Denali St., a real architectural oddity. Buses #2, 36, and 60 stop out front; bus #75 stops at C St. and 36th is within ½ block. (☎343-2975. Open M-Th 10am-8pm, F-Sa 10am-6pm; in winter also Su noon-6pm. 1hr. free.) **Post Office:** 344 W 3rd. Ave. (☎279-9188. Open M-F 10am-5:30pm.) **ZIP code:** 99510. **Area code:** 907.

█ ACCOMMODATIONS. Visitors can call **Alaska Private Lodgings** (☎888-235-2148; open M-Sa 9am-6pm) for lodgings or the **Anchorage Reservation Service** (☎272-5909) for out-of-town B&Bs (from $80). Grab a copy of *Camping in the Anchorage Bowl* (free) at the Visitors Center for crowded in-town camping, or head to nearby **Chugach State Park** (☎354-5014).

Guests take pride in the elegant kitchen and common area at the █**Anchorage Guesthouse ❶,** 2001 Hillcrest Dr., and gladly earn their keep with a chore. Take bus #3, 4, 6, 36, or 60 from downtown; get off at West High School, and go west on Hillcrest. Bikes $2.50 per hr., $20 per day. $5 key deposit. (☎274-0408. Bunks $25; private rooms $75.) Originally a commune, the **Spenard Hostel ❶,** 2845 W. 42nd Pl., still retains its original character without sacrificing cleanliness. On Spenard, turn west on Turnagain Blvd., then left onto 42nd Pl., or take bus #7. (☎248-5036. Reception 9am-1pm and 7-11pm. Chore requested; free stay for 3hr. work. $16.)

LET'S MUSH The celebrated Iditarod dog sled race begins in Anchorage on the first weekend in March. Dogs and their drivers ("mushers") traverse a trail over two mountain ranges along the mighty Yukon River and over the frozen Norton Sound to Nome. State pride holds that the route is 1049 mi., in honor of Alaska's status as the 49th state, but the real distance is closer to 1150 mi.

The Iditarod ("a far-off place") Trail began as a dog sled supply route from Seward on the southern coast to interior mining towns. The race commemorates the 1925 rescue of Nome, when drivers delivered 300,000 units of life-saving diphtheria serum from Nenana. The first race, in 1967, was a 27 mi. jaunt; today, up to 70 contestants speed each year from Anchorage to Nome, competing for a $450,000 purse.

The race has come under fire from animal rights activists due to the hardships borne by the dogs, some of whom have died en route to Nome. Nevertheless, the race goes on, and Anchorage turns out in force for the ceremonial start. For more info, contact the Iditarod Trail Committee (376-5155; www.iditarod.com). Visit the Iditarod Headquarters, Mile 2.2 Knik Rd. in Wasilla, for video presentations and a museum. Free.

ALASKA

IN RECENT NEWS

HOW'S YOUR HALIBUT?

Sport fishing for Pacific Halibut has rapidly gained popularity in Seward, but as more of the fish are caught off the shores of Alaska's ports, a subsequent decline in the fish population has been noted. The most striking evidence? Halibut charters that once took customers on an hour-long boat ride out of Seward must now travel 2 or even 3 hours to find decent fishing waters. But where have these bottom-dwelling flat fish gone?

Halibut are famous for their size; the world record catch weighed in at just over 450 lb. What people don't realize is that these "barn doors," or large halibut, play a role in determining the future survival of the species. Any halibut over 80 lb. is usually female, and the amount of eggs females lay is proportionate to their size. A 50 lb. female will produce about 500,000 eggs, but a 250 lb. female will produce 4,000,000. Keeping the big fish when they're caught can quickly lead to a decline in eggs and a subsequent decline in halibut that survive to maturity.

While there hasn't been much official action to address the decreasing number of halibut in the waters surrounding the Kenai Peninsula, many charter companies now encourage customers to release any halibut over 100 lb. Some will even give you a discount for releasing the big ones. Most knowledgeable fishers agree that the meat from smaller "chickens" (20-60 lb. fish), tastes better, anyway.

Though often more tightly packed than your knapsack, the **International Backpackers Hostel ❶**, 3601 Peterkin Ave. (☎274-3870), is centrally located. A shuttle runs to and from airport (15min.; $14 for 1, $17 for 2). A 15min. bike ride from downtown, this popular hostel rents two-wheelers for $10 per day. Towels $1, laundry $3. $10 key deposit. (☎274-3870. Dorms $15. Sites $10, $2 each additional person.)

◪ ◪ **FOOD & NIGHTLIFE.** ▨**Moose's Tooth ❷**, 3300 Old Seward, bus #2 or 36, serves pizza and brews as hearty as the climbers who tackle the nearby peak. (☎258-2537. Open mic M 9-11pm. Open M-Th 11am-midnight, F-Sa noon-1am, Su noon-midnight.) **Sweet Basil Cafe ❶**, 335 E. St., is run by the black labrador retriever/CEO Buba, who keeps the owner/chef turning out tasty treats. (☎274-0070. Open M-F 7:30am-4pm, Sa 9am-4pm.) Artsy **Snow City Cafe ❷**, 1034 W. 4th St., at L St., is famous for the best breakfast in town. (☎272-2489. Salads and big sandwiches $4-10. Live music F-Sa. Open daily 7am-4pm, W-Su also 5-9pm; reduced hours in winter.)

The brewpub revolution has hit Anchorage, and microbrews gush from taps like oil through the pipeline. Catch a flick with brew in hand at the **Bear Tooth Grill**, 1230 W. 27th St. (☎276-4500. Pints $2.50. Cover for movie $3.) The young and retro at **Bernie's Bungalow Lounge,** 626 D St., relax in one of many wingback chairs as they sip a lemon drop martini ($5), puff on a cigar ($3-10), and play a round of croquet. (☎276-8808. Open daily noon-2am; in winter 3pm-2am.) **Chilkoot Charlie's,** 2435 Spenard Rd. bus #7, has cavernous dance floors and rock music. "Koots" is the place to dance into the night; take bus #7. (☎272-1010. $1 drink specials until 10pm. Cover $2-5. Open Su-Th 10:30am-2:15am, F-Sa 11am-2:45am.)

◪ ◪ **SIGHTS & OUTDOOR ACTIVITIES.** Near town off Northern Lights Blvd., **Earthquake Park** recalls the 1964 Good Friday quake, the strongest ever recorded in North America, registering 9.2 on the Richter scale. ▨**Cyrano's Off Center Playhouse,** 413 D St., between 4th and 5th, contains a cafe, a bookshop, the stage of the **Eccentric Theatre Company,** and a cinema that screens foreign and art films. (☎274-2599. Theater in summer M-Tu and Th-Su 7pm; in winter Th-Su 7pm. Tickets $15, students $10.) At the ▨**Anchorage Museum of History and Art,** 121 W. 7th Ave., at A St., permanent exhibits of Native Alaskan artifacts and art mingle with national and international works. (☎343-4326. Open June-Aug. Su-Th 9am-9pm, F-Sa 9am-6pm; Sept.-May Tu-Sa 9am-6pm, Su 1-5pm. Tours daily at 10, 11am, 1, and 2pm. $6.50, seniors $6, under 18 free.) At the **Alaska Zoo,** Mile 2 on O'Malley Rd., Binky the polar bear became a newsmaker after mauling a tourist in 1994. (☎346-3242. Open daily 9am-6pm. $8, seniors $7, ages 12-18 $5, ages 3-11 $4.)

The 13 mi. **Tony Knowles Coastal Trail** is arguably one of the best urban bike paths in the country; in the winter, it's groomed for cross-country skiing. The serene **Chugach State Park,** cornering the city to the north, east, and south, has 25 established day hiking trails. A 15min. drive from the city center, **Flattop Mountain** (4500 ft.) is the most frequently climbed mountain in Alaska, providing an excellent view of the inlet, the Aleutian Chain, and on the rare clear day, Denali. Park at the trailhead for $5, or take bus #92 to Hillside Rd. The trailhead is a ¾ mi. walk along Upper Huffman Rd., then right on Toilsome Hill Dr. for 2 mi.; it's a 2 mi. hike to the summit. Less frequented hikes branch from the **Powerline Trail,** which begins at the same parking lot as the Flattop Trail. The **Eklutna Lakeside Biking Trail** extends 13 mi. one-way from the Eklutna Campground, off Mile 26 of the Glenn Hwy. (Rte. 1). A relatively flat dirt road, the trail follows the blue-green Eklutna Lake for 7 mi. before entering a steep river canyon, ending at the base of the Eklutna River. **Nancy Lake State Recreation Area,** just west of the Parks Hwy. (Rte. 3) at Mile 67.3, contains the **Lynx Lake Canoe Loop,** which takes two days and weaves through 8 mi. of lakes and portages, with designated campsites along the way. The loop begins at Mile 4½ of the Nancy Lake Parkway, at the Tanaina Lake Canoe Trailhead. For canoe rental in the Nancy Lake Area, call **Tippecanoe.** (☎495-6688. Canoes $33 per day, $78 per week. Shuttle free for backpackers.)

SEWARD & KENAI FJORDS ☎907

Seward serves as a gateway to the waterways and yawning ice fields of **Kenai Fjords National Park. Exit Glacier,** the only road-accessible glacier in the park, lies 9 mi. west on a spur from Mile 3.7 of the Seward Hwy. (Rte. 9). Beyond this glacier, boat cruises are the easiest and most popular way to see the park. **Kenai Fjords Tours** are informative and amusing. (☎224-8068 or 800-478-8068. Tours last 6-9½hr. $149, children $69.) **Major Marine Tours** brings along a ranger to explain wildlife and glacier facts. (☎224-8030 or 800-764-7300. $109; with seafood dinner $121.) **Sunny Cove Sea Kayaking** offers a joint trip with Kenai Fjords Tours, including the wildlife cruise, a salmon bake, kayaking instruction, and a 2½hr. wilderness paddle. (☎224-8810. 8hr. $149-169.)

🖾**Kate's Roadhouse ❶,** 5½ mi. outside town on the Seward Hwy., has clean dorms, huge continental breakfasts with home-baked goods, and a heated outhouse with flush toilet. (☎224-5888. Free shuttle service, laundry, bedding, and towels. Shared baths. Dorms $17; private rooms $60.) **Moby Dick Hostel ❶,** at 3rd Ave. between Jefferson and Madison St., has a view of Mt. Marathon. (☎224-7072. Showers and kitchen. Linen $2. Office open 9-11am and 5-10pm. $17; private room $45.) Camp at the **Municipal Waterfront Campground ❶,** on Ballaine Rd. between Railway Ave. and D St. (Open May-Sept. Sites $6; RV sites $10, with hookup $15.)

Seward is 127 mi. south of Anchorage on the scenic **Seward Hwy. (Rte. 9).** Most services and outdoor outfits cluster in the small harbor on Resurrection Bay. Across from the Visitors Center at the **Alaska Railroad** depot, trains leave for Anchorage at 6:45am in summer. (4½hr.; $55, ages 2-11 half-price.) **Katchemak Bay Transit** (☎235-3795) runs daily to Anchorage (3½hr., $35). The **Alaska Marine Hwy.** (☎224-5485 or 800-642-0066) docks at 4th Ave. and Railway St., with state-wide connections. The **Seward Chamber of Commerce** is at Mile 2 on the Seward Hwy. (☎224-8051. Open M-F 8am-6pm, Sa 9am-5pm, Su 9am-4pm.) **Kenai Fjords National Park Visitors Center** is at the small-boat harbor. (☎224-3175. Open daily 8am-7pm; in winter M-F 8am-5pm.) **Post Office:** 5th Ave. and Madison St. (☎224-3001. Open M-F 9:30am-4:30pm, Sa 10am-2pm.) **ZIP code:** 99664. **Area code:** 907.

WRANGELL-ST. ELIAS NATIONAL PARK ☎907

At 13.2 million acres, **Wrangell-St. Elias National Park** is the largest national park in the US. Beyond towering peaks and extensive glaciers, Wrangell teems with wildlife. With only two rough roads that penetrate its interior, and almost no established trails, the park's inaccessibility keeps many tourists away. **Ranger stations** lurk exclusively outside the park boundaries in Copper Center, south of Glennallen (☎822-7261; open daily 8am-6pm); Yakutat in the east (☎784-3295; open daily 8am-5pm); Chitina in the west (☎823-2205; open daily 10am-6pm); and Slana on the park's northern boundary (☎822-5238; open daily 8am-5pm). They have the lowdown on all the must-knows and go-sees of the park and sell invaluable topographical maps ($4-9). **Backcountry Connection** (☎822-5292 or 800-478-5292) runs buses daily to McCarthy from Glennallen (4hr., $70) and Chitina (3hr., $55-80). **Charter flights** from McCarthy or Nabesna start at around $60.

The more harrowing **McCarthy Rd.** plunges 60 mi. into the park from Chitina to the western edge of the Kennicott River, and the town of McCarthy. Deep in the heart of the park, McCarthy and Kennicott are quiet today, but abandoned log buildings and forgotten roads bear witness to a boom town past. A **shuttle** runs the 5 mi. road between the towns 9am-7:30pm (round-trip $10). **Wrangell Mountain Air** flies to McCarthy twice daily from Chitina and farther afield by arrangement. (☎554-4411 or 800-478-1160. Round-trip $140.) A quarter-mile before the river, the **Kennicott River Lodge and Hostel ❶** awaits with McCarthy's cheapest beds, six-person cabins, and a cozy common room. (☎554-4441, in winter 479-6822. Rooms $25; cabins $85.) Camping is free at the lot ½ mi. back along the road toward Chitina (pit toilets, no water). The food in town is expensive; bring groceries with you. **The Potato ❶**, next to McCarthy Air, serves spicy breakfast, a strong cup o' joe, and an awesome $5 spudniks and gravy. (Open daily 7:30am-4pm.)

This is the place for flightseeing in Alaska. Even a short flight to 16,390 ft. Mt. Blackburn and the surrounding glaciers offers stunning views. **Wrangell Mountain Air** makes a 35min. tour of the amazing icefalls of the Kennicott and Root Glaciers. (☎554-4411 or 800-478-1160. $60.) The best bargain is a 70min. trip up the narrow Chitistone Canyon to view the thundering Chitistone Falls and a slew of glaciers and peaks ($105 per person; min. 2 people). **Copper Oar** runs a daylong whitewater rafting trip down the Class III Kennicott River with a flightseeing jaunt back from Chitina. (☎554-4453 or 800-523-4453. $235.) **St. Elias Alpine Guides** (☎888-933-5427) lead a variety of guided hikes and explorations. The park maintains no trails around McCarthy; consult with a ranger station before setting out. Ranger stations need a written itinerary for independent overnight trips.

DENALI NATIONAL PARK & PRESERVE ☎907

Encompassing six million acres of snow-capped peaks, braided streams, and glacier-carved valleys interrupted only by a lone gravel road, Denali National Park and Preserve is not a place made for humans; nevertheless, more than a million visitors invite themselves here each year. And why not? Visitors to the park are the guests of grizzly bears, moose, caribou, wolves, Dall sheep, and wildflowers. Denali's 20,320 ft. centerpiece, known as Mt. McKinley (or simply "Denali") is the world's tallest mountain from base to peak. (Mt. Everest reaches a higher elevation but starts from the 11,000 ft. Plateau of Tibet.) Mid- to late August is the best time to visit—fall colors peak, berries ripen, mosquito season is virtually over, and September snows have yet to arrive.

▐ **TRANSPORTATION.** The **George Parks Hwy. (Rte. 3)** makes for smooth and easy traveling to the park entrance north from Anchorage or south from Fairbanks. Leading east away from the park, the gravel **Denali Hwy. (Rte. 8)** starts 27 mi. south of the park entrance at Cantwell and proceeds to Paxson, but is closed in winter. The **Alaska Railroad** (☎264-2494 or 800-544-0552; open daily 10am-5pm) stops at Denali Station, 1½ mi. from the park entrance, and runs to Anchorage (8hr., $125) and Fairbanks (4½hr., $50); reserve ahead. **Parks Hwy. Express** (☎888-600-6001) runs here from Anchorage (5hr., $39) and Fairbanks (3½hr., $54).

Only the first 14 mi. of the park road are accessible by private vehicle; the remaining 75 mi. of dirt road can be reached only by shuttle bus, camper bus, or bicycle. **Shuttle buses** leave from the Visitors Center at 5am to 6pm, pause at the almost inevitable sighting of any major mammal ("MOOOOOSE!"), and turn back at various points along the park road, such as Toklat, Mile 53 ($17); Eielson, Mile 66 ($23); Wonder Lake, Mile 85 ($30); and Kantishna, Mile 89 ($33). Most buses are wheelchair accessible. **Camper buses** ($18.50) transport only those visitors with campground or backcountry permits and move faster than the shuttle buses. Bikes are permitted on all park roads.

7 PRACTICAL INFORMATION. All travelers must stop at the **Denali Visitors Center**, ½ mi. from the Parks Hwy. (Rte. 3), for orientation. Most park privileges are first come, first served; conduct all business at the Visitors Center as early in the day as possible. (☎683-2294. Open late Apr.-late mid-May daily 10am-4pm; late May-early Sept. 7am-8pm. Entrance fee $5, good for 7 days.) **Denali Outdoor Center,** at Parks Hwy. Mile 238.9, just north of the park entrance, rents bikes. (☎683-1925. Half-day $25; full-day $40.) **Medical Services: Healy Clinic,** 13 mi. north of the park entrance. (☎683-2211. On call 24hr.) **Post Office:** 1 mi. from the Visitors Center. (☎683-2291. Open May-Sept. M-F 8:30am-5pm, Sa 10am-1pm; Oct.-Apr. M-Sa 10am-1pm.) **ZIP code:** 99755. **Area code:** 907.

⌐❑ ACCOMMODATIONS & FOOD. The ⦾**Denali Mountain Morning Hostel ❶**, 13 mi. south of the park entrance, has showers, groceries, free park shuttles, helpful outdoor advice, and outdoor gear rental. (☎683-7503. Backpacker kit $30 first day, $7 each additional day. Bunks $23, ages 5-13 $17. Semi-private and private rooms start at $50. Reservations recommended.) **Campers** must obtain a permit from the Visitors Center and may stay for up to 14 nights in the seven campgrounds lining the park road. (☎272-7275 or 800-622-7275 for advance reservations. First come, first served sites are distributed rapidly at the Visitors Center.) **Riley Creek,** the only campground open year-round, has the only dump station. Most campgrounds are wheelchair accessible.

Once you board that park bus, there is no food available anywhere. At **Black Bear Coffee House ❶**, 1 mi. north of the park entrance, the coffee is hot and strong, the muffins are fresh, and the staff is all smiles. Veggie sandwich with hot cup of soup $7. (☎683-1656. Open May-Sept. daily 7am-10pm.)

❧ FLIGHTSEEING. Oddly, the best place for flightseeing around Denali is actually in Talkeetna, 60 mi. to the south of the mountain. If the weather cooperates, these flights are worth every penny and will leave you itching for more. Flights come in two standard flavors: a 1hr. flight approaching the mountain from the south, and a 1½hr. tour that circumnavigates the peak. One-hour trips cost $100-120 per person. Landing 15-30min. on a remote glacier (often at a climbing base camp) at the base of Denali costs an additional $35-45 per person. All flights are weather-dependent, with most companies offering flights over the rugged Talkeetna Mountains to the south if Denali weather is uncooperative. Many companies, such as **Doug Geeting Aviation** (☎733-2366 or 800-770-2366) provide discounts to groups of four or five. **K2 Aviation** (☎733-2291 or 800-764-2291), **McKinley Air Service** (☎733-1765 or 800-564-1765), and **Talkeetna Air Taxi** (☎733-2218 or 800-533-2219) offer standard services, plus a variety of other specialized trips. All flight services suspend glacier landings in mid-July due to unpredictable snow conditions.

⚄ OUTDOOR ACTIVITIES. The best way to experience Denali is to get off the bus and explore the land. Beyond Mile 14 (the point which only shuttle and camper buses can cross), there are no trails. You can begin day hiking from anywhere along the park road by riding the shuttle bus to a suitable starting point and asking the driver to let you off. It's rare to wait more than 30min. to flag a ride back. **Primrose Ridge,** beginning at Mile 16, is bespangled with wildflowers and has spectacular views of the Alaska Range and its carpeted emerald valley below. A walk north from Mile 14 along the **Savage River** provides a colorful, scenic stroll through this valley. The more challenging **Mt. Healy Overlook Trail** starts from the hotel parking lot and climbs to an impressive 3400 ft. view. (5 mi. round-trip; 1700 ft. elevation gain; 3-4hr.). **Discovery hikes** are guided 3-5hr. hikes departing on special buses from the Visitors Center. Topics vary; a ranger might lead you on a cross-country scramble or a moose trail excursion. The hikes are free but require reservations and a bus ticket.

There are no trails in the backcountry. While day hiking is unlimited and requires no permit, only 2-12 backpackers can camp at a time in each of the park's 43 units. Overnight stays in the backcountry require a **free permit,** available no earlier or later than one day in advance at the backcountry desk in the Visitors Center. Type-A hikers line up outside as early as 6:30am to grab permits for popular units. Talk to rangers and research your choices with the handy *Backcountry Description Guides* and *The Backcountry Companion*, available at the Visitors Center bookstore, which also sells essential topographic maps ($4). Most zones in Denali require that food be carried in **bear-resistant food containers (BRFC),** available for free at the backcountry desk. These are bulky things; be sure to leave space in your backpack. With the park's cool, drizzly weather and many rivers, streams, and pools, your feet will get wet. **Hypothermia** can set in quickly and quietly; talk with rangers about prevention and warning signs.

FAIRBANKS ☎907

Fairbanks stands unchallenged as North American civilization's northernmost hub—witness such landmarks as the "World's Northernmost Woolworth's," "World's Northernmost Denny's," and "World's Northernmost Southern Barbecue." From here, adventuresome travelers can drive, fly, or float to the Arctic Circle and into the tundra.

⚄ PRACTICAL INFORMATION. Most tourist destinations lie within the square of **Airport Way, College Rd., Cushman Blvd.,** and **University Way.** Fairbanks is a bicycle-friendly city, with wide shoulders, multi-use paths, and sidewalks. The **airport** is 5 mi. from downtown on Airport Way. **Alaska Railroad,** 280 N. Cushman St. (☎458-6205 or 800-544-0552; open M-F 7am-3pm, Sa-Su 7-11am), runs one train per day to Anchorage ($175) via Denali ($50); service is reduced during the winter. **Parks Hwy. Express** (☎479-3065 or 888-600-6001) runs daily to Denali (1 per day, $39) and Anchorage (1 per day, $54). **Municipal Commuter Area Service (MACS),** at 5th and Cushman St., runs through downtown. (☎459-1011. $1.50; students, seniors, and disabled 75¢; day pass $3. Service M-F 7am-8pm; limited on Sa.) **Fairbanks Taxi,** ☎452-3535. **Visitor Info:** 550 1st Ave. (☎456-5774 or 800-327-5774. Open in summer daily 8am-8pm; in winter M-F 9am-5pm.) **Alaska Public Lands Info Center (APLIC),** 250 Cushman St., #1A, at 3rd. St. in the basement of the Federal Bldg. (☎456-0527. Open daily 9am-6pm; in winter Tu-Sa 10am-6pm.) **Post Office:** 315 Barnette St. (☎452-3223. Open M-F 9am-6pm, Sa 10am-2pm.) **ZIP code:** 99707. **Area code:** 907.

UM, HONEY, IS IT...COLD IN HERE? The thick blanket of snow that envelops Alaska in the winter months shields the state from the flood of tourism that washes over it in the summer. Those who brave the Alaskan winter come for the intense skiing and snowboarding opportunities... and sometimes for the luck. Japanese tradition has it that good luck will follow the couple whose marriage is consummated under the northern lights. The dead of winter thus finds Fairbanks deserted except for the locals and a few blushing Japanese newlyweds.

▐▌▐▌ ACCOMMODATIONS & FOOD. **Boyle's Hostel ❶,** 310 18th Ave., has TVs in every room and provides access to 2 kitchens. (☎456-4944. Showers and laundry. No curfew or lockout. Dorms $17; private doubles $30; outside cabins $15 per person. Monthly rates available.) **Billie's Backpackers Hostel ❶,** 2895 Mack Rd., is a somewhat cluttered but welcoming place to meet international travelers. Shower and kitchen in each room. (☎479-2034. Beds $20, sites $15.) **Chena River State Campground ❶,** off Airport Way on University Ave., is on a quiet stretch of the Chena River. (56 sites, $15.)

An artery-blocking good time fills Airport Way and College Rd. ▨**Bun on the Run ❶,** located in a trailer in the parking lot between Beaver Sports and the Marlin on College Rd., whips up the best pastries in Alaska. (Open M-F 7am-6pm, Sa 9am-4pm.) ▨**Second Story Cafe ❷,** 3525 College Rd., above Gulliver's, has the best and freshest wraps in town, plus salads, sandwiches, and veggie-friendly soups. All wraps and sandwiches $6.50. Combinations $4.75-$9.50. (☎474-9574. Open M-F 9am-8pm, Sa 9am-7pm, Su 11am-5pm.) **Gambardella's Pasta Bella ❹,** 706 2nd Ave., turns out the "Mother of all Lasagnas" for $15 in true Italian ambience. (☎457-4922. Open daily M-Sa 11am-10pm.)

◙◪ SIGHTS & SKIING. The ▨**University of Alaska Museum,** a 10min. walk up Yukon Dr. from the Wood Center, features a thorough look at the Aleut/Japanese evacuation during WWII, indigenous crafts, and Blue Babe, a 36,000 year-old steppe bison recovered from the permafrost. (☎474-7505. Open June-Aug. daily 9am-7pm; May and Sept. 9am-5pm; Oct.-Apr. M-F 9am-5pm, Sa-Su noon-5pm. $5, seniors $4.50, ages 7-17 $3.) Stand upwind of the **Large Animal Research Station,** which offers a rare chance to see baby musk oxen and other arctic animals up close. Take Farmer's Loop to Ballaine Rd. and turn left on Van Kovich; the farm is 1 mi. up on the right. (☎474-7207. Tours June-Aug. Tu, Th, and Sa at 11am and 1:30pm; Sept. Sa 1:30pm. $5, students $2, seniors $4.)

Moose Mountain, 20min. northeast of Fairbanks, grooms over 30 ski trails. Take Sheep Creek Rd. to Murphy Dome Rd., then right onto Moose Mt. Rd. (☎479-4732. Open Th-Su 10am-5pm or dusk. Lift tickets $23, ages 7-12 $18. Rentals $20, under 12 $15.) Another option, holding over 20 trails, is **Mt. Aurora Ski Land,** 2315 Skiland Rd. Take a right onto Fairbanks Creek Rd. off the Steese Hwy. (Rte. 6) at Mile 20.5 and then turn left. (☎389-2314. Open Nov.-Apr. 10am-dusk. Lift tickets $24, students and military $20, seniors and ages 13-17 $17, ages 7-12 $10, under 6 $5. Rentals $20, students, military, and seniors $15.)

♫▓ ENTERTAINMENT & NIGHTLIFE. The scene at the **Blue Loon Saloon,** 2999 Parks Hwy., ranges from gyrating with go-go dancers in cages to lounging on the couches and watching a movie. The grille serves a bar menu ($2.50-15.75) throughout the night. (☎457-5666. Cover $3. Movie M-Tu $4, W-Th $5, F-Sa $6.

FROM THE ROAD

UNEXPECTED NEW FRIENDS

In the last five minutes of the flight from Seattle to Ketchikan, I met my neighbor. She was a Sitka resident who, upon hearing that I would be in her town three weeks later, gave me her number and offered the free use of her car and her home. Being a New Yorker, I was flabbergasted and almost melted in thanks as she preceded me down the aisle. On the three minute ferry ride from the Ketchikan airport to Ketchikan proper I met John, who gave me a ride to the hostel, protested that I needn't pay for a bed, and insisted that I share his family's freshly-caught halibut dinner. Later that night, I met two pilots who offered to take me flying. And did. Four times. Two nights later I met a woman who offered to have me crash with her when I got back from a few days on Prince of Wales. I called when I got back to Ketchickan, but hung up when I got her business machine. A few hours later, I tried again, this time listening to the full message. After the typical message ended, there was a brief pause and then, "and if this is Catherine, we're at [insert address]. The house is open—please make yourself at home and we'll see you tonight." I don't mean to suggest that you cancel your hostel reservations, but people are awfully friendly here. I have never encountered such casual and natural generosity. Southeastern Alaskans thrive on sharing the wealth.

—*Catherine Gowl*

Open M-Th 5pm-1am, F-Sa 5pm-3am.) In mid-July, Fairbanks citizens don old-time duds and whoop it up for **Golden Days**, a celebration of Felix Pedro's 1902 discovery that sparked the Fairbanks gold rush. Although its relation to the actual gold rush days is questionable, the **rubber duckie race** is one of the biggest events. The Fairbanks Goldpanners play their annual **Midnight Sun Baseball Game** on the solstice itself (June 21, 2003). The game begins as the sun dips at 10:30pm, features a short pause near midnight for the celebration of the midnight sun, and ends at about 2am, in full daylight. For a true sports spectacular, see the **World Eskimo-Indian Olympics**, in mid- to late July. Native Alaskans from all over the state compete for three days in traditional tests of strength and survival. Witness the ear pull, for which sinew is wrapped around the ears of contestants, who then tug to see who can endure the most pain. Be warned: ears have been pulled off in this event. (☎ 452-6646. Daily pass $6, season pass $20.)

SOUTHEAST ALASKA

Southeast Alaska sometimes goes by "the Panhandle" or "the southeast." It spans some 500 miles from the basins of Misty Fjords National Monument to Skagway at the foot of the Chilkoot Trail. The waterways weaving through the Panhandle, collectively known as the Inside Passage, make up an enormous saltwater soup spiced with islands, inlets, fjords, and the ferries that flit among them. The absence of roads in the steep coastal mountains has helped most Panhandle towns maintain their small size and hospitable personalities.

KETCHIKAN ☎ 907

Ketchikan is Alaska's fourth-largest city (population 14,000), and it's quite easy to see that Ketchikanians *want* to live here. Ketchikan is surrounded by the sprawling Tongass National Forest and Misty Fjords National Monument, and provides an excellent home base for some of the most outstanding hiking, kayaking, fishing, and flightseeing opportunities in all of Southeastern Alaska.

◪ PRACTICAL INFORMATION. Ketchikan rests on **Revillagigedo Island** (*ruh-VIL-ya-GIG-a-doe*). The town caters to the elite, and its attractions are extremely spread out, making bike rental a wise decision. The **airport** is across from Ketchikan on Gravina Island. **Alaska Airlines** (☎ 800-225-2752) makes daily flights to Juneau. A small **ferry** runs every 30min.

from the airport to just north of the state ferry dock ($2.50). **Alaska Marine Hwy.** (☎225-6181 or 800-642-0066) sends boats from the far end of town on N. Tongass Hwy. to Juneau ($83); Sitka ($61); and Wrangell ($26). The main bus route runs a loop between the airport parking lot near the ferry terminal at one end, and Dock and Main St. downtown at the other. (Runs every 30min. M-F 5:15am-9:45pm; 1 per hr. Sa 6:45am-8:45pm, Su 8:45am-3:45pm. $1.50, students, seniors, and children free.) **Taxi: Sourdough Cab,** ☎225-5544. **Ketchikan Visitors Bureau:** 131 Front St., on the cruise ship docks downtown. (☎225-6166 or 800-770-3300. Open daily 8am-5pm.) **Southeast Alaska Discovery Center (SEADC),** 50 Main St., provides trip-planning service and info on public lands around Ketchikan, including Tongass and Misty Fjords. (☎228-6220. Open May-Sept. daily 8am-5pm; Oct.-April Tu-Sa 8:30am-4:30pm.) **Post Office:** 3609 Tongass Ave. (☎225-9601. Open M-F 8:30am-5pm.) **ZIP code:** 99901. **Area code:** 907.

⚏⚏ ACCOMMODATIONS & FOOD. The **Ketchikan Reservation Service** provides info on B&Bs. (☎800-987-5337. Singles from $69.) Because of boardwalk stairs, these accommodations aren't wheelchair accessible. The **Ketchikan Youth Hostel (HI-AYH) ❶** is at Main and Grant St. in the First Methodist Church. The social scene is skimpy since the doors close at 11pm sharp. Bring a sleeping bag for the foam mats. (☎225-3319. Common area, showers, kitchen, and free tea and popcorn every night. 4-night max. stay when full. Lockout 9am-6pm. Call ahead if arriving on a late ferry. Reservations required. Open June-Aug. $12, nonmembers $15.) **Eagle View Bed & Breakfast and Backpacker Bunks ❶,** 2303 5th Ave., is reached via Jefferson Ave. Not as cheap as the hostel, but it has free use of a kitchen, TV, sauna, BBQ, and hammocks. (☎225-5461. $25 per person.)

Campgrounds usually have stay limits of a week or two and are really out of the way. **Signal Creek ❶** sits on Ward Lake Rd. Drive north on Tongass Ave. and turn right at the sign for Ward Lake, 5 mi. from the ferry terminal. (Open May-Sept. Water, pit toilets. $10.) Anyone can camp for up to 30 days in **Tongass National Forest,** but may not return for six months after that time. Any clearing is free.

The freshest seafood swims in **Ketchikan Creek;** in summer, anglers frequently hook king salmon from the docks by Stedman St. **⚓Ocean View Restaurante ❷,** 1831 Tongass Ave., serves up enchiladas and pizza with equal gusto. The fried ice cream is a winner for dessert. (☎225-7566. Open daily 11am-11pm.) **New York Cafe ❷,** 207 Stedman St., is at the south end of Creek St. Come for the incredible soup and healthy lunch specials. (☎225-1800. Open M-F 6am-10pm, Sa-Su 6am-11pm.)

◧⚏ SIGHTS & NIGHTLIFE. Ketchikan's primary cultural attraction is the **Saxman Totem Park,** the largest totem park in Alaska, 2½ mi. southwest of town on Tongass Hwy. The **Totem Heritage Center,** up Park St., houses 33 well-preserved totem poles from Tlingit, Haida, and Tsimshian villages. It is the largest collection of authentic, pre-commercial totem poles in the US, but only a few are on display. (Open May-Sept. daily 8am-5pm; Oct.-Apr. Tu-F 1-5pm. $4.) A $10 combination ticket also provides admission to the **Deer Mountain Fish Hatchery and Raptor Center,** across the creek. (☎225-6026. Open May-Sept. daily 8am-4:30pm.)

First City Saloon, ¼ mi. north of the tunnel on Water St., is the most spacious hangout in town and liberally distributes Guinness and a variety of microbrews. (☎225-1494. Live local music Tu-Su. Open daily noon-2am.) **Ketchikan Brew Pub,** 602 Dock St., has the only beer brewed in town. With true local flavor, the owner hand-picks Sitka Spruce tips and steeps them in Spruce Tip Beer. If you bring any bottle that seals, they'll fill it for your beer-to-go. (☎247-5221. Open M-Sa 10am-2am, Su 12:30pm-2am.) **Arctic Bar,** 509 Walter St., is a hop, skip, and stagger north of the downtown tunnel. Distinguished by their copulating bears logo, this popular bar sports a deck with harbor view. (☎225-4709. Open daily until 2am.)

ALASKA

◪ OUTDOOR ACTIVITIES. From Ketchikan, a trail up the 3001 ft. **Deer Mountain** makes a good day hike. Walk up the hill past the city park on Fair St.; the marked trailhead branches off to the left just behind the dump. The ascent is steep but manageable, and on a rare clear day the walk yields sparkling views of the sea and surrounding islands. While most hikers stop at the 2½ mi. point, the trail continues above the treeline to the summit along an 8 mi. route that passes Blue Lake and leads over John Mountain to Little Silvis Lake and the Beaver Falls Fish Hatchery. This portion of the trail is poorly marked, and snow and ice are common on the peaks even in the summer; only experienced and well-prepared hikers should attempt it. For swimming, a sandy beach, and picnic tables, head to **Ward Lake** at the Signal Creek Campground. A 1¼ mi. trail circles the grassy pond.

NEAR KETCHIKAN: MISTY FJORDS NATIONAL MONUMENT
The jagged peaks, plunging valleys, and dripping vegetation of **Misty Fjords National Monument,** 20 mi. east of Ketchikan, make biologists dream and outdoors enthusiasts drool. Only accessible by kayak, boat, or float plane, the 2.3 million-acre park offers superlative camping, kayaking, hiking, and wildlife-viewing. **Camping** is allowed across the park, and the Forest Service maintains first come, first served **shelters** (free) and 14 **cabins** ($25). Contact the **Misty Fjords Ranger Station,** 3031 Tongass Ave., Ketchikan (☎225-2148), or ask the SEADC (see p. 1025) for advice.

JUNEAU   ☎907
Alaska's state capital has an air of modernity and progressiveness usually not found in the rural fishing villages of Southeast Alaska. Accessible only by water and air, Juneau is the 2nd-busiest cruise ship port in the US, after Miami. Hordes of travelers come to Juneau for the Mendenhall Glacier, numerous hiking trails, and close access to Glacier Bay, so be prepared to share the beauty.

⚐ PRACTICAL INFORMATION. Franklin St. is the main drag downtown. **Glacier Hwy.** connects downtown, the airport, the Mendenhall Valley, and the ferry terminal. The ferry and airport are both annoyingly far from the glacier and downtown. **Juneau International Airport,** 9 mi. north of Juneau on Glacier Hwy., is served by **Alaska Airlines** (☎789-9539 or 800-426-0333). **Capital Transit** runs buses from downtown to the airport and Mendenhall Glacier, with express service downtown every hr. (☎789-6901. Runs M-Sa 7am-10:30pm, Su 9am-6:30pm. Fare $1.25.) **Alaska Marine Hwy.** docks at the Auke Bay terminal, 14 mi. from the city on the Glacier Hwy., and runs to Ketchikan (18-36hr., $83) and Sitka (9hr., $30). **Taku Cab** (☎586-2121) runs to the glacier ($15), the ferry ($20), and the airport ($15). The **Visitors Center** is at 101 Egan Dr. in Centennial Hall. (☎586-2201 or 888-581-2201; www.traveljuneau.com. Open June-Sept. daily 9am-5pm; Oct.-May M-F only.) **Alaska Dept. of Fish and Game,** 1255 W. 8th St. (☎465-4112; licensing 465-2376), close to the bridge, serves your outdoor needs. (Open M-F 8am-5pm.) **Trail Hotline,** ☎856-5330. **Internet access: Public Library,** over a parking garage at Marine Way and S. Franklin St. **Post Office:** 709 W. 9th St. (☎586-7987. Open M-F 8:30am-4:30pm, Sa noon-3pm.) **ZIP code:** 99801. **Area code:** 907.

♫▢ ACCOMMODATIONS & FOOD. On a steep hill, lovely ▧**Juneau International Hostel (HI-AYH) ❶,** 614 Harris St. at 6th St., occupies a prime location. (☎586-9559. 3-night max. stay if full. Lockout 9am-5pm. Curfew midnight. Beds $10. Reservations available by phone.) **Alaskan Hotel ❸,** 167 Franklin St., downtown, has been meticulously restored to its original 1913 decor. (☎586-1000 or 800-327-9347. Kitchenettes and TVs. Laundry. Rooms $60-80; rates lower in winter.) **Mendenhall Lake Campground ❶** is about 6 mi. from the ferry terminal on Montana Creek Rd.;

take Glacier Hwy. north 10 mi. to Mendenhall Loop Rd., continue 3½ mi., and take the right fork. Bus drivers will stop within 2 mi. of camp. The 60 sites have stunning views of the glacier and convenient trail access. (Open June-Sept. Reception 7am-10:30pm. Firepits, water, flush toilets, showers, and firewood. No reservations. Sites $10, with hookup $20.) **Silverbow Bagels ❶**, 120 2nd. St., is the oldest operating bakery in Alaska, and the years of experience shine through in the quality of their food. (☎586-9866. Open M-F 7am-5:30pm, Sa 8am-4:30pm, Su 9am-3:30pm. **Back Room ❷** restaurant open for dinner.) **Fiddlehead Restaurant ❸**, 429 Willoughby Ave., has the best gourmet vegetarian options in town at the best prices. Dinner can get pricey, but cheaper options ($8-12) are still delicious. (☎586-3150. Open 7am-10pm daily.)

🎿 🎣 **SIGHTS & OUTDOOR ACTIVITIES.** The excellent **Alaska State Museum**, 395 Whittier St., leads visitors through the history and culture of Alaska's four major native groups: Tlingit, Athabascan, Aleut, and Inuit. (☎465-2901. Open June-Aug. daily 8:30am-5:30pm; Sept.-May Tu-Sa 10am-4pm. $5, under 18 free.)

The **West Glacier Trail** begins off Montana Creek Rd., by the Mendenhall Lake Campground. The five- to six-hour walk yields stunning views of **Mendenhall Glacier** from the first step to the final outlook. The 3½ mi. trail parallels the glacier through the western hemlock forest and up a rocky cairn-marked scramble to the summit of 4226 ft. **Mt. McGinnis.** At the end of Basin Rd., the easy **Perseverance Trail** leads to the ruins of the Silverbowl Basin Mine and booming waterfalls. The **Granite Creek Trail** branches off the Perseverance Trail and follows the creek to a beautiful basin 3¾ mi. from the trailhead. The summit of Mt. Juneau lies 3 mi. farther along the ridge and also offers terrific views. The shorter, steeper **Mt. Juneau Trail,** which departs from Perseverance Trail about 1 mi. from the trailhead, opens up to similar vistas. Many trails are well-maintained and excellent for mountain biking. Biking off-road is sometimes prohibited.

Tracy Arm, a mini-fjord near Juneau, is known as "the poor man's Glacier Bay," for it offers the same spectacular beauty and wildlife as the national park at well under half the cost. **Alaska Paddle Sports,** 800 6th St. (☎463-5678), provides rental kayaks, pickups and dropoffs in Glacier Bay and elsewhere, and **guided kayak tours.** In winter, the **Eaglecrest Ski Area,** on Douglas Island, offers decent alpine skiing. (☎586-5284. $25 per day, ages 12-17 $17, under 12 $12; ski rental $20/14/14.)

GLACIER BAY NATIONAL PARK ☎907

Glacier Bay was once referred to by explorer Jean François de Galaup de la Perouse as "perhaps the most extraordinary place in the world." Crystal monoliths, broken off from glaciers float peacefully in fjords, while humpback whales maneuver through the maze of the icy blue depths. Glacier Bay National Park encloses nine tidewater glaciers, as well as the **Fairweather Mountains,** the highest coastal range in the world. Charter flights, tours, and cruise ships all probe Glacier Bay, providing close encounters with glaciers, rookeries, whales, and seals. The bay itself is divided into two inlets: the westward **Tarr Inlet** advances as far as the Grand Pacific and Margerie Glaciers, while the eastward **Muir Inlet** ends at the Muir and Riggs Glaciers.

Glacier Bay provides a rare opportunity to see geological and ecological processes radically compressed. A mere two centuries ago, the **Grand Pacific Glacier** covered the entire region under a sheet of ancient ice. Severe earthquakes separated the glacier from its terminal moraine, and the glacier retreated 45 mi. in 150 years—light speed in glacial time. As a result, the uncovered ground is virgin territory, colonized by pioneering vegetation.

Getting to **Bartlett Cove,** the principle access point to the bay, is relatively easy. A plane or ferry takes visitors to **Gustavus,** and from there a taxi or shuttle (about $10) goes to **Glacier Bay Lodge** and the **Visitor Information Center,** both close to the campground in the immediate Bartlett Cove area. Wilderness camping and hiking are permitted throughout the park, though there are no trails except the two near the lodge. Hiking is very difficult in most of the park because of thick alder brush. Backcountry hiking and kayaking are possible in the Dry Bay area, as is **rafting** down the Alsek River. For info, contact the **Yakutat District Office** of the National Park Service (☎ 784-3295).

THE END. Congratulations! You've officially traveled all the way across the North American continent. Take a deep breath, go get your film developed, and get some sleep. And thanks for taking us along for the ride.

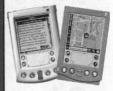

DISTANCES (MI.) & TRAVEL TIMES (BY BUS)

DISTANCES

	Atlanta	Boston	Chic.	Dallas	Denver	D.C.	L.A.	Miami	N. Orl.	NYC	Phila.	Phnx.	St. Lou.	Sa. Fran.	Seattle	Trnto.	Vanc.	Mont.
Atlanta		1108	717	783	1406	632	2366	653	474	886	778	1863	560	2492	2699	959	2825	1240
Boston	22hr.		996	1794	1990	442	3017	1533	1542	194	333	2697	1190	3111	3105	555	3242	326
Chicago	14hr.	20hr.		937	1023	715	2047	1237	928	807	767	1791	302	2145	2108	537	2245	537
Dallas	15hr.	35hr.	18hr.		794	1326	1450	1322	507	1576	1459	906	629	1740	2112	1457	2255	1763
D.C.	12hr.	8hr.	14hr.	24hr.	29hr.		2689	1043	1085	225	139	2350	845	2840	2788	526	2915	665
Denver	27hr.	38hr.	20hr.	15hr.		1700	1026	2046	1341	1785	1759	790	860	1267	1313	1508	1458	1864
L.A.	45hr.	57hr.	39hr.	28hr.	20hr.	55hr.		2780	2005	2787	2723	371	1837	384	1141	2404	1285	2888
Miami	13hr.	30hr.	24hr.	26hr.	39hr.	20hr.	53hr.		856	1346	1214	2368	1197	3086	3368	1564	3505	1676
New O.	9hr.	31hr.	18hr.	10hr.	26hr.	21hr.	38hr.	17hr.		1332	1247	1535	677	2331	2639	1320	2561	1654
NYC	18hr.	4hr.	16hr.	31hr.	35hr.	5hr.	53hr.	26hr.	27hr.		104	2592	999	2923	2912	496	3085	386
Phila.	18hr.	6hr.	16hr.	19hr.	33hr.	3hr.	50hr.	23hr.	23hr.	2hr.		2511	904	2883	2872	503	3009	465
Phoenix	40hr.	49hr.	39hr.	19hr.	17hr.	43hr.	8hr.	47hr.	30hr.	45hr.	44hr.		1503	753	1510	2069	1654	2638
St. Louis	11hr.	23hr.	6hr.	13hr.	17hr.	15hr.	35hr.	23hr.	13hr.	19hr.	16hr.	32hr.		2113	2139	810	2276	1128
San Fran.	47hr.	60hr.	41hr.	47hr.	33hr.	60hr.	7hr.	59hr.	43hr.	56hr.	54hr.	15hr.	45hr.		807	2630	951	2985
Seattle	52hr.	59hr.	40hr.	40hr.	25hr.	54hr.	22hr.	65hr.	50hr.	55hr.	54hr.	28hr.	36hr.	16hr.		2623	146	2964
Toronto	21hr.	11hr.	10hr.	26hr.	26hr.	11hr.	48hr.	29hr.	13hr.	11hr.	13hr.	48hr.	14hr.	49hr.	48hr.		2785	655
Vancvr.	54hr.	61hr.	42hr.	43hr.	27hr.	60hr.	24hr.	67hr.	54hr.	57hr.	56hr.	30hr.	38hr.	18hr.	2hr.	53hr.		4861
Montreal	23hr.	6hr.	17hr.	28hr.	39hr.	12hr.	53hr.	32hr.	31hr.	7hr.	9hr.	53hr.	23hr.	56hr.	55hr.	7hr.	55hr.	

INDEX

A

A&P editor 81
Acadia National Park,
 ME 84
Acadiana, LA 461
accommodations 42
action figures
 for which you can
  make up your own
  dialogue 286
The Adirondacks, NY 256
adventure trips 51
AIDS 41
airplanes 53
Alabama 421–433
 Birmingham 426
 Huntsville 430
 Mobile 430
 Montgomery 422
 Selma 425
 Tuskegee 424
Alaska 1015–1028
 Anchorage 1016
 Denali National Park
  and Preserve 1020
 Fairbanks 1022
 Glacier Bay National
  Park 1027
 Juneau 1026
 Kenai Fjords National
  Park 1019
 Ketchikan 1024
 Misty Fjords National
  Monument 1026
 Seward 1019
 Wrangell-St. Elias
  National Park 1020
Albany, NY 247
Alberta 1007–1014
 Alberta Badlands 1014
 Banff National Park
  1009
 Calgary 1013
 Jasper National Park

  1011
 Waterton Lakes
  National Park 714
Alberta Badlands, AB
 1014
Albuquerque, NM 839
alcohol 38
Alexandria Bay, NY 260
Alexandria, VA 322
Amarillo, TX 686
American Express 35
American Red Cross 39
American University,
 see Washington, D.C.
Amtrak 59
Anchorage, AK 1016
Ann Arbor, MI 540
Annapolis, MD 297
Antelope Island State
 Park, UT 781
Apostle Islands, WI 585
Appalachian Trail 85,
 340, 347, 370
Arapahoe/Roosevelt
 National Forest, CO 748
Arches National Park,
 UT 788
Arco, ID 700
Arizona 795–830
 Biosphere 2 828
 Bisbee 829
 Chiricahua National
  Monument 830
 Coconino National
  Forest 807
 Flagstaff 803
 Grand Canyon 795
 Havasupai
  Reservation 803
 Hopi Reservation 812
 Kaibab National
  Forest 798
 Montezuma Castle
  National Monument
  810
 Monument Valley 811

 Navajo National
  Monument 812
 Navajo Reservation
  810
 Page 814
 Painted Desert 813
 Petrified Forest
  National Park 813
 Phoenix 817
 Saguaro National
  Park 827
 Sedona 808
 Sunset Crater Volcano
  National Monument
  808
 Tombstone 828
 Tonto National Forest
  822
 Tonto National
  Monument 822
 Tucson 823
 Tuzigoot National
  Monument 810
 Walnut Canyon
  National Monument
  807
 Wupatki National
  Monument 808
Arkansas 465–467
 Helena 378
 Little Rock 466
Arlington, VA 321
Asheville, NC 384
Ashland, OR 987
Aspen, CO 756
Assateague Island, VA
 300
Astoria, OR 980
Athens, GA 413
Atlanta, GA 401
Atlantic City, NJ 261
ATM cards 35
au pair 75
Austin, TX 661
auto racing
 Daytona Beach, FL

475
Indianapolis, IN 531
auto transport
companies 65
automobile clubs 61
Avenue of the Giants, CA
933

B

B&Bs 45
backpacks 51
Badlands National Park,
SD 612
Baltimore, MD 291
Bandelier National
Monument, NM 836
Bandera, TX 662
Bandon-by-the-Sea, OR
981
Banff National Park, AB
1009
Bar Harbor, ME 82
Bardstown, KY 354
bargaining 36
Baton Rouge, LA 458
bears 48
Beaufort, SC 395
bed and breakfasts 45
Beer Can House 682
Beirut
the city, see Let's Go
Middle East 2003
the drinking game 240
Bend, OR 988
Berkeley, CA 919
bicycles 65
Big Bear, CA 875
Big Bend National Park,
TX 691
Bighorn National Forest,
WY 733
Biosphere 2, AZ 828
Birmingham, AL 426
Bisbee, AZ 829
Bismarck, ND 606
Black Canyon of the
Gunnison National Park,
CO 761
Black Hills National

Forest, SD 615
Block Island, RI 142
Bloomington, IN 532
Bodie Island, NC 388
Boerne, TX 662
Boise State University,
see Boise, ID
Boise, ID 694
Boone, NC 384
Boston, MA 105
Boulder, CO 747
Bowling Green, KY 355
Bozeman, MT 702
Branson, MO 649
Brattleboro, VT 103
Breckenridge, CO 746
Bridger-Teton National
Forest, WY 730
British Columbia 991–1004
Dawson Creek 1002
Pacific Rim National
Park 1001
Prince Rupert 1001
Vancouver 993
Victoria 999
Whistler 998
Brookings, OR 981
Brown University, see
Providence, RI
Brown, John 345
Browning, MT 713
Bryce Canyon National
Park, UT 790
Buffalo, NY 252
Burlington, VT 96
buses 59
Butt's Tubes, Inc. 347

C

Calaveras County, CA 935
Calgary, AB 1013
California 850–946
Avenue of the Giants
933
Berkeley 919
Big Bear 875
Calaveras County 935
Calistoga 925
Cascades 937

Death Valley National
Park 887
Devil's Postpile
National Monument
946
Disneyland 874
Escondido 881
Inyo National Forest 945
Joshua Tree National
Park 885
La Jolla 881
Lake Tahoe 937
Los Angeles 850
Mammoth Lakes 946
Marin County 921
Mendocino 932
Mono Lake 945
Monterey 893
Muir Woods National
Monument 922
Napa Valley 925
Orange County 872
Palm Springs 884
Palo Alto 925
Sacramento 935
San Diego 876
San Francisco 897
San Luis Obispo 891
Santa Barbara 888
Santa Cruz 894
Sierra Nevada 937
Sonoma Valley 928
Yosemite National Park
941
California Polytechnic
State University, see
San Luis Obispo, CA
Calistoga, CA 925
calling cards 52
Cambridge, MA 121
Camden, ME 85
camping 46
Canada
Eastern Canada 148–
202
Western Canada 991–
1014
Cannon Beach, OR 980
Cape Breton Island, NS
153
Cape Canaveral, FL 484

Cape Cod, MA 127
Cape May, NJ 266
Cape Vincent, NY 260
Capitol Reef National Park, UT 789
car rentals 63
Carlsbad Caverns National Park, NM 849
Carnegie Mellon University, see Pittsburgh, PA
cars
  auto transport companies 65
  automobile clubs 61
  driving permits 61
  insurance 61
  interstate driving 63
  maintenance 63
  rental 63
Cascades, CA 937
Case Western Reserve University, see Cleveland, OH
casinos
  Illinois 642
  Louisiana 448
  Mississippi 436
  Missouri 642
  Nevada 773, 776, 939
  New Jersey 263
  Ontario 539
  South Dakota 619
  Tennessee 369
Casper, WY 735
Castillo de San Marcos National Monument, FL 473
Catskill Forest Preserve, NY 245
Cavendish, PEI 162
Cedar Breaks National Monument, UT 794
Centers for Disease Control (CDC) 39
Champlain Valley, VT 99
changing money 35
Chapel Hill, NC 379
Charleston, SC 391
Charlotte, NC 383

Charlottesville, VA 335
Charlottetown, PEI 160
Chattanooga, TN 370
Cherokee Reservation, TN 369
Cheyenne, WY 735
Chicago, IL 553
Chillicothe, OH 525
Chincoteague Island, VA 300
Chippewa National Forest, MN 599
Chiricahua National Monument, AZ 830
Cibola National Forest, NM 843
Cincinnati, OH 525
Ciudad Juárez, Mexico 688
Clarksdale, MS 378
Clayton, NY 260
Clearwater, FL 509
Clemens, Samuel, see Twain, Mark
Cleveland, OH 518
Cocoa Beach, FL 484
Coconino National Forest, AZ 807
Cody, "Buffalo Bill" 732
Cody, WY 731
College of William and Mary, see Williamsburg, VA
College, Stoner see also Harper's Ferry, WV see Blazejewski, Chris
Colorado 738–768
  Arapahoe/Roosevelt National Forest 748
  Aspen 756
  Black Canyon of the Gunnison National Park 761
  Boulder 747
  Breckenridge 746
  Colorado Springs 758
  Crested Butte 761
  Denver 739
  Durango 765
  Estes Park 750

  Glenwood Springs 757
  Grand Lake 751
  Gunnison National Forest 760
  Mesa Verde National Park 767
  Pagosa Springs 767
  Pikes Peak National Forest 759
  Río Grande National Forest 760
  Rocky Mountain National Park 750
  San Juan National Forest 766
  Steamboat Springs 755
  Summit County 746
  Telluride 762
  Uncompahgre National Forest 760
  Vail 753
  White River National Forest 746, 758
  Winter Park 745
Colorado Springs, CO 758
Columbia River Gorge, OR 983
Columbia University, see New York City, NY
Columbia, SC 395
Columbus, OH 523
Concord, MA 124
Connecticut 143–147
  Hartford 143
  Mystic 146
  New Haven 144
consulates 30
converting currency 35
Conway, NH 94
Cooke City, MT 720
Cooper, James Fenimore 248
Cooperstown, NY 248
Cornell University, see Ithaca, NY
Corpus Christi, TX 684
courier flights 54
Crater Lake, OR 986
Craters of the Moon National Monument, ID 700

credit cards 35
Crested Butte, CO 761
Cumberland Island
  National Seashore, GA
  420
currency exchange 35
Custer State Park, SD 618
customs 34
Cuyahoga Valley National
  Park, OH 522

D

Dallas, TX 670
Davis, Julia 696
Dawson Creek, BC 1002
Daytona Beach, FL 474
Deadwood, SD 619
Death Valley National
  Park, CA 887
dehydration 39
Delaware 288–290
  Lewes 288
  Rehoboth Beach 289
Dempster Highway, YT
  1007
Denali National Park and
  Preserve, AK 1020
Denver, CO 739
Des Moines, IA 620
Deschutes National
  Forest, OR 988
Detroit, MI 533
Devil's Postpile National
  Monument, CA 946
Devils Tower National
  Monument, WY 734
diarrhea 40
Dinosaur National
  Monument, UT 783
disabled travelers 69
Disney World, FL 479
Disneyland, CA 874
Dixie National Forest, UT
  788
Dodge City, KS 637
Door County, WI 583
dorms 45
Drexel University, see
  Philadelphia, PA

driving permits 61
drugs 38
Dubuque, IA 625
Duke University, see
  Durham, NC
Duluth, MN 597
Durango, CO 765
Durham, NC 379
dysentery 40

E

Eastern Canada 148–202
Eastham, MA 128
Effigy Mounds National
  Monument, IA 626
El Morro National
  Monument, NM 845
El Paso, TX 688
Ely, MN 600
email 53
embassies 30
entrance requirements 30
Escondido, CA 881
Estes Park, CO 750
Eugene, OR 984
Eveleth, MN 599
Everglades National Park,
  FL 499
Evergreen State College,
  see Olympia, WA
exchange rates 35
exhaustion, heat 39

F

Fairbanks, AK 1022
False Creek, BC 998
Fargo, ND 605
Faulkner, William 433,
  437, 447, 461
featured topics
  Bank One Tower—Fort
    Worth, TX 676
  Cockfighting—Lafayette,
    LA 462
  Community Planning—
    Arcosanti, AZ 808
  Confederate Flag
    Controversies—

  Columbia, SC 396
  Enron Bankruptcy—
    Houston, TX 680
  Halibut Fishing—
    Seward, AK 1018
  Hiawatha Light Rail—
    Minneapolis-St. Paul,
    MN 590
  Highway Construction—
    Boston, MA 106
  Literary Readings—New
    York, NY 235
  Mayor Buddy Cianci—
    Providence, RI 138
  Michelangelo Drawing
    Discovery—New York,
    NY 228
  Police Brutality—
    Cincinnati, OH 526
  Racial Unease—
    Montgomery, AL 422
  Response to
    September 11—
    Moncton, NB 158
  Scopes Monkey Trial—
    Dayton, TN 364
  Underage Drinking—
    Washington, D.C. 320
female travelers 67
festivals
  Albany, NY 248
  Albuquerque, NM 834
  Ann Arbor, MI 542
  Apostle Islands, WI 587
  Asheville, NC 386
  Ashland, OR 987
  Aspen, CO 756
  Austin, TX 668
  Baltimore, MD 296
  Beaufort, SC 395
  Black Hills, SD 616
  Boise, ID 696
  Boulder, CO 749
  Breckenridge, CO 747
  Browning, MT 713
  Buffalo, NY 253
  Burlington, VT 99
  Calgary, AB 1014
  Casper, WY 735
  Charlottesville, VA 338
  Chattanooga, TN 372

Cheyenne, WY 736
Chicago, IL 569
Crested Butte, CO 762
Dallas, TX 673
Daytona Beach, FL 475
Denver, CO 744
Des Moines, IA 623
Detroit, MI 538
Dodge City, KS 637
Eugene, OR 985
Fairbanks, AK 1024
Fargo, ND 606
Fort Worth, TX 676
Gainesville, FL 513
Garberville, CA 933
Grand Rapids, MN 601
Halifax, NS 152
Hannibal, MO 643
Helena, AR 378
Houston, TX 682
Indianapolis, IN 531
Iowa City, IA 624
Jackson, WY 730
Kansas City, MO 648
Key West, FL 506
Knoxville, TN 367
Lafayette, LA 465
Lancaster County, PA 281
Laramie, WY 738
Lenox, MA 136
Lincoln, NE 632, 633
Louisville, KY 353
Macon, GA 417
Memphis, TN 378
Miami, FL 498
Milwaukee, WI 578
Minneapolis, MN 596
Missoula, MT 707
Mobile, AL 432
Montgomery, AL 424
Montréal, QC 178
Natchitoches, LA 461
New Haven, CT 146
New Orleans, LA 452
Newport, RI 142
Oklahoma City, OK 654
Omaha, NE 630
Pella, IA 623
Philadelphia, PA 277
Pine Hill, NY 246

Portland, ME 80
Portland, OR 979
Prince Rupert, BC 1002
Québec City, QC 184
Red Lodge, MT 705
Roswell, NM 848
San Antonio, TX 661
San Francisco, CA 916
San Juan Island, WA 963
Santa Fe, NM 835
Savannah, GA 420
Seattle, WA 958
St. Paul, MN 596
Tampa, FL 509
Telluride, CO 763
Toronto, ON 194
Traverse City, MI 546
Tulsa, OK 652
Virginia Beach, VA 335
Williamstown, MA 136
film
  Canada 29
  United States 19
film festivals
  Austin, TX 916
  Fargo, ND 606
  Halifax, NS 153
  Newport, RI 142
  Portland, OR 979
  San Francisco, CA 916
  Seattle, WA 958
  Telluride, CO 763
  Toronto, ON 194
The Finger Lakes, NY 250
"fire in the hole" 722
Fire Island, NY 244
Flagler College, see St. Augustine, FL
Flagstaff, AZ 803
Flaming Gorge National Recreation Area, UT 785
Florida 468–516
  Cape Canaveral 484
  Castillo de San Marcos National Monument 473
  Clearwater 509
  Cocoa Beach 484
  Daytona Beach 474
  Everglades National

  Park 499
  Fort Lauderdale 487
  Gainesville 511
  Key Largo 502
  Key West 503
  Orlando 475
  Palm Beach 485
  Panama City 513
  Pensacola 515
  St. Augustine 471
  St. Petersburg 509
  Tampa 507
  Walt Disney World 479
  West Palm Beach 485
flowers, suggestive, see O'Keeffe, Georgia
Forests, see **National Forests**
Fort Lauderdale, FL 487
Fort Pulaski National Monument, SC 420
Fort Worth, TX 675
Franconia Notch, NH 92
Fredericksburg, TX 663
Fredericksburg, VA 327
Freeport, ME 85
frostbite 39
Fundy National Park, NB 157

G

Gainesville, FL 511
Gallup, NM 844
gambling, see casinos
Gardiner, MT 720
gay travelers 68
George Washington National Forest, VA 342
Georgetown University, see Washington, D.C. 305
Georgia 400–421
  Athens 413
  Atlanta 401
  Cumberland Island National Seashore 420
  Savannah 418
  St. Mary's 420
Gettsyburg, PA 281

Gila Cliff Dwellings National Monument, NM 846
Gila National Forest, NM 846
Ginsberg, Allen 235
Glacier Bay National Park, AK 1027
Glacier National Park, MT 709
Glen Canyon National Recreation Area, UT 814
Glenwood Springs, CO 757
GO25 card 34
Golden Access Passport 47
Golden Age Passport 47
Grand Canyon, AZ 795
Grand Haven, MI 545
Grand Lake, CO 751
Grand Marais, MN 602
Grand Rapids, MI 543
Grand Staircase-Escalante National Monument, UT 792
Grand Strand, SC 398
Grand Teton National Park, WY 724
Granville Island, BC 998
Great Smoky Mountains National Park, TN 367
Gros Morne National Park, NF 165
Guadalupe Mountains National Park, TX 687
Gunnison National Forest, CO 760
Guttenberg, IA 625

H

Halifax, NS 151
halls of fame
Alabama Sports, AL 429
American Police, FL 498
Baseball, NY 249
Cowgirl, NM 835
Fishing, FL 491
Georgia Music, GA 416

Georgia Sports, GA 417
Hockey, ON 193
International Bowling, MO 641
Marine, MI 551
Mountain Biking, CO 762
Oklahoma Jazz, OK 652
Olympic, AB 1013
Pro Football, OH 523
Rock and Roll, OH 521
Ski, CO 754
St. Louis Cardinals, MO 641
US Hockey, MN 599
Women's Basketball, TN 366
The Hamptons, NY 244
Hannibal, MO 643
Harpers Ferry, WV 345
Hartford, CT 143
Hatteras, NC 388
Havasupai Reservation, AZ 803
health 39
Helena, AR 378
Helena, MT 701
Hells Canyon, OR 989
Hemingway, Ernest 219, 505, 506, 549, 550, 565, 696, 698, 720
hepatitis 40
Hiawatha National Forest, MI 552
hiking equipment 49
history
   Canada 27
   United States 8
hitchhiking 67
HIV 41
holidays 24
Holland, MI 545
Hopi Reservation, AZ 812
hostels
Albuquerque, NM 841
Anchorage, AK 1017
Ashland, OR 987
Atlanta, GA 403
Austin, TX 665
Banff National Park, AB 1009

Bar Harbor, ME 82
Bend, OR 988
Bodie Island, NC 388
Boise, ID 695
Boulder, CO 748
Breckenridge, CO 747
Buffalo, NY 252
Burlington, VT 97
Calgary, AB 1013
Cape Breton Island, NS 154
Capitol Reef National Park, UT 790
Charlottetown, PEI 161
Chicago, IL 558
Clearwater, FL 510
Columbia River Gorge, OR 983
Conway, NH 94
Crested Butte, CO 762
Deadwood, SD 619
Denali National Park, AK 1021
Denver, CO 741
Detroit, MI 536
Durango, CO 765
El Paso, TX 690
Eugene, OR 985
Everglades National Park, FL 500
Fairbanks, AK 1023
Fort Lauderdale, FL 489, 490
Fundy National Park, NB 157
Gettysburg, PA 282
Glacier National Park, MT 711
Glenwood Springs, CO 757
Grand Lake, CO 751
Halifax, NS 151
Harpers Ferry, WV 346
Hartford, CT 143
Houston, TX 679
Jackson, WY 729
Jasper National Park, AB 1011
Juneau, AK 1026
Ketchikan, AK 1025
Key West, FL 505

Knoxville, TN 365
Lake Placid, NY 258
Lake Tahoe, CA 938
Las Vegas, NV 772
Lincoln, NE 631
Los Angeles, CA 854
Madison, WI 580
Marin County, CA 923
Memphis, TN 373
Miami, FL 495
Milwaukee, WI 574
Minneapolis, MN 591
Monterey, CA 893
Montréal, QC 171
Mt. Rainier National
  Park, WA 973
New Orleans, LA 442
New York City, NY 209
Niagara Falls, NY 254
Niagara Falls, ON 254
North Conway, NH 94
Olympia, WA 961
Olympic National Park,
  WA 965
Orange County, CA 873
Ottawa, ON 199
Pacific Rim National
  Park, BC 1001
Philadelphia, PA 270
Phoenix, AZ 819
Pine Hill, NY 246
Pittsburgh, PA 284
Port Townsend, WA 964
Portland, OR 975
Québec City, QC 181
Sacramento, CA 935
San Antonio, TX 658
San Diego, CA 878
San Francisco, CA 899
San Luis Obispo, CA 891
Santa Barbara, CA 889
Santa Cruz, CA 895
Savannah, GA 419
Seattle, WA 953
Seward, AK 1019
Shenandoah National
  Park, VA 339
St. Augustine, FL 472
St. Ignatius, MT 708
St. John's, NF 163
St. Louis, MO 638

St. Petersburg, FL 510
Summit County, CO 746
Tampa, FL 508
Taos, NM 837
Thousand Island
  Seaway, NY 260
Toronto, ON 191
Truth or Consequences,
  NM 845
Tucson, AZ 825
Vancouver, BC 995
Vashon Island, WA 961
Victoria, BC 999
Washington, D.C. 307
Waterton Lakes
  National Park, AB 714
West Yellowstone, MT
  720
Whistler, BC 999
Wrangell-St. Elias
  National Park, AK 1020
Yarmouth, NS 151
Yosemite, CA 943
Zion National Park, UT
  793
hotels 44
Houston, TX 676
Huntsville, AL 430
Hyannis, MA 127
hypothermia 39

I

Idaho 693–700
  Arco 700
  Boise 694
  Craters of the Moon
    National Monument
    700
  Ketchum 696
  Sawtooth National
    Recreation Area 698
  Stanley 698
  Sun Valley 696
identification 34
Iditarod Trail, AK 1017
Île-d'Orléans, QC 185
Illinois 553–573
  Chicago 553
  Springfield 571

Immigration and
  Naturalization Service
  (INS) 72
immunizations 39
Indian Reservations, see
  Native American
  Reservations
Indiana 529–533
  Bloomington 532
  Indianapolis 529
Indiana University, see
  Bloomington, IN
Indianapolis, IN 529
insurance 41, 65
Intercourse, PA 279
International Student
  Identity Card (ISIC) 34
International Teacher
  Identity Card (ITIC) 34
International Youth
  Discount Travel Card 34
Internet 53
interstates 63
Inyo National Forest, CA
  945
Iowa 620–627
  Des Moines 620
  Dubuque 625
  Effigy Mounds National
    Monument 626
  Guttenberg 625
  Iowa City 624
  Madison County 623
  McGregor 625
  Okoboji 627
  Pella 623
  Prairie City 623
  Sabula 625
  Spirit Lake 627
  Winterset 623
Iowa City, IA 624
Iron Range, MN 599
ISIC card 34
Ithaca, NY 250
ITIC card 34

J

Jackson, MS 433
Jackson, WY 729

Jamestown, VA 332
Jasper National Park, AB 1011
Jewel Cave, SD 618
Johnson City, TX 663
Jones, John Paul 299
Joplin, Janis 910
Joplin, Scott 641
Joshua Tree National Park, CA 885
Julliard School of Music, see New York City, NY
Juneau, AK 1026

K

Kaibab National Forest, AZ 798
Kansas 633–636
  Dodge City 637
  Kansas City 644
  Lawrence 636
  Lebanon 633
  Wichita 634
Kansas City, KS 644
Kansas City, MO 644
Kenai Fjords National Park, AK 1019
Kennebunk, ME 81
Kennebunkport, ME 81
Kennedy, John F. 673
Kentucky 349–359
  Bardstown 354
  Bowling Green 355
  Lexington 356
  Louisville 352
  Mammoth Cave National Park 355
  White Hall 358
Kerrville, TX 662
Ketchikan, AK 1024
Ketchum, ID 696
Keweenaw Peninsula, MI 552
Key Largo, FL 502
Key West, FL 503
Kisatchie National Forest, LA 460
Kit Carson National Forest, NM 837

Klamath Falls, OR 986
Kluane National Park, YT 1006
Knoxville, TN 365
kosher travelers 70
Kouchibouguac National Park, NB 159

L

La Jolla, CA 881
Lafayette, LA 463
Lake Champlain, VT 99
Lake Placid, NY 257
Lake Powell, UT 814
Lake Superior National Forest, MN 601
Lake Tahoe, CA 937
Lakeshores, see National Lakeshores
Lancaster County, PA 279
Laramie, WY 738
Las Vegas, NV 771
Lawrence, KS 636
Lebanon, KS 633
Lebanon, NH 103
Lenox, MA 136
lesbian travelers 68
Lewes, DE 288
Lexington, KY 356
Lexington, MA 123
Lexington, VA 343
Lighthouse Route, NS 150
Lincoln, Abraham 572
Lincoln, NE 630
literature
  Canada 28
  United States 15
Little Big Horn National Monument, MT 702
Little Rock, AR 466
Livingston, MT 704
Long Island, NY 243
Los Alamos, NM 836
Los Angeles, CA 850
Louisiana 439–465
  Acadiana 461
  Baton Rouge 458
  Kisatchie National Forest 460

  Lafayette 463
  Natchitoches 459
  New Orleans 439
  Louisiana State University, see Baton Rouge, LA
Louisville, KY 352
Lunenburg, NS 150
Lyme disease 40

M

Mackinac Island, MI 548
Madeline Island, WI 587
Madison County, IA 623
Madison, WI 579
mail 51
Maine 78–85
  Acadia National Park 84
  Bar Harbor 82
  Camden 85
  Freeport 85
  Kennebunk 81
  Kennebunkport 81
  Mt. Desert Island 82
  Ogunquit 81
  Portland 79
  Wells, ME 81
Mammoth Cave National Park, KY 355
Mammoth Lakes, CA 946
Manistee, MI 545
Manson, Charles 910
Manteo, NC 388
Manti-La Sal National Forest, UT 789
Marin County, CA 921
Martha's Vineyard, MA 131
Maryland 290–303
  Annapolis 297
  Assateague Island 300
  Baltimore 291
  Ocean City 302
Massachusetts 104–137
  Boston 105
  Cambridge 121
  Cape Cod 127
  Concord 124
  Eastham 128

Hyannis 127
Lenox 136
Lexington 123
Martha's Vineyard 131
Nantucket 133
North Adams 135
Plymouth 125
Provincetown 129
Salem 125
Williamstown 136
McGill University, see
Montréal, QC
McGregor, IA 625
Medicine Bow National
Forest, WY 737
Medina, TX 662
memorials
Civil Rights Memorial,
AL 423
Crazy Horse, SD 617
Fort Clatsop National
Memorial, OR 980
Franklin Delano
Roosevelt Memorial,
D.C. 313
Hemingway Memorial,
ID 698
Holocaust Memorial, FL
497
Iwo Jima Memorial, VA
321
Jefferson Expansion
Memorial, MO 640
Jefferson Memorial,
D.C. 313
Korean War Memorial,
D.C. 313
Lincoln Memorial, D.C.
313
Mary Tyler Moore 591
Mt. Rushmore 616
National War Memorial,
ON 200
Oklahoma City National
Memorial, OK 654
Vietnam Veterans
Memorial, D.C. 313
Volunteer Firemen, CA
908
Wright Brothers
National Memorial, NC

389
Memphis, TN 372
Mendocino, CA 932
Mesa Verde National
Park, CO 767
Mexico
Ciudad Juárez 688
Tijuana 881
Michigan 533–553
Ann Arbor 540
Detroit 533
Grand Haven 545
Grand Rapids 543
Hiawatha National
Forest 552
Holland 545
Keweenaw Peninsula
552
Mackinac Island 548
Manistee 545
Petoskey 550
Sault Ste. Marie 551
Traverse City 546
Upper Peninsula 550
Middlebury College, see
Middlebury, VT
Middlebury, VT 99
mileage chart 1030
Milwaukee, WI 573
Minneapolis, MN 588
Minnesota 588–602
Chippewa National
Forest 599
Duluth 597
Ely 600
Eveleth 599
Grand Marais 602
Lake Superior National
Forest 601
Minneapolis 588
Soudan 599
St. Paul 588
Voyageurs National
Park 600
minority travelers 69
Mississippi 433–439
Clarksdale 378
Jackson 433
Oxford 437
Vicksburg 435
Missoula, MT 705

Missouri 637–650
Branson 649
Hannibal 643
Kansas City 644
St. Louis 637
Misty Fjords National
Monument, AK 1026
Moab, UT 786
Mobile, AL 430
Moncton, NB 158
money 35
Mono Lake, CA 945
Monongahela National
Forest, WV 347
Montana 701–715
Bozeman 702
Browning 713
Cooke City 720
Gardiner 720
Glacier National Park
709
Helena 701
Little Big Horn National
Monument 702
Livingston 704
Missoula 705
Polson 708
Red Lodge 704
St. Ignatius 708
West Yellowstone 720
Whitefish 713
Montana State
University, see
Bozeman, MT
Montauk, NY 244
Monterey, CA 893
Montezuma Castle
National Monument, AZ
810
Montgomery, AL 422
Montréal, QC 166
Monument Valley, AZ 811
motorcycles 65
Mt. Desert Island, ME 82
Mt. Hood, OR 982
Mt. McKinley, see Denali
National Park and
Preserve, AK
Mt. Rainier National Park,
WA 972
Mt. Rushmore, SD 616

INDEX

Mt. St. Helens, WA 968
Mt. Tremper, NY 245
Mt. Vernon, VA 322
Muir Woods National
  Monument, CA 922
music
  Canada 28
  United States 18
  Myrtle Beach, SC 398
  Mystic, CT 146

N

Nantucket, MA 133
Napa Valley, CA 925
Naropa University, see
  Boulder, CO
Nashville, TN 359
Natchitoches, LA 459
National Forest info 48
National Forests
  Arapahoe/Roosevelt,
    CO 748
  Bighorn, WY 733
  Black Hills, SD 615
  Boise, ID 695
  Bridger-Teton, WY 730
  Chippewa, MN 599
  Cibola, NM 843
  Coconino, AZ 807
  Deschutes, OR 988
  Dixie, UT 788
  George Washington, VA
    342
  Gila, NM 846
  Gunnison, CO 760
  Hiawatha, MI 552
  Inyo, CA 945
  Kaibab, AZ 798
  Kisatchie, LA 460
  Kit Carson, NM 837
  Lake Superior, MN 601
  Manti-La Sal, UT 789
  Medicine Bow, WY 737
  Monongahela, WV 347
  Mt. Baker-Snoqualmie,
    WA 970
  Mt. St. Helens, WA 968
  Olympic, WA 961
  Pikes Peak, CO 759

Río Grande, CO 760
San Juan, CO 760, 766
Santa Fe, NM 836
Shoshone, WY 724
Tongass, AK 1025
Tonto, AZ 822
Uinta, UT 783
Uncompahgre, CO 760
White Mountain, NH 89
White River, CO 746, 758
Willamette, OR 985
National Historic Sites
The Alamo, TX 659
Cave and Basin, AB
  1010
Chaco Canyon, NM 844
Fort Raleigh, NC 389
Fort Sumter, SC 394
Halifax Citadel National
  Historic Park, NS 152
Harpers Ferry, WV 347
Herbert Hoover, IA 626
Hopewell Culture
  National Historical
  Park, OH 525
Independence National
  Historical Park, PA 272
Lincoln Home, IL 572
San Antonio Missions
  National Historical
  Park, TX 659
San Juan National
  Historical Park, WA 963
Valley Forge National
  Historical Park, PA 279
Vicksburg, MS 436
National Lakeshores
Apostle Islands, WI 585
Indiana Dunes, IN 571
Pictured Rocks, MI 551
Sleeping Bear Dunes,
  MI 545
National Monuments
Bandelier, NM 836
Castillo de San Marcos,
  FL 473
Cedar Breaks, UT 794
Chiricahua, AZ 830
Craters of the Moon, ID
  700
Devil's Postpile, CA 946

Devils Tower, WY 734
Dinosaur, UT 783
Effigy Mounds, IA 626
El Morro, NM 845
Fort Pulaski, SC 420
Gila Cliff Dwellings, NM
  846
Grand Staircase-
  Escalante, UT 792
Jewel Cave, SD 618
Little Big Horn, MT 702
Misty Fjords, AK 1026
Montezuma Castle, AZ
  810
Mt. St. Helens, WA 968
Muir Woods, CA 922
Navajo, AZ 812
Petroglyph, NM 843
Scotts Bluff, NE 632
Sunset Crater Volcano,
  AZ 808
Tonto, AZ 822
Tuzigoot, AZ 810
Walnut Canyon, AZ 807
White Sands, NM 847
Wupatki, AZ 808
National Park info
  Golden Access
    Passport 47
  Golden Age Passport 47
National Parks
Acadia, ME 84
Arches, UT 788
Badlands, SD 612
Banff, AB 1009
Big Bend, TX 691
Black Canyon of the
  Gunnison, CO 761
Bryce Canyon, UT 790
Cape Breton Highlands,
  NS 154
Capitol Reef, UT 789
Carlsbad Caverns, NM
  849
Charlottetown, PEI 161
Crater Lake, OR 986
Cuyahoga Valley, OH
  522
Death Valley, CA 887
Denali, AK 1020
Everglades, FL 499

Fundy, NB 157
Glacier Bay, AK 1027
Glacier, MT 709
Grand Canyon, AZ 795
Grand Teton, WY 724
Great Smoky
  Mountains, TN 367
Gros Morne, NF 165
Guadalupe Mountains,
  TX 687
Jasper, AB 1011
Joshua Tree, CA 885
Kenai Fjords, AK 1019
Kluane, YT 1006
Kouchibouguac, NB 159
Mammoth Cave, KY 355
Mesa Verde, CO 767
Mt. Rainier, WA 972
North Cascades, WA
  970
Olympic, WA 965
Pacific Rim, BC 1001
Petrified Forest, AZ 813
Rocky Mountain, CO 750
Saguaro, AZ 827
Shenandoah, VA 338
Voyageurs, MN 600
Waterton Lakes, AB 714
Wind Cave, SD 617
Wrangell-St. Elias, AK
  1020
Yellowstone, WY 715
Yosemite, CA 941
Zion, UT 793
**National Recreation
Areas**
Flaming Gorge, UT 785
Golden Gate, CA 906
Hells Canyon, OR 989
Lake Mead, NV 775
Missoula, MT 707
Oregon Dunes, OR 981
Sawtooth, ID 698
National Seashores
Assateague Island, MD
  301
Canaveral, FL 485
Cape Hatteras, NC 389
Cumberland Island, GA
  420
Gulf Island, FL 515

Padre Island, TX 685
National Wildlife Refuges
Chincoteague, VA 302
Merritt Island, FL 485
Missisquoi, VT 99
Pea Island, NC 390
Prarie City, IA 623
Rachel Carson, ME 81
**Native American
Reservations**
Blackfeet Indian
  Reservation, MT 713
Cherokee Reservation,
  TN 369
Havasupai Reservation,
  AZ 803
Hopi Reservation, AZ
  812
Leech Lake Indian
  Reservation, MN 599
Navajo Reservation, AZ
  810
Navajo National
  Monument, AZ 812
Navajo Reservation, AZ
  810
Nebraska 627–633
Lincoln 630
Omaha 628
Scotts Bluff National
  Monument 632
Nevada 769–777
Lake Tahoe 937
Las Vegas 771
Pyramid Lake 777
Reno 775
New Braunfels, TX 662
New Brunswick 155–159
Fundy National Park 157
Kouchibouguac
  National Park 159
Moncton 158
Saint John 155
New Hampshire 87–95
Conway 94
Franconia Notch 92
Lebanon 103
North Conway 94
Pinkham Notch 91
Portsmouth 87
White Mountain

National Forest 89
New Haven, CT 144
New Jersey 261–266
Atlantic City 261
Cape May 266
New Mexico 830–849
Albuquerque 839
Bandelier National
  Monument 836
Carlsbad Caverns
  National Park 849
Cibola National Forest
  843
El Morro National
  Monument 845
Gallup 844
Gila Cliff Dwellings
  National Monument
  846
Gila National Forest 846
Kit Carson National
  Forest 837
Los Alamos 836
Petroglyph National
  Monument 843
Roswell 848
Sangre de Cristo
  Mountains 835
Santa Fe 831
Santa Fe National
  Forest 836
Taos 836
Truth or Consquences
  845
White Sands National
  Monument 847
New Orleans, LA 439
New River Gorge, WV 341
New York 203–261
The Adirondacks 256
Albany 247
Alexandria Bay 260
Buffalo 252
Cape Vincent 260
Catskill Forest Preserve
  245
Clayton 260
Cooperstown 248
The Finger Lakes 250
Fire Island 244
The Hamptons 244

Ithaca 250
Lake Placid 257
Long Island 243
Montauk 244
Mt. Tremper 245
New York City 205
Niagara Falls 253
Phoenicia 246
Thousand Island
 Seaway 259
New York City, NY 205
New York University, see
 New York City, NY
Newfoundland 162–165
 Gros Morne National
  Park 165
 St. John's 163
Newport, OR 981
Newport, RI 140
newspapers
 Canada 29
 United States 23
Niagara Falls, NY 253
Niagara Falls, ON 255
North Adams, MA 135
North Carolina 378–390
 Asheville 384
 Bodie Island 388
 Boone 384
 Chapel Hill 379
 Charlotte 383
 Durham 379
 Hatteras 388
 Manteo 388
 Ocracoke 388
 Outer Banks 387
 Raleigh 379
 Research Triangle 379
 Roanoke Island 389
 Winston-Salem 382
North Carolina State
 University, see Raleigh,
 NC
North Cascades National
 Park, WA 970
North Central Michigan
 College, see Petosky, MI
North Conway, NH 94
North Dakota 603–610
 Bismarck 606
 Fargo 605

Theodore Roosevelt
 National Park 608
North Dakota State
 University, see Fargo,
 ND
Northwestern Michigan
 College, see Traverse
 City, MI
Northwestern State
 University, see
 Natchitoches, LA
Northwestern University,
 see Chicago, IL
Nova Scotia 148–155
 Cape Breton Highlands
  National Park 154
 Cape Breton Island 153
 Halifax 151
 Lighthouse Route 150
 Lunenburg 150
 Yarmouth 150

O

O'Keeffe, Georgia 314,
 362, 834
Ocean City, MD 302
Ocracoke, NC 388
Ogunquit, ME 81
Ohio 517–529
 Chillicothe 525
 Cincinnati 525
 Cleveland 518
 Columbus 523
 Cuyahoga Valley
  National Park 522
Ohio State University, see
 Columbus, OH
Ohiopyle State Park, PA
 287
Oklahoma 650–654
 Oklahoma City 652
 Tahlequah 652
 Tulsa 650
Oklahoma City, OK 652
Okoboji, IA 627
Olympia, WA 961
Olympic National Forest,
 WA 961
Olympic National Park,

WA 965
Omaha, NE 628
Ontario 185–202
 Niagara Falls 255
 Ottawa 196
 Stratford 196
 Toronto 187
 Windsor 539
Oral Roberts University,
 see Tulsa, OK
Orange County, CA 872
Oregon 974–990
 Ashland 987
 Astoria 980
 Bandon-by-the-Sea 981
 Bend 988
 Brookings 981
 Cannon Beach 980
 Columbia River Gorge
  983
 Crater Lake 986
 Deschutes National
  Forest 988
 Eugene 984
 Hells Canyon 989
 Klamath Falls 986
 Mt. Hood 982
 Newport 981
 Portland 974
 Three Capes Loop 980
 Wallowa Mountains 989
 Willamette National
  Forest 985
Orlando, FL 475
Ottawa, ON 196
Outer Banks, NC 387
Oxford, MS 437

P

Pacific Rim National
 Park, BC 1001
Padre Island, TX 685
Page, AZ 814
Pagosa Springs, CO 767
Painted Desert, AZ 813
Palm Beach, FL 485
Palm Springs, CA 884
Palo Alto, CA 925
Panama City, FL 513

parasites 40
Park City, UT 782
passports 32
Pei, I.M. 673
Pella, IA 623
Pennsylvania 266–287
  Gettysburg 281
  Lancaster County 279
  Ohiopyle State Park 287
  Philadelphia 266
  Pittsburgh 283
  Valley Forge 278
Pensacola, FL 515
Petoskey, MI 550
Petrified Forest National
  Park, AZ 813
Petroglyph National
  Monument, NM 843
Philadephia, PA 266
Phoenicia, NY 246
Phoenix, AZ 817
phone cards 52
pickpockets 38
Pigeon Forge, TN 372
Pikes Peak National
  Forest, CO 759
Pinkham Notch, NH 91
Pittsburgh, PA 283
Plymouth, MA 125
Polson, MT 708
Port Renfrew, BC 1001
Port Townsend, WA 964
Portland, ME 79
Portland, OR 974
Portsmouth, NH 87
Prairie City, IA 623
Prince Edward Island 160–
  162
  Cavendish 162
  Charlottetown 160
  Prince Edward Island
    National Park 162
Prince Edward Island
  National Park, PEI 162
Prince Rupert, BC 1001
Prince, see Minneapolis,
  MN
Providence, RI 137
Provincetown, MA 129
Pyramid Lake, NV 777

Q

Québec 166–185
  Île-d'Orléans 185
  Montréal 166
  Québec City 178
Québec City, QC 178

R

rabies 40
radio
  Canada 29
  United States 23
Raleigh, NC 379
Rapid City, SD 614
Red Cross 39
Red Lodge, MT 704
Rehoboth Beach, DE 289
Reid, Bill 997
Reno, NV 775
Research Triangle, NC 379
Rhode Island 137–143
  Block Island 142
  Newport 140
  Providence 137
Rhode Island School of
  Design, see Providence,
  RI
Richmond, VA 323
Río Grande National
  Forest, CO 760
Roanoke Island, NC 389
robbery 38
Rockwell, Norman 643
Rocky Mountain National
  Park, CO 750
Rocky Mountain oysters
  742
Ron Jon Surf Shop, see
  Cocoa Beach, FL
Roswell, NM 848
RVs 51

S

Sabula, IA 625
Sacramento, CA 935
safety 37
Saguaro National Park,

AZ 827
Saint John, NB 155
Salem, MA 125
Salt Lake City, UT 778
San Antonio, TX 656
San Diego, CA 876
San Francisco, CA 897
San Juan Islands, WA 962
San Juan National Forest,
  CO 766
San Luis Obispo, CA 891
Sangre de Cristo
  Mountains, NM 835
Santa Barbara, CA 888
Santa Cruz, CA 894
Santa Fe National Forest,
  NM 836
Santa Fe, NM 831
Saratoga, WY 737
Sault Ste. Marie, MI 551
Savannah, GA 418
Sawtooth National
  Recreation Area, ID 698
scams 38
scenic drives
  Apache Trail, AZ 822
  Blue Ridge Parkway 342
  Buffalo Bill Cody, WY
    724
  Cape Hatteras National
    Seashore, NC 389
  Centennial, WY 728
  Chief Joseph, WY 724
  Going-to-the-Sun Road,
    MT 712
  Great River Road, IA 625
  Icefields Parkway, AB
    1011
  North Cascades
    Highway, WA 970
  North Fork, WY 724
  North Shore Drive, MN
    601
  Northern Michigan
    Shore, MI 549
  San Juan Skyway, CO
    764
  Snowy Range, WY 737
  Texas Hill Country Drive,
    TX 662
  U.S. 101, OR 980

Scotts Bluff National Monument, NE 632
Seashores, see National Seashores
Seattle, WA 948
Sedona, AZ 808
Selma, AL 425
senior travelers 68
Seward, AK 1019
sexually transmitted diseases 41
Shakespeare festivals
    Asheville, NC 386
    Ashland, OR 987
    Boise, ID 696
    Boulder, CO 749
    Dallas, TX 674
    Garberville, CA 933
    Houston, TX 682
    Kansas City, MO 648
    Louisville, KY 354
    Montgomery, AL 424
    New York City, NY 233
    Omaha, NE 630
    Stratford, ON 196
Shenandoah National Park, VA 338
Sheridan, WY 732
short-term work
    Minneapolis, MN 590
    Apostle Islands, WI 586
    Block Island, RI 143
    Duluth, MN 597
    Rapid City, SD 615
    Salt Lake City, UT 782
    St Paul, MN 590
    St. Louis, MO 638
Shoshone National Forest, WY 724
Showtime, Synergy! 528
Sierra Nevada, CA 937
Sioux Falls, SD 611
skiing
    California 946
    Colorado 753
    Montana 707
Sleeping Bear Dunes, MI 545
Soleri, Paolo 74, 808
solo travelers 67
Sonoma Valley, CA 928

Soudan, MN 599
South Carolina 390–400
    Beaufort 395
    Charleston 391
    Columbia 395
    Fort Pulaski National Monument 420
    Grand Strand 398
    Myrtle Beach 398
South Dakota 610–619
    Badlands National Park 612
    Black Hills National Forest 615
    Custer State Park 618
    Deadwood 619
    Jewel Cave 618
    Mt. Rushmore 616
    Rapid City 614
    Sioux Falls 611
    Wind Cave National Park 617
Southern Methodist University, see Dallas, TX
Spinal Tap 630
Spirit Lake, IA 627
sports
    Canada 29
    United States 23
Springfield, IL 571
St. Augustine, FL 471
St. Ignatius, MT 708
St. John's, NF 163
St. Louis, MO 637
St. Mary's University, see Halifax, NS
St. Mary's, GA 420
St. Paul, MN 588
St. Petersburg, FL 509
STA Travel 54
Stanford University, see Palo Alto, CA
Stanley Park, BC 997
Stanley, ID 698
STDs 41
Steamboat Springs, CO 755
Stowe, VT 101
Stratford, ON 196
Sullivan, Louis 562
Summit County, CO 746

Sun Valley, ID 696
Sunset Crater Volcano National Monument, AZ 808

T

Tahlequah, OK 652
Tampa, FL 507
Taos, NM 836
taxes 36
telephones 52
television
    Canada 29
    United States 22
Telluride, CO 762
Temple University, see Philadelphia, PA
Tennessee 359–378
    Chattanooga 370
    Cherokee Reservation 369
    Great Smoky Mountains National Park 367
    Knoxville 365
    Memphis 372
    Nashville 359
    Pigeon Forge 372
terrorism 37
Test of English as a Foreign Language (TOEFL) 72
Texas 655–692
    Amarillo 686
    Austin 661
    Bandera 662
    Big Bend National Park 691
    Boerne 662
    Corpus Christi 684
    Dallas 670
    El Paso 688
    Fort Worth 675
    Fredericksburg 663
    Guadalupe Mountains National Park 687
    Houston 676
    Johnson City 663
    Kerrville 662
    Medina 662

New Braunfels 662
Padre Island 685
San Antonio 656
theft 38
theses
  Brenna's 297
  Megan's, see Let's Go 2005
  Scott's 531
Thousand Island Seaway, NY 259
Three Capes Loop, OR 980
ticks 40
Tijuana, Mexico 881
tipping 36
Tombstone, AZ 828
Tonto National Forest, AZ 822
Tonto National Monument, AZ 822
Toronto, ON 187
trails, long
  Juan de Fuca Marine 1001
trains 56
transportation 53
  airplanes 53
  bicycles 65
  buses 59
  cars 61
  motorcycles 65
  trains 56
travel agencies, budget and student 54
traveler's checks 35
traveling alone 67
Traverse City, MI 546
trees, self-possessed 414
Truth or Consequences, NM 845
Tucson, AZ 823
Tulsa, OK 650
Tuskegee University, see Tuskegee, AL
Tuskegee, AL 424
Tuzigoot National Monument, AZ 810
Twain, Mark 144, 366, 643, 935, 945

U

Uinta National Forest, UT 783
Uncompahgre National Forest, CO 760
United Nations 221
United States Naval Academy, see Annapolis, MD
University of Alaska, see Fairbanks, AK
University of British Columbia, see Vancouver, BC
University of California-Berkeley, see Berkeley, CA
University of California-Los Angeles, see Los Angeles, CA
University of California-Santa Cruz, see Santa Cruz, CA
University of Chicago, see Chicago, IL
University of Cincinnati, see Cincinnati, OH
University of Colorado, see Boulder, CO
University of Florida, see Gainesville, FL
University of Illinois at Chicago, see Chicago, IL
University of Iowa, see Iowa City, IA 624
University of Kansas, see Lawrence, KS
University of Miami, see Miami, FL
University of Michigan, see Ann Arbor, MI
University of Montana, see Missoula, MT
University of Nebraska-Lincoln, see Lincoln, NE
University of New Brunswick at Saint John, see Saint John, NB
University of New Mexico (UNM), see Albuquerque, NM
University of North Carolina, see Chapel Hill, NC
University of Oregon, see Eugene, OR
University of Ottawa, see Ottawa, ON
University of P.E.I, see Charlottetown, PEI
University of Pennsylvania, see Philadelphia, PA
University of Pittsburgh, see Pittsburgh, PA
University of Portland, see Portland, OR
University of South Carolina, see Columbia, SC
University of Texas at Austin, see Austin, TX
University of Toronto, see Toronto, ON
University of Utah, see Salt Lake City, UT
University of Vermont, see Burlington, VT
University of Virginia, see Charlottesville, VA
University of Washington, see Seattle, WA
University of Windsor, see Detroit, MI
University of Wisconsin-Madison, see Madison, WI
University of Wyoming, see Laramie, WY
Upper Peninsula, MI 550
Utah 777–795
  Antelope Island State Park 781
  Arches National Park 788
  Bryce Canyon National Park 790
  Capitol Reef National Park 789
  Cedar Breaks National

INDEX

Monument 794
Dinosaur National
Monument 783
Dixie National Forest
788
Flaming Gorge National
Recreation Area 785
Glen Canyon National
Recreation Area 814
Grand Staircase-
Escalante National
Monument 792
Lake Powell 814
Manti-La Sal National
Forest 789
Moab 786
Park City 782
Salt Lake City 778
Uinta National Forest
783
Vernal 783
Zion National Park 793

V

Vail, CO 753
Valley Forge, PA 278
Vancouver, BC 993
Vashon Island, WA 961
vegetarian travelers 70
Vermont 95-104
Brattleboro 103
Burlington 96
Champlain Valley 99
Lake Champlain 99
Middlebury 99
Stowe 101
Vernal, UT 783
Via Rail 59
Vicksburg National
Military Park 436
Vicksburg, MS 435
Victoria, BC 999
Virginia 322-341
Alexandria 322
Arlington 321
Assateague Island 300
Charlottesville 335
Chincoteague Island
300

Fredericksburg 327
George Washington
National Forest 342
Jamestown 332
Lexington 343
Mt. Vernon 322
Richmond 323
Shenandoah National
Park 338
Virginia Beach 333
Williamsburg 330
Yorktown 332
Virginia Beach, VA 333
Visa 35
visas 33, 72
Voyageurs National Park,
MN 600

W

Wake Forest University,
see Winston-Salem, NC
walking tours
Calle Ocho—Miami, FL
498
Chinatown—Vancouver,
BC 996
monuments—
Washington, D.C. 316
pub crawling—Tempe,
AZ 820
SoHo shops—New York,
NY 232
Wall Drug 612
Wallowa Mountains, OR
989
Walnut Canyon National
Monument, AZ 807
Walt Disney World, FL 479
Warhol, Andy 286
Washington 947-973
Mt. Rainier National
Park 972
Mt. St. Helens 968
North Cascades
National Park 970
Olympia 961
Olympic National Forest
961
Olympic National Park

965
Port Townsend 964
San Juan Islands 962
Seattle 948, 961
Washington University,
see St. Louis, MO
Washington, D.C. 304
Waterton Lakes National
Park, AB 714
Wells 81
West Palm Beach, FL 485
West Virginia 345-348
Harpers Ferry 345
Monongahela National
Forest 347
New River Gorge 341
West Yellowstone, MT 720
Western Canada 991-
1014
Western Union 36
Whistler, BC 998
White Hall, KY 358
White Mountain National
Forest, NH 89
White River National
Forest, CO 746
White Sands National
Monument, NM 847
Whitefish, MT 713
Whitehorse, YT 1004
Wichita, KS 634
wilderness 48
wildlife 48
Wildlife Refuges, see
National Wildlife
Refuges
Willamette National
Forest, OR 985
Williams College, see
Williamstown, MA 136
Williamsburg, VA 330
Williamstown, MA 136
Wind Cave National Park,
SD 617
Windsor, ON 539
Winston-Salem, NC 382
Winter Park, CO 745
Winterset, IA 623
Wisconsin 573-588
Apostle Islands 585
Door County 583

Madeline Island 587
Madison 579
Milwaukee 573
women travelers 67
work permits 72
Wrangell-St. Elias
  National Park, AK 1020
Wright, Frank Lloyd 22, 74,
  287, 544, 565, 572, 582,
  819, 821
Wupatki National
  Monument, AZ 808
Wyoming 715–738
  Bighorn National Forest
  733
  Bridger-Teton National
  Forest 730
  Casper 735
  Cheyenne 735
  Cody 731

Devils Tower National
  Monument 734
Grand Teton National
  Park 724
Jackson 729
Laramie 738
Medicine Bow National
  Forest 737
Saratoga 737
Sheridan 732
Shoshone National
  Forest 724
Yellowstone National
  Park 715

Y

Yale University, see New
  Haven, CT
Yarmouth, NS 150

Yellowstone National
  Park, WY 715
Yeshiva University, see
  New York City, NY
YMCAs 44
Yorktown, VA 332
Yosemite National Park,
  CA 941
youth hostels, see **hostels**
Yukon Territory 1004–1007
  Dempster Highway 1007
  Kluane National Park
  1006
  Whitehorse 1004
YWCAs 44

Z

Zion National Park, UT
  793

PDAs & Travel

LG
LET'S GO

(it's not what you're thinking)

Let's Go City Guides are now available for Palm OS™ PDAs. Download a free trial at http://**mobile.letsgo.com**

MAP INDEX

Alaska 1015
Alberta 1008
Albuquerque 839
Ann Arbor 540
Appalachian Trail 86
Atlanta 406
  Greater Atlanta 405
Austin 664
Baltimore 292
Boston 108
British Columbia & the Yukon Territory 992
Burlington 97
California 851
Cape Cod & Islands 126
Charleston 391
Chicago 555
  Downtown 557
Cincinnati 528
Cleveland 520
Dallas 671
Denver 740
Detroit 534
Eastern Canada 149
El Paso (with Ciudad Juárez) 689
Florida Peninsula 469
Fort Lauderdale 488
Grand Canyon 796
Great Lakes 518
Great Plains 604
Houston 678
  Museum District 678
Kansas City 645
La$ Vega$ 774
Los Angeles & Vicinity 852
  Westside 859
Madison 579
Memphis 374
Miami 493
  South Beach 495
Mid-Atlantic 204
Milwaukee 575

Minneapolis/St. Paul 589
Montréal 168-169
Nashville 360
National Parks of Utah 788
New England 77
New Orleans 441
  Downtown 446
New York City (Manhattan) 206
Ontario & Upstate New York 186
Orlando Theme Parks 477
Ottawa 197
Pacific Northwest 948
Philadelphia 268
Phoenix 818
Pittsburgh 285
Portland 976
Richmond 324
Rocky Mountains 694
Salt Lake City 778
San Antonio 657
San Diego 877
San Francisco 901
San Francisco Bay Area 919
Santa Fe 831
Seattle 950-951
South 350-351
Southwest 770
St. Louis 639
Texas 655
Toronto 188
Tucson 824
United States xvi-xvii
  Chapters (and Canada) vi
  National Park System xviii-xix
  Transportation Network xv
Vancouver 994
Vieux-Québec 179
Washington, D.C. 306
Yellowstone & Grand Teton
  National Parks 716
Yosemite 942

MAP LEGEND

✚	Hospital	✈	Airport	🏛	Museum
🚓	Police	🚌	Bus Station	♠	Hotel/Hostel	Park
✉	Post Office	🚂	Train Station	⛺	Camping	
(i)	Tourist Office	⚓	Ferry Landing	🍴	Food & Drink	Beach
$	Bank	▲	Mountain	🛍	Shopping	
⚑	Embassy/Consulate	♨	Theater	★	Entertainment	Water
■	Site or Point of Interest	📖	Library		Nightlife	
☎	Telephone Office			💻	Internet Café	
				········	Pedestrian Zone	

The Let's Go compass always points NORTH.